M000193998

The ENCYCLOPEDIA
of CHRISTIANITY

Volume 1
A–D

The

of

Volume 1

editors

translator and English-language editor

statistical editor

foreword

WILLIAM B. EERDMANS PUBLISHING COMPANY
BRILL

ENCYCLOPEDIA CHRISTIANITY

A–D

Erwin Fahlbusch
Jan Milič Lochman
John Mbiti
Jaroslav Pelikan
Lukas Vischer

Geoffrey W. Bromiley

David B. Barrett

Jaroslav Pelikan

GRAND RAPIDS, MICHIGAN / CAMBRIDGE, U.K.
LEIDEN / BOSTON / KÖLN

Originally published in German as
Evangelisches Kirchenlexikon, Dritte Auflage (Neufassung)
© 1986, 1989, 1992, 1996, 1997
Vandenhoeck & Ruprecht, Göttingen, Germany

English translation © 1999 by
Wm. B. Eerdmans Publishing Company and
Koninklijke Brill NV

Published jointly 1999 by
Wm. B. Eerdmans Publishing Company
255 Jefferson Ave. S.E., Grand Rapids, Michigan 49503
and by
Koninklijke Brill NV
Leiden, the Netherlands

All rights reserved. No part of this publication may be reproduced,
translated, stored in a retrieval system, or transmitted in any form
or by any means, electronic, mechanical, photocopying, recording
or otherwise, without prior written permission from the publishers.

Printed in the United States of America

05 04 03 02 01 00 99   10 9 8 7 6 5 4 3 2 1

Library of Congress Cataloging-in-Publication Data

Evangelisches Kirchenlexikon. English.
    The encyclopedia of Christianity / editors, Erwin Fahlbusch . . . [et al.];
  translator and English-language editor, Geoffrey W. Bromiley;
  statistical editor, David B. Barrett; foreword, Jaroslav Pelikan.
      p.   cm.
  Includes index.
  Contents: v. 1. A–D.
  ISBN 0-8028-2413-7 (cloth: v. 1.: alk. paper)
    1. Christianity — Encyclopedias.   I. Fahlbusch, Erwin.
II. Bromiley, Geoffrey William.   III. Title.
BR95.E8913   1999
230′.003 —DC21   98-45953
                                   CIP

Brill ISBN 90 04 11316 9

Contents

List of Entries

This list does not include headings that simply refer the reader to a cross-reference.

Abbot, Abbess
Abortion
Abortion Counseling
Abraham
Absolute, The
Acathistus
Acclamation
Acculturation
Achievement and Competition
Acoemetae
Act
Action Theory
Acts of the Apostles
Adam
Adiaphora
Adulthood
Adventists
Aesthetics
Afghanistan
Africa
African Theology
Afro-American Cults
Aggression
Agnosticism
Agrapha
Albania
Alchemy
Alexandria
Alexandrian Theology
Algeria
All Africa Conference of
 Churches
All Saints' Day
Allegory
Alpha and Omega
Altar
Altötting
Amen
Amnesty International
Amos, Book of
Anabaptists
Analogy

Analytic Ethics
Analytic Philosophy
Ānanda Mārga
Anaphora
Anarchy
Ancestor Worship
Anchorites
Angel
Anglican Communion
Angola
Animals
Animism
Anointing
Anonymity
Anselm
Anthropology
Anthroposophy
Antichrist
Antimodernist Oath
Antinomian Controversies
Antinomy
Antioch
Antiochian Theology
Anti-Semitism, Anti-Judaism
Anti-Trinitarianism
Anxiety
Apocalypticism
Apocatastasis
Apocrypha
Apologetics
Apologists
Apophatic Theology
Aporia
Apostasy
Apostle, Apostolate
Apostles' Creed
Apostolic Churches
Apostolic Fathers
Arameans
Archaeology
Archetype
Archimandrite

Argentina
Arianism
Aristotelianism
Ark of the Covenant
Armenia
Armenian Apostolic Church
Arminianism
Arnoldshain Conference
Ascension of Christ
Asceticism
Asia
Asian Theology
Assembleias de Deus no Brasil
Assemblies of God
Assurance of Salvation
Astrology
Asylum
Athanasian Creed
Athanasius
Atheism
Athos
Atonement
Augsburg Confession
Augsburg, Peace of
Augustine
Augustine's Theology
Augustinians
Australia
Austria
Authority
Autocephaly
Autogenic Training
Autonomy
Ave Maria
Axiom
Azerbaijan
Babylonian and Assyrian
 Religion
Baha'i
Bahamas
Bahrain
Bangladesh

LIST OF ENTRIES

LIST OF ENTRIES

Foreword

In every field of thought and scholarship there come moments when it is time to summarize the present state of research and reflection and thereby to provide a starting point for the next stage. In the natural sciences and some of the mathematically oriented social sciences, where the usual medium of publication is the scientific paper, disseminated as quickly as possible, these moments represent the opportunity to put out a book; but in the humanities, where the full-length scholarly article and the monograph are still dominant, they are an opportunity to put together a reference work: a manual, a collection of scholarly essays, a dictionary, or even an entire encyclopedia.

Quite apart from the symbolic or real import of the year 2000, this is such a moment for the serious study of Christianity as a historical and a contemporary phenomenon, and the *Encyclopedia of Christianity* is the outcome of a serious scholarly effort to supply both a summary and a starting point. For in one branch of theology after another, the investigations and the debates of the generations since the Second World War now permit, indeed demand, a job of scholarly cartography, not to arrest the continuing development of the discipline but to facilitate it. And the articles in this encyclopedia have been able to take good advantage of that situation, by putting old and seemingly irrelevant questions into a new light and by examining new questions — and new answers — that have come out of the changed situation of Christian faith and obedience at the end of the second millennium. Although eventually I had to withdraw from the editorial board of the German *Evangelisches Kirchenlexikon,* on which the *EC* is based, because of the assignment of delivering the Gifford Lectures, followed by my election as president of the American Academy of Arts and Sciences, I was able to join with my colleagues of that board in the planning and design of the set. We reviewed one comprehensive list of article titles after another — typically, the German word for such a list was *Stichwörterverzeichnis* — asking whether that was still the category to which a reader of the twentieth (or twenty-first!) century would naturally turn for information and guidance.

One of the most striking such changes is the truly global character of the Christian faith at the conclusion of the twentieth century. Ever since the command to carry the gospel "into all the world" and to "make disciples of all nations," Christianity has aspired to be universal: one of the earliest marks of the church, an attribute that found its way into many of the major creeds, was "catholic," meaning universal. The early legends about the twelve apostles described them as traveling to all the corners of the then-known world. But it was only the then-known world. With the modern voyages of discovery, ancient peoples, ancient civilizations, and ancient religions became part of the European and the Christian consciousness, as well as the objects of Christian missions, above all in what the late historian of the expansion of Christianity and my Yale colleague Kenneth Scott Latourette called "the great century" of missions, the nineteenth. Yet it was not until the century which followed that the full implications of this development became clear. In one article after another of the *EC,* the reader will be caught up short by the reminder of a Christian belief or practice or organizational form that reflects an Asian or African or Latin-American cultural context and that both enriches and challenges conventional Western understandings of what it means to be Christian. Indeed, the very titles of many of the articles themselves present such a challenge, as even a cursory review of the entries will show.

But what has happened to the Christian movement during the twentieth century is not only globalization; "the great new fact of Christian history" has been the cluster of experiences, insights, and shocks associated with the term "ecumenical." As applied, for example, to the first seven "ecumenical" councils of the church, that term used to refer to the Mediterranean world, to the Christian *imperium Romanum* governed by a Christian emperor, and to the five historic patriarchates inherited from the early church. The twentieth-century process of redefining the word "ecumenical" has left its mark on every Christian group, and no traditional conviction or problem has remained unaffected. From a concern of various Protestant churches to reexamine their historic divisions and differences in the light of Scripture and in the light of their rediscovery of one another, the ecumenical movement has gone on to engage the participation, with varying mixtures of caution and enthusiasm, of Roman Catholic and Eastern Orthodox partners in the conversation; and that too has left its imprint on these pages. It is a useful, if rather sobering, exercise to flip at random through the *EC,* reading first an article with a geographic designation, then one with a theological title, but seeing in each of them a "strange new world."

Nor should the reader of these volumes forget that its editors and contributors, like their predecessors in every century of Christian history, are conscious participants in the culture and outlook of their own time. I suspect that, for many readers, one of the unexpected differences between the great German and French theological encyclopedias of the past, on which we have all depended, and the *EC* is its reliance on the methodology of the various social sciences: Max Weber and Ernst Troeltsch are present in these articles, even when their names do not appear in the bibliography. Also among those present are the considerably less sympathetic modern interpreters of Christianity, Karl Marx and Sigmund Freud. As a result of this serious but critical involvement of the *EC* in the spirit and methodology of our time, it will certainly be far more accessible and useful than earlier works were to those readers who do not regard themselves as members of any Christian group or church but who want to know and understand Christian beliefs and teachings. It should therefore also commend itself to public libraries and to school libraries at every educational level from elementary school to university.

Being something of a reference book freak, I have since my student days been surrounding myself in my study with general and specialized encyclopedias, foreign language lexica, and dictionaries of many other kinds, which (at least so far) no electronic resources have successfully replaced. Whether I am engaged in my own scholarly research in the primary sources or simply reading within or beyond my own discipline, I feel insecure without the ever present help of "hunt-and-find" works that will give me, more or less instantaneously, a bibliographic reference, a statistic, a date, a name, or a definition. Reference works such as the *EC* quickly become indispensable for that "hunt-and-find" purpose (if only when working on the Sunday crossword puzzle). But it is gross neglect of a major intellectual resource, and of a great personal pleasure, to leave it at that. Over and over, I turn to my reference works in order to get a conspectus that will enable me to review, with a mixture of reminder and new insight, some area of human endeavor or speculation. I have been doing just that with the German version as the individual volumes have appeared, and now I shall be able to do it even more easily and even more profitably with the English *EC*. It is a great indoor sport, and I heartily recommend it.

JAROSLAV PELIKAN
Yale University

xii

Publishers' Preface

The William B. Eerdmans Publishing Company and E. J. Brill are pleased to introduce the *Encyclopedia of Christianity* — a five-volume work that addresses the current, broad interest in Christianity and religion. Comprehensive, up to date, reflecting the highest standards in scholarship yet intended for a wide range of readers, the *EC* describes the Christian faith and community as it exists today in its myriad forms and also in its relation to the core apostolic tradition throughout the 2,000 years of Christian history. The *EC* also looks outward beyond Christianity, considering other world religions and philosophies as it paints in broad strokes and fine the overall religious and sociocultural picture in which the Christian church now finds itself as it moves into a new millennium.

Describing Christianity in its *global context,* the *EC* is a fully international work, with articles written by scholars from many countries and cultural backgrounds. Separate articles for every continent and for over 170 countries present both the history and the current situation of the Christian faith in all its rich spiritual and theological diversity around the world. A number of articles discuss Christian theology in its various regional expressions (e.g., African, Asian, Latin American, North American), the perspectives of these regional theologies on central doctrines and practices (e.g., Baptism, Marriage and Divorce), and even Christian Spirituality throughout the world. Other articles highlight different branches of theological and religious study (e.g., Exegesis, Biblical; Philosophy of Religion; Practical Theology; Sociology of Religion; Systematic Theology), different theologians and their thought (e.g., Augustine, Calvin, Schleiermacher), and various religiosocial perspectives of Christian theology (e.g., Black, Feminist, Liberation). Additional presentations — such as those on Pentecostalism and the Independent Churches of Africa — highlight the vitality of Christianity in many Third World settings.

In order to show readers ecumenical perspectives beyond their own ecclesiastical frameworks, the *EC,* firmly committed to a universality rooted in the Reformation tradition, embraces Christianity in its widest *ecumenical context.* Major articles detail the history, thought, and practice of Anglicans, Orthodox, Protestants, and Roman Catholics. In addition, articles on Christology, eschatology, worship, and numerous other subjects include separate sections on the views and practices of each of these major Christian traditions. Further articles give an account of many other groupings of Christians (from Adventists to Augustinians, Black Churches to Free Church, the Church of South India to the Ethiopian Orthodox Church, Athos to the Taizé Community), as well as of important movements within Christianity and deriving from it (e.g., Jansenism, the Oxford Movement, Unitarians). International ecumenical bodies receive their own focus — in articles on the World Council of Churches, the Lutheran World Federation, the World Evangelical Fellowship, and many more such organizations. These studies collectively highlight the manifold relationships among churches in both theological dialogue and practical cooperation.

A highly useful feature of the *EC* is the comprehensive statistical information provided by David B. Barrett, today's leading statistician of Christianity around the world. These data are presented in the boxes and tables printed with each of the country and continent articles. For the milestone A.D. 2000, Barrett gives — country by country and continent by continent — the latest, best estimates of affiliation among the major world religions and of church association within Christianity itself. In addition, the *EC* presents the latest U.N. statistics for population, growth rate, population density, birth and death rates, fertility rate, infant mortality rate, and life expectancy. These religious and nonreligious data together provide readers with a comprehensive statistical snapshot of each country and continent and of the world as a whole at the turn of the millennium. (See the Introduction below for a detailed explanation of all statistics.)

In its portrayal of Christianity, the *EC* also takes into account the current *sociocultural context,* including other world religions, secular philosophies, cultural trends, and political and economic forces that define our modern age. Articles on these topics describe the multivalent setting in which Christianity today must maintain a credible witness to the ancient gospel. From Abortion, Atheism, and Autonomy to Islam, Modernity, and Psychoanalysis, *EC* articles chart the contemporary sociocultural and religious world.

The *EC* also presents Christianity in its rich *historical context,* starting with the biblical tradition and reflecting how the apostolic tradition developed and how the church has throughout its history sought to keep faith with its traditions while engaging the world around it. Exploring these themes are articles presenting every book of the Bible, key biblical figures, and the life of the early church in their intellectual and religious contexts (e.g., Babylonian and Assyrian Religion; Church Fathers; Gnosis, Gnosticism; Hellenism), church councils (from Nicaea I to Vatican II), the creeds and other important declarations (from the Apostles' Creed to the Barmen Declaration), and the church's contribution to culture (e.g., Church Architecture, Literature and Christian Tradition, Theology of History). A number of major articles address also mission work by all branches of Christianity and its impact on the non-Western world. Enhancing the *EC*'s coverage of the historic Christian faith is its series of over 70 biographies. These pieces offer important personal windows into the preceding two millennia, from the earliest days of the church (e.g., Athanasius and Chrysostom), through the medieval and Reformation periods (e.g., Hildegard of Bingen, Martin Luther, Menno Simons), and into the 19th and 20th centuries (e.g., Leo XIII and Martin Luther King Jr.).

In the course of presenting Christianity in these several contexts, the more than 1,700 articles of the *EC* address a wide range of subjects. Besides the categories noted above, separate entries inform readers about such matters as the following:

- academic disciplines of special interest to religious and theological studies (e.g., Archaeology; Linguistics)
- church practices (e.g., Blessing; Church Discipline; Eucharist)
- church titles and officeholders (from Abbot, Abbess to Worker-Priests)
- documents and practices of specific Christian traditions (e.g., Bulls and Briefs; Gospel Song; Starets).

- the impact of modern technology on the church (e.g., Distance Education; Electronic Church)
- important nonchurch organizations (e.g., Amnesty International; International Council of Christians and Jews)
- key terms of other religious traditions (e.g., Cabala; Karma; Shia, Shiites)
- personal religious devotion (e.g., Devotional Literature; Piety)
- philosophical issues and schools (e.g., God, Arguments for the Existence of; Islamic Philosophy; Kantianism)
- relations between Christianity and other major religions and philosophies (e.g., Hinduism and Christianity; Marxism and Christianity)
- the transmission and use of the books of the Bible (e.g., Bible Manuscripts and Editions; Bible Study; Bible Versions)
- worldwide concerns (e.g., Disarmament and Armament; Genocide; Racism)
- the older (e.g., Continuing Education; Old Age)
- the younger (e.g., Religious Instruction; Youth Work)
- — even the unexpected (e.g., Cannibalism; Word Square).

The *Encyclopedia of Christianity* is based on the third revised edition of the *Evangelisches Kirchenlexicon: Internationale theologische Enzyklopädie* (Göttingen: Vandenhoeck & Ruprecht, 1986-97) and is its authorized English-language edition. The first edition of the *EKL,* edited by Heinz Brunotte and Otto Weber, appeared in the 1950s. The current, altogether new edition has taken into account more recent theological and ecclesiastical developments and, reflecting those developments, has stressed, even more than did the original edition, the Christian faith in its current sociocultural and global setting. As the editors note in their foreword to the first volume of the new *EKL,* "The challenges of our time and the problems of contemporary Christian life provide the investigative framework in which the manifold tradition of the gospel is presented." The *Encyclopedia of Christianity* not only has tailored the articles of the current *EKL* to better suit the requirements of an English readership but has taken the international commitment of the *EKL* even further by adding articles of special interest to our English readers (e.g., Assemblies of God, Civil Rights Movement), by expanding other articles to give more complete coverage (e.g., Christian Art now includes a section on contemporary art; Public

Health covers the latest AIDS perspectives), and by adding articles on the newest independent nations. In addition, the *EC* throughout expands and updates the original *EKL* article bibliographies — in particular, by adding more recent works in English.

It is our pleasure, finally, as the publishers of the English edition of the *EKL,* to acknowledge and express our gratitude for the visionary work of Professor Erwin Fahlbusch and his four coeditors — Professors Jan Milič Lochman, John Mbiti, Jaroslav Pelikan, and Lukas Vischer — in producing the third edition of the *EKL* and in working closely with the preparation of the *EC.* Also, by providing numerous suggestions regarding the outlines of articles and by proposing authors to write them, by their critical review of the manuscripts and suggestions for their improvement, and through their willingness to step into the breach to write a number of articles themselves, the eighteen Consulting Editors have made a significant contribution to the *Encyclopedia.* Professor Fahlbusch has presided tirelessly over this immense, long-term project, pushing authors and editors alike toward the highest critical standards. In Arndt Ruprecht, of Vandenhoeck & Ruprecht, Professor Fahlbusch had the blessing and support of a publisher whose vision and commitment equaled his own. And over the years, V&R house editors Brigit Bender-Junker,

Katja Fiedler, Britta Hübner, Wolfgang G. Roehl, Notger Slenczka, Ekkehard Starke, and Dietrich Voorgang have done much to shape the volumes of both the *EKL* and the *EC.* The editorial team, together with the adviser colleagues Professors Jürgen Roloff and Rudolf Smend, as well as Reinhilde Ruprecht of Vandenhoek & Ruprecht, helped to oversee the translation and adaptation process, working with their English-language counterparts to keep the *EC* in line with the original encyclopedic, ecumenical, and international commitment.

For the English edition of this work, we are deeply indebted to our own successive coordinating editors, Edgar W. Smith Jr., who assisted his German colleagues in evaluating the manuscripts submitted, and Craig Noll, who, along with Ed Smith, tailored and augmented the German articles and assigned new articles to suit the needs of an English readership. They were helped at key points by advisers Mark Noll, Thomas Hoyt, and Douglas Stott. The final tribute is to English-language editor Geoffrey Bromiley, whose knowledgeable and felicitous work as *EKL* translator and wise counsel as *EC* editor crown a lifetime devoted to bringing significant publications (German and otherwise) to the English-reading public.

THE PUBLISHERS

Introduction

This introduction provides a brief guide to the editorial conventions followed throughout the *Encyclopedia of Christianity,* as well as to the statistical information specially prepared for the *EC* by David Barrett.

ALPHABETIZATION

Articles are arranged alphabetically word by word (not letter by letter), with hyphens and apostrophes counted as continuing the single word; all commas are ignored. For example:

> Antiochian Theology
> Anti-Semitism, Anti-Judaism
> . . .
> Augsburg Confession
> Augsburg, Peace of
> . . .
> Calvin, John
> Calvinism
> Calvin's Theology
> . . .
> Church Year
> Churches of Christ

STATISTICS

The *EC* includes separate articles for each of the six major areas (formerly "continents") currently recognized by the United Nations (i.e., Africa, Asia, Europe, Latin America and the Caribbean, Northern America, and Oceania). It also presents separate articles for all independent countries of the world, omitting only those whose population, according to U.N. estimates for 1995, is less than 200,000 (e.g., Andorra, Nauru).

Accompanying each country article is a standard statistical box with the following format:

Argentina

	1960	1980	2000
Population (1,000s):	20,616	28,094	37,032
Annual growth rate (%):	1.55	1.51	1.19

Area: 2,780,400 sq. km. (1,073,518 sq. mi.)

A.D. *2000*
Population density: 13/sq. km. (34/sq. mi.)
Births / deaths: 1.90 / 0.78 per 100 population
Fertility rate: 2.44 per woman
Infant mortality rate: 20 per 1,000 live births
Life expectancy: 74.2 years (m: 70.6, f: 77.7)
Religious affiliation (%): Christians 92.9 (Roman Catholics 90.2, Protestants 5.9, indigenous 5.4, marginal 1.4, unaffiliated 1.1, other Christians 0.6), nonreligious 2.2, Muslims 2.0, Jews 1.5, other 1.4.

The demographic information in these boxes is taken from the *World Population Prospects: The 1996 Revision* (New York [United Nations], 1998). Depending on the presentation in U.N. tables, figures for 1960, 1980, and 2000 are either for that year alone or for a five-year period beginning with that year. In each case where the United Nations provides three estimates, the medium variant estimates are cited. Information on country area is taken from the *1996 Britannica Book of the Year* (Chicago, 1996). For countries like Argentina, where the birth rate minus the death rate (1.12 per 100 population) does not equal the annual growth rate (1.19), the difference is due to migration — in this case, *into* the country.

David Barrett, editor of the *World Christian Encyclopedia* (New York, 1982) and president of Global Evangelization Movement, Richmond, Virginia, has provided all the information on religious affiliation in the statistical boxes. In the first place, the boxes present the breakdown of overall religious affiliation for each country, using the following sixteen categories:

atheists — persons professing atheism, skepticism, or disbelief, including antireligious (opposed to all religion)

Baha'is — followers of the Baha'i World Faith, founded in the 19th century by Bahā' Allāh

Buddhists — followers of any of the branches of Buddhism; worldwide, 56 percent are Mahayana (northern), 38 percent Theravada (Hinayana, or southern), 6 percent Tantrayana (Lamaism)

Chinese folk religionists — followers of the traditional Chinese religion, which includes local deities, ancestor veneration, Confucian ethics, Taoism, divination, and some Buddhist elements

Christians — followers of Jesus Christ, either affiliated with churches or simply identifying themselves as such in censuses or polls

Confucianists — non-Chinese followers of Confucius and Confucianism, mostly Koreans in Korea

Hindus — followers of the main Hindu traditions; worldwide, 70 percent are Vaishnavas, 25 percent Saivas, 3 percent Saktas, 2 percent neo-Hindus and reform Hindus

Jews — adherents of Judaism

Muslims — followers of Islam; worldwide, 83 percent are Sunnites, 16 percent Shiites, 1 percent other schools

new religionists — followers of Asian 20th-century new religions, new religious movements, radical new crisis religions, and non-Christian syncretistic mass religions, all founded since 1800 and most since 1945

nonreligious — persons professing no religion, nonbelievers, agnostics, freethinkers, dereligionized secularists indifferent to all religion

Shintoists — Japanese who profess Shinto as their first or major religion

Sikhs — followers of the Sikh reform movement arising out of Hinduism

spiritists — non-Christian spiritists, spiritualists, thaumaturgists, medium-religionists

Taoists — followers of the religion developed from the Taoist philosophy and from folk religion and Buddhism

tribal religionists — primal or primitive religionists, animists, spirit-worshipers, shamanists, ancestor-venerators, polytheists, pantheists, traditionalists, local or tribal folk-religionists

The country boxes list each religious group that numbers at least 1.0 percent of the population of that county; any groups that number 0.9 percent or less of the population are grouped together under "other." Because of rounding, the totals of all the religious groups in a country may not equal 100.0 percent.

Second, for the category "Christians," the infor-mation in the boxes shows in parentheses the breakdown by ecclesiastical bloc, using the following seven categories:

Anglicans — persons in a church that is in fellowship with the archbishop of Canterbury, especially through its participation in the Lambeth Conference; Episcopalians

indigenous — Christians in denominations, churches, or movements who regard themselves as outside of mainline Anglican/Orthodox/Protestant/Roman Catholic Christianity; autonomous bodies independent of foreign origin or control (e.g., Independent Charismatic Churches [Braz.], house church movement [China], isolated radio believers [Saudi Arabia], Zion Christian Church [S.Af.], Vineyard Christian Fellowship [U.S.])

marginal — followers of para-Christian or quasi-Christian Western movements or deviations out of mainline Protestantism, not professing Christian doctrine according to the classic Trinitarian creeds (i.e., Apostles', Nicene) but often claiming a second or supplementary or ongoing source of divine revelation in addition to the Bible (e.g., Christian Scientists, Jehovah's Witnesses, Mormons, Unitarians)

Orthodox — Eastern (Chalcedonian), Oriental (Pre-Chalcedonian, Non-Chalcedonian, Monophysite), Nestorian (Assyrian), and nonhistorical Orthodox

Protestants — persons in churches that trace their origin or formulation to the 16th-century Reformation and thus typically emphasize justification by faith alone and the Bible as the supreme authority, including (1) churches in the Lutheran, Calvinistic, and Zwinglian traditions; and (2) other groups arising before, during, or after the Reformation (e.g., Waldenses, Bohemian Brethren, Baptists, Friends, Congregationalists, Methodists, Adventists, Pentecostals, Assemblies of God)

Roman Catholics — persons in a church that recognizes the pope, the bishop of Rome (with the associated hierarchy), as its spiritual head

unaffiliated — professing Christians not associated with any church

As with the different religions, so for the different types of Christians, any group that numbers at least 1.0 percent of the population of the country is listed. Any groups of Christians that number 0.9 percent or less of the population are included together under "other Christians." Because of rounding, the totals of all the individual Christian groups may not equal the total percentage of Christians. In some cases (as in the Argentina box above), because of double counting, the percentages of the individual Christian groups total more than the country-wide percentage of Christians.

Accompanying each major area article are three tables that list most of the information appearing in the individual country statistical boxes. The first table displays demographic information; the second, data on overall religious affiliation; the third, data on church affiliation. The religion tables list separately the twelve most popular religions worldwide (i.e., the above list of sixteen minus Baha'is, Confucianists, Shintoists, and Taoists), with all the others accounted for under "Other." In the tables showing ecclesiastical breakdown, all Christians are counted in one of the seven categories (or, in cases of double counting, in more than one category). The tables of religion and of Christianity report country by country all adherents of a religious position or Christian grouping that total at least 0.1 percent of the population. In addition, all tables present totals for the major area as a whole, as well as for each region that U.N. statistics distinguish within the major area. (The tables accompanying "Africa," for example, show totals for the whole continent; for the regions of eastern, middle, northern, southern, and western Africa; and also for each country that has a separate article in the *EC*.) Finally, for purposes of comparison, relevant figures for the whole world appear as the top row of each major area table.

CROSS-REFERENCES

A variety of cross-references aid the reader in locating articles or specific sections of articles. One type appears as a main title, either (1) making clear where a subject is treated or (2) indicating the exact article title. For example:

(1) **Aid** → Christian Development Services; Development 1.4

Anathema → Confessions and Creeds

(2) **Ancient Church** → Early Church

Ancient Oriental Churches → Oriental Orthodox Churches

Other cross-references appear within the text of articles. Those referring to other sections of the present article have the form "(see 1)," "(see 3.2)."

Cross-references to other articles cited as such appear (3) within parentheses in the text, following a cross-reference arrow and using the exact spelling and capitalization of the article title, and (4) on a separate line after the text proper and before the bibliography. In both cases, multiple cross-references are separated by semicolons, and only a single, initial arrow is used. Items cross-referenced within the text of an article normally do not also appear following the text of the article.

(3) In the latter part of the 20th century some churches in the United States and Europe have tried to revive the right of church asylum for some refugees whom the government refused to recognize as political refugees (→ Sanctuary 1; Resistance, Right of, 2).

As such, dance rejects an antibiblical dualism (→ Anthropology 2.3 and 3.2; Soul).

The Roman Catholic Church reacted negatively, placing Beccaria's book on the Index (→ Censorship; Inquisition 2). Then in the 19th century F. D. E. Schleiermacher (1768-1834; → Schleiermacher's Theology) criticized theologically the theory of retribution.

(4) → Anglican Communion 4; Clergy and Laity; Consensus 4; Councils of the Church

→ Catholicism (Roman); Church 3.2; Lay Movements

→ Communities, Spiritual; Ethics 2; Monasticism 3.2.2; Property, esp. 3.2-3

Finally (5), cross-references also appear within the flow of the text, with an arrow appearing before a word or phrase that points clearly (but not necessarily exactly) to the title of another article. Specific sections referred to are indicated by section marks and numbers in parentheses. Normally (6), the exact name of an article is used if a specific section is cited.

(5) The extension of the problem to political matters makes it necessary to define the relations between the obedience of → faith (§3), → freedom (§2), and → reason.

In the controversy with the → Pelagians Augustine's main concern was to show that grace is not limited to external aids like the → law (§§3.1-2) or the teaching and example of Christ.

Jewish → proselyte baptism incorporates the baptized not only into the religious fellowship but also into God's → covenant → people. This matter is relevant in the dialogue between Israel and the → church (§§1.4.1.3, 2.1, 5.5.3).

(6) . . . the 19th-century → apocalyptic movement in the United States.

vs. . . . the 19th-century apocalyptic movement (→ Apocalypticism 3) in the United States.

BIBLIOGRAPHIES

Within a bibliography (or separate section of a bibliography), entries are ordered first by author, then by title (disregarding an initial article in any language). Successive articles by the same author(s) are separated by semicolons.

In individual bibliographic entries, the names of series are included only if the title is omitted (typically only for biblical commentaries). For works appearing both in a non-English language and in English translation, normally only the English title is cited.

Consulting Editors

Ulrich Becker *Education*
Eugene L. Brand *Liturgy; Worship*
Faith E. Burgess *Women's Studies/Issues*
Carsten Colpe *Religious Studies*
Hans-Werner Gensichen *Asia; Mission Studies*
Martin Greschat *Biographies; Church History*
Heimo Hofmeister *Philosophy*
Hubertus G. Hubbeling† *Philosophy*
Anastasios Kallis *Orthodoxy*
Leo Laeyendecker *Sociology*

Ekkehard Mühlenberg *Church History*
Hans-Jürgen Prien *Latin America*
Dietrich Ritschl *Systematic Theology; Ethics*
Jürgen Roloff *New Testament*
Joachim Scharfenberg† *Practical Theology; Psychology*
Traugott Schöfthaler *Sociology*
Rudolf Smend *Old Testament*
Albert Stein *Law; Church Law*

Contributors

Gottfried Adam, *Würzburg, Ger.*
Confirmation
Samuel Akle, *Paris*
Benin
Barbara Aland, *Münster, Ger.*
Bible Versions
Christoph Albrecht, *Berlin*
Bells; Cantata; Canticle; Choir
Horst Albrecht, *Preetz, Ger.*
Congregation 2
Ruth Albrecht, *Hamburg*
Anchorites; Basilian Monks
Fritz Erich Anhelm, *Rehburg-Loccum, Ger.*
Church Conference Centers 3
Marianne Awerbuch, *Berlin*
Anti-Semitism, Anti-Judaism

S. J. Kenneth Baker†, *Bradford, Eng.*
Comoros
Heinrich Balz, *Berlin*
Acculturation
Josep M. Barnadas, *Cochabamba, Bol.*
Bolivia
James Barr, *Oxford*
Biblical Theology 1
Paul Bassett, *Kansas City, Mo.*
Church of the Nazarene
Gaetano Benedetti, *Basel, Switz.*
Despair
Hans Dieter Betz, *Chicago*
Corinthians, Epistles to the
Ana María Bidegain de Urán, *Bogotá, Col.*
Colombia

WOLFGANG A. BIENERT, *Marburg, Ger.*
Benedictines; Cluny, Order of

KARL-HEINRICH BIERITZ, *Rostock, Ger.*
Communication 5

MANFRED BIERSACK, *Vechelde, Ger.*
Cuius regio eius religio

HELMUT BINTZ, *Bad Boll, Ger.*
Devotional Literature 3

KLAUS BLASCHKE, *Kiel, Ger.*
Church Finances 1

KLAUSPETER BLASER, *Lausanne, Switz.*
Culture and Christianity

EDITH L. BLUMHOFER, *Chicago*
Assemblies of God

OTTO BÖCHER, *Mainz, Ger.*
Disciple

HANS JOCHEN BOECKER, *Wuppertal, Ger.*
Book of the Covenant; Decalogue

RICHARD BOECKLER, *Stuttgart, Ger.*
Diakonia

HANS-KURT BOEHLKE, *Kassel, Ger.*
Cemetery

COENRAAD M. BOERMA, *Geneva*
Development Education

ALBERTO BONDOLFI, *Zurich*
Death Penalty

H. R. BOUDIN, *Brussels, Belg.*
Belgium

HERMANN BOVENTER, *Bergisch Gladbach, Ger.*
Church Conference Centers 1-2

FRANÇOIS BOVON, *Cambridge, Mass.*
Ascension of Christ

PAUL BOYER, *Madison, Wis.*
Apocalypticism 4.5

HUGO BRANDENBURG, *Appelhülsen, Ger.*
Catacombs

EGON BRANDENBURGER, *Schlangenbad, Ger.*
Anthropology 2

HANNS CHRISTOF BRENNECKE, *Erlangen, Ger.*
Arianism

BEATUS BRENNER, *Bensheim, Ger.*
Bonifatiuswerk

GEOFFREY W. BROMILEY, *Santa Barbara, Calif.*
Cranmer, Thomas

MICHAEL VON BRÜCK, *Munich*
Caste

WALTER L. BÜHL, *Munich*
Culture 5

JAN-ADOLF BÜHNER, *Ravensburg, Ger.*
Angel 1

WOLF-DIETRICH BUKOW, *Cologne*
Anarchy

EBERHARD BUSCH, *Göttingen, Ger.*
Barmen Declaration; Barth, Karl; Confessing
Church; Darmstadt Declaration

GOTTFRIED BUTTLER, *Darmstadt, Ger.*
Continuing Education

JAMES R. BUTTS, *Sonoma, Calif.*
Agrapha

ALASTAIR V. CAMPBELL, *Dunedin, N.Z.*
Confession of Sins

FRANCINE CARDMAN, *Cambridge, Mass.*
Cyprian of Carthage

SUSANNA BEDE CAROSELLI, O.S.S.G., *Grantham, Pa.*
Christian Art 1-9

J. DAVID CASSEL, *Hanover, Ind.*
Cyril of Alexandria

KEITH W. CLEMENTS, *Bristol, Eng.*
Congregationalism 2

CARSTEN COLPE, *Berlin*
Afghanistan; Ānanda Mārga; Animism;
Bhagwan Shree Rajneesh; Cao Dai; Cyprus;
Devil; Divine Light Mission

JAMES H. CONE, *New York*
Black Theology

JAMES L. CRENSHAW, *Durham, N.C.*
Creation 2

JONAS N. DAH, *Buea, Camer.*
Cameroon

KARL-FRITZ DAIBER, *Hannover, Ger.*
Anonymity; Custom

ERNST DAMMANN, *Pinneberg, Ger.*
Africa

JOSEPH DAN, *Jerusalem*
Cabala

J. G. DAVIES†, *Birmingham, Eng.*
Altar; Dance

RICHARD R. DE RIDDER, *Pasadena, Calif.*
Church Discipline 3

VOLKMAR DEILE, *Bonn*
Conference of European Churches

KLAUS DEPPERMANN†, *Freiburg, Ger.*
Apocalypticism 4.1-4

ERIKA DINKLER–VON SCHUBERT, *Heidelberg, Ger.*
Cross

HEINRICH DÖRING, *Munich*
Christology 4; Church 3.2

BERND T. DRÖSSLER, *Erfurt, Ger.*
Consecration; Constitution

DONALD F. DURNBAUGH, *Elizabethtown, Pa.*
Brethren Churches; Church 3.6

KARL W. ECKERMANN, O.E.S.A., *Vechta, Ger.*
Augustinians

OSWALD EGGENBERGER, *Zurich*
Apostolic Churches; Christian Science

CONTRIBUTORS

HEINER GROTE†, *Bensheim, Ger.*
  Abbot, Abbess; Bulls and Briefs; Cardinal;
  Dimissorial; Diocese
WOLFGANG GRÜNBERG, *Hamburg*
  City 3; Congregation 2
DIETER GRUNOW, *Mülheim, Ger.*
  Bureaucracy
GUSTAVO GUIZZARDI, *Padua, It.*
  Class and Social Stratum
COLIN E. GUNTON, *London*
  Atonement 3
ROBIN GURNEY, *Geneva*
  Conference of European Churches
VIGEN GUROIAN, *Baltimore*
  Armenia
HANS HAFERKAMP†, *Bremen, Ger.*
  Achievement and Competition
ROBERT HANHART, *Göttingen, Ger.*
  Apocrypha 1; Daniel, Book of
YAP KIM HAO, *Singapore*
  Christian Conference of Asia
GUNNAR HASSELBLATT†, *Berlin*
  Djibouti
JENS HAUSTEIN, *Jena, Ger.*
  Dance Macabre
ROBERT D. HAWKINS, *Columbia, S.C.*
  Church Music; Church Musicians
FRIEDEMANN HEBART, *Bayreuth, Ger.*
  Australia
HANS-GÜNTER HEIMBROCK, *Frankfurt*
  Creativity
MARTIN HEIN, *Kassel, Ger.*
  Bishop, Episcopate 1-4
WOLFGANG HEIN, *Hamburg*
  Dependence
HERIBERT HEINEMANN, *Bochum, Ger.*
  Canon Law; Codex Iuris Canonici 1-3; Curia
KLAUSJÜRGEN HEINRICH, *Vienna*
  Blessing 1-6
HEINZ JOACHIM HELD, *Hannover, Ger.*
  Argentina
JOAN M. H. J. HEMELS, *Malden, Neth.*
  Communication 1-4
REINHARD HEMPELMANN, *Berlin*
  Christadelphians
PATRICK HENRY, *Collegeville, Minn.*
  Benedict of Nursia
ALASDAIR I. C. HERON, *Erlangen, Ger.*
  Arminianism; Calvinism; Canon 3; Church 3.5;
  Covenant 3; Descent into Hell
NICOLAUS C. HEUTGER, *Hannover, Ger.*
  Cistercians

JOHN F. HINNEBUSCH, O.P., *Washington, D.C.*
  Dominic
OSKAR VON HINÜBER, *Freiburg, Ger.*
  Bhagavad Gita; Bhakti; Buddhism
NORMAN A. HJELM, *Wynnewood, Pa.*
  Christian Communication; Christian Publishing
PETER HOCKEN, *Northampton, Eng.*
  Charismatic Movement
ERIKA M. HOERNING, *Berlin*
  Biography, Biographical Research
HEIMO HOFMEISTER, *Heidelberg, Ger.*
  Analytic Philosophy; Anthropology 4;
  Categorical Imperative
KARL HOHEISEL, *Bonn*
  Alchemy; Anthroposophy; Astrology
GÜNTER HOLE, *Ravensburg, Ger.*
  Depression
TRAUGOTT HOLTZ, *Halle, Ger.*
  Christological Titles
ANTON G. HONIG, *Kampen, Neth.*
  Dutch Missions
GÜNTER HOPPE, *Bad Honnef, Ger.*
  Development 2
FRIEDRICH WILHELM HORN, *Mainz, Ger.*
  Creation 3.1-4
HUBERTUS G. HUBBELING†, *Groningen, Neth.*
  Aesthetics; Aporia; Axiom; Dialectic;
  Dogmatism 1
BRITTA HÜBENER, *Mannheim, Ger.*
  Beguines
WOLFGANG HUBER, *Berlin*
  Church and State 2; Conscience 2
HANS HÜBNER, *Göttingen, Ger.*
  Covenant 2; Demythologizing
MELVIN D. HUGEN, *Grand Rapids*
  Counseling 5
DAVID G. HUNTER, *St. Paul, Minn.*
  Chrysostom, John
PETER HUNZIKER, *Basel, Switz.*
  Consumption
HEINZ HUSSLIK, *Vienna*
  Categories
DOUGLAS JACOBSEN, *Grantham, Pa.*
  Civil Rights Movement
BERND JANOWSKI, *Tübingen, Ger.*
  Atonement 1
RANDAL M. JELKS, *Grand Rapids*
  Black Churches 1
PAUL JENKINS, *Basel, Switz.*
  Cape Verde
JACOB JERVELL, *Årnes, Nor.*
  Acts of the Apostles; Adam

CONTRIBUTORS

E. C. JOHN, *Bangalore, India*
Church of South India

MANFRED JOSUTTIS, *Göttingen, Ger.*
Dogmatism 2

FRANK OTFRIED JULY, *Stuttgart, Ger.*
Agnosticism

HANS-GERNOT JUNG†, *Kassel, Ger.*
Bishop, Episcopate 1-4

ANASTASIOS KALLIS, *Münster, Ger.*
Anaphora; Christology 3

ANDREAS KARRER, *Tutzing, Ger.*
Conciliarity

MARTIN KARRER, *Wuppertal, Ger.*
Anointing 2; Antichrist; Apostle, Apostolate

HANS-BERNHARD KAUFMANN, *Münster, Ger.*
Christian Education

THOMAS KAUFMANN, *Munich*
Bucer, Martin; Calvin, John

WERNER KELLER, *Cologne*
Classicism

OTTO KIMMINICH, *Regensburg, Ger.*
Asylum

LOUIS L. KING, *Nyack, N.Y.*
Christian and Missionary Alliance

JACK DEAN KINGSBURY, *Richmond, Va.*
Beatitudes

HANS G. KIPPENBERG, *Bremen, Ger.*
Apocalypticism 1; Dualism

HUBERT KIRCHNER, *Berlin*
Creed of Pius IV

STEFFEN KJELDGAARD-PEDERSEN, *Copenhagen*
Antinomian Controversies; Crypto-Calvinism

VERENA KLEMM, *Hamburg*
Baha'i

DAVID W. KLING, *Coral Gables, Fla.*
Beecher, Lyman

HINRICH KNITTERMEYER†, *Bremen, Ger.*
Aristotelianism 1

KLAUS KOCH, *Hamburg*
Apocalypticism 2-3

MARTIN KOSCHORKE, *Berlin*
Abortion 2; Abortion Counseling

BEATE KÖSTER, *Münster, Ger.*
Bible Manuscripts and Editions 3

ULRICH KÜHN, *Leipzig, Ger.*
Church 3.4

FRANK KÜRSCHNER, *Hamburg*
Angola

ULI KUTTER, *Göttingen, Ger.*
Carnival 3

PETER KUZMIČ, *Osijek, Croatia*
Bosnia and Herzegovina; Croatia

AUGOUSTINOS LABARDAKIS, *Bonn*
Church Growth 3.2

LEO LAEYENDECKER, *Bunnik, Neth.*
Denomination 6

GARY LAND, *Berrien Springs, Mich.*
Adventists

PETER LANDAU, *Munich*
Corpus Iuris Canonici

GEORG LANGGÄRTNER†, *Würzburg, Ger.*
All Saints' Day

WALTER L. LARIMORE, M.D., *Kissimmee, Fla.*
Birth Control

SUNG-HEE LEE-LINKE, *Mühlheim an der Ruhr, Ger.*
Abortion 1

MARTIN LEINER, *Mainz, Ger.*
Depth-Psychological Exegesis

JOACHIM LELL†, *Bensheim, Ger.*
Arnoldshain Conference

ANZA A. LEMA, *Dar es Salaam, Tanzania*
Burundi

BILL J. LEONARD, *Winston-Salem, N.C.*
Baptism 3; Baptistery

HERMANN LICHTENBERGER, *Münster, Ger.*
Apocrypha 2

WOLFGANG LIENEMANN, *Bern, Switz.*
Disarmament and Armament 2

ANDREAS LINDEMANN, *Bielefeld, Ger.*
Colossians, Epistle to the

FRIEDRICH-WILHELM LINDEMANN, *Berlin*
Counseling Centers, Christian

POUL GEORG LINDHARDT, *Skødstrup, Den.*
Denmark

CHRISTOPH LINK, *Erlangen, Ger.*
Church Government 5.1; Collegialism

JAN MILIČ LOCHMAN, *Basel, Switz.*
Apocatastasis; Apostles' Creed 1-3; Assurance of
Salvation 1-2; Atheism

PAUL LÖFFLER, *Lębork, Pol.*
Conversion 1

ARCHBISHOP LONGIN, *Düsseldorf, Ger.*
Cherubicon; Diptych

BRIGITTE LUCHESI, *Berlin*
Bangladesh; Bhutan

ULRICH LUZ, *Bern, Switz.*
Christology 1

WILLIAM McKANE, *St. Andrews, Scot.*
Abraham

ELSIE ANNE McKEE, *Princeton*
Deacon, Deaconess

INGE MAGER, *Hamburg*
Corpora doctrinae

MANFRED MARQUARDT, *Reutlingen, Ger.*
Assurance of Salvation 3

HEINER MARRÉ, *Essen, Ger.*
Church Finances 2

PETER MASER, *Münster, Ger.*
Cathedral; Choir Stalls; Christian Art 10-11

ALBERT MAUDER†, *Bad Kleinkirchheim, Aus.*
Doxology

GERHARD MAY, *Mainz, Ger.*
Athanasian Creed; Augsburg Confession;
Augsburg, Peace of

HELMUT MAYER, *Munich*
Doubt 1

HANS MAYR, *Esslingen, Ger.*
Communities, Spiritual

JOHN MBITI, *Burgdorf, Switz.*
All Africa Conference of Churches; Biblical
Theology 2.3; Burkina Faso

EGINHARD P. MEIJERING, *Oegstgeest, Neth.*
Apostles' Creed 4; Dogma, History of

GUILLERMO MELÉNDEZ, *San José, C.R.*
Costa Rica

UTE MENNECKE-HAUSTEIN, *Jena, Ger.*
Devotional Literature 1-2

OTTO MERK, *Erlangen, Ger.*
Canon 2

FRIEDEMANN MERKEL, *Münster, Ger.*
Church Dedication; Devotion, Devotions

HELMUT MERKEL, *Osnabrück, Ger.*
Charisma 1

BRUCE M. METZGER, *Princeton*
Bible Manuscripts and Editions 2

JÖRG METZINGER, *Mainz, Ger.*
Cathedral

JOSEF METZLER, O.M.I., *Rome*
Catholic Missions

HARDING MEYER, *Strasbourg, Fr.*
Christian World Communions

MANFRED MIDDENDORF, *Münster, Ger.*
Action Theory

CHRISTIANE MÖHLE-KÖHNKEN, *Kiel, Ger.*
Behavior, Behavioral Psychology

HUBERT MOHR, *Tübingen, Ger.*
Divination 1-3

CHRISTIAN MÖLLER, *Heidelberg, Ger.*
Church Growth 1.1

SABINE MÖLLERS, *Mainz, Ger.*
Crypt

AMEDEO MOLNÁR†, *Prague*
Bohemian Brethren

CHRISTOPH MORGENTHALER, *Muri (Bern), Switz.*
Dream

PAUL C. E. MORRIS, *London*
Church Discipline 4

DIETZ-RÜDIGER MOSER, *Munich*
Carnival 1-2

MICHAEL MOXTER, *Frankfurt*
Cynicism

EKKEHARD MÜHLENBERG, *Göttingen, Ger.*
Apologists; Catena; Chapel; Christology 2;
Docetism

KAREN L. MULDER, *Jackson, Tenn.*
Christian Art 12

GERHARD MÜLLER, *Erlangen, Ger.*
Confessions and Creeds 1-2

RICHARD A. MULLER, *Grand Rapids*
Beza, Theodore

RUDOLF WOLFGANG MÜLLER, *Hannover, Ger.*
Capitalism

HUBERTUS MYNAREK, *Odernheim, Ger.*
Christian Community, The

LUDWIG NAGL, *Vienna*
Critical Theory

WOLF-DIETER NARR, *Berlin*
Democracy 1-2

KARL NEUMANN, *Göttingen, Ger.*
Childhood

WILHELM H. NEUSER, *Ostbevern, Ger.*
Basel Confession; Calvin's Theology

WOLFGANG NIKOLAUS, *Vienna*
Cartesianism; Conscience 1

OTHMAR NOGGLER, O.F.M., *Munich*
Cuba

PEDER NØRGAARD-HØJEN, *Nivå, Den.*
Codex Iuris Canonici 4

FREDERICK W. NORRIS, *Johnson City, Tenn.*
Athanasius

GERARD O'DALY, *London*
Augustine's Theology

HEINRICH OTT, *Riehen, Switz.*
Dialogue 2

JOHN W. PADBERG, S.J., *St. Louis, Mo.*
Bellarmine, Robert

CHRISTOPHOROS PAPAKONSTANTINOU, *Münster,
Ger.*
Athos; Autocephaly

DAMASKINOS PAPANDREOU, *Geneva*
Church 3.1

ALEXANDER PATSCHOVSKY, *Constance, Ger.*
Cathari

HENNING PAULSEN†, *Hamburg*
Apostolic Fathers

CLIFFORD PAYNE, *Geneva*
Caribbean Conference of Churches

HANS PEETERS, *Bathmen, Neth.*
Bourgeois, Bourgeoisie 1-3

CONTRIBUTORS

LOTHAR PERLITT, *Göttingen, Ger.*
Covenant 1; Deuteronomy, Book of

URS PESCHLOW, *Göttingen, Ger.*
Baptistery; Basilica

ALBRECHT PETERS†, *Ziegelhausen, Ger.*
Dogma

STEPHAN H. PFÜRTNER, *Marburg, Ger.*
Celibacy of the Clergy

RICHARD V. PIERARD, *Terre Haute, Ind.*
Church Struggle; Civil Religion

DIETRICH PIRSON, *Munich*
Church Law 1-5

PETER PLANK, *Würzburg, Ger.*
Acathistus; Archimandrite; Catholicos

MICHAEL PLATHOW, *Heidelberg, Ger.*
Church Membership 1

JÜRGEN-ECKARDT PLEINES, *Karlsruhe, Ger.*
Chance

ROLF J. PÖHLER, *Stuttgart, Ger.*
Adventists

HORST G. PÖHLMANN, *Wallenhorst, Ger.*
Apologetics

HANS-JÜRGEN PRIEN, *Cologne*
Assembleias de Deus no Brasil; Brazil; Costa
Rica

HANS-JÜRGEN PUHLE, *Frankfurt*
Conservatism 1

KARLHEINZ REBEL, *Rottenburg am Neckar, Ger.*
Distance Education

HANS-DIETHER REIMER†, *Stuttgart, Ger.*
Adventists

GUSTAV REINGRABNER, *Vienna*
Austria

JOHANNES RENGER, *Berlin*
Babylonian and Assyrian Religion

KARL RENNSTICH, *Bad Urach, Ger.*
Corruption

HENNING GRAF REVENTLOW, *Bochum, Ger.*
Dietary Laws

ERROLL F. RHODES, *New York*
Bible Manuscripts and Editions 1-2; Bible
Societies; Bible Versions

HERMANN RIESS†, *Korntal, Ger.*
Diaspora

JOHN B. RIJSMAN, *Tilburg, Neth.*
Cognition

GUENTHER C. RIMBACH, *Riverside, Calif.*
Baroque

JOACHIM RINGLEBEN, *Göttingen, Ger.*
Culture Protestantism

DIETRICH RITSCHL, *Heidelberg, Ger.*
Act; Aggression; Anthropology, Overview, 3;
Anxiety; Apostasy; Authority; Autogenic
Training; Biblicism; Christology, Overview, 5-6;
Conflict; Congregation 4; Counseling 1-4

ADOLF MARTIN RITTER, *Heidelberg, Ger.*
Chalcedon, Council of; Church 2.2

ANTJE ROGGENKAMP-KAUFMANN, *Munich*
Catherine of Siena

WOLFGANG G. RÖHL, *Stuttgart, Ger.*
Demons

JAN ROHLS, *Munich*
Confessions and Creeds 3

JÜRGEN ROLOFF, *Erlangen, Ger.*
Catholic Epistles; Church 2.1; Church
Government 1; Congregation 1

HELMUT ROSCHER, *Hamburg*
Crusades

JEAN-PAUL ROULEAU, *Quebec*
Congregation 3

GEOFFREY ROWELL, *Oxford*
Church 3.3

ENNO RUDOLPH, *Heidelberg, Ger.*
Causality

ARNDT RUPRECHT, *Göttingen, Ger.*
Christian Publishing

TODOR SABEV, *Geneva*
Bulgaria

DIETER SACKMANN, *Reutlingen, Ger.*
Church Growth 1.2

DIETRICH SATTLER, *Hamburg*
Christian Communication

GERHARD SAUTER, *St. Augustine, Ger.*
Dialectical Theology

WALTER SAWATSKY, *Elkhart, Ind.*
Belarus

ANGELIKA SCHADE, *Frankfurt*
Achievement and Competition

PETER SCHÄFER, *Berlin*
Circumcision

BERNHARD SCHÄFERS, *Karlsruhe, Ger.*
City 2

JOACHIM SCHARFENBERG†, *Kiel, Ger.*
Commune

RAINER SCHERSCHEL, *Trier, Ger.*
Ave Maria

JOHANNES SCHILLING, *Kiel, Ger.*
Altötting; Catechismus Romanus; Devotional
Images; Discalced Friars; Donation of
Constantine

PAUL SCHMIDLE, *Freiburg, Ger.*
Charity

GABRIELE SCHMIDT, *Düsseldorf, Ger.*
Buddhism and Christianity

GÜNTER R. SCHMIDT, *Erlangen, Ger.*
Didactics

WERNER H. SCHMIDT, *Bonn*
Anthropology 1

HANS-CHRISTOPH SCHMIDT-LAUBER, *Vienna*
Benediction; Days of Prayer and Repentance

HANS SCHNEIDER, *Marburg, Ger.*
Antimodernist Oath; Bible Societies;
Conciliarism; Councils of the Church

CHRISTOPH SCHNEIDER-HARPPRECHT, *São
Leopoldo, Braz.*
Consolation, Comfort

UDO SCHNELLE, *Halle, Ger.*
Baptism 1

THADDEUS A. SCHNITKER, *Münster, Ger.*
Acclamation; Alpha and Omega; Amen;
Blessing 7; Book of Common Prayer; Dove

WOLFGANG SCHOBERTH, *Bayreuth, Ger.*
Death; Doubt 2

ULRICH SCHOENBORN, *Marburg, Ger.*
Biblical Theology 2.5

TRAUGOTT SCHÖFTHALER, *Bonn*
Anthropology 5

HANS-MICHAEL SCHOOF, *Birkenfeld, Ger.*
Botswana

WALTER SCHÖPSDAU, *Bensheim, Ger.*
Catholic Action; Conversion 2

LUISE SCHOTTROFF, *Kassel, Ger.*
Biblical Theology 2.6

WILLY SCHOTTROFF†, *Kassel, Ger.*
Curse

LOTHAR SCHREINER, *Wuppertal, Ger.*
Contextual Theology

OSMUND SCHREUDER, *Nijmegen, Neth.*
Bourgeois, Bourgeoisie 4

GREGORY SCHUFREIDER, *Baton Rouge, La.*
Anselm

FRIEDER SCHULZ, *Heidelberg, Ger.*
Church Year

EDUARD SCHÜTZ, *Hamburg*
Baptist World Alliance; Baptists

WERNER SCHWARTZ, *Frankenthal, Ger.*
Allegory; Analytic Ethics; Antinomy; Casuistry;
Deontology; Duty

FRIEDRICH SCHWEITZER, *Tübingen, Ger.*
Development 3

ECKART SCHWERIN, *Schwerin, Ger.*
Catechist

THEODOR SEIFERT, *Wimsheim, Ger.*
Archetype

ALF SEIPPEL, *Dortmund, Ger.*
Community Service

FRANK C. SENN, *Evanston, Ill.*
Christmas

RUDOLF SMEND, *Göttingen, Ger.*
Bible Manuscripts and Editions 1; Canon 1;
Deuteronomistic History

HERIBERT SMOLINSKY, *Freiburg, Ger.*
Catholic Reform and Counterreformation

STEPHEN R. SPENCER, *Dallas*
Dispensationalism

HERMANN SPIECKERMANN, *Hamburg*
Anointing 1; Arameans

ANNELIESE SPRENGLER-RUPPENTHAL, *Hamburg*
Church Orders; Church Registers

REINHART STAATS, *Kiel, Ger.*
Acoemetae; Asceticism

PAUL STADLER, *St. Gallen, Switz.*
Central African Republic; Chad

JOSEPH B. STANFORD, M.D., *Salt Lake City*
Birth Control

PETER STAPLES, *Utrecht, Neth.*
Anglican Communion

EKKEHARD STARKE, *Duisburg, Ger.*
Animals; Despair; Discipleship 2

ALBERT STEIN, *Brühl, Ger.*
Baptism 5; Clergy and Laity; Delegation;
Dispensation

JÜRGEN STEIN, *Bremen, Ger.*
Compromise

HERMANN STEINKAMP, *Münster, Ger.*
Adulthood; Base Community

MARTIN STÖHR, *Siegen, Ger.*
Church in a Socialist Society

FRITZ STOLZ, *Männedorf, Switz.*
Ark of the Covenant

GEORG STRECKER†, *Göttingen, Ger.*
Discipleship 1

THEODOR STROHM, *Heidelberg, Ger.*
Democracy 3

GERLINDE STROHMAIER-WIEDERANDERS, *Berlin*
Baptismal Font

PETER STUHLMACHER, *Tübingen, Ger.*
Atonement 2

JOSEF SUDBRACK, *Munich*
Contemplation

GIANFRANCO TELLINI, *Edinburgh*
Confession of Sins

EUGENE TESELLE, *Nashville*
Augustine

WERNER THIEDE, *Berlin*
Church of Scientology

WINFRIED THIEL, *Bochum, Ger.*
Amos, Book of

NIKOLAUS THON, *Bochum, Ger.*
Church Government 4; Church Membership 2

EDWARD E. THORNTON, *Louisville, Ky.*
Clinical Pastoral Education

MADY A. THUNG, *Dreiberger-Rijsenburg, Neth.*
Church 4

PETER VON TILING, *Hannover, Ger.*
Church Law 6

BERNHARD TÖNNES, *Bergisch Gladbach, Ger.*
Albania

KÁROLY TÓTH, *Budapest*
Christian Peace Conference

HANS G. ULRICH, *Erlangen, Ger.*
Adiaphora; Confession of Faith

KARL-HEINZ UTHEMANN, *Munich*
Byzantium

CHARLES VAN ENGEN, *Pasadena, Calif.*
Church Growth 2.1-2, 5

HOWARD J. VAN TILL, *Grand Rapids*
Creationism

A. J. VANDERJAGT, *Groningen, Neth.*
Aristotelianism 2

MARLIN VANELDEREN, *Geneva*
Bishop, Episcopate 5

HANS VAN DE VEEN, *Amsterdam*
Child Labor

TIMO VEIJOLA, *Helsinki, Fin.*
David

MARIE VEIT, *Marburg, Ger.*
Christians for Socialism

RUURD VELDHUIS, *Groningen, Neth.*
Absolute, The; Deism; Dialogue 1

HANS VÖCKING, *Frankfurt*
Algeria

THEOPHIL VOGT, *Zollikerberg, Switz.*
Bible Study

RAINER VOLP, *Mainz, Ger.*
Cathedral; Church Architecture

JACQUES D. J. WAARDENBURG, *Lausanne, Switz.*
Cultic Meal; Cultic Purity

FALK WAGNER, *Vienna*
Analogy

RUDOLF G. WAGNER, *Heidelberg, Ger.*
Charismatic Religion; China; Confucianism

GEOFFREY WAINWRIGHT, *Durham, N.C.*
Baptism 2

HANS WALDENFELS, *Bonn*
Buddhism and Christianity

ROY WALLIS, *Belfast, N.Ire.*
Charisma 2

ANDREW F. WALLS, *Edinburgh*
British Missions; China Inland Mission

W. REGINALD WARD, *Durham, Eng.*
Dissenters

DAVID LOWES WATSON, *Nashville*
Church Growth 4

HANS-RUEDI WEBER, *Tentena, Indon.*
Church Growth 2.1

HERMANN WEBER, *Frankfurt*
Censorship; Censures; Church and State 1

PAUL WEE, *Geneva*
Commission of the Churches on International
Affairs

KLAUS WEGENAST, *Bern, Switz.*
Catechesis; Catechism

ALFONS WEISER, *Vallendar, Ger.*
Community of Goods

DOROTHEA WENDEBOURG, *Tübingen, Ger.*
Cappadocian Fathers

GUNTHER WENZ, *Munich*
Anti-Trinitarianism

ULRICH WICKERT, *Berlin*
Alexandria; Alexandrian Theology; Antioch;
Antiochian Theology

THOMAS WILLI, *Greifswald, Ger.*
Chronicles, Books of

GLEN G. WILLIAMS†, *Geneva*
Conference of European Churches

EBERHARD WINKLER, *Halle, Ger.*
Church Growth 3.1

WILLIAM L. WIPFLER, *New York*
Dominican Republic

WOLFGANG WISCHMEYER, *Mühlacker, Ger.*
Archaeology 2

DIETMAR WYRWA, *Berlin*
Donatists

SEIICHI YAGI, *Tokyo*
Biblical Theology 2.4

CHRISTOS YANNARAS, *Athens*
Apophatic Theology

HERBERT ZDARZIL, *Vienna*
Culture 1-3

WALTHER C. ZIMMERLI, *Brunswick, Ger.*
Criticism

HARTMUT ZINSER, *Berlin*
Dead, Cult of the

Abbreviations

Abbreviations generally follow those given in the *Journal of Biblical Literature* "Instructions for Contributors." For those not listed there, the abbreviations in the second edition of S. M. Schwertner's *Internationales Abkürzungsverzeichnis für Theologie und Grenzgebiete* (Berlin, 1992) are used; for works of theology or related fields not listed in either source, new abbreviations have been formed.

Writings listed below under the section "Early Church Writings" include those of writers through Augustine.

BIBLICAL BOOKS, WITH THE APOCRYPHA

Gen.	Genesis	Hab.	Habakkuk
Exod.	Exodus	Zeph.	Zephaniah
Lev.	Leviticus	Hag.	Haggai
Num.	Numbers	Zech.	Zechariah
Deut.	Deuteronomy	Mal.	Malachi
Josh.	Joshua		
Judg.	Judges	Add. Est.	Additions to Esther
Ruth	Ruth	Bar.	Baruch
1-2 Sam.	1-2 Samuel	Bel	Bel and the Dragon
1-2 Kgs.	1-2 Kings	Ep. Jer.	Epistle of Jeremiah
1-2-3-4 Kgdms.	1-2-3-4 Kingdoms	1-2 Esdr.	1-2 Esdras
1-2 Chr.	1-2 Chronicles	4 Ezra	4 Ezra
Ezra	Ezra	Jdt.	Judith
Neh.	Nehemiah	1-2-3-4 Macc.	1-2-3-4 Maccabees
Esth.	Esther	Pr. Azar.	Prayer of Azariah
Job	Job	Pr. Man.	Prayer of Manasseh
Ps.	Psalms	Sir.	Sirach / Ecclesiasticus / Wisdom of Jesus, Son of Sirach
Prov.	Proverbs		
Eccl.	Ecclesiastes	Sus.	Susanna
Cant.	Canticles / Song of Solomon / Song of Songs	Tob.	Tobit
		Wis.	Wisdom of Solomon
Isa.	Isaiah		
Jer.	Jeremiah	Matt.	Matthew
Lam.	Lamentations	Mark	Mark
Ezek.	Ezekiel	Luke	Luke
Dan.	Daniel	John	John
Hos.	Hosea	Acts	Acts of the Apostles
Joel	Joel	Rom.	Romans
Amos	Amos	1-2 Cor.	1-2 Corinthians
Obad.	Obadiah	Gal.	Galatians
Jonah	Jonah	Eph.	Ephesians
Mic.	Micah	Phil.	Philippians
Nah.	Nahum	Col.	Colossians

ABBREVIATIONS

1-2 Thess.	1-2 Thessalonians	Jas.	James
1-2 Tim.	1-2 Timothy	1-2 Pet.	1-2 Peter
Titus	Titus	1-2-3 John	1-2-3 John
Phlm.	Philemon	Jude	Jude
Heb.	Hebrews	Rev.	Revelation

OLD TESTAMENT PSEUDEPIGRAPHA

2-3 Apoc. Bar.	Syriac, Greek *Apocalypse of Baruch*	Ep. Arist.	*Epistle of Aristeas*
		Jub.	*Jubilees*
Apoc. Mos.	*Apocalypse of Moses*	Pss. Sol.	*Psalms of Solomon*
1-2-3 Enoch	Ethiopic, Slavonic, Hebrew *Enoch*	T. Jud.	*Testament of Judah*

EARLY CHURCH WRITINGS, WITH NAG HAMMADI TRACTATES

Augustine
Conf.	*Confessions*
De bapt.	*De baptismo contra Donatistas*
De cat. rud.	*De catechizandis rudibus*
De lib. arb.	*De libero arbitrio*
De Trin.	*De Trinitatae libri quindecim*
Enarr. in Ps.	*Enarrationes in Psalmos*
In Evang. Iohan.	*In Evangelium Iohannis tractatus*
Barn.	*Barnabas*

Basil the Great
De Spir. S.	*De Spiritu Sancto*
Ep.	*Epistulae*
1-2 Clem.	*1-2 Clement*

Clement of Alexandria
Strom.	*Stromateis*

Cyprian of Carthage
De eccl.	*De ecclesiae catholicae unitate*
Ep.	*Epistulae*

Cyril of Jerusalem
Cat.	*Catecheses*
Dial. Sav.	*Dialogue of the Saviour*
Did.	*Didache*

Eusebius
Hist. eccl.	*Historia ecclesiastica*
Gos. Heb.	*Gospel of the Hebrews*
Gos. Pet.	*Gospel of Peter*
Gos. Phil.	*Gospel of Philip*
Gos. Thom.	*Gospel of Thomas*
Herm. Vis.	*Hermas, Vision(s)*

Hippolytus
Haer.	*Refutatio omnium haeresium*
Trad. apos.	*Traditio apostolica*

Ign. [Ignatius]
Eph.	*Letter to the Ephesians*
Magn.	*Letter to the Magnesians*
Phld.	*Letter to the Philadelphians*
Rom.	*Letter to the Romans*
Smyrn.	*Letter to the Smyrnaeans*
Trall.	*Letter to the Trallians*

Irenaeus
Adv. haer.	*Adversus omnes haereses*

Jerome
In Hiez. comm.	*In Hiezechihelem commentarii*

Justin Martyr
Apol.	*Apologia*
Dial.	*Dialogue with Trypho*

Marcellus of Ancyra
Frg.	*Fragments*

Origen
Comm. in Rom.	*Commentarii in Romanos*
In Exod. hom.	*In Exodum homiliae*
Sel. in Ezech.	*Selecta in Ezechielem*

Pol. [Polycarp]
Phil.	*Letter to the Philippians*

Rufinus, T.
De princ.	*De principiis*
Hist. eccl.	*Historia ecclesiastica*

Socrates Scholasticus
Hist. eccl.	*Historia ecclesiastica*

Tertullian
Adv. Marc.	*Adversus Marcionem*
De bapt.	*De baptismo*
De cor.	*De corona*
De praescr. haeret.	*De praescriptione haereticorum*
De res. car.	*De resurrectione carnis*

DEAD SEA SCROLLS AND RELATED TEXTS
("1Q" indicates a document found in Qumran Cave 1, etc.)

CD	Cairo (Genizah text of the) *Damascus (Document)*	1QSa	Appendix A *(Rule of the Congregation)* to 1QS
1QH	*Hôdāyôt (Thanksgiving Hymns)*	4Q243	Text no. 243 (see *Discoveries in the Judean Desert*) from Cave 4
1QIsaᵃ	First copy of Isaiah		
1QM	*Milḥāmāh (War Scroll)*	4QFlor	*Florilegium* (or *Eschatological Midrashim*)
1QpHab	*Pesher on Habakkuk*		
1QS	*Serek hayyaḥad (Rule of the Community, Manual of Discipline)*	4QPBless	*Patriarchal Blessings*
		11QPsᵃ	First copy of Psalms
		11QTemple	*Temple Scroll*

ORDERS AND TRACTATES IN MISHNAIC AND RELATED LITERATURE

b.	Babylonian Talmud	*Ned.*	*Nedarim*
m.	Mishnah	*Šabb.*	*Šabbat*
t.	Tosepta	*Sanh.*	*Sanhedrin*
'Abot	*'Abot*	*Yad.*	*Yadayim*
B. Bat.	*Baba Batra*		

OTHER RABBINIC WORKS

'Abot R. Nat.	*'Abot de Rabbi Nathan*	*Pesiq. R.*	*Pesiqta Rabbati*
Gen. Rab.	*Genesis Rabbah*	*Tg. Ps.-J.*	*Targum Pseudo-Jonathan*

OTHER ANCIENT, MEDIEVAL, AND EARLY MODERN WRITINGS

Abbo		Descartes, R.	
Ikk.	*Ikkarim*	*Med.*	*Meditationes de prima philosophia*
Apuleius			
Met.	*Metamorphoses*	Diogenes Laertius	
Aristotle		*Peri biōn*	*Peri biōn dogmatōn kai apophthegmatōn*
Cat.	*Categoriae*		
Eth. Nic.	*Ethica Nicomachea*	Firmicus Maternus	
Metaph.	*Metaphysica*	*Err. prof. rel.*	*De errore profanarum religionum*
Pol.	*Politica*	Hobbes, T.	
Top.	*Topica*	*De corp.*	*De corpore*
Augs. Conf.	Augsburg Confession	*De hom.*	*De homine*
Calvin, J.		Horace	
Inst.	*Institutes of the Christian Religion*	*Sat.*	*Satirae*
		Hume, D.	
Cano, M.		*Inquiry*	*An Inquiry concerning Human Understanding*
De locis theol.	*De locis theologicus*		
Cicero		Iamblichus	
De div.	*De divinatione*	*De vit. Pyth.*	*De vita Pythagorica*
Tusc.	*Tusculanae disputationes*	Isidore of Seville	
		Etym.	*Etymologies*

ABBREVIATIONS

John of Damascus		
Hom. transfig.	*Homilia in transfigurationem Domini*	

Josephus
Ag. Ap.	*Against Apion*
Ant.	*Jewish Antiquities*
J.W.	*Jewish War*

Juvenal
| *Sat.* | *Satirae* |

Livy
| *Annals* | *The Annals of the Roman People* |

Locke, J.
| *Essay* | *An Essay concerning Human Understanding* |

Maimonides, M.
| *More* | *More nevukhim* |

Melanchthon, P.
| *Treatise* | *Treatise on the Power and Primacy of the Pope* |

Ovid
| *Met.* | *Metamorphoses* |

Palamas, Gregory
| *Antirrh.* | *Contra Gregoram antirrhetici* |

Philo
| *De spec. leg.* | *De specialibus legibus* |

Plato
Phdr.	*Phaedrus*
Phlb.	*Philebus*
Plt.	*Politicus*
Resp.	*Respublica*
Ti.	*Timaeus*

Plutarch
| *De Is. et Os.* | *De Iside et Osiride* |

Pseudo-Dionysius
| *De eccl. hier.* | *De ecclesiastica hierarchia* |

| Schmalk. Art. | Schmalkald Articles |

Spinoza, B.
| *Tract. theol.-pol.* | *Tractatus theologico-politicus* |

Tacitus
| *Ann.* | *Annales* |

Thomas Aquinas
| *Summa c. Gent.* | *Summa contra Gentiles* |
| *Summa theol.* | *Summa theologiae* |

MODERN PUBLICATIONS AND EDITIONS

AA	I. Kant, *Gesammelte Schriften* (Berlin Akademie Ausgabe)
AAfN	*Annuaire de l'Afrique du Nord*
AAS	*Acta apostolicae sedis*
AB	Anchor Bible
ABD	*Anchor Bible Dictionary*
ABG	*Archiv für Begriffsgeschichte*
ACO	*Acta conciliorum oecumenicorum*
AcOr	*Acta orientalia*
ACQR	*American Catholic Quarterly Review*
ACW	Ancient Christian Writers
ADLR	*Abingdon Dictionary of Living Religions*
AEcR	*American Ecclesiastical Review*
AFP	*Archivum Fratrum Praedicatorum*
AHC	*Annuarium historiae conciliorum*
AHP	*Archivum historiae pontificiae*
AISIG	*Annali dell'Istituto Storico Italo-Germanico in Trento*
AJBI	*Annual of the Japanese Biblical Institute*
AKathKR	*Archiv für katholisches Kirchenrecht*
AKuG	*Archiv für Kulturgeschichte*
AmA	*American Anthropologist*
AnBoll	*Analecta Bollandiana*
ANET	*Ancient Near Eastern Texts*
ANRW	*Aufstieg und Niedergang der römischen Welt*

ARG	*Archiv für Reformationsgeschichte*
ARG.L	*ARG Beiheft: Literaturbericht*
ArPh	*Archives de philosophie*
ARSoc	*Annual Review of Sociology*
ARSSR	*Annual Review of the Social Sciences of Religion*
ARW	*Archiv für Religionswissenschaft*
ASR	*American Sociological Review*
ASSR	*Archives des sciences sociales des religions*
Aug(L)	*Augustiniana* (Louvain)
BEFEO	*Bulletin de l'École Française de l'Extrême-Orient*
BenM	*Benediktinische Monatsschrift*
BG	Berlin Gnostic Codex
BHH	*Biblisch-Historisches Handwörterbuch*
Bib	*Biblica*
BIDW	*Die Bibel in der Welt*
BJS	*British Journal of Sociology*
BK	*Bibel und Kirche*
BMCL	*Bulletin of Medieval Canon Law*
BNTC	Black's New Testament Commentaries
BRN	*Bibliotheca reformatoria Neerlandica*
BSKORK	*Bekenntnisschriften und Kirchenordnungen der nach Gottes Wort reformierten Kirche*

BSLK	Bekenntnisschriften der evangelisch-lutherischen Kirche
BSOAS	Bulletin of the School of Oriental and African Studies
BSRK	Bekenntnisschriften der reformierten Kirche
BT	Bible Translator
BTZ	Berliner theologische Zeitschrift
BUBS	Bulletin of the United Bible Societies
ByZ	Byzantinische Zeitschrift
CA	Current Anthropology
CAr	Cahiers archéologiques
Cath(M)	Catholica (Münster)
CBC	Cambridge Bible Commentary
CBQ	Catholic Biblical Quarterly
CCen	Christian Century
CChr.SA	Corpus Christianorum, Series Apocryphorum
CD	K. Barth, Church Dogmatics
CE	Catholic Encyclopedia
CGG	Christlicher Glaube in moderner Gesellschaft
CH	Church History
CHR	Catholic Historical Review
ChrTo	Christianity Today
ChW	Christliche Welt
CIC	Codex Iuris Canonici
CistSQ	Cistercian Studies Quarterly
CMCS	Cambridge Medieval Celtic Studies
CNT	Commentaire du Nouveau Testament
Conc(D)	Concilium (German ed.)
COst	Der christliche Osten
CovQ	Covenant Quarterly
CP	Classical Philology
CPG	Clavis patrum Graecorum
CR	Critical Review of Books in Religion
CRef	Corpus Reformatorum
CrossCur	Cross Currents
CScR	Christian Scholar's Review
CSSH	Comparative Studies in Society and History
CTJ	Calvin Theological Journal
CTM	Concordia Theological Monthly
D	H. Denzinger, Enchiridion symbolorum
DACL	Dictionnaire d'archéologie chrétienne et de liturgie
DAN	Documenta anabaptistica Neerlandica
DArt	Dictionary of Art (Grove's)
DBSup	Dictionnaire de la Bible, Supplément
DCB	Dictionary of Christian Biography
DCE	Dictionary of Christian Ethics
DDC	Dictionnaire de droit canonique
DECH	Dictionary of English Church History

DEM	Dictionary of the Ecumenical Movement
DH	Denzinger-Hünermann, Enchiridion symbolorum (37th ed., 1991)
DMA	Dictionary of the Middle Ages
DOP	Dumbarton Oaks Papers
DR	Downside Review
DSp	Dictionnaire de spiritualité, ascétique et mystique
DTC	Dictionnaire de théologie catholique
EAR	Encyclopedia of American Religions
EDNT	Exegetical Dictionary of the New Testament
EI	Encyclopaedia of Islam
EKKNT	Evangelisch-katholischer Kommentar zum Neuen Testament
EKL	Evangelisches Kirchenlexikon (1st ed., 1956-59)
ELC	Encyclopedia of the Lutheran Church
EncBio	Encyclopedia of Bioethics (rev. ed.)
EncChr	Encyclopedia of Christianity
EncE	Encyclopedia of Ethics
EncHB	Encyclopedia of Human Behavior
EncHI	Encyclopedia of Human Intelligence
EncJud	Encyclopaedia Judaica
EncPh	Encyclopedia of Philosophy
EncRel(E)	Encyclopedia of Religion (ed. M. Eliade)
ER	Ecumenical Review
ERE	Encyclopaedia of Religion and Ethics
ErJb	Eranos Jahrbuch
ESL	Evangelisches Soziallexikon
EStL	Evangelisches Staatslexikon
ETR	Études théologiques et religieuses
EuA	Erbe und Auftrag
EvDia	Evangelische Diaspora
EvT	Evangelische Theologie
ExpTim	Expository Times
FC	Fathers of the Church
FiHi	Fides et historia
FirstT	First Things
FR	Felix Ravenna
FZPhTh	Freiburger Zeitschrift für Philosophie und Theologie
GOTR	Greek Orthodox Theological Review
GRLH	Garland Reference Library of the Humanities
G2W	Glaube in der 2. Welt
HAT	Handbuch zum Alten Testament
HCE	Handbuch der christlichen Ethik
HCEC	HarperCollins Encyclopedia of Catholicism
HDG	Handbuch der Dogmengeschichte
HDRG	Handwörterbuch zur deutschen Rechtsgeschichte

HDThG	Handbuch der Dogmen- und Theologiegeschichte	JCH	Journal of Contemporary History
HFTh	Handbuch der Fundamentaltheologie	JChS	Journal of Church and State
HIsl	Handwörterbuch des Islam	JEH	Journal of Ecclesiastical History
HKAT	Handkommentar zum Alten Testament	JEPTA	Journal of the European Pentecostal Theological Association
HKG(J)	Handbuch der Kirchengeschichte (ed. H. Jedin)	JES	Journal of Ecumenical Studies
HLR	Harvard Law Review	JHKGV	Jahrbuch der hessischen kirchen-geschichtlichen Vereinigung
HNT	Handbuch zum Neuen Testament	JJRS	Japanese Journal of Religious Studies
HNTC	Harper's New Testament Commentaries	JJS	Journal of Jewish Studies
HOK	Handbuch der Ostkirchenkunde	JK	Junge Kirche
HPhG	Handbuch philosophischer Grundbegriffe	JKGV	Jahrbuch des kölnischen Geschichtsvereins
HPs	Handbuch der Psychologie	JMLB	Jahrbuch des Martin-Luther-Bundes
HPTh	Handbuch der Pastoraltheologie	JPaCo	Journal of Pastoral Counseling
HPTh(G)	Handbuch der praktischen Theologie (Gütersloh)	JPC	Journal of Pastoral Care
		JPh	Journal of Philosophy
HRG	Handbuch der Religionsgeschichte	JPsT	Journal of Psychology and Theology
HRP	Handbuch der Religionspädagogik	JRAI	Journal of the Royal Anthropological Institute of Great Britain and Ireland
HT	History Today		
HThG	Handbuch theologischer Grundbegriffe	JRH	Journal of Religious History
HTKNT	Herders theologischer Kommentar zum Neuen Testament	JRT	Journal of Religious Thought
		JSNT	Journal for the Study of the New Testament
HTR	Harvard Theological Review		
HTTL	Herders theologisches Taschenlexikon	JSSR	Journal for the Scientific Study of Religion
HUCA	Hebrew Union College Annual	JTSA	Journal of Theology for Southern Africa
HWP	Historisches Wörterbuch der Philosophie	JVK	Jahrbuch für Volkskunde
HZ	Historische Zeitschrift	JWKG	Jahrbuch für westfälische Kirchengeschichte
IBMR	International Bulletin of Missionary Research		
		KAT	Kommentar zum Alten Testament
ICC	International Critical Commentary	KatBl	Katechetische Blätter
ICom	Ius commune	KAV	Kommentar zu den Apostolischen Vätern
IDB	Interpreter's Dictionary of the Bible		
IDBSup	Supp. vol. to IDB	KEK	Kritisch-exegetischer Kommentar über das Neue Testament
IESS	International Encyclopedia of the Social Sciences		
		KJV	King James Version
IJRS	Internationales Jahrbuch für Religionssoziologie	KM	Die Katholischen Missionen
		KO	Kirche im Osten
IKaZ	Internationale katholische Zeitschrift	KP	Der Kleine Pauly. Lexikon der Antike
IKRS	Internationaler Kongreß für Religionssoziologie	KSL	Katholisches Soziallexikon
		KuD	Kerygma und Dogma
IKZ	Internationale kirchliche Zeitschrift	KuK	Kirche und Kunst
ILR	International Labour Review	KuKi	Kunst und Kirche
ILRef	Im Licht der Reformation. Jahrbuch des Evangelischen Bundes	LÄ	Lexikon der Ägyptologie
		LCI	Lexikon der christlichen Ikonographie
IRM	International Review of Missions	Leit.	Leiturgia. Handbuch des evangelischen Gottesdienstes
ISBE	International Standard Bible Encyclopedia (rev. ed.)		
		LitWo	Liturgisch woordenboek
ITS	Indian Theological Studies	LJ	Liturgisches Jahrbuch
JAC	Jahrbuch für Antike und Christentum	LMA	Lexikon des Mittelalters
JAF	Journal of American Folklore	LMTG	Lexikon missionstheologischer Grundbegriffe
JASt	Journal of Asian Studies		
JBL	Journal of Biblical Literature	LPGL	Lampe, Patristic Greek Lexicon
JBTh	Jahrbuch für biblische Theologie	LQ	Lutheran Quarterly

LR	Lutherische Rundschau	NZM	Neue Zeitschrift für Missionswissenschaft
LRR	Liturgy of the Roman Rite	NZSTh	Neue Zeitschrift für systematische Theologie
LS	Louvain Studies	ÖAKR	Österreichisches Archiv für Kirchenrecht
LTJ	Lutheran Theological Journal (Adelaide)	OCP	Orientalia Christiana periodica
LTK	Lexicon für Theologie und Kirche	OCtP	Oxford Companion to Philosophy
LuJ	Luther-Jahrbuch	ODCC	Oxford Dictionary of the Christian Church (3d ed.)
LuthCyc	Lutheran Cyclopedia	ODPB	Ostdeutsches Pastoralblatt
LuthW	Luther's Works, "American Edition" (55 vols.; St. Louis and Philadelphia, 1955-76)	ÖEH	Ökumenische Existenz heute
LV(L)	Lumière et vie (Lyon)	OER	Oxford Encyclopedia of the Reformation
LWF.R	Lutheran World Federation Report	OGE	Ons geestelijk erf
Mansi	Sacrorum conciliorum nova et amplissa collectio (ed. J. D. Mansi et al.)	ÖL	Ökumenelexikon
		ÖR	Ökumenische Rundschau
MD	La Maison-Dieu. Revue de pastorale liturgique	OrChr	Oriens Christianus
		OR(E)	L'osservatore romano (Eng. ed.)
MdKI	Materialdienst des Konfessions-kundlichen Instituts, Bensheim	Orien.	Orientierung
		OrSuec	Orientalia Suecana
MDÖC	Materialdienst der Ökumenischen Centrale	OS	Ostkirchliche Studien
		ÖTBK	Ökumenischer Taschenbuchkommentar zum Neuen Testament
MEZW	Materialdienst. Evangelische Zentralstelle für Weltanschauungsfragen		
		OTL	Old Testament Library
MGG	Musik in Geschichte und Gegenwart	OxyPap	The Oxyrynchus Papyri
Missi	Missi. Missionnaires de la Compagnie de Jésus	ÖZS	Österreichische Zeitschrift für Soziologie
		PastPsy	Pastoral Psychology
MNTC	Moffatt New Testament Commentary	PBSR	Papers of the British School at Rome
MOFPH	Monumenta Ordinis Fratrum Praedicatorum historica	PG	Patrologia Graeca
		PhTh	Philosophy and Theology
MonS	Monastic Studies	PL	Patrologia Latina
MQR	Methodist Quarterly Review	PPP	Praxis der Psychotherapie und Psychosomatik
MTZ	Münchener theologische Zeitschrift		
Mün.	Das Münster	PrJ	Preußische Jahrbücher
MySal	Mysterium salutis	PTh	Pastoraltheologie
NCB	New Century Bible	PThI	Pastoraltheologische Informationen
NCBC	New Century Bible Commentary	QGDOD	Quellen und Forschungen zur Geschichte des Dominikanerordens in Deutschland
NCE	New Catholic Encyclopedia		
NEBrit	New Encyclopaedia Britannica		
NHC	Nag Hammadi Codices	QGPRK	Quelle zur Geschichte des Papsttums und des römischen Katholizismus
NHThG	Neues Handbuch theologischer Grundbegriffe		
		RAC	Reallexikon für Antike und Christentum
NICNT	New International Commentary on the New Testament	RB	Revue biblique
		RBén	Revue bénédictine de critique, d'histoire et de littérature religieuses
NovT	Novum Testamentum		
NPL	Neues pädagogisches Lexikon (5th ed.)	RBK	Reallexikon zur byzantinischen Kunst
NPNF	A Select Library of (the) Nicene and Post-Nicene Fathers of the Christian Church	RBS	Regulae Benedicti studia
		RDL	Reallexikon der deutschen Literaturgeschichte
NRSV	New Revised Standard Version		
NSHE	New Schaff-Herzog Encyclopedia of Religious Knowledge	RE	Realencyklopädie für protestantische Theologie und Kirche
NTD	Das Neue Testament Deutsch		
NTS	New Testament Studies	Ref.	Reformatio. Evangelische Zeitschrift für Kultur und Politik
Numen	Numen: International Review for the History of Religions		
		RelS	Religious Studies

ABBREVIATIONS

Ren.	Renovatio. Zeitschrift für das interdisziplinäre Gespräche	THAT	Theologisches Handwörterbuch zum Alten Testament
RfR(StM)	Review for Religious (St. Mary's, Kans.)	ThBer	Theologische Berichte
RFS	Revue française de sociologie	Theol(A)	Theologia (Athens)
RGG	Religion in Geschichte und Gegenwart (3d ed.)	THKNT	Theologischer Handkommentar zum Neuen Testament
RhM	Rheinische Merkur/Christ und Welt	ThPr	Theologia practica
RoJKG	Rottenburger Jahrbuch für Kirchengeschichte	ThViat	Theologia viatorum
		TLZ	Theologische Literaturzeitung
RQ	Römische Quartalschrift für christliche Altertumskunde und Kirchengeschichte	TPQ	Theologisch-praktische Quartalschrift
		TQ	Theologische Quartalschrift
RSPT	Revue des sciences philosophiques et théologiques	Tr.	Traditio: Studies in Ancient and Medieval History, Thought, and Religion
RSR	Recherches de science religieuse	TRE	Theologische Realenzyklopädie
RTL	Revue théologique de Louvain	TRev	Theologische Revue
SB	Sources bibliques	TRT	Taschenlexikon Religion und Theologie
SBAW	Sitzungsberichte der Bayerischen Akademie der Wissenschaften	TRu	Theologische Rundschau
		TS	Theological Studies
SC	Sources chrétiennes	TSSI	Textbook of Syrian Semitic Inscriptions
SCJ	Sixteenth Century Journal: A Journal for Renaissance and Reformation Students and Scholars	TTZ	Trierer theologische Zeitschrift
		TWAT	Theologisches Wörterbuch zum Alten Testament
SEAJT	South-East Asia Journal of Theology	TZ	Theologische Zeitschrift
SecCent	Second Century	US	Una Sancta. Rundbriefe für interkonfessionelle Begegnung
SJT	Scottish Journal of Theology		
SM	Sacramentum mundi. Theologisches Lexikon für die Praxis	VC	Vigilae Christianae
		VF	Verkündigung und Forschung
SM(E)	SM (Eng. ed.)	VSVD	Verbum Societatis Verbi Divini
Soc.	Sociologus	VT	Vetus Testamentum
SocAn	Sociological Analysis	WA	M. Luther, Werke. Kritische Gesamtausgabe (Weimarer Ausgabe)
SocComp	Social Compass		
SoR	Sociology of Religion	WA.TR	WA Tischreden
StCan	Studia canonica	WCE	D. Barrett, ed., World Christian Encyclopedia
StEnc	Study Encounter		
StGen	Studium generale	WD	Wort und Dienst
StGra	Studia gratiana	WDCS	Westminster Dictionary of Christian Spirituality
StL	Staatslexikon		
StLeib	Studia Leibnitiana	WJP	Wiener Jahrbuch für Philosophie
StMed	Studi medievali	WK	Weltkirche
StMiss	Studia missionalia	WKL	Weltkirchenlexikon
StMR	St. Mark's Review (Canberra)	WLuth	Works of Martin Luther, "Philadelphia Edition" (6 vols.; Philadelphia, 1930-43)
StPatr	Studia patristica: Papers Presented to the International Conference on Patristic Studies		
		WM	Wörterbuch der Mythologie
StZ	Stimmen der Zeit	WPKG	Wissenschaft und Praxis in Kirche und Gesellschaft
SVTQ	St. Vladimir's Theological Quarterly	WzM	Wege zum Menschen
TAPhS	Transactions of the American Philosophical Society	ZAW	Zeitschrift für die alttestamentliche Wissenschaft
TDNT	Theological Dictionary of the New Testament	ZBK	Zürcher Bibelkommentar
		ZBKG	Zeitschrift für bayerische Kirchengeschichte
TDOT	Theological Dictionary of the Old Testament	ZDPV	Zeitschrift des deutschen Palästina-Vereins
TGl	Theologie und Glaube	ZDT	Zeitschrift für dialektische Theologie

ZEE	*Zeitschrift für evangelische Ethik*	ZNW	*Zeitschrift für die neutestamentliche Wissenschaft*
ZEvKR	*Zeitschrift für evangelisches Kirchenrecht*	ZRG	*Zeitschrift für Rechtsgeschichte*
ZGDP	*Zeitschrift für Göttesdienst und Predigt*	ZSRG.K	*Zeitschrift der Savigny-Stiftung für Rechtsgeschichte — Kanonistische Abteilung*
ZGSRW	*Zeitschrift für die gesamte Strafrechtswissenschaft*		
ZKG	*Zeitschrift für Kirchengeschichte*	ZTK	*Zeitschrift für Theologie und Kirche*
ZM	*Zeitschrift für Missionswissenschaft*	ZVK	*Zeitschrift für Volkskunde*
ZMiss	*Zeitschrift für Mission*	ZZ	*Zwischen den Zeiten*
ZMR	*Zeitschrift für Missionskunde und Religionswissenschaft*		

STATES AND PROVINCES

Ala.	Alabama	Mont.	Montana
B.C.	British Columbia	N.C.	North Carolina
Calif.	California	Nebr.	Nebraska
Colo.	Colorado	N.H.	New Hampshire
Conn.	Connecticut	N.J.	New Jersey
D.C.	District of Columbia	N.S.W.	New South Wales
Del.	Delaware	N.Y.	New York
Fla.	Florida	Okla.	Oklahoma
Ga.	Georgia	Ont.	Ontario
Ill.	Illinois	Oreg.	Oregon
Ind.	Indiana	Pa.	Pennsylvania
Kans.	Kansas	R.I.	Rhode Island
Ky.	Kentucky	S.C.	South Carolina
La.	Louisiana	Tenn.	Tennessee
Mass.	Massachusetts	Tex.	Texas
Md.	Maryland	Va.	Virginia
Mich.	Michigan	Vt.	Vermont
Minn.	Minnesota	Wash.	Washington
Mo.	Missouri	Wis.	Wisconsin

GENERAL

adj.	adjective	can(s).	canon(s)
Akkad.	Akkadian	cent.	century
anniv.	anniversary	cf.	*confer,* compare
Arab.	Arabic	chap(s).	chapter(s)
Aram.	Aramaic	Chin.	Chinese
art.	article	cm.	centimeter(s)
Aus.	Austria	Col.	Columbia
Austral.	Australia	col(s).	column(s)
b.	born	comm.	commentary
Belg.	Belgium	C.R.	Costa Rica
bk.	book	d.	died
Bol.	Bolivia	Den.	Denmark
Braz.	Brazil	ed.	edited by, edition, editor
ca.	*circa,* about, approximately	e.g.	*exempli gratia,* for example
Camer.	Cameroon	EKD	Evangelische Kirche in Deutschland

ABBREVIATIONS

Eng.	England, English	N.Z.	New Zealand
esp.	especially	orig.	original, originally
est.	estimate	OT	Old Testament
ET	English translation	P	"Priestly" source (P^G, Priestly
etc.	*et cetera,* and so forth		*Grundschrift* ["basic material"];
exp.	expanded		P^s, secondary Priestly source)
f	females	p(p).	page(s)
fasc.	fascicle	par(s).	paragraph(s)
fem.	feminine	part.	participle
Fin.	Finland	pl.	plural
fl.	*floruit,* flourished	pl(s).	plate(s)
Fr.	France, French	P.N.G.	Papua New Guinea
frg(s).	fragment(s)	Pol.	Poland
FS	Festschrift	Port.	Portuguese
ft.	foot, feet	pt.	part
Ger.	German, Germany	pub.	publication, published
Gk.	Greek	Q	hypothetical source of material common
ha.	hectare(s)		to Matthew and Luke but not found in
Heb.	Hebrew		Mark
ibid.	*ibidem,* in the same place	q(q).	question(s)
i.e.	*id est,* that is	repr.	reprinted
in.	inch(es)	rev.	revised (by, in)
Indon.	Indonesia	Russ.	Russian
It.	Italian, Italy	S.Af.	South Africa
Jap.	Japanese	sc.	*scilicet,* namely
km.	kilometer(s)	Scot.	Scotland
L	material in Luke not found in Matthew	sing.	singular
	or Mark	Skt.	Sanskrit
Lat.	Latin	Sp.	Spain, Spanish
lit.	literally	sq.	square
LXX	Septuagint	St.	Saint
M	material in Matthew not found in Mark	supp.	supplement, supplementary
	or Luke	Switz.	Switzerland
m	males	Tibet.	Tibetan
m.	meter(s)	trans.	translated by, translator
masc.	masculine	Turk.	Turkish
Mex.	Mexico	U.K.	United Kingdom
mi.	mile(s)	U.N.	United Nations
MS(S)	manuscript(s)	U.S.	United States
n(n).	note(s)	v(v).	verse(s)
Neth.	Netherlands	var.	variant (reading)
NGO(s)	nongovernmental organization(s)	Vg	(Latin) Vulgate
N.Ire.	Northern Ireland	vol(s).	volume(s)
no.	number	vs.	versus
Nor.	Norway	Yid.	Yiddish
NT	New Testament	YMCA	Young Men's Christian Association
		YWCA	Young Women's Christian Association

The ENCYCLOPEDIA
of CHRISTIANITY

Volume 1
A–D

A

Abbot, Abbess

The words "abbot" and "abbess" come from Aram. *abba* (father). Abbots and abbesses are the heads of independent cloisters, especially Benedictine; an abbot may also be the head of an abbey church. Many abbots and abbesses, who are often esteemed as highly as bishops, have made their mark as missionaries, pioneers, preachers, poets, scientists, and territorial rulers. They typically receive an oath of obedience from those under them.

The abbot general, or abbot president, is the head of a group of monasteries. The head of the confederated Benedictines, elected for 12 years, has the title "abbot primate." Abbots nullius (lit., abbots "of no [sc. place]"), or leaders of abbeys not under the jurisdiction of the local bishop, were appointed by the pope to have episcopal jurisdiction or special privileges in their own small territories; after 1976, no new such abbeys were to be established. Titular abbots have only the title of abbeys that no longer exist. A few Reformation churches have continued the title in perpetuation of ancient rites.

Bibliography: T. FRY, O.S.B., ed., *RB 1980: The Rule of St. Benedict in Latin and English, with Notes* (Collegeville, Minn., 1981) 322-78 • A. VEILLEUX, O.S.B., "The Abbatial Office in Cenobitic Life," *MonS* 6 (1968) 3-45.

HEINER GROTE†

Abortion

1. Medical, Biblical, and Historical Survey
2. Legal Aspects and Ethical Discussion

1. Medical, Biblical, and Historical Survey

1.1. The term "abortion" refers to the intervention, usually in the first three months, in the process of the development of human life in a mother's body, with the intention of ending the pregnancy prematurely.

1.2. Abortion, as far as we know, has been practiced in all ages and almost all places for different reasons. Over the centuries, the methods used, which vary across countries and cultures, have included physical force, medicine, and magic, applied both internally and externally.

Modern medicine is concerned to avoid risk in performing abortions, preferring the suction method to curettage in the early months and inducing premature birth in later months. Newer hormonal methods like the "abortion pill" RU 486, which has been tested in some countries and which requires a high level of involvement by medical staff, or the injection of prostaglandin reduce the risk of immediate infection or bleeding or of later infertility. Abortion still poses some threat to a woman's health, as indeed continuation of pregnancy might also. The measure of risk depends heavily on following proper procedures, good aftercare, and the informed consent and attitude of the one undergoing the abortion.

1.3. The Bible deals with the subject of abortion only indirectly or incidentally. Exod. 21:22-25 decrees that if a violent conflict between two men causes a woman to miscarry, payment must be made to her husband, since wives, children (→ Women; Childhood), and the fruit of the womb were considered the husband's property. If the pregnant woman herself is injured, the ancient Near Eastern *lex talionis* applies. The present version of this Exodus text makes a clear distinction between the fetus and the pregnant woman, even as Jer. 1:5 and Luke 1:40-44 (which mentions the child leaping in Elizabeth's womb) allow us to see in the fetus a full human being from the first (as in → Thomism). → Paul condemns the practice of pagan magic in the → primitive Christian community (Gal. 5:20; cf. Rev. 9:21; 21:8; 22:15), using the term *pharmakeia*, which can denote abortion or contraception.

Against the background of an → anthropology that views the human being as a totality made in God's image and of a worldview that esteems the family and regards progeny as a → blessing, we may see in the commandment not to murder (→ Decalogue) a general protection of human → life, including that of the fetus before birth.

1.4. Along these lines, Christianity clearly distinguished itself at the outset from the pagan world around, which to a large extent permitted abortion and the exposing of children, or even approved such action in the economic or social interests of the state (Plato, Aristotle; → Greek Philosophy). The author of the *Epistle of Barnabas* (ca. A.D. 130) wrote that one must not kill a child by abortion or kill the newborn (19.5). Beginning in the fifth century, penitential books (e.g., the second book of St. Finnian on penance) impose specific penalties for contraception and abortion. The Trullan Synod of 692, which was normative on the issue for many years, condemned abortion as the killing of children and imposed the same penalties for both.

For many centuries Christian theology debated the question when human life begins, or, more precisely, when an embryo has a → soul. Under the impact of Greek ideas (including the dualism of body and soul, the divine origin of the soul, and Aristotle's belief that the male embryo gains a soul at 40 days, the female at 80), it adopted categories of thought that still influence → moral theology (→ Ethics 2-5). The debate has influenced various disciplinary measures taken by the church. Thus Sixtus V (1585-90) threatened to excommunicate anyone who aided contraception (*Effraenatum* [1588]; → Canon Law;

Church Discipline). Gregory XIV (1590-91) lifted penalties against those who aborted a fetus not yet 40 days old.

The → Reformers did not differ essentially from church tradition in this matter. M. → Luther (1483-1546; → Luther's Theology) regarded procreation as divine service and thus sought protection for the fruit of the womb (WA 6.247). J. → Calvin (1509-64; → Calvin's Theology) clearly opposed abortion in his exposition of Exod. 21:22, arguing that the child in the womb is already human.

In the first half of the 20th century, however, Protestant → social ethics, discussing → Vatican statements (e.g., Pius XI's → encyclical *Casti conubii* [1930]) and possible conflict between the life of the mother and that of the unborn, reached a nuanced interpretation of the command not to kill (see → Barth in *CD* III/4; → Dialectical Theology). From approximately 1970 the insight that → punishment does not stop abortions, as well as new thinking on the position of women, has led to a more discriminating understanding of the whole issue of abortion.

→ Feminism lays the main stress on a woman's → autonomy and → responsibility for her own body as an expression of her → human dignity, viewing these factors as independent of the decision for or against abortion.

SUNG-HEE LEE-LINKE

2. Legal Aspects and Ethical Discussion

2.1. The ancient world did not impose penalties for abortion. Only under Christian influence did abortion come to be punished as murder. Liberalization, which began gradually with the elimination of the → death penalty at the end of the 18th century, reached a provisional conclusion in the legal reforms enacted in various countries. In most of the former socialist states between 1955 (USSR) and 1972 (East Germany), women achieved a right to abortion with their integration into the labor force. For want of alternatives (i.e., contraceptive devices), abortion became in effect a means of → birth control and of government population control in lands like China.

In the West some legalizing of abortion took place after 1967 (in Great Britain and in some states in the United States), with limits and in certain situations such as those involving danger to the mother's life, rape, or serious defects in the fetus (→ Abortion Counseling). The U.S. Supreme Court case *Roe v. Wade* (1973) was a landmark decision in the West, though it has provoked strong efforts to modify or reverse it. The situation is not uniform in the → Third World, ranging from strict prohibition in Roman Catholic and Islamic countries to toleration or even the promotion of abortion to control population.

2.2. In ethical discussion of abortion we must distinguish two issues that are often blurred in the usually passionate public debate. The first is that of evaluation, the second that of effective prevention.

In evaluation, most people — even women — are against abortion. Abortion means the irrevocable termination of a developing human life. Yet there is similar opposition to forcing a woman to continue an unwanted pregnancy against her declared will and then having to care for the child for decades, for this situation involves an irrevocable intrusion into her own life. The right of the one party to full development of life may thus be in conflict with the same right of the other party.

There is a unique bond between the mother and the unborn child, the fetus being part of the mother and unable to develop without her, yet at the same time an independent human being. This bond is the root of the extreme tension when conflict arises, and there is no way to relax the tension or to reach compromise. The need to be unequivocal and to avoid feeling the impotence that irreconcilable principles involve has forced the partners in debate into unbalanced positions such as the reducing of life to no more than biological existence, the playing down of the killing of the fetus or of the burden imposed on the mother, and the leveling of distinctions between life before and after birth. Polarization usually follows.

The traditional Roman Catholic prohibition of abortion and artificial contraceptive measures may appear to be theologically and morally conclusive, but in the context of urban industrialization (→ City 2) it is unworkable, loses credibility, and cannot escape the charge of deriving from a patriarchal imposing of decisions on women and children (→ Sexism). Jesus' expounding of the commandment not to murder as a command to promote life (Matt. 5:21-22; → Sermon on the Mount; see Luther's Small Catechism) makes it possible to avoid allocating individual → guilt and instead to see that social conditions that hamper life, and therefore society as a whole, are responsible for the dilemma (S. Keil).

Since we can reach a viable solution only with, and not against, the woman or married couple, perhaps the best prerequisites for responsible decision and psychological follow-up on the decision made are → trust in the woman's or couple's ability to be responsible and to use the appropriate measures. Comparison of places that have more liberal legal provisions with those that are more restricted supports this view. Nevertheless, it may be felt that with the growing threat of overpopulation, a fundamentally new appraisal of abortion is needed.

Bibliography: On 1.1-3: GENERAL COUNSEL OF THE UNITED CHURCH OF CANADA, *Contraception and Abortion* (Toronto, 1980) • M. J. GORMAN, *Abortion and the Early Church: Christian, Jewish, and Pagan Attitudes in the Greco-Roman World* (New York, 1982) • H. HEISS, *Die künstliche Schwangerschaftsunterbrechung* (Stuttgart, 1967) • J. HURST, *The History of Abortion in the Catholic Church* (Washington, D.C., 1983) • NCCC IN THE U.S.A., *Abortion: A Paper for Study* (New York, 1973) • PRESBYTERIAN–ROMAN CATHOLIC CONSULTATION, *Ethics and the Search for Christian Unity* (Washington, D.C., 1980) • H. RINGELING and H. S. RUH, eds., *Schwangerschaftsabbruch. Theologische und kirchliche Stellungnahmen* (Basel, 1974) • P. STALLSWORTH, ed., *The Church and Abortion: In Search of a New Ground for Response* (Nashville, 1994) • G. TATTRIE, *Abortion: A Christian Perspective* (Toronto, 1984).

On 1.4 and 2.2: W. BRENNAN, *The Abortion Holocaust* (St. Louis, 1983) • H. DÄUBLER-GMELIN and R. FAERBER-HUSEMANN, *§218. Der tägliche Kampf um die Reform* (Bonn, 1987) • U. EIBACH, *Experimentierfeld: Werdendes Leben* (Göttingen, 1983) • C. FRANCOME, *Abortion Freedom* (Boston, 1984); idem, *Abortion Practice in Britain and the United States* (London, 1986) • F. M. FROHOCK, *Abortion: A Case Study in Law and Morals* (London, 1985) • C. GILLIGAN, *In a Different Voice* (Cambridge, Mass., 1982) • B. W. HARRISON, *Our Right to Choose: Toward a New Ethic of Abortion* (Boston, 1983) • C. HEYWARD, *Our Passion for Justice: Images of Power, Sexuality, and Liberation* (New York, 1984) • T. W. HILGERS and D. J. HORAN, eds., *Abortion and Social Justice* (New York, 1972) • A. F. IDE, *Abortion Handbook: The History, Clinical Practice, and Psychology of Abortion* (3d ed.; Las Colinas, Tex., 1988) • S. KEIL, "Leben fördern–ethische Überlegungen zu Schwangerschaftsabbruch aus evangelischer Sicht," *Schwangerschaftskonflikt-Beratung* (ed. M. Koschorke and J. Sandberger; Göttingen, 1978) 327-38 • M. KOSCHORKE, "Schwangerschaftskonflikt und Schwangerschaftskonflikt-Beratung," *ThPr* 26 (1991) 192-206 • P. LAMBRECHT and H. MERTENS, *Small Family–Happy Family. Internationale Bevölkerungspolitik und Familienplanung in Indien* (Münster, 1989) • J. T. NOONAN, ed., *The Morality of Abortion* (Cambridge, Mass., 1977) • H. POETTGEN, ed., *Die ungewollte Schwangerschaft. Eine anthropologische Synopsis* (Cologne, 1982).

On 2.1: A. ESER and H. A. HIRSCH, eds., *Sterilisation und Schwangerschaftsabbruch* (Stuttgart, 1980) • A. ESER and H. G. KOCH, eds., *Schwangerschaftsabbruch im internationalen Vergleich* (Baden-Baden, 1988) • I. L. GARFIELD and P. HENNESSY, eds., *Abortion: Moral and Legal*

Perspectives (Amherst, Mass., 1984) • E. KETTING and P. VAN PRAAG, *Schwangerschaftsabbruch. Gesetz und Praxis im internationalen Vergleich* (Tübingen, 1985).

MARTIN KOSCHORKE

Abortion Counseling

1. Definition
2. Variables
3. Dynamics and Goals
4. Training
5. Institutions

1. Definition

Abortion counseling is the counseling of women who contemplate or have decided upon having an abortion, with a view to making sure that they are aware of all the options and consequences. Some places insist that counseling must occur before an abortion is in fact performed. Social workers may offer advice on the possibilities of assistance or adoption, should the final decision be not to have the abortion. Physicians can give information on what precisely the procedure involves. Psychologists can give psychological preparation to help the women deal with possible adverse reactions. Christians opposed to abortion run their own counseling centers with a view to dissuading women from having an abortion and guiding them through the alternatives. Legal advice might also be needed and offered regarding the conformity of a given abortion to existing laws.

2. Variables

The legal situation in Western countries varies widely. It extends from regulations based purely on time (e.g., in Sweden, Denmark, Austria, eastern Europe, and the United States), with the actual limits varying between 10 and 28 weeks; to regulations based de facto on length of pregnancy, though accompanied by legal regulations addressing the question of which cases may appropriately be terminated (England, Netherlands, France, Italy); to regulations conceived more broadly (Switzerland) or narrowly (recently Poland) that deal with the circumstances in which a pregnancy could be terminated. This varying situation is reflected by the various prescribed counseling procedures, including more or less intensive gathering of medical information (Sweden, Denmark, eastern Europe), an agreement between the woman and the physician (Netherlands), medical examination (Switzerland, England), briefing with a nonmedical counselor regarding alternative solu-

tions to abortion (France), and encouragement to choose solutions that avoid abortion itself (Italy). The course of events in each individual case depends largely on how the particular physician or counselor deals with the law and the existing regulatory procedures.

3. Dynamics and Goals

Abortion counseling takes place in a complex situation, hard for outsiders to follow, that involves individual, family, and social → conflicts and ambivalence. At a time when they are in need of physical protection, → women may often see themselves as fully unprepared for the crisis, frequently in connection with tensions with a → partner or → family or a threat to → career (→ Vocation) or even personal → identity. Tension in such conflicts can be well-nigh unbearable. One → life stands opposed to another, one part of the woman to another. Within a short time she must make a decision that is irreversible, but also one on which her own life and plans and well-being, and sometimes those of others, may depend for decades or for life. No matter which way the decision goes, it is against the woman herself. Neither choice can soften the conflict or the polarization that marks current public and ethical debates. The woman must carry the tension in her own body.

The first goal of a counselor is to convey understanding to those affected in this existential crisis, conceding ambivalence and allowing for feelings of total impotence. The counselor's role is to help the woman to make an independent, responsible decision and then to follow through with it in the face of → depression, self-reproach, guilt feelings, the rejection of the previously unwanted child (→ Childhood), and anger at a partner (→ Guilt). The art of abortion counseling is to transform what may in some countries be an obligatory interview into a counseling session characterized by openness, trust, and an attitude of confidence. For the counselor to try to influence motivation directly clearly is an obstacle in this regard, for it would mean depriving the pregnant woman of the capability of making her own decision in this situation, in which responsibility for the decision regarding the child is hers. Pressure usually produces defensiveness and prevents openness. The Vatican and some other churches require that counseling undertaken by their institutions should certainly open up the ethical issues and make known both the alternatives to abortion and other planning options.

4. Training

Abortion counseling demands specialized competence in such matters as psychological counseling,

4

→ crisis intervention, social work, and family planning. It also demands personal flexibility and the ability to work under pressure. Those who engage in counseling in Christian institutions must be able to put their work in their church context. In many cases this approach may mean that they meet with misunderstanding and suspicion. Thorough and ongoing training and a willingness to be held accountable (→ Supervision) are needed for this difficult task.

5. Institutions

Abortion counseling may be public or private, denominational or nondenominational. Since the churches have a duty to promote and protect life, they have had a strong involvement in this field from the outset (→ Pastoral Care). Roman Catholic and many Protestant institutions make it their aim not only to respect the conscientious decision of the woman but also to act as advocate for the unborn child. Their services are thus more often sought by women whose inclination it is to keep the child.

As part of the counseling, churches and Christian groups may also provide financial and material help to pregnant women to supplement any help given by state or local authorities. Since the majority of women seeking material help are those not wishing to have an abortion, the reduction in abortion statistics is accompanied by an increasing involvement in general pregnancy counseling, prophylaxis, and sex education, as well as a decrease in abortion counseling in the narrower sense.

Groups that strongly oppose abortion should be prepared not only to offer counseling against it but to advise on options and to make them possible with practical support, including financial support. In the United States in 1997, for example, Care Net, the crisis pregnancy ministry of the Christian Action Council (founded 1975), offers such services through its 450 pregnancy care centers nationwide. An additional 2,500 centers in the United States provide similar counseling and services.

→ Anthropology; Autonomy; Birth Control; Emancipation; Ethics; Forgiveness; Human Dignity; Medical Ethics; Poverty; Sexual Ethics

Bibliography: Beratung im Schwangerschaftskonflikt. Eine Stellungnahme der Kammer der EKD für Ehe und Familie (Hannover, 1990) • S. CALLAHAN, "Counseling Abortion Alternatives: Can It Be Value-Free?" America 165/5 (1991) 110-13 • E. KAUSCH, Soziale Beratung Schwangerer (Berlin, 1990) bibliography • M. KOSCHORKE and J. F. SANDBERGER, eds., Schwangerschaftskonfliktberatung (Göttingen, 1978) • F. MATTHEWS-GREEN, Real Choices: Offering Practical, Life-Affirming Alternatives to Abortion (Portland, Oreg., 1994) • P. J. RIGA, "Counseling and the Abortion Issue," JPaCo 17 (1982) 44-55 • J. R. RZEPKA, "Counseling the Abortion Patient: A Pastoral Perspective," PastPsy 28 (1980) 168-80.

MARTIN KOSCHORKE

Abraham

1. Biblical Tradition
2. History of Research
    2.1. Historical Assessment
    2.2. Form-Critical and Historical Analyses
3. Abraham in the NT

1. Biblical Tradition

The biblical stories of Abraham occur only in Genesis, chaps. 11 (origins and call) through 25 (death). Together, they are the source of the figure of Abraham that is referred to elsewhere in the biblical tradition and in the thought of the church — namely, the ancestor of the people of Israel who received God's promises and lived in faithful obedience to God. As Abram, he responded to God's command and moved to a distant country, where God promised that he would become the ancestor of a great nation. He prospered in Canaan, but his wife, Sarai, had no children. She thus proposed that Abram have a child by her handmaid, Hagar, who ultimately bore a son, Ishmael. God repeated the promise of descendants through Sarai, made a covenant with Abram that required circumcision, and changed their names to Abraham and Sarah. Despite their old age, the two had a son, → Isaac. Sometime later, God, as a test of Abraham's faith and obedience, commanded him to sacrifice Isaac. Abraham agreed, but at the last moment God prevented the sacrifice of Isaac. Thus the promise of descendants was maintained, and Isaac became the forefather of great peoples, including the later Israelites, while Ishmael, who had been sent away after Isaac's birth, became the forefather of neighboring peoples, including the Arabs.

Elsewhere in the OT Abraham is mentioned with reference to the main themes of these stories: as the first of the forefathers by whom both the people of Israel and their God are identified (e.g., Exod. 3:6) and as the initial recipient of the promises that maintain the hope of that people (e.g., Deut. 9:27; Isa. 51:2).

2. History of Research

According to the predominant critical viewpoint, the stories in Genesis 11–25 rest on ancient oral traditions that now appear in the three main written sources of the → Pentateuch, especially J. An exception is the later chap. 14, in which Abraham has a role markedly different from that which he plays in the three main sources. In J, the main theme is the promise of Gen. 12:1-3, whose climax is that all the nations on earth will be blessed in Abraham. In E, Abraham is a model for believers. In P, reflecting the impact of the exile, he is the recipient of the covenant promise (chap. 17), which guarantees the preservation of Israel in spite of every threat.

2.1. *Historical Assessment*

In the historical assessment of Abraham in OT research, there are two basic positions.

2.1.1. One is to view him as a fictitious figure and the stories about him (→ Patriarchal History) as legends contributing to the history of seminomadic culture. On this view the stories about Abraham do not come from Canaan but were brought in by the Israelites as recollections of an earlier culture (H. Greßmann, H. Gunkel).

2.1.2. The predominant view sees in Abraham a historical person, a seminomadic sheikh, with a clan and connections with Mesopotamia, who came to Canaan from Haran in the first half of the second millennium B.C. While O. Eißfeldt supported this view almost solely on the basis of the OT material, other scholars (W. F. Albright, R. de Vaux) used the findings of archaeology, especially the Mari, Nuzi, and Amarna texts from the second millennium, to support the reliability of the biblical texts. In contrast, some scholars have protested that the biblical stories show marked divergence from historical reality (T. L. Thompson, J. Van Seters).

2.2. *Form-Critical and Historical Analyses*

2.2.1. A. Alt and after him M. Noth took another view — that Abraham was the founder of a clan-cult (the God of Abraham or shield of Abraham, Gen. 15:1) before the conquest. His descendants brought the cult to Canaan, where it became an essential constituent of Yahwism. Since this cult alone stands at the heart of the tradition about Abraham, it is impossible to reconstruct a biography of Abraham or to say anything about his personal religion. Noth's special contribution is to have shed light on the place of Abraham in the Pentateuchal tradition. As Noth saw it, Abraham was integrated into this tradition later than → Isaac or → Jacob but became more important, attracting to himself traditions that were originally connected with the other two. Paradoxically, the last became the eldest, the father in connection with the original element of promise in the patriarchal cult.

2.2.2. Building on Noth, R. E. Clements has shown how J forged a link between Abraham and → David. The promise of the land to Abraham was fulfilled with the secure possession of Canaan that David achieved. The traditions about Abraham came from Hebron, where the Calebites linked them to Yahwism, and then moved on to Jerusalem, where they influenced the theology of David's → monarchy forged in the royal court and temple.

3. Abraham in the NT

While some NT passages continue the OT patterns (Luke 19:9; Rom. 11:1), others speak disparagingly of people who claim Abraham as their ancestor (Matt. 3:9; Luke 3:8; John 8:39), in criticism of Jewish religious pride. Also, Abraham is presented in the NT as a model of obedience (Jas. 2:21) and faith (Heb. 11:8-17). Paul uses the concept of Abraham's faith, contrasting Abraham's covenant with God and the covenant of → Sinai, with its orientation to the → law. The faith of Abraham is the trust that God reckons as → righteousness, a righteousness that is attained by faith alone (Rom. 4:3). Also, intertestamental elaboration of the figure of Abraham is reflected in the NT. He is an eschatological figure, related to the state of the righteous dead (Luke 16). Exod. 3:15 is used as evidence for resurrection (Matt. 22:31-32).

Bibliography: A. Alt, "The God of the Fathers," *Essays on OT History and Religion* (Oxford, 1966) 1-77 • O. Betz, "Ἀβραάμ," *EDNT* 1.2-4 • R. E. Clements, *Abraham and David: Genesis 15 and Its Meaning for Israelite Tradition* (London, 1967) • O. Eissfeldt, "Achronische, anachronische und synchronische Elemente in der Genesis," *Kleine Schriften* (Tübingen, 1968) 4.153-69 • W. McKane, *Studies in the Patriarchal Narratives* (Edinburgh, 1979) • M. Noth, *A History of Pentateuchal Traditions* (Englewood Cliffs, N.J., 1972) • T. L. Thompson, *The Historicity of the Patriarchal Narratives: The Quest for the Historical Abraham* (New York, 1974) • J. Van Seters, *Abraham in History and Tradition* (New Haven, 1975) • H. Weidmann, *Die Patriarchen und ihre Religion im Lichte der Forschung seit Julius Wellhausen* (Göttingen, 1968) • W. Zimmerli, *1. Mose 12– 25: Abraham* (Zurich, 1976).

WILLIAM McKANE

Absolute, The

The word "absolute" comes from the Lat. *absolutus* (loosed, completed). Taken negatively, it means the unconditioned — in metaphysics, as distinct from the finite and conditioned; in epistemology, as distinct from the indefinite and relative; and in ethics, as distinct from the provisional and only partly valid.

Taken positively, in metaphysics it represents the complete and perfect being on which all that exists depends, the ground that sustains all things, the final goal toward which all reality strives. It may also be understood immanently as the totality of being, which embraces all that is and which in principle is accessible to human → reason, or transcendentally as ultimate reality, which both surpasses and underlies human being and thought (→ Immanence and Transcendence). In epistemology, the transcendental view stressing the negative character of the knowledge of the absolute leads easily to → agnosticism or fideism. The immanent view has led to a suspicion of projection and → illusion because it has been thought that the necessary linking of human knowledge to a specific place rules out the identity of being and thought. In ethics, the absolute can point to the fact that moral norms are not dependent on human conventions but are objectively valid. It can signify the priority of moral duty over other considerations (e.g., prudential) or denote the unrestricted nature of moral → duties and rights.

Although there is no exact linguistic equivalent in Greek, the idea of the absolute is unmistakably present in the concept of the *archē* (pre-Socratics), in the idea of the → good that transcends all being (Plato), in the concept of substance (Aristotle; → Aristotelianism), and in the idea of the one (Plotinus; → Platonism). The Latin fathers (→ Church Fathers) began to use *absolutum* for God (→ Tertullian *Adv. Marc.* 2.5; → Jerome *In Hiez. comm.* 16.48-49). Materially, → Anselm (1033-1109) equates God and the absolute. Kant (1724-1804) links human knowledge to the conditions of time and space; hence the absolute can function only as a regulative principle of thought in the sphere of theoretical reason. Only in the practical knowledge of moral obligation does it manifest itself. The modern understanding of the concept has been much influenced by its treatment in German idealism, as in Fichte (the ego as the absolute principle of philosophy), Schelling (the absolute as the end of all antitheses in the philosophy of identity, the total "indifference" of being and thought), and Hegel (reality as an unfolding of absolute spirit in history; → Hegelianism). Criticism of idealism often carries with it disparagement of the concept of the absolute. In → Kierkegaard (1813-55) reason has no access to the absolute, but a relation to it is possible in the decision at which one arrives in existential → despair (→ Existentialism). For others the absolute is simply a mistake, a mystification, or a meaningless word with no empirical content. E. Lévinas has suggested a new approach. For him, the absolute comes to us as a summons in the revelation of the radically other in the face of our neighbor.

Bibliography: W. CRAMER, *Das Absolut und das Kontingente* (2d ed.; Frankfurt, 1976) • J. H. FINDLAY, *Ascent to the Absolute* (New York, 1970) • G. HUBER, *Das Sein und das Absolut* (Basel, 1955) • P.-J. LABARRIÈRE, "L'homme et l'absolu," *ArPh* 36 (1973) 209-23, 353-71 • E. LÉVINAS, *Totality and Infinity* (Pittsburgh, 1969) • J. MÖLLER, *Der Geist und das Absolut* (Paderborn, 1951) • I. TRETHOWAN, *The Absolute and the Atonement* (New York, 1971).

RUURD VELDHUIS

Absoluteness of Christianity → Theology of Religions

Absolution → Confession of Sins

Acathistus

The Acathistus (from Greek, meaning "not [sung] sitting"), a Byzantine hymn to the Virgin Mary sung while standing, takes the form of an alphabetic acrostic and is thought to have been first composed by Romanus Melodus (6th cent.). The original served as a model for many similar hymns, especially in Russia. At times having considerable influence in the West, the Acathistus has been illustrated in picture-cycles since the 14th century.

→ Mariology; Mary, Devotion to

Bibliography: A. CHADZINIKOLAU, "Akathistos Hymnos," *RBK* 1.94-96 • G. DÉVAI, "Akathistos–Prooemia in Byzantine Musical MSS in Hungary," *Studies in Chant* 1 (1966) 1-3 • G. G. MEERSSEMANN, *Der Hymnos Akathistos im Abendland* (2 vols.; Fribourg, 1958-60) • J. SZÖVÉRFFY, *A Guide to Byzantine Hymnography* (Brookline, Mass., 1978) 1.116-35 (bibliography) • I. THOMAS, "Akathistos," *NCE* 1.228 • T. VELMANS, "Une illustration inédite de l'Acathiste et l'iconographie des hymnes liturgiques à Byzance," *CAr* 22 (1972) 131-65 • E. WELLESZ, "The 'Akathistos,'" *DOP* 9-10 (1956) 141-74; idem, *The Akathistos Hymn* (Copenhagen, 1957).

PETER PLANK

Acclamation

"Acclamation," from the Lat. *acclamo* (applaud, cheer, shout), denotes shouts, often intensified by repetition, that express the cheers, praises, thanks, demands, or devotion of individuals or crowds. Examples occur in the NT *(amēn, allēlouïa, marana tha, hōsanna,* and also *Kyrios Iēsous).* They occur also in connection with the election of → bishops and → popes *(ad [per] multos annos, axios),* and there are examples at → councils and → synods *(anathema).* In antiquity and in the Middle Ages rulers received acclamations on special occasions. All Eastern and most Western → liturgies include acclamations in such forms as "amen," "hallelujah," "Kyrie eleison," and *dignum et justum (est).* We also find longer examples, as in the words of institution "We proclaim your death, O Lord. . . ." Contemporary church musicians work at finding suitable musical settings for acclamations.

Bibliography: E. H. KANTOROWICZ, *Laudes regiae: A Study in Liturgical Acclamations and Medieval Ruler Worship* (Berkeley and Los Angeles, 1946) • H. GRAF REVENTLOW et al., "Formeln, liturgische," *TRE* 11.252-71 (extensive bibliography).

THADDEUS A. SCHNITKER

Acculturation

1. Concept
2. Forms of Acculturation
3. Criticism

1. Concept
In 1935 American anthropologists first used "acculturation" as a technical term to denote a basic shift in one or more cultures that have experienced direct and long-term contact with each other. In contrast to the *diffusion* of individual cultural traits over time, acculturation is a subject of strictly empirical description. It is also to be differentiated from → *socialization,* in German sometimes called *Enkulturation,* and from *inculturation,* which, in recent Catholic missiology, has the much wider meaning of incarnating Christianity in a given culture. Sometimes *assimilation* is contrasted with acculturation, but more commonly it is seen as a form of acculturation. Although applied universally, acculturation as a subject of anthropology belongs primarily to the age of uncontested → colonial domination by the Western nations. With the challenging of this domination, the concept inevitably came under criticism.

2. Forms of Acculturation
Acculturation is "free" when those concerned decide which elements of a given culture to incorporate into their own without coming under the military or political sway of the givers (who typically are Western). Examples of free acculturation include Japan, modern Mexico, and the kingdoms in precolonial West Africa. Much more common and more extensively researched is directed, or "unfree," acculturation, which typically occurs under military pressure. In this case we find three responses: assimilation, blending, and resistance.

Assimilation designates the most radical change. A → minority loses its previous cultural → identity to the dominant culture of the social majority. Examples that have been studied in the United States include the descendants of African → slaves, the original → Indians, and European immigrants. In Germany the children of guest workers provide an example.

Blending as the fusion of one culture with a more dominant one is a more common ethnological and sociological response. Essential features of the former culture (e.g., family structure or language) persist in spite of the adaptation. In part, new cultures emerge that differ both from Western and from traditional cultures, as has happened in Indonesia, Africa, and Mexico. The religious aspect of such intermingling is usually called → syncretism if it involves the great religions (→ Buddhism; Buddhism and Christianity; Islam). Either the original message is effectively acculturated (i.e., adapted), or it loses its distinctives through complete incorporation into the established culture.

Resistance (reaction) as a subject of → ethnology focuses on "nativistic movements" in Oceania, Africa, and America. These politico-religious struggles against Western dominance kindle the enthusiasm of those who are threatened, but resistance is doomed to failure because of the relative weakness of their cultures' military and economy.

3. Criticism
Criticism of the concept of acculturation focuses on its obscuring of the realities of colonialism, domination, and subjection (G. Leclerc, R. Bureau). Either the concept is rejected philosophically (P. J. Hountondji), or it is defined more narrowly in economic terms (M. Kohler).

In missiology the question of culture and acculturation is taken up both self-critically and apologetically. Christian mission must take other cultures seriously, but it also must view itself as involving a legitimate and normal process of acculturation (E. A. Nida, L. J. Luzbetak). Profound changes in religion within biblical history may themselves be regarded as acculturation (K. Rennstich). In the non-Western churches that are the product of mission, the problem has been reformulated and at times radicalized into the question of cultural contextualization and the identity of the faith. Special missiological discussion in the United States finds in acculturation, along with linguistics and cybernetics, a main aspect of communication and accordingly investigates its conditions. At the center stands the sender (or messenger), the person who brings the Christian message to the non-Christian culture as a whole. In a way that is both critical and complementary, a European approach puts at the center the recipient of the message as a person in whom faith develops from its beginning. In every culture hermeneutics and the appropriation of faith must follow communication. Thus in every culture, including those of the West, acculturation of the Christian faith is an open and ongoing process.

Bibliography: H. BALZ, *Theologische Modelle der Kommunikation* (Gütersloh, 1978); idem, *Where the Faith Has to Live: Studies in Bakossi Society and Religion* (pt. 1, Basel, 1984; pt. 2, Berlin, 1995) • R. BUREAU, *Péril blanc. Propos d'un ethnologue sur l'Occident* (Paris, 1978) • P. J. HOUNTONDJI, *African Philosophy* (Bloomington, Ind., 1983) • M. KOHLER, *Akkulturation in der Südsee* (Frankfurt, 1982) • G. LECLERC, *Anthropologie et colonialisme* (Paris, 1972) • L. J. LUZBETAK, *The Church and Cultures* (Techny, Ill., 1963; 5th ed., 1988) • B. MALINOWSKI, *The Dynamics of Culture Change* (New Haven, 1945) • E. A. NIDA, *Customs and Cultures* (New York, 1954); idem, *Message and Mission* (New York, 1960) • K. RENNSTICH, *Mission und wirtschaftliche Entwicklung. Biblische Theologie des Kulturwandels* (Munich, 1978).

HEINRICH BALZ

Achievement and Competition

1. An essential feature of modern → industrial societies is the principle of achievement, toward which the → organization of both social relations and individuals is oriented. Such a society is characterized primarily by the fact that its basic organizational goal is the maximizing of production and therefore of the gross national product. A second feature is that the members of this type of society themselves desire and seek achievement. Third, material and social opportunities should be distributed in accordance with individual achievement, and all should have equal chances to improve themselves.

Competition is the rule and the standard of achievement in market-structured industrial societies (→ Economy). "Achievement" in these settings means productive or useful work, or the resultant

market product. Competition stimulates the individual will to achieve when opportunities are in principle equal, as in an achievement society. The principles of achievement and competition are thus closely intertwined. In a functioning competitive society economic → power (§1) is widely dispersed. Yet competition has a tendency to disregard the weak and thus can ultimately destroy itself. Restrictions of competition that prevent the formation of monopolies are thus necessary to maintain fair competition.

2.1. Various definitions are given of the complex term "achievement," which we cannot discuss fully in all its aspects and facets (G. Hartfiel). Since, however, the abandonment of precision and clarity in the use of the terms has complicated the whole discussion, contributing to a certain emotionalizing of the issues, we must persist in the search for a clear definition of "achievement."

In physics, "achievement" may be used for work done in a particular time. In economics it refers to the capital, labor, technological knowledge, space, raw materials, and means of production put to work in a specific period. It is not a suitable term for questions of → sociology, → psychology, or → anthropology, since it relates to the product or result of work and not to the social, psychological, or cultural processes involved. Thus far no generally accepted sociological definition has been found. In the theory of sociological → action, society and its members face up to the problems of life, to defects, and to the struggle for a better life; actions that meet these ends are achievement (H. Haferkamp 1990). Achievement relations will usually be power relations. Good achievers and action groups have more potential than those that are not. Disruptions in these relations occur when more achievement is ascribed to some than is actually the case.

2.2. Economic competition involves the establishing or maintaining of a market in which suppliers and consumers can meet and in which prices are set freely according to supply and demand.

3. It is clear that very early, in order to solve various problems of life, human beings had to be → socialized as achieving beings. It is also clear that the intensity of the will to achieve depends on many inner and outer factors. The principles of achievement and competition find their true development as principles of social formation and as individual orientations only as a result of impulses from religious and philosophical ideas, economic conditions, and → revolutionary challenges, which in Europe from around 1500 helped to mobilize individual activity.

3.1. A new understanding of → vocation and work arose in → Protestantism. M. → Luther (1483-1546; → Luther's Theology) maintained that, with regard to the soul's → salvation, secular activity is in principle equal to religious activity, since vocation, as calling, means service before and to God. With our work we are to cooperate with God in giving shape to the → kingdom of God in this world. J. → Calvin (1509-64; → Calvin's Theology; Predestination), with his ascetic → ethics, was of decisive significance in the promotion of the achievement principle, as M. → Weber (1864-1920) showed in his *Protestant Ethic and the Spirit of Capitalism.* Weber found that the most authentic representatives of the → Puritan spirit were the traders and farmers of North America (→ Bourgeois, Bourgeoisie), whose individualistic striving for achievement paved the way for → capitalism, which ultimately no longer needed the support of religious ideas.

3.2. Economic → liberalism also helped to promote the principle of achievement. Asking whether certain laws underlie life in society, Adam Smith (1723-90) described the so-called market mechanism. He transferred to the market the anthropological and psychological assumptions of Scottish moral philosophy, namely, that self-interest and → reason are fundamental to human nature and that, insofar as these can operate freely, they mobilize activity and promote the common good. The market, then, is in a state of equilibrium when all economic subjects may freely compete. Since the market sees to it that there is an optimum achievement capability, Smith thought it necessary, if natural forces were to be released, to set aside all the traditional rules and relations that hamper the economic activity of the individual.

4. Related to the principles of achievement and competition are concepts of a just distribution of material and social opportunities and of a free market that is open to all. These concepts, however, have not worked out very well in history. Thus K. → Marx (1818-83; → Marxism 2-3), among others, showed that fundamentally the surging ethos of achievement created very different conditions for wage earners (→ Proletariat) and for entrepreneurs. For the latter, market success on the basis of monetary skill and a striving for profit might be a measure of the ability to achieve, but for those dependent on wages, achievement meant extensive and intensive labor, split up piecemeal into partial functions for the sake of efficiency and thus wrested from a meaningful context. To keep production costs down, entrepreneurs also paid the lowest possible wages, and

workers had to be content with these if they were not to fall victim to → unemployment. Even the organizing of → labor unions (→ Labor Movement) did not always offer adequate protection in this regard. These disproportionate achievements demonstrated very clearly the antagonism between the two → classes that Marx described extensively in *Das Kapital,* over against which he proposed a → socialist society.

5. Criticism of the achievement society and, above all, of the inhumane consequences (→ Humanity) of exaggerating the achievement principle has never been wanting. Steps have been and are being taken to limit the negative results. Some countries have set up a principle of socialism as an additional principle of distribution. This involves active state intervention to establish justice when the possibility of achievement is reduced because of age, sickness, or ill health. → Conflicts that arise in a situation of competition have given rise to reflection on values such as creative coresponsibility for one another, → solidarity with all people, and the protection of the disadvantaged.

Bibliography: K. M. BOLTE, *Leistung und Leistungsprinzip. Zur Konzeption, Wirklichkeit und Möglichkeit eines gesellschaftlichen Gestaltungsprinzips* (Opladen, 1979) • H. BRAUN, *Leistung und Leistungsprinzip in der Industriegesellschaft. Soziale Normen im Wandel* (Freiburg, 1977) • COUNCIL OF THE PROTESTANT CHURCH OF GERMANY (EKD), *Leistung und Wettbewerb. Sozialethische Überlegungen zur Frage des Leistungsprinzips und der Wettbewerbsgesellschaft* (3d ed.; Gütersloh, 1982) • W. FUCHS et al., eds., *Lexikon zur Soziologie* (Opladen, 1973) • A. H. GUNNEWEG and W. SCHMITHALS, *Achievement* (Nashville, 1978) • H. HAFERKAMP, *Soziales Handeln. Theorie sozialen Verhaltens und sinnhaften Handelns, geplanter Handlungszusammenhänge und sozialer Strukturen* (Opladen, 1990); idem, *Soziologie der Herrschaft. Analyse von Struktur, Entwicklung und Zustand von Herrschaftszusammenhängen* (Opladen, 1983) • E. E. HAGEN, *On the Theory of Social Change* (Homewood, Ill., 1962) • G. HARTFIEL, introduction to *Das Leistungsprinzip. Merkmale–Bedingungen–Probleme* (ed. idem; Opladen, 1977) *Einleitung* • D. C. MCCLELLAND, *The Achieving Society* (Princeton, 1961) • K. MARX, *Capital: A Critique of Political Economy* (New York, 1977) • A. SCHADE, *Der Weg zur Gleichheit. Thesen und Daten zum Abbau sozialer Ungleichheiten* (Frankfurt, 1987) • H. SCHOECK, "Ist Leistung unanständig?" *Das Leistungsprinzip. Merkmale–Bedingungen–Probleme* (ed. G. Hartfiel; Opladen, 1977); idem, *Soziologisches Wörterbuch* (8th ed.; Freiburg, 1974) • A. SMITH, *Inquiry into the Nature and Causes of the Wealth of Nations* (London,

1776; New York, 1965) • M. Weber, *The Protestant Ethic and the Spirit of Capitalism* (6th ed.; London, 1962).

Hans Haferkampt and Angelika Schade

Acoemetae

"Acoemetae," meaning "those who do not sleep," designates certain monks in and around Constantinople who, divided into two choirs and using various languages (Greek, Latin, and Syriac), sang God's praises without ceasing. Long before the Benedictines, they observed the seven → hours of prayer. Their founder was Alexander (d. ca. 430), who began his work in Mesopotamia and → Antioch and who in 426 was driven out of Constantinople on account of Messalianism. In 428 the group founded the monastery of Gomon, then Irenaeon. The history of the famous Studios monastery in Constantinople also begins with them. Siding with Rome in 484, they provoked an early schism between East and West (→ Heresies and Schisms). In the Acoemetae's stress on the two natures of Christ, Pope John II (533-35) found an occasion for repudiating them as → Nestorians.

Bibliography: "Acoemetae," *ODCC* 10-11 • G. Dragon, "La vie ancienne de S. Marcel l'Acémète," *AnBoll* 86 (1968) 271-321 • R. Riedinger, "Akoimeten," *TRE* 2.148-53 • E. G. M. J. de Stoop, ed., *Vita Alexandri* (Paris, 1911) • E. Wölfle, *Hypatios. Leben und Bedeutung des Abtes von Rufiniane* (Frankfurt, 1986).

Reinhart Staats

Act

The term "act" figures in the philosophical analysis of becoming, of the phenomenon of change. Parmenides (d. after 480 B.C.) regarded all change as appearance, while Heraclitus (ca. 500 B.C.) considered all that is unchanged as appearance. Aristotle (384-322 B.C.) made an extensive analysis of becoming in his doctrines of substance and accident, *dynamis* and *energeia*, potency and act. These doctrines were greatly refined in medieval → metaphysics, especially by → Thomas Aquinas (1224/25-74), who related them to the doctrines of God and creation.

A potency seems to precede every act (e.g., the power to think precedes the act of thought). Hence → Scholasticism called "act," thus viewed, *actus secundus* (in contrast to *potentia activa*). The principle that precedes the act, which a potency can shape (e.g., stone in sculpture), is called *actus primus*. Only

for God is there no such thing as mere possibility or unactivated potency; he is *actus purus*. At this point controversies broke out in later Scholasticism that neo-Thomism (→ Thomism) took up. At this point, too, Protestant theology entered in with its criticism. The concept also occurs in the psychology of act and experience (A. Meinong, F. Brentano) and, in a related sense, in the phenomenology of E. Husserl (intentionality), the ontology of N. Hartmann, and the analysis of ethical judgments.

→ Neoscholasticism; Ontology; Phenomenology

Bibliography: B. Aune, *Reason and Action* (Boston, 1977) • D. Charles, *Aristotle's Philosophy of Action* (Ithaca, N.Y., 1984) • J. B. Lotz, "Akt," *HPhG* 1.28-31 • D. Schlüter, "Akt, Potenz," *HWP* 1.134-42.

Dietrich Ritschl

Acta Sanctorum → Lives of the Saints

Action Theory

1. Antiquity and Middle Ages
2. Modern Period
3. Present-Day Discussion
   3.1. Sociology
   3.2. Anthropology
   3.3. Analytic Action

The term "action theory" denotes various philosophical and scientific attempts to analyze and interpret human action. In a narrower sense it refers to the present intensive conceptual and empirical effort to clarify the supposedly necessary components of any action as a complex event. A key question is whether and to what extent human action can be distinguished from behavior (→ Behaviorism). In a broader sense the term applies to traditional positions in → philosophy and → science, insofar as they imply a theory of act, and to more recent proposals for a → practical theology and a → pastoral theology that are empirically oriented and framed in terms of a science of action.

1. Antiquity and Middle Ages
Ancient and medieval philosophies always linked human action to a theory of the good, just, and happy life, referring to concepts and problems that have shaped discussion right up to the present day. Thus in Plato (427-347 B.C.; → Platonism) we find *autarkeia*, the right ordering of the → soul that expresses itself in the striving for the → good and that

is a condition for fulfillment of the true → self (*Phlb.* 67A; *Ti.* 68C; *Plt.* 443C-E). Aristotle (384-322 B.C.; → Aristotelianism) considered the → teleological structure of human action, which manifests itself in → reason's choice *(proairesis)* of means to achieve the end (*Eth. Nic.* 1111B, 1112B-1113A; *Metaph.* 1025B). In → Augustine (354-430) we find the role of the will in pursuit of happiness and the related → freedom in action (*De Trin.* 13.20.25; *Conf.* 10.21.31; *De lib. arb.* 3.255; → Augustine's Theology). → Thomas Aquinas (1224/25-74) distinguished between *actiones humanae* (human actions) and *actiones hominis* (actions of a person; behavior) (*Summa theol.* I of II, q. 1, art. 1; → Thomism). A general feature in all these approaches is that reason has a constitutive role in characterizing an activity as an action.

2. Modern Period

The feature of a general theory of action that led to later intensive interest in the topic of human action came to light for the first time in English → empiricism, which shows that the largely unexplained phenomenon of human action embraces many complex problems in → ethics, → epistemology, political philosophy, and → anthropology, and also that answers to central questions in these disciplines can be expected from an analysis and conceptual clarification of action. In deliberate opposition to traditional ideas, with their speculative content and orientation to everyday human life, modern discussions have sought a theory of human action according to the model of natural science.

Self-preservation functions as a quasi-mechanistic principle of nature whose effects on action precede any influence exerted by reason. On the basis of this principle, one may distinguish three models of action in T. Hobbes (1588-1679): (1) the model of the emotionally determined action as a necessary effect from within the activity of the emotions, with a causal nexus extending from the object to cognitive representation, on to emotion, to the engagement of nerves, and finally to bodily movement (*De corp.* 25.12); (2) the model of the determined act of will, an act in which the deed is merely the phenomenal expression of the will, which in its own turn is dependent on deliberation; and (3) a model on the basis of natural law, in which reason plays the role of mediator between the telos of self-preservation, on the one hand, and concrete action, on the other (*De hom.* 12.1).

For J. Locke (1632-1704), the desire to avoid uneasiness and to attain happiness directs the will as an innate practical principle (*Essay* 2.21.31; → Fate and [Good] Fortune) and mediates between the general principle of self-preservation and actions. Not for the first time, but with particular clarity, we find the vital insight — which is essential to action that is morally and legally relevant — that if an act of will precedes action, lack of such an exercise of will can also be a form of action (ibid. 2.21.28).

D. Hume's (1711-76) penetrating criticism of the epistemologically naive acceptance by contemporary philosophy and science of the universal validity of → causality in → nature not merely was applicable to the sphere of human action but found in such action a special paradigm in formulating a psychophysical problem that is still under discussion. That is, if we presuppose a strict determinism in nature that is independent of all → experience, what does it mean to propose a mental cause for a material effect (e.g., a physical movement), such as is at issue in talk about human action (*Inquiry* 7.1)?

In answer to Hume, I. Kant (1724-1804; → Kantianism) tried to save the freedom of action on the premise of the general validity of causality by distinguishing between the *Ding an sich* (the thing-in-itself) and the phenomenon (*Critique of Pure Reason*, B19-20). As a phenomenon, an act is subject to all the laws that obtain in nature (esp. that of causality), but as the effect of a spontaneous activity of the will, as an intelligible action, it can at least be thought of as free (ibid., B27, B561ff.; *Foundations of the Metaphysics of Morals*, AA 4.446-63). Kant, however, did not try to develop a general theory of action, although recent investigations (F. Kaulbach) have sought to establish the thesis that the principle of action is basic to Kant's whole philosophy. They thus find in it an important starting point for the development in modern discussion of a morally neutral concept of action on a transcendental basis (G. Prauss 1983).

3. Present-Day Discussion

The development of the theme in the 20th century follows two directions. On the one hand, a theory of action is developed out of the specific epistemological interest of the human sciences (→ sociology, → psychology, etc.), which regard action as a basic category of inquiry (M. → Weber, A. Gehlen). On the other hand, a theory of action is regarded as a natural subject of interdisciplinary study (see Lenk 1980, 9-11), with input from such varied academic fields as → logic, systems theory, → analytic philosophy, transcendental philosophy, linguistic philosophy, social science, psychology, → hermeneutics, and behavioral research, and which is only loosely linked to the philosophical tradition. In either case, the theory of action involves the aim of working out a position in the problems and tasks confronting individual disciplines and philosophy and in clear opposition to the traditional metaphysics of act (behaviorism).

3.1. Sociology

Of fundamental importance in constructing a new theory of human action is the sociology of Max Weber (1864-1920), which is essentially a theory of social action. Its goal is to interpret this action and thus to explain its course and effect. Action is viewed as conduct that actively or passively is given subjective → meaning. Social action has a meaningful reference to the conduct of others, to which it is oriented. Purposive-rational action is the ideal type used by Weber, against which concrete action is measured; with regard to the economy of means to achieve a given end, such action possesses the highest possible certainty and clarity.

Asking what "meaning" signifies in the context of action, Alfred Schütz (1899-1959) distinguishes between (1) action taking place as such *(actio)* and aiming at a specific form of a completed event (action), and (2) this action *(actum)* itself as that which is generated by acting. The meaning or point of action resides in the preliminary plan of an action (the intended result), and it is precisely here that action differs from behavior. The temporal mode characterizing action in the purposive-rational meaning thus determined is that of the past. The projection or plan of such action anticipates action as the result attained by acting and thus as a fully specific event that has already occurred.

3.2. Anthropology

In the anthropology of Arnold Gehlen (1904-76), action is the basic category in interpreting cultural achievement and thus in explaining the human ability to survive. Action is the changing of reality according to an idea of it. Defects in the conditions of human existence are changed into chances for maintaining life. The general condition on which human action is possible is the fact that impulses can be restrained. There is thus the gap between a need and satisfying it; into this gap action comes, both inward (thought as a testing of action) and outward. Action finds security in → institutions, which ease the burden of developing motives and making decisions in each new situation.

3.3. Analytic Action

Among the most important modern impulses toward a general theory of action, especially in clarification of problems in semantics (A. C. Danto) and logic (G. H. von Wright), is work in the sphere of analytic philosophy. Borrowing from the refusal of L. Wittgenstein (1889-1951) to distinguish between willing and acting, and from his idea of language games as the union of speech and action, analytic theory of action asserts that an act can be explained only from the intention of the one who performs it (G. E. M. Anscombe) or from a causality, of which the intention is only a special instance in the sense of asserting logical reasons for the act (D. Davidson). In contrast, the close link between speaking and acting leads to an explanation of speech (→ Language) in terms of action, according to which so-called performative statements (e.g., commands and promises) are not true or false but either succeed or fail (J. L. Austin). On the basis of structural identity in the sense of regulated conduct, this link also leads to a theory of speech as a subpart of a theory of action (J. Searle).

Bibliography: G. E. M. Anscombe, *Intention* (Oxford, 1957) • J. L. Austin, *How to Do Things with Words* (Cambridge, Mass., 1962) • M. Brand, *Intending and Acting* (Cambridge, Mass., 1984) • R. Bubner, *Handlung, Sprache und Vernunft* (2d ed.; Frankfurt, 1982) • R. S. Burt, *Toward a Structural Theory of Action* (New York, 1982) • A. C. Danto, *Analytical Philosophy of Action* (Cambridge, 1973) • D. Davidson, "Actions, Reasons, and Causes," *JPh* 60 (1963) 685-700 • A. Gehlen, *Der Mensch* (13th ed.; Wiesbaden, 1986) • C. Ginet, *On Action* (Cambridge, 1990) • A. I. Goldman, *A Theory of Human Action* (Princeton, 1970) • F. Kaulbach, *Das Prinzip Handlung in der Philosophie Kants* (Berlin, 1978) • H. Lenk, ed., *Handlungstheorien interdisziplinär* (4 vols.; Munich, 1977-81) • G. Meggle and A. Beckermann, eds., *Analytische Handlungstheorie* (Frankfurt, 1985) bibliography • C. J. Moya, *The Philosophy of Action* (Cambridge, 1990) • J. Pörn, *Action Theory and Social Science* (Dordrecht, 1977) • G. Prauss, *Kant über Freiheit als Autonomie* (Frankfurt, 1983); idem, ed., *Handlungstheorie und Transzendentalphilosophie* (Frankfurt, 1986) • A. Schütz, *Der sinnhafte Aufbau der sozialen Welt* (2d ed., Frankfurt, 1981) • J. Searle, *Speech Acts* (Cambridge, 1969) • R. Taylor, *Action and Purpose* (Atlantic Highlands, N.J., 1980) • J. E. Tomberlin, ed., *Action Theory and Philosophy of Mind* (Atascadero, Calif., 1990) • M. Weber, *Economy and Society: An Outline of Interpretive Sociology* (2 vols.; Berkeley, Calif., 1978; orig. pub., 1922) • G. H. von Wright, *Handlung, Norm und Intention* (Berlin, 1977).

Manfred Middendorf

Acts of the Apostles

1. Author

Acts is the second part of the Lukan document, with the Gospel of John separating the two in the canon. According to ancient Christian tradition, the author is the physician Luke, a coworker of → Paul (Col. 4:14). The author's interest focuses on Paul, his mission, and his fate (Acts 9; 11; 13–28). Arguments against authorship by a coworker are the biographical defects and the lack of specific features of Pauline theology. Nevertheless, the author shows a good knowledge of the nonpolemical, "catholic" Paul whom we know from marginal observations in the Epistles. Hence he might very well have come from the Pauline circle.

2. Structure

The structure follows the geographic theme of 1:8. The first part of the book (1:1–8:4) deals with the → primitive Christian community in Jerusalem. The second part (8:5–15:35) treats the mission to Samaria, the beginnings of the Gentile mission, the first work of Paul, and the apostolic council. The third part (15:36–19:20) covers Paul's mission to Asia Minor and Europe. The final part (19:21–28:31) deals with the prosecution of Paul in Jerusalem and Rome.

3. Sources

The author had extensive but disparate sources at his disposal. First, he had oral information, reports, and traditions. These account for the fact that he includes stories of the reception of the message as well as its proclamation. Then he had some written materials (esp. in the first parts) that we can no longer reconstruct because they have been worked over so much both linguistically and theologically. Finally, he had the "we source," which in the later parts describes the routes and sites of some of Paul's missionary work.

4. Text

We have two sharply divergent versions of the text, the Egyptian (Alexandrian) and the Western. The latter, represented especially by Codex Bezae Cantabrigiensis (→ Biblical Manuscripts), is a deliberate editing of the original, dating from the second century. A distinctive feature is its attempt to soften the Jewish-Christian character and to make the work more Gentile Christian and catholic by stressing Jewish guilt. Especially important is the ethical re-

working of the cultic decree of the apostolic council (15:20, 29; 21:25).

5. Style

The style gives evidence of great linguistic and narrative skill. Using variety and vividness, the author tells his story in lively incidents and details instead of settling for mere reports and abstract theological expositions (Acts 2:10-11; 17; 20). He uses the Greek of the LXX as well as the Koine, or common speech, of his day (→ Greek Language).

6. Historical Significance

Acts is a unique source for information about the beginnings of Christianity. Although fragmentary, it gives us information about the primitive community, the first mission outside Jerusalem in various parts of the world, the work of Paul, and the church situation in the author's day. The author is well informed about the political, religious, and social conditions in → Palestine and is acquainted with legal procedure, for example, in the case brought against Paul (chaps. 21–28). As a historian, he works theologically and sees events in terms of God's direction of history. He works over his traditions conservatively, especially the "liberal" ones involving criticism of the law, the temple, and Israel. He has been unjustifiably disparaged, especially for his depiction of Paul, which in many features is correct, if selective.

7. Theology

The author's theology is expressed in the form of charismatic-prophetic interpretations of Scripture (2:16-21, 25-36; 3:13-16, 22-26; 4:25-28; 5:30-31; 7; 13:17-22; 15:15-18). It comes to expression in the preaching of the apostles, especially Peter and Paul. Manifestations of the Spirit such as → miracles confirm this preaching (2:43; 3:1-8; 5:12; 6:8; 9:32-42; 13:4-12; 15:12; 16:16-26; 19:11-12; 20:7-12; 28:9). The main theme is the restoration of God's people by the Messiah Jesus (2:22-24, 27-33, 38-39; 3:13-21; 15:15-17). The promises come to fulfillment above all in the church as the true and → penitent Israel.

The church as the people of the Spirit consists primarily of converted Jews who accept the Messiah of Israel (see again 2:22-24, 27-33, 38-39; 3:13-21; 15:15-17). The rise of the true eschatological Israel is depicted in terms of mass conversions of the Jews (2:41; 4:4; 5:14; 6:1, 7; 9:42; 12:24; 13:43; 14:1; etc.). To this Israel of the Spirit (2:17-21) the → Gentiles are added, which the author regards as a fulfillment of the divine promises (Luke 24:44-47; Acts 1:6, 8; 2:39; 3:25; 10–11; 13:42-48; 15:7-8, 14-17). As a fulfillment of Scripture, the Gentile mission can be seen to be God's work and initiative (10–11; 15:7-8). Impenitent Israel — the synagogue — is cut off from God's people because it rejects the Messiah Jesus (13:46).

The church is the direct continuation of the history of God's people that begins with → Abraham (Luke 1:67-75; Acts 7). The promised → salvation comes through the work of the God of the patriarchs (3:13-15; 5:30; 7:32, 46; 13:17) and through the Messiah Jesus. The death of Jesus by itself does not have → atoning significance. Reconciliation means that God turns in → love to his people and restores them in grace. Salvation comes only through God's → grace, with forgiveness of sins through Christ's → resurrection (2:38; 3:19-26; 4:12; 13:39; 15:11).

Because the → law is a mark of the people of God, the → church sees to its observance. The primitive community is faithful to the law (6:11, 13-14; 10:14, 28; 11:3, 8; 21:21). So too is Paul (18:18; 21:24; 22:3; 23:5; 24:14-16; 25:8; 28:17). Fixed cultic traditions are adopted, but the law is expounded in terms of the first commandment — namely, obedience to the one God of Israel (7:38-43). → Jewish Christians keep the whole law, but only parts of the law are made binding on Gentile Christians (15:20, 29; 21:25). The sayings criticizing the → temple, Israel, and the law, which the author knows from the tradition, he repudiates as false accusations (6:11-14; 21:21, 28; 22:3).

A widespread theory is that Luke could have written Acts to solve the problem of the delay in the → parousia, with the help of the idea of epochs in salvation history. The history of Jesus is the middle of time, and the end will come in a → future that cannot be calculated. The author is aware of the delay, but it is indeed not theologically decisive for him. The events of the resurrection and ascension of the Messiah Jesus, along with the outpouring of the Spirit, mean that the last days have dawned (2:17; 17:31). The events of the end time involve a historical process in which the promises come to successive fulfillment, ending with the return of the Messiah Jesus. Already the promises have been fulfilled in part (2:17, 33; 13:32-33; 15:16-18). In a future that is probably near, they will come to complete fulfillment with the → apocatastasis (1:11; 3:19-21; 17:30-31; 23:6; 24:15, 21; 26:6-8; 28:20). The author regards history as a long period of time on which one can look back (15:7, 9, 14, 19; 3:21; cf. chap. 7 and 13:16-23). In contrast, now that the end time has begun, one is not to expect any very prolonged future (2:17-21).

8. Apostolic Council

At the heart of Acts stands the apostolic council of 15:1-29. Having accepted for some time a Gentile mission that was not under the law (10:34-35; 11:1-18; 13–14; Galatians 1–2), the church faced demands that Gentile Christians should receive → circumcision and observe the law (15:1, 5). The issue is that of the place of the law in the church, which was resolved with the apostolic decree (15:1, 29; 21:25). A fundamental part of the law is laid on the Gentiles, but they are free regarding the rest. Paul maintains (Galatians 2) that the council recognized that the Gentile mission was not under the law and that no obligations were put upon Gentiles. He neither mentions the decree nor takes it as a guide. It is undoubtedly historical, but perhaps it belongs to some other occasion than that of Acts 15 and Galatians 2. For Luke the council and the decree support the idea that the church is the end-time Israel. What influences Paul, however, is the battle for his independent apostolate.

Bibliography: F. Bovon, *Luke the Theologian* (Allison Park, Pa., 1987) • C. Burchard, *Der dreizehnte Zeuge* (Göttingen, 1970) • H. Conzelmann, *The Theology of St. Luke* (New York, 1960) • M. Dibelius, *Studies in the Acts of the Apostles* (London, 1956) • E. J. Epp, *The Theological Tendency of Codex Bezae Cantabrigiensis in Acts* (Cambridge, 1966) • E. Haenchen, *The Acts of the Apostles* (Philadelphia, 1971) • M. Hengel, *Acts and the History of Earliest Christianity* (Philadelphia, 1979) • J. Jervell, *Luke and the People of God* (Minneapolis, 1972) • G. Lohfink, *Die Sammlung Israels. Eine Untersuchung zur Lukanischen Ekklesiologie* (Munich, 1975) • R. Maddox, *The Purpose of Luke-Acts* (Göttingen, 1982) • E. Plümacher, *Lukas als hellenistischer Schriftsteller* (Göttingen, 1972) • P. Vielhauer, "On the 'Paulinism' of Acts," *Studies in Luke-Acts* (ed. L. E. Keck and J. L. Martyn; Nashville, 1966) 33-50 • U. Wilckens, *Die Missionsreden der Apostelgeschichte* (Neukirchen, 1961; 3d ed., 1974).

Jacob Jervell

Adam

In the OT *'ādām* is a collective term for humanity, a term for the individual, and finally a proper name (Genesis 1–11). Adam stands in a special relation to God, created by him and bearing his image. Adam is the crown of → creation (§2) and has almost divine rank (e.g., 1:26-27; 5:3). He is a social being, and God gives him dominion over the rest of creation (1:26-28; 2:18-20). Yet limits are set for him as a creature. He is fully dependent on God and is mortal. The story of the fall (chap. 3) elucidates the essential limitation. Transgression of God's command brings → guilt and → punishment (§2), though without lessening God's goodness.

In Jewish theology Adam, on the one hand, is created glorious, great, and immortal (Sir. 49:16; *b. Sanh.* 38d). He is the ancestor of Israel, a patriarch and a → high priest (Wis. 10:1; *Gen. Rab.* 24:2). On the other hand, his → sin (§1) corrupts the good creation, brings → death to his descendants, and threatens the existence of → Israel (4 Ezra 3:7, 21; 7:118; *2 Apoc. Bar.* 17:3; 23:4; 48:42-43).

In the NT Adam plays a theologically significant role only in the Pauline writings. Paul uses Adam to show the cosmic meaning of the Christ-event, which overcomes the fateful consequences of Adam's transgression of the command. Through Adam death and sin came into the world, creation was given up to vanity, and human beings became totally unable to keep the → law (Rom. 5:12-14; 7:7-12; 8:22; 1 Cor. 15:22, 45). Christ as the "second" or "last" Adam is the true image of God (2 Cor. 4:4). In him, through the → righteousness of God, the life that Adam forfeited is granted to all (Rom. 5:12-21). The risen and exalted Christ bears the image of the heavenly man and therefore the image of the eschatological humanity issuing from the → resurrection (1 Cor. 15:45-49). The rest of the NT has only a few allusions to Adam, which give no evidence of systematic elaboration (Luke 3:38; 1 Tim. 2:13-14; Jude 14).

In many of the mythological systems of → Gnosticism we find speculations about Adam in relation to anthropogenesis and → soteriology. As the heavenly primal man, Adam is an emanation of the original divine principle. As the earthly man, Adam is a creature of the Demiurge, but the life-giving divine Spirit has been breathed into him, and an image of the heavenly Adam is imprisoned in him (BG 35:3-5; 48:1ff.; Hippolytus *Haer.* 5.7.7; 5.19.13ff.). The divine Spirit in us is the presupposition of redeeming knowledge (→ Epistemology) of our imprisonment in the world and of our divine origin. This knowledge grants liberation for return to the heavenly home.

In the → Koran, Adam is the first unbeliever, yet he also is the elect servant of Allah (3:33; 20:122). The foundation is thus laid for the separation of the righteous from sinners at the judgment.

Bibliography: C. K. BARRETT, *From First Adam to Last* (New York, 1962) • K. BARTH, *CD* IV/1, 504-13 • O. BETZ et al., "Adam," *TRE* 1.414-37 • E. BRANDEN-BURGER, *Adam und Christus* (Neukirchen, 1962) • J. JEREMIAS, "Ἀδάμ," *TDNT* 1.141-43 • J. JERVELL, *Imago Dei* (Göttingen, 1960) • B. SCHALLER, "Ἀδάμ," *EDNT* 1.27-28 • H.-M. SCHENKE, *Der Gott "Mensch" in der Gnosis* (Göttingen, 1962) • R. SCROGGS, *The Last Adam* (Philadelphia, 1966).

JACOB JERVELL

Addiction → Substance Abuse

Adiaphora

1. "Adiaphora," from the Gk. pl. *adiaphora* (cf. Lat. sing. *indifferens*), denotes things that are indifferent. A broad range of usage for what is permitted or what is between permission and proscription has helped to determine its historical significance.

The term occurs in the → ethics of antiquity, especially in → Stoicism. The Stoics tried to see how things that encounter us or acts that we perform have a moral significance that is not intrinsic to them. Christian ethics adopted the term but used it in many different ways as it faced problems relating to specific places and developments. Common to the usage as a whole, the concept sets a limit to what may be justified in terms of Christian ethics.

2.1. In Christian ethics the term determines the range of biblical guidance insofar as this is understood as a comprehensive instruction for the Christian life. Adiaphora are matters in secular life for which the Bible gives no specific guidance.

2.2. The term fixes the range of a morality that consists of commands and prohibitions. As considered in ethical textbooks, adiaphora are things that are permitted or things that fall between command and prohibition. Over against them, some have maintained the comprehensive nexus of moral → duty (F. D. E. → Schleiermacher). Protestant ethics has largely followed the latter view and has thus maintained a Christian → freedom that exempts no sphere of life from moral accountability. Only marginally is it asked whether a "free area" — as, for example, in art — can exist (e.g., W. Trillhaas).

2.3. The fundamental problem arises when Christian freedom in all its scope is viewed as freedom from works. One might include all that we experience and do within such a freedom, which in turn is needed if any of our deeds is to be morally relevant before God. In such a view, adiaphora cannot refer to morally indifferent things but simply to all things without distinction. This position avoids both antinomianism and the binding of freedom to a specific morality. This is how we are to understand M. → Luther's "freedom of a Christian." The lordship of Christians over all things rests on their all having the same value for → righteousness before God. The evaluation of all things then relates to whether they give offense to the faith of others (see Romans 14; 1 Corinthians 8–10). The criterion is the need of the neighbor. In this context there can be no regard for distinctions in moral validity.

2.4. Church ordinances (ceremonies) are paradigms by which to test Christian freedom, a point that textbooks of → dogmatics discuss. Luther understood the validity of church rulings in terms of Christian freedom. In the first adiaphora controversy a debate about this question arose between the position of P. → Melanchthon (1497-1560) and the → Gnesio-Lutherans, especially M. Flacius (1520-75), writing in his *Liber de veris et falsis adiaphoris* (1549). Flacius's opinion is expressed in FC 10 in the statement that in the case of confession (i.e., when it is necessary under persecution to confess evangelical teaching for the sake of the truth of the → gospel), church ordinances are also included. An application of this understanding to moral or political matters is not in view. This application comes in the more precise usage of the phrase → *status confessionis* only in the 19th century (→ Church Struggle). The question of the obligatoriness of church ordinances also brings to mind the broader question of the theological significance of church order. This has been a decisive question since the German church struggle.

3. The extension of the problem to political matters makes it necessary to define the relations between the obedience of → faith (§3), → freedom (§2), and → reason. What is "reasonable" for Christians can be understood only in light of freedom, which is not based on equating "reasonable" and "ethically indifferent." Those who ask whether a decision about what is ethically reasonable could ever contradict what is taken as the truth of the gospel must not assume that guidance for all actions can be derived directly from the gospel. To establish such a contradiction would require theological judgment. No view of Christian ethics leads to the conclusion that political decisions would be indifferent in regard to Christian freedom.

Bibliography: K. BAIER, *The Moral Point of View* (Ithaca, N.Y., 1958) • J. GOTTSCHICK, "Adiaphora," *RE* 1.168-79 • T. GRAEBNER, *The Borderland of Right and Wrong* (5th ed.; St. Louis, 1938) • C. L. MANSCHRECK, "The Role of Melanchthon in the Adiaphora Controversy," *ARG* 48 (1957) 165-82 • G. MAURACH and K. ALAND, "Adiaphora," *HWP* 1.83-85 • M. SCHLOEMANN, "Der besondere Bekenntnisfall. Begriffsgeschichtliche und systematische Beobachtungen zum casus confessionis vor, in und nach Daressalam 1977," *Politik als Glaubenssache? Beiträge zur Klärung des Status Confessionis im südlichen Afrika und in anderen soziologischen Kontexten* (R. Bertram et al.; ed. E. Lorenz; Erlangen, 1983) 48-98

• W. TRILLHAAS, "Adiaphoron. Erneute Erwägung eines alten Begriffs," *TLZ* 79 (1954) 457-62; idem, *Ethik* (3d ed.; Berlin, 1970) • B. J. VERKAMP, *The Indifferent Mean: Adiaphorism in the English Reformation to 1554* (Athens, Ohio, 1977).

HANS G. ULRICH

Admonition → Parenesis

Adoptionism → Trinity

Adult Education → Continuing Education

Adulthood

Legally, psychologically, philosophically, and theologically, "adulthood" is the term for those who have reached a stage or time in the → development of the subjectivity of the human → person.

In law adulthood confers such rights as the right to vote or to enter into contracts, but it also exposes one to penalties, since coming of age carries with it → responsibility and expectation of a certain type of conduct. Basic here is the psychological premise and observation that in the process of → socialization, we become increasingly capable of internalizing → norms and roles and thus of keeping the elementary laws of social interaction (→ Development 2; Society).

We find a similar usage in → education. Adulthood, or maturity, is the comprehensive goal of educational processes. In contrast to the common view of education as a preparing of individuals to participate in human affairs (→ Humanity) and controlling → nature, the emphasis in critical eductional theory falls on the need to free the individual from social pressures and blinders (→ Consumption; Manipulation; Mass Media).

Current educational and political debates often discuss the theme under the slogan of → emancipation, but in reality they are part of the struggle for a view of humanity (→ Anthropology; Modern Period) that embodies the Promethean idealism cf the → Enlightenment. Against this view, which finds pregnant expression in I. Kant's (1724-1804) famous formula that we use our understanding without direction from anyone else (→ Autonomy; Kantianism), we find two opposing emphases.

First is the insight into the power of the otherness of reason (H. Böhme and G. Böhme), which serves as criticism of a one-sided stress upon → reason in the concept of adulthood. Second, in criticism of the → individualism involved, it is pointed out that individual adulthood is doomed to destruction (H. J. Heydorn, 119), where this is invoked to validate the principle of liberal capitalism (→ Liberalism); we achieve adulthood only in concert with all or else not at all.

In regard to the concept of adulthood, Christianity has a double function, as does → religion in general. On the one hand, there is no doubt that most attempts to achieve individual adulthood have also been directed against the church and religious → institutions insofar as these tend to act as (oppressive) guardians and teachers. On the other hand, Christianity over its history has contributed to social and individual emancipation; repeatedly it has resisted social movements that threaten individual development.

Theology is actively at work on the problems of adulthood in such contexts as → autonomy and creaturehood (→ Creation), liberation and redemption (→ Soteriology).

→ Church Membership; Human and Civil Rights; Identity; Initiation Rites

Bibliography: H. BÖHME and G. BÖHME, *Das Andere der Vernunft* (Frankfurt, 1983) • E. H. ERIKSON, ed., *Adulthood* (New York, 1978) • H. J. HEYDORN, *Zu einer Neufassung des Bildungsbegriffs* (Frankfurt, 1972) • I. KANT, "What Is Enlightenment?" (1783), *Foundations of the Metaphysics of Morals and What Is Enlightenment?* (trans. L. W. Beck; Indianapolis, 1959) 85-92 • W. KERN and C. LINK, "Autonomie und Geschöpflichkeit," *Christlicher Glaube in moderner Gesellschaft* (Freiburg, 1982) 18.101-48 • S. B. MERRIAM and M. C. CLARK, *Lifelines: Patterns of Work, Love, and Learning in Adulthood* (San Francisco, 1991) • T. RENDTORFF, "Emanzipation und christliche Freiheit," *Christlicher Glaube in moderner Gesellschaft* (Freiburg, 1982) 18.149-79 • E. E. WHITEHEAD and J. D. WHITEHEAD, *Christian Life Patterns: The Psychological Challenges and Religious Invitations of Adult Life* (Garden City, N.Y., 1979).

HERMANN STEINKAMP

Adveniat → Relief Organizations

Advent → Church Year

Adventists

1. History
2. Organization, Structure, and Activities
3. Doctrine and Worship

Adventism began as a 19th-century apocalyptic movement (→ Apocalypticism 3) in the United States. It led directly to the development of the Advent Christian Church, the Church of God of the Abrahamic Faith, and, the largest of the Adventist denominations, the Seventh-day Adventist Church (SDA). Other groups influenced by, but less directly connected with, Adventism include the → Jehovah's Witnesses and the → Worldwide Church of God.

1. History
During the first half of the 19th century the United States experienced an evangelical religious revival known as the Second Great Awakening. Postmillennialism (→ Millenarianism) was a dominant theme of this revival, characterizing both mainstream churches and revivalists such as A. Campbell (1788-1866), while other forms of millennialism appeared among the Shakers, → Mormons, and John Humphrey Noyes's → Oneida Community. By the 1820s W. Miller (1782-1849), a farmer in upstate New York, developed a premillennialism that was very similar to, but apparently independent of, contemporary British premillennialism. On the basis of Daniel 8, Miller calculated that Christ would return (→ Parousia) in 1843/44 — a specific time prediction that differentiated him from other millennialist thinkers — and began publicly preaching this belief in 1831. He thus started Adventism, a broad revival movement that at first (ca. 1839-44) embraced many Christian circles.

At its peak, Adventism broke with the existing churches, regarding them as the Babylon of Revelation because of their growing opposition to Miller's teaching. After the Great Disappointment of October 22, 1844, the movement's last significant predicted date for Christ's coming, some Adventists found an explanation for the delay. They related Dan. 8:14 to Hebrews 8–9, concluding that the final ministry of Christ began on October 22, 1844, in the heavenly sanctuary and avails for the purifying of the church (the "investigative judgment"). At the same time, J. Bates (1792-1872), a former ship captain, advanced the doctrine of the eschatological restoration of the biblical day of rest (→ Sabbath), which he had taken over from a small group of Seventh Day Baptists. His writings convinced the young Adventist itinerant preacher J. White and his visionary wife,

E. G. White (1827-1915). Mrs. White, who was understood in terms of the "spirit of prophecy" of Rev. 19:10, played a decisive role in consolidating the SDA after 1846. The main SDA doctrines are expectation of Christ's coming (the Advent hope), sanctification (the present as an age of judgment), and the Sabbath (as a seal of the end-time community). Michigan churches formed the first state conference in 1862, and a General Conference was organized the following year. The first official missionary went to Europe in 1874. The actual founder of the mission in Europe, from 1886 on, was the gifted L. R. Conradi (1856-1939). In 1932 Conradi left the SDA to join the Seventh Day Baptists.

2. Organization, Structure, and Activities

In 1994 the SDA was at work in 204 countries, with a total worldwide membership exceeding 7.5 million. The annual rate of growth is between 6 and 7 percent. Over three-quarters of the members now live in Asia, Africa, and Latin America. The formerly separatist American sect has thus become a worldwide church that enjoys general recognition, engages in mission, and carries out humanitarian aid activities.

The base of the organization is the local church, which is led by elders, a church board, and a full-time pastor, who is typically theologically well trained and who is appointed by the local conference (a regional association of churches). Local conferences, in turn, are grouped into union conferences, which are grouped into divisions, the officers of which are part of the General Conference, whose staff is elected every five years at a meeting of delegates and which directs the church worldwide from Silver Spring, Maryland. Biblical tithes and other gifts supply the finances. The level of giving surpasses that of most churches. Apart from mission abroad, among the missionary and evangelistic activities especially worthy of note are publishing, radio and television programs (*Voice of Prophecy* and *It Is Written*), lectures and conferences on evangelism, Bible courses, and correspondence courses (The Bible Speaks). Welfare, medical, and educational work has also been developed in a way that is surprising in what began as an apocalyptic fellowship. Across the globe there are many hospitals, sanatoriums, clinics, courses to stop smoking, programs for the blind, health-food workshops, and over 5,500 schools.

3. Doctrine and Worship

The SDA confesses the Trinitarian and Christological faith of the early creeds, espouses the Reformation doctrines of → justification and grace, and stresses the exclusive authority of Scripture for life and teaching. In addition, it has its own distinctive tradition with its OT and apocalyptic features.

3.1. The SDA does not try to calculate when the end will come, but it does believe that the end time dawned in 1844. Appealing to God's plan for salvation history as they take it from the Bible, Seventh-day Adventists expect a certain sequence of apocalyptic events in which Satan will play a great role as a power against God (→ Devil).

3.2. To the → biblicist approach corresponds a relatively strong emphasis on the OT, whose ordinances and events are regarded as foreshadowings of the Christian → order of salvation and salvation history. Hence at many points the SDA understands the NT in the light of the OT. (More recently there has been a change in this regard.)

3.3. With a → Calvinistic root, the SDA's thinking on the law and its ordinances has led to the adoption of many OT rules in life and diet, thereby opening itself to the charge of legalism. The main theological point here is the understanding of the → Decalogue as reflecting the basic moral law given to the race at creation.

3.4. The Sabbath commandment (i.e., the one relating to the seventh day, or Saturday) has thus become a central point whereby Advent belief may be known and demonstrated. Although the exegetical and historical arguments of the SDA may not convince non-Adventist theologians, the religious zeal with which the group honors the Sabbath is impressive.

3.5. The SDA rejects natural immortality, favoring instead a conditionalist view in which immortality is given at the resurrection, which occurs at Christ's second coming. It is given only to the saved, who spend the next 1,000 years in heaven. The wicked are resurrected at the end of this millennium, only to be destroyed completely in the cleansing of the earth before the creation of "a new heaven and a new earth."

3.6. The Magna Carta of Adventist proclamation is the threefold angel message of Rev. 14:6-12, which is the basis for the SDA's ecclesiological self-understanding. It is the remnant end-time community (Rev. 12:17), whose obedience of faith marks it off from the world, which is under the dominion of the devil, and from a worldly church. The result is a separatist program that has slowly been softened by numerous encounters with other Christians and churches on the mission field and in humanitarian work. Among some present-day Adventist theologians one may detect a trend toward a certain ecumenical openness and to critical questioning of what is specifically Adventist, especially in respect to the role of E. G. White.

3.7. Influenced by the American health reform movement of the 1830s and 1840s (itself part of the general religious and social reform of the period), E. G. White made health a major element of SDA belief and practice. She promoted vegetarianism and drugless therapies and helped establish abstinence from alcoholic beverages and tobacco as requirements of the Adventist faith. Later in the 19th century, medical doctor J. H. Kellogg (1852-1943), director of the Battle Creek (Mich.) Sanitarium, tirelessly promoted health reform by writing books, developing new therapies, and inventing health foods. The most notable of these foods was Corn Flakes, which started the breakfast-food industry in Battle Creek.

Adventist worship has pietist and revivalist features. It consists of Bible discussion (mostly in small groups), prayer, music, and preaching. Stress falls on → conversion (§1) and personal faith. Infant → baptism is thus rejected. Baptism (or rebaptism upon entry into the church) is by immersion with the Trinitarian formula. Four times a year Adventist churches administer the Lord's Supper (interpreted in a Reformed sense; → Eucharist), using unleavened bread and nonalcoholic wine, preceded by → foot washing (see John 13).

Bibliography: SDA sources: SDA Bible Commentary (10 vols.; rev. ed.; Washington, D.C., 1976) vol. 10 serves as "encyclopedia" of the SDA • *Seventh-day Adventists Answer Questions on Doctrine* (Washington, D.C., 1957) • *Seventh-day Adventists Believe. . . . A Biblical Exposition of 27 Fundamental Doctrines* (Washington, D.C., 1988) • E. G. WHITE, *Testimonies for the Church* (9 vols.; 1855-1909; Mountain View, Calif., 1948).

Periodicals: Adventecho (formerly *Zionswächter; Adventbote*) (Hamburg, 1895-) • *Adventist Heritage: A Journal of Adventist History* (Riverside, Calif., 1974-) • *Review and Herald* (Washington, D.C., 1850-) • *Spectrum: Journal of the Association of Adventist Forums* (Takoma Park, Md., 1969-).

Criticism: H. BLOOM, "Seventh-day Adventism: Health, Prophecy, and Ellen Harmon White," *The American Religion: The Emergence of the Post-Christian Nation* (New York, 1992) 147-58 • A. HOEKEMA, *The Four Major Cults* (Grand Rapids, 1963) 89-169; idem, *Seventh-day Adventism* (Grand Rapids, 1972) • K. HUTTEN, *Seher, Grübler, Enthusiasten* (12th ed.; Stuttgart, 1982) 35-79 (bibliography) • W. MARTIN, *The Truth about Seventh-day Adventism* (Grand Rapids, 1960) • H. OBST, *Apostel und Propheten der Neuzeit* (2d ed.; Berlin, 1981) 194-236 • H.-D. REIMER, "Endzeitgemeinde im Wandel," *MEZW* (1973) 218ff. • H.-D. REIMER and O. EGGENBERGER, . . . *neben der Kirchen* (4th ed.; Constance, 1985) bibliography 179-217 • M. SCHMIDT and J. BUTSCHER, "Adventisten," *TRE* 1.454-62.

Other works: M. BARKUN, *Crucible of the Millennium: The Burned-over District of New York in the 1840s* (Syracuse, N.Y., 1986) • M. BULL and K. LOCKHARD, *Seeking a Sanctuary: Seventh-day Adventism and the American Dream* (San Francisco, 1989) • E. N. DICK, *William Miller and the Advent Crisis* (Berrien Springs, Mich., 1994) • R. A. DOAN, *The Miller Heresey, Millennialism, and American Culture* (Philadelphia, 1987) • L. E. FROOM, *Movement of Destiny* (Washington, D.C., 1971) • O. GMELING, *Christus der Herr im Glauben und Leben der STA* (Hamburg, 1965) • C. E. HEWITT, *Midnight and Morning* (Charlotte, N.C., 1983) • G. R. KNIGHT, *Millennial Fever and the End of the World: A Study of Millerite Adventism* (Boise, Idaho, 1993) • G. LAND, ed., *Adventism in America: A History* (Grand Rapids, 1986) • K. F. MUELLER, *Die Frühgeschichte der STA* (Marburg, 1969) • R. L. NUMBERS and J. M. BUTLER, eds., *The Disappointed: Millerism and Millenarianism in the Nineteenth Century* (Bloomington, Ind., 1987) • G. PADDERATZ, *Conradi und Hamburg. Die Anfänge der deutschen Adventgemeinde* (Hamburg, 1978) • A. L. WHITE, *Ellen G. White* (6 vols.; Washington, D.C., 1982-86).

ROLF J. PÖHLER, HANS-DIETHER REIMER†, and GARY LAND

Aesthetics

1. Concept
2. Characteristics
3. Criteria
4. Tasks
5. Religion

1. Concept

Traditionally "aesthetics" has been defined as the science of the beautiful. The word comes from the Gk. adjective *aisthētikē* (from the verb *aisthanomai,* meaning "perceive, experience"), with which a noun is understood such as *technē* (art) or *epistēmē* (knowledge). *Aisthētikē epistēmē* was thus originally the science of perception. Then the adjective took on the sense of giving direct pleasure in contemplation or → imagination — that is, beautiful, charming, and so forth.

A. Baumgarten (1714-62) first used the term "aesthetics" to denote the science of the beautiful. Today, however, people may speak of aesthetic experience in relation to what is sublime, tragic, or even ugly. This makes a modern definition extremely difficult. At a minimum one might say that aesthetics is the science of what is experienced aesthetically, with such experience involving the beautiful or something analogous.

2. Characteristics

In contrast to moral experience, aesthetic experience imposes no obligation. Whereas the → good implies duties, the beautiful does not. The beautiful does not need to be useful or to have a goal. Furthermore, aesthetic experience intensifies the feeling for life. Aristotle (384-322 B.C.) pointed out that the experience of tragedy induces a catharsis of the emotions. Art alone is not the object of aesthetics. Nature, too, can be experienced aesthetically.

3. Criteria

What gives an object aesthetic worth? We must distinguish here between special criteria that apply only to a specific art form and general criteria that are universally applicable. Various theories have arisen. One formal criterion is that the structure of an object must display *unity in diversity*. Chaos and monotony alike are contrary to an aesthetic experience. A second important criterion is *wealth of association*. Formally considered, ugly ruins can awaken associations and can thus be experienced as beautiful. A third criterion is the idea of *what is normal* (I. Kant). Some call this the concept of the standard model or the criterion of typical beauty. What is beautiful or aesthetically valuable is what conforms to its type or standard. Another aesthetic value is *indirectness*. An indirect rather than a direct communication of → meaning is calculated to affect us aesthetically. Any artistic expression stands in the context of rules of interpretation and inference by which it acquires its meaning. Many works of art can thus be experienced in many different senses.

Aesthetic evaluation of an object depends on which criteria we use. What is common to them all is that complicated structures are seen, difficulties in perception are overcome, and associative or rational conclusions are drawn that extend the mental or spiritual horizon.

4. Tasks

Besides the more speculative task, several problems need attention. First is the problem of the social significance of aesthetic value, or the problem of the relation of the artist to society. Another problem is that of interpretation. Should we consider a work of art in and of itself, or in its historical context? Is the interpretation of its author normative, or is it only one of many possible interpretations? Third are the problems of classification, including the question

whether we can have aesthetic experiences with the senses of smell or taste. A fourth problem is that of the relation between art and morals (→ Ethics). According to Plato (427-347 B.C.) and L. Tolstoy (1828-1910), works of art have aesthetic worth only if they also meet moral criteria. The churches, too, have often held this view, which was also found in the Communist understanding of art in terms of socialistic realism. A final important question is whether aesthetic values are objective or subjective. Here we also come up against the question of the → truth or verification of a work of art. Thinkers in both aesthetics and religious philosophy have often made a structural comparison between aesthetic and religious → experience. In both, a generally recognized verification causes difficulties if it claims more than subjective validity.

5. Religion

The usual approach to aesthetics and → religion is by way of art and religion. The relation has been variously interpreted in the course of history. In what are called primitive cultures the unity of art and religion is much greater than in so-called modern cultures. In the former, → dance, song, → images, and so forth are both an expression of artistic creation and a part of the religious ritual. Gradually, however, people began to separate the spheres of life, including the spheres of art and religion. To this → secularization of art corresponded a partial criticism of many art forms, and even hostility to them on the part of Christian churches. Dancing and the theater in particular came under criticism, and some literary products were classified as dangerous to religion. For the most part the reasons for criticism were moral, especially when it was a matter of human → sexuality.

Yet other than moral reasons also played a role. The prohibition of images often arose from the belief that the holy transcends every form. Many musical instruments were banned from the → liturgy because of their association with profane activities (→ Sacred and Profane). Not only in Christianity has such antagonism between religion and art occurred (→ Christian Art). As is well known, → Islam forbids images. Plato censured the poet Homer because he gave far too human a depiction of the gods, and → Buddhism and → Hinduism restrict the freedom of artistic creation with religious rules.

Any enmity between art and (Christian) religion is not intrinsic to either. The churches have gradually learned to respect the → autonomy of art. Nevertheless, one cannot deny that → theology has developed its understanding of ethics much more fully than it has of art and aesthetics. Its relation with art and aesthetics, however, is particularly important when we realize that aesthetic experience is more than a nonbinding experience of the beautiful. If it enriches life, then reflection on its relation to religion and → faith is inescapable. Certainly there is a need here for religious criticism. If aesthetic experience can enrich life and have a therapeutic function, art can be a rival of religion and become a kind of substitute religion. It also may be a first step on the way to religion. By reason of its structural similarity, aesthetic experience can pass over into religious experience. Art is also important in its bearing on theodicy. Suffering often results in an intensifying of life that shows structural similarity to aesthetic experience.

Finally, one must consider that → Jesus had a much more positive relation to aesthetic experience than might be suggested by the legalistic religion that Christianity as well as → Judaism has often become. Later thinking and preaching about God have often been couched only in moral terms, and the aesthetic aspects of the biblical message forgotten. Many problems are still present in this area. Working out a theological aesthetics is an important project that has thus far been largely neglected.

Bibliography: T. W. ADORNO, Aesthetic Theory (London, 1984) • H. U. VON BALTHASAR, The Glory of the Lord: A Theological Aesthetics (7 vols.; San Francisco, 1982-91) • R. BOHREN, Daß Gott schön werde. Praktische Theologie als theologische Ästhetik (Munich, 1975) • T. EAGLETON, The Ideology of the Aesthetic (Oxford, 1990) • W. P. ECKERT, G. ROHRMOSER, and H. SCHRÖER, "Ästhetik," TRE 1.544-72 • H.-G. GADAMER, Truth and Method (2d rev. ed.; New York, 1990) • K. E. GILBERT and H. KUHN, A History of Esthetics (rev. ed.; Bloomington, Ind., 1953) • N. HARTMANN, Ästhetik (Berlin, 1953) • H. G. HUBBELING, "Das Heilige und das Schöne. Gerardus van der Leeuws Anschauungen über das Verhältnis von Religion und Kunst," NZSTh 25 (1983) 1-19 • H. KÜNG, Art and the Question of Meaning (New York, 1981) • G. VAN DER LEEUW, Sacred and Profane Beauty (New York, 1963) • H. R. ROOKMAAKER, Art Needs No Justification (Leicester, Eng., 1978) • N. A. SCOTT JR., ed., The New Orpheus (New York, 1964) • W. TATARKIEWICZ, History of Aesthetics (ed. C. Barrett; 3 vols.; The Hague, 1970) • N. WOLTERSTORFF, Art in Action: Toward a Christian Aesthetic (Grand Rapids, 1980).

HUBERTUS G. HUBBELING†

Afghanistan

Afghanistan became a separate kingdom under Aḥmad Shāh Durrāni (ruled 1747-73), who, as an

	1960	1980	2000
Population (1,000s):	10,775	16,063	25,592
Annual growth rate (%):	2.27	–2.02	2.84

Area: 652,225 sq. km. (251,825 sq. mi.)

A.D. 2000

Population density: 39/sq. km. (102/sq. mi.)
Births / deaths: 4.67 / 1.84 per 100 population
Fertility rate: 6.30 per woman
Infant mortality rate: 143 per 1,000 live births
Life expectancy: 47.5 years (m: 47.0, f: 48.0)
Religious affiliation (%): Muslims 99.5, other 0.5.

officer of Nāder Shāh of Persia, left the army and was able to build his small Pashtuni state on the subjection of various ethnic groups in northeast Iran and central Asia. About 90 percent of the present-day population are rural peasants or → nomads. Approximately 78 percent belong to the → Sunni branch of → Islam, 20 percent are → Shiites, and 1 percent are Ismailis. The rest consist primarily of → Hindus, → Sikhs, adherents of traditional religions (the tribes in Nuristan), and a small number of Jews and Christians.

In July 1973, a coup overthrew Afghani king Zahir Shah, beginning a turbulent two decades that so far has failed to lead to political stability. A second coup in April 1978 ousted President Mohammad Daud, leading to the establishment of a pro-Soviet government. Troops from the USSR invaded Afghanistan in December 1979, occupying major cities until their final withdrawal in February 1989. The invasion provoked fierce resistance by rebel Muslim tribesmen, known collectively as the *mujahidin*. Their activity led ultimately to the collapse of the Communist regime in April 1992. Since that time, armed clashes among the various rebel groups have continued intermittently, preventing a recovery of the shattered economy and complicating the resettlement of the estimated seven million people who have had to flee their homes.

There are probably less than 1,000 indigenous Christians in Afghanistan, living mostly in cities. As a group, they are not organized in churches and cannot look back on a continuous history but only on sporadic missionary efforts. Thus in 1811-18 the Baptists translated the NT into Pashto, which with Dari (a form of Persian) is the national language. These efforts were unsuccessful or were officially repressed, partly by Russian colonial rule in Turkistan, partly by the British East India Company, and then, after liberation from British tutelage, by King Amānollāh Khān (1919-29).

Other Christians in the country are either immigrants or people temporarily in the country as technicians, merchants, trade representatives, diplomats, tourists, developers, or archaeologists, with their families, mostly from western Europe or North America, with some Russians and Asians. At the height of aid programs this group reached several thousand, not counting Russians and Indians. Almost all the aliens lived in Kabul. There official services (Roman Catholic) took place only in the Italian embassy chapel. Others worshiped in private houses. Only a few ministers were present, and these had come into the country with other jobs as teachers or in the medical assistance program. Alongside the Anglican and (since 1962) German congregations, an international Community Christian Church was founded in 1962. In 1971, in Kabul, this group succeeded in putting up the only church structure in the country (without a tower), but two years later this church was demolished by order of the government. In 1994 missionaries were not officially permitted, although the government welcomed the 70 Christian relief workers in the country.

Bibliography: A. BONNER, *Among the Afghans* (Durham, N.C., 1987) • H. S. BRADSHER, *Afghanistan and the Soviet Union* (2d ed.; Durham, N.C., 1985) • V. GREGORIAN, *The Emergence of Modern Afghanistan: Politics of Reform and Modernization, 1880-1946* (Stanford, Calif., 1969) • A. HYMAN, *Afghanistan and Soviet Domination, 1964-83* (New York, 1984) • L. B. POULLADA, *Reform and Rebellion in Afghanistan, 1919-1929* (Ithaca, N.Y., 1973).

CARSTEN COLPE

Africa

1. General Survey

1.1. *Population and Economic Potential*

With an area of 30.4 million sq. km. (11.7 million sq. mi.) and a population estimated to reach 820 million in 2000, Africa is the second largest continent (after Asia) and is less densely populated than either Asia or Europe. The continent may be roughly divided into (1) the Arab and Islamic countries in the northern one-third and (2) the African countries in the other two-thirds. The various countries manifest pronounced variations in density and area. Burundi and Rwanda, for example, each have over 600 people per sq. km., while Botswana, Libya, and Namibia have less than 10. Again, large countries like Algeria, Sudan, and Zaire each cover over 2.3 million sq. km. (0.9 million sq. mi.) and have relatively low density, but half of the more than 50 African states crowd into only one-tenth of the land mass.

Economic production and per capita income also vary widely. Some countries (e.g., Botswana and Gabon) have experienced extraordinary growth (also Zimbabwe after the war of liberation in 1980), but in other states the economy has stagnated, if not regressed severely (e.g., Ivory Coast and Rwanda). Many countries do not produce enough food to sustain themselves and, for both agricultural and internal structural reasons, must import food. Approximately four-fifths of all Africans are engaged in agriculture, but together they account for only 19 percent of Africa's gross national product. Mining is a key part of the economy. Mining productivity, however, has not kept pace with population growth. South Africa, Zimbabwe, and Kenya are centers of regional economy. Elsewhere only Nigeria, with its oil production, is of economic significance. Development is making no visible impact, nor is there progress in social areas (→ Third World).

1.2. *Social and Political Structure*

Modern Africa is a product of its own tradition and of the consequences of colonialism. The northern region was shaped earlier by foreign invasion and the advance of → Islam. In other areas a development began in the 18th and 19th centuries that altered the continent in many ways. The determinative factors include colonial rule, the opening up of trade and commerce, Christian → missions, the influx of secular thinking, and finally the rise of African nationalism and → Marxist propaganda with the end of the colonial era. The results of the colonial period are still evident in state boundaries, official languages (French, English, and Portugese), and economic, social, and cultural infrastructures.

Whereas imperial acts and colonial caprice could hold things together and put off unsolved problems, national governments find great difficulty in forging viable states through all the crises of integration and stabilization. Tanzania and Zambia have tried a form of African socialism (common ownership of land, socially oriented norms of conduct, forms of rural democracy, etc.). In other countries (e.g., Kenya) a capitalist economy has set in. In a few cases the form of ancient monarchy also survives (e.g., Swaziland). By 1995, Western democratic forms of government were being reintroduced in many countries. A one-party system with its authoritarian structure, which argues that opposition is dangerous to the state, contradicts the African tradition, which entrusts leadership to older and more experienced people. Below the surface older ideas persist. Ancient tribal law, for example, would call for a death sentence for witchcraft or black → magic, and a minister of health would put a medicine man on the same professional level as a scientifically trained physician.

1.3. *Trends*
In the middle of the 20th century, Africa achieved formal independence from its colonial masters. As has happened so often in its history, however, it is still a target of foreign powers. Its economic dependence in particular has made it a disturbed continent beset by many problems: the poverty of uprooted people, social conflicts, and the struggles of competing groups. In the 1990s fierce ethnic warfare erupted in Liberia and Rwanda. The great need is for common solutions to problems and for African self-awareness, but other interests and priorities prevail with the growth of armies and mounting expenditures for arms. Nevertheless, the situation is not simply a matter of dealing with easily recognizable factors such as climate, limited resources, economic competition, opposing interests and ideologies, foreign alliances, corruption, and incompetence. More fundamental is the tension in almost every situation between two factors — the thinking of old Africa on the one hand, and scientifically logical and critical thinking on the other. This dilemma creates problems in every area. For Africans it will be decisive whether they can consciously make changes and achieve a synthesis between the old and the new.

2. The Religious Situation
2.1. *Statistics*
In Africa there were originally tribal religions reflecting the respective forms of the economy (hunting, agriculture, cattle raising). From the first century, Christianity spread in North Africa and reached up the Nile to Ethiopia. Islam came into northern Africa in the seventh century, then moved southward and by sea on to the coast in East Africa. Today Islam dominates the North and Northeast. With its linking of religious, social, and political factors, and its ability to integrate elements of tribal religion, Islam has successfully maintained itself and even made ad-

vances. It is still spreading into many parts of Africa. Its yearly rate of growth has been estimated at 2.5 percent, which is about the same as the natural population growth. In the southern two-thirds of Africa, Christians are a majority. Their number is increasing annually at about 3.5 percent, and they now make up over 45 percent of the total population. In addition, there are still many adherents of the traditional tribal religions, which are experiencing something of a renaissance in many places.

2.2. *A Holistic View of Life*
Africans typically view life holistically. → Religion, accordingly, is a significant factor in African life. Africans make no sharp distinction between transcendence and → immanence or between the religious and the secular; magic and religion permeate daily life. Bushmen use magic to ensure success in hunting, peasants perform rites for rainmaking and to protect against poor crops or pests, and cattle raisers follow cultic rules for milking and slaughtering. This integrated perspective encompasses material as well as intellectual culture, including everyday handwork (e.g., pottery, weaving, and forging), elaborate wood carving, social and ritual dancing, and the popular poetry of myths, sagas, fairy stories, and songs.

In social relations the clan, tribe, and age group are fundamental; they provide the context for communal thinking and action. The circle of life offers security and protection, for each person has a specific role within the whole. Ethics is tribal ethics. There is a firm bond with ancestors, established by rituals and maintained even in the changed conditions of urban life.

There is a religious order to work, daily successes and failures, and all the events and phases of biological life. Besides an awareness of natural relations, there is also a sense of dependence on personal and impersonal forces. Africans assume the reality of supernatural powers — for example, in sickness and healing, when calling on the medicine man for help.

2.3. *Significance of Tribal Religions*
The tribal forms of religion in part are practiced overtly and in part live on unconsciously in daily life, with different expressions in rural areas and in the cities. The traditional religions change with changing conditions, and many a tradition has assumed the much weaker form of a mere custom. Yet even when the older religious ideas and norms lose their binding force, they still have an influence in modern African societies. The attraction that the older, emotionally charged religious ideas and rituals still have for Africans is reflected in the steady influx into new religious movements and African churches (→ Independent Churches). Even the churches that missionaries have

Africa in A.D. 2000: Demography

	Population (1,000s)	Annual Growth Rate (%)	Population Density (per sq. km. / mi.)	Births / Deaths (per 100 pop.)	Fertility Rate (per woman)	Infant Mortality Rate (per 1,000 live births)	Life Expectancy (years)
World total	6,091,351	1.27	45 / 116	2.13 / 0.86	2.66	51	66.9
Africa	819,910	2.54	27 / 70	3.70 / 1.16	4.86	77	55.9
Eastern Africa[a]	**255,500**	**2.75**	**40 / 103**	**4.13 / 1.38**	**5.54**	**89**	**51.4**
Burundi	6,974	2.49	251 / 649	4.01 / 1.52	5.76	105	49.3
Comoros	612	2.95	329 / 851	3.86 / 0.91	5.03	72	59.5
Djibouti	687	2.43	30 / 77	3.67 / 1.37	4.98	97	52.3
Eritrea	3,809	2.36	32 / 84	3.71 / 1.35	4.88	87	52.1
Ethiopia	66,175	3.06	58 / 151	4.46 / 1.41	6.46	96	52.4
Kenya	30,340	2.55	52 / 135	3.53 / 0.98	4.30	57	57.4
Madagascar	17,395	3.04	30 / 77	3.91 / 0.87	5.21	68	60.5
Malawi	10,984	2.51	93 / 240	4.53 / 2.03	6.18	130	42.5
Mauritius	1,177	1.05	577 / 1,493	1.79 / 0.64	2.21	13	72.7
Mozambique	19,563	2.47	24 / 62	4.06 / 1.59	5.62	101	48.9
Rwanda	7,674	2.37	291 / 755	4.11 / 1.74	5.45	113	45.1
Somalia	8,697	3.17	14 / 35	4.67 / 1.51	6.46	103	51.0
Tanzania	33,687	2.71	36 / 93	3.91 / 1.20	5.06	72	53.8
Uganda	22,459	2.95	93 / 241	4.75 / 1.80	6.47	101	44.2
Zambia	9,133	2.49	12 / 31	4.07 / 1.59	5.01	90	45.5
Zimbabwe	12,423	2.11	32 / 82	3.40 / 1.29	4.17	60	50.8
Middle Africa[b]	**95,385**	**2.85**	**14 / 37**	**4.13 / 1.29**	**5.57**	**84**	**53.8**
Angola	12,781	3.04	10 / 27	4.53 / 1.64	6.18	112	49.0
Cameroon	15,129	2.73	32 / 82	3.78 / 1.06	4.90	51	58.2
Central African Rep.	3,640	2.12	6 / 15	3.61 / 1.49	4.59	89	50.6
Chad	7,270	2.37	6 / 15	3.95 / 1.59	5.13	106	49.5
Congo (Brazzaville)	2,982	2.72	9 / 23	4.05 / 1.34	5.45	87	52.3
Equatorial Guinea	452	2.41	16 / 42	3.87 / 1.46	5.13	98	52.0
Gabon	1,235	2.45	5 / 12	3.50 / 1.28	4.99	77	57.5
Zaire	51,749	2.98	22 / 57	4.22 / 1.21	5.78	82	54.7
Northern Africa[c]	**175,037**	**1.90**	**21 / 53**	**2.60 / 0.69**	**3.23**	**46**	**66.5**
Algeria	31,599	2.15	13 / 34	2.67 / 0.51	3.32	37	70.2
Egypt	68,119	1.73	68 / 177	2.40 / 0.65	2.97	43	68.1
Libya	6,387	3.20	4 / 9	3.79 / 0.60	5.44	45	67.6
Morocco	28,854	1.54	63 / 163	2.18 / 0.60	2.55	41	68.6
Sudan	29,823	2.17	12 / 31	3.25 / 1.08	4.23	64	57.0
Tunisia	9,837	1.60	60 / 155	2.16 / 0.56	2.59	31	70.9
Western Sahara	289	2.58	1 / 3	2.86 / 0.76	3.51	53	63.9
Southern Africa	**52,887**	**2.13**	**20 / 51**	**2.87 / 0.74**	**3.62**	**45**	**66.1**
Botswana	1,619	2.10	3 / 7	3.29 / 1.19	4.06	50	52.5
Lesotho	2,294	2.46	76 / 196	3.41 / 0.95	4.51	63	60.8
Namibia	1,733	2.35	2 / 5	3.44 / 1.09	4.55	54	57.1
South Africa	46,257	2.09	38 / 98	2.80 / 0.70	3.52	43	67.4
Swaziland	984	2.61	57 / 147	3.40 / 0.79	4.07	56	62.5
Western Africa[d]	**241,102**	**2.72**	**39 / 101**	**4.02 / 1.31**	**5.47**	**81**	**53.3**
Benin	6,222	2.90	55 / 143	4.03 / 1.08	5.37	73	57.1
Burkina Faso	12,057	2.78	44 / 114	4.42 / 1.63	6.05	89	47.5
Cape Verde	437	2.26	108 / 281	2.88 / 0.62	3.23	36	68.2
Gambia	1,244	2.07	116 / 301	3.65 / 1.58	4.81	112	49.0
Ghana	19,928	2.71	84 / 216	3.64 / 0.94	4.85	65	60.0
Guinea	7,861	2.86	32 / 83	4.53 / 1.65	6.07	114	48.5
Guinea-Bissau	1,180	1.98	33 / 85	3.89 / 1.91	5.05	123	45.3
Ivory Coast	15,144	2.32	47 / 122	3.57 / 1.29	4.55	78	52.3
Liberia	3,256	3.25	33 / 85	4.40 / 1.16	5.86	101	59.5
Mali	12,559	2.91	10 / 26	4.44 / 1.53	6.10	138	50.0
Mauritania	2,580	2.47	3 / 6	3.65 / 1.19	4.66	83	55.5
Niger	10,805	3.17	8 / 22	4.68 / 1.52	6.54	105	50.5
Nigeria	128,786	2.73	139 / 361	3.97 / 1.25	5.48	70	54.4
Senegal	9,495	2.59	48 / 125	3.90 / 1.31	5.18	56	53.3
Sierra Leone	4,866	2.20	68 / 176	4.41 / 2.21	5.62	146	41.1
Togo	4,676	2.63	82 / 213	3.98 / 1.36	5.58	78	51.6

Note: Because of rounding, population figures for the regions and the major area as a whole may not equal the sum of their constituent parts.

[a]Figures include former British Somaliland, Mayotte (Fr.), Réunion (Fr.), Seychelles. [b]Figures include São Tomé and Príncipe. [c]Figures include Spanish North Africa. [d]Figures include St. Helena (U.K).

Africa in A.D. 2000: Religious Affiliation (as percentage of population)

	Christians	Muslims	Hindus	Non-religious	Chinese Folk Religionists	Buddhists	Tribal Religionists	Atheists	New Religionists	Sikhs	Jews	Spiritists	Other
World total	33.1	20.0	12.8	12.7	6.3	5.9	4.1	2.4	1.6	0.4	0.2	0.2	0.3
Africa	46.4	40.3	0.3	0.7	—	—	11.9	0.1	—	—	—	—	0.3
Eastern Africa[a]	61.4	21.0	0.5	0.4	—	—	16.2	—	—	—	—	—	0.5
Burundi	92.2	1.4	0.1	0.1	—	—	6.2	—	—	—	—	—	—
Comoros	1.2	98.1	—	0.1	—	—	0.5	—	—	—	—	—	0.1
Djibouti	5.4	93.2	—	1.3	—	—	—	—	—	—	—	—	0.1
Eritrea	43.8	51.0	—	4.6	—	—	0.6	—	—	—	—	—	—
Ethiopia	59.1	30.2	—	0.2	—	—	10.4	—	—	—	—	—	0.1
Kenya	79.4	7.3	0.5	0.1	—	—	11.2	—	—	0.1	—	—	1.4
Madagascar	50.8	2.0	0.1	0.3	0.1	—	46.6	—	—	—	—	—	0.1
Malawi	76.9	14.6	0.2	0.2	—	—	7.8	—	—	—	—	—	0.3
Mauritius	32.8	17.0	42.9	3.1	1.4	0.2	0.2	0.1	—	0.2	—	—	2.1
Mozambique	38.3	10.5	0.2	0.5	—	—	50.4	0.1	—	—	—	—	—
Rwanda	82.0	7.8	0.2	—	—	—	9.8	—	—	—	—	—	0.2
Somalia	1.8	97.9	—	—	—	—	0.1	—	—	—	—	—	0.2
Tanzania	50.9	31.7	1.0	0.3	—	0.1	15.5	0.1	—	—	—	—	0.4
Uganda	89.3	5.3	0.8	0.7	—	—	3.7	0.1	—	—	—	—	0.1
Zambia	82.9	1.1	0.1	0.3	—	—	13.7	0.1	—	—	—	—	1.8
Zimbabwe	67.4	0.7	0.1	1.0	—	—	30.1	0.2	—	—	—	0.1	0.4
Middle Africa[b]	82.6	9.1	0.1	0.5	—	—	7.2	0.1	—	—	—	—	0.4
Angola	94.8	—	—	0.8	—	—	4.2	0.2	—	—	—	—	—
Cameroon	54.7	21.4	—	0.4	—	—	23.1	0.1	—	—	—	—	0.3
Cen. African. Rep.	68.9	15.7	—	0.8	—	—	14.3	—	—	—	—	—	0.3
Chad	25.5	57.8	—	0.1	—	—	15.5	—	—	—	—	—	1.1
Congo (Brazzaville)	90.8	1.3	—	2.3	—	—	4.8	0.1	0.2	—	—	—	0.5
Equatorial Guinea	88.3	4.1	0.1	3.2	—	—	1.9	1.9	—	—	—	—	0.5
Gabon	90.8	4.7	—	0.9	—	—	3.0	0.1	0.5	—	—	—	—
Zaire	95.9	1.1	0.2	0.5	—	—	1.9	—	—	—	—	—	0.4
Northern Africa[c]	9.3	87.5	—	1.1	—	—	1.9	0.1	—	—	—	—	0.1
Algeria	0.2	96.7	—	3.0	—	—	—	—	—	—	—	—	0.1
Egypt	16.0	83.4	—	0.5	—	—	—	0.1	—	—	—	—	—
Libya	3.9	95.4	0.1	0.2	—	0.3	—	—	—	—	—	—	0.1
Morocco	0.6	98.2	—	1.0	—	—	—	—	—	—	0.1	—	0.1
Sudan	16.1	71.7	—	1.0	—	—	11.1	0.2	—	—	—	—	—
Tunisia	0.5	98.9	—	0.5	—	—	—	—	—	—	—	—	0.1
Western Sahara	0.3	99.3	—	0.4	—	—	—	0.1	—	—	—	—	—
Southern Africa	81.8	2.1	2.2	2.1	—	0.1	10.5	0.2	—	—	0.3	—	0.7
Botswana	61.6	0.2	0.2	0.2	—	—	37.1	—	—	—	—	—	0.7
Lesotho	92.6	0.1	0.1	0.2	—	—	6.3	—	—	—	—	—	0.7
Namibia	92.3	—	—	1.3	—	—	5.7	—	—	—	0.1	—	0.6
South Africa	81.5	2.4	2.5	2.3	—	0.1	9.9	0.2	—	—	0.4	—	0.7
Swaziland	86.9	0.7	0.2	1.2	—	—	10.7	—	—	—	—	—	0.3
Western Africa[d]	35.5	47.3	—	0.4	—	—	16.7	—	—	—	—	—	0.1
Benin	33.3	19.6	—	0.2	—	—	46.6	0.1	—	—	—	—	0.2
Burkina Faso	19.2	49.8	—	0.8	—	—	30.2	—	—	—	—	—	—
Cape Verde	94.4	2.9	—	1.5	—	—	1.1	—	—	—	—	—	0.1
Gambia	4.1	87.0	—	0.6	—	—	7.5	—	—	—	—	—	0.8
Ghana	57.7	20.1	—	0.3	—	—	21.8	—	0.1	—	—	—	—
Guinea	4.4	67.4	—	0.2	—	—	28.0	0.1	—	—	—	—	—
Guinea-Bissau	11.1	41.6	—	1.6	—	—	45.5	0.2	—	—	—	—	—
Ivory Coast	31.7	30.6	0.1	0.4	—	—	37.1	—	—	—	—	—	0.1
Liberia	39.5	16.0	—	1.7	—	—	42.5	—	—	—	—	—	0.3
Mali	2.0	82.4	—	0.1	—	—	15.5	—	—	—	—	—	—
Mauritania	0.7	98.7	—	0.1	—	—	0.5	—	—	—	—	—	—
Niger	0.7	91.2	—	0.1	—	—	8.1	—	—	—	—	—	—
Nigeria	45.8	44.0	—	0.3	—	—	9.9	—	—	—	—	—	—
Senegal	5.7	87.5	—	0.3	—	—	6.3	—	—	—	—	—	0.2
Sierra Leone	11.4	46.3	0.1	2.1	—	—	40.0	—	—	—	—	—	0.1
Togo	49.4	19.0	—	0.2	—	—	30.8	—	—	—	—	—	0.6

Note: A dash represents a value of less than 0.05 percent. Because of rounding, horizontal totals may not equal 100.0.

[a]Figures include former British Somaliland, Mayotte (Fr.), Réunion (Fr.), Seychelles. [b]Figures include São Tomé and Príncipe. [c]Figures include Spanish North Africa. [d]Figures include St. Helena (U.K.).

Africa in A.D. 2000: Church Affiliation (as percentage of population)

	Total Christians	Roman Catholics	Indigenous	Protestants	Orthodox	Unaffiliated	Anglicans	Marginal
World total	*33.1*	**17.6**	**6.2**	**5.8**	**3.7**	**1.5**	**1.0**	**0.5**
Africa	*46.4*	**15.7**	**10.9**	**11.2**	**4.5**	**3.2**	**3.4**	**0.4**
Eastern Africa[a]	*61.4*	**19.9**	**8.1**	**13.5**	**10.5**	**5.3**	**4.6**	**0.3**
Burundi	92.2	66.7	0.4	12.8	—	10.5	3.1	—
Comoros	1.2	0.9	0.1	0.2	—	—	—	—
Djibouti	5.4	1.5	—	—	3.8	0.1	—	—
Eritrea	43.8	3.7	0.2	0.6	31.0	8.4	—	—
Ethiopia	59.1	0.8	1.7	12.8	36.9	7.0	—	—
Kenya	79.4	25.1	24.7	20.9	3.0	4.1	6.3	0.2
Madagascar	50.8	22.4	2.9	20.7	—	3.0	1.6	0.2
Malawi	76.9	21.4	17.3	24.6	—	10.6	1.8	1.3
Mauritius	32.8	26.9	0.3	11.5	—	0.7	0.4	0.3
Mozambique	38.3	15.6	9.0	11.3	—	1.7	0.5	0.4
Rwanda	82.0	50.8	1.9	20.8	—	0.6	7.8	—
Somalia	1.8	0.2	0.1	—	1.5	0.1	—	—
Tanzania	50.9	26.7	2.2	12.9	—	6.4	4.2	0.1
Uganda	89.3	47.4	3.5	3.0	0.2	6.1	29.2	—
Zambia	82.9	32.3	19.3	22.3	0.1	3.2	3.4	3.8
Zimbabwe	67.4	9.3	36.4	12.1	0.1	6.6	2.4	0.6
Middle Africa[b]	*82.6*	**46.0**	**18.2**	**19.3**	—	**5.2**	—	**0.9**
Angola	94.8	75.1	7.7	15.7	—	0.3	—	1.2
Cameroon	54.7	28.8	4.1	13.4	—	7.9	—	0.5
Central African Rep.	68.9	22.3	10.3	16.2	—	20.0	—	0.2
Chad	25.5	7.8	1.0	14.7	—	2.0	—	—
Congo (Brazzaville)	90.8	45.3	10.7	18.4	—	15.9	—	0.5
Equatorial Guinea	88.3	81.6	4.4	3.5	—	1.3	—	0.5
Gabon	90.8	70.0	17.0	21.9	—	2.1	—	0.7
Zaire	95.9	49.9	28.4	23.0	—	4.6	—	1.2
Northern Africa[c]	*9.3*	**1.8**	**0.4**	**0.6**	**5.8**	—	**0.7**	—
Algeria	0.2	0.1	0.2	—	—	—	—	—
Egypt	16.0	0.4	0.3	0.8	14.4	—	—	—
Libya	3.9	1.0	0.3	0.1	2.4	0.1	—	—
Morocco	0.6	0.1	0.5	—	—	—	—	—
Sudan	16.1	9.1	0.7	1.4	0.6	0.2	4.2	—
Tunisia	0.5	0.1	0.4	—	—	—	—	—
Western Sahara	0.3	0.1	0.2	—	—	—	—	—
Southern Africa	*81.8*	**9.9**	**41.9**	**26.7**	**0.4**	**5.7**	**5.1**	**0.5**
Botswana	61.6	4.8	26.9	11.1	—	17.9	0.7	0.3
Lesotho	92.6	41.4	13.1	14.4	—	18.7	4.7	0.3
Namibia	92.3	25.1	12.1	54.8	—	5.2	6.4	0.5
South Africa	81.5	8.1	44.6	27.0	0.4	4.5	5.3	0.6
Swaziland	86.9	5.6	56.5	13.8	—	8.6	1.7	0.7
Western Africa[d]	*35.5*	**10.5**	**11.8**	**9.8**	—	**0.9**	**4.9**	**0.6**
Benin	33.3	24.5	3.4	3.9	—	1.2	—	0.3
Burkina Faso	19.2	11.2	0.6	7.5	—	—	—	—
Cape Verde	94.4	88.7	0.3	4.0	—	—	—	1.5
Gambia	4.1	2.6	0.7	0.3	—	0.2	0.2	—
Ghana	57.7	12.8	14.8	20.3	—	7.1	1.1	1.6
Guinea	4.4	1.3	0.7	0.6	—	1.8	—	—
Guinea-Bissau	11.1	8.1	2.9	1.1	—	0.3	—	—
Ivory Coast	31.7	14.5	10.8	5.6	0.2	0.5	—	0.2
Liberia	39.5	4.6	13.5	12.3	—	8.9	0.8	0.3
Mali	2.0	1.0	0.1	0.9	—	—	—	—
Mauritania	0.7	0.6	0.1	—	—	—	—	—
Niger	0.7	0.2	0.3	0.2	—	—	—	—
Nigeria	45.8	11.1	17.6	12.7	—	0.1	9.0	0.6
Senegal	5.7	5.5	0.2	0.1	—	—	—	—
Sierra Leone	11.4	3.5	3.6	3.8	—	0.9	0.5	0.1
Togo	49.4	35.7	2.6	6.8	—	1.9	—	9.0

Note: A dash represents a value of less than 0.05 percent. Because of rounding, horizontal totals of the individual Christian groups may not equal the total percentage of Christians. Also, Christians in some countries are counted in more than one category, in which case the total of the individual groups may exceed the overall percentage of Christians.

[a]Figures include former British Somaliland, Mayotte (Fr.), Réunion (Fr.), Seychelles. [b]Figures include São Tomé and Príncipe. [c]Figures include Spanish North Africa. [d]Figures include St. Helena (U.K.).

founded incorporate popular traditions into their congregational life. One should not underestimate the significance of the traditional religions for African Christianity.

3. African Christianity

3.1. *Diversity and Growth*

African Christians belong to many churches, with the various confessions arising from European and American missions. Roman Catholic missions led to the development of a native → hierarchy beginning in 1950, which by 1992 included 15 African cardinals and 404 bishops. The over 100 million Roman Catholics live in 65 archdioceses and 337 dioceses.

The work of Protestant missionary societies of various provenance has led continuously since World War I to the rise of autonomous national churches that mirror the confessional diversity of the sending countries. Besides over 25 million Anglicans, there are more than 90 million Protestants, primarily Baptists, Methodists, Lutherans, and Reformed. There are an estimated 34 million Christians of the Orthodox churches of Egypt and Ethiopia. Completely reliable statistics are not available, particularly in the case of the thousands of "independent" churches that have arisen since 1819. The estimated membership in the year 2000 of these indigenous churches is close to 90 million, many of whom also nominally belong to traditional churches.

The rapid and consistently strong growth of African Christianity is striking. The proportion of Christians to the total population has grown from 9 percent (ca. 10 million) in 1900 to around 45 percent (ca. 200 million) in 1980, and is projected to rise to 46.4 percent (ca. 380 million) by 2000. Reasons for this growth include the changes in the traditional social pattern, as well as the fine work of Christian missions (including their educational and medical programs). We find more awareness today of the material and intellectual losses in earlier development, yet we should remember that a Christian renewal of African society can remedy the results of colonial changes. The African mind with its orientation to the present world can combine what is social and secular with what is intellectual and religious into a unique totality.

3.2. *The African Legacy and Christianity*

Economic and political changes and trends and the potential of traditional African religion provide more than just the external setting for African Christianity. Social relations and the tribal religions still have their influence in all the churches shaped by the various confessions. Africans who believe that God created humanity in his image cannot think of this God as weak and ignorant, poor and helpless. The credibility of the Christian church is tied to its addressing social and economic conditions; spiritual life cannot be separated from economic need. The life situation and the characteristically holistic sense demand a uniquely African form of the Christian message.

3.2.1. The → Roman Catholic Church finds in both its doctrine and its practice a point of access for Africanizing its message. Dogmatically it can use the incarnation as a theoretical model for the integration of what is specifically African. Along with the veneration of Mary and the → saints and other forms of piety, the church can find room for the traditional veneration of → ancestors and other practices. The danger of syncretic foreign infiltration is always present. It has proved hard to enforce the Western view of → marriage (§2.7) in the face of the tradition of polygamy, to claim unconditional authority for → celibate priests, or to apply restrictive Roman Catholic rules to the behavior of an active laity. Many have longed for an African council that would stress the connection between evangelizing and human development and that would sanction the presentation of the faith in African thought-forms and categories.

3.2.2. → Protestant churches especially emphasize one's personal relation to God, private and detailed study of the Bible, and action according to ethical norms for which one is personally responsible. Such an emphasis leads to a problem in the relation of individuals to their community. According to African notions the group (whether tribe or clan) shapes all thought and action in both religious and social life. But Protestant missionary work has presupposed that conversion to Christian faith would involve an individual decision, that is, a personal confession in → baptism after catechetical instruction (→ Confession of Faith). The individual determination of converts has had to prove itself daily in a different faith-world. The result could be negative if they failed to become adequately incorporated into their → congregation.

Personal and collective independence could not always be restricted to the religious sphere. A striving for political autonomy corresponds to the awakening of individual religious responsibility. The Bible not merely legitimizes engagement in political goals and social concerns but demands this very activity. The result is sometimes a switch of Protestant church members to political and socioreligious movements and the participation of many Christians in liberation movements (e.g., in SWAPO, the South West African People's Organization). A danger here is that the church may limit itself to a purely social and political function and fail to fulfill its overall task. Without social and political relevance, however, African Christianity cannot convincingly live out its confession of Christ.

3.3. Problems and Tasks

At first, missionary Christianity brought European forms to Africa. The more Christianity put down roots into Africa, the greater became the need for indigenization (→ Acculturation). An → African theology provides the answer, engaging aspects of the African religious and intellectual world, but not in the form of a situational theology like what is called → black theology. What cannot be conceded is to be distinguished from what is variable as → adiaphora. The basis of the Christian faith as it is laid down in the → Apostles' Creed is not to be reinterpreted or replaced. But the structure and government of the church, the incorporation and cooperation of the laity, and the forms of → liturgy, → preaching, and education can all be African. The charismata of 1 Corinthians 12 can also find a place, with the gift of healing enjoying special importance. No less necessary is the gift of discerning spirits, in view of the thousands of religious movements and sects, which one may often call post-Christian and which for the sake of indigenization have often surrendered or unacceptably relativized fundamental Christian truths. Problematic, too, is the common reemergence of the pre-Christian religious past in the second and third generations. Many Christians, for example, maintain an allegiance to their ancestors.

3.4. Ecumenical Developments

Attempts to achieve an organizational unity of African Christians face almost insuperable difficulties. In their multiplicity, however, the Christians can show the greatness of the body of Christ, even as they try to solve in concert the problems that crowd in upon them. The → All Africa Conference of Churches — to which the Roman Catholic Church does not belong — was founded in 1963 as an ecumenical organization to undertake common tasks. The Roman Catholic bishops' conferences provide regional organizations for North, East, Central, West, and South Africa, and they have also set up a symposium of conferences for Africa and Madagascar. The Ecumenical Association of African Theologians was founded in Accra in 1977 with the goal of developing a → theology reflecting a distinctly African basis and speaking to the African situation. Another ecumenical union of African theologians came into being in May 1983 — the Ecumenical Association of African Theologians in Southern Africa. This organization seeks to develop African theologies, to encourage cooperation between theologians of different regions and denominations, and to contribute to → dialogue with other religious societies.

Bibliography: C. AKE, *A Political Economy of Africa* (Harlow, Essex, 1981) • D. BARRETT, ed., *WCE* (statistics, bibliography) • H. BAUMANN, *Die Völker Afrikas und ihre traditionellen Kulturen* (2 vols.; Wiesbaden, 1975-79) • H. BETTSCHEIDER, *Das Problem einer afrikanischen Theologie* (St. Augustin, 1978) • E. BEUCHELT, *Die Afrikaner und ihre Kulturen* (Berlin, 1981) • K. E. BLEYLER, *Religion und Gesellschaft in Schwarz-Afrika* (Stuttgart, 1981) • C. COQUERY-VIDROVITCH, *Africa: Endurance and Change South of the Sahara* (Berkeley, Calif., 1988) • R. CORNEVIN and M. CORNEVIN, *Geschichte Afrikas von den Anfängen bis zur Gegenwart* (Stuttgart, 1980) • E. DAMMANN, *Die Religionen Afrikas* (Stuttgart, 1963); idem, *Die Übersetzung der Bibel in afrikanische Sprachen* (Munich, 1975) • J. D. FAGE, *An Atlas of African History* (London, 1978) • E. W. FASHOLÉ-LUKE et al., eds., *Christianity in Independent Africa* (Bloomington, Ind., 1978) • R. GIBELLINI, ed., *Paths of African Theology* (Maryknoll, N.Y., 1994) • R. HALLETT, *Africa since 1875* (Ann Arbor, Mich., 1974) • B. HEINE, T. SCHADEBERG, and E. WOLFF, *Die Sprachen Afrikas* (Hamburg, 1981) • R. HOFMEIER and M. SCHÖNBORN, *Politisches Lexikon Schwarz-Afrika* (2d ed.; Munich, 1984) • INTERNATIONAL SCIENTIFIC COMMITTEE FOR THE DRAFTING OF A GENERAL HISTORY OF AFRICA, *A General History of Africa* (ed. J. Ki-Zerbo et al.; 8 vols.; Berkeley, Calif., 1981-) • E. ISICHEI, *A History of Christianity in Africa* (Grand Rapids, 1995) • H. JUNGRAITHMAYR and W. J. G. MÖHLIG, *Lexikon der Afrikanistik* (Berlin, 1983) • W. MANSHARD, *Afrika südlich der Sahara* (6th ed.; Frankfurt, 1980) • J. S. MBITI, *African Religions and Philosophy* (New York, 1969; 2d ed., Portsmouth, N.H., 1990); idem, *Bible and Theology in African Christianity* (New York, 1986); idem, *Introduction to African Religion* (2d ed.; Portsmouth, N.H., 1992) • MISSIONSWISSENSCHAFTLICHES INSTITUT MISSIO, *Theologie im Kontext* (Aachen, 1980- [biannually]) • E. J. MURPHY, *History of African Civilization* (New York, 1972) • J. MURRAY, ed., *Cultural Atlas of Africa* (New York, 1981) • D. NOHLEN and F. NUSCHELER, eds., *Handbuch der Dritten Welt,* vol. 4, *West-Afrika und Zentral-Afrika;* vol. 5, *Ost-Afrika und Süd-Afrika;* vol. 6, *Nord-Afrika* (3d ed.; Hamburg, 1993) • G. C. OOSTHUIZEN, *Post-Christianity in Africa* (Grand Rapids, 1968) • H.-D. ORTLIEB and J. ZWERNEMANN, *Afrika zwischen Tradition und Fortschritt* (Hamburg, 1980) • P. PRADERVAND, *Listening to Africa* (New York, 1989).

ERNST DAMMANN

African Independent Churches → Independent Churches

African Theology

1.1. In view of the geographic, ethnic, and linguistic diversity of Africa, the idea of a single African theology has been long debated. Setting aside the great theologians of North Africa (→ Tertullian, → Cyprian, and → Augustine), we note that concern for an independent African theology is only a few decades old. Geographically this sphere of an African theology embraces the territory south of the Sahara; in content it embraces the theological work of the Christian churches of Africa. It is not a theology that has arisen within the traditional African religions.

1.2. With J. Mbiti, we may distinguish three main forms of an African theology: oral, symbolic, and written. The most extensive is the oral theology that one finds in hymns, → preaching, → prayer (§1), and catechetical instruction. Symbolic theology covers the various attempts to express theological contents in art, drama, ritual (→ Initiation Rites 1), → dancing, and painting. Written theology embraces the work of specialists in books and journals.

1.3. In basic orientation also there are three varieties. One theology recognizes the traditional religions and the proclamation of the → gospel in them. A critical theology sees the totality of the social, economic, and political reality of Africa against the background of the Christian → revelation (§1). Finally, there is the → black theology of South Africa, which, inspired by the experiences of North American blacks (esp. J. Cone), wrestles with oppression and → racism.

1.4. Prerequisites for the development of an independent African theology include, first, the great growth of African → Independent Churches during the present century. In the search for African identity the idea of being African or black plays a large role. The translation of the Bible (either complete or in part) into some 600 African languages has also been one of the most significant preconditions for all forms of African theology (→ Bible Versions). In addition, an emphasis on the importance of context (including religious, cultural, and social backgrounds) has facilitated the development of an incarnational African theology (→ Contextual Theology). The notion that African theology may be an independent theology presupposes a theological pluralism that does not accept the idea of a universal theology.

2. With respect to their sources, African theologians differ in giving precedence either to the biblical revelation or to the cultural and religious legacy of Africa itself. An ecumenical conference of African theologians in Accra in 1977 listed various sources as follows: (1) the Bible and the Christian heritage, (2) African anthropology and cosmology, (3) African traditional religions (→ Guinea 2), (4) Independent African churches, and (5) other African realities (racism, oppression, etc.). This list includes no explicit reference to the theological legacy of the Western churches (→ Acculturation); some African theologians (e.g., E. W. Fasholé-Luke) in fact put this source last.

3.1. The most important question for African theology is that of African identity. African theologians often speak about their "anthropological poverty," the lack of recognition of their distinctive humanity, and the loss of their language, culture, and religious tradition in the colonial period. These things are for them an open wound that the achievement of political independence has not yet succeeded in healing.

3.2. Efforts to determine the detailed contents of African theology are dominated by the problem of African identity. One sees this connection in Christology, in which the place of Jesus Christ among the → ancestors is investigated. One also sees it in the discussion of ideas of → God, prayer, → sacrifice (§1), the concept of life, → initiation, and notions of the afterlife in the traditional religions of Africa. The decision to pursue an incarnational theology (under the slogan that we must Africanize Christianity, not Christianize Africa) has far-reaching implications for → liturgy, proclamation, church organization, and, not least, the understanding of → marriage (§2.7) and → family. It is critical that an African theology wrestle with the African elements in such phenomena as faith healing, → exorcism, and the belief in spirits.

3.3. The problem of → racism has been a special concern of the black theology of South Africa. Yet African theologians increasingly must face questions of economic → dependence, political incompetence, urbanization, and → secularization, which they cannot answer merely by appealing to the traditional religious and cultural ideas of Africa.

4.1. Africa is still weak in theological institutions that can train theological teachers. Priority must be given to the building up of theological faculties, both Roman Catholic and Protestant (→ Theological Education 3).

4.2. Many leading African theologians have come together in the Ecumenical Association of African Theologians (1977), which published the *Bulletin de théologie africaine* (1979-85) and the Ecumenical Association of African Theologians in Southern Africa (1983). Other ecumenical or confessional groups of

African theologians meet on a regular basis or have formed their own associations, such as those of African exegetes and moral theologians.

5.1. One of the main problems facing African theology is that writing is not done in African languages but in English, French, or Portuguese. In a continent in which 50 percent of the population is illiterate, this means that published books and journals reach only relatively few readers.

5.2. The almost 10,000 → Independent African churches with their 35 million adherents (1995) show how little African the main churches are and underline the urgency of the task of Africanizing and hence the importance of a truly African theology.

→ All Africa Conference of Churches

Bibliography: O. BIMWENYI-KWESHI, *Alle Dinge erzählen von Gott. Grundlegung afrikanischer Theologie* (Freiburg, 1982) • A. A. BOESAK, *Farewell to Innocence* (Maryknoll, N.Y., 1977) • B. BUJO and J. O'DONOHUE, *African Theology in Its Social Context* (Maryknoll, N.Y., 1992) • E. W. FASHOLÉ-LUKE, "Footpaths and Signposts to African Christian Theologies," *SJT* 34 (1981) 385-414 • INSTITUTE OF MISSIOLOGY, Missio: *Theology in Context* (Aachen, 1985- [biannually]) • E. ISICHEI, *A History of Christianity in Africa* (Grand Rapids, 1995) • E. MARTEY, *African Theology* (Maryknoll, N.Y., 1993) • J. S. MBITI, *African Religions and Philosophy* (New York, 1969); idem, *Bible and Theology in African Christianity* (Oxford, 1986) • B. MOORE, ed., *Theologie in Afrika* (Göttingen, 1973) • J. PARRATT, *Reinventing Christianity: African Theology Today* (Grand Rapids, 1995) • G. PARRINDER, *Religion in Africa* (Harmondsworth, 1969) • J. S. POBEE, *Toward an African Theology* (Nashville, 1979); idem, ed., *Exploring Afro-Christology* (New York, 1992) • T. SUNDERMEIER, ed., *Christus, der schwarze Befreier* (Erlangen, 1973) • I. TÖDT, ed., *Theologie im Konfliktfeld Südafrika. Dialog mit M. Buthelezi* (Stuttgart, 1976).

GEORG EVERS

Afro-American Cults

1. At the heart of African American cults stands the → experience of a superhuman presence. A deity or spirit or God's Spirit seizes believers, through whom he speaks and acts. This seizure is introduced and ritually directed by rhythms, drums, songs, dances, and offerings, for there is a fear of uncontrolled possession (→ Dance; Sacrifice 1; Ecstasy).

2. African American cults arose through 350 years of → slavery.

2.1. The slaves wanted from their religion what their memory preserved. They used it in their burial rites, hoping for rebirth in Africa. They used it in → magic directed against their masters. They used it in countermagic, to check magicians. They used it to worship African gods and their own → ancestors and helpers.

2.2. The Christian owners did not tolerate African rites. Most of them had no interest in making Christians of their slaves, however, saying that Africans were like animals, without a → soul and rebellious if baptized (→ Black Churches 1). Some Protestant congregations excluded slaves from the → church and hindered → missionaries, who assured whites that the slaves would be more obedient as Christians. Roman Catholics passed laws demanding their speedy → baptism and instruction, but there were often too few → priests to do the work of instruction (→ Catechesis).

3. These cults were and are found in tropical America. About 50 percent of all the slaves from Africa — 4.5 million — were taken to South America, 3.5 million to Brazil alone. Some 40 percent went to the Caribbean, 7 percent to British North America, and the others to Central America.

4. The cults changed with time.

4.1. A variety of cults arose throughout the New World.

4.1.1. In America the slaves combined various African religions. Often one would dominate, such as that of the Fon in the → voodoo cult of Haiti and New Orleans or that of the Yoruba in the Shango cults of Brazil, Trinidad, and Grenada.

4.1.2. In all cases the slaves had to practice the cult in secret. Only runaways (Span. *cimarrones,* Eng. *maroons*) could develop their faith freely at a distance from whites. In Roman Catholic areas the slaves would often form religious fraternities and take part in → processions. On Christian feast days they would secretly worship in African fashion and disguise their deities as → saints. In Cuba, for example, such a cult is called Santería. (Santería was in the news in 1993 when the U.S. Supreme Court overturned an ordinance enacted by a suburb of Miami, Florida, that had sought to ban the ritual killing of animals by the cult.)

4.2. The freeing of slaves brought the freeing of their religion.

4.2.1. It was now seen that the Christian element was not just a mask, for the slaves retained it. But they also became open to new influences. In Jamaica, Kumina (meaning "possessed by ancestors") developed after a revolt in 1760. Slaves there achieved their freedom in 1834, and in 1860 a Protestant revival swept over the island. From this arose Pukkumina, led by faith healers and comparable in significance to voodoo in Haiti.

4.2.2. Not all the influences were Christian. After emancipation, free workers came from Africa. Around 1850, some 1,000 landed on Grenada, and 7,000 Yoruba on Trinidad, all with working contracts. They brought a new emphasis on their religious practice.

4.2.3. In Brazil the Bantu slaves formed Macumba, with Candomblé the most African of its sects. Spiritism came around 1880 and became the pillar of a new religion, → Umbanda, which is Brazilian with African elements. A similar spiritist religion is Maria Lionza in Venezuela, though its African components are now secondary.

4.2.4. Others linked up with the original longing of the slaves for Africa, the promised land of some → spirituals. When Haile Selassie (1892-1975) became emperor of Ethiopia in 1930, new hope sprang up in Jamaica. As → Ras Tafari, he was their god; Ethiopia was their home, and return there was redemption.

5. The path that begins with the beliefs of slaves and then moves on to the religion of emancipated slaves, which is mostly open also to poor whites, ends in a sense with the Pentecostals (→ Black Churches 2). Another path, ending with spiritists, is trodden by rich and poor alike. Cults for Africans alone have become increasingly rarer.

Bibliography: W. Bascom, *Shango in the New World* (Austin, Tex., 1972) • R. Bastide, *The African Religions in Brazil: Toward a Sociology of the Interpenetration of Civilizations* (Baltimore, 1978) • U. Fischer, *Zur Liturgie des Umbandakultes* (Leiden, 1970) • R. Flasche, *Geschichte und Typologie afrikanischer Religiosität in Brasilien* (Marburg, 1973) • B. Gates, ed., *Afro-Caribbean Religions* (London, 1980) • L. Hurbon, *Dieu dans le vaudou haïtien* (Paris, 1972) • A. Métraux, *Voodoo in Haiti* (New York, 1972) • F. Otiz, *Hampa Afro-Cubana: Los Negros Brujos* (Madrid, 1906) • A. J. Raboteau, *Slave Religion: The Invisible Institution in the Antebellum South* (Oxford, 1978) • A. Ramos, *The Negro in Brazil* (2d ed.; Washington, D.C., 1951) • G. E. Simpson, *Black Religions in the New World* (New York, 1978) • R. Tallant, *Voodoo in New Orleans* (2d ed.; New York, 1962) • L. Weingärtner, *Umbanda* (Erlangen, 1969).

Hans-Jürgen Greschat

Aggression

1. Concept
2. Theological Tradition
3. Theories
4. Conclusion

1. Concept

No single, comprehensive psychological theory of aggression can encompass the various phenomena covered by the term "aggression." Three theories or groups of theories are most commonly cited, namely, impulse theory, frustration theory, and learning theories. But even this division is finally imprecise and not very helpful because of the overlapping of some features and many unanswered questions. The theories rest on deductions from questions put to empirically perceptible attitudes of aggression and operate unavoidably with basic anthropological presuppositions that at least influence the approach one takes to understanding the origin, outworking, evaluation, and removal of aggression. If, reflecting popular usage, the concept of aggression is to include such diverse phenomena as the activities of a bird in defense of its nest, those of a child at play, the destructive rage of a tyrant and his henchmen, the successful activity of a businessperson, the assault of a rapist, and the self-attack of a desperate person driven to → suicide, then we can see that a single theory could hardly be adequate.

2. Theological Tradition

Similarly, we cannot deduce a single explanation of such different phenomena from biblical → exegesis and the theological tradition (e.g., from the doctrine of → sin). Sin and aggression are no more equivalent than are the (Augustinian) doctrine of original sin and the psychological theory of an inborn instinct of aggression. Nevertheless, a biblically oriented theology can perhaps have a clarifying and integrating function when it relates the various theories to the implied → anthropologies (→ Biblical Theology 2). In this way what the Bible says about sin and the biblical insights and commands regarding → love, → freedom, and → trust can be relevant, unlike in older discussions between → psychology and theology, which were typically hostile.

3. Theories

3.1. One theory that calls for critical notice is the doctrine of concupiscence, which derives largely from → Augustine. This is the theory of an inherited self-seeking that, through the envy originally implanted by the temptation of Satan, becomes destructive aggression.

3.2. The impulse theory of A. Adler (1870-1937) and S. Freud (1856-1939) seems to harmonize with Augustinian doctrine, but in reality it is more akin to the insights of S. → Kierkegaard (1813-55) into → anxiety. Adler postulated his theory in 1908, when Freud had merely projected it in principle; only under the impact of World War I (1914-18) did Freud develop his theory of an impulse of destruction or aggression that is innate like the → libido and that is always destructive, in contrast to Adler's emphasis on self-preservation.

Later psychoanalysis has generally not accepted the theory of a death wish. It has retained, however, the idea of an aggression that is understood quantitatively almost like a substance (or hydraulically like a fluid that may be displaced or dammed up) and that fuses with the libido. In fact, this (pessimistic) theory has proved itself practical countless times in → psychotherapy, but it is sharply contested by the learning schools.

3.3. The learning or behaviorist schools also criticize the theory of K. Lorenz (1903-89), who (only in this matter) appeals to Freud and finds aggression in animals as a basic instinct in (1) preserving the species, (2) selecting partners, and (3) protecting young. Lorenz finds the center of human aggression in the limbic system (i.e., the oldest parts of the cerebrum, the mesocortex and allocortex). We cannot train away the instincts of aggression, only ritualize them (in sports, military maneuvers, etc.). By engaging in or watching harmless acts of aggression, we can reduce the instinctive potential for aggression in a kind of catharsis. Thus children can work off aggression by watching scenes of violence on television. (This theory of catharsis draws the strongest criticism from the schools of social psychology and psychoanalysis.)

3.4. An alternative both to psychoanalysis and social learning is frustration theory (J. Dollard et al.), which first appeared in 1939. On this view the frustration of vital needs or impulses leads to aggression. Only a → society and → education free from repression will produce strong people free from aggression. This theory supplements the others at essential points, but the results of permissive education and experimental research on anger and bad temper seem to refute it.

3.5. The various theories of (social) learning appeal to many experiments (esp. on animals) and make a confident claim to universal validity. On this view aggression is not innate but learned; hence it can be unlearned. Learning occurs through conditioning, with both so-called operant conditioning (reinforcement for success) and modeling (the observation of aggression increases aggression) playing important roles in the theory. This (optimistic) theory may explain one form of aggression, but it fails to account for self-aggression, social aggression, and brutality such as that of terrorism or genocide.

3.6. A variation on this theory is the thesis that held sway for some time (e.g., in Marxism) that some primitive cultures were originally free from aggression. (See M. Mead's writings on Samoa.) Modern → ethnology no longer accepts this assertion.

4. Conclusion

If the psychoanalytic theory of aggression seems to have the greatest integrative force (because its explanation is more differentiated than that of other theories), this is only insofar as it may function as an aid to therapy and → pastoral care, not as an anthropological system that is closer to biblical faith than the other theories. Aggression is not identical with → evil, and its sublimation and acceptance are not finally the same as freedom and → forgiveness, important as they are for life in society.

→ Force and Nonviolence; Psychology; Terrorism

Bibliography: A. ADLER, *Der Aggressions-Trieb im Leben und in der Neurose* (Leipzig, 1908) • J. DOLLARD et al., *Frustration and Aggression* (7th ed.; New Haven, 1947) • D. FREEMAN, *Margaret Mead and Samoa: The Making and Unmaking of an Anthropological Myth* (Cambridge, Mass., 1983) • S. FREUD, *Civilisation and Its Discontents* (London, 1930) • F. HACKER, *Materialen zum Thema Aggression* (Vienna, 1972) • W. W. HARTUP and J. DE WIT, eds., *Origins of Aggression* (The Hague, 1978) • K. S. LARSEN, *Aggression Myths and Models* (Chicago, 1976) • K. LORENZ, *On Aggression* (New York, 1966) • A. MUMMENDEY, "Aggressives Verhalten," *Psychologie der Motive* (ed. H. Thomae; Göttingen, 1983) 321-403 (extensive bibliography, 403-39) • W. PANNENBERG, "Aggression und die theologische Lehre von der Sünde," *ZEE* 21 (1977) 161-73; idem, *Anthropology in Theological Perspective* (Philadelphia, 1985) 142-53 • G. ROCHLIN, *Man's Aggression* (Boston, 1973) • H. SELG, "Aggression," *Handbuch psychologischer Grundbegriffe* (ed. T. Herrmann; Munich, 1977) 15-26 • A. STORR, *Human Aggression* (New York, 1968) • D. ZILLMANN, *Hostility and Aggression* (Hillsdale, N.J., 1979).

DIETRICH RITSCHL

Agnosticism

The word "agnosticism" (related to Gk. *agnōsia*, "not knowing") was coined as a technical term by the English scientist T. H. Huxley (1825-95). It denotes an attitude that refuses to recognize knowledge that is not logical or empirical. In particular, agnosticism denies the claim that → God is knowable. In general, it might be called metaphysical abstention.

The problem raised by agnosticism was present even before Huxley coined the term. The earlier tradition of → skeptical thinking includes positions that since Huxley's day we might call agnosticism. Philosophically Huxley, who was influenced by a sense of scientific → progress, could appeal to modern → metaphysical criticism. He found this in the philosophy of Hume and the criticism of Kant (→ Kantianism), who fixed the boundaries of possible knowledge. The works of W. Hamilton (1788-1856), who reduced all human knowledge to the sphere of the conditioned, had a decisive impact. The English theologian H. L. Mansel (1820-71) offered his own interpretation of Hamilton when he espoused an epistemological agnosticism with the apologetic intention of defending Christian → faith against unjustified epistemological claims. The term "agnosticism" quickly became an important catchword, often as an ideological judgment. This was especially true in 19th-century England. One might refer to H. Spencer (1820-1903), L. Stephen (1832-1904), and J. Ward (1843-1925).

Agnosticism came under criticism from the → Roman Catholic Church, which pointed to the natural knowledge of God, as well as from such diverse thinkers as F. → Nietzsche, F. Engels, and F. Mauthner, who rejected its implied refusal to take sides. In logical → positivism and → analytic philosophy agnosticism develops into metatheological agnosticism (see A. J. Ayer), which makes the point that the → atheistic denial of God's existence is also epistemologically undemonstrable. How vaguely and diversely "agnosticism" is employed today may be seen from its use in reference to thinkers like A. Camus, B. Russell, A. Malraux, and J. Améry, who either call themselves agnostics or are interpreted as such. H. R. Schlette has diagnosed an "aporetic agnosticism" that is linked to the relapse into emotional atheism and marked by the present-day experience of → secularization.

Bibliography: R. A. ARMSTRONG, Agnosticism and Theism in the Nineteenth Century (New York, 1977; orig. pub., 1905) • A. J. AYER, Language, Truth, and Logic (London, 1936) • S. BUDD, Varieties of Unbelief: Atheists and Agnostics in English Society, 1850-1960 (London, 1977) • R. W. HEPBURN, "Agnosticism," EncPh 1.56-59 • T. H. HUXLEY, Collected Essays (vol. 5; repr., New York, 1970) • B. LIGHTMAN, The Origins of Agnosticism: Victorian Unbelief and the Limits of Knowledge (Baltimore, 1987) • F. MAUTHNER, Wörterbuch der Philosophie (2 vols.; repr., Zurich, 1980) • K. NIELSEN, Philosophy and Atheism (Buffalo, N.Y., 1985) • H. R. SCHLETTE, Aporie und Glaube (Munich, 1970) esp. 36-72; idem, ed., Der moderne Agnostizismus (Düsseldorf, 1979) • K.-D. ULKE, Agnostisches Denken im viktorianischen England (Freiburg, 1980) with good bibliography.

FRANK OTFRIED JULY

Agnus Dei → Mass

Agrapha

"Agrapha" is a term used for sayings of Jesus not recorded in the NT Gospels. The word means "unwritten things" and presupposes that such sayings come from oral tradition that is independent of the canonical writings.

1. The following ancient sources contain agrapha: (1) some textual variants of the NT → Bible MSS (e.g., D after Luke 6:5); (2) NT writings outside the Gospels (e.g., Acts 20:35); (3) early apostolic and patristic works up to the third century (e.g., Clement of Alexandria Strom. 1.24.158); (4) papyrus fragments outside the NT (e.g., OxyPap 1224); and (5) later Jewish-Christian and Christian Gnostic writings (e.g., Gos. Heb., Gos. Thom., and Dial. Sav. [NHC 3.5]; → Apocrypha; Nag Hammadi).

2. Most agrapha have no significance in the quest for the historical Jesus, since they were shaped by the theological and dogmatic interests of the later church (→ Early Church). Furthermore, in the Hellenistic Roman period it was customary for disciples and adherents of esteemed teachers to create new sayings and attribute them to the teachers, so that even when they are not oriented to specific polemical or dogmatic concerns, the authenticity of the agrapha is always debatable. Even what seem to be authentic sayings of Jesus might well be the product of his disciples.

It is quite possible, however, that some agrapha reflect early dominical traditions. Thus investigation of the Coptic Gospel of Thomas suggests that certain material in it is older than the canonical Gospels, arose independently of them, and perhaps even includes genuine, otherwise unknown sayings of Jesus.

Bibliography: J. A. FITZMYER, "The Oxyrhynchus Logoi of Jesus and the Coptic Gospel according to Thomas," TS 20 (1959) 505-60 (extensive bibliography) • O. HOFIUS, "Agrapha," TRE 2.103-10 (extensive bibliography) • J. JEREMIAS, Unknown Sayings of Jesus (2d ed.;

London, 1964) • H. KOESTER, "Apocryphal and Canonical Gospels," *HTR* 73 (1980) 105-30, esp. 112-19 • G. W. MACRAE, "The Gospel of Thomas: *Logia Iesou?*" *CBQ* 22 (1960) 56-71 • E. M. YAMAUCHI, "Agrapha," *ISBE* 1.69-71.

JAMES R. BUTTS

Aid → Christian Development Services; Development 1.4

AIDS → Public Health

Albania

	1960	1980	2000
Population (1,000s):	1,611	2,671	3,493
Annual growth rate (%):	2.99	2.07	0.70
Area: 28,748 sq. km. (11,100 sq. mi.)			

A.D. *2000*
Population density: 122/sq. km. (315/sq. mi.)
Births / deaths: 1.88 / 0.63 per 100 population
Fertility rate: 2.35 per woman
Infant mortality rate: 28 per 1,000 live births
Life expectancy: 71.6 years (m: 68.8, f: 74.8)
Religious affiliation (%): Muslims 40.4, Christians 32.3 (Roman Catholics 15.5, Orthodox 14.7, unaffiliated 1.0, other Christians 1.2), nonreligious 17.1, atheists 10.0, other 0.2.

In 1967 Albania declared itself officially an → atheistic state, the first such in the world. It closed all of its 2,169 → mosques and churches and even prohibited the use of private religious symbols (e.g., crosses and icons). Not until 1990 was the prohibition on religious activities revoked; legislation in April 1991 stated that Albania was a secular state that observes "freedom of religious belief and creates conditions in which to exercise it." Of the approximately 1.4 million Muslims, approximately 80 percent are → Sunnites, and 20 percent are members of the → Shiite dervish order of Bektashi. Among the Muslims we find both Sunnite sects (Kadri, Tidshani, Rifai, and Sadi) and Shiite sects (Halveti and Rrufai).

Albania was Christianized as early as the second century. When the Roman Empire was divided in 395, Albania came under the administrative rule of Constantinople but the ecclesiastical → jurisdiction of Rome (until 733). After the schism of 1054 (→ Heresies and Schisms) northern Albania went to Rome, having been reconverted to Catholicism by 1250.

With the Turkish invasion at the end of the 15th century, → Islam gradually became a dominant factor in Albania. The Ottoman government recognized the patriarch of Constantinople as the spiritual head of Orthodox Christians, but Albania's Roman Catholicism suffered severe setbacks. The low point occurred between 1850 and 1880, when only a few isolated priests were active, and Catholics commonly went underground. Thanks to the protective supervision of Austria-Hungary over all Roman Catholics in the Ottoman Empire, Roman Catholicism then recovered until the end of the 19th century. Socially the Roman Catholic Church was especially active in schools (→ Jesuits; Franciscans; Education 4), which even Muslims could attend.

The → Orthodox Church suffered in the 19th century from severe tensions between the Greek and Albanian clergy. In 1923 Fan Noli (1882-1965), the leader of the Albanian Orthodox Church in America, declared the Orthodox Church of Albania to be → autocephalous. He met with opposition especially from the archdiocese of Gjirokastër and the diocese of Korçë and was → excommunicated by the patriarch of Constantinople. In 1937 a synod of orthodox bishops under the presidency of Archbishop Kristofor Kisi adopted self-government. In 1940 a synod of the two Italian Albanian dioceses with the Byzantine Rite and Greek language in Lungro (Cozenza), Calabria, and Piana degli Albanesi in Palermo, Sicily, along with the Basilians of Badia Greca di Grottoferrata on the one hand and the orthodox bishop of Berat, Albania (Agathangiel Çançe), on the other, attempted a → union with Rome. When the Communists seized power, Archbishop Panteleimon of Gjirokastër and Bishop Evlogios of Korçë (both Greeks born in Albania) fled the country, and the last links with the patriarchate of Constantinople were broken.

Beginning in 1944, all religious groups were subject to bloody persecutions. The clergy of both Christian churches — and also of the Bektashi — were almost completely extirpated. The property of all religious societies (which amounted to only 1.2 percent of the usable land area of Albania) was confiscated, along with the church schools, orphanages, printing presses, and libraries. All orders were forbidden, and foreign priests were excluded. In 1948-49 Orthodox archbishop Kisi was forced into a union with Moscow, which ultimately failed.

Since the election of a non-Communist government in March 1992, Albania has been open to the presence and work of religious agencies. Muslims as well as the Orthodox and Roman Catholics have been working hard to reassert their presence in areas where they formerly were strong. By the end of 1992 the Catholics had appointed 2 archbishops (to Durrës and Shkodër) and ordained 67 priests. The Ecumenical Patriarchate in Istanbul also had appointed a Greek bishop (since there were no longer any Albanian bishops alive) as exarch of the Albanian Orthodox Church.

Bibliography: J. K. BIRGE, The Bektashi Order of Dervishes (London, 1937) • G. GIACOMO, Banishing God in Albania: The Prison Memoirs (San Francisco, 1988) • E. K. KEEFE et al., Area Handbook for Albania (Washington, D.C., 1971) • A. SCHNYTZER, Stalinist Economic Strategy in Practice (Oxford, 1982) • B. TÖNNES, Albanien. Der erste atheistische Staat der Welt (Zollikon, 1978); idem, Sonderfall Albanien. Enver Hoxhas "eigener Weg" und die historischen Ursprünge seiner Ideologie (Munich, 1980) • T. WINNIFRITH, ed., Perspectives on Albania (London, 1992).

BERNHARD TÖNNES

Albigenses → Cathari

Alchemy

Since the ninth and tenth centuries the Gk.-Arab. word alchēmeia has denoted the attempt to change base metals into silver and gold. This effort has been more than a mere curiosity in the history of science and technology, however, for in alchemy the smelting, alloying, and tinting of metals have been linked with the belief that one can help what is thought of as living nature achieve its quickest possible development and fulfillment. It was probably in Alexandria in the second century B.C. that popular traditions of this kind became joined with metallurgical techniques that had been practiced from ancient times, especially in Egypt. This connection, along with the viewpoint of Greek natural philosophy (→ Philosophy of Nature) that processes of transition are qualitative changes in an unchanging substratum, did not at first reduce the work to a pure → symbol, in defense of which suspicious religious and philosophical forms were used. From the outset, however, it meant that alchemy had the character both of a manufacturing technique and of a spiritual craft.

The first document of Greek-Egyptian alchemy is the fragmentary Physika kai mystika of Pseudo-Democritus, which suggests already its two-sided character. This work deals with the reduction of lead to "amorphous black," which by the laws of sympathy

and antipathy, by way of white and yellow, unites with other materials to form a noble metal. Over the whole process stands the principle that "one nature rejoices over another, . . . masters [and] conquers another."

In the handbook by Zosimos in the third and fourth centuries A.D., which supplanted all others and became the main source for later ones, matter goes through states that are denoted by the colors of the ingredients. But the original state, like the final one (the philosophers' stone, which supposedly can change any metal into gold), cannot be equated with any known material and defies definition. Instead, minerals are treated as living things that suffer and die and mate and are resurrected. It is not known what → experience the adept describe as the attainment of the stone, which not only can change metals but also can heal and unite opposites. Nevertheless, the moral qualities required of the adept show that the alchemist achieves personal fulfillment with the ennobling of metals. Related to its having initiates, alchemy derives from → revelation (§1), guards its secrets from the uninitiated, and considers work on metals as a theurgic process.

The alchemy of the Arabs largely abandoned these mystery aspects (→ Mystery Religions) in favor of pure → causality, but the pendulum swung the other way in the European Middle Ages. Even when Paracelsus (1493-1541) in particular turned away from making gold to preparing medical pharmaceutics, alchemy still survived through the 18th century. Its scientific foundations slowly eroded, and finally a replacement came with chemistry. Yet the religious or spiritual side blossomed afresh in pansophy, in the natural philosophy of J. A. Comenius (1592-1670), and, along with other esoteric teachings, in theosophical and → occult movements (e.g., → Rosicrucians; Freemasonry).

Most representatives of alchemy were superficially loyal to the church and practiced their craft in this spirit, but already in the Middle Ages they had departed from the biblical, Christian foundation with their concept of the purification of the world and humanity solely with the help of the forces of → creation (§1). According to Paracelsus, this was the crystallizing core of → theosophical speculations, and it stood opposed to Lutheran orthodoxy. C. G. Jung (1875-1961) regarded the symbolism of alchemy — with inadequate historical backing — simply as an expression of human self-development. Outside the West, we find in certain strands of Chinese → Taoism and Tantric → Buddhism and Hinduism an alchemy that corresponds at many points to that of the West in aim, practice, and symbolism.

Bibliography: M. ELIADE, *The Forge and the Crucible: The Origins of Alchemy* (New York, 1971) • S. S. HARTMAN and J. TELLE, "Alchemie," *TRE* 2.195-227 (extensive bibliography) • E. J. HOLMYARD, *Alchemy* (Harmondsworth, 1957) • A. PRITCHARD, *Alchemy: A Bibliography of English-Language Writings* (London, 1980) • G. SCHOLEM, "Alchemie und Kabbala," *ErJb* 46 (1977) 1-96.

KARL HOHEISEL

Alcoholism → Substance Abuse

Alexandria

1. Alexander the Great (336-323 B.C.) founded this city in 331 B.C. as a port on the west coast of the Nile Delta. Its position guaranteed its importance as a center of trade and commerce. The Ptolemies (323-30 B.C.) moved the site of government from Memphis to Alexandria. The Egyptian queen Cleopatra (51-30 B.C.) received support first from Caesar (100-44 B.C.) and then from Antony (d. 30 B.C.), in what was Alexandria's most prominent period politically. During the Roman Empire, Alexandria was the seat of a provincial governor. The Islamic Arabs conquered Alexandria in A.D. 642. Thereafter it looked commercially eastward to India.

2. Alexandria was conceived as a Hellenistic → city, and thus its population was mixed (→ Hellenism). Various groups, mostly Greek-speaking, counterbalanced the Egyptians. These groups included surprisingly many (Greek-speaking) Jews, who, without being confined to a ghetto, lived predominantly in two districts of their own. They made up two-fifths of the total population, which has been calculated at about one million in the first century B.C.

3. Alexandria was a city of worldwide importance. Under the Ptolemies it became a metropolis of Greek culture. Ptolemy II Philadelphus (283-246 B.C.) founded an academy with two libraries. The larger of these in the Museion, containing some 700,000 scrolls, perished in flames under Caesar. The smaller in the Sarapeion was destroyed by fanatical monks in A.D. 391. We owe to Alexandrian scholars (e.g., Eratosthenes, Aristophanes, and Aristarchus) the transmission of the texts of Greek antiquity in purified form. Precise scholarship was a goal of Callimachus, Theocritus, and other writers. Alexandria also took the lead in various arts and sciences.

4. As in other cities, the Jews formed virtually an autonomous corporation *(politeuma)*. At the time of Augustus (27 B.C.–A.D. 14) an ethnarch administered justice for them according to their own laws. This privilege did not include full citizenship, which would have required worship of the city gods.

At times the Jews of Alexandria lived in considerable tension with both pagans (→ Gentiles, Gentile Christianity) and Christians. We see this in their history from the restrictions imposed by Claudius (A.D. 41-54) in A.D. 41 to their expulsion by Metropolitan → Cyril (412-44). These difficulties, however, did not prevent them from having great historical significance as intellectual mediators between Judaism and the Hellenic world, on the one hand, and primitive Christianity and the Greco-Roman church, on the other. Thus the Greek translation of the OT (the LXX), which was made under the Ptolemies, became the Bible of the primitive church and of the Greek fathers, as well as the basis of translations into Latin (→ Church Fathers; Bible Versions). Philo (b. 15-10 B.C., d. A.D. 45-50), who as both exegete and religious thinker was an outstanding representative of the → synagogue of Alexandria, had little influence on → Judaism but, through → Alexandrian theology, exerted a strong influence on the → church.

5. Baptized Jews seem to have brought Christianity to Alexandria. According to legend, John Mark, a disciple of the apostles, founded the Alexandrian church. Many leaders of → Gnosticism flourished in Alexandria during the first half of the second century (e.g., Basilides and Valentinus). With these as debating partners, the Jews in the background, and an atmosphere characterized by the fusion of faith and culture (*pistis* and *paideia*), the church's → theology in Alexandria quickly developed into a scientific system that in its way has not been surpassed (Pantaenus, Clement, and → Origen, around the year 200).

The experimental freedom of these beginnings led later in many different dogmatic directions, including Christological subordinationism (Dionysius the Great [d. ca. 265] and Arius [d. 336]), Nicene orthodoxy (Alexander [d. 328], → Athanasius [d. 373], and Cyril), and → Monophysitism (Dioscorus, the successor of Cyril [444-51]). The ecclesiastical position of Alexandria, whose sphere of influence, according to canon 6 of Nicaea (325), embraced Egypt, Libya, and the Cyrenaican Pentapolis, is mentioned in an imperial edict dated A.D. 380. The bishop of Alexandria was a guardian of the faith no less than was the bishop of → Rome. One of his tasks was to fix the date of Easter in annual Easter letters. By the fifth century the Monophysite → Coptic Orthodox Church had split off, setting up its patriarchate in Alexandria.

Bibliography: Y. AMIR, *Die hellenistische Gestalt des Judentums bei Philon von Alexandrien* (Neukirchen, 1983) • H. I. BELL, *Jews and Christians in Egypt* (London, 1924) • H. T. DAVIS, *Alexandria, the Golden City* (2 vols.; Evanston, Ill., 1957) • E. M. FORSTER, *Alexandria: A History and a Guide* (Garden City, N.Y., 1961) • C. D. G. MÜLLER and H. WEISS, "Alexandrien," *TRE* 2.248-64 (bibliography) • W. W. TARN, *Hellenistic Civilisation* (London, 1927; 3d ed., 1952).

ULRICH WICKERT

Alexandrian Theology

1. We can distinguish two phases in the theology of Alexandria. The older phase was one of free experimentation; later, in spite of its basic significance for all → theology, it came under the suspicion of → heresy and official condemnation. The later phase was one of orthodox maturity; it provided a rigid framework for the legacy of the earlier period, thus ensuring the steady course of dogmatic history.

2.1. The real merit of the first phase is that, after the tentative beginnings of the early → apologists and → Irenaeus (ca. 130-ca. 200), it succeeded in harmonizing the primitive Christian traditions with the philosophical achievements of the Greeks, thereby establishing a Christian metaphysics. The synthesis of biblical faith and Greek thought that the Hellenistic → synagogue had made (Philo [d. A.D. 45-50]) formed its background, and the Gnosticism that flourished in Alexandria participated in the dialogue and debate. The → allegorical method, which was inherited ultimately from the → Stoics and made it possible to find a deeper "pneumatic" (quasi-philosophical) sense in the literal words of the Bible, greatly facilitated this whole process. As Alexandrian theology developed, it proved decisive that metaphysical traditions were not just adopted selectively but, because of a sense of the nearness of Christ that was grasped in an awareness of faith, were vitally transformed "from within," turned around, and given a new direction. The thinking of antiquity thus gained a new future, and Christianity acquired metaphysical depth.

2.2. In the early theology of Alexandria we must distinguish between individual leaders and their hearers, on the one hand, and the church's catechetical school, which gave simple Christian instruction, on the other. The free teachers entered into exacting debate with Hellenistic culture and philosophy (→ Greek Philosophy). The philosophical and theological school of which → Origen was for a time the head (before 230) finally came under the jurisdiction of the bishop.

2.3. The first teacher in Alexandria whose name we know was Pantaenus (ca. 180). Clement (d. ca. 215) achieved great significance as an unusually erudite and open-minded scholar who in → Platonic fashion mixed seriousness and playfulness in his predominantly apologetic writings. Origen (d. ca. 254) dug much deeper in the absoluteness of faith. He was the first to establish theology as a scholarly discipline. In ceaseless activity he focused on textual criticism, exegesis, dogmatics (which he established formally for the first time), and preaching. Origen thought along such Greek lines that he could view the cosmic drama as a cycle (Heraclitus) bringing us back to a lost beginning (with universal restoration). He had to flee to Caesarea to escape his bishop, and he finally was condemned by the Fifth Ecumenical Council at Constantinople in 553 under Emperor Justinian (527-65; → Councils of the Church).

3.1. → Athanasius (archbishop 328-73) systematized the new insights of the early teachers of Alexandria. Yet this self-sacrificing champion of Nicaea (who was exiled five times) was also a thinker in his own right in the field of → Christology (§2). Borrowing from Irenaeus, he explained the incarnation of the Logos in a way that left traces in → Anselm (d. 1109) and the → Heidelberg Catechism (1563). In good Greek fashion, he depicted God himself as in a dilemma between creation and fall. The vicarious death and → resurrection of Christ formed the only way out (→ Incarnation).

3.2. → Cyril (archbishop 412-44) made it his main aim to combat the Antiochene Nestorius (d. ca. 451) and to defend for → Mary the title *theotokos* (adopted at the Council of → Ephesus in 431). Antiochene theology based its Christology on the man → Jesus and conceived of the divine Logos as also dwelling in him. Alexandrian theology, in contrast, began with the Logos (its Platonic legacy) and set the → person of the Logos under the conditions of the humanity of Jesus. Mary had to be called the mother of God, not man, because she had given birth to him who is God. M. → Luther (1483-1546) agreed with Cyril's position.

Bibliography: B. ALAND, ed., *Gnosis* (FS H. Jonas; Göttingen, 1978) • B. ALTANER and A. STUIBER, *Patrologie* (9th ed.; Freiburg, 1980) • U. BERNER, *Origenes* (Darmstadt, 1981) • J. C. MCCLELLAND, *God the Anony-*

mous: A Study in Alexandrian Philosophical Thought (Cambridge, 1976) • E. MOLLAND, *The Conception of the Gospel in the Alexandrian Theology* (Oslo, 1938) • C. D. G. MÜLLER and H.-F. WEISS, "Alexandrien," *TRE* 2.248-64 • J. E. L. OULTON and H. CHADWICK, eds., *Alexandrian Christianity: Selected Translations of Clement and Origen* (Philadelphia, 1954) • M. SCHÄR, *Das Nachleben des Origenes im Zeitalter des Humanismus* (Basel, 1979) • R. V. SELLERS, *Two Ancient Christologies: A Study in the Christological Thought of the Schools of Alexandria and Antioch in the Early History of Christian Doctrine* (London, 1954) • C. T. WALDROP, *Karl Barth's Christology: Its Basic Alexandrian Character* (Berlin, 1984) • D. WYRWA, *Die christliche Platonaneignung in den Stromateis des Clemens von Alexandrien* (Berlin, 1983).

ULRICH WICKERT

Algeria

	1960	1980	2000
Population (1,000s):	10,800	18,740	31,599
Annual growth rate (%):	1.98	3.10	2.15
Area: 2,381,741 sq. km. (919,595 sq. mi.)			

A.D. 2000
Population density: 13/sq. km. (34/sq. mi.)
Births / deaths: 2.67 / 0.51 per 100 population
Fertility rate: 3.32 per woman
Infant mortality rate: 37 per 1,000 live births
Life expectancy: 70.2 years (m: 68.7, f: 71.8)
Religious affiliation (%): Muslims 96.7, nonreligious 3.0, other 0.3.

The modern state of Algeria forms the central section of Maghreb, the Arabic term for North Africa. It is bordered by Tunisia on the east, Morocco on the west, and the Mediterranean on the north. To the south it borders Libya, Niger, Mali, and Mauritania. With 2.4 million sq. km. (920,000 sq. mi.), Algeria is the second largest country in Africa, after Sudan. Since 1962, when the country achieved its independence, the population has increased by roughly three and a half times.

Some 96 percent of the people are → Sunni Muslims in the Malikite tradition. About 0.4 percent of the population belong to the Ibadi sect of Muslims. As of the year 2000 there are estimated to be approximately 30,000 Roman Catholics, with a much smaller number of Protestants.

From the 2d to the 7th centuries there was a flourishing Christian church, distinguished for its theologians and → martyrs. Internal conflicts (e.g., → Do-

natists) and the Arab-Islamic conquest in the 7th century destroyed the church. Since the 16th century there have been some Christian enclaves (in 1509 Oran came under the Archdiocese of Toledo). Under the Ottoman Empire, merchants, slaves, and prisoners formed a small Christian community that from 1646 to 1827 was entrusted to a vicar-general with his seat in Carthage. In the 19th century a "second" church came into being with French → colonialism, which remained a foreign church, never succeeding in setting up a national church within the Islamic population by means of → mission (the Protestant North Africa Mission and the Roman Catholic White Fathers). It came to an end with the exodus of Europeans in the aftermath of decolonization.

The Roman Catholic Church, which has divided Algeria into three dioceses, is the strongest Christian group. It has churches and chapels in many towns and oases. Although it enjoys a kind of acceptance, it has no official legal status, for Algerian law grants no official status to any non-Islamic religious group. The Ministry of the Interior has given the church the status of an "association." This enables it to hold property and to engage in its own activities. The Ministry of Religious Affairs supervises its property and members.

The very few Protestants have come together supradenominationally and supranationally in the Protestant Church of Algeria. This group has the same legal status as the Roman Catholic Church. It has places of worship in the cities of Algiers, Oran, and Constantine. In Algiers there is also an → Anglican Church on the site of the British embassy. The return of Algeria to the Arab world has brought many people from the Middle East to help in its development. Thus today we also find the Russian and Greek Orthodox Church, and a relatively large number of Coptic Christians (→ Coptic Orthodox Church), groups the Algerian state largely ignores. Evangelical and Free Church groups are also quietly active in Algeria. The Protestant Church of Algeria is too small to work with the → World Council of Churches as an independent church. It has membership in various international organizations, through the Reformed Church of France.

Along with pastoral care for Christian guest workers, which is marked by an ecumenical spirit, the various churches devote much energy and concern to living out their → solidarity with the Algerian people. Caritas (Roman Catholic) and Recontre et Développement (Protestant) are at work in the social sphere (e.g., for children with mental and physical handicaps; → Charity). They aid in development and cooperate with state institutions in social service.

They form a well-organized church of foreigners made up of Europeans, Africans, and Arabs. The only nationals are a few nationalized Algerian-French, some nationalized priests and members of orders, and an unknown number of Christian women who have married Algerians.

Few accurate statistics are available regarding the various Berber peoples, who perhaps compose one-third or more of the total population. Particularly among the Kabyle group of Berbers, relatively large numbers of people have in recent years embraced an evangelical faith.

Bibliography: D. BARRETT, ed., WCE 136-38 • P. BOUR-DIEU, The Algerians (Boston, 1961) • J. DÉJEUX and H. SANSON, Algérie 1980, église en terre d'Islam (1980) • R. FACÉLINA, Théologie en situation. Une communauté chrétienne dans le Tiers-Monde (Algeria, 1962-74) (Strasbourg, 1974) • H. D. NELSON, ed., Algeria: A Country Study (Washington, D.C., 1986) extensive bibliography • H. SANSON, Christianisme au miroir de l'Islam. Essai sur la rencontre des cultures en Algérie (Paris, 1984); idem, "Statut de l'église catholique au Magrebh," AAfN (Paris, 1979) 381ff. • U. SCHOEN, "Vom Leben und Sterben der Kirchen in Nordafrika," Radiokolleg Kirchen in Afrika (ed. W. Usorf and W. Weisse; Erlangen, 1979) 19-26.

HANS VÖCKING

Aliens → Foreigners

All Africa Conference of Churches

The 380 million African Christians (2000 est.) constitute 46.4 percent of the total population (as compared with only 9.2 percent in 1900). Statistically the southern two-thirds of Africa is predominantly Christian, while the northern third is predominantly Islamic (→ Islam). The proportion of the population practicing traditional African religion is declining.

The rapid growth of Christianity since 1900 rests on the ministry in the 19th century of overseas → missionaries (→ Mission), the work of African Christians as evangelists and missionaries (→ Evangelization), the translation of the Bible or Bible portions into 613 African languages (as of 1996; → Bible Versions), a deeper encounter with African religion, and a sense of independence in the postcolonial era (→ Colonialism). As a result of missionary work, African Christians belong to many denominations, and in the course of time many native → Independent Churches and church groups have come into being (over 9,000 in 1995).

According to its constitution, the All Africa Conference of Churches (AACC), which was founded in 1963, "is a fellowship of churches which confess the Lord Jesus Christ as God and only Saviour according to the Scriptures and therefore seek to fulfill together their common calling to the glory of the one God, Father, Son, and Holy Spirit." In 1994 the AACC comprised 147 member churches and related councils (→ National Councils of Churches) in 39 countries. It has its headquarters in Nairobi (Kenya) and a regional office in Lomé (Togo). Member churches include the → Orthodox Church, the → Anglican Communion, → Reformed, → Lutheran, and other Protestant churches, and independent churches. The → Roman Catholic Church, though not a member, sometimes cooperates. Many evangelical churches and missions have refused to join the AACC for theological reasons or out of suspicion, and they remain aloof from it (→ Evangelical Missions; Evangelical Movement).

The tasks of the AACC include evangelization, informing society about the concerns of the church, service, the seeking of → unity, programs of study and research, the promoting of contacts and exchanges of views among the churches, the coordination of material, personal, and intellectual efforts, and aid for the churches in training its employees, leaders, pastors, and members. In the process the AACC tries to promote the independence of the churches and the development of → African theology.

To achieve its goals the AACC has three programs: (1) study, research, and program coordination; (2) finance and administration; and (3) communication. From its formation AACC has aided six million → refugees, immigrants, and stateless persons in many African lands. It is interested in international affairs and demands liberation, → human rights, justice, and → reconciliation. Its structures and programs are very similar to those of the → World Council of Churches in Geneva, with which it is closely related.

A full assembly is held every five to seven years (Kampala 1963, Abidjan 1969, Lusaka 1974, Nairobi 1981, Lomé 1987, and Harare 1992). Each assembly has had a Christological theme.

Bibliography: AACC, The Church in Changing Africa (New York, 1959); idem, Drumbeats from Kampala (Report of the First Assembly, Kampala, Uganda, April 20-30, 1963; London, 1963); idem, Engagement (Report of the Second Assembly, Abidjan, Ivory Coast, 1969; Nairobi, 1970); idem, Follow Me . . . Feed My Lambs: Nairobi 1981 (Report of the Fourth Assembly, Nairobi, Kenya, August 2-12, 1981; Nairobi, 1982); idem, The

Struggle Continues (Nairobi, 1975); idem, *A Time for Self-Reliance: A.A.C.C., 1975-78* (Nairobi, 1975) • *AACC Magazine* (formerly *AACC Bulletin;* quarterly) • H. E. FEY, ed., *A History of the Ecumenical Movement,* vol. 2, *The Ecumenical Advance, 1948-1968* (2d ed.; Geneva, 1986) 73-79 • M. RAFRANSOA, *Église d'Afrique, qui es-tu?* (Lausanne, 1983) • R. SAKALA and N. N. NKU, eds., *You Shall Be My Witnesses* (Nairobi, 1988).

JOHN MBITI

All Saints' Day

The Christian veneration of saints began with the honoring of martyrs. All Saints' Day thus began as the Feast of All Holy → Martyrs. This feast is first mentioned in A.D. 359 by Ephraem Syrus (ca. 306-73) in one of his hymns for May 13. In Antioch about the year 380, → Chrysostom (ca. 347-407) preached a sermon in honor of "all the saints who anywhere on earth have suffered martyrdom." He did so on the Sunday after → Pentecost, which the Greek Orthodox Church has retained as the Sunday of All Saints. In → Rome May 13 took on special significance when in 609 or 610 Boniface IV (608-15) dedicated the Pantheon, which Emperor Phocas (602-10) had handed over to him, as a church "in honor of the Virgin Mary and all martyrs." Thereafter the day was celebrated in annual remembrance of the dedication.

The commemoration of martyrs was extended to include that of all saints when Gregory III (731-41) dedicated a chapel with this name in St. Peter's. Yet the idea of honoring all the saints together seems to have originated in Ireland and then spread by way of England. It is in this context that we first find the term "All Saints' Day" used for November 1, which had been licentiously observed in Ireland as a New Year festival, and which the church reshaped with its own regimen of → fasting and feasting. Finally, Gregory IV (827-44) induced the Frankish ruler Louis the Pious (814-40) to introduce All Saints' Day on November 1 throughout his kingdom. Only in the later Middle Ages, however, did the feast gain its dominant position as the autumn Easter. It did so by virtue of its proximity to All Souls' Day (November 2), which featured reception of the sacrament and an → indulgence.

→ Church Year

Bibliography: LitWo 1.100-103 (bibliography) • M. PERHAM, *The Communion of Saints* (London, 1980) • C. SMITH, "All Saints, Feast of," *NCE* 1.318-19.

GEORG LANGGÄRTNER†

All Souls' Day → All Saints' Day

Allegory

Allegory is an artistic or linguistic form that expresses something different (Gk. *allēgoreō*) from what it states directly. In art it represents that which cannot be represented directly, usually in a complex picture that carries individual features (personification). In literature it is a story in which a second complex of meaning may be discerned behind the literal one. In interpretation one decodes the individual elements, which have the character of → metaphors, and reconstructs the whole on the level of the second intended meaning. In this respect an allegory differs from a → symbol, which in a narrative points to an additional meaning with which it stands in an intrinsic relationship that can be grasped intuitively, and from a → parable, in which the story must be metaphorically understood as a whole and not in its individual features.

Allegory offers religion an indirect way of speaking whereby it can express what it cannot say simply, or preserve secrecy by means of the concealing nature of the expression. In the OT we find allegories predominantly in the prophetic and → apocalyptic writings (Ezekiel 16; 17; 34; Daniel 7; also Ps. 23; 80:8-19). In the NT allegories occur as allegorical expositions of the parables of Jesus (Mark 4:13-20; Matt. 13:36-43, 49-50), in Paul (Rom. 11:17-24; 1 Cor. 3:10-15; 12:12-27), and in John (John 10:1-18; 15:1-8). In → Judaism (Philo) and the early and medieval church (→ Origen), biblical texts that were not originally so intended were expounded allegorically so as to arrive at a spiritual sense.

Bibliography: A. FLETCHER, *Allegory: The Theory of a Symbolic Mode* (Ithaca, N.Y., 1965) • R. M. GRANT, *The Letter and the Spirit* (New York, 1957) • R. P. C. HANSON, *Allegory and Event: A Study of the Sources and Significance of Origen's Interpretation of Scripture* (Richmond, Va., 1959) • J. C. JOOSEN and J. H. WASZINK, "Allegorese," *RAC* 1.283-93 • G. KURZ, *Metapher, Allegorie, Symbol* (Göttingen, 1982) • S. L. WAILES, *Medieval Allegories of Jesus' Parables* (Berkeley, Calif., 1987) • H. WEDER, *Die Gleichnisse Jesu als Metaphern* (Göttingen, 1978).

WERNER SCHWARTZ

Alpha and Omega

Alpha and omega are the first and last letters of the Greek alphabet (A and Ω, or in art mostly A and ω).

They are a title for God in Rev. 1:8; 21:6 (cf. Isa. 41:4; 44:6) and for Christ in Rev. 22:13 (cf. 1:17; 2:8). They symbolize the fact that God, or Christ, embraces all things.

A and Ω found their greatest use during the 3d to the 6th centuries in → patristics and Christian art. With few exceptions, they referred to Christ and bore witness to his consubstantiality with the Father in opposition to → Arianism. They usually occur with a → cross or Christogram. In the Middle Ages we find them in depictions of the majesty of the Lord as well as on the Host, on Easter candles, and on → bells. This symbolism disappeared in the 16th century, but → Romanticism rediscovered it.

Bibliography: G. KITTEL, "ΑΩ," *TDNT* 1.1-3 • *LMA* 1.455 (bibliography).

THADDEUS A. SCHNITKER

Altar

1. The word "altar" derives from Lat. *altare* or *altaria,* which come from *altus,* meaning "high." Lat. *ara* (from Gk. *airō,* "raise") has the same connotation; it is the Vg word for *bōmos* (from *bainō,* "lift up"). In the LXX *bōmos* is used of heathen altars precisely because they were on high places, whereas *thysiastērion,* "place of sacrifice," is used of the OT → tabernacle (§1) and temple altars. This distinction corresponds respectively to the Heb. *bāmâ* versus *mizbēaḥ.*

2.1. The etymology points to two fundamental aspects of the altar: (1) it is a structure raised above the ground, both to avoid pollution and to bring it nearer to the abode of the gods in the heavens; and (2) it is used for offerings to these deities. An altar is thus an object of liturgical furniture upon which gifts are deposited, slaughtered, or burned; as such, it is found in the majority of world religions.

2.2. In early Hebrew practice, the altar was made of natural materials, either earth or unhewn rock (Exod. 20:24-25). Later, bronze and other metals were allowed (1 Kgs. 8:64).

2.3. The location of the altar was determined by an appearance of Yahweh (e.g., at Shechem, Gen. 12:6-7) or by divine order (Deut. 12:5, 13-14). Other religions, such as those of the Greeks and Romans, usually placed altars inside their temples, which were regarded as divine dwelling places.

3. The NT terminology reproduces that of the LXX, using *bōmos* for the altar to an unknown god in Athens (Acts 17:23) and *thysiastērion* to refer to the Jewish temple (e.g., Matt. 5:23) and to the heavenly altar in the Apocalypse (Rev. 6:9). The usage of the latter term defies certain interpretation only in Heb. 13:10. Neither term appears in a eucharistic context, where *trapeza,* "table," appears instead (1 Cor. 10:21).

4.1. Beginning around A.D. 110, however, "altar" appears with reference to the Communion table (Ign. *Phld.* 4). Many → church fathers (e.g., → Origen) were prepared to use *thysiastērion* in this way because they interpreted the Eucharist in sacrificial terms, in effect thus repudiating the idea of an altar as a place of bloody sacrifice.

4.2. During the → Reformation, although M. → Luther continued to use "altar," other Reformers such as J. → Calvin, U. → Zwingli, and the leaders of the Church of England reverted to "table" in strong reaction to any idea that the Eucharist involves a reimmolation of Christ. They also wanted to emphasize the character of the Lord's Supper as a fellowship meal.

5.1. In the period before the Council of → Nicaea, the Eucharist also took place in private homes, where the altar had the shape of a table. It had from one to nine legs, depending upon taste, and was oblong or semicircular.

5.2. With the development of the cult of the → saints and of devotion to their → relics, there was a change in the sixth century from an open to a solid altar, from a table to a boxlike cube to enclose the sacred remains. If an altar was erected over the tomb of a → martyr, a shaft connected the two that was accessible through a grill (or *fenestella*) on the side of the altar facing the nave.

5.3. Consequently, there was a growing preference for stone as the material to be used in altars. This was due also to the practice of celebrating the Eucharist on tombs. Finally, the use of materials such as marble spread with such rapidity that in 517 the Council of Epaon in Burgundy prohibited wooden altars entirely (can. 26).

5.4. At the time of the Reformation, impelled by doctrinal motives, many churches reverted to wood. To Luther, however, stone altars were merely items of furniture, the use of which was permissible "until they are used up or we are pleased to make a change" ("The German Mass" [1526]).

6. Altars for bloody sacrifices can be very large, depending upon how many animals are to be killed at one time. For example, the altar of Zeus at Pergamum, now in Berlin, has a foundation measuring

36.44 × 34.20 m. (119.55 × 112.20 ft.). The Christian altar, however, is on a more human scale, since it holds only the materials for Communion. Since such an altar could appear insignificant in a large church, the practice began in the fourth century of covering it with a small dome (known as a ciborium or baldachin), supported by columns. The altar usually was placed freestanding between the nave and the apse, although at times it stood in the center of the nave.

7.1. The one officiating at the Eucharist normally faced the congregation across the table, and so no object was placed on it other than a chalice and paten. In time, as the division between → clergy and laity became more pronounced, the leader changed his position; in the Middle Ages he faced east with his back to the congregation. Even so, it was not until the 12th century that the Roman Catholic Church allowed crosses. Candlesticks and flowers had to wait until the 17th century. Protestants were less willing to follow suit, doing so only by the 19th century.

7.2. The same change of position affected the place of the altar. It no longer needed to be freestanding and was often located against the rear wall of the sanctuary. In Eastern Orthodox churches it has remained freestanding, but it is shielded from view by the → iconostasis. Eastern Orthodoxy has also preserved the early custom of having only one altar per church.

7.3. Protestant churches, wanting the faithful to gather around the Lord's Table, insisted on making it freestanding once again. Calvin was typical when in 1541 he removed the altar, rood screen, and choir in St. Pierre, Geneva, and had a table carried in only on Communion days. In Holland and in Scotland the altar became a table large enough to seat a dozen or more, so that groups could come up and take their places as at a proper meal. In England a wooden table was carried forward from the east end into the center of the choir on eucharistic occasions, but in the 17th century, to avoid profanation, it was once again anchored against the rear wall and provided with a rail. In the same century Lutheranism brought together at the east end its three liturgical foci of altar, → pulpit, and → baptismal font. Congregationalists and → Baptists, with their great emphasis upon preaching, adopted a dominant pulpit at the east end, with the result that the table lost its prominence entirely.

7.4. At the present day, under the influence of the liturgical and → ecumenical movements, there is a tendency to speak of an altar table and to give it once again the importance it had in the early basilicas, while paying attention also to the equal importance of the ministry of the Word.

Bibliography: K. W. BOLLE et al., "Altar," *NCE* 1.343-52 • J. BRAUN, *Der christliche Altar in seiner geschichtlichen Entwicklung* (2 vols.; Munich, 1924) • C.-M. EASMAN, "Altar," *EncRel(E)* (1987) 1.222-27 • J. MILGROM and B. M. LERNER, "Altar," *EncJud* 2.760-71 • C. E. POCKNEE, *The Christian Altar* (London, 1963) • P. POSCHARSKY, "Die Geschichte des christlichen Altars," *KuK* (1972) 24-29 • C. H. RATSCHOW, A. STUIBER, and P. POSCHARSKY, "Altar," *TRE* 2.305-27 • G. WEBB, *The Liturgical Altar* (2d ed.; London, 1939).

J. G. DAVIES†

Altötting

Altötting, Bavaria, is an important site of pilgrimage in honor of Mary. The town, which has a chapel going back to the eighth century, has long been a favorite resort of the nobility. After reports of miracles in about 1489, the pilgrimage developed under the patronage of the dukes of Bavaria, attracting travelers from Bohemia, South Tirol, and Italy as well as Bavaria. The → Reformation and → Enlightenment, however, threatened to end it.

P. Canisius (1521-97), M. Eisengrein (1535-78), and, later, J. M. Sailer gave it fresh impetus. Albert V (1550-79) did much to promote it. A new church was built in 1910-12. Pope John Paul II recognized its importance by visiting it on November 18-19, 1980.

→ Mary, Devotion to; Popular Religion

Bibliography: R. BAUER, *Bayerische Wallfahrt Altötting* (2d ed.; Munich, 1980) • O. WIEBEL-FANDERL, *Die Wallfahrt Altötting* (Passau, 1982).

JOHANNES SCHILLING

Amen

The word "amen" (Gk. *amēn*, from Heb. *ʾāmēn*) means "so it is." Except in sayings of Jesus, "amen" is a response to something that has just been said. Expressing his supreme authority, Jesus introduces his teachings with "(very) truly [*amēn (amēn)*] I tell you. . . ." In Rev. 3:14 "Amen" is a self-designation of Christ (cf. 2 Cor. 1:20).

In both Judaism and Christianity "amen" is one of the most important words in the congregation's participation in → worship. The → eucharistic prayer ends with "Amen," and the believer responds with "Amen" after receiving Communion (→ Eucharist). In the Middle Ages the priest, choir, and preacher used "Amen" in self-response, which M. → Luther found objectionable. The liturgical movements of the 20th century have restored "Amen" to its proper place as congregational → acclamation.

Bibliography: A. JEPSEN, "אָמַן *'āman,*" *TDOT* 1.320-23 • J. JEREMIAS and G. KRAUSE, "Amen," *TRE* 2.386-402 (bibliography) • M. R. E. MASTERMAN, "Amen," *NCE* 1.378 • H. SCHLIER, "Ἀμήν," *TDNT* 1.335-38.

THADDEUS A. SCHNITKER

Amnesty International

Amnesty International (AI), an international organization that is independent of governments, political parties, → ideologies, economic interests, and religions, plays a special role in the worldwide struggle for human rights. It does this particularly in cases of political imprisonment, working for the release of men, women, and children who are detained because of their political convictions, color, sex, race, culture, or religion, or who for these reasons are subjected to other physical restrictions, provided that they have neither used nor advocated → force. AI regards such people as nonviolent prisoners of conscience. It asks for fair and speedy trials for all political prisoners — irrespective of the question of force — and pleads for political prisoners who are being held without accusation or due process. The organization unreservedly opposes the → death penalty, → torture, and all other cruel, inhuman, or degrading treatment or punishment of all prisoners. It acts on the basis of the → United Nations' Universal Declaration of Human Rights, along with other international agreements.

To sustain the lofty claims that AI makes for itself demands that it maintain a high degree of credibility in its work. It thus strives to maintain nonalignment, independence, and impartiality. It does not classify governments or keep a black list or rank offenders against human rights. It adopts no position vis-à-vis political, economic, or ideological systems. Objectivity and the greatest possible completeness of information are decisive for the credibility of its work. Its secretariat in London has a special information division that gathers and evaluates reports from many sources. Wherever possible, AI does research on site, observes trials, visits prisoners, and intervenes with the representatives of governments. It never publishes anything anonymously but takes full responsibility for all the facts that it reports.

AI's practical work (appeals, publication, care for prisoners and their families, etc.) is done by volunteer groups. It is financed solely by the donations of members and supporters and does not accept grants from public funds for special purposes. Founded in 1961 by British attorney P. Benenson, AI in the early 1990s had over one million members, subscribers, and donors all over the globe. It had 48 national sections and was working with some 6,000 volunteer groups in 74 countries. Between 1991 and mid-1992, AI had adopted or investigated more than 43,500 cases. In 1977 AI received the Nobel Peace Prize.

Bibliography: The Amnesty International Handbook (ed. M. Staunton, S. Fenn, and Amnesty International U.S.A.; Claremont, Calif., 1991) • *Amnesty International Report* (London, appears annually) • E. LARSEN, *A Flame in Barbed Wire: The Story of Amnesty International* (New York, 1979) • D. PEERMAN, "A Map of Horrors and a Conspiracy of Hope," *CCen,* November 5, 1986, 963-64 • J. POWER, *Amnesty International: The Human Rights Story* (New York, 1981).

HELMUT FRENZ

Amos, Book of

1. Amos, the first of the writing prophets, came from Tekoa in Judah. Although a herdsman and a grower of figs, not a professional prophet, Amos was a man of broad outlook who did not lack means or education. A call from God took him out of his daily round and sent him to do prophetic work in the northern kingdom. He came there about 760 B.C. and in Bethel and Samaria, perhaps also Gilgal, proclaimed the inevitable fall of → Israel. Denounced and expelled, he seems to have gone back to Judah after hardly a year of activity.

Amos's coming occurred at the time of Israel's final prosperity. The weakness of the → Arameans and Assyrians allowed Jeroboam II (787-747 B.C.) to engage temporarily in a foreign policy of expansion. The period of peace led to an economic blossoming, which made a life of luxury possible for the upper classes at the expense of the poor. But Aramean and Ammonite raids on Gilead in East Jordan heralded a new decline.

2. The Book of Amos contains some former collections, the first of which is a cycle of sayings against foreign people in 1:3–2:16 (of which only 1:3-8; 1:13–2:3, 6-9, 13-16 may be authentic). This cycle ends with a strong word against Israel. A collection of sayings follows in chaps. 3–6. Then there is a cycle of five visions in 7:1-9; 8:1-3; 9:1-4. It seems unlikely that Amos himself was the immediate source of all the texts. With H. W. Wolff we might suppose that followers of Amos used some written notes of the prophet (1:3–2:16; 3–6*; 7:1-8 + 8:1-2 + 9:1-4),

adapting and enlarging them. The next stage of read-action was likely a Bethel interpretation that is oriented to the reforms of Josiah (639-609 B.C.). A → Deuteronomistic and a post- Deuteronomistic redaction gave the book its ultimate form. K. Koch, however, thinks there might have been a longer oral tradition of clusters of sayings that were made into a book in → Jerusalem in the 7th century B.C. Certainly the final form is postexilic.

3. The message of Amos is a radical one of disaster: "The end has come upon my people Israel" (8:2). This calamity may be depicted as drought, earthquake, or military defeat and deportation. Judgment falls because of Israel's failure in human relations. Amos's proclamation is uniquely dominated by social criticism, with closely connected charges of worship that has become self-seeking and of a corrupt legal system. Shocking, too, is his rejection of the people's reliance on the tradition of election, the gift of the promised land, and the exodus (3:2; 2:9; 9:7). Instead of being the basis of privilege or of security for Israel, these blessings bring special → responsibility. They thus prove Israel's guilt and bring on destruction. Ruin is ineluctable; there is no glimmer of → hope. No other prophetic book contains such a radical No to the existence of Israel. Amos's school softens it or weakens it by admonitions (5:14-15). The Deuteronomistic redaction in the time of the exile uses it as the reason for judgment, which had taken place in 587 B.C. The post-Deuteronomistic redaction adds the hope of salvation (9:11-15).

→ Prophet, Prophecy

Bibliography: F. I. ANDERSEN and D. N. FREEDMAN, *Amos* (New York, 1989) • G. BARTCZEK, *Prophetie und Vermittlung* (Frankfurt, 1980) • R. B. COOTE, *Amos among the Prophets* (Philadelphia, 1981) • J. JEREMIAS, *Der Prophet Amos* (Göttingen, 1995) • K. KOCH et al., *Amos. Untersucht mit den Methoden einer strukturalen Formgeschichte* (3 vols.; Kevelaer, 1976) • L. MARKERT, "Amos / Amosbuch," *TRE* 2.471-87 (extensive bibliography) • R. MARTIN-ACHARD, *Amos. L'homme, le message, l'influence* (Geneva, 1984) • J. L. MAYS, *Amos* (Philadelphia, 1969) • M. E. POLLEY, *Amos and the Davidic Empire* (Oxford, 1989) • R. SMEND, "Das Nein des Amos," *EvT* 23 (1963) 404-23 • G. V. SMITH, *Amos* (Grand Rapids, 1989) • H. W. WOLFF, *Amos the Prophet* (Philadelphia, 1973); idem, *Joel and Amos* (Philadelphia, 1977).

WINFRIED THIEL

Amphictyony → Tribes of Israel

Anabaptists

1. Term
2. Threefold Origin
3. Groups
4. Theological Positions

1. Term

"Anabaptist" is a term used for groups in the age of the → Reformation that baptized adults instead of infants (→ Baptism). The term, which strictly means "rebaptizer," was contested by the groups themselves, who denied that infant baptism was real baptism. It had been used in the → early church for the → Donatists (→ Heretical Baptism) and remained in use in English to distinguish these groups from the later → Baptists. Today, however, it is more common to speak of "radical reformers" or "left-wing reformers."

In the 5th century, rebaptizing could be punished by death, and the code of Justinian (527-65), which was still in effect in much of Europe as late as the 16th century, demanded for conviction only that the fact of rebaptizing be proved. The term had a defamatory sense in the Reformation period, being used to refer to many religious dissenters, even some who did not practice baptism at all (→ Spiritualism; Anti-Trinitarianism). The various groups called themselves Brethren in Christ, Chosen in the Lord, Companions in Tribulation, Poor in Spirit, and other names, rejecting the term of opprobrium used by their opponents.

2. Threefold Origin

The many different groups of Anabaptists may be seen against the background of their threefold origin.

2.1. The first rebaptism at the time of the Reformation took place in Zurich on January 21, 1525, when the priest George Blaurock (ca. 1491-1529) had himself baptized by Konrad Grebel (ca. 1498-1526), son of a patrician. Then Grebel baptized Felix Mantz (ca. 1500-1527) and others. Though the authorities at once took action, the first Anabaptist community was formed in the next few days at the fishing village of Zollikon, outside Zurich. The reasons for its formation were complex. The theology of U. → Zwingli (1484-1531) provided the intellectual framework — on the one hand, through his early relativization of infant baptism, and, on the other, through his increasing caution about immediately implementing the new insights of the Reformation in church and society. There was also an economic problem relating to interest, → tithes, benefices, and the obligations of village communities to monasteries, foundations, and the city of Zurich. Finally, the conflict also had political dimensions related to peasant unrest (→ Peasants' War). C. A. Peter has shown that Carlstadt (ca. 1480-1541) played an early role, though we must not view him as the father of the movement.

The measures the Zurich authorities took against the Anabaptists helped to spread the movement to German Switzerland and to southern Germany and Austria. The original goal of influencing the society as a whole failed with the collapse of the peasant movement and the great Zurich disputation of November 1525. Instead, Grebel's view prevailed. Already in a letter to Thomas Müntzer (ca. 1489-1525) in the fall of 1524, he had envisioned a minority church. This view found classic expression in the Schleitheim Confession (or "Brotherly Union of a Number of Children of God concerning Seven Articles"), a confession written by Michael Sattler (burned at the stake in 1527) that was adopted at Schleitheim near Schaffhausen in February 1527 (→ Reformers 2.1.3).

2.2. As a follower of Müntzer and ardent colporteur of his works, Hans Hut (ca. 1490-1527) had already become familiar with his criticism of infant baptism. After the battle of Frankenhausen and Müntzer's death in May 1525, Hut sought the more zealously to serve the legacy of his teacher. He did not abandon this goal when he met Anabaptists and had himself baptized on Pentecost 1526 in Augsburg by Hans Denck (ca. 1495-1527), who was inclined to mysticism and → pacifism.

Hut was the most successful Anabaptist missioner in Franconia, Bavaria, and Austria. His strongly mystical theology was also influenced by expectation of the immediate inbreaking of the → kingdom of God (→ Millenarianism; Mysticism). In preparation, he preached "the gospel of all creatures." He had in view the purifying suffering that is ordained for all creation and that is identical with the → cross of Christ. With baptism, his followers received the sign of the Greek letter tau on their foreheads to seal them for final redemption (Rev. 9:4).

2.3. In 1530 Melchior Hoffmann (ca. 1500-ca. 1543), a furrier from Schwäbisch-Hall, took the movement from Strasbourg to the → Netherlands (§1.4.1), where it spread quickly. He, too, thought God's kingdom was imminent, expecting it to be set up in Strasbourg after a last decisive battle. He thus went there in 1533. Of vital importance for him was a sense of endowment with the Spirit conferred by God on his messengers who carry the → gospel. The community, the bride of Christ, was simply a receptor for those who were won for the gospel. Like Hut, Hoffmann died in prison.

3. Groups

The formation of viable Anabaptist communities followed a relatively simple pattern. Conflict with the authorities and the churches supported by them resulted, where possible, in a retreat underground or into a more or less tolerated minority church that saw itself as a "church under the cross" and that survived under conditions of → separatism.

3.1. This change took place in Switzerland by the end of 1525. Strong persecution forced the Anabaptists into the mountains and forests. As the Swiss Brethren, they differentiated themselves from rival groups in southern Germany, such as the churches founded by Pilgram Marpeck (ca. 1495-1556), whose mystical and biblicist → piety made them less inclined to separatism.

3.2. The Anabaptists who fled to Tyrol (e.g., Jörg Blaurock) were also considered revolutionary, provoking strong countermeasures from traditionalists. Many found refuge in Moravia. Here Anabaptist pacifist groups were at work (as opposed to those who stressed the right of self-defense), and they adopted sharing of goods in communities. Taking their name from Jakob Hutter of Tyrol (burned at the stake in 1536), they formed the largest group of Anabaptists, with some 20,000 members (→ Hutterites). They not only prospered but were able to turn into practical piety the mystical revolutionary tradition of Hut.

3.3. The Anabaptist regime in Münster (January 1534 to July 1535) was the disastrous climax of Hoffmann's movement. It aimed to set up an emperor and empire, not merely founding a city of God but bringing in God's kingdom directly, after extirpating the ungodly. When the reign of terror collapsed and the leaders (Jan Mathys, Jan van Leiden, and Bernd Rothmann) were killed or executed, the movement seemed to have dug its own grave. Hoffmann's work, however, had laid a broader foundation.

From those who escaped from Münster and others, various groups were formed, including two of importance: the → Mennonites and the Jorists. In 1536 → Menno Simons (1496-1561) abandoned his Roman Catholic priesthood in Witmarsum, Friesland, and in 1537 was elected an → elder among the Anabaptists. With the help of Dirk and Obbe Philips, Adam Pastor, and Leenaert Bouwens, Menno founded a chain of fellowships from Amsterdam to Danzig, all unarmed.

David Joris (ca. 1501-56) gathered his followers into secret groups and recognized the official church, thus escaping persecution.

4. Theological Positions

4.1. Because of differences in origin and aims,

Anabaptist teaching was not uniform. In retrospect, the initiation of believers' baptism implied separation of → church and state, dissolution of the concept of Christendom, and the concept of a → free church. Almost everywhere they appeared, however, the Anabaptists initially aimed at changing society as a whole; only reluctantly did they accept the role of a pacifist, minority church separate from the world.

The sense of living in the last days, intermingled with apocalyptic and millennial notions (→ Apocalypticism 4.3), played an important role. → Church discipline was also central. For Hoffmann and the Mennonites, such discipline was primarily a means to keep the community pure as the bride of Christ (→ Excommunication 2). In Germany, however, the rule of Christ (Matt. 18:15-17) had an indispensable pedagogical function in upbuilding the community. There were differences, too, in evaluation of the Bible, with spiritualizing of the text existing alongside → biblicism (→ Spiritualism). It is not surprising that much feuding took place among the various Anabaptist groups.

4.2. At first (1525-29), the Anabaptist movement attracted not only laity but also many theologians, clergy, and intellectuals. Some like Balthasar Hubmaier (1485-1528), Ludwig Hätzer (ca. 1500-1529), and H. Denck played an active role. Later members, however, were mostly peasants and artisans. Only a few theologians or people of higher social status were supporters.

The Anabaptists disparaged the theology of the schools. Yet they defended their faith wherever they could in protests, public discussions, disputations, or prison. Sometimes they disputed matters of faith and biblical exposition in pamphlets and books, such as in the controversies between Hubmaier and Zwingli, Micronius and Menno, Dirk Philips and Sebastian Franck. For the most part, however, they accepted the differences. They realized the need to be left alone, for often, especially in traditionalist areas, they were dealt with harshly. By 1539, in German-speaking territories alone, the Anabaptists had recorded 780 → martyrs.

4.3. The spiritual life of the Anabaptists found expression in hymnbooks, tracts, confessions, and devotional letters and chronicles. Martyrology played a particularly important role. One may rightfully speak of an Anabaptist theology of martyrdom.

Bibliography: H. J. HILLERBRAND, *Anabaptist Bibliography, 1520-1630* (St. Louis, 1991) over 6,000 entries.

Primary sources: M. BAUMGARTNER, *Die Täufer und Zwingli. Eine Dokumentation* (Zurich, 1993) • S. CRAMER and F. PIJPER, eds., *BRN* 2, 5, 7, 10 • H. FAST, ed., *Der linke Flügel der Reformation* (Bremen, 1962) • INSTITUTE OF MENNONITE STUDIES, *Classics of the Radical Reformation* (vols. 1-6; Scottdale, Pa., 1973-92) • A. E. MELLINK, ed., *DAN* 1-3, 5-6 • L. VON MURALT, H. FAST, and M. HAAS, *Quellen zur Geschichte der Täufer in der Schweiz* (vols. 1-2, 4; Zurich, 1952-74) • R. STUPPERICH, ed., *Die Schriften Bernhard Rothmanns* (Münster, 1970) • VEREIN FÜR REFORMATIONSGESCHICHTE, *Quellen zur Geschichte der (Wieder-) Täufer* (16 vols.; Leipzig and Gütersloh, 1930-88) • G. H. WILLIAMS and A. M. MERGAL, eds., *Spiritual and Anabaptist Writers: Documents Illustrative of the Radical Reformation* (London, 1975) • A. J. F. ZIEGLSCHMID, ed., *Die älteste Chronik der Hutterischen Brüder* (Ithaca, N.Y., 1943).

Secondary works: H. S. BENDER, *Conrad Grebel* (Goshen, Ind., 1950) • G. A. BENRATH, "Die Lehre der Täufer," *Die Lehrentwicklung im Rahmen der Konfessionalität* (ed. B. Lohse et al.; Göttingen, 1980) 611-58 • T. BERGSTEN, *Balthasar Hubmaier: Anabaptist Theologian and Martyr* (ed. W. R. Estep Jr.; Valley Forge, Pa., 1978) • C. BORNHÄUSER, *Leben und Lehre Menno Simons. Ein Kampf um das Fundament des Glaubens (etwa 1496-1561)* (Neukirchen, 1973) • S. B. BOYD, *Pilgram Marpeck: His Life and Social Theology* (Durham, N.C., 1992) • C. P. CLASEN, *Anabaptism: A Social History, 1525-1618: Switzerland, Austria, Moravia, South and Central Germany* (Ithaca, N.Y., 1972) • K. DEPPERMANN, *Melchior Hoffman: Social Unrest and Apocalyptic Visions in the Age of Reformation* (ed. B. Drewery; Edinburgh, 1987) • H.-J. GOERTZ, *Religiöse Bewegungen in der frühen Neuzeit* (Munich, 1993); idem, *Die Täufer. Geschichte und Bedeutung* (2d ed.; Munich, 1988); idem, ed., *Umstrittenes Täufertum: 1525-1975* (2d ed.; Göttingen, 1977) • H.-J. GOERTZ and W. KLASSEN, eds., *Profiles of Radical Reformers: Biographical Sketches from Thomas Müntzer to Paracelsus* (Kitchener, Ont., 1982) • J. F. G. GOETERS, "Die Vorgeschichte des Täufertums in Zurich," *Studien zur Geschichte und Theologie der Reformation* (FS E. Bizer; Neukirchen, 1969) 239-81 • I. B. HORST, *The Radical Brethren: Anabaptism and the English Reformation to 1558* (Nieuwkoop, 1972) • K.-H. KICHHOFF, "Das Phänomen des Täuferreiches zu Münster, 1534/35," *Der Raum Westfalen* (vol. 6/1; ed. H. Aubin and F. Petri; Münster, 1989) 277-422 • W. KLAASSEN, ed., *Anabaptism Revisited: Essays on Anabaptist/Mennonite Studies in Honour of C. J. Dyck* (Scottdale, Pa., 1992) • M. LIENHARD, "Die Wiedertäufer," *Die Geschichte des Christentums* (vol. 8; Freiburg, 1992) 122-90 • U. LIESEBERG, *Studien zum Märtyrerlied der Täufer im 16. Jahrhundert* (Frankfurt, 1991) • W. O. PACKULL, "The Beginnings of the Hutterian Brethren: The Storm and Stress of Early Communitarian Anabaptism, 1527-1556" (MS; 1993); idem, *Rereading Anabaptist Beginnings* (Winnipeg, 1991) • J.-G. ROTT and S. L. VERHEUS, eds., *Täufertum und radikale Reformation im 16. Jahrhundert* (Baden-Baden, 1987) • J. Séguy, *Les assemblées Anabaptistes-Mennonites de France* (Paris, 1977) • J. M. Stayer, *The German Peasants' War and Anabaptist Community of Goods* (Montreal, 1991) • J. M. Stayer, W. O. Packull, and K. Deppermann, "From Monogenesis to Polygenesis: The Historical Discussion of Anabaptist Origins," *MQR* 49 (1975) 83-121 • G. K. Waite, *David Joris and Dutch Anabaptism, 1524-1543* (Waterloo, Ont., 1990) • G. H. Williams, *The Radical Reformation* (3d ed.; 2 vols.; Kirksville, Mo., 1992) • J. H. Yoder, *Täufertum und Reformation im Gespräch* (Zurich, 1968).

Heinhold Fast

Analogy

1. Definition
2. History
3. Modern Discussion
4. Theological Evaluation

1. Definition

In general the word "analogy" means correspondence or similarity between two or more entities that are neither completely the same nor completely different. Scientifically the term is used *(analogia nominum)* with reference not only to the comparable things themselves but also to the relations within which they may be said to be comparable. Hence analogy takes on its strictest form as proportionality *(analogia proportionalitatis:* a : b = c : d; e.g., 9 : 3 = 6 : 2). The difference between this and simple proportion *(analogia proportionis)* is that the analogy here involves not a relation between two entities but a relation between two relations.

2. History

2.1. The strict view of analogy finds its origin in the mathematics of the Pythagorean school. But more generally Parmenides (d. after 480 B.C.) and Heraclitus (ca. 540-ca. 480 B.C.) were already discussing analogy, although Plato (427-347 B.C.) was the first to use the term as a philosophical concept, doing so to bring to light correspondences in the cosmos, as well as between and within the ontic and noetic spheres, with the help of three- and four-membered proportions (→ Platonism).

Aristotle (384-322 B.C.) followed the Pythagorean view of analogy when he applied it as a similarity of relations to the fields of → ethics and → metaphysics. Although Aristotle defined proportionality alone as analogy, we also find in him an early form of the analogy of attribution *(analogia attributionis),* which was developed especially in → Scholasticism (→ Aristotelianism). Such analogy does not posit any specific relational correspondence but expresses the relation to a first principle, upon which all the rest depends (e.g., for something to be "healthy," some notion of "health" is necessary).

2.2. → Thomas Aquinas (1224/25-74) applied this form of analogy to the relation between God and the world, which, in a further development of the Platonic and Neoplatonic thought of participation, he viewed as a causal relation. The relation between the divine being and the multiplicity of being arises when what is said about finite being is seen in its dependence on the divine origin.

2.3. Thomas espoused an autonomy of analogy as midway between a univocal relation and complete difference (→ Thomism). Duns Scotus (ca. 1265-1308), however, shattered this understanding by showing that analogy itself presupposes a univocal element (→ Scotism). Kant (1724-1804) in turn destroyed the ontological basis of the metaphysical and theological concept of analogy by arguing that the rational idea of God attained from the relation of the conditioned to the unconditioned does not include the knowability or definability of God's intrinsic being (→ Kantianism). Thus, although the existence of God can undoubtedly be thought of by analogy with the objects of experience, it cannot be thought of as really given but only as an idea that is thought.

2.4. A different use of analogy informed the important work of the English bishop Joseph Butler (1692-1752). His *Analogy of Religion* (1736) was a response to the deism of his day. It rested on a recommendation of probabilities, whereby Butler tried to show, first, that Christianity was not unreasonable and, second, that both nature and revelation pointed in the direction of traditional Christianity. The work was a central feature of British theological discussion for over 150 years and is still used with respect today.

3. Modern Discussion

In the 20th century E. Przywara (1889-1972) and neo-Thomism have gone beyond the concept of the *analogia entis* (analogy of being) that was introduced by T. Cajetan (1469-1534). Along the lines of the Fourth Lateran Council (1215), they regard the analogy between Creator and creature as a similarity that involves a greater dissimilarity. This view overthrows the intention of analogy, which by reason of its univocal element seeks to integrate what is dissimilar into what is similar.

Without doing full justice to Przywara's understanding, K. → Barth (1886-1968), in his rejection of every form of → natural theology, criticized the *analogia entis* for using the ontic similarity between Creator and creature as a basis on which to construct a natural knowledge of God apart from divine → revelation. Barth replaced the *analogia entis* by the *analogia fidei* (analogy of faith; see Rom. 12:6), which he grounded in God's revealing action. As for the divine likeness of humanity, Barth anchored this analogy in the inner-Trinitarian being of God as an *analogia relationis* (→ Trinity). He also developed the similarity between divine and human work as an *analogia operationis*.

4. Theological Evaluation
The logical difficulties (3) and the criticisms of Scotus and Kant (2.3) have cast doubt on the applicability of analogy to the relation between God and the world. If analogy is grounded in the divine → act alone, the relative autonomy of the creature seems to be suspended. But if analogy is upheld in its strict form as analogy of proportionality, the alleged comparability of divine and creaturely relations seems to presuppose a univocal element that relativizes the absoluteness of God.

Bibliography: H. U. von Balthasar, *The Theology of Karl Barth* (New York, 1971; orig. pub., 1951) • K. Barth, *CD* I/1, 184ff., 259ff.; II/1, 58ff.; III/1, 164ff.; III/2, 184ff.; III/3, 42ff. • J. Butler, *The Analogy of Religion, Natural and Revealed, to the Constitution and Course of Nature* (3d ed.; Charlottesville, Va., 1986; orig. pub., 1736) • C. Cunliffe, ed., *Joseph Butler's Moral and Religious Thought* (Oxford, 1992) • R. M. McInerny, *The Logic of Analogy: An Interpretation of St. Thomas* (The Hague, 1961) • B. Mondin, *The Principle of Analogy in Protestant and Catholic Theology* (2d ed.; The Hague, 1968) • W. Pannenberg, *Analogie und Offenbarung. Eine kritische Untersuchung der Geschichte des Analogiebegriffs in der Gotteserkenntnis* (Heidelberg, 1955); idem, "Zur Bedeutung des Analogiegedankens bei Karl Barth," *TLZ* 78 (1953) 17-24 • E. Przywara, *Analogia entis. Metaphysik* (Einsiedeln, 1962) • L. B. Puntel, *Analogie und Geschichtlichkeit* (vol. 1; Freiburg, 1969) extensive bibliography • Thomas Aquinas, *Summa c. Gent.* 1.32-34 • J. Track, "Analogie," *TRE* 2.625-50 (extensive bibliography).

FALK WAGNER

Analytic Ethics

1. Concept
Analytic ethics denotes the treatment of ethics within British analytic philosophy as this has been pursued from the beginning of the 20th century. Unlike the mainstream of traditional moral philosophy, analytic ethics does not try to work out a system of principles so as to give valid guidance to acts and judgments and thus to tell us in practice what we ought to do. Instead, it engages in a theoretical analysis of moral phenomena on the level of → language, examining the sentences in which moral statements are made and the meanings of the terms they use (e.g., "good," "bad," "right," and "ought"). Its concern is to analyze moral discourse, its elements and interconnection, and to show on what conditions its statements can claim universal validity and how they may be supported and justified. It is thus in essence → metaethics.

2. Trends
Although there is a great measure of agreement about the object and method of the philosophical treatment of ethics, the results of the analyses differ widely, as do the underlying assumptions.

2.1. Intuitionism (G. E. Moore) regards the basic moral values as simple qualities that cannot be analyzed but merely reveal themselves to the → intuitions of the moral subject (→ Good, The). It rejects all equation of moral predicates with nonmoral predicates (e.g., "good" with what brings happiness or is pleasing or is in accord with God's will). Such equations contain a naturalistic fallacy, it is argued, as descriptive statements illegitimately become → normative statements. Here note Hume's distinction between what is and what ought to be.

2.2. Emotivism (A. J. Ayer and C. L. Stevenson) applies to ethics the strict criteria of verification imposed by logical → positivism. Moral principles have no cognitive meaning. Their sole significance is to express emotions and attitudes, or to evoke them in others.

2.3. Prescriptivism (R. M. Hare) starts with Wittgenstein's criterion of verification, according to which the meaning of a word is to be found in its use. Moral discourse includes both descriptive elements and prescriptive elements. The → logic of imperatives, however, does not let its moral principles be reduced to purely descriptive statements. Its premises always contain an imperative that can be applied universally, that is, to all situations that are alike in the relevant aspects.

2.4. Many authors direct their attention expressly to the logic of moral discourse. They ask what good reasons there are for decisions and judgments and analyze supposedly rational arguments in practical discourse with a view to describing the rationality of morality (S. E. Toulmin, K. Baier, P. H. Nowell-Smith, J. Rawls, and M. G. Singer). Alternatively, they outline a → deontic logic that formalizes the function and rationality of moral usage (G. H. Wright).

2.5. Neonaturalism or descriptivism gets behind criticism to naturalism, rejects the reduction of morality to a formal treatment, and stresses the inalienable character of the specifically moral criteria of morality. These criteria correspond to basic human needs and ultimately show a judgment or action to be good (G. J. Warnock, P. Foot, and G. E. M. Anscombe). This position thus rejects every kind of ethical → relativism.

3. Present Discussion
Intuitionism and emotivism are outdated. Debate continues among the other views. Still at issue are the meaning of moral concepts and the justification of moral principles. How far, for example, can material criteria, formal procedures, or the principle of universal application demonstrate the rationality of moral discourse? In the process of supporting a moral decision, is there finally a decision of principle that ultimately has its basis only in the lifestyle and outlook of the moral subject (R. M. Hare and P. F. Strawson)? What significance do moral subjects and their self-understanding have for ethics (S. Hampshire), or as a means of bridging the gap between "is" and "ought"? In this discussion the linguistic restriction of analytic ethics is largely surmounted. On the level of normative ethics, to which analytic ethics returns, the question is whether to justify moral decisions by their results (→ Teleology; Utilitarianism) or by specifically moral qualities.

4. Analytic Ethics and Theological Ethics
Analytic ethics deals with the basic philosophical questions of ethics that precede practical, normative ethics. This concern can help theological ethics to clarify its own foundations, to fix its position within ethics, and to formulate what is distinctive to it. If we adopt the metaethical position that moral decisions finally have their basis, not in unchangeable principles, but in underlying convictions or outlook, then interesting perspectives result for a Christian ethics that finds its impulse, measure, and foundation in the stories of the Christian tradition that live on among Christians.

Bibliography: H. Biesenbach, *Zur Logik der moralischen Argumentation* (Düsseldorf, 1982) • D. Birnbacher and N. Hoerster, eds., *Texte zur Ethik* (Munich, 1976) • W. K. Frankena, *Ethics* (Englewood Cliffs, N.J., 1963) • G. Grewendorf and G. Meggle, eds., *Seminar: Sprache und Ethik* (Frankfurt, 1974) • S. Hauerwas, *Vision and Virtue: Essays in Christian Ethical Reflection* (Notre Dame, Ind., 1974) • S. Hauerwas and A. MacIntyre, eds., *Revisions: Changing Perspectives in Moral Philosophy* (Notre Dame, Ind., 1983) • K. Nielsen, "Ethics, History of" and "Ethics, Problems of," *EncPh* 3.100-134 • G. Outka and J. P. Reeder jr., eds., *Religion and Morality* (Garden City, N.Y., 1973) • I. T. Ramsey, ed., *Christian Ethics and Contemporary Philosophy* (London, 1966) • W. Schwartz, *Analytische Ethik und christliche Theologie* (Göttingen, 1984) • K. Ward, *Ethics and Christianity* (London, 1970).

Werner Schwartz

Analytic Philosophy

1. Name
   1.1. Rise and Spread
   1.2. Founders and Representatives
2. Method and Goal
   2.1. Logical Atomism
   2.2. Logical Empiricism
   2.3. Linguistic Philosophy

1. Name
The term "analytic philosophy" derives from its methodology. Its aim is to arrive at the truth, meaning, and significance of statements by analysis of → language and usage.

1.1. *Rise and Spread*
Analytic philosophy arose in Great Britain at the beginning of the 20th century. It did so in reaction to English → idealism and its interpretation of Hegel (→ Hegelianism). Under the influence of the Vienna Circle and Wittgenstein, it moved on from logical atomism to logical → empiricism and then to linguistic philosophy or phenomenalism. Outside Great Britain it became dominant in the United States and spread also in Scandinavian countries. After the end of World War II, although logical empiricism tried to regain its influence in Germany, interest in the philosophical approach of Wittgenstein led to the spread of linguistic philosophy and to concern with it throughout most of Europe.

1.2. *Founders and Representatives*
To the early period of logical atomism belong especially G. E. Moore (1873-1958) and B. Russell (1872-1970). Logical empiricism and the Vienna Circle include M. Schlick (1882-1936) and R. Carnap (1891-1970), as well as O. Neurath, F. Waismann, V. Kraft,

B. Juhos, C. G. Hempel, H. Feigl, and H. Reichenbach. The most significant representative of the linguistic trend is L. Wittgenstein (1889-1951), with G. Ryle and J. L. Austin also noteworthy.

2. Method and Goal

From the very outset analytic philosophy is concerned with doing linguistic criticism with the goal of accepting only those statements whose truth can be demonstrated.

2.1. *Logical Atomism*

Moore and Russell shared the conviction that one must distinguish between the logical and the grammatical forms of language and that grammar alone does not suffice to differentiate true statements from false. Moore took the view that for philosophy this defect can be remedied by recasting its statements into ordinary language. There we can test the logical form by whether or not the statements are in keeping with common sense. Russell, in contrast, pleaded for the construction of an ideal logical speech that would be free from contradictions, as projected in his *Principia Mathematica*. This division led to linguistic phenomenalism and logical empiricism.

2.2. *Logical Empiricism*

With the aim of getting beyond metaphysics, logical empiricism makes the question of truth expressly the subject of reflection. Its starting point is that knowledge of the truth-value of a statement is not possible without knowing the circumstances in which it can be true. Under the influence of the Vienna Circle (a group of students and scholars interested in philosophy that gathered originally around M. Schlick, professor of philosophy at the University of Vienna, and that, as a result of the political situation, did their work mostly in the United States in the 1930s), logical empiricism proceeded by examining only those conditions to which one can apply an empirical criterion of meaning or principle of verification.

This position underwent later modification, not because of dissatisfaction with the principle, but because it did not prove possible to establish the meaningfulness of the principles of knowledge (principles of inquiry, protocol, or basis) by way of empirically demonstrable statements. Recognizing the impossibility of equating statements with structures of reality, Carnap elaborated a theory of formal language in which he developed the theorizings of Russell and the insights of F. L. G. Frege (1848-1925) into a theory of inductive → logic. The decisive advantage of formal language over natural language is that it does not talk about things (e.g., as in "the table is brown"), but about words (e.g., by showing that

"table" is the word for a thing). Yet the important question of determining the relation between speech and reality — one that demands the establishment of a criterion of verification — does not really become meaningless when such a distinction is made, for in fact the reference to reality, which has no relevance for formal speech itself, is subject to a specific standpoint, namely, physicalism.

Logical empiricism is more often called logical → positivism (§1). This label emphasizes the connection with phenomenalism and the denial that the psychological is an independent class of phenomena alongside the physical during the early phase of logical empiricism.

2.3. *Linguistic Philosophy*

This approach was shaped by the works of Wittgenstein: his *Tractatus Logico-Philosophicus* and especially his *Philosophical Investigations*. The *Tractatus*, which is committed to → empiricism, evaluated afresh the significance of ideal and ordinary language. It thus prepared the way for the linguistic turn of the third period of analytic philosophy. It begins with the structural equation of language and reality and thus finds the meaning of a statement in what it represents. Scientific language is an isomorphic representation of reality, but not in the sense of Russell, who with his ideal language wanted to describe a primarily nonlinguistic reality. When we cannot get behind language, it takes on the character of constituting reality in a way that reminds us of the transcendental philosophy of Kant (→ Kantianism). Skepticism of ordinary language remains, declaring that all questions of → ethics, → religion, and → aesthetics — the classic problems of life — are meaningless and unanswerable. Yet there is no claim that they express no reality. Instead, it is argued that they are unclear in their use of words.

The implicit, empiricist principle of verification that governs the *Tractatus* is less prominent in the *Philosophical Investigations,* in which a pluralism of language games replaces the concept of an ideal language. These games prove to be true within the sphere of their functioning, so that analysis of a given use can replace verification by means of a structurally equivalent scientific language. The distinction between the grammatical and logical forms of a statement that was so important in the early period of analytic philosophy is supplemented by a distinction between superficial grammar and deep grammar in which the issue is the connection between the object and the word that seeks to express it. Linguistic thought, then, no longer has recourse to an ideal language that controls and constructs the rules of usage but sees in language use itself the means of purging ordinary speech of errors. The difficulties in the *Tractatus* opened the door to this insight, for they made it clear that determining the relation that the theory of representation presupposes between language and reality can be done and verified only by ordinary language and not by ideal language. The functioning language game provides a basis on which language as a pragmatic life-form ensures its own meaning. Thus the problem areas that logical empiricism called metaphysics, and that Wittgenstein called mystical in the *Tractatus,* become amenable again to philosophical treatment.

The lifting of the linguistic veto in the *Philosophical Investigations* brought the need for fresh reflection on fundamental issues and also for asking such questions as that of the relation of languages that express only certain aspects of → experience to those that claim to grasp the totality of reality (e.g., the language of religion or of philosophy). The problem of the interdependence of language games and the development of → analytic ethics, → philosophy of history, → aesthetics, and so forth also widened the range of the philosophical disciplines within analytic philosophy, so that there is hardly a philosophical issue that now lies outside the sphere of linguistic analysis.

Bibliography: Primary sources: R. CARNAP, *Der logische Aufbau der Welt* (Berlin, 1928) • G. E. MOORE, *Philosophical Studies* (London, 1922) • M. SCHLICK, *Gesammelte Aufsätze, 1926-1936* (Vienna, 1938) • L. WITTGENSTEIN, *Philosophical Investigations* (2d ed.; New York, 1958); idem, *Tractatus Logico-Philosophicus* (London, 1988).

Secondary works: G. E. M. ANSCOMBE, *An Introduction to Wittgenstein's Tractatus* (London, 1959) • M. J. CHARLESWORTH, *Philosophy and Linguistic Analysis* (Pittsburgh, 1959) • E. HEINTEL, *Einführung in die Sprachphilosophie* (Darmstadt, 1972) • H. HOFMEISTER, *Truth and Belief: Interpretation and Critique of the Analytical Theory of Religion* (Boston, 1990) • V. KRAFT, *Der Ursprung des Neopositivismus* (Vienna, 1968) • K. LORENZ, *Elemente der Sprachkritik. Eine Alternative zum Dogmatismus und Skeptizismus in der analytischen Philosophie* (Frankfurt, 1971) • C. A. VAN PEURSEN, *Phenomenology and Analytical Philosophy* (Pittsburgh, 1972) • W. SCHULZ, *Wittgenstein. Die Negation der Philosophie* (Pfullingen, 1967) • E. TUGENDHAT, *Traditional and Analytical Philosophy* (Cambridge, 1982) • B. WILLIAMS and A. MONTEFIORE, eds., *British Analytical Philosophy* (London, 1966).

HEIMO HOFMEISTER

Anamnesis → Eucharistic Prayer

Ānanda Mārga

Meaning "way of blessedness" in Sanskrit, Ānanda Mārga is the name of a Hindu reforming movement that was started in 1955 at Jamalpur, in Bihar, India. Its originator was Prabhata Ranjana Sarkar (b. 1921), who called himself Shree Ānanda-murti, and to whom his followers attached a further title "shree." With the Ānanda he thought of himself as a member of the classical Vedanta triad *sat* (being), *chit* (thought), and *ānanda* (bliss), which, as attributes of Atman or Brahman, compose the true nature of humanity and the universe. He could thus make it his goal to reactivate → Yoga, on which comparable tendencies in other cultures could build. The great model for taking over the whole system of meditation lay already in the founder's reinterpretation of Tantra-Yoga, which gave its concepts a new and often spiritualizing and folk-etymological sense with a basis in modern views of psychology, physiology, and energy. Generally retaining the Sanskrit-Hindu terminology, he translated his teaching into the languages of over 100 countries. The organization includes five grades of spiritual perfection. Every integrated personality is finally to be helped to perfection. To this end, with the related dietetics, the translation of partially achieved mental liberation into social activity (involving kindergartens and other schools, rehabilitation centers, and disaster relief), and a political theory and organization (his so-called Progressive Utilization Theory), the movement has harnessed the aspirations of many people, including young people, for happiness and making the world a better place.

→ Fate and (Good) Fortune

Bibliography: W. AHRENS, *Die Weisheit der Tantralehre* (Mainz, 1977) • W. AHRENS and J. WEILER, *16 Punkte zur Selbstverwirklichung von Shrii Shrii Anandamurti* (Mainz, 1976) • S. S. ANANDAMURTI, *Ein Führer zu menschlichem Handeln* (2d ed.; Mainz, 1975) • P. R. SARKAR, *Baba's Grace* (2d ed.; Willow Springs, Mo., 1988).

CARSTEN COLPE

Anaphora

From Gk. *anapherō* (lift up, lead back), "anaphora" strictly denotes relation, connection, reference, report, appeal, and, in theological usage, offering or sacrifice (cf. Heb. 7:27; 13:15). It is thus used to bring out the meaning of the eucharistic action (→ Eucharist). This is the offering of a → sacrifice (§3) in reflection of the original sacrifice, the unique sacrifice of Christ (Heb. 10:12), which finds representation in the eucharistic celebration.

In a narrower liturgical sense the Anaphora is the core of Eastern → liturgies, corresponding to the canon *(canon actionis)* in the West. Less commonly the term may denote the eucharistic celebration, the liturgical form, entry in the register of → diptychs, or, in the Syrian Rite, the great vellum that covers the cup and paten (→ Syrian Orthodox Church).

Bibliography: A. BAUMSTARK, "Anaphora," *RAC* 1.418-27 • W. H. FRERE, *The Anaphora, or Great Eucharistic Prayer* (London, 1938) • R. C. D. JASPER and G. J. CUMING, *Prayers of the Eucharist: Early and Reformed* (3d ed.; Collegeville, Minn., 1990) • A. RÜCKER, "Das große Dankgebet in den orientalischen Meßliturgien," *ODPB* 12 (1941).

ANASTASIOS KALLIS

Anarchy

1. Anthropologically, "anarchy" refers to forms of society with no central authority or law. In social history it refers to libertarian social movements. In social philosophy it refers to an antiauthoritarian, antidogmatic theory that competes with socialist and Communist traditions — that is, anarchism. In → ideological criticism it refers to a polemical construct that has been used since the days of Plato (→ Platonism). Anarchy raises ethical (→ Force and Nonviolence), theological (→ State), and ecumenical (→ Third World) questions.

2. The anthropological basis of anarchy has been developed in social → anthropology.

2.1. In an investigation of the political systems of Africa, M. Fortes and E. E. Evans-Pritchard succeeded in discovering a developed form of → society that is organized in segments with no central authority.

2.2. C. Sigrist and others have found many other examples of this "regulated anarchy" both within and outside of Africa. Such anarchy builds on a unilinear tribe that unites with other groups to form a complex system in an amphictyony (a union based on shared religious or other interests). This form of organization has great staying power and can offer strong resistance to integration into societies with a central government.

2.3. Regulated anarchy often existed alongside other social forms and was only gradually transformed into a centralized system such as a monarchy (→ Colonialism). Some of its constitutive elements (lineage, custom, and the calendar) would be retained and continue to influence daily life. Anarchy

may be adduced in criticism of civilization (S. Diamond) and in demonstration of a primal egalitarianism (Sigrist, W.-D. Narr).

3. Social movements to reestablish anarchy have existed from the 19th century. They become significant in social crises.

3.1. We find precursors of such movements in the popular, egalitarian regional uprisings of the → Middle Ages and the early → modern period, when the mainly rural population resisted the increasing pressure of central authorities. These tensions occurred in about 1200 and 1400 in France and later involved the radical reformers of the Reformation and, from 1640, the Levelers in England. A religious element entered into the criticism of government and law.

3.2. The anarchist movements of the 19th century were libertarian-socialistic, and they arose in left-wing circles (→ Socialism). They may be seen in debate with → Marx (→ Marxism), in the French National Assembly of 1848, in literary activity, and in the → proletarian international. In 1872 the libertarian and authoritarian socialists split. The Belgian, Swiss, Italian, and Spanish anarchists then concentrated on spectacular acts of terrorism. Only later, by way of the trade unions, did they again join the workers' movement.

3.3. After 1905 most left-wing revolutionaries came under the influence of the anarcho-syndicalists. Ultimately, however, the Communistic socialists won out with revolutions in Russia and the Ukraine. Fascism crushed the anarchists in Italy and Spain (1931-36). In Latin America, China, and Japan they merged into the Communist parties. But from the time of the Paris antiauthoritarian movement in 1968, libertarian elements have revived, criticizing the → state, bureaucracy, and parties.

4. Anarchist theory has gone through various phases. First was an individualistic conception in W. Godwin and P.-J. Proudhon (*Qu'est-ce que la propriété* [1840]), followed by a collective-socialist view in M. A. Bakunin (*Dieu et l'état* [1871]) and a utopian-activist understanding in S. G. Nechayev and P. A. Kropotkin (*Paroles d'un révolté* [1885]). Then came the anarcho-syndicalism of Voline (pseudonym of W. M. Eichenbaum, who wrote *La révolution inconnue* [1917]), N. I. Machno, G. Landauer, and E. Mühsam in Russia and Germany, and that of R. Mella and D. A. de Santillan (*El organismo económico de la Revolución* [1936]) in Spain and elsewhere.

4.1. Proudhon (1809-65), the founder of anar-

chism, advocated an individualistic view, as did
M. Stirner (1806-56). Proudhon criticized morality,
law, → religion, → family, and property and
demanded a federalism based on the voluntary organization of all members of society. Stirner
grounded his definition of anarchy in an absolute
individuality and thus rejected all → institutions. He
did permit unions, however, in personal self-interest.

4.2. Bakunin (1814-76) offered the clearest explanation of anarchy. In contact with Marx and
Proudhon, he developed from a Pan-Slavic patriot
into a revolutionary, → atheistic, libertarian socialist.
He made a radical demand for the abolition of all
ancient institutions, including all rights, in order to
make possible a revolutionary, autonomous association that would resist all dictatorship, whether from
below or above. There would be no privileges in the
institutions that would then be established.

4.3. At the end of classic anarchism stood Nechayev (1847-82), who activated the → revolutionary
elements. As in the case of Kropotkin (1842-1921),
circles of conspirators prepared the way for acts of
terrorism. Anarchism recovered from this aberration
only by going back to Bakunin.

5. Anarchy is of ethical interest because of its libertarian conception, including nonviolence, equal
rights, and no taxation. Yet in its criticism of authority, it is hostile to the church. The use of revolutionary force to end force is as a whole less problematic
than is its use to establish authoritarian socialism.
Anarchy is interesting theologically as a challenge to
develop antiauthoritarian and antidogmatic movements in the Judeo-Christian tradition (→ Dogma;
Dogmatics). Regulated anarchy is important ecumenically because it occurs regularly in the → Third
World and demands completely new and indigenous
forms of religious reflection.

Bibliography: Primary sources: M. A. BAKUNIN, *Selected
Writings* (ed. S. Cox and O. Stevens; New York, 1974);
idem, *Statism and Anarchy* (New York, 1990; orig. pub.,
1873); idem, *Werke* (6 vols.; Leiden, 1961-65) • S. DOL-
GOFF, ed., *Bakunin on Anarchy* (New York, 1972) • P. J.
PROUDHON, *Oeuvres complètes* (33 vols.; Paris, 1968-76);
idem, *Selected Writings of Pierre-Joseph Proudhon* (ed.
L. S. Edwards; New York, 1969).

Secondary works: U. BERMBACH, *Rätedemokratische
Versuche im 20. Jahrhundert* (Darmstadt, 1984) • J. CAT-
TEPOEL, *Der Anarchismus* (Munich, 1979) • P. ELTS-
BACHER, *Anarchism* (New York, 1960) • D. GUÉRIN, *An-
archism: From Theory to Practice* (New York, 1970) •
J. JOLL, *The Anarchists* (New York, 1966) • F. KRAMER
and C. SIGRIST, eds., *Gesellschaften ohne Staat* (2 vols.;
Frankfurt, 1978) • M. NETTLAU, *Der Anarchismus von
Proudhon zu Kropotkin* (Berlin, 1927) • E. OBERLÄNDER,
ed., *Der Anarchismus* (Olten, 1972) • A. RITTER, *The
Political Thought of Pierre-Joseph Proudhon* (Princeton,
1969) • C. SIGRIST, *Regulierte Anarchie* (Frankfurt,
1979).

WOLF-DIETRICH BUKOW

Anathema → Confessions and Creeds

Ancestor Worship

1. The phrase "ancestor worship" comes from an era
when Europeans ruled over foreign cultures and religions. The Spaniards spoke of it as the *culto de los
antepasados.* Missionaries deplored it as a sin against
the first commandment (→ Decalogue). The term is
still in vogue, perhaps because Europeans accuse
others of the sin and can feel that they are above
reproach. But people of those other cultures — including the Christians among them — feel misunderstood and insulted by the term.

Such misunderstandings grow out of mistaken
comparisons. Thus the Polynesian Maoris speak of
atua. There is no exact equivalent for this term, and
so Westerners variously translate it "ancestor," "chieftain," or even "God." Among the Maoris, however,
the concept of *mana* is closer to the biblical idea of
God than is that of *atua.* Similar mistakes are common among Europeans everywhere.

2. People are born into many religions. It thus depends on one's parents and ancestors what ideas of
God and humanity one has, and what → rites and
→ prayers one learns from childhood. The race, tribe,
or family is thus bound up with the religion. The
religions of neighbors and their families may be different, but they do not rate as erroneous or wrong.
Blood relatives and their ancestors form closed religious societies that one can enter only by birth or
adoption. One may also be converted to some religions. World religions are open to people of every
tribe. They have no place for clans or tribes or people
of a particular descent. They use models that are
accepted by all people everywhere. The ancestors
must be spiritual, not physical.

In comparing physical and spiritual ancestors, we
may discover similar religious functions. Both kinds
have a spiritual influence (to the degree that there is
belief in a transcendent → life in the present). Ancestors in the one type of religion and → saints in
the other serve as helpers in times of acute need.

Ancestors in the one case and → angels (§1) in the other punish evildoers and lead them to conversion.

Both kinds of ancestors work spiritually. The dead whom one has known personally live on in recollection, whether parents, grandparents, chiefs, tribal priests, pastors, bishops, or popes. Those long dead work through tradition. They have set up religious forms or reformed them. They may be physical ancestors in tribal religions or the spiritual progenitors of exegetical schools, religious orders, confessions, and so forth. They serve as models in life or as authorities in times of → doubt. They awaken feelings of proud obligation and loving fellowship in believers.

Bibliography: H.-J. GRESCHAT, Manu und Tapu (Berlin, 1980) • M. GRIAULE, Schwarze Genesis (Freiburg, 1966) • LIN YUTANG, My Country and My People (New York, 1935) • J. S. MBITI, African Religions and Philosophy (2d ed.; Portsmouth, N.H., 1990) • W. MÜLLER, Indianische Welterfahrung (Frankfurt, 1981).

HANS-JÜRGEN GRESCHAT

Anchorites

Anchorites (from Gk. *anachōreō,* "separate oneself, withdraw") form the basic impulse of monasticism. From the end of the third century, male and female anchorites left the civilized world both outwardly and inwardly to meet with God in the isolation of the desert. → Athanasius (ca. 297-373) describes the life of an anchorite in his *Vita Antonii,* and the *Vita of Syncletica* tells us about a female anchorite. The *Apophthegmata patrum* gives us an insight into the world of the anchorites, who lived either alone or in small groups. Cenobitic monasticism ultimately became a serious rival of the anchorites. Modern → Roman Catholicism has experienced a revival of anchorites and hermits.

Bibliography: S. BONNET and B. GOULEY, Gelebte Einsamkeit. Eremiten heute (Freiburg, 1982) • D. J. CHITTY, The Desert a City: An Introduction to the Study of Egyptian and Palestinian Monasticism under the Christian Empire (Oxford, 1966) • K. HEUSSI, Der Ursprung des Mönchtums (repr., Aalen, 1981) • F. VON LILIENFELD, Spiritualität des frühen Wüstenmönchtums (Erlangen, 1983) • A. K. WARREN, "Anchorites," OER 1.35-36; idem, Anchorites and Their Patrons in Medieval England (Berkeley, Calif., 1985).

RUTH ALBRECHT

Ancient Church → Early Church

Ancient Oriental Churches → Oriental Orthodox Churches

Angel

1. Biblical
  1.1. OT
  1.2. Hellenistic Judaism
  1.3. NT
2. Dogmatic

1. Biblical

1.1. *OT*

The word "angel" (Lat. *angelus,* Gk. *angelos*) is a general term for two groups of beings that the OT clearly differentiates. Heb. *mal'āk* (messenger) lies behind the term.

1.1.1. The phrase *mal'ak YHWH 'ĕlōhîm* denotes the messenger, representative, or emissary of God. This kind of angel does not belong permanently to the heavenly world and has no wings. In case after case the form is human (e.g., Genesis 16; 18; 28; 32; Exodus 3; Numbers 22–23; Judges 6; 1 Kings 19; 2 Kings 1). There is not always a plain distinction between God and his messenger (Gen. 18:1, 2, 8, 10, 14, 18-22; Judg. 6:12-24; 13:3-21), for the sender is directly linked to the one he sends. According to Ezek. 1:26 and Gen. 1:26, the angel who appears in human form is the mantle of → Yahweh. From the standpoint of religious history the popular, historicizing, nonmythological realism of the stories in which angels appear is particularly striking.

1.1.2. The → temple at Jerusalem took over from the cultic and cosmic symbolism of the Canaanites another group of heavenly beings (1 Kgs. 22:19-22; Job 1:6-12; Ezek. 1:10), the cherubim (Heb. *kĕrûbîm;* cf. the griffin of German mythology) of 1 Kgs. 6:27 and 8:6. The seraphs (Heb. *śĕrāpîm*) of Isaiah 6, the "burning ones," are winged serpents that perhaps correspond to heavenly fire, the symbol of total purity. Yahweh rides or sits on the former. The cultic symbolism signifies a crossing of this world and the next. The predicate *YHWH ṣĕbā'ôt* (Lord of the heavenly host [i.e., of the stars?]) in 1 Sam. 1:3; 4:4; Jer. 8:3 has cultic-cosmic significance.

1.1.3. The angel as God's messenger belongs to the sphere of God's historical direction of → Israel, whereas the other heavenly beings are symbols of a cultic-cosmic view of the world. Only in a few passages does the OT bring the two groups together under the one term *mal'āk* (Ps. 103:20; 104:4; 148:2; Job 4:18; 33:23).

1.2. Hellenistic Judaism. This period of → Judaism manifested a more developed angelology.

1.2.1. The angels fulfill God's overruling of history (either as messengers or as guardian angels). They execute divine judgment (as advocates or accusers) and, as fallen angels, have control over → evil. Above all, they surround God's throne as heavenly worshipers. They thus preserve and mediate relevant heavenly and eschatological knowledge (*Jub.* 10:10ff.; *1 Enoch* 1:2; 10:3; 17ff.). The holy angels have special significance for the → Qumran community as a source of heavenly knowledge as well as a forum of cultic and eschatological fellowship with God. Jewish → mysticism fully developed the latent possibilities for practical → magic. A special chief angel is God's companion, the heavenly → high priest and scribe. Called Michael, Metatron (throne companion?), or Yahoel, he is found also in the form of the Son of Man.

1.2.2. The Jewish teaching about angels thrives on the antithesis of holy and profane (→ Sacred and Profane), expressed in the categories of above and below. The holy person, traditionally the → priest, may mix with heavenly beings (Zech. 3:7). This leads to a → soteriology in which redemption is understood as the achievement of an angel-like fellowship with God (*1 Enoch* 60:2).

1.3. *NT*

The NT presupposes the OT and Jewish teaching about angels.

1.3.1. Angels are representatives of the heavenly world and interpret earthly processes against their heavenly, eschatological background (→ Eschatology 2). They appear frequently in the infancy stories, the stories of the resurrection and ascension, and in the Book of Revelation. These occurrences bring to light this main, interpretive function. In a priestly setting the infancy stories intermingle cultic motifs, with angels as representatives of the heavenly sphere, hymns as cultic songs, and a sex-transcending purity as priestly or angel-like purity. In the stories of the resurrection and ascension, angels bring out the significance of Jesus' transition to the heavenly world as the basic datum of the Christian cultus. Revelation views angels as the forum of the heavenly cultic world, from which eschatological eternity becomes accessible for the community of the Son of Man, who is now enthroned amid angels (Revelation 1; 3:5; 4; 14:6, 10).

1.3.2. By → resurrection, exaltation, and heavenly, eschatological lordship, Jesus Christ (→ Christology 1) is in a form of spirit that far excels that of the angels (Phil. 2:9-11; Eph. 1:21; Heb. 1:4). This "above the angels" Christology of the NT has deep roots in Jesus' teaching about the Son of Man. Already during his earthly course he is mysteriously related to the vice-regent of God who rules over angels. Hence → Jesus does not need the usual guardian angels (though cf. Luke 22:43; John 1:51). This ancient Son of Man Christology gives Christological significance to angelological attributes (immortality, transcending of sexuality, heavenly holiness). We find traces of these attributes in the earthly life of Jesus — in his celibacy, in his baptism and transfiguration (= sanctification), and in the announcement of his resurrection. According to Matt. 18:10 and Mark 12:25, this Christology suggests a doctrine of redemption that aspires to a heavenly being like that of the angels. The baptized acquire in faith a share in the Spirit-glory of the heavenly Christ and stand with him above the angels (Rom. 8:9-11, 17-18, 21, 29-30; 1 Cor. 3:16; 2 Cor. 3:17; 5:1, 5-6; Phil. 3:21; Heb. 1:14; 2:6-18). Because NT Christology, pneumatology (→ Holy Spirit 1.2), and → soteriology (§1) are so deeply rooted in the biblical and early Jewish teaching about angels, we should take seriously the presupposed separation into above and below, holy and profane, heavenly-eschatological and earthly-corruptible as a challenge to the monistic view of the world that is current today (E. Peterson).

Bibliography: L. Boros, *Angels and Men* (New York, 1977) • F. F. Church, *Entertaining Angels* (San Francisco, 1987) • C. F. Dickason, *Angels, Elect and Evil* (Chicago, 1975) • O. Keel, *Jahwe-Visionen und Siegelkunst* (Stuttgart, 1977) • U. Mann et al., "Engel," *TRE* 9.580-99 (extensive bibliographies) • J. Maritain, *The Sin of the Angel* (Westminster, Md., 1959) • E. Peterson, *The Angels and the Liturgy* (London, 1964) • H. Röttger, *Mal'ak Jahwe–Bote von Gott* (Frankfurt, 1978) • P. Schäfer, *Rivalität zwischen Engeln und Menschen* (Berlin, 1975) • J. Strugnell, "The Angelic Liturgy at Qumran," *Congress Volume, Oxford, 1959* (Leiden, 1960) 318-45 • M. Werner, *Das Entstehung des christlichen Dogmas* (2d ed.; Bern, 1953) • C. Westermann, *God's Angels Need No Wings* (Philadelphia, 1979).

Jan-Adolf Bühner

2. Dogmatic

Belief in angels is typically, though not uniquely, biblical. It is a belief in the existence of personal beings that, like humans, were created by God but that have their own spiritual quasi-corporeality and also enjoy → immortality. Along with fallen angels, → demons, and Satan (→ Devil), the angels are part of the unseen world. They form a sphere between God and us and are instruments of God's governing of the world, though (as evil angels) they also act as forces of seduction.

→ Thomas Aquinas (1224/25-74; → Thomism) took up this whole dimension into his → ontology of the world (*Summa theol.* I, qq. 50-64, 106-14). In the modern → Roman Catholic Church the belief that at → baptism (§2) every Christian acquires a special guardian angel plays an important role. With its belief in the survival of the → soul (§2) and in its purification in purgatory, Catholic teaching consistently highlights the spiritual dimension of the world. In the → Orthodox Church a main reason for belief in angels is the (ancient) view that earthly → worship is a reflection of heavenly worship and a concelebration with it; angels are the beings that offer heavenly worship. With its emphasis on Christ, Reformation theology rejects any veneration of angels or → saints (Schmalk. Art. 2.2). Yet M. → Luther (1483-1546) maintained a belief in angels as executors of the divine rule and also as guardian angels (see his evening blessing).

In the → Reformed Church J. → Calvin (1509-64) curbed the belief in guardian angels with his thesis that God has not entrusted his care of us to a single angel but that all the angels in concert watch over each of his people (cf. → Barth, *CD* III/3, 517). Modern Protestant dogmatics takes belief in angels more seriously than was done in the 19th century (see ibid., 378). This is especially true in the case of K. Barth (1886-1968). → Barth did not teach an ontology of angels but stressed their function of proclamation and witness (ibid., 461).

The belief in angels is helpful in several ways. First, it gives expression to the invisible world. The Nicene Creed, for example, mentions God as the Creator of heaven and earth, of things seen and unseen. Second, it represents the threat to human existence as conflict with satanic powers and forces, but it also mentions angels as defense against these. Luther commented about the angelic watch (WA 32.115ff.; 37.152). Third, it expresses human receptivity. God, we may say, gives us good thoughts by way of angels. Finally, it bears witness to the special providence that rules over each of us. Without bringing angels into its doctrinal and liturgical statements, theology could not do full justice to its subject matter. A loss of the concept of angels would be detrimental to the spiritual dimension, belief in which distinguishes Christian faith from → atheism and → materialism.

Bibliography: G. DAVIDSON, *A Dictionary of Angels* (New York, 1967) • L. HEISER, *Die Engel im Glauben der Orthodoxie* (Trier, 1976) • W. KRUMONIG, *Engel* (Berlin, 1963) • U. MANN, *Das Wunderbare. Wunder, Segen und Engel* (Gütersloh, 1979) • K. ONASCH, *Kunst und Liturgie der Ostkirche in Stichworten* (Leipzig, 1981) • K. RAHNER, "Engel," *HTTL* 2.120-25.

HANS-GEORG FRITZSCHE†

Anglican Communion

1. Organization
2. Expansion
3. Statistics
4. Ecumenical Relations

The Anglican Communion is a worldwide fellowship of Episcopal churches that recognizes the archbishop of Canterbury as its spiritual head. He is ex officio chairman of the Lambeth Conference of Bishops, which from 1867 has been meeting every ten years. (The 1998 conference was at Canterbury, attended by 750 bishops.) The archbishop is primus inter pares (i.e., first among equals).

1. Organization

1.1. The Anglican Communion is episcopal but not hierarchical. Its national churches resemble the → autocephalous churches of Orthodoxy and the → Old Catholic churches, with which it has been in full communion since the Bonn Agreement of 1931. It is also in communion with episcopal Lutheran churches in Scandinavia and several independent Catholic churches in Spain, Portugal, and the Philippines.

1.2. Its faith and order are based on the Bible and the teachings of the "undivided" church (i.e., the church up to → Chalcedon, 451). Evangelical and Catholic revivals in the 19th century strengthened the identity of its Protestant (Low Church) and Catholic (High Church) wings. The → liturgical movement and biblical theology movement have more recently strengthened its central core (Broad Church). The British and North American churches have also been affected by liberal and radical movements, especially among intellectuals.

From 1957 onward, most Anglican provinces have revised their liturgies at least once; for example, Hong Kong and Macao did so in 1957, the United States in 1977, and Australia in 1978. In 1980 the *Alternative Service Book* appeared in England; in 1982, in Scotland; and in 1984, in Ireland, Wales, and Canada. For all provinces, however, the distinctive Anglican style of → worship is still based upon the → Book of Common Prayer (1662).

1.3. In addition to the Lambeth Conference, there is also an Anglican Consultative Council that meets every two years (from 1971) and that includes laity and priests. Every two years (beginning in 1979) the primates meet for discussions. Earlier Pan-Anglican Congresses (1908, 1954, and 1963 in Toronto) have been discontinued. Since 1980 there has been an international doctrinal commission. The main theological problems now are the → ordination of women (only in November 1992 did the Church of England decide to ordain women), the practice of → baptism (§5) and → confirmation and admission to the → Eucharist, divorce and remarriage (→ Marriage and Divorce), and → Christology (e.g., the conflict in England in 1977 over John Hick's *Myth of God Incarnate;* → Theology in the Nineteenth and Twentieth Centuries 4.2).

None of these international bodies has the juridical power to legislate for the 29 independent member churches (1994) and the extraprovincial dioceses that come under the jurisdiction of the archbishop of Canterbury (e.g., Bermuda, Hong Kong, and Korea). But neither are resolutions of the Lambeth Conference lightly discarded.

2. Expansion

2.1. Outside England, Wales, and Ireland (Scotland is a special case because the Presbyterian Church of Scotland is the official state church), episcopal oversight was traditionally exercised by the bishop of London, beginning about 1630. The expansion of the British Empire, the extension of commercial interests, and the work of the missionary societies (→ British Missions) so increased the number of overseas congregations that central jurisdiction could not possibly work in practice.

2.2. After the British Parliament passed the Colonial Bishops Act in 1786, it became legally possible to send bishops overseas. Anglican bishops thus were sent to Canada (1787), India (Calcutta, 1814), Australia (1836), and New Zealand (1841). Meanwhile, Scottish Anglicans consecrated Samuel Seabury (1784) for the Protestant Episcopal Church in the United States. The first dioceses were far too large and were soon subdivided. They quickly developed into full metropolitan sees with their own liturgies, primates, and → synods.

Outside England, Anglican church law was never incorporated into state law. The parliaments of the new dominions thus did not have the legal power to veto ecclesiastical legislation enacted by Anglican Church provinces, but they did have the duty to ensure that the legal rights of both the Anglican Church and the other denominations were not violated. That

is why these churches pioneered liturgical revision and synodic government. They were never politically dependent upon England or even upon their own parliaments. But in the early stages they were financially dependent upon the missionary societies and the funds of the London-based Colonial Bishops' Council.

The main problem in the mid-19th century was not to liberate the colonial churches but rather to give the Anglican Communion an identity and a focus of unity, an issue that was largely resolved by the Lambeth Conference of 1867. Nevertheless, national churches refused to surrender their own (de facto) powers of jurisdiction.

2.3. Continental Europe is a special case. British soldiers who fought alongside the Dutch in the War of Dutch Independence (1567-1648) formed their own congregations (e.g., in Utrecht and other commercial centers). Mass → tourism in the 19th and 20th centuries led to the establishment of seasonal chaplaincies, and entry into the ECC brought many more English expatriates to the Continent. The bishop of London finally surrendered his historical → jurisdiction over the Continent in 1980. The Anglican Diocese in Europe is now part of the Province of Canterbury.

2.4. Anglicanism has also penetrated into Japan, Korea, South America, and the francophone countries of central Africa. When the → Third World colonies became independent in the 1950s and 1960s (→ Colonialism), two major institutions remained intact: cricket and the Anglican Communion. Three factors were decisive: the use of local languages in the liturgy, the rapid education of local clergy, and the lack of a central power to enforce uniformity.

3. Statistics

Statistics for each country can be found in the *WCE*, which estimates the number of affiliates in 1985 at 68 million. The 1983 edition of the *Church of England Handbook* gave a figure of about 65 million for those who "describe themselves as Anglicans." The problem here is one of definition rather than arithmetic, especially in England, where the question of definition is absolutely crucial. In 1962 there were 27 million baptized Anglicans in England. Of this number, 9.8 million were confirmed, 2.7 million were officially registered as electors of local parochial officials, and only 2.3 million received Holy Communion at Easter. Barrett counted 65 million "affiliates" in 1980 and gives estimates for 1985 (68 million) and 2000 (83 million).

In 1998 Barrett and Johnson estimated that in the year 2000 there would be 55.5 million "members," a category that is more precisely defined than "affiliate" or "adherent." The overall annual growth rate of 1.3 percent conceals considerable losses in Europe and North America and substantial gains in the Third World. The 1995 Church of England Handbook lists 29 church provinces and 299 dioceses in more than 165 countries, together with more than 300 dioceses that are either in → united churches or in other churches already in full communion with the Church of England.

4. Ecumenical Relations

4.1. All Anglican churches are members of the → World Council of Churches and are usually members of → national councils.

Participation in the ecumenical movement is on the basis of the Chicago-Lambeth Quadrilateral (1888), which elaborated four elements to be honored in any plans for reunion with other churches: (1) the OT and NT as the revealed → Word of God; (2) the → Nicene Creed as the basis of the Christian faith; (3) the dominical sacraments of → baptism and the → Eucharist; and (4) the historic episcopate.

4.2. Since 1920 the national churches have been involved in → dialogue with other → Reformation churches. In the Anglican–Roman Catholic International Commission (ARCIC), the Anglican Communion is also in dialogue with the → Roman Catholic Church. (ARCIC-I began in 1969, with its final report in 1982; ARCIC-II began in 1983.) National synods have long been in dialogue with the → free churches, but church → union plans have often been rejected. The Church of England rejected the → Methodists and the Reformed Church in 1982 (→ Reformed and Presbyterian Churches), and Canadian Anglicans have repeatedly broken off talks with the United Church. In 1995 the Church of England was negotiating full communion with Lutheran churches in Germany, Iceland and Finland, and the newly independent Baltic states in accordance with the terms of the Meissen and Porvoo agreements. Similar negotiations are also in progress in the United States. The basic problem is church order, that is, → reception of nonepiscopal ministries (→ Offices, Ecclesiastical), as well as the papal office (→ Pope, Papacy) and other issues. Full communion with united churches in the → Third World (India, Pakistan) was also difficult to achieve, although Anglicans took part in these unions (→ Church of South India).

Bibliography: D. B. BARRETT and T. M. JOHNSON, "Annual Statistical Table on Global Mission: 1998," IBMR 22 (January 1998) 26-27 • C. O. BUCHANAN, Modern Anglican Liturgies, 1958-1968 (Oxford, 1968); idem, Further Anglican Liturgies, 1968-1975 (Bramcote, Nottingham, 1975); idem, Latest Anglican Liturgies, 1976-1984 (London, 1985) • N. EHRENSTRÖM and G. GASSMANN, Confessions in Dialogue (3d ed.; Geneva, 1975) • G. R. EVANS and J. R. WRIGHT, eds., The Anglican Tradition: A Handbook of Sources (London, 1991) • H. R. MCADOO, Being an Anglican (Dublin, 1976) • E. G. MOORE, An Introduction to English Canon Law (Oxford, 1967) • S. NEILL, Anglicanism (4th ed.; New York, 1977) • J. F. PUGLISI, A Bibliography of Interchurch and Interconfessional Theological Dialogues (Rome, 1984) • W. L. SACHS, The Transformation of Anglicanism from State Church to Global Communion (Cambridge, 1993) • P. STAPLES, The Church of England, 1961-1980 (Utrecht, 1981) • A. M. G. STEPHENSON, Anglicanism and the Lambeth Conferences (London, 1978) extensive bibliography • S. W. SYKES, ed., Authority in the Anglican Communion (Toronto, 1987) • S. W. SYKES and J. E. BOOTY, eds., The Study of Anglicanism (Philadelphia, 1988) • J. W. C. WAND, Anglicanism in History and Today (London, 1961).

PETER STAPLES

Angola

	1960	1980	2000
Population (1,000s):	4,816	7,019	12,781
Annual growth rate (%):	1.45	2.63	3.04
Area: 1,246,700 sq. km. (481,354 sq. mi.)			

A.D. 2000
Population density: 10/sq. km. (27/sq. mi.)
Births / deaths: 4.53 / 1.64 per 100 population
Fertility rate: 6.18 per woman
Infant mortality rate: 112 per 1,000 live births
Life expectancy: 49.0 years (m: 47.4, f: 50.6)
Religious affiliation (%): Christians 94.8 (Roman Catholics 75.1, Protestants 15.7, indigenous 7.7, marginal 1.2, other Christians 0.3), tribal religionists 4.2, other 1.0.

1. Missionary History
2. Churches in Angola
   2.1. The Roman Catholic Church
   2.2. The Protestant Churches
   2.3. The Independent Churches
3. Interconfessional Cooperation
4. The Ecclesiastical and Social Situation in Angola

1. Missionary History

In 1482 the Portuguese sailor Diogo Cão was the first European to set foot on what is now Angola. To mark the occasion Cão erected a stone pillar in honor of the Portuguese king and himself 150 miles south of the modern city of Lobito. On the Congo River he made contact with the kingdom of the Congo, which extended over the south of modern Zaire and the north of modern Angola. The capital was in São Salvador do Congo (modern Mbanza Congo), in northern Angola. Relations between Portugal and the Congo were at first on terms of equality. Diplomatic contacts were set up, the kings exchanged over 20 letters, and trade began. But soon Portuguese military superiority and marine monopoly led to one-sided dependence and finally to crass exploitation and the collapse of the kingdom of the Congo.

The Christianizing of southern Zaire and northern Angola began in 1491 with the arrival of the first Roman Catholic missionaries. These won the later King Afonso for Christianity, and during his reign he did much to spread Christianity to his kingdom. His son was consecrated a → bishop at → Rome in 1518 and then returned to his homeland. From 1512 a *regimento,* or special agreement, governed the relations between Portugal and the Congo. This opened the Congo to Portuguese trade, and the Portuguese promised in turn to educate the Africans and to build churches. But as the agreement began to be implemented, the missionary efforts of the Portuguese receded into the background, and cultural hostility and economic exploitation increased. The slave trade (→ Slavery 2) in particular became a central concern in Portuguese policy. Afonso very politely reminded the Portuguese king in letters that their common Christian → faith was not compatible with the conduct of the Portuguese. In one letter he said concerning the Portuguese merchants and slave traders: "They capture [the people] and then sell them. So great, sire, is their corruption and viciousness that our land is well on the way to depopulation. . . . What we need from your realm are simply priests and teachers who will give instruction in our schools, and no goods apart from wine and flour for the Holy Sacrament."

But the royal court in Lisbon and the merchants were interested in slaves and profit, not in the well-being of the people of Angola. Congregations in the parts where slaves were hunted were no longer able to pay their pastors. Finally, the pastors were even paid from the proceeds of slave sales, as the slave traders paid a "baptism tax" for each slave. When the slave trade declined in this part of Africa, the income from this tax also declined. In the 18th and 19th centuries Christianity was in retreat in Angola. As in the case of Portuguese → colonial rule, church work was limited to the coastal areas.

In 1865 the Fathers of the Holy Spirit were entrusted with missionary work in Angola. By 1890 they had built four mission centers and had set out to establish new congregations in the interior. Only after World War II, however, did many areas first see Roman → Catholic missions. By the time of Angola's independence in 1975, the Roman Catholic proportion of the population had risen to over 50 percent.

2. Churches in Angola
2.1. *The Roman Catholic Church*
During the period of Portuguese colonialism this church never freed itself from a close relation to the state. Educational work was limited for the most part to the sphere of primary schools (→ Education 3). Neither state nor church trained an educated national leadership, unlike the practice, for example, in the British colonies. The result was that until the 1970s, Europeans alone were discharging virtually all leadership tasks in the churches. Not until 1970 was a national bishop again consecrated, more than 450 years after the consecration of the first Angolan bishop. The close cooperation with the colonial rulers and the paucity of national leaders were serious handicaps for the Roman Catholic Church when independence came.

2.2. *The Protestant Churches*
At the coming of independence, Protestant churches were more favorably placed than were the Catholics. The closely allied government and Catholic Church had only reluctantly allowed Protestant missions, hampering them and sometimes preventing them altogether, so that even today some animosity remains. British Baptists built the first Protestant mission station in São Salvador in 1878. The Bacongo, who lived in this area and in neighboring Zaire, were very largely Christianized by the time of independence. The Evangelical Mission to Angola (→ Evangelical Missions) was an independent missionary group that also worked among the Bacongo; the Canadian Baptists took over its work in the 1950s. After the uprising of 1961 some 400,000 Bacongo fled to neighboring Congo (now Zaire).

Protestant missionary societies worked among specific groups or in specific areas with little overlapping. Thus beginning in 1885, the Methodists concentrated on the Kimbandu in an area east of Luanda, the capital, where they established about 100 schools. Various missions were active in the large territory of the Ovimbundu in central Angola (e.g., the United Church of Canada, the Swiss Reformed Church, the → Pentecostals, and the → Adventists). All these churches built many schools and thus helped to educate at least a small minority of the African population.

The small Protestant churches of Portugal confined their work mostly to the provision of pastoral care for Portuguese residents in Angola. Only in Huambo (Nova Lisboa) did Baptists begin missionary work among Angolan nationals.

2.3. *The Independent Churches*

These groups play a less significant part than in neighboring countries like Zaire because of the repressive measures used during the colonial period. The → Independent Churches, which are growing rapidly, can trace their origin for the most part to adjacent countries. → Kimbanguism, which belongs to Zaire, has gained 40,000 followers among the Bacongo in northern Angola. The church of the prophet Simon Toco grew in Angola when the colonial rulers of Congo banished him to Angola and he did missionary work in the northern part of the country. Although the colonial rulers of Angola banned Toco in many areas, this attention only resulted in his gaining more adherents for his church. Some smaller Independent Churches have spread into Angola from Zambia and Zimbabwe.

3. Interconfessional Cooperation

Fourteen churches work together in the Conselho Angolano de Igrejas Evangélicas (Angolan Council of Evangelical Churches). This council was founded in 1977 and aims to promote joint work by the churches, to contribute to the unity of the churches, and to represent the interests of the churches before the state and the world. Gatherings normally take place every two years, and an ongoing executive committee handles decisions between meetings. Among its programs are a lending fund, an income program, and aid for refugees. At the regional level, ecumenical committees and centers promote cooperation. A center for theological and cultural studies has been founded in Lobito that holds courses for pastors and other → church employees, seminars in congregation building for young people and women, and courses for teachers at theological institutions, doing so in very simple conditions.

4. The Ecclesiastical and Social Situation in Angola

The most important Protestant churches in Angola include the Evangelical Congregational, Christian Brethren, Methodist, Evangelical Church of Southwest Angola, Seventh-day Adventist, and Assemblies of God. All these churches suffer from a lack of trained workers and resources (including even a shortage of duplicating paper). In view of the great distress in Angola, they face serious diaconal tasks, which they are trying to handle with the aid of their ecumenical partners.

The restrictions placed by the Portuguese rulers on the independent and other non–Roman Catholic churches were strengthened by the popular uprising of 1961. Even before the revolt, Methodist and Baptist missionaries had criticized existing economic and political relations, and Protestant schools had contributed to the emancipation of African Angolans. António Agostinho Neto, for example, the leader of the independence movement MPLA (Movimento Popular de Libertação de Angola, or Popular Liberation Movement of Angloa) and later the president, was the son of a Methodist minister. After the fighting began, five Methodist missionaries were imprisoned, and several national Protestant pastors and teachers were shot by soldiers. During the bloody colonial war some in the Roman Catholic Church began to have doubts about its link to a repressive state, but only with independence did it adopt an autonomous position and stress national forms of Christian life.

Independence came after 15 years of intense warfare, during which the military struggles between the hostile political groups took a daily toll. By 1975 the MPLA had gained control of the central government but was contested by the nationalist group UNITA (União Nacional para a Independência Total de Angola, or National Union for the Total Independence of Angola), which controlled much of the countryside. The cold war fueled the conflict, with the USSR and especially Cuba aiding the MPLA, and the West and South Africa supporting UNITA. A peace agreement was finally brokered in 1991, which led to popular, multiparty elections held in September 1992. The MPLA was victorious at the polls, but when UNITA refused to accept the election results, the civil war resumed with increased severity. By the end of 1993, UNITA controlled well over half of the country. Further moves were taken in 1995 to form a government of national unity and to stop armed clashes between supporters of both parties.

In spite of the ongoing effects of the fighting and the very poor economic situation, the Roman Catholic Church has been able to stabilize and develop its membership and work. Thus in the early 1990s it numbered 1 cardinal, 12 bishops, and 383 priests. The → lay movement Legio Mariens is working hard to bring young people back to the faith. In many congregations new core community groups have arisen (→ Base Community). Adopting the traditional forms of the meeting of elders, they discuss biblical texts, specific social problems, and possibilities of action.

For all groups, it is the unstable political and military situation that most severely hampers the churches' work and poses great problems for Christians. Most of the church leaders try to adopt a neutral attitude toward the actual conflicts and hope that the church can make a contribution to → reconciliation.

Bibliography: D. BARRETT, ed., *WCE* 141-44 • A. BOAVIDA, *Angola: Five Centuries of Portuguese Exploitation* (Richmond, B.C., 1972) • G. BRÖNNER and J. OSTROWSKY, *Die angolanische Revolution* (Frankfurt, 1976) • T. COLLELO, ed., *Angola: A Country Study* (3d ed.; Washington, D.C., 1991) • B. DAVIDSON, *In the Eye of the Storm: Angola's People* (Garden City, N.Y., 1972) • P. KIVOUVOU, *Angola. Vom Königreich Kongo zur Volksrepublik* (Cologne, 1980) • M. KUDER, *Angola. Eine geographische, soziale und wirtschaftliche Landeskunde* (Darmstadt, 1971) • J. A. MARCUM, *The Angolan Revolution* (2 vols.; Cambridge, Mass., 1969-78).

FRANK KÜRSCHNER

Animals

1. Biblical Data
2. Church History
3. Religion
4. Philosophy
5. More Recent Themes

1. Biblical Data

The biblical texts present no unitary view of animals. We find the motif of human peace with animals, as well as the recognition that animals have been tamed but also destroyed and killed, and that animals destroy and kill one another.

1.1. In the OT the evaluation of animals includes the understanding (1) that they are creatures of God and thereby human partners (Gen. 1:20-28; 2:18-20) and (2) that they have their essential significance in the → covenant God made with his → creation. The task of giving names to animals (2:19) presupposes both their identity and their dignity. The idea that they were not given to the first humans merely as food (1:29-30) gives evidence of a peace with them that was broken only by → sin. Recent exegesis of Gen. 9:1-3 (K. Koch, J. Ebach) has shown that this original peace was not entirely removed by subsequent events. Yet we must note that during → Israel's nomadic existence, wild animals were a threat to them and their herds, so we can legitimately view animals as both companions and enemies (B. Janowski, U. Neumann-Gorsolke, and U. Gleßmer).

It should be noted, too, that many OT narratives had a background in Babylonian, Assyrian, and Sumerian myths and cults in which nature is often supreme, even a godhead, before which we humans are helpless. Dedemonizing this numinous quality of animals — which occurred when names were given to animals, thus making them familiar to us — seems to many exegetes to be an important step in the liberation of humans from a numinous nature.

1.2. The NT includes anthropocentric references to animals (1 Cor. 15:32; 2 Pet. 2:12). Also, in Rom. 8:19-22 it contains a central theological text for the ethics of animals, one that includes them as part of God's creation, which stands in need of redemption. The Pauline comment that "the whole creation has been groaning" (v. 22) has been largely ignored in church history and the history of theology (see E. Gräßer).

It is recorded that Jesus dealt with animals in an uninhibited way. On the one hand, he ate animals that had been killed; on the other hand, he lived with wild animals (Mark 1:12-13). In the → Sermon on the Mount he compares favorably the moment-by-moment life of animals with the future-oriented worries and plans of humankind. Such orientation to the future — criticized by Jesus in Matt. 6:25-34 — was (and is) often regarded in philosophical and theological → anthropology as the specific factor that shows human superiority to the animals. It is also used as an ideological justification for performing painful experiments on animals but not on humans (G. Patzig).

2. Church History

In church history and the history of theology, animals play a very minimal role. The only significant voice is that of → Francis of Assisi (1181/82-1226), who lovingly called them little brothers or brother animals and taught and lived out their significance for the unity of creation. (On Easter 1980 John Paul II named Francis the patron and protector of nature and the environment.) Seven centuries later A. → Schweitzer (1875-1965) took a similar view with his → ethics of reverence for life.

There are also a few positive references to animals in the writings of → Thomas Aquinas (1224/25-74) and M. → Luther (1483-1546), but they do not have central importance. More recent discoveries (e.g., by W. Schoberth) point to approaches toward a comprehensive view of creation in, for example, the work of J. G. Hamann (1730-88) and F. C. Oetinger (1702-82).

3. Religion

Various ideas toward animals appear in non-Christian religions and cultures. Animals have no souls in → Confucianism, which has no ethical problem with killing and eating them. Indifference to nonhuman life has met with criticism in Europe and the United States when the issue of eating dogs and cats arises. → Buddhism, however, places a very high ethical and legal value on animals. The basis for this position is the assumption that all life — explicitly including humans — can be reincarnated in various forms of creaturely existence. A person thus could be → reincarnated in his or her next life as an animal, which leads to a radical renunciation of animal killing. For this reason many Buddhists (e.g., in India) live as vegetarians.

4. Philosophy

4.1. Philosophical positions became increasingly important in giving animals value both in Europe and later in the United States. A decisive paradigm shift took place in the early → modern period.

Aristotle (384-322 B.C.; → Aristotelianism) understood human beings as living beings that had additional qualities, including political, in forming the commonwealth; cognitive, in using → reason; and emotional, in the capacity for laughter. The → Stoics and the → Scholastics understood animals as capable of feeling.

A fundamental break came with R. Descartes (1596-1650; → Cartesianism), who in his *Discours de la méthode* (1637) compared animals to machines, with both totally lacking reason or feelings. People relate to animals only mechanically and can draw no conclusions about their pain or other feelings, since animals have no understanding. The decisive point is that animals do not feel pain, and hence using them in experiments is legitimate.

For I. Kant as well (1724-1804; → Kantianism), animals are outside the realm of ethical reflection, for we have no → duties toward them. In his work "Über den mutmaßlichen Anfang des Menschengeschlechts" (On the alleged origin of the human race), Kant, expounding Genesis 2–6, projected a human power over animals obtaining already in → primeval history when he interpreted Gen. 3:21 as follows: "The fourth and final step that reason took in elevating humans completely above animals was that humans (however darkly) understood that humans themselves were the true purpose of nature, and nothing living on earth could be a rival for them. The first time someone said to the sheep, 'Nature has given the pelt you are wearing to me and not to you,' and took it from him and wore it himself (v. 21), he was becoming aware of a privilege that by nature he had over all animals, which he no longer saw as fellow creatures in creation but as means and instruments left to his own will for achieving his own arbitrary goals" (AA 8.114). In Kant this prerogative of humans over animals is limited ethically only by a prohibition of excessively cruel dealings with animals, dealings that would result in humans themselves becoming morally crude, which would be contrary to our duty to ourselves and others (*The Metaphysics of Morals,* pt. 2, §17).

In J. G. Fichte (1762-1814; → Idealism 4) animals are regarded as property that we may dispose of as we wish, not limited by Kantian ethics or any other restriction. Fichte's idea, still with us today, is typical: humans, being gifted with reason, dominate all nonhuman creatures and may use them as they will. The disastrous → ecological results of this understanding of nature, which make cosmology into anthropology or anthropocentricity, have only just begun to be appreciated in our own times.

4.2. Philosophical approaches give animals a higher significance insofar as the limitation and finitude of human reason are appreciated. An example here is G. W. Leibniz (1646-1716), who with his concept of monads gave reason only a partial capacity for knowledge. He ascribed feeling to animals, as well as a capacity for pain, memory, and a → soul.

Along similar lines is A. Schopenhauer (1788-1860), who saw sympathy as the moral basis of all ethics. In sharp antithesis to Descartes, he asserts there is a "boundless egoism innate in every animal, even the smallest and humblest; this amply proves how perfectly they are conscious of their self, as opposed to the world, which lies outside it" (219). F. → Nietzsche (1844-1900) universalized the will for → life in such a way that life is ultimately the will for → power. He contested the prerogative of humans on the basis of reason, comparing humans to "animals that have lost their instincts." In radically questioning the principles and postulates of Western → metaphysics, he pointed out that every perception and knowledge (→ Epistemology) is one of perspective and that all deception regarding oneself is a lie ("On Truth and Falsity in the Ultra-Moral Sense," 2.173ff.).

In the tradition of this criticism of dominance and reason are M. Horkheimer (1895-1973) and T. W. Adorno (1903-69), who consider the alienation of humans from nature as part of the dialectic of the → Enlightenment (→ Critical Theory), which absolutized and ideologized the way that nature can be used by human reason (or, in M. Heidegger's terms, by technology). Human reason, then, is turned here into its opposite. On these presuppositions animals became simply matter.

The contradictions and implications of such an

imperial anthropology have come under discussion in recent works of various philosophers such as J. M. Bocheński, a Polish Dominican and logician who fundamentally disputes any essential superiority of humans over animals (*Gegen den Humanismus* [1980]), and ethicists such as the Australian P. Singer, who rejects the assumption of an ethical superiority of one species over another. For Singer, no approach is free of contradiction or can be universalized.

5. More Recent Themes

Since roughly 1960 the theme of the ethics of animals has claimed increasing interest. Secular analyses and actions concentrate mainly on concrete misunderstandings, but theological discussion starts in the context of the theology of → creation. Remembering Schweitzer's postulate of reverence for life, it develops the insight that nonhuman life represents, not material that we can use as we like, but creatures of God who must not be exposed to unnecessary pain (G. M. Teutsch, G. Altner). Three basic principles are normative: (1) the avoidance of pain, suffering, or damage; (2) respect and consideration for all life; and (3) creaturely dignity (Teutsch, 5-6). Essential themes and positions are as follows.

5.1. Christian faith believes that God is the "Creator of heaven and earth," has made all things, and has a place for them. Creatureliness and finitude are their essential common properties.

5.2. God's → reconciliation with the cosmos (2 Cor. 5:18-19), which is also called a new creation (v. 20), is not limited exclusively to human beings but rather is universal (Romans 8). The result is that nonhuman creation remains an object of God's salvific activity. In order to make this dimension visible within the sphere of the church as well, churches in various countries have for several years sponsored worship services and blessings for animals. Even though such activities are a matter of theological dispute, they do attempt to make manifest the unity of God's creation and to acknowledge animals as the object of church actions.

5.3. God's universal reconciling action makes possible for Christians a new relation to the world (→ Worldview), which D. → Bonhoeffer (1906-45) called "the structure of responsible life." This approach, rooted in → responsibility, has been well received in → theology, → social ethics, and → philosophy. Its core thesis is the postulate of the self-limitation of the strong in favor of the weak. In animal ethics this position means that we consciously renounce any dominion over animals that would bring them suffering and death.

5.4. A duty of care as an ethical implication of ruling over the earth raises the issue of killing animals. Those who advocate a blanket forbidding of killing stress that we must respect the vulnerability of God's creation. An ethically less rigid position stresses the need to avoid inflicting pain (e.g., in keeping animals in zoos and in killing them), criticizes mass efforts to kill animals, and pleads for a respectful caring for them (as the German Catholic bishop's conference did in 1993 in its declaration on responsibility toward animals). There is also a warning against the overconsumption of animal flesh and a reminder that animals are not a status symbol, for example, in the case of the skins of snakes or crocodiles, of furs, or the eating of frogs or turtles, which often cause indescribable pain to animals. Protectors of animals also set a ban on private hunting and sports that cause animals pain (bullfighting, rodeos, cockfighting, etc.).

5.5. Sustaining natural species has come increasingly into public attention and ethical reflection. As species die out daily, awareness arises that destruction of our natural world fundamentally harms ourselves and our future on the earth. Protecting animals is a consequence of protecting humanity, whether for the ecological preservation of creation or for peaceful dealings with other creatures.

This awareness is a matter of national mentality. The measures taken in Scandinavian countries and in Switzerland are a model. They are growing in strength in the United States (with its debates about animal rights) and Germany. There is more indifference in Mediterranean lands, and especially in the → Third World and Fourth World, where the export of rare and often protected animals is a cause of ruthless dealings with animals.

5.6. Animal experiments are much debated. Many advocate forbidding them for frivolous reasons, but their use in medicine is a theme of controversial discussion (→ Medical Ethics 4). Those who favor such experiments appeal to possible medical progress and a supposed "higher" right to use animals for this purpose. Opponents point out that experimental results obtained from animals are frequently not applicable to humans at all.

A Christian ethics of animals states fundamentally that animal experiments violate the defenseless. It notes that most of these experiments involve unimaginable cruelty and thus questions very critically their justifiability, often in the face of an all too easily defended "freedom of teaching and research," which particularly at the universities is used to legitimate terrible pain. A question in theological ethics is whether it is valid to delegate our own pain to other creatures who are helpless. The answers will not merely be in the realm of medical ethics but are set against the background of a universal ethics of a reconciled creation that is not limited to one's own species but that takes responsibility for preserving the holiness of all of God's creation in faith and action.

Bibliography: G. ALTNER, *Naturvergessenheit. Grundlagen einer umfassenden Bioethik* (Darmstadt, 1991) • J. BERNHARDT, *Die unbeweinte Kreatur. Reflexionen über das Tier* (Munich, 1961) • J. M. BOCHEŃSKI, "Gegen den Humanismus," *Vom Sinn des Lebens und über die Philosophie* (ed. D. von Gabler; Freiburg, 1987) 147-65 • D. BONHOEFFER, *Ethics* (New York, 1964) • R. BRANDT, ed., *Kirchliche Erwägungen zur Diskussion über Tierschutz* (Frankfurt, 1993) • G. CARSON, *Men, Beasts, and Gods: A History of Cruelty and Kindness to Animals* (New York, 1972) • M. DAMIEN, *L'animal, l'homme et Dieu* (Paris, 1978) • DEUTSCHE BISCHOFSKONFERENZ, *Zukunft der Schöpfung–Zukunft der Menschen* (Bonn, 1980) • J. EBACH, "Bild Gottes und Schrecken der Tiere. Zur Anthropologie der priesterlichen Urgeschichte," *Ursprung und Ziel* (Neukirchen, 1986) 16-47 • E. FULDA, "Rechte der Tiere. Zur ethischen Vertretbarkeit von Tierversuchen," *Die Natur ins Recht setzen* (ed. M. Schneider and A. Karrer; Karlsruhe, 1992) 181-228 • E. GRÄSSER, "Das Seufzen der Kreatur (Röm 8, 19-22). Auf die Suche nach einer 'biblischen Tierschutzethik,' " *JBTh* 5 (1990) 93-117 • B. JANOWSKI, U. NEUMANN-GORSOLKE, and U. GLESSMER, eds., *Gefährten und Feinde der Menschen. Das Tier in die Lebenswelt des alten Israel* (Neukirchen, 1993) • H. KIRCHHOFF, *Sympathie für die Kreatur. Mensch und Tier in biblischer Sicht* (Munich, 1987) • K. KOCH, "Gestaltet die Erde, doch heget das Leben. Einige Klarstellungen zum *dominum terrae* in Gen 1," *"Wenn nicht jetzt"* (FS H.-J. Kraus; Neukirchen, 1983) 23-36 • C. LINK, "Rechte der Schöpfung. Argumente für eine ökologische Theologie," Schneider and Karrer, *Die Natur ins Recht setzen*, 87-104 • A. LINZEY, *Animal Rights: A Christian Assessment of Man's Treatment of Animals* (London, 1976); idem, *Animal Theology* (London, 1994) • C. A. MAGEL, *A Bibliography on Animal Rights and Related Matters* (Washington, D.C., 1981) • K.-M. MEYER-ABICH, "Frieden mit den Tieren," *Mehr Rechte für die Tiere* (ed. K. Franke; Hamburg, 1985) 7-22 • F. NIETZSCHE, *The Complete Works* (ed. O. Levy; Edinburgh, 1909-13) • F. NIGGEMEIER, "Umwelt, Natur, Tierschutz," *Wörterbuch der Religionssoziologie* (Gütersloh, 1994) • W. PANGRITZ, *Das Tier in dem Bibel* (Munich, 1963) • G. PATZIG, "Ethische Aspekte von Tierversuchen," *Chima* 39 (1985) 373-76 • T. REGAN, *The Case for Animal Rights* (Los Angeles, 1983) • T. REGAN et al., "Animal Welfare and Rights," *EncBio* 1.158-93 • R. RYDER, *Victims of Science: The Use of Animals in Research* (London, 1978) • W. SCHOBERTH, *Geschöpflichkeit in die Dialektik der Aufklärung* (Neukirchen, 1994) • A. SCHOPENHAUER, *The Basis of Morality* (London, 1903; orig. pub., 1841) • A. SCHWEITZER, *Kultur und Ethik* (Munich, 1923) • P. SINGER, *Animal Liberation: A New Ethics for Our Treatment of Animals* (New York, 1980); idem, *Practical Ethics* (Cambridge, 1979) • C. A. SKRIVER, *Der Verrat der Kirchen an den Tieren* (Munich, 1967) • H. STEFFAHN, *Menschlichkeit beginnt beim Tier* (Stuttgart, 1987) • G. M. TEUTSCH, *Mensch und Tier. Lexikon der Tierschutzethik* (Göttingen, 1987) bibliography; idem, *Tierversuche und Tierschutz* (Munich, 1983) • J. C. WHORTON et al., "Animal Research," *EncBio* 1.143-58 • G. ZOEBE, *Das Tier im Recht* (Frankfurt, 1962).

EKKEHARD STARKE

Animals, Symbolism of → Symbolism of Animals

Animism

Georg Ernst Stahl (1660-1734), a German physician and chemist who established the phlogiston theory, used the term "animism" from the → psychology of the early modern period, wanting as a doctor to give scientific form to the classical identification of the life principle and the → soul. The English anthropologist Edward Burnett Tylor (1832-1917) then took it over from Stahl, proposing it in a lecture to the Royal Asiatic Society in London in 1867 as a substitute for the term → "fetishism" to denote more clearly "the state of mind which sees in all nature the action of animated life and the presence of innumerable spiritual Beings." In his two-volume *Primitive Culture* (London, 1871; 2d ed., 1873; 4th ed., 1903; 5th ed., 1913), Tylor developed this concept in chaps. 11-17.

In animism, Tylor saw a belief in the soul that was natural for primitive peoples (a "defined minimum of religion"). He did not clearly distinguish this "philosophy" from his own theory of the cosmos. For him, animism was a primal and basic view deriving from such things as breathing, dreaming, the heartbeat, the blinking of the eye, visions, and apparitions. These everyday activities led quite early to the doctrines that organic and inorganic → nature has a soul and that the personal soul leaves the bodies of animals and humans at → death. Associated ideas are ancestor worship, the transmigration of souls, and the grounding of cosmic processes in the activity of spirits. This last thought developed into a belief in the gods of → polytheism relating to every area of life, then to a hierarchy of these gods, and finally to the supremacy of one God (→ Monotheism). The form of primitive perception finds parallels in sensory epistemologies and in the concept of the soul both in the doctrine of ideas and in theories concerning the body and soul. Similarly, the unity of the essentially monotheistic idea of God finds a parallel in the concept of spirit in the → philosophy of religion.

Tylor's impressive proposal found broad and varied acceptance in anthropology (G. A. Wilkens), psychology (W. Wundt), sociology (H. Spencer), religion (N. Söderblom), and the study of antiquity (E. Rohde). Criticism focused on the substantiality or → identity of the "soul" (A. E. Jensen) and the dating of belief in the soul early in human history, where instead we find belief in one God or a supreme God (A. Lang). Attempts were made to define the hypothetical early findings more exactly as "preanimism" or "animatism" (R. R. Marett), or as dynamism (A. van Gennep), which would better describe the fact that natural objects have life or are endowed with magical force. The opposition to evolutionism (→ Evolution), which was closely related to animism, applied to animism, too, especially by pointing out how recent were the tribal views with which Tylor started. Today, the noun "animism" is avoided because the concept suggests a total system in which belief in the soul is dominant. The adjective "animistic" may still be used to denote an ethnologically demonstrable sphere that embraces not only the spirits of the elements, mountains, trees, animals, and ancestors but also demons, "soul-birds," and the like.

Bibliography: K. W. BOLLE, "Animism and Animatism," *EncRel(E)* 1.296-302 • F. GÖLZ, *Der primitive Mensch und seine Religion* (Gütersloh, 1963) • K. E. MÜLLER, "Animismus," *HWP* 1.315-19 • E. A. NIDA and W. A. SMALLEY, *Introducing Animism* (New York, 1959) • G. K. PARK, "Animism," *NEBrit* (15th ed., 1992) 26.537-40 • I. PAULSON, Å. HULTKRANTZ, and K. JETTMAR, *Die Religionen Nordeurasiens und der amerikanischen Arktis* (Stuttgart, 1962) • P. RADIN, "Introduction to the Torchbook Edition," *Primitive Culture* (E. B. Tylor; New York, 1958) 1.ix-xv, 2.ix-xvii • P. M. STEYNE, *Gods of Power: A Study of the Beliefs and Practices of Animists* (Houston, 1989) • E. B. TYLOR, *Primitive Culture* (2 vols.; New York, 1871) chaps. 11-17.

CARSTEN COLPE

Anointing

1. OT
2. NT

1. OT

In the Near East, anointing is almost as essential as eating and drinking, with the three often occurring together in cuneiform texts. We also find anointing in many cultic and legal records. In the OT the main Hebrew word for "anointing" is *māšaḥ*, with *šemen* used most often for "oil."

Although anointing appears in OT texts of various provenance (e.g., Gen. 28:18; Exodus 40), its primary emphasis is in connection with the appointing of the king (e.g., 2 Sam. 2:4; 5:3). In → David's dynasty anointing quickly established itself as a separate action (1 Kgs. 1:39; 2 Kgs. 11:12; 23:30), a sign of change in legal status and of cultic consecration. For anointing at the beginning of the → monarchy as a predestinating act, see 1 Sam. 9:16 and 10:1 (for → Saul) and 16:3, 12-13 (for David). It is not wholly clear whether or to what extent anointing was practiced in the North (though note Jehu's anointing in 1 Kgs. 19:16; 2 Kgs. 9:6, etc.).

Anointing resulted in the current king's being called the Anointed (*māšîaḥ*, "Messiah"; → Messianism). This concept appears especially in the traditions about Saul and David (1 Sam. 2:35; 16:6; 24:6, 10, etc.) and in the Psalms (2:2; 20:6; 89:38, 51, etc.). The passages, many of which are from postexilic times, suggest that the title arose in the period of the middle or late — but not the early — monarchy. When the Davidic dynasty came to an end, the title was applied to Cyrus (Isa. 45:1), the patriarchs (Ps. 105:15), and the → high priests (Lev. 4:3, 5, 16; 6:22; see also Exodus 29–30; Leviticus 8). Texts like Zechariah 4, which speak of both a priestly and a kingly "anointed" (lit. "sons of oil"), gave rise in later → Judaism to differently nuanced messianic → hopes.

→ Cultic Purity

Bibliography: W. GRUNDMANN et al., "χρίω," *TDNT* 9.493-527 • E. KUTSCH, *Salbung als Rechtsakt im Alten Testament und im Alten Orient* (Berlin, 1963) • T. N. D. METTINGER, *King and Messiah* (Lund, 1976) 185-232 • K. SEYBOLD, "מָשַׁח *māšaḥ* / מָשִׁיחַ *māšîaḥ*," *TWAT* 5.46-59.

HERMANN SPIECKERMANN

2. NT

In the time of → Jesus the anointing of the Judean → monarchs had been at an end for some 600 years, and that of the → high priests for some 200 years (see 1). The focus of religious anointing (with oil or other substances) was now on the → temple with its holy of holies (perhaps the "anointed," according to Dan. 9:26b LXX) and on → sacrifices. Anointing (or being anointed) was the most powerful expression of belonging and consecration to God.

If a dead person was in a house, oil became unclean there (11QTemple 49:12; → Cultic Purity); yet the bones remaining after corruption could be anointed, which protected against final alienation from God. The Essenes (→ Qumran) avoided anointing completely (Josephus *J.W.* 2.123). The surrounding Greco-Roman world related religious anointing to God's presence and used it widely in idol worship, in daily rites, and at death to help the deceased's passage to Hades (the ointment being applied with a spatula).

This usage provides the background for the accounts of Jesus' being anointed. In Luke 7:36-50 the → love of the sinful woman, triggered by → forgiveness, leads to her anointing of Jesus; freedom from moral stain is no longer a precondition. At Bethany (Mark 14:3 and par.) the anointing of the head is a distinguishing mark (cf. Ps. 23:5). It causes offense (Mark 14:4-7, 9). In the Hellenistic sphere it is seen as an anointing for burial (v. 8; → Funeral) to overcome remoteness from God before death. In contrast, the women at the tomb who want to anoint Jesus learn that he has not remained in Hades (Mark 16:1; John 19:40 corrects to a more Jewish view).

In this context the title "Anointed" (i.e., "Christ") means not only that Jesus was anointed with the Spirit and power for his special ministry (Acts 10:38) but also that he was closer to God than even the temple holy of holies (see Mark 14:61, after v. 58). Traditions of sacrificial (Heb. 9:28) and personal anointing (→ Messianism) come together here in a reinterpreted form (→ Christological Titles 3.1). It is a Greco-Roman thought that divinely granted anointing confers deity on one who has been redeemed from humanity (Ovid *Met.* 14.605ff.). Christianity does not go as far; Christ (the anointed) does not lose humanity.

In 2 Cor. 1:21 the apostle describes Christians as anointed by God to enable them to stand firm in Christ, with the Spirit in the heart as a guarantee. In 1 John 2:20-27 anointing by the Holy One (the Holy Spirit?) gives knowledge of the truth and protects against the falsehoods of antichrist. Jas. 5:14-16 instructs elders to pray over the sick and anoint them with oil, perhaps as a physical remedy or a religious tradition (cf. Mark 6:13; Luke 10:34; cf. *Apoc. Mos.* 9:3; 13:2); healing is promised to the prayer of faith.

Apart from spiritual anointings and the anointing of the sick, the NT does not refer to the anointing of Christians in general, or of church ministers specifically for service. Ritual development of anointing began in the church in about 200. One or more sacraments of anointing arose among → Gnostics. In the orthodox churches anointing found a place at → baptism and → confirmation (→ Initiation Rites 2). Unction has also become, and still is, an important → rite (→ Pastoral Care of the Sick; Sacrament). The anointing of kings since the Middle Ages recalls the Davidic tradition.

Bibliography: H. G. GAFFRON, "Studien zum koptischen Philippusevangelium unter besonderer Berücksichtigung der Sakramente" (Diss., Bonn, 1969) • W. GRUNDMANN et al., "χρίω," *TDNT* 9.493-580 • P. HOFMEISTER, *Die heilige Öle in der morgen- und abendländischen Kirche* (Würzburg, 1948) • M. DE JONGE, "Messiah," *ABD* 4.777-88; idem, "The Use of the Word 'Anointed' in the Time of Jesus," *NovT* 8 (1966) 132-48 • M. KARRER, *Der Gesalbte. Die Grundlagen des Christustitels* (Göttingen, 1991) bibliography • G. KOCH, "Anointing of the Sick," *Handbook of Catholic Theology* (ed. W. Beinert and F. Schüssler Fiorenza; New York, 1995) 9-14 • K. RAHNER, *The Anointing of the Sick* (Collegeville, Minn., 1975).

MARTIN KARRER

Anonymity

1. In ordinary speech, "anonymity" refers to the concealing of one's name, to remaining nameless, thus avoiding being questioned as a → person. Anonymity is both a protection and a threat. By it individuals escape the control of a → group or → society and protect themselves against attack by a collective. Anonymity is also a mark of individualizing, a loss of the social relations that belong to the wholeness of the person, a loss of rootage in society. The consequences might be loneliness, → substance abuse, the threat of → suicide, or crime.

2. Sociology seldom deals with anonymity. The word appears most often in criticism of modern society as a mass society (→ Masses, The) that promotes anonymity and leads to the loss of personal relations. Statements about it occur in research into cities. Life in the → city is called a life in anonymity (E. Pfeil). In 1903 G. Simmel (1858-1918) pointed out that most interpersonal encounters in an urban setting demand that individuals take defensive measures. They cannot give themselves to others with the same

openness or intensity as they can in smaller, more manageable social units.

The relations subsumed under the concept of anonymity can be better understood if one attempts to grasp the interactions in which individuals encounter one another in limited areas of interest (A. F. Vierkandt). The introduction of the concept of role by the American sociologist R. Linton (1893-1953) made possible a precise description of these social contacts. Individuals often meet others with only a limited spectrum of expectation, in specific positions, with particular social roles. For each such meeting only the role expectations are significant. The differentiation of social relations, and especially the distance between home and job in cities, enhances the orientation to role. In the domestic sphere the many social relations in which individuals stand can no longer be perceived. This leads to the impression of anonymity.

3. The positive aspect of anonymity lies in the higher measure of personal → freedom that it allows. For example, anonymity makes privacy possible, and it frees from personal commitments (→ Individualism). Such freedom, however, may have its negative consequences. If individuals are seen only in certain limited roles, they are no longer adequately perceived as persons within the normal, well-rounded scope of human relationships. Even in cities, however, there is no marked tendency toward anonymous social relations. On the one hand, the trend is promoted by certain forms of housing (e.g., by suburbs and highrises). On the other hand, in older parts of cities, with a more stable population, one may find intensive relationships that reduce anonymity. Again, cities have many → institutions that strengthen the social relations of individuals, for example, associations, church fellowships, and civic groups that promote common interests and foster formal and informal relationships. Modern discussion has pointed to the significance of the neighborhood (R. Gronemeyer and H.-E. Bahr).

Related phenomena may be seen in culture criticism and in more in-depth research into cities as a typical expression of industrial societies. But only up to a point is the charge of anonymity relevant to life in modern cities.

Bibliography: H. P. BARTH, Die moderne Großstadt (Reinbek, 1969) • J. FRIEDRICHS, Stadtanalyse (Reinbek, 1977) • E. GOFFMAN, Behavior in Public Places (New York, 1963) • R. GRONEMEYER and H.-E. BAHR, eds., Nachbarschaft im Neubaublock (Weinheim, 1977) • P. S. HAWKINS, Civitas: Religious Interpretations of the City (Atlanta, 1986) • R. E. PARK, The City (Chicago, 1925) • E. PFEIL, Großstadtforschung (2d rev. ed.; Hannover, 1972) • G. SIMMEL, "Die Großstädte und das Geistesleben," Die Großstadt (Dresden, 1903).

KARL-FRITZ DAIBER

Anselm

Anselm is a pivotal thinker in the history of medieval philosophy. He is both the heir of → Augustine and the father of → Scholasticism, although there is a tendency to regard his thought primarily in view of that to which it led. As such, he is typically remembered as the originator of a strictly rational theology, most evident, perhaps, in his traditional identity as the creator of the ontological argument for the existence of God. There can be no doubt, however, that Anselm was also a successor to the legacy of → monasticism as well as to the → mysticism that is characteristic of medieval thought.

Born in Aosta, Italy, in 1033, he found his way as a wandering scholar to the → Benedictine monastery at Bec, which he entered at the age of 27. Three years later he was made prior, and the writings from this period, from 1063 to 1078, reflect that responsibility. These works, which include his Monologion (1076) and Proslogion (1077-78), are intensely contemplative, as are the → prayers and → meditations that he wrote at this time. Each has as its format a style of presentation suited to the interests of one who is "striving to elevate his own mind to the contemplation of God" (preface to Proslogion).

After 1078, when Anselm became → abbot, his writings shift their orientation, taking on a more pedagogical character. These works include De grammatico, a kind of medieval introduction to → logic, and the dialogues On Truth and On Free Will (1080-85) as well as the later On the Fall of the Devil (1085-90). Precisely what led to this transition in his thought is hard to say, although his new job was clearly devoted more to administration than to contemplation. Similarly, one might conclude that his late, most clearly → apologetic works — like The Letter on the Incarnation of the Word (1092-94), Why Did God Become Man? (1097-98), On the Virgin Birth and Original Sin (1099-1100), On the Procession of the Holy Spirit (1102), On the Sacraments of the Church (1106-7), and On the Harmony of the Foreknowledge, Predestination, and the Grace of God with Free Choice (1107-8) — all reflect his role as archbishop of Canterbury, an office that Anselm held from 1093 until his death in 1109. Whatever the reason, even the titles of these various texts give an indication of the transition that is taking place in his thought: from the early *Monologion,* in which the solitary meditator reasons about the essence of divinity in the quiet of his private contemplation, to those writings addressed not only to more doctrinal issues but to the world at large.

This transition in Anselm's own thought not only anticipated but aided the change that took place in medieval philosophy as it moved from the monastery to the → university. The key to understanding Anselm's work as historically transitional, however, lies in appreciating the way in which his own argumentative rigor can lend legitimacy to a certain → rationalistic strain in medieval religious thinking precisely because it was grounded in the visionary forms of thought that were authoritative at his time.

This appreciation is required most of all in approaching Anselm's famous ontological proof for the existence of God (→ God, Arguments for the Existence of). Properly interpreted, this argument must be shown to combine logical rigor with mystical insight, as it depends upon a specific vision of God that is founded upon the practice of rational meditation. This understanding is made clear by the format of the *Proslogion,* which surrounds its famous argument with prayers for a vision of God, although it is usually lost sight of when the argument is extracted from the context of the philosophical prayerbook in which it originally appeared.

On a larger scale, the reintroduction of the works of Aristotle in the 12th century (→ Aristotelianism), which led to a more discursive than intuitive view of the nature of reason, coupled with the transition from the monastery to the university, rather quickly placed Anselm's thought out of context. This is not to deny that certain aspects of his work survived these historic changes — indeed, they may even have been enhanced by them. The problem is that only certain elements were emphasized and thrived in the new world of scholastic thought. As such, much of Anselm's work, like his famous argument, was subject to a kind of dislocation as it was transported from the prayer cell to the logic class, where it has, at least in philosophical circles, remained ever since.

Bibliography: K. Barth, *Fides quaerens intellectum: Anselm's Proof of the Existence of God* (Richmond, Va., 1960) • M. J. Charlesworth, *St. Anselm's Proslogion* (New York, 1965) • Eadmer, *The Life of St. Anselm* (New York, 1972) • J. Hopkins and H. Richardson, *Anselm of Canterbury* (3 vols.; Lewiston, N.Y., 1974-76) • J. Leclercq, *The Love of Learning and the Desire for God* (Bronx, N.Y., 1982) • G. Schufreider, *Confessions of a Rational Mystic: Anselm's Early Writings* (West Lafayette, Ind., 1994) • R. W. Southern, *St. Anselm and His Biographer* (Cambridge, 1963).

Gregory Schufreider

Anthropology

Overview
1. OT Anthropology
   1.1. Individual Anthropology
   1.2. Social Anthropology
2. NT Anthropology
   2.1. Basic Points
   2.2. Clarifications
   2.3. Terminology
3. Theological Anthropology
   3.1. Thematic Definition
   3.2. Historical Development
   3.3. Eastern Orthodoxy
   3.4. Theological Alternatives
   3.5. Remaining Ecumenical Tasks
4. Philosophical Anthropology
   4.1. Word and Concept
   4.2. History and Methodology
   4.3. Themes
5. Social Anthropology
   5.1. Concept
   5.2. Explicit and Implicit Models
   5.3. Relation to Self and the World

Overview

Theological anthropology is systematic reflection on human nature and destiny (→ Human and Civil Rights) in the light of the biblical witness. As a classic theological discipline (→ Dogmatics), anthropology holds an important place. It does not simply challenge the various anthropological sciences, nor does it necessarily transcend or endorse them. Insofar as these → sciences say true things about humanity, theological anthropology regards their findings neither as competition nor as threat but accepts them as thematic enrichment, warning, and delimitation. Various writers debate, however, whether it should (1) pursue an enterprise wholly its own, (2) limit itself to critical inquiry into the various anthropological sciences, or (3) find points of contact only in → ethics. The importance of nontheological disciplines and certain theological reasons argue against the first course. Its own cognitive contents argue against the second position. Tending to refute the third are the extensive insights of Jews and Christians into human dignity, → freedom, and the limitations of creaturehood.

Theological anthropology faces severe methodological tasks if it is to tread the narrow path between a dilettante dabbling in alien disciplines (or the scorning of their results) and a self-denying limitation to relevant, critical comments. At stake is no less than the theological understanding of → truth. Theological anthropology must arrive at a coherent integration of both prescientific and scientific knowledge of humanity. In so doing, it need not come into serious tension with → psychology, psychosomatic medicine, or biological or ethnological anthropology. It is more likely to clash, however, with the various forms of philosophical anthropology, which often seek integration themselves, either one-sidedly on the basis of one of the disciplines or comprehensively in orientation to one or another broad movement of thought, such as historical, idealistic, positivist, or → Marxist systems (→ Philosophy of History; Idealism; Positivism). Theological anthropology will properly enter into debate with these other systems of philosophical integration. In the process, the biblical witness to God's view of the human race will be a constant warning not to lose sight of the fact that humanity ultimately — and concretely — means both → men and → women, children and adults (→ Childhood; Adulthood), the healthy as well as the sick and those with → handicaps, the weak and the strong.

Bibliography: G. ALTNER, *Zwischen Natur und Menschengeschichte* (Munich, 1975) • J. C. ECCLES, *The Human Mystery* (New York, 1979) • H. FISCHER, ed., *Anthropologie als Thema der Theologie* (Göttingen, 1978) • C. FREY, *Arbeitsbuch Anthropologie* (Stuttgart, 1979) • W. PANNENBERG, *Anthropology in Theological Perspective* (Philadelphia, 1985) • C. F. VON WEIZSÄCKER, *Der Garten des Menschlichen. Beiträge zur geschichtlichen Anthropologie* (Munich, 1977).

DIETRICH RITSCHL

1. OT Anthropology

1.1. *Individual Anthropology*
The OT not only speaks about the people of Israel but also contains general insights into humanity, though without developing any explicit, comprehensive anthropology. Basic statements about the human race occur especially in Genesis 1–11 (→ Primeval History), the → Wisdom literature (e.g., Prov. 16:1-2, 9; Job 4:17; Ecclesiastes), and elsewhere (e.g., Exod. 4:11; Deut. 8:3; 1 Sam. 16:7; Mic. 6:8; Ps. 103:15). Always at issue in the OT is our standing before God: "What are human beings that you are mindful of them?" (Ps. 8:4).

1.1.1. In using such terms as "soul," "spirit," "heart," and "body," the OT denotes not specific human parts but the whole person from various standpoints. It views the parts of the body and its functions and activities as a whole. → "Soul" *(nepeš),* originally "mouth" (Isa. 5:14) and "breath," denotes the life that slips away with → death (Gen. 35:18; 1 Kgs. 19:4; cf. "spirit" in Ps. 104:29-30 and Job 34:14-15). A human being, made up of earth and the divine breath, does not *have* body and soul but *is* a living soul (Gen. 2:7), a living being, a → person, an individual. "Soul" often also denotes feelings — for example, impatience and especially desire (Gen. 34:2-3), that is, orientation to something: "As a deer longs for flowing streams, so my soul longs for you, O God" (Ps. 42:1; cf. 63:1; 130:5-6). In this regard a person may stand over against its own self in such a way as to engage in dialogue with it: "Why are you cast down, O my soul?" (Ps. 42:5; cf. 103:1).

Spirit *(rûaḥ)* also has the primary sense of breath or wind. It too denotes living force (Gen. 7:15, 22; 1 Sam. 30:12), then mood or emotion (1 Kgs. 10:5; 21:5), and especially the ability to do something (Exod. 31:3; Judg. 3:10; Num. 24:2; etc.).

Like the spirit, the heart *(lēb)* can be the seat of feelings (Isa. 7:2; Prov. 15:13; 24:17); more commonly, it is the seat of understanding, insight, → reason, and planning: "The human mind [*lēb*] plans the way, but the LORD directs the steps" (Prov. 16:9; also Isa. 6:10; 1 Kgs. 3:9, 12). The smiting of the heart (1 Sam. 24:5) is the smiting of the conscience. The heart is thus the inner part that is hidden from others but open to God (1 Sam. 16:7; Ps. 139:23-24; cf. 51:10). God tests the minds and hearts (Ps. 7:9; Jer. 11:20; etc.) — that is, the thoughts and feelings.

Finally, human beings both have and are flesh *(bāśār),* that is, bodies: "In God I trust; . . . what can flesh do to me?" (Ps. 56:4; also v. 11 and Jer. 17:5). In most instances this term suggests weakness and mortality: "All people [*bāśār*] are grass" (Isa. 40:6-7; also Gen. 6:3 and Ps. 78:39).

1.1.2. The time between birth and death, with its → joy and → suffering, is not in our hands (Eccl. 3:1-8). We may understand both good and bad experiences in terms of faith in the one God (Exod. 4:11; Eccl. 7:14; Job). As life is God's → creation (Genesis 1–2; Ps. 36:9; etc.), so death is not just "the way of all the earth" (1 Kgs. 2:2; also Job 14) but God's disposing (Psalm 90; 104:29; etc.). As a rule, death is a limit for fellowship with God (Isa. 38:18-19), but from the confession of God's power even over → death or → hell (1 Sam. 2:6-7; Amos 9:2; Ps. 139:8), the OT can imply that fellowship with God continues after death (Ps. 22:30; 49:15; 73:23-26; Isa. 25:8; Dan. 12:2).

1.2. Social Anthropology

1.2.1. In the nomadic period and after more permanent settlements, the clan seems to have been the basic social structure. Evidence exists (Josh. 7:14; cf. 1 Sam. 10:19-21) of a progression from individual to household (with the father at the head) to clan (led by the elders) to tribe. The extended family of three to four generations (see Exod. 20:5; Leviticus 18), the clan, the tribe, and the whole people regarded themselves as the children of the one father (corporate personality). By Israelite law (as distinct from Canaanite law), the landed inheritance, the basis of the clan's existence (see Mic. 2:2), was inalienable (1 Kings 21). With the → monarchy (with its attendant standing army and civil service) and the integration of former Canaanite city-states, there gradually came about the negative social changes that the message of the → prophets reflects. The increasing gap between rich and poor was contrary to legal practice, which provided for the upholding of the → family, for example, through purchase by the next of kin (Ruth 4; Jer. 32:6-9; Lev. 25:24-28), release from slavery after seven years (Exod. 21:1-11; see also Leviticus 25), the prohibition of interest (Exod. 22:25), and care for the poor (Lev. 19:9-18; etc.).

In a much simplified way, we can divide the population into four groups: (1) in the towns, civil and military officials, merchants, and artisans; (2) in rural areas, free landowners who had the four great rights to → marriage, worship, → war, and justice (L. Köhler); (3) people who owned no land, such as day laborers and aliens (Exod. 22:21); and (4) slaves (Exod. 21:1-11; Deut. 15:12-18), who shared the seventh day of rest from → work (Exod. 20:10; see also 12:44) and could take on honorable tasks (Genesis 24). In the exilic and postexilic periods the father's house (Ezra 1:5) and the institution of the elders (Jer. 29:1; Ezekiel 20; Ezra 5:9; etc.) again acquired decisive importance.

1.2.2. The OT contains promises for every group (Joel 2:28-29; cf. Jer. 31:34) and indeed for all humanity (Isa. 2:2-4; 40:5; Zeph. 2:11; etc.). Every person, whether male or female (→ Men; Women), is a creature of God and made in God's image (Gen. 1:26-28). This teaching has ethical implications (9:6). Knowing the wickedness of the human heart from youth up (Gen. 6:5; 8:21; Jer. 13:23; etc.; → Sin), the OT also contains the appropriate request: "Create in me a clean heart, O God, and put a new and right spirit within me" (Ps. 51:10; cf. Ezek. 36:26-27).

Bibliography: R. ALBERTZ, "Mensch II," *TRE* 22.464-74 (bibliography) • A. R. JOHNSON, *The Vitality of the Individual in the Thought of Ancient Israel* (Cardiff, 1949; 2d ed., 1968) • L. KÖHLER, *Hebrew Man* (Nashville, 1957) • B. LANG, ed., *Anthropological Approaches to the OT* (London, 1985) • G. PIDOUX, *L'homme dans l'Ancien Testament* (Neuchatel, 1953) • J. W. ROGERSON, *Anthropology and the OT* (Atlanta, 1979) • W. H. SCHMIDT, "Anthropologische Begriffe im Alten Testament," *EvT* 24 (1964) 374-88; idem, *Einführung in das Alte Testament* (5th ed.; Berlin, 1995) §32 • W. SCHOTTROFF, "Soziologie und Altes Testament," *VF* 19/2 (1974) 46-66 • W. THIEL, *Die soziale Entwicklung Israels in vorstaatlicher Zeit* (Berlin, 1980; 2d ed., 1984/85) • R. DE VAUX, *Ancient Israel: Its Life and Institutions* (2d ed.; London, 1973) • H. W. WOLFF, *Anthropology of the OT* (Philadelphia, 1981).

WERNER H. SCHMIDT

2. NT Anthropology

2.1. Basic Points

NT anthropology rests on a theological and Christological interpretation of world experience. According to the Jesus tradition, our perverted life (→ Sin) has brought us under the threat of the → wrath of God, as announced in prophetic and eschatological proclamation (inherited by way of John the Baptist). Against this background the opportunity of accepting God's royal dominion is announced and personally represented. In the various presentations of the NT, theological anthropology develops in increasingly strong recognition of Jesus, and reflection upon him, as the prototypical guarantor and mediator of eschatological → salvation. NT anthropology is thus a partial aspect of NT → soteriology ($1), → Christology, and ecclesiology (→ Church 2.1).

2.2. Clarifications

Applying the modern term "anthropology" to the NT is a dubious procedure. The NT is motivated neither by the questions of philosophical anthropology nor especially by those of empirical anthropology (considered in terms of either the humanities or the natural and social sciences). The following sections highlight the distinctive features of NT anthropology.

2.2.1. In the ancient world human beings do not appear primarily as individuals. They are incorporated into various theologically defined groupings, including the people of God (the children of Abraham, Matt. 3:9-10), the "nations" (i.e., the Gentiles), "this evil generation" (→ Q), or the universal community, either with → Adam in sin and → death, or with those who are in fellowship with Christ in → righteousness and the promise of life (1 Cor. 15:21-22; Rom. 5:12-21). As all people stand related to something — for example, sin or the → law as a way of life or death (Romans 7) — so believers as those who are freed from bondage are not just autonomous individuals. They belong to their exalted and heavenly Lord. As persons, they are his body *(sōma)*, members of (the body of) Christ (1 Cor. 6:12-17). Their bodies compose a "temple," that is, a holy place in which God dwells in a manifestation of his Spirit. The divine King rightfully claims the place of dominion and honor (vv. 19-20), which results in the people's salvation. Misconduct in the church (e.g., on the part of its officers) is thus sacrilege and has corresponding eschatological consequences (3:16-17). The wicked person, according to a formula from the sacred law of the OT, is to be driven out of the community (5:13), for such persons damage and threaten it as a whole (vv. 6-8). In serious cases the offender may be committed to Satan (for the destruction of the flesh) so that the spirit (i.e., the → self that survives death) may finally be saved (vv. 1-5).

People are presented as responsible individuals in the accusation of guilt (Romans 2), in the offer of an opportunity of salvation by faith (10:9-13; cf. Matt. 13:44-50), and at the judgment (1 Cor. 3:12-15; Rom. 2:11-16; John 5:24-29; Matthew 25).

2.2.2. For the most part, social relations are limited to, or deliberately focused on, the *ekklēsia* (assembly, church) of God (a term for the true people of God), first within the religious and legal unit of the Jewish community, then, after persecution or expulsion, in independent mixed communities of Jews and Hellenists. Here, too, especially in the Pauline sphere, we find insiders and outsiders (1 Cor. 5:12-13). After initial struggles (1 Thess. 2:15-16; Galatians 2; Acts 15), the community becomes wide open for → mission, aiming at the salvation of the nations or the cosmos (the world of humanity). Through → baptism as a rite of → initiation, believers become members of the saved community, the people of God, the body of Christ. Relationships within this sphere are close and intensive, even in battles for the → truth, with respect to both conduct and teaching (Matt. 5:17-20; 7:15-20; Acts 15; Galatians 2; Philippians 3; 2 Corinthians 10–13; 1-2 John; Revelation 2–3).

The heart of the strict maxims of social conduct is the upbuilding *(oikodomē)* of the *ekklēsia* with a view to attaining final salvation (e.g., 1 Corinthians). This is also the impulse behind admonition and exhortation (1 Thess. 2:10-12 and the Epistles generally). There is an intensive concern for brotherly love, that is, for promoting the good of others. In → Paul this love extends also to outsiders (see Matt. 5:43-46), but with a characteristic limitation (Gal. 6:10).

Social models are mostly taken from the common world of experience, mediated for the most part by Hellenistic Judaism. (Note the lists of virtues and vices, the → household rules, and Wisdom → ethics [§2], e.g., in James.) Yet the holiness of the *ekklēsia* gives its people their specific basis and form, as does Christology (Phil. 2:1-11; 1 Cor. 11:1; Rom. 15:2-3, 7-13; Matt. 25:31-46). The latter greatly influences traditional models governing the household of antiquity, including the relations of women and men, children and parents, slaves and masters (Col. 3:18-25; Eph. 5:22–6:9; 1 Pet. 2:18–3:7). The phrase "in Christ" goes furthest in basically removing distinctions, for all are one in him (Gal. 3:27-28).

Little is said about secular society. Positively, political institutions simply function to uphold the divine order (Rom. 13:1-7; 1 Pet. 2:13-17). An urgent need arose to understand persecution. On the one hand, opponents had to be met in the spirit of Christ, even under → suffering (Mark 13:9-13; Matt. 5:38-42; Rom. 12:17-21; 1 Pet. 3:13-22). On the other hand, not merely for lack of any other possibilities but also for theological reasons, concern for → evil was to be left to the royal lordship of God or his Messiah King (Rom. 12:19), who would execute judgment and restore order to the world. In times of oppression his coming was awaited with longing (note the prayer "Marana tha," 1 Cor. 16:22; see also Rev. 22:20) and gave the courage to persevere in suffering (Mark 13:13; 1 Pet. 4:12-19; Heb. 10:32–12:11; Rev. 21:7).

2.2.3. With regard to the cosmic dimensions of human life, there is constant reflection on such problems as sickness, suffering, and death, not so much as cosmic events (cf. 1 Cor. 15:42 with v. 56), but within traditional models of thought (Mark 2:1-12; 1 Cor. 11:30-34; Rom. 5:12-21; 6:23). The problems are worked through to a Christological solution (Rom. 6:23; Mark 3:27; Luke 11:20; Matt. 9:35-38; Rev. 21:4; John 11). Further reflection on a Christological basis may be found in 2 Cor. 4:7-12; 12:7-10; Rom. 8:18-39; Heb. 2:14-18; John 9. We find nothing of the (limited) empirical and philosophical tradition of → Hellenism along the lines of the Jewish contemporary Philo, with his effort to combine it with the theological tradition. Obviously there was no need for anything of this sort in the early period as there was in the Hellenistic Jewish diaspora of → Alexandria.

2.3. *Terminology*

The terminology of anthropology in the narrower sense is extremely varied and for the most part not very precise in the NT. There is no uniformity even in individual writers such as Paul. The → Synoptists (Luke is at times an exception) adopt a simple terminology following the tradition of the OT and Judaism. In the Pauline literature we find Hellenistic terminology adapted via Hellenistic → Judaism (*nous = esō anthrōpos;* → Conscience; Reason). John uses such traditional terms as "heart," "soul" for ego (10:24; 12:27) and for earthly life (12:25), and "body" for corpse (19:38), but he has no sharply differentiated anthropological terminology. According to John, we live in the tension of encroaching spheres of life and are exposed to the forces they emit both for evil and for good. These are the spheres of darkness and light, below and above, the cosmos and God's heavenly world, the devil and God, flesh and Spirit, death and life.

Under the influence of the OT and Judaism, *kardia* (heart) is the (hidden) inner life, the center of thought and aspiration (Mark 7:6, 21-23; John 13:2; 1 Cor. 4:5), of → grief, trouble, or → joy (John 14:27; 16:6, 22), and of → anxiety (2 Cor. 2:4).

The Hellenistic (Platonic) antithesis of body and soul is not particularly relevant (→ Platonism). The combination of body and spirit (1 Cor. 7:34) or of spirit, soul, and body (1 Thess. 5:23) is rare and does not indicate adoption of a fundamental dichotomy or trichotomy but represents a naive reference to the totality from various aspects. The term "body" refers to the personal, concrete, earthly mode of being. It is mortal because of sin (Rom. 8:10), a victim of death as the power of destruction (7:24), but capable of being raised again insofar as God's Spirit dwells within it (8:11). Like "spirit," "soul," or "flesh," "body" can be parallel to "I" (6:12-19), but so too can "flesh" (1 Cor. 5:5). Thus the body is not simply identical with the ego but highlights only one aspect of it. The point is that we do not just have bodies but live in bodily fashion. The passage 1 Cor. 15:44-49 only seems to be opposed to this, for we are what we bear. If the I as body is tied to a place, as *pneuma* (spirit) it can also be present and at work elsewhere (1 Cor. 5:3).

Psychē (→ soul) usually denotes earthly life (Mark 8:35, 37) along OT lines (1 Cor. 15:45). It thus stands for this aspect of the ego (2 Cor. 12:15; Rom. 16:4). As life, it can be parallel to body and linked to concern for food and drink (Matt. 6:25). What is decisive is life (*psychē*) before God (Mark 8:36). In times of severe persecution and martyrdom (from the 2d cent. B.C.), this insight led in early Judaism to the concept of resurrection or, as a variation, to that of life after death before God (e.g., *1 Enoch* 108). In this life the self as a person lives on as a totality, but in another mode, as soul or (more often) spirit (Rev. 6:9; 20:4; 1 Cor. 5:5; Heb. 12:23). Popular Platonic and later Gnostic presuppositions present an obvious threat to this concept (cf. 1 Corinthians 15). Thus the idea of resurrection prevails, not in the sense of

flesh and blood, nor of a corresponding psychic body, but along the lines of a pneumatic body (vv. 44-49).

Sarx (flesh) denotes the earthly, creaturely sphere. We derive from it and belong to it. It is limited, weak, and transitory. It is also a place of temptation (Mark 14:38; John 6:63; Rom. 1:3-4; 6:19; Heb. 5:7). It always stands opposed to the (primarily inaccessible) spiritual sphere of God, with which beings of earth (1 Cor. 15:47-48), brought to live as flesh (v. 45), can have no contact (v. 50). The word is morally neutral insofar as flesh, or being in the flesh, is not necessarily tied to sin (Heb. 5:7-8; John 1:14). In fact, however, flesh is under the rule of sin (*sarx hamartias,* Rom. 8:3). Thus to be fleshly is to be sold into slavery under sin (7:14). Salvation is liberation from false dominion and training in another dominion that promises life (5:12-21; 7-8; Galatians 5; 1 Cor. 15:21-22). But inasmuch as the earthly body — or its members, as its concrete expression (Rom. 7:5) — serves sin with its various passions and thus has fallen victim to death, redemption is liberation out of or from this earthly, psychic body (Rom. 7:24; cf. 1 Cor. 15:49, 51c, 53-57).

This understanding of anthropology uses in part the vocabulary of demonology ("indwell," "rule") and in part that of dualistic Wisdom. The latter uses contrasting spatial statements (e.g., once in the flesh or → Adam, now in the Spirit or Christ; the Spirit or Christ replacing sin in us) as well as the idea of a garment. Thus, for example, the old self or the body of sin or the flesh with its passions and desires is crucified (Rom. 6:6) or put off (Col. 3:5, 9; Eph. 4:22), and the new self or Christ is put on (Gal. 3:27-28; Col. 3:10-11; Eph. 4:24). "Old" and "new" in this context have specific meanings in the NT.

Parallel to the earthborn person of flesh (*psychē zōsa* in Gen. 2:7) is the remarkable idea of the psychic person or body (1 Cor. 2:14; 15:44-49). This concept hardly made sense on Greek presuppositions. It denotes the totality of the person as belonging and oriented to earth and as closed to God's world and excluded from it.

Bibliography: K. A. BAUER, *Leiblichkeit–das Ende aller Werke Gottes. Die Bedeutung der Leiblichkeit des Menschen bei Paulus* (Gütersloh, 1971) extensive bibliography • E. BRANDENBURGER, *Fleisch und Geist. Paulus und die dualistische Weisheit* (Neukirchen, 1968) • R. BULTMANN, *Theology of the NT* (2 vols.; New York, 1951-55) • W. GUTBROD, *Die paulinische Anthropologie* (Stuttgart, 1934) • R. JEWETT, *Paul's Anthropological Terms* (Leiden, 1971) • E. KÄSEMANN, *Leib und Leib Christi* (Tübingen, 1933); idem, "On Paul's Anthropology," *Perspectives on Paul* (London, 1971) 1-31 •

C. F. D. Moule, *Man and Nature in the NT* (London, 1964).

Egon Brandenburger

3. Theological Anthropology

3.1. *Thematic Definition*

Throughout most of church history there was no single theological anthropology. Rather, the church developed a series of traditionally related individual themes deriving, on the one hand, from ancient philosophy (e.g., body and → soul, freedom of the will and → freedom in general, → immortality and the problem of → evil) and, on the other hand, from authentic biblical tradition (the image of God, → sin [§3], the original human state, → forgiveness, repentance and → penitence, the old and the new humanity, → justification, etc.). In classical theology the question of the human soul dominated the field that we now call anthropology, though it embraced more than we might expect. Only relatively recently have questions of → evolution, → aggression, → sexuality, and genetic engineering as well as such critical issues as the unity of the race and its survival in face of → racism and the moral perils of → armaments, world → hunger, and → ecological irresponsibility become genuine themes of theological reflection.

3.2. *Historical Development*

Undoubtedly it was a remarkable achievement of the early church to work out a doctrine of the historical origin and goal of humanity in which the relation to God and to God's history was central. With this doctrine as a base, the church could then speak about evil and the hope of ultimately escaping it. In turn, it could then relate bondage and freedom dialectically and then could reasonably hope to pass on from the "old man" to the new. This was the messianic element that would later take secular form as the possibility of → revolutions.

In the → early church the overcoming of the → Gnostic disparagement of the body — even if the victory was not complete — was an important step that we today are inclined to underestimate because of → Augustine's (354-430) crass emphasis on concupiscence (→ Augustine's Theology). The Fathers conceived of God's relation to us mainly as a relation to the soul. They thus attached such unduly large significance to the debate over whether we inherit the soul (and sin) from our parents and ancestors (traducianism) or whether each soul is created afresh by the Creator (creationism, even in the form of preexistent souls), a question that occupied even the Reformers. The disparagement of the body, however, was in no sense as radical as in Gnostic or Neoplatonic movements, especially since the Aristotelian (→ Aristotelianism) conception of form and matter enabled and even compelled medieval theology to relate soul and grace to body and nature (→ Scholasticism).

The Reformers did not finally abandon this approach, though they tried to impress upon their anthropology the primary concept of redemption, and thus we find in them (esp. M. → Luther) less emphasis on the philosophical definition of human nature and more emphasis on the grace of → justification. But medieval problems returned in Protestant → orthodoxy (§§1-2), often in their older form, and the original questions of inherited or actual sin (even a sinful substance), of human → guilt, of the immortality of the soul (as distinct from resurrection), of traducianism versus creationism, and so forth all finally went unanswered. In the end they were ignored as new value came to be placed on human → reason and → autonomy in the philosophical and theological thinking of the → Enlightenment.

3.3. *Eastern Orthodoxy*

The Eastern church (→ Orthodox Church) developed its own anthropology apart from the Western church, using the distinction that → Irenaeus (d. ca. 200) drew between the surviving image of God and the likeness that was lost at the fall as the starting point for a richly developed doctrine of human divinization (*theōsis* or *theopoiēsis*). The specific feature of Eastern anthropology is the (Neoplatonic) distinction between the invisible heavenly soul and the visible earthly body that has been "cast out of paradise into the present world" (Liturgy of Basil). "Afflicted with the curse, the soul is bidden to reflect on its divine origin and imperishable home . . . as a supraterrestrial being" (liturgy for Sunday evening worship). People are living → icons of God, or God in microcosm. Our adoption as God's children by the Son in the → Holy Spirit leads to transfiguration, or divinization, whereby, in union with Christ, we surrender our individuality in favor of a new → identity and personhood. To praise the triune God who does this for us is the point and purpose of life: "I will sing to my God as long as I live."

3.4. *Theological Alternatives*

Six distinctive (but not mutually exclusive) types of theological anthropology might be distinguished as follows.

3.4.1. The doctrine of → *theōsis,* or transfiguration, in Eastern Orthodoxy is the first. From an ecumenical standpoint one might ask whether this is not simply the Eastern way of stating the doctrine of justification.

3.4.2. The concept of nature and grace is the classic type in Roman Catholicism. It rests on the doctrine of the image of God and attaches much importance to the philosophical definition of human nature.

3.4.3. The doctrine of the image of God occurs in both Roman Catholicism and Protestantism. It finds in creation or the incarnation a basis for humanity, for human dignity and destiny, as well as for → human rights.

3.4.4. The doctrine of justification (with an appeal to Paul) takes a central place in Reformation, and especially Lutheran, anthropology.

3.4.5. K. → Barth (1886-1968) especially championed a Christological basis for theological anthropology. For Barth, the only valid way to deduce anthropology is from the reality of Christ. The humanities can make no cognitive contribution to theological anthropology.

3.4.6. A final anthropology starts with the humanities and finds in Jesus Christ the telos. This is the anthropology of education (J. G. → Herder [1744-1803]) of humanity or the evolution of human nature for the → future, for openness to religion, as the race moves toward its destiny in the interplay of planning and experience, of developing individuation and increasing differentiation of (social) → institutions. W. Pannenberg has offered the most impressive exploration of this alternative.

3.5. *Remaining Ecumenical Tasks*
Along with the methodological task of integrating the various branches of anthropology with theological anthropology, the following problems remain: (1) systematically interpreting the historical differences in theological anthropology (cf. 3.4.1-6); (2) determining the significance of modern → ego psychology and the understanding of the → self and → identity, also in relation to the right to change; (3) inquiring into the relation between sickness and → health or normality; (4) evaluating the stages in human life, including childhood, → work, retirement, and death; (5) considering the relation between evil, → aggression, and genetic engineering; (6) finding the true basis of human rights; (7) balancing individuals and institutions; and (8) fixing the relation between the unity of the → church and that of the race.

Bibliography: K. BARTH, *CD* III/2 • E. BRUNNER, *Man in Revolt* (Philadelphia, 1947) • H. GOLLWITZER, *Krummes Holz–Aufrechter Gang* (9th ed.; Munich, 1982) • R. L. HART, *Unfinished Man and the Imagination* (New York, 1968) • R. NIEBUHR, *The Nature and Destiny of Man* (2 vols.; New York, 1941-43) • W. PANNENBERG, *Anthropology in Theological Perspective* (Philadelphia, 1985) • O. H. PESCH, *Frei sein aus Gnade. Theologische Anthro-*
pologie (Freiburg, 1983); idem, ed., *Einheit der Kirche–Einheit der Menschheit* (Freiburg, 1978) • G. THEISSEN, *Biblical Faith: An Evolutionary Approach* (Philadelphia, 1985).

DIETRICH RITSCHL

4. Philosophical Anthropology
4.1. *Word and Concept*
The word "anthropology," coined from Gk. *anthrōpos* and *logos,* took on its present meaning in German philosophy during the 16th century. Whether the definition of humanity takes place within → metaphysics under the title of philosophical anthropology or, as is more usual in Anglo-Saxon countries, as a part of → ethnology, the position of humanity in → nature, → society, and history governs the investigation. The philosophical perspective lies in the mode of putting the questions. What is attempted is not merely a description of the empirical facts of human existence but the grounding of what is said in a claim to supra-empirical universality.

4.2. *History and Methodology*
Until the → modern period the attempt to define human nature occurred within the context of a total interpretation of being (→ Ontology). Criticism of the metaphysical tradition and the attempt to find a new basis for philosophy resulted in the construction of anthropology as an independent discipline within it. Ignoring questions of the final ground of being, it aims to tell people about themselves, about their past and their → future. Philosophically established especially by R. Descartes (1596-1650) with his fixing of the ego as a self-existing being (→ Cartesianism), anthropology became a doctrine of human nature (O. Casmann). In the movement from Descartes by way of T. Hobbes (1588-1679) to I. Kant (1724-1804), human bodily nature increasingly became the central object of inquiry. For Kant, anthropology nevertheless remained a marginal discipline within philosophy. It had lesser rank than → ethics or the philosophy of history because its teaching, although ordered by philosophy, rested on → experience (→ Kantianism).

Only under the influence of the → philosophy of nature of the later F. W. J. von Schelling (1775-1854) did anthropology become a fundamental philosophical discipline. Yet even as late as the rise of German → idealism, its methodology was guided by the insight that only self-reflection distinguishes us from animals and that the question of human nature can find an answer only in the context of the basic Kantian questions of metaphysics (What can I know? What should I do? What may I hope?). L. A. Feuerbach (1804-72), turning aside from transcendental metaphysics, advanced the thesis that we are to understand human beings as humanity, as the → absolute. This led to the demand that we make humanity, including nature as its basis, the universal object of philosophy and that we replace philosophy with anthropology. Uniting with Feuerbach only in his criticism of metaphysics, K. → Marx (1818-83), followed by → Marxist philosophy, integrated anthropology into the philosophy of history.

Modern philosophical anthropology brought a new methodological orientation beginning with the publication of M. Scheler's *Die Stellung des Menschen im Kosmos* in 1928, the year that also saw the appearance of H. Plessner's *Die Stufen des Organischen und der Mensch*. Along the lines of W. Dilthey's program of an immanent understanding of humanity, speculative anthropology is broken off here by a methodological appeal to biological facts. The result is a strong biologizing of anthropology, and the question of human nature yields to that of the suitability of human conduct. For Scheler, "spirit" remains as the principle that cannot be traced back to the natural revolution of life and that differentiates human beings from other living things by their openness to the world and by their personhood.

Also for H. Plessner and A. Gehlen, openness to the world is a central anthropological category. Plessner begins with human "ec-centricity," that is, the ability to get out of one's own center and view oneself from outside. Gehlen views human beings as biologically inferior to animals, although he finds compensation in their artistic nature (i.e., in → language and → culture). In his anthropo-biological sketch Gehlen is interested solely in the conditions of human existence, viewing all human functions from the standpoint of self-preservation.

Thinkers like M. Heidegger, G. Lukács, B. Bollnow, and E. Heintel assessed critically the methodological change initiated by Scheler and warned against a philosophically inadequate understanding of human existence and of the place of humanity in nature and history as a result of too strong an influence of biology. They also criticized the neglect of reflection on the presuppositions on which modern anthropology was grounding the validity of its statements, which it also regarded as an answer to the question What may I hope?

4.3. Themes
Although there has been a change in methodology, the central themes are still the same as in Aristotle's (384-322 B.C.) *De anima, Ethica Nicomachea, Politica,* and *Rhetorica* (→ Aristotelianism). Anthropology still deals with the relation between → reason and impulse, intellect and volition and emotion, the special position of humanity, and the relation between spirit and body. Investigation continues into anthropological characteristics, nature, temperament, physiognomy, and sexuality, along with differences of nationality and race.

Bibliography: O. CASMANN, *Psychologica anthropologica sive animae humanae* (Hanau, 1594) • R. DESCARTES, *Treatise on Man* (Cambridge, Mass., 1972) • L. FEUERBACH, *The Essence of Christianity* (New York, 1957) • A. GEHLEN, *Man, His Nature and Place in the World* (New York, 1988) • I. KANT, *Anthropology from a Pragmatic Point of View* (The Hague, 1974) • H. PLESSNER, *Die Stufen des Organischen und der Mensch* (3d ed.; Berlin, 1975; *Gesammelte Schriften* [vol. 4; Frankfurt, 1981]) • M. SCHELER, *Man's Place in Nature* (New York, 1961).

HEIMO HOFMEISTER

5. Social Anthropology
5.1. Concept
Anthropology offers a scientific depiction of humanity and its understanding of the self and the world. English social anthropology covers most of the same ground (G. Lienhardt). American cultural anthropology and French social and cultural anthropology fall under → ethnology, but in both cases there is much overlapping with other social approaches (C. R. Ember and M. Ember; M. Harris; C. Lévi-Strauss; J.-P. Colleyn). In Germany, anthropology is interdisciplinary, including insights from ethnology, ethology, → psychology, → pedagogy, → sociology, → philosophy, → theology, and biology.

The scope of anthropology is apparent in the series World Anthropology (from 1975), which now includes more than 100 volumes (see the survey by S. Tax). For a more philosophical account one might turn to the seven-volume *Neue Anthropologie,* edited by H.-G. Gadamer and P. Vogler. Modern anthropology warns against anthropological constants that are formulated without clear criteria, as almost all statements about humanity rest on theories about historically dominant forms of society, so that they are implicitly normative (K. Holzkamp). Anthropology is the self-reflection of social and cultural scholarship on a biological basis and on normative contents in specific historical and political situations. It builds on the ideas of humanizing nature and culture that have been developed since the → Enlightenment (A. Honneth and H. Joas, 16).

5.2. Explicit and Implicit Models
The older "psychology of peoples" (E. Beuchelt), which adopted S. Freud's (1856-1939) idea of similarities between the primitive and the neurotic, was oriented to the model of the cultural development of

both the individual and the society. American research into culture and personality rejected this → evolutionary optimism and made a plea for the equal validity of culture-specific modal personalities and national characters (V. Barnouw). In sociology, pessimistic thinking from the time of M. → Weber (1864-1920) supported the thesis that modern → capitalism trains and creates the subjects that it needs. From the time of W. von Humboldt (1767-1835), pedagogical concepts were based on the idea of shaping personality to the cultural ideals of the upper classes (H. Blankertz), which resulted ultimately in nationalistic aberrations (H. Gaudig).

Today, ideals and → norms have more or less disappeared from sociological depictions. Empirical studies rely on abstractions as they examine humankind from the standpoint of economics, sociology, or psychology (R. Dahrendorf; K. Holzkamp; → Experience; Social Science). The difficulties of such reductionism appear most clearly in educational theory. From the time of J. Dewey (1859-1952), reformers have replaced the old ideals with the demand for action-oriented learning in a democratic society. However, reflection on the relatively free-thinking, free-willing, free-evaluating, and free-acting ego, which is not content merely to meet external demands, was inevitable (H. Roth).

5.3. *Relation to Self and the World*
Modern thinking about humanizing faces a twofold requirement. Wrestling with the thesis of a behavioral structure common to humans and animals (→ Aggression), it also must take into account the ethological (K. Lorenz; D. Morris) and sociobiological (D. P. Barash) approaches to humanizing. It also must deal with the scope, validity, and implicit normativity of neutrally formulated models of human development. In this regard J. Piaget (1896-1980) and G. H. Mead (1863-1931) offer examples of individuals learning and developing → identity in a balance between assimilation and accommodation and between role-taking and role-making (H. Ginsburg and S. Opper; L. Krappmann). Traditionally, ethnology has considered such issues by investigating cultural diversity.

Anthropology can no longer be limited to testing anthropological constants. It cannot be denied that aggression is common to humans and animals or that thought develops in the stages formulated by Piaget, but this admission in no way devalues research on the learning of various modes of aggressive behavior (A. Bandura and R. H. Walters) or the many different forms of → reason (T. Schöfthaler and D. Goldschmidt). Through entering into interdisciplinary dialogue, anthropology must retain the idea that there is always a human potential that can introduce changes in culture and → society. Anthropology is thus fundamental to critical thought concerning modern belief in progress, which has been shaped sociologically through keeping alive both the memory and the idea of a rich variety of possibilities of development, both individual and social.

Bibliography: A. Bandura and R. H. Walters, *Adolescent Aggression* (New York, 1959) • D. P. Barash, *Sociobiology and Behavior* (New York, 1977) • V. Barnouw, *Culture and Personality* (4th ed.; Homewood, Ill., 1985) • E. Beuchelt, *Ideengeschichte der Völkerpsychologie* (Meisenheim, 1974) • H. Blankertz, *Die Geschichte der Pädogogik* (Wetzlar, 1982) • J.-P. Colleyn, *Éléments d'anthropologie sociale et culturelle* (5th ed.; Brussels, 1988) • R. Dahrendorf, *Homo Sociologicus* (London, 1973) • C. R. Ember and M. Ember, *Cultural Anthropology* (6th ed.; Englewood Cliffs, N.J., 1990) • D. Freeman, *Margaret Mead and Samoa: The Making and Unmaking of an Anthropological Myth* (Cambridge, Mass., 1983) • H.-G. Gadamer and P. Vogler, eds., *Neue Anthropologie* (7 vols.; Stuttgart, 1972-75) • H. Gaudig, *Die Idee der Persönlichkeit und ihre Bedeutung für die Pädagogik* (Leipzig, 1923) • H. Ginsburg and S. Opper, *Piaget's Theory of Intellectual Development* (3d ed.; Englewood Cliffs, N.J., 1988) • M. Harris, *Cultural Anthropology* (New York, 1983) • K. Holzkamp, "Verborgene anthropologische Voraussetzungen der allgemeinen Psychologie," *Neue Anthropologie* (vol. 5; ed. H.-G. Gadamer and P. Vogler; Stuttgart, 1973) 237-82 • A. Honneth and H. Joas, *Social Action and Human Nature* (Cambridge, 1988) • L. Krappmann, *Soziologische Dimensionen der Identität* (5th ed.; Stuttgart, 1978) • C. Lévi-Strauss, "The Place of Anthropology in the Social Sciences," *Structural Anthropology* (London, 1968) 1.346-81 • R. G. Lienhardt, *Social Anthropology* (2d ed.; London, 1971) • K. Lorenz, *The Foundations of Ethology* (New York, 1981) • M. Mead, *Coming of Age in Samoa: A Psychological Study of Primitive Youth for Western Civilization* (7th ed.; New York, 1968) • D. Morris, *The Naked Ape* (New York, 1980) • W. Pannenberg, *Anthropology in Theological Perspective* (Philadelphia, 1985) • P. Parin, "Der Beitrag ethnopsychoanalytischer Untersuchungen zur Aggressionstheorie," *Die Psyche* 27 (1973) 237-48 • A. Parsons, "Is the Oedipus-Complex Universal?" *Personalities and Culture* (ed. R. C. Hunt; 2d ed.; Austin, Tex., 1977) 352-99 • H. Roth, *Pädagogische Anthropologie* (2 vols., 5th ed.; Hannover, 1984) • T. Schöfthaler and D. Goldschmidt, eds., *Soziale Struktur und Vernunft* (Frankfurt, 1984) • S. Tax, ed., *World Anthropology* (The Hague, 1980) follows a broader, social-research concept of anthropology.

Traugott Schöfthaler

Anthroposophy

1. Development
2. Basic Ideas
3. Practical Implications

T. Vaughan first introduced the term "anthroposophy" at the beginning of the 18th century in the title of a book. Rudolf Steiner (1861-1925) adopted it to advance his Adyar → theosophy.

1. Development

Steiner was born on February 27, 1861, in Kraljevec, which was then in Austria, near the Hungarian-Croatian border. Early in life he had → spiritist and → occult experiences. He was also attracted by the solemnity of Roman Catholic worship and by the exact sciences. As a student of nature and literature at Vienna, he developed his mental powers in such a way as to arrive at a higher reality embracing both matter and spirit. Reinforced by encounters with an otherwise unknown herb gatherer and a theosophist, he went to Weimar, where from 1890 to 1897 he devoted himself to editing the writings of J. W. von Goethe (1749-1832) on natural science.

Personal problems that are still obscure drove Steiner in following years to editing the *Magazin für Literatur* (until 1900) and lecturing in the Workers' Educational College in Berlin (until 1905), as well as to a meditative-visionary encounter with the figure of Christ (→ Meditation; Visions). In spite of strong reservations about the Eastern slant, the high evaluation of spirit in the Theosophical Society moved him to join the recently formed German section, which he served as general secretary from 1902. Steiner believed most emphatically that Christ represented a unique turning point in human history, as his three *Evangelienzyklen* (Gospel cycles; 1908 and 1910) and *Geheimwissenschaft im Umriß* (Secret knowledge in outline; 1910) make clear. Obstinacy on both sides forced Steiner out of the esoteric school of the Theosophical Society in 1907. When he rejected the proclamation of Krishnamurti as world savior, A. Besant (1847-1933) expelled him from the society altogether.

The founding of the Anthroposophical Society in 1913 marked a break only externally, for Steiner himself regarded all previous writings and addresses as basic to anthroposophy. Also in 1913 his desire for a worthy setting for the performance of the mystery plays he had composed after 1910 led to the founding of the Goetheanum at Dornach near Basel. From here he directed the societies founded in various European countries and turned his understanding of the world and humanity to practical account in more and more fields. He sketched an order of service in 1921 and the next year founded the → Christian Community. In 1923 he set up the Universal Anthroposophical Society to maintain unity among anthroposophists. He died on March 30, 1925. The complete edition of Steiner's speeches and writings, which began appearing in Dornach in 1955, numbers thus far about 300 volumes.

2. Basic Ideas

Steiner's anthroposophy is expounded in different ways by the many groups into which the movement has split. Its overall aim is to bring us to live out consciously our involvement in world development on the basis of the continued development of our powers of will and spirit. According to Steiner's anthropology, the human ego not only unites lifeless and animated → nature with higher spiritual planes but manifests in this life the consequences of previous existences and prepares the way for those that follow in accordance with the dominant part of being (→ Reincarnation). According to his cosmology, the earth itself, in a process that elevates the material to the spiritual, goes through seven stages, each of which is divided into seven periods.

Christ as a cosmic being is an integral part of this speculation regarding the epochs of the world. To lead humanity out of a threatened relapse into the material, he incarnated himself in a corporeality prepared for him by Zoroaster and Buddha. The doctrine of the boy Jesus as derived from lines tracing back both to Solomon and to Nathan, which Steiner developed from the two biblical genealogies of Jesus, served to present the biblical Christ as the incarnation of both. From Christ, especially through the event of Golgotha, emanated decisive thrusts for the development of innate human powers that would bring humanity to maturity. As a spiritual teacher and student, Steiner regarded it as his chief task to make people aware of these connections. The esoteric Christianity for the sake of which he extolled an exoteric (or public) Christianity is based partly on the Bible but mainly on traces of cosmic development (accessible only to Steiner) in the so-called Akasha Chronicle (→ Esotericism).

3. Practical Implications

Even more than through the Anthroposophical Society, the repercussions of Steiner's speculations can be seen in their various applications. The introduction of eurythmics had a stimulating effect on art and therapeutic pedagogy. With the help of the Waldorf educational system (named after the director of a cigarette factory who set up the first school of this kind in Stuttgart), Steiner sought to train his students to be independent and also morally and artistically well developed, keeping strictly to his postulated seven-year phases of development. In the area of medicine and therapeutic pedagogy he regarded sickness and disturbances of development as the maladjustment of essential parts of human nature, which he tried to overcome by the intensive concern of the doctor or counselor for the patient and by the use of natural means of healing. In agriculture the biodynamic methods he propagated involved a rejection of artificial fertilizers and the use of cosmic forces; he advocated natural fertilizers in preparation of the soil and observation of the phases of the moon in sowing. His program of a self-sufficient, independent organization of cultural, legal, and political or economic life (his so-called threefold social integration) has led to few long-lasting practical results.

Bibliography: O. BARFIELD, *Romanticism Comes of Age* (2d ed.; Middletown, Conn., 1967) • S. C. EASTON, *Man and World in the Light of Anthroposophy* (2d ed.; Hudson, N.Y., 1989) • K. HUTTEN, *Seher, Grübler, Enthusiasten* (12th ed.; Stuttgart, 1982) 687-720 • G. A. KAUFMANN, ed., *Fruits of Anthroposophy* (London, 1922) • R. A. McDERMOTT, "Anthroposophy," *EncRel(E)* (1986) 1.320-21; idem, ed., *The Essential Steiner* (San Francisco, 1984) • H. RELLER, *Handbuch Religiöse Gemeinschaften* (Gütersloh, 1978) 502-29 • H. RINGGREN, "Anthroposophie," *TRE* 3.8-20.

KARL HOHEISEL

Antichrist

The term "antichrist," which occurs in the NT only in 1 John 2:18, 22; 4:3; 2 John 7, was coined by primitive Christianity and presupposes the title "Christ" (→ Christological Titles). Not found in → Paul's letters, "antichrist" represents an → eschatological formulation of the second generation of Christians, who faced both internal and external opposition to the Christ, whom they proclaimed as Lord. In the first century there was still no single term for the immanent eschatological opponent of God, Christ, and the church community. Thus 2 Thess. 2:1-12 refers to "the man of lawlessness," "the son of destruction." Mark 13:22 expects several pseudo-Christs and pseudoprophets. The Book of Revelation (e.g., chaps. 12–13) uses the image of two beasts dependent on the dragon. The focus is on the first as the counterpart of Christ. Besides variation in the terms used (cf. also *Did.* 16.4), there are also differences in their characterization. In 1-2 John opponents who have gone out from Christianity rank as antichrists, but in Revelation 13 and 17 the anti-Roman thrust gives a political accent.

The conceptual variety that we find in the early statements prevents us from seeking the background in an existing antichrist myth, even though the statements may well derive from older traditions. Among these is a well-developed idea of → Judaism, namely that of ungodly eschatological rulers and kingdoms, for which Ezekiel 38–39 prepared the ground, which was fostered by the experience of the rule of Antiochus IV Epiphanes (d. 164 B.C.; see Daniel 2; 7–9; 11) and which was developed further in the → pseudepigrapha (see *2 Apoc. Bar.* 36–40; 4 Ezra 5). Revelation 12–13 displays many of the features of an eschatologized → myth of conflict with the chaos dragon.

In the early and medieval church (→ Early Church; Middle Ages 2) the various notions of an adversary all met in the figure of antichrist. First put together about 950 by Adso (d. 992) in a *Vita,* the legend went far beyond the biblical statements. Its application varied from age to age. In the Investiture Controversy the tradition of antichrist as a secular ruler dominated criticism of the empire, but in criticism of the church (from the time of the → Donatists), the main concept was that of an opponent and his adherents within the church. A favorable reference of the *katechon* (restraining factor) of 2 Thess. 2:6 to the civil power also made it possible to emphasize the function of secular government vis-à-vis antichrist. The idea of an antichrist within the church was applied both to the main church and to heretics, and finally to the → pope. The figure of antichrist has thus consistently been a difficult one in the teaching of the church.

The → Reformation presupposed medieval developments. Yet M. → Luther (1483-1546) arrived independently at an equation of the papacy with antichrist. The sole consideration for him was the claim of the papacy to supremacy and the keys. With this claim it perverted the → gospel and showed itself to be the opponent of 2 Thess. 2:4 (Schmalk. Art. 2.4 etc.). This view quickly became common in Protestant → theology and polemics (see → Calvin *Inst.* 4.7.24-25; J. Foxe; J. → Knox), and for many years it thwarted ecumenical discussion.

After the period of → orthodoxy and → Pietism the figure of antichrist lost much of its luster. It gained new prominence with F. → Nietzsche (1844-1900), who in his later work (*Der Antichrist* [1895]) used the figure of antichrist to combat the decadent morality that he found supremely in Christianity (independently taken up by R. J. Sorge). Fruitful use of the concept was again made in the conflict with National Socialism (J. Roth; → Fascism). The term "antichrist" plays little role in contemporary dialogue.

Bibliography: W. Bousset, The Antichrist (London, 1896) • D. Brady, The Contribution of British Writers between 1560 and 1830 to the Interpretation of Revelation 13:16-18 (Tübingen, 1983) • R. K. Emmerson, Antichrist in the Middle Ages (Manchester, 1981) • S. S. Hartmann et al., "Antichrist," TRE 3.20-50 (extensive bibliography) • G. C. Jenks, The Origins and Early Development of the Antichrist Myth (Berlin, 1991) • F. Nietzsche, The Antichrist (London, 1928) • J. Roth, Antichrist (New York, 1935) • R. J. Sorge, Antichrist. Dramatische Dichtung (1925; repr. in Werke [vol. 1; Nürnberg, 1962]).

MARTIN KARRER

Anti-Judaism → Anti-Semitism, Anti-Judaism

Antimodernist Oath

In 1910 Pope Pius X (1903-14) required all Roman Catholic priests to take the Antimodernist Oath (→ Motu proprio Sacrorum antistitum) in rejection of the errors of → modernism. It also had to be taken before taking higher order (→ Consecration) or institution to office. Non-Catholics viewed its introduction as evidence of Roman Catholic backwardness and intolerance. In the long run, the oath could not suppress the problems raised by modernism. In 1967 a new Professio fidei became obligatory, replacing the oath with a general confession of the church's teaching.

Bibliography: Primary sources: DH 3537-50 • J. Neuner and H. Roos, The Teaching of the Catholic Church (Staten Island, N.Y., 1967) 64-74 • Pius x, "Sacrorum antistitum," ACQR 35 (1910) 712-31 • "Professio fidei 1967," QGPRK 2/1 (1972) no. 1356.
Secondary works: J. Mausbach, Der Eid wider den Modernismus (Cologne, 1911) • H. Mulert, Antimodernisteneid (Halle, 1911). See also the bibliography in "Modernism."

HANS SCHNEIDER

Antinomian Controversies

1. The question of the place and function of the law in penitence, the Christian life, and Christian proclamation often caused strife during the course of the Lutheran → Reformation (§1.3) up to the Formula of Concord. The debate between Martin → Luther (1483-1546) and his follower Johann Agricola (1494-1566) of Eisleben might be viewed as an antinomian controversy in the narrower sense. Always presupposed by the disputants is the importance of the Reformation discovery of the distinction (variously understood) between → law and → gospel (→ Luther's Theology).

1.1. Historians have found a prelude to the antinomian controversy in the Salhausen debate (1524) concerning the teaching method of the preacher Dominicus Beyer. Both alone and with Johannes Bugenhagen (1485-1558) and Philipp → Melanchthon (1497-1560), Luther supported Beyer in his view that we must preach the law both for external discipline and common → peace and also for the making known of → sin, without which the gospel cannot be accepted as such (WA 15.222-29).

1.2. To back the sin-disclosing function of the law, the Wittenberg theologians quoted Luke 24:47 and John 16:8. From these passages, however, Agricola deduced that the knowledge of sin and repentance springs only from proclamation of the gospel. For him law and gospel become states in the Christian → life that are statically and formally distinguished from one another, just as the NT message of Christ has put an end to the period of the OT → covenant. Thus the gospel takes over the sin-disclosing function of the law and becomes the principle of the Christian life in → penitence. Not to leave Christians alone with the law as an accuser has been finely depicted as Agricola's concern.

1.3. On this basis Agricola protested against Melanchthon's Saxon Visitation Articles (1527), which stressed preaching the law and repentance before the message of → grace and → faith. In his Instruction to Visitors and Pastors (WA 26.202.32–203.4), Luther issued a compromise formula that is not wholly satisfying.

1.4. A decade later (1537), with the publication of some anonymous theses formulating Agricola's concern, Luther began an uncompromising campaign against Agricola. In six series of theses (1537-40) and three disputations (1537-38), he attacked the antinomians, as he called Agricola and his followers (WA 39/1.334-584). In 1539 his Against the Antinomians appeared (WA 50.461-77). The debate brought to light a basic and unbridgeable gulf in the understanding of Scripture on the subject of penitence and therefore of human reality. According to Luther, Agricola did not see that we are always sinners and hence can never leave behind us the law, which continually discloses sin. As distinct from Agricola, Luther espoused a dynamic and functional

80

distinction between law and gospel. God is the Lord of this distinction in human life, and the gospel is unequivocally and exclusively a word of → consolation.

2. Paradoxically Melanchthon and his supporters, the Philippists, adopted an antinomianism similar to that of Agricola with their thesis that the gospel is a message of repentance *(doctrina poenitentiae)*.

3. After Luther's death the significance of the law in the → sanctification of Christians came into dispute. Over against Melanchthon and the Philippists, → Gnesio-Lutherans like A. Poach (1516-85), A. Otho (1505-83), A. Musculus (1514-81), and M. Neander (1525-95) contested a special, third use of the law — a *tertius usus* — in the regenerate. They thus came to be called antinomians, even though they obviously differed from Agricola. The Formula of Concord rejected the antinomianism of Agricola, Melanchthon, and the Philippists in article 5. In article 6 it taught a *tertius usus*, at least superficially, if not substantively.

Bibliography: M. BRECHT and R. SCHWARZ, eds., *Bekenntnis und Einheit der Kirche* (Stuttgart, 1980) • D. D. HALL, ed., *The Antinomian Controversy, 1636-1638: A Documentary History* (Middletown, Conn., 1968) • G. HAMMANN, "Nomismus und Antinomismus innerhalb der Wittenberger Theologie von 1524-1530" (Diss., Bonn, 1952) • S. HAUSAMMANN, *Buße als Umkehr und Erneuerung von Mensch und Gesellschaft* (Zurich, 1975) • W. JOEST, *Gesetz und Freiheit* (4th ed.; Göttingen, 1968) • G. KAWERAU, *Johann Agricola von Eisleben* (repr., Hildesheim, 1977) • S. KJELDGAARD-PEDERSEN, *Gesetz, Evangelium und Buße* (Leiden, 1983) • J. ROGGE, *Johann Agricolas Lutherverständnis* (Berlin, 1960) • M. SCHLOEMANN, *Natürliches und gepredigtes Gesetz bei Luther* (Berlin, 1961) • W. YOUNG, "Antinomianism," *EncChr* 1.270-78.

STEFFEN KJELDGAARD-PEDERSEN

Antinomy

The word "antinomy" denotes the rationally irreconcilable contradiction between two equally well-grounded laws or statements. After I. Kant (1724-1804; → Kantianism), antinomies have been based on the contrariety of the laws of human reason as it traces back everything conditioned to the unconditioned and yet views every condition as itself conditioned, or finally based on the tension between the empirical world and the world of the unconditioned that is posited in → metaphysics and → epis-

temology (→ Dialectic). → Dialectical theology has tried to resolve this tension in talk about God with the help of the concept of → paradox. Analytic → philosophy of religion takes over from formal → logic the distinction between various linguistic steps (object language and metalanguage) or various linguistic games (L. Wittgenstein).

Bibliography: M. COHEN, "Antinomies," *OCtP* 40 • I. U. DALFERTH, *Religiöse Rede von Gott* (Munich, 1981) • N. FERRÉ, *Language, Logic, and God* (New York, 1961) • N. HINSKE and W. VON KUTSCHERA, "Antinomie," *HWP* 1.393-405 • J. TRACK, *Sprachkritische Untersuchungen zum christlichen Reden von Gott* (Göttingen, 1977).

WERNER SCHWARTZ

Antioch

1. Whereas → Alexandria was founded by Alexander the Great (356-323 B.C.), Antioch belonged to the age of his successors (→ Hellenism). Seleucus I Nicator, ruler of the Seleucid Empire from 305 to 280 B.C., founded Antioch in honor of his father, Antiochus, around 300 B.C. on the Orontes River, 22 km. (14 mi.) from the Mediterranean. He adorned it with colonnades and fine buildings and made it the capital of Syria. Meeting point of many important roads and close to the port of Seleucia, Antioch soon became a great center of trade. After a short period of Armenian rule (83-66 B.C.), Pompey (106-48 B.C.) captured it; from 64 B.C. it was the capital of the Roman province of Syria. After many changes under the emperors, Zenobia of Palmyra ruled it from A.D. 267 to 272. In 540 Antioch was destroyed by the Persian king Khosrow I (531-79); Justinian (527-65) rebuilt it and gave it the new name Theopolis (City of God). The Arabs seized it in 638.

2. As a Hellenistic settlement, Antioch had a varied population. Most of its residents were Greeks (from Athens and Macedonia), but there were also Jews, Syrians, and other nationalities. Greek was the main language, with Aramaic also spoken. Antioch was the third largest city in the Roman Empire, after → Rome and Alexandria.

3.1. Culturally, Antioch could not compare with Alexandria. It did, however, have Libanius (d. ca. A.D. 393), an important rhetorician who was a pagan traditionalist and an admirer of Emperor Julian the Apostate (361-63). Libanius's students included many of the leading → church fathers.

3.2. Antioch provided a bridgehead for early

Christian expansion. Hellenistic Jewish Christians who had been driven out of → Jerusalem began the Gentile mission there (Acts 11:19-30). Believers were first called Christians in Antioch (v. 26). Antioch was the site of the controversy between → Paul and → Peter concerning table fellowship between Jewish and Gentile Christians (Gal. 2:11-16).

3.3. In Bishop Ignatius (martyred ca. A.D. 107), Antioch produced the most sharply defined among the → Apostolic Fathers. In a characteristically Syrian form, the idea of the universal church was already emerging with Ignatius. Around the year 180 Bishop Theophilus represented the first generation of truly theological → apologists in Antioch. An important event took place about 232, when the great Alexandrian → Origen (ca. 185-ca. 254) came to the city to give instruction to the emperor's mother, Julia Mamea, who was known for the wide range of her interests.

3.4. Antioch acquired a theological character of its own through its bishop, Paul of Samosata, whose teaching was condemned by a council in 268 on account of his → Christology. As an official under Zenobia, Paul succeeded in remaining bishop until 272. In these years he began to teach Lucian (martyred in 312), who became an important disputant with the Alexandrians and the founder of the Antiochian school. Lucian taught Arius (ca. 280-336), and thus there are links between Lucian and the Arian controversy, which caused the Antiochian (Meletian) schism (330-414).

This complicated affair, which involved → Athanasius (ca. 297-373) and Basil the Great (ca. 330-79), resulted from the deposing and exiling of the Nicene Bishop Eustathius (d. ca. 337) in 330 (→ Arianism). His successor, Melitius (d. 381), who leaned toward orthodoxy, was removed by Emperor Constantius II (337-61) in favor of a strict Arian. Paulinus of Antioch (d. ca. 388), however, leader of the Eustathians, was consecrated bishop. The complicated ebb and flow of the struggle ended only when all the people involved had died.

The Council of Antioch (341) also figured in the Arian controversy. Dominated by the Arians under their leader Eusebius of Nicomedia (d. ca. 342), this council ratified the condemnation of Athanasius and Marcellus of Ancyra (d. ca. 374). The death of Eusebius, who had become bishop of Constantinople, prevented a schism between East and West.

3.5. Antiochian theology became very important in the fourth century, suffered a reverse with Nestorius (d. ca. 451), but then made a compromise with Alexandria and exerted a normative influence on the → Chalcedonian Definition of 451. Yet, in another instance of Antioch's ability to change sides, the patriarch Severus of Antioch (d. 538) was a leading → Monophysite (→ Nestorians). The appearance of a figure like the stylite Simeon (d. 596) in the neighborhood of Antioch shows that a mere survey of theological schools cannot adequately characterize the dominant → piety.

→ Early Church; Heresies and Schisms

Bibliography: R. DEVREESSE, *Le patriarcat d'Antioche depuis la paix de l'église jusqu'à la conquête arabe* (Paris, 1945) • G. DOWNEY, *Ancient Antioch* (Princeton, 1963) • R. M. GRANT, "Jewish Christianity at Antioch in the Second Century," *RSR* 60 (1972) 97-108 • G. M. HADDAD, *Aspects of Social Life in Antioch in the Hellenistic-Roman Period* (New York, 1949) • F. W. NORRIS and B. DREWERY, "Antiochien," *TRE* 3.99-113 (bibliography) • D. S. WALLACE-HADRILL, *Christian Antioch: A Study of Early Christian Thought in the East* (Cambridge, 1982).

ULRICH WICKERT

Antiochian Theology

1. A contrast is usually made between the theologies of → Antioch and of → Alexandria. Whereas the latter was for the most part confined to a single place, the former, at its height, affected many bishops scattered through the eastern (Greek-speaking) half of the empire. Alexandrian theology favored → Platonism and allegorizing, but Antiochian theology inclined to Aristotle (→ Aristotelianism) and honored the literal sense of Scripture. The Antiochian school was not oriented to historical criticism in the modern sense. Its exegetical method (and the related polemic against Alexandria) was bound up with its different style of → dogmatics. The Alexandrians sought to fuse Greek → metaphysics into Christian thinking, but the (later) Antiochians, building on this effort, showed more concern for salvation history (→ Theology of History). They thus preferred → typology (on a Hebrew model) and an ecclesiastically more correct → eschatology (§3).

2. We may divide Antiochian theology into three periods, although these do not represent strictly sequential phases of development.

2.1. It is hard to define exactly the dogmatic position of Paul of Samosata (bishop of Antioch 260-72). He seems to have taught a Logos Christology in some sense, thus anticipating the golden age of Antiochian theology. For Paul, however, the → incarnation brought an impersonal Logos into contingent union with the man → Jesus. Paul was definitely an original thinker; we should not be too hasty in linking such an individualist with specific traditions or schools.

2.2. Lucian of Antioch (ca. 240-312), who died a martyr's death, may be compared with the great Alexandrians of an earlier period and ranks as the founder of the Antiochian school. Yet we must distinguish him from the later theologians of Antioch in the fourth and fifth centuries. Whereas the latter thought in Nicene terms, Lucian taught very consistently the subordinationism of the pre-Nicene era, which, through his disciple Arius (a presbyter at Alexandria, d. 336), was to plunge the church into the → Arian controversy. → Origen (ca. 185-ca. 254), in spite of subordinating the Son, still had affirmed his essential closeness to the unbegotten Father. Lucian, finding a reasonable basis in the divine will, viewed the (personally conceived) Logos as caused (i.e., created out of nothing). Lucian's widely circulated recension of the Bible revealed his exacting scholarship, as did his exegetical work, which was oriented to the literal sense.

2.3. With Diodore (d. ca. 390), who was first a presbyter in Antioch and then bishop of Tarsus, a school developed that deserves the name "Antiochian" in a narrower sense. Diodore's historico-grammatical exposition of Scripture caused him to take note of historical events outside the Bible, for example, the intermingling of peoples in the age of → Hellenism and the Augustan → peace as a presupposition for the success of the Christian mission.

Diodore's pupil Theodore, bishop of Mopsuestia in Cilicia from 392 to 428, was an outstanding exegete and systematic theologian. For Theodore, the Antiochian Christology of separation — in which the Logos and an otherwise ordinary man come together, thus making the unity of Christ's person problematic — does not arise solely out of the dogmatic need to ensure the reality of → salvation by an untruncated human nature of Jesus. With the → philosophy of antiquity, Theodore looked to spirit, → soul (§2), and body in us as the representatives of all the stages of cosmic being. For this reason the second → Adam had to be both true God and true man. An important feature in Theodore was his fine exegetical work on Paul, through which he mediated the apostle to the Greek East. → Augustine (354-430) performed a similar function in the Latin sphere.

A contemporary of Theodore was the famous preacher John → Chrysostom (patriarch of Constantinople, 398-404). A farsighted churchman and a pastor of insight and gentleness, Chrysostom demanded a scholarly Antiochian exegesis from his congregation and succeeded brilliantly in his efforts. Persecuted by Theophilus of Alexandria (d. 412), Chry-

sostom was sent into exile and died on the way, his last words being, "God be thanked for all things."

The fate of Nestorius (d. ca. 451) was also a tragic one in the controversy over the title *theotokos* (bearer of God).

Theodoret of Cyrrhus (ca. 393-ca. 460) deserves credit for having worked toward the union that brought a compromise between Antioch and Alexandria at → Chalcedon in 451.

→ Christology; Early Church

Bibliography: B. ALTANER, *Patrology* (2d ed.; New York, 1961) • B. ALTANER and A. STUIBER, *Patrologie* (9th ed.; Freiburg, 1980) • V. CORWIN, *St. Ignatius and Christianity in Antioch* (New Haven, 1960) • A. GRILLMEIER and H. BACHT, *Das Konzil von Chalkedon* (vol. 1; Würzburg, 1951) • F. W. NORRIS and B. DREWERY, "Antiochien," *TRE* 3.99-113 (bibliography) • C. C. RICHARDSON, *The Christianity of Ignatius of Antioch* (New York, 1967; orig. pub., 1935) • R. V. SELLERS, *Two Ancient Christologies* (London, 1954) • D. S. WALLACE-HADRILL, *Christian Antioch: A Study of Early Christian Thought in the East* (Cambridge, 1982) • U. WICKERT, *Studien zu den Pauluskommentaren Theodors von Mopsuestia* (Berlin, 1962).

ULRICH WICKERT

Anti-Semitism, Anti-Judaism

1. Antiquity
2. Middle Ages
3. Modern Period

1. Antiquity

The Jews in antiquity aroused hostility in the pagan world. Their exclusiveness incurred the charge that they hated the rest of the world. It was said that the gods had rejected them and that they were a race of slaves, contentious and obstinate. People found their cultic practices abhorrent. Whereas pagan Rome practiced toleration, the new world power of the church (→ Early Church) found it impossible to deal in the same way with so obvious a demarcation and even rejection. As heralds of the new age and true interpreters of the Hebrew Bible, Christians became antagonists of the Jews, who regarded their understanding of the Bible as the result of an ancient tradition deriving from revelation, enriched by various writings, and defined in such a way as to make impossible transition to a faith that meant abolition of the → law, understanding of Christ as the *vera lex* (true law), and the fulfillment of redemption.

The refusal of the Jews to take the step into the new age revived the pagan charge of obstinacy —

now raised, however, not as rhetorical defamation but as material accusation. Every biblical philippic of God or the → prophets bore witness to future punishment. The vehemence of the attacks revealed the existential conflict felt by the young church. The religion of "God's cast-off people" had a strong attractive force that believers sought to counter by defamation and denunciation. Israel, it was said, has "the forehead of a whore" (Jer. 3:3), its temple has become "a den of robbers" (Jer. 7:11), its cult and prayers are offensive, it is guilty of deicide. Even the most obstinate *judaizantes* (Judaizers) in the cities of the Roman Hellenistic world had to avoid visiting the → synagogue, having dealings with Jews, or speaking of the Bible in a Jewish sense. The ecclesia was the *verus Israel* (true Israel), with which God had made a new → covenant.

2. Middle Ages

Under the tension of religious self-assertion on both sides, interrupted at times by some expedient → toleration on the part of both secular and spiritual rulers, the story of the Jews in the Middle Ages is one of suffering, including forced baptisms, persecutions, and threats to life and property, all provoked by Jewish exclusiveness and prosperity and justified by repeated arguments against the Jews and → Judaism. The promise of final salvation for the Jews (Rom. 11:26) seemed to run contrary to the Jews' resistance. Theological justification needed to be found for such a promise to those guilty of deicide. → Augustine argued that the Jews were necessary to believing Gentiles as witnesses to the Jews' own iniquity and the Gentiles' truth (*Enarr. in Ps.* 58.1.21-22).

The promise of salvation occurs in defenses of the Jews, in attacks upon them, and in religious controversies. It is linked with the Christian view that they are allowed to exist like Cain, leading an uncertain life and bearing an eternal mark because of their wicked act. One sometimes catches a more conciliatory note in art and in the discussions of learned divines. The depiction of the synagogue in the Strasbourg cathedral — as a statue of great beauty, the veil over her eyes transparent as though she would awaken any moment — leaves the impression that it embodies the eschatological hopes of the period (→ Eschatology 3). Theologically the conclusion was reached that guilt could not attach to the Jews for the crucifixion of Jesus. The crucifixion, → resurrection, and → ascension, after all, were the main elements in the event of salvation. Thus the Jews had enriched the world; their act was part of the divine plan (Lanfranc and → Anselm). But such individual insights could not offset the church's fear of the in-

fluence of the Jews over Christians — a fear that came to expression in many conciliar decrees.

On threat of → excommunication, Christians were forbidden to eat with Jews or to participate in Jewish services, while Jews were commanded not to leave their houses during Holy Week, since they would seem to mock Christ if they appeared on the streets during → processions. Both religious and social unease manifested itself in this line of argument. Thus when a ninth-century archbishop complained of the insolence of the Jews, this gave evidence of the social and economic position of the Jews in his city, which he regarded as a threat to his people because the Jews enjoyed the favor of the emperor. Agobard of Lyons (ca. 769-840) closed a missive with a wordy theological argument showing how intolerable was the situation.

The church grew stronger during the centuries that followed, and the age of faith that ensued seemed to provide the necessary and constantly renewed justification for Jewish persecutions. During the → Crusades troops or townspeople thought they should fight the enemies of Christ in nearby lands before fighting the infidels in the Holy Land. Peter the Venerable, → abbot of → Cluny, advised Louis VII of France to despoil the Jews in order to finance a crusade. The kings of England and Spain expelled the Jews from their domains in 1290 and 1492 respectively. Zealous monks preached hatred of the Jews. The same pious words always masked the underlying social or economic motives.

At times conflicts between councils and guilds engulfed the Jews. Outbreaks of plague gave rise to the accusation that Jews were poisoning the wells. The dramatic appearance of wandering → flagellants stirred up religious → ecstasy. Such things all caused mass hysteria, and against this background we can understand the 14th-century persecutions in almost every German city. The constant defamation of a group that is forced to live separately leads to demonization. Christians accused the Jews not merely of poisoning wells and desecrating the Host but also of ritual murders. As those who had put Christ to death, the Jews were the very opposite of what human beings ought to be — in fact, they were personifications of the devil. On into the → modern period, → fear, hate, and envy, augmented by superstition, exposed the Jews to every possible irrational accusation, with unspeakable sufferings as a result. Economic and religious factors were the two forces that determined the status and destiny of the Jews in the Middle Ages.

Religious zeal motivated → Innocent III (1198-1216) to fight against heretical movements and thus to make degrading decrees (e.g., requiring distinctive clothing) in an effort to check a Judaizing influence on heretics (→ Heresies and Schisms). He also felt called to keep alive the church's teaching on → slavery (§1) as a divine judgment on the Jews "because they crucified the Lord" (*Etsi Judeos* [1205]). It was thus in keeping with the spirit of the age that under Frederick II the *servi Dei* (slaves of God) became simultaneously the *servi camerae* (slaves of the state). From a status of privilege, the Jews plunged into one of total dependency. As Jews, they could neither hold land nor engage in trade, hence they had to take to finance. The Jew as haggling usurer completed the bedeviled picture. To deal in money was to "judaize" (→ Bernard of Clairvaux).

Nevertheless, the Jews were still the people of the Bible. Disputations showed that they knew their book and that arguments could not convince them. Later antiquity already had charged them with telling useless tales about God and → angels. The Fathers complained that they put more faith in the teachings of their → rabbis than those of God (→ Jerome and Augustine). In the 12th century Peter the Venerable called the → Talmud a book of dark secrets that contains blasphemous ideas proving the stupidity and inhumanity of the Jews. During the centuries that followed, those arguing against the Jews no longer confronted them with biblical quotations but cited Talmudic sayings that allegedly bore witness to their infamy and their hatred of Christ. The earliest recorded burning of the Talmud took place in Paris in the middle of the 13th century. The treatment of the Talmud as a devilish work became a central element in modern hatred of the Jews.

3. Modern Period

Mercantilism and the → Enlightenment ushered in the modern period for the Jews but did not end the antagonism between Jews and Christians. They simply gave it a new vocabulary, which added a new and no less dangerous dimension. Since the battle now was no longer for the true faith but for consolidation of the nation-state and civil order (→ Nation, Nationalism; Bourgeois, Bourgeoisie), which in the spirit of the Enlightenment demanded toleration in matters of faith, a need arose for new terms in conflict with the Jews. It was no longer a matter of → baptism or → conversion (§1) but of → "emancipation" (i.e., civil equality) and "assimilation" (i.e., integration into Christian society). For the Jews, however, "assimilation" simply meant the tearing down of economic and social barriers that separated them from other people. The misunderstanding soon became apparent. Christian society demanded also the

tearing down of religious barriers — in fact, the abolition of Judaism, as by → baptism (§2).

The Jewish question assumed the form: What are the Jews, a people or a religion? As a people within a people, the Jews would have made no demands. But toleration in the sense of G. E. Lessing (1729-81) and M. Mendelssohn (1729-86) remained the inheritance of only a single generation. The Christian state of the 19th century, like the church of the Middle Ages, required religious self-immolation as the price of assimilation.

The explosive power of the emancipation debate is evident in the position taken toward the Jewish question by theoreticians like Bruno Bauer (1809-82) and Karl → Marx (1818-83), whose dubious formulations reappeared in cruder and more aggressive form in many writings hostile to the Jews in these and later years. Their religion and nature would force the Jews — they themselves admitted it — to live apart. Their nature made them Jews, not human beings like others. "If they wanted to be free, they would confess a free religion . . . enlightenment . . . free humanity" (Bauer). The work of Marx shows that enlightenment did not necessarily give a true understanding of Judaism. Society, Marx argued, must succeed in changing the "nature of the Jews," in getting rid of their financial activity and its presuppositions, in making such things impossible for them. Both by religion and nature (their religion is the "polytheism of the many needs"), they are "hucksters"; their worldly God is money. Marx thus concluded: "The social emancipation of the Jew is the emancipation of society from Judaism." The medieval charge that to take interest is to Judaize was absolutized here and became an element in economic theory.

In the opening decades of the 19th century, economic changes shattered the basis of life in the cities but opened up new opportunities of gain for Jews. A search for intellectual refuge accompanied the economic and political instability, and in Germany this goal came to expression in an excessive nationalism. As many saw it, Jews were the reason for the instability. They were aliens without roots. Anti-Jewish works of the time depict them as "corrupters of the nation" and "bread stealers"; they controlled half of the capital in Frankfurt (Fries, 1816). They can only be barely tolerated in a Christian state. They must not be allowed to serve in the army, because only "Germans may fight beside Germans." Their descent makes them a "state within the state" (Rühs, 1816).

The attack then became broader. "Christianity and the German people" supposedly formed a unity, leaving no place for Jews. The emancipation laws of 1869 and 1871 rested less on moral conviction or a changed understanding of Judaism than they did on ideas of → progress and political reason. They did not end the agitation, especially when bitterness after the crash of the exchange and the economic crisis raised the question of guilt, with the answer being found in "Jewish" → liberalism. A new factor came into the equation: Jewish politics; Jews became seen as opponents. The Talmud bears witness not merely to superstition and contempt for Christians, as in the Middle Ages, but to the enmity of the Jews against all other peoples (Rohling).

The step to popular hatred of the Jews had now been taken, and the new term "anti-Semitism," first used in 1879 by W. Marr, came into use. An "Anti-Semitic Catechism" listed the harmful activities of the Jews in the economy, the press, politics, and finance (T. Fritsch). Hatred of the Jews assumed the form of an → ideology. As a product of natural law, Jews could not be changed; they stood opposed not to Christianity but to Germanic culture. "Tough and powerful Judaism" was "Judaizing the society" and threatened a weakened Germany. The doctrine of racial inequality (A. Gobineau) made anti-Semitism a closed system of thought. Now there were either members or outcasts. Thus the Jewish question now became a question of race, custom, and culture (E. K. Dühring, 1881). The phrases "Jewish liberalism," "Jewish features," and the "inferior Jewish race" became a stock part of the vocabulary. Everything that might be held in common between Jew and Gentile was eliminated. Christ became an anti-Semitic Aryan, and the Bible was said to be a history of glorification of the Jews. The new religion was that of racial anti-Semitism. The Jews had become defenseless.

A parallel movement demanded that the Jews, "the masters of Germany," should be expelled from economic life and the press. The appeal at court, in the army, and among the nobility and students was always to "the German spirit" (A. Stöcker, 1879). With the argument that "the Jews are our misfortune," there developed a national hostility as a result of vehement antiliberalism (H. von Treitschke). Racialism was not yet common in these circles, for they demanded, "The Jews should become Germans" (von Treitschke). The reply that they already were (T. Mommsen) represented the voice of reason at this time. Resentment and the denial of social reality, however, fostered national visions of the future inspired by romantic dreams of the past and longings for it — for a settled social order, a national religion, and the simple life of the artisan and the worker on the land. As many writings of the period testify, these longings went hand in hand with violent revulsion to contemporary society. In this world of thought the Jews were the cause of everything hateful, the personification of the modernism that must be contested, of industrialism, high finance, and liberalism. The Jews "had enslaved Germany," planting their own banner in place of German individuality (H. S. Chamberlain). They had made it Jewish (P. de Lagarde). Their "alien Asiatic nature" was incompatible with Germany and Christianity.

Medieval hatred of the Jews still survived. It was now directed, not against their obduracy, but against their different spirit, which had robbed them of any awareness of the significance of the suffering Savior (Chamberlain). Jeremiah, who in despair sought a refuge in the desert (Jer. 9:2) to hide from his people, gave us the true picture of the Jew in the Bible that the Talmud had filled out (Chamberlain). The link between Judaism and Christianity finally snapped with the claim that the Jews did not adhere to the religion of the Bible. Their religion supposedly was made up of the → Mishnah, the Talmud, and philosophical teachings alien to the OT. "In the midst of a Christian world," it was argued, "they are Asiatic pagans." Their law and culture have the force of "atavism." "Forged by Talmudic training," their "racial pride" has grown. The two things have resulted in internationalism and the striving for world dominion; thus "either we include them, or we exclude them totally" (Lagarde).

The antithesis to assimilation is obvious. The Jews are unalterable, and full mingling is therefore impossible. Even if "spirit can conquer race" (Lagarde), and Germanness is not a matter of blood (Geblüt) but of temperament (Gemüt), this does not alter the total negation of the Jews. In their case blood and spirit become one and the same. The claim that the Jews were Judaizing the country adopted Marx's equation of Judaism with finance. It would have a future impact by separating the Jewish spirit from the Jews as people (W. Sombart). Anti-Semitism supposedly became a matter of reason, not emotion. Anti-Semites were not Jew haters (Lagarde). Anti-Semitism would last as long as the earth endures, but it did not have to be accompanied by hatred or scorn for the Jews (Sombart). The Jew as an abstraction of counterhumanity had become an integral part of a nation-redeeming ideology, a new religion. The Jew as the "agent of corruption" was the destroyer (Lagarde). Humanity in the traditional sense had lost its validity when confronted with the Jew and had to be overcome. Humanity, it was said, is our guilt, and individuality is our task. We reject the jelly of humanity as unpalatable along with the spirit of the century that is simply that of the liberal newspapers (Lagarde). Such statements were calculated to justify a policy that built on the theory of glorifying Aryans and demonizing cohumanity.

After surveying the whole range of anti-Jewish and anti-Semitic utterances, we can only conclude that the sense of humanity in the Christian West was poisoned by the demonized picture of the Jews. In every age the Jew as thus depicted was available as a scapegoat in every social, political, or economic crisis, no matter what experience should otherwise have taught.

Bibliography: W. BÖHLICH, ed., *Berliner Antisemitismusstreit* (Frankfurt, 1965) • H. S. CHAMBERLAIN, *Foundations of the Nineteenth Century* (2 vols.; 2d ed.; New York, 1977; orig. pub., 1899) • B. ELIAV, "Anti-Semitism," *EncJud* 3.87-160 (information on anti-Semitism in other countries, esp. eastern Europe) • T. FRITSCH, *Handbuch der Judenfrage* (Leipzig, 1944) expansion of 1887 "Antisemiten-Catechismus" • H. GRIEVE, *Geschichte des modernen Antisemitismus in Deutschland* (2d ed.; Darmstadt, 1988) • P. DE LAGARDE, *Deutsche Schriften* (4th ed.; Munich, 1940) • K. MARX, "On the Jewish Question" (1843), *Karl Marx, Frederick Engels: Collected Works* (trans. R. Dixon et al.; New York, 1975ff.) 3.146-74 • P. W. MASSING, *Rehearsal for Destruction: A Study of Political Anti-Semitism in Imperial Germany* (New York, 1949) • T. MOMMSEN, *Auch ein Wort über unser Judentum* (4th ed.; Berlin, 1880) • P. G. J. PULZER, *The Rise of Political Anti-Semitism in Germany and Austria* (New York, 1964) • K. H. RENGSTORF and S. VON KORTZFLEISCH, eds., *Kirche und Synagogue. Handbuch zur Geschichte von Christen und Juden* (2 vols.; Stuttgart, 1967-70) • M. SIMON, *Verus Israel: A Study of the Relations between Christians and Jews in the Roman Empire (135-425)* (Oxford, 1986) • W. SOMBART, *A New Social Philosophy* (Princeton, 1937); idem, *Die Zukunft der Juden* (Leipzig, 1912) • E. STERLING, *Judenhaß. Die Anfänge des politischen Antisemitismus in Deutschland, 1815-50* (Frankfurt, 1969) • F. STERN, *The Politics of Cultural Despair: A Study in the Rise of the Germanic Ideology* (Berkeley and Los Angeles, 1961) • H. VON TREITSCHKE, "Unsere Ansichten," *PrJ* (1879).

MARIANNE AWERBUCH

Anti-Trinitarianism

In church polemics all opponents of the → dogma of the Trinity may be called anti-Trinitarians. Usually, however, the term applies only to those movements at the time of the → Reformation that, in defense of

monotheism (→ God), declared the orthodox doctrine of the → Trinity to be contrary to Scripture and reason. Their grouping together in history should not cause us to overlook the fact that the 16th-century anti-Trinitarians belonged to various traditions. Along with the Anabaptists, we find especially those who were under the influence of → nominalism or → humanism. Substantive differences (there were modalists, subordinationists, and adoptionists) combined from the very first with persecutions to prevent any solid organization.

Espoused quietly by individual Anabaptists, anti-Trinitarian ideas spread in humanist circles in Upper Italy and Switzerland, especially after M. Servetus (ca. 1511-53) developed the first systematic criticism in his *Christianismi restitutio* (1553). F. Sozzini (Socinus; 1539-1604) founded an anti-Trinitarian church that embraced those of unitarian views in Transylvania, where they still survive, and in Poland, where a tolerant nobility granted refuge to those driven out of Italy. Sozzini supplied them with a common confession on the basis of a rational → biblicism. From the middle of the 17th century Socinianism in Poland suffered at the hands of the Counter-Reformation (→ Catholic Reform and Counterreformation), but its ideas had an impact through → Arminianism and → deism and helped to prepare the ground for the Enlightenment. The tradition of anti-Trinitarianism led to the formation of new churches from the end of the 18th century with the development of a nondogmatic Christianity in English and North American → Unitarianism.

Bibliography: G. A. BENRATH, "Antitrinitarier," *TRE* 3.168-74 • D. CANTIMORI, *Italian Heretics of the Sixteenth Century* (Cambridge, Mass., 1979) • R. DÁN and A. PIRNÁT, eds., *Antitrinitarianism in the Second Half of the Sixteenth Century* (Budapest, 1982) • E. M. WILBUR, *A Bibliography of the Pioneers of the Socinian-Unitarian Movement* (Rome, 1950); idem, *A History of Unitarianism* (2 vols.; repr., Boston, 1969) • P. WRZECIONKO, ed., *Reformation und Frühaufklärung in Polen. Studien über den Sozinianismus und seinen Einfluß auf dem westeuropäischen Denken im 17. Jahrhundert* (Göttingen, 1977).

GUNTHER WENZ

Anxiety

Anxiety is an emotion that functions on different levels. Any adequate definition must therefore take account of these levels, explaining and distinguishing them, and finally weaving them philosophically or theologically into an → anthropological whole. Concepts of anxiety depend on the interrelationship between these levels, even when they are viewed as a totality. The way of viewing the distinction between normal and pathological forms of anxiety also plays an important part in the construction of helpful concepts of anxiety. Should we regard → neurotic anxieties as extreme forms of normal anxiety, but psychotic anxieties as qualitatively different? Or is it more meaningful to consider further distinctions? Finally, we must distinguish between individual anxiety and group anxiety, partly so as to understand how collective anxiety affects individuals.

1. Physiologically, one may describe and measure the reactions of people to threatening external (social) and inner stimuli, though thus far it has not been possible to determine clearly the relation, independently of particular persons and situations, between such stimuli and the psychodynamic (personal-subjective) dimensions. There is undoubtedly a connection between what is experienced and the physiologically measurable hyperactivities or aversion structures of specific parts of the brain and other organs, which results in increased action of the heart, a rise in blood pressure, dilation of the pupils, and measurable effects on digestion, the skin, and the nervous system. But the findings of physiology, medical → psychology, and behavioral research regarding standard reactions, the learning and unlearning of anxiety (with reference to and in distinction from animals), and the mastering of one's inner life and environment are all partly contested and, in the eyes of critical observers, may be grouped in different schools. Finally, it is not clear how we can really control reactions in conflict or flight, evasive and defensive attitudes, or conversions from anxiety to psychic or somatic symptoms (phobias, compulsions) in individuals or groups. At this point different concepts of the ego are significant, a factor that emerges in discussions between neurophysiologists, psychologists, and philosophers.

2. If we ignore the older behaviorism, the experimental psychology of consciousness at the turn of the century, then we may say that psychodynamic models, especially psychoanalysis, offer the best hope of an integrated explanation of anxiety. But here too we find competing theories, with some interesting developments. Thus S. Freud (1856-1939), though he wanted to maintain a physiological model, began (1895) by finding the cause of anxiety (and the neurosis of anxiety) in an under-utilized and frustrated → libido. Later (1932), however, he reversed the relation, finding anxiety itself

the cause of repression. This was the result of his new concept of the → ego.

Anxiety is unmastered dependence. It may be real anxiety in face of the external world, involving something foreseeable or a present trauma. It may be the neurotic anxiety of the unconscious. Or it may be the anxiety of conscience, of the superego. Freud's differentiated theory is linked to his schema of desire and its opposite as emotions, and again it has physiological dimensions. Others (e.g., J. Cohen) developed it further. Also helpful and influential was F. Riemann's distinction of four basic forms of anxiety: (1) in schizoid personalities: fear of self-giving, of self-loss or dependence; (2) in depressive personalities: fear of self-becoming, isolation, or exposure; (3) in impulsive personalities: fear of change; and (4) in hysterical personalities: fear of the inevitable, the definitive, or loss of freedom. All anxiety belongs to one or another of these groups; it is a sign of sickness only when present to pathological excess.

3. How may these scientific and psychological findings be integrated with philosophy and theology? Certain philosophical classifications are close to those of behavioral research and overlap with those of → psychoanalysis, for example, the concept of anxiety as basic to existence (M. Heidegger), or of existential anxiety and meaninglessness (J.-P. Sartre), or of anxiety as related to → aggression, → death, and → freedom. Yet there is not any real overlapping, nor even any adequate mutual understanding, particularly because on all sides — most strongly that of theology — there is an obvious fear that the specific task and line of inquiry will be taken over and relativized.

4. → Theology should deal with anxiety, not so much in terms of individual authors and concepts (P. → Tillich [1886-1965] is rightly included), but in order to find help as it seeks to give aid and comfort in → pastoral care, → counseling, → preaching, and public service. If believers have done much harm with their individual anxieties and ideological rigidity, in every age they have also given much help in both life and death to a world afflicted with anxiety (→ Pastoral Care of the Dying). Their theories of anxiety have not really been trying to rival or to transcend secular theories, even though this might often seem to be so. Critically using all possible insights into the causes and functions of individual and collective anxiety, they must apply theology to the healing mission of all believing Jews and Christians. In this regard real anxiety needs sober analysis, pathological anxiety needs loving therapy, and anxiety in face of

God and the → future needs the preaching of → hope.

Bibliography: N. Birbaumer, "Angst," *Handbuch psychologischer Grundbegriffe* (ed. T. Herrmann; Munich, 1977) 27-38 • J. Cohen, *The Lineaments of Mind in Historical Perspective* (Oxford, 1980) • S. Freud, *Inhibition, Symptoms, and Anxiety* (New York, 1990) • D. Fröhlich, "Perspectiven der Angstforschung," *Psychologie der Motive* (ed. H. Thomae; Göttingen, 1983) 110-321 • A. Heigl-Evers and F. Heigl, "Trauma und Signal," *PPP* 2 (1982) 83-96 • S. Kierkegaard, *The Concept of Anxiety* (Princeton, 1980) • K. König, *Angst und Persönlichkeit* (Göttingen, 1981) • J. Moltmann, *Experiences of God* (Philadelphia, 1980) • F. Riemann, *Grundformen der Angst* (Munich, 1995) • P. Tillich, *The Courage to Be* (New Haven, 1952).

Dietrich Ritschl

Apartheid → Racism

Apocalypticism

1. Scope

1.1. *Definition*

Apocalypticism, which was forged within the Judeo-Christian tradition, comprises a literary genre, a set of eschatological concepts, and a world-renouncing lifestyle. Apocalypticism differs from → eschatology, → millenarianism, and → messianism. Eschatology reflects on the end of the old aeon, apocalypticism on the way to the new aeon. Millenarianism appeals to the vision of a millennium without → work or government, apocalypticism to an otherworldly lifestyle. Messianism counts on a personal redeemer, apocalypticism on an impersonal order. Apocalypticism is present when concepts of a radically new universal order are given literary form and expressed in → ethical daily life. It occurs also in religious traditions outside → Judaism (see 2) and Christianity (see 3).

1.2. *Other Religions*

1.2.1. *Hinduism*

In Hindu writings (the Mahābhārata and the Purāṇas) the world goes through four yugas (ages), during which conditions gradually worsen, including a decline in morals and a disruption of → nature. Kalkin, an avatar of Vishnu, comes at the end of the last age (the kali yuga), traverses the world on a white horse, destroys the wicked, and ushers in a new → golden age. After thousands of such processes (mahāyugas), the destruction of the cosmic system follows (→ Hinduism).

1.2.2. *Buddhism*

In → Buddhist writings (e.g., the Anagātavamsa) Buddha is asked about the → future. He replies that at the end of time the Maitreya (the coming fifth Buddha) will appear. A righteous world ruler will precede him and will join him with his household. The → state will then disappear. Those who want to be reborn at this time (→ Reincarnation) must merit it by good works.

1.2.3. *Zoroastrianism*

Zoroastrianism produced several apocalypses. These incorporated the expectation of a new end-time creation into a (Babylonian) doctrine of cosmic ages (12,000 years divided into four periods). The millennium of Zoroaster (9,000 to 9,999) will be followed by those of his sons Ushētar and Ushētarmāh (the 11th and 12th millennia). Then, at the end, the Saoshyant — another son of Zoroaster — will bring in a creation without sickness, old age, → death, enmity, injustice, tyranny, → heresy, or wickedness. The Druj (lying demon) will then be vanquished. Those who have been faithful to the true religion of Zoroaster will reap the benefits (→ Iranian Religions).

1.2.4. *Islam*

Islamic religion quickly integrated into the oral tradition of Muḥammad (ca. 570-632) the prophecy that at the end of the days, when the world is full of unrighteousness, a righteous teacher (Mahdi) will come from God and fill it with → righteousness again. No independent apocalyptic literature developed, but popular thinking concerned itself with the signs of the times, which led to *fitnah*, or internal conflict. Many Islamic revolutionaries have sought legitimation by appealing to this prophecy (→ Islam).

Bibliography: ASSR 53/1 (1982) several articles on apocalypticism • C. COLPE, "Eschatologie," *WM* 4.333-40 • H. DESROCHE, *The Sociology of Hope* (London, 1979) • D. HELLHOLM, *Apocalypticism in the Mediterranean World and the Near East* (Tübingen, 1983) • R. KLOPPENBORG, "The Place of Maitreya in Early and Theravāda Buddhism and the Conditions of Rebirth in His Time," *Proceedings of the 30th International Congress of Human Sciences in Asia and North Africa, South Asia* (Mexico City, 1982) 3.37-48 • A. A. SACHEDINA, *Islamic Messianism: The Idea of Mahdi in Twelver Shi'ism* (Albany, N.Y., 1981).

HANS G. KIPPENBERG

2. The OT and Early Judaism
2.1. *Extent and Origin*

The general concept of apocalypticism that has arisen in biblical scholarship during the last 150 years is connected with the discovery of a literary genre called apocalypse. Apocalyptic writings are those that resemble John's Revelation, or Apocalypse (from which the term derives). John's Apocalypse differs from other NT writings by its use of an ambiguous symbolic language that is filled with mythological allusions and that very dramatically depicts the imminent end of the world and its succeeding renewal. Extensive → visions and auditions form its basis. Daniel in the OT and various pseudepigrapha such as the Ethiopic *Enoch,* the Syriac *Apocalypse of Baruch,* 4 Ezra, and *Apocalypse of Abraham* belong to the same literary type. Related are the testaments of OT men of God, such as *Testaments of the Twelve Patriarchs, Testament of Abraham, Testament of Job, Jubilees,* and especially *Sibylline Oracles* from the writings of the Greek diaspora. Qumran includes works like the pseudo-Daniel fragments and *Melchizedek* (Cave 11). NT pseudepigrapha include *Apocalypse of Peter* and *Apocalypse of Paul,* as well as parts of *Hermas* and some works from → Nag Hammadi. This genre includes also some parts of biblical books, such as the Isaiah apocalypse (chaps. 24-27) and the Synoptic apocalypse in Mark 13 and parallels. Some exegetes (e.g., P. D. Hanson) go further and find apocalyptic writings in Joel, Proto- and Deutero-Zechariah, Ezekiel, and Trito-Isaiah.

All the apocalypses except Revelation are pseudepigraphic, that is, fictitiously ascribed to an early author (cf. Deuteronomy and Ecclesiastes), which makes possible the presentation of a good deal of the historical material in the form of (fulfilled) prophecy. But this may not be the only reason for ascribing the works to others. The reasons for pseudonymity have been much discussed, but no consensus has been reached. Did the works come from specific synagogues that claimed Enoch, Daniel, or a similar hero as their patron saint? Or did the author view himself as the "extended personality" of such a man of God?

Most of these writings lay claim to a canonical status that is accepted in part in → Qumran (Ethiopic *Enoch* and *Jubilees*) and the NT (see Jude 14). The rabbis, however, rejected all these works, perhaps because of their importance in the two revolts against Rome, which should not be repeated, perhaps also in opposition to Christianity. They did so with such rigor that none of the works has survived within → Judaism. The church also held aloof from this type of literature. Fortunately, part of it was preserved in the Eastern churches, especially in Ethiopia.

Such works appeared mainly between the third century B.C. and the third century A.D. This has led to the view that a movement of apocalypticism formed the soil for the writings in this period, and that they came from circles that rejected the dominant trends of the Hasmonean and Herodian eras and of the early rabbis (→ New Testament Era, History of). With regard to their setting, contradictory theories have been advanced, since the writings themselves offer no sure clues. Some scholars trace apocalypticism back to a branch of the → Pharisees, others to their opponents. Or were the authors more often simply the silent minority? Others suggest that → scribes concerned about Wisdom were their authors. Besides the thesis of a sectarian conventicle opposed to the ruling → theocracy (O. Plöger and P. D. Hanson), there is the opposite thesis of a priestly origin (J. C. H. Lebram).

The tendency today is to ascribe apocalypticism to the Hasideans and Essenes and their followers, although the Qumran Essenes were firmly opposed to specific apocalyptic ideas. Since the sociological question is unclear for the OT time period, it is hard to decide how far → John the Baptist, → Jesus, and the → primitive Christian community adopted apocalyptic presuppositions from their background.

2.2. Main Ideas

In contrast to what the current use of the adjective "apocalyptic" might suggest, no writer of apocalypses merely proclaims pessimistically the imminent destruction of the world. These writings carry the sense of being at the beginning of the end time, which will bring an unprecedented collapse of human government and the drama of cosmic overthrow. The authors perceive in the previous course of history the reason for the woes of the end time. Above all, however, they are convinced that a new creation will follow. To convey this message they use a series of concepts that do not occur in the OT but that are found in the NT. The relation between Jesus and, on the one hand, primitive Christianity and, on the other, late Israelite apocalypticism has thus become a subject of considerable discussion, especially since E. Käsemann in 1970 made the provocative statement that apocalypticism is "the mother of all Christian theology." The following subsections summarize the essential concerns of apocalypticism.

2.2.1. Creation and Human Power

Unlike most of the OT books, apocalypses postulate an ongoing political history that is directed by non-Israelite powers right up to the Roman emperors and that falls victim to increasing degeneracy. This teaching leads to the doctrine of four kingdoms, namely, that by divine foreordination (after the end of an independent → monarchy in Israel), four empires successively rule humanity, beginning with the Assyrian (1 Enoch 89) or Babylonian (Daniel 2) and ending with the Hellenistic (Daniel) or Roman (4 Ezra and NT). From the last kingdom will come a final ruler as → antichrist, and he will surpass all his predecessors in arrogance and wickedness (Dan. 7:24-26; 8:9-12; 11:21-35; etc.). The relation between worldly rule and divine rule is not uniformly assessed. It vacillates between the attributing of imperial government to divine appointment (Dan. 2:37-38) and a sharp → dualism (Revelation 13).

2.2.2. The Community of the Righteous

This community is in the minority. It is always in danger, standing under the threat of death because of its confession (Daniel 3; 6; 11:33). It represents the true people of the → covenant, which is no longer the same as visible → Israel but consists solely of the wise and the righteous. Apocalypses are written to encourage the members of this community to faithfulness and patience under the tribulations of the end time. The unspeakable → sufferings show that the coming eschatological change is near and that immediate conversion is necessary for all who are still

wavering. One explanation of the apostasy of the majority is the anthropological belief that there is an evil seed in the race that only a few resist (4 Ezra).

2.2.3. Numbers

The times are set numerically from creation. In these calculations the number 7 is predominant (Dan. 9:24-27; 1 Enoch 89; 91:11-17; 93:1-10; Revelation 6; 8; 16), but mysterious numbers like 2,300, 1,290, and 1,335 also play a role (Dan. 8:14; 12:11-12; cf. Rev. 11:3). Such numbers show that God is in control of the times. This line of thought has brought the charge of determinism against the apocalyptic view of history. It must be stressed, however, that the freedom of individual decision is never questioned.

2.2.4. Angels and Demons

The course of history depends not merely on the (saving) providence of God and (mostly negative) historical personages. The real driving forces belong to a metahistory that points to a suprahistory alongside the real foreground history. This suprahistory is directed by → angels and demons. These groups stand in a hierarchical relation to their heads, the archangels and the → devil (Belial, Satan; see 1 Enoch 6–36).

2.2.5. The Eschatological Turning Point

The critical moment comes with a sudden divine intervention that brings earthly evil to an inexorable end, along with the whole process of human action and rule, thus causing → sin to vanish (Dan. 9:24). There follows the → resurrection of the righteous, or of exemplary righteous and sinners, or of all the dead; next, at a cosmic forum (→ Last Judgment), occurs a final judgment according to works. The wicked will be condemned to eternal flames, but the justified will be transfigured and will shine like the stars of heaven (12:1-3). The justified will gain a share in the → kingdom of God, which now breaks into the earthly sphere (2:44) and which is understood as the new aeon or the aeon of aeons (7:18 etc.). According to a hermeneutical principle that equates the first time with the last, → paradise will then return. Indeed future → salvation will far surpass it in good things. In particular, it will bring about a dwelling of God among his people.

2.3. The Background in Prophecy or Wisdom

OT scholars are not sure where to find the background of apocalypticism in the tradition. Its works can hardly go back to the → law, but some like to trace them back to the early stories of Genesis or even more so to the prophetic writings. The writers of apocalyptic, however, do not see themselves as prophets but rank themselves among the wise (Dan. 2:12, 18, 48; cf. maśkîlîm in 12:3) or claim to be scribes (sofer/safar, 1 Enoch 12:3-4; 15:1; 92:1; 4 Ezra

40:50). Taking up a suggestion of G. Hölscher, G. von Rad has thus ruled out an origin in prophecy as "impossible" and has found in apocalypticism an encyclopedic concern of Wisdom that develops into a hybrid, universal gnosis. P. von der Osten-Sacken has opposed this view. American scholarship defends a prophetic derivation. The main argument against von Rad is that in the preapocalyptic period the Wisdom books up to Sirach show no interest in eschatology.

2.4. *The Historical Problem*

From the time of the *Erläuterungen zum Neuen Testament aus einer neu eröffneten morgenländischen Quelle* (1775) by J. G. → Herder (1744-1803), the suspicion has been stubbornly present, and has prevailed from time to time in exegesis (cf. the → history-of-religions school), that apocalypticism as a literary and intellectual phenomenon has its roots in Zoroastrianism (→ Iranian Religions). According to Greek accounts, the belief in an eschatological resurrection of the dead is in fact attested there as early as the fourth century B.C. The idea of four successive world empires also seems to be native to Iran (J. W. Swain). Although apocalypses were preserved in Iran only since the Middle Ages, some of them, like the *Bahman-Yasht* or the *Oracles of Hystaspes*, might go back to the early Hellenistic period (G. Widengren). The uncertainty surrounding the sources prevents us from arriving at any definitive conclusions.

3. The NT

One of the debated themes in modern exegesis is the question of the extent of apocalypticism in the NT. Because of gaps in our knowledge of the sources, it is still unclear what ought to be called apocalyptic in the strict sense in the primitive Christian period. Some ideas, like expectation of the resurrection, the last judgment, and the concept of the two aeons, might well have arisen in apocalyptic circles, but they have obviously undergone much broader development. In the scholarly literature the question of apocalyptic influence on the → Synoptic tradition and → Paul figures prominently. The following sections mention only some of the points discussed.

3.1. *John the Baptist*

At the beginning of the NT John the Baptist manifests a central apocalyptic concern with his preaching of repentance and imminent judgment. With his baptism for remission of sins, however, he introduces a motif that is alien to any known apocalypses.

3.2. *Jesus*

It is hard to define the relation of Jesus to apocalypticism, since decisions will vary according to opinions concerning the authenticity of his sayings in the Synoptics. Yet we can hardly deny that he proclaimed an imminent invasion of this world by the kingdom of God, along with the resurrection of the dead and separation at the last judgment (Mark 1:15). But this teaching implies apocalypticism, for rabbinic Judaism thought that God's royal dominion was present already in the law. The parables of the *basileia* are also relevant in this connection (cf. the parables of growth in 4 Ezra 4:27-32). The same applies to the vision of Satan fallen from heaven (Luke 10:18). This passage shows that Jesus views his own age as the final period of this aeon. He thus ascribes to his own person a decisive function that goes beyond anything that other apocalyptists claim (in spite of *1 Enoch* 71, where → Enoch is the Son of Man). Confession of him today will decide how the angels act at the judgment (Luke 12:8). Jesus can anticipate by his word (Mark 2:5) the eschatological forgiveness of sins (Dan. 9:24). He can purify the → temple, an action that apocalyptists (*1 Enoch* 90:28-29) regard as inappropriate. When he casts out demons, it may be seen that the kingdom of God is present already (Matt. 12:28-29). Like the apocalyptists, Jesus pays heed to the signs of the times (Luke 21:25-28); unlike them, however, he forbids calculation (Luke 17:20).

3.3. *The Evangelists*

The Evangelists have as a basis not only the teaching of Jesus, which is characterized by comparison and contrast with apocalypticism, but also the experience of Jesus' violent end on the → cross and the succeeding → Easter event, which may be understood against the background of apocalyptic ideas of resurrection. (The resurrection of an individual within the present aeon, however, cannot be integrated into apocalypticism.) Since the end of the earthly Jesus does not coincide with the incursion of the kingdom of God, as the message of Jesus had led his disciples to expect, there now must be some explanation of the time that has suddenly opened up between Easter and the end of the world. How else can this be construed but apocalyptically? This leads the different Evangelists to inject different apocalyptic motifs into their accounts.

For *Mark*, Jesus came when the time that God had predetermined was fulfilled (1:14-15). This coming thus began the messianic age, which (according to later apocalyptic and rabbinic teaching) belongs to the end of this aeon and means a restoration of the kingdom of → David for Israel (11:9-10). There then ensues the rule of the Son of Man in a transformed aeon. After the resurrection Jesus is expected at the → parousia with a very different power from previously (14:62). An eschatological sketch is given of the intervening gloomy time (chap. 13).

Matthew draws the lines even more strongly. First there is the fulfilling of the times on the basis of the periods of sevens (1:2-17), then the return of Jesus as Son of Man and World Judge (25:31-46). *Luke* has a similar depiction in 21:25-38. For *John,* the phrase "Son of Man" on the lips of Jesus refers always to the future form of his person after its glorifying through the cross and resurrection, but the last judgment and the aeonic change are less prominent. The Prologue perhaps represents a development of the apocalyptic → myth of Wisdom (= Logos), which sought a home on earth but did not find it even in Israel (*1 Enoch* 42, contra Sirach 24), finding it finally by means of the → incarnation.

3.4. *Paul*

Paul avoids such concepts as "kingdom of God" and "Son of Man" and extols Jesus Christ with the non-apocalyptic title "Kyrios" (→ Christological Titles). Yet he sets the Christ-event in a historical frame of an apocalyptic type. This aeon is wicked (Gal. 1:4). With the coming of Jesus after a period fixed by God (4:4), the end time dawns (1 Cor. 10:11). We may now expect the crushing of Satan, the parousia of Christ in a great end-time drama, and the judgment of fire (1 Thess. 4:14-15; 2 Thess. 1:5-10; Rom. 16:20; 1 Cor. 3:13, 15). Paul goes beyond pre-Christian apocalypticism when he regards the community as the beginning of the future aeon, the eschatological temple (2 Cor. 6:16), and the site of the new creation (2 Cor. 5:17; Rom. 5:12-14).

For the rest of the present aeon, Jesus as the Kyrios who frees us for the obedience of faith terminates the intervening period of the dominion of the law over Israel (Rom. 5:20; 10:4). This is an original Pauline conception that seems to have been evoked by the distinctive revelation of Christ to him on the Damascus road, which Acts 9, 22, and 26 depict in apocalyptic colors. It goes beyond apocalypticism to the extent that it involves the disclosure of a person, not a new teaching. Similarly transcended is the historical background of Paul's doctrine of justification by faith. The establishment of eternal righteousness is a decisive eschatological act that possibly in Dan. 9:24-27 and in the images of *1 Enoch* 48:6-7; 49:2; 60:2 is related to the coming of the Son of Man (P. Stuhlmacher). Yet the idea of a justification of the wicked and its coupling with the crucifixion of Jesus go far beyond any literary models.

3.5. *Revelation*

This work manifests a broad influx not merely of apocalyptic ideas but of apocalyptic forms with heavenly-earthly dialogues, visions, and mythological metaphors. It differs from earlier and laters works in the same genre by its renunciation of pseudo-nymity. Nor is there any depiction of earlier history. With mythical colors Revelation gives successive depictions of the final drama of the history of this aeon up to the resurrection, the → Jerusalem that comes down from heaven, and the renewal of the world.

Other Christian authors followed in the same tracks. There thus arose a Christian apocalypticism (→ Pseudepigrapha), of which the *Apocalypse of Peter* is the first example. How close Christian circles came to later Israelite apocalypticism, and how much they even identified themselves with it, may be seen from the fact that they alone preserved the works of the latter. Furthermore, it is often unclear whether the authors or redactors of these works are Christians or Jews (note *Sibylline Oracles, Testaments of the Twelve Patriarchs,* and *Apocalypse of Abraham*). Christian apocalypses typically depict the destruction of the world and the coming promised land in wilder colors than any Israelite or Jewish apocalypticism, which may be because they came from marginal social groups (e.g., *Apocalypse of Paul* 22ff.).

Bibliography: General: J. J. COLLINS, ed., *Apocalypse: The Morphology of a Genre* (Missoula, Mont., 1979) • P. D. HANSON, "Apocalypticism," *IDBSup* 28-34 • P. D. HANSON, A. K. GRAYSON, J. J. COLLINS, and A. Y. COLLINS, "Apocalypses and Apocalypticism," *ABD* 1.229-92 • D. HELLHOLM, ed., *Apocalypticism in the Mediterranean World and the Near East* (2d ed.; Tübingen, 1989) • K. KOCH, *The Rediscovery of Apocalyptic* (London, 1972) bibliography • K. KOCH and J. M. SCHMIDT, eds., *Apokalyptik* (Darmstadt, 1982) bibliography • G. LANCZKOWSKI, J. LEBRAM, K. MÜLLER, and A. STROBEL, "Apokalyptik / Apokalypsen I-IV," *TRE* 3.189-257 (bibliography) • H. H. ROWLEY, *The Relevance of Apocalyptic* (3d ed.; London, 1963) • J. M. SCHMIDT, *Die jüdische Apokalyptik* (2d ed.; Neukirchen, 1976) • W. SCHMITHALS, *The Apocalyptic Movement* (Nashville, 1975) • G. WIDENGREN, *Iranische Geisteswelt* (Gütersloh, 1961) texts.

OT: J. H. CHARLESWORTH, *The OT Pseudepigrapha,* vol. 1, *Apocalyptic Literature and Testaments* (Garden City, N.Y., 1983) texts • J. J. COLLINS, *The Apocalyptic Imagination* (New York, 1984) • S. K. EDDY, *The King Is Dead: Studies in the Near Eastern Resistance to Hellenism* (Lincoln, Nebr., 1961) • P. D. HANSON, *The Dawn of Apocalyptic* (Philadelphia, 1975) • K. KOCH, " 'Adam, was hast du getan?' Erkenntnis und Fall in den zwischentestamentlichen Literatur," *Glaube und Toleranz* (ed. T. Rendtorff; Gütersloh, 1982) 211-42; idem, "Spätisraelitisches Geschichtsdenken am Beispiel des Buches Daniel," *HZ* 193 (1961) 1-32 • J. T. MILIK, *The Books of Enoch: Aramaic Fragments of Qumrân Cave 4*

(Oxford, 1976) • G. W. E. NICKELSBURG, *Jewish Literature between the Bible and the Mishnah* (Philadelphia, 1981) • P. VON DER OSTEN-SACKEN, *Die Apokalyptik in ihrem Verhältnis zu Prophetie und Weisheit* (Munich, 1969) • O. PLÖGER, *Theocracy and Eschatology* (Oxford, 1968) • G. VON RAD, *OT Theology* (vol. 2; Edinburgh, 1965) • D. RÖSSLER, *Gesetz und Geschichte* (Neukirchen, 1960) • D. S. RUSSELL, *The Method and Message of Jewish Apocalyptic, 200 B.C.–A.D. 100* (London, 1964; repr., 1980) • J. SCHREINER, *Alttestamentlich-jüdische Apokalyptik* (Munich, 1969) • J. W. SWAIN, "The Theory of the Four Monarchies: Opposition History and the Roman Empire," *CP* 35 (1940) 1-21 • P. VOLZ, *Die Eschatologie der jüdischen Gemeinde im neutestamentlichen Zeitalter* (2d ed.; Hildesheim, 1966).

NT: J. BAUMGARTEN, *Paulus und die Apokalyptik* (Neukirchen, 1975) • R. BULTMANN, *The Presence of Eternity: History and Eschatology* (New York, 1957) • W. HARNISCH, *Verhängnis und Verheißung der Geschichte. Untersuchungen zum Zeit- und Geschichtsverständnis im 4. Buch Esra und in der syrischen Baruchapokalypse* (Göttingen, 1969) • E. KÄSEMANN, "The Beginnings of Christian Theology," *NT Questions of Today* (Philadelphia, 1969) 82-107 • U. LUZ, *Das Geschichtsverständnis des Paulus* (Munich, 1968) • N. PERRIN, *Rediscovering the Teaching of Jesus* (London, 1967) • P. VIELHAUER, "Apocalyptic in Early Christianity: Introduction," *NT Apocrypha* (vol. 2; ed. E. Hennecke and W. Schneemelcher; Philadelphia, 1966) 608-42.

KLAUS KOCH

4. In Church History

4.1. *Historical Significance*

In church history apocalypticism usually expressed the → hope of movements of social protest or of persecuted religious → minorities. Faced with the threat of disintegration, Protestant → orthodoxy (§§1-2) also saw its time in apocalyptic terms. Only at the end of the confessional wars did apocalypticism take the weaker form of an immanent hope of better times in the future (P. J. Spener). During the → Enlightenment, rational criticism of a futurist cosmic eschatology reduced apocalypticism to a phenomenon found only among marginal groups (→ Adventists; Jehovah's Witnesses; Pentecostal Churches). Because of their social basis, apocalyptic movements usually went hand in hand with militant anticlericalism. They often accused tyrannical authorities of being the beast of Revelation. They were equally critical of the feudal social order. Very often, therefore, these visions include the ideas of the destruction of the ungodly, the abolition of private property, and a 1,000-year reign of peace (→ Millenarianism) with

no class distinctions. In connection with anticlericalism we find a disparagement of Scripture and the → sacraments, the belief in new direct revelations, and the leadership claims of inspired prophets and prophetesses who justify their special position by identification with eschatological roles (→ Elijah; Enoch).

4.2. *The Middle Ages*

The triumph of the → church over paganism in the 4th century dampened the apocalyptic mood of early Christianity, which had reached its climax in → Montanism. Under the influence of → Augustine (354-430), who rejected belief in a 1,000-year reign as a "carnal error," the early Middle Ages repudiated eschatological interpretations of the present. Only in the 12th century, with the Investiture Controversy, did apocalyptic thinking enjoy a new upsurge. In particular, the prophetic vision of the Calabrian abbot Joachim of Fiore (ca. 1135-1202) made a strong impact on later heretical apocalyptic movements. Joachim differentiated three stages in history: (1) the age of the Father under the → law (§1), in which the order of the married rules; (2) the epoch of the Son under the → gospel, in which the order of the → priests oversees the discipline of God's people; and (3) the coming age of the Holy Spirit, in which monks offer the model of a brotherly spirit. The Holy Spirit will imprint an everlasting gospel on the hearts of believers so that they no longer need the direct guidance of the clergy. During the transition from the second age to the third (ca. 1260), the → antichrist will try in vain to block the new order by persecuting the saints.

This optimistic vision of an egalitarian, Spirit-filled → society brought a revolutionary element into the political thinking of the later Middle Ages. The radical spiritual wing of the → Franciscans developed this aspect further in its fight against the papacy. Joachim's ideas also influenced such movements of revolt as those of the Apostolici (Fra Dolcino [d. 1307]) and the → Hussites. The Great Schism (1378-1417), the decline of the papacy, and the failure of the conciliar movement strengthened end-time expectations in the 14th and 15th centuries (→ Heresies and Schisms).

4.3. *The Reformation*

After 1518, when he came to view the → pope as the → antichrist, M. → Luther lived in constant expectation of the last day. Before the end, however, he counted on a collapse of Rome and an extensive propagation of the gospel newly discovered by him. Yet he never expected the final triumph of the → Reformation. He feared that with the unmasking of antichrist, ungodliness would reach a peak in the world with the triumph of Epicureans and atheists

(WA 10/1/2.93-120). He did not think that the Book of Revelation should be interpreted literally and rejected calculations based on it. He also rejected new direct revelations and did not expect that the saints would enjoy an earthly reign of peace.

Apocalyptic expectations were constitutive for the left wing of the Reformation, especially for militant groups among the → Anabaptists. These groups focused on the gathering of a pure church whose outward sign was adult → baptism. With this pure church would come the destruction of the ungodly and a reign of peace in which believers would be free from the fear of tyranny and exploitation. Reception of the Spirit as the fruit of a testing period would make believers into sinless saints who could receive illumination directly. Under the pressure of the imminent → Peasants' War, Thomas Müntzer (ca. 1489-1525) had already developed various important aspects of this apocalypticism. His follower Hans Hut (ca. 1490-1527; → Hutterites) linked these ideas to German Anabaptism. The underground communities founded by him quickly fell apart after the death of their leader, but Melchior Hoffmann (ca. 1500-ca. 1543) achieved a new, demagogic fusion of apocalypticism, spiritualism, and Anabaptism. Under the influence of the so-called Strasbourg prophets, Hoffmann changed his original peaceful apocalypticism into a militant ideology. The authorities were to extirpate the established clergy and thus prepare the world for the coming of the Lord in 1533 (→ Parousia).

Favored by severe economic crises, the Melchiorites flourished in Strasbourg, East Friesland, and Holland. When the authorities would not accept the role of apocalyptic avengers and Hoffmann himself was imprisoned, the Melchiorite movement split into a pacifist wing and a revolutionary wing. The latter, under the leadership of John Mathys (d. 1534) and John of Leiden (ca. 1509-36), seized power in Münster in 1534. The introduction of polygamy and common ownership (→ Community of Goods), and especially the collapse of this Anabaptist kingdom in 1535, discredited the militant form of apocalypticism during the centuries that followed.

4.4. The Confessional Age and Pietism
The Thirty Years' War cast such gloom on the historical sense of Lutheran orthodoxy that an imminent end of the world came to be expected without preceding improvement. This was in contrast to the apocalypticism of the revolutionary Independent Puritans in England, who in the Civil War period (1642-51) counted on a "latter-day glory" before the evening of the world. In Lutheranism itself P. J. Spener (1635-1705) in his *Pia desideria* (Pious

desires; 1675) was the first to break with historical pessimism (→ Theology of History). On the basis of NT promises that had not yet been fulfilled, he foretold the fall of the papal antichrist, purer doctrine among Protestant Christians, and the → conversion (§1) of Jews and pagans (→ Gentiles, Gentile Christianity). Separatist → Pietism returned to a belief in the Millennium and a coming universal reconciliation (→ Apocatastasis). The theology of J. A. Bengel (1687-1752) made a fresh attempt to view all world history in the light of Revelation, with the date of Christ's second coming being fixed at 1836. Apocalyptic ideas of history revived again in the age of the French Revolution and the various spiritual awakenings (→ Revivals). J. H. Jung-Stilling (1740-1817) thought he discerned the onset of messianic troubles in the hostile religious policy of the Jacobins and the destruction of the Holy Roman Empire by Napoleon (1803-6; → Antichrist).

Bibliography: B. W. BALL, *A Great Expectation: Eschatological Thought in English Protestantism to 1660* (Leiden, 1975) • N. R. C. COHN, *The Pursuit of the Millennium* (2d ed.; London, 1970) • K. DEPPERMANN, *Melchior Hoffman: Social Unrest and Apocalyptic Visions in the Age of Reformation* (Edinburgh, 1987) • H. U. HOFMANN, *Luther und die Johannes-Apokalypse* (Tübingen, 1982) • R. A. KNOX, *Enthusiasm: A Chapter in the History of Religion* (5th ed.; Oxford, 1961) • B. McGINN, *Visions of the End* (New York, 1979) • G. MAIER, *Die Johannesoffenbarung und die Kirche* (Tübingen, 1981) • G. MÄLZER, *Johann Albrecht Bengel. Leben und Werk* (Stuttgart, 1970) • M. REEVES, *The Influence of Prophecy in the Later Middle Ages* (Oxford, 1969) • K. H. SCHWARTE, R. KONRAD, and G. SEEBASS, "Apokalyptik / Apokalypsen V-VII," *TRE* 3.257-89 (bibliography) • B. TÖPFER, *Das kommende Reich des Friedens* (Berlin, 1964) • J. WALLMANN, *Philipp Jakob Spener und die Anfänge des Pietismus* (2d ed.; Tübingen, 1986).

KLAUS DEPPERMANN†

4.5. North America
The Puritans of the Massachusetts Bay Colony shared the apocalyptic expectations that pervaded English Puritanism, especially during the English Civil War and the Commonwealth. Increase Mather, his son Cotton Mather, and other New England divines immersed themselves in eschatology, sometimes anticipating that the New Jerusalem (Rev. 21:2) would arise in America. During the Great Awakening of the 1740s, Jonathan → Edwards (1703-58) speculated that the revivals sweeping America heralded the onset of the Millennium.

The American Revolution and the emergence of

an independent United States gave rise to a secularized apocalypticism, promulgated by Timothy Dwight and others, in which the new nation would lead the world toward a millennial state. In various guises, this civic millennialism would profoundly shape American thought for the next two centuries. Meanwhile, in the 1830s, a self-taught itinerant of New York State, William Miller (1782-1849), on the basis of his reading of the Book of Daniel, began to preach the second coming of Christ "about the year 1843." Other Millerites set a precise date: October 22, 1844.

The Millerite fiasco discredited date-setting, creating a receptive climate for the dispensational teachings of the Englishman J. N. Darby (1800-1882), a founder of the Plymouth Brethren. Darby viewed the present "church age" as devoid of prophetic significance except for the "signs of the times" portending the approaching end. The church age, Darby taught, will end with the rapture, when true believers will meet Christ in the air, followed by the antichrist's seven-year rule (i.e., the tribulation), the second coming and the battle of Armageddon, Jesus Christ's 1,000-year earthly reign ("the kingdom age"), and the last judgment. C. I. Scofield (1843-1921) embedded Darby's dispensationalism in his vastly influential *Scofield Reference Bible,* first published in 1909. Lutheran and Reformed groups remained firmly amillennial, liberal Protestant denominations and Social Gospel advocates embraced a secularized and reformist postmillennialism, and premillennialism flourished among evangelical, fundamentalist, and Pentecostal groups.

After World War II itinerant evangelists, radio and television preachers, and scores of paperback writers offered variants of Darby's scheme. Hal Lindsey's *Late Great Planet Earth* (1970), a popularization of dispensationalism, outsold all other nonfiction books published in the United States in the 1970s. Using biblical prophecy to find meaning and order in history, popularizers found a place in their end-time scenarios for the atomic bomb, the Soviet Union, the emergence of Israel in 1948, the European Common Market, the rise of multinational and computerized economic order (foretold, they taught, in Rev. 13:16-18), and the environmental crisis. All these were seen as signs of the approaching end. As the 20th century closes, apocalypticism remains vigorously alive in American popular religion.

Bibliography: P. BOYER, *When Time Shall Be No More: Prophecy Belief in Modern American Culture* (Cambridge, Mass., 1992).

PAUL BOYER

Apocatastasis

The term "apocatastasis" (Greek for "restitution, recovery"; = Lat. *restitutio,* the restoration of all things, universal reconciliation) was coined in ancient → philosophy. It occurs in the NT only in Acts 3:21, and there not in a technical sense. Church tradition quickly adopted it to sum up the thrust of such NT passages as Col. 1:20; 1 Cor. 15:21-28; Rom. 5:18; 11:32, namely, that the saving will of God, eschatologically realized in Jesus Christ, will finally reach even the last of sinners. All will be → reconciled; all will be saved. When developed as a doctrine of universal reconciliation, apocatastasis was soon contested, and the → teaching office of the church expressly rejected it in view of what the NT has to say about the twofold outcome of salvation history (Council of Constantinople [553]). Yet the idea was never forgotten, and it found supporters in every age. Among the Fathers we may mention → Origen (d. ca. 254), Gregory of Nazianzus (d. 389/90), and Gregory of Nyssa (d. ca. 395; → Church Fathers; Origenism). Through such thinkers it found an echo in Eastern orthodoxy both among great theologians and in → popular religion.

Apocatastasis was strongly represented among supporters of the left wing of the → Reformation (§1.6; H. Denck and the → Anabaptists). It may be found especially in → Pietism (J. A. Bengel and F. C. Oetinger). Very impressive is the plea for it made by the two Blumhardts. J. C. Blumhardt (1805-80), who accepted the idea only after resolving vexing inner conflicts, found in it an implication of the cross: "Good Friday proclaims a general pardon to the whole world" (→ Theologia crucis). For his son C. F. Blumhardt (1842-1919), apocatastasis is the basic accent of the whole → gospel: "To teach a hell in which God has nothing more to say is to negate the whole gospel." Both emphasized the social implication of the gospel (cf. the → Social Gospel of W. → Rauschenbusch in America). Apocatastasis offers a prospect of → hope for the world. In this sense it has been at work as an eschatological and social motif in modern theology. It found a warm supporter in E. Staehelin (1889-1980). Karl → Barth (1886-1968) also reflected on it with considerable sympathy, although without making it into a theory of universal salvation, arguing that we cannot set limits either for God's → love or for his → freedom.

"The person who does not believe [apocatastasis] is an ox, but the person who teaches it is an ass." This saying of the Pietist C. G. Barth (1799-1862) is not a superficial bon mot but a wise commentary. The NT carries two accents. The one is on judgment, on the possibility of damnation, on a twofold outcome. The other is on God's transcendent love. We cannot combine the two under a common denominator in a single doctrine, nor can we slight either one. We do not control the divine economy, neither should we stabilize the tension. In the light of the deeds, → passion, and → resurrection of Jesus Christ, the last word of the gospel, which contains both a Yes and a No, is an unequivocal Yes.

Bibliography: K. BARTH, *CD* II/2 • F. BURI, J. M. LOCH-MAN, and H. OTT, *Dogmatik im Dialog* (vol. 1; Güters-loh, 1973) • H. CHADWICK, "Origin, Celsus, and the Resurrection of the Body," *HTR* 41 (1948) 83-102 • E. DEÁK, *Apokatastasis: The Problem of Universal Salva-tion in Twentieth Century Theology* (North York and Don Mills, Ont., 1979) • G. MÜLLER, *Apokatastasis pan-ton: A Bibliography* (Basel, 1969) • J. A. T. ROBINSON, *In the End, God* (London, 1950) • E. STAEHELIN, *Die Wiederbringung aller Dinge* (Basel, 1960) • A. J. VISSER, "A Bird's-Eye View of Ancient Christian Eschatology," *Numen* 14 (1967) 4-22.

JAN MILIČ LOCHMAN

Apocrypha

1. OT Apocrypha

1.1. *Concept*

In common parlance, the term "Apocrypha" is used for the books or parts of books that appear in the Alexandrian canon of the LXX translation but are not found in the Masoretic canon. On the basis of the former tradition the → Roman Catholic Church recognized these books as canonical from the Third Council of Carthage (397) and today ranks them as deuterocanonical. The designation of these books as Apocrypha in the churches of the → Reformation goes back to 1520 to Carlstadt (ca. 1480-1541). When M. → Luther included the books (apart from 1 Es-dras, 3 Maccabees, and the Prayer of Manasseh) in the first full edition of his translation of the Bible in 1534, he added the explanation that, although he did not regard them as equal to Scripture, they were still books that it was good and profitable to read. The original meaning of the term (from Gk. *apokryptō,* "hide"; *apokryphos,* "hidden") is debated. The prob-able reference is to secret writings that were meant only for the wise (cf. 4 Ezra 14:45-47 and the → pseudepigrapha). Only later did the word take on the connotation of what is spurious or false.

1.2. *Form*

Essentially the Apocrypha embraces the same literary genres as the canonical writings, namely, narrative or history, proverbial wisdom, and poetry. The dif-ference does not lie in the introduction of new forms but in the handling of the old. The boundary be-tween Palestinian works that were originally written in Hebrew or Aramaic and Hellenistic works that were originally written in Greek is unclear at some points.

1.3. *Contents*

1.3.1. *First Esdras*

This book (= Vg 3 Esdras) contains parts of 2 Chronicles, Ezra, and Nehemiah, along with some independent material originally written in Greek, namely, an account of the contest that leads to the exaltation of Zerubbabel by Darius and the end of the exile (3:1–5:6). The main differences from the canonical tradition are (1) that by putting Ezra 2:1–4:5 after 4:24, the first return under Zerubbabel comes in the time of Darius I (king 521-485 B.C.) and (2) that the proclamation of the → law by Nehemiah (Neh. 7:73–8:13) comes directly after Ezra's restoration (Ezra 7–10). The purpose of the compilation is the definitive establishment of the cultus at Jerusalem; it was begun under Josiah and completed under Ezra.

1.3.2. *First Maccabees*

This work is the Greek version of a lost Hebrew or Aramaic original. It tells the story of the Seleucid persecutions under Antiochus IV Epiphanes (175-164 B.C.) and his successors, and of the resistance of the loyal Maccabees and their supporters from the accession of Antiochus in 175 to the high priesthood of John Hyrcanus under Antiochus VII (138-129 B.C.) around 134 B.C. The introductory reminder of Alexander the Great and the strife between his successors (1:1-9) set the story under the concept of the four empires of Daniel. The depiction follows OT models but with more emphasis on human heroism.

1.3.3. *Second Maccabees*

This work is the epitome of the lost five-volume work of Jason of Cyrene. It was originally written in Greek and narrates events from the incursion of Heliodorus into the → Jerusalem → temple under Seleucus IV (187-175 B.C.) up to the victory of Judas Maccabeus over Nicanor in 160 B.C. The main theme is the preservation of the people and the → sanctuary (desecration in 5:11-20 and 6:1-2, reconsecration in 10:1-8, and deliverance from a new threat in 15:34). The two introductory festal letters (originally in Hebrew?) serve the same purpose with their summons to observe the Feast of Hanukkah (1:1-9; 1:10–2:18). The religious persecutions seem to be due in part to intrigues among the priests. The most significant theologoumena are the hope of resurrection (7:11, 14; 14:46), creation out of nothing (7:28), and suffering as expiatory punishment (7:18, 32). The main distinction from 1 Maccabees is the transition from history to legend, for example, in martyrdom (6:18–7:42) and supraterrestrial phenomena (3:24-40; 5:1-4; cf. 15:11-16).

1.3.4. *Third Maccabees*

In its theme of religious persecution, this book is similar in content to 1 and 2 Maccabees; formally its prose style is similar to that of 2 Maccabees. The story itself belongs to the pre-Maccabean period of the Ptolemies. Ptolemy IV Philopator (221-205 B.C.), after his victory over Antiochus III (223-187) at Raphia in 217, was divinely prevented from entering the sanctuary at Jerusalem. He then tried to avenge

himself on the Jews of → Alexandria by forcing them to participate in the cult of Dionysus, but in vain, since on three occasions he was prevented by similar visitations. The work may contain historical reminiscences, but it undoubtedly presupposes Seleucid persecutions and perhaps also later events up to the Roman period.

1.3.5. *Judith*

This book was probably written originally in Hebrew or Aramaic. In legendary form it combines OT saga, actual history (→ Historiography), and novel in the style of antiquity. Nebuchadnezzar (king of Babylon 605-562 B.C.) wants to punish the western territories for not assisting him in his campaign against the Mede Arphaxad. Hard pressed through the siege of the city of Bethulia, the Jews are saved by Judith, who beguiles and assassinates Holofernes, the enemy general. The background of the Persian period may be seen in the fact that the return from exile has already taken place, and also in the names of Holofernes and the chamberlain Bagoas, who were generals under Artaxerxes III (359/58-338). No historical kernel has yet been discovered.

1.3.6. *Tobit*

This short story carries legendary motifs (e.g., that of the grateful dead). The main theme is that of the rewarding of faithfulness. The Naphtalite Tobit (Tobias in the Vg) is one of those who were deported to Nineveh under Shalmaneser V (727-722 B.C.). When he must appear before Sennacherib (704-681) because he has buried executed Jews, he flees. His nephew Ahikar intercedes for him under Esarhaddon (680-669), and Tobit returns, but at the same time he goes blind, and Sarah, the daughter of his cousin Raguel in Ecbatana, is persecuted by the demon Asmodeus, who slays seven of her suitors before marriage. The common prayer of Tobit and Ahikar receives an answer in the sending of the angel Raphael, who, unrecognized, accompanies Tobit's son Tobias to Media and, by means of the viscera of a fish, grants him the power to free Sarah, his intended wife, from the demon, and to cure his father's blindness. The story, which incorporates proverbial wisdom in the Ahikar tradition, has been handed down in various textual forms. The most important of these contain a longer version (Codex Sinaiticus and Vetus Latina), a shorter form (most of the Greek MSS), and an independent short form (the Vg), which according to → Jerome (ca. 345-420) was originally in Aramaic. Aramaic fragments from → Qumran have been proved to be a translation of the longer version.

1.3.7. *Additions to Esther*

The nine additions to Esther may be described as a

Hellenistic interpretation of the Greek text. Their most significant intent may be seen in (1) the fictional shaping, (2) the supposed documentation, and (3) the theological interpretation. The first set includes the dream of Mordecai at the beginning (A1-11/1:1a-l), its interpretation at the end (F1-10/10:3a-k), the conspiracy against Ahasuerus-Artaxerxes (A12-17/1:1m-r), and Esther's audience with the king (D1-16/5:1a-f, 2a-b). The documentation mentioned is the edict against the Jews (B1-7/3:13a-g) and its revocation (E1-24/8:12a-x); the theological interpretation appears in the prayers of Mordecai (C1-11/4:17a-i) and Esther (C12-30/4:17k-z). The colophon (after F10/10:3l) describes the text as a Greek translation by Lysimachus of Jerusalem and as a festal letter for the Feast of Purim.

1.3.8. *Additions to Daniel*

Two stories added to Daniel have the aim of presenting Daniel as a God-fearing sage after the manner of Daniel 1–6. In the story of Susanna he is the righteous judge who vindicates an unjustly calumniated woman, and in the story of Bel and the Dragon he is a wise man of true faith who unmasks idolatry as a deception. Woven into the canonical book — probably first in the two Greek forms of the text — are the prayer of Azariah (3:24-50), which is a popular complaint, and the prayer of the three in the fiery furnace (3:51-90), a → hymn. These serve the same goal of theological interpretation.

1.3.9. *Prayer of Manasseh*

This individual song of complaint embellishes the original text of 2 Chr. 33:12-20, which tells of Manasseh's repentance and deliverance. In one Vg MS it is integrated into the text of 2 Chronicles; in the rest of the tradition, into the Odes, which are appended to the Psalms.

1.3.10. *Baruch and the Letter of Jeremiah*

These works, which are put with Jeremiah and Lamentations in the LXX canon, are embellishments of two main themes in the prophecy of Jeremiah: submission to the yoke of Babylon and condemnation of idolatry. The Book of Baruch consists of songs of various types. It is introduced by the story that after Baruch read the book to the Jews in the exile, they collected money to pay for → sacrifices in Jerusalem for the life of Nebuchadnezzar and his son Belshazzar. The Letter of Jeremiah, which according to the preface is a copy of a letter sent by Jeremiah to Jews who were marked for deportation to Babylon, combines material from the letter to the exiles of 598 B.C. in Jeremiah 29 (LXX 36) with the attack on idols in 10:1-16.

1.3.11. *Sirach*

The Hebrew original of Sirach (Lat. Ecclesiasticus), a good part of which was found in the Cairo → Genizah in 1896, and more recently at Qumran and Masada, gives evidence of two textual forms that are preserved in part in the Greek tradition. The Greek translation, which according to the prologue was made in the 38th year of Ptolemy (VIII) Euergetes (132 B.C.), comes from the author's nephew. The form is that of proverbial wisdom, the content that of practical wisdom. It thus is similar to the → Wisdom literature of the canonical OT (Proverbs), the only difference being the relative one that proverbs of related content are more closely grouped together in Sirach. A more essential difference arises in the hymns to wisdom at the beginning (1:1-20), in the middle (chap. 24), and at the end (51:13-30), which define wisdom itself by equating it with the → law. After a period of wandering, wisdom finds a home in → Israel (24:7-8; cf. chap. 23). Necessarily, then, it is linked to history, as in the praise of famous ancestors in 44:1–50:26.

1.3.12. *The Wisdom of Solomon*

Originally written in Greek, this book defines apocryphal wisdom in the same way as Sirach does in Hebrew. Wisdom as a virtue of the just stands in contrast to the folly of the wicked (chaps. 1–5). It is the supreme possession of kings (6–9) and is a force at work in history (10–19). In origin and nature it is the wisdom of Israel. The personification of wisdom and the divine Word (18:15-16), as well as its hypostatization as a mediator between God and the world (cf. Proverbs 8–9), is oriented to its operation in the history of Israel.

Bibliography: R. H. CHARLES, *The Apocrypha and Pseudepigrapha of the OT in English* (2 vols.; Oxford, 1913) • E. J. GOODSPEED, *The Apocrypha: An American Translation* (repr., New York, 1969) • E. KAUTZSCH, ed., *Die Apokryphen und Pseudepigraphen des Alten Testaments* (2 vols.; repr., Hildesheim, 1962) • B. M. METZGER, *Introduction to the Apocrypha* (New York, 1965) • H.-P. RÜGER, "Apokryphen I," *TRE* 3.289-316 (bibliography) • D. S. RUSSELL, *The Method and Message of Jewish Apocalyptic* (London, 1964) • J. ZIEGLER and R. HANHART, eds., *Septuaginta. Vetus Testamentum Graecum* (Göttingen, 1965-84) Greek text.

ROBERT HANHART

2. NT Apocrypha

The NT Apocrypha are writings that stand alongside the canonical works in form and claim but that were not received into the canon. They adopt and reshape the NT genres and traditions, although for the most part with no historical basis. The earliest use of "apocryphal" (from Gk. *apokryphos*) had the positive meaning "revealing of hidden secrets." Much later the term received the connotation "spurious; not authentic."

2.1. Gospels

The canonical Gospels do not rule out the writing of other gospels but in fact gave rise to a whole crop of them. In some cases only fragments of these non-canonical works have survived. This fact is connected with their suppression by the mainline church, which meant that they could persist only in heretical circles (→ Heresies and Schisms). It is also connected with what is in part their fantastic character. Besides the Infancy Gospels and the *Epistula apostolorum,* only the *Gospel of Thomas* from the → Nag Hammadi findings (which also contain several incomplete gospels) has survived intact.

2.1.1. Gospel Fragments

Fragments of early gospels are known through MS findings in Egypt. They include the Papyrus Egerton 2 (mid-2d cent.), which combines elements from the Synoptics and John with apocryphal materials. The two pericopes preserved in *OxyPap* 840 (an address of Jesus and a debate about purity) are in the style of the Synoptics. One is a sheet of parchment that was probably used as an amulet. The Fayûm Fragment is a short form of Mark 14:27, 29-30.

2.1.2. Jewish-Christian Gospels

From references and fragmentary quotations in the Fathers, we know three Jewish-Christian gospels. The *Gospel of the Nazarenes,* which is dependent on Matthew and manifests the character of a Synoptic, has novella-like features and might be called "a targumic version of the canonical Matthew" (P. Vielhauer). Its original language might have been "Hebrew" (i.e., Aramaic or Syriac), and its origin might be dated in the first half of the second century in Coele-Syria (modern Bekáa Valley in Lebanon).

The *Gospel of the Ebionites* is dependent on the → Synoptics. It has → Gnostic features and was written in Greek in the first half of the second century in Transjordan.

The *Gospel of the Hebrews* — an ancient title — was at first almost as voluminous as Matthew. It represents an independent type of gnosticizing → Jewish Christianity. → James plays a special role. It arose in the first half of the second century and was the gospel of Greek-speaking Jewish Christians in Egypt.

2.1.3. Gospel of the Egyptians

There is good evidence for the existence of this gospel, but it has not survived. It was the gospel of Gentile Christians in Egypt and was written in the first third of the second century. It bears no connection to the Coptic *Gospel of the Egyptians* from Nag Hammadi.

2.1.4. Gospel of Peter

→ Origen (ca. 185-ca. 254) and Eusebius (ca. 260-ca. 340) both refer to this gospel but without giving any of the text. A find in Egypt in 1886/87 is identical with it; it contains parts of the account of the passion and the resurrection. The gospel presupposes the four canonical Gospels but does not try to harmonize them. Instead, it offers a new presentation. It stresses the miraculous element and is strongly mythological but not → Docetic. It perhaps was composed in Syria in the second half of the second century.

2.1.5. Infancy Gospels

These gospels are primarily concerned to amplify and embellish the scanty canonical traditions about the childhood of Jesus. To this end they also include vitae of → Mary and → Joseph (§2).

2.1.5.1. The *Protevangelium of James* was much read in the → early church and even later in the East. It primarily is the story of Mary. Serving to glorify her, it is a predecessor of later lives of Mary. The oldest MS (Bodmer V) dates from the third or fourth century, and the work was written in the second half of the second century. It is not related to the works from Nag Hammadi that bear the name of James.

2.1.5.2. The *Infancy Gospel of Thomas* was a very popular and widespread work, telling the story of the childhood of Jesus up to the age of 12. It depicts → Jesus as a powerful and capricious prodigy with all the features of a supernatural wonder-worker and teacher. It probably comes from Gentile Christian circles in the second century and bears no relation to the Nag Hammadi *Gospel of Thomas.*

2.1.6. Conversations of the Risen Lord with His Disciples

These works present secret teachings as revelations of the risen Lord to his disciples. Many of the texts are Gnostic, but others (e.g., the Freer Logion in the inauthentic Marcan ending) are not.

The *Epistula apostolorum* was an unknown work before its discovery in 1895 and its publication in 1912 (editio minor) and 1919 (editio maior; see W. Schneemelcher, 205ff.). The Greek text was lost, but the Coptic MS, although incomplete, presents a better text than the Ethiopic MS. It probably dates from the second century in Egypt. The text takes the form of a letter sent by the 11 apostles to Christians everywhere, warning them against the false apostles Simon and Cerinthus. The 11 inform their readers about the revelations that Christ imparted to them after his → resurrection. The work is anti-Docetic and anti-Gnostic. Further works of this genre may be found specially among the discoveries at Nag Hammadi.

The form of dialogue and the use of a question-

and-answer scheme show that these conversations between the risen Lord and his disciples are in genres familiar to the → philosophy and scholarship of antiquity.

2.2. Acts

Because the → apostles were accepted as guarantors of the authentic tradition, works were written in their names as well as about them. Five important writings come from the second and third centuries. They are much better preserved than the apocryphal gospels, for the apocryphal acts never competed with the canonical Acts in the way that the apocryphal gospels did with the canonical Gospels.

2.2.1. Acts of Peter

This work is the oldest of the apocryphal acts, written between about 180 and 190; about two-thirds of its original volume has been preserved. By divine command → Peter comes to → Rome to reestablish the church there after its disruption by Simon Magus. He defeats Simon and finally suffers martyrdom for his preaching of chastity.

2.2.2. Acts of Paul

This work is dependent on *Acts of Peter*. Written about 200, it depicts the acts of → Paul on a journey from Damascus to Rome. Parts of this fictional account with strongly Encratitic tendencies have been handed down independently, namely, the apocryphal correspondence with the Corinthians (anti-Gnostic), the acts of Paul and Thecla, and the martyrdom of Paul. In this writing, Paul suffers repeated persecutions for his preaching of chastity and is ultimately martyred on account of his proclamation of Jesus Christ as king.

2.2.3. Acts of Andrew

This work focuses on Peter's brother. It was at first more voluminous but has been handed down only in fragmentary and much-edited form. It depicts a fictional journey from Pontus to Achaia. Andrew preaches abstemiousness, which leads to his martyrdom. For two days and nights, however, he preaches from the cross, showing himself to be a righteous, wise, and ascetic philosopher. The *Acts of Andrew* is not Gnostic but is influenced by Hellenistic philosophy.

2.2.4. Acts of John

This work, supposedly authored by a companion of John, depicts the wonderful ministry of the son of Zebedee, especially in → Ephesus. Erotic-ascetic features accompany the preaching of chastity in a novella-like presentation (→ Asceticism), and the miraculous deeds give John supernatural stature. John dies a peaceful death. Approximately two-thirds of this work, which was condemned in 787, have been preserved. Gnostic proclamation shows that it was at home in Gnostic circles.

2.2.5. Acts of Thomas

This work has been completely preserved in Syriac and Greek. It recounts in 13 "acts" the work and preaching of the apostle in India, where he ultimately suffers martyrdom. Thomas is an ascetic who preaches abstinence and performs astonishing → miracles. Among the elements inserted (including sermons, prayers, and liturgical texts), the Song of the Pearl in particular depicts the way of redemption. This song is surely to be taken in a Gnostic sense, even though the Gnostic character of the work as a whole has been contested. There are some connections with the Nag Hammadi *Gospel of Thomas*.

2.3. Epistles

2.3.1. Jesus and Abgar

The apocryphal epistles include a supposed correspondence between Jesus and King Abgar of Edessa (Eusebius *Hist. eccl.* 1.13; 2.1.6-8). They were written to validate the "orthodox" claim of the church of Edessa.

2.3.2. Paul and Seneca

Paul and the → Stoic philosopher Seneca (d. A.D. 65) were contemporaries, and both were in Rome under Nero (54-68). These facts led to the writing of a fictional correspondence between the two in which each expresses admiration for the other.

2.3.3. Laodiceans

Prompted by Col. 4:16, a Laodicean letter was written that was attributed to Paul.

2.3.4. Pseudo-Titus

This is an ascetic admonition probably written in the fifth century.

2.4. Apocalypses

In the tradition of Jewish apocalypticism, early Christianity adopted this genre, both canonically in Revelation and noncanonically in the → Apostolic Fathers (*Hermas*).

2.4.1. Ascension of Isaiah

This reworking and expanding of a Jewish writing is notable among apocalypses.

2.4.2. Apocalypse of Peter

Written about 130, this work gives express depictions of → hell and → paradise with an admonitory intent.

2.4.3. Apocalypse of Paul

This work, dating from the end of the fourth century and deriving its inspiration from 2 Cor. 12:1-7, reveals secrets concerning → heaven and hell. Dante (1265-1321) made use of the apocalypses of Peter and Paul in his *Divine Comedy*.

The NT apocryphal writings have no value as historical sources, but they do offer us a glimpse of popular literature and religious life during the first centuries of the Christian era. If one compares the apocryphal tradition with the canonical tradition, the striking feature is the restraint of the latter regarding miracles and depictions of judgment.

Bibliography: ANRW 2.25.4 • CChr.SA (Turnhout, 1983-) • J. H. CHARLESWORTH, *The NT Apocrypha and Pseudepigrapha* (Metuchen, N.J., 1987) • M. DIBELIUS, *Geschichte der urchristlichen Literatur* (repr., Munich, 1990) • E. HENNECKE and W. SCHNEEMELCHER, eds., *NT Apocrypha* (vol. 2; Philadelphia, 1966) • M. R. JAMES, *The Apocryphal NT* (repr., Oxford, 1980) • H. KOESTER, *Introduction to the NT* (vol. 2; Philadelphia, 1982) • W. SCHNEEMELCHER, ed., *NT Apocrypha* (vol. 1; Cambridge, 1991) • P. VIELHAUER, *Geschichte der urchristlichen Literatur* (Berlin, 1975) • R. M. WILSON, "Apokryphen des Neuen Testaments," *TRE* 3.316-62 (extensive bibliography).

HERMANN LICHTENBERGER

Apologetics

1. Definition
2. New Concepts
   2.1. Up to World War I
   2.2. After World War I
3. Theological Significance

1. Definition

Apologetics, the teaching of defense (apology) or defensive scholarship, is the thoughtful interaction of Christian faith with contemporary teachings and → ideologies that are opposed to the → gospel. Since misuse has led to the discrediting of the term in Roman Catholic → neoscholasticism and neo-Protestantism (→ Protestantism 1.3), other terms have replaced it, such as "missionary theology," "eristics," and → "fundamental theology." The last term is current especially in Roman Catholic theology, but also in Protestant theology, sometimes in the broader sense of theological prolegomena (G. Ebeling, W. Joest, and P. Knauer).

Many scholars distinguish apologetics from → dogmatics and → moral theology (→ Ethics), since it addresses the public rather than the church, and also because it argues more strongly or even exclusively from reason than from → revelation (using what has been called sectoral understanding). Others do not see it as a separate discipline but view it as an aspect of (→ systematic) theology, namely, one involving an integral understanding. An immanent apologetics tries to link up with the positive motifs in other branches of thought, whereas a transcendent apologetics takes up its own defensive and offensive position. A reactive apologetics responds to the demands of the age, but a principial apologetics,

which depicts positively the nature of Christianity (F. D. E. → Schleiermacher and K. → Rahner), enters into dialogue with its age as a matter of principle.

Classic Roman Catholic apologetics distinguishes three fields of apologetics: *demonstratio religiosa, Christiana,* and *catholica (ecclesiastica).* The first is an apologetics for religion in general against its opponents. The second is an apologetics for the Christian religion against non-Christian religions, and the third is an apologetics for Roman Catholicism against those who are not Roman Catholics. The first deals with the general philosophical question, the second with the religious question, and the third with the confessional question (→ Ecumenical Theology). Protestantism, too, discerns three similar areas. From the time of the → Enlightenment and → secularization, apologetics has often been equated generally with the philosophy of religion and distinguished from the theology of polemics or of controversy (i.e., the internal debate between the gospel and error).

2. New Concepts
2.1. *Up to World War I*

Apologetics in the stricter sense dates only from the Enlightenment (B. → Pascal, G. W. Leibniz, J. Butler, J. G. → Herder, C. Wolff, et al.), although there are earlier forms in Protestant → orthodoxy (§§1-2), the Middle Ages, and especially the → early church (→ Apologists). After Schleiermacher's reorganization of theology, the prolegomena of traditional dogmatics came to be replaced by a comprehensive doctrine of the principles of religious philosophy, starting with the concept of religion and assessing the place of Christianity within the history of religion. Thus the → philosophy of religion or apologetics became an independent discipline. It has the task of providing a basis for dogmatics in the philosophy of religion. It does not try to prove the truth of Christianity, as traditional apologetics did. Instead, it tries to formulate its nature. It finds a point of contact in the religious disposition, in the human feeling of absolute dependence on a sustaining power, in our ability to see every individual thing as part of a whole. It views religion as an autonomous field, the transmoral and transrational field of contemplation and feeling.

Starting along these lines with Schleiermacher, and accepting Kant's distinction of faith and knowledge, the apologetics of neo-Protestantism and Roman Catholic → modernism has often assumed that religion is independent of proofs or counterproofs because it is instead a matter of → experience and life. In Roman Catholicism the Tübingen school (J. S. Drey, J. E. Kuhn, and J. A. Möhler) gave apologetics a new thrust, as did J. H. → Newman (1801-90) and, later in France, M. Blondel (1861-1949) and others, with their immanent apologetics. In Protestant apologetics F. C. Baur (1792-1860) defended Protestantism against Möhler's symbolics, and many writers took part in the debates about materialism and Darwinism (J. H. A. Ebrard, A. Baumstark, et al.), especially A. Tholuck, a theologian of the awakening, and C. E. Luthardt, a neo-Lutheran, who were the most widely read apologists of their age. These two were influenced by the tradition of Schleiermacher, which bases the certainty of faith on experience rather than on proofs.

Starting from biblical theology, K. Heim (1874-1958) offered a typical apologetics of transcendence and delimitation. Facing the 19th-century argument that miracles are impossible because they claim to break through the closed causal nexus of the world, he tried to weaken it with the thesis that miracles cannot break through it because it is broken in any case (appealing to a kind of → relativity theory). In contrast, → liberal theology and → culture Protestantism represent an immanent apologetics, with a point of contact evident, for example, in E. → Troeltsch (1865-1923) and H. Stephan (1873-1954). Troeltsch started with the religious a priori and found in the modern age with its relativizing of reality a growing longing for the absolute. Stephan thought that the Christian faith transcended the goals of other → worldviews. Regarding the reality of God as the primal and sole reality, he brought it inescapably into life and in this way met the longing of our world and gave it final meaning.

2.2. *After World War I*

Traditional apologetics was radically challenged in Protestant theology by Karl → Barth and his → dialectical theology, and in Roman Catholic theology by the theology of reconstruction (R. Guardini, K. Adam, H. de Lubac, E. Przywara, and K. Rahner). It had lost credibility because of its defensive and advocatory mentality (Doerne). It not infrequently took the form of a self-righteous triumphalism, which not only sought to prove the superiority of Christianity or a Christian confession but also aimed to establish the church and extend its power.

In Roman Catholicism A. Lang, K. Rahner, J. B. Metz, and others took the new paths of an immanent apologetics, leaving behind the neoscholastic separation of nature and supernature. Whereas the apologetics of neoscholasticism had tried to prove supernatural faith on the plane of → reason, Lang argued that apologetics should try to awaken a readiness for faith in us moderns by showing that faith is a fulfillment of needs and tendencies already present within

us. In Rahner's transcendental theology, the world does not have a supernatural addition but itself aims at the absolute point, which is God (cf. de Lubac and P. Teilhard de Chardin). God is the totality, the infinite horizon, transcending all our immanent goals. Orientation to God and his grace is a constitutive part of our nature, not something that is externally posited for us; we have a "supernatural existential." In a very different way Metz linked up with human hopes in his → political theology of the subject. Whereas traditional apologetics was concerned about objects rather than subjects, an "apologetics of → hope" (see 1 Pet. 3:15) ought to show that God has called us to be subjects. The hermeneutical apologetics of E. Biser and W. Kasper took a similar direction in its effort to show that faith and modern thought have a common vocabulary and understanding.

In Protestant theology K. Barth, K. Aland, and H. Thielicke advocated a more transcendent apologetics, but E. Brunner, the later D. → Bonhoeffer, and especially P. → Tillich and W. Pannenberg favored an immanent apologetics. According to Barth, one cannot win non-Christians for Christianity by first taking up a non-Christian position alongside them. The debate between faith and reason can take place only in the sphere of the church, since there is in us no natural point of contact. The Word of God verifies itself. Hence there is only a subsequent apologetics, not an apologetics that first establishes the Word. Brunner discerned in God's general revelation (Rom. 1:19-20; 2:14-15) a natural point of contact for the message. Eristics, or missionary theology, first identifies itself with the hearers, entering into their need and confusion and skepticism and longing. Without this bonding, the message cannot become existentially relevant for them (cf. R. Bultmann).

The later Bonhoeffer condemned thinking in two spheres, or division into secular and religious fields. There is only one sphere, he said, for the incarnation of God united God and the world. Theology, then, has the task of speaking about God in a secular way, of providing a nonreligious interpretation of the Christian faith. Tillich, too, in his apologetic or responsive theology, attempted to answer modern questions from the message, which could be done only with his conceptual means, using the method of correlation. He thus presupposed common ground with those who put the questions. Otherwise theology could not take the questions seriously and could not give authentic answers. The point of contact for Tillich — as distinct from Bonhoeffer — was the concept of religion, as that which applies to us unconditionally. Like Rahner, Pannenberg has defined human beings as limited creatures that can fulfill their destiny only fragmentarily in their finite existence; they thus must ask concerning the whole, the totality of meaning — that is, God.

3. Theological Significance

Apologetics cannot be viewed sectorally but only integrally — as a function of systematic theology. As principial and immanent, it is in all its three fields an answer. It thus is properly not a defense or an attack but an intellectual diakonia that → love demands, in contrast to a disputatious project of overbearing power. Love does not seek itself but others (1 Cor. 13:5) and identifies itself with them (9:20-22). It does so in order to win them to Christ (vv. 20-23). It must really answer the questions of those who think differently, not simply toy with the issues after the manner of an apologetics of accommodation. Given the relativistic view of truth common to our age, unrestricted witness must be borne to the truth claim of the gospel even in the third, interconfessional sphere. The common challenge of mass → atheism, which is perhaps the most important dialogue partner of apologetics in the modern debate, does tend to unite the confessions with a new urgency. In the work of the church, the place of a public apologetics that is understood as an intellectual diakonia lies in → continuing education and especially in pastoral visitation.

Bibliography: K. ALAND, *Apologie der Apologetik* (Berlin, 1948) • K. BARTH, *CD* I/1, 26; II/1, 5 • E. BISER, *Glaubensverständnis. Grundriß einer hermeneutischen Fundamentaltheologie* (Freiburg, 1975) • D. BONHOEFFER, *Ethics* (New York, 1964); idem, *Letters and Papers from Prison* (New York, 1972) • E. BRUNNER, *Dogmatics* (vol. 1; Philadelphia, 1950) • A. DULLES, *Apologetics and the Biblical Christ* (Mahwah, N.J., 1963); idem, *A History of Apologetics* (London, 1971) • W. JOEST, *Fundamentaltheologie* (Stuttgart, 1974) • P. KNAUER, *Der Glaube kommt vom Hören* (6th ed.; Freiburg, 1991) • A. KOLPING, *Fundamentaltheologie* (3 vols.; Münster, 1967-81) • H. KÜNG, *Does God Exist? An Answer for Today* (New York, 1980) • H. LAIS, *Probleme einer zeitgemäßen Apologetik* (Vienna, 1956) • A. LANG, *Fundamentaltheologie* (2 vols.; 4th ed.; Munich, 1967-68) • C. E. LUTHARDT, *Apologie des Christentums* (2 vols., Leipzig, 1864-67) • J. B. METZ, *Faith in History and Society* (New York, 1980) • W. PANNENBERG et al., *Grundlagen der Theologie–ein Diskurs* (Stuttgart, 1974) • H. G. PÖHLMANN and W. BRÄNDLE, *Religionsphilosophie* (Gütersloh, 1982) • K. RAHNER, *Foundations of Christian Faith* (New York, 1978) • J. RATZINGER, *Theologische Prinzipienlehre* (Munich, 1982) • F. SCHLEIERMACHER, *The Christian Faith* (2 vols.; New York, 1963; orig. pub., 1821-22); idem, *On Religion* (Cambridge, 1988) • A. THOLUCK, *Die Lehre von der Sünde und vom Versöhner* (Gotha, 1823; 6th ed., 1836; 9th ed., 1871) • P. TILLICH, *Systematic Theology* (vol. 1; Chicago, 1951) • E. TROELTSCH, *Gesammelte Schriften* (vol. 2; Tübingen, 1913).

HORST G. PÖHLMANN

Apologists

The early Christian writers who defended the Christian faith became known as apologists. The first apologies were legal defenses directed to the Roman emperors in the second century. Many of the names of the authors are known, and we have full copies of the apology addressed by Aristides to Hadrian (117-38) and of that of Justin Martyr to Antoninus Pius (138-61). The plea of Athenagoras to Marcus Aurelius (161-80) is similar. The literary form, which was influenced by the current persecutions, reached its height in the North African → Tertullian (ca. 160-ca. 225). It then faded out, merging into the stories of → martyrs.

From the very first, the literary form served also as public propaganda for Christianity, and it could thus adopt other rhetorical devices. Justin Martyr defended the Christian understanding of the Bible against the Jews in a dialogue, and Minucius Felix (3d cent.) showed how to win over a pagan partner in debate. We also find the open letter, as in the anonymous *Letter to Diognetus* (end of the 2d cent.). Justin's disciple Tatian (in → Rome up to 172) wrote a protreptic, or exhortation, to the Greeks, around the year 180 Antiochian bishop Theophilus used the same form, and Clement of Alexandria (d. ca. 215) wrote a tractate under the title *Protreptikos*. During the last persecution, the rhetorician Lactantius (ca. 250-ca. 325) wrote an apology that was also an exhortation to conversion.

The more the refuting of pagan ideas became predominant, the closer a defense of Christian truth came to religious philosophy. Athenagoras proved the resurrection of the dead along such lines. In such circumstances, however, the apology can no longer be defined in terms of a literary genre; rather, the goal of refuting non-Christian allegations becomes determinative. This is particularly true of the debate of → Origen (ca. 185-ca. 254) with the Platonic philosopher Celsus and of the arguments against Porphyry (ca. 232-ca. 303) and Julian the Apostate (emperor 361-63). → Augustine's *City of God*, which was written to meet the accusation that the ancient gods had avenged their neglect by bringing about the sack of Rome by the Goths in 410, entered into dialogue with the whole tradition of antiquity.

The apologists Aristides, Justin Martyr, and Athenagoras claimed for themselves the title "philosopher," thus indicating whom they wished to answer and convince. They had to dispel the popular allegations that Christians were guilty of atheism, cannibalism, and incest. But since the best defense is attack, prominence was given to criticism of pagan myth and worship. The arguments were not new but were taken over from the Greek tradition of the Epicureans and skeptics (→ Greek Philosophy). The attack on the cultus that could be found in the biblical → prophets also offered indirect parallels. Before the Christians were on the scene, the Jews had used similar arguments, especially Philo of Alexandria (d. A.D. 45-50) in his work *On the Contemplative Life*. Hellenistic → Judaism provided an apologetic model both in negative criticism and in the presentation of a positive case.

Although the intellectual achievement of the apologists is not outstanding, the history of theology must find a proper place for them. What began as an attempt at refutation became the starting point for what was at first an incomplete dialogue. → Monotheism and the demand for a righteous life (→ Virtue) found much in common with the → philosophy of antiquity. The apologists could thus refer expressly to this commonality in their doctrine of → God; as a result, the Christian idea of God began to adapt itself to the Platonic tradition. For the apologists, the Son of God was the Logos of God, who created the world and who permeates it and sustains it. Through him the knowledge of God has been revealed to Christians. He gave himself historical form in Jesus, and therefore, as Justin Martyr said, a saving knowledge of God is available even to simple and uneducated people. This argument demonstrates the contrast with an aristocratic → Platonism, as the debate between Origen and Celsus illustrates. The Logos teaching of the apologists showed Christian → theology how it could make a well-considered claim to truth over against the philosophy of antiquity. The → Arian controversy would require the apologists to make a further distinction from this philosophy.

Bibliography: G. BARDY, "Apologetik," *RAC* 1.533-45 • L. W. BARNARD, "Apologetik I," *TRE* 3.371-411 (extensive bibliography); idem, *Justin Martyr* (Cambridge, 1967) • H. CHADWICK, *Early Christian Thought and the Classical Tradition* (Oxford, 1966) • J. GEFFCKEN, *Zwei griechische Apologeten* (Leipzig, 1907) • E. J. GOODSPEED, *Die ältesten Apologeten* (Göttingen, 1914) • R. M. GRANT, *Greek Apologists of the Second Century* (Philadelphia, 1988) • R. P. C. HANSON, *Tradition in the Early Church* (London, 1962) • A. VON HARNACK, *History of Dogma* (vol. 2; New York, 1961) chap. 4 • A. HAUCK, *Apologetik in der alten Kirche* (Leipzig, 1918) • W. JAEGER, *Early Christianity and Greek Paideia* (Cambridge, Mass., 1961) • M. SIMON, *Verus Israel* (New York, 1966).

EKKEHARD MÜHLENBERG

Apology → Augsburg Confession

Apophatic Theology

1. Basis
2. Significance
3. In the Church
4. Theological Implications

1. Basis

A theology is "apophatic" if it recognizes that a knowledge of the → truth rightfully goes beyond a given linguistic formulation or a detailed conceptual account. Even → atheists may know that the God of the church is a triune God (→ Trinity), and they may have studied the appropriate chapter in Christian dogmatics. But such knowledge itself does not mean that they know the triune God of the church in person.

1.1. Apophatic theology does not equate knowledge with individual experience, with subjective apprehension, or with individual mystical discovery; rather, knowledge involves personal participation in the common experience of the church as a whole (→ Epistemology). Thus this knowledge can never be said to be definitive. It is a dynamic participation of each individual in the whole church. It imparts itself as do life, speech, nurture, beauty, and eros.

1.2. Apophatic theology does not refuse to formulate the truth of the church. It uses both the affirmative way (saying what God is) and the negative way (saying what God is not). In both forms of expression, however, it finds only a delimiting, a description, or a sign of the truth.

1.3. The text of Holy Scripture, the decisions of ecumenical councils, and the writings of the Fathers are definitive truth that the church as a whole recognizes. They thus constitute a boundary that must not be crossed. They do so, not as an abstract ideological principle or a theoretical → axiom, but as a sign of the distinction between the experience of the church and the repudiation of this experience in → heresy.

Thus knowledge of the truth presupposes a fixed delimitation of the truth but does not stop there. Knowledge is equated with the experience, and with participation in the experience, of formulating and describing the truth.

2. Significance

The terms of reference define the distinctive conceptual content that theologians of the undivided church ascribed to the term "apophatic," which the Eastern → Orthodox Church still ascribes to it in accordance with this tradition. Linguistically the term is identical with the *via negativa* (negative way), for it comes from the verb *apophēmi*, "reject, say no to."

2.1. The distinctive conceptual content that Christian theology has given the term was by no means alien to the epistemology of → Greek philosophy. As is well known, Heraclitus related truth to participation in the common meaning *(koinos logos)* that makes life in society possible. We are rational because we share in this common meaning, not because we are equipped with the possibility of achieving an individual understanding. Democritus, too, noted that meaning defines the nature of things, namely, the way in which they are for common experience.

2.2. This apophatic epistemology was predominant in all Greek philosophy in the classical period. For Plato (→ Platonism), knowledge was achieved only in contemplation *(theōria)*, or the viewing of truth with the eyes of the soul. It was thus a participation in its object. For Aristotle (→ Aristotelianism), correct thinking was an appropriate defining and structuring of concepts and syllogisms (→ Logic), but knowledge amounted to more than this, being achieved in rational contemplation. The → soul is what arrives at the concept that makes knowledge possible, and the soul is the whole person.

3. In the Church

The first systematic formulation of the principles and presuppositions of apophatic theology in the church appeared in the writings of Dionysius the Pseudo-Areopagite in the fifth century. These principles and presuppositions may be summed up as follows.

3.1. Apophatic theology neither denies nor adulterates the content of common terms. It does not reject the use of syllogisms, nor does it deny their methodological correctness. It uses both the positive and the negative ways, as well as a synthesis of both.

3.2. A pure, apophatic formulation of theology is pictorial. Concepts transcend one another and thus make it possible for us to go beyond their obvious meaning. Conceptual antitheses also make it possible

for us to grasp the truth that must be expressed not merely with pure thought but with the whole person. They speak about supradivine deity, knowledge in nonknowing, the nameless name, the ineffable word, and so forth. The antithetical use of terms transcends their obvious meaning and creates a picture (as in poetry) that uses words to elucidate a truth that is beyond words.

3.3. Between God the Creator and his creatures there is an → analogy and a causal relation comparable to that between cause and effect. But these relations give rise, not to definite and positive knowledge of God, but to a reflection of the truth of God. Analogous reduction and the causal relation enable us merely to determine the existence of God but not to know the nature or substantial (hypostatic) distinctiveness of this existence.

4. Theological Implications

The apophatic theology of the Orthodox Church differs from the apophatic philosophy of Greek antiquity inasmuch as it presupposes and expresses an → ontology that has as its center the truth of a person. The starting point of what exists is not some divine being that can easily be objectified as a concept or a known object. It is a person that is the basis of its own essence or nature. This person actualizes its nature as substance, hypostasis, and real existence, eternally begetting the Son and sending forth the → Holy Spirit. God exists as the → freedom of a personal fellowship of love (1 John 4:16). He outwardly demonstrates his mode of being (i.e., love) as a personal Trinity by doing the work of creation and seeing to its preservation and salvation.

4.1. The two ontological distinctions of (1) nature and person and (2) nature and energies form the basis of apophatic theology. We do not know God's nature, but we do know his person, which, like the human person that is created in his image, manifests itself in its energies, that is, in the works of will, → reason, love, and creative power. We know the person only in the fact of a relation that constantly mediates knowledge but never exhausts it.

4.2. The ontology as well as the epistemology of apophatic theology identifies the actualizing of both existence and knowledge with the fact of the relation. We experience this relation dynamically in the stages of fellowship, participation, love, and eros.

→ Negative Theology

Bibliography: V. LOSSKY, *The Mystical Theology of the Eastern Church* (2d ed.; Crestwood, N.Y., 1976) • J. PIEPER, *The Silence of St. Thomas* (New York, 1957) • D. TURNER, *The Darkness of God: Negativity in Christian*

Mysticism (Cambridge, 1995) • C. Yannaras (Giannaras), *Person und Eros. Eine Gegenüberstellung der Ontologie der griechischen Kirchenväter und der Existenzphilosophie des Westens* (Göttingen, 1982); idem, *Philosophie sans rupture* (Geneva, 1986); idem, *La théologie de l'absence et de l'inconaissance de Dieu* (Paris, 1971) • J. D. Zizioulas, *Being as Communion: Studies in Personhood and the Church* (Crestwood, N.Y., 1985).

Christos Yannaras

Aporia

Gk. *aporia* literally denotes the absence of a way. In a figurative sense it stands for a difficulty, principally one in philosophy. An aporia arises when in a philosophical argument a material or conceptual contradiction appears. According to Plato (427-347 b.c.), the fundamental aporia of human knowledge is that we cannot possibly engage in the search for → truth (*Meno* 80D-81E), for either we know the truth and do not need to seek it, or we do not know it and do not know where or how to seek it (→ Platonism). For many thinkers (e.g., S. → Kierkegaard and M. Polanyi), this Platonic aporia has been the starting point for new approaches; it is still a matter for discussion.

In Aristotle (384-322 b.c.) the dialectical discussion of opposing arguments serves to heighten our awareness of the problem and in this way hastens a solution (→ Aristotelianism). In modern philosophy N. Hartmann (1882-1950) consciously took up the matter by giving methodological priority to discussion of the aporia.

Bibliography: N. Hartmann, *Grundzüge einer Metaphysik der Erkenntnis* (5th ed.; Berlin, 1965) • S. Kierkegaard, *Philosophical Fragments* (Princeton, 1985) • M. Polanyi, *The Tacit Dimension* (New York, 1966).

Hubertus G. Hubbeling†

Apostasy

The → early church distinguished between apostates and the weak who gave way under pressure. Until the Decian persecution (250/51), apostasy, like murder and adultery, ranked as an unforgivable → sin. Then (against Novatian protests) penances were introduced (→ Penitence), and in later → canon law distinctions were made. In contrast to → heresy, apostasy was defined as a voluntary lapse from the Christian faith (1917 CIC 1325.2) or the Catholic faith (can. 646), or as a willful renunciation of orders or ordination vows (1983 CIC 751, 1364). Excommunication followed automatically.

Whereas at an earlier time questions of ecclesiastical and secular sanctions were important, today, if one wants to speak about apostasy at all, the main questions are those of → church membership, → truth, and → lifestyle.

→ Church Discipline; Lapsi

Bibliography: N. T. Ammerman, "Schism: An Overview," *EncRel(E)* 13.98-102 • J. L. Boojamra, "Schism: Christian Schism," ibid. 102-7 • H. G. Kippenberg, "Apostasy," ibid. 1.353-56 • F. X. Murphy, "Schism, History of," *NCE* 12.1131-32 • P. Roche, B. Chudoba, and E. D. McShane, "Heresy, History of," ibid. 6.1063-69 • K. Rudolph, "Heresy: An Overview," *EncRel(E)* 6.269-75 • J. B. Russell, "Heresy: Christian Concepts," ibid. 276-79 • A. Scheuermann, "Apostasie," *LTK* (2d ed.) 1.733-34.

Dietrich Ritschl

Apostle, Apostolate

1. History of the Term "Apostle"
2. Adoption by Christianity
3. Development in Paul
4. Further Development
    4.1. In the Pauline School
    4.2. In Luke
    4.3. In First Clement and Ignatius
5. Christ as Apostle

In the NT the term "apostle" denotes someone who is sent. "Apostolate" designates the task and authority of an apostle.

1. History of the Term "Apostle"
In pre-Christian Greek the word *apostolos* relates to the act of sending or to an object that is sent. The idea of a person who is sent is rare in classical Greek; in the papyri it occurs later. There the emphasis on someone who is commissioned suggests a link with the ancient Near Eastern office of the emissary, in which the envoy authoritatively represents the one who commissioned him. This thought stands behind the only use in the LXX (3 Kgdms. 14:6). It became a fixed concept in the Jewish sphere only when the state and temple had collapsed (→ Israel) and a central authority sent official messengers to the → diaspora to make visitations and discharge other tasks. The word used for these envoys, however, was never *apostolos* but the Aramaic *šaliăḥ*, perhaps because Christians had in the meantime taken over the Greek equivalent.

2. Adoption by Christianity

The official use in Judaism was preceded by the Christian development of the term "apostle," but the Semitic concept of the envoy formed the context. This concept is the basis of John 13:16, of the version of the sending of the disciples in Mark 6:7-13, 30, and of the temporary formation of a *community apostolate* in Paul's sphere of activity. Paul himself valued those apostles who were commissioned and authorized by the congregations (2 Cor. 8:23; Phil. 2:25). Yet he differentiated his own apostolate as one derived from Christ (Gal. 1:1).

Other lines of thought that are less dependent on the Semitic practice were at work here. One of these was that of a *pneumatic, charismatic, wandering apostolate,* with proclamation and signs through the power of the Spirit as its center. The tradition behind Acts 14 (cf. 13:1-3) relates Paul and Barnabas to this kind of apostolate. Although Paul later criticized wandering apostles severely (2 Corinthians 10–13), they continued their work for some time (Rev. 2:2; *Did.* 11.3-6).

A second and older line of thought in an independent Christian understanding of the apostolate had its basis in *appearances of the risen Lord.* The result was a more restricted group in both time and persons. → Jerusalem was its center (Gal. 1:17-19), Andronicus and Junia(s) perhaps belonged to it (Rom. 16:7), and Paul was the last to be brought into it (1 Cor. 15:8). This circle of apostles was thus larger than the group of the 12 → disciples of Jesus, who probably also received their calling and mission from the risen Lord and who came into the thinking of the church as the 12 apostles (Matt. 10:2; Rev. 21:14; Luke).

3. Development in Paul

Paul integrated the two lines of a wandering apostolate and an apostolate based on resurrection appearances in his unfolding of the apostolate as a personal commissioning by the risen Lord for the service of the → gospel and the upbuilding of the church. Paul believed that his own calling and sending had their basis in a revelation of Christ (Gal. 1:15-16), to whom also his weakness and sufferings as an apostle united him (1 Cor. 4:9-13). He was set apart to proclaim the gospel (Rom. 1:1), into whose mighty and saving operation he was drawn. Mighty works were thus part of his own apostolate (2 Cor. 12:12; Rom. 15:19). His apostolate was universal in scope, and he aimed to spread the obedience of faith among all the → Gentiles (Rom. 1:5). At the same time, he maintained his connection with the individual congregations founded by him (1 Cor. 9:1-

2). He was for them the first bearer of a divine function in the church (along with others, 1 Cor. 12:28). When necessary, he could give them stern directions and enter into sharp debate with them (1 Cor. 5:1-5; Gal. 1:6-9).

4. Further Development

4.1. *In the Pauline School*

How influential Paul's view of the apostolate was may be seen in works in which he is the apostle par excellence. Consider especially the → Pastoral Epistles, which link teaching with his apostolate and proclamation, so that he is the guarantor of its truth (1 Tim. 2:7; 2 Tim. 1:11). Ignatius (*Eph.* 12.2 and *Rom.* 4.3) and Polycarp (*Phil.* 3.2; 9.1) later emphasize Paul's ranking as an apostle. In Asia Minor we also find the idea (cf. 1 Cor. 12:28) that, along with the (primitive Christian) → prophets, the apostles were the foundation of the church, since they had by revelation an insight into the mystery of Christ (Eph. 2:20; 3:5; cf. Rev. 18:20).

4.2. *In Luke*

In his own way, Luke to some extent developed a similar concept. With his generation he looked back on the apostles as normative figures for the church's tradition and teaching (Acts 2:42). In order to achieve a direct link to Jesus, however, he limited the circle to the → Twelve. The apostles had to have been with → Jesus from the beginning of his work up to his → ascension. They thus had to be witnesses of both his life and his → resurrection (Acts 1:21-22; cf. Luke 6:13 etc.). Luke, then, promoted the concept of the 12 apostles directing the → primitive Christian community (Acts 6:2-6 etc.) and validating the early stages of its mission (8:14-25; 15:22-29). He could not include Paul in this circle, even though he rated him highly as a witness whom the Lord himself had commissioned (22:15; 26:16).

4.3. *In First Clement and Ignatius*

At the end of the first century, the apostles of the first generation had become the decisive authority figures for Christians (see also Jude 17 and 2 Pet. 3:2). They could therefore be adduced in authorization of other → offices in the church. Thus Ignatius serves as a model for the presbyters (*Trall.* 3.1 etc.), and in *1 Clem.* 42.1-5 and 44.1-2 we find a hierarchy that leads from God to Christ to the apostles, who then appoint → bishops and → deacons.

5. Christ as Apostle

Heb. 3:1 expresses the concept of Jesus as an apostle, the priestly envoy of God par excellence. This thought, however, did not undergo further development. Justin Martyr (*Apol.* 1.12.9 etc.) used the term "apostle" for Jesus in a different sense, which perhaps gives evidence of → Gnostic influence. Surprisingly, in spite of his Christology of sending, John made no use of the concept.

Bibliography: F. Agnew, "On the Origin of the Term *Apostolos,*" *CBQ* 38 (1976) 49-53; idem, "The Origin of the NT Apostle-Concept: A Review of Research," *JBL* 105 (1986) 75-96 • C. K. Barrett, *The Signs of an Apostle* (Philadelphia, 1970) • S. Brown, "Apostleship in the NT as a Historical and Theological Problem," *NTS* 30 (1984) 474-80 • J.-A. Bühner, *Der Gesandte und sein Weg im vierten Evangelium* (Tübingen, 1977) • K. Haacker, "Verwendung und Vermeidung des Apostelbegriffs im lukanischen Werk," *NovT* 30 (1988) 9-38 • K. Kertelge, "Das Apostelamt des Paulus, sein Ursprung und seine Bedeutung" (1970), *Grundthemen paulinischer Theologie* (Freiburg, 1991) 25-45 • G. Klein, *Die zwölf Apostel. Ursprung und Gehalt einer Idee* (Göttingen, 1961) • G. Lüdemann, *Paul, Apostle to the Gentiles* (Philadelphia, 1984) • H. Merklein, *Das kirchliche Amt nach dem Epheserbrief* (Munich, 1973) • L. Oberlinner, "Die Apostel und ihre Nachfolger," *Anpassung oder Widerspruch* (L. Oberlinner and A. Vögtle; Freiburg, 1992) 9-39 • K. H. Rengstorf, "Ἀπόστολος," *TDNT* 1.407-47 • J. Roloff, *Apostolat–Verkündigung–Kirche. Ursprung, Inhalt und Funktion des kirchlichen Apostelamtes nach Paulus, Lukas und den Pastoralbriefen* (Gütersloh, 1965) • J. Roloff, G. G. Blum, F. Mildenberger, and S. S. Hartmann, "Apostel / Apostolat / Apostolizität," *TRE* 3.430-83 • W. Schmithals, *The Office of Apostle in the Early Church* (Nashville, 1969) • R. Schnackenburg, "Apostles before and during Paul's Time," *Apostolic History and the Gospel* (ed. W. W. Gasque and R. P. Martin; Grand Rapids, 1970) 287-303 • G. Schneider, "Die zwölf Apostel als 'Zeugen.' Wesen, Ursprung und Funktion einer lukanischen Konzeption," *Lukas, der Theologe der Heilsgeschichte* (Königstein, 1985) 61-85 • J. H. Schütz, *Paul and the Anatomy of Apostolic Authority* (London, 1975).

Martin Karrer

Apostles' Creed

1. History and Setting
2. In the Tradition of the Reformation
3. Its Nature
4. Debate

1. History and Setting

The Apostles' Creed, an early confession (→ Confession of Faith), was first referred to as the *Symbolum apostolorum* in a letter from the Council of Milan (390) to Pope Syricius (384-99). According to an ancient tradition, its text arose from an attempt by the → apostles to formulate a common → rule of faith, with each apostle contributing a statement. This story, told by T. Rufinus (ca. 345-411), is merely a legend, but it does illustrate the high esteem in which the text was held.

The setting of the Apostles' Creed was early Christian → baptism. Statements of faith in interrogatory form were set before candidates for baptism, who had to profess belief in them. From such questions, connected declaratory texts developed in the course of the third century. The Symbolum Romanum (→ Old Roman Creed) was particularly important; with some additions, this finally became the present-day Apostles' Creed. Under the influence of the ecclesiastical policies of the Carolingians, its *textus receptus* found its way into the Roman → liturgy. It thus became the central confession of Western Christendom. In the Eastern churches it never achieved universal validity, since the → Nicene Creed was normative for them.

2. In the Tradition of the Reformation

The → Reformers accepted the Apostles' Creed. M. → Luther (1483-1546) praised it as a brief and true summary of the faith. J. → Calvin (1509-64) described it as a kind of compendium and epitome of the faith. J. A. Comenius (1592-1670) took a similar view when he said that none other is so brief or pithy, nor so excellently embraces what is decisive. Yet there were criticisms, especially within post-Reformation → orthodoxy (§1), which felt the lack of some of its cherished themes, such as original → sin, → justification, repentance (→ Penitence), and → sanctification. Liberal → Protestantism contested in particular the apostolicity of the creed. Debates occurred in several countries in the 19th century regarding the creed's binding nature. In many (but not all) Protestant churches the Apostles' Creed has found an established place in liturgy and instruction, as well as in → ordination.

3. Its Nature

The first and last words, "I believe" and → "Amen," point the way to a vital understanding of the Apostles' Creed. We are not offered here a theory, an unfolding of divine secrets, or mere information. Instead, witness is given that can be understood only as an act of participating and expressing faith in the → promise. This rule of faith is not a magical text, nor is it an intrinsic guarantee of → salvation. We receive in it the essence of the → gospel as praise in which we may join, as invitation and encouragement to stand together in the common Christian venture.

Bibliography: K. Barth, *Credo* (New York, 1936); idem, *Dogmatics in Outline* (London, 1949) • D. L. Holland, "The Earliest Text of the Old Roman Symbol: A Debate with Hans Lietzmann and J. N. D. Kelly," *CH* 35 (1965) 262-81 • J. N. D. Kelly, *Early Christian Creeds* (3d ed.; London, 1972) • J. M. Lochman, *The Faith We Confess: An Ecumenical Dogmatics* (Philadelphia, 1984) • W. Pannenberg, *The Apostles' Creed in the Light of Today's Questions* (Philadelphia, 1972) • J. Ratzinger, *Introduction to Christianity* (New York, 1970).

JAN MILIČ LOCHMAN

4. Debate

The → Reformers viewed the → Apostles' Creed as a correct summary of the teaching of the → apostles, although they left open the question of whether it actually came from the apostles themselves. Like the early dogma of the → Trinity and → Christology, so the Apostles' Creed, from the time of P. → Melanchthon (1497-1560), was regarded as useful in interconfessional approaches (G. Calixtus). For this reason → orthodoxy (§1.4, e.g., as defended by A. Calovius and A. Quenstedt) viewed it with some skepticism, since it did not mention typical Reformation concerns like the → justification of sinners.

Enlightenment theologians like G. E. Lessing (1729-81) argued that the church was not built on Scripture but on the Apostles' Creed. (In the time of the → early church, a similar position was held by → Tertullian.) In the conflict between orthodoxy and rationalism, the Apostles' Creed was a means to weaken the confessional character of theology. In the 19th century the situation changed, with criticism of the Apostles' Creed, now commonly recited at worship, being regarded as criticism of the substance of the faith. After the → union between Lutherans and Reformed, controversies arose through the refusal of pastors to recite the creed. The most famous case was that of C. Schrempf (1860-1944) in 1892, in which A. Harnack (1851-1930) played a role. Although Harnack's criticism was well considered and moderate, it annoyed both the theological left (the Protestantenverein) and the theological right (orthodoxy). Harnack appreciated the confession of God the Father and Jesus Christ the Lord (→ Confession of Faith), but he missed any reference to the earthly life of Jesus and was critical of the → virgin birth. Criticism of the creed either focused on some details while accepting others, or it was directed against the whole idea of compulsory confession. So-called → dialectical theology seemed at first to value again the importance of the creed, but the discussion

that it initiated on the nonobjectifiability of faith, on historiography and history, and on → demythologizing took up critical concerns in the creed and pushed controversy about the creed itself into the background.

Bibliography: H. M. Barth, "Apostolisches Glaubensbekenntnis II," *TRE* 3.554-66 (bibliography) • A. von Zahn-Harnack, *Der Apostolikumstreit des Jahres 1892 und seine Bedeutung für die Gegenwart* (Marburg, 1950).

EGINHARD P. MEIJERING

Apostolic Churches

1. Catholic Apostolic Church
2. New Apostolic Church
3. Other Apostolic Churches

The phrase "apostolic churches" designates several different churches that have reintroduced the office of → apostle: the Catholic Apostolic Church, the New Apostolic Church, and various other churches and groups. The several bodies differ in significant ways.

1. Catholic Apostolic Church

Around 1830 there was an outbreak of charismatic gifts (tongues, prophecy, and healing; → Charisma; Charismatic Movement) in certain revivalist Bible circles in England and Scotland. The central figure in this movement was the Scottish minister Edward Irving (1792-1834). In expectation of the imminent return of Jesus Christ (→ Eschatology; Millenarianism; Parousia), a prophetic word called for "the restoration of the divine order of the church," with 12 apostles. By 1835 the 12 apostles had been named, and various prophets, angels, priests, and deacons (see Revelation 2–3) were called. The apostles divided different countries among themselves, and through their efforts some 300 congregations were established.

In place of the hoped-for one, holy, catholic, apostolic church of the end time, however, there simply developed another ecclesiastical movement. The death of the first apostles led the rest to the conviction in 1855 that the return of Jesus Christ was not imminent after all, and thus they made no new apostolic appointments. The last apostle died in 1901. According to the Catholic Apostolic constitution, the flow of the → Holy Spirit was thus interrupted. → Ordination, sealing (i.e., the imparting of the Holy Spirit to believers), and the fullness of the → liturgy were thus abandoned. The congregations could no longer grow.

In 1995 about 110 congregations remain in Germany, 12 in England, and 9 in Switzerland. They still have a litany and divine service with readings. For the sacraments and other aspects of congregational life, the members have joined Protestant churches.

2. New Apostolic Church

The New Apostolic Church arose when the apostolic college of the Catholic Apostolic Church did not appoint any more apostles after 1855. On his own initiative, the "angel-prophet" Heinrich Geyer (1818-96) began to call new apostles in northern Germany. This move led to considerable tension and ultimately schism. In 1863 the church was organized as the Universal Christian Apostolic Mission; the present name was adopted in 1907.

The church has somewhat fewer than eight million members in all parts of the world (1995 est.; 400,000 in Germany, 35,000 in the United States). World headquarters are in Zurich, Switzerland. The guidance of the church is in the hands of over 230 apostles, presided over by the chief apostle. The church publishes various journals, including *Our Family, Word of Life,* and *New Apostolic Review,* as well as an official paper. It has largely replaced its Catholic Apostolic inheritance with its own practices and insights.

The fourth of the ten articles of faith is that the Lord Jesus rules his church by living apostles until his coming again and that he has sent — and continues to send — his apostles with the tasks of teaching, forgiving sins in his name, and baptizing with water and the Holy Spirit. The chief apostle is his representative on earth. In him and the other apostles Christ does his present work in the world. In descending order, bishops, elders, evangelists, congregational elders, pastors, congregational evangelists, priests, deacons, and subdeacons are the other offices in the church (→ Offices, Ecclesiastical).

The New Apostolic Church has three → sacraments: infant → baptism, the Lord's Supper each Sunday (→ Eucharist), and sealing, which none but the apostles can administer. Only the holders of the main offices rank as true expositors of the Bible and in virtue of their office as preachers of God's Word for the day. It is they who appoint the other officers.

The church expects the imminent return of Jesus Christ and the first → resurrection (§2). In the related and terrible intervening time, which will end with the defeat of Satan (→ Devil), the only ones to be preserved will be those who belong to God's people — as defined by membership in the New Apostolic Church. After the second resurrection will follow God's final judgment (→ Last Judgment) and the new creation (Rev. 21:1-4).

The New Apostolic Church views itself not merely as the direct continuation of the first apostolic church but also as God's only redemptive work on earth. By the word of the apostles and their sealing, it itself is prepared for the divine future as no other church is. Being the only true church, it holds aloof from other churches. They in turn regard the New Apostolic Church as a sect, believing that, according to the Bible, only Jesus Christ, and not any church officeholder, has full power and authority to mediate salvation.

3. Other Apostolic Churches

In the course of time, because of disagreements with the office of chief apostle, over a dozen groups have broken away from the New Apostolic Church. These groups have usually given up the office of chief apostle but have preserved the main features of the office of apostle. Of the various churches, the most important in 1995 are the Apostolic Office of Jesus Christ (20,000 members in Germany), the Reformed Apostolic Congregational Union (40 congregations in Germany), Het Apostolisch Genootschap (26,000 members in Holland), the Union of Apostolic Christians (1,000 members in Switzerland), and the Apostolic Fellowship (8,000 members in Germany). Several apostolic congregations have also joined together in a Union of Apostles of the Apostolic Churches (30,000 members).

Bibliography: Catholic Apostolic Church: R. A. DAVENPORT, *Albury Apostles: The Story of the Body Known as the Catholic Apostolic Church* (2d ed.; Birdlip [Glos.], 1973) • *EAR* (5th ed.) no. 2093 • C. G. FLEGG, *"Gathered under Apostles": A Study of the Catholic Apostolic Church* (Oxford, 1992) • E. IRVING, *Collected Writings* (5 vols.; London, 1864-65) • P. E. SHAW, *The Catholic Apostolic Church* (New York, 1946).

New Apostolic Church: F. O. BURKLIN, "The New Apostolic Church," *Dynamic Religious Movements* (ed. D. J. Hesselgrave; Grand Rapids, 1978) 67-81 • *EAR* (5th ed.) no. 2114 • *Questions and Answers concerning the New Apostolic Church* (Frankfurt, 1978) • G. ROCKENFELDER, *Geschichte der Neuapostolischen Kirche* (Frankfurt, n.d.; new ed., 1968).

General: EAR (3d ed. supp.) 73-75 • O. EGGENBERGER, *Die Neuapostolischen* (Munich, 1953) • F. W. HAACK, *Neuapostolische Kirche* (6th ed.; Munich, 1992) • H. OBST, *Apostel und Propheten der Neuzeit* (3d ed.; Berlin, 1990) 20-175 • H. D. REIMER and O. EGGENBERGER, eds., . . . *neben den Kirchen* (10th ed.; Constance, 1992) 258-84.

OSWALD EGGENBERGER

Apostolic Council → Acts of the Apostles

Apostolic Fathers

1. The Phrase

The phrase "Apostolic Fathers" goes back to a 1672 Paris edition prepared by J.-B. Cotelier entitled *Ss. Patrum qui temporibus apostolicis floruerunt . . . opera.* This work contained *Barnabas, 1 and 2 Clement,* the epistles of Ignatius and Polycarp, *Martyrdom of Polycarp,* and Hermas. Although the historicity is debatable, the phrase has secured a place in historical study. It now applies also to *Didache,* the *Epistle to Diognetus,* the *Quadratus Fragment,* and the fragments of Papias.

2. The Writings

2.1. *Didache*

The work called *The Didache,* or *The Teaching of the Twelve Apostles,* was discovered only in 1873 and was published in 1883. It has come to be regarded as of crucial importance for the history of early Christianity (→ Primitive Christian Community). The first part contains teaching on the two ways (the way of life and the way of death, 1–6), followed by directions for → baptism, → fasting, → prayer, and the → Eucharist (7–10). Chaps. 11–15 contain regulations for teachers, (itinerant) → apostles, and → prophets, as well as instructions for the Lord's Day and for the selection of → bishops and → deacons. The work closes with a brief apocalypse (16). The *Didache* might be called a church rule and was formative as such. One cannot say when or where it was written, since there are no external criteria by which to judge. Chaps. 11–15, however, suggest that it belongs to the first half of the second century. The extent of its greatest impact suggests Egypt or Syria as the place of origin.

2.2. *Barnabas*

Dated between 130 and 150, this work has been traditionally assigned to the Barnabas who was the companion of → Paul. It does not mention the author, however, nor does it reveal its place of origin (Egypt?) or its background. *Barnabas* falls into neat divisions. After a short introduction (1), the first section uses allegorical and typological → hermeneutics to appropriate the OT for the church (2–17). Then chaps. 18–20 contain teaching on the two ways (of light and of darkness), which is very similar to that in the *Didache,* while chap. 21 brings the work to a conclusion. *Barnabas* is a theological tractate in epistolary form, its aim being to mediate perfect knowledge (1.5) to believers. This knowledge consists of the Christian interpretation of the OT in sharp antithesis to → Jewish theology. The work owes less to → dialogue with a Jewish partner than to debates within the church on the appropriate use of the OT.

2.3. *Clement*

2.3.1. *First Clement*

The history of the text and influence of *1 Clement* bears witness to the rank and significance that the → early church accorded it. Written from the church of Rome to the church of Corinth, it seems to have been composed by an important person (traditionally — and probably — St. Clement I of Rome). Its background is the → persecution at the end of the reign of Domitian (96/97). It has a simple structure. After the introduction (1–3), chaps. 4–39 contain general → parenesis, 40–58 address the disorders at Corinth that are the real occasion of writing, and an extended conclusion in 59–65 contains as its climax the prayer of 59–61. This book intervenes in a controversy at Corinth in which younger members had ousted → elders. The author criticizes their action with exhortations and the theologoumenon of the divine origin of office (42). *First Clement* was able to make good its claim and hence to shape history.

2.3.2. *Second Clement*

The work called *2 Clement* was not written by St. Clement, nor is it a letter. Stylistically, it rather alludes to the diatribe and thus assumes a homiletic character. In content, it begins by emphasizing → Christology as → soteriology (1–2). The admonitions in chaps. 3–8 characterize human conduct in response to salvation, with a special stress on doing. In 9–12 the author attacks doubts about the → resurrection and the church's → eschatology. In calls for repentance in 13–18, → ecclesiology (14, with links to gnosticizing motifs) holds a special place. Chaps. 19–20 conclude the work. The traditions cited and their handling suggest a date in the middle of the second century; there are few clues as to the place of origin.

2.4. *Ignatius*

The epistles of Ignatius had a major influence in the → early church. They consist of four letters that Ignatius, → bishop of → Antioch, wrote from Smyrna (to the churches of → Ephesus, Magnesia, Tralles, and → Rome) and three letters that he wrote from Troas (to the churches at Philadelphia and Smyrna, and to Bishop Polycarp [ca. 70-ca. 166]). The letters contain many references that are theologically and historically important. Their → theology is oriented to the direct access to → salvation that Ignatius will achieve in martyrdom. In contrast to this yearning is the presence of salvation in the churches (through the Eucharist!). Direct consequences follow for Christology, which is essentially conceived of soteriologically, and emphasis falls on ecclesiology. Central here is the concept of → unity, with the foundation being laid for the episcopal office and the idea of the catholic → church.

2.5. *Polycarp*

2.5.1. *Philippians*

This essentially parenetic work is full of admonitions (4–6, → household rules; 6–7, polemics and exhortation). Some inner textual tensions in the letter suggest that it combines two earlier letters, the first consisting of chap. 13 (and 14?), the second essentially of 1–12. Polycarp has noticeably little theological individuality (esp. in contrast to Ignatius). The work consists primarily of a collection of traditional motifs.

2.5.2. *Martyrdom of Polycarp*

This work shows that the person of Polycarp was of great significance for the church in Asia Minor. The text has probably been worked over theologically and revised several times. Written from the church of Smyrna to that of Philomelion (in Phrygia), it describes the death of Polycarp, with echoes of the passion of Jesus and reservations about voluntary martyrdom (→ Montanism). Legendary features become prominent at the end, and for this reason doubts arise as to the date given in 21.1. If it is correct, the death of Polycarp took place in 156 (or 155).

2.6. *Shepherd of Hermas*

This work takes its name from the figure who came to Hermas to communicate a divine message to him. It contains 5 → visions, 12 mandates, and 10 similitudes (→ Parable). It acquired great → authority in the → early church by reason of its teaching on repentance. For Hermas the issue was that of the possibility of repentance even for those who have been baptized. The work thus steers a middle course between ethical claim and historical experience, with immediate implications for the understanding of the church. In addition to its basic thrust Hermas integrates elements of different types, the apocalyptic tradition playing an important part. The text arose in Rome between 140 and 150 and was composed by a certain Hermas, perhaps the brother of Pope Pius I (ca. 140-ca. 154).

2.7. *Epistle to Diognetus*

This work is essentially a defense of Christianity with a focus on worship of God, love of neighbor, and the Christian ethos. It resembles other apologies (→ Apologists) but also shows traces of Pauline influence. There can be no certainty about author, date, or place, but a date in the second half of the second century is possible.

2.8. *Quadratus Fragment and Papias of Hierapolis*

The *Quadratus Fragment*, an apology belonging to the period 120-30, is addressed to Emperor Hadrian (117-38). Only a fragment has survived. At its heart stands a reference to witnesses to Christ. Around the year 130 Papias wrote five books called *Logiōn Kyriakōn exēgēseis* (Expositions of the oracles of the Lord), of which only fragments have survived. These are particularly important with regard to the rise of the Gospels (→ Literature, Biblical and Early Christian, 2). They also give us a glimpse of the process by which the tradition took written form in the second century. Because of Papias's chiliastic tendencies, later generations came to view him with suspicion (→ Millenarianism).

Bibliography: R. BRÄNDLE, *Die Ethik der "Schrift an Diognet"* (Zurich, 1975) • H. VON CAMPENHAUSEN, *Bearbeitungen und Interpolationen des Polykarpmartyriums* (Heidelberg, 1957) • K. P. DONFRIED, *The Setting of Second Clement in Early Christianity* (Leiden, 1974) • J. A. FISCHER, *Die Apostolischen Väter* (Munich, 1956) texts with translations • F. X. FUNK and K. BIHLMEYER, eds., *Die Apostolischen Väter* (Tübingen, 1956) text edition without *Hermas* • R. M. GRANT et al., eds., *The Apostolic Fathers: A New Translation and Commentary* (6 vols.; New York, 1964-65) • A. VON HARNACK, *Die Lehre der zwölf Apostel* (Leipzig, 1886) • P. N. HARRISON, *Polycarp's Two Epistles to the Philippians* (Cambridge, 1936) • D. HELLHOLM, *Das Visionenbuch des Hermas als Apokalypse* (Lund, 1980) • KAV • O. KNOCH, *Eigenart und Bedeutung der Eschatologie im theologischen Aufriß des erstens Clemensbriefes* (Bonn, 1964) • U. H. J. KÖRTNER, *Papias von Hierapolis* (Göttingen, 1983) • K. LAKE, trans., *The Apostolic Fathers* (2 vols.; Cambridge, Mass., 1945-46) • J. B. LIGHTFOOT, *The Apostolic Fathers* (repr., New York, 1950) • J. MUILENBERG, *The Literary Relations of the Epistle of Barnabas and the Teaching of the Twelve Apostles* (Marburg, 1929) • C. OSIEK, *Rich and Poor in the Shepherd of Hermas* (Washington, D.C.,

1983) • H. Paulsen, *Studien zur Theologie des Ignatius von Antiochien* (Göttingen, 1978) • J. Reiling, *Hermas and Christian Prophecy* (Leiden, 1973) • P. Schaff, *The Oldest Church Manual Called the Teaching of the Twelve Apostles* (Edinburgh, 1885) • W. R. Schoedel, *Ignatius of Antioch* (Philadelphia, 1985) • K. Wengst, *Tradition und Theologie des Barnabasbriefes* (Berlin, 1971) • M. Whittaker, ed., *Der Hirt des Hermas* (2d ed.; Berlin, 1972).

Henning Paulsen†

Apostolic Succession → Bishop, Episcopate

Arabic Philosophy → Islamic Philosophy

Arameans

The Arameans (Heb. and Aram. *'ărām, 'ărammî, 'rm;* Akkad. *aramu, arimu,* etc.) left an important legacy in the Near East until well into the Christian era, namely, the Aramaic language, which belongs to the West Semitic group and is closely related to Hebrew. The OT contains several passages in Aramaic (Gen. 31:47; Ezra 4:8–6:18; 7:12-26; Jer. 10:11; Dan. 2:4b–7:28); the Hebrew text itself also contains various Aramaisms. Widespread from around the eighth century B.C., Aramaic became an official language in the Persian Empire and, with its many dialects, long remained the dominant language in the Near East.

This development is remarkable enough, for it would be an exaggeration to call the Arameans a people. Scattered in a number of tribes, they organized a number of ephemeral city-states. Neither in archaeology nor in literature have they left behind any heritage worth noting. Their native territory was the Syrian-Arabian desert (Tadmor, or Palmyra), from which they moved out into the neighboring regions of the Fertile Crescent (Amos 9:7 does not help us to be more specific). As far as we can tell, this expansion became historically relevant only with the so-called Aramaic migration in the last quarter of the second millennium.

The result of this migration was that many tribes, including the Israelites and Arameans, took over territory and founded cities in Syria and Palestine. The OT has preserved a recollection of this common origin in the names, genealogies, and stories of Genesis (10:22-31; 11:10-26; 12–36; cf. *'ărammî 'ōbēd* in Deut. 26:5, whose date and meaning are much disputed, but which seems to say that Israel's first ancestor was a wandering Aramean). Even until a later

date it was recognized that in the early period the patriarchs had lived in Aram-naharaim (Gen. 24:10) or Paddan-aram (Gen. 25:20; 28:2, 5-7, etc.).

From the founding of states to the eighth century, the story of the Aramean city-states (Sam'al, Hamath, Aram-Damascus, etc.) and tribes (Bīt-adini [cf. Beth-eden, Amos 1:5]; Lāqê, Hindānu, Sūhu, etc.) was essentially one of conflict with the Assyrians and → Israel, first with Tiglath-pileser I (ca. 1100 B.C.), then with David (2 Sam. 8:3-8; 10:6-19), then with the Assyrian kings of the ninth century. In 853 at Qarqar a coalition under the king of Damascus gained a temporary victory over Shalmaneser; Ahab (871-852 B.C.) was a member of this coalition. This rare agreement stands in contrast to numerous threats of the Arameans to the northern kingdom (1 Kgs. 15:16-22; 20; 22; 2 Kgs. 8:7-15; 13:14-25; Amos 1:3-5).

The rise of Assyria to the status of a world power from 745 inevitably brought about the destruction of the Levantine Aramean states (see 2 Kgs. 15:29-30). As a result of the war between Syria and Ephraim (733/32; cf. 2 Kgs. 16:5-9; Isaiah 7, etc.), Damascus, the last Aramean city-state, lost its political independence. Strangely enough, however, this did not destroy the ethnic power of the Arameans. On the contrary, the infiltration of native populations by Aramean tribes, which started from Babylon, led to a relentless Aramaizing of Mesopotamia; among the Achaemenids of Persia, for example, Aramaic was easily understood and enjoyed a prominent position. Among the Jews of Palestine, Aramaic became the language into which the Bible was translated (i.e., the Targums) when Hebrew was no longer understood (→ Bible Versions). Aramaic became the native speech of the Jews, and hence the language that Jesus spoke. We find Aramaic words transcribed into Greek in the NT too, though it is hardly likely that there were Aramaic originals for many passages in the Gospels.

Bibliography: K. Beyer, *Die aramäischen Texte vom Toten Meer* (Göttingen, 1984) bibliography • H. Donner and W. Röllig, *Kanaanäische und aramäische Inschriften* (3 vols.; 3d ed.; Wiesbaden, 1971-76) • E. G. H. Kraeling, *Aram and Israel; or, The Aramaeans in Syria and Mesopotamia* (New York, 1918) • E. Lipiński, R. Degen, and H. P. Rüger, "Aramäer und Israel/Aramäisch," *TRE* 3.590-613 (bibliography) • A. Malamat, "The Aramaeans," *Peoples of OT Times* (ed. D. J. Wiseman; Oxford, 1975) 134-55 • H.-P. Müller, "Die aramäische Inschrift von Deir 'Allā und die älteren Bileamsprüche," *ZAW* 94 (1982) 214-44 • W. T. Pitard, *Ancient Damascus: A Historical Study of the Syrian City-State from Earliest Times until Its Fall to the Assyrians in 732 B.C.* (Winona Lake, Ind., 1987) • M. F. UNGER, *Israel and the Aramaeans of Damascus: A Study in Archaeological Illumination of Bible History* (Grand Rapids, 1957) • H. WEIPPERT and M. WEIPPERT, "Die 'Bileam'-Inschrift von Tell Dēr 'Allā," *ZDPV* 98 (1982) 77-103.

HERMANN SPIECKERMANN

Archaeology

1. Biblical Archaeology
   1.1. Task
   1.2. Methods
   1.3. Historical Chronology (Epochs)
   1.4. Biblical Archaeology and
       Biblical Scholarship
2. Christian Archaeology

1. Biblical Archaeology
1.1. *Task*

The task of biblical archaeology is to investigate the history of settlement and culture of → Palestine. This task demands the reconstruction of the history of settlement and the recovery of artifacts by surface exploration and excavation, followed by the collection and interpretation of the artifacts with a view to exhibiting the material culture in the different epochs.

Surface exploration involves taking an inventory of whatever remains may still be present. Ruined buildings are seldom available. A site usually consists of a heap of ruins called a tell (Arab. *tall;* pl. *tulul*). By its form a tell can be easily distinguished from a natural hill. A settlement that has existed only for a short time and that differs little from the surrounding country is called a *ḥirbe*. Surface fragments make a preliminary dating possible.

Archaeological excavation serves the purpose of investigating a ruined site systematically. Since only parts of a tell or ḥirbe can be uncovered, the aim is to proceed in such a way as to unfold the whole history of the settlement and to achieve as comprehensive a picture as possible of the material culture. The style of building is the decisive mark of a layer of settlement, or stratum. The sequence of strata provides the history of settlement, while the architecture and artifacts give evidence of the material culture.

The combined artifacts of a given epoch make possible a reconstruction of the cultural history. As a direct expression of everyday life, the material culture offers a glimpse into the conditions, habits, and powers of expression of the people of the epoch in question. Thus biblical archaeology does not concern ancient → Israel alone but embraces all preceding cultures and neighboring peoples.

1.2. *Methods*

Special methods of excavation have been developed. Since the work in general destroys the object being studied, these methods must be oriented to the objective investigation and critical testing of the results. The guiding principle of stratigraphy is to understand each stratum and its total findings in distinction from the strata that precede and follow. The methods employed must thus ensure not merely that the findings relate to the buildings uncovered but also that the sequence of strata is established in every detail.

Parallel to the development of methods of excavation has been a development of ceramic chronology. Since each period has its own form of pottery, each stratum can be dated with the help of the pottery. The chronological arrangement of the pottery of different eras has been promoted with the help of dated findings, especially from Egypt, and by the relating of individual strata to historical events that are known from the sources.

1.3. *Historical Chronology (Epochs)*

Chronologically, biblical archaeology begins with the Neolithic Age (8000-4000 B.C.), during which the land began to be settled and villages were founded. Since there was no writing, however, the culture belongs to prehistory. In this epoch a transition to agriculture and cattle breeding, as well as the making of pottery, led to decisive cultural developments that formed the basis of all further advance. Metallurgy began during the Chalcolithic Age (4000-3150 B.C.). Another crucial change came with the transition to → city life during the Early Bronze Age (3150-2350 B.C.) After the Middle Bronze Age I (2350-1950), the cities were refounded by new settlers during the Middle Bronze Age II and the Late Bronze Age (1950-1200 B.C.). The destruction of the original Canaanite civilization during this last period has not yet been sufficiently explained.

The Iron Age (1200-332 B.C.) was the age of the newly settled Israelites and their neighbors. In accordance with the historical development, one may divide this age into three periods: that before the monarchy (Iron Age I, 1200-1000 B.C.), that of the monarchy (Iron Age II, 1000-587 B.C.), and that of the Babylonian and Persian hegemony (Iron Age III, 587-332 B.C.). There has been debate about including the Hellenistic and Roman periods, which began with the conquest by Alexander the Great (336-323 B.C.) in 332 B.C. and which ended with the accession of Constantine (306-37) in the East in A.D. 324. Since the development of → Judaism and the rise of Christianity fall in this period, one may include it in biblical archaeology in the broader sense.

A depiction of the history of civilization takes us far beyond ancient Israel in both space and time. Yet there is a close connection with biblical studies (→ Exegesis, Biblical), for the OT is the most important source for the history of the land during the Iron Age. Although biblical archaeology and biblical research may be pursued as independent disciplines, a close relationship exists between them.

1.3.1. Archaeological research gives us better historical knowledge. As excavations show, historical processes are usually more differentiated than written sources would suggest. Thus archaeological results can and should be used in our account of the history of Israel.

1.3.2. The study of objects, which has been part of biblical archaeology from the very beginning, constitutes an indispensable part of material exegesis. The types of houses, palaces, vessels, weapons, pottery, and jewelry of Israel and surrounding nations can all be documented from many rich discoveries.

1.3.3. The material civilization that the findings illustrate, as a concrete expression of life, will often provide a much larger picture than the written tradition. As a source of its own in many spheres of daily life, biblical archaeology offers its own view of the world of ancient Israel.

1.4. Biblical Archaeology and Biblical Scholarship

The relation between biblical archaeology and biblical scholarship has long been hampered by the preconception that biblical archaeology ought to prove the truth of the biblical tradition. This assumption has sometimes led to incorrect interpretations and identifications. A more comprehensive understanding of the task of biblical archaeology as the investigation into the history of settlements and of material culture has replaced this one-sided focus on providing proofs for the course of biblical history. This approach avoids the danger of trying to confirm specific biblical events by archaeological excavation or interpreting specific findings in the light of a particular understanding of the text. A comparison can be made between the biblical tradition and the archaeological findings only when both disciplines have studied their material with all the methods at their disposal. Typically, what emerges is a mutually complementary relationship. Since the textual tradition is very restricted in view of the great range of biblical history, biblical archaeology takes on added importance with its steadily increasing number of artifacts and individual findings. It thus contributes decisively to a widening of the horizon of biblical scholarship.

Bibliographies: Bibliography up to 1878: R. RÖHRICHT, *Bibliotheca geografica Palaestinae* (new ed., with Introduction by D. H. K. Amiran; Jerusalem, 1963); bibliography from 1878 to 1945: P. THOMSEN, *Die Pälastina-Literatur* (7 vols.; Leipzig and Berlin, 1908-72); bibliography up to 1980: E. K. VOGEL, "Bibliography of Holy Land Sites . . . ," *HUCA* 42 (1971) 1-96 (also published separately) • E. K. VOGEL and B. HOLTZCLAU, "Bibliography of Holy Land Sites II," *HUCA* 52 (1981) 1-92 (also published separately).

Other literature: Y. AHARONI, *The Archaeology of the Land of Israel* (Philadelphia, 1982) • W. F. ALBRIGHT, *The Archaeology of Palestine* (3d ed.; Gloucester, Mass., 1971) • R. AMIRAN, *Ancient Pottery of the Holy Land* (Jerusalem, 1969) • E. ANATI, *Palestine before the Hebrews* (London, 1963) • H. A. BEN-TOV, *The Archaeology of Ancient Israel* (New Haven, 1992) • F. FRITZ, *Einführung in die biblische Archäologie* (Darmstadt, 1985) • K. M. KENYON, *Archaeology in the Holy Land* (5th ed.; Nashville, 1985) • H.-P. KUHNEN, *Palästina in griechisch-römischer Zeit* (Munich, 1990) • A. MAZAR, *Archaeology of the Land of the Bible, 10,000-586 B.C.E.* (New York, 1990) • P. R. S. MOOREY, *A Century of Biblical Archaeology* (Cambridge, 1991) • H. WEIPPERT, *Palästina in vorhellenistischer Zeit* (Munich, 1988) • G. E. WRIGHT, "The Archaeology of Palestine," *The Bible and the Ancient Near East* (ed. G. E. Wright; Garden City, N.Y., 1961) 73-112.

VOLKMAR FRITZ

2. Christian Archaeology

Scientific interest in the monuments of early Christianity developed in → Rome during the Counter-Reformation (→ Catholic Reform and Counterreformation). A piety oriented to history and stamped by the → Renaissance and → humanism created an archaeological → apologetics. In his posthumous *Roma sotteranea* (1634) the Maltese A. Bosio (ca. 1575-1629) depicted the world of the → catacombs with their paintings, sarcophagi, and inscriptions. With an orientation to Rome and an interpretation of the findings in terms of dogmatic history, a new collection of Roman material was made in the 19th century, begun by G. B. de Rossi (1822-94), continued by J. Wilpert (1857-1944), which included mosaics and church paintings.

Since the monuments of early Christianity proved to be an increasingly important source for the history of piety, the confessional restriction eventually disappeared. Christian archaeology established itself as a special branch of church history in many German

Protestant universities and faculties of divinity, especially Berlin. From the beginning of the 20th century, late antiquity also began to be of interest from the standpoint of the history of art. Christian archaeology was integrated with the art of Hellenistic Roman antiquity and the Byzantine and Western art of the Middle Ages. As a history of the art of late antiquity, it increasingly found a place in other than theological faculties (→ Theological Education). But the relation to questions of church history still demanded interdisciplinary investigation. The description, siting, and dating of monuments necessarily led to historical interpretation in the broad field of interaction between antiquity and Christianity.

Christian archaeology deals with all the objects that Christians made and used. The main sites are in Mediterranean and neighboring countries; the earliest monuments are from the third century. With one exception — the accidentally preserved house church of Dura-Europos — they are all funerary in character. From the time of Emperor Constantine (306-37) we have church buildings and their decoration, with mosaics only from the Theodosian era. The Christianizing of the Roman Empire enabled Christians to use almost all forms of art during the fourth century (e.g., the illustration of books as well as ivory carvings and work in clay and metal). From the first, Christian (biblical) themes may be found in a traditional world that is religiously neutral. Beginning in the age of Justinian, other traditions of antiquity were adopted with increasingly distinctive accents.

Bibliography: C. ANDRESEN, *Einführung in die christliche Archäologie* (Göttingen, 1971) • F. W. DEICHMANN, *Einführung in die christliche Archäologie* (Darmstadt, 1983) • W. H. C. FREND, *The Archaeology of Early Christianity: A History* (London, 1996) • A. GRABAR, *Early Christian Art* (New York, 1969); idem, *The Golden Age of Justinian* (New York, 1967) • W. F. VOLBACH and M. HIRMER, *Early Christian Art* (New York, 1961).

WOLFGANG WISCHMEYER

Archetype

C. G. Jung (1875-1961) introduced the concept of archetype into → psychology and → psychotherapy. In his work with patients Jung was struck by the similarity of personal ideas and fantasies (→ Imagination) to images and motifs that occur in fairy tales and myths and that have been for centuries the themes of meditation and practice in ritual festivals, → visions, and sacred pictures and texts. Such images and motifs have been handed down as tribal lore, creation stories, stories of the end of the world, mystery cults (→ Mystery Religions), or depictions of the gods. They are similar in both content and form.

Archetypes correspond to these images psychologically as structural elements of the "collective unconscious," as human being's human nature, as the preformed psyche that comes to fresh expression in each individual. They are possibilities, orientations, and potentialities that are present in all of us in an order and number that is conditioned by → evolution and significant for the survival of the species. They form the presupposition of every life and determine its goal. They are an important unifying element in human society; experience of their power and form overcomes all barriers. They are characterized by the high value of a numinous experience, by universality, by a leading and guiding function such as we find in great → dreams or in the life of Brother Nicholas of Flüe, in the legend of the Holy Grail, in the mandalas, or in symbolism.

Archetypes have practical significance for analytic psychotherapy and the theory of curing → neuroses. The required living out of archetypal images in personal analysis (e.g., in dreams) links patients with vital forces from which they have been cut off by harmful social influences, so that they are afraid of them instead of finding in them a vital basis of self-confidence. In such images they encounter the source, the protected circle or square (the ancient Greek temenos); they find a relation to a tree or to the Great Mother, or they come back to God by way of the divine child as an inner opposite. The healing, if dangerous, forces of the subconscious may be discerned, the archetypal image gives them form, and it makes possible a differentiated experience and awareness of the → energy of → life. They are an inner opposite with which the "I" must wrestle and may not identify itself; if it did, the result would be a psychotic or a political fanatic who is identical with a great idea and hence depersonalized (e.g., an apostle of morality).

In content, archetypes relate to all the great areas and elements of life, such as the relationship between two persons, the birth of a child, man and woman (→ Men; Women), mother and → father, the meaning and goal of life, the I and the → self, → nature and God. They are the great instruments of the psyche that point to the → future. Relating to them consciously is life sustaining, for it brings healing and promotes development.

Bibliography: W. BAUER et al., *Lexikon der Symbole* (4th ed.; Munich, 1988) • C. G. JUNG, "Concerning Mandala

Symbolism," *The Collected Works* (Princeton, 1968) 9.355-90; idem, "On the Nature of the Psyche," ibid. 8.159-234; idem, "Psychological Aspects of Mother Archetypes," ibid. 9.73-110 • C. G. JUNG et al., eds., *Der Mensch und seine Symbole* (12th ed.; Düsseldorf, 1991) • E. NEUMANN, *The Great Mother* (Princeton, 1972) • T. SEIFERT, *Lebensperspektiven der Psychologie* (Olten, 1981).

THEODOR SEIFERT

Archimandrite

"Archimandrite" (from Greek roots meaning "head of a sheepfold [*mandra*]") refers to a dignitary ranking below a → bishop. It was used from the 4th century for certain heads of monasteries (Orthodox or united with Rome). After the 6th century it was reserved for leaders of groups of monasteries and at first restricted to certain → abbots. Since the 18th century the title has been conferred on other monks or unmarried priests only loosely connected to the monastic state (as a rhasophore, or novice), either in an honorary way or as a promotion on the way to the episcopal office.

→ Orthodox Church

Bibliography: P. de MEESTER, *De monachico statu iuxta disciplinam Byzantinam* (Rome, 1942) • J. PARGOIRE, "Archimandrite," *DACL* 1.2739-61 • V. POSPISHIL, "The Archimandrite," *Diakonia* (Bronx, N.Y.) 13 (1978) 214-31 • M. WOJNAR, "De archimandritis basilianis in metropolia Kioviensi (1617-1882)," *Ius populi Dei* (FS R. Bidagor; Rome, 1972) 2.343-423.

PETER PLANK

Architecture → Church Architecture

Argentina

1. History
2. The Churches
   2.1. The Roman Catholic Church
   2.2. Protestantism and the Organization of Evangelical Churches
3. The Protestant Churches
4. Interdenominational Cooperation
5. Non-Christian Religions

Argentina is a republic with 22 provinces and the eastern half of the territory of Tierra del Fuego. It is the second largest country in Latin America (after Brazil) and has a relatively slow rate of population

	1960	*1980*	*2000*
Population (1,000s):	20,616	28,094	37,032
Annual growth rate (%):	1.55	1.51	1.19
Area: 2,780,400 sq. km. (1,073,518 sq. mi.)			

A.D. 2000

Population density: 13/sq. km. (34/sq. mi.)
Births / deaths: 1.90 / 0.78 per 100 population
Fertility rate: 2.44 per woman
Infant mortality rate: 20 per 1,000 live births
Life expectancy: 74.2 years (m: 70.6, f: 77.7)
Religious affiliation (%): Christians 92.9 (Roman Catholics 90.2, Protestants 5.9, indigenous 5.4, marginal 1.4, unaffiliated 1.1, other Christians 0.6), nonreligious 2.2, Muslims 2.0, Jews 1.5, other 1.4.

growth (1.7 million in 1869, 17.2 million in 1950, 22.3 million in 1965, 28.1 million in 1980, and an estimated 37.0 million in 2000). In 2000 its estimated population is the fourth highest, following that of Brazil, Mexico, and Colombia.

1. History

Argentina was influenced by Spanish civilization after its discovery in about 1515, but for long it remained outside the main centers of power in Peru and Mexico. It gained increasing importance and self-awareness in the 18th century through the development of oceanic trade and the ideas of the → Enlightenment. After formal declaration of independence in 1816 and the establishment of the constitution in 1853, and following a period of inner confusion and conflicts, Argentina opened its gates to mass immigration, chiefly from Europe (primarily from Italy, Spain, Poland, Ireland, and Germany), but also from the Near East and Far East. Its economy then blossomed, and the foundations of its industry were laid. Democratic forces emerged in the first decades of the 20th century, but the coming of the worldwide depression in 1930 initiated a time of political unrest and the struggle for a just economic and social order under the first presidency of Juan Perón (1946-55). A military coup forced Perón into exile in 1955; further military takeovers occurred in 1962, 1966, and 1976. There were also strong guerrilla movements, especially after 1969. A "dirty war" (1976-83) against them cost tens of thousands of lives, including between 15,000 and 30,000 "disappeared," and was accompanied by a severe economic crisis. On April 2, 1982, Argentina invaded and captured the Falkland Islands (Sp. Islas Malvinas), considered illegally occupied by Britain since the time of independence, but six weeks later it was forced to surrender the islands to a British military task force. Argentina returned to democracy in 1983, but political consolidation is still incomplete. Economic problems (including an inflation rate of over 6,000 percent in 1989) continue as severe impediments to national stabilization.

2. The Churches

With the immigration of the 19th century, churches, religions, and religious groups of all kinds entered this traditionally Roman Catholic country. The constitution guarantees religious freedom, yet it grants the "Roman, Apostolic, and Catholic Church" a special position as the religion supported by the → state (→ Church and State). The Protestant churches, which represent approximately 8 percent of the total population, have arisen either through (European) immigration, missionary work (mostly North American), or independently. Eastern and Oriental Orthodox churches and congregations also are found in Argentina. All churches that are not Roman Catholic must be registered by the state.

2.1. *The Roman Catholic Church*

After the declaration of independence, under the influence of England and the North American example, and with the encouragement of Protestant forces, an anticlerical → liberalism became dominant in ruling circles in Argentina. From the beginning of the 20th century, however, the → Roman Catholic Church came to be increasingly recognized and effective as a social and intellectual power. In 1992 it had 13 archbishops and 49 dioceses, churches and chapels in 2,459 parishes, 1,384 primary schools, 964 high schools, and 10 universities. In its service were 5,923 → priests, 11,612 sisters, 1,079 brothers, and 2,126 seminarians. There were 589,000 baptisms in 1992.

The Catholic Church has been very conservative in reaction to the anticlerical spirit of the founding period of the republic, and with the (transitory) introduction of divorce (→ Marriage and Divorce) and of secular schools under Perón in 1954/55, it came into conflict with the government. Things improved, however, with the demands of church renewal following → Vatican II and with their implementation by the second conference of Latin American bishops at Medellín, Colombia (1968; → Latin American Council of Bishops). Liturgical renewal, the thinking of → liberation theology, pastoral work oriented to actual problems (so-called *pastoral popular*), and concern for social rights have all come together in many places in the struggle for a new Catholicism. Through the power of the → gospel, this renewed church will deal with both spiritual and social conflicts in a unified and healing way. In the movement

known as Priests of the Third World, the readiness for social criticism has found its plainest but also its most contested expression. During the military dictatorship of 1976-83, the national bishops' conference and individual bishops came out publicly with criticisms of the political and economic situation.

2.2. *Protestantism and the Organization of Evangelical Churches*

In the early 1990s there were some 170 Protestant → denominations. The largest were the National Union of Assemblies of God (415,000 adherents) and the Assemblies of God (indigenous, with 211,000 adherents). The next largest Protestant groups were the Visión del Futuro, the Christian Brethren, the Christian Assemblies, and the Seventh-day Adventists, which had a major evangelistic and diaconal impact (e.g., through the provision of schools and hospitals in remote areas).

"Transplanted" *(iglesias del trasplante)* or "historical" churches owe their origin to immigration or missionary work. In addition, there are the independent churches and congregations that have arisen and are characterized by splits or by the work of Charismatic leaders (→ Charismatic Movement). Efforts to secure evangelical cooperation are long-standing. The goal is more effective evangelism, a common championing of interests (e.g., freedom of belief) in relation to the government, and cooperation in theological education, publishing, and social work. A new attempt to unite evangelical forces who would accept the challenge of political responsibility within a democratic framework came in 1982 with the formation of the Alianza Cristiana de las Iglesias Evangélicas de la República Argentina (ACIERA, Christian Alliance of Argentine Evangelical Churches). This alliance numbers thousands of congregations, including → Baptists, independents, and Pentecostals. Other associations of Pentecostals include Confederación Evangélica Pentecostal (CEP), Federación de Iglesias Pentecostales Autónomas (FIPA), and Confederación de Iglesias Pentecostales de la República Argentina (CIPRA).

Important earlier interdenominational organizations include the → Bible Society (founded in 1818, uniting some 40 churches and societies), the Federación Argentina de Iglesias Evangélicas (FAIE, Argentine Federation of Evangelical Churches, with 30 member churches, founded in 1959; previously the Evangelical Confederation of La Plata, with the churches of Paraguay and Uruguay, founded in 1939), the Billy Graham Society (an evangelistic fellowship of 3,200 churches and congregations of all kinds), and Union Theological Seminary in Buenos Aires (Facultad Evangélica de Teología). The seminary had Waldensian and Methodist beginnings in Uruguay in 1884 and Argentina in 1901. It became a theological seminary for several churches in 1917 and then in 1969, along with the Facultad Luterana de Teología (founded in 1955 in José C. Paz, a town in the greater Buenos Aires area), formed the Instituto Superior Evangélico de Estudios Teológicos (ISEDET). Among the many other evangelical centers of theological training are the Instituto Bíblico Buenos Aires and the Pentecostal Instituto Bíblico Río de la Plata.

3. The Protestant Churches

We consider here seven evangelical churches that have arisen from immigration, and then five others that are the fruit of missionary work.

3.1. The → Anglican Church dates from 1825 and has some 85 congregations and an active missionary work among → Indians in the North.

3.2. The (Scottish) Presbyterian Church dates from 1829 and consists of one large congregation with nine preaching stations.

3.3. The Evangelical Church of the River Plate dates from 1899; until 1965 it was the German Evangelical La Plata Synod. Originating among German-speaking immigrants, its first congregation was established in Buenos Aires in 1843. Russian-German congregations were set up in the province of Entre Rios from 1878. New waves of immigrants came after 1918, 1933, and 1945. Bilingual church work began early, which has moved toward a clear dominance of the national language today. Following the tradition of the united churches from Germany, its congregations can generally be considered Lutheran, with significant Reformed emphasis (also embracing congregations in Paraguay and Uruguay). In 1994 there were 50,000 members in 156 congregations.

3.4. The Evangelical Waldensian Church has been in Argentina since 1859 and has joined forces with congregations that have been in Uruguay since 1857. Like the Evangelical Church of the River Plate, it is a signatory of the → Leuenberg Agreement. It comprises ten congregations.

3.5. The Argentine Reformed Church (deriving from the Dutch Reformed Church) dates from 1889 and includes immigrants from South Africa in 13 congregations.

3.6. The Argentine Evangelical Lutheran Church (belonging to the Missouri Synod) dates from 1905 and consists mainly of German immigrants. It oversees the Concordia Theological Seminary and more than 260 congregations.

3.7. The Evangelical Congregational Church (from 1924) arose among Russian-German congregations of the German Evangelical La Plata Synod and is now linked to the United Church of Christ. It has 150 congregations.

3.8. The Evangelical Methodist Church dates from 1836 and is strongest in the cities. It did vigorous evangelistic work toward the end of the 19th century, is active in social criticism, and has led in ecumenical cooperation. It has 101 congregations.

3.9. The Baptist churches have worked since 1878 in many parts of the country and now have about 700 congregations and an important seminary in Buenos Aires (Seminario Internacional Bautista). Most of them are in fellowship with the U.S. Southern Baptist Convention.

3.10. The Evangelical Church of Disciples of Christ has resulted from the missionary work of the Disciples of Christ (→ Christian Church [Disciples of Christ]) and has eight congregations.

3.11. The United Evangelical Lutheran Church developed through missionary work by American Lutherans from 1908. The first congregation was founded in Buenos Aires in 1920 and became independent in 1948. The church supported the Lutheran Theological Seminary in José C. Paz from 1955 to 1969, and since World War II it has included many immigrant congregations (Estonians, Latvians, Slovaks, Hungarians, and Germans). It has 33 congregations.

3.12. There are many independent evangelical and Pentecostal churches and, since the late 1980s, a growing charismatic and neopentecostal movement. The Adventists estimate their membership at 60,000 in 500 congregations. The Free Brethren have about 1,000 congregations. The classic Pentecostals include the Union of the Assemblies of God, with possibly 3,000 congregations; the Christian Assemblies, with 750; the Assemblies of God, with 554; and the Church of God (Cleveland, Tenn.), with 495. The Visión del Futuro with 780 congregations and the Ondas de Amor y Paz with 120 belong to the neopentecostal movement, as do the Church of the Kingdom of God and the Universal Church of Jesus Christ from Brazil, which have recently been planting congregations in Argentina.

4. Interdenominational Cooperation

From the first, the evangelical churches in Argentina have taken a lead in the → ecumenical movement in Latin America. Continental evangelical conferences were held in Buenos Aires in 1949 and 1969, which led in 1982 to the formation of the → Latin American Council of Churches. The theological school in Buenos Aires (ISEDET) has gained recognition far beyond its supporting churches and the boundaries of Argentina as a leading center of theological and ethical teaching and research for Latin American Protestantism. In recent years the so-called historic churches have grown much closer together and are seeking ways to promote increasingly closer cooperation. The tasks set by political events (refugees from Chile in 1973 and problems of human rights under military dictatorships), and also by social need, have been tackled in concert by the evangelical churches, in part together with the Roman Catholics. Possibilities of evangelical–Roman Catholic encounter exist both in the field of theological dialogue and at the congregational level (e.g., the Week of Prayer for Christian unity and various diaconal activities).

5. Non-Christian Religions

The largest Jewish community in Latin America, over half a million and organized in about 300 different institutions, lives in Argentina, especially in the area of Buenos Aires, with important synagogues in the major cities. By the year 2000, it is estimated that the Muslim population will number over 700,000 ($\rightarrow$ Islam). New religions and spiritist movements also call for notice ($\rightarrow$ New Religions; Spiritism).

Fewer than 100,000 descendants of the original Indian inhabitants still live in the North and the Southwest. In the 1870s the native Pampa Indians in the South and the Guaycurúes in the North were victims of $\rightarrow$ genocide as a result of the "conquest of the wilderness" by General Julio A. Roca, a tragedy that occurred even as immigrants were streaming into the country. Missionary work among the remaining Indians seeks to teach them to help themselves and to maintain their own cultural traditions, although many, especially in the North, have become syncretistic Pentecostals.

Bibliography: D. BARRETT, ed., *WCE* 147-51 • T. BEESON and J. PEARCE, *Vision of Hope: The Churches and Change in Latin America* (Philadelphia, 1984) • A. FRIGERIO, ed., *El pentecostalismo en la Argentina* (Buenos Aires, 1994) • V. W. LEONARD, *Politicians, Pupils, and Priests: Argentine Education since 1943* (New York, 1989) • J. L. MECHAM, *Church and State in Latin America* (rev. ed.; Chapel Hill, N.C., 1969) • E. F. MIGNONE, *Witness to the Truth: The Complicity of Church and Dictatorship in Argentina, 1976-1983* (Maryknoll, N.Y., 1986) • D. P. MONTI, *Presencia del Protestantismo en el Río de la Plata durante el Siglo XIX* (Buenos Aires, 1969) • H. J. PRIEN, *Die Geschichte des Christentums in Lateinamerika* (Göttingen, 1978) • W. L. VILLALPANDO, ed., *Las Iglesias del Trasplante* (Buenos Aires, 1970) • H. WYNARCZYK, P. SEMAN, and M. DEMAYO, *Panorama actual del campo evangélico en la Argentina. Un estudio sociológico* (Buenos Aires, 1994).

HEINZ JOACHIM HELD

Arianism

Arianism is the teaching of the Alexandrian presbyter Arius (ca. 280-336) and his supporters. It arose originally in reaction to the $\rightarrow$ Christology of the apologists.

To preserve both $\rightarrow$ monotheism and the deity of Christ, the $\rightarrow$ apologists had adopted the philosophical idea of the Logos, and $\rightarrow$ Origen (ca. 185-ca. 254), making use of ontological $\rightarrow$ Platonic $\rightarrow$ categories, had attributed autonomy to the Logos/Christ as a hypostasis, or ousia, subordinate to God ($\rightarrow$ Ontology). Rejecting the Monarchian views of the Trinity of which he accused his bishop Alexander in 318, Arius applied the teachings of Origen in a radical way. As he saw it, God alone is God; in terms of negative Platonic predicates for deity, God is unbegotten, eternal, and without beginning or change. Christ is distinct from God, created out of nothing by the will of God (Arius cited Prov. 8:22 as a biblical proof), not eternal, yet created before all time or the world; in spite of his creaturehood, he is the world's mediator and redeemer.

Excommunicated in 319, Arius found supporters, including Eusebius of Nicomedia and Eusebius of Caesarea. By the time Constantine (emperor 306-37) became ruler in the East in 324, the Arian controversy had split the $\rightarrow$ church in practice. Constantine, who wanted uniform worship as a basis for the welfare of the empire, exerted himself to achieve a nontheological solution, but these efforts failed. In $\rightarrow$ Antioch in the winter of 324/25, Arius and his friends were condemned for the first time outside Egypt, but a final decision concerning Eusebius of Caesarea (ca. 260-ca. 340) was passed on to a larger council that had been planned. At the invitation of Constantine, the first ecumenical council met at $\rightarrow$ Nicaea in May 325 to settle the order and organization of the developing imperial church ($\rightarrow$ Early Church). Arius and two of his loyal followers were $\rightarrow$ excommunicated and banished. Eusebius, however, was rehabilitated, and an anti-Arian confession was adopted that rejected the idea that the Son is a creature. It excluded any ontological differentiation by using the term *homoousios* (of one substance), which had not hitherto been used in a Trinitarian sense.

Outwardly Nicaea had restored unity, but the strict supporters of Nicaea soon found themselves in conflict with the emperor's desire for ecclesiastical peace, especially → Athanasius (ca. 297-373), who became archbishop of → Alexandria in 328. On the narrower theological question, a debate ensued between those who supported three hypostases along the lines of Origen and those who supported one hypostasis along the lines of Nicaea (e.g., Marcellus of Ancyra, d. ca. 374). Arius himself ceased to play any significant role.

After the death of Constantine, his empire was divided among three of his sons. Constantius II (d. 361), who ruled the East, favored the → Origenists and Arians. Constantine II (d. 340) and Constans I, however, favored Athanasius and Marcellus, who also found support in the West. The Council of Sardica (342) sealed the de facto division of the church.

Constans's murder in 350 changed the ecclesiastical situation. Athanasius now seemed to be the main obstacle to the pacification that Constantius was seeking. By imperial command he was condemned at the Councils of Arles (353) and Milan (355), and he had to flee from Alexandria. Nevertheless, the Origenists began to divide into three different parties — the Homoeans, the Homoiousians, and the Anomoeans. At the end of the 350s the emperor favored the Homoeans, who were now the only real Arians, and who taught a biblicist theology of subordination that rejected any theorizing about hypostasis or substance, saying of the Son only that he is like the Father according to the Scriptures *(homoios kata tas graphas)*.

The Homoiousians, in the tradition of Origen and Eusebius, championed a theology of three hypostases that regarded itself as anti-Arian. Rejecting the Sabellian-sounding *homoousios*, they described the Son as *homoiousios* (like the Father). Around Aëtius (d. ca. 366) and Eunomius (d. ca. 394) arose the group known as the Anomoeans or the Eunomians, whose interest was philosophical, who continued the radical thinking of Arius, and who from the first were persecuted as heretical. The Homoean policies of the emperor (see the Councils of Rimini and Seleucia in 359) brought the Homoousians and the Homoiousians closer together, and the result was a neo-Nicene formula that distinguished between *ousia* and *hypostasis*, using the former for the unity in the Godhead and the latter for the members of the Trinity *(mia ousia, treis hypostaseis)*. As defined at the Synod of Alexandria (362), it thus ended the debate between those who argued for one hypostasis and those who argued for three hypostases.

The Homoeans, who were protected by Valens (378) in the East and were few in number in the Nicene West (Milan, Illyria), came under persecution as heretics (→ Heresies and Schisms) when Theo-dosius I (347-95) became emperor. Yet they experienced a literary blossoming in the fifth century, and the Christian Goths under Ulfilas (ca. 311-83) joined forces with them (→ Germanic Mission). The Goths then mediated this form of Christianity to the Germans who moved into the empire, and it faded out only in the seventh century when the eastern Goths and Vandals were overthrown and the western Goths had been won to → Catholicism.

Bibliography: L. Abramowski, "Dionys von Rom († 268) und Dionys von Alexandrien († 264/5) in den arianischen Streitigkeiten des 4. Jahrhunderts," *ZKG* 93 (1982) 240-72 • M. R. Barnes and D. H. Williams, eds., *Arianism after Arius: Essays on the Development of the Fourth-Century Trinitarian Conflict* (Edinburgh, 1993) • H. C. Brennecke, "Erwägungen zu den Anfängen des Neunizänismus," *Oecumenica et Patristica* (ed. D. Papandreou, W. A. Bienert, and K. Schäferdick; Stuttgart, 1989) 241-52; idem, *Hilarius von Poitiers und die Bischofsopposition gegen Konstantius II* (Berlin, 1984); idem, "Lucian von Antiochien," *TRE* 21.474-79; idem, "Nicaea I, ökumenische Synode von 325," *TRE* 24.429-41; idem, *Studien zur Geschichte der Homöer* (Tübingen, 1988) • F. Dinsen, "Homoousios" (Diss., Kiel, 1976) • R. C. Gregg, ed., *Arianism: Historical and Theological Reassessments* (Philadelphia, 1985) • R. C. Gregg and D. E. Groh, *Early Arianism: A View of Salvation* (Philadelphia, 1981) • R. P. C. Hanson, *The Search for the Christian Doctrine of God: The Arian Controversy, 318-381* (Edinburgh, 1988) • C. Kannengiesser, "Arianism," *EncRel(E)* 1.405-6 • T. A. Kopecek, *A History of Neo-Arianism* (2 vols.; Cambridge, Mass., 1979) • W. Löhr, "Arius redivivus? Ein Jahrzwölft Arianismusforschung," *TRu* 55 (1990) 153-87; idem, *Die Entstehung der homöischen und homöusianischen Kirchenparteien. Studien zur Synodalgeschichte des 4. Jahrhunderts* (Tübingen, 1986) • R. Lorenz, *Arius judaizans?* (Göttingen, 1979) • C. Markschies, *Ambrosius von Mailand und die Trinitätstheologie* (Tübingen, 1995) • M. Meslin, *Les Ariens d'Occident, 335-430* (Paris, 1967) • J. Pelikan, *The Christian Tradition*, vol. 1, *The Emergence of the Catholic Tradition (100-600)* (Chicago, 1971) • A.-M. Ritter, "Arianismus," *TRE* 3.692-719 (bibliography) • E. Schwartz, "Zur Geschichte der alten Kirche," *Gesammelte Schriften* (vol. 4; Berlin, 1960); idem, "Zur Geschichte des Athanasius," *Gesammelte Schriften* (vol. 3; Berlin, 1959) • M. Simonetti, *La crisi ariana nel IV seculo* (Rome, 1975) • C. Stead, "Homoousios," *RAC* 16.364-433 • J. Ulrich, *Die Anfänge der abendländischen Rezeption des Nizänums* (Berlin, 1994) • R. Williams, *Arius: Heresy and Tradition* (London, 1987).

Hanns Christof Brennecke

Aristotelianism

1. Philosophy of Aristotle

1.1. *Works*

Aristotle (384-322 B.C.) edited personally only the so-called exoteric (or popular) works — the dialogues of the academic period (*Eudemus* etc.) and the *Protrepticus,* which give evidence of an unequivocal → Platonic period — and also the dialogue *On Philosophy,* which on account of its criticism of the doctrine of ideas has been assigned to the years in Assus as a "programmatic work" (W. Jaeger). These writings may be only partially reconstructed from quotations in the Hellenistic philosophers and the Fathers.

We owe the real teaching works after his death to his student and disciple Theophrastus (ca. 372-ca. 287 B.C.), who possibly revised them. It was only in the first century B.C. that Andronicus of Rhodes arranged and edited them under the traditional headings of logic, physics, and ethics, putting physics first and then metaphysics, or as Aristotle sometimes called it, "first philosophy." The logical writings *(Organon)* contain *Categories, On Interpretation, Prior Analytics, Posterior Analytics, Topics,* and *Sophistical Refutations.* To the treatises on nature belongs the work *On the Soul.* The *Metaphysics* consists of 14 books that are separated in time and to some extent overlap. Of the ethical writings the *Nicomachean Ethics* and probably the earlier *Eudemian Ethics* are genuine, and positive conclusions have been reached also for the *Greater Ethics.* Here we may also mention the *Politics* and a collection of constitutions, of which only that for Athens survives. We may also add the fragmentary *Poetics* and the *Rhetoric,* at least part of which is genuine.

1.2. *Teaching*

1.2.1. Aristotle was the first to establish formal → logic (i.e., the doctrine of the deductive and inductive syllogism), a doctrine of categories that went beyond the merely "rhapsodical" (Kant's term), and the principle of contradiction (as distinct from a relative antithesis). In the *Organon* he also paid constant attention to the boundaries of logic and → ontology.

1.2.2. Whereas the various disciplines deal with specific aspects of being, metaphysics — the first philosophy — deals with being as such. Aristotle distinguishes four ways of this investigation: essential (or formal), material, efficient (or moving), and final. Only when taken together do they bring us to the heart of the matter. The material principle differs from the others because it represents pure receptivity, being according to its potentiality, yet not as an undifferentiated mass but as that which awaits specific actualization. In contrast, the essential principle is that which forms or shapes receptivity. Aristotle spoke of *eidos* (that which is seen; form), which is not ideal essentiality but that which gives essence its specificity. What is brought out of mere existence into specific existence also involves the principle of movement — of becoming, perishing, changing, and especially spatial movement. The fact that all movement points back to something unmoved may well be the theological basis of the metaphysics (W. Jaeger; → God, Arguments for the Existence of, 2). We see this plainly in the fourth principle, which as the goal and the → good knits all being together in a → teleological order.

On the one hand, Aristotle stresses the development from the inorganic, by way of the organic but perishable, and then the moved but imperishable heavenly bodies, to the deity as the immaterial and eternally self-thinking reality. On the other hand, the legacy of the later Plato (→ Platonism) indicates the downward path, on which all nondivine being is understood as an *analogia entis,* that is, an → analogical reflection of the being that is fully actualized in → God (§3.5) alone. This ensures for us the priority of theory over practice.

1.2.3. The physics, or second philosophy, is above all a doctrine of movement. As such, it is linked to time and number, but also to becoming, perishing, and qualitative transition. The ether embraces the traditional four elements in a circular movement, which is the most perfect. The → soul (§2) as the entelechy of the body rises up in steps. First there is the purely vegetative soul of plants, then the soul of animals, which can feel, desire, and move. Finally, we have the human soul, which is both thinking and immortal. This soul is one in its multiplicity of inner possibilities. As a thinking soul, it also acts and directs. It is the center of being that permeates all the rest.

1.2.4. Ethics is defined in terms of the center. The → virtues are the mean of extremes assigned to them. Happiness is the supreme good, and action attains it only with self-purification for pure contemplation of the divine being. On the downward path, also contemplated here, Aristotle describes the human being as a political entity *(zōon politikon)* who should find the right mean in political order. Specifically, monarchy, aristocracy, or *politeia* is opposed to tyranny, oligarchy, or democracy.

1.2.5. The *Poetics* and *Rhetoric* contain Aristotle's famous dictum that tragedy seeks to heighten and relax both fear and pity in the audience. This statement, however, is only an incidental formulation in the treatment of the nature of art as *technē* and the proposed mediation between human nature and destiny. With M. Heidegger, we may regard the *Rhetoric* as the first systematic hermeneutics of everyday life together.

HINRICH KNITTERMEYER†

2. History of Aristotelianism
2.1. *Antiquity*
The Peripatetic school under Theophrastus developed and refined Aristotelianism. The Hellenistic schools used Aristotelian logic, epistemology, and linguistics in clarification of their own doctrines. Epicurus (341-270 B.C.) made use of Aristotelianism in his theory of the will (→ Greek Philosophy). In later antiquity Plotinus (ca. 205-70), Porphyry (ca. 232-ca. 303), Proclus (410 or 412-85), and Boethius (ca. 480-524) all tried to harmonize the theories of Plato and Aristotle. They prepared the way for the Platonized Aristotelianism of the Middle Ages. Porphyry's commentary on the *Categories,* for example, underlies the debate about universals (→ Scholasticism).

2.2. *Middle Ages*
The Latin Middle Ages up to about the 12th century knew only the logical works of Aristotle, chiefly through the Latin translation by Boethius. After the translation of the most important works of Aristotle from Arab and Greek sources, three trends developed in the Aristotelianism of the 13th century: (1) Neoplatonic and Augustinian theology used Aristotelian terminology; (2) a moderate Aristotelianism took shape in the thought of Albert the Great and → Thomas Aquinas; and (3) Siger de Brabant adopted a radical Aristotelianism.

Albert the Great and Thomas Aquinas stressed the possibilities of natural theology (metaphysics) independently of revealed theology. In ethics Thomas made a careful distinction between natural and theological virtues (→ Thomism). Radical Aristotelianism espoused a philosophical monopsychism and the doctrine of the eternity of the world. Aristotelianism, both moderate and radical, was condemned at Paris and Oxford in 1277 in regard to its basic problems: matter as a principle of individuation; the theory that intelligences constitute independent species; the idea that *sophia* is the direct cause of the action of the will. The condemnation was not final,

however, and did not for long prevent the definitive differentiation of natural theology from the monism of Neoplatonic and Augustinian science and philosophy.

There were similar debates in the Jewish and Islamic thought of the Middle Ages (→ Jewish Philosophy; Platonism; Islamic Philosophy). Disciples of Aristotelianism over against (Neo-)Platonism were Abraham ibn Daud (ca. 1110-ca. 1180), M. Maimonides (1135-1204), al-Fārābī (ca. 878-ca. 950), and Averroës (1126-98). These all influenced the Latin West. The → Renaissance was predominantly Platonic. In ethics, however, Aristotelianism underlay the civic → humanism of L. Bruni, and P. Pomponazzi relied on Aristotelianism in his doctrine of the → soul.

2.3. *The Reformation and Modern Times*
The 16th-century Reformers tended to be cautious with regard to Aristotelianism. P. → Melanchthon (1497-1560), however, developed an Aristotelianism modified by Stoicism, and a humanistic synthesis between Aristotle and Plato was sought in France (by J. Lefèvre d'Étaples and others). In England, Oxford supported Aristotelianism, but Cambridge upheld Ramism and Platonism. Dutch Calvinists (→ Calvinism) used Aristotelianism as a starting point for their resistance to the skepticism of Descartes (→ Cartesianism).

Although the influence of Aristotelianism declined because of the criticism of → Scholasticism, many universities and church institutions did not stop teaching Aristotelian philosophy. The work of Aristotle played an important part in the early stages of the thought of G. W. Leibniz and G. W. F. Hegel (→ Hegelianism). Interest in Aristotle received a strong impetus from the editing of his works by the Prussian Academy of Sciences (1831-70). The Didon edition (1848-70) appeared at the same time in France, along with the editions and translations of the "collection des Universités de France." W. D. Ross, who prepared an English translation in the 20th century, also stimulated interest in the analytic philosophy of Aristotle.

Bibliography: Primary sources: J. BARNES, ed., *The Complete Works of Aristotle* (2 vols.; Princeton, 1984) • I. BEKKER, ed., *Aristotelis opera* (5 vols.; Berlin, 1831-70) • O. GIGON, ed., *Aristotelis opera* (5 vols.; Berlin, 1960-87) • R. MCKEON, ed., *The Basic Works of Aristotle* (New York, 1941) • V. ROSE, ed., *Aristotelis . . . fragmenta* (2d ed.; Stuttgart, 1967) • R. WALZER, ed., *Aristotelis dialogorum fragmenta* (Florence, 1934).

Secondary works: D. J. ALLAN, *The Philosophy of Aristotle* (2d ed.; London, 1978) • E. BIGNONE, *L'Aristotele perduto e la formazione filosofica di Epicuro* (Florence, 1936) • *The Cambridge History of Later Medieval Philosophy* (New York, 1982) pt. 2, "Aristotle in the Middle Ages" • *The Cambridge History of Renaissance Philosophy* (New York, 1988) • I. DÜRING, *Aristotle in the Ancient Biographical Tradition* (Göteborg, 1957) • W. K. C. GUTHRIE, *A History of Greek Philosophy,* vol. 6, *Aristotle: An Encounter* (2d ed.; Cambridge, 1983) bibliography • W. W. JAEGER, *Aristotle: Fundamentals of the History of His Development* (rev. ed.; Oxford, 1948) • F. E. PETERS, *Aristotle and the Arabs* (New York, 1968) • C. B. SCHMITT, *Aristotle and the Renaissance* (Cambridge, Mass., 1983).

A. J. VANDERJAGT

Ark of the Covenant

The ark was a portable → sanctuary of the Israelites, a wooden chest that could be carried on poles. According to the later, but probably accurate, information in Exod. 25:10, it measured about $125 \times 75 \times 75$ cm. ($50 \times 30 \times 30$ in.). According to common scholarly opinion, the ark appears for the first time in the Shiloh temple as part of the priestly cultus. It was lost in the war against the Philistines but was regained and brought to a neighboring sanctuary (1 Samuel 4–6). Later → David, probably in order to integrate religious traditions from the North with his national cultus, brought it to → Jerusalem, where it was at first still used in war (see 2 Sam. 15:24-26) and later probably in → processions (Psalm 132). Under → Solomon it found a place in the temple and remained there until being lost or destroyed with the capture of the city in 587 B.C.

Contemporary scholarship debates the early history and original functions of the ark. It was either a nomadic sanctuary with special significance in war or a Canaanite cultic object (e.g., a divine throne). The transfer to Yahweh occurred in Shiloh, and its being "called by the name of the LORD of hosts who is enthroned on the cherubim" (2 Sam. 6:2) occurred either there or, more probably, in Jerusalem. In any case, in the earlier times the ark was seen as a direct and salvific, but also dangerous, embodiment of the divine presence. Later it was, with the cherubim, the throne of Yahweh in the Holy of Holies in the Jerusalem temple (1 Kings 8). In Deut. 10:1-5 and in → Deuteronomistic thought, the idea arose that the ark had contained the tables of the → law (→ Decalogue), but whether it actually contained anything is uncertain.

Bibliography: G. HENTON DAVIES, "Ark of the Covenant," *IDB* 1.222-26 • J. JEREMIAS, "Lade und Zion. Zur Entstehung der Ziontradition," *Probleme biblischer Theologie. Gerhard von Rad zum 70. Geburtstag* (ed. H. W. Wolff; Munich, 1971) 183-98 • W. LOTZ, M. G. KYLE, and C. E. ARMERDING, "Ark of the Covenant," *ISBE* 1.291-94 • J. MAIER, *Das altisraelitische Ladeheiligtum* (Berlin, 1965) • P. D. MILLER JR. and J. J. M. ROBERTS, *The Hand of the Lord: A Reassessment of the "Ark Narrative" of 1 Samuel* (Baltimore, 1977) • J. MORGENSTERN, "The Ark, the Ephod, and the 'Tent of Meeting,'" *HUCA* 17 (1942-43) 153-266 • R. SCHMITT, *Zelt und Lade als Thema alttestamentlicher Wissenschaft* (Gütersloh, 1972) • C. L. SEOW, "Ark of the Covenant," *ABD* 1.386-93 (bibliography).

FRITZ STOLZ

Armament → Disarmament and Armament

Armenia

	1960	1980	2000
Population (1,000s):	1,867	3,096	3,662
Annual growth rate (%):	3.32	1.51	0.60

Area: 29,800 sq. km. (11,500 sq. mi.)

A.D. *2000*

Population density: 123/sq. km. (318/sq. mi.)
Births / deaths: 1.40 / 0.80 per 100 population
Fertility rate: 1.70 per woman
Infant mortality rate: 23 per 1,000 live births
Life expectancy: 71.6 years (m: 68.2, f: 75.0)
Religious affiliation (%): Christians 88.4 (Orthodox 82.7, Roman Catholics 4.4, other Christians 1.3), nonreligious 6.2, atheists 4.0, Muslims 1.4.

On September 23, 1991, the Parliament of the former Soviet Socialist Republic of Armenia declared Armenia a sovereign state, thus marking a new and as yet undetermined future for the nation and the → Armenian Apostolic Church. Present-day Armenia is a small nation, with an ethnic makeup of 96 percent Armenians and 4 percent minorities, including Russians, Kurds, Greeks, Jews, Yezidis, and Assyrians. The Armenian people trace their history back over 2,500 years. Through most of that time they have inhabited not only the southern Caucasus but much of eastern Anatolia. Armenia has often come under foreign rulers, including Byzantines, Persians, Arabs, Ottomans, and Russians. Nevertheless, Armenians have maintained a distinct civilization rooted in the early Christianization of the people.

The → conversion (§1) of the Armenian people was achieved through the labors of St. Gregory the

Enlightener, under whose influence King Tiridates III made Christianity the official religion of the kingdom, with the consequent founding in 314 of the Armenian church — called the Armenian Apostolic Church. Thus Armenia was the first country in which Christianity was made the officially established religion — one year after Constantine promulgated the Edict of Milan. A traditional conversion date of 301 is still honored officially by the church, however, and the 1,700th anniversary of this date will be celebrated at the turn of the millennium.

The ethnic distinctiveness of Armenians and rejection of the two-natures Christological formula of the Council of → Chalcedon (451) have subjected the Armenian Church to accusations of → Monophysitism and estranged it from greater Byzantine Orthodoxy (→ Orthodox Church). The Armenian church has kept its independence, despite attempts by Byzantines and Latins to absorb it and its people. The Ottoman invasions in the 14th and 15th centuries put an end to the sovereign Lower Armenian kingdom of Cilicia in 1375. Thus began the steady deterioration and weakening of the Armenian church as a theological and ecclesial entity.

Through the millet system the Ottoman rulers made the Armenian → patriarch of Constantinople an administrative arm of the central authorities. When one speaks of the lost freedom of the churches under Ottoman rule and the increased identification of Armenian, Greek, and other churches with the prevailing ethos, one must include also a process of → secularization of ecclesial life and a heightened survivalist mentality. This mind-set persisted into the modern period. But the greatest harm done to the Armenian church and people commenced with pogroms of Armenians in the late 19th century that culminated with the Ottoman Turkish → genocide of Armenians during the First World War. At least a million and a half Armenians lost their lives as the result of these pogroms and massacres, and the institutional framework of the church in Turkey (monasteries, schools, seminaries, etc.) was destroyed.

After a brief period of independent Armenian statehood (1918-20), the portion of Armenia that had been under Russian control became the smallest of the Soviet republics. Early and severe persecution of the Armenian church eased eventually as the Soviets recognized the usefulness of the church for propaganda purposes and for its relations with the large and prosperous Armenian diasporas in Europe and in North and South America.

During the long reign of Vasken I (1955-94), the See of the Patriarch and Catholicos of All Armenians in Echmiadzin made some strides toward recuperation from the devastating consequences of the genocide and bloody first years of Bolshevik massacres and Stalinist atrocities. Large-scale physical repairs and additions were made to Echmiadzin, as it also took on the semblance of a functioning ecclesiastical center. However, as late as 1972 the Armenian church had only 6 → bishops, 8 monks, about 30 → archimandrites and roughly 100 → priests in all of the Soviet Union. These served about 4 million Armenians. Even in 1990 there were only 33 operating churches in the whole of Armenia; while that number has increased, it still remains small. During the Soviet period, the church produced no significant theology, although it was engaged fairly continuously in the modern → ecumenical movement.

On April 9, 1995, Karekin I became the new catholicos, the 131st in a line of leaders stretching back to the fourth century. This ecumenically minded leader of the Armenian Church quickly moved to establish more cordial relations with other churches. And in December 1996 Karekin I made a historic visit to the Vatican and met with Pope John Paul II. The Armenian catholicos and the pope issued a joint declaration that included a common Christological formulation agreeable to both churches, attempting to overcome their historic disagreement over the teaching of the Council of Chalcedon.

Political and natural events of 1987-95 made a special impact upon contemporary Armenian religious life. Historic Armenian claims to the autonomous region of Nagorno-Karabakh, just across the border in neighboring Azerbaijan, intensified in the late 1980s with reports of → human rights violations and the ensuing massacres of Armenians in Sumgait and Baku, the capital of Azerbaijan. In 1988, during massive political protests against Moscow and Azerbaijan, a deadly earthquake struck Armenia, claiming between 25,000 and 50,000 lives. These events, the accelerating armed conflict between Armenians and Azeris in Nagorno-Karabakh, together with growing prospects of independence, aroused new interest in religion as people sought answers to their suffering and an anchor of hope for the future.

The Armenian church was not adequately prepared for these turns in events. While it administered the sacrament of → baptism to increasing numbers, it lacked the resources needed to educate; not enough was done to reach out to the people in their need in the villages and cities. By the early 1990s increased numbers of Seventh-day → Adventists, → Mormons, → Pentecostals, and Hare → Krishna and → Transcendental Meditation sects became active in Armenia. Meanwhile, the traditional minority Armenian Protestant → evangelical movement, which dates back to the 19th century, gained strength, and the → Uniate Catholic Church claimed as many as 30,000 adherents in 1995.

The Armenian Apostolic Church felt threatened and sought protection and special privileges from the government, which led to the passage of the Law on Freedom of Conscience and Religious Organizations in 1991. While it declared the principles of freedom of religious expression and separation of → church and state, the law nevertheless set limits on → proselytism by other churches and granted the Armenian church special privileges that amount to a quasi-establishment status. The full consequences of this law have yet to be worked out. The exact nature of the relationship of church and state in post-Soviet Armenia awaits definition.

Bibliography: J. DE MORGAN, *Histoire du peuple arménien* (Paris, 1919) • V. GUROIAN, *Faith, Church, Mission: Essays for Renewal in the Armenian Church* (New York, 1995) • R. G. HOVANNISIAN, *Armenia on the Road to Independence: 1918* (Berkeley, Calif., 1967) • C. S. MOURADIAN, *De Stalin à Gorbachev. Histoire d'une république soviétique: L'Arméniens* (Paris, 1990) • T. NERSOYAN, "The Armenian Church," *EncRel(E)* 1.413-17; idem, *Armenian Church Historical Studies* (New York, 1996) • M. ORMANIAN, *The Armenian Church* (London, 1912) • K. V. SARKESSIAN, "The Armenian Church," *Religion in the Middle East* (2 vols.; Cambridge, 1969) 1.482-520 • R. G. SUNY, *Looking toward Ararat: Armenia in Modern History* (Bloomington, Ind., 1993).

VIGEN GUROIAN

Armenian Apostolic Church

This is the most widespread → Monophysite church. Of about 4 million members worldwide, some 3.5 million live in Armenia, 440,000 in Georgia, and the rest in other countries of the former Soviet Union, as well as the United States, Turkey, and Iran. The heartland of the church is Armenia, where the → catholicos resides in the ancient monastery of Echmiadzin, Armenia.

The broad dispersion of this much-tested church has taken place in the course of a lengthy history. Even before Constantine (emperor 306-37), ancient Armenia between the Caucasus and Mesopotamia had accepted Christianity as the state religion when it was brought to them by Greek and Syrian missionaries (esp. Gregory the Illuminator, who worked in the second half of the third century and after whom the Armenians were often called Gregorians). From the fifth century onward there developed a national church that had its own Armenian alphabet and soon had its own translation of the Bible (→ Bible Versions). At the Council of Dvin (506, or perhaps somewhat later) the church adopted Monophysitism and rejected the → Chalcedonian Definition of 451; in 522 it adopted its own calendar.

The sufferings of the Armenian people began with the end of the Roman Empire when Persian, Arab, and finally (after 1071) Turkish armies overran the country. Most of the people fled to neighboring Cilicia and in 1080 founded there the kingdom of Cilicia, or Little Armenia, with the church as its spiritual guide. When this kingdom broke up under the attack of the Mamlukes and the catholicate in Sis (the capital of Cilicia) was restricted in its functions, the catholicate in Echmiadzin in approximately 1443 became the center of the Armenian Church. In the Russo-Turkish War of 1829 Echmiadzin came under Russian rule. From 1918 to 1920 it was the capital of a small independent Republic of Armenia, and it is now the seat of the chief patriarch and catholicos of all the Armenians. During World War I Armenians under Turkish rule were the victims of severe pogroms. Those who escaped fled from Little Armenia. In 1921 the catholicate in Sis was expelled and relocated in Antelias, near Beirut (Lebanon). This move led to a complex jurisdictional system that has experienced internal friction.

In their → liturgy the Armenians have adopted Latin customs, for example, in the use of unleavened bread for the Eucharist. Since the veneration of → images has never played a special role among them, a curtain has replaced the reredos. The liturgical language is Old Armenian. The → Uniate churches include Armenians in union with Rome.

Along with the catholicates of Echmiadzin and Sis, there are now patriarchates in Jerusalem and Istanbul that recognize the Echmiadzin catholicos as the supreme patriarch. On April 4, 1995, His Holiness Karekin II, catholicos of All Armenians in Echmiadzin, was enthroned on Palm Sunday, April 9, as Karekin I. In an unusual gesture, Levon Ter-Petrosyan, president of the Armenian Republic, endorsed Karekin II just before the election. The new catholicos's election and enthronement aroused great expectations and hopes for a revitalized and more ecumenically minded church, since the new spiritual leader of the Armenian church has been a respected ecumenist. His election also brought the promise of ending the long-standing jurisdictional dispute between the Holy See of Echmiadzin and the Holy See of Cilicia, which has divided the Armenian church around the world.

Bibliography: AGATHANGELOS and R. W. THOMSON, *History of the Armenians* (Albany, N.Y., 1976) • L. ARPEE, *A History of Armenian Christianity from the Beginning to Our Own Time* (New York, 1946) • G. H. CHOPOURIAN, *The Armenian Evangelical Reformation: Causes and Effects* (New York, 1972) • T. E. DOWLING, *The Armenian Church* (2d ed.; New York, 1970) • E. F. K. FORTESCUE and S. C. MALAN, *The Armenian Church* (New York, 1970) • H. R. GAZER, *Die Reformbestrebungen in der Armenisch-Apostolischen Kirche im ausgehenden 19. und im ersten Drittel des 20. Jahrhunderts* (Göttingen, 1995) • F. HEYER, ed., *Die Kirche Armeniens* (Stuttgart, 1978) • MANOUKIAN, *Agopik und Armen. Documenti di architettura Armena* (10 vols.; Milan, 1974-80) • J. DE MORDAN, *The History of the Armenian People* (Boston, 1965) • C. D. G. MÜLLER, *Geschichte der Orientalischen Nationalkirchen* (Göttingen, 1981) • K. SARKISSIAN, *The Council of Chalcedon and the Armenian Church* (London, 1965).

ERWIN FAHLBUSCH

Arminianism

Jacobus Arminius (1560-1609, from 1603 professor at Leiden) rejected the Calvinist doctrine of predestination. → Salvation, he taught, certainly depends solely on God's → grace, but we receive from God the → freedom to receive this grace or to reject it. Thus his view was more Erasmian and humanistic than Reformed. His opponents accused him of Socinianism (→ Unitarians) and semi-Pelagianism (→ Pelagianism). In 1604 he engaged in public debate with his colleague Franciscus Gomarus (1563-1641), who championed a supralapsarian doctrine of predestination. The struggle lasted until the death of Arminus, and its effects continued for some years after.

In 1610 the Dutch statesman Jan van Oldenbarnevelt (1547-1619) presented to the States General of Holland a remonstrance drawn up by Jan Uytenbogaert (1557-1644). Among the leading Remonstrants were the theologian Simon Episcopius (1583-1643) and the jurist Hugo Grotius (1583-1645). In opposition to absolute → predestination the Remonstrants affirmed five articles: (1) God has predestined those who believe for blessedness; (2) Christ died for all; (3) saving faith is the product of human free will; (4) God's grace is not irresistible; and (5) it is an open possibility that believers may fall away from their salvation. The conflict widened with the publication of the counterremonstrance of Gomarus in 1611.

The controversy initially had an ecclesiastical focus, for libertine trends had an influence among the Remonstrants. There was also a political element, for Oldenbarnevelt represented the interests of the provinces, especially Holland, against the centralizing tendency of the stadtholder Maurice of Nassau (1567-1625). This interrelation of theology and politics protected the Remonstrants for a time, but it finally led to their total defeat. For some years Oldenbarnevelt blocked the calling of a national council aimed at the Remonstrant minority, but his policy of peace with Spain and alliance with France stirred up increasing opposition both at home and abroad. Maurice wanted an alliance with England, whose king, James I (1603-25), was a resolute opponent of Arminianism. He also wanted continued war against the Spaniards, who were threatening the southern Netherlands.

Oldenbarnevelt and Grotius were arrested in 1618. The Synod of Dort (1618-19) condemned the Remonstrants point by point, declaring that (1) election does not depend on faith; (2) Christ's death achieves salvation only for the elect; (3) human nature is totally corrupt on account of → sin; (4) conversion is the work of God alone; and (5) the elect will assuredly persevere. The synod did not make the supralapsarianism of Gomarus an article of faith, but the reaction was a plain affirmation of Reformed → orthodoxy. In 1619 Oldenbarnevelt was executed on a charge of high treason, and the Remonstrants lost all official recognition and were banished. They founded the Remonstrant Brotherhood with a confession drawn up by Episcopius in 1622; this group still exists as a minority church in the Netherlands.

In the later history of theology Arminianism became a negative or delimiting concept. For orthodox Calvinists it denoted a semi-Pelagian error, while those who called themselves Arminians thought of it primarily as an expression of their opposition to the Calvinist doctrine of grace or to → Calvinism. High Anglican Arminians of the 17th century such as Archbishop W. Laud (1573-1645) fought against the → Puritans and saw Arminianism in terms of a state church (Erastianism), which was totally alien to the views of Arminius. In the 18th century John → Wesley (1703-91) described his Methodist preaching of the goal of Christian perfection as Arminian. Here again the decisive factor was less a direct link to Arminius or the Remonstrants than it was rejection of a Calvinism that had become dry and rigid. The concern of Arminius to look afresh at a doctrine of predestination that had become much too abstract, viewing it in light of Christ and faith, was less well represented by such movements than by modern Re-

formed theology itself, though with considerable course corrections (see K. → Barth, *CD* II/2, 67ff.).
→ Calvin's Theology

Bibliography: C. BANGS, *Arminius: A Study in the Dutch Reformation* (Nashville, 1971) • A. W. HARRISON, *Arminianism* (London, 1937); idem, *The Beginnings of Arminianism to the Synod of Dort* (London, 1926) • G. J. HOENDERDAAL, "Arminius / Arminianismus," *TRE* 4.63-69 • H. LADEMACHER, *Geschichte der Niederlande* (Darmstadt, 1983) 100-109 • J. MOLTMANN, *Prädestination und Perseveranz* (Neukirchen, 1961) 127-37 • R. A. MULLER, *God, Creation, and Providence in the Thought of Jacob Arminius: Sources and Directions of Scholastic Protestantism in the Era of Early Orthodoxy* (Grand Rapids, 1991) • A. P. F. SELL, *The Great Debate: Calvinism, Arminianism, and Salvation* (Worthing, Eng., 1982) • H. A. SLAATTE, *The Arminian Arm of Theology: The Theologies of John Fletcher, First Methodist Theologian, and the Precursor, James Arminius* (Washington, D.C., 1977).

ALASDAIR I. C. HERON

Arnoldshain Conference

1. Founding and Goal
2. History and Mode of Operation

1. Founding and Goal

The Arnoldshain Conference, named for the Evangelical Academy of Arnoldshain in the Taunus Mountains, Germany, and the theses that it drew up on the → Eucharist in 1957, is an independent working fellowship of leading personalities in the Evangelische Kirche der Union (EKU) and its member churches, in other union churches, in the Reformed churches in northwest Germany and Lippe, and in the Evangelical Lutheran Church in Oldenburg. Representatives of the Evangelical Church in Württemberg and of the → Reformed Alliance also participate by invitation. The declared aim is agreement in essential matters of church life and action, with a view to helping the Evangelische Kirche in Deutschland (EKD) more fully to be the church. An essential part of the goal was reached with the resolution of the EKD synod at Worms in 1983 that between the member churches there is church fellowship along the lines of the concord of Reformed churches in Europe (→ Leuenberg Agreement). There is also pulpit and table fellowship. The constitution of the EKD has been altered accordingly.

2. History and Mode of Operation

After the founding of the EKD in 1948, the confessional Lutheran churches (apart from Württemberg and Oldenburg) formed the United Evangelical Lutheran Church in Germany (VELKD), a united church with pulpit and table fellowship, and with a governing → bishop and church office. The other member churches of the EKD, following some earlier approaches, then began looking for ways to overcome confessional and other differences. For this purpose they found useful the common experiences of unions and of the → Confessing Church, as well as dialogues (→ Ecumenical Dialogue) on the Lord's Supper in the years 1947-67.

After preliminary talks between representative leaders, the Arnoldshain Conference was set up with a basic declaration between April 6 and July 20, 1967. This document states that the confessional distinctions of the Reformation period could no longer separate the churches, that the members of the Arnoldshain Conference regarded the EKD as the church, that they would strive for full table fellowship according to the Arnoldshain theses (→ Eucharist 5), that they would mutually recognize ordinations in their various churches, and that they would pledge to deal in concert with all essential questions of church life. The Arnoldshain Conference does not see itself either as a union of the EKD and member churches or as an umbrella for all the churches. It views its coordinating task, not in terms of organization, but more in terms of fostering responsible → dialogue, also with confessional alliances, especially the VELKD. On February 14, 1969, the churches of the Arnoldshain Conference united in pulpit and table fellowship, and their synods followed suit in the years thereafter. Delegates of the Arnoldshain Conference participated in the Leuenberg Agreement and in the Lima statement *Baptism, Eucharist, and Ministry,* issued in 1982 by the Faith and Order Commission of the → World Council of Churches.

Bibliography: Bekenntnis und Bekennen im Gottesdienst (Hamburg, 1978) • P. M. BRETSCHER, trans., "The Arnoldshain Theses on the Lord's Supper," *CTM* 30 (1959) 83-91 • A. BURGSMÜLLER and R. BÜRGEL, eds., *Die Arnoldshainer Konferenz, ihr Selbstverständnis* (2d ed.; Bielefeld, 1978) • A. BURGSMÜLLER and R. FRIELING, eds., *Amt und Ordination im Verständnis evangelischer Kirchen und ökumenischer Gespräche* (Gütersloh, 1974) • *Der Dienst von Pfarrern und "Mitarbeitern"–Empfehlungen zur Neuordnung der Dienste in der Gemeinde* (1975) • *Gemeinsame theologische Erklärung zu den Herausforderungen der Zeit* (1971) • *Gottesdienst anläßlich der Eheschließung zwischen einem evangelischen Christen und einem Nichtchristen* (1975) • E. GRISLIS, "Arnoldshain Theses on the Lord's Supper in Recent Discussion," *LQ*, 3d ser., 13 (1961) 333-55 • *Möglichkeiten und Grenzen der politischen Betätigung der Kirche und ihrer Mitarbeiter* (Neukirchen, 1982) • "Muster einer Ordnung für Lehrverfahren und Visitationsordnung," *Abl. EKD* 1976, nos. 43 and 44 • *Ordination. Gottesdienstordnungen für Ordination und Einführung* (Gütersloh, 1972 and 1976) • *Pluralismus in der Kirche, Chancen und Grenzen* (1977) • *Stellungnahme zur Reform der Grundordnung der EKD* (1972) • T. F. TORRANCE, "The Arnoldshain Theses on Holy Communion," *SJT* 15 (1962) 4-21.

JOACHIM LELL†

Art → Christian Art

Ascension of Christ

1. Luke is the only NT author to tell the story of the ascension (which is mentioned in *Barn.* 15:9 and *Gos. Pet.* 9:35-42, as well as in the Old Latin codex Bobiensis [MS *k*] at the beginning of Mark 16:4). There are two short accounts, whose surprising differences can be explained by their respective literary functions.

The first account, at the end of Luke (24:50-53), focuses on → Jesus blessing his → disciples (note the repetitions in vv. 50 and 51) and parting from them at the end of his life. The disciples, who feel protected, fall down before the risen Lord in worship and then return to the city full of joy. In the second account, at the beginning of Acts (1:9-11), the focus is on the disciples and their anxiety (with mention of their looking in all three verses). In this account Jesus is torn from them, the cloud serving as both vehicle and shield. In this version "two men" (→ Angel) are present and talk with the disciples about the → parousia.

2. The two accounts, which in vocabulary, style, and theme are clearly redactional, are a historicizing of — or, more precisely, an attempt to put into narrative form — the → Easter motif of exaltation, which was very widespread in the primitive Christian community and which was usually expressed in liturgical, biblical terms (exaltation and session at God's right hand, announced in Ps. 110:1) and celebrated as an invisible reality. In these accounts, however, the event is made visible, and the → apostles become eyewitnesses. Thus a question arises: Did the crossover from hymnic confession (→ Confession of Faith) to narrative come from Luke (G. Lohfink), or could he have been using earlier traditions (F. Hahn)?

3. Apart from the answer to such questions, the variety of Luke's means of expression calls for comment. In Luke 24 the author uses the motif of final parting (cf. that of the patriarchs) and expresses continuity by means of the → blessing. In Acts 1 he uses the motif of transport and apotheosis, which brings about a break between the hero and his followers (cf. Romulus in Livy *Annals* 1.26). Luke, or the tradition that he embodies, is thus using conventional themes to depict a unique event in salvation history: the exaltation of Jesus the Lord to the right hand of God.

4. Distinct from the ascension, which was visible to the disciples and attested only by Luke, Christ's exaltation is a widespread creedal element in the NT. Christ's victory over death could be expressed by several categories, particularly the resurrection and the exaltation. If, as we have seen, the ascension is a later development, the exaltation is an early belief to which NT creed formulas and hymnic passages bear witness.

In a traditional sentence attributed to the apostle Peter, we find the expression "being therefore exalted [*hypsōtheis*] at the right hand of God" (Acts 2:33; or perhaps the dative phrase here could better be translated instrumentally: "by the right hand of God"). The first epistle attributed to the same Peter is filled with kerygmatic and hymnic expressions. It is therefore not surprising to find not a narrative of Christ's ascension but homologous expressions of Christ's exaltation, for example, in 1 Pet. 3:22: "who has gone into heaven and is at the right hand of God." In Phil. 2:6-11 Paul uses an early Christian hymn with the triumphant confession, "Therefore God also highly exalted [*hyperypsōsen*] him" (v. 9). The motif of Christ's elevation is also embedded in the Johannine tradition, and the evangelist meditates upon it: "So must the Son of Man be lifted up [*hypsōthēnai*]" (John 3:14; see also 8:28; 12:32, 34). An unusual hymn is quoted in 1 Tim. 3:16, which ends, "Believed in throughout the world, taken up in glory." The verb for "taken up" here is *analambanō*, which Luke uses for the ascension in Acts 1:2 and 11. Luke also uses the verbs "carry up" (*anapherō*, Luke 24:51) and "lift up" (*epairō*, Acts 1:9).

→ Resurrection

Bibliography: F. BOVON, *Luke the Theologian: Thirty-Five Years of Research (1950-1985)* (Allison Park, Pa., 1987) 170-77 • J. G. DAVIES, *He Ascended into Heaven: A Study in the History of Doctrine* (London, 1958) • B. K. DONNE, *Christ Ascended: A Study in the Significance of the Ascension of Jesus Christ in the NT* (Exeter, 1983) • F. HAHN, "Die Himmelfahrt Jesu. Ein Gespräch mit Gerhard Lohfink," *Bib* 55 (1974) 418-26 • G. LOHFINK, *Die Himmel-fahrt Jesu. Untersuchungen zu den Himmelfahrts- und Erhöhungstexten bei Lukas* (Munich, 1971) • M. C. PAR-SONS, *The Departure of Jesus in Luke-Acts: The Ascension Narratives in Context* (Sheffield, 1987) • G. SCHNEIDER, *Die Apostelgeschichte* (vol. 1; Freiburg, 1980) 195-211 • P. TOON, *The Ascension of Our Lord* (Nashville, 1984).

FRANÇOIS BOVON

Asceticism

1. The Concept and Its Present Significance
2. The NT and the Early Church
3. The Reformation and the Modern Period

1. The Concept and Its Present Significance

1.1. Asceticism is a basic concept in the history of European civilization. In Greek antiquity from the fifth century B.C., "asceticism" denoted bodily self-control on the part of athletes and likewise the exercise of moral restraint on the part of philosophers. It rests primarily on the voluntary decision of individuals and entails the temporary or indefinite renunciation of certain pleasures or activities that are otherwise available, all in order to achieve a suprapersonal goal. In this sense asceticism has been rediscovered in the present age. According to S. Freud (1856-1939), all civilization is built on self-restraint. In fact, neither art nor science can be productive without it.

The striving for technical and economic → progress might also be called a secular form of asceticism (P. Chaunu). According to C. F. von Weizsäcker, the → future demands the constant development of new forms of self-control. It is doubtful, however, whether the democratic asceticism that Weizsäcker wanted can be broadly achieved in view of the widespread popular revolt against asceticism, at least as long as certain enlightened democratic maxims remain firmly rooted in our sense of what is right in a modern → society, for example, the protection of private property (J. Locke) or the proclamation in the U.S. Declaration of Independence that the pursuit of happiness is an "unalienable" right. Movements of protest nevertheless arose in North America and Europe in the 1960s, calling for an end to unlimited control over private property, to unregulated dominion over → nature, and to → weapons of mass destruction. These movements may be regarded as signs of a new sense of asceticism.

The understanding of asceticism as it has developed in the course of the history of Christianity may contribute to our understanding of contemporary attitudes, allowing us to critique them. Sport, for example, has both ancient and modern Christian roots (Puritanism in England and America but also Christian military preparatory training in Germany, which, as F. Jahn and E. M. Arndt have pointed out, has influenced the theory of sport in socialist lands). In the quest for superior achievement, sport loses its suprapersonal goals. The same thing happens in the "asceticism of preservation" (R. Bohren), manifested in a consuming attention to one's bodily hygiene, or in a view of employment as simply a means of increasing one's personal possessions.

1.2. Asceticism is a leading concept in Christian → ethics. To be sure, the term has increasingly gone out of use in Protestant theology since the 17th century (G. Voetius, *Exercitia pietatis,* 1644), but it now calls for more notice in Protestant groups and communities (→ Taizé Community) as well as at conferences. Increasing regard is also paid to it in theological teaching.

D. → Bonhoeffer's work *The Cost of Discipleship* (1937) represented a new beginning, with its reflection on basic ascetic principles. Yet Bonhoeffer's work subordinated the ultimate to the penultimate, and the arcane discipline to "the world come of age"; it thus demanded asceticism in the world. Bonhoeffer also revealed a leaning toward the new Roman Catholic understanding. On August 21, 1944, he wrote, "Again and again we must immerse ourselves at great length and very quietly in the life, actions, passion, and death of Jesus." Such a statement basically involves a narrow view of asceticism as spiritual discipline (inward and spoken → prayer, → penitence, the reading of spiritual works, and sacramental reflection). Bonhoeffer's observation that many Protestant circles cannot understand spiritual exercises, asceticism, meditation, or contemplation (made in his *Ethics*) remains relevant here.

After 1945 the American church, with the encouragement of the Lutheran World Federation, adopted → stewardship — that is, the careful, responsible use of one's time, abilities, and material possessions — as a model of virtue. Such an emphasis, however, has not gained acceptance in the church as a whole.

The concept of asceticism has never met with opposition in → Orthodoxy (§3) or → Roman Catholicism, but it usually has had a narrower sense in Roman Catholic moral theology. In contrast, K. → Rahner's distinction of three forms of asceticism — moral, cultic (ritual), and mystical — offers a new scholarly and ecumenical clarification of the term, for it recognizes that the three forms are not necessarily Christian, and also that Christian asceticism means particularly a penitent, personal, voluntary anticipation of death along the lines of orientation to Christ's passion. Typical of a Roman Catholic non-ritual understanding is the new view of → pilgrimages, according to which relics are not the goal so much as the pilgrimage itself, which receives its meaning from the pilgrims' march as the wandering people of God.

2. The NT and the Early Church

In the NT and the early church, as in antiquity at large, asceticism meant personal discipline, including renunciation. There was not as yet any distinction between general and special asceticism. Every form of asceticism that was significant in church history was present already in the NT.

2.1. Jesus demanded that his followers give up riches, → money, and possessions (Luke 16:19-31). His command to the rich young ruler (Mark 10:17-31) and his words to his disciples as he sent them on their mission (Matt. 10:5-15) often led to popular movements of ascetic poverty, such as the → anchorites in Egypt connected with Anthony, the monastic houses of Basil (4th cent.), and "apostolic poverty" in the High Middle Ages (the Waldenses, Franciscans, and mendicant orders). In contrast, the demonizing and total negation of earthly possessions among the Gnostics, Manichees, and Spiritual Franciscans were sometimes condemned as violating the church's rightful diaconal task (Matt. 25:31-46; cf. Cyril of Jerusalem). Thus in 1323 John XXII (1316-34) responded to movements espousing poverty by condemning the thesis that Jesus and the → apostles had no property.

A special form of apostolic poverty was the wandering asceticism that derived from Jesus' words in Matthew 10 and that was found already in the early church. This peregrination in the Irish-Celtic and Anglo-Saxon churches early in the Middle Ages played a decisive part in the Christianizing of central and western Europe.

2.2. According to → Jesus, sexual asceticism can be required "for the sake of the kingdom of heaven" (Matt. 19:12). → Paul rated celibacy higher than → marriage (1 Corinthians 7). The central position of widows (sometimes called the altar of God) under the church's care in the first centuries had a basis in sexual ethics as well as in love (1 Timothy 5). From the second century the ideal of virginity was widespread (cf. Rev. 14:4 and the Thecla cult). From the fourth century it had a Christological basis in the virgin birth of Jesus (first plainly attested in Cyril of Jerusalem and Gregory of Nyssa), and from the

Council of → Ephesus (431) it increasingly found a → Mariological basis.

Even asceticism that was radically hostile to sexuality (e.g., as taught by → Origen and → Augustine) remained consciously aloof from Neoplatonic asceticism in that it regarded marriage as commanded for Christians. Up to the fourth century, however, widowers and widows were commonly forbidden to contract a second marriage. This prohibition bears witness to the exceptionally high regard for monogamy on the basis of the sayings of Jesus in Matt. 5:31-32 and Mark 10:2-12. Yet in opposition to Gnostic and Manichaean hostility to the body, and to the Montanist and Messalian practice of an ascetically motivated cohabitation (→ Subintroductae) on the basis of Gal. 3:28, the church defended both marriage and ecclesiastical → monasticism.

2.3. Prayer as one of the constant elements in the history of Christian piety developed into a special form of asceticism in monasticism. In the *Life of Anthony* by → Athanasius (ca. 297-373), we meet for the first time the clear connecting of prayer and → work that later characterized Benedictine monasticism. Thus work *(ergon)* could be understood as *parergon* (bywork, or subordinate business). Monasticism also included an asceticism of prayer that cultivated constant prayer (1 Thess. 5:17) and regarded prayer as the supreme → virtue (Macarius Simeon). The short prayer that people frequently made to Jesus (in the formula of Mark 10:47; cf. Matt. 6:5-15; Luke 18:1-8) became a leading form in Orthodoxy, at least from the → hesychast movement of the 14th century. It sometimes had a revelation of light as its goal (the light of Tabor, according to Matt. 17:1-8).

2.4. Another form of asceticism is the avoidance of outside cultural influences, which could be defended from the example of the apostles, who were simple and uneducated people (Acts 4:13; 1 Cor. 4:10-13). Here we could cite → Tertullian (d. ca. 225) and his attack on academic instruction, or the anti-intellectualism of → Francis of Assisi (d. 1226) and Elizabeth of Thuringia (1207-31). In → Byzantium and Slavic Christianity this form of the simple life created the figure of the fool for Christ's sake (Simeon Salos; cf. Dostoyevsky's *Idiot*). The opposition to culture that is found in some modern sects and groups (e.g., the → Jehovah's Witnesses) is not ascetic but is aimed against the → Enlightenment and → rationalism.

2.5. → Fasting was liturgically normative from the second century. According to *Didache* and *Hermas*, Wednesday and Friday were the fast days. There was also fasting before baptism (mentioned by Justin Martyr), and from the third century, the 40 days before → Easter became a general fast. These developments show a ritualizing tendency that is in tension with the rule given by Jesus, which stresses the hidden nature of fasting (Matt. 6:16-18) and which also endorses joyful feasting as long as the bridegroom is present (Mark 2:18-19; Matt. 11:19). The promotion of physical abstention can lead to an extremely popular misunderstanding of Christian asceticism (cf. the → stylites, or pillar saints, and Syrian monasticism).

2.6. The Middle Ages saw an increase in both the regimen and the extent of asceticism. Particularly momentous was the distinction (on the basis of 1 Cor. 7:25 Vg) between a precept and a counsel. The former, like one of the Ten Commandments (→ Decalogue), is binding for all Christians. The latter, however, is an additional demand — for example, for a life according to the → Sermon on the Mount, which can produce works of supererogation in → heaven but is fully possible only in a state of perfection. From the time of → Scholasticism these counsels were equated with the monastic vows of poverty, chastity, and → obedience. The distinction, and the form of monasticism related to such vows, was virtually unknown in Eastern monasticism.

From the 6th to the 13th century, Western civilization was shaped by the predominance of the → Benedictine and related orders (Gorze, Cistercians; → Cluny). The ascetic norms of the Benedictine Rule (obedience to the → abbot, silence, → humility, stability of residence, work, and → hours of prayer) shaped the history of mission in Europe. The Benedictine Rule also depicted asceticism as *militia Christi* (see Ephesians 6), which in the age of the → Crusades could take the form of knightly service in orders. The spiritual asceticism of meditation, which involved the external memorizing and internal reflecting on a biblical text (cf. Ps. 1:2), and which M. → Luther also practiced, came to the Middle Ages from J. Cassian by way of the Benedictine Rule.

A special medieval form distinct from the lay asceticism of the Eastern church was priestly celibacy. As early as Pope → Gregory I (590-604), the Western distinction between social and private asceticism (the active life vs. the contemplative life; cf. Luke 10:38-42) was supposed to find a synthesis in the secular priesthood (or the so-called mixed life). This resulted in a demand for priestly celibacy, which Boniface in particular promoted in Germany and which finally became a Roman Catholic law in 1074.

Also Western is an orientation of asceticism to the sacrament of penance (→ Penitence), which we owe to Irish monasticism. Penitential books that prescribed fines for particular offenses required a high

ascetic sense from the laity. The best known of these, which Gregory I inspired, and which modified an ancient monastic doctrine of eight offenses (from Evagrius Ponticus and John Cassian), took the view that there are seven mortal sins that make penance absolutely obligatory. From the days of High Scholasticism these sins were listed as pride, sloth *(accedia)*, lust, anger, gluttony, envy, and covetousness. Finally, another distinctively Western idea was that social service and material sacrifices, especially monetary gifts, could serve as penances (→ Indulgence). In the history of Western piety, then, especially from the time of Francis, penance and asceticism meant much the same thing.

3. The Reformation and the Modern Period

The → Reformation repudiated medieval asceticism at essential points: the two-stage ethics reflected in monastic vows, an exclusive orientation to penance, the meritoriousness of works, and the classification of sins. Any charge of ethical indifference, however, especially with regard to Luther's doctrine of justification, is quite unfounded, as one may see from Luther's *Sermon on Good Works, Address to the German Nobility,* and catechisms. In detail, the Reformation promoted a new understanding of bodily discipline, including fasting (as an external bodily discipline; see Luther's Small Catechism and Augs. Conf. 26), but especially work, → vocation, marriage, obedience to parents, teachers, and rulers, and social responsibility, as well as prayer and → meditation in Bible reading. The observance of Sunday in Lutheranism was less an observance of the whole day than it was in → Calvinism, but in both it meant an obligation to take part in the → worship of God.

The Protestant declericalizing of morality and its extension to Christian people as a whole under the principles of the priesthood of believers and evangelical → freedom helped to develop the Protestant middle class (→ Bourgeois, Bourgeoisie), with the manse as a model. One may thus understand the ethos of evangelical Christianity as a renewal of the lay asceticism of primitive Christianity. The ethics of the → Pastoral Epistles and the → household rules (M. Dibelius) was already essentially a lay asceticism. The characterizing of Protestant ethics as a this-worldly asceticism is apt, but it is doubtful whether modern capitalism can be understood as an expression of Puritan mentality (as M. → Weber tried), especially since the values of the Enlightenment had a much greater impact on it (see 1).

Finally, → Pietism and the revival movements in Europe and North America developed rich forms of ascetic life, often reaching back to older monastic asceticism (J. Arndt, G. Arnold, and J. → Wesley). We can only conclude, then, that the claim that Protestantism has no asceticism is simply a one-sided depiction of neo-Protestantism in distinction from medieval and Pietist asceticism (see A. Ritschl, *Christian Perfection,* 1874). Nevertheless, one should not overlook the fact that up to the middle of the 20th century, the term "asceticism" had almost vanished from Protestant ethics, surviving only occasionally in such forms as meditation and private → devotion.

It is perhaps the task of a new Protestant asceticism to depict the unity of private and social conduct in the unity of the person of Jesus Christ and, in so doing, to pay heed to the primacy of personal commitment as a basic insight of Christian asceticism. The sayings of Jesus about discipleship provide the norm, combining self-denial and self-discovery, witness *(martyria)* and confession *(homologia)* (Matt. 10:32 and par.; Mark 8:31-38; Luke 14:26-27). Social asceticism, which nowadays is represented organizationally in the → diakonia of the church, and especially a secular form of democratic asceticism (see 1), cannot function without a readiness for personal sacrifice. Historical asceticism engages in a religious comparison that highlights the distinctive features of an asceticism that is based on Christian → discipleship. One of its distinctive characteristics is its nonritual and noncultic nature.

Bibliography: E. Benz, *Die protestantische Thebais* (Mainz, 1963) • R. Bohren, *Fasten und Feiern* (Neukirchen, 1973) • D. Bonhoeffer, *The Cost of Discipleship* (5th ed.; New York, 1960) • P. Chaunu, *Le refus de la vie* (Paris, 1975) • S. Elm, *"Virgins of God": The Making of Asceticism in Late Antiquity* (Oxford, 1994) • K. S. Frank, ed., *Askese und Mönchtum in der alten Kirche* (Darmstadt, 1975) • E. Geldbach, *Sport und Protestantismus* (Wuppertal, 1975) • B. Lohse, *Mönchtum und Reformation* (Göttingen, 1963) • P. Nagel, *Die Motivierung der Askese in der alten Kirche und der Ursprung des Mönchtums* (Berlin, 1966) • K. Rahner, "Passion and Asceticism," *Theological Investigations* (vol. 3; Baltimore, 1967) 58-85 • W. J. Shiels, ed., *Monks, Hermits, and the Ascetic Tradition* (Oxford, 1985) • E. Troeltsch, *The Social Teaching of the Christian Churches* (2 vols.; Louisville, Ky., 1992) • C. F. von Weizsäcker, "Gehen wir einer asketischen Weltkultur entgegen?" *Deutlichkeit* (Munich, 1981) 56-86 • V. L. Wimbush and R. Valantasis, eds., *Asceticism* (New York, 1995).

REINHART STAATS

Asia

1. Social, Political, and Economic Situation
2. The Religions of Asia
3. Christianity in Asia
   3.1. History of Christianity
   3.2. The Christian Churches and Their Work
   3.3. Cooperation of the Protestant Churches
   3.4. Ecumenical Dialogue

1. Social, Political, and Economic Situation

1.1. Asia (which, according to current United Nations definitions, does not include Russia) covers an area of 31.9 million sq. km. (12.3 million sq. mi.) and in A.D. 2000 is estimated to have a population of 3.7 billion people. Of all continents, it is both the largest (embracing 21 percent of the world's total area) and the most populous (61 percent of all people). The People's Republic of China itself, with 1.26 billion people, has a bigger population than Europe (729 million) and Latin America and the Caribbean (515 million) combined. For some years China has been successful in limiting its population growth. By 2000 India is expected to be the second country surpassing a billion in population. By that date, Indonesia should have 213 million, and Pakistan 156 million. These four countries alone would be home to 71 percent of all Asians. Asia, the cradle of humanity and of great cultures and religions, for all its centuries of history is a continent of → youth. Three-fourths of its people are under 40 years of age; nearly half are under 21. In most of the countries the economy is mainly agricultural. If we disregard Japan (the world's third greatest industrial power), South Korea, Taiwan, Singapore, and China's recently acquired Hong Kong, approximately two-thirds of the people work on the land. The effects of the → colonial past, the lack of skills, and the unjust conditions of the present economic system make it more difficult for Asia to develop its own industries.

1.2. Since the end of World War II Asia has gone through great political, social, and intellectual upheavals. The search for modernization and humanization, for economic and social justice, for nationality and political independence, has had different results in the different countries. The People's Republic under Mao Zedong (1893-1976), through many conflicts and inner tensions, tried to develop a Chinese → socialism. This system has experienced major changes under the present leadership. The development of Japan into a leading industrial and trading nation has led to its being regarded by many Asians as a First World country, with doubts cast on its Asian identity. India has long been called the

Asia in A.D. 2000: Demography

	Population (1,000s)	Annual Growth Rate (%)	Population Density (per sq. km. / mi.)	Births / Deaths (per 100 pop.)	Fertility Rate (per woman)	Infant Mortality Rate (per 1,000) live births)	Life Expectancy (years)
World total	**6,091,351**	**1.27**	**45 / 116**	**2.13 / 0.86**	**2.66**	**51**	**66.9**
Asia	**3,688,535**	**1.26**	**116 / 299**	**2.05 / 0.76**	**2.50**	**49**	**67.7**
Eastern Asia	**1,483,111**	**0.66**	**126 / 326**	**1.40 / 0.73**	**1.78**	**29**	**72.1**
China	1,260,751	0.70	132 / 341	1.43 / 0.72	1.80	32	71.0
Japan	126,428	0.12	335 / 867	1.03 / 0.91	1.48	4	80.3
Mongolia	2,736	2.00	2 / 5	2.60 / 0.60	2.98	46	67.7
North Korea	23,913	1.22	195 / 504	1.78 / 0.56	2.10	19	73.2
South Korea	46,883	0.72	472 / 1,223	1.39 / 0.67	1.65	8	73.5
Taiwan	22,401	0.70	619 / 1,604	1.47 / 0.61	1.80	32	71.0
South-central Asia	**1,495,977**	**1.42**	**139 / 361**	**2.19 / 0.69**	**2.58**	**39**	**67.6**
Afghanistan	25,592	2.84	39 / 102	4.67 / 1.84	6.30	143	47.5
Bangladesh	128,310	1.73	869 / 2,252	2.67 / 0.87	2.88	67	60.7
Bhutan	2,032	2.59	43 / 112	3.77 / 1.19	5.42	91	55.7
India	1,006,770	1.45	318 / 824	2.29 / 0.85	2.74	65	64.1
Iran	76,429	2.60	47 / 121	3.13 / 0.54	4.23	35	70.8
Kazakhstan	16,928	0.45	6 / 16	1.69 / 0.84	2.10	31	69.2
Kyrgyzstan	4,543	0.86	23 / 59	2.31 / 0.69	2.84	35	69.2
Maldives	302	3.23	1,014 / 2,628	3.85 / 0.63	6.02	40	66.7
Nepal	24,347	2.39	165 / 428	3.35 / 0.96	4.47	70	59.8
Pakistan	156,007	2.59	177 / 459	3.32 / 0.68	4.54	65	66.1
Sri Lanka	18,821	1.07	287 / 743	1.78 / 0.60	2.10	13	74.1
Tajikistan	6,398	1.90	45 / 116	2.82 / 0.64	3.57	51	68.5
Turkmenistan	4,479	1.82	9 / 24	2.58 / 0.69	3.21	51	66.3
Uzbekistan	25,018	1.82	56 / 145	2.58 / 0.62	3.13	39	68.8
Southeastern Asia[a]	**521,983**	**1.69**	**116 / 301**	**2.54 / 0.83**	**3.09**	**64**	**64.0**
Brunei	326	1.66	57 / 146	1.80 / 0.32	2.40	8	76.3
Cambodia	11,207	1.86	62 / 160	2.92 / 1.06	4.10	90	56.6
Indonesia	212,565	1.31	111 / 287	2.09 / 0.71	2.37	39	67.3
Laos	5,693	2.80	24 / 62	3.95 / 1.16	5.92	76	56.0
Malaysia	22,299	1.74	67 / 175	2.21 / 0.47	2.86	9	73.2
Myanmar	49,342	1.61	73 / 189	2.49 / 0.88	3.00	65	62.6
Philippines	75,037	1.80	250 / 648	2.56 / 0.54	3.24	30	69.8
Singapore	3,587	1.03	5,596 / 14,523	1.30 / 0.53	1.79	5	78.1
Thailand	60,495	0.69	118 / 305	1.58 / 0.70	1.74	25	70.0
Viet Nam	80,549	1.51	243 / 630	2.15 / 0.63	2.53	32	69.4
Western Asia[b]	**187,463**	**2.13**	**38 / 99**	**2.71 / 0.60**	**3.58**	**36**	**70.3**
Armenia	3,662	0.60	123 / 318	1.40 / 0.80	1.70	23	71.6
Azerbaijan	7,828	0.72	90 / 234	1.70 / 0.66	2.10	30	71.8
Bahrain	618	1.65	890 / 2,306	1.72 / 0.38	2.54	16	73.8
Cyprus	608	0.98	103 / 266	1.55 / 0.75	2.24	6	78.3
Georgia	5,418	0.02	78 / 201	1.38 / 0.99	1.90	21	73.6
Iraq	23,109	2.86	53 / 138	3.40 / 0.54	4.80	39	69.4
Israel	4,982	1.56	244 / 633	1.88 / 0.64	2.53	6	78.3
Jordan	6,330	3.04	71 / 184	3.47 / 0.43	4.70	25	71.0
Kuwait	1,966	2.18	110 / 286	1.93 / 0.24	2.44	12	76.7
Lebanon	3,289	1.45	321 / 833	2.06 / 0.62	2.41	25	71.0
Oman	2,717	3.90	9 / 23	4.20 / 0.39	6.63	21	72.0
Palestine	2,070	3.93	332 / 859	4.37 / 0.45	7.41	31	69.3
Qatar	599	1.56	52 / 136	1.84 / 0.44	3.44	14	72.7
Saudi Arabia	21,661	3.07	10 / 25	3.32 / 0.39	5.43	18	72.9
Syria	16,126	2.46	87 / 226	2.92 / 0.45	3.58	28	70.2
Turkey	65,732	1.39	84 / 218	2.03 / 0.64	2.30	36	70.5
United Arab Emirates	2,444	1.69	29 / 76	1.83 / 0.33	3.12	12	75.9
Yemen	18,118	3.49	34 / 88	4.36 / 0.87	6.99	68	60.5

Note: Because of rounding, population figures for the regions and the major area as a whole may not equal the sum of their constituent parts.

[a]Figures include Timor. [b]Figures include Northern Cyprus.

Asia in A.D. 2000: Religious Affiliation (as percentage of population)

	Christians	Muslims	Hindus	Non-religious	Chinese Folk Religionists	Buddhists	Tribal Religionists	Atheists	New Religionists	Sikhs	Jews	Spiritists	Other
World total	33.1	20.0	12.8	12.7	6.3	5.9	4.1	2.4	1.6	0.4	0.2	0.2	0.3
Asia	8.3	22.9	21.0	16.7	10.3	9.6	4.0	3.2	2.7	0.6	0.1	—	0.6
Eastern Asia	7.7	1.3	—	38.1	24.7	12.6	4.4	7.1	3.0	—	—	—	1.1
China	7.0	1.5	—	42.7	28.3	8.4	4.3	7.8	—	—	—	—	—
Japan	3.6	0.2	—	10.4	—	54.5	—	3.0	26.2	—	—	—	2.1
Mongolia	1.3	5.1	—	31.4	0.4	23.0	30.0	8.8	—	—	—	—	—
North Korea	2.3	—	—	55.8	0.1	1.5	12.3	15.6	12.6	—	—	—	—
South Korea	40.9	0.2	—	1.6	0.1	14.9	16.2	0.1	15.3	—	—	—	10.7
Taiwan	7.1	0.4	—	4.2	50.1	20.8	0.3	0.2	6.9	—	—	—	10.0
South-central Asia	4.3	34.9	51.1	1.8	—	1.7	3.9	0.3	—	1.5	—	—	0.5
Afghanistan	—	99.5	0.4	—	—	—	—	—	—	—	—	—	0.1
Bangladesh	0.6	86.1	12.0	0.1	—	0.6	0.6	—	—	—	—	—	—
Bhutan	0.5	1.0	21.2	0.2	—	73.6	3.5	—	—	—	—	—	—
India	5.3	11.9	72.1	1.4	—	0.7	5.5	0.2	—	2.2	—	—	0.7
Iran	0.9	97.9	0.1	0.3	—	—	—	—	—	—	—	—	0.8
Kazakhstan	20.7	39.3	—	29.5	—	0.1	0.2	10.0	—	—	0.1	—	0.1
Kyrgyzstan	9.2	65.8	—	18.5	—	0.5	0.3	5.5	—	—	0.1	—	0.1
Maldives	0.1	99.1	0.1	—	—	0.6	—	—	—	—	—	—	0.1
Nepal	1.6	4.0	76.2	0.3	0.1	8.2	9.4	0.1	—	—	—	—	0.1
Pakistan	2.3	96.2	1.2	0.1	—	0.1	0.1	—	—	—	—	—	—
Sri Lanka	7.9	9.0	11.7	2.1	—	68.4	—	0.5	—	0.3	—	—	0.1
Tajikistan	2.1	85.5	—	10.6	—	0.1	0.1	1.4	—	—	0.1	—	0.1
Turkmenistan	2.9	88.0	—	8.0	—	—	—	1.0	—	—	0.1	—	—
Uzbekistan	1.3	78.5	—	17.0	—	0.2	0.2	2.7	—	—	0.2	—	—
Southeastern Asia[a]	21.4	26.8	2.0	3.6	2.2	27.2	4.8	1.3	10.3	—	—	—	0.4
Brunei	8.7	64.4	0.7	1.0	3.2	8.9	11.0	—	—	—	—	—	2.1
Cambodia	0.7	2.3	0.3	2.4	4.7	85.0	4.0	0.2	0.3	—	—	—	0.1
Indonesia	13.6	55.4	3.5	2.2	1.4	0.9	2.3	0.2	20.6	—	—	—	—
Laos	2.7	0.3	0.1	4.6	1.5	48.2	41.3	1.2	0.2	—	—	—	—
Malaysia	9.0	47.6	7.4	0.5	23.5	6.7	3.0	0.2	1.5	0.2	—	—	0.4
Myanmar	8.4	2.1	1.8	0.8	0.3	72.2	12.7	0.1	—	—	—	—	1.6
Philippines	89.7	6.3	—	0.6	0.1	0.1	2.7	0.2	—	—	—	—	0.3
Singapore	13.0	18.3	5.4	4.7	41.4	14.5	—	0.1	1.8	0.4	—	—	0.4
Thailand	1.9	6.9	0.4	2.2	0.8	84.8	2.2	0.2	—	—	—	—	0.6
Viet Nam	8.3	0.8	—	13.8	0.9	48.4	8.8	7.1	11.5	—	—	—	0.4
Western Asia[b]	7.6	86.7	0.4	2.5	—	0.1	—	0.3	—	—	2.2	—	0.2
Armenia	88.4	1.4	—	6.2	—	—	—	4.0	—	—	—	—	—
Azerbaijan	5.3	84.4	—	9.6	—	—	—	0.4	—	—	0.4	—	—
Bahrain	11.2	81.5	6.4	0.5	—	0.1	—	—	—	—	0.1	—	0.2
Cyprus	94.1	1.0	—	4.0	—	—	—	0.8	—	—	—	—	0.1
Georgia	60.5	19.4	—	16.9	—	—	—	2.8	—	—	0.4	—	—
Iraq	3.2	96.0	—	0.5	—	—	—	0.2	—	—	—	—	0.1
Israel	6.1	12.5	—	4.2	—	—	—	0.8	—	—	76.2	—	0.2
Jordan	5.3	92.3	—	1.8	—	—	—	0.3	—	—	—	—	0.3
Kuwait	8.0	89.9	0.8	0.9	—	—	—	—	—	0.1	—	—	0.3
Lebanon	52.9	42.6	—	3.4	—	—	—	1.0	—	—	0.1	—	—
Oman	3.7	88.4	5.9	0.2	—	0.8	—	—	—	0.7	—	—	0.3
Palestine	11.0	70.5	—	5.8	—	—	—	0.1	—	—	12.6	—	—
Qatar	13.0	79.8	2.7	2.3	—	2.0	—	0.1	—	—	—	—	0.1
Saudi Arabia	4.2	93.3	1.2	0.5	0.1	0.3	0.1	—	0.1	0.2	—	—	—
Syria	9.0	87.7	—	3.1	—	—	—	0.2	—	—	—	—	—
Turkey	0.5	97.1	—	2.1	—	0.1	—	0.1	—	—	—	—	0.1
United Arab Emir.	12.1	74.6	7.7	0.9	—	2.0	—	0.1	0.1	0.2	—	—	2.3
Yemen	0.2	98.9	0.7	0.1	—	—	—	0.1	—	—	—	—	—

Note: A dash represents a value of less than 0.05 percent. Because of rounding, horizontal totals may not equal 100.0.

[a]Figures include Timor. [b]Figures include Northern Cyprus.

Asia in A.D. 2000: Church Affiliation (as percentage of population)

	Total Christians	Roman Catholics	Indigenous	Protestants	Orthodox	Unaffiliated	Anglicans	Marginal
World total	*33.1*	**17.6**	**6.2**	**5.8**	**3.7**	**1.5**	**1.0**	**0.5**
Asia	*8.3*	**3.1**	**3.8**	**1.4**	**0.4**	**0.2**	—	**0.1**
Eastern Asia	*7.7*	**0.8**	**6.1**	**0.7**	—	**0.1**	—	**0.1**
China	*7.0*	0.6	6.3	—	—	—	—	—
Japan	*3.6*	0.4	1.1	0.5	—	0.9	0.1	0.7
Mongolia	*1.3*	—	0.2	0.9	0.1	0.1	—	—
North Korea	*2.3*	0.3	2.0	—	—	—	—	—
South Korea	*40.9*	7.9	17.3	19.8	—	0.9	0.2	1.9
Taiwan	*7.1*	1.3	2.2	1.8	—	1.6	—	0.2
South-central Asia	*4.3*	**1.4**	**1.4**	**1.2**	**0.5**	—	—	—
Afghanistan	—	—	—	—	—	—	—	—
Bangladesh	*0.6*	0.2	0.3	0.2	—	—	—	—
Bhutan	*0.5*	—	0.3	0.2	—	—	—	—
India	*5.3*	1.7	1.9	1.7	0.3	—	—	—
Iran	*0.9*	—	0.1	—	0.7	0.2	—	—
Kazakhstan	*20.7*	2.1	0.8	0.2	16.5	1.1	—	—
Kyrgyzstan	*9.2*	0.1	0.8	0.4	6.4	1.6	—	—
Maldives	*0.1*	—	—	0.1	—	—	—	—
Nepal	*1.6*	—	1.5	0.1	—	—	—	—
Pakistan	*2.3*	0.9	0.6	0.8	—	—	—	—
Sri Lanka	*7.9*	6.8	0.5	0.6	—	0.1	0.3	—
Tajikistan	*2.1*	0.1	0.1	0.4	1.6	—	—	—
Turkmenistan	*2.9*	0.1	0.2	0.1	2.3	0.3	—	—
Uzbekistan	*1.3*	0.2	0.2	0.2	0.7	—	—	—
Southeastern Asia[a]	*21.4*	**14.7**	**5.0**	**4.1**	—	**0.5**	**0.1**	**0.2**
Brunei	*8.7*	1.8	2.8	2.3	—	0.3	1.5	—
Cambodia	*0.7*	0.2	0.3	0.2	—	—	—	—
Indonesia	*13.6*	3.0	4.3	6.2	—	0.1	—	—
Laos	*2.7*	1.0	0.9	0.8	—	—	—	—
Malaysia	*9.0*	3.4	0.7	2.9	—	1.1	0.8	—
Myanmar	*8.4*	1.3	0.9	5.9	—	0.1	0.1	—
Philippines	*89.7*	83.1	20.5	4.4	—	3.0	0.2	1.2
Singapore	*13.0*	4.9	2.4	4.2	0.1	0.3	0.9	0.2
Thailand	*1.9*	0.5	0.7	0.6	—	—	—	—
Viet Nam	*8.3*	6.8	0.5	0.9	—	—	—	—
Western Asia[b]	*7.6*	**1.9**	**0.7**	**0.1**	**5.0**	**0.1**	—	—
Armenia	*88.4*	4.4	0.8	0.4	82.7	—	—	0.1
Azerbaijan	*5.3*	0.1	0.1	—	5.1	—	—	—
Bahrain	*11.2*	4.4	4.5	0.9	0.5	0.3	0.6	—
Cyprus	*94.1*	1.6	—	0.8	89.3	0.2	0.5	1.6
Georgia	*60.5*	0.8	0.8	0.5	56.9	1.4	—	—
Iraq	*3.2*	1.1	1.4	—	0.6	0.1	—	—
Israel	*6.1*	3.0	2.1	0.5	0.5	0.1	—	—
Jordan	*5.3*	0.6	1.7	0.2	2.8	—	0.1	—
Kuwait	*8.0*	4.2	3.3	0.1	0.3	0.1	—	—
Lebanon	*52.9*	42.4	4.3	0.8	15.9	0.1	—	0.3
Oman	*3.7*	2.0	0.7	0.2	0.7	0.1	0.1	—
Palestine	*11.0*	1.6	6.1	0.2	2.8	0.1	0.2	0.1
Qatar	*13.0*	6.7	3.0	1.0	0.3	0.7	1.4	—
Saudi Arabia	*4.2*	3.4	0.4	0.2	0.2	0.1	—	—
Syria	*9.0*	2.2	0.6	0.3	5.8	—	—	—
Turkey	*0.5*	0.1	0.1	0.1	0.3	0.1	—	—
United Arab Emirates	*12.1*	5.5	2.1	0.5	3.3	0.4	0.4	—
Yemen	*0.2*	—	0.1	—	0.1	—	—	—

Note: A dash represents a value of less than 0.05 percent. Because of rounding, horizontal totals of the individual Christian groups may not equal the total percentage of Christians. Also, Christians in some countries are counted in more than one category, in which case the total of the individual groups may exceed the overall percentage of Christians.

[a]Figures include Timor. [b]Figures include Northern Cyprus.

greatest Western-style → democracy in Asia. But the tensions in this country of so many different ethnic groups and religions (e.g., Hindus against Muslims) have become so strong that they are threatening its inner stability. Numerous other Asian countries have also had their share of internal strain, as long-standing ethnic grievances and religious intolerance have also polarized the political scene in Pakistan, Afghanistan, Bhutan, Cambodia, China, Indonesia, and Myanmar, and especially the Philippines (Muslims against Christians) and Sri Lanka (Buddhist Sinhalese against Hindu Tamils).

1.3. The rapid growth of population confronts Asia with massive problems. The battle against → poverty and → hunger is being lost, in spite of many successes in agriculture (e.g., the "green revolution" in India). In addition, the economic → dependence and exploitation of Asia persist, even after the achievement of political independence. In spite of great efforts to stay neutral in the political, ideological, and economic conflicts of the great power blocs, Asia has been the theater of great wars (Viet Nam, Cambodia, Iran and Iraq, Afghanistan, and, on the largest scale, the 1991 Gulf War against Iraq). These conflicts have produced millions of → refugees who, as the "boat people" or those in camps in Pakistan and Thailand, are still awaiting a worthwhile life. The ideological struggles between socialist and capitalist systems often serve in Asia as an excuse for the violation of → human rights, for oppression and → torture, and for increasing militarization. A special problem is the position of women in Asia (→ Sexism 3), who are trying to escape from their traditional subjection but who are often degraded to the level of sex objects as a result of modern → tourism.

2. The Religions of Asia

2.1. All the great religions had their origin in Asia. Respect for → religion, for → popular piety (→ Popular Religion), for → meditation, for → monasticism, and for → pilgrimage are typical in Asia. → Buddhism, which arose in India in the sixth century B.C., spread over all Southeast Asia. The branch of Buddhism known as Theravada (meaning "doctrine of the elders") is predominant in Sri Lanka, Thailand, Cambodia, Laos, and Myanmar, while Mahayana Buddhism is traditionally the strongest religious force in Viet Nam, China, and Japan. Islam, which began in Arabia, spread from there to Pakistan, Bangladesh, Malaysia, and India. Indonesia, with almost 120 million adherents, is the country with most Muslims. Of Asia's 775 million Hindus, nearly 95 percent live in India, with small groups also in Sri Lanka, Pakistan, Bangladesh, Malaysia, and Indone-

sia. → Shinto is limited to Japan. Confucianism occurs in China, Korea, and Japan, but how far it is a religion and how far an → ethics (§1) has been a debated issue for centuries. Special Asian religions are the → Baha'i (mainly in Iran and Israel) and the → Sikhs (India). Christianity, with slightly over 300 million adherents, forms a minority of only 8 percent of the population. The Philippines alone contributes 67 million Christians, 62 million of them Roman Catholics.

2.2. In the progress to nationhood, the religions have played an important role for many countries (e.g., Islam for Pakistan, Buddhism for Sri Lanka, and → Hinduism for India). During the Cultural Revolution (1966-69) in China a massive attempt was made to instill the religious philosophy of Marxism and to extinguish the influence of religion, particularly → Taoism, Buddhism, Islam, and Christianity. Although the temples, churches, and sacred writings were destroyed, the influence of the religions could not be broken. The Chinese government ultimately restored → religious liberty in order to secure control once again of the religions and of expanding popular piety. Islam, moving out from Iran by way of Pakistan, Indonesia, Malaysia, and the Philippines, has shown great vitality, with an estimated 800 million adherents in 1997. The renaissance of Islam gives evidence of many integralist features that make cooperation and → dialogue with Muslims difficult (→ Islam and Christianity). Since World War II Japan has seen the development of many → new religions, including Tenrikyo (first started in 1860), Rissho Koseikai, Soka Gakkai, Perfect Liberty Kyodan, and many others. These are syncretistic, fusing Shintoist, Buddhist, and Christian elements. In Japan they have won over 30 million followers, or a quarter of the population.

2.3. The role of the religions in Asia is ambivalent with respect to the underdevelopment of the various countries. On the one hand, the religions are responsible for the patience, lethargy, and → fatalism with which poverty, oppression, and exploitation are accepted as unavoidable. Some forms of discrimination (e.g., the → caste system in India) may be traced back to religious factors. On the other hand, in debate with the Marxist criticism of religion, Asian theologians (see declaration no. 21 of the Ecumenical Association of Third World Theologians at Geneva, 1984) have pointed out that the religious traditions of Asia have also displayed humanizing elements and inspired movements of liberation.

Modern efforts at reform in the religions of Asia bring out very well their twofold character, for they vacillate between (1) acceptance of modern ideas in

→ technology, science, and politics and (2) the rejection of these ideas and a return to uncritical fundamentalism. The religions of Asia have gained some influence in Europe and North America in movements of → meditation (e.g., → Zen Buddhism and → Yoga) and, more broadly, in the so-called → youth religions (the Unification Church, or Moonies, the Hare Krishna movement, and → transcendental meditation).

3. Christianity in Asia
3.1. *History of Christianity*
The development of Christianity in Asia is marked by several phases and breaks. As a religion that began in Asia Minor, Christianity came early to India, certainly by the 4th century if one discounts the Indian mission of the apostle Thomas as legendary. → Nestorian Christians reached China in the 7th century, translated the Bible, and gained many adherents under the leadership of the Persian monk A-lo-pen, as shown in the Hsi-an monument (discovered in 1625). Islamic expansion in the 7th and 8th centuries broke and forestalled the influence of Christianity in Asia until the Portuguese and Spanish colonization in the 16th and 17th centuries. In spite of attempts to adapt Christianity to the cultural and religious customs of Asia (such as by M. Ricci in China and R. de Nobili in India), Christianity now seemed to be an alien religion, closely tied to the colonialism and imperialism of European powers. The only exceptions in southern and eastern Asia seem to be the Philippines, South Korea, and Indonesia.

Protestant → mission began in India and Indonesia as early as the 17th century, but in most of the countries of Asia only in the middle of the 19th century, the main centers then being China, Korea, Japan, and India. Political upheavals such as the Chinese revolution and the achievement of independence by many countries caused some withdrawal of European and American missionary activity and an emphasis on the responsibility of the national churches for their own life and mission (see the three-self movement in → China [§§2-3]; → Christology 5). The churches of Asia, both Protestant and Roman Catholic, have their own missionary societies and organizations for the propagation of the faith.

3.2. *The Christian Churches and Their Work*
The Christian churches of Asia are a small minority (although up from 2 percent in 1900 and 5 percent in 1970) who live out the message and bear their witness in contexts that vary widely in culture, religion, and politics. Their main task is to give themselves an Asian look, to develop an Asian Christian identity in church life, → piety, → liturgy, and →

theology (→ Asian Theology). As demanded by the poverty and exploitation of the masses, the churches, though limited in numbers, have made great efforts to make a contribution to development, both by giving aid and also by seeking structural changes in society. Of particular importance have been study centers devoted to the theme of religion and society, for example, in India, Sri Lanka, South Korea, the Philippines, and Hong Kong.

Closely related to problems of economic development are questions of human rights, civil liberty, and participation in the shaping of society. In this regard the churches defend the people who live under authoritarian regimes. In the educational field, the influence of Christians has been out of proportion to their numbers (→ Education 3, 4). This is a disputed field because of the great financial resources that it ties up and that often come from Western churches abroad. The churches have also played a major role in health care (establishing hospitals, leprosariums, dispensaries, etc.) and in work on behalf of refugees.

3.3. *Cooperation of the Protestant Churches*
The churches are the product of missionary work by several European and American societies, and their confessional diversity reflects the divisions of the home churches. To promote cooperation among the Protestant churches of Asia, the East Asian Christian Conference was founded at Kuala Lumpur in 1959. In 1973 this became the more comprehensive Christian Conference of Asia (CCA), with 86 member churches from 17 countries (including Australia and New Zealand). The China Christian Council is not yet a member of the CCA, but it succeeded in 1991 in becoming a member of the → World Council of Churches.

At the regular general assemblies (every five years, with the most recent gatherings in Seoul [1985], Manila [1990], and Colombo [1995]), the work of the CCA in the various programs for youth work, women's work, urban-industrial mission, social work, and study programs for theological education and research is evaluated, and new incentives are given to coordinate the activities of the member churches. Yap Kim Hao, then the general secretary, formulated its priorities as follows at Penang in 1981: (1) the challenge of science and technology; (2) → faith, ideology, and political vision in Asia; (3) the challenge of rural awakening and urban renewal; and (4) the search for a new Asian identity. His successors as general secretary — Park Sang Jung (1985-90) and John Victor Joseph (1990-) — have continued and deepened the work of the conference.

In 1974 the churches of the Middle East founded

the → Middle East Council of Churches, with head-quarters in Beirut. Transnational work in the Protestant sphere corresponds to that of the Roman Catholic Federation of Asian Bishops' Conference, which was founded in Manila in 1970. By its programs for mission, interreligious dialogue, and the social apostolate, the conference has done much to awaken a sense of common problems in the Asian sphere. More than 25 percent of the bishops of Asia have taken part in the programs of the social apostolate. The transnational boards of the Christian churches of Asia all wrestle with the cultural, religious, and political diversity of the vast Asian context and the resultant tensions and different positions. In a relatively short time they have helped to make the voice of the Christians of Asia heard in other international bodies such as the → World Council of Churches, the world confessions, and the corresponding Roman Catholic councils.

3.4. Ecumenical Dialogue

Dialogue has now become intensive among the Christian churches of Asia. In spite of long being rivals in mission, Protestants and Roman Catholics now enjoy close contacts at every level and have developed various forms of institutional cooperation. Increases in denominational splintering have occurred in South Korea and the Philippines, but other movements are fostering closer cooperation or unity. In 1947, the → Church of South India was formed, and in 1970 the Church of North India. Political pressure led in 1941 to a church union in Japan (Kyodan), though this partially broke up when the war ended. Protestant developments in the churches of China are of particular interest. Here the Chinese Christian Council is trying to forge a truly united church out of the enforced ending of denominational divisions.

On the way to an Asian Christianity, dialogue with the religious traditions of Asia plays an important part. India has some 50 Protestant and Roman Catholic centers for dialogue between → Hindus and Christians. In Japan close contacts between Buddhists and Christians exist in centers for dialogue, where adherents discuss questions of the nature of humanity, of meditation, and of work for peace (e.g., in the World Conference of Religions for Peace). Intensive contact with Muslims takes place in India, Indonesia, and the Philippines, though the influence of a militant and fundamentalist Islam often hampers this dialogue.

Talks have occurred between the CCA and the Catholic Federation of Asian Bishops' Conferences with the goal of forming an Asian Ecumenical Committee as a common structure to strengthen the cooperation between the various Christian churches

in Asia. In many Asian countries the Catholic Church has become a full member of the → national council of churches.

The political realities (e.g., regarding national security) often hinder dialogue with other ideologies, especially → Marxism. In China, where the Christians have much experience of life and of surprising survival in a socialist state, there has been little wrestling with socialism on the ideological level. Christians have decided to support the modernizing of China while maintaining their ideological distinction from Marxism. In North Korea the church has been silenced and has disappeared from view. In Viet Nam and Cambodia it is going through periods of persecution.

Bibliography: T. BALASURIYA, *Planetary Theology* (Maryknoll, N.Y., 1984) • W. BÜHLMANN, *The Church of the Future: A Model for the Year 2001* (Maryknoll, N.Y., 1986) • D. J. CHO, ed., *New Forces in Missions: The Official Report of the Asia Missions Association* (Seoul, 1976) • F. CLARK, *An Introduction to the Catholic Church of Asia* (Manila, 1987) • J. M. COLACO, ed., *Jesus Christ in Asian Suffering and Hope* (Christian Conference of Asia Sixth Assembly, May 31-June 9, 1977; Singapore, 1977) • P. DIGAN, *Churches in Contestation: Asian Christian Social Protest* (New York, 1984) • ÉCHANGE FRANCE-ASIE, *L'Asie en chiffres, 1982* (Paris, 1982) • C. M. EDSMAN, *Die Hauptreligionen des heutigen Asiens* (Tübingen, 1976) • *The Far East and Australasia, 1991* (London, 1991) • R. E. HEDLUND, ed., *World Christianity*, vol. 3, *South Asia* (Monrovia, Calif., 1980) • Y. C. LAK, ed., *Doing Theology with Cultures of Asia* (no. 6; Singapore, 1988) • D. C. E. LIAO, ed., *World Christianity*, vol. 2, *Eastern Asia* (Monrovia, Calif., 1980) • *Living in Christ with People* (Christian Conference of Asia Seventh Assembly, Bangalore, May 18-28, 1981; Singapore, 1981) • D. NOHLEN and F. NUSCHELER, eds., *Handbuch der Dritten Welt*, vol. 7, *Südasien und Südostasien;* vol. 8, *Ostasien und Ozeanien* (3d ed.; Hamburg, 1994) • K. RAJARATNAM and A. A. SITOMPUL, *Theological Education in Today's Asia* (Theological Education and Training for Witness and Service Held in Manila, Philippines, October 21-24, 1976; Madras, 1978) • G. B. ROSALES and C. ARÉVALO, eds., *For All the Peoples of Asia: Federation of Asian Bishops' Conferences Documents from 1970 to 1991* (Maryknoll, N.Y., 1992).

GEORG EVERS

Asian Theology

1.1. Since Asia contains so many peoples, languages, cultures, religions, and philosophies, a blanket concept like Asian theology has unavoidably been contested. Nevertheless, it increasingly has gained acceptance in the latter part of the 20th century as a term to distinguish theological work done in Asia from that of Europe, Africa, or Latin America.

1.2. In Asia, which is the home of various world religions, the Christian churches are a very small minority. Asia is a continent in social upheaval in which the problems of → poverty, oppression, violations of human rights, and repressive governments dominate the social, political, and economic context.

2.1. A common feature of Asian theological method is the decision to pursue theology contextually. Practitioners wish to reflect theologically on the pluralism of the historical, cultural, religious, and social environment in the light of → revelation.

2.2. According to A. Lambino, contextual factors allow us to distinguish three forms of Asian theology. First we have → dialogue between Christianity and a particular Asian → culture, where "culture" embraces language, thought forms, insights, and values. In this expression of Asian theology we find efforts to apply the principles of yin and yang, to take into account the Asian understanding of harmony and nature, and in the doctrine of → God to use Asian categories such as change and unity instead of the traditional concepts of → Greek philosophy.

Next we have dialogue with the living religions and religious traditions of Asia. Here it is a matter of determining the saving significance of Buddhism, Hinduism, or Islam. In encounter and exchange with representatives of the other great religious traditions, the questions of → Christology demand new answers.

Finally, we have wrestling with the social, political, and economic problems of Asia. This aspect has been called the Asian form of → liberation theology, since the term "liberation" has replaced the original term → "development."

2.3. Another approach to Asian theology, critical of the previous outline, comes from the → evangelical camp. According to B. R. Ro, one must distinguish four types of Asian theology: (1) the syncretistic theology of interreligious dialogue; (2) the theology of accommodation, which has been attempted since the time of M. Ricci; (3) a situational theology, such as that of K. Kitamori; and (4) a biblically oriented theology, which, it is argued, alone does justice to Asian needs.

3.1. A feature of Asian theology is the priority given to practice over orthodoxy. The Asian view is that the first thing in religion is an obligation to act. At issue is spiritual experience and discipline (→ Ethics), which give historical concreteness to religious → truth. Fixing religious truth solely in → dogmatic formulations runs contrary to this unity of → experience, action, and word.

3.2. People themselves, with their experiences and distinctive humanity, are the main sources of Asian theology. The → popular religion of Asians itself contains an implicit theology.

3.3. The extrabiblical holy writings of the religions of Asia form another source. The problem of two histories (biblical revelation and other Asian scriptures), raised prominently at Tambaram in 1938 in the World Missionary Conference debate between H. Kraemer and P. Chenchiah, has never been settled.

4.1. The main themes of Asian theology may be summarized under four heads: (1) the Christological question of the uniqueness of Jesus Christ as Redeemer; (2) the whole sphere of social justice (→ Righteousness, Justice), liberation, and → political theology; (3) questions of the → acculturation of Christianity in Asia, which touches on several themes such as popular piety, ecclesiastical forms, the → family, and society; and (4) dialogue with Asian religions and religious traditions.

4.2. Within the three main streams of an Asian theology one may distinguish regional theologies. Minjung (simple people) theology has become familiar in South Korea; it has made the oppression and suffering of Korean peasants and fishermen the object and subject of theological work. Two trends may be distinguished in the Philippines: Filipino theology (L. Mercado and E. Rivera), which on the basis of religious and historical factors is seeking to develop a → contextual theology; and the rather stronger Philippine liberation theology, which is wrestling with economic and political questions. Theology in mainland China might soon secure a special position with its attempt to develop a postconfessional Chinese theology that will serve as the basis for a united Chinese Christian church and could thus have great ecumenical significance.

5. Theological organizations play an important role in the development of an Asian theology. The Christian Conference of Asia includes the Commission for Theological Concerns and the Association of Theological Institutions of South-East Asia. Both groups organize regular conferences and days for study. Since 1983 the Programme for Theology and Cultures in Asia has organized seminar workshops under the heading "Doing Theology with Asian Resources,"

with the aim of developing new forms of an inculturated Asian theology. The Roman Catholic Church,
through its Federation of Asian Bishops' Conferences
(FACB), sponsors activities in the areas of interreligious dialogue, missionary responsibility, lay
apostolate, and the social apostolate. In 1986 the
Theological Advisory Commission of the FACB was
founded to address theological problems concerning
all Asian churches. The Asian branch of the Ecumenical Association of Third World Theologians has also
had a great influence.

Special mention should be made of conferences
of Asian theologians at Wennapuwa (1979), Hong
Kong (1984), and Suambo, Korea (1989). The issues
of Asian women and feminist theology are taken up
by Asian women theologians at various international
conferences and centers like the Asian Women's Resource Center in Korea and the Institute of Women's
Studies in Manila and by publications like the journal
In God's Image (1981-).

Bibliography: G. H. ANDERSON, ed., *Asian Voices in
Christian Theology* (Maryknoll, N.Y., 1976) • H. CHUNG,
*Struggle to Be the Sun Again: Introducing Asian Women's
Theology* (Maryknoll, N.Y., 1991) • D. J. ELWOOD, ed.,
What Asian Christians Are Thinking (Quezon City, 1976)
• J. ENGLAND and C. LEE, eds., *Doing Theology with
Asian Resources* (Auckland, 1993) • J. GNANAPIRAGASAM
and F. WILFRED, eds., *Being Church in Asia: Theological
Advisory Commission Documents, 1986-1992* (Manila,
1994) • A. G. HONIG, "Trends in Recent Asian Theol-
ogy," *Exchange* 32/33 (1982) 1-75 (bibliography) •
M. KATOPPO, *Compassionate and Free: An Asian
Woman's Theology* (Maryknoll, N.Y., 1980) • K. KITA-
MORI, *Theologie des Schmerzes Gottes* (Göttingen, 1972)
• K. KOYAMA, *Water-Buffalo Theology* (London, 1974) •
A. LAMBINO, "Zur theologischen Methode in der
Kontextualisierung. Kritik an einigen asiatischen An-
sätzen," *ZMR* 65 (1981) 1-13 • A. PIERIS, *An Asian The-
ology of Liberation* (Maryknoll, N.Y., 1988) • S. RAYAN,
"Um einen neuen Entwurf theologischer Praxis in
Asien," *Orien.* 48 (1984) 42-45, 56-58, 64-66 • S. SAMAR-
THA, *One Christ–Many Religions: Toward a Revised
Christology* (Maryknoll, N.Y., 1991) • C. S. SONG, *Third-
Eye Theology: Theology in Formation in Asian Settings*
(Maryknoll, N.Y., 1979) • R. SUGIRTHARAJAH, ed., *Fron-
tiers in Asian Christian Theology: Emerging Trends*
(Maryknoll, N.Y., 1994) • M. M. THOMAS, *The Acknowl-
edged Christ of the Indian Renaissance* (Madras, 1970) •
F. WILFRED, *Sunset in the East? Asian Challenges and
Christian Involvement* (Madras, 1991) • For ongoing
bibliography, see the biannual publication *Theology in
Context* of the Institute of Missiology Missio, Aachen
(1985-).

GEORG EVERS

Assembleias de Deus no Brasil

1. History
2. Church Structures
3. Faith and Life

1. History

The history of the Pentecostal movement in Brazil,
which is now its worldwide center, goes back to the
year 1910, when the foundations were laid for the
Congregação cristã do Brasil (CCB) and the Assembleias de Deus no Brasil (ADB), the largest Latin
American → Pentecostal church today. The CCB
arose out of a split from the Presbyterian church in
São Paulo, the ADB by a split from the Baptist church
in Belém, to which two Swedish immigrants to the
United States, Gunnar Vingren and Daniel Berg, who
had been gripped by a revival movement of the Spirit
in the Baptist churches in Chicago, had been specifically called in 1910. After learning Portuguese in the
→ Baptist church in Belém, Vingren and Berg
preached redemption and the baptism of the Spirit
with great eloquence and steadfastness, always with
the support of Scripture (esp. appealing to Acts 2:38).
On June 2, 1911, Celina de Albuquerque, after five
days of → prayer, received the baptism of the Spirit.
But then in a service on June 10 there was controversy
with the commissioned preacher, which ended with
the exclusion of the two Swedes and their 18 followers
(E. Conde). Thus the history of the ADB began.

In 1913 the first Brazilian was ordained: Absalão
Piano. Henceforth, the number of workers and the
missionary efforts increased greatly, the work spreading to Amazonia and then in the 1920s to the industrial and coffee-growing areas. Large congregations were founded in Rio de Janeiro, São Paulo, and
Pôrto Alegre, and the inland areas were opened up.
In 1930 a number of preachers of the Igreja de Cristo
de Mata Grande, Alagoas, an → evangelical church
of North American origin, joined the ADB, which
then had 14,000 members.

The growth of the Pentecostal movement accelerated with the economic crisis of 1929/30 and then
again after 1950. The ADB itself grew from 120,000
in 1949 to 678,000 baptized with the Spirit in 1971.
In 1990 it numbered 14 million adherents in 85,000
congregations. (In 1990 the CCB had 3.1 million
adherents in over 15,000 congregations.) By 1997 the
number of ADB members had risen to 20 million.
From this remarkable expansion Conde draws the
weighty historico-theological conclusion: "To gain
the regard and admiration that it enjoys today, a
movement that from the first was contested, hated,
despised, slandered, misrepresented, and excom-

municated cannot be moved and guided by human ideas and forces, but must have God himself as the center that inspires and promotes it" (p. 9).

2. Church Structures

The local congregations of the ADB are autonomous, but they work together organizationally through annual regional conferences, a national conference, and common enterprises like the publishing house in Rio with its paper *Mensageiro da Paz* (Messenger of peace), Bible institutes for the training of pastors, and cooperation with the Brazilian → Bible Society. In accordance with the congregational structure (→ Congregationalism), each congregation is also a missionary mother church, forming and nurturing daughter churches (→ Filiation). In the associated churches presbyters (→ Elder) serve as lay workers under the direction of the pastor. To deal with social questions there are → deacons. → Tithing as a means of financing the congregations promotes missionary expansion among the descendants of Mediterranean immigrants and African slaves.

3. Faith and Life

In accordance with its basic teachings (cf. Conde's summary with H. Meyer, 39-40), the ADB stresses brotherly → unity in Christ, the redeeming work of Christ, and the collective and individual work of the Holy Spirit. By a declaration of the National Conference in 1962, it cannot cooperate with other denominations and confessions in the → ecumenical movement without a firm confession of faith, although this has now been done by a free Pentecostal church, O Brasil para Cristo, which is under the leadership of Manoel de Mello (who left the ADB). In 1990 this church had approximately two million adherents in 5,000 congregations. It joined, and later left, the → World Council of Churches.

The basic doctrines of the ADB include biblical → fundamentalism, which places the Bible above → conscience and → reason, but does not regard it as contrary to reason; redemption by → grace through repentance (→ Penitence) and → faith; baptism by immersion; the baptism of the Spirit, with accompanying signs such as → glossolalia; sanctification; spiritual healing; expectation of Christ's return; and the → resurrection of the dead. Prayer plays an essential role in worship. Along with testimonies it imparts the message that God is mighty, Jesus saves, and the Holy Spirit is present. Testimonies — which follow the pattern of curse, sin, ecstasy, conversion, blessing, and redemption — contribute emotionally to the mutual strengthening of faith.

Following a strictly → dualistic thinking, the church teaches that one can belong either to the Pentecostal movement or to the world, which stands under condemnation. According to the Puritan → ethics that is customary in traditional Protestant denominations, ADB *crentes* (believers) abstain from alcohol, tobacco, dancing, and the use of makeup. The change of lifestyle at conversion is so radical that *crentes* have been much sought after as workers on account of their strong sense of duty.

Sociologically, the expansion of the Pentecostal movement is a religious answer to the social uprooting and the consequent lack of cohesiveness that came with the intensive restructuring of the agrarian and urban sectors in Brazil. The Pentecostal faith is a religion of the poor like → popular Catholicism or the → Umbanda cult (→ Afro-American Cults). It is a form of symbolic protest against the ruling social system. But it does not release any forces for changing the system, since the collective work of → prayer in worship steers *crentes* into sharing in the values of the symbolic world, which represents a denial of the world of daily experience. In this symbolic world they are the elect of the Lord who receive → sanctification from him and expect the imminent establishment of his → millennial rule.

Bibliography: D. BARRETT, ed., *WCE* 186-95 • E. CONDE, *História das Assembleias de Deus no Brasil* (Rio de Janeiro, 1960) • W. J. HOLLENWEGER, *Pentecostalism: Origins and Developments Worldwide* (Peabody, Mass., 1997); idem, *The Pentecostals* (3d ed.; Peabody, Mass., 1988) • G. U. KLIEWER, *Das neue Volk der Pfingstler* (Frankfurt, 1975) • C. LALIVE D' EPINAY, *Haven of the Masses* (London, 1969) • H. MEYER, "Die Pfingstbewegung in Brasilien," *EvDia* 39 (1968) 9-50 • B. MUNIZ DE SOUZA, *A experiência da salvação* (São Paulo, 1969) • P. A. RIBEIRO DE OLIVEIRA, "Movimentos carismáticos na América Latina. Uma visão sociológica," *Cuadernos ISER* 5 (1975) 36-48 • V. SYNAN, *The Holiness-Pentecostal Tradition: Charismatic Movements in the Twentieth Century* (2d ed.; Grand Rapids, 1997) esp. 134-35 • E. WILLEMS, *Followers of the New Faith* (Nashville, 1967).

HANS-JÜRGEN PRIEN

Assemblies of God

1. History
2. Missions
3. Institutions and Polity
4. Women's Roles
5. Recent Trends
6. The Worldwide Assemblies of God Fellowship

1. History

The Assemblies of God was formed in April 1914 at a convention in Hot Springs, Arkansas, attended by some 300 ministers and laypersons associated with the emerging Pentecostal movement. Approximately 120 of these men and women were delegates from scattered → Pentecostal congregations who felt concerned about the future of American Pentecostalism. They shared a distrust of established denominations and sought to establish a structure that would facilitate limited cooperation as well as accountability without diminishing congregational autonomy. They called the entity they created the General Council of the Assemblies of God. The degree of consensus made a statement of faith seem unnecessary. The group voted to coordinate support for foreign missions and Bible school education and to issue credentials to would-be evangelists, missionaries, and pastors who met certain qualifications. They also announced their intention to discountenance errors in doctrine and practice.

The organizing statement (1914) does not identify specific doctrines or practices but lists a general intention to exclude error. Some of the issues that agitated among Pentecostals in those years included baptism in Jesus' name, marital purity, abstinence from pork, direction by prophecy (whom to marry, where to live, all sorts of day-to-day decisions), direction by tongues (→ Glossolalia), and interpretation of tongues. Doctrinal issues debated included the meaning and timing of sanctification, rebaptism "in the name of Jesus," → millenarianism, speaking in tongues as the "initial physical evidence" of the → baptism (§2.1) with the Holy Spirit, and the necessity of the baptism with the Holy Spirit (must one have this baptism in order to be saved? do those who are not so baptized have the Holy Spirit?).

From its inception, the Assemblies of God was somewhat broader than the handful of other existing Pentecostal denominations. Those tended to be regional, and most had existed before opting to embrace Pentecostal teaching. By contrast, the Assemblies of God was formed as a Pentecostal fellowship, and from its beginning the Assemblies of God was national in scope. It was also somewhat more diverse than were other Pentecostal groups. Its leaders had been trained in various schools and had participated in different church networks before their Pentecostal sympathies drew them together.

In 1916 serious dissension over the → Trinity led the General Council to exclude Oneness (or Jesus Only) advocates from the council. The doctrinal crisis prompted the adoption of a Statement of Fundamental Truths. The statement endorsed such basic Christian doctrines as the → incarnation, → justification by faith, the substitutionary → atonement (§3), Christ's physical → resurrection, and the premillennial return of Christ. It also affirmed divine → healing and the baptism with the Holy Spirit, evidenced by speaking in tongues. After review, all credentials were reissued in 1917, and the Assemblies of God began a long period of steady growth. Over the years, the growth of bureaucracy resulted in the transformation of a loose fellowship into a full-fledged denomination (see 3).

2. Missions

From the outset, the Assemblies of God supported a growing foreign → missions (§1) program. A handful of delegates at the 1914 founding General Council were missionaries, and the concerns that led to the calling of that General Council included the need for accountability and system in channeling support to the growing number of Pentecostal missionaries. In 1927 Noel Perkin, a British-born former missionary in Argentina, accepted full-time responsibility for the Assemblies of God missions program. His personal influence proved decisive to the emergence and development of a systematic and far-reaching program. He oversaw the preparation of missions manuals, the development of promotional materials, and the creation of an administrative structure able to define and implement the denomination's missionary vision. He also encouraged the planting of indigenous churches and the implementation of → partnership rather than missionary ownership of Assemblies of God efforts abroad. Perkin's efforts were expanded after 1959 under the supervision of his successors, J. Philip Hogan and Loren Triplett.

As missionary planning progressed, other denominational programs undertook to support missionary goals by fund-raising, literature production, and the provision of various forms of support and supplies. By the 1990s, virtually every department of the Assemblies of God in some way contributed through its programs to the denomination's missionary outreach. If there is a single organizing and integrating principle in the Assemblies of God, it is probably foreign missions.

By the mid-1990s, Assemblies of God annual world ministries giving approached $200 million. More than 1,700 missionaries in 140 countries as well as hundreds of Bible institutes and extension programs gave the Assemblies of God considerable presence abroad.

In general, Assemblies of God work in other countries is organizationally separate from the American Assemblies of God. Worldwide, each General

Council is responsible for affairs only in its own region (which usually coincides with its national boundaries). While some of these sister organizations had their origins in American Assemblies of God missionary work, others did not. The Assemblies of God of Great Britain, for example (founded in 1924), has never had any formal ties to the U.S. Assemblies of God. In Brazil, another mission relinquished its work to the Assemblies of God, thereby creating the nucleus of what by 1997 had become the largest Assemblies of God organization in the world (→ Assembleias de Deus no Brasil). In some places abroad (e.g., Brazil and Korea), the Assemblies of God has been strikingly successful; in other places (e.g., Japan, Greece, France, Muslim countries in North Africa, Chile), 70 years of efforts have yielded little visible result. American Assemblies of God leaders seek to foster fraternal relations among national General Councils and to encourage participation in a worldwide Assemblies of God fellowship. The ability of U.S. leaders to accomplish such cooperation has been uneven at best.

3. Institutions and Polity

In the United States, the Assemblies of God supports 18 educational institutions (→ Education 4), including accredited Bible colleges, nonaccredited Bible institutes, and a seminary. Its denominational organ, the *Pentecostal Evangel,* has a weekly circulation of over 200,000. American Assemblies of God adherents worship in some 12,000 congregations. The average congregation has 115 members, although the denomination has numerous congregations with membership in the thousands. In 1997 the denomination reported that 14.7 percent of its members were Hispanic, 1.4 percent black, 3.0 percent Asian and Pacific Islander, and 1.5 percent Native American.

The Assemblies of God is organized into 57 districts, each of which ordains and disciplines ministers. Each district is governed by a district council and headed by a district superintendent. These district superintendents, plus two elected representatives from each district, compose the denomination's general presbytery, a legislative body that meets annually. Every two years, all ordained ministers meet as the General Council of the Assemblies of God, which is the denomination's highest governing body.

The size, scope, and resources of the Assemblies of God have assured it a leadership role in Anglo-American Pentecostalism. It was a charter member of the → National Association of Evangelicals, helped found the Pentecostal Fellowship of North America, and played a formative role in the emergence of the Pentecostal World Conference. In 1994 it helped plan the Pentecostal-Charismatic Churches of North America, a new and more inclusive ongoing Pentecostal forum.

4. Women's Roles

While women have always enjoyed considerable cultural authority in American Pentecostalism, they have never had significant institutional voice. The Assemblies of God has ordained women as pastors since 1935, but only 3 percent of Assemblies of God pastors are female, and no woman has served on the denomination's governing boards or in the general presbytery. Many congregations preclude women from serving as deacons. In the American Assemblies of God, the backlash against secular → feminism combines with sympathy for the political, moral, and social agenda of the new Christian Right to keep the issue of female institutional authority sensitive. In local congregations, however, women often predominate in the pews, exercise spiritual gifts, and pour their energies into congregational programs. Questions about ordination and institutional leadership are clearly too narrow to examine the extent of women's roles in the Assemblies of God.

5. Recent Trends

During the 1970s, the Assemblies of God (especially its Hispanic districts) grew rapidly. By the mid-1980s, however, growth had slowed dramatically. In the past decade, denominational leaders have placed particular emphasis on urban outreach programs while summoning the denomination to a celebration of the distinctively Pentecostal parts of its heritage. Renewed emphases on signs and wonders, speaking in tongues as the "uniform initial evidence" of the baptism of the Holy Spirit, healing, and the premillennial return of Christ characterize calls for reappropriation of elements of historic Pentecostalism that seemed threatened by decades of partnership with American evangelicals and interaction with the charismatic renewal (→ Charismatic Movement).

Some Assemblies of God leaders have felt that too many congregations mute their worship distinctives in order to attract more people. Highly structured services often have replaced spontaneous, longer gatherings in which people took time to "tarry" in prayer after the services. The → church growth (§5) movement has also influenced the general view of success. Some bemoan the apparent loss of a sense of standing apart from evangelicals, while others sense a greater degree of acceptance and influence. Leaders have attempted to redirect adherents toward → days of prayer and fasting and evangelism.

6. The Worldwide Assemblies of God Fellowship

The global explosion of Pentecostal forms of Christianity in the past decade contributed to the international growth of the Assemblies of God. The World Assemblies of God Fellowship (organized in 1989 as part of the denomination's decade-long evangelization program for the 1990s) became a primary vehicle for reporting and nurturing expressions of renewal in Assemblies of God units around the world. In 1994 leadership passed from the denominational offices in Springfield, Missouri, to Seoul, Korea. David Yonggi Cho, pastor of Yoido Full Gospel Church in Seoul (with 750,000 members in 1995, it has been billed as the world's largest church), the first non-Western leader of the association, hosted a mass meeting of Pentecostals in Seoul in September 1994, during which satellite hookups facilitated the participation of an estimated 10 million people in a single prayer meeting.

In 1995, after Seoul (where Cho's church accounts for some three-fourths of Assemblies of God adherents in Korea), the next largest Assemblies of God congregation (with 345,000 members) was in São Paulo, Brazil. Of the ten largest Assemblies of God congregations in that year, eight were in Brazil and two were in Korea. In Africa, LaBorne Assembly of God in Kinshasa, Zaire, headed the list with 12,000 members. In Madras, India, New Life Assembly of God was attracting some 6,000 adherents. Remarkable successes in Brazil have not been routinely replicated in the rest of Latin America, just as the large membership in Korea has not translated into significant presence in other Asian nations.

Bibliography: E. L. Blumhofer, *Restoring the Faith: The Assemblies of God, Pentecostalism, and American Culture* (Champaign, Ill., 1993) • G. B. McGee, *This Gospel Shall Be Preached* (2 vols.; Springfield, Mo., 1986-89) • W. Menzies, *Anointed to Serve* (Springfield, Mo., 1970) • V. Synan, *The Holiness-Pentecostal Tradition: Charismatic Movements in the Twentieth Century* (2d ed.; Grand Rapids, 1997).

Edith L. Blumhofer

Assurance of Salvation

1. Biblical Framework
2. Assurance and Security
3. Theological Aspects
4. Present Situation

1. Biblical Framework

"Faith is the assurance of things hoped for, the conviction of things not seen" (Heb. 11:1). This classic NT definition covers the whole field of the Christian striving for assurance of salvation. → Faith as the response to → salvation, as its appropriation, is not something that we see or have. It is a pilgrimage (Phil. 3:12). It is unthinkable without the element of the "not yet" (see 1 Cor. 13:12). It is not skeptical vacillation, however, or a nomadic course of life with no goal. As hopeful confidence and well-founded conviction, faith struggles for assurance of salvation. What is the basis of that assurance? The NT → apostles had before them the experience of the OT → prophets and very soon their own experience. The basis lies, not in the faithfulness of God's people, but in the faithfulness of God, in the validity of his promises. "If we are faithless, he remains faithful — for he cannot deny himself" (2 Tim. 2:13). God's unequivocal Yes to us in Jesus Christ (2 Cor. 1:18-20) is the basis of assurance of salvation in the NT. Paul knew very well the ambiguity of Christian existence, yet in the light of God's Yes he could say, "For I am convinced that neither death, nor life, . . . will be able to separate us from the love of God in Christ Jesus our Lord" (Rom. 8:38-39).

2. Assurance and Security

In the course of dogmatic history a distinction has rightly been made between *certitudo* (assurance of salvation, grounded in the → promise) and *securitas* (a certainty that relies on visible or ascertainable validation).

A longing for security early gripped the church. The self-serving and self-assuring strategies of the *homo religiosus* became common. Through objective forms (the sacraments or church dictates) as well as subjective forms (mystical or experiential), attempts were made to find evidences of salvation and in this way to guarantee assurance for oneself or one's church. One of the essential battles of the → Reformers was against such attempts. Assurance of salvation became a central theme for the → Bohemian Brethren in their struggle to show a lukewarm church its need of salvation, for M. → Luther in his conflict with → temptation, for the Reformed in the problem of the invisibility of election. By means of the practical syllogism some of the Reformed tried to find, not salvation, but signs of election. In general, however, the Reformers plainly set biblical assurance *(certitudo)* in opposition to every striving for security. As Luther put it, his theology could speak with assurance because it pointed away from the self, because it set us outside the self, so that we would not rely on our own powers, conscience, experience, person, or works, but on that which is outside us, namely, on the promise and truth of God, which cannot deceive us (WA 40/1.585).

→ Hope; Order of Salvation; Predestination; Soteriology

Bibliography: K. BARTH, *CD* IV/3b • M. C. BELL, *Calvin and the Scottish Theology: The Doctrine of Assurance* (Edinburgh, 1985) • E. BRUNNER, *Erlebnis, Erkenntnis und Glaube* (Zurich, 1921) • H. GOLLWITZER, *Krummes Holz–aufrechter Gang* (Munich, 1970) • H. J. IWAND, *Rechtfertigungslehre und Christusglaube* (2d ed.; Munich, 1961) • J. MOLTMANN, *Prädestination und Perseveranz* (Neukirchen, 1961).

JAN MILIČ LOCHMAN

3. Theological Aspects

Assurance of salvation as the firm conviction of believers that now and in the future they are in fellowship with God (Rom. 8:16-17, 38-39; 2 Cor. 1:20-22) is a central theme in the Reformation doctrine of faith (see 2) and a point of controversy with Roman Catholic teaching. The latter (→ Trent) holds expressly that no one can know with certainty of faith, apart from a special revelation, whether he or she has attained God's → grace (§3), or whom God has elected (DH 1533-34, 1540). But Protestants believe with → Luther that we may indeed know whether we have attained God's grace (WA 2.249). Because the Roman Catholic doctrine of → justification demands that those who are redeemed by grace should cooperate in their own salvation (R. Schnackenburg), their own weakness and ill-preparedness leave them anxious and fearful about their final blessedness (DH 1533-34). Their assurance of salvation is nurtured by the grace that is sacramentally mediated by the church, but unbelief or entrenched sin may render this ineffective (→ Church 3.2). Present-day Roman Catholic theology, however, lays more stress on the fact that faith does not receive its assurance or redeeming force from itself but from that to which it relates, namely, the Word of God (P. Knauer).

Protestant theology finds in the → gospel, shown to be God's → Word by the inner witness of the Holy Spirit, the basis of assurance of salvation. Neither → doubt nor → temptation can block this salvation; rather, they simply set it in a constant process of reassuring and confirming (G. Ebeling). More strongly than Lutherans, the Reformed tie assurance of salvation to assurance of election. The older Protestant → dogmatics (→ Orthodoxy 1-2) upheld and developed the Reformation statements about assurance of salvation, but in → Pietism, → Methodism, and to some degree Anglican evangeli-

calism, experience became more important. Like Luther, A. H. → Francke (1663-1727) and J. → Wesley (1703-91) had experienced the certainty of the divine grace that alone can justify, and they also preached it. For Wesley, the direct witness of the Holy Spirit, along with the indirect, confirmatory evidence of God's development of the fruits of the Spirit, assures believers that they are children of God (Sermons 10 and 11).

4. Present Situation

The fragility of faith in → God demands today with a new urgency, and under changed presuppositions of thought, an exposition of the conditions under which assurance of salvation is possible (G. Ebeling, W. Pannenberg, E. Jüngel, W. Härle, and E. Herms). Another challenge has come to both Reformation and Roman Catholic theology from the → liberation theologies of the Third World (→ Third World Theology), which refuse to restrict justification to its traditional individualistic interpretation (L. Boff) and move it toward a new experience of God by sharing in God's historical work of liberation. It should be noted in this regard that both a false security that resists the obedience of faith and an uncertainty that makes salvation dependent on human efforts threaten the assurance of salvation. In any context, such assurance can be understood only as a revelation of the truth of the gospel granted by the working of God in faith.

Bibliography: L. BOFF, *Liberating Grace* (Maryknoll, N.Y., 1979) • G. EBELING, "Gewißheit und Zweifel," *Wort und Glaube* (vol. 2; Tübingen, 1969) 138-83 • R. FRIELING, *Befreiungstheologien. Studien zur Theologie in Lateinamerika* (Göttingen, 1984) • B. HÄGGLUND, "Heilsgewißheit," *TRE* 14.759-63 (bibliography) • W. HÄRLE, "Krise in theologischer Sicht," *WzM* 29 (1977) 408-16 • W. HÄRLE and E. HERMS, *Rechtfertigung. Das Wirklichkeitsverständnis des christlichen Glaubens* (Göttingen, 1980) • E. JÜNGEL, "Gottesgewißheit," *Entsprechungen: Gott–Wahrheit–Mensch. Theologische Erörterungen* (2d ed.; Munich, 1986) 252-64 • P. KNAUER, *Der Glaube kommt vom Hören* (6th ed.; Bamberg, 1991) • J. MÍGUEZ BONINO, *Doing Theology in a Revolutionary Situation* (Philadelphia, 1975) • W. PANNENBERG, "Insight and Faith," *Basic Questions in Theology* (vol. 2; Philadelphia, 1971) 28-45 • R. SCHNACKENBURG and E. STAKEMEIER, "Heilsgewißheit," *LTK* (2d ed.) 5.157-60 • H. WALDENFELS, ed., *Theologen der Dritten Welt* (Munich, 1982) • J. WESLEY, *The Works of John Wesley,* vol. 1, *Sermons I, 1-33* (Nashville, 1984) • C. W. WILLIAMS, *John Wesley's Theology Today* (London, 1969).

MANFRED MARQUARDT

Assyrian Religion → Babylonian and Assyrian Religion

Astrology

In contrast to astronomy, which operates mechanistically, astrology rests on the conviction that the character and destiny (→ Fate and [Good] Fortune) of people can be decisively affected by the position of the stars at the moment of their birth. Only heavenly bodies that may be seen with the naked eye are relevant: the sun, the moon, the planets, and the "houses" to which these belong in the zodiac. Fixed stars outside the zodiac may figure in the calculations in a supplementary capacity. The demonstrable physical influence of heavenly bodies (esp. the sun) on terrestrial processes, and therefore indirectly on human behavior, plays no part in astrology.

Western astrology comes from Babylonian observation of the heavens (→ Babylonian and Assyrian Religion). Seven planets were distinguished, among which were counted the sun and the moon, and the path of the sun and the other planets through their 12 "lodging-places," which were named after striking constellations. The Greeks transmitted the details of this lore. At first the planets seemed to have had secular names according to their prominent features, but later these were replaced by names from the Greco-Roman pantheon (→ Greek Religion; Roman Religion). In connection with the signs of the zodiac as primary indicators of specific situations (such as those involving → friendship, → marriage, or → vocation), these divine names were the final basis of links between the constellations and human destinies.

Neither the Copernican revolution nor considerable shifts in position since the first development of astrology are taken into account. The main objection that the influence of the stars would rule out any freedom of human choice has always been countered with the slogan that the stars incline but do not compel. New efforts to find a theoretical basis for the idea of birth horoscopes — astrologers themselves have always rejected collective weekly horoscopes — have branched off into the world of psychology. Along the lines of C. G. Jung (1875-1961), this approach seeks to explain astrology as an exposition of the self that from a mythical age had been projected on the heavens and that serves character analysis rather than the foretelling of future events. In spite of the coincidence that is often invoked in favor of acausal connections, this reduction to the purely psychological, which is at least the tacit conviction of many followers of astrology in relating the stars to the course of the world, has as little to support it as the widespread effort of modern astrology to establish historicophilosophical schemas (→ Philosophy of History) in accordance with signs of the zodiac.

Astrology, which crosses the boundaries of all ages and cultures, has formed the link between natural science and other disciplines in various periods and not merely in the European Middle Ages and the early → modern period. Its ultimately subjective nature may be seen in the fact that in India, China, and the Arab world the same stars have very different names and characters. Often the moon is selected as the basis of calculation, its course and the "houses" are fixed only in analogy with the zodiac, and contradictory principles of interpretation are laid down as a basis. But since astrology has its roots in a deterministic, closed → worldview, it clashes foundationally with the Christian belief in creation. Nevertheless, Christians in Europe and North America daily read their horoscopes in innumerable books and newspapers, often valuing them for the help and orientation they provide.

Bibliography: P. BESKOW et al., "Astrologie," *TRE* 4.277-315 (bibliography) • I. P. CULIANN, "Astrology," *EncRel(E)* 1.472-75 • F. CUMONT, *Astrology and Religion among the Greeks and Romans* (New York, 1967; orig. pub., 1912) • H. S. LONG, "Astrology," *NCE* 1.986-88.

KARL HOHEISEL

Asylum

1. Definition
2. Religious Origin
3. History
4. Church Law
5. International Law

1. Definition
"Asylum" as a legal term means protection against persecution. Qualifiers used with the word indicate to whom, where, and how this protection is given. *External* (territorial) asylum is granted to a foreigner or stateless person. *Internal* asylum is granted only at specific places; for the most part, it now is only of historical interest. *Diplomatic* asylum by regional → international law is permissible only in South America.

2. Religious Origin
The origin of the word (from Gk. *asylon,* what may not be seized) shows that it first denoted an object

or place that provided protection for anyone who reached it while being pursued. The protection lay in the holiness of the object or place (e.g., a sacred grove; → Sacred and Profane; Altar; Temple), which outranked any earthly power. Literature leaves us in no doubt as to the religious origin of asylum. The OT makes clear that → refugees were received and protected in the → tribes of Israel (Ps. 146:9; Deut. 10:18; 26:11, 13).

3. History

Even in antiquity, the religious character of asylum declined, and its political character became stronger. The Greek city-states granted asylum on their own authority and maintained it as a right (→ Jurisprudence) against other powers. In so doing, they brought about an epochal change. From being a right of the persecuted, asylum became a right of the society that granted protection, which in turn led to its politicizing. It is noteworthy that → Rome granted asylum but insisted that other powers surrender political refugees. Thus the practice arose of granting asylum to nonpolitical refugees but not to political refugees.

In modern times (→ Modern Period 2), in the age of absolutism, this practice led to an arbitrary manipulation of asylum by rulers, who might grant asylum for political reasons but take a dim view of the asylum granted by others. After a time, however, the institution of asylum revived with religious conflicts, which produced the first great movements of refugees in modern times. Receiving banished coreligionists was regarded as a → duty. The first legal treatises on asylum appeared in the 17th century (Mylerus ab Ehrenbach, *Tractatus de iure asylorum* [Stuttgart, 1663]; Paolo Sarpi, *De iure asylorum, liber singularis* [Venice, 1683]). In the 18th century a major development occurred in the law of asylum with its restriction to those suffering political persecution. This brought about the end of internal asylum, which during the Middle Ages and the first centuries of the modern period had been granted for the most part in churches and monasteries.

4. Church Law

A restriction of the church law of asylum was attempted during the Roman Empire. Theodosius I (379-95) excluded criminals and state debtors from asylum in 392 but two years later lifted the exclusion in the case of criminals. In the process he expressly recognized ecclesiastical asylum, as did several later decrees, for example, those of Honorius in the West in 409 and 419, as well as those of Theodosius II in the East in 431 and 439. In the Middle Ages the church's

law found backing in the bishops' right to intercede *(pium officium intercedendi),* that is, the right to intercede with the ruler and the courts for those who had sought asylum in a church. Rulers also granted certain churches and monasteries express privileges of asylum. The church itself tried to avoid excesses. Thus the constitution *Cum alias* (1591) of Pope Gregory XIV (1590-91) forbade asylum for certain crimes. Civil legislation gradually limited and then abolished altogether asylum in churches and monasteries (Holy Roman Empire 1507 and 1532, Sweden 1528, France 1539, England 1697, Austria 1787, Prussia 1794, Switzerland 1798, Spain 1835, Italy 1850). Roman Catholic Church canon law originally included rules for asylum (1917 CIC 1197). The 1983 CIC, however, contains no comparable ruling.

In the latter part of the 20th century some churches in the United States and Europe have tried to revive the right of church asylum for some refugees whom the government refused to recognize as political refugees (→ Sanctuary 1; Resistance, Right of, 2). This so-called sanctuary movement received support from a number of Catholic and Protestant churches but generally failed to change government policy in the matter.

5. International Law

In international law states have retained the right to grant asylum. Those who suffer political persecution, however, have no subjective right to asylum. Even the Geneva convention on refugees (July 28, 1951) grants no such right. It simply regulates the legal status of refugees to whom a sovereign → state has granted asylum. Nevertheless, it has at least established that when a sovereign state does grant asylum, all other states, including that from which the refugees come, must recognize it and not treat it as an unfriendly act against the country of origin. This position was confirmed by the Declaration on Territorial Asylum adopted by the General Assembly of the United Nations on December 14, 1967. As of 1995, all efforts to include the right to asylum in international human rights instruments, such as the International Covenant on Civil and Political Rights, have failed.

Bibliography: A. GRAHL-MADSEN, *Territorial Asylum* (London, 1980) • O. KIMMINICH, *Grundprobleme des Asylrechts* (Darmstadt, 1983) • V. LIEBER, *Die neuere Entwicklung des Asylrechts im Völkerrecht und Staatsrecht* (Zurich, 1973) • G. LOESCHER, ed., *Refugees and the Asylum Dilemma in the West* (University Park, Pa., 1992) • M. R. H. LÖHR, *Das Asylwesen im Alten Testament* (Halle, 1930) • G. MACEAIN, ed., *Sanctuary: A Resource Guide for Understanding and Participating in the Central*

American Refugees' Struggle (San Francisco, 1985) • D. A. MARTIN, ed., *The New Asylum Seekers: Refugee Law in the 1980s* (Boston, 1988) • R. MARX, *Eine menschenrechtliche Begründung des Asylrechts* (Baden-Baden, 1984) • H.-I. VON POLLERN, *Das moderne Asylrecht* (Berlin, 1980) • N. G. SLATER, ed., *Tensions between Citizenship and Discipleship: A Case Study* (New York, 1989) • H. TREMMEL, *Grundrecht Asyl. Die Antwort der christlichen Sozialethik* (Freiburg, 1992).

OTTO KIMMINICH

Athanasian Creed

This creed, which is known as the *Quicunque vult,* from its opening words, is a pregnant summary of the doctrine of the → Trinity and → Christology. Written in Latin, it does not come from → Athanasius (ca. 297-373) but originated instead in southern Gaul or Spain at the end of the fifth century or beginning of the sixth. Works from the fifth to the seventh centuries contain echoes of it. Perhaps Caesarius of Arles (d. 542) knew it in his time. Around the time of the Council of Autun (670) it is plainly attested as the creed of St. Athanasius.

The first part of the statement presents a simplified version of → Augustine's (354-430; → Augustine's Theology) doctrine of the Trinity (with the procession of the Spirit from the Father and the Son; → Filioque). The second part teaches the full deity and humanity of Christ (→ Chalcedon, Council of) and the unity of his person, closing with statements about his death and → resurrection and the general resurrection and judgment (→ Eschatology).

From the 8th century in the West the Athanasian Creed was used in the → hours of prayer, and from the 13th century it gained acceptance as a third creed alongside the Apostles' and Nicene Creeds. The Eastern church knew it only in the Middle Ages in debates about the *filioque*. The Lutheran Book of Concord, following the Western tradition, recognized it as a third ecumenical symbol. The Reformed → confessions of the 16th century also stressed its → authority. The Anglican Church adopted it for use at Morning Prayer. In the 20th century, however, it has had a much reduced theological and liturgical role (→ Liturgy).

Bibliography: The Book of Concord (ed. T. G. Tappert; Philadelphia, 1959) 19-21 • R. J. H. COLLINS, "Athanasianisches Symbol," *TRE* 4.328-33 • J. N. D. KELLY, *The Athanasian Creed* (London, 1964) • D. WATERLAND, *A Critical History of the Athanasian Creed* (Cambridge, 1727; new ed., Oxford, 1870; repr., 1980).

GERHARD MAY

Athanasius

1. Life
2. Theology

1. Life

Born in → Alexandria about 297, Athanasius evidently knew both Greek and Coptic, and neither suffered nor saw → persecution. At an early age he was attached to the house of Alexander, → bishop of the metropolis. Made a deacon about 318, Athanasius accompanied the → patriarch to the Council of → Nicaea in 325 and acted as his secretary there. When Alexander died in 328, Athanasius succeeded him and led portions of the Egyptian church until his own death on May 2, 373.

We know from his writings, supportive church historians, and antagonists like the → Arian historian Philostorgius that Athanasius's leadership was often disputed. Some decried his election. He lived long within an age of great theological upheaval and short-lived emperors; ecclesiastical politics was the order of the day. Athanasius was accused of mistreating Egyptian Meletians by using armed people who beat, even killed, some of them. Charged with killing Arsenius and using the dead man's hand in magic, Athanasius's supporters found and produced Arsenius alive with both hands intact. Athanasius's ability to discover Arsenius, formerly hidden away in Egypt by his opponents, and to produce him at the trial indicates that he had well-disciplined and widely spread followers who could foil such a plot.

Frequent cries of misconduct suggest that the bishop used political power whenever he had an opportunity. He was rebuked at least once for apparently saying he would shut off grain shipments to the rest of the empire in order to stop Arians. → Synods at Tyre in 335, Serdica in 343, and elsewhere raised such issues, with the result that for 20 years he had few supporters in the East outside of Egypt.

At Tyre Athanasius lost his see and was exiled to Trier. When Constantine died, he returned to Alexandria in 337, only to be forced to flee toward → Rome in 339. Julius of Rome backed him, but Athanasius did not return to Egypt until 346, with Constans's support. Constantius II tired of his antics, and thus Athanasius disappeared into the Egyptian desert in 356 among friendly monks. On the death of Constantius in 361, Athanasius returned to Alexandria. Julian sent him away in 363, but he came back soon after Julian was slain. Athanasius's last exile was under Valens from late 365 until early 366.

2. Theology

Athanasius was the rock who stood against Arius and the non-Nicenes. His early *De incarnatione* and *Contra gentes* defended a view of the → incarnation that insisted on the full divinity of Christ, usually in scriptural terms as in his later *Contra Arianos*. He grasped the center of Christian faith and on occasion cited the liturgical practice of → baptism into the Father, Son, and Holy Spirit as an argument against the Son and the Spirit being creatures. Yet at times he misrepresented his foes and thus must be referred to with great care as a source for their positions.

After 362 he defended the *homoousios* of the → Nicene Creed of 325, but not particularly well. His influence has nevertheless been great. The fourth-century → Cappadocians, who developed more sophisticated Trinitarian language and attributed thoughts and actions to the human Jesus, honored Athanasius as a touchstone of faith. → Cyril of Alexandria in the fifth century held Athanasius in such affection that the formula *mia physis* (one nature [of Jesus Christ]), which actually came from Apollinarian forgeries under Athanasius's name, became central to his struggles with Nestorius (→ Nestorians).

Athanasius is still honored by both East and West. His exiles in the West allowed him to teach his sense of the incarnation and to introduce Eastern → monasticism through his presence and his *Vita Antonii*. May 2 is his feast day among both Roman Catholic and Eastern Orthodox Christians.

Bibliography: D. ARNOLD, *The Early Episcopal Career of Athanasius of Alexandria* (Notre Dame, Ind., 1991) • T. BARNES, *Athanasius and Constantius: Theology and Politics in the Constantinian Empire* (Boston, 1993) • H. I. BELL, *Jews and Christians in Egypt* (vol. 6; London, 1924) • *CPG* 2090-2309 • G. DRAGAS, *St. Athanasius contra Apollinarem* (Athens, 1985) • P. FRIES and T. NERSOYAN, *Christ in East and West* (Macon, Ga., 1987) • R. P. C. HANSON, *The Search for the Christian Doctrine of God: The Arian Controversy (318-381)* (Edinburgh, 1988) • C. KANNENGIESSER, *Athanase d'Alexandrie évêque et écrivain. Une lecture de traités Contre les Ariens* (Paris, 1983); idem, ed., *Politique et théologie chez Athanase d'Alexandrie* (Paris, 1974) • H. G. OPITZ, *Athanasius' Werke* (Berlin, 1934-41) • G. C. STEAD, "Rhetorical Method in Athanasius," *VC* 30 (1976) 121-37.

FREDERICK W. NORRIS

Atheism

1. Definition and Typology
2. Change of Significance
3. Theological Consequences

1. Definition and Typology

In antiquity, Gk. *atheos* described those who questioned the ruling religion and its gods. Thus not only the → materialist Epicurus (341-270 B.C.) but also the philosophical believer Socrates (d. 399 B.C.) could be accused of atheism. Similarly Jews and Christians often appeared to be atheists to religious contemporaries.

In the modern sense of godlessness or a general denial of God, the term "atheism" first occurs in European thought in the 16th and 17th centuries. We must distinguish various kinds of atheism, for the term is a fluctuating one with many layers of meaning. Theoretical atheism, for example, results from a nonreligious → worldview (as in materialistic thinkers of the French → Enlightenment such as P.-H. D. d' Holbach or in the German Monistenbund and other freethinking circles). Practical, or nonarticulated, atheism is action without reference to God, although perhaps without outright denial of God. Programmatic atheism fights against religion as an alienation and demeaning of humanity (L. A. Feuerbach and F. → Nietzsche). Political atheism seeks to free those who are exploited by a combination of throne and altar (K. → Marx and V. I. Lenin; → Marxism and Christianity), with the → ideological purpose of acquiring totalitarian power over the souls of citizens by forcibly eliminating the "uncertainty factor" of God (as in Stalinism and Neo-Stalinism). Psychologically motivated atheism regards religion as → illusion, into which the race can project its oldest, strongest, and most compelling desires (S. Freud). Existential atheism arises out of the experience of → suffering or the drive for unconditional → freedom (A. Camus and J.-P. Sartre). The kind of secularism that rejects meaning is an extreme form of atheism. Finally, in criticism of traditional → theism, a theological concept of atheism speaks of an atheistic belief in God (→ God Is Dead Theology).

2. Change of Significance

In its various senses atheism has become a challenger and even partner that theology and the church must take seriously. This is something relatively new. During most of its history the church has taken it for granted that the human race is almost self-evidently religious. We see this in the Bible. The real challenge to Jewish and primitive Christian faith comes from the religiosity of pagans (as superstition), not from godlessness. This has been the religious and cultural rule up to the → modern period, as atheists have been the odd exception. During the last few centuries, however, the situation has changed for theology and the church.

The process of → secularization has led to secularism, the grounding of this world in itself on the basis of the dogma of immanence: Our cosmos and history know no transcendence. More and more people seem to be finding in atheism a more attractive existential possibility than any form of religiosity. In this respect we must distinguish between a methodological atheism and an atheism of worldview. It is one thing to think that God never occurs within his → creation as a measurable object for → science, so that we may and should pursue research on the methodological premise that there is no God. It is a very different thing to let this premise become the fixed dogma of a worldview and to present scientific atheism as a philosophical system (→ Social Systems) or a fundamental existential attitude.

3. Theological Consequences
For theology the progress of atheism in the modern world means that it increasingly must view atheism, not only religion, as the backdrop for its talk about God. This change perhaps makes its task more difficult, but by no means impossible. Experiences in the formerly Communist countries of Eastern Europe are instructive and encouraging in this regard. The question of God and attempts at a credible answer by no means proved to be outdated or irrelevant in those intentionally atheistic societies. Rather, for many in those countries — and for many honest atheists today — they arise with a new intensity. God is not totally dead (V. Gardavsky). To the God of the Easter story those who live and think within a religious framework are not thereby nearer than those who live and think within one that is atheistic. The gospel is for atheists too (J. L. Hromádka).

Bibliography: H. M. BARTH, *Atheismus–Geschichte und Begriff* (Munich, 1973) • M. J. BUCKLEY, *At the Origins of Modern Atheism* (New Haven, 1987) • R. B. CUNNINGHAM, *The Christian Faith and Its Contemporary Rivals* (Nashville, 1988) • C. FABRO, *God in Exile* (Westminster, Md., 1968) • V. GARDAVSKÝ, *God Is Not Yet Dead* (Harmondsworth, 1973) • H. GOLLWITZER, *Krummes Holz–aufrechter Gang* (Munich, 1970) • J. L. HROMÁDKA, *Gospel for Atheists* (Geneva, 1965) • H. LÜBBE and H. M. SASS, eds., *Atheismus in der Diskussion* (Munich, 1975) • P. MASTERSON, *Atheism and Alienation: A Study of the Philosophical Sources of Contemporary Atheism* (Harmondsworth, 1973) • F. MAUTHNER, *Der Atheismus und seine Geschichte im Abendlande* (4 vols.; Berlin, 1920-23; repr., Hildesheim, 1963) • R. C. SPROUL, *If There Is a God, Why Are There Atheists? A Surprising Look at the Psychology of Atheism* (Minneapolis, 1978).

JAN MILIČ LOCHMAN

Athos

Athos is a mountain on one of the three spurs of the Chalcidice peninsula in northeast Greece. With the foundation of the first monastery, known later as the Great Lavra, in the middle of the ninth century by St. Athanasius the Athonite, Athos (from 1064 officially Hagion Oros, or "Holy Mountain") developed under the protection and with the support of the Byzantine emperors and other orthodox rulers into a self-governing center of Orthodox monastic life. The Fourth Crusade (1204) and the → Palamitic conflict brought times of crisis to Athos.

Monastic life was at first cenobitic, as it is in most of the houses to this day. But political changes and the impoverishment of the monasteries favored an idiorrhythmic (or self-regulating) life from the middle of the 16th century on into the 18th. In the early 1990s there were 20 monasteries, with almost 1,500 resident monks.

Bibliography: S. KADAS, *Mount Athos* (Athens, 1980) • L. MAMALAKIS, *To Hagion Oros (Athos) dia mesou tōn aiōnōn* (Thessaloníki, 1971) • *Le millénaire du Mont Athos, 963-1963* (2 vols.; Chevetogne, 1963-64) • J. J. NORWICH and R. SITWELL, *Mount Athos* (New York, 1966) • P. SHERRARD, *Athos: The Holy Mountain* (London, 1982).

CHRISTOPHOROS PAPAKONSTANTINOU

Atonement

1. OT and Judaism
2. NT
3. Systematic Theology

1. OT and Judaism
1.1. Atonement is a central concept in biblical theology. Along with the traditional misunderstanding of appeasing an angry deity, the penal definition of making good an offense and the viewing of the cultus as a human work have impeded a more relevant approach. In the OT, atonement breaks the nexus of → sin and its evil consequences by "chan-

neling the baneful influence of the → evil into an → animal that died vicariously for the man (or for the cultic object). Expiation was thus not a penalty, but a saving event" (G. von Rad, 271). The basis of cultic atonement is blood as the bearer of → life, which has been given by → Yahweh (Lev. 17:11).

Etymologically, Heb. *kipper* (expiate, make atonement) most likely derives from Akkadian, but two possibilities are open: Akkad. *kuppuru* and Arab. *kaffara*. We find various rites of atonement such as the killing of the heifer in Deut. 21:1-9 and the purification ceremony in Isa. 6:6-7. Note also the various terms structuring the lexical field, including the synonyms and antonyms in Isa. 27:9, Jer. 18:23, and Neh. 4:5, as well as the parallelism in P (→ Pentateuch) of *kipper* with the verbs *ḥiṭṭēʾ* (free from sin) and *ṭihar* (cleanse).

1.2. In noncultic examples, four groups of themes affected the understanding of the root: → reconciliation between humans (Gen. 32:20; 2 Sam. 21:3, etc.), Yahweh's atoning action (Deut. 21:8a; 1 Sam. 3:14; Isa. 6:7, etc.), the action of an intercessor (Exod. 32:30; Num. 16:46-47; 25:13), and the redemption of a forfeited life by offering an equivalent (Exod. 21:30; Num. 35:31-32, etc.). The concept and the term apparently belonged originally to the sphere of sacral law (Deut. 21:8b; 2 Sam. 21:3) or civil law (Exod. 21:30) and played a role in defining forms of social conduct (Gen. 32:20). Atonement might have the meaning here of ransom, or "equivalent of a life." Constitutive for noncultic usage is the context of the human experience of → guilt. When damage is done to the lives of the individuals or society, only a specific act of atonement can break the nexus of sin and evil and thus work for → salvation.

1.3. From the days of the middle monarchy (Exod. 32:30; Deut. 21:8a; Isa. 6:7; 22:14) and the exile (Jer. 18:23; Ps. 78:38; 79:9; possibly also Deut. 32:43), we find *kipper* used theologically in the sense of forgiveness. In the (post-)exilic period (Ezekiel 40–48; secondary P strata), the rites of atonement — under a return to preexilic conditions — finally became the heart of the cultus (Isa. 6:7; possibly also Ps. 65:3), which we can see from the expiatory quality of almost all offerings (sin, guilt, and burnt offerings; → Sacrifice) and many rites (e.g., priestly consecrations, Lev. 8:34 and par.; cathartic bird → rites, Lev. 14:53). The disaster of 587 B.C. brought a sharper sense of sin and responsibility to → Israel (§1). In new reflection on the course of national history, P^G, in his Sinai account (Exod. 24:15–Num. 10:10), succeeded in assuring Israel of the nearness of Yahweh, even though it no longer had the → temple, giving concrete form to this certainty through the concept of the tent of meeting (for → Luther, the → "tabernacle" [§1]).

The cultic theology of the atonement was later (P^S) formulated in Leviticus. Fundamental elements included the primary purification and making atonement of the temple (Ezek. 43:20; 45:18-19), the laying of hands on the sacrificial animals and sprinkling blood on the horns of the altar (note the so-called little blood rite of Lev. 4:25, 30, 34), and the connection of atonement with the formula of → forgiveness (Lev. 4:31 etc.). Laying on of hands has indicatory (or designatory? R. Rendtorff, D. P. Wright, J. Milgrom) significance. Since those who make the offering after committing an unwitting offense thus identify themselves with the offering, the death of the animal really symbolizes their own death. In contrast to the eliminatory rite of the scapegoat in Lev. 16:10, 21-22 (which seems to derive from a ritual practiced in southeastern Anatolia and northern Syria), the point here is not the transferring of the substance of sin to a ritual bearer (K. Koch, R. Rendtorff) but the symbolic offering up of the lives of the guilty in the sacrifice of the animal (again note the relation of blood and life in Lev. 17:11).

The cultic climax is the great Day of Atonement (Leviticus 16; cf. 23:27-28; 25:9), when the → high priest sprinkles the sacrificial blood on the *kappōret* (place of atonement) within the tent of meeting (Lev. 16:14-15). This act makes atonement possible with the God who is believed to be present there.

1.4. According to Isa. 52:13–53:12, future salvation comes to Israel by the → Servant of the Lord interposing his life as an *ʾāšām*, or guilt offering (53:10). To understand this process, we must note not only the internal references in 53:2-10aβ but also the legal background of the term (compensatory law? it exhibits cultic connotations for the first time only in Leviticus 4–5 P^S) and the use of the root *ʾšm* (obligatory satisfying of guilt, R. Knierim). Isa. 53:2-6 and 7-10aβ address these issues most directly. They refer to the obligation incurred by the guilty — in this case, Israel — to resolve their guilt. The issue in Deutero-Isaiah (→ Isaiah, Book of, 3.2), then, and also in the first three Servant Songs, is the deliverance of Israel (cf. 49:5-6 with 44:21-22). But only a life that is not guilty can accomplish what is needed, which the Servant offers in a unity of action with Yahweh (53:10a), thus releasing Israel from its bondage to guilt. Without this offering, it would be caught in the nexus of its own act and its penalty. Yahweh has this matter fall on the Servant in such a way that the Servant interposes his own life as a guilt offering for others (vv. 6b, 10a), and the "many"/"we" is changed from within. In the suffering of the Servant they recognize their own guilt and accept it in confession (vv. 4-6; → Confession of Sins).

1.5. The year A.D. 70 was decisive for the concept of atonement in ancient → Judaism. In the destruction of the second temple, Israel lost the place where its sins were expiated. Typical of rabbinic theology is the saying of Johanan ben Zakkai (d. ca. A.D. 80) to the effect that deeds of love are cultically equivalent to atonement (’Abot R. Nat. 4.5). For all the various means of atonement — → prayer, → fasting, alms, → suffering, → death, the Day of Atonement — expiation occurs only in connection with repentance (tĕšûbâ; → Penitence).

Qumran shows similar tendencies, such as its replacing the temple cultus with → Torah piety. In its view of atonement, the → Qumran community in part adopts OT ideas (God as subject of atonement: 1QS 2:8; 1QH 4:37; CD 2:4-5, etc.) and in part introduces new ideas, for example, that as a "spiritual temple" the community itself is equivalent to the cultus and in this function can make atonement for itself (1QS 5:6) and "for the land" (i.e., for Israel; 1QS 8:6, 10, etc.). Sayings about purity and atonement find their substantive center in cultic symbolism (which connects the cultic and cosmic orders), which also shaped the understanding of the sanctuary of the (Essenic?) Temple Scroll.

→ Covenant; Cultic Purity; Priest, Priesthood; Punishment 2; Wrath of God

Bibliography: On 1.1-3: H. GESE, "The Atonement," Essays on Biblical Theology (Minneapolis, 1981) 93-116 • F.-L. HOSSFELD, "Versöhnung und Sühne. Neuere Anstöße zur Wiederaufnahme eines biblischen Themas," BK 41 (1986) 54-60 • H. HÜBNER, "Sühne und Versöhnung. Anmerkungen zu einem umstrittenen Kapitel biblischer Theologie," KuD 29 (1983) 284-305 • B. JANOWSKI, "Auslösung des verwirkten Lebens. Zur Geschichte und Struktur der biblischen Lösegeldvorstellung," ZTK 79 (1982) 25-59; idem, Sühne als Heilsgeschehen. Studien zur Sühnetheologie der Priesterschrift und zur Wurzel KPR im Alten Orient und im Alten Testament (2d ed.; Neukirchen, 1994) • K. KOCH, "Sühne und Sündenvergebung um die Wende von der exilischen zur nachexilischen Zeit," EvT 26 (1966) 217-39 • B. LANG, "כִּפֶּר kipper" etc., TDOT 7.288-303 • B. A. LEVINE, In the Presence of the Lord: A Study of Cult and Some Cultic Terms in Ancient Israel (Leiden, 1974) 55-77, 123-27 • O. LORETZ, Leberschau, Sündenbock, Asasel in Ugarit und Israel (Altenberge, 1985) 35-57 • F. MAASS, "כפר kpr pi. sühnen," THAT 1.842-57 • J. MILGROM, "Atonement in the OT," IDBSup 78-82 • G. VON RAD, OT Theology (vol. 1; New York, 1962) • R. RENDTORFF, Leviticus (Neukirchen, 1985) 32-48 • A. SCHENKER, "Sühne statt

Strafe und Strafe statt Sühne!" Sühne und Versöhnung (ed. J. Blank and J. Werbick; Düsseldorf, 1986) 10-20; idem, Versöhnung und Sühne. Wege gewaltfreier Konfliktlösung im Alten Testament. Mit einem Ausblick auf das Neue Testament (Fribourg, 1981) • D. P. WRIGHT, The Disposal of Impurity: Elimination Rites in the Bible and in Hittite and Mesopotamian Literature (Atlanta, 1987) • D. P. WRIGHT, J. MILGROM, and H.-J. FABRY, "סָמַךְ sāmak / שְׁמִיכָה śᵉmîkāh," TWAT 5.880-89.

On 1.4: E. HAAG, "Das Opfer des Gottesknechts (Jes 53,10)," TTZ 86 (1977) 81-98 • H.-J. HERMISSON, "Der Lohn des Knechts," Die Botschaft und die Boten (FS H. W. Wolff; Neukirchen, 1981) 269-87 • R. KNIERIM, "אָשָׁם ’āšām Schuldverpflichtung," THAT 1.251-57 • E. KUTSCH, Sein Leiden und Tod–unser Heil (Neukirchen, 1967) • O. H. STECK, "Aspekte des Gottesknechts in Jes 52, 13–53, 12," ZAW 97 (1985) 36-58 • H. W. WOLFF, Jes 53 im Urchristentum (Giessen, 1984).

On 1.5: B. JANOWSKI and H. LICHTENBERGER, "Enderwartung und Reinheitsidee," JJS 34 (1983) 31-62 • E. LOHSE, Märtyrer und Gottesknecht (2d ed.; Göttingen, 1963) • J. NEUSNER, "Geschichte und rituelle Reinheit im Judentum des 1. Jahrhunderts n. Chr.," Kairos 21 (1979) 119-32; idem, The Idea of Purity in Ancient Judaism (Leiden, 1973).

BERND JANOWSKI

2. NT

2.1. In their treatment of atonement, the NT authors wrote from the traditions of → Israel. For them, cultic and noncultic acts of atonement alike involved sacrificial dedication to the holy (→ Sacred and Profane). Symbolically linked here were the vicarious offering up of life, the establishing of a new relation with God, and → sanctification (or new creation; → Symbol). Blood as the carrier of → life is an essential means of atonement (see Lev. 17:11).

2.2. In his mission, → Jesus of Nazareth came as the messianic Son of Man in total filial → obedience (Luke 4:1-13 and par.), even to death on the cross, in which he perceived the will of God (Mark 9:31 and par.). In terms of Isa. 43:3-4 and 53:10-12, he understood his death to be an atoning, vicarious offering of his life, his life being an equivalent (i.e., a ransom) for the forfeited life of the "many" (Mark 10:45 and par.). In the course of his so-called cleansing of the temple (Mark 11:15-17), Jesus took the place of the daily sacrifice (cf. Exod. 29:38-42; J. Ådna). At his parting → Passover in Jerusalem he devoted himself to death for the people of the 12 tribes. As the → Twelve ate of the broken bread and drank from the one cup, they became one with Jesus, who gave himself for them; in virtue of his shed blood of the → covenant, a place opened up for them at the end-time banquet in God's presence (cf. Mark 14:22-25 with Exod. 24:1-11 and Isa. 24:23; 25:6-10; → Eucharist).

2.3. With the → resurrection of Jesus and his → ascension to God's right hand, his atoning death was seen to be confirmed and put into effect by God (cf. Rom. 4:25 with Isa. 53:11-12). It thus became a formula already in the → primitive Christian community that "Christ died for our → sins in accordance with the scriptures" (1 Cor. 15:3; cf. Isa. 53:11-12). The accounts of the → passion and eucharistic traditions also developed a set form in community use. The church saw in the crucifixion even greater fulfilling of Lev. 16:12-17. To show his saving → righteousness and faithfulness to his people, God "publicly appointed [Jesus] to be the place of atonement by virtue of his blood" (Rom. 3:25). For the early Christians, Good Friday became the great eschatological Day of Atonement (J. Roloff).

2.4. → Paul accepted the (Jerusalem) gospel (1 Cor. 15:1-11) and made the atonement tradition the basis of his message of justification and reconciliation. The atonement, which in free → grace God himself made by the crucifixion of Jesus, is the real foundation that makes possible the → justification of all who believe in Jesus (Rom. 3:21-26). God made his own Son an offering for sin and gave him up to death (2 Cor. 5:21; Rom. 4:25; 8:3, 32; cf. Isa. 53:11-12). The life of the sinless Son of God is the ransom, in virtue of which the ungodly are redeemed and bought back once and for all from the dominion of sin (1 Cor. 6:20; cf. Gal. 4:5; 1 Pet. 1:18-19). Atonement is here "a coming to God through the judgment of death" (H. Gese), with access being opened up to God.

Parallel to justification, as Paul puts it in 2 Cor. 5:17-21 and Rom. 5:1-11, God → reconciled the world to himself by the death of Jesus. The point is that God thus ended the enmity between sinners and their Creator that sin had caused. Justification and reconciliation by Christ bring about new creation and sanctification for creatures that are freed in this way from their → guilt (1 Cor. 1:30; 2 Cor. 5:17; Rom. 8:30). As "divine word-signs" (J. Brenz), → baptism and the → Eucharist offer a share in atonement by Christ's blood and open up fellowship with God in accordance with the New Covenant of Jer. 31:31-34 (1 Cor. 6:11; 10:16-17; 11:23-26; Rom. 6:1-14; 8:1-17).

2.5. In the Pauline school, the atoning act of God through the blood of the cross (i.e., Jesus' vicarious self-offering) may be lauded as the event that gives → peace, stability, and redemption to all → creation (Col. 1:15-20; Eph. 1:7-10; → Soteriology). The early community, consisting of Jews and Gentiles, is prototypical. It owes its existence in peace with God and with each other to the act of atonement, and in terms of Mic. 5:5 it confesses Christ as "our peace" (Col. 1:11-14; Eph. 2:11-22). The → Pastoral Epistles gave precision to their → monotheistic confession (1 Tim. 2:5-6) by consciously appealing to Mark 10:45 (Matt. 20:28) and the theology of atonement.

2.6. Like Rom. 3:25, Hebrews speaks of the even greater fulfilling of the supreme Jewish expiatory cultus by Jesus, the heavenly → high priest according to Ps. 110:4 (Heb. 5:5-10; 6:20; 7:17, 21). Priest and victim at once (→ Sacrifice), Jesus entered the heavenly Holy of Holies with his own blood and made atonement once and for all for sinners before God (6:19-20; 7:26-27; 9:11-28; 10:12-14). Seated at God's right hand, he intercedes for believers (4:14–5:10; 9:24; cf. Rom. 8:26, 34). Since expiatory offerings atone only for unintentional offenses (Leviticus 4), the atoning death of Jesus does not cover willful lapsing from → faith; a second repentance thus seems to be "impossible" (6:4-8; 10:26-31; → Penitence).

2.7. Also in the Johannine writings, the atonement tradition plays a Christologically central role. In Revelation, Jesus is the victorious messianic ram and also the daily sacrificial lamb (Exod. 29:38-42) that in love has redeemed sinners from the whole earth with his blood and given them a share in God's dominion (1:5-6; 5:6-14; 7:14; 12:11; → Kingdom of God).

In 1 John 2:2 and 4:10 the expiation of all sin is the purpose and goal of the mission of Jesus, in which we see the love of God revealed. It seems, then, that a theology of atonement lies behind John 1:29; 3:16; 10:11; 11:50; 13:10 (see also 1 John 1:7); 15:13; 17:19; 19:34-35. In 6:55-56 partaking of the flesh and blood at the Eucharist relates to fellowship with the risen Jesus. Because of his death, Jesus is an advocate for his people before God (1 John 2:1-2; John 17; cf. Rom. 8:26, 34 and Heb. 9:24).

→ Forgiveness

Bibliography: J. ÅDNA, "Jesu Kritik am Tempel" (Diss., Tübingen, 1993) • F. BÜCHSEL and J. HERRMANN, "Ἵλεως κτλ.," *TDNT* 3.300-323 • L. GOPPELT, *Theology of the NT* (2 vols.; ed. J. Roloff; Grand Rapids, 1981-82) • W. HAUBECK, *Loskauf durch Christus. Herkunft, Gestalt und Bedeutung des paulinischen Loskaufmotivs* (Giessen, 1985) • M. HENGEL, *The Atonement: A Study of the Origins of the Doctrine in the NT* (London, 1981) • O. HOFIUS, "Sühne und Versöhnung. Zum paulinischen Verständnis des Kreuzestodes Jesu," *Versuch, das Leiden und Sterben Jesu zu verstehen* (ed. W. Maas; Munich, 1983) 25-46 • J. Jeremias, *The Eucharistic Words of Jesus* (2d ed.; London, 1966); idem, *Jesus und seine Botschaft* (Stuttgart, 1976) • E. Lohse, *Märtyrer und Gottesknecht. Untersuchungen zur urchristlichen Verkündigung vom Sühntod Jesu Christi* (2d ed.; Göttingen, 1963) • L. Morris, *The Apostolic Preaching of the Cross* (3d ed.; Grand Rapids, 1982) • R. Pesch, *Das Abendmahl und Jesu Todesverständnis* (2d ed.; Freiburg, 1981) • J. Roloff, "Ἱλαστήριον," *EDNT* 2.185-86 • P. Stuhlmacher, *Jesus of Nazareth–Christ of Faith* (Peabody, Mass., 1993); idem, "Das Lamm Gottes–eine Skizze," *Geschichte–Tradition–Reflexion* (vol. 3; ed. H. Cancik, H. Lichtenberger, P. Schäfer; Tübingen, 1996) 529-42; idem, *Versöhnung, Gesetz und Gerechtigkeit. Aufsätze zur biblischen Theologie* (Göttingen, 1981).

Peter Stuhlmacher

3. Systematic Theology

3.1. According to the doctrine of the atonement, the work of Christ takes its meaning from the removal of an objective barrier standing between God and humankind as the result of human → sin. It therefore presupposes that God's offended holiness must be expiated or the breach of the → law requited by a human act of restitution. The work of Christ is understood as a substitutionary or vicarious act, in which he does before God and on behalf of others that which they are unable to do for themselves. This act is to be distinguished from → reconciliation, which, as the restoration of a right human relation to God, is understood to be the purpose of atonement.

According to some conceptions of the work of Christ, in which he serves chiefly as an example of the → love of God or an example of godly life, reconciliation is achieved without substitutionary work. Such "exemplarist" theories take their direction from Peter Abelard (1079-1142; → Nominalism 2) and have been influential since the beginnings of modernity. Socinian (after F. Sozzini [Socinus; 1539-1604]) criticism of the idea of transferred penalty that underlay many post-Reformation developments of the doctrine was taken up more recently by I. Kant and F. D. E. → Schleiermacher, followed later in the 19th century by A. Ritschl. They developed the idea of Jesus as an example to be followed, an emphasis that comes into English-language theology in America through the work of Horace Bushnell (*The Vicarious Sacrifice* [1866]), and in England through Hastings Rashdall, who stressed atonement through the moral effect of the whole of Christ's life and death.

3.2. The foundations of the classical doctrine of the atonement were laid by the patristic writers (→ Church Fathers), for example, by → Athanasius (ca. 297-373), who in *De incarnatione* employed forensic, sacrificial, and military imagery in his account of the saving significance of Jesus (→ Soteriology). In the early Middle Ages, however, Christ's work came to be understood in terms of a rescue of humankind from the → devil, who was held to have gained legal power over them. It was against the irrationality of this view that → Anselm of Canterbury (1033-1109; → Nominalism 3) devised the first systematic theology of atonement. Sin, as a breach of universal justice (→ Righteousness, Justice), was an objective offense against God of infinite weight and must be punished unless an alternative could be found. That was provided by God, who, not wishing his work of → creation to come to nothing, in Christ offered a creative alternative, "satisfaction." The human achievement of Jesus was to offer to God the Father, in his life and death, a gift — a → sacrifice (§3) — of infinite worth, counterbalancing the effect of sin.

3.2.1. The → Reformers reshaped the doctrine in a more explicitly biblical form by focusing it through Paul's doctrine of → justification and stressing more strongly the love of God. Gustav Aulén has argued that in M. → Luther we find a return to what he calls the classical idea of atonement theology, namely, that the cross of Jesus represents a titanic struggle in which God overcame the → devil. More influential, however, certainly in generating exemplarist reaction, was Luther's view that on the cross Christ was loaded with the weight of the sins of the human race.

Over against the Reformers, the Council of → Trent, building on → Thomas Aquinas's (1224/25-74; → Thomism) development of Anselm, stressed the merit earned by Christ on the cross and communicable to the believer, especially through the → Mass. Against the Reformation view of the complete forgiveness of sin, the → Roman Catholic Church teaches that sinners must continue to atone for their sins, in this world and after death in purgatory. In recent times, however, there has been a change of emphasis. Juridical conceptions have given way (e.g., in the teaching of the Second → Vatican Council) to the view that by the death and → resurrection of Jesus, God overcame → evil and made humanity a new → creation (§4).

3.2.2. Protestantism after the → Reformation is more diverse. The formalization of the doctrine, in close connection with the doctrines of penal substitution (→ Punishment) and atonement of the elect only, brought the doctrine into some disrepute. In the 19th century, the Scottish theologian John

McLeod Campbell (1800-1872), taking account of the elements of truth in modern criticism of the evangelical tradition, taught a more universal and liberal doctrine and so prepared the ground for Karl → Barth (1886-1968), who reshaped the doctrine by placing the emphasis on the atonement as divine self-giving, in which God as man exercises judgment by refusing to judge ("the Judge judged on our behalf," *CD* IV/1, 556). In this way he conflated atonement and reconciliation and emphasized the universal dimensions of the atonement, which he understood as the realization of an eternal → covenant. After Barth, the doctrine has been little discussed, although there are now signs of a revival of interest, often centering on the theology of sacrifice (J. McIntyre).

→ Augustine's Theology; Calvin's Theology; Dialectical Theology; Grace; Luther's Theology

Bibliography: ANSELM OF CANTERBURY, *Cur Deus Homo* (1098?) • G. AULÉN, *Christus Victor: An Historical Study of the Three Main Types of the Idea of the Atonement* (London, 1970) • K. BARTH, *CD* IV/1 • J. M. CAMPBELL, *The Nature of the Atonement* (London, 1878) • R. FEENSTRA and C. PLANTINGA, eds., *Trinity, Incarnation, Atonement* (Notre Dame, Ind., 1989) • P. FIDDES, *Past Event and Present Salvation* (London, 1989) • C. E. GUNTON, *The Actuality of Atonement* (Edinburgh, 1988) • J. McINTYRE, *The Shape of Soteriology* (Edinburgh, 1993) • H. RASHDALL, *The Idea of Atonement in Christian Theology* (London, 1925) • A. RITSCHL, *A Critical History of the Christian Doctrine of Justification and Reconciliation* (Edinburgh, 1872) • H. STEINDL, *Genugtuung* (Freiburg, 1989) • S. W. SYKES, ed., *Sacrifice and Redemption: Durham Essays in Theology* (Cambridge, 1991).

COLIN E. GUNTON

Augsburg Confession

1.1. The Augsburg Confession arose out of the political and ecclesiastical situation of the years 1529 and 1530. After making peace with Pope Clement VII (1523-34) and King Francis I of France (1515-47), Emperor Charles V (1519-56), who had left the empire in 1521 for a long sojourn in Spain, could again turn his attention to its affairs. In the interest of his other international political goals, he was looking for a solution to the theological disputes. He was ready for a tactical arrangement with the Protestant states without being willing to surrender too much of his orthodox Catholic position. The friendly summons on January 21, 1530, to the Diet of Augsburg suggested that the emperor would listen to both sides of

the confessional debate and try to reach an impartial solution. In response, the elector John of Saxony (1525-32), seeking written support for the ecclesiastical changes in his territory, had the Wittenberg theologians prepare an opinion, the (textually disputed) Torgau Articles. A summary of Protestant doctrines existed in the Schwabach Articles from 1529.

The elector came to Augsburg on May 2. Since M. → Luther (1483-1546) was considered an outlaw and had to stay behind in Coburg, P. → Melanchthon (1497-1560) became the spokesman for the Protestant theologians at the diet. His was the task of developing the apology for the elector. Luther approved a draft on May 15, but whether it contained doctrinal articles as well as those dealing with church practices has been debated. In any case, doctrinal articles had to be included at Augsburg. J. Eck (1486-1543) had attacked the → Reformers as heretics (→ Heresies and Schisms) in his 404 Articles, and in the middle of May word came that the emperor had rejected the Schwabach Articles, which the elector had forwarded to him at Innsbruck. These articles, the Marburg Articles, the Visitation Instructions of 1528, and Luther's confession of faith at the end of his work "The Lord's Supper" (1528) all served as a basis for the doctrinal articles.

In the middle of June the elector approved the signing of the confession by other rulers, and the text was revised accordingly. Finally, the Saxon chancellor G. Brück (1483-1557) composed the skillful and self-assured preface expressing readiness for agreement with the other states but, in case of disagreement, appealing to the general council that the emperor desired.

This apology for the Saxon Reformation became a comprehensive Protestant confession (→ Confession of Faith). It was signed by the elector John and his son John Frederick (1532-47); George, margrave of Brandenburg-Anhalt (1515-43); Philip, landgrave of Hesse (1518-67); the dukes of Lüneburg; Wolfgang, prince of Anhalt (1492-1566); and the cities of Nuremberg and Reutlingen. Cities that followed U. → Zwingli's (1484-1531) doctrine of the Eucharist remained aloof. On June 25 the confession was read at the diet in German, and then it was given to the emperor in both the Latin and German versions. The two texts, which are not exactly the same at every point, were to parallel one another. Both had official status.

1.2. The history of the Augsburg Confession explains its division into two parts — one dealing with the chief articles of the faith (1-21), the other with the reform of abuses (22-28). Article 2 on original → sin is put between the articles on the Trinity and

Christology, which lead to the doctrine of → justification. This doctrine is addressed in articles 4-6 under the heads of "Justification," "The Office of the Ministry," and "The New Obedience." Articles 7-8 then deal with the → church, 9-13 with the sacraments (including confession and repentance), 14-16 with spiritual orders and civil government, and 17 with Christ's return to judgment (→ Last Judgment). Articles 18-19 on free will and the cause of sin are expansions of 2, while 20-21 on → faith and good works and the veneration of → saints develop 4-5. The more explicit and sharper articles of the second part deal with the Lord's Supper (22; → Eucharist), the marriage of priests (23), the Mass (24), confession (25), → fasting and other ecclesiastical ordinances (26), monastic vows (27), and the authority of bishops (28).

The aim of the confession is to show that the Wittenberg → Reformation agrees with Scripture and the one true church. Catholicity is supported by the articles that teach the early doctrines of the Trinity and Christology (→ Early Church), by the express rejection of early → heresies and the → Anabaptists, and by the (milder) repudiation of the Zwinglian doctrine of the Lord's Supper (art. 10). The doctrine of justification forms the heart of the Augsburg Confession. God's saving act through Christ makes possible the receiving of forgiveness of sins by faith. God gives faith through the work of the Holy Spirit by Word and sacrament. This emphasis provides the setting for an exposition of the doctrine of the church and the sacraments. The doctrine of justification also colors the discussion of the spiritual and secular orders, excluding the righteousness of works and offenses against any of God's commands. To say that the complaint against the Roman church concerned only a few abuses that had crept in since the age of → Scholasticism (Augs. Conf., between arts. 21 and 22) is to render the whole confession innocuous. The confession proper does not deal with the question of the authority of the → pope, and the Apology only touches on it. Melanchthon, however, did take up the issue in his *Tractatus de potestate et primatu papae* (Treatise on the power and primacy of the pope; 1537).

1.3. The Augsburg Confession quickly became a doctrinal standard in the Protestant church. As a test of what was evangelical in the Peace of Augsburg (1555; → Augsburg, Peace of) and the Peace of Westphalia (1648), it also took on legal significance. It has always been the most important confessional statement of → Lutheranism. In spite of its official character, however, Melanchthon constantly revised it. A Greek translation was prepared for talks with the

Eastern church. The Latin version of 1540, the so-called *Confessio Augustana variata*, occupies a special position. On the commission of the League of Schmalkald, Melanchthon prepared a new revision for the approaching conversations with traditionalists. In his alteration of article 10 on the Eucharist he took into account the agreement reached in the Wittenberg Concord of 1536. After much controversy the → Formula of Concord in 1577 declared that only the 1530 text was normative. In the ecumenical discussions of the 20th century the ecumenical role of the Augsburg Confession has been rediscovered, but the → Roman Catholic Church has not yet acted on a proposal (made by V. Pfnür in 1974) that it should recognize the confession.

2.1. At Augsburg a commission of Catholic theologians worked out a *confutatio* of the Augsburg Confession, which was read as the emperor's reply to it on August 3, 1530. The text was at first withheld from the Protestants to prevent their responding. Conversations were then held that produced some reconciliation, but these finally broke down. When failure was looming, Melanchthon wrote the Apology of the Augsburg Confession, on the basis of notes by J. Camerarius (1500-1574) and others, although the emperor on September 22 in fact refused to receive it. The Apology was meant to show that the Confutation had not refuted the Augsburg Confession. A new and expanded version, based on Melanchthon's receipt of a copy of the Confutation, appeared in print in April/May 1531. Justus Jonas (1493-1555) made a free translation of this into German.

2.2. The Apology follows the structure of the confession. Responding explicitly to the objections of the Confutation, it elucidates and defends each article of the Augsburg Confession. The extensive treatment of justification is the heart of the Apology. Against the view of the Confutation that both faith and good works are required for justification (cf. Gal. 5:6), the Apology sharply champions justification by faith alone. The attention devoted to both effective and forensic justification (i.e., to both making righteous and pronouncing righteous) in the Apology results in a comprehensive elaboration of the basic statement of the Apology that faith alone justifies. Along with the Augsburg Confession proper, the Apology of the Confession has achieved the rank of a confessional statement in Lutheranism.

Bibliography: Primary sources: "The Augsburg Confession (1530)" and "Apology of the Augsburg Confession (1531)," *The Book of Concord* (ed. T. G. Tappert; Philadelphia, 1959) 23-96 and 97-285 • P. MELANCH-

THON, "The Augsburg Confession (1530)," *A Melanchthon Reader* (trans. R. Keen; New York, 1988) 97-125.

Secondary works: F. BENTE, *Historical Introduction to the Book of Concord* (St. Louis, 1965) • J. A. BURGESS, ed., *The Role of the Augsburg Confession: Catholic and Lutheran Views* (Philadelphia, 1980) • H. FAGERBERG, *A New Look at the Lutheran Confessions (1529-1537)* (St. Louis, 1972) • L. GRANE, *The Augsburg Confession* (Minneapolis, 1981) • E. ISERLOH, ed., *Confessio Augustana und Confutatio. Der Augsburger Reichstag 1530 und die Einheit der Kirche* (Münster, 1980) • G. KRETSCHMAR, "Die Confessio Augustana Graeca," *KO* 20 (1977) 11-39 • B. LOHSE et al., "Augsburger Bekenntnis, Confutatio und Apologie," *TRE* 4.616-39 (bibliography) • W. MAURER, "Confessio Augustana variata," *ARG* 53 (1962) 97-151 = *Kirche und Geschichte. Gesammelte Aufsätze* (vol. 1; Göttingen, 1970) 213-66; idem, *Historical Commentary on the Augsburg Confession* (Philadelphia, 1986) • H. MEYER and H. SCHÜTTE, eds., *Confessio Augustana–Bekenntnis des einen Glaubens. Gemeinsame Untersuchung lutherischer und katholischer Theologen* (Paderborn, 1980) • V. PFNÜR, *Einig in der Rechtfertigungslehre? Die Rechtfertigungslehre der Confessio Augustana (1530) und die Stellungnahme der katholischen Kontroverstheologie zwischen 1530 und 1535* (Wiesbaden, 1970) • J. M. REU, *The Augsburg Confession* (St. Louis, 1983; orig. pub., 1930) • J. VON WALTER, "Der Reichstag zu Augsburg," *LuJ* 12 (1930) 1-90.

GERHARD MAY

Augsburg, Peace of

The Peace of Augsburg, promulgated on September 25, 1555, regulated the coexistence of confessions in the German Empire and gave Protestants who followed the → Augsburg Confession (i.e., Lutherans) permanent legal security. It was arranged at the Augsburg Diet among the various states in agreement with King Ferdinand. The emperor, Charles V (1519-56), remained aloof for reasons of conscience. It was meant as a temporary political settlement until religious agreement could be reached, although no time limit was set. In effect, the peace of the empire was extended to include the religious dispute. The states or their rulers could choose the religion for themselves and their territories (→ Cuius regio eius religio). Subjects who were unhappy with the religion of their territory had the right to emigrate for religious reasons.

In addition to the provisions of the peace, Ferdinand decreed that ecclesiastical princes who changed their religion would forfeit their rights (the so-called *Reservatum ecclesiasticum*). Furthermore, the king promised that Protestants could maintain representatives in Catholic ecclesiastical territories (the *Declaratio Ferdinandea*), although this pledge was short lived. He also insisted on a parity in the imperial cities that favored the Roman Catholics.

By territorializing the question of faith, the Peace of Augsburg strengthened federalism in the empire. On the Protestant side, state churches and secular → church government became entrenched. Controversies about interpreting the Peace of Augsburg helped to cause the → Thirty Years' War. In spite of its defects and limitations, however, the Peace of Augsburg formed the most thoroughgoing and permanent regulation of confessional coexistence in the 16th century. The Peace of Westphalia (1648) only modified it. This confessional partition of Germany exerted an influence until well into the 20th century.

Bibliography: Primary sources: K. BRANDI, ed., *Der Augsburger Religionsfriede vom 25. September 1555* (2d ed.; Göttingen, 1927) • E. WALDER, *Religionsvergleiche des 16. Jahrhunderts* (2d ed.; Bern, 1960).

Secondary works: W. P. FUCHS, "Der Augsburger Religionsfrieden von 1555," *JHKGV* 8 (1957) 226-35 (bibliography) • M. HECKEL, *Staat und Kirche nach den Lehren der evangelischen Juristen Deutschlands in der ersten Hälfte des 17. Jahrhunderts* (Munich, 1968) • G. PFEIFFER, "Der Augsburger Religionsfriede," *TRE* 4.639-45 • M. SIMON, *Der Augsburger Religionsfriede* (Augsburg, 1955) • L. W. SPITZ JR., "Particularism and Peace: Augsburg, 1955," *CH* 25 (1956) 110-26 • H. TÜCHLE, "The Peace of Augsburg: New Order or Lull in the Fighting?" *Government in Reformation Europe, 1520-1560* (ed. H. J. Cohn; New York, 1971).

GERHARD MAY

Augustine

1. Early Life and Conversion
2. Churchman and Writer

1. Early Life and Conversion

Augustinus, whose two other names are uncertain (some MSS add the name Aurelius), was born November 13, 354, in the small city of Tagaste, Numidia, in North Africa (present-day Souk-Ahras, in northeastern Algeria). He had at least one brother, Navigius, and a sister, whose name we do not know. His mother, Monica, was a pious if conventional Christian. His father, Patricius, was a member of the council, thus a leading citizen, though not wealthy; although Augustine's comments about his father's morals and religion are generally negative, he became a catechumen when Augustine was 16. The family supported Augustine's education in Tagaste, Madauros, and then Carthage. In Carthage he took a mistress, who bore him one son, Adeodatus. (Adeodatus died at the age of 16, probably about 389.)

Augustine tells how, at the age of 19, he read Cicero's *Hortensius,* which aroused in him a lifelong enthusiasm for the life of → philosophy (understood as a quest for wisdom). The first result was that he took an interest in → Manichaeanism, not as a different religion but as a more reasonable form of Christianity.

After teaching grammar in Tagaste (374-75?) and rhetoric in Carthage (375-83), Augustine went to Rome. In 384 he took a position as rhetorician in the city of Milan (then the residence of the Western emperor), being recommended for the job by Symmachus, one of the last champions of paganism. In Milan Augustine became acquainted with the bishop, Ambrose, and returned to the → Roman Catholic Church through a combination of factors — recognition of the authority of the Bible and the church, discovery of the Neoplatonist philosophy of Plotinus (→ Platonism), and resolution of a conflict over → marriage and → celibacy. His "conversion" (described and interpreted in *Conf.* 8) came in August 386. He spent the autumn on retreat with friends and family members in Cassiciacum, near Milan; several of his "dialogues" report the discussions there. He was baptized in Milan the next Easter (April 24/25, 387).

2. Churchman and Writer

Deciding to lead a contemplative life (at once "philosophical" and "monastic" in character) in Africa, Augustine journeyed with his mother to Rome. Monica died in the port city of Ostia, and Augustine remained in Rome for some months, becoming acquainted with the Christian community there. In the autumn of 388 he returned to Tagaste and set up a contemplative community on the family estate. His writings during this period are devoted to a refutation of the Manichaeans (esp. their theory of evil) and to exploring, in Platonist fashion, various modes of ascent toward God.

On a visit to Hippo, a seaport city, Augustine entered the church and was prevailed upon to accept → ordination as a presbyter (early 391; → Elder). He set up a voluntary community for members of the clergy and soon wrote a "rule" that became influential in the West because it combined monastic discipline with pastoral "care of souls." The remainder of his life was linked with Hippo and his new responsibilities as presbyter and (from 396) bishop. He participated in the Councils of Hippo (393) and Carthage (397), which helped establish the → canon of the NT in the West. He joined and led the polemic against the → Donatists, making important contributions to the theory of the → sacraments and the unity of the church. During the controversy with the Donatists he came to justify political measures against religious error. He was the chief prosecutor before an imperial commission in June 411, which led to the official proscription of the Donatists.

As a bishop, Augustine spent much time judging private disputes — a function permitted to bishops by Constantine and his successors — and interceding with officials. His ethical thinking was always dominated by an emphasis on → love, primarily for God, then for others "in God." Almost alone in antiquity, he opposed lying, no matter how justifiable it might seem, as a misuse of speech and human association.

During the years 398-400 Augustine began several major works — *Against Faustus* (on the relation of the OT to the NT), his *Literal Interpretation of Genesis,* and *The Trinity.* The sack of Rome by the Goths under Alaric (August 410) offered the occasion for beginning his largest work, *The City of God,* finished in 426 or 427.

Augustine was slowly drawn into the → Pelagian controversy (→ Grace), and his zeal increased after Pelagius wrote in defense of the freedom of the will and was exonerated (as a result of his equivocation, Augustine thought) by a synod in Diospolis in Palestine. Two African councils in 416 condemned the teachings of Pelagius, and Innocent, bishop of Rome (402-17), agreed. When his successor, Zosimus (417-18), vacillated, Augustine and his party persuaded the emperor to condemn the Pelagians for their allegedly radical social views. Subsequently the conflict intensified on both sides.

During these years there was a parallel but distinct controversy over the relation of faith and works, forgiveness and purification, leading Augustine to enunciate the beginnings of a doctrine of → purgatory (more accurately, a suffering that purifies through the frustration of wrongful desires), which was more fully developed during the Middle Ages. He also dealt with other "nondogmatic" issues such as funerary practices, intercession for the dead, and the indispensable place of almsgiving in penance.

After 418 Augustine took care to complete several series of expository sermons and retouched a number of sermons (mostly on moral themes) for written circulation as treatises. His *Corrections* (Lat. *Retrac-*

tationes), written in 426/27, are a record and reevaluation of most of his literary output.

Augustine's life and writings form a bridge from a period of religious → pluralism to the "Christian establishment" under Theodosius I and his sons, and then to a Europe dominated by the new barbarian kingdoms. Gothic incursions, which began in 378, led to the sack of Rome in 410. The Vandals crossed into North Africa in 427 and besieged Hippo in May or June 430. On August 28, 430, while the city was still under siege, Augustine died, reciting the penitential psalms.

Bibliography: Summaries of Augustine's life: G. BONNER, "Augustinus (uita)," *Augustinus-Lexikon* 1.519-50 • P. BROWN, *Augustine of Hippo: A Biography* (Berkeley and Los Angeles, 1967) • O. PERLER, *Les voyages de saint Augustin* (Paris, 1969) tabulation on pp. 430-77 • O. DU ROY, "Augustine," *NCE* 1.1041-58 • P.-P. VERBRAKEN, *Études critiques sur les sermons authentiques de saint Augustin* (The Hague, 1976).

Dating of sermons and writings: A.-M. LA BONNARDIÈRE, *Biblia Augustiniana* (Paris, 1960-); idem, *Recherches de chronologie augustinienne* (Paris, 1965); idem, *Saint Augustin et la Bible* (Paris, 1986).

Recently discovered letters: J. DIVJAK, ed., *Lettres 1*-29** (Paris, 1987) • R. B. ENO, trans., *St. Augustine: Letters, Volume 6 (1*-29*)* (ed. J. Divjak; Washington, D.C., 1989) • *Les lettres de Saint Augustin découvertes par Johannes Divjak* (Paris, 1983).

EUGENE TeSELLE

Augustine's Theology

1. Introduction

→ Augustine (354-430) left behind no systematic theology. His unique influence in the Western church rests on many works that he wrote for a variety of purposes — some biographical *(Confessions),* others apologetic *(City of God),* speculative *(On the Trinity),* ecclesiastical, or polemic. The basic thrust of his theology may be seen from his main concerns, which the following sections describe.

2. Ethics, Faith, and Knowledge

Already in his early works Augustine advocated traditional philosophical views. True happiness is open to all in principle and may be achieved only in our best, or intellectual, part. In later writings, Augustine modified this view to say that we cannot fully achieve happiness in this life; it is not actualized in a bodiless condition of the mind but in that of the resurrected body of the saint. To be happy is to enjoy God, to direct the will to him as the supreme goal, and in heaven to see God. Every act should be oriented to this end, and every object used as a means to achieve it.

The origin of → evil lies in the perverted orientation of the will that makes the created being an end. Neither love of self nor love of neighbor, then, is ultimately for its own sake, but with a view to enjoying God, though one can speak of joy in the Lord in relation to keeping the command to love one's neighbor.

The ability to act morally presupposes an understanding of our place in the hierarchy of being. Augustine's concept of knowledge and → truth is simply an application of Neoplatonism (→ Epistemology) in the service of Christianity. We cannot be perfectly happy without a knowledge of the truth. The same God whose beauty we love is enjoyed by intuitive, though rational, vision. The objects of knowledge in the narrower sense are transcendental and immutable ideas that include the formal causes of things and the criteria by which we make logical or ethical judgments. These can be communicated by the senses but are directly perceived only by → reason. They are to be equated with the divine wisdom, by whose inner teaching they are accessible to us.

The precondition of knowledge is gracious illumination by God. For Christians, knowledge follows → faith as its completion. The starting point of knowledge is the → authority of → revelation (§2) and of the teaching that is found in Holy Scripture and church tradition. Faith is rational, and this view is the basis of the view that faith is enough for salvation. Yet the demand for the greatest possible understanding of what is believed is deeply rooted in the nature of reason. To the extent that what is known and what is believed are one and the same, knowledge can replace the authority of faith (though genuinely so only in the future life).

3. God, the Trinity, and Christ

Augustine's theology is more theocentric than Christocentric. His concept of God went through three phases: (1) → Manichaean, with a mutable deity partly immanent in the cosmos; (2) → Stoic, with an immanent, infinite, material, but immutable being; and finally (3) → Platonic, with the transcendent, immaterial God. God's existence and essence are identical with one another and also with his attributes. His knowledge and will are eternally unchangeable. His omniscience includes knowledge of temporal events. The world was created by his will, and its historical course is directed by it. Since both his knowledge and his will are timeless, they are not affected by temporal events.

God is perfect → life, truth, and wisdom. The last is identified with the → Word of God and therefore with the second person of the → Trinity (§1). This does not mean, however, that the Son has qualities that the Father and the Holy Spirit do not share. By nature and substance the Trinity is perfect unity. The distinction of persons is to be understood in terms of their inner relations. The mystery of trinity in unity is elucidated by the → analogies of different capacities in the one individual mind (e.g., memory, understanding, and will). Augustine thus derives his doctrine of the Trinity not so much from salvation history as from ontological considerations with the help of psychological analogies. Yet he proves it from Scripture, and it is in harmony with the conciliar orthodoxy of the late fourth century.

The incarnate Christ, fully God and fully man, is a person whose rational soul links together the divine Word and a human body in a union that is analogous to that of spiritual and material substances (soul and body) in human beings. Because of the → virgin birth the human nature of Christ was free from original → sin (§3) and its consequences. He is thus the absolute model of the person who is saved and predestined by grace (a conclusion Augustine seldom affirms explicitly).

4. Creation

The world, which was created by God's will, is good because of his goodness. It was formed out of nothing in the first moment of time according to eternal ideas in God. The six days of the → creation story are to be taken figuratively. In the initial moment both the actual (→ angels, the soul of Adam, the inorganic world) and the potential (other living creatures) were present, the latter in the form of rational or causal seeds that would achieve actuality as the world progressed. This process of development covers the entire world order according to the providence of God (including suffering, insofar as it is a punishment for sin).

With regard to the origin of the souls of those created after → Adam, Augustine vacillates between creationism and traducianism without ever coming to a final decision. He equates the divine likeness with our spiritual and moral nature. The → soul, though mutable, is immortal. Loss of the divine likeness is to be understood ethically.

5. Sin and Grace

When Augustine abandoned the Manichaean idea of an evil substance that is in constant conflict with the → good, both in the cosmos and in individuals, he adopted the Neoplatonic insight that all beings are on a scale of goods. Free will, which is present in all rational creatures (angels and humans), is a good that can be misused. It is thus the sole cause of evil. Although angels were created with a will exclusively oriented to the good, since there was nothing evil in God's original creation, one section of them, and the whole of humanity as represented by Adam, turned aside from God. Underlying → sin is self-love, the pride *(superbia)* that wants to be as God.

By sharing Adam's → guilt, all people suffer its consequences of ignorance, death, and concupiscence, that is, the general attempt to find satisfaction in material things. Concupiscence expresses itself especially in sexual desire. By the act of procreation, which is linked necessarily to desire, original sin is passed down. → Baptism (§2) can cancel the guilt of concupiscence, but its effects are present even in true Christians. We are not deprived of free will, but of ourselves we are unable to will the good without the help of God. (This is Augustine's later view; earlier, he held to a kind of synergism.) The humanity that would otherwise be condemned to eternal death is thus saved by the → grace of God and not by its own merits. God's will is irresistible, but his grace is adjusted to the state of the recipient. Acceptance of grace is thus dependent on the will of the recipient, which God has prepared. True → freedom arises out of total subjection to the divine power.

In the controversy with the → Pelagians Augustine's main concern was to show that grace is not limited to external aids like the → law (§§3.1-2) or the teaching and example of Christ. It is an inner power, a gift of the Holy Spirit to the elect, whose → identity (unknown to us) is fixed by God's timeless and unsearchable → righteousness. Predestination to the good and the related perseverance are thus an expression of divine mercy upon a human race that was condemned to perdition.

6. Ecclesiology and the Sacraments

Augustine's ecclesiology developed out of the African tradition that crystallized especially in the controversy with the → Donatists. On the one hand, the church is the visible universal fellowship of baptized Christians, the institution that alone mediates → salvation, the universality of which distinguishes it from all localized schismatics. On the other hand, the church is also the invisible fellowship of angels and the elect. The unity of the church as the body of Christ (with Christ the head and Christians the members) is maintained by the presence within it of the Holy Spirit, who sheds abroad his love. Against the Donatists Augustine argues that the earthly historical church consists of a mixture of both good and bad. The latter are members only in appearance, but until the → last judgment they will be in the church in its present form, which is that of a pilgrim fellowship subject to sin.

The supreme church court for Augustine is the plenary council. Its rulings, however, are neither absolute nor infallible or irreformable. The question of the primacy of → Rome does not arise for Augustine. For him → Peter represents the whole church. Augustine gives precedence to Rome, relying on its authority (e.g., in the Pelagian controversy), but he does not regard it as sovereign. He derives church authority, not from persons, but from the truth of Scripture and from tradition as we have it in the rule of faith.

The sacraments are primarily Christ's sacraments, so their validity does not depend on the worthiness of the celebrant. A schismatic can confer the mark that is impressed upon the recipient in baptism or → ordination, hence these sacraments need not be repeated upon entry into the church. A valid administration, however, is savingly efficacious only within the church.

Augustine understands the outward form of the sacraments Platonically as the visible sign of an inner, spiritual reality. The signs can have many meanings. Thus baptism signifies both cleansing and grace, regeneration and faith, whether real or hoped for. The Eucharist is taken both realistically and symbolically (as an expression of the fellowship of the church united in the body of Christ). The eucharistic sacrifice is a present celebration of the self-offering of Christ and its renewal; it is also the self-offering of the people of God as the mystical body of Christ.

7. Asceticism and Monasticism
→ Asceticism is a means to overcome concupiscence and to promote love of God and → neighbor. It is best practiced in a fellowship of like-minded people whose celibacy and renunciation of worldly possessions are the best presuppositions for a life that is regulated by → prayer, → meditation, physical labor, and apostolic action. Typical of Augustinian → monasticism (→ Augustinians) is moderation in

asceticism and an ecclesiological orientation. The monastic community is a model of the church, founded on the basic law of love, and it is the most appropriate form of life for the clergy.

8. Hermeneutics
In the early works Augustine distinguishes between the historical and the prophetic aspects of Scripture. In the later Augustine, however, this distinction yields to the insight that all the canonical books, seen from the standpoint of the → history of salvation, are both historical and prophetic. Through Scripture, which is the supreme authority, the author, inspired by divine illumination, conveys its inner meaning. In spite of their limited knowledge and means of expression, the → prophets and → apostles are still reliable interpreters of the events that they record.

Scripture has a significatory character. Exegesis must expound the signs of Scripture aright by using the knowledge and techniques of the liberal arts according to the church's traditional teaching and rule of faith. A given scriptural passage can be taken either literally or allegorically, and it can have multiple senses (→ Hermeneutics).

9. History and Eschatology
The willful act of the fallen angels is irreversible. The "city of the devil" will thus always be separate from the "city of God" and in opposition to it. But Augustine relates the two concepts (which finally rest on the polarity between → Jerusalem and Babylon in the OT) to contrasting ethical goals rather than to specific institutions. The city of God consists of those who give precedence to love of God; the devil's, to those who are governed by love of self.

The fall of Adam corresponds on the earthly level to that of the angels. Both cities are thus present in world history. The city of God is represented by Abel, by → Israel as the elect people of the old → covenant (§1), and especially by the church. The devil's or the world's city is represented by certain earthly societies, though it is not equated with the institution of the political state. A state is just as worthy as the goals that it sets for itself. In every human society one can find signs of unity and inner peace. In spite of its earthly goals, the Roman republic reflects political virtues.

The Roman Empire after Constantine is Christian only to the extent that it displays Christian virtues and protects true religion against heretics and the adherents of other religions. Augustine makes no equation of → church and state. Both cities reach their eschatological form (as the fellowship of God and the saints and that of the devil and the damned) after the end of the world, the → last judgment, and the → resurrection of the body.

10. Augustinianism

Augustinian teaching posed the basic dogmatic questions of medieval theology up to the middle of the 13th century. Those holding opposing opinions appealed equally to Augustine's authority, especially his doctrine of grace. Philosophical Augustinianism dominated speculative thinking (regarding knowledge and enlightenment, as well as psychology) between the times of → Anselm (1033-1109) and Bonaventure (ca. 1217-74), in the case of the latter in combination with Aristotelian theories. The Franciscan struggle with → Thomistic teaching ended in victory for the latter.

The doctrine of grace and predestination lived on in the 14th century, especially in J. → Wycliffe (ca. 1330-84). The theocratic tendency of late medieval political Augustinianism (i.e., the idea that just rule is connected with a ruler who is sanctioned by the church) had little to do with the views of Augustine himself. Augustine influenced M. → Luther's (1483-1546) understanding of Paul, and Luther used Augustine's anti-Pelagian works against → scholastic theology. Other reformers like Carlstadt (ca. 1480-1541) and J. → Calvin (1509-64) took up Augustine's doctrine of grace independently. Augustinian theology experienced its last true revival in the 17th century, in → Jansenism.

Bibliography: C. Andresen, ed., Bibliographia Augustiniana (2d ed.; Darmstadt, 1973); idem, ed., Zum Augustin-Gespräch der Gegenwart (2 vols.; Darmstadt, 1975-81) • G. Bonner, St. Augustine of Hippo: Life and Controversies (Norwich, 1986) • P. R. Brown, Augustine of Hippo: A Biography (Berkeley and Los Angeles, 1967) • H. Chadwick, Augustine (New York, 1986) • U. Duchrow, Christenheit und Weltverantwortung. Traditionsgeschichte und systematische Struktur der Zweireichelehre (2d ed.; Stuttgart, 1983) • É. Gilson, The Christian Philosophy of St. Augustine (New York, 1983) • A. Schindler, G. Leff, U. Bubenheimer, and M. Schmidt, "Augustin / Augustinismus," TRE 4.645-723 (extensive bibliographies) • E. TeSelle, Augustine the Theologian (London, 1970) • A. Zumkeller, Augustine's Ideal of the Religious Life (New York, 1986).

Gerard O'Daly

Augustinians

1. The term "Augustinians" denotes members of religious orders that appeal to the order composed by Augustine (354-430). (The → Dominicans, Premonstratensians, and others appeal to the same order.) An express Augustinian orientation appears in their names (Augustinian Canons, Augustinian Hermits, Augustinian Recollects, Augustinian Discalced, Augustinian Assumptionists, and Augustinian Eremitesses).

2. The germ of Augustinian → monasticism in Europe did not lie in → Augustine's monastic foundations in Africa but in the rule that he composed in approximately 397. Objections to the authenticity of this rule must now be viewed as blunted. The heart of the rule comes from Augustine, though Ivo of Chartres (ca. 1040-1115) perhaps wrote the introductory sentence. The lifestyle and ideal of the → primitive Christian community in Jerusalem (Acts 4:32-35) served as a model for Augustine's specific rules. Commitment to God in → discipleship of Christ leads to concern for the welfare of others.

3. The Augustinian Canons seem to be the oldest group. In 1256 Pope Alexander IV (1254-61) merged the Italian Hermits into an order known as the Hermits of St. Augustine (O.E.S.A.), which today calls itself the Order of the Hermit Friars of St. Augustine (O.S.A.).

3.1. Founded to exercise → pastoral care in the cities, this order extended across Europe by the end of the 13th century. Reforming congregations tried to combat the decline in discipline in the 14th century. One of these in Germany was the Saxon Congregation, whose vicar was Johann von Staupitz (1468/69-1524) and which numbered Martin → Luther (1483-1546) as a member. The order reached its greatest numerical strength in the 18th century, when there were 20,000 Augustinian friars. In the early 1990s, there were 3,000 Augustinians in 515 houses in 27 provinces.

3.2. The basic democratic structure of the order gained approval in 1290 and was revised in 1968. At the head of the order is a prior general, at the head of each province a provincial prior, and at the head of each convent a prior. All these have advisers. For all more important matters there are conventual, provincial, and general chapters.

3.3. The stress on study as a basis of the order meant that it produced its own theological school. Giles of Rome (ca. 1245-1316), Gregory of Rimini (d. 1358), and Hugolin of Orvieto (d. 1373) took up the thought of Augustine and developed it, regarding → theology as a discipline that should empower one for love of God. In their teaching on → grace (§3) they stressed the work of God and resisted contemporary trends that laid more emphasis on the capacities of human nature. It may be assumed that several of the doctrines espoused by the Augustinian school influenced Luther in his development. G. Seripando (1492/93-1563) at → Trent, H. Noris (1631-1704) and G. L. Berti (1696-1766) in controversy with M. Baius (1513-89), and C. O. Jansen (1585-1638) all worked on a historical understanding of Augustine (→ Jansenism). In the 20th century various institutes (e.g., the Augustinus Institute at Würzburg, Germany) have taken up the concerns of the school in a rather different form.

3.4. In the 20th century the main contribution of the order is in pastoral work of all kinds. Members dedicate themselves to youth education, foreign missions, and advancement of learning through teaching and scholarly research.

Bibliography: C. ANDRESEN, *Bibliographia Augustiniana* (Darmstadt, 1962; 2d ed., 1973) • T. J. VON BAVEL, "The Evangelical Inspiration of the Rule of St. Augustine," *DR* 93 (1975) 83-99 • "Bibliographie historique de l'ordre de Saint Augustin, 1945-1975," *Aug(L)* 26 (1976) 39-301 • A. BORROMEO, "Augustinians," *OER* 1.100-101 • J. GAVIGAN, *The Augustinians from the French Revolution to Modern Times* (Villanova, Pa., 1989); idem, *The Austro-Hungarian Province of the Augustinian Friars, 1646-1820* (3 vols.; Rome, 1975-77) • R. GAVOTTO, *The Prior General: The Principle of Unity in the Order of St. Augustine* (Rome, 1973) • E. GINDELE et al., *Bibliographie zur Geschichte und Theologie des Augustiner-Eremitenordens bis zum Beginn der Reformation* (Berlin, 1977) • D. GUTIÉRREZ, *The Augustinians,* vol. 1, . . . *in the Middle Ages, 1256-1356;* vol. 2, . . . *in the Middle Ages, 1357-1517;* vol. 3, . . . *from the Protestant Reformation to the Peace of Westphalia, 1518-1648* (Villanova, Pa., 1979-84) an official history • A. KUNZELMANN, *Geschichte der deutschen Augustinereremiten* (7 vols.; Würzburg, 1969-76) • B. RANO, *The Order of St. Augustine* (Rome, 1975) • L. VERHEIJEN, *The Rule of Our Holy Father St. Augustine: Bishop of Hippo* (Villanova, Pa., 1976) • A. ZUMKELLER, *Augustine's Ideal of the Religious Life* (New York, 1986).

On Augustinian nuns: M. J. HEIMBUCHER, *Die Orden und Kongregationen der katholischen Kirche* (vol. 1; 4th ed.; Paderborn, 1980) 565-71 • W. HÜMPFNER, "Augustinerinnen," *LTK* (2d ed.) 1.1088-89 • B. RANO, "Agostiniane," *Dizionario degli Instituti di Perfezione* (1974) 1.155-92 (see also articles on the individual orders in the *Dizionario*) • A. WIENAND, ed., *Das Wirken der Orden und Klöster in Deutschland,* vol. 2, *Die weiblichen Orden, Kongregationen und Klöster* (Cologne, 1964) 190-219.

KARL W. ECKERMANN, O.E.S.A.

Australia

	1960	*1980*	*2000*
Population (1,000s):	10,274	14,565	18,832
Annual growth rate (%):	2.06	1.42	1.04

Area: 7,682,300 sq. km. (2,966,200 sq. mi.)

A.D. 2000

Population density: 2/sq. km. (6/sq. mi.)
Births / deaths: 1.35 / 0.77 per 100 population
Fertility rate: 1.89 per woman
Infant mortality rate: 6 per 1,000 live births
Life expectancy: 78.8 years (m: 76.1, f: 81.7)
Religious affiliation (%): Christians 79.7 (Roman Catholics 26.6, Anglicans 21.5, unaffiliated 18.2, Protestants 14.7, indigenous 8.9, Orthodox 4.3, marginal 1.4), nonreligious 14.6, atheists 1.7, Buddhists 1.3, Muslims 1.0, other 1.7.

1. Socioreligious Context
2. The Christian Churches
  2.1. Statistics
  2.2. The Roman Catholic Church
  2.3. The Anglican Church
  2.4. The Uniting Church
  2.5. The Orthodox Churches
  2.6. The Lutheran Church
3. Interconfessional Relations
4. Church-State Relations
5. Non-Christian Religions
  5.1. The Aborigines
  5.2. Judaism
  5.3. Islam

1. Socioreligious Context

Without a review of the socioreligious context, it is hardly possible to understand the uniqueness of the Australian churches.

1.1. Australia was much influenced by → secularism. People did not come to Australia for reasons of faith but to found a British penal colony. Religious faith was employed as an instrument of moral repression. Later immigrants came mostly for political or economic reasons. As a highly industrialized urban society, Australia shares the secularism of all Western countries. From the very beginning, churches in Australia have had to fight for their life on the margins of society. These trends are reflected in the statistics. In 1986, a census revealed that 12.7 percent of the people say they are nonreligious (6.7 percent in 1971), and 12.3 percent left the question of their religion unanswered (6.1 percent in 1971). Overall church attendance has declined from 35 percent in 1966 to 12 percent in 1990.

1.2. Apart from the Aborigines, now numbering about 250,000 (down from an estimated 300,000 in 1790), Australia is a land of immigrants, at first mostly from Great Britain, after 1947 from the mainland of Europe, then from Asia. Among the 16.8 million people counted in the 1991 census, 3.9 million (23 percent) were born outside of Australia. The largest groups had come from the United Kingdom (1.2 million) and continental Europe (1.1 million), with 763,000 from Asia and 287,500 from New Zealand. These all brought their own beliefs with them. Imported → pluralism is thus a common feature of Australian Christianity. Into the 20th century the denominations existed mainly in national groupings that had brought traditional forms from their countries of origin. The Orthodox Church grew a good deal by immigration after 1950, but in almost every canonical and noncanonical shade as centers of national and cultural → identity. Thus ecclesiastical and confessional controversies have been on the agenda from the very first. Religious pluralism has prevented the churches from exercising any lasting influence on the country's cultural development.

1.3. The churches have special problems because of the great distances. Thus around 1950, for example, the attitude of Australian → Baptists to the → World Council of Churches (WCC) varied from state to state.

1.4. Most Australians indicate that they believe in God (81 percent in 1983). Publicly, however, they view religion as a private matter and grant it at most the role of a guardian of morals.

1.5. New waves of immigration strengthened the religious-cultural pluralism. They laid upon the churches tasks for which they were not prepared. Yet ecclesiastical and ecumenical institutions were founded to care for immigrants. Thus the immigration division of the National Council of Churches in Australia (NCCA), which is affiliated with the WCC, has taken care of more than 80,000 people since 1950.

1.6. The great problems with which the churches in Australia have always had to wrestle (e.g., the isolation and indifference of the settlers, the chronic lack of personnel and resources, and the need to set up independent church structures) have meant that the organization of the churches has had to be shaped more by pragmatic than by theological considerations. This pragmatism still characterizes church life.

2. The Christian Churches

2.1. Statistics

According to estimates for the year 2000, nearly half the people of Australia are Roman Catholics (26.6 percent, vs. 26.3 percent in 1966) or Anglicans (21.5 percent, vs. 33.5 percent in 1966). The only other substantial group is the Uniting Church, which the → Methodists, Presbyterians, and Congregationalists formed in 1977. In 1993 the Uniting Church, along with those Presbyterians that did not join, accounted for 11.2 percent of the population. No other denomination can muster more than 4 percent of the population. Of all religious groups only Muslims, the Orthodox, → Pentecostals, and → Jehovah's Witnesses are growing faster than the population.

2.2. The Roman Catholic Church

Various factors have had a decisive impact on → Roman Catholicism in Australia, including early discrimination against the Irish, mutual distrust (until ca. 1960) between Roman Catholics and Protestants, the effect of the Irish model of Catholicism in Australia, the impact of the archbishops Cardinal Moran (in Sydney until 1911) and Mannix (in Melbourne until 1963), the Irish inclination to practical → piety, a massive building program that claimed almost all available resources up to 1970, and finally the struggle to secure state support for church schools. In protest against the secular ethos of the state, the church very quickly began to set up its own parochial schools, which have now become a prominent feature of the Roman Catholic system. In 1982 the church had 1,698 parochial schools.

The position of the church changed dramatically after World War II with the immigration of over one million Roman Catholics from southern Europe. → Vatican II was a decisive turning point for Australian Roman Catholicism, as it opened the door to new theological dialogue and improved the whole ecumenical climate. Roman Catholicism remained conservative in Sydney and Melbourne, but there were strong social and ecumenical impulses in the other archbishoprics. At several levels Roman Catholics now work together with other Christians (e.g., in a development program in the NCCA). From 1967 the church has been engaged in multilateral and bilateral dialogue, for example, with the Anglicans and Lutherans. From 1964 it has been active in world relief. The Project Compassion Appeal raised over $A2 million in 1983 (→ Relief Organizations).

2.3. The Anglican Church

This church was at first part of the Church of England. An Australian bishopric was created in Sydney in 1836. Only in 1962, after lengthy negotiations, did the Anglican Church in Australia become independent. Australia never developed a state-church system, but the Anglican Church long enjoyed a favored status. Today there are 24 dioceses led by a primate. Not until 1966 did an Australian occupy this position. In 1992 the Anglican Synod approved the ordination of women.

The church engages in active missionary work, especially among the Aborigines and in the Pacific. At the ecumenical level it has played a leading role, especially in Melbourne. Yet it must not be ignored that a persistent → conservatism, as well as doctrinal differences between the → Evangelicals, who have been dominant in Sydney since 1854, and the → High Church party, which is strongly represented in Brisbane and Adelaide, have made bilateral → dialogue much more difficult.

2.4. *The Uniting Church*

In 1977, after 50 years of negotiation, three churches came together to form the Uniting Church in Australia (UCA); these churches themselves were in part the result of previous unions. Although Presbyterianism has made a stronger theological impact on the UCA than Methodism, it is a matter for regret that about one-third of all Presbyterians have failed to join. The UCA consists of seven synods with 3,200 congregations. Some $A1.25 million are raised each year for missionary enterprises reaching as far as Taiwan and Latin America. The UCA works together with other churches in missionary work in Asia and the Pacific. It maintains larger welfare centers in all the capital cities. Since the UCA regards itself as one part of a process leading to church → unity, it takes ecumenical cooperation seriously at every level.

2.5. *The Orthodox Churches*

These embrace almost all the Chalcedonian and non-Chalcedonian churches and include canonical churches as well as various independent national churches, resulting in a complicated ecclesiastical picture of many small and partly divided churches in national groupings. From 1979 a conference of all canonical orthodox churches (SCCOCA) began trying to coordinate the individual churches. The largest church is the Greek Orthodox, which has an archbishopric in Sydney (founded in 1924) and over 100 congregations.

It is estimated that the Orthodox in Australia now number almost 800,000 members, or 4.3 percent of the estimated 2000 population of 18.8 million (1.5 percent in 1961). Since there is still preoccupation with integrating immigrants, these churches have thus far generally not had wider impact.

2.6. *The Lutheran Church*

Among the churches the Lutherans are something of an exception. They alone came to Australia for reasons of faith (in 1838), in protest against the Prussian Union. They alone have divided on theological grounds since coming to Australia. In spite of their differences, their confessional orientation has remained determinative, which was the uniting factor that led to the formation of the Lutheran Church of Australia (LCA). The LCA reported 114,000 baptized members in 1983. This relatively small body has developed a great circle of influence. It maintains 46 primary schools and 11 high schools or colleges and has done what is in many respects pioneering work among the Aborigines in central Australia. Although one of the churches that formed the LCA was a founding member of the → Lutheran World Federation in 1947, it had to leave in 1966 to make the union possible. Because of remaining theological tensions it has not proved possible thus far to extend the union to other churches, including some that are Lutheran. In spite of the high level of theological education, theological impulses are underdeveloped in many areas of church life. The LCA nevertheless engages in useful bilateral dialogues.

3. Interconfessional Relations

→ Ecumenism in Australia has its roots especially in the youth movement and student movement at the end of the 19th century. The Australian Council of the WCC was formed in 1946 and became the Australian Council of Churches in 1960 and, in 1994, the National Council of Churches in Australia. The NCCA has allowed the churches to remain in direct ecumenical contact. A World Week of Prayer for Christian Unity began in 1954 in which churches that are not members of the NCCA have joined. Today the NCCA includes almost all the main Protestant churches as members along with eight Orthodox churches. Roman Catholics, Lutherans, and Baptists work along with it, sometimes only at the local level. Along with carrying on theological dialogues (e.g., with Roman Catholics from 1967 to 1972), the NCCA has worked especially on behalf of world peace and the Aborigines.

In February 1991 the WCC held its seventh assembly in Canberra. A total of 842 delegates attended from 317 member churches, focusing on the theme "Come, Holy Spirit — Renew the Whole Creation."

4. Church-State Relations

4.1. The Anglican Church initially enjoyed the same relation to the state as in England. A state proposal in 1836 to found schools in which → pastors could give → religious instruction to children of their own denomination foundered on Protestant opposition. The principle of nonconfessional schools prevailed in 1847. Church-state relations changed between 1872 and 1895 as the principle of free secular education was accepted for all the colonies, along with an obligation to provide schooling and the termination of state support for church schools.

4.2. This development strongly influenced the definitive settlement of church-state relations. According to article 116 of the Constitution of the Australian Commonwealth (1901), no religion is to be either favored or hampered. A situation thus developed for the Australian churches that is akin to the free church system in the United States.

4.3. In 1963 the Commonwealth decided to support even church schools financially. In 1981 it finally ruled that such support is not unconstitutional. As part of a program of development for the Aborigines in the Northern Territory, the government also granted certain subsidies to church missions.

5. Non-Christian Religions

In 1981, non-Christian religions represented only 1.4 percent of the population, including 35,000 Buddhists. By 1990, the comparable figure was about 2.8 percent.

5.1. *The Aborigines*

The reawakening self-awareness of the Australian Aborigines runs parallel to a scholarly recognition that the land and environment are religious entities for them. In a conscious return to their religious-cultural origins, many Aborigines are now trying to recapture the link between land and tribe. Thus they often see no conflict between their acquired Christian faith and their hereditary culture. But for others, as a 1981 WCC team report shows, contact with Christianity has meant the loss of their traditional cultural legacy and alienation from their own people. The churches are now trying to help Aborigines to regain their heritage.

5.2. *Judaism*

→ Judaism has been present in Australia since 1820, with the first → synagogue founded in Sydney in 1844. With a strong influx from Europe after 1933, Jews now number about 90,000, or 0.5 percent of the population. Along with Orthodox Jews, who have synagogues and schools especially in Sydney and Melbourne, Reform Jews maintain temples in Melbourne (1937) and Sydney (1939), to which some 20 percent of practicing Jews belong. Although anti-Semitism is virtually unknown in Australia, there are no formal contacts with the Christian churches.

5.3. *Islam*

→ Islam came to Australia in 1860 with the so-called Afghans (Indian, Iranian, and Afghan camel drivers), who built several → mosques (e.g., in Adelaide around 1890). Muslims today are mostly immigrants from Mediterranean countries, especially Turkey, and from Pakistan (coming primarily from 1959 to 1975)

and Arabic-speaking countries. In 1981 there were officially 77,000 Muslims in Australia; by 2000, upward of 190,000. Mostly → Sunnites or → Shiites, they have built mosques in Brisbane (1970), Melbourne (1976), and Sydney (1978). Contact between Islam and Christianity is still in its early stages.

Bibliography: A. W. BLACK and P. E. GLASNER, eds., *Practice and Belief: Studies in the Sociology of Australian Religion* (Sydney, 1983) bibliography • J. D. BOLLEN, *Australian Baptists: A Religious Minority* (London, 1975); idem, *Religion in Australian Society* (1973) • F. ENGEL, "The Strengths and Weaknesses of the Ecumenical Movement in Australia," *StMR* 89 (March 1977) 14-18 • D. HARRIS, D. HYND, and D. MILLIKAN, eds., *The Shape of Belief: Christianity in Australia Today* (Homebush West, N.S.W., 1982) bibliography • S. P. HEBART, "Australien und Neuguinea," *Kirchengemeinschaft: Kirche und Abendmahl* (vol. 2; Berlin, 1969) 72-98; idem, "Some Specific Aspects of Lutheran Identity," *LTJ* 15 (1981) 86-91 • A. HVIDTFELDT, G. LANCZKOWSKI, and W. METZNER, "Australien," *TRE* 4.755-68 • *IRM* 68 (January 1979) • K.-P. KOEPPING, "Religion in Aboriginal Australia," *Religion* 11 (1981) 367-91 (survey of research) • M. MASON, ed., *Religion in Australian Life: A Bibliography of Social Research* (Bedford Park, South Australia, 1982) • H. MOL, *Religion in Australia: A Sociological Investigation* (Melbourne, 1971) • P. J. O'FARRELL, *The Catholic Church and Community: An Australian History* (4th ed.; Kensington, N.S.W., 1985) • C. PATOCK, "Die Ostkirche in Australien," *OS* 27 (1978) 174-200 • *StMR* 107 (September 1981) • M. SCHILD, "Christian Beginnings in Australia," *LTJ* 15 (1981) 69-78; idem, "Lutheran Confessions and Australian Diaspora," *LTJ* 13 (1979) 57-67; idem, "Luthertum im Spannungsfeld des australischen Pluralismus," *JMLB* 25 (1978) 130-44 • I. W. R. SHEVILL, ed., *The Orthodox and Other Eastern Churches in Australia* (Townsville, Queensland, 1975) • T. G. H. STREHLOW, *Central Australian Religion* (Bedford Park, South Australia, 1978) • B. WILSON, *Can God Survive in Australia?* (Sutherland, N.S.W., 1983).

FRIEDEMANN HEBART

Austria

1. Sociopolitical Framework
   1.1. Political Order
   1.2. State-Church Relations
2. Churches
   2.1. Roman Catholic
   2.2. Protestant
   2.3. Orthodox

	1960	1980	2000
Population (1,000s):	7,048	7,549	8,292
Annual growth rate (%):	0.62	0.02	0.30

Area: 83,858 sq. km. (32,378 sq. mi.)

A.D. 2000

Population density: 99/sq. km. (256/sq. mi.)
Births / deaths: 0.95 / 1.02 per 100 population
Fertility rate: 1.42 per woman
Infant mortality rate: 6 per 1,000 live births
Life expectancy: 77.5 years (m: 74.4, f: 80.6)
Religious affiliation (%): Christians 89.8 (Roman Catholics 76.8, Protestants 5.0, unaffiliated 4.4, Orthodox 2.1, other Christians 1.5), nonreligious 6.5, Muslims 2.4, other 1.3.

1. Sociopolitical Framework

1.1. Political Order

Austria, a republic since 1918, consists of eight states and the city of Vienna. At least 95 percent of the people speak German. There are minorities of Slovenes, Turks, Poles, Croatians, Serbs, Kurds, and Hungarians, including a sizable number of guest workers. The end of the Hapsburg Empire, of which Austria is a remnant, created a crisis that found expression in the desire for union with Germany. The forcible union of 1938 and the liberation of 1945 quenched that desire. A positive appreciation of → democracy developed, though the role of → political parties came under criticism after 1984. From 1950 onward, two parties dominated. The Greens made a modest appearance in 1987, and a protest vote in favor of German nationalism followed. The economy is no longer predominately agrarian.

1.2. State-Church Relations

As a result of → Catholic reforms, and even after → tolerance was granted to Protestants and the Orthodox in 1781, the → Roman Catholic Church has remained supreme in Austria under special protection of the state. Only in 1867 were freedom of conscience and → religious liberty guaranteed (→ Human and Civil Rights). Yet the state still plays a role by way of recognition of religious societies (→

Church and State). General laws passed in 1868 and 1878 regulate their external relations. There is a → concordat with the Roman Catholic Church (1934, supplemented in 1960), as well as special laws for Protestants (1961) and the Orthodox (1967; → Denomination). With regard to the Jews, the relevant law from 1890 is still valid. Since 1868, religious education has been offered, directed, and supervised by the churches (→ School and Church). Public education is the rule, but churches may have their own schools, for which they receive support (→ Education 4). In 1939 a state law regulated the financing of churches, which is a matter for the churches themselves to handle. Legally recognized churches are corporations under public law.

2. Churches

2.1. Roman Catholic

The Roman Catholic Church is the largest communion, though its share of the population dropped from 93.7 percent in 1910 to 80.4 percent in 1992 (6.3 million). In 1992 there were 3 archbishops, 19 bishops, and 3,090 parishes. In 1995 there were 4,094 priests (vs. 6,500 in 1962); their average age was over 60. There are approximately 220 male → monastic communities and 850 female (→ Orders and Congregations).

Because of its link to the monarchy and later to a political party, the Roman Catholic Church used to be more of an → institution than a true fellowship, but all that changed after 1939. With the coming of World War II, a sense of community was kindled, and fuller church commitment emerged. After the war, however, the number attending on Sundays dropped — from 39 percent in 1949 to 22 percent in 1990. In spite of religious convictions (professed by 75 percent of the people), there is much dissent from the church's moral positions (some 100,000 favoring → abortion, the → suicide rate being 25.7 per 100,000, and 71 percent supporting death with dignity).

The church plays a large part in public and cultural life. Yet conflicts developed after 1970, first with specific social groups, then within Roman Catholicism itself. Cardinal Franz König's proposed opening up of the church resulted in a church conference in 1983. But the related papal visit (→ Pope, Papacy) and strongly contested appointments of bishops showed that there would be problems. Within the church, conflicts arose regarding student and → youth work, the recognizing of democracy, respect for marginal groups, and problems in → social and → sexual ethics. In general there has been a revival of traditional forms of → piety (→ Mary, Devotion to, 1; Pilgrimage; Popular Religion), yet in 1990 a joint pastoral letter from the bishops not only subscribed to the basic principles of the church's social ethics but made notable pronouncements on the duties of Christians (and the church) in a pluralist → society. For all the protests, there is a great readiness to accept the church's → rites. Nevertheless, 30,000 members leave the church each year (→ Church Membership 5), which typically does not mean complete separation from the church's ritual and legal precepts. Of all → weddings (→ Marriage and Divorce), 80 percent are performed in church.

2.2. Protestant

Protestantism developed fairly peacefully in the 19th century, but then a period of unrest followed after 1900 and affected both its growth and its self-understanding. Periods of conversions (e.g., 1900-1903, when the slogan "Free from Rome" was popular, and 1934-38; → National Church Movements) and the settlement of refugees resulted in a growth that was undone by later reverses. About 3,000 members leave each year, and additions (some 800) do not make up the loss. The exodus is due to the weak external presence of the church and defective early religious instruction, but also to a prevalent → individualism in the church. This feature is not restricted to the transitional liberal generation but obtains also where neo-Pietist convictions have replaced traditional → Pietism.

Austrian Protestantism is marked by a homogeneity that is strengthened by its unified presbyterial → church government and by a uniform ministry that originally allowed regional and social variations and differences in belief. Protestantism still has its own strongholds, where the numbers of members fluctuate least (e.g., Carinthia and Upper Austria).

The Protestant churches are → minorities. Some 345,000 of the evangelicals are Lutherans; the next largest group is the 15,000 Reformed (→ Lutheran Churches; Reformed and Presbyterian Churches). The former, the Protestant Church of the Augsburg Confession, has seven districts and 185 parishes; the latter, the Protestant Church of the Helvetic Confession, has 9 parishes. The two churches share their confessions, and there are mixed congregations. Though they have distinct organizations (→ Synod), they present a common front to the world outside. In 1995, the majority of the pulpits (292 out of 317) were filled or cared for.

The coming of neo-Pietist evangelical ideas (→ Evangelical Movement) was greatly aided by pastors who had been ordained after approximately 1960, when there was a lack of university-trained ordinands. It resulted in a loss of confessional sense and erased distinctions from new religious movements. Because other modes of church work were not successful (→ Church Growth 3.1), evangelicalism became most important, even though it made some other problems worse. The main problem was that of polarization fueled by intolerance over differences and causing unattractiveness, at least as compared with other religious groups. The weakening of theological work might also be cited. Again, one might refer to the retreat from → society and secular → responsibility, though some resisted this trend. Enhanced diaconal work hardly offered adequate compensation (→ Diakonia), serving as it did congregational activities rather than diaconal institutions. What the future holds is open to question, especially as Lutheran-Reformed differences are also increasing (→ Denomination).

2.3. Orthodox

The Toleration Edict of 1781 allowed the non-Uniate Orthodox (→ Orthodox Church) to form their own congregations. Guest workers added to these after 1945, so that by 1965 there were congregations of five national Orthodox churches (Bulgarian, Greek, Romanian, Russian, and Serbian) and three → Oriental Orthodox churches (Armenian, Coptic, and Syrian). All these enjoy legal recognition.

2.4. Old Catholic

The → Old Catholic Church received legal recognition in 1877. It grew after 1934 and now has around 20,000 members in 412 parishes, with a bishop and council at the head.

2.5. Free Churches

Of the → free churches, the → Methodists (recognized in 1956) have some 2,200 members in eight congregations; the → Baptists, → Mennonites, and → Anglicans have smaller numbers. The Evangelical Church and Methodists have enjoyed intercommunion since 1990. Population changes after 1945 brought gains to the free churches, and liberal recognition by the → state (or an active use of legal provisions) permits an intensive congregational life supplemented in some instances by an aggressive practice of → mission (→ Church and State 1).

3. Transdenominational Organizations

The Ecumenical Council of Churches in Austria (founded 1958; → National Councils of Churches) has 14 member churches, including, since 1994, the Roman Catholics; the Baptists, the Austrian Bible Society, and 8 other churches and groups have observer status. Much of the ecumenical work is done in such agencies, along with radio preaching and a weekly ecumenical service, held each Sunday morning beginning in 1967.

A Protestant–Roman Catholic commission was formed in 1966 to try to deal with practical issues dividing the churches. When a theological commission failed to make progress, regional conversation groups were started. A Roman Catholic–Reformed conversation group followed.

In 1986 an Old Catholic–Protestant special committee standardized the rules of guest participation at Communion. An invitation in 1988 by the two Protestant synods to Roman Catholics to share Communion on a guest basis was not accepted.

The Evangelical Alliance originally worked only in Vienna and was strongly Pietist. Neo-Pietist evangelical groups, now active in its leadership, have extended its programs and the geographic scope of its operations. The alliance now sponsors a variety of transdenominational activities (→ World Evangelical Fellowship; Transdenominational Movements).

4. Non-Christian Religions

4.1. *Judaism*

The Toleration Edict of 1782 and 19th-century laws opened the way out of the → ghetto for Jews (→ Judaism). Up to 1938 they held a special position in Vienna, where they outnumbered Protestants, though many sought assimilation by → conversion (§1). Between 1886 and 1912 there were 9,300 → baptisms of Jews; between 1913 and 1922, another 2,900 became Protestants.

After 1918, the number of → synagogues in Vienna increased, and eastern Jews began to change the character of Austrian Judaism. In 1937 there were some 200,000 Jews in Austria. Expulsions and executions under Hitler reduced the number considerably (→ Holocaust). In spite of later resettlement, the flight of Hungarian Jews to Vienna, and immigration from other countries after 1945, the number of Jews never again exceeded 10,000; by 1981 it had fallen to 7,123. There are congregations in Vienna, Innsbruck, Graz, Linz, and Salzburg. The end of the 20th century has seen both an increase in the number of Jews and a reemergence of a latent → anti-Semitism.

4.2. *Islam*

Following the annexation of Bosnia, → Islam received recognition in Austria (1912). After 1918, however, there were no longer any Muslim groups in the country. Only with the arrival of guest workers from Turkey and southern Yugoslavia (after 1970) did the numbers of Muslims increase sharply, from 0.3 percent of the population in 1971 to 2 percent in 1991 (159,000). Formal recognition as a religious society came in 1979; in the 1980s a → mosque was built in Vienna. Islamic centers now exist in Vienna and Vorarlberg. The restriction to a single → rite was

lifted in 1988, thus opening the way for the free development of varied Islamic groups.

4.3. *Buddhism*

In 1983 → Buddhism received recognition. The Buddhist Union has some 8,000 members, many of them Austrian novices.

4.4. *Sects*

Legal recognition came to the → Mormons in 1956. The occupying powers opened the way for them after the war; in 1990 they had 4,100 members.

→ Jehovah's Witnesses were present in Austria before 1938. After being largely eliminated under National Socialism, they regrouped after 1947. They are estimated to have 38,000 members. The New → Apostolic Church enjoys recognition but has hardly more than 1,000 members.

Many → Pentecostals and fundamentalists flooded into Austria after 1970. Some have secured a footing and found a base of operations in the Evangelical Alliance. They penetrate mainline churches and seek to win adherents there.

5. Exodus from Churches

Various forces have encouraged Austrians to leave the churches (→ Atheism; Religion, Criticism of). The "Free from Rome" movement began in 1900, and a → freethinker movement replaced it after 1918, reaching a high point after 1939. The first movements were influential only in specific strata (middle class or artisan; → Class and Social Stratum). They worked mainly in the cities and the Upper Styrian industrial area. Some church members returned after 1945, but soon the exodus continued, becoming very large by 1968. In 1981, 6 percent of the people (450,000) professed no church membership, which was no doubt the case also for some of the 80,000 who did not answer the question of church affiliation. Since then at least 25,000 have left the churches each year. In 1991, a total of 672,000 (8.6 percent) reported no religious allegiance.

Bibliography: D. Barrett, ed., *WCE* 157-61 • H. Bogensberger, *Die katholische Kirche in Österreich* (Brussels, 1985) • H. Bogensberger and P. M. Zulehner, "Austria," *Western Religion: A Country by Country Sociological Inquiry* (ed. H. Mol; The Hague, 1972) 47-66 • W. M. Johnston, *The Austrian Mind: An Intellectual and Social History, 1848-1938* (Berkeley and Los Angeles, 1972) • P. Karner, *Der ökumenische Rat in Österreich. Schematismus, Statut, Texte, Information* (Vienna, 1986) • E. K. Keefe et al., *Area Handbook for Austria* (Washington, D.C., 1976) • A. Khol, G. Ofner, and A. Stirnemann, eds., *Österreichisches Jahrbuch für Politik* (Vienna, 1977-) • D. Knall, ed., *Auf den Spuren einer*

Kirche. Evangelisches Leben in Österreich (Vienna, 1987) • T. PIFFL-PERCERVIC, ed., *Kirche in Österreich. Berichte, Überlegungen, Entwürfe* (Graz, 1979) • H. PREE, *Österreichisches Staatskirchenrecht* (Vienna, 1984) • K. STEINER, ed. *Modern Austria* (Palo Alto, Calif., 1981) • P. M. ZULEHNER, *Die Religion im Leben der Österreicher* (Vienna, 1981).

GUSTAV REINGRABNER

Authority

1. Concept
2. Typology
3. Discussion
4. New Developments

1. Concept

It is not surprising that the understanding of authority has greatly changed over the centuries in popular speech and philosophical, theological, legal, and educational reflection. The phenomenon of authority is too close to our self-regard, our anxieties and hopes, to remain static in conception. It is all the more interesting, then, that the Roman distinction between *potestas* (of the government) and *auctoritas* (of the senate and individuals) has persisted in modern sociological and political thought (→ Sociology). Power is something enforced (by law in a constitutional state), but authority depends on recognition by the subjects and their confidence in those who wield it, whether this is a matter of reason or of trust. Thus authority has rightly been called a relational concept. The etymology of the Latin term has no bearing, but it is important that Greek had no equivalent. It may be asked, then, whether the later extension of the term "authority" — even to the OT and NT — has not been confusing. Thus there is in Hebrew no equivalent, and even the NT *exousia* denotes the creative power of God at work in the words and works of Jesus or the → apostles, the mighty power that liberates the listening → congregation. This conception relates only indirectly to the Roman and the later Western concept of authority.

2. Typology

"Authority" is certainly close to "power." We see this connection in all the usual classifications of types of authority. Thus we have personal or primary authority (in small groups) versus formal or secondary authority (in organizations with specific purposes); the authority of rule (by privilege, e.g., of birth) versus that of office (which is revocable, functional, and judged by performance); personal versus institutional authority; the distinction between traditional, legal, and charismatic authority (M. → Weber; → Charisma); finally, following I. M. Bocheński, epistemic authority (which cannot be delegated and rests on confidence in those who have it) versus deontic authority (which can be delegated and is accepted pragmatically for the sake of reaching a goal).

Whereas people can be hungry for power without being hungry for authority, almost all the above types can be perverted into a claim to power and dominion, whether by a misuse of trust or by a disregard for the limits of competence. In spite of the increasing differentiation of the spheres of life, these dangers are always present. They are especially acute in totalitarian systems that trace all authority to a single source (E. Amelung).

3. Discussion

It is debatable whether the distinction that the → Enlightenment made between individual → reason and the acceptance of authority is mistaken (H.-G. Gadamer) or is finally correct (J. Habermas). Gadamer argues that the acceptance of genuine authority is itself an act of reason (cf. Bocheński). Popular discussion of authority, authoritarian government, antiauthoritarian education, and so forth deals with the same set of problems. It goes back finally to → Augustine (354-430), who took an unfortunate and momentous step when he distinguished between authority and reason. Whereas even the philosophers of later antiquity would derive proof from venerable texts *ex autoritate*, Augustine stood for the priority of the authority of the church over one's own theological reason.

Discussion of authority and reason continued throughout the Middle Ages both in theology and in politics, often in terms of papal versus imperial *potestas* and authority. It is not surprising that the Enlightenment (even prior to the French → Revolution) set out to do battle with this understanding of authority. Authority was now viewed as a fatal antithesis to personal maturity. The development of the Reformation understanding of Scripture had also done harm, for although the doctrine of the inner witness of the Holy Spirit offered a theological safeguard against the church's striving for power, the older Protestant doctrine of the authority of Scripture did not resolve the conflict. Even today in the English-speaking world the concept of the authority of Scripture plays an important, but not wholly constructive, role (→ Biblicism).

4. New Developments

In psychology and the theory of → psychotherapy the concept of authority is limited to its use in the central problem of the → father figure. It rightly occurs in → ethnology and the analysis of modern social structures and male leadership. In common parlance, authority has unfortunately lost the marks of a relational concept. This development makes the important search for genuine authorities and models much more difficult.

→ Exegesis, Biblical; Scriptural Proof; Social Partnership; Solidarity

Bibliography: Especially helpful, in view of the great number of publications in various disciplines, are encyclopedia articles: S. I. BENN, "Authority," *EncPh* 1.215-18 • C. A. VON HEYL, "Autorität," *ESL* 114-16 • J. MIETHKE, R. MAU, E. AMELUNG, and H. BEINTKER, "Autorität," *TRE* 5.17-51 (extensive bibliograhpy) • W. VEIT, H. RABE, and K. RÖTTGERS, "Autorität," *HWP* 1.724-34 • M. WAIDA, "Authority," *EncRel(E)* 2.1-7.

Other literature: I. M. BOCHEŃSKI, *Was ist Autorität?* (Freiburg, 1974) • H. VON CAMPENHAUSEN, *Ecclesiastical Authority and Spiritual Power in the Church of the First Three Centuries* (Stanford, Calif., 1969; repr., Peabody, Mass., 1997) • G. R. EVANS, *Problems of Authority in the Reformation Debates* (Cambridge, 1992) • G. HARTFIEL, ed., *Die autoritäre Gesellschaft* (Cologne, 1969) • B. DE JOUVENEL, *Sovereignty: An Inquiry into the Political Good* (Cambridge, 1957) • G. KREMS and R. MUMM, eds., *Autorität in der Krise* (Regensburg, 1970) ecumenical contributions • H. J. KÜHNE, *Schriftautorität und Kirche* (Göttingen, 1980) • N. LASH, *Voices of Authority* (London, 1976) • J. K. S. REID, *The Authority of Scripture* (London, 1957) • A. K. RUF, *Konfliktfeld Autorität* (Munich, 1974) • H. J. TÜRK, ed., *Autorität* (Mainz, 1973) collection of interdisciplinary essays.

DIETRICH RITSCHL

Autocephaly

"Autocephaly," from Gk. *autos* (self) and *kephalē* (head), denotes the decentralized form of organization in the Orthodox Church that recognizes self-determination in each sphere of jurisdiction. An autocephalous church is one that enjoys total independence canonically and administratively; it elects its own bishops and own head (whether "patriarch," "archbishop," or "metropolitan"). The overall Orthodox Church is thus not a single constitutional unit (→ Church Government) but a spiritual fellowship of the various autocephalous churches, which are united by a common → faith, church law, and → liturgy. Through the metropolitans and → dioceses from which the ancient → patriarchates derived, the local churches developed an external structure

through synods that more or less reflect territorial, cultural, or political areas. In principle, however, the territorialism that confers autocephaly has no inherent validity in its application; it is not a canonical necessity any more than national unity is.

The formal and substantive conditions for autocephaly are (1) pastoral practicality, (2) a declaration of the will of the whole body (both laity and → clergy), and (3) a desire of the churches concerned for autocephaly. Ecumenical councils originally decided all the questions connected with autocephaly. When it became impossible to call these, their tasks fell to the Ecumenical Patriarchate of Constantinople, which made decisions on questions of autocephaly within the Orthodox family or on the raising of autocephalous churches to the patriarchate.

A canonical ruling on the question of autocephaly still is needed that will be valid for the whole of Orthodoxy. It is expected from a future → Pan-Orthodox council.

Bibliography: A. SCHMEMANN, "A Meaningful Storm: Some Reflections on Autocephaly, Tradition, and Ecclesiology," *SVTQ* 15 (1971) 3-27 • P. TREMPELAS, "Archai kratēsasai en tȩ anakēryxei tou autokephalou," *Theol(A)* 28 (1957) 5-22.

CHRISTOPHOROS PAPAKONSTANTINOU

Autogenic Training

After 1920 J. H. Schultz developed an autosuggestive, easily learned, and concentrated system of training that he presented in 1932 in his work *Das Autogene Training*. It is used in → psychotherapy (though not much in the United States) as a means of coping with physiological or psychosomatic disturbances, but it is also commonly used in the world of sports and art as a method of relaxation and concentration. It is meant to be practiced three times a day, in reclining or sitting positions.

Autogenic training brings physiological functions such as circulation, the vascular system, and the pulse rate under control; in this way it resembles → Yoga. In its formal purposes and especially in its advanced level, it is close to techniques of → meditation. It might be more helpful than has thus far been recognized in → counseling, → pastoral care, and the learning of → prayer.

Bibliography: G. EBERLEIN, *Gesund durch das Autogene Training* (Düsseldorf, 1973) • H. LINDEMANN, *Überleben im Streß–Autogenes Training* (Munich, 1979) • W. LINDEN, *Autogenic Training: A Clinical Guide* (New

York, 1990) • W. Lutke, ed., *Autogenic Training: In Honor of Johannes Heinrich Schultz on the Occasion of His Eigthieth Birthday . . . June 20, 1964* (New York, 1965) • J. H. Schultz, *Das Autogene Training* (17th ed.; Stuttgart, 1982); idem, *Übungsheft für das Autogene Training* (18th ed.; Stuttgart, 1977) • J. H. Schultz and W. Lutke, *Autogenic Training: A Psychophysiologic Approach in Psychotherapy* (New York, 1959) • K. Thomas, *Praxis der Selbsthypnose des Autogenen Trainings* (3d ed.; Stuttgart, 1972).

Dietrich Ritschl

Autonomy

1. Concept
2. Significance

1. Concept

"Autonomy," derived from Gk. *autos* (self) plus *nomos* (law), means establishing one's own law. It became a technical term in Thucydides (5th cent. B.C.), who used it to describe a city under foreign domination that was allowed to make its own internal laws. It was again used as a term in political law in the 15th century to denote the independence of a tribe, group (confession), or → institution (e.g., a university) within a superior community. This precise sense in political law has remained to the present day. "Autonomy" must be strictly distinguished from "sovereignty," a term of recent development (J. Bodin), which denotes the full legal independence of a → state both internally and externally. I. Kant (1724-1804) distinguished autonomy from autarchy and did not equate it with → freedom.

2. Significance

Today the notion of autonomy has gained academic as well as legal significance. Kant paved the way by formulating the antithesis of autonomy and heteronomy (→ Kantianism). For Kant, autonomy maintained its original meaning even in a philosophical sense, denoting the establishing of one's own inner law under the overlordship of another. Autonomy means that the will determines its own law independently of external conditions — but not in antithesis to the moral law. Indeed, it sets its own law in harmony with the moral law and in subjection to it. Hence Kant never spoke about autonomy over against God. In Kant, heteronomy does not mean inner determination by God or by the moral law that shows itself to be given by God; rather, it is determination from outside by things or persons (even though these in turn may be sent by God).

This differentiated and precise understanding of autonomy and heteronomy was not accepted. Either Kant's thought was wrongly adopted with a threefold autonomy of impulse, choice, and arbitrariness (J. F. Fries), or it was interpreted as an absolute autonomy (G. W. F. Hegel), which was fiercely contested (F. von Baader). In the main, however, a repudiation of autonomy prevailed (e.g., by J. F. Herbart and A. Schopenhauer). Only K. Fischer, who initiated neo-Kantianism around 1860, paid careful heed to autonomy. Since then the term has come into common use, especially in → ethics (§1; with a double autonomy of principle and person in N. Hartmann, though not M. Scheler) and sociology (M. → Weber). As a central Kantian category, "autonomy" finally meant the full self-determination and self-assertion of the individual over against any alien determination (H. Marcuse), including that of God. Interpretations of autonomy in Kant have mostly overlooked the original distinction (G. Prauss).
In antithesis to this (false) understanding of autonomy, theology even before 1850 formulated the theonomy of the moral law (F. Probst), according to which God is the author of the final and absolutely binding → norms of human life (C. Schrempf). Later theologians tried to formulate a theonomy that would transcend autonomy without prejudice to it (P. → Tillich). On the Roman Catholic side the thesis of an autonomous morality (A. Auer) evoked the counterthesis of an ethics of faith (B. Stoeckle), against which others defended the compatibility of autonomy and theonomy (F. Böckle). Recourse to Kant would support a theological case for autonomy and make the term "theonomy" unnecessary; Kant did not use it and would have found it unthinkable.

The later 20th century has seen a new spread of the term "autonomy," especially in the political sphere (by equating it with sovereignty) and in natural science (as in speaking of "autonomous experiments" in weightlessness in space). Autonomy has thus lost its sharp contours. It would be constructive to return to its original signification in Kant, namely, the definition of autonomy as self-determination within the framework and in free acceptance of the morality that is not under human control. In this sense autonomy would be a critical corrective of emancipation, where this concept is taken to mean absolute freedom.

Bibliography: A. Auer, *Autonome Moral und christlicher Glaube* (Düsseldorf, 1971) • C. L. Coulter, "Moral Autonomy and Divine Commands," *RelS* 25 (1989) 117-29 • E. Feil, *Antithetik neuzeitlicher Vernunft. "Autonomie-Heteronomie" und "rational-irrational"* (Göttingen, 1987) • L. Froese, "Autonomie," *NPL* 1.61-62 • R. Gibbs,

"Fear of Forgiveness: Kant and the Paradox of Mercy," *PhTh* 3 (1989) 323-34 • K. Hilpert, *Ethik und Rationalität* (Düsseldorf, 1980) • W. Kern and C. Lenk, "Autonomie und Geschöpflichkeit," *Christlicher Glaube in moderner Gesellschaft* (vol. 18; ed. F. Böckle et al.; Freiburg, 1982) 101-48 • G. E. Michalson, "Moral Regeneration and Divine Aid in Kant," *RelS* 25 (1989) 259-70 • C. J. Pinto de Oliveira et al., *Autonomie* (Freiburg, [1978]) • R. Pohlmann, "Autonomie," *HWP* 1.701-19 (bibliography) • G. Prauss, *Kant über Freiheit als Autonomie* (Frankfurt, 1983) • C. Schrempf, *Die christliche Weltanschauung* (1890), *Gesammelte Werke* (vol. 5; Stuttgart, 1931) 1-74 • *TQ* 161 (1981) pt. 1 (on autonomy) • M. Welker, *Der Vorgang Autonomie* (Neukirchen, 1975).

ERNST FEIL

Auxiliary Saints → Saints, Veneration of

Ave Maria

Ave Maria (Lat. "Hail, Mary") is the title of any → prayer based on Luke 1:28, 42. These verses were a subject of "meditation," or repeated recitation, in early → monasticism. Those who could not manage the Psalms were permitted in the early Middle Ages to replace 150, 50, or 10 psalms by an equal number of Paternosters and later of Ave Marias as an allotment of penance or of prayer. The use of rosaries developed by addition of phrases pertaining to the life of Jesus. Many important composers have set the Ave Maria to music.

→ Mary, Devotion to

Bibliography: N. Ayo, *The Hail Mary: A Verbal Icon of Mary* (Notre Dame, Ind., 1994) • "Hail Mary," *ODCC* 729-30 • R. Scherschel, *Der Rosenkranz–das Jesusgebet des Westens* (Freiburg, 1979; 2d ed., 1982) 45-90 • H. Thurston, "The Origins of the Hail Mary," *Familiar Prayers: Their Origin and History* (ed. P. Grosjean; London, 1953) 90-114.

RAINER SCHERSCHEL

Averroism → Islamic Philosophy

Awe → Reverence

Axiom

The term "axiom" comes from the Gk. *axioō* (deem worthy), a verb the Greeks used in many senses. From the time of Aristotle (384-322 B.C.) it became a technical term to denote logical and philosophical principles that one accepts without further proof (→ Aristotelianism). Conclusions must follow from premises, which must themselves be proved. But since this process could go on forever, we must start with certain basic principles, or axioms, for which one cannot ask for further proof.

Traditionally a distinction has been made between axioms, which must be self-evident if they are to be accepted as principles, and postulates, which are not self-evident but may be accepted as principles on which to construct a logical or philosophical system. Modern → logic no longer makes this distinction because one may freely select an axiom without demanding evidence for it. Another important distinction is between the axiom, as a logical principle, and the rule, which tells us how to work with logical principles. Logical systems without rules are not possible, but systems with rules but no axioms (systems of natural inference) are possible.

→ Middle Axioms

Bibliography: I. M. Bocheński and A. Menne, *Grundriß der Logistik* (Paderborn, 1954) • H. C. M. de Swart and H. G. Hubbeling, *Inleiding tot de symbolische logica* (Assen, 1976) • W. V. Quine, *Methods of Logic* (4th ed.; Cambridge, Mass., 1982).

HUBERTUS G. HUBBELING†

Azerbaijan

	1960	1980	2000
Population (1,000s):	3,895	6,161	7,828
Annual growth rate (%):	3.22	1.59	0.72
Area: 86,600 sq. km. (33,400 sq. mi.)			

A.D. *2000*
Population density: 90/sq. km. (234/sq. mi.)
Births / deaths: 1.70 / 0.66 per 100 population
Fertility rate: 2.10 per woman
Infant mortality rate: 30 per 1,000 live births
Life expectancy: 71.8 years (m: 68.0, f: 75.3)
Religious affiliation (%): Muslims 84.4, nonreligious 9.6, Christians 5.3 (Orthodox 5.1, other Christians 0.2), other 0.7.

Azerbaijan is a Transcaucasian republic bordering on the Caspian Sea. Two parts of its territory have been claimed by neighboring Armenia: the Nakhichevan Autonomous Republic, an exclave to the southwest separated from the rest of Azerbaijan by a strip of

Armenia; and the Nagorno-Karabakh Autonomous Region, an area wholly within Azerbaijan populated largely by Armenians. Tensions in Nagorno-Karabakh became violent in February 1988 and continued so until May 1994, when a cease-fire mediated by Russia was signed by the warring parties. During this time an estimated 18,000 people were killed and 25,000 wounded, with more than one million Azerbaijanis becoming → refugees.

According to a national census, Azerbaijan's population in 1989 was 7.0 million, divided among the Turkic Azerbaijanis (82.7 percent), the Indo-European Russians (5.6 percent) and Armenians (5.6 percent), the Caucasian Lezgians (3.2 percent), and smaller groups of other foreign and indigenous minorities. In 1989 Azerbaijanis constituted 95.9 percent of Nakhichevan, and Armenians 76.9 percent of Nagorno-Karabakh. Since 1990, large numbers of Russians and Armenians have emigrated from Azerbaijan.

Azerbaijan possesses rich oil and mineral reserves. In the early 20th century, it was the world's leader in oil production and was the birthplace of the oil-refining industry. In 1996 Azerbaijan was part of two multinational consortia to develop several offshore oil fields in the Caspian Sea. Production of iron and steel as well as growth of grains and cotton represent other important factors in the country's economy.

Ancient Azerbaijan, home of the Scythian tribes, was part of the Roman Empire. It subsequently was conquered by the Arabs (642) and then largely absorbed by the Seljuk Turks when they entered the region in the 11th century. In the following centuries the Persians and Russians struggled for control of the region, with the Treaty of Turkmenchai (1828) dividing the area into a southern part (controlled by Persia and, ultimately, modern-day Iran) and a northern part (controlled by Russia). Following the October 1917 revolution in Russia and the collapse of the Ottoman Empire, the northern part of Azerbaijan declared its independence in May 1918. In April 1920, however, the Red Army invaded Azerbaijan, that same month establishing the Soviet Republic of Azerbaijan.

Modern Azerbaijani independence was declared a second time on August 30, 1991, by the Azerbaijani Supreme Soviet, an action approved by voters in January 1992. In September 1993 Parliament ratified an earlier decision to join the → Commonwealth of Independent States. In November 1995 voters approved a new constitution that replaced the Soviet version (with subsequent amendments). The consti-

tution declares the Azerbaijan Republic to be a democratic, secular state, headed by a president, who enjoys wide-ranging executive powers.

The religious affiliation of the people of Azerbaijan mirrors the country's ethnic divisions. In 1993 Muslims composed 88 percent of the population (62 percent → Shiites, 26 percent → Sunnis), with the balance divided mainly between the Russian → Orthodox Church and the → Armenian Apostolic Church. A small community of Polish and Armenian Catholics exists near Baku, the capital.

Azerbaijan endured particularly severe religious repression in the 1930s, including the destruction of mosques and religious sites and the killing of local religious leaders. The gaining of independence, however, as well as the recent fighting with Christian Armenia, has led to a Muslim resurgence. For partnership in the region, Azerbaijan has turned not so much to Iran, with which it shares ethnic and Shiite ties, as to Turkey, with which president Heydar Aliyev in February 1994 signed a ten-year treaty of friendship and cooperation.

Bibliography: T. Atabaki, *Azerbaijan: Ethnicity and Autonomy in Twentieth-Century Iran* (New York, 1993) • L. Chorbajian, P. Donabedian, and C. Mutafian, *The Caucasian Knot: The History and Politics of Nagorno-Karabagh* (Atlantic Highlands, N.J., 1994) • T. Dragadze, "Islam in Azerbaijan: The Position of Women," *Muslim Women's Choices: Religious Belief and Social Reality* (ed. C. Fawzi El-Solh and J. Mabro; Providence, R.I., 1995) 152-63 • B. Frelick, *Faultlines of Nationality Conflict: Refugees and Displaced Persons from Armenia and Azerbaijan* (Washington, D.C., 1994) • T. Goltz, *Azerbaijan Diary: A Rogue Reporter's Adventures in an Oil-Rich, War-Torn, Post-Soviet Republic* (rev. ed.; Armonk, N.Y., 1998) • Human Rights Watch, *Azerbaijan: Seven Years of Conflict in Nagorno-Karabakh* (New York, 1994) • J. Nichol, "Azerbaijan," *Armenia, Azerbaijan, and Georgia: Country Studies* (ed. G. E. Curtis; Washington, D.C., 1995) 79-148 • R. G. Suny, ed., *Transcaucasia, Nationalism, and Social Change: Essays in the History of Armenia, Azerbaijan, and Georgia* (Ann Arbor, Mich., 1996) • T. Swietochowski, *Russia and Azerbaijan: A Borderland in Transition* (New York, 1995); idem, *Russian Azerbaijan, 1905-1920: The Shaping of National Identity in a Muslim Community* (New York, 1985) • D. A. Trofimov, *Islam in the Political Culture of the Former Soviet Union: Central Asia and Azerbaijan* (Hamburg, 1995) • L. L. Wiesner, *Privatisation in Previously Centrally Planned Economies: The Case of Azerbaijan, 1991-1994* (Frankfurt, 1997).

THE EDITORS

B

Babylonian and Assyrian Religion

The civilizations of ancient Mesopotamia, whose written traditions have come down to us in Sumerian and Akkadian, played an important role in the development of the Near East from the end of the fourth millennium B.C. onward. In the course of history, the peoples of Syria and Palestine, among them → Israel and Judah, were particularly subjected to Mesopotamian influence (esp. in the first half of the first millennium).

At the beginning of the fourth millennium the peoples of southern Mesopotamia lived in village settlements, supported by irrigation-based agriculture, the raising of cattle, fishing, and hunting. During the fourth millennium cities developed that included imposing structures, among them some that fulfilled cultic functions. From the middle of the third millennium, with the rise of a growing textual tradition in Sumerian (a language that does not belong to any known linguistic family), we encounter a large and varied anthropomorphic pantheon (→ Polytheism) that personified the natural and cultural forces on which life in Mesopotamia rested. Each city had its own pantheon, usually headed by a god — more rarely a goddess. Other gods, usually related genealogically, were subject to this chief deity. In many cases these other gods might stand at the head of other local pantheons, but with political subjugation to a ruling city-state, they assumed subordinate roles. The hierarchy of deities thus reflected the prevailing political structure.

From the middle of the third millennium the infiltration of → Semitic → nomads affected religious developments in Mesopotamia. These nomads brought with them gods that were not tied to any one place — including the moon god Sin, the sun god Shamash, the goddess Ishtar (= the Phoenician goddess Astarte), and the weather god Adad — which were all worshiped in other Semitic religions under the same names. As the residents and intruders lived and grew together, their religious ideas fused.

When the city-state of Babylon expanded into a territorial state under → Hammurabi (18th cent. B.C.), its city god Marduk became the supreme god in Hammurabi's realm. The creation myth *Enuma elish* explains Marduk's supremacy in mythological terms. According to the myth, Marduk conquered and slew Tiamat, the representative of an older generation of gods. Marduk formed heaven and earth from her cloven body. The other gods then made him their overlord. In this role he became the dominant figure in Babylonian religion in the first millennium B.C.

Another state arose in northeastern Mesopotamia with its center at Ashur and with a god of the same name. From the end of the second millennium the Assyrians conquered northern Mesopotamia, northern Syria, and finally → Palestine. Economic needs were the reason for their expansion, which found

177

ideological justification as the mountain god Ashur was transformed into a god that claimed dominion over the whole earth. In this respect Assyrian religion, focused on Ashur, and Babylonian religion, in which the notion of a god that rules the whole world was only in its infancy, are clearly distinct. There were also important cultic differences. It is therefore not entirely appropriate to speak of a single Babylonian-Assyrian religion.

Textual discoveries from Mari on the Middle Euphrates (18th cent. B.C.) are sometimes adduced as confirmation of the biblical stories of the patriarchs (→ Patriarchal History). Such a connection, however, is historically and methodologically unsound. Nevertheless, these texts do enable us to understand OT → prophecy, especially in its ecstatic form, as a phenomenon that was present in Syria-Palestine and Upper Mesopotamia, as we learn also from Egyptian sources and other texts of later antiquity.

The accounts of Sumerian, Babylonian, and Assyrian religion relate mostly to the official cult, which involved feasts, offerings, votive offerings, hymns, → prayers, statues of the gods, cult buildings, and a hierarchically organized → priesthood (§1). Between the monarchy and the gods there was a close connection, which derived from the original function of the monarch as administrator of the territory belonging to the god or temple (third millennium). Later (beginning of the second millennium) we find the concept that the gods themselves inaugurated the monarchy. Ritual acts bestowed divine legitimation upon the individual ruler at the time he assumed office. The ruler represented the entire community before the gods in the cult. On their part, the gods guaranteed the welfare of the state. Only with qualifications, however, can we apply the idea of divine rule to this phenomenon, at least in its narrower formulation (e.g., Y. Egnell).

→ Myths deal with the gods' creation of the world, of the entire community, and of civilization. The gods established and upheld the cosmic order. Offenses against this order provoked divine wrath and punishment. Human beings were created to serve the gods (Atrahasis myth). Mesopotamians conceived their gods as part of a multitude of deities. People see their gods' power limited by the character of the natural phenomenon that they embody, by their position in the pantheon, and by the extent and significance of the political unit that they represent. The Gilgamesh epic, whose beginnings reach back to the third millennium, contains reflections on human experience with the phenomenon of → death. The attempt of the royal hero to achieve eternal life fails. He lives on only through the fame of his deeds. The epic also incorporates the story of the flood, which we find first in the Atrahasis myth (17th cent. B.C.) and which shows remarkable parallels to the flood story in Genesis 6–8.

Personal names are an important witness to religious ideas that are not directly connected to the official cult. They express experiences and expectations such as one finds at the occasion of a child's birth: thanks for the birth of a son after older siblings have died; prayer for protection from the many hazards of life; praise to a specific (guardian) god for assistance and help. Such a god was usually one of lower rank whose name is seldom given. Experiences like sickness or natural disaster were mostly attributed to → demonic forces that one sought to avert by conjurations. This task fell to → exorcists (§1), who were not priests but trained experts like those who could interpret the → future by inspecting entrails and observing astronomical and other omens (→ Astrology). These learned experts represent a distinctly rational element in Babylonian and Assyrian religion (J. Bottéro; A. L. Oppenheim).

A one-sided interpretation of the OT with the help of newly discovered sources from ancient Mesopotamia led to emotional reactions at the beginning of the 20th century (such as the so-called Babel-Bible debate). Today the unique traditions of the OT are seen in the context of the civilizations of Syria and Palestine, which for their part were influenced by the political and cultural developments of the ancient Near East as a whole.

Bibliography: J. Bottéro, Mesopotamia: Writing, Reasoning, and the Gods (Chicago, 1992) • J. J. A. van Dijk, "Sumerische Religion," HRG 1.431-96 • I. E. S. Edwards, C. J. Gadd, and N. G. L. Hammond, The Cambridge Ancient History (3 vols.; Cambridge, 1970-91) • Y. Egnell, Studies in Divine Kingship (Oxford, 1943) • B. J. Foster, Before the Muses: An Anthology of Akkadian Literature (Bethesda, Md., 1993) • T. Jacobsen, The Harps That Once . . . : Sumerian Poetry in Translation (New Haven, 1987); idem, The Treasures of Darkness: A History of Mesopotamian Religion (New Haven, 1976) • J. Laessøe, "Babylonische und assyrische Religion," HRG 1.497-525 • A. L. Oppenheim, Ancient Mesopotamia (2d ed.; Chicago, 1977).

JOHANNES RENGER

Baha'i

1. The Baha'i religion arose in the 19th century in Iran out of the reforming movement of 'Alī Moḥammad (1819/20-50), known as the Bāb, which

was directed against the orthodoxy of the → Shiite clergy (→ Islam). Its founder, Bahā' Allāh (1817-92), whose name means "glory of God," declared that he was a follower of the traditional → prophets (§1) seeking to actualize in his own time the spirit of their teaching. He gave written form to his humanitarian, cosmopolitan concept in *Al-Kitab al-Aqdas,* or Most Holy Book. After his death in exile in Palestine, his son 'Abd ol-Bahā' (1844-1921) and the latter's grandson Shogi Effendi (1897-1957) successively developed the concept and gained an increasing following by worldwide missionary travels. Although the Baha'i religion developed out of → Islam and is phenomenologically related to it, it may be considered an independent world religion.

2. According to the theology of Baha'i, humanity arose from a spark out of the depths of the divine will. It stands in a covenant relation with the one, absolutely transcendent God, whose prophets have strengthened and renewed this relation by → revelations in the successive epochs. The cycle in which the prophets of → monotheistic religions and the spiritual masters of the Indian religions were sent ended with the Bāb. Bahā' Allāh saw himself as the renewer promised in their → eschatology. Under his guidance, the world would enter a new period after a long age of decline. In the spirit of his preaching, further prophets adapted to historical change would bring spiritual rebirth to the race. Essential both to the progress of salvation history and to the → immortality of the individual → soul (§1) is → faith in God and → obedience to those he sends. → Heaven and → hell are allegories for spiritual and moral nearness to God or distance from him. The way to universal → peace lies only in a global fellowship of nations in which → toleration, freedom from → prejudice, and equality of opportunity are accepted. → Religion, working with science, will empower the striving for unity. A common → language will make its attainment easier, and a world court will control it.

3. The structures of the future global fellowship are reflected in the administration of the Baha'i religion, which is democratically elected on both the local and the national levels. The Universal House of Justice in Haifa (Israel) is the administrative and legal center, directed for the time being by an indirectly elected board. There are no → clergy, and the cultus includes only → prayers (§1) and readings from the sacred scriptures of all religions. Places of worship are open to people of every religion.

In 1993 there were National Spiritual Assemblies in 165 countries, comprising 20,000 local spiritual assemblies. To date the writings of the Baha'i religion have been published in over 800 languages. Though their teaching demands loyalty to the → state, some 300,000 followers are not officially recognized in Iran, their country of origin. Iran finally prohibited their institutions in 1983, when it also began executing Baha'is (→ Death Penalty). There are also many Baha'is in India, and a large number in the United States, where the headquarters are at the Mother Temple of the West in Wilmette, Illinois.

Bibliography: C. J. ADAMS, "Bahā'ī," *ADLR* 87-89 • A. BAUSANI, "Bahā'īs," *EI* 915-18 • J. BJORLING, *The Bahā'ī Faith: An Historical Bibliography* (New York, 1985) • W. S. HATCHER and J. D. MARTIN, *The Bahā'ī Faith: The Emerging Global Religion* (San Francisco, 1984) • R. H. STOCKMAN, *The Bahā'ī Faith in America,* vol. 1, *Origins, 1892-1900* (Wilmette, Ill., 1985) • F. VAHMAN, "Baha'ismus," *TRE* 5.115-32.

VERENA KLEMM

Bahamas

	1960	1980	2000
Population (1,000s):	110	210	302
Annual growth rate (%):	4.96	1.96	1.39

Area: 13,939 sq. km. (5,382 sq. mi.)

A.D. 2000

Population density: 22/sq. km. (56/sq. mi.)
Births / deaths: 1.72 / 0.52 per 100 population
Fertility rate: 1.95 per woman
Infant mortality rate: 12 per 1,000 live births
Life expectancy: 74.8 years (m: 71.5, f: 78.1)
Religious affiliation (%): Christians 92.7 (Protestants 59.6, Roman Catholics 16.9, Anglicans 8.9, unaffiliated 7.1, indigenous 6.6, marginal 2.2, other Christians 0.1), nonreligious 5.1, spiritists 1.4, other 0.8.

1. General Situation
2. Religious Situation

1. General Situation

The Commonwealth of the Bahamas, a West Indies nation independent since July 10, 1973, comprises an archipelago of 700 islands and over 2,000 cays and rocks extending southeastward from off the coast of Florida in the United States to just north of Haiti. Not more than 30 islands are inhabited, with the population divided ethnically between Afro-Caribbean (85 percent) and Euro-American (15 percent, largely from Great Britain, Canada, and the United States). The official language of the Bahamas is English, which reflects the dominant role of the British in the history of Bahamian contacts with Europeans.

The first European contact, though, was with the Spanish-financed Christopher Columbus, whose first landfall in the New World, in October 1492, was the Bahamas (traditionally, at San Salvador Island). Columbus noted the peaceful inhabitants — the Arawak, or Lucayans — whom later Spanish explorers carried off to Cuba and Hispaniola for work in gold mines. So thorough was this depopulation that the Bahamas was virtually uninhabited from 1520 until 1648, when a group of English → Puritans arrived from Bermuda seeking a place of religious freedom. They established a colony on an island they named Eleuthera (cf. Gk. *eleutheria,* "freedom"). In 1656 another group of English immigrants arrived from Bermuda, settling on an island they named New Providence, whose main city, Nassau (so named from 1695), eventually became the Bahamian capital.

Forced to deal with the problem of pirates, who were preying on Spanish galleons carrying booty home from the New World, the British made the islands a Crown colony in 1717. Except for brief periods of control by U.S. forces (1776) and by the Spanish (1782-83), the Bahamas was ruled continuously by a series of British governors until internal self-government was introduced in January 1964, and full independence nearly a decade later. The primary force for political change was the Bahamas' first → political party — the Progressive Liberal Party (1953) — which ultimately was successful in urging an end to segregation and white minority rule. Under the leadership of Lynden O. Pindling, the party held power from 1967 to 1992.

Economically and socially, the Bahamas has been influenced in various ways by the United States. At the time of the American Revolution (esp. 1783-85), several thousand Loyalists fled to the Bahamas, bringing with them up to 4,000 slaves, in the process doubling the white population and tripling the number of blacks. The black population further increased between 1808 and 1838, during which time the Royal Navy landed approximately 3,000 blacks captured from slave ships destined for the United States. Under the terms of the United Kingdom Emancipation Act, all slaves in the Bahamas were freed in August 1834. The Bahamas twice enjoyed major (albeit temporary) economic boosts from events in the United States: first, as a haven for Confederate blockade-runners during the U.S. Civil War (1861-65), and then as a center for rum-running to the U.S. coast during the period of Prohibition (1920-33).

In the 20th century, the Bahamas seems to have found its economic niche in → tourism. Through 1995, the Bahamas was the principal tourist destination in the Caribbean, with 90 percent of the visitors arriving from the United States. According to estimates by the World Bank, in 1994 the Bahamas had the highest per capita income of any Caribbean country.

Of concern for the future development of tourism, however, is the country's ongoing struggle to control illegal drug-trafficking. In November 1984 a government commission reported on the rising problem of illicit drugs (which are intended mainly for the U.S. market), indicating that money from the drug trade had thoroughly permeated the Bahamian society and economy. Members of Parliament and of the cabinet have been implicated, and in 1995 the government announced the creation of a special police unit to tackle the related problem of the increase in violent crime in New Providence.

The Bahamas has had to deal with the political pressures internal to Cuba and Haiti in the form of → refugees who arrive on its shores. In 1994 the government announced stepped-up efforts to deport the estimated 40,000 Haitian immigrants who were then residing illegally in the islands.

2. Religious Situation

The → Anglican Church was part and parcel of English colonization efforts in the Bahamas from the earliest days. By the mid-19th century, however, → Dissenters had engaged in a struggle for full legal recognition, which led ultimately to the disestablishment of the Anglican Church in 1869. Under the constitution promulgated in 1973 at the time of independence, freedom of religion is carefully defined and explicitly guaranteed.

From 1648 to 1800, the Anglican Church represented virtually the only Christian group ministering in the Bahamas. In the late 1700s the arrival of several thousand Loyalists from the United States gave a large boost to its membership. According to the 1990 census, the Anglicans and the → Roman Catholic Church each represented 16.0 percent of the population, both behind the → Baptists (31.2 percent).

The Baptist Missionary Society of Great Britain first sent missionaries to the Bahamas in the middle of the 19th century. They were joined in 1951 by Southern Baptist missionaries from the United States (M. C. Symonette). Approximately two dozen other Protestant groups exist in the Bahamas, including → Methodists (from 1786), Seventh-day Adventists (1909; → Adventists), Church of God (Cleveland, 1910; → Churches of God), Church of God of Prophecy (1923), → Assemblies of God (1928), → Salvation Army (1931), → Churches of Christ (1952), and → Church of the Nazarene (1971).

Roman Catholic mission work in the Bahamas began in the mid-19th century, with the first permanent mission beginning in 1891, by → Benedictine priests from the United States. A prefecture was established in 1929, which became a vicariate in 1941. In 1995 the Bahamas comprised the Diocese of Nassau, which was suffragan to the Archdiocese of Kingston in Jamaica. The bishop participates in the Antilles Episcopal Conference, which has its headquarters in Trinidad and Tobago.

Ten Christian denominations compose the Bahamas Christian Council, which was founded in 1948. Its unusually broad membership includes Anglicans, Baptists, Brethren, Greek Orthodox, Lutherans, Methodists, Pentecostals, Roman Catholics, Salvation Army, and Seventh-day Adventists.

The Bahamas is also home to small groups of Baha'is, Jehovah's Witnesses, Jews, and Muslims. In addition, several thousand Bahamians identify with no religious group. A noteworthy feature of Bahamian culture is the widespread practice of Obeah (even by many church members), an adaptation of African spiritism involving sorcery and magic ritual (→ Voodoo).

→ Colonialism 2; Slavery; Substance Abuse

Bibliography: P. ALBURY, *Paradise Island Story* (London, 1984) • D. BARRETT, ed., *WCE* 161-63 • C. J. BARRY, *Upon These Rocks: Catholics in the Bahamas* (Collegeville, Minn., 1973) • P. G. BOULTBEE, comp., *The Bahamas* (Oxford, 1989) bibliography • D. W. COLLINWOOD and S. DODGE, eds., *Modern Bahamian Society* (Parkersburg, Iowa, 1989) • M. CRATON and G. SAUNDERS, *Islanders in the Stream: A History of the Bahamian People* (vol. 1; Athens, Ga., 1992) • C. A. HUGHES, *Race and Politics in the Bahamas* (Queensland, 1981) • R. W. KAY, "Church Growth and Renewal in the Bahamas" (Diss., Fuller Theological Seminary, Pasadena, Calif., 1972) • T. O. MCCARTNEY, *Ten, Ten the Bible Ten: Obeah in the Bahamas* (Nassau, 1976) • D. G. SAUNDERS, *Slavery in the Bahamas, 1648-1838* (Nassau, 1985) • M. C. SYMONETTE, *Baptists in the Bahamas: An Historical Review* (El Paso, Tex., 1977).

THE EDITORS

Bahrain

1. General Situation
2. Religious Situation

1. General Situation

The State of Bahrain is an archipelago nation lying along the Arabian Peninsula in the Persian Gulf.

	1960	1980	2000
Population (1,000s):	156	347	618
Annual growth rate (%):	4.04	3.51	1.65
Area: 694 sq. km. (268 sq. mi.)			

A.D. *2000*

Population density: 890/sq. km. (2,306/sq. mi.)
Births / deaths: 1.72 / 0.38 per 100 population
Fertility rate: 2.54 per woman
Infant mortality rate: 16 per 1,000 live births
Life expectancy: 73.8 years (m: 72.1, f: 76.3)
Religious affiliation (%): Muslims 81.5, Christians 11.2 (indigenous 4.5, Roman Catholics 4.4, other Christians 2.3), Hindus 6.4, other 0.9.

Roughly two-thirds of the population are Bahrainis, with the remainder resident foreign workers (→ Foreigners 2), divided among Asians (13 percent, mostly Indians and Pakistanis), other Arabs (10 percent, mainly Palestinians, Egyptians, and Saudis), Iranians (8 percent), and smaller groups of Europeans.

The main island, Bahrain, is linked to Saudi Arabia by a 25-kilometer (15-mi.) causeway, and by shorter causeways to the other main islands, Muharraq and Sitra. Oil production, which began in 1934 and became a major Bahraini industry, became less significant over the years; by the 1970s, oil reserves had been largely depleted. By the 1990s, however, Bahrain had diversified its economy, becoming a major center in the Gulf for industrial, banking, and financial services.

Burial mounds have been found on Bahrain dating from the Sumerian period of the third millennium B.C., and written records concerning the archipelago exist in accounts of ancient Persian, Greek, and Roman writers. It was conquered for → Islam in the seventh century and later was controlled by the Portuguese (1521-1602) and the Persians (1602-1783). In 1783 Sheikh Ahmad bin Al Khalifah ousted the Persians. In an unbroken line since that time, sheikhs of the Al (family) Khalifah have ruled the country.

Under the terms of an 1861 protective treaty with Great Britain, the government of Bahrain was shared between the ruling sheikh and a British adviser. This protectorate status continued until August 15, 1971, when Sheikh Isa bin Sulman Al Khalifah signed a treaty of friendship with Britain. That same day he declared Bahrain's independence, and the next day named himself emir. A constituent assembly subsequently produced a new constitution, ratified in June 1973, providing for a National Assembly consisting of 14 members of the cabinet (appointed by the emir) and 30 other members elected by popular vote. Elections were duly held in December 1973. In August 1975, however, Emir Isa dissolved the assembly. Since that time, the emir has ruled virtually as an absolute monarch, advised by his cabinet and a 30-member Consultative Council.

2. Religious Situation

Since the time of the Muslim conquest, Islam has been the de facto official religion of Bahrain. The ruling Khalifah family, as well as the majority of leading Bahrainis in the urban areas, are → Sunnis. The majority of the native population, however, are → Shiites, as are the sizable number of Iranian expatriates. Sunni-Shiite tensions ignited in late 1994, when a prominent Shiite cleric — Sheikh Ali Salman — was arrested after publicly urging a restoration of the constitution and the National Assembly. His arrest led to riots and a countrywide imposition of martial law. Relations had not noticeably improved by 1997, although Emir Isa bin Sulman Al Khalifah did initiate some face-to-face dialogue with Shiite leaders.

Non-Muslim religious groups are allowed to function solely as the government's concession to the foreign workers resident in Bahrain. The → Roman Catholic vicariate apostolic of Arabia was erected in 1875; in 1991 it embraced approximately 30,000 adherents. The Arabia Mission of the Reformed Church of America began a medical dispensary in Bahrain in 1896, from which arose a hospital and the present-day National Evangelical Church (1,600 adherents in 1990). The Christian presence in Bahrain also includes groups of → Anglicans, Orthodox (→ Orthodox Church), → Pentecostals, and Mar Thomas adherents (→ Syrian Orthodox Churches in India).

In 1990 approximately 6 percent of the population was → Hindu, representing about half of the expatriate Indian community.

Bibliography: A. AL-KHALIFA and M. RICE, eds., *Bahrain through the Ages: The History* (London, 1993) • H. IBN I. AL-KHALIFA, *First Light: Modern Bahrain and Its Heritage* (London, 1994) • D. BARRETT, ed., *WCE* 163-64 • M. A. FAKHRO, *Women at Work in the Gulf: A Case Study of Bahrain* (London, 1990) • S. A. HANNA, *A Modern Cultural History of Bahrain* (Manama, 1991) • HUMAN RIGHTS WATCH, *Bahrain: Routine Abuses, Routine Denial: Civil Rights and the Political Crisis in Bahrain* (New York, 1997) • F. I. KHURI, *Tribe and State in Bahrain: The Transformation of Social and Political Authority in an Arab State* (Chicago, 1980) • F. H. LAWSON, *Bahrain: The Modernization of Autocracy* (Boulder, Colo., 1989) • J. B. NUGENT and T. THOMAS, eds., *Bahrain and the Gulf: Past Perspectives and Alternative Futures* (New York, 1985) • P. T. H. UNWIN, comp., *Bahrain* (Oxford, 1984) bibliography • A. WHEATCROFT, *The Life and Times of Shaikh Salman bin Hamad Al-Khalifa: Ruler of Bahrain, 1942-1961* (London, 1995).

THE EDITORS

Bangladesh

	1960	1980	2000
Population (1,000s):	51,419	88,221	128,310
Annual growth rate (%):	2.52	2.37	1.73

Area: 147,570 sq. km. (56,977 sq. mi.)

A.D. 2000
Population density: 869/sq. km. (2,252/sq. mi.)
Births / deaths: 2.67 / 0.87 per 100 population
Fertility rate: 2.88 per woman
Infant mortality rate: 67 per 1,000 live births
Life expectancy: 60.7 years (m: 60.6, f: 60.8)
Religious affiliation (%): Muslims 86.1, Hindus 12.0, other 1.9.

Bangladesh, a republic in southern Asia, encompasses the territory of what was formerly Indian East Bengal and the Sylhet district of Assam. After the partition of British India in 1947, it formed the eastern part of the Islamic state of Pakistan before it achieved its independence in 1971. The vast majority of the people (97 percent) are Bengalis; the largest minority groups are Urdus (600,000), Chakmas (352,000), Hindis (346,000), Burmese (231,000), and Biharis (230,000).

The Bengalis are nearly all → Sunnite Muslims, but there is a → Shiite minority in the cities. Hinduism suffered losses due to the flight of refugees to West Bengal after 1947 and during the civil war of 1971-72. Yet it is the religion with the second-largest number of adherents. Although Buddhism has been in the region a long time, less than 1 percent of the total population now confesses it. Traditional tribal religions may be found among the Garo, the Santal, and tribes of the Chittagong Hill Tracts. Christians, who form a small minority, mainly comprise low-caste Hindus (→ Caste) and members of tribal groups (esp. the Bawm, Pankhu, Garo, Oraon, Mahili, and Khasi).

The Roman Catholic Church. Although Roman Catholic missionaries were at work in Portuguese trading settlements as early as the 16th century, the first → diocese was set up only in 1886. By 1992 there were five dioceses, all with national bishops, though three-fourths of the clergy were still from abroad. The church's main support is in the cities, especially in the capital, Dhaka, whose residents include Portuguese.

Protestants. The Anglo-Saxon → Baptists were the first Protestant denomination to undertake work in Bengal, led by W. Carey, who first arrived there in 1793. Today as the Baptist Union of Bangladesh, they are the strongest Protestant group. There is also a Bangladesh Baptist Union led by missionaries from Australia, New Zealand, and the United States. Australian Baptists also support an independent Mymensingh Garo Baptist Convention. Presbyterians (→ Reformed and Presbyterian Churches) and → Anglicans came together in 1970 and formed one diocese in the Church of Bangladesh. Other Protestant groups include the Northern Evangelical Lutheran Church (1867) and the Church of Sylhet.

Ecumenical Organizations. The Bangladesh National Council of Churches (BNCC), first formed as the East Pakistan Christian Council, unites four Protestant denominations and various smaller groups. Since the civil war it has done much relief work. The Bangladesh Ecumenical Relief and Rehabilitation Services came into being in 1972 with support from the BNCC, Roman Catholics, and the state. A Christian Medical Association helps to coordinate the churches' medical program.

After independence, the Republic of Bangladesh was declared a secular → socialist state (→ Secularization). Religious freedom was one of the principles of the constitution of 1972. In 1988 Islam was declared to be the state religion, which has led to heightened tensions between Muslims and followers of other religions. Religious freedom, however, continues to be constitutionally protected.

Bibliography: D. BARRETT, ed., *WCE* 164-76 • P. McNEE, *Crucial Issues in Bangladesh: Making Missions More Effective in the Mosaic of Peoples* (Pasadena, Calif., 1976).

BRIGITTE LUCHESI

Baptism

Overview
1. Biblical Data
   1.1. Primitive Practice
   1.2. Paul
   1.3. Colossians and Ephesians
   1.4. Synoptic Gospels
   1.5. Acts
   1.6. Johannine School

Overview

In Christianity, baptism — either by plunging in water or by sprinkling with it — represents the first act of incorporation "into Christ" and into the fellowship of the → church. Further acts of incorporation are → confirmation (→ Initiation Rites 2) and the → Eucharist. Other religious societies have similar rites (→ Initiation Rites 1). Jewish → proselyte baptism incorporates the baptized not only into the religious fellowship but also into God's → covenant → people. This matter is relevant in the dialogue between Israel and the → church (§§1.4.1.3, 2.1, 5.5.3; → Jewish-Christian Dialogue).

The biblical texts (see 1) give evidence of the first baptismal practice and reflect the special character of baptism and of its significance for the life of believers and the church. But the further history of baptism and of theological reflection on it (see 2) shows that in spite of its uniqueness, and perhaps because of it, differences in understanding and practice arose. Different interpretations have been important (→ Anabaptists; Baptists; Pentecostal Churches) and still persist (see 3 and 4). They are a problem in the → ecumenical movement (see 2.3).

As is true in the history of → mission, baptism is again functioning as a test of Christian identity, both for churches in countries affected by → secularization and for those of the → Third World (§2; → Third World Theology; see 2.4). Discussion of the development of baptismal practice in the United States (see 3) and the change in practice in Germany (see 4) brings to light the problems and tasks that obtain and the concern to meet the challenge that baptism poses. The perspective of church law (see 5) enables us to see what the churches have in common in their orders and which issues are still unresolved.

ERWIN FAHLBUSCH

1. Biblical Data

The basis of all NT statements about baptism and the related practice is the historical fact of the baptism of Jesus by John the Baptist (Mark 1:9 and par.). Even if Jesus himself did not baptize (see John 4:1-2), if the command in Matt. 28:18-20 belongs to a later time, and if the NT texts give evidence of a very broad background in tradition and the history of religion, still it is the baptism of Jesus in the Jordan that explains why, from the first, baptism was a normative rite of → initiation in the → primitive Christian community. Ritual washings (→ Cultic Purity) at → Qumran, → proselyte baptism, and the washings in some mystery cults (→ Mystery Religions) show some similarities, but they cannot be accepted as the historical presupposition and source of primitive Christian baptism.

1.1. Primitive Practice
Continuity with John's baptism may be seen in some typical features of primitive Christian baptismal practice. Early Christian baptism is not self-baptism but is *administered by a baptizer* (see 1 Cor. 1:14, 16; Acts 8:38; 10:48). Like John's baptism, it is *a once-for-all act*, unlike the ritual washings in ancient → Judaism and pagan → Hellenism. As a rule, it *involved immersion in running water* (see Acts 8:38; *Did.* 7). It was also, like John's baptism, a baptism *for the* → *forgiveness of* → *sins* (Mark 1:4; Acts 2:38; see also 1 Cor. 6:11; Rom. 3:25) and thus had an → eschatological and → soteriological dimension.

In two ways, however, it differs from John's baptism. It views the Christ-event as the eschatological event of → salvation that is present in baptism "in the name of Jesus" (see 1 Cor. 1:13, 15; Gal. 3:27; Acts 2:38; 10:48). Furthermore, it is related to the giving of the Spirit (see 1 Cor. 12:13; Mark 1:8; Acts 1:5; 11:16; → Holy Spirit).

1.2. Paul
The significance of baptism for Paul may be seen in his adoption of existing traditions (see 1 Cor. 1:30; 6:11; 12:13; Gal. 3:26-28; Rom. 3:25; 4:25; 6:3-4).

Rom. 6:3-4 is particularly important, for it brings baptism into analogy with ideas in the Hellenistic mystery religions (Apuleius *Met.* 11.23.8; Firmicus Maternus *Err. prof. rel.* 22) by describing baptism as a sacramental experiencing of the death of Jesus, with the consequence of a death to sin and an ensuing life in → righteousness.

Baptism is central in three ways for Paul's ecclesiology (→ Church 2.1). First, it is the sacrament of the *unity of the* → *congregation* (1 Cor. 1:10-17; 12:13; Rom. 12:5). Second, the *gift of the Spirit* and the beginning of the new Christian life are associated with baptism (1 Cor. 6:11; 12:13; 2 Cor. 1:21-22; Gal. 5:24-25; Rom. 5:5). Third, in baptism believers attain the *exalted state of Christ.* Paul firmly links his "in Christ" to baptism (Gal. 3:26-28; 1 Cor. 1:30; 2 Cor. 5:17a; Rom. 6:11).

Paul views one's existence in the church as deriving from baptism; he is aware of being committed and empowered by God's action in it to do God's will in the church and in the world. In his → ethics, baptism is the place of forgiveness of sins, endowment with the Spirit, and the beginning of the new life in Christ. As such, it is of great importance. Baptism also figures largely in his soteriology, for it involves for individual Christians the real, historical fulfillment of the liberation from the flesh, sin, and death that has been set forth in Christ.

1.3. Colossians and Ephesians
Although in Rom. 6:3-4 Paul avoids the idea of a → resurrection achieved in baptism, we find this thought in Col. 2:11-12. We do not see here the eschatological reservation typical of Paul (e.g., see 1 Cor. 13:12; 2 Cor. 5:7; Phil. 2:12). The *eschata* are spoken of here in the past tense.

1.4. Synoptic Gospels
In the → Synoptics the baptism of Jesus is the paradigm of Christian existence (Mark 1:9-11 and par.), for already at his baptism the Son of God was beginning to follow the path of → obedience to the will of God. Current practice by the end of the first century reflects the command to baptize in Matt. 28:18-20. Baptism here is a normative initiation rite linked necessarily to salvation. As a sacrament of deliverance signifying liberation from past sins and worldly powers and the making possible of a new Christian life, it plays the same role in Eph. 4:5; 5:26; 1 Pet. 1:3, 23; 3:21; Heb. 6:2; Titus 3:5.

1.5. Acts
The Acts of the Apostles bears witness to the central place of baptism in the history of early Christian → mission. Programmatically, → Peter's pentecost sermon ends in 2:38 with the call for baptism (see v. 41), to which Paul's practice later corresponds (16:14-15,

33; 18:8). Luke closely associates the → laying on of hands, the conferring of the Spirit, and baptism, with laying on of hands either preceding baptism (9:17-19) or following it (8:4-25; 19:1-7). A decisive point is the linking of the apostolic laying on of hands to the gift of the Spirit.

1.6. Johannine School

Also in the Johannine writings, baptism is a normative initiation rite (John 3:22, 26; 4:1). On this view it follows Jesus' own practice, so that what is said about its nature in John 3:5 or 1 John 2:20, 27 is only to be expected. As elsewhere in the NT, baptism and the gift of the Spirit are primary data of Christian existence (along with John 3:5-6; 6:63a, see esp. 1 John 2:27; 3:24; 4:13; 5:6-8). The nonsacramental interpretation of John by R. Bultmann (1884-1976) is exegetically debatable. The original setting of many of these texts might well have been liturgical (→ Worship 1.3), although we cannot reconstruct primitive baptismal → liturgies.

1.7. Significance

Baptism in the NT is in many ways the starting point and basis of central ecclesiological, ethical, pneumatological, anthropological, and soteriological statements. The fact that NT theology is not uniform does not reduce the fundamental significance of baptism relative to God's historical action and the beginning of the Christian life. Baptism is primarily God's act, for God promises his own presence in it. Prior conditions do not have to be met by candidates, and to that extent one may see in the baptism of infants an appropriate practice that is not in conflict at heart with Paul's doctrine of baptism and → justification. The → grace of God put into effect by Christ breaks through in baptism and may be received in grateful faith.

Texts and archaeological findings give evidence of an interest in washings in the Qumran community. There the cleansing and sanctifying of the devout is above all the work of the Holy Spirit of God, who brings one under subjection to the laws of God. Only on such a premise do the daily baths avail that novices must take during a year of testing (see 1QS 2:25–3:12; 5:13; 6:16-17).

Baptism was important in → Gnostic groups as well, with lustrations and baptisms attested among the Naasenes, Sethians, and Valentinians. Baptism confers on Gnostics the spirit of immortality, redemption, and resurrection and makes them pneumatics. For full evidence of this view, see *Gos. Phil.* (NHC 2.3).

→ Anointing; Apostle, Apostolate; Blessing; Circumcision; Conversion; Discipleship; Eucharist; Rite; Vow

Bibliography: G. BARTH, *Die Taufe in frühchristlicher Zeit* (Neukirchen, 1981) • M. BARTH, *Die Taufe–ein Sakrament?* (Zurich, 1951) • G. R. BEASLEY-MURRAY, *Baptism in the NT* (Grand Rapids, 1988; orig. pub., 1962) • D. BRIDGE and D. PHYPERS, *The Water That Divides* (Leicester, Eng., 1977) • O. CULLMANN, *Baptism in the NT* (Philadelphia, 1978; orig. pub., 1951) • G. DELLING, *Die Taufe im Neuen Testament* (Berlin, 1963) • W. F. FLEMINGTON, *The NT Doctrine of Baptism* (London, 1948) • N. GÄUMANN, *Taufe und Ethik* (Munich, 1967) • H. HALTER, *Taufe und Ethos* (Freiburg, 1977) • L. HARTMANN, *Auf den Namen des Herrn Jesus. Die Taufe in den neutestamentlichen Schriften* (Stuttgart, 1992) • R. SCHNACKENBURG, *Baptism in the Thought of Paul* (New York, 1964) • U. SCHNELLE, *Gerechtigkeit und Christusgegenwart. Vorpaulinische und paulinische Tauftheologie* (Göttingen, 1983; 2d ed., 1986) • G. WAINWRIGHT, *Christian Initiation* (London, 1969) • A. J. M. WEDDERBURN, *Baptism and Resurrection* (Tübingen, 1987).

UDO SCHNELLE

2. History and Theology

2.1. Unity and Differences

Christianity has consistently practiced baptism as a water rite administered in the name of the → Trinity for admission into the church. However, churches and theologians have differed over the relation between it and other ceremonies in the process of → initiation (§2), as well as over the proper subjects and authorized ministers of baptism.

In particular, they have differed over the sign for the gift of the Holy Spirit, over the propriety of infants as recipients of baptism, and over the authenticity of baptism given by those considered heretics and schismatics (→ Heresies and Schisms). The roots and some early manifestations of these differences are found in the NT (see 1). Such differences over baptism may be the product of differences in understanding the ways of God's saving action, the nature and content of → faith, and the composition of the church.

Modern ecumenism has sought to discover and emphasize the commonalities in rite and understanding that persist across the differences in the doctrine and practice of baptism (see 2.3). Such commonalities will, it is hoped, help toward mutual recognition among divided communities that claim the name of Christian and thus contribute to the reintegration of churchly → unity.

2.2. The Rite in History

2.2.1. The Early Church

Justin Martyr (ca. 100-ca. 165) gives a short account

of baptism in chaps. 61 and 65 of his *First Apology*. The most detailed description of Christian initiation in the pre-Constantinian period appears in the *Apostolic Tradition* of Hippolytus. This presumably Roman document of the early third century contains all the main features that persist in the baptismal process and at the same time hints at future problems. Similar evidence for the central elements, together with his own theological interpretations, can be drawn from → Tertullian, especially his treatise *On Baptism*.

After their seriousness had been vouched for, inquirers into the Christian faith were admitted to a catechumenate that, according to Hippolytus, normally lasted three years (→ Catechesis). This period of instruction and testing included lessons in Scripture and morals, exorcisms, and regular → prayer. As the time drew near for their baptism (which would typically take place at Easter; see Tertullian *De bapt.* 19), "the chosen" underwent a more intense preparation, including daily exorcisms and "hearing the gospel." On the day before their baptism, the elect received an → exorcism at the hands of the → bishop.

At the end of the Paschal Vigil (→ Easter 2), in a place apart from the congregation, prayer was said over the water (see also Tertullian *De bapt.* 4), which was to be "flowing" (*Did.* 7.1). Hippolytus orders that "they shall baptize the little children first. And if they can answer for themselves, let them answer. But if they cannot, let their parents answer or someone from their family." Here is clear evidence of early baptisms on the basis (humanly speaking) of vicarious faith and family solidarity. Yet, Tertullian advised against the baptism of small children (*parvuli*), precisely on account of the hazards to which it exposed the sponsors of later rebellious godchildren (*De bapt.* 18).

→ Origen (ca. 185-ca. 254; → Origenism) believed that "the church has received a tradition from the → apostles to give baptism even to small children [*parvulis*]" (*Comm. in Rom.* 5.9; *PG* 14.1047). By the fifth century, the baptism of infants had become the dominant practice throughout the church, in association (esp. in the West) with the doctrine of original sin, which the practice both reflected and fortified (→ Augustine's Theology; Sin 3.2).

After the candidates had undressed, Hippolytus reports that they were bidden by a presbyter to renounce Satan (→ Devil) and then were anointed with the oil of exorcism. Another presbyter took over at the water, placing his hand upon each candidate's head and applying the water to the candidate each time upon affirmative response to three questions: "Do you believe in God the Father Almighty . . . in Christ Jesus, the Son of God . . . and in the Holy Spirit . . . ?" (→ Confession of Faith 1; Rule of Faith). Immediately afterward, the candidates were anointed with the oil of thanksgiving and then entered the assembly of the faithful.

There the bishop extended his hand over them and said a prayer whose various linguistic versions name the particular action or presence of the Holy Spirit either in reference to the water baptism that had just taken place or as the requested result of the very act that was now occurring: "Lord God, who granted these the remission of sins by the washing of regeneration of the Holy Spirit, send upon them your grace that they may serve you . . ." (Latin text of Hippolytus *Trad. apos.*), or "Lord God, who granted these the remission of sins by the washing of regeneration, fill them with your Holy Spirit, and send upon them your grace . . ." (Oriental versions). This difference gains in significance in the light of later debates concerning the moment or sign of "the gift of the Spirit," a question that would become particularly acute when the Western church, by a gradual process, split the unitary rite of initiation into "baptism" and "confirmation" (→ Initiation Rites 2.2.2).

Next, according to Hippolytus, the bishop anointed the head of each one, saying, "I anoint you with holy oil in God the Father Almighty and Christ Jesus and the Holy Spirit," "sealed" them on the forehead, then gave them the → kiss of peace. The reservation of several initiatory acts to the bishop — laying on of hands, prayer, anointing of the forehead, sealing, and kiss — would become a factor in the "disintegration" (J. D. C. Fisher) of the Western rite, when the bishop's "completion" had to be awaited after a clinical baptism or the baptism of infants by the parish priest alone or in the admission of people to the church after a heretical or schismatic baptism (→ Initiation Rites 2.3.1).

Thereupon, says Hippolytus, the newly baptized were allowed to join for the first time in the prayers of the faithful and to exchange the kiss of peace with them. They also took part in the Eucharist for the first time, receiving not only bread and wine but also water (as a sign of inward washing) and milk and honey (symbolizing entry into the promised land; see also Tertullian *De cor.* 3).

Tertullian sums up the purpose and effects of the main ceremonies of baptism thus: "Flesh is washed, that the soul may be cleansed; flesh is anointed, that the soul may be consecrated; flesh is sealed, that the soul may be fortified; flesh is shadowed by the imposition of the hand, that the soul may be enlightened by the Spirit; flesh feeds on the body and blood of Christ, that the soul also may fatten on God" (*De res. car.* 8).

Further patristic evidence for the rites of Christian initiation and their meaning comes from the later fourth and the fifth centuries, principally from the catechetical lectures given to the candidates or neophytes by bishops such as Cyril (or John) of Jerusalem, John → Chrysostom of Antioch and Constantinople, Ambrose of Milan, → Augustine of Hippo, and Theodore of Mopsuestia.

2.2.2. *The East*

From the third-century *Didascalia apostolorum* it appears that Christian initiation in Syria took place in two stages (2.39). The first stage sounds like the dual ceremony of the "apotaxis" (turning from Satan) and "syntaxis" (adhesion to Christ and the Holy Trinity), which now appears in the Byzantine rite of baptism but which may earlier have been separated from it by a catechumenate. The most striking feature of the early Syrian practice, however, as it is reflected in the *Didascalia* (3.12), the *Acts of Judas Thomas,* and the *Apostolic Constitutions* (3.16-18; 7.22), occurs in the second stage, or "seal." There an anointing for the conveyance of the Holy Spirit immediately *precedes* water baptism, the water rite being understood in terms of rebirth and filiation, and eucharistic Communion follows.

Syria also appears to be the home of the declaratory formula spoken by the minister ("I baptize you in the name of the Father and the Son and the Holy Spirit"), which spread first to Egypt (see the early 4th-cent. *Canons of St. Hippolytus* 19) and later to Spain, Gaul, and Rome. In reverse, a *post*baptismal anointing for the gift of the Holy Spirit appears to have spread from Rome via Jerusalem to Antioch and Constantinople by the late fourth century, together with a recovery of the Pauline emphasis on participation in Christ's death and resurrection through the water baptism, and leading to a reinterpretation of the prebaptismal unction as cathartic and apotropaic, as in the West.

The rite of Constantinople came to dominate the Byzantine East. Scarcely changed for 1,500 years, the rite has been preponderantly administered to infants and at a single stroke, with sponsors speaking for infants, as also for "the mute or barbarians." The catechumenate is compressed into an initial ceremony of admission, four exorcisms, the "apotaxis" and "syntaxis," with profession of the → Niceno-Constantinopolitan Creed, and a prayer for the baptismal grace of renewal and enlightenment.

The order of baptism proper begins immediately with the consecration of the water by an anaphoral prayer that includes an invocation of the Holy Spirit. The candidate is anointed on brow, breast, and back with "the oil of gladness." Baptism takes place by triple submersion in the water, the priest saying, "The servant of God N. is baptized in the name of the Father and of the Son and of the Holy Spirit." The newly baptized is dressed in the white "tunic of righteousness." The priest then gives thanks for baptism and prays for the gifts of the seal of the Holy Spirit and participation in the Eucharist. Chrismation then takes place with the holy myron, the priest anointing the various parts of the body from the forehead down and saying at each anointing, "The seal of the gift of the Holy Spirit." Priest, sponsor, and neophyte process around the → baptismal font, to the singing of Gal. 3:27. A reading from the apostle (Rom. 6:3-11) and the gospel (Matt. 28:16-20) betrays the fact that the eucharistic liturgy used to be taken up at this point. Communion is in fact received by the neophyte at the next opportunity. Meanwhile the baptismal robe and the neophyte's body are "washed," and the priest, in a Byzantine peculiarity, makes a cruciform cut of the neophyte's hair, signifying dedication to the glory of God. The entire rite may be administered by presbyters, but the use of episcopally consecrated myron at the chrismation is to be observed.

2.2.3. *The Medieval West*

From the late fourth century and throughout the fifth and sixth centuries, we learn more features of the catechumenate and the proximate preparation for baptism, including the giving of salt (the "salt of wisdom") the "scrutinies" (consisting of exorcisms and of examinations to test for the removal of the devil), the "delivery" *(traditio)* and "return" *(redditio)* of the creed and of the Lord's Prayer (whereby these texts were taught, explained, learned, and repeated), and the "effeta," a polyvalent ceremony modeled in a somewhat slapdash way on Mark 7:31-37. A letter of Pope Innocent I to Decentius of Gubbio makes clear the Roman insistence on reserving the second postbaptismal anointing (of the brow) to the bishop for the conveying of the Spirit (*PL* 56.515); this became an important factor in the separate development of "confirmation."

As in the East, the baptism of infants eventually became the heavily preponderant practice in the West also, and the rite came to be administered usually by parish priests. There could therefore develop a considerable interval, sometimes of years, between baptism and episcopal "confirmation" (interpreted as "strengthening for the fight" or "for preaching to others the same gift as we have received in baptism"). Confirmation became an occasion for catching up on the catechetical instruction that had been lacking to those baptized as infants and for professing the faith that sponsors had earlier professed on one's behalf. At first, infants continued to receive Communion immediately after baptism, but by the 12th century, scrupulous respect for the eucharistic elements was leading priests to limit infants to the liquid element only, so that when, by the next century, it became more and more common for the eucharistic chalice to be withheld from the laity in general (→ Clergy and Laity), the decline in the practice of communicating baptized infants was accelerated.

2.2.4. *The Modern West*

The Protestant → Reformers inherited a split pattern of infant baptism and later catechesis/confirmation and Communion. They largely got rid of the more "material" features — apart from the water — of the medieval rites of initiation. Lutherans and Anglicans retained the proxy profession of faith by sponsors on behalf of infants, while Calvinists appealed rather to the analogy with → circumcision and did not call for the family to "speak for" the child. All the magisterial Reformers emphasized catechism for children at the age of understanding, but it was the Anglicans who retained the strongest form of confirmation as both a personal profession of faith and an imposition of episcopal hands with prayer for the sevenfold gift of the Holy Spirit. The Roman Catholic Church continued to baptize predominantly infants, with confirmation and First Communion following at a distance and in a sequence that varied with varying pastoral reasoning over the generations and according to geography.

The entire structure of Christendom, whether in its Catholic or in its Protestant forms, was called into question by the more radical reformers. Their intended return to primitive Christianity included baptism only on personal profession of faith. (They were able to restore initial catechesis to its prebaptismal place.) Called Anabaptists by others, they claimed not to be rebaptizing but to be administering the first authentic baptism to people who had received the rite in infancy. From continental Europe and from Britain, "believer-baptists" spread to North America, where they have thrived (→ Baptists; Mennonites). While a position of baptism solely on personal profession of faith has sometimes been accused by magisterial Protestantism of perennial → Pelagianism and modern → individualism, a number of otherwise unlikely 20th-century theologians have shown sympathy with it (e.g., K. → Barth, E. Brunner, E. Jüngel, J. Moltmann).

In the 20th-century liturgical movement the revision of initiation rites in the second half of the century manifests a number of significant features. The most striking achievement has been the Roman Catholic *Ordo initiationis Christianae adultorum*

(1972), which returned to the great rites and writings of the late 4th century, and even more significantly perhaps to the pre-Constantinian *Apostolic Tradition* of Hippolytus, in reconstituting a full and complex process of initiation. The steps go from → evangelization through a multistaged catechumenate to enrollment for baptism, the ceremonies immediately preparatory to the water, renunciation of Satan, Trinitarian profession of faith, water baptism, anointing, confirmation (normally by the bishop, with imposition of hands and prayer for the sevenfold gift of the Holy Spirit, signation of the forehead with episcopally consecrated chrism, and utterance of the "Eastern" formula, "N., be sealed with the gift of the Holy Spirit"), eucharistic Communion, and postbaptismal catechesis on the → sacraments.

Revisions of baptismal rites have taken two different directions as far as the baptism of infants is concerned. In the Roman Catholic *Ordo baptismi parvulorum* (1969), the questions are put to the parents and godparents, not as though addressed to the child, but concerning their own faith and on the express understanding that they will raise their wards in the faith and bring them to confirmation and Communion. This pattern comes close to that long customary among Methodists and the Reformed. In contrast, Anglicans and Lutherans have sought to make as little distinction as possible in their revised baptismal rites between baptism of adults and baptism of infants.

Many Protestant churches have introduced a Paschal Vigil service modeled after the Roman Catholic one, which since the revision of 1951-55 has included a renewal of baptismal vows (→ Easter 3.5). Other forms of baptismal renewal (such as the annual "covenant service," which → Methodism has had since its beginnings) have also increased in popularity and apparently meet a particular need felt for the reaffirmation of Christian identity in the difficult circumstances of a declining Christendom.

2.3. *Baptism and the Ecumenical Movement*

Issues of Christian initiation have constituted both a promise and a problem in the 20th-century → ecumenical movement. The widest-ranging current account is found in the so-called Lima text of the → World Council of Churches Faith and Order Commission, entitled *Baptism, Eucharist, and Ministry (BEM)*, and in the churches' responses to that document (ed. M. Thurian).

2.3.1. Positively put, many have regarded the persistence of what they take to be a "common baptism" as one of the continuing factors of → unity across divisions; it can be seen as a foundation and impulse for efforts toward the reintegration of the one church. This position has been adopted by many Anglicans, Lutherans, and Reformed who consider some historic divisions at least as internal to the church as a whole. It also characterizes the decree on → ecumenism of → Vatican II (*Unitatis redintegratio* 22), even though the → Roman Catholic Church makes a more restrictive identification between itself and the church as such (see *Lumen gentium* 8.2). It does admit, however, that people "who believe in Christ and have been properly baptized are put in some, though imperfect, communion with the Catholic Church" (*Unitatis redintegratio* 3, cf. *Lumen gentium* 15).

Other participants in the ecumenical movement, however, have been less willing to grant the major premise of an existing common baptism. This has been particularly true of Baptists and of Orthodox. With Baptists and some other Protestants, the question is that of the proper *subjects* of baptism. Are infants properly baptized? At stake here is the proper relation between → grace and "the faith that believes" — instantiated in the theme of sacramental efficacy. With Orthodox, the question is that of the proper *ministrant* of baptism. Is it baptism when the heterodox or schismatics perform the rite? At stake here is the proper relation between grace and "the faith that is believed" — instantiated in the theme of sacramental validity.

2.3.2. Ritually, *BEM* affirms a "common baptism" by the simple declaration that "baptism is administered with water in the name of the Father, the Son and the Holy Spirit" ("Baptism," par. 17). (This commonality may be put at risk by those churches that, especially under feminist criticism, allow the use of other "names"; → Feminist Theology 3.5.) Then also, while "Christians differ in their understanding as to where the sign of the gift of the Spirit is to be found, . . . all agree that Christian baptism is in water and the Holy Spirit" (par. 14). Drawing on the Scriptures and traditional liturgies, *BEM* describes baptism as "participation in Christ's death and resurrection (Rom. 6:3-5; Col. 2:12); a washing away of sin (1 Cor. 6:11); a new birth (John 3:5); an enlightenment by Christ (Eph. 5:14); a re-clothing in Christ (Gal. 3:27); a renewal by the Spirit (Titus 3:5); the experience of salvation from the flood (1 Pet. 3:20-21); an exodus from bondage (1 Cor. 10:1-2) and a liberation into a new humanity . . . (Gal. 3:27-28; 1 Cor. 12:13)" (par. 2; see also pars. 3-7).

2.3.3. Ritually, the issue of sacramental efficacy comes to expression in the question of the mutual compatibility between the three main patterns of Christian initiation that have developed in Christian history: (1) the "Eastern" practice, whereby baptism, chrismation/"confirmation" (pneumatologically understood), and First Communion are administered in a single rite, and predominantly to infants; (2) the "Western" pattern, whereby, in both its Catholic and its Protestant variants, baptism in infancy is followed by confirmation (with a Catholic emphasis on the gift of the Spirit or a Protestant emphasis on profession of faith) and Communion, in whatever order, after a shorter or longer interval; (3) the "baptist" pattern, whereby baptism and admission to the Lord's Table take place only upon personal profession of faith.

BEM and the international Reformed-Baptist dialogue have addressed themselves, with very similar results, to the "Western" versus "baptist" controversy: a common stress is placed upon the priority of divine grace and the necessity of human response in faith (*BEM*, "Baptism," pars. 8-10), and upon the location of baptism in the church as the community of faith (pars. 11-12). Less directly, *BEM* faces the question of the "Eastern" versus the other patterns. Not only "baptists" but most "Westerners" have difficulty with an initiation that does not at some point include a personal confession of faith; "Easterners," however, find it difficult to understand why most of the West denies Communion to baptized children. In a reconciling way, *BEM* acknowledges that "baptism needs to be constantly reaffirmed" and encourages the "renewal of baptismal vows" (par. 14, comm. *c*); it faces the "Western" churches with the question of infant Communion (ibid., *b*), yet in so doing puts at risk the growing understanding typified by the Baptist-Reformed dialogue.

2.3.4. Ritually, the question of sacramental validity shows itself in the manner in which a church receives into membership and/or admits to Communion people baptized in other communities. The Eastern churches have remained closest to → Cyprian of Carthage in making heretics or schismatics undergo full initiation on → conversion (§2) to Orthodoxy; even when, in an exercise of "economy," the converted receive only a penitential/pneumatological chrismation, the Orthodox take care not to endorse any value the previous baptism may have had before the person's conversion.

The Roman church long followed Augustine in not repeating baptism for a convert already baptized elsewhere (for always "it is Christ who baptizes") but considering the efficacy of such baptism as at best doubtful until the person was converted to Catholicism. The Council of → Trent regarded as "true baptism" all baptism performed with water in the name of the Trinity and "with the intention of doing what the church does"; if converts from Protestantism were given "conditional baptism," it was for fear that their original baptism might have excluded the intention to regenerate. Although that practice has largely ceased, Protestants are still required to receive Catholic confirmation.

Many pedobaptist Protestant churches are content to receive members from other churches simply "by transfer" and an affirmation of adhesion to their own doctrine and discipline (often after a period of instruction). Believer-baptist churches usually require baptism on profession of faith of a person who has hitherto undergone the rite only as an infant. Rules by which churches offer occasional eucharistic hospitality also bear on the recognition of baptism (→ Eucharist 5).

2.4. Cultural Issues

Baptism, or the entire process of initiation, is proving a test case for Christian or ecclesial identity in (1) the areas of old Christendom that are now undergoing → secularization, (2) parts of the world where the faith has been more recently planted (→ Third World 2), and (3) encounters with other → religions (→ Theology of Religions).

2.4.1. Secularization

In Europe, and in different ways in the United States, Canada, and Latin America, the social presence of Christianity has been eroded to varying degrees by → modernity. A single example of sacramental statistics may be given from the Church of England (→ Anglican Communion): The number of infant baptisms among Anglicans per 1,000 live births in the general population fell from 672 in 1950 to 554 in 1960, to 466 in 1970, to 365 in 1980, to 275 in 1990; over the same period the ratio of people aged 15 and over who received Communion at Easter declined from 6.2 percent in 1950 (2 million out of 32.32 million in this age bracket) to 4.0 percent in 1990 (1.55 million out of 39 million; *Church of England Year Book 1995*, 170-71). In an effort to close the gap between the number of the baptized (which is in any case shrinking) and the number of practicing Christians, some Anglicans are calling for greater discipline in baptismal use, while others stress baptism as an instrument of evangelization and reject any move that might seem to turn the Church of England into a mere "voluntarist association," such as they consider the → free churches to be.

2.4.2. Inculturation

In many cultures in Africa and the Pacific, young people go through rites of passage as → initiation into social units. Debates among → missionaries and in national churches (→ Third World 2.5) have continued as to whether such rites are compatible with Christian rites of catechumenate, baptism, and con-

firmation; whether the Christian and the local initiations are mutually exclusive; or whether Christian practice may adopt, adapt, and integrate at least certain features from the indigenous ceremonies.

Such questions may focus, for example, on personal names. Sometimes the baptized have been required to take names from the Bible or the calendar of saints; sometimes they have been allowed to retain local names, although these often carry indigenous religious freight; sometimes vernacular names have been created by the baptized that show a more active effort to transform the native culture. To adjust baptism to cultural distinctives, Filipino Benedictine A. J. Chupungco suggests that "distinctive elements" from "native initiation ceremonies" may, when purged of → superstition, "add local color to the revised rite of baptism"; they "can root the sacrament of baptism in the people's initiatory traditions and thus enrich their understanding of it" (*Liturgies,* 125-39; *Liturgical Inculturation,* 134-74).

2.4.3. Encounters with Other Religions

In its response to *BEM,* the → Church of South India indicates some of the issues that arise in connection with baptism amid a culture that is deeply imbued with religious values other than Christian. Thus, "some feel that repetition of baptism or re-baptism is not contrary to the Indian religious practice of dipping in sacred rivers." However, it is also asserted that "in the present situation in India, baptism is a great disadvantage to the poorer sections of the community. Privileges that are given to the scheduled → castes and scheduled tribes and privileges stop as soon as a person becomes a Christian by baptism." Posed here, from two different directions, is the question of the distinctiveness of the Christian faith and the church. Could it indeed be true — what the response of the Church of South India apparently wants to discountenance — that "baptism somehow implies moving from one culture to another" (→ Culture and Christianity)?

Bibliography: G. AUSTIN, *Anointing with the Spirit: The Rite of Confirmation–the Use of Oil and Chrism* (New York, 1985) • P. F. BRADSHAW, "Christian Initiation: A Study in Diversity," *The Search for the Origins of Christian Worship: Sources and Methods for the Study of Early Liturgy* (New York, 1992) 161-84 • R. BURNISH, *The Meaning of Baptism: A Comparison of the Teaching and Practice of the Fourth Century with the Present Day* (London, 1985) • A. J. CHUPUNGCO, *Liturgical Inculturation* (Collegeville, Minn., 1992); idem, *Liturgies of the Future: The Process and Methods of Inculturation* (New York, 1989) • B. FISCHER, *Redemptionis mysterium. Studien zur Osterfeier und zur christlichen Initiation* (Paderborn,

1992) • J. D. C. FISHER, *Christian Initiation: Baptism in the Medieval West* (London, 1965); idem, *Christian Initiation: The Reformation Period* (London, 1970) • C. JONES, G. WAINWRIGHT, and E. YARNOLD, eds., *The Study of Liturgy* (rev. ed.; New York, 1992) 111-83 ("Initiation") • A. KAVANAGH, *The Shape of Baptism: The Rite of Christian Initiation* (New York, 1978) • D. MOODY, *Baptism: Foundation for Christian Unity* (Philadelphia, 1967) • M. ROOT and R. SAARINEN, eds., *Baptism and the Unity of the Church* (Grand Rapids, 1998) • E. SCHLINK, *The Doctrine of Baptism* (St. Louis, 1972) • A. SCHMEMANN, *Of Water and the Spirit: A Liturgical Study of Baptism* (Crestwood, N.Y., 1974) • M. SEARLE, *Christening: The Making of Christians* (Collegeville, Minn., 1980) • A. STENZEL, *Die Taufe. Eine genetische Erklärung der Taufliturgie* (Innsbruck, 1958) • K. STEVENSON, *The Mystery of Baptism in the Anglican Tradition* (Norwich, 1998) • M. D. STREGE, ed., *Baptism and Church: A Believers' Church Vision* (Grand Rapids, 1986) • M. THURIAN, ed., *Churches Respond to BEM* (6 vols.; Geneva, 1986-88) • G. WAINWRIGHT, *Christian Initiation* (Richmond, Va., 1969) • E. C. WHITAKER, *The Baptismal Liturgy* (London, 1965; 2d ed., 1981); idem, *Documents of the Baptismal Liturgy* (London, 1960; 2d ed., 1970) • WORLD ALLIANCE OF REFORMED CHURCHES, *Baptists and Reformed in Dialogue* (Geneva, 1984) • WORLD COUNCIL OF CHURCHES, *Baptism, Eucharist, and Ministry* (Geneva, 1982); idem, *Baptism, Eucharist, and Ministry, 1982-1990: Report on the Process and Responses* (Geneva, 1990); idem, *Becoming a Christian: The Ecumenical Implications of Our Common Baptism* (Geneva, 1997).

GEOFFREY WAINWRIGHT

3. Baptism in the United States

3.1. *Colonial Period and Nineteenth Century*

Colonial Christians brought to the Americas particular European attitudes and practices regarding baptism. In the colonial period the → conversion (§1) and baptism of Native Americans were a major concern of many of the earliest Christian settlers. Priests and monks established missions and, with mixed success, baptized converts, afterward offering brief instruction. In the early 17th century → Franciscans baptized as many as 86,000 Indians in New Mexico.

Protestant immigrants, however, confronted new challenges to their traditional baptismal theology. New England → Puritans continued to practice the baptism of infants while bestowing full church membership only on those who made a → confession of faith in adulthood. Problems developed, however, when baptized infants reached adulthood but were unable to confess conversion. Although they might

be moral and God-fearing, they were considered unconverted and were unable to present their own children for baptism. The famous Half-Way Covenant of 1662 was one response to this dilemma. It permitted the baptism of those infants whose parents were unconverted but required a profession of faith before they could receive church membership or the Lord's Supper (→ Eucharist). In the southern colonies, Anglicans also retained infant baptism, but a shortage of clergy and the distance between settlements meant that many children went unbaptized for years. Colonial Anglicans were among the first religious groups to evangelize and baptize → slaves.

Religious revivals of the 18th and 19th centuries brought many new converts into the churches. With → religious liberty, denominations old and new were forced to compete for members. Such competition led to a renewal of biblical primitivism, the claim that one tradition was closest to the original NT church. Preachers of various → denominations debated which of their traditions was most biblical. Methodist (→ Methodism) circuit rider Peter Cartwright (1785-1872) declared that the Baptists made so much ado about immersion that "the uninformed would suppose that heaven was an island and the only way to get there was by swimming." Alexander Campbell (1788-1866) claimed to have restored biblical Christianity based on simple → faith and immersion baptism "for the remission of sins" (Acts 2:38).

3.2. *Baptists*

→ Baptists, the first immersionists in America, often mocked as Dunkers or Dippers, were frequently harassed by religious establishments in colonial New England and Virginia. Roger Williams (ca. 1603-83) established the first Baptist church in America, in Providence, Rhode Island (1639), following his exile by Massachusetts Puritans (→ Baptists 1). On the 19th-century frontier, Baptists were known for their preaching, the democracy of their churches, and their outdoor baptisms. These were dramatic events carried out in streams and rivers with the congregation gathered on the banks singing hymns, weeping, or shouting while converts and preachers, often dressed in white, entered the water. Afterward, the new believer was welcomed with open arms by the waiting community. It was a powerful and picturesque → symbol.

Baptists often spoke of baptism and the Lord's Supper as ordinances, commanded by Christ for the church. Some Baptist groups (e.g., Primitive, Old Regular Baptists) added foot washing as a third ordinance, usually observed along with the Supper.

Baptist competition with other denominations influenced the development of a specific form of biblical primitivism known as Old Landmarkism (from Prov. 22:28). Landmarkists claimed that only Baptist churches constituted the true church of Christ, with Baptists alone holding the authority to administer baptism and the Lord's Supper. Theirs was the only valid church order preserved since the NT era. All other religious groups were merely "societies" and had no direct ties to the → primitive Christian community. Claiming the only true baptism, Landmark Baptists rejected what they called alien immersion (i.e., baptism in non-Baptist churches). They denied the validity of infant baptism and required the immersion (or reimmersion) of any who had been baptized outside the Baptist fold. Many contemporary Baptist churches demand immersion for those who come from other Christian communions.

Another serious question for Baptists involved the appropriate age for baptism. Early Baptists in England and America promoted baptism of adult believers. By the late 19th and early 20th centuries, many Baptists began to encourage the baptism of children. This was particularly true in the Southern Baptist Convention, the largest Protestant denomination in the United States. This lowering of the baptismal age is due to several factors. First, it is a result of Baptist efforts to nurture children in the faith. Second, since infants and young children were considered under grace, the question arose as to the time when they became morally and spiritually accountable. Many believe that as children reach the "age of accountability," when they are responsible to God, they become candidates for conversion and baptism. This idea has led to the baptism of large numbers of children, some even under the age of six.

Some Baptist groups continue to baptize only adults or adolescents. Among the → Calvinistic Old Regular Baptists the average is around 30 or 40, while for the more evangelistic Missionary Baptists the average age at baptism is between 12 and 16. Some rural Baptist congregations continue to hold outdoor immersions, but most churches have indoor baptismal pools (→ Baptistery). The ordinance (sacrament) is usually administered during the Sunday → worship service. Candidates and ministers often wear white robes as a sign of purity and new life. Candidates may make a simple oral confession of faith in Jesus Christ, followed by a common minister's rubric such as, "Upon your profession of faith in our Lord and Savior Jesus Christ, I baptize you in the name of the Father, the Son and the Holy Spirit." Early Baptists in Europe and America sometimes practiced the → laying on of hands as a sign of the Holy Spirit. That ritual is not widespread among Baptists in the 20th century.

3.3. *The Present Situation*

Baptism by immersion is also practiced by various other Christian denominations in the United States. These include certain branches of the → Mennonites, numerous → Pentecostal churches, → Adventists, and the various segments of the Restorationist tradition.

3.3.1. Pentecostal denominations such as the Assemblies of God and the Church of God (Cleveland, Tenn.) developed a baptismal theology that included two types of baptism. The first involved water baptism by immersion as a sign of conversion. The second baptism is known as the baptism of the Holy Spirit, outwardly expressed not with water but with → glossolalia. This event follows conversion and is evidence of another transforming experience in the life of the Christian.

3.3.2. The → ecumenical movement of the 20th century increased → dialogue among the denominations regarding the nature of baptism, its mode, and its meaning in American churches. While most communions retained traditional forms — infant baptism, sprinkling, affusion, or immersion — dialogue has focused on the recognition of baptism across denominational lines (see 2.3). The 1960s and 1970s were also a time of liturgical revision (→ Liturgy 6.3) characterized by new forms for baptism and the Lord's Supper among Lutherans and United Methodists, while Roman Catholics and Episcopalians gave renewed emphasis to baptism as "a radical, life-changing, revolutionary experience of conversion into the faith" (W. Willimon, 120-21). Although Roman Catholics retain infant baptism as normative for those nurtured in the church, they too are now ready to give baptism by immersion to adults. In fact, many newly constructed Roman Catholic churches include baptismal pools.

3.3.3. A kind of popular ecumenism is evident in the growth of so-called megachurches, a phenomenon in American ecclesiology near the end of the century. Megachurches are congregations of several thousand members organized around a charismatic pastor-administrator, providing specialized programs for selected subgroups, and employing specific business-marketing techniques. Megachurches tend to minimize denominational differences and appeal to persons reared in various Christian traditions. Many of these churches thus honor various baptismal modes and practices, often minimizing or at least reformulating the role and meaning of baptism in the congregation. Most permit baptism of infants and adults by sprinkling or immersion. As one megachurch pastor in Detroit, Michigan, observed, "We don't want baptism to become a barrier that would keep anyone away from Christianity" (M. Marty, 663).

In spite of such comments, it is possible that American Christians are on the verge of a theological and liturgical rediscovery of baptism. In an increasingly secular environment, American Christians are called upon to affirm and enact the doctrines and rituals that give identity to Christian community.

Bibliography: S. AHLSTROM, *A Religious History of the American People* (New Haven, 1972) • P. CARTWRIGHT, *The Autobiography of Peter Cartwright* (New York, 1856) • H. DORGAN, *Giving Glory to God in Appalachia* (Knoxville, Tenn., 1987) • M. E. MARTY, "M.E.M.O.," *CCen,* July 1-8, 1992, 663 • D. J. WEBER, *The Spanish Frontier in North America* (New Haven, 1992) • W. WILLIMON, *Word, Water, Wine, and Bread* (Valley Forge, Pa., 1980).

BILL J. LEONARD

4. Baptism in Germany

4.1. *Changes*

Infant baptism (except within the Jewish population) was long taken for granted in Germany as part of normal → family life. In the second half of the 19th century this situation perhaps was no longer true in some working-class areas in the large → cities, but it was only in the 1970s that this form of baptismal practice could no longer be assumed. A change in parental attitudes rather than any dogmatically based criticism produced the shift in practice.

4.1.1. The number of so-called later baptisms of children between the ages of 1 and 14 rose from 7 percent in 1963 to 12 percent in 1989, with 27 percent in West Berlin. → Confirmation instruction came to be linked with baptism, and the denominations practicing so-called believers' baptism in many cases offered it at the age for confirmation. Even those baptized early no longer received the → sacrament immediately upon birth. The baptism of adults was still rare (2 percent of all baptisms in 1989). In the former East Germany antichurch propaganda from the mid-1950s onward greatly reduced the number of those who desired baptism, and only a minority of young people there are now baptized. In sum, infant baptism is no longer the obvious rule, and with so many young people leaving the church, it is not likely to become so again in the near future.

4.1.2. Some of the responsibility for the change rests on policies relating to → church and state (§1), especially in the East, that mean → church membership itself is no longer something that is taken for granted. As analysis shows (C. Grethlein), changes in baptismal practice reflect changes in the motivation of a desire for baptism. Traditional guidance is less important. Baptism represents deliberate choice. The decline of attachment to a traditional family and the increase of formal training that is often linked to mobility strengthen the trend. Research suggests that baptism has lost its significance as a threshold. Generational caution is also a factor in a society of high risk (see H. O. Wölber [1913-89]). Hence the desire to have a child baptized often expresses openness to faith rather than conviction. New pastoral approaches are needed as a result.

4.1.3 The situation is dramatically different in the former East Germany. There most of the people are unbaptized, and have been so for two or three generations. This situation has produced a deep skepticism — even to some extent an aversion — toward the church and religion, all as a result of the 40-year-period of government atheistic propaganda.

4.2. *New Approaches in Practical Theology*

The changes sketched above, along with criticisms of the way → occasional services are commonly handled, have produced proposals for renewal that are based on experience.

4.2.1. In 1973 R. Leuenberger described the tension between the → church's teaching and the human situation, which resulted in baptism undertaken primarily because of wishes to conform, rather than out of conviction. He suggested a longer, obligatory catechumenate for parents as a criterion of selection in the national church. C. Gabler, C. Schmid, and P. Siber, in the context of experience in Swiss congregations, then proposed models of group conversations on baptism for parents that would be shorter and voluntary.

4.2.2. Alongside these proposals directed primarily at the baptism of infants and small children, and together with a suggested blessing of infants, came the radical demand that only older children of nine or ten should receive baptism (R. Stuhlmann). This proposal aimed at lessening the tension between the biblical understanding of baptism and popular expectations, while also taking into account how much children can experience. A question arises whether this proposal does not stress the cognitive side of baptism too heavily.

4.2.3. In both content and method the 1989 Berlin Conference on Baptism opened up new vistas. It viewed baptism as "the sacrament of the new → creation" linked to → ecology. P. Cornehl thus argued that there should be an open age for baptism and that forms should be worked out in keeping with the candidates' different situations. In some ways, however, the creative possibilities stood only loosely related to baptism.

4.2.4. A 1993 study then equated the invitation to

baptism with an invitation to life. It took into account the great variety we find in congregations and at the same time tried to offer a congregational model that is plainly to be identified as Christian. Under the stimulus of baptism-oriented congregational structure in Norway, it tried to show at what points in church work there is a vital reminder of baptism and the offering of an invitation to it. The cross, the name, the hand, water, and light were listed as the five basic → symbols of baptism that provide a model that makes possible a clear relating of the biblical message to life in the modern world. From the example of the → early church, the suggestion was made that we should find accepted times for baptism (→ Easter), link it to the → Eucharist, and develop forms that engage all the senses. The thorny question of → godparents went unanswered.

A second volume was published in 1995, containing recommendations concerning the introduction of baptism for older children and confirmands. It also attempts to address issues specific to the former East Germany.

4.2.5. In general, baptism has again become an important issue in → practical theology. Yet, while we find new and interesting approaches cybernetically, congregationally, and liturgically, in terms of → pastoral care our understanding of baptism has not progressed much except for the preparation of the person to be baptized or his or her parents. The discovery of baptism as an aid in pastoral counseling probably presupposes insight into the power of baptism of the sort that is actually more intimated than really being practiced as it looks back to the early church and as it deals with modern theories of ritual and symbols.

→ Identity; Initiation Rites; Socialization 4

Bibliography: R. BLANK and C. GRETHLEIN, eds., *Einladung zur Taufe. Einladung zum Leben* (Stuttgart, 1993-95) • P. CORNEHL et al., "Auf dem Weg zur Erneuerung der Taufpraxis. Thesen zum 23. Deutscher Evangelischer Kirchentag," *ZGDP* 8 (1990) 20-22 • C. GÄBLER, C. SCHMID, and P. SIBER, *Kinder christlich erziehen* (Berlin, 1979) • C. GRETHLEIN, *Taufpraxis heute* (Gütersloh, 1988) • INSTITUTT FOR KRISTEN OPPSEDING, *Dåpspraksis og dåpsopplæring i den norske kirke* (Bjørkelangen, 1982) • R. LEUENBERGER, *Taufe in der Krise* (Stuttgart, 1973) • C. LIENEMANN-PERRIN, ed., *Taufe und Kirchenzugehörigkeit* (Munich, 1983) • R. ROOSEN, *Taufe lebendig. Taufsymbolik neu verstehen* (Hannover, 1990) • U. STEFFEN, *Taufe* (Stuttgart, 1988) • R. STUHLMANN, "Kindertaufe statt Säuglingstaufe," *PTh* 80 (1991) 184-204 • H.-O. WÖLBER, *Religion ohne Entscheidung* (Göttingen, 1959).

CHRISTIAN GRETHLEIN

5. Church Law

5.1. *General Features*

The baptismal command of Matt. 28:19 represents a basic biblical directive in → church law. It governs the rule in all Christian churches (E. Wolf) and thus gives baptism a significance that transcends all denominational boundaries. The law of baptism precedes all the other main provisions of church law (H. Dombois), even though it may itself be influenced by denominationally specific thinking on the subject.

5.2. *Roman Catholics*

The → Codex Iuris Canonici (1983) of the → Roman Catholic Church finds in baptism a → sacrament that by an indelible mark incorporates a person into the → church (§3.2.4) and opens the door to the other sacraments (cans. 204, 849). All the baptized are Christians and always remain so; as such, they are subject to divine law, even though they leave the church. They are obliged to keep only the church's laws (can. 11). Those who, as catechumens, ask for baptism are already in relation to the church (can. 208).

Rules govern comprehensively the administration of baptism (cans. 849-78). Prerequisites are instruction in the case of adults (→ Catechesis 2.1; Catechism 3) and, in the case of children, the instructing of parents and → godparents, who have a part to play in the Christian → education that must follow. Normally → bishops, → priests (§3), or → deacons administer baptism, especially parish priests (→ Pastor, Pastorate, 1 and 2.2.1) or those appointed by them. With their official permission (→ Dimissorial) other ordained ministers may also perform the baptism. Any persons may give → emergency baptism, even the unbaptized and unbelievers, as long as they intend to do what the church does and observe the prescribed form. This form requires dipping in or pouring of clean water and the use of the → Trinitarian formula. The preferred time is a → Sunday or → Easter Eve. Infants should receive baptism in the first few weeks of life. The priest may delay it only if there is no hope of Catholic teaching. The proper place for baptism is the font. Records of baptisms are kept in → church registers.

5.3. *Orthodox and Anglicans*

Church law (§4.2-3) does not greatly differ for the Orthodox and the Anglicans. Orthodoxy, however, requires trine immersion in pure, natural water and allows sprinkling only in case of sickness or water shortage. → Anointing (confirmation) with episcopally consecrated oil follows at once (see 2.2.2). The Church of England (→ Anglican Communion) prescribes signing the candidate with the sign of the →

cross immediately after baptism (strongly opposed by Puritans in the 16th and 17th centuries), and also requires three godparents. Baptisms preferably occur as part of Sunday worship in the presence of the congregation.

5.4. *Protestants*

Most Protestant churches follow similar rules. Baptism admits a person to → church membership. The basic baptismal confession (→ Confession of Faith) suffices for those changing denominations, except in cases of renunciation of membership or → conversion (§2).

Rules relating to infant baptism have become more relaxed in → Reformed and → united churches. Delay no longer comes under → church discipline but is now accepted, even in the case of ordained ministers if there are conscientious objections. Christian education is offered to unbaptized children, and their church membership may even be recognized, perhaps by means of a ceremony such as blessing (see 4.2.2). A disputed point is whether such children, if receiving instruction, should be admitted to the → Eucharist as confirmands or in youth groups. These steps are all in the direction of the believers' baptism of the → Baptists and some → free churches.

5.5. *Ecumenical Questions*

As regards the → Roman Catholic Church, ecumenical questions are not so acute now that this church demands conditional baptism of converts only where there is serious doubt as to the validity of their earlier baptism (1983 CIC 869.2). The church regrets but understands the fact that some other churches require only witnesses and not godparents (can. 874.2). Problems still arise because where there is danger of death, baptism may be given to the children of non–Roman Catholic parents (can. 868.2), but Roman Catholic parents might be punished if they let their children receive non–Roman Catholic baptism (can. 1365). Canonists are trying to find an ecumenically acceptable interpretation.

Protestant churches recognize each other's baptisms as long as they meet the basic requirements of the baptismal procedure, something they find not to be the case, for example, in the baptism of the → Christian Community. In light of the variant forms in some African churches and the doubts expressed by Baptists and free churches concerning the validity of infant baptism, the 1982 Lima Declaration (see 2.3) urges all the churches involved to reconsider the practical aspects of their positions. Some common practice (i.e., some kind of ecumenical baptism) might be possible in the case of → mixed marriages (→ Wedding Ceremony).

Bibliography: W. AYMANS and K. MÖRSDORF, "Kanonisches Recht," *Lehrbuch aufgrund des Codex Iuris Canonici* (vol. 1; Paderborn, 1991) 288-307 • *Canons Ecclesiastical Promulgated by the Convocations of Canterbury and York in 1964 and 1968* (London, 1969) B21-25 • P. F. X. COVINO, "The Post-Conciliar Infant-Baptism Debate in the American Catholic Church," *Worship* 56 (1982) 240-60 • R. H. DOMBOIS, *Recht der Gnade* (2 vols.; Witten, 1969; Bielefeld, 1974) 1.296-362; 2.219-22 • H. FROST, *Strukturprobleme evangelischer Kirchenverfassung* (Göttingen, 1972) 67-68 • E. A. HIEROLD, "Taufe," *Handbuch des katholischen Kirchenrechts* (ed. J. Listl et al.; Regensburg, 1983) 659-79 • P. KRÄMER, *Kirchenrecht* (vol. 1; Stuttgart, 1992) 79-84 (Roman Catholic) • T. LORENZEN, "Baptism and Church-Membership: Some Baptist Positions and Their Ecumenical Implications," *JES* 18 (1981) 561-74 • N. MILAS, *Das Kirchenrecht der morgenländischen Kirche* (2d ed.; Mostar, 1905) 490-92 • E. G. MOORE, *An Introduction to English Canon Law* (Oxford, 1967) 67-70 • A. STEIN, *Evangelisches Kirchenrecht* (3d ed.; Neuwied, 1992) • G. WENDT, "Rechtsstellung des Gemeindeglieds," *Das Recht der Kirche* (vol. 3; ed. G. Rau, H.-R. Reuter, and K. Schlaich; Gütersloh, 1994) 22-28 • E. WOLF, *Ordnung der Kirche* (Frankfurt, 1961) 530-34 • WORLD COUNCIL OF CHURCHES, *Baptism, Eucharist, and Ministry* (Geneva, 1982).

ALBERT STEIN

Baptism, Emergency → Emergency Baptism

Baptism, Heretical → Heretical Baptism

Baptismal Font

The baptismal font (Lat. *piscina* [tank, basin] or *fons baptismalis*) is a receptacle of stone, metal, or wood that holds the water consecrated for use in → baptism. As long as immersion was the rule in the early church, baptism took place in open water or in a large bath in a separate → chapel, the *baptisterium* (→ Baptistery), or in the atrium of the → basilica. Its shape was round or polygonal.

In missionary areas baptism by affusion became common, and hence a freestanding font became possible. Yet immersion was customary into the 16th century, though small fonts were adequate because infant baptism had become the rule. From the 15th century onward, affusion increasingly established itself in the West. Since this manner demanded less water, bowls and other implements for pouring came into use, these being set in the fonts.

In the Middle Ages the font was placed at the entrance of churches (i.e., the west end), though it often appeared in the *capella regia* (a chapel within a Romanesque church, mostly in Germany, used by the king or a prince or any other honored person). A curious custom was to put the font toward the north side, with a special door by which the exorcised demon could exit to a northern, unconsecrated part of the churchyard. → Reformation churches prefer to put the font in front of the altar in clear view of all the congregation. The Puritans in England had strong objections to fonts as unbiblical, though the basins they preferred hardly seemed to be more biblical. Fonts and dippers often were decorated symbolically with depictions representing baptismal promises, Christ's baptism, the water of life, or the four rivers of Paradise.

Bibliography: R. BAUERREISS, *Fons sacer* (Munich, 1949) • S. BEDARD, *The Symbolism of the Baptismal Font in Early Christian Thought* (Washington, D.C., 1951) • F. BOND, *Fonts and Font Covers* (London, 1908) • J. G. DAVIES, *The Architectural Setting of Baptism* (London, 1962) • A. GABLER, "Taufkufen und Taufkessel im einstigen Bereich des Bistums Augsburg," *Mün.* 27 (1974) 137-41 • A. GOMMEL, *Tauf- und Abendmahlsgeräte aus evangelischen Kirchen in Württemberg* (Stuttgart, 1969) • A. HENZE, "Das Taufbecken in Freckenhorst," *Mün.* 3 (1950) 25-30 • A. REINLE, *Die Ausstattung deutscher Kirchen im Mittelalter* (Darmstadt, 1980) 32-39 • S. A. STAUFFER, *On Baptismal Fonts: Ancient and Modern* (Washington, D.C., 1994).

GERLINDE STROHMAIER-WIEDERANDERS

Baptist World Alliance

The Baptist World Alliance arose in 1905 in London as an alliance of Baptist unions and now has its headquarters near Washington, D.C. According to its constitution, it seeks to represent the essential unity of Baptists in the Lord Jesus Christ, to strengthen brotherhood, and to promote the spirit of fellowship, service, and cooperation among its members. It does not infringe upon the independence of the participating congregations and unions. It holds a world congress every five years. Its main work takes place in study commissions and relief activities. In 1992 its fellowship included 165 conventions and unions with 37.8 million members in 146,000 churches, most in North America. Only a few of the unions belong to the → World Council of Churches. Conversations have been held with the → World Alliance of Reformed Churches and are planned with other churches.

Bibliography: F. T. LORD, *Baptist World Fellowship: A Short History of the Baptist World Alliance* (Nashville, 1955) • *1992 Yearbook of the Baptist World Alliance* (Washington, D.C., 1992) • W. B. SHURDEN, *The Life of Baptists in the Life of the World: 80 Years of the Baptist World Alliance* (Nashville, 1985) • C. W. TILLER, *The Twentieth Century Baptist: Chronicles of the Baptists in the First Seventy-Five Years of the Baptist World Alliance* (Valley Forge, Pa., 1980).

EDUARD SCHÜTZ

Baptistery

Originally the term *baptisterium* denoted the basin in the *frigidarium* (cold bath) of the Roman baths. From the fourth century it came into use for the *piscina* (Lat. for "tank, basin"), or baptismal church. Other names were *balneus* and *loutron* (bath) and, among Christians, *phōtistērion* (enlightenment). From the third century certain cultic places were set apart for the purpose of → baptism. In keeping with the form and situation of the *piscina*, these were often round or octagonal with surrounding pillars, upper lighting, and a cupola. Such forms derived from the architecture of Roman baths and palaces. We also find square rooms with an apse containing the pool. As a rule, the baptistery was an annex to the atrium (forecourt) or to the narthex (entrance hall), or in the side aisle of the cathedral, parish church, or monastic church (→ Church Architecture). As infant baptism replaced adult baptism, the → baptismal font replaced the baptismal pool in churches.

Many Protestant denominations in the United States and elsewhere (e.g., Baptists, Disciples of Christ, various Pentecostal groups) still practice baptism by total immersion. In their churches the baptistery is not a separate building or room but a tank large enough to hold the water needed for immersion, often located behind the pulpit or choir area. In many rural American churches the wall behind the baptistery includes a mural depicting landscapes of the river Jordan. More recently, some new or refurbished Roman Catholic churches in the United States (e.g., the Cathedral of the Assumption in Louisville, Ky.) have included baptisteries for use in the total immersion of adults.

Bibliography: J. G. DAVIES, *The Architectural Setting of Baptism* (London, 1962) • F. W. DEICHMANN, "Baptisterium," *RGG* (3d ed.) 1.867-69 • A. KHATCHATRIAN, *Les baptistères paléochrétiens* (Paris, 1962); idem, *Origine et typologie des baptistères paléochrétiens* (Mulhouse, 1982) • F. X. MURPHY, "Baptistery," *NCE* 2.74-75.

URS PESCHLOW and BILL J. LEONARD

Baptists

1. Name and History

The name "Baptist" was originally a derogatory name used by opponents who wanted to call attention to the Baptists' distinctive practice of believers' baptism. Baptists themselves would have preferred to be known more as a congregational movement than as a baptismal movement.

The Baptists developed in England out of English → Puritanism, or more strictly out of → Congregationalism, which formed congregations independent of the state and the state church (→ Separatism). The Baptist impulse probably came by way of the → Mennonites, who baptized by pouring.

Because of persecution, some Separatists emigrated to Holland, where in 1609 the first Baptist congregation began under the leadership of J. Smyth (ca. 1554-1612). Some of this first congregation soon returned home, forming the first Baptist church on English soil in the London suburb of Spitalfields (1611/12) under the lawyer T. Helwys (ca. 1550-ca. 1616). Accepting → Arminianism, they taught the universal reconciliation of the race by God in Christ, which individual Christians ratify by their → faith. This group came to be called General Baptists. Alongside them there developed the Particular Baptists, who, under the influence of Calvinism, taught the reconciliation of specific people whom God has predestined to salvation (→ Calvin's Theology). From 1640 onward this latter group baptized by immersion, which they made obligatory in the London Confession (1644). The General Baptists also adopted immersion, and it is now the universal custom among Baptists. In the 19th century the two groups came together in a union, having settled their conflict about → reconciliation and predestination.

In general, the Baptists supported Oliver Cromwell (1599-1658), but they championed freedom of conscience and of the press (see J. Milton). At the Restoration (1660), they suffered persecution. For example, J. Bunyan (1628-88) was in prison when he wrote his *Pilgrim's Progress,* which became one of the most widely circulated books of edification (→

Devotional Literature 2). The awakening associated with → Methodism in the 18th century and the preaching of Baptist pastor C. H. → Spurgeon (1834-1892) in the 19th century helped the spread of the Baptists. The founding of a missionary society by W. Carey (1761-1834) played an essential part in initiating the "century of Protestant missions" (K. S. Latourette).

In North America Roger Williams (ca. 1603-83) founded the first Baptist congregation in Providence, Rhode Island, in 1639. He established this colony on a basis of → religious liberty. The Great Awakening in the 18th century and the Second Great Awakening in the 19th century brought rapid growth to the Baptists in America. Baptist lay preachers were most successful in the new and freer areas of the West, where they had no preexisting religious traditions to contend with. They were particularly successful in the South among both the black (→ Black Churches 1) and the white population.

In 1845 Baptists in America divided over the issue of → slavery (§3). This resulted in the creation of the more socially conservative Southern Baptist Convention and the Northern (or, from 1950, the American) Baptist Convention, which has been more open to modern theological movements and has contributed to them (e.g., W. → Rauschenbusch and the → Social Gospel; H. Cox). The Southern Baptist Convention — the largest Baptist entity anywhere in the world — is no longer limited to the American South but has penetrated into the North and the West, and even, through a vigorous foreign mission program, around much of the world. While the Northern (American) Baptist Convention was racked by fundamentalist controversies and schisms in the 1920s and 1930s, the Southern Baptist Convention managed to postpone these theological battles until the 1980s and 1990s. In these later decades, the seminaries and the mission boards frequently have become the focal points for struggles between the "moderates" and the "conservatives." Historic Baptist commitment to religious liberty and the priesthood of the believer has to some degree been compromised in the course of this continuing and partisan activity.

Black Baptists began to form their own denominational structures in the second half of the 19th century. By 1994 they were gathered largely in three groups: the National Baptist Convention, U.S.A., Inc. (8.2 million members); the National Baptist Convention of America (3.5 million); and the Progressive National Baptist Convention (2.5 million). These three groups represent by far the largest group of Christian Afro-Americans in the United States. Baptist African Americans, including M. L. → King Jr.

(1929-68), A. Young (b. 1932), and J. Jackson (b. 1941), were prominent in the civil rights movement of the 1960s, which had links to the earlier Social Gospel movement.

In continental Europe the Baptists owe their origin to J. G. Oncken (1800-1884) of Varel in Oldenburg, Germany. Oncken had come to know the free churches when serving as assistant to a merchant in Scotland and England. He came to Hamburg as an agent of the Continental Society, distributing Bibles and tracts and setting up private meetings for edification. In 1825, with the Lutheran pastor J. W. Rautenberg (1791-1865), he started the first → Sunday school in St. Georg. In 1834 he and six others had themselves baptized by B. Sears, an American professor of theology, and founded the first Baptist church. Oncken's extensive missionary travels and the sending out of workers — often journeymen — laid the basis for the modern Baptist movement in Europe.

The most notable growth was in Russia. The Russian Baptist Union (1884), with ties to Oncken, and the Union of Evangelical Christians (1908), with ties to English Baptists, both grew after 1905 and especially after the 1917 revolution. By 1927 the former had some 500,000 adherents, the latter, more than 4 million. The two groups combined in 1944, forming the All-Union Council of Evangelical Christians–Baptists. There also were also 15,000 Baptist *Initsiativnikis* who refused to be officially registered by the government of the USSR.

2. Numbers

The → Baptist World Alliance was founded in 1905, and by 1992 its fellowship included 165 conventions/unions from 98 countries with some 146,000 member churches. The number of baptized adherents (not counting children and friends) is estimated at 37.8 million (Europe 0.7 million, Asia and the Pacific 2.6, North America 30.6, South America 1.3, Africa 2.3, and Central America and Caribbean 0.3).

3. Doctrine

3.1. For Baptists, Holy Scripture is the only rule of faith and practice.

3.2. Baptists recognize no binding → confessions. Yet they have continually drawn up confessions to state their faith.

3.3. The church of Jesus Christ is a church of believers. As in the NT, faith is viewed both as a gift of God and as a human decision. Calling, → conversion (→ 1), and → regeneration are important factors in → soteriology. Church discipline is consistently practiced.

3.4. Faith and baptism go together. God begins his work with the proclamation of the → gospel as his saving word. Faith receives this word. Baptism follows as a confession of Christ (→ Confession of Faith) that the candidates make to God and others. Baptists describe in different ways the work of the triune God in baptism. They have a traditional reserve with regard to all sacramentalism, but their NT exegetes have taught them to stress afresh the work of God in baptism as Christ instituted it. They thus can say that those who receive baptism come to participate in the dying and rising again of Jesus Christ (→ Resurrection) and are appropriated to him as their Lord, receiving the gift of the → Holy Spirit to equip them for their new life of → discipleship, of imitating Christ. They are incorporated into the body of Christ and thus are received into the local congregation.

3.5. From the → Reformation, Baptists learned to place high value on the priesthood of all believers, which they see as fundamental to the Christian community as it has been founded by its Lord. Christ's community is for Baptists a charismatic community. → Charisma and office are not antithetical. Spiritual gifts and offices alike promote the gathering and expression of the community of Jesus Christ. In church decisions Baptists aim at → consensus, which they can recognize as a work of the Holy Spirit. A special feature is that they try not to wound the → conscience of individual Christians.

3.6. The community of Jesus Christ is always the local congregation. This does not mean that Baptists say nothing about the → church universal. They regard each local congregation as a manifestation of the one body of Christ.

4. Church and State

Baptists support the separation of → church and state and contend for → religious liberty. They distinguish this from toleration, which favors one church and simply bears with others. Very early, then, they took up the slogan "A free church in a free state." State and → society must make room both for belief and unbelief, for God alone is Judge. The Baptist and free church plea for freedom of belief, conscience, and assembly has helped to shape the modern → pluralist society. It does not mean, however, that Christian faith must be restricted to a private sphere, as one may easily see in church relations in the United States, the land preeminently of → free churches.

5. Mission and Evangelism

Baptists regard → mission and → evangelism as ongoing tasks of both the local church and individuals.

W. Carey and other Baptists pointed the way at the beginning of the modern missionary movement, and they have given stimulus to evangelism, especially mass evangelism (most notably, in the persons of D. L. → Moody, R. A. Torrey, and B. Graham). Oncken's slogan "Every Baptist a missionary" typifies the Baptist sense of mission and of a refusal to distinguish between home and foreign missions.

6. Catechumenate
Christian education (particularly the Sunday school) plays an important part. The growing generation should become familiar with the Christian faith through children's work and youth work. A personal decision of faith is needed for baptism, for which there is no fixed age. The churches also arrange Bible classes for adults, with Christian maturity as the goal.

7. Church Life and Worship
→ Worship stands at the heart of church life. It focuses on preaching and employs no set liturgy. The Lord's Supper is usually administered once a month. While this was once mainly a commemoration, it is now seen as the supper at which Christ awaits his own people at his table, though there is not any reflection on the nature of his presence. Baptism is the only other ordinance (not sacrament) recognized by Baptists.

Baptists support their work by freewill offerings, often representing a tithe, or 10 percent, of their income (→ Church Finances). Each congregation makes its own decisions and rules its own affairs through a board and the congregational meeting, in which all members have a voice and a vote. For full-time work the congregation typically calls an ordained pastor, who is often trained at a theological seminary or sometimes at a university with a final period at seminary. In America, formal education was lax in much of the 18th, 19th, and even 20th centuries. The → ordination of women is customary in some unions, but not in all (e.g., not in the Southern Baptist Convention).

Baptists prefer to have comprehensive congregations. Thus the average membership in Germany is between 100 and 750, with more than one pastor for larger congregations. In the United States, urban congregations may number in the thousands. In some churches average attendance at worship involves as much as 75 percent of the members. Congregations are characterized by many special-interest groups, which help individuals find a spiritual home in the churches.

8. Ecumenical Relations
Baptists have generally recognized and expressed their relationship to Christians of other → denomi-

nations. They did this especially through the Evangelical Alliance (→ World Evangelical Fellowship). Oncken was at the first meeting in London in 1846. At the local and national level Baptists often take part in working groups and church councils. In Europe most Baptist unions belong to the → Conference of European Churches (CEC). Only 16 Baptist unions (only 5 in Europe), however, belong to the World Council of Churches (WCC). At the world level, there is theological → dialogue between the Baptists and the → World Alliance of Reformed Churches, also the → Roman Catholic Church (from 1984). Thus far, only in the Church of North India have Baptists been ready to unite with churches that baptize infants, but the effects of this union may be seen in the WCC Lima declaration on baptism (par. 12 and commentary). In some instances one finds open fellowship, that is, the receiving of Christians from other churches into a Baptist church without baptism. In the United States, the Southern Baptist Convention has generally refrained from active ecumenical involvement.

9. Social Structure
Baptists were recruited at first from every social stratum (e.g., dockworkers in Hamburg, slaves in the United States, the industrial → proletariat in England or Brazil). But there is an unmistakable upward thrust, which is perhaps connected with the democratic structure of the churches, with education, and with church discipline. Today the Baptists are drawn mostly from the lower and middle classes (so esp. the Southern Baptists in the United States), but with an elite leadership. Four presidents of the United States (Harding, Truman, Carter, and Clinton) and one president of Liberia (Tubman) have emerged from their ranks as political leaders.

Bibliography: G. BALDERS, *Theurer Bruder Oncken* (Wuppertal, 1978) • R. DONAT, *Das wachsende Werk* (Kassel, 1960); idem, *Wie das Werk begann. Entstehung der Baptistengemeinden in Deutschland* (Kassel, 1958) • W. GUTSCHE, *Westliche Quellen des russische Stundismus* (Kassel, 1956) • J. D. HUGHEY, *Die Baptisten* (Kassel, 1959); idem, ed., *Die Baptisten* (Stuttgart, 1964) • W. KAHLE, *Der ostslawische Protestantismus in Rußland und der Sowjetunion* (Wuppertal, 1978) • J. LEHMAN, *Geschichte der deutschen Baptisten* (3d ed.; Kassel, 1923) • H. LUCKEY, *Johann Gerhard Oncken und die Anfänge des deutschen Baptismus* (Kassel, 1958) • W. L. LUMPKIN, *Baptist Confessions of Faith* (Philadelphia, 1959) • H. B. MOTEL, ed., *Glieder an einem Leib. Freikirchen in Selbstdarstellungen* (Constance, 1975) • P. J. PARIS, *The Social Teaching of the Black Churches* (Philadelphia, 1985) •

K. PARKER, *Baptists in Europe: History and Confessions of Faith* (Nashville, 1982) • R. G. TORBET, *A History of the Baptists* (2 vols.; Valley Forge, Pa., 1973) • J. WASHINGTON, *Frustrated Fellowship: The Black Baptist Quest for Social Power* (Macon, Ga., 1988) • G. WESTIN, *Der Weg der freien christlichen Gemeinden durch die Jahrhunderte* (Kassel, 1956).

EDUARD SCHÜTZ, with EDWIN S. GAUSTAD

Barbados

	1960	1980	2000
Population (1,000s):	231	249	264
Annual growth rate (%):	0.39	0.29	0.32
Area: 430 sq. km. (166 sq. mi.)			

A.D. 2000
Population density: 615/sq. km. (1,592/sq. mi.)
Births / deaths: 1.34 / 0.85 per 100 population
Fertility rate: 1.73 per woman
Infant mortality rate: 8 per 1,000 live births
Life expectancy: 77.1 years (m: 74.5, f: 79.4)
Religious affiliation (%): Christians 97.0 (Protestants 33.3, Anglicans 28.1, unaffiliated 21.2, indigenous 7.1, Roman Catholics 4.4, marginal 2.7, other Christians 0.2), Baha'is 1.2, other 1.8.

1. General Situation
2. Religious Situation

1. General Situation

The independent island nation of Barbados occupies the easternmost land mass in the West Indies. Archaeological evidence indicates that Arawak Indians maintained permanent settlements there beginning approximately A.D. 1000. First contacts with European explorers occurred probably in the early 1500s, when the Spanish landed in Barbados to seek slaves for their gold mines in Hispaniola. By the mid-1500s, no Indians remained, nor did a party of 80 English settlers under Henry Powell encounter any inhabitants when they established the first European settlement in 1627. Unlike any other island of the Caribbean, Barbados never changed hands from its original colonizer until it gained its own independence — on November 30, 1966. To a large extent, British traditions have remained part of the country's cultural fabric.

The early settlers established a parliament in 1639. About this time, they switched crops from tobacco and cotton to sugarcane, which led in turn to a major transformation from a society of mediocre smallholdings to a booming plantation economy. Laborers were required to work the plantations, for which the white planters turned to slaves imported from West Africa. The following two centuries witnessed a great increase in the relative number of blacks on Barbados — from only 1,000 out of 26,000 (1640) to 85,000 out of 100,000 (1834, the year slavery was abolished). This trend has continued to the present, with 96 percent of the population African or mixed African and Caribbean, and 4 percent European in 1994.

The prospering Barbadian economy survived the end of → slavery, although sociologically the white planter-merchant oligarchy long maintained its dominance at the expense of the improvement of the lot of the black majority. Workers' riots on Barbados in 1937 led to changes in British West Indian colonial policies, which in turn led to the entrance of black reformers into Barbadian politics and to a vibrant trade union movement (→ Labor Unions). Universal adult suffrage was achieved in 1951, ministerial government in 1954, and full internal self-government in 1961. Political equality, however, has not led to equality of access to economic power, for the three mainstays of the economy in the 1990s — tourism, agriculture, and manufacturing — are still largely controlled by the white minority (R. B. Potter and G. M. S. Dann, xxiii-xxiv).

Even in the 18th century, Barbados gained a reputation as a desirable tourist haven, originally because of its allegedly curative waters and moderate climate. (In 1751 George Washington, on his only journey outside what later became the United States, accompanied his half-brother Lawrence to Barbados for the relief of Lawrence's tuberculosis.) Subsequently the country has cultivated its image as "Little England" (maintaining, for example, its preference for the Anglican Church and for cricket), with the result that by the 1980s, → tourism accounted for as much as one-half of the gross national product.

2. Religious Situation

The largest religious group in Barbados is the → Anglican Church, with which 32.9 percent of the people identified themselves in the 1990 census. The constitution of 1966 declares that the people "acknowledge the supremacy of God," even as it grants complete freedom of conscience with respect to religious belief. From the earliest days, the Anglican Church was the established state church, with complete disestablishment occurring only in 1977.

The first religious groups to arrive after the Anglicans were the → Moravians (1765) and the → Methodists (1788), each of which sent missionaries to work among the slave population. The Methodists were the first to teach slave children to read and write, a program that was vigorously resisted by the white planters, who viewed slave → literacy as socially dangerous.

Between approximately 1890 and 1920, churches planted by mainly black Baptist, holiness, and Pentecostal missionaries from the United States were warmly embraced by poor blacks on Barbados. For the working classes of the black community, "the revivalist church emerged as expressive of their general rejection of the established Anglican church and other 'white-controlled' denominations. It also symbolised the denial by villagers that social respectability could only be gained by conformity to the dominant Anglicanism, and confirmed that some workers saw social legitimacy in terms of their own autonomous expressions" (G. Gmelch and S. B. Gmelch, 153). The most important of these groups were the Christian Mission (it began work in Barbados in 1891), → Salvation Army (1898), Pilgrim Holiness (1911), Church of God (Anderson, 1912), and Church of God (Cleveland, 1917 — later called the New Testament Church of God; → Churches of God).

At the time of the 1990 census, the four largest Christian groups after the Anglicans were the holiness and Pentecostal groups (collectively 12.6 percent), → Methodists (5.9 percent), Seventh-day → Adventists (4.5 percent), and Roman Catholics (4.4 percent).

In 1972 the Barbados Council of Evangelical Churches came into being, embracing 16 different church traditions, from conservative evangelical to WCC-oriented clergy. The regional → Caribbean Conference of Churches (CCC), founded in 1973, has its headquarters in Bridgetown, the Barbadian capital. The CCC, which comprises over 30 groups of Christians, includes representatives from all branches of Christendom.

Barbados has smaller groups of Baha'is, Muslims, and Hindus. Of concern to some is an increasing → materialism and → secularism, no doubt fostered by the growing national emphasis on tourism (Potter and Dann, xviii).

→ Colonialism 2; Holiness Movement; Pentecostal Churches; Roman Catholic Church

Bibliography: H. M. BECKLES, *A History of Barbados: From Amerindian Settlement to Nation-State* (Cambridge, 1990); idem, *Natural Rebels: A Social History of Enslaved Black Women in Barbados* (New Brunswick, N.J., 1989); idem, *White Servitude and Black Slavery in Barbados, 1627-1715* (Knoxville, Tenn., 1989) • T. CALLENDER and L. CALLENDER, *Concerns concerning the Co-caine Culture in Barbados and the Caribbean* (Bridgetown, Barbados, 1988) • S. R. CATWELL, *The Brethren in Barbados: Gospel Hall Assemblies, 1889-1994* (St. George, Barbados, 1995) • K. DAVIS, *Cross and Crown in Barbados* (Frankfurt, 1983) • G. GMELCH and S. B. GMELCH, *The Parish behind God's Back: The Changing Culture of Rural Barbados* (Ann Arbor, Mich., 1997) • J. S. HANDLER, *The Unappropriated People: Freedmen in the Slave Society of Barbados* (Baltimore, 1974) • W. P. HANDWERKER, *Women's Power and Social Revolution: Fertility Transition in the West Indies* (Beverly Hills, Calif., 1989) • F. A. HOYOS, *Barbados: A History from the Amerindians to Independence* (2d ed.; London, 1992) • D. I. MITCHELL, ed., *New Mission for a New People: Voices from the Caribbean* (New York, 1977) describes the work of the CCC • R. B. POTTER and G. M. S. DANN, *Barbados* (Oxford, 1987) bibliography.

THE EDITORS

Barmen Declaration

1. The "Theological Declaration on the Present State of the German Evangelical Church," or Barmen Declaration, was formulated by K. → Barth (1886-1968), H. Asmussen (1898-1968), and T. Breit (1880-1966). Barth was its theological father. At the first confessing synod of the church at Barmen-Gemarke on May 31, 1934, it was unanimously adopted by 139 delegates from 25 state and provincial churches. The boldness of the synod in rejecting the legitimacy of the → church government and regarding itself as truly representing the church formed its backbone and became the spiritual center of resistance for the → Confessing Church.

The Barmen Declaration was directed against the threat to the church posed by the so-called → German Christians. This group, which the state supported as part of its effort to eliminate all opposition, had by 1933 achieved a great deal of power in the churches and was now flooding them with teachings tied to National Socialist ideology, namely, an "authentically German belief in Christ" and an affirmation of the "divine ordering of race, people, and nation" (from a German Christian publication of June 6, 1932). According to the Barmen Declaration, in accepting such teachings, the → church ceases to be the church. With such a statement the Barmen Declaration was protecting itself implicitly against the temptation of much wider church circles to sympathize with German Christian doctrines. It was thus a fundamental self-purification for a church that was either under attack or afflicted with uncertainty regarding its innermost character.

2. The Barmen Declaration contains six theses, each consisting of a biblical text followed by a statement of confession and of repudiation. According to thesis 1, Jesus Christ is the one → Word of God, which rules out "other happenings and powers, images and truths as divine → revelation." It thus rejects the normativity of the regimens that were important for the German Christians. But it also rejects the intellectual presupposition of neo-Protestantism, the form of Reformation Christianity that stands closely related to the culture and intellectual movements of the → modern period, especially the → Enlightenment and → idealism (→ Protestantism).

Thesis 2 tells us that this Word has two aspects. It is God's "pledge of the forgiveness of all our sins" but also "God's mighty claim on our whole → life." The latter means "deprivatizing" (E. Wolf) in the lives of Christians in the sense that even in their public → responsibilities, they may not stand under the command of any authorities alien to Christ.

Theses 3, 4, and 6 draw the conclusion that the church can stand only under one master, not two, and that it must let its message and order be determined by him alone and not by "dominant ideological and political convictions." It is a fellowship of brethren, its offices are ministries, its message to all people is God's free → grace.

Thesis 5 affirms that the → state cannot be "the single and total order of human life" to which one is blindly subject. Rather, it is established and limited by "divine arrangement . . . to provide for justice and → peace." The church is not an organ of the state but must remind it of God's kingdom, command, and righteousness and therefore of the responsibilities of both rulers and ruled. The Barmen Declaration said nothing about the Jewish question, an omission that was clearly at odds with the mentality of the times (→ Anti-Semitism, Anti-Judaism; Holocaust).

3. In its aftermath, the Barmen Declaration has raised three questions.

3.1. Does a common statement by the Lutheran, Reformed, and United churches constitute a union? By its common confessing, the Barmen Declaration does not exclude different confessions, nor does the fact of different confessions exclude a common confessing. While Lutherans stressed the former aspect (H. Sasse), in the eyes of many the common confession of the gospel in a particular situation presupposed a united evangelical church. Out of regard for the Lutherans, however, the question was left open.

3.2. Is the Barmen Declaration a confession? Lutheran delegates denied that it was because it was directed, not against false teaching, but against a political threat to the church, and also because it ran contrary to the Lutheran distinction between → law and → gospel (P. Althaus). Even so, although it simply calls itself a theological declaration and not a full statement of doctrine, like the early confessions or the Reformation confessions, it claims in fact to be a decision that the church has taken on the basis of doctrine. In the face of fundamental error, the church confesses the norm of its proclamation to be binding (D. → Bonhoeffer and K. Barth).

3.3. Was the declaration also a political word? Not directly so, for it was directed theologically against a → political theology and its fusing of National Socialist ideology and → faith. Yet it was indirectly political, as its opponents saw much more clearly than many of its confessors. For it broke with the line of previous confession, which had enabled people to combine resistance to state intervention in the church with acceptance of the → fascist state itself. It set forth a criterion for the true state and pointed out that it is the church's task to remind us of this criterion.

4.1. Opposition to the Barmen Declaration came in the form of the Ansbach Recommendation of June 11, 1934. Drafted by Lutherans grouped around W. Elert (1885-1954), it was something the German Christians could largely accept. In eight theses this document speaks not of one Word but of two — law and gospel, with an emphasis on law. It lays on Christians the obligation of obedient integration into such orders as race and state. Unlike the Barmen Declaration, it endorsed the National Socialist state on these grounds.

4.2. After the war many German churches adopted the Barmen Declaration; the Netherlands Reformed Church and the Presbyterian Church (U.S.A.) have also numbered it among their traditions. It has also influenced the → Church of South India, the church's struggle against → racism in Africa, and → liberation theology in South America.

Bibliography: R. AHLERS, The Barmen Theological Declaration of 1934 (Lewiston, N.Y., 1986) • H. ASMUSSEN, Barmen! (Munich, 1935) • C. BARTH, Bekenntnis im Werden. Neue Quellen zur Entstehung der Barmer Erklärung (Neukirchen, 1979) • K. BARTH, Texte zur Barmer Theologischen Erklärung (Zurich, 1984) • A. BURGSMÜLLER and R. WETH, eds., Die Barmer Theologische Erklärung. Einführung und Dokumentation (3d ed.; Neukirchen, 1984) • A. C. COCHRANE, The Church's Confession under Hitler (Philadelphia, 1962) • K. IMMER, ed., Bekenntnissynode der Deutschen Evangelischen

Kirche Barmen 1934. Vorträge und Entschließungen (Wuppertal-Barmen, 1934) • J. H. LEITH, ed., *Creeds of the Churches* (Atlanta, 1963) 517-22 • H. G. LOCKE, ed., *The Barmen Confession: Papers from the Seattle Assembly* (Lewiston, N.Y., 1986); idem, ed., *The Church Confronts the Nazis: Barmen Then and Now* (Lewiston, N.Y., 1984) • G. NIEMÖLLER, *Die erste Bekenntnissynode der Deutschen Evangelischen Kirche zu Barmen* (2d ed.; Göttingen, 1984) comprehensive description, documentation, and bibliography • E. WOLF, *Barmen* (3d ed.; Munich, 1984).

EBERHARD BUSCH

Baroque

1. Definition
2. Connections with Humanism
   2.1. Concept of Reality
   2.2. Concept of Humanity
   2.3. Concept of Poetics
   2.4. Function of Language
3. Baroque Poetics
   3.1. From Simplicity to Multiplicity
   3.2. Striving for Completeness
   3.3. Variation
   3.4. Complexity and Obscurity
   3.5. Imagination and the Involvement of the Reader
   3.6. Thinking in Scale and the Baroque Metaphor
   3.7. Passions
4. Art, Music, Philosophy, and Science
   4.1. Garden Architecture and the Extended Metaphor of the Garden
   4.2. Palace and Theater
   4.3. Church Architecture
   4.4. Painting
   4.5. Music
   4.6. Science and Philosophy

1. Definition

The term "baroque" denotes a style and a period between approximately 1580 and 1720 or even up to 1760. The → Enlightenment introduced the word in a derogatory sense for the architecture of the High Renaissance, meaning something that was bizarre or against the classical rules. Soon it came to be used also for music and literature, where it had the sense of bombastic, affected, or unnatural. Not until the end of the 19th century were there hesitant attempts at rehabilitation (H. Wölfflin), followed by efforts to use the term in a value-free manner. In spite of much objective research, such a shift has not been wholly successful.

The word "baroque" actually has found only partial acceptance, and some influential scholars (e.g., B. Croce, E. R. Curtius, and R. Wellek) would rather totally discard it. Some critics favor restricting it to Roman Catholic phenomena or see it as part of a manneristic style that belongs to no particular epoch. Many western European literary historians use categories that apply only to the literature of their own countries. The term occurs only sporadically in history and philosophy. In what follows, however, we shall try to show that it is both possible and rewarding to give a synopsis of the European baroque. In doing so, we will have to extend the above-mentioned temporal boundaries and include basic concepts of the → Renaissance, for the age of the baroque is the second phase of → humanism.

2. Connections with Humanism
2.1. *Concept of Reality*
Between the early Renaissance and the later baroque, the intellectual world of Europe had a common view of nature and reality. With its central perspective and doctrine of constant proportions, the Renaissance revolutionized the presentation of all visible things and inferred from the proportionality of the microcosm the existence of a similar order in the whole creation (L. B. Alberti [1404-72]). Two principles are frequently quoted: "to understand numbers is to understand all things" (Plato), and God has "ordered all things by measure, → number, and weight" (Wis. 11:21). As above, one makes it a point to refer both to antiquity and to the Bible.

2.2. *Concept of Humanity*
Humankind is the one chaotic element in an otherwise perfect world. Humans have fallen and are slaves to all passions from → Adam onward. "In nature there's no blemish but the mind," as W. Shakespeare (1564-1616) later put it. The forces and impulses to which the human being is subject thus assume paramount importance. The analysis of human nature constitutes the very center of the works of C. Salutati (1331-1406), D. → Erasmus (1469?-1536), J. L. Vives (1492-1540), and N. Machiavelli (1469-1527).

Important baroque figures are F. Bacon (1561-1626), J. Lipsius (1547-1606), B. Gracián y Morales (1601-58), and the French moralists. The goal of practical philosophy is the golden mean. This harmonious balance of → reason and emotion shows the significance of the concept of proportion not only for the outer world but for the inner one as well. Cicero, Plutarch, and Seneca are studied for their discriminating inquiries into matters psychological or moral. Like the ancients, humanists prefer so-called open forms, letters, dialogues, and so forth.

Biblical rules are often regarded as far too general or unsubtle. "The world cannot be governed by the Lord's Prayer," we read in the sayings of P. Winckler (1630-86).

2.3. *Concept of Poetics*
From the poetics of Plato (→ Platonism) to the end of the Enlightenment, all artistic products are considered to be imitations. There is thus no true originality and no plagiarism, for artists merely imitate what → nature has created beforehand. Ideal imitation, however, is not mere copying but the creative transformation of a model (H. Rüdiger). An often-used baroque illustration is that of the bee changing nectar into its own honey.

2.4. *Function of Language*
Another agreement of humanism and baroque concerns the role of → language. The Word stands at the beginning of Christian → revelation, and nothing compares with it in importance. However, the rediscovered ancient books of rhetoric play a major role also; they show a way to better the individual and society. As L. Bruni (ca. 1370-1444) puts it, "Rhetoric raises *homo naturalis* onto the level of *homo civilis*." Many prominent humanists wrote books of rhetoric, including P. → Melanchthon (1497-1560), J. C. Scaliger (1484-1558), J. du Bellay (ca. 1522-60), G. Puttenham (d. 1590), and P. Sidney (1554-86). There was also a veritable flood of works on poetics.

3. Baroque Poetics
3.1. *From Simplicity to Multiplicity*
Lines of transition from Renaissance humanism to baroque are difficult to draw. What is new in the age derives from the way in which the preceding epoch developed between 1350 and 1600. The Renaissance had been a rebirth of intellectual activity in all fields of knowledge. The age of the baroque can be said to appear when, after 150 years of research in all fields, the originally assumed simplicity and symmetry of the harmonious world order had been found to be multifaceted, many-layered, and full of complexities. To be sure, this realization did not shake the foundations of faith. It rather reinforced the belief in a Creator who had endowed the world with *größtmöglicher Mannigfaltigkeit* (the greatest possible multiplicity), as G. W. Leibniz (1646-1716) defined it at the end of the epoch.

3.2. *Striving for Completeness*
New in baroque, then, is an emphasis on fullness and a claim to handle every theme without leaving any gaps. One tries to get the whole knowledge of the age onto a common denominator. Typical are the many book titles that promise exhaustive treatment, such as *Janua linguarum, oder Pflanzgarten aller Sprachen*

und Wissenschaft (Gate of tongues, or a sampler of all languages and knowledge; 1631), *The Compleat Angler* (1653), or *Ausführliche Beschreibung aller und jeder denckwürdiger Geschichten* (A detailed account of each and every notable event; 1635). The predilection for exhaustive treatment and sheer number led to the founding of libraries and museums. On the level of the individual, the ideal person was the polyhistor or pansoph, both words referring to universal wisdom and knowledge.

3.3. *Variation*
Baroque as a whole is the art of permutation (Q. Kuhlmann [1651-89]). Variety is introduced so as to display the many facets of → creation and to bring to light their correspondences. The greatest poet is the one who is best at unfolding the wealth of aspects and perspectives. Everything in baroque is at least two-sided. Titles offer a springboard to the world of intellect (W. Flemming), for example, *Catharina von Georgien, oder Bewehrete Beständigkeit* (Catherine of Georgia, or fortified constancy; 1657); *America, or the Untravelled Parts of Truth* (1650).

In echo poems, nature or a divine voice replies to human questions. Since language is given by nature, every word contains something of the essence of the thing described by it. This is the reason for the serious poetic play with anagrams, acrostics, and palindromes. This view explains also the importance of the play on words in J. Donne (1572-1631), G. Marino (1569-1625), L. de Góngora y Argote (1561-1627), and the Nürnberg poets. Ausonius (ca. 310-ca. 395) offers a model for the writing of centones (i.e., the method of making new texts out of a patchwork of quotations, or of being original by imitating). There are particularly many Virgil or Bible centones. Pattern poems — texts whose typographic form reflects the poem's content — illustrate the Horatian dictum *ut pictura poesis* (let a poem be a picture), for word and figure are brother and sister (M. Opitz [1597-1639]).

In accordance with the goal of describing a world of plenitude, many authors and artists create multipurpose works. Thus the *Orbis sensualium pictus* (The visible world in pictures; 1658) of J. A. Comenius (1592-1670) is a multimedia experiment, being at once a Latin primer, a tractate on world order, and an educational picture book. Clocks of the 17th century do not just show time but often also contain mechanical displays, ranging from playing music to showing moon phases or other reminders of transience. (The clock is also a concrete emblem of a world order that is controlled from one central point.) G. Herbert (1593-1633) composed a poem on the coconut, lauding it as a universal fruit that one can both eat and drink, and which is also suitable for making clothes or supplying building materials. J. Harington (1561-1612) says that the aim of his work is "with one kinde of meate and one dish to feed divers tastes." Finally, G. P. Harsdörfer (1607-58) writes in an epigram that a word deserves praise when it contains many other words and thus covers the content of a whole page. In the light of such features W. Hausenstein finds the essence of baroque in the simultaneity of actions.

3.4. *Complexity and Obscurity*

Because the world order transcends all human → categories, we often find the topic of the interpenetration of the obvious and the hidden, or of mystery and revelation. "Lux est umbra Dei," writes Sir Thomas Browne (1605-82); what is light for us is mere shadow for God. As already in the work of Nicholas of Cusa (1401-64), → truth arises from what we do *not* know. One of the most common theatrical techniques is that of the play-within-the-play, which depicts truth in illusion and vice versa. It appears, for example, in the work of P. Calderón de la Barca (1600-1681), Ben Jonson (1572-1637), T. Middleton (1570?-1627), and J.-B. Molière (1622-73). "We play and are played," says J. Balde (1604-88). Collections of apothegms show a predilection for doublings of consciousness, as in mental reservations, in self-deception, or inattention in → prayer. Biblical stories of pious deception (e.g., those involving Abraham and Jacob) are also greatly liked. Furthermore, there are long series of cases of self-reference and examples of the paradoxicality of almost everything.

3.5. *Imagination and the Involvement of the Reader*

Almost all baroque poetics demands the cooperation of the reader. B. Kindermann (1636-1706) asks the reader to reflect, imagine, and investigate. Palinodes in word and picture demand decisions. Emblems, apothegms, and epigrams assume the discernment of the reader. The whole system of rhetoric is designed to involve and activate the audience. The *carmen emblematicum* (emblematic poem) and the emblem book without pictures can be considered the culminating point of that procedure. As in modern conceptual art, readers must evoke the picture for themselves. In the same way Shakespeare asks the public to imagine scenes that are not to be shown (see Prologue to *Henry V*). Riddles are often-used means of ensuring the reader's participation. According to Aristotle, poets in general are makers of riddles. Active reception depends on the imagination, and praise of the imagination is the theme of many poems and treatises. It allows us to be present even when absent (D. Czepko [1605-60]) and turns a virtual reality into the true experience of supreme happiness. (See E. Dyer's [1543-1607] poem "My Mynd to Me a Kingdom Is.")

3.6. *Thinking in Scale and the Baroque Metaphor*

Already in the medieval doctrine of the → analogy of being, the images of microcosm and macrocosm are evoked, in which everything small is part of an all-encompassing divine. The baroque use of the old → metaphor arises both from more sophisticated methods of observation and from a changed concept of the macrocosm. On the one hand, G. Bruno (1548-1600), B. Spinoza (1632-77), and G. W. Leibniz extol the much-extended realm of the new astronomy. On the other hand, there are unmistakable cases of agoraphobia. This fear of open spaces appears, for example, in some metaphysical poets (M. Nicholson). B. → Pascal (1623-62) speaks of a double infinity — that of the great and that of the small — which in both directions remains equally incomprehensible. Everywhere dominant is now a thinking that is oriented to the interchange between dimensions of knowledge (→ Epistemology).

It is no surprise, then, that the characteristic baroque styles — the one using brevity, the other amplification — reflect the epoch's preference for thinking in terms of scale and proportion. The immediate basis for the development of the new diction is the most widely used textbook in Europe, Erasmus's *De copia verborum* (On the abundance of words). Generations of students of Latin learned from this work the techniques of condensing and elaborating themes and topics. The method originated with Quintilian (ca. 35-ca. 100) but was not, until the baroque, recognized as the foundation of all intellectual activity. When condensing, one describes the essence of a matter, using as few words as possible, without ever repeating oneself. In elaboration, abundance is the key word. One explores all possible meanings and connotations of a subject matter without leaving anything out. Both methods as a whole enable us to denote the multiformity of the world and its wealth of relationships. Routine school exercises of these styles by juveniles differ only qualitatively from the acumen of an accomplished baroque concetto or the grandeur of a multiperspectival dramatic monologue. Brevity is the root of the development of precise individual metaphors, while amplification is the starting point for all extended metaphors.

Consider two brief examples. In the drama *Papinianus* (1659) by Gryphius (= A. Greif [1616-64]), a Roman jurist is executed after he refuses to exonerate Emperor Caracalla from a charge of fratricide.

C. Wernicke (1661-1725) condensed this five-act drama into a two-line epigram: "Es muß der Rechtsgelahrte wehlen eins von beiden / Entweder Unrecht sprechen oder Unrecht leiden" (The legal scholar must do one of two things / either decide a case unjustly or suffer unjustly himself). This can be called a precise condensation, since Wernicke's summary of the play is the dilemma, the minimum structure, and the heart of every tragedy. S. von Birken's (1626-81) *Truckene Trunkenheit* (Dry drunkenness) offers another form of brevity. It sums up in two words the contents of a treatise on tobacco. Contained in the metaphor is the claim that there is a physical equivalence between the partaking of alcohol and that of tobacco. Birken describes the moment when someone who has given up smoking for a long time first takes another drag and experiences a feeling of giddiness, which is akin to intoxication.

Whereas the extended metaphor was previously thought to be useless or bombastic, the 20th century showed that it had a real function (M. Black and E. Topitsch). Extended metaphors like that of world harmony, the garden, or the world theater serve as filters or lens to draw attention to what the age found important. Theoreticians in the 17th century were well aware of the significance of the two forms of metaphor. According to Harsdörfer, metaphor is the lever that lifts us out of the morass of ignorance.

3.7. *Passions*

Next to the praise of creation, the passions are the second great theme of baroque art and literature. From the apothegm to the courtly novel, they are central in every genre. Examples from the stage include Ben Jonson's *Volpone* (1606), dealing with greed; Molière's *Tartuffe* (The impostor; 1669), with hypocritical → piety; *Hamlet* (1603), with vacillation; and *La fuente ovejuna* (1612-14) of Lope de Vega (1562-1635), with honor. The notes to D. C. von Lohenstein's (1635-83) *Agrippina* (1665) identify lust and ambition as the main themes. In modern terms, → libido comes here into conflict with → power, or S. Freud with A. Adler. There are many other anticipations of modern topics, such as the following question: Are emotions and passions accessible to reason, or are they blind impulses and incurable diseases of the soul? Pessimistic answers have their origin in Seneca and → Stoicism, optimistic answers in the NT and Aristotle (→ Optimism and Pessimism).

4. Art, Music, Philosophy, and Science

4.1. *Garden Architecture and the Extended Metaphor of the Garden*

The baroque garden contains all the key concepts of the age. It is usually called the French garden and was developed by A. Le Nôtre (1613-1700). Examples can be found all over Europe (Versailles, Belvedere in Vienna, Hannover-Herrenhausen). The landscape of the formal baroque garden displays a love of multiple perspectives and varied panorama. The geometrically divided parterre, with its similar but different patterns, shows the like within the unlike. Among flowers there is a preference for those of great variety, such as tulips and narcissi. Everywhere water is used for artistic purposes. Canals and ponds with standing water give off reflections, but the flowing elements of the fountains become moving ornaments and show the baroque's fascination with immaterial substances (R. Alewyn).

Palace and garden enhance one another. Natural flowers outside are complemented by those on the inside. Flowers and leaves thus appear on tapestries and inlaid wood of furniture, on tiles and china, on tablecloths and bookbindings. Even within the books we find flower-decorated capital letters. The symbolism of garden and flower unfolds itself in details of this sort. For humanity has come from the Garden of Eden, and even its pagan counterpart, Arcadia, is a gardenlike landscape. Every flower is a geometric miracle of order. J. Lipsius extols the garden as the place where one can live in peace of mind. St. → Teresa of Ávila (1515-82) depicts the progress of the soul in garden images. P. Gerhardt (1607-76) lauds the garden of the world with its narcissi and tulips, comparing it to the garden of Christ, in which the soul constantly blooms. The labyrinth or maze, a part of every baroque garden, also becomes the theme of literary works (J. A. Comenius, *The Labyrinth of the World*). The maze symbolizes → life. Down on earth, one can lose one's way, but God, from above, sees chaos changing to geometric order. The Enlightenment uses baroque garden imagery even as terms of condemnation. J. C. Gottsched's (1700-1766) *Critische Dichtkunst* (1730) contains an antibaroque chapter entitled "Of Flowery Speech." Even today, in German and English, "flowery language" is a pejorative expression.

4.2. *Palace and Theater*

The starting point of all garden perspectives is the palace, in which an absolute ruler resides. All the means that sacred art uses to glorify God (→ Christian Art) are applied here to the one who maintains earthly order. The palace contains suites that end with mirror walls and infinity. Mirror cabinets, ceiling frescoes, and illusory architecture give the impression of widening space. Often a smaller palace corresponds to a larger one (e.g., Grand and Petit Trianon, Nymphenburg and Amalienburg). Because the ruler must display his power, everything is theatrical and designed for spectators. Feudal splendor requires festivals with claims to totality. These often include protracted fireworks and even horse ballets. Plays glorify the rulers, some of whom (e.g., Louis XIV [king of France, 1643-1715] and Leopold I [Holy Roman emperor, 1658-1705]), in a living demonstration of the play-within-the-play, take the parts of rulers on the stage. Here and in many dramas of the period, we find the extended metaphor of the world theater.

4.3. *Church Architecture*

Baroque churches have imposing facades and often dominate the surrounding area (St. Peter's in → Rome; the Benedictine Abbey in Melk, Austria; the monastery church of Banz, near Bamberg). The most overpowering effect, however, is inside. Here interconnected ellipses open up new space; niches, side passages, and interior columns hide the outer walls, and these effects, reinforced by the play of light and shade, create the impression of an unlimited interior space (H. Wölfflin). Architectural parts, decorated stucco, and paintings merge with one another; the cupola has a window to eternity; and ceiling paintings end with a vista of infinity. Two-dimensional choir screens display illusionistic perspectives (e.g., in the cathedral of Lucerne and the monastery of Einsiedeln), and trompe l'oeil effects may be found even in very small inlaid-wood fillings in choir pews (e.g., in Banz and Zwiefalten). Since the aim is to evoke admiration or astonishment, this architecture has been called rhetorical (A. Blunt). Because the illusions have been worked out mathematically and the emotional responses calculated in advance, one may also speak of mathematical → mysticism. Art materials appear often to be dematerialized, with marble seeming to float in the form of clouds or smoke, and gilded metal giving the impression of rays of light. Here too there is a coincidence of appearance and reality.

The greatest baroque architects in Italy were G. Bernini (1598-1680), F. Borromini (1599-1667), and G. Guarini (1624-83); in France, F. Mansart (1598-1666) and C. Le Brun (1619-90); in Germany and Austria, J. Fischer von Erlach (1656-1723), J. L. von Hildebrandt (1668-1745), and B. Neumann (1687-1753). Some of the best sculptors were P. Puget (1620-94), B. Permoser (1651-1732), A. Schlüter (1664?-1714), and again Bernini.

4.4. *Painting*

Systematic investigations into → iconography have brought to light hidden layers of meaning in many baroque paintings, for example, in the work of M. M. Caravaggio (1573-1610) and J. Vermeer (1632-75). Behind the realism of kitchen and market scenes or still lifes of treasures and flowers, we can now discern allegorical pointers to vanity or transience, to love, and to gluttony or concupiscence. With Jan Brueghel the Elder (1568-1625), who combined in his still lifes hundreds of kinds of flowers of every season, we have again a concrete example of the period's striving for plenitude and abundance.

Paintings within paintings on painted walls (e.g., by P. P. Rubens [1577-1640] and D. Velázquez [1599-1660]) are counterparts of the play-within-the-play and bring out the symbolic intentions of a work. The so-called studio and gallery paintings also display baroque characteristics. David Teniers the Younger (1610-90), for example, combined miniature copies of a vast gallery of works of art into new paintings. This procedure, showing the role of brevity and amplification in the arts, is also a painterly equivalent of the cento. Brevity is the main feature of the caricature, invented by Bernini and the Carracci brothers (Agostino C. [1557-1602] and Annibale C. [1560-1609]). The caricature abbreviates and reduces a whole picture to a few strokes.

Also typical is the use of optical instruments to reduce proportions. Thus Velázquez used a convex mirror, and Canaletto (= G. A. Canal [1697-1768]) and Vermeer a camera obscura. As in literature, representation of the passions is a main goal, which artists accomplish by painting facial expressions and body language (e.g., in *Remorse of St. Peter* by G. de la Tour [1593-1652]). On the border with science, we find anamorphic pictures with two levels of projection.

4.5. *Music*

Baroque has been called the age of the continuo, or figured bass, which gives an outline of the accompaniment for vocal and instrumental works with several parts. Its fundamental nature is one of improvisation, demonstrating the coexistence of rules and freedom.

Baroque is also the age of variation. Since variation is part of every musical work, one must think of such masterpieces as J. S. Bach's (1685-1750) *Musikalisches Opfer* (Musical offering). It contains typical baroque forms of variation, including a "crab," or retrograde, canon; a perpetual canon (i.e., one that can go on indefinitely without a break); an enigmatic canon; and two whose themes are presented "augmented" or "diminished" (i.e., the values of the notes of the theme are doubled or halved). Baroque music also contains examples of musical mazes, "vice versa" sonatas, patchwork canzones, and echo arias. M. Praetorius (1571-1621) arranged basic and ornamental instruments in a hierarchy. At the top is the multipurpose → organ, which comprehends in it all the others.

Multiplicity obtains also in the choice of genres. There is in the first place the opera. Its secular forms are the opera seria (C. Monteverdi [1567-1643], G. F. Handel [1685-1759], and A. Scarlatti [1660-1725]) and the opera buffa (G. Pergolesi [1710-36]). Its spiritual sister is the → oratorio (G. Carissimi [1605-74], H. Purcell [1659-95], and H. Schütz [1585-1672]). Opera fuses music, drama, and acting into a totality. → Dance is added in the opéra ballet (J.-B. Lully [1632-87]). With its various wings and backdrops, the baroque stage has several vanishing points (G. da Bibiena [1625-65]). Theater machinery makes it possible to produce the effects of fire, lightning, and water. Operas and church → cantatas use the interplay of word-related recitative and the passion of the arias. Besides the composers already mentioned, the most important are A. Vivaldi (1678-1741), D. Buxtehude (1637-1707), M. A. Charpentier (1634?-1704), F. Couperin (1668-1733), A. Corelli (1653-1713), and J. P. Rameau (1683-1764).

4.6. Science and Philosophy

The science of baroque is still simultaneously natural philosophy (→ Philosophy of Nature). In philosophical systems, order is given as a synthesis, and solutions are equally mathematical and metaphysical (e.g., in B. Spinoza's *Ethica in ordine geometrico demonstrata* [1677]). G. W. Leibniz's preestablished harmony and R. Descartes's (1596-1650) proof of the equivalence of space and number derive from the spirit of thinking in correspondences. From the preoccupation of Leibniz with the problem of a universal algebra of reason and of a universal language of mathematics stems his discovery of dyadics, an arithmetic with only two numbers (1 and 0), which is the basis of modern computer technology. There is also his discovery of the infinitesimal calculus, which makes it possible to grasp continuous changes or variations mathematically.

The age was obsessed with the infinite. The telescope and the microscope are therefore symbolic inventions. R. Hooke's (1635-1703) *Micrographia* (1665), the first book on the very small, compares God's creations with some manmade products. Under a microscope, the polished sharpness of a needle can be seen as pockmarked, blunt, and irregular. Hooke therefore calls human → work mere bungling. Only nature has dimensions of true depth.

Treatises of the 17th century that contrast the certainty of reason and inner truth with the unreliability of sense impressions decide that conclusive proof always rests on concepts. Thus the philosophy of Descartes begins with the *cogito;* Galileo (1564-1642) calls the Copernican discovery, which was the result of thinking, "rape of the senses." Because

baroque → rationalism investigates the nature of human perception, it finds relativities and illusions in what seemed to be the fixed laws of perspective. Pascal shows that even the method of mathematics is one of defining by means of the indefinable. In his work, however, as everywhere in the epoch, oxymora and paradoxes again and again are turned into proofs of the divine *adumbratio.* God conceals many things from us. Paradoxes merely bring to light the all-encompassing greatness of his creation.

Bibliography: R. ALEWYN and K. SÄLZLE, *Das große Welttheater. Die Epoche der höfischen Feste in Dokument und Deutung* (Hamburg, 1959) • W. BARNER, *Barockrhetorik* (Tübingen, 1970) • M. BAUR-HEINHOLD, *Theater des Barocks. Festliche Bühnenspiele im 17. und 18. Jahrhundert* (Munich, 1966) • G. BAZIN, *The Baroque: Principles, Styles, Modes, Themes* (Greenwich, Conn., 1968) • M. BLACK, "Metaphor," *Models and Metaphors* (Ithaca, N.Y., 1962) • A. BLUNT, ed., *Baroque and Rococo* (London, 1978) • A. BUCK, *Die humanistische Tradition in der Romania* (Bad Homburg, 1968) • K. O. CONRADY, *Lateinische Dichtungstradition und deutsche Lyrik des 17. Jahrhunderts* (Bonn, 1962) • J. DYCK, *Ticht-Kunst. Deutsche Barockpoetik und rhetorische Tradition* (Bad Homburg, 1966) • W. FLEMMING, *Deutsche Kultur im Zeitalter des Barocks* (Frankfurt, 1970) • W. JENS, "Rhetorik," *RDL* 3.432-56 (extensive bibliography) • J. R. MARTIN, *Baroque* (London, 1977) • H. A. MILLER, *Baroque and Rococo Architecture* (New York, 1967) • G. C. RIMBACH, "Das Epigramm und die Barockpoetik," *Jahrbuch der deutschen Schillergesellschaft* (vol. 14; Stuttgart, 1970) • H. RÜDIGER, "Die Wiederentdeckung der antiken Literatur im Zeitalter der Renaissance," *Geschichte der Textüberlieferung der antiken und mittelalterlichen Literatur* (vol. 1; ed. M. Meier, F. Hinderman, and A. Schindler; Zurich, 1961) 511-80 • I. SCHEITLER, *Das geistliche Lied im deutschen Barock* (Berlin, 1982) • S. SITWELL, *Baroque and Rococo* (New York, 1967) • R. STAMM, ed., *Die Kunstformen des Barock-Zeitalters* (Bern, 1956) • E. TOPITSCH, *Vom Ursprung und Ende der Metaphysik* (Vienna, 1958).

GUENTHER C. RIMBACH

Barth, Karl

Karl Barth, who was born on May 10, 1886, at Basel and who died there 82 years later (on December 10, 1968), was one of the most important Protestant theologians of the 20th century. His father, Fritz, was a disciple of A. Schlatter at Bern, his mother a descendant of H. Bullinger and a relative of J. Burckhardt. The philosopher Heinrich Barth and the Calvin scholar Peter Barth were his brothers. In 1913 he married Nelly Hoffmann, and they had five children, of whom Markus became a NT scholar and Christoph an OT scholar.

Studying theology at Bern, Berlin, Tübingen, and Marburg, Barth broke away from the mild → pietism of his home and subscribed to the → liberalism of A. Harnack and W. Herrmann. He helped to edit the journal *Die Christliche Welt* with M. Rade. As an assistant pastor at Geneva, he preached from Calvin's rostrum. Then as pastor at Safenwil from 1911 to 1921, he turned to → religious socialism.

With his commentary on Romans (1919), however, Barth ushered in a new theological epoch. In it he called for a turning aside from anthropocentricity, arguing that God is always alien to all our religious and cultural thinking. From 1921 to 1935 Barth taught → dogmatics at Göttingen, Münster, and Bonn. With E. Thurneysen, R. Bultmann, E. Brunner, and F. Gogarten he entered into a working partnership whose theology, by reason of its form, came to be known as → dialectical, and which published the journal *Zwischen den Zeiten*. The heart of this theology was God's → Word to us. The circle broke up over the question whether some human preunderstanding is necessary if we are to understand this divine Word, or whether clarification can come only as we reflect on the presupposition that God himself gives us in his Word.

The latter position, to which his work on → Anselm gave added depth, became the starting point for Barth's main achievement: his 12-volume *Church Dogmatics* (1932-67). In this series, which includes many exegetical, theological, and historical excursuses, he tackles the themes of dogmatics and → ethics from the one standpoint that Jesus Christ is the fulfillment of God's → covenant with his people Israel and also with us, who, created by him, have been → reconciled to him and to one another by him, and thus liberated for maturity. He deals with → predestination, for example, solely in terms of the gospel because it is God's self-determination for fellowship with sinners and on this basis their own self-determination for fellowship with God and his people. In antithesis to the emancipating of ethics from theology he stresses the fact that God as the gracious God also commands. He sees us as transgressors of the divine command only in the light of God as Reconciler. He looks at → creation only in terms of God's gracious affirmation of his creatures in Christ, for it was for this affirmation that God made them. This involves a rejection of → natural theology. Over against a conception of → freedom as freedom to decide at will, Barth interprets it as a

freedom for and in fellowship. Humanity, then, is cohumanity. In its work, the church, which stands under the sign of response to God's Word, with a resultant criticism of the sacramental concept, is challenged to accept solidarity with the world (and thus to view political activity as service of God).

Confronting the church's readiness to compromise with National Socialism, Barth in 1933 wrote *Theologische Existenz heute*, in which he summoned the church to render obedience to God alone. He thus helped to found the → Confessing Church, which constituted itself at the Synod of → Barmen in May 1934 with a theological declaration that Barth composed. Because of his opposition to the National Socialist regime, Barth was dismissed and became a professor at Basel in 1935, where he taught until 1962.

Having first called for resistance to the National Socialists, especially because of their → antiSemitism, Barth advocated a liberating reconciliation after 1945: first in relation to Germany; then in church relationships, playing a part in the → ecumenical movement, especially at the Amsterdam assembly in 1948; then in the cold war; and finally in old age in relations between rich and poor countries, and always in the background in relations with nonChristian religions. In the United States in 1962 he argued for "a theology not of liberty, but of freedom." He had a fruitful influence on → Vatican II and visited the Vatican in 1966. It is as hard to survey his many works as it is to review the many interpretations of them. His theology set up international standards. After his death, however, a reaction began against his Christocentric theology as scholars became interested afresh in questions of self-defined humanity in dialogue with non-Christian thought. In support of this trend, appeal is often made to a theology of the → Holy Spirit, which at the last Barth himself also had in view, although in another sense.

Bibliography: Primary sources: Church Dogmatics (Edinburgh, 1936-69; orig. pub., 1932-67) • *Epistle to the Romans* (Oxford, 1935; orig. pub., 1919; 2d ed., 1922) • *Gesamtausgabe* (Zurich, 1971ff.).

Secondary works: H. U. von BALTHASAR, *The Theology of Karl Barth* (New York, 1971; orig. pub., 1951) • *Bibliographie Karl Barth* (vol. 1; ed. H.-A. Drewes and M. Wildi; Zurich, 1984), works of Barth; (vol. 2; ed. M. Wildi; Zurich, 1992), works about Barth • E. BUSCH, *Introduction to the Theology of Karl Barth* (Grand Rapids, 1979); idem, *Karl Barth: His Life from Letters and Autobiographical Texts* (Philadelphia, 1976) • E. JÜNGEL, *Barth-Studien* (Zurich, 1982) • W. KRECK, *Grundentscheidungen in Karl Barth's Theologie* (Neukirchen, 1978) • T. H. L. PARKER, *Karl Barth* (Grand Rapids, 1970).

EBERHARD BUSCH

Base Community

The phrase "base community," used especially in the → Roman Catholic Church and its theology, has become a programmatic term in theological and ecclesiastical controversies about congregational and church reform. It also denotes a church community defined empirically that, for all the individual differences — local, national, and spiritual — shares such features as self-organization, emphasis on koinonia, the active participation of all members in the congregational process, and the relating of the church program to the concrete, historical, → everyday, sociopolitical needs of the → congregation.

National and regional conditions for the development of base communities differ widely. In Latin America, where base communities are most numerous, two conditions seem to be the most prominent. The first is the acute shortage of priests, which especially in rural areas encourages self-help (e.g., services without priests led by lay catechists). The second is the decision of some church leaders to side with the poor (→ Poverty) in their struggle against → hunger and oppression. When "base" is thus equated with the lower classes, the movement in Latin America has strongly political aspects. → Liberation theology regards it as the essence of a rediscovery of the church (L. Boff). Base communities are the place of active solidarity. In practicing the ideal of koinonia, the church enjoys fresh experiences of "ecclesiogenesis."

In Asia and Africa, though without either the same critical attitude toward the church or the same definite political goals, base communities arise mainly out of a shortage of priests. The structure of the small local community accords well with the African tradition of local orientation to the family or clan. In practice, it does not quite fit in with the canonical principle of the parish. The officeholder who can give absolution and consecration is more and more an itinerant priest (R. Kleiner), while the true function of parish leadership falls on the *bakambi,* the lay leaders elected by the congregation.

The base communities in Europe arose for these reasons primarily in Italy (e.g., the well-known example at Isolotto) and Spain. In western Europe (France, Belgium, the Netherlands) and eastern Europe other forces have been at work that are critical of the hierarchy and are aiming at freedom: a new

self-awareness on the part of the laity (→ Lay Movements) inspired by → Vatican II and an attempt to make the impulses of the Latin American movement fruitful in the First World.

Though many of the communities are ecumenical, the base community is essentially a phenomenon in the Roman Catholic world. This fact is explained by the need to "catch up" with other Christians in achieving a universal priesthood and by the epochal change from a hierarchical and centralist view of the → church (§3.2) to one that is oriented to the leading concept of the people of God. Yet this explanation does not sufficiently take into account the need to see the rise of the base community in a nonecclesiastical historical context, namely, that of modern, social, grassroots movements (→ Ecology; Feminist Movement; Peace Movement). To this extent the failure of the movement to develop in the Protestant churches stands in need of explanation from the standpoint of the sociology of religion.

Debates about the base community focus on the question whether it defines itself as inside or outside the constitutional church. Theological reflection, which is only just beginning, seems to be developing ecclesiological contours. There is a stress on fellowship (as distinct from anonymous relations in the larger parish). The weight shifts from a sacramental and clerical axle to a different type of church that now rests on the Word and the laity (L. Boff). Also emphasized is an experience-related → theology and → spirituality that reflects social and political practice.

Bibliography: L. BOFF, *Ecclesiogenesis: The Base Communities Reinvent the Church* (Maryknoll, N.Y., 1986) • P. J. BRENNAN, *Re-imagining the Parish: Base Communities, Adulthood, and Family Consciousness* (New York, 1991) • N. COPRAY et al., eds., *Die andere Kirche. Basisgemeinden in Europa* (Wuppertal, 1982) • H. FRANKEMÖLLE, ed., *Kirche von unten. Alternative Gemeinden* (Mainz, 1981) • R. KLEINER, *Basisgemeinden in der Kirche* (Graz, 1976) • S. TORRES and J. EAGLESON, eds., *The Challenge of Basic Christian Communities* (Maryknoll, N.Y., 1981).

HERMANN STEINKAMP

Basel Confession

In 1534 the city council of Basel adopted a confession in order to distinguish Reformation teaching more clearly from that of Roman Catholics and → Anabaptists. Its author was Oswald Myconius (1488-1552), a friend of U. → Zwingli (1484-1531) and the leader of the Basel church. He based it on the synodal confession of J. Oecolampadius (1482-1531).

The 12 articles are short and clear. Article 1, which describes God in terms based on the early doctrine of the → Trinity (§2), states that before the → creation of the world God elected us to eternal → life (→ Predestination). Article 2 states that because of the fall (→ Sin 3; Primeval History), we have all fallen under condemnation unless the Spirit of God restores us. According to article 3, the covenant manifests God's care for us. Article 4 affirms that we share the inheritance of God through Christ. It confesses Christ in terms taken from the early church and his work in the words of the → Apostles' Creed. The Holy Spirit is the Spirit of Christ, whom he has sent to his → disciples.

Article 5 deals with the Holy Spirit and the → church separately, as in the creed and J. → Calvin (1509-64). The church is the gathering of believers in the Spirit. These accept Christ's → atoning death and prove their faith in works of love. → Sects and the monastic life are rejected. Article 6 describes the Lord's Supper along the lines of Zwingli as a meal of thanksgiving, proclamation, and fellowship, but also with H. Bullinger (1504-75) as the "food of believing souls to eternal life," with Christ being "present" to them in the supper. The enclosing of Christ's body in the bread is rejected, along with its adoration. The final articles deal with → church discipline for "betterment" of life (7), secular authorities (8), the righteousness of works (9), the → last judgment (10), Roman Catholic ceremonies (11), and the Anabaptists (12).

The city of Mühlhausen adopted the confession (except for art. 7) in 1537. Until 1826 it was read from the → pulpit in Basel on the Wednesday before → Easter. After 1871, the council no longer enforced it.

→ Helvetic Confession

Bibliography: A. C. COCHRANE, ed., Reformed Confessions of the Sixteenth Century (Philadelphia, 1966) 89-111 • K. R. HAGENBACH, Kritische Geschichte der Entstehung und Schicksale der ersten Baslerkonfession (Basel, 1827; 2d ed., 1857) • E. F. K. MÜLLER, Die Bekenntnisschriften der reformierten Kirche (Leipzig, 1903) 95-100 • W. H. NEUSER, "Oswald Myconius," HDThG 2.202-3 • P. SCHAFF, "The First Confession of Basle, A.D. 1534," The Creeds of Christendom (6th ed.; 3 vols.; New York, 1931) 1.385-88 • R. STAUFFER, "Das Basler Bekenntnis von 1534," Ecclesia semper reformanda (ed. H. R. Guggisberg and P. Rotach; Basel 1980) 28-49 • N. P. TANNER, ed., Decrees of the Ecumenical Councils (2 vols.; London, 1990) 1.453-513.

WILHELM H. NEUSER

Basel, Council of → Reform Councils

Basilian Monks

The rules of Basil the Great (ca. 330-79; → Cappadocian Fathers) were meant as spiritual reading for individual monks, not as the rule of an order. Eastern monks live according to this tradition, but they properly should not be called Basilians, as is commonly done. Basilian monasteries and congregations arose only under Western influence in the Eastern churches in union with → Rome. In Italy (even today in the abbey Grottaferrata) and Spain, Greek monks have been called Basilians from the 12th century. In Poland and Lithuania various Basilian congregations have existed from the 16th century and have had great cultural influence. The → Melchite Church includes Basilian orders of various branches.

Bibliography: P. J. FEDWICK, St. Basil the Great and the Christian Ascetic Life (Rome, 1978) • M. B. GALLONE, I Basiliani. Monachesimo greco nella storia, nella religione e nelle arti (Bari, 1973) • J. GRIBOMONT, "Basilian Monasticism," NCE 2.148-49 • E. F. MORISON, St. Basil and His Rule: A Study in Early Monasticism (London, 1912) • A. G. WELYKYJ, ed., Litterae Basilianorum in terris Ucrainae et Bielarusae (2 vols.; Rome, 1979).

RUTH ALBRECHT

Basilica

In antiquity the term "basilica" denoted a rectangular hall, usually divided by pillars and used for various purposes. From the fifth century A.D. its main use was for churches. When official permission was given to build churches under Constantine (306-37), this form was commonly chosen, adopted from secular, rather than pagan, sacral architecture. If the details were borrowed from Roman places of assembly, the structure as a whole was something new: a rectangular building, divided by colonnades into a broader and elevated nave with windows and (at least two) narrower and lower side aisles, usually with a semicircular apse in the east. An atrium, or porch, and narthex were put at the western entrance. There were only a few later innovations to meet liturgical needs (→ Liturgy), such as the crypt and the transept.

The development and spread of the basilica began after Constantine. In the fifth century it became the dominant type in all Christianized lands, often with local variations such as pillars, galleries, and a triple sanctuary. In the Middle Ages the basilica remained the basic form of the Christian church in the West. In the → Byzantine Empire, however, we also find domed churches.

Bibliography: F. W. Deichmann, *Einführung in die christliche Archäologie* (Darmstadt, 1983) • L. Marchetti and C. Bevilacqua, *Italian Basilicas and Cathedrals* (Novara, 1950) • J. B. W. Perkins, "Constantine and the Origins of the Christian Basilica," *PBSR* 22 (1954) 69-90 • G. Stanzl, *Längsbau und Zentralbau als Grundthema der frühchristlichen Architektur* (Vienna, 1979) • L. M. White, *Building God's House in the Roman World* (Baltimore, 1990).

Urs Peschlow

Beatitudes

The beatitude, or "makarism," is a literary form commonly beginning with the word "blessed" (Gk. *makarios*) and constituting some declaration of good fortune for persons. Familiar to Greek literature in both the classical and Hellenistic periods, it is most often used to extol persons considered to be happy according to the ideals of → Greek philosophy (e.g., those attaining wealth, honor, wisdom, or → virtue).

In the OT, beatitudes appear almost exclusively in the Psalms and → Wisdom literature, where they mainly serve the purpose of ethical exhortation. God, the giver of all blessedness, confers his blessings on those who do his will and follow the precepts of the wise (Ps. 112:1; Prov. 8:32-33). The blessings themselves tend to make for worldly well-being and include such rewards as those of → life (Prov. 8:34-35), prosperity (Ps. 1:1-3; → Fate and [Good] Fortune), posterity (Ps. 128:1-3), and the joys of worshiping (Ps. 65:4) and trusting in (Jer. 17:7-8) God.

Jewish → apocalyptic literature includes beatitudes that are not only this-worldly in character but also → eschatological. Eschatological beatitudes pronounce blessing on persons in distress (e.g., *3 Apoc. Bar.* 10:6-7) and are sometimes associated with woes (e.g., *1 Enoch* 99:10-15). The promise they affirm is end-time vindication and participation in the world to come (e.g., Dan. 12:12-13). The purpose of these beatitudes is to console and to give assurance of salvation.

The NT contains 44 beatitudes, with 28 appearing in Matthew and Luke and the rest in John (2), → Paul (3), James (2), 1 Peter (2), and the Apocalypse (7). In structure, NT beatitudes seldom appear in the form *makarios hos (tis)* (blessed is he who), which is found so frequently in Greek literature and the LXX (e.g., Matt. 11:6 = Luke 7:23). This form of beatitude lends itself well to a description of this-worldly bliss.

Instead, in NT beatitudes the predicate adjective *makarios* is generally coupled with a noun or substantival participle or adjective, and a reason clause may follow (e.g., "Blessed are those [you] who hunger, because . . ."). This form of beatitude is eschatological; it evaluates present circumstances in light of the → future and promises end-time salvation. In substance, it envisages history as nearing its end and announces the reversal of conditions (e.g., the poor will inherit the kingdom).

These beatitudes are, in fact, indicative of the distinctive message of → Jesus, who proclaimed the nearness of the eschatological → kingdom of God. As evidence that Jesus made use of the eschatological beatitude, one can point to the five or six sayings of Jesus that Matthew and Luke inherited and have in common (Luke 6:20b, 21, [22]; 7:23; 10:23; 12:43). Furthermore, the eschatological beatitude is typical of the → gospel of the early church, which announced the imminent coming of the exalted Jesus for salvation and condemnation (→ Parousia). The church thus not only preserved beatitudes from Jesus but also created new ones (cf. Matt. 5:3-12 with Luke 6:20b-22; → Sermon on the Mount). For Jesus and the church, beatitudes are powerful words of proclamation assuring those who hear them that God himself is their ultimate → hope of salvation.

→ Parenesis

Bibliography: H. D. Betz, *Essays on the Sermon on the Mount* (Philadelphia, 1985) 17-36; idem, *The Sermon on the Mount* (Minneapolis, 1995) 91-153 • I. Broer, *Die Seligpreisungen der Bergpredigt* (Bonn, 1986) • C. H. Dodd, "The Beatitudes: A Form-Critical Study," *More NT Studies* (Grand Rapids, 1968) 1-10 • J. Dupont, *Les Béatitudes* (Brugge, 1958) • R. A. Guelich, "The Matthean Beatitudes: 'Entrance Requirements' or Eschatological Blessings?" *JBL* 95 (1976) 415-34; idem, *The Sermon on the Mount* (Waco, Tex., 1982) • W. Käser, "Beobachtungen zum alttestamentlichen Makarismus," *ZAW* 82 (1970) 225-50 • C. Keller, "Les 'Béatitudes' de l'Ancien Testament," *Hommages à W. Vischer* (Montpellier, 1960) 88-100 • G. Strecker, *The Sermon on the Mount* (Nashville, 1988) 24-47 • H. Windisch, *The Meaning of the Sermon on the Mount* (Philadelphia, 1951).

Jack Dean Kingsbury

Beecher, Lyman

Lyman Beecher, an American Congregational and Presbyterian clergyman, revivalist, reformer, and educator, was born on October 12, 1775, and died on January 10, 1863. He graduated from Yale College

(1797) and then studied theology under Timothy Dwight. Under Dwight's influence, Beecher was "baptized into the revival spirit" of America's Second Great Awakening (1790-1835). Indeed, Beecher's life epitomized the many sides to the awakening and its profound impact for American history. An irrepressible man of boundless energy, Beecher combined the → Puritan legacy of seeking to transform the world with American → democratic notions of freedom and faith in human → progress.

Like so many of his generation of evangelical pastors, Beecher moved often and comfortably within the northern Presbyterian-Congregationalist orbit. His first pastorate was a Presbyterian charge at East Hampton, Long Island (1799-1810), where his calls to → conversion (§§1-2) and social activism established him as a leading "presbygationalist." In 1810 he accepted a call to the Congregational church of Litchfield, Connecticut. Beecher capitalized on an area where → revivals had flourished for over a decade by bringing to fruition the conception that most distinguished the evangelical resurgence of the next half-century, namely, linking personal spiritual transformation through revival with moral reform and social benevolence. A whirl at the center of the institutional side of the awakening, Beecher rallied the spiritually regenerate to reform manners, abstain from alcohol, support Bible societies, and end → Sabbath-breaking. For 15 years, beginning in 1813 with the formation of the Beecher-inspired Connecticut Society for the Reformation of Morals, the state was the nation's most important reform center. Nevertheless, it remained a bastion of religious and political → conservatism, and Beecher, as a member of the "Standing Order," defended the state's support for the Congregational establishment. With the finality of legal disestablishment in 1818, however, he enthusiastically endorsed the new → voluntarism as a tonic to the health of the churches.

In 1826 Beecher left Litchfield for Hanover Street Congregational Church in Boston. Here he attacked New England → Unitarianism primarily through revival tactics. At the same time, he quarreled with Charles → Finney over the latter's "new measures" revivalist tactics. Beecher pledged to keep Finney from coming to Boston, but he later retreated and even welcomed the great revivalist to Boston as a champion of evangelical religion and reform.

In 1832, convinced that America's future growth lay west of the Hudson River, Beecher accepted an invitation to become president of Lane Seminary, as well as to pastor the Second Presbyterian Church, both in Cincinnati, Ohio. His *Plea for the West* (1835)

articulated the potential for continued Protestant expansion, but it also expressed alarm over the increasing Catholic presence in the West. Beecher's fears of a "popish plot" to capture America found a receptive audience during a visit to Boston in 1834, where his anti-Catholic diatribes led indirectly to mob action and the burning of an Ursuline convent in nearby Charlestown.

Beecher's early years in Cincinnati were tumultuous. For some, he was not sufficiently radical on social issues; for others, he was not sufficiently conservative theologically. His commitment to the gradual (and not immediate) abolition of → slavery did not go far enough for the 40 "Lane Rebels," who left the seminary in 1834. Beecher's optimistic view of the will prompted conservative Presbyterians to accuse him of departing from the → Westminster Confession. In 1835 he was tried for heresy but cleared of the charges. These setbacks aside, Beecher continued to link evangelical → Calvinism with moderate reform.

Retiring from the pastorate in 1843 and from the presidency of Lane in 1850, Beecher spent the remainder of his life writing and lecturing. Throughout the 19th century and well into the 20th, Beecher's commitment to activism, reformism, and to the grand vision of a righteous empire endured among Protestants. His children, most notably Harriet Beecher Stowe and Henry Ward Beecher, left their own indelible mark on American culture.

Bibliography: Primary sources: Autobiography of Lyman Beecher (2 vols.; ed. B. Cross; Cambridge, Mass., 1961) • *Works* (Boston, 1852-53).

Secondary works: H. W. BOWDEN, *Dictionary of American Religious Biography* (Westport, Conn., 1977) • M. CASKEY, *Chariot of Fire: Religion and the Beecher Family* (New Haven, 1978) • J. W. FRASER, *Pedagogue for God's Kingdom: Lyman Beecher and the Second Great Awakening* (Lanham, Md., 1985) • S. HENRY, *Unvanquished Puritan: A Portrait of Lyman Beecher* (Grand Rapids, 1973).

DAVID W. KLING

Beguines

The Beguines were various ascetic and religious communities of women not under vows that arose chiefly in the Low Countries in the 13th century. The origin and meaning of the term "Beguine" are unclear, but it probably had a connotation of heresy.

As part of the movement in response to urban poverty and to limitations of religious life among women, the Beguines tried to achieve the ideals of chastity, evangelical poverty, and the contemplative life. Social impulses (including economic, legal, and cultural discrimination against women) as well as religious factors (esp. the goal of an apostolic life outside the → orders, which increasingly opposed associations of houses for women) played an important part. These religious women, who did not belong to approved orders or take permanent → vows, lived together in convents and shared in a → community of goods. Unmarried, widowed, or married, they earned their living by manual labor but also had many intellectual and spiritual interests.

In the beginning of the 13th century the Beguines spread from what is now Belgium to Holland, France, and Germany. Although Pope Honorius III (1216-27) in 1216 orally recognized them as a community without approved rule or monastic practices, the Beguines fell increasingly under suspicion of → heresy. Some of them were in fact open to mystical influences. Although the majority remained orthodox, they were a source of irritation to the clergy (as a lay movement) and to the guilds. Eventually, some of them joined existing orders (mostly mendicants), and others were attacked as heretical by the → Inquisition. The Beguines experienced a short revival as a consequence of the Counter-Reformation (→ Catholic Reform and Counterreformation), but by the 19th century the movement had no practical significance.

The male equivalent of the Beguines were the Beghards, who never became more than a marginal movement in numbers or importance. They came mostly from the lower classes, sustained themselves more by begging than by work, and were much more susceptible to heresy than the Beguines. By the 14th century, they were virtually extinct.

Bibliography: J. GREVEN, Die Anfänge der Beginen (Münster, 1912) • H. GRUNDMANN, Religiöse Bewegungen im Mittelalter (2d ed.; Darmstadt, 1961); idem, "Zur Geschichte der Beginen im 13. Jahrhundert," AKuG 21 (1931) 296-320 • S. HARKSEN, Die Frau im Mittelalter (Leipzig, 1974) • G. KOCH, Frauenfrage und Ketzertum im Mittelalter (Berlin, 1962) • R. E. LERNER, "Beguines and Beghards," DMA 2.157-62; idem, The Heresy of the Free Spirit in the Later Middle Ages (Berkeley, Calif., 1972) 35-60 • E. W. MCDONNELL, The Beguines and Beghards in Medieval Culture, with Special Emphasis on the Belgian Scene (2d ed.; New York, 1969) • D. PHILLIPS, Beguines in Medieval Strasburg: A Study of the Social Aspect of Beguine Life (Stanford, Calif., 1941) • S. SHAHAR, The Fourth Estate: A History of Women in the Middle Ages (London, 1983) • R. W. SOUTHERN, Western Society and the Church in the Middle Ages (Harmondsworth, 1970) 319-31.

BRITTA HÜBENER

Behavior, Behavioral Psychology

1. Definition
2. Research
3. Deviance
4. Therapy

1. Definition

Originally the word "behavior" referred to any form of physical activity of living creatures that, as distinct from psychological processes, could be objectively seen (with appropriate instruments) or measured by external observers. This classical definition was later expanded when a distinction was made between open and concealed conduct. The former is physical activity as just defined, whereas the latter involves what is not observed but may be concluded on the basis of that which is either open or known by introspection (N. Birbaumer and H. P. Huber, 514). Hence today processes of experience are viewed as examples of concealed behavior, especially processes of cognition such as imagining and thinking, as well as emotions, motives, and the processes of attribution.

2. Research

2.1. Research into behavior in the narrower sense — for example, comparative study, reflex theory, and the theoretical conceptions of learning as these apply to behaviorism — is limited to the study of outward and objectively observable (i.e., "open") behavior. Comparative research, or ethology (developed by W. Craig, K. Lorenz, N. Tinbergen, E. Holst, and others), systematically describes and classifies inherited and genetically specific behavior (esp. of animals), interprets it in terms of → evolution, analyzes its physiological and regulatory principles, and examines the processes of inheritance (J. R. Nitsch). Reflex theory, deriving from the works of the Russian physiologists V. M. Bekhterev (1857-1927) and I. Pavlov (1849-1936), attempts to trace all psychological contents (→ Soul 3) back to physiological reflexes. Behaviorism, founded by J. B. Watson (1878-1958) and developed further in 1938 by B. F. Skinner (1904-90; → Social Science), deals with reflex theory, especially with learned behavior, studying such behavior not in its natural → environment but under laboratory conditions, thereby trying to explain the nexus of stimulus and response (Nitsch). According to behaviorism, conduct arises through experience; learning is meant to be conditioning. Two such forms are typically distinguished: classical conditioning and operant (or instrumental) conditioning.

2.1.1. The principle of classical conditioning is that

a neutral stimulus is associated repeatedly with a so-called unconditioned stimulus, that is, one that triggers a quite specific response. A repeated presentation of this combination leads to the previously neutral stimulus becoming a conditioned stimulus, it alone now being able to produce the same response as the unconditioned stimulus. Pavlov's well-known experiments with dogs provide the model. The sight of meat causes the dogs to salivate. When the sight of meat (the unconditioned stimulus) is then connected repeatedly with the sound of a gong (the neutral stimulus), eventually the sound alone will produce the same salivation (the conditioned response).

Many aspects of, for example, the rise and persistence of neurotic (e.g., phobias; → Neurosis) and psychosomatic (e.g., asthma) disturbances might be described and explained at least in part by the principle of classical conditioning. Moreover, the knowledge gained by experiments in classical conditioning is the basis of many methods of behavior therapy (see 4.1).

2.1.2. The second form of simple learning is *operant conditioning*, which derives from the work of E. L. Thorndike (1874-1949). In 1898 he formulated his law of effect, which states that if a response to stimuli includes behavior whose consequences are satisfactory, the individual will tend to repeat the behavior; if the consequences are annoying or harmful, the individual will tend not to repeat the behavior. This type of learning can be called learning by results. Skinner's conditioning experiments indicated that, put simply, behavior is contingently modified by reward or punishment. The most important findings are that the longer the reinforcement of the learning, or conditioning, is postponed, the longer the process of learning (conditioning) will take and the weaker the conditioning will be. If the reinforcement of the desired behavior comes too late, the conditioning will not occur at all. Rather, some other element of behavior occurring between the desired behavior and the reinforcement will be reinforced and thus learned.

In both classical and operant conditioning, the time interval between behavior and its reinforcement is of great importance. Consider, for example, the origin of → superstition. A particular behavior perhaps once preceded a certain pleasant (or unpleasant) consequence, which thus encourages the person to repeat the behavior more frequently (or avoid it more carefully). For both kinds of conditioning, a reinforcement that is delayed or that is indicated unclearly slows the learning process; interestingly enough, this kind of inconsistent reinforcement

at the same time makes the relevant behavior resistant to extinguishing. Postponed and unsystematic reward influences human behavior in many ways (e.g., in → education). Here, however, we also must consider other kinds of learning, as for instance concept learning and learning through reason.

Operant principles are also part of the methods employed in behavior therapy today (see 4.1), and they also play an important role in the attempt to explain the persistence of physical and psychological disturbances. Phobias (→ Fear 2) could be mentioned here. Those with phobias receive reinforcement both from active avoidance of the adverse circumstances and from the social attention they receive because of the problem (H. Reinecker).

2.2. Academic criticism of behaviorism starts with the fact that it pays attention only to externally observable and measurable *open* behavior. The concealed behavior that can be measured only indirectly but is still important and interesting is an object of cognitive → psychology (§4), which developed in opposition to the behaviorist paradigm and is still a great influence in psychology today. Its main themes are that research into cognitive and emotional-motivational processes will better explain and predict human behavior. Cognitive psychology is concerned to interpret actively the stimuli around us in the light of what we have at our disposal through earlier experiences (cognitive schema), such as how ideas and attributions arise and how, finally, the transformed stimuli influence behavior. The cognitive theory is most important in therapy, for cognitively oriented therapists try to modify the thinking processes of their patients in such a way as to influence their emotions and finally their behavior (E. Fürntratt; G. C. Davison and J. M. Neale; see 4.2).

2.3. Exchange theorists in → social psychology focus on the results and concepts of learning theory, for they describe social behavior as a function of its consequences (i.e., its rewards and punishments; G. Mikula, 274), whereby in the case of social interaction, these consequences are the behavior of others. This school postulates that (1) only such interactions will be repeated that are rewarding to the partner, (2) voluntary relations will be entered into only if rewards are anticipated, and (3) the maintenance and development of relations that are already present are determined by the rewards they actually offer. A → hedonistic principle is at work here, for we strive to achieve what is pleasant and to avoid what is unpleasant, that is, to achieve the maximum in rewards and the minimum in costs.

On the basis of Skinner's behaviorism, G. C.

Homans (1961) argued that human beings repeat an exchange and extend it to other fields if it is rewarding for them. He postulated the following theses: (1) the more often a certain action of a person is rewarded, the more likely that person will engage in the action; (2) if a person's actions in past encounters with a certain stimulus were rewarded, the person will be more inclined to engage in the same or similar action the more closely the present situation of stimulus resembles that past one; (3) the more valuable the results of an action are, the more likely it will be repeated; and (4) the more often a reward has been obtained in the recent past, the less valuable it will be for every additional unit of reward.

The central thesis of R. W. Thibaut and H. H. Kelley is the mutual dependence of interaction partners in achieving positive results. The maintenance and development of interaction depend on the outcomes, that is, the difference between the expected rewards and the actual costs. The standard of comparison, or the standard of comparison for alternatives, is at the heart of the matter. The attractiveness of an interaction depends on this level, which determines at which point an interaction is considered satisfactory and attractive. The greater the degree to which the outcome surpasses the standard of comparison, the more satisfied the person will be with the interaction. If it falls below the level, it can still be maintained as long as it does not fall below the standard of comparison for alternatives, which indicates the level of outcomes of the next-best alternative. This is why people maintain interactions, even though they may be unsatisfactory.

2.4. Certain problematic forms of behavior like alcoholism, the use of drugs, or excessive smoking (→ Substance Abuse) are often reactions that are learned according to the theories of learning or behaviorism and persist because they soothe tensions. People know that in the long run they are faulty acts that cause harmful consequences. Must not the extremely negative results outweigh the relatively mild easing of stress? The reality of reward and → punishment (§3), measured by its influence on certain behavior, declines, however, with greater temporal distance from the reaction. A small but immediate reward is more effective than one that does not directly follow the reaction. Similarly, punishment that follows days, weeks, or months later has far less enduring impact than one that follows immediately. Thus a brief relief of tension after a wrong line of conduct is an immediate and fairly effective reinforcer. By contrast, longer-term consequences often do not dissuade such behavior, for they come only long after the enjoyment has passed.

3. Deviance

As a general category for various forms of behavior such as delinquency and suicide, social sciences use the term "deviance." Common to all the forms that are characterized as deviant is that most of a certain segment of the population regard them as unusual, inappropriate, or dangerous (H. Keupp). To say that people and their behavior are abnormal is inseparably bound up with certain social and cultural consequences (Davidson and Neale, 52). Contemporary research into deviancy seeks to demonstrate how the normal and the abnormal presuppose each other. This problem is at the heart of the interactionist theory of deviance taught by H. S. Becker, known by the designation "labeling perspective" (Keupp).

Theoreticians of learning have reduced the distinction between normal and abnormal behavior. They begin with the fact that deviant behavior is learned like most of the rest of human conduct. They thus concentrate on those particular learning processes that lead to inappropriate behavior in order to discover possibilities for treating such behavior. From the standpoint of cognitive psychology, a certain schema of perception and interpretation concerning the stimuli around us is responsible for deviance (Davison and Neale).

4. Therapy

The behavior therapy developed since the 1960s represents an attempt to apply the results of experimental psychology to change ways of conduct that are inappropriate or that cause → suffering. In this manner behavior therapy tries to provide their clients with more effective ways of dealing with life.

4.1. The procedure of systematic desensitization developed by J. Wolpe rests on the principle of counterconditioning and is successfully used to deal with anxiety. Patients first learn deep muscular relaxation, and then, in a state of deep relaxation, they can review situations that normally cause them great anxiety. But since → anxiety and relaxation do not mix, anxiety is increasingly reduced. Over the course of these sessions, clients work on the hierarchy of anxiety from the bottom up, learning to tolerate increasingly difficult situations (Davison and Neale, 641). To carry over what is learned in therapy into daily life, patients are given homework between sessions, being advised to place themselves into situations that involve more and more anxiety, which they are to overcome through the techniques of depth-relaxation they have learned. This so-called in vivo confrontation has in the meantime become a decisive element in handling disturbances of anxiety and panic (→ Psychotherapy).

The findings of operant conditioning by Skinner have produced methods of behaviorist therapy. Systematic reinforcement by reward builds up the desired behavior, and ignoring, or negative reinforcement, can eliminate behavior that is not desired. Such methods have proved useful, for example, in dealing with faulty behavior in children, whereby a therapist works with parents and others (e.g., teachers) at changing their practices of reinforcement (Davison and Neale).

4.2. The results of cognition research (see 2.2) lead to methods of so-called cognitive restructuring, by which we understand quite generally a change of the particular models of thought that are believed to be the cause of emotional disturbance or disturbed behavior (Davison and Neale, 658).

The rational-emotive therapy of A. Ellis focuses on what are known as inappropriate inner guiding principles of a disturbed person (e.g., "I must always be perfect in order to be loved"). Through rational observation, this therapy seeks to make them superfluous and to replace them with a more realistic view of the counselee's own person and the world.

The cognitive theory of A. T. Beck rests on his observation that many — and especially → depressive — disturbances are caused by negative views of the self, the environment, and the future, which often are based on faulty logic. An example is the so-called overgeneralization that draws comprehensive conclusions from individual — and perhaps trivial — incidents. With clients, therapists must be concerned to track down and examine every false interpretation of the world that plunges the clients deeper into depression and to replace it by a more satisfactory view ("collaborative empiricism"; see Davison and Neal, 663).

In addition to these methods, behaviorist therapy has access to many other promising techniques such as, for example, training by role models (→ Play) and the learning of models, training in self-assertion, and training in solving social problems. In clinical practice a therapist will use one method after or alongside another so as to address as many controllable variables as possible ("broad-band theory"; see Davison and Neale, 671).

Bibliography: N. Birbaumer and H. P. Huber, "Verhalten und Erleben," *Handbuch psychologischer Grundbegriffe* (ed. T. Herrmann, P. R. Hofstätter, H. P. Huber, and F. E. Weinert; Munich, 1977) 513-20 • L. Blöschl, "Verhaltensmodifikationen und Verhaltenstherapie," ibid. 520-27 • G. C. Davison and J. M. Neale, *Abnormal Psychology: An Experimental Approach* (4th ed.; New York, 1986) • E. Fürntratt, "Behaviorismus," *Handwörterbuch Psychologie* (Weinheim, 1992) 54-59 • G. C. Homans, *Social Behavior: Its Elementary Forms* (New York, 1961) • E. Jaeggi, "Verhaltenstherapie," *Handwörterbuch Psychologie,* 531-35 • H. Keupp, "Abweichendes Verhalten," ibid. 4-10 • A. Maslow, *The Farther Reaches of Human Nature* (New York, 1971) • G. Mikula, "Psychologische Theorien des Austausches," *Theorien der Sozialpsychologie,* vol. 2, *Gruppen- und Lerntheorien* (ed. D. Frey and M. Irle; Bern, 1985) 273-305 • J. R. Nitsch, "Verhaltung und Handlung," *Handwörterbuch Psychologie,* 525-30 • H. Reinecker, *Grundlagen der Verhaltenstherapie* (Munich, 1987) • D. N. Robinson and R. B. Edwards, "Behaviorism," *EncBio* 1.229-38 • B. F. Skinner, *Science and Human Behavior* (New York, 1953) • R. W. Thibaut and H. H. Kelley, *The Social Psychology of Groups* (New York, 1959) • E. L. Thorndike, *Animal Intelligence* (Washington, D.C., 1889) • D. Wendt, *Allgemeine Psychologie* (Stuttgart, 1989).

Christiane Möhle-Köhnken and Dieter Frey

Belarus

	1960	1980	2000
Population (1,000s):	8,190	9,659	10,284
Annual growth rate (%):	0.99	0.69	−0.23

Area: 207,595 sq. km. (80,153 sq. mi.)

A.D. *2000*
Population density: 50/sq. km. (128/sq. mi.)
Births / deaths: 1.03 / 1.28 per 100 population
Fertility rate: 1.40 per woman
Infant mortality rate: 13 per 1,000 live births
Life expectancy: 70.5 years (m: 65.4, f: 75.6)
Religious affiliation (%): Christians 73.9 (Orthodox 50.6, Roman Catholics 14.0, unaffiliated 6.2, Protestants 1.9, indigenous 1.2, other Christians 0.1), nonreligious 21.3, atheists 3.9, other 0.9.

1. General
2. Orthodox, Catholics, and Uniates
3. Protestants

1. General

The Belarusians, who include the ancient Krivichi and Dregovichi of the central and western regions of Kievan Rus, have often been overlooked but yet have achieved remarkable influence. Usually part of some larger political state, though retaining their own language or four basic dialects, the Republic of Belarus finally came into being in 1991 and became a member of the Commonwealth of Independent States (CIS). Its capital, Minsk, also became the capital of the CIS. Geographically, Belarus has a largely flat terrain. Belarusian became the official language for a population that in the 1989 census was divided ethnically among Belarusians (77.9 percent), Russians (13.2 percent), Poles (4.1 percent), Ukrainians (2.9 percent), Jews (1.1 percent), and some others. ("Belarusian" is the current international spelling for peoples also known as Belorussians, Byelorussians, White Russians, Baltorussians, White Ruthenians, Radzimichi, Dregovichi, Viatichi, and Krivichi; the last four are ancient tribal groups whose dialects are still distinct.)

2. Orthodox, Catholics, and Uniates

Having accepted Christianity in 988 as part of Kievan Rus, the Belarus gained the designation "White Russians" because they managed to avoid paying tribute to either the Tatars in the East or the Lithuanians in the West. Sometime after 1250, however, the Belarusians sought the protection of the emergent Grand Duchy of Lithuania, placing themselves in vassalage. Old Slavonic, which evolved into Belarusian, became the official language of the Lithuano-Belarusian state. After 1386, when Grand Duke Jogaila married Jadwiga, queen of Poland, thus uniting two states, a slow decline in Belarusian influence began. It remained the language of the lower classes, but the Orthodox Christian culture (→ Orthodox Church) now faced increased → Roman Catholic influence.

A third major confessional influence emerged in 1596 when the Union of Brest-Litovsk (a Belarusian city) established what came to be known as the → Uniate Church, or Eastern Rite Roman Catholic. In essence, Slavic Orthodox Christians accepted the primacy of the Roman pontiff in exchange for permission to retain their own liturgy in the vernacular and a married priesthood. Intended as a reunion of Eastern and Western Christianity, Uniates became a distinctly separate church structure caught between the politics of East and West. When Poland was partitioned (1772, 1793, 1795) and taken over by the Austrian, German, and Russian empires, the Belarusian territory largely disappeared into the Russian Empire. The Uniate Church was swallowed up into Russian Orthodoxy, although some of the faithful continued to practice in secret. After World War I and the Treaty of Brest-Litovsk, the changed border between the USSR and Poland resulted in most Belarusians being part of Poland and becoming the predominant ethnic group in the region of Polesia. Retaken by the Soviets in 1943, it became the

Belorussian Republic, fully integrated into the USSR, and also into the Russian Orthodox Church again. Only in 1990 were there indications of a developing national self-consciousness.

The Belarusian territory, like Poland itself, became a place of shelter for Jews from eastern Europe (→ Diaspora 1). The so-called Pale of Settlement (stemming from decrees of Russian empress Catherine the Great in 1783, 1791, and 1794), beyond which Jews were not permitted to move in the Russian Empire, bordered Belarus. As a result, by World War II, Jews represented 10.4 percent of the population in Polesia. Over 80 percent of these were killed after 1941 by Einsatzgruppen (task forces) B and C in northern and southern Belarus, respectively, to hasten the "final solution" of the Jewish "problem." Two other tragedies associated with Belarus were the mass executions in 1941 at Khatyn and Kurapaty, where over 1,000 people were killed and buried in mass graves on the order of L. P. Beria, and the Chernobyl nuclear disaster of 1986, which left radioactive damage in over three-fourths of Belarusian territory. Thus the history of major European events during the past millennium requires a Belarusian subtext.

A general history of the Russian Orthodox Church can serve as a history for the Belarusian Orthodox, since the majority of the population is still largely Orthodox. The Belarusian Orthodox story is not merely one of subjugation to empire. The bishops and the metropolitan sent to Minsk served Soviet policies of pacification of conquered peoples by facilitating their religious worship. Starting with Nikolai, and more obviously later with Metropolitan Filaret of Minsk, Belarusian churchmen headed the External Affairs Department of the Russian Orthodox Patriarchate and exerted major influence within the church and abroad. David Marples has noted that the official Soviet interpretation of World War II (namely, to highlight the high casualty rate) "may have served to enhance loyalty to the Soviet Regime, and to establish a pivotal role for Belarus as one of the republics to have suffered most from the evil" (p. 5). This role included keeping the church under control and, more broadly, shaping the direction the entire Russian Orthodox Church and Evangelical Christians–Baptists took during the Soviet era. One might say that by subordinating themselves to the larger body, the Belarusians played a significant, larger role. That observation fits the career patterns of several politicians as well as leaders of the evangelical Protestant movement.

Church life in Belarus under the Soviets was similar to that within the USSR as a whole. By 1958 the Diocese of Minsk had officially registered 967 parishes. With the Khrushchevian attack on religion, this number was reduced to 423 by 1966, continuing to decline to only 370 parishes in 1986. During the next five years of glasnost and perestroika, renewed registration of parishes became possible, and thus by 1991 the number had risen to 610. By 1994 there were already 850 parishes within the diocese.

With Belarus's declaration of sovereignty in July 1990, a new era began of uncertainty and even conflict between Roman Catholics and Orthodox. Jan Zaprudnik suggested that Catholics were identified with Polishness, with a Latin and Western orientation, whereas Orthodoxy was identified with the Russians. In his estimate, 7.5 million of 10.1 million in 1993 were Orthodox-leaning, with about 1 million Catholics. To counter the religio-nationalist schisms that so troubled the Ukraine since 1990, the Russian Orthodox Patriarchate gave Metropolitan Filaret of Minsk the title "exarch of Minsk."

For its part, the Vatican shocked the Orthodox by creating several bishoprics in the former Soviet Union, including making Cardinal Kazimierz Swiatek head of the 341 parishes in Belarus, where in 1996 the Catholics claimed two million adherents (*G2W* 24/1 [1996] 10).

Finally, it is uncertain how many will reassert their Uniate allegiance, since a forced "reunion" with Moscow at L'viv in 1946 has been rejected by Uniate leaders. Since that date, Uniate Christians made repeated efforts to recover their legal right to exist, which was finally granted in 1989, just before Mikhail Gorbachev visited the Vatican. A separate, legal Greek Catholic (Uniate) Church has resulted in conflicts over return of church buildings and has drastically decimated Orthodox strength in western Ukraine. The estimates of possible Uniate adherents in Belarus range from a mere 33,000 to at least one-third of Orthodox parishes.

3. Protestants

Belarus also has a minority Protestant history, which began with the Hussite Reformation when Jerome of Prague, a follower of Jan → Hus (ca. 1372-1415), came to teach in Vitebsk for two months in 1413. Many young men then went to study at the University of Prague. Between 1517 and 1525 Georgi (Frantsiska) Skorin of Polotsk translated the Bible into Belarusian, heavily influenced by M. → Luther's translation. The Orthodox Church rejected the translation. By 1535 a Calvinist-oriented church had opened in Slutsk and was supported by wealthy magnates. This Reformed, or Calvinist, Protestantism (→ Calvinism) declined after 1596 in the face of strong Catholic persecution.

The memory of earlier Protestantism had its effect after the mid-19th century, when free churches, or neo-Protestantism, emerged in Belarus. Some influence came from peasants seeking work in Russia and southern Ukraine who experienced Baptist or other evangelical Christian worship and returned as evangelists. Polish Baptists moved to Belarusian territory after 1915 and started churches. Still other poor Belarusians emigrated to America, were converted, and returned to influence their relatives. Of key significance were Bible colporteurs at the end of the 19th century selling copies of Scripture in Belarusian and organizing churches. Also in Belarus the group "Churches of Christ" emerged in 1924, led by K. I. Yaroshevich. This union, which claimed 70 churches by 1939, was later absorbed into the Belarusian part of the All Union Council of Evangelical Christians–Baptists (AUCECB). → Pentecostals who had emerged in the interwar years were part of a united evangelical union in Poland. After 1945 they too were forced to join the AUCECB, with the Belarusian representative Pan'ko playing a more prominent role than did those from the Ukraine.

When the Khrushchevian pressures came, the AUCECB in Belarus experienced a serious split, with a breakaway group organizing itself in 1966 as the Council of Churches of Evangelical Christians–Baptists (CCECB). By 1988 the AUCECB had recovered its influence and claimed 195 churches, 39 of them newly registered since 1980. The largest Protestant alternative was a very loose union of 26 autonomous CCECB churches, all but two registered since 1980, the largest of which is a church in Brest with over 1,000 members. Forced to adapt their formerly centralized administration to the virtual independence of the "independent states" of the CIS, the AUCECB renamed itself the Euro-Asiatic Federation of ECB Unions.

The Pentecostals, the autonomous Evangelical Christians–Baptists, and the CCECB churches have retained association status with similar bodies in the former Soviet Union and receive financial and training support from mission and service agencies from the West. The Belarus ECB Union is an active member of the European Baptist Federation.

Although statistics are incomplete, all confessional bodies have concentrated since 1990 on church building projects, evangelism, and charity ministries to assist the many nonreligious persons looking for values after the political and ideological collapse of the → atheistic Soviet state. The major concern for Orthodox, Catholic, and Protestant free churches is the preparation of → clergy through the establishment of theological schools. A second concern is the publication of religious literature in the new official language, Belarusian (although most Belarusians in fact have no trouble reading Russian).

Bibliography: "Belorusskoe bratstvo," *Istoriya evangel'skikh khristian–baptistov v SSSR* (Moscow, 1989) chap. 3 • R. Crampton and B. Crampton, *Atlas of Eastern Europe in the Twentieth Century* (London, 1996) • N. Davis, *A Long Walk to Church: A Contemporary History of Russian Orthodoxy* (Boulder, Colo., 1994) • I. S. Lubachko, *Belorussia under Soviet Rule, 1917-1957* (Seattle, Wash., 1993) • D. R. Marples, *Belarus: From Soviet Rule to Nuclear Catastrophe* (New York, 1996) • J. S. Olsen, L. B. Pappas, and N. J. Pappas, "Belarusian," *An Ethnohistorical Dictionary of the Russian and Soviet Empires* (Westport, Conn., 1994) • "Republic of Belarus–Crushing Civil Society," *Human Rights Watch* (Helsinki) 9/8 (August 1997) • V. Rich, "Belarus: Nation in Search of a History," *Index on Censorship* (1991) • N. P. Vakar, *Belorussia: The Making of a Nation* (Cambridge, Mass., 1956) standard history • J. Zaprudnik, *Belarus: At a Crossroads in History* (Boulder, Colo., 1993) • J. Zaprudnik and H. Fedor, "Belarus," *Belarus and Moldova: Country Studies* (Washington, D.C., 1995) 1-91.

Walter Sawatsky

Belgium

	1960	1980	2000
Population (1,000s):	9,153	9,852	10,257
Annual growth rate (%):	0.67	0.01	0.12

Area: 30,528 sq. km. (11,787 sq. mi.)

A.D. 2000

Population density: 336/sq. km. (870/sq. mi.)
Births / deaths: 1.09 / 1.09 per 100 population
Fertility rate: 1.69 per woman
Infant mortality rate: 6 per 1,000 live births
Life expectancy: 77.9 years (m: 74.6, f: 81.1)
Religious affiliation (%): Christians 88.3 (Roman Catholics 81.9, unaffiliated 3.3, Protestants 1.3, other Christians 1.8), nonreligious 5.6, Muslims 3.7, atheists 1.8, other 0.6.

1. Churches
2. Interdenominational Dialogue
3. Church and State
4. Non-Christian Religions

1. Churches

1.1. In the last decades of the 20th century, the → Roman Catholic Church has shown renewed vitality,

a revived Christian consciousness. A newly kindled love for the Bible brought with it a return to the original sources of Scripture. The abandoning of Latin in the liturgy brought a renewal that promoted the participation of believers in the services. New methods of → catechesis were meant to strengthen the interest of young people. The church owed its upswing mainly to the integration of the laity (→ Lay Movements) into church life. It gradually lost its official character and won the confidence of its members by showing more understanding for human problems. It showed itself open to a freer → spirituality.

As almost everywhere in western Europe, however, the church bemoaned the decline in attendance at Sunday → worship. In 1950 about 50 percent of Belgians were at mass, but in 1976 only 30 percent. Many sociologists explain this decline in terms of the rejection of an official church by the younger generation. The improvement of social relations has also perhaps brought indifference with it. This might be one cause for changes in religious motivation and the rise of many smaller groups. But a more impersonal → technology has also led to a certain religious nostalgia.

Parallel to the decline in attendance has been a growth in organizations such as schools, youth movements, unions, health insurance companies, hospitals, journals, and a political party. Neither the sharp decline in attendance and the smaller decline in baptisms, weddings, and burials nor the debates within the church have affected the religious consciousness, according to sociological studies. But there has been an obvious reaction to most of the sociocultural elements of → Catholicism. The concern to be present in the world even outside educational and charitable institutions raises among an increasing number of Roman Catholics the question whether → dialogue with non-Christians will not be necessary in pluralistic organizations.

Under the leadership of Cardinal G. Danneels, archbishop of Mechlin-Brussels since 1980, the Roman Catholic Church has addressed modern problems, combining theological competence with a readiness to compromise (the latter often extolled as a national virtue). The church has sometimes appeared to embrace a curious mixture of old theology and new sociology.

Pope John Paul II came to Belgium in June 1995 for the beatification of Father Damien, a missionary among lepers at Molokai, Hawaii. This visit highlighted a growing estrangement of Belgian Catholics from the pontiff, whose strict declarations about birth control, priestly → celibacy, and divorce have antagonized many of the faithful. The United Protestant Church of Belgium (UPCB) declined an invitation to attend the ceremony, finding the event contrary to the gospel.

1.2. Belgian → Protestantism also went through a process of development during the latter part of the 20th century. Although religious freedom is fully protected legally, social acceptance of Protestants as a minority church has been less complete. As a result of the movement of Pan-Protestantism, the UPCB, founded in 1979, has brought together the traditions of the Presbyterian, Methodist, Reformed, and Lutheran Churches, as well as the Belgian branch of the Dutch Gereformeerde Kerken (→ Reformed and Presbyterian Churches 4.1). The UPCB is in fact a microcosm in which the tendencies of world Protestantism coexist. Orthodoxy with fundamentalist overtones is represented, as are less dogmatic liberal opinions and all positions in between. This church is striving to witness as a Christian body, not without tensions when prompted to issue declarations with ethical or political implications.

The death of the beloved King Baudouin (ruled 1951-93), who, driven by genuine Christian conviction, had shown interest in Protestantism, generated a general upsurge of loyalty to the Crown. After his impressive funeral service, the Belgian people rallied around his brother, Albert II.

On the eve of the founding of this united church, a multilingual service was held on November 4, 1978, attended by a delegate of the king as well as representatives of sister churches abroad. This church remains a member of the → World Council of Churches (WCC), the → World Alliance of Reformed Churches, the Methodist World Council, and the → Conference of European Churches.

Organized in 1942, the Protestant Theological Faculty, which enjoys widespread recognition in Belgian universities, has contributed significantly to intellectual growth in Belgian Protestantism by training many pastors and religious teachers. Its intercontinental outreach includes a doctoral program for Zairian professors and the upgrading of the Faculté de Théologie protestante de Butare (Rwanda), whose staff has been killed or disbursed and its buildings ransacked during the tragic upheaval in this country.

Links with → Lutheranism go back to the first two Reformation martyrs, who were burned to death in Brussels in 1521. Danish, Norwegian, and Swedish churches have been founded in Brussels.

1.3. Besides the UPCB, Belgium has free churches that originated in revivalist movements started by groups from abroad. Engaged in missionary outreach, they are often jealous of their respective brands of theology and reject the concerns and structures of the WCC. Cooperating with the UPCB in religious education in state schools and in various chaplaincies, they nevertheless are very reticent about joining conversations aiming at church unity, which the UPCB considers its vocation. Its synod has invited the free churches to discuss the present situation. The participation in overall solidarity about common concerns seems to be superseded by an impatience to share power.

The most important free churches are the → Pentecostal churches, → Baptists, → Plymouth Brethren, and → Mennonites. The Mission Évangélique Belge developed into a church in 1962 when eight of its congregations formed a fellowship of free churches, to which 33 congregations now belong.

1.4. The → Anglican Church, present in Belgium since the 17th century, has six congregations.

1.5. The → Orthodox Church came to Belgium in 1885 with the founding of a Russian chapel. It grew when Russian immigrants came to Belgium in 1917. With the settling of eastern European refugees of the Orthodox confession since 1945 and the coming of Greek migrant workers, it grew further and now has an estimated 50,000 members.

2. Interdenominational Dialogue

2.1. In Belgium relations between the denominations can be described as good. The monastery of Chevetogne, founded in 1925, has played a significant role in → dialogue. Since the Mechlin conversations the Roman Catholic Church has had friendly relations with the Anglican Church. Examples of positive relations were the address given by Cardinal Suenens at a session of the Protestant church and the presence of the papal nuncio at the opening sessions of the Protestant faculty. An example of interfaculty cooperation was the publication of the study *Luther Today* on the initiative of the dean of the Catholic theological faculty of Louvain-la-Neuve, with contributions from the professors of both faculties. The Catholic and Protestant churches, along with German-speaking Protestant congregations, recognize one another's baptism. One of the most important ecumenical prayer services took place on May 19, 1973, in St. Michael's Cathedral, Brussels. The participants were more concerned to raise support for the → Third World than to promote their own well-being.

2.2. The Protestant church has refrained from direct missionary work among Jews, but at the same time it has shown a great concern to obviate misunderstandings and to study the common sources of

Christianity and Judaism. Exchanges are taking place in Antwerp, Brussels, and Ostend, and also among the Sisters of the Holy Virgin of Zion. → Jewish-Christian dialogue also profits from the study of theological questions by the interuniversity Institutum Judaicum, which holds regular colloquia and meetings.

3. Church and State

3.1. Since gaining its independence from the Netherlands in 1830, Belgium has recognized four denominations — Catholic, Protestant, Anglican, and Eastern Orthodox — as well as the Jewish faith. According to article 117 of the constitution, the state gives financial support to ministers. Local councils give legal guarantees and make it possible to cover deficits (→ Church Finances). State, provincial, and local funds can be used for the building or repair of church property. Islam gained recognition in 1974, and the state now also pays the salaries of some imans.

3.2. For a long time the → lay movement sought the separation of church and state. It now works for a confessional-type acknowledgment from the state. Various movements came together on July 3, 1969, to form a Center for Lay Action and a Unie Vrijzinnige Vereinigingen, both under the Central Lay Council. The minister of justice supplied funds for this organization for the first time in 1981.

3.3. Apart from chaplaincies in the armed forces, hospitals, and prisons, it is in → religious instruction that the special relation to the state is plain. Parents of students at state schools can choose for their children Catholic, Protestant, Jewish, or Muslim teaching, or they can choose a nondenominational → moral education. Church boards and synods may nominate candidates for teaching positions to the ministers of education.

4. Non-Christian Religions

4.1 In numbers → Islam is the strongest single religious body after Roman Catholicism. Since there has been no religious census since 1846, reliable figures are not available. As a result of the massive immigration of guest workers, it is estimated that in 2000 there will be over 350,000 Muslims, with perhaps only half practicing their religion. The settling of these immigrants in particular communities and city wards provoked incidents of → racism. Efforts were made at the national level, however, to guarantee Muslims the free exercise of their religion. A first Muslim center was founded in Brussels in 1963. On May 7, 1978, the Oriental pavilion in Conquantenaire Park was declared to be an Islamic Cultural Center. King Baudouin, along with Saudi Arabian ruler Caleb, attended the opening. A large mosque was built there, and there are about 100 smaller meeting places throughout the country.

4.2. The formerly large Jewish community was decimated by the → Holocaust and now numbers less than 30,000, mostly in the cities. A focus of unity for the different branches is the Central Council of the Jewish Communities of Belgium. In making the Jewish heritage known, several Jewish elementary and secondary schools play an important part, as do sporting, cultural, and charitable organizations and the Martin Buber University Institute for Jewish Research.

4.3. In a society increasingly pluralistic, the Christian churches in Belgium have tended to move closer to each other. Engulfed in progressing secularism, the Roman Catholic Church has shed its triumphalistic approach to society and considers the former "heretics" to have become today's "separated brothers." The Protestant church is developing an awareness of its role as a link between a more tolerant Roman Catholicism and lay humanism, which intended to make its mark on a wider public. The latter movement, which previously sought complete separation of church and state, now accepts state subsidies similar to those received by the churches. It has opened Maisons de la Laïcité in several Belgian towns.

Bibliography: R. ANDRÉ, "Religion, Secularism, and Politics," *Modern Belgium* (ed. M. Boudart, M. Boudart, and R. Bryssinck; Palo Alto, Calif., 1990) • R. AUBERT, *150 ans de vie des églises* (Brussels, 1980) • D. BARRETT, ed., *WCE* 169-73 • J. BILLIET, "Religion and the Institutionalization of Different Subcultures," *Religion and Social Change* (ed. J. Aranguren et al.; Lille, 1975) 345-51 • H. R. BOUDIN, *De Léopold Ier à Jean Rey. Les protestants en Belgique de 1839 à 1989* (Brussels, 1990) • H. R. BOUDIN and M. BLOK, *Synodaal gedenkboek–Mémorial synodal, 1839-1992* (Brussels, 1992) • J. ESTRUCH, "L'église réformée de Belgique," *Soc Comp* 16 (1969) 387-94 • F. HOUTART, "Belgium," *Western Religion: A Country by Country Sociological Inquiry* (ed. H. Mol; The Hague, 1972) 67-82 • G. VAN LEEUWEN, "Der belgische Protestantismus im Prozeß der Neuorientierung," *Diaspora,* 1974, 66-79 • E. PICHAL, *De Geschiedenis van het Protestantisme in Vlaanderen* (Antwerp, 1975) • L. VOYÉ, "Situation religieuse des catholiques en Belgique II: De l'adhésion ecclésiale du catholicisme socio-culturel en Wallonie," *Acta 15e IKRS* (Venice, 1979).

H. R. BOUDIN

Belize

	1960	*1980*	*2000*
Population (1,000s):	93	146	242
Annual growth rate (%):	2.81	2.56	2.26

Area: 22,965 sq. km. (8,867 sq. mi.)

A.D. 2000

Population density: 11/sq. km. (27/sq. mi.)
Births / deaths: 2.75 / 0.39 per 100 population
Fertility rate: 3.14 per woman
Infant mortality rate: 27 per 1,000 live births
Life expectancy: 75.7 years (m: 74.2, f: 77.1)
Religious affiliation (%): Christians 90.7 (Roman Catholics 66.1, Protestants 19.1, Anglicans 3.9, indigenous 2.4, marginal 2.3, unaffiliated 1.5), Baha'is 3.0, Hindus 2.5, Jews 1.0, other 2.8.

Formerly British Honduras (to 1973), Belize lies between Guatemala and Mexico on the Caribbean coast of Central America. From the middle of the 17th century British traders exploited the coast from Campeche to Belize, cutting timber (for dyeing) and building factories. After 1680 Spanish pressure forced the British out of the Yucatán peninsula and into the stretch of coast in Belize between the Río Hondo and the Río Belize. With the Dallas-Clarendon agreement they secured control over a territory enlarged from 6,000 to 20,000 sq. km. (2,300 to 7,700 sq. mi.). In 1859 Guatemala recognized British sovereignty on the condition that the British link Guatemala City and Belize at their own cost. So far they have not fulfilled this condition.

In 1981 Belize became an independent state with a parliamentary constitution, but British troops remained, protecting it against Guatemalan claims. In April 1993 Belize and Guatemala signed a nonagression pact. Britain then announced that by the end of 1994, all its troops would be removed from the country. Agricultural exports (sugar, citrus fruits, bananas, cocoa) are the basis of Belize's economy, but → tourism is also a major source of foreign exchange. Most of the people are descendants of African slaves, mestizos, and → Indians. Only 2 percent of the population is white, but it largely forms the upper class.

Approximately 90 percent of the nation's inhabitants are Christians. Two-thirds of these are Roman Catholic, followed by Seventh-day Adventists, Anglicans, Methodists, Assemblies of God, Nazarenes, Baptists, and 20 other denominations. From 1957 the Belize Council of Churches (with eight member churches and four associate bodies) has served as an interfaith organization. Its churches are involved especially in → development (§1), education, and health services.

Belize is a secular → state and by law treats all the churches equally. It has no diplomatic relations with the Vatican. Other religious groups (with estimated percentage of the population in the year 2000) include Bahai's (3.0), Hindus (2.5), Jews (1.0), spiritsts (0.8), Muslims (0.6), Buddhists (0.4), and tribal religionists (0.1).

Bibliography: A. C. BURNS, *A History of the British West Indies* (London, 1954) • J. MATA GAVIDIA, *Anotaciones de historia patria centroamericana* (Guatemala City, 1969) • M. RODRIGUEZ, *Central America* (Englewood Cliffs, N.J., 1965) • J. E. S. THOMPSON, *Maya History and Religion* (Norman, Okla., 1970).

THE EDITORS

Bellarmine, Robert

Robert Bellarmine (b. Montepulciano, Tuscany, October 4, 1542; d. Rome, September 17, 1621) was one of the best-known and most widely published Roman Catholic theologians of the post-Reformation period. He entered the Society of Jesus in 1560, began the study of theology at Padua in 1567, and in 1569 went to Louvain both as student and as professor. There he began his lectures on → Roman Catholic teachings then under attack by the → Reformers. In 1576 he was appointed to the chair of controversial theology at the Roman College, later the Gregorian University. His lectures over the next decade resulted in his most important work: the three-volume *Controversies* (1586-93), or *Disputationes de controversiis Christianae fidei adversus huius temporis haereticos* (Lectures concerning the controversies on the Christian faith against the heretics of the present time). In 20 editions over the next centuries, it was the most comprehensive Roman Catholic reply to the central theological questions raised by the Protestant Reformers. Bellarmine's treatment of the nature and characteristics of the → church was especially influential on Catholic thought on the subject.

Rightly known as a defender of Roman Catholic positions, Bellarmine nonetheless stood firm against Pope Sixtus V's personal attempt at editing the official version of the Latin Vg Bible and was later put in charge of the revision that became the Catholic Church's received text of the Scriptures for the next several centuries. Only the death of Sixtus V kept the → pope from putting the *Controversies* itself on the Index of Forbidden Books; Sixtus thought that Bellarmine's opinions therein unduly restricted the pope's temporal jurisdiction.

After serving in Paris as theological adviser to the papal legate sent to help untangle the question of Henry IV's succession to the French throne, Bellarmine returned to Rome to serve as spiritual director for the young → Jesuits at the Roman College and for the seminarians of the English College. He was then briefly head of the former institution before going to Naples as superior of the Jesuit province there. In 1597 Pope Clement VIII chose him as his personal theological adviser and in 1599 made him a → cardinal. Meanwhile Bellarmine had published his immensely successful *Catechism,* eventually translated into 62 languages. He was also involved in producing the *Ratio studiorum,* the plan of studies by which the hundreds of Jesuit schools around the world were governed for the next several centuries. In 1602 the pope, who did not take advice well, neither from his friends nor even from the counselors he himself had chosen, temporarily exiled Bellarmine from Rome by appointing him archbishop of Capua, where he became a model of the reforming bishop envisioned by the Council of → Trent.

Pope Paul V called Bellarmine back to Rome to become a member of the papal → curia in 1605. As a result, over the next 16 years he became much involved in internal and external church affairs. Among them were the resolution of the dispute between → Dominicans and Jesuits over the question of divine → grace, the bitter quarrel between the Vatican and Venice over respective secular and religious rights, and the act of James I of England "for the better discovery and repressing of Popish Recusants," by which Catholics were to take a loyalty oath that in parts involved denial of Catholic doctrine.

As a member of the Holy Office, Bellarmine was indirectly involved in the first part of the Galileo case in 1616. As an admirer of Galileo, he helped avoid an explicit condemnation at that time but, far too strongly and incorrectly committed to a literal meaning of Scripture passages that seemed to imply the geocentric nature of the universe, he wanted Galileo to treat heliocentrism not as fact but as theory, since it seemed irreconcilable with the Bible.

In the later years of his life Bellarmine wrote several devotional treatises on the Christian life and Christian spirituality (→ Devotional Literature). They were deeply indebted to Scripture, to the fathers of the church, and to the traditions of his religious family, the Society of Jesus. The most famous of them were *The Art of Dying Well* and *The Mind's Ascent to God by the Ladder of Created Things.* These little treatises were immensely popular. The last named, for example, went through about 60 editions in four languages.

Bibliography: Primary sources: The Louvain Lectures and the Autograph Copy of His 1616 Declaration to Galileo (Rome, 1984) • *Opera omnia* (Naples, 1862) • *Spiritual Writings* (New York, 1989) contains "The Mind's Ascent to God by the Ladder of Created Things" and "The Art of Dying Well" • *Treatise on Civil Government* (Westport, Conn., 1980).

Secondary works: R. BLACKWELL, *Galileo, Bellarmine, and the Bible* (Notre Dame, Ind., 1991) • J. BRODRICK, *Robert Bellarmine, 1542-1621* (2 vols.; London, 1950); idem, *Robert Bellarmine: Saint and Scholar* (Westminster, Md., 1961) condensed and largely rewritten version of the previous item • E. A. RYAN, *The Historical Scholarship of St. Robert Bellarmine* (New York, 1936).

JOHN W. PADBERG, S.J.

Bells

Bells were forged in the most varied cultural circles once the art of metallurgy had been mastered. Little bells were partly used to decorate garments (also as amulets?) (see Exod. 28:33-35); large bells were poured from prebiblical times. They came in various shapes, but cup-shaped bells became the most popular because they gave out the best sound. The favorite metal was bronze (four parts copper to one part tin). Christian use of bells began in the East (→ Orthodox Church). In the West their liturgical use began in monasteries to call the monks to prayer (→ Hours, Canonical). English bell-ringers have developed an elaborate system of chimes, used especially at festivals.

Bibliography: A. L. BIGELOW, "Bells," *NCE* 2.259-63 • S. M. COLEMAN, *Bells: Their History, Legends, Making, and Uses* (Detroit, 1971; orig. pub., 1928) • W. ELLERHORST, *Handbuch der Glockenkunde* (Weingarten, 1957) • H. HICKMANN and C. MAHRENHOLZ, "Glocke," *MGG* 5.267-91 (extensive bibliography) • P. PRICE, "Bell," *The New Grove Dictionary of Music and Musicians* (Washington, D.C., 1980) 2.424-37. CHRISTOPH ALBRECHT

Benedict of Nursia

In his *Second Dialogue,* the earliest notice we have of the life of Benedict of Nursia, Pope → Gregory the Great (590-604) concludes his tale of miracles and wonders with a simple direction: "Anyone who wishes to know more about [Benedict's] life and character can discover in his *Rule* exactly what he was like as an abbot, for his life could not have differed from his teaching." Nevertheless, as biographical sources, both the *Second Dialogue*, written a half-century after Benedict's death, and the *Rule* itself, require caution.

One reason Benedict's life is not noticed in contemporary documents is that → monasticism was already by his time a 200-year tradition of bewildering variety. He would have appeared to be simply one among many who sifted through countless options to organize motifs and themes into a coherent, manageable way of life. His "originality" is characteristic of the late patristic and early medieval period: no one wanted to say anything new, so originality consisted in weaving the old into new patterns. His way, because of its balance, could easily have escaped notice. The *Rule* reflects suspicion of spectacular → asceticisms as well as of accommodations to ease and luxury. Above all, the *Rule* implies suspicion of the capacity of any rule to anticipate all circumstances. In contrast, the *Rule of the Master*, now nearly universally regarded as one of Benedict's main sources, is almost obsessive in its attention to the minutiae of → everyday life. To imagine Benedict intentionally revising the *Rule of the Master* is to get a sidelong glance at a supremely effective legislator of the monastic life who was profoundly skeptical of legalism.

The previous two paragraphs presuppose a decision about a historical question that has been vexed in recent decades: Is the Benedict praised by → Gregory the Great actually the author of the *Rule* that has been attributed to him for more than a millennium? There is no proof that can stand up to the most strident skepticism, especially since it is highly unlikely that Pope Gregory and his monastic colleagues actually organized their life according to what we know as the *Regula Benedicti*. But in that era there probably was not a monastery anywhere that based its life on a single rule. Monastic tradition was a shelf of books, from which a community would pick and choose. Gregory's *Dialogue* seeks to tell more about God's direct action through the agency of Benedict than about Benedict's career on the human plane, but the story is sufficiently plausible and circumstantial to persuade nearly all critics today to include among historical facts the existence, approximate dates, general vicinity, and authorial activity of Benedict of Nursia.

Benedict was born about 480 in Nursia, in the mountains northeast of Rome. He was sent to → Rome for school, where he experienced a religious → conversion and renounced the world. In a pattern that can be seen already in the earliest Christian monastic → biography, the *Life of Anthony* attributed to → Athanasius of Alexandria, the newly committed ascetic spent time with holy men of good reputation, then retired to utter solitude. After three years alone, Benedict headed a group who turned out to be "false monks," and in desperation he returned to Subiaco, his earlier retreat, where numerous disciples joined him. There he founded 12 → monasteries of 12 monks each. After this system was well established, Benedict left with some disciples and founded a true cenobitic monastery on Monte Cassino, 80 miles south of Rome. Pope Gregory says that Benedict's sister, Scholastica, established a monastery for women near Monte Cassino, and that brother and sister met annually to discuss spiritual matters. Benedict died about the year 547.

The *Rule* reflects Benedict's humility, his moderation, and his conviction that the main work of the monk is the *opus Dei*, the daily regimen of common → prayer, and meditative, reflective reading *(lectio divina)*. From an ecumenical perspective, the most striking feature of Benedict's piety is its grounding in Scripture. There are 321 citations of the Bible in the 73 chapters of the *Rule*, including references to every NT book except Colossians, Philemon, 2 Peter, and 3 John. The history of the church reveals few leaders whose vision of the Christian life is more deeply imprinted than Benedict's by the word of Scripture.

Bibliography: T. Fry, O.S.B., ed., *RB 1980: The Rule of St. Benedict in Latin and English, with Notes* (Collegeville, Minn., 1981) esp. 73-79 and bibliography, xxxii-xxxvi • P. Henry, "Rule of Benedict: Charter for Ecumenism," *Mid-Stream*, 1993, 59-69 • J. McCann, *St. Benedict* (New York, 1937; rev. ed., 1958) • O. Zimmermann, trans., *St. Gregory the Great: Dialogues* (New York, 1959). See also the bibliography in "Benedictines," esp. the items by A. de Vogüé.

Patrick Henry

Benedictines

1. The term "Benedictine" applies in a general sense to all monks who live communally according to the rule of Benedict of Nursia (ca. 480-ca. 547). More narrowly Benedictines are members of a Benedictine confederation set up in 1893 by Pope → Leo XIII (1878-1903). To this group belong 21 autonomous congregations with some 9,000 male members and 18,500 female members under an abbot primate in → Rome (*Catalogus monasteriorum OSB* 17 [1990]).

2. → Benedict composed the rule that would decisively shape Western → monasticism originally for

his own → monastery at Monte Cassino (after 529). After the destruction of this house in 577, the rule apparently became accepted in Rome. From there, often in combination with other rules, especially that of Columbanus (ca. 543-615), it spread to the Franks and (in mixed form) to England. Whether the monks whom → Gregory the Great (pope 590-604) sent to England brought the Benedictine rule is debated. But by the picture that Gregory drew of the Italian man of God and wonder-worker Benedict (*Dialogues,* bk. 2), he promoted the influence of his legacy. Toward the end of the seventh century the rule prevailed in England, and by means of the Anglo-Saxon mission in close connection with Rome (St. Boniface, d. 754), it also became the dominant rule on the mainland of Europe. Charlemagne (d. 814) made it the norm for all the monasteries in his empire.

3. Apart from later political influences, the reasons for the rapid spread of the rule lie in the rule itself. Sharing the common monastic tradition, it is distinguished positively from other contemporary rules by its strict but, at the same time, moderate → asceticism, its pedagogical wisdom, its clarity of form, and its great adaptability. A first vow is that of constancy, that is, perseverance in vocation and membership in the community. (The *stabilitas loci,* or vow to remain till death attached to the monastery of the monk's profession, was emphasized somewhat later.) Another vow is to keep the convent's order, which involved such conditions as no private property, silence, → prayer, → humility, and chastity. Finally, there is the vow of → obedience to the abbot as the vicar of Christ. For his part, the abbot, after the manner of a Roman father, must see to the interests of the community as though it were his own family. After an early church model, the rule achieves a balance of prayer and → work. (Only in the later Middle Ages do we encounter the slogan *Ora et labora.*) The obligation of study and the receiving of boys *(pueri oblati)* — which the → Cistercians later abandoned — opened the door to academic and educational work.

4. In the Carolingian kingdom the Benedictine monastery became a state-supported cultural force with its schools, libraries, and workshops, but the movement came increasingly to depend on those in positions of power in church and state (→ Proprietary Church). The reforming and unifying of the Benedictines by Benedict of Aniane (ca. 750-821) (achieved in 817 at the Council of Aachen) led to the development of Western orders. The 10th-century reforms emanating from → Cluny, Gorze, Hirsau, and other places did not seek merely to renew monastic life by an emphasis on liturgical life (such as adding choral services) but also aimed at freeing it from secular and ecclesiastical influence. To accomplish this, houses with a common rule banded together in the 11th century under central leadership and papal protection.

At the same time, Italy saw a linking of the eremitic and Benedictine lifestyles by the Camaldolesians and Vallombrosans. The → Cistercians attempted a radical renewal in the 12th century. As distinct from the Cluniacs, they held that a strict observance of the Benedictine Rule meant → asceticism, → poverty, and manual labor. By a strict system of → filiation they set up the first monastic order, which achieved a great deal of freedom from feudal ties.

The blossoming of the Benedictines in the 11th and 12th centuries was followed by stagnation and decline in the 13th. The mendicants now took the lead, fitting in better with the new, city-oriented social situation. Reform movements in the 15th century led to the founding of some new congregations (e.g., Bursfelde), but soon the → Reformation closed down almost half the Benedictine monasteries in Europe. They continued only in Roman Catholic countries. By its significant scholarly achievements the Congregation of St. Maurus (formed in Paris in 1618) gained special renown in the 17th and 18th centuries.

5. The French → Revolution and → secularization (§4) in 1803 almost obliterated the Benedictines, but they staged an astonishing revival with the → restoration and → Romanticism. They contributed to liturgical renewal at Solesmes (1832), Beuron (1863), and Maria Laach (1892). The upsurge of missionary activity in the age of colonial expansion also included the Benedictines, who linked up with early traditions (→ Catholic Missions; Colonialism). The Congregation of the Missionary Benedictines of St. Ottilia (1883) has joined with other Benedictines, both male and female, in missionary work around the world. Concern for → liturgy, → patristics, biblical → exegesis, → mission, and supporting the → ecumenical movement (Chèvetogne, Niederaltaich; → Una Sancta Movement) is a mark of the modern Benedictines.

6. The story of women Benedictines is related to that of the rule. Houses for women as well as men early adopted the rule in a slightly modified form. The beginnings of this development go back to Scholastica (d. ca. 543), Benedict's sister, who handed over the direction of her convent to her brother. The victory of the rule in England in the seventh and eighth centuries and the resultant mission on the Continent led to the establishment of houses for women, sometimes linked to those for men under the headship of an abbess.

The women's houses suffered from the eclipse at the end of the Carolingian kingdom but also enjoyed revival with the reforms of the 10th and 11th centuries. But they played little part in the association of houses under Cluny. Toward the end of the 12th century many previously independent houses for women linked to the movement of poverty secured official recognition only by adopting the Benedictine Rule, which enjoined both commitment to the contemplative life and strict confinement. During the Reformation the women's houses put up the strongest resistance to disbanding. New branches of women Benedictines arose in France in the 17th century, devoted partly to contemplation and partly to educational work. The rise of monasticism in the 19th century affected women too, and there are now more women Benedictines than men, either engaged in educational, missionary, or cultural work, or devoted to contemplation and worship. But today, as always, they must rely on the support of a male Benedictine or a secular priest in their spiritual life (for the Mass and sacraments).

7. The Benedictine Rule became the basis of all Western monasticism, not merely because of its great adaptability, its moderate asceticism, and its balance of prayer, work, and study, or contemplation and action, but also because of its close linkage to the → spirituality rooted in the early church and finally in the Bible. This explains its influence on new evangelical → congregations that seek forms of Christian life in fellowship that are tested, biblically based, and ecumenically open. As the rule understands itself, it must always keep to the biblical witness in its practical application of a consistent discipleship of Christ, never becoming an independent rule for some extraordinary Christian lifestyle.

→ Orders and Congregations

Periodicals: BenM (from 1919; since 1959, *EuA*) • *RBén* (1884-) extensive bibliography • *RBS* (1972-).

Bibliography: P. BATSELIER, ed., *Benedictus. Eine Kulturgeschichte des Abendlandes* (Geneva, 1980) • K. S. FRANK, "Benediktiner," *TRE* 5.549-60 • S. HILPISCH, *Geschichte der Benediktinerinnen* (St. Ottilien, 1951) • G. HOLZHERR, *Die Benediktsregel* (2d ed.; Einsiedeln, 1982) • B. JASPERT, *Bibliographie der Regula Benedicti, 1930-1980. Ausgaben und Übersetzungen* (Hildesheim, 1983); idem, *Studien zum Mönchtum* (Hildesheim, 1982) • L. VON MATT and S. HILPISCH, *St. Benedict* (London, 1961) • I. P. MÜLLER, *Atlas O.S.B.* (2 vols.; Rome, 1973) • F. RENNER, "Benediktusregel," *TRE* 5.573-77 • P. SCHMITZ, *Histoire de l'Ordre de saint Benoît* (6 vols.; Maredsous, 1942-49) • A. DE VOGÜÉ, "Benedikt von Nursia," *TRE* 5.538-49; idem, *Community and Abbot in the Rule of St. Benedict* (2 vols.; Kalamazoo, Mich., 1979-88); idem, *The Rule of St. Benedict: A Doctrinal and Spiritual Commentary* (Kalamazoo, Mich., 1983).

WOLFGANG A. BIENERT

Benediction

A benediction, from the Lat. *benedicere* (praise, bless, consecrate), was originally praise directed to God (Heb. *bĕrākôt*, LXX *eulogia* and then *doxologia*), whether in the form of public → worship, house (table) fellowship, or individual → prayer. The → Eucharist (from Gk. *eucharisteō*, be thankful, return thanks) took its name from this practice. The NT supplemented Jewish eulogies (→ Eulogia) by the wishing of grace *(charis)* and by formulas of greeting and blessing.

In the church there developed blessings of persons (at worship, official acts, → ordinations, installations, etc.), of things (churches, sacred vessels, → images, → cemeteries, also houses, bridges, fields, carriages, flags, animals, etc.), and of cultic materials (esp. oil, fire, candles, palms, baptismal water, holy water, and wedding rings). Roman Catholic tradition regards most benedictions as sacramental, but after → Vatican II it again linked them to common worship and proclamation of the Word with an orientation to the people rather than being predominantly reserved for → priests (→ Sacramentals). The Protestant tradition has been more restrained and has always kept in mind the essential connection between praise, intercession, and → blessing.

Bibliography: J. BAUMGARTNER, ed., *Gläubiger Umgang mit der Welt* (Freiburg, 1978) • *Benediktionale* (Einsiedeln, 1978) • L. COLEMAN, "Benediction," *The Apostolical and Primitive Church* (Philadelphia, 1871) 373-88 • W. H. DOLBEER, *The Benediction* (Philadelphia, 1907) • *Liturgy and Agenda* (St. Louis, 1936) • R. TATLOCK, *An English Benedictional: Translated and Adapted from the Leofric Missal* (Westminster, 1964).

HANS-CHRISTOPH SCHMIDT-LAUBER

Benedictus → Canticle

Benin

	1960	1980	2000
Population (1,000s):	2,237	3,459	6,222
Annual growth rate (%):	1.66	3.03	2.90

Area: 112,680 sq. km. (43,500 sq. mi.)

A.D. 2000

Population density: 55/sq. km. (143/sq. mi.)
Births / deaths: 4.03 / 1.08 per 100 population
Fertility rate: 5.37 per woman
Infant mortality rate: 73 per 1,000 live births
Life expectancy: 57.1 years (m: 54.8, f: 59.6)
Religious affiliation (%): tribal religionists 46.6, Christians 33.3 (Roman Catholics 24.5, Protestants 3.9, indigenous 3.4, unaffiliated 1.2, other Christians 0.3), Muslims 19.6, other 0.5.

The West African country of Benin, on the Gulf of Guinea, is one of the poorest nations in the world. Formerly named Dahomey, it achieved independence in 1960 after 60 years as a colony of France. It received its new name, the People's Republic of Benin, after a military coup in 1972 and the proclamation of Marxism-Leninism as its ideology in 1975. In December 1989 the leadership officially renounced Communism, which led to multiparty elections in March 1991.

The population of Benin consists of over 50 ethnic groups. The largest of the ethnolinguistic groups are the Fon (2.0 million), followed by the Yoruba (610,000), Adja (560,000), Bariba and Houéda (430,000 each), and Somba (330,000).

The economy is agricultural, with cotton and oil palm products as the most important exports. Industry is poorly developed. Though Benin is virtually self-supporting agriculturally, the extremely rapid growth in population (3.2 percent for the period 1988-93) is becoming increasingly problematic. Already Benin has a high level of unemployment, especially among more highly qualified artisans.

1. The largest Christian church in Benin is the Roman Catholic Church, with over one and a half million adherents. Over 400,000 belong to the Protestant and → Independent Churches together.

1.1. The first Roman Catholic chapel was set up by the Portuguese in 1680. French and Portuguese priests served there in the 17th and 18th centuries. Only after 1860, however, did missionary work begin in earnest, with the Société des missions africaines de Lyon. The composition of a → catechism by Msgr. Steinmetz marks the beginning of the spread of

Roman Catholicism in Benin. The first seminary was founded in Ouidah in 1914, and in 1929 a large one was set up with the help of the → Diocese of St. Gall, whose name it still bears. The first national → priest, Father Mouléro, was ordained in 1928. The archbishopric of Cotonou was formed in 1955, and the first African archbishop appointed in 1960. At his instigation a Cistercian monastery was founded at Parakou.

Roman Catholicism has found its main support in the cities, among the elite, and in the southern half of the country, especially among the Fon, Mina, Adja, and Gun. Work in the North has run up against many difficulties. Along with evangelism there are various social institutions that have given Roman Catholicism a sure footing. A Benin committee of several missionary societies has been set up, consisting of African Christians and having the task of financing Christian work and promoting vocations to the priesthood in religious schools.

1.2. Prominent among non-Catholic Christians in Benin are the Methodists, the Pentecostals, the Sudan Interior Mission, and the → Independent Churches.

1.2.1. The Methodist Church, which derives from British Methodism, began in 1843 with two visits of Pastor Thomas B. Freeman to King Guézo. In about 1924 the district of West Africa was formed under the oversight of the Society of Methodist Missions in London. In 1965 it came under the leadership of the first Benin pastor, Georges Ghéyongbé. The church has a general synod consisting of seven regional synods and three ambitious projects of evangelism. Its social and diaconal activities (→ Diakonia) include an agricultural project in Savé, an information service, a center for admission and education, a special program for women, and a theological school that serves the three countries of Benin, Ivory Coast, and Togo. Pastor Y. Henry is the president of the general synod (1985).

The center of Methodist work was originally the territory of the Gun in the South, but the work has now spread to the Fon in the interior and to the tribes in the North. Believers who have been won by evangelism but who still cling to tribal traditions create severe problems for the Methodists. The issue of how to deal with polygamy has been particularly difficult to resolve (→ Marriage and Divorce 2.7).

1.2.2. The Pentecostals and the U.S.-based Sudan Interior Mission have done the most evangelism in the North. The Pentecostals differ from others by not baptizing infants (→ Baptism) and thus by using only the proclamation of the Word in evangelism. Their congregations are organized at the local level and have no higher links (hence the name "Assemblies of God").

The Sudan Interior Mission opened its first two stations in 1947. It then set up schools and boarding schools and began medical work. It has also undertaken the translation of the Scriptures into the language of the North. Books and tracts are printed in Nigeria and distributed from there. The mission's headquarters is in Nigeria.

1.2.3. There are many Independent Churches in Benin, such as the Église du Christianisme Céleste (1947) and the Chérubins et Séraphins arrivés du Nigeria (1933). The independent Methodist church Eledja broke off from the Methodist Church in 1927, and the national church Bodawa split off from the Anglican Church of Nigeria. These divisions were primarily over polygamy.

2. In ecumenical relations, the Methodists took the lead in uniting all Protestant groups in a national Interfaith Council. This council works with the Roman Catholics in Bible translation and on the committee of the → Bible Societies. Relations between the Methodists and the Roman Catholics are fraternal.

3. With regard to church-state relations, Benin is a secular → state. Up to 1974 the state subsidized the church's educational work and tolerated religious instruction in its schools. In 1976, however, the state nationalized church schools, though cooperating to some extent in appointing teachers. While Benin was following an explicitly Marxist-Leninist ideology (1974-89), tensions existed between the churches and the state. Free, multiparty elections in 1991 have led to a lessening of tensions and complete religious freedom.

4.1. Other religions in Benin include primarily the → tribal religions, the largest single bloc of religious affiliation in the country (→ Guinea 2). Practices of these religions include voodoo, especially among the Fon of Abomey. Characteristic of these religions are fellowship with the gods in their various manifestations and a permanent need to know their will and to consult them through oracles.

4.2. Islam claims close to 20 percent of the population. The Yoruba and Hausa brought it to the south among the Nagot, and the Dendi of Niger brought it to the north among the Fulani, Dendi, and Bariba.

Between the tribal religions and the Christian churches there are no formal relations. Yet → syncretism plays some part. Islam holds significant → dialogue with the Methodist Church. Christians and

Muslims have initiated some common projects of development, which they are now pursuing. Young Methodist pastors are well equipped to engage in the dialogue that takes place within the Islam in Africa Project.

Bibliography: D. Barrett, ed., *WCE* 175-77 • R. Cornevin, *La République populaire du Bénin* (Paris, 1981) • J. Egharevba, *A Short History of Benin* (Ibadan, 1968) • R. Home, *City of Blood Revisited: A New Look at the Benin Expedition of 1897* (London, 1982).

Samuel Akle

Bernard of Clairvaux

Born to minor nobility at Fontaines-les-Dijon, Bernard (1090-1153) entered the recently founded "New Monastery" of Cîteaux (Burgundy, Fr.) in 1112, bringing with him some 30 friends and relatives whom he had persuaded to leave careers and families in the world. The eloquence, persuasiveness, and persistence behind this accomplishment marked his entire life. Three years later, Bernard, then 24 or 25 years old, led a band of "White Monks" to a new foundation at Clairvaux (Valley of Light) in Champagne. From this abbey, by the → Cistercian system of affiliation, nearly half the monasteries of the Cistercian order were founded, at sites from Scotland and Norway to Spain and the Holy Land. Bernard's early monastic zeal undermined his health, causing him within a few years to be separated from his community and opening the way to a public career as spokesman for the reform papacy and reformed → monasticism that took him frequently away from the → monastery.

Possessed of a poetic Latin style, Bernard began his literary career about 1124/25. His first treatise, *The Steps of Humility and Pride,* was an ironic inversion of the steps of → humility listed in chap. 7 of the *Rule* of St. → Benedict. At about the same time, while quarantined apart from his community, he composed *Four Homilies on "And the angel was sent,"* on the place of Mary in Christian devotion. To defend the austere Cistercians against charges of innovation and smugness, he penned two works on the respective observances of → Benedictines and Cistercians: Letter 1, a public document ostensibly addressed to his nephew Robert, who had deserted the harsh life at Clairvaux for the more comfortable routine at → Cluny (to which he had, in fact, been pledged by his parents in infancy), and a satiric *Apologia.* Between 1126 and 1135, his first theological work on a burning question of the day, *Grace and Free Choice,* was composed, as was a work entitled *In Praise of the New Knighthood* for the newly founded Knights Templar.

For the papal chancellor Bernard composed the book *On Loving God*. Sometime before 1144, an older and mellower Bernard revisited the question of monastic observances in *On Precept and Dispensation*. His vision of the reformed church under saintly episcopal and contemplative papal governance found expression in his biography of the monk-missionary bishop of Armagh, and friend of Clairvaux, Malachy O'Morgair (d. 1152), and in public advice to the Cistercian pope, Eugenius III, *Five Books on Consideration*.

During his lifetime several of his sermons and sermon series circulated, including a sermon "On Conversion," delivered originally at Paris and later expanded; sermons on the liturgical year (→ Church Year), on various subjects *(De diversis);* and sermons on the OT Song of Solomon *(Sermones in Cantica canticorum)*. In these last, 86 sermons composed between 1135 and his death in 1153 provide a verse-by-verse commentary up to Cant. 3:1. Unpolished outlines of other works have survived as *Parables* and *Sententiae* (Opinions). Some 500 letters, written between 1116 and 1153, also circulated and attest to the influence Bernard had on persons at every level of medieval society, from emperors and popes to clergy, religious, scholars, and nobles. They collectively articulate his vision of the Christian life as a freely willed and loving response to God's → love and the → grace that makes human response possible.

Still dictating, polishing, and revising his works on his deathbed, Bernard exercised an enormous influence on contemporaries and on subsequent generations of Latin readers. Many works were translated into vernacular languages, and Bernard's name was applied to a number of non-Bernardine compositions. In the 16th century, John → Calvin, Martin → Luther, and the English → Reformers both knew his work and incorporated into their own his thought on a number of points, not least on the governance of the church, on grace, and on Scripture.

A champion of Innocent II in the so-called Anacletan papal schism, Bernard was soon enlisted as a spokesperson for the reformed and reforming papacy and thus was propelled into a public career that kept him on the road for much of his life. Wherever he traveled — throughout France, to the empire (Germany), and into Italy — Cistercian monasteries sprang up in his wake. Although he himself never accepted preferment, many Cistercian monks were elevated to the episcopate, and one, Eugenius III, to the papacy (1145-53) because of Bernard's influence. In his capacity as papal spokesman, he advocated the

Second, ultimately disastrous, → Crusade in France, the Low Countries, and the Rhineland — a duty his embarrassed official biographers insisted he undertook only on obedience and at the repeated urgings of the king, bishops, and Eugenius himself.

A representative of the patristic-monastic tradition of theology in which Scripture study and prayerful personal experience lead to insight, Bernard was twice drawn into confrontations with emerging academic "pre-Scholastic" theologians. At the insistence of a friend, he attacked Peter Abelard (1079-1142), a "new theologian" propounding a "new theology" without, in Bernard's opinion, due regard for Scripture or → tradition, and secured Abelard's condemnation at the Synod of Sens in 1140. Eight years later, Bernard attempted unsuccessfully to secure the condemnation of the philosopher Gilbert of Poitiers. Bernard, "the last of the Fathers," has, as a result, been unfairly set in the popular mind in opposition to analytic theology.

Even before his death in 1153, Bernard's monks had begun an official Life with an eye to securing his canonization through the newly forming proper Roman channels. When their first request failed, perhaps because too many people remembered and did not particularly approve of Bernard's activities, they busied themselves retouching his biography, increasing the miraculous and explaining the controversial. On January 18, 1174, Bernard was officially canonized by Pope Alexander III.

Bibliography: Primary sources: J. LECLERCQ, O.S.B., and H. M. ROCHAIS, *Sancti Bernardi opera* (8 vols.; Rome, 1957-79) replaces Mabillion • J. MABILLION, *Sancti Bernardi abbatis clarae-vallensis . . . opera omnia* (4th ed.; 2 vols. in 4; 1939; repr. in *PL* 182-85 [1978; orig. pub., 1879]). Translations of the works of Bernard are being produced by Cistercian Publications, Kalamazoo, Mich., in the Cistercian Fathers Series (1970-).

Secondary works: J. DE LA CROIX-BOUTON, *Bibliographie Bernardine, 1891-1957* (Paris, 1958) • L. JANAUSCHECK, *Bibliographia Bernardine* (Vienna, 1891; repr., Hildesheim, n.d.) • J. LECLERCQ, *Bernard of Clairvaux and the Cistercian Spirit* (Kalamazoo, Mich., 1976) • E. MANNING, *Bibliographie Bernardine, 1957-1970* (Rochefort, 1972) • J. R. SOMMERFELDT, ed., *Bernardus Magister: Studies in Honor of the Nonacentenary of the Birth of Bernard of Clairvaux* (Kalamazoo, Mich., 1993).

E. ROZANNE ELDER

Bethel

Founded in Germany in 1867, Bethel is an institution dedicated to Christian charitable work (→ Inner

Mission). Its founding came as J. Bost (1817-81), leader of the French diaconal institution La Force (→ Diakonia), shared a personal experience.

A group of Bielefeld businessmen, theologians, and politicians acquired property, called the Württemberg teacher Johannes Unsöld (1843-1934), and opened a place of healing and care with epileptic youngsters. Rapid growth came after 1872 with the calling of Friedrich von Bodelschwingh (1831-1910), who united a faith that turned to the world in helping love, a talent for organization, and an impelling sense of expectation (→ Eschatology) that the Lord would redeem the captives of Zion (Psalm 126, the Bethel psalm). There developed a fellowship of workers and those with → handicaps that made Bethel one of the happiest places in the land.

At the outset, the workers were → deaconesses of the motherhouse of Sarepta and deacons of the house of Nazareth (founded in 1877). Care, therapeutic aids, schooling, handicrafts, community life, and varied worship were all designed to create an environment in which the handicapped would have room to develop. Besides epileptics, Bethel took in the mentally ill or retarded, the educationally disadvantaged, and marginal groups. Branches were set up in Eckardtsheim (1882), Freistatt (1899), Lobetal (1905), and Homborn (1958). Focused on those in need of help, the fellowship was able to undertake various broader enterprises such as the bringing of unused land into cultivation, providing homes for workers, mission in East Africa (→ German Missions), student hostels, and a church school (→ Theological Education).

The youngest son of Bodelschwingh, Fritz von Bodelschwingh (1877-1946), took over the direction of Bethel in 1910. The world wars, severe economic inflation, political problems, the → church struggle, and Hitler's ordering of → euthanasia made it a difficult period for him. Yet he built up the medical and educational work with a general hospital, a hospital for children, gymnasia, and special schools. To combat unemployment, a retraining program and a settlement project were started in 1927.

After 1945/46, reconstruction, adaptation to new methods of treatment (an epileptic clinic and research, special schools, etc.), changes in support, and the need to work out new structures of leadership posed serious tasks for the development of Bethel and its adjustment to the demands of the new age. Today a circle of friends supports the work by donations.

Bibliography: F. von Bodelschwingh, *Ausgewählte Schriften* (ed. A. Adam; 2 vols.; Bielefeld, 1980) • W. Brandt, *Friedrich von Bodelschwingh, 1877-1946. Nachfolger und Gestalter* (Bielefeld, 1967) • A. Funke, *Friedrich von Bodelschwingh* (Hamburg, 1980) • M. Gerhardt and A. Adam, *Friedrich von Bodelschwingh* (2 vols.; repr., Bielefeld, 1980) • B. Gramlich, *Friedrich von Bodelschwingh. Werk und Leben* (Stuttgart, 1981) • I. Ludolphy, trans., "Bodelschwingh, Father and Son," *ELC* 1.314-15.

Alex Funke

Beza, Theodore

Theodore Beza (or de Bèze), the protégé, colleague, biographer, and successor of J. → Calvin (1509-64), was born on June 24, 1519, at the castle of Vézelay in Burgundy, where his father was the governor. At the age of five he was given into the care of his uncle, Nicholas de Bèze, who brought the boy to Paris and eventually entrusted his education to the humanist scholar Melchior Wolmar, of Orléans. Beza lived and studied with Wolmar from 1528 to 1534. In May of 1535 Beza matriculated at the University of Orléans, where he studied → law. Upon receiving his degree in 1539, he moved to Paris with the intention of practicing law. His early humanistic training, cultured tastes, scholarly and poetic abilities, social station, and relative wealth, however, led him away from the law. In 1548 he published *Juvenalia*, a set of Latin poems, which brought him considerable repute in literary circles.

On recovering from a serious illness in 1549, Beza charted a new direction for his life. Most of his biographers also credit the influence of Beza's first teacher, Wolmar, both for the change of heart and for the espousal of the cause of reform, which followed shortly. Beza relinquished the several ecclesiastical benefices that had enabled him to live as an independent scholar and left Paris for Geneva. There he declared himself Protestant, married his mistress, and began an association with Calvin that lasted until the latter's death. In November 1550 Beza accepted the position of professor of Greek in the academy at Lausanne. At this time he completed a sacred drama, *Abraham sacrifiant,* in which he contrasted Reformed and Roman Catholic views of → faith.

While at Lausanne, Beza protested the French persecution of the → Waldenses, became embroiled in controversy over the Lord's Supper (→ Eucharist), wrote *De haereticis a civili magistratu puniendis* (1554) and the famous *Tabula praedestinationis* (1555), and published the first edition of his highly influential *Annotationes in Novum Testamentum* (1556). The first of these works placed Beza in the forefront of Calvin's defense against dissident voices who had been punished or ejected from Geneva for their religious views. The second treatise, despite its brevity, has associated Beza with the development of a strict doctrine of double → predestination among the Reformed. Beza's *Tabula* indeed has a clarity of argument and a precision in its use of distinctions (such as that between the eternal decree and its execution in time or between reprobation and damnation), but it cannot be identified either as a prospectus for a full system of theology or as a primary cause of Reformed → scholasticism (§6). The third work drew on Beza's humanistic training and assured him a preeminent status among Reformed translators and exegetes. It consists in a carefully collated Greek text, the Vg, and Beza's own translation, followed by annotations in which Beza argues his translation against those of D. → Erasmus (1469?-1536) and Calvin and other extant Latin translations and in which he offers brief theological commentary. Much of the substance of the translation and its theological annotations were rendered into English in the various editions of the Geneva Bible.

Beza's *Confession de la foy* (1558), written at the time of his arrival in Geneva to serve as professor in the academy, not only presented his theology as a whole but also stated so precisely the Reformed critique of Roman Catholicism that it exercised considerable influence in its time. It was rendered into Latin by Beza himself (1561) and was printed in England both in its original Latin and in English translation. With minor emendation, it was adopted as a confessional standard by the Hungarian Reformed Church in 1562.

In 1559 Beza assumed the post of rector at the newly reconstituted Academy of Geneva and became a close adviser to Calvin. Beza's literary work continued in his artful completion (1560) of the French metrical psalter begun by Clément Marot (ca. 1497-1544). In 1561 he represented the French and Swiss Reformed at the Colloquy of Poissy, called by the advisers of the young Charles IX in order to resolve some of the religious tensions in the kingdom of France. Although the colloquy ended without resolution of any of the debated issues, Beza emerged as a leader of the Reformed movement. When Calvin died in 1564, Beza succeeded him as the leader of the Reformation in Geneva.

At this point, Beza gave up his post as rector of the academy to Nicholas Colladon and succeeded Calvin as moderator of the Company of Pastors, a post that he held until 1580. Beza also continued Calvin's support of the French Reformed Church, serving as moderator of the National Synod of 1571

and participating actively in debates over polity and the Lord's Supper. In 1586 he represented the Reformed at the Montbéliard Colloquy, significant both for its political impact on the Reformed population of Montbéliard and for its identification of the major Christological, predestinarian, and eucharistic problems dividing the Reformed and the Lutherans. One of the results of the colloquy was further debate over predestination, which spilled over into Bern. Beza participated in that debate as well, helping to resolve the doctrine in a Reformed direction in 1587.

Although Beza's later years saw a waning of energies, he retained his post as professor of theology until 1597. He was also lively enough to engage in debate with the young Francis de Sales (1567-1622), who visited Geneva in 1597, with the pope's blessing, in the unrealistic hope of converting Beza to Roman Catholicism. Beza died peacefully on October 13, 1605.

As recent scholarship has indicated, Beza was not, as once argued, the author of a predestinarian system of theology, nor was he responsible for a major deviation in the development of the Reformed tradition. He did bring a precision of statement and definition to Genevan theology that contributed to the development of Reformed orthodoxy and the rise of Protestant scholasticism, but primarily he should be remembered as a great linguist and exegete who provided a solid textual foundation for the Reformed understanding of the NT and as a stable focus, in the line of Calvin, for the faith and practice of the Genevan Reformation in the late 16th century.

Bibliography: H. M. BAIRD, *Theodore Beza: The Counsellor of the French Reformation, 1519-1606* (New York, 1899) • P.-F. GEIZENDORF, *Théodore de Bèze* (Geneva, 1967) • H. HEPPE, *Theodor Beza: Leben und ausgewählte Schriften* (Elberfeld, 1861) • R. W. A. LETHAM, "Theodore Beza: A Reassessment," *SJT* 40 (1987) 25-40 • T. MARUYAMA, *The Ecclesiology of Theodore Beza: The Reform of the True Church* (Geneva, 1978) • R. A. MULLER, *Christ and the Decree: Christology and Predestination in Reformed Theology from Calvin to Perkins* (Grand Rapids, 1988) • J. RAITT, *The Colloquy of Montbéliard: Religion and Politics in the Sixteenth Century* (New York, 1993); idem, *The Eucharistic Theology of Theodore Beza: Development of the Reformed Doctrine* (Chambersburg, Pa., 1972).

RICHARD A. MULLER

Bhagavad Gita

The Bhagavad Gita, or "Song of the Blessed One [i.e., Krishna]," is a Sanskrit religiophilosophical didactic poem in 18 songs, constituting part of the sixth book of the → Mahābhārata.

Krishna, an avatar (→ Incarnation 1) of the god Vishnu, presents the Bhagavad Gita to the hero Prince Arjuna, for whom he acts as charioteer, when the latter hesitates to fight his own relatives. According to the teaching of Krishna, Arjuna has the task of acting according to the duties of his → caste; as a Kshatriya (ruler or warrior), he is thus bound to fight. Knowing the all-sustaining, self-resting Krishna-Vasudeva, the wise must act without regard for their own advantage or disadvantage. When they see this, then with the help of the love of God (→ Bhakti), they will attain redemption in the form of union with God.

We know only the outlines of the history of the Bhagavad Gita, which in its oldest strata goes back to the first centuries B.C. Various philosophical reflections have flowed into it, and these have led to widely different expositions, both old and new, as may be seen from the commentaries of philosophers of the different schools, and also from the influence on trends in neo-Hinduism (→ Hinduism). In the West the Bhagavad Gita came to be known from the Latin translation of A. W. Schlegel (1823).

Bibliography: W. M. CALLEWAERT and S. HEMRAJ, *Bhagavadgītānuvāda: A Study in the Transcultural Translation* (Ranchi, 1983) • F. EDGERTON, *The Bhagavad Gītā: Translated and Interpreted* (2 vols.; Cambridge, Mass., 1972) • R. GARBE, *Die Bhagavadgītā* (2d ed.; Leipzig, 1921; repr., Darmstadt, 1978) • P. HUBERT, *Histoire de la Bhagavad Gītā* (Paris, 1949) • B. S. MILLER, trans., *The Bhagavad-Gita: Krishna's Counsel in Time of War* (New York, 1986) • R. N. MINOR, ed., *Modern Indian Interpreters of the* Bhagavadgītā (Albany, N.Y., 1986) • R. OTTO, *Die Lehrtraktate der Bhagavadgītā* (Tübingen, 1935) • R. C. ZAEHNER, *The Bhagavad Gītā, with a Commentary Based on the Original Sources* (2d ed.; Oxford, 1972).

OSKAR VON HINÜBER

Bhagwan Shree Rajneesh

"Bhagwan Shree Rajneesh" is the guru name of Rajneesh Chandra Mohan (1931-81). It combines with the given name "Rajneesh" the appellative "Bhagwan," commonly used in India for gods, demigods, and holy men (from Skt. *bhag(a)van,* meaning "reverend" or "divine"), and the title "Shree."

Rajneesh was born in Kuchwada (Madhya Pradesh), India, on December 11, 1931. On March 21, 1953, he experienced the "other reality," which his philosophy enabled him to interpret as God, truth, dharma, tao, and so forth. He deepened the experi-

ence by techniques of → meditation, mostly of the Jaina and Tantra variety, which contributed finally to his own dynamic method. He developed the method further with the help of insights from modern → psychotherapeutic schools and from an understanding of the global history of mind and spirit. He then taught in ashrams in Bombay (1969-74) and Poona (1974-81), and then in various places in the United States. He founded Rajneesh Puram, Oregon, which later disbanded when he was deported.

In India Rajneesh presented his teaching in all-morning lectures that transposed the listeners into trancelike conditions by their almost rhapsodic delivery. He held out the possibility of deconditioning the → self with its drives (sex, aggression, death). The way to achieving this state was by personal initiation with the giving of a new name, strengthened by encounter and meditation groups, sensitivity and bioenergetic courses, dynamic training, and various therapies.

There are approximately 75 centers in the world, visited annually by 350,000 people, including 75,000 sannyasins (initiates). The latter include prominent artists and writers, along with migrant workers. To forestall misrepresentation after the death of the master in 1981, the movement was centralized as a religion (Rajneeshism), with a priesthood, calendar, → rites, and a stable financial structure.

Bibliography: Bhagwan's discourses have been published in approximately 350 volumes (English, with some Hindi), of which 88 are translated into 11 other languages.

Secondary works: J. S. GORDON, *The Golden Guru: The Strange Journey of Bhagwan Shree Rajneesh* (Lexington, Mass., 1987) • F.-W. HAACK, *Die "Bhagwan"-Rajneesh-Bewegung* (2d ed.; Munich, 1983) • K. P. HORN (Swami Prem Deepen), "Rebellion gegen den Verstand? Eine sozial-wissenschaftliche Untersuchung über deutsche Neo-Sannyasins in Poona" (Diss., Berlin, 1982) • V. JOSHI, *The Awakened One: The Life and Work of Bhagwan Shree Rajneesh* (San Francisco, 1982) • D. MURPHY, *The Rajneesh Story: The Bhagwan's Garden* (West Linn, Oreg., 1986) • K. STRELLING, *The Ultimate Game: The Rise and Fall of Bhagwan Shree Rajneesh* (San Francisco, 1987).

CARSTEN COLPE

Bhakti

"Bhakti," a Sanskrit word originally meaning "distribution" (from the verb *bhaj,* "allot; revere [God]"), has come to mean also "dedication" or "love [of

God]." It denotes a devotional movement in → Hinduism that arose in the sphere of Vaishnavism. Its roots go back to the pre-Christian era, but as a way of salvation it is found only from the eighth and ninth centuries A.D. in the teachings of the holy men called the Alvars in southern India. With the → Bhagavad Gita, its most important basic text is the Sanskrit Bhāgavata-Purāṇa.

According to the way of Bhakti *(bhakti-mārga)*, love of God rather than knowledge leads to redemption. Believers must have a constant awareness of God and let all their thoughts and acts be determined by him. In this way they can overcome the effect of → karma and the distinction between → castes. Aids to focusing on God are hearing *(śravaṇa)* his praise, extolling him *(vandana)*, constantly thinking of him *(smaraṇa)*, and serving him *(sevana)* by good works in his name. Believers may stand in a varied relation to God, for example, as a slave *(dāsa)* or beloved *(ratibhāva)*, the → love between Krishna and Radha being an expression of the erotic form of this love of God.

When Bhakti spread to northern India, Brahman orthodoxy embraced it only with some hesitation. The Brahman Caitanya (1485-1533) of Bengal, however, became one of its most important champions. For nearly 25 years he went through northern India as an inspired preacher of Krishna mysticism. Honored already in his lifetime as an avatar (→ Incarnation) of Vishnu, he entrusted to his disciples in Vrindavan near Mathura the theology and writing of what became the Caitanya movement, a → sect that still persists (→ Krishna Consciousness, International Society for).

Bhakti religion has not been restricted to Vaishnavism in its development but has also influenced Saiva sects. It has been suspected that Christianity had some impact on Bhakti Hinduism.

Bibliography: R. K. BARZ, *The Bhakti Sect of Vallabhācārya* (Canberra, 1982) • M. DHAVAMONY, *The Love of God according to the Śaivasiddhānta* (Oxford, 1971) • W. EIDLITZ, *Die indische Gottesliebe* (Olten, 1955); idem, *Kṛṣṇa-Caitanya. Sein Leben und seine Lehre* (Stockholm, 1968) • A. J. GAIL, *Bhakti im Bhāgavatapurāṇa* (Wiesbaden, 1969) • F. HARDY, *Viraha-Bhakti: The Early History of Krishna Devotion in South India* (Delhi, 1983) • J. LELE, ed., *Tradition and Modernity in Bhakti Movements* (Leiden, 1981) • F. MALLISON, "Les littératures dévotionnelles de l'Inde septentrionale prémoderne," *BEFEO* 79 (1992) 293-98; 80 (1993) 331-41 • R. OTTO, *Die Gnadenreligion Indiens und das Christentum* (Munich, 1930).

OSKAR VON HINÜBER

Bhutan

	1960	1980	2000
Population (1,000s):	868	1,292	2,032
Annual growth rate (%):	1.83	2.32	2.59

Area: 47,000 sq. km. (18,150 sq. mi.)

A.D. 2000
Population density: 43/sq. km. (112/sq. mi.)
Births / deaths: 3.77 / 1.19 per 100 population
Fertility rate: 5.42 per woman
Infant mortality rate: 91 per 1,000 live births
Life expectancy: 55.7 years (m: 54.1, f: 57.4)
Religious affiliation (%): Buddhists 73.6, Hindus 21.2, tribal religionists 3.5, Muslims 1.0, other 0.7.

Bhutan (Tibet; Druk-Yul, "Dragon Kingdom") is an independent kingdom in the eastern Himalayas. The primary ethnic groups are the Bhote (50 percent) and the Nepalese (35 percent), with smaller percentages of many others (including Assamese, Loba, and Lepcha). About two-thirds belong to the "red cap" sect of Lamaistic → Buddhism (the Drukpa group of the Karyud school), which is the state religion. Most of the rest are → Hindus, primarily Nepali settlers in the south and southwest of Bhutan. Immigration from Nepal has been forbidden since 1959. A small percentage of the people are adherents of → tribal religions, with an even smaller percentage of Muslims (→ Islam; Sunni, Sunnites).

The total number of Christians is very small, estimated at approximately 10,000. The only recognized Christian community, located at Phuntsholing (from 1965), is that of Salesians (→ Orders and Congregations). In 1626 two → Jesuit missionaries passed through Bhutan on their way to Tibet, but apparently no missionary efforts followed, and even today the state forbids → conversion (§1) to Christianity. Most of the Christians are Indians working in schools and institutions for development. Roman Catholics among them come under the → bishop of the Diocese of Darjeeling in India. With state approval the Salesians and Jesuits opened three schools for Buddhist scholars in 1965. The Protestant Eastern Himalayan Church has some village schools in the West. Otherwise, Protestants have no approved organization. Some Protestant missions have concentrated on working with Bhutanese who live across the Indian border in West Bengal.

Bibliography: D. BARRETT, ed., *WCE* 179-80 • G. L. HARRIS et al., eds., *Area Handbook for Nepal, Bhutan, and*

Sikkim (2d ed.; Washington, D.C., 1973) • R. RAHUL, *Modern Bhutan* (New York, 1972).

BRIGITTE LUCHESI

Bible Exegesis → Exegesis, Biblical

Bible Manuscripts and Editions

1. OT MSS
   1.1. Background
   1.2. Ancient Bible MSS
   1.3. Medieval Bible MSS
2. NT MSS
   2.1. The Oldest Extant MSS
   2.2. Noteworthy Uncials
   2.3. Important Minuscules
3. Printed Editions

1. OT MSS

1.1. *Background*

In antiquity the materials used for Bible MSS were leather, parchment, and papyrus. The parchment was prepared from the skins of sheep, goats, antelopes, and other animals. Papyrus, which was made from the pith of the papyrus plant that grows in the marshes of the Nile, was imported from Egypt but usually did not last long in damp climates.

The usual form for a literary document was the scroll (see, for example, Jeremiah 36; *Ep. Arist.* 177), especially for Jewish Scriptures used in worship services. In Christian circles scrolls were supplanted by the codex, or MS book. Writing was in ink (Jer. 36:18; cf. *Ep. Arist.* 176) with a reed pen (Jer. 8:8?). Deluxe parchment codices were dyed purple and written with silver or gold ink. Some were decorated with illuminated initials and pictures of scenes and of persons mentioned in the text.

The first script used in Israel was the Phoenician or Old Hebrew script, but this was generally replaced after the exile by the Aramaic square script. The Samaritan script developed from the Old Hebrew (→ Samaritans); the earliest surviving MSS of the Samaritan → Pentateuch are from the Middle Ages. Religious literature that formed the OT undoubtedly existed in Israel during the monarchy and from the time of the exile, although there is no direct evidence of this. There are only letters and inscriptions written on various materials (besides those mentioned, esp. stone, clay tablets, and potsherds).

1.2. *Ancient Bible MSS*

Until 1947 the oldest known witness to the text of

the Hebrew Bible was the Nash Papyrus, which was found in Egypt in 1902 and is now at Cambridge. It is a small sheet containing the → Decalogue and the Shema (Deut. 6:4-5), from perhaps the second century B.C.

After 1947 the caves at → Qumran, as well as at Masada, Wadi Murabbaʿat, and Naḥal Ḥever, yielded a great number of Bible MSS, mostly fragmentary, representing all the canonical books of the Hebrew Bible except Esther, and also some noncanonical books. These must come from the period before the Jewish revolt of A.D. 66-70 or that of A.D. 132-35, and some are considerably older (2d or even 3d cent. B.C.). Of special importance are the complete Isaiah scroll from Cave 1 of Qumran (1QIsa^a), the Psalm scroll from Cave 11 (11QPs^a), and the Minor Prophets scroll from Wadi Murabbaʿat. The materials used are leather or parchment and occasionally papyrus. The Old Hebrew script is sometimes found. Evaluation of the findings, which reveal a text close to the MT but sometimes also to the LXX and the Samaritan, is still in progress.

1.3. *Medieval Bible MSS*

The earliest medieval Bible MSS of the OT are the numerous fragments found at the end of the 19th century in the → genizah (i.e., a chamber housing discarded MSS) of the → synagogue of Old Cairo, which have been relocated for the most part in Cambridge and Oxford. The oldest of these seem to come from the sixth, or even fifth, century A.D. The consonantal text shows traces of the Masoretic additions in a variety of forms and at various stages. The work of the Masoretes was crowned and fixed in the great MSS of the Tiberian families Ben Asher and Ben Naphtali. The most important are the following:

Cairo Prophets (C, for *codex prophetarum Cairensis*, in *Biblia Hebraica Stuttgartensia* [BHS]). Containing the prophetic writings, this codex was written in 895 by Moshe ben Asher and is now in the possession of the Karaite community in Old Cairo.

Petersburg Codex of the Prophets (BHS V^p). This work, from the year 916, belongs to the Firkowitsch collection in St. Petersburg, the greatest collection of Hebrew biblical MSS.

Aleppo Codex. This contains virtually the whole of the OT (the beginning and the end are lost). Written in 930 by Shelomo ben Buyaʿa and provided with pointing and Masoretic notes by Aaron ben Moshe ben Asher, it was kept in Aleppo probably since the end of the 14th century and is now in Jerusalem. It was adopted as the textual base for the Hebrew University Bible undertaken in 1965.

Leningrad Codex (BHS L). This codex of the complete OT was copied in 1008 from the MSS of

235

Aaron ben Moshe ben Asher and is the textual base of the third edition of R. Kittel's *Biblia Hebraica* (1937) and of the BHS.

Erfurt Codices. These date from the 11th to the 14th centuries and are now in Berlin. They have been traditionally associated with Ben Naphtali.

The variants between the various Bible MSS were assiduously assembled in the 18th century (B. Kennicott, 1776/80; J. B. de Rossi, 1784/88). Because of the care with which the Masoretes standardized the text, these variants involve largely formal matters and rarely affect the sense of the text, unlike the situation found among NT MSS.

→ Masorah, Masoretes; Qumran

Bibliography: Textus: Annual of the Hebrew University Bible Project (Jerusalem, 1960-) • E. Tov, *Textual Criticism of the Hebrew Bible* (Minneapolis, 1992) • E. WÜRTHWEIN, *The Text of the OT* (2d ed.; Grand Rapids, 1995).

RUDOLF SMEND, with ERROLL F. RHODES

2. NT MSS

Older NT MSS have few or no marks of punctuation, and the text runs almost without any break between words. The style of writing is called uncial or majuscule because of its large, simple letters derived from the formal style of inscriptions. About the beginning of the ninth century, a new handwriting style became popular — the minuscule, or rapid cursive script of the professional medieval scribe. Also in later MSS, paragraph marks and chapter divisions were introduced. Occasionally Byzantine copies were provided with musical neumes for the cantillation of the Scripture lesson at → worship.

According to the latest official list (1994, maintained by the Institut für neutestamentliche Textforschung at Münster) of NT Greek MSS, numbers have been assigned to 99 papyri, 306 uncial MSS, 2,856 minuscule MSS (the earliest dated minuscule is from A.D. 835), and 2,403 lectionaries, making a total of 5,664 items. Only 61 of these contain the entire NT. Whether MSS contain the whole or only parts of the NT, the order of books in most copies is the same: Gospels, Acts, Catholic Epistles, Pauline Epistles (with Hebrews between 2 Thessalonians and 1 Timothy), and Revelation. Only a few late Bible MSS are dated; the age of the others must be ascertained from careful examination of characteristic features of the handwriting.

2.1. *The Oldest Extant MSS*

The oldest surviving MSS are the following, all written on papyrus:

$\mathfrak{p}^{46}$: Chester Beatty Biblical Papyrus II, about A.D. 200, now at Dublin; contains portions of ten epistles of → Paul (Hebrews appears after Romans).

$\mathfrak{p}^{52}$: part of a leaf from the first half of the 2d century, now at Manchester; preserves John 18:31-33, 37-38, the oldest fragment of NT text.

$\mathfrak{p}^{66}$: Bodmer Papyrus II, about A.D. 200, now at Geneva; contains John 1–16 almost complete and fragments of the remaining chapters.

$\mathfrak{p}^{75}$: Bodmer Papyri XIV and XV, 3d century, now at Geneva; contains most of Luke and more than half of John.

$\mathfrak{p}^{87}$: a leaf from the 3d century, now at Cologne; preserves Phlm. 13-15 and 24-25.

2.2. *Noteworthy Uncials*

Noteworthy uncials on parchment include the following:

ℵ: Codex Sinaiticus, 4th century, now in the British Library, London; contains the complete NT followed by *Barnabas* and a large portion of the *Shepherd of Hermas.*

A: Codex Alexandrinus, 5th century, now in the British Library, London; lacks Matthew up to 25:6, as well as some leaves of John and 2 Corinthians.

B: Codex Vaticanus, 4th century; lacks the concluding pages (from Heb. 9:14 onward, which includes 1-2 Timothy, Titus, Philemon, and Revelation).

C: Codex Ephraemi, 5th century, now at Paris; a palimpsest MS (erased in the 12th cent. and the sheets rewritten with Greek writings of St. Ephraem, a 4th-cent. Syrian church father) of a small portion of the OT and approximately ⅝ of the NT, from which almost all of the original text has been able to be recovered.

D: Codex Bezae, 5th century, now at Cambridge University; a Greek and Latin MS of the Gospels (in the sequence Matthew, John, Luke, Mark) and most of Acts; it presents a form of the text that frequently differs from that of other MSS (in Acts the text is about 8 percent longer than the generally accepted text).

W: Codex Washingtoniensis, 4th or 5th century MS; contains the Gospels (in the sequence Matthew, John, Luke, Mark) and presents variegated types of text, as though copied from portions of several different MSS.

2.3. *Important Minuscules*

We list here seven of the more noteworthy minuscules:

1: 12th century, at Basel; contains the NT except Revelation; as established by K. Lake (d. 1946), it belongs to a family of MSS that preserves a text like that current in Caesarea in the 3rd and 4th centuries.

13: 13th century, at Paris; contains the Gospels,

with the pericope John 7:53–8:11 after Luke 21:38; as identified by W. H. Ferrar (d. 1871), it belongs to a family of MSS that are descendants of an archetype from Calabria.

33: 9th century, at Paris; contains the entire NT except Revelation; often called "the queen of the minuscules," it preserves a type of text like that of B and ℵ.

461: the earliest dated minuscule MS (A.D. 835), now at St. Petersburg; contains only the Gospels.

565: 9th-century deluxe copy of the Gospels, now at St. Petersburg, written in gold letters on purple vellum; at the end of Mark it has a colophon stating that it was copied and corrected "from the ancient manuscripts at Jerusalem."

700: 11th-century MS of the Gospels, now in the British Library; at Luke 11:2 in the → Lord's Prayer it reads "Thy Holy Spirit come upon us and cleanse us" instead of "Thy kingdom come."

1739: 10th-century MS, now on Mount → Athos; contains Acts and the Epistles in a form of text like that used by → Origen (ca. 185-ca. 254).

Bibliography: K. ALAND, *Kurzgefaßte Liste der griechischen Handschriften des Neuen Testaments* (2d ed.; Berlin, 1994) • K. ALAND and B. ALAND, *The Text of the NT* (2d ed.; Grand Rapids, 1989) • B. D. EHRMAN and M. W. HOLMES, eds., *The Text of the NT in Contemporary Research* (FS B. M. Metzger; Grand Rapids, 1995) • B. M. METZGER, *MSS of the Greek Bible* (New York, 1981); idem, *The Text of the NT* (3d ed.; New York, 1992).

BRUCE M. METZGER, with ERROLL F. RHODES

3. Printed Editions

Early editions of Hebrew Bibles for academic use include those published in Soncino in 1488 and Brescia in 1494, the Michaelis Bible of 1720, and the Oxford Bible of 1776-80. In this century the most important have been R. Kittel's *Biblia Hebraica* (1906; 3d ed., 1937) and the *Biblia Hebraica Stuttgartensia* (1977; 4th ed., 1990).

The first Greek NT was that of D. → Erasmus (1469?-1536), printed in Basel in 1516. Especially influential were the Bibles of the Stephanus printers (1503-59), particularly the 1550 and 1551 editions. In the 17th century the Elzevier editions (1624-78) and that of J. Fell (1675) are noteworthy, and in the 18th we should mention editions of J. A. Bengel (1734), J. J. Wettstein (1751/52), and J. J. Griesbach (1775-77). The NT of C. von Tischendorf appeared in 1841, followed by editions of B. F. Westcott and F. J. A. Hort (1881), Eberhard Nestle (1898, rev. Erwin Nestle in 1927), and H. von Soden (1902-13).

Under the editorship of K. Aland, the Nestle text has become the standard NT text. It is identical with the United Bible Societies NT (1966; 4th ed. [= 27th Nestle-Aland ed.], 1993), which is widely used in the English-speaking world. In 1997 the first fascicle appeared of the *Novum Testamentum Graecum. Editio Critica Maior* (vol. 4/1, *The Epistle of James*), a publication of the Institute for New Testament Textual Research in Münster, edited by B. Aland, K. Aland†, G. Mink, and K. Wachtel.

Bibliography: K. ALAND and B. ALAND, *The Text of the NT* (2d ed.; Grand Rapids, 1989) • P. W. COMFORT, ed., *The Origin of the Bible* (Wheaton, Ill., 1992) • S. L. GREENSLADE, ed., *The Cambridge History of the Bible* (vol. 3; Cambridge, 1963) • E. WÜRTHWEIN, *The Text of the OT* (Grand Rapids, 1979).

BEATE KÖSTER

Bible Societies

1. Bible societies are organizations for the distribution of the Bible. The foundations of the Bible society movement may be traced to the Reformation understanding of the Bible as the sole authority in matters of faith and to the concept of the priesthood of all believers. This understanding led to → Luther's translation of the Bible into German and to similar undertakings for other languages. The demand of → Pietism for the wider circulation of the Word of God (P. Spener) spurred increased distribution of the Scriptures and inspired the founding of a Bible institute at Halle by K. H. von Canstein (1710). Cost-effective procedures (e.g., keeping the type in place) and the reinvestment of profits made possible inexpensive editions that even poorer people could afford. The development of Protestant nations as maritime powers, together with the rise of evangelical movements and → missions in the 18th century, led to the production of → Bible versions in non-European languages such as Massachusetts (complete Bible in 1663), Tamil (NT, 1715), Malay (Bible, 1735), Sinhalese (Gospels, 1739), Dakhini (NT, 1758), Greenland Eskimo (NT, 1766), and Mohawk (Mark, 1787).

2.1. All the Bible societies that arose in the 19th century found an example and inspiration in the British and Foreign Bible Society (BFBS), which was founded in London in 1804. In its first 15 years this society distributed 1.5 million Bibles in 13 European and 5 non-European languages. It was followed within 15 years by more than 40 similar societies in

Europe, including those founded in 1806 (Ireland), 1812 (Finland, Hungary, and Württemberg), 1814 (Denmark, Netherlands, and Sweden), 1815 (Iceland), and 1816 (Norway and Poland). Like the British society, and in cooperation with it, the later ones were essentially laypersons' organizations, and they were for the most part interconfessional. Thus their work became an important area of ecumenical encounter.

2.2. In the United States the earliest Bible society was founded at Philadelphia (1808), quickly followed by many others, including those of New York and Massachusetts (1809). In 1816 a total of 31 local societies joined together to form the American Bible Society (ABS). Some local societies continued as independent institutions, at the same time cooperating closely with the national body. The original New York Bible Society (NYBS) dissolved in 1828, but a series of later institutions adopted its name. The society incorporated in 1866, expanded its program in 1970 to include Bible distribution in Latin America, changed its name to the NYBS International, and moved to New Jersey. In the meantime it undertook sponsorship of the conservative New International Version (NIV; NT in 1973, Bible in 1978). In 1982 it became known as the International Bible Society and later moved to Colorado.

3.1. From their beginnings the Bible societies pursued a missionary outreach, with agents in the British colonies (→ Colonialism) and an extension of activity along with the advance of mission. During the 20th century there has been increasing cooperation in their missionary work. Societies have now been formed by the churches of the → Third World. These are growing rapidly and vigorously as they attempt to satisfy their national needs. Technical and financial support is offered by the United Bible Societies (UBS). The work of the societies has contributed extensively to translating into the national languages, an exercise that wrestles profoundly with cultural self-understanding. Increasingly, attention is being given to nonprint media and nondoctrinal helps for readers. For illiterate groups audio Bibles have been developed (on tape), drawing both on linguistic skills and on expertise in modern communication techniques.

3.2. In a dispute about the → Apocrypha (1824-26), the British society, at the urging of the Scottish Presbyterians, resolved to distribute only Bibles without the Apocrypha and not to support societies that took a different course. The BFBS maintained this policy until the increase of interconfessional cooperation in the mid and late 20th century.

4. In Roman Catholic areas the response to Bible societies has been ambivalent, ranging from imitation (e.g., in Germany) to hostility (→ Syllabus of Errors). A change came at the end of the 19th century, an important basis being the dogmatic affirmation by → Vatican I of the teaching authority of the → pope as the supreme hermeneutical court. → Leo XIII (1878-1903), who established the Pontifical Biblical Commission in 1902 to promote and supervise Bible study, sanctioned Bible reading in officially approved editions. In Italy in 1902 the later Benedict XV (1914-22) set up the Holy Society of St. Jerome to see to the distribution of the Bible, which as pope he championed in his → encyclical *Spiritus Paraklitus* (1920). In the next decades many countries saw a Roman Catholic Bible movement (often along with the → liturgical movement). Pius XII (1939-58) supported its aim in his encyclical *Divino afflante Spiritu* (1943). *Lumen gentium,* Vatican II's dogmatic constitution on the church, also supported the necessity and value of Bible reading and distribution.

In 1968 the Pontifical Secretariat (from 1989, the Pontifical Council) for Promoting Christian Unity and the UBS joined in issuing *Guiding Principles for Interconfessional Cooperation in Translating the Bible.* Today there is vigorous cooperative activity in ecumenical Bible translations in Europe, America, and the Third World. In 1996 the UBS was engaged in 681 Bible translation or revision projects throughout the world, 190 of which represented the cooperative efforts of Roman Catholics and Protestants.

5.1. In 1946 the delegates of 13 Bible societies from 12 nations (Czechoslovakia, Denmark, Finland, France, Germany, the Netherlands, Norway, Poland, Sweden, Switzerland, the United Kingdom, and the United States) met in Elfinsward, England, to coordinate their efforts and resources as the United Bible Societies. This institution has since grown to comprise more than 140 national societies and offices, now organized in four major regions: Africa, Asia and the Pacific, Europe and the Near East, and the Americas. The individual societies are independent and interconfessional. They are not organs of the churches, although they have close personal and financial ties with them. The UBS cooperates with the → World Council of Churches and International Missionary Council (→ Mission), and they also draw support from bodies that hold aloof from the → ecumenical movement, mostly fundamentalist or evangelical, since these are also interested in circulating the Bible (e.g., World Gospel Crusade, New Testament Pocket League; → Fundamentalism; Evangelical Movement).

5.2. The purpose of the Bible societies is to make the Holy Scriptures readily available to all people throughout the world in languages that they clearly understand and at prices that they can easily afford. They not only publish and distribute affordable Bibles but also promote Bible translation and revision projects with financial help, specialist assistance, and publications such as the *Bible Translator* and the series Helps for Translators. In order to avoid denominational controversy, their Bibles are printed without doctrinal notes or commentary. Increasingly, however, the preparation and propagation of aids to Bible reading are viewed as important.

The distribution of the Bible takes place through volunteers, churches, and bookshops and also through workers of the Bible societies engaged in mission and → evangelization. Specially trained Bible missionaries are at work in some countries. The UBS offers a forum for the member societies to coordinate their resources in strategic planning, to engage in international cooperative efforts, and to meet the demands of special crises with mutual assistance. Regular ecumenical and regional gatherings are held, as well as special conferences, regional consultations, and training seminars.

5.3. In 1996 the UBS achieved a total distribution of 19.4 million Bibles, 12.2 million New Testaments, and 22.2 million Bible portions. They also issued 476.9 million selections for beginners and new readers. The number of languages in the world is estimated to be around 7,000; the number of these into which at least a part of the Bible has been translated has now reached 2,167, with work in progress in nearly 500 others.

Bibliography: Periodicals: BIDW (1951-) • BT (1950-) • BUBS (1950-), esp. *The UBS at Forty* (= no. 144/145 [1986]).

Other works: J. Barr, *The Bible in the Modern World* (London, 1973) • G. Hammer et al., *Die Luther-Bibel. Entstehung und Weg eines Volksbuches* (Stuttgart, 1980) • E. Hoffmann-Aleith, *Die älteste Bibelanstalt der Welt* (Witten, 1972) • B. Köster, *Die Lutherbibel im frühen Pietismus* (Bielefeld, 1984) • C. Lacy, *The Word-Carrying Giant: The Growth of the American Bible Society* (South Pasadena, Calif., 1977) • W. von Loewenich, *Der moderne Katholizismus vor und nach dem Konzil* (Witten, 1970) • E. M. North, *The Ministry of the Bible Societies Today* (New York, 1954).

Hans Schneider, with Erroll F. Rhodes

Bible Study

1. Concept
2. History
3. Forms and Contents
4. Didactic Steps and Methods
5. Worldwide Significance

1. Concept

Bible study in the churches is the group study of individual texts or whole books of the Bible by church members. The goal is the people's participation in biblical exposition, the promotion of their theological maturity (→ Adulthood), and the grassroots building up of the congregation (→ Church Growth 1.1). Bible study usually takes the form of discussion.

2. History

The beginnings of Bible study may be found in the Bible hours of the Dutch Reformed tradition (from 1550) and later in → Pietist gatherings. In Germany in 1883, Bible circles began in high schools and then spread worldwide in student movements (→ World Student Christian Federation), which led to the adoption of a discussion format. Later there came extension to the congregations with adult Bible classes, Bible weeks, Bible schools, and so forth. Most congregations now offer their members some form of Bible study.

3. Forms and Contents

In Bible study, participants learn how to understand the text objectively and how to relate it to their own situations. Members play an important part in this → hermeneutical task. The tension between text and situation leads to discussion and gives rise to the main forms of Bible study.

3.1. Bible study may be oriented to specific themes. For a given theme a particular text may be chosen and approached in dialogue form.

3.2. Bible study may also deal with specific texts. This is the most common form in group study. The essential task is to lead to dialogue between the message of the text and the → experience of the readers. For this purpose there needs to be a clear understanding of the role of the reader and the role of the participants.

3.3. Bible study may also focus on connected passages or the text of the whole Bible. This form is appropriate, not only in Bible schools, but increasingly for church members, when so many have so little knowledge of the Bible. Individuals may do it on their own with aids, or they may work in seminars.

3.4. Bible study may also be done in larger groups, as at Bible days or Bible weeks. This approach requires not only a new willingness of the group to work and think together but also a new structuring of the presentations.

4. Didactic Steps and Methods

Since the Bible is increasingly being neglected by today's society at large, a more intensive approach is needed if people are to grasp its message and integrate it into their own lives. It has proved helpful to follow three steps, adopting specific methods for each step. The first step is simply to go to the text and discover it, with members expressing their own feelings, evaluations, and projections in relation to it. Methods include illustration, repetition, and silent interaction.

The second step is to focus on the text itself. Members now get close to the text to see how it is constructed and what it is saying. Methods include questioning, comparison, and input from the leader.

The third step is to go on from the text and appropriate it. At this stage the Bible interacts with the personal and social situation of the participants, opening up for them new experiences of life and salvation in the everyday world. Methods include role playing, group delineation, and writing (e.g., diaries, letters, or prayers).

5. Worldwide Significance

Bible study is assuming increasing significance in the churches of Asia, Africa, and Latin America, especially in → base communities, because it helps to train lay workers and congregational leaders. In distinction from the literary traditions of the West, Bible study in these other areas typically makes more use of oral, symbolic, and artistic forms (→ Iconography), including the use of narrative, carved or painted figures, gestures, → dancing, and the acting out of the biblical contents in liturgical drama. In this way the Bible is evocative, suggesting pictures and → symbols, as well as leading to vision and meditation.

Bibliography: H. BARTH and T. SCHRAMM, *Selbster-fahrung mit der Bibel* (Munich, 1977; 2d ed., 1983) • D. EMEIS, *Bibelarbeit praktisch* (Freiburg, 1994) • KATHOLISCHES BIBELWERK, *Praktische Bibelarbeit heute* (Stuttgart, 1973; 2d ed., 1974) • W. LANGER, ed., *Handbuch der Bibelarbeit* (Munich, 1987) • C. MESTERS, *Vom Leben zur Bibel–von der Bible zum Leben* (2 vols.; Mainz, 1983) • A. STEINER and V. WEYMANN, *Gleichnisse Jesu* (3d ed.; Basel, 1986); idem, *Jesus-Begegnungen* (4th ed.; Basel, 1984); idem, *Psalmen* (Basel, 1982); idem, *Wunder Jesu* (2d ed.; Basel, 1982) • T. VOGT, *Bibelarbeit* (Stuttgart, 1985); idem, *Bibelseminar für die Gemeinde* (Zurich, 1982; 5th ed., 1984) • H.-R. WEBER, *Experiments with Bible Study* (Geneva, 1981) • W. WINK, *The Bible in Human Transformation* (Philadelphia, 1973).

THEOPHIL VOGT

Bible Versions

1. General

Bible versions are subject to the same rules of translation as other texts, but with some qualification because of their special character. For the modern translator, it must first be determined which form of the text should serve as the basis for translation: the earliest attested form, or the form established by → Masoretic scholars in the 9th/10th century for the Hebrew Bible and the standard text of 16th-century Renaissance scholarship for the Greek NT. Then it must be decided whether to aim for a literal reproduction of the chosen original text or to prepare an idiomatic rendering in the receptor language. This decision will depend on the extent to which one views the text as verbally inspired in a fixed, sacred language or as a message that can be communicated between diverse cultures. Finally, there is the consideration of how long a particular translation can continue to serve effectively in a given language. This will determine the desirability of revision and whether or not a translation once made (whether it be the Latin Vg, the Syriac Peshitta, Luther's German

Bible, or the English King James Version) should be regarded as immune to change.

Bible versions have always proved to be linguistically creative. They have helped to establish the written language of many peoples, making a deep impact on its literary forms.

2. Antiquity
2.1. *LXX*

In antiquity, Bible versions of the Jewish world must be distinguished from those of the Christian world. To the first group belongs the most important of the early translations of the Scriptures, called the Septuagint (LXX). The name derives from a legendary account, dating to approximately 100 B.C., according to which 70 (or 72) translators agreed independently and unanimously on a Greek rendering of the OT, which was then received as authoritative by all Jews both in → Palestine and throughout the diaspora. Thus the LXX was reputedly declared to be the standard translation for → Judaism.

Historically, the LXX served the Greek-speaking Jews in Egypt in the third and second centuries B.C. who were no longer acquainted with Hebrew. It was not the work of a single translator but is characterized by a marked variety of literary style. Yet it is also marked by a common concern to communicate the message of the OT thought-world in a form that Greek-speaking Jews would understand. Its historical impact was immense. It mediated to the Greeks an appreciation of Jewish thought that made it possible for many → Gentiles to become sympathetic with, and even convert to, Judaism. It thus prepared the ground for a Christian → mission to Greek-speaking peoples throughout the → Roman Empire.

In the first two centuries A.D., the LXX was the Scripture of Christians. It influenced the style of the authors of the NT writings, which by approximately 200 came to be viewed as canonical along with the OT (i.e., the LXX; → Canon). Because of this development the Jews abandoned the LXX in the second century A.D. For the communities of the → diaspora several new Greek translations were made to replace it, each of which served a different purpose: the literal rendering of Aquila (ca. 130), which was appreciated for its extreme fidelity to Hebrew idiom; the good Greek version of Symmachus (ca. 170), which could still differentiate itself from Christian Scriptures; and the revision by Theodotion (end of the 2d cent.) of an anonymous earlier Greek translation. These have all come down to us only in fragmentary form.

The different recensions and renderings of the OT, of which these are only the most important, as well as the variations in the current text of the LXX,

led the Christian scholar → Origen (ca. 185-ca. 254), around 230-40, to attempt a correction of the LXX according to the Hebrew original. For this purpose he assembled in his Hexapla the four above-mentioned translations, the Hebrew text, and a transliteration of the Hebrew into Greek. He placed these in six parallel columns and then corrected the LXX text, using marks to show what it had omitted or added to the original. This Hexapla recension had a great influence on later MSS of the LXX (→ Bible Manuscripts and Editions).

2.2. *Aramaic Targums*

After the exile, Aramaic became the common speech of Palestine. As a result, many Palestinian Jews no longer were able to understand the OT in its original Hebrew form. There thus arose the Aramaic Targums (translations), which were read at synagogue → worship following the reading of the → Torah in Hebrew. These "translations" were at first oral, but they soon became fixed in written form. The different Targums are for the most part paraphrases and interpretations. They are therefore valuable as witnesses to the contemporary understanding of the Scriptures. Many have been lost. Of those that have survived, the oldest, which come from the pre-Christian era, are among the → Qumran discoveries. These Palestinian Targums must be distinguished from the Targums officially edited in Babylonia in the fifth century A.D., as the latter have a fixed text that agrees with the orthodox Jewish interpretation and is close to the traditional Hebrew text (*Targum Onqelos* and *Targum Jonathan*).

2.3. *Languages of the Roman Empire*

The Christian faith spread at first in the → Greek language. Only around the year 200 did translations of its Scriptures begin to be made into the more important regional languages of the Roman Empire, especially Latin, Syriac, and Coptic. These new versions exhibit a similar pattern of development. First came early translation attempts, of which only traces have survived. Then corrections were made, and finally a revised form became the standard text for speakers of the language.

2.3.1. *Latin*

The Old Latin (Vetus Latina) has survived only in a few MSS and in the Scripture quotations found in writings of the → church fathers. It possibly came from North Africa (at the earliest ca. 180, first plainly attested ca. 250 in the works of → Cyprian). Its first purpose was to provide a Latin rendering for the Greek text of the Holy Scriptures that was read at Christian worship.

The Vulgate goes back to the work of → Jerome (ca. 345-420), who at the behest of Pope Damasus I

(366-84) began to revise or retranslate the Gospels in 383. The rest of the NT books followed, though Jerome himself possibly did not do all of them. The Vg OT was at first based on the Hexapla LXX, but then Jerome prepared a fresh translation from the Hebrew text. At first the complete Vg circulated alongside the various Old Latin versions, but gradually it replaced them and finally became the definitive text of the Latin Bible.

In a new revision by Alcuin (ca. 732-804), the Vg served as the authoritative Latin text of the Middle Ages. This was essentially reproduced in the official Roman edition published after the Council of → Trent under the authority of Pope Clement VIII in 1592, which remained the official text of the Catholic Church until 1979. At that time the Pontifical Biblical Commission issued a new Vg (rev. 1986), based on modern critical scholarship.

2.3.2. Syriac

Syriac is the Aramaic dialect of Edessa. The mission in Syria opened with Tatian's harmony of the Gospels, known as the Diatessaron, which was probably first written in Greek but quickly translated. The Old Syriac (Vetus Syra) version, whose beginnings go back to the third century, could not supplant this well-loved text. Only around 450 did the Peshitta, a new version based on the authoritative Greek text, establish itself among all Syriac-speaking Christians. This version is still the accepted text among their successors, the Christians of the → Syrian Orthodox Church. It is uncertain whether the Peshitta of the OT was produced in Jewish or in Jewish-Christian circles. At any rate it is much older than the Peshitta of the NT, has the form of a Targum, and is not the work of a single translator.

Only in → Monophysite Syrian circles do we find translation work that goes beyond the Peshitta, with a tendency to assimilate the version to the inspired Greek text. Bishop Philoxenus of Mabbug (ca. 440-523) commissioned the so-called Philoxenian version of the NT in 508/9 (now lost), which Thomas of Harkel (= Heraclea) greatly revised in 616. Along with Thomas, and in connection with him, Paul of Tella (7th cent.) translated the Hexapla version of the LXX, taking over Origen's critical marks and expanding them to indicate textual variants. Thomas of Harkel employed a similar system, so that both versions are very valuable for textual research.

2.3.3. Coptic

"Coptic" is a general term for Egyptian dialects of the Christian era. Christian mission came early to Egypt in the Greek language, which enjoyed widespread use in Lower Egypt. With the rapidly growing monastic movement at the end of the third and

fourth centuries, a need arose for the Bible in the popular national dialects. Possibly the translation was done at first orally, and only later written down. There were probably several translations, or at least partial translations, in the main dialects (Sahidic and Bohairic), which then were standardized. Significant new findings have helped us trace the tradition of the Coptic Bible, the OT of which has not been fully preserved. A great number of MS fragments have survived; only when these have been examined and evaluated will it be possible to tell the full history of Coptic Bible translation.

2.4. Others

Besides the important Christian Bible versions of the early period, there are also several other versions that were not made directly from the Greek but from earlier translations and that for the most part have experienced several revisions. Thus we have the Armenian Bible (for which an alphabet had to be devised), which was translated from the Syriac at the beginning of the fifth century. A Georgian version was made from a form of the Armenian obviously earlier than the one that has been preserved. The Ethiopic Bible comes from the fifth/sixth century and goes back to the Greek original, with influence also from the Coptic version. The Arabic versions date to the Islamic period and derive for the most part from the Syriac and Coptic. Fragments of the translation of the NT into Nubian and Middle Iranian (ca. 6th cent.) round out the picture of the early Christian mission to the Near East and Africa. The rise of → Islam put a halt to many of these early advances. Forward-looking in contrast was the first translation into a Germanic language, the Gothic version by Ulfilas in the middle of the fourth century (the OT only in part), which was made from the Greek Koine.

3. Middle Ages

In the West the Vg, in the text edited by Alcuin, was dominant for the University of Paris, which had a decisive influence in the High Middle Ages. Yet there were also translations or partial translations into the national languages. A part of the Gospel of John was reputedly translated into Early Old English by the Venerable Bede in the 8th century, and the Lindisfarne Gospels of the 7th/8th century contain a Late Old English interlinear gloss that was added in the mid-10th century. John → Wycliffe promoted a Middle English rendering of the whole of the Vg in the 14th century. The Psalms were translated into Dutch in the 9th and 10th centuries, and the NT in about 1390. Translations into the Scandinavian languages in the High and Late Middle Ages have been preserved only in fragments. The full Bible appeared in French and Provençal at the end of the 13th century after an earlier ban on translation for fear of the → Waldenses, who had made a demand for translations. A lay movement, then the mendicant and preaching orders, the → Franciscans and → Dominicans, sponsored an Italian version in the 13th century. This century also saw versions in Spanish and Catalan.

During the same period in the East, the church carried on vigorous missionary work. This produced an early Slavic version from the 9th century on the basis of a Koine text that was accepted in → Byzantium. Translation work continued throughout the Slavic sphere up to the 16th century. In 1499 a first collection of all the biblical books in Old Church Slavonic was made, the OT being partly translated from the Vg. We also find Czech and Polish versions in the pre-Reformation period. Nor should one forget the late medieval Jewish renderings of the OT into Yiddish and Spanish (Jewish-Spanish Ladino), which were in use up to the 19th and 20th centuries.

4. Reformation and Modern Period

Bible translation and revisions proceeded at a new pace from the → Reformation onward, for which the following three reasons are mainly responsible: (1) the attempt of the Reformation churches to orient Christian faith more strictly to the Bible, (2) the new possibilities of dissemination by the discovery of printing, and (3) the humanist summons "Back to the sources" (→ Humanism), which aroused a stronger interest in the original sources, especially the original Greek texts. From the beginning of the 18th century, revisions of the Reformation renderings began, though these ran into various difficulties.

New versions appeared in all the languages and linguistic areas mentioned in §3 above. In the lands affected by the Reformation, these had particular significance and influence as the basis for a national literature. There were also many new translations for which in some cases a written language had to be created, as in the early period and the Middle Ages.

4.1. *English*

In England, William Tyndale (1494?-1536) was the first to translate the NT from the Greek, but because of opposition he had to publish his work in Germany (1525 and 1534). The first complete Bible to be published without restriction was that of Miles Coverdale (1488?-1569). Revised combinations of Tyndale's work with that of Coverdale appeared in 1539 as the Great Bible, and in 1568 as the Bishop's Bible. The latter was the basis of a further revision compared anew with the original languages and with the competing Geneva Bible to produce the Authorized, or

King James, Version (AV/KJV) of 1611. The Rheims-Douai Bible (Rheims, NT 1582, Douai, OT 1609-10), an official Roman Catholic translation of the Latin Vg, was revised by Richard Challoner, bishop of London (1738-52), and became the standard version for English-speaking Catholics. The KJV exercised the greatest influence on English literature, unchallenged (but with corrected editions issued in 1762 at Cambridge and in 1769 at Oxford) until the → modern period, when it was itself revised in 1881 (NT) and 1885 (OT), appearing as the Revised Version (RV).

Significant versions in the modern period include those by James Moffatt (NT 1913, Bible 1924) and by Edgar J. Goodspeed and J. M. Powis Smith (NT 1923, Bible 1935), which led to the revision of the RV as the Revised Standard Version (NT 1946, Bible 1952) and the New Revised Standard Version (1989). There also were independent translations such as the New English Bible (NT 1961, Bible 1970), further updated as the Revised English Bible (1989), the Good News Bible (NT 1966, Bible 1976) in "common language," the Contemporary English Version (NT 1991, Bible 1995), and such conservative evangelical versions as the Amplified Bible (1965), the Modern Language Bible (New Berkeley Version, NT 1945, Bible 1969), and the New American Standard Bible (NT 1963, Bible 1971), which have been largely superseded by the New International Version (NT 1973, Bible 1978).

Noteworthy modern Roman Catholic versions include Ronald Knox's translation in England of the Latin Vg (1955). Following the encyclical *Divino afflante Spiritu* (1943), which authorized translations from the original languages, the Jerusalem Bible (1966) appeared, emulating the French 1954 edition (the former was revised in 1985 on the basis of the French 1973 revision), as did, in America, the New American Bible (1970).

Jewish translations were made in England by A. Benisch (1861) and M. Friedlander (1881), and in America by I. Leeser (1854, English rev. in 1865), the standard Jewish version until the publication of the Jewish Publication Society Bible (1917). This translation has now been replaced by the New Jewish Version (1985).

4.2. *German*

The earliest German translations consist of glosses of the Lord's Prayer; the first partial translation was a version of the Gospel of Matthew (ca. 800, Monsee-Wiener Fragments), followed by the Old High German Harmony of the Gospels of Tatian (Fulda, 9th cent.), culminating in learned commentary-translations in the 14th century, still focused on biblical poetry and mostly based on the Latin Vg. Before the Reformation,

14 mostly anonymous versions were published in High German and 4 in Low German.

Martin → Luther's translation (NT 1522, Bible 1534) inaugurated a new era of translation, using the original languages for the whole Bible (for the NT a Strasbourg edition of the Greek of → Erasmus, for the OT the 1494 Brescia edition of the Hebrew) and giving priority to the comprehension of the reader. Constantly revising his work and seeking the counsel of others (e.g., P. → Melanchthon and J. Bugenhagen), Luther forged a German style that contributed profoundly to the formation of the written language. The results may be seen in the first revision of 1541 and then in the final editions of 1545 and 1546.

Luther's version had a pervasive influence on the German Reformation and on other Bible versions of the Reformation period. Roman Catholic Bible versions (by H. Emser, J. Dietenberger, and J. Eck) were largely reactions to Luther but also borrowed from him. The Reformed Zurich Bible began as a revision of Luther's NT (1524) and his earlier OT books, but when the rest of the Wittenberg OT took so long, it proceeded independently in a group supervised by Leo Juda, with a first important revision in 1540. There were many subsequent revisions, the latest being in 1931 and 1954, the Gospels and Psalms in 1996. A very literal rendering by the Reformed theologian J. Piscator (1546-1625) in 1602-4 did not meet with much approval, but it continued to be printed in Switzerland until 1848.

The Luther Bible became a kind of textus receptus for German Lutheranism throughout the 16th and 17th centuries. Only toward the end of the 17th century was revision ventured (by J. Dieckmann and J. Pretten). In the 18th century → Pietism undertook a conservative revision (J. R. Hedinger 1704) and even retranslation, partly on theological and devotional grounds (N. L. von → Zinzendorf 1739, the Berleburg Bible 1726-42), partly on textual grounds (J. A. Bengel 1753).

New versions in the 19th and 20th centuries followed the originals more accurately (W. De Wette 1809-14, E. Kautzsch 1888-94, C. H. von Weizsäcker 1875, H. Menge 1926), sought a more faithful rendering of what was regarded as the verbally inspired text (Elberfeld Bible 1871, NT rev. 1974, OT 1985), or aimed at greater intelligibility for readers (F. Pfäfflin 1939; A. Schlatter 1954; J. Zink, NT 1965, OT selection 1967; U. Wilckens 1970). *Die Gute Nachricht* (NT 1967, OT 1983, rev. ed. 1997) offered a rendering in everyday speech. Roman Catholics also attempted many new translations in the 19th and 20th centuries (J. F. von Allioli 1837; J. Ecker 1903; O. Karrer, NT 1950; Pattloch Bible 1956; Her-

der Bible 1965), finally resolving this multiplicity of translations by its union version *Einheitsübersetzung* (NT 1979, Bible 1980).

The 19th and 20th centuries also saw Jewish renderings. The best known of these are the editions by M. I. Landau (1833-37), L. Zunz (1837), and L. Philippson (1854); the impressive work of M. Buber and F. Rosenzweig (1925-37; rev. ed., 1954-62); and that of H. Torczyner (Tur-Sinai) (1935-58).

4.3. *Dutch*

In Holland the first Dutch NT was based on the Latin Vg, but the Luther Bible was soon translated (NT 1523, Bible 1526). Through a series of revisions in 1558 ("Biestkins Bible"), 1648 (A. Visscher), 1750 (N. Haas), 1823 (J. T. Plüschke), and 1951 (Netherlands Bible Society), it has remained the text of the Dutch Lutherans. The Dutch Reformed Church Bible of 1556 (J. Gheylliaert) was based on the German Zurich Bible. G. van Wingen's 1561-62 version ("Deux Aes Bible") was generally preferred until the States General version of 1637, which is still in use (latest rev. 1977).

4.4. *Scandinavian Languages*

The Reformation also saw new renderings in all the Scandinavian countries, and revisions followed. A *Danish* NT appeared in 1524, and the whole Bible (C. Pedersen) in 1550. A new translation from the Greek appeared in 1607 (H. P. Resen, rev. H. Svaning), which became the standard Bible in Danish. The present official Bible of the National Danish Church is the revision of 1992, authorized by Queen Margarethe II.

Norway, united until the 19th century to Denmark, used the Danish Bible up to the beginning of the 20th century. A revision in Riksmål was issued in 1930 and was further revised in 1988.

A rendering of the NT on the basis of the original text appeared in *Swedish* in 1526, and the OT followed in 1541. These came together as the renowned Gustav Vasa Bible, which has had a profound influence on Swedish literature, culture, and piety. Minor revisions were made already in the 16th century, and the result was the Charles XII Bible of 1702. This remained the standard text until the 1917 Bible of Gustav V.

4.5. *Romance Languages*

The effect of the Bible on the literature and culture of the Romance languages was less significant than in that of the Germanic languages. Most significant was the impact upon *French* of the work done by Pierre Robert, called Olivetan (ca. 1506-38), a cousin of J. → Calvin, who translated the Bible from the original languages in 1535. Significant revisions were made by D. Martin (1707), J.-F. Ostervald (1744),

L. Segond (1874-80, rev. 1975), and the Synodal version (1910). In Roman Catholic France the 1530 translation (from the Vg) of J. F. Stapulensis (ca. 1455-1536) played a decisive part; the Port-Royal version ("de Sacy," 1667-95) was popular among Protestants as well as Catholics. Recent Catholic versions include those of A. Crampon (1904), the monks of Maredsous (1950, rev. 1968), and the *Bible de Jérusalem* (1954, rev. 1973). Significant recent versions include the *Traduction œcuménique* (1975) and the *Français courant* common-language version (1982). The Jewish version by S. Cahen (1831-51) was superseded by the French Rabbinate version of 1906 (rev. 1966); A. Chouraqui's independent version (1975-77) includes both Testaments.

The first printed *Italian* Bible was by N. Malerbi (1471) based on the Latin Vg, but the humanist A. Brucioli published a translation from the original languages in 1530-32. The most important Protestant Italian version was that of G. Diodati (1576-1649) in 1607 (made from the original texts), which Italian Protestants still use in revised form (the last revision was the Versione Riveduta of 1994). The standard Roman Catholic Bible was long that of A. Martini (1769-81), based on the Latin Vg; more recent Catholic versions have been produced by the Cardinal Ferrari Society (1929), the Pontifical Biblical Institute (1958-65), and the Italian Episcopal Conference (1971). Ecumenical versions include the *Bibbia Concordata* (1968) and an interconfessional common-language version (1985).

C. de Reina (ca. 1520-94) published a *Spanish* translation in Basel in 1569 that was revised by C. De Valera in 1602, but this was not disseminated in Spain until the 19th century. Frequently revised (most recently in 1960 and 1995), it remains the popular Protestant Bible. The first Bibles produced in Spain were the Catholic versions of F. Scio (1793) and F. T. Amat (1825). More recent versions include those of E. Nacar and E. Colunga (1944), J. M. Bover and F. Cantera (1947), E. M. Nieto (1961), J. A. Ubieta (1967, based on the French Jerusalem Bible), R. Ricciardi (1971), and L. A. Schökel and others (1975, rev. 1982). Ecumenical publications include the Bible by S. De Ausejo and F. De Fuenterrabia (1975) and the Bible Society common-language version, *Dios habla hoy* (1979).

In *Portuguese* J. F. d'Almeida, a Reformed preacher in Batavia, published the NT in Amsterdam in 1681; his OT was not published until 1751 in Tranquebar, India, by the Danish Bible Society. Revised repeatedly (most recently in 1917 and 1958), it remains the popular Protestant Bible. A common-language version was published by the Bible Society

of Brazil in 1988. The first Bible published in Portugal was the Catholic version by A. P. de Figuereido (1781), based on the Latin Vg. More recent versions are those by M. Soares (1930-34, from the Latin Vg), the Catholic Biblical Center of São Paolo (1959, from the French Maredsous version), L. Garmus (1983, from the New American Bible), and an ecumenical version by the Portuguese Bible Society (NT 1978, Bible 1993).

The first edition of the *Catalan* Bible (1478) fell victim to the Inquisition; only a single page survives. Apart from the NT by J. Prat (1832), no further translations appeared until the 20th-century editions of the Monserrat Benedictines (1926-66, 1970), the Catalan Biblical Foundation (portions 1968), and the United Bible Societies (Bible 1993).

The first *Galician* Bible was the Roman Catholic X. F. Lago version (NT 1980, Bible 1989, rev. 1992).

The *Romanian* Scriptures (Gospels 1561, NT 1648, Bible 1688) were printed in the Cyrillic alphabet until 1860. Today the D. Cornilescu version (1921) is the Protestant version; the Orthodox version is that of V. Radu and G. Pisculescu (1938, rev. 1968 and 1975).

4.6. *Slavic Languages*

The *Old Church Slavonic* version traditionally ascribed to Sts. Cyril and Methodius of the 9th century remains the standard Bible of the Russian Orthodox Church (first printed 1581, rev. 1633, 1712, 1751). Its influence was pervasive among Slavic translations, the earliest of which was the Czech Hussite version (NT 1475, Bible 1488; later replaced by the Kralice Bible of 1579-94; a new Roman Catholic version appeared in 1925, and an ecumenical version in 1979). The 16th century saw the publication of Bibles in Polish (the Lutheran Seklucyan NT of 1553; the Calvinist "Brest Bible" of 1563, rev. 1632 as the Danzig version; the Roman Catholic J. Wujek version of 1593/1599, rev. 1935, 1962; the Millennium Version of 1965, rev. 1971, is now the official Roman Catholic text) and Slovenian (the Lutheran P. Truber, NT 1582, and J. Dalmatin, OT 1584, rev. A. Chraska 1914; a Roman Catholic version by A. A. Wolf based on the German Allioli version appeared in 1859, and an ecumenical version in 1961, rev. 1974), as well as a NT in Serbo-Croatian (J. Dalmatin and S. K. Istrianin 1562-63) in the Glagolitic script. While the first complete Bible (Vuk S. Karadžić and G. Daničić 1868) is still popular in both Serbian (Cyrillic script) and Croatian (Roman script), other Croatian versions include the Protestant L. Bakotić version (1933), the Roman Catholic I. E. Sarić version (1942), and the ecumenical Stvarnost version (1968).

Other Slavic languages received the Scriptures

later, including Ukrainian (P. A. Kulisch, NT 1880, Bible 1904; Y. Levitsky, NT 1921, Bible 1930; I. Ohienko, NT 1939, Bible 1962), modern Russian (Synod Version, NT 1823, Bible 1875; a colloquial version by K. Logachev, NT 1989, Bible 1993), Bulgarian (NT 1840, Bible 1871), Byelorussian (NT 1931, Bible 1973), and Slovak (Roman Catholic J. Palkovič, Bible 1832, and J. Donoval, Bible 1926; Lutheran J. Rohaček, Bible 1936, and V. Cobrda, Bible 1978).

4.7. Uralic Languages

The first *Finnish* NT was translated from Luther's German by the Reformed pastor M. Agricola in 1548. The 1632 version, sponsored by Queen Christina and based on the original languages, has remained through successive revisions (latest 1938) the standard Finnish Bible; an ecumenical version was recently published by the Finnish Bible Society (NT 1989, Bible 1992).

The *Hungarian* Vizsoly Bible (1590) by the Reformed pastor G. Károlyi has served as the Protestant Bible (latest rev. 1975) and has had a dominant influence on Hungarian culture comparable to that of the King James Version. Catholic Bibles include the traditional G. Csipkes version of the Latin Vg (1626) and a new version by A. Szöreny and others (1976) made from the original languages and based on the French Jerusalem Bible.

4.8. Other Languages

From the 17th century and especially the 18th century onward, missionary work greatly encouraged Bible translations into non-European languages. The first modern missionary version of the whole Bible was that of the New England Congregationalist pastor J. Eliot (1604-90) on behalf of the Massachusetts → Indians. German Pietists B. Ziegenbalg and J. P. Fabricius produced the first Asian version with their Tamil Bible in India (NT 1715, OT 1727). From 1800 on, W. Carey (1761-1834) and his companions at Serampore, India, aimed to translate the Bible into every Oriental language. The → Bible societies have since pursued this goal systematically.

5. The Present

Since the mid-20th century, Bible translation has focused on two principal tasks: (1) revision and fresh translation for the historic churches of Europe and America and (2) initial translations for the younger churches of the Third World and the mission fields. The methods used in the process have undergone such refinement that one can speak of *new* methods. The very different languages, feelings, and ideas of the peoples of Africa and Asia, and the sociolinguistic differences of dialects in the languages of the Old World, have made it necessary to pay more attention

to the individual recipients of Bible translations than ever before. The aim has been to achieve the best possible functional (rather than formal) balance between fidelity to the original languages of the Scriptures and fidelity to the idiom of new receptor languages. Sociolinguistics, communication theory, structural linguistics, semiotics, and → ethnology on the one side, exegetical skills and textual research on the other, all help to achieve this goal. Computer technology has also facilitated immeasurably the processes of revising translations and of preparing new ones.

Perspectives have become increasingly ecumenical in the sharing of techniques and resources. The Wycliffe Bible Translators and the United Bible Societies (UBS) have played a leading part in the task. Roman Catholic scholarship participated in formulating the *Guiding Principles for Interconfessional Cooperation in Translating the Bible* (1968, rev. as *Guidelines* in 1987). Translation work is now done as far as possible by nationals, supported by consultants. The UBS has issued various aids (e.g., low-cost critical editions of the Hebrew, Greek, and Latin Scriptures; the periodical *Bible Translator;* and a series of handbooks for translators).

There are an estimated 7,000 languages in the world. By 1996, parts of the Bible had been put into 2,167 of these, 355 of which have entire Bibles, and 880 the complete NT. In terms of geographic distribution, parts of the Bible have been translated into 613 languages in Africa, 535 in Asia, 372 in Australia and the South Pacific, 193 in Europe, 376 in Latin America, and 75 in North America, as well as 3 international languages (Esperanto, Interlingua, and Volapük). Revisions are also underway in almost all the major languages.

Bibliography: The Cambridge History of the Bible (3 vols.; Cambridge, 1963-70) • E. A. NIDA, *The Book of a Thousand Tongues* (London, 1972) • L. O. SANNEH, *Translating the Message: The Missionary Impact on Culture* (Maryknoll, N.Y., 1989) • P. C. STINE, *Bible Translation and the Spread of the Church: The Last Two Hundred Years* (Leiden, 1990) • UNITED BIBLE SOCIETIES, *Scriptures of the World* (New York, 1997).

BARBARA ALAND, with ERROLL F. RHODES

Biblical Theology

1. Concept and History
   1.1. Concept
   1.2. History
   1.3. Recent Developments
   1.4. Conclusion

1. Concept and History

1.1. *Concept*

"Biblical theology" is not one single and simple concept, for it may be understood variously, depending on what is set in contrast with it:

1.1.1. Biblical theology may be contrasted with dogmatic theology. It lies on the level, and uses the methods, of biblical scholarship (→ Exegesis, Biblical), rather than the level and the methods of → dogmatics. The difference has been stated thus: biblical theology, which is descriptive and historical, seeks to state the theology implied by the biblical books themselves, while dogmatics is normative and seeks to define what is to be believed.

1.1.2. Alternatively, the stress may be placed on the component "theology": biblical theology then means that the Bible is studied not merely historically or phenomenologically but with a truly theological interpretative purpose.

1.1.3. The stress may be placed upon the logical and conceptual structures used in theology. In that case biblical theology suggests a theology that works with biblical concepts and biblical logic, as against one that works with philosophical concepts, with Hellenic logic, or with modern schemes of thought.

1.1.4. The stress may be placed upon the distinctiveness of the Bible as against its religiohistorical background and environment. Although many similarities in detail are to be admitted, biblical theology, by seeing the overall shape of the biblical witness, makes clear its distinctive character.

1.1.5. The stress may lie upon the inner coherence of the Bible as against the meaning of its parts. In contrast to theologies of OT or NT, or of particular strata such as the → Prophets, → apocalyptic or → Paul, biblical theology is understood as showing the unity of the Bible and the necessary interdependence of its various component parts.

1.2. *History*

1.2.1. The idea of a biblical theology may be said to go back to the → Reformation, with its conviction that Scripture alone is the source and criterion of doctrine. But traditional Protestant theology developed into a complex scholastic system; though stressing biblical → inspiration, it strayed far from biblical styles and thought forms and became heavily didactic and confessionalistic. In contrast with such scholastic systems, the more → pietistic trends stressed the simplicity and directness of the Bible's own speech. A biblical theology founded upon the Bible's own speech might be considered as a department or even a groundwork of dogmatics. Or indeed it could seem to be a higher form of dogmatics, for what could be better in principle than a theology that worked with the very language of Scripture?

1.2.2. This same distinction was transformed, however, by the rise of historical consciousness, for it then came to be said that biblical theology was in essence historical description, leaving aside didactic and normative considerations. The distinction between biblical theology and dogmatics on this basis was classically formulated by J. P. Gabler (1787). Many of the works entitled "Biblical Theology" (of OT or of NT) published throughout the 19th century purported to be valid historical accounts of religion and theology in biblical times, prepared without regard to dogmatics. Yet biblical theology in this sense, even when insisting on its freedom from traditional dogmatics, was influenced by theological, philosophical, and cultural assumptions. It was often less purely historical and more like theology than the theory of the subject allowed.

1.2.3. The 20th century, especially from the '20s and '30s on, saw a reaction against what the historical study of the Bible seemed to have done. It seemed to have been overwhelmingly analytic; it separated the Bible into numerous rather unconnected strands; it overstressed the common elements between the Bible and its cultural environment; it overvalued the process of development; it failed to provide truly theological interpretation. In contrast, theologies of the OT and NT came to be written that sought to state the common elements between the strata, to delineate the total profile of the OT or NT, to distinguish them from the thought of surrounding cultures, and to provide a result that was more truly theological. Opinion was moving in the direction stated in 1.1.2, namely, that biblical study must become truly theological. This move stood in parallel with the rise of the → dialectical theology.

1.2.4. In the English-speaking world during 1945-60, the central emphasis was often as in 1.1.3: the entire Bible was animated by the distinctive Hebrew way of thinking, which in later theology had often been distorted by the acceptance of Greek categories. The NT must therefore be interpreted in the Hebrew categories deriving from the OT and not according to the Greek categories of its environment. Attempts to prove this relationship through linguistic arguments, however, ultimately foundered.

1.2.5. So-called → history of salvation thought was also central in this period. It was supposed to be characteristic of Hebrew thinking, unknown to the extrabiblical world, strange to → philosophy and poorly appreciated by dogmatics, but common to the entire Bible and thus the basis of its inner unity. It also supported a revived interest in → typology as a link between OT and NT, for it was suggested that typology, unlike → allegory, worked with historical correspondences.

The dominance of history as a theological category, however, also ran into difficulties. On the one hand, salvation history did not dominate all the Bible equally; on the other hand, the → theology of history had more important roots in the ancient Near Eastern and Greco-Roman environments than biblical theology had granted. With the loss of assurance in the primacy of salvation history, the older biblical theology fell into some degree of decline. The support of dialectical theology was less manifest; in contrast, philosophical theology, the history of religions, historical criticism, and the study of the environing cultures all seemed to be reviving. If there was to be a biblical theology, new lines for its guidance would have to be worked out.

1.3. *Recent Developments*

1.3.1. Some regarded these difficulties as signs of the "decline and fall" of biblical theology and even pronounced the discipline to be dead. Such a judgment, however, should probably be considered premature. There are several indications that it is likely to remain very much alive.

1.3.2. For one thing, many of the major works of OT and NT theology seemed not to be vulnerable to the criticisms that fell upon the more general arguments of biblical theology. They were solid works that embodied comprehensive scholarly strength, such as the NT theology of R. Bultmann (1884-1976) and OT theologies like those of W. Eichrodt (1890-1978) and G. von Rad (1901-71). The decline of biblical theology, if there really was such a decline, seemed not to carry these works away with it.

These works, however, seemed to create difficulties for biblical theology. Bultmann perceived several different theologies within the NT; he left the message of → Jesus somewhat on the margin as a presupposition of NT theology rather than as a part of it; he did little to provide an integral connection between OT and NT. Von Rad saw no single theology of the OT but a multiplicity of different traditions, each with its own essential → kerygma. Yet the ability to reactualize traditions in a new situation, which was central to the entire process, applied also to the relation between OT and NT. This approach, while achieving a connection with the NT, seems to abandon the attempt to produce an inner coherence for the OT itself in terms of content. Might this be an indication that biblical theology, in the terms in which it had been conceived, was impossible?

1.3.3. To these considerations, we should add that there had always existed a certain opposition to the whole idea of a biblical theology. Enthusiasts for biblical theology tended to resent such opposition and to discount it as a purely historicist and analytic approach that refused to see the Bible as a whole. This attitude, however, ignored the fact that there were genuinely theological arguments against the idea of biblical theology. For it may well be argued that the main content of the NT, and still more that of the OT, is not theology in any proper sense of the word, even if it provides material for theology and calls for theological explanation. Again, it can be argued that the problems that biblical theology has set for itself cannot be answered without the inclusion of dogmatic considerations. This could mean that the idea of a biblical theology working independently of dogmatics is unrealistic.

1.3.4. Nevertheless, the production of works in biblical theology has continued and been fruitful. In OT theology there was a pause after von Rad, as if he had brought a stage in the development of the subject to an end. But in the 1970s a new series began to appear, by W. Zimmerli (1972), G. Fohrer (1972), C. Westermann (1978), S. Terrien (1978), and R. E. Clements (1978). On the whole, these theologies seem in general terms to return to something more like Eichrodt's design, which seeks a comprehensive statement of the faith of the OT as a whole. This revives the question of the "center" around which such a theological statement may be organized (R. Smend).

The drive at all costs to differentiate biblical theology from the history of religions seems to have diminished or disappeared. Several workers in biblical theology also wrote works in the history of religions and treated sympathetically within biblical theology the questions that arose from that other side. W. H. Schmidt (1968) expressly described his book as lying between a history of Israelite religion and an OT theology. Fohrer's OT theology shows an openness to the sort of questions that were asked in the older "liberal" scholarship. There is no reason to doubt that this now-classic line of theologies of OT and NT will continue to develop.

1.3.5. A more radical proposal for the reconstruction of biblical theology comes from B. S. Childs. Convinced of the collapse of the older "biblical theology movement," he argued that the canon of Scripture was the basis upon which a new biblical theology could be created. The canon is the normative context for understanding within the church. Historical scholarship is legitimate but is a quite separate matter. The emphasis should lie not on the reconstruction of earlier stages, nor on that which "lay behind" the text and to which the text referred, but on the text as it stands in its final canonical form.

1.3.6. The canon is important also in the proposal of H. Gese. The emphasis here lies on the inner coherence of the entire Bible (see 1.1.5). Although theologies of the OT or NT might strive to establish connections with the other Testament, this could not succeed so long as only one Testament was taken as the starting point. Biblical theology must begin and end with the entire Bible; OT and NT together form one closed corpus of tradition, one continuum, within which change, growth, and development take place. The process of tradition history is accompanied by the process of → revelation history. The apocryphal and apocalyptic books are an essential part of this stream of tradition; it was a mistake that the Protestant churches excluded them from the canon. In NT times the canon was not yet closed, and it was the NT as the telos that completed the continuum of → tradition and also effectively created the OT in bringing it to a conclusion. There is therefore no "canon within the canon" but a variety of tradition streams that can be understood only through their interdependence with other traditions. Similar concepts, working from the NT side, are maintained by P. Stuhlmacher.

Against these positions, however, considerable criticism has been voiced. According to these critics, the OT and NT cannot really be viewed as one continuum of tradition; separate theologies of the OT and NT remain the more proper approach; Gese's views of the canon are untenable both historically and theologically.

1.3.7. Another interesting approach comes from H. H. Schmid, who lays the emphasis upon → creation. The older biblical theology (e.g., von Rad) had treated creation as secondary to the historical acts of redemption. For Schmid, however, creation theology is primary. Similarly, as against the older biblical theology that sought to distance the OT from ancient Near Eastern religion, the involvement of the OT in that religious environment is of positive theological importance. The dominant background of OT thought and faith was the conception of a comprehensive world order related to creation; it is when seen against this background that the theology of history has meaning.

Such ideas constitute a reversal of the older pro-

gram of biblical theology (1.1.4). Schmid, however, sees them as providing the horizon within which various NT themes (→ Justification; Forgiveness; Peace) are meaningful. This approach thus provides a perspective on the unity of the Bible. But characteristic biblical notions are seen as "transformations of general human presuppositions of thought" and "solutions of general basic human problems." Thus in this form of biblical theology — unlike most others — the Bible does not form a distinct world of thought but is set firmly within the general constitution of human thought.

1.3.8. A somewhat similar direction is seen in the work of U. Luck, who sees biblical theology in correlation with the perception of reality (Wirklichkeitserfassung). Biblical tradition tries to cope in three ways with the tension between expectation and experience: (1) the institutional mode, (2) the historical mode, and (3) the "intellectual" mode. None of these succeeds in overcoming the tension, and the way out must lie in the apocalyptic → hope for a new era in which → righteousness governs.

These newer directions are likely to be criticized for transforming biblical theology into something like general religious consciousness and implications of human → experience. It is not likely that they can be simply dismissed on this ground, however; they seem to mark out a significant and positive new direction for biblical theology to explore.

1.4. Conclusion

The general field of biblical theology remains both alive and lively; it promises much interesting progress in coming years. The most central and challenging question under discussion remains that of the relation between the OT and the NT. The underlying problem that most requires clarification, however, is that of the relation between biblical theology and dogmatics.

Bibliography: J. Barr, *Biblical Faith and Natural Theology* (Oxford, 1993); idem, "Biblical Theology," *IDBSup* 104-11; idem, *The Semantics of Biblical Language* (2d ed.; London, 1962) • R. Bultmann, *Theology of the NT* (2 vols.; New York, 1951-55) • B. S. Childs, *Biblical Theology in Crisis* (Philadelphia, 1970); idem, *Biblical Theology of the Old and New Testaments* (Minneapolis, 1993); idem, *OT Theology in a Canonical Context* (Philadelphia, 1985) • R. E. Clements, *OT Theology: A Fresh Approach* (London, 1978) • G. Ebeling, "The Meaning of 'Biblical Theology,'" *Word and Faith* (London, 1963) 79-97 • W. Eichrodt, *Theology of the OT* (2 vols.; Philadelphia, 1961-67) • G. Fohrer, *Theologische Grundstrukturen des Alten Testaments* (Berlin, 1972) • J. P. Gabler, *Oratio de iusto discrimine theologiae bi-*

blicae et dogmaticae regundisque recte utriusque finibus (1787; ET in J. Sandys-Wunsch and L. Eldredge, "J. P. Gabler and the Distinction between Biblical and Dogmatic Theology: Translation, Commentary, and Discussion of His Originality," *SJT* 33 [1980] 133-58) • H. GESE, *Essays on Biblical Theology* (Minneapolis, 1981); idem, *Vom Sinai zum Zion. Alttestamentliche Beiträge zur biblischen Theologie* (Munich, 1974) • U. LUCK, *Welterfahrung und Glaube als Grundproblem biblischer Theologie* (Munich, 1976) • M. OEMING, *Gesamtbiblische Theologien der Gegenwart. Das Verhältnis vom Alten Testament und Neuen Testament in der hermeneutischen Diskussion seit Gerhard von Rad* (2d ed.; Stuttgart, 1987) • G. VON RAD, *OT Theology* (2 vols.; New York, 1962-65) • H. REVENTLOW, *Problems of Biblical Theology in the Twentieth Century* (Philadelphia, 1986) • H. H. SCHMID, *Altorientalische Welt in der alttestamentlichen Theologie* (Zurich, 1974) • W. H. SCHMIDT, *The Faith of the OT* (Oxford, 1983; orig. pub., 1968) • R. SMEND, *Die Mitte des Alten Testaments* (Zurich, 1970) • P. STUHLMACHER, *Historical Criticism and Theological Interpretation of Scripture: Toward a Hermeneutics of Consent* (Philadelphia, 1977) • S. TERRIEN, *The Elusive Presence: Toward a New Biblical Theology* (New York, 1978) • C. WESTERMANN, *Elements of OT Theology* (Atlanta, 1982; orig. pub., 1978); idem, ed., *Essays on OT Hermeneutics* (Richmond, Va., 1964) • W. ZIMMERLI, *OT Theology in Outline* (Atlanta, 1978; orig. pub., 1972).

JAMES BARR

2. Biblical Theology in Context
2.1. *Problem*

The phrase "biblical theology in context" refers to the theological interpretation of the Bible relative to the challenges and situations Christians must live up to in a given place, country, or region (→ Contextual Theology). It calls attention to the great variety in the exposition and application of the OT and NT Scriptures, showing that the Bible can be read and understood in different ways, even though there is widespread agreement on the basic questions of biblical → exegesis. The different interpretations of biblical texts reflect the various cultural presuppositions of the churches, as well as their wrestling with social and political relations and other religions or worldviews. Over against tradition, such an approach to biblical theology draws attention to the fact that new theological insights into the OT and NT witness can arise out of direct experience with the Bible in daily Christian life as well as out of the critical confrontation of biblical texts with contemporary questions and trends.

The context that affects the theological interpretation of the Bible and that characterizes its diversity enriches the → hermeneutical process, that is, the interplay of address and questioning that the biblical text mediates, or that readers direct to the authors. In this process readers accept that what the biblical witnesses proclaim as God's word and interpret as his revealing, judging, and saving action in history possesses → authority and is significant as the biblical tradition. At the same time, the current life situation — with all its various dimensions and open questions — shapes the perspective in which the biblical witness is read and expounded. Biblical theology in context is thus the multifaceted attempt to enter into the process of exposition that the biblical authors began and, in spiritual concert with those early witnesses, to continue theological interpretation in the various situations of life. In this interpretative process neither the universally recognized authority of the Bible nor the commonly applied rules of exposition will necessarily lead to the same results.

From this standpoint the question of the authority of the Bible is a complex one. We must remember the special character of the biblical texts (as witness to divine → revelation; → Word of God); the varied and changing nature of the situation; the historical, dogmatic, and confessional dimensions of the problem; and the factor of the operation of the → Holy Spirit in the process of exposition. The question of the authority of the Bible bears decisively on the → hermeneutical problem, the significance of the → canon, the relation between the OT and the NT, the central point of reference in Scripture, and the contribution of human → experience and understanding of reality. The attempts at biblical theology in context make it plain that there can be no avoiding hermeneutical perspectives that are conditioned by the situation, and that the question of the authority of the Bible cannot be separated from the process of its interpretation.

In the sections that follow we show first how the problem is taken up in ecumenical studies. We then consider selected examples from Africa, Asia, and Latin America, and finally theological interpretation from feminist standpoints.

2.2. *Ecumenical Aspect*

2.2.1. The present → ecumenical movement binds together in a search for → unity more than 300 churches that differ both by tradition and present-day experience. It recognizes Holy Scripture as the basis and norm of Christian faith and life. At the same time, it realizes that the actual significance of the Bible in the teaching and life of the churches is not everywhere the same. There is both committed Bible study and also difficulty in dealing with the Bible and alienation from certain biblical texts. In biblical study, answers and orientation are sought in the face of confusion and pressure. Thus there is both a sense of distance from the biblical authors and the discovery of their unquestionable relevance. Yet there are also differences in the method of approach, in the understanding of the OT and NT, and in the inferences drawn from the biblical testimonies for the church's proclamation and its attitude to actual social and political questions. At this point confessional factors play a part (e.g., the meaning of → tradition, the function of the → teaching office, the validity of → confessions and → dogmas), as do the respective traditions of thought, varied interests, and social and cultural conditions.

The ecumenical movement, then, considers the Bible as the common reference point and source of Christian faith and also affirms that the given context plays an important role in determining its theological interpretation. In its concern for unity, though, the movement must answer several questions. How can the churches give a concerted and credible witness on the basis of the Bible? How can they find a common answer to the questions of the modern world? How can they give an authoritative form to their own fellowship?

2.2.2. In its ecumenical studies and conferences, the Faith and Order Commission of the → World Council of Churches has addressed the problem of the authority of the Bible and an appropriate theological interpretation that also takes into account the varied situation of Christians and the churches. A report published from Wadham College, Oxford, entitled *Guiding Principles for Interpretation of the Bible* (1949), stresses a biblical theology that (1) links historical interpretation of the biblical texts with a Christocentric, confessing theology and (2) understands the OT and the NT in their unity as credible witness to the divine salvation history. A conference at Montreal in 1963 took up the issue of the relation between Scripture and tradition, which churches evaluate differently. The formulated consensus refers to the tradition of the gospel in Scripture but leaves open the question of hermeneutical principles.

A study entitled "The Significance of the Hermeneutical Problem for the Ecumenical Movement" was presented at a conference at Bristol in 1967. It laid the groundwork for widespread agreement in basic exegetical questions and in the description of the hermeneutical process. It recognized tensions, contradictions, and differences in the OT and NT writings and explained this variety, which makes theo-

logical understanding of the Bible more difficult, in terms of varied human testimony arising in varied historical situations. Thus the question of the authority of the Bible remained acute.

A report entitled "The Authority of the Bible," discussed at Lyons in 1971, understands authority as a relational concept. The Bible manifests its authority by seeking free acceptance as a witness to encounter with the living God, by being actually experienced in, and yet also transcending, human experience. From the first its theological interpretation has stood in a living process of exposition and appropriation by the church. The report makes it clear that different historical situations do not merely permit different interpretations of the biblical witness — they require them. It highlights the problem of the abiding identity of the gospel in temporal change.

A consultation in 1977 at Loccum, Germany, considered the report "The Significance of the OT," which dealt with the relation between the OT and the NT. It emphasizes that the OT is an integral and inalienable part of the Bible that must not simply be interpreted Christologically. The OT is also important in dialogue with → Judaism (→ Jewish-Christian Dialogue) and with other religions (→ Islam and Christianity), as was stressed in a 1978 meeting in Bangalore, India. The document drawn up there ("Common Account of Hope") bears witness that the faith and → hope mediated by the biblical witness as a whole bind the churches together, even though multiplicity and distinction still remain in theological interpretation and contextual conditions.

Bibliography: E. Flesseman-van Leer, ed., *The Bible: Its Authority and Interpretation in the Ecumenical Movement* (Geneva, 1980).

Erwin Fahlbusch

2.3. Africa

2.3.1. In 1900 there were 113 partial or complete translations of the Bible into African languages (→ Bible Versions). By 1985 there were 550 translations, with work in progress in approximately 300 additional languages. Similarly the number of Christians grew from around 10 million in 1900 to 238 million by 1985, with projections to nearly 400 million in 2000. The Bible is one of the main factors in the rapid spread of Christianity in Africa. In the 1960s African theologians began to formulate their own biblical theology (→ African Theology).

2.3.2. Biblical religion and the religious and cultural life of Africa contain many points of contact. African theologians describe these as cultural continuity with the Bible, such as the creation story and early Jewish history as it appears in the Pentateuch and the Books of Joshua and Kings, the Wisdom literature and poetry, the general cultural traditions of the OT, and the teachings of Jesus (esp. the → parables). Of special interest are themes from the history and religion of → Israel, ideas of → God, → prophecy, the role of → nature (esp. the land and seasons), and the relation of the individual to society, redemption, and → eschatology. In this comprehensive complex of themes the OT commands more attention than the NT (at least to judge from current publications). Themes like the → kingdom of God and questions of inspiration and biblical criticism have stirred less interest. To understand the choice of themes one should note that the theological thinking of Africa is mostly handed down orally. As in the early church, Africans have an oral theology. A written theology will be a subsequent development.

2.3.3. The situation of African Christianity today is studied in the light of the biblical message. It includes the political questions that afflict many African nations, → racism, corruption, injustice (→ Righteousness, Justice), the attitude to nature, the role of the churches in the African context, ethical questions (→ Ethics; Social Ethics 4), and — not least — what is called → development (§1). Theologians from all the great churches of the African continent (→ Anglicans, the → Roman Catholic Church, → Reformed churches, the → Orthodox Church, et al.) take part in studies of such themes. Like those in other areas of African theology, they are published in such non-African languages as English, French, and Portuguese, thus enabling Africans to communicate across the many linguistic boundaries.

2.3.4. Preaching in African churches uses the whole Bible, mostly in translation into the local languages. The few collections of sermons manifest a specific theological interest in the teaching and deeds of Jesus (esp. his healings), the understanding of → sin and redemption, personal ethics, and expectations of a speedy end to the world and consummation of → eschatological → hope. There are only a few African commentaries on the Bible, and these are as a rule oriented strongly to Western theological schools, though the writings on the NT might reflect the standpoint of the African churches.

2.3.5. Many Christians in Africa, in studying the teaching and practice of the churches that have developed out of → missionary work and leadership, have measured them by the Bible as the sole normative authority for the life of Christians. Often they have found them wanting. They hold aloof from the mission churches and form their own churches, known as → Independent or Indigenous churches

(→ Kimbanguist Church). These groups stress certain parts of the Bible, for example, → healings, the role of the → Holy Spirit, legalism (the OT and the Books of Matthew and James, all from an African standpoint), ritual (from both the OT and African life), or → symbols. A comprehensive African theology must address the distinctive features of these churches.

→ Contextual Theology; Third World; Third World Theology

Bibliography: D. B. BARRETT, "The Spread of the Bible and the Growth of the Church in Africa," *BUBS* 128-29 (1982) 5-18 • K. A. DICKSON, *The History and Religion of Israel* (London, 1969); idem, *Theology in Africa* (London, 1984) • K. A. DICKSON and P. ELLINGWORTH, eds., *Biblical Revelation and African Beliefs* (3d ed.; London, 1972) • K. ENANG, *Salvation in a Nigerian Background* (Berlin, 1979) • R. GIBELLINI, ed., *Paths of African Theology* (Maryknoll, N.Y., 1994) • E. B. IDOWU, *Job: A Meditation on the Problem of Suffering* (Ibadan, 1977) • L. KALUGILA, *The Wise King* (Lund, 1980) • U. LINK-WIECZOREK, "Neulesen der Bibel im Kontext afrikanischer Theologie," *MdKI* 45/6 (1994) 116-19 • J. S. MBITI, *Bible and Theology in African Christianity* (Nairobi, 1985); idem, "The Biblical Basis for Present Trends in African Theology," *African Theology en Route* (ed. K. Appiah-Kubi and S. Torres; Maryknoll, N.Y., 1979) 83-94; idem, *NT Eschatology in an African Background* (London, 1971) • T. A. MOFOKENG, *The Crucified among the Crossbearers: Towards a Black Christology* (Kampen, 1983) • B. MOORE, comp., *Black Theology* (2d ed.; Atlanta, 1974) • N. I. NDIOKWERE, *Prophecy and Revolution* (London, 1981) • J. S. POBEE, *Toward an African Theology* (Nashville, 1979) • H. SAWYERR, *Creative Evangelism* (London, 1968) • D. TUTU, *Versöhnung ist unteilbar. Biblische Interpretation zur Schwarzen Theologie* (Wuppertal, 1985) • H. W. TURNER, *Profile through Preaching* (London, 1965).

JOHN MBITI

2.4. *Asia*

2.4.1. In this section we focus primarily on Japan as we consider biblical theology in an Asian context, for Japan offers a good model of the encounter and confrontation of East and West. In the case of Japan, biblical theology operates in a country in which (1) Christianity is not well known, (2) the Christian church is still heavily dependent on Europe and the United States, and (3) a rich → Buddhist tradition flourishes. The works of biblical theology in Japan thus fall into three types represented by the following three scholars.

Zenda Watanabe (1885-1978), an OT scholar,

dealt with questions of the Bible, the → canon, and the significance of historical criticism for the canon (→ Exegesis, Biblical). He found testimony in the whole Bible to salvation history, which by the shattering of human autonomy points us to Christ. He thus developed a method of drawing testimonies to Christ from the whole Bible and presenting them in diverse, yet systematic, form.

Masao Sekine (b. 1912), another OT scholar, worked in the European (esp. German) tradition of OT scholarship, yet with an independent turn. He made his own translation of the OT, exegeted the OT writings, and elucidated biblical terms in the light of biblical theology. Finding the essence of the → prophets' message to be the breaking and renewing of the relation between God and his people, he applied concepts developed by Japanese philosopher H. Tanabe (1885-1962) to his own analysis of the prophetic act. This synthesis shows his openness to the national tradition. In the history of Israel, Sekine sought to trace anticipations of the Christian → revelation, an approach that guided all his OT theology.

Seiichi Yagi (b. 1932), a NT scholar, has seen a profound relation between Christianity and Buddhism, and especially between → Paul and Shinran (1173-1262), a Buddhist reformer who preached a kind of justification by faith alone, but also between → Jesus and → Zen. He has sought to develop terms in religious philosophy that would give relevant expression to the main issue in both religions (in Pauline terms, dying to the world, being in Christ, and walking according to the Spirit). In his view, NT theology does not aim merely to explain the NT understanding of existence but supremely to interpret NT Christology in a way that is intelligible to non-Christians, or at least Buddhists (→ Buddhism and Christianity).

2.4.2. In India, insofar as it is characterized by → Hinduism, the Jesus of the Gospels (esp. John's gospel), is a sympathetic figure. Even in terms of Christian theology, he has been successfully interpreted in Hindu terms. The Hindu tradition, however, has sometimes called the OT into question.

→ Asian Theology; Hinduism and Christianity

Bibliography: Japan: AJBI (1975-) • Y. FURUYA, ed., A History of Japanese Theology (Grand Rapids, 1997) • C. MICHALSON, Japanese Contributions to Christian Theology (Philadelphia, 1960) • M. SEKINE, The History of the Religion and Culture of Israel (in Japanese) (Tokyo, 1952); idem, The Thinkers of Ancient Israel (in Japanese) (Tokyo, 1982) • Z. WATANABE, The Canonicity of the Bible (in Japanese) (Tokyo, 1949); idem, Interpretation of the Bible (in Japanese) (Tokyo, 1954); idem, Theology of the Bible (in Japanese) (Tokyo, 1963) • S. YAGI, Contact Points between Buddhism and Christianity (in Japanese) (Kyoto, 1975); idem, Paul/Shinran, Jesus/Zen (in Japanese) (Kyoto, 1983).

India: R. BOYD, An Introduction to Indian Christian Theology (Madras, 1975) • L. LEGRAND, "Indian Lines of Approach to the Bible: A Seminar," ITS 20 (1983) 368-69 • G. M. SOARES-PARBHU, Wir werden bei ihm wohnen. Das Johannesevangelium in indischer Deutung (Freiburg, 1984) • P. T. THOMAS, ed., The Works of Vengal Chakkarai (vol. 1; Bangalore, 1981).

SEIICHI YAGI

2.5. Latin America

2.5.1. An elementary concern of → liberation theology is reflection on the faith — specifically, the faith promoted among the poor of Latin America as they interact with the Bible and with their everyday reality.

2.5.2. In church → base communities the Bible has acquired a new position, for it no longer stands solely on the side of knowledge and power. The poor have discovered that the Word of God is the story of their own history. They thus understand their own experiences in relation to the basic events of the Bible, such as the exodus, the conquest, the exile, calling and discipleship, proclamation of the kingdom of God, the → cross, and → the resurrection of Jesus. Life is the place where the liberating God reveals himself (e.g., 1 Sam. 2:1-10; Luke 1:46-55) and gives a prophetic task to the poor. By a dialogic treatment of the text (E. Cardenal), the Bible becomes a living book for the community instead of a dead history of the past. To promote understanding, it is related to the wisdom of experience, → spirituality, and the intuitive closeness of the poor to metaphor. Dealing with the themes of biblical theology (e.g., → Poverty; Righteousness, Justice; Hope; Sin; Reconciliation) initiates a process in the course of which a sense of freedom and a readiness for conflict replace apathy. In this way the Bible provides a vocabulary for the poor to express themselves confidently in theological writings and in the spoken theology of songs, festivals, and community encounters.

2.5.3. Scholarly exegesis, which in the Latin American context no longer views itself merely as an extended arm of European ideas or as the dispenser of a closed revelation, has acquired a new → hermeneutical consciousness through this approach. The history of Jesus of Nazareth becomes the paradigm and enables us to see the → incarnation of the liberating God in the passion story of the poor. Biblical theology becomes unequivocal in its presupposition that the semantics of the → gospel is not contextually neutral. Exegesis can learn from the fact that the poor are "co-natural" with the Bible (C. Mesters), without having to cease being an advocate for the text and for traditions of exposition.

2.5.4. Biblical theology questions traditional church structures and thereby provokes criticism. The high place given to biblical interpretation facilitates and strengthens ecumenical cooperation. Since a biblical theology that is oriented to liberation knows, in S. J. Croatto's phrase, the *reserva de sentido* (reservoir of meaning) of the biblical texts, it enjoys → eschatological perspectives that enable it to tolerate enthusiastic reception, criticism, or political defamation.

Bibliography: E. CARDENAL, ed., *The Gospel in Solentiname* (4 vols.; Maryknoll, N.Y., 1982) • S. J. CROATTO, "Befreiung und Freiheit. Biblische Hermeneutik für die 'Theologie der Befreiung,'" *Lateinamerika: Gesellschaft–Kirche–Theologie* (vol. 2; ed. H.-J. Prien; Göttingen, 1981) 39-59; idem, *Biblical Hermeneutics: Toward a Theory of Reading as the Production of Meaning* (Maryknoll, N.Y., 1987) • G. GORGULHO, "Hermeneútica bíblica," *Mysterium liberationis* (vol. 1; ed. I. Ellacuria and J. Sobrino; Madrid, 1990) 169-200 • G. GUTIÉRREZ, *A Theology of Liberation* (2d ed.; Maryknoll, N.Y., 1988) • *Lateinamerikanische Exegese* (= *EvT* 51/1 [1991]) • C. MESTERS, *Abraham und Sara* (Neukirchen, 1984); idem, *Die Botschaft des leidenden Volkes* (Neukirchen, 1982); idem, *Vom Leben zur Bibel–von der Bibel zum Leben* (2 vols.; Mainz, 1983) • J. SOBRINO, "Der Gott des Lebens wird sichtbar bei Jesus von Nazaret," *Die Götzen der Unterdrückung und der befreiende Gott* (ed. H. Assmann; Münster, 1984) 63-110.

ULRICH SCHOENBORN

2.6. Feminist Perspectives

2.6.1. In the early stages of the feminist movement in the 19th century, wrestling with the meaning of the Bible played an important role. The *Woman's Bible* published by Elizabeth Cady Stanton offers a historicocritical reading of selected biblical texts from the standpoint of women's liberation. In → feminist theology the Bible is an object of both criticism and identification. The theologically interested feminist movement has promoted feminist Bible reading among the laity and scholarly feminist Bible study, also related to the lay movement.

2.6.2. Objects of feminist criticism are the patriarchal view of → God, androcentric → language, the suppression of female → spirituality (§4), lack of emphasis on the role of women in the development

of Christianity, and the theology of → Paul and post-Pauline Christianity. It has also been pointed out that the history of the transmission and interpretation of the Bible (→ Exegesis, Biblical) has led to other → sexist emphases in the Christian reception of the Bible. Positive emphasis is given to outstanding women in the history of Israel and primitive Christianity (esp. Mary Magdalene), and especially → Jesus, whose words and acts give no evidence of patriarchalism or the oppression of women (in contrast to his first interpreters, the writers of the Gospels, who consistently speak an androcentric language and at least partially support patriarchal structures of domination).

2.6.3. The methods of feminist Bible interpretation, insofar as they involve historical questions, are in the broadest sense those of historical criticism, though they do justice both to the context of the Bible and to that of modern interpreters (→ Contextual Theology). Since in present-day biblical scholarship in western Europe and North America, historicocritical research largely neglects social history (i.e., the question of the context of the Bible), historical method itself creates a gap between the feminist reading of the Bible at this level and prevailing biblical scholarship (→ Sociohistorical Exegesis).

2.6.4. In spite of great differences in approach, the various feminist readings of the Bible always have much the same goals. They are trying to discover an integrated picture of God with the help of the Judeo-Christian tradition and in criticism of it. Thus feminist theology makes critical demands upon almost every biblical text material that do not remain on the periphery of existing tradition. The idea of God and the theological thinking of, for example, Paul are from the outset so hierarchical and patriarchal that there can be no accepting them without substantive criticism. Feminist theology is not content apologetically to reconstruct Paul's theology and to ascribe patriarchalism to post-Pauline development alone. The goal of feminist theology is not to set a matriarchal counterpart over against patriarchal theology but to formulate a comprehensive theology that will do justice to → women and → men, black and white, hungry and wealthy. It thus must always begin its inquiry "below," with the oppressed. With this goal it agrees with the heart of the biblical tradition in both the OT and the NT.

2.6.5. Thus far the feminist interpretation of the Bible in Germany and western Europe has met with only a lukewarm reception. In learned commentaries, virtually the only concession widely made is that Junia, whom Paul calls an apostle in Rom. 16:7, was a woman. Certain publications try to neutralize feminist insights by a kind of antifeminist apologetic for the Bible. Only gradually are the implications for Bible translation and liturgical language being accepted.

The main point of difference between the dominant theology in scholarship and in the church and the feminist reading of the Bible probably lies in the sensitivity of the latter to hierarchical relationships. The experience of dependence and oppression, at least when one becomes conscious of it, generates resistance to a theology that takes its place on the side of oppression.

Bibliography: B. BROOTEN, Women Leaders in the Ancient Synagogue (Chico, Calif., 1982) • H. JAHNOW et al., Feministische Hermeneutik und Erstes Testament (Stuttgart, 1994) • E. KÄHLER, Die Frau in den paulinischen Briefen (Zurich, 1960) • E. MOLTMANN-WENDEL, ed., Frauenbefreiung. Biblische und theologische Argumente (3d ed.; Munich, 1982) • C. A. NEWSOM and S. H. RINGE, eds., The Woman's Bible Commentary (Louisville, Ky., 1992) • L. M. RUSSELL, ed., The Liberating Word: A Guide to Non-Sexist Interpretation of the Bible (Philadelphia, 1976) • L. SCHOTTROFF, Let the Oppressed Go Free: Feminist Perspectives on the NT (Louisville, Ky., 1993); idem, Lydia's Impatient Sisters: Feminist Social History of Early Christianity (Louisville, Ky., 1995) • L. SCHOTT-ROFF and M.-T. WACKER, eds., Von der Wurzel getragen. Christlich-feministische Exegese in Auseinandersetzung mit Antijudaismus (Leiden, 1995) • E. SCHÜSSLER-FIORENZA, In Memory of Her: A Feminist Theological Reconstruction of Christian Origins (New York, 1983); idem, ed., Searching the Scriptures, vol. 1, A Feminist Introduction; vol. 2, A Feminist Commentary (New York, 1993-94) • E. C. STANTON, ed., The Woman's Bible (2 vols.; New York, 1895-98; repr., 1974) • P. TRIBLE, God and the Rhetoric of Sexuality (Philadelphia, 1978); idem, Texts of Terror: Literary-Feminist Readings of Biblical Narratives (Philadelphia, 1984) • U. WINTER, Frau und Göttin (Fribourg, 1983).

LUISE SCHOTTROFF

Biblicism

The imprecise term "biblicism" is commonly used disparagingly (cf. "historicism") to denote a particular way of dealing with the Bible, especially the expectation that it can be transposed directly into modern thought forms or lifestyles. European theologians who attempt to classify types of biblicism — for example, into broader and narrower forms (W. Wiesner), or into a theoretical and doctrinaire form, a practical and programmatic form, and a salvation-

history form (G. Gloege) — have failed to make the term more precise. Similarly, attempts to distinguish various manifestations of the term have not been successful (H. Karpp, TRE).

Sometimes the term is used simply to mean a strict reference to the Bible. More often it refers to occasions when ardent believers displace or completely relativize → dogmas and doctrines; when the Bible is held to disclose not only truths of faith (→ Revelation 2.2) but also historical, ethical, and political information and → norms that may be gained from no other source; when, even if the Bible is studied philologically (→ Exegesis, Biblical), direct deductions are sought for answering modern questions; when the Bible is thought to form a totality over against other texts, and its readers can seek in it a divine system, whether religious or secular.

This list of characteristics allows us to view fundamentalism (→ Inspiration) as a special case of biblicism that is very influential in English-speaking churches and the → Third World. The distinction between biblicism and biblical theology is sometimes difficult. We always need the latter, but does it not also tend to minimize theological reflection and displace doctrine? → Narrative theology also seems to be a reduction of theology's doctrinal structure by turning to the biblical stories and retelling them. The problem (→ Hermeneutics) is whether we must make the Bible relevant, or whether we must show the relevance of our own time to the OT and the NT, which we cannot do without theological concepts and theories (i.e., doctrines). Yet systems and doctrines lie concealed in biblicism itself. No one can answer the question of the meaning of the Bible by the simple slogan "The Bible alone."

Representatives of viewpoints that might be called biblicistic appear regularly in church history. Besides the → Puritans we might mention the Württemberg Pietists (J. A. Bengel, F. C. Oetinger, and later J. T. Beck) and G. Menken (1768-1831), as well as certain forms of → dispensationalism. One could also mention M. Kähler's (1835-1912) criticism of biblicism as historicism, though — following A. Schlatter (1852-1938) — we should not include Kähler among the biblicists. It might be asked whether we gain much from these examples, or whether they offer any support for an ecumenically helpful understanding of the Bible.

Bibliography: J. BARR, Fundamentalism (London, 1977) • C. B. BASS, Backgrounds to Dispensationalism (Grand Rapids, 1960) • D. A. CARSON and J. D. WOODBRIDGE, eds., Hermeneutics, Authority, and Canon (Grand Rapids, 1986) • A. DORNER, "Bibliolatry," ERE 2.615-18

• H. KARPP, "Das Aufkommen des Begriffs 'Biblizismus,'" *ZTK* 73 (1976) 65-91; idem, "Biblizismus," *TRE* 6.478-84 (extensive bibliography) • M. E. MARTY and R. S. APPLEBY, eds., *Fundamentalisms Observed* (Chicago, 1991) • E. SCHOTT and G. GLOEGE, "Biblizismus," *RGG* (3d ed.) 1.1262-63 • W. WEIBLEN, "Biblicism," *ELC* 1.307-9 • W. WIESNER, "Biblizismus," *EKL* (2d ed.) 1.515-16.

DIETRICH RITSCHL

Biography, Biographical Research

1. General
2. New Research
3. Conversions

1. General

The scholarly handling of biographical material has a century-old tradition in sociology (Paul). Biographical materials serve as valuable sources for research in → ethnology and → psychology. They are aids in documenting and interpreting the processes of modern social history and in researching → everyday life in various cultures and spheres of life. As distinct from quantitative, empirical → social science, which uses questionnaires, graphs, and a variety of investigative techniques in proving its hypotheses and testing its theories, biographical research works qualitatively. The three most important achievements of qualitative procedures are (1) appropriate sociological description, (2) hermeneutical understanding, and (3) the construction of hypotheses and theories.

Sociological biographical research examines the impact of an individual life and in so doing focuses on breaks, transitions, and passages of status in order to work out models that will show the active influence of the past on the → future. Major changes or breaks like → conversion (§1) form a point of contact with theology (see 3). Such models that are oriented to the whole course of a person's life can support a broader basis of interpretation. A basic presupposition of such research is that a person's age and sex are equally important as structural indicators of social action.

2. New Research

2.1. Cohort research tries to see what effect historical changes (including → war, as well as inflation, breakdown of a political system, and technological advance) have on the typical development of certain cohorts (e.g., social climbing through education) (Elder).

2.2. The sociology of age-stratification examines the various social conditions that differentiate age-groups and their role. Thus the existence of a longer period of adolescence (→ Youth) and the isolation of the elderly (→ Old Age) are structural features of modern → industrial society (Riley, Johnson, and Foner; Döbert and Nunner-Winkler).

2.3. The sociology of the life course in the narrower sense investigates changes in the course of life and in planning during typical transitions (e.g., education, parenthood, and employment). As in 2.1, it distinguishes biographical tracks (e.g., those of upward mobility, or social-class differences between generations) (Kohli 1978).

2.4. Biographical research works on the basis of life histories or sections of life histories that exist as narrative texts. It investigates the connections between the so-called objective events of life paths (the interfacing of age-group, social class, economic cycles, crises, and historical events) and the subjective direction on the basis of personal experiences (Bude). It also investigates the impact of objective events in various lives (see Niethammer's study of oral history) and the construction of the subjective gestalt from individual experiences. People's taking stock of themselves and developing their personal perspectives both result from and determine what goes on around them (Kohli 1978 and 1980).

2.5. Psychological research into intelligence at different ages shows that (1) age-groups have distinctive levels of intelligence and (2) exceptions to these levels are sociological rather than biological. The old thesis of a rise and fall in competence as life goes on is mere prejudice. Intelligence changes its structure with increasing experience, and its achievements owe more and more to expertise. At every age level it may also be influenced by training (Baltes).

3. Conversions

The radical changes from one life-orientation to another (identity changes) that are often called conversions in autobiography have thus far been only tentatively explored (psychoanalytically by Rangell). In efforts to find common features in → Augustine's *Confessions* (→ Augustine's Theology) and the autobiographies of → Pietism, it has been shown that the sharp contrasting of life before and after conversion serves, on the one hand, to give assurance of one's own role and conflicting social expectations and, on the other, to leave biographical alternatives open.

A typical result of the establishment of a new identity is the change of style from a very personal autobiography to a memoir that describes the harmony between the personality and the new sphere of life (Neumann, Leitner, and Misch). Largely unanswered, however, are questions as to the actual extent of the change of identity and the possibility of its reversal (→ Identity). Attempts have been made to understand conversions that are directed from outside, for example, by entry into closed sectarian circles (→ Sects), or brainwashing as the exchange of one loyalty for another (Strauss). The fact that belief in providence plays a role in many stories of conversion is seen as the biographical outworking of a change of loyalty of this kind. It is an open question to what extent conversions are unique events and to what extent they are merely particularly striking examples of the general problem of overcoming the crises of life and the related conflict of → autonomy and alien control, of shaping and constructing social reality (Berger and Luckmann).

Bibliography: P. B. BALTES, "Intelligenz im Alter," *Spectrum der Wissenschaft*, May 1984, 46-60 • P. L. BERGER and T. LUCKMANN, *The Social Construction of Reality: A Treatise in the Sociology of Knowledge* (Garden City, N.Y., 1966) • H. BUDE, "Rekonstruktion von Lebenskonstruktionen–eine Antwort auf die Frage, was die Biographieforschung bringt," *Biographie und soziale Wirklichkeit* (ed. M. Kohli and G. Robert; Stuttgart, 1984) 5-28 • R. DÖBERT and G. NUNNER-WINKLER, *Adoleszenzkrise und Identitätsbildung* (Frankfurt, 1975) • G. H. ELDER JR., "Age Differentiation and the Life Course," *ARSoc* 1 (1975) 165-90 • M. KOHLI, ed., *Soziologie des Lebenslaufs* (Darmstadt, 1978) • H. LEITNER, *Lebenslauf und Identität* (Frankfurt, 1982) • G. MISCH, *A History of Autobiography in Antiquity* (London, 1950; 4th ed., 1974) • B. NEUMANN, *Identität und Rollenzwang. Zur Theorie der Autobiographie* (Frankfurt, 1970) • L. NIETHAMMER, ed., *Lebenserfahrung und kollektives Gedächtnis: Die Praxis der "oral history"* (Frankfurt, 1980) • S. PAUL, *Begegnungen* (2 vols.; Hohenschäftlarn, 1979) • L. RANGELL, "Die Konversion," *Psyche* 23 (1969) 121-47 • M. W. RILEY, A. JOHNSON, and A. FONER, *Aging and Society,* vol. 3, *Sociology of Age Stratification* (New York, 1972) • A. L. STRAUSS, *Mirrors and Masks: The Search for Identity* (1968; 3d ed., London, 1977).

ERIKA M. HOERNING

Biological Weapons → Weapons

Birth Control

1. Historical Overview of Fertility and Family Planning
2. Biomedical Overview of Birth Control Methods
3. Demographic Overview of Family Planning
4. Social History and Issues
5. Moral Issues and Perspectives
6. Positions of Specific Religious Traditions

1. Historical Overview of Fertility and Family Planning

Prior to the development of modern methods of family planning, key determinants of fertility rates in most societies included age at → marriage and breast-feeding. Historical evidence suggests, however, that in at least some societies, fertility was less than would have been expected from these two factors alone (A. Omran, 275; S. Szreter, 704). Potential mechanisms for explaining this phenomenon are not fully clear but seem to have included both coitus interruptus (withdrawal) and abstinence for periods of time. → Abortion and infanticide have also been practiced for centuries, but their impact on fertility rates is unclear.

Attempts to control fertility by other means go back to antiquity. For instance, the ancient Egyptians used vaginal pessaries made of honey, herbs, and other substances, including crocodile dung (W. Robertson, 152). Various herbal preparations for both topical use and systemic ingestion were used in ancient times and were continued through the Middle Ages. These were probably somewhat spermicidal. Similarly, condoms made from animal parts (such as goat bladders) were used by the Romans. Condoms became more widespread in the mid-1800s, when they began being made of rubber. The diaphragm appeared at about the same time. The intrauterine device (IUD) started being widely used in the 1930s, as did surgical sterilization in the 1950s. Oral contraceptives became available in the early 1960s, and long-acting hormonal contraceptives, by injection or by implant, followed.

Meanwhile, the timing of ovulation in the menstrual cycle was first described in 1930, which led to the development of calendar rhythm. Basal body temperature to determine the time of fertility and infertility became used in the 1940s. The single most reliable biological sign of fertility — the vaginal discharge of cervical mucus — began to be used together with basal body temperature in the 1950s (the "sympto-thermal method") and independently in the 1960s (the "ovulation method").

2. Biomedical Overview of Birth Control Methods

A biomedical summary of birth control methods appears in the accompanying table. Pregnancy rates during "perfect" use imply no error on the part of the user and reflect the biological capacity of a

Birth Control Methods

	Pregnancy rate during perfect use[a]	Pregnancy rate during typical use[a]	Continuation rate at one year[a]	Mechanism(s) of action[b]	Responsible for use
No method	NA	85-89	NA	NA	NA
Coitus interruptus	4	14-19	?	II	man
Barrier methods					
Condom (male)	3	7-16	63	II	man
Condom (female)	5	21	?	II	woman
Diaphragm	6	10-22	58	II	woman
Spermicide	6	13-30	43	II	woman
Hormonal methods					
Combined oral contraceptives	0.1	3-25	72	I, II, III	woman
Progestin-only pills	0.5	4-30	60-70	I, II, III	woman
Depo-Provera	0.3	0.4	70	I, II, III	woman
Norplant	0.9	0.9	85	I, II, III	woman
Intrauterine device (IUD)	0.6-0.8	3-5	80	II, III	woman
Surgical sterilization					
Tubal ligation (female)	0.4	0.4	100	II	woman
Vasectomy (male)	0.1	0.1	100	II	man
Natural family planning[c]					
Calendar rhythm (outdated)	9	10-30	?	IV	both
Sympto-thermal method	1	3-20	70	IV	both
Ovulation method	1	2-20	65-79	IV	both

Source: Adapted from Hatcher et al.
Note: NA = not applicable.
[a]Rates per 100 women for one year.
[b]I = prevents ovulation; II = physically prevents sperm from reaching egg (may include effects on cervical mucus blocking sperm transport); III = may prevent implantation of a zygote (after fertilization); IV = avoids presence of sperm when egg is present.
[c]These methods can also be used to achieve pregnancy. The use of the ovulation method to achieve pregnancy seems to be about 67 percent per menstrual cycle.

method to avoid pregnancy. Pregnancy rates during "typical" use include pregnancies that may be due to user error or inconsistent use. Continuation rates after one year reflect both procreative intentions (e.g., deciding to achieve pregnancy) and acceptability of the method in terms of its side effects, expense, and so forth. Pregnancy rates during typical use and continuation rates vary widely, depending on who is using the method and on the respective motivations of the partners; figures can vary considerably from those in the table.

Research is ongoing to develop new methods of contraception, including new spermicides, easily reversible sterilization procedures, and vaccinations conferring "immunity" to pregnancy. In natural family planning, urine test kits are being developed that are sensitive to the hormones of the menstrual cycle, which may prove to be reliable in determining the exact time of fertility.

3. Demographic Overview of Family Planning

Among women in the United States who were potentially able to get pregnant in 1988, the most commonly used method to avoid pregnancy was the oral contraceptive (28 percent), followed by female sterilization (25 percent) and the (male) condom (13 percent). That the statistics are collected by women, not men, reflects a cultural attitude that family planning is primarily the woman's responsibility.

Breast-feeding remains an important contributor to reduced rates of fertility in societies where the prevalence of the use of family planning is 70 percent or less. If breast-feeding is continued for 1.5 years or more, births are generally spaced over two years apart (M. Kent). In many developing countries ($\rightarrow$ Third World), however, breast-feeding rates, as well as the duration and frequency of feeding, are decreasing in response to Westernization influences. Often the decline in breast-feeding precedes the adoption of contraception, causing a temporary increase in the fertility rate until contraceptives are introduced to offset the effects of decreased breast-feeding (D. Smith 1985).

Decreases in population growth and average number of children per woman in many countries of the world seem to be directly related to the adoption of modern methods of family planning, which in turn is usually highly correlated with increased education of the population, particularly of women (R. Bulatao et al., 830). At least one country (Mauritius in Africa) has reduced its fertility rate to near replacement level, with a relatively large percentage of the population (20 percent) using natural family planning.

4. Social History and Issues

In general, laws and social policy in developed countries have evolved from forbidding or discouraging contraception to toleration and then active promotion of it (J. Reed, 447). For example, in 1873 the U.S. Congress passed the Comstock Law, which prohibited the use of the mails for transporting "articles for immoral use." This and similar laws were often enforced through the 1930s to prosecute those who distributed contraceptives or contraceptive information (C. Wood and B. Suitters, 238). In contrast, today there is government funding for family planning services, both in the United States and throughout the world.

In the early 1900s a number of activists began working to make means of birth control available and widely accepted among the general public. Among the best known of these are Marie Stopes (1880-1958) in England and Margaret Sanger (1879-1966) in the United States. To some, Sanger was a visionary and courageous woman who helped liberate women worldwide through giving them the means to control their fertility (E. Chesler, 639). Others have criticized her for having multiple sexual partners outside of marriage, abandoning her children, and making statements implying that marriage is bondage (R. Marshall and C. Donovan, 371). Along with many others, she vigorously promoted a eugenic philosophy (the idea that only the most fit in society should reproduce). Sanger's organizational legacy is Planned Parenthood, which continues to be a major force for the spread of contraception (and abortion) throughout the world.

Within Christianity, there was virtually universal, fundamental rejection of birth control until the 1930 Lambeth Conference of the Church of England (→ Anglican Communion), which adopted a resolution stating that where there was a "moral obligation to limit or avoid parenthood . . . the primary and obvious method is complete abstinence from intercourse (as far as may be necessary)" but that "where there is a morally sound reason for avoiding complete abstinence . . . other methods may be used." Soon afterward, Pope Pius XI issued *Casti connubii,* an → encyclical that reiterated the Catholic opposition to artificial contraception but allowed for periodic abstinence within marriage. Virtually all

other Christian churches followed the path initiated by the Anglican Church. Thus, the use of contraception within marriage has been reviewed and approved by the Congregational Christian Churches (1931), Protestant Episcopal Church (1946), Evangelical and Reformed Church (1947), Lutheran Church (1954), Methodist Church (1956), and United Presbyterian Church (U.S.A.) and → World Council of Churches (1959) (J. Rohr). In 1968, amid widespread speculation that the Catholic Church would change its views on the basis of the new method of the oral contraceptive pill, Pope Paul VI issued the encyclical *Humanae vitae,* which reiterated the Catholic stand against artificial contraception but allowed for the use of natural family planning within marriage for sufficiently serious reasons. This encyclical was widely criticized and rejected by many Catholics, including clergy (J. Smith, 425).

A critical distinction remains between the acceptance of contraception by most Christian groups and the championing of contraception by secular institutions: the church, by and large, still holds that contraception should be used only within marriage, whereas many secular institutions that have promoted birth control (such as Planned Parenthood) promote the concept of "responsible → sexuality" as being only optionally linked to marriage. Additionally, many if not most Christian bodies continue to reject abortion, while most secular institutions consider it an integral part of the family planning alternatives (R. Hatcher et al., 730).

While the motivating factor for couples in the use of family planning is usually their own family circumstances, most of the current driving force behind governmental and institutional efforts to promote family planning comes from concerns of overpopulation, as articulated by Thomas Malthus (1766-1834) in the early 1800s. The idea that the world population is rapidly outgrowing its resources is accepted as fact by most scholars today, although not universally so. Some have questioned the scientific basis of the overpopulation arguments, contending that the crusade to reduce population growth diverts attention from more important issues of economic equity and social justice (J. Kasun, 225; B. Hartmann).

Fueled by the concern of overpopulation, major efforts to promote contraception on an international level have come from corporate philanthropists. John D. Rockefeller III (1906-78), for example, established the Population Council in 1952. This and similar organizations have subsequently done much to promote the use of contraception in developing countries, often with questionable approaches (B. Mass, 287). One example is the case of Puerto

Rico, where women were subjected to mass experimentation with early, test versions of the birth control pill without adequate informed consent, and reports of adverse side effects (which were numerous and sometimes severe, at least with the early formulations) were suppressed (A. B. Ramírez de Arellano and C. Seipp, 219).

Despite the widespread availability of contraception (and abortion) in the United States today, almost 60 percent of pregnancies are felt to be unintended (S. S. Brown and L. Eisenberg). The percentage for teenage pregnancies is even higher. One interpretation of this situation is that contraception is not used widely enough and needs to be promoted more vigorously (ibid.). An alternative interpretation is that the widespread use of contraception, especially outside of marriage, may actually contribute to "contraceptive failure" and unintended pregnancies. Evidence for this point of view comes from studies showing that federally funded family planning clinics are associated with both higher pregnancy rates and lower birth rates (S. E. Weed and J. A. Olsen; Olsen and Weed; J. D. Forrest, A. I. Hermalin, and S. K. Henshaw). There are similar concerns about whether encouraging "responsible sexuality" (contracepted intercourse and sexual activity other than intercourse) outside of marriage contributes to the spread of sexually transmitted diseases (G. C. Griffin).

5. Moral Issues and Perspectives

Feminist perspectives on the issue of contraception are diverse. Two main and somewhat contradictory ideas exist: first, that birth control is a great boon to help women control their own body and be free of the biological tyranny of unwanted pregnancy (L. Gordon, 570); second, that many of the modern methods of contraception put women at unnecessary risk for the sake of population control (B. Seaman, 258; Hartmann). With many of the methods, the onus for preventing a pregnancy and for the associated health effects falls entirely on the woman.

A key moral issue relative to some of the birth control methods is the issue of preventing births versus preventing conception. For those who are morally opposed to abortion, this issue raises the crucial question of when life begins. Although there is no definitive medical evidence one way or the other, there is evidence to suggest that some methods may (sometimes, at least) exert their effects after conception (H. D. Croxatto et al.; S. Killick, E. Eyong, and M. Elstein). There is no question that the currently touted "morning-after pill" regimens often act after conception (D. A. Grimes and R. J. Cook). Thus, there is the potential for a gray area between abortion and

some methods of contraception. Often, contraception is touted as the way to reduce abortion demand. However, it is also possible that the widespread use of contraception, particularly outside of marriage, could increase sexual activity, increase "contraceptive failures," and increase demand for abortion. In the United States, over half of those who obtain abortions were using contraception at the time they became pregnant (S. K. Henshaw and K. Kost).

Many advocates for "reproductive health" have argued that abortion must be an integral part of any family planning program. There was a concerted effort to codify a statement to this effect at the International Conference on Population and Development sponsored by the World Health Organization in Cairo in 1994, but it was blocked by an alliance of the Vatican, predominantly Roman Catholic nations, and predominantly Muslim nations. Another key element of the Cairo report was that all family planning should be offered and received completely voluntarily. However, this ideal is not necessarily implemented in all cases, as attested by the coercive population policy currently in place in China.

Another key moral question regarding birth control regards the very nature of sexuality and its link with procreation. Is the link between sexual union and procreation God-given and sacred, or is it a feature of nature that can and should be subdued by the will of human beings? The answer to this question makes a distinction among some of the methods of family planning. On the one hand, the ideal (and nonexistent) method of artificial contraception, as pursued by medical research, would make the link between sexual intercourse and procreation completely and utterly voluntary, without any side effects. On the other hand, the methods of natural family planning do not seek to alter in any way the natural consequences of sexual activity; they merely take advantage of the naturally occurring (e.g., God-ordained) cycles of fertility and infertility, either to achieve or to avoid pregnancy.

6. Positions of Specific Religious Traditions

As noted earlier, the → Roman Catholic Church has consistently opposed artificial contraception, but it considers the use of natural family planning within marriage to be justifiable for "just reasons . . . not motivated by selfishness" (*Catechism,* §2368). In the United States, however, Catholics are nearly indistinguishable from the rest of the population in terms of their use of contraception, and have been so for a number of years (C. Goldscheider and W. D. Mosher, 1988, 1991).

The Orthodox tradition (→ Orthodox Church),

while holding that sexual expression is to be reserved for marriage, has mixed opinions on the issue of the use of contraception within marriage. Some Orthodox theologians hold all contraception to be wrong, as abortion, but some hold that it is the totality of the marriage relationship that needs to be open to life, and not necessarily every act of intercourse (S. Harakas, 190).

As noted above, virtually all → Protestant denominations have authoritatively decided that birth control, practiced within marriage, is allowable and even, with proper motives, to be commended (J. Melton and N. Piediscalzi, 203; M. Marty, 173). There is a need to balance a responsibility for seeking to conceive with a receptivity to the grace of God in a "surprise" pregnancy (K. Vaux, 149). Couples also must consider very carefully the finality of the choice of sterilization (D. Smith 1986, 103). Choices about contraception need to be considered in the light of being generous, rather than selfish, with family size, and seeking to have the healthiest possible family (E. Holifield, 198). Some have gone as far as to suggest that since sexual union often occurs outside the boundaries of marriage, the use of contraception in those instances can reduce the chance of suffering among unwanted children (ibid.).

Jewish thought (→ Judaism) on contraception has centered on the need for a proper act of sexual intercourse to fulfill the purpose of the husband and wife being joined together as one flesh (Gen. 2:24) and on the need for ejaculation to occur only in the vagina. Hence coitus interruptus is unacceptable. Some Jewish scholars have interpreted this conclusion to mean that a condom would be unacceptable because it would impede full genital contact and deposition of semen, whereas a diaphragm (and, by extension, any other method that did not impede the deposition of semen in the vagina) would be permissible (D. Feldman, 322).

In → Islam, there is a long tradition of allowing and perhaps even encouraging contraception within marriage. Numerous Islamic texts from the Middle Ages describe methods for barrier and even abortifacient approaches to contraception. It was held that God, if he chose, was able to overrule any human effort to contracept, so human efforts were permissible. On the subject of abortion, there has been a divergence of opinion. While all have agreed that the fetus becomes a human being after the fourth month of pregnancy, some have felt that abortion before that time is permissible, and others have not (Omran, 275; B. Musallam, 176).

→ Genetic Counseling; Medical Ethics; Reproductive Research; Sex Education; Sexual Ethics

Bibliography: S. S. Brown and L. Eisenberg, *The Best Intentions: Unintended Pregnancy and the Well-Being of Children and Families* (Washington, D.C., 1995) • R. Bulatao, R. Lee, P. Hollerbach, and J. Bongaarts, "Determinants of Fertility in Developing Countries: Fertility Regulation and Institutional Influences," *Studies in Population* (vol. 2; New York, 1983) • *Catechism of the Catholic Church* (New York, 1994) • E. Chesler, *Woman of Valor: Margaret Sanger and the Birth Control Movement in America* (New York, 1992) • H. D. Croxatto, S. Diaz, M. Pavez, and H. B. Croxatto, "Histopathology of the Endometrium during Continuous Use of Levonorgestrel," *Long-Acting Contraceptive Delivery Systems* (ed. G. I. Zatuchni, A. Goldsmith, J. D. Shelton, and J. J. Sciarra; Philadelphia, 1984) 290-95 • D. Feldman, *Marital Relations, Birth Control, and Abortion in Jewish Law* (New York, 1978) • J. D. Forrest, A. I. Hermalin, and S. K. Henshaw, "The Impact of Family Planning Clinic Programs on Adolescent Pregnancy," *Family Planning Perspectives* 13 (1981) 109-16 • C. Goldscheider and W. D. Mosher, "Patterns of Contraceptive Use in the United States: The Importance of Religious Factors," *Studies in Family Planning* 22/2 (1991) 102-15; idem, "Religious Affiliation and Contraceptive Usage: Changing American Patterns, 1955-82," ibid. 19/1 (1988) 48-57 • L. Gordon, *Woman's Body, Woman's Right* (New York, 1990) • G. C. Griffin, "Condoms and Contraceptives in Junior High and High School Clinics — What Do You Think?" *Postgraduate Medicine* 93 (1993) 21-38 • D. A. Grimes and R. J. Cook, "Mifepristone (RU 486) — An Abortifacient to Prevent Abortion?" *New England Journal of Medicine* 327/15 (1992) 1088-89 • S. Harakas, "Health and Medicine in the Eastern Orthodox Tradition," *Health/Medicine and the Faith Traditions* (ed. J. Wind; New York, 1990) • B. Hartmann, *Reproductive Rights and Wrongs: The Global Politics of Population Control* (Boston, 1995) • R. Hatcher, J. Trussell, F. Stewart, et al., *Contraceptive Technology* (New York, 1994) • S. K. Henshaw and K. Kost, "Abortion Patients in 1994-1995: Characteristics and Contraceptive Use," *Family Planning Perspectives* 28 (1996) 140-47 • E. Holifield, "Health and Medicine in the Methodist Tradition," *Health/Medicine and the Faith Traditions* (ed. M. Marty and K. Vaux; New York, 1986) • J. Kasun, *The War against Population: The Economics and Ideology of Population Control* (San Francisco, 1988) • M. Kent, "Breastfeeding and Birth Rates," *Populi* 9 (1982) 44-55 • S. Killick, E. Eyong, and M. Elstein, "Ovarian Follicular Development in Oral Contraceptive Cycles," *Fertility and Sterility* 48 (1987) 409-13 • *Lambeth Conference 1930* (London, 1930) • R. Marshall and C. Donovan, *Blessed Are the Barren: The Social Policy of Planned Parenthood* (San Francisco, 1991) • M. Marty, "Health and Medicine in the

Lutheran Tradition," *Health/Medicine and the Faith Traditions* (ed. M. Marty and K. Vaux; New York, 1983) • B. Mass, *Population Target: The Political Economy of Population Control in Latin America* (Brampton, Ont., 1976) • J. Melton and N. Piediscalzi, *The Churches Speak on Sex and Family Life* (Detroit, 1991) • B. Musallam, *Sex and Society in Islam* (Cambridge, 1983) • J. A. Olsen and S. E. Weed, "Effects of Family-Planning Programs for Teenagers on Adolescent Birth and Pregnancy Rates," *Family Perspective* 20 (1987) 153-70 • A. Omran, *Family Planning in the Legacy of Islam* (New York, 1992) • M. Polican et al., "Fertility Control," *EncBio* 2.818-47 • A. B. Ramírez de Arellano and C. Seipp, *Colonialism, Catholicism, and Contraception: A History of Birth Control in Puerto Rico* (Chapel Hill, N.C., 1983) • J. Reed, *The Birth Control Movement and American Society: From Private Vice to Public Virtue* (Princeton, 1983) • W. Robertson, *An Illustrated History of Contraception* (Park Ridge, N.J., 1990) • J. von Rohr, "Christianity and Birth Control," pt. 2, "Protestant Views," *CCen,* October 19, 1960, 1209-12 • B. Seaman, *The Doctor's Case against the Pill* (Alameda, CA, 1995) • D. Smith, "Breastfeeding, Contraception, and Birth Intervals in Developing Countries," *Studies in Family Planning* 16 (1985) 154-63; idem, "Health and Medicine in the Anglican Tradition," *Health/Medicine and the Faith Traditions* (ed. M. Marty and K. Vaux; New York, 1986) • J. Smith, *Humanae Vitae a Generation Later* (Washington, D.C., 1991) • S. Szreter, *Fertility, Class, and Gender in Britain, 1860-1940* (Cambridge, 1996) • K. Vaux, "Health and Medicine in the Reformed Tradition," *Health/Medicine and the Faith Traditions* (ed. M. Marty and K. Vaux; New York, 1984) • S. E. Weed and J. A. Olsen, "Effects of Family-Planning Programs for Teenage Pregnancy — Replication and Extension," *Family Perspective* 20 (1987) 173-95 • C. Wood and B. Suitters, *The Fight for Acceptance: A History of Contraception* (Aylesbury, Eng., 1970). See also the bibliography in "Reproductive Research."

Joseph B. Stanford, M.D., and
Walter L. Larimore, M.D.

Bishop, Episcopate

1. Rise
2. Forms
3. Disruption and Continuity
4. Spiritual Leadership
5. Ecumenical Developments

1. Rise

In distinction from → Jewish Christianity, whose leaders were the 12 apostles and local elders (Acts 11:30; 15:2, 4, 22-23, etc.), the Pauline churches gradually developed a constant leadership consisting of bishops and deacons (Phil. 1:1). In secular Greek the term for bishop *(episkopos)* denoted the work of supervision or administration. Bishops, then, exercised administrative oversight over congregational life. A later stage finds reflection in Acts 20:17, 28; 1 Pet. 5:1-5; 1 Tim. 3:1-7; Titus 1:5-9, which shows that the Jewish-Christian eldership had merged with the Gentile Christian episcopal order. Thus in the Pastoral Epistles the bishop (always sing.) belongs to the college of → elders but has the primary function of preserving and propagating apostolic teaching (Titus 1:9).

First Clement followed up on this understanding, tracing the episcopate directly to regular appointment by the → apostles and thus introducing for the first time the thought of apostolic succession (44.2-3). The precedence of the bishop took institutional form in the church's hierarchy in the form of the monarchical episcopate, to which Ignatius bears witness in the territories of Syria and Asia Minor in approximately A.D. 107. For Ignatius the bishop represented God and thus took first place in the → congregation (*Magn.* 6.1), with no restrictions on his work.

In the period that followed, opposition to heresy made the theory of apostolic succession a normative one for the episcopate (→ Irenaeus; Tertullian). Consecrated and acknowledged by neighboring bishops, the bishop formed part of an unbroken line that could be traced back to the apostles. This connection made him a true successor of the apostles in his office. It also made him an expression and guarantor of the apostolicity, unity, and truth of the → church. Thus the episcopate became constitutive for the church's existence. The development of the monarchical episcopate became universal in the third century. The bishop united in his own person the church's supreme didactic, sacerdotal, and judicial offices.

2. Forms

The legal recognition of the bishop's primacy under Constantine (306-37) strengthened the external position of the bishop, and the establishment of a territorial structure (→ Diocese) enhanced his influence locally. At the same time, the church, borrowing from political divisions, set up provinces with metropolitans at their head (called archbishops from the 6th cent.). Special honor was paid to sees that could claim apostolic foundation, which were called patriarchates. The Roman episcopate then claimed jurisdictional primacy over all other bishoprics (esp.

under Popes Damasus I [366-84] and → Leo I [440-61]). As a result, the Western sees all became subject to the papacy (→ Pope, Papacy), but the East rejected the idea (→ Jurisdiction, Ecclesiastical).

Supported by the Byzantine Empire, the patriarchate of Constantinople (after 518 called the Ecumenical Patriarchate) tried to achieve jurisdictional supremacy, but it was accorded only a precedence of honor. The ecumenical council of all bishops was presumed to have final → authority. The principle of episcopal equality has ever since been a determinative one for the Orthodox view of the episcopate. In → autocephalous churches bishops rule in their own sees and form in concert the Holy Synod of the hierarchy, which makes all basic decisions for the church.

In the Latin church right up to modern times the further development of the episcopate was shaped by resistance to the intrusion of secular influence in the Middle Ages and by an ongoing struggle to establish a position over against the papacy. In spite of the dogmatic definition of the pope as the universal bishop in 1870, this question was not settled until → Vatican II set up a collegial structure of supreme authority. On this view, the supreme direction of the church as a whole lies with the college of bishops in fellowship and agreement with the pope as their head (see 1983 CIC 336). The principle of collegiality takes effect in bishops' conferences, which bring the bishops of a country or territory together in common discharge of their pastoral tasks (can. 447).

The individual bishop is by divine right a successor of the apostles; in virtue of his office he represents the unity of the church in his diocese. He possesses in it the real power of consecration and jurisdiction except insofar as this is reserved for the supreme ecclesiastical authority. He does so in three ways. As pastor, he directs the church's life; as teacher, he proclaims the truths of the faith and guards their integrity; and as → priest, he dispenses the mysteries of God as a means for promoting the → sanctification of the faithful (cans. 375-402). In his ministry he may have coadjutor bishops or assistant bishops (i.e., titular bishops with no jurisdiction of their own). The appointment or confirmation of a bishop is a matter for the pope, as is the arranging of his → consecration.

3. Disruption and Continuity

The view of the episcopate at the → Reformation was not uniform. In accordance with the doctrine of the ministry held by J. → Calvin (1509-64), the episcopate disappeared in most of the Reformed churches, although it was still valued in the Lutheran sphere.

Like all the Reformers, however, the Lutherans rejected the idea of the divine right and special character of bishops. The bishop's office should be primarily one of preaching, → visitation, and → ordination (Augs. Conf. 28). Yet in Germany, except in a few cases, the introduction of this kind of episcopate failed because the existing bishops would not give up their secular powers as princes. The consolidation of the Reformation was in the hands of evangelically minded "estates of the empire," who claimed the right to instigate reforms as early as 1526, and who as "emergency bishops" regulated church affairs by visitations, the appointment of → superintendents, and the setting up of consistories. In 1555 spiritual jurisdiction and all episcopal rights finally passed into the hands of the provincial rulers, who thus became the real bishops in their own territories.

Different political conditions in northern Europe, however, meant that an evangelical episcopate continued in Sweden and Finland without any breach of apostolic succession. In the → Anglican Church, too, the episcopate maintained a historical succession (the so-called historical episcopate), and from the end of the 19th century the Lambeth Conference, a gathering of all Anglican bishops, became an effective sign of the continuity of the church in the apostolic faith. The Brethren communities (→ Moravian Church) struck out in new directions in the 18th century with their view of the episcopate as a priestly office but not one of leadership. American Methodism entrusted the bishop, chosen by the synod, with the direction of the church's work in each jurisdiction. In Prussia in the 18th and 19th centuries attempts were made to reintroduce the episcopate with the naming of titular bishops, but these efforts met with no success.

4. Spiritual Leadership

After the abolition of the secular episcopate in Germany in 1918, the Protestant churches had the chance to develop a new episcopate according to their own theological insights. They did not succeed at first in uniting the orientation to preaching that M. → Luther (1483-1546) had recommended with the newer synodal understanding and the consistorial character of church leadership. The office of the general superintendent could not inherit the secular episcopate directly because it was still too much in its shadow. The new church constitutions followed the model of the democratic state constitution (→ Church Government). The power of leadership fell to the → synods, but these viewed themselves as common jurisdictions whose structures did not embrace the preaching office. The episcopate favored by the → German Christians copied the leadership principle of National Socialism (→ Fascism). The church thus relapsed into dependence on the ideologized state (→ Church Struggle).

In opposition to the German Christians, the → Barmen Declaration (1934) related the order of the church to its message. It formulated the basic principle of a spiritual leadership. The church's offices are subordinate to the ministry that is entrusted and commended to the whole church. From 1945 on, this principle made possible the development of a synodal episcopate in the church orders of the Lutheran or Union churches. Synods were to be spiritual and not just jurisdictional assemblies. Their members represented the pastors and congregational leaders. As the "witnessing organ of the hearing church" (the province of Saxony, 1947), the synod would take into account the priesthood of all believers (Luther). The significance of the preaching office for the being of the synodal church as the church was recognized, and this office was integrated into the synodal episcopate in a presbyterial-synodal constitution.

Within the framework of the synod, and accepting the classic tasks involved in being the "pastor of pastors" (i.e., ordination and visitation), the episcopate now also discharged the tasks of a "pastor of the church" (i.e., having the right to preach in any pulpit and to handle pastoral letters, public relations, and ecumenical contacts). Some constitutions gave concreteness to this spiritual leadership by giving precedence to the bishop in the church's direction and constitution and by making the bishop a member of the synod. In larger churches the episcopate thus found support in corresponding officers at the regional level. In all their variety, however, the new synodal constitutions shared a common concern to fashion a spiritual direction that would allow for dialogue between officeholders and congregations at the larger level.

Bibliography: H. VON CAMPENHAUSEN, Ecclesiastical Authority and Spiritual Power in the Church of the First Three Centuries (Stanford, Calif., 1969; repr., Peabody, Mass., 1997) • Catechism of the Catholic Church (New York, 1995) • E. R. FAIRWEATHER and R. F. HETTLINGEN, Episcopacy and Reunion (London, 1953) • H. E. FEINE, Kirchliche Rechtsgeschichte. Die katholische Kirche (Weimar, 1950; 5th ed., Cologne, 1972) • G. GASSMANN, Das historische Bischofsamt und die Einheit der Kirche in der neueren anglikanischen Theologie (Göttingen, 1964) bibliography • C. JENKINS and K. D. MACKENZIE, eds., Episcopacy, Ancient and Modern (London, 1930) • K. LEHMANN and W. PANNENBERG, eds., Lehrverurteilungen–kirchentrennend? vol. 1, Rechtfertigung, Sakramente und Amt im Zeitalter der Reformation und heute (Freiburg, 1988) • W. MAURER, Die Kirche und ihr Recht (Tübingen 1976) • G. F. MOEDE, The Office of Bishop in Methodism (Zurich, 1964) • J. NEUMANN et al., "Bischof," TRE 6.653-97 (bibliography) • K. RAHNER and J. RATZINGER, The Episcopate and the Primacy (New York, 1962) • H. SCHAUF, Das Leitungsamt der Bischöfe (Munich, 1975) • D. STONE, Episcopacy and Valid Orders in the Primitive Church (London, 1926) • W. TELFER, The Office of a Bishop (London, 1962) • A. WEISER et al., "Bischof," LTK (3d ed.) 2.481-92.

MARTIN HEIN and HANS-GERNOT JUNG†

5. Ecumenical Developments

The question of episcopacy has been a central and difficult one in the ecumenical quest for a convergent understanding of ministry on the way to that "mutual recognition of ministries" that is regularly identified as a sine qua non for realizing the visible unity of the church. Among the most divisive elements of the question are those centering on the role of the episcopacy in ensuring the transmission of the apostolic faith and the conviction in some churches that only ordination by a bishop in apostolic succession can confer the power to consecrate a valid → Eucharist.

The Lambeth Quadrilateral (1888) included as one of the four elements that Anglicans consider essential for bringing about the reunion of divided churches the "historic episcopate, locally adapted in the method of its administration to the varying needs of the nations and peoples called of God into the unity of his church" (see 3). This approach functioned well in the uniting of episcopal and nonepiscopal churches on the Indian subcontinent, of which the ecumenically most notable case was the formation of the → Church of South India in 1947. The plan for this union did not call into question the authenticity of the previously exercised ministry of those nonepiscopal churches that constituted it, nor did it require reordination.

Multilateral discussions in the Faith and Order Commission of the → World Council of Churches (WCC) have regularly addressed the question of episcopacy, especially in the process leading to the 1982 Lima text Baptism, Eucharist, and Ministry (BEM). A statement entitled "The Holy Eucharist" from the Bristol conference of 1967 suggested that episcopally ordered churches should give more attention to the values found in the "charismatic" and "extraordinary" ministries of nonepiscopal churches, that the latter in turn should reconsider ecumenically "the value of the commonly accepted ministry of the early church and of pre-Reformation times," and that both should reexamine whether "pre-Reformation" and "Reformation" ministries do not in fact preserve "a measure of hidden identity," despite their very different appearances. A statement entitled "The Ordained Ministry" from Louvain 1971 appealed to the Second → Vatican Council in identifying new lines of historical and theological research calling into question some of the traditional approaches to determining the validity of ministry.

The *BEM* text itself urged recovery of the "threefold ministry" of bishops, presbyters (→ Elder), and → deacons, suggesting that this "may serve today as an expression of the unity we seek and also as a means for achieving it" ("Ministry," par. 22). It sets forth the role of bishops as "representative pastoral ministers of oversight, continuity and unity" (par. 29) and underscores their leadership in → mission, in relations with the wider church, and in the orderly transfer of ministerial → authority. At the same time, it speaks of an increasing recognition in episcopal churches that "a continuity in apostolic faith, worship and mission has been preserved in churches which have not retained the form of historic episcopate" (par. 37) and calls on nonepiscopal churches to recognize episcopal succession "as a sign, though not a guarantee, of the continuity and unity of the church" (par. 38). Several reports at the fifth world conference on Faith and Order (Santiago de Compostela, 1993) emphasized the need to reopen joint ecumenical historical and theological research on the question of episcopacy, also in connection with its links to the question of primacy.

The issue of episcopacy has also been dealt with in several international bilateral dialogues — in particular, those involving Roman Catholics and Anglicans (beginning most notably with the first Anglican–Roman Catholic International Commission, 1970-81), Roman Catholics and Lutherans (from 1967), and Roman Catholics and Reformed (from 1968). Inevitably the debate has centered on the understanding of apostolic succession and the relationship of the episcopal ministry to the primacy of the Roman See. There has been a fruitful interaction between multilateral discussions in the framework of the WCC and the bilateral dialogues.

Drawing on the *BEM* document, the 1984 → consensus text *In Quest of a Church of Christ Uniting*, drafted by the U.S. Consultation on Church → Union (COCU), proposes a continued threefold ordering of ministry and suggests that bishops in such a united church would stand in continuity with the historic ministry of bishops and invite recognition from all parts of the universal church. No particular theory about episcopacy or episcopal succession would be required of the constituting churches, but the effort would be made to appropriate creatively existing → traditions.

→ Anglican Communion 4; Clergy and Laity; Consensus 4; Councils of the Church

Bibliography: T. F. BEST and G. GASSMANN, eds., *On the Way to Fuller Koinonia: Official Report of the Fifth World Conference on Faith and Order, Santiago de Compostela, August 1993* (Geneva, 1994) • CONSULTATION ON CHURCH UNION, *Covenanting toward Unity: From Consensus to Communion* (Princeton, 1984); idem, *In Quest of a Church Uniting* (Princeton, 1984) • L. VISCHER and H. MEYER, eds., *Growth in Agreement: Reports and Agreed Statements of Ecumenical Conversations on a World Level* (Mahwah, N.J., 1984) • G. WAINWRIGHT, "Reconciliation in Ministry," *Ecumenical Perspectives on the BEM* (ed. M. Thurian; Geneva, 1983) 129-39 • WORLD COUNCIL OF CHURCHES, *Baptism, Eucharist, and Ministry* (Geneva, 1982).

MARLIN VANELDEREN

Black Churches

1. In the United States
   1.1. Introduction
   1.2. Beginnings in the Colonial Era
   1.3. 1800-1860: The Rise of the Independent African American Church
   1.4. 1860-77: The Civil War and Reconstruction
   1.5. 1877-1915: The Church at Its Nadir
   1.6. 1915-65: Urbanization and the Struggle for Civil Rights
   1.7. 1965-Present
2. The African Diaspora
   2.1. Variety of African Expressions
      2.1.1. Background
      2.1.2. Multiformity and Contextuality
      2.1.3. African Diaspora in Britain
   2.2. Historical and Theological Insights
      2.2.1. Contribution to the Church Universal
      2.2.2. Organization
      2.2.3. Different Concept of the Holy Spirit
      2.2.4. Freedom from Fundamentalism
      2.2.5. Same Biblical Language but Different Realities
      2.2.6. Danger of Further Exploitation
   2.3. Ecumenical Significance

1. In the United States

1.1. *Introduction*

Black churches in the United States represent a group of diverse congregations and historic denominations that have been fostered by, and are representative of, American Christians of African descent. African American denominations, like the majority of churches in the United States, are overwhelmingly Protestant, falling into three broad categories of → Baptist, → Methodist, and → Pentecostal. Although African Americans have enduring historic relations within Roman Catholicism and the more confessional (Reformed, Lutheran, and Anglican) strands of Protestantism, only a small percentage of the communicants in these traditions are African Americans. Despite the small representation of African Americans in these Christian traditions, it is important to note that African Americans, as one of the oldest immigrant groups in the United States, have belonged to every Christian denomination in the country.

The common understanding of the African American Church, which arose during the early years of the → black theology movement, focuses primarily on the three historic denominations. This article, however, uses an expanded definition of the African American Church that includes a variety of Protestants as well as Roman Catholics. This article views the African American Church as an institutional mirror of the collective struggles of African Americans for civic, political, and cultural freedoms. Central to all African Americans churches has been the desire to serve, protect, and instruct their communicants to the end that they become free of oppressive social control, whether in worship or in the society as a whole. The broad coalition of divergent denominations and traditions whose central aim has been to promote the freedoms of African Americans composes what we define as the African American Church.

1.2. *Beginnings in the Colonial Era*

Christianity was not readily accepted by the first enslaved African immigrants to the British colonies. They either rejected Christianity or were justifiably suspicious of it because of its relationship to their enslavement (→ Slavery 2). The various ethnic groups that survived the Middle Passage across the Atlantic from West and Central Africa to North America continued their practices of African traditional religion under the adverse conditions of slavery or experienced the destruction of their native spiritual moorings. Simply stated, the teachings of the Christian church were not welcomed into various slave communities because the "old Gods of Africa,"

though wounded, still lived in the worldview of the slaves.

Concurrent with the slaves' attitudes toward Christianity was the understanding of many slaveholders that it could be detrimental to their interests. They contended that the sacraments of baptism and Communion might confer a recognition of humanity on slaves that would interfere with the practice of slavery itself. This belief diminished as evangelical Protestantism spread throughout the slaveholding elite and as Southern plantation economy became economically dominant. Under these conditions Christianity began to be seen as a stabilizing influence on slaves. Instruction in the Christian faith, it was believed, would make the enslaved more dutiful. Slaveholders, at the encouragement of clergy, began making their slaves attend worship and receive instruction in the tenets of their respective churches. This shift in attitude by slaveholders, accompanied by the 18th-century revivalism known as the Great Awakening (→ Revivals 2.1), and the birth of the first full generation of native-born African Americans, helped to foster a more receptive view of Christianity by both slaveholder and slave.

One explanation for the new attitude toward Christianity by slaves can be found in the theology of evangelical Protestantism that spread from New England to Georgia in the 18th century. Evangelical Protestantism as expressed by the Baptists and Methodists somewhat improved the status of American slaves. The theological emphasis on equality and a personal relationship to God no doubt helped slaves claim a certain amount of freedom denied to them in the general society. Both the Methodists and the Baptists, with their lack of emphasis upon formally educated clergy, allowed African American slaves to become preachers, evangelists, and class leaders. The social location of Baptist and Methodist ministries among the middle and the lower-middle classes deeply influenced slaves, who were at the margins of colonial society.

The other factor to which we can attribute the receptivity of Christianity by slaves was the evangelical emphasis on conversion, sanctification, and holiness. This emphasis provided an avenue for African Americans to express African traditional religion in a new tongue. The emotional aspects of revivalism seemed congruent with the African experiences of ritual spirit-possession. The evangelical emphasis on personal salvation also provided individual slaves with a modicum of personal freedom, expressed in enthusiastic worship.

Scholars have intensively studied the extent to which African Americans fully accepted Christianity or the extent to which Christianity was synthesized with African religious understandings. The present scholarly consensus is that African religious beliefs were synthesized with Christianity, creating a unique African American Christian tradition. There is no scholarly consensus, however, in the evaluation of how deeply African religiosity self-consciously survived the slave experience. Numerous studies of African Americans in anthropology, archaeology, and the arts suggest that Africanisms survived and were influential in the American culture as a whole. For instance, recent archaeological discoveries of slave cemeteries have shown that slaves were buried in patterns akin to African traditions, that is, with bodies facing the East. Historians have also begun to study the ways in which African worldviews shaped colonial America's evangelical piety. What is now being discussed is the fluidity in the acculturation process among competing cultural groupings in the colonial era of North America, and how Africans, Europeans, and native peoples influenced one another.

1.3. *1800-1860: The Rise of the Independent African American Church*

Until the 19th century, Christianity spread gradually and unevenly among African American slaves. The African slave trade continued to bring new immigrants who practiced African traditional religions or Islam, which hindered the missionary work of both Anglo-American and African American evangelists. Christianity achieved religious hegemony among African Americans with the demise of the transatlantic slave trade in 1807 and the rise of 19th-century slave codes that sorely restricted the independent gatherings of slaves. The slave codes prohibited the beating of drums and other practices associated with African traditional religions. These codes arose in response to slave revolts to protect Anglo-Americans, who in some instances were outnumbered by the slave population, as well as to protect the financial interests of the slaveholding elite. Similar to European peasants of the time, African American slaves by the end of the 18th century were being Christianized.

By the end of the 18th century, African Americans in the northeastern region of the United States had begun organizing independent churches. While slavery had been abolished in New England and Middle States like Pennsylvania by 1787 and prohibited in the Northwest Ordinance, the status of African Americans living in these regions remained in doubt. As one historian described them, "They were neither slave nor free." However, in their struggle for independence and recognition, they began to assert themselves in controlling the context in which they worshiped.

It must be remembered that the context for worship among African American Christians at this time was biracial. In both slaveholding and nonslaveholding states, blacks and whites attended the same churches, a phenomenon that would not disappear until the Reconstruction era. Although evangelicals promoted egalitarianism, and for a short time actually stated it as church policy, their social practices increasingly reflected the hierarchical and oppressive relationships found in the general society. African Americans thus were forced to endure degradation even in worship by being forced into separate sanctuary space and different ritual times from those of their Anglo-American counterparts.

By 1787, therefore, African American Baptists began the move to establish independent congregations in Virginia and Georgia. For instance, in 1783 George Liele (ca. 1750-1820), an African American convert and evangelist, had begun preparing the groundwork for the establishment of the first African Baptist Church in Savannah, Georgia. Throughout the North and South, independent congregations began to spring up among African Americans. From the 1790s to the 1840s, independent Protestant congregations were developed that served the unique needs of African American Christians. While these churches grew in the North and the South, those organized by Northern freedpersons developed the furthest. The best example is that of Richard Allen (1760-1831), a former slave in Philadelphia who refused to have a segregated Sabbath for African Americans in St. George Methodist Church. Allen and his colleague Absalom Jones formed the Free African Society and then the Bethel Church in 1794. Later Allen went on with other independent Afro-Methodist congregations to establish the African Methodist Episcopal denomination in 1816. Similarly, in New York City, Peter Williams was able to establish the African Methodist Episcopal Zion denomination in 1822.

This period saw a veritable explosion among freedpersons in establishing independent congregations, including the Joy Street Baptist Church of Boston (1805), the First African Presbyterian in Philadelphia (1808), and the Abyssinian Baptist Church of New York City (1809). These congregations and their leaders were self-consciously ethnic, giving their institutions the name "African" or names symbolic of freedom such as "Concord" and "Canaan." These churches and many of their biracial counterparts became the chief religious, political, and cultural organizations of the African American community. Additionally, the 19th-century independent African American churches situated the African American clergy as the representative religiopolitical leadership of the community, a practice continued even today.

While Northern freedpersons formed churches, the vast majority of African Americans remained enslaved in the South. Christian worship among slaves occurred in two ways: first, attendance in biracial congregations, in which slaves, nonslaveholders, and slaveholders worshiped together, led by white clergymen; second, in secretive gatherings of various slave communities to worship in fields, led by slave preachers. While there were African American independent congregations throughout the South, these remained restricted to the small number of freedpersons and under the tight scrutiny of the larger white religious establishment. Biracial churches stressed all the tenets of evangelical piety, including personal sinfulness, judgment, dutifulness to Scripture, obedience, and charity. When slaves worshiped among themselves, the service included many of the same theological themes as did its more restricted counterpart; however, a greater emphasis was placed on OT themes of the exodus and a Christology of deliverance. The shape of African American churches remained in this pattern until the end of the Civil War.

1.4. *1860-77: The Civil War and Reconstruction*
The U.S. Civil War ended slavery as a political institution. The discord of the war gave African Americans in the South freedom to worship among themselves. Slaves during the war quickly seized the opportunity to form prayer groups or establish regular worship. By the war's end in 1865, many former slaves were ready to establish their own congregations. Over the 14-year period known as Reconstruction (1863-77), not only did former slaves attain formal declaration of their constitutional rights as citizens, including (male) suffrage and equal protection under the law along with limited educational opportunities, but they also moved en masse to establish their own churches. It was within this period that African Americans, despite contrary white opinion, developed and established churches among themselves. The African Methodist Episcopal (AME) and African Methodist Episcopal Zion denominations, as well as independent Baptist congregations, grew rapidly in this period throughout the South. No doubt many of these churches would not have been established without the assistance of Northern white abolitionists and missionaries, who aided former slaves in the founding of institutions of higher education and elementary schools as well as churches, but historical scholarship is being revised to show

that the initiative in the South for independent African American churches and denominations was taken by African Americans themselves.

1.5. *1877-1915: The Church at Its Nadir*
Historian Rayford Logan describes the period 1877-1901 in American history as the nadir in the status of American blacks. In this period the United States witnessed the retrenchment of abolitionist hopes and the hardening of white attitudes toward blacks ($\rightarrow$ Racism). America's racialization had numerous causes, such as the long economic depression of the 1870s and 1890s, the withdrawal of Union troops from the South in 1877 and the subsequent reestablishment of many of the former slaveholding elite in political power by 1900, the growth of large industry and ruthless labor competition brought on by the hordes of immigrants from southern and eastern Europe, the xenophobic response of nativism and its justification in social Darwinist thought by the Anglo-American elites — all of which undermined the citizenship rights of African Americans.

By the turn of the 20th century, segregation by custom or law influenced every area of American life. In this climate of racial hostility the African American church did what it has always done to protect its members from the hostility of the larger society. African American elites, agrarian workers, and artisans alike experienced this nadir. In this period every U.S. denomination with African American members began the formation of "separate but equal" congregations. Amid the turmoil, Afro-Baptists coalesced and in 1895 organized the largest African American denomination, the National Baptist Convention, U.S.A., Inc. (8.2 million members in 1994).

Internally, African American churches concerned themselves with the religious education of their members, stressing a Booker T. Washington–like accommodation to the difficulties of American society. Following the lead of the country's growing imperialism, African American church leaders worried about the fate of Africa and sent missionaries there. Other church leaders such as Bishop Henry McNeil Turner, an AME bishop, and Alexander Crummell, an Episcopal priest, espoused nationalism and a return to Africa as solutions to the plight of African Americans. Many more church leaders took the middle ground, taking up the fight for civil rights by helping found organizations such as the National Association for the Advancement of Colored People (NAACP) (1909) to advocate on their behalf. Yet, among most African American churches the struggle was to secure a place to worship and mediate the hostile and violent world on behalf of their beleaguered members. Although historical scholarship in this area is growing, from the perspective of African Americans it remains small.

1.6. *1915-65: Urbanization and the Struggle for Civil Rights*

Between 1915 and 1965, two events, or processes, shaped the course and the Christian witness of the African American Church: urbanization and the quest for civil rights. World War I brought the temporary cessation of European immigration. This cessation, accompanied by the eroding agricultural economy among small farmers, tenant farmers, and sharecroppers, gave African American agricultural workers the room to find new forms of labor in America's cities. By the end of World War I a massive population shift from Southern farmlands to Southern and Northern cities had begun. This shift, abetted by racial hostility, fostered large central-city congregations among Baptists and Methodists and smaller congregations among Roman Catholics and confessional Protestants. Catholics and Protestants alike became concerned with the growing ranks of urban dwellers. African American "proletariatization," as one historian describes African American class formation in Northern industrial cities, also gave impetus to the churches' becoming more politically engaged and oriented to social service. Here as elsewhere the research remains insufficient. Historical monographs are still needed on various congregations and their contribution to African American working-class life.

Additionally, the migration gave rise to Pentecostal and Spiritualist churches, which ranged from Holy Rollers and storefront churches to denominations such as the Church of God in Christ. In many cities storefront churches became havens for newly arrived migrants attempting to adjust to urban life. The role of women in these congregations has not yet been adequately studied. While African American women have played significant roles in every aspect of African American Church life, a fact not sufficiently expressed in historical writings, it is within the Pentecostal and Spiritualist tradition that women were notably able to have an expanded leadership role as evangelists, preachers, and healers, at least in the early part of the 20th century.

No doubt the greatest accomplishment of this era of the African American Church was the struggle waged for civil rights. From the formation of organizations such as the NAACP and the National Urban League (1910) to the election of African American politicians, the African American Church was the seedbed from which all political action sprang. In this sense it continued to play its historic role as the center of African American politics. The scholarly literature on this aspect of the African American Church has now grown tremendously, primarily through studies done about or around the advent of Martin Luther → King Jr. (1929-68) and the civil rights movement in the South between 1955 and 1965. Historical writings on the period before the King years are steadily progressing, offering a broader interpretation of the vitality and resourcefulness of the African American Church during the hitherto silent years of the "Negro revolution."

1.7. *1965-Present*

Since 1965 the greatest influence on the African American Church has been the development of the black theology movement as articulated by theologians James Cone and Gayraud Wilmore. This movement, conjoined with the black power movement and the black studies movement (1965-75), initiated serious academic scholarship regarding the life of the African American Church by its own people. Union Theological Seminary of New York, where James Cone has taught, continues to play a valuable role in this effort. Black theology is a partisan and political theology that seeks to reinterpret Christian theology in cultural terms that affirm African Americans in all aspects of their lives. Broadly speaking, black theology has moved from being solely an Afro-Baptist and Methodist theology to becoming an ecumenical effort. Confessional Protestants and Roman Catholics of African descent have also articulated the central claim of black theology, namely, that African American liberation is the starting point of doing theology in their reformulation of a European theological heritage. More important, black theology as well as Latin American → liberation theology has brought the African American Christians' struggle together with that of other oppressed people around the world. This has been particularly significant in the case of South Africa, where apartheid has dominated the lives of black South Africans just as racism has curtailed the lives of African Americans. Black theology has mobilized a new generation of scholars and clergy, whose mature writings we still await.

The African American Church continues to mirror the multiple experiences of the African American community in its struggle for civic, personal, and social freedoms. For the first time since the 19th century, however, the church is experiencing open religious competition from Islam, other religious faith expressions, and → secularism. Additionally, the church is faced with social stratification, dividing the African American middle class and working class from the poor. In spite of these new trials, the African American Church continues overall to hold the loyalty and promote the aspirations of the African American community.

Bibliography: Africanism in African American Christianity: L. BARRETT, *Soul Force: African Heritage in Afro-American Religion* (Garden City, N.Y., 1974) • M. J. HERSKOVITS, *The Myth of the Negro Past* (Boston, 1958) • J. E. HOLLOWAY, *Africanism in American Culture* (Bloomington, Ind., 1990) • S. WALKER, *Ceremonial Spirit Possession in Africa and Afro-America* (Leiden, 1972).

Studies of slave religion: E. D. GENOVESE, *Roll, Jordan, Roll: The World the Slaves Made* (New York, 1974) • A. J. RABOTEAU, *Slave Religion: The Invisible Institution in the Antebellum South* (New York, 1978) • M. SOBEL, *Trabelin' On: The Slave Journey to an Afro-Baptist Faith* (Westport, Conn., 1979); idem, *The World They Made Together: Black and White Values in Eighteenth-Century Virginia* (Princeton, 1987).

Twentieth-century sociological profiles of the African American church: E. F. FRAZIER, *The Negro Church in America* (New York, 1963) • C. E. LINCOLN and L. MAMIYA, *The Black Church in the African-American Experience* (Durham, N.C., 1990) • B. E. MAYS and J. W. NICHOLSON, *The Negro Church* (New York, 1933; repr., 1969).

General historical studies: K. L. DVORAK, *An African-American Exodus: The Segregation of the Southern Churches* (Brooklyn, N.Y., 1991) • C. V. R. GEORGE, *Segregated Sabbaths: Richard Allen and the Emergence of the Independent Black Churches, 1760-1840* (New York, 1973) • R. LOGAN, *The Betrayal of the Negro, from Rutherford B. Hayes to Woodrow Wilson* (New York, 1965; orig. title: *The Negro in American Life and Thought: The Nadir, 1877-1901*) • R. E. LUKER, *The Social Gospel in Black and White: American Racial Reform, 1885-1912* (Chapel Hill, N.C., 1991) • P. J. PARIS, *The Social Teachings of the Black Church* (Philadelphia, 1985) • G. S. WILMORE, *Black Religion and Black Radicalism: An Interpretation of the Religious History of Afro-American People* (Maryknoll, N.Y., 1986) • G. S. WILMORE and J. H. CONE, *Black Theology: A Documentary History, 1966-1979* (Maryknoll, N.Y., 1979) • C. G. WOODSON, *The History of the Negro Church* (Washington, D.C., 1921).

Denominational studies: Baptist: L. FITTS, *A History of Black Baptists* (Nashville, 1985) • M. SOBEL, *Trabelin' On: The Slave Journey to an Afro-Baptist Faith* (Westport, Conn., 1979) • J. M. WASHINGTON, *Frustrated Fellowship: The Black Baptist Quest for Social Power* (Macon, Ga., 1986).

Methodist: R. ALLEN, *The Life Experiences and Gospel Labor of the Right Reverend Richard Allen* (repr., New York, 1960) • O. H. LAKEY, *The History of the CME* (Memphis, Tenn., 1985) • H. V. RICHARDSON, *Dark Salvation: The Story of Methodism As It Developed among Blacks in America* (Garden City, N.J., 1976) • C. E. WALKER, *A Rock in a Weary Land: The AME Church during the Civil War and Reconstruction* (Baton Rouge, La., 1982).

Pentecostal: I. MACROBERTS, *The Black Roots and White Racism of Early Pentecostalism in the U.S.A.* (New York, 1988).

Presbyterian: A. MURRAY, *The Presbyterians and the Negro* (Philadelphia, 1966) • I. PARKER, *The Rise and Decline of the Educational Program for Black Presbyterians of the United Presbyterian Church, U.S.A.* (San Antonio, Tex., 1977).

Roman Catholic: C. DAVIS, *The History of Black Catholics in the United States* (New York, 1990).

RANDAL M. JELKS

2. The African Diaspora

2.1. *Variety of African Expressions*

2.1.1. *Background*

The term "African diaspora" was coined by African American scholars in black history (G. S. Wilmore and others) to describe the scattering of Africans in many countries as the historical consequence of (1) the transatlantic slave trade, (2) the conditions of → slavery and the encounter between white and black communities, and (3) the subsequent → racism perpetuated in the Northern Hemisphere. Theologically, the term therefore denotes the historical reality and present experience of people of African descent on both sides of the Atlantic. Although they now reside in different continents, still they demonstrate "a certain kind of religious orientation as the result of the coming together of African and European cultures" under quite specific conditions; in worship, organization, and theologizing they reveal "consistent patterns" (Wilmore) not destroyed under these conditions but, rather, influencing the host societies. Melville Herskovits, in searching for the cultural forces surviving in the African diaspora, developed a new ethnohistory by mapping out a scale of African retentions from Latin America to the Caribbean, the southern parts of the United States, and the free blacks of the northern United States and Canada. Descendants of African and African-Caribbean immigrants into modern Britain may be, geographically and historically, the furthest extension on these scales. However, the intensity of their religious experience, especially among African-Caribbean immigrants and settlers and those related to black indigenous headquarters, is still informed and supplied by African culture and religion (see 2.1.3).

2.1.2. *Multiformity and Contextuality*

Independent black churches comprise diverse theological traditions, liturgies, leadership patterns, and social and ecumenical activities. These are determined by the degree of nearness to and distance from Africa, by the character of migration, by the kind of attachment to the present location, by the sociopolitical and economic environment, and by the degree of synthesis with Western-white Christian elements. In 1955 Henry van Dusen, who first encountered such multiformity of Adventist, Pentecostal, and Holiness movements in the Caribbean, spoke prophetically of a "new reformation" and called it "the third mighty arm of Christianity," after Eastern → Orthodoxy (§3) and Western missions (i.e., → Roman Catholicism and → Protestantism). He recognized in it the "sovereign unpredictability" of the Holy Spirit and warned against considering it a merely transitional phenomenon. David Barrett paid tribute to this development in his *World Christian Encyclopedia* by identifying these new bodies among the established churches of the 223 countries of the earth. These → Independent Churches presently show the highest growth rate within Christianity worldwide (S. M. Burgess and G. B. McGee, 816-17; → Pentecostal Churches 1).

2.1.3. *African Diaspora in Britain*

The → United Kingdom (§2.3) today is the unique example of the African diaspora in Europe (R. I. H. Gerloff 1992, 1.48-55). From 1952, with the start of black mass migration into Britain, it has developed into a meeting point of at least 12 different expressions of black Christianity from other continents. They have brought with them their own → spirituality (§2), theologies, cultural expressions, organizational structures, and understanding of → mission and → ecumenism. Largely now combined in African and African-Caribbean councils of churches, they regard themselves as independent partners of the British churches, with some participating in the "new instrument" — the Council of Churches for Britain and Ireland, established in 1990.

The 12 theological families are listed here in roughly chronological order, relating to their history overseas:

The oldest are *independent African American churches* such as the African Methodist Episcopal Church and the African Methodist Episcopal Zion Church (see 1.2; → Methodist Churches 2.3). These churches, which protested against inequality and racial discrimination within American Protestantism, reached England via South Africa and the Caribbean.

The → *Sabbatarians* are represented in three different streams: the Seventh Day Baptists, the Seventh-day Adventists, and Sabbatarian Pentecostals. These groups interpret the → Sabbath as the symbol of freedom from oppression and social injustice. They came to Europe via the Caribbean and the United States.

The → *Holiness movement* arose from primitive Wesleyanism, which separated from American Methodism in 1843 on the issues of the abolition of slavery, emancipation of women (→ Sexism), commitment to the poor (→ Poverty), and nonhierarchical structures of the church. It found its way via the Caribbean.

The *Revivalists* (Jamaica) created the first synthesis between African cultural symbols and the Christian message. Similarly, the *Spiritual Baptists* (Trinidad, St. Vincent, Grenada, and Guyana) blended African traditional religion with Christianity and are still very active and flourishing in the London area.

The Pentecostal movement, which forms by far the largest group of African-Caribbean Christians, traces its inspiration back to the intercultural and interracial Azusa Street Revival of 1906-9 in Los Angeles under William J. Seymour. It is divided into three different theological families. One is the *Trinitarian Pentecostals,* represented primarily by the Church of God tradition (→ Churches of God). Entering Britain via the Caribbean, they are in the process of freeing themselves from the legacy of white control.

The second group is the *Oneness,* or *Apostolic, Pentecostals* (e.g., the First United Church of Jesus Christ Apostolic), which grafted themselves into the cultures of the black urban poor in North America (→ Ghetto) and the villages "up in the hills" in Jamaica and other Caribbean islands. Teaching a dynamic non-Trinitarian theology, they form the second largest group of African-Caribbean Christians in Britain.

The third group of Pentecostals is the so-called *Latter Rain movement.* Theologically influenced by American healing evangelists, it lays special emphasis on healing and "spiritual power."

The *African Indigenous Churches,* which arrived in Europe from West Africa, are divided into Nigerian (Yoruba) and Ghanaian (mainly Akan) congregations, with only a few being multicultural. They emphasize African cultural symbols such as dreams and → visions, prayer for → healing, shouting, → dancing, and water symbolism, combined with social and ecumenical commitment. These churches belong mainly to the Aladura movement (e.g., the Aladura International Church; the Cherubim and Seraphim United Council of Churches; → Nigeria 2.4) and to the Ghanaian prophetic churches (e.g., the Musama Disco Christo Church; → Ghana 2.4).

In 1973 the *Ras Tafari* movement initiated efforts

to bring the → Ethiopian Orthodox Church into existence in Britain, which it accomplished in 1974 through the instrumentality of young African-Caribbean radicals and in conjunction with the Ethiopian World Federation.

Black *Anglo-Catholics* gained access to historic Christianity by adopting apostolic succession (→ Bishop, Episcopate 1; High Church Movement 3.1).

African charismatic congregations, a new type linked globally to the charismatic renewal (→ Charismatic Religion), are attracting increasingly large numbers of modern, educated Africans.

Finally, insofar as "black" can refer to all people from the Two-Thirds World, we could mention the great variety of *Asian Christian fellowships.*

2.2. Historical and Theological Insights

Study of the churches of the African diaspora, and generally of oral cultures within Christianity, is relatively new. Research into black Pentecostalism, which forms the greater part of the African diaspora in Britain, began only in the 1970s. Until then, white historians of the Pentecostal and → charismatic movements evaluated Pentecostalism only from their limited literary and racist perspectives. The Birmingham school under Walter J. Hollenweger introduced quite different historical and theological insights (→ Pentecostal Churches; Charismatic Religion). Historical ignorance and cultural arrogance of Western Christians led to their describing churches that are part and parcel of world Christianity as → sects and cults. Misinterpretations still circulate — such as the supposed otherworldliness or the predominance of → fundamentalism in black majority churches — for which there is little or no basis in the faith or social life of groups, which arise from a history of exploitation and suffering. African American scholars have therefore spoken of the "black oblivion" (E. Lincoln, 145) — the invisibility of communities of African heritage in white-dominated societies.

The historical and theological insights gained since the 1970s can be summarized in the following six subsections.

2.2.1. Contribution to the Church Universal

The churches of the African diaspora have been, and still are, a contribution of the African scene to the universal church (J. S. Tinney, 4-6), representing the spiritual and sociopolitical departure of black Christians from physical and cultural bondage. In the Pentecostal movement, an African oral culture became the pioneer of a worldwide movement. Similar interactions could be observed in the past in the North American great → revivals (§2.1) or the Jamaica Revival of 1861/62, when Christian and Afri-

can elements entered a fruitful symbiosis or a fresh articulation of reality.

Discoveries in black culture and black religion (see works by W. E. B. DuBois, Z. N. Hurston, and M. J. Herskovits) have indicated that the African heritage was never lost in the lives of the slaves, even when languages, family bonds, and ethnic belongings were destroyed. Interwoven with biblical symbols, it contributed, rather, to the physical and spiritual survival of a people. This is immensely relevant for an understanding of the "interculturation" of a religion (→ Acculturation 3; Culture and Christianity 3). "Spirit possession" under oppression, the "exodus" through the wilderness into the "promised land," the integrity of human feelings in the "furnace" of suffering, the liberation of language in "pentecost," the body-mind relationship in healing, → worship (§5.1) as an all-embracing experience — these all manifest a biblical renaissance. American sociologists have called it "the revitalization of the pan-human capacity for supra-rational, → ecstatic experience" (L. P. Gerlach and V. H. Hine 1970, 204).

2.2.2. Organization

Origins, proliferation, and growth of the churches of the African diaspora on both sides of the Atlantic are due to "movement organization," or organizational structures that are quite different from those of the white, established Christian bodies, five features of which deserve mention (see Gerlach and Hine 1968).

They form a *reticulate* (or polycephalous) *organization,* linked together by a variety of personal, structural, and ideological ties. It is not linear or bureaucratic but can be likened to a cellular organism and, like life itself, cannot be suppressed. They form a *mission that travels along preexisting daily social relationships* such as family, friendship, village or island community, trade or work companionship, and shared migration and suffering. There is *charismatic leadership,* which signifies responsibility moving from the bottom up, identification with the needs of the people, spiritual maturity, and the "ability to make the charisma of each individual flow freely through the ranks of the movement." The structures convey a *change-oriented and action-motivating message* that is not abstract but can be easily communicated both verbally and nonverbally, through words, music, dance, or body language. They stand for *opposition against the existing order* (i.e., for resistance against inhuman forces), for grassroots communities, and for the personal worth and power of each individual. The Azusa Street Revival can also be understood as such a mission, a stroke "against the highbrow tendency" of black intellectuals and their alienation from the impoverished masses (H. Eley, in Z. N. Hurston 1987, 318; Gerloff 1992, 1.123).

2.2.3. *Different Concept of the Holy Spirit*

The churches of the African diaspora share with all Christians the biblical foundation of faith in the → gospel of Jesus Christ. Especially in their modern developments and expressions, however, they represent a different concept of the → Holy Spirit (§2) from that of traditional theologies. In the view of these churches, the Spirit of God is first and foremost a living power, or "power in participation," the power of the continued interdependence of all creatures. It is a "traveling power" from generation to generation and continent to continent, not just in the church but also in the world. As in the epiclesis of the ancient church, it "renews the face of the earth." The rebellion that white members of the early Pentecostal movement staged against the "crude negroism of the Southland" (C. F. Parham, in R. M. Anderson, 190) arose not only from cultural, racial, and social differences but also from different pneumatological understandings. White Christians repeatedly have distanced themselves from the "fanatical" expressions of black or integrated worship, attempting to deprive the Spirit experience of its bodily accompaniments. In contrast, almost all black independent churches today have become charismatic.

Only the black Oneness, or Apostolic, Pentecostals (see 2.1.3), however, have so far developed a new "black" pneumatology (→ Trinity). For them, God is *one* — Creator, Liberator, and Indwelling Power. The God who traveled with → Israel through the wilderness bore the wounds of the oppressed in → Jesus of Nazareth. The God who worked through Jesus can also dwell in us and inspire us to even greater works. Such a pneumatology is rooted, quite true to the NT, in a Spirit Christology that perhaps, in the post-Hellenistic era, offers better categories for the Christian message than the traditional Logos → Christology (§§2, 5, and 6.7). Jesus becomes the Emancipator, or the "Deliverer of humanity" (J. Cone) in us — the embodiment of → Love, which is constitutive for all → black theologies from W. J. Seymour to M. L. → King Jr.

2.2.4. *Freedom from Fundamentalism*

Partly from ignorance, but more so from lack of access to different resources, the churches of the African diaspora have been taken captive by fundamentalist tendencies. However, black Christians have been slowly but persistently freeing themselves from these disastrous white overlays. White, rational fundamentalism, which preserves the status quo, is something totally different from the faith of people who struggle against racism or (in the case of black

women) against the combination of racism, sexism, and classism (→ Class and Social Stratum); resist all class divisions; act and preach through self-help projects; care for the identity of their youth; and, as they do in Britain, speak out against social injustice in church and society (→ Righteousness, Justice). If anything, theirs is a "liturgical fundamentalism" (J. Barr), poetry that preserves the beauty of the traditional words in worship and theology that is led by the "fundamentals" of the gospel and not by the superimpositions of foreign categories.

2.2.5. *Same Biblical Language but Different Realities*

The churches of the African diaspora use the same biblical → symbolic language as their traditional western European counterparts. These stories, paradigms, and images, however, represent quite different realities. We can clearly grasp this difference from comparing sermons, forms of worship (→ Liturgy), congregational lifestyles (→ Congregation), and sometimes contradictory attitudes to social and ecumenical issues. Any interaction between cultures, and in particular between dominant and subordinate ethnic groups, is a power struggle. The early Pentecostal movement, which was integrated, was an attempt to overcome these struggles by the power of the Spirit. This effort implies learning from the different realities behind the same words. It means considering racism in a Christian community as sin, a violation of the very gospel entrusted to it, and a "spiritual monstrosity" (R. C. Lawson, in Gerloff 1992, 1.102), not just a question of one's preference, an unimportant spot on the garment of faith (→ Status confessionis).

2.2.6. *Danger of Further Exploitation*

The churches of the African diaspora have been the forerunners of the Pentecostal and charismatic movements, on the one hand, and, on the other, of pop culture. The religion and music of Africans in the New World (→ Gospel Song; Spirituals) were the two areas that the slave masters could not control, exploit, or commercialize. They formed the heart of the black church as the source of spiritual, cultural, and sociopolitical survival. In the 20th century, however, the white charismatic movement and the → mass media run the risk of further exploitation of black elements. By integrating them into their respective systems, by manipulating and instrumentalizing them, they often deprive them of their genuine message and content. Almost all black independent congregations therefore emphasize that they are not "disco churches." All these communities lay primary emphasis on holiness and love, with only secondary stress on → glossolalia and healing miracles.

2.3. Ecumenical Significance

The ecumenical significance of the African diaspora lies in at least five directions.

2.3.1. The African diaspora signifies that multiformity and contextuality of all theologies (→ Contextual Theology) and religions are necessary. It challenges us to accept questions and answers from other cultures as theologically and spiritually relevant for ourselves. The → ecumenical dialogue of the future will no longer be the debate among the historical churches but between North and South, black and white, rich and poor. On this issue depends the relevance of the → ecumenical movement.

2.3.2. The African diaspora demonstrates different organizational patterns that obviously correspond to the needs of the young and the marginalized and counteract the rigidity of traditional institutions and denominations. "Mission," or recruiting to a movement (→ Church 5), follows not abstract channels but human relationships and communities, an approach that signals → friendship. In this way, religions have helped people to survive humanely in a technologically manipulated world (→ Technology).

2.3.3. The African diaspora manifests a biblical renaissance that is rooted in the material, social, and political reality of the poor (→ Bible Study 5; Biblical Theology 2.3; Poverty). The "blackout" of non-Western interpretations of the Hebrew Bible and the NT has deprived European church language of its symbolic power. Only congregations that offer → experience (§2.2.5) instead of → dogmas, life testimonies instead of logical arguments, friendship instead of rational treatises, songs instead of complicated books, can recapture the power of the biblical Word (→ European Theology 1.1; Word of God).

2.3.4. The African diaspora highlights issues of social justice. In behalf of the next generation, it struggles against economic recession, political powerlessness, → unemployment, underachievement, poor housing conditions, and illness (→ Health and Illness). In a world of increased racial and cultural polarization and so-called ethnic cleansing, the diaspora makes clear the basic choice of direction for our society: toward an apartheid nation of injustice and hopelessness, or toward shalom, in which each person shares in the resources of the earth. In their undivided message of love, black churches can help societies become aware of the destructive forces in our midst.

2.3.5. Finally, the African diaspora demonstrates the existential character of → faith. People of an oppressive past, an almost hopeless present, and a future that seems to render them redundant still carry love for → life under these adverse conditions.

In times when → wars and catastrophes cause Europeans to lose their faith, this contribution of an indestructible → trust in the kindness of God (H. Mitchell) is perhaps the most important gift that black Christians can give to white people today.

→ African Theology; Third World Theology

Bibliography: R. M. ANDERSON, *Vision of the Disinherited* (Oxford, 1979) • J. BARR, *Fundamentalism* (London, 1977) • D. BARRETT, ed., *WCE* • L. E. BARRETT, *Soul Force: African Heritage in Afro-American Religion* (Garden City, N.Y., 1974) • M. W. BECKWITH, *Black Roadways* (Chapel Hill, N.C., 1929; repr., New York, 1969) • A. M. BRAZIER, *Black Self-Determination* (Grand Rapids, 1969) • S. M. BURGESS and G. B. McGEE, eds., *Dictionary of Pentecostal and Charismatic Movements* (Grand Rapids, 1988) • J. H. CONE, *The Spirituals and the Blues* (New York, 1972) • W. E. B. DuBois, *The Souls of Black Folk* (New York, 1969; orig. pub., 1905) • H. P. VAN DUSEN, "Caribbean Holiday," *CCen,* August 17, 1955, 946-48 • N. L. ERSKINE, *King among the Theologians* (Cleveland, 1994) • M. J. GAXIOLA-GAXIOLA, "The Unresolved Issue: A Third-World Perspective on the Oneness Question," *Probing Pentecostalism* (Oklahoma City, Okla., 1987) • L. P. GERLACH and V. H. HINE, "Five Factors Crucial to the Growth and Spread of a Modern Religious Movement," *JSSR* 7 (1968) 23-40; idem, *People, Power, Change: Movements of Social Transformation* (Indianapolis, 1970) • R. I. H. GERLOFF, "The Holy Spirit and the African Diaspora: Spiritual, Cultural, and Social Roots of Black Pentecostal Churches," *JEPTA* 14 (1995) 85-100; idem, *Partnership in Black and White* (London, 1977); idem, *A Plea for British Black Theologies: The Black Church Movement in Britain in Its Transatlantic Cultural and Theological Interaction, with Special References to the Pentecostal Oneness (Apostolic) and Sabbatarian Movements* (2 vols.; Frankfurt, 1992) • R. I. H. GERLOFF and H. VAN BEEK, eds., *Report of the Proceedings of the Consultation between the World Council of Churches . . . and African and African-Caribbean Church Leaders in Britain* (Geneva, 1996) • S. D. GLAZIER, ed., *Perspectives in Pentecostalism* (New York, 1980) • M. J. HERSKOVITS, *The Myth of the Negro Past* (Boston, 1944; 2d ed., 1958) • W. J. HOLLENWEGER, *Pentecost between Black and White* (Belfast, 1974); idem, *Pentecostalism: Origins and Developments Worldwide* (Peabody, Mass., 1998); idem, *The Pentecostals* (Minneapolis, 1972) • Z. N. HURSTON, *Jonah's Gourd Vine* (London, 1987); idem, *The Sanctified Church* (Berkeley, Calif., 1926; 2d ed., 1983) • C. E. JONES, *Black Holiness* (Metuchen, N.J., 1987) • J. A. B. JONGENEEL, ed., *Experiences of the Spirit* (Frankfurt, 1991) • C. E. LINCOLN, *The Black Church since Frazier* (New York, 1974) • I. MACROBERT, *The Black Roots and White Racism of Early Pentecostalism in the USA* (New York, 1988) • H. H. Mitchell, *The Recovery of Preaching* (London, 1977) • J. C. Richardson, *With Water and Spirit: A History of Black Apostolic Denominations* (Washington, D.C., 1980) • G. E. Simpson, *Black Religions in the New World* (New York, 1978) • J. S. Tinney, "Exclusivist Tendencies in Pentecostal Self-Definition: A Critique from Black Theology," *JRT* 36 (1979) 32-49 • G. S. Wilmore, *Black Religion and Black Radicalism* (2d ed.; Maryknoll, N.Y., 1983).

ROSWITH I. H. GERLOFF

Black Theology

1. Theological Discipline and Historical Roots
2. Central Theses and Positions
3. Black Theology in South Africa.
4. New Developments

1. Theological Discipline and Historical Roots

1.1. The term "black theology" first appeared as a description of a theological movement in the United States with the publication of James H. Cone's *Black Theology and Black Power* in 1969 (→ North American Theology 8). Its meaning was derived from a community of African American clergy and laypersons (→ Black Churches 1) who were struggling to understand the meaning of their identity as *black* and *Christian* in the white → racist society of America, which also claimed to be Christian and the leader of the free world. If the Christian faith has nothing to do with black people's struggle for justice (→ Righteousness, Justice), as implied in the common silence of American white theologians regarding → slavery and oppression, how then is it possible for African Americans to affirm their identity as being both black and Christian? What does the → gospel of Jesus Christ have to do with the black struggle for → freedom in a society that refused to acknowledge African Americans as human beings? These were the questions that initiated the development of a black theology of → liberation (§1).

As a theological discipline, black theology arose out of the → civil rights and black power movements of the 1950s and 1960s (→ Human and Civil Rights), as defined by the life and work of Martin Luther → King Jr. (1929-68) and Malcolm X (1925-65). The meaning of the word "black" in black theology was derived from the black nationalist philosophy of Malcolm X. The meaning of the term "theology" in the phrase was derived from Martin Luther King. The idea of a black theology came into being as black, politically active clergy attempted to reconcile Chris-

tianity and black power, Martin Luther King and Malcolm X. (e.g., G. S. Wilmore).

1.2. The historical roots of black theology, however, go back to the beginning of African slavery in the United States and the founding of the independent African American → Baptist and → Methodist churches in the late 18th and early 19th centuries. The central theological claim of black theology is that the God of the exodus, of the prophets, and of → Jesus can be known only in the struggles of the poor for liberation. *Christian* theology, therefore, is language about God's liberating activity in the world on behalf of the freedom of the oppressed. Any theology that fails to give an essential place to God's liberation of the oppressed is not Christian. It may be philosophical and have some relation to Scripture, but it is not Christian, for the word "Christian" connects theology inseparably to God's will to set the captives free.

2. Central Theses and Positions

Because the public meaning of the Christian gospel has been almost exclusively identified with the dominant cultures of white Americans and Europeans (→ Culture and Christianity 2 and 4; European Theology 1), who are primarily responsible for the victimization of blacks and other colored peoples throughout the world (→ Colonialism; Colonialism and Mission), African American theologians of the 1960s concluded that many Christian → symbols had to be radically transformed and redefined in the light of the struggles of the poor for freedom. They thus began to speak of a *black* theology of liberation (Cone 1970; J. D. Roberts), referring to God and Jesus as black (→ Christological Titles) in order to emphasize the divine → solidarity with the oppressed (Cone 1975). Instead of turning to the white theologians of America and Europe for an analysis of the gospel, African Americans began to reread the Bible in the light of their own history and culture, as well as the contemporary black liberation struggles (→ Contextual Theology 2).

3. Black Theology in South Africa

3.1. Black theology emerged in South Africa during the early 1970s in the context of black resistance to apartheid. Although it was influenced by theological and political developments in the United States, it developed its own distinctive characteristics in South Africa (→ Africa 3.3; African Theology 1.3-4). Like black theology in the United States, black theology in South Africa identified God's liberation of the oppressed as the heart of the Christian gospel. Archbishop Desmond Tutu and Alan Boesak were among the early, well-known exponents of black theology. Other important interpreters include Takatso A. Mofokeng, Simon S. Maimela, and Itumeleng J. Mosala.

3.2. Unlike some U.S. black theologians, several South African black theologians gradually moved away from the idea of a black theology to a stress on contextual theology, putting African identity at the center (→ African Theology 3.1) and emphasizing their struggle to create a nonracial society (→ Salvation 6.3). Many progressive white theologians joined black theologians in the Institute of Contextual Theology and together wrote the Kairos Document (issued in September 1985), the most widely disseminated theological assessment critical of South Africa's political crisis created by the system of apartheid. They spoke of the need for a prophetic theology that would denounce the evils of apartheid and announce the good news of liberation, a just society free of racial, economic, and political oppression.

4. New Developments
Although black liberation theology in the United States arose independently of → liberation theology (§2) in Latin America, both theologies receive their identity from their solidarity with the poor of their communities. The chief difference between them has been black theology's focus on race oppression and Latin American theology's focus on → class exploitation.

Since the 1980s, black theology has developed in three important directions, featuring (1) the rise of "womanist theology," (2) the emergence of new voices in biblical → exegesis, and (3) the return to the religion of African slaves.

4.1. Since African American women were invisible in the black male liberation theology, even in white → feminist theology, black women broke their silence and began to speak of womanist theology. They borrowed the term "womanist" from Alice Walker's *In Search of Our Mother's Gardens* (1983), where she defined it as "a black feminist" who is "committed to survival and wholeness of entire people, male and female." While black male theologians emphasized the biblical theme of liberation as defined by the exodus, prophets, and Jesus, womanist theologians emphasized the theme of survival as defined by the biblical character Hagar, whom God, in contrast to the Israelite slaves, did not liberate (D. S. Williams). Womanist theologians do not deny the importance of liberation as a biblical theme in the African American community but point out that it is not the only theme in the Bible and the African American community (K. G. Cannon). Also present,

especially among women, in the Scripture and in the black experience is the theme of survival. Womanist theology critiques black liberation theology for failing to take seriously the experience of African American women in their discourse about God, as they have suffered from discrimination for sex and class as well as race (→ Feminism; Sexism).

4.2. Although the biblical message of liberation defined the center of black theology from its beginning, academically trained biblical scholars were few in number. But since the publication of Cain H. Felder's groundbreaking work *Troubling Biblical Waters: Race, Class, and Family* (1989), African American biblical scholars have begun to reread the Bible in light of the themes of liberation and justice and the "racial motifs in the biblical narratives." *Stony the Road We Trod: African American Biblical Interpretation* (1991), edited by Felder, represents five years of collaboration among African American biblical scholars. In discovering an African presence in the Bible that white biblical scholars have either ignored or marginalized, the authors challenge the Eurocentric focus of biblical scholarship (→ European Theology 1).

4.3. The third development in black theology is being shaped by a second generation of young black theologians who are seeking to deepen black theology by returning to its sources in the slave narratives, sermons, prayers, songs, and folklore (→ Gospel Song; Spirituals). *Cut Loose Your Stammering Tongue* (1991), edited by Dwight Hopkins and George Cumming, is their major text; like the work of black biblical scholars, it too is the result of several years of collaboration. Hopkins has also published *Shoes That Fit Our Feet: Sources for a Constructive Black Theology* (1993). Both books identify the religion and culture of African slaves as the most important starting point for shaping the future direction of black theology.

Black women and men in all theological disciplines have begun a creative conversation and are working together for the improvement of the quality of life in the African American churches and community. Black theology arose out of → black churches and continues to be closely linked with them. In the African American community, the struggle for liberation and survival is not alien to the black religious community but rather is an essential part of it.

Bibliography: A. Boesak, *Farewell to Innocence* (Maryknoll, N.Y., 1976) • K. G. Cannon, *Black Womanist Ethics* (Atlanta, 1988) • J. H. Cone, *Black Theology and Black Power* (New York, 1969); idem, *A Black Theology of Liberation* (Philadelphia, 1970; 20th anniv. ed., with critical reflections by D. S. Williams et al., Maryknoll, N.Y., 1990); idem, *For My People* (Maryknoll, N.Y., 1984); idem, *God of the Oppressed* (San Francisco, 1975); idem, *The Spirituals and the Blues* (New York, 1972) • J. H. Cone and G. S. Wilmore, eds., *Black Theology: A Documentary History*, vol. 1, *1966-1979;* vol. 2, *1980-1992* (Maryknoll, N.Y., 1979-93) • K. B. Douglas, *The Black Christ* (Maryknoll, N.Y., 1994) • C. H. Felder, *Troubling Biblical Waters: Race, Class, and Family* (Maryknoll, N.Y., 1989); idem, ed., *Stony the Road We Trod: African American Biblical Interpretation* (Maryknoll, N.Y., 1991) • J. Grant, *White Women's Christ and Black Women's Jesus* (Atlanta, 1989) • D. Hopkins, *Black Theology. USA and South Africa: Politics, Culture, and Liberation* (Maryknoll, N.Y., 1989); idem, *Shoes That Fit Our Feet: Sources for a Constructive Black Theology* (Maryknoll, N.Y., 1993) • D. Hopkins and G. Cumming, eds., *Cut Loose Your Stammering Tongue* (Maryknoll, N.Y., 1991) • T. A. Mofokeng, *The Crucified among the Crossbearers: Towards a Black Christology* (Kampen, 1983) • B. Moore, *The Challenge of Black Theology in South Africa* (Atlanta, 1973) • I. J. Mosala, *Biblical Hermeneutics and Black Theology in South Africa* (Maryknoll, N.Y., 1989) • J. Parratt, *Theologiegeschichte der Dritten Welt. Afrika* (Munich, 1991) bibliography • J. D. Roberts, *Liberation and Reconciliation: A Black Theology* (Philadelphia, 1971) • T. Sundermeier, ed., *Zwischen Kultur und Politik. Texte zur afrikanischen Theologie und Schwarzen Theologie* (Hamburg, 1978) • E. Townes, ed., *A Troubling in My Soul: Womanist Perspectives on Evil and Suffering* (Maryknoll, N.Y., 1993) • D. M. Tutu, *Hope and Suffering* (Grand Rapids, 1984) • D. Williams, *Sisters in the Wilderness: The Challenge of Womanist God-Talk* (Maryknoll, N.Y., 1993) • G. S. Wilmore, *Black Religion and Black Radicalism* (Garden City, N.Y., 1972; 2d ed., Maryknoll, N.Y., 1983) • T. Witvliet, *The Way of the Black Messiah* (London, 1987).

James H. Cone

Blessing

1. Term
2. OT
3. NT
4. History
5. Signs
6. Significance
7. The Papal Blessing

1. Term

In contrast to → cursing, the concept of blessing denotes a reason for success in → life, either immediately or continuously. It promises power that will enhance the → good and give mastery over life by the averting of what is harmful. The action of blessing consists of the word of blessing and related gestures such as the → laying on of hands, the lifting up of hands, or making the → sign of the cross.

2. OT

The OT relates the fulfilling of → promises of blessing and the actual force of any pronouncing of blessing to the power of → Yahweh (Gen. 12:1-3; Numbers 22–24). Only occasionally in stories of the patriarchs do we get any suggestion of a blessing working autonomously (Genesis 27; → Patriarchal History). To impart blessings to the larger cultic community, certain persons are given special empowerment, for example, charismatic leaders (Exod. 39:43; Josh. 14:13; → Charisma), kings (2 Sam. 6:18; 1 Kgs. 8:14, 55; → Monarchy in Israel) and priests (Lev. 9:22), to whom alone there finally falls the task of dispensing cultic blessing (Sir. 50:20-21). Yet despite this development, the practice of private blessing (Gen. 9:26-27; 27:23-29) still remained in force (Sir. 3:8-9) after the time of the patriarchs. There might also be blessings at meeting (e.g., in greetings) or parting. But blessing was not just a wish or request. It would also take the form of praise and thanksgiving, as at meals. We still see in blessing the original unity of the cultic and the → everyday (e.g., Deuteronomy 28).

For all the variations, blessing in the OT finally involves always an awareness or recognition of the promise of Yahweh to uphold his → creation (§2) and his → covenant. The efficacy of a blessing thus stands always under the freedom of God, which we cannot control. Related to this understanding is the most essential cultic form of blessing in Num. 6:24-26, which is formulated as a wish or petition. In its present form the Aaronic blessing and its etiologic context in Num. 6:22-23, 27 probably was drafted for the Jerusalem priesthood and was used as the climax of the whole act of blessing (Sir. 50:20-21). In the Jerusalem → temple it was given daily by the priests at the morning and evening offerings (→ Sacrifice), and at morning → worship (§1.2) in the synagogue it came between the 18th and 19th benedictions of the main prayer, the *těpillâ*. Still given daily in Jerusalem, it is restricted to feast days in the → diaspora (→ Jewish Practices), though fathers, on returning from the → synagogue to begin celebration of the → Sabbath at home, dispense it to their children.

The essential link between blessing and greeting may be seen in ancient formulas like "The Lord be with you" (Judg. 6:12; Ruth 2:4) or "Peace be to you" (Judg. 19:20; 1 Sam. 25:6).

3. NT

In the NT we still find traditional Jewish formulas of blessing and greeting (John 20:19, 21, 26; Luke 1:28; 2 Thess. 3:16), but they are changed in the Epistles (2 Tim. 4:22a), often expanded to include a wishing of → grace (2 Tim. 4:22b). Hellenistic influence is apparent here. The blessing is also given an introduction and a conclusion, usually binitarian (e.g., Rom. 1:7; 1 Cor. 1:3) or Christological (Rom. 16:20b; 1 Cor. 16:23, etc.). This is the practice in most NT epistles.

At meals we find the OT Jewish practice of table blessing in the form of thanks and praise to God (Mark 6:41 and par.; 14:22 and par.; Luke 24:30; 1 Cor. 11:24; → Eucharist 2.2; Eulogia). For other blessings of → Jesus (Mark 10:13-16 and par.; Luke 24:50-51), we do not have the formula but only gestures like the laying on or lifting up of the hands (Mark 10:16; Luke 24:50). In light of these examples — as well as other passages such as Matt. 10:12-13 and par.; Gal. 3:8-9, 13-14; and Acts 3:25-26 — we may say of the NT as a whole that it basically modifies, but does not abrogate, the OT view of blessing as Yahweh's constant intervention in history through what he has done in Christ. Blessing is now oriented to the saving work of Christ, and it confirms a relation to the → salvation that will be fully actualized only eschatologically (Matt. 25:34; → Eschatology).

4. History

Almost without exception, Christian churches have used forms of salutation (see 2 and 3) and episcopal prayers of blessing in their → worship. In the West these soon assumed a succinct and pregnant form. Fixed formulas developed and found increasing use, and after the 11th century, in view of the importance of the sacrament of the altar, they largely came after, rather than before, Communion. The simple Trinitarian concluding blessing that has now become the most essential formula of blessing in the Roman Catholic → Mass appeared for the first time in 1230. M. → Luther (1483-1546) and U. → Zwingli (1484-1531) at first retained this but later recommended the Aaronic blessing, which, besides the → Enlightenment and → rationalism, has been determinative in the → Lutheran churches. The Roman Mass of 1970/1974 (→ Liturgical Books) contains not only the final Trinitarian blessing but 20 other blessing formulas, among them the Aaronic, along with many blessing prayers for special feasts and seasons in the → church year.

In contrast to the Trinitarian opening blessing ("In the name of the Father and of the Son and of the Holy Spirit"), the closing blessing marks the transition from worship to everyday life, and it binds the two together by basically promising the divine presence that has been experienced in Word and → sacrament and by asking for God's protection and help in personal life. Blessing has the same function also for transition situations in life, which the churches give to those affected.

Roman Catholics also bless material objects, including gifts of nature and products of technology. Similar on the Protestant side is the blessing of produce at → harvest festivals. Also in this category are acts of consecration, for example, of church buildings (→ Church Dedication), institutions, and liturgical vessels, as well as of schools, public buildings, and bridges, though in practice these are not strictly blessings (→ Benediction; Sacramentals). In English-speaking Protestant churches, the practice of blessing palm branches, water, and houses has increased.

The ancient constitutive aspects of blessings — namely, the intervention that is sought from God and the praise that is offered to him — may be seen especially at the celebration of the → Eucharist when the → eucharistic prayer is used. The epiclesis as an invoking of the Holy Spirit upon the communicants and the anamnesis as a recollecting of God's saving act in Christ to make it present actualize these two aspects. In the Eucharist, with its linking to an act of blessing by word and elements, we have the basis of blessings at meals in Protestant → piety, at least where there is a eucharistic understanding.

5. Signs

The gesture of laying on of hands, to which the Bible bears frequent witness (see 3; also Gen. 48:14; Acts 8:17; 2 Tim. 1:6), comes into play in many blessings at → occasional services, at which Roman Catholics and others also use oil, → holy water, and → incense. If the blessing is passed on to many people at once, the uplifting of the hands replaces the laying on of hands (see 3; also Lev. 9:22; Sir. 50:20).

In the Middle Ages the → sign of the cross, known from the earliest days of Christianity, became the decisive gesture of blessing and was used at the concluding blessing, the consecration of the eucharistic elements, → ordination, and official actions and dedications. In the 14th century it became customary to end the increasingly popular Corpus Christi processions (→ Eucharistic Spirituality) with an act of blessing, at which the sign of the cross was then made with the monstrance (→ Liturgical Vessels). In Roman Catholic practice relative to these so-called sacramental blessings, we also find the sign of the cross being given with a reliquary (→ Relics) or an actual small cross.

6. Significance

Whereas the emphasis in the East lay on the doxological aspect of blessings (→ Orthodoxy 1; Liturgy 2), the West oriented blessing to God's relation to us and its real outworking in the divine promise and our petitions.

The new Roman Catholic benedictional relativizes denominational differences by stressing the need for the → Word of God, ceremonies that Christians share in common, and the personal use of consecrated things in accordance with a Protestant understanding of blessing (1 Tim. 4:4-5).

→ Rite; Sacramentality

Bibliography: S. Ben-Chorin, *Betendes Judentum* (Tübingen, 1980) • R. Berger et al., "Gestalt des Gottesdienstes," *Gottesdienst der Kirche* (ed. H. B. Meyer et al.; Regensburg, 1987) 30-39 • H. W. Beyer, "Εὐλογέω κτλ.," *TDNT* 2.754-65 • *The Congregation's Life: Proposed Services to Be Included in a Book of Worship (United Church of Christ)* (St. Louis, 1982) • J. G. Davies, ed., *A New Dictionary of Liturgy and Worship* (London, 1986) • P. Evdokimov, *Das Gebet der Ostkirche* (Graz, 1986) • K. Frör, "Salutationen, Benediktionen, Amen," *Leit.* 2.569-97, esp. 587-92 • A. C. Myers, "Bless," *ISBE* 1.523-24 • *Occasional Services: A Companion to the Lutheran Book of Worship* (Minneapolis, 1982) 183-91 • J. G. Plöger, "Vom Segen des Herrn," *Gott feiern* (ed. J. G. Plöger; 2d ed.; Freiburg, 1980) 275-93 • H. Graf Reventlow et al., "Formeln, liturgische," *TRE* 11.252-71; • P. Schäfer, R. Deichgräber, and J. G. Davies, "Benediktionen I-III," *TRE* 5.560-73 • H.-C. Schmidt-Lauber, "Gesten / Gebärden, Liturgische," *TRE* 13.151-55; idem, "Segnungsfeiern als ökumenischer Gottesdienst," *Heute segnen* (ed. A. Heinz and H. Rennings; Freiburg, 1987) 84-93 • F. Schulz, "Segnungen in evangelischer Sicht," ibid. 72-83 • C. Westermann, *Der Segen in der Bibel und im Handeln der Kirche* (Munich, 1986).

KLAUSJÜRGEN HEINRICH

7. The Papal Blessing

The term "papal blessing" is used in two senses. It refers to the blessing that the pope pronounces *urbi et orbi* (over the city of → Rome and the whole earth); it carries with it a full → indulgence. Second, it refers to the extreme unction that each priest may give at the hour of → death with confession of guilt and penance (→ Penitence); a full indulgence is again linked to it.

The papal blessing arose in connection with the rites of penance as the remission of all penalties when death was imminent (11th cent.), and Benedict XIV (1740-58) extended it considerably. Rules governing it appear in the celebration of sacraments for the sick (nos. 102 and 122) and in 1983 CIC 530.3.

→ Corpus Iuris Canonici; Pope 1

Bibliography: A. Adam and R. Berger, *Pastoralliturgisches Handlexikon* (Freiburg, 1980) • A. Franz, *Die kirchlichen Benediktionen im Mittelalter* (2 vols.; Graz, 1960; orig. pub., 1909).

THADDEUS A. SCHNITKER

Blind, Missions to the → Medical Missions

Bohemian Brethren

Around 1458 the Czech nobleman Gregory gathered around him a group that was called the Brotherhood of the Law of Christ, made up for the most part of the remnants of the → Hussite Taborites. This group soon came to be known as the Bohemian Brethren. Theologically they were influenced by the writings of the pacifist Peter Chelčický (ca. 1390-ca. 1460); in organization, they borrowed from the so-called Faithful Brethren, itinerant Waldensian preachers trained by the Taborites.

The young brotherhood survived two waves of persecution under King George of Podebrady (1420-71). In 1464 they formulated their goals in the Reichenau agreement. Then in 1467 they established their own priesthood, which completed the break both with Rome and with the Hussite church. Waldensians who in 1480 fled from Brandenburg to Bohemia and Moravia joined forces with them.

The concern of the Bohemian Brethren to retain rural ways of life prevented them from winning support in the towns and among the nobility. After Gregory's death in 1474, however, their aversion to city life began to weaken. Lukáš of Prague (d. 1528) initiated the change. Under him the Bohemian Brethren deliberately ended their first stage in 1495. The "Great Party" became autonomous and gave the brotherhood a fixed form with the doctrine of → justification by → faith, a → church order, and rules of worship. They moved into the towns and enlarged their membership, in spite of being declared illegal in 1508. They sought contacts outside; a friendly discourse between M. → Luther (1483-1546) and Lukáš reached its high point in 1523.

After the death of Lukáš the Bohemian Brethren finally opened themselves up to the nobility. Under the inspiration of the Protestant princes in Germany, nobles within the Bohemian Brethren sponsored their confession before king and provincial diet in 1535 and took part in the revolt of the estates against the Hapsburgs in the Schmalkaldic War of 1546/47. The victory of the emperor resulted in executions and confiscations, and many went into exile in Poland. In Moravia, Jan Blahoslav (1523-71) was able to continue work on philological study of the Bible and hymns.

After the Consensus Sandomiriensis (or Concord of Sandomierz) in 1570, the Polish Bohemian Brethren finally merged with the Reformed Polish and Lithuanian Church in approximately 1630. In Moravia they joined with Utraquists who favored P. → Melanchthon (*Confessio Bohemica*, 1575) to form a united church that gained official recognition in 1609. After the failure of the revolt of 1618, however, the Hapsburg Ferdinand II (1578-1637) rooted them out from all territories under the Bohemian crown. The ordinary members went underground; by 1628 all their preachers were in exile. In 1632, while in exile, J. A. Comenius (1592-1670) became the last bishop of the Czech Bohemian Brethren.

Of the émigré Bohemian Brethren, only the Polish branch retained relative independence, with D. E. Jablonski (1660-1741), grandson of Comenius, as its bishop from 1699. Jablonski also served as a Reformed court preacher in Berlin. After Jablonski's death J. G. Elsner (1717-82) became bishop. His Czech Reformed congregation in Berlin prepared a new edition of the Confession and Catechism (1748), and also of the hymnbook of Comenius (1753).

In Hungary the remnants of the Bohemian Brethren found a place in the Reformed Church, first in Skalica, then in Réca, near Bratislava. In about 1760 an attempt by the émigré Johann Slerka to reorganize the diaspora in Hungary, Silesia, and Prussia failed. More successful was the founding of Herrnhut (1722) by German-speaking Bohemian Brethren from Moravia. But these largely surrendered their own distinctiveness under the influence of the strong personality of the pietistically inclined Count N. L. von → Zinzendorf (1700-1760).

By 1781 the secret illegal remnants of the Bohemian Brethren in Bohemia and Moravia would accept either the Helvetic or the → Augsburg Confession. Their own confession enjoyed no legal recognition. Attempts to secure this in 1848, the year of revolutions, and then again ten years later, did not succeed. Only in the late winter of 1918, with the collapse of the Hapsburg monarchy, could the two tolerated churches unite and readopt their ancient confession. There thus came into being the Evangelical Church of the Bohemian Brethren, with a presbyterian-synodal constitution. This church now has some 300 congregations in Bohemia and Moravia. The seat of its synodal council is in Prague, where the Comenius Faculty of Theology (from 1919) sees to the continuation of the tradition.

Gregory had been convinced by P. Chelčický that the true church must always be a minority on the narrow road of discipleship. Christians should not try to achieve social or cultural security, and the church should renounce the Constantinian legacy. → Faith, → love, and → hope constitute the essence of Christianity. These three correspond, he said, to the essential things, the gracious divine initiatives (the Father's grace, the Son's merit, and the Spirit's gifts). They are helped by what he called the useful things: Scripture, → preaching, the → sacraments, and discipline. The national Bohemian Brethren groups (→ Moravian Church) have only a servant function, whereas Christ's church is universal and supranational. The theology of Lukáš set the direction up to the time of Comenius. In 1534 the Bohemian Brethren abandoned the rebaptism of converted adults (→ Anabaptists; Baptism); they also abandoned belief in the seven sacraments.

Bibliography: P. Brock, "Bohemian Brethren," *NCE* 2.636; idem, *The Political and Social Doctrines of the Unity of Czech Brethren in the Fifteenth and Early Sixteenth Centuries* (The Hague, 1957) • J. Gonnet and A. Molnár, *Les Vaudois au Moyen Age* (Turin, 1974) • F. Machilek, "Böhmische Brüder," *TRE* 7.1-8 • J. T. Müller, *Geschichte der Böhmischen Brüder* (3 vols.; Herrnhut, 1922-31) • E. Peschke, *Kirche und Welt in der Theologie der Böhmischen Brüder* (Berlin, 1981) • R. Rícan and A. Molnár, *Die Böhmischen Brüder* (Berlin, 1961) • M. Spinka, "Peter Chelčický, the Spiritual Father of the *Unitas Fratrum,*" *CH* 12 (1943) 271-91 • M. L. Wagner, *Peter Chelčický: A Radical Separatist in Hussite Bohemia* (Scottdale, Pa., 1983) • J. K. Zeman, *The Anabaptists and the Czech Brethren in Moravia, 1526-1628: A Story of Origins and Contacts* (The Hague, 1969).

Amedeo Molnár†

Bolivia

1. Peoples and Politics
   1.1. History
   1.2. Social History
2. Christian Churches
   2.1. Roman Catholic Church
   2.2. Historic Protestant Churches
       2.2.1. Baptists
       2.2.2. Methodists
       2.2.3. The Evangelical Christian Union
       2.2.4. Other Groups
       2.2.5. Evangelical Expansion

3. Relations among the Churches
   3.1. Evangelical Churches
   3.2. Roman Catholic and Evangelical Churches
4. Relations between Church and State
   4.1. Roman Catholics and the State
   4.2. Evangelicals and the State
5. Other Religious Groups

	1960	1980	2000
Population (1,000s):	3,351	5,355	8,329
Annual growth rate (%):	2.24	1.92	2.15

Area: 1,098,581 sq. km. (424,164 sq. mi.)

A.D. *2000*

Population density: 8/sq. km. (20/sq. mi.)
Births / deaths: 3.05 / 0.82 per 100 population
Fertility rate: 3.92 per woman
Infant mortality rate: 56 per 1,000 live births
Life expectancy: 63.6 years (m: 61.9, f: 65.3)
Religious affiliation (%): Christians 94.4 (Roman
Catholics 90.7, Protestants 7.4, indigenous 1.9,
marginal 1.8, other Christians 0.7), Baha'is 3.4, non-
religious 1.0, other 1.2.

1. Peoples and Politics

The topography of Bolivia ranges from the High
Andes (4,000-7,000 m. / 13,100-23,000 ft.) through
the inland valleys (2,200-3,000 m. / 7,200-9,800 ft.)
to the eastern lowlands (150 m. / 500 ft.). In 1997
urban dwellers accounted for 57.5 percent of the
population. Ethnically and culturally there are three
main groups: the Quechuas (30 percent), the Aymaras (25 percent), and the mestizos, or "mixed"
(25-30 percent). There are also several smaller, Indian groups (approximately 200,000 total). Politically
the country is a constitutional centralist republic
with a president at the head.

1.1. *History*

Historically Bolivia was independent under its ancient civilizations until 1535, when it became a
Spanish colony. In 1825, after a long war of freedom,
it gained its independence. In April 1952 the Bolivian
national revolution took place, which led to efforts
at a significant social revolution. However, Bolivia's
long history of coups and revolutions (over 200 between 1825 and 1985) have generally kept it from
realizing true stability. Since 1985 there have been
successive democratic governments, which holds out
a promise for improvement.

1.2. *Social History*

Bolivia, a country marked by profound ethnic and
cultural diversity, has not yet developed beyond what
we might call internal colonialism, which is supported by all organized, ruling, political forces. How
to develop a national consciousness remains an open
question, which should not be eclipsed by the issue
of imperialist dependence stressed by the traditional
Left. A further key social issue for Bolivia is the removal of its dependence on the cocaine trade. (Currently, about half the world's cocaine is grown in
Bolivia.)

2. Christian Churches

The expansion of Spanish → colonialism in America
brought Christianity to Bolivia at the end of the 16th
century. Until the end of the 19th century, the →
Roman Catholic Church represented the only Christian missionary force among the Indians. Later other
churches began work, and various denominations
and religious groups have come into the country.

2.1. *Roman Catholic Church*

The first missionaries reached present-day Bolivia
around 1540, but until the 1560s followed no specific
plan. In 1552 the bishopric of La Plata was founded,
but it had no resident bishop until 1563. In 1605 the
sees of La Paz and Santa Cruz were separated from
this jurisdiction, and this move established the
diocesan structure of the colonial period. The same
period saw the founding of almost 50 monasteries
(e.g., of the → Franciscans, → Dominicans, Mercedarians, → Augustinians, and → Jesuits). These became centers of ecclesiastical and cultural growth.
The Peruvian Provincial Councils regulated pastoral
activity in the 16th century, and later those of Char-
cas (1629-1774) along with some seven diocesan synods. The true missionary cell was the *doctrina* (missionary pastorate). Under the supervision of one or
more members of the orders, and later a diocesan
priest, this represented the decisive sphere of religious → acculturation, which affected → catechism,
→ preaching, the → liturgy, and sacramental practice. Only the Jesuits played an important part in
education with their grammar schools and the university St. Francis → Xavier of La Plata. After the
colonial regime had stabilized the boundaries that
ensured its actual control of the territory, the church
usually worked only in this area. But this restriction
was broken by the → conversion (§1) of the Mojo
and Chiquito (from the end of the 17th cent. to 1768)
by the Jesuits, and of the Apolobamba and Chiri-
guano by the Franciscans.

After the trauma of independence the church
slowly regained its power. The Franciscans took the
lead, reestablishing and extending their → mission
schools. The Jesuits returned in 1881, the Salesians
came in 1896, the Lazarists in 1905, the Redemp-
torists in 1910, and the Lasallians in 1912. Various

women's orders, which had been limited to the contemplative life in the colonial era, now took up the work of teaching and the care of the sick.

Roman Catholicism, which was never fully restored under the republic, was officially disestablished in 1961. It continues to enjoy unofficial recognition as the state church, but it is increasingly being challenged by liberal legislation permitting freedom of belief, by the attrition and absence of its lay members from public life, by the increasing lack of vocations to the priesthood, by the evangelistic zeal of Protestants, and by → Marxist propaganda. The official reaction to this crisis at the end of the 20th century was threefold: (1) the use of foreign personnel (priests and nuns); (2) dependence on increasing sums of capital to finance operations; and (3) the freezing and opposing of tendencies toward the Indianizing of culture and the mobilizing of the Indian people, with a simultaneous restriction of any public activity apart from the representations of the → hierarchy to the successive governments. In 1992 the Roman Catholic Church had 922 priests, 192 brothers, and 1,945 sisters.

2.2. Historic Protestant Churches

2.2.1. Baptists

A. Reekie, a Canadian pastor, came to Oruro in 1898, but his work proceeded slowly. A. Baker began work among the Aymaras in 1913. The Baptists opened the first Protestant church in Bolivia at Oruro in 1923. In 1936 the mission adopted the name Unión Bautista Boliviana (UBB, Baptist Union of Bolivia). The Canadian Baptist Mission joined the UBB in 1973. The UBB has a theological seminary at Cochabamba and a radio station La Cruz del Sur (The Southern Cross) at La Paz. It 1990 it numbered approximately 30,000 adherents.

2.2.2. Methodists

From 1891 the Methodists had a preacher in Oruro, who went to La Paz in 1901. After freedom of belief became legally established, the Methodist Episcopal Church of the United States took up missionary work. In 1907 F. Harrington founded the Instituto Americano (a high school) in La Paz, and another in Cochabamba in 1912. In those early days, conversions were rare but were not the central concern. Missionary work was begun among the Aymaras, and growth followed after 1952. In 1969 the churches declared their autonomy and took the name Iglesia Evangélica Metodista en Bolivia (Evangelical Methodist Church of Bolivia). This church, which in 1990 numbered 31,000 adherents in 150 congregations, is marked by sensitivity to local sociopolitical problems, an ability to adjust to the Latin American context, and an interest in liberation theology.

2.2.3. The Evangelical Christian Union

From 1903 the Allan family lived in Bolivia, where, with support from England, Australia, and New Zealand, they founded the Bolivian Indian Mission (BIM) for the → evangelizing of the Indians. After 1916 the BIM became dependent on support from the United States. Its first centers were in San Pedro de Buenavista and Cochabamba. It worked especially among the Quechuas in eastern Bolivia. The Unión Christiana Evangélica (UCE) came into existence in 1950 on the basis of the BIM, and after 1959 it was followed by the South American Evangelical Union (though the BIM still continues as a supporting society). Growth accelerated after 1952, with some 67,000 adherents in 1990. Organizationally the union has sought decentralization and autonomy vis-à-vis foreign missionary societies.

2.2.4. Other Groups

One group that merits special mention is the Iglesia Nacional Evangélica Los Amigos (INELA, Friends National Evangelical Church), which arose out of the Cuaquero mission from Oregon in 1931. This has maintained itself as an Aymara church and has enjoyed spectacular growth, from 75 members in 1929 to 22,000 in 1990. It renounced all foreign support in 1963. The Assemblies of God have also seen rapid growth. Beginning work in 1946 and ministering predominantly among the Aymaras, they grew from 300 in 1950 to 55,000 in 1990. It is the only Pentecostal church of significance.

Seventh-day Adventists came to Bolivia in 1907; by 1920 their mission to the Aymaras had begun to see fruit. They have grown to become the largest Protestant denomination, with 68,000 adherents in 1990. Among the Protestants, the Adventists are isolated and have not been without conflict.

2.2.5. Evangelical Expansion

Although full statistics are lacking, evangelicals in Bolivia have manifested dramatic growth, from 250 in 1916 to 17,000 in 1952 to approximately 320,000 members in 1990 (with perhaps an equal number of nonmember adherents).

3. Relations among the Churches

3.1. Evangelical Churches

Cooperation among evangelical churches has been difficult because of the tendency of missions to form enclaves and because of the differences in denominational and national traditions. Several efforts, however, deserve mention: the Conferencia Regional para Bolivia (La Paz, 1916), which apportioned areas among the missions; the Conferenzia de Obreros Evangélicos Nacionales (La Paz, 1935); preparatory steps toward the formation of a Consejo Evangélico de Bolivia (National Council of Churches, 1941), which ultimately failed; the Iglesias Unidas of La Paz, Cochabamba, and Santa Cruz, which share pastors.

Wishing to keep intact their respective dogmatic traditions, churches have typically resisted the establishment of synodal structures. This difficulty became clear at the time of the forming of the fundamentalistically oriented (→ Fundamentalism) Asociación Nacional de Evangélicos (ANE) in 1965 and the ecumenically oriented Asociación Nacional de Evangélicos de Bolivia (ANDEB) in 1966. Yet evangelicals have cooperated in some areas, such as the translation and dissemination of the Bible (United → Bible Societies, with help from Adventists and Roman Catholics), theological education (the Asociación Boliviana de Educación Teológica — ABET, which shares information), social action (the Comisión Boliviana de Acción Social Evangélica — COMBASE, and the Alfabetización y Literatura — ALFALIT), and evangelistic crusades (including, since 1965, the ambitious program of Evangelism-in-Depth).

3.2. Roman Catholic and Evangelical Churches

Historically, relations between Catholics and evangelicals have been stormy, with frequent misunderstandings as well as incidents even of missionaries murdered and churches attacked. Only after → Vatican II have some mutual efforts emerged, such as cooperation in Bible translation and joint membership in Iglesia y Sociedad en América Latina (ISAL).

4. Relations between Church and State

4.1. Roman Catholics and the State

After the passing of the law declaring freedom of belief in 1906, the Roman Catholic Church ceased to be the state church but still enjoys very high regard. Bolivia had never ratified a → concordat with the Vatican but has regulated relations by pacts and agreements, including the Convección Misionera in 1957, establishing → military chaplaincies in 1958, and granting the church freedom from customs dues in 1964.

4.2. Evangelicals and the State

Missionaries have been content with the guarantee of freedom of belief, although in a few cases they have made arrangements for special projects (e.g., in health and education).

5. Other Religious Groups

→ Mormons, → Jehovah's Witnesses, and → Baha'is also are represented in Bolivia. With 69,000 adherents, the Mormons are as numerous as any single Protestant group. All three engage in intensive propagation. → Spiritism of Brazilian origin also deserves mention. Finally, there are many new syncretistic groups, centered in villages or even individuals, which have blended indigenous beliefs and Christian components, and which reflect the mentality, religiosity, and culture of many segments of the population, both urban and rural. Neither the Roman Catholics nor the Protestants have so far developed effective ministries with such groups.

Bibliography: M. Arias, "El protestantismo," *Presencia* 6/8 (1975) 181-89 • J. M. Barnadas, *La iglesia católica en Bolivia* (La Paz, 1976) • W. T. Boots, "Protestant Christianity in Bolivia" (Diss., Washington, D.C., 1971) • *Guía Eclesiástica. Bolivia 1981* (La Paz, 1981) • K. E. Hamilton, *Church Growth in the High Andes* (Lucknow, 1962) • R. A. Hudson and D. M. Hanratty, eds., *Bolivia: A Country Study* (3d ed.; Washington, D.C., 1991) • O. E. Leonard, *Bolivia: Land, People, and Institutions* (Washington, D.C., 1952) • P. Madeyski, "Das Entwicklungsland Bolivien und seine Kirche" (Diss., Mannheim, 1970) • J. L. Mecham, *Church and State in Latin America* (2d ed.; Chapel Hill, N.C., 1966) • Q. Nordyke, *Animistic Aymaras and Church Growth* (Newberg, Oreg., 1974).

Josep M. Barnadas

Bonhoeffer, Dietrich

Dietrich Bonhoeffer (1906-45) was a German Lutheran theologian, → pastor, and → martyr. A member of the large and prominent Berlin family of Karl Bonhoeffer and Paula von Hase, Bonhoeffer first studied at Tübingen, then took his doctorate in theology at Berlin, where he studied with A. Harnack, K. Holl, and R. Seeberg. Early allied with Karl → Barth's theological movement, Bonhoeffer thought independently, yet continued to read Barth and contact him personally at crucial periods in his life. He traveled to Rome and North Africa (1924), served a pastorate in Barcelona (1928-29), and had a postdoctoral fellowship at Union Theological Seminary, New York (1930-31), where he studied with Reinhold → Niebuhr, became a friend of Paul Lehmann, and was deeply impressed by African American Christianity (→ Black Churches 1).

Becoming a lecturer in theology at Berlin in 1931, Bonhoeffer was also active in the ecumenical movement and, from the outset, an uncompromising opponent of National Socialism, especially the ideological corruption of the churches and Nazi → anti-Semitism. Absent from the → Barmen Synod while serving a German congregation in London (1933-35), Bonhoeffer was a leader in the → Confessing Church and director of its theological seminary in Finkenwalde. After the Gestapo closed the seminary, and concerned about how his → pacifism and refusing military service would affect the church, he accepted an invitation by Niebuhr and Lehmann to New York in 1939. He quickly returned to Germany, however, convinced that he must share the fate of his nation during war in order to contribute to its reconstruction in peace.

Through family contacts he joined the resistance circle around Canaris in the German military intelligence, used his ecumenical contacts to bring important information about the resistance movement to Allied church and government leaders, and supported the plans to assassinate Hitler. Shortly after his engagement to Maria von Wedemeyer in 1943, he was imprisoned in Tegel Prison, Berlin, on April 5. After the failure of the July 20, 1944, assassination attempt, Hitler ordered reprisals that killed several thousand resisters, including three members of Bonhoeffer's family; he himself was hanged in Flossenbürg on April 9, 1945.

A widely influential theologian whose writings have been translated into many languages, Bonhoeffer, in his dissertation, entitled *Sanctorum Communio*, showed his alignment with Barth's theology of → revelation but also his own characteristic emphasis on the human, social, and temporal impact of God's revelation. The church as "Christ existing as community" is simultaneously a reality of revelation and a sociological form. Bonhoeffer interpreted the church as part of a larger "Christian social philosophy," insisting that all Christian doctrines have a "social intention."

Act and Being, Bonhoeffer's *Habilitationsschrift,* revealed his philosophical sophistication in exploring the theological import of the transcendental and → ontological traditions. After these early systematic works, most of Bonhoeffer's writings during the 1930s were more occasional, covering ecumenical essays and addresses, church politics, → ethics, → exegesis, sermons, and → pastoral theology. *Creation and Fall* and *Christ the Center* derived from university lectures in 1932-33, while *Life Together* reflected the discipline of the Finkenwalde community. Most influential during Bonhoeffer's lifetime was his *Cost of Discipleship.* Largely a meditation on the → Sermon on the Mount, it argues that → faith and → obedience are two inseparable moments in the life of Christian → discipleship; its attack on "cheap grace" reflects the struggle of Christians in Germany to remain faithful as well as Bonhoeffer's own personal commitment.

Two posthumous works have also been very influential. The incomplete *Ethics,* written during Bon-

hoeffer's resistance work, presents a Christocentric contextual ethic especially concerned with how Christian → responsibility and → freedom engage issues of public life. His *Letters and Papers from Prison* had a catalytic effect in the 1960s like the earlier *Romans* of Barth and Bultmann's contemporary → demythologizing proposal. In response to the increasing power of humanity in the Western world and other secular developments, Bonhoeffer analyzed the decay of "religion" as a marginal segment of life rooted in weakness and dependency, sketching a "nonreligious" interpretation of Christianity modeled on the freedom of Jesus in "being for others."

Bibliography: Primary sources (collected works): Dietrich Bonhoeffer Werke (17 vols.; Munich and Gütersloh, 1986ff.) German critical edition • *Dietrich Bonhoeffer Works* (Minneapolis, 1995-) English edition, two volumes published to date: *Act and Being* (1996); *Life Together / Prayerbook of the Bible* (1995) • G. B. KELLY and F. B. NELSON, eds., *A Testament to Freedom: The Essential Writings of Dietrich Bonhoeffer* (rev. ed.; San Francisco, 1995).

Primary sources (monographs in English translation): Christ the Center (San Francisco, 1978) • *The Cost of Discipleship* (New York, 1995) • *Creation and Fall / Temptation* (New York, 1966) • *Ethics* (New York, 1995) • *Fiction from Prison* (Philadelphia, 1981) • *Letters and Papers from Prison* (New York, 1972) • *Love Letters from Cell 92* (Nashville, 1995) • *No Rusty Swords* (New York, 1965) • *Sanctorum Communio* (New York, 1964) • *Spiritual Care* (Philadelphia, 1985) • *True Patriotism* (New York, 1973) • *The Way to Freedom* (New York, 1966).

Secondary works: E. BETHGE, *Dietrich Bonhoeffer: Theologian, Christian, Contemporary* (London and New York, 1970) • E. FEIL, *Bonhoeffer Studies in Germany: A Survey of Recent Literature* (Philadelphia, 1997); idem, "Standpunkte der Bonhoeffer-Interpretation," *TRev* 64 (1968) 1-14; idem, ed., *Internationale Bibliographie zu Dietrich Bonhoeffer* (Gütersloh, 1997) • W. W. FLOYD JR. and C. J. GREEN, *Bonhoeffer Bibliography: Primary Sources and Secondary Literature in English* (Evanston, Ill., 1992). For secondary literature in English, see especially studies by J. Burtness, K. Clements, T. Day, A. Dumas, E. Feil, W. Floyd, J. Godsey, C. Green, J. de Gruchy, D. Hopper, G. Kelly, R. Lovin, C. Marsh, J. Moltmann, H. Ott, and L. Rasmussen. The *Newsletter* of the International Bonhoeffer Society, English Language Section, publishes an annual bibliography update.

CLIFFORD GREEN

Bonifatiuswerk

Founded in 1849 as the *Bonifatiusverein,* the Bonifatiuswerk is a German Roman Catholic charitable organization for pastoral care among the → diaspora in Germany. With some 500,000 members, it promotes spiritual vocations, provides transportation for pastoral work, and supports the building of churches and educational centers, always in the form of help for self-help. Its work has spread to the Scandinavian countries, including Iceland. It also promotes interdenominational dialogue, helped to found the Johann-Adam-Möhler Institute at Paderborn, and distributes four newsletters about the diaspora situation (with a total circulation of 1.4 million copies). Associated societies are the Bonifatiuswerk der Kinder (1894), the Katholische Diaspora-Kinderhilfe (1885), the Diaspora MIVA (1949, for transportation aid), and the Akademische Bonifatius-Einigung (1876).

Bibliography: Bonifatiusblatt (Paderborn, since 1852) • GENERALVORSTAND DES BONIFATIUSVEREINS, *In heiliger Sendung–100 Jahre Diaspora-Arbeit* (Paderborn, 1949) • *Handbuch des Bonfatiuswerkes* (Paderborn, 1964) • A. I. KLEFFNER and W. WOKER, *FS zum 50jährigen Bestehen des Bonifatiouswerks* (Paderborn, 1899).

BEATUS BRENNER

Book of Common Prayer

The Book of Common Prayer is the most common name of the prayer book used in the → Anglican Communion in regular → worship (§2). Along with the Bible, it has something of the status of a standard of faith among Anglicans.

The Book of Common Prayer is a product of the English → Reformation (§2.4) and may be compared with the service books of other Reformation churches. It was first introduced in 1549 under the leadership of Archbishop T. → Cranmer (1489-1556) in order to provide the English church with a suitable order of worship. It included morning and evening prayer, the Psalms, a lectionary, the → Eucharist, the litany, offices for → baptism and confirmation (→ Initiation Rites), a → catechism, and orders for → marriage, visitation of the sick, → funerals, thanksgiving after childbirth, and commination (→ Penitence). An order for the ordination of → deacons, → priests, and → bishops (the so-called ordinal) was added in 1550. The book was established by law rather than by the church courts.

A second book followed in 1552 by parliamentary enactment. The contents, which now included the ordinal, were overall much the same. However, because of criticism both by conservatives and by those on the side of reform who had been influenced by U. → Zwingli (1484-1531) and J. → Calvin (1509-64), the structure of the services and the text and rubrics were so greatly altered that the theology expressed in the book differs radically at certain points from that of the 1549 book, as all the changes were definitely in a Protestant direction. In 1553 the Catholic Mary Tudor (1553-58) came to the throne, and with the gradual re-Catholicizing of England, the Book of Common Prayer was abandoned and the Latin liturgy restored. Under Elizabeth (1558-1603), however, the 1552 Book of Common Prayer was restored in 1559, with three alterations, again attaining official liturgical rank by act of Parliament. The strong opposition of the Puritans both to the → authority of the church and to various rites could not overthrow the established liturgical order either under Elizabeth or under James I (1603-25), who brought out a new edition in 1604.

The growing strength of the Puritan middle class and the influence of the Scottish Presbyterians finally succeeded in abolishing the monarchy and episcopate in 1644 and at the same time in making the Book of Common Prayer illegal, replacing it by the Directory for Public Worship. After the Restoration (1660), however, Parliament in 1662 restored the book in essentially its previous form, although enlarged and modernized. With amendments to permit minor alterations, the law of 1662 made the Book of Common Prayer the single, legal prayer book in the Church of England, a status it enjoyed until 1975. The Church of England (Worship and Doctrine) Measure (1974, No. 3) gave the church for the first time the right to issue liturgical books on its own authority as long as the 1662 edition could also still be used.

Attempts were made in 1927-28 to get a revision through Parliament, which were unsuccessful because of suspected "Romanizing" tendencies. The failure of this effort provided an occasion for thinking more deeply about the meaning and shape of liturgy and ultimately led, on the basis of liturgical and theological studies associated with the → liturgical movement, to the use of alternative texts, beginning in 1965 (all with parliamentary sanction). Experience with these texts led to the composition of an Alternative Service Book (1980) for ten years of trial use in the worship of the Church of England. This gave the church two prayer books that differ considerably in underlying theology as well as ritual.

The life span of the Alternative Service Book was later extended another ten years to give some space for setting up experiments leading to a liturgical form that is suitable for the third millennium. Additional services have in the meantime been authorized by the General Synod.

From 1789 we must distinguish different forms of the Book of Common Prayer, since at that time the Episcopal Church in the United States adopted its own prayer book. In the 20th century most of the member churches of the Anglican Communion have brought out their own revisions, so that today we must speak of the Books of Common Prayer. The 1979 revision by the American Episcopal Church has given both the Anglican Communion and all Western churches a new standard, for it has been called the finest achievement of the modern liturgical movement (G. Wainwright). The same holds true for the 1985 Book of Alternative Services of the Anglican Church of Canada. Future revisions will have to measure themselves by these books.

Bibliography: F. E. BRIGHTMAN, *The English Rite* (2 vols.; 2d ed.; London, 1921) • C. O. BUCHANAN, T. LLOYD, and H. MILLER, eds., *Anglican Worship Today* (London, 1980) • G. J. CUMING, *A History of Anglican Liturgy* (2d ed.; London, 1982) the standard work • G. J. CUMING and S. G. HALL, "Book of Common Prayer," *TRE* 7.80-83 • M. J. HATCHETT, *Commentary on the American Prayer Book* (New York, 1981) • T. A. SCHNITKER, *The Church's Worship: The 1979 American Book of Common Prayer in a Historical Perspective* (New York, 1989).

THADDEUS A. SCHNITKER

Book of the Covenant

The Book of the Covenant, which comprises Exod. 20:22–23:19 (or perhaps through 23:33), is the oldest legal code in the Pentateuch. It takes its name from Exod. 24:7 (although it is an open question whether the phrase here refers specifically to the material of the earlier chapters). In the present text the Book of the Covenant is related to the events at Sinai, being put between the theophany depicted in 19:1–20:21 and the covenant described in 24:1-11. Special theological importance is thus ascribed to it.

The heading in Exod. 21:1 introduces the specific provisions, but a prologue precedes this in 20:22-26. A series of sacral regulations that relate materially to the prologue concludes the book in 23:10-19. The passage 23:20-33 is an epilogue.

Along with the sacral framework the Book of the Covenant contains legal provisions that vary greatly in form and content. Casuistic rules regarding slaves, liability, property, and various types of injury are given. Then from 21:12 — and especially from 22:16 — we have very different laws that A. Alt (1883-1956) called apodictic. At points these contain additions, especially → parenetic comments, such as at 22:21 and 23:9.

The time and manner of development of the Book of the Covenant are much debated. A likely date is between the conquest and the formation of the state (A. Jepsen; → Israel).

Bibliography: H. J. BOECKER, *Recht und Gesetz im Alten Testament und im Alten Orient* (2d ed.; Neukirchen, 1984) esp. 116-53 • F. CRÜSEMANN, *Tora* (Munich, 1992) esp. 132-234 • R. J. FOLEY, "Book of the Covenant," *NCE* 2.698-99 • A. JEPSEN, *Untersuchungen zum Bundesbuch* (Stuttgart, 1927) • E. OTTO, *Wandel der Rechtsbegründungen in der Gesellschaftsgeschichte des antiken Israel* (Leiden, 1988) • S. M. PAUL, *Studies in the Book of the Covenant in the Light of Cuneiform and Biblical Law* (Leiden, 1970) • L. SCHWIENHORST-SCHÖNBERGER, *Das Bundesbuch* (Berlin, 1990).

HANS JOCHEN BOECKER

Bosnia and Herzegovina

	1960	1980	2000
Population (1,000s):	3,180	3,914	4,338
Annual growth rate (%):	1.32	1.04	0.10
Area: 51,129 sq. km. (19,741 sq. mi.)			

A.D. *2000*
Population density: 85/sq. km. (220/sq. mi.)
Births / deaths: 1.04 / 0.82 per 100 population
Fertility rate: 1.40 per woman
Infant mortality rate: 12 per 1,000 live births
Life expectancy: 74.0 years (m: 71.3, f: 76.7)
Religious affiliation (%): Muslims 72.8, Christians 23.7 (Orthodox 14.1, Roman Catholics 9.2, other Christians 0.5), nonreligious 2.3, atheists 1.2.

Bosnia (the northern part) and Herzegovina (the southern part), situated in the Balkan Peninsula, was recognized as an independent country in 1992. The country is bordered to the north and southwest by Croatia, and to the east and south by Serbia and Montenegro. The Slavs settled this area in the seventh century. In 1991 the main groupings of Bosnia and Herzegovina's population were Bosnian Muslims (43.7 percent), Bosnian Serbs (31.3 percent), and Bosnian Croats (17.3 percent). All the main Bosnian ethnic groups are of South Slavic origin. These figures were radically affected by the war in Bosnia, which started in 1992 and caused extensive displacement and casualties. By 1995 an estimated 200,000 people had been killed and more than 2 million made refugees.

The Romans occupied this area in the first century B.C. In A.D. 395 it became part of the Western Roman Empire. Since the Great Schism in 1054, it has remained under the jurisdiction of the Roman Catholic Church. Christianity was introduced to the regions near present-day Bosnia and Herzegovina as early as the first century, through the apostle Paul's missions. The organized forms of Christianity were sporadically established in Bosnia and Herzegovina itself in the pre-Slavic ages. Yet the impact of Christianity on Bosnia was minimal until the tenth century because of its geographic isolation as a land-locked, mountainous region.

In the Middle Ages Bosnia was a separate kingdom and the last of the South Slavic provinces to lose its independence. In the 12th century, "Ban" Kulin, the Bosnian sovereign, laid the foundations for an autonomous Bosnian church, independent of both Rome and Byzantium. This church is often identified by historians as a dualistic Manichaean sect called the Bogomils (meaning "beloved by God"). However, the contemporary native sources prefer the term *Krstiani,* which simply means "Christians." Ban Kulin himself, as well as many subsequent rulers of Bosnia, were Krstiani and claimed that they were "good Catholics." In 1340 the Franciscans organized the Vicariate of Bosnia to reestablish Roman Catholicism across the country.

In the 15th and 16th centuries the religious history of Bosnia and Herzegovina took another turn when the Turks extended their control over Bosnia (1463) and Herzegovina (1482). With the occupation came widespread conversions to Islam, largely for economic or political reasons and particularly among the Krstiani, whose Bosnian church was weakened after the fall of the Bosnian Kingdom. In the subsequent centuries the Krstiani completely disappeared as a separate and distinct religious group. During the Turkish invasion many Catholic Bosnian Croats escaped to Croatia, and after the fall of Serbia to the Turks in 1389, Orthodox Christian Serbs in a large number found refuge in Bosnia and Herzegovina.

When the Turks were defeated in the late 19th century, tensions arose in Bosnia between the Croats, who welcomed the new Austro-Hungarian rule in 1878, and the Bosnian Muslims and Serbs, who opposed it. Tensions exploded in 1914 in the Bosnian capital, Sarajevo, when a Serbian nationalist assassinated the Austro-Hungarian archduke. This event was the infamous spark that ignited World War I.

At the close of the war in 1918, Bosnia and Herzegovina became a part of the newly established southern union called the Kingdom of Yugoslavia, ruled by a Serbian monarch. During World War II the country was incorporated into the independent state of Croatia. After the war Bosnia and Herzegovina was recognized as one of the six republics of the Communist-ruled Yugoslavia. The Bosnian citizens coexisted in peace until shortly after the collapse of Communism in 1990. After the breakup of Yugoslavia in 1991, Bosnian Croats and Muslims joined in support of independence of Bosnia and Herzegovina in 1992. Bitter conflict broke out, however, when Bosnian Serbs, with support from Serbia, moved militarily to seize 70 percent of Bosnian land in an effort to join Serbian-populated areas of Croatia and of Bosnia and Herzegovina into a "Greater Serbia." The war and the Serbs' tactic of "ethnic cleansing" affected Bosnian Muslims most severely.

Serbs who favored the war have used the old European idea of "the defense of the Christian West" to gain sympathy for their fight against "the onslaught of fundamentalist Islam." But for most Bosnian Muslims the term "muslim" is not primarily a religious designation; it is the way they identify themselves culturally. Since the 1961 census the official distinction has been made for Muslims with a capital *M* as "Muslims in the ethnic sense." These "Muslims" include many atheists, as well as some of other religious affiliation. On the other side are Muslims with a lower case *m,* or "muslims in the religious sense." These Muslims are Sunnis of the Hanafite rite. Various sects and dervish orders were more numerous and more popular in the past. The connection these Muslim orders had with the medieval Krstiani, who also had monastic organizations, must not be overlooked. An Islamic seminary opened in Sarajevo in 1977.

Before World War II Sarajevo was home to 104 Muslim mosques and also 5 synagogues (four were Sephardic and the other, Ashkenazic). Jewish adherents constituted 12 percent of the city's population. The Sarajevo Haggadah is very famous. During the Holocaust, however, the Jewish community in Bosnia was almost completely exterminated.

Roman Catholics also have two seminaries in Sarajevo, and in 1994 the archbishop was promoted to the rank of cardinal. There have been four Croatian translations of the Bible, each originating in Bosnia. Medjugorje, the site of reported apparitions of the Virgin Mary, is situated in southwest

Herzegovina. The Catholic population declined after World War I, when many left Bosnia.

In contrast, the Orthodox Christian population in Bosnia and Herzegovina increased in the period between the two world wars but then declined after World War II. Before the Second World War there was one Serbian Orthodox seminary in Sarajevo. Eastern Herzegovina is predominantly Orthodox.

Protestantism arrived in Bosnia with the Austrians, who established the first Lutheran communities in the country. Only a few of these communities still exist today. Bosnia and Herzegovina has fewer Protestant believers than any other country in Europe. All the Protestants in Bosnia and Herzegovina together (mostly Seventh-day Adventists, Lutherans, Pentecostals, and Baptists) total only 0.1 percent of the population.

Bibliography: R. ALI and L. LIFSCHULTZ, eds., *Why Bosnia? Writings on the Bosnian War* (Stoney Creek, Conn., 1993) • T. BRINGA, *Being Muslim the Bosnian Way: Identity and Community in a Central Bosnian Village* (Princeton, 1995) • G. S. DAVIS, *Religion and Justice in the War over Bosnia* (New York, 1996) • J. FINE, *The Bosnian Church: A New Interpretation* (Boulder, Colo., 1975) • F. FRIEDMAN, *The Bosnian Muslims: Denial of a Nation* (Boulder, Colo., 1996) • N. MALCOLM, *Bosnia: A Short History* (New York, 1994) • M. PINSON, ed., *The Muslims of Bosnia-Herzegovina: Their Historic Development from the Middle Ages to the Dissolution of Yugoslavia* (2d ed.; Cambridge, Mass., 1996) • M. A. SELLS, *The Bridge Betrayed: Religion and Genocide in Bosnia* (Berkeley, Calif., 1996) • E. WERBER, *The Sarajevo Haggadah: The Study* (Sarajevo, 1988).

PETER KUZMIČ

Botswana

Overview
1. Christian Churches
   1.1. Survey
   1.2. Church Life
   1.3. Ecumenical Relations
2. Church and State
3. Other Religions

Overview

Botswana is one of the least densely populated countries of Africa. This country on the sandy Kalahari plateau in southern Africa has had an extremely high rate of population growth (3.4 percent between 1988 and 1993), which was cause for concern. The dominant ethnic group is the Batswana (95 percent).

Botswana gained its independence from Great

	1960	1980	2000
Population (1,000s):	480	906	1,619
Annual growth rate (%):	2.68	3.46	2.10

Area: 581,730 sq. km. (224,607 sq. mi.)

A.D. 2000
Population density: 3/sq. km. (7/sq. mi.)
Births / deaths: 3.29 / 1.19 per 100 population
Fertility rate: 4.06 per woman
Infant mortality rate: 50 per 1,000 live births
Life expectancy: 52.5 years (m: 51.2, f: 53.6)
Religious affiliation (%): Christians 61.6 (indigenous 26.9, unaffiliated 17.9, Protestants 11.1, Roman Catholics 4.8, other Christians 0.9), tribal religionists 37.1, other 1.3.

Britain in 1966 and since that time has functioned as a relatively stable, multiparty democracy. The most important economic pursuits are mining, which is almost totally under the control of multinational corporations, and agriculture, which does not produce enough to feed the people. Livestock processing, oriented strongly to the export market, represents a major component of the economy. Economically Botswana is very dependent on South Africa, for example, for the import of technology and food, and for the supply of migrant workers, who, with an unemployment rate estimated officially at 35 percent, are unable to find work in Botswana.

1. Christian Churches
1.1. *Survey*
There are about 150 state-registered Christian groups. Membership figures are not reliable. Often membership of a tribe will be equated with that of a → church (e.g., the Bamangwato as United Congregational, the Bamalete as Lutheran, and the Bakgatla as Dutch Reformed). The biggest group are African indigenous churches, many having come into existence in Botswana. In a time of extreme cultural change, the presence of pre-Christian religious forms and a strong sense of group identity seem to allow the members of these indigenous churches to express both release and protest. Their numbers grow constantly, especially among those with little education.

Some churches are the result of Western missionary work (→ Mission). When Botswana ceased to be a British protectorate and became an independent → state in 1966, the Roman Catholic, Anglican, and Lutheran churches organized themselves as independent bodies or autonomous dioceses with African bishops; also becoming organized then were the Dutch Reformed Church and the United Congregational Church of Southern Africa (UCCSA). In some cases there were lengthy controversies between congregations in Botswana and church leaders in South Africa. In the case of the Evangelical Lutheran Church in Botswana (ELCB), these still continue in the 1990s. In 1978, when negotiations broke down, most of the Lutherans in Botswana registered as an Independent Church, but the leaders of the Evangelical Lutheran Church in Southern Africa (Botswana Diocese) reacted with judicial steps and pressure to stop personal and material support for the ELCB churches.

Missionary work began in Botswana in the first half of the 19th century. Missionaries came from neighboring countries, often when wars caused people groups to move (e.g., different tribes of the Batswana and the Herero). The call for missionaries arose in part through military considerations, especially because of the desire for weapons. Early missionary work was carried on by the London Missionary Society (LMS, including, in the 1840s, the earliest missionary journeys of D. Livingstone; the work was continued later by the UCCSA) and by the German Hermannsburg Mission (HM). Other German missionary societies expanded across the border into Botswana, including the Rhenish, Berlin, and Bleckmar missions. Roman Catholics began work in 1928 with the purchase of a farm by the German Father Rittmüller, O.M.I.

In 1857 the whole Bible was translated into Setswana. This was chiefly the work of R. Moffat (LMS) in South Africa and was the first complete translation of the Bible into an African language south of Ethiopia. In the 19th century several chieftains were won to Christianity, which led to serious conflicts within their tribes. Missions "from above" led to many traditional practices being abandoned or restricted (→ Initiation Rites). Khama III was baptized by H. C. Schulenburg (HM) in 1860, and as the ruler (1872-1923) of the most powerful tribe (Bamangwato), he implemented radical reforms that made Christianity practically the state religion (such as morning prayers at court; a national day of prayer for rain; thanksgiving for harvest; the prohibition of work or travel on Sunday; the prohibition of alcohol; the replacement of counselors by missionaries; the reform of laws of property, inheritance, and marriage in favor of women and the underprivileged).

1.2. Church Life

In the congregations women's organizations play a leading part, as do → elders and evangelists because of the relative lack of pastors. The congregations are mostly small and scattered, and the costs of travel are heavy because of the distances and poor roads. As a

rule, mission churches receive support from groups in South Africa or other foreign countries. In the → Independent Churches prominent features are → dancing, rapture, prophecy, public processions, baptisms in rivers and similar natural settings, and healings. All too often, such features have obscured the significant contributions of the Independent Churches in the fields of educational and social work.

1.3. Ecumenical Relations

The churches cooperate in mission work, in → evangelization, in educational work (also for → adults), in disseminating the Bible, in training for jobs in the churches, in providing various services, in hospitals and medical care, and in development projects, such as agriculture, crafts, trade, water supplies, and care for refugees. They are helped in this regard by missionary organizations and an ecumenical → diakonia. An important instrument is the Botswana Christian Council (BCC; → National Councils of Churches), founded in 1966, which is also represented in the → All Africa Conference of Churches and the → World Council of Churches. The 25 member churches of the BCC include the Roman Catholics and 11 African Independent Churches. Its goals are → development (§1; e.g., slum clearance) and theological education. The Botswana Theological Training Programme (BTTP) is a member of the BCC. This offers extension courses for laity, evangelists (→ Evangelization), and → pastors in English and Setswana. The BCC also engages in religious broadcasting, has an urban and industrial mission in the mining town of Selebi-Phikwe, and does work on behalf of refugees. It also supports a pioneering mission to the Hambukushu refugees who have settled in Etsha in northern Botswana. There also is a union of medical missions and a Bible society. Also in Botswana are Bread for the World, Misereor, and the → Lutheran World Federation (esp. on behalf of refugees; → Relief Organizations).

2. Church and State

The state registers churches and their constitutions according to the law governing societies. Fifteen are exempt from control. The constitution guarantees freedom of worship; furthermore, all school curricula provide for → religious instruction. A department of → theology (→ Theological Education) and → religious studies at the state-run → University of Botswana has four teaching positions and trains religious teachers and pastors. Courses lead to the B.A. and M.Th. degrees. In cooperation with the BTTP, extension studies lead to a diploma. Missionaries have often served as speaker in Parliament. Pastors have served as state officials. The government for its part expects the churches to contribute significant aid toward development. Christian faith and hope are invoked on national occasions such as the installation of chiefs, occasions of national mourning, and days of prayer for rain.

3. Other Religions
→ Islam and → Hinduism have a place only in the larger cities. Few nationals belong to them. → Baha'i has gained a surprising following among the Tswana, albeit rather small in absolute numbers. Traditional religions are those of the Batswana, Kalanga, Herero, and Basarwa. In the main centers of population they have little influence as a result of the prevailing modern lifestyle. The religion of the Batswana recognizes the creator-god Modimo, which has no images. Everyday life is influenced by the respectful intercourse of the living with their ancestors. Christians often observe ancestral customs (→ Guinea 2), and "Modimo" is the Christian name for God. → Magical practices are increasing in the cities. Traditional healers have a national organization.

Bibliography: J. M. CHIRENJE, *A History of Northern Botswana, 1850-1910* (Rutherford, N.J., 1977) • G. M. SETILOANE, *The Image of God among the Sotho-Tswana* (Rotterdam, 1976) • T. TLOU and A. CAMPBELL, *History of Botswana* (Gaborone, 1984).

HANS-MICHAEL SCHOOF

Bourgeois, Bourgeoisie

1. Etymology and Semantics
2. Background of the Rise of the Bourgeois Class
3. Bourgeois Society
4. The Bourgeoisie and Christianity

1. Etymology and Semantics
The word "bourgeois," in its earliest meaning as a burgher, is related to the medieval Ger. *burg,* or fortified place. Out of fortified places, cities in medieval times began to develop, in which (as they were later known) the bourgeois came to play an increasingly important role. The → city came into its own as certain groups of people — later collectively labeled the bourgeoisie — freed themselves from feudal ties, achieved economic power, and secured a measure of political → autonomy. The burgher, or the bourgeois, is the person who lives in a city and there enjoys a legally secure place. At first every city dweller was a bourgeois, but an oligarchy developed in the 12th century; since then the term "bourgeois" has been applied more specifically to this economic and political elite.

The age of absolutism saw considerable restriction of the autonomy of cities. Princely armies took over the duties of defense. In the cities, the bourgeois typically became an obedient subject, a responsible parent, and usually was fairly wealthy.

French thinkers in the 19th century talked about the active "citizen" of liberal views who was politically mature and who espoused the ideas of the French Revolution. Conservatives, however, rejected such a person as a traitor to the naturally or divinely given class system that history also validates (→ Conservatism). Marxism then introduced the concept of ideology, according to which the city dweller is the "bourgeois," the epitome of the → capitalistic exploiter. On this view there could be no true "citizens" before the social revolution. Thus the term "bourgeois" became the center of stormy debate during the 19th century. The threatened nobility used it as a term of opprobrium, while → Romantics found it useful in taking aim at the narrow-minded philistine.

"Bourgeois" and "bourgeoisie" as terms are still ambivalent. The meaning attached to them depends on the ideological and historical context and also on the user's intellectual and political assumptions. Social science has attempted to speak more generally of members of the middle class, but not with complete success. As used perhaps most broadly (and as used below), "bourgeois" refers to a person who is economically independent in production, trade, or the creation of capital.

2. Background of the Rise of the Bourgeois Class
The history of the term "bourgeois" points us to the social conditions that led to the rise and development of the European bourgeoisie. In cities, where artisans and merchants set up markets for the exchange of goods and established an independent jurisdiction, some citizens owned land, had their own houses, and arranged their own businesses. People who met these three conditions and who had lived in a walled city for a year and a day could become known publicly as "bourgeois."

Gradually the bourgeoisie managed to undermine the feudal agrarian economy and to replace it with a system based on the production and exchange of goods. The development of the economic power of the bourgeois soon had political and legal consequences. They became relatively independent of the nobility, throwing off feudal obligations and developing early democratic administrative structures. Their independence and political equality, however, were short lived. In the 13th and 14th centuries oligarchic patrician families seized political power in almost all European towns, although for a time, revolutionary movements of renewal on the part of the *arti minori* (small artisans and merchants) resisted this development.

From the 16th to the 18th century, centralization robbed the bourgeois of much of their political power. They were, however, offered positions in the army, the administration of justice, government, and the treasury, and it became possible for them to enter the nobility. Rulers worked out the system of ennobling in order to maintain a balance between the nobility and the middle class. This particularly French phenomenon came to an end in 1789. The French bourgeoisie achieved by ideology and force what the English middle class had achieved a century earlier by the Glorious Revolution. The German bourgeoisie did not succeed in imitating their neighbors, for their revolution of 1848 failed.

3. Bourgeois Society

The phrase "bourgeois society" is strongly loaded. The preference now in English is to speak of "middle class society," and the usage in German follows suit. The hope is to avoid the ambivalence of the term "bourgois," replacing it one without such negative connotations.

The bourgeois form of society might be characterized as follows. Its economy rests on the principle of supply and demand, on free enterprise, and on the profit motive (→ Achievement and Competition). Mass production and mechanization in large factories are the rule. The political order promotes equality before the law, inalienable basic rights, and a constitutional system with responsible government supported by an extensive → bureaucracy. The social order involves relative divisions and the functioning of institutions. Individuals enjoy great freedom compared with the experience in the older collectives. Achievement determines individual status. Urban conglomerates, strongly developed infrastructures, and extensive → communication networks are further features. The culture of the bourgeois society is strongly → individualistic and hence → pluralistic. The future is more important than tradition, this world than the next.

This sketch must be regarded, of course, as only a model. In fact, the middle-class societies of the West have all undergone modernization in their own ways. Thus Germany in the 19th century developed a bourgeois economic system without political → democracy. Marxism repudiates such a society because it means the dictatorship of the capitalist bourgeoisie, the antagonistic division of classes, and alienation by

the hostile force of labor (→ Work). → Conservatism criticizes especially the decay of traditions, the fragmenting of human relations, and the resultant intellectual lawlessness.

Many historical and sociological works have tried to evaluate what we here call bourgeois culture in its broadest sense. But the descriptions differ according to the age described, the country researched, and the specific groups within the middle class investigated. Yet there is one common feature. From the time of its rise, the bourgeoisie has helped to determine social, economic, and political structures. When it fought and vanquished entrenched powers and economic relations, bourgeois culture might be called dynamic and even revolutionary. But once it achieves power and economic success, the middle class chooses peace, order, and security. Historians and sociologists such as W. Sombart, M. → Weber, A. von Martin, and E. Barber have all pointed to this trend in bourgeois culture in the course of history.

More narrowly, people often use the term "bourgeois culture" (culture in the sense of theater, literature, and painting) to characterize artistic expression that focuses on the moral excellence, outward status, and political stability of the middle class. We find such drama in Dutch prose in the 17th century and then in the French and German theater of the 18th and 19th centuries. In general such artistic expression occurs in periods when the middle class has achieved economic success.

Bibliography: E. BARBER, *The Bourgeoisie in Eighteenth-Century France* (Princeton, 1967) • N. ELIAS, *Über den Prozeß der Zivilisation* (Bern, 1969) • B. GROETHUYSEN, *Die Entstehung der bürgerlichen Welt- und Lebensanschauung in Frankreich* (Halle, 1927) • M. GUGEL, *Industrieller Aufstieg und bürgerliche Herrschaft* (Cologne, 1975) • L. KOFLER, *Zur Geschichte der bürgerlichen Gesellschaft* (Neuwied, 1971) • G. KÖHLER et al., "Bürgertum," *TRE* 7.338-54 (extensive bibliography) • E. KOHN-BRAMSTEDT, *Aristocracy and the Middle Classes in Germany* (London, 1937) • W. MESCHKE, *Das Wort "Bürger." Geschichte seiner Wandlungen in Bedeutungs- und Wertgehalt* (Greifswald, 1952) • H. PEETERS, *Burgers en Modernisering* (Deventer, 1984) • W. SOMBART, *Der Bourgeois. Zur Geistesgeschichte der modernen Wirtschaftsmenschen* (Munich, 1927) • M. WEBER, "Die protestantische Ethik," *Archiv für Sozialwissenschaft und Sozialpolitik* 20-21 (1904-5).

HANS PEETERS

4. The Bourgeoisie and Christianity

The relation between the bourgeoisie and religion is ambivalent. Opposing feudalism, the European bourgeoisie disputed the absolutist claims of the church, as well as its intellectual traditionalism and ideological support for the absolute state. The English → deists, the French rationalists (→ Enlightenment), and the German critics of religion were not very close to Christianity. Closer was the so-called petite bourgeoisie, though the latter sometimes turned to the → free churches and sectarian movements. Max → Weber has rightly underlined the pluralism of bourgeoisie religion.

What we now call bourgeois religion arose only in the 19th century as the impoverished proletariat retreated into spiritual apathy and societal distrust, and as activists in the → labor movement took up the weapon of the Marxist criticism of religion. The churches then began to rely more heavily on the middle classes, which out of understandable self-interest turned themselves to religion, especially in France. The middle classes thus began to dominate church organization, its policy and ministry. In this way the main features of bourgeois religiosity began to emerge.

This religiosity promoted the values and virtues of marriage and family life and legitimated material welfare and social advance. It favored the maintenance of public order and offset the forces of social unrest and → revolution. Criticized already by S. → Kierkegaard, this bourgeois religiosity ran into new theological criticism in the decades after World War II. In the opinion of the critics, bourgeois religiosity robs Christianity of its messianic and eschatological power, and consequently the church cannot be an agent of societal change in favor of the lowly and oppressed along the lines of the → Sermon on the Mount. It has to give room to the "grassroots religiosity" of voluntary communities at the basis of the church that try to develop the social dimension of the gospel in modern society (→ Base Community).

Findings of social research, however, indicate that we no longer can speak simply of a general and strong affinity between the middle classes and the church. This may be true in France and Spain, but not in Italy and no more in Germany and the Netherlands. For some decades a better-educated portion of the middle class has left the church, so that in effect the various classes show no special pattern in their church attachment, with the exception that, sometimes, the lower classes are closer to religion and church. Similarly, the supremacy of the middle class on church committees was weakened. Research has also shown that ministers, especially the younger among them, do not preach bourgeois religiosity any longer and therefore do not always represent their congregations but live in open or secret conflict with them, supported by some theologians and members of the upper-middle class.

In spite of these findings, we cannot dismiss the concept of bourgeois religion out of hand. National surveys in several European countries show that those who stick more closely to supernatural beliefs and are more attached to the church also emphasize more strongly the so-called middle-class virtues. They champion family life, marriage, the traditional role of women, and the protection of life (→ Abortion). They are more content with existing conditions of life and the status quo of society, are more likely to vote for law and order, and are less concerned to exercise civil liberties. They are more inclined to label themselves as → conservatives, and at elections they vote more for the center and the right wing. When the belief dimension of this middle-class religiosity is compared with the organizational dimension of church allegiance, it can be pointed out that the former has a much heavier causal weight than the latter.

Religiosity, then, can be defined as a significant cultural force, mostly conservative, in both the private and the public spheres, and especially in politics. This cultural force is more or less operative in all social classes, but somewhat stronger among the lower ones. It is not incorrect, then, to speak of bourgeois religiosity so long as one does so with balance, with feeling for history, and with a sense of its different influence in the various fields of human life.

→ Civil Religion

Bibliography: P. EICHER, *Bürgerliche Religion* (Munich, 1983) • P. EESTER, L. HALMAN, and R. DE MOOR, eds., *The Individualizing Society: Value Change in Europe and North America* (Tilburg, 1994) • A. FELLING, J. PETERS, and O. SCHREUDER, *Dutch Religion: The Religious Consciousness of the Netherlands after the Cultural Revolution* (Nijmegen, 1991); idem, *Religion im Vergleich: Bundesrepublik Deutschland und Niederlande* (Frankfurt, 1987) • B. GROETHUYSEN, *Die Entstehung der bürgerlichen Welt- und Lebensanschauung in Frankreich* (Halle, 1927) • H. MCLEOD, *Religion and the People of Western Europe, 1789-1970* (Oxford, 1981) • K. MARX and F. ENGELS, *On Religion* (Chico, Calif., 1982) • J. B. METZ, *Jenseits der bürgerlichen Religion* (Munich, 1980) • E. PIN, *Pratique religieuse et classes sociales* (Paris, 1956) • E. POULAT, *Église contre bourgeoisie* (Paris, 1977) • Y. SPIEGEL, ed., *Kirche und Klassenbindung* (Frankfurt, 1974) • M. WEBER, *Economy and Society: An Outline of Interpretive Sociology* (3 vols.; New York, 1968; orig. pub., 1922) 2.468-500.

OSMUND SCHREUDER

Brazil

	1960	1980	2000
Population (1,000s):	72,757	121,672	169,202
Annual growth rate (%):	2.96	2.12	1.18

Area: 8,547,404 sq. km. (3,300,171 sq. mi.)

A.D. 2000

Population density: 20/sq. km. (51/sq. mi.)
Births / deaths: 1.89 / 0.72 per 100 population
Fertility rate: 2.10 per woman
Infant mortality rate: 38 per 1,000 live births
Life expectancy: 68.3 years (m: 64.5, f: 72.4)
Religious affiliation (%): Christians 91.3 (Roman
Catholics 89.8, Protestants 19.0, indigenous 16.1,
marginal 1.0, other Christians 0.2), spiritists 4.7,
nonreligious 2.6, other 1.4.

1. History, Society, Economy, and State
2. Missions, Roman Catholic Structures, and
   Evangelization
3. Protestantism and Ecumenism

1. History, Society, Economy, and State

P. A. Cabral (1467/68-1520) discovered Brazil for
Portugal in 1500. The name came from its first export, brazilwood (from Sp. *brasa*, "live coals"), which
was in demand on account of its red dye. After hesitant beginnings, the settlers expanded in the →
colonial period, and in the 19th and 20th centuries
pushed far beyond the boundaries set by the Treaty
of Tordesillas in 1494. In 1822, under Pedro I (1822-
31) of the house of Braganza, Brazil achieved total
independence from Portugal. At the end of the long
rule of Emperor Pedro II (1840-89), the final abolition of → slavery in 1888 led to a military coup that
abolished the monarchy and, in 1889, established
Brazil as a republic.

The military has ever since claimed to be a moderating force in Brazilian politics, taking control in
1930, 1945, and 1964, with the last period of domination lasting until 1985. In the → revolution of 1964
it took full power and proceeded to govern under a
democratic facade. In conflict with guerrilla organizations, it gave dictatorial powers to the president in
1968 and suspended the right of habeas corpus. It
changed the constitution in 1979, giving the president the right to govern by decree. An amnesty for
political offenders made possible the return of many
→ refugees in 1979. Reputedly free elections took
place in November 1982, but these were not fully
representative because city populations were at a pro-
portional disadvantage and only 69 percent of the

adults had the right to vote (the 31 percent who were
illiterate were excluded). And then, even though the
opposition party won an absolute majority, the presidential system did not allow it to form a government.

Although the military was not yet ready to permit
a direct vote in the choice of a new president, in 1985
surprising shifts in the electoral body led to the selection of the opposition candidate, Tancredo Neres, the
first civilian president in 21 years. In spite of his
sudden death (from natural causes) before taking
over the presidency, the process of democratization
continued under the newly elected vice-president
José Sarney, who succeeded him. Since the beginning
of the 1990s, corruption scandals have rocked congress. The most prominent victim has been Collor
de Mello, the first president elected directly by the
people, who resigned in 1992 at the beginning of
impeachment proceedings against him. Elections in
October 1994 brought finance minister F. H. Cardoso to the presidency, by the widest popular margin
in Brazil since 1945.

In area, Brazil is larger than the contiguous 48
U.S. states. It is both the largest and most populous
country in Latin America. Until the 18th century,
settlement was mostly confined to the coast and the
river systems. With the discovery of gold and diamonds in Minas Gerais, however, and the attraction
of a new wave of Portuguese settlers, there was an
increasing move into the interior, helped particularly
by the large number of German, Italian, Polish,
Spanish, and Japanese immigrants (some 3.8 million
between 1890 and 1942).

In 1970, for geopolitical, economic, and strategic
reasons, the military adopted the Trans-Amazon
Project, with a view to "winning" the last frontiers
and settling the → Indian question. In 1500 there
were an estimated 3-5 million Indians in Brazil. By
1910, when the Indian Protection Service (SPI) was
founded, the number had dwindled to 500,000, apart
from those who as *caboclos* (mestizos) had mixed in
with the national population. The stated aim of the
SPI was to facilitate the nonviolent integration of the
Indians. By 1980 the number of Indians was down
to 220,000 or 230,000, some in reservations, and
some still living in → freedom. Currently, the
National Indian Foundation (FUNAI), which replaced the corrupt SPI (but which itself is also subject
to the same corruption), is subject to the Ministry of
the Interior, whose goals are determined solely by
economic considerations. Indians who disrupted the
opening up of the land are to be integrated and →
acculturated and used as far as possible as a source
of cheap labor. Anthropologists, ethnologists, the

Roman Catholic Conselho Indigenista Missionario (CIMI, Indigenous Mission Council, founded in 1972), and some evangelical missionaries have tried to prevent the → genocide of the Indians and to secure their right of self-determination, especially their right to adequate land. But they have long since lost their voice in FUNAI. The new Brazilian constitution of 1988 has indeed strengthened the rights of the indigenous population. Congress, however, has failed to abide by a constitutional provision requiring the establishment of the *reservas indigenas* by October 1993.

Besides the Indians, imported African slaves have also been sacrificed to the opening up of the interior. Some 3-4 million Africans were shipped to Brazil between 1550 and 1850, when British pressure and the campaign for abolition ended the slave trade. Further millions of Africans are estimated to have lost their lives either in the course of capture or through the terrible conditions on shipboard in the slave trade with America. Those who survived were physically branded by the secular power, baptized by the church (→ Baptism), and thus integrated into a slave-owning society. The final abolition of slavery in 1888 brought freedom but also economic misery, since the slaves had no education, and no provision was made for their integration into a society whose much-vaunted racial tolerance and democracy new sociological investigation has classified as a myth (→ Racism). The descendants of the Indians and Africans who have intermingled with one another and with European settlers are even today the most deprived and exploited substratum of the population.

Unjust land ownership is a serious problem. Productive use of the land available for cultivation is frustrated by the structure of landholdings. Large holdings of over 1,000 ha. (4 sq. mi.) of land account for 43 percent of the arable land. Such holdings, however, involve only 1 percent of the total of all landholdings and only 3 percent of the total number of agricultural workers. In contrast, small holdings up to 10 ha. (25 acres), which together represent only 3 percent of the arable land, make up 52 percent of all landholdings and employ 42 percent of the agricultural workforce. Existing laws for agrarian reform have never been seriously implemented. Large-scale agro-industrial enterprises sell most of their products abroad. Small- and middle-level operations are the main source of food for the country's internal needs. Millions of landless people (the *semterras*) roam the rural regions, often victims of unfair expropriation. Various ecumenical pastoral land commissions try to help these unfortunates.

A related problem is inadequate land develop-

ment, which has led to an increasing flight from the land (a rural population of 54 percent in 1960, but only 25 percent in 1993). As a result the large cities have grown inordinately, with São Paulo increasing from 5.7 to 16.5 million, and Rio de Janeiro from 4.2 to 10.2 million, during the years 1968-95. Even a forced industrialization could not keep pace with the rural exodus and the growth of the population in the creation of new jobs. The results are mass unemployment, poor living quarters for millions, broken families, migrant children and young people, and an increased rate of juvenile crime.

The much-lauded economic miracle in Brazil at the beginning of the 1970s did lead to some increase in the gross national product, but hardly more than 60 percent of the working population could be integrated into the economic cycle, and the legal minimum wage remained very low at an estimated $70 a month. The distribution of income was so unequal that in 1980 the bottom 20 percent of the population received only 2 percent of the national income, while the top 20 percent received 67 percent — and this with an inflation rate that reached almost 200 percent in 1983, averaged 731 percent between 1985 and 1992, and reached 1,009 percent in 1992. After the introduction of the *real* in the second half of 1994, however, the inflation rate was less than 3 percent monthly. With foreign credit the regime financed pharaonic development schemes (irrigation, the Trans-Amazon Project, nuclear power stations), but these have simply done much more environmental damage. For example, the deforested, arid region of the northeast hinterlands suffered a seven-year drought that by 1983 had left 3.5 million dead of hunger. Such schemes have made Brazil the biggest debtor nation in the world, with $121 million in external debt at the end of 1992. In addition, drug-related crime is presently the fastest-growing problem.

2. Missions, Roman Catholic Structures, and Evangelization

The → Jesuits carried the main missionary burden in Brazil until their expulsion in 1759. The first group came in 1549 under M. da Nóbrega (1517-70). At their urgent request a → bishop was sent in 1552 to Salvador Bahia. Church structures were only feebly developed in the colonial period. In 1575 a prelacy for all of southern Brazil was established at Rio de Janeiro (which became a diocese in 1676), 11 years after the expulsion of French settlers banished the Franciscans from the area. In 1676 the bishopric of Bahia was elevated to a metropolitan see.

The bay of Rio was the site of the first three Protestant → martyrdoms in the New World — Calvin-ists whom the Roman Catholic commander N. de Villegaignon (1514-71) executed, in spite of a guarantee of religious freedom. In the 17th century the Dutch attempted to settle in northeastern Brazil and establish a Protestant church and → mission. They were expelled in 1654, and in 1676/77 the sees of Olinda and Maranhão were founded. Pará was then founded in 1719, and São Paulo and Mariana in 1745. The right of patronage, which lasted until the separation of church and state in 1890, tied the official church closely to the Portuguese or Brazilian crown.

In something of a simplification, one might say that the → cathedral chapters and most of the → orders represented the interests of the colonists and that only the Jesuits sought the welfare and salvation of the Indians. Rising no higher than the colonists was the government, which moved to protect the Indians, ostensibly on Christian and humanitarian grounds, only insofar as the settlers' economic inter-ests were not affected. For this reason the Jesuit In-dian *aldeias* (villages of converted Indians) never had the same significance as the similarly intended *reduc-ciones* (→ Reductions) in Paraguay.

From 1655 to 1661, António Vieira (1608-97) se-cured the peaceful coexistence of some 100,000 In-dians with the settlers under Jesuit supervision in Maranhão. Although this arrangement was approved at Lisbon, a revolt of Portuguese settlers put an end to it, and Vieira and other Jesuits were sent back to Portugal. Such events severely damaged the credi-bility of missionary work among the Indians right up to the 20th century, and it was only in 1972 that the CIMI began to restore it (e.g., see its monthly *Porantim*).

Even less credible was missionary work on behalf of the slaves. These were mostly put under priests who had neither the linguistic nor the theological equipment for the task and depended totally on the local *fazendeiros* (farmers), who served as their pa-trons. Under the cover of Christian saints, whom they nominally adopted, the slaves often continued their traditional cults. There thus developed syn-cretistic cults like → Umbanda or Macumba (→ Afro-American Cults), in which millions of nominal Roman Catholics currently have their religious home, while millions of the middle and upper classes became adherents of → spiritism when the → posi-tivism of the second half of the 19th century had alienated many of the educated people from the Roman Catholic Church. In 1945 the Catholic Apos-tolic Church of Brazil split off from Rome; in 1978, it numbered 2 million members.

More significant evangelistically than → Catholic Action or the Eucharistic Congresses have been the 90,000 or so → base communities that sprang up in the 1960s and that regard themselves as the church of the people. These communities have created a new sensitivity in matters of church and society among some 3 million Roman Catholics, to some extent in cooperation with the basic instructional programs of 116 Roman Catholic radio stations, dealing with lit-eracy, hygiene, social problems, and agriculture.

After the 1960s the National Conference of Brazil-ian Bishops (CNBB), with more than 300 bishops, began to address national challenges much more boldly, speaking out on such issues as → human rights, democratization, land reform, and economic justice. This activism led to expulsions of foreign → priests, on whom the church was heavily dependent because of the lack of national clergy, along with imprisonments of priests and laity, and also some assassinations, by which the right-wing extremists hoped to intimidate the progressive wing of the church. The Catholic Church in Brazil nevertheless persisted courageously, attempting to put into prac-tice the resolutions of the general conferences of the Latin American Council of Bishops (CELAM) from Medellín (1968) and Puebla (1979). Brazilians such as Archbishop H. Câmara of Olinda and Recife and Cardinal P. E. Arns of São Paulo and Cardinal A. Lorscheider of Fortaleza, who was for a time presi-dent of CELAM, became leading figures in Latin American Roman Catholicism.

Through the practice of filling vacant seats of bishops with conservative or even reactionary successors (a practice common in the pontificate of John Paul II), the balance in the CNBB has shifted noticeably. Nevertheless the declarations of the an-nual conferences of the CNBB have continued to reflect a strong commitment of the bishops to social reform. Thus the 1991 CNBB lamented abortions, homicides among the 7-8 million street children, the inequitable distribution of wealth, the often degrad-ing level of wages, and inadequate education (30 mil-lion Brazilians are illiterate; many children leave school before the eighth grade and are semiliterate).

When in the early 1990s the Brazilian government acquiesced in the demands of the International Monetary Fund without having developed any coordinated economic policy of its own, the 1992 CNBB criticized its policies, contending that "liber-alizing," "deregulation," and "privatization" would lead to a broader deterioration of the armed forces, to greater social destabilization, and ultimately to a new social apartheid. Realistic estimates for the year 2000 project 14.2 million unemployed and 23.9 percent of the population in a condition of misery, with annual earnings of less than $600 per capita.

The 1993 CNBB demanded far-reaching reforms of government institutions in order to eradicate corruption. A 1993 declaration of the chairman of the CNBB referred to the acute AIDS problem in Brazil, which has the second highest number of AIDS cases on the American continent (after the United States). In 1994 the permanent council of the CNBB published an open letter praising the role of the church base communities and encouraging their work.

3. Protestantism and Ecumenism

Among the churches of immigrants are some → Orthodox churches, which together include 173,000 adherents. The immigration of mostly Protestant Germans, beginning in 1824, led to the establishment of Protestant churches and, between 1886 and 1912, to the formation of four synods, which united in 1950 as the Federation of Synods and in 1968 as the Evangelical Church of Lutheran Confession in Brazil (850,000 members in 1990), the largest Lutheran church in Latin America. Because of a shortage of clergy among the German immigrants, the Missouri Synod was able to get its foot in the door. In 1904 it founded a district, from which the Evangelical Lutheran Church of Brazil eventually developed (216,000 members in 1990).

Anglo-American missionary work in Brazil commenced in the first half of the 19th century with the work of colporteurs of the → Bible societies. In this way the foundations were laid for the Evangelical Christian Congregational Church (1855, with 50,000 members in 1996), the Presbyterian Church of Brazil (1859-69, with 350,000 members in 1996), and the Independent Presbyterian Church of Brazil (92,000 in 1996). An Anglican foreign congregation in Rio de Janeiro (1810) led to the formation of the Episcopal Anglican Church of Brazil (70,000 members in 1991), while the Methodist Church of Brazil was founded in 1870 (132,000 adherents in 1990).

Protestantism in Brazil developed through the natural growth of the traditional denominations and through free church missions, for example, that of → Baptists (from 1871), whose convention (1.4 million adherents in 1990) is the fastest-growing apart from the Pentecostals, also the → Salvation Army, the → Mennonites, the → Adventists (900,000 in 1990), a number of Faith Missions, and the Pentecostals.

Included among the Pentecostals are six large churches — Assemblies of God (with 14 million adherents in 1990, the largest Protestant church in Latin America; → Assembleias de Deus no Brasil),

Universal Church of the Kingdom of God, Christian Congregation in Brazil, God Is Love, Brazil for Christ, and International Church of the Foursquare Gospel — and more than 100 smaller churches. Of the estimated total of 26 million Protestants in Brazil in 1990, fully 88 percent were members of a Pentecostal group. (Other estimates show a lower total of Protestants, with the share of Pentecostals at 70 percent.) Brazil for Christ is the first Pentecostal church in Brazil to join the → World Council of Churches.

The Pentecostal movement, as a kind of popular Protestantism, is related to → popular Catholicism. In this form, Protestantism has taken root in the impoverished and marginalized masses. For the most part, however, Pentecostal leaders have not addressed social problems. (The colorful Benedita da Silva, who comes from the Favelas of Rio de Janeiro and who works for the Labor Party, is clearly an exception.) For many Pentecostals, concerns about their personal experience of the power of God, the gifts of the Holy Spirit, and issues of eschatology have been allowed to erode any inclination for practical social action. This tendency may be related to the fact that the Pentecostal movement came to Brazil from the United States through two Swedes who had aligned themselves with the white U.S. Pentecostals. (In the United States in 1908 the white Pentecostals separated themselves from the black Pentecostals, who were strong social critics; → Black Churches 2.) Finally, since World War II, conservative, mostly fundamentalistic evangelical bodies from the United States influenced by the church growth movement have proliferated in Brazil.

The historic churches have increasingly made use of radio and television, as have the Pentecostal churches, which has been one means of confirming their status in society. The group God Is Love in particular has utilized radio and television and owns its own network of radio stations. Both the Evangelical Pentecostal Christian Church and the Universal Church of the Kingdom of God have developed into U.S.-style electronic churches.

Cooperation among Protestants, which began with the founding of the Confederação Evangélica do Brasil in 1933, lost much of its significance under the shadow of Roman Catholic ecumenism after → Vatican II. The fruits of joint ecumenical work are to be seen in Evangelical-Catholic Bible translation, common organizations for development, pastoral cooperation, and the pioneering formation in 1982 of the National Council of Christian Churches in Brazil (CONIC), which includes Catholics, Christian Reformed, Episcopalians, Lutherans, and Methodists.

Bibliography: R. A. ALVES, *Protestantismo e repressão* (São Paulo, 1979) • D. BARRETT, ed., *WCE* 186-95 • T. C. BRUNEAU, *The Church in Brazil: The Politics of Religion* (Austin, Tex., 1982); idem, *The Political Transformation of the Brazilian Catholic Church* (Cambridge, 1974) • E. B. BURNS, *A History of Brazil* (New York, 1970) • B. W. DIFFIE, *A History of Colonial Brazil, 1500-1792* (Melbourne, Fla., 1987) • G. FREYRE, *New World in the Tropics* (New York, 1963); idem, *Order and Progress: Brazil from Monarchy to Republic* (New York, 1970) • H. HANDELMANN, *Geschichte von Brasilien* (ed. G. Faber; Zurich, 1987; orig. pub., 1860) • J. F. HAUCK, H. FRAGOSO, J. O. BEOZZO, K. V. D. GRIJP, and B. BROD, *História da igreja no Brasil. Segunda época: A igreja no Brasil no século XIX* (Petrópolis, 1980) • E. HOORNAERT, R. AZZI, and K. V. D. GRIJP, *História da igreja no Brasil. Primeira época* (Petrópolis, 1977) • F. IGLÉSIAS, *Trajetória política do Brasil, 1500-1964* (São Paulo, 1993) • K. S. LATOURETTE, *A History of the Expansion of Christianity,* vol. 3, *Three Centuries of Advance;* vol. 5, *The Great Century in the Americas, Australasia, and Africa* (New York, 1943, 1945; repr., Grand Rapids, 1970) • W. LIEHR, *Katholizismus und Demokratisierung in Brasilien* (Saarbrücken, 1988) • S. MAINWARING, *The Catholic Church and Politics in Brazil, 1916-1985* (Stanford, Calif., 1986) • L. MORITZ SCHWARCZ, *O espetáculo das raças. Cientistas, instituições e questão racial no Brasil, 1870-1930* (São Paulo, 1993) • H.-J. PRIEN, *Evangelische Kirchwerdung in Brasilien* (Gütersloh, 1989); idem, *La historia del cristianismo en América Latina* (Salamanca, 1985); idem, ed., *Lateinamerika: Gesellschaft, Kirche, Theologie* (vol. 1; Göttingen, 1981) • W. R. READ, *New Patterns of Church Growth in Brazil* (Grand Rapids, 1965) • W. R. READ and F. A. INESON, *Brazil 1980* (Monrovia, Calif., 1973) • D. C. REILY, ed., *História documental do protestantismo no Brasil* (São Paulo, 1984) • F. C. ROLIM, *Pentecostais no Brasil* (Petrópolis, 1985) • R. SOUTHEY, *History of Brazil* (3 vols.; 1822; 2d ed., New York, 1969) • G. P. SÜSS, *Volkskatholizismus in Brasilien* (Munich, 1978) • D. G. VIEIRA, *O protestantismo, a maçonaria e a questão religiosa no Brasil* (Brasília, 1980).

HANS-JÜRGEN PRIEN

Bread for the World → Relief Organizations

Brethren Churches

Several religious organizations in the United States have chosen the biblical designation "Brethren." Although diverse in origin, they share a basic → bibli-

cist orientation. None of them is related to the Plymouth Brethren (→ Dispensationalism).

1. One of the older movements of this sort is the Church of the Brethren, which originated in central Germany in 1708. Its eight founding members had moved from a radical → Pietist position within their Reformed and Lutheran churches to separatism heavily influenced by → Anabaptism through contact with German → Mennonites. Their first minister was Alexander Mack (1679-1735) from Schriesheim near Heidelberg. The group called itself simply Brethren, but the people were known by outsiders as the Neutäufer (New Baptists) because of their baptism of adult converts. The movement expanded in the earldom of Wittgenstein, where it was formed, and also formed daughter congregations in the Büdingen area (Marienborn), Eppstein (Palatinate), Altona (near Hamburg), and Krefeld (Lower Rhine).

2. It was from Krefeld that the first group of Brethren migrated to North America in 1719, establishing a congregation in 1723 in Germantown, north of Philadelphia. Later congregations in colonial America were planted in other parts of Pennsylvania and in New Jersey, Maryland, Virginia, and the Carolinas. By 1770 there were perhaps 1,500 Brethren. As one of the historic → peace churches, the Brethren experienced some persecution in 1776 because of their refusal to enter the cause of the American Revolution (→ Pacifism).

In the 19th century the Brethren expanded with the westward movement in the new nation, creating strong rural settlements in Ohio, Indiana, Illinois, Iowa, Missouri, Kansas, Oregon, and California. By the last third of the 19th century, members were found coast to coast, with few Brethren in the South (because of the earlier slavery system) and none in New England (because of the path of migration and the Puritan intolerance of sects). Traveling → elders worked to keep → denominational unity despite the increasing distances; the yearly "Big Meeting," or Annual Conference, held in varied local settings, settled many issues of doctrine and practice. However, tensions built up around issues such as higher education, church publications, and the salaried ministry (heretofore, all ministers were self-supporting). The result was a three-way split in 1881-83.

3. A conservative faction (the Old German Baptist Brethren) withdrew, and a progressive faction (the Brethren Church) was expelled. Each numbered about 5,000 members. The large central body, known for legal purposes as the German Baptist Brethren,

numbered 60,000. In 1908 it took the name Church of the Brethren, as few of its members still spoke the German language. Freed from the internal tensions of the 1880s, the Church of the Brethren expanded rapidly with foreign and home mission programs, colleges, and charitable institutions such as orphanages and homes for the elderly. By 1983 membership had grown to 170,000.

Brethren mission activity flourished in India (after 1894), China (1908), Nigeria (1922), and Ecuador (1948). The church in China was dissolved during the Communist revolution, the church in Ecuador joined the United Evangelical Church of Ecuador in 1965, and the church in India joined the United Church of North India in 1970. The Nigerian church has experienced a tide of growth, attaining a membership of 40,000 by 1981. During World War II, the energies of the Church of the Brethren centered on assistance to its members who were in alternative service as → conscientious objectors. This effort was enlarged after 1945 with an ambitious worldwide program of relief and rehabilitation. Brethren helped to begin many agencies such as Christian Rural Overseas Program, Church World Service, the Heifer Project, International Christian Youth Exchange, and others.

4. In the late 1930s the Brethren Church suffered schism, resulting in the formation of the Fellowship of Grace Brethren Churches. By 1983 this group had 42,000 members, which surpassed the Brethren Church with its 17,000 members. Earlier, in 1926, a small group that had taken the name Dunkard Brethren withdrew from the Church of the Brethren, seeking to preserve a plainer lifestyle.

Whereas the Church of the Brethren is an active member of the National and → World Council of Churches (WCC), the other Brethren bodies are opposed to ecumenism. Since 1948 the Church of the Brethren has had its European offices in the WCC headquarters in Geneva. Its national office is at Elgin, Illinois. The denominational periodical is the *Messenger;* the scholarly journal *Brethren Life and Thought* is published on behalf of the church.

Although noncreedal, the Brethren have always held to the basic tenets of Protestant Christianity. Besides the distinctive practice of threefold immersion of confessing believers (→ Baptism), the Brethren observe a "love feast" that includes foot washing, a fellowship meal, and Communion (→ Eucharist). Anointing for spiritual and physical health is another ordinance.

5. A similar religious group is the Brethren in Christ, known informally until 1863 as the River Brethren.

It originated around 1780 in Lancaster County, Pennsylvania, under the influence of revivalism (→ Theology of Revivals) among Swiss Mennonites. Some of its practices were evidently taken from the Brethren, with whom some of its members unsuccessfully sought baptism. Small offshoots of the movement are the Old Order River Brethren ("Yorkers"), the United Zion Children, and the United Zion Church. In 1983 there were 16,200 members in these movements.

6. A like-named movement with different antecedents, the Evangelical United Brethren Church, was formed in 1946 from the Evangelical Church and the United Brethren Church. In 1968 it in turn merged with the Methodist Church to form the United Methodist Church (→ Methodist Churches). All of the movements share a Wesleyan orientation. When the Pietist-influenced Evangelical Association and the United Brethren in Christ were formed in the late 18th century, they were closely aligned with the Methodists but, because of their German ethnic background, remained separate.

Bibliography: D. F. DURNBAUGH, ed., *The Brethren Encyclopedia* (3 vols.; Philadelphia, 1983-84); idem, ed., *The Church of the Brethren, Past and Present* (Elgin, Ill., 1971) • F. NIEPER, *Die ersten deutschen Auswanderer von Krefeld nach Pennsylvanien* (Neukirchen, 1940) • F. A. NORWOOD, *The Story of American Methodism* (Nashville, 1974) • H. RENKEWITZ, *Hochmann von Hochenau (1670-1721)* (Witten, 1969) • D. R. STOFFER, "The Background and Development of Thought and Practice in the German Baptist Brethren (Dunker) and the Brethren (Progressive) Churches (c. 1650-1979)" (Ph.D. diss., Fuller Theological Seminary, 1980) • C. O. WITTLINGER, *Quest for Piety and Obedience* (Nappanee, Ind., 1978).

DONALD F. DURNBAUGH

Brethren of the Common Life

Like the Canons of Windesheim, the Brethren of the Common Life was a product of the *devotio moderna* (modern devotion) inspired by G. Groote (1340-84). This community traces its origin to clergy and laity who, in Deventer in 1380/81, without official vows or an approved rule, came together in a communal spiritual life. Their goal was to promote their own edification and, by their example and teaching, to further the → salvation of others. They lived mainly by their own work, including the production of books. Organized by Florentius Radewijns (1350-1400), their life was in some cases merely a first stage toward monastic life, but in Holland, Belgium, northern France, and Germany they found many imitators who took a permanent resolve to live a "devout" life. H. von Ahaus (d. 1439) helped them to spread in many parts of Germany, beginning at Münster in 1401, moving to the Rhineland (e.g., Cologne in 1401 and 1416), then to Hesse (e.g., Königstein in 1467), Mosel (e.g., Trier in 1499), and Württemberg (e.g., Dettingen and Tübingen in 1482).

Although the Brethren of the Common Life, as well as sisters who followed a similar pattern, lived a nonworldly life and displayed a → spirituality shaped by the spirit of the NT and the Fathers, they were repeatedly accused of ignoring conciliar rulings and founding a new order without an approved rule. Nevertheless, by pointing to the tradition of a semi-religious life, they defended themselves more successfully than did the → Beguines and Beghards. They approximated more and more the monastic and canonical life, the houses in Württemberg under G. Biel (d. 1495) more rapidly than those of the Northwest, where Hildesheim under P. Dieburg (d. 1494) retained its original character, leading M. → Luther (1483-1546) to recognize the validity of its life without rule or → vows.

In Germany the Brethren of the Common Life maintained itself until the 18th and 19th centuries, not merely in houses that remained Roman Catholic (Cologne, Münster, Emmerich, Wesel), but also in the Protestant house at Herford.

Bibliography: K. Elm, "Die Brüderschaft vom gemeinsamen Leben," *OGE* 59 (1985) 470-96 • J. van Engen, ed., *Devotio Moderna: Basic Writings* (New York, 1988) • A. Hyma, *Brethren of the Common Life* (Grand Rapids, 1950); idem, *The Christian Renaissance: A History of the "Devotio Moderna"* (rev. ed.; Hamden, Conn., 1965) • S. Kettlewell, *Thomas à Kempis and the Brothers of the Common Life* (2d ed.; London, 1885) • W. Leesch, E. Persoons, and A. G. Weiter, eds., *Monasticon Fratrum Vitae Communis* (2 vols.; Brussels, 1977-79) • R. R. Post, *The Modern Devotion: Confrontation with Reformation and Humanism* (Leiden 1968) • G. Rehm, *Die Schwestern vom gemeinsamen Leben im nordwestlichen Deutschland* (Berlin, 1985) • A. G. Weiler and W. Persoons, *G. Grote en de devotio moderna* (Nijmegen, 1984).

KASPAR ELM

Breviary → Hours, Canonical

British Missions

1. Origins
2. Nineteenth-Century Developments
3. Missions and Imperialism
4. The First World War and After
5. The Last Stage

1. Origins

British missions were born in the theoretical ideals of the English Commonwealth of the 17th century and later were given new directions by the American colonies and the reconversion of the Scottish Highlands. They were driven by the → Moravian example and an eschatology that stressed that "the earth shall be full of the knowledge of the Lord as the waters cover the sea" (Isa. 11:9) before the return of Christ. The Evangelical Revival (→ Revivals 2.2) provided the religious dynamic, and the economic and technological development of 19th-century Britain provided the outlets.

1.1. Some key British mission institutions had their origin at the turn of the 17th and 18th centuries.

1.1.1. Thomas Bray (1656-1730) organized the Society for Promoting Christian Knowledge (SPCK) in 1699, and the Society for the Propagation of the Gospel in Foreign Parts (SPG) in 1701. These had royal charters and involved the bishops in their management. The early SPG concentrated on providing "orthodox clergy" for the American colonies. Despite Bray's wider vision, few missionaries reached black slaves or American → Indians. Young John → Wesley (missionary in Georgia, 1735-37) tried but failed. Thomas Thompson (d. 1773) was exceptional in visiting the slaves' African homeland. After American independence, Bishop Beilby Porteus tried in vain to redirect the society's work toward plantation blacks.

1.1.2. From 1709, the SPCK channeled funds to the king of Denmark's German missionaries in Tranquebar, India, and after 1727 those who worked in British-administered territory were designated SPCK missionaries.

1.1.3. The Honourable Society in Scotland for Propagating Christian Knowledge attempted to remodel Highland culture. It combined preaching in Gaelic with education in English. This model influenced later Scottish educational missions in India. The society developed parallel work in North America, with David Brainerd being one of its missionaries.

1.2. Between 1790 and 1810 groups influenced by the Evangelical Revival in all the Protestant traditions began to form societies for → evangelization overseas. The Particular (i.e., Calvinistic) Baptists were the first, in 1792. The society was originally based on the local colleagues of the chief founder and first missionary, William Carey, not on the leading churches of the denomination.

1.2.1. "The Missionary Society" (later the London Missionary Society, LMS) was founded by leading Evangelicals in 1795. It was intended to be interdenominational, with new converts to determine their own church government. → Congregationalists could accept this principle more easily than others and tended always to predominate in the society.

1.2.2. Several Scottish towns set up societies on LMS lines. In 1796 the Church of Scotland General Assembly prevented any official recognition of these societies while refusing any initiative of its own. The decision was influenced by the association of the missions cause with Evangelicals, seceders, and political radicals, together with the belief that "civilization" must precede evangelization. The main Scottish societies were eventually subsumed within the Free Church of Scotland and the United Presbyterian Church.

1.2.3. Evangelical → Anglicans had little confidence in the official societies, SPG and SPCK, but they were not willing to breach church discipline by forming a partnership with → Dissenters in the LMS. In 1799 they founded the Church Missionary Society for Africa and the East (CMS). Its earliest missionaries were German Lutherans. The bishops neither supported nor censured this mission effort.

1.2.4. The Methodist Conference appointed preachers to the Caribbean from 1769, and Wesley's lieutenant, Thomas Coke, campaigned for overseas missions. Missionary societies grew on local initiatives until in 1818 the conference constituted the Wesleyan Methodist Missionary Society (WMMS). This was the only new English mission closely linked with the organization of its parent denomination.

1.2.5. The British and Foreign Bible Society (BFBS), founded in 1804, was inspired by home needs and then extended overseas. By encouraging translation and facilitating production of vernacular Bibles, it (and later the National Bible Society of Scotland) assisted and sometimes instigated the work of other missions. Churchmen and Dissenters could unite in Bible societies, and while Evangelicals took the lead, other churchmen could support it without embarrassment.

2. Nineteenth-Century Developments

Evangelicals pioneered the new missions, but by 1830 church and public opinion were generally favorable. Pressure to identify British rule in India with Christianity made the government establish a bishopric in Calcutta in 1813. Moderates and Evangelicals in the Church of Scotland combined to commission a missionary of the church, Alexander Duff, in 1829. Emigration was taking British people abroad, and in New Zealand and South Africa emigrants lived next to non-Christian peoples. More bishoprics were founded, and the SPG initiated missionary, as well as pastoral, work. Vigorous bishops like G. A. Selwyn of New Zealand and Robert Gray of Cape Town sought to establish a church framework over both types. The Universities' Mission to Central Africa (UMCA), founded 1859, applied Tractarian theories of episcopacy to missions by sending a bishop with the first mission party.

2.1. By the middle of the century British missions were securely established, mostly in voluntary societies on broadly denominational lines. Their "civilizing" role was publicly recognized. They achieved modest successes — small Christian states like Sierra Leone and Samoa — but not dynamic growth. Against this background new missions emerged that were nondenominational, nonclerical, often international, and concerned with extending the evangelizing role of missions. They reflected new currents in evangelical piety, stressing individual decision for Christ, self-surrender, direct reliance on God for finances, sometimes the expected return of Christ, and often the lamentable fate of the unconverted heathen. The → China Inland Mission (CIM), founded in 1865, was the first and most important of many.

2.2. A great missionary expansion occurred between 1880 and 1914. While some new societies used missionaries without education or training, the older societies received for the first time an influx of highly educated young people. The Student Volunteer Movement became a major source of missionary leadership. Much of the new missionary force was female, explained in part by the opening of professions to women, the declericalizing of missions by the new societies, and the recognition that certain mission tasks could be done only by women.

2.2.1. Specialist medical missions were increasingly used from the 1840s where evangelistic access was difficult ("heavy artillery," one commentator called them). The Edinburgh Medical Missionary Society was formed to train mission doctors. High standards were often achieved, but advances in medicine made medical missions proportionately very expensive.

2.2.2. British missions before 1914 were overwhelmingly Protestant. An English mission, the Mill Hill Fathers, was formed in 1866 partly to ease Catholic access to British colonies, but in its early years it needed foreign recruits, mainly Dutch.

3. Missions and Imperialism

The relationship between missions and other British interests is complex. Official opinion was cautious or hostile toward the early missionary movement, especially for fear of its provoking religious reaction in India. In midcentury "Christianity, commerce, and civilization" were held to work together in Africa, but elsewhere missionaries and traders frequently saw each other as opponents. In the imperial period (i.e., after 1880) British missions generally welcomed the establishment of British power or protection and certainly inculcated loyalty to it. However, the missionaries were sometimes disillusioned by the outcome, often believing that official policy was biased against them in favor of Islam.

Missions frequently mobilized government and public opinion at home and on the field on humanitarian concerns (e.g., the slave trade), unchristian practices by Britain (e.g., the official opium trade in China), or the implications of British policy overseas (e.g., regarding the Central African Federation in the 1950s).

4. The First World War and After

The war greatly and permanently reduced the supply of missionaries while increasing commitments with the removal of German staff. The World Missionary Conference of 1910 resulted in new machinery for international and intermission consultation. In both areas J. H. Oldham became the outstanding British figure. The Conference of British Missionary Societies (since 1978, the Conference for World Mission, CFWM) was founded in 1912.

The postwar economic depression ensured that missionary enterprise could not return to the scale envisaged before. In Africa, however, the increased readiness of British colonial administrations to finance approved educational work and the insistent African demand for education caused even the evangelistically oriented missions to become heavily involved in schools.

5. The Last Stage

The purpose of missions as enunciated by Henry Venn (CMS secretary, 1841-72) and generally acknowledged (at least in theory) was the formation of self-governing, self-supporting, self-propagating churches. To the theological, financial, and logistic factors introduced by the world wars, the depression, and the ecumenical movement were added the missionary evacuation of China, the achievement of the → Church of South India, the political independence of the Asian and African nations, and the consciousness of recession from Christianity in Britain. Clearly, any future missionary role would be purely ancillary to the new churches of the southern continents. (Some identified a renewed role in primary evangelization in minority or "hidden" ethnic groups — witness the growth of the Wycliffe Bible Translators, British branch.)

5.1. In 1984, the CFWM, now largely integrated with the British Council of Churches (BCC), had 21 full and 17 associate members. The Evangelical Missionary Alliance (EMA) provided services for some 70 societies, some of them also members of the CFWM. The EMA missions, while increasingly recognizing the social demands of the gospel, insist on the primacy of the evangelistic task; few are linked to a specific church or → denomination or have any other connection with the BCC.

5.2. As postimperial Britain grew self-absorbed, British missions promoted awareness of wider issues — of race, poverty, and justice — a role not always popular with church members. They have also linked British churches and those of the southern continents. At present they face a new test: can structures originally developed for *giving* grow into instruments for *receiving* and *sharing* the total resources of the world church?

→ Acculturation; Colonialism; Colonialism and Mission; Mission

Bibliography: E. A. ALEXANDER, *The First Generation: Early Leaders of the Baptist Missionary Society in England and India* (London, 1937) • A. E. M. ANDERSON-MORSEHEAD and A. G. BLOOD, *History of the Universities' Mission to Central Africa* (3 vols.; London, 1955-58) • D. BAKER, ed., *Religious Motivation* (Oxford, 1978) articles by A. Porter (349-65) and A. F. Walls (339-48) • H. J. CNATTINGIUS, *Bishops and Societies* (London, 1952) • J. A. DE JONG, *As the Waters Cover the Sea* (Kampen, 1970) • N. GOODALL, *A History of the London Missionary Society, 1895-1945* (London, 1954) continues Lovett • E. G. K. HEWAT, *Vision and Achievement, 1796-1956* (London, 1960) • G. HEWITT, *The Problems of Success: A History of the Church Missionary Society, 1910-1942* (London, 1971) continues Stock • W. R. HOGG, *Ecumenical Foundations* (New York, 1952) • E. M. JACKSON, *Red Tape and the Gospel* (Birmingham, 1980) • K. S. LATOURETTE, *A History of the Expansion of Christianity* (vols. 5-7; New York, 1943-45; repr., Grand Rapids, 1970) • R. LOVETT, *The History of the London Missionary Society, 1795-1895* (2 vols.; London, 1899) continued by Goodall • S. C. NEILL, *A History of Christian Missions* (11th ed.; Harmondsworth, 1986) • L. NEMER, *Anglican and Roman Catholic Attitudes on Missions* (St. Augustin, 1981) • C. F. PASCOE, *Two Hundred Years of the SPG* (2 vols.; London, 1901) • W. J. SHEILS, ed., *The Church and*

Healing (Oxford, 1982) articles by A. F. Walls (287-97) and C. P. Williams (271-85) • W. R. Shenk, *Henry Venn, Missionary Statesman* (Maryknoll, N.Y., 1983) • E. Stock, *History of the Church Missionary Society* (4 vols.; London, 1899-1901) continued by Hewitt • H. P. Thompson, *Into All Lands: The History of the Society for the Propagation of the Gospel in Foreign Parts, 1701-1950* (London, 1951) • J. Van den Berg, *Constrained by Jesus' Love* (Kampen, 1956) • A. F. Walls, "Missionary Vocation and the Ministry," *NT Christianity for Africa and the World* (ed. M. Glasswell and E. W. Fasholé-Luke; London, 1974) 141-56 • M. Warren, *The Missionary Movement from Britain in Modern History* (London, 1965); idem, *Social History and Christian Mission* (London, 1967).

Andrew F. Walls

Brotherhoods → Communities, Spiritual

Brunei

	1960	1980	2000
Population (1,000s):	82	193	326
Annual growth rate (%):	4.51	2.89	1.66

Area: 5,765 sq. km. (2,226 sq. mi.)

A.D. 2000
Population density: 57/sq. km. (146/sq. mi.)
Births / deaths: 1.80 / 0.32 per 100 population
Fertility rate: 2.40 per woman
Infant mortality rate: 8 per 1,000 live births
Life expectancy: 76.3 years (m: 74.2, f: 78.9)
Religious affiliation (%): Muslims 64.4, tribal religionists 11.0, Buddhists 8.9, Christians 8.7 (indigenous 2.8, Protestants 2.3, Roman Catholics 1.8, Anglicans 1.5, other Christians 0.3), Chinese folk religionists 3.2, Confucianists 1.7, nonreligious 1.0, other 1.1.

The sultanate of Brunei (official name: Negara [State of] Brunei Darussalam) is a small enclave on the northwestern coast of Borneo. It is bordered by the South China Sea and, on land, is surrounded entirely by Sarawak, an eastern state of Malaysia. In 1997 the sultan was Sir Muda Hassanal Bolkiah Mu'izzadin Waddaulah, who, upon succeeding his father in October 1967, became the 29th ruler in a single family of sultans tracing back to Sultan Mohammed (reigned 1405-15), the first Brunei leader to embrace → Islam.

According to the official census, in 1991 the population of Brunei was 260,000. The largest ethnic group was Malay (approximately 65 percent), which included many of the tribal people who had converted to Islam. Other major groups were the Chinese (20 percent), most of whom were resident foreign workers (→ Foreigners 2), and tribal peoples (5 percent), primarily the Iban. The remainder largely comprised expatriates, mainly British, Koreans, and Filipinos involved in the oil industry, as well as a Gurkha battalion maintained by the sultan for protection of the oil and gas fields.

Brunei's robust economy, fueled primarily by its exploitation of large reserves of petroleum and natural gas, discovered in 1929, has given the country one of the highest standards of living in Asia. In October 1995 Brunei joined the World Bank and International Monetary Fund, in part to find help in reducing its reliance on earnings from oil. Nearly 30 percent of all national expenditures are designated for → social services, as Brunei citizens enjoy free medical services, assistance programs for the poor, and free education at all levels. Schools are taught using Malay, Mandarin Chinese, or English.

Little is known of the early history of the Brunei Sultanate. By the time Magellan anchored his ships off Brunei in 1521, however, the fifth sultan, Bolkiah, controlled almost all of Borneo, several neighboring islands, and the Sulu Archipelago (part of modern-day Philippines). The arrival of the Portuguese and then the Dutch in the 16th century led to a reduction in the sultan's sphere of control, a decline that continued through the 19th century, when the British became more involved in the region. In 1888 Brunei signed a treaty putting itself under British protection. Except for a period of occupation by Japan (1941-45), direct British oversight continued for almost a century. Following friendly negotiations with Great Britain in 1979, as well as nonaggression assurances by Brunei's powerful neighbors Malaysia and Indonesia, Brunei became a fully independent state on January 1, 1984, that same year joining the → United Nations, the Association of South East Asian Nations (ASEAN), the Commonwealth, and the Organization of the Islamic Congress.

In September 1959, during Brunei's status as a British protectorate, a constitution was promulgated conferring supreme executive authority on the sultan, to be assisted and advised by four constitutional councils. In 1962, after a massive rebellion in Brunei and other parts of Borneo was crushed with the aid of British troops, Sultan Sir Omar Ali Saifuddin III invoked a provision of the constitution allowing him to assume emergency powers for two years. Parts of the constitution have been held in abeyance ever since. As of 1997 there was no legislature, and national elections had not been held since 1968. Every second year since 1962, the sultans have declared a renewal of emergency rule.

Along with a stabilization of Brunei's political fortunes has come increasingly zealous support of Islam, the country's official religion. The Sultan Omar Ali Saifuddin Mosque in the capital, Bandar Seri Begawan, completed in 1958 at a cost of US$5 million, is one of the largest and most impressive mosques in the Far East. In 1990 the government began widespread promotion of Melayu Islam Beraja (Malay Islamic monarchy), a traditional formulation of Bruneian values especially prepared for Malay Muslims, and urged closer adherence to Islam. In January 1991 Brunei banned the entry of alcohol into the country; later in the year the government expelled most Catholic priests and nuns. In 1992 the celebration of Christmas was prohibited, as was the importation generally of religious teaching material or scriptures such as the Bible. Women have been urged to wear the traditional *tudong* (Muslim headdress) when appearing in public.

In the 1991 census, Muslims accounted for 67 percent of the population. Indigenous ethnic groups (approximately 5 percent) represented mainly animists. Other religions existed in Brunei solely by virtue of the various nonnative communities present. They included Buddhists (13 percent in 1991) and Christians (10 percent), the latter divided fairly evenly between → Roman Catholics and → Anglicans. The remainder consisted of practitioners of other Chinese religions and those claiming no religion at all.

→ Colonialism 2; Tribal Religions

Bibliography: A. ALI, *From Penury to Plenty: Developement of Oil Rich Brunei, 1906 to Present* (Perth, Austral., 1996) • A. G. J. CHALFONT, *By God's Will: A Portrait of the Sultan of Brunei* (New York, 1989) a study of the current sultan • G. C. GUNN, *Language, Power, and Ideology in Brunei Darussalam* (Athens, Ohio, 1997) • B. A. HAMZAH, *The Oil Sultanate: Political History of Oil in Brunei Darussalam* (Seremban, 1991) • B. A. HUSSAINMIYA, *Sultan Omar Ali Saifuddin III and Britain: The Making of Brunei Darussalam* (New York, 1995) • L. A. KIMBALL, *Alam Brunei: The World of Traditional Brunei Malay Culture* (Bellingham, Wash., 1991) • S. C. E. KRAUSSE and G. H. KRAUSSE, *Brunei* (Oxford, 1988) bibliography • K. MULLINER and J. A. LENT, eds., *Brunei and Malaysian Studies: Present Knowledge and Research Trends on Brunei and on Malaysian Anthropology, Mass Communication, and Women's Studies* (Williamsburg, Va., 1994) • J. ROONEY, *The Good News: A History of the Catholic Church in East Malaysia and Brunei, 1880-1976* (London, 1981) • G. E. SAUNDERS, *A History of Brunei* (New York, 1994) • R. TYLER, *Brunei Darussalam: The Making of a Modern Nation* (Bandar Seri Begawan, 1996).

THE EDITORS

Bucer, Martin

Modern research has rightly come to see in Martin Bucer (1491-1551) one of the main leaders of the → Reformation. Educated at the famous Schlettstadt grammar school, he became the reformer of the imperial city of Strasbourg. Having first made an intensive, Thomistically oriented study of → Scholastic theology, he then came under the lasting influence of the → humanism of D. → Erasmus (1469?-1536). His crucial experience, however, was his encounter with M. → Luther (1483-1546) at the Heidelberg Disputation (1518), which led to his adopting a theology of → justification linked to the anti-Pelagian → Augustine (354-430; → Augustine's Theology). Renouncing his monastic vows, he undertook two brief pastoral charges, married in token of his acceptance of the Reformation, and then in 1524 took up ministry in the capital of Alsace, on which Reformation writings and Lutheran preaching had already made a strong impact. Along with a reforming circle that included especially Matthäus Zell (1477-1548), Wolfgang Capito (1478-1541), and Caspar Hedio (1494/95-1552), Bucer influenced the development of the church in Strasbourg until the Augsburg Interim of 1548 forced him into exile in England. There, until his death, he played an important role as professor of theology at Cambridge, as consultant for the 1552 revision of the prayer book, and as the author of *On the Kingdom of Christ*, a guideline for the comprehensive reform of English society that he presented to the young King Edward VI (1547-53).

As exegete, theologian, and translator of Luther, Bucer did much to promote the Reformation both by direct debate with traditionalists and by influencing officials and public opinion. He was at first strongly Lutheran, but the outbreak of eucharistic controversies in 1524 found him moving away from the position advocated by Luther and J. Bugenhagen (1485-1558), which focused so strongly on the bodily presence of Christ in the bread and wine (→ Eucharist). Instead Bucer made a vital contribution to the formation of a front in southern Germany. Although he had an irenic intention and disagreement with Luther was painful for him, he combined with Capito to write anonymous and pseudonymous tracts and to issue edited translations of Luther and Bugenhagen in opposition to their eucharistic teaching. Close to U. → Zwingli (1484-1531) and J. Oecolampadius (1482-1531) both personally and in his ideas, Bucer must be regarded with them as a father of the Reformed family of → confessions. With Peter Martyr (1500-1562), Bucer fortified the Anglican reformers in the Reformed eucharistic teaching that became the decisive issue in the Marian persecution and the official position in the 1571 Articles.

At the 1530 Diet of Augsburg the Tetrapolitan Confession, drawn up by Bucer and Capito, was an attempt at mediation with the Lutherans. Along with Bucer's Greater Catechism it became binding in Strasbourg in 1534. Political concerns (the threatened military isolation of Strasbourg) combined with personal and theological interests to drive Bucer into further efforts at mediation, which achieved some success with the 1536 Wittenberg Concord, though it did not gain Swiss support. In the 1540s he was active in conversations with the Roman Catholics, but his tendency to solve irreconcilable differences by → compromise won him no friends. In the meantime, however, he successfully organized church life in Strasbourg; promoted reformation in many other cities, such as Augsburg and Ulm; served ably as preacher, pastor, and city consultant; and taught biblical → exegesis at the newly founded academy.

Although Bucer, like other Reformers, strongly opposed the → Anabaptists, he tried to find a place for their zeal for sanctification by forming Christian fellowships and establishing → church discipline, while at the same time making it a concern to win over Anabaptists for the mainline Reformation. In this regard he not only was a pioneer of → Pietism but also influenced J. → Calvin (1509-64) during his Strasbourg years, helping also to give shape to Calvin's doctrines of the sacraments and election and to his vision of the church and its role in a Christian society. By way of Calvin, as well as by his other contacts in person or by letter, Bucer contributed to the development of the Reformation in many European countries, especially Holland and France, along with England.

In his last years at Cambridge, to which he went at the invitation of T. → Cranmer (1489-1556), Bucer struggled against an unfavorable climate and poor health. He died in time to avoid the persecution. Under Mary Tudor (1553-58) he suffered posthumous martyrdom when his remains were solemnly dug up and burned.

Bibliography: Primary sources: C. HUBERT, ed., Martini Buceri scripta Anglicana fere omnia (Basel, 1577) ·
M. LEUTZ, ed., Briefwechsel Landgraf Philipps des Großmüthigen von Hessen mit Bucer (3 vols.; repr., Osnabrück, 1965) · F. ROTT, ed., Correspondance de Martin Bucer (Leiden, 1979ff.) · R. STUPPERICH, ed., Martin Bucers Deutsche Schriften (Gütersloh, 1960ff.) · F. WENDEL et al., eds., Martini Buceri opera Latina (Paris and Leiden, 1954ff.).

Secondary works: M. GRESCHAT, Martin Bucer (Munich, 1990) · T. KAUFMANN, Die Abendmahlstheologie der Strassburger Reformatoren (Tübingen, 1992) · J. MÜLLER, Martin Bucers Hermeneutik (Gütersloh, 1965) · J. V. POLLET, Martin Bucer. Études sur la correspondence (2 vols.; Paris, 1958-62); idem, Martin Bucer. Études sur les relations de Bucer avec les Pays-Bas, l'Électorat de Cologne et l'Allemagne du Nord (2 vols.; Leiden, 1985) · W. P. STEPHENS, The Holy Spirit in the Theology of Martin Bucer (Cambridge, 1970) · W. VAN T'SPIJKER, The Ecclesiastical Offices in the Thought of Martin Bucer (Leiden, 1996) · D. F. WRIGHT, "Martin Bucer (1491-1551) in England," Anvil 9 (1992) 249-59; idem, ed., Martin Bucer: Reforming Church and Community (Cambridge, 1994).

THOMAS KAUFMANN

Buddhism

1. Sphere
2. Sources
3. Teaching
4. Monastic Community
5. History

1. Sphere

The sphere of Buddhism embraces a great part of Asia but has suffered serious reductions through the centuries. In India itself it died out after 1200, and it was suppressed or destroyed in China (after 1947), in Tibet (after 1950), and in Viet Nam, Cambodia (where there have been signs recently of a revival), and Laos (from the middle of the 1970s). Theravada Buddhism still flourishes in Sri Lanka, Myanmar, and Thailand, and other forms exist in Nepal, Japan (→ Zen), Korea, and in some areas of the former Soviet Union. The end of the 19th century saw a new wave of → mission with the founding of the Maha Bodhi Society (1891) in India. This society moved into America and Europe in the 20th century.

2. Sources

Most of the writings of Buddhism, composed in Indian languages like Sanskrit, have been preserved only in Chinese or Tibetan translations. Buddha expressly permitted the proclamation of his teaching in the respective vernaculars. Only the canon of the Theravada school has been completely preserved. It was composed in Pali and has been handed down in Southeast Asia and Sri Lanka under the name "Tipiṭaka" (Skt. *tripiṭaka*, "three baskets"). It comprises the Vinaya Piṭaka (Basket of Discipline), with rules for the monastic life of monks and nuns; the Sutta Piṭaka (Basket of Teachings); and the obviously much later Abhidhamma Piṭaka (Basket of Concepts). It was probably written down for the first time in Sri Lanka in the first century B.C. on the basis of centuries-old oral tradition. A near-canonical text is the Milinda-panha (questions of Milinda), a dialogue with the Indo-Greek king Menander.

The Pali canon was expounded in commentaries (*aṭṭhakathā*, "explanation"), which were given their present form by Buddhaghosa in the fifth century A.D. Around these has clustered an extensive exegetical literature. The works of Buddhism in Tibetan translation have been collected in Kanjur and Tanjur (→ Tibetan Religions). Chinese Buddhists have made many translations since the first century A.D., the exact date of which is very important for the chronology of Buddhist literature. Fragments of old translations have been preserved in central Asian languages such as Sogdian, Sakian, and Tocharian.

3. Teaching

3.1. Buddha (which in Sanskrit means "awakened"; cf. Tibet. *saṅs-rgyas*, Chin. *fo*, Jap. *butsu[da]*) is the title of a series of preachers of salvation, of whom no two can be contemporary. The historical Buddha — Siddhārtha Gautama (in Pali: Siddhattha Gotama), also called Śākyamuni (Sage of the Sakyas) — was from Kapilavastu (present-day Piprahva) and was born in what is now Rummindei, Nepal. He died at the age of eighty around 480 B.C. according to the longer chronology of Buddhism, or around 380 B.C. according to the shorter chronology. The traditional version of Theravada Buddhism puts his attaining of nirvana (Skt. *nirvāṇa*, "extinction, blowing out") in the year 544 B.C. (The 2,500-year anniversary of this event was celebrated in 1956.) The career of all the Buddhas, who bear the 32 marks of a great man (e.g., wheels on the hands and feet), is identical except for places and persons.

The parents of Buddha were of the Kshatriya (warrior) caste. His mother died seven days after his birth. According to legend, at the age of 29 he had disturbing encounters with an old man, a sick man, a dead man, and an ascetic on four separate journeys, which caused him to forsake his life of luxury in the palace, his wife, Yaśodharā, and his son, Rāhula, for a homeless existence. His two teachers, Āḷāra Kālāma

and Uddaka Rāmaputta, whose views could not convince him, introduced him to the practice of → Yoga. Sitting under an *aśvattha*, or pipal, tree *(Ficus religiosa)* at Uruvela in Buddh Gaya (a small town in present-day Bihar, in northeast India), Buddha attained enlightenment on his own by perceiving "origination in dependence" (explained below), after warding off the attacks of his opponent Māra (death), who sought to prevent his enlightenment.

After initial hesitation because of the difficulty of making his dharma, or teaching, understood, Buddha preached his first sermon, the Dhammacakkappavattana-sutta ("Setting in motion the wheel of law"), in the Deer Park at Sarnath, near modern Varanasi, Uttar Predesh. He began by presenting his teaching to five disciples, the first monks, expounding on the four noble truths, thus rejecting the idea of becoming a *pratyeka-buddha* ("Buddha only for himself"; Pali *pacceka-buddha*), immediately entering nirvana as Buddha without teaching.

The order of the further events in the life of Buddha has been difficult to ascertain. He died of food poisoning near Kuśinagara (modern Kasia, east of Gorakhpur). His body was burned, and stupas were set up over his relics.

3.2. In his teaching Buddha seeks escape from entanglement in samsara (Skt. *saṃsāra*, "cycle of rebirth"), the cycle of birth, suffering, and death resulting from one's → karma — the force generated by one's good and evil deeds. This cycle is regarded as *duḥkha* (sorrow, suffering, imperfection; Pali *dukkha*). The entanglement, which is explained by the "origination in dependence" (Skt. *pratītya-samutpāda*, Pali *paṭicca-samuppāda*), is described as a series of 12 interrelated concepts. On the basis of (1) ignorance arise (2) habitual tendencies, the impulses of the will that lead to a new birth. Then comes (3) consciousness, the object of which is (4) name and form and (5) the six spheres of the sense organs (the senses and their objects), each of which is the presupposition of the next. There is (6) contact with sensory objects, from which come (7) feelings, and with them the (8) thirst for → reincarnation. This leads to the (9) grasping of what is mistakenly thought to be the ego. There is thus a renewed (10) becoming, (11) birth, and then (12) old age and death.

In this series of concepts, which Buddha himself regarded as hard to understand, an older series that builds on the idea of thirst (Skt. *tṛṣṇā*, Pali *taṇhā*) merges with a later one that extends it. The latter is more sharply defined philosophically and begins with the concept of ignorance, that is, of lack of insight into the four noble truths. Buddha elaborated these truths in his first sermon: the noble truth of suffering (caused by the cycle of birth), that of the origin of suffering (the desire for fresh rebirth), that of the removal of suffering (involving the removal of this desire), and that of the way that leads to the removal of suffering. This way is described very generally as the noble Eightfold Path, which involves right insight, thinking, speech, conduct, livelihood, striving, mindfulness, and concentration.

The way of salvation taught by Buddha applies only to monks who leave secular life to grasp the four noble truths through the way of → meditation. By so doing, they achieve the nonexistence of their own → person, which, according to the teaching of Buddha, is composed of five constituents: physical forms, feelings/sensations, ideas/knowledge, dispositions/impulses, and consciousness. They thus put an end to origination in dependence and reach nirvana as the goal of salvation. This alone has reality. Unlike things and experiences, nirvana is not composed (*saṃskṛta*) of innumerable individual, impersonal factors of existence (i.e., of dharmas).

3.3. In Hinayana Buddhism, or the "lesser vehicle" (Skt. *hīnayāna*, at present often called Theravada, "teaching of the elders"), the monk seeks to become "arhat" (one who is fit or worthy), that is, to reach nirvana himself on the basis of the teaching of Buddha. In Mahayana Buddhism, or the "great vehicle" (Skt. *mahāyāna*), however, a doctrine has developed since the first century A.D. that puts less emphasis on personal salvation. Bodhisattvas (i.e., future Buddhas) may postpone their own final entrance into nirvana in order to create good karma to be shared with others and thus, through a transfer of merit, deliver as many people as possible from the cycle of birth.

Mahayana Buddhists typically distance themselves from the human nature of Buddha, which Hinayana Buddhists always emphasize. Buddhism has adopted the doctrine of trikaya, or the three bodies of the Buddha. The *dharmakaya*, or transcendent body of doctrine that constitutes the true Buddha, is hidden. The body that is visible only to bodhisattvas, the *sambhogakaya*, is that which evolves from the enjoyment of the saving deeds of a Buddha. Buddha appears to people in his *nirmanakaya* (i.e., phantom body, or body of transformation).

In Mahayana Buddhism two philosophical schools have developed. In both the doctrine of emptiness is worked out, building on texts that refer to the perfection of wisdom (*prajñāpāramitā*). In the Madhyamika school, the empirical world and nirvana are the same, for both are viewed as empty. The second, or Yogacara school, which had great influ-

ence on Buddhist logicians, teaches that the phenomenal world exists only in the human mind.

3.4. The Vajrayana (lit. "vehicle of the diamond") school arose in the late phase of Buddhism. It seeks the way of redemption with the aid of → esoteric, → magical, and erotic practices.

4. Monastic Community
With his preaching at Varanasi, Buddha founded a sangha, or monastic community. After much hesitation he added to this an order of nuns, which came to an end centuries ago. Prospective monks serve two years as a novice (*sāmaṇera*). If the parents approve and the monastic community gives its unanimous consent, ordination (*upasaṃpadā*) as a monk (Skt. *bhikṣu*, Pali *bhikkhu*) follows, with the handing over of the three robes (*tricīvara*) and the alms bowl (*pātra*).

In older Buddhism no single organization embraced all monks. Monks would all gather in one place twice a month to recite the approximately 220 precepts of the pratimoksha (Skt. *prātimokṣa*, Pali *pātimokkha*, "that which is binding"), the code governing the common life of the community. This gathering could also independently execute all judicial acts (ordination, punishments, etc.). Only later, as in modern Thailand, did the order develop a hierarchical system with a *saṅgharāja*, or chief monk, at the head.

Buddhist monks initially lead a wandering life but soon settle into monasteries (*vihāra*). They are under obligation to live by begging for alms.

5. History
5.1. To give support to the monastic community after the nirvana of Buddha, tradition says that in the year of his death the Vinaya and the Sutta Piṭaka were put together at a council in Rajagriha (in modern Bihar). Debates about the Vinaya led repeatedly to new councils, the historicity of some of which is contested. As tradition has it, a second council was held in Vaishali (also in Bihar), at which time the elders (Skt. *sthavira*, Pali *thera*) broke off from the Mahasanghika school, which constituted the majority. This is traditionally regarded as the beginning of the formation of 18 schools. The sixth and most recent council of Theravada Buddhism took place at Rangoon in 1956.

5.2. Archaeology is an important source for the history of Buddhism in India, as are accounts of Chinese Buddhist pilgrims. Only in Sri Lanka is there a comprehensive history of the community, the form of the Mahāvaṃsa (Pali for "great chronicle").

5.3. One of the most significant promoters of

Buddhism was the Maurya ruler Aśoka in the 3d century B.C. In his day Buddhism spread beyond India to Sri Lanka. From the 1st century A.D. Buddhism was in China, and from there it moved to Viet Nam, and in the 6th century to Japan by way of Korea. It spread to Tibet in the 7th century and from there to Mongolia in the 16th century. The historical details of its spread into Southeast Asia (Thailand, Myanmar, and Cambodia) are obscure.

In India itself during the first millennium A.D. → Hinduism increasingly replaced Buddhism, which was finally ousted with the beginning of Islamic conquests (→ Islam) in the 13th century.

Bibliography: H. BECHERT, *Buddhismus, Staat und Gesellschaft* (3 vols.; Frankfurt, 1966); idem, ed., *When Did the Buddha Live? The Controversy on the Dating of the Historical Buddha* (Delhi, 1995) • H. BECHERT and R. GOMBRICH, eds., *The World of Buddhism* (London, 1984) • H. DUMOULIN, *Buddhism in the Modern World* (New York, 1976) • E. FRAUWALLNER, *History of Indian Philosophy* (2 vols.; New York, 1974); idem, *Die Philosophie des Buddhismus* (3d ed.; Berlin, 1969) • H. VON GLASENAPP, *Buddhistische Mysterien* (Stuttgart, 1940) • S. HANAYAMA, *Bibliography on Buddhism* (Tokyo, 1961) • W. KIRFEL, *Symbolik des Buddhismus* (Stuttgart, 1959) • E. LAMOTTE, *History of Indian Buddhism* (Louvain, 1988) • S. LÉVI et al., eds., *Hôbôgirin. Dictionnaire encyclopédique du bouddhisme d'après les sources chinoises et japonaises* (Paris, 1929ff.) • G. P. MALALASEKERA, ed., *Encyclopaedia of Buddhism* (Colombo, 1961ff.) • H. OLDENBERG, *Der Buddha. Sein Leben, seine Lehre, seine Gemeinde* (13th ed.; Munich, 1961) • F. E. REYNOLDS, *Guide to Buddhist Religion* (Boston, 1981) • G. SCHOPEN, *Stones, Bones, and Buddhist Monks: Collected Papers on the Archeology, Epigraphy, and Texts of Monastic Buddhism in India* (Honolulu, 1997) • A. K. WARDER, *Indian Buddhism* (Delhi, 1970) • Y. YOO, *Buddhism: A Subject Index to Periodical Articles in English, 1728-1971* (Metuchen, N.J., 1973) • E. ZÜRCHER, *The Buddhist Conquest of China* (2d ed.; Leiden, 1972).

OSKAR VON HINÜBER

Buddhism and Christianity

The first references to relations between Buddhism and Christianity come from Clement of Alexandria (ca. 150-ca. 215; see *Strom.* 1.15.71.6). Information about Buddhism may be found in the letters and journals of Francis → Xavier (1506-52) and other Jesuit missionaries. True dialogue between Buddhism and Christianity began when the lands of Asia opened themselves to the West and Christian missionary work led to the development of a new religious self-awareness in Asia (→ Mission). The World Parliament of Religions in 1893 initiated an encounter between Buddhism and Christianity along these lines. D. T. Suzuki (1870-1966), a participant, became the first significant interpreter of Mahayana Buddhism to the West.

In its declaration on the relation of the church to non-Christian religions *(Nostra aetate)*, Vatican II offered a brief introduction of individual religions and their religious experiences. It stated that the various forms of Buddhism express radical dissatisfaction with the transitory world and teach a way whereby people may either attain a state of full liberation with a devout or trusting mind or achieve supreme enlightenment, either by their own efforts or with higher aid. The council took note of the doctrine of the four noble truths and also of the distinction between Theravada Buddhism and Mahayana Buddhism with its division into the → Zen Buddhism of meditation and Amida Buddhism of belief. In opposition to the common interpretation of Buddhism as a religion without God, Vatican II puts Buddhism among the world religions.

In the → World Council of Churches (WCC), interreligious dialogue has been inspired especially by S. J. Samartha. Interreligious conversations took place in Ajaltoun, Lebanon (1970), Geneva (1972), Bangkok (1973), Colombo (1974), Nairobi (1975), and Chiang Mai, Thailand (1977). Issues have been discussed at most of the subsequent WCC meetings (e.g., Vancouver 1983 and Canberra 1991). A further area of common work between Buddhism and Christianity is the World Conference of Religions for Peace in Kyoto (1970), Lyons (1974), Princeton (1979), and Nairobi (1984). At these meetings representatives of various religious traditions tried to find ways in which the religions could work together to secure → peace, justice (→ Righteousness, Justice), and → human dignity.

In addition to practical questions of cooperation, important themes of → dialogue include the relation between Buddha and → Jesus, the question of God and human understanding (divine self-emptying/kenosis and self-actualizing in *anattā*, non-I, or selflessness), the world and the understanding of history, redemption and → karma, personal or human dignity and impersonality, and Buddhist → meditation and Christian → spirituality. The Roman Catholic Secretariat for Non-Christians has been involved in the discussion of such themes.

Bibliography: J. A. CUTTAT, *Asiatische Gottheit, Christlicher Gott* (Einsiedeln, 1971) • H. DUMOULIN and J. C.

MARALDO, eds., *Buddhism in the Modern World* (New York, 1976) • A. FERNANDO, *Buddhism and Christianity: Their Inner Affinity* (Colombo, 1981) • C. GEFFRÉ and M. DHAVAMONY, eds., *Buddhism and Christianity* (New York, 1979) • P. O. INGRAM and F. J. STRENG, eds., *Buddhist-Christian Dialogue* (Honolulu, 1986) • W. L. KING, *Buddhism and Christianity* (London, 1963) • J. MAY, "Kleine Beiträge zum Vergleich zur Verständigung," *ZMR* 66 (1982) 58-66 • G. MENSCHING, *Buddha und Christus–ein Vergleich* (Stuttgart, 1978) • S. J. SAMARTHA, *Courage for Dialogue: Ecumenical Issues in Interreligious Relationships* (Maryknoll, N.Y., 1981); idem, ed., *Dialogue between Men of Living Faiths* (Geneva, 1971) • D. T. SUZUKI, *Mysticism: Christian and Buddhist* (New York, 1957) • H. WALDENFELS, *Faszination des Buddhismus* (Mainz, 1982).

HANS WALDENFELS and GABRIELE SCHMIDT

Bulgaria

	1960	1980	2000
Population (1,000s):	7,867	8,862	8,306
Annual growth rate (%):	0.83	0.22	–0.48

Area: 110,994 sq. km. (42,855 sq. mi.)

A.D. 2000

Population density: 75/sq. km. (194/sq. mi.)
Births / deaths: 1.02 / 1.40 per 100 population
Fertility rate: 1.45 per woman
Infant mortality rate: 14 per 1,000 live births
Life expectancy: 72.1 years (m: 68.8, f: 75.6)
Religious affiliation (%): Christians 80.7 (Orthodox 77.7, indigenous 1.2, Protestants 1.2, Roman Catholics 1.1, other Christians 0.2), Muslims 12.0, nonreligious 4.8, atheists 2.4, other 0.1.

1. Historical Context
2. The Bulgarian Orthodox Church
3. The Roman Catholic Church
4. Protestant Churches
5. Muslims
6. Other Religious Groups
7. Church and State

1. Historical Context

On the Balkan Peninsula the Christianizing of the Slavs (→ Slavic Mission) began in Bulgaria. With a civilization that flourished under the influence of Christian Slavonic Orthodoxy, Bulgaria played a significant role in the development of contacts between the Christian East and West.

The Bulgarian state was founded in 681. Up to the tenth century, with its feudal economic, military, and political power, it was a worthy rival of → Byzantium, the Frankish kingdom, and the German Empire. Christianity came to Bulgaria in the sixth and seventh centuries, affected the Turkish governing class (the Proto-Bulgars), and became the official religion in 865, forging an independent culture and art. Moral and legal norms, worship and customs, the use of the Slavic-Bulgarian language as the language of liturgy (known as Old Bulgarian or Old Church Slavonic), the development of the written language (with Cyrillic characters developed from the Greek alphabet with added characters for Slavic sounds), and the promotion of a Christian national literature all helped to overcome ethnic and social distinctions and to nurture a sense of Bulgarian nationality.

With the recognition of an independent → patriarchate in 927, the Bulgarian church became the first national church in eastern Europe. The Bogomil movement, named for the priest Bogomil in the tenth century, contended for an apostolic lifestyle. It spread throughout the Balkans (→ Cathari), with its religious and social ideas influencing pre-Reformation development even in the West. Early Bulgarian culture, promoted in the ninth and tenth centuries by the literary and philosophical schools in Pliska, Preslav, and Ohrid, had an influence not only in the Balkans and Russia but over the whole of Europe. The struggle of the Bulgarian church for → autocephaly over against the Ecumenical Patriarchate of Constantinople, along with the competition between Constantinople and Rome for supremacy in Bulgarian territories, resulted in great tension between these ecclesiastical centers and helped to bring about the schism of 1054.

Bulgaria reached the zenith of its economic, political, cultural, and ecclesiastical development in the 13th century, when it stretched from the Black Sea to the Aegean and Adriatic coasts. It had cultural and commercial contacts as far away as Dubrovnik, Venice, and Genoa. Latin influence led to a brief union of the Bulgarian church with Rome. The golden age ended with the onslaught of the Muslim Turks.

From 1396 to 1878 Bulgaria was under the Ottoman yoke. The church lost its autocephaly and fell under the jurisdiction of the Constantinople patriarchate. Revolts against Turkish rule failed. Yet the → Renaissance and the → Enlightenment, along with religious and social revolutionary movements, had an impact on life in Bulgaria and strengthened the desire for national, ecclesiastical, and political independence. It is in this context that we are to understand the rise of the Roman Catholic Church in the

17th century and the formation of Protestant denominations in the middle of the 19th. The battle of the Bulgarian church for autocephaly ended in 1870, when a state decree proclaimed the establishment of an autonomous Bulgarian exarchate, to which the patriarchate of Constantinople replied with schism. The goal remained the economic, cultural, ecclesiastical, and political independence of the country.

In the period up to the socialist revolution of 1944, the church took an active part in the life of the people. The era of → socialism brought significant economic, social, and cultural changes. A law decreed the separation of church and state in 1949. The changes affected religious confession, the church's influence on society, the methods of Christian proclamation, and the practical forms of church life.

In December 1989 the Communist rule began to end, as the National Assembly abolished the Communist Party's sole right to govern. A new constitution was promulgated in July 1991, and in October of that year a non-Communist government was elected. The constitution guarantees freedom of religion, with Eastern Orthodoxy given a place of prominence as the "traditional religion in Bulgaria."

2. The Bulgarian Orthodox Church

2.1. The schism of 1870 ended on February 22, 1945, with the recognition of autocephaly. A people's church council restored the patriarchate in 1953. There are now 11 dioceses, each under a metropolitan, with a Holy Synod over them under the presidency of the Bulgarian patriarch. A council elects the patriarch, a board consisting of ordained and non-ordained persons deals with general questions, and an upper council handles financial matters.

In addition to the 11 dioceses in Bulgaria there are 2 foreign dioceses (the Diocese of North and South America and Australia and the Diocese of West Europe). Parishes in Istanbul, Budapest, Vienna, Bucharest, London, Munich, Brussels, Stockholm, and Paris also come under the jurisdiction of the Bulgarian Orthodox Church. Each diocese is divided into smaller administrative units, of which there are now 58 in all. Each deanery is then subdivided into parishes.

The church experienced a schism in 1992 when three metropolitans acted contrary to the patriarch in establishing a separate synod in Bulgaria. Mediation efforts in September 1992 by the ecumenical patriarch of Constantinople were unsuccessful.

2.2. In its church life the Bulgarian Orthodox Church focuses on worship, preaching, lectures, the dissemination of the Bible (new editions in 1982 and 1991), and Christian literature. Its goal is church and family education, moral and spiritual unity and piety among the people, and the maintaining of peace. The religious law of 1949 described the Bulgarian Orthodox Church as "the traditional confession of the Bulgarian people" and as a democratic people's church (art. 3).

2.3. Organizationally the Bulgarian Orthodox Church in 1992 had 2,600 parishes, 1,700 priests, 400 monks and nuns, and 3,700 churches and chapels. It also has two seminaries and two theological faculties, as well as a synodal press for journals and theological writings. It owns land, farms, and workshops for church goods. It also has a synodal organization for building churches.

2.4. The church has steadily built up ecumenical relations with other Christian communions in the country. Representatives have attended every important international and regional ecumenical conference from the early part of the 20th century. Stefan Zankow (1881-1965) made important contributions to basic ecclesiological problems, to the Orthodox conception of the → unity of the church, to the role of nontheological factors, and to the relation of faith and life. In movements within the → World Council of Churches (WCC) for the international friendship of churches, and in the → World Student Christian Federation, note should be taken of the efforts of the archimandrite Stefan, Bishop Paisij, Prof. N. Glubokovskij, and Grigor Latinov. The Bulgarian Orthodox Church became a member of the WCC in 1961 and has worked with its various committees and commissions. It helped to found the → Christian Peace Conference and became a member of the → Conference of European Churches (CEC). In the 1920s it established good relations with the → Anglican and → Old Catholic churches. It has helped in preparations for a Pan-Orthodox Church Council and participates in conversations with the ancient Eastern and many non-Orthodox churches.

At the regional level it engages in bilateral dialogue with Protestant churches, for example, with churches in Germany and Hungary. To coordinate ecumenical activities there is a special board that has representation on the Holy Synod and that is responsible both for ecumenical relations and for all interchurch contacts. Great strides have been made in local ecumenicity, for example, in preparation for an ecumenical translation of the Bible, or in permitting non-Orthodox students to attend the theological academy St. Clement of Ohrid. Recently, however, ecumenism has lost some of its vigor.

3. The Roman Catholic Church

3.1. Settlers from Dubrovnik and Saxony at the

time of Ottoman rule founded the first churches of the Latin Rite in Bulgaria. In the 16th and 17th centuries they enjoyed protection and religious care from Rome. Up to the middle of the 17th century almost all Bogomils and Pavliks in northern and southern Bulgaria were converted to Roman Catholicism. The church took part in the movement for independence and in the spread of Bulgarian literature during the 17th century. At the end of the 19th century and the beginning of the 20th it set up schools, boarding schools, hospitals, orphanages, and other institutions. The Western Rite is organized in two dioceses: the Diocese of Sofia and Plovdiv (35,000 adherents in 1993) and the Diocese of Nikopol (20,000 adherents).

3.2. The Roman Catholic Church with Eastern Rites (→ Uniate Churches) became very active in the middle of the 19th century. In its journal *Bulgaria* it even called on the people to join Rome and throw off the dominion of the patriarchate of Constantinople. In the 19th and 20th centuries it engaged in educational and social work to sustain and strengthen its parishes. In recent decades it was headed by the apostolic exarch of Sofia; in 1997 it claimed over 100,000 adherents.

4. Protestant Churches

In the second half of the 19th century American → Congregationalists and → Methodists, Russian → Baptists, and → Adventist immigrants from the Crimea came to Bulgaria. American → Pentecostals of Russian origin followed in 1921. With their missionary zeal, their disseminating of the Bible, their religious journals and books, and their schools and welfare organizations, these groups won many adherents and set up several churches in the cities. Their activities have kept these churches going, and membership has grown in some places. In the early 1990s the largest groups were the Union of Evangelical Pentecostal Churches (43,000 affiliated), the Bulgarian Church of God (30,000), and the Union of the Churches of the Seventh-day Adventists (8,000). The membership of Protestant churches is growing continuously.

5. Muslims

Bulgarian Muslims, mostly of Turkish origin, live in the northeast part of the country. Along with the 820,000 (1992) Turkic Muslims and the 300,000 Pomaks (i.e., Bulgarians who were forcibly won over to Islam and assimilated), there are also Muslims among the over 500,000 Gypsies (→ Roma) and the 6,000 Tatars. The Turkish Islamic population is gradually coming out of its isolation, but the Ot-

toman tradition is still a powerful factor that easily provokes negative emotional reactions among ethnic Bulgarians. Yet the old idea that Muslims may not live and work with Christians has been overcome. In the new social and political conditions Muslims, like the members of other religious groups, are subject to the influence of → secularization. Nevertheless, they cling fast to their traditional religious practices, which the state recognizes. In the mid-1990s the number of mosques was growing rapidly.

6. Other Religious Groups

Other religious groups in Bulgaria include the Armenian Apostolic Orthodox Church (10,000 adherents in 1992), as well as smaller Russian and Romanian Orthodox congregations. There is also a small Jewish community.

7. Church and State

At first, church-state relations in Bulgaria followed the model of → Byzantium, which influenced the whole of the Orthodox East. Yet harmonious cooperation remained an impracticable ideal. After the liberation of Bulgaria from the Ottoman yoke, caesaropapist tendencies increased as, in a movement of secularization, the government tried to interfere in the life of the church. The church defended its internal independence and thus came frequently into conflict with the state.

In the Communist epoch, legislation formally guaranteed to all citizens the freedom of conscience, religion, and worship. In 1948, however, Catholic schools and institutions were abolished and foreign religious were banned. All church activity was under close surveillance or control by the government.

Under the new constitution of 1991, freedom of conscience and belief is reaffirmed. The state provides 17 percent of Orthodox Church funds. No church, however, may operate a school or college (other than a theological institution) or may organize a youth movement. Religious education remains a challenge.

Bibliography: T. Beeson, *Discretion and Valour* (3d ed.; Philadelphia, 1982) • H. Christov, *Bulgaria: 1,300 Years of History* (in Bulgarian) (Sofia, 1980) • Ecumenical Division of the Holy Synod, *Churches and Confessions in the People's Republic of Bulgaria* (in Bulgarian) (Sofia, 1975) • A. Johansen, *The Bulgarian Orthodox Church* (London, 1965) • T. Sabev, "Évolution et originalité de l'église local de Bulgarie," *Église locale et église universelle* (Geneva, 1981) • A. de Santos Otero and F. Heyer, "Bulgarien," *TRE* 7.363-75 (bibliography) • I. Snegarow, *A Brief History of the Modern Orthodox Churches* (in Bulgarian) (vol. 2; Sofia, 1946) 1-91 •

S. Zankow (or Tsankov), *The Bulgarian Orthodox Church from the Independence of Bulgaria until the Present* (in Bulgarian) (Sofia, 1939); idem, *The Ethical Reality and Function of the Church* (in Bulgarian) (Sofia, 1948); idem, *The Internal Situation of the Bulgarian Orthodox Church* (in Bulgarian) (Sofia, 1933); idem, *Die Verfassung der Bulgarischen Orthodoxen Kirche* (Zurich, 1918) introduction, 1-40, has a history of the church, with bibliography.

Todor Sabev

Bulls and Briefs

Bulls and briefs are unofficial titles for papal deeds, edicts, and orders, especially before the appearance of *Acta sanctae sedis* (1865-1908). They represent communications of supreme significance from the standpoint of doctrine and canon law, as well as more localized directions and grants to individuals. They have defined dogma, established law (→ Canon Law), given decisions, set up or transformed bishoprics, confirmed orders and congregations, pronounced beatification and sainthood, appointed bishops and patrons, conferred benefices, privileges, and honors, and threatened or pronounced bans and → excommunications.

In form, bulls are generally documents in a long, vertical format; briefs are usually broadsides with a single fold.

Bulls (Lat. *bulla*, "capsule") are named for the round seal of gold and/or silver metal or embossed lead that, from the 11th century, bore on the one side the name of the → pope issuing the bull and on the other the heads of the apostolic princes → Peter and → Paul. The seal and the document itself were connected with silk or hempen cords. After 1878 a red seal came into use, and the lead seal was reserved for only the most solemn communications. The term "bull" is used today only infrequently (e.g., sometimes for the articles of incorporation of a new bishopric), and then not in any consistent, technical sense.

"Briefs" designates papal parchment letters executed in relatively simple style and dealing with matters of lesser importance.

Written in Latin in antique calligraphy or printed in selected typographic styles, bulls and briefs are collected and reprinted in so-called *bullaria*. They are identified according to the opening words *(arenga)* of their text.

Bibliography: R. L. Poole, "Bulls, Papal," *DECH* 72-74 • H. Thurston, "Bulls and Briefs," *CE* 3.52-58; idem, "Bulls and Briefs," *ERE* 2.891-97.

Heiner Grote†

Bureaucracy

1. Term
2. Scientific Analysis
3. Bureaucracy and the Church

1. Term

The first use of the term is ascribed to the French Physiocrat J.-C.-M. V. de Gournay (1712-59), who used it critically for absolutist government by means of civil servants. From the beginning of the 19th century it has been used for the hierarchical, monocratic organization of officialdom that, following Napoleon's administrative reforms in France, was also introduced into other countries. In its further development both the word and what it denotes have remained somewhat ambivalent. It can refer negatively to a kind of domineering quality or positively, as formulated for example by Max → Weber (1864-1920), to government structure that is rational and efficient. The term may also be used neutrally. Popular usage reflects many nuances, with "bureaucracy" referring variously to rational organization, government by officialdom, public administration, a type of organization, and inefficiency and waste.

2. Scientific Analysis

Sociologically, bureaucracy denotes a type of → organization. Weber has described the following features: official, trained personnel; separation of office and person; hierarchical system of posts with directives and controls; formal division of labor and specialization; explicit rules for carrying out tasks; and putting everything in writing and keeping records for internal and external control. Weber's ideal type of a bureaucratic organization has been developed as a model of rule by law and as the most effective way of carrying out the tasks of administration.

Anglo-Saxon sociologists in particular have tested empirically the working principle and various features of bureaucracy. Their results confirm the dominant view that, to varying degrees, state organizations all show bureaucratic characteristics and that these may develop likewise in private enterprises, political parties, church organizations, and labor unions. The scope or degree of bureaucracy has been studied with respect to efficiency, in an attempt to fashion optimal structures for specific tasks. It has become clear that hierarchical structures and the detailed regulation of every process hinder rather than promote real input from specialists. The efficiency of an organization is dependent on a careful balancing of structural requirements and the freedom that leaves room for the motivation and active involvement of members of the organization (esp. the professionals).

Empirical tests are also important in the → democratic validation and control of this form of administration from a legal and rational standpoint. It needs to be asked especially whether state bureaucracy is a genuine instrument of government in a democratic system or whether bureaucracy has in fact become an independent and uncontrollable factor on its own. In a rather different form the same question must be put to nonpolitical bureaucratic organizations. At issue is the potential alienation between those who lead the organization (officials, professionals, or representatives) and their members, customers, and clients. As early as 1911 R. Michels described such alienation as the iron law of oligarchy.

New discussion has started with the various manifestations of bureaucracy in all social spheres. It has analyzed the interdependence between state and nonstate bureaucracy and developments along the lines of bureaucratizing and de-bureaucratizing. Such research into modern forms and expressions of bureaucracy can lead to important insight for the practical mastering of social problems as social institutions encounter crises of confidence and validity (→ Church; State), and as everyday life becomes more difficult to control and regulate.

3. Bureaucracy and the Church
Analysis of the conceptual relation between bureaucracy and state government and administration has enabled us to see similar phenomena in other social spheres, particularly the church. Thus the Roman Catholic Church, with its structured hierarchy, differentiated internal structure, and dogmatic rules (→ Dogma), might be called the oldest bureaucratic organization still in existence. But bureaucracy can be found similarly in all religious organizations insofar as they implement or copy the secular structures of government (cf. the uniting of civil, military, and ecclesiastical powers in the pharaohs, as well as the respective bureaucracies in state churches, churches that function as separate legal corporations, and those that exist in societies with full separation of church and → state). Since the work of E. → Troeltsch, the different degrees of bureaucracy and administration in church organizations have been related especially to the contrast between church and → sect, with the former showing more of the features of bureaucracy, the latter fewer.

Applying the writings on bureaucracy to church organizations runs into at least two problems. First, in asking about the efficiency of bureaucratic organizations and the necessary conditions, we have to ask what church organizations are supposed to be doing. The relevant theological controversies (cf. the various church views stressing missions, institutional structures, or appropriate church functions) show that such investigations involve theological presuppositions that are often unconscious. In criticizing bureaucratic elements in different church organizations and proposing alternatives, writers often adopt concepts and formulas from secular management without sufficiently taking into account the differences between religious and commercial organizations. (On this point, see some American literature as well as the work of L. Paul. Note that C. R. Hinings and M. A. Thung try to do justice to specific theological and religious factors.)

Second, there is a widespread public idea, even prejudice, that all the problems of alienation in church organizations are due to bureaucracy. In examining the question of what elements of bureaucracy may be avoided or not, we need to distinguish carefully between (1) phenomena of bureaucratic organizations per se and (2) institutional rigidities that have their roots elsewhere.

Bibliography: M. ALBROW, *Bureaucracy* (New York, 1970) • G. BORMANN and S. BORMANN-HEISCHKEIL, *Theorie und Praxis kirchlicher Organisation* (Opladen, 1971) • K. GABRIEL and F. X. KAUFMANN, *Zur Soziologie des Katholizismus* (Mainz, 1980) • C. R. HININGS and B. D. FOSTER, "The Organization Structure of Churches: A Preliminary Model," *Sociology* 7 (1973) 93-106 • H. JACOBY, *The Bureaucratization of the World* (Berkeley, Calif., 1973) • F. X. KAUFMANN, *Kirche begreifen. Analysen und Thesen zur gesellschaftlichen Verfassung des Christentums* (Freiburg, 1979) • T. LEUENBERGER and K.-H. RUFFMANN, eds., *Bürokratie* (Bern, 1977) • N. LUHMANN, "Die Organisierbarkeit von Religionen und Kirchen," *Religion im Umbruch* (ed. J. Wössner; Stuttgart, 1972) 245-85 • R. MICHELS, *Political Parties: A Sociological Study of the Oligarchical Tendencies of Modern Democracies* (Gloucester, Mass., 1978) • L. PAUL, *The Deployment and Payment of the Clergy* (London, 1964) • H. J. PRATT, "Bureaucracy," *EncRel(E)* 2.568-71 (bibliography) • P. F. RUDGE, *Ministry and Management* (London, 1968) • R. P. SCHERER, *American Denominational Organization* (Pasadena, Calif., 1980) • K. A. THOMPSON, *Bureaucracy and Church Reform* (Oxford, 1970) • M. A. THUNG, "Organizing Religion: An Exercise in Applied Sociology," *ARSSR* 1 (1977) 145-66 • E. TROELTSCH, *The Social Teaching of the Christian Churches* (2 vols.; Louisville, Ky., 1992) • M. WEBER, *Economy and Society: An Outline of Interpretive Sociology* (2 vols.; Berkeley, Calif., 1978; orig. pub., 1922).

DIETER GRUNOW

Burial → Funeral

Burkina Faso

	1960	1980	2000
Population (1,000s):	4,452	6,909	12,057
Annual growth rate (%):	1.80	2.64	2.78

Area: 274,400 sq. km. (105,946 sq. mi.)

A.D. 2000

Population density: 44/sq. km. (114/sq. mi.)
Births / deaths: 4.42 / 1.63 per 100 population
Fertility rate: 6.05 per woman
Infant mortality rate: 89 per 1,000 live births
Life expectancy: 47.5 years (m: 46.6, f: 48.4)
Religious affiliation (%): Muslims 49.8, tribal religionists 30.2, Christians 19.2 (Roman Catholics 11.2, Protestants 7.5, other Christians 0.6), other 0.8.

1. General Situation
2. Religious Situation

1. General Situation

Burkina Faso, known before August 1984 as Upper Volta, is a landlocked country in West Africa, bordered on the north by Niger and Mali, and on the south by Benin, Togo, Ghana, and Ivory Coast. The northern and northeastern regions, belonging to the Sahel zone, are very dry and abandoned to the advance of the desert. The vegetation is mainly grassland and savanna, with some thick forest patches in the South. The southern region has more rain, which comes in two seasons a year (May–June and September–October), with dry seasons between. Temperatures range from 15° C (59° F) in November through March to 42° C (108° F) in March through May.

Burkina Faso includes over 70 distinct ethnolinguistic groups, with the largest being the Mossi (49 percent), Fulani (8 percent), and, with about 7 percent of the population each, the Mandé, Bobo, Gourounsi, and Gourmantché.

Only 10 percent of the land is arable. About five-sixths of the population live on subsistence farming, growing millet, maize, rice, beans, sweet potatoes, and yams for local consumption, and cotton, sesame, peanuts, sugarcane, pineapples, and tobacco for export. Cattle, sheep, goats, horses, and donkeys are raised.

The original inhabitants of Burkina Faso were hunters, but they were later replaced by agricultural peoples. The Mossi arrived from the East, probably in the 13th century, and established five main states.

Their states opposed French colonial expansion in the 1880s until the beginning of the 20th century, when they were subdued and made part of French West Africa. In 1947 the territory became a separate entity and in 1960 an independent nation. The army took over the government in 1965, 1980, and 1987. The last coup established the current regime, which restored limited democracy in the early 1990s. Ouagadougou, the capital, is situated in the center of the country. The second largest city is Bobo-Dioulasso, an important rail link between Ouagadougou and the Ivory Coast.

2. Religious Situation

African religion (→ Guinea 2) evolved in Burkina Faso, as in other parts of the continent, without a founder. It is practiced among all the peoples of Burkina Faso; the majority of the Komono, Minianka, Birifor, and Dorosie still adhere strongly to it, having resisted both Islam and Christianity.

Islam was rejected for many centuries by the peoples of Burkina Faso, but it began to penetrate the country in the 18th century. During the French colonial period, it is said to have experienced harassment. After independence, however, it made rapid expansion, especially in urban areas. It is presently growing rapidly in some areas.

Christianity arrived in 1900 with the Roman Catholic White Fathers (→ Catholic Missions), who established themselves in Ouagadougou a year later. As more → missionaries arrived, the process of → evangelization gained momentum. First converts were severely persecuted, but an indigenous congregation (→ Orders and Congregations), Soeurs de l'Immaculée-Conception, was established in 1922, and Soeurs de l'Annonciation in 1948. The first African → priests were ordained in 1942. A large number of converts from African religions join the → Roman Catholic Church each year. Roman Catholic lay groups (→ Clergy and Laity) are very active; under their organization Communauté Chrétienne de Haute-Volta was established in 1970. In 1992 there were eight → dioceses, 452 priests, and 305 seminarians. The Episcopal Conference of Burkina Faso and Niger has its headquarters in Ouagadougou. The church turned over its schools to the state in 1969 but continues to direct several colleges, has a number of medical centers, and runs development projects.

Protestant missionaries of the Assemblies of God (→ Pentecostal Churches) arrived in Burkina Faso from America in 1919 and were joined by others from France. As a result of their work, an autonomous church, Assemblées de Dieu en Haute-Volta, was established in 1955. Its activities in → Sunday school and literature have increased the number of members. By 1990 the Assemblies of God had over 1,600 congregations with 270,000 affiliated. Other Protestant work includes churches of the Christian and Missionary Alliance (48,000 adherents), the Evangelical Church Association (30,000), the Apostolic Mission (14,000), and the Baptist Convention (associated with the U.S. Southern Baptist Convention; 11,000). Indigenous churches (9 groups, with 10,000 members in 1990) are presently small but have recently shown a high rate of growth.

In 1973 the Roman Catholic Church had 687 missionaries from the Western world and 50 from Africa. Protestants had 121 missionaries from the Western world (mainly the United States and Canada) and 15 from Africa and Korea. In 1990 there were a total of 579 Catholic and 364 Protestant missionaries.

The Fédération des Églises et Missions Évangéliques (FEME, formed in 1961) is a member of the Association of Evangelicals of Africa and Madagascar (AEAM) with headquarters in Nairobi (Kenya). The Roman Catholic and Protestant churches broadcast programs over the government Radiodiffusion-Télévision Burkina. Otherwise no ecumenical relations or activities are reported in Burkina Faso. According to Burkina Faso's constitution, all religious creeds are respected and granted appropriate rights.
→ African Theology

Bibliography: P. ADAMSON, "Ideas in Action: The Rains. A Report from a Village in Yatenga, Upper Volta," The State of the World's Children, 1982-83 (ed. J. P. Grant; Oxford, 1982) 45-128 • African Encyclopedia (London, 1974) • S. ANDERSON, ed., Thomas Sankara Speaks: The Burkina Faso Revolution, 1983-87 (New York, 1988) • Les Assemblées de Dieu en Haute-Volta: 50ᵉ anniversaire (Ouagadougou, 1971) • "Burkina Faso," Africa South of the Sahara, 1993 (22d ed.; London, 1993) 179-94 • J. R. DE BENOIST, "Upper Volta," NCE 14.474 • W. EATON, "Upper Volta," Cultural Atlas of Africa (ed. G. Speake; New York, 1981) 143 • L'Eglise Catholique en Afrique occidentale et centrâle (19th ed.; Paris, 1993-94) • D. M. McFARLAND, Historical Dictionary of Upper Volta (London, 1978) • E. P. SKINNER, "Christianity and Islam among the Mossi," AmA 60 (1958) 1102-19 • STATISTISCHES BUNDESAMT WIESBADEN: LÄNDERBERICHT, Statistik des Auslandes Länderbericht Burkina Faso (Wiesbaden, 1988).

JOHN MBITI

Burma → Myanmar

Burundi

	1960	1980	2000
Population (1,000s):	2,941	4,130	6,974
Annual growth rate (%):	1.77	2.79	2.49

Area: 27,816 sq. km. (10,740 sq. mi.)

A.D. 2000

Population density: 251/sq. km. (649/sq. mi.)
Births / deaths: 4.01 / 1.52 per 100 population
Fertility rate: 5.76 per woman
Infant mortality rate: 105 per 1,000 live births
Life expectancy: 49.3 years (m: 47.6, f: 51.0)
Religious affiliation (%): Christians 92.2 (Roman Catholics 66.7, Protestants 12.8, unaffiliated 10.5, Anglicans 3.1, other Christians 0.5), tribal religionists 6.2, Muslims 1.4, other 0.2.

Overview
1. Christian Missions
2. Interdenominational Organizations
3. Church and State

Overview

Burundi is a small, landlocked country of East Africa, bordered by Rwanda, Tanzania, and Zaire. Its people are of the Hutu (85 percent), Tutsi (14 percent), and Twa (1 percent) tribes and are mainly peasant farmers. The minority Tutsis have traditionally been the politically dominant tribe. Its culture remained largely uninfluenced by the outside world until toward the end of the 19th century, when Christian missionaries began to arrive and build schools. The social structure was hierarchical and patrilineal, with family and clan as the focus of community life. Traditional religion taught belief in one God (called Imana), as well as the influence of ancestral spirits (→ Tribal Religions; Ancestor Worship; Guinea 2). Today, the vast majority of the people of Burundi are Christian, with smaller numbers in African traditional religions and in Islam. Also there are Hindu, Buddhist, Baha'i, and Jewish minorities. These last groups, however, are mostly of nonindigenous origin and make little or no attempt to gain converts.

Burundi became independent from Belgium in 1962, but the military has ruled from 1966 until the first democratic presidential elections in June 1993. Since 1972, ethnic tensions between Burundi's majority Hutus and the minority Tutsis have led to hundreds of thousands of deaths and to over a million people being displaced from their homes. Severe internal tensions have continued into the mid-1990s, with the Hutus in control of the government and the

Tutsis controlling the military, and both having to cope with the problems of large numbers of refugees from Rwanda, which has struggled with the same interethnic problem.

1. Christian Missions

The first attempt to reach Burundi with the gospel was in 1879, with the arrival of two Catholic White Fathers from France. However, it was not until 1912 that mission stations were permanently established. The fact that a viable German colonial administration was established in Burundi in 1896 contributed to this success.

Although the White Fathers were protected by the German administration, it was with the coming of the Belgian administration (→ Colonialism) that they gained considerable power and were given financial subsidies for their educational and medical work. The → Roman Catholic Church grew tremendously during the 1920s and 1930s. In 1992 it accounted for about 60 percent of the whole population, making Burundi one of the most Catholic nations in the continent of Africa.

Among the first Protestants to establish mission stations in Burundi were the Bethel Lutheran missionaries (1907) and the Neukirchner Missionsgesellschaft (1911). Both groups had to leave Burundi when the country was occupied by Belgian soldiers in 1916 (→ German Missions).

After the Second World War there were renewed Protestant missionary efforts. The Seventh-day Adventists were among the first, and by 1990 had some 44,000 adherents.

The next group was the Danish Baptist Church. They gradually took over the stations formerly established by the Lutheran and the Neukirchner missionaries. They had less success than the Adventists, however.

In 1932 the American Free Methodist Church began work, in cooperation with the Baptist missionaries. Their adherents numbered about 70,000 by 1990.

In the early 1930s the Kansas Yearly Meeting of → Friends began work at another former German station. Currently there are approximately 9,500 adherents.

The Church Missionary Society started work in Burundi at almost the same time as the Friends. The result of their work is the Protestant Episcopal Church of Burundi, which by 1990 had become the second largest Protestant church in the country, with 143,000 adherents.

Missionaries of the Swedish Pentecostal Church arrived in Burundi in 1935 from Zaire. They started to evangelize in the south of Burundi. Their work led to the formation of the Church of Pentecost (→ Pentecostal Churches), which became the largest Protestant church in the country (425,000 adherents in 1990).

Smaller groups were the World Gospel Mission, which started work in 1939 but made slow progress, and the World Grace Testimony Society, which carried on ministries during the 1940s but later handed over their work to the Immanuel Mission (→ Plymouth Brethren).

2. Interdenominational Organizations

The Alliance of Burundi Protestant Churches was founded in 1935. The member churches were able to coordinate their respective spheres of work, thus avoiding future conflicts. Also, the alliance could have more influence with the government than individual churches could. In 1985 the alliance had five member churches: the Baptist Church, the Episcopal Church, the Friends, the Methodists, and the World Gospel Mission. Other churches that did not join still cooperate with the alliance on some projects, such as teacher training institutions.

Since 1967, → dialogues have been held between Protestant churches and the Roman Catholic Church, and there is growing ecumenical collaboration among the churches in Burundi.

3. Church and State

Relationships between the colonial governments and the missionary societies were good. Missionaries were given government protection and in turn provided significant services in the areas of education, medical services, and agricultural → development (§1). These activities were subsidized by the Belgian administration.

In 1969, a meeting between government and church representatives dealt with some issues of concern. Following this, the churches summoned their members to cooperate with the government to reduce ethnic tensions in the country. In spite of this effort, the violence has continued to the present time.

Unfortunately, the churches in Burundi have not been free of blame for the social and political strife that has arisen between the Tutsi and the Hutu. The Roman Catholic Church tended to support the Hutu, while the Protestant churches tended to favor the Tutsi. During the upheavals of 1972, the Tutsi bishops had more freedom to speak than did the Hutu leaders. In 1972, 1973, and 1977 the government expelled a number of white missionaries.

In 1985 the government arrested several Catholic priests as well as the archbishop of Gitega, and also expelled many foreign missionaries. It later took over the administration of several Catholic seminaries. After 1987 a measure of religious freedom was restored, with missionaries being allowed to return.

Bibliography: D. B. BARRETT, *Schism and Renewal in Africa* (Nairobi, 1968); idem, ed., *African Initiatives in Religion* (Nairobi, 1977); idem, ed., *WCE* 205-7 • E. H. CHILSON, *Ambassador of the King* (Wichita, Kans., 1943) • L. O. EVANS, ed., *Emerging African Nations and Their Leaders* (Chicago, 1964) • D. HOHENSEE, *Church Growth in Burundi* (Pasadena, Calif., 1977) • K. S. LATOURETTE, *A History of the Expansion of Christianity*, vol. 7, *Advance through Storm* (New York, 1945; repr., Grand Rapids, 1970) • R. LEMARCHAND, *Rwanda and Burundi* (London, 1970) • J. S. MBITI, *African Religions and Philosophy* (London, 1969); idem, *Concepts of God in Africa* (London, 1970).

ANZA A. LEMA

Byzantium

1. General Features
2. Historical Epochs
    2.1. Early (324/330-634)
    2.2. Middle (635-1204)
    2.3. Late (1204-1453)
3. Theology
    3.1. Post-Nicene Patristics
    3.2. Iconoclastic Controversy, Macedonian Renaissance, Dialectic, the "Panoply," and Palamism
4. Aftermath of Defeat

1. General Features

G. Ostrogorsky has pointed out that Roman statecraft, Greek culture, and Christian faith are the main sources of Byzantine development. These forces found outward expression in the concentration of the Roman Empire in the East with its new center on the Bosporus. Their synthesis gave rise to Byzantium, whose inhabitants called themselves Romans. Its constitutive phase was the period from the victory of Constantine (306-37) in 324 to the claim of Constantius II (337-61) to supreme dominion. It resulted, on the one hand, from the mastering of a world economic crisis, which had meant above all the end of the old city culture, and, on the other hand, from the abandoning of attempts to restore old Rome (as under Decius, emperor 249-51) or Hellenistic tradition (as under Diocletian, emperor 284-305) in favor of forces that from the late second century had moved ever more clearly in historically new directions. On this basis Christianity had received recog-

nition as *religio licita* and, under a *do ut des* — tit for tat — mentality, had increasingly been favored within the scope of Roman cultic thinking. This trend integrated the episcopally constituted church (→ Episcopalianism) into the reality of the empire and its political conception.

The antagonism of the imperial claim against the political civilization of the East, which found support in the pagan citizenry, led to sharp conflict in the fourth century. In this situation the Christians supported the idea of one empire, of the unity of the oikoumene — especially under Julian the Apostate (361-63) — thus giving a political dimension to their opposition to → pagans (→ Gentiles, Gentile Christianity).

The idea of Rome and its claim to universal dominion, the hierarchical Neoplatonic idea of the rule of the one over the many (→ Platonism), and the monarchical thinking of what had become the Christian tradition came together in a kind of syndrome to produce the Byzantine ideology of empire and emperor. On this basis religiopolitical forms of the cult arose that viewed the "Christ-loving" emperor as a representation of the divine (thus *proskynēsis*, obeisance, was appropriate). Yet the ideology had no directly normative function for the political reality. According to the unwritten but historically influential constitutional sense of the Byzantine state, the emperor as living embodiment of law was subject to the laws of humanity and human criticism. The → state was *res publica* and not a matter of private will. Hence the emperor was restricted by the will of the forces that supported him — the senate, the people (with their political parties), and the army — forces that, according to their economic and political importance, established the reality of imperial power.

The church's hierarchy, especially the patriarch of Constantinople and representatives of the interests of → monasticism, could also set limits to imperial power, though normally they were at the service of the will of an emperor who was only too close to them. The concept "caesaropapism," the typically Byzantine blending of secular and spiritual power that Justinian I (527-65) had described as a symphony guaranteed by the emperor (preface to his *Novella* 6), is only partly correct. At the same time the theory of a "political Dyophysitism" finds no support in the sources. The idea of a tension in principle between the two powers was alien in the East.

Furthermore, Byzantium never knew a clerical class with a monopoly of education and common standards. In Byzantium the conviction that by entering the ministry or a → monastery one would finally forgo any state office was also politically influential. The → culture of intellectuals was firmly committed to pagan wisdom, to the feeling for life articulated in its → myth and its Logos. In general, Byzantium had no interest in promoting the Christian confession (→ Confession of Faith) as something new and different from the tradition of antiquity. The pre-Christian past of the Byzantines included the idea that "true → philosophy" could be expressed in a life of seclusion and contemplation, such as the Christian monks and contemplatives later demonstrated, and thus the → "worldview of even the secular inhabitants of Byzantium had a place for such an expression of Christianity" (H.-G. Beck).

2. Historical Epochs

2.1. Early (324/330-634) By the early epoch we mean the period from the founding of Constantinople (324/330) to the beginning of the Arab invasions (634). The cultural centers at this time were → Alexandria, → Antioch, and Constantinople.

2.1.1. In the fourth century Byzantium ruled from the Euphrates to Britain, but barbarian invasions eventually reduced its territory to the eastern Mediterranean and the Near East.

2.1.2. Justinian I (527-65) succeeded in reconquering Italy, Africa, and southern Spain. But with the settling of the Lombards in Italy (568) and the Slavs in the Balkans (ca. 580), only the exarchates of Carthage and Ravenna in the West, as well as southern Italy, Sicily, and Thessalonica, remained under Byzantine control.

2.1.3. The long-standing battle with Persia on the eastern frontier was finally lost, as the Persians captured Armenia, Cilicia, and Syria (613), then → Palestine (614) and, after an attack on Constantinople itself (615-16), Egypt (619). Emperor Heraclius (610-41) implemented some social and military reforms in Asia Minor that would undergird the future strength of Byzantium. The main point was the creation of indigenous peasant-soldiers for the military districts and their armies, which would be typical in the middle epoch. In these districts, as in the exarchates, all power, including civil power, was in the hands of the military. Nevertheless, after exhausting itself in its victory over the Persians (629-31), Byzantium could not stop the victorious march of Caliph Omar (634-44).

2.2. Middle (635-1204)

In ten years the Arabs altered the picture throughout the Mediterranean world, thus initiating the middle epoch, which lasted until the 12th century.

2.2.1. Byzantium concentrated itself as a military state in Asia Minor and Thrace. It lost the exarchates (Carthage in 698, Ravenna in 751) and had to defend itself against the Arabs, who besieged Constantinople in 674-78 and 717, as well as the Bulgars, who after 680 became increasingly menacing.

2.2.2. Under the Macedonian dynasty (867-1056) Byzantium was again able to push back the eastern frontier to the Euphrates, to win back Syria, Armenia, and, for a short time, Palestine. It also managed to shore up its rule in southern Italy and the Balkans. With a new inner strength, this state reached its greatest size under Basil II (976-1025).

2.2.3. Nevertheless, when the senate, high officials, and intellectuals in the capital achieved domination over politics and the emperor, Byzantium became unable to withstand the Normans in Italy, the Hungarians in the Balkans, and especially the Seljuks, nor could it stop Croatia and Zeta from becoming vassals of the papacy.

2.2.4. The military aristocracy achieved power with the Comnenus dynasty (1081-1185). It managed to secure Byzantium from outside threats, especially against the desire of the → crusaders for land, but it prepared the way for internal and ultimately outer collapse under the Angelus dynasty (1185-1204) by promoting centrifugal forces, such as the extensive possessions made possible by the *pronoia* system (i.e., giving absolute possession of property in exchange for the landholders' supplying a varying number of troops).

2.3. Late (1204-1453)

The late epoch began in 1204 with the capture of Constantinople by the crusaders and ended with the Ottoman capture of the city on May 29, 1453.

2.3.1. The true victor in 1204 was the Venetian doge Enrico Dandalo (1192-1205), who established a Latin kingdom with the → feudal system of the Frankish states on Greek soil. Byzantium lived on in Epirus (in northern Greece) and Asia Minor, where the Lascaris kingdom organized itself for reconquest in Nicaea, and also in Trebizond (present-day Trabzon), where a kingdom of the Comnenus family was established in 1204 that survived until 1461.

2.3.2. Michael VIII Palaeologus (1259-82), the founder of the last dynasty, recaptured Constantinople in 1261. In the same year he made an alliance with Genoa against Venice. By diplomatic means, including the Union of Lyons (1274), he forestalled the enemies of Byzantium, especially Charles of Anjou (1265-85), whose harsh rule provoked the so-called Sicilian Vespers in 1282, which aided the Byzantine cause.

2.3.3. After Michael's death Byzantium shrank to a small state. In about 1320 it lost Asia Minor, apart from a few strongholds, to the Turks, led now by the

Ottomans. At the same time the Serbs under Stephan Dušan (1331-55) and the Bulgars spread across the Balkans. In Byzantium itself civil war raged, with a revolution in Thessalonica. Byzantium survived into the 14th century only because of the onslaught of the Mongols under Timur (Tamurlane, 1336-1405), who in 1402 defeated the Ottoman Sultan Bayezid I (1389-1402) at Ankara.

3. Theology

The political history and geography of Byzantium are reflected in its theology.

3.1. Post-Nicene Patristics

The beginnings of Byzantine theology are identical with post-Nicene → patristics.

3.1.1. From the standpoint of dogmatic history, the earliest theological focus (4th cent.) was the controversy about the deity of the Logos and the Spirit, which the hypostatic teaching of the → Cappadocians finally settled. In the fifth century the focus was on the two natures of Christ, with debate on the nature of the union in Christ between the Logos and human existence. At the Council of → Ephesus (431) a breach took place with Christianity beyond the eastern frontier (→ Nestorians), and at → Chalcedon (451) a boundary was defined to exclude the → Monophysite confession of Egypt and Syria, whose inspiration was → Cyril of Alexandria (d. 444).

3.1.2. A strict Chalcedonianism based on the so-called *Tome* of → Leo the Great (440-61), and located chiefly in the West, tended to lay more stress on the two natures of Christ than on their unity. In response there developed at the time of Justinian I a mediating position oriented to Cyril and today called neo-Chalcedonianism. This provided the religious policy of the emperor with compromises that seemed calculated to win over the Monophysite Near East and Egypt to a united imperial church, and it became dogma at the Second Council of Constantinople (553).

3.1.3. Under Emperor Heraclius (610-41), on the basis of his proposal that the two natures of Christ had a single will (Monothelitism) and a single operation (Monenergism), unions were achieved in Armenia (626) and Egypt (633). Little came of these, however, because of the Arab invasions.

3.2. Iconoclastic Controversy, Macedonian Renaissance, Dialectic, the "Panoply," and Palamism

With the consolidation of the middle Byzantine state, the imperial church opted for union with → Rome and Western Christianity at an ecumenical council in Constantinople in 680-81. It adopted as a dogma the Dyothelitism espoused by Maximus the Confessor (ca. 580-662) but rejected the idea of a single personal, or hypostatic, will in Christ.

3.2.1. Under Justinian I, in 543, the church had rejected the → Origenism connected with the Platonizing spirituality of Evagrius Ponticus (ca. 346-399). But between the seventh and ninth centuries Evagrian mysticism, and with it monastic mentality, with its desire for direct knowledge of God, was integrated into the → church. Maximus the Confessor in particular had made this possible with a synthesis that transformed both mysticism and the hierarchical thinking of Paul the Areopagite (6th cent.).

Externally this period is known as that of the iconoclastic controversy (726-843), which was unleashed in former imperial territories now ruled by → Islam but which rested on traditions in Christianity itself (→ Images). Both parties could appeal to practice, to Christological arguments, and to ecumenical synods (in 754 the iconoclastic Council of Hiereia, in 787 the Council of Nicaea). The most important theologian to defend images in the 8th century came from the caliphate and did his work there. This was John of Damascus (ca. 655-ca. 750), who summarized theology in his "Exposition of the Orthodox Faith," a work that later had a strong influence, especially in the West during the 12th century. The main contestants when iconoclasm sprang to life again in 815 were the patriarch Nicephorus I (806-15, d. 829) and his adversary, the monastic zealot Theodore of Studios (759-826), who achieved a significant victory in the debate for the → orthodoxy (§3) of Byzantine monasticism, which for centuries would be joined to the cenobitic ideal, and in this form was integrated into the life of the church.

3.2.2. From the standpoint of the West, the age of the Macedonian renaissance is known for the → *filioque* controversy. The Latins had inserted this phrase into the creed, probably as early as the Council of Toledo (589). In so doing, they began a struggle that lasted from Photius (patriarch 858-67 and 877-86) to Michael I Cerularius (patriarch 1043-58) and led to the schism between East and West. This schism is usually dated from July 16, 1054, when Cardinal Humbert of Silva Candida (d. 1061) placed a → bull of excommunication on the → altar of Hagia Sophia, but contemporaries did not find the matter quite so clear-cut, nor do Byzantine historians (→ Heresies and Schisms). Photius had already challenged the Roman claim to primacy. Up to the rediscovery of this argument by Cerularius, the *filioque* had dominated the controversy, along with differences of rite and discipline (e.g., over the use of unleavened bread, the insistence on → celibacy, and Saturday fasting). In the ninth century the Slavic mission of Cyril (ca.

827-69) and Methodius (ca. 815-85) and conflict that arose over their relation to the German hierarchy further exacerbated the tension between East and West.

But polemics, whether that of the Photians, that against Islam, or that against the Paulicians and Bogomils, formed only part of the theological production of the period. Homiletic and hagiographic literature was at a high point. The vitae in the ten-volume *Menologion* of Simeon Metaphrastes (10th cent.), both in content and in form, became paradigmatic for Byzantium. Arethas (ca. 850-944), bishop of Cappadocian Caesarea (present-day Kayseri), was an exegete of particular philological interest. He had apologetic works of the ancient authors copied, a collection that has been partially preserved. Simeon the New Theologian (949-1022) was an important mystic who influenced later mysticism with his views of sensory-spiritual → experiences open to all who properly pursue them.

3.2.3. In the 11th century Byzantium turned increasingly to the past. In theological literature we find philosophical, largely Platonic, interests, along with a revival of the art of dialectical persuasion (→ Dialectic) based on Aristotle.

3.2.4. In the age of the Comnenus and Angelus dynasties, the usual type of theological work was the "panoply," or "armor" — a collection of the arguments of → tradition against all heresies. Noteworthy in this genre is the *Summa* of Neilos Doxopatres (first half of the 12th cent.), though this is an independent achievement of systematics. One emperor above all, Manuel I Comnenus (1143-80), loved to take part in theological controversies. He believed that Christianity and Islam had the same view of → God. He also regarded → astrology as compatible with the Christian faith. His theological adviser, Nicholas of Methone (d. 1165), wrote against a revival of the pagan Neoplatonist Proclus (410 or 412-85) in the Byzantium of the time.

The capture of Constantinople by the Latins (1204) and the setting up of a Latin → hierarchy to which the Greeks were subject aroused great bitterness and hatred that produced anti-Latin polemics, except in the most sophisticated theologian of the Nicene kingdom, Nicephorus Blemmydes (1197-ca. 1272). Barriers were thus erected that blocked all future attempts at union.

3.2.5. The 14th century was governed by the conflict about what is called → Palamism. Through the work of Gregory of Sinai (d. 1346), the methods of → mysticism and → prayer (§2.4) propagated by Simeon were adopted on Mount Athos. Because of its ideal of rest *(hēsychia)*, this mystical movement

came to be called → hesychasm. Gregory Palamas (ca. 1296-1359), resisting the attacks of Barlaam the Calabrian (d. 1350), who used Aristotelian dialectic, tried to give this a speculative basis that he thought was oriented to the patristic tradition. Gregory started with the conviction that, along the lines of → apophatic (negative) theology, God's being is beyond all comprehension or mystical experience in both the present and the future age. Only God's uncreated energies — which are distinct from the begetting of the Son and the procession of the Spirit, and therefore from the divine essence, not only for human knowledge but also "in reality" — may be experienced by us and may be seen like the uncreated light of the Mount of Transfiguration, which is identical with the → grace of God. In Gregory's view, not even the saints in the future age will attain a vision of the divine essence.

This theological speculation, especially with the question of method that it raised, was sharpened with the circulation of the works of → Thomas Aquinas (1224/25-74; → Thomism), which Demetrius Cydones (ca. 1324-ca. 1398) translated. It was over the theological speculation, not over the practice of the hesychasts, that the Palamites divided from the anti-Palamites. The controversy abated at the turn of the 15th century, but insofar as attempts are now made to equate → Orthodoxy and Palamism, it has a new relevance in ecumenical conversations.

4. Aftermath of Defeat

With the Ottoman victories, an ethical and theological renewal began in Byzantium. This came to expression, for example, in the apology of Emperor Manuel II (1391-1425) against Islam. Writing for and against the idea of reuniting with the Western church, as proposed in the Council of Florence (1439), occupied the most significant theologians of the time. Adherents included Isidore of Kiev (ca. 1385-1463) and Bessarion (1403-72); opponents of union included Markos Eugenikos (ca. 1392-1445) and George Scholarius (ca. 1405-ca. 1472), who, as Gennadius II, was the first patriarch under Turkish rule. All these were men of universal culture, and their legacy, along with that of George Gemistus Plethon (ca. 1355-1452), opened up a new future with the Platonic academy of Florence.

Bibliography: H.-G. Beck, "The Byzantine Church from 886 to 1054," *The Church in the Age of Feudalism* (F. Kemp et al.; New York, 1969) 404-25; idem, "The Byzantine Church: The Age of Palamism," *From the High Middle Ages to the Eve of the Reformation* (H.-G. Beck et al.; New York, 1970) 488-520; idem, "The Early

Byzantine Church," *The Imperial Church from Constantine to the Early Middle Ages* (K. Baus et al.; New York, 1980) 421-514; idem, *Kirche und theologische Literatur im byzantinischen Reich* (Munich, 1959) • G. EVERY, *The Byzantine Patriarchate, 451-1204* (2d ed.; London, 1962) • J. M. HUSSEY, *The Orthodox Church in the Byzantine Empire* (New York, 1986) • A. P. KAZHDAN, ed., *The Oxford Dictionary of Byzantium* (3 vols.; New York, 1991) • G. OSTROGORSKY, *History of the Byzantine State* (New Brunswick, N.J., 1969) • G. PODSKALSKY, *Theologie und Philosophie in Byzanz* (Munich, 1977) extensive bibliography.

KARL-HEINZ UTHEMANN

— C —

Cabala

1. Term
2. Spread
3. Teaching

1. Term

Cabala (also spelled cabbala, cabbalah, kabala, kabbala, and kabbalah) means "tradition" — more specifically, "esoteric, mystical tradition." It is the common name for the most important school of Jewish → mysticism, which flourished from the late 12th century to the 19th, mainly in Christian Europe and the Middle East. The early cabalists in medieval Europe relied on ancient Jewish (→ Judaism) mystical traditions known as *Hekhalot* (heavenly palaces) and *Merkabah* (chariot) mysticism and on the traditions of the ancient cosmological work *Sefer Yetzirah* (Book of creation). The most important characteristic of cabala is the central concept of the ten *sefirot* (numbers, or divine emanations), which together represent pleroma (i.e., divine fullness of being) in most cabalistic systems. This concept is found for the first time in the anonymous work *Sefer ha-bahir* (Book of brightness), edited in southern Europe in the last decade of the 12th century. The symbols of this work served as a basis for later circles and schools of the cabalists.

2. Spread

The earliest cabalists known to us belonged to the circles of Jewish lawyers in Provence, in southeastern France. The most prominent among them was Rabbi Isaac the Blind (d. 1235), the son of the great leader and → Halakist Rabbi Abraham ben David (ca. 1125-98). From this early center cabala spread first to northern Spain, especially to Gerona, where a circle of mystics was active in the first half of the 13th century under the leadership of Naḥmanides (ca. 1195-1270). During the 13th century several other groups of cabalists produced bodies of mystical literature in Spain.

The most important cabalistic work is *Sefer hazohar* (Book of splendor), written by Rabbi Moses de León (1250-1305) in the last quarter of the 13th century. The *Zohar* was written as a pseudepigraphic work, attributed to the ancient sages of antiquity, in the form of a classical homiletical commentary on the → Pentateuch and other biblical books. De León wrote it mainly in Aramaic, inventing an artificial style for presenting this work.

Under the influence of the *Zohar,* cabala became more and more central to Jewish medieval culture, spreading from Spain to Italy, Germany, and the Middle East. Until the 16th century, however, only small circles of mystics dealt with it. It became a prominent, and then dominant, element of Jewish religion only after the catastrophe of the expulsion of the Jews from Spain in 1492.

In the 16th century a great center of mystical study was established in Safed, north of the Sea of

Galilee in Israel, where the most influential school of cabala developed around the teachings of Rabbi Isaac ben Solomon Luria (called ha-Ari, "the Lion"; 1534-72). He formulated a fiercely mythological, dualistic symbolism that expressed the feelings of all Judaism following the intense sense of exile after the expulsion.

Two modern Jewish movements developed mainly on the basis of cabalistic symbolism and theology: Shabbetaianism, or belief in the self-proclaimed messiah Shabbetai Tzevi (1626-76; → Messianism), and → Hasidism, based on the teachings of Rabbi Israel ben Eliezer, known as Ba'al Shem Tov (Master of the Good Name; ca. 1700-1760), in eastern Europe.

3. Teaching

Early cabala up to the 16th century dealt mainly with the description of the → creation of the world, and especially the → emanation of the divine *sefirot*. The cabalists believed that mystical knowledge of the divine process of emanation and creation would help them to achieve closeness and communion with God by retracing the steps by which present plurality emerged from ancient unity. The cabala of Luria and his successors tended to emphasize messianic redemption rather than ancient genesis. Cabalistic mythology described the Godhead as including male and female elements (the female power was known as the *shekhinah*, the divine presence), and sexual symbolism played a significant part in many cabalistic works. Some of the greatest cabalists, especially De León and Luria, developed → dualistic symbolisms, describing an evil pleroma that is in mythical struggle against the good one. Many → Gnostic characteristics can be found in cabala from the book *Bahir* to present-day Habad Hasidism.

The early cabalists often wrote ethical works, relying on their mystical symbolism. This tendency became central after the 16th century, when most Hebrew ethical and homiletical works were based on cabalistic ideas. Because of the impact of this literature, cabala was popularized and became central to Jewish everyday life, with the result that Jewish rituals and ethical values became identified with mystical symbols.

→ Jewish Philosophy; Jewish Theology

Bibliography: J. DAN, *The Teachings of Hasidism* (New York, 1982) • J. DAN and F. TALMAGE, *Studies in Jewish Mysticism* (Cambridge, 1980) • M. IDEL, *Kabbalah: New Perspectives* (New Haven, 1988) • G. SCHOLEM, *Das Buch Bahir* (Leipzig, 1923); idem, "Kabbalah," *EncJud* 10.490-654; idem, *Major Trends in Jewish Mysticism* (3d ed.; New York, 1961); idem, *On the Kabbalah and Its Symbolism* (New York, 1965); idem, *On the Mystical Shape of the Godhead: Basic Concepts in Kabbalah* (New York, 1991); idem, *Origins of the Kabbala* (Princeton, 1987); idem, *Sabbatai Sevi: The Mystical Messiah* (Princeton, 1977) • I. TISHBY et al., eds., *The Wisdom of the Zohar* (3 vols.; Oxford, 1989).

JOSEPH DAN

Caesaropapism → Empire and Papacy

Calendar → Church Year

Calvin, John

Born July 10, 1509, at Noyon in northern France, John Calvin became one of the most influential of the second generation of → Reformers. His work was of significance throughout Europe and beyond. His theological development, confessional importance, ecclesiastical consolidation, and international training of reformers were lasting impulses throughout his life and for ages to come.

The son of a notary in the bishop's secretarial service who was excommunicated for financial conflicts with the church in 1528, Calvin was at first destined for a career in the church. Between approximately 1523 and 1527/28 he took an arts degree at Paris, among other colleges attending the Collège de Montaigu, which was famed for ascetic strictness, and where D. → Erasmus (1469?-1536), F. Rabelais (ca. 1483-1553), and → Ignatius Loyola (1491-1556) were educated. Possibly his first patristic and humanistic studies gave him an early contact with Reformation ideas. When he gained his master's degree, his father sent him to study law at Orléans, but in 1531, when his father died, he went back to study the classical *studia humaniora* at Paris. Between 1533 and 1534, under the influence of Protestant scholars in Paris, he underwent a sudden → conversion (§1) that, like the apostle Paul's, meant also a call to service. The "placard" affair of 1534 brought persecution to the Protestants, and Calvin began to live a wandering life that in 1536 took him to exile in Switzerland.

In March of 1536 he published in Basel his *Christianae religionis institutio* (ultimately known in English as *Institutes of the Christian Religion*), which he republished in successive and enlarged editions in 1539, 1543, 1550, and finally 1559, as well as French editions in 1541 and 1560. He based his work on the Lutheran catechism but extended it to cover all

Christian doctrines, thereby offering a Reformed → orthodoxy (§2) that would be of unbroken historical significance for the Reformed faith. He dedicated the work to Francis I (1515-47) of France but aimed especially to strengthen the Protestant movement in his own country and to make the Reformation ecclesiastically and politically acceptable.

The year 1536 was important, too, for during what was meant to be a one-night stay in Geneva, he was challenged by the fiery reformer G. Farel (1489-1565) to take part in the work of reformation that had been initiated there so far. Calvin became a theological teacher with no official ordination. Between 1536 and 1538 he was active as a preacher and an organizer, introducing the *Ordonnances ecclésiastiques* in 1538. A conflict with the city council, stemming from Calvin's and Farel's insistence on enforcing strong discipline, led to their banishment.

From 1538 to 1541 Calvin lived in Strasbourg, where his close but not uncritical contact with M. → Bucer (1491-1551) was decisive for his theological development. In his doctrine of → predestination, understanding of the Eucharist, pneumatology, ecclesiology, and theology of the → covenant, we can everywhere see Bucer's influence. Calvin was in charge of the French community in the imperial city and also taught at the famous school of Johannes Sturm (1507-89). He fashioned his community in accordance with the liturgical and ecclesiastical ordinances that were then in vogue in Strasbourg. The period also brought him into contact with leading representatives of the German Reformation, especially P. → Melanchthon (1497-1560).

Supporters of Farel and Calvin in Geneva, who had gained the upper hand politically, invited Calvin to return to the city. He thus came back in 1541 and spent the rest of his life there. A lasting mark of his church organization, which he owed in part to Strasbourg, was the → church discipline that he put in the hands of pastors and elders. Giving favor to no one, it sought — and in large measure achieved — a strict discipline of the whole community. It was the source of resistance on the part of many leading citizens, however, against the dominance of what were in part alien clergy. The supporters of Calvin finally gained a complete victory in 1555 and consolidated their position on the consistory.

Calvin was also concerned about doctrine. He had weekly conferences in which pastors were asked to expound the Bible. His aim was to strengthen pure doctrine. He was not concerned about minor differences, but he regarded public attacks on the whole system as intolerable and took every effort to avoid them. M. Servetus (ca. 1511-53), who came to Geneva as a known publisher of books attacking the → Trinity, was arrested and put to death with Calvin's consent. He served as a warning against heresy that would undermine the whole of Christian doctrine and Christian life.

Among the more important fruits of Calvin and his teachings was the Geneva Academy (later the University of Geneva), founded in 1559. It served as a most influential source of international instruction in the life and doctrine of Calvin and the Reformed faith. Calvin also maintained extensive correspondence with leaders throughout central and western Europe.

By the Consensus Tigurinus (1549), a statement on the → Eucharist made with the Swiss and German Protestantism that was under U. → Zwingli's (1484-1531) and then H. Bullinger's (1504-75) influence, Calvin essentially reached a confessional position that would become the mark of the Reformed faith. The departure here from a purely symbolic presence of Christ at the Eucharist did not lead, as he hoped, to greater understanding with the Lutherans, but it did provide a coherent and lasting position within Protestantism, as we see from his debate with the Hamburg theologian J. Westphal (ca. 1510-74). Lutheranism in the second half of the 16th century found in Calvin and his successor T. → Beza (1519-1605) implacable opponents. The development of double predestination by Calvin and Beza brought new Protestant divisions beyond the Eucharist and → Christology, heightening the doctrinal differences that separated the two confessions.

Calvin died on May 27, 1564, leaving behind a varied work that uses patristic (esp. Augustinian) and philosophical sources and that rests on a solid knowledge of medieval → Scholasticism. His many Bible commentaries, which use the principles of humanistic philology, informed Reformed exegesis for centuries. His sermons, not yet fully published, bear testimony, like his exegesis, to an intensive concern both to exhibit his doctrinal principles and to mediate the practice of → piety. In the ethics of the state, society, and economics within the political and economic processes of the new age, his role is a disputed one. His theological importance is tied to the attempted systematization of Christian doctrine. In the doctrine of predestination; in his simple, eschatologically grounded distinction between an → immanent and a transcendent eternal work of salvation, resting on Christology and the sacraments; and in his emphasis upon the work of the Holy Spirit in producing the obedience of faith in the regenerate (the *tertius usus legis*, or so-called third use of the law), he elaborated the orthodoxy that would have a lasting impact on Reformed theology. Indeed, no one was more influential than Calvin in giving permanent shape to this theology or in developing the Reformed as a distinct confessional type.

Bibliography: Calvin bibliographies: P. DE KLERK, ed., "Calvin Bibliography 1972," *CTJ* 7 (1972) 221-50 (henceforth published annually in the November issue) • A. ERICHSON, *Bibliographia Calviniana* (Brunswick, 1900; 2d ed., Nieuwkoop, 1960) • D. KEMPFF, *A Bibliography of Calviniana, 1959-1974* (Leiden, 1975) • W. NIESEL, *Calvin Bibliographie, 1901-1959* (Munich, 1961).

Primary sources: J. CALVIN, *Institutes of the Christian Religion* (Philadelphia, 1960); idem, *Opera quae supersunt omnia* (59 vols.; Brunswick, 1863-1900); idem, *Opera selecta* (5 vols.; Munich, 1926-52); idem, *Theological Treatises* (Philadelphia, 1954); idem, *Tracts and Treatises* (3 vols.; Grand Rapids, 1958) • R. F. WEVERS, *A Concordance to Calvin's Institutio 1559* (6 vols.; Grand Rapids, 1992).

Secondary works: W. J. BOUWSMA, *John Calvin: A Sixteenth-Century Portrait* (New York, 1988) • E. DOUMERGUE, *Jean Calvin, les hommes et les choses de son temps* (7 vols.; Lausanne, 1899-1927; repr. 1969) • E. A. DOWEY JR., *The Knowledge of God in Calvin's Theology* (New York, 1952) • R. C. GAMBLE, ed., *Articles on Calvin and Calvinism* (14 vols.; New York, 1992) • A. GANOCZY, *The Young Calvin* (Philadelphia, 1987) • W. DE GREEF, *The Writings of John Calvin* (Grand Rapids, 1993) • R. C. HANCOCK, *Calvin and the Foundations of Modern Politics* (Ithaca, N.Y., 1989) • I. J. HESSELINK JR., *Calvin's Concept of the Law* (Allison Park, Pa., 1992) • A. E. MCGRATH, *A Life of John Calvin: A Study in the Shaping of Western Culture* (Oxford, 1990) • W. A. MUELLER, *Church and State in Luther and Calvin* (Garden City, N.Y., 1965) • W. NIESEL, *The Theology of Calvin* (Philadelphia, 1958) • T. H. L. PARKER, *Calvin's Preaching* (Edinburgh, 1992) • R. S. WALLACE, *Calvin, Geneva, and the Reformation* (Edinburgh, 1988) • F. WENDEL, *Calvin: Origins and Developments of His Religious Thought* (Durham, N.C., 1987).

THOMAS KAUFMANN

Calvinism

1. Term
2. The Influence of Calvin
3. Calvinism as a Theology
4. Implications in Other Fields

1. Term

Calvinism is not to be equated either with John → Calvin's theology or with that of the → Reformed churches in general, though the latter are especially influenced by it. In the narrower sense the term denotes the main forms of classic Calvinism as they arose in the 16th and 17th centuries. In the broader sense it stands for the outworking of Calvinistic impulses that, in spite of many changes, may still be detected in the Reformed tradition and in other communions like the → Anglican, in the → Methodist churches, and among the → Baptists. In contrast, there were, and still are, Reformed churches that were influenced less by Calvin than by other Reformers like U. → Zwingli and H. Bullinger or in which the Calvinist legacy was combined with that of other Reformers, such as P. → Melanchthon in Germany, or Bullinger and M. → Bucer in England (→ Reformation). Calvinism, then, can hardly be identified with a single → denomination or confession. Rather, it is a broad driving force in → Protestantism that has also had an important influence on culture and society.

2. The Influence of Calvin

The influence of → Calvin (1509-64) on Calvinism was important in two areas — theology and polity — though neither was simply adopted unchanged. Instead, an attempt was made to develop the theology and to adjust the new order of church life to different situations than that in Geneva.

2.1. Theologically, especially in the last edition of the *Institutes* (1559), Calvin offered a general survey of Christian → dogmatics that set the full scholarship of → humanism in the service of theology. In spite of inner tensions (which, however, gave the work great dynamic energy), his presentation was particularly well adapted to influence future generations. The basic themes of the survey appear repeatedly in Calvinism: the glory of → God; the corruption of human nature by the fall; the possibility and actuality, on the basis of God's → revelation, of a true, twofold knowledge of God — first as Creator, and then as Redeemer in Jesus Christ (→ Christology); the → law of God as the standard of the Christian life grounded in → justification and → sanctification; the → Holy Spirit as the bond of union with Jesus Christ; God's eternal counsel as the final basis of election and reprobation (→ Predestination); the → authority of the → Word of God in and over the → church; and the urgent summons to restore the true face of the church. These themes still characterize the Calvinist outlook, the related → piety, and the resultant approach to life and sense of responsibility.

2.2. The Genevan church, which was largely the work of Calvin, was marked by independence, a focus on preaching God's Word, concern for theological and academic education and culture, and a strong sense of social responsibility. Many people saw it as the ideal model of an authentic church fellowship that might be copied even in very different political situations. Already in the 16th century there thus arose in France the Calvinist → Huguenot church, which was able to survive for decades even in the face of a mostly hostile absolutist state. Territorial churches also arose in German areas like the Palatinate, East Friesland, and the Lower Rhine, though it was only with the Peace of Westphalia (1648) that the Reformed confession received official recognition (→ Thirty Years' War). In Hungary, too, there was a widespread Calvinist church, in spite of much discrimination against it by the state. In the Netherlands the Calvinist state church was closely linked to the struggle for independence against Spain. In Scotland the national church was Calvinist. In England there was a strong Calvinist strand in the national church, which made its mark on English and North American → Puritanism (→ Church and State).

These churches had very different constitutions. Calvinism produced Presbyterianism, and English Puritanism led to → Congregationalism. Churches with both forms of government from every continent are now represented in the → World Alliance of Reformed Churches. Furthermore, there is no single, universally binding Reformed → confession (→ Confessions and Creeds). Instead, we find many confessions from different areas and periods, though some of these can claim classic significance, including the → Heidelberg Catechism, the → Westminster Confession, and, in this century, the → Barmen Declaration.

Similarly the Reformed churches have many different forms of → worship, those in central Europe being especially sober and simple. Among the impulses given by Calvin that still largely characterize Reformed churches are the strong emphasis on → preaching, the singing of psalms, and, not least, the important role of the office of presbyters or elders (→ Offices, Ecclesiastical).

Features that were neglected for many years but have recently been rediscovered include an active concern for the → unity of the church on the basis of the evangelical message, and an emphasis on the centrality of the → Eucharist in worship. If the history of the Reformed churches up to approximately 1850 was largely one of schism and disruption, in the 20th century these churches have increasingly given themselves to the task of Christian reunification.

3. Calvinism as a Theology

The theology of Calvinism has developed in many forms and schools that are not easily differentiated, being more like interconnected trends within a single, varied tradition. The distinctions were to a large extent evoked by the dynamic of the development of the tradition itself. Along with inner tensions deriving from Calvin and from other Reformation influences, the differences rest largly on ongoing preoccupation with Holy Scripture, on the differing importance accorded to predestination, and on the adoption of different philosophical views.

From the outset there was debate within Calvinism between those who championed the → logic and → metaphysics of Aristotle (→ Aristotelianism) and those who espoused the empirically oriented, antimetaphysical logic of Petrus Ramus (1515-72). Later the disciples of Johannes Cocceius used the philosophy of René Descartes (1596-1650) as a basis for theology (→ Cartesianism), and in later Puritanism John Locke (1632-1704) had a great influence, as did Thomas Reid (1710-96) in the Princeton theology. Calvinism was fairly heavily concerned with empirical, anthropological, and epistemological questions, and it attempted with such means to understand and present the theological material as systematically as possible.

3.1. In the period of classic Calvinism, four main forms are usually distinguished.

3.1.1. Reformed → orthodoxy (§2) began after Calvin's death with his successor at Geneva, Theodore → Beza (1519-1605), and extended to France, England, and especially Holland. It made the doctrine of double predestination the ruling principle of dogmatics, which was affirmed by the Synod of Dort (1618-19) in opposition to → Arminianism. After the synod Arminianism ranked as a particularly dangerous error along with Socinianism (→ Unitarians), which came from Poland.

3.1.2. The German Reformed tradition adopted a milder position. Preeminently expounded in the Heidelberg Catechism, it was also influenced by Melanchthon and for this reason was stamped as Crypto-Calvinism by the → Gnesio-Lutherans. The differences from → Lutheranism — which were important only in central Europe and related to predestination, the Eucharist, and Christology (→ Extra calvinisticum) — were reconciled in the → Leuenberg Agreement of 1973.

3.1.3. Federal theology (→ Covenant 3) began with an emphasis on the covenant concept in the German Reformed tradition, was developed by British theologians, and came to full flower in Cocceius's *Summa doctrinae de foedere et testamento Dei*

(Comprehensive treatise on the doctrines of the covenant and testament of God; 1648). Cocceius's dramatic biblical theology, which was clearly oriented to eschatology, prepared the ground for modern historicocritical biblical scholarship (→ Exegesis, Biblical) and at the same time powerfully influenced German → Pietism.

3.1.4. Finally, Puritanism stressed the subjective and practical dimension of faith in opposition to the rather rigid objectivism of orthodoxy. Its fusion with the more orthodox tradition of Scottish Presbyterianism found classic expression in the Westminster Confession (1647).

3.2. In the modern period since about 1700, classic Calvinism has been largely superseded by the → Enlightenment, which it essentially initiated thanks to its humanistic impulse. Reformed theology and the Reformed churches were revitalized in the 19th century, for example, through the efforts of F. D. E. → Schleiermacher in Germany, T. Chalmers in Scotland, the Mercersburg theology of J. Nevin and P. Schaff in the United States, and the new interest in the Reformed tradition among German theologians such as H. Heppe.

In addition, movements arose in the Netherlands and the United States that could rightly be called neo-Calvinist because they consciously went back to Calvin but also tried to develop a contemporary and relatively comprehensive Calvinist worldview. In the Netherlands, Abraham → Kuyper (1837-1920) was the center of an ecclesiastical, political, and cultural movement that was influenced by → Romanticism and popular thinking, the representatives of which sought both a Christian logic and a Calvinistic view of law and politics.

In the United States, Princeton Theological Seminary became the center of a Calvinism that, on the one hand, adopted the dogmatics of the Genevan theologian Franciscus Turretinus (1623-87) and, on the other, promoted a scientific, inductive exegesis of Holy Scripture. The last prominent representative of this school was Benjamin Warfield (1851-1921). Louis Berkhof (1873-1957) also espoused a moderately conservative Calvinism of the same type, one that is still widespread today in the Anglo-Saxon world. Theologians who have championed Calvinism in a broader sense include Schleiermacher, Emil Brunner (1889-1966), and especially Karl → Barth (1886-1968), whose *Church Dogmatics* has in many ways given radically new shape to the legacy of Calvinism.

4. Implications in Other Fields

Writing about Calvinism in 1956, O. Weber noted that its proponents were motivated by an urge, generated by the certainty of election, to represent the honor of God in the church and the world and to show God the thanks that was due to him as praise. Its vision was, quite simply, to shape things holistically. It could not remain a matter for theologians alone. The very doctrine of election gave new validity to human dignity in politics, economics, and culture, and it also meant an understanding of Christian action as goal oriented, namely, toward the kingdom of God (see *EKL*, 1st ed., 1.662-63).

Implications of this kind are to be seen especially in politics, science, and economics, though the inner connection between the theological concern and the practical implications is sometimes obscure and even contested. This may be seen particularly in the thesis first advanced by Max → Weber in 1904 that Calvinism gave rise to the spirit of modern → capitalism by promoting both a work ethic and an ascetic lifestyle. Theologians and economic historians have largely rejected the thesis, but sociologists commonly view it as correct in principle. If we want to uncover the spiritual forces behind social history, the thesis is plausible, but if we look more closely at the fundamental theological concern of Calvinism or the historical development of economic capitalism, at most we can establish a positive relation to Calvinism only in some geographic areas.

Much clearer are the relations of Calvinism to natural science, especially in the great epoch of the 17th century. Huguenots and Puritan scientists played an especially significant part in the development and spread of science in England, Holland, and France. The new spirit of empirical, critical research with its ability to break through traditional modes of thinking by observation, experiment, and new theorizing spread from theology and biblical exegesis to the field of the "book of nature." Although we cannot say that Calvinism gave birth to modern science, we must recognize the fruitful inner connection between the two.

The influence of Calvinism is perhaps clearest in politics. Calvinism had no inclination to regard the political sphere as autonomous after the pattern of the Lutheran → two-kingdoms doctrine. It was itself eminently political, and it was often confronted with direct political challenges. Significant political theories and programs such as those of Johannes Althusius (1557-1638), Hugo Grotius (1583-1645), and Jean-Jacques Rousseau (1712-78) were largely influenced by Calvinism, the idea of → natural law being especially prominent in Grotius, that of the → covenant in the other two. The concept of → human and civil rights developed in English Puritanism, and

American Puritanism was the breeding ground of →
democracy.

Bibliography: General: J. GUHRT, ed., *100 Jahre Reformierter Bund* (Bad Bentheim, 1984) contributions on
German Calvinism, 1884-1984 • J. H. LEITH, *Introduction to the Reformed Tradition* (Atlanta, 1977) rather
thematic, offers an excellent overview • J. T. McNEILL,
The History and Character of Calvinism (2d ed.; London,
1973) the classic historical presentation • A. A.
VAN SCHELVEN, *Het Calvinismus gedurende zijn bloei-
tijd* (2 vols.; Amsterdam, 1943-51) standard work •
J. STAEDTKE, *Reformation und Zeugnis der Kirche*
(Zurich, 1978) collected essays on many aspects of Reformed theology.

On 2: K. HALASKI, ed., *Die reformierten Kirchen*
(Stuttgart, 1977) • P. JACOBS, *Theologie reformierter
Bekenntnisschriften in Grundzügen* (Neukirchen, 1959)
• E. F. K. MÜLLER, *Die Bekenntnisschriften der reformierten Kirche* (Leipzig, 1903) still the standard collection of
Reformed confessions from the 16th to the 19th centuries • W. NIESEL, ed., *Bekenntnisschriften und Kirchenordnungen der nach Gottes Wort reformierten Kirche*
(3d ed.; Zurich, 1938) • L. VISCHER, ed., *Reformed Witness Today: A Collection of Contemporary Reformed Confessions* (Bern, 1982).

On 3: L. BERKHOF, *Systematic Theology* (Grand
Rapids, 1932) • H. FAULENBACH, *Weg und Ziel der
Erkenntnis Christi* (Neukirchen, 1973) on Cocceius •
R. W. GREEN, ed., *Protestantism and Capitalism: The
Weber Thesis and Its Critics* (Boston, 1959) • H. HEPPE
and E. BIZER, *Reformed Dogmatics* (London, 1950) •
R. T. KENDALL, *Calvin and English Calvinism to 1649*
(Oxford, 1979) • E. M. KLAAREN, *Religious Origins of
Modern Science* (Grand Rapids, 1977) • A. KUYPER, *Dic-
taten dogmatiek* (Kampen, 1910) • A. KUYPER JR., *De
Band des Verbonds* (Amsterdam, 1906) • J. M. LOCHMAN
and J. MOLTMANN, eds., *Gottes Reich und Menschen-
rechte* (2d ed.; Neukirchen, 1977) • W. H. NEUSER,
"Dogma und Bekenntnis in der Reformation. Von
Zwingli und Calvin bis zur Synode von Westminster,"
Die Lehrentwicklung im Rahmen der Konfessionalität (ed.
B. Lohse et al.; Göttingen, 1980) 165-352 • B. B. WAR-
FIELD, *Biblical Doctrines* (New York, 1929); idem, *Calvin
and Calvinism* (2d ed.; Grand Rapids, 1981).

ALASDAIR I. C. HERON

Calvin's Theology

1. The Institutes

John → Calvin's main work, *Institutio Christianae
religionis,* ultimately appearing in English as *Institutes
of the Christian Religion,* is the most significant →
dogmatics of the Reformation period. It is more systematic and comprehensive than either the *Loci*
(1521ff.) of P. → Melanchthon (1497-1560) or the
True and False Religion (1525) of U. → Zwingli
(1484-1531; → Zwingli's Theology). It was intended
as "a necessary aid to study" (1539 preface), as "a key
and door" to Holy Scripture (1541 preface).

1.1. *1536 Edition*

In 1536, at the age of 27, Calvin gained sudden fame
with the first edition of the *Institutes.* Following the
overall outline of M. → Luther's (1483-1546) Small
Catechism, Calvin's little book dealt with the main
topics of the catechism in four chapters: first the
Decalogue (law), then the Apostles' Creed (gospel),
then the Lord's Prayer, and finally the → sacraments.
Two apologetic chapters were appended on the five
false sacraments of the Roman church and on Christian → freedom, ecclesiastical power, and civil
government. Repetitions give evidence of a certain
systematic insecurity, but polished language and
pregnant terminology characterize the work. Serving
as a preface was a letter to King Francis I of France
(1515-47) in which Calvin brilliantly defended the
French Protestants and the whole → Reformation
against the charges of revolutionary novelty and
political disruption. This letter would introduce the
succeeding editions, which led by many additions
and changes to the definitive 1559 edition.

1.2. 1539 Edition

The second edition of 1539 appeared in Strasbourg, with the subtitle "At [in] length truly corresponding to its title." There were now 17 chapters, covering such new topics as repentance (→ Penitence), → justification, good works, the OT and NT, → predestination, and → providence. Calvin now took up themes of the apostle → Paul, especially in Romans; in 1540 he published a commentary on this epistle. The distinctive feature of Calvin's theology was now apparent — a concern for the sanctification of all of life. Already in 1536 Calvin had begun with the knowledge of God and the knowledge of self *(cognitio Dei et hominis)*, which are indissolubly connected. In chaps. 1 and 2 of the 1539 edition, he discussed this subject at length.

1.3. 1543 and 1550 Editions

The 1543 edition introduced two subjects that were at issue in debates with Roman Catholics in 1540 and 1541: monastic → vows and → tradition. There were now 21 chapters, and three more were added in 1550.

1.4. Final 1559 Edition

The famous last, fully revised edition appeared in 1559. Its four parts correspond very generally to the articles of the → Apostles' Creed. Following → Augustine (354-430), Calvin made a break in the third article, stating that we cannot believe *in* the church; we can only believe *that* it is. Yet it is hard to divide the third article consistently into a third and a fourth, for in speaking about the church, we necessarily speak again about the work of the → Holy Spirit. Calvin entitled book 3 "The Way in Which We Receive the Grace of Christ," and book 4 "The External Means or Aids by Which God Invites Us into the Society of Christ and Holds Us Therein." There are now 80 chapters.

1.5. French Editions

Calvin's practice was to publish a French edition (in 1541, 1545, 1551, and 1560) some years after each Latin one. The translations into French are his own. They rank high from a literary standpoint and, like Luther's translation of the Bible, had a powerful influence on the development of the national tongue.

2. Calvin's Theology in the Institutes

The final form of the *Institutes* provides the clearest picture of Calvin's theology. His commentaries and sermons are also important, but the *Institutes* is still the supreme work, for the ordering of the topics represents Calvin's ripest insights.

2.1. Book 1: The Knowledge of God

In this first book, two thoughts intersect that are basic to Calvin's theology and that pervade the whole work. On the one hand, he binds together the knowledge of God and the knowledge of the self, showing that the one conditions the other. On the other hand, there is a twofold knowledge of God, as Creator and as Redeemer. The doctrine of → sin relates the two thoughts (2.4 and 2.6).

The natural knowledge of God the Creator leads to true self-knowledge: "I speak only of the primal and simple knowledge to which the very order of nature would have led us if Adam had remained upright" (1.2.1). Calvin ascribes to us a knowledge *(sensus)* of deity and a natural insight *(intuitus naturalis)*, but he also stresses that we always pervert this knowledge of God because we are sinners. Following Cicero (106-43 B.C.) in *De natura deorum* (1.16.43), Calvin accepts a rational proof of God (→ God, Arguments for the Existence of), since God is known among all peoples *(e consensu gentium)*. But we turn this knowledge into false worship and idolatry (1.3.1). God created us upright, but we were not grateful to him (1.5.3-4). Calvin praises the human achievements of technology, civilization, and science, yet the natural light of understanding *(lumen naturalis)* is only a small spark compared with the light of grace (1.5.14). We constantly rob God of his honor. The natural order on its own, therefore, cannot lead us to a knowledge of the Creator and Sustainer. Only Scripture, God's revealing Word, can do so. Like spectacles, it discloses nature to us as the order of creation (1.6.1). External proofs confirm the authority of Scripture (1.8), but the basis of this authority is Scripture's own self-authentication: "God alone is a fit witness of himself in his Word" (1.7.4). Only the internal (or hidden) witness of the Holy Spirit can give certainty regarding the → authority of Scripture. This doctrine of the *testimonium Spiritus Sancti internum* (or *arcanum*) is a new creation of the Reformation. But we must not separate the witness of the Spirit from the Word of Scripture (as the → Anabaptists and radical reformers tended to do).

Since Scripture offers a sufficiently clear picture of God, a warning must be added against idolatry (chaps. 10-12) and the veneration of → images (chap. 11). From Scripture we may infer the doctrine of the → Trinity (§2; see chap. 13). The doctrine of providence brings book 1 to a close (chaps. 16-18). Calvin emphasizes that although God uses the deeds of the wicked, he is not the author of sin.

2.2. Book 2: Christology

The full title of book 2 is "The Knowledge of God the Redeemer in Christ, First Disclosed to the Fathers under the Law, and Then to Us in the Gospel." Calvin begins with the themes of the fall, original sin, and free will (chaps. 1-5), which lead to → Christology (chaps. 6-17). This account begins with the old → covenant (§1). From the beginning of the world God made a covenant of grace with us; the old covenant, then, contains the gospel in the form of hope for the coming of Christ the Mediator. This is why a book on the knowledge of God the Redeemer in Christ deals with the → law in its three uses. The law convicts the sinner *(usus elenchticus),* upholds society *(usus politicus),* and guides believers *(usus in renatis).* Whereas the first use is the most important for Luther, the third is for Calvin, whose theology is oriented to sanctification. Nevertheless, Calvin avoids a new legalism. He distinguishes the "naked law" *(lex nuda)* of the OT from the "clothed law" *(lex vestita)* of the NT, that is, the law as it is clothed with Christ and valid only in him (2.7.2).

An exposition of the Ten Commandments follows, and then a distinction between the OT and the NT, for inclusion of the old covenant in Christology demands an elucidation of the relation between the revealing Christ and the incarnate Christ. For Calvin, the former is related to the latter as reflection is to reality, substance to related form, positive to comparative ("clear" and "clearer"), bondage to freedom, and particular to universal → salvation (chap. 11). Calvin's doctrine of the threefold → office of Christ expresses the transition from the OT to the NT. To the traditional two offices of king and priest he adds a third, that of prophet (2.15.1-2). He likes the title "Mediator," which speaks of → reconciliation between God and humankind (chap. 12) and which also permits him to include the early church doctrine of the divine and human natures of Christ (chap. 13). The work of the Mediator rounds off his Christology and → soteriology (chaps. 16-17).

In contrast to Luther, who stresses the → incarnation of God, Calvin stresses the divine majesty of Jesus. In his commentaries, for example, he finds it hard to think of Jesus sleeping in the storm, for his deity could only be awake. (M. Dominicé gives other instances.) The early doctrine of the two natures, which is itself of speculative origin, leads him into further speculation. Since the divine nature of Jesus is the Logos (John 1), itself an independent person, Calvin can think of the divine nature of Jesus as outside *(extra)* the assumed humanity (→ Eucharist 3.3). In the eucharistic controversy with J. Westphal (ca. 1510-74), this concept allows him to teach the presence of Christ only according to his divine nature (→ Extra calvinisticum).

2.3. *Book 3: The Doctrine of Grace*

This book has the title "The Way in Which We Receive the Grace of Christ: What Benefits Come to Us from It, and What Effects Follow." More notable than the contents is the logical order in which they come. Melanchthon and Luther (→ Luther's Theology) had put the law before the → gospel, repentance before → faith, and so forth. Calvin reverses this order. For Calvin, repentance comes from the gospel, and consequently it follows faith. We thus have the following sequence in the *Institutes:* Holy Spirit, faith, repentance, attack on the Roman Catholic doctrine of penance (chaps. 1-5; → Penitence). Then follows the doctrine of sanctification (chaps. 6-10) and justification (chaps. 11-18), which is viewed as a norm and corrective relative to the preceding doctrines. Christian freedom, prayer, assurance of election, and hope of the resurrection are further developments and fruits of faith (chaps. 19-25).

The doctrine of predestination (chaps. 21-24) is clearly not Calvin's central doctrine but serves to establish the certainty of faith. It is thus prominent, and we may ask whether it can fulfill its allotted function. But it does not stand at the beginning of the dogmatic system as it does in Zwingli or T. → Beza (1519-1605). Nevertheless in Calvin, who took over the doctrine from Augustine (→ Augustine's Theology), predestination does tend to burst through the soteriological-Christological framework. Election to eternal salvation or perdition at the last judgment (Romans 9) takes place before the foundation of the world (Eph. 1:4), and therefore the doctrine of predestination stands in tension with the preaching that leads to faith and with the universality of reconciliation in Christ. Calvin, however, does not counterbalance election and reprobation. As P. Jacobs has noted, in Calvin's treatment, each is a boundary rather than a territory whose surface is fully described.

2.4. *Book 4: The Church, the Means of Grace, and Civil Government*

Under the title "The External Means or Aids by Which God Invites Us into the Society of Christ and Holds Us Therein," Calvin in book 4 discusses the → church, the means of grace, and civil government.

Calvin does not spend long on the invisible church, which is known only to God. His interest is more on the concrete → congregation that is built up by preaching, the sacraments, and → church discipline. The Word and sacrament are inalienable marks of the church *(notae ecclesiae,* 4.1.8-12). Calvin frequently quotes Augs. Conf. 7 but stresses the hearing of God's Word by the community (4.1.9). He has in mind faith and obedience, as well as their promotion by church discipline. As in Luther, the Word and its proclamation are the "scepter of Christ." They are thus the decisive mark of the church. In a letter to J. Sadolet (1539) Calvin enumerates four marks, adding church discipline and ceremonies that serve God's people at worship to the Word and sacrament.

A notable feature of Calvin's theology is his detailed development of an evangelical → church order contrasting sharply with the Roman Catholic understanding of the church (chaps. 2-13). On the whole, church organization was neglected in → Lutheranism, but Calvin worked out an order that was no less strong than that of the church of Rome. This organization made evangelical life possible in Roman Catholic lands and gave it stability in the face of the Counter-Reformation (→ Catholic Reform and Counterreformation). Calvin's order included four church offices — pastor, elder, (religious) teacher, and deacon (→ Offices, Ecclesiastical, 1.2). He thought that the other offices mentioned in the NT were only for NT times (chap. 3).

Calvin put less stress than Luther did on the idea of the priesthood of all believers. He emphasized the authority of the preacher and was inclined to call → ordination a sacrament (4.14.20). He strictly regulated the tasks, calling, and supervision of office-holders. Preachers and → elders are in charge of church discipline. Discipline is thought of in terms of aid rather than punishment; in accordance with the model in Matt. 18:15-17, it always begins with admonitions. There is to be no prying into secret sins. Church discipline applies only to public sins that cause offense (chap. 12).

Calvin's teaching on the sacraments follows the Augustinian distinction between Word and sign (chap. 14). The two sacraments serve to confirm faith. Calvin joins Luther in defending infant → baptism (chaps. 15-16). In his doctrine of the Lord's Supper, Calvin faults Zwingli for undervaluing the sign, and Luther for overvaluing it (→ Eucharist). He teaches a spiritual presence of Christ (P. Jacobs). By the Holy Spirit, Christ in heaven is present to believers at the Eucharist. Faith is the presupposition of sacramental reception. Calvin rejects the sacrifice of the Mass and the idea that there are seven sacraments (chaps. 18-19).

The chapter on → church and state (4.20) brings the work to a close. Calvin distinguishes between spiritual and civil government *(duplex regimen Dei)* but does not separate them as Luther does (→ Two Kingdoms Doctrine). God's glory must be the goal of secular government too. Calvin prefers aristocracy ("the rule of the best men") to either monarchy or democracy (4.20.8).

2.5. *Method*

Even today the method underlying Calvin's theology has not been fully clarified. In his investigation early this century, H. Bauke put an end to the one-sided search for a doctrinal root or center, some overarching material or formal principle. Calvin's mode of thinking is much more varied and complex. J. Bohatec characterized Calvin's theology as a "theology of the diagonal." By this helpful figure he meant that Calvin relates the theologies of his contemporaries as a diagonal links the four sides of a rectangle, and in this way makes them all more fruitful. F. L. Battles found in Calvin a true/false principle in the sense that the true constantly divides again into true and false (what he called "fractioning off"). Further research is necessary.

The conflict in 1934 between → Barth and Brunner concerning a point of contact in Calvin brought a new spate of work on Calvin. Beginning in 1974, the International Congress for Calvin Research, which meets every four years, has given a boost to Calvin studies.

3. Importance

3.1. *Exposition of Scripture*

Calvin's expository work is still held in high regard. His commentaries (which cover all of the NT except Revelation, as well as many of the OT books) exegete the text precisely, succinctly, and in a way that is useful to readers. For Calvin, the text is the word of Spirit-filled prophets and apostles, but it is not free from error or contradiction. The doctrine of the internal testimony of the Holy Spirit prevents him from formalizing assurance of faith in the verbal inspiration of the Bible, as post-Reformation → orthodoxy would try to do.

3.2. *Geneva Academy*

At Calvin's prompting, the Geneva Academy was founded in 1559, and it served as a nursery for Calvinist theology. It trained pastors for the congregations of → Huguenots and for succeeding generations of evangelical officeholders. Theodore Beza was its first rector. Famous students included C. Olevianus (1536-87), P. van Marnix (1540-98), and John → Knox (ca. 1513-72).

3.3. *Geneva Catechism*

This work was translated into several languages and influenced the → Heidelberg Catechism. After Calvin's death → Calvinism split into two schools, that of Ramism and that of Aristotelianism, but Calvin himself remained the preeminent theological authority in European Calvinism. The *Institutes* were published until well on in the 17th century, even if only in selections or with commentaries.

3.4. *The Doctrine of Predestination*

In a letter to Calvin in 1555 Beza suggested that creation, the fall, and reconciliation should all be subordinated to the eternal divine decree of predestination. Calvin's answer has not been preserved. Beza, H. Zanchi (1516-90), and others later began to think through and build up the doctrine of predestination logically. They put it at the head of the dogmatic system, thereby loosening the close connection Calvin had given it with Christology and pastoral care.

3.5. Eucharistic Controversy

As one of the Strasbourg clergy (1536-40), Calvin was pledged to the Wittenberg Concord (1536) and remained aloof from the controversy surrounding the → Eucharist. In 1539 he wrote a conciliatory work entitled *Little Tractate on the Sacred Supper.* In the Consensus Tigurinus (1549) he entered into a wide-ranging agreement with the eucharistic teaching of H. Bullinger (1504-75) so as to make things easier for his followers in Vaudois. When the Hamburg pastor J. Westphal attacked the Consensus Tigurinus in 1552, Calvin became drawn into a eucharistic debate. He overestimated the moderating influence of Melanchthon, with whom he was in correspondence. Attempts at conciliation failed. Contrary to Calvin's own wishes, this controversy cemented the confessional division in Protestantism.

3.6. Servetus

The burning at the stake of the → anti-Trinitarian M. Servetus (ca. 1511-53) has unjustly brought upon Calvin the charge of being a narrow-minded inquisitor. Calvin's participation as a plaintiff and as one of the theological assessors was consistent with the general attitude of the time toward notorious heretics (→ Heresies and Schisms).

Servetus is important historically for his discovery of the pulmonary circulation of blood. He got himself in trouble, however, for regarding himself as a final authority with a divine commission. In accordance with contemporary civil law, he was condemned for blasphemy — specifically, for rejecting the Holy Trinity and infant baptism. On a positive note, the Servetus incident helped provoke public demand for the abolition of the death penalty for heretics.

3.7. The Right of Resistance

In the *Institutes* Calvin grants the right of → resistance only to royal princes and to lesser magistrates. Private individuals must be ready to suffer for their faith and call upon God for help.

The persecutions in France, however, were intolerable. After the massacre of Vassey (1562), the first Huguenot war broke out. The murder of the Huguenots in Paris on St. Bartholomew's Eve (1572) led several writers to advocate the sovereignty of the people and a right of resistance to the king (T. Beza, F. Hotman, H. Languet, P. du Plessis-Mornay). Even private individuals were granted this right. In his

Politica (1603) the Emden legal scholar J. Althusius developed ideas of monarchomachism (i.e., legitimizing resistance against a monarch who commits acts held to be unlawful), which Roman Catholic theoreticians as well as Scottish and French Calvinists shared.

3.8. The Presbyterial Office

Calvin's greatest influence came through the revolutionary innovation of giving the so-called laity a share in church government (→ Presbyterianism). Luther and → Bucer had already wanted to use elders in the congregations, but either these had not been regarded as full officeholders, or churches generally had not appointed them. Oecolampadius of Basel, in a famous address to the council in 1530, had proposed to entrust elders with the discipline of the church. Calvin, however, was the first to develop the doctrine of the presbyterial office (as part of his doctrine of four offices), which he introduced into the Geneva constitution of 1542 *(Ordonnances ecclésiastiques).* He fought for the consistory's independence of the City Council, finally winning the battle in 1561.

Government by presbytery and synod appeared in a pure form in the Huguenot Constitution of 1559. It then made its way into Scotland, Holland, and the refugee churches of southern and western Germany. It prevailed in the Reformed (and Lutheran) free churches in Kleve-Jülich-Berg-Mark, and from there with only minor alterations it came into the Rhenish-Westphalian Constitution of 1835, which is the model for all evangelical → church orders in Germany today. From Scotland, this form came to the United States, especially in → Congregationalism.

3.9. Human Rights, the Constitutional State, and Democracy

No conclusive answer can be given to the question of how far Calvinism prepared the way for civil and human rights, the constitutional state, and → democracy. We clearly exaggerate, however, if we call Calvin the father of modern democracy.

3.10. Capitalism

It is likewise a mistake to trace back → capitalism to Calvin. Max → Weber (1864-1920) based this thesis on the practical syllogism that inferred faith and divine election from good works. Calvin taught the practical syllogism only in the framework of biblical statements and never related it to predestination. Nor are there any instances in 17th-century Calvinism of explicit support for the thesis that economic success is a proof of individual election.

There is a grain of truth, however, in the second thesis that Calvinists practice a secular → asceticism that results in economic success. Calvin himself was very open to economic innovations and made various proposals in Geneva along these lines. Thus (unlike Luther) he opposed the medieval prohibition of interest, though he did think that interest rates should not exceed 5 percent.

Bibliography: Calvin bibliographies: P. De Klerk, "Calvin Bibliography," annually in *CTJ* (from 1971) • A. Erickson, "Bibliographia Calviniana," *CR* 87 (1900) 460-586 • D. Kempff, *A Bibliography of Calviniana, 1959-1974* (Leiden, 1975) • W. Niesel, *Calvin-Bibliographie, 1901-1959* (Munich, 1961) • R. Peter and J.-F. Gilmont, *Bibliotheca calviniana. Les ouevres de Calvin publiées au XVIe siècle* (3 vols.; Geneva, 1991-).

Editions of Calvin's works: P. Barth, W. Niesel, and D. Scheuna, eds., *Joannis Calvini opera selecta* (5 vols.; Munich, 1926ff.) • *CR* 29-87 (1863-1900, repr. 1964) • *Ioannis Calvini opera omnia* (Geneva, 1992-) • *Supplementa Calviniana. Sermons inédits* (Neukirchen, 1936ff.).

Translations of Calvin's works: J. T. McNeill and F. L. Battles, eds., *Institutes of the Christian Religion* (2 vols.; Philadelphia, 1960) • D. W. Torrance and T. F. Torrance, eds., *Calvin's NT Commentaries* (Grand Rapids, 1960) • D. F. Wright, ed., *Calvin's OT Commentaries* (Grand Rapids, 1994-).

Secondary works: W. Balke, *Calvin and the Anabaptist Radicals* (Grand Rapids, 1981) • J. Bohatec, *Calvins Lehre von Staat und Kirche* (2d ed.; Aalen, 1968) • M. Dominicé, ed., *L'humanité de Jésus d'après Calvin* (Paris, 1933) • E. A. Dowey, *The Knowledge of God in Calvin's Theology* (New York, 1952) • A. Ganoczy, *Ecclesia ministrans. Dienende Kirche und kirchlicher Dienst bei Calvin* (Freiburg, 1968) • W. de Greef, *Calvijn en het Oude Testament* (Groningen, 1984) • P. Jacobs, *Prädestination und Verantwortlichkeit bei Calvin* (2d ed.; Darmstadt, 1968) • R. M. Kingdon and R. D. Linder, eds., *Calvin and Calvinism: Sources of Democracy?* (Lexington, Mass., 1970) • B. C. Milner, *Calvin's Doctrine of the Church* (Leiden, 1970) • W. H. Neuser, "Calvin und der Calvinismus," *Die Lehrentwicklung im Rahmen der Konfessionalität* (ed. B. Lohse et al.; Göttingen, 1980) 238-306; idem, ed., *Calvinus theologus. Die Referate des Europäischen Kongresses für Calvinforschung: 1974* (Neukirchen, 1976); idem, ed., *Calvinus ecclesiae doctor. Die Referate des Internationalen Kongresses für Calvinforschung: 1978* (Kampen, 1980), *1982* (Frankfurt, 1984), *1986* (Budapest, 1988), *1990* (Grand Rapids, 1994), *1994* (forthcoming) • W. Niesel, *The Theology of Calvin* (2d ed.; Grand Rapids, 1980) • W. Nijenhuis, "Calvin," *TRE* 7.568-92 • T. H. L. Parker, *Calvin's Doctrine of the Knowledge of God* (2d ed.; Grand Rapids, 1959) • D. Schellong, *Das evangelische Gesetz in der Auslegung Calvins* (Munich, 1968) • S. E. Schreiner, *The Theater of His Glory: Nature and the Natural Order in the Thought of John Calvin* (Durham, 1991) • H. Schützeichel, *Die Glaubenstheologie Calvins* (Munich, 1972) • R. Stauffer, *Dieu, la création et la providence dans la prédication de Calvin* (Bern, 1978) • T. F. Torrance, *Calvin's Doctrine of Man* (2d ed.; Grand Rapids, 1972) • R. S. Wallace, *Calvin's Doctrine of the Christian Life* (2d ed.; Tyler, Tex., 1982) • F. Wendel, *Calvin: The Origins and Development of His Religious Thought* (3d ed.; London, 1978) • E. D. Willis, *Calvin's Catholic Christology: The Function of the So-Called Extra Calvinisticum in Calvin's Theology* (Leiden, 1966).

Wilhelm H. Neuser

Cambodia

	1960	1980	2000
Population (1,000s):	5,433	6,498	11,207
Annual growth rate (%):	2.45	2.66	1.86
Area: 181,916 sq. km. (70,238 sq. mi.)			

A.D. *2000*
Population density: 62/sq. km. (160/sq. mi.)
Births / deaths: 2.92 / 1.06 per 100 population
Fertility rate: 4.10 per woman
Infant mortality rate: 90 per 1,000 live births
Life expectancy: 56.6 years (m: 55.1, f: 57.9)
Religious affiliation (%): Buddhists 85.0, Chinese folk religionists 4.7, tribal religionists 4.0, nonreligious 2.4, Muslims 2.3, other 1.6.

1. General
2. Missionary History
3. Church and State
4. Buddhism

1. General

Cambodia, formerly known as the People's Republic of Kampuchea, is located in Southeast Asia, on the Indochina Peninsula. Some 85 percent of its population are Theravada → Buddhists. Ethnically, approximately 85 percent of the people are Khmer, 6-10 percent are Vietnamese, 3 percent Chinese, 2 percent Cham, plus much smaller percentages of several other groups.

2. Missionary History

2.1. The Roman → Catholic mission was initiated from Malacca in 1555 by the → Dominicans Gaspar da Cruz (d. 1570) and Sylvester Azevedo (d. 1576). Only in the 17th century, however, were mission stations opened, with a Buddhist priest becoming one of the first Christians. About 1770 P. Levasseur translated the → catechism into the Khmer language. By 1842 there were four churches with 222 members. The apostolic prefecture was established in Phnom Penh in 1850 and was made a vicariate in 1924.

The first ordination of a Vietnamese priest took place in 1888, the first of a Khmer only in 1957. Between 1888 and 1970 a total of 163 priests were ordained (156 Vietnamese, 5 Khmer, and 2 Chinese); only a few could preach in Khmer. The Roman Catholic Church was mainly Vietnamese and European up to 1970. It ran 50 primary schools, four middle schools, two hospitals, day care centers, community centers, and homes for the handicapped.

In the aftermath of the coup in 1970 of General Lon Nol (1913-85) and his anti-Vietnamese policy, some 40,000 Christians were killed, churches were burned down, and church schools were closed. Many Roman Catholics fled to Viet Nam. By 1973 only 29 priests were left in the country. The 17,000 remaining Christians stayed in areas liberated from the Khmer Rouge. In the zone to the west under Lon Nol, Roman Catholicism was held to be too Vietnamese and found little support. The fall of Phnom Penh and the seizure of power by Pol Pot and the Khmer Rouge in 1975 led to the expulsion of European → missionaries. The remaining Khmer and Vietnamese Roman Catholics were forced out of the cities of Phnom Penh and Battambang and scattered all over the country. From 1979 until 1990, when religious freedom was reestablished, a general persecution greatly weakened the church.

In 1992 there were 18,000 baptized Roman Catholics, most of whom were Vietnamese. At that time 16 → priests were serving in 14 parishes.

2.2. Protestant missions were started in 1922 by the Christian and Missionary Alliance (C&MA), which made a great contribution to Bible translation in Cambodia. The C&MA had its center at Phnom Penh, where it began to build up the Église Évangélique Khmere. By 1964 there were 13 churches in 9 of the 17 provinces, and by 1970 there were some 20,000 Protestant Christians in Cambodia. The C&MA also worked among the Muong Biet and Kuoy (Kui) in the Northeast.

Because of the strong pro-West orientation of the C&MA, all foreign missionaries had to leave in 1965 except Jean Clavaud, the pastor of the French Reformed congregation (→ Reformed and Presbyterian Churches). Since the C&MA had a broader Khmer base and cooperated with the Lon Nol regime, which soon acquired a Western orientation, many missionaries were able to return in the years 1970-75. They focused on relief work and → evangelization until a

fresh evacuation was necessary in 1975. Many Christians then fled to Thailand. Those who remained were ravaged by mass executions (perhaps as many as 3 million), hunger, and sickness, especially malaria, between 1975 and 1979. Rebuilding commenced in the 1980s with the help of the → Christian Conference of Asia, which seeks a more ecumenical profile. Some 30 Protestant relief organizations from Europe, North America, and Australia, along with the → World Council of Churches, after years of providing help for refugees and disaster and famine relief, have since 1985 intensified their efforts at improving medical care, industry, and agriculture and at providing an adequate water supply. The larger Protestant groups that have come to Cambodia since World War II include the → Adventists and the Christian Mission in Many Lands (Plymouth Brethren). Only after 1990 were Christians allowed to worship openly.

3. Church and State

Relations between → church and state in Cambodia between 1947 and 1970 were affected by a change in the royal constitution in 1956. Buddhism was the state religion, but article 8 granted religious liberty. All religious groups were under the Ministry of Religious Affairs, which cooperated especially with representatives of the two Buddhist orders appointed by the king. The king also named the Islamic leader. Other religious communities were considered a "private matter." Lon Nol's constitution in 1972 also recognized Buddhism as the state religion but could not prevent the monks from remaining attached to the exiled regime of Norodom Sihanouk. After 1975 religious liberty obtained officially, but monks were forced to stop begging and to participate in national reconstruction. Monasteries were closed between 1975 and 1979, and many monks died. After 1979 the monasteries reopened and were able to play a part in educational and cultural work.

A new constitution was promulgated in September 1993. It proclaims the state to be a multiparty, liberal democracy, in which Cambodian citizens have full right of freedom of belief. It follows earlier constitutions in naming Theravada Buddhism the state religion.

4. Buddhism

In ancient Cambodia from the 9th century, Buddhism was influenced by the *devarāya,* or cult of the god-king. This practice was a fusion of Mahayana Buddhism and → Hindu Brahmanism, as may be seen especially in the pantheon of Angkor-Wat (→ Temple) with its Hindu and Buddhist deities and godlike persons. Only in the 13th century did Siamese monks bring Theravada Buddhism to Cambodia, which was finally accepted in 1321 by King Jayavarman Paramesvara (1327-36).

→ Asian Theology; Taoism and Chinese Popular Religion

Bibliography: D. BARRETT, ed., *WCE* 429-32 • H. BECHERT, *Buddhismus, Staat und Gesellschaft in den Ländern des Theravada-Buddhismus* (vol. 2; Wiesbaden, 1967) • H. BECHERT and R. GOMBRICH, eds., *The World of Buddhism: Buddhist Monks and Nuns in Society and Culture* (New York, 1984) • N. CHOMSKY, *At War with Asia: Essays on Indochina* (New York, 1970) • G. GIESENFELD, *Land der Reisfelder. Vietnam, Laos, Kampuchea* (3d ed.; Cologne, 1981) • G. HILDEBRAND and G. PORTER, *Cambodia: Starvation and Revolution* (New York, 1976) • M. KREILE, "Kampuchea," *Handbuch der Dritten Welt,* vol. 7, *Südasien und Südostasien* (3d ed.; Hamburg, 1994) 345-60 • E. MYSLIVIEC, *Punishing the Poor: The International Isolation of Kampuchea* (Oxford, 1988) • K. J. SCHMIDT, *Leben im Reisfeld. Reportagen aus Vietnam, Laos, und Kampuchea* (Wuppertal, 1984) • O. WEGGEL, *Indochina. Vietnam, Kambodscha, Laos* (Munich, 1987).

WOLFGANG GERN

Cameroon

	1960	1980	2000
Population (1,000s):	5,296	8,655	15,129
Annual growth rate (%):	2.10	2.84	2.73

Area: 475,442 sq. km. (183,569 sq. mi.)

A.D. *2000*

Population density: 32/sq. km. (82/sq. mi.)
Births / deaths: 3.78 / 1.06 per 100 population
Fertility rate: 4.90 per woman
Infant mortality rate: 51 per 1,000 live births
Life expectancy: 58.2 years (m: 56.9, f: 59.6)
Religious affiliation (%): Christians 54.7 (Roman Catholics 28.8, Protestants 13.4, unaffiliated 7.9, indigenous 4.1, other Christians 0.5), tribal religionists 23.1, Muslims 21.4, other 0.8.

1. General Situation
2. Religious Situation
  2.1. The Coming of Christianity
    2.1.1. Missions
    2.1.2. Protestant Churches
    2.1.3. Roman Catholic Church
  2.2. Interdenominational Organizations
    2.2.1. Church Union
    2.2.2. Federation of Churches and
        Missions

  2.3. Church and State Relations
  2.4. The Church and Islam

1. General Situation

Cameroon is at the crossroads of Central and West Africa. Historically it has experienced the rule of Germans (Kamerun), French (Cameroun), and British (Cameroon). It took its name from the 15th-century Portuguese naming of the mouth of the Wouri River in Duala as Rio dos Camerões (Shrimp River). Cameroon is an ethnic and linguistic hodgepodge, with more than 100 different ethnic groups (some would distinguish 500 separate groups) speaking a total of over 250 languages. The larger groups include the Bamileke (1.7 million), Fulani (1.1 million), and Mandara (400,000). Pygmies live in the southern forests. The official languages are French and English.

2. Religious Situation

2.1. *The Coming of Christianity*

2.1.1. *Missions*

The first Christian → mission to Cameroon was launched in 1845 by the London Baptist Missionary Society (→ British Missions), which had begun work in Jamaica in 1814. The idea of the → evangelization of Africa arose among freed slaves, who cooperated with the home mission in London. Between 1841 and 1844 different teams arrived in the West African island of Fernando Póo. These missionaries opposed the → slave trade and ritual murders. Alfred Saker (d. 1880) immediately embarked on a translation of the Bible into the Duala language. The NT came out in 1862 and the OT in 1872.

In 1852 Fernando Póo came fully under Spanish influence, and → Roman Catholicism was declared the sole religion of the island. With the choice of becoming Roman Catholic or leaving, the Protestant groups chose to leave. In 1858 Saker's group went to Cameroon on the mainland and founded Victoria.

In 1884 Germany colonized Cameroon, and soon thereafter the Basel Mission began work there (→ Colonialism; German Missions 1.2). In 1886 the first four missionaries arrived to take over the mission field of the London Baptist Missionary Society, which moved its work south to present-day Gabon. The Basel Mission quickly ran into major difficulties with the existing church when it pressed for uniformity in all its congregations, a policy that led to an early split on the part of Bethel in 1888 and Victoria in 1889.

Before World War I the mission had penetrated 300 km. (185 mi.) inland. In most villages that asked for help, schools and churches were established. Many native helpers were used in this work, although their training was sufficient only to help them to carry out the essential directions of the missionaries. Two factors accounted for the rush into the hinterland: the southward penetration of Islam and the aggressive Roman → Catholic mission into the interior.

With the division of Cameroon between French and British rule in 1919, the field of the Basel Mission was split as well. The part under French rule was handed over to the Paris Mission (→ French Missions). Both churches deriving from the work of the Basel Mission became autonomous in 1957 under the names of the Presbyterian Church in Cameroon and the Église Évangélique du Cameroun. While some aid is still received from the founding missions in the form of funds and personnel, the burden of evangelization and administration now falls on Cameroonians.

2.1.2. Protestant Churches

The Presbyterian Church in Cameroon works mainly in the two anglophone provinces. Like that of other → denominations, its witness takes various forms. Through → education (§3) at primary and secondary levels, it assists the → state in training for responsible citizenship. Various activities, many of them interdenominational, are connected with the department for women's work. There is also a department for → youth work. The medical services offered by the various denominations include health centers, hospitals, leprosy settlements, and primary health care posts.

Cameroon is basically an agricultural country. The church accordingly has centers for the training of youth in modern methods of increasing food production and self-subsistence. Church centers serve as lay institutes from which secular and religious activities are organized to train the laity to participate fully in the ministry of the church in society. The laity thus has a sense of the priesthood of all believers, and many laypeople preach regularly. There are also teacher training colleges, theological colleges, and seminaries. Christian life in the congregations is dominated by a search for indigenization in → dance, → hymnody, drama (→ Religious Drama), and → sacraments (→ Acculturation; African Theology).

Cameroon is a secular state that guarantees religious freedom. Over 20 Protestant churches and missions are presently at work in Cameroon. In 1990 the ones claiming the most adherents were Église Évangélique du Cameroun (EEC; 500,000 affiliated), Presbyterian Church in Cameroon (PCC; 250,000), Église Presbytérienne Camerounaise (EPC; 200,000), Cameroon Baptist Church (106,000), the Union of Baptist Churches of Cameroon (86,000), and Evangelical Lutheran Church of Cameroon (83,000).

2.1.3. Roman Catholic Church

The Roman Catholic → Order of the Pallotines started its mission in Cameroon in 1890. German colonial politicians at first viewed Roman Catholic missions skeptically. Once in Cameroon, the Pallotines saw their mission as one of complementing colonial politics. Under the leadership of Heinrich Vieter (1853-1914), the first → bishop of Cameroon, the Roman Catholics opened 15 mission stations before World War I. With the coming of the Sacred Heart Fathers in 1910, mission work extended to northern Cameroon, where the apostolic prefecture of Adamawa was founded in 1912. The first native priests were ordained in 1935.

Roman Catholic work did not suffer as much during World War I as the Protestant work did. In 1916 the Holy Ghost Fathers from France took over when the German Pallotines were expelled. In 1922 they were joined by the Mill Hill Fathers from England, who concentrated their work in British Cameroon. The educational system was used as a major instrument for → conversion (§1) by both Roman Catholic and Protestant missions.

In 1992 the Roman Catholic Church had in its service 4 archbishops and 18 bishops in 18 → dioceses. Statistically, Roman Catholics in Cameroon represent approximately twice the number of all Protestants put together. There is no cooperation with Protestants. A national bishops' conference oversees the church, while → synods govern the Protestant churches.

2.2. Interdenominational Organizations

2.2.1. Church Union

In 1922 the Basel Mission Church in southern Cameroon (now the PCC) joined the Christian Council of Nigeria (→ National Councils of Churches). Member denominations of the council included Anglicans, Methodists, and Presbyterians. In 1956 the PCC became a full member of the Church Union Committee of Nigeria. In 1964 a Church Union Committee of Cameroon was formed in Kumba. The founding member churches were the PCC, the EEC, and the EPC.

In order to instill the idea of church → union in Christians of the various member churches, a Church Union Sunday was designated. On that day, a single biblical text was to be used in all the churches, and information on developments in church union talks was to be communicated. In addition, a Church Union Constitution was drawn up for study in all the churches, yearly retreats (→ Meditation) were organized for selected pastors, student weekends were organized that rotated yearly among the colleges, and a united theological college was planned for Duala. For various reasons the final project has never been executed, but in 1961 a Protestant Faculty of Theology was opened in Yaoundé, the capital, for the higher training of the clergy of the French-speaking churches of West and Central Africa (→ Reformed and Presbyterian Churches).

2.2.2. Federation of Churches and Missions

In 1943 missionary societies operating in equatorial Africa founded a federation for the purposes of → evangelization. They named it the Federation of Evangelical Churches and Missions in Cameroon and Equatorial Africa and located it in Yaoundé. Political developments in Cameroon after 1961 forced the federation to limit its operation to churches in Cameroon. In 1969, therefore, the name was changed to Federation of Evangelical Churches and Missions in Cameroon.

The federation's goals are to reinforce the ties between the churches and missions, to develop their activities, and to coordinate their efforts for evangelization and Christian service in Cameroon. Membership is open to churches and missions that are recognized by the state, have been in operation in Cameroon for at least five years, unanimously recognize the Holy Scriptures as the sole authority for faith and teaching, accept the → Apostles' Creed, and respect the convictions and administrative and liturgical forms of the other members. The council of the federation has many duties, such as representing the members and their institutions before the public authorities. In 1990 the federation had ten member churches.

2.3. Church and State Relations

Cameroon, a secular state, respects religious values but favors no particular religion. The church participates in nation building through humanitarian and welfare services in the fields of education and health. While all Christians are expected to carry out their civic duties, clergy wishing to enter politics must resign their church appointment.

2.4. The Church and Islam

Over one-fifth of the people of Cameroon are actively or nominally Muslim. Christianity and Islam have lived side by side without much interference in each other's domain. In the 1970s, however, when Christian missions penetrated the Muslim North, they met with strong resistance. In 1959 an Islam in Africa project was founded with headquarters in Ibadan, Nigeria. Its aims were to intensify the study of Islam and to take action to present the gospel to Muslims. This project extended its activities to Cameroon when Protestant churches decided in 1972 to open a

similar center at Ngaoundéré. Theological institutions were encouraged to include Islam as a discipline in their curriculums. Some churches set pastors aside for work among Muslims, and writers began to publish on Islam. Thus far, however, there has been no real dialogue between Christians and Muslims (→ Islam and Christianity).

Bibliography: J. N. DAH, "Missionary Motivations and Methods: A Critical Examination of the Basel Mission in Cameroon, 1886-1914" (Diss., Basel, 1983) • M. W. DELANCEY, *Cameroon: Dependence and Independence* (London, 1989) • W. KELLER, *Zur Freiheit berufen. Die Geschichte der Presbyterianischen Kirche in Kamerun* (Zurich, 1981) • L. E. KWAST, *The Discipling of West Cameroon: A Study of Baptist Growth* (Grand Rapids, 1971) • W. SCHLATTER and H. WITSCHI, *Geschichte der Basler Mission* (vols. 3-5; Basel, 1965) • J. VAN SLAGEREN, *Les origines de l'Église Évangélique du Cameroun* (Leiden, 1972).

JONAS N. DAH

Campus Crusade for Christ → Student Work; Youth Work

Canada

	1960	1980	2000
Population (1,000s):	17,909	24,593	30,679
Annual growth rate (%):	1.88	1.07	0.75
Area: 9,970,610 sq. km. (3,849,674 sq. mi.)			

A.D. 2000
Population density: 3/sq. km. (8/sq. mi.)
Births / deaths: 1.15 / 0.78 per 100 population
Fertility rate: 1.68 per woman
Infant mortality rate: 6 per 1,000 live births
Life expectancy: 79.4 years (m: 76.5, f: 82.4)
Religious affiliation (%): Christians 80.5 (Roman Catholics 45.4, Protestants 12.9, unaffiliated 9.5, indigenous 6.6, Anglicans 2.6, Orthodox 2.1, marginal 1.4), nonreligious 9.8, Chinese folk religionists 2.5, atheists 1.7, Jews 1.3, Muslims 1.1, Hindus 1.0, Sikhs 1.0, other 1.1.

1. Christian Churches
2. Collaboration among Christians
3. Church and State
4. Non-Christian Groups

1. Christian Churches

1.1. The → Roman Catholic Church (over 12 million adherents in 1994) is almost equally divided between Canada's two chief linguistic components. Roughly 6 million, mainly in the province of Quebec, descend from French settlers who were already in what is now Canada before cessions to Britain in 1713 and 1763. In English-speaking areas the Irish have traditionally been the dominant group, but the tendency of immigrants from Italy, Poland, Portugal, and the Philippines to choose English as their language of adoption is rapidly changing this situation. Ukrainians, largely from the former Austrian province of Galicia, are allowed their own Eastern Rite and have their own eparchy (130,000 adherents) centered at Winnipeg.

1.2. The United Church of Canada (3.0 million adherents in 1991, the date of all figures given below) was formed in 1925 by the → union of → Methodists, Presbyterians (→ Reformed and Presbyterian Churches), and → Congregationalists. The last two groups were mainly British immigrants, Presbyterians chiefly from Scotland and Ireland, and Congregationalists in small numbers from England.

The Methodists converted most of their members in the late 18th century. In 1968 the United Church absorbed the Canada Conference of the Evangelical United Brethren Church, a small body of German background that originated from Methodist-style → revival on the U.S. frontier.

1.3. The Anglican Church of Canada (2.1 million adherents) takes seriously its participation in the worldwide → Anglican Communion. Although it retains a certain prestige from its earlier connections with an imperial religious establishment, its membership today is distinguished more by an English (and sometimes Irish) background than by upper-class status.

1.4. The Presbyterian Church in Canada (636,000 adherents) continues the witness of a large minority within its denomination that declined to enter the United Church. It claims, as does the United Church, to stand in legitimate succession to the Presbyterian Church as it existed before 1925. It tends to be more cautious than the United Church in its pronouncements on social and economic issues, but it participates fully in most ecumenical activities.

1.5. The → Lutheran churches (636,000 adherents) have been handicapped in the past by division into separate jurisdictions. In 1986, however, the union of the Lutheran Church of America, Canada Section, and the Evangelical Lutheran Church of Canada brought most Canadian Lutherans into the Evangelical Lutheran Church in Canada. The Lutheran Church–Canada, associated with the Missouri Synod in the United States, remains separate. While some Lutherans settled in Nova Scotia as early

as 1750, → Lutheranism became a major force only with massive immigration in the 20th century.

1.6. The → Baptists (633,000 adherents) look to origins in Britain, the United States, and the Continent but owe many of their members to conversion. They are especially strong in the Maritime Provinces, where revival among settlers from New England in the late 18th century represented their initial growth. While Baptist congregations are completely autonomous, the Canadian Baptist Federation (with 240,000 people affiliated) and the Fellowship of Evangelical Baptist Churches (110,000) provide vehicles of consultation for those of more liberal and more conservative approaches respectively.

1.7. Other Protestant → denominations fall mainly into two categories. Some have been introduced by immigrants and continue to appeal mainly to them or their descendants. The → Mennonites (229,000 adherents, including several groups) and the Christian Reformed (84,000, including all Reformed groups) are the only ones of this type to have attained relatively large size. Canada also now is home to most of the world's → Hutterites and perhaps all of its practicing Doukhobors (→ Friends, Society of).

The other category consists of churches that are more active in recruiting new members. Some of these groups are growing rapidly. Most numerous are the → Pentecostal churches (the Pentecostal Assemblies of Canada has 400,000 adherents, the Pentecostal Assemblies of Newfoundland 40,000), the → Salvation Army (112,000), and → Christian and Missionary Alliance (59,000). Other larger groups include the → Jehovah's Witnesses (168,000) and the → Mormons (100,000).

1.8. The Eastern Orthodox Church (650,000 adherents), present from the early 20th century, draws upon a variety of ethnic groups from eastern Europe and the eastern Mediterranean. The largest groups are the Greek Orthodox Church and the Ukrainian Orthodox Church of Canada; smaller groups include the Romanian, Serbian, Coptic, Antiochian, Armenian, and Byelorussian Orthodox Churches. Canadian Orthodox cling to their traditional autocephalous churches, showing little inclination as yet to set up a unified national church using English in the liturgy.

1.9. Since 1844 Canadian Protestant churches have participated in overseas → missions, setting up stations in Oceania, Asia, Africa, and Latin America. Practically all of these have given rise to independent churches operating in partnership with their former sponsors. In recent years both Roman Catholics and conservative evangelicals have overtaken the traditional Protestant churches in the extent of their operations; the Sudan Interior Mission, one of the largest of the → faith mission type, was founded mainly on Canadian initiative. In missions among the → Indians and Inuit, too, the more traditional churches have been joined in recent years by the Pentecostals and other newer groups (→ North American Missions).

1.10. Until comparatively recent years the vast majority of Canadians have belonged to a relatively small number of religious groups. This pattern corresponded to the manner in which Canada developed as a nation. The founders conceived their task as a transplanting rather than a renewing of civilization, with a resulting downplaying of innovation. Moreover, a small and scattered population spread over a vast area could not afford a multiplicity of religious organizations.

1.11. In conformity with this pattern, the major churches have inclined to the inclusiveness of a → people's church, basing themselves on ethnic or social constituencies more than on rigorously enforced confessional standards. This inclusiveness has long been both the strength and the weakness of the Anglican Church, which holds within a single communion disparate elements ranging from near-Roman to outright Reformed. It has been equally characteristic of the United Church, which seeks to be open to Canadians of various beliefs and traditions.

1.12. In Canada, as elsewhere, this flexible stand has been challenged in recent years by a growing number of conservative evangelicals (→ Evangelical Movement), who believe in the inerrancy of Scripture (→ Biblicism; Fundamentalism), insist on the necessity for salvation of explicit Christian profession (→ Confession of Faith), and oppose any relaxation of sanctions against breaches of traditional morality (→ Conservatism 2). Some look to the → Holy Spirit for such charismatic gifts as speaking in tongues (→ Glossolalia) and miraculous → healing. Conservative evangelicals have grown to a considerable extent at the expense of the more traditional churches. The nation's three largest Protestant/Anglican bodies, which in 1941 accounted for 42 percent of the population, were by 1991 reduced to 22 percent.

1.13. Far outnumbering conservative evangelicals, however, are more than three million Canadians who have recorded no religious preference. The existence of such a large group of unchurched is a relatively new phenomenon in a country that once prided itself on having one of the world's highest proportions of church attenders. One even encounters at times a hostility to the church that is seldom evident in the United States. For the most part, how-

ever, the falling off of participation in religious activities seems to reflect a sense that the church is irrelevant to the spiritual "quests" in which many individuals are involved. The number who openly identify with any form of "new age" religion, however, is negligible.

1.14. There remain roughly 80 percent of Canadians who state a preference for some Christian church, and to these must be added 628,000 who list themselves simply as Protestants and 275,000 others who profess themselves Christians without adding further labels. The average age of many congregations suggests that nostalgia may be a factor, but a ready supply of candidates for ministry indicates that the Christian gospel retains its power to appeal to youth. A considerable number of those who come forward for ministry, often converts (→ Conversion 1) with little church background, conceive their task as that of offering good news of personal salvation. Many others, moved by concern for human needs, find in the gospel chiefly a dynamic for exposing unjust systems of → sexism, → racism, and elitism and for resisting threats to human existence. The necessity for concerted action is driving the churches to a renewed examination of their basic convictions.

2. Collaboration among Christians

Especially since the formation of the Evangelical Alliance in 1846 (→ World Evangelical Fellowship), Canadian Protestants have welcomed proposals for tangible manifestations of Christian unity. Among early results were the consolidation of fragmented Protestant denominations into national units and the foundation of a number of nondenominational agencies. Formal interdenominational cooperation was inaugurated early in the 20th century through the Christian Social Council of Canada and the Religious Education Council of Canada.

2.1. In 1944 the Canadian Council of Churches (→ National Councils of Churches) came into being. The present membership consists of the Anglican Church of Canada, → Armenian Holy Apostolic Church, Baptist Convention of Ontario and Quebec, → Christian Church (Disciples of Christ), → Coptic Orthodox Church in Canada, Ethiopian Orthodox Church, Evangelical Lutheran Church in Canada, Greek Orthodox Church (Archdiocese of North and South America), Polish National Catholic Church of Canada, Presbyterian Church in Canada, Reformed Church of America in Canada (Ontario Classis), Religious Society of Friends (Canada Yearly Meeting), Salvation Army (Canada and Bermuda), Ukrainian Orthodox Church, and United Church of Canada. The British Methodist Episcopal Church and the

Canadian Conference of Catholic Bishops are associate members. A number of nondenominational and interdenominational agencies have affiliated status. The council has been handicapped by the unwillingness of constituent churches to entrust to it more than fairly routine activities.

2.2. The churches composing the Canadian Council, except the Baptists, the British Methodist Episcopals, the Salvation Army, and the Ukrainian Orthodox Church, are also members of the → World Council of Churches, either directly or as constituents of larger bodies. The international contacts it provides have had a special appeal in a country that has difficulty in maintaining a distinctive identity in the shadow of a powerful neighbor. Like other ecumenical institutions, however, it seems to inspire less enthusiasm than it did a few years ago.

2.3. The union that produced the United Church in 1925 reflected the desire for a more unified Christian witness to a nation with a scattered and mixed population. In 1943 an Anglican initiative led to negotiations with the United Church that were expanded in 1969 to include the Christian Church (Disciples of Christ). Principles of Union were approved in 1965, and a Plan of Union presented in 1973 with the unanimous concurrence of a joint commission. In 1975, however, the Anglicans withdrew, and in 1985 continuing negotiations between the United Church and the Disciples broke down.

2.4. Other forms of collaboration are in a healthier condition, although perhaps more at the national than at the local level. A favored form of cooperation is the "coalition," or ad hoc task force, which could almost be considered a Canadian contribution to the ecumenical movement. Such coalitions typically deal with particular problems or concentrate on the needs of particular parts of the world. Among the most active are Project Ploughshares, which has a particular concern for peace, and the Taskforce [sic] on the Churches and Social Responsibility. Council members belong to most of these coalitions, as does the Roman Catholic Church.

2.5. Theology in Canada is now essentially an ecumenical endeavor. Most candidates for ministry of the four largest churches, including the Roman Catholic, are educated in ecumenical centers. Theological scholars and students of these traditions are thus brought into daily contact with one another.

3. Church and State

Since the middle of the 19th century all religious bodies have been regarded as equal before the law and dependent on their own resources. The "wall of separation" between church and state so insisted upon in the United States has, however, been much more permeable in Canada. The clergy perform the great bulk of → marriages, and in Quebec they keep the registers of births, marriages and deaths. Chaplains to the armed forces are appointed on the advice of the churches (→ Military Chaplaincy).

3.1. Government and religion have intersected most conspicuously, and at times most controversially, in relation to → education. In Newfoundland each religious denomination maintains its own schools. Quebec has Roman Catholic and Protestant systems, although it is moving to systems based on language. Ontario, Saskatchewan, and Alberta have both inclusive public schools and publicly financed Roman Catholic schools. Most provinces make some provision for religious exercises and voluntary religious instruction. Most also make grants, directly or indirectly, to denominational universities and theological colleges.

3.2. Beyond such legalities the churches have considered themselves custodians of the national conscience, especially since, until the adoption of a Charter of Rights in 1982, the Canadian constitution consisted almost entirely of provisions for the allocation of powers between the central government and the provinces. At one time they concentrated on matters of personal morality such as → Sunday observance, abstinence from alcoholic beverages, and probity in business and government. In recent years, opinions have become increasingly polarized over moral issues. Most of the churches that traditionally dominated Canadian society now emphasize social and economic justice while moving toward greater permissiveness in personal behavior. The more conservative churches vigorously reassert the need for moral rigorism and absolute standards.

4. Non-Christian Groups

Until the 20th century the non-Christian population of Canada consisted almost entirely of a few Jewish concentrations (→ Judaism) in the larger cities, some Chinese laborers, and a much diminishing number of Indians and Inuit holding to their ancestral traditions. With the arrival of many → Hindus, → Sikhs, → Buddhists, Muslims (→ Islam), and → Baha'is since World War II, however, it is evident that Canada is now a country of many religions and that Christianity can no longer expect a privileged status. In 1991 the largest of these non-Christian groups were the Jews (numbering an estimated 318,000), Muslims (253,000), Buddhists (163,000), Hindus (157,000), and Sikhs (147,000). In some cases, churches have begun to initiate formal → dialogue both with the newly arrived religions and with the native peoples, who are reasserting the validity of many of their aboriginal beliefs and practices.

→ North American Theology

Bibliography: C. P. ANDERSON, T. BOSE, and J. I. RICHARDSON, eds., Circles of Voices: A History of the Religious Communities of British Columbia (Lantzville, B.C., 1983) • S. CRYSDALE and L. WHEATCROFT, eds., Religion in Canadian Society (Toronto, 1976) • J. W. GRANT, The Church in the Canadian Era (rev. ed., Burlington, Ont., 1988) • R. T. HANDY, A History of the Churches in the United States and Canada (Oxford, 1976) • H. MOL, Faith and Fragility (Burlington, Ont., 1985) • M. NOLL, A History of Christianity in the United States and Canada (Grand Rapids, 1992) • G. A. RAWLYK, ed., Amazing Grace: Evangelicalism in Australia, Britain, Canada, and the United States (Montreal, 1994) • P. SLATER, ed., Religion and Culture in Canada (Waterloo, Ont., 1977) • B. G. SMILLIE, ed., Visions of the New Jerusalem: Religious Settlement on the Prairies (Edmonton, 1983).

JOHN WEBSTER GRANT

Cannibalism

When he was in Cuba, Christopher Columbus (1451-1506) heard of some "Canibales" (cf. Lat. canis, "dog") who ate human flesh. In fact these were Caribs (Columbus mistook the r for n), ancient inhabitants of the Caribbean, but "cannibalism" became the common term for eating human flesh.

Cannibalism was common in primitive times, and it has occurred in tribal cultures, in World War II prison camps, and in many places where victors have triumphantly eaten the livers of their enemies in front of clicking cameras. Friends as well as foes have been eaten — the dead, the fallen, the slaughtered, and the sacrificed (→ Human Sacrifice). People eat others because they are starving, because they desire novelty, because they hate or love the dead, or because they believe that in this way they will gain extraordinary magical or sacred powers. In some cultures they eat the dead so as to restore harmony in a society in which there is discord.

Cannibalism is accepted or rejected on political, social, moral, and religious grounds. But emotion is often stronger than argument. Those who thirst for revenge forget good manners. Those who are choked by abhorrence will not listen to reasoning. Christian Maoris whose ancestors joyfully feasted on their enemies experience a painful aversion to the → Eucharist.

→ Cultic Meals; Totemism

Bibliography: W. ARENS, The Man-Eating Myth (Oxford, 1980) • F. BOEHM, Formen und Motive der Anthropophagie (Vienna, 1932) • P. BROWN and D. TUZIN, eds., The Ethnography of Cannibalism (Washington, D.C., 1983) • M. JOSUTTIS and G. M. MARTIN, eds., Das heilige Essen (Stuttgart, 1980) • E. VOLHARD, Kannibalismus (repr., New York, 1968).

HANS-JÜRGEN GRESCHAT

Canon

1. The OT Canon
    1.1. Presuppositions and Preparatory Stages
    1.2. The Hebrew Canon
    1.3. Other Forms of the OT Canon
2. The NT Canon
    2.1. Presuppositions and Preparatory Stages up to Approximately A.D. 150
    2.2. Early Development
    2.3. The Closing of the NT Canon
    2.4. Conclusion
3. Doctrine of the Canon
    3.1. Criteria of Canonicity
    3.2. Critical Significance of the Canon

1. The OT Canon

1.1. Presuppositions and Preparatory Stages

Long before the OT writings became canonical in any strict sense (measuring up to a kanōn, i.e., a standard or rule), many of them claimed and received an authority that was already related to canonicity and that logically prepared the way for it. → Priests, → prophets, and wise men spoke with great, if not final, authority. Many of their sayings were remembered and gave instruction and direction to later generations, even if in changed or supplemented form. The experience of the Babylonian exile was of decisive significance, for it confirmed the prophets' intimations of judgment and led to the comprehensive collecting and interpreting not only of the prophetic traditions but also of the legal and historical traditions. These underwent constant change over the years, but they had gradually been taking on a fixed form, so that new interpretation followed in writings based upon the older ones, namely, the Priestly document and the work of the Chronicler. In these writings the impulses of the prophets were still influential, even where they had been neutralized.

The history of the canon — or better, perhaps, its prehistory — begins in the cultic reforms of King Josiah. These rested on the finding of the Book of the Law in the → temple in 622 B.C. Along similar lines, the people later pledged themselves to the law that Ezra brought back with him from exile (in 458 B.C.?). In both cases we are not sure exactly what happened or what was the Book of the Law at issue. Yet it is fairly certain that the Law, or the Pentateuch, which was developed from it and understood in the light of it, was the starting point and basis for the formation of the canon. The Pentateuch alone was the Holy Scripture that the community of the → Samaritans adopted or retained when it split off from orthodox Judaism, and at first only this Law was translated into Greek (→ Bible Versions 2). The Prophets were then added to the Law because they were regarded as its interpretation and also had authority in their own right. The fact that the Book of Daniel was not numbered among them shows that this part of the canon was closed by the second century B.C. Toward the end of the same century the translator of Sirach (→ Apocrypha) refers in his preface to the Law and the Prophets and the other books that have come down from the Fathers. Here we have mention of the three parts of the later canon, although as yet the third part has no name, let alone any fixed content (cf. also Luke 24:44).

1.2. The Hebrew Canon

According to a widespread view, the Hebrew canon was fixed at the end of the first century A.D. by a synod in Jamnia (Jabneh), in Gaza, then the site of the Sanhedrin. But the → Mishnah simply records the tradition that a vote favored the "hand-defiling" canonicity of Canticles and Qoheleth (*Yad.* 3:5). There was thus debate as to the details of the third part of the canon. But the essentials had been settled, and soon the details would be too.

Around A.D. 95 the Jewish writer Josephus had mentioned 22 books that the Jews accepted as reliable and that contained the ordinances of God (*Ag. Ap.* 1.7-8). These books had been written by prophets in the time from → Moses to the Persian king Artaxerxes. Moses wrote 5, the prophets who followed him 13, and 4 others contained hymns and rules of life. After Artaxerxes (i.e., Ezra) the true succession of the prophets had failed, so that what had been written since did not have the same reliability.

The account in the apocalyptic 4 Ezra (14) is to the same effect. It tells us that after God's law had been burned, Ezra was inspired by the Holy Spirit to dictate 24 books for promulgation and 70 others that were restricted to the wise. The 24 seem to be identical with the 22 of Josephus, who in all probability had combined Ruth with Judges and Lamentations with Jeremiah. The Babylonian Talmud (*b. B. Bat.* 14b-15a) then gives us the classic number, sequence, and authorship, dividing the canon into the three

parts of Law, Prophets, and Writings. The distinction made in Ezra meant that an obviously later writer like Sirach remained outside the canon, whereas disputed works like Canticles and Qoheleth could be accepted under the name of → Solomon.

1.3. Other Forms of the OT Canon

Differences in both contents and order came when the Christian church adopted the LXX. The order in the Hebrew canon reflects the process of historical development. In contrast, the LXX deliberately reshaped the canon in such a way as to take books out of the third and last part, the Writings, and insert them where they seem to fit in naturally with the others (e.g., Ruth after Judges, Chronicles and Ezra-Nehemiah after Kings, and Daniel among the Prophets). It also moved the Prophets from the middle of the OT to the end as the eschatological equivalent of the great block of historical works at the beginning.

To these divisions (historical, poetic, and prophetic) other works were now appended that for various reasons had not found their way into the Hebrew canon. They were later called the → Apocrypha and were accorded a different degree of canonicity. The → pseudepigrapha formed another nonhomogeneous group. For the most part the LXX and Vg did not include these writings, but they achieved — and still enjoy — validity in various churches, especially in the East.

Bibliography: R. BECKWITH, *The OT Canon of the NT Church and Its Background in Early Judaism* (London, 1985) • J. BLENKINSOPP, *Prophecy and Canon* (Notre Dame, Ind., 1977) • K. F. R. BUDDE, *Der Kanon des Alten Testaments* (Giessen, 1900) • B. S. CHILDS, "The Exegetical Significance of Canon for the Study of the OT," *Congress Volume, Göttingen, 1977* (Leiden, 1978) 66-80; idem, *Introduction to the OT as Scripture* (Philadelphia, 1979) • E. E. ELLIS, *The OT in Early Christianity: Canon and Interpretation in the Light of Modern Research* (Tübingen, 1991) • S. Z. LEIMAN, *The Canonization of Hebrew Scripture: The Talmudic and Midrashic Evidence* (Hamden, Conn., 1976) • J. A. SANDERS, *Torah and Canon* (Philadelphia, 1972) • A. C. SUNDBERG, *The OT of the Early Church* (Cambridge, Mass., 1964) • G. WANKE, "Bibel I: Die Entstehung des Alten Testaments als Kanon," *TRE* 6.1-8 (bibliography).

RUDOLF SMEND

2. The NT Canon

2.1. Presuppositions and Preparatory Stages up to Approximately A.D. 150

2.1.1. From the very beginning, primitive Christianity focused on its experience of → salvation, in the proclaiming and teaching of which the new norm of the Kyrios showed itself (1 Thess. 4:15; 1 Cor. 7:10; 11:23-26; 15:1-11; cf. John 18:9, 32; Acts 20:35, etc.). This was set forth by the → apostles as an inspired authority that bore witness to the unity of the earthly and the risen Lord. It was thus an unconditional norm alongside the "Holy Scripture" that was the OT (see 1). The scope of this new norm might be seen in the critical reception of Scripture (2 Cor. 3:6-18) and in the resultant norm of those who bore the Lord's commission (see 1 Cor. 7:25, 40; Gal. 1:7-17; Eph. 4:1; 1 Tim. 5:14; 6:13-21; Heb. 10:26-27; 13:18-22; 3 John 5-10; → Hermeneutics).

2.1.2. The new situation of salvation did not demand a supplementing of the OT writings but rather the expounding of the saving event. This was done first in the oral apostolic tradition, which found its first written form in the letters of → Paul. Parallel to the apostolic development of the → kerygma, and largely independent of it, a process of oral tradition about Jesus was emerging.

If the apostolic writings were passed around and read at → worship (Col. 4:16; 1 Thess. 5:26-27; 2 Cor. 13:12; Rom. 16:16; cf. Heb. 11:32; 1 Pet. 5:14), and if a collection of Paul's letters might well have been made by the end of the first century (in Asia Minor; cf. 1 Pet. 3:15-16), neither this collection nor the gospels that were written by the last decades of the first century (Mark, Matthew, Luke, and John) are to be regarded as some kind of new "Holy Scripture." Both the oral traditions about Jesus and the legacy of the apostles (including fictional apostolic works) are geographically widely scattered witnesses that reflect the theological concerns of churches that were now consolidating themselves, that differed greatly in many respects, but that were all united in their faith in Christ.

2.1.3. The sources up to the first half of the second century lead to no very solid conclusions. First Clement (A.D. 96) knows Romans, 1 Corinthians, and Hebrews. Ignatius (ca. 35-ca. 107) is acquainted with Romans, 1 Corinthians, and Ephesians. The evidence from both suggests that collections of apostolic writings (by Paul) were to hand, but there is no mention as yet of any collecting or liturgical reading of the Gospels, nor is there any sure testimony to individual gospels. Ignatius refers to the gospel and the Lord, while Polycarp (ca. 70-ca. 166) mentions, along with the OT, the proclamation of the Lord and the apostles, and he obviously knows the epistles of Paul, 1 Peter, Matthew, and Luke. Papias (ca. 60-130) combines with the living testimony of the Lord a discussion of the composition of Matthew and Mark.

Other witnesses point in the same direction, though we do not yet have a canon of four gospels.

If Tatian (ca. 120-73) composed his Diatessaron before his excommunication, this would give us a basic canon of the four gospels in the first half of the second century. Second Clement (ca. 150) knows Matthew and Luke, and he refers to the apostles and a gospel as recognized authorities alongside the OT. As the history of primitive Christianity stretched on, these uncertainties produced the need for a twofold "Scripture" (→ Apostolic Fathers; Apologists).

2.2. *Early Development*

2.2.1. With Justin Martyr (ca. 100-ca. 165) a collection of gospels came into liturgical use (after 150) as a normative entity alongside the OT, and perhaps also an apostolic writing (Revelation; he does not mention Paul's epistles). Bit by bit, then, a new canon was crystallizing in two parts.

2.2.2. A push was given to this development when the heretic Marcion (d. ca. 160; → Marcionites), who was excommunicated in about 144, drew up for his own community a collection of Scriptures that purged the Jewish → law, that thus ruled out the whole of the OT, and that included only Luke and ten of Paul's epistles (not the Pastoral Epistles). Marcion's exclusion of some of Paul and his division of the collection stimulated, but did not initiate, the church's own work of canonical development and delimitation. Marcion posed for the → church the question of a single Christian Bible. At the same period a clear-cut restriction of the new collection was needed in defense against → Montanism.

2.2.3. Regarding the sources, we have some not very clear references to Tatian's Diatessaron in the Gnostic Valentinians (Heracleon and Ptolemaeus) and the apologist Athenagoras (ca. 180). Along with the rejection of apocryphal writings, these and other witnesses give evidence of the formation of a twofold "NT" canon, as one might call it, on the basis of a list of the writings of "the old covenant/testament" composed around 180 by Melito of Sardis.

2.2.4. Around 200 the three leading theologians — → Irenaeus (d. ca. 200), → Tertullian (d. ca. 225), and Clement of Alexandria (d. ca. 215) — with only slight variations, bear witness to a twofold NT canon consisting of 4 gospels, 13 letters of Paul, Acts, 1 John, and Revelation (6 → Catholic Epistles and Hebrews are still contested). This collection corresponds substantially to the oldest Roman list, the Muratorian Canon (late 2d cent.), which includes 2 John, Jude, Wisdom, and the Apocalypse of Peter, but not 1 Peter, Hebrews, James, or 3 John. The dominant motif in the drawing up of this canon seems to have been the defining of a normative list for the *ecclesia catholica*, though the process of selection for the apostolic part is not yet complete.

2.3. *The Closing of the NT Canon*

The development of the church's relationship with the state hastened the development of the canon in the Greek, Latin, and Syrian churches.

2.3.1. By way of → Origen (ca. 185-ca. 254), learned discussion of the canon in about 250 produced the following threefold classification in individual Greek churches: (1) *homologoumena:* the 4 gospels, 13 Pauline epistles, 1 Peter, 1 John, Acts, and Revelation; (2) *amphiballomena,* or writings in doubt, whose canonicity depended on a majority vote of the congregations: 2 Peter, 2-3 John, and Hebrews (James, Judes, and Barnabas counted as canonical); and (3) *pseudē:* the Gospel of the Egyptians, the Gospel of Thomas, and the gospels of Basilides and Matthias.

The main list of the sixth-century Codex Claromontanus (D^p) shows that in the third century there was still some discussion of Barnabas, Hermas, Acts of Paul, and Apocalypse of Peter (missing are 1-2 Thessalonians, Hebrews, and, certainly as an oversight, Philippians). The third-century papyrus $\mathfrak{p}^{72}$ contains Jude and 1-2 Peter. The three-way classification of Eusebius of Caesarea (ca. 260-ca. 340) — into *homologoumena, antilegomena,* and nonsensical and impious works — shows that there was still some uncertainty regarding the apostolic part and gives evidence of a lively debate about Revelation from the time of Dionysius of Alexandria (d. ca. 265).

Several lists from the fourth century contain 26 works in the NT canon (Revelation as the 27th was still contested). In the 39th Paschal Letter (367) of → Athanasius (ca. 297-373), the NT canon contains 27 books in the following order: the four gospels, Acts, the seven catholic epistles (James, 1-2 Peter, 1-3 John, and Jude), 14 epistles of Paul (Hebrews, after 2 Thessalonians and before the Pastoral Epistles and Philemon), and Revelation. (In the Greek church, Revelation found full acceptance only in the 10th cent.)

2.3.2. The Latin church closed the canon more quickly on the whole, but the canonical validity of five catholic epistles and Hebrews was disputed for a time. Novatian (ca. 200-257/58) recognized only the four gospels, Acts, 13 epistles of Paul, 1 John, and Revelation. → Cyprian (ca. 200-258) in North Africa also included 1 Peter. Others who also did not recognize Hebrews include Tertullian, Ambrosiaster (an otherwise unknown 4th-cent. author), and Pelagius (ca. 354-after 418). Hebrews, James, and Jude are missing from the North African canon (Kanon Mommsen; ca. 360).

Only under Greek influence and the sponsorship of → Jerome (ca. 347-419/20) did the canonical definition of Athanasius become fully acceptable in the West. The Synod of Hippo Regius (393), confirmed by that of Carthage (397), received Hebrews among the Pauline Epistles, but only at a synod in 419 was it described expressly as the 14th epistle of Paul. From the fifth century onward the canon was closed and accepted in the Latin church.

2.3.3. From A.D. 170 to 200 we find the first statements about the canon in the Syriac-speaking region of Christianity, though according to the *Doctrina Addai* (a legend from the early 5th cent.), only a very limited NT collection was recognized along with the OT (the Gospels, Pauline Epistles, and Acts). Especially at an earlier time Tatian's Diatessaron was used instead of the four gospels. The Pauline Epistles include Hebrews but not Philemon. The Catholic Epistles and Revelation are missing, but 3 Corinthians finds canonical recognition.

A Syrian list from about 400 has four gospels, Acts, and Paul's Epistles (including Philemon, but not 3 Corinthians). At this time the Diatessaron was still widely used. With the Peshitta (early 5th cent.) there is an attempt at approximating the canon of the Greek church: four gospels, Acts, 14 epistles of Paul (including Hebrews), James, 1 Peter, and 1 John (but not the other catholic epistles or Revelation). The → Nestorians defended this 22-book canon, but the West Syrian Monophysites came closer to the Greek canon after the Council of Ephesus (431), especially in the Philoxenian version of the Bible, commissioned in 508 by Bishop Philoxenus of Mabbug (ca. 440-523), and in the Harklean version, completed in 616. These versions included 2-3 John, 2 Peter, and Revelation, although the attitude to all of these books, as well as to James, was still ambivalent.

The → Coptic → Monophysite Church added 1-2 Clement and the eight books of the *Apostolic Constitutions.* The Ethiopians also added various apocryphal books.

2.4. *Conclusion*

A distinctive feature of the development of the NT canon is that the → early church paid particular regard to apostolic authorship in defining the canon. By dividing the canon into the Gospels and the apostolic part, they brought the incomparably new thing of the Christ-event and its attestation into a correlation of norm and Scripture. Also, they recognized their common biblical responsibility in the controversy with Marcion. The formation of the NT canon itself can be explained only in terms of the history of primitive Christianity, its development into the early church, and the determinative motives in this process.

Bibliography: Primary sources: The Apostolic Fathers (many editions) • Eusebius, *Ecclesiastical History* (many editions) • H. Merkel, *Die Pluralität der Evangelien als theologisches und exegetisches Problem in der Alten Kirche* (Bern, 1978) • E. Preuschen, *Analecta II. Kürzere Texte zur Geschichte der Alten Kirche und des Kanons* (2d ed.; Tübingen, 1910) • W. Schneemelcher and R. M. Wilson, eds., *NT Apocrypha* (2 vols.; Louisville, Ky., 1991-92).

Secondary works: K. Aland, "Die Entstehung des Corpus Paulinum," *Neutestamentliche Entwürfe* (Munich, 1979) 302-50; idem, "Methodische Bemerkungen zum Corpus Paulinum bei den Kirchenvätern des zweiten Jahrhunderts," *Kerygma und Logos* (FS C. Andresen; Göttingen, 1979) 29-48 • H. von Campenhausen, *The Formation of the Christian Bible* (Philadelphia, 1972) • B. Childs, *The NT as Canon: An Introduction* (Philadelphia, 1985) • W. R. Farmer, *Jesus and the Gospel: Tradition, Scripture, and Canon* (Philadelphia, 1982) • H. Gamble, *The NT Canon: Its Making and Meaning* (Philadelphia, 1985) • F. Hahn, "Die Heilige Schrift als älteste christliche Tradition und als Kanon," *EvT* 40 (1980) 456-66 • E. Käsemann, ed., *Das Neue Testament als Kanon* (Göttingen, 1970) • W. G. Kümmel, *Introduction to the NT* (Nashville, 1975) 475-510 (bibliography) • D. Lührmann, "Gal. 2:9 und die katholischen Briefe. Bemerkungen zum Kanon und zur *regula fidei,*" *ZNW* 72 (1981) 65-87 • B. M. Metzger, *The Canon of the NT: Its Origin, Development, and Significance* (New York, 1987) • K.-H. Ohlig, *Die theologische Begründung des neutestamentlichen Kanons in der Alten Kirche* (Düsseldorf, 1972) • H. Paulsen, "Die Bedeutung des Montanismus für die Herausbildung des Kanons," *VC* 32 (1978) 19-52 • A. Sand, *Kanon. Von den Anfängen bis zum Fragmentum Muratorianum* (Freiburg, 1974) • W. Schmithals, "Die Sammlung der Paulusbriefe," *ThViat* 15.111-22 • W. Schneemelcher, "Bibel III: Die Entstehung des Kanons des Neuen Testaments und die christliche Bibel," *TRE* 6.22-48 (bibliography) • U. Schnelle, *Einleitung in das Neue Testament* (Heidelberg, 1994) 401-18 (bibliography).

Otto Merk

3. Doctrine of the Canon
3.1. *Criteria of Canonicity*

The early church was relatively clear about the criteria for canonicity. With regard to the OT, the church accepted the canon that → Judaism had adopted by the beginning of the second century A.D. As for the NT, the church received what was held to be apostolic as canonical, although it was not until the fourth and fifth centuries that the NT canon was defined and universally accepted. In spite of justifiable doubts whether everything that was accepted was really apostolic, a comparison of the NT writings with contemporary competitors shows that the early church was guided by a good sense of what was authentic.

3.2. *Critical Significance of the Canon*

The canon took on new critical significance at the end of the → Middle Ages and especially during the → Reformation, when striking differences could be seen between Scripture and the teaching and practice of the church. With a new sharpness, Scripture as God's Word was distinguished from the → tradition of the church and even set in opposition to it. The search for a theology based on the Bible began in earnest. The question of the nature and purpose of the age-old canon became acute again. The → Reformers did not find it sufficient merely to stress the external, objectively given → authority of Scripture. They also emphasized its content — the good news of Jesus Christ and the dynamic of the divine Word, which in the power of the Spirit awakens → faith and in so doing bears witness to itself. A one-sided stress on the external authority of Scripture, often bound up with a theory of → inspiration that was more pagan than biblical, led to various forms of → biblicism and → fundamentalism in later → Protestantism.

The main developments in 20th-century Protestant theology are closer to the real concerns of the Reformation. One has been the attempt in historico-critical biblical investigation (→ Exegesis, Biblical) to trace the history and discover the meaning and purpose of the biblical text. Another, following the work of F. D. E. → Schleiermacher (1768-1834) at the beginning of the 19th century, is to relate the biblical message directly to the basic experiences of human existence. Finally, K. → Barth (1886-1968) has taught → dogmatics to listen to Scripture as the witness to the self-revelation of God (→ Revelation 1), both anticipating and echoing the one Word that was incarnate in Jesus Christ.

These three trends cannot be brought under a common denominator. In mutual dialogue and critical debate, however, they seem to show what is the best way forward. The canon did not fall ready-made from heaven but arose as a historical witness to God's saving work in history. Christian theology cannot avoid it. Yet the message of the canon, not the canon itself, must direct its steps.

Bibliography: J. Barr, *Holy Scripture: Canon, Authority, and Criticism* (Philadelphia, 1983) • K. Barth, *CD* I/2, 457-660 • W. R. Farmer and D. M. Farkasfalvy, *The Formation of the NT Canon* (New York, 1983) •

H. Karpp, "Bibel IV," *TRE* 6.48-93 (bibliography) • E. Käsemann, ed., *Das Neue Testament als Kanon* (Göttingen, 1970) • W. G. Kümmel, *The NT: The History of the Investigation of Its Problems* (Nashville, 1972) • W. Schneemelcher, "Bibel III," *TRE* 6.22-48 (bibliography).

Alasdair I. C. Heron

Canon Law

1. The term "canon law" refers to the study of church law ("canon" is a ruling by the church). It is a theological discipline using the methods of jurisprudence to ensure the orderly life of the → church as an institution based on the will of Jesus Christ. It has the task of inquiring critically into prevailing church law (→ Codex Iuris Canonici [CIC]), analyzing and presenting the meaning and purpose of the statutes, warning against potentially harmful directions, and promoting legal development (→ Law). It has a dogmatic branch (the exposition of existing law) and a historical branch (research into its historical development), a distinction made from the time of U. Stutz (1868-1937). The role of canon law as a theological discipline has been explained in papal statements, for example, the Apostolic Constitution *Sapientia Christiana* of April 15, 1979. There is usually a chair of → church law on Roman Catholic faculties. Faculties or institutes of canon law exist at Munich, Lublin, Washington, D.C., Strasbourg, Rome, Louvain, Salamanca, and Pamplona.

2. Historically we may identify six periods in the development of canon law. First was the period of preparation and collection (up to about 1140). Materials were gathered from Holy Scripture, early church orders, the → church fathers, local or ecumenical synods and → councils, and papal decisions (decretals). Magister Gratian (d. ca. 1160) arranged and reconciled these materials (Concordia Discordantium Canonum, or Decretum Gratiani). His work became the basis of canonical study.

Next was the classical period, up to John Andreae (1271-1348). This was the age of the decretists (who worked with Gratian's Decretum) and the decretalists (who worked with later papal decretals and their continued development).

The postclassical age followed (1350-1550). This focused on collecting the responses *(responsa)* and counsels *(consilia)* of the popes and papal courts. Of special importance were the penitentiaries (→ Penitence), which produced a mixture of moral theology and canon law. Important in this effort were

Raymond of Penafort (ca. 1180-1275), Panormitanus (1386-1445), and John of Turrecremata (1388-1468). The end of this period saw the completion of the Corpus Iuris Canonici, which contained Gratian's Decretum and other papal collections, the Liber Extra of Gregory IX, the Liber Sextus of Boniface VIII, the Clementines (the Liber Septimus issued by Clement V), the Extravagantes of John XXII, and the Extravagantes Communes.

Then came the neoclassical period (→ Trent to the 1917 CIC), when there was movement away from Germanic law but also a renewed interest in systematization. Historical scholarship also made an impact on the presentation of church law. On the historical side, several Protestants made important contributions, including A. L. Richter (1808-64), P. Hinschius (1835-98), E. Friedberg (1837-1910), and U. Stutz. Roman Catholics prominent in such efforts included F. Walter (1794-1879), G. Phillips (1804-72), R. von Scherer (1845-1918), J. B. Sägmüller (1860-1942), and E. Eichmann (1870-1946).

The fifth period is from 1917 to the revision of 1983. Canon law now set out to expound and interpret and interact critically with the CIC, which was published on May 27, 1917, by Benedict XV (1914-22). Important in this process was the work in Germany by Eichmann, A. M. Koeniger, N. Hilling, H. Barion, H. Flatten, K. Mörsdorf, A. Scheuermann, A. M. Stickler, J. Creusen, J. Beyer, and U. Navarette. Also important were the efforts of P. Gaspari in Rome, A. Vermeersch in Louvain, L. M. Örsy in Washington, D.C., J. Gaudemet in Paris, R. Sobanski in Warsaw, P. J. M. Huizing in Nijmegen, and R. Metz in Strasbourg. The reform undertaken by → Vatican II was also the occasion of serious work in canon law.

The final period was inaugurated by the 1983 revision of CIC. The new volume was published by John Paul II on January 25, 1983. In its contents and organization, the 1983 CIC is based on the teachings of Vatican II and also reflects the reception of the council as well as subsequent church legislation.

→ Church 3.2; Roman Catholic Church

Bibliography: J. M. Buckley, "Canon Law," *NCE* 3.29-34 • J. A. Coriden, T. J. Green, and D. E. Heintschel, *The Code of Canon Law: A Text and Commentary* (New York, 1985) • J. H. Erickson, *The Challenge of Our Past* (New York, 1991) introduction to canon law in Orthodoxy • G. May, "Kirchenrechtswissenschaft und Kirchenrechtsstudium," *Handbuch des katholischen Kirchenrechts* (ed. J. Listl et al.; Regensburg, 1983) 71-82 • G. May and A. Egler, *Einführung in die kirchenrechtliche Methode* (Regensburg, 1986) • K. Mörsdorf,

Lehrbuch des Kirchenrechts auf Grund des Codex Iuris Canonici . . . (vol. 1; 12th ed.; Munich, 1967) 33-42 • J. H. PROVOST, "Canon Law," *EncRel(E)* 3.69-72 • A. M. STICKLER, "Kanonistik," *LTK* (2d ed.) 5.1289-1302 (bibliography) • C. VOGEL et al., "Canon Law, History of," *NCE* 3.34-50 • S. WOYWOD and C. SMITH, *A Practical Commentary on the Code of Canon Law* (rev. ed.; New York, 1963).

HERIBERT HEINEMANN

Canon Law, Code of → Codex Iuris Canonici

Canon Law, Corpus of → Corpus Iuris Canonici

Canonical Hours → Hours, Canonical

Cantata

The cantata (It. *cantata,* choral piece with several movements, as distinct from the purely instrumental sonata), which was developed in Italy in the 17th century, involves an alternation of arias and recitatives. It achieved central importance in Protestant → church music in the 17th and 18th centuries, especially in combination with biblical passages and hymns (also songs), though after 1700 increasingly with free texts as well.

As an exposition of texts with musical figures, symbols, impressions, and stimuli, the cantata has a place in → worship alongside → preaching. The composition of cantatas reached a climax with the work of J. S. Bach (1685-1750), who for the most part used the classic form, involving an introductory chorus (often based on a biblical text), alternation of recitatives and arias, and a concluding chorale.

→ Choir; Motet; Oratorio; Passion Music; Requiem

Bibliography: W. BLANKENBURG, "Der mehrstimmige Gesang und die konzertierende Musik im evangelischen Gottesdienst," *Leit.* 4.661-718 • F. BLUME, *Protestant Church Music: A History* (New York, 1974) • N. FORTUNE et al., "Cantata," *New Grove* 3.694-718 (bibliography) • R. JAKOBY, *The Cantata* (Cologne, 1968) • C. WOLFF, *The New Grove Bach Family* (New York, 1983).

CHRISTOPH ALBRECHT

Canticle

In ancient tragedy the *canticum* was a monologue with flute accompaniment. In later Latin, *canticum* became a general term for a song. In the church the term at first came into use for very different kinds of songs, but later it was limited to OT and NT canticles used for the most part in the → hours of prayer. In particular, three NT canticles came into liturgical use: the Magnificat, or Song of Mary (Luke 1:46-55); the Benedictus, or Song of Zacharias (Luke 1:68-79); and the Nunc Dimittis, or Song of Simeon (Luke 2:29-32).

From the early days of the monastic hours of prayer in the fourth and fifth centuries, several OT texts as well as the Psalms came to be known and used as canticles, for example, the Song of Moses (Exodus 15) and the Song of the Three Children in the fiery furnace (Additions to Daniel). The rule of St. → Benedict of Nursia (ca. 480-after 547) in 530 (→ Benedictines) firmly anchored the canticles in the hours of prayer. They then found their way into the → Mass as well. OT canticles are still sung at the Easter Vigil (→ Church Year; Holy Week).

The Lutheran Church took over the use of canticles at matins (Benedictus), vespers (Magnificat), and compline (Nunc Dimittis), and in the Anglican Church they serve as alternatives to psalms after the lessons at morning prayer (Song of the Three Children and Benedictus) and evening prayer (Magnificat and Nunc Dimittis). Since the canticles have the same poetic form as the Psalms (parallelism), they are sung to similar chants.

Bibliography: H. GOLTZEN, "Der tägliche Gottesdienst," *Leit.* 3.99-294 • A.-G. MARTIMORT, ed., *Introduction to the Liturgy* (Shannon, 1968) • J. MEARNS, *The Canticles of the Christian Church, Eastern and Western, in Early and Medieval Times* (Cambridge, 1914) • H. SCHNEIDER, *Die altlateinischen biblische Cantica* (Beuron, 1938) • B. STÄBLEIN, "Canticum," *MGG* 2.770-71 • M. VELIMIROVIĆ, R. STEINER, and N. TEMPERLEY, "Canticle," *New Grove* 3.723-26 • P. WAGNER, *Ursprung und Entwicklung der liturgischen Gesangsformen* (3d ed.; Leipzig, 1911).

CHRISTOPH ALBRECHT

Canticles → Song of Solomon

Cantor → Church Musicians

Cao Dai

Cao Dai is the religion of the Vietnamese god Cao Dai, whose name means "great palace." The full self-designation is (Dai-Dao) Tam-Ky Pho-Do, or "(Great Way of) the Third Forgiveness of God." Along this way, the unity of all religions is to be recovered, a unity that had already been divided in a "first forgiveness" under the forerunners of Confucius, Lao-tzu, and Buddha Sakyamuni, and then in a "second forgiveness" under these founders themselves plus Jesus Christ. Around this focus, many in the then disintegrating Vietnamese society of Cochin China sought to find themselves again. This province, along with the protectorates of Annam and Tonkin and the kingdom of Cambodia, had come under French Indochina from 1887 (→ Colonialism). In this constellation the ancient tendency of the province toward syncretism fostered the birth of this new organized religion.

One of the most important participants was Ngo Van Chieu (1878-1926), who was brought up in the Taoist tradition and educated in a French secondary school. Ngo, an immigration official, had the first Cao Dai vision in 1920. Also participating were several French → spiritist circles, the most important of which were Pham Con Tac, Cao Quynh Cu, and Cap Huai Sang, in which writing mediums received messages reputedly from Cao Dai and great human figures such as René Descartes, Joan of Arc, Victor Hugo, Louis Pasteur, William Shakespeare, Vladimir Lenin, and many poets and philosophers from the Chinese-Vietnamese tradition, especially Meng-tzu (4th cent. B.C.), Ly Thai Bach (7th cent. A.D.), Nguyen Binh Khiem (16th cent.), the revolutionary and statesman Sun Yat-sen (1866-1925), and more than 60 others. Another important leader was Le Van Trung (1875-1934), who, as a Saigon businessman and former adviser to the colonial government, had a flair for organization.

The task of formally founding and spreading the movement fell to the Taoist "jade-king" Ngoc-Hoang-Thuong De, who in part was regarded as identical with Cao Dai and hence with the Yahweh of the Hebrews, with the Unknown God and Father of Jesus Christ, with Christ himself, and with the other founders of the second forgiveness. Ngoc was also seen as the model of the head of an earthly fellowship, who ought then to be enthroned as pope.

The official inauguration of the movement, with some 100 charter members, took place on September 7, 1926. In 1927 it set up its sacred seat in Tay Ninh, northwest of Saigon, in a cathedral built by a former Roman Catholic engineer.

As its numbers increased, Cao Dai filled its teaching with new, syncretistic content. From → Buddhism it adopted the idea of "origination in dependence," a semi-Hindu transmigration of souls, samsara, nirvana (understood as paradise), and → meditation; from → Taoism, which had many sects in the country, a tendency toward → mysticism, → magic, and the uniting of opposites; from → Confucianism a sense of → authority, altruism, tradition, and rites; from Roman Catholicism the duty of → mission and models of → hierarchy; and from animistic village cults the conviction that the worship of natural forces and lower spirits could be combined with the invocation of higher spirits and human heroes. Caodaist congregations formed in other cities of the region between the Mekong delta, Da Nang, and Pnompenh. Between 1927 and 1954 the membership of Cao Dai rose to over two million.

According to their various political convictions, Caodaist sects took part in the various regional conflicts of the 20th century — the Japanese-French war of 1943-45, the war of independence against the French in 1946-54, and the Viet Nam War of 1964-75. They fought both for and against the Viet Minh and the Viet Cong. After Communist North Viet Nam took over, the Caodaists could no longer function as an autonomous, visibly practicing society. The Committee of Religious Affairs had to split into two parts, the northern being represented at Hanoi, the southern at several smaller places. They could probably exploit both their socialist and their esoteric possibilities, but thus far (to the end of 1984) there is no evidence that they have done so.

Bibliography: V. L. OLIVER, Caodai Spiritism: A Study of Religion in Vietnamese Society (Leiden, 1976); idem, "Caodaism: A Vietnamese Socio-Religious Movement," Dynamic Religious Movements (ed. D. J. Hesselgrave; Grand Rapids, 1978) 273-96 • P. RONDOT, "Der Caodaismus," Kairos 9 (1967) 205-17 • M. SARKISYANZ, "Caodaismus," TRE 7.628-36 • R. SMITH, "Introduction to Caodaism," BSOAS 33 (1970) 335-59, 573-89 (bibliography) • R. WÜNSCHE and D. WEIDEMANN, Vietnam, Laos und Kampuchea (Berlin, 1977) • J. S. WERNER, Peasant Politics and Religious Sectarianism: Peasant and Priest in the Cao Dai in Viet Nam (New Haven, 1981).

CARSTEN COLPE

Cape Verde

	1960	1980	2000
Population (1,000s):	196	289	437
Annual growth rate (%):	3.07	1.37	2.26

Area: 4,033 sq. km. (1,557 sq. mi.)

A.D. 2000

Population density: 108/sq. km. (281/sq. mi.)
Births / deaths: 2.88 / 0.62 per 100 population
Fertility rate: 3.23 per woman
Infant mortality rate: 36 per 1,000 live births
Life expectancy: 68.2 years (m: 67.0, f: 69.0)
Religious affiliation (%): Christians 94.4 (Roman Catholics 88.7, Protestants 4.0, marginal 1.5, other Christians 0.3), Muslims 2.9, nonreligious 1.5, tribal religionists 1.1, other 0.1.

1. General Situation
2. Religious Situation

1. General Situation

Cape Verde is a volcanic archipelago of 15 islands, lying 620 km. (385 mi.) from the West African mainland. The first Portuguese discoverers (ca. 1460) found the islands uninhabited. The present mestizo, Creole-speaking population is descended from Portuguese settlers and African slaves, the first of whom were brought to Cape Verde about 1500.

Climatically, Cape Verde is almost continuously under the influence of the northeast trade winds and thus belongs to the Sahel zone. Repeated periods of catastrophic drought can be documented from the late 18th century to the present day. Only about 15 percent of the total land area is suitable for agriculture. The sea is rich in fish, but the fishing industry is very backward.

The economy as a whole is also backward, with an average annual income of only $760. The resident population is smaller than the total émigré population, well over half of whom live in the United States (many are descendants of Cape Verdeans who went to New England as whalers). Other main centers of settlement are Angola and Portugal, where Cape Verdeans act to some extent as substitutes for Portuguese guest workers in other European Union countries.

Exports equal only about 10 percent of Cape Verde's imports, and local agricultural production often as little as 10 percent of the country's food needs. Accounts remain in balance, however, partly because of private transfers from Cape Verdeans outside the country and partly because of massive food aid.

Cape Verde was a Portuguese possession until gaining its independence in 1975. From 1963 PAIGC, the Liberation Movement for Guinea-Bissau and Cape Verde, led by the Cape Verdean Amilcar Cabral, fought a guerilla war in Guinea-Bissau. The postliberation unity of these two very different areas ended with the Guinea-Bissau coup of 1981.

Its constitution of 1981 made Cape Verde a one-party state. In 1990 the national assembly revised the constitution to allow for multiple parties, with the first free presidential election held in 1991.

2. Religious Situation

Cape Verde is predominantly → Roman Catholic. The first seminary for indigenous → priests was founded in 1570, though the first indigenous → bishop was consecrated only in 1975. The church plays an active role in social development through Caritas Cabo-Verdeana. With independence in 1975, the Catholic Church lost its privileged position. The state is secular, with freedom of religion.

The only significant Protestant group is the Church of the Nazarene (→ Perfectionists), which started work in the islands in 1903. In 1990 it had 9,000 adherents in 23 congregations.

Bibliography: E. BAUMANN et al., eds., *Der Fischer Weltalmanach* (Frankfurt, 1990) • B. DAVIDSON, *The Fortunate Isles: A Study in African Transformation* (Trenton, N.J., 1989) • R. HOFMEIER and M. SCHÖNBORN, eds., *Politisches Lexikon Africa* (3d ed.; Munich, 1987) • S. MAY, *Tourismus in der Dritten Welt. Von der Kritik zur Strategie: Das Beispiel Kapverde* (Frankfurt, 1985) 206-52 • *New African Yearbook–West and Central Africa, 1985-6* (New York, 1986) 36-39 • C. SHAW, *Cape Verde Islands* (Oxford, 1990) bibliography • *Weltkirche* (Aachen, 1985) 123-30.

PAUL JENKINS

Capital and Labor → Social Partnership

Capital Punishment → Death Penalty

Capitalism

1. Term
2. Development
3. Criticism

1. Term

1.1. The word "capitalism" has often been a highly controversial one, not only in political contexts but also in sociology and academia generally, though much less so in English, Italian, and Japanese circles than, for example, in Germany. The word has often been used to make accusations, and thus it has become regarded as an → ideological term. Nazism demagogically equated it with Western countries ("capitalist plutocracy") or with the Jewish population (*jüdisches Wucherkapital*, "Jewish usury capital"). After the fall of the Soviet empire and state socialism, the word "capitalism" seems to have fallen somewhat out of favor, having been perceived as an antithesis to state socialism. In contrast, some have argued that only now, with the progressive globalization of the market economy, has capitalism fully come into its own.

Underlying all such uses are social, political, and academic debates, with their competing points of view. Stress may fall positively on the dynamic of capitalism in developing industry and popular well-being or in promoting individual freedom. Negatively, one may also highlight the fact that capitalism gathers material wealth, knowledge, political influence, and so forth at two opposite poles (doing so both in the sense of different classes and in the sense of developed vs. backward countries). Some will point out that state intervention can reform or direct capitalism, while others insist on the need for a revolution. In a positive sense, we find such terms as "free [or social] market economy," "free economy" (or "free society"), "modern society," and "Western → industrial society." In terms of epochs, capitalism is contrasted with → feudalism, with preindustrial or premodern society, and with communist or → socialist society. Its beginnings are usually found in the early industrial revolution in Britain, though earlier the emphasis is on noneconomic aspects.

1.2. Capitalism is a social system (→ Society) in which one part of the activity that is necessary for the preservation of life is set aside and subjected to market forces. Profit by the production of goods and services in independent enterprises, and by trading them with the aim of increasing capital, is a primary goal, and the increase of national wealth (both principal and income) is a concomitant result. The orientation to profit in individual businesses leads to a neglect of broader interests (e.g., the neglect of the environment; → Ecology). The market process is subject to the vacillation of booms, recessions, and crises generally (→ Unemployment). Those engaged in the process can be classified according to their typical roles: *executives* (originally coinciding with owners of capital), issuing commands according to the necessities of increasing capital, and *dependent laborers*, who follow those commands but who act

without any means of their own (→ Work). We thus get such antitheses as those between capitalists and the proletariat and between entrepreneurs and wage-slaves.

1.3. Another side to life is outside capitalism per se and only recently and partially recognized by it, namely, that of the usually unpaid support roles of caring for and comforting the tired, exploited, and redundant participants in the capitalist process, along with children, the aged, and those with intellectual → handicaps. Such work has typically been assumed to be the lot of women and the churches. A further aspect of noncapitalistic life is the work done in direct self-support in gardens, the home, or small farms.

1.4. In addition, there is paid work outside capitalism, for example, in education, medicine, law, the police, and the armed forces, inasmuch as these fields are organized by the public and do not involve the issue of profit, being financed by taxes.

2. Development
Essential factors in the rise and development of capitalism, still important in modernization today, are as follows.

2.1. First is the existence of a market and → money along with freedom from social and political restraints that are typical of traditional societies (such freedom achieved either by legal or by violent means), as well as related institutions such as banks and trading rights (see 2.2) and civil law (see 2.3).

2.2. Next, people with the proper "spirit of capitalism" (Weber) are required — namely, those with an inner drive to work hard and to act rationally for one's own advantage, both industrial entrepreneurs and wage laborers. Max → Weber (1864-1920), contra Karl → Marx (1818-83), emphasized the importance of religious attitudes in this regard. In some forms of → Puritanism (→ Calvinism), material gain might be seen as a mark of election (→ Predestination), and hard work and restraint of desires fostered as evidence of victory over → sin in a rational lifestyle. Strict objectivity relative to the self led to a systematic reduction of expenditure (rationality principle), and there was rationalization in every sphere. Weber cites the greater development in Protestant countries and sectors as compared with the hampering effects of → Roman Catholicism and its stronger attachment to → feudalism. Reference is also made today to the influence of → Confucianism on capitalism (e.g., in Japan, Korea, and Taiwan).

2.3. Another factor is the modern → state (set up as a → bureaucratic state on the European continent, in Japan and elsewhere, and developing more gradually and partially in the United States) to safeguard conditions of a market economy. These conditions include (1) internal peace maintained by a monopoly of → force and criminal law; (2) reliable behavior of market participants by legal procedures; (3) a guarantee of private property and other constitutional restrictions of the executive; (4) a defined territory defended (or expanded) by armed forces, tariffs, and so forth; (5) institutions or minimum standards in many fields, such as weights and measures, money and banking, language, and education; (6) possibly an economic policy favorable to the development of capital; (7) possibly social legislation, including insurance systems against the risks of income losses from old age and sickness; and (8) a taxation system to provide funds for these purposes. One may observe in many backward or underdeveloped countries (such at least from the point of view of capitalist development) the more or less successful founding or refounding of such institutions.

2.4. Also important is modern science and its rationality, especially as objective and value-free natural science (see 2.2). Neutral with respect to → norms, devoted only to the search for truth, natural science with its artificial empiricism promotes a similar empiricism in industrial production, with market forces eliminating any enterprise incapable of incorporating the results of research.

2.5. A controversial matter is the relation of capitalism to the noncapitalist world (e.g., colonies, developing countries; → Third World). Capitalism claims to be a global system, and today to a large extent we have a global market. The capital amassed by conquest, exploitation, and → slave labor played a crucial part in the rise of capitalism. Technological and financial advantages enable developed states to control the underdeveloped by military, political, and economic means, including → colonialism, imperialism, culture (e.g., through the Hollywood film industry), tariffs, intervention, and international institutions (→ Dependence). Note must also be taken of the newly developed countries (e.g., South Korea) and the countries on the threshold of development (e.g., Brazil). At the lower end of the scale are many impoverished countries (e.g., in Africa), where the traditional economy has collapsed but where no steps are being taken toward capitalist development, resulting in social catastrophes like civil wars and famine (once again opening a traditional field of service for well-meaning church relief organizations; → Hunger). The more optimistic theories of capitalist development expect all countries to eventually "take off" and close the gap, at whatever human (and environmental) cost. The more pessimistic ones expect ever fiercer competition among countries, and with a growing distance between winners and losers, with all the concomitant struggles.

3. Criticism

The above sections include criticism of capitalism, which was controversial because of the plight of labor in Europe in the 19th century (note mention of the *soziale Frage,* "social problem") and the fear of revolutions after 1848/49.

3.1. Capitalism came under particular criticism and accusation from labor (→ Labor Movement). The most influential analysis was developed by Marx, whose starting point was a criticism of religion (→ Religion, Criticism of; Marxism). As the fetish was the god of primitive people, though in fact only the result of their activity and their dreams, so capital is the true god of the presumably enlightened people of capitalist society, resulting from their individual activity, exchange of goods, and so forth. Thus they treat the apparent facts of capitalist economy with a superhuman, godlike objectivity. Those who are (or should be) the subjects of their own lives thus have been turned into objects — namely, objects of capital (→ Money 1). And capital, which should be the object of sensible human activity, has instead turned into the mighty subject, into the true god, tossing its objects into crises and devastation, gathering some of them around the pole of wealth and power, but many more around the pole of poverty and ignorance. In the labor movement, however, Marxism made one side of the alienation (i.e., material poverty) the theme of its protest. As poverty has declined, it is therefore not surprising that the movement has lost force (see 2.3).

The churches have long tended either to steer clear of capitalism or to accept it, though accepting the job of alleviating the ills it has caused. Some of them are now perceiving the problems that capitalism involves in the light of the difference between the wealthy North and the poverty-stricken South.

3.2. The → Roman Catholic Church for the most part has not endorsed capitalism. With its precapitalist relations and interests, it was opposed to the → Enlightenment and → liberalism, but it also developed quickly a perception of social misery and a sensitivity to the noneconomic presuppositions of capitalism. The special status of labor and orientation to the common good are major themes in papal pronouncements (cf. also the writings of O. von Nell-Breuning; → Social Ethics; Sociology). Often we see a clear preference for guilds (or similar corporations in fascist states, e.g., in Spain in the 1940s).

The weak integration of Roman Catholicism into

capitalism facilitated the most influential criticism of capitalism in the 1970s, that of Latin American → liberation theology, with its roots in European theology and the → base communities of Latin America (cf. the Bishops' Conferences at Medellín in 1968 and Puebla in 1979). This theology, which takes a stand for the poor of the continent, opposes the capitalist global economy. It stands for its own cultural identity over against the consumerism of the North (→ Consumption). The base communities are self-organized and are strongly oriented to the Bible. Typically rejecting Eurocentric ecclesiasticism and theology, this movement has had an impact in North America (→ Pastoral Letters) and Europe and elsewhere.

3.3. The Protestant churches (→ Lutheran Churches; Reformed and Presbyterian Churches) have been more supportive of the development and function of capitalism, especially the free churches in England and the United States, which often openly advocate it. (In this regard there is a theory that a pluralist → democracy is not possible without a free economy and vice versa.) Lutheranism with its traditionalism did not actively foster capitalism. With its support for property, however, it checked any criticism of capitalism as a system (→ Social Systems), and with its orientation to the state, it tended to hinder the rise of social opposition. This explains the alienation of labor from Protestant churches in Europe. At the same time, the church was always ready to support social legislation on behalf of the underprivileged.

In the latter part of the 20th century, → ecumenical theology began to modify this conservatism. From the standpoint of social effectiveness, however, phenomena like C. F. Blumhardt (1842-1919), the 1925 Stockholm conference on Life and Work, K. → Barth (1886-1968) and his systematic criticism, the church's discovery of alienation in industry (H. Symanowski), and *Church and Society* (1966) have not had major effect.

→ Achievement and Competition; Bourgeois, Bourgeoisie; Class and Social Stratum; Development 1; Economics, Ethics of; Political Theology; Poverty; Proletariat; Religious Socialism; Service Society

Bibliography: D. Bell, *The Cultural Contradictions of Capitalism* (New York, 1976) • R. Benne, *The Ethic of Democratic Capitalism: A Moral Reassessment* (Philadelphia, 1981) • H. Braverman, *Labor and Monopoly Capital: The Degradation of Work in the Twentieth Century* (New York, 1974) • V. A. Demant, *Religion and the Decline of Capitalism* (London, 1952) • M. Friedman, *Capitalism and Freedom* (Chicago, 1962) • B. Griffiths, *The Creation of Wealth* (London, 1984) • D. A. Hay, *Economics Today: A Christian Critique* (Grand Rapids, 1989) • R. B. McKenzie, *The Fairness of Markets: A Search for Justice in a Free Society* (Lexington, Mass., 1987) • E. Mandel, *Late Capitalism* (London, 1975) • K. Marx, *Capital* (3 vols.; Moscow, 1965-67); idem, *Early Writings* (trans. R. Livingstone and G. Benton; New York, 1975) • O. von Nell-Breuning, *Arbeit vor Kapital. Kommentar zur Enzyklika "Laborem exercens" von Johannes Paul II* (Vienna, 1983); idem, *Kapitalismus kritisch betrachtet* (Freiburg, 1974) • R. J. Neuhaus, "John Paul's 'Second Thoughts' on Capitalism," *FirstT* no. 41 (March 1994) 65-67 • M. Novak, *The Spirit of Democratic Capitalism* (New York, 1982) • H. M. Robertson, *Aspects of the Rise of Economic Individualism* (Cambridge, 1933) • A. Smith, *The Wealth of Nations* (11th ed.; 3 vols.; London, 1995; orig. pub., 1776) • H. Symanowski and F. Vilmar, *Die Welt des Arbeiters. Junge Pfarrer berichten aus der Fabrik* (Frankfurt, 1963) • R. H. Tawney, *Religion and the Rise of Capitalism* (London, 1926) • M. Weber, *The Protestant Ethic and the Spirit of Capitalism* (New York, 1958).

Rudolf Wolfgang Müller

Cappadocian Fathers

The term "the three great Cappadocian Fathers" refers collectively to the three Eastern → church fathers (all from the region of Cappadocia in central Asia Minor) who completed the development of the early doctrine of the → Trinity and also provided decisive initiatives for the theology and practice at least of the Eastern church: Basil the Great of Caesarea (d. 379), his brother Gregory of Nyssa (d. ca. 395), and their friend Gregory of Nazianzus (d. 389/90). Amphilochius of Iconium (d. 395) is sometimes included in this group.

The Trinitarian teaching of the Cappadocian Fathers achieved two things: Based on the teaching of → Athanasius (d. 373), but with more consistency, they developed an understanding of the → Holy Spirit that unequivocally placed him on a level with the Father and the Son — in Nicene terms, that implied his being *homoousios* with them (→ Niceno-Constantinopolitan Creed).

They also managed to solve in a widely acceptable way a problem that, in the aftermath of the Council of Nicaea (325), had divided the opponents of Arius (ca. 280-336; → Arianism), namely, how the *homoousia* between Father and Son relates to their distinctness. Taking the formula of Nicaea as their starting point, the Cappadocian Fathers showed a concern for the distinctness of Father and Son (and

Spirit) that had been part of Trinitarian teaching since → Origen (ca. 185-ca. 254; → Origenism) and adopted the reference to "three divine hypostases" advocated by that tradition. According to the Cappadocian Fathers, the terms *ousia* and *hypostasis*, which until then had universally been seen as being synonymous, were now to be distinguished, with *ousia* referring to the oneness, *hypostasis* to the three-ness in God.

This solution ultimately prevailed, not least because in the second phase of the Arian controversy, after an alliance had formed against the neo-Arians (Anomoeans), who taught that the Son is totally unlike the Father, it managed to unite the parties that advocated the deity of the Son (original Nicenes, Homoiousians). The Cappadocian Fathers worked out the relation between the two terms within the framework of the realism of the → Platonic universals. Accordingly, the one concrete *ousia* is seen as being present in each specific *hypostasis*. The three hypostases must be distinguished insofar as each has its own individuality *(idiotēs)*, its own characteristic *(gnōrisma)*, and its own mode of being *(tropos hyparxeōs)* in which it possesses the common *ousia*: the Father in the mode of unbegottenness *(agennēsia)*, the Son in the mode of begottenness *(gennēsia)*, and the Spirit in the mode of procession *(ekporeusis* or *probolē*, with variants as to the participation of the Son). Each hypostasis has its own, noninterchangeable relation with the other hypostases, in which it also acts outwardly together with them.

The Cappadocian Fathers' understanding of the Trinity became the basis of the teaching of the second ecumenical council, namely, the First Council of Constantinople (381). In the Latin West their formulation was adopted in the translation *una substantia–tres personae*, though within the framework of the Latin tradition and seen through the prism of its own understanding.

The Cappadocian Fathers also contributed to → Christology in its progress toward the Definition of → Chalcedon (451) by insisting, especially against Apollinarius of Laodicea (ca. 310-ca. 390; → Christology 3.2.3), on the integrity of the humanity of Christ and by beginning to apply their Trinitarian terminology to Christology. Their contributions to specific themes like the doctrine of → God and his works and attributes, the doctrine of → creation, and → eschatology (→ apocatastasis in Gregory of Nyssa) were also very influential in the later history of dogma.

The Cappadocian Fathers exerted a similar influence on the development of the ideas and forms of → spirituality (→ Monasticism). Finally, it should be mentioned that the Cappadocian Fathers, all of whom enjoyed the highest level of education available at their time, were to a great extent responsible for the transmission of the culture of antiquity within the Christian context. Their efforts at mediation resulted in the adoption of the treasures of antiquity into the educational syllabus (Basil), the development of Christian rhetoric (Basil and Gregory of Nazianzus), the fostering of Christian literature (Gregory of Nyssa), and the establishment of a comprehensive link between the Christian faith and classical philosophy (Gregory of Nyssa).

→ Early Church

Bibliography: On the doctrine of the Trinity: H. DÖRRIES, *De Spiritu Sancto. Der Beitrag des Basilius zum Abschluß des trinitarischen Dogmas* (Göttingen, 1956) • K. HOLL, *Amphilochius von Ikonium in seinem Verhältnis zu den großen Kappadoziern* (2d ed.; Darmstadt, 1969) • A. M. RITTER, "Dogma und Lehre in der alten Kirche," *HDThG* 1.3.4 • D WENDEBOURG, *Geist oder Energie. Zur Frage der innergöttlichen Verankerung des christlichen Lebens in der byzantinischen Theologie* (Munich, 1980) chap. 4.

On the relationship of antiquity and Christianity: H. DÖRRIES et al., eds., *Gregor von Nyssa und die Philosophie* (Leiden, 1976) • P. J. FEDWICK, ed., *Basil of Caesarea: Christian, Humanist, Ascetic* (2 vols.; Toronto, 1981) • R. C. GREGG, *Consolation Philosophy: Greek and Christian* Paideia *in Basil and the Two Gregories* (Cambridge, Mass., 1975) • M. HARL, ed., *Écriture et culture philosophique dans la pensée de Grégoire de Nysse* (Leiden, 1971) • W. W. JAEGER, *Early Christianity and Greek Paideia* (Cambridge, 1961) • R. R. RUETHER, *Gregory of Nazianzus: Rhetor and Philosopher* (Oxford, 1969).

Other studies: P. J. FEDWICK, *The Church and the Charisma of Leadership in Basil of Caesarea* (Toronto, 1979) • P. M. GREGORIUS, *Cosmic Man–the Divine Presence: The Theology of St. Gregory of Nyssa (ca. 330 to 395 A.D.)* (New York, 1988) • A. MEREDITH, *The Cappadocians* (Crestwood, N.Y., 1995) • A. M. RITTER, *Das Konzil von Konstantinopel und sein Symbol* (Göttingen, 1965) • D. F. WINSLOW, *The Dynamics of Salvation: A Study in Gregory of Nazianzus* (Cambridge, Mass., 1979).

DOROTHEA WENDEBOURG

Capuchins → Franciscans

Cardinal

"Cardinal" is the title of the highest dignitaries below the → pope in the → Roman Catholic Church. Cardinals were originally → priests of the principal churches (sing. *cardo*) in or near Rome, from whom the pope sought help in leading the whole → church. The beginnings of the College of Cardinals date back to the 12th century. The ranks of cardinal bishops, cardinal priests, and cardinal deacons reflect this origin. In the last few centuries the → patriarchs of the → Uniate churches of the East have also become cardinal bishops.

The number of cardinals was fixed at 70 by Sixtus V in 1586. → John XXIII (d. 1963) increased it to 144 so as to internationalize the college and make it more representative. Paul VI raised the number to 145 in 1973, and in 1985 John Paul II set the figure at 152. By a decree of 1975 the election college for a new pope includes a maximum of 120 cardinals. At age 80, cardinals lose their privilege of participating in papal elections, but they do keep their honorary rank.

The cardinals are appointed (or technically: created) by the pope. They must be priests and must receive episcopal consecration (→ Bishop, Episcopate; Ordination) if they have not already undergone this rite. They form a papal senate and are the pope's supreme counselors and fellow workers. Sometimes they represent the pope personally *(legatus a latere).* They enjoy → jurisdictional and liturgical privileges, as well as privileges of protocol. Most of them are leaders of important dioceses. Curial cardinals hold the highest positions at the → curia. When there is a papal vacancy, they act during the interregnum.

Bibliography: 1983 CIC 349-59 • H. G. Hynes, "Cardinal II: Canon Law of," *NCE* 3.105-6 • S. Kuttner, "Cardinals: The History of a Canonical Concept," *Tr.* 3 (1945) 129-214 • P. Leisching, "Die Kardinäle," *Handbuch des katholischen Kirchenrechts* (ed. J. Listl et al.; Regensburg, 1983) 277-81 • K. F. Morrison, "Cardinal I: History of," *NCE* 3.104-5.

Heiner Grote†

Cargo Cult

1. "Cargo cult" refers to a religious group that believes that material wealth can be gained through the exercise of proper ritual worship. The word "cargo" in this phrase refers to various goods of European origin (e.g., dishes, knives, rice, canned food, glass beads, razor blades, hydrogen peroxide, rifles, axes, and cotton goods) and the money with which to buy such items. Believers in the cult typically have no access to such goods but expect that they will soon acquire them supernaturally.

2. The cults belong to Melanesia, though there are similar phenomena in other cultures (e.g., the spirit dance of the → Indians and the prophetic movements among Africans). From the end of the 19th century, cargo cults have been reported in many of the islands between New Guinea and Fiji, and the numbers have been growing since World War II. (Some identify any mixing of material and religious hope as a cargo cult, but this usage of the phrase is overly broad.)

3. Cargo cults usually begin with the appearance of → prophets. These announce the near approach of cargo and threaten severe punishments on whites and unbelieving Melanesians. The prophets require believers to make a complete break with their former life. Some move elsewhere in order to escape judgment. Others have destroyed their goods, including crops and domestic animals, so as to be ready for the new things soon to come.

4. In the face of contact with the dominant Europeans, old values became worthless, new ones were an insoluble riddle, but the cargo cults had an answer: The whites are superior because of their cargo. Originally the Melanesians regarded the whites as superhuman. They called them gods or spirits and gave the objects they brought a similar label, calling them spirit-tables, spirit-knives, and so forth. Later they saw that the whites were only human, but they still regarded whites as superior, although full of contradictions. The whites flaunted their material advantages and yet preached Christ-like self-sacrifice; they did not admit their own guilt but made the Melanesians feel guilty. Why, then, should not the Melanesians themselves also have cargo?

Baptized Melanesians have expected cargo from the Christian God as a sign of racial equality with their white "fellow Christians." Disappointed, they begin to mistrust the whites even more. Many turn back from the new God to old saviors, expecting cargo from their own ancestors. These had once been deceived by the whites and had let "the secret" be stolen. Others believe their ancestors still send cargo but accuse the whites of foiling the process by changing the address.

Cargo cults are nevertheless convinced that there are some whites who will help them set up a new order of life in which believers will become new people. Cargo is a symbol of their → hope. True life will begin with its coming.

Bibliography: K. Burridge, *Mambu: A Melanesian Millennium* (London, 1960); idem, *New Heaven, New Earth* (Oxford, 1969) • G. Cochrane, *Big Men and Cargo Cults* (London, 1970) • I. Leeson, *Bibliography of Cargo Cults and Other Nativistic Movements in the South Pacific* (Sydney, 1952) • W. E. Mühlmann, *Chiliasmus und Nativismus* (Berlin, 1961) • F. Steinbauer, *Melanesische Cargo-Kulte . . .* (Munich, 1971) • P. Worsley, *The Trumpet Shall Sound* (London, 1957).

Hans-Jürgen Greschat

Caribbean → Latin America and the Caribbean

Caribbean Conference of Churches

1. Origin
2. Organization
3. Challenges

1. Origin

The Caribbean Conference of Churches (CCC) was inaugurated in November 1973 in Kingston, Jamaica. Its roots can be traced directly back to a consultation of mainline Protestant churches in Puerto Rico in 1957 on future ecumenical cooperation within Caribbean countries, which led to the establishment of the Caribbean Committee on Joint Christian Action (CCJCA) in 1959. CCJCA served as a catalyst for much ecumenical activity, including Christian → education, family life education, → youth work, and → communication. In 1968 it helped to spawn a new body, Christian Action for Development in the Eastern Caribbean (CADEC), to enable the churches of the eastern Caribbean to play a greater role in the social and economic development of their countries.

CADEC organized the now-historic Caribbean Ecumenical Consultation for Development at Chaguaramas, Trinidad, in November 1971. This meeting proved to be a watershed event in the entire history of the Caribbean church. Never before in Caribbean history had such a widely representative body of Christians come together for any purpose. There were 250 participants representing the four language areas — Spanish, English, French, and Dutch — from 22 countries. Addressing the theme "Justice, Liberation, and the Christian Gospel," the consultation was sharply critical of most Caribbean governments for pursuing wrong models of social, economic, and political development. The church, too, was criticized for its role in sanctifying the status

quo. The impact of this consultation upon the region unquestionably shaped the character of the CCC in its early years.

2. Organization

There were 18 founding member churches, among them the Antilles Episcopal Conference of the → Roman Catholic Church. The CCC thus became the first regional ecumenical body in the world with the Roman Catholic Church as a founding member. By 1988 the number of member churches had grown to 33 from all four language groups, including all the major confessional families — → Anglicans, → Baptists, → Methodists, Orthodox (→ Orthodox Church), Reformed (→ Reformed and Presbyterian Churches), Roman Catholics, and the → Salvation Army. The CCC seeks to serve the churches of the Caribbean in the cause of unity, renewal, and joint action; without prejudice to its autonomy, it wishes to promote collaboration with the → World Council of Churches, the Roman Catholic Church, and other bodies.

A quinquennial assembly, which is the CCC's highest decision-making body, elects three presidents and a Continuation Committee, which serves as an executive committee and meets twice a year. Operating from its headquarters in Barbados and three subregional offices in Jamaica, Antigua, and Trinidad, the CCC develops programs dealing with theological reflection and conscientization, projects (community action and organization), and communications. CCC publishes a monthly newspaper, *Caribbean Contact*.

3. Challenges

Two major challenges face the CCC: (1) how to overcome the ambivalence of its member churches toward it, due in large part to the "progressive" stance taken by the CCC leadership on most controversial political questions; and (2) how to integrate the churches of the Spanish- French- and Dutch-speaking countries more fully into the movement. Though still a relatively new organization, the CCC has established itself as one of the strongest and most credible voices for Pan-Caribbeanism within the region.

Bibliography: Caribbean Ecumenical Consultation for Development, *Called to Be* (Bridgetown, Barbados [CADEC], 1972) • R. W. M. Cuthbert, *Ecumenism and Development: A Socio-Historical Analysis of the Caribbean Conference of Churches* (Bridgetown, Barbados [CCC], 1986) • K. Davis, *Mission for Caribbean Change: Caribbean Development as Theological Enterprise*

(Frankfurt, 1980) • D. I. MITCHEL, ed., *New Mission for a New People: Voices from the Caribbean* (New York, 1977) work of the CCC; idem, *With Eyes Wide Open: A Collection of Papers by Caribbean Scholars on Caribbean Christian Concerns* (Bridgetown, Barbados [CADEC], 1973).

CLIFFORD PAYNE

Carmelites → Orders and Congregations

Carnival

1. Terminology
2. Theological Context and Debate
3. German Fasnacht

1. Terminology
"Carnival" refers to pre-Lenten celebrations in Catholic countries. Signifying the abolition of fleshly pleasures, it derives from the equivalent terms *carnislevamen, carnisprivium, carnetollendas, carnelevale,* and *carnevale* (lit. "Farewell, flesh!"). In the Catholic mission areas of Japan, the word for carnival is *shanikusai* (or, "rejection of the flesh"). Only the Latin term "bacchanalia," referring to the Roman feast of Bacchus (the wine god), clearly reflects the character of the modern carnival.

2. Theological Context and Debate
The beginning of the carnival period varies from country to country and from region to region. Lasting, for example, for six days before Ash Wednesday, the time of feasting is in some sense the celebration of an anticreation. Carnival celebrations have taken root in Belgium (since 1394, in Binche), Brazil (a four-day celebration in Rio de Janeiro), Italy (in Venice, six months of celebrating in the 18th cent., now 12 days), Trinidad and Tobago (featuring a daylong competition among calypso bands), the United States (most notably, the New Orleans Mardi Gras festival), and elsewhere.

As an outgrowth of the urban mission of the 13th century, the idea of the carnival is based on the Augustinian model of two cities (→ Augustine's Theology). We could say that the carnival allows (or perhaps encourages) a fellowship of cupidity in the city of the devil, that is, in a world of fools, in contrast to the fellowship of love in the city of God. Essential elements — such as depictions of the ship of fools, figures of the devil and fools, and allegories of sin — are based on the transferring of this model to the Christian calendar, with the help of the → lectionary

passages from Luke 18:31-43 and 1 Corinthians 13 on the Sunday before Lent. The potential value of this contrast perhaps explains why, in spite of earlier prohibitions, Benedict XIV (1740-58) in 1748 strictly forbade the abolition of this devil's feast in Roman Catholic lands, although he opposed its excesses. From a Roman Catholic standpoint, it made sense to make it easy for believers to choose between the world of the devil and that of God by a demonstration of folly, in this way pointing them to the good.

On the Protestant side, however, the value of such a decision was contested because of the view that Christians are always both righteous and sinners (M. → Luther's *simul iustus et peccator*) and that they can be justified by faith alone (→ Luther's Theology). Luther's view of → church and state as → two kingdoms, each divinely ordained in its own right, also made it impossible to relate → Augustine's model to liturgical seasons. As Continental 16th-century church orders show, the feast was thus abolished in the Protestant world for theological reasons. Relics survived in England, however, in Shrovetide customs, which included revels at court, pancakes and pancake races, cockfighting, horseplay among university students, and the holly boy and ivy girl in rural areas.

Bibliography: U. ECO, V. V. IVANOV, and M. RECTOR, *Carnival!* (ed. T. A. Sebeok; Berlin, 1984) • G. VON GYNZ-REKOWSKI, *Der Festkreis des Jahres* (2d ed.; Berlin, 1985) 116-35 • W. MEZGER, *Narrenidee und Fastnachtsbrauch* (Constance, 1991) • D.-R. MOSER *Bräuche und Feste im christlichen Jahreslauf* (Graz, 1992); idem, "Perikopenforschung und Volkskunde," *ZVK,* 1984.

DIETZ-RÜDIGER MOSER

3. German Fasnacht
In Germany *Fasnacht* or *Fastnacht* (Eve of the fast; cf. Scots *fasterneen;* or perhaps derived from *faseln,* "talk nonsense") is a term attested from the early 13th century. The festivities are now mostly organized by societies and guilds. Officials are deposed, children are let out of school, balls and processions are held, and the so-called freedom of fools finds expression in legal → anarchy. Wearing masks denotes exchange of roles and extension of → identity. In the area of the Alemannic dialects (the German spoken in southwestern Germany, Alsace, and Switzerland), the carnival begins on Epiphany (i.e., January 6). In Cologne and the Rhineland, it begins earlier, on November 11.

→ Church Year; Popular Catholicism; Popular Religion; Religious Folklore

Bibliography: S. GLOTZ, ed., *Le masque dans la tradition européenne* (Binche, Belg., 1975) • J. KÜNZIG, *Die alemannisch-schwäbische Fasnet* (1950; Freiburg, 1980) • W. KUTTER, *Schwäbisch-alemannische Fasnacht* (Künzelsau, 1976) • M. MATTER, ed., *Rheinischer Karneval* (Bonn, 1978) • D.-R. MOSER, *Fastnacht–Fasching–Karneval. Das Fest der "Verkehrten Welt"* (Graz, 1986) • N. SCHINDLER, "Karneval, Kirche und verkehrte Welt," *JVK*, n.s., 7 (1984) 9-57.

ULI KUTTER

Cartesianism

1. Term
2. René Descartes
   2.1. Life
   2.2. Main Theses
      2.2.1. Methodology
      2.2.2. Epistemology
      2.2.3. Doctrine of God
      2.2.4. Physics
      2.2.5. Metaphysical Dualism
      2.2.6. Ethics
   2.3. Main Works
3. The Development of Cartesianism
   3.1. The Main Trends
   3.2. Occasionalism
   3.3. The End of Cartesianism
4. Cartesianism Today

1. Term

"Cartesianism" is the term for the philosophical and scientific teaching of Dutch, French, and German thinkers in the 17th century who adopted and developed the thinking of René Descartes. The main features of Cartesianism were Descartes's rationalistic method, his axiomatic *sum cogitans,* his mechanistic explanation of the world, and his metaphysical dualism (see 2.2).

2. René Descartes

2.1. *Life*

Descartes was born into a wealthy aristocratic French family in 1596 at La Haye, Touraine. After a scholastically shaped education at the Jesuit college of La Flèche, he first took up life in society at Paris, then gained experience as an officer and by extensive travel in Europe. From 1629 he led a retiring life in various places in Holland, concentrating on his academic work. Then in 1649, at the prompting of the Swedish queen, he moved to Stockholm, where he died a year later.

2.2. *Main Theses*
2.2.1. *Methodology*

Determinative for his philosophical and scientific work was his own analytic geometry, from which he derived his ideal of clear and distinct perception. In seeking to explain something, he would first break it down into its basic elements, then reconstruct it in a synthesis.

2.2.2. *Epistemology*

From → doubt of all the contents of knowledge, Descartes achieved the insight that the only thing we cannot doubt is doubt itself. But because doubt is a mode of thought, the thesis is true that "I think, therefore I am" *(Cogito, ergo sum).* I can thus be certain of my reality as a thinking being *(res cogitans).*

2.2.3. *Doctrine of God*

Apart from the *sum cogitans,* the existence of God is also beyond doubt. Along with an ontological proof (→ God, Arguments for the Existence of), Descartes advanced the argument that the idea of God as a perfect being cannot come from us who are imperfect, but only from God himself.

2.2.4. *Physics*

Because God will not deceive us in our perception, we can be sure of the reality of the sensory world as an extended thing *(res extensa).* All change in the bodily world can be explained mechanically. Living beings, too, are simply machines.

2.2.5. *Metaphysical Dualism*

Res cogitans and *res extensa* are essentially different substances that cannot have any direct impact on one another. Hence both perception and action need the help of God *(concursus Dei).*

2.2.6. *Ethics*

Descartes's not very influential ethics is a system of emotions corresponding to mechanical processes in human bodies.

2.3. *Main Works*

Descartes is best known for his *Discours de la méthode* (Discourse on method; 1637), *Meditationes de prima philosophia* (Meditations on first philosophy; 1641), and *Principia philosophiae* (Principles of philosophy; 1644).

3. The Development of Cartesianism
3.1. *The Main Trends*

The Dutch physiologist H. de Roy (1598-1679), the French thinkers J. Rohault (1620-72) and P.-S. Régis (1632-1707), and the German J. Clauberg (1622-65), whose metaphysics prepared the way for occasionalism (see 3.2), worked primarily on the scientific aspects of Cartesianism. The teaching of Descartes made a special impact on the → Jansenists of Port Royal, where A. Arnauld (1612-94) and P. Nicole

(1625-95), in their *Logique, ou l'art de penser* (Logic, or the art of thinking; 1662), developed an influential → logic on the basis of Descartes's methodology. Occasionalism may be regarded as a systematic development of the teaching of Descartes; philosophically it is the most important form of Cartesianism. Metaphysical → dualism is its starting point. A. Geulincx (1624-69) and N. Malebranche (1638-1715) were its main representatives; the latter's *La recherche de la vérité* (Search after truth; 1675) is considered its leading work.

3.2. *Occasionalism*

The occasionalists understand the relation between *res extensa* and *res cogitans* in analogy to that between two synchronized clocks. Bodily processes only occasionally are causes of things of the mind and establish no causal relation with it, the true cause of the latter being divine operation on the basis of "occasions" in the physical world (e.g., fire as an occasion for the sensation of warmth). The same applies to the → soul as the cause of bodily processes. Descartes never explained satisfactorily the origin of ideas from outside *(ideae adventitiae)*. According to Malebranche, they arose in Platonic-Augustinian fashion from the participation of the human *res cogitans* in God and in the archetypes of ideas that are present in him (→ Platonism).

3.3. *The End of Cartesianism*

The metaphysical dualism of Cartesianism came to an end, on the one hand, in the → monism of Spinoza (→ Spinozism) and, on the other, in the revival of the Aristotelian concept of the entelechy (→ Aristotelianism) in the monad of Leibniz. The reduction of reality to processes that can be explained mechanically and rationally came under criticism in G. B. Vico's → philosophy of history and in → Pascal's reference to the intuitive and emotional logic of the heart that one cannot reduce to the *esprit géométrique*.

4. Cartesianism Today

The *sum cogitans* of Descartes represents the origin of transcendental philosophy, or at least of the philosophical defense of the trust in the power of intelligence that is determinative in modern science and → technology. (This German interpretation is often rejected by French authors as too rationalistically subjective, neglecting as it does the link of Descartes with the tradition of → Scholasticism.) Contemporaries were already criticizing the absolutizing of a mechanical view of the world and the ignoring of human historicity and the Aristotelian concept of the entelechy (see 3.3), and this still seems to be a weakness in Cartesianism. The problem with Cartesianism from the standpoint of religious philosophy and theology is that it overlooks completely the dimensions of → revelation and soteriology, reducing God's role to that of a mediator between *res extensa* and *res cogitans*.

→ Enlightenment; Epistemology; Immanence and Transcendence; Rationalism; Reason; Subjectivism and Objectivism

Bibliography: J. J. BLOM, "A Systematic Study of the Mind-Body Relation according to Descartes" (Diss., Columbia University, 1975) • R. DESCARTES, *Philosophical Writings* (2 vols.; ed. J. Cottingham, R. Stoothoff, and D. Murdoch; Cambridge, 1985) • É. GILSON, *Études sur le rôle de la pensée médiévale dans la formation du système cartésien* (5th ed.; Paris, 1984; orig. pub., 1930) • H. GOUHIER, *La pensée religieuse de Descartes* (Paris, 1924; 2d ed., 1973) • M. GUEROULT, *Descartes selon l'ordre des raisons* (Paris, 1953) • K. JASPERS, *Descartes und die Philosophie* (Berlin, 1937; 4th ed., 1965) • A. J. KENNY, *Descartes* (New York, 1968) • J. LAPORTE, *Le rationalisme de Descartes* (Paris, 1945; 2d ed., 1950) • T. M. LENNON et al., eds., *Problems of Cartesianism: Studies in the History of Ideas* (Kingston, 1982) • C. LINK, *Subjektivität und Wahrheit. Die Grundlegung der neuzeitlichen Metaphysik durch Descartes* (Stuttgart, 1978) • W. RÖD, *Descartes' erste Philosophie* (Bonn, 1971) • G. SEBBA, *Bibliographia Cartesiana: A Critical Guide to the Descartes Literature, 1800-1960* (The Hague, 1964) • H. THIELICKE, *The Evangelical Faith*, vol. 1, *Prolegomena: The Relation of Theology to Modern Thought-Forms* (Grand Rapids, 1974) • R. A. WATSON, *The Breakdown of Cartesian Metaphysics* (Atlantic Highlands, N.J., 1987).

WOLFGANG NIKOLAUS

Carthusians → Orders and Congregations

Cartography → History, Auxiliary Sciences to, 8

Caste

Caste (Port. *casta*, "race, lineage"), which is fundamental to → Hinduism, rests on the idea of ritual purity (→ Cultic Purity). It is also a socially and historically conditioned way of organizing → society with a religious sanction.

1. Caste is based on racial distinction (the Sanskrit word for caste, *varṇa*, means "color"), which resulted from centuries-long struggles between the light-

skinned Aryan conquerors and the dark-skinned original inhabitants. It is also based on a class and guild system that, through regional, economic, and religious differentiation into an ever-increasing number of subsidiary groups *(jāti)* today numbering more than 3,000, generated a rigid and pitiless order, yet one that confers → identity and social security. If *jāti* is the local endogamous group, *varṇa* is the general category. The two can sometimes be in contradiction. Caste affects marriage, food, clothing, vocation, ritual, language (including one's name), and general cultural behavior.

2. Religious sanction is given to caste by creation myths (Rigveda 10.90.12). With the self-sacrifice of the primal universal god *(Puruṣa)*, the main castes were formed from the parts of his body (mouth = *brāhmāṇa*, priests; arms = *kṣatrīya*, kings and officials; bones = *vaiśya*, merchants; feet = *śūdra*, landless peasants and servants). Through karma, the fate of birth is the result of the past, for which the individual is responsible. In this way → hierarchy is rationalized.

→ Buddhism attacked the injustice of the caste system. → Islam and → Sikhism reject it but are influenced by the caste mentality. Christians, too, find it hard to overcome the notion; this difficulty has led to conflict about caste in missionary strategy (→ Hinduism and Christianity).

There is some mixing of caste in certain Hindu sects, in mass pilgrimages to transregional cultic sites, in following a guru who, because of his holiness of life, transcends caste distinction as a sannyasin, and as a result of modernization, industrialization, and the → mass media. Yet there are conservative reactions that strengthen caste consciousness by caste unions *(sabha)* that even cut across religious boundaries.

3. The untouchables — that is, those without caste — are the scandal of the caste system (→ Pariahs). Though attacked by reformers (esp. M. Gandhi) and outlawed by the state, this evil persists. The Indians who are in this category (about 120 million in 1996) are not allowed to enter temples or to use communal wells or inns. They also suffer from economic exploitation. Government attempts to help them have provoked resistance from the higher castes and have often led to violence.

It seems as though the caste system can never be abolished as long as it grants identity and social security to individuals and therefore a stability that, in the present unsettled social climate, can be achieved in no other way.

→ Reincarnation

Bibliography: L. M. Dumont, *Gesellschaft in Indien. Die Soziologie des Kastenwesens* (Vienna, 1976) • J. H. Hutton, *Caste in India* (7th ed.; Cambridge, 1983) • M. N. Srinivas, *Caste in Modern India* (Bombay, 1962).

Michael von Brück

Casuistry

1. The term "casuistry" denotes the methodical process of bringing individual, real-life cases under the established → norms of a discipline or → worldview or → ethics. It has its roots in → law. As in Roman and English law, general rules are developed on the basis of individual cases; these general rules in turn are applied to individual cases. The same procedure may then be adopted in other spheres in which human conduct is evaluated according to fixed norms. We find it in almost all religions in connection with ideas of → sin and purification, as well as in broad ethical traditions.

2. Rabbinic → Jewish theology sought to lay down in detail the type of conduct that was commanded in the → Torah and discussed in the → Mishnah and → Talmud. As far as possible, its aim was to rule out offenses against the commands of God. It thus developed a full casuistry with a law (→ Halakah) regulating individual cases. Tensions in the Torah and rabbinic exposition became the theme of constant debate.

3. The beginnings of a Christian casuistry may be detected in the NT when the law of Christ gives rise to specific directions (Gal. 6:2; → Law 2; Parenesis). The influence of → Stoicism and the OT tradition as well as the pastoral need to give concrete instruction on how to live as a Christian in a pagan setting resulted in ethical sketches along casuistic lines (e.g., by → Tertullian and Ambrose).

From the time of the 6th-century penitentiaries, the church worked out a penitential practice in which casuistry helped priests to determine appropriate penance for offenses. In the later Middle Ages penitential *summae* regulated ethics. → Scholasticism probed more deeply into the principles of ethics, but from the 17th century a casuistry developed in Roman Catholicism that claimed to be able to decide individual cases, especially borderline issues, by the logical deduction of general principles based on → natural law. This was the mark of classical → moral theology up to the 19th century.

Roman Catholic moral theology today integrates casuistry, as a process by which to make ethics concrete, into a total system of Christian ethics.

4. Casuistry has always run into criticism because it is in danger of reducing ethical demands to a minimum (B. → Pascal). In general, Protestant theology rejects it, although the English Puritans of the 16th and 17th century produced several notable casuists, supremely William Ames (1576-1633). To its basic anthropological understanding that we are in personal encounter with God there corresponds in the ethical sphere a stress on personal → responsibility that rules out tight regulation. In consequence, however, Protestant theological ethics runs the risk of not being able to give Christian behavior any specific content and making ethical discussion arbitrary. The clearest example of this danger appeared in the 1950s, in the stir about "situation ethics."

This experience and ecumenical conversations have thus raised again the → metaethical question as to what role specific ethical directions in the biblical tradition (e.g., the → Decalogue or the → Sermon on the Mount) might have in the Christian discussion of ethics. With the help of casuistry, a material ethics will perhaps develop in the ecumenical context. Vigorous research in practical fields (e.g., → medical ethics) and lively international debate with the Anglo-Saxon tradition may give urgency to these questions.

→ Action Theory; Analytic Ethics; Duty; Emotive Theory of Ethics; Freedom

Bibliography: K. BARTH, *CD* III/4, 5-15 • V. A. DEMANT, "Casuistry," *DCE* 47-49 • A. DENECKE, *Wahrhaftigkeit. Eine evangelische Kasuistik* (Göttingen, 1972) • K. GOLDAMMER, E. L. DIETRICH, and J. KLEIN, "Kasuistik," *RGG* (3d ed.) 3.1166-71 • A. R. JONSEN, "Casuistry," *EncBio* 1.344-50 • A. R. JONSEN and S. E. TOULMIN, *The Abuse of Casuistry: A History of Moral Reasoning* (Berkeley, Calif., 1988) • J. KLEIN, "Moralsystem," *HWP* 6.192-99 • E. LEITES, ed., *Conscience and Casuistry in Early Modern Europe* (Cambridge, 1988) • R. C. MORTIMER, *Elements of Moral Theology* (London, 1947) • K. L. SPRUNGER, *The Learned Doctor William Ames* (Urbana, Ill., 1972) • T. WOOD, *English Casuistical Divinity during the Seventeenth Century* (London, 1952).

WERNER SCHWARTZ

Catacombs

1. "Catacomb" refers to the underground Christian → cemeteries (§4) in → Rome, as well as in Naples

and Syracuse, which consist mainly of a network of passages, the walls along which contain hundreds of simple tombs *(loci)*, with chambers *(cubicula)* for more lavish interment (including vaulted tombs, or *arcosolia*) or as family burial plots. The wall tombs are shut off with brick or marble, on which there might be inscriptions, often with only the names of the dead. Light shafts *(lucernaria)* provided air and illumination and also served to mark important graves (e.g., of → martyrs). The ancient name was *coemeterium,* and the passages were called *cryptae.* The term "catacombs," documented from the ninth century, derives from *ad catacumbas,* the name of the locality above the catacombs of St. Sebastian on the Appian Way.

2. The origin of the catacombs in Rome dates from the late second or early third century. Literary sources show that the motive behind them was the desire for separate Christian cemeteries, combined with the Christian duty of seeing to the burial of the many poor believers. Archaeology shows that the layers of tufa, which are easy to excavate, provided the opportunity to establish large community cemeteries at low cost beneath the ground and outside the city walls.

As burial grounds, the catacombs served for the cult of the dead and of martyrs. They never served as places of refuge in times of → persecution. By the fourth century, the tombs and cult of the martyrs led to the development of very large cemeteries, sometimes over 12 km. (7 mi.) long and containing thousands of graves. From the fourth century, under the Constantinian dynasty, cemetery basilicas were built above the catacombs or in their neighborhood to serve the eucharistic cult of the dead and the martyrs. From the fifth century the catacombs were used mainly for veneration of the tombs of martyrs (→ Saints, Veneration of). In the early seventh century we have the first recorded instances of the removal of → relics from the catacombs to city churches. The catacombs, even those of St. Sebastian, then became deserted and fell into oblivion until rediscovered in the Counter-Reformation.

3. About 70 catacombs of different lengths are known in Rome, having a total length of about 170 km. (105 mi.) and an estimated 800,000 graves. The oldest Christian cemetery is Area 1 of the Callistus catacombs on the Appian Way, which is named for the first superintendent, who was appointed by Pope Zephyrinus (198-217). Most of the martyr popes of the third century were buried there (papal vault). Nearby are smaller, originally private cemeteries also

of the early third century (of Domitilla, Priscilla, Praetextatus, etc.), which quickly grew in size and came into the possession of the Christian community.

As a rule, only a few tombs carry artistic decoration. Among them, in the Lucina vaults and Area I of the Callistus catacombs, are the oldest examples of Christian art from the early third century. Several examples of Christian painting from the later third and fourth centuries appear in the *cubicula* of the Marcellinus and Petrus catacombs. The small private catacombs on the Via Latina, which were discovered in 1956, are fully painted and include many OT themes that were previously unknown in Christian → iconography (→ Christian Art).

The catacombs of Rome were a genuine Christian creation arising out of the needs of the community and the social and economic situation prevailing in the city. No forerunners or models have been found elsewhere. Only the smaller Jewish catacombs in Rome, which arose at much the same time, are comparable. These obviously developed in response to similar needs and conditions.

The oldest of the Naples catacombs go back to the early third century. As in the case of the catacombs in Syracuse and Hadrumetum (modern Sousse) in Tunisia, most of the graves come from the fourth century.

Bibliography: H. BRANDENBURG, "Katakomben I: Christliche Katakomben," *LTK* (3d ed.) 5; idem, "Überlegungen zu Ursprung und Entstehung der Katakomben Roms," *Vivarium* (FS T. Klauser; Münster, 1984) 11-49 • J. G. DECKERS et al., *Die Katakomben "Santi Marcellino e Pietro." Repertorium der Malereien* (3 vols.; Münster, 1987) • E. GATZ, ed., *Die römischen Katakomben und ihre Wirkungsgeschichte* (= *RQ* 89 [1994]) • E. R. GOODENOUGH, "Catacomb Art," *JBL* 81 (1962) 113-42 • L. HERTLING and E. KIRSCHBAUM, *Die römische Katakomben und ihre Märtyrer* (2d ed.; Vienna, 1955) • L. REEKMANS, "Recherches récentes dans les cryptes des martyres romains," *Martyrium* (Louvain, 1995) 31-70; idem, *Die Situation der Katakombenforschung in Rom* (Opladen, 1979); idem, "Zur Problematik der römischen Katakombenforschung," *Boreas* 7 (1984) 242-60 • J. STEVENSON, *The Catacombs: Life and Death in Early Christianity* (Nashville, 1985) • P. TESTINI, *Archeologia cristiana* (2d ed.; Bari, 1980); idem, *Le catacombe e gli antichi cimiteri cristiani in Roma* (Bologna, 1966) • J. M. C. TOYNBEE, *Death and Burial in the Roman World* (Ithaca, N.Y., 1971; repr., Baltimore, 1996) 199-244.

HUGO BRANDENBURG

Catechesis

1. Term and History

1.1. "Catechesis" is the term for the instruction in the Christian → faith that is connected with baptismal preparation or administration (→ Baptism). The underlying Greek word *katēcheō*, "teach by word of mouth" (originally used in drama), acquired in primitive Christianity the sense of communicating the content of the faith by instruction (1 Cor. 14:19; Gal. 6:6; Acts 18:25, etc.). In Heb. 6:1-2 the content is listed: "repentance from dead works and faith toward God . . . baptisms, → laying on of hands, → resurrection of the dead, and eternal judgment" (→ Last Judgment). Catechesis also included moral injunctions (e.g., Eph. 5:22–6:9; Col. 3:18–4:1) and other Bible texts. The reference in *2 Clem.* 17:1 is clearly to baptismal instruction.

1.2. Many examples of baptismal catechesis may be found in the → early church. The catecheses of → Augustine (354-430; *De cat. rud.*) are very impressive. He sets the whole → history of salvation before the candidates, describing the goal as one of leading from faith by way of → hope to → love. For Augustine, catechesis must pay attention to candidates' language as well as their knowledge and readiness to understand. Along with the catechesis for which teachers were responsible, the early church also had house catechesis for those already baptized.

1.3. In the Middle Ages, catechesis for individuals was less common. Instead there was elementary catechesis, for example, for tribes that became Christian en masse (→ Germanic Mission). The content consisted of the creed (→ Confession of Faith), the → Lord's Prayer, and sometimes the → Decalogue. The Synod of Paris (825) ruled that → godparents and parents should give instruction to baptized children. Catechesis occurred also in penance (→ Penitence), in the form of giving lists of sins and → virtues (E. Paul, 1.25ff.). Although we have expositions of the creed from the ninth century, memorization of the tradition was probably the main form of catechesis in the Middle Ages. This changed only in the later Middle Ages with the → Bohemian Brethren and the humanists (→ Humanism), such as D. → Erasmus (1469?-1536), who demanded the instruction of all baptized children, along with testing whether they knew the value of baptism and were ready to confirm it.

1.4. The Reformers paid great attention to catechesis. After many attempts to give written form to Protestant truth, M. → Luther (1483-1546) in 1529 published his Large Catechism (for theologians and pastors) and his Small Catechism (for *Hausväter,* "heads of households"), which would fix the content of catechesis for centuries. Still the main stress was on pure memorization, though with some explanation. Terms were defined, summaries given, and the teachers encouraged to ask questions. Luther supplemented the → catechism with biblical stories confirming it. Methodologically, the Reformers followed humanist rules and the question-and-answer schema of medieval penitential practice.

New methods came in only with pedagogical reformers like W. Ratke (1571-1635) and J. A. Comenius (1592-1670), who asked among other things for pictorial presentations of the → truth and for attention to the ability of the students to understand. Comenius's application of the catechism and the Bible to Christian living and dying was an early intimation of → Pietism, for which the main aim of catechesis was → edification (→ Devotional Literature) and the bettering of life. But even Pietism could not free catechesis from the prison of sterile memorization.

J. B. Basedow (1723-90) was the first to suggest an alternative to rote memorizing, namely, independent reflection that leads to knowledge, and he gave practical direction along these lines in his *Grundriß der Religion* (1764). J. G. → Herder (1744-1803) expounded Luther's Small Catechism in this way (1800). The next 150 years presented a confusing picture of catechesis, with changing aims both with and without the traditional catechisms.

2. Roman Catholic, Orthodox, and Free Church Views

2.1. On the → Roman Catholic side, the Council of → Trent brought a renewal of catechesis, often following Reformation models. The → orders were of great significance in catechesis, as were the catechisms of P. Canisius (1521-97) and R. → Bellarmine (1542-1621). During the → Enlightenment the catechism was enriched by vivid stories from the Bible and lives of the → saints. Roman Catholic truth and the Christian lifestyle were to be successfully communicated by this means. At this period the catechesis of both confessions moved from the church and the home into the school. The original catechism was no longer at the center but biblical history variously applied. Thus the problem became that of relating the Bible to teaching and → religious instruction to church catechesis.

2.2. → Orthodox churches of the 18th century and the Protestant → free churches made use of catechisms in their catechesis. In Orthodoxy, catechesis covered the → creed; the virtues of → prayer, → fasting, and almsgiving; the four cardinal virtues (prudence, temperance, fortitude, and justice); and a doctrine of → sin.

The free churches laid great stress on different forms of → evangelization for children and young people and on the → Sunday school along with the day school. Ordinary church members ran the Sunday school. Its pioneer was R. Raikes (1736-1811) in England. By the early 19th century it had spread to all parts of the world (esp. the United States, Germany, Holland, Switzerland, and virtually all mission fields). Along with initial instruction in the Bible and church teaching, its aim was to lead to a personal decision of faith.

3. Catechesis Today

Catechesis is still one of the inalienable tasks of the church. Differences arise concerning the aim, the relation between faith and → experience, the importance of the human sciences, and the understanding of the church that underlies the catechism. But catechesis still has the task of communicating valid tradition (the history of salvation, confessions, hymns, etc.), of leading to a decision for Christ, and of building up the core community.

Social developments brought other aims to the fore around 1970, including various confrontations between the world of experience and the Christian tradition, → communication as an occasion for meetings between people in situations of action and conflict in which the → gospel might have aid to offer, and occasions for fellowship in service groups. Next to the traditional contents of catechesis, those addressed have become the most important object of instruction. New forms of catechesis (involving projects, practical exercises, etc.) are customary. The common aim is to set present-day reality in the light of faith and to facilitate encounters with model Christians. The problems are different when religious education is given in the school.

For many people, → ecumenical learning is also important, which involves training in the ability to handle conflict and achieve → consensus in conciliar striving for the truth (→ Conciliarism). Concretely, this approach entails a readiness to enter into the experience of others beyond superficial → pluralism or an overhasty leveling down of differences. It thus demands a removal of national, cultural, and denominational limitations.

How important catechesis is for the churches may

be seen from → Vatican II (1962-65), for example, in its statement on Christian education and its call for a renewal of catechesis. We see it also in the corresponding Catechetical Directory (1971), the documents *Evangelii nuntiandi* (1975) and *Ad populum Dei nuntius* (1978), the fourth bishops' synod on catechesis (1977), and the apostolic exhortation *Catechesi tradendae* (1979). Note might also be taken of the working paper of the synod of German bishops on the theme (1974), which initiated a lively discussion of the content and method of catechesis. In the Roman Catholic sphere catechesis embraces not only the Bible and catechism but also instruction in the liturgy, the sacraments, prayer, ethics, the symbols, and much else. Among Protestants there has also been much discussion of religious education and preparation for → confirmation. More recently, discussion especially in the Catholic Church has focused less on people and more on the preservation of what is truly Christian. This development has led to a call for a new, authoritative catechism.

4. Adult Catechesis

Today there once again is talk about the need for adult catechesis. The orientation is not so much to a correct understanding of the faith as to dialogic understanding and a mutual communication of faith and reality in which the recipients and their problems are taken seriously. E. Lange (1927-74) called for adult catechesis as a "school for the language of freedom" where people would confront their analysis of reality with the unredeemed promises of the Bible, with a view, for example, to changing society. New forms of → Bible study are becoming increasingly important.

5. Catechesis in the Third World

In the → Third World, catechesis long consisted simply of relying on European or American catechisms that largely ignored the context of other cultures and religions (→ Acculturation). In this regard much has changed during the last decades. Under the slogan of contextualization, there is now serious reflection on the shape of Christian faith under the conditions of a specific society, a specific culture, and specific religious ideas (→ Contextual Theology). This awareness entails distancing oneself from what we could call a colonial catechesis (→ Colonialism and Mission). There are interesting examples from Asia, Africa, and Latin America.

→ Catechist; Christian Education; Initiation Rites; Religious Education Theory

Bibliography: G. ADAM, *Der Unterricht der Kirche* (3d ed.; Göttingen, 1984) • G. ADAM and R. LACHMANN, eds., *Gemeindepädagogisches Kompendium* (2d ed.; Göttingen, 1994) • G. BIEMER, "Katechese," *NHThG* (1st ed.) 2.272-85 (bibliography) • P. C. BLOTH, ed., *Christenlehre und Katechumenat in der DDR* (Gütersloh, 1975) • T. BÖHME-LISCHEWSKI and H.-M. LÜBKING, *Engagement und Ratlosigkeit* (Bielefeld, 1995) • L. BOPP, "Katechese," *LTK* (3d ed.) 5.1303ff. • M. C. BRYCE, *Pride of Place: The Role of the Bishops in the Development of Catechesis in the United States* (Washington, D.C., 1984) • M. VAN CASTER, *Themes of Catechesis* (London, 1967) • A. EXELER, *Katechese in unserer Zeit. Themen und Ergebnisse der 4. Bischofssynode* (Munich, 1979); idem, *Wesen und Aufgaben der Katechese* (Freiburg, 1966); idem, *Zur Freude des Glaubens hinführen. Apostolisches Schreiben "Über die Katechese heute" Johannes Pauls II.* (Freiburg, 1980) • F. FRICKE, *Luthers Kleiner Katechismus in seiner Einwirkung auf die katechetische Literatur des Reformationsjahrhunderts* (Göttingen, 1898) • I. GREEN, *The Christian's ABC: Catechisms and Catechizing in England, c. 1530-1740* (Oxford, 1996) • T. H. GROOME, *Christian Religious Education: Sharing Our Story and Vision* (New York, 1982) • G. HANSEMANN, *Katechese nach dem Konzil* (Graz, 1967) • D. JANZ, *Three Reformation Catechisms: Catholic, Anabaptist, Lutheran* (New York, 1982) • D. KLOSE, *Kirchliche Entwicklungsarbeit als Lernprozeß der Weltkirche* (Zurich, 1984) • F. KÖSTER, *Afrikanisches Christsein* (Zurich, 1977) • E. LANGE, *Sprachschule für die Freiheit* (Munich, 1980) • G. MORAN, *Religious Education as a Second Language* (Birmingham, Ala., 1989) • W. NASTAINCZYK, *Katechese, Grundfragen und Grundformen* (Paderborn, 1983) • E. PAUL, *Geschichte der christlichen Erziehung* (Freiburg, 1993-95) • J. M. REU, *Dr. Martin Luther's Small Catechism: A History* (Chicago, 1929) • P. SCHAFF, *The Creeds of Christendom* (6th ed.; 3 vols.; New York, 1931) • SEKRETARIAT DER DEUTSCHEN BISCHOFSKONFERENZ, *Stufen auf dem Glaubensweg. Handreichung zu Fragen des Katechumenats in der BRD* (Bonn, 1982) • G. S. SLOYAN, *Shaping the Christian Message: Essays in Religious Education* (Glen Rock, N.J., 1963) • G. STRAUSS, *Luther's House of Learning* (Baltimore, 1978) • T. F. TORRANCE, *The School of Faith: The Catechism of the Reformed Church* (London, 1959) • K. WENEGAST and G. LÄMMERMANN, *Gemeindepädagogik* (Stuttgart, 1994).

KLAUS WEGENAST

Catechism

1. Term
2. Reformation Catechisms
3. Roman Catholic Catechisms
4. Modern Catechisms
5. Catechisms in the Third World

1. Term

The term "catechism" comes from the Greek by way of the Late Lat. *catechizo*. It refers to the process of oral instruction for → baptism (→ Catechesis). When infant baptism replaced adult baptism, the term came to be used for Christian education in general. From the time of the → Reformation it has also been a term for published works summarizing Christian faith and Christian life.

Today there is uncertainty as to whether a catechism is meant for teaching or for learning, for children or for adults, for memorizing or as an argumentative introduction to the → faith in the face of opposition, as a dogmatic and deductive statement or as a proclamatory and situational statement. Yet even today the catechism is designed to make known the rudiments of the faith and to lead to confession (→ Confession of Faith), being presented in a form that takes account of the faith and life of those addressed.

2. Reformation Catechisms

The catechism as a written genre is older than the Reformation, but it was M. → Luther (1483-1546) who established it. He viewed the catechism with its questions and answers in terms of → preaching that is to be heard and learned. In 1525 he collected the Ten Commandments (→ Decalogue), the Apostles' Creed, and the → Lord's Prayer in the *Kurze Form.* In this respect he was copying the Children's Questions (1502) of the → Bohemian Brethren. Luther added material on the → sacraments in 1528. His Large Catechism (April 1529) dealt with the commandments, creed, Lord's Prayer, baptism, and → Eucharist, as did also his Small Catechism for Common Pastors and Preachers (May 1529). The new edition of June 1529, the *Enchiridion,* added a form of confession and some prayers. Luther managed throughout to emphasize theologically the doctrine of → justification.

Before and alongside Luther, P. → Melanchthon (1524), J. Bugenhagen (1525), J. Brenz (1527/28), A. Althamer (1528), and many others wrote catechisms. When Luther's work achieved confessional status, however, there was room for new catechisms only in response to specific instructional needs. Yet as early as the 16th century there are examples of the free handling of Luther's text, and from the 17th century attempts to replace it, from P. J. Spener's *Erklärung* of 1677 to the *Versuch* of D. → Bonhoeffer and F. Hildebrandt in 1932. From the middle of the 19th century, efforts were made to revise the Small Catechism and establish a uniform text (e.g., in 1884, 1931, and 1951). Such revisions,

however, could no longer accomplish what Luther had in mind.

Thus far there is no substitute for Luther. In the → Lutheran churches of North America and the → Third World, Luther's Small Catechism (sometimes the Large) is still the basis of instruction for → confirmation. In many cases these catechisms are the only written materials available for → Christian education.

In the → Reformed churches the *Katechismus-Tafel* of L. Jud (1525) was the first catechism. Jud also wrote the *Catechismus* of 1534, in which the pupil asks the questions, and that of 1535, in which the teacher does the questioning. Also important were the *Gesprächbüchlein* (1526) of J. Bader of Landau, the *Kurtz schrifftliche Erklärung* of M. → Bucer (1534), Bucer's *Kürtzer Catechismus* (1537, dealing with the creed, Lord's Prayer, Decalogue, and sacraments), and H. Bullinger's *Catechesis pro adultoribus scripta* (1561), which has 294 questions.

In Geneva → Calvin published his *Instruction et confession de foy* in 1537 and the Geneva Catechism in 1541/42. The latter dealt with → faith, the → law, the command of love, → prayer, the Word, and the sacraments, with 373 questions that were meant for a year's preaching. The → Heidelberg Catechism of 1563, which also had a section on the power of the keys, achieved great popularity. Even today, many Reformed churches base their youth instruction on a simplified form of the Heidelberg Catechism.

In England Nowell's Catechism (1563), the Prayer Book Catechisms (1549, 1604), and the Westminster Larger and Shorter Catechisms (1647) played a leading role, the last also in Scotland and the whole Presbyterian world. Reformed catechisms tended to become textbooks of → dogmatics and ethics rather than simple manuals for parents or → pastors, but they provided a solid theological grounding to those who took them seriously. The Heidelberg Catechism achieved symbolic status in many Reformed churches in 1618.

During the 19th century Germany saw some so-called Union catechisms, which tried to combine the Lutheran and Reformed positions. Between 1836 and 1928 Baden adopted these catechisms as textbooks.

3. Roman Catholic Catechisms

3.1. The Reformation stirred the → Roman Catholic Church to catechetical activity. Important German catechisms dealing with the five main heads were those of G. Witzel (1535) and J. Dietenberger (1532). But a breakthrough came only with *Summa doctrinae Christianae* of P. Canisius (1554) and the controversial *Parvus catechismus catholicorum* of

1559. The less controversial → Catechismus Romanus (1566) and the Catechism of → Trent, which deals with the five main heads, are both significant. R. → Bellarmine's Catechism (1597/98) was translated into 56 languages.

E. Augér (1563) wrote a catechism for France, as did J. M. de Ripalda (1616) for Spain. J. B. Bossuet struck a new note with his 1687 catechism, providing it with theological introductions. So did C. Fleury (1683), who included biblical texts, and F. A. Pouget (1702), who allowed for age differences among those addressed.

In Germany K. von Felbiger (1774) and K. von Deharbe, whose work was adopted in every → diocese except Rottenburg, aimed at completeness. Noteworthy also is the moralizing catechism of C. von Schmid (1836), the more elementary catechism of J. B. Hirscher (1842, 1854), the catechism of T. Mönnich (1925), and the catechism of the German bishops (1955), which uses the question-and-answer form and is strongly oriented to the Bible. Later catechisms in 1978 and 1980 are hampered by their language from establishing effective → communication between the faith and modern → youth.

In the United States the Baltimore Catechism of 1885 was influential, while in Holland the Dutch Catechism of 1966 broke new ground with its narrative form and controversial opinions; it received approval in 1968. The Irish Keenan's Catechism of 1870 emphatically rejected papal infallibility as a Protestant calumny but then was hurriedly changed after Vatican I.

Fundamentally the Roman Catholics lack a convincingly relevant catechism. Nor does the so-called universal catechism (Catechism of the Catholic Church, published in French in 1992, in German in 1993, and in English in 1994), which would be binding for all Catholics, really help. It too has been unable to solve the problems attaching to the substantively and personally appropriate mediation and inculturation of faith. The larger the circle is of persons a catechism must address, the less likely it will succeed in doing justice to the various cultures and situations. Because faith can arise only in specific contexts, however, universal catechisms are from the outset beset with problems.

3.2. In their catechisms, → Orthodox Churches add many things to the traditional main points, including teaching on the gifts of the Spirit, the nine fruits of faith, eschatology, and → the Beatitudes. Important catechisms are the Confessio Orthodoxa of P. Mogila (1640) and the Large and Small Catechisms of V. Philaret (1839, 1840). In the Greek world catechisms are published under such titles as Holy Catechesis or Christian Didascalia. In the United States an important adult catechism is the New-Style Catechism on the Eastern Orthodox Faith for Adults (1977); note also the family catechism Dieu est vivant (God is alive; 1979).

4. Modern Catechisms

The Dutch Catechism of 1966 represents a new generation inasmuch as it was designed for adults rather than children and does not follow the usual deductive course but deals with arguments and problems and leaves many questions open. In five parts — entitled "Existence–A Mystery," "The Way to Christ," "The Son of Man," "The Way of Christ," and "The Way to Consummation" — the faith is discussed in relation to life. Along similar lines is the 1973 Neues Glaubensbuch of J. Feiner and L. Vischer, an ecumenical attempt to give a coherent account of the faith (with chapters "The Question of God," "God in Jesus Christ," "The New Man," "Faith and the World," and "Open Questions between the Churches"). The Evangelical Adult Catechism was published in 1975, and in 1985 the Catholic Adult Catechism, which gives an account of the faith but is also witness to it. An adult catechism for Roman Catholics also came out in the United States (1975), as did the Italian Signore, da chi andremo? (1981), part of a series for various ages, as well as Pierres vivantes (rev. ed., 1984), and many short formulas offering help to believers in today's modern world.

New attempts at catechisms for children are Il catechismo dei bambini in Italy (1973) and the German Erzähl mir vom Glauben (1984) and Textbücher für Kinder (n.d.). A common feature in these new catechisms is that they do not present faith as identical with unchanging doctrine but as something that must be discovered and proved afresh in the ongoing encounter between tradition and experience. This basic theological insight was obscured for many years as the actual expositions of Luther or the Heidelberg Catechism were viewed as eternal truth, even as efforts were made to adjust them to changed situations.

New expositions of classic catechisms, such as → Barth's exposition of the Geneva Catechism and Heidelberg Catechism (1949) and the expositions of Luther's Small Catechism by G. Dehn (1939) and J. Schieder (1933), have again given prominence to the important insight that exposition must constantly seek to say old things in new ways as the situation of faith and life changes. These new catechisms have succeeded in making it clear that exposition alone is not enough if we are to give expression to the faith in the modern world.

5. Catechisms in the Third World

In the Third World, with its low rate of literacy, crushing poverty, and continuing oppression, it is not the classic catechism or the compendium of beliefs that sums up the faith but a book like *Vamos caminando* (Let's go walking) from Peru. Also from Peru comes the children's book *Buscamos el camino* (Let's seek the way), from Nicaragua *The Gospel of the Peasants of Solentiname*, and from Brazil C. Mester's *From Life to the Bible*. All these attempts to *tell* the faith are linked directly to the need and hope of liberation (→ Liberation Theology). The social context and a directly understood language of the Bible have led here to testimonies of individual faith, in connection with the theology of liberation. Similar attempts to present Christian faith contextually have been made in the Philippines, India, and various African countries (→ Contextual Theology).

→ Base Community; Catechist; Formula of Concord

Bibliography: K. Barth, *The Faith of the Church* (2d ed.; New York, 1963); idem, *The Heidelberg Catechism for Today* (Richmond, Va., 1949) • G. J. Bellinger, "Katechismus," *LTK* (3d ed.) 5.1311-15 • H. Brandt, ed., *Die Glut kommt von unten. Texte einer Theologie aus der eigenen Erde* (Neukirchen, 1981) • *Catechism of the Catholic Church* (New York, 1994) • W. Chroback, ed., *Der Katechismus von den Anfängen bis zur Gegenwart* (Munich, 1987) • O. Clément, ed., *The Living God: A Catechism for the Christian Faith* (2 vols.; Crestwood, N.Y., 1989) • F. Cohrs, *Die evangelischen Katechismusversuche vor Luthers Enchiridion* (repr., 5 vols. in 2; Hildesheim, 1978) • *Dossier sul catechismo degli adulti* (Bologna, 1981) • G. J. Dyer, ed., *An American Catholic Catechism* (New York, 1975) • D. Emeis and K. H. Schmitt, *Handbuch der Gemeindekatechese* (Freiburg, 1986) • L. Fendt, "Katechismus," *EKL* 2.561-66 • H. J. Fraas et al., "Katechismus," *TRE* 17.710-44 • P. Freire, *Pedagogy of the Oppressed* (10th ed.; New York, 1974) • J. Gevaert, *Dizionario di catechetica* (Turin, 1986) • *Der Heidelberger Katechismus 1563* (Lemgo, 1984; German-Latin ed., Zurich, 1983) • J. Hofinger, "Katechismus," *LTK* (2d ed.) 6.45-50 • L. Karrer, *Der Glaube in Kurzformeln* (Mainz, 1978) • W. Kasper, ed., *Einführung in den katholischen Erwachsenenkatechismus* (Düsseldorf, 1985) • E. W. Kohls, ed., *Evangelische Katechismen der Reformationszeit vor und neben Luthers Kleinem Katechismus* (2d ed.; Gütersloh, 1980) • J. L. Leith, ed., *Creeds of the Churches* (2d ed.; Atlanta, 1977) • Lutheran World Federation, *Report of the Studies on Confirmation, Luther's Catechism, and Catechetical Materials* (Geneva, 1983) • G. Mastrantonis, *A New-Style Catechism on the Eastern Orthodox Faith for Adults* (St. Louis, 1977) • J. B. Metz and E. Schillebeeckx, eds., *World Catechism or Inculturation?* (Edinburgh, 1989) • E. Meueler, *Katechismus und Curriculum* (Düsseldorf, 1972) • E. Paul et al., *Katechismus—Ja? Nein? Wie?* (Zurich, 1982) • A. Peters, *Kommentar zu Luthers Katechismen* (5 vols.; Göttingen, 1990-94) • H. B. Pöhlmann, ed., *Unser Glaube* (Gütersloh, 1986) 527-770 (Luther's Large and Small Catechisms) • J. Ratzinger, *Evangelische Katechese* (Cologne, 1995) • G. S. Sloyan, "Catechism," *NCE* 3.225-31 • H. W. Surkau, "Katechismus II," *RGG* (3d ed.) 3.1179-86 • R. Virkkunen, *Confirmation in the Lutheran Churches Today* (Geneva, 1986) • C. Wackenheim, *La catéchèse* (Paris, 1983) • C. Weismann, *Eine kleine Biblia. Die Katechismen von Luther und Brenz* (Stuttgart, 1985).

Klaus Wegenast

Catechismus Romanus

The Catechismus Romanus is the authoritative catechetical response of the Council of Trent (1545-63) to the main catechisms of the Reformers (G. J. Bellinger). It was planned in the first sessions of → Trent but could not be completed while the council was meeting. The council thus gave the task, along with its preparatory labors, to Pope Pius IV (1559-65), who entrusted the work in 1564 to a commission of former council members under the presidency of his nephew Carlo Borromeo (1538-84). After various revisions the first edition came out in September/October 1566 in Rome. It bore the title *Catechismus ex decreto Concilii Tridentini, ad Parochos, Pii V Pont. Max. jussu editus* (Catechism of the Council of Trent for parish priests, issued by order of Pope Pius V). Overall, the purpose of the catechism was to guide the clergy in their preaching and teaching of the laity. A work was originally planned for laity and children as well (somewhat along the lines of → Luther's Small Catechism), but this came to nothing.

This first official catechism issued by the Roman → curia, which followed the *Professio fidei Tridentina* (DH 1862; → Creed of Pius IV), remained in force until the 20th century, being superseded only by the *Catechism of the Catholic Church* (French ed., 1992; English ed., 1994). Although frequently commended by the teaching office, the Catechismus Romanus does not have the status of a formal definition of faith.

The four parts of the catechism deal with the Apostles' Creed, the sacraments, the Ten Commandments, and prayer (esp. the Lord's Prayer). With a focus on these points, it covers the whole range of →

dogmatics and → ethics. Unlike other catechisms of the period (e.g., those of Canisius or Augerius), it avoids debate with party opinions or the controversial teachings of the → Reformers.

The Catechismus Romanus underwent much revision in later editions and was even put in question-and-answer form. By now there have been over 500 Latin editions and more than 300 editions in translations into approximately 20 languages.

Bibliography: G. J. BELLINGER, *Bibliographie des Catechismus Romanus . . . , 1566-1978* (Baden-Baden, 1983); idem, "Catechismus Romanus," *TRE* 7.665-68; idem, *Der Catechismus Romanus und die Reformation* (Paderborn, 1970) bibliography • R. I. BRADLEY, *The Roman Catechism in the Catechetical Tradition of the Church* (Lanham, Md., 1990) • J. A. McHUGH and C. J. CALLAN, trans., *Catechism of the Council of Trent for Parish Priests* (issued by order of Pope Pius V; 3d ed.; Ruzal, Philippines, 1974).

JOHANNES SCHILLING

Catechist

1. Term
2. History
3. The Present

1. Term

The term "catechist" (from Gk. *katēcheō*, "instruct") occurs in the NT only in Gal. 6:6. It means the same as *didaskaloi*, "teachers," who in 1 Cor. 12:28 and Eph. 4:11 are grouped by Paul among charismatics and who had the task of instructing those who sought baptism in the fundamentals of the faith. In the course of proclamation the catechist was responsible especially for instructing and accompanying (→ Catechesis) baptized and unbaptized children (→ Baptism).

2. History

The spread of Christianity called for a catechumenate and the office of catechist. As the church developed, the catechumenate changed. The office of catechist disappeared, being replaced by that of → bishops and other clergy. In the → early church the catechetical schools put their stamp on → Alexandrian theology and that of Antioch (→ Antiochian Theology). Different forms of catechetical teaching remained important for centuries, but the office of catechist was not revived. In Germany, however, it reemerged with the → Confessing Church. Discussions after the → Barmen Declaration (1934) were the basis for the

development of religious education under church auspices, which was the church's responsibility in the later East Germany (1945).

3. The Present

3.1. In Germany, religious education is given in the public schools, the details of which are determined by the respective provinces and churches. This was always the case for West Germany, while East German churches as early as 1945 appointed as catechists former religious education teachers and members who had been trained in catechetical seminaries. The ministry of catechists became increasingly one of supporting children in their individual and social situations. The catechist was essentially a pastoral reference person for parents and families. Even after 1990, when religious education was added to the public school curriculum with reunification, catechists continued their ministry of religious instruction in the territorial churches of former East Germany.

3.2. In other countries, too, there are catechetical workers (either salaried or unpaid volunteers), such as → Sunday school teachers. Their work and function are determined by church-state relations, access to public or church schools, instruction in church or at home, and other factors. Church schools carry much of the burden of Christian education in Asia and Africa, but organized Christian education may not be permitted in some countries. The training of catechetical workers centers on → Christian education, Bible studies, and the use and preparation of teaching materials. Smaller churches (e.g., in India) cannot give the training that does justice to the practical demands.

It is of interest that women are mostly engaged in catechetical work in Western countries (even in the → Roman Catholic Church), while men are more prominent in Africa and Asia. In the Lutheran Church in Poland celibate women theologians and catechists give instruction and perform other tasks. In Hungary specially trained catechists are mostly volunteers. In Tanzania catechists are identical with evangelists (→ Evangelization 3.1.2). Trained as theologians, they give religious instruction, teach in Sunday school, equip the people (→ Clergy and Laity), and largely fill the role of pastor. In Lutheran and some other churches of North America, seminary-trained teachers may be active as catechists. In most churches, however, catechetical workers are not set apart, inducted, or commissioned in a special liturgical action for the ministry for which they are responsible. They often perform their ministry without adequate support from parents, families, or the church.

→ Catechism; Christian Education; Education; Offices, Ecclesiastical; Religious Educational Theory; Religious Socialization; Theological Education; Youth Work

Bibliography: J. HENKYS and G. KEHNSCHERPER, "Die Unterweisung," *HPTh* 3.7-139 • P. LEHTIÖ, *Religionsunterricht ohne Schule* (Münster, 1983) • D. REIHER, "Der katechetische Dienst und die gemeindepädagogische Dimension," *Die Christenlehre* 32 (1979) 107-10; idem, *Religion in der Schule. Entwicklungen-Auseinandersetzungen–Regelung in der ostdeutschen Ländern von 1989 bis 1991* (Frankfurt, 1992) • E. SCHWERIN, "Kirchliche Arbeit mit Kindern und Konfirmanden in der Kirchen der DDR," *Glaube im Dialog. 30 Jahre religionspädagogischer Reform* (FS H. B. Kaufmann; Gütersloh, 1987) 217-28 • A. SHORTER and E. KATAZA, eds., *Missionaries to Yourselves: African Catechists Today* (Maryknoll, N.Y., 1972) • R. VIRKKUNEN, ed., *Teachers in Christian Education* (Geneva [Lutheran World Federation], 1986).

ECKART SCHWERIN

Categorical Imperative

1. Term
2. Formulations

1. Term

I. Kant (1724-1804) used the term "categorical imperative" to designate the absolute character of the moral law. The law must be stated in terms of an imperative, for the human will is not "holy," that is, not fully in accord with → reason (→ Kantianism). In practical morality the categorical imperative is necessarily and universally valid (i.e., it is an a priori); it is stronger than the "hypothetical imperative" (e.g., the rules of what is apt or the precepts of cleverness), which describes the more limited relation between end and means.

2. Formulations

The most important formulation is that we should act only according to maxims that we might also wish to become universal law (*Groundwork of the Metaphysic of Morals; Werke* 4.421). In this way the will also ought to be able to view itself as universally legislative with its maxims (4.434). We must act in such a way that both in our own person and in that of any other, we use humanity as an end and never as a mere means (4.429).

The categorical imperative is binding because it is a constituent of → freedom. "Thus freedom and unconditional practical law reciprocally imply each other" (*Critique of Practical Reason; Werke* 5.29); "the categorical imperative is the *ratio cognoscendi* of freedom, and freedom the *ratio essendi* of the moral law" (5.4). The categorical imperative is the law of freedom (→ Autonomy), and as such it may be formulated only in form and not in content. Thus the categorical imperative cannot deduce the unconditional necessity of an action from looking merely at a specific end, but only from whether or not a given end promotes or hinders the achievement of freedom as the possible freedom of all. The categorical imperative is to be distinguished from the "rule of subsumption," which determines the correspondence between moral law and specific maxims. The categorical imperative takes individual shape as → conscience, which for its part is both the law and its application.

Many have criticized the categorical imperative for being so formal a principle of ethical action, from G. W. F. Hegel (1770-1831) to F. → Nietzsche (1844-1900) and M. Scheler (1874-1928). Anglo-Saxon moral philosophy also criticized it. How far the criticism is valid can be decided only by comparing Kant's transcendental ethical approach with other attempts to lay a similarly broad foundation for → ethics. Various other formulations have been suggested in continuation of Kant's categorical imperative, such as those of H. Jonas.

→ Criticism; Deontology; Duty; Enlightenment; Norms

Bibliography: L. W. BECK, *A Commentary on Kant's Critique of Practical Reason* (Chicago, 1960) • H. JONAS, *The Imperative of Responsibility: In Search of an Ethics for the Technological Age* (Chicago, 1985) • I. KANT, *Critique of Practical Reason* (trans. L. W. Beck; New York, 1993; orig. pub., 1788); idem, *Groundwork of the Metaphysic of Morals* (trans. H. J. Paton; New York, 1964; orig. pub., 1785); idem, *Werke* (ed. Preußische Akademie der Wissenschaften; Berlin, 1910ff.) • H.-J. PATON, *The Categorical Imperative* (6th ed.; London, 1967) • M. G. SINGER, *Generalization in Ethics* (London, 1963).

HEIMO HOFMEISTER

Categories

1. Aristotle (384-322 B.C.) introduced the Greek word *katēgoria* into philosophy (→ Aristotelianism). Aristotle's categories, used in analysis of the parts of a sentence, had the aim of distinguishing between sense and nonsense (*Cat.* 1b25ff.; *Top.* 103b20ff.). Aristotle distinguished ten fundamental predicates, or "categories": substance, quality, quantity, relation, space, time, position, state, activity, and passivity.

Since, as the Greeks understood it, being manifests itself in the Logos, the logical types of predication are also ontological principles of being. This means that the analysis of parts of a sentence by categories is grounded in being and that the categories are moments in the presupposed mediation of being and thought. For R. Descartes (1596-1650), the correspondence of being and Logos became a problem (→ Cartesianism); the result was questioning whether the categories embrace the whole sphere of reality.

2. This question could find an answer only as I. Kant (1724-1804) transcendentally deduced the categories from the functions of judgment (→ Kantianism). For Kant, the categories were the true root concepts of pure understanding (*Critique of Pure Reason*) that structure the world of possible → experience. Kant derived the categories from the forms of judgment, which, with those of perception (space and time), constitute the whole sphere of experience. If errors resulted for Aristotle from the confusion of categories, they did so for Kant through the illegitimate use of categories outside the sphere of possible experience. The categories are basic to the world of experience, but they take an idealistic and subjectivist turn because of the → epistemological presuppositions.

3. The categories had a critical and instrumental character from Aristotle to Kant, but for G. W. F. Hegel (1770-1831; → Hegelianism) they became relative moments of the coming of → reason to itself. Hegel combines being and thought by postulating knowledge as being and by finding the basic history of being in the transition from the categories of being *in* itself to the categories of being *for* itself. In Hegel's categories, thought has itself for an object in the way that it makes itself, precisely as relation-to-object, into an object.

4. Thinking about categories now takes place in the field of tension between Aristotle and Kant, and it thus leads from the universality of principles that can no longer be deduced to individual axioms that we construe as we please.

The theoretical relevance of the problem leads from H. Rickert's (1863-1936) distinction between methodological and constitutive categories to E. Husserl's (1859-1938) formal and regional categories and displays a shift of the problem from transcendental → logic to → ontology. In → analytic philosophy the categories again have a critical function. A critical linguistic philosophy (e.g., of F. L. G.

Frege, B. Russell, A. N. Whitehead, or R. Carnap) reaches the categories by working back from logical mathematical concepts to a few basic concepts.

Bibliography: E. FINK, *Hegel* (Frankfurt, 1977) • E. HUSSERL, *Logical Investigations* (2 vols.; London, 1970) • I. KANT, *Critique of Pure Reason* (trans. N. K. Smith; New York, 1987; orig. pub., 1781; rev., 1787) • F. A. TRENDELENBURG, *Geschichte der Kategorienlehre* (1846; repr., Hildesheim, 1963) • A. N. WHITEHEAD and B. RUSSELL, *Principia Mathematica* (4th ed.; 3 vols.; Cambridge, 1957).

HEINZ HUSSLIK

Catena

The Latin word *catena,* "chain," designates a form of Bible commentary that lists extracts from older commentaries for each verse. The catena first developed in the sixth century and became very common in → Byzantium. Its purpose was to give a handy summary of biblical tradition. Much of the Greek exposition of the → early church has come down to us only in catenas. The catena is related to the florilegium, which assembled quotations from the Fathers on dogmatic topics. In the Middle Ages the Latin church in the West developed the biblical gloss as a counterpart, the aim of which was to interpret individual words.

→ Scriptural Proof

Bibliography: H.-G. BECK, *Kirche und theologische Literatur im Byzantinischen Reich* (Munich, 1959) see index under "Katenen" • "Catena," *ODCC* 300 (bibliography) • *CPG* 4.185-259, C1-C179 (overview, with bibliography) • R. DEVREESSE, "Chaînes exégétiques grecques," *DBSup* 1.1084-1233 • H. LIETZMANN, *Catenen* (Freiburg, 1897) • E. MÜHLENBERG, "Katenen," *TRE* 18.14-21 • C. O. SLOANE, "Catenae, Biblical," *NCE* 3.244-46.

EKKEHARD MÜHLENBERG

Cathari

1. Name
2. Origin
3. Spread
4. Organization

1. Name

The name "Cathari," from Gk. *katharos* (pure), in popular etymology derives from "cat" as a symbol of the devil. At first applying only to German members, it became more widely used until the beginning of the 13th century. Till that time, other names were in use, such as "Albigenses" in France, "Patarines" in Italy, as well as "Manichees."

In both geographic spread and political status, the Cathari were the most important Western sect. They appeared in Cologne as early as 1143 and moved quickly into southern France and upper and middle Italy. They were viewed as such a threat by the Roman church and the related secular rulers that a → crusade was launched against them — the Albigensian Crusade (1209-29). From 1231, the → Inquisition was believed to be necessary to combat them. Because of persecution they ceased to be politically important from the middle of the 13th century. The Cathari disappeared from Germany after 1233, from France by 1330, and from Italy around 1400.

2. Origin

In its origin Catharism was not a Western movement. It came from Bulgaria, where a priest named Bogomil (mid-10th cent.) had preached a rigorous ethical → asceticism to the lower nobility, peasants, and lesser clergy. This went hand in hand with criticism of the church and an underlying → dualistic worldview, in which only God and the superterrestrial world are good, the terrestrial world being evil and created by the → devil.

After the conquest of Bulgaria by Basil II (976-1025), the Bogomile sect gained a foothold in Byzantium, where its dualistic teaching was developed on the basis of the → Manichaean and → Gnostic writings of late antiquity. But soon there was a division on the nature of their dualism. The moderate dualism of the older Bogomiles found in the creator of this world, the lord of Genesis and the Mosaic → law — indeed, of the whole of the OT — only the older (or younger) son of God who had fallen away from God. The more radical wing, however, made Satan equal with God and spoke of two primal principles. Both trends preached the fall of angels, linking it to the doctrine of the transmigration of souls. Practical consequences of these beliefs were the sect's emphasis on vegetarianism and its condemnation of marriage.

3. Spread

In this divided form the Bogomile religion spread to the west by the middle of the 12th century, where it underwent an independent development. Its attraction lay less in its dualistic → worldview than in the strictly ascetic lifestyle of its leaders, called "good men." This lifestyle corresponded to the widespread need for a renewal of the apostolic life that later found expression in the various poverty movements, such as the Humiliati, the → Waldenses, and the → Beguines.

The mendicant orders (→ Dominicans; Franciscans) became the rivals of the Cathari and similar movements and were charged with the church's defense against them. By the 1170s the dualism of the Cathari had become fully known to both adherents and opponents. The resultant polemical debate brought to light the incompatibility of the teaching of the Cathari with Christian doctrine, which worked against the survival of the sect no less than did the clear inferiority of its mythical thinking to the rational intellectualism of → Scholasticism.

4. Organization

Already by 1167 the Cathari had organized themselves as a church with fixed bishoprics and an efficient → hierarchy. The sect consisted of (1) hearers, who still needed conversion; (2) believers, who were already converted; and (3) the elect or perfect, the leaders. In its fully developed form the episcopal system had a → bishop at the head; then his delegate and future successor, the "older son"; then this son's delegate and presumptive successor, the "younger son." Under these were the deacons, who had the duty of caring spiritually for simple believers. Rites, attested from an early stage, included → baptism of the Spirit for novices and those who would later become perfect (the later so-called *consolamentum,* "consolation," or → laying on of hands), a breaking of bread analogous to the → Eucharist, and later penitential ceremonies.

Making the movement increasingly into a church helped to give it stability but also contributed to its ossification. Important in this regard was the crass distinction made between ordinary believers and the perfect. This meant that in the sect itself, an elite with a high moral claim stood apart from the rank and file, whose lifestyle did not differ noticeably from that of the church, which was condemned so severely. Socially the Cathari came mostly from the urban middle classes; only in southern France did the nobility give strong support, and there alone has a vital memory of the sect survived, which has resulted today in the stirring of a neo-Cathari movement.

→ Heresies and Schisms; Middle Ages 2

Bibliography: C. T. Berkhout and J. B. Russell, *Medieval Heresies: A Bibliography, 1960-1979* (Toronto, 1981) nos. 213-709 • A. Borst, *Die Katharer* (Stuttgart, 1953) • J. Duvernoy, *Le catharisme* (2 vols.; Toulouse, 1976; 2d ed., 1979) • H. Grundmann, *Bibliographie zur Ketzergeschichte des Mittelalters (1900-1966)* (3d ed.; Rome, 1967) nos. 119-328 • E. Le roy Ladurie, *Montaillou, village occitan de 1294 à 1324* (Paris, 1975) • J. H. Mundy, *The Repression of Catharism at Toulouse: The*

Royal Diploma of 1279 (Toronto, 1985) • L. PAOLINI, *L'eresia a Bologna fra XIII e XIV secolo,* vol. 1, *L'eresia catara alla fine del duecento* (Rome, 1975) • G. ROTTENWÖHRER, *Der Katharismus* (3 vols.; Bad Honnef, 1982-90); idem, *Unde malum? Herkunft und Gestalt der Bösen nach heterodoxer Lehre von Markion bis zu den Katharern* (Bad Honnef, 1986) • S. RUNCIMAN, *The Medieval Manichee* (Cambridge, 1947) • J. SUMPTION, *The Albigensian Crusade* (London, 1978) • W. L. WAKEFIELD, *Heresy, Crusade, and Inquisition in Southern France, 1100-1250* (London, 1974).

ALEXANDER PATSCHOVSKY

Cathedral

Since the tenth century, the *ecclesia cathedralis* has been the bishop's church, as it still is in France, Spain, England, and Sweden. The term "cathedral" (Gk. *kathedra;* Lat. *cathedra*) originally meant "seat," then "teaching chair [of the bishop]." In the Eastern Orthodox Church the cathedral is the main church of a city, though the term is not used in the Russian Orthodox Church. In Germany, *Dom* (from Lat. *domus ecclesiae,* "house of the Christian community") or *Münster* (cf. Eng. "minster") is often used instead of the cognate *Kathedrale.*

In the → Roman Catholic Church the approval of the → pope is needed for elevation of a church structure to the rank of a cathedral (which is inferior to that of the four great basilicas of → Rome; see 1983 CIC 504). In a cathedral the → bishop cooperates with the chapter (i.e., the body of canons responsible for the cathedral) in arranging special services and → ordinations (→ Worship).

→ Middle Ages 1; Minster

Bibliography: B. J. COMASKEY, "Cathedral," *NCE* 3.247-48 • R. NAZ, "Églises cathédrales," *DDC* 5.228-33 • O. VON SIMSON, *The Gothic Cathedral: The Origins of Gothic Architecture and the Medieval Concept of Order* (New York, 1956) • H. THOROLD, *Collins Guide to Cathedrals, Abbeys, and Priories of England and Wales* (London, 1986).

RAINER VOLP, JÖRG METZINGER, and PETER MASER

Catherine of Siena

The Italian mystic Caterina di Benincasa was born in humble circumstances in Siena, Italy, in 1347. Early in life, visionary experiences led her to take a vow of virginity. Around 1364/65 she became a Dominican → tertiary. She received a spiritual education and became the center of a circle comprising both religious and laity. Highly cultured Tuscan men and women supported Catherine, who was unskilled in writing and who, in 1370, began expressing her "political" thinking. In light of her experiences, she offered insightful criticism of the monastic life.

After an invitation to see the chapter general of the → Dominicans in Florence in 1374, Raymond of Capua was appointed her confessor. He served as both secretary and listener and, as master general (after 1382), introduced her reforming views into the Dominican order. He later wrote a biography of Catherine.

Between 1375 and 1378 Catherine went on several journeys that took her to Pisa, to the papal court at Avignon (in the summer of 1376), to Florence, and to Siena. With no great success she called for a → crusade, and she also tried to resolve various disputes. Historians are unsure to what extent she caused Gregory XI (1370-78), to return to Rome in January 1377. There can be no question, however, about her influence on his successor, Urban VI (1378-89). After the beginning of the Great Schism in 1378, Catherine made Rome the focal point of her activities. She died there on April 29, 1380. Pius II declared her a saint on June 29, 1461.

Most of Catherine's political activities are recorded in her 382 letters in Italian taken down by dictation. Between 1370 and 1376, seeing the evident impossibility of her Avignon project, she called for the crusade in the hope of converting unbelievers and liberating the Holy City, hoping in the process to purify Christians and reform the church. Her prophetic and visionary involvement brought her into touch with the works of → Hildegard of Bingen (1078-1179) and with Bridget of Sweden (ca. 1303-73). She threatened the rulers of the day, both spiritual and temporal, with the → wrath of God, but she also reminded them of the boundless → love of the crucified Christ in her appeals to them to play their proper part.

In confrontation with the people of Florence, Catherine styled Gregory XI the "true Christ on earth." There was an → apocalyptic element in her judgment on the antipope Clement VII (1378-94), who seemed to her to be an incarnation of the → devil. She found justification in her → visions for this and similar judgments. The 26 prayers of hers that have come down to us represent only a fraction of her actual prayers and were obviously recorded by those present at her → ecstatic experiences. Her private revelations, along with the fact that she was speaking as a woman in a church that did not allow women to speak in public, served as a contributory factor to her relatively late canonization.

In her letters, and especially in her *Dialogue of Divine Providence* (1377-78), a dialogue between herself and God, Catherine developed her ideas on → spirituality and ecclesiology. The redeeming work of Christ is central here. Orientation to the suffering Christ caused her to insert herself into Christ's sacrifice by a heart's exchange. In the process, like other women mystics, she stresses her eucharistic hunger and depicts the church as a garden that is sprinkled with the blood of Christ. The → pope is in charge of this treasure, which priests are charged to distribute, even though they may prove unworthy of their task. But Catherine inveighs against false adoration of the Host and clearly argues for reception by the laity in both kinds. Her final letters from Rome bear witness to a certain impotence and resignation, for she thinks that only the mercy of God can overcome the schism.

Catherine's thinking moves chiefly in the circle of the Dominican observations movement, which opposed the elite of the order (who, by tradition, were intellectually oriented). Earlier research focused onesidedly on her political activities. With the discovery of how widespread the phenomenon of women mystics was in Europe, however, her religious thought has now come increasingly to the forefront.

Bibliography: Primary sources: CATHERINE OF SIENA, *The Dialogue* (trans. S. Noffke; New York, 1980); idem, *The Letters of St. Catherine of Siena* (trans. S. Noffke; Binghamton, N.Y., 1988); idem, *Le orazioni* (ed. G. Cavallini; Rome, 1978) • RAYMOND OF CAPUA, *The Life of St. Catherine of Siena* (trans. G. Lamb; New York, 1960).

Secondary works: G. ALBERIGO, "Katharina von Siena," *TRE* 18.30-34 • *Atti del simposio internazionale cateriniano-bernardiniano* (ed. D. Maffei and P. Nardi; Siena, 1982) includes bibliography of items in English • M. JEREMIAH, *The Secret of the Heart: A Theological Study of Catherine of Siena's Teaching on the Heart of Jesus* (Front Royal, Va., 1995) • S. NOFFKE, *Catherine of Siena: Vision through a Distant Eye* (Collegeville, Minn., 1996) • M. REEVES, *The Influence of Prophecy in the Later Middle Ages: A Study on Joachimism* (Oxford, 1969) • *Temi e problemi nella mistica femminile trecentesca* (Todi, 1983) • A. VAUCHEZ, "Heiligung in der römischen Kirche," *Die Geschichte des Christentums,* vol. 6, *1274-1449* (Freiburg, 1991) 518-48 • M. F. WINDEATT, *St. Catherine of Siena: The Story of the Girl Who Saw Saints in the Sky* (Rockford, Ill., 1993) • L. ZANINI, *Bibliografia analitica di s. Caterina da Siena dal 1901 al 1950* (new ed.; Rome, 1971).

ANTJE ROGGENKAMP-KAUFMANN

Catholic Action

1. Task
2. Development
3. Present Manifestations

1. Task

Catholic Action, an organized religious activity in which ordinary church members (→ Clergy and Laity) participate in the church's mission on the basis of a special commissioning by the → hierarchy, is the official lay apostolate of the → Roman Catholic Church (so declared by a speech of Pius XII on October 5, 1957). The commissioning is viewed as making their action *(actio catholicorum)* that of the church itself *(actio catholica).*

According to the deeper understanding of the church at Vatican II, the content of the lay apostolate is everything that members contribute, in virtue of their participation in the threefold office of Christ, to the achieving of the church's goal in → evangelization and → sanctification (→ Mission) and also in Christian penetration of the world by building up the temporal order. In this last task, the laity act on their own responsibility as citizens, not in the name of the church or the hierarchy (*Gaudium et spes* 43, 76). The work of Catholic Action proper, however, is restricted to the church's apostolic goal. It is participation in the work of the hierarchical apostolate, oriented to evangelizing and sanctifying and to the formation of a Christian conscience (*Apostolicam actuositatem* 20).

2. Development

Historically, Catholic Action originated in the church's reaction to its own loss of power and to the decline generally in faith (e.g., at the time of the French Revolution; → Papal States; Secularization). Its home is in Roman Catholic countries that allowed for missionary and social involvement but not for political involvement, given the climate of the → Syllabus of Errors (1864), which was hostile to reform.

In Germany and Switzerland the propagation of *actio catholica* by Pius XI (in his 1922 encyclical *Ubi arcano* and in a letter to Cardinal Bertram on November 13, 1928) affected the many church → societies and associations that, especially after their experiences in the struggle for Christian → labor unions (1900-1912), were not prepared to be restricted to mere participation in the hierarchical apostolate. Here, Catholic Action became a principle of action with no specific organizational consequences. In Italy and Latin America, Catholic Action was organized by gender and by age (e.g., in Italy in 1954 it registered 285,000 men and 597,000 women, as well as 557,000 young men and 1.2 million young women).

There were variations in local expression based on common interests as awareness grew of the social causes of secularization. In France the Jeunesse Ouvrière Chrétienne (founded in Belgium in 1925; → Worker-Priests) and the Action Catholique Ouvrière opted for → socialism, though without leaving Catholic Action. The bishops tolerated this alignment as a temporary decision made by the members of Catholic Action themselves.

3. Present Manifestations

The strict tying of Catholic Action to the hierarchy (due in part to the situation under Italian → fascism) was relaxed with the new formula of Pius XII, who spoke of cooperation with, rather than participation in. Vatican II, while not imposing any organizational form, did list four characteristics: orientation to the church's apostolic goal (see 1), an authentic lay character, organization as an organic body, and action taken under the supervision of the hierarchy, which can also give an express mandate (*Apostolicam actuositatem* 20). Where the hierarchy judges these marks to be present, organizations can call themselves Catholic Action without having to conform to any specified form. Such an approach enables Catholic Action to link the power of the laity to the work of the pastor in a variety of contexts. This concept of the church, on which the classic formulation of Catholic Action rests (Paul VI, in a speech on August 11, 1971), has run into criticism in → liberation theology because it suggests a merely surface universality of the church that is inattentive to social tensions.

→ Catholicism (Roman); Church 3.2; Lay Movements

Bibliography: Y. CONGAR, *Lay People in the Church: A Study for a Theology of Laity* (rev. ed.; Westminster, Md., 1985) • "Decree on the Apostolate of Lay People (*Apostolicam Actuositatem*)," *Vatican Council II: The Conciliar and Post-Conciliar Documents* (rev. ed.; Grand Rapids, 1992) 766-98 • F. KLOSTERMANN, "Der Apostolat der Laien in der Kirche," *HPTh* 3.586-635 (bibliography) • J. NEWMAN, *What Is Catholic Action?* (Dublin, 1958) • W. ZAUNER, "Die Katholische Aktion," *TPQ* 125 (1977) 37-47.

WALTER SCHÖPSDAU

Catholic Apostolic Church → Apostolic Churches

Catholic, Catholicity

1. Term and Usage
2. Catholicity as a Mark of the Church
3. Ecumenical Discussion and Protestant Catholicity

1. Term and Usage

The word "catholic" (Gk. *katholikos,* "relating to the whole, comprehensive," from *katholou,* "on the whole, generally") has appeared often in philosophy from the time of Plato and Aristotle (→ Greek Philosophy). Theology adopted it in the lexical sense and developed its basic meaning with reference to the → church, its teaching, and its members.

1.1. Though it does not occur in the NT, "catholic" as a predicate used of the church is found in Ignatius of Antioch (ca. 35-ca. 107), who distinguishes between the whole church, where Christ is, and the partial or local church, where the bishop appears, and relates the two (*Smyrn.* 8.2). Clement of Alexandria (ca. 150-ca. 215) uses the term in the sense of "true" (*Strom.* 7.17.106-7). It is also a synonym for "authentic" in the Muratorian Canon (late 2d cent.; → Canon 2.2.4). Beginning in the third century, "catholic" became an attribute of the church in the debate with heretical trends (→ Heresies and Schisms), though it does not appear in the → Old Roman Creed, and it took the sense "orthodox" (i.e., conforming to right faith; see the anathemas of → Nicaea and cans. 8, 9, and 19). As a statement of faith in the confession (→ Confession of Faith), as a claim and program in opposition to heretics and schismatics, and as an assertion of orthodoxy against error, the expression has taken on a confessional character. The religious edict of 380 under Theodosius the Great gave legal protection to the *ecclesia catholica* (*religio licita;* → Byzantium 1).

1.2. Theological interpretation from the time of → Augustine (354-430; → Augustine's Theology) has given the term the sense not merely of comprehensiveness and orthodoxy but also of geographic universality, numerical greatness, and consensus of belief. Vincent of Lérins (d. before 450) proposed as a kind of test of catholicity "that which has been believed everywhere, always, and by all" (*Commonitorium* 2.3). We thus arrive at a geographic, numerical, temporal, and historical catholicity.

1.3. After some early clarification by → Irenaeus (d. ca. 200) and → Cyprian (d. 258), more precision was given to the word "catholic" by the addition of "Roman" in the 12th century. This development was the result of the ideology of the Gregorian reform (→ Gregory VII, *Dictatus papae* [1076] nos. 1 and

26) and the need to reject ecclesiological errors among the → Cathari and → Waldenses. The Councils of → Trent and → Vatican I (→ Roman Catholic Church) emphasized the claim of Rome to be the one catholic church. Although Vatican II avoided the expression "Roman Catholic," it maintained the equation (see 2.2).

2. Catholicity as a Mark of the Church

The one ancient and undivided catholic church broke apart with the mutual excommunications of Pope Nicholas I (863) in Rome and Patriarch Photius (867) in Constantinople, and with the final East-West schism of 1054 (→ Byzantium 3.2). The idea of catholicity lived on in both camps, however, as both the Orthodox and the Roman Catholic continued to claim to be truly catholic. The formation of confessions in the 16th century particularized the idea of catholicity, and the formula *Sancta catholica apostolica Romana ecclesia* (Vatican I, DH 3001; → Creed of Pius IV, DH 1868) documented this fact.

2.1. As the → Orthodox Church sees it, the term "catholicity" has a quantitative aspect (no limitation of time or space) and a qualitative aspect (the wholeness of the church as the body of Christ, the fullness of its divine-human life, and the → grace of the Holy Spirit and truth granted to it). The accent in the catholicity of the church is on the work of God in Christ and the → Holy Spirit. This work unites believers by the power of mutual love and integrates them into the mystical body of Christ. External or quantitative catholicity (universality) results from the love that crosses all boundaries and from the church's divine commission to proclaim → salvation to the whole world. Either way, the church's → unity finds expression here.

The unity embraces both the earthly and the heavenly church and unites past saints with present-day believers and future witnesses. The catholicity of one faith and one love manifests itself in local churches as eucharistic fellowships. Believers share in these as members of specific local churches, and the bishops, as leaders of local eucharistic fellowships, demonstrate the catholicity of the church by witnessing to the catholic faith and by expressing their collegiality.

The term *sobornost* (*sobor* means "gathering") is used in 19th-century Russian Orthodox theology to express this catholicity. It contains the thought of → conciliarity and denotes the essential unity between believers, bishops, and (local) churches in the life of the → church (§3.1).

2.2. In the Roman Catholic definition of catholicity, the apologetic use of this *nota characteristica* as a mark of distinction (i.e., the teaching that only in

the Roman Catholic Church is catholicity present) has given way since Vatican II to the aim of facilitating dialogue with those of other views and valuing and accepting their share in → truth and → sanctification (see *Lumen gentium* [*LG*] 15; *Unitatis redintegratio* 2-4). Along with freedom from limitation of time or space and openness in principle to all people, the qualitative elements are stressed, namely, catholicity as the fullness of truth and the blessings of salvation, as the crown of all that is true and beautiful and good in creation, and as totality and completeness.

For Catholics, however, catholicity is still tied to the dogmatic thesis that it is Roman, even though the cultural and sociological sense of "Roman" is no longer significant in description (on the primacy of the *Romanus pontifex,* see *LG* 8, 18, 22, 23, 25; → Hierarchy; Pope). A Christological and pneumatological approach finds the catholicity of the church in the fact that it is sacramental (*sacramentum mundi;* → Catholicism [Roman] 3.2). The unity, the community structure of the people of God, the college of bishops, and the vast number of local churches all display the catholicity of the undivided church (*LG* 13, 22, 23), though catholicity is still an uncompleted task. With catholicity as a leading motif, the claim is made that the true church of Christ finds manifestation (*subsistit,* see *LG* 8; → Church 3.2) in the church united under the pope. Distinguishing this group from other denominations are the abiding catholic element as a concrete principle (H. Schlier), the Roman church's aspects of mystery (H. U. von Balthasar), and the catholic way of thinking, that is, the "law of the polar tension of the 'both-and'" (L. Scheffczyk; → Catholicism [Roman] 3.4).

2.3.1. On the Reformation view, the catholicity of the church is a theme of confession, an attribute of the church that is believed (see the third article of the creed). It is one of the promises of Christ under which the church stands, and thus it has an → eschatological character. This catholicity finds its basis and criterion in the → gospel of Christ, which, as good news for the whole world, promises God's love and → grace to believers (→ Justification), the proclamation of which by Word and sacrament and by active witness is the task of the churches in every time and place and sphere of life. Catholicity aims at a holy Christian people that believes in Christ and that spiritually, not bodily, gathers together in this one faith (→ Luther, WA 50.624 and 626; → Calvin *Inst.* 4.1-12). In this people it is manifest and known wherever God's Word is preached in its purity and the sacraments are administered according to Christ's institution (Augs. Conf. 7; *Inst.* 4.1.9).

This definition covers both the qualitative and the quantitative aspects, both the inward and the outward. Expression is also given both to the universality of the divine action through Christ and the Holy Spirit and to the reality of this salvation in particular local churches, both of which are aspects of catholicity. According to this understanding, catholicity is not an attribute of the church. What is at issue is witness to a divine reality and the task of giving expression to the universality and the fellowship of true believers (*ecclesia spiritualis*) in the individual churches (*singulae ecclesiae*) and also in their totality (*ecclesia universalis*).

2.3.2. In later ecclesiological reflection and theorizing (→ Church 3.3-6) and in the constituting of the various Protestant churches, the Reformation emphases and their balance could not always be strictly maintained. They became mixed with secular motifs and ecclesiastical interests and were weakened as the denominations perpetuated themselves. Thus they either suffered ossification with concentration on the ecclesiastical → institution and its structural elements, or they evaporated in the inwardness of individual → piety (→ Pietism).

The emphases of the Reformation continued in the conflict regarding the true church and the false and in the tense synthesis of Catholic and Reformed in → Anglicanism, which aims at "comprehensiveness" (→ Church 3.3). They also play a part in the efforts at → union and reunion, which, beginning even in the 16th century, have tried to move beyond denominations. In all this we have a demonstration and confirmation that the church's catholicity is an implication of the gospel and that it thus stands in need of interpretation and of being lived out in the practice of → discipleship. According to H. Berkhof, "The church is summoned to become what it is."

3. Ecumenical Discussion and Protestant Catholicity

3.1. From the first, catholicity has been a theme and problem of the → ecumenical movement. The understanding and usage here have been in keeping with the traditional meaning and the views of the participating churches, with the ecumenical goals furnishing the accents. The Fourth Assembly of the → World Council of Churches (WCC), in Uppsala (1968), articulated the theological theme under the pressure of conflicts that tend to tear apart the web of the church's common life and demand political and social involvement. Thus catholicity is described as a gift of the Spirit that is already present in the church and as a task that must be discharged in the struggle for the unity of the whole church and the unity of the human race.

The study document "Catholicity and Apostolicity" (1968) of a joint working group of Roman Catholic and WCC representatives also stresses catholicity as divine gift but also calls for human change of ways, referring to its dynamic character. The local churches as parts of a universal koinonia are called upon to actualize the catholicity of the church day by day. The Commission on Faith and Order dealt with the theme of the unity of the church and the unity of humanity at Louvain in 1971. The newly articulated understanding of catholicity has remained a basic note in further WCC conferences. It is the basis of the demand that the catholicity of the church be practiced and declared in conciliarity as a constant structure.

3.2. N. Söderblom (1866-1931) helped to bring the idea of a Protestant catholicity into ecumenical discussion. He recalled the message of justification, which frees us for unconditional service for God and finds concrete form in service to the world. It can bring about a real catholicity as those who are justified by faith come together in common action (Life and Work). Söderblom asked for an ecumenical council that might articulate this goal with spiritual authority.

For F. Heiler (1892-1967), however, Protestant catholicity denotes an inner uniting of Protestant Christianity and the Roman Catholic Church, a synthesis of the imperishable values of both forms, that is, a church whose soul is Protestant and whose body is Catholic. This ideal gave shape to the → High Church movement and is still influential in so-called Catholicizing groups, in Protestant communities, in the → Una Sancta movement, in liturgical reform (→ Liturgical Books), and in the efforts that working committees (→ Ecumenical Theology) are making to achieve → consensus.

Bibliography: On 1: W. BEINERT, *Um das dritte Kirchenattribut. Die Katholizität der Kirche im Verständnis der evangelisch-lutherischen und der römisch-katholischen Theologie der Gegenwart* (2 vols.; Essen, 1964) bibliography • Y. CONGAR, "Die Wesenseigenschaften der Kirche," *MySal* 4/1.357-502.

On 2: H. U. VON BALTHASAR, *Katholische Aspekte des Mysteriums* (Einsiedeln, 1985) • Y. CONGAR, "Kirche und Romanität," *Die römische-katholische Kirche* (ed. W. Löser; Frankfurt, 1986) 47-87 • J. DANTINE, *Die Kirche vor der Frage nach ihrer Wahrheit. Die reformatorische Lehre von der "notae ecclesiae" und der Versuch ihrer Entfaltung in der kirchlichen Situation der Gegenwart* (Göttingen, 1980) • A. DULLES, *The Catholicity of the Church* (Oxford, 1985) • T. Nikolaou, "Die Grenzen der Kirche in der Sicht der Orthodox Katholischen Kirche," *ÖR* 21 (1972) 316-32 • L. Scheffczyk, *Katholische Glaubenswelt* (2d ed.; Aschaffenburg, 1978) • H. Schlier, "Das bleibend Katholische," *Cath(M)* 24 (1970) 1-21 • P. Steinacker, *Die Kennzeichen der Kirche* (Berlin, 1982) bibliography • G. Thils, *Les Notes de l'église dans l'apologétique catholique depuis la Reforme* (Gembloux, 1937) • H. Wagner, "Aspekte der Katholizität," *Cath(M)* 30 (1976) 55-68 • S. Zankow, "Sobornost oder Katholizität der Kirche," *IKZ* 52 (1962) 108-12.

Anglicanism: E. S. Aboot et al., *Catholicity: A Study in the Conflict of Christian Traditions in the West* (London, 1947) • S. F. Allison et al., *The Fullness of Christ* (3d ed.; London, 1960) • R. N. Flew and R. E. Davies, *The Catholicity of Protestantism* (4th ed.; London, 1953) • G. Tavard, *La poursuite de la Catholicité. Études sur la penseé anglicane* (Paris, 1965).

On 3: H. Berkhof, *De katholiciteit der kerk* (Nijmegen, 1962) • N. Goodall, ed., *Bericht aus Uppsala 1968* (Geneva, 1968) • R. Groscurth, ed., *Katholizität und Apostolizität* (Göttingen, 1971) • L. Mudge, *One Church: Catholic and Reformed* (London, 1963) • K. Raiser, ed., *Löwen 1971* (Stuttgart, 1971) • L. Vischer, V. Borovoy, and C. Welch, "The Meaning of Catholicity," *ER* 16 (1963/64) 24-42.

Protestant Catholicity: H. Asmussen and W. Stählin, eds., *Die Katholizität der Kirche* (Stuttgart, 1957) • E. Kinder, "Evangelische Katholizität," *KuD* 6 (1960) 69-85 • R. Paquier, *Vers la catholicité évangélique* (Lausanne, 1935) • A. Rössler, "Paul Tillichs Programm einer evangelischen Kirche," *ÖR* 35 (1986) 415-27 • N. Söderblom, "Die Aufgabe der Kirche, Internationale Freundschaft durch evangelischer Katholizität," *Die Eiche* 7 (1919) 129-36.

Erwin Fahlbusch

Catholic Conference → German Catholic Conference

Catholic Epistles

Since the third century the term "Catholic Epistles" has been used for the seven NT letters other than Hebrews that are not part of the Pauline collection (Eusebius *Hist. eccl.* 2.23.24-25). Originally the term seems to have been coined for 1 John (Dionysius of Alexandria; Eusebius 7.25.7), which, because it was not addressed to any church in particular, was thought to be directed to the whole church and thus universally binding (i.e., "Catholic"; → Catholic, Catholicity). The description was then transferred to the whole seven, although in some cases (e.g., 2-3 John), the basic criterion hardly applies.

The order of the Catholic Epistles is the same in the Greek and Latin Bibles (→ Canon 2): James, 1-2 Peter, 1-3 John, and Jude. Canon criticism led M. → Luther (1483-1546) to change the order in his NT to 1-2 Peter, 1-3 John, James, and Jude (→ Luther's Theology).

Bibliography: M. Dibelius and H. Conzelmann, *The Pastoral Epistles* (Philadelphia, 1972) • H. Koester, *Introduction to the NT,* vol. 2, *History and Literature of Early Christianity* (Philadelphia, 1982) 297-305 • W. G. Kümmel, *Introduction to the NT* (trans. H. C. Kee; Nashville, 1975) 366-87 (bibliography).

Jürgen Roloff

Catholic Missions

1. Theological Basis
2. Goal
3. Hierarchy/Leadership
4. Statistics
5. Workers
6. Supporting Mission-Aid Societies
7. Modern Characteristics

1. Theological Basis

The → Roman Catholic Church regards the fulfillment of its commission from Christ — namely, the completion of his work on earth, through the aid of the Holy Spirit, of making all people his disciples (Matt. 28:19) — to be not just one activity among others but its true nature, just as burning is the essential quality of fire (E. Brunner). The church (§3.2) actualizes itself by engaging in → mission. In the words of John Paul II, mission is the proper name of the church. This thought occurs repeatedly in the documents of → Vatican II, for example, in *Lumen gentium* and *Ad gentes.* The whole church is missionary. All believers must have a share in the work of propagating the faith.

Mission, or → evangelization, embraces the whole person — body, soul, and environment (culture) — including both intellectual and material development. To separate these for the sake of mission or to play them off against one another is a schizophrenic undertaking, for "the human being to be evangelized is not an abstraction but is subject to social and economic conditions" (Paul VI, *Evangelii nuntiandi* 31).

2. Goal

We must distinguish between the immediate and the more distant, or final, goal of evangelization. The immediate goal can be described in various ways, such as proclaiming or propagating the faith, making disciples, or integrating individuals into the saving will of God. The final goal is the planting and confirming of the visible church, of a tightly knit and stable indigenous church within the fellowship of the universal church. As Pius XII saw it, "The object of missionary activity . . . is to bring the light of the Gospel to new races and to form new Christians. However, the ultimate goal of missionary endeavor, which should never be lost sight of, is to establish the Church on sound foundations among non-Christian peoples, and place it under its own native Hierarchy" (*Evangelii praecones* §22).

This rooting and planting among all groups of people on earth must be done "in the same way that Christ by his incarnation committed himself to the particular social and cultural circumstances of the men among whom he lived" (*Ad gentes* 10; → Incarnation 3). There is an indication here of an important element in the missionary method by which the goal of mission is reached. In another place *Ad gentes* speaks of the meeting of cultures as follows: "Whatever goodness is found in the minds and hearts of men, or in the particular customs and cultures of peoples, far from being lost is purified, raised to a higher level and reaches its perfection, for the glory of God, the confusion of the demon, and the happiness of men" (§9).

3. Hierarchy/Leadership

The → pope bears primary responsibility for propagating the faith, along with the bishops. The collegiality of bishops with one another and the pope, which Vatican II emphasized, is nowhere more clearly expressed than in the area of propagating the faith.

Since 1622 direct responsibility for mission and direction of Catholic missions has been in the hands of the Congregation for the Propagation of the Faith (from 1988, the Congregation for the Evangelization of Peoples), which was set up expressly for this purpose (→ Curia). The most urgent task of this body has been to separate the church's missionary activity from the colonial policies of the European powers (→ Colonialism and Mission). Its duty also is to build up in each country a national clergy, to appoint national bishops, to found national churches, and to publish national literature (see the missionary press in Rome). It also must see to the maintaining of the faith by organizing → pastoral care in the → diaspora and must maintain → dialogue with other Christian bodies with a view to restoring church → unity. The countries of the Eastern church and parts of northern Europe and North America have until recently thus been under its supervision. Its final duties relate to bishops' conferences, the Secretariate (from 1989, the Pontifical Council) for Promoting Christian Unity, and the Congregation for the Oriental Churches.

Vatican II reaffirmed the authority of the Congregation for the Propagation of the Faith over mission and all missionary activity and enlarged its membership by adding 12 missionary bishops, 4 generals of missionary orders, and 4 national presidents of papal mission agencies. Regular plenary sessions discuss all questions of mission and establish general guidelines for it.

The most striking and significant contribution of the central authority to the progress of world mission in the last decades has been the promotion of the independence of the mission churches by putting church leadership in national hands, by establishing proper church → hierarchy, and by aiming at inculturation or contextualization (→ Acculturation; Contextual Theology). Its work, however, is far from completed. In many lands (e.g., in Asia) the mission churches still seem to be alien bodies. The task of the local hierarchy and theologians is to find and construct their own ways of thinking and their own forms of church life, order, and perhaps even organization. The missionary congregation in Rome, which has outlined the vision and framework for this development, will not stand in the way of new experiments or the search for new methods.

4. Statistics

On January 1, 1995, the Roman world mission consisted of 963 church branches, 152 archdioceses, 693 dioceses, 66 apostolic vicariates, 43 apostolic prefectures, and 9 other districts. The division into vicariates and prefectures, which was so long typical, is now only marginal; the common pattern of organizing in terms of → dioceses and archdioceses is presently the norm in mission churches as well. It is a historical error to maintain that the Congregation for the Propagation of the Faith invented the system of vicariates and prefectures and made it the basis of its mission policy. Right from the start, the congregation wanted normal church organization in the mission churches. Because of the resistance of patrons, however, who insisted on the right of presentation to the episcopal office, Rome was forced to use the tactic of instituting titular dioceses.

5. Workers

Since the whole church is missionary, all believers are responsible for spreading the faith (→ Catholic Action; Lay Apostolate). As in the primitive church, lay missionaries now play an important part. The male and female orders, however, still do most of the work, aided by world priests, especially from the time of *Fides donum* (1957), the mission encyclical of Pius XII. Some missionary orders were founded only to do missionary work, including the Missions Étrangères de Paris, the Gesellschaft des Göttlichen Wortes (Steyler Missionaries), and the White Fathers. Other orders include mission in their programs along with pastoral and educational work, such as the → Franciscans, → Dominicans, and the → Jesuits. Hundreds of women congregations also render outstanding missionary service. The orders have an advantage that we must not underestimate, namely, their international composition and membership, which enables them to do missionary work, not as a national undertaking, but as an undertaking of the worldwide church. National religious orders also exist in almost all the 963 missionary churches.

6. Supporting Mission-Aid Societies

Believers who cannot serve as lay missionaries can have a share by their prayers and gifts in the auxiliary work of propagation done by four papal agencies: one founded in Lyons in 1822, now known as Missio in Germany (→ Relief Organizations); Holy Childhood Association (Pontifical Association of the Holy Childhood), founded in Paris in 1843 with a view to kindling a concern for worldwide mission among children; a society founded in France in 1889 to promote and support national clergy; and the union of priests and members of orders, founded in Italy in 1916. The main aim of all these societies is to foster a universal missionary spirit among all of God's people.

New statutes approved in 1980 include the following perspectives: "Created by the initiative of the churches of the old Christian tradition to sustain the works of the missionaries in non-Christian religions, the Pontifical Mission-Aid Societies have become an instrument of the universal church and of each particular church. . . . Since the church is totally missionary, the duty of evangelization falls on each church and each of its members." These societies "procure for the young churches indispensable help while safeguarding the respect which is their due. They invite these young churches to make every effort to become progressively self-sufficient."

7. Modern Characteristics

Characteristic of Catholic missions today is the fundamental separation of missions from colonial politics, the indigenization of mission churches, the setting up of apostolic delegatures and nunciatures, the new appreciation of cultures and the great world religions, and a new missionary → spirituality and concern. Other issues that are now to the fore are aid in → development, cultural and social work, the translation of Scripture, the promoting of native art and music, and liturgical adjustment. These are the main concerns today, though some of them are by no means new. Many may be found in the missionary program of the Congregation for the Propagation of the Faith in the 17th century. The knotty problems of the rites question were solved in the Asian churches in the 1930s (→ Liturgy 5.2), and after Vatican II the work of adjusting liturgical rites to local customs went into high gear. Leadership today is mostly in native hands.

The future of all Christian mission depends to a large extent on church unity, without which the Christian message loses its credibility. Division among Christians thus seems to be the main obstacle to successful propagation of the faith.

→ German Missions; Mission 3; Theology of Religions

Bibliography: Missions bibliography: Bibliografia missionaria (begun in 1933 by J. Rommerskirchen, continued by W. Henkel, in association with J. Dindinger, N. Kowalsky, and J. Metzler) bibliography of missions literature that appeared during the course of a year • *Bibliotheca missionum* (30 vols.; begun by R. Streit, continued by J. Dindinger, J. Rommerskirchen, N. Kowalsky, and J. Metzler; 1916-74) scholarly missions bibliography containing Catholic missionary literature since the Middle Ages.

Journals: KM (1973-) • *NZM* (1945-) • *StMiss* (1943-) • *Worldmission* (1950-) • *ZM* (1911-).

Other literature: W. R. BURROWS, ed., *Redemption and Dialogue: Reading Redemptoris Missio and Dialogue and Proclamation* (New York, 1993) • A. DA SILVA RÊGO, *Curso de missionologia* (Lisbon, 1950) • S. DELACROIX, ed., *Histoire universelle des missions catholiques* (4 vols.; Paris, 1956-59) • *Dizionario di missiologia* (ed. professors of the Pontifical Urban University [Rome]; Bologna, 1993) • S. KAROTEMPREL, ed., *Following Christ in Mission: A Foundational Course in Missiology* (Bombay, 1995) • K. S. LATOURETTE, *A History of the Expansion of Christianity* (7 vols.; New York, 1937-45) • J. METZLER, "Die jungen Kirchen in Asien, Afrika und Ozeanien," *HKG(J)* 7.769-820; idem, ed., *Sacrae Congregationis de Propaganda Fide Memoria Rerum. 350 Jahre im Dienste der Weltmission, 1622-1972* (3 vols.; Freiburg, 1971-76) extensive bibliography • F. MONTALBAN, *Manual de historia de las misiones* (Bilbao, 1952) • A. MULDERS, *Missiologisch bestek. Inleiding tot de katholieke missiewetenschap* (Hilversum, 1962) • S. NEILL, *A History of Christian Missions* (London, 1965) • A. ROCHE, *In the Track of the Gospel: An Outline of the Christian Apostolate from Pentecost to the Present* (New York, 1953) • H. SCHÜTTE, ed., *Mission nach dem Konzil* (Mainz, 1967) • A. SEUMOIS, *Introduction à la missiologie* (Schöneck-Beckenried, 1952); idem, *Théologie missionnaire* (5 vols.; Rome, 1973-81).

JOSEF METZLER, O.M.I.

Catholic Reform and Counterreformation

1. Terms
2. Historical Survey

1. Terms

1.1. The Göttingen jurist J. S. Pütter (1725-1807) seems to have been the first to use the term "counterreforms" for the recatholicizing of territories by force on the basis of the principle → *cuius regio eius religio* (→ Augsburg, Peace of). L. von Ranke (1795-1886), M. Ritter (1840-1923), and E. Gothein (1853-1923) then gave the term a more comprehensive significance. Since it might still suggest the suppression of → Protestantism by force and a purely defensive movement, it could hardly commend itself for adoption among Roman Catholic historians (→ Historiography). These emphasized instead the idea of Catholic reform and restoration.

The Protestant historian W. Maurenbrecher (1838-92) drew attention to a genuine Catholic reformation in the later Middle Ages and early modern period. Further studies produced clear evidence of such a reformation in Italy and Spain, and attempts were made to downplay the influence of the → Reformation on Roman Catholic renewal. In 1946 H. Jedin (1900-1980) combined the two concepts in the formula "Catholic reform and counterreformation," seeing the former as the inner presupposition of the latter, but not denying the influence of the Reformation on the development and activities of the Roman church. In this way he tried to do justice both to the continuity of reform and to the new quality of the epoch under the impact of the Reformation.

1.2. Despite widespread acceptance, debate continues regarding this double concept. Three issues are prominent: the question of value judgments, the relation between reform and counterreformation, and the serviceability of the concept to describe an age. With respect to the first issue, there is a danger of viewing the Counter-Reformation as a negative phenomenon oriented solely to delimiting and restricting. We thus could overlook the positive aspects, which include modernization, adjustment to a changed → society, theological clarification, and the intensifying of → piety.

On the second matter, the issue is one of chronological and material priority. The sequence reform and counterreformation, or Reformation (1517-55) and Counter-Reformation (1555-1648), fails to note that the two run together from at least as early as 1520/21 and does not do justice to what was taking place in Europe as a whole. Materially the question is whether the Counter-Reformation did not destroy valuable currents of a reform that was (1) irenic and Erasmian and/or (2) Catholic and dedicated to evangelism, the variety, inner dynamic, and independence of which Italian research has demonstrated. An important point along these lines is that the measure of what is catholic (→ Catholic, Catholicity) should not be taken solely from the Council of → Trent.

With respect to the third issue — whether we may speak of the age of Catholic reform and counterreformation — many scholars plead for a different perspective and propose that we call this the confessional age. Perhaps a solution to these problems lies in working out more fully the complexity of the Counter-Reformation, which was subject to the pressure of historical demands and hence had to change parts of the Catholic reform, with which it coexisted from the 1520s. Together the two were undoubtedly a leading theme in the history of the Roman church, even though one might subordinate them to the title "confessional age," which has established itself on a more comprehensive level.

2. Historical Survey

2.1. Catholic reform rested on the late medieval desire for reform, which did not exist within the church alone but embraced all Christianity. Driven by the most varied motives — ranging from general dissatisfaction with the church system to criticism in particular of the church's leadership, fiscal policy, and devotional practice, to what was often an economically motivated anticlericalism — critics clamored for a reform of the whole church, head as well as members. Possible sources for Catholic reform include the *devotio moderna,* → humanism with its return to Scripture and the → church fathers (stimulated esp. by D. → Erasmus [1469?-1536]), the related return to the gospel while discounting of individual achievements (→ Evangelism), the return in theology to the older → Scholasticism and the orientation to a practical theology of piety (e.g., J. de Gerson [1363-1429]), and the returning of the → orders to their original rules. Typical are the movements toward an inner individual piety and the orientation to an active apostolate.

The → reform councils of Constance (1414-18) and Basel (1431ff.) and the Fifth Lateran Council (1512-17; → Councils of the Church) addressed religious concerns but had no lasting impact. The actual movement of reform arose instead primarily from individual groups within orders like the Observants (→ Franciscans) and the active fraternities in Italy (e.g., the Oratory of Divine Love) — as well as new orders like the Theatines, Somascans, Barnabites, Capuchins, Ursulines, and → Jesuits, evangelistic circles in France and Italy, and reform bishops like L. Giustiniani (1381-1455) — all quite apart from initiative on the part of great institutions like the → curia and the papacy (→ Pope, Papacy). An additional problem was that although there was a tendency toward more inwardness and a new theology and → ethics, as may be seen in Erasmus, the movements never became ones of mass proportion. In Spain, however, the reforming Cardinal Jiménez de Cisneros (1436-1517) achieved success with the help of the state church — a cooperation that pointed the way to the future.

2.2. With the Reformation, which was in the same stream of renewal and saw itself as the true reform, a new situation developed. An inner connection was seen between the need for reform in the church and the new movement (e.g., Hadrian VI, 1522-23), and intensification came on the territorial level (e.g., in Bavaria, in the duchy of Saxony, and through the Regensburg text of 1524) at the same time that defensive and repressive measures were taken in reply to the Reformation.

The more strongly the Reformation took doctrinal and practical shape (→ Church Orders), the more radical became Catholic reform, which in Germany was often the work of theologians influenced by humanism (e.g., G. Witzel). This reponse involved collections of sermons, → catechisms, and liturgical texts. It aimed at a solid instruction of the → clergy. In its more irenic and compromising form it returned to Scripture and the Fathers in the search for a principle of reform that would serve the cause of unity in religious colloquies. In this regard, however, it met with no success.

It would finally be the championing of reform by the papacy (Paul III, in 1536-37), along with the Council of Trent (1545-63), that created a permanent link between Catholic reform and the Counter-Reformation. Rejecting Protestantism, the council formulated Roman Catholic doctrine, sought a unity of doctrine and life in its reforming decrees, and called for intensive pastoral care.

The orientation to countering the Reformation was strengthened in 1542 by the founding of the Roman → Inquisition and then by the pontificate of Paul IV (1555-59), who favored reform but not the council. There thus developed a new confidence that involved much more than a mere mechanical implementing of the decrees of Trent. Devotional practice followed the later medieval tradition but with a decided emphasis on its Roman Catholic character. Humanism was transposed into a scholastic humanism and made to serve the relevant goals (→ Polemics) and the desire for a positive theology (e.g., in church history). In the process it lost its breadth with the exclusion of the gospel as well as the Erasmians. In particular the Jesuits, with their roots in Spanish Catholic reform and their special concern for the Counter-Reformation, developed in their schools, universities, and pastoral work a humanistic view of the person that included great emphasis on the potentiality of the will.

The → liturgy was reformed and Romanized. The training of the clergy was slowly improved. Religious education was strengthened by catechisms, sermons, and missions (esp. through the Capuchins). Art (e.g., paintings and theater) was put in the service of the new church ethos. A leading part was played by the → nuncios and by bishops like C. Borromeo (1538-84) and Francis de Sales (1567-1622), whose example others followed. → Visitations helped to establish the new norms at the parish level. It is hard to prove, however, that now for the first time there was a full-scale Christianizing, as J. Delumeau suggests.

No less decisive than this strictly controlled inner renewal was the close association of the church with the territorial princes, without which success would not have been possible. The church-supported side of the Counter-Reformation, which involved political force, was actively championed by the princes through the suppression of minorities, expulsions, and, in extreme cases, religious wars (→ Thirty Years' War). Politically these measures were frequently bound up inextricably with opposition to the nobles and estates. They resulted in a confessional absolutism.

The Counter-Reformation succeeded in France (→ Huguenots), the Hapsburg lands, Bavaria, and Poland (→ Unitarians). It failed in England, in Scandinavia, and, in the struggle for Dutch independence, in Holland. The dissensions in Protestantism and the lack of decisive leaders in German → Lutheranism were of great help. Socially the thrust of the Counter-Reformation toward unity and discipline involved a modernizing trend that might be seen as an adjustment to changed conditions. The older Catholic reform was not totally suppressed, but it was restricted.

Broad disagreements nevertheless remained, extending from French *humanisme dévot* on the left to the Counter-Reformation in Bavaria on the right (→ Baroque). A confessionalizing developed in the Roman Catholic Church (→ Denomination), which it shared with other churches, so that by the end of the 17th century both Catholic reform and the Counter-Reformation had ended, both as partial cause and as constituent part of the comprehensive age of confession.

→ Catholicism (Roman)

Bibliography: C. ALBERIGO and P. CAMAIANI, "Katholische Reform und Gegenreformation," *SM* 2.1078-1107 (extensive bibliography) • R. BIRELEY, *The Counter-Reformation Prince* (Chapel Hill, N.C., 1990) • J. DELUMEAU, *Catholicism between Luther and Voltaire: A New View of the Counter-Reformation* (Philadelphia, 1977) • H. O. EVENNETT, *The Spirit of the Counter-Reformation* (ed. J. Bossy; Notre Dame, Ind., 1970) • H. JEDIN, *Geschichte des Konzils von Trent* (4 vols.; Freiburg, 1949-76); idem, ed., *HKG(J)* vols. 4-5 • G. MARON, "Katholische Reform und Gegenreformation," *TRE* 18.45-72 (bibliography) • S. MARSHALL, ed., *Women in Reformation and Counter-Reformation Europe* (Bloomington, Ind., 1989) • B. MOELLER, ed., *Die Kirche in ihrer Geschichte* (vol. 3, pt. 1; Göttingen, 1975) • M. R. O'CONNELL, *The Counter-Reformation: 1559-1610* (New York, 1974) • J. C. OLIN, ed., *The Catholic Reformation: Savonarola to Ignatius Loyola* (repr., New York, 1992) • J. W. O'MALLEY, ed., *Catholicism in Early Modern History: A Guide to Research* (St. Louis, 1988) • P. PRODI, "Il binomio jediniano 'riforma cattolica e contro riforma' e la storiografia italiana," *AISIG* 6 (1980) 85-98 • A. PROSPERI, "Catholic Reformation," *OER* 1.287-93 • W. REINHARD, "Reformation, Counter-Reformation, and the Early Modern State: A Reassessment," *CHR* 75 (1989) 383-404 • W. REINHARD and H. SCHILLING, eds., *Die katholische Konfessionalisierung* (Münster, 1995) • M. VENARD and H. SMOLINSKY, eds., *Die Zeit der Konfessionen* (Freiburg, 1992) • R. B. WERNHAM, ed., *The Counter-Reformation and Price-Revolution: 1559-1610* (Cambridge, 1968) • A. D. WRIGHT, *The Counter-Reformation: Catholic Europe and the Non-Christian World* (London, 1982). For bibliographies, see *AHP* 1ff. (1963ff.) and *ARG.L* 1ff. (1972ff.).

HERIBERT SMOLINSKY

Catholicism (Roman)

1. Term and Phenomenon
2. Research
3. Dogmatic Elements
4. Catholicism and Protestantism

1. Term and Phenomenon

1.1. Whereas the phrase → "Roman Catholic Church" denotes a specific Christian organization (→ Church 3.2; Hierarchy; Church Government), we may use the word "Catholicism" for a historical form of Christianity that culturally and socially transcends any single ecclesiastical form. In both personnel and substance, it is still closely related to the → Roman Catholic Church. It embodies expressions of the church's life, work, and organization. We may consider Catholicism the range of forms in which that church manifests itself. Yet the two are not completely identical. Catholicism is preceded by objectifications of the content of faith that are expressed in liturgical life (→ Liturgy), in a social corporation with its own law (→ Church Law), in doctrine, and in pastoral practice (→ Pastoral Care).

The historical form of Catholicism is subject to various contextual conditions and possibilities in different times and places. It is dependent on the nature and range of the visible social presence of church members in culture and society, on their numbers and abilities, and on their desires and hopes against the background of daily experience. Hence the profile of Catholicism results not merely from the situation within the church itself but also from social, economic, cultural, and legal relations and developments in a given region and epoch, and from the adoption or criticism of forms of thinking, life, and conduct that themselves are subject to other influences.

If we reduce Catholicism to the doctrinal positions of Roman Catholicism (K. Adam) or regard the contingent historical development in terms of the self-understanding of this church as *sacramentum mundi* (K. → Rahner), then Catholicism is both timebound and timeless in a contextually dependent process and manifestation of what is catholic. As Catholicism develops and actualizes the essential catholicity of the church (→ Catholic, Catholicity), which is the same in substance in every age (W. Kasper), it shows itself to be an active and influential force in history.

If Catholicism is seen historically within the sphere of intellectual competition and the clash of worldviews, it assumes the form of an → ideology (K. G. Steck), one component in the schema of modern ideological thinking (J. Ratzinger). Sociologically it might be viewed as a subsociety or → subculture (U. Altermatt and K. Gabriel). Theological criticism can describe it as a scandal (J. Klein).

No matter how we look at it, we must take note that Catholicism is not a uniform entity and does not in every case measure up to its normative character. From one country to another or one cultural sphere to another across the centuries, it has different features in accordance with the various political, social, and cultural conditions and the particular goals and interests of its partisans, so that we must speak of different forms of Catholicism. These different forms may misrepresent, obscure, restrict, alienate, or exaggerate the underlying substance — that is, the fundamental catholicity of the church (W. Kasper).

1.2. A phenomenological approach perceives the different faces of Catholicism and also, in addition to differences in definition, notes differences in form and content.

1.2.1. One may speak about Catholicism as a *historical construct* only from the time of the → Reformation and Counter-Reformation (→ Catholic Reform and Counterreformation). This viewpoint presupposes the formation of confessional churches (→ Denomination) and leads to an antithesis between Catholicism and → Protestantism. Besides internal church developments and trends that are indicated by the dogmatic and organizational consolidation of the Roman Catholic Church, as well as the development of a baroque Catholicism and aloofness from the surrounding world (→ Modern Church History 1.1-2), the historical context includes the changing of the feudal social order of the → Middle Ages into one that is pluralist (→ Modern Period) and in which the various spheres (state and politics, economy and industry, culture and scholarship, church and religion, everyday life and family) are more distinct and autonomous.

Against the background of social differentiation, from the early 19th century onward Catholicism appears as the specific social form of the Roman Catholic tradition (F. X. Kaufmann), especially clearly where Roman Catholics are a minority (as in Germany, Switzerland, and Holland, but not in the British Commonwealth or the United States), where they form their own milieu, and where they engage in political, social, and cultural activities. From a historical perspective that takes into account the loss of church powers and privileges through → secularization, the resultant centralization and intellectual revival (→ Curia; Pope, Papacy; Vatican Council I and II 1), the conflict between → church and state in various European countries (→ Concordat; Papal

States), the political struggles in many areas (university, schools, marriage laws; → Kulturkampf), and the rejection of errors (→ Syllabus of Errors), Catholicism seems to be a Roman Catholic movement. It has had a persistent impact on political relations and developments, especially in an → Ultramontanist direction (H. Hürten).

1.2.2. *Political Catholicism* is the term for efforts to train church members politically, to work for church rights in the political sphere, to bring the principles of a Roman Catholic worldview to bear on political events, and to maintain these principles against contrary views. Beginning in the middle of the 19th century, Catholicism in this sense organized itself in Germany in many church → societies and associations (→ German Catholic Conference), achieved parliamentary representation, and founded → political parties.

1.2.3. Related to political Catholicism is *social Catholicism,* which also first took the form of societies and led to the formation of Christian → labor unions. It was marked by social criticism in opposition to → socialism and Communism, on the one hand, and by capitalist economic practices, on the other (→ Capitalism; Liberalism). It featured charitable work (→ Charity) and efforts to implement the insights and programs of Roman Catholic social teaching (→ Social Ethics).

1.2.4. Under the name of *cultural Catholicism,* societies were founded to pursue Roman Catholic interests in scholarship, art, and literature and to enable both institutions and individuals to give publicity to Roman Catholic ways of thinking (→ Christian Publishing; Literature and Christian Tradition; Mass Media). From the first beginnings in 19th-century → Romanticism there were many differences in form, influence, theme, and intention according to the different situations in different countries. Because of its impact on French culture, the literary movement of *renouveau catholique,* which included L. Bloy, P. Claudel, C. Péguy, G. Bernanos, and F. Mauriac, is especially noteworthy. → Vatican II made the communication of Roman Catholic belief in every culture (→ Acculturation) a special goal and pastoral task and thus broadened this whole perspective.

1.2.5. *Liberal Catholicism* is the term for postulates and actions that aim to separate church and state in Roman Catholic lands (H. F. R. Lammenais [1782-1854]); to encourage → freedom of conscience, press, and education; and to ensure a free church (C. F. R. Montalembert [1810-70]). Such Catholicism seeks to mediate between Roman Catholic traditions and the consciousness of the age

(A. Rosmini [1797-1855] and G. Bonomelli [1831-1914]). Although often condemned by the papacy (e.g., in *Mirari vos* [1831] and in the Syllabus [1864]), these liberal longings remained powerful and to some extent found a positive echo in Vatican II (esp. *Gaudium et spes* [*GS*]).

1.2.6. The aims and goals of all the above forms of Catholicism came together in *reform Catholicism*, which at the end of the 19th century and the beginning of the 20th tried to open up Roman Catholic tradition to academic and cultural progress and opposed the reigning neoscholasticism (F. X. Kraus, H. Schell, A. Ehrhard, C. Muth, F. von Hügel, M. Sangnier, A. Fogazzaro, et al.). The reforming goals concerned the structure and discipline of the church (curia and papacy, as well as the issues of → celibacy and → censorship), theological questions (biblical criticism and historical research), → liturgy (including liturgical diversity; → Liturgical Movements), political and social cooperation (Christian democracy and socialism), and a return to religious Catholicism (Kraus and Schell).

In North America, reforming ideas (e.g., freedom of conscience and action), along with a high estimation of the American way of life and the demand for dogmatic reinterpretation, came to expression in the form of Americanism (founded by I. T. Hecker [1819-88]). Reform Catholicism took a very definite turn as → modernism, with its so-called *théologie nouvelle* coming under suspicion as neomodernism. → Leo XIII (1878-1903) rejected Americanism (*Testem benevolentiae* [1899]). In opposition to the culmination of reform Catholicism in modernism, which was considered the sum of all heresies, Pius X (1903-14) published a new syllabus (*Lamentabili sane exitu* [1907]), issued a solemn condemnation (*Pascendi dominici* [1907]), and imposed the → Anti-Modernist Oath. Pius XII (1939-58) then rejected the *théologie nouvelle* (*Humani generis* [1950]). Yet the questioning and stirrings toward reform could not finally be suppressed. Vatican II had to accept the presence of the modern world in the church. The earlier demands are visible behind its many structural and pastoral reforms. But John Paul II sets clear limits for the progressive forces and thus tries to preserve the substance and stability of the Roman Catholic → tradition.

1.2.7. The terms *critical Catholicism* and *left-wing Catholicism* characterize forward-looking groups that oppose the latent restoration of the official church, take up urgent social and political themes (→ Peace; Peace Movement; Human and Civil Rights; Women), and work for changes in the church's structure and practices (in the areas of

celibacy, the role of the laity, the ministry of women, and life in → base communities).

Congregational Catholicism is another term that puts the emphasis on rather different problems. It advocates the acceptance of the local → congregation (the parish) as the spiritual and social center of church members and its cultivation as the soil that will prepare the members for secular life.

Modern Catholicism, with all its internal tensions, is enriched by the variety of new spiritual movements that have taken hold in many places. Alongside them we still find the older → Catholic Action (which may have different names and forms in different countries in response to different needs). This movement, which is officially commended, supported, and controlled, seeks to organize the active presence of the laity within earthly realities (Paul VI) and to promote the Christian penetration of every sphere of life (see *Apostolicam actuositatem* [*AA*] from → Vatican II; → Lay Apostolate).

Vatican II did more than just encourage progressive Catholics in their activities. It also provoked a traditionalist movement among the laity, supported by like-minded clergy (e.g., Archbishop Lefèbvre), that has contested the reforms of the council through groups such as Una Voce and Movement for Church and Papacy.

1.2.8. The various forms of *national Catholicism* enlarge the picture, which we sketch here only selectively. Coming out of a defensive subculture, British Catholicism has become a domesticated denomination controlled by competing elite progressives and traditionalists. French Catholicism is no longer a cohesive system but has become pluralistic. German Catholicism maintains its institutional stability and strength, but its sense of identity has been weakened, and it seems to have lost some of its attractiveness. Dutch Catholicism suffers from the tense coexistence of a church from above and a church from below. Italian Catholicism has become a minority socially but is finding a new sense of identity and a profile of its own. Spanish Catholicism suffers from antagonistic tendencies, a lack of joy in faith, and, as elsewhere, increasing aloofness from the official church. In Poland national Catholicism seems to be still intact. It does not rest so much on organizational stability or activity but owes its continuity to a union of church and family that maintains and promotes Roman Catholic tradition and links it to patriotic ideas.

North American Catholicism manifests much the same changes and trends that exist in western Europe. U.S. Roman Catholicism, once a church of immigrants and a missionary church, lived in a ghetto and had monolithic features. But it has now broken out of its isolation, has become pluralistic, and may be described as do-it-yourself Catholicism (in A. M. Greeley's phrase, "Catholicism on your own terms").

Chinese Catholicism has developed in a surprising and notable way. The Catholic Patriotic Association was founded in 1957, and then in 1980 the state approved also the formation of the Chinese Catholic Church Administrative Commission and the Chinese Catholic Bishops' Conference. The three organizations constitute a specific form of Catholicism as the Chinese church. This association is independent of the Vatican and nationally oriented. It elects and consecrates its own bishops, has colleges to give theological and pastoral instruction and to kindle patriotic sentiment, and gives the members (including women) a part in the ministry. Roman Catholics loyal to the papacy — who meet in house, or underground, churches — avoid open conflict.

How Catholicism may develop in other lands and continents in what were originally mission churches, or what social form it will take in different cultural and social contexts, is always an open question. In Latin America, where a third of the world's Roman Catholics live, the struggle between traditional and progressive forces has not yet been resolved. In the Philippines (65 percent Roman Catholic in 1990), which is dominated by social conflicts, a minority is attempting to bring about a change of thinking among church members.

1.2.9. *Anglo-Catholicism* is the term for a controversial movement that arose in the Church of England in the middle of the 19th century, one attempting to renew the legacy of the → church fathers and the Anglican tradition (→ Oxford Movement; Theology in the Nineteenth and Twentieth Centuries 4.1). It was influenced by the thinking and piety of Roman Catholicism and took the form of ritualism in its church practice. Yet it was also open to liberal ways of thought without succumbing to → modernism (see 1.2.5 and 1.2.6). Later it came under the influence of sociopolitical ideas (→ Social Movements). It suffered from → conversions (§2) to Rome, more notably, J. H. → Newman (1801-90) and H. E. Manning (1808-92), who both became cardinals.

1.2.10. *Sociohistorical Catholicism* represents additional social and regional varieties of Catholicism (→ Social History). This aspect deals with the → "people's church," which involves not just an organization or the movement of an elite but an anonymous mass of nominal members. Catholicism in this sense comprises the social and cultural realities of specific times and places. Institutionally (sacramentally) mediated → spirituality and → norms and contents of doctrines are here adjusted to specific ways of life, with their respective opportunities and needs.

→ Popular religion of this type exists wherever the Roman Catholic Church assumes different contours according to time, place, situation, and historical development, whether in western Europe, Latin America, Africa, or Asia, or whether in different centuries. It changes in nature, strength, rank, and significance according to contextual conditions and relations, as a comparison makes clear, for example, between the church in an industrialized nation and in a Latin American country. In the former case, a national church typically offers the opportunity to develop and practice pastoral concepts (→ Evangelization), while in the latter it is the starting point for action aimed at social change and for giving a place to theological reflection (→ Liberation Theology). In both cases the total picture has a particular accent and is brought into an ongoing process.

2. Research

2.1. When we distinguish between Catholicism and the Roman Catholic Church, Catholicism as an object of research presupposes, on the one hand, a collective confessional mentality that finds expression in modes of thought, life, and conduct; on the other, it involves a social grouping that seeks effective representation. These two elements give it contours when we look at it in relation to confessional practices against the background of modern societies. Research after World War II has focused on the total picture and studies it in its many forms and specific contextual involvements and purposes.

2.2. Historical research may concentrate on the concrete historical, cultural, or theological form in which the Roman Catholic Church manifests itself socially and philosophically in a given time and place; on an analysis of interdependencies, events and processes, and changes of sentiment and conduct that are important in some way (culturally, socioeconomically, politically, or ecclesiastically); on various individual factors or elements (organizational-legal, theological, spiritual, etc.) that contribute their own accents to the total picture; or on the biographies of individuals who represent Catholicism in culture, learning, politics, and society. To do justice to the complexity, interdisciplinary cooperation is needed. Many publications record the progress of research.

2.3. Sociology, which seeks to develop a → sociology of Catholicism with a primarily pastoral orientation (→ Sociology of Churches), views the Catholic tradition of Christianity as a characteristic social form, as a specific answer to the challenge of modern social development (K. Gabriel and F. X. Kaufmann). The macrosociological perspective studies the organization of church members against the background of pluralist societies. Research follows the different sociological approaches. In an attempt to expound the macrophenomenon, the focus is on (1) past and present church history, which mediates tradition and continuity, but also confessional distinctiveness and controversy; and (2) contemporary (national) societies with their political, cultural, and economic features and changes. Note is taken of the church's own forms of organization, relations, and individual orientations, though these are not the object of special analysis. The development of the modern social system (→ Society) has raised the question whether Catholicism may not be approaching its end as a specific social form (K. Gabriel). Studies thus far have concentrated on the Dutch and German spheres.

2.4. The social history of Catholicism is a complex subject that has thus far received little attention. The rediscovery of popular religion and the related interest in the "people's church" might help to stimulate research. Study of the multidimensional phenomenon of such a church will give breadth to what has thus far been more restricted historical and sociological research. Information on Catholicism as popular religion might result in what U. Altermatt has called a sociohistorical alternative.

3. Dogmatic Elements

3.1. Historically and sociologically it is natural to find in the groupings, developments, and trends of secular and ecclesiastical history the conditions for the rise, orientation, development, and profiling of Catholicism. In this context we may evaluate the reality and significance of the historical and social form of Catholicism (including its specific manifestations). Nevertheless, an adequate understanding of Catholicism demands that we look also at the dogmatic elements of the Roman Catholic tradition, since we must view these as constitutive of Catholicism in its total spectrum.

3.2. From its own standpoint the Roman Catholic Church claims to be the *sacramentum mundi*, that is, the sign and instrument for the most intimate union with God and for the unity of the whole race (*Lumen gentium* [*LG*] 1). This self-understanding includes the knowledge, gained through faith, that the church and the world are different but not antithetical, that the world needs the church and is the recipient and goal of its ministry, and that there is a difference between the human development of the world and the church's actualizing of the kingdom of God, between culture and evangelization, between society and the church. Along with these differences, however, we must also believe in their unity on the basis of God's universal will to save, of his → grace.

The Roman Catholic Church seeks to discharge its mission as a ministry of healing and sanctification by its sacramental presence and its secular activity. This task presupposes that the social nexus of the church (its → institution, organization) can represent the presence and communion of salvation, that it has the proper organs for communicating salvation, and that by this sacramentality, as the earthly form of the work of the Holy Spirit, as the visible form of invisible grace (DH 1639), it can effectively pass on → salvation in constant encounter and communication with the world.

In relation to Catholicism these ecclesiological theses mean that, both theoretically and practically, the church is in principle what makes Catholicism possible in the contingency of history. Only on the premise of the church's understanding of itself and the world, of its saving mission and its relation to the world, can Catholicism be a legitimate form of expression for the Roman Catholic tradition. Catholicism has its place solely in the secular nexus (in culture, society, etc.). This distinguishes it from the church. In relation to the saving mission, it has a function that relates it to the church's worship. These two features characterize its ecclesial relation.

3.3. The "salvific mission of the Church to the world" involves "the common priesthood of the faithful" (*LG* 30 and 10; see also 9-17, 30-38). Discharge of the task is not controlled merely by the content of the message of salvation. It is fundamentally related to the → hierarchical structure of the people of God, which makes a distinction in kind and not merely in degree between the general priesthood of all believers and the → priesthood of the hierarchical ministry, yet also relates them to each other (*LG* 10.2). Although the task is to be performed by both → clergy and laity, these two are differently qualified and thus participate in their own distinctive ways. Members of the clergy, set apart by priestly and episcopal → ordination, have authority and power (→ Teaching Office). Pastors are "shepherds of the faithful and also recognize the latter's contribution and charisms that everyone in his own way will, with one mind, cooperate in the common task" (*LG* 30).

The laity, furnished with the grace of → baptism and various spiritual gifts (→ Charisma), have a "secular character" that is "proper and peculiar" to them (*LG* 31.2). The laity have been given a "special vocation: to make the Church present and fruitful in those places and circumstances where it is only through them that she can become the salt of the earth" (*LG* 33.2). Their model in this regard is Mary, the queen of the apostles (*AA* 4.10; → Mary, Devotion to). In this structurally imposed and dogmatically justified division of work, which corresponds to the logic of the above understanding of the church and the world, the lay apostolate has its basis. For the Christian penetration of secular society, which is a third goal along with evangelization and sanctification, the church depends on the laity. The laity "ought to take on themselves as their distinctive task [the] renewal of the temporal order," to which the church would otherwise have no access (*AA* 7; see also *GS* 76).

This position of the laity and their specific secular mission are basic to Catholicism. On the one hand, they assume a specific profile through the varied forms and contents of the lay apostolate. Included is the personal apostolate (see *AA* 28-32), which finds its sphere of action in every life situation, in → family, → vocation, → leisure time, and social engagements. Included, too, is the group apostolate (see *AA* 18-22), which works through groups and societies on the local and regional levels and also through national and international organizations.

On the other hand, the practicing of the faith and the shaping of life and conduct by the laity also make possible many shifting and, to some extent heterogeneous, expressions of Catholicism. These are integrated into the complexity of earthly reality and exposed to its dynamic. The secular character and competence of the laity influence their understanding and action, blur traditional pictures of leadership and models of conduct, create tensions with official concepts and goals, and sometimes lead to conflicts with the hierarchy. The ambivalence innate in the nature and secular existence of the laity leaves its mark on Catholicism, points up both its relation to the church and its distinction from it, and gives it meaning and significance.

3.4. Roman Catholicism views in a specific way the relations between the nature of the church and its concrete task, between its being and its function, between pneumatic character and religious organization, between church and world, between universal priesthood and hierarchical priesthood.

The model of thought is the → incarnation, in which the Word became flesh. The dogmatic formula of → Chalcedon interprets the unity of deity and humanity as one that undergoes "no fu-

sion, no change, no division, no separation" (→ Christology 2). The term "and" links the deity and humanity linguistically but does not denote a summation. Rather, it represents a relation that (1) safeguards the distinctiveness of both but (2) expresses a totality in which the qualitative difference is seen to be mediated, the creaturely distance bridged, and the confrontation reconciled; as a result, the relation (3) is such that one element might become the objectifying of the other. The word "and" thus denotes a unity that can be presented as that of sign and thing signified (→ Sacrament) and actualized as a unity of → representation and that which is represented.

Roman Catholic thinking applies this model to various relations (e.g., Christ and the church, grace and → nature, → faith and works, → love and → law, church and world). Often, then, the model is described as typically "catholic." Fulfilling the church's commission may be seen, for example, as an objectifying of the hidden nature of the church, as a visible presence of the believed mystery of salvation. The church itself can be conceived as a sacrament, and its social nexus can be designated with the task of displaying and continuing the goal and content of the incarnation (*LG* 8, 52). The thought of unity validates the hierarchical structure of the church and the need for visible representation in the pope as the vicar of Christ (*LG* 19.2) and in each → bishop standing in Christ's place and acting in his person (*LG* 21). This arrangement requires representation as a guideline for action, in which Christ meets us and that which is present but invisible takes visible form.

The model thus has essential relevance for Catholicism. It is the basis of its distinctiveness and gives it its task. In the relation between the church and Catholicism, the latter is a distinct and differentiated entity, and yet it seems to be embedded in the comprehensive totality, so that by its sociological form and varied activities, it can create an objective expression for the presence of Christ and the lordship of God in the church. It has its own sacramentality as it does the work of permeating the temporal order like leaven and sanctifying the world. Its apostolic mission is to be an effective representative of communion with God and communion of believers. This is what makes it so important for the self-presentation of the church and for its strategy.

3.5. Relative to these dogmatic elements in the Roman Catholic tradition, Catholicism is a reflection and characteristic manifestation of the "catholic," which denotes universality, presupposes a specific attitude of mind, and claims universal relevance. To people today this seems to be folly, arrogance, and intolerance (H. U. von Balthasar). The effectiveness of Catholicism, then, depends necessarily on its plausibility and its ability to communicate in society.

4. Catholicism and Protestantism

On the Roman Catholic view the specific historico-sociological form has always been made into what it aims to present, namely, the one true church of Christ. It is the expression of the mystery that it believes (see LG 8). It is here that Catholicism finds its place, discharges its inalienable function, and has a share in the program and goal of the ongoing presence of Christ. The dogmatic approach sees Catholicism as a dynamic and functional way of expressing the Roman Catholic claim. This makes it a distinctive and lasting phenomenon.

Historically and sociologically, however, it is a contingent form of but one part of the Christian tradition. Other forms of other partial traditions may be found and described (e.g., Protestantism). The specific features of the different forms can be compared and contrasted.

In a theological presentation that takes the historical and sociological data into account, Catholicism is a specific expression of the confessional dominance and historical dynamic of the Roman Catholic Church. The confessional features and their concrete manifestations give evidence of differences and antitheses when Catholicism and Protestantism are set in juxtaposition, thus indicating a need for comparative studies (→ Ecumenical Theology), opening the door to → polemics and showing the need for → dialogue.

The denominational character of Catholicism is fixed in principle by the Roman Catholic understanding of the church and the world and the corresponding aims and models of thought and action (see 3). Protestantism displays similar denominational features. For it, however, the church is not in principle the condition of its possibility (see 3.2). Its different ecclesial relation (→ Church 3.4-6) means that dogmatically it gives precedence to the universal priesthood; it is oriented to the world; it displays pluriformity, movement, and change; and it seeks effective identity rather than representation (→ Early Catholicism). The result is that Protestantism has a completely different denominational character. The point is that the difference between it and Catholicism lies in the understanding of the church. The different conceptions of the church provide the basis for comparison and contrast (→ Catholic, Catholicity 2).

Bibliography: Term; general nature: H. U. von Balthasar, *Katholische Aspekte des Mysteriums* (Einsiedeln, 1985) • P. W. Carey, *The Roman Catholics in America* (Westport, Conn., 1996) • E. Fahlbusch, *Kirchenkunde der Gegenwart* (Stuttgart, 1979) • U. von Hehl and H. Hürten, eds., *Der Katholizismus in der Bundesrepublik Deutschland, 1945-80* (Mainz, 1983) bibliography • K. Lehmann, F. X. Kaufmann, and K. Conzemius, "Katholizismus," *EStL* 1.1486-1507 (bibliography) • W. Löser, ed., *Die römisch-katholische Kirche* (Frankfurt, 1986) • R. P. McBrien, ed., *The HarperCollins Encyclopedia of Catholicism* (New York, 1995) • *NCE* • *LPGL*, s.v. "Καθολικός" • K. Rahner, *The Shape of the Church to Come* (New York, 1974) • J. Ratzinger, *Das neue Volk Gottes* (Düsseldorf, 1972) • L. Scheffczyk, *Katholische Glaubenswelt* (Aschaffenburg, 1977) • C. Schmitt, *Römischer Katholizismus und politische Form* (2d ed.; Munich, 1925; repr., Stuttgart, 1984).

Historical form: J. Aretz et al., eds., *Zeitgeschichte in Lebensbildern. Aus dem deutschen Katholizismus des 20 Jahrhunderts* (6 vols.; Mainz, 1973-85) • E. Barbier, *Histoire du catholicisme libéral et du catholicisme social en France* (5 vols.; Bordeaux, 1923) • R. N. Flew and R. E. Davis, eds., *The Catholicity of Protestantism* (London, 1950) • M. P. Fogarty, *Christian Democracy in Western Europe* (London, 1957) • T. Gannon, ed., *World Catholicism in Transition* (London, 1988) • A. Hastings, ed., *Modern Catholicism: Vatican II and After* (London, 1991) • E. Heinen, *Staatliche Macht und Katholizismus in Deutschland* (2 vols.; Paderborn, 1969-79) • P. Hughes, *The Faith in Practice: Catholic Doctrine and Life* (London, 1938) • D. T. Jenkins, *The Nature of Catholicity* (London, 1942) • A. Langner, ed., *Katholizismus, nationaler Gedanke und Europa* (Paderborn, 1985) • K. E. Lönne, *Politischer Katholizismus im 19. und 20. Jahrhundert* (Frankfurt, 1986) • T. L. Loome, *Liberal Catholicism, Reform Catholicism, Modernism* (Mainz, 1979) • W. Loth, *Katholiken im Kaiserreich. Der politische Katholizismus in der Krise des wilhelminischen Deutschland* (Düsseldorf, 1984) • R. P. McBrien, *Catholicism* (3d ed. in 1 vol.; London, 1994) • A. Rauscher, ed., *Der politische und soziale Katholizismus in Deutschland, 1803-1963* (2 vols.; Munich, 1981-82); idem, ed., *Probleme des Konfessionalismus in Deutschland seit 1800* (Paderborn, 1984).

Regional expressions: U. Altermatt, *Der Weg der Schweizer Katholiken ins Ghetto* (3d ed.; Fribourg, 1995) • A. Favale, *Movimenti ecclesiali contemporanei* (Rome, 1980) • C. A. Fracchia, *Second Spring: The Coming of Age of U.S. Catholicism* (San Francisco, 1980) • G. Gallup and J. Castelli, *The American Catholic People: Their Beliefs, Practice, and Values* (New York, 1987) • T. M. Gannon, ed., *World Catholicism in Transition* (New York, 1988) • G. Gorschenek, ed., *Katholiken und ihre Kirche in der Bundesrepublik Deutschland* (Munich, 1976) bibliography • B. GOULEY, *Les catholiques français aujourd'hui. Survol d'une peuple* (Paris, 1977) • A. M. GREELEY, *The American Catholic* (New York, 1977) • J. J. HENNESSEY, *American Catholics* (New York, 1981) • J. HITCHCOCK, *Catholicism and Modernity: Confrontation or Capitulation?* (New York, 1979) • M. P. HORNSBY-SMITH, *Roman Catholics in England* (Cambridge, 1987) • H. HÜRTEN, *Kurze Geschichte des deutschen Katholizismus, 1800-1960* (Mainz, 1986) • H. JEDIN and J. DOLAN, eds., *History of the Church* (10 vols.; New York, 1980) • L. KARRER, *Aufbruch der Christen. Das Ende der klerikalen Kirche* (Munich, 1989) • W. KASPER, "Zur Lage der katholischen Kirche in Deutschland," *IKZ Communio* 17 (1988) 64-72 • F. KLOSTERMANN et al., *Kirche in Österreich* (2 vols.; Vienna, 1966) • R. MALEK and M. PLATE, eds., *Chinas Katholiken suchen neue Wege* (Freiburg, 1987) • R. MEHL, *Le catholicisme français dans la société actuelle* (Paris, 1977) • T. MURPHY and G. STORTZ, eds., *Creed and Culture: English-Speaking Catholics in Canadian Society, 1750-1930* (Montreal and Kingston, 1993) • A. STOECKLIN, *Schweizer Katholizismus. Eine Geschichte der Jahre 1925-75 zwischen Ghetto und konziliarer Öffnung* (Einsiedeln, 1978) • P. WARNIER, *Nouveaux témoins de l'église, les communautés de base* (Paris, 1981).

Popular piety: J. BAUMGARTNER, ed., *Wiederentdeckung der Volksreligiosität* (Regensburg, 1979) in this volume, see esp. U. Altermatt, "Volksreligion–neuer Mythos oder neues Konzept? Anmerkungen zu einer Sozialgeschichte des modernen Katholizismus," 105-24 • J. M. BONINO, "Popular Piety in Latin America," *The Mystical and Political Dimension of the Christian Faith* (ed. C. Geffré and G. Guttiérez; New York, 1974) 148-57 • J. P. CHINNICI, *Living Stones: Catholic Spiritual Life in the United States* (New York, 1989) • M. N. EBERTZ and F. SCHULTHEIS, eds., *Volksfrömmigkeit in Europa* (Munich, 1986) • K. KENNELLY, ed., *American Catholic Women* (New York, 1989) • K. RAHNER, ed., *Volksreligion–Religion des Volkes* (Stuttgart, 1979) • W. SCHIEDER, ed., *Volksreligiosität in der modernen Sozialgeschichte* (Göttingen, 1986).

Other studies: K. GABRIEL and F. X. KAUFMANN, eds., *Zur Soziologie des Katholizismus* (Mainz, 1980) bibliography • F. X. KAUFMANN, *Kirche begreifen. Zur Soziologie des Katholizismus* (Mainz, 1979) • O. KÖHLER, "Die Ausbildung der Katholizismen in der modernen Gesellschaft," *HKG(J)* 6/2.195ff. (bibliography) • H. MAIER, *Schriften zu Kirche und Gesellschaft* (3 vols.; Freiburg, 1983-86) • G. SCHMIDTCHEN, *Protestanten und Katholiken. Soziologische Analyse konfessioneller Kultur* (Bern, 1973) • K. G. STECK, "Katholizismus und Neuzeit," *TRu* 44 (1979) 1-35, 285-318 (bibliography).

ERWIN FAHLBUSCH

Catholicism, Popular → Popular Catholicism

Catholicos

Of Antiochian origin, "catholicos" is the title of some Orthodox or ancient Eastern archbishops (→ Bishop, Episcopate) who have supervision over scattered and relatively independent areas. Among the Jacobites in Persia, the term "maphrian" is also found.

Where full autonomy is achieved or claimed, the title is associated with that of → patriarch in the Orthodox Church of Georgia and the Assyrian Church of the East. It is used alone for the leaders of the Malankara Orthodox Syrian Church and of the Armenian Apostolic Church. Among the Armenians today the catholicos ranks above a mere patriarch.

→ Armenian Apostolic Church; Nestorians; Offices, Ecclesiastical; Oriental Orthodox Churches; Orthodox Church

Bibliography: D. ATTWATER, *The Christian Churches of the East* (2 vols.; Milwaukee, Wis., 1961-62) • K. H. MAKSOUDIAN, *Chosen of God: The Election of the Catholicos of All Armenia from the Fourth Century to the Present* (New York, 1995) • D. G. C. MÜLLER, "Stellung und Bedeutung des Katholikos — Patriarchen von Seleukia-Ktesiphon im Altertum," *OrChr* 53 (1969) 227-45 • R. G. ROBERSON, *The Eastern Churches: A Brief Survey* (5th ed.; Rome, 1995) • M. TAMARATI, *L'église géorgienne des origines jusqu'à nos jours* (Rome, 1910) 348-413 • A. P. URUMPACKAL, *The Juridical Status of the Catholicos of Malabar* (Rome, 1977).

PETER PLANK

Causality

1. Classic Definition
2. Antiquity
3. The Modern Period

1. Classic Definition

The term "causality" is used to identify a natural event or action as the effect of a cause. In conflict with the → skepticism of D. Hume (1711-76), the principle that all that happens has a cause has been a basic epistemological formula from the time of I. Kant (1724-1804). Strictly speaking, its general validity became possible and meaningful only with Kant's → epistemology. According to Kant, causality is one of the necessary conditions of the possibility of → experience (→ Kantianism). As a pure concept a priori, it precedes experience. We interpret an event as causally determined because we already have the idea of causality and apply it to the event by way of explanation. In this way Kant answers Hume's provocative thesis that there are no a priori concepts.

In Hume's view, causality is a result of experience. As the mind sees various similar events that follow each other in time, a belief arises that causes us to understand the things that occur later as effects of those things that occur earlier (→ Empiricism). Hume thus interprets psychologically that which is in Kant a necessity of thought. Common to both, however, is the fact that they define causality as a structure of processes that are ascribed to things by the subject and hence that do not belong to them as such. According to Kant, this is true of all objects of experience and therefore of the whole world of objects.

2. Antiquity

Whereas modern → philosophy views causality in the strictly causal terms of efficient cause, the philosophy of antiquity developed a whole series of causes to explain being, becoming, and change. In → Greek philosophy Aristotle (384-322 B.C.; → Aristotelianism) developed the theory of cause into a system. The origin of any particular things can be explained as the result of four operative causes: (1) the material cause, which describes the raw material from which the thing is made; (2) the formal cause, which accounts for the specific form of the thing; (3) the efficient cause, which is the causative agent (in art, the artist; in nature, nature itself), and (4) the final cause, which identifies the purpose for which the thing is made. In this way Aristotle united the various competing theories of tradition. In particular, atomistic philosophy (Democritus and Leucippus) and → Platonic → teleology were brought constructively into the system of four causes. The former had viewed matter or its atomistic elements as the primary cause of being, while for Plato (427-347 B.C.), eidetic being was the basis and goal of material things. Aristotle tried to relate to one another the various forms of causality. He also tried to solve the conflict between → freedom and necessity by integrating artistic causality into the system.

3. The Modern Period

In → Scholasticism the development of the proofs of God (→ God, Arguments for the Existence of) found a use for causal thinking that we do not find in Aristotelian philosophy. R. Descartes (1596-1650) used the doctrine of the greater degree of perfection of the cause relative to the effect as an argument in his proof of God (→ Cartesianism). Our idea of a most perfect being is itself an effect. In respect of existence, the cause has to be more perfect than the effect. The most perfect being thus exists as an efficient cause. Unsolved by Descartes is the problem of the causal relation between the immaterial and the material world or the working of the will on bodies.

Occasionalist philosophy (N. Malebranche), with its doctrine of occasional causes or divine interventions, simply brought with it new difficulties, against which G. W. Leibniz (1646-1716) sought to react. Without constructing a formal proof of God, Leibniz made use of the thesis that the cause must be more perfect than the effect. He linked this idea to the teleological mode of thinking prefigured in Greek philosophy. The visible world of phenomena results from immaterial power-centers — the monads — whose preestablished harmony is guaranteed by God's constant upholding. In the act of → creation God made the world as the best of all possible worlds. Along the lines of genetic information, the monads keep the law by which events take place in the world. There is no need for an occasional deus ex machina.

In the English-speaking world the Anglican bishop George Berkeley (1685-1753) and the American Congregationalist minister Jonathan Edwards (1703-58) developed views of causality similar to Malebranche's. Both posited God as the central preserver of ordinary causality, both feared the spread of a dehumanizing, universal mechanistic causation, and both were bypassed rather than refuted in their respective regions.

In the age that followed, however, a cleft remained between natural causality in the mechanistic sense and the unconditional autonomous causality of freedom. Here again Kant's philosophy represents a final ratification. Nature and → reason, necessity and freedom — these stand over against each other like two different systems of causality.

This dualistic disposition between nature and freedom results from the fact that Kant uses the concept of causality not only to describe the processes of nature but also to designate the initiative of freedom. His use in the two cases, however, is very different. The causality of nature is conditioned, or contingent; that of freedom is unconditioned. "Unconditioned" means that freedom is conceived as the capacity to initiate independently a series of natural phenomena, that is, of acts. It is on this thesis that Kant bases his → ethics (§1.3) and his exposition of reason as an autonomous moral court. Acts are natural processes that can be traced to a supernatural, intelligible cause. With the concept of act Kant tries to harmonize the sphere of natural processes with that of human actions, namely, history. He fully executes this program of harmonization in his *Critique of Judgment,* in which he attempts to relate to the concept of nature a teleology analogous to that found in historical acts. In this way the Aristotelian distinction between efficient and final cause recurs within the framework of the philosophy of subjectivity.

More recently, discussion of the problem of causality has been enduringly altered by developments in the natural sciences. → Quantum theory has shaken the notion of classical causal determinism insofar as from the state of a closed physical system obtaining at time t_1, one can now calculate the state of that same system at time t_2, but only according to the criteria of probability. Although calculations for the determinative data of such a system (e.g., the location and momentum of a particular object) are made according to the standards of classical physics, the simultaneous, exact measurement of such data in the case of, say, a particular electron or photon, is no longer possible. The idea of full causal determinism as we find it in classical physics has now become a marginal theory. We have no theory yet that will allow us to integrate into a single system the dimensions and boundaries of classical physics and those of particle physics. Whether the principle of causality in Kant's sense is still valid would depend on the development of such a theory.

→ Logic; Relativity Theory

Bibliography: W. E. ANDERSON, ed., *Jonathan Edwards: Scientific and Philosophical Writings* (New Haven, 1980) • É. GILSON, *From Aristotle to Darwin and Back Again* (Notre Dame, Ind., 1984) • I. KANT, *Critique of Judgment* (trans. J. C. Meredith; Oxford, 1973) • L. KRÜGER, ed., *Erkenntnisprobleme der Naturwissenschaften* (Cologne, 1970) • T. O'CONNOR, ed., *Agents, Causes, and Events* (New York, 1995) • A. SCHOPENHAUER, *Über die vierfache Wurzel des Satzes vom zureichenden Grunde* (2d ed.; ed. M. Landmann and E. Tielsch; Hamburg, 1970) • W. A. WALLACE, "Aquinas and Newton on the Causality of Nature and of God: The Medieval and Modern Problematic," *Philosophy and the God of Abraham* (ed. R. Long; Toronto, 1991). In Krüger's volume, see esp. E. Scheibe, "Ursache und Erklärung," 253ff.; W. Stegmüller, "Das Problem der Kausalität," 156ff.; and C. F. von Weizsäcker, "Die Einheit der Physik als konstruktive Aufgabe," 372ff.

ENNO RUDOLPH

CELAM → Latin American Council of Bishops

Celibacy of the Clergy

1. History
2. Theology
3. Sociology
4. Within the Catholic Church
5. Ecumenical Significance

1. History

The word "celibacy" derives from the Lat. *caelibatus,* which, as used by Cicero, Seneca, Suetonius, and others, refers to the unmarried state of both men and women. Its historical appropriation by theology and the church, however, has been largely unexplored. The word had no great currency even as late as the → Middle Ages. According to the → Codex Iuris Canonici of 1983, it denotes the duty of clergy "to observe perfect and perpetual continence [from sexual relations] for the sake of the kingdom of heaven" (can. 277.1). → Institutional history far anticipated actual linguistic development.

The NT attests no obligatory link between ordination and celibacy (1 Tim. 3:2, 12; Titus 1:6), and celibacy was thus a voluntary matter for Jesus' disciples (Matt. 19:12; 1 Cor. 9:5; → Discipleship). Yet early church movements such as → monasticism found motivation in both the OT and the NT.

The first institutional steps were taken at the Council of Elvira (ca. 306), which called upon → bishops, → priests, and → deacons (→ Consecration) to refrain from sexual relations with their wives and to have no more children (can. 33). The rules met with no full acceptance until the 11th century, when the holding of daily → Eucharists (→ Eucharistic Spirituality) in the West and an acceptance of the OT restriction against sexual relations before encounter with the holy (e.g., Lev. 15:16-33; 22:4-7; 1 Sam. 21:4-6) seem to have prompted wider acceptance of celibacy (→ Sacred and Profane; Marriage and Divorce 3.3.1). The → Orthodox Church widely resisted such developments, particularly at the Synod of Constantinople in 691 (can. 13; → Councils of the Church). Only following Lateran II in 1139 did the Latin church fully adopt the rule, and even then it was frequently ignored. The → Reformation churches reacted violently against the public scandal that the rule caused, developing an incisive theological protest (Carlstadt; → Luther 1521; → Augsburg Confession 23; Apology 23; → Luther's Theology) that became linked with a broad exodus from the state of monks and priests. To thwart this development, the Council of → Trent in 1563 condemned all who asserted that virginity or celibacy is no better or more blessed *(melius ac beatius)* than marriage (DH 1810). It is often thought that the council was here establishing a dogmatic position. The text does not support this interpretation, however, and shows that it was rather a pastoral and practical direction to clergy who were wavering.

2. Theology

Theological discussion of celibacy has been renewed in recent decades. → Vatican II attempted a more nuanced language than Trent, stressing that celibacy "is not demanded of the priesthood by its nature. This is clear from the practice of the → primitive Christian community and the tradition of the Eastern Churches" (*Presbyterorum ordinis* 16; → Priest, Priesthood, 3.3). Yet it did not really go beyond the → ideology of values that marriage is a less perfect state than celibacy. Four ecclesiastical reasons were given:

1. Exposition of 1 Corinthians 7:33 reveals that unmarried clergy "can adhere more easily to Christ with an undivided heart" (1983 CIC 277.1).
2. Clergy can also "more freely dedicate themselves to the service of God and humankind" (ibid.).
3. Celibate clergy are also an eschatological sign, since their celibacy gives evidence of "the arrival of a new world" (Paul VI, §34).
4. An additional motivation, one often dominant in → tradition, also remains effective. In this view, only sexual abstinence constitutes "perfect chastity" (Pius XII, §23). For clergy to engage in sexual relations makes them cultically unclean (→ Cultic Purity) and subdues their spirit to carnal desires. It thus is inconsistent with an encounter with the holy.

This pattern of reasoning shows that the future of celibacy in the church can be decided only theologically. Yet pastoral needs — for example, of countering a lack of priests and of meeting spiritual needs of many congregations (→ Roman Catholic Church 7.3) — are not unimportant.

The critical principle, however, can only be the NT doctrine of justification as rediscovered by the Reformation, according to which no achievement makes a person more perfect, purer, or freer than any other in the sight of God, our undivided offering of the heart taking place only in faith (→ Law and Gospel). Only on this basis can we reach agreement that faith makes a married relation a good gift of God and that, whether married or unmarried, we can render service to both God and others.

3. Sociology

The theological crisis alone can also help us appreciate the findings of → sociology, instead of, as has hitherto been the case, largely suppressing them. Analysis of this crisis by no means reveals celibacy to be an institution benefiting the free ministry of the church. It gives evidence instead that it is a central steering instrument of power of the religious system, working against open → communication. For sociologically, celibacy led to the establishment of a clerical class that separated its members from the rest of the people — the *laos*, the laity (→ Clergy and Laity). The consequences of this social isolation are multifaceted.

From the perspective of social → anthropology, this isolation often imposes heavy burdens on the clergy, leading to anxieties in dealing with "the world," especially in relationship with women, or to loneliness, especially of the elderly. From the perspective of → group dynamics, celibacy prompted clergymen to separate themselves in the manner of (male) fraternities. As a functional system (→ Social Systems), it has created a power elite excluding all others from positions of → power or the responsibility of leadership. The economic and social dependence of the clergy also subjects them to manipulation by those who hold central power. The dominance of male celibates has particularly subjected women to repression in both the church and society (→ Feminist Movement; Feminist Theology; Ordination).

Within the Roman Catholic Church, celibacy has long been a topic excluded from open sociological research and theological discussion. On the one hand, the church → hierarchy has made the subject taboo, and on the other, clergy are reluctant to share their personal conflicts even with close friends (S. H. Pfürtner 1992, 52ff.). Their real views and actual conduct constitute what A. W. R. Sipe has called a secret world. The first empirical, long-time study (from 1960 to 1985), involving 1,500 American priests, shows that only 2 percent reached "achieved celibacy," and only 6-8 percent a certain stability. The others all deviated, with 20 percent involved in stable heterosexual relations, 10 percent experimenting, and 10 percent living homosexually (ibid., 262ff.). Critical lay members and theologians within Catholicism claim that this wide gap between norm and actuality, between public ideal and private practice, damages the credibility of the charismatic gift of celibacy "for the sake of the kingdom of heaven" (Matt. 19:12) in both the historical past and today. From a sociopsychological and therapeutic perspective, E. Drewermann has drawn attention especially to the negative effect celibacy has on personal → identity.

4. Within the Catholic Church

Protest within the Catholic Church is usually directed not against the NT gift of celibacy (1 Cor. 7:7, 32-40) but against compulsory celibacy, that is, against its institutional coupling with the priestly office. The argument is that one who chooses the charisma must do so voluntarily and must be able to continue in it in freedom. Clergy whose development prevents them from identifying now with the gift often feel oppressed in their moral identity by the church institution. They appeal to the freedom of → religion and of conscience that was solemnly accepted at → Vatican II (→ Conscience; Human and Civil Rights). In the meantime, numerous international support groups of Catholic priests and their wives have developed. Such groups contain around 80,000 members (J. Kerkhofs), many of whom would continue in their office if freed from celibacy.

Historical comparison shows that despite the continued validity of the law of celibacy, some movement is discernible within Catholicism. A clear shift in values has taken place in congregations, with an increasing number of members saying they preferred or at least would not in principle reject a married priest. Vatican II addressed the question of priestly consecration of married *viri probati* (tested men in faith and conduct). Despite the Vatican's continued intransigence, the demand that the issue be addressed further has not diminished even within the hierarchy itself, since the increasing dearth in the number of priests is becoming an ever more urgent matter. As recently as 1985, only 157,000 of the 368,000 Roman Catholic congregations in the world had a resident priest (Kerkhofs, 3).

Individual bishops' conferences, for example, the Swiss, have implemented tolerant compromises with married priests; to the extent the latter have remained loyal to the church and so desire, they can continue to serve in church administration, adult education, or religious instruction. The only thing they are not allowed to do is preside at the celebration of the Eucharist. Finally, the Vatican still practices, albeit with considerable obstacles, laicization as begun by Paul VI (1963-78), that is, the legal-ecclesiastical demotion of a priest, in response to his urgent petition, back to the status of a layperson.

5. Ecumenical Significance

The decoupling of celibacy and the priesthood will probably be of great ecumenical significance. According to J. Lortz (2.62, 272), attempts at reaching a consensus failed at Augsburg in 1530, not least because of the dispute concerning priestly marriage and lay chalice. Lutheran reform stressed the gift as worthy of praise (Apology of Augs. Conf. 23) and merely rejected viewing it as merit in earning justification or as something to be imposed legally. Evangelical Christianity has developed in part a new understanding of free celibacy (→ Marriage and Divorce 3.5.1), as seen at → Taizé and in other spiritual → communities (§1; I. Reimer). As a free charisma, it can still have spiritual power and social validity in the Roman Catholic world as well.

Bibliography: J. Blenkinsopp, *Celibacy, Ministry, Church* (New York, 1968) • R. Cholij, *Clerical Celibacy in East and West* (Leominster, Eng., 1988) • G. Denzler, *Das Papsttum und der Amtszölibat,* vol. 1, *Die Zeit bis zur Reformation;* vol. 2, *Von der Reformation bis in die Gegenwart* (Stuttgart, 1973-76) • E. Drewermann, *Kleriker. Psychogramm eines Ideals* (5th ed.; Olten, 1990) • C. Frazee, "The Origins of Clerical Celibacy in the Western Church," *CH* 41 (1972) 149-67 • A. Karlstadt, *De coelibatu, monachatu et viduitate* (Wittenberg, 1521) • J. Kerkhofs, "Neue Formen des kirchlichen Dienstes und verheiratete Priester," *Mitteilungsblatt der Vereinigung katholischer Priester und ihrer Frauen eingetragener Verein* 5 (1988) 3-14 (see also the entire issue) • F. Klostermann, *Gemeinde ohne Priester? Ist der Zölibat eine Ursache?* (Mainz, 1981) • R. Kottje, "Das Aufkommen der täglichen Eucharistiefeier in der Westkirche und die Zölibatsforderung," *ZKG* 2 (1971) 218-28; idem, "Zur Geschichte des Zölibatsgesetzes," *Ehelosigkeit des Priesters in Geschichte und Gegenwart* (ed. R. Kottje et al.; Regensburg, 1970) 9-24 • H. Lea, *History of Sacerdotal Celibacy in the Christian Church* (4th ed.; London, 1932; repr., New York, 1966) • B. Lohse, *Mönchtum und Reformation. Luthers Auseinandersetzung mit dem Mönchsideal des Mittelalters* (Göttingen, 1963) • J. Lortz, *Die Reformation in Deutschland* (2 vols.; 3d ed.; Freiburg, 1948) • M. Luther, "De votis monasticis" (1521), WA 8.323-35; idem, "Vom ehelichen Leben" (1522), WA 10/2.275-304 • S. Ozment, "Marriage and the Ministry in the Protestant Churches," *Celibacy in the Church* (ed. W. Bassett and P. Huizing; New York, 1972) 39-56 • Paul vi, "Sacerdotalis caelibatus" (June 24, 1967), *The Papal Encyclicals* (5 vols.; ed. C. Carlen; Raleigh, N.C., 1981) 5.203-21 • S. H. Pfürtner, *Sexualfeindschaft und Macht. Eine Streitschrift für verantwortete Freiheit in der Kirche* (Mainz, 1992); idem, "Das Zölibatsgesetz–die Probe aufs Exempel. Zum Disput zwischen Holland und Rom," *Macht, Recht, Gewissen in Kirche und Gesellschaft* (Zurich, 1972) 215-23 • Pius xii, "Sacra virginitas" (March 25, 1954), *The Papal Encyclicals,* 4.239-53 • I. Reimer, "Bruderschaften und Kommunitäten," *EStL* 1.285-87 • E. Schillebeeckx, *Christliche Identität und kirchliches Amt. Plädoyer für den Menschen in der Kirche* (Düsseldorf, 1985) • R. Schoen-

HERR, "Holy Power? Holy Authority? and Holy Celibacy?" Bassett and Huizing, *Celibacy in the Church*, 126-42 • A. W. R. SIPE, *A Secret World: Sexuality and the Search for Celibacy* (New York, 1990) • G. SLOYAN, "Biblical and Patristic Motives for Celibacy of Church Ministers," Bassett and Huizing, *Celibacy in the Church*, 13-29 • H.-J. VOGELS, *Celibacy: Gift or Law? A Critical Investigation* (Tunbridge Wells, 1992).

STEPHAN H. PFÜRTNER

Cemetery

1. The Word
2. Definition
3. Forms
   3.1. Europe
   3.2. North and South America
   3.3. Africa
   3.4. Asia
4. Development in the Christian West
   4.1. Origin of the Christian Cemetery
   4.2. The Medieval Churchyard
   4.3. Protestantism
   4.4. The Secular Cemetery

1. The Word

The word "cemetery" comes from a Greek word meaning "dormitory" or "sleeping chamber" and denotes the final resting place of our body.

2. Definition

Legally, the cemetery is an institution for public burial. With → secularization it has come into communal or private hands. Churches also administer places for burial in many lands. Burial may take place either in graves or in vaults.

3. Forms

3.1. *Europe*

3.1.1. In central and northern Europe we find communal, private, and church cemeteries, but there are few differences in practice. In cities the trend toward the large central cemetery (widespread in the 19th and early 20th centuries) has been reversed in favor of a smaller cemetery in each district that can also serve as a park for recreation and that is frequently integrated into green belts. The cemetery may be laid out geometrically in garden form, or it may take the form of a park or wood. The great increase in cremation (e.g., 21 percent in Germany and 60 percent or higher in the cities) has brought changes with the burial or setting aside of urns. Ashes are scattered in

Scandinavian countries, Holland, and England. In the last two countries coffins are buried over one another. The number of graves determines the nature of the cemetery, and we often find mass conformity. Gravestones predominate over markers of metal or wood. War cemeteries follow their own rules.

3.1.2. In Britain and Ireland, along with the community and private cemetery, we find traces of Celtic influence, especially in burial within monasteries or monastic ruins. In Britain 80 percent of the dead are cremated, and the ashes are scattered in gardens of remembrance, the names being listed in memorial chapels or on tablets on trees or plants.

3.1.3. In western Europe and the Mediterranean lands the cemetery is mostly in the hands of the community, but we see Roman influence in the stones, buildings, and the necropolis, the best-known example being the Père-Lachaise Cemetery in Paris. Coffins and urns may be found in wall niches, and there are also vaults in northern France, Belgium, and Luxembourg.

In Spain and Portugal we find the communal cemetery, the denominational cemetery, the monastic cemetery, and the necropolis, with wall niches and vaults. The Italian cemeteries are literally monumental (note the *cimitero monumentale* in Milan, Bergamo, or Genoa), with their colossal architecture and rich decoration. Graves are status symbols, social rank being denoted by the mausoleum, the niche grave, and the earth grave. In Greece, as in Italy, we see the latent influence of antiquity. Cities like Athens have class cemeteries and family graves. In the case of earth burials, the bones are placed in ossuaries after some years.

3.1.4. Some countries of eastern and southeastern Europe have → Islamic cemeteries, along with stone vaults with photographs of the dead on the markers. In Slavic countries the influence of the → Orthodox Church is evident. There also are examples of popular art in carved and painted wooden markers, for example, in Hungary, Bulgaria, and Romania.

3.2. *North and South America*

3.2.1. The United States and Canada mostly follow the Anglo-Saxon tradition, though other immigrants have had an influence. U.S. cemeteries are mostly private and have thus been commercialized. Parklike cemeteries disguise the reality of death. In some cases a "vertical" cemetery avoids graves, as in the Greenwood Bible Mausoleum of San Diego, California. In some parts of northern Canada and Alaska the original inhabitants retain their native burial customs.

3.2.2. The influence of the Spanish and Portuguese colonizers is predominant in Central and

South America, though there are also instances of → ancestor worship.

3.2.3. Australia has followed British traditions, with the rural-type cemetery and upright grave-stones.

3.3. Africa

The great religious communions have determined the forms taken by the cemetery in Africa. In South Africa and other former colonial areas, the traditions of Christian Europe are evident. Black Africans have made their own contribution, with their graves being mostly covered. In West and Central Africa the nature religions and ancestor worship determine the forms of burial. In many parts of Africa, especially in the East and the North, the Islamic tradition is dominant. The cemetery is outside the township as a collection of graves, usually covered. A city like Cairo has a giant necropolis that has been in use for centuries, with elaborate buildings and mosques and simple earth graves in between. Different cultures have produced different types of graves, including graves in huts, rock, cliffs, rivers, trees, and platforms. We also find cremation and exposure of the dead.

3.4. Asia

3.4.1. In the Middle East, → Palestine is a land of cemeteries. → Jerusalem is a magnet for Jews (→ Judaism), who long to be gathered there to their fathers and there to await the Messiah; for Christians, whose Messiah worked there and was crucified and buried there; and for Muslims, whose prophet, Muḥammad, began there his journey to heaven. The graves of Jews and Muslims, covered with stones, are inviolable. Christian cemeteries and graves with their crosses and steles are always enclosed. Traditionally, Jewish cemeteries in Israel with graves, not vaults, consist of bare earth, although immigrants from Europe have brought new ideas. Since Jewish law requires that burying grounds be outside the city, those within the city have walls, and the city is thus "outside."

In Arab lands Islamic cemeteries predominate, often fenced with stones. The graves are so arranged that the head of the deceased, turned to the right, looks to Mecca. The graves are furnished with stones, stone slabs, bricks, or dried mud to give them the shape of tombs. There are usually steles at the head or feet, often inscribed with passages from the Koran.

3.4.2. Customary in central Asia is the Islamic necropolis with richly ornamented mausoleums and mosques, though we also find the individual mau-soleum, as well as wall-encircled Islamic cemeteries with earth graves oriented toward Mecca.

3.4.3. Northern India, once ruled by the Mongols, boasts Islamic monuments such as the Taj Mahal, as well as walled cemeteries deriving from central Asia. The corpses of prominent → Hindus are burned on funeral pyres, if possible near sacred rivers, especially the Ganges, into which the ashes are then scattered. → Buddhists also generally burn their dead. The ashes may be committed to the water, but there are also cemeteries in which to place them, often near sanctuaries or monasteries. Burial is also possible, for example, for lamas who may enter Nirvana but who want to stay tied to earth. Particularly holy lamas are buried more than once. Other Buddhist customs, seldom used, also help make cemeteries superfluous, such as the throwing of the body into a river or its dissection and abandonment to vultures. Buddhism also influences the practices in Sri Lanka, and Islam those in Indonesia and Malaya, though here we also find traditional ancestor worship with symbolic wooden figures of ancestors. In the predominantly Roman Catholic Philippines, cemeteries sometimes have burial niches; there are also lawn cemeteries after the American pattern.

3.4.4. Buddhism has had an impact on Indochina and China. The cemeteries of Buddhists, and also of → Confucianists and → Taoists, can be large, and the graves often give evidence of ancestor worship; the stone pavement of family graves, often symboliz-ing rotation and rebirth, may be as much as 150 sq. m. (1,600 sq. ft.) in area. In the → syncretism of Chinese beliefs, elements of ancestor worship may stand alongside ideas of survival and → regeneration. In the cemetery the living have intercourse with the dead. The Communist system has suppressed ances-tor worship in China. Cremation is promoted, and 85 percent of the cities and 40 percent of the rural areas now have crematoria.

Buddhism and → Shinto are influential in Japan, and ancestor worship, which does not allow the reuse of graves, is very important. Stone monuments crowd in upon each other, usually with pedestals on which to place offerings for the guardians of dead souls. The urge to communicate with ancestors makes these cemeteries busy places. In Tokyo lack of room has led to the building of skyscrapers in which to place caskets of ashes.

4. Development in the Christian West
4.1. Origin of the Christian Cemetery

The burial practices of the Christian West (→ Funeral) developed mainly out of the traditions of the Bible and Israel, along with those of ancient Greece and Rome. The OT tells of family graves and individual graves in rocky gardens near the houses (Gen. 23:17, 20; 1 Kgs. 2:10; 11:43; 2 Kgs. 9:28; 23:30; 2 Chr. 32:33), or of common burial places for aliens (pilgrims) called fields of blood (Matt. 27:8). Cremation was regarded as shameful (2 Kgs. 23:16). Christ's grave was in a rock sepulchre in a garden near Gethsemane (John 19:41-42). Since the NT gives no directions regarding burial of the dead, the early churches, remembering Christ's burial, following OT customs, and expressing their belief in the → resurrection, buried the dead in caves, graves, vaults, or → catacombs. They called these resting places for the dead *cemeteria* or *dormitoria*. From an early date special honor was paid to the tombs of → martyrs.

4.2. The Medieval Churchyard

As Christians began to seek salvation through physical nearness to → saints and their intercession and that of the congregation, burial came to take place in and around churches, first in the narthex, then in the churchyard. The church thus became the focus of Christian burial, places outside city walls were abandoned, and the private plot gave way to the common cemetery of the family of faith. Christian → eschatology relating to the communion of saints determined the arrangement of the churchyard. Graves were oriented to the church and the → altar. Parish churches, and later monasteries and the churches of the Hospitallers, had the right to bury (Lat. *sepultura* = "burial"). Toward the end of the 14th century, because of the plague, city churchyards became too small, and burying grounds were set up outside the cities. Churchyards and cemeteries had rights of asylum and thus became places of jurisdiction.

4.3. Protestantism

The Protestant cemetery is not *res sacra* in the Roman Catholic sense, but → Luther described it as virtually so and advocated its dedication with Bible reading and prayer (WA 27.375). With the abandonment of the intercession of saints, the veneration of relics, and the veneration of saints as mediators, the altar in the parish church lost its importance for the salvation of the dead and therefore as a focus for graves. Thus Luther could recommend the siting of cemeteries outside cities. He suggested that edifying epitaphs, texts, and hymns be put on the graves.

4.4. The Secular Cemetery

The age of the → Enlightenment and → secularization saw the final replacement of the cult-related churchyard with the more hygienic and aesthetic cemetery. As towns assumed more and more functions, a rapid communalizing of the cemetery ensued. The churchyard gave place to the publicly or privately administered cemetery, whose hygienic character was more important than its apotropaic character. Funeral chapels took the place of parish churches. The natural science of the Enlightenment, enthusiasm for antiquity (→ Classicism), and anticlericalism combined to encourage cremation, which led to the building of crematoria (Milan in 1876, Gotha in 1878). Conscious inquiry into burial practices, along with cultural concerns, led to the protection of monuments and concern for local customs. The growth of cities made necessary much larger cemeteries with far more funeral plots. At the same time, attempts have been increasingly made to coordinate cultural and economic requirements.

In the immediate future, it seems that the large cemetery of the traditional type will be the norm, conforming in its practices to a pluralistic society. Cremation will continue to gain ground, but slowly. The task of the churches in this area is to determine whether they are simply to reflect a pluralistic consumer society or to be genuine places of Christian proclamation, whether in their own churchyards or in the public or private cemetery.

Bibliography: R. Auzelle, *Dernières demeures* (Paris, 1965) • K. Bauch, *Das mittelalterliche Grabbild: Figürliche Grabmäler des 11.-15. Jahrhunderts in Europa* (Berlin, 1976) • H.-K. Boehlke, *Das Bestattungs- und Friedhofswesen in Europa* (Vienna, 1977); idem, *Friedhofsbauten–Kapellen, Aufbahrungsräume, Feierhallen, Krematorien* (Munich, 1974); idem, *Der Gemeindefriedhof–Gestalt und Ordnung* (2d ed.; Cologne, 1972); idem, ed., *Vom Kirchhof zum Friedhof* (Kassel, 1984); idem, ed., *Wie die Alten den Tod gebildet–Wandlungen der Sepulkralkultur, 1750-1850* (Mainz, 1979) • H.-K. Boehlke and M. Belgrader, "Friedhof," *TRE* 11.646-53 • J. Gaedke, *Handbuch des Friedhofs- und Bestattungsrechts* (5th ed.; Cologne, 1983) • A. Hüppi, *Kunst und Kultur der Grabstätten* (Olten, 1968) • P. M. Küsters, *Das Grab der Afrikaner* (Vienna, 1921/22) • E. Panofsky, *Grabplastik* (Cologne, 1964) • O. Valentien and J. Wiedemann, *Der Friedhof* (2d ed.; Munich, 1963).

HANS-KURT BOEHLKE

Censorship

Censorship refers broadly to the changing or suppressing of thoughts and actions that a society believes are detrimental to the common good. In the context of the → Roman Catholic Church, censorship involves the official examination and approval of both the production and the distribution of printed works before and after their publication (so-called pre- and post-censorship). According to contemporary Roman Catholic → canon law, "the pastors of the Church have the duty and the right to be vigilant lest harm be done to the faith or morals of the Christian faithful through writings or the use of the instruments of social communication; they likewise have the duty and the right to demand that writings to be published by the Christian faithful which touch upon faith or morals be submitted to their judgment; they also have the duty and right to denounce writings which harm correct faith or good morals" (1983 CIC 823.1). This principle has been strictly limited in practice, for only books of Scripture (can. 825), → liturgical books (826.1 and 2), prayer books for public or private use (826.3), catechisms and books for catechetical instruction (827.1), and religious books for school instruction (827.2) now require permission to print (from the apostolic see, bishop's conferences, or the ordinary). For the rest, the CIC merely recommends presenting all other theological works to the local chief pastor (827.3).

These regulations are only a remnant of the 15th-century imprimatur that was still current in 1917 CIC 1385-94. Objections were leveled especially against the *Index librorum prohibitarum* imposed in 1564 following Trent (the first Roman Index appeared in 1559 under Paul IV), which from 1571 to 1917 was overseen by the Congregation of the Index, created by Pius V (1566-72; → Inquisition 2). The decree of the Congregation of the Faith (→ Curia) put an end to the Index and to prohibited works (1917 CIC 1399) on November 15, 1966.

In the secular world, prohibiting censorship is a basic principle of liberal constitutions (→ State 5). For example, in Germany the only challenge is (1) to protect young people and (2) to ban books that are libelous in character.

Bibliography: G. ANASTAPLO, "Censorship," *NEBrit* (15th ed., 1991) 15.619-26 • J. GREEN, ed., *The Encyclopedia of Censorship* (New York, 1990) • A. HAMANN, "Zur rechtsgeschichtlichen Entwicklung des Verhältnisses von staatlicher Zensur und Kunstfreiheit," *Verwaltungsarchiv* 75 (1984) 15-37 • H. HEINMANN, "Schutz der Glaubens- und Kirchenlehre," *Handbuch des katholischen Kirchenrechts* (ed. J. Listl et al.; Regensburg, 1983) 567-78, esp. 569ff. • L. HOFMANN, "Der Index der verbotenen Bücher," *TTZ* 64 (1955) 205ff. • H. LACKMANN, *Die kirchliche Bücherzensur nach geltendem kanonischem Recht* (Cologne, 1962) • G. MAY, "Die Aufhebung der kirchlichen Bücherverbote," *Ecclesia et Ius* (FS A. Scheuermann; ed. K. Siepen et al.; Munich, 1968) 547-71 (bibliography) • G. H. PUTNAM, *The Censorship of the Church of Rome and Its Influence upon the Production and Distribution of Literature* (2 vols.; New York, 1967; orig. pub., 1906-7) • P. RAABE, ed., *Der Zensur zum Trotz. Das gefesselte Wort und die Freiheit in Europa* (Weinheim, 1991).

HERMANN WEBER

Censures

1. Catholic Canon Law
2. History

1. Catholic Canon Law

In the → church law of the → Roman Catholic Church, censures are → punishments imposed by the church primarily in order to restore delinquents to obedience (and which are thus to be remitted if the latter abandon their contumacy; 1983 CIC 1358, in connection with 1347.2). By contrast, expiatory (vindication) penalties serve primarily the retribution of a punishable deed (cans. 1336ff.). Canon law knows three punishments: excommunication, interdict, and suspension. All three, depending on the offense, are imposed either automatically with the offense or by a sentence; beyond this, there is also the possibility of announcing automatic imposition. Excommunication involves (1) prohibiting any service in the celebration of the Eucharist (→ Mass) or other liturgical acts, (2) forbidding giving or receiving of the sacraments and → sacramentals, and (3) prohibiting the discharge of any ecclesiastical offices, services, or tasks and of exercising any position of leadership (1331.1). One on whom an interdict has been imposed is subject to the first two restrictions (1332). In both cases the sentence may be made heavier if the censure has been imposed or declared to be already in effect (1331.2 and 1332). Suspension applies only to the → clergy. It forbids any acts of ordination or leadership and the exercise of any rights or duties connected with office (1333.1; → Laicization; Consecration).

2. History

Censures developed over many years of history. Especially as the Roman Church sees it, church discipline already applied to the → primitive Christian community, though with no clear-cut penalties (→ Acts of the Apostles; Jurisdiction, Ecclesiastical). Excommunication is the oldest form still practiced and, since the end of the 4th century, has meant the loss of membership privileges rather than exclusion from the church (→ Church Membership 5). Suspension and the interdict arose about the same time. Canon law in the 13th century distinguished between these penal forms as *poenae medicinales,* on the one hand, and *poenae vindicativae,* on the other, though not with the clearly defined difference that we find later.

In → Reformation churches — apart from the Church of England (→ Anglican Communion), which imposes excommunication on essentially a medieval basis (Thirty-Nine Articles of 1562, no. 33)

— there is no basis for independent church punishment as a means to protect social discipline within the church (C. Link), and there is thus no system of punishments corresponding to canon law. Instead, the church, spiritually understood, adopts church discipline as a part of the power of the → keys that is given to Christ's church, administered by spiritual leaders with the help of the → congregation (§4.2; M. → Luther) or by the → elders (J. → Calvin). At the center of both the → Lutheran and the → Reformed churches, excommunication means banning especially from Communion (→ Eucharist). Differently than in canon law, this does not involve censure grounded in church authority, but rather a declaration of the loss of membership in the spiritual church brought about by the banned person's own conduct. Subsequent development, however, shows they did not in fact maintain this stance, for in both the Lutheran consistory (17th cent.) and the Reformed tradition (since the 16th cent.), church discipline was variously secularized into consistorial or congregational justice, often accompanied by harsh penalties.

In modern Protestant discipline, penal elements deal above all with clerical offenders and with regulations involving church life and worship. The question of heresy, however, has largely been detached from disciplinary law and has become a matter of doctrinal debate, which itself is free of any disciplinary character.

→ Codex Iuris Canonici

Bibliography: General: R. PAHUD DE MORTANGES, Zwischen Vergebung und Vergeltung. Eine Analyse des kirchlichen Straf- und Disziplinarrechts (Baden-Baden, 1992) • H. SCHILLING, ed., Kirchenzucht und Sozialdisziplinierung im frühneuzeitlichen Europa (Berlin, 1994).

Roman Catholic Church: J. A. CORIDEN, T. J. GREEN, and D. E. HEINTSCHEL, eds., The Code of Canon Law: A Text and Commentary (New York, 1985) 893-941 • W. M. PLÖCHL, Geschichte des Kirchenrechts (5 vols.; 2d ed.; Vienna, 1960-70) 1.97-199, 252-54, 422-25; 2.374-400 • W. REES, Die Strafgewalt der Kirche. Das geltende kirchliche Strafrecht–dargestellt auf der Grundlage seiner Entwicklungsgeschichte (Berlin, 1993) • R. STRIGL, "Kirchenstrafen," Handbuch des katholischen Kirchenrechts (ed. J. Listl et al.; Regensburg, 1983) 923-50, esp. 934ff.

Anglican Communion: R. VON FRIEDEBURG, "Anglikanische Kirchenzucht und nachbarschaftliche Sittenreform: Ref. Sittenzucht zwischen Staat, Kirche und Gemeinde in England, 1559-1642," Schilling, Kirchenzucht und Sozialdisziplinierung, 153-82.

Protestant churches: S. L. GREENSLADE, Shepherding the Flock: Problems of Pastoral Discipline in the Early Church and the Younger Churches Today (London, 1967)

• J. H. LEITH and H.-J. GOERTZ, "Kirchenzucht," TRE 19.173-91 • P. G. LINDHARDT, "Church Discipline," ELC 1.505-9 • C LINK, "Kirchenzucht," EStL 1.1782-87 • E. WOLF, Ordnung und Kirche (Frankfurt, 1961) 599-601.

HERMANN WEBER

Central African Republic

	1960	1980	2000
Population (1,000s):	1,534	2,313	3,640
Annual growth rate (%):	1.78	2.31	2.12

Area: 662,436 sq. km. (240,324 sq. mi.)

A.D. 2000

Population density: 6/sq. km. (15/sq. mi.)
Births / deaths: 3.61 / 1.49 per 100 population
Fertility rate: 4.59 per woman
Infant mortality rate: 89 per 1,000 live births
Life expectancy: 50.6 years (m: 48.1, f: 53.2)
Religious affiliation (%): Christians 68.9 (Roman Catholics 22.3, unaffiliated 20.0, Protestants 16.2, indigenous 10.3, other Christians 0.2), Muslims 15.7, tribal religionists 14.3, other 1.1.

1. General Situation
2. Religious Situation

1. General Situation

The Central African Republic, a landlocked country, has French as its official language, with Sango a trade language spoken by most of the population. Other main languages correspond to the country's various ethnic groups; the largest are Baya, Banda, and Mandja. After the French gained control of the area in the late 19th century, the region was called Ubangi-Shari; later the area was incorporated into the Afrique Équatoriale Française (→ Colonialism). On August 13, 1960, it gained independence as the République Centrafricaine. General André Kolingba assumed power in 1981 through a bloodless coup. He ruled until the country's first parliamentary election, on September 19, 1993, when Ange Félix Patassé became the new head of state for the next six years. The Movement for the Liberation of the Central African People won the election and put what had been the dominating unity party since 1987 in a minority position.

Education is well developed in the country. The country's single university is in Bangui; there also are higher technical and agronomic centers. The economy is concentrated on agriculture and diamond mining. The major exports are coffee, diamonds, wood, wool, rubber, and peanuts. The most important trading partners are France, Belgium, and Luxembourg, as well as other members of the European Union. The majority of the population practices subsistence farming, raising millet, peanuts, rice, maize, and bananas (→ Third World 1.3).

2. Religious Situation

Over two-thirds of the people of the Central African Republic identify themselves as Christians. Almost one-sixth claim to be Muslims, with a slightly smaller percentage practicing tribal religions.

2.1. Among Christians, in 1990 approximately 57 percent were Protestant (704,000), 41 percent Roman Catholic (580,000), 1.7 percent members of African Independent Churches (36,000), and 0.3 percent in marginal groups.

2.1.1. The beginnings of Protestant Christianity go back to 1920/21, when missionaries of the Baptist Mid-Missions came from the Belgian Congo and began work in Bangassou and Rafai in the Southeast. They then spread westward and set up missions in Fort Sibut and Fort Crampel, working mostly among the Banda, Mandja, and Nzakara. In 1921 the first missionaries of the American → Brethren Church arrived, who set up hospitals, clinics, and Bible schools. In 1923, coming from the Sudan Mission, Lutherans began work (→ Lutheran Churches), which was later taken over by American Lutherans and Norwegians. In 1966 ten different denominations were active. The most important are the Église Évangélique des Frères, Église Baptistes, and Union des Églises Baptistes (→ Baptists). The Église Évangélique Centrafricaine broke away from the Brethren Churches. In 1956 a separatist movement in the Baptist Mid-Missions at Fort Crampel under the charismatic Pastor Boymanja led to the formation of the Comité Baptiste. This church gained state recognition and the cooperation of French and Swiss missionaries of the Coopération Évangélique Mondiale. Other independent churches, mostly from Zaire and including the → Kimbanguist Church, are at work in Bangui and other larger centers. The translation of the Bible (→ Bible Versions) began in 1927; today there are versions in seven languages.

2.1.2. The first mission of the → Roman Catholic Church was to Bangui in 1894. The Capuchins, → Dominicans, Marists, and sisters of the → Franciscans and the Holy Spirit, with sisters of St. Paul de Chartres (→ Orders and Congregations), all cooperated. There was no indigenous religious congregation. Today there are nine bishops in the archbishopric of Bangui, which has five → dioceses. A *pro nuntius* (→ Nuncio) represents the Vatican. In 1992 there were 85 diocesan priests and 169 priests of orders, 82 monastic brethren and 301 sisters, 101 lay missionaries, and 3,741 catechists. Charitable work is done in 134 institutions. The church has established large initiatives for the development of the people, especially for women (the *Animation rurale des femmes*), for whom a large-scale program has been set up since 1963.

2.2. No ecumenical → national Christian council or similar organization exists. Since 1974 most Protestant churches have worked with the Association des Églises Évangéliques de l'Afrique. Catholics work with the association in Bible translation. The Faculté de Théologie Évangélique de Bangui, a school of theology begun in 1976, is open to all denominations.

2.3. The Central African Republic maintains the principle of separation of church and state. Schools are mostly run by the state, though private schools and religious instruction outside school are permitted. The state everywhere supports the church's development projects.

2.4. Other religions have become a minority in most tribes (→ Guinea 2; Tribal Religions), although the Binga pygmies have preserved their religious inheritance. Of the various traditional religious movements, the Nzapa ti Azande movement is recognized by the state as an authentic African religion. → Islam is supported by non-Africans in the cities and by the → nomads in the North, but it has had little success among the general population.

→ Africa; African Theology; Social Ethics

Bibliography: D. Barrett, ed., *WCE* 220-22 • P. Kalck, *Central African Republic* (Oxford, 1993).

Paul Stadler

Chad

1. General Situation
2. Religious Situation

1. General Situation

The inland African nation of Chad includes three climatic zones with different peoples and cultures. In the wastes of the North live → nomads with their herds. In the Sahel, once the home of important kingdoms, nomads and herders live together. The South is the home of peasants, joined in clans. The dominant people here are the Sara, who show openness to modern development.

The complex history of Chad reaches back to the sixth century. From 1900 to 1960 it was under French rule (→ Colonialism). From 1965 onward, various

	1960	1980	2000
Population (1,000s):	3,064	4,477	7,270
Annual growth rate (%):	1.69	2.29	2.37

Area: 1,284,000 sq. km. (495,755 sq. mi.)

A.D. 2000

Population density: 6/sq. km. (15/sq. mi.)
Births / deaths: 3.95 / 1.59 per 100 population
Fertility rate: 5.13 per woman
Infant mortality rate: 106 per 1,000 live births
Life expectancy: 49.5 years (m: 48.0, f: 51.0)
Religious affiliation (%): Muslims 57.8, Christians 25.5 (Protestants 14.7, Roman Catholics 7.8, unaffiliated 2.0, indigenous 1.0), tribal religionists 15.5, Baha'is 1.1, other 0.1.

ethnic groups fought for supremacy. The nationalist Hissène Habré seized and held power from 1982 to 1990, and with international recognition he endeavored to give peace and national identity to his country. In 1990 Idriss Déby came to power in a coup d'état, and he sought to give Chad a democratic government. A new constitution was adopted in 1995 that mandated free parliamentary and presidential elections. The national languages are French and Arabic, with Chad Arabic as a language of the people. In addition, more than 100 other languages and dialects are spoken. Chad's chief crop is cotton; the country has deposits of salt and uranium. Long drought periods (→ Hunger), however, have forced many of the residents to move to neighboring countries.

2. Religious Situation

2.1. Protestant beginnings go back to 1925. The Sudan United Mission (→ North American Missions) in the South has the largest church, the Église Évangélique du Chad. There are also → Baptist, → Mennonite, → Lutheran, and Evangelical churches. Because of government pressure, no viable → Independent African Churches have been possible. Protestant projects and programs, especially for the rural population, contribute to → development (§1) of the country. By steady → evangelization, the Protestant churches enjoy slow but constant growth, even in unfriendly areas such as the prefecture of Guéra.

2.2. The → Roman Catholic Church is today a dynamic fellowship of Christians who, perhaps through the sufferings of the civil war, have become bearers of hope for Chad. Beginning in the South in 1929, they now have five → dioceses, one of them led since 1987 by the first Chad bishop. → Base communities and diocesan councils for pastoral care

work together to give form to an African lifestyle (→ Acculturation). The diocesan office of development has many projects, especially involving land. In 1983 the Diocese of N'Djamena introduced a new organization for development, independent of church structures, which seeks to serve all peoples for social justice and total development.

2.3. In the Republic of Chad, a secular state, religious organizations can work unhindered. President François Tombalbaye (1960-75) attempted a cultural revolution (1973-75), which claimed many victims among Protestant Christians, including pastors. President Hissène Habré, however, recognized the contribution of the churches to the country's rebuilding and development and was interested, too, in the forging of harmonious relations between Muslims and Christians (→ Islam and Christianity). Present tensions between French speakers and Arabic speakers point to a certain pressure toward a stronger form of Islamic life.

→ Africa; African Theology; Social Ethics

Bibliography: M. AZEVEDO, ed., Cameroon and Chad in Historical and Contemporary Perspectives (Lewiston, N.Y., 1990) • M. BAAR and L. BAAR, Tschad. Land ohne Hoffnung? Erlebnisbericht einer 25 jährigen Aufbautätigkeit im Dangaleat-Stamm (Bad Liebenzell, 1985) • D. BARRETT, ed., WCE 222-24 • J. L. COLLIER et al., Chad: A Country Study (Washington, D.C., 1990) • G. J. NGANSOP, Tchad. Vingt ans de crise (Paris, 1986) • Le Tchad profond (= Missi 53/1 [1987]).

PAUL STADLER

Chalcedon, Council of

1. Historical Importance
2. The Definition
3. Other Rulings
4. Ecumenical Significance

1. Historical Importance

The Council of Chalcedon (modern Kadiköy, a district of Istanbul on the eastern shore of the Bosporus) holds a place of preeminence among the imperial or ecumenical → councils of the early church that dealt with Christological questions (→ Christology). Made possible by a change in the leadership of the Roman Empire, according to the plan of the new rulers (Marcian and Pulcheria), it had the main purpose of reversing the decisions of the Council of Ephesus of 449, which had provoked a storm of anger in the West. (Pope → Leo I [440-61] called it the robber council.) It was also designed to put an authoritative end to the dogmatic discord caused by Nestorius and the Constantinopolitan abbot Eutyches (→ Nestorians; Monophysitism). It would do this by getting as many of the bishops as could be assembled to subscribe to a confession that would embody doctrinal agreement.

2. The Definition

The council opened on October 8, 451, and sat for approximately three weeks. From the West only four papal legates and two North African bishops (probably refugees from the Vandal attack) attended. The most important achievement of the council was in fact its confession. Against what was at first the strong opposition of the council, imperial commissaries, who firmly controlled the proceedings, worked persistently to draft this and secure its passage. In its key statement it confesses "one and the same Son, our Lord Jesus Christ . . . truly God and truly man; . . . one and the same Christ, Son, Lord, only-begotten, acknowledged in two natures which undergo no confusion, no change, no division, no separation; at no point was the difference between the natures taken away through the union, but rather the property of both natures is preserved and comes together into a single person and a single subsistent being; he is not parted or divided into two persons, but is one and the same only-begotten Son, God, Word, Lord Jesus Christ."

The traditional historical view is that this statement must be interpreted as a compromise between Antiochene and Alexandrian Christology (→ Antiochene Theology; Alexandrian Theology). In other words, it is the answer of the West to the problems of the East. In strict language, and with no attempt at metaphysical speculation, it tries to achieve a mean of faith in Christ and to set aside extremes on both sides.

More accurately, however, we have here only one clear quotation from an older Western document, the Tome of Leo I, which he sent to Patriarch Flavian of Constantinople on June 13, 449. In this document, indirectly at least, the pope did justice to one of the main concerns of the Antiochenes, namely, the safeguarding of true humanity of Christ. For the rest, the Christological formula of Chalcedon in 451 echoes the Alexandrian Christology of unity in the interpretation of → Cyril (d. 444). Its strength and attractiveness rest on the fact that better than any other Christological definitions, it tries to uphold the unity of the biblical picture of Christ and to anchor the historical act of salvation firmly in God. In so doing, it also answers to a fundamental concern of piety.

3. Other Rulings

Chalcedon also dealt with many financial, disciplinary, and constitutional questions. Several of its resolutions addressed the issue of the integration of → monasticism into the fabric of the church (cans. 4, 16, 23, 24); others dealt with the integration of the church into the empire. The latter include canon 28, adopted at the end of the council and in the absence of the Roman legates, which soon proved significant in alienating Rome from the churches of the East. Appealing to canon 3 of the First Council of Constantinople (381), this 28th canon of Chalcedon defined the privileges of the church of Constantinople, doing so on purely political grounds.

4. Ecumenical Significance

In protest against canon 28, Rome almost went over to the camp of the foes of Chalcedon. Ultimately, however, it remained one of the staunchest supporters of the → dogma. The churches of the → Reformation later inherited this loyalty.

In contrast, the East found far too far-reaching the agreement with the Roman-Antiochene Christology of separation, especially in the clause "the property of both natures is preserved and comes together into a single person," which is the only sure quotation from Leo in the Chalcedonian Definition. Thus the Council of Chalcedon did not bring the peace that had been expected from it. On the contrary, it finally caused a first great confessional split in Christianity (→ Heresies and Schisms). This development in turn weakened the Christian empire of → Byzantium, and as a result the Christian populations of the Monophysite territories in Syria, Palestine, and Egypt eventually passed almost without a struggle under the domination of → Islam.

Bibliography: ACO 2 (2d ed.; 1962) • M. ASHJIAN, ed., "The Reception of the Council of Chalcedon by the Churches," ER 22 (1970) 348-423 • P. T. CAMELOT, Ephesus und Chalcedon (Mainz, 1963) • A. J. FESTUGIÈRE, Éphèse et Chalcédoine (Geneva, 1982/83) • P. T. R. GRAY, The Defense of Chalcedon in the East (Leiden, 1979) • P. GREGORIOS, W. H. LAZARETH and N. A. NISSIOTIS, eds., Does Chalcedon Divide or Unite? Towards Convergence in Orthodox Christology (Geneva, 1981) • A. GRILLMEIER, Christ in Christian Tradition, vol. 1, From the Apostolic Age to Chalcedon (451) (2d ed.; London, 1975) • A. GRILLMEIER and H. BACHT, eds., Das Konzil von Chalcedon (5th ed.; 3 vols.; Würzburg, 1979) • A. DE HALLEUX, "La définition christologique à Chalcédoine," RTL 7 (1976) 3-23, 155-70 • A. M. RITTER, "Das Konzil von Chalcedon," HDThG 1.261-70 • R. V. SELLERS, The Council of Chalcedon: A Historical and

Doctrinal Survey (London, 1953) • N. P. TANNER, ed., *Decrees of the Ecumenical Councils* (2 vols.; London, 1990) 1.75-103.

ADOLF MARTIN RITTER

Chance

1. Definition
2. Logical Status
3. Organization and Systematic Classification
   3.1. Chance in Mathematics and Physics
   3.2. Chance and Practical Actions
   3.3. Chance in Art
   3.4. Chance and Finite Life

1. Definition

In the meaning familiar to us, the word "chance" refers to an unexpected and incalculable event ("pure chance") encountering a person from the outside *(eventus)* and intervening in that person's → life in the sense of fortune or misfortune (→ Fate and [Good] Fortune). As such, chance eludes human knowledge and will, and it thus is often attributed to an arbitrary or divine power, at whose disposal one's life-path stands.

The word's history, however, points in a different direction. The spatially understood element of chance or encounter developed first into a concept of that which fell to a person as a *habitus* of nature, or of that which comes deservedly to a person (such as regular, legitimate income). Only after the philosophical distinction between *substantia* and *accidens* (Gk. *ousia* and *symbebēkos*) in its scholastic coloring had become part of this language game did the word change, by way of the volitional-metaphysical understanding of late-scholastic theology (→ Metaphysics; Scholasticism), into the meaning customary today. In the process, elements of German → mysticism exerted a certain influence, ultimately turning "chance," originally understood spatially and naturally, into a fateful or divine dispensation altering the very foundations of life.

2. Logical Status

Considered formally, that which is accidental both theoretically and practically is the individual or absolutely isolated element with no discernible relationship to the universal. As such, it does not submit to rationally comprehensible rules, to mathematical or physical laws, or to any all-encompassing principle of → reason, as whose emanation or necessary constituent part it might be manifested. Viewed in this way, chance or the accidental resists all empirical

comprehension by way of the categories of the understanding, and all derivation from any unified principle of reason.

This understanding stands juxtaposed philosophically with the quantitative tripartite division of all rational judgments into individual, particular, and universal, a conception itself based on a different understanding of judgments and concepts. Without reflecting on anything like immediate faith or intellectual perception, we understand the universal as always standing over against the individual and the particular, whereby the concrete concept (e.g., the relationship between body and soul) resists both any isolation of the object (atomism of the concept) and any absolute universalization (despotism of the concept). Instead, it delimits itself against both arbitrary metaphysics and against vulgar → nominalism of the late scholastic variety.

3. Organization and Systematic Classification

Commensurate with the → Aristotelian division of philosophy into theoretical, practical, and aesthetic judgments, a similarly differentiated understanding of chance emerges with regard to the natural-philosophical (→ Philosophy of Nature), the ethical-theoretical (→ Action Theory), and the → aesthetic.

3.1. *Chance in Mathematics and Physics*

Both the unavoidable use of irrational numbers and the analogous application of relational determinatives (→ Analogy) to materially different phenomena gave rise to a remnant that would not fit into established, logical relationships. To that extent, this remnant was attributed to chance, even though in other respects one did indeed reckon with it. This complex also included acknowledgment of optical or acoustic relationships whose harmony could not be expressed in purely mathematical or physical relations (e.g., the well-tempered scale). Here chance is something unavoidably added to abstract judgment, yet something that eludes any purely rational understanding (in terms of mathematics and physics), without for that reason being arbitrary. The concept acquires this same meaning when applied to the determination of internally organized, self-driven → nature (organic and animal life). Neither externally focused description nor any purely abstract concepts or single-cause explanatory models (→ Teleology) are able to comprehend nature's internal purposiveness *(autarkeia)* and self-movement *(energeia)* with respect to its internal organization and functional relationships or its actual course of development or end-status.

3.2. *Chance and Practical Actions*

The part of our own nature that is involved in deciding, on the basis of clear and accountable reasoning, what is to be either done or not done voluntarily *(hēkon)* is the object of practical consideration *(bouleusasthai)*; in their own turn, these considerations are what make possible theoretical, pragmatic, and ethical decisions that endure with respect to common reason. The capacity for practical judgment, however, is only one of the presuppositions required for successful action; this must be accompanied by an ethically disposed character *(hēxis)* and by favorable circumstances *(eutychia)* contributing to this success. Insofar as these circumstances cannot be predicted or must be created by the individual, that which "falls to us" by chance (undeserved or unmerited) does also play a role in the evaluation of a deed *(praxis)* and of human work *(ergon)*.

3.3. Chance in Art

The → experience of the accidental in → everyday life and in the reflective consideration of the natural and moral world, amid what are always finite conditions of will and volition, is expanded by taste *(gustus)* in the evaluation of what we call "beautiful works of art" insofar as a more essential meaning is extracted from the element of the contingent or even the incidental *(symbebēkos)*. Whereas technical actions and the production of purposive products and their use are valued with regard to their external usefulness and success in addressing the needs of existence, artistic → play *(praxis)* and the generation of works *(poiēsis)* that do not (or do not primarily) serve to satisfy natural needs and finite interests are internally purposive. Here — especially with respect to the fertile imagination *(ingenium)* — the focus is on a productive freedom within the act of artistic creation and on the internal purposiveness and beauty of artistic works insofar as these neither follow simple nature *(physei)* nor submit to the pressures of dominant conceptual and intellectual habits or to conceptually fixed rules of judgment.

3.4. Chance and Finite Life

Compared with the utter regularity and enduring character of the things, beings, and processes that are subject to the universal laws of nature and that eternally repeat themselves, all finite life, along with all its individual acts and self-conceived works of art, seems fleeting and threatened by decay. The vagaries attaching to the various conditions of the spirit, and even more the dependence of all action on external conditions that are beyond the power of human beings — all this makes human life, deeds, and works seem bathed in the twilight of the accidental and the transitory. Precisely this element of chance, however, over against the complete determination of nature, first creates the possibility of engaging in meaningful action and kindles the flame of artistic representa-

tion that, as the expression of reason itself, both survives the genius that created it and endures through time.

Bibliography: K. BARTH, *CD* III/3, 161ff. • P. ERBRICH, *Zufall. Eine naturwissenschaftliche Untersuchung* (Stuttgart, 1988) • G. GIGERENZER et al., eds., *The Empire of Chance: How Probability Changed Science and Everyday Life* (Cambridge, 1989) • I. HACKING, *The Emergence of Probability: A Philosophical Study of Early Ideas about Probability, Induction, and Statistical Inference* (Cambridge, 1975); idem, *The Taming of Chance* (Cambridge, 1990) • J. MONOD, *Chance and Necessity* (New York, 1971); idem, *The Necessity of Being* (London, 1973) • J.-E. PLEINES, ed., *Zufall, teleologisches Argument in der Philosophie* (Würzburg, 1991) • W. WINDELBAND, *Die Lehren vom Zufall* (Berlin, 1870).

JÜRGEN-ECKARDT PLEINES

Chapel

The designation "chapel" derives from the place that housed the royal Frankish relic, namely, half of the cape (Lat. *cappella*) of St. Martin of Tours (ca. 316-97). Although chapels conceived as sacred spaces in citadels and castles were actually part of the overall concept, independent cultic spaces, normally with an → altar, were also called chapels (e.g., baptismal chapels, → baptisteries, funerary chapels) and were constructed usually in the shape of a cross or as a central edifice. The initial architectonic result of the veneration involving altars (→ Saints, Veneration of), influenced by the Cluniac reform (→ Cluny, Order of), were the chancel chapels and, beginning with the late Middle Ages, the aisle chapels. Worship structures not legally bearing the designation "church" can also be called chapels.

In England so-called chapels of ease were built for the convenience of parishioners who lived too far away from the parish church. "Chapel" became the usual term for a dissenting place of worship (e.g., Baptist or Methodist chapels). Within the mainline church, proprietary chapels (e.g., in England in the 18th and 19th centuries) were built or maintained privately. Such chapels did not have the usual rights or restrictions of parishes.

→ Cathedral; Church Architecture; Minster

Bibliography: J. FLECKENSTEIN, *Die Hofkapelle der deutschen Könige* (2 vols.; Stuttgart, 1959-65) • H. LECLERCQ, "Chapel de Saint Martin," *DACL* 3.381-90; idem, "Chapelle," *DACL* 3.406-28 • K. LINDLEY, *Chapels and Meeting Houses* (London, 1969) • P. J. MULLINS,

"Chapel," *NCE* 3.452-53 • H. SAALMAN, *Medieval Archi-tecture: European Architecture, 600-1200* (2d ed.; New York, 1965) • O. VON SIMSON, *The Gothic Cathedral: Origins of Gothic Architecture and the Medieval Concept of Order* (3d ed.; Princeton, 1988) • E. H. SWIFT, *Roman Sources of Christian Art* (New York, 1951).

EKKEHARD MÜHLENBERG

Chaplain, Military → Military Chaplaincy

Chapter → Cathedral

Charisma

1. The NT
   1.1. Term
   1.2. Paul
      1.2.1. Basic Meaning
      1.2.2. Specific Sense
   1.3. First Peter and the Pastoral Epistles
2. The Sociology of Religion
   2.1. Term
   2.2. Attributions
   2.3. Charismatic Authority
      2.3.1. Ideal Type
      2.3.2. Change
   2.4. Significance for Religious Sociology

1. The NT

1.1. *Term*

The term "charisma" occurs in Hellenistic Jewish writings only in textually uncertain passages. It finds broad attestation for the first time in → Paul and in works influenced by him. It is rare in secular Greek, being used only from the second century A.D. in the basic sense of "gift," "present," or "charitable act."

1.2. *Paul*

1.2.1. *Basic Meaning*

We occasionally find the basic meaning "gift" in Paul (Rom. 1:11; 6:23). More specifically, we also find the sense "gift that comes from God's act of salvation" (e.g., 1 Cor. 1:7; 2 Cor. 1:11; Rom. 5:15-16). This usage echoes the *charis* (grace) that is central for Paul.

1.2.2. *Specific Sense*

The term eventually denotes "gracious gift of the divine Spirit" in the controversy with the Corinthian enthusiasts (1 Corinthians 12–14). Here Paul develops a doctrine of charisms that — as its adop-tion in Rom. 12:3-8 shows — characterizes the Christian → congregation in a fundamental sense.

Some Christians in Corinth wanted to discern the Spirit's working only in → ecstatic phenomena, espe-cially → glossolalia. Pneumatics were thus rivaling one another at worship. Paul radically criticizes this view. God's Spirit primarily manifests himself, not primarily in extraordinary experiences such as pagan cults might also offer, but in confession of Jesus as Lord (1 Cor. 12:2-3).

For Paul, too, there are spiritual gifts, but he calls these *charismata*, rather than the usual *pneumatika*, and as parallels for the term he employs "ministries" and "miraculous divine operations." The Spirit gives a charisma, not to confer distinction on an in-dividual, but to edify the community. One and the same Spirit gives different charismata, some of which seem to be supernatural, others ordinary (1 Cor. 12:8-10, 28; Rom. 12:7-8). The → apostles, → proph-ets, and teachers are also bearers of charismata.

Paul illustrates the need for different charisms by a comparison drawn from popular philosophy: the image of the body and its members. By → baptism and the → Eucharist, believers belong to the body of Christ. Like a human organism, the Lord's body con-sists of many members, which can fulfill the mission that God has laid upon the → church only as they work together in orderly fashion. Thus the concept of the charisma embraces every aspect of the church's life.

If Paul refers to higher charisms, he does not imply that these have greater worth before God, but he has in view their value for the life of the commu-nity in the temporal world. → Love alone has sote-riological relevance. Love, then, is the criterion in the exercise of the charisms (1 Corinthians 13). Paul strongly plays down the glossolalia that the Corinthi-ans rated so highly (chap. 14). In the lists of charisms in Romans 12 there are no ecstatic phenomena at all. Instead, Paul gives prominence to the ministry of leading and ruling the community, to love of neigh-bor, and to the proclamation of the Word.

1.3. *First Peter and the Pastoral Epistles*

In 1 Pet. 4:10 "charisma" is a general term for keryg-matic and diaconal gifts in the community. In the → Pastoral Epistles the term has the narrower sense of the official charisma that leaders of the community receive by the → laying on of hands (1 Tim. 4:14; 2 Tim. 1:6).

Bibliography: U. BROCKHAUS, *Charisma und Amt* (Wup-pertal, 1972) • C. DUQUOC and C. FLORISTAN, eds., *Charisms in the Church* (New York, 1978) • F. HAHN, "Charisma und Amt," *ZTK* 76 (1979) 419-49 • E. KÄSEMANN, "Ministry and Community in the NT," *Essays on NT Themes* (London, 1964) 63-94 • H. SCHÜR-

MANN, "Die geistlichen Gnadengaben in den paulinischen Gemeinden," *Ursprung und Gestalt* (Düsseldorf, 1970) 236-67 • A. VANHOYE, "Charism," *Dictionary of Fundamental Theology* (ed. R. Latourelle and R. Fisichella; New York, 1994) 103-8.

HELMUT MERKEL

2. The Sociology of Religion

2.1. *Term*

The term "charisma" was developed as a tool for the social-scientific study of religion by the sociologist Max → Weber, who used it to refer to possession of, or by, extraordinary powers of a supernatural or superhuman kind.

2.2. *Attributions*

In this sense, charisma can be attributed to objects as well as to people. Places, statues, or → icons may be believed to manifest supernatural powers. Charisma may be a pervasive attribute of individuals, as with the magician (→ Magic), or an occasional experience, as in displays of "gifts of the Spirit" in → Pentecostal churches.

2.3. *Charismatic Authority*

2.3.1. *Ideal Type*

Weber describes the ideal type in dealing with forms of authority. Charismatic leaders exercise authority on the basis of the personal devotion of followers, who regard the leaders as endowed with superhuman or otherwise exceptional powers or qualities, which are considered divine in origin or exemplary. Typical charismatic leaders are messiahs (→ Messianism) and radical prophetic innovators. The leader demands → obedience on the basis of his or her mission, offers a new way of life, divulges a new truth or revelation, and imposes on the followers obligations that differ from those of the prevailing order. Charismatic authority is exercised on the basis of the leader's revelation rather than on the basis of tradition or rational considerations. It breaks with → everyday routine and is highly unpredictable. Administration is conducted through a personally appointed staff of disciples selected for their own charismatic endowment or their intense commitment to the leader, rather than their technical competence. Duties and responsibilities are only vaguely delimited, and the leader intervenes at will in the conduct of administration.

2.3.2. *Change*

Unconstrained by normal conventions and expectations, the leader may change policy or practice frequently. Such a leadership style will seem arbitrary and erratic to the outside observer, but followers often experience it as liberating and inspired. Charisma is inherently unstable and precarious. Belief in the supernatural → inspiration or superhuman power of the leader will weaken in the face of continuing setbacks or signs of failure.

The charisma itself is exposed to weakening as a movement goes on. Growth leads to the emergence of impersonal mechanisms of coordination and supervision. Followers grow older and seek more security or a more predictable future for themselves or their children. The continuation of a movement demands more predictable sources of finance. Administrators establish routine operating procedures of greater efficiency than the ad hoc commands of the leader. Those appointed to administrative office entertain hopes of preserving their authority, income, and style of life; they seek some form of tenure of office.

The development of structures of regulations, of rights among appointed officials, and of dependence upon a routinized economic base and formalized procedures constrains the leader's capacity for arbitrary behavior and dramatic changes in doctrine or policy. In this way charismatic government tends to take a calculable form as routine, whether in a more traditional or a more legal and rational way. The charisma then either disappears entirely or becomes a more attenuated or specialized feature of a traditional or → bureaucratic role.

2.4. *Significance for Religious Sociology*

The concept of charisma has been of major significance in the → sociology of religion because of the insight it has offered into the emergent stage of religious → development in a wide variety of cultures and historical periods. Although beset by many ambiguities, the concept remains valuable, applicable to many of the new religions that appeared in the West in the 1960s and 1970s, as well as to the origins of major world religions.

Bibliography: D. F. BARNES, "Charisma and Religious Leadership: An Historical Analysis," *JSSR* 17 (1978) 1-18 • A. GODIN, *The Psychological Dynamics of Religious Experience* (Birmingham, 1985) • W. J. HOLLENBERGER, *The Pentecostals: The Charismatic Movement in the Churches* (Minneapolis, 1972) • V. LANTERNARI, *The Religions of the Oppressed: A Study of the Modern Messianic Cults* (New York, 1963) • E. A. SHILS, "Charisma, Order, and Status," *ASR* 30 (1965) 199-213 • M. WEBER, "Charisma and Its Transformation," *Economy and Society: An Outline of Interpretive Sociology* (2 vols.; Berkeley, Calif., 1978; orig. pub., 1922) 2.1111-56; idem, "Charismatic Authority and Charismatic Community," ibid. 1.241-45; idem, *On Charisma and Institution Build-*

ing: Selected Papers (ed. S. N. Eisenstadt; Chicago, 1968)
• B. R. WILSON, *The Noble Savages: The Primitive Origins of Charisma and Its Contemporary Survival* (Berkeley, Calif., 1975).

ROY WALLIS

Charismatic Movement

1. Definition and Terminology

The term "charismatic movement" refers to the currents of → revival and renewal resulting from a transforming spiritual experience generally termed "baptism in the Spirit," which is associated with the reception and contemporary availability of the spiritual gifts of 1 Cor. 12:8-10 (esp. prophecy, → healing, and → glossolalia). While baptism in the Spirit and the spiritual gifts also characterize the Pentecostal movement, the charismatic movement with its many different strands is clearly distinct in theological framework, patterns of fellowship, and sociocultural ethos.

The term "charismatic movement" was coined by H. Bredesen and J. Stone in 1963 to designate what was at first called neo-Pentecostalism, that is, the occurrence of Pentecostal-type blessing within the historic Protestant denominations. This was the general connotation of "charismatic movement" in the mid-1960s. By the late 1960s, however, there were independent groups and ministries, often calling themselves nondenominational, that identified more with the charismatic movement than with Pentecostalism per se. These nondenominational currents, which spread in the 1970s and mushroomed in the 1980s, are now generally recognized as part of the overall charismatic movement, in which we may distinguish three major strands: (1) charismatic renewal in the historic Protestant churches (from the 1950s); (2) charismatic renewal in the Roman Catholic Church (from 1967); (3) charismatic renewal in the independent sector (from the late 1960s). In 1988 the

numbers of those active in these three groups were estimated, respectively, at 10.9 million, 10.1 million, and 17.4 million.

2. Beginnings

The early stirrings of the charismatic movement lie in the 1950s in the United States, the Netherlands, and the United Kingdom, although only in the early 1960s did they enter public consciousness and acquire visibility as a movement. Important influences in its origins, all of which were operative in the 1950s, were groups praying for revival (e.g., Nights of Prayer for Worldwide Revival in the United Kingdom), circles ministering divine healing (e.g., the London Healing Mission, the key role of Agnes Sanford, often — despite its official disapproval — within the milieu of the Order of St. Luke in the United States), people studying the Book of Acts (e.g., the Methodist Tommy Tyson in North Carolina), and contact with Pentecostals (e.g., the healing campaigns of T. L. Osborn in the Netherlands and the major influence of the Full Gospel Business Men's Fellowship International; → Pentecostal Churches). Some people and groups became charismatic without any evident outside influence.

The public emergence of a distinct movement occurred in the United States through national publicity in 1960 concerning the Episcopal priest Dennis Bennett (then of Van Nuys, Calif., and later of Seattle) and in Britain in 1963 through another Anglican priest, Michael Harper. Other major publicizing factors were David Wilkerson's biographical book *The Cross and the Switchblade* (1963) and John Sherrill's *They Speak with Other Tongues* (1964). Between 1962 and 1965 the charismatic movement spread to New Zealand, Germany, Kenya, South Africa, and Australia.

Like the meetings of Pentecostals, charismatic meetings were characterized by vocal praise, lengthy preaching or teaching, personal testimonies, and personal ministry. From the start, there was a strong lay character about the charismatic movement, with an emphasis on "every-member" ministry. This practice favored the discovery and use of gifts independent of ministerial → ordination, though the mainline charismatics continued to recognize ordained ministry.

Charismatic renewal in Protestant traditions tended to produce either overtly charismatic congregations or congregations with a charismatic flavor, while charismatic Roman Catholic renewal typically gave rise to prayer groups, intentional (often covenant) → communities, and centers for ministry and healing.

3. Developments Worldwide
3.1. *North America*
Between the mid-1960s and the late 1970s, the charismatic movement spread rapidly in the United States, helped by the homogeneity of language and culture, media publicity, mass conventions, and the influence of the Full Gospel Business Men's Fellowship. Since 1988, the impact of the movement has been uneven, except in the independent sector, which has continued to grow steadily.

Charismatic renewal in the mainline churches has generally struggled to have a significant influence on church life. Often just tolerated, sometimes given a limited welcome, charismatic renewal has lost many of its supporters to Pentecostal and independent charismatic churches, especially from Presbyterian, United Methodist, and Baptist ranks. In the 1990s an increasing → liberalism in the liturgical churches has intensified the struggle of loyal charismatics. Some Episcopalians have joined the Charismatic Episcopal Church, formed in 1992 by former independent charismatics and Pentecostals.

The spread of the charismatic movement to the Roman Catholic Church in 1967 produced a powerful new thrust toward church renewal, the beginning of Life in the Spirit seminars to prepare people for the baptism in the Spirit, and the establishment of local and national service committees for the renewal movement. This pattern soon spread to the Catholic renewal in other countries and influenced other major denominations in the United States such as the Episcopalians and Lutherans to establish their own renewal agencies.

Charismatic Roman Catholic renewal was marked in its early years by the forceful influence of the covenant communities, especially Word of God (Ann Arbor, Mich.) and People of Praise (South Bend, Ind.). Divisions between such communities and the challenge of those favoring parish renewal, represented particularly in the Association of Diocesan Liaisons, led to a more diverse but weakened charismatic Catholic renewal.

The tradition that has been most positively influenced by charismatic renewal seems to be the Mennonite/Anabaptist churches, whose denominational leaderships have taken the charismatic movement more seriously. Until recently, charismatic renewal among → Episcopalians has maintained momentum, strengthening the evangelical strands in the Episcopal Church.

At its beginning, opposition to the charismatic movement was least in the Roman Catholic Church and greatest among the Presbyterians, in the Lutheran Church–Missouri Synod, and among the Orthodox. However, a leading Presbyterian scholar, John A. Mackay, with positive memories of Pentecostalism in Latin America, defended the Presbyterian charismatics and urged his church to study the question, leading to the important *Report on the Work of the Holy Spirit,* received by the United Presbyterian Church in 1978. The Lutheran Church–Missouri Synod has taken somewhat longer to come to terms with charismatic renewal, as have the Holiness churches such as the → Church of the Nazarene, which opposed the Pentecostal movement at its beginning.

The independent, or nondenominational, groupings first came into prominence in the early 1970s with the impact of Christian Growth Ministries, based in Fort Lauderdale, Florida. Led by Derek Prince, Bob Mumford, Don Basham, Charles Simpson, and Ern Baxter, the group produced the magazine *New Wine* (1969-86) and until the mid-1970s were the main exponents of so-called discipleship teaching. Their teaching and practice became controversial, and the mid-1970s saw much effort in the United States to repair strained relationships and to moderate heavy forms of authority.

The independent charismatics have tended to form networks linked more by personal bonds between the leading pastors than by creed or style of church government. Their patterns of organization reflect secular patterns from the world of business enterprise, with the possibility of simultaneous association with more than one network. The major networks include International Convention of Faith Ministries (Tulsa, Okla.), Fellowship of Covenant Ministers and Churches (Mobile, Ala.), Liberty Fellowship (Birmingham, Ala.), People of Destiny International (Gaithersburg, Md.), and Vineyard churches (Anaheim, Calif.). In the United States, independent charismatics outnumbered all "denominational" charismatics by the early 1990s (14 million vs. 6 million).

The interdenominational character of the charismatic movement was fostered by major events such as the Kansas City conference of 1977. This ecumenical dimension weakened in the 1980s, though the formation of the North American Renewal Service Committee (1985) and their organizing of interchurch congresses (New Orleans, 1987; Indianapolis, 1990; Orlando, 1995) have given a new impetus. The monthly magazine *Charisma* serves all constituencies, coming out of a Pentecostalism reanimated through the charismatic movement plus a strong nondenominational impulse.

3.2. *Europe*
Charismatic renewal in European Protestant churches

has been uneven. Variations reflect (1) church situations (minority churches may accept charismatic renewal as an agent of growth, as do, for example, the Baptists in France), (2) experience of revival movements (charismatic renewal is often stronger in regions with a history of revival, such as the Lutheran Church of Finland and the Evangelical Church in Wurttemberg), and (3) quality of leadership (Anglican charismatic renewal in England has benefited from responsible leadership, esp. of D. Watson [1933-84]). Charismatic renewal has had less impact on → Methodism than on the Reformation churches. The renewal in the Evangelical Lutheran Church has been gaining ground, despite some defections to the independent sector.

The charismatic movement in France has been marked by the rise of strong communities (Emmanuel, Chemin Neuf, Lion de Juda [now Béatitudes], and Pain de Vie) that have spread to many other countries, especially in Africa. In Italy, the charismatic Roman Catholic renewal attracts huge numbers to its annual convention in Rimini. In Ireland it has faded; it is relatively small in Spain and Portugal. In Germany, theology has played a larger role, with a theological commission having been formed for charismatic Catholic renewal.

In Scandinavia, charismatic renewal has been strongest in Finland and Norway and weakest in Denmark. Lutheran renewal has struggled generally with the antienthusiastic strain in → Luther's heritage.

The independent sector has grown the fastest. Britain has many networks, of which the largest are Pioneer (led by G. Coates), New Frontiers (led by T. Virgo), and Salt and Light (led by B. Coombs). The Ichthus churches of R. Forster have integrated charismatic and social concerns with a strong ministry to the inner city. The British independent sector has strong outreach to other lands and has pioneered the worldwide March for Jesus, held annually especially in the capital cities of the world.

3.3. *Africa*

Since the 1970s sub-Saharan Africa has seen extensive spiritual revival that is mainly Pentecostal/charismatic. The largest growth has occurred in new independent churches, mostly at the expense of the older churches. The new churches combine charismatic features known to African religion (healing, visions, dreams, dance, prophecy, emphases on power and immediacy to God) with a Western evangelical theology. They reject the African → Independent Churches as syncretistic.

Faced with loss of their members to Independent Churches or to independent Pentecostal/charismatic churches, the historic churches either see the charismatic renewal as a way of containing experiential enthusiasm or as a danger exacerbating this hemorrhage (a fear evident in Zambia in the forced resignation of the Roman Catholic Archbishop Msgr. E. Milingo).

In South Africa, where the independent surge has been more studied, there have been an estimated 1,000 new churches with 140,000 adult members. The biggest explosion is probably in Nigeria, where megachurches coexist with home fellowships. In the historic churches, charismatic Roman Catholic renewal is found throughout Catholic Africa (Anglo, French, and Portuguese); Anglican charismatic renewal has expanded since the late 1980s with the aid of Sharing of Ministries Abroad (SOMA) missions; Lutheran renewal is strong in Tanzania, as is renewal among Presbyterians in Nigeria.

3.4. *Asia*

Several Asian countries have seen an explosive growth of the charismatic movement, especially Korea (with major Methodist and Presbyterian charismatic congregations), the Philippines, and Indonesia. Anglican charismatic renewal has been strong in Singapore. Charismatic Roman Catholics have been strong in the Philippines and parts of Malaysia, as well as in South India, where vast crowds follow the healing ministry of Father M. Naikomparambil. Independent churches are mushrooming in many eastern Asia countries, including China, with the Hope Churches led by K. Chareonwongsak having an evangelistic impact in Thailand.

3.5. *Latin America*

The charismatic movement in Latin America has developed amid fears and concerns aroused by the rapidly growing Pentecostal movement. The first signs of charismatic renewal among Protestants (called Renovacion) came in Brazil in the early 1960s, but the new charismatic groupings (Presbyterian, Methodist, Baptist) all became new → denominations. Since then, Protestant Renovacion has been slight, either cautious or underground, except among some Lutherans in Brazil and Anglicans in the Southern Cone. Argentina is now seeing dramatic Pentecostal/charismatic growth, especially in the independent sector.

Charismatic Roman Catholic renewal came via North American missionaries and the visits of ecumenical teams in 1971/72. The Catholic Church in Latin America has greater difficulty than the church in Europe and North America in accepting and encouraging lay leadership, despite the shortage of priests (→ Clergy and Laity). Charismatic Catholic renewal now totals 50 million participants in the widest sense and is strongest in Brazil (a recent report cites 4 percent of active Catholics), Colombia (base of the Encuentro Carismático Católico Latino-Americano, the charismatic Catholic renewal structure for Latin America), Dominican Republic, and northern Mexico.

3.6. *Australia and New Zealand*

New Zealand has seen extensive charismatic renewal since 1965; it has been strong among Baptists, Presbyterians, Anglicans, some Brethren, with the group Youth with a Mission playing an important role. The charismatic movement in Australia has been widespread, but it lacks cohesion and strong leadership. Neither country has a big independent charismatic sector.

4. Points of Tension

Four issues continue to dominate discussion about the charismatic movement:

1. Differences of vision. Is it wiser to renew the historic churches, or should new charismatic churches be formed? Should the renewal be integrated into the church, or should there be a vision of an ecumenical, charismatic renewal? Are there apostles and prophets today?

2. The Spirit and the Word. Can doctrine be based on biblical narrative as well as teaching? What is the role of → experience and the role of → prophecy and its relation to the Bible (note the "signs and wonders" message of J. Wimber).

3. Theologies of healing and prosperity. Does God will to heal all sickness? What is the place of → suffering in the Christian life? What about the "positive confession" teaching of certain U.S. televangelists?

4. Demonology. Can the born-again have → demons? What is the relation between natural and preternatural causes? Are there territorial spirits?

Despite the tensions, the charismatic renewal provides a unique point of interaction between historic churches and more fundamentalist groups.

5. Reception

Charismatic renewal has found easier acceptance in the Roman Catholic Church than in most Protestant churches. The reasons include more space for movements within a Catholic framework; divisive struggles in churches with more democratic and representative structures, and the familiarity of popular Catholic piety with the miraculous and the supernatural.

Among Protestants, liturgical traditions tend to find charismatic renewal less threatening to their identity. Charismatic congregations in denominations emphasizing local autonomy (e.g., the → Baptists) can easily disaffiliate and join independent networks.

The greatest opposition has come from conservative evangelicals fearing charismatic subjectivity as a threat to the objective Word of God. Evangelical-charismatic tension was much reduced in the 1980s, aided by greater charismatic maturity and by the impact of "power evangelism" (preaching of the Word, accompanied by visible signs). The term "third wave" was coined by Peter Wagner of Fuller Seminary to describe those evangelicals who accepted charismatic gifts without any doctrine of second blessing. Since 1994, charismatic renewal has been boosted by the so-called Toronto blessing, a controversial movement accompanied by many revivalistic phenomena (→ Laughing and Crying) that has spread to many countries from the Toronto Airport Christian (formerly Vineyard) Fellowship, though also coming from other leaders and centers.

6. International Structures

The first world-level structure was the International Catholic Charismatic Renewal Office (founded in Rome in 1975), which sponsors regular international conferences. Anglican charismatics have formed SOMA International, with national branches to promote short-term intercultural mission. The only interchurch world structure is the International Charismatic Consultation on World Evangelization (1989), organizer of the Brighton Congress (1991).

Bibliography: A. BITTLINGER, ed., *The Church Is Charismatic* (Geneva, 1981) • L. CHRISTENSON, ed., *Welcome, Holy Spirit* (Minneapolis, 1987) • Y. CONGAR, *I Believe in the Holy Spirit* (vol. 2; New York, 1983) • P. GIFFORD, ed., *New Dimensions in African Christianity* (Nairobi, 1992) • M. HÉBRARD, *Les charismatiques* (Paris, 1991); idem, *Les nouveaux disciples dix ans après* (Paris, 1987) • P. HOCKEN, "Charismatic Movement," *Dictionary of Pentecostal and Charismatic Movements* (ed. S. M. Burgess and G. B. McGee; Grand Rapids, 1988) 130-60; idem, *The Glory and the Shame* (Wheaton, Ill., 1994); idem, *The Strategy of the Spirit?* (Guildford, 1996); idem, *Streams of Renewal* (2d ed.; Exeter, 1997); idem, ed., *Pneuma* 16/2 (1994) • J. N. HORN, *From Rags to Riches* (Pretoria, 1989) • C. E. HUMMEL, *Fire in the Fireplace* (Downers Grove, Ill., 1993) • C. E. JONES, *The Charismatic Movement* (2 vols.; Metuchen, N.J., 1995) • K. MCDONNELL, *Presence, Power, Praise* (3 vols.; Collegeville, Minn., 1980) • K. MCDONNELL and G. MONTAGUE, *Christian Initiation and Baptism in the Holy Spirit* (Collegeville, Minn., 1991) • K. POEWE, ed., *Charismatic Christianity as a Global Culture* (Columbia,

S.C., 1994) • R. Quebedeaux, *The New Charismatics II: How a Christian Renewal Movement Became a Part of the American Religious Mainstream* (San Francisco, 1983) • T. Smail, N. Wright, and A. Walker, *The Love of Power and the Power of Love* (Minneapolis, 1994) • F. Sullivan, *Charisms and Charismatic Renewal* (Ann Arbor, Mich., 1982).

Peter Hocken

Charismatic Religion

1. Features
2. Concept
3. Sources
4. Extensions of the Concept

1. Features
In → religious studies, the phrase "charismatic religion" applies to thousands of religious movements that have the following five features.

1. They arise in times of cultural, economic, or national crisis (→ Crisis Cult).
2. They are founded and directed by → prophets (often women), whose direct mandate from the Supreme Being (by → visions, → dreams, etc.) the adherents recognize.
3. The vision, often symbolically, shows the reason for the crisis and intimates divine help in the renewing of the world under the leadership of the prophet.
4. The vision contains elements of a "higher" religion (e.g., Christianity or → Islam), such as subjection to the one God, a rigorous break with → superstition, repentance (→ Penitence), or monogamy.
5. Only adherents will have a part in the new world; unbelievers and enemies will be destroyed.

2. Concept
The concept of a charismatic religion (→ Charisma) derives from the Christian tradition. Max → Weber (1864-1920) has defined it as a movement with charismatic (as distinct from traditional or rational) leadership. It is also commonly described as messianic (→ Messianism), prophetic, chiliastic (→ Millenarianism), nativist, revivalist, and fanatic. It has also been defined as a movement in which salvation is expected.

3. Sources
Charismatic religions are best known from the → colonial and postcolonial epoch, in which they manifest a reaction to Christian and colonial de-

mands. For example, Simon Kimbangu's Ngunza (prophets) movement (→ Kimbanguist Church), which started in 1921, expected a → golden age after driving out the whites; or the various Melanesian → cargo cults awaited the return of the dead laden with Western goods (cargo), and an ensuing golden age with no whites. In the → Taiping Rebellion in China (1850-64), however, adherents saw themselves after the model of the children of Israel. They took up arms against the Manchu "barbarians" and sought friendship as equals with their "Christian brethren across the sea." Other cults, like the North American Peyote cult (founded in the late 1880s by the American Indian Wovoka, also known as Jack Wilson), have created a new cultic fellowship among estranged → Indian tribes and largely refrain from denunciations of whites.

4. Extensions of the Concept
Ongoing research and further developments have brought two extensions of the concept. First, from the earliest times there have been charismatic movements on the margin of the great religions. In the case of → Taoism, one may see this in the Yellow Turbans (China, 2d cent. A.D.) or the movements led by the descendants of Lao-tzu. Also in China, many movements declared the coming of Buddha Maitreya and with it the end of the old *kalpa* (cycle) and the beginning of the new (e.g., the Eight Trigram uprising of 1815). In → Islam, expectation of the coming of the Mahdi has inspired charismatic movements from the 12th century, some of them in reaction to Western pressure (e.g., the Babi movement, beginning in 1844, from which the → Baha'i religion arose), as well as various charismatic movements in Bengal.

Second, the development of → new religions with the characteristics of charismatic movements in industrialized countries during recent decades (e.g., Soka Gakkai in Japan; the → Unification Church, or Moon movement, in Korea and the United States; → Bhagwan in India and the United States) shows the attractiveness of such movements in times of disorientation and anomie.

Bibliography: J. Bak and G. Benecke, eds., *Religion and Rural Revolt* (Manchester, 1984) • C. Colpe, "Cargo-Kulte," *TRT* 1.240-42; idem, "Krisenkulte," ibid. 3.158-60; idem, "Das Phänomen der nachchristlicher Religion in Mythos und Messianismus," *NZSTh* 9 (1967) 42-87 • S. Fuchs, *Rebellious Prophets: A Study of Messianic Movements in Indian Religions* (Bombay, 1965) • G. Guariglia, *Prophetismus und Heilserwartungs-Bewegungen als völkerkundliches und religionsgeschicht-*

liches Problem (Vienna, 1961) • V. LANTERNARI, *Die religiösen Freiheits- und Heilsbewegungen underdrückter Völker* (Neuwied, 1966) • W. MÜHLMANN, *Chiliasmus und Nativismus* (Berlin, 1961).

RUDOLF G. WAGNER

Charity

Caritas (Eng. "charity"), the Latin equivalent for the NT Greek word *agapē*, denotes Christian → love, which is grouped with → faith and → hope. Caritas is primarily the love of God manifested in Jesus Christ, and then it is love for others. In the popular sense of charity, it denotes the church's organized relief work, which, along with proclamation (teaching) and worship, is an essential function.

→ Relief Organizations

PAUL SCHMIDLE

Chemical Weapons → Weapons

Cherubicon

The cherubicon is an Orthodox liturgical hymn that is sung in the course of the divine → liturgy of John → Chrysostom and Basil the Great. The name refers to the cherubim, who, mentioned throughout the OT (e.g., Gen. 3:24), are a choir of → angelic beings. The cherubicon, which is sung while the offerings are carried from the side table to the altar, goes back to the third century. It was introduced into the liturgy in 574. The symbolic essence is that participants in the liturgy mystically join with the cherubim in singing "Hallelujah" as the apostle John heard it in heaven (Rev. 19:4).

The musical style of the cherubicon has changed considerably in the course of the centuries. On some days in the Christian year (e.g., the Thursday and Saturday of Holy Week, and in the liturgy of the presanctified gifts; Church Year), a special wording replaces the usual text.

Bibliography: A. BAUMSTARK, *Der Cherubimhymnus und seine Parallelen. Eine Gattung frühchristlicher Meßgesänge des Morgenlandes* (Munich, 1911); idem, "Der 'Cherubshymnus' und seine Parallele," *Gottesmime* 6 (1911/12) 10-22 • D. E. CONOMOS, *Byzantine Hymnography and Byzantine Chant* (Brookline, Mass., 1984); idem, *Byzantine Trisagia and Cheroubika of the Fourteenth and Fifteenth Centuries: A Study of Late Byzantine Liturgical Chant* (Thessaloníki, 1974) • H.-J. SCHULZ, *The Byzantine Liturgy: Symbolic Structure and Faith Expression* (New York, 1986) • M. M. SOLOVEY, *The Byzantine Divine Liturgy: History and Commentary* (Washington, D.C., 1970).

ARCHBISHOP LONGIN

Child Labor

1. The Problem
2. The Struggle against Child Labor

1. The Problem

Although child labor usually takes place publicly, a wall of silence typically surrounds it. Parents are mostly silent out of shame that → poverty forces them to exploit their children. Employers are silent out of anxiety lest they lose a cheap and malleable work force. Authorities often close their eyes, even though most countries have enacted legislation against employing juveniles. Finally, the children themselves are silent because often they do not know to whom to turn. These factors make it hard to gain reliable information about the extent of the phenomenon. Also, the definition of child labor varies from country to country, as it does in its usage by the various international organizations.

According to 1996 estimates of the International Labour Organization (ILO), "in the developing countries alone, there are at least 120 million children between the ages of 5 and 14 who are fully at work, and more than twice as many (or about 250 million) if those for whom work is a secondary activity are included. Of these, 61 per cent are found in Asia, 32 per cent in Africa, and 7 per cent in Latin America" (*Child Labour,* 7). The report also mentions the practice of slavery or child bondage in South Asia, Southeast Asia, and West Africa. In addition, it estimates that there are 1 million child prostitutes in Asia, with growing numbers also in Africa.

Even in → industrial societies, child labor is not altogether a thing of the past. In the United States, for example, at least 290,000 children were illegally employed in 1997 (1998 Associated Press report, based on U.S. Department of Labor statistics). Of this number, approximately 130,000 were aged 14 or 15, and 60,000 were younger than 14.

Nevertheless, most of the working children are to be found in the → Third World. Some 20 to 30 million children are part of India's work force. Thus in the cigarette and match factories in Sivakasi (Tamil Nadu), 45,000 of 100,000 workers are under 15. A typical working day for children in the Third World may last as long as 14 hours. Children in Brazil literally have to eat off and on the streets. In Thailand dealers entice children from the villages into → prostitution. In Morocco and Pakistan the rapid growth of the carpet industry is largely due to the busy fingers of children. In various countries children are forced to earn money in agriculture, in housework, or on the streets as shoe cleaners, newspaper sellers, or beggars.

Apart from the fact that children, and often their families, survive through this work, there is hardly anything positive to say about child labor. In fact, it hampers the → development of poor countries. Cheap child labor results in → unemployment and poorer working conditions for adults. Children leave school and their family too soon, before they have had the chance to mature intellectually or psychologically. Daily work makes quasi adults out of them and finally condemns them to unemployment, since they do not have the opportunity to train for a proper job.

Work is also physically and psychologically hard for children. It is heavily mechanized and goes at a fast pace. It often involves handling sharp and dangerous objects and poisonous substances. Workplaces may be very hot and have a great deal of dust and noise. Because of unsafe conditions, lack of experience, fatigue, and the fact that the machines are not made for children, there is typically a high accident rate. Sex discrimination (→ Sexism) is common. Girls are often given the most tedious and exhausting tasks with less regard for their right to education, and they have to endure lower wages and longer working hours.

Children often work in small, unregistered concerns in a market characterized by stiff competition (→ Achievement and Competition), instability, and seasonal fluctuation. The advantages of child labor in these circumstances lie in a cheap working force, the possibility of hiring and firing at will, and the avoidance of unionization.

2. The Struggle against Child Labor

In most countries children under a certain age may not be legally employed, and special rules govern which children may work. The problem is one of enforcement. Inspection is inadequate in most countries, and thus child labor is accepted de facto.

History shows that the fight against child labor is futile if a society does not accept the premise of its cruelty. UNICEF began worldwide action on behalf of street children in 1985. This program aimed at setting a four-hour maximum of work each day with an equivalent number of hours at school. ILO has developed programs for children in formal working sectors and seeks worldwide ratification of conventions forbidding dangerous and extremely exploitative work and demanding a minimum age of 12. Thus far, however, few countries have signed the conventions. The ILO study *(Combatting Child Labour)* presents extensive research findings on child labor in various Third World countries and gives examples of national programs.

UNICEF has the same aims as ILO and seeks UN agreement on an International Convention on the Rights of the Child. Increasingly, other organizations are also fighting against extreme forms of child labor such as prostitution and dangerous and unsanitary work in industry.

→ Childhood; Development 2; Education; Family 1.7; Work; Youth

Bibliography: A. BEQUELLE and J. BOYDEN, eds., *Combatting Child Labour* (Washington, D.C., 1988) • J. BOYDEN and A. HUDSON, *Children, Rights, and Responsibilities* (London, 1985) • *Child Labour — A Briefing Manual* (International Labour Conference, 69th session; Geneva, 1983) • A. FYFE, *All Work and No Play: Child Labor Today* (U.K. Trades Union Congress; London [U.K. Committee for UNICEF], 1985) • ILO, *Annotated Bibliography on Child Labour* (Geneva, 1986); idem, *Child Labour: Targeting the Intolerable* (Geneva, 1996); idem, *The Emerging Response to Child Labour* (Geneva, 1988); idem, *Towards a Global Programme of Action on Child Labour* (Geneva, 1985) • INTERNATIONAL CONFEDERATION OF FREE TRADE UNIONS, *Breaking Down the Wall of Silence: How to Combat Child Labour* (Brussels, 1986) • M. LANSKY, "Child Labour: How the Challenge Is Being Met," *ILR* 136 (1997) 233-57 • G. RODGERS and G. STANDING, eds., *Child Work, Poverty, and Underdevelopment: Issues for Research in Low-Income Countries* (Geneva, 1981) • UNICEF, *The State of the World's Children, 1997* (Oxford, 1997) • U.S. DEPARTMENT OF LABOR, *International Child Labor Problems* (Washington, D.C., 1990) • WORLD HEALTH ORGANIZATION, *Children at Work: Special Health Risks* (Washington, D.C., 1990).

HANS VAN DE VEEN

Childhood

1. Definition
2. Child Development
3. Changing Views of Childhood
4. Socialization

1. Definition

Childhood is usually defined as the first stage in the human life cycle, as the age up to the attainment of puberty. Division is normally made into infancy, early childhood, preschool, and school age. The phase between the onset of puberty and adulthood is called → youth or adolescence. From the standpoint of ages in the life cycle, childhood is the period of the ability and need to learn, of malleability, and of → education. It has thus been the object of varied philosophical and political concerns and the theme of many academic disciplines, including biology, medicine, law, history, and, increasingly, the media and culture.

2. Child Development

Every age of human culture has expressed a concern for the upbringing and education of children. The distinctiveness of childhood as a specific form of humanity has been brought to light, however, only with the development of → pedagogy (i.e., since the 17th cent.). Thus far there is no uniform or generally accepted theory of the process of child development. At the same time, analysis of the macro- and microstructures of the processes of → development and → socialization has progressed to such a degree in the last hundred years, and has undergone such a change in social evaluation, that knowledge of the processes of child development has now become a constituent part of everyday knowledge.

In contrast to the older theories of child development, advanced by W. L. Stern (1871-1938), O. Kroh (1887-1955), A. Busemann (1887-1968), and M. J. Langeveld (1905-89), which view the specific abilities of the child and the phases of its development or maturing primarily in the light of the goal of adulthood, later theories of the development of personality (→ Person) see the interplay of physical, cognitive, emotional, and sociomoral abilities in a far more differentiated way and from the standpoint of the structure of competence in action. The works of S. Freud (1856-1939), G. H. Mead (1863-1931), and their followers contain investigation of the emotional structure and the importance of interaction with parents and the environment, while J. Piaget (1896-1980), L. Kohlberg (1927-87), and their disciples stress the developmental logic of the operative, cognitive, and sociomoral ability to solve problems. E. H. Erikson's (1902-94) theory of phases tries to integrate the inner psychological structure and social experiences into a concept of psychosocial → identity.

3. Changing Views of Childhood

Since the 1960s the history as well as the → anthropology of childhood has been of primary interest. In his work *Centuries of Childhood: A Social History of Family Life*, originally published in 1960, P. Ariès described the new status of adult-child relations in the middle-class → family after the dissolution of the larger family in the 17th and 18th centuries. The new status of childhood created for the child a relative → autonomy on the basis of an emotionalized and individualized attitude of adults to children, but it has brought added discipline and dependence. In his psychohistorical researches, L. de Mause has tried to integrate the change described by Ariès (from prebourgeois to bourgeois childhood) into the whole history of childhood, which is seen as the continuing progress of concern and moral responsibility for children on the part of adults.

Children and childhood change as the social status of adults changes. Ideas of childhood as a world of its own also change. If, as N. Postman sees it, the influence of modern → mass media involves a complete blurring of the life spheres of adults and children, then we can expect to see the extinction of childhood. Sociohistorical investigation of changes in the socioeconomic, spatial, and cultural spheres of modern society (→ Industrial Society) and the associated change in the → everyday life and culture of children seem to indicate, however, that it is overhasty to announce the end of childhood on the basis of analyses of crises in the system and orientation of modern mass society (→ Masses, The).

4. Socialization

The principle that precedence must be given to the nature of the child and his or her needs, because the child can claim a relative autonomy vis-à-vis the demands of society and protection against functional incorporation, is normative now as always for the status of children in modern society. On the basis of comparative studies across cultures, there are clear signs that this status is beginning to establish itself in the so-called developing countries (→ Third World) through extension of the period of education and upbringing. The historical change to the relative autonomy of the child as a leading sociohistorical idea may be seen not least of all in changes in family socialization.

In the dynamics of family socialization one of the most important dimensions — that of religious → socialization — also has a place. The concern of the churches to communicate the Christian → faith to the next generation by religious education should not be restricted to reducing the contents of faith to the level of an elementary child. Religious education as an aid in developing a child's self-awareness and self-worth is not in the first instance a matter of making the child familiar with contents but rather of mediating the experience of being unconditionally wanted and recognized.

→ Aggression; Child Labor; Creativity; Development 3; Father; Love; Men; Play; Trust; Women; Youth Work

Bibliography: P. Ariès, *Centuries of Childhood: A Social History of Family Life* (New York, 1962) • R. Döbert, J. Habermas, and G. Nunner-Winkler, eds., *Entwicklung des Ich* (2d ed.; Königstein, 1980) • D. Elschenbroich, *Kinder werden nicht geboren. Studien zur Entstehung der Kindheit* (2d ed.; Bensheim, 1980) • E. H. Erikson, *Identity and the Life Cycle* (2d ed.; New York, 1980) • H.-J. Fraas, *Glaube und Identität. Grundlegung einer Didaktik religiöser Lernprozesse* (Göttingen, 1983) • B. Hassenstein, *Verhaltensbiologie des Kindes* (Munich, 1973) • J. M. Hawes et al., "Children," *EncBio* 1.350-78 • U. Herrmann et al., *Bibliographie zur Geschichte der Kindheit. Jugend und Familie* (Munich, 1980) • K. Hurrelmann and D. Ulich, eds., *Handbuch der Sozialisationsforschung* (Weinheim, 1980) bibliography • J. Kagan, *The Nature of the Child* (New York, 1984) • L. Kohlberg, *Zur kognitiven Entwicklung des Kindes* (Frankfurt, 1974) • M. J. Langeveld, *Studien zur Anthropologie des Kindes* (Tübingen, 1956) • L. de Mause, ed., *The History of Childhood* (New York, 1974) • N. Mette, *Voraussetzungen christlicher Elementarerziehung. Vorbereitende Studien zu einer Religionspädagogik der Kleinkindalters* (Düsseldorf, 1983) • K. Neumann, ed., *Kindersein. Zur Lebenssituation von Kindern in modernen Gesellschaften* (Göttingen, 1981) bibliography • J. Piaget and B. Inhelder, *The Psychology of the Child* (New York, 1969) • N. Postman, *The Disappearance of Childhood* (New York, 1982) • U. Preuss-Lausitz et al., *Kriegskinder, Konsumkinder, Krisenkinder. Zur Sozialisationsgeschichte seit des 2. Weltkrieg* (Weinheim, 1983) • R. Spitz, *Vom Säugling zum Kleinkinder* (4th ed.; Stuttgart, 1974) • I. Weber-Kellermann, *Die Kindheit. Kleidung und Wohnen. Arbeit und Spiel* (Frankfurt, 1979).

Karl Neumann

Children of God

1. Development and Teaching
2. Organization and Practice
3. Status

"Children of God" is the self-designated name for a youth religion that grew out of the California Jesus People movement under the leadership of David Berg (1911-94, also known as Moses, Mo, Moses David, and Father David). Inspired by the visions of his mother, Virginia Brandt-Berg, a prophetess in the Pentecostal sect Church of the Open Door, radio evangelist Berg founded the Children of God in 1968 along with Revolutionaries for Christ and Teens for Christ.

1. Development and Teaching
As a morally strict, eschatological group of penitents, the Children of God at first found a welcome among established churches. Berg's own daughter Faith began a mission to Germany with a Jesus Festival at Herne in 1971.

Later, however, other churches withdrew their approval because of the Children of God's autonomous organization, its harsh dealings with new converts (including deprogramming, rebaptism, and a "forsake-all" policy), and its increasing substitution of new revelations of the Spirit for the Bible. After 1972 the matter of Berg's revelations became more drastic as he started teaching → prostitution as a means of salvation, a sacrament, and an aid to mission (labeled flirty fishing, or FFing). This development might be regarded as a libertinistic exaggeration of the original Pentecostal assurance of salvation (now taking the form of self-assurance), which no sin can threaten.

2. Organization and Practice
In 1969 fifty "bishops" were ordained at Montreal and other places. In 1978, however, Berg replaced the hierarchy with his own direct dictatorship. In spite of fluctuations, membership has continued to rise (climbing from 50 in 1968, to 4,500 in 1975 and 9,000 in 1994). For prostitution, which is called sexual mission, there are mobile "families of love," that is, two or three adults and children, sometimes in trailers or with "escort service." A tithe of the income goes to headquarters. Every year some 20,000 flirty fishing contacts are recorded. To make first contacts, radio missions (known as Music with a Meaning) now exist in several continents. The group claims to have ceased the practice of flirty fishing in 1987.

3. Status
The Children of God come from a Christian Pentecostalist background. Today, however, they are an independent religion based on new revelation, not unlike a secret society. Berg's writings and the comics depicting him (together called the "Mo-Letters") have canonical status for the Children of God. After Berg's death, his second wife, Maria, became head of the movement.

→ Youth Religions

Chile

Chile

Bibliography: D. B. BERG [Moses David], *The Basic Mo Letters* (Geneva, 1976); idem, *The FF-er's Handbook* (N.p., January 1977) • F.-W. HAACK, *Die neuen Jugendreligionen* (22d ed.; Munich, 1983) • R. HAUTH, *Die Kinder Gottes–Weg und Irrweg einer Jugendsekte* (5th ed.; Munich, 1979) • J. MAXWELL, "COG Founder Berg Dead at 75," *ChrTo*, January 9, 1995, 57 • W. D. PRITCHETT, *The Children of God/Family of Love: An Annotated Bibliography* (New York, 1985) • L. D. STREIKER, *The Cults Are Coming* (Nashville, 1978) • D. E. VAN ZANDT, *Living in the Children of God* (Princeton, 1991) • S. A. WRIGHT, *Leaving Cults: The Dynamics of Defection* (Washington, D.C., 1987).

THOMAS GANDOW

Children's Church Service → Sunday School

Chile

	1960	1980	2000
Population (1,000s):	7,608	11,147	15,211
Annual growth rate (%):	2.39	1.55	1.18

Area: 756,626 sq. km. (292,135 sq. mi.)

A.D. *2000*

Population density: 20/sq. km. (52/sq. mi.)
Births / deaths: 1.82 / 0.57 per 100 population
Fertility rate: 2.35 per woman
Infant mortality rate: 12 per 1,000 live births
Life expectancy: 76.0 years (m: 73.0, f: 79.0)
Religious affiliation (%): Christians 89.0 (Roman Catholics 76.0, indigenous 27.9, marginal 3.3, Protestants 3.0, unaffiliated 1.1, other Christians 0.3), nonreligious 7.2, atheists 2.5, other 1.3.

1. Land
2. History
3. Roman Catholic Church and State to 1973
4. Protestantism
5. Ecumenism
6. Churches after 1973
7. Non-Christian Religions

1. Land

Chile stretches 4,300 km. (2,650 mi.) along the western coast of South America. It is a narrow country, averaging only 176 km. (109 mi.) across, lying between the Pacific and the inland countries, with the Andes Mountains as its eastern border. Approximately 70 percent of the Chileans are mestizo (mixed Spanish and Indian), 20 percent European, 7 percent Amerindian, with the remainder miscellaneous ethnic groups. There is a strong concentration in the cities; Santiago had 5.1 million inhabitants in 1992. Rich in raw materials (e.g., nitrate and copper), Chile is one of the most prosperous countries in Latin America. Yet it is dependent on market prices, and it has an unbalanced, export-oriented economic structure. It thus suffers from chronic → unemployment and shortage of work. The reversal of agrarian reforms and the ending of social programs after 1973 also adversely affected the social situation of the lower classes.

2. History

The Araucas (→ Indians, American) defended their independence against the Incas south of the Bío-bío River. From the middle of the 16th century, they also resisted Spanish invasion (Santiago was founded in 1541; → Colonialism), remaining independent until the 19th century. At first governed from Lima, Chile was under the control of only 60 landowners. It acquired a captain-general of its own in 1778 and became constitutionally independent in 1818. The constitutions of 1833 and 1925 made it a model South American democracy.

It took its present shape toward the end of the 19th century with the subjugation of the Araucas and the conquest of the northern provinces of Antofagasta and Tarapacá (in the so-called Nitrate War of 1879-84). With the British-financed development of nitrate, the present-day economic pattern came into being of foreign dependence and a relatively strong middle class with an apparatus of government financed by profit sharing and more vigorous → consumption that trade made possible.

In the middle of the 20th century an increasingly urgent demand arose for economic and social reform. The Democracia Cristiana, inspired by Catholic social teaching (→ Social Ethics 3), attempted a Christian "third way" between → conservatism and → socialism under the presidency of Eduardo Frei (1964-70). The government of the socialist Unidad Popular followed with Salvador Allende as president (1970-73), often identified as the world's first freely elected Marxist head of state. A military coup overthrew Allende in 1973, with help from the United States. It left unanswered the question whether the reforms begun under the two governments would have succeeded.

The military rulers, led by General Augusto Pinochet, assumed wide-ranging powers and imposed strict economic and political controls. In a plebiscite in 1988, the people rejected Pinochet's bid to become president. The current democratically elected government is seeking to resolve the deep divisions and social inequities that plague Chilean society.

3. Roman Catholic Church and State to 1973

The history of the → Roman Catholic Church in Chile corresponds in its double character to its history in the rest of Latin America (→ Colonialism and Mission). As the church of the Spanish colonialists, which followed hard on the conquest (the bishopric of Santiago was founded in 1559), it justified the attack on the Araucas and their enslavement. Yet as the church of mission, it also tried to win the original inhabitants by the work of the → orders and to protect them against infringements. Missionary work is now done competitively by the Capuchins and Protestant missions (e.g., the Misión Araucana of the English South American Missionary Society).

With independence in 1818, the Roman Catholic Church had to reconstitute itself. The constitution of 1833 recognized it as the only legitimate state church. In the 19th century, however, it gradually relinquished its legal privileges and its monopoly of education and religion. The law of 1865 allowed people of other faiths to practice their religion privately and to establish their own schools (→ Education 4). Later the first evangelical societies received state recognition. From 1875 the English congregation to Valparaiso had legal status, from 1877 the Église de l'Union, from 1886 the German Evangelical congregation in Santiago, and so forth. The state recognized the first Pentecostal church in 1929. Finally, the constitution of 1925 separated church and state, with article 100 guaranteeing the free exercise of any religion (→ Religious Liberty). The constitution did not eliminate inequalities. The Roman Catholic Church still had the status of a public legal corporation and could regulate its legal relations under a special arrangement. In contrast, the Protestant churches were private societies subject to civil law.

The Roman Catholic Church had political influence from the 19th century through the conservative National Party of landowners and entrepreneurs. But the social aspect of Christian teaching gained strength, and the churches extended their work to include educational, medical, and welfare services. Their social teaching developed slowly from pure paternalism and eventually sought more active participation of the poorest classes. The new social involvement showed itself in support for the social legislation of 1925, and it took shape in the Democracia Cristiana, which was formed by politicians from the circles of → Catholic Action. This party attempted to modernize Chilean society by the humanizing of socioeconomic structures without challenging the dependent → capitalism. The Roman Catholic Church offered another sign of this involvement, which was based on a comprehensive concern for inner reform in view of widespread alienation from the church, by handing over church lands to landless farm workers in 1962.

The failure of Frei's Christian Democratic government led to internal disruption. Many Roman Catholics supported the socialist reforms of the Unidad Popular of Allende. (The first meeting of the Latin American → Christians for Socialism took place in Santiago in 1972.) But others viewed the Marxist program of the Unidad Popular with great skepticism and welcomed the military coup of 1973.

4. Protestantism

The first Protestant congregations in Chile in the 19th century, consisting of foreigners and European immigrants, met with stiff opposition from the Roman Catholic Church. Eventually, however, the liberalizing of the state's religious policies made European and North American missions possible. The result was the rise of the national or Creole Pentecostal churches, which developed out of Methodist congregations. Their spread shows that Protestantism has made an impact on the masses. Proclamation is done by proletarian groups that view themselves as members of a national church.

Protestantism expanded in three phases. During the first phase (essentially one of immigration), the so-called historical churches appeared: Anglican (from 1830), Lutheran (1846), and Presbyterian (1872; → Reformed and Presbyterian Churches). The second phase brought the so-called younger churches with pronounced missionary goals: Methodists (1877), the Mission Église du Seigneur (1913), Seventh-day Adventists (about 1890), and Baptists and → Salvation Army (1909).

The third phase saw the rise of the Pentecostal churches, emerging especially out of the younger churches. In 1990 the largest Pentcostal groups were the Iglesia Metodista Pentecostal (from 1910, with 720,000 affiliated in 1990), the Iglesia Pentecostal de Chile (1942, with 570,000 in 1990), and the Iglesia Evangélica Pentecostal (1932, with 400,000 in 1990). In 1990 perhaps 25 percent of the population were Protestants or indigenous Christians. The numbers increased strongly from 1970 to 1973, stagnated from 1974 to 1979, and took another leap upward after 1980. Such facts support the theory that the number of Protestants rises in times of serious political and economic crises.

5. Ecumenism

Not until just before World War II were attempts made to create ecumenical bodies, including the Concilio Evangélico de Chile, to which the Methodists, Baptists, Presbyterians, and some Pentecostals belong — in all, some 42 churches with approximately 42,000 members. This council was meant at first to promote missionary campaigns, but after 1958 it took on political and economic significance by distributing American agricultural surpluses through World Church Services. Other church unions were founded for economic, political, and other reasons, including El Nuevo Consejo Evangélico Nacional, El Consejo Evangélico Independiente, and El Consejo Chileno de Iglesias Evangélicas Fundamentalistas. Later the Confederación Única de Iglesias Evangélicas de Chile came into being, with 50 churches and some 20,000 members, as well as the Associación de Iglesias Evangélicas de Chile, an ecumenical organization comprising some eight important historical church groupings.

The membership of the Fraternidad Ecuménica de Chile includes Roman Catholics, some Pentecostals, the Anglicans, Methodists, some Baptists, and the Salvation Army. The → Orthodox Church has about 25,000 members in Chile.

6. Churches after 1973

In 1973 a decisive phase began of bitter theological and political debate in the churches and between various Christian movements regarding the role of the churches and Christians in society. Many Protestant church leaders were at first won over with the courting of the minority churches by the Pinochet regime. They signed a declaration of solidarity favoring the junta in December 1974 and sang a Te Deum in honor of Pinochet (who was present) in the "cathedral" of the Iglesia Metodista Pentecostal.

The most serious conflict concerning the role of the churches under the military regime came in the Evangelical Lutheran Church in Chile (ELKC). Its membership included many of the landowning middle and upper classes, as well as many upper-class and lower-middle-class industrialists, whose interests had been challenged by the socialist-oriented measures of the Allende government. When, therefore, Provost Helmut Frenz defended → human rights against the systematic attacks of the military government, he ran into heavy criticism from an important part of the membership, which saw in the new regime the savior of landed interests. The political and theological conflict led to a split in the ELKC and to the expulsion of Frenz at the instigation of the regime.

After the coup the Roman Catholic and Protestant churches formed ecumenical organizations to aid the poor, the oppressed, and the persecuted. A National Council of Cooperation for Peace formed in 1973 brought together some Protestants, the Roman Catholics, the Orthodox, the Jews, and others and played a decisive role in the defense of human rights. Under persistent pressure from the government, the Roman Catholic Church accepted the council's dissolution in 1975 but founded at the same time a vicariate for solidarity that carried on much of the work of the dissolved committee. Other ecumenical organizations help → minorities, the unemployed, debarred students, persecuted intellectuals, and others in conscientiously discharging the church's social task.

7. Non-Christian Religions

Significant non-Christian religions in Chile are the Indian → tribal religions (some 180,000 Araucas, Aymaras, Quechuas, and other animist groups) and → Judaism, with an estimated 0.2 percent of the population in the year 2000. Others include → Baha'i, → Islam, → Buddhism, the Moon movement (→ Unification Church), and → Krishna. Apart from the Jewish synagogues, these groups have no positive relations with the Christian churches.

Bibliography: Adveniat Dokumente-Projekte 12, *Evangelium, Politik, Sozialismus* (Essen, 1972) • F. Araneda Bravo, *Breve historia de la iglesia en Chile* (Santiago, 1968) • D. Barrett, ed., *WCE* 226-30 • R. J. Hunt, *Among the Araucarians of Southern Chile* (London [South American Missionary Society], 1930) • J. B. Kessler, *A Study of the Older Protestant Missions and Churches in Peru and Chile* (Goes, 1967) • *Kirche in Chile* (Aschaffenburg, 1976) • G. U. Kliewer, *Das neue Volk der Pfingstler* (Bern, 1975) • C. Lalive d'Epinay, *Haven of the Masses* (London, 1969) • A. Noggler, "Chile," *Lateinamerika: Gesellschaft–Kirche–Theologie* (vol. 1; ed. H. J. Prien; Göttingen, 1981) 220-72; idem, *Vierhundert Jahre Araukanermission* (Schöneck, 1973) • D. Nohlen, "Chile," *Handbuch der Dritten Welt,* vol. 2, *Südamerika* (3d ed.; Hamburg, 1992) 177-218 • H.-J. Prien, *Die Geschichte des Christentums in Lateinamerika* (Göttingen, 1978) • S. Silva, *Glaube und Politik. Herausforderung Lateinamerikas. Von der christlichen inspirierten Partei zur Theologie der Befreiung* (Bern, 1973) • B. H. Smith, *Church and Politics in Chile* (Princeton, 1981) • W. Weischet, *Chile. Seine länderkundliche Individualität und Struktur* (Darmstadt, 1970) • E. Willems, *Followers of the New Faith: Protestantism and Cultural Change in Brazil and Chile* (Nashville, 1967); idem, "Religiöser Pluralismus und Klassenstruktur in Brasilien und Chile," *IJRS* 1 (1965).

Antonio Faundez

Chiliasm → Millenarianism

China

	1960	1980	2000
Population (1,000s):	649,948	986,526	1,260,751
Annual growth rate (%):	2.07	1.38	0.70

Area: 9,572,900 sq. km. (3,696,100 sq. mi.)

A.D. *2000*

Population density: 132/sq. km. (341/sq. mi.)
Births / deaths: 1.43 / 0.72 per 100 population
Fertility rate: 1.80 per woman
Infant mortality rate: 32 per 1,000 live births
Life expectancy: 71.0 years (m: 69.2, f: 73.0)
Religious affiliation (%): nonreligious 42.7, Chinese folk religionists 28.3, Buddhists 8.4, atheists 7.8, Christians 7.0 (indigenous 6.3, other Christians 0.7), tribal religionists 4.3, Muslims 1.5.

1. The Churches in China

The first verifiable presence of Christianity in China came via Nestorian missionaries, who entered China from the Middle East in the mid-7th century. Their work effectively ended by the 9th century, although traces of Nestorianism survived until the 14th. The first Western missionary was John of Monte Corvino (1247-1328), a Franciscan, whose efforts were nullified by the advent of the Ming dynasty in 1368. Between 1552 and the mid-1800s, the Jesuits, and later also other orders, sent missionaries to China. Although they collectively aided in China's gaining of Western scientific learning, they left no permanent Christian presence.

The arrival of Christian missionaries in the 19th century occurred in the context of China's increasing humiliation before the Western powers, who progressively forced their way into the country's interior. Through the vicissitudes of the Opium Wars, the turn-of-the-century political and cultural disintegration, the period of the republic under Sun Yat-sen

(1866-1925), the occupation of the Japanese during World War II, and the takeover of the Communists, the church managed to achieve modest growth, in 1949 claiming approximately 1 percent of the population (3.3 million Catholics and 1.8 million Protestants). The prominent status achieved by some Christians, as well as the modern educational and welfare institutions begun by missionaries (esp. Protestants), attracted some of the Chinese elite, thus magnifying the influence of the Christians beyond what their numbers alone might have indicated.

1.1. Protestant Churches

During the period of open missionary work in the early 20th century, Protestant groups often succeeded in overcoming confessional distinctions among themselves. For example, in 1912 four independent Anglican churches formed the Holy Catholic Church of China; 20 missionary groups of the Lutheran Church, mostly from the United States, formed the Lutheran Church of China in 1917; the Church of Christ in China united Presbyterians, English → Baptists, the Canadian United Church, the United Brethren in Christ (→ Brethren Churches), and a Methodist denomination (→ Methodist Churches); and three English and four American Methodist missions were united by home reunions. The → China Inland Mission, which operated in outlying areas and had 86,000 members in 1949, and the → YMCA, the → YWCA, and various theological seminaries enjoyed interdenominational support.

1.2. National and Independent Churches

As a protest against administrative, financial, and spiritual control of the churches from abroad, national churches arose in China. The Jesus Church (1917) stressed the direct experience of faith, literal exposition of the Bible, faith → healing, and signs (→ Glossolalia). In 1949 it had over 100,000 members, some outside China. The Christian Meeting Place, or Little Flock movement, with 70,000 members and 700 churches in 1949, rejected → ordination and church → organization in favor of lay → evangelization. The Jesus Family, with 141 families and 6,000 members in 1949, adopted → ecstatic forms of religious expression from a Methodist community. Its members lived in communal-type "families," with sharing of goods (→ Community of Goods) and autocratic leadership.

The largest expression of national churches is the current house church movement, discussed in section 3 below.

1.3. Roman Catholic Church

In its 20th-century missions to China, the → Roman Catholic Church concentrated particularly on rural areas, where there were several self-contained Roman Catholic villages.

The conflict over foreign control of the Chinese churches went back to the 19th century (→ Taiping Rebellion). The founding of national churches and the accusation that Christianity was a foreign religion favored efforts to make the church's leadership indigenous or Chinese. In 1949 there were approximately 2,700 Chinese priests and 3,100 foreign priests.

Beginning in 1949, Communist persecution of Catholic personnel and institutions was particularly systematic. Over 5,000 foreign missionaries were expelled, and all Chinese religious, clergy, and hierarchy were arrested, imprisoned, or otherwise harassed. Nearly 4,000 Catholic schools were closed, plus hundreds of hospitals, dispensaries, and orphanages.

2. Churches and Political Development

The attitude of the churches to the revolution of 1949 was not uniform. Some churches, along with groups like the YMCA and YWCA, followed the → Social Gospel, with its stress on the social responsibility of the church. Such groups could more easily support the program of the Communist regime. Churches with state-church traditions inclined toward cooperation, while fundamentalist groups and the Roman Catholic Church opposed the new government, sometimes openly. In contrast to the Buddhist and Muslim religions (→ Islam), which had long since been indigenous to China, the Christian churches had to defend themselves against the charge of being simply outposts of Western imperialism. Beginning in 1950, the Korean War meant the cut-off of all foreign monies to Chinese churches, which led to a financial crisis in many churches.

The Communists sought to bring the Christian church under their complete control through their Three-Self Patriotic Movement (TSPM), whereby churches were to cut all ties with the West, demonstrated through their becoming completely self-supporting, self-governing, and self-propagating. In the widespread nationalism or patriotism of the period, Protestant churches themselves often took more radical efforts to make themselves indigenous. After discussions with Jou Enlai, they also published the *Christian Manifesto* in 1950. Its author was the Social Gospel champion Y. T. Wu, secretary of the YMCA, who linked the development of the church to that of society. On his view, the Roman Catholic Church belonged to → feudalism and the Protestant Church to capitalism, both of which needed significant reform for the purposes of → socialism. The manifesto

described the contribution of the missions as not unworthy, but it accepted the charge that they were tied to imperialism. By 1953 some 400,000 Protestants had signed it.

The TSPM became formally organized as the official church organ and worked together with the Bureau for Religious Affairs. It supported a harsh campaign against "counterrevolutionaries" who were using the cloak of religion. This campaign resulted in long prison sentences for some prominent Protestants. Criticism of the three-self movement in China came especially from fundamentalists. The same was true abroad. English and German church leaders accepted the need for some flexibility, but American Protestants spoke of betrayal.

The exodus of Roman Catholic missionaries was largely complete by 1951. After 1950 there were three-self efforts in individual congregations, although in general the Catholic Church resisted becoming part of the TSPM. The bishops who remained issued a manifesto of their own in 1951. This document affirmed the patriotic attitude of Roman Catholics but charged the three-self movement with being incompatible with Roman Catholic principles. The 1954 encyclical *Ad Sinarum gentes* confirmed this position. The imprisonment of some dignitaries, the cooperative attitude of others (e.g., Bishops Li Wei-guang of Nanjing and Alfonse Zhang of Beijing), and finally the more liberal attitude of the government after 1957 led to the founding of the National Catholic Patriotic Association (CPA) as a church independent of the Vatican. By the end of 1961, the government was firmly in control of the organized Christian church in China — of the Protestants through the TSPM, and of the Catholics through the CPA.

But there was still considerable resistance. The campaign against the right in 1958 led to attacks on leading Protestants, and the almost military regulation of life during the Great Leap Forward (1958-60) emptied the churches. In Beijing total church attendance sank to below 500. The denominations joined forces to keep 65 churches open and to maintain their work. Elsewhere there were similar efforts at unity among evangelical churches and organizations (→ Evangelical Movement).

3. The Present Situation

3.1. *New Developments in Church-State Relations*

The situation became less tense in the following years, and contacts with the outside world were restored. Yet the position of the churches does not yet seem to have been consolidated. During the Cultural

Revolution (1966-76) all churches were closed. The house church, a traditional form of Chinese Christianity, quickly became the most important and widespread form of church life and piety. In Nanjing, for example, there soon were 25 such groups, and 30,000 copies of a home-teaching program for → lay preachers were in circulation. In Roman Catholic villages the laity assumed the spiritual leadership.

With the beginning of more open cultural policies and greater exposure to other countries in 1979, the Bureau for Religious Affairs reopened. Leaders of the three-self movement who had been sent to the countryside for retraining came back to the cities, as did also their critics. The Cultural Revolution had left behind a younger generation for whom Communist ideals were often simply a means whereby to justify political repression, factional strife, and self-seeking. Even within the Communist youth movement, the revolution had raised penetrating questions about the meaning of life.

The result was a rapid requickening of what had been thought to be an almost completely dead Chinese Christianity. Between 15,000 and 20,000 Protestants a week came into the reopened churches in Shanghai. In 1981 some 3,000 people took part in a → pilgrimage to the Church of St. Maria in Sheshan, near Shanghai. The Bureau of Religious Affairs estimated the number of Roman Catholics and Protestants to be over three million in 1982. Older and very young people were in the majority. A survey in Hangchow showed that of 1,500 who went to church, only 500 had been baptized before the Cultural Revolution. Theological seminaries were reopened. The financing of the churches came from receipts from former church property.

Along with the two patriotic three-self organizations, more purely religious bodies were formed in 1980 with the China Christian Council under Bishop Ding and the Catholic Council of Bishops in China. The constitution of 1982 laid down the conditions of → religious liberty, expressly forbidding the use of pressure either for or against any confession of faith. The same section also dealt with counterrevolutionary activity under the guise of religion.

3.2. *Ecclesiastical and Theological Developments*
The particular conditions in China did not allow the production of any rich theological writing. Worship in all the churches follows the pre-1949 model (in Roman Catholic churches, it is in Latin). Protestant theologians from China speak of a postdenominational epoch in which common experiences have overcome ancient divisions.

In theological orientation the Social Gospel model is still influential, but China is in a postrevolutionary situation, and a theology of liberation (→ Liberation Theology) is less relevant for this environment than a theology of reconciliation after the long years of conflict. The cosmic Christ is the crown of all → creation, in whom all people, including atheists, have a share. In Chinese Roman Catholic theology the emphasis is on the founding of an independent Chinese church on the model of earlier communities. (The bishops and cardinals that are elected in China itself are not recognized by the Holy See.)

Nothing is known of any dialogue between Chinese Christians and → Marxists (→ Marxism and Christianity). Among other great religions, Buddhism in the Lamaist form is predominant in Tibet and in the Mahayana form among the Han people of China, while Islam is common especially among the minority peoples in the Northwest. In 1993 there were an estimated 71 million Buddhists and 28 million Muslims in China.

A sharper persecution of Christian movements outside the three-self movement soon followed the restoration of official church institutions. Many Roman Catholics loyal to the Vatican, including two bishops, were imprisoned, and strict measures were taken against nonecclesiastical fundamentalist groups. An internal party document of 1983 demanded that Protestants support four basic principles: (1) Marxism, Leninism, and the ideas of Mao Zedong; (2) the democratic dictatorship of the people; (3) party leadership; and (4) socialism. It also demanded self-commitment and forbade worship outside official services as well as preaching by unauthorized evangelists (→ Evangelization). Possibly this document was directed less against the house churches of Protestant Christians than against the "Shouting Group," a → revival movement initiated by Witness Lee, later of Los Angeles. Nevertheless, some local party officials used it as an occasion to initiate proceedings against house churches as illegal assemblies, even though official writings had given them a positive evaluation.

Although accurate figures of the current number of Chinese claiming membership in a Christian group are not available, fairly conservative estimates in 1990 showed 60-70 million Christians (or approximately 6 percent of the estimated 1990 population of 1.155 billion people). The Christians were divided roughly into 47 million affiliated with unofficial house churches, 11 million with TSPM churches, 5 million Catholics loyal to Rome, and 4 million Catholics belonging to CPA churches.

→ Asian Theology

Bibliography: R. C. BUSH, *Religion in Communist China* (Nashville, 1970) • J. CHAO, ed., *The China Mission Handbook: A Portrait of China and Its Church* (Hong Kong, 1989) • J. K. FAIRBANK, *China: A New History* (Cambridge, Mass., 1992); idem, *The Great Chinese Revolution, 1800-1985* (London, 1987) • F. P. JONES, *The Church in Communist China* (New York, 1962); idem, ed., *Documents of the Three-Self Movement* (New York, 1963) • F. M. KAPLAN and J. M. SABIN, *Encyclopedia of China Today* (3d ed.; London, 1982) • R. P. KRAMERS, "China," *TRE* 7.747-60 (bibliography) • G. MALMQUIST, "Die Religionen Chinas," *HRG* 3.1-68 • G. N. PATTERSON, *Christianity in Communist China* (Waco, Tex., 1969) • PONTIFICAL URBAN UNIVERSITY, CENTER FOR CHINESE STUDIES, *China Bulletin* (1979-) • J. L. SCHERER, ed., *China: Facts and Figures Annual* (vol. 5; Gulf Breeze, Fla., 1982) • K. H. TING et al., *Chinese Christians Speak Out* (Beijing, 1984).

RUDOLF G. WAGNER

China Inland Mission

1. Background
2. Origins
3. Development
4. Characteristics

1. Background

Until 1842 the Chinese Empire resisted all European penetration. The Anglo-Chinese War (1839-42) opened five "treaty ports," where missions quickly established residence (→ Colonialism and Mission). By 1860 Western powers had secured more ports, European rights of travel, and certain concessions to religious toleration and foreign protection of missionaries (→ Mission).

By this period, the missionary movement was accepted by the main Protestant churches. Most missionary societies were organized on a national and denominational basis and worked in several fields; → missionaries were normally ordained ministers. Financing missionaries was becoming difficult when the opening of China created new demands.

2. Origins

The Chinese Evangelization Society (CES) began in response. James Hudson Taylor (1832-1905), English CES missionary, had adopted the teachings of George Müller, English pastor and orphanage founder, on specific prayer and complete trust in God for material needs. By contrast, CES was continually in debt. Taylor resigned and practiced faith principles as an independent missionary. In 1860 his health collapsed, and he returned to Britain.

No mission responded to his concern for China's unevangelized provinces, so in 1865 Taylor founded the China Inland Mission (CIM) to reach the entire Chinese Empire. It embodied "faith principles" (→ Faith Missions): no debts, no public appeals for funds, no stated salaries, and reliance on God through → prayer for all needs.

3. Development

Taylor's first target — 24 workers with their financial support, two for each missionless province and for Mongolia — was achieved within a year. Later targets, including 70 workers in 1881 and 100 in 1886, were also reached. By 1895, CIM had 641 missionaries, or 40 percent of all Protestant missionaries in China. Expansion brought conflict with Chinese officials; Western officials also complained, feeling responsible for enforcing treaty protection, which CIM did not seek. More CIM missionaries died in the anti-Western Boxer Rebellion (1900) than did those of any other mission. In 1929, despite economic depression, CIM called for 200 new missionaries. Withdrawal before the Japanese and Communist advances was slow.

CIM missionaries left China between 1950 and 1953 and began work elsewhere in Asia. In 1965 the name of the organization was changed to Overseas Missionary Fellowship (OMF), recognizing that the mission now included Asian missionaries working outside their own countries. In 1990 OMF was working in over 20 countries, including Thailand, the Philippines, Japan, Taiwan, Indonesia, Singapore, and the United States.

4. Characteristics

CIM strictly subordinated medical and other institutional work to evangelism and avoided the involvement in higher education characteristic of missions in the Chinese revolutionary era. It sought missionary identification with Chinese life (Chinese dress was usual in Taylor's lifetime) but did not stress church planting or indigenous ministry. It repudiated foreign protection and declined indemnities for the Boxer attacks. Opposition to British-led opium traffic was its only openly political concern.

The CIM was interdenominational. Missionaries of one church background were grouped together, so that some work belonged to Anglican dioceses, while others reflected Presbyterian or Baptist polity. CIM recruited internationally, from Europe, North America, and Australasia, and it gave sectors of its work to associated missions such as the Liebenzeller Mission

(→ German Missions) and the Scandinavian Alliance Mission (→ Scandinavian Missions). The director (Taylor and his successors) was based in China, not Europe. No single national church was ever formed.

CIM accepted women, whether wives of missionaries or not, as missionaries in their own right. It accepted candidates with less education and training than older missions required, but it demanded proven competence in Chinese. An enthusiastic home constituency was served by skillfully directed publications. CIM inspired many other "faith missions," though few followed it completely.

→ British Missions

Bibliography: A. J. BROOMHALL, *Hudson Taylor and China's Open Century* (7 vols.; London, 1981-89) • J. H. KANE, "The Legacy of J. Hudson Taylor," *IBMR* 8/2 (1984) 74-78 • K. S. LATOURETTE, *A History of Christian Missions in China* (New York, 1929) • L. T. LYALL, *A Passion for the Impossible* (2d ed.; London, 1976) • J. C. POLLOCK, *Hudson Taylor und Maria* (Giessen, 1966) • J. H. TAYLOR, *China: Its Spiritual Need and Claims* (3d ed.; London, 1890); idem, *A Retrospect* (London, 1875).

ANDREW F. WALLS

Choir

The Greek word *choros* meant the place where a round dance was danced, the round dance itself, or the group that danced it. For a group of singers Latin adapted the loanword *chorus* for use in → worship, and the group then gave its name to its place in the church. Both in the church and in secular settings, groups from ancient times have come together to make music on a higher level than that of the general public.

In the earliest days of Christianity the choir had something of the function of the chorus in ancient drama, taking part in the action as representatives of the people and commentators on what was happening. The heavenly worship that the seer witnessed in Revelation, which one might regard as a projection of the earthly worship of his day, is characterized essentially by choral songs (chaps. 4, 5, 14, 19) that represent the → acclamations of the → congregation. On a Christian view, the choir leads the congregation and is commissioned by it.

With the gradual reduction of the role of the congregation in both the Eastern and the Western Rites, the choir finally assumed all its functions. The → Roman Catholic Church ended this false development only with Vatican II, although the function of the congregation had already been restored with the revival of the Easter Vigil in 1951. The Reformation churches tended to neglect the significance of the choir with their emphasis on congregational singing. To a great extent, the choir lost its liturgical function, becoming a mere luxury at great festivals.

Paul's order that women should keep silence in the church (1 Cor. 14:34) was never applied to congregational singing but only to choirs. On this ground choirs were mostly made up of men and boys up to the 18th century. School choirs and city choral societies also excluded women. J. Mattheson in 1716 was a pioneer in letting women sing in church at Hamburg. Only hesitantly did Protestant and later Roman Catholic choirs follow his example.

In England, college and cathedral choirs set the essential choral pattern from the time of Henry VIII. In the 18th century G. F. Handel (1685-1759) brought the → oratorio — a form that came from Italy — to full flower. Whereas → Orthodox churches sing unaccompanied, not allowing instrumental music, the Western churches have been more open in this regard. Instrumental support has been the rule since the rise of part singing in the 17th century. The choir may participate in three ways: singing antiphonally with the congregation, adding an introductory piece, or taking over parts of the → liturgy from the celebrant or the congregation.

→ Church Music; Gregorian Chant

Bibliography: W. BLANKENBURG, "Chor," *MGG* 2.1230-65 (bibliography); idem, "Der mehrstimmige Gesang und die konzertierende Musik im evangelischen Gottesdienst," *Leit.* 4.661-718 • P. ENSRUD, "Choir," *ELC* 1.399-401 • M. PIERIK, *The Song of the Church* (New York, 1947) • E. A. WIENANDT, *Choral Music of the Church* (New York, 1965).

CHRISTOPH ALBRECHT

Choir Stalls

Choir stalls are seats in cathedrals or monastery chapels that are reserved for participants in choral worship (→ Hours, Canonical). They are usually arranged lengthwise in the choir in two rows. Their arrangement reflects the monastic rule and the hierarchical principle of the separation of priests and people. The rows of seats, with sidewalls, are either open or separated. On the underside the seats have supports (*misericordia*) to lean on when standing. From the Romanesque period (→ Middle Ages 1), the backs (*dorsalia*), canopies, *misericordia*, armrests, and sides were richly and often imaginatively decorated.

Bibliography: "Choir Stalls," *Oxford Companion to Christian Art and Architecture* (ed. P. Murray and L. Murray; New York, 1996) 101-2 • H. SACHS, *Chorgestühl* (Leipzig, 1964) • H. SCHINDLER, *Chorgestühle* (Munich, 1983) • C. TRACY, *English Gothic Choir-Stalls, 1200-1400* (Woodbridge, Suffolk, 1987).

PETER MASER

Chrism → Anointing

Christadelphians

Christadelphians (meaning "Christ's brothers," with allusion to Heb. 2:11) are fellowships that claim to have kept the early Christian faith in its original and unfalsified form (→ Primitive Christian Community). They arose from the teachings of John Thomas (1805-71), a doctor who emigrated from England to the United States and who originally joined Thomas Campbell and his son, Alexander (→ Christian Church [Disciples of Christ]; Churches of Christ). In studying Scripture, Thomas concluded that there were profound differences between the Bible and the traditional doctrines and confessions of the church. He separated himself from his former friends and in 1844 began spreading his discoveries in America and Europe, especially through his monthly newspaper *Herald of the Future Age.*

Christadelphian doctrine, which claims to be fully biblically based (→ Biblicism), begins with its belief that the original gospel was falsified when it moved out of the OT Jewish world into the world of Hellenic culture (→ Hellenism 3). It stresses the continuity of the OT Jewish tradition, even to the point of making a sevenfold lampstand its central liturgical symbol. For Christadelphians, the doctrine of the → Trinity is an illegitimate Hellenizing and a loss of Christian authenticity. They likewise reject the → immortality of the → soul, → hell as a place of eternal torment, and the personality of Satan (→ Devil). → Jesus is the promised Messiah, born of the Virgin → Mary, but he is not preexistent (→ Christological Titles; Messianism). Those who confess faith in his name are baptized by immersion (→ Baptism). A central doctrine is expectation of the coming kingdom of the Messiah, namely, that Jesus on his physical return will establish a 1,000-year earthly kingdom, reigning from → Jerusalem (→ Millenarianism). A further doctrinal conviction, over which there is continuing controversy among Christadelphians, is that at the end of the millennium all those who have died — believers and unbelievers — will be resurrected to judgment, at which time God will clothe his own with immortality and repay the godless with annihilation.

Christadelphian → devotion centers on daily Bible study and weekly meetings. Members take no part in elections, military service, political office, or political life generally. Christadelphian churches, called ecclesias, are congregationalist, with no pastor or central organization.

In 1995 there were an estimated 50,000 Christadelphians worldwide. They are in mostly small congregations in about 100 cities in North America, in 80 cities in Australia, and in more than 30 other countries, especially Latin America and Africa. England is the main European center, with relatively large numbers also in Germany.

→ Adventists; Free Church; Fundamentalism; Unitarians

Bibliography: "Christadelphians," *EAR* nos. 842, 855 • K. HUTTEN, *Seher, Grübler, Enthusiasten* (12th ed.; Stuttgart, 1982) • C. H. LIPPY, *The Christadelphians in North America* (Lewiston, N.Y., 1989) • F. S. MEAD and S. S. HILL, *Handbook of Denominations in the United States* (10th ed.; Nashville, 1995) 91-92 • H. TENNANT, *The Christadelphians: What They Believe and Preach* (Birmingham, 1986).

REINHARD HEMPELMANN

Christengemeinschaft → Christian Community, The

Christian and Missionary Alliance

1. Origin and Aims
2. Extent and Size
3. Beliefs

1. Origin and Aims

The Christian and Missionary Alliance (C&MA) was organized in 1887 as an interdenominational deeper-life and missionary movement (→ Mission). The founder was Dr. A. B. Simpson, a Presbyterian minister from New York City. He was an eloquent and persuasive preacher whose ministry, books, and periodicals rapidly gained for the C&MA an international reputation. Simpson was also an innovator. In 1882 he launched the first illustrated missionary magazine and the first Bible institute in North America. *The Alliance Witness* and Nyack College have had an unbroken history since that time. In 1884 Simpson inaugurated the missionary convention, as well as the "faith-promise pledge" for raising missionary funds.

2. Extent and Size

Within five years of the society's founding, over 300 Alliance missionaries had entered 12 countries. Besides the more than 50 countries it now serves, it has worked in 15 others. Its missionaries planted the first churches in the provinces of Hunan and Kwangsi, China. In Palestine, they constructed the first American church in Jerusalem. They started the first gospel churches in Viet Nam and Cambodia. In Venezuela and Ecuador, they dedicated the first Protestant chapels. In 1990 the Alliance had over 1,100 active → missionaries, with work carried on in over 200 languages and dialects on every continent. Because of the indigenous church policy adopted in 1927, all national churches are self-governing and self-supporting. Some of the national church organizations — notably those in Japan, Hong Kong, Thailand, India, the Philippines, and Argentina — have sent and are supporting their own missionaries to other countries.

3. Beliefs

Theologically the Alliance stands firmly upon the essentials of evangelical faith (→ Evangelical Movement). It is unswervingly loyal to the authority and inerrancy of the Holy Scriptures (→ Inspiration; Exegesis, Biblical). It particularly emphasizes the role of the Holy Spirit in holiness of life and power for service. Over the years, C&MA has gradually evolved from an interdenominational agency into a → denomination, yet its particular and special purpose remains the same.

Worldwide, considerable emphasis is given to the publication and distribution of Christian literature. In 1993 in its overseas outreach, the Alliance sponsored 70 Bible correspondence courses, 365 weekly radio programs in 47 languages, and 59 Bible colleges and theological seminaries.

In 1993 there were almost 1,950 Alliance churches in North America, with approximately 300,000 members. Overseas there were approximately 15,000 churches, with a total of 2.1 million members.

Bibliography: R. B. EKVALL, After Fifty Years (1939) published by Christian Publications, Camp Hill, Pa. • J. H. HUNTER, Beside All Waters (1964) • Missionary Atlas (1964) • R. L. NIKLAUS, All for Jesus (1986) fullest coverage; idem, To All Peoples (1988) • S. J. STOESZ, Understanding My Church (1983) • A. E. THOMPSON, Life of A. B. Simpson (1920) • A. W. TOZER, Wingspread (1943).

Other works: Alliance Life (1882-) • H. E. DOWDY, The Bamboo Cross (New York, 1964) • R. T. HITT, Cannibal Valley (New York, 1962).

LOUIS L. KING

Christian Art

1. Early Christianity
2. Byzantium
3. The Early Medieval West
4. The Romanesque and Gothic
5. The Renaissance
6. The Protestant and Catholic Reformations
7. The Baroque and Rococo
8. The Enlightenment and Neoclassicism
9. The New World
10. Nineteenth Century
11. Twentieth Century
12. Contemporary

The phrase "Christian art" may encompass any of the following: art (for the purposes of this article, inclusive of architecture) produced by Christians, art produced for Christians, or art with themes or uses that may be identified as Christian. Different historical periods saw various combinations of the above. In the earliest centuries of Christianity, art was produced for Christians but not necessarily by Christians or on distinctly Christian themes (which had not yet appeared); in the → Middle Ages all three characteristics were true, and in contemporary art Christian themes are often used symbolically or associatively in works for secular display by artists who claim not to be religious. Between the third and the 18th centuries, most art was Christian in all three senses of the word.

1. Early Christianity

In the two centuries after the death of Christ, Christianity developed a complex theology, rites of → initiation and celebration, and advanced systems of administration, → communication, and → pastoral care. Christian writers and thinkers produced profound and sophisticated apologias, → hymns, homilies, and → dialogues. It is therefore all the more striking that almost nothing has survived from those 200 years that may be securely identified as Christian art. Scholarly explanations for this absence have included the adherence of early Christians, many of whom were Hellenized Jews, to the Mosaic proscription against the making of images (Exod. 20:4); a sense of impermanence because of a present hope in the Second Coming (→ Parousia); and a romanticized view that Christians were constantly subject to persecution in all parts of the empire and could not risk an open display of faith.

Archaeological, documentary, and visual evidence, however, suggests that Christians of the first two centuries did commission art, including architecture, but much has been destroyed, and what has survived may not be recognized as Christian because it is indistinguishable from the art of its larger → culture, from which the converts freely adapted, a practice recommended by the theologian Clement of Alexandria (ca. 150–ca. 215) in his advice as to what → symbols a Christian might chose for a signet ring. Many of the symbols scratched on first- and second-century Christian ossuaries unearthed in Israel — crosses, ships, plows, stars, trees, and serpents — had a significance to religions far more ancient than Christianity; perhaps only the fish (Gk. *ichthys,* used as an acronym for "Jesus Christ, Son of God, Savior") and the Chi-Rho (from the first two letters of "Christ" in Greek) are indisputably Christian. Even early visual references to Christ are borrowed. He appears in the guise and with the attributes of Orpheus, Apollo, Dionysus, Sol Invictus (the Invincible Sun), and the ubiquitous Good Shepherd (→ Images of Christ), the last image dating back thousands of years in Mediterranean culture.

Although some Roman → catacombs or aboveground tombs may have been decorated with Christian themes in the first half of the third century, the oldest extant monument that may be securely dated is in an eastern outpost of the empire, Dura-Europos on the Euphrates: a house adapted for Christian worship around 240 (→ House Church), including a → baptistery painted with imagery drawn from the Old and New Testaments; it includes the earliest known images of Christ's miracles (the wall paintings are in the Yale University Art Gallery, New Haven). A coeval house-synagogue in the same section of Dura is even more lavishly (and skillfully) painted with OT narratives, figures, and symbols; this and the discovery of figural mosaic floors in early → synagogues in Israel, Jordan, and Syria suggest that, despite scriptural prohibitions, Jews outside Jerusalem were accustomed to use visual imagery and may have influenced their Christian neighbors, many of whom had been raised as Jews.

In the Roman catacombs, walls and ceilings of the niches and chambers of wealthier families were painted in the later third century with images of the Good Shepherd, commemorative banquets known as *refrigeria* (a continuation of a pagan custom), and a large repertory of OT figures in peril, such as Jonah, Noah, and Daniel, narratives prominent in both Jewish and Christian writings as examples of divine

→ salvation. These figures are often *orans* (lit. "praying"), with hands raised in an ancient pose of adoration. Early depictions of Christ focus on significant actions rather than a recognizable physiognomy, especially his → baptism and → miracles (as miracle worker, he is often depicted with a magician's wand). The marble sarcophagi of the well-to-do depicted many of the same themes, the story of Jonah being particularly popular, not just because of the → typology of Jonah's three days in the whale (which Christ likened to his own death in Matt. 12:40), but because the cast-up Jonah could be depicted as a classical nude adapted from a pagan favorite, the sleeping Endymion. The style of this funerary art fits into the Roman mainstream — especially a sketchy, "impressionistic" technique and the compartmentalization of wall surfaces — but it is usually not of the first quality.

Christians originally met for worship in houses and later gathered in larger adapted structures such as covered markets (possibly San Crisogono, Rome, early 4th cent.). There is documentary evidence that in the Eastern empire, where → conversion (§§1-2) was more widespread and → persecution less frequent, there were buildings openly erected for Christian worship.

In less than 70 years Christianity went from a persecuted cult to the official religion of the empire. Though this change began with Emperor Galerius's edict of toleration in 311, the pivotal episode was the conversion of his successor, Constantine, after a miraculously inspired victory in 312 over Maxentius, his coemperor in the West. Not surprisingly, as Christians were freed from the threat of persecution, themes of peril gradually disappeared from funerary art, to be replaced by representations of Christ's power and grandeur. The central panels of the sarcophagus of the prefect Junius Bassus, from 359 (Vatican Grottoes, Rome), depict Christ's triumphal entry into Jerusalem and his enthronement upon the universe. The quality of Christian art also improved with the importance and wealth of Christian patrons.

The most profound impact of the new status of Christianity was on architecture. Christians again borrowed, in this case, the secular → basilica (lit. "hall of the king"), which had served the Greek and Roman world for purposes as varied as social gatherings and legal proceedings. With a long central nave flanked by single or double aisles, and with the → altar set in a curved apse that would have contained the statue of the emperor, the basilica was ideal for the large crowds of new converts and the increasingly elaborate processional liturgies based on imperial ceremonial; the earliest built was San Giovanni in

Laterano, → Rome, on property given to the bishop of Rome by Constantine in 313.

Another type of building adapted for Christian use was a round structure derived from tombs of ancient rulers and heroes, now fittingly used to commemorate the site of the → martyrdom or burial of a → saint. A variant of this form was the octagonal baptistery, inspired by both temples and public baths, and often equipped with a hydraulic system similar to those in the baths. A striking conflation of the central-plan and basilican structures is San Lorenzo Maggiore in Milan (ca. 370), which greatly influenced later architecture in Italy and possibly Constantinople.

The floors of these vast buildings were often paved with stone mosaics in figural or decorative patterns, and the wall surfaces were frequently sheathed with marble at the lower level and covered above with glass mosaics, such as the depiction of Christ enthroned among the apostles in the apse of Santa Pudenziana, Rome (ca. 390). Christ's appropriation of the attributes and powers of the pagan gods in this and other depictions may indicate a deployment of imagery against the → Arian heresy, which disputed the full divinity of the Son.

Most of the early Western images of Christ depict him as a long-haired, clean-shaven young man, probably a reference to the eternally youthful pagan gods, but the gradual influx of MSS from the East, especially Syria, introduced the bearded, middle-aged Christ who was to become universally familiar. The first known monumental cycle of the life and → passion of Christ was commissioned by an Arian, the Ostrogoth king Theodoric, as a series of mosaics in the Church of Sant'Apollinare Nuovo (494-526), Ravenna, a Byzantine outpost on the eastern Italian coast. In these mosaics, as in fourth-century "Passion" sarcophagi, Christ dominates the other figures and is never shown in situations involving humiliation or suffering; even in the earliest extant depiction of the Crucifixion, an ivory plaque from approximately 400 from northern Italy (British Museum, London), Christ is fully awake and in no discomfort. Painted images of the Crucifixion, first in Syria and then in Rome, show him dressed in a sleeveless purple *colobium*, the garment of an Eastern aristocrat.

The extant art of early Christian North Africa, although for the most part less sophisticated (the fabled glories of Christian → Alexandria not having survived), includes striking Coptic (Egyptian) figural textiles and the so-called Fayumic portraits, exquisite painted likenesses in the tradition of Roman realism bound into mummy wrappings. King Ezana of Ethiopia was converted to Christianity not long after Constantine, but because of the wholesale destruction of Ethiopian art and architecture by Islamic invaders, most of the remaining monuments date no earlier than the 10th and 11th centuries. They include the remarkable churches of Lalibela, a reconstruction of the sites of the Holy Land, carved from the living rock, and vibrant murals and altarpieces that transform motifs from European art with great → iconographic originality, such as the Covenant of Mercy, a pact between Christ and his much-venerated mother.

2. Byzantium

When Constantine in 324-25 moved the capital of the empire eastward to the small town of → Byzantium, renamed Constantinople, he initiated a massive campaign of building there and, under the supervision of his mother, Helena, at hallowed sites in the Holy Land, most notably the Church of the Holy Sepulcher in Jerusalem (328-36), a large complex of a basilica linked to a round martyrium, enclosing the traditional sites of both Golgotha and Jesus' tomb. Although sculpture had become rare in the Christian empire, probably because of a concern over idolatry, mosaic decoration flourished for centuries, as did painting with encaustic on wood panels of images of Christ, the Virgin Mary, and the saints. These → icons (lit. "images") were understood to be derived directly or indirectly from likenesses of the originals miraculously made or inspired during their lifetime or shortly thereafter; thus icon painters changed the types of faces and narratives as little as possible over the centuries. Veneration was given not to the images but, through the images, to the originals; their strict frontality promoted contact with the viewer, while their rigid posture and golden surroundings reminded observers of their dignity and otherworldly nature.

Many of Constantine's churches were replaced by those of his sixth-century successor Justinian, whose greatest architectural achievement was the Church of the Holy Wisdom (Hagia Sophia) in Constantinople (532-37), designed by a mathematician and an engineer and melding the basilica and round church into a huge, light-filled space whose dome seems to float high above the floor. The exuberant mosaic decoration of Justinian's day can best be seen in Ravenna, especially in the Church of San Vitale, where Justinian and his empress, Theodora, are depicted as they bring their gifts to the altar (ca. 547). Byzantine artists also produced a dazzling variety of luxury objects in ivory, precious metals, jewels, and enamels for liturgical, ceremonial, and personal use, some featuring scenes from pagan → mythology.

Several forms of Christianity declared heretical by the bishop of Rome and the patriarch of Constantinople continued to flourish in the East (→ Heresies and Schisms), especially among the armies of the empire, until the heretics outnumbered the orthodox. Even many of the short-lived imperial dynasties held heretical views. In several of these systems it was blasphemous to represent Christ because it was beyond human ability to perceive and depict his all-encompassing divinity. For a while the factions lived in an uneasy balance, but in 726 the iconophobes gained sufficient power to initiate the so-called Iconoclastic Controversy, which, except for a short period of restoration of images (780-815), lasted until 843. Icons were destroyed, mosaics and mural paintings were whitewashed, and some who refused to cease venerating or creating icons were put to death. Only the isolation of monasteries like St. Catherine's on the → Sinai Peninsula saved early icons, such as the extraordinary sixth-century Sinai Christ.

The next centuries saw ambitious programs of church and monastic architecture not just in the capital but throughout the Eastern empire, especially Greece, Sicily, the Balkans, and finally Russia, which converted to Christianity in approximately 990. In the decoration of these churches a uniform hierarchy is evident. Christ and attendant angels are in the highest architectural zones, proceeding downward through the Virgin, the apostles, scenes from the life of Christ, and finally lesser saints on the lowest registers of the walls. A final flourishing of Byzantine culture for several centuries before the fall of Constantinople (1453) saw in art a new humanity, a display of emotion, and a more naturalistic depiction of figures in space, such as is demonstrated in the Constantinopolitan Church of St. Savior in Chora (Kariye Camii, early 14th cent.). These trends were continued and developed by the icon painters of the Balkans and Russia, culminating in the art of the early 15th-century monk Andrey Rublyov, in graceful images evocative of great tenderness.

3. The Early Medieval West

Although the spirituality and discipline of the monastic → communities of Ireland and Scotland were inspired by Eastern → ascetics, their art was a blend of many sources, including the spiral and interlace patterns and animal art of the Illyrians, Celts, and successive Germanic tribes, the color and form of Roman glass and "barbarian" enamel, the content of Byzantine MSS, and their own iconographic originality. These diverse elements were combined in illuminated MSS, carved stones, and precious metal in which a mastery of technique and love of color, material, and calligraphic line all but overwhelm the content. In the distinctive gospel books, such as the Book of Kells, possibly produced on Iona (ca. 800; Trinity College, Dublin), although the illuminators included images of Christ and the Virgin, the greatest attention was devoted to dense ornamental fantasies and depictions of the Evangelists or their symbols, whom the Celtic peoples revered as the bards of Christianity. This Hiberno-Saxon culture was crucial for the history of Christian Europe. As Celtic monks like Columbanus traveled to reconvert the ravaged regions of Europe, they brought with them their art and their love of learning to reestablish a Christian culture at centers such as Luxeuil, Bobbio, and St. Gall.

European tribes gradually ceased their peripatetic existence. The Franks, having defeated the Moors in 732, established a vast kingdom including much of western Europe, achieving a stability in which the arts could flourish. Their king, Charlemagne, crowned emperor by the → pope in 800, saw himself as both the successor to Constantine and the rival of the emperor in Constantinople. His advocacy of education and patronage of the arts reflected his grand designs, and his octagonal palace chapel at Aachen (792-805) was deliberately patterned after earlier imperial structures in the Byzantine world. In the many scriptoria founded in his empire, illuminators copied earlier MSS brought from Italy and Byzantium, depicting toga-clad Evangelists in classical landscapes. There were important developments in the arts, including the emergence of regional styles, such as the distinctive linear energy of the school of Reims (the Ebbo Gospels, 816-35; Bibliothèque Municipale, Épernay) and the development of an influential monastic "master plan" in the annotated scheme for the rebuilding of St. Gall (ca. 820).

The influence of imperial patronage was noticeable, particularly in the prevalent image of Christ. MSS and relief sculpture depicted him enthroned, crowned, and surrounded by a "court" of evangelists, prophets, and → angels. In the art produced under the Ottonian successors to the Carolingian emperors, however, the untouchable imperial Christ began to lose ground to imagery that spoke to the larger population. Evolving perhaps from folk art, and increasingly reflected in → devotional literature, were images of the suffering Savior, a tormented and twisting or bloated and dead life-sized figure of Christ on the → cross, such as the crucifix of Archbishop Gero of Cologne (969-76; Cathedral, Cologne). Other works presented a more human interaction of figures, as on the bronze doors of St. Michael's in Hildesheim (ca.

1015), commissioned by Bishop Bernward, who was greatly influenced by the art of Roman antiquity. The churches themselves were beautifully proportioned — the exterior a complicated massing of blocks and towers (often featuring apses at both the east and west ends), the interiors white or gray with accents in colored stone or painted decoration on a flat wooden ceiling.

4. The Romanesque and Gothic

The architecture of the later 11th and 12th centuries was labeled Romanesque in the 19th century because it was considered a debased re-creation of that of ancient Rome, which it resembled primarily in scale and the use of the arch and vault. Much of the art and architecture was inspired or motivated by a new movement of peoples, this time on → pilgrimage and → crusade. While people had always traveled to the Holy Land, the pilgrimage gained in popularity after its introduction by Celtic monks in the seventh century as a → penitential practice. When Jerusalem became inaccessible, many Europeans set out for Compostela in northwestern Spain, legendary site of the tomb of St. → James the Great (in Spanish, Santiago). → Monasteries situated along the routes, especially in France, expanded to care for the travelers, and large monastic churches rose to house holy → relics, whose presence guaranteed lucrative offerings. The churches, basilican in plan, evolved a more complex system of aisles and ambulatories so that crowds could visit various altar-shrines without disturbing the → Mass in the → choir area. Wide expanses of walls and ceilings were decorated with fresco cycles, and architectural elements were carved with biblical and symbolic scenes, natural motifs, and fabulous monsters. The tympana of the three western portals were often carved, the central being → apocalyptic in nature, such as the *Last Judgment* at Autun (1130-35) and the *Commissioning of the Apostles* at Vézelay (1120-32). Flattened, elongated figures, distorted by a spiritual energy, snake down pilasters and around column capitals. In the monastic churches of large → orders, such as the → Benedictines of → Cluny (Cluny III, 1095-1130), the elaborate liturgical life of the community required more subsidiary altars and side chapels, increasing the spatial complexity of the interiors and the massing of exterior forms.

The booty brought back from the Crusades inspired European artisans to produce magnificent reliquaries and liturgical objects of precious metals and jewels and illuminated MSS of decorative splendor. There were critics of this wealth and magnificence, chief among them → Bernard of Clairvaux, who in 1127 denounced the waste of vast sums that might have been spent on the poor, declaring images in church and cloister a hindrance to contemplation of the divine. The opposing view was embodied by Abbot Suger, who saw in the contemplation of the rich and the precious a path to God. In enlarging the choir of the Carolingian basilica of Saint-Denis just outside Paris, the traditional burial place of French monarchs, Suger's masons incorporated in 1140-44 a more complex system of vaulting previously developed in sites as varied as Sant' Ambrogio in Milan (10th-12th centuries), Speyer Cathedral in Germany (1082-1106), and Durham Cathedral in England (1093-1130), in what is regarded as the first example of "Gothic" architecture, a label conferred later by those who believed it an outlandish, "barbarian" style. In a structural system of great sophistication using complex ratios and symbolic numbers, the enormous weight of stone roofs and towers could be distributed into patterns of stress channeled into columns and piers; churches rose to a greater height, more complex spaces were vaulted, and expanses of wall, no longer load-bearing, could be punctured by large windows. The colored and painted glass inserted in these openings and the exterior sculpture, which expanded to encrust entire facades, presented a rich iconography of biblical and historical narrative. The medieval → Scholastics saw the complexity of Gothic → cathedrals as an embodiment of their rational system of → philosophy and → theology and, at the same time, as the echo on earth of the heavenly Jerusalem.

During this time artists traveled throughout Europe following building opportunities, and thus styles and techniques were transmitted throughout the continent. Each region developed its own variation on the Gothic style: Italian churches were wider and lower, English more rectangular, German simpler in massing of internal spaces and external forms. A change in direction was also evident. Even as illuminators and glass painters emphasized two-dimensional ornamental patterns, sculptors began to employ a more naturalistic, three-dimensional style reminiscent of ancient sculpture, as in the Visitation group (1225-45) on the west portal of Reims Cathedral.

Painting in medieval Italy was still very much in the Byzantine style of rigid figures rendered as flattened decorative surfaces. This period saw the birth of the altarpiece. As priests turned their backs on the congregation to obscure the mystery of transubstantiation (promulgated in 1215), the frontal was moved behind and above the altar, where it increased in size and complexity, as in Duccio's double-sided *Maestà* (1308-11) in the Cathedral of Siena.

The early 14th century felt the stirring of an interest in antiquity. The Pisani family from southern Italy carved a series of marble pulpits in Tuscany influenced by ancient Roman sarcophagi, and Giotto painted frescoes of figures with weight and presence, seen in natural and expressive postures, reflecting the more popular → spirituality preached by the mendicant orders and an interest in religious drama from which some of his themes seem to be taken (Arena Chapel, Padua, 1305-6). Although Sienese artists such as Duccio and Simone Martini preferred a more linear surface elegance, they too began to depict saints as human beings in naturalistic settings engaged in the minutia of everyday life. This trend was checked, however, by the outbreak of bubonic plague in 1348-50 and subsequent natural disasters, which were responsible for the death of leading artists and convinced the depleted population of Europe that God had struck them down for pride and presumption. Art reflected this conclusion by a return to more conservative, antinaturalistic styles and traditional subjects, with a concentration on penitential themes.

5. The Renaissance

The establishment in northern Europe in the 14th and 15th centuries of lay communities devoted to a life of humility and simplicity, such as the Brothers and Sisters of the Common Life, fostered an atmosphere in which the everyday was sanctified by its dedication to the service of God and humanity. This attitude made possible the work of the Flemish painters of the 15th century, in which the archangel Gabriel could appear to the Virgin Mary in a cozy Flemish parlor full of the accoutrements of a middle-class home (the *Merode Triptych,* by Robert Campin, 1425-30; The Cloisters, New York). Each ordinary object, however, was an example of "disguised symbolism"; a vase of lilies referred to the Virgin's purity, a glass of water to her intact virginity. The artists' perfection of the oil technique enabled the use of translucent glazes, which suggested depth where before there had been only surface, and could reproduce the effects of natural and supernatural light, long regarded as the most divine of all natural phenomena. Many works contained striking likenesses (rare in medieval art) of their self-contained commissioners, who showed no shyness at being introduced to the Virgin and Child by their patron saints. Novel depictions of ancient themes appeared, such as the image of the Virgin kneeling in adoration of her newborn child, from a vision (ca. 1370) of St. Bridget of Sweden. This representation of the Nativity was transmitted throughout Europe in a matter of years, thanks to peripatetic artists, the beginnings of art collecting, and the production of woodcuts and block books, which traveled easily and were accessible to a wider segment of the population.

A similar interest in naturalism and attitude of self-assurance appeared among the painters of Italy (who eventually adopted the oil technique for themselves, while continuing to work in the far less flexible mediums of fresco and tempera). The age of → humanism, however, in which "man was the measure of all things," is mistakenly seen as a secular culture. Religious subjects still dominated, the church was still the primary commissioner of art and architecture, and the new interest in the classical past inspired similar themes that referred, albeit subtly, to Christian iconography (such as allusions to the Virgin Mary in Sandro Botticelli's *Birth of Venus,* ca. 1481; Uffizi, Florence) or illustrated exemplary morality. While → Renaissance scholars praised human achievement and Renaissance artists reveled in the beauty of the human form, all acknowledged that humanity was created in the image of God and that to seek to express human perfection in art was to praise the Creator.

Also seen as reflective of the mind of God were the structural and mathematical systems, such as symbolic ratios, geometry, and one-point and aerial perspective, that began to invade and govern the world of the artist and architect. Churches, basilican or round, were designed in spatial modules based on human proportions whose ratios were carefully calculated; the circular form of a church or chapel was seen as an embodiment of divine perfection and eternity (although these buildings served primarily a commemorative rather than parochial function because of the liturgical complications of a centrally placed altar). Architects and sculptors measured Roman remains, and painters marveled at newly excavated wall paintings and pored over ancient descriptions of lost Greek masterpieces. Inspired by a conviction that the ancients had possessed the secret of perfect form and proportion, "experts" wrote treatises on the theory and practice of every aspect of art, defining the ideals and setting down rules. Raphael, who followed the rules, was considered to have reached perfection itself. Still, all this re-creation of antiquity was channeled primarily into the production of religious art and architecture. Clerics regarded painting and sculpture as valuable didactic tools, commissioning works that conveyed specific messages (such as the paean to papal authority on the walls of the Sistine Chapel, 1482) or supplied the population with images of their indispensable → patron saints as exemplars of → piety and good conduct.

Thanks to a system of apprentices and journeymen, a single workshop could turn out paintings, sculpture, architectural designs, decorated furniture, metalwork, and even textiles. Invention and adaptation played an equal role. Bramante's first plan (1506) for the new St. Peter's in Rome is nearly identical to architectural sketches by Leonardo da Vinci, who was working in Milan at the same time, and both resemble the fourth-century Milanese church of San Lorenzo. Artists also rose in stature from servile artisans to sought-after professionals. The work and personality of Michelangelo, the first truly independent artistic spirit, influenced artists in the second quarter of the 16th century, when political chaos, eccentricity, and boredom with Raphael and the "rules" were channeled into a style later called Mannerism, which prized artifice, elegance, and erudition. In the paintings and sculpture of Bronzino, Pontormo, Rosso Fiorentino, Gianbologna, and Cellini, elongated figures strain and twist, forms and shapes shift and confuse, colors are not of the natural world, and many themes that seem religious are otherwise unidentifiable. This Mannerist tradition formed the mature style of the later 16th-century Cretan icon painter Domenikos Theotokopoulos, known by his adopted country of Spain as El Greco, whose first contact with Italian art had been the large, light- and color-filled religious canvases of Venetian Renaissance painters such as Titian and Tintoretto, commissioned by the wealthy confraternities of that city.

6. The Protestant and Catholic Reformations

The themes of → suffering and compassion were still very much present in German art. On the eve of the → Reformation, Mathias Grünewald painted a multipaneled altarpiece (1510-15; Musée Unterlinden, Colmar) for the monastery of St. Anthony Abbot at Isenheim, in which the agonized figure of the crucified Christ was afflicted with the same disfiguring disease as the patients cared for by the monks. The Reformation itself had an enormous impact on the arts in German-speaking lands. Many of the Protestant leaders were iconoclastic, and artists and architects, deprived of patronage, either changed professions or, like Hans Holbein the Younger, emigrated. Ulrich → Zwingli in Zurich, besides banning religious art, supervised teams who closed medieval churches and, in a few days' time, opened them to reveal a whitewashed interior from which all statues, images, and figurative stained glass had been removed. Zwingli himself operated not out of a hatred of art but out of too great a love for it — he found it distracted him from → worship. Martin →

Luther, in contrast, acknowledged the value of religious art as a didactic tool and opposed those who would "cleanse" churches in a destructive manner. His close friend Lucas Cranach the Elder and the latter's son Lucas the Younger were the only artists who attempted to capture Protestant doctrine in visual imagery, painting scenes of → grace freely given, such as Christ with children and with the woman taken in adultery. Albrecht Dürer, who worked for both Catholic and Protestant patrons, sympathized with Luther, produced prints that illustrated the ideas of → Erasmus and other Christian humanists, and attempted in his late works, such as the *Four Apostles* (1523; Pinakothek, Munich), to create a Protestant art that would rival the "old art" in monumentality, but no artists of stature followed his lead.

There is evidence that John → Calvin was initially of Luther's mind — that images might be left in churches as long as their function was didactic — but he soon changed his view, probably not so much because of the danger of idolatry as because of the people's tendency toward intercessory prayer directed to or through the images in an attempt to alter circumstances that Calvin believed already determined. Although he subsequently banned images and discouraged the building of churches as useless good works, he, like both Luther and Zwingli, was against the violent destruction of images and the vandalism of religious buildings.

Calvin's followers were extremely iconoclastic, and their influence may be seen in the severe, undecorated churches of 17th-century Holland, Switzerland, England, Scotland, and the Huguenot territories of France, where the primary objects were the clarity of the Word and the visibility of its preacher. Indeed, architecture in the early Reformation consisted of adaptation rather than innovation. Once "cleansed" of imagery, the interiors of churches were reorganized to eliminate elevated or distinct areas restricted to the clergy; the people sat on four sides of the → pulpit, which, symbolizing the → Word of God, was most prominent. The only other fixed furniture might be a simple Communion table, and the only image acceptable to those who allowed images at all was the Last Supper. The only notes of color were coats of arms and painted organ shutters. Even when imported elements of the Italian and French Renaissance and baroque were later absorbed into English architecture by Inigo Jones, Christopher Wren, and their followers, they were used more as applied decoration than as structural determinants, resulting in the elegant, restrained style still perceived as Protestant.

In Catholic countries the reforms resulted in, if anything, a greater attention to art and architecture. The Council of → Trent (1545-63) saw the value of art as a means to inspire devotion and recommitment to the → Roman Catholic Church, as long as the authorities could control the content. Avoidance of titillating forms and subjects was demanded; strict adherence to scriptural passages was required. The Venetian Veronese, for example, was called before the → Inquisition for including dwarves, animals, and Germans in a huge painting of the Last Supper (now titled *Christ in the House of Levi,* 1573; Accademia, Venice). The art produced in this period was, ironically, extremely sensual, as saints of both sexes, often almost nude, writhed in luminescent scenes of → ecstasy or grisly scenes of martyrdom, a feature that could be justified by the call of → Ignatius Loyola to involve all the senses in acts of devotion. Decorative complexes combining painting, sculpture, and architecture, such as Bernini's *Ecstasy of St. Theresa* (1645-52; Santa Maria della Vittoria, Rome), resulted in a sort of carefully calculated religious theater. At the other extreme, the devout if profligate Caravaggio painted the humble people of Rome as saints and sinners in canvases full of deeply internalized spirituality, dramatic in their own way for the abrupt contrasts of light and shadow.

The basilica was still the dominant architectural form, but now, richly decorated with gilding, stucco, and illusionistic ceiling paintings that seemed to explode into heaven itself, the architecture was only one element in a multimedia liturgical experience, in which sight lines and acoustics were much improved. Some architects like Borromini experimented in smaller churches with ovals and interlocking spatial forms; these spaces were fashioned primarily not for liturgies but for the adoration of the Sacrament or the veneration of relics.

7. The Baroque and Rococo

In Spain, which had retained its medieval spirituality, artists such as Francisco de Zurbarán and Diego Velázquez painted stark, realistic canvases of saints lost in devotion, commissioned by the powerful religious orders, while sculptors carved life-sized polychromed figures or elaborate retables whose intricacy mirrored the sculptural incrustation of church facades. In Catholic Flanders, which was under Spanish control, the huge religious canvases of Peter Paul Rubens, such as those for the Cathedral of Antwerp (early 17th cent.), pulse with life and color, as figures tumble over one another, although he preferred historical → allegories that could display his erudition. The younger Anthony van Dyck, working in Italy and England, settled into a more somber style in which religious themes were rendered with tenderness and deep feeling. Italian decorative painters of the later 17th and 18th centuries, such as Giovanni Battista Tiepolo, migrated into Catholic Bavaria and Austria and inspired the extraordinary rococo churches in which painting, sculpture, and architecture lose their separate identities and flow into a riotous, light-filled ensemble.

The other half of the Netherlands, Protestant Holland, rebelled and declared its separation from Spanish control in 1581. Although Dutch churches were stark and undecorated, religious themes were still acceptable to private patrons as a variant of the much-esteemed category of history painting. As the wealthy middle class grew (→ Bourgeois, Bourgeoisie), so did the demand for pictures for the home, resulting in "specialty" painting, primarily secular in content; there is evidence, however, that still lifes, landscapes, interiors, and genre scenes were intended to warn of worldly vanity and the evanescence of earthly delights. A few artists painted religious subjects, often stylistically and thematically influenced by Caravaggio's work, transmitted to Holland through the artists of Catholic Utrecht. Rembrandt, whose religious themes were a matter of personal choice, went from a flashy, Rubensian style as a young man to the introspection and psychological insight of his late paintings and prints, such as the *Return of the Prodigal Son* (ca. 1665; Hermitage Museum, St. Petersburg).

France, a Catholic country many of whose artists and artisans were Protestants, produced an art unlike that of other cultures. An intellectual fascination with antiquity led many of its artists to present mythological and historical themes as a golden age of moral perfection (Nicolas Poussin) or idyllic beauty (Claude Lorrain). Poussin, painting Christian themes as well, developed strict principles for the suitability of compositional elements, resulting in canvases whose appeal is (and was meant to be) primarily cerebral and paving the way for the strict codification of the art academies of 18th-century Europe. As the aristocratic patrons of art became less interested in morality and intellectual pursuits, religious imagery was largely abandoned for themes of earthly love and frivolity in the enchanting works of François Boucher, Clodion, Jean-Honoré Fragonard, and Antoine Watteau. The → Revolution, whose proponents perceived the church as part of the oppressive ruling class, fostered a virulent anticlericalism, and religious themes all but disappeared, to be replaced by an advocacy of secular morality in the depiction of ancient and contemporary history, as in the works of Jacques-Louis David.

8. The Enlightenment and Neoclassicism

The → Enlightenment of the late 17th and 18th centuries finally accomplished the → secularization of Europe. Science, philosophy, and a new passion for antiquity dominated cultural pursuits; the clerical establishment was no longer the primary patron of art and architecture. As religion became a personal rather than cultural concern, so did religious themes in art become a personal choice of patron or sometimes even of artist. It was almost impossible to install figural stained glass in Protestant churches, and programs of public religious decoration were rare, one of the few being Benjamin West's Chapel of Revealed Religion (begun 1780) for George III, an effort to foster a renaissance of religious art. The commission was never installed because of the king's worsening health, and the paintings were dispersed. But religious themes had become so ingrained that artists representing secular subjects often fell back upon traditional depictions, especially scenes that had come to stand as a clearly recognized paradigm for profound emotion. In West's *Death of General Wolfe* (1770; National Gallery of Canada, Ottawa) and the prison death scene from William Hogarth's *The Rake's Progress* (ca. 1734; Soane Museum, London), each artist borrowed for his central group the image of lamentation over the dead Christ.

→ Church architecture was more in demand than religious themes in painting and sculpture. As a result of the Great Fire of London in 1666, Christopher Wren rebuilt St. Paul's Cathedral (1675-1710) and more than 50 city parish churches. But in this cathedral, as in many other Continental churches, the forms of dome and portico and the very articulation of wall surfaces were borrowed from classical temples (presaging an outburst of eclectic revival styles in 19th-cent. Europe and America), and Wren's parish churches were singled out more for the architectural accomplishment of their ingenious accommodation to odd-shaped urban lots and the inventiveness of their plans than for any religious sensibility.

9. The New World

In the Americas, Christian art and architecture reflected the customs of immigrating groups modified in form and material by indigenous art and accommodation to new climates and circumstances. Spanish and Portuguese communities in what would become the West Indies, Florida, the southwestern United States, and Central and South America built adobe mission churches, usually long, aisleless halls, whose white walls were often decorated with exuberant mural paintings and elaborate carved and gilded altars, sometimes brought from "civilization," more often executed by native artists. → Missions in Central and South America adapted huge walled temple precincts, furnishing them with a series of covered altars for processional liturgies and outdoor Masses, inspired by the older rites of the native populations.

→ Puritan English settlers of New England, in a deliberate rejection of the architecture of the → Anglican Church that had persecuted them, built meetinghouses of a high order of craftsmanship, the exteriors of which were identical to domestic architecture. Fixed pews, the lack of a central aisle, and an elevated pulpit demonstrated the primacy of God's Word and a rejection of ceremony. Anglicans in the Virginia Tidewater, Catholics in Maryland, and Dutch, German, and French settlers in New York, northern New England, and Canada built small churches like the village parishes of their native countries. Except for paintings and sculptures of indifferent quality brought by the Marylanders, there was almost nothing in the way of visual imagery. Dutch settlers were permitted to have paintings in their homes of the scenes from their illustrated Bibles, while the → Moravians had a number of fairly accomplished artists, such as John Valentine Haidt, who, true to German tradition, depicted harrowing scenes of Christ's Passion. Until the 19th century, accomplished North American artists, such as West and John Singleton Copley, who wished to depict religious themes, left for Europe, where they usually remained for their entire careers.

Bibliography: General works: J. Cook, "Sources for the Study of Christianity and the Arts," *Art, Creativity, and the Sacred* (ed. D. Apostolos-Cappadona; new ed.; New York, 1995) • Jane Dillenberger, *Style and Content in Christian Art* (New York, 1965; repr., 1986) • John Dillenberger, *A Theology of Artistic Sensibilities: The Visual Arts and the Church* (New York, 1986) • S. Kostof, *A History of Architecture: Settings and Rituals* (2d ed., rev. G. Castillo; New York, 1995) • M. R. Miles, *Image as Insight: Visual Understanding in Western Christianity and Secular Culture* (Boston, 1985) • L. Murray and P. Murray, *The Oxford Companion to Christian Art and Architecture* (Oxford, 1996) • G. Schiller, *Iconography of Christian Art* (2 vols.; Greenwich, N.Y., 1971).

Early Christianity and Byzantium: M. Gough, *The Early Christians* (New York, 1961) • A. Grabar, *Christian Iconography: A Study of Its Origins* (Princeton, 1968) • R. Krautheimer, *Early Christian and Byzantine Art and Architecture* (4th ed.; Baltimore, 1987) • R. Milburn, *Early Christian Art and Architecture* (Berkeley, Calif., 1988) • L. Ouspensky, *Theology of the Icon* (2 vols.; vol. 1 rev. ed.; Crestwood, N.Y., 1992) • L. Ouspensky and V. Lossky, *The Meaning of Icons* (rev. ed.;

Crestwood, N.Y., 1982) • S. Runciman, *Byzantine Style and Civilization* (New York, 1987) • O. von Simson, *Sacred Fortress: Byzantine Art and Statecraft in Ravenna* (Princeton, 1987) • L. M. White, *The Social Origins of Christian Architecture* (2 vols.; Baltimore, 1990).

Medieval, Renaissance, and Baroque: H. Belting, *Likeness and Presence: A History of the Image before the Era of Art* (Chicago, 1994) • W. Braunfels, *Monasteries of Western Europe: The Architecture of the Orders* (Princeton, 1972; repr., New York, 1993) • M. Camille, *The Gothic Idol: Ideal and Image-Making in Medieval Art* (New York, 1989) • C. Christensen, *Art and the Reformation in Germany* (Columbus, Ohio, 1979) • J. Dunkerton et al., *Giotto to Dürer: Early Renaissance Painting in the National Gallery* (New Haven, 1991) • C. Garside, *Zwingli and the Arts* (New Haven, 1966) • P. Humfrey and M. Katz, eds., *The Altarpiece in the Renaissance* (Cambridge, 1991) • P. Lasko, *Ars Sacra, 800-1200* (2d ed.; New Haven, 1995) • M. A. Lavin, *The Place of Narrative: Mural Decoration in Italian Churches, 431-1600* (Chicago, 1990) • É. Mâle, *Religious Art in France* (ed. H. Bober; 3 vols.; Princeton, 1978-86) • H. van Os et al., *The Art of Devotion in the Late Middle Ages in Europe, 1300-1500* (Princeton, 1994) • O. von Simson, *The Gothic Cathedral: Origins of Gothic Architecture and the Medieval Concept of Order* (3d ed.; Princeton, 1989) • T. Verdon and J. Dally, eds., *Monasticism and the Arts* (Syracuse, N.Y., 1984) • T. Verdon and J. Henderson, eds., *Christianity and the Renaissance: Image and the Religious Imagination in the Quattrocento* (Syracuse, N.Y., 1990) • R. Wittkower and I. Jaffe, *Baroque Art: The Jesuit Contribution* (New York, 1972). The above sources deal primarily with the intersection of art and Christianity. Much on Christian art in general appears in art-historical surveys and in works on individual artists.

Susanna Bede Caroselli, C.S.S.G.

10. Nineteenth Century

Art in the 19th century stands under the dictum of G. W. F. Hegel (1770-1831), who declared that it gives sanctity to humanity, to the heights and depths of the human spirit, to what is human in all its joys and sorrows, to human strivings, acts, and destiny. From the standpoint of art, the century began in 1780 and ended between 1905 and 1918. It was an age of transition in which, for the first time, an opposition art confronted the official art of the academy. This was finally connected with the fact that a dialectical view of the world was replacing a hierarchical view. The → Marxist description of the century — as a time in which everything is pregnant with its contrary — may be seen in art too.

Autonomous art served the self-reflection of the artists, and with its negation of traditional ties, it thus needs explanation. Artists took on quasi-religious functions, viewing their creations as confession and themselves as priests or even martyrs. The individualizing of artistic work broke up art into a series of personal achievements. Art became a matter of → conscience and confession that could no longer define any "supreme content" or "supreme beauty"; it was accused of being formless and chaotic by academicians, which tried to present only the true and the → good. An urge for authenticity made the process of creating the work a decisive element in its meaning or content (expressionists).

Artistic ability and self-reflection carried with them the danger of exaggeration. As free artists encountered the public, also trying to woo them by new, popularizing techniques (e.g., lithography, fine art printing, and photography), the problem of kitsch became acute and proved a constant menace in Christian art. This was more or less unavoidable in face of the "loss of center" (H. Sedlmayr) and the attempt to create an "earthly paradise" (W. Hofmann).

In a situation in which the traditional view of things (→ Worldview) was destroyed and art achieved the freedom to redefine its themes, formal means, and → symbols, Christian art reacted in a predominantly retrospective way. The → classicism of the academies, which became increasingly → naturalistic, culminated in historical paintings. In 1841 T. F. Vischer hailed such paintings as a substitute for religious painting, which had now come to the end of the road: "We must paint history. History is the religion of our time."

Christian → iconography was increasingly ignored. It finally became so marginalized that one could not determine the Christianity of this art by iconographical statistics. P. → Tillich's ultimately ahistorical declaration that a still life by Cézanne or a tree by van Gogh has more of the quality of holiness than a picture of Jesus by Uhde must also be regarded as problematic.

The 19th century began with the religious iconoclasm of the French Revolution. Its classicism transposed and profaned the schemata of Christian art, and classicism outside France to a large extent avoided religious pictures. Only in → Romanticism do we see an attempt to revive Christian art. Along with individual painters like W. Blake (1757-1827) in England and E. Delacroix (1798-1863) in France, the German Romantics were the ones who especially tackled religious themes. P. O. Runge (1777-1810) tried to unite biblical Christianity and panentheistic nature → mythology. Contemporaries found in his

Times of Day the most significant attempt at a total work of Romantic art. The artist avoided "looking inquisitively at the past" so as not to hamper "a productive faith in the future." Related in many ways was the work of C. D. Friedrich (1774-1840), who gave a religious dimension to landscape painting. This sacralizing of the secular and secularizing of the sacred was at once felt to be a problem. B. von Ramdohr decried the presumption of landscape painting, which "slunk" into churches and "crept" onto altars.

In contrast to this early Protestant Romanticism of northern Germany, the later Romantics consciously followed tradition. The Nazarenes turned against classicism and preferred the old German masters and early Italians. Such an ideal helps explain the fact that 13 German painters had converted to Roman Catholicism in Rome by 1819. Through a later, less well-controlled liking for the restorative trends of the epoch, and a certain mawkishness of presentation because of a superficial adaptation of Raphael (1483-1520), the Nazarene attempt to renew Christian painting failed, and the general evaluation of the movement, which had a counterpart in the Pre-Raphaelites in England, suffered accordingly.

The late Nazarene style undoubtedly affected the understanding of art in many church circles, and thus the works of J. F. Overbeck (1789-1869), F. Pforr (1788-1812), P. von Cornelius (1783-1867), J. Schnorr von Carolsfeld (1794-1872), and P. Veit (1793-1877) merit unprejudiced appraisal. L. Richter (1803-84) is a case apart. He was in close contact with the Nazarenes but found an independent, popular, and nonconfessional way of expressing himself.

→ Realism and → impressionism virtually eliminated religious themes. There are exceptions in the work of W. Leibl (1844-1900), A. von Menzel (1815-1905), F. von Uhde (1848-1911), H. Thoma (1839-1924), and E. von Gebhardt (1838-1925). One can come to different conclusions on the attempt to make biblical events contemporary by naturalistic means, but it provided a model for many decades, for example, in religious education. At the end of the epoch, the fin de siècle, only a few artists dealt with religious themes. Worth noting are the fantasies of O. Redon (1840-1916) and J. Ensor (1860-1949), the paintings of P. Gauguin (1848-1903) (*Yellow Christ* in 1889, *Ave Maria* in 1891), and especially the work of V. van Gogh (1853-90), who dreamed of a renewal of Christian art and by → expressionistic exaggeration forced a → panentheistic confession upon the depiction of → nature.

In → church architecture the efforts of neoclassicism were essentially unproductive, while in Roman-

ticism, → historicism became the fate of the 19th century (F. Wieacker). Along with fantastic plans that were quite impracticable, we simply have an adaptation of traditional models. The buildings of K. F. Schinkel (1781-1841) show independent power; he revived the classical cupola with his Nikolai Church (1830) at Potsdam. The Eisenach Regulation of 1861 made Gothic obligatory for Protestant churches. The trend recognizable here found its best achievements in the restoration and completion of medieval works (such as the Cologne Cathedral in 1842). Christian art as a whole reproduced the main problems of the period, namely, the reconciling of faith and science and the relation of the church to Christianity. One may thus regard it as "a genuine expression of the age" (H. Jursch).

11. Twentieth Century

The cleft between the church and artists in the 20th century, which reflects the antithesis between the → church and contemporary → culture, makes it doubtful whether one can talk any longer about Christian art. Religious themes occur marginally, often very impressively (e.g., in the work of E. Nolde, G. Rouault, E. Barlach, and M. Chagall).

The development of → church architecture has continued steadily. At the end of the 19th century it was already breaking free from the chains of historicism, adopting contemporary styles and rethinking the theological foundations. After 1918 it took up new ideas (e.g., the forward-looking plans of O. Bartning), which only the adoption of new techniques and materials made possible. Worth noting is the temporary church structure that Bartning inaugurated in 1945, which was accepted as a valid approach and had wide-ranging consequences. The various churches now being built try to do justice to the different tasks of modern → congregations (community centers), and yet in their variety they still try to give architectural form to the basic views of the congregations. Church building still commands public interest, inasmuch as people appreciate striking statement in architectural form.

In art, one notes deep-seated uncertainties in both theology and the views of the congregation. At the congregational level people are content with what is often in the last resort a very conventional if technically competent → utilitarian art, while theology gives evidence of increasing attempts to enter into fresh dialogue with artists. Theologians need to cultivate a solidarity with the questions that artists ruthlessly pose: the questions of truth, of the desacralizing of the world, of an openness in principle that does not shrink from total venture, of support for the oppressed, and of the experience of remoteness from God. "Faith and artistic intelligence have been brought close together again. Without the universal claim of art, the church ossifies in a false conservatism. Conversely, without the church's basic and restrictive word of → salvation, the artist's venture threatens to become fixed in perennial revolution. Neither → conservatism nor → revolution has any foundation of its own. The task is to enter into liberating → dialogue" (H.-E. Bahr).

Bibliography: Nineteenth century: W. Hofmann, *C. D. Friedrich, 1774-1840* (Munich, 1974); idem, *Das irdische Paradies* (2d ed.; Munich, 1974) • G. Metken, *Die Präraffaeliten* (Cologne, 1974) • H. Schindler, *Nazarener* (Regensburg, 1982) • H. Sedlmayr, *Verlust der Mitte* (Salzburg, 1947).

Twentieth century: H.-E. Bahr, *Poiesis* (Stuttgart, 1961) • J. Begbie, *Voicing Creation's Praise: Towards a Theology of the Arts* (Edinburgh, 1991) • M.-A. Couturier, *Das Religiöse und die moderne Kunst* (Zurich, 1981) • J. Dillenberger, *A Theology of Artistic Sensibilities: The Visual Arts and the Church* (New York, 1986); idem, *The Visual Arts and Christianity in America* (New York, 1989) • W. A. Dyrness, *Christian Art in Asia* (Amsterdam, 1979); idem, *Rouault: A Vision of Suffering and Salvation* (Grand Rapids, 1971) • A. Lehmann, *Afroasiatische christliche Kunst* (Konstanz, 1967) • G. Rombold, *Der Streit um das Bild. Zum Verhältnis von moderner Kunst und Kultur* (Stuttgart, 1988) • H. R. Rookmaaker, *Modern Art and the Death of a Culture* (London, 1970) • W. Schmied, ed., *Zeichen des Glaubens–Geist der Avantgarde* (Stuttgart, 1980) • H. Schnell, *Der Kirchenbau des 20. Jahrhunderts in Deutschland* (Munich, 1973); idem *Zur Situation der christlichen Kunst der Gegenwart* (Munich, 1962) • H. Schwebel, *Autonome Kunst im Raum der Kirche* (Hamburg, 1968); idem, *Glaubwürdig* (Munich, 1979) • R. Volp, *Das Kunstwerk als Symbol* (Gütersloh, 1966).

Peter Maser

12. Contemporary

For the church at large, "Christian art" connotes such a broad variety of skill levels and content that it ceases to be a category; for many academicians, the classification ceased to exist shortly after the → Enlightenment. To complicate matters, "spiritual art," as represented at a significant exhibition in 1986 at the Los Angeles County Museum of Art ("The Spiritual in Art"), excludes the validity of a specifically "Christian" contribution but applauds the generic cosmic → spirituality (§1.3) of James Turrell, Robert Irwin, or Barnet Newman, among others. Recent artistic trends confuse the issue further by appropriating Christian → symbols and themes from a plethora of religious imagery, in quixotic pursuit of self-validating → experiences. Also, artists who profess Christianity often prefer to avoid inclusion in an infamous fraternity that, to them, signifies a trite, vestigial, or reactionary body of art that has spoken weakly, if at all, to contemporary culture.

To this day, the only modern artist of international fame who openly professed a personal faith is the French → Roman Catholic Georges Rouault (1871-1958). A full-bodied discussion about the efficacy of modern art between the Vatican and Roman Catholic clerics arose long before the issue came under renewed scrutiny in Protestant circles; the Catholic dialogue is partially preserved in the publication *L'art sacré* (Paris, 1935-54). Dominican father Marie-Alain Couturier became convinced that by applying the genius of Europe's modern artists to liturgical settings, regardless of personal convictions, the church's identity in the postwar years would be revitalized. This "Sacred Arts Movement" eventually drew works by H. Matisse, F. Léger, M. Chagall, G. Richier, J. Lipchitz, and even P. Picasso into sanctuaries built after World War II, culminating to some extent in the de Menil family's sponsorship of Houston's ecumenical Rothko Chapel (1964-71). Couturier also instigated Le Corbusier's unique and organically shaped church in Ronchamp, France (1955), still considered by many architects as one of the most important structures of the 20th century (→ Expressionism; Church Architecture 5). Renewed commitment to the contemporary arts is represented today by the Museum of Contemporary Religious Art (MOCRA), based in St. Louis, Missiouri, or the Center for Contemporary Art at St. Peter's, Cologne, both founded by → Jesuit art historians.

Attempts to attain a unified Protestant aesthetic theory have most frequently arisen from the Reformed or Calvinistic traditions through the late Hans R. Rookmaaker (Free University, Rotterdam), Calvin Seerveld (Institute of Christian Studies, Toronto), and Nicholas Wolterstorff (Yale University, New Haven, Conn.). Exhorting artists to interact fearlessly with culture, Reformed theology nevertheless equated the expression of universal → truth with aesthetic beauty (→ Calvinism 4). Clearly this approach did not meet Christians who desired to master abstraction, minimalism, conceptualism, or other modern vocabularies, nor those who opted to express the themes of → suffering, → despair, and the fallen state of creation.

For the sole purpose of establishing validity for artistic praxis, supporters of the arts founded hundreds of Christian arts groups, fellowships, performance companies, schools, newsletters, and parachurch organizations in the 1970s and 1980s. Groups in London and Washington, D.C., set examples for vital fellowships in New York City, Los Angeles, Sydney, Johannesburg, Mainz, Barcelona, and Tokyo. Though many such groups ceased operation after a decade, their cumulative effect was to advance the discussion beyond whether Christians could ever participate in postmodern art (→ Postmodernism 2) to the point of proposing specific guidelines for how they could affect their own cultural milieu and serve God.

Consequently, churches now increasingly support arts-related exhibitions, festivals, and conferences. Protestant colleges have funded improved and expanded arts departments, inviting professional, non-conventional artists to mentor hundreds of undergraduate art majors. College-based groups like Christians in the Visual Arts (Minneapolis), Christians in the Theatre Arts (Greenville, S.C.), and the International Christian Dance Fellowship (Sydney) now maintain extensive databases, organize regional conferences to showcase new works and teaching methodologies, and procure funding for significant projects. Umbrella groups like Christians in the Arts Networking, Inc. (founded 1983, Arlington, Mass.) actively track the overwhelming growth of arts activity. Christian Artists Europe (Rotterdam) exercises considerable political influence with European trade unions (→ Labor Unions); a mixed-race antiapartheid group of musicians and performers called Friends First toured the world as an example of racial collaboration during the height of South Africa's political crisis (→ Racism 2); Creative Ministries International (Sydney) has sought to place Christians of the most competitive musical abilities in top public performance venues; and Société Internationale des Artistes Chrétienne (France) and Das Rad (Germany) are two of the groups seeking to improve the quality of liturgical art.

Outside a Western context, the issue of preserving indigenous integrity in the arts, yet syncretizing regional art forms with Christian messages, remains unresolved and is represented by a tremendous disparity of aesthetic niveaux. Balinese, Philippine, and Indian Christians have melded gospel content to traditional dance and theater forms and won top honors in their cultures; African tribal imagery in woodcarving and woodcuts has been by turns recuperated or reinvented to portray majesty, power, or the animus of the soul in the Christian sense. The Association of Christian Asian Artists (Kyoto) and the Traditional Media Unit of the International Christian Media Commission (Auckland, Seattle) organize regular conferences to showcase the communicative efficacy of time-honored art forms. Christians have also contributed vitally to the contemporary art scene, occasionally at the highest professional echelons; Ugandan theater, South African township art exhibits, Native American painting, Mexican murals, and Australian aboriginal ceremonies are all experiencing rejuvenation at the hands of indigenous believers. Ethnographically diverse approaches to → aesthetics frequently cross-fertilize Western Christians who seek a more meaningful involvement in the wider world community (e.g., Bay Area Christian Artists Network, Berkeley, Calif.; → Acculturation).

The common denominator across all cultures is that an independent and dynamic fluorescence of arts activity innovated by Christians is slowly, imperceptibly rebuilding the efficacy of the arts in society at a time when, in the West, the loss of artistic values is being lamented and, elsewhere, indigenous traditions are increasingly threatened by the relentless pressures of internationalization and modernization.

→ Culture and Christianity

Bibliography: Quarterly journals: ARTS: The Arts in Religious and Theological Studies (ed. W. Yates; New Brighton, Minn., 1989-) • *Image: Journal of the Arts and Religion* (ed. G. Wolfe; Denville, N.J., 1992-).

Other works: J. BEGBIE, *Voicing Creation's Praise: Towards a Theology of the Arts* (Edinburgh, 1991) • M.-A. COUTURIER, *Sacred Art* (Austin, Tex., 1983) • J. DILLENBERGER, *Image and Spirit in Sacred and Secular Art* (New York, 1987) • M. MILES, *Image as Insight: Visual Understanding in Western Christianity and Secular Culture* (Boston, 1985) • G. E. VEITH, *State of the Arts: From Bezalel to Mapplethorpe* (Westchester, Ill., 1991).

KAREN L. MULDER

Christian Charity → Diakonia

Christian Church (Disciples of Christ)

1. Origin and Aims
2. Development

1. Origin and Aims

1.1 The beginnings of the Disciples of Christ movement lay peculiarly in the time and space of America's 19th-century frontier. There the nation provided the liberty, the frontier the opportunity, and the century the dream of apostolic purity. The first generation of the new nation seized religious liberty as though it were a challenge to be met with all the energy and creativity of which human imagination was capable. The 1820s and 1830s saw a host of experiments — millennial, utopian, transcendental (→ Transcendentalism), and mundane — all designed to show that "separation of → church and state" was no abstract constitutional principle but a concrete reality upon which to build. The resulting "voluntarism" led some to believe that proliferation of denominations and schism had gone too far; the seamless robe of Christ was being ripped into countless pieces. Thus, out of the very diversity that America spawned came a major theme of the Disciples' message: unity. Beyond all the labels, banners, and competing → sects, cannot there be simply a fellowship, a discipleship, that needs no other designation than "Christian"? As Alexander Campbell asked in 1835, "Was there at any time, or is there now, in all the earth, a kingdom more convulsed by internal broils and dissensions, than what is commonly called the church of Jesus Christ?"

1.2. The frontier likewise provided the second essential ingredient to the movement: opportunity. Free from long-standing → traditions, → liturgies, and → authorities, men and women on this new frontier could start their church along entirely new lines. No → bishop interfered, no board advised, no civil authority had to be either placated or consulted. For Christian evangelicals (→ Evangelical Movement) on the American frontier, one authority was needful and sufficient: the Bible. All could read it, or could have it read or preached to them; and all could learn therefrom everything essential for life here and hereafter. In a favorite phrase of the Disciples movement, "Where the Scriptures speak, we speak; where they are silent, we are silent."

1.3. The third driving force of this made-in-America denomination was the vision of apostolic purity: that is, restoring the church of the NT by casting off all the corruptions of centuries of compromise and modification. The 19th century believed strongly in → progress, but for some, progress could come only by turning backward, by a "restoration" of all that had been buried or lost. To reproduce this ancient and primitive church, one must follow the Bible faithfully, meticulously, as blueprint and guide. The grand assumption was that if all followed the same book in the same spirit, then all would end up, theologically and ecclesiastically, at the same point. Thus an affirmation of the unity of the church, the authority of the Bible, and the purity of the apostolic period would result in a truly Christian church that could and would gather all others unto it.

2. Development

2.1. Major spokesmen Alexander Campbell (1788-1866) and Barton Stone (1772-1844) started separate movements that merged as one in the 1830s. Stone worked chiefly in the frontier state of Kentucky, while Campbell moved out from western Pennsylvania into the mountainous regions of West Virginia and the newer frontier of Indiana. The movement continued to be strong in the freshly opened areas of Ohio, Tennessee, Missouri, Indiana, and Illinois. Although this Christian church resisted all hierarchical structure, it managed to grow rapidly in a region where results were more important than the credentials of old tradition. Within half a century of their origin, Disciples numbered about one-half million, passing the one million mark early in the 20th century.

2.2. Ironically, a movement dedicated to overcoming denominational division and strife ended up by creating not one new denomination but three: the Disciples of Christ (1.0 million members in 1994), the Christian Churches (1.1 million), and the → Churches of Christ (1.7 million). The Disciples, the most liberal and most ecumenical of the three branches, had by mid-20th century moved into mainstream Protestantism. The Churches of Christ, the most conservative and most sectarian, continued to search for a denominational identity and focus. In between these two groups, the Christian Churches still called for a restoration of the primitive church but found themselves associating more and more with other groups similarly motivated. Unity, which remained a dream for all three, seemed even further removed in the 1990s than it had been in the 1830s.

Bibliography: W. E. GARRISON and A. T. DE GROOT, The Disciples of Christ: A History (St. Louis, 1948) • D. E. HARRELL JR., A Social History of the Disciples of Christ (2 vols.; Atlanta, 1973) • R. T. HUGHES and C. L. ALLEN, Illusions of Innocence: Protestant Primitivism in America (Chicago, 1988).

EDWIN S. GAUSTAD

Christian Communication

1. Concept and Goals
2. History
3. Europe and North America
4. Third World and Ecumenical Cooperation

1. Concept and Goals

By means of communication media, the church seeks to help all people and to bring them "to the knowledge of the truth" (1 Tim. 2:4). The → church in its communications work disseminates information concerning the many facets of church life, interprets patterns and motives for Christian action in the world, encourages the adoption of a Christian lifestyle, and provides forums for reflection and debate on issues of importance to its message and mission. Thus the church makes use of → communication media to relate the biblical message to social, political, and cultural interests; to articulate the reconciling power of the → gospel; and to help the church itself both to deepen its fellowship (communio) and to participate in public discourse concerning the common good. These media are often directed to special groups and peoples.

The use of the media by the church has been explored both ecumenically and by particular church families. The decree *Inter mirifica* of Vatican II (1963) and the subsequent papal instruction *Communio et progressio* (1971) both stress the function of the press, film, and television as means of social communication and the right of the church to develop its own media. The aim of social communication is that through a variety of means, people should develop a deeper sense of fellowship (*Communio et progressio* 8). The Roman Catholic view is that the church media serve both the search for truth and the finding of truth. Social communication thus has a Christological basis, since according to the pastoral instruction Christ was a master of communication who has given to Christians in their discipleship a duty of bearing witness to the faith and taking an active part in the life and happenings of their contemporary world (ibid. 20).

Global ecumenical and denominational thinking on media and communication has in recent years reflected discussions between the communication units of the → World Council of Churches (WCC), the World Association for Christian Communication (WACC), and the → Lutheran World Federation (LWF). In 1981 at Versailles, France, these three organizations sponsored a consultation that produced a discussion paper, "The Search for Credible Christian Communication," which subsequently was circulated among some 400 churches, media, institutions, and individuals. The paper described itself as "an invitation to the churches to join a journey towards a new understanding of their communication opportunities in the 1980s." Discussions such as these were basic to several major statements within the next years, most notably "Credible Christian Communication" (WCC, 1983) and "Principles of Christian Communication" (WACC, 1986).

2. History
The beginnings of the use of communication media

appear in the primitive church. The letters of the apostle → Paul and the Gospels are primary and demonstrate how the original oral → proclamation developed into a variety of written genres.

Media in the modern sense date from the invention of printing by movable type by Johannes Gutenberg (d. 1468). This advance made possible the mass production of Bibles, devotional material, and pamphlets and aided the spread of the Reformers' work in a way and to an extent never before enjoyed by a religious movement. The first Protestant periodicals in Germany appeared in the 18th century, while planned communication with a missionary motive arose in the 19th century in both Europe and North America under the influence of pietistic, → revival, and → inner mission movements. The media used were at first restricted to tracts and periodicals.

At the end of the 20th century, Christian communication makes use of the whole range of contemporary media: books and printed materials, films, cassettes, recordings, radio, television, video, and computerized technologies. Moreover, virtually all church and Christian bodies have specialized departments for both communication and public relations that avail themselves of these media in order to meet the needs of particular audiences and groups. The greatest communication challenge of the present is certainly for the churches to understand, evaluate, develop, and make use of the technologies that are opening "cyberspace" to the contemporary world.

3. Europe and North America
In April of 1997 a joint statement on Christian communication was released in Germany by the Evangelical Church in Germany (EKD) and the Roman Catholic German Bishops' Conference entitled "Chancen und Risiken der Mediengesellschaft" (Opportunities and risks of the media society). This ecumenical statement assessed the general media situation in its anthropological, social, ethical, and technological dimensions.

The EKD has professionally developed communication agencies. A press service, the Evangelische Pressedienst (EPD), founded in 1910 and now centered in Frankfurt, distributes information about the life and work of the church and its institutions, about ecumenical activities, and about societal issues that impinge on the life of the church. In 1997 the EKD released its own comprehensive communication strategy paper, "Mandat und Mark. Perspektiven evangelischer Publizistik" (Mandate and market: Perspectives in Protestant communication), the result of a three-year study. The paper defines a larger role for Christian communication within the media marketplace, a goal that increasingly requires commercial viability and technical excellence. Such communication must increasingly be aimed at particular audiences: "Church communication guided by institutional interests will not be successful; it can be successful only if it is consistently aimed at its target groups."

Roman Catholic communication work in Germany is carried out in close cooperation with the Pontifical Council for Social Communications and with the Centrum Internationale Catholicum in Rome. There is also in Germany a press service of the conservative *evangelikale* movement (IDEA).

Almost all the European churches publish newspapers, journals, and books. Most also have access to radio and television, frequently with the privilege of special transmission on state-controlled media. In most of these countries radio stations transmit brief daily devotions that reach a wide public, and Sunday church services are viewed by many (→ Devotion, Devotions; Worship).

After years of state restrictions, churches in the former socialist countries are now beginning to make use of contemporary media with the assistance of global Roman Catholic, Protestant, and ecumenical communication agencies (→ Church in a Socialist Society). From 1982 through 1994, the LWF supported the Information Service of European Lutheran Minority Churches (IDL), a news service in Eastern Europe. This extremely important press service, located first in Budapest and then in Vienna, became in effect the only source for ecumenical church news and information behind the Iron Curtain.

In the United States and Canada, church communication media reflect both the organizational and the denominational variety of Christianity and the countries' high standards of communication. All the larger church bodies have periodicals and contribute, frequently on an ecumenical basis, to radio and television broadcasting. The work of denominational and ecumenical communication agencies is supplemented by lay and other organizations (→ Lay Movements) whose members are natural recipients of the communicated message. National associations of religious press, broadcasters, and public relations experts function actively on an interfaith basis. The → National Council of the Churches of Christ in the USA, the largest and oldest ecumenical organization in the United States, has in the course of its history approved several important statements regarding aspects of Christian communication. Notable among

these statements have been "Global Communication for Justice" (1993), "The Churches' Role in Media Education and Communication Advocacy" (1995), and "Churches and the News Media" (1996).

Peculiar to North America has been the widespread use of television, not least in the service of conservative Christian causes. Names of so-called televangelists — such as Pat Robertson, who heads the Christian Broadcasting Network; Jerry Falwell, of the *Old-Time Gospel Hour;* and Jim Bakker, who, until faced with legal problems in 1987, was the celebrated host of the *PTL* [Praise the Lord] *Club* — are widely known in Christian communication circles. The largest of these television enterprises transmit 24 hours a day to all parts of the United States. Programs include → healing and → prayer as well as preaching and services of worship. They are also marked by clearly political advocacy, almost uniformly conservative in nature. This → "electronic church" has no members, does not found local congregations, and relies on viewers' gifts for major support. It owes its success to the entrepreneurial talents of its preachers and the renaissance of → fundamentalism in the United States.

An alternative form of television communication is represented by the Faith and Values Network (originally known as VISN), an interfaith venture in which many U.S. and Canadian mainline churches participate. This cable TV network offers family and news programming as well as educational, social, and artistic programs reflecting the concerns of America's religious communities. Additionally, in 1997 the Public Broadcasting Service began a regular television program concerning matters of faith and ethics in American life.

4. Third World and Ecumenical Cooperation

Whereas in Europe and North America the main task of church communication is to support the proclamation of the Christian message and to bring about → dialogue between the church and a public that is still largely under Christian influence, the emphasis in other parts of the world is on → evangelization and mission, on concerns of development education and nation building, and on maintaining the Christian presence in societies where the predominant religions are non-Christian. In these contexts the media play a crucial role in the development of indigenous cultures and political systems (→ Culture and Christianity), and churches have, with increasing frequency and depth, taken the responsibility to make substantive contributions through the media to these developments.

The WCC and Christian World Communions

such as the → Roman Catholic Church, the LWF, the → World Alliance of Reformed Churches (WARC), and the Anglican Consultative Council support ecumenically coordinated and financed projects in Asia, Africa, and Latin America that include radio, publishing houses, information and audiovisual services, and journals, as well as television and computerized media. These technological media are increasingly combined with the support of culturally indigenous alternative and group media. A well-known example of this work was the major project of the LWF — Radio Voice of the Gospel (RVOG), an enterprise of educational and religious broadcasting that, with ecumenical participation, covered the African continent and beyond. Established in 1957 in Addis Ababa, Ethiopia, RVOG ceased operation in 1977, when it was nationalized by the then Marxist revolutionary government of Ethiopia.

The WCC and Christian World Communions have extensive programs of studies and documentation intended primarily for their member churches. The WCC, LWF, and WARC, together with the Conference of European Churches, support the Ecumenical News Service (ENS), which from its headquarters in Geneva provides ecumenical news and information of concern to churches throughout the world. In other cases individual sponsoring organizations provide news services to their own constituencies, as, for example, the LWF's *Lutheran World Information,* which appears regularly in both English and German editions. All of these services feed and thus support regional ecumenical news and information services in Asia, Africa, and Latin America.

The Roman Catholic Church has an extensive program that supports communication in Third World churches, largely through its Pontifical Council for Social Communications. UNDA (International Catholic Association for Radio and Television), centered in Brussels, and UCIP (International Catholic Union for the Press), centered in Geneva, are instrumental in this work.

The largest ecumenical and global agency for Christian communication is the World Association for Christian Communication, with its main offices located in London. This organization was founded in 1975, but its origins go back at least 25 years earlier to predecessor bodies such as the World Committee for Christian Broadcasting and the Agency for Christian Literary Development. Linking several hundred organizations in seven regions, WACC works together with Protestant, Roman Catholic, and Orthodox churches and other Christian and media groups throughout the world in support of communication projects of the most varied kinds. Addi-

tionally, WACC sponsors global projects that (1) study and support the full participation of women in media, (2) offer a thorough and positive evaluation of the UNESCO "MacBride Report," which proposed a New World Information and Communication Order, and (3) generally raise questions concerning communication as an issue in globalized society. WACC publishes the highly respected quarterly journal *Media Development,* and it has sponsored two international congresses: "Communication and Community" (Manila 1989) and "Communication and Human Dignity" (Mexico City 1995). The stated "bias" of WACC is toward communication issues in the Third World, believing that such a bias is now "the most valid interpretation of Christ's teaching."

→ Information; Mass Media

Bibliography: B. ARMSTRONG, *The Electric Church* (Nashville, 1980) • C. ARTHUR, ed., *Religion and the Media: An Introductory Reader* (Cardiff, 1993) • P. BABIN, with M. IANNONE, *The New Era in Religious Communication* (Minneapolis, 1991) • C. G. CHRISTIANS and G. GJELSTEN, eds., *Media Ethics and the Church* (Kristiansand, 1981) • *The Church and Media: Statements from the National Council of the Churches of Christ in the USA* (New York, 1997) • F.-J. EIKERS, ed., *Kirche und Publizistik. Dreizehn Kommentare zur Pastoralinstruktion "Communio et Progressio"* (Paderborn, 1972) • W. F. FORE, *Television and Religion: The Shaping of Faith, Values, and Culture* (Minneapolis, 1987) • R. GEISSENDÖRFER, *Zum Mandat der evangelischen Publizistik* (Frankfurt, 1975) • P. G. HORSFIELD, *Religious Television: The American Experience* (New York, 1984) • P. LEE, ed., *The Democratization of Communication* (Cardiff, 1995) • D. LOCHHEAD, *Shifting Realities: Information Technology and the Church* (Geneva, 1997) • M. LUNDGREN, *Proclaiming Christ to His World: The Experience of Radio Voice of the Gospel, 1957-1977* (Geneva, 1983) • S. MACBRIDE et al., eds., *Many Voices, One World: Communication and Society, Today and Tomorrow. Towards a New More Just and More Efficient World Information and Communication Order* (London, 1980; repr., 1988) the "MacBride Report" • G. MEHNERT, *Evangelische Presse. Geschichte und Erscheinungsbild von der Reformation bis zur Gegenwart* (Bielefeld, 1983) bibliography • M. MUGGERIDGE, *Christ and the Media* (Grand Rapids, 1977) • P. A. SOUKUP, ed., *Christian Communication: A Bibliographical Survey* (New York, 1989) • *Statements on Communication by the World Association for Christian Communication* (London, 1990) • L. I. SWEET, ed., *Communication and Change in American Religious History* (Grand Rapids, 1993).

DIETRICH SATTLER and NORMAN HJELM

Christian Community, The

1. The Christian Community (Ger. *Christengemein-schaft*) is the name and claim of a movement that seeks to bring Christianity to fulfillment by a new → reformation. It sees itself as the driving force of the "third epoch" — the first being that of a suprapersonal but unfree cultus (→ Catholicism [Roman]), the second that of the loss of the cultus and restriction to the personal alone (→ Protestantism). In the third epoch the suprapersonal, spiritual aspiration of free people will find cultic expression in the renewed sacramentalism of the Christian Community.

2.1. The development and many of the basic doctrines of the Christian Community are hardly conceivable without R. Steiner (1861-1925) and his → anthroposophy. In 1921 Steiner called for (1) the proclamation of the living word without outdated ecclesiastical language, (2) the setting up of free communities outside existing church forms, and (3) the building up of fellowship by cultic acts to offset an overemphasis on doctrine and → dogma.

The Christian Community was founded on September 16, 1922, with F. Rittelmeyer conducting the first consecration at the anthroposophy center at Dornach near Basel. Previously a Lutheran pastor, Rittelmeyer became the first supreme leader. His successors, E. Bock and R. Frieling, had both been Protestant theologians.

The Christian Community spread especially in cities and among intellectuals. Branches formed throughout Europe and then after World War II in the United States, Canada, South America, and South Africa. In 1941 the National Socialists proscribed it in Germany. In the United States, the Christian Community has been established since 1948. It has spread particularly on the East Coast, wherever anthroposophical societies are located.

2.2. The Christian Community considers itself the first Christian fellowship consistently to follow the principle of freedom of doctrine and confession (E. Bock). Neither priests nor members are under obligation to confess anthroposophy, which provides the context and the instrument of thought for the teaching and especially the cultus. God is the almighty spiritual-physical Godhead, the ground of all being. Christ, as the son born in eternity and the ruler in the realm of the sun, is the chief spiritual being. After a long process of influencing humanity by oracles and mysteries, he incarnates himself in the Lucan Jesus (born of David's son Nathan), who after 12 years unites the Matthean Jesus (born of David's son Solomon) to himself. In the central mystery of Golgotha the blood of the incarnate sun-spirit Christ permeated the earth, which by this first great communion was claimed and filled by the spiritualized powers of Christ for final, higher development. By his → incarnation and sacrificial death, Christ is the primal sacrament on which rest the seven → sacraments of the Christian Community: → baptism, confirmation (→ Initiation Rites), penance (→ Penitence), → marriage, ordination, consecration, and extreme unction. At many points the understanding and celebration of the sacraments differ considerably from their practice in the churches.

2.3. The ethical claim of the Christian Community is based on a certain elitist sense. This results from the conviction of having grasped the mystical sense of Holy Scripture, recognized the anthroposophical and Christosophical → truth of Christianity, and become a member of the third and spiritual church. At the heart of the ethical struggle is the task of developing a spiritual personality in the course of a world process of "redemption," which is viewed partly in emanative terms and partly in evolutionary terms.

2.4. Organizationally, the Christian Community is congregational in its local structure. Its central organization features the "circle of seven," which includes a "supreme leader" and two "chief leaders." The congregations have "pastors" (i.e., ordained priests), with lay members to help them. The office of the supreme leader is in Stuttgart, with Sussex, England, the home of a theological training center. Community publications in English include the *New York Newsletter* and the *Christian Community Journal* (England).

In 1989, there were ten congregations in the United States and two in Canada. The total number of members in Europe, Africa, and America does not exceed 120,000. There also are many friends and sympathizers.

3. How the Christian Community views its relations to anthroposophy, on the one hand, and, on the other, to Christian churches is not wholly clear.

3.1. Anthroposophy has influenced the community's mode of thinking and orientation, but it views anthroposophy as only a preparatary stage of church expression. It has no formal connection with anthroposophy, although many people are members in both.

3.2. In relation to the mainline churches, the Christian Community does not view itself as a → sect or alternative denomination, and therefore it does not demand withdrawal of → church membership (§5), but it stresses its own freedom of teaching and confession. Its worship as an act of consecration is the center at which all true Christians may be united (Rittelmeyer). Participation is open to anyone.

3.3. In Germany, the group's country of origin, the → Roman Catholic Church totally rejects the Christian Community. The relationship of the Evangelical Church in Germany (EKD) is more nuanced. Positive aspects are valued, and its Christianity is not denied. Yet its baptism is not accepted as Christian baptism (as of a decision in May 1949), and the recommendation of a study commission that it be received into the → World Council of Churches was refused (December 1950). The reason for this critical attitude is the belief that the Christian Community sees itself as offering a new source of revelation alongside the historic Christian heritage.

Bibliography: Primary sources: E. Bock, *Die neue Reformation* (Stuttgart, 1953); idem, *Was will die Christengemeinschaft?* (Stuttgart, 1960) • R. Frieling, *Vom Wesen des Christentums* (Stuttgart, 1948) • F. Rittelmeyer, *Christus* (Stuttgart, 1937); idem, *Die Menschenweihehandlung* (Stuttgart, 1926).

Secondary works: "Anthroposophical Society," *EAR* (5th ed.) no. 1570 • G. Bichlmair, *Christentum, Theosophie und Anthroposophie* (Vienna, 1950) • E. F. Derry, *Seven Sacraments in the Christian Community* (2d ed.; London, 1966) • K. Eberhardt, ed., *Was glauben die andern?* (2d ed.; Gütersloh, 1978) • K. Hutten, *Seher, Grübler, Enthusiasten* (11th ed.; Stuttgart, 1968) • H. Mynarek, *Religiös ohne Gott? Neue Religiosität der Gegenwart in Selbstzeugnissen* (Düsseldorf, 1983) • H. Reller, ed., *Handbuch religiöse Gemeinschaften* (2d ed.; Gütersloh, 1979) • O. Simmel, "Anthroposophie und Christentum," *StZ* 149 (1951) 175-84 • W. Stählin, ed., *Evangelium und Christengemeinschaft* (Kassel, 1953) • K. von Stieglitz, *Die Christosophie R. Steiners* (Witten, 1955); idem, *Rettung des Christentums? Anthroposophie und Christengemeinschaft* (Witten, 1965) • G. Wachsmuth, *The Life and Work of Rudolf Steiner* (New York, 1955).

Hubertus Mynarek

Christian Conference of Asia

1. Scope
2. Founding
3. Basis of Membership
4. Goals
5. Tasks
6. Methods

1. Scope

The Christian Conference of Asia (CCA) is a regional ecumenical association of Christian churches and national church councils (→ National Councils of Churches). It comprises more than 100 member churches and 15 national councils. Its territory stretches geographically from Pakistan in the West to Japan in the East. In the South it includes Australia and New Zealand.

2. Founding

Church representatives planned for a council of Asian Christians at a meeting at Prapat (Indonesia) in March 1957. It was officially founded at Kuala Lumpur (Malaysia) in May 1959. Delegates from 48 churches and councils took part in the founding meeting of the East Asia Christian Conference. In 1973 the name was changed to Christian Conference of Asia.

3. Basis of Membership

The basis of membership is confession of the Lord Jesus Christ as God and Savior according to "the witness of Holy Scripture and the resultant attempt to fulfill the calling expressed therein to the one God, Father, Son, and Holy Spirit."

4. Goals

The CCA promotes the common work of the churches and council of Asia within the framework of the worldwide → ecumenical movement (→ World Council of Churches [WCC]). It is sustained by the belief that God's purpose for the church in Asia is that as a fellowship it should be obedient to him and do his will in the world.

5. Tasks

The CCA has set itself six tasks. It seeks to (1) develop a convincing Christian answer to the demands of Asia's changing societies; (2) gain information on the possibilities and promotion of common efforts in Christian missionary work (→ Mission) in Asia; (3) encourage Asian contributions to Christian thinking, worship, and action throughout the whole world; (4) develop mutual awareness, fellowship, sharing, and relationships to other regional conferences and to the WCC; (5) promote study and action in the fields of evangelization, → diakonia, social and human development, and internal relations; and (6) stimulate initiatives and efforts in the direction of more forceful Christian life and action.

6. Methods

To achieve its goals the CCA has set up nine committees for special programs: mission and evangelization (including → dialogue); education; youth; women; internal affairs (including → human rights); development and diakonia (including health questions); urban rural missions (including problems of race and minorities); theology (including faith and order); and → communications. These committees are responsible to a central committee made up of elected representatives from all the countries and meeting every year. A popular assembly is normally held every five years and is the chief legislative body.

The CCA publishes the bimonthly *CCA News,* which gives information concerning ecumenical happenings and matters concerning Asia. Circular letters, reports, and books deal with individual programs. The central secratariat of CCA is located in Hong Kong.

→ Asian Theology

Bibliography: T. ARAI and T. K. THOMAS, "Christian Conference of Asia," *DEM* 151-53 • Y. K. HAO, *From Prapat to Colombo: History of the Christian Conference of Asia, 1957-1995* (Hong Kong, 1995).

YAP KIM HAO

Christian Development Services

1. International Background
2. Ecumenical Responses and Structures
3. Problems

1. International Background

In 1960 the → United Nations initiated a decade-long program of → development, which, by means of a strategy of economic aid and with the help of such special agencies as the United Nations Conference on Trade and Development (UNCTAD) and the Food and Agriculture Organization (FAO), was designed to abolish → poverty. Disenchantment, however, soon set in. In 1969 the Pearson Report described the alarming results of the "trickle-down" process and showed the need for a second decade of development. Economic growth and wealth would not come down from above. They simply manifested and strengthened the central power of → industrial societies and their means of production, along with the concentration of wealth and the power of economic decision in the hands of a few concerns in → Third World countries.

2. Ecumenical Responses and Structures

This recognition also came to expression in the pronouncements of the → World Council of Churches (WCC), for example, at the World Conference on Church and Society (Geneva, 1966) and at the fourth assembly (Uppsala, 1968), and of the Roman Catholic Church, such as in the bishops' conference at Medellín (1968; → Latin American Council of Bishops) and the encyclical *Populorum progressio* (1968). Both sides stressed the theme of social justice (→ Righteousness, Justice), both as a goal and as a means to self-help. Particularly sobering was the insight that economic and industrial → progress organized "from above" (e.g., President J. F. Kennedy's Alliance for Progress, formed in 1961 to aid Latin America) simply boosted the "development of underdevelopment" (see A. G. Frank's theory of dependence). The process of "economic uncoupling" in some Third World countries (see D. Senghaas and others) had little influence on the world economy, but it opened the door to some basic local and regional movements that aimed at economic, political, and cultural independence.

2.1. In 1970, at the instigation of the Uppsala assembly, the WCC established the Commission on the Churches' Participation in Development (CCPD). Earlier that year, a consultation entitled "Ecumenical Assistance to Development Projects" was held in Montreux, Switzerland. The common aim was to change the traditional relation between donors and recipients, to share → power in the decision-making process, and to foster the greatest possible participation of all stakeholders. The practice of the commission was shaped by studies of the churches' role in the process of development and by the promotion of groups and group contacts to support the economically underprivileged in their work for justice and independence. The first five years saw the establishment of the Ecumenical Development Co-operative Society, the Ecumenical Development Fund, and a CCPD network, which made favorable credits possible and gave greater control over decisions to the recipients. In the donor churches a process was initiated to increase awareness and educate members in their responsibility for the central task. It was proposed that the wealthier churches should donate 25 percent of their available development resources to this work of education in their own lands.

After the second Montreux consultation in 1974, a study process entitled "The Church and the Poor," which was promoted by C. I. Itty of India and J. de Santa Ana of Uruguay, put to the commission, the WCC, and the member churches the question as to the theological status of the poor and their liberation in the life of the churches (→ Liberation Theology), as well as the practical contribution that the churches were ready and willing to make in the battle against injustice. "Liberation" was now the new name for development (J. Míguez Bonino, Argentina). After the fifth WCC assembly at Nairobi (1975), the commission supported the concern to reorient political → ethics toward the search for a "just, participatory, and sustainable society," in place of the traditional concept of a "responsible society" (popular since the first assembly in Amsterdam in 1948). A 1982 study of transnational concerns was the practical result of the reorientation. This study raised the question of the power and accountability of the relevant corporations. After the sixth WCC assembly at Vancouver (1983), the financial system came under ecumenical criticism (1985), and later there was a hearing on the debt crisis at Berlin (1988). With these moves the search for basic change in the structure of the existing economy intensified (→ Economics, Ethics of).

2.2. The WCC Commission on Inter-Church Aid, Refugee, and World Service (CICARWS), which was founded in 1945 as a department for rebuilding and interchurch aid, has increasingly devoted itself to development programs and projects. In the 1970s, in connection with the so-called moratorium debate (esp. at Bangkok 1973, a world conference on mission and evangelism), the overall system of development was revised to feature block grants and favored independent decision making on the part of the recipients. A 1977 WCC conference in Glion, Switzerland, questioned critically the restriction inherent in the system of "sharing" material goods (called resource transfer). The WCC study entitled "Ecumenical Sharing of Resources," also prompted by CICARWS, led ultimately to an ecumenical conference ("Koinonia: Sharing Life in a World Community") held in 1987 at El Escorial, Spain. The result was a commitment to aim at "a new understanding of sharing," one including trade in → solidarity with and for one another.

2.3. A body dealing with *s*ociety, *d*evelopment, and peace — SODEPAX — linked the WCC to the papal commission *Justitia et Pax* (1968-80). SODEPAX quickly lost its function as a bridge, however, when in 1972 it became clear that the Roman Catholic Church would not become a member of the WCC in the foreseeable future. Yet it made important contributions in the question of Northern Ireland (1973), by the formation of the Asian Cultural Forum on Development (1975), and in ecumenical discussion of a new world economic order (1976-78).

In the → Lutheran World Federation a commission and division for world service took up the issue of development. This includes a project-oriented Community Development Service (from 1952) and

a relief agency (from 1947). Helping refugees and the victims of drought is an important part of this aid.

In 1965 in Brussels, Roman Catholics formed Coopération Internationale pour le Développement et la Solidarité (CIDSE) to unite 14 Catholic development organizations. It gives support to over 20 organizations in Europe, North America, and Australia. Also in Brussels since 1990 has been the Association of Protestant Development Organizations in Europe, which coordinates the work of member organizations. In 1971 Pope Paul VI (1963-78) founded the pontifical council "Cor unum," a forum of representatives from Third World bishops' conferences who discuss the work of the church and the → orders in → mission, relief, and development aid.

3. Problems
The following questions highlight the main problems facing Christian development services. How can changing and improving the living conditions at the local and regional levels tie in with and contribute to the needed macroeconomic structural changes? How far should Christian development services seek → dialogue, common learning, and cooperation with groups outside the churches that have the same goals? Will the claim to solidarity and sharing among equals be adequately worked out in practice? How will the disbursing of state moneys by Christian development services affect the integrity of the churches' contribution? These questions call for theological discussion and openness to change. In the framework of a just → stewardship, they demand that the antithesis of cooperation and control be overcome.

→ Ecumenical Movement; Ecumenical Theology; Relief Organizations

Bibliography: K.-H. DEJUNG, *Die ökumenische Bewegung im Entwicklungskonflikt, 1910-1968* (Stuttgart, 1973) • R. D. N. DICKINSON, *Entwicklung in ökumenischer Sicht* (Frankfurt, 1975); idem, *Poor, Yet Making Many Rich* (Geneva, 1983) • U. DUCHROW, *Weltwirtschaft heute–ein Feld für bekennende Kirche?* (Munich, 1986); idem, ed., *Geld für wenige oder Leben für alle?* (Oberursel, 1989) • *Empty Hands* (Geneva, 1980) • J. LISSNER, *The Politics of Altruism* (Geneva, 1977) • K. RAISER, ed., *Ökumenische Diakonie–eine Option für das Leben* (Stuttgart, 1988) • J. DE SANTA ANA, *Gute Nachricht für die Armen* (Wuppertal, 1979); idem, ed., *Towards a Church in Solidarity with the Poor* (Geneva, 1980) • W. R. SCHMIDT, ed., *Catalysing Hope for Justice* (Geneva, 1987) • K. SRISANG, ed., *Perspectives on Political Ethics* (Geneva, 1983).

WOLFGANG GERN

Christian Education

This increasingly important concept embraces all the educationally relevant phenomena, processes, and tasks associated with the founding and growth of Christian congregations (→ Church Growth; Congregation). It concerns the congregation viewed as a sphere of education and relevant learning processes and comes under the general rubric of → religious instruction. Its development has been promoted by various challenges, interests, and motives and stands closely related to the history of the relationship between the church and its educational work. Christian education engages in discussion of the relations between → theology and → pedagogy, and also between the church and educational institutions and those who work in them.

As a development of the catechumenate, Christian education involved an attempt to develop a structured education for which the church would be responsible. The aim was to offer a full Christian education to children and young people and to introduce and integrate them into full church membership (K. Hauschildt, 61).

After World War II, adults were increasingly included, and closer links were forged with other forms of church ministry (→ Youth Work). The total catechumenate formed a framework for the goal of total education at home and at school, confirmation instruction occupying a central place. The main workers were the → pastor, catechists, congregational assistants, and Christian teachers.

In 1974 E. Rosenboom posed the demand for a new definition of the relation between theology and pedagogics. He argued that the local congregation is properly the subject of education rather than the church as a whole, for it is here that the church takes concrete shape. The congregation is a place of learning with opportunities for growth and development.

The initial thesis is that God's saving work in Jesus Christ precedes all instruction in the congregation. The idea of church education shows that church growth must also be viewed as a matter involving education. Rosenboom thus demanded systematic reflection on educational practice in the church as a learning center. This view strengthened the need for other functions and qualifications apart from those of the minister, and especially the need for educational assistants. The participation of the church in its own learning processes and the ability of those responsible to share and cooperate thus took on great importance for church growth. The task of Christian education is to combine differentiation with integration in a total concept of con-

gregational education. The congregation itself is both the subject and object of its own life and learning (Rosenboom, 57).

Christian education, then, raises the question of coordinating variously qualified workers (→ Church Employees), accredited teachers in some cases, special church teachers in others. K. E. Nipkow took a further step when he argued that congregational education cannot be initiated and organized from above without the assent and cooperation of the members. This view assumed that education is not a one-sided influencing of children and young people by adults (→ Childhood; Youth), for it is the relations set up by adults that constitute "the real problem of education" (Nipkow 1990, 31-32). Instead, education should be viewed as a basic relation between generations. It can be achieved only by mutual learning. In the Christian tradition it means learning to live and believe in common before God. A further point for Nipkow, in agreement with ecumenical discussion, was that learning ideally is grounded less in learning than it is in the life of the congregation, in a lifestyle, in an experienced faith, in a lived-out Christian fellowship and → spirituality.

In the 1980s discussion focused on the connection between life, faith, and learning. On the basis of Paul's view of the church as Christ's body, the congregation was depicted as a sphere of learning encompassing not only traditional congregational offerings but also the activities and initiatives of individual Christians and groups. The aim was to accept and promote the abilities of all members, to encourage open discussion and exchange, and to foster various learning projects. Impulses were thus set in motion to create a more sharing church in which the role and ministry of the pastor would still be important, but they would be exercised in cooperation with groups and coworkers who are qualified educationally, diaconally, musically, and administratively.

There have been similar developments in Roman Catholicism. Under the slogan "Congregational catechesis," an answer has been found to the shortage of priests and the increasing need for religious education. Catechesis has been rediscovered as a congregational task, with the common life of Christians as the locus of learning. Led by theologians, mature Christians (as lay catechists or confirmation aides) help to prepare children and young people for participation in the sacraments. The catechetical instruction of children and adults has taken on increasing importance with the help of congregations and societies.

Since the early 1990s Christian education has increasingly focused on questions addressing congregations' own self-understanding and understanding of their commission in view of changes in society at large. What is known as the second phase of Christian education has thus focused on the tendency toward individualization, on the increasing orientation toward one's own immediate life sphere, and on the altered presuppositions of the processes of Christian education itself.

Some theoretical and practical issues still call for discussion. The first is the relation between the local congregation and the church at large. Different positions are taken that directly affect the structure of church growth as the place of Christian education. Social, political, and theological conflicts must be dealt with in common learning processes, and possible forms of communicative learning must be found and developed. Also to be explored is the relation to the local church of ministries and organizations specializing in a particular service. Another part of the learning task is to develop regional and individual → confessions and devotional traditions, and to foster a sense of the worldwide fellowship of Christians and the common ecumenical responsibility of the churches for → peace, justice (→ Righteousness, Justice), and the conservation of creation (→ Ecumenical Learning).

The second issue is that of the linking of the various stages of life to the experience of faith. More regard is now paid to the different phases of life and the related approach to faith. For encounter with God, the relation of children to parents and adults is decisive as an emotional event, a development of a common language, an experience of → conscience, and a challenging of thought. For young people, adults, and older people the question of God has a different setting. What does this mean for the offerings and ministries of the local church and its relationship with → family, school, and the working world?

The third matter is that of evaluating qualifications and spiritual competence. Christian education adopts the Reformation recognition of the priesthood of all believers. It emphasizes the equality of various congregational offices and ministries and thus calls for strenuous efforts to perceive and take seriously what are often hidden gifts and abilities in the congregation. New thought must be given to defining the pastor's role and self-understanding in a sharing congregation as compared to that of the laity and nontheological coworkers.

A final issue is that of the relation between educational offerings and the task of proclamation. Here profound consideration needs to be given to the inner link between the task of education and the traditional view of proclamation. In particular, much more attention must be paid to the training or advanced training of theological and educational assistants.

→ Continuing Education; Education 4; Family Education

Bibliography: G. ADAM and R. LACHMANN, eds., *Gemeindepädagogisches Kompendium* (2d ed.; Göttingen, 1994) • F. BARTH, ed., *Gemeindepädagogik im Widerstreit der Meinungen. Ringvorlesung der Evangelischen Fachhochschule im Sommersemester 1989* (Darmstadt, 1989) • R. BLÜHM et al., *Kirchliche Handlungsfelder. Gemeindepädagogik, Pastoralpsychologie, Liturgie, Kirchenmusik, Kirchenbau und kirchliche Kunst der Gegenwart* (Stuttgart, 1990) • M. C. BOYS, *Educating in Faith: Maps and Visions* (San Francisco, 1989) • COMENIUS-INSTITUT, *Arbeitshilfen, Materialien und Studien zur Gemeindepädagogik* (9 vols.; Gütersloh, 1985-95) • R. DEGEN, *Gemeindeerneuerung als gemeindepädagogische Aufgabe. Entwicklungen in den evangelischen Kirchen Ostdeutschlands* (Münster, 1992); idem, *In der Gemeinde Leben lernen. Gemeindeaufbau als gemeindepädagogische Aufgabe* (Berlin, 1989) • R. DEGEN et al., eds., *Mitten in der Lebenswelt. Lehrstücke und Lernprozesse zur zweiten Phase der Gemeindepädagogik; Dokumentation des Ersten Gemeindepädagogischen Symposiums in Ludwigshafen/ Rhein* (Münster, 1992) • K. FOITZIK, *Gemeindepädagogik. Problemgeschichte eines umstrittenen Begriffs* (Gütersloh, 1992); idem, ed., *Lebenswelten Erwachsener. Zweites Gemeindepädagogisches Symposium; Beiträge und Reaktionen* (Münster, 1994) • J. W. FOWLER, *Becoming Adult, Becoming Christian: Adult Development and Christian Faith* (San Francisco, 1984); idem, *Stages of Faith: The Psychology of Human Development and the Quest for Meaning* (San Francisco, 1981) • K. O. GANGEL and W. S. BENSON, *Christian Education: Its History and Philosophy* (Chicago, 1983) • E. GOSSMANN and H. B. KAUFMANN, eds., *Forum Gemeindepädagogik. Eine Zwischenbilanz* (Münster, 1987) • C. GRETHLEIN, *Gemeindepädagogik* (Berlin, 1994) • T. H. GROOME, *Christian Religious Education: Sharing Our Story and Vision* (San Francisco, 1980) • P. JARVIS and N. WALTERS, eds., *Adult Education and Theological Interpretations* (Malabar, Fla., 1993) • H. B. KAUFMANN, with E. GOSSMANN, *Nachbarschaft von Schule und Gemeinde* (Gütersloh, 1990) • V. A. McCLELLAND, ed., *Christian Education in a Pluralist Society* (London, 1988) • N. METTE, "The Christian Community's Task in the Process of Religious Education," *The Transmission of the Faith to the Next Generation* (ed. N. Greinacher and V. Elizondo; Edinburgh, 1984) 69-75 • G. MORAN, *Religious Education Development* (Minneapolis, 1983) • K. E. NIPKOW, *Bildung als*

Lebensbegleitung und Erneuerung. Kirchliche Bildungs-verantwortung in Gemeinde, Schule und Gesellschaft (Gütersloh, 1990) • E. ROSENBOOM, "Gemeindepäda-gogik–eine Herausforderung an die Kirche," *Leben und Erziehen durch Glauben* (Gütersloh, 1978) 55-71 • M. RUHFUS, *Diakonie-Lernen in der Gemeinde. Grund-züge einer diakonischen Gemeindepädagogik* (Rothen-burg, 1991) • E. SCHWERIN, ed., *Gemeindepädagogik. Lernwege der Kirche in einer sozialistischen Gesellschaft. Gemeindepädagogische Ansätze, Spuren, Erträge* (Mün-ster, 1991).

ELSBE GOSSMANN and
HANS-BERNHARD KAUFMANN

Christian Labor Unions → Labor Unions, Christian

Christian Peace Conference

1. Founding and Goal
2. Organization
3. Guidelines
4. Recent Changes

1. Founding and Goal

The Christian Peace Conference (CPC) was founded in Prague in 1958 under the leadership of several important theologians and church leaders, including Joachim Beckmann, Josef Hromádka, Hans-Joachim Iwand, Martin → Niemöller, Werner Schmauch, Hel-mut Gollwitzer, and Heinrich Vogel. Its headquarters are in Prague. It is an ecumenically oriented move-ment inspired by the → gospel of peace. It seeks the establishment and safeguarding of → peace, social justice and a life of dignity for all, and the settlement of disputes on the basis of peaceful coexistence and the renunciation of → force. It formerly was at work in some 90 countries and had contacts with churches not represented in → World Council of Churches (WCC) bodies (e.g., in Viet Nam and North Korea). It is registered with the → United Nations as a non-governmental organization.

2. Organization

2.1. Churches, Christian societies, groups, and in-dividuals could all be members if they agreed with the aims and were ready to support them.

2.2. The work of the CPC was done through various commissions and study groups.

2.3. Every three to seven years or so there was an All Christian Peace Assembly, the main instrument

of the CPC. It discussed relevant theological, ecu-menical, and international peace problems and es-tablished guidelines for the work of the CPC. Thus far six assemblies have been convened — in 1961, 1964, 1968, 1971, 1978, and 1985.

2.4. Since 1975 there have been regional branches: in Asia (India), begun in 1975; in Africa (Sierra Leone), in 1977; and in Latin America (Mex-ico), in 1978. The CPC has had regular contacts with liberation movements like the Palestine Liberation Organization (PLO) and South West Africa's Peace Organization (SWAPO).

3. Guidelines

3.1. The CPC was founded during the years of the cold war for various reasons: recognition of Christian failure in two world wars; the need of the churches for peace as this had emerged in the → ecumenical movement; the challenge posed to the churches by → socialist societies; and developments in the Third World. Avoidance of nuclear war (→ Weapons; War) is the main goal, but peace and justice are seen to be related, hence the interest in liberation movements and in dialogue between East and West. A particular concern has been dialogue between Christians and → Marxists, with the aim of setting up a credible witness of the church to the world, especially in so-cialist countries.

3.2. The CPC worked closely with the WCC and other ecumenical organs (→ All Africa Conference of Churches; Conference of European Churches) and also was open to contacts with secular organizations.

4. Recent Changes

In view of the recent political changes in central and eastern Europe, the CPC leadership issued a state-ment in December 1989. It declared, in part, "The leadership of the CPC believes that our movement had an important mission to fulfill, in that it became an ecumenical forum for the churches in Eastern Europe and in other parts of the world where social-ist states had been established, and it tried to make visible the presence of the Christian faith in these countries. It is true that during the difficult period of the cold war and in an atmosphere of strong ideological pressure, the CPC accepted some com-promises, made mistakes, and in some cases gave way to pressure. We need to do penance for this and to alter our methods of working and our terminology in the future, in the spirit of the new challenges of our times."

In 1990 the activities of the movement were con-siderably reduced. It now maintains a small office in Prague and publishes the *CPC Information* in English and German six times a year. An International Coordination Committee meets regularly. The Women's Desk is active, as are the regional committees in Europe, Asia, and Latin America.

Bibliography: Asian Christian Peace Conference (Prague, 1986) • Christian Involvement in the Promotion of Liberation, Peace, and Justice (Prague, 1985) • Christian Women Call for Peace (Prague, 1975) • Equal before God: CPC Essays on Anti-Racism (Budapest, 1982) • God Calls: Choose Life! (Papers of the Sixth All Christian Peace Assembly; Prague, 1985) • God Calls to Solidarity (Papers of the Fifth All Christian Peace Assembly; Prague, 1978) • Set Asia Free for Peace, with Justice and Dignity for All (Prague, 1985) • K. Tóth, Living as a Christian in Today's World (Prague, 1981).

KÁROLY TÓTH

Christian Political Parties → Political Parties

Christian Publishing

1. Definition
2. History
3. Development and Organization
4. Conservative Religious Publishing in the United States
5. Problems and Prospects

1. Definition

Christian (or, more frequently, *religious*) *publishing* is an autonomous literary activity that supplements the oral witness to the Christian faith and is "addressed to man in his total situation" (mandate of the Christian Literature Fund [subsequently, as the Agency for Christian Literature Development of the World Council of Churches, a founding partner of the World Association for Christian Communication], 1963). It is particularly suited for purposes of presenting the Christian message in depth, making possible concentrated theological study, fostering devotional life (→ Devotion, Devotions), spreading new and accurate information, and stimulating free reflection on matters of faith, → vocation, and the life of society. Literary programs of any kind obviously presuppose → literacy, and it is important to note that Christian publishing in many societies is often marked by a literacy component.

2. History

Publishing in the modern sense began with the invention by Johannes Gutenberg (d. 1468) of printing by means of movable type. In Gutenberg's Germany the → Reformation was marked by the spread of Christian literature in the vernacular; well-known printers were Hans Lufft at Wittenberg and Johan Froben at Basel. Religious writings represented a large segment of all publications in the first two centuries of printing: out of all German titles published before 1700, about 30 percent were of Protestant origin and about 15 percent of → Roman Catholic origin. Roman Catholic → missions founded printing establishments early in many countries: Goa, India (1556), America (1584), Japan (1590), and the Congo (1624). In Europe only a few firms survived the → Thirty Years' War (1618-48), including Cambridge University Press (1583), which began its publication of Bibles with the Geneva Bible of 1591, and Kösel Verlag in Kempten (1593, now in Munich).

After the Reformation, significant religious movements contributed to the establishment of exemplary publishing firms. → Pietism gave rise in Halle to the "orphanage bookshop" of A. H. → Francke (1698), which among other things introduced fixed prices, and also to the von Canstein Bible House, which initiated the printing of inexpensive Bibles in large quantities. The Society for Promoting Christian Knowledge (SPCK) was founded by five Anglican laymen in London in 1698; its commitment to the publication of literary, theological, liturgical, and educational materials continues to the present through daughter institutions in all parts of the world. In 1712 SPCK supplied the first Protestant printing press in India for the Danish Halle Mission. The English → revivals produced both the Religious Tract Society (1799), which in 1935 merged with affiliates to become the United Society for Christian Literature, and the British and Foreign Bible Society (1804), which subsequently provided the pattern for many similar → Bible societies throughout the world.

The spread of various confessional churches in the United States led to the founding of a number of denominational publishing houses, beginning in 1789 with the Methodist Book Concern, now Abingdon Press, headquartered in Nashville, Tennessee. Organized Presbyterian publishing began in 1838 and, after several consolidations, has been centered since 1988 in the work of Westminster/John Knox Press in Louisville, Kentucky (→ Presbyterianism). Lutheran publishing began in a number of places: the Henkel Press in New Market, Virginia, in 1806; in Rock Island, Illinois, in 1855 (the Augustana Book Concern, 1889); and in Philadelphia, Pennsylvania, in 1855. After mergers in 1962, Lutheran publishing took its chief identity as Fortress Press in Philadelphia; since 1989, when Fortress joined with the Augsburg Publishing House, it has been centered in Minneapolis, Minnesota, as Augsburg Fortress Publishers. The Lutheran Church–Missouri Synod owns the Concordia Publishing House, which was founded in 1869 in St. Louis, Missouri (→ Lutheran Churches).

As a result of similar impulses, free church publishing houses were founded in Germany and Switzerland by the → Baptists, → Plymouth Brethren, and Methodists (→ Methodism); these include J. G. Oncken (1828) and K. Brockhaus (1853). It is important to note that in Europe, Protestant publishing has been centered in privately owned enterprises rather than, as in much of American religious publishing, church-owned houses. Lutheran and Reformed awakenings in 19th-century Europe resulted in various tract societies, bookshops, and publishing houses founded for the purposes of mission, → diakonia, and → Christian education: in Germany, Calwer Verlag, which arose from a tract society in 1836, and C. Bertelsmann, which was founded in 1835. The Bärenreiter Verlag, also in Germany, arose in 1924 on the basis of renewed interest in → church music.

In Britain, Hodder & Stoughton began its program of religious publishing in 1868, and the modern → evangelical movement lay behind the establishment of Inter-Varsity Press in 1935. The Student Christian Movement Press (incorporated as SCM Press in 1929) was actually developed at the end of the 19th century out of the Student Volunteer Movement (→ Student Work), which was itself inspired by the great modern ecumenist John R. Mott (1865-1955). The global → ecumenical movement has also produced other publishing enterprises, such as WCC Publications, part of the → World Council of Churches in Geneva (1948), La Aurora in Buenos Aires (1926-92), and the joint trading arm of Christian publishing houses in Japan, Nikki Han in Tokyo (1968), which provides Christian books to more than 200 non-Christian bookshops.

Dating from only 1906 but currently the fastest growing movement in 20th-century Christianity, Pentecostalism, despite its emphasis on oral rather than printed witness, is now producing not only much popular literature but also first-generation academic theology. Such work is published in Latin America, where the movement is strongest, as well as in Asia and the Northern Hemisphere. Significant periodicals include *Pneuma: The Journal of the Society for Pentecostal Studies* (Fresno, Calif., 1979-) and the *Journal of Pentecostal Theology* (Sheffield,

Eng., 1992-); a recent promising addition is the *Asian Journal of Pentecostal Studies* (Baguio City, Philippines, 1998-).

The → Enlightenment gave rise to the phenomenon of the periodical, which has subsequently taken such varied forms as theological journals, missionary magazines, books of daily readings (→ Devotional Literature 3), and calendars. The first Christian journal, which was particularly concerned with missions, was founded in Dresden in 1701. The first newspaper of any kind in India was produced in 1818 in Bengali by the great missionary William Carey.

The publication of academic theology was first undertaken by private firms: in Germany, Vandenhoeck & Ruprecht (1735), J. C. Hinrichs (1791), J. C. B. Mohr (Paul Siebeck) (1801 and 1878); in the United Kingdom, T. & T. Clark (1828) and SCM Press in London. In the United States, Wm. B. Eerdmans (1911), Harper (now HarperCollins) from 1926, and a number of denominational and ecumenical publishers — notably Fortress Press, Westminster/John Knox Press, and Trinity Press International (1989) — were also early concerned with the publication of serious theology, a commitment that continues. A significant number of university presses — Oxford, Cambridge, Princeton, Yale, and Chicago, to name several — have distinguished themselves in the English-speaking world by strong programs of theological publishing. Extremely important in the publication of scholarly work for the academic study of religion has been the program in the United States of Scholars Press, formed over the course of the 1970s by a number of learned societies in American universities and theological faculties, most notable being the American Academy of Religion and the Society of Biblical Literature. Scholars Press, in Atlanta, Georgia, focuses on the publication of dissertations and series of specialized research works in a wide variety of academic areas that impinge directly or indirectly on the study of religion. Its program is by no means restricted to Christianity or other Western religious traditions.

During its existence, the Theological Education Fund (1958-77) promoted theological publishing in the → Third World, being helped largely by distribution through organizations such as World Christian Books. In Asia, Africa, and Latin America, theological publishing — originally often of translations of European and North American works, but now of original work from Third World contexts — is expanding through independent, church-related, and internationally affiliated firms. The annual *Buchmesse* at Frankfurt has become a location for interchange between publishers and consequently the internationalization of markets. The World Association for → Christian Communication annually provides at the Frankfurt Book Fair an opportunity for selected younger publishers from Asia, Africa, and Latin America to engage in training programs and seminars concerning both the philosophy and the techniques of international religious publishing.

There are some Roman Catholic publishing firms marked by a long history — such as the German firm Aschendorff (1720, Münster) — but it was the renewal of the church and the papacy in the 19th and 20th centuries that provided the most important impulses for contemporary Catholic publishing. In Germany such publishing has also included vigorous programs centered in journals (Bachem, 1818, and Schöningh, 1847). Roman Catholic publishing in Asia and Africa has emphasized journals rather than books. Thus in Africa in 1980 there were 242 Roman Catholic periodicals, compared with only 131 Protestant periodicals, although there were only 33 Catholic publishers, compared with 208 Protestant houses. Roman Catholic publishing has also been marked by global institutions and translation programs (esp. Herder, 1801), by the international publishing and marketing of Catholic encyclopedias, children's books, and specialized works, as well as by an emphasis on the development of library programs (the Borromeo Society, 1844).

Private trade publishers as well as organizations sponsored by religious → orders have in recent times provided the chief vehicles for Roman Catholic publishing, especially in the United States (Paulist Press [1866], Crossroads [Herder, 1957], Continuum [an imprint of Crossroads from 1980 and subsequently independent], Ignatius Press [1978]) and in the United Kingdom (Darton, Longman & Todd [1959]). Increasingly, however, in these countries the academic and devotional lists of such publishers as SCM Press, T. & T. Clark, Fortress Press, Eerdmans, Continuum, and Trinity Press International have become thoroughly ecumenical, providing major outlets for both Protestant and Roman Catholic authors. Roman Catholic religious orders have also set up presses with specific theological or programmatic emphases, such as those of the social justice movement of the 19th century, the → liturgical movement from the 1920s, the reforms of Vatican II (e.g., the international series *Concilium*), and → liberation theology (e.g., Orbis Books, founded in 1972 by the Maryknoll order).

Extremely significant changes in Christian publishing have taken place in recent years in eastern Europe and China. The disintegration of the Soviet Union and its satellite empire (1989-91) opened the way for countless new religious activities within both the older states and the newly created nations located in the territory of the former USSR. In Russia extremely depressed economic conditions and the lack of viable distribution systems continue to hinder large-scale expansion, but there nevertheless are many new religious publishing ventures, very often found in local areas and often undertaken by single individuals with computer capabilities. Particular dioceses, monasteries, lay organizations, and even local parishes of the Moscow Patriarchate (Orthodox) have undertaken the republication of liturgical, catechetical, and theological literature, often with subsidies from Western Christian organizations. Prominent among several newly founded independent Orthodox publishing houses in Russia is one established by the Alexander Men Society (→ Orthodox Church) after the 1990 death of Men, an Orthodox priest and theologian. An important Christian magazine, *Istina i Zhizh'* (Truth and life), is a Roman Catholic initiative, although it is also notable for the active participation of ecumenically minded Orthodox priests and laity. Baptists in Russia are prolific in their production of evangelistic tracts.

Roman Catholic publishing particularly has become stronger since the early 1990s in Belarus, Croatia, the Czech Republic, Hungary, Lithuania, Poland, Slovakia, Slovenia, and the Ukraine. Reformed publishing efforts have increased mainly in Hungary and the Czech Republic; new Lutheran initiatives have arisen in Hungary, Estonia, Latvia, and in both the German-speaking and the Finnish-speaking communities within Russia. With international support, the → Armenian Apostolic Church opened its first modern printing and publishing house in 1996.

In China, in spite of internationally noted tensions caused by the ambiguous policy of the government toward religious institutions, Christian publishing and distribution initiatives have nevertheless grown remarkably, especially since the death of Chairman Mao in 1976. In 1985 with the consent of the Chinese government, the international United Bible Societies helped establish a large printing house for the publication of Bibles (the Amity Foundation, Nanking), and in its first decade this house published and sold nearly 13 million complete Bibles and portions of Scripture. In cooperation with the China Christian Council, this house also has published more than 4 million hymnals and 2.6 short catechisms, mainly for new believers in Christianity. Notable among a growing number of publications in China is the magazine *Tian Feng* (Heavenly wind), which in 1994 had a monthly circulation in excess of 100,000, and the *Nanjing Theological Review,* which has attained international respect as a source for Chinese theological insight (→ Asian Theology). More and more evangelistic tapes and other Christian educational materials are also being produced. Hong Kong, especially before being handed over to China in 1997, has provided a great deal of published material in Chinese, being home to about 30 Christian publishers, 40 Protestant bookstores, and three Christian newspapers (two Protestant and one Roman Catholic). Most of these Hong Kong institutions represent conservative movements within Christianity. Hong Kong also has a program designed for the translation of serious international theological work into Chinese languages.

3. Development and Organization

Religious publishing around the world is marked by broad differences in professional structure, development, and organization. In Europe and North America the infrastructure for religious publishing is professionally well developed — as, for example, in the United States, where over 600 firms publish approximately 3,500 to 4,000 religious titles each year, representing some 6.5 percent of all titles published, and these are sold through more than 3,000 bookstores; or in Germany, where nearly 2,500 religious titles are published annually by about 200 firms, representing 4-5 percent of all titles published. Sales are chiefly through 300 Christian bookstores. In many parts of Asia, Africa, and Latin America, Christian publishing is well developed — as, for example, in South Korea, where Christian titles represent about 8 percent of all titles published, Japan (2 percent of all books published are Christian in content), Indonesia (where BPK, the Protestant publishing house in Jakarta, is one of the largest in all Asia), India, Nigeria, Ghana, Kenya, Argentina, Brazil, and Mexico. The situation is predictably different and far more difficult in Islamic nations, which often have no more than a single bookshop, and in countries marked by programmatic suppression of Christian activities by Communism (e.g., North Korea) or by fundamentalistic forces within Islam (e.g., Iran, Sudan, and Saudi Arabia).

In Germany, Austria, and Switzerland important organizations of religious publishers and distributors include the Vereinigung evangelischer Buchhändler und Verleger (United Evangelical Booksellers and Publishers, founded in 1886 and bearing its current name since 1925) and the Verband katholischer Verleger und Buchhändler (Union of Catholic Publishers and Booksellers, founded in 1906, with its present name since 1951). These two organizations engage in joint advertising and career education on an ecumenical basis, with the regular participation of more conservative religious publishers.

In North America the Christian Booksellers' Association (see 4) sponsors an annual trade convention that includes a highly developed program of professional education. The association has also helped found similar organizations in at least five other countries. Two organizations important in overall U.S. religious publishing are the Evangelical Christian Publishers Association (ECPA, 1974) and the Protestant Church-Owned Publishers Association (PCPA, 1951). Membership in the former group, in 1997 numbering 194 organizations, is restricted to publishers whose programs express views consistent with the association's conservative statement of faith. The second group, composed exclusively of publishers owned and controlled by American Protestant churches, is by no means strictly to be identified with *evangelical* Christianity. A similar organization, the Catholic Book Publishers Association (1987), has a membership of over 180 organizations, including more than 70 publishers.

Organizations similar to the Christian Booksellers Association, though smaller, exist outside of North America, including some in the Third World, where nearly all Protestant publishers cooperate with → national Christian councils. Other organizations with affinities to the world of religious publishers include the ecumenical Christian Literature Society in Madras, India (founded as the Madras Religious Tract and Book Society in 1818, with its present name since 1981), the Centro de Comunicación in Mexico City, and the Chinese Christian Literature Council in Hong Kong (established in Shanghai in 1887 as the Christian Literature Society and in Hong Kong since 1951 with its present name). Common centers for training in publishing, among other fields of → communication, are found, for example, in India, Kenya, and Zambia. The World Association for Christian Communication (WACC) maintains an important program of global education in publishing, oriented primarily toward the need of Third World publishers and centered in activities at the annual Frankfurt *Buchmesse.*

4. Conservative Religious Publishing in the United States

In the United States the publishing of conservative — evangelical — Christian books is a billion-dollar business that deserves special attention. In 1870 Fleming H. Revell, brother-in-law of evangelist

Dwight L. → Moody, launched, at Moody's urging, a publishing company for the production of → Sunday school material. Two years later Revell turned to the publication of books, and by 1890 he had become the U.S. leader in the production of such books. He established evangelical publishing as predominantly a nondenominational, lay-oriented, profit-making enterprise.

The pattern set by Revell was followed rapidly and successfully by others. In 1875 David C. Cook, a Chicago businessman, founded a company to publish *Our Sunday School Quarterly* and other educational materials. In 1901 the company was moved to Elgin, Illinois, where it has remained, under family leadership, now being known as Cook Communication Ministries. In like manner, Daniel S. Warner, influenced by holiness revivals, in 1881 started the Gospel Trumpet Company for the publication of periodicals, and in 1906 that company, already identified with book publishing, moved to become part of the Church of God (Anderson, Ind.; → Churches of God). Since 1962 it has been known as Warner Press. Moody himself established the Bible Institute Colportage Association to distribute paperback books produced for him by his son-in-law, Fleming Revell. In 1941 that association became officially affiliated with the Moody Bible Institute in Chicago, at which time it divided into Moody Press and the Colportage Department (now Moody Literature Ministries).

Grand Rapids, Michigan, is known in the United States as a center of Dutch Reformed Christianity. In 1911, after immigrating to the United States from the Netherlands and for a time attending Calvin Theological Seminary in Grand Rapids, William B. Eerdmans established a firm for the distribution of Dutch theological works. Soon thereafter he began the publication of original American works of theology. The firm has continued under William B. Eerdmans Jr. as a major publisher not only of Reformed theology but in recent years also as a publisher of serious and progressive ecumenical works for a wide variety of readers, specialists and laity. In 1931, after working for the senior Eerdmans, two of his nephews branched out to form, also in Grand Rapids, Zondervan Publishing House, which became a large publisher of Bibles and conservative Christian books. A third important Christian publisher in Grand Rapids is Baker Book House, founded in 1939 by Herman Baker, also a Dutch immigrant.

After World War II the number of evangelical presses in the United States increased dramatically. Noteworthy among more recently founded such publishers have been InterVarsity Press (1947, with earlier connections with its U.K. counterpart), Word Books (1951, Waco, Tex.), Multnomah Press (1970, Portland, Oreg.), and Tyndale House (1972, Wheaton, Ill.). Thomas Nelson Publishers (Nashville), in 1998 the world's largest Bible publisher, was the result of a merger in 1969 of Royal Publishing, a relatively small Bible publisher founded in 1961, and Thomas Nelson, a venerable publisher of Bibles founded in Edinburgh in 1796. It is worth noting that the publication of Bibles is a highly specialized area of religious publishing with unique translation, production, and distribution requirements. Bibles are virtually always published in collaboration with Bible societies and/or national councils of churches. Tyndale House, through the publication of its own paraphrase of the Bible prepared by its founder, Kenneth N. Taylor, *The Living Bible,* which by 1996 had sold 40 million copies, was itself a kind of watershed in conservative Christian publishing in America, bringing evangelical publishing to the attention of the broader reading public and drawing countless new buyers into Christian and general bookstores.

Several of the larger of these evangelical publishers have been taken over by secular publishers and corporations. Word Books was purchased by the American Broadcasting Company (ABC) in 1974, which subsequently became a part of the entertainment conglomerate Capitol Cities; Word is now a part of Thomas Nelson Publishers. After becoming a public company in 1976, Zondervan was bought in 1988 by Harper & Row (now HarperCollins Publishers) and thus became part of News Corporation Ltd., the international communications enterprise controlled by Rupert Murdoch.

An important arm of the conservative religious publishing effort in the United States is the Christian Booksellers Association (CBA), founded in 1950 at the initiative of several publishers and booksellers in the Chicago area. The association, headquartered in Colorado Springs, Colorado, comprises 2,800 member bookstores and more than 750 product and service suppliers. It is host to an annual international convention that regularly draws over 12,500 retailers, publishers, music companies, and other product suppliers.

Much recent American evangelical publishing has been built around the writing of extremely popular authors and their books. The evangelist Billy Graham has been of great importance in this regard, and a book by → dispensationalist Hal Lindsey, *The Late Great Planet Earth* (1973), sold over 10 million copies, breaking the U.S. sales record for a single religious book held for decades by *In His Steps,* Charles Sheldon's novel of 1897. Yet even with the popularity of such evangelical authors, total religious book sales slowed in the United States in the 1980s to half the annual growth rate of the 1970s. It appears, however, that the emergence of new, popular evangelical authors has stimulated a new growth phase in the late 1980s and 1990s.

5. Problems and Prospects

Many issues facing publishers of Christian books and other religious materials are perennial: the identification of suitable and relevant topics, the identification of new authors, the integrity of relationships between publishers and church communities, and new realities created by the modern ecumenical movement. Other issues, though also perennial, are now taking on radically new forms: the opportunities presented by the technologies of the electronic and computer ages, the relation of book publishing to other media ("Does the book have a future?"), and the hard economic realities posed by competitive forces in the new information age (→ Mass Media). These problems are transformed and heightened in both the emerging countries of eastern Europe and in the so-called Two-Thirds World of Asia, Africa, and Latin America. In the Southern Hemisphere especially, the task of equipping and training authors, editors, business and production managers, and distribution specialists is enormous. Throughout the world, in varying forms, obstacles to relevant publishing are being set up by economic difficulties (lack of resources, inflation), political restrictions (trade policies, censorship), cultural deprivations (small language groups, insufficient literacy), and even internal tensions within the Christian community (historical divisions, ideological conflicts).

In the late 1980s a major American study, supported by the Lilly Endowment of Indianapolis, Indiana, and entitled "The Role of Denominational Presses in the Publication of Theological Books" was undertaken, led by Barbara Wheeler, president of Auburn Theological Seminary in New York City, and Christopher Walters-Bugbee, then editor of the periodical *Books and Religion*. This study, completed in 1988 but not yet adequately pursued or even noted among church leaders, scholars, and publishers, raised questions relevant to the task of publishers of religious books in a wide variety of settings — denominational, ecumenical, independent, academic, evangelical, and interfaith. The report was marked by melancholy conclusions concerning the content and purpose of ecclesially oriented theological publishing, such as that "few denominational officials regard theological publishing as a critical element in their church's mission," and that such leaders do not

see "the present challenge confronting the mainline denominations" as fundamentally theological. These conclusions, far-reaching indeed, are most pressing in respect to religious publishing. Responsible religious publishing requires new patterns of partnership between publishers, authors, scholars, and leaders of religious communities.

Even the question "What is a religious book?" is not being clearly answered. Some publishers answer that question by reference to "whatever is authentically human." Others restrict religious publishing to the classic texts of religious traditions or to programmatic concerns of religious communities. The classification of "self-help books" as religious books is indeed problematic, even though prevalent among both publishers and distributors. Similarly, many publishers are unable adequately to identify markets (laity, clergy, academic) for elements within publishing lists.

Questions such as these — economic, technological, cultural, theological, and professional — have caused many to question the future viability of religious publishing as it has been known since the 16th century. They impinge not only on established patterns of religious publishing in Europe and North America but also on the developing mission and vocation of such publishing in the Southern Hemisphere. At the present time realism requires that imaginative and professional solutions to "problems" must determine "prospects" in respect to viable and dedicated Christian publishing.

Bibliography: J. S. DUKE, *Religious Publishing and Communications* (White Plains, N.Y., 1981) • F. J. EILERS, *Christliche Publizistik in Afrika* (Steyl, 1974); idem, ed., *Communication Directory — Africa* (Paderborn, 1980); idem, ed., *Communication Directory — Asia* (Paderborn, 1982) • *Der evangelische Buchhandel* (Stuttgart, 1961) • A. GILMORE, *Agenda for Development: The Future of Third World Christian Publishing* (London, 1996) • L. G. GOSS and D. M. AYCOCK, eds., *Inside Religious Publishing* (Grand Rapids, 1991) • C. LIENEMANN-PERRIN, *Training for a Relevant Ministry* (Madras and Geneva, 1981) on the Theological Education Fund • R. N. OSTLING, "Evangelical Publishing and Broadcasting," *Evangelicalism and Modern America* (ed. G. Marsden; Grand Rapids, 1984) 46-55 • Q. J. SCHULTZE, ed., *American Evangelicals and the Mass Media* (Grand Rapids, 1990) in this volume, see esp. M. Fackler, "A Short History of Evangelical Scholarship in Communication Studies," 357-71 • L. I. SWEET, ed., *Communication and Change in American Religious History* (Grand Rapids, 1993) in this volume, see esp. E. J. O'Brien, "American Christianity and the History of

Communication: A Bibliographic Probe," 355-479 • B. G. WHEELER, "Theological Publishing: In Need of a Mandate," *CCen*, November 23, 1988, 1066-70 (the entire 1988 report, *A Study of the Role of Denominational Presses in the Publication of Theological Books,* is available from the Lilly Endowment, Indianapolis).

No single source comprehensively presents either the history or the current situation of Christian publishing. The most recent lexicon article, admittedly Eurocentric, is that by D. FAUQUET-PLÜMACHER, "Buch, Buchwesen III," *TRE* 7.275-90 with detailed bibliography. Current information on China and Third World countries can be secured from the WACC (London), and on eastern Europe from *Glaube in der Zweiten Welt* (Zollikon, Switz.).

ARNDT RUPRECHT and NORMAN A. HJELM

Christian Science

1. Rise
2. Teaching
3. Healing
4. Worship

1. Rise

In the early 1860s the American Mary Baker Eddy (1821-1910) reported that she was cured of a nervous disorder with physical manifestations by a healer named P. P. Quimby (1802-66) in Belfast, Maine. She connected a further healing in 1866 with Matt. 9:2, and according to her own statements, she came to the view that the life of the spirit is the only reality. She produced her main work, *Science and Health, with Key to the Scriptures (SH),* in 1875. The Christian Scientists Association was founded in 1876, and then in 1892 a new central organization called The First Church of Christ, Scientist, was formed in Boston. In the early 1990s there were about 3,000 churches, associations, and high school unions in 68 countries. The Christian Science Publishing Company in Boston, founded in 1898, publishes a newspaper *(Christian Science Monitor)* and journals *(Herald of Christian Science,* in 13 languages, and *Christian Science Journal).* Each church has an official reading room with Christian Science literature.

2. Teaching

Jesus was the first to "demonstrate" the power of Christian Science *(SH,* 110, line 25), and now in the modern age M. B. Eddy has been enabled to continue it. She summarized her understanding of truth in the following four principles of divine metaphysics:

1. God is All-in-all.
2. God is good. Good is Mind.
3. God, Spirit, being all, nothing is matter.
4. Life, God, omnipotent good, deny death, evil, sin, disease. — Disease, sin, evil, death, deny good, omnipotent God, Life (113.16-21).

Furthermore, "Spirit, God, is infinite, all. Spirit can have no opposite" (278.10-11). Matter, wickedness, sin, sickness, and death — all alike are mental illusion.

The founder's mental or spiritual exegesis of Scripture is normative. At the heart of the NT we do not find the death and → resurrection of Jesus Christ; rather, "the central fact of the Bible is the superiority of spiritual over physical power" (131.10-11). Hence biblical statements have a different meaning for Christian Science than for all the churches (→ Exegesis, Biblical). Creation is the unfolding of mental ideas, redemption is liberation "from all error, physical and mental" (132.25-26), grace is not God's all-embracing mercy but the fact that Jesus shows us the new way. According to Eddy, the petition "Thy kingdom come" means "Thy kingdom is come; Thou art ever-present" (16.30-31). The supreme → prayer (mental) "is not one of → faith merely; it is demonstration" (16.3-4). Christ is "the divine image, idea" (333.26) — the idea of God, ideal truth, as Jesus himself first demonstrated.

3. Healing

Christian Science lays great stress on the → healing of the sick. According to its basic concepts, sickness has no reality. For the Christian Science healer, "sickness is a dream from which the patient needs to be awakened" (417.20-21). The healer or practitioner must first free patients from their → fear and make them see that they are indeed liberated from sickness and danger (411.27-28). Christian Science rejects the idea that this is a matter of suggestion. *SH* even holds out the possibility of "mental surgery" (402.6).

Worldwide, some 3,000 full-time healers are at work, devoted to healing through prayer. Only in an emergency may medical help be sought.

4. Worship

Christian Science worship consists of hymns, prayers, and responsive readings from the Bible and *SH.* There is no → preaching. → Baptism is spiritualized as "purification from all error" (35.19), and hence it is not celebrated. Neither is the Eucharist per se. Twice a year there is a Communion, but it consists of quiet absorption into union with God. Membership includes belonging to one of the churches (→

Church Membership). Ecumenical relations have never been pursued.

There have been some splits. J. W. Doorly (1878-1950), a former president of the mother church, and M. Kappeler developed their own understanding and gained some adherents after being expelled from the church.

Bibliography: Primary sources: M. B. EDDY, Manual of the Mother Church (Boston, 1936; orig. pub., 1895); idem, Science and Health, with Key to the Scriptures (Boston, 1994; orig. pub., 1875) • I. C. TOMLINSON, Twelve Years with Mary Baker Eddy (Boston, 1945).

Secondary works: C. S. BRADEN, Christian Science Today: Power, Policy, Practice (Dallas, 1958) • S. GOTTSCHALK, The Emergence of Christian Science in American Religious Life (Berkeley, Calif., 1973) • K. HUTTEN, Seher, Grübler, Enthusiasten (Stuttgart, 1950; 14th ed., 1989) 382-401 (bibliography) • S. E. KNEE, Christian Science in the Age of Mary Baker Eddy (Westport, Conn., 1994) • H.-D. REIMER, Metaphysisches Heilen. Eine kritische Darstellung der "Christlichen Wissenschaft" (Stuttgart, 1966) • H. RELLER, ed., Handbuch Religiöse Gemeinschaften (Gütersloh, 1978; 3d ed., 1985) 253-64.

OSWALD EGGENBERGER

Christian World Communions

Toward the end of the 19th century and the first half of the 20th, worldwide denominational communions began to be founded. The first was the → Anglican Communion (1867, the first Lambeth Conference), followed by the → Reformed Alliance (1877). The original term "worldwide alliances" was found to be unsuitable, and since 1979 the usual term has been "Christian World Communions" (CWCs). A self-definition from 1962 reads: "These bodies have this in common: (1) that their member churches share together not only the general tradition which is common to all Christian churches, but also specific traditions which have grown out of spiritual crises in the history of the church; (2) that they desire to render witness to specific convictions of doctrinal or ecclesiological character which they consider to be essential for the life of the whole church of Christ."

Since 1958 there has been an annual meeting of secretaries of the CWCs, which serves as a communication link. The groups represented are the Anglican Communion, → Baptist World Alliance, → Friends World Committee for Consultation, General Conference of Seventh-day → Adventists, → Lutheran World Federation, → Mennonite World Conference, → Old Catholic Churches (Utrecht Union), → Orthodox Church (→ Ecumenical Patriarchate and Moscow Patriarchate), → Reformed Alliance, → Reformed Ecumenical Council, → Roman Catholic Church (through the Pontifical Council for Promoting Christian Unity; → Curia 1.2.4), → Salvation Army, World Convention of the Churches of Christ (Disciples; → Christian Church [Disciples of Christ]), and → World Methodist Council.

Finally, CWCs represent the organizational and structural expression for Christian confessions as spiritual and ecclesiastical realities. Three concerns are typical. First, they see themselves as the one, catholic, and apostolic church, each existing in a specific form. It is evident to them that the one apostolic faith and the one catholic church exist in many different forms (→ Catholic, Catholicity). Second, they live with the conscious awareness of the historical continuity and deep rootedness of their faith. In a particular way they thus represent a spiritual inheritance in its meaning for faith and witness today. Third, in the CWCs the universality of Christian fellowship finds special expression, even though each individual member church represents only a partial realization of it. They thus strongly stand for the Christian faith and fellowship that transcends all geographic, ethnic, cultural, political, and national boundaries (→ Ecumenism).

According to the aims usually stated in their constitutions, CWCs seek not only to foster the fellowship and cooperation of their own member churches but also to promote and participate in the all-embracing → ecumenical movement. One important form of fulfilling this ecumenical duty is that of bilateral dialogues (→ Ecumenical Dialogue), in which many of the CWCs are engaged. Relations with the World Council of Churches (WCC) were at first strained, even though most (though not all!) denominations were members of the council. The reason was that the CWCs represented a form of Christian → unity that allowed a place for denominational differences (→ Denomination 4-5) The concept of "unity with reconciled differences" (→ Unity 3.2), as developed by the CWCs, reduces their view to a formula. The justification of such a view of Christian unity was recognized by the WCC only after some hesitation (→ Ecumenical Movement 4). More recently, however, the relation between CWCs and the WCC has been one of partnership or mutual support.

Bibliography: A. J. VAN DER BENT, "Christian World Communions," DEM 156-59 • H. E. FEY, "Confessional Families and the Ecumenical Movement," A History of the *Ecumenical Movement*, vol. 2, *The Ecumenical Advance, 1948-1968* (ed. H. E. Fey; 2d ed.; Geneva, 1986) 115-42 • Y. Ishida, H. Meyer, and E. Perret, *The History and Theological Concerns of World Confessional Families* (=LWF.R, August 1979) • M. Kinnamon and T. F. Best, eds., *Called to Be One in Christ: United Churches and the Ecumenical Movement* (Geneva, 1985) • H. Meyer, "Weltweite Christliche Gemeinschaften," ÖL 1260-66.

HARDING MEYER

Christians for Socialism

1. Founding
2. Worldwide Scope
3. Agenda

1. Founding

The Christians for Socialism movement was started in Santiago, Chile, in April 1971. Beginning in 1967, many groups of Latin American priests had taken up the cause of the poor (→ Poverty). Their experience of mass misery had led them from reformism, which brought no amelioration, to the demand for a Latin American → socialism. This experience was the root of → liberation theology.

After the triumph of the Unidad Popular in Chile in 1970, the hardening middle-class opposition, which laid claim to the Christian tradition, made it necessary to publicize the new Christian identity, the cooperation of Christianity and → Marxism. This was done by the founding of Christians for Socialism and the publication of its confession, *We Are Committed to Socialism,* which contained the decisive sentence: "To be a Christian is to be in solidarity." This document unleashed a campaign of defamation on the part of the opposition press and also led to a lively theological debate within the church. Counterarguments included the incompatibility of Christianity and socialism and the one-sided and intolerant understanding of solidarity. A pastoral letter from the bishops stressed the danger to the church's unity. A group of theological professors at the Catholic University, however, supported Christians for Socialism.

On April 23-30, 1972, the first Latin American Congress of Christians for Socialism took place in Santiago, with over 400 delegates from 28 countries. Its final statement formed the basis for the world movement, recognizing class conflict as a fact on a global scale (given the alliance of imperialism and middle-class nationalism or fascist dictatorship; → Class and Social Stratum). It also affirmed that the logic of politics impels toward → revolutionary change, noting the convergence of radical faith and radical political engagement and understanding faith as a critical and dynamic force in the revolutionary process.

2. Worldwide Scope

Christians for Socialism soon spread to Europe, with a group forming in Spain in 1973. It was preceded by various movements of reform and protest such as the → base communities in Florence and Holland and the ecumenical group Politisches Nachtgebet in various countries, the latter forming the basis for Christians for Socialism in Germany and Holland (Arnhem, 1973). In central and western Europe, members of Christians for Socialism come from the middle class and engage strongly in both ecclesiastical and theological criticism.

Groups also exist in some of the cities of the United States and Canada. The first world congress in Quebec in 1975, in a final statement, supported the Santiago theses, adding more detailed political and economic analysis.

3. Agenda

The fall of Chile's S. Allende on September 11, 1973, and the setting up of a military dictatorship showed that parliamentary majorities are not sufficient to achieve a socialist structure. Unresolved questions include the following: Who can bring about the needed change? What form will socialism take? What can Christians contribute? European congresses in 1976, 1979, and 1983, and the world congress at Barcelona in January 1984, which had as its theme "Christians in Liberation Movements," took up these questions. Since there is no central direction, individual groups develop their own understanding of socialism and Christianity independently. The mode of operation is that of open discussion.

→ Marxism and Christianity

Bibliography: Christians for Socialism, Münster Group, *Zur Rettung des Feuers* (Münster, 1981) • L. Ossa, *Christliche Basis-Gemeinden und die Zuspitzung sozialer Auseinandersetzungen in Chile* (Frankfurt, 1977) • D. Sölle and K. Schmidt, eds., *Christen für den Sozialismus* (2 vols.; Stuttgart, 1975).

MARIE VEIT

Christmas

1. The birthdays of rulers were celebrated in the → Roman Empire, even after their deaths. Christians

naturally felt inclined to honor the birth of their *Kyrios* (→ Christological Titles). In the East the commemoration of Christ's nativity was January 6, the beginning of the solar year. This Feast of Epiphany celebrated especially Jesus' baptism. When Epiphany spread to the West, it celebrated the visit of the Magi to the Christ child (Matthew 2). About 330 the Roman church assigned December 25 as the birth of Christ. By the turn of the fifth century, the Roman practice was gradually becoming universal. Where both December 25 and January 6 were observed, this created a season of 12 days (→ Church Year).

It has been thought that the Roman date of December 25 was chosen for the nativity of Christ to counter the festival of the Invincible Sun *(Natale solis invicti)*, which Emperor Aurelian (269/70-75) established on December 25, 274, in honor of the Syrian sun god Emesa. It is more likely, however, that the December 25 date for the birth of Christ stems from the tradition of commemorating both the conception (annunciation) and death of Christ on March 25.

2. In the Roman tradition three → masses were celebrated on Christmas Eve and Christmas Day: *missa in nocte* (midnight), *missa in aurora* (dawn), and *missa in die* (during the day). The Gospels of these masses are the angelic announcement (Luke 2:1-14), the visit of the shepherds (Luke 2:15-20), and the → incarnation (John 1:1-18). The masses are often said to symbolize Christ's threefold birth (of the Father, of Mary, and in believers).

In Spain and Gaul a season of preparation for Christmas called Advent developed. Regulations on → fasting issued by Bishop Perpetuus of Tours (d. 490) called for three days of fasting per week from St. Martin's Day (November 11) to Christmas. This "St. Martin's Lent" was really a 40-day fast in preparation for baptism on Epiphany. Because this was a penitential season, the Gloria and Alleluia were dropped from the Mass, and purple → vestments were worn. The theme was repentance in preparation for the second coming of Christ in judgment (→ Parousia). In Rome there developed a two-week preparation for Christmas centered on the annunciation, with focus on the historical nativity of Christ. These two Western traditions were merged to produce the four-week season of Advent, which combines the second coming, the ministry of → John the Baptist, and the annunciation. In the Roman → liturgy the Alleluia was never dropped during Advent, and in more recent times the season has been seen as one of → hope rather than → penitence.

3. A number of popular customs developed around Advent and Christmas (→ Popular Religion). Advent customs include the Advent wreath, which originated in Germany in the 16th century; Advent calendars, which also originated in Germany; preparing the manger, from France; and Advent plays, such as the Search for an Inn (*Herbergesuchen* in Germany, *Posada* in Spain). Christmas customs have included the singing of carols (→ Hymnody); the nativity scene, or crèche (attributed to St. → Francis of Assisi); Christmas lights and fire (including the Yule log); the Christmas tree, which originated in Germany, perhaps as a blending of the Yule tree and the paradise tree used in the 11th-century paradise play; Christmas plays and pageants; greeting cards; gift exchanges; and special ethnic foods and drinks.

A number of special observances developed in connection with reveling during Christmas week, including the Feast of Fools *(Festum Fatuorum)*, the Feast of the Ass *(Festum Asinarium)*, and the Feast of the Boy Bishop on Holy Innocents' Day (December 28). The Reformation churches and the post-Tridentine papacy (→ Trent, Council of) discouraged these revels. German Lutherans (→ Lutheranism) focused on a thoughtful devotion to the Christ child and celebrated Christmas in a deeply spiritual way in churches and homes.

The English → Puritans, however, went as far as to abolish Christmas. In 1642 church services and civil celebrations were forbidden on December 25, and in 1647 Parliament ordered the abolition of Christmas and other holy days. This was enforced in spite of popular resistance to these measures, but Christmas was revived with the restoration of the monarchy in 1660. Puritan ideas were influential in early America and contributed to the secularization of Christmas, including the tradition of Santa Claus. In the American colonies the Dutch Sinter Klaas became Santa Claus, and the Visit from St. Nicholas was transferred from December 5 to Christmas Eve. Puritan aversion to → saints days and bishops resulted in modifying Santa's appearance so that he much more resembles the god Thor from Nordic mythology than the early fourth-century St. Nicholas.

→ Hymn

Bibliography: A. ADAM, *Das Kirchenjahr mitfeiern. Seine Geschichte und seine Bedeutung* (Freiburg, 1979) • W. P. DAWSON, *Christmas: Its Origins and Associations* (London, 1902) • H. LECLERCQ, "Crèche," *DACL* 3.2.2021ff. • L. MACKENSEN, "Geschichte des Weihnachtsbaumes," *Deutscher Kulturatlas* (Berlin, 1919) • H. MANG, *Unsere Weihnacht* (Innsbruck, 1927) • T. J. TALLEY, *The Origins* of the Liturgical Year (New York, 1986) • F. X. WEISER, Handbook of Christian Feasts and Customs (New York, 1952).

FRANK C. SENN

Christological Titles

1. Christological Titles as a Clue
   to Early Christian Faith
2. Son of Man
3. Other Titles
   3.1. Christ (Messiah)
   3.2. Lord
   3.3. Son of God
   3.4. Logos
   3.5. Son of David
   3.6. End-Time Prophet
   3.7. Servant of the Lord, High Priest, Lamb
4. The One Faith in Christ
   and Christological Titles

1. Christological Titles as a Clue
   to Early Christian Faith

The Christological titles offer an important clue to early Christian faith, though they do not disclose it fully. Early → Christology was essentially functional, being expressed preferably in short (confessional) statements. The titles play an important role in such statements, giving them a specific framework and horizon.

2. Son of Man

Most strongly connected with the earthly → Jesus is the title "Son of Man." This is true no matter how we answer the critical questions that its use poses. Apart from Acts 7:56, it occurs only in sayings of Jesus (in Rev. 1:13 and 14:14 the title as such is not intended). It is widely distributed and in all strata (Q, Mark, M, L, John). Since there is no obvious point (e.g., the development of confessions) from which it could have entered so broadly into the Jesus tradition, we must trace its original use back to Jesus himself. Its spread stays remarkably within the limits noted.

In all the writings that have come down to us, "Son of Man" is a title. We have to reckon with the possibility that it was so already in Semitic usage and that Jesus used br 'nš as a title. In so doing, he related apocalyptic expectation (Dan. 7:13; 1 Enoch 37–71; 4 Ezra 13) to his own ministry (→ Apocalypticism). He was perhaps counting upon his suffering leading to his exaltation as Son of Man. The approaching fate of the world, whose end is

imminent, is bound up with him (see Luke 9:26 and par.; Matt. 19:28).

At least the starting point for the development of sayings about the coming, suffering, and present Son of Man may be found in Jesus himself. The post-Easter tradition took up the equation of Jesus with the Son of Man, intensified it, and thus underlined its significance for → eschatological salvation and judgment. This strange title could not play an independent Christological role, at least at first and in its original use.

3. Other Titles
3.1. Christ (Messiah)

The title "Christ" (i.e., "Messiah," "Anointed") quickly became a name for Jesus. It so characterized the primitive community that members came to be known as Christians (Acts 11:26; Tacitus Ann. 15.44; cf. 1 Pet. 4:16; Acts 26:28; also Mark 9:41). Jesus himself obviously did not accept it (Mark 8:29-33) because it was connected with the traditional Jewish hope of salvation, with special stress on national liberation. Yet the inscription on the cross (Mark 15:26) and the case against Jesus show that he was regarded and executed by the Romans as a messianic pretender. This historical fact brings the title into close affinity to the passion.

In general, "Christ" quickly came to function as a distinctive name. This process is presupposed in Paul. It likely took place outside of the world of Palestinian Judaism. Here "Christ" could be regarded as a very general designation for the promised bringer of eschatological salvation. That this savior had come in Jesus was the basic content of missionary proclamation, which focused on his → death and → resurrection.

3.2. Lord

The title "Lord" opens up Christology very radically to theological impulses from the world around. It is not a Jewish messianic title. Yet 1 Cor. 16:22 shows that it was known already to the Aramaic-speaking community. Expressions such as "the brothers of the Lord" and "the Lord's brother" (1 Cor. 9:5 and Gal. 1:19; cf. 1 Cor. 7:10, 12, 25; 9:14) suggest that even the earthly Jesus might have been respectfully addressed as Lord.

Essentially the Hellenistic → synagogue must have developed the title Christologically. By way of the Hellenists (see Acts 6), its influence extended very early to the Jerusalem congregation. This may be seen from the confessional statement that Paul adopted in 1 Cor. 8:6. In line with Hellenistic Jewish explanations of God's working in the world, the Lord is there related to God the Creator as the mediator of creation. What is confessed, then, is both the deity of the Christ and the unity of God. The personalizing of the mediator of creation goes hand in hand with the historicity of Christ Jesus.

The relating of the Lord Jesus to God makes it possible to transfer to him OT references to "the Lord" (= Yahweh). This opens up new dimensions for Christology but also ties it to the OT (note the hymn adopted by Paul in Phil. 2:6-11). The adoption of the title "Lord" likely is also promoted by its pagan use. As we see from the basic confession "Jesus is Lord" (1 Cor. 12:3; Rom. 10:9), "Lord" quickly becomes a comprehensive Christological title (cf. also the adj. form in 1 Cor. 11:20 and Rev. 1:10). In Paul especially it often carries also an element of personal claim and demand.

3.3. Son of God

The title "Son of God" obviously has much the same origin as the title "Lord." It has not been found as a fixed messianic title in the Jewish sphere (though cf. 4QFlor 1.10-11; 4Q243 2.1). The "sending" formula in Rom. 8:3-4; Gal. 4:4; John 3:16-17; 1 John 4:9, however, points us to the Hellenistic synagogue and its view of God's work in the world. The confession taken up in Rom. 1:3-4 is oriented to OT prophecies. These two elements in connection with the history of Jesus, especially his sense of sonship and his self-giving to death, make up the content of the title. Because it can involve an ontological relation to God, it achieves clear dominance in the development of Christology.

Pagan influences are relatively late and peripheral. In Mark the concept is still wholly functional. It has a genetic basis in Matthew and Luke. Essentially in the form "the Son" it serves in John (and also in Hebrews) to establish the nature of Jesus, although obviously with a → soteriological goal. In general the title raises the question of the relationship of Christ to God.

3.4. Logos

The title "Logos" ("word") occurs only in the Prologue to John (1:1, 14). This traditional hymn interprets the nature and way of the preexistent One in terms of Hellenistic Jewish ideas about divine wisdom (Sir. 24:1-22 [23]; 1 Enoch 42). In the Logos, the world meets the God who gives it meaning but whom it has evaded by taking its own way. But the Incarnate One is not merely called Logos. He is Jesus Christ, the only Son (KJV: the "only begotten Son") from the Father (John 1:14, 18).

3.5. Son of David

The title "Son of David" is seldom used, but the related idea is old and widely attested. The title was common in Palestinian → Judaism, especially among the → rabbis. An end-time Davidic Messiah was widely expected. The use of the title in Matthew and the significance of David in the infancy stories in Matthew 1–2 and Luke 1–2 (cf. also Acts 13:22-23) give evidence of the debate with Judaism concerning the messiahship of Jesus. In the confession in Rom. 1:3-4, descent from David defines the messiahship of the earthly Jesus (cf. Mark 12:35-37). As a result of the separation from Judaism, the title necessarily lost its importance.

3.6. End-Time Prophet

Expectation of an end-time prophet like → Moses is connected with Deut. 18:15, 18. It is especially characteristic of the → Samaritans. It is expressly adopted in the addresses in Acts 3:22-23 and 7:37, which reflect the tradition. We also find it in John 6:14 and 7:40 (cf. also 1:21, 25). Probably the related messianic concept had more impact in the earlier period. The influence of Moses typology on Christology (esp. in Matthew) supports this view. But the title could not achieve any greater acceptance, since it lacked sharpness and clarity for wider groups.

3.7. Servant of the Lord, High Priest, Lamb

These titles occur rarely or only in specific works. "Servant of the Lord" is an old title occurring only in Acts 3:13, 26; 4:27, 30 (cf. Matt. 12:18). The underlying idea of the servant of Isaiah 53 and elsewhere in Deutero-Isaiah had considerable influence, but the title was not comprehensive enough. It has perhaps been incorporated into "Son of God."

The titles "High Priest" (in Hebrews) and "Lamb" (in Revelation) represent Christological-soteriological interpretations that have been given the status of titles in individual writings.

4. The One Faith in Christ and Christological Titles

The central titles "Lord" and "Son of God" have a related history from the standpoint of both origin and tradition. Interrelations may also be presupposed between "Son of God" and "Son of Man." None of the others seems able to claim exclusive validity.

The various titles plainly developed early in a theologically scattered community that tried to integrate various presuppositions in the light of the Christ-event. In the process, the cooperation of Palestinian disciples with those who were won from Hellenistic Judaism was clearly of special significance. The different titles do not appear to be in competition with one another as the representatives of divergent theologies.

→ Christology 1; Jesus

Bibliography: W. BOUSSET, *Kyrios Christos: A History of the Belief in Christ from the Beginnings of Christianity to Irenaeus* (Nashville, 1970; orig. pub., 1913) • O. CULLMANN, *The Christology of the NT* (London, 1959) • F. HAHN, *The Titles of Jesus in Christology: Their History in Early Christianity* (New York, 1969) • M. HENGEL, *The Son of God: The Origin of Christology and the History of Jewish-Hellenistic Religion* (Philadelphia, 1976) • S. KIM, *The "Son of Man" as the Son of God* (Tübingen, 1983) • W. KRAMER, *Christ, Lord, Son of God* (Naperville, Ill., 1966) • W. G. KÜMMEL, *Jesus der Menschensohn?* (Stuttgart, 1984) • B. LINDARS, *Jesus Son of Man* (London, 1983) • W. LOHMEYER, *Gottesknecht und Davidsohn* (2d ed.; Göttingen, 1953) • L. SABOURIN, *The Names and Titles of Jesus* (New York, 1967). See also the relevant articles in *EDNT* and *TDNT* and the bibliographies in "Christology 1" and "Jesus."

TRAUGOTT HOLTZ

Christology

Overview

Overview

Christology is systematic reflection on the basis and significance of the apostolic witness to Jesus Christ, along with its expression and application throughout the history of the church. It has long been a classic part of theological teaching. It seeks to fashion explicit statements that can be tested and used in close connection with other central areas of Christian doctrine (e.g., → Church; Anthropology; Justification; Hope; Ethics; Pastoral Theology). It begins, however, with implicit as well as explicit Christological statements. The distinction is significant because it does justice to an important empirical distinction in the way of talking about Jesus Christ.

Most of the sayings about Jesus or Jesus Christ in the NT are *implicitly* Christological. Also implicitly Christological, in contrast to the academic development of Christology in the fifth century, was the theology of the early → church fathers when they dealt with → salvation, the → church, and even the → Trinity (§1). Implicit, too, in every age has been the Christology of → preaching, → liturgy, → doxology, → hymns, → pastoral care, and ethical appeals. The Christology of the → Third World is unquestionably implicit unless it has only adopted formulations from European and American confessions.

Explicit Christological formulations presuppose implicit statements. Explicit Christology undoubtedly brings a depth of insight into the person and work of Jesus Christ. It also grants an unmistakable security of → communication among believers, a solidity of teaching. Yet it also brings some constriction. This element showed itself for the first time in the early church when the many implicit Christologies of the NT experienced an unalterable, drastic reduction in the classic Christological formulas of the Council of → Chalcedon (451).

Both the depth and the restriction of explicit Christology result from academic theological reflection and the formation of schools. This connection was plainly visible even before the split between East and West (→ Orthodoxy 3) and before the breakup of the Western church after the → Reformation into different confessions (→ Denomination). To be sure, Christology was not the only reason for the formation of schools or confessions, but at least secondarily, difference in Christology has marked the differences among Christian denominations.

458

If we consider this development from an ecumenical angle, it is not surprising that the classic Christology of the early church, which historically underlies all the churches and confessions, takes on today a wholly new importance. In the → ecumenical movement (→ Ecumenical Theology), the explicit Christology of the early church is again valued very highly. Classic Christology had never been pushed onto the margin in English-speaking churches to the degree that it was in German-speaking theology. It was still to a large extent a point of reference (often almost normatively) for new work in explicit Christology (→ Theology in the Nineteenth and Twentieth Centuries 4.2). This basic attitude has now become typical on ecumenical commissions, not least through the influence of Orthodox members, for whom the → dogma of the early church has always been indisputable. It remains to be seen whether the churches of the Third World will produce explicit Christologies of another type, perhaps freely drawing afresh on the implicit Christologies of the NT.

Bibliography: H. DEMBOWSKI, Einführung in die Christologie (Darmstadt, 1976) • W. KASPER, Jesus the Christ (London, 1976) • KONFERENZ EUROPÄISCHER KIRCHEN, Europäische Theologie herausgefordert durch die Weltökumene (Geneva, 1976) • J. McINTYRE, The Shape of Christology (London, 1966) • H. OTT, Die Antwort des Glaubens (Stuttgart, 1972; 3d ed., 1981) pt. 4 • V. C. SAMUEL, The Council of Chalcedon Re-examined (Madras, 1977) • E. SCHWEIZER, Jesus (London, 1971); idem, Jesus, the Parable of God: What Do We Really Know about Jesus? (Allison Park, Pa., 1994).

DIETRICH RITSCHL

1. Christology in the NT

1.1. The State of Research

Christology in the NT is not yet teaching about Christ. Rather, it presents an interpretation of Christ, with a reference to the present, in the various modes of → proclamation, → parenesis, → confession of faith (§1), recollection, and narrative. In the study of NT Christology since about 1965, three basic tendencies may be observed. First, the individual → Christological titles are not clues to different Christologies (as had been claimed by F. Hahn; R. Fuller), since they overlap and supplement one another in many ways (H. R. Balz). Second, more strongly than previously, Jesus is now seen again as the source not merely of implicit Christology but of direct Christological statements (e.g., L. Goppelt). Finally, the narrative concepts of the Gospels (we might call them Christo-"logical") claim special interest, as well as conceptual Christological statements.

1.2. Jesus

There is still widespread agreement that Jesus did not identify himself explicitly with the theopolitical, messianic hopes of → Judaism connected especially with the titles Christos, huios Dauid (Son of David), and huios theou (Son of God). Yet one can be fairly certain that he spoke about the Son of Man, for only thus can we explain the many occurrences of this title, almost all of them in sayings of Jesus. Was he only referring to someone else as the coming Son of Man (perhaps after the manner of → John the Baptist?), thus indirectly pointing to the significance of his sending (see esp. Luke 12:8-9; 17:26-30; e.g., Hahn)?

It is difficult, however, not to relate to Jesus himself the sayings that speak about the present activity of the Son of Man (Luke 7:33-34; 9:58), or to understand the saying about the judgment of fire that he must bring on the earth (Luke 12:49-50) as an analogy to his encoded identification with the coming world-judge. We are rather to suppose, then, that in a concealed way Jesus was referring to himself as the Son of Man (e.g., Goppelt). This implies that he must have expected his exaltation in some way (Luke 13:32-33; cf. the exaltation of Enoch as Son of Man in 1 Enoch 70–71), at least by the time he was accepting death as part of his mission. Consistent with this view is the fact that the death of Jesus is no longer seen as a historical accident but as a fulfillment of his mission that he deliberately embraced (H. Schürmann). For this reason, rather than because of the embarrassment it raised for Christians, it became a center of Christology after → Easter. Christology, then, is essentially an adoption and deepening of the claim of Jesus himself.

Also important for primitive Christianity was the fact that the contemporaries of the earthly Jesus frequently regarded him as a prophet, a category that Jesus deepened and transcended (e.g., Luke 11:31-32). Important, too, was Jesus' addressing of God as Father, which was felt to be special and became the impulse for post-Easter references to Jesus as Son. Finally, even more important for the narrative Christology of the Gospels was the way in which Jesus set his own work in the light of the dawning kingdom of God (e.g., Luke 11:20; 17:21; cf. the parables of contrast). Less secure are older and newer attempts to relate Jesus to the Suffering Servant of Isaiah 53 (e.g., H. Patsch) or to find a basis for the → atoning death of Jesus in the Lord's Supper (→ Eucharist) and therefore in Jesus himself (P. Stuhlmacher). Yet it is still true that at essential points primitive Christian Christology has a basis already in Jesus himself.

1.3. The Post-Easter Community

The above considerations show that Bultmann's thesis that Easter is "the original and all-decisive datum of Christology" (H. F. Weiß, 89) is doubtful, or at least needs to be made more precise. Might one say that Easter is the origin of Christology but not its (historical) beginning? Since the NT accounts of the appearances and the kerygma of 1 Cor. 15:3-5 all tell how people were changed or commissioned by encounter with the risen Lord, one might regard the Easter experiences as a divine empowering to continue the work of Jesus. Part of this view is acceptance of Jesus' understanding of himself. But Easter, and the ensuing prophetic experience of the Spirit, also mean that Jesus is the living Lord. Thus the Christian communities did not just stop at the self-understanding of Jesus but constantly tried to express in their own words the meaning of Jesus for them. Hence post-Easter Christology contains a strong element of innovation.

Where the communities found the terms and concepts for their new attempts at Christological statements has naturally given rise to much debate. The following thesis might perhaps command broad agreement. The new and deeper Christological concepts developed as the communities thought about Jesus *in the light of the Bible*. Without the OT, there would be no Christology. The linguistic world in which they read and understood the OT was that of contemporary Judaism, which was diverse and already permeated by → Hellenism. In modern research there is a clear tendency to give much greater weight to the Jewish background of NT Christological statements than to a purely Hellenistic or even Gnostic background. But the material criterion for Christological statements was the work of Jesus. Precisely in such new Christological predications as that of "Son of God" or "Messiah" or even *sophia* (see 1 Cor. 1:18-25), it is plain how traditional ideas were alienated when set in the light of Jesus.

Much debated is the question of to what extent we must take into account different cycles of tradition and different community Christologies in primitive Christianity (e.g., H. Köster), or at least how far we must reckon with two basically different Christological types — a kerygmatic Christianity marked by the death and → resurrection of Jesus (→ Paul and the other NT Epistles), and a Jesus Christianity oriented to his earthly life (Gospels). The overlappings between these spheres (John's gospel and the kerygmatic Epistles of John; Luke-Acts and the related → Pastoral Epistles in the Pauline sphere) advise caution. What is generally true is that in kerygmatic confessions and → acclamations, the community was saying who Jesus is *now*. The Epistles (besides Paul, esp. Colossians and Ephesians, but also Hebrews, 1 Peter, and 1 John) expound the confession situationally. The Gospels, however, say who the Jesus is that the communities confess in the → kerygma (cf. Goppelt, 2.27-28). Narrative and confession thus stand related from the outset (cf. 1 Cor. 15:3-7; Phil. 2:6-11; Acts 10:38-42; 1 Pet. 3:18-22). This connection does not rule out the fact that in the primitive community there were different emphases and relatively different cycles of tradition conditioned by different backgrounds, different knowledge of Jesus, different experiences, and so forth.

1.4. *The Gospels*

The Gospels narrate who the Jesus of the kerygma is. The oldest → gospel developed out of the insight that we can understand isolated traditions about Jesus only in the light of the whole story, culminating in his passion and resurrection. One sees here already the material closeness of the Gospels to Christological confession. Another important point is that the confessional title "Son of God" is central in all the Gospels (Mark 1:1, 11; 15:39; Matt. 1:1; 1:21–2:23; 3:17–4:11; 27:43, 54; Luke 1:32-35; John 1:18; 20:31).

The individual gospels stress the divine sonship of Jesus differently. Mark emphasizes that one can grasp it only in the light of the passion and in → discipleship. The "ethical" evangelist Matthew, in his Christological introit, speaks about the → obedience of the Son of God (3:13–4:11). Both gospels are obviously telling the story of Jesus transparently for their own audiences — Mark tracing the general inability to understand the passion, Matthew developing the story for the community as the story of "God with us" (1:23; 28:20).

Luke, however, unfolds the story of Jesus the Son of God as an event that goes beyond Easter to be "fulfilled among us" (Luke 1:1). For Luke, the time of Jesus that is now gone by is not an isolated time of salvation in the midst of history. Rather, the ascended Jesus is the one who is active in the time of proclamation after his death; even the so-called time of the church is the time of Jesus.

John's gospel differs from the → Synoptics by taking up the idea of the preexistence of Jesus, which was widespread in Hellenistic → Jewish Christianity as an expression of his transcendent significance (cf. in Judaism the preexistence of Wisdom and the → Torah, and in Christianity Phil. 2:6-11 and Col. 1:15-20), and in the form of a hymn to the Logos, making it a prologue to the gospel. In connection with a dualistically accented worldview (→ Dualism), the Son of God becomes the only Son sent by the otherworldly Father, and the death of Jesus becomes a paradoxical victory over the world. John, then, stands at the head of important later developments and makes possible an unfolding of the concept of incarnation (first emphasized in 1 John), a consistent rejection of the world that Christ has overcome (Christian → Gnosis), and a fresh interpretation of Christology in the categories of ontology and substance in the → early church.

1.5. Paul

Paul well illustrates the way in which kerygmatic Christology becomes applicative Christology and not merely a subject of isolated theological reflection. This statement involves a modification of the basic thesis of Bultmann that Paul's Christology is always also → soteriology. Paul does not so much expound Christology in general existential structures of being as he rather applies it to concrete human experiences and situations in the church. Precisely in his Christology Paul shows that primarily he is a theologian anchored in the tradition of the church. He gives concrete form to the fundamental kerygmatic statements of the tradition. Even when he engages in independent reflection, he presupposes these principles as given (e.g., in his discussion of → justification [§1], or in his use of the phrases *en Christō* [in Christ] and *sōma Christou* [body of Christ]).

On the one hand, Paul's independence shows itself in the selection of traditions. Especially important to him are the kerygma of the atoning death, the Hellenistic Jewish interpretation of Christ as preexistent, Christ's sending as a cosmic event, and dying with Christ in → baptism. On the other hand, his independence also shows itself in his Christology of the cross. The focusing of all the statements about the death of Jesus on the → cross made possible for Paul a fundamental antithesis to the → law as a way of salvation (see Gal. 3:13), a polemical interpretation of the Christ-event as the end of all human claims (1 Cor. 1:18-25; justification), and an existential relating of Christ's death to the → suffering of Christians with Christ (Gal. 6:14; 2 Cor. 4:10; Phil. 3:10). Paul hardly referred to the work of the earthly Jesus but found it summed up in his death (see Phil. 2:6-9). The interpretation of the salvific meaning of the death of Jesus (e.g., in what is said about justification) gives substantive evidence of profound convergence with the heart of Jesus' own proclamation.

1.6. Summary

NT interpretations of Christ took up Jesus' own claim and expounded it in an unusually rich and creative way. The claim, and the potential for freedom found in Jesus, constantly made possible new ways of saying who Jesus was for the Christian community. The possibilities supplemented one another rather than being mutually exclusive. There are only a few attempts at a critical function of Christology,

namely, in Paul (the cross) and in 1 John (the → incarnation), but in both cases the criticism is directed against the total life of opponents of Christianity, not merely against a "wrong" Christology.

In all the gospels, traditions about Jesus as a part of the history of the Son of God were related to the present, and in all primitive Christianity they were used to a greater or lesser degree as verification or exemplification of the proclamation of Christ (see G. Stanton). Matthew and Luke especially make it clear that with increasing temporal distance, these traditions became increasingly important for the identification of → faith.

Bibliography: H. R. BALZ, *Methodische Probleme der neutestamentlichen Christologie* (Neukirchen, 1967) • R. BULTMANN, *Theology of the NT* (2 vols.; New York, 1951-55) • J. ERNST, *Anfänge der Christologie* (Stuttgart, 1972) • R. FULLER, *The Foundations of NT Christology* (New York, 1965) • L. GOPPELT, *Theology of the NT* (2 vols.; Grand Rapids, 1981-83) • E. HAHN, *The Titles of Jesus in Christology: Their History in Early Christianity* (New York, 1969) • M. HENGEL, *The Son of God: The Origin of Christology and the History of Jewish-Hellenistic Religion* (Philadelphia, 1976) • J. D. KINGSBURY, *The Christology of Mark's Gospel* (Philadelphia, 1983) • H. KÖSTER, "Grundtypen und Kriterien frühchristlicher Glaubensbekenntnisse," *Entwicklungslinien durch die Welt des frühen Christentums* (H. Köster and J. M. Robinson; Tübingen, 1971) 191-215 • C. F. D. MOULE, *The Origin of Christology* (Cambridge, 1977) • H. PATSCH, *Abendmahl und historischer Jesus* (Stuttgart, 1972) • K. RAHNER and W. THÜSING, *Christologie–systematisch und exegetisch* (Freiburg, 1972) • H. SCHÜRMANN, *Jesu ureigener Tod* (2d ed.; Freiburg, 1976) • G. STANTON, *Jesus of Nazareth in NT Preaching* (Cambridge, 1974) • P. STUHLMACHER, *Reconciliation, Law, and Righteousness: Essays in Biblical Theology* (Philadelphia, 1986) 1-67 • H. WEDER, *Das Kreuz Jesu bei Paulus* (Göttingen, 1981) • H. F. WEISS, *Kerygma und Geschichte* (Berlin, 1983). See also the bibliographies in "Christological Titles" and "Jesus."

ULRICH LUZ

2. Christology in the History of Dogma

2.1. "Classical Christology"

2.1.1. The expression "classical Christology" has come down to us as part of the heritage of the 19th century and refers to any Christology that acknowledges in an unbroken fashion the Christological → dogma of the → early church as formulated at the Council of → Chalcedon (451). The basic formula professes one and the same Christ, who is of one substance with God the Father as regards his deity, and of one substance with us human beings as regards his humanity. Although he is acknowledged in two natures, "the property of both natures is preserved and comes together into a single person and a single subsistent being [*sōzomenēs tēs idiotētos hekateras physeōs kai eis hen prosōpon kai mian hypostasin syntrechousēs / salva proprietate utriusque naturae et in unam personam atque subsistentiam concurrente*]." As interpretative aids, letters from Cyril of Alexandria and from Pope Leo were included with the Definition. "Classical Christology," however, does not really constitute a self-enclosed unity, exhibiting rather an animated history burdened with problems prompted primarily by four factors.

First, the Definition of Chalcedon was too controversial ever to enjoy universal acceptance (e.g., among the older national churches of the Near East). Even when accepted, it was not spared additional emendations (e.g., at the Councils of Constantinople in 553 and 680-81).

Second, its excessively abstract nature prevented it from incorporating in any effective fashion the various Christologies under discussion by the participants at the time (Alexandrians, Orientals/Antiochenes, and the Latin West), or, conversely, from excluding subsequent, differently accentuated Christologies (Byzantine Orthodox Christologies, medieval and Roman Catholic Christologies, Lutheran Christologies, Reformed Christologies).

Third, the Definition — and along with it the entire tradition following upon the Christology of the ancient church — has since the → Enlightenment been subjected to incisive questioning, which, while indeed generating various answers (e.g., from F. D. E. → Schleiermacher and D. F. Strauss), has at the same time been unable to prompt any universal and absolute rejection (e.g., mediating theology, E. Brunner, K. → Barth).

Fourth, today's theologians do not really agree in their understanding of the meaning of the various Christological models deriving from the time of the early church, and it is thus a matter of debate whether the pre-Chalcedonian development of Christology really can be taken as an anticipation of, or preparation for, the dogma.

2.1.2. Throughout its history, "classical Christology" has held fast to the list of heretics generated by the early church (→ Heresies and Schisms), and these censures had the effect of delimiting from the outside the parameters within which Christological reflection could move, contributing thus to the self-enclosed nature of "classical Christology." Ever since the time of → Pietism and the → Enlightenment, and even into the present, the decisions reached by

the early church have been the subject of ever-renewed discussions that, while touching on the attachment of various confessions to tradition, nevertheless also have sought, within the center of Christian theology, a more penetrating understanding of the fundamental statements and convictions of faith (e.g., the positive portrayal of the → Nestorians in the → dogmatic histories of → liberal theology, or the discovery of neo-Chalcedonianism in Roman Catholic scholarship). In the second century — though also unequivocally, albeit with less differentiation, as early as Ignatius of Antioch (d. ca. 107; → Apostolic Fathers) — it became clear that although Christ does indeed belong to God, he was at the same time a real human being with a real human history (birth, suffering, and death), a conviction relegating → Docetism to the status of a heresy.

We can no longer determine the extent to which, or even how long, the notion was yet entertained that Christ was a normal, ordinary human being, though one filled by the Spirit of God (at → baptism or, alternatively, perhaps also at the → virgin birth); in any event, by the end of the second century this particular view could be abandoned as Jewish (→ Irenaeus [ca. 130-ca. 200]), the blame being put on the → Ebionites. It reenters the discussion around the turn of the second/third centuries, when the so-called Monarchians (→ Trinity) were searching for a way out of the dilemma that faith in the God Christ posed for → monotheism, and Paul of Samosata (deposed 268) later came to epitomize every heresy that did not ascribe preexistent divine sonship to the human being Jesus.

This complex of problems surrounding the preservation of monotheism also includes forms of Sabellianism, named after Sabellius, whom the Roman bishop Callistus condemned (ca. 220) for having considered Jesus to be merely a different form of the one God, that is, a kind of temporary revelatory mode (hence the alternative term "modalism"). Tertullian (d. ca. 225) objected that according to this understanding, God the Father was himself crucified and suffered (hence the heretical designation "Patripassianism"), an argument that was quite convincing because it demonstrated the incompatibility of this view both with the impassibility implied in the concept of → God and with the gospel accounts themselves (cf. Mark 15:34).

2.1.3. "Classical Christology" presents itself as revelatory theology (→ Revelation). That is, in Jesus Christ, God is revealing himself, and this revelation can variously involve his essence, his → grace, and his will. In its deeper structure, this Christology takes as its point of departure the assertion that Jesus

Christ reveals God only because he, Jesus, is himself God before his revelation, that is, preexistently. Although this notion is making a presupposition that is actually to be grounded by the doctrine of the Trinity, the notion itself is not really reflected in Christology, since this particular Christology is concerned only with clarifying that the deity revealed in Jesus Christ is one in substance with God — an assertion that in fact also means identical in substance. The decisive point here is that this understanding excludes any notion of gradations of divine being that extend through stages of increasingly lesser divinity down into the human realm. It was the rejection of → Arianism that definitively elevated to the status of a confession the assertion that there is but one ontological distinction, namely, that between the uncreated and the created, and thus between God and the world of human beings. The logical core of the argument against the Arians, formulated by → Athanasius (d. 373), declared that Christ must be God by nature *(physei)* to be able to impart to created, mortal human beings a share of that divine imperishability inherent in himself. Because God's own salvific activity (→ Soteriology) must now be portrayed in the person of Jesus Christ, the soteriological argument — one deriving, by the way, from → Platonic philosophy — comes to constitute the foundation of Christology.

The course of dogmatic history has seen the ebb and flow of various points of emphasis within Christological reflection. For example, whereas the early church conceived Christology primarily as the event of God becoming man (→ Incarnation), the Latin West — influenced by Augustine (→ Augustine's Theology) — addressed it as the presupposition for the justification effected by the merits of Christ as the God-Man. Reformation theology then understood Christology largely as the doctrine of the mediator who, as the representative of human beings, took their → sins upon himself; this notion itself then provided the point of departure for the doctrine of the person of the God-Man, one that by addressing the questions of the Enlightenment also allowed the question of preexistence to be held in abeyance for the moment while it profited from advances made by research into the "life of → Jesus." Strictly speaking, however, this also constituted a break with what we understand as "classical Christology" (cf. A. Ritschl and W. Herrmann).

2.2. Early Church Christology

The basic model of early church Christology goes back to Athanasius, who wrote the first tractate with the title *De incarnatione*, bringing theological traditions into a form that may be called classical.

2.2.1. Both Irenaeaus and Origen (ca. 185-ca. 254) developed significant Christological models before that of Athanasius. Because Irenaeus adopted from Justin Martyr (→ Apologists) the identification of the preexistent Christ with the Logos, that is, with the mediator of creation, he was able to view Christology within the broader arc of salvation history extending from the → creation of human beings to their → eschatological consummation. The guiding principle at the creation of human beings was the likeness of God (→ Anthropology). Although Christ — the Logos of God — is indeed the image of God, he did not appear to human beings in any historically perceptible form at creation, but rather only after human beings had undergone a period of guided maturation. The fact that the image of God actually became incarnate made it possible for human beings to approach or to approximate God's own likeness in themselves, and to achieve the consummation of creation. This mode of becoming increasingly like God, of approximating God's own likeness in oneself (sometimes called *theopoiēsis*), provided the point of reflection for Christology in the early church.

Although this process of becoming increasingly like God within oneself actually represents a Platonic philosopheme *(homoiōsis theǭ)*, the Christians went beyond philosophy in asserting that the goal of this process has itself been revealed in the visible world of sensory perception, that is, in history. It is of only secondary significance to the Christological train of thought at work here, however, that this Christology — one ultimately bound up with the Platonic doctrine of knowledge of the → good — is also drawing connections with sacramental doctrine, and that the Holy Spirit is of course the one who bestows the personal power requisite for achieving this divine likeness. All this becomes abundantly evident in Origen (→ Origenism), since his Christology — despite any speculative queries regarding the actual possibility of an incarnation of the Logos of God — understands Jesus as the one who reveals what lost humanity should become. Jesus, a soul completely united with the Logos in corporeal actuality, is the lowest stage of this process of becoming like God, and it is upon this stage, as upon virtuous action, that the progressive path begins along which a person can come to know and see God (see Matt. 5:8).

2.2.2. Insofar as Athanasius was addressing Greek pagans, he completely incorporated into his own presentation the mode of thought characterizing Platonic → epistemology. Through sin, human beings lost the imperishability bestowed in knowledge of God and were given over to corruption, and it is the incarnation that now renews this knowledge of God.

Although the Logos is itself present in the created world insofar as it lends to the individual things of the world their unity as cosmos (kosmos = sōma), the sinful self-centeredness of human beings conceals any knowledge of this unity as established by the Logos. For this reason, such knowledge of God is now renewed by the Logos's own act of entering into an individual body (sōma) and demonstrating visibly that it is the Logos itself that vivifies the human body, giving it life. The Christological formula reads commensurately: the Logos or God in the body.

Because Athanasius also argued against the Arians that God's action in the incarnation has redeemed humanity from the corruption of perishability, he is conceiving this incarnation as the acceptance of humanity, as its union with God, and thereby also as the transformation of humanity into a status of imperishability. Because Athanasius presents the universal functionality of salvation within the framework of the incarnation, this doctrine was referred to as the "doctrine of physical redemption" (W. Herrmann and A. Harnack). Salvation in its efficaciousness is indeed clarified by means of the incarnation; here the → Cappadocians, Cyril of Alexandria (d. 444), and the → Monophysites all followed the lead of Athanasius.

2.2.3. Apollinarius of Laodicea (ca. 310-ca. 390) went beyond Athanasius in posing the question of the conceptual possibility of the incarnation in and of itself. After all, the incarnated Christ is allegedly a unity, and the coincidence of his deity and his humanity should be conceivable. The heretical danger here was that one might understand the human being Jesus as merely a prophet filled by the Spirit of God, that is, as a person not really qualitatively different from any other human being. Apollinarius responded to this with a formulation asserting that the incarnate Jesus is actually "a nature that has become a physical body." The Incarnate One, however, did not possess any capacity for human → reason that might contradict God; rather, the Logos itself, in the incarnation, took a body already informed by a soul.

This idea was rejected, and it was formulated against Apollinarius in accordance with incarnational Christology: "What is not assumed is not redeemed," meaning that a human being in the entirety of its humanity must have been taken in the incarnation. The Antiochenes (→ Antiochene Theology) developed this line of anti-Apollinarian argumentation further by asserting that, commensurate with the notion of grace prompting the incarnation in the first place, a human being was adopted in the incarnation as God's Son because of having been "pleasing

to God." There was an inclination to view God's redemptive activity toward us human beings as anticipated or prefigured in this humanity that the Logos adopted, a situation leading Nestorius (d. ca. 451) to understand this adopted humanity as a distinct person. For this he was accused of having spoken about a preexistent Son of God as well as about a second Son of God, one adopted by grace, and this notion was condemned at the Council of Ephesus (431), though the Eastern Syrian Church in Persia did remain loyal to his Christology.

2.2.4. If one bears in mind that the Christology of incarnation also seeks to bring to expression an understanding of the work of redemption, the Definition of Chalcedon understandably could not satisfy the Eastern churches, just as it was also in tension with the portrait of Jesus presented in the Gospels. The heirs of Cyril of Alexandria (→ Alexandrian Theology) rejected the Definition of Chalcedon because its conception of the unity of human nature with God did not adequately affirm the reality of that unity and thus ran the risk of undercutting the process through which the participant element of humanity is elevated to divine status (→ Monophysites). Although the opposing party, mockingly called Dyophysites, triumphed, it still had to accept the anhypostasia of human nature, the result being that Christology was now no longer in a position to render an accurate account of the appropriation of salvation. In a futile attempt to counter the Monophysites, the concept of hypostasis was now defined as meaning the "independent status of self" in which the human nature of the Incarnate One receives its individuality (enhypostasis; cf. the Second Council of Constantinople in 553). Over against what must thus be termed a Cyrillic interpretation of Chalcedon (neo-Chalcedonianism), however, the condemnation of Monothelitism (at Constantinople in 680-81) resulted in the attribution of a distinct will to Christ's human nature, though Christ's human will was admittedly to be conceived as completely permeated by his divine will. It was John of Damascus (d. ca. 750) who then balanced these contradictory correctives of Chalcedon in his own doctrine of the mutual exchange of characteristics (perichōrēsis); this determined the subsequent understanding of Christ in Byzantine Orthodoxy.

2.3. Christology in the Latin Middle Ages

2.3.1. Pope → Leo I (440-61) had a hand in the victory of the "Dyophysite" majority. From the time of Tertullian's controversy with the Monarchians, the Latin West had access to fixed Christological formulas: two natures, one substance or person. In Augustine, this notion of a personal unity of the two natures acquires clear and unequivocal contours, as well as over and above this a theological content of its own. The notion determining the thinking of both Leo and the subsequent period was that the divine person Christ engaged his own humanity as an instrument of action for the sake of redemption, and in this situation Christ's human nature is conceived as being wholly passive and essentially determined only by sinlessness (the virgin birth!), while Christ himself acts in his capacity as the divine Word. Chalcedon was thus quite correct in committing itself to the *anhypostasia* of the human nature.

2.3.2. Anselm of Canterbury (1033-1109) introduced a new element into Christology. Attention is now focused on the realization that although it is human beings themselves who must make satisfaction for human sin, only God is actually able to do so. This makes it necessary for a person distinct from God to act, that is, the second person of the Trinity (Christ as the God-Man), though at the same time it implies that Anselm is speaking about an actual human being who owes this satisfaction, and thus not merely about human nature. Here an element of insecurity regarding the dogma becomes evident, and in the 12th century this led to various controversies resulting in a renewal of Nestorianism. That is, Anselm's doctrine of satisfaction postulated merits on the side of Christ that he could not offer as God, that thus had to be ascribed to him as a human being. Similar inclinations to emphasize the activity of the human being that is united with the deity in the Incarnate One can also be found in Abelard (1079-1142), indeed even in Thomas Aquinas (1224/25-74) and in the school of Duns Scotus (ca. 1265-1308; → Thomism; Scotism; Scholasticism).

The concept of the hypostatic union, according to which human nature receives its own personal individuality in the Logos, did not really offer a full solution. Despite all the splitting up of concepts into "scholastic" isolated questions, it should be pointed out that in the doctrine of the person of Christ, theological → anthropology was expounded exemplarily and even ontologically (Christ as the second → Adam and the new human being). For example, the idea of hypostatic union was also supposed to explain that human personhood comes to completion in unity with God and that grace is granted to human beings in their personal unity with Christ. This also provided an opening for the various forms of Christ → mysticism, forms presupposing the human being Christ, either as a man elevated to beatific vision or as a man humiliated in → suffering. Christology now became a statement about the mediation of grace.

2.4. Reformation Christology

2.4.1. All the Reformers accepted the Christological dogma of the first four councils, asserting in addition that they had no controversy with the traditionalists regarding this doctrine. Nevertheless, the emphases shifted so extremely that Reformation Christology developed into a confessional controversy, especially between the Lutheran and Reformed traditions, of which the latter in this case went along with Roman Catholic polemics. Although the eucharistic controversy precipitated the debate (→ Eucharist), the debate as such was not limited to that sphere.

2.4.2. The Reformation doctrine of redemption "by grace alone" presupposes as its foundation the notion of "Christ alone" (*solus Christus;* → Reformation Principles). The concept of the mediator now moves to the center, and the confession is now "one person in two natures." The new shift in emphases over against tradition becomes evident in three separate points: (1) Christ is to be defined solely by his capacity as mediator, and in this capacity he is the second person of the Trinity; (2) Christ's capacity as mediator relates solely to our → salvation (*pro nobis*) and consists exclusively in God's own self-surrender to us human beings; and (3) the soteriological constitution of Christ's person is presented in the doctrine of the → office of Christ. (After becoming a formal doctrine of dogmatics first in J. → Calvin, this then passed into the common possession of Protestant → orthodoxy [§2].) The intention of understanding Christ's sole mediatorship as a function of this complete and total "pro nobis" made possible the abbreviated formula: "To know Christ is to know his benefits" (P. Melanchthon). More accurately, however, we should speak of the Christological premise of the notion of "by faith alone," since the personal act of trust commits itself to a person, and in that person is granted fellowship with God.

2.4.3. Lutheran and Reformed doctrine went separate ways in addressing the question of how exclusively faith is actually bound to the incarnate Jesus, that is, to the actual presence of Christ's humanity. U. → Zwingli (→ Zwingli's Theology) understood the humanity that Christ incorporated into his own person as a pledge of human salvation, a pledge that after the → ascension is then retained in heaven. By contrast, Calvin (→ Calvin's Theology) and his tradition maintained that since it is the unity of the human and divine nature in the person of Christ that actually constitutes God's fellowship with human beings, this unity constitutes the real ground of faith, though the mode of Christ's presence is provided by the Spirit — the same Spirit with which the humanity of Christ was anointed (→ Extra calvinisticum).

M. → Luther (→ Luther's Theology) and his loyal followers (esp. J. Brenz and M. Chemnitz) insisted that through the incarnation we must believe and teach the presence of Christ fundamentally and continually in the unity of the two natures. Whereas both Zwingli and Calvin asserted that the human nature united with Christ died on the → cross, Luther preached and taught that it was God himself who faced death and died in our place; because both natures are combined in Christ — so Luther's argument — we must relate every statement to his whole person. Commensurately, omnipresence (ubiquity) is to be ascribed to the humanity of Christ as well (→ Eucharist 3.3). Hence it is not just God whom human beings encounter in Christ, nor simply the merciful God, but rather the *Deus incarnatus,* that is, the concrete God who has taken the human being into fellowship with himself. This assertion takes us back to the Christology of incarnation (the miracle of Christmas); and the theological intention of speaking about a qualitatively new presence of God is comparable to what we find in Athanasius.

2.4.4. Luther's doctrine of personal union *(unio hypostatica)* probably attests to a more profound understanding of what Calvin wanted to express in his own doctrine of the prophetic office of the mediator. This personal union of the two natures resulting in the one person Christ is the basis for the exchange of attributes *(communicatio idiomatum).* Humanity is exalted to divine majesty, and the deity is informed into humanity. In contradistinction to Reformed doctrine, strict Lutherans maintain that the incarnation itself constitutes, not abasement, but rather the exaltation of humanity to fellowship with God. The act of true abasement (see Phil. 2:7) actually falls to the mediator (→ Kenosis), whose own humanity, for the sake of taking upon itself human sin and death in self-sacrificial → obedience, refrains from making use of the communicated divine attributes in its own behalf *(status exinanitionis).* Hence in a controversy that raged from 1616 to 1624, the Tübingen theologians, polemically called Cryptics, voted their agreement with the Formula of Concord (art. 8) against the theologians of Giessen, who insisted that the divine attributes had genuinely been put aside or divested (kenosis), the consequence of which made Jesus into a normal, ordinary human being. The participation of humanity in the majesty of divine rule comes to light in the → ascension of the transfigured Lord *(status exaltationis).*

2.5. *Post-Enlightenment Christology*

2.5.1. The → Enlightenment prompted such a crisis in "classical Christology" that its repristination never succeeded. Three contributing factors can be cited: (1) empirically oriented → reason rejected the miraculous element in the gospel accounts of Jesus; (2) critical reason put an end to → metaphysics; and (3) autonomous reason only conditionally accepted revealed morality. F. D. E. Schleiermacher (1768-1834) suggested one way out of the difficulty, G. W. F. Hegel (1770-1831) another.

2.5.2. Schleiermacher moved the person of Jesus into the center of attention. Because the Christian community presupposes a historical initiator, Schleiermacher ascribed to the person of Jesus a prototypical consciousness of God, opening up thereby the possibility not only of writing a life of Jesus but also of basing Christology on Jesus' ethical self-consciousness in the fashion then actually carried out by A. Ritschl (1822-89). Because of its metaphysical categories, the conceptual terminology of "classical Christology" was ultimately abandoned in favor of focusing on ethical categories, and this type of Christology reached a crisis in W. Herrmann (1846-1922). G. Thomasius (1802-75) represented a middle way, trying with the aid of the doctrine of kenosis to adjust the framework of classical Christology so as to allow Jesus to be understood as having had a human self-consciousness.

2.5.3. Hegel's speculative idea that God must be conceived together with the human being was subsequently subjected to various theological developments (e.g., P. K. Marheineke [1780-1846]), and the notion of the God-man in which the idea enters into history was brought into historical connection with "classical Christology" (cf. F. C. Baur and I. A. Dorner).

When D. F. Strauss (1808-74) wrote that the biblical Jesus is but a myth produced by the believers of Jesus themselves, he rocked theological conventions. While today there is no longer absolute skepticism about a historical Jesus, the realization that the historical figure of Jesus might be a distant stranger (A. → Schweitzer) touches at the foundations of dogmatic Christology.

Bibliography: J. Baur, "Auf dem Wege zur klassischen Tübinger Christologie. Einführende Überlegungen zum sogenannten Kenosis-Krypsis-Streit," *Theologen und Theologie an der Universität Tübingen* (ed. M. Brecht; Tübingen, 1977) 195-269 • I. A. Dorner, *Entwicklungsgeschichte der Lehre von der Person Christi* (pt. 1, 2d ed., Stuttgart, 1845; pt. 2, Berlin, 1853-56) • W. Elert, *Der Ausgang der altkirchlichen Christologie* (Berlin, 1957) • A. Gilg, *Weg und Bedeutung der altkirchlichen Christologie* (2d ed.; Munich, 1961; orig. pub., 1936) •

A. GRILLMEIER, *Jesus der Christus im Glauben der Kirche* (vol. 1; Freiburg, 1979; 2d ed., 1982) • A. GRILLMEIER and H. BACHT, eds., *Das Konzil von Chalkedon. Geschichte und Gegenwart* (3 vols.; Würzburg, 1951-54; 2d ed., 1962) • A. M. LANDGRAF, *Dogmengeschichte der Frühscholastik* (vol. 2, pts. 1-2; Regensburg, 1953-54) • J. LIÉBAERT, *Von der apostolischen Zeit bis zum Konzil von Chalcedon* (Freiburg, 1965) • F. LOOFS, "Christologie," *RE* 4.16-56 • T. MAHLMANN, *Das neue Dogma der lutherischen Christologie. Problem und Geschichte seiner Begründung* (Gütersloh, 1969) • O. RITSCHL, *Dogmengeschichte des Protestantismus* (vol. 4; Göttingen, 1927) • A. SCHWEITZER, *The Quest of the Historical Jesus: A Critical Study of Its Progress from Reimarus to Wrede* (New York, 1968; orig. pub., 1906) • N. P. TANNER, ed., *Decrees of the Ecumenical Councils* (2 vols.; London, 1990) • C. WELCH, *God and Incarnation in Mid-Nineteenth-Century German Theology* (New York, 1965).

EKKEHARD MÜHLENBERG

3. Christology in Orthodox Theology

The differences in theological methodology between East and West have often led to the misunderstanding that Orthodox theology found the definitive form of Christology in the Definition of → Chalcedon (451). Later Christological debates in the Byzantine sphere are regarded as offshoots of Chalcedon, and the Christological arguments in the iconoclastic controversy (→ Images) as the application of a fixed, conservative Christology. This view fails to see that in the → Orthodox Church, Christology is not primarily the subject of abstract speculation. It arises from the liturgical world of → prayer, → meditation, and → asceticism and leads to soteriology, which in essence is Christology. In the iconoclastic controversy the old Christological arguments were cited, but what finally mattered was the soteriological dimension of the incarnation, the reality of theophany, the restoration of the divine image, and the bringing back of the cosmos to God (see John of Damascus, *Hom. transfig.* 18 [*PG* 96.573A-B]).

The Byzantine theologians continued this tradition, especially Gregory Palamas (ca. 1296-1359; → Palamism), who in the incarnation as the hypostatic union of divine and human nature saw the basis of → salvation and the beginning *(aparchē)* of human deification (→ Theosis; cf. *Antirrh.* 3.6.13, 170.25-31 [ed. P. Chrestou]). Western theologians have often denied that Christology holds this central place in Byzantine mysticism, and especially in the theology of Palamas (see H.-G. Beck, 367, with reference to K. Holle, and on this G. Podskalsky). But without

Christology the theology of the mystical vision of God would have no theological basis. The development of Orthodox → spirituality by way of Simeon the New Theologian (d. 1022), Gregory Palamas, Maxim Grek (d. 1556), and Seraphim of Sarov (d. 1833) to the lay figures N. Gogol (d. 1852) and A. Chomiakov (d. 1860) and even the critic N. Kasandsakis (d. 1957) shows that Christology is the center of Orthodox faith and thought, for which the mystery of Christ is an existential experience of salvation.

For Byzantine theology, Christology figured in a distinct set of questions in speculative theology that were politically necessary with non-Chalcedonian churches throughout the medieval period and later. Thus at the beginning of the 11th and 12th centuries the philosopher John Italus and his disciple Eustratios of Nicaea joined in discussion of the psychology of the human Christ, and their strong emphasis on the human aspect of Christology was rejected as → heresy. Another sharp debate in the 12th century focused on whether John 14:28 ("the Father is greater than I") relates to the distinction of natures in Christ.

From the end of the 19th century Russian theologians have repeatedly appealed to modern psychology in debates with Protestant theologians aimed at clarification of the Chalcedonian Definition. Finally, the beginning of the 20th century saw a typical Orthodox debate regarding the divinity of the name of Christ. This raised all the basic questions that Byzantine theology had discussed in different contexts without ever finding convincing answers.

Monothelitism and Monergism failed to achieve the desired compromise with non-Chalcedonians, for they did not overcome the distinction of Christological viewpoints. Emphasis on the deity of Christ marked the mode of thinking of both parties, as well as that of the East in general. The Third Council of Constantinople in 680-81 condemned post-Chalcedonian, pro-Monophysite constructions, but it maintained the asymmetry inherent in the nature of the divine-human union in Christ, giving priority to the divine will in Christ (see Mansi 11.637). The West has often misunderstood this approach, which is still valid in Orthodox Christology on the basis of the NT and the Fathers, charging the East with a Monophysite disparagement of Christ's humanity (P. Jungmann, K. Adam, and, in response, M. Lot-Borodine, 668).

On this point there is obviously a fundamental difference between the standpoints of East and West. The West focuses more on the humanity of Christ, on the earthly life and death of Jesus, whereas the East views the mystery of the incarnation as a

theophany and hence sees it in the light of the →
resurrection, which is the basis of salvation. Orthodox → piety and theology are controlled by Paul's
awareness that "if Christ has not been raised, then
our proclamation has been in vain and your faith has
been in vain" (1 Cor. 15:14). This spirit permeates
especially the Easter hymns of the Orthodox Church,
which extol → Easter as the feast of feasts and think
of the passion and death of Christ with all the confidence of resurrection. Iconography reflects this
view in protraying the crucified Christ with open
eyes.

The period of Western alienation from Orthodox
theology (17th-19th centuries) disrupted this tradition, but 20th-century theologians have taken it up
again, pointing to the immanent danger of Christo-
monism and projecting an integrated Trinitarian
Christology that does justice to the mystery of the
incarnation (V. Lossky, G. Florovsky, N. Nissiotis, et
al.). They do not view the work of the incarnate
Logos as an isolated action of one of the persons of
the Trinity but relate it to the Father and the → Holy
Spirit, who proceeds from the Father and whom
Christ sends into the world to complete the work of
redemption. This is also the answer of Orthodoxy to
the tendency to treat Christology as an abstract, an-
thropocentrically oriented theological theme in
which the divine origin retreats into the background
and we have a kind of anthropomorphic Monophysitism with far-reaching consequences for an understanding of the church and its function.

Orthodox academic dogmatics holds fast to the
Chalcedonian Definition, which makes dialogue difficult with non-Chalcedonian churches (→ Oriental
Orthodox Churches). In essence, the latter have an
orthodox Christology but do not accept Chalcedon.
The ontological vocabulary leads the discussion into
a dead end, out of which a liturgical, mystical Christology that is oriented to the Trinity might well lead,
especially when the traditions have so much in common.

→ Orthodoxy 3

Bibliography: H.-G. Beck, *Kirche und theologische Literatur im byzantinischen Reich* (Munich, 1959; 2d ed.,
1977) • S. Bulgakov, *Du Verbe Incarné (Agnus Dei)*
(Paris, 1943) • P. Evdokimov, *Christus im russischen
Denken* (Trier, 1977) • G. Florovsky, *Anatomia prob-
lēmatōn tēs pisteōs* (Thessaloníki, 1977) • M. Fouyas,
*The Person of Jesus Christ in the Decisions of the Ecumeni-
cal Councils: A Historical and Doctrinal Study with the
Relevant Documents Referring to the Christological Relations of the Western, Eastern, and Oriental Churches*
(Addis Ababa, 1976) • P. Gregorios, W. H. Lazareth,
and N. A. Nissiotis, *Does Chalcedon Divide or Unite?
Towards Convergence in Orthodox Christology* (Geneva,
1981) • P. Joannou, "Der Nominalismus und die
menschliche Psychologie Christi. Das Semeioma gegen
Eustratios von Nikaia (1117)," *ByZ* 47 (1954) 369-78 •
V. Lossky, *The Mystical Theology of the Eastern Church*
(2d ed.; Crestwood, N.Y., 1976) • M. Lot-Borodine,
"Initiation à la mystique sacramentaire de l'Orient,"
RSPT 24 (1935) 664-75 • J. Meyendorff, *Christ in East-
ern Christian Thought* (Crestwood, N.Y., 1975) • N. Nis-
siotis, *Die Theologie der Ostkirche im ökumenischen
Dialog. Kirche und Welt in orthodoxer Sicht* (Stuttgart,
1968) 64-85 • "Non-Official Ecumenical Consultation
between Theologians of the Oriental Orthodox
Churches and the Roman Catholic Church," *Wort und
Wahrheit* (Vienna [Ecumenical Foundation "Pro
Oriente"], 1972) 1-184 • "Papers and Discussions be-
tween Eastern Orthodox and Oriental Theologians, the
Bristol Consultation, July 25-29, 1967," *GOTR* 13 (1968)
121-320 • G. Podskalsky, "Gottesschau und Inkarna-
tion. Zur Bedeutung der Heilsgeschichte bei Gregorios
Palamas," *OCP* 35 (1969) 5-44 • C. Schönborn, *Die
Christus-Ikone* (Schaffhausen, 1984) • B. Schultze,
"Problemi di teologia presso gli ortodossi, Cristologia,"
OCP 9 (1943) 135-70; idem, "Der Streit um die Gött-
lichkeit des Namens Jesu in der russischen Theologie,"
ibid. 17 (1951) 321-94 • "Unofficial Consultation be-
tween Theologians of Eastern Orthodox and Oriental
Orthodox Churches, August 11-15, 1964, Papers and
Minutes," *GOTR* 10 (1964/65) 1-160 • T. Uqbit, *Current
Christological Positions of Ethiopian Orthodox Theolo-
gians* (Rome, 1973).

Anastasios Kallis

4. Christology in Roman Catholic Discussion

Until the 20th century, Roman Catholic Christology
was dominated by the ontological categories of the
early church and High → Scholasticism (→
Scotism; Thomism). The age of the → Enlightenment disrupted this tradition, first, with attempts to
interpret the Christ-event in anthropological and
ethical concepts and then, in the 19th century,
with Christological concentration on the problem
of the self-consciousness of Jesus (A. Günter and
H. Schell). A glance at present-day texts indicating
ecumenical consensus or convergence shows that
Christological questions play no central part in interdenominational → dialogue (W. Breuning, 191-
92). Most of the Christological problems now under
discussion within Roman Catholicism either have
transdenominational significance or have been
raised by Protestant theology. On the Roman Catholic side, four (overlapping) groups of questions are
evident.

4.1. *Exegesis and Dogmatics*

The debate here aims to clarify the sometimes tense relation between historical-critical research (→ Exegesis, Biblical) and the dogmatic statements of the → teaching office (→ Dogma). Can the conclusions of the former be made compatible with the latter? In answer to such a question it is pointed out that (1) dogmatic development can and must show its material basis in what is called implicit, pre-Easter Christology (K. → Rahner, 243-52; E. Schillebeeckx, 95-240) and (2), in spite of all the discontinuity (e.g., in the → death and → resurrection of Jesus), one must assume a permanent continuity between the Jesus of history and the Christ of faith (Schillebeeckx, 482-93; J. Blank, 11-92). The idea of the development of dogma is accepted as a legitimate unfolding of the historically demonstrable claim and self-understanding of Jesus; this approach applies already to the NT books (see 1). The related question as to the appropriate method of Christological reflection — Christology from above or from below (W. Kasper in L. Scheffczyk, 141ff.) — cannot be given a single answer (A. Schilson and W. Kasper, 135), though there is a plain preference for starting with the historically accessible humanity of Christ (see Schillebeeckx, 32; H. Küng, 145-65; Rahner, 291ff.).

4.2. *Tradition and Interpretation*

The question of the relation between dogma or church → tradition, on the one hand, and modern reinterpretation, on the other, forms a second problem area in modern Roman Catholic Christology. No one doubts today that dogmatic formulations are historical in principle, though this does not mean that we have to draw the relativistic conclusions that are often feared (e.g., in the debate with → modernism).

The historicity of dogma means that it must always be open to fresh interpretation (Breuning, 195ff.; Rahner, 279-98; Schillebeeckx, 494-504; Schilson and Kasper, 139ff.). The aim of such expositions of the Christ-mystery is to show the responsibility of the Christian faith in face of modern challenges. They set forth the content of the Christological dogma of the incarnate God in the framework of typically modern experiences of reality and → worldviews (see Rahner, 206-11) — for example, in the perspective of a transcendental starting point that seeks to show the correspondence between humanity and the being of Christ (→ Immanence and Transcendence), or, in Rahner's terms (180-202), interpreting Christology within an evolutionary view of the world. Schillebeeckx (509-98), Küng (411-63), and Kasper take other approaches.

For all the differences, the common feature is an attempt to relate the message of Christ to modern experience of the self and the world. The story of Jesus, which is inseparable from his person, is our human story. In it God's self-impartation to us manifests itself. The norm of such fresh interpretations is the witness to Christ in Holy Scripture, on the one hand, and, on the other, the church's tradition (Scheffczyk, 13). To some extent, the former is played off critically against the latter (see Küng, 126-44). The attempt to expound the content of Scripture in accordance with the age comes into conflict with the claim of the teaching office that it accompanies the transmission of the witness to Christ critically and authoritatively (see Küng). The controversy in this area broadly reflects the tension typically existing between church → authority and academic freedom.

4.3. *Past and Present*

At least from the time of A. → Schweitzer's work on the quest of the historical Jesus, the strangeness of the historical Jesus has caused → hermeneutical problems for all of Christology. Yet the strangeness that arises out of the distance between past and present might be viewed as an opportunity to maintain the nondeducible claim of the message of Jesus in every age. This line of thought shows clearly that Christology has more to tell us than any → anthropology (Kasper, 61; Schilson and Kasper, 145).

A Christology from within (E. Biser) tackles the problem in another way. The broad and ugly ditch between past and present is overcome by existentially experienced contemporaneity with Jesus, who as helper is also the help itself (S. → Kierkegaard) and makes successful humanity possible (Biser, 246ff.).

4.4. *Jesus and the Church*

Clarification of the relation between Jesus and the → church poses a final problem in modern Roman Catholic Christology. The tendency today in speaking of the founding of the church is not to point to specific acts (e.g., Matt. 16:18), as in traditional *demonstratio catholica* (Blank, 122-46). Instead, the church is viewed as the sacramental mode of Christ's presence in the Holy Spirit (Rahner, 308ff.), with a basis in the total Christ-event. Thus the church is the decisive place of encounter with Christ, though with no need to postulate that it is the only place where the Spirit of Christ is present (Rahner, 303-12).

Church proclamation, → liturgy, and charity are signs and instruments (*Lumen gentium* 1) of the → love of God for us as this is manifested in Christ. But the boundaries of this love are not identical with those of the organized fellowship of the church (as → Vatican II allows). Against this background, interpretations of Jesus outside the church or Christianity (e.g., those of Jews or Marxists), for all their imperfection, make it possible, in self-critical openness, to overcome traditional constructions (Fries in Scheffczyk, 71ff.). This is happening especially in → political theology.

The consensus in modern Roman Catholic theology is that Christology (1) must be historically determined (i.e., faith in Christ has a concrete aspect), (2) must be given universal expression (in a Christologically oriented, historical, and personal ontology), and (3) must be soteriologically oriented (i.e., the being and significance of Christ are indissolubly united; see Kasper, 20-26).

Bibliography: E. Biser, Der Helfer. Eine Vergegenwärtigung Jesu (Munich, 1973) • J. Blank, Jesus von Nazareth. Geschichte und Relevanz (Freiburg, 1972) • W. Breuning, "Christologische Bemühungen in der katholischen Theologie," Einführung in die Christologie (ed. H. Dembowski; Darmstadt, 1976) 191-211 • P. Hünermann, Jesus Christus. Gottes Wort in der Zeit. Eine systematische Christologie (2d ed.; Münster, 1997 • W. Kasper, Jesus der Christus (1974; ET Jesus the Christ [London, 1976]) • H. Küng, Christ Sein (1974; ET On Being a Christian [Garden City, N.Y., 1976]) • K.-J. Kuschel, Born before All Time? The Dispute over Christ's Origin (London, 1992) • K.-H. Ohlig, Fundamentalchristologie. Im Spannungsfeld von Christentum und Kultur (Munich, 1986) • K. Rahner, Grundkurs des Glaubens. Einführung in den Begriff des Christentums (1976; ET Foundations of Christian Faith: An Introduction to the Idea of Christianity [New York, 1978]) • L. Scheffczyk, ed., Grundfragen der Christologie heute (2d ed.; Freiburg, 1978) • E. Schillebeeckx, Jesus. Die Geschichte von einem Lebenden (Freiburg, 1974; 7th ed., 1980) • A. Schilson and W. Kasper, Christologie im Präsens. Kritische Sichtung neuer Entwürfe (Freiburg, 1974).

HEINRICH DÖRING

5. Christology in the Third World

In the churches of the so-called Third World (→ Third World Theology), Christologies that differ from classic Christology, or that break away from the influence of the theology of European or American missions, exist as yet only in embryonic form. The traditional churches that are the product of → mission, and many of the numerous → independent churches (not least the postdenominational three-self movement in China), cling conservatively to traditional Christology. This is also true of Orthodox and Roman Catholic churches in the Third World.

In contrast, implicit Christological statements and fresh presentations may be found in great num-

bers and variety, especially in art and poetry, as well as in the Christological concretion of the hope of liberation (→ Liberation Theology) and the acceptance of suffering (e.g., in minjung theology in Korea and Japan). In view of the inseparability of thought and life, symbol and ritual, and the unity of experience and teaching in African cultures, or the precedence of practice over abstract doctrine in Asian cultures, can we realistically expect Third World churches to develop explicit Christologies? Perhaps their resort to new, implicit presentations in practice, myth, ritual, poetry, and art — sometimes connected with spontaneous, provocative theses on the part of some authors — may be regarded as a long-needed criticism of the Western understanding of propositional truth and "pure" doctrine.

These new presentations, which often contain harsh and even unjust criticism of the academic theology of Europe and America, may be classified as follows.

5.1. A Christus Victor Christology

Jesus Christ conquers → demons and → evil. Although a marginal emphasis in Asia, this concept is central in African churches. For J. Pobee (not without his African critics), Jesus is a chieftain and progenitor, and as such the mediator between God and us. According to H.-J. Margull (1925-82), the oppressed in the messianic Independent Churches often want a Christianity without offense. They view Jesus Christ more as conqueror than as crucified. They also view Christ the Victor eschatologically. If Africans could open up their futureless understanding of time (J. Mbiti), they would see the final victory of Christ eschatologically within the framework of traditional African piety and its concern for victory over evil powers (→ Eschatology 6).

5.2. A Christology of the Passion

This implicit Christology in Africa arises from the amplification of the legend that Simon of Cyrene, who carried the cross of Jesus, was an African (e.g., in the → Kimbanguist Church). In art and poetry, too, this motif plays a role in Africa (T. Sundermeier), though less in preaching and didactic theology.

In Asian churches the supraindividual significance of Christ's passion is central in piety and theology. Christ suffers with all people and is a symbol for their suffering (minjung). What he has experienced, we also must experience in order to attain to → resurrection. Resurrection in some political contexts can also mean liberation. In Japan — also motivated by criticism of the ethics of Confucianism — there is a strong leaning toward → kenotic Christology, that is, the idea that God did not just cover or conceal his power in the coming and suffering of

Jesus but actually surrendered it. In the cultural context of → Hinduism, the Christian theologians of India in particular have made the particularity and uniqueness of Jesus as fellow sufferer an important theme. In the context of East Asia, C. S. Song has upheld the uniqueness of Jesus but left open in principle the free transferring of other paradigms from the history of Israel and the church (the exodus, the Davidic kingdom, the exile, and events in Christian history).

5.3. A Christology of the Cosmic Christ

Rather in the background today stands a revised concept of the cosmic dimensions of Christ championed by the American theologian J. Sittler (1961) in New Delhi. This had found much acceptance, since it fits in with the interests of Indian and Far Eastern religious traditions and Christians living in those areas. Matthew Fox has written broadly on themes relating Christology, spirituality, and the environment.

5.4. The Black Christ as Liberator

→ Black theology (§3), which has spread from the United States to South Africa, in part to black Africa, and in a modified form to Australia and the churches of the Pacific, contains essentially two Christological theses and a central problem. The theses relate to the linking of the exodus of God's people with the coming of Christ as a divine event for all oppressed peoples, and to the important theological truth that Christ is fully (also racially) one with all those who believe in him. The problem is that of the compatibility of the second thesis with the indispensable insight that Jesus was a Jew, that his human nature, viewed enhypostatically as classic Christology says, was that of a specific Jewish man, who cannot be "general man" (as possibly in Alexandrian Christology), white for whites, yellow for those who are yellow, and black for blacks. Black theology inclines to a symbolic understanding of Jesus as Christ and Liberator for the nations.

Undoubtedly many of these new expressions of implicit Christology in the churches of the Third World appear in the categories of traditional Christology. Some of them also have parallels in Christological positions and criticisms within European church history. Such observations, though, should not lead us to undervalue the implicit Christologies of the Third World or their critical value for the whole church.

→ African Theology; Asian Theology; Black Theology; Contextual Theology; Liberation Theology; Third World Theology

Bibliography: D. Elwood, ed., Wie Christen in Asien denken. Ein theologisches Quellenbuch (Frankfurt, 1979) • M. Fox, The Coming of the Cosmic Christ: The Healing of Mother Earth and the Birth of a Global Renaissance (San Francisco, 1988); idem, Wrestling with the Prophets: Essays on Creation, Spirituality, and Everyday Life (San Francisco, 1995) • J. Pobee, Toward an African Theology (Nashville, 1979) • H. Rücker, Afrikanische Theologie, Darstellung und Dialog (Innsbruck, 1985) • T. Sundermeier, Das Kreuz als Befreiung. Kreuzesinterpretationen in Asien und Afrika (Munich, 1985) bibliography • M. M. Thomas, The Acknowledged Christ of the Indian Renaissance (Madras, 1970) • M. Welling, "Asiatische Theologie im Werden" (Diss., St. Augustin, 1982) • C. Wright and L. Fugui, eds., Christ and South Pacific Cultures (Suva, Fiji, 1985).

Dietrich Ritschl

6. Christology in Dogmatics

→ Jewish-Christian dialogue, which after a silence of almost 2,000 years has begun in American, Dutch, and German theology, is examining again the central thesis of Christology that Jesus is the fulfillment of the promise given to → Israel. How is it that, not the → Mishnah or the → Talmud, but the → apostles and the → church fathers are the legitimate continuation of the history of Israel, the history of God with his people (as Christian theologians often put it)? Backing up this statement, or qualifying it, is the task of Christology.

A radical solution, which was already a problem in the early church (in the criticism of Marcion in the 2d cent.) and which German theology has constantly considered, is the denial of the internal connection between Israel and the coming of Jesus. Affirming the connection, however, does not automatically result in a uniform Christology. Ideas of fulfillment (of the promises to Israel) and also of history differ too much to achieve total uniformity.

The big differences in Christologies that accept the central thesis of Jesus as fulfillment may be explained by the initial differences in starting point. Should we begin with the witness to the historical → Jesus, with the celebration of the risen Lord in primitive communities, with present-day faith in Christ, with the promises to Israel, or with the effective history of Jesus? Or should we take a → Trinitarian course, asking about the person of the God-man and determining more fully the relation between the two natures? All these approaches can be defended.

Explicit Christology seeks to give reasons for its detailed statements, listening to the varied, implicitly Christological witness of the NT and to believers throughout the centuries, and measuring them by the whole Bible, by questions about the Jews, and by cosmic disasters, from the death of a child to Auschwitz. Surveying this task of explicit Christology, we sketch the following six issues, which will also help to relativize a question that academic theology often discusses too much, namely, that of the relation between (explicit) Christology and the doctrines of → justification and → reconciliation (which are ultimately only of didactic interest).

6.1. *Expectations of Christus praesens*

Believers in all ages have worshiped Jesus Christ as one who is present. In his name they have prayed, blessed, healed, preached, forgiven one another, and discharged their whole → diakonia in the hope of his presence. They have ventured their statements about Jesus in recollection of earlier hopes and their fulfillment. They rely on promises. They thus interpret his presence as something other than mere recollection of a loved one who is now dead. They rest on the fact that he makes himself present in a special way corresponding to the characteristic mode of his absence after his death. The classic answers regarding the mode of this presence — for example, in the → Word of → preaching, in the Spirit or gifts of the Spirit (→ Charisma; Pneumatology), in the → sacraments, in works of → love, in personal → prayer, in → suffering, in expectation of the establishment of his future → righteousness (→ Kingdom of God) — do not exclude one another. But their one-sided or exclusive tendencies have become typical marks of different denominations or of various trends in the church (e.g., a kerygmatic theology of the Word, sacramentalism, the → Social Gospel, → Religious Socialism, mysticism).

Left open in these basic positions is the Trinitarian question as to the subject of the presence. Is it the Spirit of God (as in some NT epistles), or is it the spiritual body of the risen Christ (→ Resurrection)? Does the humanity of Jesus participate in some way in the presence (→ Eucharist 3; Ubiquity), or is Christ present only in the church? (Different conceptions of this latter possibility in the thought of, e.g., F. D. E. → Schleiermacher and D. → Bonhoeffer ["Christ existing as community"] demonstrate the breadth of Christological interpretations.) Widely different, too, are the explicit Christologies of those who begin in principle with the question of *Christus praesens,* such as Eastern → Orthodoxy (§3), M. Kähler (1835-1912), K. → Barth (1886-1968), and R. Bultmann (1884-1976).

6.2. *The Coming of Jesus*

It is uncontested that through the coming of Jesus of Nazareth, a community came into being that confessed in different ways that this coming (and going) of Jesus was of central significance not only for them but for all Jews and Gentiles, and thus for all people everywhere. Also uncontested is the fact that the primitive community (and the later church) said much more about Jesus than he said about himself (see 1). The question of the legitimacy of this extension (on the basis of OT and later Jewish hopes) is a central one in Christology. It is ultimately the question of God in Jesus. All theologians accept this. But they differ sharply on whether Christology should start here.

The older quest for the historical Jesus (→ Exegesis, Biblical, 2) wanted to find out how Jesus "really was." On conceptual grounds it linked up in the 19th century with the (idealistic) question of what is lasting and eternal in Jesus, who did not come properly alive in the meager findings of historical research. In contrast, with similar but extended methods, the → history-of-religions school presented what was strange and Oriental about Jesus as distinct from what is familiar and might serve as a lasting model. M. Kähler's famous work of 1892, and especially A. → Schweitzer's (1875-1965) great historical discussion of the quest for the historical Jesus (1906), brought the quest provisionally to an end. Occasional attempts to continue it seemed to be anachronistic and irrelevant.

In the German-speaking sphere at least, the dominance of the newer form-criticism of the NT had become too strong, as had that of → dialectical theology, which on similar grounds but for different reasons did not regard the older approach as appropriate in the case of the NT documents. Only in the 1950s did a "new quest" for the historical Jesus begin with E. Käsemann, J. Robinson, and others. Deleting the pre-Easter Jesus from theology and Christology was regarded as exposed to the danger of exaggeration. Continuity between Jesus' own claim, whether found in his destiny (E. Fuchs) or in his conduct, and the later predications of the primitive community had always to be unconditionally the theme of Christology, the "new quest" claimed.

Anglo-Saxon theology had always maintained this connection, though it had not been through the purifying fire of historical criticism as German-speaking theology had in the 19th century, or at least the results of this criticism had not shaken the churches so severely (→ Theology in the Nineteenth and Twentieth Centuries 4). The same point applies even more to preconciliar Roman Catholic theology, which had never fully given up the question of the historical Jesus in either theology or church teaching. For this reason believers in Anglo-Saxon and Roman Catholic churches are much more familiar with the names and (legendary) biographies of the people around Jesus and the apostles than are those of the ("Pauline"-) Protestant churches of Europe.

Two decisive questions call for our attention in the "new quest" for the historical Jesus. The first is whether we can and must talk about Jesus' mission, or whether he was self-appointed, a righteous man of the people whom God (in adoptionist fashion) vindicated and exalted. The second is how we can talk ("anhypostatically") about his uniqueness in such a way that the Christological vocabulary might not validly be applied to others (e.g., Socrates or Martin L. → King). These questions condition each other. They become the more acute the more clearly we see the minimal lifestyle of Jesus. He had no possessions, was unmarried, and made no claim to self-fulfillment or development of his personality. Yet this Jew with his minimal lifestyle gave maximal attention to God and other people. Along these lines, he undoubtedly revealed → God and not himself (→ Revelation 2.3 and 2.6). The revelatory significance of the coming of Jesus must be strictly qualified relative to the OT, Israel's knowledge of God, and the extension of the vocabulary of witness in the primitive community. W. Pannenberg finds in Jesus' resurrection, but not in his coming, the first intimation of the revelation that will take place only at the end of history.

The term → "incarnation," which is much too heavily freighted in academic theology, has come in for radical criticism in English theology in J. Hick's volume *The Myth of God Incarnate* (though many of the arguments are out of date). In fact, Jewish-Christian dialogue needs to test the concept afresh. The English discussion, however, did not consider the extension of Israel's promise to the Gentiles in the coming of Jesus.

6.3. *Who Is Jesus Christ?*

The quest for the nature of the God-man in classic Christology was harshly criticized in the 19th century by A. Ritschl (1822-89) and his school, with an anti-metaphysical thrust, especially regarding the answers of → Chalcedon (451). Modern theology, however, has other linguistic instruments at its disposal, and behind the systems that made use of such current concepts as nature, person, substance, and hypostasis, with ramifications like anhypostasis, enhypostasis, and communication of attributes (see 2.2.4), it can often discern abiding and central Christological insights. This is also true of the older Protestant doctrines of the states of humiliation and exaltation (→ Orthodoxy), or of Christ's concealment or self-emptying (see 2.4.4). Finally, classic Christology did not merely pose the *how* question of the natures and their union. It also had in view the *who* question of

the Christ who is glorified in → worship (§§1-2). (D. Bonhoeffer distinguished between these two questions.)

We must not reproach classic Christology for using scholastic terms and the implied → metaphysics, for no theology can escape the theorizing of its day. Our real complaint against it is twofold: (1) it reduced the broad possibilities that the NT offers for developing explicit Christologies to the single question of the simultaneous presence of God and man in Jesus, and (2) it abstracted this question from the context in which it should have arisen, namely, God's history with Israel.

Classic Christology thus contains no basis for the coming of Jesus, no reference to his link with Jews and → Gentiles, to the present Christ, or to the hope of Jews and Gentiles. If the primitive community achieved a significant, legitimate gain of vocabulary relative to Jesus, at Chalcedon the church suffered a striking loss. Classic Christology nevertheless has an important corrective function, warding off erroneous concepts, and an important communicative function, promoting ecumenism. The explicitly Christological essays of Protestant, Catholic, and Orthodox authors that critically adopt classic Christology have made this value abundantly plain in the last decades.

6.4. *The Significance of Christ's Coming*

This issue, which asks what is changed by his coming, is that of → reconciliation. On a primary level that is dominant in the liturgical service, believers celebrate the reconciliation of God and humanity. (According to the satisfaction theory, Christ's work, passion, and death accomplished, more broadly, the reconciliation of all people and indeed of the world.) On a secondary level, believers look for perceptible historical signs of reconciliation, and they themselves try to establish such signs in the personal, social, and political spheres (→ Ethics; Social Ethics), and then in → ecological responsibility (→ Environmental Ethics) to animals, plants, and all of creation. They do all this with the knowledge, and shame, that the church has brought infinitely much conflict, anxiety, implacability, and ecological irresponsibility into the world, as though nothing new had resulted from the coming of Jesus.

Modern Christology also considers more strongly than previously God's suffering with those who are exploited and deprived of their rights, the poor and helpless. Thus the ancient Roman Catholic concern (in the → Mass) to repeat Christ's sacrificial death (→ Eucharist) has taken on a new actuality, as has that of the suffering people of God (e.g., at Auschwitz; → Holocaust). God himself "experiences" a history in the death of Jesus and the suffering of humanity (→ process theologians, but also other authors).

6.5. Resurrection, Cross, and Incarnation as Retrospective Theological Concepts

We may understand, but we must also regret, the reduction of the story of Jesus in the NT to these three terms, which quickly became autonomous in theology, thus leading to such absurd expressions as "the cross demands," "the resurrection prevents," "the incarnation forbids," and the like. For all the assurances to the contrary, making these three concepts into separate themes — and the third is the most dubious — has led to one-sided thinking, so that we find in church history typical theologies and confessions of the incarnation, cross, or resurrection.

Positively, we can also see in one movement a challenge to others, or a correction of them, as in the helpful German discussion of the cross (→ Theologia crucis) and the resurrection (see bibliography). Mutual challenges of this kind are also ecumenically fruitful, for such great communions as the → Anglicans, the Lutherans (→ Lutheran Churches), and the → Orthodox Church (also to a limited extent the → Reformed churches) easily link themselves respectively to theologies of the incarnation, the cross, and the resurrection. The concepts as such will always be merely auxiliary in a retrospective interpretation of the theme of Christology.

6.6. The Tragic in the Light of Christology

Protestant theology has always steered clear of the concept of the tragic, as though it belittled in some way Christ's perfect work. After Auschwitz, Dresden, Viet Nam, and the political and economic dictatorships of our age, however, we now think with a new helplessness about the Christological implications of the irrevocable suffering and destruction of individuals and whole nations. At this point we cannot fail to hear the Christological question of the relation between what we might call the metaphysical significance of the coming of God in Jesus of Nazareth and the historical effectiveness of this coming. We have here a test for the hope that is based on Christ, which occupies a central position in dialogue with → Marxism (→ Marxism and Christianity) and the world → religions. What does it mean that Jesus Christ has overcome death and the world?

6.7. Remaining Tasks

None of the Christological tasks that the implicit Christologies of the church have set for theology has been finally completed, especially those that theology has set for itself. In particular, we discern the following tasks today. First, in dialogue with Jews, we need to support the basic Christological thesis that the coming of Jesus is a fulfillment of the promises. Second, we need to relate what is said about Jesus Christ to the Trinity, justifying theologically the statements about God that undoubtedly underlie every Christology. Next, in the interests of ecumenism, we need a comprehensive reinterpretation of classic Christology and the Christological traditions of the great churches. Fourth, we need to deal with the impact of implicit Christologies from the Third World. Finally, we need a courageous interpretation of the theme of Christology in the light of the disasters and sufferings of our world.

→ Christological Titles; Docetism; Easter; Eschatology; Eucharist; Holy Spirit; Justification; Reconciliation; Resurrection; Soteriology; Trinity 2

Bibliography: J. ALFARO et al., Das Christusreignis (= MySal 3/1) • D. J. BAILLIE, God Was in Christ (London, 1947) • K. BARTH, CD IV/1 • E. BETHGE, Dietrich Bonhoeffer: Theologian, Christian, Contemporary (London, 1970) • D. BONHOEFFER, "Christologie-Vorlesung, 1933," Gesammelte Schriften (vol. 3; ed. E. Bethge; Munich, 1960) 166-242 • G. EBELING, Dogmatik des christlichen Glaubens (vol. 2; Tübingen, 1979) • M. GOULDER, ed., Incarnation and Myth: The Debate Continued (London, 1979) • J. HICK, ed., The Myth of God Incarnate (London, 1977) • M. KÄHLER, The So-Called Historical Jesus and the Historic, Biblical Christ (Philadelphia, 1964) • G. B. KELLY and F. B. NELSON, eds., A Testament to Freedom: The Essential Writings of Dietrich Bonhoeffer (rev. ed.; San Francisco, 1995) • B. KLAPPERT, ed., Diskussion um Kreuz und Auferstehung (Wuppertal, 1967; 5th ed., 1981) • J. MOLTMANN, The Crucified God: The Cross of Christ as the Foundation and Criticism of Christian Theology (New York, 1974) • S. M. OGDEN, The Point of Christology (San Francisco, 1982) • W. PANNENBERG, Jesus, God, and Man (Philadelphia, 1968) • D. RITSCHL, The Logic of Theology (Philadelphia, 1987) • E. SCHILLEBEECKX, Jesus. Die Geschichte von einem Lebenden (Freiburg, 1974; 7th ed., 1980) • A. SCHWEITZER, The Quest of the Historical Jesus: A Critical Study of Its Progress from Reimarus to Wrede (New York, 1968; orig. pub., 1906) • P. TILLICH, Systematic Theology (vol. 2; Chicago, 1957).

DIETRICH RITSCHL

Chronicles, Books of

1. In Hebrew, the Books of Chronicles are commonly known as dibrê hayyāmîm, "events of the days." → Jerome (d. 420) gave them the more precise title "Chronicles of All the Divine History," which led to our present-day title "Chronicles." In the Vg, how-

ever, Jerome retained the LXX title *Paralipomena* (things passed over, omitted), referring to things left out of Samuel and Kings. This view, which is oriented exclusively to → Deuteronomistic history, hardly does justice to the aims of the Books of Chronicles, which span the whole period from the spread of humanity across the earth, by way of the settlement of the → tribes of Israel in the land, their uniting by → David, the establishment of the cultus in → Jerusalem, and the account of the Davidic dynasty, to the deportation of the people from the land.

The full extent of the contents of the two books may be seen in their clear *arrangement,* which supports a single authorship. In 1 Chronicles 1–9 we have genealogies relating to the settlement of human families, especially the tribes of Israel. These lists are not merely an introduction to the entity of Israel but form the basis of it. Chaps. 10–29 then tell the story of David's uniting of Israel and founding of the Levitical cultus and his own dynasty in Jerusalem. In 2 Chronicles, chaps. 1–9 present the construction and dedication of the temple at Jerusalem by Solomon, and chaps. 10–36 tell of the preservation of the Davidic legacy through the Davidic kings up to the exile. We do injury to this self-contained scheme if we view 1-2 Chronicles merely as part of a larger historical work that includes Ezra and Nehemiah. The investigations of scholars like S. Japhet and H. G. M. Williamson offer various considerations — language, ideas of history, technical matters relating to the tradition — that favor a rejection of this thesis.

2. The purpose of the far-ranging *retelling* (R. Mosis) is to show that the postexilic cultus at Jerusalem does not rest solely on the → Pentateuch, with its strong priestly orientation, but may appeal to David, by way of the Levites as the guardians of genuine Israelite and especially prophetic teaching and practice, for giving the people a larger spiritual and material share in worship. Primarily, then, the motivation of Chronicles is an internal Jewish one; with their emphasis on the praise of God, the books point in the same direction as the titles of the Psalms. The books are not an apology for Judaism (W. Rudolph), and in their exposition it is not necessary to introduce the developing controversy with the → Samaritans. The prophetic and national role of the Levites (G. von Rad) is not played off against the cultus but is seen to have been anchored in it by David. The depiction of history may be characterized as an interpretation (T. Willi) of the older tradition of the Pentateuch and Deuteronomy. The books thus prepare the way for an → apocalyptic method of depiction (P. Welten).

3. On the basis of the theme of the books and their place in the history of thought, the time of composition may be put in the later Persian epoch. The Davidic kingship is presented as a prototype of Achaemenid engagement for Israel and the Jerusalem temple cult. The significance of Chronicles lies in the fact that in the history of Israel's tradition these books mark the transition from a collection of writings to Scripture. Interpretation and performance are the way to safeguard the divine word, to which they give a decisive place even in → worship. More than the books themselves, their example influenced Jewish exegesis and worship, and consequently the NT message of the Son of David, which carries a clear reference to 1 Chronicles 1–3 in Matthew 1.

Bibliography: Commentaries: S. Japhet (OTL; London, 1993) • W. Rudolph, (Tübingen, 1955) • H. G. M. Williamson (NCBC; Grand Rapids, 1982).

Other works: S. Japhet,. *The Ideology of the Book of Chronicles and Its Place in Biblical Thought* (Frankfurt, 1989); idem, "The Supposed Common Authorship of Chronicles and Ezra-Nehemiah Investigated Anew," *VT* 18 (1968) 330-71 • R. Mosis, *Untersuchungen zur Theologie des chronistischen Geschichtswerkes* (Freiburg, 1973) • M. Noth, *The Chronicler's History* (Sheffield, 1987) • G. von Rad, *Das Geschichtsbild des chronistischen Werkes* (Stuttgart, 1930) • G. Steins, *Die Chronik als Abschlußphänomen* (Weinheim, 1995) • K. Strübind, *Tradition als Interpretation in der Chronik* (Berlin, 1991) • P. Welten, *Geschichte und Geschichtsdarstellung in der Chronik* (Neukirchen, 1973) • W. M. L. de Wette, *Kritischer Versuch über die Glaubwürdigkeit der Bücher der Chronik, mit Hinsicht auf die Geschichte der mosaischen Bücher und Gesetzgebung* (Halle, 1806) • T. Willi, *Die Chronik als Auslegung* (Göttingen, 1972); idem, *Juda–Jehud–Israel. Studien zum Selbstverständnis des Judentums in persischer Zeit* (Tübingen, 1995) • H. G. M. Williamson, *Israel in the Books of Chronicles* (Cambridge, 1977).

Thomas Willi

Chrysostom, John

John of Antioch (ca. 347-407), surnamed Chrysostom, "Golden-mouthed," was → bishop of Constantinople and the greatest preacher of the patristic era. Born and raised at Antioch in Syria, the son of Christian parents of the educated upper class, John received the finest rhetorical education available, under the distinguished pagan sophist Libanius. Rejecting a career in law or in the imperial service, John chose to enter the clergy. He was baptized by Bishop Melitius (ca. 367), became a lector, and devoted himself to Scripture study under Diodore of Tarsus in a → monastery near → Antioch. From Diodore, Chrysostom learned the characteristically Antiochene emphasis on historical and grammatical → exegesis.

Beginning in 372, John's ecclesiastical career was interrupted for several years while he pursued the ascetic life in the hills near Antioch. Four years were spent in the company of an elderly Syrian monk; John then withdrew to a cave, where he lived in complete solitude for two years. The harshness of his ascetic regimen, however, damaged John's health, and he eventually returned to the city and the clerical life (378). He soon advanced to the order of → deacon (381) and presbyter (386; → Elder). This period marked the beginning of John's extraordinary career as a writer and preacher.

Upon returning to the city, John immediately threw himself into intense literary activity. Several of his earliest works were concerned with defending the monastic and ascetic ways of life against pagan and Christian critics. *A Comparison between a King and a Monk, Against the Opponents of the Monastic Life, On Virginity, Against Remarriage, On Compunction,* and his letters *To a Young Widow* and *To the Lapsed Monk Theodore* are among the works that testify to the young John Chrysostom's continued enthusiasm for → asceticism in this early period of his life.

John's attitude toward → monasticism, however, was not uncritical, for he was aware of the moral dangers that confronted Christian ascetics. He composed two books attacking "spiritual marriage," the practice of unmarried ascetics living together as brother and sister. He also had to face the problem of mental or spiritual illness among the monks (*To Stagirios Suffering from a Demon*).

During this early period John also composed several apologies in defense of Christianity (*On St. Babylas against the Greeks* and *Demonstration against the Jews and Greeks That Christ Is God*). John's apologies were directed specifically against the recent pagan revival of the emperor Julian and the continued support of → Hellenism by Libanius. Somewhat later (386) John delivered a series of eight sermons entitled *Against Judaizing Christians,* which show that his → apologetic concern with both Judaism and Hellenism continued well into his presbyterate.

As presbyter, Chrysostom turned his attention increasingly toward the life and problems of ordinary Christians in the city of Antioch. Among his most famous writings is the treatise *On Vainglory and the Proper Way to Raise Children,* a work that is virtually unique in → patristic literature for the careful attention it gives to the problem of → Christian education. The book contains a blistering attack on the lifestyle

and values of the Antiochenes, as well as advice on how Christian parents might use Bible stories to mold the character of their children. At Antioch John also composed a six-book treatise *On the Priesthood,* a discussion of the difficulties and duties of the episcopate.

The vast bulk of John's work during his years as presbyter (386-98) consisted of sermons addressed to the people of Antioch. There are cycles on particular themes, such as the seven panegyrics *In Praise of St. Paul;* a series of dogmatic sermons *On the Incomprehensibility of God,* directed against a group of radical Arian Christians in the city; and a series of 21 Lenten sermons, the *Homilies on the Statues,* occasioned by a riot in the city in 387 during which a mob destroyed the images of the emperor and his family. In the last series John took the opportunity to remind his congregation of the importance of repentance, as well as to argue that the emperor's clemency (which John attributes to the intervention of the bishop Flavian and the monks) is a sign of the superiority of Christianity over paganism.

At Antioch, Chrysostom also delivered sermons on Genesis, Isaiah, the Psalms, Matthew, John, and most of the Pauline corpus. His preaching bears the stamp of his rhetorical education under Libanius, as well as his exegetical formation under Diodore. On the one hand, his sermons abound with images and topoi from the rhetorical handbooks. John himself tells us that his congregation expected a display of verbal pyrotechnics in no way different from that of secular orators. On the other hand, John is most interested in applying the biblical texts to the spiritual and moral lives of his congregation. For John, the Bible offered patterns of the moral life for the imitation of the Christian community.

In 398 John was forced to accept consecration as bishop of Constantinople. His inability to deal tactfully with the imperial court, especially the empress Eudoxia; his frustrated attempt to reform the clergy of Constantinople; and the jealousy of Theophilus, bishop of the rival see of → Alexandria, twice led to his deposition and exile. John wrote many letters during this period, including a famous series to Olympias, deaconess in Constantinople. John died in exile on September 14, 407, at Comana, an obscure village of Pontus in Asia Minor.

Bibliography: Biographies: PALLADIUS, *Dialogue on the Life of St. John Chrysostom* (trans. R. T. Meyer; New York, 1985) • SOCRATES SCHOLASTICUS *Hist. eccl.* 6.2-23; 7.25-45.

Primary sources: ACW 31, 45 • FC 33, 41, 68, 72-74 • *NPNF* 9-14 • *PG* 47-62 • SC 13, 28, 50, 79, 103, 117, 125, 138, 188, 272, 277, 300, 304, 346, 348.

Secondary works: T. E. AMERINGER, *The Stylistic Influence of the Second Sophistic on the Panegyrical Sermons of St. John Chrysostom* (Washington, D.C., 1920) • C. BAUR, *John Chrysostom and His Time* (trans. M. Gonzaga; 2 vols.; Westminster, 1959) • D. C. BURGER, *A Complete Bibliography of the Scholarship on the Life and Works of St. John Chrysostom* (Evanston, Ill., 1964) • R. E. CARTER, "The Chronology of St. John Chrysostom's Early Life," *Tr.* 18 (1962) 357-64 • E. A. CLARK, *Jerome, Chrysostom, and Friends: Essays and Translations* (New York, 1979) • A. J. FESTUGIÈRE, *Antioche païenne et chrétienne. Libanius, Chrysostome et les moines de Syrie* (Paris, 1959) • D. G. HUNTER, *A Comparison between a King and a Monk / Against the Opponents of the Monastic Life: Two Treatises by John Chrysostom* (Lewiston, N.Y., 1988) • M. L. W. LAISTNER, *Christianity and Pagan Culture in the Later Roman Empire* (Ithaca, N.Y., 1951) • J. H. W. G. LIEBESCHUETZ, *Barbarians and Bishops: Army, Church, and State in the Age of Arcadius and Chrysostom* (Oxford, 1990) • L. MEYER, *Saint Jean Chrysostome. Maître de perfection chrétienne* (Paris, 1933) • E. NOWAK, *Le chrétien devant la souffrance. Étude sur la pensée de Jean Chrysostome* (Paris, 1972) • O. PASQUATO, *Gli spettacoli in S. Giovanni Crisostomo. Paganesimo e cristianesimo ad Antiochia e Costantinopoli nel IV secolo* (Rome, 1976) • A. M. RITTER, *Charisma im Verständis des Johannes Chrysostomos und seiner Zeit* (Göttingen, 1972) • R. L. WILKEN, *John Chrysostom and the Jews: Rhetoric and Reality in the Late Fourth Century* (Berkeley, Calif., 1983).

DAVID G. HUNTER

Church

1. Subject, Tasks, and Problems of Ecclesiology

1.1. *The Church of Faith*

The early → confessions, following the NT, relate the church to the → Holy Spirit as an object of the faith that is the Spirit's work ("I believe in the Holy Spirit, the holy church . . ."). The → Niceno-Constantinopolitan Creed characterizes the church as one, holy, catholic, and apostolic, while the → Apostles'

Creed speaks of "the holy catholic church, the communion of saints." Theological reflection in dogmatics develops these statements of faith into the doctrine of the church (ecclesiology). According to the insight of faith, dogmatics defines the church variously as the mystical body of Christ, a divine-human organism, a sacramental fellowship, a fellowship of faith, a fellowship of experience and communicating, a fellowship of → discipleship of Christ, and more. This ecclesiological development finds its orienting data primarily in the distinctive marks of the church set forth in the creed. Yet it also takes into account differences between the essence and the form of the church, with a tendency to find the essential church in the visible church, and to equate the two. As a consequence of the various confessional contexts and their respective implications (→ Denomination), a variety of doctrines about the church have evolved (see 3).

1.2. The Empirical Church

The church as object of belief is correlated with a multifaceted reality of church that can be experienced and observed empirically, both historically and in its everyday appearances. That is, the concept and the reality of the church do not correspond with each other; "church" thus refers to statements of faith and doctrine as well as to the details of external appearances, to concepts and practices, to collective expressions of faith and their → spirituality. "Church" likewise involves a social corporation with its members, the fact of different churches with their divergent views of themselves, and issues of social effectiveness and contextual factors.

The ordinary uses of the term "church" embrace these manifold aspects. The term can denote the building (→ Church Architecture) or the services held there ("going to church"; → Worship). It can also be used for representative figures (→ Offices, Ecclesiastical) or for the church membership as a whole. "Church" can also stand for an agent of public action in the social, cultural, and political spheres. It can be used for worldwide Christianity in all its colorful variety. In empirical study, which observes the manifestations of the church as an object of belief, and in the usage that calls what is manifested the church, the church is truly a complex phenomenon that takes different forms and that can be variously experienced, used, and understood.

1.3. The Uniqueness of the Phenomenon

The multifarious nature of the church highlights its uniqueness. The church combines a transcendental reference, which is the subject of faith, with immanent factors and actions that can be perceived empirically. It links a sacred sphere, which is distinct from its environment, with the secular world of the usual and the everyday (→ Sacred and Profane). It presents itself in the plurality and particularity of real historical structures and organizations (→ Orthodox Church; Roman Catholic Church; Lutheran Churches; Reformed and Presbyterian Churches; Free Church; United and Uniting Churches, etc.). In their own ways, often in competition or conflict with one another, these various groups pass on the Christian faith and also, in different ways, function as social, cultural, and political factors in the nexus of society. The phenomenon of the church is characterized by fundamental disparity and inner tensions that seem inherent. Its ambivalence makes possible many different definitions and explanations and permits antinomies and alternatives both theoretical and practical.

1.4. Tasks, Problems, and Framework of Ecclesiology

In view of the ambivalence of the phenomenon, a relevant ecclesiology must present both the dogmatically normative premise and the empirical reality in a way that allows us to explain the conditions leading to the distinctive phenomena and to make intelligible the legitimacy and reality of the actual forms. In any methodological survey, we must focus on what the church really means, what distinguishes it, what function it discharges, where it is to be found, and what significance it has in the secular context.

1.4.1. The above task involves some fundamental ecclesiological problems.

1.4.1.1. First, we have the difference and the relation between the church of faith and the church of the empirical world. The former, as a work of the Holy Spirit, is a given that precedes faith; it cannot be ignored for reasons of praxis or institutionalizing, and it is accessible and perceptible only to → faith. The latter, as a collective expression of faith, is a historical entity that can be studied from many different angles. Its social form is distinguished by particular structures, conventions, and tasks and is open to scholarly reflection.

1.4.1.2. Second, there is the discrepancy between the assertion of the unity and universality of the church (→ Catholic, Catholicity) and the fact that there are many particular churches (→ Denomination). The confession bears witness to the church's unity, which is the motivation and goal of → ecumenism (→ Ecumenical Movement). The different churches, however, which have arisen in different historical situations and sociocultural contexts (and are still arising, esp. in the → Third World [§2]) and which all appeal to the → gospel of Jesus Christ, give it denominational expression, cling to their respective denominational → identity, and defend their various understandings theologically and institutionally.

1.4.1.3. Third, there is the commonly neglected problem, which logically precedes the previous two, of developing the basic insight of faith that allows for the possibility of the church in the first place. This insight finds formulation in the OT statement that in → Israel, → Yahweh chose a people for himself (→ Predestination) and also in the broader NT explanation that this election, oriented to salvation in Jesus Christ, is manifest in the church of Jews and Gentiles (see 2.1.2). Here we have the basis and purpose of the church. The church as the people of election owes its existence to God's turning to us. It has the task of giving expression to the will of God in concrete forms of human coexistence. The reality of election (D. Ritschl) cannot be seen in relation to the church alone but must include Israel as well. An inalienable relationship between Israel and the church exists, for both claim God's turning to them, even though today, unreconciled, they confront one another (→ Jewish-Christian Dialogue).

To these traditional ecclesiological themes we may add two others as we widen the dogmatic discussion phenomenologically, looking more closely at the church as it is.

1.4.1.4. Fourth, we must consider the fact of the church's internal disagreements. There is tension and conflict, for example, between so-called charismatic and traditional Christianity (note the movements for lay emancipation; → Counterculture; Lay Movements) or between academic theology and the church → bureaucracy and → hierarchy. This dissonance exists also as a loss of unity between personal religion and the institutionalized church (→ Transdenominational Movements), between the ecclesiastical and the social orientation of church members (who may sense a distance between themselves and the official church establishment; → Religion, Personal Sense of).

Such discord may be compared with the fractures that have occurred in church history over conflicting expressions of the Christian message (→ Heresies and Schisms). They seem to be possible and even legitimate when the saving message of Jesus Christ affects human existence in a comprehensive way, forces those whom it addresses to make an inner decision and an outer confession, and thrusts believers into personal and social action. Because of its transcendence, uniqueness, uncontrollability, and dynamic, however, the message cannot be fully grasped in the appropriation and actualization of salvation. It evades all attempts by its recipients to normalize, objectify, or regulate it in dogma, doctrine, order, and practice.

In this line of thought, it is altogether plausible that specific actions and beliefs of individual believers may conflict with the self-description of the believing society in its life and teaching. An individual confessional preference in → everyday life is subject to specific contexts and experiences, whereas a collective confession must be guided by transcendent interests and references (→ Salvation [Overview]). This fact makes the ecumenical or denominational question (the unity of the church and plurality of denominations) an ecclesiological problem from another angle. Universality is a mark and claim of the message of salvation, but its outworking in the decision of faith of individual people is particular, so that the plurality and variability of the church can be justified as a reflection of the constant and tension-laden difference between the (timeless) message of salvation and the (individual and collective) witness of faith, expressed historically.

1.4.1.5. Fifth, we must consider the church's inadequacy in the sociocultural nexus of → society, where it exists with its own claim and task (→ Evangelization; Mission). This is certainly a relevant factor from the standpoint of church history. We see plainly today that the church's own estimate of its rank and importance differs greatly from the way in which it is actually regarded in the secular world. As a religious fellowship, it is liable to the general, society-wide criticism of religion (→ Religion, Criticism of) and thus has lost much of its credibility and forfeited its social function. It is now in competition with other attempts to find → meaning, with other → religions and worldviews.

The church has not succeeded in bringing its communication of the faith into harmony with scientific insights and developments (→ Evolution; Progress; Worldview), with → anthropological data (→ Development 3), or with the needs of concrete life-relationships (→ Salvation 6-7). Traditional church → norms and values do not seem to measure up to the demands of the age (→ Ecology; Ethics; Human and Civil Rights; Peace; Sexuality; Women). From the standpoint of the Christian claim and actual relations, it is hardly sufficient to appeal to the necessary historicity of the church. Internal criticism and contradiction, as well as the many external challenges, including the question of the church's ability to deal with the issues of human life (→ Lifestyle), raise a basic theological problem (→ Fundamental Theology) involving both the conditions of the transcendental, timeless church and the legitimacy and relevance of the immanent, time-bound church.

In theological discussion today, ecclesiological problems are seen from many angles: the dialectic of → charisma and → institution, the unity and plurality of the church (→ Pluralism 2), the → congregation (§§2-4) and its maintenance (→ Church Growth), → secularization and opposing trends (→ Charismatic Movement; Evangelical Movement; Fundamentalism; New Religions), the complex of Christianity and culture, the missionary task of the church (→ Mission; Political Theology), a → theology of religions, and typological comparisons between the territorial church (→ People's Church), → civil religion, and → base communities. Often dominant in this connection are dogmatic explanatory models (→ Covenant 3; Incarnation 3; Justification, Doctrine of; Law and Gospel) rather than the basic data of scientific anthropology, the constitutive importance of which for an ecclesiology appropriate to the phenomenon of the church is unrecognized and neglected.

1.4.2. A realistic ecclesiology that avoids → dogmatism requires a procedure that focuses on the uniqueness of the phenomenon of the church, attempts to understand its disparity and ambivalence, and makes possible the solving of the basic problems indicated above. Various approaches are needed to do justice to the many factors and dimensions. The overall framework must include integrative observation and a realistic study of its various contexts, and it must be open to new insights and the interaction of others.

Approaching the church historically (see 2), we consider the NT statements about the church originating from the message of salvation that Jesus proclaimed, which gives us a hint already of the problems of claim and reality, of universality and particularity. Then we must note the significant structures and theories in the course of the church's history, out of which arises the question of continuity and change.

Approaching the church theologically (see 3), we note the various denominational ecclesiologies that deal with the nature and form of the church and that — on a confessional basis — make dogmatic statements expounding, safeguarding, communicating, and applying what the creeds say about the church. Studying such ecclesiologies makes us realize that the church of belief (like faith itself) can be grasped only through its manifestations in the life and teaching of believers and, furthermore, that theological explications will differ.

The unavoidable phenomenological element brings to light many problems that must be reflected in an integrative view, which we simply list here. First,

in expounding the ecclesiological statement of the creed, the problem of → truth and interest arises with reference to the interpretation of Jesus' message of salvation. Second, in safeguarding the statement in doctrine, order, and practice, there is the problem of → identity and continuity, of the original statement and its later development. Third, as regards communication then and now, the problem is that of history and of the modern relevance of that history, with the former based on the contingent sociocultural context of the early witnesses. Finally, in developing an application that has regard to both → tradition and the modern situation, the problem arises of overcoming dissonance and contingence with reference to church members and their practice as they attempt to deal with the complex reality of present-day challenges.

Approaching the church sociologically (see 4), we view it as a social and institutionalized form of the Christian religion that is appropriately subject to social analysis (→ Organization; Pastoral Sociology; Sociology; Sociology of Churches; Sociology of Religion). We must note the shifting relations between church (religion) and → society that are part of the distinctive phenomenon of the church (see 1.3), and then the different functional achievements of the church as a system of faith and action that masters and shapes existence (→ Communication; Diakonia; Evangelization; Pastoral Care; Theology).

Also coming under review are the church's organizational structures and social forms (→ Hierarchy; Bureaucracy; Church Government), including its ministers (→ Offices, Ecclesiastical; Priests; Pastor, Pastorate), → authority, spheres of action, and internal processes. Attention is paid also to church members, including their recruitment (→ Church Membership), social status (→ Class and Social Stratum), participation in church life, and public roles (→ Communication; Socialization; Education; Political Parties; School and Church). The sociological approach, which notes differences among denominations in their respective functions and attitudes, helps provide a realistic view of the church and is of relevance in tackling all the ecclesiastical questions indicated.

Finally, we need to look at modern trends that, either negatively or positively, influence traditional views of the church and show that the church is in transition (see 5). Of note here are contextualization (→ Contextual Theology; Third World 2; Church in a Socialist Society; Independent Churches), reforming and alternative movements (→ Base Communities), charismatic and → social movements, confessionalization (→ Denomination; Evangelical

Movement; Traditionalist Movement; Fundamentalism), and ecumenical processes (ecumenism, ecumenical and transdenominational movement, → local ecumenism, interdenominational and interreligious → dialogue). Processes of this kind reveal the problems that we must face in our present situation. Account must also be taken of the Jewish-Christian relation, the basic theological questions of which have been open for some time, and which demands ecclesiological rethinking in light of the → Holocaust and the founding of the State of Israel (→ Jewish-Christian Dialogue 6; Israel 2). The emergence of a plethora of ecclesiological insights, with their various competing interests and agendas, calls for special consideration. Critical investigation can lead to discussion that points toward evangelical universality (see 1.4.1) and also toward → conciliarity and interaction as constant features of our church life (see 5.5). As regards the relation between the church and Israel, we must realize that the common faith-experience of election as God's people calls for → reconciliation.

Bibliography: J. DANTINE, *Die Kirche vor der Frage nach ihrer Wahrheit* (Göttingen, 1980) • E. FAHLBUSCH, "Grunddaten und Typen christlicher Gemeinschaften," *Kirchenkunde der Gegenwart* (Stuttgart, 1979) • W. HUBER, *Kirche* (Stuttgart, 1979; 2d ed., Munich, 1988) • E. HÜBNER, *Theologie und Empirie der Kirche* (Neukirchen, 1985) • W. KERN et al., eds., *HFTh* • P. VON DER OSTEN-SACKEN, *Christian-Jewish Dialogue: Theological Foundations* (Philadelphia, 1986) • T. RENDTORFF, ed., *Charisma und Institution* (Gütersloh, 1985) • D. RITSCHL, *The Logic of Theology* (Philadelphia, 1987) • G. SAUTER, "Kirche als Gestalt des Geistes," *EvT* 38 (1978) 358-69 • P. STEINACKER, *Die Kennzeichen der Kirche. Eine Studie zu ihrer Einheit, Heiligkeit, Katholizität und Apostolizität* (Berlin, 1982) • P. VAN BUREN, *Discerning the Way: A Theology of the Jewish-Christian Reality* (New York, 1980) • C. WELCH, *The Reality of Church* (New York, 1958) • H. ZIRKER, *Ekklesiologie* (Düsseldorf, 1984).

ERWIN FAHLBUSCH

2. Historical Aspects

2.1. NT

2.1.1. Term

Originally the term *ekklēsia* was a political one, denoting an assembly of free people who are qualified to vote (Acts 19:39) or, more generally, a public assembly (vv. 32, 41). The specifically Christian use, however, is not fully in line with this meaning. The attempt to explain the word etymologically from the

parts *ek* (out from) and *kaleō* (call) as indicating the gathering of those who are called out (from the world) would also be misleading. Rather, its background can be found in the OT and apocalyptic → Judaism. When the → primitive Christian community in Jerusalem called itself the *ekklēsia tou theou* (church of God; cf. Gal. 1:13), it was probably translating the Aramaic *qěhal el* (1QM 4:10; 1QSa 1:25). If so, it reflects the community's awareness of being the company of those called as the center and core of the end-time people of God. The simple *ekklēsia* is always implicitly defined by the genitive phrase "of God" (e.g., see 1 Cor. 14:4; Phil. 3:6) and can be taken as a shortened form of the full *ekklēsia tou theou*.

2.1.2. Jesus

A debated issue is the relation of the pre-Easter Jesus to the church. The consensus in modern scholarship is that Jesus neither directly founded the church nor even indirectly envisaged or prepared for its emergence after his death. In support, it is argued that since Matt. 16:18 and 18:17 are secondary, the term *ekklēsia* does not occur in the pre-Easter tradition. Jesus also expected the imminent end and made → Israel the exclusive aim of his ministry.

Debated, too, is the measure of continuity between the pre-Easter work of Jesus and the post-Easter church (→ Easter). Is the church a replacement for Israel when the attempt of Jesus to gather his people failed, with continuity lying not in the nation but in the person of Jesus as the one who gathers and calls (W. G. Kümmel)? Is the company of → disciples that Jesus gathered the holy remnant of Israel, which, after Easter and along the line of salvation history (→ History of Salvation), broadens out into the church and a redeemed humanity (K. L. Schmidt)? Or is the church, according to the will of Jesus, the gathered and renewed Israel in its end-time breadth and fullness?

In favor of the last view is the programmatic width and inclusiveness with which Jesus addressed Israel. He was not aiming merely to restore Israel as it was then but to re-create it → eschatologically according to the will of God. Also pointing in this direction are the appointment of the Twelve as a sign of the renewal of the 12 tribes in eschatological fullness (Matt. 19:28) and Jesus' turning to tax collectors and sinners, in which room is made for God's claim upon winning and assembling even the most marginal members of his people.

A necessary correlate of the proclamation of the → kingdom of God is the concept of a people in which the name of God is so hallowed that his → salvation advances and takes shape in concrete human relationships (Luke 11:2). Jesus seems to have set his death in the context of the promotion of this salvation in Israel. Celebrating the Last Supper with the Twelve, he dedicated to them, as the symbolic representatives of Israel, his expiatory death "for many" (Mark 14:24; → Atonement), that is, for all the members of the people of God, thus opening up a new possibility of life in the fellowship of salvation.

2.1.3. *The Primitive Community*

A decisive factor in the self-awareness of the Jerusalem community was the conviction that God had introduced the end time with the → resurrection (§1) of Jesus from the dead and that the time had thus come to complete the gathering of Israel, which Jesus had begun. The leading disciples, especially Peter with the Twelve, settled in → Jerusalem shortly after the last appearance in Galilee and there began their public witness (see the story of pentecost in Acts 1–2). This decision involved an ecclesiological program. Jerusalem was the center of Israel, the place of salvation. It was there that the assembling of God's people was to be expected. This city was the goal of the end-time pilgrimage of the nations. After Easter there doubtless were groups of disciples in Galilee, but the true rise of the church was in Jerusalem.

Most important were the experiences of the working of the Spirit in the church (→ Holy Spirit), which were viewed as the fulfillment of OT promises for the time of salvation (Acts 2:16-21; Gal. 3:2-5; 4:6-7; → Promise and Fulfillment) and as a manifestation of the lordship of the exalted Christ. Incorporation into Christ's sphere of lordship and subjection to the power of the Spirit were by → baptism (§1) into the name of Jesus Christ (Acts 2:38). The Spirit-effected eschatological holiness and purity of the church found visible expression in its rigorist ethos. Disciplinary measures were seen as acts in which the Holy Spirit himself defended his lordship against those who transgressed the norms (Acts 5:1-11; 1 Cor. 5:1-5; → Church Discipline).

Very early, a central problem was that of the relation of the church to Israel. Two experiences needed to be worked out theologically. First, the refusal of most Israelites to believe in Christ called into question the church's claim to be the end-time gathering of all Israel. Second, the winning of God-fearers (Acts 10:1–11:18) and → Gentiles to → faith as a result of the → mission of Hellenistic → Jewish Christians (Acts 11:19-24) showed that the idea of an exclusive tie of the church with Israel was a fiction that was not in keeping with the facts. The apostolic council (ca. 48; → Acts of the Apostles §8) gave fundamental recognition to believing Gentiles as members of the church without having to submit to the → law or → circumcision. It thus accepted them as members of the → people of God (Gal. 2:1-20). Such acceptance, however, did not solve the eschatological problem.

2.1.4. *Paul*

By linking ecclesiology to the message of → justification, Paul brought basic theological elucidation. Starting with the antithesis of Christ and law, he showed that God's saving eschatological will took plain form in the nonlegalistic gospel and therefore that acceptance of the Gentiles into church membership by faith alone without the law was not just a marginal possibility but represented a valid expression of the church (Gal. 3:10-14; → Law and Gospel). In this way → Paul did not dissolve the relation between the church and Israel but defined it afresh from an eschatological standpoint. Believing Gentiles are the church as they are planted into the people of promise (Rom. 11:17-24).

Elsewhere in Paul, too, there are new accents as he reflects on the church, for example, the stress on the ecclesiological function of his apostolic office (1 Cor. 1:1-2; Rom. 1:5, etc.; → Apostle, Apostolate). As a messenger of the risen Lord, Paul so presents the → gospel that the community arises as a historical association that is concretely shaped by it. Paul views the relation of the church to Christ in terms of the image of the body of Christ (1 Corinthians 12), an image that is no doubt related to the → Eucharist (10:16). By liturgical participation in the gift of the sacrament (→ Worship 1), the church achieves participation in the vital functioning of Jesus Christ in the sense of the reciprocal ministry of all the members.

2.1.5. *Later Writings*

Theological reflection on the church became very important in the later NT writings. Along with the question of the relation to Israel, we also have that of the → identity of the church in its future and that of the relation to the state (→ Church and State) and non-Christian society. Various answers were given.

2.1.5.1. The theme of the church and Israel occurs in Matthew and Revelation, which come from the Jewish-Christian tradition. These advocate the radical-substitution view that Israel has lost its status in salvation history and the church has replaced it. Luke, however, shares with Ephesians the thought that the goal of salvation history is the coexistence of Jews and Gentiles in the church (see Eph. 2:11-14).

2.1.5.2. The question of preserving the church's identity is answered by a strong emphasis on → tradition and ministry (→ Offices, Ecclesiastical). The apostles, including Paul, are the basis and norm in both cases. The apostolic tradition is the foundation of the church (Eph. 2:20). The main task of church leaders is to keep this tradition, to pass it on, and to ward off error (1 Tim. 6:20). The Johannine writings, however, with their strong theological advocacy of early Christian prophecy (→ Prophets), point to the abiding presence of the prophetic Spirit as the authoritative interpreter of the exalted Christ for the church (John 14:26). Matthew grounds the identity of the church in its → obedience to the commands of Jesus the → messianic teacher (7:24-27; 28:20).

2.1.5.3. In the Pauline tradition the church's relation to the state and society is cautiously positive. The church can at least count on the fact that the public witness of its life will win people and bring about change. The → Pastoral Epistles go furthest in this regard by giving the → incarnation of the church a moral teaching role vis-à-vis the world at large (Titus 2:11; 3:4).

The Johannine writings, however, find a sharp antithesis between the church and society (see John 15:18; 1 John 3:13). The same is true about Revelation, which strongly emphasizes that there can be no compact (Rev. 12:17) between the city of God, whose common life is determined by the presence of God (Revelation 21), and the "great city," the social entity that is characterized by enmity against God and his rule (chaps. 13, 17).

Bibliography: R. E. Brown, *The Churches the Apostles Left Behind* (New York, 1984) • H. Frankemölle, *Jahwebund und Kirche Christi* (Münster, 1974) • J. Hainz, *Ekklesia. Strukturen paulinischer Gemeinde-Theologie und Gemeinde-Ordnung* (Regensburg, 1972) • G. Heinz, *Das Problem der Kirchenentstehung in der deutschen-protestantischen Theologie des 20. Jahrhunderts* (Mainz, 1974) • K. Kertelge, "Die Wirklichkeit der Kirche im Neuen Testament," *HFTh* 3.98-121 • W. Klaiber, *Rechtfertigung und Gemeinde. Eine Untersuchung zum paulinischen Kirchenverständnis* (Göttingen, 1982) • W. G. Kümmel, "Jesus und die Anfänge der Kirche," *Heilsgeschehen und Geschichte* (ed. E. Gräßer et al.; Marburg, 1965) 289-309 • G. Lohfink, *Wie hat Jesus Gemeinde gewollt?* (Freiburg, 1982) • K. Müller, ed., *Die Aktion Jesu und die Re-Aktion der Kirche. Jesus von Nazareth und die Anfänge der Kirche* (Würzburg, 1972) • J. Roloff, "Ἐκκλησία," *EDNT* 1.410-15 • K. L. Schmidt, "Ἐκκλησία," *TDNT* 3.487-536 • R. Schnackenburg, *The Church in the NT* (New York, 1966); idem, *God's Rule and Kingdom* (New York, 1963) • W. Schrage, " 'Ekklesia' und 'Synagoge,' " *ZTK* 60 (1963) 178-202 • K. Stendahl, "Kirche II," *RGG* (3d ed.) 3.1297-1304 (bibliography) • G. Theissen, *Studien zur Soziologie des Urchristentums* (Tübingen, 1979) • W. Trilling, *Das wahre Israel. Studien zur Theologie des Matthäus Evangeliums* (Munich, 1964).

Jürgen Roloff

2.2. Historical Constructs and Theories

2.2.1. Early Church Structures

The history of Christianity very quickly displayed astonishing variety in every sphere of life, including views of the church and its functions (see 2.1). In the later NT period — for example, in the Pastoral Epistles and the Johannine writings (i.e., the Gospel and Epistles of John, and Revelation) — we find very different developments. In the age that followed, an increasing trend toward uniformity is apparent. The model is essentially the Lukan one of the great church. In the process, the official element (→ Offices, Ecclesiastical) and the associated → authority soon came to predominate. The result institutionally — though at different paces in different regions — was the establishment of the presbyterate and, some decades later, of monarchical episcopacy (i.e., one → bishop in each congregation). This basic structure, which underwent various administrative changes but was firmly in place by the middle of the third century, became the basis of all "Catholic" offices (see 3.1-2).

2.2.2. Apostolic Fathers

If we consider the theory of the church in this light, Christianity in its → eschatological alienation from the world (see *Did.* 9.4; Pol. *Phil.* 9.2) seems to be a fellowship of believers following a → piety of observances similar to that of Jewish synagogue circles. This is true, even though all sense of the ongoing link in the → history of salvation between the church and Israel had soon vanished. Fear of false teachers (→ Heresies and Schisms) had become more important than missionary outreach (→ Mission) to the world. This generalization applied even to the martyr bishop Ignatius of Antioch (d. ca. 107), theologically the most significant of the Apostolic Fathers.

Ignatius tried to guard against seduction by all kinds of heretics by telling the churches to rally round their bishops. The bishop is the one who administers the → Eucharist, and he embodies in his own person the right sacramental theology, the right theology of suffering, and the right → Christology. Those who participate in the bishop's Eucharist and know its saving power cannot possibly think that the → suffering of Christ was a mere appearance (see Ign. *Trall.* 7.2; *Phld.* 7; *Smyrn.* 8.2; → Docetism).

In contrast, → Gnosis has no place for ecclesiology, at least in theory. This is only logical, for on the view that the way to knowledge of God is by self-knowledge — indeed, that the two are identical — a religious → solipsism arises in which the individual, sure of direct access to God, is self-sufficient. In practice, the Christian Gnostics seem to have regarded the church as a building of many stories, the most attractive of which was their own (J. Kunze, 344).

2.2.3. *The Gnostic Crisis*

The coming together of the church during the course of the Gnostic crisis in the second century, which restored the → unity that the church had almost lost, took place under the sign of a return to the original understanding of the person of → Jesus Christ. This rule of faith was now given a wider setting and justified by the NT → canon (§2), the fixed collection of writings from the → primitive community in the span between → Peter, → James, Stephen, and → Paul. But there was still no organizational expression of church unity apart from the mutual giving of the → peace, the treatment of fellow Christians as brethren, and the extending of hospitality (→ Tertullian *De praescr. haeret.* 20.8.9).

The theoretical basis of organization was broadly and firmly laid in the third century, not least by → Cyprian of Carthage (ca. 200-258), whose ecclesiology, formed in conflict with the schisms resulting from the different ways of treating lapsed Christians after the → persecutions, would make a lasting impact. Cyprian was the first early church theologian to advance a restrictive doctrine of the unity of the catholic church. He based this view unequivocally on the episcopal office, though for him its nature and mystery *(sacramentum unitatis)* transcended this → hierarchical structure, as may be seen especially from his work *De ecclesiae catholicae unitate*. Two of his formulations impressed themselves indelibly on the consciousness of Western Christianity: first, the well-known thesis that outside the church there is no salvation (*De eccl.* 6; cf. *Ep.* 52.1, 55.24, 71.1, 73.21, 74.7-8); then, the statement that no one can have God as Father, and thus be a Christian, who does not have the church as mother (*De eccl.* 6).

2.2.4. *The Patristic Golden Age*

This episcopal church of early Catholicism, which showed its independence in the age of persecution by not letting mass apostasy shake its self-understanding and then, after the persecutions, generously providing penance (→ Penitence) for the fallen and thus opening up to them the possibility of restoration, succeeded in making a public breakthrough long before the great change that came with Constantine, who became Western emperor in 312 and emperor of West and East in 324. By deliberately renouncing the way of "regression" (e.g., as done by Clement and → Origen; → Alexandrian Theology), it prepared itself inwardly for this change, so that the implications of the change were less serious than one might have expected for both its self-understanding and its structures. In its → monas-

ticism, the church had a corrective for obvious → secularization. This was more important for the inner adherence of the masses than the concessions that were made to → popular piety (e.g., in the form of veneration of → saints and the cult of → relics). The church might acquire a taste for → power, but it could still be seen as a manifestation of heavenly working (see Ambrose *In Lucam* 3.38).

The theologians and liturgies of the East expressed more strongly than those of the West the fact that → worship represents a unity between heaven and earth, between the visible and the invisible (see 3.1). The ecclesiology of the East is uniquely defined and gripped by the theme of human deification (→ Theosis) and is very much under the influence of the Christological controversies of the fifth century (→ Christology 2.2). Finally, in the East (at the latest with Anastasius Sinaita at the beginning of the 8th cent.), we see a certain transfer of spiritual leadership and the exercise of the → power of the keys to penance from the hierarchical priesthood to the monks, who become the real clergy (Y. Congar, 1.47).

2.2.5. *Augustine*

→ Augustine (354-430) was particularly influential in the development of Western ecclesiology. He worked out his concept of the church in debate with the → Donatists of North Africa and in the broader context of the relation between the heavenly and earthly cities (*civitas Dei, civitas terrena*). Leading elements in the concept are a theology of catholicity (→ Catholic, Catholicity), which includes the geographic aspect, as well as the idea that Christ is the true subject of all the church's sacramental activity, and this not merely as the source of a transmissible power to ordain (e.g., *In Evang. Iohan.* 5.18; → Consecration). The sacraments are valid wherever there is faith and the form that Christ appointed, though they are profitably received — that is, savingly — only in the unity of the church, to which alone the → Holy Spirit is promised (e.g., *De bapt.* 1.1.2, 4.17.24).

A first problem in this view is that Augustine hardly does justice to Donatism and its vital interest in the indissoluble relation between the confession of faith and the confession of act as a constitutive element in the being of the church (A. Schindler, 307). The main liability, however, is the clear distinction Augustine draws between the inward and the outward, spirit and office, law and spirituality, which in many cases amounts almost to separation (ibid., 303; → Augustine's Theology).

2.2.6. *The Middle Ages*

In the → Middle Ages in the West, the main concern was addressing the problems raised by Augustine. But when the works of Dionysius the so-called Pseudo-Areopagite (see Acts 17:34), a Greek or Syrian author of the late 5th and early 6th century, became available in translation to Latin theology, the Areopagite hierarchy with its sublime and explicit clericalism exerted a wide influence. This reached its peak in the 13th and 14th centuries and may be seen in the fact that → Thomas Aquinas (1224/25-74; → Thomism) ascribed to the sacrament of priestly → ordination not only the transferring of sacramental character but also the communication of sanctifying → grace, that is, grace that effects a real change in the recipient (*Summa theol. Supp.*, q. 35, art. l, ad 2).

Under the impact of Dionysius, the question was discussed in the high and late Middle Ages whether the office of bishop represents an order *(ordu)* of consecration superior to that of the office of elder, that is, whether episcopal ordination confers a special character. This question was an urgent one because in the Dionysian system, a higher rank in the hierarchy claimed a higher perfection. By nature, position, and rank, the hierarch (bishop) can be consecrated and deified in divine things and in turn pass on to those beneath him, according to their rank, a share in this holy deification that God has infused into him (*De eccl. hier.* 1.2).

What is finally at issue comes out unmistakably in the → bull *Unam sanctam* (1302) of Boniface VIII, which shows more plainly than much else what the clericalist implications are of the apparently otherworldly thinking of the Pseudo-Areopagite and its focusing on the return of the → soul to God. For when Boniface argued that not all things in the world are directly ruled by God, but that the lowest are brought back to the divinely willed order by the intermediate, and when he concluded that it is necessary for salvation that all of humanity should be subject to priestly authority, and finally to the Roman bishop (→ Pope, Papacy), this was to take the Areopagite principles out of their original context (which dealt with the doctrine of mystical ascent by the mediation of the cultus and hierarchy) and to apply them to the sphere of law and church politics.

More than just these curial tendencies in the interests of papal centralization seriously imperiled the Augustinian synthesis. It was endangered no less by → spiritualist movements, which from time to time were of great influence in reaction to the predominant → institutionalism and sacramentalism. Note, for example, the → Cathari, the → Waldenses and spiritual → Franciscans, the followers of John → Wycliffe (ca. 1330-84) and his works on the church and the papacy, and the followers of Jan → Hus (ca. 1372-1415; → Hussites). Such movements sought a new fellowship that stressed an apostolic lifestyle, not rank, merit, or office (Y. Congar, 1.130-31).

Involved here were impulses of → nominalism, the main theological and philosophical trend of the later Middle Ages. Along the lines of the writing of William of Ockham (ca. 1285-1347) on church politics, nominalism made a basic distinction between power relating to the eternal and spiritual and power relating to the earthly and temporal. It emphasized that Christ has made the pope the earthly representative not of his divine and eternal power but only of the ministry that has been committed to us by his → incarnation, with corresponding responsibility for the whole Christian body (note Occam's work, probably in early 1347, on the power of emperors and popes). Certainly some features of church law are part of divine law, for God himself has given them, and they are not subject to human jurisdiction. Fundamentally, however, the church's organization must be judged by the same standards as a political organization (see 3.2.2; → Conciliarism).

2.2.7. *The Reformation*

→ Reformation criticism made common cause with that of the later Middle Ages but also went beyond it. All the → Reformers rejected the → sacrificial character of the → Mass (which demanded a → priest in the literal sense), the sacramental character of ordination, the distinction between → clergy and laity (which went back to the canonist Gratian [d. by ca. 1160], who had seen them as two types of Christians, or even as two different peoples within the one church), and the hierarchical structure of the church (which demanded a new definition of the relation between priests and bishops). But different nuances quickly appeared, for example, in the way in which some Reformers appealed to the biblical testimony to the royal priesthood of the → congregation and related the office of → proclamation (or offices, to which some, who received their actual "consecration" in baptism, are called, therein not only to proclaim the Word itself but also to dispense baptism, the Eucharist, and absolution) and the universal priesthood (see A. M. Ritter, 92ff.). Different definitions were also given of who constituted the church. Is it the assembly of believers, of the called, or of the elect?

2.2.7.1. For Martin → Luther (1483-1546; → Luther's Theology; see 3.4) the priesthood of all believers (in a living relation to the preaching office) was simply an implication of → justification by faith alone. In Philipp → Melanchthon (1497-1560), however, it no longer had any role and hence received no place in the → Augsburg Confession. With his increasing stress on the visible, institutional side of the

church, Melanchthon gave a different answer from
Luther to the question where the true church is to be
found and who belongs to it. Luther began with a
stronger sense that the true church and the false are
mixed together in the one church body, so that the
true church is a hidden church. Melanchthon, however, put the stress more and more strongly on the
gathering of the called, which is the visible church
(note the *Loci communes* [1521], as well as his 1559
dogmatics [*Studienausgabe* 2.2.474]). This gathering,
which also embraced the unregenerate, was distinguished by the pure preaching of the gospel, the administration of the sacraments as God appointed
them, and due → obedience to the office of preaching
the gospel (*Examen ordinandorum* [1552, *Studienausgabe* 6.212, cf. 286]).

Similar external, institutional marks occur in the
ecclesiology of the post-Tridentine controversialist
Robert → Bellarmine (1542-1621; → Polemics), for
whom the church was a human fellowship just as
visible and palpable as that of the Roman people, the
French kingdom, or the Republic of Venice. In contrast, the essential marks of the church for Luther
were the → Word of God, baptism, Eucharist, the
keys, the preaching office, → prayer, public praise of
God and thanksgiving, and the cross and suffering
(see pt. 3 of his *Von den Konziliis und Kirchen* [Of
councils and churches; 1539]).

2.2.7.2. John → Calvin's (1509-64; → Calvin's
Theology; see 3.5) understanding of the church has
its roots in the doctrine of → predestination. The
church in the true sense is the invisible fellowship of
those who are elect in Christ. Yet Calvin's primary
interest is in the visible church as the "mother of all
the godly" (*Inst.* 4.1 title). One must be a member of
this church to be a member of the true church, the
gathering of the predestined. With respect to the visible church, Calvin distinguishes between the true
church and the false in the same way as Melanchthon
does. In his ecclesiology he also has a doctrine of four
offices instituted by Christ: pastor, teacher, → elder,
and deacon, with pastor as most important (→ Calvin's Theology, 2.4). → Church discipline is entrusted to the elders (or rulers), with assistance from
the state, as necessary. In emphasizing the concept of
fellowship as well as certain legal aspects, Calvin became influential in England and Holland. He thus
had a broader influence on world Protestantism than
did German → Lutheranism, which tended to ossify
in the territorial churches.

2.2.7.3. Tendencies toward the → free church
view (see 3.6) appeared in the early Zurich Reformation, especially among those who first supported and
then increasingly opposed the work of Ulrich →

Zwingli (1484-1531; → Zwingli's Theology). After
the break with Zwingli and the disaster of the
Peasants' War, the Schleitheim Confession (1527),
the oldest and most important of the → Anabaptist
confessions, unmasked the illusion then current in
Christendom that the Christian and the civil communities were identical. Schleitheim argued for separation from the world. In strict adherence to the
Bible alone, it demanded a life in accordance with
the perfection of Christ, making use of → excommunication (appealing to Matthew 18) in such a way
that no tolerance would be shown for open sin. After
those who escaped persecution gained a footing in
Holland, England, and eastern and southern Europe,
they put into practice their ideas of community and
community order, ultimately having a decisive influence on Christianity and church life in America (→
Baptists; Friends, Society of; Mennonites).

2.2.8. *The Modern Period*
The period that followed was marked by the discrepancy between the universality of the church, as theology described it, and the particularity of the
church, as expressed in the multiple → denominations (§2) that resulted from the Reformation. It was
marked also by the danger of ideological alienation
through institutionalism, as well as through → individualism. The father of Lutheran → Pietism, Philipp Jakob Spener (1635-1705), tried to avoid this
alienation by incorporating certain fundamental
Anabaptist ideas into Lutheranism. In stressing common features of life and doctrine, especially as regards the Reformed Church, he became the "father
of all German union theology" (E. Hirsch, 2.131). At
the same time, Spener saw, with an appeal to Luther,
that the establishment and zealous exercise of the
spiritual priesthood was one of the most important
challenges to the overinstitutionalized and clerical-
ized church life of his day, and also a basic prerequisite for renewal of the pastorate.

At any rate, a countermovement was already at
work, namely, religious individualism, which, drawing on medieval spiritualism and neo-Catholic →
mysticism, finally began to affect the Protestant
masses in the age of Pietism and the → Enlightenment. To the isolating inwardness of piety that
marked this tendency, the large church inevitably
seemed problematic, and membership in it of no
great religious significance. In this regard F. D. E. →
Schleiermacher (1768-1834; → Schleiermacher's
Theology) could make no real difference, even
though he helped to put discussion of the church on
a different level in the 19th century; for good reason
he has been called the church father of that century.
With the new significance given to the church, the

way was opened for the independence of the church over against the state (→ Church and State) as this finally took shape in Germany during the Weimar Republic. Otto Dibelius (1880-1967) gave this situation programmatic expression in his catchword "century of the church."

In the → church struggle, the multifaceted understanding of the church that Schleiermacher had pioneered in the 19th century could no longer be upheld. The Barmen Declaration (1934) defined the realm of the church as "the community of brethren in which Jesus Christ presently works in the Word and sacraments through the Holy Spirit" (thesis 3). It went beyond the Augsburg Confession and its purely functional concept in article 7 by asserting the communal aspect. At the same time, Barmen clearly rejected any tendency to let someone else decide on the constitutional form of the church or to treat external order as a matter of secondary concern.

Ecumenical discussion (→ Ecumenical Movement; Ecumenical Theology) of the foundations and basic questions of ecclesiology has been weakened both by faulty developments within Protestantism and by the fact that the → Roman Catholic Church, through fits and starts, developed and promoted the idea of the papacy and finally made it a → dogma at → Vatican I (1869-70). Yet Roman Catholic theology, sensing that the epoch of counterreformation in the church has come to an end and that it has secured what was at stake in the controversies with Protestantism, has now again embraced without inhibition the concept of universal priesthood (→ Lay Apostolate; Lay Movements). This concept has become the dogmatic basis of, for example, attempts at liturgical reform (→ Liturgical Movements).

At any rate, all denominations and church groups and fellowships are as yet only on the way toward the one, holy, catholic, apostolic church. In the church today perhaps at best half of all biblical truth finds expression, yet we could say that what seems most essential has indeed been grasped: the inalienable and irreplaceable character of personal faith and the ministry of unity (→ Ecumenism) and the dimension of worship, seen in the indissoluble relation between the confession of faith and the confession of actions (cf. Donatism, Third World churches; see 5).

→ Catholic Reform and Counterreformation; Early Church; Middle Ages 2; Modern Church History; Theology in the Nineteenth and Twentieth Centuries

Bibliography: C. ANDRESEN, *Die Kirchen der alten Christenheit* (Stuttgart, 1971) • H. VON CAMPENHAUSEN, *Ecclesiastical Authority and Spiritual Power in the Church of the First Three Centuries* (Stanford, Calif., 1969; repr., Peabody, Mass., 1997) • Y. CONGAR, *Die Lehre von der Kirche. Von Augustinus bis zum abendländischen Schisma* (Freiburg, 1971); idem, *Vom abendländischen Schisma bis zur Gegenwart* (Freiburg, 1971) • P. DABIN, *Le sacerdoce royal des fidèles dans la tradition ancienne et moderne* (Paris, 1950) • R. F. EVANS, *One and Holy: The Church in Latin Patristic Thought* (London, 1972) • E. HIRSCH, *Geschichte der neuern evangelischen Theologie* (vol. 2; 3d ed.; Gütersloh, 1964) • J. KUNZE, *Glaubensregel, Heilige Schrift und Taufbekenntnis* (Leipzig, 1894) • R. MURRAY, *Symbols of Church and Kingdom: A Study in Early Syriac Tradition* (Cambridge, 1975) • A. PETERS, "Die Barmer Theologische Erklärung und das Luthertum," *Die lutherischen Kirchen und die Bekenntnissynode von Barmen* (ed. W. D. Hauschild; Göttingen, 1984) 319-59 • J. C. PLUPE, *MATER ECCLESIA: An Enquiry into the Concept of the Church as Mother in Early Christianity* (Washington, D.C., 1943) • H. RAHNER, *Symbole der Kirche. Die Ekklesiologie der Väter* (Salzburg, 1964) • A. M. RITTER, *Wer ist die Kirche? Amt und Gemeinde im Neuen Testament, in der Kirchengeschichte und heute* (Göttingen, 1968) • A. SCHINDLER, "Augustins Ekklesiologie in den Spannungsfeldern seiner Zeit und heutiger Ökumene," *FZPhTh* 34 (1987) 295-309 (with an important Augustine bibliography) • P. STOCKMEIER, "Kirche unter den Herausforderungen der Geschichte," *HFTh* 3.122-52 (bibliography).

ADOLF MARTIN RITTER

3. Theological Aspects
3.1. *Orthodox Ecclesiology*
3.1.1. *Basic Concept*

In orthodox ecclesiology, in accordance with a concept that is basic to the biblical and patristic tradition, the church is defined by nature and essence as the body of Christ in history that takes shape in time and space and is the basis of the → kingdom of God. All the other descriptions that appear in Holy Scripture and the patristic tradition are to be understood only in relation to the ecclesiology of the body of Christ as an authentic description of the church. From this angle the → Orthodox Church underscores the perichoresis (i.e., interconnectedness) of the mystery of Christ and the mystery of the church.

The Christocentric understanding of the mystery of the church (→ Christology 3) also gives expression to the → Trinitarian dimension of the church. For in the church everything is done by the Father through the Son in the → Holy Spirit. The unbreakable connection between the mystery of Christ and the mystery of the church comes out clearly in the doctrine of the preexistence of the church. On this view the church "was created the first of all things . . . and for her sake was the world established" (*Herm. Vis.* 2.4.1).

The constitution of the body of Christ finds fulfillment in the → history of salvation in the → unity of believers in the body of the church. By this unity they are fellow members *(sysōmoi)* of the body of Christ. They are those who have grown up together with Christ *(symphytoi)*. By divine → grace, they thus participate in the life of Christ.

This incorporation takes place through the work of the Holy Spirit in → baptism, → anointing, the Holy → Eucharist, and the other → sacraments (mysteries). On the one hand, the church is signified in the sacraments; on the other hand, the sacraments of the church dispense divine grace to believers. Thus the church is "the fullness of him who fills all in all" (Eph. 1:25).

3.1.2. *Marks of the Church*

The Christocentric → ontology of the church is the characteristic feature of Orthodox ecclesiology. On the basis of this criterion Orthodox theology evaluates even the qualities specified in the → Niceno-Constantinopolitan Creed, which speaks of the one, holy, catholic, and apostolic church.

3.1.2.1. The church of Christ is one, for the body that the Logos of God took in the → incarnation is one, and so is the Head of this body, Jesus Christ (Eph. 4:4-7). The source of this unity of the church is the unity of the Holy Trinity in the whole mystery of the incarnation, by which the unity of the one body of Christ is achieved. This view rules out the rise of a plurality of ecclesial bodies. In this spirit the Holy Eucharist is celebrated in the Orthodox Church as a realization and revelation of this unity of the life of the church. The church defines its relation to church communions outside itself as one of either *communio (koinonia)* or *necommunicatio (akoinonisia)*.

3.1.2.2. This Christocentric unity of the body of the church, by which believers are related in the Holy Spirit to one another and to their divine Head, also defines the holiness of the church, for the incarnate divine Son and Logos "loved the church and gave himself up for her, in order to make her holy," so that the church might be "holy and without blemish" (Eph. 5:25-27). By nature, the church is thus holy in Christ, for it represents the perfect and absolute holiness of the Holy Trinity. The presence of sinful members (→ Sin) within the church does not affect its natural holiness, for the task of the church is the equipping of the saints. The "holiness without which no one will see the Lord" (Heb. 12:14) is the work of the Holy Spirit, who knits the body together, quickens it, and gives divine grace to believers in order to upbuild them in the church as a chosen race, a royal priesthood, a holy nation (1 Pet. 2:9).

3.1.2.3. The unity and holiness of the church also define its catholicity (→ Catholic, Catholicity), which may be seen wherever there is an authentic realization of the one body of Christ — that is, wherever the one, constant Eucharist is celebrated. This localization of catholicity does not rule out the catholicity of God's worldwide church; rather, it confirms it by the criterion of the → identity of the experience that is lived out in Christ. The universality of the church is a dynamic component of its catholicity, but it is not the decisive factor, for the catholicity of the local church is fully experienced in its ongoing Eucharist. As the whole Christ is offered at every altar table at a eucharistic assembly and is likewise offered in the worldwide church, so the catholicity of the local church is manifested in the worldwide church, and vice versa. Hence the relation between catholicity and universality is a question of the identity of all and not a cumulative relation of parts to the whole, for the whole is Christ.

3.1.2.4. The unity, holiness, and catholicity of the church are confirmed by the criterion of its apostolicity, that is, by the continuous and authentic life and experience of the apostolic → tradition, according to the epigrammatic formulation of Vincent of Lérins (d. before 450): "that which has been believed everywhere, always, and by all." In the Orthodox tradition the mind of the church is expressed and confirmed through its → synodal self-understanding in local or ecumenical → councils.

Synodal confirmation of the catholic witness of local churches takes place by the diachronic apostolicity (i.e., the historic witness of the apostles and apostolicity) and the synchronic catholicity (i.e., the contemporary fullness) of the worldwide church of God. In this sense the council (synod) is a manifestation of the total church, for "the name of the council is 'church,' and the church has the name 'assembly' [*ekklēsia synodou onoma*]." On the basis of the synodal self-understanding of the Orthodox Church, it can say that the whole body speaks with → infallibility, for it is knit together by the Holy Spirit and led into all truth. The same cannot be said for any individual → bishop or even the collective body of bishops.

Synodally, the church exists as the organic fullness of the body and certainly not independently of it or apart from it. Orthodox ecclesiology thus sees the bishop as having a right to participate in the synod as the visible head of a local ecclesial body whose mind he is summoned to express at the synod. This right is not merely given to him ex officio. Hence the canons categorically forbid both episcopal → consecration in cases where there is no bishopric for the candidate and participation in the synod by bishops who are not at the head of local churches.

The criterion of Christocentric ontology, which rests on an understanding of the church as the one and only body of Christ, also defines the Orthodox view regarding (1) the relation of the local church to the worldwide church, (2) the unity of the ecclesial body and the limits of the church, (3) the experience of the gifts of grace that the Holy Spirit dispenses in the church, and (4) the synodal activity of the local church and the one worldwide ecclesial body.

→ Orthodoxy 3

Bibliography: Centre orthodoxe du Patriarchat oecuménique, Église locale et église universelle (Chambésy, 1981) • G. Florovsky, "The Catholicity of the Church," Bible, Church, Tradition: An Eastern Orthodox View (Belmont, Mass., 1972) 37-55; idem, Le corps du Christ vivant. Une interprétation orthodoxe de l'église universelle (Neuchâtel, 1948) 9-57 • A. Kallis, "Kirche V: Orthodoxe Kirche," TRE 18.252-62 (bibliography) • I. Karmiris, A Synopsis of the Dogmatic Theology of the Orthodox Catholic Church (Scranton, Pa., 1973) • N. Nissiotis, Die Theologie der Ostkirche im ökumenischen Dialog. Kirche und Welt in orthodoxe Sicht (Stuttgart, 1968) • D. Papandreou, "Orthodoxie und Ökumene," Gesammelte Aufsätze (ed. W. Schneemelcher; Stuttgart, 1986) • P. Trembelas, Dogmatique de l'Église Orthodoxe Catholique (vol. 2; Chevetogne, 1967) • T. Ware, The Orthodox Church (rev. ed.; London, 1993) • J. D. Zizioulas, Being as Communion: Studies in Personhood and the Church (Crestwood, N.Y., 1985).

Damaskinos Papandreou

3.2. Roman Catholic Ecclesiology

Among the central images and concepts with which the Roman Catholic Church tries to express its self-understanding (e.g., body of Christ, → people of God), the sacramental concept (→ Sacrament) now has a leading role. In the relevant documents of → Vatican II, the first council to attempt a comprehensive definition of the nature of the church, the Catholic Church views itself as a sacrament, "a sign and instrument . . . of communion with God and of unity among all men" (Lumen gentium [LG] 1). This characterization opens up perspectives for answering some basic questions that have been important for Roman Catholics both before and after the council.

3.2.1. Divine and Human Character

In the light of the basic sacramental concept, there can no longer be any serious talk of an uncritical and unqualified equation of the church's divine and human elements, such as seems to be suggested in some traditional formulations that make it harder to achieve ecumenical solutions (→ Ecumenical Movement) to ecclesiological problems. On the Roman Catholic view, the church is not absolutely identical with Christ or with the divine → grace that is seen to be victorious in him, though the latter does find effective expression in sign, in and through the church. Hence the relation between ecclesiology and → Christology is one of analogy, not identity.

The visible church serves the Spirit of Christ in analogy to the way in which the human nature assumed in the → incarnation serves the divine Logos (LG 8). The historically known and socially constituted fellowship of believers cannot, then, be abstracted from its visibility; rather, it serves as an effective sign of the grace of God. This basic ecclesiological decision sheds light on other significant relations, for example, that between the church and the → kingdom of God, which is one of representation; or that between → institution and event, which is to be understood in the sense of a "functionalizing" of the institutional through events. Interpretation of the traditional body-soul analogy (→ Soul 2) moves in the same direction.

3.2.2. Hierarchy and the People of God

Modern Roman Catholic ecclesiology now views the whole people of God as having a share in the saving mission of Christ (→ Salvation), and thus it no longer ascribes decisive significance to the distinction between → clergy and laity. The difference between specific and universal priesthood is set against the background of the sacramental function of the whole people of God (see LG 10; → Hierarchy; Jurisdiction, Ecclesiastical). The structural distinctions are supported neither for merely positivist reasons (because of their revealed character) nor for purely sociological reasons (because of their general utility or even necessity). They manifest a relation that is constitutive for → faith, namely, the interconnection between Word and sacrament, which are imparted exclusively through pronouncement. Questions of authority and power must also be answered within the believing fellowship of → communication and in terms of the ministering character of this fellowship and its basic sacramental structure.

As regards the obedient service that must be rendered to God in faith and → love, → Mary, the Mother of God, is the type of the church, the model of its true nature (LG 63-64). Mary has this central role in the Roman view of the church because she is the figure of proper response, evoked by the Lord of the church himself, to the love of God that is granted to us in him. Because Mary is the personal and "real" symbolic core of the church, Roman Catholic theology finds in her a concrete model of being made conformable to Christ.

The promise that throughout the centuries the church as a whole will remain in the truth of Christ (→ Infallibility) is inseparable on a Roman view from the teaching authority of the → pope and the college of bishops. The one-sided emphasis on the papacy that resulted from Vatican I has been overcome by the stressing and including of the episcopal office (→ Bishop, Episcopate) at Vatican II, though clarification is still needed. In their own understanding, the pope and bishops are not above the message that has been entrusted to the church for transmission. With a fidelity to the basic revelation attested by the Bible — a fidelity that is effected and attested by the Holy Spirit — they hand this message down. In this regard, too, the ministry (→ Offices, Ecclesiastical) has a servant character. How far the functions and powers associated with the papacy in the course of history are really an inalienable part of the biblically based ministry of Peter is a matter for discussion in ecumenical → dialogue today. Since the Roman Catholic Church views itself in principle as *ecclesia semper reformanda* (a church always to be reformed), the present form of this ministry (including the papal office) cannot claim to be of divine right (see 2.2.6).

3.2.3. *Symbolic and Instrumental Sacramentality*
The question whether the church is to be seen as simply a signifier and anticipation of → eschatological salvation or exclusively as an instrument of its manifestation in the → history of salvation involves a false alternative. Stress on the church's character as a sign tends to view God also working outside the visible limits of the church, while a theological model that focuses on the church as instrument tends to put the stress on the mediating of salvation.

Though sign and instrument represent different ecclesiological emphases, they do not necessarily exclude one another (W. Beinert). On a sacramental understanding, the sign has efficacy; it can impart that which it signifies. The church as a sign, however, cannot claim to impart what it signifies in an exclusive way that negates any other possibility of impartation (→ Sacramentality).

3.2.4. *Membership*
To belong to the visible church in the true sense is to be incorporated into it by means of "the profession of faith, the sacraments, ecclesiastical government, and communion" (*LG* 14; → Church Membership 1). In a broader sense, the church encompasses all humanity, "called by God's grace to salvation" (*LG* 13). To avoid confusion, it is apt to speak of different

possible levels of relationship or even membership (see *LG* 13). On a Roman view, the church in the full sense subsists in this church (*LG* 8).

The formula that outside the church there is no salvation can no longer be viewed as raising an exclusive claim that limits the church to the particular members of a specific socially organized society and ruling out all others. Naturally this line of argument is possible only on the sacramental view of the church. Reinterpretation of the marks of the church, which in the age of the Counter-Reformation (→ Catholic Reform and Counterreformation) were seen as criteria of exclusion, is also demanded within this framework.

3.2.5. *Church and World*
The traditional danger of ecclesiological self-centeredness is avoided by clearly defining the church in terms of its function relative to the world's salvation. What characterizes the church is not a triumphalist self-assertion but a servantlike continuation of the pro-existence of Christ on behalf of a world that is yearning for salvation. This task can be properly fulfilled only when a clear distinction is made between the church and the world (→ Church and State). In this regard the Roman Catholic understanding finds in → secularization, not the collapse of the church in the modern world, but the opportunity for it to grasp and once again achieve its true significance on the basis of a clearer distinction. In dialogue with the various religions, → ideologies, and sciences, it regards itself not merely as one that gives and advises but also as one that receives. Only thus can it fulfill its task as a sign that is lifted up among the nations (DH 3014).

→ Catholic, Catholicity; Catholicism (Roman)

Bibliography: G. ALBERIGO, Y. CONGAR, and H. J. POTT-MEYER, eds., *Kirche im Wandel. Eine kritische Zwischenbilanz nach dem Zweiten Vatikanum* (Düsseldorf, 1982) • W. BEINERT, "Die Sakramentalität der Kirche im theologischen Gespräch," *ThBer* 9 (1980) 13ff. • Y. CONGAR, *Diversity and Communion* (London, 1984); idem, *Die Lehre von der Kirche. Von Augustinus bis zum abendländischen Schisma* (Freiburg, 1971); idem, *Vom abendländischen Schisma bis zur Gegenwart* (Freiburg, 1971) • "Dogmatic Constitution on the Church (*Lumen Gentium*)," *Vatican Council II: The Conciliar and Post-Conciliar Documents* (rev. ed.; Grand Rapids, 1992) 350-426 • H. DÖRING, *Grundriß der Ekklesiologie* (Darmstadt, 1986) • P. KNAUER, *Der Glaube kommt von Hören. Ökumenische Fundamentaltheologie* (Graz, 1977) • H. KÜNG, *The Church* (New York, 1967) • K. RAHNER, *Foundations of Christian Faith: An Introduction to the Idea of Christianity* (New York, 1978) • J. RATZINGER, *Das neue Volk*

Gottes. *Entwürfe zur Ekklesiologie* (Düsseldorf, 1969) •
J.-M. R. TILLARD, *Church of Churches: The Ecclesiology of
Communion* (Collegeville, Minn., 1992).

HEINRICH DÖRING

3.3. *Anglican Ecclesiology*
3.3.1. *Doctrinal Basis*
→ Anglican ecclesiology is often characterized as a
reformed Catholicism (→ Catholic, Catholicity). By
this is meant a dual affirmation of continuity with
the primitive church in → faith, → sacraments, and
ministry (→ Offices, Ecclesiastical), but also an acknowledgment of the → Reformation heritage, repudiating the claims of the papacy (→ Pope, Papacy)
and stressing the supremacy of Scripture.

Unlike the churches of the Reformation on the
continent of Europe (→ Lutheran Churches; Reformed and Presbyterian Churches; see 3.4-5), Anglicanism is not a strongly confessional church (→
Denomination 2). In addition to the Thirty-Nine
Articles, it has historically appealed to the → Book
of Common Prayer (1549, 1552, 1559, and 1662) as
a doctrinal as well as a liturgical (→ Liturgy) norm,
though in recent decades liturgical revision has in
certain respects relegated the prayer book to a more
subordinate position, yet leaving it as one of the official touchstones of doctrine.

This doctrinal status of the prayer book reflects
the characteristic Anglican standpoint of thinking
in terms of the sacramental worshiping community
and an episcopally ordered ministry as defining
church identity. The Lambeth Quadrilateral of 1888
(→ Anglican Communion 4.1), which set out from
an Anglican perspective the essentials for a reunited
Christian church, still represents the characteristic
Anglican emphases, stressing (1) the Scriptures as
"containing all things necessary to salvation" and as
being the rule and ultimate standard of faith; (2)
the → Apostles' Creed and the → Niceno-Constantinopolitan Creed as the sufficient statement of
Christian faith; (3) the sacraments of → baptism
and the → Eucharist (esp. §3.3); and (4) the historic
episcopate (→ Bishop, Episcopate).

3.3.2. *Ecclesiology*
In its ecclesiology, as in other areas of theology, Anglicanism has emphasized the complementary authority of Scripture, → tradition and → reason. "It
professes the faith uniquely revealed in the Holy
Scriptures and set forth in the catholic creeds, which
faith the Church is called upon to proclaim afresh in
each generation" (canon C5 of the Church of England, "Of the Declaration of Assent"); to that faith

"the historic formularies of the Church of England
bear witness." Doctrine is grounded in Scripture, the
liturgical and doctrinal tradition of the church draws
out the implications of Scripture, and reason has its
part to play as a God-given gift whereby both the
church corporately and individual believers may be
led into a right assessment of Christian → truth.

Maintaining that there is no distinctive Anglican
doctrine (though there may be a characteristic Anglican theological method and outlook), Anglican
ecclesiology has been characterized by a concern for
comprehensiveness and has often stressed Anglicanism as the *via media* (middle way) or "bridge church"
standing between → Roman Catholicism and →
Protestantism. This polarity has meant that within
Anglicanism there exist schools of theology and
churchmanship stressing respectively "Catholic" and
"Protestant" understandings of the church, as well as
"central" or "liberal" viewpoints. Anglican usage of
the terms "Catholic" and "evangelical" is frequently
nuanced in ways that do not precisely match their
use within other theological traditions.

3.3.3. *Organization*
As the "mother church" of the Anglican Communion, the Church of England has a special position
within Anglicanism; also, it is the only Anglican
church to be established as a state church (→ Church
and State). The churches of the Anglican Communion are frequently described as a family, with the
individual churches being independent but sharing
a common history and traditions, though with increasing local variations in liturgical practice. The
archbishop of Canterbury, as primus inter pares
among the Anglican primates, has a role analogous
to that of the ecumenical → patriarch in Orthodox
ecclesiology. The definition of a church as "Anglican"
can simply be that it is a church in communion with
the See of Canterbury.

Concern with the concept of primacy has marked
recent Anglican discussions, both ecumenically (notably the discussions of the Anglican–Roman Catholic International Commission with the → Roman
Catholic Church; → Ecumenical Movement) and
structurally by the institution of → Primates Meetings within the Anglican Communion as a way of
maintaining → unity and fellowship. Tensions within
the communion (notably over the → ordination of
women, which threatens a commonly accepted ministry, particularly now that some Anglican churches
consecrate women to the episcopate) have been in
part responsible for this development. These developments have also been addressed at the Lambeth
Conferences of all Anglican diocesan bishops, held
every ten years, which have had an important role of

guidance in matters of faith and morals within the Anglican Communion, though possessing no executive authority (→ Church Law).

Beginning with Anglican churches outside England, and now in the Church of England itself, → synodic government has enabled elected representatives of the → clergy and the laity to share responsibility for the government of the church with the bishops, though the distinct roles of the different orders are recognized by the procedure of voting "by houses." Different Anglicans evaluate in different ways the relation of bishops to the synod and give synodic decisions different weight in the determination of theological issues.

→ Anglicanism has never claimed to be the true church, and indeed has often spoken of itself as but a branch of the one, holy, catholic, and apostolic church. Many Anglicans would maintain that the churches that have preserved the historic episcopate most truly reflect the apostolic pattern of Christian faith and life, but there are disputes among Anglicans as to whether episcopacy belongs to the *esse* of the church or simply to its *bene esse* (its "very essence" vs. its "proper existence"). Ecumenical negotiations have often foundered on the difficulties of reconciling the ministries of nonepiscopally ordered churches with the Anglican ministry.

→ High Church Movement; Oxford Movement

Bibliography: CHURCH OF ENGLAND, DOCTRINE COMMISSION, *Christian Believing: The Nature of the Christian Faith and Its Expression in Holy Scripture and Creeds* (London, 1976) • *Doctrine in the Church of England (1938): The Report of the Commission on Christian Doctrine Appointed by the Archbishops of Canterbury and York* (ed. G. W. H. Lampe; London, 1938; repr., 1982) • D. EDWARDS, *What Do Anglicans Believe?* (London, 1974) • G. GASSMANN, *Das historische Bischofsamt und die Einheit der Kirche in der neueren anglikanischen Theologie* (Göttingen, 1964) • H. H. HARMS, ed., *Die Kirche von England und die anglikanische Kirchengemeinschaft* (Stuttgart, 1966) • M. KELLER-HÜSCHEMENGER, *Die Lehre der Kirche im frühreformatorischen Anglikanismus* (Gütersloh, 1972) • J. MACQUARRIE, *Theology, Church, and Ministry* (London, 1986) • S. NEILL, "Anglikanische (Kirchen-) Gemeinschaft," *TRE* 2.713-23 • W. NIESEL, *The Gospel and the Churches: A Comparison of Catholicism, Orthodoxy, and Protestantism* (Philadelphia, 1962).

GEOFFREY ROWELL

3.4. Lutheran Ecclesiology

3.4.1. Basis

Basic to Lutheran ecclesiology is the thesis that the church is "the assembly of all believers among whom the gospel is preached in its purity and the holy sacraments are administered according to the gospel" (Augs. Conf. 7). In this conception, a personal spiritual element is crucial. The church is made up of saints in the sense of those who are → justified by → faith, a view in keeping with M. → Luther's (1483-1546) understanding of the church as a holy people (→ Luther's Theology). → Institutional elements, however, are also essential, especially gathering for the teaching of the → gospel and for the → sacraments.

What is at issue is the → proclamation that makes the church the church, since in it the justifying Word of the gospel goes forth (note Luther's statement that the church is a creature of the Word). The sacraments are also constitutive for the church as means of → grace. The assembly of believers is where proclamation and the celebration of the sacraments take place. The church is thus a → worshiping assembly, with → preaching and the sacraments as its distinctive "marks." The Lutheran view, then, does not relate solely to the invisible church. Yet there is tension in it, as we see from article 7 of the Apology of the → Augsburg Confession. Does the church consist only of believers, or of all those who have a part in proclamation and sacraments — or all who are baptized (→ Baptism)? Note that this article 7 distinguishes between the church "properly speaking" and the church in the broader sense.

In the later P. → Melanchthon (1497-1560), as distinct from Luther, the stress falls more and more on the institutional side (the church as *coetus scholasticus*, "an institution of learning"). The tension mentioned has produced various definitions right up to our own day, including the church as *coetus baptizatorum* (assembly of the baptized; W. Elert following A. Vilmar, F. J. Stahl, et al.), or the church as *communio sanctorum* (communion of saints) as distinct from Christendom (P. Althaus following T. Harnack et al.). This tension exists in the persistent antithesis of established church versus believers' church. In this matter the idea of degrees of membership might be helpful (C. Lienemann-Perrin; → Church Membership).

According to the Nicene Creed, the church is the one, holy, catholic, and apostolic church. In the Lutheran view, → unity is the true spiritual unity (Apology 7.31) that finds expression in → consensus in proclamation of the gospel and celebration of the sacraments. In the light of the event of justification, holiness is the ever new power of divine → forgiveness and renewal. "Catholicity" (→ Catholic, Catholicity) denotes the historical continuity and objective universality of the church, which the Lutheran churches also claimed from the very outset, in contrast to Roman exclusiveness (see 3.2; → Roman Catholic Church). Apostolicity means continuous fidelity to apostolic teaching.

3.4.2. *Understanding of Ministry*

On the Lutheran view, spiritual preaching (Augs. Conf. 5, "The Office of the Ministry"), being established by God, is a necessary part of the church. → Ordination is to the ministry of publicly proclaiming the gospel and administering the sacraments. Luther in his ecclesiological writings speaks often of ministries (pl.), while Melanchthon and the confessions refer only to the one ministry. Such a ministry can also be exercised on the regional level as the office of → bishop (Augs. Conf. 28).

Today, as in the NT and Luther, there is emphasis on the plurality of ministries (→ Offices, Ecclesiastical). Ordination to the pastorate is to a specific office (→ Pastor, Pastorate), which has many features (public, relating to the whole → congregation, serving the cause of unity, and leadership). There is as yet no adequate Lutheran theology of the episcopal office (in the context of synodal and collegial → church government; see 2.2.7.1).

3.4.3. *Present Situation*

Current Lutheran ecclesiology sees a need to supplement the classic Lutheran view of the church in two ways. First, it seems necessary to state clearly that the ethos of mutual → love and → responsibility is of the essence of the church as a work of the gracious action of God that constitutes it. At issue is an objective ethos of love (W. Elert) characterized as a committed fellowship (P. Althaus) or as a brotherhood (J. Wiebering).

Second, the dimension of sending (→ Mission) has now become significant for the Lutheran understanding of the church. That the church is a decisive social factor (→ Church and State) with a public responsibility was self-evident to the → Reformers (within the still existent *corpus Christianum*), and it has been the subject of fresh reflection today (W. Huber). But the church is now also seen as an instrument of God's mission to the non-Christian world (G. Vicedom and the idea of *missio Dei*); in the context of a secular society (→ Secularization), the church is understood and described as a fellowship of witness and service. Discussions of its missionary structure have played a special part in this regard (W. Krusche). D. → Bonhoeffer's (1906-45) idea of "the church for others" has been adopted, contrary to the tendency toward a stabilization of national churches.

3.4.4. *Situation outside Germany*

The Scandinavian Lutheran churches face the problem of change in the face of the persistence, if not inflexibility, of the state church. Declining baptisms and the increasing withdrawal of church members (→ Church Membership 5) mean that the church may no longer represent the majority of the people. The connection with the state, which varies from country to country, is a continuing issue. In → Sweden (§5), for example, a series of constitutional changes has strengthened the role of local parishes in church affairs, giving them greater voice in the appointment of bishops and affirming their right of taxation.

In North America the development of the Lutheran churches has been characterized by movements toward → union, which have produced the American Lutheran Church (1960), the Lutheran Church in America (1962), and, most recently, the Evangelical Lutheran Church in America (1988). The dimension of the universal church and the question of the leadership of the regional church (episcopacy) have increasingly entered ecclesiological discussion (e.g., in debates with the → fundamentalism of the still separate Lutheran Church–Missouri Synod). Important themes in the ecclesiology of North American Lutheranism are the ecumenical, the missionary, and the social tasks of the church.

In the → minority situation in eastern Europe, there is a strong, historically conditioned preoccupation with the Roman Catholic majority (e.g., in Austria and Poland; cf. also Italy), as well as a link to ethnic minorities (e.g., in Romania and Russia). We find the same situation in Latin America, where there are also approaches to → liberation theology (cf. the Methodist J. Míguez Bonino), leading to a growing link between the reforming element and the self-understanding of progressive Roman Catholics. In Africa and Asia, Lutherans function in a non-Christian religious background. The associated need for ecumenism is an important factor.

3.4.5. *The Ecumenical Context*

With the → ecumenical movement of the 20th century, the question of church unity takes a different form for Lutheran ecclesiology than it did in the 16th century. After the relatively recent encounters with other → denominations (§2), Lutherans deny that a specific structure of ministry (e.g., apostolic succession of bishops) is a necessary condition of unity. The insight is also growing that, despite the assertion in Augs. Conf. 7 that identical ceremonies do not represent a condition for true church unity, still some common structural elements must be present for overall church unity (e.g., conciliar assemblies, some form of the Petrine office). In this regard, the model of "reconciled difference" has been developed, as adopted by the → Lutheran World Federation at Dar es Salaam in 1977. This view accepts the necessity and possibility of permanent plurality (of constitutions, forms of worship, and doctrinal formulations) within a full church fellowship. In this plurality, formerly unreconcilable antitheses will be reconciled by the removal of misunderstandings and the development of fresh interpretations.

→ Orthodoxy 1; Protestantism; Reformation

Bibliography: I. ASHEIM and V. R. GOLD, eds., *Kirchenpräsident oder Bischof?* (Göttingen, 1968) • A. S. BURGES, ed., *Lutheran Churches of the Third World* (Minneapolis, 1970) • W. HUBER, *Kirche* (Stuttgart, 1979; 2d ed., Munich, 1988) • L. S. HUNTER, ed., *Scandinavian Churches* (London, 1965) • W. KRUSCHE, *Schritte und Markierungen* (Berlin, 1972) • U. KÜHN, *Kirche* (Gütersloh, 1980) • C. LIENEMANN-PERRIN, ed., *Taufe und Kirchenzugehörigkeit* (Munich, 1983) • W. LOHFF and L. MOHAUPT, eds., *Volkskirche–Kirche der Zukunft?* (Berlin, 1977) • B. LOHSE et al., eds., *Die lutherische Kirche, Geschichte und Gestalten* (2 vols.; Gütersloh, 1976) • W.-D. MARSCH, *Institution im Übergang* (Göttingen, 1970) • J. MÍGUEZ BONINO, *Doing Theology in a Revolutionary Situation* (Philadelphia, 1975) • *The Ministry of the Church: A Lutheran Understanding* (New York [Lutheran Council in the U.S.], 1974) • E. C. NELSON, ed., *The Lutherans in North America* (Philadelphia, 1975) • J. PELIKAN, *Spirit versus Structure: Luther and the Institutions of the Church* (New York, 1968) • V. VAJTA, ed., *Die evangelisch-lutherische Kirche* (Stuttgart, 1977); idem, ed., *The Gospel and the Ambiguity of the Church* (Philadelphia, 1974) • G. VICEDOM, *Missio Dei. Einführung in eine Theologie der Mission* (Munich, 1958) • F. K. WENTZ, *Lutherans in Concert: The Story of the National Lutheran Council, 1918-1966* (Minneapolis, 1968) • J. WIEBERING, "Kirche als Bruderschaft in der lutherischen Ekklesiologie," *KuD* 23 (1977) 300-315 • R. C. WOLF, *Documents of Lutheran Unity in America* (Philadelphia, 1966).

ULRICH KÜHN

3.5. Reformed Ecclesiology

The family of Reformed churches includes both presbyterian and congregational (→ Congregationalism) forms of church government. In this section we shall deal only with the former, which is most common. (On the latter, see 3.6.)

3.5.1. Theological Aspects

Theologically, the Reformed understanding of the church has a Trinitarian and Christocentric anchor, is oriented to the → history of salvation, and has an → eschatological reference. The proper subject of

church history in its temporal expression is not the church as an → institution but is exclusively the triune God — Father, Son, and Holy Spirit (→ Trinity), revealed as Creator, Reconciler, and Redeemer. Jesus Christ himself, the → incarnate Son of the Father, "gathers, defends, and preserves" his church (Heidelberg Catechism, q. 54). The church is "the community of brethren [and sisters] in which Jesus Christ presently works in the Word and sacraments" (Barmen Declaration 3).

The salvation history (→ History of Salvation) of God with his chosen people began in the OT as a history of judgment and → grace. Hence the OT has exemplary significance for Reformed ecclesiology. As the constitution of the Reformed Church in Germany puts it, on the Reformed view, it is a task of the church to seek encounter and reconciliation with the people of Israel (1988). All that the church does must have as its goal the preparing of people for the coming → kingdom of God as this is dramatically depicted, for example, in Revelation 21.

In classic Reformed theology these insights are linked to the doctrine of → predestination and to the distinction between the visible and the invisible church. The size of the invisible church is known only to God, for he alone knows whom he has elected. The distinction does not mean that the order of the visible church is regarded as unimportant (see 2.2.7.2 and 3.5.3).

3.5.2. Orienting Data

Within this framework, Reformed ecclesiology has a catholic, Reformation, and congregational orientation. For the Reformed the church is the one, holy, catholic (i.e., universal), and apostolic church. As the first of the Articles Declaratory of the Constitution of the Church of Scotland (1921) puts it, "The Church of Scotland is part of the Holy Catholic or Universal Church; worshiping one God Almighty, all-wise and all-loving, in the Trinity of the Father, the Son, and the Holy Ghost, the same in substance, equal in power and glory. The Church of Scotland adheres to the Scottish Reformation; receives the Word of God which is contained in the Scriptures of the Old and New Testaments as the supreme rule of faith and life; and avows the fundamental doctrines of the Catholic Faith founded thereupon."

Reformed ecclesiology is also a Reformation ecclesiology inasmuch as it confesses the central insights of the → Reformation of the church in Europe in the 16th century as M. → Luther (1483-1546) stated them and as U. → Zwingli (1484-1531; → Zwingli's Theology) and J. → Calvin (1509-64; → Calvin's Theology) developed and applied them. It is congregationally oriented to the extent that it understands and values the local → congregation, gathered around the Word and → sacrament, as the local fellowship of the pilgrim → people of God.

3.5.3. *Form of the Church*
A distinctive feature of Reformed ecclesiology is that it pays particular attention to the form of the Christian communion both locally and extralocally. This concern emerged quite early in the course of the Swiss Reformation, first in Zwingli's Zurich, then more fully in Calvin's Geneva. Along with the pure → preaching of the → Word of God and the due administration of → baptism and the → Eucharist according to their divine institution, discipline or → church order (§2.2) was often regarded as the mark of a genuine church. The reference was not merely to → church discipline in the traditional sense but also to the form of ministry (→ Offices, Ecclesiastical) and to government by presbytery and synod, whether at the local, regional, or national level.

A pioneer in this regard was Calvin. Although most Reformed churches today do not have the kind of discipline that Calvin had in Geneva (and many other churches for centuries afterward), and although Calvin's division of the ministry into the four offices of pastor, teacher, → elder, and → deacon (→ Calvin's Theology 2.4) did not fully establish itself, nevertheless the inclusion of elders with pastors in local, regional, and national church government is a typical feature in Reformed constitutions and has been followed in many other Protestant churches.

In the → ecumenical movement today, along with the → synodal principle, Reformed ecclesiology offers the only viable alternative to episcopacy (→ Bishop, Episcopate) as we find it in the Orthodox Church (see 3.1), the → Roman Catholic Church (see 3.2), and the → Anglican Communion (see 3.3). The only national Reformed church of any size with an episcopal form of government is the Hungarian, which was forced to adopt this form by the Austrian rulers. Similar attempts by other absolutist rulers (e.g., in Great Britain in the 17th cent.) were successfully defeated after a long struggle. The result today is that many Reformed Christians have only a negative view of the term "bishop," particularly when the reference is to the bishop of Rome (→ Pope, Papacy). As the Synod of Emden (1571) succinctly put it in the first of its articles on church order: "No church, pastor, elder, or deacon should have precedence or power over other churches, pastors, elders, or deacons, but should steer clear of any appearance thereof or occasion thereto."

3.5.4. *Social Significance*
The family of → Reformed churches is a worldwide one, with each church also being stamped by its own history. Common Reformed concerns have done much to shape not merely the church but indeed the whole of Western → society. Without this contribution, modern → democracy would hardly be conceivable, let alone feasible. It must not be overlooked, however, that in a → pluralist society, Reformed ecclesiology can easily degenerate into a kind of lack of breadth that opens the door to sectarianism (→ Sect). This has happened in the past when division has come over supposed basic principles, such as in Holland, Great Britain, the United States, and Germany.

An opposing movement has sought the unity, not merely of Reformed churches, but of all Christian churches. This led to the formation of the → World Alliance of Reformed Churches and contributed to the founding of the → World Council of Churches. In all this it is clear that for the Reformed churches to survive, they cannot merely cling to their own → tradition. The summons that now confronts them is to make the Reformed legacy fruitful by taking up with new zeal the theological task of being the church of the Word of God that is addressed to all people.

→ Calvinism; Orthodoxy 2; Protestantism

Bibliography: K. BARTH, *CD* IV/1, §62; IV/2, §67; IV/3b, §72 • E. BRUNNER, *The Misunderstanding of the Church* (London, 1952) • E. GELDBACH, *Ökumene in Gegensätzen* (Göttingen, 1987) • K. HALASKI, ed., *Die reformierten Kirchen* (Stuttgart, 1977) • E. JAY, *The Church: Its Changing Image through Twenty Centuries* (2 vols.; London, 1977-78) • C. LINK, U. LUZ, and L. VISCHER, *Sie aber hielten fest an die Gemeinschaft. . . . Einheit der Kirche als Prozeß im Neuen Testament und heute* (Zurich, 1988) • G. MACGREGOR, *Corpus Christi* (Philadelphia, 1958) • E. MCKEE, *Elders and the Plural Ministry: The Role of Exegetical History in Illuminating John Calvin's Theology* (Geneva, 1988) • J. T. MCNEILL, *The History and Character of Calvinism* (New York, 1954) • M. PRADERVAND, ed., *A Century of Service: A History of the World Alliance of Reformed Churches, 1875-1975* (Grand Rapids, 1975) • O. WEBER, *Foundations of Dogmatics* (vol. 2; Grand Rapids, 1983) §10.

ALASDAIR I. C. HERON

3.6. *Free Church Ecclesiology*
3.6.1. *Concept and Historical Presuppositions*
The term "free church" emerged in the 1890s in England, but the reality began in 1525 with the → Anabaptists (see 2.2.7.3). English → Dissenters, including → Baptists, → Congregationalists, Presbyterians (→ Reformed and Presbyterian Churches), and → Methodists (→ Methodism), emphasized the central feature of the free church, namely, its voluntary (→

Church Membership) and self-supporting (→ Church Finances) nature as a "gathered church," as opposed to a state or established church. Though they originally were part of this development, Presbyterians (with their Calvinist connections) and Methodists (with their Anglican origin) are not free churches in the fuller and stricter sense. Despite having certain features in common with free churches, Presbyterians and Methodists do not share the characteristic free church emphasis on discipleship, nor do they have the same church offices or nonliturgical style of worship.

Most scholars agree that evangelical Anabaptism of the 16th century was the first free church movement, although some prefer to begin with the → Waldenses (12th cent.) or the Unitas Fratrum (15th cent.; → Bohemian Brethren). Anabaptism combined elements of medieval Catholic → piety with Protestant doctrines to form a new "third force" in Christendom. Because they were perceived as subversive of good order, Anabaptists were suppressed alike by Catholics and Protestants. Some survived in a few areas by strategies of withdrawal and continual migration.

The → Pietist → revival movement within the → Lutheran churches (see 3.4) and Reformed churches (see 3.5) of the late 1600s and 1700s also produced free churches. The renewed → Moravian Church founded at Herrnhut in 1727 became an ecumenically minded → minority with a worldwide → mission. The Brethren, who began in central Germany in 1708, and several communitarian groups (the Inspired, Harmonists, and Zoarites in Ohio; → Separatism) also emerged from 18th-century → Pietism. Other free churches were created in Europe in protest against interference in church affairs by government leaders. After 1817, for example, when Prussian rulers forced the union of Lutherans and Reformed and altered liturgical forms (→ Liturgy), recalcitrant clergy and laity created several independent church bodies. New entities also resulted from the extensive revival movement of the 19th century initiated by the Continental Society (led by R. Haldane and H. Drummond) and the Brethren movement (led by J. N. Darby; → Plymouth Brethren).

3.6.2. Characteristics

The voluntary nature of membership in a covenanted → congregation has already been noted as central to the free church. One problem with this identification is that a number of modern nations maintain the separation of → church and state, which means that, in some sense, *all* ecclesiastical bodies located in such countries could be called free churches, including the → Orthodox Church and → Roman Catholic

Church. Some therefore prefer the more precise term "believers' church," coined by Max → Weber (1864-1920) for the "community of personal believers of the reborn, and only those." Conferences have been held in North America to refine this concept. Another way to distinguish helpfully between church types is to note the following other identifying characteristics of the free church.

3.6.2.1. First comes discipleship. Living → faith for the free churches has never been a matter merely of sacramental participation (→ Sacraments), assent to creeds (→ Confessions and Creeds), or liturgical correctness (→ Liturgy); rather, it is an obedient focus on following Jesus Christ. H. S. Bender described → discipleship as "the transformation of the entire way of life of the individual believer and of society so that it should be fashioned after the teachings and example of Christ" (42-43).

3.6.2.2. Next comes the primacy of Scripture above tradition. Scriptural authority is primary for the free churches. In this regard they understand themselves as following the Reformers' doctrine of *sola Scriptura* (→ Reformation Principles); the difference is that they see themselves as living out the principle more consistently. They are more radical in rejecting the authority of church → tradition, and while maintaining the unity of the Bible, they hold that the OT should be read in the light of the NT. The free church depends on the working of the Holy Spirit to help it exegete the Bible (→ Exegesis, Biblical) in the "hermeneutic community" (J. H. Yoder).

3.6.2.3. A third characteristic is the desire to restore the church as a community of saints. This core principle of Anabaptists and later free churches represents the intent to recover "the life and virtue of the True Church" of → primitive Christianity (F. H. Littell). Apostolicity for the free church means being true to the → apostles, not → institutional continuity.

3.6.2.4. Another emphasis is on the priesthood of all believers. Although free churches have developed patterns of discerning and affirming pastoral and other leadership, they place great stress upon the ministry of all members (→ Offices, Ecclesiastical). Likewise, they dissent from double standards of respect and morality that set clergy apart from laity (→ Clergy and Laity), particularly attacking the sacerdotalism upon which such distinctions are based (→ Priest, Priesthood).

3.6.2.5. Separation from the world and service to the world are also important. Free churches stress the narrow way of strict ethical conduct and teach that members should not be of the world, though living in it. At the same time, they are active in expressions of mutual aid to support both the material and spiritual needs of their fellows and the broader → society. Widely known for varied ministries of philanthropy and relief to the needy and suffering, they have also been leaders in spreading the → gospel to the world. The history of → mission is to no little extent the history of free church activity, from the sacrificial journeys of early Anabaptists to the mission societies of today.

→ Religious Liberty

Bibliography: H. S. BENDER, "The Anabaptist Vision," The Recovery of the Anabaptist Vision (ed. G. F. Hershberger; Scottdale, Pa., 1957) 29-54 • E. H. BROADBENT, The Pilgrim Church (London, 1931) • H. DAVIES, The English Free Churches (London, 1952) • D. F. DURNBAUGH, The Believers' Church: The History and Character of Radical Protestantism (New York, 1968; 3d ed., 1985) • C. J. DYCK, An Introduction to Mennonite History (3d ed.; Scottdale, Pa., 1993) • J. L. GARRETT JR., ed., The Concept of the Believers' Church (Scottdale, Pa., 1969) • U. KUNZ, ed., Viele Glieder–ein Leib (Stuttgart, 1963) • F. H. LITTELL, The Free Church (Boston, 1957) • P. MEINHOLD, Ökumenische Kirchenkunde (Stuttgart, 1962) • H. B. MOTEL, ed., Glieder an einem Leib. Die Freikirchen in Selbstdarstellung (Konstanz, 1975) • E. E. PAYNE, The Free Church Tradition in the Life of England (London, 1944; 4th ed., 1965) • J. D. WEAVER, Becoming Anabaptist: The Origin and Significance of Sixteenth-Century Anabaptism (Scottdale, Pa., 1987) • G. A. WESTIN, The Free Church through the Ages (Nashville, 1958).

DONALD F. DURNBAUGH

4. Sociological Aspects

4.1. Concept

Since the word "church" can have many meanings in colloquial speech (e.g., established church, local church, church building, worship service; see 1.2), the sociological use demands the most accurate definition possible. In this context we do best to speak of "a" church or "several" churches so as to avoid confusion with theological concepts, which mostly relate to "the" one church, the object of faith. This usage may seem to contradict the classic use of church as an ideal type (M. → Weber). In that approach, however, "church" is only one subtype in a broader typology, in which it is the opposite of → "sect." "Church" and "sect," then, are abstract mental constructs that help us order the many → institutionalized forms of the Christian religion and thus allow for generalizations.

The concept "church," then, indicates a community that dispenses → grace (→ Sacrament) under the leadership of a → priestly caste and functions as an institution that includes all the members of a population. "Sect," in contrast, indicates a voluntary organization of believers who seek to actualize → salvation in their personal lives instead of expecting it from officially granted means of grace. Using this typology, one could formerly speak of one type of church, but now many elaborate typologies have been developed in which the subtype "church" is but one of many; only in their plurality can justice be done to the variety of religious institutions in history.

The American J. M. Yinger, for example, who has developed very elaborate typologies, avoids the single word "church" altogether. According to the extent that historical religious institutions either accept or critically confront the social order, he has divided them into "established churches," "universal churches," "established sects," and "radical sects," thus assuming a continuum with many intermediate forms.

4.2. Tasks and Problems

Whereas typologies focus on the differences between various institutionalized Christian groups, other studies deal with common features and problems. The word "church," then, is a collective noun that also points to empirical social structures (→ Social Science). Various levels of inquiry are thus possible, which are taken up with different theoretical perspectives. On the macrolevel, the variety of relations to the constellation of → power in → society is investigated (e.g., support, legitimation, or, its opposite, protest, as well as many intermediate forms of → compromise). Pioneers in this field were K. → Marx (1818-83), F. Engels (1820-95), and M. Weber (1864-1920). Along these lines, sociological studies have tackled the question of how various social strata relate to various churches (H. R. Niebuhr, N. J. Demerath III, L. Pope, et al.; → Class and Social Stratum), or how established churches have lost contact with the working classes (K. S. Inglis, G. Kehrer, E. R. Wickham; → Labor Movement). Following É. Durkheim (1858-1917), inquiry can also be made into the (changing) social functions of churches. Since the 1950s the → sociology of churches has pursued this issue on the local, regional, and national levels (J. Freytag, K.-F. Daiber). The tendency has been to look at → secularization as a loss of functions by the churches (J. P. Kruyt, P. Smits).

On the microlevel, inquiry is made into the various forms of member participation and the different degrees of commitment (W. Menges and N. Greinacher, H. Carrier). The primary interest here is in the variety of forms (see J. Freytag and T. Rendtorff, who suggest the illuminating term "distant membership"). At present the focus is on withdrawal from the church (→ Church Membership 5) and participation in alternative forms of church life (A. Feige, T. Schmieder, K. Schumacher). Less note is taken of the questions why the churches generally fail to attract the younger generation in Europe and what other ways of passing on Christianity might be found (F. X. Kaufmann).

Between the macrolevel and the microlevel, inquiry is made into churches as → organizations. This approach also gives important impulses for the linkage between the two other levels and for considering problems of church practice, as well as those of power structures and of ecumenical efforts at reunion. There is a close relation between the organizational forms of various church types, their roles in society, and the way in which members participate in each type (P. F. Rudge, M. A. Thung). Formal and theologically validated church constitutions seldom reflect the actual structure of → authority (P. M. Harrison). The interests of church officials in maintaining the differences between the various churches are an obstacle to reunion (→ Ecumenical Movement), even where members no longer regard the differences between → denominations as important (note P. L. Berger's market model of ecumenical processes).

These and other practically relevant insights are gained from the sociology of organizations. Likewise, church rigidity or possibilities of change can be considered in terms of the theory of → bureaucracy (K. A. Thompson) or in terms of the alienation that always takes place over time as a result of the institutionalization of religious leadership (→ Offices, Ecclesiastical), religious experience (rituals, symbolism), forms of community life (church constitution), and religious beliefs (dogmas; T. F. O'Dea). Schisms (→ Heresies and Schisms) and the rise of sects are often explained along these lines (L. Laeyendecker). Adopting the sociological perspective on churches as social structures thus brings to light tensions and dilemmas that can deepen theological understanding and elucidate practical problems.

→ Pastoral Sociology; Sociology; Sociology of Religion

Bibliography: P. L. BERGER, "A Market Model for the Analysis of Ecumenicity," *Social Research* 30 (1963) 77-93 • H. CARRIER, *Psycho-sociologie de l'appartenance religieuse* (Rome, 1960) • K.-F. DAIBER, *Volkskirche im Wandel* (Stuttgart, 1973) • G. DAVIE, *Religion in Britain since 1945: Believing without Belonging* (Oxford, 1994) • N. J. DEMERATH III, *Social Class in American Protestantism* (Chicago, 1965) • F. ENGELS, "The Peasant War in Germany," *Karl Marx, Frederick Engels: Collected Works* (trans. R. Dixon et al.; New York, 1975ff.) 10.397-482 • A. FEIGE, *Kirchenaustritte. Eine soziologische Untersuchung von Ursachen und Bedingungen* (Gelnhausen, 1977); idem, *Kirchenmitgliedschaft in der Bundesrepublik Deutschland* (Gütersloh, 1990) • R. FINKE and R. STARK, *The Churching of America, 1776-1990: Winners and Losers in Our Religious Economy* (New Brunswick, N.J., 1992) • J. FREYTAG, *Die Kirchengemeinde in soziologischer Sicht. Weg und Ziel empirischer Forschungen* (Hamburg, 1959) • P. M. HARRISON, *Authority and Power in the Free Church Tradition: A Social Case Study of the American Baptist Convention* (Princeton, 1959) • K. S. INGLIS, *Churches and the Working Classes in Victorian England* (London, 1963) • F. X. KAUFMANN, *Kirche begreifen. Analysen und Thesen zur gesellschaftlichen Verfassung des Christentums* (Freiburg, 1979) • G. KEHRER, *Das religiöse Bewußtsein des Industriearbeiters* (Munich, 1967) • D. M. KELLEY, *Why Conservative Churches Are Growing* (Macon, Ga., 1986) • J. P. KRUIJT, *De onkerkelijkheid in Nederland* (Groningen, 1933) • L. LAEYENDECKER, *Religie en conflict. De zogenaamde sekten in sociologisch perspectief* (Meppel, 1967) • K. MARX, "Contribution to the Critique of Hegel's Philosophy of Law," *Karl Marx, Frederick Engels: Collected Works* (trans. R. Dixon et al.; New York, 1975ff.) 3.175-87 • W. MENGES and N. GREINACHER, eds., *Die Zugehörigkeit zur Kirche* (Mainz, 1964) • D. O. MOBERG, *The Church as a Social Institution* (2d ed.; Grand Rapids, 1984) • H. R. NIEBUHR, *The Social Sources of Denominationalism* (Magnolia, Mass., 1984; orig. pub., 1929) • T. F. O'DEA, *The Sociology of Religion* (Englewood Cliffs, N.J., 1966) • L. POPE, *Millhands and Preachers* (New Haven, 1942) • T. RENDTORFF, *Die soziale Struktur der Gemeinde* (Hamburg, 1958) • P. F. RUDGE, *Ministry and Management: The Study of Ecclesiastical Administration* (London, 1968) • T. SCHMIEDER and K. SCHUMACHER, eds., *Jugend auf dem Kirchentag. Eine empirische Analyse* (Stuttgart, 1984) • P. SMITS, *Kerk en stad. Een godsdienstsociologisch onderzoek met inbegrip van een religiografie van de industriestad Enschede* (The Hague, 1952) • K. A. THOMPSON, *Bureaucracy and Church Reform: The Organizational Response of the Church of England to Social Change, 1800-1965* (Oxford, 1970) • M. A. THUNG, *The Precarious Organisation: Sociological Explorations of the Church's Mission and Structure* (The Hague, 1976) • M. WEBER, *Economy and Society: An Outline of Interpretive Sociology* (2 vols.; Berkeley, Calif., 1978; orig. pub., 1922) • E. R. WICKHAM, *Church and People in an Industrial City* (London, 1957) • R. WUTHNOW, *The Restructuring of American Religion: Society and Faith since World War II* (Princeton, 1988) • J. M. YINGER, *Religion in the Struggle for Power* (Durham, N.C., 1946; 2d ed., 1961).

MADY A. THUNG

5. The Church in Transition

5.1. *The Present-Day Phenomenon*

The present picture of the church shows it to be in transition. This has always been true (see 2.2). There was transition from the martyr church to the imperial church (→ Early Church 2), just as the East-West schism represented transition (→ Heresies and Schisms). The rise of → denominations (§2) as a result of the → Reformation introduced a time of transition, as did our entering the century of the church (→ Modern Church History; Theology in the Nineteenth and Twentieth Centuries). In all these instances the changes were linked to intellectual and sociopolitical crises, conflicts, or transitions. Analogies are plain to see.

If we speak of the church in transition today (K.-F. Daiber, G. Alberigo), of structural change (K. → Rahner), of a crisis, of the need for a paradigm shift (H. Küng), of tension and change in the ecumenical fellowship (E. Geldbach, K. Raiser), we must connect these diagnoses with parallel phenomena and processes in society as a whole. We see here the dynamic of the evolution of civilization (H. Lübbe) and its many manifestations, which affect the conditions and relationships of human life in various ways, both positive and negative. We see a change in the form of global complexity and an increasing rate of change (N. Luhmann). The limits of growth seem to have been reached as → progress threatens life (D. Meadows). The scientific revolution and structural social change are calling for a paradigm shift (T. S. Kuhn, N. Luhmann). The new unintelligibility (*Unübersichtlichkeit*, J. Habermas), the discomfort with modernity (P. L. Berger), and the transition from a society of growth to one of risk (U. Beck) all raise the need for reduction, for new models and orientations.

In relation to ecclesiological problems, however, there is not merely parallelism to society or participation in its change. The church in transition and societal transition correspond at a fundamental level; the reconstruction of modern society affects deeply the function of the church. The church, as a segment of society, exists under secular conditions that impinge on both its outer relations and its inner experiences and thinking. We must therefore examine the contents of dogmatic definitions and the organizational structures and pastoral activity of the church (1) as they are surrounded by changes and crises in other spheres of life, (2) as they become involved in changes in the psychological and cognitive structures of modern consciousness, and (3) as they are of relevance to the entire secular nexus.

5.2. *Ecclesiological Problems*

The phenomena that bear witness to change in the church and that indicate an ecclesiological problem have been listed above in section 1.4. We can evaluate each one in relation to (1) theological reflection on the basis, goal, form, and marks of the church and its dogmatic definition as a fellowship of tradition, understanding, and action; (2) efficiency of the community of faith, as measured by success in spiritual → communication and by a sense of permanence and stability in the course of the church members' everyday life; (3) the church functioning in its sociocultural environment to communicate the Christian message of salvation in its twofold relevance — to the experience and understanding of the world, and to conditions that will promote life-sustaining coexistence with humanity at large; and (4) an ecumenical intercommunication of particular churches that presupposes and respects differences in teaching, structure, → piety, and practice but that aims at a web of relationships in which there will be contextual participation in the universal, saving message of Jesus and mutual influence, both cognitive and practical.

5.3. *Situation as an Ecclesiologically Relevant Context*

For the reasons stated in 5.1, this evaluation of phenomena will be in the context of a diagnosis of the age or specific situation. Relevant in this regard is the insight that social transformation concerns the external conditions and relationships of life, as well as our mental attitude and consciousness. These are in mutual interaction, together defining the situation of modernity (P. L. Berger), though with differences of degree from country to country and society to society.

The churches are immersed in this interaction in every respect, which involves their physical place and existence, their members, those with whom they seek to communicate, their forms of organization and activities, their interrelations, and their relations with the non-Christian world. To the extent that the church regards its situation as threatening and bandies about slogans like "survivability" and "expedience," the changes noted will be perceived as negative.

The situation as thus described is the ecclesiologically relevant context. At first sight the thesis that the churches are subject to the conditions of their milieu and are thus contextually determined might seem to be trivial. Yet, as we look deeper, we find many significant implications and consequences.

5.4. *Implications and Consequences*

5.4.1. First, we must remember that crisis, change,

and reconstruction are all normal in history. As elements in history, they are the object of historical writing and interpretation (→ Historicism; Theology of History). To define them as such, we need to see what comes before and after and to point out the relations. They are of interest as everyday phenomena because they help us question ordinary life and provide a context for defining everyday situations. Historical study makes us aware that human life is exposed to change. Analysis of the complex reality of the everyday shows how much change there is in life, including its psychological and cognitive structures.

In general, then, history and everyday life imply variability. More specifically, the church as a historical entity and a factor in the everyday world, along with its concepts, theories, organizational structures, and activities, is subject to change. It may wish to avoid or deny this fact, both ecclesiastically and theologically, or it may declare it to be illegitimate. Variability, however, is inevitably a mark of the church.

5.4.2. The attempt to escape, deny, or invalidate change is based on the recognition of faith that the → grace of God that is revealed in the saving message of Jesus is unchangeable. The witness to it, its objectification in the church, and its theological exposition all seek to affirm that → revelation is not variable. They present it and try to validate it as given → truth. Yet we must point out that what is unchangeable is neither conceivable, nor can it be reproduced in the conditions and changes of everyday life. This fact marks the abiding distinction between God and the world (humanity). Dissatisfaction with reality as we now find it is the condition of change, and consummation — the wholeness of reality — is the goal of the change for which we → hope (→ New Self).

5.4.3. The fundamental variability of the church has implications for the ecclesiological problems indicated (see 1.4.1 and 5.2). First, it means that the collective practice of faith that is the theme of theological reflection can be overthrown by new forms or led back by older ones to an earlier stage. It is thus limited. That is, we must recognize *particularity* also as a mark of the church. It unavoidably makes divergent ecclesiologies possible. It restricts the validity of dogmatic definitions of the church's basis, goal, form, and character, leaving such matters open in principle. Like other marks of the church listed in the creeds, however, its opposite — universality — may be asserted at most ideologically (→ Ideology 2).

Second, the changeability of the church rules out any normativity. We might establish certain norms dogmatically on the basis of faith, with faith itself as a reason and argument against → doubt. But the fact that we have churches (in the pl.), which is due to the church's inevitable variability, contradicts the ideal construct. Differentiations are possible. The individual churches are distinguished by their *confessionality* (→ Denomination 5) and can be defined by their specific achievements. In both cases we have evidence of the church's variability.

Third, to be able to establish change, we must know what is changing. A definition of the situation is essential (see 5.3). If the situation is one of crisis in the ordering of life and in experience of the world, with an accompanying demand for what is valid today, this is the context in which the church must take up the function that it claims in the sociocultural nexus, showing therein its relevance. In accordance with its own intention, its communication and presentation of the Christian message of salvation must be situational, taking account of what is valid today, if it is both to hold fast to the gospel on the one hand and to make it relevant on the other. This *contextuality* is thus the church's qualification. If it tries only to insist on what is ultimately valid, it will fail to discharge its function and be untrue to its own existence. Contextuality is thus a mark of the church corresponding to its variability.

Fourth, the particularity, confessionality, and contextuality of the churches are the reason for its *plurality*. Reflected here is the dissatisfaction with the existing situation that is the condition of variability (see 5.4.2) but also the difference between the saving message of Jesus and the witness of believers, which makes plurality possible and seems to give it validity (see the fourth problem listed in 1.4.1). Plurality, then, is also a mark of the church. It shows itself in a worldwide Christian process whereby churches interact as free and equal partners within a conciliar structure (→ Conciliarity). In interchurch relations plurality means competition and conflict, but it also holds out the possibility of mutual accommodation and → solidarity. In relations with the secular society that are directed at the whole inhabited earth (the oikoumene) and that take in the whole of reality, the church can prove itself by inherent models of service and action that transcend everyday life (§4.3.2).

5.5. *Concept, Value, Form, and*
         Function of the Church

Traditional ecclesiologies usually follow the dogmatic norms laid down in the creeds, mentioning → unity, holiness, catholicity (→ Catholic, Catholicity), and apostolicity as the church's marks. The church is defined as a unique fellowship unlike all other collective structures (→ Society). Doctrinal definitions and ecclesiological development must adhere to these norms. But the norms are true only on the level of abstract reflection, which ignores the actual historical foundations of the real churches and their specific place, time, and situation. This approach reveals little of the complexity of the phenomenon of the church.

A phenomenological approach avoids this reduction and removes the pressure of norms. It looks at the phenomenon of the church from various angles (historical, theological, sociological, and situational), thus providing a frame of reference that reveals the real, empirically verifiable marks of the church (see 1.4.2). In ecclesiological reflection that can do justice to the phenomenon, these marks are relevant for grasping the concept, relevance, form, and function of the church.

5.5.1. The term "church" is multidimensional (see 1.1-3). It embraces different elements, the relations between them, and variations based on time and place. An increase in these elements and their variety, relations, and changes cannot be ruled out. Hence a conceptual definition must always be dependent on the social reality. It is possible only within a theory of the church that focuses on the church's present form or on a descriptive listing of specific features (regional spread, form of organization, etc.).

5.5.2. The structural wealth of the church, which indicates its status in the relation between God and humankind, is the content of the saving message of Jesus and is that to which the church owes its distinctiveness (see 1.3) and ongoing existence. It reflects the complexity of our human world. But this advantage is subject to a certain restriction. Whereas God is ultimately beyond our human perception (the term "God" being definable only in the reflection of believers), the church is open to observation as the social locus and agent of the message of salvation. Because it is so manifold, however, the structural wealth of the church, like the complexity of our human world, can be grasped only selectively. This unavoidable fact means that ecclesiology, which formulates the church's self-understanding, can draw on only a partial view of the church. No single church, then, on the basis of its orthodoxy, can lay claim to the ancient axiom of → Cyprian that outside the church there is no salvation. It must always acknowledge that other ways of salvation are possible (→ Theology of Religions).

5.5.3. The concrete form of the church, including its piety, worship, spiritual communication, organizational structure, and collective functions, will not continue unchanged. This contingency is not due merely to the contextual conditions in which individual churches developed. It is unavoidable also for fundamental theological reasons. The complexity of persons and relations (God as Father and Creator, Son of God and Son of Man, Holy Spirit; → Trinity),

which is viewed as the divine economy in the three articles of the creeds, and which is attested as the reality of faith, is as such inaccessible to us. Hence manifesting it in the practice of faith calls for a reduction that will make it selectively accessible. This takes place in images, fantasies, symbols, stories, myths, interpretive models, doxologies, practices, and institutions against the background of secular experience, as we see clearly enough in the history of the church and its dogmas or doctrinal statements.

This complexity, however — which, theologically speaking, results from God's electing activity, and which is the subject of faith as the people of God assembled from both Jews and Gentiles — can be communicated only in narrative, parable, and metaphor as → hope, and in the perspective of → promise and fulfillment. In the concrete form of the people of God, it is reduced to an aspect that distinguishes between the church and Israel and for various reasons does not grasp the whole. We have not yet seen the end of the contingent form of the church that presents itself in the multiplicity of worldwide Christianity.

The communication process of real churches in which each affects the other and all view understanding with the Jews as God's people as an urgent matter, fails to reach its goal or to be relevant to its situation if it simply falls back on tradition, raises the old question of confirmation, or seeks an answer in convergence and → consensus. This communication takes place in contemporary conditions and thus has the chance to find and develop new forms of the church. It can listen to the Fathers, and yet it still can leave tradition behind with what seem to be its inalienable institutions. It can orient its thinking and action to modern experiences and the prevailing situation. Yet even in what is valid today, it can persevere in the message of salvation for Jews and Gentiles.

5.5.4. The church discharges its function as the congregations or churches in a given place (particularity) live out and give shape to the saving message of Jesus in accordance with their own experience of faith (confessionality) and in relation to the demands of the everyday world (contextuality), seeking in this way to give multiple expression to the universality of the gospel (plurality). Whether and how far the transmission and expression of faith by the church succeed in meeting contemporary demands depend, on the one hand, on the message leading to a realistic form and, on the other hand, on an ecclesiological concept that can offer a realistic and feasible solution to the basic theological problems indicated in section 1.4 above.

Bibliography: G. ALBERIGO, Y. CONGAR, and H. J. POTT-MEYER, eds., *Kirche im Wandel. Eine kritische Zwischenbilanz nach dem Zweiten Vatikanum* (Düsseldorf, 1982) • E. AMELUNG, ed., *Strukturwandel der Frömmigkeit* (Stuttgart, 1972) • G. BAADTE et al., eds., *Neue Religiosität und säkulare Kultur* (Graz, 1988) • U. BECK, *Risk Society: Towards a New Morality* (London, 1992) • P. L. BERGER et al., *The Homeless Mind: Modernization and Consciousness* (New York, 1973) • K.-F. DAIBER, *Volkskirche im Wandel* (Stuttgart, 1973) • E. FAHLBUSCH, "Abschied von der Konfessionskunde. Überlegungen zu einer Phänomenologie der universalen Christenheit," *Evangelisch und Ökumenisch* (ed. G. Maron; Göttingen, 1986) 456-93; idem, *Einheit der Kirche–eine kritische Betrachtung des ökumenischen Dialogs* (Munich, 1983) • C. GEFFRÉ, ed., *Théologie et choc des cultures* (Paris, 1984) • E. GELDBACH, *Ökumene in Gegensätzen* (Göttingen, 1987) • J. HABERMAS, "Das neue Unübersichtlichkeit," *Kleine politische Schriften* (vol. 5; Frankfurt, 1985) 30-56 • H. J. HÖHN, *Kirche und kommunikatives Handeln. Studien zur Theologie und Praxis der Kirche in der Auseinandersetzung mit den Sozialtheorien N. Luhmanns und J. Habermas'* (Frankfurt, 1985) • L. KARRER, *Aufbruch der Christen* (Munich, 1989) • F. X. KAUFMANN et al., eds., *Religion, Kirche und Gesellschaft in Deutschland* (= *Gegenwartskunde* 37 [1988]) • P. KOSLOWSKI, *Die postmoderne Kultur. Gesellschaftlich-kulturelle Konsequenzen der technologische Entwicklung* (Munich, 1987; 2d ed., 1988) • T. KUHN, *The Structure of Scientific Revolutions* (2d ed.; Chicago, 1970) • H. KÜNG and D. TRACY, eds., *Paradigm Change in Theology: A Symposium for the Future* (New York, 1989) • P. LENGSFELD, ed., *Ökumenische Theologie* (Stuttgart, 1980) bibliography • H. LÜBBE, *Religion nach der Aufklärung* (Graz, 1986) • N. LUHMANN, *Funktion der Religion* (Frankfurt, 1977) • D. MEADOWS et al., *Die Grenzen des Wachstums* (Stuttgart, 1972) • K. RAHNER, *Strukturwandel der Kirche als Aufgabe und Chance* (Freiburg, 1972) • K. RAISER, *Ökumene im Übergang* (Munich, 1989) • D. RITSCHL, *The Logic of Theology* (Phladelphia, 1987) • M. WELKER, *Kirche ohne Kurs?* (Neukirchen, 1987).

ERWIN FAHLBUSCH

Church and State

1. Legal Aspects

From the standpoint of modern constitutional states, the problem of church and state is part of the broader problem of organized → religion and the state. For historical reasons, the issue is normally discussed as that of "church and state." The problem arises only where, at least conceptually, a distinction may be made between political government and the religious order and thus between political and religious organization. The Christian church first made possible a "duality of orders," for "as a religiously exclusive, eschatological entity subject finally only to its Lord" (P. Mikat), it necessarily contradicted the single order of the → Roman Empire, which in the tradition of antiquity combined political and religious elements. Since then, the relationship of church and state — closer at some times and more distant at others — has been a basic theme in Western history. Cultures that are controlled by religion but that do not raise up → hierarchies (and hence religious organizations clearly differentiated from the political) do not experience the problem (e.g., → Islam). We may rightly say, then, that "the relation of church and state in the sense of a confrontation of the secular order and legally independent religious societies is unique to the Christian West" (A. von Campenhausen).

1.1. Historical Development

Primitive Christianity and the Christian community of the first centuries (→ Primitive Christian Community) respected the state of antiquity as an order that God had ordained (e.g., see Romans 13 and Mark 12:17, "Render unto Caesar . . .") but opposed the pagan state religions and refused to participate in → emperor worship. The bloody → persecutions that resulted (→ Martyrs) did not arrest the spread of Christianity. In A.D. 313 the edicts of Constantine (306-37; → Donation of Constantine) and Licinius (308-24) gave Christianity equal status with the traditional pagan state religions (Edict of Milan). Two generations later, in 380, Theodosius I (379-95) made Christianity the sole state religion.

The result in the Eastern empire — where it was justified as a "symphony" of church and state — was a close relation between the secular and the spiritual kingdoms under the rule of the emperor. This traditional relation persisted in the → Byzantine Empire up to its collapse, and also in Russia up to the end of the czars in the 20th century (→ Orthodox Church; Orthodoxy 3).

In the West, however, a similar linking of secular and spiritual → authority in the person of the ruler never established itself. In theory, the church clung consistently to its autonomy. Pope Gelasius I (492-96) gave classic formulation to the two-swords theory. The world is ruled by two independent forces — the church (represented by the → pope; → Empire and Papacy) and the king or emperor.

In practice, neither power could remain independent. The alliance of the Franks and the papacy (→ Pope, Papacy), expressed through the donation of Pepin in 754 and the coronation of Charlemagne in 800 (→ Middle Ages 2), made the two authorities dependent on one another and led to the establishing of territorial churches (→ Proprietary Church), the granting to overlords of various rights over the churches, and the giving of secular powers to bishops and abbots appointed by rulers.

In contrast, the movement of church reform from the 10th century to the 12th, involving in particular → Gregory VII, → Bernard of Clairvaux, and → Thomas Aquinas (→ Middle Ages 1; Thomism), postulated a basic distinction between the powers. It nevertheless held to the primacy of the pope even in the secular realm, thereby placing the spiritual kingdom above the secular. On this view, God gave both swords to the church. "The pope himself wields the spiritual sword, and the princes wield the secular sword on behalf of the church and at the direction of the pope" (Campenhausen). In the → Investiture Controversy (Canossa [1077], Concordat of Worms [1122]) and in developments of the 12th and 13th centuries, the church managed to make good this claim. Boniface VIII (1294-1303) stated it again in the bull *Unam sanctam* in 1302. A short time later, however, papal supremacy suddenly collapsed, and the power of the church fell into decay.

Untouched by these historical changes, the idea remained that Christendom is a *res publica Christiana*, with church and state as the *ecclesia universalis et politica*, two powers within the one spiritual and secular entity. The two orders in concert bear responsibility for maintaining the unity of the faith. Even the → Reformation brought no essential change. With his → two-kingdoms doctrine, M. → Luther (1483-1546; → Luther's Theology) offered a starting point for a secular validation (not defined spiritually) of the secular order, much more strongly than did J. → Calvin (1509-64; → Calvin's Theology). Calvin held to a more theocratic theory of the state, in essence remaining true to the medieval concept of the *corpus Christianum*. Luther, however, also gave Christian rulers a religious role, making them responsible for upholding the unity of the faith. In keeping with this position, the Peace of Augsburg (1555; → Augsburg, Peace of) and then the Peace of Westphalia (1648; → Thirty Years' War) legally recognized two, and later three, main confessions linked to specific territories. The idea of two imperial partners in religion thus persisted, and with them the medieval notion of the *unum corpus Christianum* (K. Hesse).

Fundamental changes came only with the → Enlightenment in the second half of the 18th century as → human and civil rights were established, especially → religious liberty, and as states were set up that were secular and neutral with respect to denominations and then to religion in general. These developments as we now find them in all democratic constitutional states, even where remnants of state churches survive, have resulted in a separation of spiritual and secular government and the dissolution of the *corpus Christianum* (→ secularization).

1.2. Present Situation

In spite of parallels in historical development, there are differences between one constitutional state and another regarding church and state relations, though in fact they are relatively small. For all the deviations, the Western democracies show "clear approximations to a type of order in which individual and corporate religious freedom is secured and church and state work loyally together in areas in which their tasks touch on one another or overlap" (Hesse). We may differentiate four legal models.

1.2.1. Hostile Separation

The model of hostile separation seeks to banish religion and the church from public life. This model, in different degrees of intensity, was featured in the states of eastern and southern Europe when they were under Communist control, most notably in Albania, where, between 1967 and 1990, religion was proscribed altogether. Now, however, this model has disappeared from the scene.

The legislation in these states is now coming closer to the Western model, as we see, for example, in the laws in Hungary enacted in January 1990 relating to the church and to the freedom of conscience and religion, or in the law of the Supreme Soviet that set up religious freedom in the former USSR in October 1990, or in the Russian law of November 1990 pertaining to religion. The last two examples, in distinction from the laws in other eastern European nations (e.g., Hungary), indicate a clear separation of church and state. The new Polish constitution of

1997 now regulates the relation between church and state in a similar fashion. Since 1990, especially in Russia, reactionary trends have appeared that tend strongly to restore the monopoly of the Orthodox Church. In 1997 President Yeltsin, after various marginal corrections, signed a more restrictive religious law that had been first passed by the Duma in 1993 (and in 1997 in slightly altered form) favoring the Orthodox Church. In Poland a concordat with the Vatican was proposed in 1993 that was broadly accommodating to the Roman Catholic Church, particularly in → marriage laws. Only at the beginning of 1998 did the Polish Seym finally approve this concordat as proposed.

1.2.2. *Separation*

In the West the United States and France (apart from Alsace-Lorraine) illustrate models of separation of church and state, each coming from a different historical root. The system in France rests on anticlerical laws of separation in 1905, whereas the forbidding of any establishment of religion in the First Amendment (1791) of the U.S. Constitution is not in any way hostile to religion. Indeed, it safeguards its free exercise. In the interests of the neutrality of the state regarding religion, there is to be no state religion or financial support for religious societies. But religions and churches enjoy full freedom of development. They also play a part in → civil religion, and state ceremonial has a religious tinge.

For all its different roots, separation has followed a similar course in France. Here again religions and churches have no institutional support from the state. But cooperation is not ruled out in specific matters, and the churches have full freedom in public life as well as the narrower religious sphere.

1.2.3. *Establishment*

The older establishment model, though with variations, persists in Protestant northern Europe. The → Anglican church is the established church in Great Britain, as is the → Lutheran Church in Sweden, Norway, Finland, Denmark, and Iceland. But the religious freedom of minorities of other beliefs is not affected. In Britain, Parliament and the Privy Council still have some authority in matters of church order and doctrine, but the state gives no financial support, and it receives guidance either informally or formally through the church's synod. In spite of many attempts at reform and much criticism even from within the churches, no radical changes have thus far been made in any of these countries, nor is significant change likely in the foreseeable future. Sweden is an exception, however, for there a committee on church and state relations in 1994 proposed a constitutional change aimed at far-reaching separation, though for

constitutional reasons no action can be expected before 1998.

In Italy and Spain, relations between church and state are regulated by the → concordats of 1984 and 1976/1979, respectively, which essentially overturned existing structures. Here we now have approaches that represent a fourth, or intermediate, model of separation, such as appears also in Germany, Austria, some of the Swiss cantons, and Alsace-Lorraine.

1.2.4. *Intermediate Separation*

West Germany set up a system of religious liberty and of self-determination for the churches, within legal limits. Churches and religious societies are corporations of public law if this has been their prior status, and others have similar rights if they meet certain conditions. The status gives the clergy and church officials the right to take part in rendering public services and to raise taxes on the basis of civil tax lists. The church and religion still maintain a public presence in state institutions, and religious instruction is given in public schools. Similarly, religion has a place in the armed forces, hospitals, and prisons. The role of theological faculties in colleges is also guaranteed by the constitutions of some of the individual states. The system has been called one of "limping separation" (U. Stutz) or "balanced separation" (E.-W. Böckenförde). Following reunification, it was expanded without qualification to include the area of the former East Germany.

Scotland, too, has a balanced structure by an act passed in 1921 that secures for the national church full freedom "within the sphere of spiritual government and jurisdiction" and "doctrinal statement," while acknowledging "the divine appointment and authority of the civil magistrate within its own sphere."

1.3. *Basic Positions*

The → Codex Iuris Canonici of 1983 contains the decisive Roman Catholic statements regarding the relation of the church to the state. Like → Vatican II with its recognition of religious liberty, the CIC retains finally the concept of church and state as two sovereign entities *(societates perfectae)*. Christ has established the church free and independent of all secular authority and given it all the rights it needs to discharge its task. Only the church itself in its sovereignty can say what these rights are, but "it knows that in many cases its claims run up against limits set by the laws of state" (Mikat; → Jurisdiction, Ecclesiastical).

Under the influence of the two-kingdoms doctrine of Luther, Protestants recognize the responsibility of the state in the secular sphere and with it the "dynamic global responsibility of the Christian"

(Mikat). Reformed theology and → dialectical theology (K. → Barth) have stressed the lordship of Christ, and the later 20th century has seen a growing tendency to draw from the claims of the → gospel directions for specific actions in the political sphere. Along with traditional Roman Catholic conceptions of the church and some misunderstandings of the two-kingdoms doctrine has arisen the danger of a new clericalism (→ Political Theology). Respect for the order of state is not linked to any specific form. In spite of some traditional Lutheran objections, → democracy has received unanimous recognition (e.g., by the Evangelical Church in Germany [EKD]).

Orthodox churches speak of a "symphony" theology, which supports a close connection with the state, which was true even in former Communist countries, especially the → Soviet Union. There the church, even though separate, was in many areas an instrument of state policy. Changes have come with the end of Communism, although the ultimate outcome is impossible to foresee.

In distinction from Christian churches, which in different ways all see a separation in principle, Islam posits a unified Islamic society. In such a society, the state itself (not some distinct religious organization) has the responsibility of upholding Islamic law (→ Islam 4). On this ground we can understand the hostility of Islam to democratic constitutional states, such as in an Islamic country like Turkey, and the present-day trend toward Islamic fundamentalism in lands like Iran and Algeria.

→ Canon Law; Church; Church Law; Church Membership; Church Orders; Church in a Socialist Society; Church Struggle; Cuius regio eius religio; Islam and Christianity; Modern Period; Papal States; Pluralism; Politics; State; Theocracy; Toleration; Zwingli's Theology

Bibliography: General: K. HESSE and H. E. J. KALINNA, "Kirche und Staat," EStL 1.1546-85 (full bibliography) • P. MIKAT, C. LINK, A. HOLLERBACH, and P. LEISCHING, "Kirche und Staat," StL 3.467-511 • J. F. WILSON, ed., Church and State in America: A Bibliographical Guide (2 vols.; New York, 1986).

On 1.1: H. E. FEINE, Kirchliche Rechtsgeschichte (5th ed.; Cologne, 1972) • W. P. FUCHS, ed., Staat und Kirche im Wandel der Jahrhunderte (Stuttgart, 1966).

On 1.2: A. VON CAMPENHAUSEN, Staatskirchenrecht (3d ed.; Munich, 1996) 385-426 • "Developments in the Law: Religion and the State," HLR 100/7 (1987) 1606-1781 • J.-D. KÜHNE, "Wandlungen des Staatskirchenrechts im ehemaligen Ostblock," Recht in Ost und West 35 (1991): 135-40 • O. LUCHTERHANDT, "Neuere Entwicklungen der Religionsgesetzgebung in Osteuropa," ZEvKR 35 (1990) 283-318 • S. V. MONSMA and J. C. SOPER, The Challenge of Pluralism: Church and State in Five Democracies (Lanham, Md., 1997) on Australia, England, Germany, the Netherlands, and the United States • J. E. NOWAK, R. D. ROTUNDA, and J. N. YOUNG, Constitutional Law (4th ed.; St. Paul, 1991) 1157ff. • R. WEILER, "Zur Entwicklung der Beziehung von Kirche und Staat in Europa nach dem Zusammenbruch des Kommunismus," Für Staat und Recht (Berlin, 1994).

On 1.3: W. ENDE and U. STEINBACH, eds., Der Islam in der Gegenwart. Entwicklung und Ausbreitung, Politik und Recht, Kultur und Religion (2d ed.; Munich, 1989) esp. 155-467 • G. GÖBEL, Das Verhältnis von Kirche und Staat nach dem Codex Iuris Canonici des Jahres 1983 (Berlin, 1993) • E. HAMMERSCHMIDT, reports on the Orthodox churches, e.g., in IKZ 83 (1993) 65-100 • J. LISTL, Die Aussagen des CIC von 25. Januar 1983 zum Verhältnis von Kirche und Staat (Münster, 1985) 9-37 • Die Neuordnung des Verhältnisses von Staat und Kirche in Mitteleuropa (Münster, 1995) • T. ROBBINS and R. ROBERTSON, eds., Church-State Relations: Tensions and Transitions (New Brunswick, N.J., 1987) • H. SIMON, "Das Verhältnis von Kirche und Staat nach der Lehre der evangelischen Kirche," Handbuch des Staatskirchenrechts der BRD (vol. 1; Berlin, 1974) 189-212.

HERMANN WEBER

2. Theological Aspects

2.1. The Problem

Theologically, the problem of the relation between church and state is part of the wider problem of the relation between the church and the secular order, or the public domain. Often the theme has been discussed solely as that of the confrontation of church and state because the secular order is equated with the state and because the state is seen as standing in for → society in general. In some countries, too, it is the state that has taken the church under its protection and exercised special supervision over it. Thus theology has dealt with the issue in this narrower context, as may be seen in the interpretation of the → two-kingdoms doctrine of M. → Luther (1483-1546; → Luther's Theology) or the Reformed doctrine of the sovereignty of Christ.

In distinction, we need today to put the theme in the broader context of the relation of the church to secular orders and to the forms of such orders. From this angle the state is only one of many social → institutions. Protestant understanding has typically oriented itself to the main topic of → freedom. We must ask what the consequences are of constitutionally guaranteed freedom, and also what the global

→ responsibility of Christians is as a result of their freedom. From the standpoint of the state, a basic matter is recognition of → religious liberty and therefore of neutrality in religious affairs. From that of the church, the responsible political cooperation of individual Christians and the public duty of the church are of fundamental importance. Theologically, the relation of church and state is one that can be affirmed when there is religious freedom for all and when the independence of churches and religious societies and their public activity are guaranteed.

For many years discussion was on the level of particular states and national churches. But this focus was in keeping neither with the church's understanding of itself as a fellowship that transcends national boundaries nor with increasing state interdependence. Hence revision is called for along ecumenical lines that will transcend any Eurocentric view. Even the multireligious European states must now take into greater account the position of non-Christian religious groups (→ Theology of Religions).

2.2. Biblical Basis

Theological reflection on the issue must begin with the central biblical texts. Less attention is usually paid to the OT, though the → Torah as comprehensive instruction deals with the relation to secular institutions, and the → prophetic (§2) tradition demands criticism of the effects of political → power.

Four NT texts are most commonly cited: the saying of Jesus about the tribute money (Mark 12:17 and par.), Paul's call for → obedience to the secular powers (Rom. 13:1-7), Peter's statement that we must obey God rather than any human authority (Acts 5:29), and the depiction in Revelation of the demonic state as the beast from the abyss (Rev. 13:1-8; → Apocalypticism; Demons). These texts come from different situations and in their intentions carry different accents. They support neither an unconditional obedience of individuals to the state nor the church's unrestricted loyalty to it.

The passages set the church's relation to the state in a twofold light. They affirm the state, not for its own sake, but for that of its task. Hence the state loses its legitimacy if it abandons its specific task and raises a totalitarian claim to the obedience of citizens (→ Bourgeois, Bourgeoisie). The Christian relation to the state is thus one of critical loyalty that may in some cases involve disobedience and → resistance.

This basic thrust of a Christian political → ethics (→ Social Ethics; Politics 3) is critical for the relation between church and state. Under the conditions of the Constantinian alliance of church and state (→ Donation of Constantine; Early Church), however, it has often been pushed into the background. Various

movements did criticize the Constantinian order, as may be seen in Petr Chelčický (ca. 1390-ca. 1460) and the → Bohemian Brethren who were his followers, or in the → peace churches. Only in the 20th century, however, have the mainline churches begun to adopt this concept of critical loyalty.

2.3. Roman Catholic Church

The Roman Catholic → teaching office (§1) developed a full concept of the relation between church and state. Under the sign of neo-Thomism (→ Neoscholasticism), → Leo XIII (1878-1903) proposed a comprehensive understanding of the relation. His thesis was that God has entrusted the care of the human race to both institutions. Their different goals define the boundaries between them. The one cares for secular welfare, the other for divine → salvation. We have in this concept of two *societates perfectae* a continuation of a classic line that goes back by way of R. → Bellarmine (1542-1621) and → Thomas Aquinas (1224/25-74; → Thomism) to the two-swords teaching of Pope Gelasius (492-96) and the two-cities teaching of → Augustine (354-430; → Augustine's Theology).

Experiences with 20th-century → totalitarianism, the opening up to → pluralist and → democratic constitutional states, and movements of theological renewal in → Roman Catholicism have resulted in modifications of Roman Catholic teaching on the church-and-state relation. The conception of Leo XIII has not been explicitly abandoned, but it has been profoundly modified. These changes have involved the recognition of freedom of religion and secular autonomy and the insight that cultural, social, and political factors, which demand theological study, affect the relation between church and state in different parts of the globe (→ Roman Catholic Church 4). Against this background a readiness for service in the world has gained in importance as compared with a rigid distinction between institutional spheres of influence. The theologies of → liberation have promoted this → contextual investigation in the era after → Vatican II, although the utterances of the teaching office have shown a tendency toward retardation.

2.4. Greek and Russian Orthodoxy

In the traditions of Greek and Russian → Orthodoxy (§3), the Byzantine origins have left a relatively lesser role for the autonomous church in its relations with the state. The concept of the "symphony" of the secular and spiritual powers is still normative. In the face of the danger of the secularization of the church, the stress falls on its spiritual character. Balance is sought between the vertical relation to God and the horizontal relation to others.

2.5. *Reformation Churches*

The Reformation churches never achieved a unified doctrine of the relation to the state, but the distinction between God's spiritual and secular government was a basic insight to which they always appealed (→ Reformation 1.3 and 3). Luther never worked out the distinction comprehensively but made use of it in various contexts when specific counsel was needed. He laid just as much emphasis on the distinction as on the connection between God's modes of government. The secular arm indeed must use → force to check the results of → sin, but its actions still come under the commandment of → love. Luther's view does not enable us to arrive at any general conception of how the Christian state should be run under the direction of the church. Indeed, he brought against any attempts in this direction the accusation (not always justified) of fanaticism and legalism (→ Two Kingdoms Doctrine).

U. → Zwingli (1484-1531; → Zwingli's Theology) and J. → Calvin agreed with Luther in differentiating the two realms but added a new emphasis. Warning against the danger of making peace with false gods, they stressed Christ's presence outside the sphere in which the → gospel is preached and hence his rule even in the political sphere.

American developments show that this concept can go hand in hand with a large-scale separation of church and state. In the spirit of the Christian → Enlightenment, the United States forged a system of mutual autonomy and respect in which recognition of religious freedom still leaves the churches room for independent and public activity.

With the development of modern secular states (→ Modern Period; Secularization) in Europe, the Lutheran and Reformed positions became more sharply opposed for a time than they were during the Reformation period. The two-kingdoms teaching gave neo-Lutheranism (→ Lutheranism) a view that at times included the autonomy of the political. Countering this conclusion, the Reformed emphasized Christ's sovereignty, from which no sphere of life is exempt.

We might argue that the Barmen Declaration of 1934 (→ Church Struggle; Confessing Church) overcame this rift in principle, even while it is sometimes set forth more sharply. Thesis 2 expressly affirms the insight that in every sphere of life Christians are under both the gracious promise and the claim of Jesus Christ, and it rejects the idea of the autonomy of the political.

Against this background, thesis 5 recognizes the inalienable significance of the distinction between the two realms. The state derives its dignity from its divine institution that imposes on it the duty of ensuring law and → peace. Discharging this duty necessarily involves the threat and the use of force. In place of an autonomous order of state, this view defines the state functionally. The church, in turn, must remind us "of God's kingdom, God's commandment, and righteousness, and thereby the responsibility of rulers and ruled." It thus envisions a distinction and relation between church and state that K. → Barth (1886-1968; → Dialectical Theology) depicted in the pregnant image of two concentric circles (a figure not wholly free of problems).

On this basis the declaration rejected both state totalitarianism and the church's usurping of the state's duties. This drawing of the boundaries is of lasting significance. Further work is needed, however, in light of changed conditions. The relation of church and state to social situations common to both of them, the place of the church in a pluralist democracy, and the material significance of law and → peace as determinative tasks for the state all stand in need of more precise definition. Theological scholarship and ecclesiastical evaluation alike must address this matter.

2.6. *Ecumenical Movement*

From the first, the relation between church and state has been a basic theme of the → ecumenical movement. It was treated especially at the Life and Work conferences at Stockholm in 1925 and Oxford in 1937, which set the global fellowship of Christians above national loyalty. The First Assembly of the → World Council of Churches, at Amsterdam in 1948, formulated the concept of the "responsible society" as an agreed formula for the churches' political responsibility. Global changes resulting from the end of → colonialism threw doubt on the formula, as the World Conference on Church and Society (Geneva 1966) showed in its discussions of a → theology of revolution.

Later ecumenical approaches have focused less on the distinction between the church and the national state and more on the responsibility of Christians within the one humanity, contending for a "just, participatory, and sustainable society" (beginning in 1975) and for "justice, peace, and the integrity of creation" (from 1983). New changes with the collapse of Communist regimes (→ Socialism) in the late 1980s have forced the ecumenical movement to deal in a new way with the problems of state organization and identity. A key theme in ecumenical responsibility that has now come to the fore is that of the universal validity of elementary human rights.

→ Church; State; State Ethics; Theology in the Nineteenth and Twentieth Centuries

Bibliography: H. Abromeit and G. Wewer, eds., *Die Kirchen und die Politik* (Opladen, 1989) • J. C. Bennett, *Christians and the State* (New York, 1958) • E.-W. Böckenförde, *Kirchlicher Auftrag und politisches Handeln. Analysen und Orientierungen* (Freiburg, 1989) • A. Burgsmüller, ed., *Zum politischen Auftrag der christlichen Gemeinde (Barmen II)* (Gütersloh, 1974) • U. Duchrow, *Christenheit und Weltverantwortung. Traditionsgeschichte und systematische Struktur der Zwei-Reiche-Lehre* (Stuttgart, 1970; 2d ed., 1983); idem, ed., *Zwei Reiche und Regimente. Ideologie oder evangelische Orientierung? Internationale Fall- und Hintergrundstudien zur Theologie und Praxis lutherischer Kirche im 20. Jahrhundert* (Gütersloh, 1977) • W. J. Everett, *Gottes Bund und menschliche Öffentlichkeit* (Munich, 1991) • H. Falcke, *Die unvollendete Befreiung. Die Kirchen, die Umwälzung in der DDR und die Vereinigung Deutschlands* (Munich, 1991) • R. B. Fowler, *Religion and Politics in America* (London, 1985) • T. Friebel, *Kirche und politische Verantwortung in der sowjetischen Zone und der DDR, 1945-1969* (Gütersloh, 1992) • T. Gauly, *Kirche und Politik in der BRD, 1945-1976* (Bonn, 1990) • G. Göbel, *Das Verhältnis von Kirche und Staat nach dem Codex Iuris Canonici des Jahres 1983* (Berlin, 1993) • A. D. Hertzke, *Representing God in Washington: The Role of Religious Lobbies in the American Polity* (Knoxville, Tenn., 1988) • W. Huber, *Folgen christlicher Freiheit. Ethik und Theorie der Kirche im Horizont der Barmer Theologischen Erklärung* (Neukirchen, 1983); idem, *Kirche und Öffentlichkeit* (Stuttgart, 1973; 2d ed., Munich, 1991) • W. Joest, *Der Friede Gottes und der Friede auf Erden* (Neukirchen, 1990) • E. Jüngel, *Mit Frieden Staat zu machen. Politische Existenz nach Barmen V* (Munich, 1984) • P. I. Kaufman, *Redeeming Politics* (Princeton, 1990) • C. Lienemann-Perrin, *Die politische Verantwortung der Kirchen in Südkorea und Südafrika. Studien zur ökumenischen politischen Ethik* (Munich, 1992) • H. Maier, M. Honeker, and J. Isensee, *Die Verantwortung der Kirche für den Staat* (Münster, 1991) • E. Mechels, *Kirche und gesellschaftliche Umwelt. Thomas–Luther–Barth* (Neukirchen, 1990) • R. Niebuhr, *Christian Realism and Political Problems* (New York, 1953) • T. Rendtorff, ed., *Charisma und Institution* (Gütersloh, 1985) • W. Schrage, *Die Christen und der Staat nach dem Neuen Testament* (Gütersloh, 1971) • C. Stückelberger, *Vermittlung und Parteinahme. Der Versöhnungsauftrag der Kirchen in gesellschaftlichen Konflikten* (Zurich, 1988) • J. F. Wilson, *Church and State in America: A Bibliographical Guide* (2 vols.; New York, 1986-87) • World Council of Churches, *Church and State–Opening a New Ecumenical Discussion* (Geneva, 1978).

Wolfgang Huber

Church Architecture

1. Term
2. Beginnings and Development in Late Antiquity
3. Middle Ages in the West
4. Renaissance, Reformation, Mannerism, Baroque
5. Modern Times

1. Term

To speak theologically and architectonically about church architecture is to reflect on all the places in which Christians meet in the name of → Jesus for cultic services and → catechesis, table fellowship and the exchange of gifts and ministries. These include not only parish churches and centers but also churches associated with baptisteries, houses, castles, cemeteries, and pilgrimage sites; → cathedrals; → crypts; and → chapels in villages, castles, high-rises, colleges, universities, and retreat centers, as well as at crossroads and along hiking paths, in airports, and at exhibitions; also temporary meetings places such as living rooms, exhibition halls, stadiums, and public squares. Furthermore, the following selected examples frequently constitute merely parts of larger central sites (early Christian house churches, → monasteries, etc.), often causing us to forget that Christians basically have sought to assemble in every possible spatial context, including domiciles (unconsecrated private houses, niches, → catacombs, etc.), halls (usually conceived as such from the perspective of the history of art), and the court (worship services in public squares, though also arcades and church spaces exhibiting the character of an agora).

Extant buildings are fragments of comprehensive life processes; as such, they are generally of at least as much informational value as the theological literature of a period; they usually predate the expression of contemporary theological systems in the same way as art does. Church architecture conditions the situations of worship and, as a nonliterary but complex text with a rich → hermeneutical claim, crystallizes many of the media of a period. It reveals many dimensions that, as we learn from other sources, illuminate the interplay of functions (→ Liturgy; Diakonia). The relation between → religion and contemporary → culture at large, however, is brought out less by depicting idealized high points of the various styles (Romanesque, Gothic, etc.) than by taking note of the changes and cultural interactions, innovations and reform, whose witnesses are more difficult to grasp precisely because they have frequently been destroyed.

2. Beginnings and Development in Late Antiquity

The first Christians met in the → temple (→ Jerusalem) and → synagogue, and → Paul preached on the Areopagus, but the chief model was that of the meal that Jesus had with his disciples in a private house (Matt. 26:20-46; Acts 2:42; → Eucharist 2). Christians themselves, not the place they meet in, are called by Paul the temple of God, of which Christ is the foundation (1 Cor. 3:11-15). The goal is the *oikodomē* (→ Edification) of the fellowship as a model of → love for all people (14:26). Hence in the initial centuries of the Christian era, rooms and residences were at first used for meeting on a temporary basis. Wealthier believers then gave these over to the assembly ("title churches"), which in → Rome were named after the patron. → Baptisms, too, which were not celebrated every Sunday, represented high points. The rooms were arranged as needed, commensurate with their use for celebratory meals and baptisms.

Evidence of the development from a temporary meeting place to a church center exists in the so-called house of Christians at Dura-Europos on the Middle Euphrates (ca. A.D. 230). Arranged around an atrium in the usual style, the rooms were used as well as the atrium itself. This house church included a large room, formed by the removal of a partition, and a smaller baptismal room with a ritual bath under a ciborium, with paintings from the OT and NT in the latter. In the house church found in Qirk Bizzeh in Syria (early 4th cent.), a large room has a bema, or platform for the holy table, in the middle. The double church at Aquileia (also early 4th cent.) has a center with three larger rooms, one with supporting pillars to give three naves. The rooms, which also served as dwellings, were used for the Eucharist, baptism, and catechesis. When Christianity gained recognition in the Roman Empire, basilicas, baptisteries, and memorial churches were built.

Typical features of the basilica, which had models both in the covered forum and in the imperial and private basilicas, included the impression of freedom given by the raftered ceiling (later by the coffered ceiling), as compared with Roman vaulted architecture; a certain lightness of construction; the perspective of horizontal movement achieved by the rows of pillars; and, above all, a formative will oriented exclusively from the perspective of the interior. The almost equally large atrium (narthex with fountains) and the liturgical center in the middle of the nave; the place for singers, itself encompassed by the congregation and with a separating lattice screen (*cancelli*; → Pulpit); and ambos for Bible readings all give

evidence that the → "sanctification" of the community was still the point of departure for the design. At the narrower side of the transept was the Communion table, and behind this in the semicircle of the apse were seats for the presbyters (→ Elder) and leaders. The basilica, originally viewed as provisional, was vital, with functional changes, to the development of church architecture in the West.

Symmetrically focused edifices, attested in all the forms that can be superimposed onto a circle (symmetrical cross, square, various other polygons), generate through their lack of any linearly oriented perspective a spatial experience of rest, on the one hand, but also of universal priesthood, on the other *(circumstantes)*. Used as churches for baptisms, burials, and commemorations (e.g., S. Stefano Rotondo in Rome), the central room, with a cupola over each crossarm and in the center, became the main form of church architecture in the → Orthodox Church.

The combination of length and centrality, as in fourth-century St. Gereon in Cologne and sixth-century Hagia Sophia in Constantinople, sought to harmonize movement and rest. Around the entire Mediterranean basin many types developed in combination. For churches in the East the cross cupola church (in the shape of a Greek → cross) was typical.

We can view the development of Orthodox churches as an attempt to integrate the Byzantine liturgy and its architectural models into various cultural contexts. The → iconostasis does not separate as sharply as the rood screen does in the West, for the doors and → icons of the former are part of the common liturgy. An Orthodox church as a whole symbolizes the eternal divine view of the world, so that between → paradise to the east and the → last judgment to the west, the center of the church offers an open stage for the cultic action that the iconostasis expresses theologically. The symbolizing of the liturgical mystery is at the center. As a rule, the western side of the church approximates more closely the main basilica. This style influenced the West, just as later the Western Renaissance left traces in Russian church architecture.

3. Middle Ages in the West

Little remains of the wooden churches of the second half of the first millennium, though a few survive in England. From the beginning of the second millennium, stave churches appeared in Norway. Not following Continental patterns, these churches reflected the influence of the old Norwegian royal hall. The Carolingian renaissance established the stone edifice, setting a standard with the imperial palace in Aachen.

More uniformly, strongly, and monumentally than the forerunner St. Vitale in Ravenna, a conscious attempt was made to copy late antiquity, with far-reaching consequences.

At the time of Byzantine iconoclasm (→ Images 3.2), the interiors of the buildings were richly painted. With the growth of a more material view of the Eucharist, the central edifice expanded into a larger chancel (e.g., the arcade and radiating chapels of St. Martin in Tours); the western portion was expanded, and commensurate with the increasing significance of the emperor, so was the west chancel. Again in accordance with the tradition of the basilica schema, the intersection of transept and nave produced the square shape characterizing the entire Middle Ages (§1). This square shape, strengthened by vaulting, offered a new feeling of statuary and material space. The Romanesque style (ca. 1000-1300), which developed in Germany, northern France, and England, reached a climax in its alternating support structures (pillars and columns), in what is known as the bound system (two smaller squares in the aisle corresponding to the square in the main nave), in the cross (groined) vaulting, and in the emphasized nave intersection (central tower). The so-called imperial cathedrals at Mainz, Worms, and Speyer, with a double apse (representing two powers) and doubled transept-nave intersections, acquired thus six towers, symbols of the tension between spiritual and temporal orders. For the first time, the exterior structure was also differentiated (pilaster strips, galleries); inside, the increasing play of light and shadow as well as emergent lofts and galleries *(triforium)*, enhanced by painting and sculptures, rivaled the splendor of sixth-century Ravenna. This was the age of early → Scholasticism and of the → Crusades, the latter affecting imperial, → monastic and courtly (knighthood) circles. Early reform movements (→ Cluny, Order of) oriented themselves to the fourth-century basilica (Cluny II [981]) but also demonstrated increasing → hierarchical power (Cluny III [1089], by the middle of the 12th century, had five naves, two transepts, many chapels, and eight towers). More radical reforming movements (→ Cistercians) simply tried to retain what was essential for a liturgical gathering, with no adornment except a belfry.

Gothic church architecture originated in the Ile-de-France in approximately 1140. It used buttresses, thus opening up the walls for windows. Characteristic features include a conception of the entire interior space as a unity rather than as a sum of individual rooms; an enhancement of vertical spatial elements (with the aid of cross-grained arches); an attempt to render the material world transparent (through the integration of richly segmented architectural elements, diaphanous towers, glass walls, and rose windows); the open display of technical aids as well, such as external pillar buttresses and flying buttresses, as well as ornamental architectural elements such as finials, gables, and turrets. Interpretations of these structures as "Scholasticism in stone" or as a "copy of heaven" were subject to the general architectural conception, according to which (commensurate with → Augustine's view) the edifice itself was to render the divine model visible. As a nexus of elements distributed in units — rhythmically ordered, and composed of number, measure, and weight — the church reflects the bosom of nature itself, which harbors the pure relations or the pure structure that God is (Augustine *De lib. arb.* 2.16).

Gothic spread with regional variations to England, Germany, Spain, Scandinavia, and Italy. In England we find the perpendicular and Tudor style (ca. 1530-1600). Germany developed a distinctive brick Gothic with broadly conceived wall surfaces and enormous rooms, and also churches specifically designed for → preaching, with aisles of equal height and walls perceived as load-bearing elements. The roomy, agoralike church — in which there might be many masses simultaneously (→ Mass) and also, near a pillar in the main nave, a place where monks could preach — prepared the way positively for movements of reform and indeed the → Reformation.

4. Renaissance, Reformation, Mannerism, Baroque

The architecture of the → Renaissance, which originated in Florence and Mantua through the work of Leon Battista Alberti (1404-72), composed its spatial aspects from the perspective of the cube. Spaces reflecting sensuous presence and balanced beauty could seem large even when small, and visually accessible even when large, yet they still could force differentiated and mystical-individual liturgical activities into a comprehensible conception of unity. The enclosure of the intersection of transept and nave in the vaulted cupola, as well as the use of the Byzantine Greek cross, the scalloped cupola, and the half-dome over the cube itself, demonstrated the aesthetic ideal of an internally resting, practical harmony. Under the tensions that developed in the 16th century, the originally Platonic idealism (note Brunelleschi's cathedral cupola in the Santa Maria del Fiore in Florence [1421]) and the impulses of → humanism disintegrated between liturgical tenaciousness and renewal, between scientific research and irrational political decisions, between a formative will with artistically subjective inclinations, on the one hand, and international ones, on the other.

So-called Mannerism mixed the central and basilican forms, developing them with great fervor (e.g., St. Peter's, Rome) or used architecture as a rhetorical means of expression and laid the foundations of the age of the → baroque. The Gesù in Rome (1568-84) became the prototype of Roman Catholic church architecture, which now liked to subordinate the basilican congregational area to the pillar of light above the area around the → altar. The cupola vault became an attractive and later a decorated symbol of → heaven. The idea of a unified space in movement was developed by G. Bernini (1598-1680), Michelangelo (1475-1564), and F. Borromini (1599-1667); also by adopting pre-Christian elements from Central America, Borromini tried to evoke a sense of infinity in the body of the edifice by using flexion and curvature in vertical wall segments.

In Spain Manneristic architecture became the symbol of a theocratic, monarchical order from which, with exotic ornamentation, Roman architecture declared the supremacy of Rome over the American and Asian colonies. In France this type of church architecture was subject to the cool calculation and transparent rationality of secular power (note the Invalides, a cupola church patterned after St. Peter's). Baroque churches were only an interlude on the way to classicism.

In England the ornamental style of the Renaissance overlapped the traditionalism of lavish late Gothic. The fire of London (1666) resulted in fine buildings that were economical, bright, and rational; they appeared in various shapes: rectangular, multiangled, oval, or round. Usually these had fronts with classical pillars in a humanistic synthesis of reason and emotion. They served as models for many churches in New England and the colonies. Eventually they were supplemented by the places of prayer built by many → denominations. With St. Paul's of London (1675-1710), the most impressive example of Protestant church architecture in the world, the Church of England (→ Anglican Communion) demonstrated the union of → church and state in a way that both harked back to antiquity and set a worldwide standard.

Germany adopted the Renaissance only hesitantly (e.g., the Fugger burial chapel in Augsburg [1518]), but the ideas of the Reformation made a lasting impact. As we read in the *Reformatio ecclesiarum Hassiae* (1526), all believers were to attend public prayer and reading and were to partake diligently of the Lord's Supper. These exercises were now moved to the middle of the church so that all of both sexes could

both learn and sing together and glorify God's name, for all have become priests in Christ. As in the first century, presbyters and liturgists were to gather on one side and the congregation on the other around the altar, effectively canceling out the material sacral quality of the chancel of the Middle Ages. In the Castle Church at Stuttgart (1553) the → organ was put above the altar, the → baptismal font (cf. also Torgau [1544]) was put in the middle of the nave, and the celebrant was behind the altar. Even when elements were borrowed from the late Gothic structural schema, the centralizing function of the altar and font caused considerable change (Lauenburg [1508/1600], Wolfenbüttel [1608], Bückeburg [1615]) and led eventually to restructuring (Freudenstadt [1601/1608]). The introduction of seats led to a need for lofts and a repositioning of the pulpit.

The Reformed developed two traditions (→ Reformed and Presbyterian Churches; Church 3.5). Even more plainly than U. → Zwingli (1484-1531; → Zwingli's Theology), J. → Calvin (1509-64; → Calvin's Theology) desired a weekly Communion. Nevertheless, the appropriation of medieval buildings in the regions of the Netherlands and Switzerland led to a separation between the weekly preaching service on Sunday (in the nave) and the special celebrations of the Eucharist at the great tables in the chancel (Zurich: "seated communion"; Netherlands: coming forward in groups of twelve); cf. the Great Church at Emden (1455/1520). A second tradition established the custom of using the central area (Lyon [1564], La Rochelle [1577], Rouen [1601]; Double Church in Hanau [1622-54]; double cloverleaf church: New Church in The Hague [1649/1655]). Even the basilican form was conceived as a single space, the altar and pulpit being either in the middle or a bit to one side, though surrounded by pews that could be removed for Communion (Westerkerk in Amsterdam [1620-31], Huguenot Church in Charenton [1623], Wädenswil [1764]).

The great building activity following the → Thirty Years' War drew from the experiences of this time of upheaval (churches in the half-timbered style), though also from previous creative models (Nooderkerk in Amsterdam [1620-22]) and the new theories of J. Furttenbach (1591-1667) and L. C. Sturm (1669-1719). In particular, variations on the central area sought to bring more people close to the liturgical center. Devices included variations on the Greek cross (Schweidnitz [1657-58], Hirschberg [1709/1718]), the circle extended in the manner of a cross (G. Bähr [1666-1738]; e.g., the Frauenkirche in Dresden [1722]), though also the oval (Egidienkirche, Nürnberg [1711]), the cloverleaf (Parochial-kirche, Berlin [1695/1703]), five conches (Neue Kirche, Berlin [1708]), the triangle, square, centered rectangle, polygons, L-shape, or integrated naves (Grossenhain [1748]; the Jerusalem Church and Petrikirche, Berlin; St. Michael's, Hamburg [1751/1762]). An independent culture of half-timbered churches of high quality developed especially in Hesse. Like the larger churches, these primarily were meant to be family churches and could be closed during the week when family devotions were held. The same was true of the meeting places of the Herrnhut community (→ Moravian Church).

In Germany, the Roman Catholic baroque style was focused more strongly on its representative function; characteristic architects included Fischer von Erlach (1656-1723), J. L. von Hildebrandt (1668-1745), and K. I. Dientzenhofer (1689-1751). While the brothers C. D. (1686-1739) and E. Q. (1692-1750) Asam transformed this space into a *theatrum sacrum* in an illusive sense as well (St. Nepomuk, Munich), B. Neumann (1687-1753) tried to evoke a feeling of infinite being without illusive devices by employing the idea of spatial movement in round and oval forms (Wallfahrtskirche Vierzehnheiligen [1743-75]); the brothers D. (1685-1766) and J. B. (1680-1758) Zimmermann used color and light to create a sense of floating (Wallfahrtskirche, Wies [1746]).

5. Modern Times

Classical church architecture (→ Classicism) countered the playful culture of the rococo with elements of religious dignity by drawing on ideas from the temple architecture of antiquity. F. Weinbrenner (1766-1826) built both the Protestant and the Roman Catholic churches in Karlsruhe (1807 and 1808). K. F. Schinkel (1781-1814) reinforced this through the idea — representing a Protestant interpretation — of setting the pure central area in the axis of the Greek cross, "as opposed to the longitudinal Roman Catholic church" (as expressed in the plans for renovating the Berlin cathedral [1815]). The people are situated in the arena under the cupola, and the altar is in the middle, while the pulpit is quite justifiably envisioned as being in the upper and thus rear tiers. But this plan was not adopted, nor was the warning of G. Semper (1803-79) heeded that there should be adherence to the Reformation. Instead an epoch bent on restoration adopted Romanesque and Gothic styles, and later that of the Renaissance, seeking religious identification in forms without regard to content. In contrast to the eras imitated, the rooms were now filled with pews, and the central focus was now the middle section leading to the elevated altar.

A new sacred architecture developed that made dignity its goal. The so-called Eisenacher Regulativ of 1861 set the guidelines for territorial churches in Germany, in which this "dignity" became the measure drawn from the historically developed styles, "above all the Romanesque and Gothic"; at the same time, qualified art was proscribed (individual "artistic taste" and the free adaptation of Christian motifs). Inferior representatives of church architecture around the world propagated both this notion and the ponderous features of the Victorian style. Resistance arose with the so-called Wiesbaden Programme of 1891, which called for a fusion of the central and longitudinal forms (with a pulpit altar) in favor of the congregational concept (e.g., J. Otzen's Wiesbaden Ringkirche [1892-94]). An architectural congress at Dresden in 1906 demanded an opening up of church architecture to modern styles and art and an orientation to function, with the liturgy serving as architect (C. Gurlitt and P. Brathe).

New materials made renewal possible (Saint-Jean de Montmartre [1894-1901], with A. de Baudot [1834-1915] as architect), but a consistent reappraisal of function and form came only when the principles of liturgical reform joined forces with the modern movement in architecture, as in the Unitarian church of Oak Park, Illinois, by F. L. Wright (1867-1959), the design for a star-shaped church (1923) or the steel church at the Pressa Exhibition in Cologne in 1928 by O. Bartning (1883-1959), A. Perret (1874-1954) in Le Raincy near Paris (1923), D. Böhm (1880-1955) in Mainz-Bischofsheim and Neu-Elm (1926), T. Fischer (1862-1938) near Munich, R. Schwarz (1897-1961) in Aachen, and F. Metzger (1898-1973) in Lucerne. Though authentic modern church architecture began in Germany, the exile of significant architects spread their ideas abroad, for example, in the United States. From there, with the help of Bartning, Böhm, and Schwarz, they quickly took hold again in shattered Europe after 1945.

Internationally there are now five critical areas for modern church architecture. One result of the new relation between form and function — that is, between the authenticity of the builder and the appropriateness to the task — has been that architectural pilot projects and religious impulses have mutually influenced and enhanced one another. In this spirit F. L. Wright built the Florida Southern College chapel in Lakeland in 1940 and a Unitarian church in Madison, Wisconsin, in 1947; Eliel Saarinen (1873-1950) a Lutheran church in Minneapolis in 1951; his son Eero Saarinen (1910-61) the MIT chapel in Cambridge, Massachusetts, in 1951; O. Niemeyer the Franciscus church of Pampulha, Brazil, in 1943; K. Sijmons the Advent Kerk in The Hague in 1955; and K. and H. Siren the church at the Polytechnical Institute Otanieniu, Finland (1957); A. Aalto (1898-1976) the Vnosksenniska Church in Imatra, Finland (1959), and other churches, most recently in Piola, Italy (1977); Le Corbusier (1887-1965) the Wall-fahrtskirche in Ronchamp, France (1955); E. Eiermann (1904-70) the Matthew Church in Pforzheim (1953) and the Kaiser-Wilhelm-Memorial Church in Berlin (1957); H. Striffler the Versöhnungskirche (Church of Reconciliation) in Dachau (1964-67), L. Mies van der Rohe (1886-1969) the chapel at the Illinois Institute of Technology (1956), and R. Senn the Thomas Church in Basel (1954), as well as the chapel of the → World Council of Churches in Geneva (1960). More recently (→ Postmodernism), significant representatives include H. Stubbins, the church of St. Peter on New York's 54th Street (1975), and P. Johnson's Ecumenical Chapel at Turacher Höhe, Austria (1975).

Second, the more significant representatives of qualified projects for emergency or crisis situations (→ Third World) include O. Bartning's serial program for some 50 emergency churches after 1947 (with variations according to local conditions), as well as the churches of E. Steffann (from 1943), R. Senn (from 1950), and L. Kroll (Froidmont, Belg. [1976]). Some theologians have recognized the great importance of church architecture in → mission areas since the 1920s (Toradya Church, Sangalla, Indon. [1929]; Yambem congregation in Ngase-galatu, New Guinea [1937-38]; circular cottages in Zaire; Church of John the Baptist in Eldoret, Kenya, among others). Others worthy of mention include the church of Nova Huta as well as many anonymous builders of cottages for the → diaspora in the former Soviet Union, in South America, and in Africa.

Third, the need to integrate art has led many architects to provide it themselves or to replace it with a plastic, in part late-expressionistic architecture. In this regard, note the work, for example, of Le Corbusier, G. Böhm (in Neviges [1968]), G. Michelucci (in Florence [1963]), W. M. Förderer (in Mannheim [1967]), and J. Lackner. Artists, too, have built their own churches, such as H. Matisse (1869-1954) in Venice (1950) and F. Wotruba (1907-75) in Vienna Mauer (1976). Architects have also integrated independent art (e.g., F. Grundmann and L. Kallmeyer), although the lack of education on the side of theologians and church leaders has typically thwarted the use of authentic art in churches.

Fourth, congregational centers promoting the life and edification of the people must take into account differences in culture and integration into the church. The "agora" layout (outer rooms, foyers, and cultic areas free of fixed seating) is typical, as is the making possible of heightened → communication and → contemplation, such as by adding niches and rooms for work and → meditation. The churches cited meet functional needs without being purely functional. Important architects in this regard are W. Fohrer, H. H. von Busse, K. Wimmenauer, O. A. Gulbransson, and H. Schaedel in Germany; B. Huber and E. Gisel in Switzerland; R. Rainer, O. Uhl, and F. Schuster in Austria; and J. J. Exner, H. H. Hjertholm, H. Castrén, and R. Bergh in Scandinavia. G. and G. Bylefeld, M. Krug and B. van der Minde, M. Förderer, and H. Hollein have built ecumenical complexes, for example, in Groningen (1972), Hagen-Helfe (1976), and Buchholz (1976).

Fifth, one of the most important current tasks of church architecture is that of adapting old buildings to new situations. This may involve reshaping for new forms of liturgy (e.g., Christ Church in St. Louis [1960], Lübeck Cathedral [1972]), or spaces may have to be divided or reduced (Marthakirche, Berlin [1970]; Nikolaikirche, Potsdam [1976]). The ensemble may have to be put to a new use (Heilig-Kreuzkriche, Berlin), or sold for nonchurch purposes (in Dordrecht, Holland).

To conclude, complex processes take place in each church building, each with its own theological value. The church itself suffers if builders and architects do not see the needs of the time and thus hamper the interplay of liturgical, diaconal, and catechetical procedures. In every age the church requires places for meeting, and shaping them authentically and relevantly is part of the event itself. Church building today must take into account the five issues mentioned above.

→ Christian Art; City; Iconography; Minster; Symbol 4

Bibliography: O. Bartning, Vom neuen Kirchenbau (Berlin, 1919); idem, Vom Raum der Kirche (Bramsche, 1958) • R. Beck al., eds., Die Kunst und die Kirchen (Munich, 1984) • H.-K. Boehlke, Friedhofsbauten (Munich, 1974) • H. Brandenburg et al., "Kirchenbau," TRE 18.421-528 • P. Brathe, Theorie des evangelischen Kirchengebäudes (Stuttgart, 1906) • D. J. Bruggink, Christ and Architecture (Grand Rapids, 1965); idem, When Faith Takes Form: Contemporary Churches of Architectural Integrity in America (Grand Rapids, 1971) • R. Bürgel, Raum und Ritual (Göttingen, 1994); idem, ed., Bauen mit Geschichte (Gütersloh, 1980) • A. Christ-

Janer and M. Mix Foley, *Modern Church Architecture* (New York, 1962) • J. G. Davies, *The Secular Use of Church Buildings* (Birmingham, 1968) • Deutsche Gesellschaft für christliche Kunst, *Kirchenbau in der Diskussion* (Munich, 1973) • R. Disse, *Kirchliche Zentren* (Munich, 1974) • Evangelische Kirche in Berlin-Brandenburg, *Neue Nutzungen von alten Kirchen* (Berlin, 1988) • J. Furttenbach, *Gottes-Dienst-Gebäu* (Augsburg, 1653) • R. Giewselmann, *Neue Kirchen* (Stuttgart, 1972) • M. Görbing et al., eds., *Planen, Bauen, Nutzen. Gemeindezentren* (Giessen, 1981) • W. C. Huffman and S. A. Stauffer, *Where We Worship* (Minneapolis, 1987) • G. Jedlicka, *Die Matisse-Kapelle in Vence* (Frankfurt, 1955) • *KuKi* (1925-) • R. Kuehn, *A Place for Baptism* (Chicago, 1992) • G. Langmaack, *Evangelischer Kirchenbau im 19. und 20. Jahrhundert* (Kassel, 1971) • R. Lee, ed., *The Church and the Exploding Metropolis* (Richmond, Va., 1965) • R. S. Lindstrom, *Creativity and Contradiction: European Churches since 1970* (Washington, D.C., 1988) • F. Lingenbach, *Architectura religiosa en climas cálidos* (Estrella, 1975) • M. Mauck, *Shaping a House for the Church* (Chicago, 1990) • H. Muck, "Kirchenbau," *Lexikon der Pastoraltheologie* (1972) 260-61; idem, *Der Raum. Baugefüge, Bild, und Lebenswelt* (Vienna, 1986) • S. Muri, *Norske Kyrker* (Copenhagen, 1971) • M. C. Neddens and W. Wucher, *Die Wiederkehr des Genius Loci. Die Kirche im Stadtraum–die Stadt im Kirchenraum* (Wiesbaden, 1987) • P. P. Regamey, *Kirche und Kunst im XX. Jahrhundert* (Graz, 1954) • L. Ridderstedt, *Kyrkan bygger vidare* (Katrineholm, 1974) • L. E. Schaller, *Planning for Protestantism in Urban America* (New York, 1965) • S. Scharfe, *Dorfkirchen in Europa* (Königstein, 1973) • H. Schnell, *Der Kirchenbau des 20. Jahrhunderts in Deutschland* (Munich, 1973) • R. Schwarz, *The Church Incarnate* (Chicago, 1958; orig. pub., 1938) • O. H. Senn, *Evangelischer Kirchenbau im ökumenischen Kontext* (Basel, 1983) • L. C. Sturm, *Vollständige Anweisung aller Arten von Kirchen* (Augsburg, 1718) • M. Takenaka, *The Place Where God Dwells: An Introduction to Church Architecture in Asia* (Hong Kong, 1995) • H. Turner, *From Temple to Meeting House: The Phenomenology and Theology of Places of Worship* (The Hague, 1979) • R. Volp, "Umgang mit Raum und kirchliches Bauen," *HPTh(G)* 3.225-37 • R. Volp and H. Schwebel, eds., *Ökumenisch planen* (Gütersloh, 1973) • C. M. Werner, *Das Ende des "Kirchen"-Baus* (Zurich, 1971) • J. F. White, *Protestant Worship and Church Architecture* (New York, 1964) • P. W. Williams, *Houses of God: Region, Religion, and Architecture in the United States* (Urbana, Ill., 1997) • W. Wucher, ed., *Alte Kirchen–Räume der Zukunft* (Giessen, 1984).

RAINER VOLP

Church Base Community → Base Community

Church Conference Centers

1. Origin and Development of the Concept
2. Work and Importance
3. Worldwide Scope

1. Origin and Development of the Concept

Church conference centers were set up in West Germany after World War II as places of discussion in the encounter between the church and the world. These institutions understand themselves to be church forums for intellectual discussion with the problems of the age in the tension between religious faith and the secularized world.

1.1. Church conference centers owe their origin and development to a memorandum that Helmut Thielicke (1908-86) drew up in 1942 in the middle of the → church struggle. A link was made to the Evangelical Weeks held by the → Confessing Church during the Third Reich. In Bad Boll in 1945, Eberhard Müller (1906-89) held a conference for lawyers and economists that embodied the idea of dialogue between the church and the world, doing so against the background of the bitter experience of the church struggle. In 1946 Müller formulated the Bad Boll program as follows: "It is not enough for the church merely to preach. In give and take, and without avoidance, it must meet modern doubt and within it bear witness to the authority of the divine Word."

1.2. After 1945, Protestants took the lead in founding church conference centers. The → Roman Catholic Church, however, did not simply imitate the idea of conference centers, since it was able to draw on the tradition of Catholic associations and academic societies (→ Societies and Associations, Ecclesiastical). For example, Romano Guardini (1885-1968) held "working weeks" at Burg Rothenfels from the 1920s. Also, Carl Muth's (1867-1944) journal *Hochland,* founded in 1905, helped Catholicism (→ Catholic, Catholicity) address modern culture. A broad program of → continuing education, in part aimed at specific groups, had indeed been initiated from the time of the → Kulturkampf. These developments all converged after 1945 in Roman Catholic conference centers.

1.3. After 1945, → ecumenism increasingly shaped the programs of such centers (→ Ecumenical Movement). Protestant conference centers tend to be places of encounter at the forefront of → faith; focusing on contextually and temporally specific topics, they address controversial contemporary issues with forms of encounter in "stations" drawn from real life and with an eye on finding concrete answers to concrete questions. In contrast, Catholic centers are typically more concerned with the encounter between faith and knowledge as scholars reexamine and reformulate the foundations of faith. Such centers are also concerned with recommunicating knowledge and with training leaders for the church and its associations, while at the same time providing a framework for the work of adult education. Protestant centers have been more independent; Roman Catholic centers vary greatly in size, program, and level of autonomy.

2. Work and Importance

By the end of the 1950s, throughout Germany 14 Protestant conference centers had arisen in quick succession, the oldest being those at Bad Boll and Arnoldshain (Hesse and Nassau). These centers belong to a federation that is now international and includes some 80 centers and institutes in Europe. Roman Catholics sponsor 22 institutions; the oldest, at Stuttgart-Hohenheim, was founded in 1950, and others followed soon after. The center in Bavaria (1957) plays a leading role.

→ Education

Bibliography: H. BOVENTER, "Der Auftrag der katholischen Akademien," *StZ* 198 (1980) 808-16; idem, ed., *Evangelische und katholische Akademien. Gründerzeit und Auftrag heute* (Paderborn, 1983) • H. KALLENBACH, "Geschichte der evangelischen Akademien," *Geschichte der Erwachsenenbildung* (vol. 4; ed. F. Pöggeler; Stuttgart, 1975) 197-208 • LEITERKREIS DER EVANGELISCHEN AKADEMIEN, *Der Auftrag evangelischer Akademien. Ein Memorandum* (Bad Boll, 1979) • F. MESSERSCHMIDT, "Geschichte der katholischen Akademien," *Geschichte der Erwachsenenbildung* (vol. 4; ed. F. Pöggeler; Stuttgart, 1975) 208-18 • E. MÜLLER, *Bekehrung der Strukturen* (Zurich, 1973) • H. STORK, ed., *Mut zur Verständigung. 25 Jahre evangelischer Akademien in Loccum* (Göttingen, 1977).

HERMANN BOVENTER

3. Worldwide Scope

An ecumenical association of European church conference centers was founded in 1956. Originally consisting of 15 institutions, all Protestant, in 1989 it included some 80 Roman Catholic, Orthodox, and Protestant houses from 15 countries (Austria, Czechoslovakia, Denmark, Finland, France, Germany, Great Britain, Greece, Italy, the Netherlands, Norway, Portugal, Spain, Sweden, and Switzerland). Offerings ranged from adult education to → communities and retreat centers. The work described above in sections 1 and 2 is more distinctive of church conference centers in the German-speaking sphere.

The ecumenical → lay movement is a common historical link. A European lay conference was held in Bad Boll in 1951, followed in 1952 by one in Buffalo, New York, for North America. After the → World Council of Churches (WCC) 1954 Evanston Assembly, conference centers were founded at Bossey and Geneva. International problems like → racism, a new economic order, and militarism have come up for discussion (→ Ecumenical Movement). At the conference in Järvenpää (Finland) in 1983, a public document was prepared on the theme of risking peace in Europe. The perspective then was that of Europe as a whole, not just western Europe, and after regional forums in Scandinavia and in central and southern Europe, a common peace forum was held at Driebergen (Netherlands) in 1987. This prepared the way for the ecumenical assembly at Basel in 1989 on the theme of peace with justice, as 29 church or church-related organizations at work on the European level held hearings.

Networks on common themes have been set up between the different centers, for example, on → youth, → women, and Europe. These reflect ecumenical and social discussion and prepare the way for conferences. Consultations also accompany the dialogue between East and West. In southern Europe, important issues are → tourism and cultural identity.

Similar associations of lay conference centers exist in Asia, Africa, North America, and the Caribbean. Individual centers are also operating in Latin America, the Pacific, the Middle East, and Australia. They are all linked to the WCC division dealing with renewal and community life. They set up interregional training programs for coworkers and meet in world consultations organized by a joint committee.

→ Education

Bibliography: F. E. ANHELM, *Diskursives und konziliares Lernen. Politische Grenzerfahrungen, Volkskirche und evangelische Akademien* (Frankfurt, 1988) • ÖKUMENISCHE VEREINIGUNG DER AKADEMIEN, *Raum für Frieden. Ein Beitrag zum konziliaren Prozeß für Gerechtigkeit, Frieden und Bewahrung der Schöpfung* (Bad Boll, 1988) • W. SIMPFENDÖRFER, ed., *The New Fisher Folk: How to Run a Church-Related Conference Center* (Geneva, 1988) • WORLD COUNCIL OF CHURCHES, *Directory of Ecumenical Conference Centers* (2d ed.; Geneva, 1994).

FRITZ ERICH ANHELM

Church Dedication

"Church dedication" refers to the solemn consecration of a newly built or restored church building (→ Church Architecture) to the use for which it was designed.

Over the years, the Western church developed a complicated, extended, and highly symbolic ritual of dedication that assumed fixed form in the Roman pontifical of 1475 and that retained its validity until a first simplification in 1961 (L. Eisenhofer, 2.448ff.). Pursuant to the resolutions of → Vatican II the church published *Ordo dedicationis ecclesiae et altaris* (1977). One form of church dedication includes a → procession with → relics to the new church, the handing over of the building to the → bishop, whose taking possession can find symbolic expression in the inscribing of the Greek and Latin alphabet on a cross of ashes on the church floor. Then follows aspersion (→ Holy Water) of the congregation, the → altar, and the church walls and the liturgy of the Word of God (→ Worship). After the → litany comes the placing of the altar relics, followed by the prayer of dedication, the → anointing and → incensing of the altar and walls, and the solemn lighting of the lights. The → Mass of dedication reaches its climax in the First Communion (→ Eucharist). By church law it is usually the diocesan bishop who should conduct the dedication (1983 CIC 1206; cf. 1217-18).

In the → Orthodox Church, too, church dedication is a legal act embellished with solemn ritual (K. Onasch, 210).

In spite of Reformation criticism of the Roman ritual (Schmalk. Art. 3.15), Protestant churches have their own special ceremonies of church dedication. As a rule, the congregation takes solemn leave of the old site and then moves to the new house of God. The keys are handed over at the church door. The altar and crucifix (→ Cross), the → baptismal font, the → pulpit, the → organ, and the → bells are then consecrated to the service of God.

From an early period the church dedication came to be commemorated each year. Later there was regional consolidation, from which folk festivals developed that today often give little evidence of their true origin.

Bibliography: J. D. Crichton, *The Dedication of a Church* (Dublin, 1980) • *LRR* • R. W. Muncey, *A History of the Consecration of Churches and Churchyards* (Cambridge, 1930) • K. Onasch, *Kunst und Liturgie der Ostkirche in Stichworten* (Vienna, 1981).

Friedemann Merkel

Church Discipline

1. History
2. Germany
3. United States
4. Church of England

1. History

In the course of church history, church discipline has sought to fashion and safeguard Christian living as a response to the preached Word. It falls somewhere between Christian → ethics and → church law.

NT statements form the starting point for discipline within the church, for example, the dominical saying in Matt. 18:15-18 concerning the settlement of disputes among Christians, or the saying about the power of the keys in Matt. 16:18-19. The primitive practice of expulsion and → forgiveness is reflected in 1 Cor. 5:1-6 and 2 Cor. 2:5-11. Church discipline relates fundamentally to the ministry (→ Offices, Ecclesiastical) and to the → congregation.

In the → early church, discipline was a means of protecting the community in times of → persecution. The → penitential system grew up in connection with the condemnation and readmission of the → Lapsi, evidence of which appears in the early penitential books. After the year 399 civil laws were added to deal with heretics, and the way was prepared for the persecution of heretics in the 12th to 14th centuries (→ Inquisition). → Canon law was concerned to separate the sacrament of penance from the church's penal system, though the lesser and greater → excommunication still had social and legal consequences.

The criticism of the → Reformers focused on this point. M. → Luther (1483-1546) wanted the church itself to be in charge of church discipline but could not accomplish this goal in the existing situation. The pastoral power of the → keys was reserved for the minister, but church discipline in the form of the lesser excommunication, which meant exclusion from the → sacraments, was in the hands of the partly secular consistory. In the 16th-century → church orders we see the impact of secular ideas of moral discipline.

Things were different in the → Reformed churches (→ Church 3.5). For many years church discipline was an essential feature in → church government. After the model of M. → Bucer (1491-1551) and J. Oecolampadius (1482-1531), followed in part in Hesse and Strasbourg, J. → Calvin (1509-64) laid the theological foundations of church discipline in his *Institutes* (4.12) and embodied it in the Genevan orders of 1541/1561, though clearly allowing a role for the city government. The preachers had the power of binding and loosing, while the → elders were actually in charge of church discipline. The French order of 1559 freed the ministers from state influence and brought the → synods into the system of church discipline, which persisted throughout the age of persecution. Church discipline took a similar course in Scotland, Holland, and western Germany. In many instances church discipline was regarded as a third note, or key, of the church, alongside the Word and the sacraments (→ Heidelberg Catechism, qq. 83-85).

In the age of → rationalism and the → Enlightenment, church discipline patently lost its influence. Changed habits of life, little affected even by → Pietism and → revivals, set moral discipline under middle-class social control, with grave offenses falling solely under state punishment. In some places church discipline was indeed revived in 19th-century church law, but it was merely a means to ensure worthy reception of the → Eucharist (see the Rhenish-Westphalia church orders of 1835). Church discipline achieved greater significance in the → church struggle of 1933-45, especially in relation to congregational orders and the right to vote, but it has been practiced only in a limited way in the changed postwar situation.

2. Germany

Formal church discipline exists today only in connection with admission to Communion, which is itself a prerequisite for holding office. Refusal of → baptism, → confirmation, → marriage (esp. remarriage), and burial (→ Funeral) is also possible. A confessional distinction is that in → Lutheran churches it is the minister, advised by church leaders, who administers discipline, while in the Reformed and the union churches (→ United and Uniting Churches), discipline is in the hands of the church leaders. The → superintendent or synod may also have a role. Specific provisions may be found in the ordinances governing the Christian life or congregational practice.

Apart from the relation to the Eucharist, however, the actual significance of church discipline is slight. In its traditional form it does not harmonize with a diaconal and missionary understanding of modern church life. The same might be said of ministerial and doctrinal discipline. Precisely for this reason the practice of → pastoral care with its disciplinary features of penance and absolution has assumed all the more importance.

Nevertheless, in some smaller groups like the → free churches and in spiritual → communities, church discipline can still have integrative force, bringing the church together and sustaining it in difficult times.

Bibliography: R. BOHREN, *Das Problem der Kirchenzucht im Neuen Testament* (Zurich, 1952) • G. EBELING, *Kirchenzucht* (Stuttgart, 1947) • T. E. FULOP, "The Third Mark of the Church? Church Discipline in the Reformed and Anabaptist Reformations," *JRH* 19 (1995) 26-42 • D. KLUGE, "Die 'Kirchenbuße' als staatliches Zuchtmittel im 15.-18. Jahrhundert," *JWKG* 70 (1977) 51-62 • J. KUHN, "Kirchenzucht und Kirchenbegriff," *ZEvKR* 9 (1962/63) 264-93 • J. PLOMP, *De kerkelijke tucht bij Calvijn* (Kampen, 1969) • A. SCHÖNHERR, *Kirchenzucht* (Gütersloh, 1966).

HERBERT FROST

3. United States

Formal categories of church discipline have all but been abandoned in mainline American churches. Members may simply leave the church altogether or transfer to a different church (→ Church Membership 4). → Excommunication from membership is rare. Pastoral → counseling of those who have erred has increased, while fear of litigation for defamation has led many evangelical → pastors and churches to avoid public announcements of those whose membership is terminated. In most denominations membership is simply allowed to lapse.

Practice varies in the rapidly growing nonmainline churches such as → Pentecostals and → Baptists. Pastors in these churches are censored and deposed when their personal life is judged contrary to the lifestyle required by Scripture. African Americans, Spanish, Asian, and Native American ethnic churches seldom exercise formal, public discipline. Pastors in these churches are expected to be skilled counselors of the erring. Overall, the pressures of the extended family are generally far more effective than public church discipline.

Bibliography: W. BRINK and R. R. DE RIDDER, *Manual of Christian Reformed Church Government* (Grand Rapids, 1987) • R. R. DE RIDDER, *The Church Orders of the Sixteenth-Century Dutch Churches* (Grand Rapids, 1981) • T. C. ODEN, *Corrective Love: The Power of Communion Discipline* (St. Louis, 1995).

RICHARD R. DE RIDDER

4. Church of England

Disciplinary proceedings against those in holy orders in the Church of England are governed mainly by the Ecclesiastical → Jurisdiction Measure of 1963, a measure passed by the General Synod of the Church of England and having the force of law. All → bishops, → priests, and → deacons are subject to the provisions of the measure, which distinguishes between (1) offenses involving matters of doctrine, ritual, or ceremony (→ Liturgy) and (2) other offenses against → church law.

4.1. Proceedings against offenses involving doctrine and → worship may be instituted only if the offense was committed within the provinces of Canterbury or York. This geographic restriction does not apply to other offenses.

Offenses relating to doctrine have been held to include → heresy, the expression of blasphemous and impious opinions contrary to the Christian religion, defaming the → Book of Common Prayer, and maintaining doctrines repugnant to the Thirty-Nine Articles.

Offenses relating to ritual and ceremony include the use of forms of service not authorized by the canon or the introduction of illegal ornaments or ceremony (→ Paraments; Vestments).

4.2. Other offenses include (1) conduct unbecoming the office and work of a cleric in holy orders, which can include dishonest, immoral, or disorderly (but not political) behavior; (2) serious, persistent, or continuous neglect of duty; (3) officiating without episcopal or other requisite permission; and (4) offenses relating to church buildings, including illegal alterations or damage.

4.3. Proceedings under the 1963 measure are commenced by way of a complaint, which must normally be presented within three years of the alleged offense. A preliminary investigation follows that can include, in prescribed cases and at the option of the parties, an interview with the bishop of the → diocese or archbishop of the province. In certain cases the bishop or archbishop may decide that proceedings should not continue. In other cases the matter will be referred to an examiner or committee, the identity of which will depend on the type of offense and the orders of the accused. The examiner or committee must decide whether or not there is a prima facie case for the accused to answer. If it decides that there is, the matter will proceed to trial by the appropriate ecclesiastical court in accordance with time limits and procedures prescribed by the 1963 measure and associated rules. The court will have powers to compel the attendance of witnesses and the production of documents similar to those of the civil courts in England and Wales.

4.4. All offenses involving doctrine, ritual, or ceremony are tried by the Court of Ecclesiastical Causes Reserved, from which appeal lies to a Commission of Review. Other cases against a priest or deacon are tried by the consistory court of the relevant diocese. Appeal lies to the appropriate provincial court (i.e., the Court of Arches in the province of Canterbury, the Chancery Court in that of York). Other cases against a bishop are tried by a Commission of Convocation, from which appeal lies to a Commission of Review.

4.5. An accused person found guilty of an offense under the 1963 measure is liable to have censure pronounced by the relevant ecclesiastical court. The censures that may be pronounced are deprivation (removal from office), inhibition (disqualification for a specified time from exercising the functions of orders), monition (an order to do or refrain from doing a specified act, breach of which constitutes an ecclesiastical offense), and rebuke. Where the censure is deprivation, deposition from holy orders may ensue. Pursuant to the Ecclesiastical Jurisdiction (Amendment) Measure of 1974, deprivation may also follow the making of certain judgments or orders in the secular courts without further trial in the ecclesiastical courts.

In addition to the disciplinary proceedings outlined above, the Incumbents (Vacation of Benefices) Measure of 1977 provides procedures enabling a priest who is an incumbent of a parish to be removed from office on grounds of serious pastoral breakdown or where the incumbent is unable adequately to minister to parishioners by reason of age or infirmity. Such removal may take place only following an inquiry by a diocesan committee or, if the incumbent so elects, by a diocesan tribunal.

→ Church Employees; Church Government; Offices, Ecclesiastical

Bibliography: Halsbury's Laws of England (vol. 14; 4th ed.; London, 1975) 129ff. • HER MAJESTY'S STATIONARY OFFICE, *Ecclesiastical Jurisdiction (Amendment) Measure* (London, 1974); idem, *Ecclesiastical Jurisdiction (Discipline) Rules* (London, 1964); idem, *Ecclesiastical Jurisdiction Measure* (London, 1963); idem, *Incumbents (Vacation of Benefices) Measure* (London, 1977).

PAUL C. E. MORRIS

Church Employees

1. Germany
2. England
3. United States

1. Germany

1.1. The underlying NT concept is that of coworkers (1 Corinthians 12; Romans 12). In the church there are many offices and functions, but individual workers with their different gifts are members of the one organic fellowship, they are equally important, and they are all responsible to him who alone is the Lord of all. The reality measures up only imperfectly to this biblical statement. In the German Protestant churches the term "church employees" tends to be used only for the nonordained, as distinct from "church administrators" (→ Civil Law and the Church).

1.2. According to the church's basic law, higher tasks are usually undertaken by officials, but in fact church employees often perform them. The legal distinction is that in the case of employees, there is a contract, which means that when disputes arise, the secular laws of employment apply. In certain points, however, the contracts create situations similar to those of officials. The biblical model of a fellowship of service became a legal principle in the Weimar Constitution, and it has thus had an impact on the law of employment both individually and collectively.

For the credibility of church employment, it is critical that church employees respect the orders of the church in their own lives. Inconsistent conduct, including withdrawal from the church, may legally lead to dismissal (→ Church Membership 5). Since church employees are in the same service and under the same Lord as church ministers, the churches in Germany, on the basis of their autonomy (→ Offices, Ecclesiastical), have refused to make wage agreements with the → labor unions and instead taken the so-called third way of cooperation.

1.3. The churches offer many different types of employment, for which in many cases they offer training in their own colleges (→ Theological Education). This is true not only of employees in the churches themselves but also of those in privately run church institutions, especially in the diaconal sphere. The various groups include educators or ministers of Christian education (→ Christian Education), church assistants (e.g., in → proclamation, → pastoral care, and edification), deaconesses (→ Deacon, Deaconess), church sisters, social secretaries, social workers, social teachers, → kindergarten teachers and helpers, → church musicians, especially organists, workers in the medical sphere as well as in general administration, in books and archives, and in the literary sphere. Others are caretakers, business managers, handymen, and chauffeurs.

1.4. Church employees have rights of representations in accordance with the church laws regulating their appointment, tasks, and powers. These norms meet the demand of Christian → ethics that they should have legal protection, in spite of the social independence of the churches. Employees of all classes in the → Roman Catholic Church have the same rights.

→ Church Law; Jurisdiction, Ecclesiastical; Pastor, Pastorate

Bibliography: D. Friedrich, *Einführung in das Kirchenrecht* (2d ed.; Göttingen, 1978) • H. Marré and J. Stüting, *Arbeitsrecht in der Kirche* (Aschendorf, 1984) • R. Richardi, *Arbeitsrecht in der Kirche* (Munich, 1984) • A. Stein, *Evangelisches Kirchenrecht* (3d ed.; Neuwied, 1992).

Herbert Ehnes

2. England

The nature of the Church of England's employment and remuneration of the clergy has evolved through its history. At present there are three types of employment: (1) → diocesan → bishops, deans and canons of → cathedrals, and beneficed clergy; (2) suffragan bishops and curates; and (3) other licensed and employed clergy and lay workers. In the first two cases, income derives largely from the church commissioners, who administer church endowments.

2.1. Diocesan bishops are elected and confirmed to a title. Deans, canons, and beneficed clergy (i.e., incumbents) are collated, or instituted to a living. Once confirmed, collated, or instituted, they become self-employed persons and can remain in that office until they attain the age of 70. By a concession of the Inland Revenue, they are treated as employed persons for the purposes of National Insurance, but in every other way they are self-employed. They can be removed from their office and the emoluments that go with it only by various disciplinary measures, such as those described in the Ecclesiastical Jurisdiction Measure (1963) or the Incumbents (Vacation of Benefices) Measure (1977), but these procedures are complex and rarely used (→ Jurisdiction, Ecclesiastical).

2.2. Suffragan bishops and other parochial clergy are believed to be self-employed, but as occasion demands, they are licensed to hold office. Suffragan bishops are commissioned by the diocesan bishop and have duties delegated to them by the commission. The diocesan bishop can revoke the commission but has no power to remove the suffragan bishop. Area bishops are also self-employed, but their duties are given to them by an instrument of the General Synod and cannot easily be revoked. Likewise, parochial clergy such as curates can have their license removed summarily by the bishop, subject to an appeal to the archbishop. Equally with the consent of the bishop an incumbent can determine his curate's curacy on six months' notice. Where this happens a curate cannot exercise his orders in that particular diocese or parish. Like suffragan bishops, curates are deemed to be self-employed except for the purposes of National Insurance. Whether such persons are really employed or self-employed in law has been challenged recently, and the position is uncertain. Some argue that the bishop's right to remove a license and the question of employment rights are separate. The matter remains to be resolved by the courts.

2.3. The remaining category are clergy employed by third parties, such as central boards, the General Synod, schools, and hospitals. In this case the license and job may be independent of one another. If the job requires a bishop's license, then clergy who otherwise function as → priests or → deacons could not be appointed to the job, though they may have a right to continue in their job. For this reason some church employers make it a condition of employment that the person has a license to an office and that if that license is withdrawn, the employment ceases.

Lay employees are in the same position as employees in the secular realm. In the case of organists (→ Church Musicians), the courts have ruled that only the hours that they play at services can be taken into account and not the hours of practice. An organist is an employee of the incumbent but is paid by the Parochial Church Council. Other offices include those of chancellor, clerk, and verger.

→ Church Law; Civil Law and the Church; Offices, Ecclesiastical

Bibliography: Halsbury's Laws of England (4th ed.; vol. 14; London, 1975) 129ff. • Pluralities Act, 1838.

DAVID W. FAULL

3. United States

In the United States, relations with church employees are governed by general law as long as there is no conflict with the First Amendment, which prohibits any religious establishment.

3.1. Title VII of the federal Civil Rights Act of 1964, the Age Discrimination in Employment Act of 1975, and the Americans with Disabilities Act of 1990 (ADA) prohibit employers with 15 or more employees, including religious organizations, from discriminating against employees on the basis of race, color, sex, national origin, disability, or age (40 to 70 years). The Federal Family Leave Act applies to churches with 50 or more employees. However, the civil courts have held that the First Amendment to

the U.S. Constitution bars enforcement of the acts on clerics and others with ministerial duties. Moreover, unlike employers generally, §702 of the 1964 act permits religious organizations to discriminate on the basis of religion in employment regardless of whether the nature of the job is ministerial. Likewise, §12113(c) of the ADA permits a religious entity to have religious preferences and to require employees to follow its tenets. Nondiscrimination legislation in the 50 states varies, and a few states do not exempt the same discriminatory employment activities by religious organizations as do the federal acts. Nondiscrimination legislation in most states prohibits employers from discriminating against employees with → handicaps who are otherwise qualified, and a few states do not exempt religious organizations from this legislation.

3.2. The civil courts in the states generally hold that an employee hired for a definite term may not be discharged before the expiration of the term without good cause. However, courts have held that such wrongful termination actions may not be brought against religious organizations by discharged clerics and others with ministerial duties.

The Federal Fair Labor Standards Act protects nonsupervisory employees by imposing overtime and minimum wage requirements, requiring equal pay for equal work regardless of sex, and restricting the employment of underage children (→ Child Labor). Religious organizations, including churches, are subject to the act insofar as its employees engage in commerce. Clerics and others with ministerial duties are exempt.

Workers' compensation laws exist in all states to assist employees injured at work, without regard to fault. Churches are not exempt in many states. The Federal Unemployment Tax Act implements cooperative federal-state programs to benefit → unemployed workers. It is financed by an excise tax on wages paid by employers. Churches and other organizations operated primarily for religious purposes, however, are exempt from this act.

The National Labor Relations Act affords nonsupervisory employees a right to join a union (→ Labor Unions). The act applies to religious organizations that engage in substantial commercial activities, but it has never been applied to a church, and clerics and others with ministerial duties are exempt. It has been applied, however, to church-operated orphanages and hospitals and, in some cases, parochial schools.

3.3. Federal law imposes an employment tax on both employers and employees to finance Social Security, Medicare, and Medicaid benefits. Nonclerical employees of a church are covered unless the church elects to become exempt by filing an application. Exemptions are available only to churches that are opposed for religious reasons to the payment of Social Security taxes. If not exempt, a church must withhold the nonclerical employee's share of the tax from each wage payment. If exempt, nonclerical employees are personally liable for the tax as self-employed individuals.

Nonclerical church employees are subject to the same income taxes as wage earners generally. The salary and wages of nonclerical church employees are subject to federal income tax withholding from each wage payment. The same applies in states imposing an income tax. Clerics are treated as self-employed individuals for income tax purposes, and they are permitted a few favorable exclusions such as a housing allowance.

Bibliography: *Abington Clergy Income Tax Guide* (Nashville [printed yearly]) • R. B. Couser, *Ministry and the American Legal System: A Guide for Clergy, Lay Workers, and Congregations* (Minneapolis, 1993) • R. Hammar, *Pastor, Church, and Law* (2d ed.; Springfield, Mo., 1991).

Carl H. Esbeck

Church Fathers

1. Definition
2. Historical Development of the Concept
3. Patristics
4. Historical Survey

1. Definition

In Christian thought since the eighth century, a church father (*pater ecclesiae*) is a teacher living within the first seven centuries (eight among the Greeks) whose teaching the → church has recognized as orthodox (→ Early Church). The four basic requirements have been orthodox doctrine, sanctity of life, agreement with the church, and antiquity. (For someone to be named a *doctor* of the church, outstanding learning is further required.) As the medieval world (→ Middle Ages) emerged out of late antiquity, the patristic era came to an end — in the East with John of Damascus (ca. 655-ca. 750), in the West with → Gregory the Great (ca. 540-604) and Isidore of Seville (ca. 560-636). In Orthodox thought the Fathers ranked especially high because they embodied the → tradition, a source of authority along with the Scriptures, and provided an alternative to papal authority (→ Pope, Papacy). The Orthodox emphasis led to a great deal of copying of ancient MSS.

The → Reformers generally found an alternative to papal authority in the authority of Scripture, but they had an extensive knowledge of the Fathers and regarded especially the earlier Fathers as important church witnesses. In 16th-century circles, both Catholic and Protestant, the publication of patristic texts was actively carried on, often with a view toward reviving ancient simplicity as against medieval complexity. Today Protestant and Catholic scholars alike generally regard the church fathers as indispensable historical witnesses to early biblical exegesis and the history of doctrine. Karl → Barth valued them but considered them subordinate to Scripture because of their human fallibility. In Anglican theology they are esteemed, but their authority is not absolute.

2. Historical Development of the Concept

The idea of an older authority called → "father" is far older than Christendom. It is found in various cultures, including Greek and Roman, and notably in the Hebrew Bible, where God is Father and the patriarchs are fathers too. The term "father" in the church is old. The apostle → Paul spoke of himself as the father of his converts (1 Cor. 4:15). In the *Martyrdom of Polycarp* this aged bishop of Smyrna (ca. 70-ca. 166) is called "the teacher of Asia, the father of the Christians" (12.2). → Origen (ca. 185-ca. 254) addressed several bishops as "papa" in his *Dialogue with Heraclides,* and the title was soon used of bishops of → Alexandria, then those of → Rome.

Without using the name "father," Christian authors of the second century claimed to adhere to the tradition of their predecessors, making the claim against the "innovations" of heretics. Just so, Platonists of the time claimed that they and not their rivals taught the authentic doctrines of Plato (427-347 B.C.). The theologian → Irenaeus (ca. 130-ca. 200) relied on the authority of earlier Christian writers, not all of them named, but he preferred to speak of the agreement (*adsensus*) of all the churches. A generation later, theologians of various schools began to pit groups against individual authorities. For example, Roman adoptionists (→ Trinity 1) held that their own doctrine was the traditional doctrine of the Roman church, recently modified by Pope Zephyrinus (198-217), while a more orthodox author named the famous second-century writers with whom he was in agreement (Justin Martyr, Miltiades, Tatian, Clement, Irenaeus, Melito; cf. Eusebius *Hist. eccl.* 5.28.4-5).

We do not expect to find an appeal to the Fathers in the writings of → Tertullian (ca. 160-ca. 225) and Origen, the leading theologians of the third century, for they were not always devoted to older traditions.

521

In the fourth century, however, the term "fathers" came to the fore.

Eusebius of Caesarea (ca. 260-ca. 340) denounced his opponent Marcellus (d. ca. 374) for rejecting "all the ecclesiastical fathers." (By "all the fathers" Eusebius meant Origen and his own friends.) According to → Athanasius (ca. 297-373; → Alexandrian Theology 3.1), all the bishops who condemned Paul of Samosata at Antioch (ca. 268; → Christology 2.1.2) were "fathers," for all rest in Christ. He says that one cannot choose some as more reliable than others or the earlier against the later. Like Athanasius, Basil (ca. 330-79) and Gregory of Nyssa (ca. 330-ca. 395; → Cappadocian Fathers) referred to the "fathers" who attended the Council of Nicaea in 325 (→ Councils of the Church).

A generation later, there was conflict over the teaching of Origen (→ Origenism). T. Rufinus (ca. 345-411) translated some of his works into Latin and occasionally corrected his theology in the light of Roman orthodoxy. He was fearful of the presbyter → Jerome (ca. 345-420), who translated more literally and attacked doctrine. The term "father" was normally reserved for bishops, but → Augustine went so far as to call Jerome a "father" (at a time when they agreed), and the Gelasian Decree speaks thus of the layman Prosper of Aquitaine (ca. 390-ca. 463), a militant defender of Augustine (354-430).

In 392 Jerome prepared his *De viris illustribus,* a compilation, mostly from Eusebius, of short notices about 135 Christian authors, including himself. He saw his forerunner in the Roman historian Suetonius (ca. 69-after 122; → Historiography), as he noted, but included few heretics in the work supposedly concerned with "all who handed down to memory anything concerning the Holy Scriptures." They proved that Christianity was not for the simple alone but included "philosophers, rhetoricians, and teachers." (A decade later Jerome advised Laeta to have her daughter read → Cyprian's works, the letters of Athanasius, and the books of Hilary of Poitiers.) Toward the end of the fifth century a certain Gennadius (fl. 470) added about a hundred more notices about approved authors in later times.

In his *Commonitorium,* Vincent of Lérins (d. before 450) lists the patristic authorities cited at the Council of → Ephesus in 431. Four Greeks came from Alexandria (Peter, Athanasius, Theophilus, and → Cyril) and three from Cappadocia (the two Gregories and Basil). In addition, there were testimonies by Popes Felix (269-74) and Julius (337-52), Cyprian of Carthage (ca. 200-258), and Ambrose of Milan (ca. 339-97). Only Cyprian represented the Fathers of the second and third centuries, since neither Origen and

Tertullian could be regarded as fully orthodox. Vincent boldly says he would rather be wrong with Origen than right with others, thus imitating Cicero's (106-43 B.C.) similar statement about Plato. Vincent does not mention Augustine but opposes aspects of his doctrine. He insists, however, that Scripture must be interpreted "in accordance with the norm of the ecclesiastical and Catholic understanding," meaning "that which has been believed everywhere, always, and by all" (*Commonitorium* 2.3; → Exegesis, Biblical). He thus appeals to ecumenicity, antiquity, and consensus, while allowing for the development of doctrine. The consensus need not be universal, for it is that of "the Holy Fathers" mentioned above, given by "the definitions and judgments of all, or nearly all, the bishops and teachers." This, too, is like Cicero's appeal to the agreement of philosophers, not people in general. But the basic appeal is to the consensus, which Cicero regarded as "a law of nature" (*Tusc.* 1.30-39).

The so-called Gelasian Decree, an anonymous sixth-century work, contains a traditional list of the orthodox councils and fathers. There are six Greek fathers (Peter of Alexandria and Gregory of Nyssa have disappeared, while John → Chrysostom [ca. 347-407] has been added; the early *Shepherd of Hermas* appears among the → Apocrypha) and six Latins, with Cyprian and Ambrose, usually named, accompanied by Hilary of Poitiers, Augustine, Jerome (*presbyter*), and Prosper (*vir religiosissimus*). There is a special place for Leo's *Tome,* read at → Chalcedon, and for all the *decretales epistolae* of the popes, as well as the more credible acts of the martyrs (→ Martyrs, Acts of the). The author lists "apocrypha" that include Eusebius's *Church History* (as translated and edited by Rufinus), Tertullian, Lactantius (whom Constantine summoned to Trier in 317 to teach his son), Julius Africanus (ca. 180-ca. 250), Clement of Alexandria (ca. 150-ca. 215), and (by mistake) Cyprian and Arnobius the Elder (3d-4th cent.). The author's reach obviously exceeded his grasp.

A comparable Greek document of doubtful orthodoxy is the seventh-century *Doctrina Patrum,* which contains 751 citations from "Fathers," beginning with "Peter from the Clementines," a dubious fragment from a fictitious document. It goes on with the Cappadocians, Cyril of Alexandria (ca. 375-444), and Athanasius but then gives an inauthentic fragment from Justin Martyr, *On Faith.* The work also provides quotations from "Ebion" (a nonexistent Jewish-Christian heretic) and Mani (216-76/77, founder of → Manichaeanism). It may have been used by the much more important John of Damascus (ca. 655-ca. 750).

3. Patristics

The study of the church fathers, not only for theology but also for literary and historical purposes, is a product of the → Renaissance and the → Reformation, and the distinction between → patristics (the literature of the Fathers) and patrology (now chiefly used of a systematic manual) comes from early Lutherans. Another distinction, from the 19th century, between early church and early Christian literature has been called in question by the modern wave of interest in → Gnosticism and other ancient heresies as providing necessary background for patristics. Though documents emanating from the heresies are not "church" and not clearly "Christian," they must be considered in relation to authors more clearly ecclesiastical and Christian.

Another distinction that remains useful is that between authentic documents and those wrongly ascribed to early authors. The problem of forgery and misattribution arose in fifth-century orthodoxy when the writings of the → "Apostolic Fathers" of the early second century fell far short of contemporary requirements. It therefore seemed necessary to neglect their authentic works and use dubious documents ascribed to such authors as Clement of Rome (pope ca. 91-ca. 101), Ignatius of Antioch (ca. 35-ca. 107), and even the early apologist Justin Martyr (ca. 100-ca. 165). This period saw the wide circulation of treatises based on late Neoplatonic theology but ascribed to the first-century Athenian Christian Dionysius the Areopagite (Acts 17:34). Any historical idea of the development of doctrine necessarily vanished, revived only at the Renaissance with fresh study of the authenticity of documents.

4. Historical Survey

4.1. The Fathers are still generally viewed as those who made major contributions to the history of Christian doctrine. The most important Greek fathers are apologist Justin Martyr, who taught at Rome in the mid-second century; the theologian and bishop Irenaeus of Lyons, who cited earlier Christian authors and used logic and Scripture against Gnosticism (late 2d cent.), and his admirer the homilist and antiheretical writer Hippolytus of Rome (ca. 170-ca. 236), who ended his life as antipope. We should not even consider the claims of most Gnostic teachers, but Valentinus (fl. 2d cent.) and some of his pupils stood much closer to the church than others did.

Numerous Alexandrian authors of greater orthodoxy (→ Alexandrian Theology) wrote about early Christian theology, among them the polymath Clement, incessant user of literature and → philos-

ophy, not to mention Valentinian writings; the great theologian Origen, interpreter of Christianity in proto-Neoplatonic terms and ultimately founder of a school at Caesarea in Palestine; and the scholar-bishop Dionysius (d. ca. 265). A certain Methodius of Olympus (d. ca. 311) wrote a dialogue in Platonic style as well as a theological treatise against Origen (late 3d cent.). Somewhat later there was an important "school of Antioch," with tendencies toward a lower → Christology and a more literal biblical exegesis (→ Antiochian Theology). Eusebius of Caesarea produced not only a chronology, a church history, and a biography of the emperor Constantine but also biblical studies and commentaries, apologetic works, and theological polemics (early 4th cent.). All these Fathers are usually styled "ante-Nicene."

As the golden age of patristic literature began, Eusebius was overshadowed by Athanasius of Alexandria, the great defender of Nicene orthodoxy, and three Cappadocian bishops of a later generation: Basil of Caesarea, Gregory of Nazianzus (d. 389/90), and Gregory of Nyssa. All reflect Christian assimilation of Greek literature, rhetoric, and philosophy, as well as the reinterpretation of Christian doctrine.

4.2. The first Latin father was Tertullian of Carthage, who became a → Montanist sectarian in his later years. He was followed by Cyprian of Carthage, militant defender of orthodoxy but admirer of Tertullian, and the apologists Arnobius and Lactantius. All these were ante-Nicene. Later authors include Hilary of Poitiers (ca. 315-ca. 367), upholder of Nicaea; Ambrose of Milan, exegete and administrator; and his convert Augustine, spiritual pilgrim, vigorous antiheretical author, and bishop of Hippo in Africa (→ Augustine's Theology). His contemporary and critic was Jerome, monk of Bethlehem and confidant of Roman noblewomen, who wrote numerous letters, controversial treaties, and commentaries, and who translated the Bible from Hebrew and Greek into Latin (the Vg; → Bible Versions).

4.3. Mention should also be made of such Syrian fathers as Aphrahat (early 4th cent.), "the Persian Sage," and Ephraem (ca. 306-73), declared a *doctor* of the → Roman Catholic Church in 1920.

Bibliography: B. Altaner, *Patrologie* (Freiburg, 1938; 7th ed., 1966) • E. Amann, "Pères de l'église," *DTC* 12.1192-1215 • E. von Dobschütz, *Das Decretum Gelasianum* (Berlin, 1912) • A. Hamann, "Patrology–Patristics," *Encyclopedia of the Early Church* (ed. A. Di Berardino; New York, 1992) 654-56 • R. P. C. Hanson, *Tradition in the Early Church* (London, 1962) • G. W. H. Lampe, *A Patristic Greek Lexicon* (Oxford, 1961-68) •

J. Quasten, *Patrology* (4 vols.; Westminster, Md., 1950-86) • W. Schneemelcher, *Bibliographia patristica* (Berlin, 1959ff.); idem, "Wesen und Aufgabe der Patristik innerhalb den evangelischen Theologie," *EvT* 10 (1950) 207-22 • M. Widmann, "Irenaeus und seine theologischen Väter," *ZTK* 45 (1957) 156-72.

Robert M. Grant

Church Finances

1. Germany
2. International

1. Germany

Suggestions for church finances appear in both the OT (Lev. 27:30) and the NT (1 Cor. 16:1; 2 Cor. 9:12). The → tithe and → Peter's Pence are familiar items from church history. → Secularization (§2) of church property began at the → Reformation; by 1803 it was complete in Germany. Since 1919 German churches have enjoyed financial autonomy.

As corporations under public law, the territorial churches, → dioceses, and smaller units control money, property, and buildings in fulfillment of their mission. Their income derives variously from endowments, fees (→ Cemetery; Kindergarten), private sources, state taxes and subsidies, as well as entrepreneurial activities (banks, lease of property, etc.). Salaries and related costs are the biggest single item in church expenditure.

→ Church and State; Church Government; Church Law; Usury

Bibliography: K. Blaschke, "Kirchliches Finanz- und Haushaltsrecht," *ZEvKR* 27 (1982) 45 • W. Lienemann, ed., *Die Finanzen der Kirche* (Munich, 1989) • J. Listl et al., eds., *Handbuch des katholischen Kirchenrechts* (Regensburg, 1983) • H. G. Nordmann, "Kirchliches Finanz- und Haushaltsrecht," *ZEvKR* 27 (1982) 155.

Klaus Blaschke

2. International

Because of biblical statements, church → tradition, and the tasks incumbent upon it, the → church accepts the principle that each member should contribute to the common financial burden for the fulfilling of common obligations. Because of various historical developments, especially in the relation of → church and state, a variety of financial structures have also developed in different countries. There are three main types: the voluntary system (e.g., United States, France, and the Netherlands), the system of mandatory contributions (Austria), and the system of church taxes (Germany, Switzerland, and Scandinavia) or partial church taxes (Italy and Spain). In practice the forms are often mixed. Income also comes from direct subsidies and from endowments. Also to be included here are countries such as Belgium and Luxembourg, where all denominations recognized by the state are financed almost entirely from the national budget, and Greece, where only the dominant Greek Orthodox Church is so supported.

2.1. The voluntary system is common in technically and economically advanced countries in which church and state are separated. In the United States, for example, the → free churches fostered the principle of voluntarism, the result being great liberality and church support. In Roman Catholic France a lay spirit led to disestablishment in 1905, with ensuing financial problems for the church. Minority churches follow the same pattern (e.g., Roman Catholics in Scandinavia or Protestants in Italy; → Diaspora; Minorities). In the mainly agrarian → Third World the younger churches are also financed in this way, though church finances are inadequate because of the → poverty of the population, and support must come from the churches of Europe and the United States (→ Development 1.4). Many Latin American churches, however, have a system of mandatory contribution by members.

2.2. The system of mandatory contributions under both state law and church law is found only in Austria, where since 1939 the churches' financial needs have been met mainly in this way. With state help the churches can recover unpaid contributions, if necessary, through the courts.

2.3. The system of church taxes obtains in countries in which church and state are organizationally separate but cooperate as equal partners for the common good. State and church taxes are collected there in an attempt to achieve greater justice in member support according to the ability to pay. Italy and Spain have seen development from a system of close liaison between state and church to state-church cooperation of free churches in free states. By treaties of 1979 and 1985, a certain percentage of personal income tax now can go directly to the churches according to the wishes of taxpayers.

2.4. Many churches also derive income from endowments and state subsidies. The Church of England (→ Anglican Communion), the → Vatican, and many churches in the United States depend heavily on endowment or investment income. Churches also receive state support for many branches of their work, for example, in education (→ kindergartens, schools, high schools, → continuing education), → youth work, work among the elderly, as well as for hospitals, chaplaincies, and the care of places of historic importance.

2.5. Church financial systems have been strongly influenced by the development of → society, relations between church and state, and overall economic development, so that one system cannot easily be transferred from one country to another. In western Europe and the United States we now see converging developments as, on the one hand, strict church-and-state separation erodes and, on the other, the historically close relation of church and state weakens. Ideas of voluntary contribution are growing where support originally came from taxes, while regular voluntary contributions are seen elsewhere as an obligation, moral if not also legal.

→ Church Government; Church Law; Codex Iuris Canonici; Peter's Pence; Proprietary Church; Tithe; Usury

Bibliography: W. Bassett, "Support of the Church by Freewill Offering," *The Finances of the Church* (ed. W. Bassett and P. Huizing; New York, 1979) 28-38 • F. R. McManus, "Solicitation of Funds and Accountability," ibid. 39-47 • H. Marré, *Die Kirchenfinanzierung in Kirche und Staat der Gegenwart* (3d ed.; Essen, 1991) 13-30; idem, "Kirchenfinanzierung international in EU-Ländern und USA," *Ren.* 52 (1996) 113ff.; idem, "Das kirchliche Besteuerungsrecht," *Handbuch des Staatskirchenrechts der Bundesrepublik Deutschland* (2d ed.; ed. J. Listl and D. Pirson; Berlin, 1994) 1.1101-47 • W. E. Pradel, *Kirche ohne Kirchenbeitrag–Mittel und Methoden kirchlicher Finanzierung, Dokumentation aus 75 Ländern* (Vienna, 1981) • G. Robbers, ed., *Staat und Kirche in der Europäischen Union* (Baden-Baden, 1995) • R. E. Vallet, *The Mainline Church's Funding Crisis: Issues and Possibilities* (Grand Rapids, 1995) • R. Wuthnow, *The Crisis in the Churches: Spiritual Malaise, Fiscal Woe* (New York, 1997).

HEINER MARRÉ

Church Government

1. Early Church Tendencies

1.1. *Two Fundamental Convictions*

Two fundamental convictions concerning the nature of the church, which are of great significance for the later development of church government, become evident in the NT writings.

1.1.1. The church has its origin in God's actions in Jesus Christ. It is *ekklēsia,* or the people of the end time chosen and sanctified by God, to whom belongs the sphere of the → sacred. Because he alone exercises his dominion over the church through the → Holy Spirit, the church does not stand at the disposal of any human control or power (1 Cor. 3:16-17). This relationship distinguishes it from all other social constructs that establish their own statutes and are able to make independent decisions concerning their purpose and goals. Only the Holy Spirit present within the church determines and shapes its life (1 Cor. 3:16). Human beings participate in the Spirit's activities in guiding the church only as the Spirit's helpers (Acts 15:28), discerning his will and following his instructions obediently. Their own activity in guiding the church has a merely *subsidiary* character.

1.1.2. The second fundamental conviction derives from the norm of service *(diakonia),* established as binding by Jesus' own conduct. Through his unconditional concern for helping others and by his renunciation of power and dominion (Luke 22:27), he provided the essential model for the commencing reign of God in its fundamental otherness from all other human structures of power and dominion. The pre-Easter fellowship of disciples was similarly obligated to this principle of service (Mark 10:42b-45); their lives were to be determined and realized, not through any struggle among themselves for power and dominion, but rather through their concern with helping one another and through their renunciation of power. This same principle of service was maintained as binding after Easter as well. Thus the NT defines in a comprehensive fashion all communal leadership functions as → diakonia (e.g., Rom. 11:13; 1 Cor. 12:5; Acts 6:4; 20:24; Rev. 2:19), that is, as the *rendering of service.* The Latin translation *ministerium,* from which English "ministry" derives, preserves this basic meaning.

1.2. *Various Early Forms*

The NT writings present a whole series of specific forms and models of church government, each of which, despite profound differences at the level of details, nonetheless tries in its own way to implement these two fundamental premises.

1.2.1. The movement of *itinerant charismatics,* who remained active in Galilee and Syria into the second century, picked up directly on the lifestyle of the pre-Easter fellowship of Jesus' disciples. Its members understood themselves as emissaries of Jesus whose authority to transmit Jesus' → proclamation was grounded in a direct, prophetic commission through the eschatologically active Spirit of God (Luke 10:16, par. to Matt. 10:40). The principle of leadership through the Spirit was actualized here in the authorization of certain individuals through the Spirit. Because we are not yet dealing with "church" in the sense of an independent, religiously grounded social structure, but rather only with an assemblage of small, dispersed groups of adherents of Jesus, one can speak only with qualification of church government in the narrower sense.

1.2.2. By contrast, an extremely influential model of church government developed in → *Jerusalem,* one that through all its various stages was shaped by the significance of this particular city as a center of the people of God. It was here that adherents of Jesus first assembled around the circle of "the Twelve" (Acts 1–2) in anticipation of the imminent eschatological consummation. Although this circle possessed primarily representative significance as the symbolic core of the → eschatological people of God, it quickly faded into the background when the mood of acute and imminent expectation disappeared; it was hardly ever a church-governmental committee in the real sense of the word.

In a second phase, individual members of the circle of the → Twelve then emerged as leadership figures whose claim to authority extended far beyond Jerusalem itself and now encompassed all Jesus' adherents as members of the eschatological people of God. At first, Cephas/Peter alone was the head of the church of Jerusalem (Gal. 1:18). A little later, we encounter a committee of three, called the pillars — James (a brother of Jesus), Cephas, and John (Gal. 2:9). Obviously, James was holding the highest rank among those three, even though he had not been one of the Twelve. Finally, in the end stage of development, it was James who for nearly two decades was the sole leader. The authority of these leaders was probably grounded and legitimized, on the one hand, by their commissioning by the resurrected Jesus himself, that is, by their calling as → apostles (1 Cor. 15:5-7) and, on the other hand, by evidence of charismatic power (→ Charisma). James was surrounded by a circle of "elders" (Acts 15:6) after the analogy of → synagogue organization.

Although this particular Jerusalem model of monarchical church government by charismatic authority was not continued directly after the death of James and the catastrophe of Jerusalem (A.D. 70), it

did continue to exert indirect influence into the second century in Antioch's notion of the one → bishop supported by a college of → elders (Ign. *Eph.* 2.2; *Magn.* 7.1, and elsewhere), as well as in Rome.

1.2.3. In contradistinction, the conception introduced by *Paul* and developed further in Pauline congregations attributed much greater significance to the local → church (§2.1). Here the motif of worship fellowship at the table of the Lord *(koinōnia)* played a central role (1 Cor. 10:16-17). When believers are fused into a fellowship of life and service through the Lord, who surrendered his own life, the church emerges as the "body of Christ," that is, as the living organism determined by the presence of Christ in the Spirit (1 Cor. 12:8-27). For Paul, church government is accordingly a function of each local assembly and is exercised by all its members in interplay with the various charismata. This conception is, of course, not democratic, but rather pneumatocratic, insofar as members of the congregation act, not in free self-determination, but rather under the guidance of the Spirit as he bestows the various charismata.

Concrete attempts at organizing local leadership structures in the Pauline congregations were first undertaken in the house churches. "Bishops and deacons" (or "overseers and helpers," Phil. 1:1), including women (Rom. 16:1), were at first probably responsible for structuring eucharistic worship and for managing offerings. During the post-Pauline period, a model advocated by the → Pastoral Epistles developed from this, one according to which the local congregation was led by one bishop (1 Tim. 3:1-7), along with a circle of → deacons (vv. 8-10). Although this bishop as the house father is accorded higher authority, the church itself being viewed in analogy to the extended family of antiquity (v. 5), still the only means for asserting this authority was correct teaching (legitimized through association with the apostle himself; 1 Tim. 4:6; 6:20). The extensive identification of the elders (*presbyteroi,* similarly mentioned in the Pastorals) with those who were chronologically elders (1 Tim. 5:17; Titus 1:6-7) was probably prompted by efforts to merge the Jewish institution of elders still present in some congregations with the institution of bishops and deacons of the Pauline congregations (cf. also Acts 20:17, 28; 1 Pet. 5:1-4). Neither the post-Pauline congregations nor any other writing in the NT envisions a threefold pattern of ministry (bishop, presbyter, and deacon).

1.2.4. The *Johannine literature* plays a special role in early Christianity. It reflects the ecclesial self-understanding of a group lacking the structure of a congregation as such but understanding itself rather as a supralocal circle of disciples whose center was occupied by a figure with prophetic-charismatic authority as portrayed in the "beloved disciple" of the fourth gospel. It understood itself as a circle of "friends" of Jesus (3 John 15), being led "into all the truth" by the Spirit sent directly by Jesus himself (John 16:13). Neither the institutional form of the church nor the problems of church government as such are taken up as themes here. The group itself, however, can be characterized as episodic; that is, whereas part of the group turned to the → Gnostic movement, the rest of its members found their way into the nascent larger church of the second century.

Bibliography: R. Banks, *Paul's Idea of Community* (Exeter, 1980) • R. E. Brown, *The Church the Apostles Left Behind* (New York, 1984); idem, *The Community of the Beloved Disciple* (New York, 1979) • F. J. Cwiekowski, *The Beginnings of the Church* (Mahwah, N.J., 1987) • B. Holmberg, *Paul and Power* (Philadelphia, 1978) • H. C. Kee, *Who Are the People of God? Early Christian Models of Community* (New Haven, 1995) • J. Roloff, *Die Kirche im Neuen Testament* (Göttingen, 1993).

Jürgen Roloff

2. Church History

The Christian churches, as expressions in this world of God's supratemporal and supraspatial acts toward his people, have developed specific forms of legally constituted organization, as have other human societies. "Church government," or "church polity," refers to the ordering of personal and collegial tasks and concrete functions in a fellowship of service. Formally it involves legal documents or the right of custom.

In the course of church history various types of church government have developed with either strongly personal or strongly collegial structures. With some oversimplification, one might say that episcopal government focuses on the → bishop, synodic government on collegial responsibility, and consistorial government on official structure, though elements of all three types typically overlap.

2.1. In the NT and the early church up to the second century, in spite of incipient legal thinking, there was no fixed form of church government. Even when expectation of the imminent end diminished (→ Eschatology), along with its charismatic features (→ Charisma), there was more of a community spirit, accompanied by a development of ministry. Slowly a threefold system of ministry emerged, involving the bishop, presbyter, and → deacon. At first the three enjoyed a collegial relation, but already in the second century the bishop, buttressed by the doc-

trine of apostolic succession, began to exercise a hierarchical superiority over the congregation and other ministers (→ Offices, Ecclesiastical). After the Edict of Milan in 313 and the merging of the early church into the imperial church (381/392), metropolitans and patriarchs came on the scene after the political model of the empire, and with the increasing authority of Rome from the end of the fourth century, leadership devolved upon the → pope. Collegial elements remained, however, in diocesan and metropolitan → synods, and after 325 in general councils (→ Nicaea, Councils of; Councils of the Church). From the fourth century onward, a different type of polity appeared also in → monasticism (→ Orders and Congregations).

2.2. After the confusion of the barbarian invasions, the papacy grew more powerful with the help of the ecclesiastical policy of France. It achieved external influence through the rise and spread of the → Papal States. The reforming popes of the 11th and 12th centuries, resisting trends in Germanic law (→ Proprietary Church) and other powerful foreign influences, established the centralized system that still exists in principle today. The → hierarchical structures (pope, archbishop, bishop) increased the separation of → clergy and laity. Nevertheless, collegial rights might still be seen in → cathedral and clergy chapters, diocesan synods, national councils, and revived ecumenical councils (from the First Lateran Council, 1123). In the 14th century → conciliarism and early → secularization by stronger rulers made inroads into the system.

2.3. In some ways, the 16th-century Lutheran → Reformation did not achieve any basic change of church government. The attempts of M. → Luther (1483-1546) to bring the local congregations and their members into responsibility for church work failed in actual practice, so the subject-object relation between → pastor and parishioners persisted. Since the bishops did not go along with the Reformation, the higher levels of church government fell into the hands of the secular rulers, an arrangement confirmed by the Peace of Augsburg (1555; → Augsburg, Peace of).

Though there might be differences in detail, church government as it found expression in the various church orders was remarkably uniform. Consistories commissioned by the rulers took charge of church affairs (e.g., in writing marriage laws). The congregations were grouped under → superintendents or deans, with general superintendents for larger areas. Ministerial synods (chapters) were merely advisory. Rationalistic theories of justification finally changed the position of the rulers from one of emergency bishops to that of framers of religious policy (→ Episcopalianism, Episcopal System; Collegialism).

2.4. Development under U. → Zwingli (1484-1531) and J. → Calvin (1509-64) was different, leading to the formation of Reformed and Presbyterian churches. Under the influence of conciliarism and city constitutions of the late Middle Ages, early models arose in Hesse (Homberg Synod 1526, Lambert of Avignon) and Strasbourg (M. → Bucer). In his *Institutes* and in church life in Geneva, Calvin then worked out the presbyterial form with the four offices of pastor, teacher, elder, and deacon (→ Calvin's Theology). The French National Synod in the *Discipline ecclésiastique* then developed a system of synods consisting of pastors and laity. At three or four levels these made formal decisions regarding the government of the church. Between meetings of the synod, the local congregation was supreme. Only gradually did standing bodies *(Moderamina)* arise to exercise ongoing leadership. No place was left for personal leadership. With variations, this became the model throughout the Reformed world (including Scotland, the Netherlands, and Germany; → Presbyterianism).

2.5. In the 19th century, because of territorial changes made at the Congress of Vienna (1815), the German territorial churches came into being, partly under the influence of → Pietism and the unions by which Lutheran consistories merged with Reformed synods. The church government in Baden (1821) and Westphalia (1835) was a model, and the other churches, partly under the influence of the 1848 → revolution, followed suit after 1870. Councils consisting of church members as well as ministers were set up in the parishes to support the ministers and to make basic decisions regarding church life and the handling of church property (→ Church Finances). At the middle level there was a superintendent, provost, or dean, along with a synod and standing committee. At the territorial church level was the consistory, with representatives of both state and church, which acted as *summus episcopus* but not without the consent of a territorial synod consisting of both ordained and nonordained members.

3. Roman Catholic Church

The worldwide → Roman Catholic Church is numerically the most important and most highly organized Christian body. It counts 1.1 billion members (1995), approximately 55 percent of all Christians around the world.

3.1. This church has a sense of being in unbroken continuity with the → apostles, in spite of various schisms in the course of church history (→ Heresies and Schisms), the most important being the breaking away of the churches of the East in the 5th and 11th centuries, and the Reformation churches in the 16th century. Since the 5th century, the constitution of the Roman church has been centered on the papacy, which gained strength with the enforcement of universal jurisdiction in the 12th century. This constitution found legal expression in the → Corpus Iuris Canonici, which came into being in the 12th to 14th centuries as the most important collection of sources. Already here the pope has the threefold power of teaching, ordination, and jurisdiction that was upheld in spite of problems both external (Babylonian captivity, Western schisms, conciliarism) and internal (the Renaissance papacy).

After the internal reforms of the 16th century (→ Catholic Reform and Counterreformation), the medieval development was continued and sharpened by the Council of → Trent (1545-63). From this, notwithstanding absolutism, secularization, and episcopalianism, there is a direct line to → Vatican I (1869-70), whose dogmatic decisions ensured the pope's hierarchical leadership, even though the Papal States were dissolved (1870). Since then there has been a distinct spiritualizing of ecclesiastical law (→ Church Law) and also of church government, despite the legal positivism that came to expression in the codification of 1917 (→ Corpus Iuris Canonici [CIC]). The predominantly pastoral → Vatican II (1962-65) strengthened this tendency, as may be seen in the 1983 CIC.

3.2. The 1983 CIC, which codifies the most important legal rulings, is more flexible than its predecessor — appropriately so, in view of the growing diversity of the worldwide church. The emphasis as regards constitutional law falls on book 2 ("The People of God," cans. 204-746), though pertinent statements may be found throughout the text.

3.3. Essentially, Roman Catholic constitutional law distinguishes three types of law: divine law, divinely created → natural law, and human law. It views the whole church as the body of Christ, the → people of God, but continues to make a significant distinction between → clergy and laity. Constitutionally the stress is not on power but on office. Three basic offices *(munera)* are elaborated, and the CIC is divided accordingly.

3.3.1. The → teaching office *(munus docendi,* bk. 3, cans. 747-833) includes → proclamation, mission, and the development of → dogma. This office is entrusted to the church as a whole but is exercised by the pope and bishops. Papal pronouncements on → faith and morals are → infallible, and so are those of bishops when they are made along with all other bishops and the pope.

3.3.2. The office of sanctifying (*munus sanctificandi*, bk. 4, cans. 834-1253) is the equivalent of the legal power of ordaining, the transmission of ministry. This right pertains primarily to the bishop, with only a restricted power of delegation. The pope's right to ordain does not differ qualitatively from that of the bishop, but since he is the universal bishop, it extends to the whole church.

3.3.3. The office of rule *(munus regendi)* concerns matters of ecclesiastical legislation (→ Church Law), church administration, and ecclesiastical → jurisdiction. At this level the pope and bishop are supreme, along with the heads of orders and free → prelates. The structures are primarily personal, but administratively we also find the → cardinals, → curia, → nuncios, → bishops' nuncios, → vicar-generals, and others. There also are the patriarch or → primate and archbishop (metropolitan), and in the → diocese the deans and parish clergy.

3.4. The whole structure also includes supplementary collegial bodies with a variety of supportive and advisory roles. At the level of central leadership is the ecumenical council. Bishops' synods offer advice. Under the pope, and primarily to deal with specific issues, there are national and continent-wide bishops' conferences and national and provincial councils. As chief lawgiver, the bishop has a diocesan synod, as well as the cathedral chapter, priests' council, and pastoral and diocesan councils. A parish council assists at the local level. The → orders and → monasteries have their own official and collegial structures.

Bibliography: J. M. BUCKLEY, "Canon Law," *NCE* 3.29-53 • S. GRUNDMANN and R. SMEND, "Kirchenverfassungen VI-VII," *RGG* (3d ed.) 3.1570-91 • P. HINSCHIUS, *Das Kirchenrecht der Katholiken und Protestanten in Deutschland* (6 vols.; Berlin, 1869-97) • C. H. LEFEBVRE, "Canon Law, Influence of Roman Law on," *NCE* 3.50-53 • J. LISTL et al., eds., *Handbuch des katholischen Kirchenrechts* (Regensburg, 1983) • K. LÜDICKE, ed., *Münsterischer Kommentar zum CIC/1983* (Essen, 1985ff.) • A. PETTEGREE, A. DUKE, and G. LEWIS, eds., *Calvinism in Europe, 1540-1620* (Cambridge, 1994) • W. M. PLÖCHL, *Geschichte des Kirchenrechts* (5 vols.; 2d ed.; Vienna, 1960-70) • "Roman Catholicism," *ODCC* 1408-9 • E. SEHLING, "Church Government," *NSHE* 3.92-96 • C. VOGEL et al., "Canon Law, History of," *NCE* 3.34-50 • E. WOLF, *Ordnung der Kirche* (Frankfurt, 1961) • A. W. ZIEGLER, *Religion, Kirche und Staat in Geschichte und Gegenwart* (3 vols.; Munich, 1969-74).

HERBERT FROST

4. Orthodox Church

The Orthodox Church is administered according to its synodic-collegial structure as a fellowship of churches and Christians. This corresponds to its basic democratic view and its self-understanding as a → church (§3.1) where no single member dominates the others. The Orthodox Church strongly affirms that the guardian of truth is the entire → "people of God" and that the church as a whole is being led "into all the truth" (John 16:13). Therefore the supreme, leading institution is not a single person but a congregation — the ecumenical → council or → synod, in which the living awareness of faith of the whole people of God finds its authentic expression. Ecumenical councils constitute the highest canonical, doctrinal, and administrative authority; they are called when very important matters affecting the faith and order of the whole church are to be decided by the *plērōma* (fullness, entity) of the church. Preparations are now being made for a "Holy and Great Council of the Orthodox Church" that will witness to and confirm the Orthodox faith in the coming millennium (→ Pan-Orthodox Conferences). Ecumenical councils can be called only if all parts of the church consent. Corresponding to them on the local or regional level are the synods of the various → autocephalous Orthodox churches, which are independent and consist of the assembly of all the bishops of the area, normally together with representatives from the clergy, the monasteries, and the laity. These local synods meet from time to time, or they may be permanent. They have the task of general administration in the territory of the autocephalous church. Under their supervision every bishop rules his own → diocese (eparchy) independently.

The office of the bishop is one of spiritual leadership (in teaching and worship) and administration. He is the witness of a tradition going back to the apostles. Some bishops have broader administrative functions, especially the head bishops of the autocephalous churches, who may be called patriarch, metropolitan, or archbishop. The bishops are supported by the → priests as local parish leaders and by the → deacons; both are specially ordained to their positions (→ Ordination).

The laity also has a share in administration of the church. Since all the baptized are members of equal value (→ Baptism; Church Membership 2), the distinction between → clergy and laity is not essential or fundamental but merely functional. Lay leaders assist the clergy at the diocesan and the congregational levels, both administratively and liturgically. Church administration involves ecclesiastical legisla-

tion, jurisdiction, finance, and matters affecting →
church employees.

→ Orthodox Church; Orthodoxy 3

Bibliography: S. BULGAKOV, The Orthodox Church (London, 1935) • A. JENSEN, Die Zukunft der Orthodoxie. Konzilspläne und Kirchenstrukturen (Zurich, 1986) • A. KALLIS, Orthodoxie — Was ist das? (Mainz, 1979) • Die Kirche und die Kirchen. Autonomie und Autokephalie (Vienna, 1980/81) • Konziliarität und Kollegialität als Strukturprinzipien der Kirche (Innsbruck, 1975) • N. THON, "Einheit in die Vielfalt. Die Kirche in die Sicht der heutigen orthodoxe Ekklesiologie," COst 38 (1983) 84-92; idem, ed., Quellenbuch zur Geschichte der Orthodoxen Kirche (Trier, 1983) • J. D. ZIZIOULAS, Being as Communion: Studies in Personhood and the Church (New York, 1985).

NIKOLAUS THON

5. Other Christian Churches

5.1. *Western and Central Europe*

In the → Lutheran and → Reformed churches of
Germany and nearby lands, the doctrine of church
government developed in sharp contrast to the
Roman Catholic concept of hierarchical jurisdiction.
Criticism was directed against the latter's supposed
necessity to salvation and its use of secular power in
the spiritual sphere. On the Reformation view, authority in the church is that of the proclamation of
the Word, the administration of the sacraments, and
the use of the → power of the keys, all by the Word
and not by force (*sine vi sed verbo*, Augs. Conf. 28).
The church has only the one spiritual office at its
disposal (→ Offices, Ecclesiastical). Therefore the
terms "bishop" and "pastor" are synonymous. However, such leadership functions of the bishop as →
visitation, → ordination, and oversight are accepted
as matters of good order. All other power is to be
exercised in Christian → freedom, and it is not necessarily tied to the spiritual office.

Since most bishops rejected the Reformation and
the Protestant view of church government, the Reformers saw no reason not to commit the government of the church to the princes as an auxiliary and
emergency service (J. Heckel) in defense against disintegration, though the princes had this function
only as leading members of the church, not as those
who wielded secular power. Only with the legal
settlement (→ Episcopalianism, Episcopal System;
Augsburg, Peace of) did the older episcopal functions of church government pass to the territorial
rulers on the basis of a secular legal title. The ruler
was the *summus episcopus*, though a leader only in
external matters (*episcopus in externis*). In practice

he worked with a consistory made up of theologians
and jurists.

The "three estates" teaching of the older Protestant orthodoxy tried to limit the concentration of
power by giving the clergy a right of cooperation.
The episcopal office survived at first in the form of
the → superintendent, who increasingly came to
serve the end of moral discipline, but who also, by
way of the general superintendent of Prussia, helped
the church toward independence in the 19th century.
The Reformed tradition moved in the same direction.
This revived the idea of leadership by synod by emphasizing the office of the presbyter, as discussed
most clearly in the Bible (→ Elder). Rhenish Westphalia set up a presbyterian system alongside the
consistory in 1835, and the system then spread to the
other territorial churches. The weakness of the secular bishop led finally to the disengagement of the
church from state government and the greater independence of its organs. Territorial church government remained, but in increasing separation from
secular government. The consistories achieved autonomy.

The secular episcopate ended with the upheaval
of 1918, but this development did not find the
churches unprepared. Constitutions after 1919 reshaped church government, nominally entrusting
supreme leadership to the synod, but with real
power in the hands of a board of leaders representing both synod and consistory. In fact the consistories, in virtue of their stability and competence,
retained their earlier authority. The episcopal question was the cause of bitter strife. Most constitutions
introduced a leading spiritual office, though not all
used the title "bishop" or gave it the same functions.
The office of the bishop was generally introduced
only after 1933; one reason, though by no means
the only one, was the general acceptance by the
church then of what we might call a Führer mentality.

Fresh thinking after the → church struggle led to
the defining of leadership in terms of the church's
commission and not primarily in terms of secular
ideas of democracy, parliamentarianism, or the separation of powers. Functionally, many organs now
shared church leadership, including pastors and lay
leaders in the congregations; synods, boards, and
leading clergy at the middle level; and a council and
administrators at the territorial level. The task was
"to lead the church in cooperative fellowship and
mutual responsibility" (art. 40.1 of the Bavarian constitution). It is to be noted that spiritual leadership
means pastoral direction by Word and sacrament.
Only to this extent is it reserved for the ministry of

the Word. All external functions of leadership are to be exercised in evangelical freedom.

Church leadership in the institutional sense is different. It is usually the task of a college consisting of the bishop, superintendent, members of the synod, and administrators. It thus unites episcopal, synodic, and consistorial elements. There are considerable differences in detail. The central place of the bishop finds expression in the fact that he exercises spiritual leadership as pastor and watchman, but he is also president of the leading council and may also be in the synod. He thus has a coordinating function.

As a whole, one may say that in spite of constitutional multiplicity and divergent traditions (→ Denomination), the differences in practice are not of crucial importance. The newer constitutions all emphatically remind all officeholders at all levels that church leadership is not primarily a matter of rule but one of ministry to the church (§§3.4-5) and its members and commission.

Bibliography: T. BARTH, *Elemente und Typen landeskirchlicher Leitung* (Tübingen, 1995) • A. VON CAMPENHAUSEN, "Entstehung und Funktionen des bischöflichen Amtes in die evangelische Kirchen in Deutschland," *ÖAKR* 26 (1975) 3-24; idem, "Kirchenleitung," *ZEvKR* 29 (1984) 11-34 • G. EBELING, *Dogmatik des christlichen Glaubens* (vol. 3; Tübingen, 1979; 2d ed., 1982) • H. FROST, *Strukturprobleme evangelischer Kirchenverfassung* (Göttingen, 1972) • M. HECKEL, "Rechtstheologie Luthers," *EStL* 2.2818-49; idem, "Reformation II," ibid. 2898-2931 • G. HOFFMANN, "Kirchenleitung I," *EStL* 1.1640-45 • C. LINK, *Die Grundlagen der Kirchenverfassung im lutherischen Konfessionalismus des 19. Jahrhunderts . . .* (Munich, 1966); idem, "Kirchenrecht (= Staatskirchenrecht)," *HRG* 2.783-825; idem, "Staat und Kirchen," *Deutsche Verwaltungsgeschichte* (ed. K. G. A. von Jeserich et al.; Stuttgart, 1983) 3.527-59; 4.459-82, 1002-16 • H. M. MUELLER, "Church Polity," *ELC* 1.519-26 • J. L. SCHAVER, *The Polity of the Churches* (6th ed.; 2 vols.; Grand Rapids, 1961) • A. STEIN, *Evangelisches Kirchenrecht* (3d ed.; Neuwied, 1992).

CHRISTOPH LINK

5.2. Scandinavia
In Denmark, Finland, Iceland, Norway, and Sweden, the Lutheran churches take a sharply different form. With slight variations, they are organized as state churches and are episcopalian, with some synodic features. The leader of the church is the king or president, and each church has its legal basis in the national constitution, laws, and ordinances. The churches have independent rights mainly in the parishes, which are divided into districts under pro-

vosts and bishops. In Sweden and Finland the archbishops of Uppsala and Turku have a certain primacy and limited powers of leadership. Pastors, provosts, and bishops are appointed by the government or the head of the church after church elections. They are in some sense state officials. To varying degrees synods function in the deaneries and dioceses, and in Iceland, Finland, and Sweden there are also church synods with limited powers of legislation, chiefly in liturgical matters. The cathedral chapters and bishops' conferences have some initiative in leadership and administration. In Iceland and Finland the same applies to the church council or extended bishop's conference, in which the laity participate.

5.3. Anglican Communion
The → Anglican Communion includes the Church of England, Anglican churches in the Commonwealth, the Episcopal Church of Scotland, the Episcopal Church in the United States, and many independent churches resulting from missionary work. Anglicans have kept the liturgical forms of → Roman Catholicism, but their theology is that of the European Reformation. A general characteristic is the strong emphasis on the episcopal office with the claim to unbroken apostolic succession (→ Church 3.3).

The Church of England is a state church with mixed episcopal and synodic features. The monarch is the temporal governor of the church, but the government and parliament have a leading voice, with some bishops being seated in the upper house. The structure of ministry is the threefold one of bishops, priests, and deacons. Control is exercised by the parochial church councils, the cathedral deans and chapters, diocesan synods, and the church assembly, which can pass laws, though these require parliamentary confirmation.

The other Anglican and Episcopal churches are in countries in which they have no state ties, so that they have great freedom in shaping their own polity. This is especially true in the United States, where the parishes have a good deal of control over their own affairs, and synods and conventions play an important role.

5.4. United States and the Third World
Church government varies greatly in the United States. Almost all → denominations have their own distinctive features, reflecting the lands of their origin. A notable characteristic is that in every confession there is an emphasis on the local congregation (→ Congregationalism), which also functions as a social entity. The Orthodox, Roman Catholics, Episcopalians, and Methodists have bishops, the Presbyterians and Lutherans rule by synods, and the → free

churches (→ Church 3.6) have looser associations in which general decisions have force only as local congregations accept them. In synods and conventions, special commissions and the general secretary exert great influence.

Worldwide, the Orthodox, Roman Catholic, and Episcopal Churches present what is to a large extent a common picture. Presbyterians and Reformed are all synodic, though with bishops in Hungary, Romania, and Spain. The Lutherans vary greatly depending on the primacy of the bishop (superintendent) or synod. In the main, the → Third World churches follow the models of the European or American mother churches, though they are tentatively striking out on their own, especially in the → base communities, with their strong spiritual dynamic.

→ Concordat; Filiation; Visitation

Bibliography: O. P. GRELL, ed., *The Scandinavian Reformation* (Cambridge, 1995) • H. H. HARMS, ed., *Die Kirche von England und die Anglikanische Kirchengemeinschaft* (Stuttgart, 1966) • W. S. HUDSON, *The Great Tradition of the American Churches* (New York, 1953) on voluntarism • L. S. HUNTER, ed., *Scandinavian Churches* (London, 1965) • P. LEISCHING, *Kirche und Staat in die Rechtsordnungen Europas* (Freiburg, 1973) • S. NEILL, *Anglicanism* (3d ed.; Harmondsworth, 1965) • *WKL.*

HERBERT FROST

Church Growth

Overview

Overview
The term "church growth" can refer to church renewal, church organizational and structural maturation, the empirically verifiable numerical growth of churches, and the theory of how and why churches grow or decline. The so-called church growth move-

ment (see 5) began in the United States in the 1960s, although not everyone who studies the dynamics of church growth and decline would consider themselves part of this movement.

Corresponding to Eng. "church growth" is Ger. *Gemeindeaufbau,* which to a large extent has become a programmatic word today in the German- speaking world. The lively *Diskussion zur Theologie des Gemeindeaufbaus* (ed. R. Weth; Neukirchen, 1986) points to differences in the understanding of this term. On the one hand, it may denote the organization of the church — its activity and the forms of its external and internal relationships. On the other hand, it may point to changes to be made in these — that is, to reform and rejuvenation in the light of new goals. This tension reflects the ecumenical diversity today in understanding the church (→ Congregation 4.3) and its tasks.

ERWIN FAHLBUSCH

1. Germany
1.1. *People's Church (Volkskirche)*
Bruno Gutmann initiated discussion of church growth with his book *Gemeindeaufbau aus dem Evangelium* (1925). Missionary work in Africa from 1903 had shown the inadequacy of earlier ideas of congregational care (E. Sulze), work (M. Schian), or organization (W. Warneck), for these put human care, work, and organization at the center. Instead, Gutmann wanted to see the community as the body of Christ grow organically from the → gospel itself, while noting and honoring what God the Creator has already structured in such traditional relationships as tribe, locality, and age-group. → Dialectical theology regarded Gutmann's understanding as too little protected against the dangers of natural theology.

The → Confessing Church, following the seventh article of the Augsburg Confession and the third thesis of the → Barmen Declaration (1934), argued that the origin, center, and goal of every congregational structure is → worship, in which the gathered community responds to authentic proclamation and administration of the sacraments in thanksgiving, confession, and prayer (J. Beckmann, 362). K. → Barth systematically developed this insight in *CD* IV/1-3, and a revision of most → church orders and liturgies (→ Liturgical Books) followed after 1945. Under inspiration from the United States, a theology of → stewardship after World War II attempted to enrich the liturgical view with a missionary view oriented to the gifts of the whole congregation and promoting a charismatic understanding of church organization and growth.

The WCC study *"The Church for Others" and "The Church for the World"* (1967), with the liturgically oriented parish in view, spoke of a morphological fundamentalism and called for the replacement of a "come-structure" by "go-structures" in which the church would move out into the world. Experiences with unstructured communities and the question "How stable is the church?" (H. Hild) showed that the ecumenical study had ignored people's real expectations. The local congregation with worship as its organizing center proved to be the "church of shortcuts" (H. Schröer), which in the long run not only is more stable but also is closer to E. Lange's concept of the "ensemble of offerings."

But the question also arose how far the church in its organization and growth should make itself dependent on popular expectations. The demand for an "evangelistic and missionary community" (T. Sorg, M. Seitz), for a "manageable" (F. Schwarz) and "inviting" (K. Teschner) church, for a "community of spiritual renewal" (W. Kopfermann), and for "church growth" (G. W. Peters) had as its aim a search for the true sources of church growth in the power of the → Holy Spirit, in an ecclesia radically different from the (established) → people's church, and in a spiritual renewal of the pastorate (→ Pastor, Pastorate) and all → church employees.

The need in discussion of church growth is to overcome false alternatives that play off congregation against → church or people's church against missionary congregation. A true people's church can still provide the opportunity for evangelistic and missionary work and is not just a comfortable cushion. In the matter of church growth, we must discover the congregation afresh as the spiritual reality of the body of Christ, which is always in the process of being built up because Christ exists as the church community in the power of the Holy Spirit and sustains his people by Word and sacrament (D. → Bonhoeffer). Paul had this event of community building in mind when he used the term *oikodomē* (e.g., 1 Cor. 3:9; 14:3-12).

Bibliography: K. BARTH, *CD* IV/1-3, *The Doctrine of Reconciliation* • J. BECKMANN, ed., *Kirchliches Jahrbuch für die Evangelische Kirche in Deutschland, 1933-1944* (2d ed.; Gütersloh, 1976) • D. BONHOEFFER, *The Communion of Saints: A Dogmatic Inquiry into the Sociology of the Church* (New York, 1963) • B. GUTMANN, *Gemeindeaufbau aus dem Evangelium* (Leipzig, 1925) • H. HILD, ed., *Wie stabil ist die Kirche? Bestand und Erneuerung. Ergebnisse einer Meinungsbefragung* (Gelnhausen, 1974)

• T. A. KANTONEN, *A Theology for Christian Stewardship* (Philadelphia, 1956) • E. LANGE, *Chancen des Alltags. Überlegungen zur Funktion des christlichen Gottesdienstes in der Gegenwart* (2d ed.; ed. P. Cornehl; Munich, 1984) • C. MÖLLER, *Lehre von Gemeindeaufbau* (vol. 1; 2d ed.; Göttingen, 1987); idem, *Seelsorglich predigen* (Göttingen, 1983); idem, *Wovon die Kirche lebt* (Göttingen, 1980) • G. W. PETERS, *A Theology of Church Growth* (Grand Rapids, 1981) • F. SCHWARZ, *Überschaubare Gemeinde* (3 vols.; Gladbeck, 1980-81) • F. SCHWARZ and C. A. SCHWARZ, *Theologie des Gemeindeaufbaus* (2d ed.; Neukirchen, 1985) • M. SEITZ, *Erneuerung der Gemeinde. Gemeindeaufbau und Spiritualität* (Göttingen, 1985) • T. SORG, *Wie wird die Kirche neu?* (Wuppertal, 1977) • R. STRUNK, *Vertrauen. Grundzüge einer Theologie des Gemeindeaufbaus* (Stuttgart, 1985) • E. SULZE, *Die evangelische Gemeinde* (Gotha, 1891) • P. VIELHAUER, *Oikodome* (2d ed.; Munich, 1978) • R. WETH, ed., *Diskussion zur "Theologie des Gemeindeaufbaus"* (Neukirchen, 1986) • E. WINKLER, "Zur Theologie des Gemeindeaufbaus," *TLZ* 111 (1986) 481-92 • WORLD COUNCIL OF CHURCHES, *"The Church for Others" and "The Church for the World": A Quest for Structures for Missionary Congregations* (Geneva, 1967).

CHRISTIAN MÖLLER

1.2. Free Churches

In the → free churches in Germany, believers are invited to commitment and → discipleship. The church community comes into being wherever the Word finds faith (W. Klaiber). A lived-out → faith is the inalienable starting point for the community. Only those who confess their faith before the → congregation can become members; only those who stay with the congregation can remain members. For the free churches, voluntariness means a free response of faith to the gospel, with all that this implies (R. Knierim). Reformation is thus extended to the structure of the church (R. Thaut).

→ Baptists and the Union of Free Evangelical Churches are congregational (→ Congregationalism). They have central instrumentalities only to help the local congregations. → Methodists have a kind of → presbyterian order. The annual conference of all pastors in an area (i.e., all the ordained elders), along with a similar number of elected laity, exercises leadership. All ministries are oriented to church growth, and all members are meant to be free to develop their particular gifts (→ Charisma). The church thus is run as a "charismatic organization" (T. Spörri).

The free churches try to make the church a place

of fellowship (W. Popkes). They chiefly represent the evangelistic type of church growth (→ Evangelical Movement), for from the outset the free churches organized themselves as missions — the congregational free churches more as representing a pure community, the → Methodist churches more as a movement of evangelization and sanctification, with emphasis on the issue of human salvation.

The voluntary contribution of the so-called laity is fundamental in understanding church growth in the free churches. The church is the mature people of God. Along with the missionary emphasis there is also a stress on → diakonia, which reveals itself in the high level of giving to charity. All church support comes from voluntary gifts, which is both a limitation and a strength (→ Church Finances).

The still unclarified relation with national churches has often led to the denouncing of free-church organizing as proselytizing. Part of the problem is that ossified thinking in the national churches regards → evangelization as unnecessary and thus dismisses basic free church concerns. From the second generation on, the free churches, too, become dependent on biological growth. The voluntary nature of → church membership can result in painful separations, for faith is not hereditary, and spiritual awakening cannot be institutionalized. Where the congregation loses sight of its revivalist background, attempts at securing binding discipleship can become legalistic. Church growth of the free churches in otherwise manageable congregations is not immune to unproductive polarizations, which can lead to an acid test. The free churches cannot accept a parochial restriction of their work or any monopolizing of proclamation. In fellowship with others, they know that they are committed to the missionary command, which sets no limits on church growth.

→ Church 3.6

Bibliography: E. GELDBACH, Freikirchen — Erbe, Gestalt und Wirkung (Göttingen, 1989) • W. KLAIBER, Rechtfertigung und Gemeinde (Göttingen, 1982) • R. KNIERIM, Entwurf eines methodistischen Selbstverständnisses (Zurich, 1960) • C. LIENEMANN-PERRIN, ed., Taufe und Kirchenzugehörigkeit (Munich, 1983) esp. article by R. Weth, 337ff. • W. POPKES, Gemeinde. Raum des Vertrauens (Wuppertal, 1984) • T. SPÖRRI, Die Lehre von der Kirche (Zurich, 1947) • R. STRUNK, Vertrauen. Grundzüge einer Theologie des Gemeindeaufbaus (Stuttgart, 1985) esp. 89ff. • R. THAUT, "Der theologische Beitrag der Freikirchen," Glieder an einem Leib (ed. H. B. Motel; Konstanz, 1975) 9-38 • A. WALKER, See How They Grow (Glasgow, 1979).

DIETER SACKMANN

2. Third World Churches

Today more than two-thirds of the world's population lives in the so-called → Third World. We find there typical people's churches (e.g., in ethnic groups and in the South Sea Islands), small minority churches (e.g., in the Islamic, Hindu, and Buddhist worlds), and a variety of relations between → church and state (from situations of persecution to state support for Christian educational programs). Amid this diversity, are there any common marks of church growth?

2.1. Challenges

2.1.1. In spite of → secularization, in Europe and North America there is still a cultural continuity between the Jewish-Christian heritage and the modern world. Third World Christians, however, have seldom met any Jews, who might provide them with living contact with the OT. Likewise, their languages and worldviews have not been shaped by Christianity. Their festivals did not originate in the → church year but in the feasts of → Islam, → Hinduism, or other religions. Thus Third World churches are often culturally isolated and in danger of living in a ghetto influenced by Western forms of thought, worship, and church. For church growth, then, the theme of the → gospel and culture is extremely important, as is also → dialogue with other religions.

2.1.2. The European parish system and other forms of ministry that developed in church history are alien to many Third World social and leadership structures. For church growth it is important to rediscover NT structures of community and worship and in the light of them to develop the forms best suited to each particular culture. In modern China and large areas of Latin America, for example, house churches and → base communities have provided the best setting for → worship, instruction, and diaconal and missionary service. In them pastorally gifted laypeople and mobile theological teachers play an important part, making necessary ongoing training of the laity and advanced theological education (e.g., through correspondence courses, congregation-based leadership formation, theological education by extension systems, and other nontraditional forms of ministry formation).

2.1.3. Third World Christians live in conditions ranging from very poor to very wealthy, from a small persecuted minority to a significant, sometimes powerful, increasingly nominal majority. Some Third World Christians live in rural communities with an essentially oral tradition. In such situations, church growth on the basis of purely literary media makes little sense. For them, the narrating and singing of biblical stories, mimes and sacramental liturgies, and a close linking of daily → work to worship are the best means of church growth. Radio and tape cassettes can also render good service.

Increasingly, however, Third World Christians are also to be found living in the exploding cities of the world, where they are involved in all types of professions and are highly literate. Leadership formation, church development, lay ministries, and living out what it means to be a Christian in every walk of life are urgent issues. Writing and publishing by Third World Christians in their own languages and in their own settings is paramount. Computer literacy is increasing, and creativity in new forms of communication, especially through the use of video technology and the arts, is evident. As everywhere, the biblical message and a concrete involvement of Christians in the world are primarily needed.

→ Biblical Theology 2; Christian Art 12; Contextual Theology; Liberation Theology; Third World Theology

Bibliography: R. ALLEN, *Missionary Methods: St. Paul's or Ours? A Study of the Church in the Four Provinces* (London, 1912) • M. BAVAREL, *New Communities, New Ministries: The Church Resurgent in Asia, Africa, and Latin America* (New York, 1983) • P. BEYERHAUS and H. LEFEVER, *The Responsible Church and the Foreign Mission* (Grand Rapids, 1964) • J. FREYTAG and H. J. MARGULL, eds., *Junge Kirchen auf eigenen Wegen* (Neukirchen, 1972) • R. FUNG, *Households of God on China's Soil* (2d ed.; Maryknoll, N.Y., 1983) • D. A. McGAVRAN, *The Bridges of God: A Study in the Strategy of Missions* (New York, 1955) • V. SØGAARD, *Media in Church and Mission: Communicating the Gospel* (Pasadena, Calif., 1993) • G. F. VICEDOM, "Gemeinde V: Gemeindeaufbau in der Mission," *RGG* (3d ed.) 2.1342-44 • WELTMISSION '85, *Ein Wort wie Feuer. Wie Christen in der Welt die Bibel lesen* (Hamburg, 1985).

HANS-RUEDI WEBER, with CHARLES VAN ENGEN

2.2 Recent Growth

An astounding development of the 20th century has been the rapid growth in the number of Christians in Africa, Asia, and Latin America. This growth has been coupled with decline in the number of active church members in Europe and North America. "The total of Christians has grown enormously [in the 20th cent.], from 558 millions in 1900 to 1,433 millions in 1980. . . . Since 1900 Christianity has become massively accepted as the religion of developing countries in the so-called Third World, Africa in particular. But no one in 1900 expected the massive

defections from Christianity that subsequently took place in Western Europe due to secularism, in Russia and later Eastern Europe due to Communism, and in the Americas due to materialism" (*WCE*, 3). This phenomenal growth has meant a shift in the center of gravity of global Christianity, away from West and North to East and South — from the industrial nations of Europe and North America to the Third World.

Most of the growth of churches in the Third World has involved groups not associated with the older historic traditions of Europe and North America. For example, Pentecostal/charismatic Christians around the globe numbered 461 million in 1998, or 23.4 percent of all Christians, up from only 6.1 percent in 1970 and 0.7 percent in 1900 (D. B. Barrett and T. M. Johnson 1998, 27). The rapid growth of Protestantism in Latin America during the last 30 years is a well-known phenomenon.

In addition to the growth of Pentecostal/charismatic churches, the 1980s and 1990s have seen a spectacular growth in the number of megachurches (i.e., churches with membership in the tens of thousands), of which there were more than 150 in 1993, according to John Vaughan. Some of these are "postdenominational" churches, that is, with little or no historic ties to older Western missionary endeavor. They often have taken on a life and nature of their own, mushrooming through home-cell and house-church development, often comprising one church numbering from several thousand to hundreds of thousands of members.

A result of this rapid expansion has been the concomitant growth in cross-cultural mission-sending from the Third World to everywhere else on the globe. In 1973 there were 203 Third World mission agencies, together sending a total of 3,404 cross-cultural missionaries (J. Wong, P. Larson, and E. Pentecost). In 1983 this number had increased to 368 Third World mission agencies, sending an estimated 13,000 cross-cultural missionaries (L. Keyes). In 1989 there were 49,300 full-time missionaries, sent by 1,094 Third World mission agencies (L. Pate). Worldwide, there was a total of 409,000 foreign missionaries in 1998, up from 62,000 in 1900 (Barrett and Johnson 1998, 27).

Bibliography: Latin American Protestant growth: D. MARTIN, *Tongues of Fire: The Explosion of Protestantism in Latin America* (Oxford, 1990) • D. R. MILLER, ed., *Coming of Age: Protestantism in Contemporary Latin America* (New York, 1994) • D. STOLL, *Is Latin America Turning Protestant? The Politics of Evangelical Growth* (Berkeley, Calif., 1990).

Megachurches: J. N. Vaughan, *The World's Twenty Largest Churches: Small Group Church Growth Principles in Action* (Grand Rapids, 1984).

Pentecostal growth: D. B. Barrett, "The Twentieth-Century Pentecostal/Charismatic Renewal in the Holy Spirit, with Its Goal of World Evangelization," *IBMR* 12 (1988) 119-29; idem, ed., *WCE* • D. B. Barrett and T. M. Johnson, "Annual Statistical Table on Global Mission: 1998," *IBMR* 22 (1998) 26-27 • M. A. Dempster, B. D. Klaus, and D. Petersen, eds., *Called and Empowered: Global Mission in Pentecostal Perspective* (Peabody, Mass., 1991) • P. Pomerville, *The Third Force in Missions* (Peabody, Mass., 1985) • E. Pousson, *Spreading the Flame: Charismatic Churches and Missions Today* (Grand Rapids, 1992).

Third World mission-sending: L. E. Keyes, *The Last Age of Mission: A Study of Third World Mission Societies* (Pasadena, Calif., 1983) • L. Pate, *From Every People: A Handbook of Two-Thirds World Missions with Directory/ Histories/Analysis* (Monrovia, Calif., 1989) • J. Wong, P. Larson, and E. Pentecost, *Missions from the Third World* (Singapore, 1973).

Charles Van Engen

3. Minority Churches in Europe

A noteworthy development of the 20th century has been the rise of free, relatively independent minority churches, dissociated from the national churches, predominantly congregationally focused, and dispersed in a diaspora form throughout Europe.

3.1. *Lutheran and Reformed*

Diaspora is a presupposition of minority churches but certainly not the goal of church growth. W. Krusche in 1973, faced with resignation on the dissolution of the → people's church in East Germany, stressed the positive possibilities offered by the new → diaspora — namely, concentrating on what is decisive and maintaining a clear profile instead of settling for an amorphous church. This was helpful, but it would be wrong to conclude that diaspora offers a better basis for church growth than the people's church. Deficiencies in personnel and resources, along with spatial isolation, make church growth difficult. The sense of being a minority, loss of heart, and an elitist self-isolation weaken missionary strength.

The historical origin of a situation of diaspora affects the conditions of church growth. Among groups like the → Waldenses or the Protestant churches in Poland, France, Spain, and Italy, where for centuries the majority has been Roman Catholic, church growth does not take the same course as it did, for example, among Protestants in former East Germany. There Protestants became a postnational church minority, with extreme differences from region to region (7 percent of the population of East Berlin were members, in contrast to 90 percent in many villages in southern Saxony, less than 20 percent in others).

The main task of church growth in the diaspora is to become independent instead of being subsidized. This was more difficult in East Germany than in older diaspora churches, in which laypeople are used to sharing responsibility. Pastoral supervision of larger areas by fewer workers proves increasingly to be unsatisfying in more than a theological sense. Inordinate physical and psychological demands are a hindrance to intensive church growth. Such growth requires the establishing and strengthening of personal relations, which will help individuals to maintain and affirm their Christianity on the job, in society, and within the family. The laity has to form and lead groups and keep them going. As the Reformed Church of Poland has said, all Christians in the diaspora must be evangelists. At the same time, every congregation needs a pastor or lay preacher, even if honorary. In France, both Lutherans and Reformed are looking for new models of church and ministry. The diaspora situation calls for mutual dependence, yet also cooperative independence, of the two.

The possibilities of church growth in the diaspora come to light when Christians accept their situation as a missionary task, equip themselves in vital diaconal groups for the communication of the gospel in word and deed, show good → stewardship in the use of the gifts entrusted to them, and overcome the danger of insulation by diaconal openness, skill in communication, and a dynamic reworking of what has been handed down to them.

Bibliography: G. Bassarak and G. Wirth, eds., *Luther und Luthertum in Osteuropa* (Berlin, 1983) • R. Bodenstein et al., eds., *Kirche als Lerngemeinschaft. Dokumente aus der Arbeit des Bundes der Evangelischen Kirchen in der DDR* (FS D. A. Schönherr; Berlin, 1981) • A. Karner, "Diaspora als Lebensform der Kirche," *EvDia* 53 (1983) 47-55 • W. Krusche, "Die Gemeinde Jesu Christi auf dem Weg in die Diaspora," *EvDia* 45 (1975) 56-82 • J. A. Overman, "The God-Fearers: Some Neglected Features," *JSNT* 32 (February 1988) 17-26 • E. Winkler, "Die neue ländliche Diaspora als Frage an die Praktische Theologie," *TLZ* 112 (1987) 161-70 • F. Winter, "Kirche in der Diaspora," *PTh* 57 (1968) 170-88.

Eberhard Winkler

3.2. Orthodox

To meet the needs of believers, Orthodox congregations have been formed by the direction of the relevant hierarchs to develop and nurture church life. The metropolitan or → bishop appoints or calls the → priests to take charge of the liturgical life, social care, → pastoral care, and religious education in the → congregations. The metropolitan also appoints or summons a church council (usually consisting of five to seven laypeople) to help the pastor in his administrative tasks.

In the 20th century, Orthodox congregations of emigrants and migrant workers and their families have been founded in central and western Europe (→ Foreigners). The number of Orthodox has thus grown considerably in this region. The churches, however, suffer from special problems and difficulties. First comes the fact of migration itself. This uproots believers from their homelands, without giving them fresh roots in the West. The fluctuations of migrants worsen the problem. The → diaspora situation results in poor, scattered congregations with no church buildings and infrequent services. Believers thus experience isolation. Even more of a problem is the encounter with Western → industrial society, the → Enlightenment, → secularization, and modern → ideologies, which both priests and people are unable to handle because they come into the encounter unprepared. Training priests in the West might offer such preparation, but thus far it has not been possible. For Orthodox who have been used to → people's churches, living with other Christian churches is also something new. They have to become accustomed to church life in ecumenical fellowship (→ Local Ecumenism). Another great problem is that of second- and third-generation Orthodox who integrate themselves into their new surroundings. They are in danger of losing their language and culture, and even perhaps their religion. The Orthodox Church, however, is ill prepared to meet this danger and to find viable church solutions. The division of congregations by nationalities is a further problem. It reflects practical and linguistic circumstances, but it has no basis in Orthodox teaching or polity.

The pastoral idea of church growth in → Orthodoxy (§3) has a theological basis. The center of Orthodox church life is → worship, the divine liturgy. Experience shows that there will be a living church wherever believers come regularly to the → Eucharist. Orthodox worship applies to the whole person and has implications for all life. It is only on this basis that people and churches can solve their problems. The eucharistic event builds up the church as the body of Christ in this world.

→ Church 3.1

Bibliography: BROTHERHOOD OF THEOLOGIANS "ZOE," A Sign of God. Orthodoxy 1964: A Pan-Orthodox Symposium (Athens, 1964) • A. KALLIS, "Orthodoxie in Deutschland," RhM, no. 11 (March 14, 1980) and no. 13 (March 28, 1980); idem, "Westliche Orthodoxie, östliche Identität," MDÖC, no. 10 (June 1986) • J. KALOGIROU, "Hē Orthodoxos diaspora kata tēn epochēn tēs Oikoumenikēs kinēseōs," Ho kosmos tēs Orthodoxias (Thessaloníki, 1968) 137-82 • A. LABARDAKIS, "Die Griechische-Orthodoxe Metropolie von Deutschland. Sorgen und Probleme einer Gastarbeiterkirche," US 30 (1975) 146-50 • N. PAPADOPOULOS, "Zur Akkulturationsproblematik griechischer Industriearbeiter in Westdeutschland: Soziale Situation. Religiosität" (Diss., Bonn, 1975) • L. A. ZANDER, Die westliche Orthodoxie (Munich, 1959).

AUGOUSTINOS LABARDAKIS

4. United States

Church growth in the United States is viewed primarily as the recruitment and assimilation of new members into local congregations. More recently the term has come to have a technical meaning as the theory and practice of strategies that are conducive to these activities (see 5).

4.1. Socioreligious Context

The understanding of ekklēsia in the United States has been conditioned by the cultural history of the country, during the course of which church membership has been viewed as a voluntary activity with a wide range of motivation and commitment. The locus of the → church has therefore been the local congregation, where membership is determined less by doctrinal affirmation than by socioeconomic and racial constituency, and where, accordingly, the duties of a → pastor or → priest include not only the spiritual welfare of a congregation but also the management of its numerical stability and growth.

This ecclesial perspective is prevalent in most → denominations and is reflected in religious demographic surveys, which suggest that, while two-thirds of the population consistently affiliate with a church or synagogue and as many as 95 percent believe in God, only 10 percent regard themselves as spiritually committed to their faith.

4.2. Evangelism and Discipleship

In the mainstream of North American church life, this discrepancy gives rise to a particular connotation for the two words most closely associated with church growth: evangelism, understood as the reaching out of the church into society in order to gather in new members; and discipleship, understood as the building up in the Christian faith of those who join the church. This broad view is flanked by denominations with a high view of the church, such as Roman Catholics and Episcopalians, who emphasize nurture and instruction in the Christian tradition; and by theologically conservative denominations, such as the Southern Baptists and the Christian Church, who stress personal → conversion (§1) both as the purpose of → evangelization and as the condition of church membership.

By contrast, there is significant movement in many denominations toward a view of church growth as the result rather than the objective of faithful Christian witness. For the most part, this movement is expressed through the creative tension of *ecclesiola in ecclesia* (a little church within the church), as for example in the United Methodist Church (9.5 million members in 1992), which fosters small discipleship groups within local congregations, patterned after the early Wesleyan class meetings.

Bibliography: J. D. ANDERSON and E. E. JONES, *The Management of Ministry: Leadership, Purpose, Structure, Community* (San Francisco, 1978) • D. BOHR, *Evangelization in America: Proclamation, Way of Life, and the Catholic Church in the United States* (New York, 1977) • *Religion in America: Fifty Years, 1935-85* (Gallup Report no. 236; Princeton, 1985) • L. E. SCHALLER, *Assimilating New Members* (Nashville, 1978) • G. C. SMITH, ed., *Evangelizing Adults* (Wheaton, Ill., 1985) • J. WALLIS, *The Call to Conversion: Recovering the Gospel for These Times* (San Francisco, 1981) • J. H. WESTERHOFF III, *Inner Growth/Outer Change: An Educational Guide to Church Renewal* (New York, 1979).

DAVID LOWES WATSON

5. Church Growth Movement

The church growth movement is one of the most significant missiological, evangelistic, and church-related movements of the 20th century. It was initiated by Donald Anderson McGavran (1897-1991), a missionary of the Christian Church (Disciples of Christ) who served in India from 1923. McGavran devoted much time and thought to the reasons for the lack of growth of the churches he worked with in India, which led to his book *Bridges of God* (1955); it has been called the Magna Carta of the church growth movement. During those years McGavran was influenced by the Student Volunteer Movement, by the writings of Henry Venn and Rufus Anderson, by the pneumatological and ecclesiological thought of Roland Allen, by the strong emphasis on strategy and ecumenical cooperation of people like John R. Mott, and by the searching questions regarding results in numerical church growth initiated by Methodist researcher J. Waskom Pickett (with whom McGavran collaborated in publishing *Church Growth and Group Conversion* [1936]).

In 1961 McGavran began the Institute of Church Growth, which in 1965 became the School of World Mission/Institute of Church Growth of Fuller Theological Seminary, in Pasadena, California. Here McGavran gathered a team of researchers and activists that became the founders and mobilizers of the church growth movement. They included A. R. Tippett (anthropology), Ralph Winter (mission history and theological education by extension), Charles Kraft (anthropology, ethnotheology, and communication), J. Edwin Orr (revival), and Arthur Glasser (mission theology). In 1970 McGavran published *Understanding Church Growth*, which became the foundational textbook of the movement.

Since the early 1970s, the church growth movement has spawned a host of new movements, church planting initiatives, institutes, magazines and other publications, and degree programs directed toward the goal of mission as originally defined by Donald McGavran: "an enterprise devoted to proclaiming the Good News of Jesus Christ, and to persuading men and women to become his disciples and responsible members of his church" (*Understanding Church Growth*, 24). Church growth advocates from Fuller Seminary were very influential at the International Congress on World Evangelization in Lausanne, Switzerland, in 1974.

Theologically, the movement emphasizes an ecclesiocentric view of mission, which should lead to a numerical growth of congregations. The ethical issue has to do with pragmatism, or a focus on the results in the actual growth of churches. Missiologically, the movement investigates the resistance or receptivity of a given culture to the gospel, as well as the specific cultural barriers that need to be overcome for conversion (T. Rainer, 35-36).

Since the mid-1970s, the church growth movement has expanded to include many new movements, involving practitioners of church growth, church planters, urban church growth specialists, church growth consultants, denominational church growth mobilizers, and advanced church growth degree programs. A major step occurred in the mid-1970s when Peter Wagner focused attention on the rapidly secularizing Western world, with emphasis on North American church growth.

In the 1970s, after critics had attacked what seemed to be the movement's excessive concern for numerical growth, Peter Wagner and Charles Kraft led the way in emphasizing a broader range of spiritual concerns. These included pneumatology, "power evangelism," physical healing, the demonic, spiritual warfare, and prayer as important factors both in considering the resistance or receptivity of target culture groups and in evaluating the internal, institutional factors of the spiritual life of congregations.

Bibliography: Writings of early church growth leaders: E. GIBBS, *I Believe in Church Growth* (Grand Rapids, 1981) • D. A. MCGAVRAN, *The Bridges of God: A Study in the Strategy for Missions* (New York, 1955); idem, *Understanding Church Growth* (3d ed.; ed. C. R. Wagner; Grand Rapids, 1990) • A. R. TIPPETT, ed., *God, Man, and Church Growth* (Grand Rapids, 1973) • C. P. WAGNER, *Church Growth and the Whole Gospel: A Biblical Mandate* (New York, 1981); idem, *Church Planting for a Greater Harvest* (Ventura, Calif., 1990); idem, *Strategies for Church Growth* (Ventura, Calif., 1987); idem, *The Third Wave of the Holy Spirit* (Ann Arbor, Mich., 1988); idem, *Your Church Can Grow: Seven Vital Signs of a Healthy Church* (Ventura, Calif., 1980) • C. P. WAGNER, W. ARN, and E. TOWNS, eds., *Church Growth: State of the Art* (Wheaton, Ill., 1986).

Secondary literature: H. CONN, ed., *Theological Perspectives on Church Growth* (Nutley, N.J., 1977) • O. COSTAS, *Christ outside the Gate: Mission beyond Christendom* (Maryknoll, N.Y., 1988) • C. F. GEORGE, *How to Break Growth Barriers* (Grand Rapids, 1993) • D. R. HOGE and D. A. ROOZEN, eds., *Understanding Church Growth and Decline, 1950-1978* (New York, 1979) • D. M. KELLEY, *Why Conservative Churches Are Growing* (New York, 1972) • R. E. LOGAN, *Beyond Church Growth: Action Plans for Developing a Dynamic Church* (Grand Rapids, 1989) • G. W. PETERS, *A Theology of Church Growth* (Grand Rapids, 1981) • T. S. RAINER, *The Book of Church Growth: History, Theology, and Principles* (Nashville, 1993) • D. A. ROOZEN and C. K. HADAWAY, eds., *Church and Denominational Growth: What Does (and Does Not) Cause Growth and Decline* (Nashville, 1993) • W. SHENK, ed., *Exploring Church Growth* (Grand Rapids, 1983) • C. VAN ENGEN, *God's Missionary People: Rethinking the Purpose of the Local Church* (Grand Rapids, 1991); idem, *The Growth of the True Church* (Amsterdam, 1981) • W. ZUNKEL, *Church Growth under Fire* (Scottdale, Pa., 1987).

CHARLES VAN ENGEN

Church in a Socialist Society

1. Issues
2. The Example of East Germany
3. Evaluation

1. Issues

The issue of the church existing in a socialist society is related in principle to that of the church coexisting with → capitalism. The latter, however, is usually not regarded as an important problem because the achievements of middle-class → revolutions have helped to ensure → freedom and participation in → religious liberty under → laws for state churches or laws defining the legal and social space in which churches may function freely.

The problem of the church in a socialist society arose only as socialist regimes seized power, which forced the church to reexamine its previous relation with capitalism or → feudalism (caesaropapism in czarist Russia, neocolonialism in Cuba, colonialism in Angola and Mozambique, oligarchy in Ethiopia). As a rule, the new rulers "punished" the churches because of their former alliance with the dominant classes (→ Class and Social Stratum). With their reorientation under socialism, the churches examined the question whether their earlier failures (e.g., as regards socialism) had removed or reduced any right to criticize the new state of affairs.

On the side of the state, reactions to the church varied from strict repression to an increasing liberalization. With the achievement of a socialist state in the Russian Revolution of 1917, the problem of the criticism of the churches and → religion, in which all socialist movements and → political parties engaged both practically and theoretically (→ Atheism; Freethinkers; Religion, Criticism of), became at once the problem of a reordering of the relations between → church and state. The model of separation of church and state and attempts to set up new regulations (except in Albania, which, from 1967, attempted to suppress all religion) or to take new measures against the churches were familiar from presocialist revolutions (e.g., France in 1789, Mexico in 1857, and Portugal in 1910). Privileges were stripped away, restriction of freedoms to the cultic sphere and cultic activities was common, and believers suffered discrimination. It is worth noting that at least on paper, all socialist constitutions (except that of Albania) allow(ed) the free exercise of religion. However, in socialist states that, following the European tradition of 19th-century → positivism, view socialism as a science and therefore "true," → conflict with adherents of religion typically occurs on many levels.

Many factors have brought about change, involving both the church, which can no longer be seen as totally dependent on the state, and governments, which have long pursued a totally statist socialism.

1.1. A first factor was the historical recognition

that the Catholic Church often played a positive role in relation to both national → identity and → emancipation (e.g., in Poland). Protestants similarly — for example, in Czechoslovakia (J. → Hus and J. A. Comenius) and Hungary (L. Kossuth, 1848) — have been champions of movements of social and democratic renewal.

1.2. The → ecumenical movement made it clear that the Christian → faith worldwide has not always been "the opiate of the people." In many cases it did not merely protest against actual misery (which K. → Marx conceded) but took action on behalf of the disadvantaged, for example in the fight against fascism and in → liberation theology, in the civil rights work of M. L. → King, and in South Africa, South Korea, and Nicaragua. The → Marxist interpretation of history, which would assign a progressive role only to primitive Christianity (→ Early Church) and the left wing of the → Reformation, has had to correct itself.

1.3. The self-understanding of socialism as a closed dogmatic and economic → system has also had to change. The collapse of the former Soviet Union and its European allies graphically illustrates the deep and fertile interaction between political theory and church life.

1.4. Movements of renewal in the churches have refuted the Marxist idea of the inevitable withering away of religion. The failure of traditional Marxism to establish an → ethics, → anthropology, or understanding of history has become evident. Like → law and → language, religion can no longer be dismissed as mere superstructure.

1.5. In virtue of their relative aloofness from the state ideology, Christian groups and churches were able to play a part in social reconstruction *(perestroika)* in Poland, Hungary, East Germany, Czechoslovakia, and, to a lesser extent, Bulgaria, Romania, and the USSR.

2. The Example of East Germany

The case of the former East Germany (DDR) well illustrates the problem of the church in a socialist society. The DDR, like other socialist states, recognized the leadership of the proletariat and the Marxist-Leninist party in article 1 of its constitution, which defined the society as socialist. Articles 20 and 39 guaranteed freedom of conscience and belief and the independence of the church. But text and reality did not always coincide. The churches and critical socialists sought a closer approximation. The Protestant churches in the DDR formed an alliance in 1969 with a view to proclaiming the gospel in a socialist society. Ten articles (1963) on the freedom and ministry of the church were the basis, attempting to define the position of the church in a socialist society. The church must take up its tasks and make use of its opportunities in any society. It must also be critical and unrestricted vis-à-vis all social systems. It must not rely on any guaranteed → authority or conferred privileges.

The first united synod at Eisenach in 1971 formulated the principle that the church must neither hold itself aloof from nor repudiate socialism; it must be the church *in* a socialist society. For different reasons speakers on behalf of both state and church rejected a socializing of the church, viewing any such equation as a mistake. The difficulties of the learning process that was thus initiated, which was oriented strongly to the → Barmen Declaration, the ecclesiology of D. → Bonhoeffer (1906-45), and the Darmstadt Declaration (1947), were addressed at later synods. Critical issues were those of → peace, → education (→ Childhood; Youth), → human rights, and state interference. The church also had to learn to see itself as a church for others (Bonhoeffer) and as a → free church instead of an established church (e.g., in matters of political and social responsibility, which had been neglected under the previous system of → church government). Considerable reduction in church programs brought a new understanding and shaping of the true Christian community.

3. Evaluation

It was unavoidable that the universal Christian and socialist views of life should come into → conflict. The contrasting positions were more obvious than in nonsocialist countries. Since, contrary to the Marxist diagnosis, the state did not wither away, in fact using its power against a church that could be free and strong only in virtue of its word and credibility, freedom from conflict could be achieved only at the cost of the church's self-surrender.

The survival of churches in socialist societies raises critical questions for churches in nonsocialist countries. Do the latter really recognize that in many cases they are → minorities? Do they accept the challenge posed by a society that is increasingly secular or dabbles in substitute religions, without being overtly hostile? Are they prepared to lose their social advantages and official privileges? The church in a socialist society might well be regarded as an attempt at → contextual theology.

→ Marxism and Christianity

Bibliography: G. Barbarini, M. Stöhr, and E. Weingärtner, *Kirchen im Sozialismus. Kirche und Staat in den osteuropäischen sozialistischen Republiken* (Frankfurt, 1977) • J. Brown, *Conscience and Captivity: Reli-*

gion in Eastern Europe (Washington, D.C., 1988) •
O. Chadwick, *The Christian Church in the Cold War*
(New York, 1992) • R. Henkys, *Gottes Volk im Sozialismus. Wie Christen in der Deutschen Demokratischen Republik leben* (Berlin, 1983); idem, ed., *Bund der Evangelischen Kirchen in der Deutschen Demokratischen Republik (Dokumente)* (Witten, 1970) • D. Pospielovsky, *The Russian Church under the Soviet Regime, 1917-1982* (2 vols.; New York, 1984) • Sekretariat des Bundes der Evangelischen Kirchen in der DDR, *Dokumente aus der Arbeit des Bundes der Evangelischen Kirchen in der Deutschen Demokratischen Republik* (Berlin, 1981) • H. Stehle, *Die Ostpolitik des Vatikans, 1917-1975* (Munich, 1975).

                                        Martin Stöhr

Church Law

1. Term
2. History
    2.1. Before the Middle Ages
    2.2. Middle Ages
    2.3. Reformation
    2.4. Modern Times
3. Basis and Standards
4. Subject Matter
    4.1. Protestant
    4.2. Roman Catholic
    4.3. Orthodox
5. Sources and Forms
6. Legislation
    6.1. Problem
    6.2. History
    6.3. Roman Catholic
    6.4. Orthodox

1. Term

The → church has to do its work in the world under secular conditions. It must present itself in the world as a historical entity, using secular means to ensure that it endures and does justice to its task. Thus it must have a specific constitution and specific standards of action for itself and its members. The term "church law" comprises all the provisions that serve the continued existence of the church and its life and work according to its commission. Yet this normative element, which is inevitably bound up with its existence in the world, has not always and everywhere been viewed as law or called church law. The qualification of the normative rules emanating from the church as church law derives from the development of law in the West, with its inclusion of the domestic rulings of the church in more general legislation.

2. History

Church law has meant various things in the history of the church. It has been variously assessed in its status, its relation to secular law, and its relation to the center of the church's activity. There is controversy as to whether church law existed from the outset at the beginning of the church's existence or whether it arose only with the development of the church. Even though we may not accept the classic position of the → Roman Catholic Church, namely, that Christ founded the church as a legally constituted entity with leaders (→ Church Government; Offices, Ecclesiastical), we cannot counter this view with the thesis that in the beginning the church had no law at all. Insofar as the church recognizes the → authority of Christ and regards the commission that he gave it as an obligation, this obligation governs its life and activity. The normative element was not imported into the church later as something that was not present at first. It developed in accordance with the necessities involved in the church's existence in history.

2.1. *Before the Middle Ages*

Though there might not originally have been any positive legal statutes, the normative side of church life soon enough took form in (1) commands regarding the lifestyle and conduct of believers; (2) rules for the administration of the → sacraments, for → worship, and for official acts (→ Occasional Services); (3) the recognition of certain apostolic writings (→ Canon); (4) the establishment and transmission of specific offices; and (5) demarcation from heretical groups (→ Heresies and Schisms). What was regarded as binding in these rules on the basis of apostolic → tradition soon became collected together. From approximately the third century the decisions of → synods were added to the normatively formulated list of regulations. At this stage the binding nature of rules within the church was completely independent of the position of the church in the legal order of the → Roman Empire.

Even when the church finally became a *religio licita*, this change did not at first affect the legal status of the → norms it recognized and followed. The church's law acquired a new status only when in the later Roman imperial period statutes were adopted by the state that related to affairs in the church. Not only did this development open up new legal possibilities for the church, but internal church relations also became a matter of state law, and its norms (esp. the rulings of ecumenical councils) were in part adopted into secular law. Its thinking also found a place in later Roman law. The qualitative difference between church law and general state law was thus erased.

2.2. *Middle Ages*

In the new types of government that arose in the early → Middle Ages (§1) as whole peoples accepted Christianity, the normative complexes connected with the Christian religion found recognition at once as a constituent part of public order. Such recognition naturally led to conflict as secular rulers sought to shape legal relations in the church and to adjust church organization to the secular system. Collections of traditional church law became especially important in this connection (→ Canon Law 2). In the early Middle Ages they especially helped to assert church tradition over against new tendencies, especially in Germanic legal thinking, and to safeguard the independence and wealth of the church. Church law became an important instrument of the church's → hierarchy in its struggle with secular rulers. This trend is particularly clear in the Pseudo-Isidorian Decretals (→ False Decretals), a collection of partly genuine and partly falsified ninth-century legal sources that later collections often recognized.

Church law again received new accents when it became an object of academic study. Gratian (d. by ca. 1160) provided a basis for this study with his Concordia Discordantium Canonum, better known as the Decretum Gratiani, a collection of traditional materials made about 1140. The Decretum discusses legal questions with relevant materials from the Bible, the → church fathers, and papal decretals. Following this lead, legal studies came to be conducted by investigating specifically ecclesiastical-legal sources according to the method of → Scholastic jurisprudence and no longer merely by simply adducing sources, behind which was seen the working of the → Holy Spirit. The study of church law now became a legal discipline. Just as, with the help of traditional Roman law, secular law was given systematic form, so also did universal church law develop on the basis of the Decretum and supplementary papal law. Church law also adopted the division of law into divine and human law.

A need thus arose for an authority that had the right both to expound human and divine law and to legislate in the human sphere. When the → pope received recognition in the high Middle Ages as the holder of *summa potestas* (supreme power; → Empire and Papacy), he acquired increasing authority to interpret and develop church law through his legislation and through assertion of his teaching authority. Church legislation no longer restricted itself to matters directly concerning the constitution and inner life of the church but rather extended to various spheres of social life in an assertion of the requirements of Christian → faith, for example, to → marriage and also to the economy in the form of a prohibition of → usury.

As shaped by papal legislation or maintained and validated by papal authority, "canon law" from the 16th century onward was collected in the → Corpus Iuris Canonici and set alongside universal secular law as it found expression in the Corpus Iuris Civilis. The legal order in the West was viewed as a whole as *ius utrumque* (law on both sides), that is, as law that does justice to the fact that public order is determined by both spiritual and secular elements and is covered by both spiritual and secular authority.

2.3. *Reformation*

The → Reformation protest against canon law was directed against the intrusion of church law into affairs that are secular by nature and also against the way in which church law burdens the → conscience by incorporating the sacramental sphere and the process of individual sanctification into the system of legal relations. For this reason the leading principle of → Lutheranism and the → Lutheran churches (→ Church 3.4) is that any legal order in the church must avoid coercing the conscience. The → church orders of the Reformation and post-Reformation periods thus try not to make expressly normative rules regarding worship, acts of ministry, or Christian lifestyle. They consist to a larger degree of admonitions and instructions about the right way to deal with the Word and sacraments. Church law simply has an auxiliary function in implementing the church's commission. It is seen as a provision, one based on considerations of purpose, in the service of commensurate biblical → proclamation and the proper administration of the sacraments. Since on this approach the church's constitution does not affect the center of its life, there was no objection in principle to leaving the corresponding regulations largely to the secular ruler.

The churches influenced by the teaching of J. → Calvin (1509-64; → Calvinism; Church 3.5; Reformed and Presbyterian Churches) were more open to the idea of a church law resting on spiritual authority. Since → church discipline was regarded as a necessary expression of the church's life, a starting point existed for a spiritual understanding of rulings of church law. Church constitutions are not just a matter for human → reason to decide. They have their basis in certain offices to which the Holy Scriptures bear witness.

2.4. *Modern Times*

A new understanding of the state developed in the age of royal absolutism. In keeping with this view, the territorial states, claiming omnicompetence, sought control over every aspect of law. An attempt was thus made to bring church law into the total legal system that the ruler controlled and guaranteed. The result was the possibility, as well as danger, that secular ideas would find an entry into church law. It is true that only in a few instances have modern states had an impact on traditional legal relations within the church. Nevertheless, church law was generally viewed as having validity within a given territory only when the ruler recognized it as such. The state's approval of church law became the decisive postulate, one vigorously contested by Roman Catholics but accepted as a valid condition by Protestants.

The → Enlightenment understood the individual church community as the corporative aggregate of believers of a given confession. This view influenced considerably the approach to church law in the Protestant world. Church law came to be regarded as a law of association oriented toward realizing the communal purpose of the particular ecclesiastical corporation. The matters to be regulated were thus reduced to those relating to the organization of the corporate life. The central action of the church in proclamation and sacramental administration and the conduct of believers as it came under the influence of their faith stood in no clearly defined relation to church law.

Gradually from the 19th century onward the supremacy that the state had claimed over the churches began to erode. The result is that today most churches are independent of the state in respect of their own legislation, as they have always been in countries with no state churches such as the United States. A clear distinction arose between church law and state church law. In general, church law is normative for the legal order of the state only to the extent that it seeks to correspond to the conditions that the state has laid down for its legal activity or to the extent that it complements the state's legislative empowerments. Only in the few countries in which the involvement of → church and state has continued (e.g., the United Kingdom and the Scandinavian countries) does church law depend on state sanction, although in practice the state has hardly any influence on the legal decisions taken by the church.

3. Basis and Standards

Church law has come to be called autonomous insofar as it is law whose validity does not depend on any outside authority. In claiming that they can develop their legal rulings independently of state cooperation, churches of necessity must set forth that particular understanding of law serving as the basis of church law. What causes and permits the church to set up a binding order? To what extent does this order have the character of law? What is the basis of the substantive standards for the churches' legal order?

These questions have been a matter for lively debate in the period after World War II, especially in German Protestantism. They were originally shaped by experiences in the → church struggle, which created the awareness that a church constitution oriented to secular standpoints can threaten the church's confessional realization of its tasks. The thesis of the → Barmen Synod — that we cannot separate the external order from the confession — pointed the way to a new understanding of church law. The theoretical discussions, however, were also largely influenced by debate with the earlier contention of R. Sohm (1841-1917), a teacher of church law, that church law is irreconcilable with the essence of the church because there is contradiction in principle between the Holy Spirit as authority in the church and law, which is characterized in the → modern period by its formal character and by the element of physical compulsion. Attempts to work out an autonomous understanding of church law were promoted by the use of various associated terms, such as "the law of grace," "the law of the neighbor," "lex caritatis" (the law of love), "brotherly Christocracy," "confessing church law," "responsive church law," and "biblical instruction." Nevertheless, no systematic Protestant concept that enjoys even marginal consensus has yet emerged, nor has there been any lasting influence of the new theoretical insights on actual practice in ecclesiastical legislation and administration.

In the Roman Catholic Church the quality and significance of church law have been questioned since → Vatican II and discussed from basic standpoints in connection with the new edition of → Codex Iuris Canonici (CIC) in 1983.

Protestant as well as Roman Catholic contributions to the discussion of the fundamentals of church law comprise various approaches, though we cannot unequivocally and exclusively attribute these to specific authors. The need for church law is often related to the fact that the church exists in the world in the form of a union of persons, and that it is thus subject to laws in the same way as any corporate body. Previously the dominant view among Roman Catholics was that the quality of the church as a society explains church law, and this view is still upheld in the new CIC (can. 204.2). Precisely the church's character as a *societas perfecta*, which it allegedly has in common with sovereign states, enables it to establish its own original legal order.

Among Protestants, too, church law is often derived from the church's character as a union of persons. This explanation — partly in terms of sociology, partly of → natural law — has now come under criticism, however, from both Protestants and Roman Catholics, since alienation might easily be the result of a recourse to secular legal patterns. Rather, the basis of church law must be endogenous, not exogenous (R. Sobanski). Theology must replace natural law as its foundation (E. Corecco).

Today Roman Catholic teaching in part takes the concept of communion as a starting point in order to illustrate the church's unique form of fellowship, which can be grasped only in terms of faith. Similar ideas have sprung up among Protestants, such as the reference to M. → Luther's (1483-1546) idea of a *lex caritatis* (J. Heckel). In this way, too, the distinctive personal relation that is an expression of the working of the Holy Spirit is seen as an appropriate basis for the fashioning of legal relations within the church.

We find a different emphasis in attempts to understand church law specifically on the basis of the church itself. The premise here is a direct relation posited between the Christian message and church law. Various points of departure are taken. Statements of substantive legal relevance might simply be derived directly from the message of the gospel. The problem of the relation between → law and gospel arises in this connection. This leads very naturally to the sphere of the so-called third use of the → law (§3), according to which believers, though trusting in justifying → grace, find the biblical imperatives helpful in dealing with their continuing sinfulness (→ Sin). In principle, the question arises as to how the individual duties supported by theological → ethics can and should be the object of church law.

A more nuanced relation between the gospel and church law occurs in the attempt to define a Christocratic basis of church law (such as by K. → Barth and E. Wolf). The idea of Christocracy does not entail specific constitutional demands or material regulations. Rather, it forms a point of orientation for individual believers and imposes on them an obligation to take account of Christ's claim to lordship in all their conduct and also in the social sphere. Negatively, this means that there can be no question of basing church law on secular standards. Positively, it means that we cannot list all the specific implications, since the lordship of Christ is a relation that governs all of one's personal life. Hence neither does Holy Scripture serve as a direct legal source, though it does offer "biblical instruction" (Wolf, A. Stein) by giving believers a basis for responsible decision. The Christian position demands that the church give visibility to its faith by its law and that its law be "confessing law." A similar postulate is that of "responsive church

law" (H. Ammer), which sees in the church's legal order not the fulfillment of abstract commands but a response to the Christian message.

A direct relation between church law and the → salvation-event is also assumed when the origin of church law is sought in the reality of the sacral sphere. This position views church law as a development of the relation an individual has with God through → sanctification. It is the same as the order of the divine → covenant with us that has been renewed in Christ. The subject of church law is not the church as the work of the Holy Spirit in the world; it is God himself who is in legal relation with the believer. Roman Catholics have tried to find a sacramental basis for church law, as has Orthodoxy (→ Orthodox Church; Church 3.1; and see 4.3 below). Among Protestants, Hans Dombois has made inquiry along similar lines.

The demand for a confessionally related church law in keeping with the specific requirements of the church often takes the form of orientation to the church's mission as the basic condition of church law. Most of the preambles to the more recent church constitutions among German Protestants (→ Church Government) describe this mission as that which validates church law and gives direction to it. By referring church law to the commission that Christ gave in his missionary command and imparted by instituting the sacraments, it is possible to hold different views. Some try to derive direct implications for the church's order from the Christian gospel; others see church law as a provision of the church that seems to be necessary for the complete fulfillment of Christ's commission. Even when church law is thus only indirectly linked to the missionary command, it is oriented solely to ecclesiastical considerations. Its normative validity can be based only on the reference to a statement of faith. Its unique legal purpose in distinction from secular law also gives a specifically spiritual component even to its material content. On this view church law cannot be viewed as an attempt adequately to express or even to safeguard through material legal means that which distinguishes the life of the church relative to its members' assurance of salvation. Church law normatively guides the constitution of the church, its actions, and the actions of its members from the standpoint of achieving an ongoing fulfillment of its mission and preserving its apostolicity.

This kind of indirect relation to the Christian message characterizes church law in the Lutheran tradition. The traditional view here — that an action of church law that accords with its mission and serves the church rests on considerations of utility and does not relate to the marks of the true church — now seems to be too one-sided because of its failure to see that some normative elements are indispensable in the interests of the church's commission.

4. Subject Matter

No single summary of the subject matter of church law fits every age or denomination. The range of what the church regulates for the sake of its mission depends to some degree on the way in which the state legislates in church matters, though the various controversial views of the status of law in the church's life and of its significance for individual sanctification also influence the selection of topics.

4.1. *Protestant*

For Protestant churches, a large and essential part of church law is organizational law, whose main purpose is to enable the church to fulfill its tasks. It covers the composition and responsibilities of the various administrative organs, the appointment of officeholders, and the various subdivisions of the church and its organs. The rules that make it possible for individual members to share in the church's mission are also part of organizational law. Church law also normalizes the regular activity of officeholders and instrumentalities.

This part of church law gives rise to many problems, for the idea must be avoided that the work of proclamation itself is the mere fulfillment of a legal → duty. There is a need, however, to bring the form and occasion and competence of this action under a norm. In worship this is usually done by means of set forms (→ Liturgical Books) that are binding only by legal decision of the church. Standards for church activity at the congregational level and for the conduct of individual congregation members are formulated in the church's rules of life, which also stipulate the conditions to be met in undertaking official church activities; to that extent, such rules do function normatively. At the same time, by describing essential elements of community life, they attempt to provide aids to orientation. The issuing of such rules was also prompted by the desire to provide a basis for church discipline, which was itself considered necessary. The rules of life do involve this purpose insofar as they also regulate the personal prerequisites for participation in official acts. In this indirect way, Protestant churches do tie the conduct of individual church members to a large extent to church norms, though in some churches special church laws do admittedly stipulate the legal conditions affecting the exercise of office. Legal rulings dealing with finance also stand indirectly in the service of the organization and work of the church, as do the rules relating to church holdings. In this sphere, however, the church is linked in part to secular law (→ Church Finances).

4.2. *Roman Catholic*

Roman Catholic church law covers all the matters that are of essential concern to the → Roman Catholic Church (→ Church 3.2), regardless of secular law. The resultant possibility of conflict between state and church law is simply accepted. Yet church law today has refrained from legislating on many matters that it dealt with earlier. It now admits that church laws, except insofar as they are an expression of divine law, can claim validity only for Roman Catholics (1983 CIC 11). In contrast to the usual subjects in Reformation churches, the sphere of Roman Catholic legislation is broader. It includes a positive legal stipulation of what are called general norms, that is, principles relative to legal forms and the application and exposition of church law. Within sacramental laws pertaining to the seven sacraments, we also find rules that govern the presuppositions and forms of marriage. Though in considerably reduced form in the 1983 CIC, Catholic church law also includes a list of offenses and an extensive law of procedure for church courts (→ Jurisdiction, Ecclesiastical). A separate section of church law deals with the rights and duties of individual believers in and toward the church (cf. the lists of civil rights in many state constitutions). Expectations of individual believers in terms of faith, lifestyle, and charitable activity are also designated as legal obligations.

4.3. *Orthodox*

The church law of the Orthodox Church is marked by a concern to show the continuity between the principles valid today and the rules *(canones)* recognized by the early church. This law deals with all matters that in the course of church history have come to be viewed as necessary additions to the commands of Holy Scripture. It does not take the form of systematic codification but exists in the form of particular collections from individual sources. Understood as development rather than new creation, this legislation came into being chiefly through the resolutions of synods, though also through the formation of a law of custom and through state legislation whose ecclesiastical validity was justified by the church's acceptance and by the partially successful integration of its organs into the secular jurisdiction. The result of the → autocephaly of Orthodox churches (i.e., their independence of one another) is that in different countries there are marked differences in the details of their inner order, though with a homogeneity of the basic structures of the church constitution. This applies especially to the hierarchical structure with the central position of the episcopal office (→ Bishop, Episcopate), to the synod as the leading organ both centrally and congregationally, and to the coparticipation of the laity (→ Clergy and Laity), especially in administration at the local level.

5. Sources and Forms

In the forms taken by legal principles today, we find many external similarities between church law and state law. Yet the process of generating law is not the same in the church as in the modern state. A mark of the development of state law today is that the territorially limited state, in virtue of the sovereignty that it claims, has made the validity of law in its territory dependent on its legislative will; it assumes a right to make laws without commitment to any universal order. Thus the law in a given territory is almost fully codified in positive statutes, with a corresponding need for legal certainty and clarity. A similar need exists to some extent relative to legal relations in the church, so that church law appears to resemble state law. This is most apparent in the legal codification of Roman Catholicism in its CIC. For the church, however, the unavoidable fixing of its law in positive statutes raises a problem. In church law the voluntaristic principle of legislation corresponding to the notion of sovereignty, and the associated noncommitment of the legislator, is inadequate. To be sure, a legally independent church may enjoy the same ability to legislate as a sovereign state. But the process of validation cannot be found in any creative legal decision of the legislating instrument. Church law derives its validity from the expectation that when the church makes rules, it acts with the assistance of the Holy Spirit.

The question of material commitment in church legislation is usually discussed from the standpoint of *ius divinum*. The Roman Catholic thesis is that divine law can be derived from natural law or from Scripture and tradition and that this divine law is both binding on church law and unchangeable. In the traditional legal thinking of Lutheranism, which views church law as the result of human reason, the idea of a *ius divinum* behind individual legal statutes or institutions is an alien one. Yet Lutheranism recognizes that church legislation is determined and restricted by elements that are beyond its control, being posited by the nature and commission of the church. Legal thinking in the Reformed Church has always been open to the thought of a *ius divinum* inasmuch as specific institutions were derived from the will of God revealed in Holy Scripture.

In church law the distinction between constitutional law and other law does not have the primary importance that it does in state law. Many churches (esp. individual Reformation churches) have indeed embodied basic and lasting legal relations in constitutions whose provisions can be changed only in special circumstances. But the content of such constitutions does not enjoy higher rank, as though we had here a law that can invalidate all other law.

Church law usually takes the form of what are officially known as church laws passed by bodies to which the constitution gives a legislative function (e.g., synods). The body that is entrusted with ongoing leadership in the church is called upon to legislate in the form of ordinances. Yet the authority of church leadership to legislate in this way, especially to legislate provisionally, is relatively broad and is not restricted to the implementation of laws, since the synods as legislative organs are able to meet only periodically. The development of binding norms in the church is not limited unconditionally to these regulated forms of legislation if true legislative power is accorded to the Holy Spirit expressing himself in the → consensus of believers. Hence we cannot exclude the possibility that formulations of a different kind (e.g., unanimous synodic resolutions) will have the force of law. The Roman Catholic Church, though, with its full codification of church law, has definitively established its legal sources and given them a rank of their own.

→ Civil Law and the Church; Concordat; Magisterium; Teaching Office

Bibliography: History of church law: H. E. FEINE, *Kirchliche Rechtsgeschichte* (4th ed.; Weimar, 1960) • G. LE-BRAS, ed., *Histoire du droit et des institutions de l'église en Occident* (16 vols. [unfinished]; Paris, 1955-) • W. M. PLÖCHL, *Geschichte des Kirchenrechts* (5 vols.; 2d ed.; Vienna, 1960-70).

Issues: H. AMMER, "Die Ordnung der Kirche," *HPTh* 1.229-97 • K. BARTH, *CD* IV/2, 676-726 • J. BOHATEC, *Calvins Lehre von Staat und Kirche* (Breslau, 1937) • E. CORECCO, *Theologie des Kirchenrechts* (Trier, 1980) • H. DOMBOIS, *Das Recht der Gnade. Ökumenisches Kirchenrecht* (vol. 1, 2d ed., Witten, 1969; vols. 2-3, Bielefeld, 1974-83) • H. FROST, *Strukturprobleme evangelischer Kirchenverfassung* (Göttingen, 1972) • J. HECKEL, *Lex charitatis* (2d ed.; Munich, 1973) • W. MAURER, *Die Kirche und ihr Recht. Gesammelte Aufsätze* (Tübingen, 1976) • D. PIRSON, *Universalität und Partikularität der Kirche* (Munich, 1965) • R. SOBANSKI, *Grundlagenproblematik des katholischen Kirchenrechts* (Vienna, 1987) • R. SOHM, *Kirchenrecht* (2 vols.; repr., Leipzig, 1923) • L. J. SPITERI, *The Code in the Hands of the Laity: Canon Law for Everyone* (New York, 1997) • W. STEINMÜLLER, *Evangelische Rechtstheologie* (2 vols.; Cologne, 1968) • E. WOLF, *Ordnung der Kirche* (Frankfurt, 1961); idem, *Rechtstheologische Studien* (Frankfurt, 1972).

Specific traditions: Protestant: A. STEIN, *Evangelisches Kirchenrecht* (3d ed.; Neuwied, 1992).

Anglican: G. R. EVANS and J. R. WRIGHT, eds., *The Anglican Tradition: A Handbook of Sources* (London, 1991) • E. G. MOORE and T. BRIDEN, *Moore's Introduction to English Canon Law* (2d ed.; London, 1985).

Catholic: J. A. CORIDEN and D. E. HEINTSCHEL, eds., *The Code of Canon Law: A Text and Commentary* (Mahwah, N.J., 1985) • P. KRÄMER, *Kirchenrecht* (2 vols.; Stuttgart, 1992-93) • J. LISTL et al., eds., *Handbuch des katholischen Kirchenrechts* (Regensburg, 1983) • G. SHEEHY et al., eds., *The Canon Law: Letter and Spirit. A Practical Guide to the Code of Canon Law* (Collegeville, Minn., 1995).

Orthodox: H. ALIVISATOS, "Das kanonische Recht der Orthodoxen Kirche," *Ekklesia* (ed. F. Siegmund-Schultze; Leipzig, 1949) 75-90 • N. MILASCH, *Das Kirchenrecht der morgenländischen Kirche* (2d ed.; Mostar, 1905).

DIETRICH PIRSON

6. Legislation
6.1. *Problem*
The church makes rules according to its own law and self-understanding. How far these rules are laws and thus have a normative legal character in the judicial sense depends upon state law, namely, upon whether or not the state recognizes them.

6.2. *History*
Early in its history, the Christian church demonstrated a remarkable tendency to pass statutes. The establishment of the NT → canon (§2) and doctrinal decisions of the early councils were essentially legislative acts. In the → Middle Ages (§2) the church achieved the status of a sovereign and rational legislative body more quickly than the community that corresponds to the modern state. In many ways → canon law influenced civil law.

The → Reformation criticized the legalizing of the church, arguing that the → preaching of the → gospel is what constitutes the church. In Reformation preaching the → law acquired a new theological function (→ Law and Gospel). Yet the Protestant churches also needed ordinances. M. → Luther (1483-1546) himself showed how these might be derived from the church's mission. The first great legislative achievements of the Reformation churches were the 16th- and 17th-century → church orders, in the development of which pastoral concerns and secular authority were influential. Under a territorial → church government, legislative activity in both the internal and the external affairs of the church passed more or less completely to the state and thus assumed forms that were borrowed from the legislative activity of the state. The parallel continued when in the 19th-century constitutional movement, and in the interest of greater autonomy, the church set up its own legislative organs.

6.3. *Roman Catholic*
In Roman church law, the right to legislate is part of the power of jurisdiction. The one who has jurisdiction (i.e., the → pope, the college of → bishops, the diocesan bishop, and the head of an order) can pass laws. All legislative activity must be within the limits set by the hierarchical order and ultimately by the *ius divinum.* The → hierarchy of legal norms comes to expression in the use of different terms such as "laws," "executive decrees," "orders," and "statutes." The general source of ecclesiastical legislation is the → Corpus Iuris Canonici. Papal laws are published in the *Acta apostolicae sedis,* those of individual churches in their official publications.

6.4. *Orthodox*
In the → Orthodox Church, only a general council can pass universally binding church laws. No such council has met since 787. Most of the legal matter is thus viewed as being of a historical nature, consisting of Holy Scripture, the decisions of the seven ecumenical → councils, and various other documents, traditions, and legal collections of the → early church. To a lesser degree, law has also been established by the synods of individual churches (i.e., episcopal synods), usually with no participation by the lesser → clergy and laity.

→ Bulls and Briefs; Collegialism; Jurisdiction, Ecclesiastical; Law

Bibliography: H. FROST, *Strukturprobleme evangelischer Kirchenverfassung* (Göttingen, 1972) 340-44 • J. LISTL and K. SCHLAICH, *EStL* 1.1689-93 • K. W. NÖRR, "Typen von Rechtsquellen und Rechtsliteratur als Kennzeichen kirchenrechtlicher Epochen," *ZEvKR* 13 (1968) 225-38. See also the bibliography in "Church Government."

PETER VON TILING

Church Membership

1. Protestant and Roman Catholic
2. Orthodox
3. Free Churches
4. United States
5. The Withdrawal of Church Members

1. Protestant and Roman Cathlic
Church membership and adherence are related to the theological and institutional understanding of the → church. Church membership has both spiritual and legal dimensions.

1.1. On the Protestant view, the church is the communion of saints instituted by the → Holy Spirit. Church membership, then, is essentially being part of the communion of saints. It begins with the work of the Holy Spirit, who brings one into this fellowship through the preaching of the → gospel. → Baptism is incorporation into the body of Christ and the → people of God. Becoming a Christian is thus the beginning of church membership. Participation in the gifts of the → Eucharist confers fellowship with other church members in anticipation of perfected fellowship with God.

The legal aspect of church membership is connected to the spiritual. The member churches of, for example, the German Evangelical Church regard baptism as a prerequisite of church membership (H. Brunotte in P. Meinhold, 173ff.). It confers both the rights and the duties of church membership. As an ecumenical → sacrament, it incorporates the baptized into the church of Jesus Christ, the universal church. Church membership is also related to individual church confession (→ Confession of Faith), entry being through baptism or through confirmation. Finally there is membership in the local church, according to where a person lives.

The rules of the various churches differ on how membership is attained and how it ends (e.g., by death, removal, or withdrawal; → Church Membership 5), as well as how membership rights may be suspended (e.g., by → church discipline). The rights include participation in worship and ministry, serving as a sponsor (→ Godparent), and voting. Duties include participation in worship, rendering diaconal and missionary service, and giving financial support by offerings or taxes.

In actual life in both church and community, there is the problem of how to understand double church membership, for example, in an evangelical fellowship and the territorial church.

1.2. On the Roman Catholic view, from R. → Bellarmine (1542-1621) to the encyclical *Mystici corporis* (June 29, 1943), church membership has been defined by the threefold cord of baptism *(vinculum liturgicum)*, confession of faith *(vinculum symbolicum)*, and church unity *(vinculum hierarchicum)* (D 2286; DH 3802-3).

Vatican II (*Lumen gentium* 14-15; *Unitatis redintegratio* 3) introduced the idea of degrees of church membership (Y. Congar; → Church 3.2.4). In free churches (see 3), there is a period of testing before acceptance, and church membership can be ended by exclusion.

1.3. The challenge of a → people's church in transition is now pointing away from early church models of church membership (involving catechumens and the baptized) and the undefined boundary of the church in the → Donatist controversy (→ Augustine *De bapt.* 5.27-28; → Augustine's Theology) to a church of open boundaries (W. Huber in C. Lienemann-Perrin, 488ff.) and degrees, or levels, of church membership (H. Frost, J.-J. von Allmen, K. → Rahner, N. N. Nissiotis). Certain pastoral and legal tasks are involved (e.g., thanksgiving after childbirth, dedication of infants — thus no sacramental baptism, through which membership in the church as the body of Christ is constituted). The way is also opened for an ecumenical law of church membership (W. Huber, 488ff.).

→ Church Law

Bibliography: C. LIENEMANN-PERRIN, ed., *Taufe und Kirchenzugehörigkeit* (Munich, 1983) 337ff., R. Weth on the free churches • H. LIERMANN, "Kirchenmitgliedschaft," *RGG* (3d ed.) 3.1493-95 • J. MEHLHAUSEN and C. LINK, "Kirchengliedschaft," *EStL* 1.1592-1604 • P. MEINHOLD, ed., *Das Problem der Kirchenmitgliedschaft heute* (Darmstadt, 1979) bibliography, 435ff.; J.-J. von Allmen, 412ff.; Y. Congar, 279ff.; H. Frost, 237ff.; N. N. Nissiotis on the Orthodox Church, 366ff.; S. W. Sykes on the Anglican Church, 391ff. • M. PLATHOW, *Lehre und Ordnung im Leben der Kirche heute* (Göttingen, 1982) • K. RAHNER, "Kirchenmitgliedschaft," *SM* 2.1209-15 • A. STEIN, "Kirche als rechtstheologisches Problem," *ZEvKR* 29 (1984) 47-62.

MICHAEL PLATHOW

2. Orthodox

In the Orthodox view, church membership rests on → baptism, with which comes incorporation into the communion of saints (Eph. 5:25-27). Directly linked to baptism, and hence significant for church membership, is → anointing with *myron* (chrism), which seals baptism, and also the first → Eucharist (§3.1).

As a rule, baptism outside the Orthodox Church is accepted as valid, and the associated membership in the church of Christ is also accepted, as long as the baptism is with water in the name of the Trinity. Also accepted is anointing in the → Oriental Orthodox churches and the Roman Catholic and → Old Catholic churches. When Protestants convert, or when separated members return to the church, the anointing is given or repeated. The common view is that the great non-Orthodox churches and their members are not separated from the fellowship of graces, the church of Christ. The NT concept of *oikonomia* (Col. 1:25; Eph. 1:10) is normative for recognition of baptism administered outside the visible boundaries of the Orthodox Church ($\rightarrow$ Economy [Orthodox Theology]).

$\rightarrow$ Church Law; Orthodox Church; Orthodoxy 3

Bibliography: G. FLOROVSKY, "O granicach," *Zhurnal Moskovskoy Patriarchii* 5 (1989) 71-73 • A. KALLIS, *Orthodoxie–Was ist das?* (Mainz, 1979) • N. MILASCH, *Das Kirchenrecht der morgenländischen Kirche* (2d ed.; Mostar, 1905) 553-60 • S. ZANKOW, *Das orthodoxe Christentum des Ostens* (Berlin, 1928) 64ff.

NIKOLAUS THON

3. Free Churches

The decisive difference between church membership in a national church ($\rightarrow$ People's Church) and in the $\rightarrow$ free churches ($\rightarrow$ Church 3.6) is that in the former it is usually assigned, and in the latter it is actively acquired. In Baptistic churches (including $\rightarrow$ Adventists, $\rightarrow$ Baptists, $\rightarrow$ Brethren Churches, $\rightarrow$ Christian Church [Disciples of Christ], $\rightarrow$ Mennonites, et al.), acceptance into the $\rightarrow$ congregation comes with believers' baptism. Where infant baptism is the rule ($\rightarrow$ Methodist Churches; Moravian Church), church membership comes later, when a personal $\rightarrow$ confession of faith can be made.

In countries with a national church, persons wishing to belong to a free church may often end up with double church membership. The German Arbeitsgemeinschaft christlicher Kirchen (Working fellowship of Christian churches), for example, has come out against this practice. Official withdrawal (see 5) from previous membership is demanded where there is a desire to change church affiliation.

As membership can be actively secured, so it may be ended by declaring one's withdrawal. A free church congregation may use the withdrawal of membership rights and duties as a disciplinary measure ($\rightarrow$ Church Discipline; Excommunication). Exclusion is not meant to be legalistic pressure but is exercised for the sake of the inner integrity of the congregation after all other pastoral possibilities have been exhausted. The appearance of a church is to a large degree determined by the issue of church membership.

Bibliography: E. GELDBACH, *Freikirchen–Erbe, Gestalt und Wirkung* (Göttingen, 1989).

ERICH GELDBACH

4. United States

Typical of Christianity in the United States are the principles of freedom of belief and separation of $\rightarrow$ church and state, and the associated religious and ecclesiastical $\rightarrow$ pluralism. These principles determine the theological and legal understanding of church membership in the United States. For $\rightarrow$ congregationalism, the congregation is a voluntary association. The territorial principle, with its concept of the local parish ($\rightarrow$ Cuius regio eius religio), thus has been replaced by the voluntary principle. A free resolve is the decisive prerequisite of church membership. Most $\rightarrow$ denominations ask for a conscious decision of faith (e.g., by confession of faith or in adult $\rightarrow$ baptism). Church membership is thus achieved, not ascribed. Reception into the church often follows the completion of special membership classes. Provisional membership may then precede full church membership, as in the $\rightarrow$ Methodist churches.

In detail, the definitions of church membership vary widely in the different denominations. Thus Baptists, with their view of baptism, regard only those who have received believers' baptism as members. Lutherans and Roman Catholics ($\rightarrow$ Lutheran Churches; Roman Catholic Church) accept baptized infants as members. Most of the other mainline churches view full membership as beginning with $\rightarrow$ confirmation. Many churches distinguish between broader church membership (inclusive membership, adherents) and strict church membership (full communicant or confirmed members). In the congregations, which often number in the hundreds, or even thousands, there are again many levels of participation. Active participation in the life of the congregation (e.g., in worship) is much higher than in Europe. It is lowest in the age group from 18 to 30.

Because of the voluntary principle the existence of the churches in the United States depends much more than in the established churches of Europe on the active participation and freewill offerings of the members ($\rightarrow$ Church Finances). Full rights of membership are usually enjoyed only by those who take part in worship, the $\rightarrow$ Eucharist, and congregational activities and who also help to finance the work of the congregation. In such cases, church membership may be dissolved by inactivity.

In practice, U.S. churches and denominations are involved in market-style competition. Winning members is a high priority and is validated theologically as "church growth." The high mobility of the population leads to a frequent crossing of denominational boundaries and to a breaking up of the socioeconomic homogeneity of many denominations. Since distinctions of confession and doctrine are not the primary marks of difference among most denominations, there is usually no obstacle to transfers of church membership.

Whereas in colonial days only 10 percent of the

people belonged to a church, today more than 50 percent belong to one of the more than 200 Christian and Jewish religious fellowships. Most of the unchurched still view themselves as believing Christians. Since the end of the 1960s the more liberal and ecumenically minded mainline churches have steadily lost members, while the evangelical and fundamentalist groups and denominations have gained in membership (→ Evangelical Movement; Fundamentalism). Many who do not participate in organized religion belong to the so-called → electronic church. In view of rapid changes in church membership in the past, no firm forecast can be given of future theological and social trends regarding church membership in the United States.

Bibliography: R. FINKE and R. STARKE, The Churching of America, 1776-1990 (New Brunswick, N.J., 1992) • GLENMARY RESEARCH CENTER, Churches and Church Membership in the United States, 1980 (Atlanta, 1982) • A. M. GREELEY, Religious Change in America (Cambridge, Mass., 1989) • D. HOGE and D. ROOZEN, eds., Understanding Church Growth and Decline: 1950-1978 (New York, 1979) • W. HUDSON, The Great Tradition of American Churches (New York, 1953) • D. M. KELLEY, Why Conservative Churches Are Growing (San Francisco, 1972) • S. E. MEAD, The Lively Experiment (New York, 1963) • H. R. NIEBUHR, The Social Sources of Denominationalism (Magnolia, Mass., 1984; orig. pub., 1929) • A. C. PIEPKORN, Profiles in Belief: The Religious Bodies of the United States and Canada (4 vols.; San Francisco, 1977-79) • PRINCETON RELIGIOUS RESEARCH CENTER, The Unchurched (Princeton, 1978) • D. B. ROBERTSON, ed., Voluntary Associations (Richmond, Va., 1966) • W. C. ROOF and W. McKINNEY, Mainline Religion: Its Changing Shape and Future (New Brunswick, N.J., 1987) • D. A. ROOZEN and C. K. HADAWAY, eds., Church and Denominational Growth (Nashville, 1993) • Yearbook of American and Canadian Churches (Nashville, 1996).

HEINRICH GROSSE

5. The Withdrawal of Church Members

The withdrawal of church members is a bigger issue in countries in which support of the established church still involves taxes or similar obligations. Forcing people to support a religious society against their will is incompatible with the religious neutrality of the modern → state. No official withdrawal of church members is necessary in countries in which there are no legal obligations.

How the churches themselves treat withdrawal of church membership depends on their understanding of the relation between the → church of Christ and the ecclesiastical organization. The closer the rela-

tion, the less withdrawal from the visible church is regarded as possible. Thus for the → Roman Catholic Church withdrawal is inappropriate and can bring with it penalties (→ Church Discipline), though the 1983 → Corpus Iuris Canonici 1124 links to it a releasing from canonical obligation (→ Marriage and Divorce). Other churches regard withdrawal, not from the church of Christ, but from the ecclesiastical organization as possible and do not disapprove of it in all circumstances. Special rules may apply when transfer is made to another church (→ Conversion 2).

Bibliography: A. VON CAMPENHAUSEN, "Der Austritt aus den Kirchen und Religionsgemeinschaften," Handbuch des Staatskirchenrechts (2d ed.; vol. 1; Berlin, 1994) 777ff. • L. CARLEN, ed., Austritt aus der Kirche–Sortir de l'église (Fribourg, 1982) • H. ENGELHARDT, Der Austritt aus der Kirche (Frankfurt, 1972) • G. ROBBERS, "Kirchenrechtliche und staatskirchenrechtliche Fragen des Kirchenübertritts," ZEvKR 32 (1987) 87ff.

HANNS ENGELHARDT

Church Music

1. Perspective
2. History
   2.1. Early Church
   2.2. After Constantine
   2.3. The East
   2.4. Gregorian Reform in the West
   2.5. The Reformation
   2.6. Eighteenth Century
   2.7. Nineteenth Century
3. Recent Developments

1. Perspective

J. S. Bach (1685-1750), describing the art of figured bass, suggested that it and all music should glorify God and recreate the mind, otherwise there is no music, only "a devilish hubbub." According to M. → Luther (1483-1546), music, understood properly, serves to proclaim the good news of God in Christ. As such, it is an *ancilla* (handmaiden), subordinate to the Word. Moreover, because of the ability of music to address and express suprarational thoughts, attitudes, and emotions related to communion with God, it serves as a vehicle for → faith and → piety.

2. History

Early Christian writers address music from four perspectives. They denounce lewd pagan entertainment for its use of music, particularly instruments; they recognize music's place in the liberal arts; they use musical images to develop arguments; and they make fleeting references to music in Christian → worship (J. McKinnon, 1ff.). Pagan music, insofar as it is self-serving and excites participants to excesses of debauchery, is contrasted with "solemn → prayers and → hymns" to God's glory and praise. Although instrumental music within a pagan context is condemned, the Christian writers do not ipso facto exclude instrumental music from Christian worship. The sources indicate, however, that unaccompanied singing is preferred because of the dangers otherwise of emotional excess and abuse. The early writers are unanimous in their opinion that Christian music serves always and only to voice divine praise and remains the constitutive mark of worship (→ Doxology).

2.1. Early Church

NT references to music are brief. → Jesus and the → disciples sang a hymn on the eve of the passion (Mark 14:26). → Paul mentions "psalms and hymns and spiritual songs" (Eph. 5:19; Col. 3:16) but provides no description of content or form. Recent scriptural research has identified hymnic and poetic forms embedded within NT texts (→ Hymn 2). Despite angelic choirs in John's apocalyptic vision, NT music appears to center on the offering of the community of faith itself, not on that of a separate, trained ensemble. The early church drew on Jewish → psalms and canticles, even while incorporating characteristics of Hellenistic culture and musical traditions, especially in its acceptance of various modes of music and views of music theory.

2.2. After Constantine

Christian worship and music developed in strikingly diverse patterns from the fourth century, the time of Constantine's acceptance of Christianity and the political establishment of the church. As the church's worship patterns became formalized, even incorporating imperial court ceremony, professional or specially trained musicians gradually ended the monopoly on music enjoyed by the early congregation (→ Church Musicians). Pseudo-Ignatius and several → councils in the fourth century identify the *psaltas* (cantor) as one of several clerical and administrative roles in worship.

The music of the post-Constantinian church developed a highly sophisticated manner of singing psalms. Old Roman chant developed initial, medial, and final cadential formulas requiring trained singers. Antiphonal psalmody was marked by contrasting sections between cantor and → choirs (e.g., the responsory in the Divine Office, the → gradual in the → Mass). The church in Milan preserves some of the earliest of these musical forms. Hymnody constitutes the other major musical genre of the early church. Prose and poetic texts written for use in churches (e.g., Gloria in Excelsis and Te Deum) quickly won permanent places in the various → liturgies.

In the West the ordinary and propers for both the Mass and the Liturgy of the Hours drew on both psalmody and a growing collection of hymns and psalmlike NT canticles (e.g., the Magnificat, Benedictus, and Nunc Dimittis). While the East continued to employ a wide variety of forms, the West formalized its liturgical celebrations into the five-part mass ordinary and the cycle of psalmody, hymns proper to time and season, and responsories. Methods for the chanting of Scripture moved beyond Jewish cantilena style to formal melodic patterns for distinguishing the various roles in the gospel accounts (those of evangelist, groups of people, and Christ).

2.3. The East

The sacking of → Rome in 475 shifted the center of ecclesial and cultural influence to → Byzantium. The Christian East, a multifaceted collection of national, relatively independent → autocephalous churches marked by elaborate, vernacular liturgies, based much of its music on Greek, Syriac, and Jewish sources. As a complement and further development of psalmody, *troparia* were composed. Originally, these were texts inserted between lines of psalms to expand and reflect upon the biblical text; they eventually became detached from the original text, resulting in independent hymnic compositions in rhythmic prose. *Kontakia,* another form deriving from Byzantine and Syrian Orthodox traditions in the fourth through sixth centuries, were short hymns in praise of saints. The *kanōn* comprised nine biblical canticles, or odes.

The early church in both East and West typically arranged musical works into specific collections or books. For the divine liturgy (Mass) of the Orthodox East as well as the Liturgy of the Hours, the *Heirmologion* contained the odes of the canon, and the *Sticherarion* included freely composed hymns, troparia, and antiphons arranged according to the church year. The *Kontakarion* contained the musically demanding kontakia.

2.4. Gregorian Reform in the West

The Gregorian reform of Western Catholic music began in the late sixth century. Growing numbers of unaccompanied unison chants were collected and systematically purged of awkward melodic movement and rhythm. The result was the smooth, ethereal style known as plainsong, or Gregorian chant, which was based eventually on eight modes, or scale patterns. Boethius (ca. 480-524) and others codified this musical system in theoretical form.

The repertoire for the Mass and Divine Office was expanded, particularly by tropes, sequences, and hymns. Tropes were original texts set to the extended melismas of chants such as the Kyrie (e.g., *Kyrie fons bonitatis*). The sequence, eventually an independent composition, began as the setting of a text to the melismatic last syllable of the Alleluia. Collected into books (known as the gradual and the antiphonal) and arranged for the church year and daily round of the Office, such music was the property of monastic communities, → cathedral and foundational churches, and the professional choir *(schola cantorum)* of the papal entourage.

The liturgies of the church, codified and arranged according to the church year (by ferial and festival days), the unchanging sections of the Mass (the ordinary), the rotation of psalmody for daily prayer with appropriate chants, and the appointed Scripture, music, and other text for specific days (the propers) eventually were recorded in sacramentaries, breviaries, and books of Gospels, Epistles, and Psalms. Although such collections of music were sung primarily by trained musicians of the church, recent musicological research has uncovered a lively folk tradition that hints at the music of popular lay devotions and pilgrimage hymns, as well as the music for mystery plays and liturgical dramas.

Organ and other instrumental music drew on vocal sources, embellishing the vocal line with ornamentation and scale passages. Voice parts multiplied, first paralleling the melody (in the organum and Ars Antiqua; e.g., in the 11th-century MS *Winchester Troper* and in the Notre Dame school) and then providing independent lines. The Ars Nova produced polyphonic → motets employing elaborate rhythmic systems.

In time, musical instruments were introduced into Christian worship. These included the → organ, which had originally been associated with secular revels. By the → Middle Ages in both East and West a veritable orchestra of string, wind, bell, and percussion instruments augmented the church's musical forces. Luther, with his conviction that music can be response as well as → proclamation (see WA 35), stands in the tradition of early Christian theoreticians, though Lutheran and Reformed theologians have debated the point in the 20th century (see W. Blankenburg and G. Harbsmeier).

2.5. *The Reformation*

While the music of the Christian East developed in an extremely conservative fashion, preserving the very early musical forms discussed, the 16th-century

→ Reformation saw a revival of devotional music of the laity, especially in hymnody, paralleling the spiritual upheavals marking the numerous reforms and sectarian movements.

2.5.1. The music of the → Roman Catholic Church enjoyed a flowering of polyphony — Flemish in the 15th century (J. d'Ockeghem and Josquin des Prez), Italian in the 16th (A. Gabrieli, G. Gabrieli, G. Palestrina, and O. di Lasso). Sophisticated compositions used Gregorian melodies and even folk tunes for Mass settings, motets, and settings of the Office (e.g., C. Monteverdi's music for Marian vespers). By the 17th century the rapidly growing popularity of Italian opera influenced not only compositional forms for the church (e.g., in use of the sequence; → Oratorio; Passion Music) but music for the Mass itself.

Orchestral accompaniments, at first only as a minimal vocal accompaniment but later as independent compositions, lavishly enriched the church's musical repertoire. → Classicism, renowned for its symphonic literature, also produced symphonic works for the church (masses by Haydn and Mozart, plus many oratorios and passions) and instrumental works to be played during the liturgy (e.g., Mozart's "epistle sonatas" for organ and strings). In France the organ played an important role in *alternatum praxis* with a Gregorian choir during the Mass as well as the Office (N.-A. Lebègue, N. de Grigny, F. Couperin, J. Titelouze, L. Marchand).

2.5.2. The Lutheran reform is marked chiefly by the central role that it gave to the vernacular, congregational hymn, chiefly through the efforts of M. Luther, P. Speratus, N. Decius, P. Nicolai, and P. Gerhardt. At the same time, Latin compositions and even liturgical forms and ceremony continued to distinguish Lutheran worship well into the 18th century (e.g., Bach mass settings and Magnificat verses by J. Pachelbel). The hymn became an essential part of all Lutheran liturgies and was understood to be both response to the saving Word and itself a proclamation of the good news. Its popularity and ability to focus congregational devotion are apparent in the brief flowering of Roman Catholic hymnody during the century (e.g., the Leisentritt Hymnal of 1567). Because hymnody was so strongly identified with the Lutheran reform, however, the Roman hierarchy soon forbade its use in the Mass. Only in the 20th century has the Catholic Church given uneasy recognition to congregational hymn singing.

Lutheran musical forces include first and foremost the → congregation. The *Kantorei,* or trained instrumentalists and vocalists, performed the more complex literature (the motet and → cantata). Under the direction of the cantor, the Lutheran musical tradition reached its golden age under H. Schütz (1585-1672), S. Scheidt (1587-1654), J. H. Schein (1586-1630), D. Buxtehude (1637-1707), and J. S. Bach.

The Lutheran tradition is perhaps the only Western tradition that is able to articulate a developed theology of music, beginning with Luther (→ Luther's Theology) and J. Walter (1496-1570). Based on the unique role of the arts in proclamation, it articulates the congregation's praise, devotion, and → meditation. There is a striking unity between the music of the laity and that reserved for the clergy, thanks to an inherent → conservatism in the tradition. Instrumental and concert music, related directly to the congregational hymn, further helped to achieve what we might call the Lutheran musical ethos. The 20th century is witnessing the tradition's recovery not only of the rich heritage of church music in the 16th-18th centuries but also of a revival of composition for organ, choir, and the instruments (H. Distler, E. Pepping, J. Bender, C. Schalk, P. O. Manz, D. Busarow). Other influences are gradually being incorporated as the tradition grows beyond its Germanic and Scandinavian roots.

2.5.3. The Calvinist reform saw a drastic reduction of musical forms and resources. J. → Calvin (→ Calvin's Theology), conservative in his estimation of music's role in worship, limited the music of the church to settings of the 150 psalms. C. Marot (ca. 1497-1544) and T. → Beza (1519-1605) aided Calvin by casting the psalms into verse so that they could be set to music. In the Calvinist theocracy, however, the arts did flourish. Even while psalm settings and associated tunes remained simple for the liturgy, composers such as L. Bourgeois (ca. 1510-after 1561) created complex, polyphonic settings for musical entertainment in the home.

Holland followed Calvin's lead, accepting psalmody and its characteristic tunes after the introduction of the Reformation.

The cautious introduction of hymnody into the Church of England was largely the result of Calvinist influences during the brief reign of Edward VI (1547-53). The exile of many theologians and reforming priests and bishops to Reformed territories during the reign of Mary Tudor (1553-58) introduced them not only to the music but to Reformed theology as well. This was brought back to Scotland after Mary's death by J. → Knox (ca. 1513-72), who established the Scottish psalm tradition.

Although much church music history has been only the record of music in cathedrals and court chapels, research is uncovering a parallel history in the small parish. Here simple psalms and hymns, occasionally accompanied by quaintly embellished settings, continued to be sung into the present century. In England the compositions of W. Byrd (1543-1623), O. Gibbons (1583-1625), T. Weelkes (ca. 1576-1623), and T. Tomkins (1572-1656) continued the Renaissance polyphonic tradition. Royal foundations and cathedrals underwrote the training and schooling of boys to sing for the daily liturgies (e.g., at the Chapel Royal, King's College). The "verse anthem," developed at this time by Gibbons and H. Purcell, took advantage of antiphonal possibilities of the divided choir, typical of English church architecture.

2.5.4. U. → Zwingli (1484-1531; → Zwingli's Theology) forbade the use of music altogether, finding theological, philosophical, and even psychological reasons for banning its use in Zurich — although seemingly tolerating it elsewhere. Zurich itself reintroduced singing soon after his death. The → Anabaptists found that hymnody served as the ideal expression not only of a fervent faith but also of the persecutions they endured. The Quakers (→ Friends, Society of), on the leftmost wing of the reforming movements, accepted no specific forms of music but rather relied on direct inspiration of the → Holy Spirit to move members to sing "spiritual songs."

2.6. Eighteenth Century

The 18th century witnessed the continued popularity of the oratorio across Europe, which moved church music out of the sanctuary and into the concert hall. Handel's works in particular laid the foundation for the singing societies of the 19th century, which provided a ready market for the choral compositions of F. Mendelssohn (1809-47). Hymnody again underwent a revival with the compositions of I. Watts (1674-1748), J. Newton (1725-1807), W. Cowper (1731-1800), and Charles Wesley (1707-88). Wesley alone penned over 6,000 hymns.

2.7. Nineteenth Century

Church music in North America was largely imported from Europe until the mid-19th century. → Moravians enjoyed a particularly rich musical tradition, continuing to compose in a conservative, "American Baroque" style and drawing on the same forces as the German Lutheran *Kantorei*.

The Cane Ridge Revival of 1803, the most famous camp meeting of the Second Great Awakening, set the direction for American "frontier religion." Drawing on the hymns of Watts and Wesley but simplifying the texts into hard-hitting religious slogans coupled with catchy tunes, the revival adopted songs that became the prototypes for the later "gospel song." Slavery, which caused increasing tension in the

19th century, gave the church yet another form — the spiritual. African influences coupled with a scriptural message of freedom produced a musical genre that voiced the hope of liberation and also provided comfort and assurance to an oppressed people.

A number of peculiar religious sects sprang up in the "new land," which represented to the religious outcast or group some degree of tolerance. The Shakers, a now-dwindling tradition that produced some of the most refined yet simple crafts, are also noted for the songs sung during their charismatic dances (e.g., "Lord of the Dance"), in which evil and sin were to be physically shaken out of the body.

In reaction to the industrial revolution, the inhumane working conditions of the poor, and a general religious laxity at the turn of the 20th century, the Social Gospel movement promulgated its program with the insistent rhythms of the gospel song (e.g., as popularized by I. Sankey). A simple "come to Jesus" appeal permeated the songs, often entwined with temperance themes. Church music of this ilk had less to do with the established church than with gospel missions. The message was intentionally simple, and also at times simplistic and shallow.

The music of African American churches has incorporated aspects of blues, jazz, ballad, and improvisation since the 19th century, all marked by enthusiastic, spontaneous participation by the entire congregation. Black preaching styles further combine song with spoken proclamation.

3. Recent Developments

The 20th century has witnessed radical changes in the direction, form, and content of church music. → Third World countries, once the passive recipients of imported culture and foreign ecclesial systems, are learning that they too have "a new song." → Roman Catholicism in particular has investigated how it as an established ecclesial body can preserve traditional music and liturgical forms but at the same time accept into its tradition music indigenous to foreign cultures (→ Acculturation).

The traditional psalmic forms, ordinary, and propers for the Mass and hours also have received fresh treatment. Going beyond the complex formulas of Gregorian chant, J. Gélineau set the Psalter to a steady beat of chord progressions over which the text is loosely arranged. The French ecumenical community → Taizé has published numerous collections of meditative and joyous chants that include solo verses sung in alternation with chordal phrases by the entire community. Drawing on simple principles of improvisation and *Gebrauchsmusik*, the style has been embraced by many traditions.

Some of the most interesting recent research in church music investigates the relationship between the scientific → language of doctrine and the experiential language of faith. Interdisciplinary studies by linguistic scholars have helped to clarify the understanding of faith of an earlier era. Congregational music can reveal much about personal and corporate piety, always an elusive subject.

→ Vatican II indirectly marked the beginning of the ecumenical era of church music (→ Ecumenical Movement). Roman Catholic composers have greatly influenced the use by other traditions of psalmody and Scripture in worship. The Lutheran "hymn of the day" is now part of Roman Catholic and Anglican experience. Evangelical → free churches and ethnic traditions have helped the more liturgical churches to breathe new life into staid liturgies. Black Roman Catholic and → Episcopal churches in particular have discovered that a charismatic influence on traditional liturgical and musical forms can be faithful to the tradition. Some degree of spontaneity has relieved a fixation on rubric exactness and propriety. Finally, ecumenical dialogues with liturgical traditions have helped free churches realize the importance of orderly, responsible proclamation (e.g., in using a common lectionary) and the value and beauty of the vast musical heritage of the church.

→ Ave Maria; Canticle; Dance; Gospel Song; Hymnbook; Hymnology; Liturgical Movements; Liturgics; Mary, Devotion to; Requiem; Spirituals; Stabat Mater dolorosa

Bibliography: W. BLANKENBURG, "Kann Singen Verkündigung sein?" *Kirche und Musik* (ed. E. Hübner and R. Steiger; Göttingen, 1969) • F. BLUME et al., *Protestant Church Music* (New York, 1974) • F. B. BROWN, *Transfiguration: Poetic Metaphor and the Language of Religious Belief* (Chapel Hill, N.C., 1983) • P. BRUNNER, "Singen und Sagen," *Pro Ecclesia. Gesammelte Aufsätze zur dogmatischen Theologie* (vol. 2; Berlin, 1966) 352-79 • H. T. DAVID and A. MENDEL, *The Bach Reader* (2d ed.; New York, 1966) • C. DEARNLEY, *English Church Music, 1650-1750* (New York, 1970) • R. DEICHGRÄBER, *Gotteshymnus und Christushymnus in der frühen Christenheit* (Göttingen, 1967) • H. W. FOOTE, *Three Centuries of American Hymnody* (Cambridge, Mass., 1940) • C. GARSIDE JR., *Zwingli and the Arts* (New Haven, 1966) • G. HARBSMEIER, "Theologie und Liturgie," *TRu*, n.s., 20 (1952) 271-93 • R. D. HAWKINS, "The Liturgical Expression of Sanctification: The Hymnic Complement to the Lutheran Concordia" (Diss., Notre Dame, Ind., 1988) • J. LASTER, *Catalogue of Choral Music Arranged in Biblical Order* (Metuchen, N.J., 1996) • P. LE HURAY, *Music and the Reformation in England, 1549-1660* (London, 1967)

• J. McKinnon, ed., *Music in Early Christian Literature* (Cambridge, 1987) • D. Power, "Two Expressions of Faith: Worship and Theology," *Liturgical Experience of Faith* (ed. H. Schmidt and D. Power; New York, 1973) 95-103 • P. Price, *Bells and Man* (Oxford, 1983) • J. Quasten, *Musik und Gesang in den Kulten der heidnischen Antike und christlichen Frühzeit* (Münster, 1930) • W. I. Sauer-Geppert, *Sprache und Frömmigkeit im deutschen Kirchenlied* (Kassel, 1984) • W. L. Smolden, *The Music of the Medieval Church Dramas* (London, 1980) • N. Temperly, *The Music of the English Parish Church* (2 vols.; Cambridge, 1979) • W. Ulrich, *Semantische Untersuchungen zum Wortschatz des Kirchenliedes im 16. Jahrhundert* (Lübeck, 1969) • E. Wellesz, *A History of Byzantine Music and Hymnography* (2d ed.; New York, 1961) • E. Wellesz and M. Velimirovic, eds., *Studies in Eastern Chant* (3 vols.; London, 1966-73) • A. Wilson-Dickson, *The Story of Christian Music from Gregorian Chant to Black Gospel* (Minneapolis, 1997).

Robert D. Hawkins

Church Musicians

The primary musicians of the church are the faithful gathered for → worship, and only by extension also → choirs, soloists, and instrumentalists. The church, understood in the NT as a charismatic community (1 Corinthians 12–14; Col. 3:16; Eph. 5:15-20), manifests its praise and thanksgiving to God in "psalms and hymns and spiritual songs." Such → doxological offerings are the common "sacrifice of praise" (Heb. 13:15) of the universal priesthood. Early Christian communities continued familiar → prayer traditions, incorporating → psalms and canticles while composing new → hymns and psalms to the Christ.

The post-Constantinian church recognized the role of "chief musician" (Lat. *cantor;* Gk. *psaltas*), that is, one who leads the → congregation in song as well as directing the choir. The cantor was soon named as a minor cleric who assumed an increasingly greater musical role in worship. Still, there is reason to assume a lively, grassroots repertoire of spontaneous, popular Christian song unrecorded by church historians.

As → liturgies became more complex, musical roles of necessity were more specifically defined. The cantor, responsible for the solo sections of antiphonal psalmody, led and shared the singing with choirs trained to render the music for various psalm tunes, chants during the liturgies, and eventually polyphonic → motets and hymn settings for the → Mass and the Divine Office. The → deacon was charged with the chanting of the gospel for the Mass, a tradition that survives to the present in Roman Catholicism. The presiding → priest was expected to render extensive musical sections of the eucharistic liturgy (→ Eucharist).

The elaborate, imperial ceremonial bestowed on the church during the Byzantine ascendancy popularized the acclamation, led by cantor *(domesticus)* and choirs. Instrumentalists were employed for → processions, although it is not clear whether they were employed also for the liturgies. Trumpets, horns, pipes, and portable organs all had fixed places in the court music, influencing the monks who reintroduced instrument making, particularly the organ, to the Christian West. At first the organist most likely helped to teach plainsong and provided pitches for singers. Later, as attitudes concerning instruments in worship shifted, more independent parts were composed for accomplished performers.

The High Middle Ages recognized the unique gifts of the composer, and churches became musical centers for learning as well as for worship. The church schools (at Notre Dame; the Flemish school under Josquin des Prez and H. Isaac; and those under A. Gabrielli in Venice, H. Schütz in Dresden, and J. S. Bach in Leipzig) gave shape to national styles. Bach's (1685-1750) aim of providing "well-regulated music" for the church envisioned the active participation of congregation, choir, organ, and instrumental ensemble. This concept is still influential in European → church music and governs the training of professional church musicians in special music schools.

The situation in England is like that on the Continent, but the main work is done in → cathedrals and college chapels, many of which have choir schools for the education of choirboys. These schools have practically disappeared from the rest of Europe, where church musicians usually work in churches, often supported by professional associations.

With specific adaptations, these traditions have been adapted to → pluralism in North America, where church musicians are most commonly trained in church-related liberal arts colleges. They also have the support of professional organizations that do research, provide further education, and maintain musical standards (e.g., the American Guild of Organists). North America has contributed the free church "song leader," who not only may be the sole musical support for worship but also serves the didactic role of "lining out" hymns for illiterate worshipers.

In Asia and Africa the churches are in transition from American and European liturgical use to independent musical forms mostly relating to hymnody (→ Hymnbook). Examples of more recent institutions for the training of church musicians and native composers are the Asian Institute for Liturgy and Music (Philippines) and the African Association for Liturgy, Music, and the Arts (Zimbabwe).

Bibliography: W. Blankenburg et al., *Leit.* 4 • W. Douglas, *Church Music in History and Practice* (2d ed.; London, 1962) • J. McKinnon, *Music in Early Christian Literature* (Cambridge, 1987) • K. F. Müller, *Der Kantor: Sein Amt und seine Dienste* (Gütersloh, 1964) • J. Quasten, *Musik und Gesang in den Kulten der heidnischen Antike und christlichen Frühzeit* (2d ed.; Münster, 1973) • G. Stiller, *Johann Sebastian Bach und das leipziger gottesdienstliche Leben seiner Zeit* (Kassel, 1970) • E. Wellesz, *A History of Byzantine Music and Hymnography* (2d ed.; Oxford, 1961) • P. Westermeyer, *The Church Musician* (San Francisco, 1988).

Robert D. Hawkins

Church of Christ, Scientist → Christian Science

Church of Georgia → Orthodox Church

Church of God → Worldwide Church of God

Church of Jesus Christ of Latter-Day Saints → Mormons

Church of Scientology

1. Origins
2. Basic Principles
3. Political and Economic Aspects, Institutions
4. Organization
5. Evaluation

1. Origins

The term "scientology," meaning "the science of science," was used as early as 1934 for the title of a book by the philosopher A. Nordenholz. It is uncertain whether the American writer L. Ronald Hubbard (1911-86), the founder of Scientology, knew this work. In Scientology, which Hubbard viewed as a kind of superscience, he aimed to liberate the human spirit by his "religious philosophy" or "technology." He did not at first organize a church. The starting point was the great success of his book *Dianetics* (1950), following which he founded a "church" in the mid-1950s: the St. Hill Manor at East Grinstead in England, which helped give the group a religious coloring. The Church of Scientology, organized in 1954 from Los Angeles, is a financially strong, worldwide organization claiming in 1988 to have seven million members (probably an exaggeration).

2. Basic Principles

The main principles of Scientology freely combine elements from the fields of the early → psychoanalysis of Sigmund Freud (1856-1939); the world of science fiction, to which Hubbard increasingly devoted himself as he grew older; and an esoteric-Gnostic and even occult-magical → tradition (→ Esotericism; Gnosis, Gnosticism; Magic; Occultism). After World War II Hubbard experienced the last of these in his alleged global travels, both practically and theoretically, in the Ordo Templi Orientis (a neo-Satanic occult order).

Dianetics (from Gk. *dia-noētikos*, "through the mind") developed against the background of numerous experiments in hypnotism. A procedure similar to → psychotherapy, it aims at producing "Clear," or a perfect person liberated from present or potential psychosomatic sicknesses or irrational aberrations. It seeks to negate destructive "engrams" (i.e., painful experiences, which, in a way similar to films, make unconscious impressions on us). According to Hubbard's theory, the brain, which is like a computer, collects these engrams in unconscious "reactive mind," and it is the task of an "auditing" process to remove them. As the one who gives dianetic "pastoral" care, the "auditor" has hypnosis-type sessions in which the aim is by pointed questions to take the "Pre-Clear" back to the past, to bring the engrams to light, and to promote a reliving of the past experiences in every detail. An aid in the process is Hubbard's "electropsychometer," or "E-meter," a device that measures skin resistance and, for scientologists, thus makes possible the direct measurement of mental energy.

When during such auditings (i.e., the reexperiencing of past traumas) scenes from what seemed to be a previous life turned up, Hubbard, against the advice of some of his coworkers, decided to include this dimension of reincarnation in his total system. With the integration of dianetics, Scientology thus became a "religious philosophy" — "religious" not so much because of a hardly discernible transcendental reference (→ Immanence and Transcendence) as because of its assertion of an → immortal and preexistent spirit, which Hubbard called Thetan and defined as the nameless and bodiless person, the unit that is conscious of its own consciousness. The aim of Scientology is to give the full → freedom that will confer on the "Operating Thetan" (OT), saved from the results of its own decisions originally made out of tedium, control not only over its own environment but also over matter, energy, space, and time. The gradient path to total freedom outlines, at the very top of the so-called bridge, 15 OT stages, whose content is not to be disclosed; the eighth stage, hitherto the highest, was made available to members in 1988.

Scientological → ethics is also concerned with the issue of control, following the principle of survival on the "eight dynamics" of reality (upward from the individual person to the family, group, humanity, and up as far as the "God-plane"). As far as the organization itself is concerned, the section "Ethics" is to "remove" from its immediate surroundings any oppositional and alien purposes. Opponents of the Church of Scientology are viewed as "antisocial," and members not functioning as desired as a "Potential Trouble Source" (PTS, to be "dealt with" using commensurate severity).

3. Political and Economic Aspects, Institutions
The aim of the Scientology Church to "clear" the planet can hardly be nonpolitical and gives evidence of → totalitarian features. In the 1980s younger followers adopted specific strategies, especially that of infiltrating the → economy. Support in this field came from the World Institute of Scientology Enterprises, which undertook to market Hubbard's management technology and indirectly to conduct the employees of the firms concerned to the "bridge." Daughter (and camouflaged) organizations of the Scientology Church — which include Narconon, Crimanon, the Commission on Offences of Psychiatry against Human Rights, the Center for Individual and Effective Learning, and the Union of Concerned Managers — also seek to influence society.

4. Organization
The Scientology Church itself is organized in steps. On the first step are several hundred "missions" worldwide. These work with the churches, which are called Orgs (i.e., organizations). Above these are "Advanced Organizations" in East Grinstead, Copenhagen, Los Angeles, and Sydney. The Flag Service Org in Clearwater, Florida, is the "most advanced church." This alone works with the Flag Ship Service Org on board the ship *Freewinds* to run the highest Operative Thetan course. The ship belongs to "Sea Org," an

organization of some 5,000 members that as a kind of fraternity plays a key role in the system. At its head is the Religious Technology Center (RTC), which holds all the rights to Scientology and dianetics.

5. Evaluation
For decades the Scientology Church has come under international criticism from the media, experts in church → sects, and many judicial authorities. It is accused of seeking → power and → money and of using methods to control the consciousness. Its status as a religion or a church is vigorously disputed. Its religious features — devotions, ceremonies, name-giving, weddings, and burials — are seen to be either sham or imitative. Because of disputes concerning its authenticity as a religion, its tax-free status has been contested. Its eagerness for profit through sale of books and the offering of successive expensive courses has claimed attention. In 1993 the U.S. Internal Revenue Service accepted its religious status; rulings in Germany (in Hamburg and Stuttgart), however, have defined it as a business.

→ EST; Youth Religions

Bibliography: J. ATACK, *A Piece of Blue Sky: Scientology, Dianetics, and L. R. Hubbard Exposed* (Secaucus, N.Y., 1990) • F.-W. HAACK, *Scientology. Magie des 20. Jahrhunderts* (2d ed.; Munich, 1991) • R. HARTWIG, *Scientology. Ich klage an!* (Augsburg, 1994) • J. HERRMANN, ed., *Mission mit allen Mitteln* (4th ed.; Reinbek, 1994) • R. KAUFMAN, *Inside Scientology: Or, How I Joined Scientology and Became Super Human* (New York, 1972) • J. G. MELTON, *Encyclopedia Handbook of Cults in America* (New York, 1986) 128-34 • R. MILLER, *Bare-Faced Messiah* (New York, 1988) • N. POTTHOFF, *Im Labyrinth der Scientology* (Munich, 1997) • H. P. STEIDEN and C. HAMERNIK, *Einsteins falsche Erben* (Vienna, 1992) • W. THIEDE, *Scientology–der Magie-Konzern. Medienpaket* (Offenbach, 1994); idem, *Scientology–Religion oder Geistesmagie?* (2d ed.; Neukirchen, 1995) • R. WALLIS, *The Road to Total Freedom: A Sociological Analysis of Scientology* (New York, 1977).

WERNER THIEDE

Church of South India

The Church of South India (CSI) resulted from the → union in 1947 of the → Anglican Church of India, Pakistan, Burma, and Ceylon; the South India United Church (SIUC); and the → Methodist Church. The SIUC itself resulted from a union of Presbyterian and Congregational churches (→ Reformed and Presbyterian Churches; Congregationalism), along with churches of the Basel Mission in South India. The CSI represented the first union in the world involving → episcopal and nonepiscopal churches. In numbers the CSI is the largest non–Roman Catholic church in India, with over two million members in 1994. It is at work in four Indian states among speakers of Tamil, Malayalam, Kannada, and Telugu, and also in Jaffna (Tamil), Sri Lanka. There are CSI diaspora congregations in the major cities in India, the Gulf countries, and the United States.

1. Early History
Protestant missionary work (→ Mission) early demanded close cooperation among Indian churches. Many national Christians felt that the multiplicity of denominations tended to be a hindrance to the → evangelization of Indians and worked for union in their country. This trend became stronger in 1905 with the formation of the National Missionary Society.

The first step to negotiations for union came in 1919 at a conference for pastors in Tranquebar, when 26 pastors of the South India Church and 7 Anglican representatives affirmed their readiness for union. On the basis of a manifesto drawn up there, the → Anglicans and the SIUC began negotiations. The manifesto took as its basis the four points of the Lambeth Quadrilateral, which listed the elements to be honored in any reunion plans: (1) Holy Scripture, (2) the → Apostles' and → Niceno-Constantinopolitan Creeds, (3) the sacraments of baptism and Eucharist, and (4) the historic episcopate, adjusted to local situations. Five years later the Methodists joined the negotiations. Agreement about the → bishop's office and the status of nonepiscopally ordained ministers (→ Offices, Ecclesiastical) was reached in 1929. The bishops would conduct new → ordinations, but ministers already in office would be recognized without further → laying on of hands. In 1941 the mother churches agreed to the draft of a constitution. On September 27, 1947, the new church began life at a solemn service in St. George's Cathedral, Madras.

2. Confessional Basis
The constitution mentions the confessional basis. First, Holy Scripture contains all that is necessary to salvation and is the supreme and decisive norm for believers. Second, the Apostles' and Nicene Creeds bear witness to the faith and help to preserve it. Third, the church can make further statements of faith as needed, as long as they are not contrary to Holy Scripture.

3. Development
Since 1947 other churches and areas have joined the CIS that were not at first ready to do so, including the Church Councils in North and South Karnataka (formerly the Basel Mission). The newly formed → dioceses and districts overlapped former denominational boundaries, and the introduction of new forms of worship also helped to speed integration. Control of the church gradually passed into the hands of nationals. The missions in Europe and the United States kept up relations with the Union for some 30 years, mostly with their respective daughter churches. But gradually the CSI came to be seen as a whole, as its own church. In spite of initial doubts about the validity of CSI orders, the Anglican Communion is now in full communion (→ Eucharist 5).

The CSI became a model for other unions, such as the Church of North India and the Church of Pakistan (which both came into being in 1970 on a similar basis and with a similar structure).

4. Organization
The organization of the CSI includes pastorates (comprising one or more congregations) and dioceses (with more than one pastorate). In 1994 there were 21 dioceses and 9,000 congregations. To understand the CSI as a model of union, it is important to grasp that there are church councils and diocesan councils made up of both clergy and laity. The church thus combines various structural elements. Representatives from all the dioceses form the → synod, the supreme ruling body. The diocesan council in each diocese has representatives of all the ministers; the president of the council and the diocesan committees is the bishop. A bishop also presides over the synod, elected by the synod as moderator for a two-year term. The CSI recognizes three offices: → deacon, presbyter (→ Pastor, Pastorate), and bishop. Women have been ordained since 1982. Only ordained ministers may administer the sacraments.

5. Worship, Church Law, Institutions
The constitution grants to each congregation the right to continue forms of worship (→ Liturgy) that it may have used previously. A need soon arose, however, for uniform liturgical texts. Services were thus introduced for the Eucharist, baptism, and ordina-

tion (in the four Indian languages). These services fused elements from the earliest Christian traditions with new forms adjusted to Indian thinking. The eucharistic liturgy has gained special recognition as an example of the integration of biblical and Reformation doctrine with early traditions.

The constitution and decisions of the synod form church law. Every communicant over 21 years of age may vote and can be elected to the synod and other bodies. The CSI took over schools, hospitals, and other missionary institutions. It has also founded new schools and vocational schools. It provides theological instruction in the theological schools of the missionary societies and in four seminaries (one for each linguistic area). → Evangelization and social work geared to development are decisive concerns. The sisters of the Order of Sisters do work as teachers, catechists, doctors, and nurses as part of the missionary work of the CSI.

6. Ecumenical Relations
The CSI is a member of the → World Council of Churches, the Indian → National Council of Churches, and the → Christian Conference of Asia. It has reached theological understanding with the Lutheran churches in conversations but has not yet achieved union. Conversations with the Mar Thomas Church (→ Syrian Orthodox Churches in India) and the Church of North India have also taken place, resulting in the formation of a joint council of the three churches.

7. Self-Understanding and Problems
The organizational unity of the CSI, whose members speak different languages and belong to different social strata and → castes, is seen as a symbol of the → unity of all Christians. One of the challenges to the CSI is to preserve this unity in the face of the tendency to fracture, which is undeniably present. The much-debated episcopal office has served as an instrument to maintain unity, even as serious questions have arisen regarding its functions and effects.

The gospel is being preached to non-Christians, and the CSI is growing and becoming more significant. → Dialogue with other religions must continue. In spite of its minority status, the CSI has made an important contribution to the solving of social problems by its broad ministry of education and development. The movement for the uplift and liberation of the Dalits (untouchables/outcastes) deserves special mention.

Bibliography: Primary sources: *The Book of Common Worship* (London, 1963; repr., Madras, 1979) • *The Constitution of the CSI* (Madras, 1952ff.) • *Renewal and Advance: Report of the CSI Commission on Integration and Joint Action, 1963* (Madras, 1963; 2d ed., 1964).

Secondary works: T. S. GARRETT, *Worship in the CSI* (London, 1958; 2d ed., 1965) • J. L. NEWBIGIN, *The Reunion of the Church* (New York, 1948) on the theological foundation of the CSI • R. D. PAUL, *Ecumenism in Action. CSI: An Assessment* (Madras, 1972); idem, *The First Decade* (Madras, 1958) • R. D. PAUL and E. C. JOHN, "Die Kirche von Südindien," *Evangelische Kirche in Indien* (ed. H. Grafe; Erlangen, 1981) 127-48 • B. SUNDKLER, *CSI: The Movement towards Union, 1900-1947* (London, 1954; 2d ed., 1960) • A. M. WARD, *The Pilgrim Church: An Account of the First Five Years of the CSI* (London, 1953).

E. C. JOHN

Church of the Nazarene

1. Summary
2. Doctrine
3. Development
4. Present Tendencies

1. Summary
The Church of the Nazarene, a denomination in the Wesleyan/Holiness tradition, in 1996 had 1.3 million members (total constituency around 3.5 million) in 12,000 congregations in 115 nations. Two-thirds of its members and congregations are in the United States, but it is striving to develop indigenous leadership at all levels everywhere. It maintains 2 postbaccalaureate theological seminaries, 8 liberal arts institutions offering baccalaureate and graduate degrees, and 41 postsecondary Bible colleges (→ Education 4). It also maintains numerous Bible institutes, one hospital, and numerous clinics. It operates a separately incorporated international → relief agency that works both independently and in cooperation with other agencies. The church's worldwide headquarters, its principal publishing house, and its music publishing company (Lillenas) are in Kansas City, Missouri. Since 1912, its official paper has been the *Herald of Holiness*, which is currently a monthly periodical appearing in separate English, Spanish, and Portuguese editions.

2. Doctrine
From its beginnings, the Church of the Nazarene has believed itself to be an authentically Protestant expression of the "one, holy, catholic, and apostolic church." It holds to an orthodox Trinitarian theology, as did each of its original constituent bodies. Histori-

cally, it is the offspring of the British Wesleyan revival and the American → holiness movement. Especially important in its Wesleyan heritage is John → Wesley's belief that Christ's → atonement provides for every believer a grace-given, grace-sustained experience of unconditional love to God and to neighbor in this life. Wesley referred often to the social dimension of the experience and set it as Methodism's purpose "to spread scriptural holiness over these lands."

Doctrinally, Nazarenes accept the interpretation of Wesley's thought developed by the American holiness movement, especially in urging believers to seek and receive the gracious gift of entire sanctification, the entry "here and now" into the life of holiness, or Christian perfection. With Wesley, they teach that this gift is received "instantaneously," subsequent to regeneration, and that the Holy Spirit is faithful to witness to the seeker that the work has been done. Like Wesley, Nazarenes emphasize the belief that this is a perfection in love, not in mind, physical condition, or insight, and that while it is always perfection, it also always admits to, and seeks, growth in grace. The model is Christlikeness, which means not only personal purity but sacrificial social concern.

Membership is restricted to persons who receive Jesus Christ as personal Savior and agree to abide by the disciplinary rules of the denomination. Positively, these are "doing good to the bodies and souls of others," "avoiding evil of every kind," and "not inveighing against the doctrines and usages" of the denomination. Negatively, they include prohibitions against smoking, use of alcohol as a beverage, membership in oath-bound secret societies, and participation in behaviors that militate against purity of heart and life.

3. Development

The holiness movement began in the vigorous, transdenominational revival of interest in Christian → perfection (→ Methodism 3), or the Higher Life, in the United States in the 1830s. Revivalistic, it called for personal, immediate, life-changing religious decision; it believed that evangelism was a primary task of the church, and it therefore saw the evangelistic elements of corporate worship as central. Of special relevance here, but not of uncontested authority in the movement, are the teachings of Phoebe Worrall (Mrs. Walter) → Palmer (1807-74), Charles G. → Finney (1792-1875), and Asa Mahan (1799-1889).

On June 13, 1867, eight pastors and one "local preacher" in the Methodist Episcopal Church, meeting at Vineland, New Jersey, organized the National Camp Meeting Association for the Promotion of Holiness (later, the National Holiness Association; still later, the Christian Holiness Association; now, the Christian Holiness Partnership). This followed a very successful camp meeting held there with the specific, but not sole, purpose of promoting the Wesleyan doctrine of Christian perfection (by now more frequently termed "holiness" or "entire → sanctification" [§3]) in revivalistic fashion. The National, as it was called, quickly became the principal engine of the movement. It remained essentially, though not exclusively, Methodist Episcopal until the early 1900s. It soon spawned a multitude of smaller holiness associations, often not so dominantly Methodist. In some, Oberlin perfectionism, emphasizing the role of the will in obtaining and retaining entire sanctification, gained considerable footing; in others, "restorationist" ecclesiologies accompanied a more or less Wesleyan understanding of Christian perfection; in still others, the revivalistic style became the norm for Christian worship in general (sometimes even to the point of neglect of the sacraments).

All of these groups engaged aggressively in evangelism, often forming congregations for those who felt unwelcome in mainline groups — even in → Methodist churches. By the 1870s, holiness people, Methodist and otherwise, were openly accusing Methodism of doctrinal and ethical compromise in its yearning for social standing and political influence. The Methodist hierarchy seldom criticized holiness preaching as such, but it responded to its often contentious holiness constituency by demanding institutional loyalty and discipline, especially in the control of itinerant holiness evangelists. As a result, from about 1885 to 1920, significant numbers of holiness clergy and laity left episcopal Methodism.

The history of the Church of the Nazarene began almost wholly within the Methodist Episcopal expression of the holiness movement. The Association of Pentecostal Churches of America, with roots going back to the formation of the People's Evangelical Church in Providence, Rhode Island, in 1887, was led primarily by disaffected Methodist preachers. The first Church of the Nazarene was established in Los Angeles, California, in 1895, by P. F. Bresee (→ Perfectionists 1), a former Methodist Episcopal pastor and presiding elder (and preacher for the National), and by J. P. Widney, M.D., a Methodist very prominent in the founding of the University of Southern California. That Los Angeles congregation soon begot a small West Coast denomination. Widney, reflecting on Christ's ministry to the poor, gave it its name. By 1907, the Nazarenes had congregations in the Midwest, and the association had spread to New York, Pennsylvania, the Cape Verde Islands, and India. The association and the Nazarenes joined in

Chicago that year as the Pentecostal Church of the Nazarene. (The denomination dropped the "Pentecostal" in 1919 to avoid being identified as a "tongues" church.)

In 1908 the Holiness Church of Christ, itself the result of a series of mergers of Methodistic and Restorationist holiness bodies in Tennessee, Alabama, and the old Southwest and led by such persons as Mary Lee Cagle and C. B. Jernigan, joined the Nazarenes. Meanwhile, the Nazarenes had established a (feeble) presence in the Southeast. The denomination was now a national body of some 10,000.

In 1898 J. O. McClurkan, a Cumberland Presbyterian holiness evangelist, organized the affiliates of his Pentecostal Mission in Nashville, Tennessee, as the Pentecostal Alliance. The alliance merged with the Nazarenes in 1915. That same year, the Pentecostal Church of Scotland also merged with the Nazarenes. This small denomination, with missionaries in South Africa, radiated from Parkhead (Glasgow) Pentecostal Church, a congregation formed in 1906 by dissidents from Parkhead Congregational Church.

Most of the merging groups came in with regularly published periodicals, schools at various levels, missionaries (including medical personnel), and such agencies as homes for unwed mothers and missions for the urban needy.

Other mergers have occurred since 1915, even to the present day, but this originating series gave the denomination its enduring character. They were critical in that they kept the doctrine and experience of entire sanctification as the rubric for unity. Flexibility and compromise (often very difficult) marked discussions concerning forms of government, → liturgies, sacramental theology, modes of baptism and of serving and receiving Communion, → millenarianism, military service, faith → healing, and behavioral norms. On the basis of the doctrine and experience of entire sanctification, the merging groups all entered with ordained women on their ministerial rolls, though the styles of ordination varied from Methodistic (Bresee's early Nazarenes) to congregational (the Holiness Church of Christ). The earliest appear to have been in late 1895 or 1896. About 20 percent of the 1908 roll of elders (ordained ministers) were women.

As the originating series of mergers gathered momentum, some thought that the new denomination would finally unite most of the holiness movement into a single church. It could not. Methodism would retain most of the holiness people. And some who believed that the Nazarenes had compromised too much in the various mergers went their own way.

Still, it has long been, next to the → Salvation Army, the largest of the Wesleyan/Holiness bodies.

The Nazarenes have deliberately undertaken a difficult path in intentionally nourishing both an ecumenical spirit and a strong denominational identity. Pastors are encouraged to participate in local ministeria, and Nazarene laity are encouraged to participate in generally evangelical endeavors. The denomination belongs to the Christian Holiness Partnership and the → National Association of Evangelicals.

4. Present Tendencies

Deliberate indigenizing of leadership by democratic processes has led to explosive membership growth outside the United States — at least 5 percent per year since 1985 — most impressively in Haiti (in 1996, approximately 65,000), Korea (36,000), Mexico (40,000), and Guatemala (27,000). Indigenous clergy and laity are increasingly pro-active in developing programs of → theological education, → social service and political understanding, and evangelism reaching beyond national and ethnic boundaries; and in translating ethical, liturgical, and lifestyle issues (e.g., styles of worship, relationships between the sexes, and modesty in dress and behavior) into local expressions. Serious efforts are underway worldwide to guarantee that choices of highest-level leadership be made without regard to gender, nationality, or ethnicity. Nazarenes have debated whether to hold together as a single-administration denomination worldwide or to proceed as a federation or fellowship of autonomous national or ethnic denominations. The former alternative is generally favored. The doctrine of Christian perfection remains central everywhere, but in some areas (e.g., Latin America, where it tends to be defined as a higher degree of pious legalism) attempts to inculcate a more Wesleyan understanding have created tensions between longer-term membership, clergy and lay, and the educational institutions and their more recent alumni.

Bibliography: CHURCH OF THE NAZARENE, "Historical Statement," *Manual* (Kansas City, Mo., 1992) 15-25 (a fine, short summary) • J. F. PARKER, *Mission to the World: A History of Missions in the Church of the Nazarene through 1985* (Kansas City, Mo., 1988) • W. T. PURKISER, *Called unto Holiness,* vol. 2, *The Second Twenty-Five Years* (Kansas City, Mo., 1983) • T. L. SMITH, *Called unto Holiness,* vol. 1, *The Formative Years* (Kansas City, Mo., 1962) • V. SYNAN, *The Holiness-Pentecostal Tradition: Charismatic Movements in the Twentieth Century* (2d ed.; Grand Rapids, 1997).

PAUL BASSETT

Church Orders

1. Early Church
2. Reformation and After
   2.1. Terminology
   2.2. Commissioning
   2.3. Influence
   2.4. Content
   2.5. Later Influence

1. Early Church

The earliest church order is probably the *Didache* (→ Apostolic Fathers 2.1). The later *Apostolic Church Order* contains the two-ways teaching and rules relating to clergy and widows. The *Didascalia apostolorum* (Teaching of the apostles), from Syria in the early third century, is mostly sermonic and only in part a church order with rulings on married couples; on the tasks of → bishops, → deacons, widows, and deaconesses; and on almsgiving, → baptism, → worship, penance (→ Penitence), and → fasting.

The *Apostolic Tradition* of Hippolytus (d. ca. 236), also from the early third century, gives rules for the election and → ordination of bishops, presbyters, and deacons; for the setting apart of → lectors, subdeacons, widows, and virgins; and for the correct practice of → laying hands on catechumens, baptism, fasting, and reception of the → Eucharist. The *Apostolic Constitutions* comes from Syria in the late fourth century. Books 1-6 consist of the Syrian *Didascalia*, book 7 is a collection of prayers of Jewish origin, and book 8 seems to be the work of Hippolytus on → graces and the church order, followed by discussion of the ordination of bishops and the so-called Clementine Liturgy.

2. Reformation and After

2.1. *Terminology*

With the coming of the Reformation, church orders replaced canon law, missals, rituals, and breviaries in Protestant cities and territories.

2.2. *Commissioning*

The commissioning of church orders was by the secular authorities, who soon began to view themselves as the sole source of human law. In a few instances the bishops (e.g., at Cologne in 1543), parishes (Leisnig in 1523), or local congregations (Hildesheim in 1544) took the lead. The city councils were the authority in the municipalities. → Free Churches (→ Church 3.6) were themselves the source of their church orders, such as in the Dutch refugee and → Huguenot congregations.

2.3. *Influence*

The various church orders often had effects far beyond their immediate jurisdiction. The work of P. → Melanchthon (1497-1560) had an important impact on electoral Saxony, and J. Bugenhagen (1485-1558) used Melanchthon's work for his own church order for Brunswick (1528), which in turn was the basis of the church orders in Hamburg (1529), Lübeck (1531), Pomerania (1535), and in part of those in Denmark (1537) and elsewhere. Chiefly Melanchthon and M. → Bucer (1491-1551) composed materials for the Cologne Reformation of 1543, which then had an influence on the English → Book of Common Prayer of 1549, in the 1552 revision of which Bucer's influence was felt.

J. → Calvin's (1509-64; → Calvin's Theology) *Ordonnances ecclésiastiques* (1541/1561) for Geneva were to some extent a model for the *Discipline ecclésiastique* of the Paris General Synod of 1559, the latter in turn becoming a model for the Articles (1571) of the Emden Reformed Synod Dutch refugee congregations. Also important in the Reformed sphere were the church orders of the Dutch in London (*Microns ordinancien* [1554/1565]) and the *Book of Discipline* (1560), which J. → Knox (ca. 1513-72) drew up for Scotland.

2.4. *Content*

The proper → proclamation of the → Word of God is the goal of Protestant church orders. Influential in this regard were children's sermons (Brandenburg-Nürnberg [1533]), Melanchthon's examining of ordinands (Mecklenburg [1552]), and the brief instruction offered by M. Chemnitz (1522-86) in the order for Brunswick-Wolfenbüttel (1569). The → Heidelberg Catechism is the most important part of the Palatinate order of 1563 (→ Confessions and Creeds). Some orders impose specific confessions, and others contain directions for worship (→ Liturgical Books). Many also contain cycles of prayer.

2.5. *Later Influence*

Various orders, such as those of Saxony (1539 and 1580), were published in later editions in the 17th, 18th, and 19th centuries. The Brunswick-Wolfenbüttel order of 1569 ceased to be valid in Wolfenbüttel in 1709 but retained its validity in most of Hannover (rev. 1615 and 1853) and was introduced into Calenberg-Göttingen in 1585. An enlarged 1660 edition of the *Discipline ecclésiastique*, edited in 1666 and also later at The Hague in 1710, was important for German Huguenot congregations. The Presbyterian system combined with traditional structures in some territorial churches.

On the basis of the → Barmen Declaration of 1934, the Reformation concept of church orders is still reflected in the territorial constitutions subsequent to World War II, such as the Evangelical

Lutheran Churches of Oldenburg (1950), the Rhineland (1952), and Westphalia (1953).

→ Church Government; Early Church; Literature, Biblical and Early Christian

Bibliography: Apostolic Fathers (ed. K. Lake; Cambridge, Mass., 1985) • P. F. BRADSHAW, A. SPRENGLER-RUPPENTHAL, and M. PLATHOW, "Kirchenordnungen," *TRE* 18.662-713 • C. DAIB, "Church Order and the Confession," *CTM* 17 (February 1946) 128-38 • H. FROST, *Strukturprobleme evangelischer Kirchenverfassung* (Göttingen, 1972) 23-24 • G. J. VAN DE POLL, *Martin Bucer's Liturgical Ideas: The Strasburg Reformer and His Connection with the Liturgies of the Sixteenth Century* (Assen, 1954) • E. SEHLING, ed., *Die evangelischen Kirchenordnungen des 16. Jahrhunderts* (Leipzig, 1902-13; Göttingen, 1955-94) • K. SICHELSCHMIDT, *Recht aus christlicher Liebe oder obrigkeitlicher Gesetzesbefehl? Juristische Untersuchungen zu den evangelischen Kirchenordnungen des 16. Jahrhunderts* (Tübingen, 1995).

ANNELIESE SPRENGLER-RUPPENTHAL

Church Registers

1. Church registers include records of local baptisms, → ordinations, official acts of the bishop and presbytery, church regulations, and accounts.

2. The keeping of church registers began in the Middle Ages. The register of Johann Ulrich Surgant (d. 1503) deserves mention, running from 1490 to 1497. With the coming of the → Reformation, a register of weddings was kept at Zwickau from 1522 and of baptisms at Hammelburg from 1527. Burial records in Nürnberg date from 1547. In Zurich a baptismal register was kept from 1526; also in 1526 U. → Zwingli (1484-1531) began keeping a wedding register.

The registers of the Dutch community in London from 1550 are especially important. The presbytery in Reformed Emden asked that a record of those admitted to the Eucharist be kept from 1563; these members constituted the core of the → congregation, which was coming under → church discipline and thus under special care of the presbytery. A decree in 1538 of Henry VIII (1509-47) initiated the keeping of church registers in England (cf. also the similar practice in Scandinavia). In its 24th session (1563), the Council of → Trent asked for the keeping of baptismal and wedding records.

From the standpoint of the → state, church registers often provided figures on which to estimate the population. France, followed by other countries, then began to keep official state records of births, marriages, and deaths. In countries where there are church taxes, official membership lists for tax purposes are based on baptismal registers, since baptism is the primary requisite of church membership. In England and other countries marriage registers are also the official state records, copies being regularly sent to the state archives.

Bibliography: H. BAIER, "Kirchenbücher," *TRE* 18.528-30 • A. VON CAMPENHAUSEN, *Münchener Gutachten* (Tübingen, 1983) 178-94 • E. SEHLING, ed., *Die evangelischen Kirchenordnungen des 16. Jahrhunderts* (Leipzig, 1902-13; Göttingen, 1955-94) • M. SIMON, "Zur Entstehung der Kirchenbücher," *ZBKG* 28 (1959) 129-42.

ANNELIESE SPRENGLER-RUPPENTHAL

Church Schools → Education 4

Church Splits → Heresies and Schisms

Church Struggle

1. Term
2. Background of the Conflict
3. The Protestant Church Struggle
4. The Role of the Roman Catholic Church
5. Connections with the Ecumenical Movement
6. Aftereffects
7. Evaluation

1. Term

The phrase "church struggle" (CS, Ger. *Kirchenkampf*) refers to the conflicts between rival factions within the German Evangelical (or Protestant) Church (GEC), as well as to their opposition to the dictates of the National Socialist state during the years of the Third Reich, 1933-45. It also applies to the → Roman Catholic Church's struggle against the Nazi Party and state, even though this was not as intense as the differences among the Protestants. Recent scholarship has made it clear that, in both cases, the churchmen were more interested in safeguarding the institutions of the church than in rousing the public against the Nazi leaders and their programs.

2. Background of the Conflict

The leaders of both churches enthusiastically welcomed Adolf Hitler's accession to power on January 30, 1933, even though it was well known that he, a baptized Catholic, had rejected whatever Christian principles he may have had. He was accepted initially because he never formally cut his ties with his church, nor was he excommunicated, and he courted support among both confessions by emphasizing nationalism (→ Nation, Nationalism) and claiming to support the church's position in the state. Although National Socialism (→ Fascism) itself was a new faith that appealed to those Germans longing for national regeneration, Hitler refrained from attacks on Christianity, since he recognized that the → masses were still attached to it and that the churches could be utilized in his quest for power. The Nazi party program affirmed its support of "positive Christianity," an undefined phrase into which one could read a variety of meanings. Actually, Hitler's attitude to the churches was political in nature. He envied Catholicism's structure and power over its adherents and had contempt for the GEC because it lacked unity and authority.

For their part, the implacable hostility of many Protestant clergymen to the democratic Weimar Republic, which they regarded as much too secular and lacking in German national feeling, made them vulnerable to the Nazis' political message. They regarded Hitler's overthrow of → democracy as a first step toward replacing the → Marxist republic with Christian rulers. His pro-moral, pro-family stance also was appealing, since he emphasized childbearing and the role of women in the home and promised to eliminate pornography, → prostitution, and → homosexuality.

A strongly pro-Nazi faction in the church, the German Christians (GCs), advocated a completely new interpretation of Christianity free of its "prescientific mentality" and old orthodoxies, a retelling that would be relevant to the needs of the new age. They called for Christian activism, following the example of the heroic Jesus, and replacement of → pietistic preaching with the church's political commitment. They saw Hitler as sent by God to redeem Germany, although in fact he despised them, as he did all the evangelical clergy. For him they were nothing more than opportunists seeking power in the church, but they could be used to disrupt the GEC.

Roman Catholics were just as quickly won over to the new regime. The bishops endorsed it, the Catholic Center Party voted for the Enabling Act in Parliament on March 23, 1933 (the measure allowing Hitler to rule by decree), and the party and Catholic trade unions voluntarily dissolved themselves. In turn, Hitler agreed to a → concordat with the Vatican, signed on July 20, 1933. It guaranteed individual Catholics the freedom to profess and practice their religion and the independence of the church organi-

zation, while at the same time sanctioning the dissolution of confessional political parties and barring the clergy from political involvement. Most churchmen refrained from open conflict with the regime, which they feared would jeopardize the privileges protected by the agreement; the Nazis, however, violated it from the very beginning.

3. The Protestant Church Struggle
On March 23, 1933, Hitler declared that his government viewed both Christian denominations as important factors in the maintenance of the national society, and he pledged to observe the existing church-state agreements and leave their rights untouched. However, extremists in the Nazi party who detested the churches ignored these promises, which Hitler upheld only as long as they suited his political tactics. A movement swept the GEC in spring 1933 calling for the unification of the 28 regional churches into one national church (Reichskirche) headed by a single Reich bishop. This goal seemed in line with Hitler's larger policy of bringing all groups under the total control of the Führer and the state. His choice for the post was Ludwig Müller (1883-1945), a military chaplain and fervent admirer. After months of turmoil, during which the GC faction attempted to occupy as many church offices as possible and promote their Nazified theology, Müller's election took place at the National Synod in Wittenberg on September 27, 1933. The GCs also set out to restructure the church along Nazi lines by introducing the Führer (leadership) principle into church government and adopting the Aryan Paragraph, which provided for the dismissal of all staff members of Jewish racial descent.

By late 1933, however, Hitler concluded that the GCs had served their usefulness and thereafter ignored them. He flatly rejected their idea of a National Socialist state church and felt that the GEC's sole function was to cater to benighted people who still had religious needs. Any church, even one that formally espoused the doctrines of Nazism, threatened to divide people's loyalties and would mean a restriction on his power. Hitler thus listened increasingly to the anti-Christian voices in the Nazi party who called for the elimination of both the GCs and their opponents in the church. With the creation in 1935 of the Ministry of Church Affairs under Hanns Kerrl (1887-1941), Reichsbischof Müller and the GCs lost all influence.

In September 1933 Pastor Martin → Niemöller formed the Pastors Emergency League to combat GC ideas in the church, especially the odious Aryan Paragraph, and thousands rallied to his side. When GC churchmen took over the administration of all the regional churches except the so-called intact churches — Württemberg, Bavaria, and five smaller ones — Niemöller and his allies set up an alternative church government structure called the → Confessing Church (CC, Ger. *Bekennende Kirche*). Its affairs were conducted by a Reich Brotherhood Council, and a national synod was convened at Wuppertal-Barmen on May 29-31, 1934, which spelled out its theological basis in the → Barmen Declaration. This declaration, largely written by Karl → Barth and Hans Asmussen, called the German church back to the central truths of Christianity and rejected the totalitarian claims of the state in religious and political matters.

The declaration was not intended as a political protest, nor did the CC plan to spearhead resistance to Nazism. It was primarily a theological document directed against the heretical teachings of the GCs. Most CC churches professed loyalty to Hitler, and their pastors refused to become involved in politics. The Lutheran tradition of respect for and submission to the ruling power had a strong hold on the GEC pastors (→ Two Kingdoms Doctrine 4), and they were not about to follow a course of political and theological "disloyalty." The CC leaders endorsed the regime's repudiation of the World War I peace treaty and foreign policy decisions. With few exceptions — most notably Dietrich → Bonhoeffer (1906-45) and Marga Meusel (1897-1953) — they were silent about Nazi anti-Jewish actions, including the notorious Nuremberg Laws on Citizenship and Race (1935) and the brutal *Kristallnacht* pogrom in November 1938 (→ Anti-Semitism, Anti-Judaism). Only in 1943 did the CC at long last openly protest actions against Jews.

The CC did not set up a rival free church but rather endeavored to defend the traditional orthodoxy of Christian faith against politically motivated innovations. Although it saw itself as the true GEC, it was deeply divided over how it would exercise this role; in 1936 the more confessional elements formed the Luther Council to protect the interests of → Lutheranism within the CC. Still, the ongoing rivalry between the GEC leadership and the CC resulted in disruption within the church. This attracted considerable foreign attention and greatly embarrassed the Nazi state, and the regime did what it could to suppress the dissidents. In 1935 Barth was expelled to his native Switzerland. Two years later Niemöller was jailed and then placed in a concentration camp as Hitler's "personal prisoner," and the heavy hand of the Gestapo was felt in CC congregations. The CC had to set up alternative seminaries when its ministerial students were denied admission to the theological faculties. But when some CC figures prepared a service of intercession to be used the Sunday before the anticipated German attack on Czechoslovakia in September 1938, the CC bishops meekly repudiated the action after the authorities denounced it.

In a speech in January 1939 Hitler mentioned the need to separate → church and state, but when the → war came, he decided to postpone final action against the GEC. However, what lay ahead could be seen in the Warthegau, a model territory in Poland where the institutional church was virtually wiped out. Churches there were converted into religious societies that could have only adult members. → Religious instruction in the schools, → youth organizations, and social welfare endeavors were forbidden. The churches had to be supported by private contributions, could possess only worship facilities, and were under total state supervision. Such Nazi hardliners as Martin Bormann and Reinhard Heydrich went even further and projected the total elimination of Christianity, an action fully in line with statements Hitler was making privately.

Some German Protestants recognized the implacable hostility of National Socialism to Christianity and became involved in the conspiracy to remove Hitler, which led to the unsuccessful attempt on Hitler's life on July 20, 1944. The Kreisau Circle, a group of high-ranking officers and army personnel led by Count Helmuth von Moltke, met regularly at his estate in Silesia to discuss the implications of tyrannicide, as well as the spiritual and other problems that would confront Germany once Hitler was gone from the scene. The most important Protestant clergyman to be involved in the conspiracy was CC pastor Dietrich Bonhoeffer, though he did so purely in his personal capacity, and as a close relative of other members. He never received encouragement or endorsement from the CC to take part in such activities, which the CC continued to regard as treasonable. In April 1942 Bonhoeffer traveled to Sweden to meet Bishop George Bell of Chichester, England, in order to convince him of the resistance movement's authenticity and sincerity, revealing to Bell the names and plans of the conspirators. Bonhoeffer was subsequently arrested in April 1943 and executed in April 1945 at Hitler's command. The failed assassination attempt led to severe measures, including the execution of several members of the Kreisau Circle.

4. The Role of the Roman Catholic Church

Although the Catholics thought they had made peace with the Nazi state and could join in the struggle for a national Christian order against Bolshevism and →

pluralism, they were drawn into the CS as well. The Nazis methodically destroyed the network of Catholic organizations in Germany and clamped down on the Catholic press and schools. Churchmen expressed alarm about the spread of the new heathenism and restrictions on their work and turned to the Vatican for help. The result was Pius XI's issuance of the encyclical *Mit brennender Sorge* (With burning anxiety), which was smuggled into Germany and read from all Catholic pulpits on Palm Sunday, March 21, 1937. This was the first major Catholic church document to criticize Nazism. It protested against the oppression of the church and called upon Catholics to resist the idolatrous cult of race and state, to stand against the perversion of Christian doctrines and morality, and to maintain their loyalty to Christ and his church. The papal letter criticized the excesses of Nazi doctrines without denouncing the regime's → totalitarianism or anti-Jewish policy, thus keeping the door open for reconciliation.

Hitler was furious, but he decided to avoid a complete break by treating the matter with silence. He knew that he had the support of German Catholic laypeople, and he simply stepped up the pressure on church activities and clergy to undermine the possibility of resistance. Pius XII, who succeeded to the papal throne in 1939, was much more cautious about criticizing actions of the Nazi regime, for he saw it as a bulwark against Communism. He also feared that an open protest, besides being ineffective, would jeopardize the position of Catholics in Germany.

The Nazis did in fact deal severely with Catholic dissent in the lower ranks, although they took no action against high church dignitaries such as Bishop Galen (1878-1946) of Münster, who openly condemned the → euthanasia program in August 1941. A few courageous clergymen stood up against the system and paid for it with their lives, such as Father Bernhard Lichtenberg (1875-1943) of Berlin, who openly prayed for the Jews, and Father Alfred Delp (1907-45), who was involved in the conspiracy against Hitler. Some Catholic laymen were involved in the plot to assassinate the Führer, most notably Count Claus von Stauffenberg, who detonated the bomb on July 20, 1944, but the hierarchy itself never called for resistance against the Nazi regime.

5. Connections with the Ecumenical Movement

The CS was a matter of great interest to the rising → ecumenical movement. The GEC had been involved in numerous ecumenical meetings and organizations, but after Hitler came to power, the church leadership tried as much as possible to keep the CS off the agenda of ecumenical concern. The foreign affairs section of the GEC, led by Bishop Theodor Heckel (1894-1967), claimed it had the exclusive right to represent the church in external matters and attempted to prevent the CC from gaining foreign support. It also tried to undermine British influence in the ecumenical movement, since their churchmen were favorably disposed toward the CC. The American ecumenical figure Charles S. Macfarland (1866-1956) and Swedish archbishop Erling Eidem (1880-1972) met with Hitler personally to try to persuade him to intervene in the CS against the GCs. Such bodies as the World Alliance for Promoting International Friendship through the Churches, Universal Christian Council for Life and Work, and Faith and Order were quite supportive of the CC's endeavor to uphold the purity of the church.

Heckel's agency effectively excluded the CC from participation in international meetings, including the Life and Work conference at Oxford in 1937 and the Utrecht meeting in 1938 that set up the provisional committee to form the → World Council of Churches. When the Ministry of Church Affairs denied passports to both the mainline and the CC groups to go to Oxford so as to avoid the appearance of two GEC delegations, Heckel's views were represented by the pliable Methodist bishop Otto Melle and Baptist leader Paul Schmidt. Still, the conference adopted a strong statement expressing sympathy with both the CC and the Roman Catholic Church in their struggles with the Nazi state. Henceforth, the GEC's relations with the ecumenical movement deteriorated, and it refused to take part in the World Council talks in 1939.

Bonhoeffer's ecumenical efforts were of particular importance. He had been named a secretary in the World Alliance's youth department in 1931, pastored German churches in London in 1933-35, and traveled extensively in Europe and North America. Thus, he knew personally many of the prominent ecumenical figures such as W. A. → Visser 't Hooft in Geneva and Bishop George Bell in England. Because of his deep involvement with the CC, the authorities forbade him to preach and publish, and in 1940 his brother-in-law Hans von Dohnanyi enlisted him for the Abwehr, an organization within the German army that brought together many of the members of the anti-Hitler resistance. He served as a courier to keep ecumenical leaders informed about the resistance, and they in turn sought support in the Allied countries for the endeavor.

6. Aftereffects

The GEC, which had been formed after World War I,

ended with the demise of the Third Reich. The Allied Control Council, adhering to the idea of → religious liberty, allowed its administrative machinery to remain intact but demanded a democratization and denazification of the church. The churches took the initiative to reorganize its leadership structures, and the Catholic Bishops' Conference in Fulda resumed its meetings in August 1945. That same month the Protestants, led by Bishop Theophil Wurm of Württemberg and including members of the CC Brotherhood Councils, met at Treysa and launched the Evangelical Church in Germany (ECG, Evangelische Kirche in Deutschland), a new body that would join together Lutheran, Reformed, and United churches. The conference also formed a Christian → relief organization to channel the assistance churches abroad were sending to Germany. The organization was finalized at a meeting in Eisenach in June 1948. The ECG was to be a confederation of churches that honored the confessional basis of its member bodies and would not interfere with their doctrine, church life, or administration. Article 1 of the constitution states that the ECG confirms the decisions made at the confessing synod of Barmen and pledges itself as Confessing church to further the experiences gained in the CC in respect to the nature, commission, and governance of the church.

The ECG leaders also met with some members of the Provisional Committee of the World Council of Churches in Stuttgart on October 18-19, 1945, to renew old friendships and resume ecumenical activity. At this meeting the ECG leaders issued the famous Stuttgart Declaration of Guilt, which admitted the failures of the German church in responding to the moral challenges of Nazism. It was a religious confession of repentance addressed to other Christians asking for their forgiveness, and it paved the way for German reintegration into the ecumenical movement.

7. Evaluation

The German church struggle raised a number of fundamental questions for the ecumenical world, such as the appropriate theological response to the forces of nationalism and racism, as well as the issues of confession (→ Confession of Faith) in → church law and polity, the Christian life in relation to politics, and, especially after the revelations of the Nazis' atrocities against the Jews, the need for a new relationship between Israel and the church. For its part, National Socialism unwittingly became the reforming force for a church that, without this chastening rod, would not have reformed itself.

→ Dialectical Theology; Modern Church History;

Theology in the Nineteenth and Twentieth Centuries 1-2

Bibliography: S. BARANOWSKI, *The Confessing Church, Conservative Elites, and the Nazi State* (New York, 1986) • V. BARNETT, *For the Soul of the People: Protestant Protest against Hitler* (New York, 1992) • F. BAUMGÄRTEL, *Wider die Kirchenkampf-Legenden* (Neuendettelsau, 1959) • J. BENTLEY, *Martin Niemöller* (New York, 1984) • D. L. BERGEN, *Twisted Cross: The German Christian Movement in the Third Reich* (Chapel Hill, N.C., 1996) • G. BESIER and G. RINGSHAUSEN, *Bekenntnis, Widerstand, Martyrium. Von Barmen 1934 bis Plötzensee 1944* (Göttingen, 1986) • E. BETHGE, *Dietrich Bonhoeffer* (New York, 1970) • A. BOYENS, *Kirchenkampf und Ökumene* (2 vols.; Munich, 1969-73) • A. C. COCHRANE, *The Church's Confession under Hitler* (Philadelphia, 1962) • J. S. CONWAY, *The Nazi Persecution of the Churches, 1933-1945* (New York, 1968) • R. P. ERICKSEN, *Theologians under Hitler* (New Haven, 1985) • F. G. M. FEIGE, *The Varieties of Protestantism in Nazi Germany* (Lewiston, N.Y., 1990) • J. FORSTMAN, *Christian Faith in Dark Times: Theological Conflicts in the Shadow of Hitler* (Louisville, Ky., 1992) • K. GOTTO and K. REPGEN, eds., *Die Katholiken im Dritten Reich* (2d ed.; Mainz, 1983) • M. GRESCHAT, ed., *Die Schuld der Kirche* (Munich, 1982) • E. C. HELMREICH, *The German Churches under Hitler: Background, Struggle, and Epilogue* (Detroit, 1979) • G. LEWY, *The Catholic Church and Nazi Germany* (New York, 1964) • F. H. LITTELL and H. G. LOCKE, eds., *The German Church Struggle and the Holocaust* (Detroit, 1974) • H. G. LOCKE, ed., *The Church Confronts the Nazis: Barmen Then and Now* (Lewiston, N.Y., 1984) • K. MEIER, *Der evangelische Kirchenkampf* (3 vols.; Göttingen, 1976-84) • C. NICOLAISEN, ed., *Documente zur Kirchenpolitik des Dritten Reiches* (2 vols.; Munich, 1971-75) • G. VAN NORDEN, *Der deutsche Protestantismus im Jahr der nationalsozialistischen Machtergreifung* (Gütersloh, 1979) • R. V. PIERARD, "Implications of the German Church Struggle for Christians Today," *CovQ* 39/1 (February 1981); idem, "Why Did German Protestants Welcome Hitler?" *FiHi* 10/2 (Spring 1978) • J. H. SCHJØRRING, *Ökumenische Perspektive des Deutschen Kirchenkampfes* (Leiden, 1985) • T. M. SCHNEIDER, *Reichsbischof Ludwig Müller: Eine Untersuchung zu Leben, Werk und Persönlichkeit* (Göttingen, 1993) • K. SCHOLDER, *The Churches and the Third Reich*, vol. 1, *Preliminary History and the Time of Illusions, 1918-1934;* vol. 2, *The Year of Disillusionment: 1934* (Philadelphia, 1987-88) • L. SIEGELE-WENSCHKEWITZ, *Nationalsozialismus und Kirche: Religionspolitik von Partei und Staat bis 1935* (Düsseldorf, 1974); idem, ed., *Theologische Fakultäten im Nationalsozialismus* (Göttingen, 1993) • F. SPOTTS, *The Churches and Politics in*

Germany (Middletown, Conn., 1973) • C. Vollnhalls, ed., *Entnazifizierung und Selbstreinigung im Urteil der evangelischen Kirche* (Munich, 1989) • G. C. Zahn, *German Catholics and Hitler's Wars* (New York, 1962) • C. Zentner and F. Bedürftig, eds., *The Encyclopedia of the Third Reich* (2 vols.; New York, 1991) • F. Zipfel, *Kirchenkampf in Deutschland, 1933-1945* (Berlin, 1965).

RICHARD V. PIERARD

Church Year

1. Term
2. Types
    2.1. Orthodox
    2.2. Roman Catholic
    2.3. Lutheran
    2.4. Anglican
    2.5. Reformed
3. Liturgical Aspects
4. Development
5. Problems and Opportunities

1. Term

The church year — a term found from the 16th century — focuses "liturgical time" on the annual recurrent cycles of liturgical Sundays and festivals. In the strict sense it pays no attention to ordinary weekdays or to the time divisions of secular society. Some liturgists prefer the term "liturgical year" (see P. L. P. Guéranger; T. J. Talley; J. Pascher); others refer to the "Christian year" (A. A. McArthur, P. G. Cobb). Related phrases from other traditions include "church year" (H. Kellner, J. A. Jungmann, A. Adam, T. Schnitzler), "the Lord's year" (J. Pinsk), "the year of salvation" (P. Parsch), and "the year of the church" (Evangelische Michaelsbruderschaft, K. B. Ritter).

The changing liturgical texts of the church year form the *proprium de tempore* (proper of time; i.e., the seasons and Sundays involved in the celebration of Easter and Christmas) and the *proprium de sanctis* (proper of holy days; i.e., specific dates of the year set apart for commemorations). The relevant days may be found in the various calendars (Roman Catholic, Lutheran Book of Worship, Anglican → Book of Common Prayer). Published calendars with traditional Christian dates combine the church year calendar with Catholic martyrs (→ Saints, Veneration of) or Protestant faithful. As the church year influences the choice of liturgical readings (→ Lectionary), so the readings have an impact on the different → Sundays. For private Bible reading, Protestants since the 19th century (G. C. Dieffenbach) have also provided daily readings covering the whole church year; the Sunday Gospels have materially influenced the choice of the weekly readings.

2. Types
2.1. *Orthodox*

The church year of the → Orthodox Church comprises the four Sundays before Lent (called the Sunday of the Pharisee and Publican, the Sunday of the Prodigal Son, Meat-Fast Sunday, and Milk-Fast Sunday), the five Sundays of Lent (with readings from Mark), and Holy Week, with its Palm Sunday, Maundy Thursday, Good Friday, and Easter Saturday. Then come → Easter Day and Easter Week, followed by the six Sundays of Easter (with readings from John, known as the Sundays of Thomas, the women with the anointing oil, the man with the paralysis, the Samaritan woman, the man born blind, and the fathers of Nicaea). The Feast of the → Ascension is celebrated 40 days after Easter (see Acts 1:3). The seventh Sunday after Easter Day is → Pentecost.

Depending on the date of Easter, there are between 32 and 37 Sundays after Pentecost, with up to 17 of these being "Matthew-Sundays" (with readings from Matthew), ending with the Sundays before and after the Feast of the Elevation of the Cross (September 14). Then come as many as 19 "Luke-Sundays" (readings from Luke), including the Sunday before and, if applicable, the Sunday after the Feast of the Birth of Christ (December 25), as well as the Sunday (if any) before the Feast of the Epiphany (January 6). Finally, there are up to 4 Sundays after Epiphany (readings from Luke and, as appropriate, Matthew) until the beginning once again of the four Sundays before Lent. The formal beginning of the church year is September 1, though there is no special feast on this day.

Other feasts include Circumcision (January 1), Presentation (February 2), Annunciation (March 25), John the Baptist (June 24), Peter and Paul (June 29), Transfiguration (August 6), Dormition of → Mary (August 15), Beheading of John (August 29), Birth of Mary (September 8), Elevation of the Cross (September 14), and Mary's Visit to the Temple (November 21). Other times of fasting are before the feasts on June 29, August 15, and December 25. Since the Julian calendar is used, 13 days must now be added to all dates to convert them to the worldwide Gregorian calendar.

2.2. *Roman Catholic*
As of 1970, the church year of the → Roman Catholic Church begins with the four Sundays of Advent, followed by the Christmas season, which lasts from December 25 to the Sunday after Epiphany. The sea-

son includes Christmas Day, with the preceding vigil; the Feast of the Holy Family (first Sunday after Christmas); the Feast of Mary, Mother of God (January 1); Epiphany; and the Feast of the Baptism of Our Lord (first Sunday after Epiphany, which is counted as the first Sunday of the year).

The season of Lent begins on Ash Wednesday, followed by the five Sundays of Lent and then Passion (Palm) Sunday, the beginning of Holy Week. The *triduum sacrum* includes Maundy Thursday, Good Friday, and Easter Saturday. The Easter season lasts for 50 days, from Easter to Pentecost. Ascension Day is celebrated on the Thursday following the sixth Sunday of Easter.

The general church year has up to 33 ordinary Sundays per year, interrupted by the Lenten and Easter periods. The last Sunday before the first Sunday of Advent is the Feast of Christ the King, which always becomes the 34th Sunday in the annual cycle.

Special days include those commemorating Stephen (December 26), the Holy Innocents (December 28), the Conversion of Paul (January 25), the Presentation of the Lord (February 2), the Annunciation of the Lord (March 25), John the Baptist (June 24), Michael (September 29), and All Saints (November 1). Other celebrations are for Trinity Sunday (first Sunday after Pentecost), Corpus Christi (the Thursday after Trinity Sunday), the → Sacred Heart of Jesus (third Friday after Pentecost), the Chair of Peter (February 22), Joseph (March 19), the Transfiguration (August 6), St. Lawrence (August 10), the Assumption of Mary (August 15), the Birth of Mary (September 8), the Triumph of the Cross (September 14), the Dedication of St. John Lateran (November 9), and the Immaculate Conception of Mary (December 8).

2.3. *Lutheran*

2.3.1. The church year of the → Lutheran churches in Germany (as of 1978) includes four Sundays in Advent, Christmas (two days, with Christmas Eve), New Year's Day (with vigil), and Epiphany. According to the date of Easter, there are up to six Sundays after Epiphany, followed by the prepassion season, with three Sundays known as Septuagesima, Sexagesima, and Quinquagesima (the last, exactly 50 days before Easter, also called Estomihi, from the beginning of the antiphon to the Latin introit, based on Ps. 31:2). The season of the passion includes Ash Wednesday (40 days before Easter), followed by six Sundays, known as Invokavit (Ps. 91:15), Reminiscere (Ps. 25:6), Oculi (Ps. 25:15), Laetare (Isa. 66:10), Judica (Ps. 43:1), and Palm Sunday (see John 12:13). Holy Week includes Maundy Thursday and Good Friday, then the two days of Easter (Easter Eve

and Easter Day), and 6 Sundays after Easter, named Quasimodogeniti (1 Pet. 2:2), Misericordias Domini (Ps. 89:1), Jubilate (Ps. 66:1), Cantate (Ps. 98:1), Rogate (named for rogations, or petitionary processions), and Exaudi (Ps. 27:7). Ascension Day falls on the Thursday after Rogate (i.e., 40 days after Easter). Next is Pentecost (two days) and Trinity Sunday, and then 22-27 Sundays after Trinity.

Special commemorations remember the apostles (as named in Acts 1), evangelists, and Mary (three days), as well as Michael (September 29), John the Baptist (June 24), and the → Reformation (October 31), these last three being observed on the nearest Sunday. The following are observed only when they fall on a Sunday: the celebrations of John (December 27), Peter and Paul (June 29), the Presentation (February 2), Stephen (December 26), the Holy Innocents (December 28), and the → Augsburg Confession (June 25).

Locally, various churches also commemorate Andrew (November 30), Thomas (December 21), Matthias (February 24), Mark (April 25), Philip and James the Less (May 3), James (July 25), Bartholomew (August 24), Matthew (September 21), Luke (October 18), Simon and Jude (October 28), the Annunciation (March 25), the Visitation (July 2), the Circumcision (January 1), All Saints (January 11), and the Conversion of Paul (January 25). (A limited revision of the church calendar is expected in 1996/97.)

2.3.2. In Scandinavia (as of 1974) the order has been revised. The three Sundays before Lent are now named the 7th and 8th after Epiphany and the Sunday before Shrove Tuesday; Trinity Sunday and the Sundays that follow are called the Sundays after Pentecost, followed in Sweden by the Sunday before Judgment Sunday and Judgment Sunday itself, or in Norway by the 27th and then the last Sunday after Pentecost. The only other feasts are those of the Annunciation (March 25), John the Baptist (June 24), Michael (September 29), and All Saints (November 1).

2.3.3. In U.S. Lutheran churches a revision in 1978 included the following changes. The three Sundays before Ash Wednesday became the 7th, 8th, and last after Epiphany (the last always being celebrated as the Transfiguration), the Sundays after Easter were renamed Sundays of Easter (2nd to 7th), and the Sundays starting with Trinity became Sundays after Pentecost, always concluding with Christ the King. The 6th Sunday in Lent is the Sunday of the Passion (Palm Sunday). New feast days are the Name of Jesus (January 1), the Confession of Peter (January 18, the beginning of the week of prayer for unity), the Conversion of Paul (January 25, end of the week of prayer), and Mary the Mother of the Lord (August 15). Lutheran churches in the United States and in Scandinavia have typically been concerned to approximate ecumenical practice in church year celebrations.

2.4. Anglican

2.4.1. In the → Anglican Communion in the United States the calendar in the Book of Common Prayer has followed the Lutheran tradition. Feasts added in 1549 were Barnabas (June 11) and Mary Magdalene (July 22; see John 20:11-18), and in 1662 Transfiguration (August 6), Birth of Mary (September 8), and Holy Cross (September 14). The U.S. revision of 1979 parallels the Lutheran revision of 1978 except that the last Sunday after Pentecost is not celebrated as the Feast of Christ the King. Additional days are dedicated to Joseph (March 19) and James the brother of the Lord (October 23).

2.4.2. In England the Alternative Service Book suggests an alternative to the traditional order on theological and didactic grounds. It devotes nine Sundays before Christmas to the first article of the creed (with OT readings), nine Sundays before Easter and the Sundays until Pentecost to the second article (the redemptive work of the Son), and the Sundays after Pentecost to the third article (the Spirit's work in the church). The stress on Trinity Sunday corresponds to the → Trinitarian concept.

The church year begins at the end of October with the ninth Sunday before Christmas. It continues to the fifth Sunday before Christmas and is followed by the four Advent Sundays, Christmas, Epiphany, and (depending on the time of Easter) 1-6 Sundays after Epiphany. Then come the 7-9 Sundays before Easter, Ash Wednesday, and the 6 Sundays of Lent, including Palm Sunday. The year continues with Easter, the 6 Sundays after Easter (Ascension Day after the fifth one), Pentecost, and Trinity Sunday, and then 18-23 Sundays after Pentecost (also numbered after Trinity Sunday). The Alternative Order omits commemoration of the Confession of Peter (January 18), Mary the Mother of the Lord (August 15), the Holy Cross (September 14), and James the Lord's Brother (October 23).

2.5. Reformed

Since the → Reformed churches wanted to link books of the Bible more closely to → preaching than could be done by the use of "dissected" (U. → Zwingli), fixed lections, the church year found no place at first, the more so as there is no biblical basis for it. According to a Palatinate ordinance of 1563, only Sundays and the great feasts Christmas, Easter, and Pentecost, along with New Year, Ascension Day, and the Sundays of Lent (called Passiontide), were to be observed. Today, however, the Reformed outside Germany have gone beyond this restriction of the church year by leaving more place for propers. Thus the Church of Scotland since 1940 has had Prayers for the Christian Year, the Dutch Reformed Church since 1955 has had *Gebeden in de volgorde van het kerkelijk jaar* (Prayers in the sequence of the church year), and the Swiss Reformed Church since 1974 has had prayers for the whole Christian year.

Among Presbyterians and Reformed in the United States the concept of the church year began to gain a footing as early as the 19th century. In churches that have formed → unions a common lectionary has now developed on the basis of the Roman Catholic *ordo lectionum* of 1969, which reveals the influence of the Anglican tradition and the ecumenical → liturgical movement. In France the liturgical texts of → Taizé have adopted the new Roman sequence (including Corpus Christi and Christ the King). Closest to the traditional church year is the worship of the French-speaking Swiss Church in its observance of the periods from Advent to the Sunday after the Epiphany and from Ash Wednesday to Pentecost (with lections). Such a calendar reflects the Roman structure.

3. Liturgical Aspects

3.1. In worship the use of changing liturgical colors in the → paraments (as well as in hangings for → altar and → pulpit; → Vestments) gives visibility to the changes in church seasons. Roman Catholics use white for the seasons of Easter and Christmas, for feasts of Christ (except for those of the passion, though it is used for Maundy Thursday), Mary, angels, and saints who are not martyrs. Red is for Pentecost and the feasts of apostles and martyrs, as well as for Palm Sunday, Good Friday, and the Feast of the Elevation of the Cross. Green is for ordinary Sundays, and violet is for Advent and Lent.

Some Protestant churches have adopted similar practices, the various colors being noted in the → liturgical books. A specifically Catholic custom is the use of red for Palm Sunday, Good Friday, and the Elevation of the Cross (Lutherans in the United States follow them in this regard), and the use of the color rose for Third Advent (Gaudete) and Fourth Lent (Laetare). Another mark of the season is the omission of Hallelujah after Ash Wednesday and the omission of the solemn Gloria (→ Mass) in Advent and Lent. (Protestants use the Gloria on First Advent as the beginning of the church year.)

The passage through the church year is marked also by special lections, introits, and → prayers of the day, and also among German and American Lutherans by special → hymns stressing the Sunday message in song. The Bible verse for the week that sometimes precedes the → blessing, as a summary of the Sunday gospel, can also extend the observance into the following week, which brings more than just Sundays under the impact of the church year.

3.2. The church year includes periods of preparation for certain Sundays and major festivals. In particular, it specifies a 40-day Lenten fast before Easter (see Exod. 24:18; 1 Kgs. 19:8; Matt. 4:2). During this season Roman Catholics especially focus on → baptism and penance (→ Penitence), and the readings on Sundays consist of the great stories from Matthew and John (the temptation, transfiguration, Samaritan woman, man born blind, and Lazarus). The common Protestant lectionary in the United States follows the same pattern. European Protestants use readings that summon us to ministry and → discipleship on the way of the passion of → Jesus. In keeping is the traditional Protestant celebration of Good Friday with the → Eucharist as a seal of forgiveness. Today → fasting has gained in importance again, even among Protestants, as a restraint from → consumption in favor of the hungry, as has the triduum.

A corresponding four-week-long period of preparation (Advent) precedes → Christmas. This has the strongly eschatological character of joyful expectation. It is a time of hallelujahs, not of mandatory fasting. Various customs accompany it. In Europe Bread for the World has made it a time of social fasting for the → Third World (see Adveniat and Misereor among Roman Catholics; → Relief Organizations). In the Latin sphere quarterly Ember Days come at the beginning of each of the main seasons, with fasts on Wednesdays, Fridays, and Saturdays. Quarterly Communions are comparable, and among German Protestants there is now a → day of prayer and repentance on the Wednesday before the last Sunday of the church year.

4. Development

4.1. A single basic structure is common to the various types of church year, from which one may ascertain its historical development. Underlying the church year are the three fundamental ecclesiastical and cultural elements for the structuring of time that are of importance beyond the Christian sphere: the date of Easter, which rests on the Jewish → Passover; the seven-day week, taken from the OT; and A.D., or fixing the calendar according to the birth of Christ, which developed in the Latin church. Since, by generally agreed reckoning, Easter always falls on a Sunday, the periods before and after are shaped accordingly

(i.e., the 40 days of Lent and the 49 days to Pentecost). Easter is movable (appearing within a 35-day time frame), but the church year as a whole has a solid anchor in December 25 as the date of the nativity and in January 1 and 6 (occurring on varied days of the week), which govern Advent and the Epiphany. To allow for the variation in the date of Easter, the Epiphany season and the Sundays after Pentecost or Trinity also vary. The unbroken weekly rhythm, however, ensures continuity. Because of the changes mentioned, however, the church year is never exactly the same from one year to the next.

4.2. Easter was celebrated from the second century. The Easter vigil was added in the fourth or fifth century; later, the ideas of triduum and the Holy Week arose, beginning with Palm Sunday, as the recollection of Christ's passion. The Easter season then extended 50 days with celebration of the post-Easter events: the ascension, 40 days after Easter (Acts 1:3); and Pentecost, 50 days after (Acts 2:1). In the fourth century, with the catechumenate preceding baptism on Easter Eve, a 40-day period of preparation developed (→ Catechesis). The adding of a pre-Lenten season (three Sundays before Ash Wednesday) perhaps took place under Eastern influence.

The Christmas season also developed in the fourth century. Epiphany (January 6) arose in the East and later was adopted in the West, with Nativity (December 25) arising in the West and being celebrated as well in the East from the sixth century. The Sundays after the Epiphany, with readings on Christ's mighty works, came to be called the Sundays after the Epiphany from the seventh century. The nativity itself had a vigil from the sixth century, and the season was extended to January 1, the day of Christ's circumcision (rather than merely New Year's Day). With further development in the fourth to the sixth centuries, the Christmas season came to include commemorations of the first martyr, Stephen, on December 26 (cf. Acts 22:20), the apostle and evangelist John on December 27, and the Holy Innocents on December 28. Commemoration of the baptism of Jesus (originally one of the readings for Epiphany) was made the concluding festival of Christmastide by Roman Catholics in 1969, the celebration being on the Sunday after the Epiphany. When Protestants in Europe and the United States made the same decision, this change achieved ecumenical status.

The Presentation and Annunciation, which are of Eastern derivation, are also regarded as part of the Christmas season today, although originally they were feasts of Mary. The day of the former (February 2), 40 days after the birth of Jesus, is based on Luke 2:22 (cf. Lev. 12:1-4). The date of the latter (March

25), nine months before the birth, is also linked to the first day of spring, which is regarded as the first day of → creation. Other feast days include that of the birth of John the Baptist, traditionally June 24, six months before the birth of Jesus (Luke 1:36), and just after midsummer.

The Feast of the Transfiguration (August 6) is perhaps connected with an interest in the stations of the cross that arose in the 10th century and was promoted by the → Crusades; it became a feast only in 1457. Holy Cross Day (September 14) is supposedly connected to the legendary discovery of the cross by Empress Helena, but it also commemorates the redemption granted by Christ's crucifixion (see 1 Cor. 1:17). The commemoration of Michael (September 29) originally related to the dedication of the church of St. Michael in Rome (5th cent.), but this and other churches with the same dedication recall the archangel of Jude 9, the protector of Israel and patron saint of the Germans (Dan. 10:13; Rev. 12:7; see also Rev. 5:11; Ps. 91:11). All Saints, which is the Sunday after Pentecost in the East and November 1 in the West, has been celebrated since the 19th century as an expression of the communion of saints.

At the Reformation the Lutherans and Anglicans retained the basic structure and feasts of the church year but gave up holidays that had no biblical basis. There thus arose a Christological calendar based on the days and feasts of the Lord and offering the opportunity to spread the teaching of the → gospel throughout the whole year. In preindustrial society, in territories that had become Protestant, some saints days achieved social significance, becoming viewed as auspicious times for sowing and harvesting, or for interest payments and municipal elections. Clearly the civil year was originally much the same as the church year, and the link has not been totally severed (note the use of B.C. and A.D. periods, the seven-day week, and the time of Easter).

5. Problems and Opportunities

For all its rich history and minutiae, the church year is secondary and not an end in itself. If it becomes a closed system and receives a kind of independent rank, it fails in two respects to fulfill its allotted function. First, it imprisons and falsifies the biblical witness, which preaching must expound and which does not tie us to a wheel of eternal recurrence but seeks to liberate us and lead us to a goal. In this regard the Reformed reservations regarding the church year were well founded and are worth noting (see Gal. 4:9-11; Col. 2:16-17, 20).

Second, the church year as a medium of the church's self-fulfillment also fails if it loses sight of human reality, and if people thus fail to participate. Modern changes in the reckoning of time (e.g., the five-day working week and two-day weekends, or longer and more varied vacation schedules) and in regular attendance at worship (esp. Europe has seen reduced church attendance and the pressure to conform to a secularized society) also call for notice. In part, Christian festivals have become legal holidays, but in some countries they have also been truncated. The church year, which puts the contents of Christian proclamation in a specific time structure, does not wholly meet the needs of present-day churchgoers.

Such pressure led as early as the time of the Enlightenment to an attempt to make the church year more relevant by replacing the biblical stories with various topics. Today, for example, we thus have politically influenced thematic worship (e.g., focusing on racial harmony). Occasional observances have also been interjected that meet the needs of → civil religion (e.g., Thanksgiving, Mother's Day, and various national holidays). Special services mark the cycle of life: confirmations and weddings, as well as memorial services. These "diaconal" services aim to meet personal and social needs. They may indeed be successful, but at the same time they are threatened with the loss of biblical substance or aim. They may well become overly emotional or engage in indoctrination. The church year can be a wholesome corrective in this regard.

The tension between the church year and the civil year, and the disruption caused by a movable Easter, is healthy, for it reminds us that reality and humanity amount to much more than our everyday circumstances. On the whole, despite their trivialization and commercialization, the great festivals constantly provoke celebration and reflection beyond the confines of the church (see P. Cornehl for a development of these ideas). The presence of an alternative schedule within our media-directed lives, the influence of childhood family experiences at the great feasts, the political dimension of Christian proclamation at these seasons (e.g., Christmas provokes thinking on → peace and → love; Holy Week, on → force and → suffering; Easter, on → hope and → life; Thanksgiving, on thanksgiving and → responsibility for creation; end of the church year, on conversion and sorrow), and, not least of all, the model of OT and Jewish festivals as family gatherings and as resistance to Baal worship are all significant. Specific points of focus such as the church year provides give constant opportunity to interact with the biblical testimony.

→ Popular Religion

Bibliography: General: A. ADAM, *Das Kirchenjahr mit-feiern* (Freiburg, 1979) • ASTRONOMISCHES RECHEN-INSTITUT IN HEIDELBERG, *Astronomische Grundlage für den Kalender (mit kirchlichem Fest- und Namenkalender)* (Karlsruhe, appears annually) • K. H. BIERITZ, *Das Kirchenjahr. Feste, Gedenk- und Feiertage in Geschichte und Gegenwart* (Berlin, 1986) • P. L. P. GUÉRANGER, *L'année liturgique* (Paris, 1841) • J. A. JUNGMANN, *Der Gottesdienst der Kirche* (Innsbruck, 1965) 199-265 • H. KELLNER, *Heortologie oder geschichtliche Entwicklung des Kirchenjahres* (3d ed.; Freiburg, 1911) • A. A. McARTHUR, *The Evolution of the Christian Year* (London, 1953) • H. AUF DER MAUR, "Feiern im Rhythmus der Zeit I," *Handbuch der Liturgiewissenschaft* (pt. 5; Regensburg, 1983) • L. H. STOOKEY, *Calendar: Christ's Time for the Church* (Nashville, 1996) • T. J. TALLEY, *The Origins of the Liturgical Year* (New York, 1986).

Specific forms: H. A. DANIEL, *Codex liturgicus ecclesiae universae* (vol. 4; Leipzig, 1853; repr., Hildesheim, 1966) 212-78 • *Der evangelische Namenkalender* (Hannover, 1984) • E. HOFHANSL and H. NAGLATZKI, eds., *Evangelisches Stundengebet. Beten im Rhythmus von Jahr und Tag* (Hannover, 1995) • J. PASCHER, *Das liturgische Jahr* (Munich, 1963) • P. H. PFATTEICHER and C. R. MESSERLI, eds., *Manual on the Liturgy: Lutheran Book of Worship* (Minneapolis, 1979) 21-77 • RUSSISCHE ORTHODOXE KIRCHE ZU DRESDEN, *Orthodoxer Kirchenkalender* (appears annually) • H. J. SCHULZ, "Liturgie, Tagzeiten und Kirchenjahr des byzantinischen Ritus," *HOK* 332-85.

History: P. G. COBB, "The History of the Christian Year," *The Study of Liturgy* (ed. C. Jones, G. Wainwright, and E. Yarnold; London, 1978) 403-31 • F. SCHULZ, "Heiligenverehrung VII," *TRE* 14.664-72; idem, "Die Ordnung der liturgischen Zeit in den Kirchen der Reformation," *LJ* 32 (1982) 1-24 • W. VOS and G. WAINWRIGHT, eds., *Liturgical Time: Papers Read at the 1981 Congress of Societas Liturgica* (Rotterdam, 1982).

Problems: P. CORNEHL, "Der Sinn der Feste und Feiertage," *WPKG* 74 (1985) 410-25 • J. GUNSTONE, "Contemporary Problems of Liturgical Time: Calendar and Lectionary," *Liturgical Time: Papers Read at the 1981 Congress of Societas Liturgica* (ed. W. Vos and G. Wainwright; Rotterdam, 1982) 74-89 • H. MAIER, "Revolutionäre Feste und christliche Zeitrechnung," *IKaZ* 17 (1988) 348-66.

Pastoral issues: J. BAUMGARTNER, *Das Kirchenjahr* (Fribourg, 1978) • G. C. DIEFFENBACH, *Evangelische Haus-Agende . . . für alle Tage des Kirchenjahres* (Mainz, 1853) • W. DÜRIG, *Das christliche Fest und seine Feier* (2d ed.; St. Ottilien, 1978) • G. KUNZE, *Das Kirchenjahr als Lebensordnung* (2d ed.; Hamburg, 1960) • P. PARSCH, *Das Jahr des Heiles* (14th ed.; Klosterneuburg, 1952/53)

• J. PINSK, *Gedanken zum Herrenjahr* (Mainz, 1963) • T. SCHNITZLER, *Kirchenjahr und Brauchtum neu entdeckt* (Freiburg, 1977).

FRIEDER SCHULZ

Churches of Christ

As an offshoot from America's Disciples of Christ movement (→ Christian Church [Disciples of Christ]), the Churches of Christ had by the beginning of the 20th century separated into an uncompromisingly distinctive "brotherhood." Taking a firm stand against the quiet, almost inevitable move from → sect to → denomination, these churches — without hierarchy or headquarters or national program — resisted modernity and ecumenicity in their ecclesiastical life. Most conspicuous was their rejection of instrumental music, of → Sunday schools, and of permanent resident pastors. Like the Disciples generally, this movement was also a product of the rural American frontier, yet with the difference that the frontier here was not midwestern but southern: Texas, Arkansas, and Tennessee dominated the early years. In later years, the Churches of Christ made deliberate efforts to break out of their regionalism, being most successful in this regard in the Far West state of California.

Like the Disciples once more, these southern church members emphasized the → authority of the NT and the urgent necessity of restoring the true churches of apostolic times. Biblical authority was proclaimed vigorously and held to tenaciously. NT precedents were appealed to repeatedly and accepted regularly, with little discussion or debate. Yet, this conservative wing of the large Restorationist movement displayed much vitality, much movement, and much promise. About two million strong (only estimates are possible; no central bureau gathers or reports membership data), the Churches of Christ have yet to settle into a distinctive mode of worship and life.

Bibliography: E. S. GAUSTAD, "Churches of Christ in America," *Religious Situation: 1969* (Boston, 1969) • S. S. HILL JR., "The Churches of Christ and Religion in the South," *Mission Magazine* 14/2 (August 1980) • R. T. HUGHES, *Reviving the Ancient Faith* (Grand Rapids, 1996).

EDWIN S. GAUSTAD

Churches of God

The label "Church of God" is among the more confusing contributions of the United States to → denominational terminology. Several quite distinct organizations claim the name, some of these finding it necessary to resort to parenthetical additions to make clear just which Church of God they are. Most of these groups do share a common background of Pentecostal interest evident in 19th- and 20th-century America. Pentecostalism traditionally emphasizes the "second blessing" of → sanctification, which is to follow sometime after the "first blessing" of justification (see Rom. 5:9). The most dramatic if not obligatory evidence of one's having received that second blessing is the gift of tongues, or → glossolalia. Pentecostal services, which tend to be spontaneous and charismatic, also often place great emphasis upon the → healing of various physical infirmities by spiritual means alone (→ Charismatic Movement).

Three specific groups within this broad stream deserve separate mention. The first in order of time is the Church of God that has its headquarters in Anderson, Indiana. Founded by Daniel S. Warner in 1881, the denomination saw itself initially as a transcender of all the divided churches, as a fellowship open to all, regardless of past affiliation or longstanding tradition. But history has a way of imposing its own logic on those → sects whose aim is to move beyond sectarianism itself. Soon Warner's movement became a church with a publishing house, → mission board, college, and seminary. By 1994 its membership had reached 215,000.

In 1886 a movement associated with the names of R. C. Spurling and A. J. Tomlinson came to rest upon an administrative foundation located in Cleveland, Tennessee. While this group did not formally adopt the name "Church of God" until 1907, it from the beginning manifested those Pentecostal emphases noted above, along with the washing of the saint's feet (→ Foot Washing) as a biblical rite just as clearly commanded as → baptism and the → Eucharist. Still a church largely of the southeastern section of the United States, this denomination by 1994 had approached a membership of 670,000. Both these Churches of God have spread to other countries. In Germany, for example, a few thousand members are in fellowship with each U.S. church.

Finally, an African American → Baptist leader, C. H. Mason, drew about him a following to which in 1897 he gave the name "Church of God in Christ." Early in the 20th century, Mason's group derived much impetus from Pentecostal revivals then occurring in southern California, the result being a steady upward curve of growth for this predominantly African American charismatic church. Following Mason's death in 1961, serious organizational and legal disputes troubled the Church of God in Christ. Within a decade, however, the church resumed its growth as well as its mission throughout the United States and even abroad (chiefly in Belize, Haiti, and Liberia). By 1994, rough estimates placed its membership at 5.5 million.

Bibliography: K. HUTTEN, *Seher–Grübler–Enthusiasten* (12th ed.; Stuttgart, 1982) 277ff., 303ff. • J. O. PATTERSON et al., *History and Formative Years of the Church of God in Christ* (Memphis, Tenn., 1969) • A. C. PIEPKORN, *Profiles in Belief,* vol. 3, *Holiness and Pentecostal* (New York, 1979) • V. SYNAN, *The Holiness-Pentecostal Movement* (Grand Rapids, 1971).

EDWIN S. GAUSTAD

Circumcision

The practice of circumcision, or the cutting off of the foreskin, was not confined to Israel and → Judaism but was common among other peoples (e.g., in Egypt; see Jer. 9:25-26). It probably arose in prehistoric times as an apotropaic act and was originally performed shortly before puberty (see Gen. 17:25). The OT refers also to the circumcision of adults (Josh. 5:2-9; Gen. 34:13-26). Only in P is circumcision made mandatory on the eighth day after birth. It thus acquires wide-ranging theological significance as a sign of the → covenant (Gen. 17:10-14).

In early Judaism circumcision was one of the most important commands. It had a national character as a theological foundation (*Jub.* 15:25-27), and it distinguished → Israel from other peoples (1 Macc. 1:15, 48; 2:46). With the intensifying of the Maccabean movement, John Hyrcanus (ruler and high priest 135-104 B.C.) and Aristobulus I (104-103 B.C.) made it a means of Judaizing, and they forced the Idumaeans (Josephus *Ant.* 13.257) and Ituraeans (13.318) to accept it. Having come to be viewed in this way as a special mark of the Jewish people, it was increasingly condemned by other peoples and became a topic of anti-Jewish polemic. Philo (d. A.D. 45-50) was the first to give hygienic as well as theological reasons for it (*De spec. leg.* 1.1-12). The attacks of Roman satirists on circumcision (Horace *Sat.* 1.9.69-70; Juvenal *Sat.* 14.104) show that it had made its way into pagan circles as well.

In early Christianity circumcision was set aside after a long discussion. → Paul reinterpreted it most thoroughly, replacing it with → baptism (Phil. 3:3; Col. 2:11-12), although → Jewish Christians obviously wanted to retain it (Gal. 6:12-16; Acts 15:1). In the Epistle of Barnabas (9:4) the Jewish practice is the object of violent Christian attacks.

Rabbinic Judaism deepened the theological understanding of circumcision as a covenant sign (*b. Šabb.* 137b) and as the Abrahamic covenant ('*Abot* 3:11). It stressed the saving efficacy of the blood (*Tg. Ps.-J.* Exod. 4:26), which was equated with the blood of the covenant (*t. Ned.* 2:6). The ongoing debate with the pagan and Christian world involved polemical discussion about the question why circumcision was not commanded of → Adam ('*Abot R. Nat.* 2.5.2C [Neusner ed.]) and why it was not contained in the → Decalogue (*Pesiq. R.* 117a).

In the Middle Ages and the modern period, Judaism maintained the theological understanding of circumcision as a covenant sign, which had an integrating function, especially in times of persecution (Maimonides *More* 3.49; Albo *Ikk.* 4.45; Spinoza *Tract. theol.-pol.* 3.54). Hygienic reasons were also advanced for it, as well as other rational arguments, such as the lowering of sexual desire. Radical efforts in the early reform movement (Frankfurt Reform Society, 1843) to declare circumcision outdated proved unsuccessful, but for the most part Reform Judaism does not insist on it when adults are converted to Judaism. The State of Israel finds both a national and a theological rationale for circumcision, so that even secularized Jews retain it.

→ Sexism 2.2

Bibliography: O. A. Koso-Thomas and J. R. Botkin, "Circumcision," *EncBio* 1.382-90 • L. V. Snowman, "Circumcision," *EncJud* 5.570-75 • H. Trimborn, ed., *Lehrbuch der Völkerkunde* (4th ed.; Stuttgart, 1971) on circumcision among primitive peoples • A. J. Wensinck, "Khitān," *HIsl* 314-17 (on circumcision in Islam) • T. E. Wiswell, "Circumcision—an Update," *Current Problems in Pediatrics* 22/10 (1992) 424-31.

Peter Schäfer

Cistercians

1. Rise

The history of the Cistercian order begins in 1098 with the founding of a tiny monastic community at Cîteaux (Lat. Cistercium) in Burgundy by Robert of Molesme (ca. 1027-1111). The second abbot of Cîteaux, Stephen Harding (ca. 1060-1134), published *Charta caritatis* (Charter of love) in 1118, the basic order of the Cistercians, which makes Cîteaux the normal cloister of the Cistercians. The abbots of the first foundations (La Ferté, Pontigny, Clairvaux, and Morimond) were all primary abbots with a special place in the order. The most important of these was → Bernard of Clairvaux (1090-1153), who from 1115 onward figured decisively in the spread of the order.

2. Development

During Bernard's lifetime some 344 Cistercian monasteries were founded, and by 1342 the number stood at 707. The Cistercians played an important role in the eastward expansion of Germany, with the Altenberg line giving rise to Lekno, Lad, and Obra in Great Poland, which for centuries maintained close relations with Cologne. Morimond, too, set up monasteries in Suleyov, Wachock, and Koprzyvnica in Little Poland. In 1171 Amelungsborn founded the Cistercian community Doberan in Mecklenburg. More or (usually) less strictly, some convents of women were also affiliated with the order (e.g., artistically impressive Wienhausen), though almost all Cistercian nunneries were not really incorporated.

The → Reformation brought the development to an end. M. → Luther (1483-1546; → Luther's Theology) married Catherine von Bora (1499-1552), of the women's branch of the order. More than half the Cistercian monasteries in Germany were abandoned; only very few many of them continued under Protestant auspices, especially Loccum. Henry VIII (1509-47) put an end to all the Cistercian monasteries in England, of which magnificent Gothic ruins remain, for example, in Fountains in Yorkshire, Rievaulx in Yorkshire, where the great preacher and prolific writer Aelred of Rievaulx (ca. 1110-67) had worked, Roche Abbey, also in Yorkshire, Tintern in Monmouthshire, Newminster in Northumberland, and Netley in Hampshire.

The strict Trappists gave the order a new impulse in the late 17th century (→ Monasteries 5.3.2; Observance), though this reformed branch, deriving from the Cistercian monastery La Trappe, in France, became an order of its own in 1892. German → secularization (1803) led to the destruction of all the Cistercian monasteries in Germany except the two convents Marienthal and Marienstern in Saxony.

3. The Rule

From the very outset, the Cistercians aimed to follow the rule of → Benedict closely (*puritas regulae;* → Benedictines 3; Orders and Congregations 2.1). They were thus reformed Benedictines, standing opposed to the richly developed monastic culture of Cluny, and sought a return to the stringent beginnings of Western monasticism (→ Middle Ages 1.3.1). Choral music was greatly simplified in comparison with that of Cluny.

4. Constitution

The Cistercians had a paternalistic, central constitution. The mother monasteries were responsible for their daughter houses by a → filiation system. Organization was tight. The father abbot visited each of his monasteries every year. And every year all the abbots gathered at Cîteaux. The order constantly tried to preserve the freedom of its monasteries from estate administration in order to keep themselves free of patronage control.

5. Liturgy

From the first, the order sought a correct form of → liturgy. It had its own rite up to 1618. The first houses tried to get the best textual version of hymns, consciously coming to follow the authentic Gregorian choral tradition, and laid value on unified choral singing within the order as a whole. The oldest known complete breviary is the Cistercian Breviary of Stephen of 1132.

6. Spirituality

The Cistercians sought to follow Jesus Christ in his poverty (→ Discipleship; Spirituality). By way of Bernard, mystical devotion to Christ was native to the order. It focused on the human figure of the one who was crucified (→ Mysticism 2.4.1). The patron of the order was → Mary, who was honored with much devotion. Even today, the Salve Regina is sung daily. Meditative reading and daily celebration of the Eucharist are still common today. Opus Dei, simple inward prayer at all times of the day, Lectio Divina, the reading especially of Scripture, and Labor manuum, or manual labor, permeated their inward life and harmoniously united solitude and fellowship (→ Benedictines 3 and 7).

7. Arts

Numerous Cistercian edifices have been preserved (e.g., Pontigny, Maulbronn, Altenberg, Haina, Wal-kenried, Amelungsborn, Loccum, and Riddagshausen in Germany). The characteristic feature of Cistercian churches, apart from the squared choir ending and the plain ridge turret, was the interior batter. The Cistercians became pioneers of Gothic vaulting techniques (→ Church Architecture 3). They all have the same basic form modeled on Clairvaux (→ Monastery 3.1). The refectory and dormitory had to be doubled. The west wing was for the conversi (lay brothers; → Clergy and Laity). Among book illustrations, the Leiden Wigalois MS from Amelungsborn is especially noteworthy.

8. Economy

The Cistercians built their monasteries in the "wilderness" and thus became pioneers in developing the land, especially in draining swamps. The work was done by conversi, who took the vows but did not keep the hours. Although the division of *ora et labora* was initially of great value, it contradicts the original intention of the Benedictine rule. The *grangia* (great farms) became an agricultural model. Cities would buy up the surplus. Hard work and moderate consumption brought great wealth (→ Middle Ages 2.3.1; Monastery 4).

9. Habit

The order's habit is the cowl, a folding garment originally gray (the natural wool color), though later it became white. This is why they are called Gray or White Monks. Except in the choir, the monks wear a black scapular, a shoulder garment with hood. Through the widespread conviction that entering the order constituted a second baptism, the habit acquired religious significance.

10. Cistercians Today

In Germany in 1888 the abbey Marienstatt, founded in 1212, was reinhabited, as was the abbey Himmerod in 1922. The only Trappist monastery in Germany is Mariawald, and the one Trappist convent for women is Maria Frieden (since 1952). There are 9 men's and 13 women's monasteries belonging to the Mehrerau Congregation (Union) in Austria.

Vigorous Trappist monasteries exist also in the United States, and these were strongly influenced by Thomas Merton (1915-68) of Our Lady of Gethsemani (Trappist, Ky.). Also important are Our Lady of New Melleray (Peosta, Iowa), Our Lady of Guadalupe (Lafayette, Oreg.), and the Holy Spirit Monastery (Conyers, Ga.). The North American monasteries aim at economic independence. An institute for Cistercian studies, which also runs the press Cistercian Publications, is located at Western Michigan University.

Bibliography: Primary sources: J. B. VAN DAMME, *Documenta pro Cisterciensis Ordinis historiae ac juris studio* (Westmalle, 1959) • F. VAN DER MEER, *Atlas de l'ordre cistercien* (Brussels, 1965) • *Sancti Bernardi opera* (ed. J. Leclercq, H. M. Rochais, et al.; 8 vols., Rome, 1957-77) • *Statuta Capitulorum Ordinis Cisterciensis, 1116-1786* (ed. J. M. Canivez; 8 vols.; Louvain, 1933-41). Cistercian Publications (Kalamazoo, Mich.) has published many primary works, including those of Aelred of Rievaulx, Baldwin of Ford, Beatrice of Nazareth, Bernard of Clairvaux, Gilbert of Hoyland, Isaac of Stella, John of Ford, and Nicolas Cotheret.

Secondary works: M. CASEY, *Athirst for God: Spiritual Desire in Bernard of Clairvaux's Sermons on the Song of Songs* (Kalamazoo, Mich., 1988) • *CistSQ* • K. ELM et al., *Die Zisterzienser. Ordensleben zwischen Ideal und Wirklichkeit* (2 vols.; Bonn, 1980-82) • P. FERGUSSON, *Architecture of Solitude: Cistercian Abbeys in Twelfth-Century England* (Princeton, 1984) • J. FRANCE, *The Cistercians in Scandinavia* (Kalamazoo, Mich., 1992) • É. GILSON, *The Mystical Theology of St. Bernard* (New York, 1940) • N. C. HEUTGER, *850 Jahre Kloster Walkenried* (Hildesheim, 1977); idem, *Das Kloster Amelungsborn im Spiegel der zisterziensischen Ordensgeschichte* (Hildesheim, 1968); idem, *Loccum. Eine Geschichte des Klosters* (Hildesheim, 1971); idem, *Zisterziensisches Wirken in Niedersachsen* (Hildesheim, 1993) • J. LECLERQ, *Bernard of Clairvaux and the Cistercian Spirit* (Kalamazoo, Mich., 1976); idem, *Women and St. Bernard of Clairvaux* (Kalamazoo, Mich., 1989) • L. J. LEKAI, *The Cistercians: Ideals and Reality* (2d ed.; Kent, Ohio, 1989); idem, *The White Monks: A History of the Cistercian Order* (Okauchee, Wis., 1953) • M. P. LILLICH, ed., *Studies in Cistercian Art and Architecture* (3 vols.; Kalamazoo, Mich., 1982-87) • T. MERTON, *The Seven Story Mountain* (New York, 1948) • L. PRESSOUYRE and T. N. KINDER, *Saint Bernard et le monde cistercien* (Paris, 1992) • H. J. ROTH and A. GROSSMANN, *Bernhard von Clairvaux an die Tempelritter* (Sinzig, 1990) • A. SCHNEIDER et al., *Die Cistercienser* (3d ed.; Cologne, 1986) • G. SCHWAIGER, ed., *Mönchtum, Orden, Klöster* (Munich, 1993) esp. 432-35 and 451-70 (bibliography) • J. R. SOMMERFELDT, *The Spiritual Teachings of Bernard of Clairvaux: An Intellectual History of the Early Cistercian Order* (Kalamazoo, Mich., 1991); idem, ed., *Erudition at God's Service* (Kalamazoo, Mich., 1987) • E. VACANDARD, *Leben des heiligen Bernhard von Clairvaux* (2 vols.; Mainz, 1897-98) • C. WADDELL, ed., Cistercian liturgy series (Kalamazoo, Mich., 1984-).

NICOLAUS C. HEUTGER

Citizen → Bourgeois, Bourgeoisie

Citizens' Initiatives → Social Movements

City

1. Biblical Aspects
    1.1. General
    1.2. Negative
    1.3. Positive
2. Sociological Aspects
    2.1. Definition
    2.2. Reasons for Development
    2.3. Phases in Development
    2.4. Further Development
3. Theological Aspects
    3.1. Church Reactions
    3.2. Problems
    3.3. Tasks

1. Biblical Aspects

1.1. *General*

Biblical history includes a rich theology of the city, which we might see as a parable of all human history and destiny in its vertical relation to God. From the first narratives in Genesis (4ff.) to their counterpart in Revelation (17ff.), the city is a central locus of the development of sinful humanity and of the drama of God's action both in a response of judgment and in an initiative of → grace and → salvation.

1.2. *Negative*

Only when the age of innocence in the garden (Genesis 2) ended with disobedience and expulsion (chap. 3) did the history of the city begin. Significantly, Cain founded the first city (4:17). → Culture and → technology seem to have arisen in the city, but negatively, it quickly became also the place of corruption, idolatry, violence, and arrogance in centers like Nineveh (10:11), Babel (11:1-9), and Sodom and Gomorrah (18:16-33). The call of → Abram was away from the city of Ur (11:31-32). Even in → Israel, predominantly a rural people, the cities became centers of intensified human → sin. → Solomon's storage cities involved forced labor; cities, including Jerusalem itself (1 Kgs. 11:7), had their idolatrous cults; and even the → temple at → Jerusalem could become the home of false practices (Ezekiel 8), which, along with the disobedience of rulers and people, brought the capital city under castigation and final judgment.

The great city-empires of the later period — Nineveh, Babylon, and Rome — display to the full the wealth, splendor, power, and beauty of the city, with the right development of human life that it makes possible, but they also reflect the pride, greed, violence, corruption, and religious aberration that beset the human race, with the attendant evils of oppression, cruelty, → poverty, and degradation (see Dan. 4:30; Isa. 13:19; Revelation 18).

In this context the city in particular comes under God's judgment (→ Wrath of God). Fire and brimstone rain down on the cities of the plain. Confusion of tongues afflicts Babel. Nineveh, although at first repentant (Jonah), falls victim finally to disaster (Nahum). The Babylonians sack Jerusalem. Babylon itself loses its empire and falls ultimately into decay. The Babylon of Revelation, for all its institutional, economic, and military strength, faces imminent destruction.

1.3. Positive

It is only one side of the story, however, that the city as the center of more intensive life serves as the symbol of the human revolt against God and the response of God in righteous power. For the city did not take God by surprise. He did not merely react to it or give up on urban humanity. In an initiative of grace he also began to work out a purpose of salvation in and through the city. An intimation might be seen in the enigmatic figure of the ruler of Salem in Gen. 14:18. The choice of Jerusalem as the place where God sets his name for his presence and → worship denotes acceptance and sanctification of the city (e.g., Psalm 48). Cities of refuge in the promised land carry a promise of salvation (Num. 35:9-15). The exiles can even be told to seek the welfare of the pagan city and pray for it (Jer. 29:7). Jerusalem is destroyed, but not without the promise of a rebuilding that God will see to be means of pagan rulers, prophets, and civil and religious leaders (Ezra and Nehemiah) recognizing and glorifying him.

In the NT too, the city has both positive and negative roles. → Jesus preaches in the cities (Luke 8:1), as well as pronouncing woes on those that reject him (Matt. 11:20-21). Foreseeing the fall of Jerusalem, he weeps over it (Luke 13:34-35). Jerusalem resists and slays the prophets, and thus the decisive event of the crucifixion and → resurrection will take place there (v. 33). The apostolic mission begins in the city (Acts 2), and the spread of the → gospel and Christian churches is by way of strategic cities, though accompanied with opposition and → suffering. As the city became the main center of alienation from God, so it became also the main center of the → reconciling event and ministry.

Significantly, then, the city and not the garden is the symbol of → eschatological consummation. The true and heavenly Jerusalem that Revelation 21-22 depicts in glowing colors differs from all human cities, yet is also a model for them, as the city of God. God does not force the race back into a pre-city mode of life. He takes up the human dream to which our earthly cities give only ambivalent realization and himself gives it the perfect form that it seeks. He banishes from this city all moral and material ills, sees to it that it needs neither defenses against human violence nor any special site for his presence and worship, and finds a place in it for all the riches of human development. Under the very sign of the city, then, God in his divine purpose of election and grace reverses the disastrous human recourse to the city and achieves definitively the goal of his own eternal plan in creating the human race.

Bibliography: J. ELLUL, *The Meaning of the City* (Grand Rapids, 1970) • D. W. GILL, "City, Biblical Theology of," *ISBE* 1.713-15.

THE EDITORS

2. Sociological Aspects

2.1. Definition

A city, or human settlement, is differentiated from a village by the following characteristics:

1. A city is larger and more compact than a village, with houses closer together and, generally until ca. 1700, with a protective outer wall.
2. A city has a relatively denser population.
3. There is little agricultural production in a city; in earlier times it was the center of military and political rule over the surrounding area.
4. A city is also the religious, cultural, and economic center for a larger or smaller surrounding area; today — as with New York, Tokyo, or London, for example — it may have global importance in respect of certain functions.
5. A city is the place where many needs are met and many forms of trade and manufacture are located (G. W. F. Hegel).

2.2. Reasons for Development

Cities arose as people began to settle from Neolithic times. For religious, cultural, military, and political reasons the centralizing of previously scattered functions was required with → temples, markets, and defenses along with water (L. Mumford). After some first beginnings, cities developed in about 3500 B.C. in Mesopotamia, → Palestine, and Syria, then in the Punjab, Turkestan, Egypt, and China. Ur, Uruk, Jericho, Babylon, Jerusalem, and Memphis/Thebes were early centers of culture that had divine city-kings (→ Monarchy in Israel).

With the rise of cities, human development

crossed a decisive threshold (→ Anthropology 5). The city alone made possible self-stabilizing and self-perpetuating cultural development (→ Culture 5) and hence cultures at a higher level. It is hard to encompass all the innovations associated with the city (see Mumford's attempt at a summary). Social innovations include the differentiation of social structure on the basis of the increasingly complex division of labor (→ Industrial Society), the fixing of functions and relations, the forming of new human types and mentalities (from urban dwellers to idlers), along with new forms of government, participation (in the Greek city-states), and local identity (e.g., as Romans).

2.3. Phases in Development
From the days of antiquity we may distinguish the following five stages.

2.3.1. Antiquity gave us our ideas of the city, of culture, of urbanity, and of civility. The cities of antiquity largely decayed with the migrations and the end of the → Roman Empire, but cities like Cologne, Trier, Paris, Milan, London, and Rome itself were early centers of Christianity in which market halls and temples became → basilicas, churches, and → monasteries.

2.3.2. In the → Middle Ages, as the Frankish kingdom was established and trade revived, new city development began to take place by the end of the 11th century, and a new type of city dweller (→ Bourgeois, Bourgeoisie) emerged in a relationship of tension with the ecclesiastical and political authorities. The rapid spread of cities across central Europe in the 12th and 13th centuries is a unique phenomenon in the history of culture. These cities developed the urban → society, → capitalism, and industrial system that are now the hallmarks of the Western city (M. → Weber).

2.3.3. The age of absolutism saw the end of the centuries-old struggle against the → autonomy of cities. With few exceptions, cities were subjugated to the territorial claims of absolute rulers or states, and a new wave of planning and founding capitals and residences began.

2.3.4. Industrialization from the beginning of the 19th century brought a complete change in the structure and significance of cities in both Europe and North America (→ Industrial Society). A global process of city development now began, and cities increasingly swallowed up surrounding villages and open country. Both the number and population of cities also increased rapidly. The enormous growth of world population since the beginning of industrialization (from 1.2 billion in 1850 to 2.5 billion in 1950 and then 6.2 billion in 2000) has taken place disproportionately in the cities. Especially in the countries of the Third World (→ Development 1), cities have not been able to assimilate the masses that have migrated to them, the result being inner city slums and surrounding shanty towns for the poor.

2.3.5. In the 20th century, industrialization has continued and brought with it a third phase of city development, or "tertiary urbanization" (R. Mackensen, 141). The tertiary sector now governs the amount and form of urbanization. Its features — combined with the spread of means of mass communication, the increasing use of the private automobile, and the separating of the place of residence from the place of work — result in the movement of people, shops, and industry to the suburbs (→ Work 5-8; Leisure).

2.4. Further Development
We cannot now foresee how cities will maintain their autonomy in the ongoing process of global urbanization, with its great differences in specific regions. Regarding the new and sprawling cities that have developed in the → Third World since 1950, we now find not only the older term "conglomeration" but also "conurbation," "megalopolis," and "megacity."

Bibliography: L. Benevolo, *Die Geschichte der Stadt* (Frankfurt, 1983) • H. Berndt, *Die Natur der Stadt* (Frankfurt, 1978) • A. Borst, *Babel oder Jerusalem? Sechs Kapitel Stadtgeschichte* (Stuttgart, 1984) • T. Chandler and G. Fox, eds., *Three Thousand Years of Urban Growth* (New York, 1974) • A. D. King, *Urbanism, Colonialism, and the World-Economy: Cultural and Spatial Foundations of the World Urban System* (London, 1990) • J. W. Konvitz, *The Urban Millennium: The City-Building Process from the Early Middle Ages to the Present* (Carbondale, Ill., 1985) • G. T. Kurian, ed., *World Encyclopedia of Cities* (2 vols.; Santa Barbara, Calif., 1993) • R. Mackensen, "Städte in der Statistik," *Die Stadt in der Bundesrepublik Deutschland* (ed. W. Pehnt; Stuttgart, 1974) 129-66 • L. Mumford, *The City in History: Its Origins, Its Transformations, and Its Prospects* (New York, 1961) • U. Petz and K. M. Schmals, *Metropole, Weltstadt, Global City. Neue Formen der Urbanisierung* (Dortmund, 1992) • B. Schäfers, "Stadt und Kultur," *Soziologische Stadtforschung* (ed. J. Friedrichs; Opladen, 1988) 95-111.

Bernhard Schäfers

3. Theological Aspects
3.1. Church Reactions
In the absence of an agreed theological or sociological concept of the city, practical theology has had to cope as best it could with the needs of the city. It has

reacted in various ways to the urbanizing trends of the past nearly two centuries.

First were diaconal and missionary initiatives (→ Diakonia; Mission). City missions were founded in Glasgow in 1826 and London in 1835, and the → Inner Mission followed their example in Germany from 1849 onward. Then came structural modernizing, new parishes, synodic reform, and construction of new churches. A third response was new forms of pastoral ministry aimed at special groups, such as prison or youth ministries. Fourth, the settlement model of social and friendship ministry developed in England, especially in working-class areas.

Fifth came initiatives in the form of → youth work, children's services, and women's and men's fellowships. A sixth initiative was autonomous educational ventures, especially in adult education. Seventh, ecumenical impulses came after 1945. These efforts have included → Jewish-Christian Dialogue, the institutionalizing of diaconal work with supporting agencies, the new understanding of mission as a structural principle, efforts at spiritual renewal, new missionary strategies, and interaction with culture in such forms as concerts.

3.2. Problems

The list in the previous section, which could easily be expanded, gives evidence of the forces now at work in urban areas and shows with what different dimensions and problems of city life the church must deal. It may be observed that comparatively little attention has been paid to art, culture, the media, or the development of a political and literary public life. The churches have maintained with one voice their claim that the Christian religion is relevant to all phases of city development. In practice, their presence in the cities has assumed a wide variety of institutional forms, reflecting broadly the social → pluralism (§§1-2) of the cities.

The dynamic of diversification in the cities continues, but not on the basis of much theological reflection. The churches and their agencies often react to the problems of urbanization with past models of action and concepts of organization, ignoring any analysis of the religious potential of city development, which indeed has rich possibilities (→ Philosophy; Sociology).

The unfathomable crisis of → modernity resulting from the political, economic, social, and intellectual crises and disasters of the 20th century has thus far not received any clear illumination from theology. F. Gogarten (1887-1967) made an attempt at theological clarification with his distinguishing of → secularization from → secularism (1953). In his Secular City (1965), H. Cox stressed the opportunities, validity, and qualities of the modern secular city (with its "disenchantment of → nature," "desacralization of politics," and "deconsecration of values"). He took a positive view of the enlarged sphere of freedom that the city gives as the place of possible progress for individual → emancipation. Later, in Religion in the Secular City (1984), he showed how religion is still of abiding importance in the development of the → postmodern city. Other interpretations point to victims of city development, such as what we lose in the form of social segregation, → poverty, and the marginalizing of the socially weak.

Prophetic criticism appears in the English study Faith in the City (London, 1985), in the → base communities in Latin America, and in the German study Menschengerechte Stadt (1984), which stresses the opportunities for children (→ Childhood) as the criterion of humane city development. For a comprehensive study of the tasks and problems from the standpoint of practical theology, see C. Bäumler's 1993 work on the church in the city.

3.3. Tasks

The various trends in urbanization find a reflection in the church, given its century-long position of power. Religious diversity corresponds to the divisions of spheres of life in the city. A result is the majority role played by → minorities, even in the religious sphere, along with the new interreligious and ecumenical tasks that this poses.

The diminution of the church's role in society does not necessarily mean a general abandoning of religion. It merely means the rejection of an institutional monopoly, moving from earlier forms of religious expression to new market-oriented organizational forms, developed further in the sphere of pastoral care and counseling. The multiplicity of religious offerings results from the claiming of religious → freedom. The city thus becomes the forum for competing strategies of education and for the struggle to achieve economic, political, and cultural → power (P. Bourdieu).

As a mirror of social tensions and possibilities, the city is a stage for all kinds of scenarios. It is the setting of local traditions, and it also reflects global problems. It is multicultural. The churches should not "emigrate" (J. Matthes) from this situation or retreat into a private sphere but should make their unique contribution to city development. In keeping with the presence of God to which their faith attests, they must act as a powerful and salutary force, even in the context of the city.

On the basis of Jewish traditions (→ Jewish Practices), the churches are to be seen as fellowships of remembrance linked to the city with their memorial days, jubilees, and city festivals. They are to present God's will to save — prophetically with timely addresses, cultically with representations, and diaconally with material aid. They must anticipate the → kingdom of God by encouragement, liberation, → reconciliation, and redemption, relying on example, not force.

Churches must face the question of their role relative to the "center" of the city, understood both geographically and ideologically. They once gave shape to this center with their understanding of → salvation and perdition, and they must still do so. City churches are important for being part of a city's history, as well as for their role in constantly expressing diaconally, spiritually, and culturally God's will to save in forms and symbols that can be publicly communicated.

The churches must also raise the question of the victims of city development, including the poor, aliens, widows, orphans, and slum dwellers. They must bring these problems to the attention of the public with community organizations (→ Community Service). This involves modifications of the parish principle (→ Congregation 2.1), networking, and institutional cooperation both locally and regionally. In time, suitable local structures need to be developed.

As organs of city life, the churches are to contend for the → future of cities, critically to decipher the spirit of the city (K. Duntze), and proleptically to give shape to the → hope of the new heaven and the new earth, for example, by an ecumenically linked system of city churches across national and denominational lines. They are to do this with a new perception also of the religious dimensions of art and culture. In this way they can give expression to the role of Christians as citizens of the heavenly Jerusalem as well as their earthly city.

Bibliography: Archbishop of Canterbury's Commission on Urban Priority Areas, *Faith in the City: A Call for Action by Church and Nation* (London, 1985) • C. Bäumler, *Menschlich leben in der verstädterten Gesellschaft. Kirchliche Praxis zwischen Öffentlichkeit und Privatheit* (Gütersloh, 1993) • H. de Bruin and W. Bröckers, *Stadt-Seelsorge* (Frankfurt, 1991) • H. Cox, *Religion in the Secular City* (New York, 1984); idem, *The Secular City* (New York, 1965) • H. W. Dannowski et al., eds., *Kirche in der Stadt,* vol. 1, *Erinnern und Gedenken;* vol. 2, *Religion als Wahrheit und Ware;* vol. 3, *Die Armen und die Reichen. Soziale Gerechtigkeit in der Stadt;* vol. 4, *Götter auf der Durchreise* (Hamburg, 1991-93) • K. Duntze, *Der Geist, die Städte baut. Planquadrat–Wohnbereich–Heimat* (Stuttgart, 1972); idem, *Die Verantwortung der Kirche für das großstädtische* *Gemeinwesen* (Frankfurt, 1993) • F. Gogarten, *Verhängnis und Hoffnung der Neuzeit. Die Säkularisierung als theologisches Problem* (Stuttgart, 1953; 2d ed., 1987) • M. Göpfert and C. Modehn, eds., *Kirche in der Stadt. Erfahrungen, Experimente, Modelle in europäischen Großstädten* (Stuttgart, 1981) • F. Green, "Urbanisierung als Herausforderung kirchlicher Strukturbildung" (Diss., Hamburg, 1992) • P. S. Hawkins, *Civitas: Religious Interpretations of the City* (Atlanta, 1986) • Kirchenamt der Evangelische Kirche in Deutschland, *Menschengerechte Stadt. Aufforderung zur humanen und ökologischen Stadterneuerung* (Gütersloh, 1984) • R. Lindner, *Die Entdeckung der Stadtkultur* (Frankfurt, 1990) • W. A. Meeks, *The First Urban Christians* (London, 1983) • L. Mumford, *The City in History: Its Origins, Its Transformations, and Its Prospects* (New York, 1961) • M. C. Neddens and W. Wucher, eds., *Die Wiederkehr des Genius Loci. Die Kirche im Stadtraum–die Stadt im Kirchenraum* (Wiesbaden, 1987) • R. Sennett, *Civitas. Die Großstadt und die Kultur des Unterschieds* (Frankfurt, 1991) • G. Winter, *The New Creation as Metropolis* (New York, 1963).

Wolfgang Grünberg

Civil Disobedience → Civil Rights Movement; Resistance, Right of

Civil Law and the Church

1. Europe
2. United States
    2.1. Church Discipline
    2.2. Confession and Counseling
    2.3. Religious Education and Proselytizing

1. Europe
To fulfill the church's mission, almost all churches in the world need ordained and nonordained workers in → proclamation, teaching, → pastoral care, → diakonia, and church administration. In some European countries the clergy are regulated by state law, such as where there are national churches (→ People's Church), as in Scandinavia, Austria, parts of Switzerland, Italy, Spain, and Portugal. In other countries, because of the separation of → church and state, as in France and the United States, they come under private law.

In Germany the clergy and administrators are under public law, but by mutual agreement, other → church employees are in private employment. The ordained clergy (→ Ordination) have a life's ministry, an ongoing one of special public significance. Arrangements are made for temporary or private appointments to prevent or lessen unemployment. The church itself has rules relating to the testing, appointment, discipline, and so forth of its leaders, and agreements with the state contain additional voluntarily accepted rules (e.g., relating to theological education).

Most clergy in the Church of England (→ Anglican Communion) are legally self-employed. They do not come under the Civil Employment Act but under church law according to the Ecclesiastical → Jurisdiction Measure of 1983. All → bishops, → priests, and → deacons are subject to the provisions of the measure.

In the → Roman Catholic Church the 1983 → Codex Iuris Canonici governs the position of the → priest. In distinction from a Protestant understanding, the CIC presents a sacramental view of priestly → consecration.

In Eastern Europe the separation of church and state meant for the most part that priests and ministers came under private law, with varying degrees of regulations. Church administrators and officials with particularly important and responsible functions were in much the same position as the parish clergy, though experiences during the → church struggle led in East Germany to allowing churches to place them under their own regulations.

→ Church Law; Residence, Duty of

Bibliography: A. von Campenhausen, Staatskirchenrecht (2d ed.; Munich, 1983) • J. Frank, "Dienst- und Arbeitsrecht," Handbuch des Staatskirchenrechts der Bundesrepublik Deutschland (Berlin, 1974/75) 1.669-725; idem, "Geschichte und neuere Entwicklung des Rechts der kirchlichen Beamten," ZEvKR 10 (1963/64) 264ff. • H.-G. Frey and E. Bahles, Dienst und Arbeitsrecht in der katholischen Kirche (Neuwied, 1989-) • J. Jurina, Das Dienst- und Arbeitsrecht im Bereich der Kirchen in der Bundesrepublik Deutschland (Berlin, 1979) • J. Listl et al., eds., Handbuch des katholischen Kirchenrechts (Regensburg, 1983) • U. Scheuner, Der Dienst in der kirchlichen Verwaltung (Kiel, 1968) • A. Stein, Evangelisches Kirchenrecht (3d ed.; Neuwied, 1992).

Herbert Ehnes

2. United States

In the United States, church employees enjoy constitutional protection, as the following examples indicate.

2.1. Church Discipline

Civil court actions concerning the → ordination, ecclesiastical appointment, discipline, or defrocking of clerics are barred by the First Amendment of the U.S. Constitution. Lacking malicious motive, defamatory information regarding a cleric may be disseminated within the agencies of a church, but it must not be communicated to those with no interest in the cleric/church relationship.

Civil court actions concerning the discipline or → excommunication of church members (→ Church Membership) are barred by the First Amendment. Church officials may be sued for injury to a member's reputation or privacy only when acting with malice concerning matters wholly outside the bounds of any interest in defining or maintaining the relationship between the church and its members. However, the law is unclear concerning civil actions alleging injury caused by actions after severance of membership.

2.2. Confession and Counseling

Communications with clergy in their priestly or pastoral capacity (→ Pastoral Care) are privileged. Testimony by clergy as to such communications can be compelled in a civil court only if the privilege is waived by the penitent. Conversely, breach of confidentiality actions may be brought if clergy disclose such communications. Civil courts do not recognize actions for injury because of bad advice suffered by persons receiving religious counseling. However, clerics charged with sexual improprieties toward counselees or children under their charge are liable for seduction or molestation.

2.3. Religious Education and Proselytizing

Because the First Amendment is a bar to requiring an individual to prove the truth of a religious teaching, → heresy is unknown to civil law. Courts may not entertain an action for fraud concerning professions of religious faith or experience. Sincerely held religious teaching that alienates spouses to a marriage or children from parents is never actionable. Nevertheless, an individual's sincerity in professing a certain religious teaching may be tested, and, if found wanting, the charlatan may be held civilly responsible. For example, deceit by a cleric concerning the intended use of solicited funds would be actionable by the donor. Deceit as to the true identity of a religious organization while proselytizing among youth has been found actionable.

→ Church Employees; Church Law; Jurisdiction, Ecclesiastical

Bibliography: L. Buzzard and T. Brandon, Church Discipline and the Courts (Wheaton, Ill., 1987) • C. H. Esbeck, "Tort Claims against Churches and Ecclesiastical Officers: The First Amendment Considerations,"

West Virginia Law Review 89 (1986) 1-114 • B. W. LYNN, *The Right to Religious Liberty: The Basic ACLU Guide to Religious Rights* (Carbondale, Ill., 1995) • W. TIEMANN and J. BUSH, *The Right to Silence: Privileged Clergy Communication and the Law* (Nashville, 1989).

CARL H. ESBECK

Civil Religion

1. Definition
2. Historical Development
3. Evolution of American Civil Religion
4. Civil Religion in Other Western Countries
5. Civil Religion outside Europe and North America
6. Criticism

1. Definition

Also known as civic, public, political, or societal religion and as public piety or religion-in-general, civil religion refers to the widely held body of beliefs or religiopolitical traits that are tied to a nation's history and destiny. It is a kind of generic faith that relates the political society as well as the individual citizen to the realm of ultimate meaning and existence. In turn, it enables the people to view their polity in a special manner, thereby providing meaningful social integration. It is in effect the operative religion of a political community — the system of rituals, symbols, values, norms, and allegiances that determines its life, invests it with meaning and a destiny, and provides it with an overarching sense of spiritual unity that transcends all internal conflicts and differences.

Civil religion is a consensus of religious sentiments, concepts, and symbols that the state utilizes — either directly or indirectly, consciously or unconsciously — for its own political purposes. This general religious faith normally encompasses the entire society, but it does not necessarily compete with the particular faiths of sectarian or → denominational groups, which can claim the allegiance of only a part of the populace. (In fact, the latter read into the civil religion whatever meaning they choose.)

As Rolf Schieder points out, civil religion actually functions on two levels. In one sense, it is a cluster of phenomena occurring in the boundary region between → politics and → religions, as illustrated by the use of religious language in constitutions and political speech, the presence of religious symbols like the Ten Commandments or crucifixes in class-

rooms and courtrooms, and the performance of religious rituals like swearing-in (oath-taking) ceremonies, the recitations of the Pledge of Allegiance to the American flag, and the communal singing of the national anthem. In a second sense, civil religion exists as theory. It is the effort to organize or systematize phenomena like those above and thereby conceptualize or explain their deeper meaning. Such a theory requires a broad understanding of religion, sociology, and political science.

2. Historical Development

The term "civil religion" assumed a life of its own after sociologist Robert Bellah published an essay in 1967 containing the oft-quoted line "There actually exists alongside of and rather clearly differentiated from the churches an elaborate and well-institutionalized civil religion in America." This statement affirmed an intimate tie between religion and politics in the very country that had pioneered the legal separation of → church and state. Looking beyond the Christian churches and other houses of worship, Bellah located a set of religious beliefs and values that guided national policy and shaped American social institutions.

At once scholars acknowledged that such a phenomenon had existed since time immemorial. The national God of ancient Israel, the public religiosity of the Greek polis, the imperial cult in Rome (→ Roman Religion), Byzantine caesaropapism (→ Byzantium 1), and the Calvinist/Puritan covenanted community were all seen as examples of a religious dimension to public life. The term itself, however, is of → Enlightenment origins, and one can argue that it reflects the Enlightenment's emphasis on religion as a secular, rational, and universal phenomenon. In fact, a figure of the time, Jean-Jacques Rousseau (1712-78), coined the phrase in his *Social Contract* (1762). It was a notion intended to aid a nondespotic government in expressing the "general will" by forming a universal society of free citizens. *Religion civile* was a conscious body of belief and practice that leaders would create and encourage, although it would be independent of both the church and the ruling class. The "dogmas" of this religion would be few and simple — the existence of a God who is intelligent and beneficent, the life to come, the happiness of the just and punishment of the wicked, the sanctity of the social contract and the laws — and it would provide persons with ultimate meaning by locating them in their society, which in turn would be located in space and history. This would be neither secular nationalism nor ecclesiastical legitimation of the state. It provided a larger moral context to measure the behavior of the body politic and restrain its tendencies toward selfish expression.

Although he did not use the term himself, Émile Durkheim (1858-1917) laid the theoretical foundation for it by affirming religion as inherent in social life. When a collection of people is a society, it exhibits a common religion. This is the positive expression of social integration. Every functioning society thus rests on a set of moral beliefs that flows from its existence and provides both its character and an overarching sense of unity. Later commentators simply replaced the word "common" with "civil."

By the 1950s and early 1960s some theologians in Germany were speaking of → "political theology" and taking a more critical and activist approach to societal problems. In contrast, American writers, both theologians and sociologists, approached the issue of "common" or "public" religion in a variety of ways. In 1974 Russell Richey and Donald Jones categorized the contrasting positions into five closely connected and often overlapping typologies of meaning. Although these were formulated to analyze American civil religion, some could be applicable to situations elsewhere.

One is civil religion as *folk religion* (→ Popular Religion). This is the common religion of Americans that emerges from the ethos and history of the folk, or, in Will Herberg's words, "the American way of life." It is an "idolatrous" faith that competes with the particularistic religions that transcend the common life of the people. The second is the *transcendent universal religion of the nation.* This is the position of Bellah as well as Sidney Mead, who labeled it "the religion of the Republic." It is a normative faith that stands in judgment on the nation and is a corrective against idolatrous tendencies in some forms of Christianity or views of government.

The third typology is *religious nationalism* (→ Nation, Nationalism). The nation itself is the object of adoration and glorification and assumes a sovereign, self-transcendent character. As the religion of patriotism, it tends strongly toward idolatry. The fourth, *democratic faith,* is the more positive form of the previous category and affirms the humane values and ideals of equality, freedom, and justice without depending on a transcendent deity or a spiritualized nation. Examples include John Dewey's "common faith" and the democracy-as-religion of J. Paul Williams. A fifth typology, *Protestant civic piety,* involves the fusion of → Protestantism and nationalism. Included here are Protestant moralism, → individualism, activism, → pragmatism, the work ethic, national destiny, and "missionizing" the world with American values.

3. Evolution of American Civil Religion

Many scholars have focused on civil religion in the United States, and they show that it draws from many sources. The → Puritan tradition provided the particularistic notion of the chosen, covenanted, and millennial nation — the "city upon a hill." From the Enlightenment came the universalistic ideas of human → equality, → freedom, peaceful → progress, and reliance on the tolerant, → deistic "god of nature." The Great Awakening (→ Revivals 2.1-2) evoked the idea of civil millennialism, in which America became the new apocalyptic hope of humankind. In the revolutionary era the notions of religious freedom and the providential God who cared for his people entered the civil religion. The evangelical and revivalistic traditions of the early 19th century contributed the concepts of → democracy, the free individual, personal → piety, and moral rectitude. At that time, the public schools and the *McGuffey Readers* served to inculcate the values of the democratic religion.

The Civil War produced the themes of sacrifice and redemption. Commemoration of national holidays with strong civil-religion components like Memorial Day and Thanksgiving began in the post–Civil War years, while the ideas of national mission and destiny gained in popularity. The great wave of "new" immigrants coming to the United States between 1880 and 1914, an emphasis on the "three great faiths" (Protestant, Roman Catholic, Jewish), and the → civil rights movement added tolerance and diversity to the mix. The cold war years saw the exaltation of the flag as the sacred object of patriotism, acceptance by Congress of "In God we trust" as the national motto (1956), and affirmation of the superiority of "our" democratic religious values over those of "godless Communism."

The Viet Nam War and social conflicts of the 1960s and early 1970s reintroduced the concept of national crisis, with writers speaking even of a third "time of trial" (after the American Revolution and the Civil War). The "national covenant," which validated the God-given, inalienable rights of Americans — the sanctity of human life, individual liberty, the pursuit of happiness, tolerance, justice, and concern for one's neighbor — seemed now to be in serious jeopardy. Could republican virtue — the public-spiritedness that encourages democratic participation in the polity — hold individual egoism and social disintegration in check?

The nation's president provided the leadership in the public faith, as Richard Pierard and Robert Linder have shown. At various times he has functioned as its pastor, priest, and even prophet, to use

Martin Marty's schema (Richey and Jones). In the prophetic mode, presidents such as Lincoln (1861-65), Kennedy (1961-63), and Carter (1977-81) assessed the nation's actions in relation to transcendent values. They called upon citizens to make sacrifices in times of crisis and to repent of corporate sins when their behavior fell short of the national ideals. As the national pastor, the president (e.g., Franklin Roosevelt [1933-45] and Eisenhower [1953-61]) provided spiritual inspiration to the people by upholding American core values and urging them to do likewise. Assuming the priestly role, such presidents as Nixon (1969-74), Reagan (1981-89), and Bush (1989-93) made America itself the ultimate reference point. They affirmed and celebrated the nation, while at the same time stroking and praising their political flock.

4. Civil Religion in Other Western Countries

For a variety of reasons, civil religion never developed in Canada. Because Canadians rejected the European tradition of church establishment without adopting the U.S. idea of church-state separation, religious liberty took on a different meaning, and the state even supported religious instruction and church-sponsored schools. Moreover, because of the linguistic and cultural differences between the founding communities, no common understanding of Canadian identity and national purpose developed. Regionalism, biculturalism, and tensions between the French Catholic and British Protestant elements inhibited the development of a Pan-Canadian identity, the prerequisite for an overall religious interpretation of the Dominion. The Protestant churches could not articulate an ideology of Canadianism acceptable to those from other religious backgrounds. In short, the "Canadian way of life" lacks shared transcendent beliefs, symbols, and values.

British scholars question whether the concept of civil religion is applicable in the United Kingdom. As it is a constitutional monarchy, the king or queen cannot articulate a civil theology in the manner of an American president. Since established churches exist that retain formal links with the Crown, any statements of civil faith would tend to be closer to Christian orthodoxy. At the same time, ethnic diversity accompanied by pressure to formulate a civil religion distinct from orthodox Christianity arose much later in Britain than it did in America. As it is, in their speeches monarchs and prime ministers express only a generalized Christianity and do not explicitly identify religion with the life of the nation. The clearest exception has been Margaret Thatcher, as illustrated by her famous speech to the Church of Scotland General Assembly in 1988. Churchmen, including the archbishop of Canterbury, seem reluctant to make claims to divine legitimacy for the country. The coronation of Elizabeth II in 1953 was the closest thing to a reaffirmation of the fundamental moral and religious values of British in this century, which some writers have seen as evidence of civil religion, but since then the monarchy has not been connected with the transcendent and mystical. Even the annual Remembrance Day (November 11) ceremony has little overt religious character.

The scholarly debate in Germany has been much more intense, particularly among theologians, sociologists, and political philosophers. Issues on the table include the distinction between civil religion and basic values (*Grundwerte*) like justice, freedom, equality, and human solidarity (Niklas Luhmann); the tension between divine → immanence and transcendence in human society; the impact of secular ideologies like → Marxism, → liberalism, and nationalism, which assert truth claims as strongly as religion ever had; national, or "cultural," Protestantism (→ Culture Protestantism), which among other things shifted the accent on Reformation theology from individual to national redemption and contributed to a particularistic, German-folkish understanding of divine purpose in the world; and secular liberal constitutional patriotism (e.g., Jürgen Habermas) versus neoconservative civil religion (e.g., Hermann Lübbe) as the left- and right-wing poles of a metapolitical legitimation of the contemporary German political system.

Several commentators have pointed to manifestations of civil religion in other European countries. John Markoff and David Regan showed that the revolutionary regime in France in 1793 replaced Christianity with a civil religion marked by a mixture of beliefs, a cult of the Supreme Being, and, later in the decade, a minimalist emphasis on Reason. The other French-style civil religion that developed in the late 19th century affirmed both the republic itself and the tradition of France as the "first daughter of the church" and focused on national greatness and universal human rights (→ Human and Civil Rights). Leo Laeyendecker contended that the Dutch republic developed a Calvinistic civil religion in the 17th century, some vestiges of which remain even in the late 1990s. Drawing upon the theoretical insights of Benedetto Croce (1866-1952) and Antonio Gramsci (1891-1937), Bellah argued that Italy possessed five civil religions coexisting with one another — peasant folk religion, Catholicism, liberalism, socialism, and activism. Ewa Morawska discovered a strong civil religion in Poland, while other writers identified civil religious traits within Finnish and Estonian Lutheranism and in Hungary.

Possibly the most wide-ranging examination of civil religion in Europe and elsewhere was a → Lutheran World Federation study project directed by Bela Harmati in 1981-87. The primary focus of the reports was the manifestation of civil religion in the various German states and Scandinavian countries, but attention was directed also to other countries, including the United States, Japan, and Indonesia. Civil-religion traits were detected even in Communist countries. Paul Mojzes and others showed that Marxism-Leninism had a distinctly religious character in the former Soviet Union, and Pierard analyzed such civil-religious practices in Communist East Germany as youth dedication, political rites with religious overtones, and the state's exploitation of the 1983 → Luther quincentenary for its own purposes.

5. Civil Religion outside Europe and North America

Scholars have identified numerous examples of civil religion in other parts of the world. In Africa, Kwame Nkrumah used it to give symbolic legitimation to the new nation Ghana, but his effort failed when he set himself up as the sole and absolute oracle of the civil religion. Julius Nyerere in Tanzania developed a political ideology based on his belief in human equality. He made this nontranscendental value an ultimate, thereby ascribing religious meaning to a secular aspect of human experience, and the concern for equality functioned like a religion in his new order. Thus the focus of Tanzanian civil religion was the socialist ideology of *ujamaa* (familyhood), which formed the basis of equality in a → pluralistic society. Mobutu Sese Seko in Zaire sought to sacralize society through his Mouvement Populaire de la Révolution, thus making it a surrogate for religion. According to Jacob Olupona, a Nigerian civil religion based on a belief in a transcendent moral order gives the country a privileged position. It seeks to identify common ground among the various religious and nonreligious groups and deny any of them official status.

Much more important is the Afrikaner civil religion in South Africa, which served as the theological underpinning for apartheid (→ South Africa 3). Most scholars recognize that → Calvinism played little part in shaping the peculiar way of life of the Dutch-speaking Afrikaners and that ideas of manifest destiny and chosenness, which are commonplace in the Western world, played a far greater role. However, as the rustic and restless Afrikaners found themselves caught in a pincer movement between the growing power of the English and the numerically superior indigenous peoples, they developed a *laager*, or fortress, mentality. The Anglo-Boer War (1899-1902) only enhanced this consciousness of the need to maintain and defend their identity.

Inspired by Reformed evangelicalism, the idea of a national church took root among the Afrikaners, while → Kuyperian neo-Calvinism contributed the concept of divinely ordained spheres in all aspects of social life, over which God must be sovereign. Romantic nationalism added the notion of an embattled people (folk) struggling to protect their racial identity. To the Afrikaners, the self-evident message of Scripture was that they were God's elect and covenant people. They now interpreted their history as that of a new Israel who in the Great Trek had fled from Egypt (the Cape) to Canaan, the promised land in the interior. There they founded a Christian republic modeled on OT Israel, where they lived separate from the alien (heathen) peoples around them and upheld the purity of their culture and God's sovereignty over it. This activist Calvinism was used to shore up Afrikaner self-respect and cultural values.

Chosenness is also a key element in the → Zionist civil religion in the modern state of Israel. This draws symbols from traditional Jewish culture and the Hebrew Scriptures that can express and foster historic and contemporary links between Judaism, the Jewish people, and the Israeli polity. It ties together Jewish peoplehood, culture, and history. Elements of this civil religion include the citizenship of Jewish people everywhere in the covenant community, the centrality of the state of Israel in the divine purpose, Jewish culture and the Hebrew language as the distinguishing marks of Israeli society, the Jewish tradition as the source of values in public life, a commitment to democracy and social justice for the Israeli population, and a strong emphasis on military security in light of the → Holocaust and the threat of the neighboring Arab states and indigenous Palestinian population to the Jewish state's very existence. The two most sacred public shrines of Israel are the Western Wall, the remaining ruin of the temple, which links people to Israel's history in the land, and the Yad Vashem Holocaust remembrance memorial, which keeps alive the spirit of resistance to all enemies of the Jewish people.

There have been various manifestations of civil religion in Asia. In the 1970s Shah Reza Pahlavi in Iran tried to use a modernized → Shia civil religion to legitimate his own power, but it failed to win over the masses, who were more committed to traditional Shiite Islam. In Sri Lanka a Buddhist civil religion developed around the rituals associated with the Temple of the Tooth in Kandy, which housed a major relic of the Buddha. It reflected the triadic relation between king, people, and religion that continued after the country had become a republic. Although the ritual dimension of this civil religion declined, the ideological aspect of it has some hold on the Buddhist public.

In Thailand a civic religion arose in the late 18th century that linked → Buddhism, the nation (both in terms of people and territory), and the monarchy and produced a degree of national integration. Markoff and Regan found a minimal sort of civil religion centered on the king in Malaysia during the 1970s. Peter Lee found evidence of a public faith in 9th-century Chinese → Confucian thought, which contributed such transcendent secular orthodoxies as male hierarchy, the mandate-of-heaven principle (which legitimated the emperor's rule), social inequality, and the giving of ultimate loyalty to the emperor.

Both Confucian and Buddhist ideas affected the formulation of civic values in Japan, as Bellah points out, but only during the late 19th and early 20th centuries did the full-blown civil-religious system of state → Shinto emerge. The government fostered a merging of the sacred ancestors of the imperial family with the localized → ancestor worship of the common people, thereby creating an ideological system that engendered a feeling of national unity and dedication. It mobilized the population for nation building, modernization, and military expansion. Participation in Shinto rituals was a "patriotic duty" of all Japanese, regardless of their personal religious convictions. The divine nation of the emperor was the kingdom of God, and the Japanese people were a chosen race who would establish this kingdom of peace and prosperity throughout Asia. The postwar "shrine Shinto" continues to sacralize Japaneseness, but clearly differentiated from the state. This is accomplished by the veneration of noble, sacred spirits *(kami)* at the shrines, which people visit at important times. The rituals and festivals promote social cohesion as well as encourage industrial and agricultural productivity.

In the independent republic of Indonesia created after World War II, a state ideology was adopted known as Pancasila. It was proposed by President Sukarno and was included in the constitution of 1945. In 1975 the teaching of "Pancasila morality" was made obligatory in primary and secondary schools, and since 1985 all social and political organizations, including Christian churches and Islamic organizations, have had to accept this ideology as the moral basis for social ethics. It consists of five *sila* (principles): (1) a belief in one Deity, (2) humanism

(i.e., human dignity), (3) the national unity of Indonesia, (4) democracy, and (5) social justice. This ideology has provided the basis for a united state, one resting on a strong ethical foundation. It also has facilitated the process of modernization and served as a means of national integration.

Looking to the south, one can find some trace of civil religiosity in New Zealand and much more in Australia, even though the influences on the latter were more liberal than Christian. According to David Parker, the transcendent elements in Australian society flowed from the antiestablishment attitude, "mateship" (a distinctly Australian emphasis on egalitarianism and fellowship), sports, and the first national testing time in World War I. The ANZAC tradition stemmed from the disastrous Gallipoli campaign in 1915, which involved a large number of Australian and New Zealand soldiers, and it mythologized the creative traditions of the people — courage, mateship, and sacrifice in the face of inexplicable hardship and sufferings. The annual commemoration on April 25 centers on a quasi-religious service held at war memorials around the country and especially the national memorial in Canberra, the greatest temple of civil religion in the country. The ANZAC observance provides the symbol and ritual to enshrine the transcendent elements of the nation's historical experience.

Moving to the other side of the Pacific, one finds that the prevalence of civil religion in Latin America is connected with the → Roman Catholic Church and the close ties that exist between church and state. In places such as Brazil and Chile, where the church came increasingly under the control of the state, the relationship was transformed into a civil religious one. In Mexico the church's position was quite ambivalent, and secular nationalism clearly predominated over religious values in public life.

6. Criticism

Some scholars question whether civil religion actually exists. The ambiguities typically surrounding the term lead many to suggest that a better term would be "legitimating myth," that the complexity of modern society, with its division into interest groups based on → class, race, religion, ethnicity, occupation, and → ideology, renders a national civil religion impossible. The groups share few collective purposes and common visions, while the individuals are typically self-centered, believing that ultimate meaning can be found only in one's personal emotional or spiritual life.

Others see civil religion as mere "culture religion" and thus idolatrous worship of the state. One can possess the "republican virtues" of responsible citizenship without requiring a religious sanction. In fact, the religious freedom that comes from a secular state enables individuals to pursue the social responsibilities once associated with religion without having to conform to an overarching standard of religious belief. Moral virtue and responsible citizenship require freedom, the full divestment of religious authority from the state.

Furthermore, it is difficult to separate the rhetoric of civil religion about covenant and mission from concepts as understood by people in Protestant churches. Images and symbols of divinity that are used to empower political agendas, such as calling a misguided nation to its "true destiny," confuse religion and politics. This terminology obscures the differences between the human and the divine and invests human institutions with an authority and implication of sanctity that belong to God alone. In fact, in countries like the United States, competing ideologies and traditions make a civil religion speaking with one voice and uniting people around common ideals utterly impossible. Religious conservatives and liberals have such widely divergent understandings of the public faith that even the unifying symbols (the flag or the Ten Commandments) have become divisive, and the national holidays, now celebrated on Mondays, have become essentially meaningless.

Social scientists in particular are uneasy about the concept of civil religion because of the enormous difficulty of doing empirical research and discovering concrete examples of it. For example, how would one develop a survey instrument that could ascertain how many Americans believe that their nation is both God's agent and yet subject to his judgment? Or what kind of terms demonstrate the existence of civil religion, and how do we measure their usage and effectiveness?

Bibliography: R. N. BELLAH, The Broken Covenant (New York, 1975) • R. N. BELLAH and P. E. HAMMOND, Varieties of Civil Religion (San Francisco, 1980) • D. R. BORG, "German National Protestantism as a Civil Religion," International Perspectives on Church and State (ed. M. Mor; Omaha, Nebr., 1993) • G. W. BRASWELL, "Civil Religion in Contemporary Iran," JChS 21 (Fall 1979) 223-46 • M. CRISTI and L. L. DAWSON, "Civil Religion in Comparative Perspective: Chile under Pinochet," SocComp 43/3 (1996) 319-38 • F. E. DEIST, "Notes on the Context and Hermeneutic of Afrikaner Civil Religion," Missionalia 19 (April 1990) 124-39 • G. GEHRIG, American Civil Religion (Storrs, Conn., 1981) • M. HONECKER, "Eschatologie und Zivilreligion," EvT 50/1 (1990) 40-55 • M. W. HUGHEY, Civil Religion and Moral Order (Westport, Conn., 1983) • JTSA 19 (June 1977) • A. E. KIM,

"The Absence of Pan-Canadian Civil Religion," SoR 54 (Fall 1993) 257-75 • H. KLEGER and A. MÜLLER, Religion des Bürgers. Zivilreligion in Amerika und Europa (Munich, 1986) • L. LAEYENDECKER, "The Problem of Civil Religion: The Case of the Netherlands," Religion as a Social Phenomenon (ed. E. Karlsaune; Trondheim, 1988) • P. K. H. LEE, " 'Civil Religion' and 'Secularization in Confucianism,'" Ching Feng 34 (January 1991) 28-50 • C. S. LIEBMAN and E. DON-YEHIYA, Religion and Politics in Israel (Bloomington, Ind., 1984) • R. D. LINDER and R. V. PIERARD, "Ronald Reagan, Civil Religion, and the New Religious Right in America," FiHi 23 (Fall 1993) 57-73; idem, Twilight of the Saints (Downers Grove, Ill., 1978) • N. LUHMANN, Funktion von Religion (4th ed.; Frankfurt, 1996) • G. R. McDERMOTT, "Civil Religion in the American Revolutionary Period," CScR 18/4 (1989) 346-62 • J. MARKOFF and D. REGAN, "The Rise and Fall of Civil Religion: Comparative Perspectives," SocAn 42/4 (1981) 333-52 • M. E. MARTY, A Nation of Behavers (Chicago, 1976) • J. A. MATHISEN, "Twenty Years after Bellah: Whatever Happened to American Civil Religion?" SocAn 50 (Summer 1989) 129-47 • S. E. MEAD, The Nation with the Soul of a Church (New York, 1975) • P. MOJZES, "Socialist Gods and God in Socialism," Dialogue & Alliance 5 (Winter 1991) 24-37 • T. B. MOODIE, The Rise of Afrikanerdom (Berkeley, Calif., 1980) • E. MORAWSKA, "Civil Religion versus State Power in Poland," Church-State Relations: Tensions and Transitions (ed. T. Robbins and R. Robertson; New Brunswick, N.J., 1987) • M. R. MULLINS, "Ideology and Utopianism in Wartime Japan," JJRS 21 (June 1994) 261-80 • J. K. OLUPONA, "Religious Pluralism and Civil Religion in Africa," Dialogue & Alliance 2 (Winter 1988) 41-48 • D. PARKER, "Civil Religion and the God of the Bible," God in Asian Contexts (ed. B. R. Ro and M. C. Albrecht; Taichung, 1988) • R. V. PIERARD, "Civil Religion in European Perspective," FiHi 22 (Fall 1990) 64-70; idem, "Civil Religiosity in a Marxist Land," CScR 22 (December 1992) 116-30 • R. V. PIERARD and R. D. LINDER, Civil Religion and the Presidency (Grand Rapids, 1980) • F. E. REYNOLDS, "Civic Religion and National Community in Thailand," JASt 36 (February 1977) 267-82 • R. L. RICHEY and D. G. JONES, eds., American Civil Religion (New York, 1974) • L. S. ROUNER, ed., Civil Religion and Political Theology (Notre Dame, Ind., 1986) • R. SCHIEDER, Civil Religion. Die religiöse Dimension der politischen Kultur (Gütersloh, 1987) • H. L. SENEVIRATNE, "Continuity of Civil Religion in Sri Lanka," Religion 14 (January 1984) 1-14 • K. A. STEENBRINK, "Towards a Pancasila Society," Exchange 18 (December 1989) 1-28 • R. C. WOOD and J. E. COLLINS, eds., Civil Religion and Transcendent Experience (Macon, Ga., 1988).

RICHARD V. PIERARD

Civil Rights → Human and Civil Rights

Civil Rights Movement

1. Background and Rise
2. High Point and Denouement

1. Background and Rise

The goal of the U.S. civil rights movement of the late 1950s and 1960s was to eliminate legal but unethical racial discrimination in the United States. This discrimination was rooted in the long history of the African American experience in the nation. Africans had been stolen from their own lands and brought to America as slaves as early as 1619. While the greatest concentration of slaves was in the South, → slavery was also allowed in the northern colonies. Despite the egalitarian rhetoric of the revolutionary era, the U.S. War of Independence (1775-83) did not substantially change the plight of the nation's black citizens. Even the Emancipation Proclamation granting freedom to slaves, announced by President Abraham Lincoln in January 1863, in the middle of the Civil War (1861-65), did little to relieve the actual conditions under which African Americans were forced to live. The white planters of the South quickly discovered that they could use and abuse black sharecroppers in almost the same way they previously had their slaves.

Through a combination of physical intimidation (enforced by white supremacist organizations like the Ku Klux Klan), public opinion, and legal action, whites in the South erected a system of so-called Jim Crow social and legal rules that ensured that African Americans remained a pliant, cooperative, and usable people. African Americans were prevented from voting, from receiving a decent education, and from entrance to many "public" facilities, including hotels, restaurants, stores, and rest rooms. A significant minority within the African American community, however, consistently opposed these restrictions. The civil rights movement of the 20th century built upon this prior legacy of resistance.

Throughout the earlier part of the 20th century, → black churches (§1), → labor unions, local "improvement" associations, and several national organizations like the National Association for the Advancement of Colored People (NAACP) had championed the cause. But the civil rights movement, which largely congealed around the figure of Martin Luther → King Jr. (1929-68), brought things together in a new way and radically heightened awareness of America's racial problems.

A number of specific events and developments paved the way for the emergence of the civil rights movement. Two of the most significant were the decision of the U.S. Supreme Court in *Brown v. the Board of Education of Topeka, Kansas* (1954) and the lynching of Emmitt Till in August 1955. *Brown v. the Board of Education* raised black hopes by declaring unconstitutional the "separate but equal" treatment of African Americans in matters of education that had been sanctioned decades earlier in *Plessy v. Ferguson* (1896). The death of Till, a teenager from Chicago visiting southern relatives in Money, Mississippi, reminded African Americans of just how different the standards of justice could be in different parts of the country. Despite the admission that they had abducted Till, the white men accused of his murder were acquitted within a month of the crime, ostensibly because Till's body was "too mangled" for positive identification to be made. Till's mother allowed pictures of the body to be published nationwide in *Jet* magazine, thus heightening interest in the systemic social injustices revealed.

The actual beginning of the civil rights movement, however, is usually associated with the refusal of Rosa Parks on December 1, 1955, to give up her bus seat for a white man in Montgomery, Alabama, as local law required. Parks was subsequently arrested, whereupon the city's black community organized itself into the Montgomery Improvement Association (MIA) and elected as its president Martin Luther King Jr., who just a year before had been appointed minister of the city's Dexter Avenue Baptist Church. A bus boycott organized by the MIA lasted for 12 months and resulted finally in the integration of Montgomery's bus lines on December 21, 1956.

Building upon his success in Montgomery, King organized the Southern Christian Leadership Conference (SCLC) in January of 1957. This organization became the backbone of the movement and guaranteed that the movement would be intimately tied to black church life, especially in the South. Not all black churches, however, supported King and the work of the SCLC. In particular, King met resistance within his own church from Joseph Jackson, the long-time president of the National Baptist Church. But many African Americans from almost every predominantly black denomination supported the movement fully.

The SCLC developed a method of direct-action campaigns designed to unite the black community and to reveal and overturn practices of discrimination in towns and cities across the South. The strategy of King and the SCLC was to publicly challenge laws and other informal practices so that the oppression and latent violence built into those structures would manifest itself in public. The black community would then need to be ready to receive that violence directed against it in a manner that would ultimately raise the guilt level of white southerners to the point where they would be forced to repent and acquiesce in the antidiscriminatory goals of the movement.

This method of social protest obviously required a tremendous amount of self-control and patience on the part of the African American population. While King himself was no gradualist in matters of race — as is evident in his "Letter from a Birmingham Jail" (1963) — he did not expect overnight results. He once said, "The moral arm of the universe is long, but it bends toward justice." To sustain the discipline and patience needed to engage in this kind of activity, the civil rights movement was fortified by constant preaching and singing. The song "We Shall Overcome" became the unofficial theme of the movement.

More than just King and the SCLC were involved in the civil rights movement. Other organizations created during this time included the Student Nonviolent Coordinating Committee (SNCC) and the Mississippi Freedom Democrat Party. The movement was also carried along by several older black organizations like the NAACP and the Congress for Racial Equality (CORE). Even groups formally opposed to the movement, like the Nation of Islam and the Black Panthers, had a positive impact in that they forced the white American population to take seriously the concerns of the civil rights movement out of fear that a more militant black freedom movement would arise if it failed.

2. High Point and Denouement

The high point of the movement came in 1963-65. In May 1963 the Supreme Court declared Birmingham's segregation ordinances unconstitutional. On August 28 King delivered his widely cited "I Have a Dream" speech to an audience of over 200,000 during the March on Washington. One year later, President Lyndon Johnson signed into law the Civil Rights Act, which included stronger provisions for federal enforcement than previous bills, overcoming attempts by southern members of Congress to block the legislation by filibuster. On December 10, 1964, King was awarded the Nobel Peace Prize. And in August 1965 the president signed the Voting Rights Bill, which passed easily in the House and Senate, despite earlier, seemingly strong opposition.

Ironically, these victories also in a certain sense signaled the end of the movement. Legally much had been changed, but socially and culturally much remained the same, and the patience that had previously sustained the movement was slowly giving way to frustration. On August 11, 1965, riots erupted in the Watts district of Los Angeles, lasting six days and leaving 34 people dead, more than 1,000 injured, and property damage estimated at $200 million, all of which became a symbol of this frustration. These tensions only increased in the years following.

A more aggressive, less patient attitude was brewing, one that found its voice during the March against Fear following the shooting of James Meredith just outside Memphis, Tennessee, on June 6, 1966. On the first day of the march Stokely Carmichael of SNCC announced: "The Negro is going to *take* what he deserves from the white man." Later in the march, a new phrase came to prominence. In response to the call "What do we want?" the shout would come back, "Black Power!"

King's message was also changing. He increasingly came to see the nation's racial problems as intricately tied together with the country's involvement in the Viet Nam War and with the most basic structures of the American economic system. At the time of his assassination in Memphis in April 1968, he was organizing a massive Poor People's March on Washington that would clearly transcend racial lines.

While most scholars would properly locate the deepest and most important roots of the civil rights movement within the American black community itself, and especially within the traditions of the black church, King had been influenced to some degree by other forces. In particular, he had learned of Mohandas Gandhi's life and message while studying at Crozer Theological Seminary (Chester, Pa.) from 1948 to 1951; in 1959 he visited India to study Gandhi's methods. At Crozer, King had also been introduced to the ideas and ideals of the → Social Gospel. Both of these models of religious social action affected King's career and, through him, the broader movement.

The legacy of the movement has been enormous. Enacted social protest, for example, is now a staple of the American political scene. Perhaps more significantly, the massive nonviolent movements toward freedom in Eastern Europe, South Africa, and China in the late 1980s were all partly inspired by the model of confrontation, suffering, and social redemption articulated so well by King and others involved in the U.S. civil rights movement.

→ Human and Civil Rights; Racism; Resistance, Right of

Bibliography: L. V. BALDWIN, *There Is a Balm in Gilead: The Cultural Roots of Martin Luther King, Jr.* (Minneapolis, 1991); idem, *To Make the Wounded Whole: The Cultural Legacy of Martin Luther King, Jr.* (Minneapolis, 1992) • T. BRANCH, *Parting the Waters: America in the King Years, 1954-63* (New York, 1988) • J. H. CONE, *Martin and Malcolm and America: A Dream or a Nightmare* (Maryknoll, N.Y., 1991) • *Eyes on the Prize*, pt. 1, *America's Civil Rights Years, 1954-1965;* pt. 2, *America at the Racial Crossroads, 1965-1985* (PBS video; Alexandria, Va., 1986-90) • D. J. GARROW, *Bearing the Cross: Martin Luther King, Jr. and the Southern Christian Leadership Conference* (New York, 1986) • M. L. KING JR., *I Have a Dream: Writings and Speeches That Changed the World* (ed. J. M. Washington, with a foreword by Coretta Scott King; New York, 1986); idem, *Where Do We Go from Here: Chaos or Community?* (Boston, 1967) • D. L. LEWIS, *King: A Biography* (2d ed.; Champaign, Ill., 1978) • H. RAINES, *My Soul Is Rested: The Story of the Civil Rights Movement in the Deep South* (New York, 1977) • H. SITKOFF, *The Struggle for Black Equality, 1954-1980* (New York, 1981).

DOUGLAS JACOBSEN

Civil Service → Conscientious Objection

CLAI → Latin American Council of Churches

CLAR → Latin American Confederation of Religious

Class and Social Stratum

The terms "class" and "social stratum" have many different meanings, deriving from their background in the history of ideas and their specialized sociological use.

Two definitions may be distinguished. In the European tradition a class is a → group of individuals who, at a given point of time in history, are in a similar economic or political position or who discharge similar functions in → society. Classes are social organisms that in certain circumstances can act as units. The boundaries between them are fixed because of differences in → power, prestige, and position in the prevailing system of production. Examples of classes are employers and employees (→ Capitalism; Work), middle class and working class (→ Proletariat), property owners and workers on the land, intellectuals, professionals, and clergy. In such

an understanding, antitheses determine class relations.

A second view sees a class as a society of individuals with similar socially relevant characteristics, which may differ according to the classification used. This view, which equates the class with the social stratum, is dominant in American → sociology. An individual may belong to several social strata, with individual abilities determining the differences. Hence the idea of social mobility (moving from one social stratum to another) is prominent. Relations between the strata are hierarchical (→ Hierarchy 2). There is an upper, a middle, and a lower stratum. → Functionalism is the main schema of theoretical interpretation.

Between these two main uses of the terms lie many others. Stress may be laid on differences in power (ruling class and subject class), or on the various dimensions of socioeconomic, cultural, and political stratification (M. → Weber [1864-1920]), which can change in independent ways. The terms are not always clearly differentiated; thus strata might denote differences within a class (skilled and unskilled workers).

The problem of distinction is not just theoretical but arises from an analysis of industrial and postindustrial society (→ Industrial Society) in which the multiplication of modes of production, the changing of social relations, and the intervention of the → state in economic and social politics bring basic alterations in the conditions of the social structure. New vocations and new classes arise (technicians and managers; → Bureaucracy). Relations in production are being detached from those in the distribution of wealth or prestige as the middle class expands. Furthermore, social changes have occurred with the growth of education and the changed status of → women. The power structure has also changed (note the rise of special-interest lobbies; → Political Parties).

In the → sociology of religion the term "strata" does not have the great importance that it does in Weber. This is because it is affected by → psychology and → anthropology, by the functionalist approach (with stress on terms like "religiosity" and "values"), and by the philosophical abstraction deriving from → Marxism. Strata often have only nominal significance, with no wider concept being attached to the term. Especially in Europe there has been research into the relations between → religion and classes or social strata (e.g., workers, farmers, women, young people), but we have no general theory regarding present relations between class, social stratification, and religion. There have been investigations of the power relations immanent in religious phenomena in some noncapitalist societies; other investigations have focused variously on new religions, social outsiders, power, and social control.

→ Achievement and Competition; Socialism

Bibliography: P. BOURDIEU, "Genèse et structure du champ religieux," *RFS* 12 (1971) 295-334 • R. DAHRENDORF, *Klassen und Klassenkonflikte in der industriellen Gesellschaft* (Stuttgart, 1957) • É. DURKHEIM, *The Division of Labor in Society* (New York, 1985; orig. pub., 1890) • A. GIDDENS, *The Class Structure of the Advanced Societies* (London, 1970) • G. GUIZZARDI, *La religione della crisi* (Milan, 1979) • F. HOUTART, *Religion et modes de production précapitalistes* (Brussels, 1980) • F. A. ISAMBERT, *Christianisme et classe ouvrière* (Paris, 1961) • K. MARX, *Capital* (3 vols.; New York, 1967-85; orig. pub., 1867) • S. OSSOWSKI, *Die Klassenstruktur im sozialen Bewußtsein* (Darmstadt, 1962) • V. PARETO, *Trattato di sociologia generale* (Florence, 1916) • T. PARSONS, "Revised Analytical Approach to the Theory of Social Stratification," *Class, Status, and Power* (ed. R. Bendix and S. M. Lipset; Glencoe, Ill., 1953) • M. W. TUMIN, *Social Stratification* (Englewood Cliffs, N.J., 1967) • M. WEBER, *Economy and Society: An Outline of Interpretive Sociology* (2 vols.; Berkeley, Calif., 1978; orig. pub., 1922).

GUSTAVO GUIZZARDI

Classicism

1. The Term
2. Weimar Classicism
3. Absolutizing Art
4. The Significance of Antiquity
5. Religiosity in Classicism
6. Classicism in the History of Music
7. Classicism in the Plastic Arts

1. The Term

The term "classicism," along with its derivatives, comes from imperial Roman tax law, where the adjective *classicus* assumed the meaning attributed to the substantive *classis* (those belonging to the highest tax bracket). Not until A.D. 165, however, does one encounter this transfer in an established form in Aulus Gellius, who speaks of the *scriptor classicus* (classical writer). For the → Renaissance and its language purists, this designation refers above all to Cicero; for the humanists north of the Alps, it is an author (studied in school) who is considered an authority. The canonization of French dramatists of the 17th century replaced the conceptual aspect of linguistic correctness and educational usefulness with

that of preeminent literary excellence. The early → Enlightenment applies the term normatively to works fulfilling in an exemplary fashion certain rules of genre; since the 18th century, and even more since the 19th, the term refers to the preeminent accomplishments of many national literatures.

The model is French classicism (*classicisme*) around 1660, which even today is viewed as the golden age of French culture and includes the participation of the court of Louis XIV (1643-1715), a strengthened national consciousness, as well as the sensibility of both the nobility and the bourgeoisie. The most esteemed genre at that time was drama. P. Corneille (1606-84) took as his point of departure a heroically idealized view of Rome; his performances addressing activities of court and state, with their (ultimately resolved) conflict between → reason and passion, greatness and self-limitation, heightened the feeling of self among his contemporaries. J. Racine (1639-99), influenced by Euripides, lent to the emotional turmoil of his figures — figures torn between honor and → love, desire and renunciation — a distanced eloquence coupled with the clarity of understanding. These two formulated the ideals of their epoch: the *grande âme* of the *honnête homme,* whom J.-B. Molière (1622-73) characterized and unmasked in his own way by elevating both the farce and the impromptu play into acceptable genres of the comedy of types and by sparing no stratum of society from his penchant for criticism.

English classicism, after the return of the Stuarts in 1660, was influenced by France. Hence it is not W. Shakespeare (1564-1616), whom Voltaire (1694-1778) rejected on the basis of a chaotic dramaturgy and Renaissance-like hyperbole, but rather A. Pope (1688-1744), J. Addison (1672-1719), and R. Steele (1672-1729) whom English literary criticism views as the representatives of its classicism: These authors fulfilled the demands of traditional rules, of exemplary control of form, and of the erudite concluding effect; as philosophizing enlighteners, they popularized the new → worldview of the early 18th century in its orientation toward the here and now.

2. Weimar Classicism

The term "classicism" can indicate epochs, values, and style. Until G. W. F. Hegel (1770-1831; → Hegelianism), classicism and Greek culture (→ Hellenism) were identical. Greek art possessed normative value for J. J. Winckelmann (1717-68), which J. G. → Herder (1744-1803) then historicized. That which is classical is thus the highest fulfillment of a stylistic ideal within a circumscribed time period; it is a historical category, but it also represents a quality of timeless features. The expression "Weimar classicism" refers (all too exclusively) to the literary and literary-theoretical works that emerged during the period of friendship between J. W. von Goethe (1749-1832) and F. von Schiller (1759-1805) in the years 1794-1805. The characteristics of this epoch include the productive appropriation of the artistic ideal of antiquity, the aestheticizing (→ Aesthetics) of reality, and — something commencing already in the early Enlightenment — an anthropocentric interpretation of the world. The aesthetic creed insists on the autonomy of art; literary works should demonstrate human constants and should be transparent with regard to what is typical, something Goethe found in → nature, and Schiller in history. The will to legislation shaped by poetics arises from an ethos focusing on proportion, equipoise, and integration into the societal whole.

In German classicism, which is temporally bound like every other epoch, the idea of → humanity and of the well-rounded personality finds its most appropriate artistic form. Its obliging themes are the "suspension" of unconditional passion in the conditional (determinative) *ordo*, and the liberation of the ideal in the individual (→ Idealism; Individualism), who founders tragically on value-blind reality. Classicism brings the Enlightenment to an end; with it, the European reception of antiquity and the "aesthetic empire of the German nation" come to an end. The designation "German classicism," used in isolated instances during Goethe's own lifetime, established itself only considerably later.

3. Absolutizing Art

Art now acquires hitherto unknown significance and dignity. It seeks to unite and address the entire spectrum of human sensibility, including thought, feeling, and will. F. G. Klopstock (1724-1803) and the Sturm und Drang period mark the beginning of the subjective expression of feeling, an expression that during the period of classicism does, however, once again take the French *haute tragédie* and genre prescriptions as its point of orientation. The new relationship with art demands a new understanding of form. C. M. Wieland (1733-1813), Goethe, and Schiller insist on the form of the literary work, which lends the appropriate dignity to content; and they insist on the forms of social → education and conduct, which any → society (after 1789) needs in times of distress. It is through → norms of artistic portrayal that one seeks to counter abnormal tendencies.

Goethe's classical style, itself the result of his journey to Italy, derives from his "pure," object-related manner of perception. Since art is "a second nature,"

its objectivity should correspond to nature's own law-bound activity. Goethe seeks "that which endures in what changes," the abiding law within fleeting appearances. Hence both as a poet and as a researcher, he focuses on the universal and typical, in which what is unique and particular is grounded.

Schiller's contribution to Weimar classicism is concentrated in his dramas and in his theory of moral-aesthetic reconciliation in the face of the self-estrangement and alienation of the modern person. Since a return to antiquity or to nature itself is blocked, it is through the medium of art that human totality and a correspondence with social reality (which itself is to be renewed) is to be established. Schiller gives both the "naive" element of antiquity and the "sentimental" element of modernity their proper due, legitimizing in the process his own relationship with reality and his own methodology over against Goethe's "Greek spirit."

4. The Significance of Antiquity

A new Renaissance began with Winckelmann, this time in Germany; antiquity became the standard for art and for true life. The apparent lightness of Greek existence, the Apollonian clarity, and the effortless certainty of its artistic creations fascinated those who had to live in a later culture. The Greek plastic arts provided a perfect model of Roman beauty; Greek poetry addressed the fundamental conflicts of the individual with the social environment; and the → myth preserved the models (such as Prometheus or Narcissus) that would remain valid, even for the cultural understanding of later times. With German classicism, the European reception of antiquity comes to an end in a pronounced condition of elective affinity.

5. Religiosity in Classicism

Whereas the Sturm und Drang period surrendered itself to → subjectivism that negated all boundaries, classicism posited dignity and proportion as well as the internally unified human being who is both reconciled with nature and active in → everyday life. A confession to the here and now is everywhere discernible. Life that reflects the radiance of art contains its → meaning and goal within itself; a person may not be a means to an end, but rather only the end or goal itself; self-education comes to completion in a humane disposition and has no need of revealed religion (→ Revelation). Classicism no longer grants unlimited → freedom; rather, it demands free self-limitation. The notion of renunciation, which already characterizes Goethe's early classicism, ethically affirms finitude and rejects the notion, inherent in the Christian religion, of → sin and → evil.

The classicists participated, each in his own way, in the process of → secularization of the 18th century: Goethe with his confession to God-nature, Schiller in his propagation of the religion of art. The Enlightenment had raised doubts concerning the belief in revelation as well as the deity of Christ (→ Christology; Trinity). In his play *Iphigenie auf Tauris,* Goethe countered the generational curse (inherited, original sin) with the notion of the inherited → virtue of the pure will, and with the → hope that human "failings" could be atoned for through humanity alone. Schiller's characters are inclined to cast off their need for redemption (→ Soteriology) along with the "duplicity" of human nature itself, duplicity that must be overcome. Like other representatives of idealism, they revered the teachings of Christ without being able to accept the doctrine of Christ.

In the meantime, Goethe elsewhere counters the de-Christianization or secularization of ecclesiastical-confessional → dogmas (such as original sin or the mediating function of Christ) with the sacralizing of life-affirming Eros, which can also assume features of Agape. Schiller's own idea of fate, which bears the physiognomy of Nemesis, ultimately serves his unique idea of theodicy, one directed toward → reconciliation in the beyond, namely, the → justification of the demise of existence through the emergence of the idea.

Except for Herder, who was himself a cleric, the representatives of the German classical epoch viewed with considerable reserve the influential orthodox theology of their own time, even though they themselves had grown up in a Protestant environment and were certainly well acquainted with the Bible. G. E. Lessing (1729-81) attacked literalist → dogmatism; for the sake of religion, Schiller rejected confessionally fixed faith. Only the *Speeches* of F. D. E. → Schleiermacher (1768-1834), a friend of the early Romantic school, again reached the "cultured" among his contemporaries, who were actually further removed from the official church than from Christianity (→ Schleiermacher's Theology).

6. Classicism in the History of Music
Here the classification of epochs largely follows the literary model. Although the term "classical" is not entirely satisfactory in the history of music either, general consensus holds that the incomparable contributions to musical culture made by F. J. Haydn (1732-1809), W. A. Mozart (1756-91), and L. van Beethoven (1770-1827) represent "Viennese classi-

cism." Freed from all material elements, from content and agenda, around 1770 the universal language of music attained its own individual expression of the experienced or yearned-for harmony of the world totality, an expression subsuming all tension and contradiction.

7. Classicism in the Plastic Arts
In German, the concept of classicism familiar in other countries serves largely as a term applied within the history of art: As early as the Augustan period, which in turn influenced Renaissance art (A. Palladio [1508-80]), the classical architecture of Greece became the model for "classicists" as a result of strict and intentional imitation that obscures all historical differences and opposition between imitation and new creation. In modern architecture, classicism (also called neoclassicism) refers primarily to the particular stylistic inclination that through Winckelmann drew on the overpowering Greek ideal of form. After approximately 1770, this emphasis became the successor to the → baroque and the rococo, corresponding as it did to the → rationalism of the age with its strict intellectual predispositions and its imperial gestures (e.g., of the Napoleonic era). German representatives include F. W. von Erdmannsdorff (1736-1800) and K. F. Schinkel (1781-1841), the latter of whom closely approximated the ancient models without surrendering himself entirely to them.

The Italian A. Canova (1757-1822) and the Dane B. Thorvaldsen (1768/70-1844), and in Germany J. G. Schadow (1764-1850), C. D. Rauch (1777-1857), and J. H. von Dannecker (1758-1841) all created sculptures in the style of an overly refined classicism.

In painting, especially in France (J.-L. David [1748-1825] and J. A. D. Ingres [1780-1867]), the classical disposition toward form was expressed with elements of heroism and monumentality, mythology, and allegory.

The term "classicism" with reference to the adoption of Greek models (or "classicist") is conceptually less vague than that of "classical" as applied to particular epochs of the arts at large, since the latter concentrates in a single term a wide variety of individual works, discontinuous developments, and diverging artistic tendencies (a simultaneity of different elements) within a single epoch.

Bibliography: W. H. BRUFORD, *Die gesellschaftlichen Grundlagen der Goethezeit* (Weimar, 1936) • H. O. BURGER, ed., *Begriffsbestimmung der Klassik und des Klassischen* (Darmstadt, 1972) • R. GRIMM and J. HER-

MAND, eds., *Die Klassik-Legende* (Frankfurt, 1971) • H. A. KORFF, *Geist der Goethezeit* (vol. 2; Leipzig, 1930) • V. LANGE, *Das klassische Zeitalter der deutschen Literatur, 1740-1815* (Munich, 1983) • T. J. REED, *The Classical Center: Goethe and Weimar, 1775-1832* (New York, 1986) • W. REHM, *Griechentum und Goethezeit* (Leipzig, 1936) • G. SCHULZ, *Die deutsche Literatur zwischen Französischer Revolution und Restauration* (vol. 1; Munich, 1983) • F. STRICH, *Klassik und Romantik oder Vollendung und Unendlichkeit* (Munich, 1922) • R. WELLEK, "The Term and Concept of Classicism in Literary History," *Aspects of the Eighteenth Century* (ed. E. R. Wasserman; Baltimore, 1965) 105-20 • E. M. WILKINSON and L. A. WILLOUGHBY, "Missing Links; or, Whatever Happened to Weimar Classicism?" *Erfahrung und Überlieferung* (Cardiff, 1974).

WERNER KELLER

Clergy and Laity

1. Historical Data
2. Roman Catholic, Orthodox, and Anglican Views
3. Reformation Understanding
4. New Ideas

1. Historical Data

The NT *laos* (people) is the whole priestly people of the community of believers in Christ (Luke 1:17; 1 Pet. 2:10; Heb. 4:9). The term *klēros* (lot, Matt. 27:35) denotes the special ministry (Acts 1:17, 26, etc.) that is at work in and for this community according to God's gracious gift (cf. 1 Cor. 12:4).

In the ministries of the → early church, with the sometimes tense relation between → charisma and office involving development from the functional to the institutional, there gradually arose a differentiation into *clergy* as the officeholders and the *laity* as the rest, who had no spiritual office. By the third century a hierarchical priesthood had developed. With the consolidation of church structures, the hierarchical structure, the special qualifications and privileges of the ministry, the differences in lifestyle and dress, and the general antithesis between the secular and the spiritual, "ordinary" church members now came to be seen as an unqualified mass. Theological reasons were later found for the distinction into two classes (e.g., in the Decretum Gratiani, ca. 1140). For example, it was seen as a copy of the divine order. It was also given canonical sanction, though not without some criticism (→ Hierarchy).

2. Roman Catholic, Orthodox, and Anglican Views

2.1. On the Roman Catholic view, the people of God represent a structured fellowship (→ Church 3.2). *Lumen gentium (LG),* the dogmatic constitution on the church drawn up at → Vatican II, differentiates between (1) the various spiritual gifts and (2) power and authority. On the one hand is the priesthood of hierarchical ministry, which has the task of leading the people of God and presenting the sacrifice of Christ in the Eucharist (*LG* 10.2; 28). On the other hand are believers who are not ordained, who differ from ordained priests "essentially and not only in degree"; these are called the laity (10.2; 31.1). Clergy are qualified by their ordination to be deacons, priests, or bishops and are dedicated to the sacred ministry by special election. The laity have a secular character and are charged with seeking God's kingdom in temporal things (31.2; *Apostolicam actuositatem* 2; → Lay Apostolate). The essential difference between clergy and laity, however, must not obscure the "true equality between all with regard to the dignity and to the activity which is common to all the faithful in the building up of the Body of Christ" (*LG* 32.3).

The 1983 CIC views both clergy and laity as sharing in different ways in the priestly, prophetic, and kingly → office of Christ (can. 204.1), though the special position of ministers, called clergy in canon law, rests on divine direction (207.1). In fellowships of evangelical counsels (e.g., in → orders), both clergy and laity can serve the saving mission of the church (207.2). Church law lays down rights and duties for both laity (224ff.) and clergy (273ff.). Special duties for the clergy include → obedience to the → pope and → bishop (273) and → celibacy (277), although the pope can grant → dispensation (291), exceptions for permanent deacons who are already married (1037). The three-tiered → sacrament of → ordination (deacon, priest, bishop) qualifies clergy for the corresponding ministries. Only a baptized man (→ Men) can validly receive ordination. → Women are not allowed to become clergy (1024), demands for which the magisterium continues to resist. When degraded (→ Laicization), clergy may no longer exercise the authority that they have indelibly by ordination (*character indelebilis,* can. 1008). They are permitted to hear confession, however, where there is danger of death (can. 976; → Penitence).

→ Church government is in the hands of the clergy alone, though the laity participate (129 and 228). At → worship, male laity may serve as → lectors or acolytes, and women may also undertake certain tasks when the need arises (e.g., because of the absence of a priest, can. 230). The laity may act as ecclesiastical judges (1421.2), as attorneys (either "the promoter of justice" or "the defender of the bond"; 1435), as administrators of funds (494 and 1282), and as advisers. The bishop can invite them to the diocesan synod (463.2). It is doubtful, however, whether such roles are enough to implement fully the vision of Vatican II.

2.2. In the → Orthodox Church the distinction between clergy and laity is one of degree and function, not one of kind. The union of the two — the fullness *(plērōma)* of the church — is essential. The distinction is occasioned by ordination, which gives deacons and priests a special place in the hierarchically structured organism of the → church (§3.1) and lays upon them special tasks in the unity of the one body of Christ (celebrating the → sacraments and cultus and → pastoral care). The function of the laity in the church's work of sanctification involves active participation in the → liturgy and in the discharge of the sacraments, for which their presence is essential. The laity also have a part in the church's teaching office, which is not the task of the clergy alone, and in passing on church teaching (e.g., in theological schools and seminaries; → Catechesis; Lay Preaching).

The distinction and unity of clergy and laity may be seen in the administrative structure of the church and its leadership. There are lay representatives at the elections of bishops, at synods, on boards and committees, in legislative and judicial proceedings, and in the handling of → church finances. According to the Orthodox tradition, the body of the church itself — the people — is the guardian of orthodoxy.

2.3. In the → Anglican Communion there is a distinction between the clergy as bearers of holy orders and the laity. The latter, however, have specific tasks as lay officers, including those of churchwarden, lay reader, vestry member, council member, synod representative, and diocesan chancellor.

3. Reformation Understanding

M. → Luther (1483-1546) abolished the theological distinction between clergy and laity with his doctrine of the priesthood of all believers. In the exercise of the common priestly privilege of ministering the Word and sacraments, however, he demanded common assent and therefore a specifically called and ordained ministry. As time passed, the earlier emphasis on the freedom of the adult congregation yielded to stress on the significance of the preaching office (→ Pastor, Pastorate). In the Lutheran confessions the universal priesthood leaves no place for a clergy but only for the spiritual office of church ministers.

Reference is made to the laity only in connection with their right to the cup (Augs. Conf. 22) and their authority to give absolution (→ Melanchthon, *Treatise* 67).

According to Reformed teaching, the various offices are rooted in the share of every Christian in Christ's gifts and treasures, which are to be used for the profit and → salvation of other members of Christ's body (→ Heidelberg Catechism, q. 55). In Reformed churches there are not only pastors but also ruling → elders, deacons, and doctors, who supplement the → preaching catechetically and by theological inquiry. In the ministry of → prophets the Wesel Assembly of 1569 found a lay ministry of the Word that augments the (ordained) preaching ministry.

The → church orders of Presbyterian and → Methodist churches (→ Reformed and Presbyterian Churches) eased the earlier distinction of clergy and laity by giving the laity many important tasks of spiritual ministry. The → Barmen Declaration found different ministries within the community of brothers (and sisters), but these are not for rule but for service to the whole community. In a duality of office and community, ministers are leaders (M. Honecker), but the laity can and must supplement what they do with their own specific gifts. All the proclamation of the ministry awaits their Amen (1 Cor. 14:16) and is exposed to their judgment. In the → church struggle (1933-45) the → Confessing Church created the office of voluntary lay preacher to care for congregations left without pastors, and a new ministry of preaching aides developed that allowed the laity to have a share in the ministry of preaching.

Preaching dialogue has also established itself, which helps to prevent the traditional concept of clergy and laity, which has semiconsciously remained in Protestantism, from hardening unwittingly into an antithesis between expert theologians and a less competent laity. The Kirchentag movement, as a → lay movement, has provided a platform for common service to the church and the public. The Lima texts (→ Ecumenical Movement) set the threefold ordained ministry of bishops, presbyters, and deacons (→ Ordination) within the calling of the whole people of God, thus helping to overcome different understandings of the ordained ministry.

4. New Ideas

In contrast to its theological basis, Protestant church law as it is practiced still differentiates somewhat between what we might call the spiritual estate and the secular estate, distinguishing those who are authorized by ordination to proclaim the Word and administer the sacraments from other members of the congregation who have a ministry in the world. In virtue of their spiritual ministry, the ordained have rights and duties that are for the most part spelled out in the terms of their employment as pastors. The danger arises, however, that ordination to a ministry of Word and sacrament will lead to an unevangelical cleavage of the congregation into clergy and laity.

Today the authorization that ordination gives for discharge of the ministry — misunderstood in part as "right of the spiritual estate" — is viewed as open equally to both men and women. It can be relinquished and lost by withdrawal from the church, renunciation, or church discipline; or with a change in vocation, it may become a nonpaid ministry. In presbyteries and synods and on church boards, theologians and nontheologians work together on equal terms. According to the rules of many synods, the latter must constitute the majority. Nontheologians may be entrusted with an honorary ministry of the Word as lay readers and preachers.

As resources dwindle, great numbers of younger, theologically trained ministers have reopened an issue that was discussed earlier in the context of church reform and → mission, namely, that of a part-time, nonstipendiary, but fully ordained ministry in cooperation with full-time pastors. These factors all go to show how unsuitable the terms "clergy" and "laity" are from a Protestant standpoint and how necessary it is to overcome the antithesis both in church law and in congregational consciousness. This can be done only as it is seen that the many spiritual gifts in a mature Christian congregation are of equal value.

→ Church Law

Bibliography: On 1: A. Faivre, The Emergence of the Laity in the Early Church (New York, 1984) • W. Kreck, Grundfragen der Ekklesiologie (Munich, 1981) • U. Kühn, Kirche (Gütersloh, 1980) • H. Küng, The Church (New York, 1967) • J. Moltmann, The Church in the Power of the Spirit (New York, 1977) • G. Rau et al., eds., Das Recht der Kirche, vol. 2, Zur Geschichte des Kirchenrechts (Gütersloh, 1995).

On 2: W. Aymans, Kanonisches Recht (Paderborn, 1991) 1.385-502 • Convocations of Canterbury and York, The Canons of the Church of England (London, 1969) • F. Heiner, Katholisches Kirchenrecht (6th ed.; Paderborn, 1912) 1.126-388 • J. Listl et al., eds., Handbuch des katholischen Kirchenrechts (Regensburg, 1983) 171-238 • E. G. Moore and T. Briden, Moore's Introduction to English Canon Law (London, 1967; 2d ed., 1985) • K. Mörsdorf, Lehrbuch des Kirchenrechts auf Grund des Codex Iuris Canonici (7th ed.; Paderborn, 1953) 1.262-542 • P. Neuner, Der Laien und das Gottesvolk (Frankfurt, 1988) • A. Rajsp, "Priester" und "Laien." Ein neues Verständnis (Düsseldorf, 1982) • J. Roloff and R. P. C. Hanson, "Amt / Ämter / Amtsverständnis IV-V," TRE 2.509-52 (bibliography) • E. Schillebeeckx, Christliche Identität und kirchliches Amt (Düsseldorf, 1985).

On 3: F. E. Anhelm, "Laie," ÖL 734-37 (bibliography) • A. Burgsmüller, ed., Kirche als "Gemeinde von Brüdern" (Barmen III) (2 vols.; Gütersloh, 1980-81) • H. Dombois, Das Recht der Gnade, vol. 3, Ökumenisches Kirchenrecht (Bielefeld, 1983) 396-408 (on Lima and Accra) • H. Fagerberg, "Amt / Ämter / Amtsverständnis VI," TRE 2.552-74 • M. Honecker, Kirche als Gestalt und Ereignis (1963) • A. Stein, Evangelische Laienpredigt (Göttingen, 1972).

On 4: H. Frost, Strukturprobleme evangelischer Kirchenverfassung (Göttingen, 1972) • C. H. Ratschow, "Amt / Ämter / Amtsverständnis VIII," TRE 2.593-622 (bibliography) • A. Stein, Evangelisches Kirchenrecht (3d ed.; Neuwied, 1992) bibliography; idem, "Ordination," Das Recht der Kirche, vol. 3, Zur Praxis des Kirchenrechts (ed. G. Rau et al.; Gütersloh, 1994) 2.1.73-117.

ALBERT STEIN

Clinical Pastoral Education

Clinical Pastoral Education (CPE) is professional education for ministry that brings theological students and ministers into supervised encounter with "living human documents" in order to develop their pastoral → identity, interpersonal competence, and spirituality. Training is given also in pastoral assessment, interprofessional collaboration, group leadership, → pastoral care and → counseling, and pastoral theological reflection.

Appearing in the 1920s, CPE began in a search for religious meaning in the personal crises requiring hospitalization and for principles of social engineering relevant to urban problems of → poverty and → family disintegration. CPE began in a mental hospital (1925), a general hospital (1930), and a cluster of social service agencies (1927).

The founders — Anton T. Boisen of Worcester, Massachusetts; William S. Keller, M.D., of Cincinnati, Ohio; and Richard C. Cabot, M.D., of Boston — adapted the methods of professional education in psychiatry, social work, and medicine, respectively. Organizations fostering CPE as an educational innovation for theological students and ministers were formed in Boston in 1930 (the Council for the Clinical Training of Theological Students), and in Cincinnati in 1927 (the Summer School in Social Service for Theological Students and Junior Clergy).

During the 1930s Helen Flanders Dunbar, M.D., and Seward Hiltner, representing the Council for Clinical Training, established a primary identity with theological education and ecumenical Christianity. Chaplain supervisors such as Russell L. Dicks developed new methods, particularly a method of conversational transcription he called the "verbatim." Others such as Carroll Wise refined the case-study methods of medicine and social work as a tool of pastoral assessment and theological reflection. A personal difference between Dunbar and A. Philip Guiles, later a professor at Andover Newton Theological Seminary, triggered the move of the Council for Clinical Training to New York City. A new organization, the New England Theological Schools Committee on Clinical Training, was formed to promote programs in the Boston area. In 1944 the group incorporated as the Institute of Pastoral Care.

Supervisors of the three groups, seminary deans and presidents, and representatives of the Federal Council of Churches met in Pittsburgh, Pennsylvania, in 1944 for the first National Conference of Clinical Pastoral Training. This event defined the goals and methods of CPE with enough consensus to set the parameters within which CPE developed during the next several decades. Then, as now, the heart of CPE was supervised encounter with "living human documents."

Agreement on standards for CPE in 1953 sustained a thrust toward organizational unity. A final merger of the Council for Clinical Training, the Institute of Pastoral Care, and two denominationally identified groups — the Lutheran Advisory Council on Pastoral Care and the Southern Baptist Association for CPE (renamed the Association for Clinical Pastoral Education) — did not occur until November 17, 1967.

Tension between the needs and values of seminaries and the clinical settings in which CPE occurs has shaped the enterprise throughout its history. At every juncture, however, CPE has identified itself as a part of theological education. CPE offers a method of interpreting human → experience, not a theological construction. The method begins within a given theological framework, examines specific ministry events or cases descriptively, enters into dialogue with the appropriate behavioral science information and the minister's own intuitive wisdom, engages in theological reflection, and then forms a pastoral assessment and plan for ministry.

At the core of CPE is the process of supervision.

Program standards, accreditation of training centers, and the certification of practitioners all revolve around the supervisory process. CPE supervision aims to foster benefit in two directions: competence in ministries to deeply troubled persons, and psychosocial and spiritual growth in those being supervised.

CPE is international in scope. Although begun in North America — the United States in the 1920s and soon thereafter in Canada — CPE took root in the years after World War II in the United Kingdom and northern Europe as well as in Southeast Asia, including New Zealand and Australia, and in Africa and South America.

International dialogue began formally in 1964. Paul Tournier and Charles Stewart sponsored a conference entitled "New Trends in Pastoral Theology" in Geneva, Switzerland. Charles Stewart and Thomas Klink initiated a second conference in 1966 at Hyde Park/Dreibergen, Netherlands. Both conferences brought together pastors with clinical experience from the United States and Dutch pastors who had trained with Chaplain Wiebe Zilstra and Heije Faber. In 1968 an international seminar was held in London under the title "New Trends in Clinical Theology and Pastoral Counseling." A series of international conferences followed with a focus on the development of CPE in Europe. European, British, and American leaders of CPE met in Arnoldsheim, West Germany (1972); Rüschlikon, Switzerland (1975); Eisenach, East Germany (1977); and Lublin, Poland (1981). A European conference continued to meet every four years, alternating with international congresses.

Beginning in 1978, an International Committee on Pastoral Care and Counseling was formed to plan an international congress. It continues to function in behalf of international encounter at professional conferences every four years. International congresses have occurred in Edinburgh, Scotland (1979), San Francisco, California (1983), Melbourne, Australia (1987), Noordwijkerhout, Netherlands (1991), and Toronto, Canada (1995). Whereas early conferences involved approximately 70 men and women, mainly from Europe and the United States, the later congresses have been truly international, with several hundred attending from all continents.

Bibliography: W. BECHER et al., eds., *Wagnis der Freiheit* (Göttingen, 1981) • S. HILTNER, *Preface to Pastoral Theology* (Nashville, 1958) • "International Conferences of Pastoral Care and Counseling," *JPC* 37 (1983) 122-26 • K. POHLY, *Transforming the Rough Places: The Ministry of Supervision* (Dayton, Ohio, 1993) • R. POWELL, *CPE: Fifty Years of Learning* (Atlanta, 1975) • J. SCHAFENBERG, "Pastoralpsychologische Aus- und Fortbildung," *Die*

Psychologie des 20. Jahrhunderts (vol. 15; Zurich, 1979) 385ff. • D. A. Schön, *Educating the Reflective Practitioner* (San Francisco, 1987) • E. Thornton, *Professional Education for Ministry: A History of Clinical Pastoral Education* (Nashville, 1970).

Edward E. Thornton

Cluny, Order of

1. The Benedictine monastery of Cluny, northwest of Mâcon in Burgundy, was founded in 910 by Duke William III of Aquitaine. In the 10th and 11th centuries it became the center of a reforming movement that began as a return to the original goals of → monasticism (i.e., renunciation of the world in anticipation of the life of paradise in adoration and praise). In the course of time, it radically changed the Christian world in the West.

2. The basis of the reform was the demand for a stricter following of the → Benedictine Rule in the tradition of Benedict of Aniane (d. 821). This demand was made in different places in the declining Carolingian kingdom (e.g., in Gorze, Lorraine). Cluny, however, occupied a special position in virtue of its freedom from both secular and religious control, which was established by its founding charter. Kings, counts, and → bishops alike were not allowed to interfere in the affairs of the monastery, which was placed under the direct protection of the pope (the → exemption was officially confirmed only in 998/99). The founder renounced all rights at its establishment.

The first abbot, Berno of Baume (910-27), was appointed by the founder, but the community itself was to elect his successor. Being independent of all external influences, which might at times include the church's own law, Cluny could live out its monastic ideals and be free for → prayer, intercession, commemoration of the dead, and acts of Christian love. The abbot thus had political freedom, which, favored by its situation outside the empire, gave Cluny far-reaching political significance, especially with the creation of associated houses.

3. The rise of Cluny began under the next abbot, Odo (927-42). By harking back to early monastic traditions, he laid the foundations for the reform of monastic life and indeed all Christian life (affecting, e.g., chivalry and the Peace of God movement). He also showed himself to be a zealous reformer. In 931 he received from the pope the privilege of putting under Cluny any monasteries that wanted to follow his reforms. This initiated a fast-growing association of monasteries.

Under three abbots who all enjoyed a lengthy tenure — Majolus (ca. 954-94), Odilo (994-1048), and Hugo (1049-1109) — the Cluniac order spread throughout western Europe and finally developed into a union of some 1,200 monasteries, abbacies, and priories that in different ways were dependent on the great abbot of Cluny. (In the empire there arose at the end of the 11th cent. the related but independent reforming center of Hirsau.) There thus developed a monastic church *(Cluniacensis ecclesia)* that was devoted to the papacy and that helped to stimulate the papal reform of the church in the 11th century (involving the battle against simony and the marriage of the clergy; → Pope, Papacy).

4. The development of Cluny is reflected in its buildings. Cluny I was built under abbot Berno (926-27) and seems to have had just one nave. Cluny II was the most influential new church structure (consecrated 981). It had three naves, and a special feature was the narthex for the assembling of processions. Under "king" Odilo, marble replaced wood. The zenith of the power of Cluny came to expression in the gigantic five-naved church begun by Hugo (1088) and consecrated in 1130 (Cluny III). This church was 187 m. long and 30 m. high (614 ft. × 98 ft.) in the middle nave, which made it the largest of all churches in the West, a distinction it long enjoyed. Its completion came in the time of the last great abbot, Peter the Venerable (1122-56), who, because of the great rise in Cluny's power and pomp, had to contend with the strong criticism of the → Cistercians.

5. The future of monasticism belonged to the type of order fashioned by the Cistercians. In the 13th century Cluny lost its exemption and came under the powerful influence of the French crown. As a result, it increasingly lost its importance. In 1567-70 Cluny was plundered by the Huguenots. The end came with the French Revolution, as the monastery was dissolved in 1790 and the buildings smashed. Today only a few ruins remain.

Bibliography: E. Badstübner, *Kirchen der Mönche. Die Baukunst der Reformorden im Mittelalter* (Berlin, 1980) • "Cluny, Cluniacs," *ODCC* 369 • K. J. Conant, *Cluny. Les églises et la maison du chef d'ordre* (Mâcon, 1968) • H. E. J. Cowdrey, *The Cluniacs and the Gregorian Reform* (Oxford, 1970) • K. S. Frank, "Cluny," *TRE* 8.126-32 (bibliography) • K. Hallinger, *Gorze-Kluny. Studien zu den monastischen Lebensformen und Gegensätzen im*

Hochmittelalter (2 vols.; Bonn, 1950-51; 2d ed., Graz, 1971) • N. HUNT, *Cluny under St. Hugh, 1049-1109* (Notre Dame, Ind., 1968); idem, comp., *Cluniac Monasticism in the Central Middle Ages* (Hamden, Conn., 1971) • J. WOLLASCH, *Mönchtum des Mittelalters zwischen Kirche und Welt* (Munich, 1973); idem, ed., *Cluny im 10. und 11. Jahrhundert* (Göttingen, 1967) sources.

WOLFGANG A. BIENERT

Codex Iuris Canonici

1. Early History
2. Contents
3. Relation to Non-Catholics
4. Ecumenical Significance

The Codex Iuris Canonici (CIC, Code of canon law) was first published on May 27, 1917, and went in effect the following year, on May 19, 1918. Following Vatican I, it codified previous church law for the first time and, in principle, claimed validity for all baptized Christians (see 3). In 1983 it was replaced by a new book of Roman Catholic law that is also called CIC and is meant for the Latin church, that is, the Western church as distinct from the Eastern. Law for the Eastern churches in communion with Rome is contained in a special code meant for them, called the Codex Canonum Ecclesiarum Orientalium (CCEO, Code of canon law of the Oriental Church), which was promulgated in 1990.

1. Early History
With the calling of → Vatican II on January 25, 1959, Pope → John XXIII (1958-63) had in mind an *aggiornamento* (adjustment, updating) of the CIC of 1917. This revision was to go hand in hand with the council and crown its work. A commission of cardinals was appointed in March 1963 to oversee the task. Pope Paul VI (1963-78) named consultants from many different nations in April 1964.

The first president of the commission was Cardinal Pietro Ciriaci, who died in December 1966. He was followed by Archbishop (later Cardinal) Pericle Felici, who had been secretary of Vatican II. When Cardinal Felici died in March 1982, the first secretary of the commission, Archbishop Rosalio I. Castillo Lara, was appointed. Because of his services, the name of Cardinal Felici is linked with the CIC of 1983, as that of Cardinal and State Secretary Pietro Gasparri (d. 1934) is with the 1917 CIC.

The question soon arose whether a basic law for the whole → Roman Catholic Church *(lex ecclesiae fundamentalis)* should precede that for the Latin church and that for Eastern churches in communion with Rome. This proposal ran into serious criticism on ecumenical grounds when drafts were made public. Until shortly before the publication of CIC, it was doubtful whether a basic law would be put into force along with the code. Since a number of the statements that had been formulated for it were included in the 1983 CIC (e.g., on the Petrine office and the basic rights of Christians) and in the CCEO, such a basic law for the whole church was no longer necessary.

The work of reforming the church's canon law rested on the 1917 CIC and the basic findings of Vatican II. The commission was appointed to scrutinize *(recognoscere)* the church's law. Its main task was to bring the basic decisions and directions of Vatican II into the new code. In doing so, it worked out principles that the Synod of Bishops had approved on the basis of positions adopted in October 1967 at its first assembly. The proposals *(schemata)* for the individual books of the code were then sent to the episcopal conferences and the curia, and after 1973, by request of the pope, to the universities, theological faculties (→ Theological Education), and generals of orders, so that these could make known their views. The Synod of Bishops, a gathering of bishops from the worldwide church that Vatican II had called for and that Pope Paul VI chartered in 1965, not only kept itself abreast of the work but expressed its own views on fundamental questions. The bulletin *Communicationes*, which had been started for the purpose in 1969, issued reports on the state of the various subcommissions that had now been initiated, as did the *Nuntia* for the CCEO.

In October 1981, some months before his death, Cardinal Felici presented the final draft of the new code to Pope John Paul II. After further deliberations and some changes, the 1983 CIC was promulgated by the apostolic constitution *Sacrae disciplinae leges* on January 25, 1983, which was 24 years after the calling of Vatican II. It came into force on November 27, 1983 — the beginning of the liturgical year, the first Sunday of Advent.

Translations were made for the various national churches, but only the Latin text is considered the authentic text. In 1984 the Pontifical Commission for the Authentic Interpretation of the Code of Canon Law was established for giving authentic interpretations of the 1983 CIC. In 1988 its name was changed to the Pontifical Council for the Interpretation of Legislative Texts, and its functions correspondingly broadened. In 1991 its oversight was extended to include also the CCEO.

2. Contents

The Latin code no longer follows the division into five books of classical Roman law, as the 1917 CIC had done, but contains seven books, which makes possible a better systematization.

Book 1 ("General Norms," cans. 1-203) contains general statements about the sphere of validity (1), the relation to previous law (5-6) and to special law (3, regarding concordats), acquired rights (4), the law itself, its coming into effect, its interpretation, and its obligatoriness. It is made clear that purely ecclesiastical laws apply only to those baptized in the Roman Catholic Church or received into it (11). This is worth noting as compared with the 1917 CIC.

Statements then follow about custom and its power to create law (23-28); about decrees and instructions and their binding force (29-34); about administrative acts and individual decrees, rescripts, privileges, and → dispensations (35-93); and about natural and legal persons (96-123). As regards natural persons, the main point is that they can have rights and duties in the church only when they are in full fellowship with it. The distinction between *communio plena* and *non plena* in relation to other churches and church communions and their members gives clear evidence of the influence of Vatican II. Book 1 also contains statements about legally significant acts (124-28), church leadership (129-44), → church offices (145-96), prescription (197-99), and chronology (200-203).

Book 2 ("The People of God," cans. 204-746) deals with constitutional issues and with groupings of churches. Its title follows the direction of Vatican II, changing from the *De personis* (On persons) of the 1917 CIC. In the introductory statements there is a very clear formulation of the relation to non–Roman Catholic churches and communions. The introductory definition of the church (204) rests on the corresponding statements of Vatican II (esp. *Lumen gentium* 8). The church of Jesus Christ "subsists" in the Roman Catholic Church. It is established and ordered as a fellowship. It is led by the successors of Peter and the bishops in communion with him, which leads to legal statements about full communion with this church.

In accordance with this general theological basis (204-7), the first part of book 2 contains definitions of the rights and duties of all Christians (208-23), of the laity (224-31), the clergy (232-93; → Clergy and Laity), personal prelacies (294-97), and "associations of the Christian faithful" (298-329). The second part deals with the → hierarchical constitution of the church, beginning with the office of the → pope and the college of bishops and going on to the → bishop, the parish priest, and other officeholders (330-572). The third part of the book deals with the institutions of the dedicated life — reminding us of the law of orders in 1917 — including secular establishments and fellowships of the apostolic life (573-746).

Under the title "The Teaching Office of the Church" (cans. 747-833), book 3 formulates the law of the church's ministry of proclamation in → preaching, → catechesis, → mission, → education (schools, universities, and faculties), the media (radio and television), and literature (→ Church Communications Media). It particularly stresses the role of the local bishop and closes with rules for the official confession of faith.

Book 4, "The Office of Sanctifying in the Church" (cans. 834-1253), deals with the church's task of sanctification and how to fulfill it. It treats the seven → sacraments (840-1165), especially → marriage (1055-1165), various other forms of worship (→ sacramental acts, → hours of prayer, → funerals, the veneration of → saints and → relics, → vows and → oaths) (1166-1204), and finally, in canons 1205-53, sacred places (e.g., churches and chapels) and times (feasts and → days of prayer and repentance).

Book 5, "The Temporal Goods of the Church" (cans. 1254-1310), deals with ecclesiastical property (→ Church Finances).

Book 6 ("Sanctions in the Church," cans. 1311-99) contains the church's penal law. It begins with general law (1311-63), with statements about → punishment, evaluation of offenses, types of penalty, and the removal of penalties. Specific laws then follow (1364-99), along with a listing of offenses with the appropriate punishments. This portion is much shorter than the 1917 CIC, as the number of punishable offenses has been reduced to a minimum.

Finally, book 7 ("Processes," cans. 1400-1752) deals with judicial procedure. After a general account (1400-1670), specific norms are given for marriage (1671-1707) and for the imposing of penalties (1717-31). Procedures are then laid down for unusual cases, such as those for nullifying a marriage (1671-91), separation from bed and board (1692-96), dissolution of a nonconsummated marriage (1697-1706), nullifying a → consecration (1708-12), recourse against administrative decrees (1732-39), and deposing or replacing parish priests (1740-52). The CIC closes with the direction that canonical equity and the salvation of souls must always be the church's supreme law. In many of its formulations the new law sees itself as a framework that can and should be filled out by episcopal conferences and local bishops. This attitude is in keeping with the statement of Vatican II about the collegiality of bishops.

3. Relation to Non-Catholics

The view of U. Stutz that according to the CIC of 1917 all non-Roman Christians are excommunicated Roman Catholics, which for a long time seemed to find support in 1917 CIC 2314, can no longer be sustained. In agreement with Vatican II, those who do not belong to the Roman Catholic Church simply are Christians who do not live in full communion with it. Thus non–Roman Catholic churches and communions are not now called "sectae" (sects), as they were in 1917, but churches and ecclesial communities that are not in full communion with the Catholic Church (e.g., 1983 CIC 463, 844.3, 908, 1124). Thus the statement about → ecumenism in Vatican II is taken up in its full sense.

Non–Roman Catholic Christians, as the express formula has it, are not subject to purely ecclesiastical law (see can. 11). Paul VI had dealt with the question of mixed marriages (see *De matrimoniis mixtis,* cans. 1124-29) in his *Matrimonia mixta* of March 1970. Thus the formulations of CIC 1917 that had burdened the relations between Roman Catholics and Protestants were blunted and legally toned down. The presuppositions for fellowship in the sacraments, especially eucharistic table fellowship (→ Eucharist 5), correspond largely to the ecumenical *Directorium* I, which the Secretariat for Christian Unity issued in May 1967. The statements now, however, are more clearly formulated (see 1983 CIC 844). The ecumenical *Directorium* II confirmed this position in 1993.

Bibliography: *Code of Canon Law: Latin-English Edition* (Washington, D.C., 1983) • J. A. CORIDEN, T. J. GREEN, and D. E. HEINTSCHEL, EDS., *The Code of Canon Law: A Text and Commentary* (New York, 1985) • J. LISTL et al., eds., *Handbuch des katholischen Kirchenrechts* (Regensburg, 1983) • K. LÜDICKE, ed., *Münsterischer Kommentar zum CIC* (Essen, 1985ff.) • N. RUF, *Das Recht der katholischen Kirche* (Freiburg, 1983) • G. SHEEHY et al., eds., *The Canon Law: Letter and Spirit. A Practical Guide to the Code of Canon Law* (Collegeville, Minn., 1995) • H. SCHMITZ, *Reform des kirchlichen Gesetzbuchs* (Trier, 1979); idem, *Tendenzen nachkonziliarer Gesetzgebung* (Trier, 1979) • H. SCHWENDENWEIN, *Das neue Kirchenrecht–Gesamtdarstellung* (Graz, 1983).

HERIBERT HEINEMANN

4. Ecumenical Significance

The 1983 CIC codifies Vatican II, especially in the spheres of ecclesiology (→ Church) and → pastoral theology. In it we can see how far the ecumenical openness that characterized the council has been put into concrete measures and possibilities of ecumenical cooperation. For this reason the CIC is very significant for the relation of the Roman Catholic Church to other confessions. In fact, it explicitly takes into account at many points the council's ecumenical change of emphasis.

Specifically, the 1983 CIC underscores the duty of the college of bishops and the apostolic see to promote the restoration of the → unity of the churches (755.1). It also charges local bishops to foster → ecumenism by acting kindly and charitably toward "those who are not in full communion with the Catholic Church" (383.3). The discussion of ecumenical questions is also a responsibility laid upon those who teach future priests (256.2), and it is the task of apostolic legates to promote relations with other churches or communions (364, responsibility no. 6). The ecumenical spirit appears also in the freedom bishops have to invite non–Roman Catholic observers to diocesan synods (463.3).

Above all, the essential viewpoint of CIC is that, along the lines of Vatican II, it no longer makes a simple equation of the Roman Catholic Church with the church of Jesus Christ. Only in the Roman Catholic Church is there access to the fullness of salvation, but outside it there are many elements of truth that impart an ecclesial character to non–Roman Catholic communions.

It is evident, however, that the demand for an ecumenical mind and praxis is put very generally. Thus the everyday ecumenical activity by which the CIC must display its credibility bears a rather different aspect. This comes out especially in a sphere that has always caused tension, that of → mixed marriages. Their regulation, on the basis of the revision carried out by Paul VI in 1970, remains ecumenically unsatisfying. Thus, even though local bishops have a right of dispensation, the ban on marrying those of another confession remains (1124-29). Similarly, there has been no reform of the canonical form of marriage in the case of mixed marriages.

Another everyday problem from an ecumenical standpoint is the lack of any fellowship in worship between the churches, as well as the refusal to admit non–Roman Catholics to Communion except in cases of emergency (→ Eucharist 5). Fundamentally, too, Roman Catholics are forbidden to take Communion in separated churches, and except for the case of the Eastern Church, Roman Catholic priests are forbidden concelebration with the clergy of churches that are not in full communion with Rome (908, 1365). The ecumenism decree (Art. 22.3) names as the reason for this prohibition the absence of the sacrament of consecration (→ Priest, Priesthood) in the separated communions.

Except in details such as the preceding, the role of the council in the CIC is ecumenically important. In contrast to the code of 1917, the council's statements have been incorporated into the definitions regarding the papacy and the bishops' college (336-41). Yet the influence of the council seems to be plainly subordinate to the power of the papacy, and for all the regard for episcopal authority, all the essential reins of power remain in papal hands. Significantly, the pope is called the vicar of Christ — for the first time in a normative legal document (331). This papocentric tendency neutralizes the conciliar structure of the Roman Catholic Church, and in the future it might fundamentally prejudice any possibility of collegial consensus. In an ecumenical context the Roman Catholic Church will lose credibility as a result. The non–Roman Catholic world again sees itself facing a papal church that links its ecumenical openness to its own self-understanding (→ Church 3.2; Unity) and follows a restorationist trend.

→ Canon Law

PEDER NØRGAARD-HØJEN

Cognition

1. Cognition as Process
2. Cognition as Content

"Cognition" is a generic term in psychology that may refer equally to the process (how) or to the content (what) of human knowledge.

1. Cognition as Process

In the earlier, more philosophically oriented psychology, "cognition" referred to the human faculty of reason as distinguished from will and feeling, but this a priori distinction is no longer maintained. For example, there now are theories about goal-directed behavior in terms of subjective probabilities and means-ends, or about emotions in terms of labeling of arousal — in other words, a mixture of cognition, motivation, and affect.

In modern experimental cognitive psychology, "cognition" refers to all the functions of the brain that contribute to human knowledge, such as attention, memory, and association. It is very typical of such an approach to look at cognition as an individual process, as the result of specific brain functions of specific individuals. Even speech in this perspective is seen as an individual function, albeit with social consequences (→ Language).

The dominant → metaphors in cognitive psychol-

ogy are artificial intelligence and formal inference models. For example, the brain is often compared to a computer, and inferential thinking compared to the causal thinking of a scientist using analysis of variance or conditional probability models. Deviations from these formal standards are defined as biases and not as genuine constructions of reality.

Quite recently, however, an important new "social" perspective on human knowledge has emerged, the so-called social constructionism. Without denying brain functions, this perspective views human knowledge as the symbolic expression of the socially coordinated activity between different individuals. Once formed, these symbolic expressions can be retained in memory and individually reproduced, but they remain social constructions nonetheless. These social constructions are not isolated concepts, but they function in stories. The study of cognition from the social-constructionist perspective thus also implies the study of language and discourse practices and entails a new face on → logic, one much more connected to a discursive regulation of activity.

2. Cognition as Content

That to which human knowledge refers and the basic vehicle of content is the concept. There has been — and still is — a great deal of discussion in psychology about the precise nature of the concept. Is it a well-defined class? Or is it a fuzzy set with loose boundaries? Does it have the properties of a schema, of prototypes? Does its meaning change with the discursive context? and so forth.

An important content-related discussion in psychology concerns the difference between nonsocial knowledge (e.g., knowledge about objects) and social knowledge (e.g., knowledge about persons — oneself and others). There are reasons to believe that self-knowledge is of a unique nature, although some would claim that such a belief rests on artifacts of the research itself.

From a social-constructionist standpoint, however, the content of cognition represents, not the inherent truth of reality, but our socially coordinated activity. Persons therefore may become objects, and objects persons, depending on the context.

→ Communication; Development 2; Socialization

Bibliography: S. T. FISKE and S. F. TAYLOR, Social Cognition (Reading, Mass., 1984) • K. GERGEN, Toward Transformation in Social Knowledge (New York, 1982) • U. NEISSER, Cognition and Reality: Principles and Implications of Cognitive Psychology (San Francisco, 1976).

JOHN B. RIJSMAN

Collect → Mass

Collegialism

According to the traditional understanding, collegialism designates a theory advanced in justification of (Protestant) territorial → church government (the last of such older theories after the territorial and episcopal systems). Unlike earlier theories, however, it includes both a sociological and a theological theory of the → church and of → church law. The basis is the view, derived from → natural law and the → Enlightenment, of the social nature of the church (as a *collegium,* as for S. Pufendorf and J. H. Boehmer). In the middle of the 18th century early collegialists (e.g., C. M. Pfaff and L. Mosheim) constructed a genuinely ecclesiastical law of church self-administration. They argued on two levels. Theologically the church, being founded by Christ, lives according to its own legal principles. In part these are inalienable as the command of God, in part they are historically variable as human decisions. The second level is that of the stricter rationality of natural law. The state cannot be expected to take over the church's understanding as a basis for its own polity. The aim of collegialism is rather to show that there can be an appropriate relation between → church and state on the basis of a religiously neutral legal order. As a corporation, the church has → autonomy in fixing its polity so as best to discharge its spiritual mission.

Like any other → society, the church is under broad state supervision concerning its external affairs, but in principle it governs its own internal affairs. If these are in the hands of the territorial ruler, this arrangement is only by a church mandate, which during the → Reformation was granted to Protestant princes in trust and was revocable. This not only grounded the institution of territorial episcopacy in a new legal title, but it also fundamentally called into question the territorial ecclesiastical authority of Roman Catholic sovereigns over the Protestant church. This deeper premise of the older system of collegialism, however, soon ran aground in the shallows of an associative legal view of the church. Although its antiabsolutist thrust could not prevail in the 18th century, it gained practical relevance in the 19th as a distinction came to be made between the political and the ecclesiastical positions of the ruler. The danger of collegialism is that it might involve an uncritical acceptance of democratic demands, the church's character as a society being made the basis of its theological self-understanding.

But from the standpoint of state church law, it has shown how the church may do its work and validate its principles within a secular commonwealth. To that extent it has laid the foundation of a free state church law.

→ Jurisprudence

Bibliography: J. BOHATEC, "Das Territorial- und Kollegialsystem in der holländischen Publizistik des 17. Jahrhunderts," *ZSRG.K* 35 (1948) 1ff. • C. LINK, *Herrschaftsordnung und bürgerliche Freiheit* (Vienna, 1979) • G. H. C. MACGREGOR, *Corpus Christi: The Nature of the Church according to the Reformed Tradition* (Philadelphia, 1959) • K. SCHLAICH, "Kirchenrecht und Vernunftrecht. Kirche und Staat in der Sicht der Kollegialtheorie," *ZEvKR* 14 (1968/69) 1ff.; idem, *Kollegialtheorie–Kirche, Staat und Recht in der Aufklärung* (Munich, 1969).

CHRISTOPH LINK

Collegiate Association for the Research of Principles → Unification Church

Colombia

	1960	1980	2000
Population (1,000s):	15,939	26,525	38,905
Annual growth rate (%):	2.99	2.07	1.47
Area: 1,141,568 sq. km. (440,762 sq. mi.)			

A.D. 2000
Population density: 34/sq. km. (88/sq. mi.)
Births / deaths: 2.13 / 0.55 per 100 population
Fertility rate: 2.51 per woman
Infant mortality rate: 30 per 1,000 live births
Life expectancy: 72.1 years (m: 69.4, f: 74.8)
Religious affiliation (%): Christians 96.7 (Roman Catholics 96.3, Protestants 2.8, indigenous 1.6, other Christians 0.9), nonreligious 1.2, spiritists 1.0, other 1.1.

1. General Situation
2. Religious Situation
   2.1. Indo-American Religions
   2.2. Christian Churches
      2.2.1. Roman Catholicism
      2.2.2. Protestant Churches
   2.3. Non-Christian Groups
   2.4. Interdenominational and Ecumenical Organizations
   2.5. Relations between State and Church

1. General Situation

The Republic of Colombia, in the extreme northwest of South America, covers the fourth largest area of any country in Latin America (after Brazil, Mexico, and Peru) and has the third largest population (2000 est.), after Brazil and Mexico. It has both a Liberal Party and a Conservative Party, each controlled oligarchically.

Though governments have mostly been civilian, Colombia has suffered from well over a century of political instability. Since *La Violencia*, the civil war from 1948 to 1958 that claimed as many as 280,000 lives, guerrilla groups such as the FARC, ELN, and ERPL have been active, along with 19 April and other smaller groups since the 1970s. During the 1980s drug dealers (many of whom are part of a regular drug mafia; → Substance Abuse) and large landholders have cooperated with the military to form so-called self-defense groups and paramilitary organizations on the extreme Right to destroy both guerrillas and left-wing and democratic groups.

A process of national dialogue began under Belisario Betancourt (1982-86), with reconciliation attempted between left-wing guerrilla forces and the government. When they were integrated into civilian life, however, many leftist leaders were assassinated by right-wing extremists and paramilitary groups. The peace process came to an end with the massacre of November 1985, when those killed included 41 members of the guerrilla group M-19 (which had occupied the Palace of Justice, seeking thereby to force the keeping of a previous agreement with the government), as well as 11 judges and some 50 other people. In the period from 1986 to 1988, country dwellers, workers, students, and intellectuals, including champions of the Communist Left and fighters for → human rights, were among those murdered. Colombia was enduring what was in effect an undeclared civil war. The situation since then has not improved noticeably, in spite of a new constitution in 1991 that was part of an effort to end the pattern of violence.

2. Religious Situtation

2.1. *Indo-American Religions*

In 1850 there were more than one million → Indians in Colombia. Making up 50 percent of the population, they were all adherents of → tribal religions. By 1950 they constituted only some 25 percent of the population, and by 1990 less than 1 percent, mostly still → animists. Regional groupings of Indians are desperately trying to defend their ownership rights to the land.

2.2. *Christian Churches*

2.2.1. *Roman Catholicism*

The → mission (§3) of the → Roman Catholic Church in what is present-day Colombia began in 1510 in Santa Maria de la Antigua del Darien, New Granada. The city of Bogotá (founded in 1538, became a diocese in 1564) quickly became the center of colonization and evangelization (→ Colonialism; Colonialism and Mission). In accordance with the → patronage system, → evangelization took place with the exploration and occupation of the country. The church grew fastest where settlers were richest and most numerous. The settlers came to the most heavily inhabited areas with the most well-developed social structures. These areas (the High Andes and the South) favored the establishment of a society that paid tribute to the Spaniards, as well as of their church.

The evangelizing of warlike Indians (Pijaos, Punches, Muzos, Armas, and Quimbayas) met with considerable opposition, as did that of tribes that during the conquest of the Antilles had fallen victim to slave traders (Cunas, Taironas, and Zenues). Alongside areas in which the original population was almost completely extirpated, there are zones with many mestizos.

During the struggle for independence (1807-24) the clergy and orders split. In general, the Creoles among them, along with the lower clergy, supported the → revolution, but the higher Spanish clergy remained loyal to the Crown, to which they were tied by the patronage system.

The main problems in the 19th century were organizing the national state and fixing the role of the various institutions. The refusal of Rome to turn over patronage to the new republics created deep-seated difficulties in the church-state relation.

At first the Colombian clergy took a liberal attitude toward independence. A change to a more spiritual, primitive Christianity was discernible. Loyalty to the king went hand in hand with support for the federal system.

Increasingly, however, the clergy sought an authoritarian regime under the tutelage of the church, which came to see itself as the sole guardian of social morality. Between 1835 and 1840 (→ Restoration; Ultramontanism), foreign clergy came into Colombia and formed the basis of support for the Conservative Party, defending the church against increasing Liberal radicalism. Liberals achieved the separation of church and state in 1853 and introduced civil marriage and divorce. In 1861 the church was disendowed, and rebellious clergy were arrested or banished. The conflict between state and church led to constant civil strife.

Concerned to structure the national economy (esp. coffee growing) for the international market, Conservatives and Liberals united from 1880 onward around a new model of Christianity in which the church would be the watchdog of the social order and the ideological overseer. This was possible on the basis of the 1886 constitution, which designated the church as the state church, and on the basis of the 1887 → concordat. Given this early history, the Colombian church has the reputation of being the most conservative of all the Roman Catholic churches in Latin America. It defended the so-called Catholic cause — the goal of preserving as Roman Catholic virtually 100 percent of the population.

More recently, a growing number of Roman Catholic priests and militant laity, especially members of labor unions, students, and intellectuals, came into conflict with the ruling oligarchy and the related section of the Roman → hierarchy. Camilo Torres (1929-66) was the best known of these. Although the second main conference of the → Latin American Council of Bishops (CELAM) at Medellín in 1968 laid the foundation for change in the church's life and practice, it found little response from the Colombian bishops. Pastoral team ministry was recommended, but as yet it is no more than a program. → Liberation theology, which some laity and monks advocated in harmony with Medellín, has been constantly suppressed.

A clerical structure characterizes the Colombian church. Toward the end of the 1960s, groups of priests like Golconda and Sal were formed. The 1970s and 1980s saw conflicts with the → Franciscans and → Jesuits, who opposed preconciliar trends that aimed to defend hierarchical privileges. During Betancourt's peace process some bishops and priests played an active part. In 1987 a great financial and economic scandal shook the church when the bank connected with the bishops' conference, La Caja Vocacional, went bankrupt. In 1987 Cardinal Alfonso Lopez Trujillo, president of the bishops' conference, tried to mediate between the guerrillas and the government, but the latter would not agree.

2.2.2. Protestant Churches

From 1819 onward, the British delegation exerted an influence on some Colombian citizens favorable to the Liberal Party and advocated the founding of a Protestant church in Colombia. In 1825 James Thomson of the British and Foreign Bible Society (→ Bible Societies 4.1), with Roman Catholic support, founded a national Bible society. It was the first to publish the NT in South America.

In the mid-19th century the Presbyterians (→ Reformed and Presbyterian Churches) — for a long time the only Protestants — took up work in Colombia. They became famous for their schools and medical centers but otherwise made little headway; by 1910 they had founded only two congregations, one in Bogotá and one in Barranquilla, each with only about 100 members. Between 1910 and 1930 other congregations were formed, which aroused little opposition from the Conservative government.

The mission of the Evangelical Alliance (→ World Evangelical Fellowship) began in 1906 with work in Venezuela, spreading from there to the east coast of Colombia. The Gospel Mission Association came from Ecuador in 1908, founded a press, and began monthly publications. The Seventh-day → Adventists arrived in 1921, the Cumberland Presbyterians in 1925, and the → Salvation Army in 1929. By 1930 the Christian and Missionary Alliance and the Scandinavian Missionary Alliance (→ Scandinavian Missions) were also at work.

During the years of Liberal government from 1930 to 1946, Protestant churches were founded unhindered and even enjoyed some government support. The Evangelical Crusade and Plymouth Brethren (→ Brethren Churches) came in 1933, the South American Native Mission in 1934, the Evangelical Lutheran Church (→ Lutheran Churches) in 1936, and, from the United States, the United Pentecostal Church (→ Pentecostal Churches) in 1936, the Southern → Baptists in 1937, and the Methodist Wesleyan Church of Colombia (→ Methodist Churches) in the same year. In 1940 churches arrived on the scene that began radio work aimed at individual settlers. The Foursquare Gospel Church and Evangelical Mission of South America came in 1942, the Interamerican Mission in 1943, the New Tribes Mission in 1944, and the Evangelical Mission of Colombia in 1945, as well as many small, independent groups.

For Protestants, as for many others in Colombia, the policy in the civil war from 1948 onward was one of suppression. Along with the thousands who were killed, 270 Protestant schools were closed, and 60 churches were destroyed. Yet the Protestant churches grew comparatively strong, increasing from 8,000 members in 1948 to 12,000 in 1953, 220,000 in 1983, and a little over 1 million in 1990. With the establishment of the National Front after La Violencia, the Pentecostals enjoyed spectacular growth. The Christian Pentecostal Church came to Colombia in 1964, the Pentecostal Church of Christ and Evangelical National Church of Colombia in 1965, and the United Pentecostal Church in 1970.

After 1960 the Protestants secured greater liberty. Many radio programs were started, including that of the conservative New Continent. Some groups, especially Pentecostals, practiced → healing. Pentecostal groups spread rapidly, especially from the 1980s onward, among marginal sectors of the population, and their political influence increased. Also, the constitution of 1991 removed the privileged position of the Roman Catholic Church. Although the preamble invokes the protection of God, all references to the Catholic Church have been deleted from the constitution, which declares all religions equal.

Protestants include both progressive and very conservative wings. Fundamentalists oppose attempts to build social awareness. They stress personal → conversion (§1) but tend to ignore collective structures and do not take class conflict seriously, seeming to believe that only a divine → miracle will solve the problems of the exploited. Interest focuses on a lifestyle that could be called either fraternal or sectarian, and social conflicts are disregarded. This view was in accord with the policy of the new American Right and the Reagan administration, which looked with favor on the missionary work of fundamentalist groups (→ Evangelical Missions). The largest of these groups is the Pentecostals; they also include the Summer Institute of Linguistics (SIL) and churches within the Evangelical Confederation of Latin America (CONELA).

The progressives, in contrast, aim at social conversion. Their goal in the social conflict is to defend the marginal and oppressed with a view to popular liberation. Mainline Protestants tend to take this view, including the churches linked to the → Latin American Council of Churches.

2.3. Non-Christian Groups
The strongest of the foreign non-Christian groups are the → Jehovah's Witnesses (117,000 adherents in 1990) and the → Mormons (76,000), with smaller numbers of Moonies, Gnostics, Followers of Aaron, → Spiritists, members of → Baha'i, → Rosicrucians, and → Hindus. The → Theosophical Society has been present since 1975 with nine lodges.

The Jews (→ Judaism), who mostly came to Colombia after World War I, have 66 → synagogues and approximately 25,000 members in the cities. Muslims (→ Islam) have also been in Colombia since the 1920s, especially in enclaves of Syrians and Lebanese. Since the founding of → Israel (§2), Islamic Palestinians have also come to Colombia. Though small in numbers, Jews and Muslims play an important part in the economic, social, and political life of the country.

2.4. Interdenominational and Ecumenical Organizations
The first ecumenical organization was the Evangelical Missionary Council, founded between 1937 and 1942. With eight missions as members, this body integrated pastoral work. The Evangelical Union of the Churches of Colombia (CEDEC) was founded in 1950 and united 20 denominations embracing 90 percent of all Protestants. Its aim was to proclaim the spiritual unity of the Protestant churches, to promote their cooperative ventures, to coordinate their work, and to represent them before agencies and to the public. In 1970 the Bogotá Union of Pastors was founded, uniting Roman priests and Protestant ministers in dialogue and prayer. Ecumenical relations were confirmed and improved after 1970 as a result of Vatican II. Yet the history of past conflicts is still a hindrance, especially in relation to church and state and the concordat.

2.5. Relations between State and Church
The 1953 concordat granted special privileges to the Roman Catholic Church. Though Protestants and other missionaries had rights, the orders had exclusive rights to evangelization and education in missionary areas. The signing of the 1974 concordat led to considerable controversy. Its opponents, especially CEDEC, criticized the articles relating to marriage and those that violate freedom of belief. Many Roman Catholics disputed the need for a new concordat. In 1975 freedom from taxation was extended to Protestant churches and Jewish synagogues. In 1988 the national government made proposals to Rome for reform of the concordat regarding marriage and divorce and → religious instruction in public schools. These issues were addressed in the concordat signed in November 1992, according to which the Vatican's legal authority over the personal lives of Colombians was greatly reduced. Provisions of this recent concordat include the legalization of divorce, the ending of obligatory Catholic education in public schools, and the canceling of the former right of priests charged with a crime to avoid trial in state courts.

→ Latin American Theology; Theology of Revolution

Bibliography: C. Abel, *Política, iglesia y partidos políticos en Colombia* (Bogotá, 1987) • E. E. Brusco, *The Reformation of Machismo: Evangelical Conversion and Gender in Colombia* (Austin, Tex., 1995) • D. Bushnell, *The Making of Modern Colombia: A Nation in spite of Itself* (Berkeley, Calif., 1993) • P. Clawson and R. W. Lee III, *The Andean Cocaine Industry* (New York, 1996) • Comissão de estudos de história da igreja na América Latina e no Caribe, *Historia general de la iglesia* (vol. 7; Madrid, 1981) • R. De Roux, *Una iglesia en estado de alerta* (Bogotá, 1984) • R. H. Dix, *Colombia: The Political Dimensions of Change* (New Haven, 1967;

2d ed., 1969) • J. E. Goff, *La persecución de los cristianos protestantes en Colombia, 1948-1958* (Cuernavaca, 1968) • D. M. Hanratty and S. W. Meditz, *Colombia: A Country Study* (Washington, D.C., 1990) • *Kirche und Entwicklung in Ekuador und Kolumbien* (Mannheim, 1972) • K. Köhler, "Entwicklung und Struktur des kolumbianischen Erziehungs- und Bildungswesens" (Diss., Bonn, 1986) • D. H. Levine, *Religion and Politics in Latin America: The Catholic Church in Venezuela and Colombia* (Princeton, 1981) • F. Ordoñez, *Historia del cristianismo evangélico* (Medellín, 1956) • A. Wilde, *Redemocratization, the Church, and Democracy in Colombia* (N.p., 1984).

Ana María Bidegain de Urán

Colonialism

1. Definition
2. European Expansion
   2.1. The Antecedents of European Expansion
   2.2. Portuguese and Spanish Colonial Empires until 1600
   2.3. Dutch, English, and French Colonial Empires until 1818
   2.4. Imperialism under the Guise of Free Trade, 1815-81
   2.5. The Period of New Imperialism, 1881-1945
   2.6. Decolonialization after 1945
3. Theories of Imperialism
4. Neocolonialism and Domestic Colonialism

1. Definition

Scholars have debated the meaning of both "colonialism" and "imperialism." Some regard colonialism as a form of imperialism, but others make a chronological distinction, relating colonialism to the period of mercantilist European empires up to the end of the 18th century and then arguing that it was absorbed by modern imperialism with the rise of the industrial revolution and → capitalism. Though both concepts are imprecise, no better alternatives are apparent.

In what follows we reject the chronological distinction on the ground that it can hardly do justice to the history of European expansion since the late Middle Ages. By "imperialism," then, we understand the extension of direct rule or indirect control over a social unit (→ Society) or → state with the aim of establishing relations of political, economic, and or social inequality between the imperialistic metropolis and the subject periphery. "Colonialism" we

understand as a special, albeit very prominent, form of imperialism. It involves direct imperialistic rule over peoples or regions, resulting in relations of inequality between the colonial power and the colonized population, which might well include colonial settlers who themselves do not enjoy full equality with the colonial metropolis. In the definition stress must fall on the establishing or maintaining of *unequal* relations, as compared with other expansion processes (e.g., migration or national aggrandizement). In practice, however, the boundaries are hard to fix, and definition becomes a matter of ideal types.

The definitions suggested above each have a universal reference, allowing them to denote not only European expansion in antiquity and the Middle Ages and also the → modern period but also similar phenomena in non-European contexts. The definitions offer a formal description of expansion processes without reference to the respective causes, unlike many competing theories of imperialism that confuse phenomena and causes in their analyses, thus contributing to conceptual confusion.

2. European Expansion

The expansion of European states beyond Europe, which began in the 15th century, is a historical event of the first rank. It decisively affected our entire world by setting up direct relations between different parts of the globe. It was linked both to great explorations and discoveries and to most dreadful atrocities, including → slavery and → genocide. With technical, economic, social, political, and intellectual → progress came naked exploitation, which is the historical basis of the present-day North-South conflict (→ Dependence; Third World). European expansion is marked by features of both growth and constriction.

There are three main phases in the history of imperialism, the boundaries between which are fluid.

Late 15th century to the end of the 18th century: the age of classic European colonialism. Prominent in this age of mercantilism was public and private commercial capital.

Early 19th century to 1945: the age of modern imperialism. Direct and indirect rule was set up through the industrial revolution and modern capitalism. The United States and Japan became new and non-European major players in this period.

After 1945: the age of decolonizing and the spread of indirect imperialistic control. Until recently, this control operated through a bipolar world-power system, one of the powers being noncapitalist.

2.1. *The Antecedents of European Expansion*

The roots of European expansion, which reach back into the Middle Ages, are to be found in the → Crusades, the reconquest of Spain and Portugal, and the expansion of the Italian trading cities in the eastern Mediterranean. The Venetians in particular successfully used the techniques of colonial rule and exploitation. For example, they made Cyprus a plantation colony run by slave labor.

The first real example of European expansion was the occupation from the 14th century onward of Madeira, the Canary Islands, and later the Azores by Portugal, Castile, and Genoa. The conquest of Ceuta at the Strait of Gibraltar by the Portuguese in 1415 gave additional impetus to this development, since it involved control of trade with North Africa. Typical features of colonialism emerged with these developments, namely, rivalries between the colonial powers, strategic preventive annexations, conflicts for access to local trade, and the colonizing of conquered territories for the production of colonial goods.

2.2. *The Portuguese and Spanish Colonial Empires until 1600*

Beginning with their occupation of the Atlantic islands and parts of North Africa, the Portuguese in the second half of the 15th century gradually worked their way down the coast of Africa to the south. Their declared aim from the 1480s onward was to find a sea route to India so as to break the Venetian trade monopoly in Asian goods. In 1498 Vasco da Gama (ca. 1460-1524) did in fact reach India. The Portuguese then began to take control by force of the developed trade in the Indian Ocean.

In 1492 Columbus (1451-1506), on the commission of the Spanish crown, sought a new route to India and discovered America. This feat initiated Spanish imperialism in the New World.

Spanish and Portuguese expansion was now along different lines, as formally recognized in the Treaty of Tordesillas (1494), which gave the Eastern Hemisphere (plus Brazil) to Portugal, and the Western Hemisphere (later also the Philippines) to Spain. In keeping with regional differences, the character of colonial rule also differed. The Portuguese set up defensive points to protect their trade, which now reached to Japan, with Goa on the west coast of India and Malacca on the Malay Peninsula being the main centers after 1510. The Spaniards, however, set up a giant colonial system in America with the conquest of Mexico (from 1519) and the Incas (from 1532).

Economically, both systems rested on a more or less developed form of crown capitalism, that is, state-controlled merchant capital. To maintain their plantations in Brazil, the Portuguese began to import African slaves in the 16th century, and the Spaniards followed suit in the Caribbean after extirpating the native population there. During the 17th century the Portuguese colonial empire in Asia largely collapsed because of Dutch and English competition, but the Spanish empire in America lasted until the 19th century, though with essentially no further expansion.

2.3. *The Dutch, English, and French Colonial Empires until 1818*

From the end of the 16th century, European wars were largely fought overseas, finally becoming global with the Napoleonic Wars. This extension of European conflicts to other parts of the world was a mark of European colonialism. As a result of the 18th-century wars, Holland and England became the new colonial powers, at the expense of the Iberian countries.

By the end of the century the Dutch had an empire consisting primarily of American possessions, the Cape of Good Hope, Ceylon, and Indonesia. The monopoly in Indonesian spice trade, which they forceably gained control of, was the basis of Dutch economic power. In contrast, the British focused first on the West Indies and North America. Gradually, however, their trading settlements in India became more important. In both India and North America the French were their main rivals, which led to a series of wars with France between 1690 to 1815. In virtue of their sea power the British emerged victorious, though losing most of their North American colonies in 1783. In compensation, they established supremacy in India between 1798 and 1819. The center of their world empire thus shifted to the east, and a new chapter in European colonialism began.

This was the period of mercantilism, the chief aim being to secure overseas trading monopolies or to break those of their competitors. The main instrument for the achievement of this purpose was the privately capitalized merchant company, which Holland and Britain both developed in trading with Asia. Mercantilist monopoly trading tended to enforce unequal trading relations, frequently even to the point of theft and plunder.

At the same time, the plantation economy developed in America, to maintain which there was a vigorous slave trade across the Atlantic. Up to the end of the 19th century at least 12½ million people were taken by force from Africa. The slave trade was part of a global trading system that led from America to Europe, from Europe to South and Southeast Asia, then back by Europe and Africa to America. Most of the profits remained in Europe.

Colonial rule took many forms. The French imposed direct state government, but the British allowed a measure of self-government in North America and ruled through the trading companies in India, as did the Dutch in Indonesia. During this period Russia was also expanding through Siberia to the frontiers of China, incorporating the conquered territories into the Russian state. Russian overseas expansion to Alaska and the West coast of North America was only tentative and temporary.

2.4. Imperialism under the Guise of Free Trade, 1815-81

With the end of the Napoleonic Wars in 1815, the industrial revolution began to affect the relations between Europe and the other continents. This was especially true because the home of this revolution, Great Britain, had no rivals in overseas access now that France had been defeated. The superior British economy and the lack of colonial competitors made it largely unnecessary to conquer further territories. The primary concern of Britain now was not to establish trade monopolies but to secure free access to markets and raw materials for British industry and investment opportunities for British capital.

Such interest led to an intensifying of what had thus far been only a marginal form of imperialism, that is, free trade imperialism. Essential to its success was the opening up and securing of markets. To this end, indirect political and economic control was usually sufficient. The motto of free trade imperialism was indirect control where possible, direct colonial rule where necessary (J. Robinson, R. Gallagher). Linked to this principle was an intensifying of gunboat diplomacy, which encouraged the native elites to collaborate with the imperial power. Another means to establish dependence was that of lending to non-European states. By this method Britain gained access to the South American market, where Spanish and Portuguese rule had collapsed in the 1820s. Gradually the Ottoman Empire, Egypt, West and North Africa, and China were opened up, and Japan by force in 1853. Other powers, especially France and the United States, were now participating.

In spite of free trade imperialism and the collapse of European colonial rule in Central and South America, European colonialism continued to expand on the basis of strategic concerns, the interests of power politics, and the subimperialist activities of locally interested parties on the colonial periphery. A growing problem now was the breakup of collaborative regimes, which often had to be replaced by direct rule. Thus Britain extended its colonial rule in South Asia by subjugating northwest India (1842), Burma (1817), and Malaya (1874), while France conquered Algeria (1830) and Indochina (1859). Britain and France also established themselves increasingly in

West Africa, and Russia continued to occupy central Asia.

New British colonies of a different kind were set up in Australia (1788) and New Zealand, where whites ousted the Maoris from 1820 onward. A new phase of European emigration was thus initiated, with some 55 million Europeans leaving the old continent between 1820 and 1920. From Australia and New Zealand there then developed a new form of subimperialism, which rivaled Britain, France, and the United States in setting up colonies in the South Pacific. At this period the government of colonies was increasingly taken over by the state. The chief example is India, which became a crown colony after the decline of the East India Company and the Mutiny of 1857-58.

2.5. The Period of New Imperialism, 1881-1945

With the seizure of Tunisia by French troops in 1881 and the occupation of Egypt by the British in 1882, a new era in modern imperialism began that saw the tempo of colonial growth increase. Lands hitherto immune, especially in Africa and Polynesia, were divided up by the colonial powers. The number of these powers also increased, with Germany, Italy, the United States, Japan, and Belgium now joining the scramble for colonial possessions.

This development had many different causes. The most important factors were the collapse of cooperative regimes in the colonies, the increasing economic and political rivalry of a growing number of industrial powers, the ease of conquest because of the technological superiority of the industrialized states, and the prestige attaching to colonial possessions at home. During this period imperialism was increasingly linked to chauvinism and militarism at home. By the end of the 19th century the growth of colonialism was at an end, for the world had largely been carved up already except for China, the heart of the Ottoman Empire, and South America, which could not be divided but were subject to an informal imperialism.

This situation increased the tensions between the colonial powers and produced a series of international crises over colonial issues: the Fashoda Incident in the Sudan involving Great Britain and France (1898), the Boer War (1899-1902), the Russo-Japanese War (1904-5), two crises in Morocco (1905 and 1911), and the Turkish-Italian War (1911-12). Colonial rivalries contributed to the outbreak of World War I, in the course of which European imperialism turned back upon Europe itself, as we see from the imperialistic war aims of the great powers.

The Versailles Treaty of 1919 brought a new division of colonial possessions. The German colonies and much of the Ottoman Empire were allocated to the victorious powers under mandate, though the United States remained aloof. A new phenomenon was the rise of the Soviet Union as an anticolonial power, though it showed no willingness to relinquish its Asian possessions. In the 1930s, imperialism gained new impetus as Italy seized Ethiopia (1935), Japan attacked Manchuria (1931) and China (1937), and Germany and the Soviets carved up Poland, the Baltic states, and other parts of eastern Europe (1939-40).

World War II saw the climax of imperialism with the radically imperialistic policies of the German Third Reich, Italy, and Japan (→ Fascism). A mark of new imperialism was the tendency to set up economically self-sufficient colonial empires protected by tariffs. Nor should we overlook the continuation of the policy of informal imperialistic penetration, which was economically more important for many powers. After the failure of the attempt to set up charter companies again in the 1880s, the system of state monopoly prevailed.

2.6. Decolonialization after 1945

World War II brought with it not only the collapse of the radically imperialist powers but also the weakening of the traditional colonial powers. Both the new superpowers — the United States and the USSR — were at least verbally opposed to colonialism. Furthermore, in most colonies stronger nationalist mass movements arose under the leadership of a new intellectual elite that wanted independence from colonial rule. Finally, colonialism came increasingly into disrepute in public opinion within the colonial powers themselves, especially when the cost of defending colonial bastions against independence movements began to outweigh the economic benefits accruing from them.

These various factors all led to a relentless process of decolonializing, which began in South and Southeast Asia. In 1947 the British found themselves forced to grant independence to India and Pakistan. Burma and Ceylon followed in 1948. The attempt of the French and Dutch to reestablish control of the territories occupied by Japan in World War II failed in savage fighting against nationalist movements. Indonesia became independent in 1949, and the French were forced to withdraw from Indochina in 1954. This development became the model for Africa. By 1965 the British, French, and Belgian colonies had gained independence either by peaceful means or by force. Portugal had to give up its colonies in 1974-75. Similar events took place in other parts of the world, so that only a few remnants of former colonial empires now remain.

Colonialism, however, has not fully ended. France still has possessions in the Pacific, the Caribbean, and Guyana, even though these are now part of the French state. Britain still has Gibraltar and (until 1997) Hong Kong, and in 1982 it fought a war to regain control of the Falkland Islands. The United States governs Puerto Rico and other islands, and Russia has not given up Siberia and other Asian territories. There are also some new cases of colonialism, such as the occupation of Western Sahara by Morocco or Israel's colonizing of Arab territories seized in 1967.

Much more important, however, was the emergence of a new form of imperialism in which formally independent states were forced to cooperate with an imperialist power or power bloc in the battle for spheres of economic and political influence. The American intervention in Viet Nam (1964-73) and the Soviet occupation of Afghanistan (1979-89) were extreme examples. Furthermore, decolonializing takes place in different ways. There might be a complete break, or the former colony might be still under the same head of state, maintaining an economic and political relationship, as in the British Commonwealth.

3. Theories of Imperialism

From the beginning of the 20th century, scholarly debate (pregnant with political undertones) has tried to identify the causes of European expansion. Yet the value of most of the theories advanced in this debate is reduced in advance by the fact that they focus chiefly on a search for the causes of new imperialist expansion. Thus in 1902 J. A. Hobson (1858-1940), under the impact of the Boer War, tried to bring to light the background of British imperialism from the second half of the 19th century. He found the reason for British expansionism in the economic and social structure of the country, which created a capitalism of the plutocracy that sought to exploit investment possibilities. Hobson, however, did not go so far as to declare this development a necessary one.

Next came the contention of the Marxist theoreticians R. Luxemburg (1871-1919) and V. I. Lenin (1870-1924). Lenin regarded imperialism as the supreme and final stage of capitalism. J. A. Schumpeter (1883-1950), however, in his work on world history, found the roots of imperialism, not in the capitalist system, but in remnants of a precapitalist stage.

Another line was followed by H. Arendt, G. Lichtheim, D. K. Fieldhouse, and others, who viewed imperialism as the result of great power rivalries intensified by chauvinism. H. U. Wehler pursued this line of thought and spoke of social imperialism, that is, of the attempt of an elite under domestic political pressure to alleviate problems at home by successful expansion abroad.

Common to all these theories, for all their merit, is the inability to explain a phenomenon like the carving up of Africa. In this regard the works of Gallagher and Robinson made real progress. Starting with an analysis of free trade, they saw imperialism as essentially the result of the collapse of informal control on the periphery. This collapse gave decisive impetus to great power rivalries and initiated a struggle for possession of strategically important territories. Lest this theory be prematurely absolutized, P. J. Cain and A. G. Hopkins rightly pointed out that important economic interests of the City of London also played a part and that modern imperialism is inexplicable without them. In fact, single theories of the cause of imperialism do not carry the debate any further. It is important that in the future we integrate the various approaches, in this way trying to take account of the whole process of European expansion.

4. Neocolonialism and Domestic Colonialism
Since the 1950s much thought has gone into understanding why imperialistic policies have continued in the age of decolonizing. The problem of the economic and often also the political dependence of most Third World countries on the industrial states, even after the achievement of formal independence, led K. Nkruma to formulate a theory of neocolonialism. He correctly observed that the former colonies are increasingly dependent and exploited through unequal trade relations, the export of capital, dependence on military aid, and the support of their own governments.

The term "neocolonialism" is unfortunate, however, for an essential feature of postcolonial imperialism is that it does not seek the restoration of colonial rule. H. Magdoff, P. A. Baran, A. G. Frank, and J. Galtung have pointed to the more rational character of this form of imperialism, which does not have to bear cost-intensive direct rule but relies largely on the more readily defended collaboration of native Third World governments.

A general restriction of imperialism to capitalist countries, however, which we also find in the theory of state-monopoly capitalism advanced by M. Dobb and P. M. Sweezy, is untenable in the light of Soviet imperialism. The theory of "internal colonialism" has also been applied to relations between whites and blacks in South Africa and the United States (→ Racism), between → Indians and whites in the United States, between Arabs and Jews in → Israel (§2), and

even between the Welsh and English in Great Britain. The development of a theory of domestic colonialism, interesting though it might be in particular cases, is still in its infancy.

→ Colonialism and Mission; Development 1; Ideology; Nation, Nationalism; Politics

Bibliography: R. VON ALBERTINI, *Europäische Kolonial-herrschaft, 1880-1940* (Zurich, 1976); idem, ed., *Moderne Kolonialgeschichte* (Cologne, 1970) • P. J. CAIN and A. G. HOPKINS, *British Imperialism* (2 vols.; London, 1993) • N. ETHERINGTON, *Theories of Imperialism: War, Conquest, and Capital* (London, 1984) • R. J. HIND, "The Internal Colonial Concept," *CSSH* 3 (1984) 543-68 • R. F. HOLLAND, *European Decolonization, 1918-1981: An Introductory Survey* (London, 1985) • F. MAURO, *Die europäische Expansion* (Stuttgart, 1984) • W. J. MOMMSEN, *Imperialismustheorien. Ein Überblick über die neueren Imperialismusinterpretationen* (Göttingen, 1977) • W. J. MOMMSEN and J. OSTERHAMMEL, eds., *Imperialism and After: Continuities and Discontinuities* (London, 1985) • J. OSTERHAMMEL, *Kolonialismus, Geschichte, Formen, Folgen* (Munich, 1995) • J. H. PARRY, *Europäische Kolonialreiche. Welthandel und Weltwirtschaft im 18. Jahrhundert* (Munich, 1972) • W. REINHARD, *Geschichte der europäischen Expansion* (4 vols.; Stuttgart, 1983ff.) • E. R. WOLF, *Europe and the People without History* (Berkeley, Calif., 1982).

STIG FÖRSTER

Colonialism and Mission

1. Methodology
2. Early Colonial Period
3. Modern Colonial Imperialism
4. Postcolonial Era

1. Methodology
The dialectic of the colonial situation (K. J. Bade), whereby colonial systems finally defeat themselves, applies also to the relation between → colonialism and → mission. It prohibits both unhistorical generalizations and overhasty ideological judgments. We must distinguish between early Iberian colonialism, that of non–Roman Catholic states after the Reformation, and that of modern imperialism, each having its own unique relation with mission. Even then, our account will be fragmentary, since we do not have the sources for a fully satisfying presentation.

2. Early Colonial Period
The medieval idea of the Christian world (→ Middle Ages), though increasingly reduced to the framework

of the national state, provided the basis for the over-lordship that the papacy gave to the Iberian rulers, namely, a synthesis embracing both a claim to colonial power and a theocratic sense of mission. On this view, the → conversion (§1) of natives presupposed subjugation to the Christian colonial power.

Mission was in many ways bound up with this system, but it also raised the question what it meant for the colonial power and the church that the heathen were to be treated as creatures of God and their right to make a free decision of faith respected (Bartolomé de Las Casas [1484-1566]). Partial alternatives like the creation of → "reductions" (i.e., South American Indian settlements organized by the Jesuits) could not permanently shatter the system, nor could the issuing of more humane rulings by the Crown or approaches to a theological ethics of colonialism. Although the → Reformation had undermined in principle both the theological and the secular legitimation of the system, similar ideas reappeared in early Dutch colonizing and in the British North American colonies, notwithstanding the warnings given by more perspicacious theologians in Holland.

John Eliot (1604-90) offered an alternative model of Christian Indian villages in Massachusetts, but this approach did not gain adherents. It was left for the fresh initiation of mission by the → Pietists, inspired by August Hermann → Francke (1663-1727) and exemplarily put into practice by the Danish-Halle Mission in South India, to overcome the pressure of a theocratic synthesis and thus to establish new presuppositions for future development.

3. Modern Colonial Imperialism

All attempts to reduce the situation in the era of modern imperialistic colonialism to a common pattern are mistaken. Different ways of defining the relation between colonialism and mission have arisen, with many variations.

3.1. It is often stated that the missionary comes first, then the consul, then the army, but this statement obscures rather than illumines. When the Basel missionary Elias Schrenk (1831-1913) pressured the British government in 1865 into finally taking over the Gold Coast, he did not appeal in any sense to the striving for colonial expansion but to the responsibility of those who owed restitution to the Africans for immeasurable injustices. Similarly, the first British missionaries in the kingdom of Buganda (northwest of Lake Victoria) summoned the (hesitant) colonial power into the country in order to suppress the → slave trade.

The situation was different in Polynesia, where in the 1840s missionaries became entangled in native conflicts and then in the rivalries of interested Western powers, so that finally they could expect a solution only from the strongest power, damaging their credibility in the process.

In 19th-century German mission, advocates of a new German colonialism like Friedrich Fabri (1824-91) were in a minority. Fabri, however, did influence the Rhenish Mission (→ German Missions) to sympathize with and support the German seizure of Southwest Africa. By 1884, when Fabri had given up the leadership, it was stated in Barmen, in opposition to every illusion, that nowhere in the heathen world has a European colony arisen without the worst of injustices, and that the Germans would hardly do any better.

3.2. Mission could profit from colonialism insofar as missionaries, as citizens of the colonial powers, could claim their protection and, in the fields of education and medicine, could cooperate with them in what were truly the best interests of the population. Yet the story of the relations between colonialism and mission is marked by frequent tensions and conflicts, for example, in relation to job training, language, and the importing of alcohol.

A painful example of the way in which mission could still profit from colonialism even vis-à-vis an autonomous state may be seen from the situation in China at the time of the unequal treaties beginning in 1842. Here France's battle for a protectorate over all Roman Catholic Christians in China led to the subjection of Chinese Christians to French → jurisdiction. Yet it also plunged mission into the rivalries of the great powers, which, like Germany, opposed their own protectorates to French policy. The integrity of mission in China suffered in consequence, with long-term effects. The different example set by James Hudson Taylor (1832-1905) with his → China Inland Mission (1865) could not prevent Christianity from being discredited in China because of its conformity to the imperialistic movement (B. Wirth).

3.3. As in China, so elsewhere we must not miss the signs of opposition to that association, even if modern mission can present no figure comparable to Las Casas. In South Africa even today the tradition lingers on of missionaries like John Philip (1775-1851), who fought against imperialistic oppression and exploitation. The hour of truth for German missions in East Africa came in 1886, when a society for mission in a national German sense began work. Gustav Warneck (1834-1910) and Franz Michael Zahn (1833-1900) opposed this effort, arguing instead that the goal of mission should be to bring to Africans their calling to be children of God and therefore our brethren (Warneck).

Even earlier, the British Church Missionary Society (→ British Missions) in Nigeria, in connection with the fight against the slave trade and slavery, had appointed a first African bishop, Samuel Ajayi Crowther (1864), over the new Niger diocese as a sign that a new sense of African identity was to arise in the new church, which the colonial powers would have to respect. This move opened up new perspectives for the relation between colonialism and mission that reached far beyond the demand for freedom for mission.

During the struggle against the alien rule of Japan in Korea (beginning in 1910), mission had the threefold task of identifying with the suffering people, renouncing outmoded religious systems, and, by a new ethos, seeking justice for the oppressed. In this way it laid the foundations for the overthrow of foreign hegemony.

4. Postcolonial Era

The hope of sociologist Albert Schäffle (1831-1903) that within a century the adoption of Western ways would lead to the demise of colonialism has proved to be illusory. The antagonism between neocolonialism and anticolonialism still stands in the way of the equality of international opportunity that is desired. Even in mission there are relics of the colonialist mentality. What is new is that today the congregations and churches of the → Third World are themselves bearers of the good news of mercy and can thus help to overcome ancient barriers and lay the foundations of a new partnership.

→ Acculturation; Colonialism; Missionary

Bibliography: K. J. BADE, *Friedrich Fabri und der Imperialismus der Bismarckzeit* (Freiburg, 1975) • T. CHRISTENSEN and W. R. HUTCHINSON, eds., *Missionary Ideologies in the Imperialist Era: 1818-1920* (Aarhus, 1982) • J. COMAROFF and J. COMAROFF, *Of Revelation and Revolution: Christianity, Colonialism, and Consciousness in South Africa* (2 vols.; Chicago, 1991-97) • J. K. FAIRBANK, ed., *The Missionary Enterprise in China and America* (Cambridge, Mass., 1974) • H.-W. GENSICHEN, "Die deutsche Mission und der Kolonialismus," *KuD* 8 (1962) 136-49 • H. GRÜNDER, *Christliche Mission und deutscher Imperialismus, 1884-1914* (Paderborn, 1982); idem, *Welteroberung und Christentum* (Gütersloh, 1992) • K. HAMMER, *Weltmission und Kolonialismus* (Munich, 1978) • J. HÖFFNER, *Kolonialismus und Evangelium* (Trier, 1969) • S. NEILL, *Colonialism and Christian Missions* (London, 1966) • H.-J. PRIEN, *Die Geschichte des Christentums in Lateinamerika, 1492-1977* (Göttingen, 1978) • B. STANLEY, *The Bible and the Flag: Protestant Missions and British Imperialism in the Nineteenth and Twentieth Centuries* (Leicester, Eng., 1990) • W. USTORF, *F. M. Zahn und der Aufbau kirchlicher Strukturen in Westafrika (1862-1900)* (Erlangen, 1989) • A. F. WALLS, *The Missionary Movement in Christian History* (Maryknoll, N.Y., 1996) • B. WIRTH, *Imperialistische Übersee- und Missionspolitik dargestellt am Beispiel Chinas* (Münster, 1968).

HANS-WERNER GENSICHEN

Colossians, Epistle to the

1. Occasion and Contents
2. Authorship
3. Features

1. Occasion and Contents

Colossians was written to a church that → Paul did not found. It was designed to strengthen the position of its founder, Epaphras (1:7-8; 4:12-13), when erroneous teaching threatened the → congregation. The first part (chaps. 1–2) contains doctrine and polemics. After the opening greeting in 1:1-2 comes an introduction (vv. 3-20), whose beginning reminds us of Phlm. 4-5. It culminates in a soteriological formula in vv. 13-14 and a hymn to Christ in vv. 15-20. In the then-and-now schema of vv. 21-23 the addressees are reminded of their → reconciliation to God and admonished to hold fast to the gospel. In 1:24–2:5 we have a picture of the suffering → apostle who has revealed God's saving act (revelation schema, 1:26-27). The polemic is introduced programmatically in 2:6-7 (see below on 2:8-23).

The second part contains parenesis (3:1–4:6). Believers are admonished to act in accordance with the reality of Christ (3:1-4). Concrete directions follow in traditional form (3:5-17 is a list of virtues and vices; 3:18–4:1, → household rules that are related to contemporary political philosophy). Further admonitions in 4:2-6 are followed by specific greetings (4:7-17), with the names being much the same as in Philemon. The letter closes with a reference to an autograph.

2. Authorship

On the surface, Colossians reveals a striking closeness to Philemon. The fact that Paul is in prison is more strongly emphasized than in Philemon or Philippians (1:24; 4:18). If Colossians is authentic, it would seem to belong to the same period as those letters (presumably written in → Ephesus), and certainly before Romans.

Theological and linguistic differences, however, distinguish Colossians from the other epistles, such as its extended clause sequences (1:9-12), strings of synonyms (1:27 etc.), and greater reliance on participial constructions (1:3-14; 2:12-13). The Pauline image of the → church as the body of Christ is changed, with Christ here the head of the body (1:18; 2:19). The → eschatology is very different: Christians are both buried *and raised* with Christ in → baptism (cf. 2:12-13 and 3:1 with Rom. 6:4-5).

If Colossians is pseudonymous, it can hardly have been written to Colossae, since that city was destroyed by an earthquake in A.D. 62 and rebuilt only much later. It is conceivable that the author is appealing to Paul and using Philemon to influence another non-Pauline church (e.g., Laodicea; see 2:1; 4:15-16; also 1:15-20 and Rev. 3:14), the true setting of the letter's fictitious account. On this view it was written after A.D. 70 and not far from the places mentioned in 4:13, perhaps Ephesus. In both theology and literary style, Ephesians is dependent upon Colossians.

3. Features
In the church addressed, an apparently flourishing heresy, which is called a → philosophy (2:8; the term embraces religious and mythical teachings) involves speculation on cosmic elements and propagates religiously motivated practices (2:16-23). This "Colossian heresy" was clearly a syncretistic religion drawing on ideas from → Judaism, → Gnosticism, and the → mystery religions (2:11, 16, 18; → Syncretism) but also having Christian components.

In opposition, Colossians declares that all additional religious practices are unnecessary and dangerous. The → salvation in Christ that is given with the Christ-event brings full victory over all powers (2:10-15). In this respect Colossians itself shows some parallels with Gnostic → soteriology. The ethical instruction follows upon the proclamation of salvation. Here Colossians follows Pauline theology, though without using the terminology of the doctrine of → justification.

Bibliography: Commentaries: M. BARTH and H. BLANKE (AB; Garden City, N.Y., 1994) • H. CONZELMANN (NTD 8; 2d ed.; Göttingen, 1981) 176-202 • J. GNILKA (HTKNT 10/1; Freiburg, 1980) • A. LINDEMANN (ZBK; Zurich, 1983) • E. LOHSE (Hermeneia, Philadelphia, 1971) • P. POKORNÝ (THKNT 10/1; Leipzig, 1987) • E. SCHWEIZER (EKKNT; 1976; ET Minneapolis, 1982) • M. WOLTER (ÖTBK 12; Gütersloh, 1993) 27-223.

Other works: C. E. ARNOLD, *The Colossian Syncretism: The Interface between Christianity and Folk Belief at Colossae* (Grand Rapids, 1996) • J. LÄHNEMANN, *Der Kolosserbrief. Komposition, Situation und Argumentation* (Gütersloh, 1971) • A. LINDEMANN, "Die Gemeinde von 'Kolossa,'" *WD* 16 (1981) 111-34 • T. W. MARTIN, *By Philosophy and Empty Deceit: Colossians as Response to a Cynic Critique* (Sheffield, 1996) • E. SCHWEIZER, "Zur neueren Forschung am Kolosserbrief (seit 1970)," *ThBer* 5 (1976) 136-89.

ANDREAS LINDEMANN

Comfort → Consolation, Comfort

Commission of the Churches on International Affairs

1. Origins and Objectives
2. Procedure
3. Ongoing Issues

The Commission of the Churches on International Affairs (CCIA) is part of the program activities of the World Council of Churches (WCC). It monitors international affairs of interest to the world fellowship of churches and assists the council in carrying out its witness in the sociopolitical sphere. Originally enjoying a large amount of autonomy within the WCC, it was later integrated in the program structure of the WCC. In 1991 it was transformed into the Board for International Affairs, located in Program Unit III (Justice, Peace, and Creation). For purposes of external relations of the council, the name "Commission of the Churches on International Affairs" was maintained.

1. Origins and Objectives
The conviction that active engagment in international affairs is an integral part of the → mission of the church undergirds the very existence of the CCIA. Its founding in 1946 in Cambridge, England, was in response to a deeply felt sense of the failure of Christian witness during the first half of the 20th century. As a joint agency of the International Missionary Council and the WCC in process of formation, it was established to serve both organizations, in the words of its charter, as a "source of stimulus and knowledge in their approach to international problems, as a medium of common counsel and action, and as their organ in formulating the Christian mind on world issues."

2. Procedure
The CCIA functions in both an internal and external direction. Internally it informs the WCC by providing background information on regional issues; ex-

ternally it makes the position of the WCC known to national churches and to governments, as well as to the → United Nations and to its various specialized agencies with which it holds consultative status. In the serial *CCIA Background Information* it publishes information intended to bring international problems to the attention of local churches for education and reflection. The daily work of the Geneva staff includes the monitoring and interpreting of → conflict situations. On occasion, public statements of the WCC on international affairs are proposed and prepared by the CCIA for possible adoption by the Assembly, the Central Committee, or the Executive Committee. The officers of the Central Committee, the moderator, and the general secretary may also make statements. Relevant member churches, councils of churches, and regional task forces are consulted. Even when adopted, statements are not legislatively binding on the member churches.

At times the CCIA makes direct appeals to governments. When it does so, it speaks either in its own name or on behalf of the WCC, but always within established policy guidelines. Occasionally the CCIA has been called upon to act as mediator between conflicting parties. This was the case in 1971 when, together with the → All Africa Conference of Churches, its mediation contributed to a successful resolution of the Sudanese civil war.

3. Ongoing Issues

The CCIA assisted in the drafting of the Universal Declaration of Human Rights as well as the Covenant on Civil and Political Rights. The CCIA called for an effective system of international inspection and control of nuclear testing and the creation of reliable international procedures for the peaceful settlement of conflicts. It has represented the WCC's call for a comprehensive treaty to ban the production and deployment of nuclear → weapons. In addition, it has issued documents for study and action on the Israeli-Palestinian conflict, the situation in Armenia, → disarmament, religious freedom, the conflict in the former Yugoslavia, the arms trade, and the application of sanctions.

→ Christian Development Services; Colonialism; Ecology; Ecumenical Movement; Human and Civil Rights; International Law; Minorities; Peace; Poverty; Religious Liberty; War

Bibliography: P. ABRECHT and N. KOSHY, eds., *Before It's Too Late* (Geneva, 1983) • A. VAN DER BENT, *Christian Response in a World of Crisis* (Geneva, 1986) • CCIA, *Christian Responsibility in World Affairs* (London, 1949) • R. FAGLY, *The First Twenty Years in Outline* (Geneva, 1967) • WCC, *CCIA Reports* (annually since 1946); idem, *Religious Freedom: Main Statements by the WCC, 1948-1975* (Geneva, 1976); idem, *The Role of the WCC in International Affairs* (Geneva, 1986) • WCC and INTERNATIONAL MISSIONARY COUNCIL, *Conference of Church Leaders on International Affairs at Cambridge* (Geneva, 1946).

See also the following articles in *CCIA Background Information* (Geneva): "Armenia: The Continuing Tragedy" (1984, no. 1) • "The Arms Trade Today" (1993, no. 1) • "East Timor" (1995, no. 1) • "Ecumenical Presence at the United Nations: Second Special Session on Disarmament" (1982, no. 3) • "Perestroika" (1988, no. 1) • "The Tragedy of Bosnia" (1994, no. 1).

PAUL WEE and DWAIN C. EPPS

Commonwealth of Independent States

The Commonwealth of Independent States (CIS) is a voluntary association that includes 12 of the 15 republics of the former Union of Soviet Socialist Republics (→ Soviet Union). Proclaiming itself a successor to the USSR in some aspects of international affairs, the commonwealth provides a framework for unified military policy, a single currency, and a single "economic space."

The Minsk Agreement of December 8, 1991, which established the commonwealth, was signed by the three Slav republics Russia, Belarus, and Ukraine. Later that month, eight other former Soviet republics also joined: Armenia, Azerbaijan, Kazakhstan, Kyrgyzstan, Moldova, Tajikistan, Turkmenistan, and Uzbekistan. Georgia was admitted as the 12th member in December 1993. After some initial hesitation about remaining in the commonwealth, the parliaments of Azerbaijan (in September 1993), Moldova (October 1993), and Georgia (March 1994) voted finally to adhere to the union.

For information about the member nations of the CIS, see the articles on the respective countries.

Bibliography: Europe World Yearbook: 1994 (vol. 1; London, 1994) 119-23 • B. HUNTER, ed., *The Statesman's Year-Book, 1994-95* (New York, 1994) 370-81 • S. WHITE, *After Gorbachev* (4th ed.; Cambridge, 1993) • S. WHITE et al., *The Politics of Transition: Shaping a Post-Soviet Future* (Cambridge, 1993).

THE EDITORS

Commune

According to Friedrich Engels (1820-95), monogamous → marriage was the historical downfall of the feminine sex, degrading → women to slavery (→ Sexism 1) and making them slaves of the lust of males (→ Sexuality) and mere instruments for the bearing of children. In response, he put forward three demands: (1) women should be reintroduced into public industry (→ Work 7); (2) → prostitution should be ended and monogamy made a reality for both men and women; and (3) the raising and education of children should be a public matter (→ Childhood; Kindergarten). In its earliest years the Soviet Union tried in grand style to put these demands into practice by ending marriage and the family as an economic unit in society, doing away with both marriage and divorce as legal institutions, and organizing and encouraging communes of both young people and workers. This experiment, however, failed miserably. Wilhelm Reich (1897-1957), probably the only author who analyzed the available material carefully, concluded that attempting to solve the anthropological problem (→ Anthropology 5) — that is, the question of the "new man" — by way of ethical rigorism simply led to a forced, authoritarian, and repressive style of community life. Hence ultimately, the interests of an obtuse state apparatus dominated life, which needed obedient soldiers, producers, and functionaries (→ Authority; Power; State).

When in the 1960s the commune movement was active again in California, West Germany, and Copenhagen, it was concerned with overcoming three fundamental difficulties: the social isolation of the nuclear family, the failure to emancipate women, and failure of the generative function in the nuclear family. The communes of the time tried to live in a politically and socially engaged larger group that would provide impulses for changing society at large in the sense of preparation for → revolution. They attempted to deal with the suppressed and exploited position of women (→ Feminism) by ending attachment to one man (which can degenerate into a view of women as possessions) and by viewing the rearing of children as a function of the larger group as a whole. By appropriating this ideological baggage, communes undoubtedly took on more than they could handle, in both theory and practice. They were unable to overcome their ghetto situation. Nor, obviously, were they really able to deal with the individual → socialization of their members. In many communes monogamous marriage and patriarchal structures reasserted themselves, a development that

society at large registered with satisfaction and a certain triumphalism.

The idea of an ideologically free commune, except in the kibbutzim in → Israel (2.2), was thus maintained only in the milieu of students or in the form of therapeutic communes for the mentally or physically → handicapped (→ Diakonia; Inner Mission; Pastoral Care 4; also → Imprisonment).

→ Counterculture

Bibliography: U. BALDENEY, H. GASCHE, and R. KUNZELMANN, eds., *Unverbindliche Richtlinien* (2 vols.; Frankfurt, 1962-63) • S. DE BEAUVOIR, *The Second Sex* (New York, 1953) • W. E. CHMIELEWSKI, L. J. KERN, and M. KLEE-HARTZELL, eds., *Women in Spiritual and Communitarian Societies in the United States* (Syracuse, N.Y., 1993) • F. ENGELS, *The Origin of the Family, Private Property, and the State* (New York, 1972; orig. pub., 1884) • E. FROMM, *Autorität und Familie* (Paris, 1936) • J. KRAUS, D. PRAUSE, and L. WIEKENS, "Auf der Suche nach neuen Gesellschaftsformen," *WzM* 22 (1970) 201-7 • W. REICH, *The Invasion of Compulsory Sex-Morality* (New York, 1971); idem, *Jugendkommunen in Sowjetrußland* (Berlin, 1931) • R. REICHE, *Sexualität und Klassenkampf* (Frankfurt, 1968) • J. SCHARFENBERG, *Die Zukunft der Familie und der Kirche* (Wuppertal, 1970) • P. A. SOROKIN, *The American Sex Revolution* (Boston, 1956) • W. R. STOKES, "Our Changing Sex Ethics," *The Family and the Sex Revolution* (Bloomington, Ind., 1964) 146-64 • B. D. ZABLOCKI, *Alienation and Charisma: A Study of Contemporary American Communes* (New York, 1980).

JOACHIM SCHARFENBERG†

Communicatio idiomatum → Christology 2.4

Communication

1. Term
2. Forms
3. Theories
4. The Church
5. Practical Theology
6. Ethics

1. Term

As a special form of social action, communication denotes the exchange of signs between a communicator and a recipient. This method of conveying meaning relates to the thinking, feelings, and acts of others. In communication science the term "communication" is normally limited to exchanges between one person or persons and another or others with the help of spoken → language, signs, and → symbols, including nonverbal. It is usual to think of the verbal elements as being auditorily perceived and primarily rationally or → cognitively processed. Nonverbal elements encompass gestures, mime, and signs and symbols that are not verbally articulated. They are for the most part visual and convey feeling. In all ages and cultures, social interaction as a basic process has played a role we can hardly overestimate. Nonliterary cultures make use of nonverbal and oral communication. With the development of the alphabet, a culture of reading and writing arose that printing enriched in the 15th century. Though most older forms of communication have not fully vanished, audiovisual → culture plays an increasingly dominant role in → industrial society.

2. Forms

We may differentiate the various forms of communication from many different angles. Three dichotomies are of fundamental importance: (1) direct versus indirect, (2) mutual versus one-sided, and (3) private versus public communication.

1. All communication is either direct (face-to-face) or indirect (at a distance of space or time or both). Signals, writing, and printed matter are older methods of indirect communication.
2. Communication is either mutual, as in conversation, or one-sided, as in a lecture or address (i.e., either with interactive exchange or not).
3. Private communication concerns only a specific person or persons; in distinction is communication to a whole mass of people, or public. The → mass media engage in public communication as a social → institution (→ Society). They do so in the form of indirect communication to a scattered public. → Preaching (see 5) and public address do not involve the same distance in space and time from the recipients.

In our industrial and → information society we cannot separate the mass media from the political, social, and technical conditions of their form of organization. Whether politically committed or superficially neutral, they represent both conservative and progressive elements, both → tradition and reform. From the standpoint of the politics of communication, there is conflict between private economic interests and the public tasks of the media. Giving material or physical form to the mass media (e.g., via paper or film) involves scientific communication practices. The press makes only an optical impact, radio and cassettes an acoustic, and films and television both.

3. Theories

The structures and functions of communication have given rise to theoretical discussion, which makes use of many sociological terms and covers a theme that demands interdisciplinary treatment. Analysis of communication generally finds four factors that form the basic scaffolding of the communication-event: someone who has something to communicate, the message itself, the means used, and one or more recipients.

The communicator is the one who has something to impart and who does it with the help of a medium that makes it accessible to others. The communicator might also be called the source or sender or producer. The recipient is the one who wants to understand the message imparted by the medium and to grasp its meaning. One might also call the recipient the consumer or addressee.

Mass media communication differs from direct interpersonal communication in being directed at a broad cross-section of the population and not just to one or more individuals. For the most part it will also involve a distance in space and perhaps also time between communicator and recipient. Again, communication will be all one-sided, with no exchange of roles and therefore no direct interaction. Communication by mass media is thus public, indirect, and unilateral, making use either of technical methods or of informal means of communication such as rumors to reach a dispersed public.

In view of the many definitions of the terms "communication" and "mass communication" and the many different aspects, no generally accepted and comprehensive theory of (mass) communication is to hand. We only have approaches to theories, especially relating to social communication processes.

As the prewar stimulus-reaction concept was abandoned, Harold D. Lasswell (1902-78), Paul F. Lazarsfeld (1901-76), and Joseph T. Klapper (1917-84) contributed to the development of a sociological theory of mass communication with an emphasis on the function of the mass media in modern society. Normative and systemative theories were central for a long time in Germany until Henk Prakke in the 1960s developed a → functionalist view. The utilitarian theory was a popular variant. The use and gratification theory was similar in the United States. On this view the main question is not what the media do with the public but what the public does with what the media offer.

4. The Church

In its decree *Inter mirifica*, → Vatican II introduced the term *communicatio socialis* for the mass media.

It claimed that the media have a social influence that the → church cannot ignore. The → Roman Catholic Church finally accepted the use of the mass media in its pastoral instruction *Communio et progressio* (1971). At Uppsala in 1968 the Protestant churches issued a statement on mass communication by the media. In the 1970s and 1980s in both Europe and the Americas attempts were made to link the theological dimensions of communication to the anthropological, sociological, cultural, and pastoral components. Specific themes in this regard that touch on both theology and communication theory include the forms of personal → piety, art and religious → experience, ritual, relations with the mass media, → popular religion, → worship, → church music, → church architecture, public work, → evangelization, church publicity and work with the media, church conferences, and → Christian art.

Bibliography: D. ABERBACH, *Charisma in Politics, Religion, and the Media: Private Trauma, Public Ideals* (London, 1995) • H. BOVENTER, *Ethik des Journalismus. Zur Philosophie der Medienkultur* (Constance, 1984) • R. BURKART, *Kommunikationswissenschaft. Grundlagen und Problemfelder* (Vienna, 1983) • *Fernsehen–Medium zur Kirche des Lebens und Glaubens?* (= *Ref.* 29/5 [1980]) • J. COLEMAN and M. TOMKA, eds., *Mass Media* (London, 1993) • B. GUNTER and R. VINEY, *Seeing Is Believing: Religion and Television in the 1990s* (London, 1994) • C. HOLTZ-BACHA, *Publizistik-Bibliographie. Eine internationale Bibliographie von Nachschlagewerken zur Literatur der Kommunikationswissenschaft* (Constance, 1985) • K. KOSZYK and K. H. PRUYS, *Handbuch der Massenkommunikation* (Munich, 1981) • W. R. LANGENBUCHER, ed., *Publizistik- und Kommunikationswissenschaft* (Vienna, 1986) • D. MCQUAIL, *Mass Communication Theory: An Introduction* (London, 1983; 3d ed., 1994) • G. MALETZKE, *Psychologie der Massenkommunikation. Theorie und Systematik* (2d ed.; Hamburg, 1978) • K. MERTEN, *Kommunikation. Eine Begriffs- und Prozeßanalyse* (Opladen, 1977) • H. PÜRER, *Einführung in die publizistikwissenschaftlichen Fragestellungen, Theorieansätze, Forschungstechniken* (2d ed.; Munich, 1981) • M. SCHMOLKE, "Kirche und Massenmedien," *HRP* 3.388-402 • P. A. SOUKUP, *Christian Communication: A Bibliographical Survey* (Westport, Conn., 1990) • D. A. STOUT and J. M. BUDDENBAUM, eds., *Religion and Mass Media: Christianity, Institutions, and Audiences* (London, 1996).

JOAN M. H. J. HEMELS

5. Practical Theology

From the standpoint of pastoral theology, the term "communication" offers the possibility of looking at the mediation of faith as an attempt to reach understanding between speakers and recipients, or preachers and hearers. One may also communicate the → gospel by such means as instruction, Bible readings, → pastoral care, or liturgical acts. The different forms of communication do not differ essentially in content or effect but have grown out of different situations of communication. As in all communication, there may be a combination of the verbal and nonverbal, for example, of Word and → sacrament combined to a common effect, and → baptism and → Eucharist may be regarded as specific modes of communicating the gospel.

In discussing the insights and methods of communication science, practical theology distinguishes between success and result. Thus one may to some degree ensure the success of a sermon (→ Preaching), but one has no final control over the result (i.e., the awakening of faith).

A further distinction is between the vertical and horizontal dimensions of communication of the gospel. If in liturgical practice we take this to mean that in its horizontal structures and processes, → worship must be in keeping with the vertical, it can involve a distortion of the communication situation that still afflicts much Protestant worship (e.g., a frontal structure, monopolizing of functions, monologic preaching, one-way flow of information, and only limited possibilities of participation). In contrast, orientation to what is meant by NT koinonia and a relating of grace (the vertical dimension) to mutual giving (the horizontal dimension) seem to be a more appropriate basis for a liturgical practice that allows all to participate actively. (See the Constitution on the Sacred Liturgy of Vatican II, *Sacrosanctum concilium* 14, 21, 27, 30, 48, etc.) According to this focus, a central structure replaces the frontal, forms of dialogic communication add to the sermon, liturgical functions are divided, and the nonverbal element is stronger, especially that which makes participation possible and communicates fellowship (→ Symbol).

Before → Vatican II the use of Latin in Roman Catholic worship permitted only limited and mostly nonverbal participation by the congregation. Popular elements thus came to underlie or overlay the official → liturgy. We now see from this model, however, how necessary it is to see liturgical communication as a complex sign-process that makes use of many means of verbal and nonverbal communication at many different levels. New light is thus shed on the theologically much-debated relation between Word and sacrament. Verbal (digital) methods of communication seem to consist for the most part of stating and imparting → cognitive contents, but nonverbal (analogical) communication methods work to form relations. Reducing the latter in favor of the Word, as Reformation churches have done, may give greater clarity to communication of the gospel, but it essentially limits the forging of relations.

In general, → prayer is primarily oriented to the vertical dimension, showing us even in the form of words that it is addressed to a transcendental Thou (→ Immanence and Transcendence) and that the speaker sets himself or herself apart from intrahuman communication. Analysis of worship as a sign-process, however, makes it plain that differentiating the vertical and horizontal dimensions in communication of the faith inadequately captures the essence of the process. Even prayer involves the realities of horizontal communication, whether we define it as speech between God and us, or whether we view it as the verbal form of a nonverbal action.

→ Proclamation

Bibliography: H.-E. Bahr, Verkündigung als Information (Hamburg, 1968) • H. Balz, "Kommunikation," LMTG 219-24 • G. Bormann, "Kommunikationsprobleme in der Kirche," Kirche und Gesellschaft (ed. J. Mathes; Reinbek, 1969) 188ff. • P. Cornehl and H.-E. Bahr, eds., Gottesdienst und Öffentlichkeit. Zur Theorie und Didaktik neuer Kommunikation (Hamburg, 1970) • B. Kappenberg, Kommunikationstheorie und Kirche. Grundlagen einer kommunikationstheoretischen Ekklesiologie (Frankfurt, 1981) • B. Klaus, ed., Kommunikation in der Kirche (Gütersloh, 1979) • H. Kraemer, Die Kommunikation des christlichen Glaubens (Zurich, 1958) • C. H. Kraft, Communication Theory for Christian Witness (Nashville, 1983) • E. Leach, Kultur und Kommunikation. Zur Logik symbolischer Zusammenhänge (Frankfurt, 1978) • G. Sauter, "Kommunikation und Wahrheitsfrage," Fides et communicatio (FS M. Doerne; Göttingen, 1970) 263ff. • G. Schiwy et al., Zeichen im Gottesdienst (Munich, 1976) • P. A. Soukup, Communication and Theology: Introduction and Review of the Literature (London, 1983) • E. Winkler, Kommunikation und Verkündigung (Berlin, 1977).

Karl-Heinrich Bieritz

6. Ethics

Communication is unavoidably a matter of → ethical concern. Even the inability to communicate a message exactly by any method poses ethical demands on both communicators and recipients. Even more so does the possibility (and reality) of abusing communication to pass on what is misleading, false, or morally harmful, along with the possibility (and reality) of receiving what is communicated in a spirit of hostility, suspicion, evil intent, perverted interest, or indeed gullibility. The demands fall on both communicator and recipient.

Communicators must consider whether they have carefully and honestly thought out what they wish to convey and how most accurately to convey it. More seriously still, they need to ask whether they are resorting to ambivalence, half-truth, deliberate misinformation or misrepresentation, or downright falsehood in a way that will deceive or mislead recipients. A further question is whether what they communicate will do harm to others, whether by destroying reputations; stirring up bigotry, hatred, or fanaticism; corrupting moral values; or offering deplorable examples of violence, cruelty, and exploitation. Those who control the → mass media face the conflict between profitability and ethical responsibility. A problem that also arises at the level of government is whether such → human rights as that of free speech can offset the evils of deceptive and harmful advertising, political slander and misrepresentation, and the perverting influence of, for example, pornographic communication.

Recipients must weigh their ethical response to what others communicate or seek to communicate. Are they open to honest and friendly attempts at communication? Are they ready for careful and unbiased discussion of opposing views or for explanations of actions that have created a rift? Do they seize on what may be careless or exaggerated as a weapon with which to resist or condemn? Conversely, do they treat with sufficient skepticism attempts to use communication to tempt them to make foolish purchases or pursue harmful courses of action? Are they prepared to close themselves off from totally unworthy communication, whether by speech, writing, film, video, or television programs, exercising their right of individual censorship?

Communication as such is neutral. Like any basic human possibility, it may be used well or badly, for good or for evil. Communication thus confronts us at every turn with a call for ethical decisions. In particular, it confronts the Christian churches with a call to set an example of the ethical use of communication, to see to it that their ministers, especially as communicators, do not abuse their office, and to instruct their members, as both communicators and recipients, to develop an ethically responsible approach to communication in personal dealings with others, in the varied areas of life in which communication plays so big a role, and in their individual hearing, reading, and watching the communication of others.

The Editors

Communications Media →
Church Communications Media

Communism → Socialism

Communities, Spiritual

1. Developments in Protestantism
2. Forms and Features

1. Developments in Protestantism

1.1 Justifiable → Reformation criticism of the medieval → monasteries and orders for merit-seeking and an emphasis on external matters effectively blocked the development within Protestantism either of biblically legitimate orders and brotherhoods such as the church had known since the Constantinian age or of → Luther's dream of a gathering of those who wished to be serious Christians (*German Mass* [1526]). Although Luther recognized the → Brethren of the Common Life and some monasteries remained (e.g., at Loccum and Amelungsborn), and although new beginnings were attempted (J. Arndt and G. Tersteegen's Pilgerhütte [Pilgrim shelter]) or made (N. L. von → Zinzendorf's → Moravian Church), ultimately an "inner → asceticism" gained acceptance.

1.2. New communities of → deacons and deaconesses in the 19th century belonged for the most part to the social or charitable sphere rather than withdrawing as separated religious communities. Where deaconesses did separate, they found in the motherhouse, which was structured along → family lines, the protection that the social → norms of the day demanded for unmarried women and hence enjoyed the freedom needed to fulfill their → vocation. This development anticipated some of the → emancipatory elements in the → feminist movement.

Things were different in England with the → High Church movement (→ Anglican Communion), which after 1841 was responsible for the founding of 114 monasteries and orders (Anglican → Franciscans, → Benedictines, etc.), of which over 50 are still in existence — for example, the Society of Sacred Mission (Kelham [1894]) and the Community of the Resurrection (Mirfield [1892]).

1.3. Germany saw a new beginning after the shattering events of World War I. In repudiation of → Culture Protestantism, communities were founded for an obligatory spiritual life after the tradition of the Pietist → revival, such as the Pfarrergebetsbruderschaft (1913), the High Church Evangelische Franziskaner-Tertiarier (1927; → Tertiaries), the Evangelisch-katholische eucharistische Gemeinschaft (1929), the Berneuchener evangelische Michaelsbruderschaft (1931), and the → Confessing Church's Kirchliche Bruderschaften (1934). In 1935-37, D. → Bonhoeffer attempted to found a community house at the seminary at Finkenwalde.

Elsewhere the Tiers Ordre protestant des Veilleurs was formed in 1923 in the French-speaking sphere, the Zoe Movement in 1915 in Greek Orthodoxy (→ Orthodox Church), the Societas Sanctae Birgittae in 1920 in Sweden, the Theological Oratorium in 1926 in Denmark, the Ordo Crucis in 1933 in Norway, the → Iona Community in 1938 in Scotland, and the Comunitá di Agape in 1947 in the Waldensian Church. Similar movements arose in the → Third World (§2) in China, Japan, Nigeria, and India (Christian ashrams; → Hinduism and Christianity).

1.4. On the soil thus prepared, a monastic spring flowed forth after World War II. Protestant orders were formed with a → celibate lifestyle for both men and women. In the French-speaking world these orders included → Taizé (1949), Pomeyrol (1948), and Grandchamp (1952); in Germany, the Christusbruderschaft (1949), the Communität Casteller Ring (1950), the Communität Imshausen (1955), and the Jesusbruderschaft Gnadental (1961); in Sweden after 1951 (→ Religious Liberty), small houses of Franciscans, → Dominicans, Carmelites, and Benedictines, as well as the Heiliggeistschwesterschaft in Uppsala (1961) and the Evangelische Marientöchter in Vadstena (1963).

1.5. The rise of these new spiritual communities did not diminish the importance of the older ones. The latter had already worked through second- and third-generation problems (e.g., loss of the original challenge and the death of the founders). New fellowships developed out of them. The Michaelsbruderschaft, for example, was the source of several, including the Ordo Pacis (1956), the retreat house Kloster Kirchberg (1958), the Ansverusbruderschaft in Hamburg (1960), the Missionsbruderschaft in South Africa (1964), and the Compagnonnage St. Michael in Alsace (1978). Some 60 larger communities and many smaller ones made up the picture, with their own crises, disbandings, and reunitings. In addition, 100 Anglican communities were formed in the 20th century, of which over 50 remain.

2. Forms and Features

2.1. As H. Dombois has pointed out, the difference between religious communities living as orders and those living in the world is not decisive (pp.

222-23). A common life can be lived in a monastery, in an external community, or in → diaspora with regular times of retreat. The so-called evangelical counsels, or counsels of perfection (i.e., poverty, chastity, and obedience), may be observed with varying degrees of strictness. → Poverty may take the form of sharing goods, of hospitality, or of a simple lifestyle with generous giving to the community. The *disponibilité* (unattachedness) of → celibacy may be practiced also in the → family. → Obedience may mean submission to an → authority, integration into a fellowship, or listening to a helper.

2.2. All spiritual communities center on frequent observance of the → Eucharist and daily canonical → hours. All also involve a rule. The thrust is toward → liturgy, → pastoral care, → meditation, spiritual exercises, theology, → diakonia, and → mission. Retreat houses cater to those on the margin of the church and those troubled in spirit.

2.3. Although we may differentiate Pietist and denominational types, there is lively exchange between them (with a common → subculture drawing them together from about 1968). Thus a High Church → Pietism has been possible (note the older → Oxford Movement). From the standpoint of church politics, we cannot categorize the orders and communities. Liturgically they seem to be → conservative, but in involvement and understanding of the church they are progressive.

2.4. Common to all the Christian communities is an ecumenical attitude. They pray for → unity and offer their facilities for international and ecumenical gatherings. Some are of mixed denominational membership; many use forms taken from other denominations (→ Ecumenical Movement).

2.5. The communities are self-conscious church movements. "We can build church only if we ourselves are church" (Michaelsbruderschaft). They avoid presenting themselves as → sects apart from the church and welcome → visitation.

2.6. The place of spiritual communities in the church is defined by the dialectic of popular parish life, on the one hand, and, on the other, by a binding lifestyle beyond that of the congregation at large. Communities are not merely legitimate in addition to the universal, regional, and local forms of the church; their absence would be an ecclesiological lack. They have an exemplary and representative function of demonstrating the committed and family life of a biblical church. The specific calling of the members, which is not for everyone, is not regarded as conferring higher status within the one body of the church.

→ Base Community; Discipleship; High Church Movement; House Church; Orders and Congregations; Spirituality

Bibliography: D. BONHOEFFER, *Life Together* (New York, 1976; orig. pub., 1939) • H. DOMBOIS, *Das Recht der Gnade,* vol. 3, *Ökumenisches Kirchenrecht* (Bielefeld, 1983) chap. 12 • H. GORNIK, *Anders leben* (Gütersloh, 1979; 2d ed., 1982) • G. HAGE et al., "Bruderschaften / Schwesternschaften / Kommunitäten," *TRE* 7.195-212; idem, ed., *Die evangelische Michaelsbruderschaft* (Kassel, 1981) • J. HALKENHÄUSER, *Kirche und Kommunitäten* (Paderborn, 1978; 2d ed., 1985) bibliography • L. MOHAUPT, ed., *Modelle gelebten Glaubens* (Hamburg, 1976) • J. O'HALLORAN, *Signs of Hope: Developing Small Christian Communities* (Maryknoll, N.Y., 1991) • *Quatember* (1936-) • T. P. RAUSCH, *Radical Christian Communities* (Collegeville, Minn., 1990) • I. REIMER, *Verbindliches Leben in Bruderschaften, Kommunitäten, Lebensgemeinschaften* (Stuttgart, 1985).

HANS MAYR

Community Churches → International Council of Community Churches

Community of Goods

The summaries in Acts 2:44-45 and 4:32-35 tell us that the → primitive Christian community in Jerusalem had all things in common as members sold land and other property and shared the proceeds according to need. This account is not exclusively historical but also has the elements of an example and an ideal. As God's people, the OT community was not to have any needy within it (Deut. 15:4). The statement that the first Christians had all things in common corresponds to Greek and Hellenistic thinking regarding personal relationships and the ideals of → friendship, common life, and the → state (Diogenes Laertius *Peri biōn* 8.10; Iamblichus *De vit. Pyth.* 30.167-69; Plato *Resp.* 462C; Aristotle *Eth. Nic.* 9.8.1168b).

As Luke depicts it, and in the underlying situation of the primitive church, the sharing of goods is not to be viewed as a legally regulated sharing of property and production, nor is it a required renunciation of private property as at → Qumran (see Acts 5:4 and 12:12). The term "communism" in describing the early church is not appropriate. Behind the relativizing of possessions and the high sense of social responsibility were impulses from the preaching of → Jesus, imminent expectation of the → parousia, economic distress, and care for the poor in → Judaism.

The sharing of possessions has been practiced in several ways through the history of Christianity, especially in → monasticism and, since the Reformation, in various other groups, especially → Anabaptists (e.g., Hutterites) or utopian communities (e.g., the Oneida Community).

→ Communities, Spiritual; Ethics 2; Monasticism 3.2.2; Property, esp. 3.2-3

Bibliography: F. F. BRUCE, *The Book of Acts* (rev. ed.; Grand Rapids, 1988) 74, 100-101 • H.-J. DEGENHARDT, *Lukas, Evangelist der Armen* (Stuttgart, 1965) • E. HAEN-CHEN, *The Acts of the Apostles* (Philadelphia, 1971) 230-41 • F. HAUCK, "Κοινός," *TDNT* 3.789-97 • T. HOYT JR., "The Poor in Luke-Acts" (Diss., Duke University, 1975) • L. T. JOHNSON, *The Literary Function of the Possessions in Luke-Acts* (Missoula, Mont., 1977) • L. E. KECK, "The Poor among the Saints in the NT," *ZNW* 56 (1965) 100-129 • B. H. MÖNNING, "Die Darstellung des urchristlichen Kommunismus nach der Apostelgeschichte des Lukas" (Diss., Göttingen, 1978) • J. ROLOFF, *Die Apostelgeschichte* (Göttingen, 1981) 89-91 • G. SCHNEI-DER, *Die Apostelgeschichte* (Freiburg, 1980) 290-95 (bibliography) • F. G. UNTERGASSMAIR, "Κοινός, κοινόω," *EDNT* 2.302-3 • N. WALTER, "Apostelgeschichte 6,1 und die Anfänge der Urgemeinde in Jerusalem," *NTS* 29 (1983) 370-93.

ALFONS WEISER

Community Service

1. Development
2. The Church and Community Service

1. Development

Community service has developed in recent decades under the leadership of America, England (settlement movement), and Holland (Opbouwwerk). But behind it is a longer history of community organization with different principles, aims, local developments, and methods (A. Dunham). Traditions of community development, social planning, social action, and citizen participation have also played a part.

Socially motivated church groups have undertaken work among → marginal groups who lack influence and are the victims of discrimination. Conscious of the limits of what they can achieve, they seek to promote self-help. Under the influence of the student movement, social criticism has also given rise to political efforts to bring about social change (→ Society). Professional social work and social education, in addition to case work and group work, also engage in historical and social criticism.

The main goal of such service is to replace alienation with self-determination. In this regard community service cannot be tied too closely to professional services, since it has become clear that emancipation cannot be imparted. Rather, only as a target group organizes itself to take responsibility and ownership for achieving its goals can it expect success.

Education is another form of community service, with the specific aim of enhancing competence. In this field it covers such topics as → pedagogy, social and political questions, and → peace education as a political process. Ernst Lange formulated for the church the idea of → continuing education oriented to conflicts.

2. The Church and Community Service

In principle the church is an ideal agent of community service. It is called to → diakonia, being charged to bear witness to Christ by word and deed and by its very form. It is meant to live on the path to life in the light of the human destiny of the freedom of God's children. Being close to human life, → church employees, → groups, and → institutions have taken part from the outset in community service, both practically and theoretically. They have naturally run into opposition from vested interests, who have charged them with operating a political diakonia or party politics. There have even been rare instances of the disciplining of those engaged in community service. Many failures may still be expected, for community service that is oriented to conflict necessarily brings the church into conflict with itself. Yet it also offers the possibility of learning, growth, and renewal.

→ Counterculture; Democracy; Politics; Social Gospel; Social Services

Bibliography: H.-E. BAHR and R. GRONEMEYER, eds., *Konfliktorientierte Gemeinwesenarbeit* (2 vols.; Gelnhausen, 1976) • A. DUNHAM, *The New Community Organization* (New York, 1970) • R. M. KRAMER and H. SPECHT, eds., *Readings in Community Organization Practice* (Englewood Cliffs, N.J., 1969) • E. LANGE, *Bildung als Problem und Funktion der Kirche* (Munich, 1980) • C. W. MÜLLER and P. NIMMERMANN, *Stadtplanung und Gemeinwesenarbeit* (Munich, 1971) • A. SEIPPEL, *Handbuch Aktivierende Gemeinwesenarbeit* (2 vols.; Gelnhausen, 1976).

ALF SEIPPEL

Comoros

	1960	1980	2000
Population (1,000s):	183	325	612
Annual growth rate (%):	2.25	3.17	2.95
Area: 1,862 sq. km. (719 sq. mi.)			

A.D. *2000*
Population density: 329/sq. km. (851/sq. mi.)
Births / deaths: 3.86 / 0.91 per 100 population
Fertility rate: 5.03 per woman
Infant mortality rate: 72 per 1,000 live births
Life expectancy: 59.5 years (m: 59.0, f: 60.0)
Religious affiliation (%): Muslims 98.1, Christians 1.2, other 0.7.

1. General Situation
2. Religious Situation

1. General Situation

Situated in the Mozambique Channel between northern Madagascar and the southeast coast of Africa, the archipelago of the Comoros comprises four volcanic islands: from northwest to southeast, Njazídja, Mwali, Nzwani (formerly called Grande Comore, Mohéli, and Anjouan respectively), and Mayotte. With its marine type of tropical climate, such subsistence crops as cassava, sweet potatoes, bananas, and upland rice are grown, although with the high density of population it remains necessary to import a major portion of the foodstuffs. Exports are derived primarily from vanilla, copra, perfume plants, and fruits. A markedly unfavorable balance of trade plagues the economy of the islands and is a factor in their heavy dependence on overseas aid.

The population is of varied origins, comprising fundamentally a mixture of mainland African, Madagascan, and Arabic elements. In the 15th century Arabs occupied Comoros, creating a separate sultanate on each island. The → slave trade increased the African component in the population. The official languages are Arabic and French, with three dialects of Comorian Swahili being widely spoken.

In 1843 France occupied Mayotte and by 1886 had gained control of the other islands. In 1914 the islands came under the administration of the French colony of Madagascar, and in 1947 they became an autonomous overseas territory of France. Internal self-government was attained in December 1961, followed on December 22, 1974, by referenda in which the three western islands voted for independence and Mayotte voted to remain with France. A unilateral declaration of independence on July 6, 1975, recognized by France at the end of the year, resulted in the establishment of the Federal Islamic Republic of the Comoros, which comprises all the islands except Mayotte, which today is a so-called territorial collectivity of France.

The republic has its capital at Moroni (30,000 in 1992), on Njazídja. Its official religion is → Islam. The basic → education remains from the French regime, but numerous → Koranic schools operate in the afternoon. The legal system represents a combination of French and Islamic law (→ Islam 4).

The island of Mayotte has an area of 232 sq. km. (144 sq. mi.), with a population of 86,000 (1992 est.). The capital Mamoundzu is a city of 12,000 (1985). French is the official language, the metropolitan franc is the monetary unit, and, in accordance with the French constitution, there is no official religion.

2. Religious Situation

In 1990, at least 98 percent of the population of Comoros were → Sunni Muslims of the Shafi'ite rite. Only about 0.5 percent were Christians, with the rest Baha'is or nonreligious. In Mayotte 97 percent are Sunni Muslims, with Christians composing most of the remaining 3 percent. Christianity has not had an appreciable demographic effect on the population of the Comoros, for most of the Christians have been expatriate French and Réunionais, with the Roman Catholics outnumbering the Protestants approximately four to one. On the declaration of independence there was a marked drop in the number of Roman Catholics with the departure of the French from the republic.

The foundation of the → Roman Catholic Church goes back to 1517, while the Protestant Église de Jésus-Christ aux Comores grew gradually with guest workers from Madagascar. It had two congregations in 1980. Since 1975 there have been contributions from the interdenominational Africa Inland Mission International in medical and educational work and through involvement with the Église de Jésus-Christ. Both Roman Catholics and Protestants have organizational links with churches in Madagascar.

→ African Theology; All Africa Conference of Churches

Bibliography: D. Barrett, ed., *WCE* 244-45 • *Britannica Book of the Year, 1996* (Chicago, 1996) 365, 393-94, 587 • J. Dresch, "Comoros," *NEBrit* (15th ed., 1991) 21.176-77 • M. Newitt, *The Comoro Islands* (London, 1984).

S. J. Kenneth Baker†

Comparative Study of Denominations →
Ecumenical Theology

Competition → Achievement
and Competition

Compromise

1. Concept
2. Meaning
3. Techniques
4. Readiness for Compromise
5. Limits

1. Concept
The word "compromise" derives from *compromitto*,
which in Roman law meant "agree on an arbiter."
Today the term indicates that parties in a → conflict
freely reach a solution by some yielding on all sides.
Compromise may be highly rated in virtue of the
principle of → consent, as in early African societies,
or it may be disparaged, as in European → feudalism.
Its high status today, especially in England, is a result
of the religious struggles of the 16th and 17th centuries and the free play of interest groups in liberal
19th-century orders.

2. Meaning
Compromise between → norms can take place
before God and the individual → conscience, for
example, in matters of self-preservation, national
defense, environmental protection, or competition.
Legislators and judges may be affected, for example,
in rules relating to → abortion. Without compromise, the problems of today would be subject to
the ethical traditions of yesterday (D. Rößler). The
supreme test of compromise occurs when conflicting
ideologies are at issue, as in the attempted historical
compromise between Christians and Communists in
Italy, or when → confessions must be reconciled, as
in church unions and mutual agreements. Compromise is the basis of ecumenical hope, or at any
rate of deeper mutual understanding (→ Ecumenical
Movement; Ecumenism).

  In everyday conflicts, compromise is a reconciliation of interests that both unites and divides
(W. Trillhaas). H. Thielicke (1908-86) viewed life as
the art of the possible, an insight suggesting that
fostering the ability to compromise is a central pedagogical task. Social groups (e.g., → political parties
and tariff partners) also seek compromise. Christian
organizations cannot refuse it in a → pluralistic mi-

lieu. Theological justification for compromise may
be found, for example, in → Luther's → two-kingdoms doctrine.

3. Techniques
Methods of compromise are meeting at the center or
making mutual concessions. The wording of the
compromise will usually provide only a superficial
cover for the problem. In → everyday life the Anglo-
Saxon technique of agreeing to disagree is useful. To
see antitheses clearly often enhances the cooperation
needed to overcome conflicting positions.

4. Readiness for Compromise
If a stalemate does not make compromise necessary,
good cooperation will often do more than making
maximum demands. The wish for prestige must not
play a role. Christian → love of neighbor and enemy
suggests compromise as an attitude of → tolerance
and respect. An → ethics of → responsibility points
in the same direction.

5. Limits
Urgent concerns and values limit compromise.
Christians see themselves in a → *status confessionis*
when they must safeguard central biblical ideas (→
Decalogue; Sermon on the Mount). Compromise
that is in any way dishonest or base is ethically unacceptable — for example, when it occurs at the cost
of a weaker third party. This is unfortunately the basis
of many apparently harmonious solutions. The →
Golden Rule of Matt. 7:12 is a good guide in making
a compromise and should be followed when other
parties are involved.

  → Democracy; International Law; Peace; Righteousness, Justice; Social Ethics; Society

Bibliography: M. BENJAMIN, "Compromise," *EncE* 1.189-
91 • J. R. PENNOCK and J. W. CHAPMAN, eds., *Com-
promise in Ethics, Law, and Politics* (New York, 1979) •
D. RÖSSLER, "Der ethische Kompromiß," *Theologie und
Wirklichkeit* (FS W. Trillhaas; Göttingen, 1974) 145ff. •
H. THIELICKE, *Theological Ethics*, vol. 1, *Foundations*
(Philadelphia, 1966) §§25-28 • W. TRILLHAAS, "Zum
Problem des Kompromisses," *ZEE* 4 (1960) 355-64.

                                                JÜRGEN STEIN

Conciliarism

"Conciliarism" is the theory that general → councils
represent the supreme church court, specifically, that
they are superior to the → pope. Its roots lie in the
discussions of medieval canonists (→ Canon Law),

especially concerning papal → immunity and responsibility. The heresy clause in the Decretum Gratiani (ca. 1140) states the principle that the pope can be judged by no one as long as he does not deviate from the faith (40.6). An extension of the concept of → heresy included → simony and persistence in schism.

In the 12th century this line of thought led to a broad discussion of the situation regarding the infallibility of the church that was promised to → Peter (Matt. 16:18) if individual popes can in fact err. Who is to decide whether a pope is guilty of heresy? The ancient maxim of Roman law that what concerns all must be approved by all, as well as the model of the → early church, pointed to a general council as the representative of the whole church. In case of conflict, some canonists were prepared to give a general council supremacy over the pope.

These discussions were fructified by the corporation theory — the idea that the church is a corporation whose head and members have authority only as they work organically together. This was first used as an argument by the college of → cardinals to justify its right to have a say. The Dominican John of Paris (or Jean Quidort, ca. 1255-1306) then related it to the whole church. The church transfers its rights to the pope as its head through his election by the cardinals, but in certain cases (involving heresy or other actions damaging to the church's well-being), it may reclaim its rights. The whole church is then represented by the cardinals or a general council. A radical democratic conciliarism of popular sovereignty was then developed by Marsilius of Padua (ca. 1280-ca. 1343), who, along with William of Ockham (ca. 1285-1347), was long regarded as the founder of conciliarism.

The Great Schism (1378-1417; → Heresies and Schisms 3) gave conciliarism practical relevance as the only way to solve the split. Its most influential champions were Konrad von Gelnhausen (ca. 1320-90), Heinrich von Langenstein (1325-97), Pierre d'Ailly (1350-1420), and Jean Gerson (1363-1429) at the University of Paris, which was a stronghold of conciliarism. At the Council of Constance (1414-18; → Reform Councils) the schism was ended with the help of conciliarism. The doctrine found classic formulation in the decrees of the council *Haec sancta* (the council's supremacy over the pope in matters of faith, church union, and church reform) and *Frequens* (the periodic holding of councils). The Council of Basel, in conflict with Pope Eugenius IV (1431-47), made a → dogma of the supremacy of the general council.

Only gradually did the papacy regain enough strength to oppose conciliarism, which was advocated by leading theologians and canonists, and which, in spite of papal prohibitions, found expression in numerous appeals to a general council.

In the → Reformation period echoes of conciliarism appeared in the call for a council. Papal fears of a revival of conciliarism were the main obstacle to the summoning of → Trent. In → Gallicanism and other → national church movements (e.g., Febronianism in Germany), conciliarism continued to make its influence felt. It has had a powerful impact, too, upon political theory and European constitutional history.

In the debates relating to → Vatican I an appeal continued to be made to conciliarism, though it fell victim to the exalting of the → infallibility and → jurisdictional primacy of the pope into a dogma. → Vatican II aroused new interest in conciliarism and resulted in attempts to integrate the new concerns ecclesiologically.

Bibliography: G. ALBERIGO, *Chiesa conciliare. Identità e significato del conciliarismo* (Brescia, 1981); idem, "Il movimento conciliare (XIV-XV sec.) nella ricerca storica recente," *StMed* 19 (1978) 913-50 • R. BÄUMER, ed., *Die Entwicklung des Konziliarismus* (Darmstadt, 1976) • A. J. BLACK, *Council and Commune: The Conciliar Movement and the Fifteenth-Century Heritage* (London, 1979); idem, *Monarchy and Community: Political Ideas in the Later Conciliar Controversy, 1430-1450* (Cambridge, 1970) • C. M. D. CROWDER, ed., *Unity, Heresy, and Reform, 1378-1460: The Conciliar Response to the Great Schism* (New York, 1977) • J. HELMRATH, *Das Basler Konzil, 1431-1449. Forschungsstand und Probleme* (Cologne, 1987) 408ff. • F. OAKLEY, "Conciliarism," *OER* 1.394-97; idem, *Council over Pope? Towards a Provisional Ecclesiology* (New York, 1969) • H. SCHNEIDER, *Der Konziliarismus als Problem der neueren katholischen Theologie* (Berlin, 1976) • B. TIERNEY, *Foundations of the Conciliar Theory* (repr., London, 1968).

HANS SCHNEIDER

Conciliarity

1. The term "conciliarity" relates to the constant inner need of the church to come together representatively in order to pray, confer, and make decisions. This process is part of the Christian tradition and serves to give expression to the → unity of the church on every level — local, regional, and global — and to maintain the quality of its life and witness relative to its origin and commission. Conciliarity is an essential mark of the church that gives it a concrete and visible structure in the form of regular or periodic assemblies. It presupposes organic unity, which is expressed in the threefold dynamic of conciliar process, concil-

iar action (→ Councils of the Church; Synod), and → reception.

2. Discussions of conciliarity were decisively influenced by the formation of the → ecumenical movement, leading to the foundation of the → World Council of Churches (WCC) at Amsterdam in 1948, and by → Vatican II (1962-65). It was then fostered by the activities of interchurch groups. After 1965 several meetings and studies of the Faith and Order Commission of the WCC explored the question of councils and conciliarity. The result at Uppsala in 1968 was the vision of a universal council that can speak again for all Christians and point the way to the future. Classic formulation to this concept of unity was given at Nairobi in 1975.

The presuppositions and characteristics of conciliar fellowship are (1) a readiness for mutual recognition as the church of Jesus Christ and therewith for the revision of existing anathemas; (2) a declaration indicating that all share in the same apostolic → faith; (3) a common understanding of → baptism, → Eucharist, and ministry (→ Offices, Ecclesiastical); and (4) agreement as to the way in which the churches are represented at a council, and as to who decides in their name. Since to a large degree these presuppositions are not yet present, the ecumenical movement is today described as a preconciliar fellowship of churches. It nonetheless is under obligation now to let the fellowship of churches toward which it is moving control what it says and does.

→ Dialogues and instruments such as → national Christian councils or → national councils of churches at all levels up to the WCC are not merely precursors of church unity but its anticipation. They may thus set aside tactical considerations and seek to prevent legitimate multiplicity from leading to schism and to make possible → conflicts that create trust and promote growth (Salamanca 1973, "Concepts of Unity and Models of Union").

3. At Vancouver in 1983 the call for unity was linked to a call for social involvement. The conciliar process or covenant of mutual commitment to justice (→ Righteousness, Justice), → peace, and the integrity of → creation will show how ready the churches are for conciliarity and will make them realize that it is by common witness that conciliarity is expressed.

→ Catholic, Catholicity; Ecumenical Theology; Utopia

Bibliography: R. BOECKLER, ed., *Interkommunion– Konziliarität. Zwei Studien im Auftrag des Deutschen Ökumenischen Studienausschusses* (Stuttgart, 1974) bibliography • "Councils, Conciliarity, and a Genuinely Universal Council," *StEnc* 10/2 (1974) • D. GILL, ed., *Gathered for Life: Official Report of the Sixth Assembly of the WCC, Vancouver, 24 July–10 August 1983* (Geneva, 1983) • E. LANGE, *And Yet It Moves: Dream and Reality of the Ecumenical Movement* (Geneva, 1979) • P. LENGSFELD, ed., *Ökumenische Theologie. Ein Arbeitsbuch* (Stuttgart, 1980) esp. 355-75 • C. LINK, U. LUZ, and L. VISCHER, *Sie aber hielten fest an der Gemeinschaft. . . . Einheit der Kirche als Prozeß im Neuen Testament und heute* (Zurich, 1988) • H. J. MARGULL, ed., *Die ökumenischen Konzile der Christenheit* (Stuttgart, 1961) • H. MEYER, " 'Einheit in versöhnter Verschiedenheit'– 'konziliare Gemeinschaft'–'organische Union.' Gemeinsamkeit und Differenz gegenwärtig diskutierter Einheitskonzeptionen," *ÖR* 27 (1978) 377-400 • D. M. PATON, ed., *Breaking Barriers, Nairobi 1975* (London, 1976) • L. VISCHER, *Ökumenische Skizzen* (Frankfurt, 1972) esp. 234-44; idem, *Veränderung der Welt–Bekehrung der Kirchen* (Frankfurt, 1976) esp. 83-106 • WORLD COUNCIL OF CHURCHES, *Councils and the Ecumenical Movement* (Geneva, 1968); idem, *Faith and Order, Louvain 1971: Study Reports and Documents* (Geneva, 1971); idem, "The Unity of the Church–Next Steps: Report of the Salamanca Consultation Convened by the Faith and Order Commission, WCC, on 'Concepts of Unity and Models of Union,' September 1973," *What Kind of Unity?* (Geneva, 1974) 119-31.

ANDREAS KARRER

Concordat

1. Term
2. History
3. Assessment

1. Term

A concordat is a treaty between the Holy See and a → state that comprehensively defines the legal position of the → Roman Catholic Church within that state (→ Church and State). The 1983 → Codex Iuris Canonici uses the terms *conventio* (can. 3) and *concordatum* (can. 365.1 n. 2). A concordat involves state as well as church → law. Although there may be debate as to the relative status of concordats, in practice civil law always take precedence over a concordat.

2. History

2.1. Medieval treaties between secular and spiritual powers dealt only with specific issues, but in view of the institutional relatedness of → church and state, they had great political significance. This is true of the

Concordat of Worms in 1122, which ended the → Investiture Controversy and was of vital interest to both → empire and papacy (→ Middle Ages 2). → National church movements produced agreements with the kings of England (Magna Carta, 1213-15) and Portugal (1238) that might be regarded as concordats.

The term "concordat" was used for the first time only when the papacy (→ Pope, Papacy), at the end of the Great Schism (1378-1417), made treaties with the five nations of the Council of Constance in 1418 (→ Reform Councils). The Princes' Concordats of 1447 guaranteed that the German princes would not enter the camp of → conciliarism. The Vienna Concordat of 1448 regulated church appointments up to 1803. The French concordats of 1472 and 1516 confirmed the relative independence of Rome for the Gallican church. Concordats were made with Spain and Portugal in the 18th century.

In the 19th century the political and territorial upheavals caused especially by the French → Revolution and → secularization (1803) necessitated a comprehensive reregulating of relations between the states and Rome. A beginning was made with the French concordat of 1801, which Napoleon (emperor 1804-15) greatly weakened with his 77 Organic Articles of 1802 (→ Gallicanism). The Bavarian Concordat of 1817 was also undercut by the religious edict of 1818.

For some Protestant states the new regulating of Roman Catholic affairs occurred through the papal circumscription → bulls, which were then promulgated as state law (Prussia 1821, Upper Rhine 1821 and 1827, Hannover 1824). The Austrian Concordat of 1855 was gradually abrogated after 1867 and fully so by 1874. Between 1860 and 1914 there were concordats with Haiti, Honduras, Nicaragua, El Salvador, Venezuela, Ecuador, Guatemala, Colombia, and Serbia.

2.2. A new era of concordats began after World War I (involving Latvia in 1922, Poland in 1925, and Romania and Lithuania in 1927). Particularly important were the so-called Lateran Treaties (including a concordat) with Italy (1929), which resolved the politically difficult Roman question that had been raised with the dissolution of the → Papal States in 1870. In Germany there were concordats with Bavaria in 1924, Prussia in 1929, Baden in 1932, and then with the whole country in 1933 (→ Church Struggle). Concordats were also signed with Austria in 1933 and Portugal in 1940.

After World War II concordats were concluded with Spain (1953), the Dominican Republic (1954), Venezuela (1964), Argentina (1966), Peru (1980), Monaco (1981), and Ecuador (1983). A "protocol"

regulated the relation with Hungary (1964) and Yugoslavia (1966). In 1964 a "modus vivendi" was signed with Tunisia, a state with a non-Christian state religion. In Austria the concordat of 1933, apart from the article on marriage law, underlies the later treaties of 1960, 1962, 1964, and 1968. The prewar concordats still hold sway in Germany (the Bavarian in a 1969 or 1974 version). New church treaties have also been signed, such as in Lower Saxony (1955), North Rhine–Westphalia (1957), Schleswig-Holstein (1957), Hesse (1960), Rhineland-Palatinate (1962), and one involving the military chaplaincy (1957). The Italian Concordat of 1929 was greatly altered in 1984.

3. Assessment

No general answer can be given to the question that has been raised a great deal recently whether the concordat is a satisfactory way of solving legally the problem of church and state. The answer depends on the different situations in different states, the role that the church and religion actually play in the lives of individuals, and therefore the extent to which state church law is a prickly legal issue. In a secular, democratic, pluralistic (→ Pluralism), and constitutional → democracy, there are certainly other ways of safeguarding and promoting the church's work. At the same time, there may still be a place for agreements by treaty that give the church a defined position in the interests of its active members.

Bibliography: Primary sources: J. LISTL, ed., *Die Konkordate und Kirchenverträge in der BRD* (2 vols.; Berlin, 1987) • L. SCHÖPPE, *Konkordate seit 1800. Originaltext und deutsche Übersetzung der geltenden Konkordate* (Frankfurt, 1964) • W. WEBER, *Die deutsche Konkordate und Kirchenverträge der Gegenwart* (2 vols.; Göttingen, 1962-71).

Secondary works: F. CONCI, *La chiesa cattolica e i vari stati* (Naples, 1954) • F. GIESE and F. A. VON DER HEYDTE, eds., *Der Konkordatsprozeß* (4 vols.; Munich, 1957-59) • E. R. HUBER, *Verträge zwischen Staat und Kirche im deutschen Reich* (Breslau, 1930) • *La institución concordataria en la actualidad* (Salamanca, 1971) • H. F. KÖCK, *Rechtliche und politische Aspekte von Konkordaten* (Berlin, 1983); idem, *Die völkerrechtliche Stellung des Heiligen Stuhles* (Berlin, 1975) • G. LAJOLO, *I concordati moderni* (Brescia, 1968) • C. S. MEYER, "Concordat," *LuthCyc* 191 • L. VOLK, *Das Reichskonkordat von 20. Juli 1933* (Mainz, 1972) • H. WAGNON, *Concordats et droit international* (Gembloux, 1935) • H. H. WALSH, *The Concordat of 1801: A Study of the Problem of Nationalism in the Relations of Church and State* (New York, 1933)

INGE GAMPL

Conference Centers → Church Conference Centers

Conference of European Churches

1. Rise
2. Members and Activities
3. Organization

1. Rise

The Conference of European Churches (CEC), the most widely recognized regional ecumenical organization for Europe, derives from the period after World War II. In the international divisions and dangerous cold-war tensions of the mid-1950s, a small group of church leaders in Eastern and Western Europe began to consider together the possibility of bringing into conversation churches in European countries separated by different political, economic, and social systems. Their aim was to enable the church to become an instrument of → peace and understanding.

Developing out of a variety of existing structures for reconciliation between the churches, a first main preparatory meeting was held in Liselund in 1957, and the first assembly of the CEC was held in January 1959 in Nyborg Strand, Denmark. Approximately 40 churches from Eastern and Western Europe were represented. A second and then third assembly were held in 1960 and 1962 (Nyborg II and III). At first there was no more than a very loose association of the churches represented, but a significant step was taken toward the formation of a regional conference of churches with the adoption of a constitution at Nyborg IV in 1964, such as was already happening in other regions of the world (→ All Africa Conference of Churches; Caribbean Conference of Churches; Christian Conference of Asia; Pacific Conference of Churches). Nyborg IV was held at sea, aboard the ship *Bornholm*, in order to overcome last-minute visa problems.

The fifth assembly (1967), at Pörtschach in Austria, decided to replace the existing part-time secretarial services with a full-time general secretariat as from April 1968. Subsequent assemblies were held at Nyborg Strand (1971), Engelberg, Switzerland (1974), Crete (1979), Stirling, Scotland (1986), and Prague (1992).

2. Members and Activities

There are now 118 member churches of CEC in all European countries. In Prague a radically revised constitution was adopted that defines the aims of the member churches of the conference: to "pursue together the path of growing conciliar understanding" and to "seek to make a common contribution to the mission of the Church, to the safeguarding of life and the well-being of all humankind" (Preamble). Member churches are from the → Anglican tradition, the Protestants (→ Lutheran Churches; Reformed and Presbyterian Churches), the → Old Catholic, and the Orthodox (→ Orthodox Church).

The → Roman Catholic Church is not a member, but there is close cooperation in virtually all activities, these being coordinated by a Joint Committee of the CEC and the Roman Catholic Bishops' Conferences in Europe (CCEE). Particularly important were a series of ecumenical meetings between CEC and CCEE. The first, at Chantilly in France (1978), had as its theme being one in order that the world may believe. The second, at Løgumkloster in Denmark (1981), discussed the joint calling to hope, ecumenical fellowship in prayer, witness, and service. The third, at Riva del Garda in Italy (1984), discussed common confession of the faith, the source of hope. The fourth, at Erfurt in East Germany (1988), took as its subject the petition "Thy kingdom come." The fifth, at Santiago de Compostela in Spain (1991), was called "At Thy Word: Mission and Evangelisation in Europe Today." In May 1995 a joint meeting was held in Assisi, Italy, between the Central Committee of the CEC and the Plenary Assembly of the CCEE.

Building on the joint work of CEC and CCEE, a European Ecumenical Assembly was held at Basel in May 1989 as part of the conciliar process of common commitment to justice, peace, and the preservation of creation (as defined in Vancouver 1983, the sixth assembly of the → World Council of Churches [WCC]). Under the heading "Peace with Justice for the Whole Creation," the concluding document lists the reasons for the → unity toward which the European churches are striving, the indissoluble link between faith and social involvement (→ Social Ethics), the → guilt of the churches that must be admitted as the beginning of the needed conversion, a vision for Europe, and recommendations and requirements for practical action. Over 600 delegates from the CEC, the bishops' conferences, ecumenical societies, associations of scientists, and action groups and movements gave shape to this assembly in a situation of increasing threat to the survival of humanity and nature in justice. It in turn was a preparatory step for the 1990 WCC convocation for justice, peace, and the preservation of creation, held in Seoul. This meeting was of special significance for European churches and Christians in virtue of its goal, its theme, its results, and its shared liturgical life. The joint CEC/CCEE meeting in May 1995 convoked a second European Ecumenical Assembly for June 1997, to be held in Graz, Austria, with the theme "Reconciliation, Gift of God and Source of New Life."

From the first there has been close cooperation between the CEC and the WCC, especially in the fields of faith and order, interchurch aid, and → human and civil rights. In some cases a division of labor is operating. Cooperation with other regional ecumenical organizations is developing, especially with the Middle East Council of Churches and the All Africa Conference of Churches.

Developments in structure have followed the diversification of activities and the increase in membership. After a first stage, which relied on frequent assemblies, in the mid-1960s assemblies were supplemented with an increasing number of consultations on specific themes, attended by 40 to 50 participants each. Some ten years later actual programs were established. A program of studies was followed by one on interchurch service, then by a human rights program, set within the framework of the Helsinki Final Acts and cosponsored by the Canadian Council of Churches and the → National Council of the Churches of Christ in the USA. Since 1986 this program has been entitled "Peace, Justice, Human Rights." A further important area of discussion is that of the role of → Islam in Europe. Other activities include interchurch service and diakonia, among others to refugees and asylum seekers, as well as women's and media work. Since 1992 a consultant has been employed to encourage and monitor the activities of the churches in the former Yugoslavia.

3. Organization

The CEC maintains only a minimal secretarial staff. The work is overseen by an eight-member Presidium and a 27-member Central Committee meeting once a year.

→ Ecumenical Movement; Ecumenical Theology; Ecumenism; European Theology; National Christian Councils; National Councils of Churches

Bibliography: Encounter at Stirling (Report of the 9th Assembly; Geneva, 1986) • *God Unites–In Christ a New Creation* (Report of the 10th Assembly; Geneva, 1992) • *Peace with Justice* (European Ecumenical Assembly; Basel, 1989).

GLEN G. WILLIAMS†, VOLKMAR DEILE,
and ROBIN GURNEY

Confessing Church

1. The Confessing Church arose in the 1930s in the Deutsche Evangelische Kirche, or German Evangelical Church (GEC), as various church groups opposed the penetration of the church by the spirit of National Socialism (→ Fascism). The Confessing Church made the claim that it alone was the true GEC.

On May 9, 1933, the Young Reformation Movement (under H. Lilje et al.) demanded the freedom of the → church from all political influence but politically accepted the new German state. In the elections of July 23, 1933, the German Christians (GC) won a major victory that initiated a process of infiltration. The state then took over control of the church (→ Church Government) with the help of *Reichsbischof* (imperial bishop) L. Müller (1883-1945).

In opposition to this development, M. → Niemöller (1892-1984) and D. → Bonhoeffer (1906-45) formed the Pastors' Emergency League in the autumn of 1933. Binding itself to the Bible and the confession (→ Confession of Faith), it resisted the state's encroachment on the church, and especially the dismissal of non-Aryan pastors on the basis of the insertion of an Aryan clause into church law. Free synods were then formed, and with Württemberg and Bavaria these joined forces in a single confessing fellowship, which declared (at Ulm, on April 22, 1934) that it alone represented the legitimate GEC. Its organ, the *Nürnberg Ausschuß*, summoned a national synod.

2. This first Confessing Synod of the GEC, held in Barmen on May 29-31, 1934, did more than oppose individual state attacks in its → Barmen Declaration. More broadly, it condemned the teaching of the GC that the National Socialist ideology of the state was binding on the church, seeing in it an illegitimate, fundamental betrayal of the church. On the basis of the emergency measure proclaimed by the synod, the Confessing Church claimed to be the one legal GEC and set up as its executive organ the National Fraternal Council.

At the second synod, in Dahlem in October 1934, the Confessing Church came even more to the attention of the national government by strengthening its emergency measure and by calling for resistance to the authority of the Reichsbischof on the ground that through that authority "the message of the church was being surrendered to the powers of this world." The Fraternal Council selected from within its ranks a Council of the GEC (comprising K. Koch, H. Asmussen, E. Fiedler, K. → Barth, and M. Niemöller).

3. Even before the third synod at Augsburg (June 1935) and the fourth and last at Bad Oeynhausen (February 1936), tensions and divisions had appeared that led to a rift. Partly these were due to the different situations in the "destroyed" churches (Prussian Union, Hessen-Nassau, Saxony, etc.) and the "intact" churches (Bavaria, Hannover, Württemberg), which maintained their existing governments. Partly, too, they were due to confessional problems.

Another ground of difference was the various ideas of what was meant by confessing. Was it a matter of maintaining the inner independence of the church? Or of bearing concrete Christian witness against the secular "powers"? Opposing views thus arose concerning cooperation with state authorities and political allegiance. The conservative intact churches drew together in opposition to the radical Dahlem wing (which included Niemöller and Barth, who had moved to Basel in 1935). In 1936 they formed the Council of the Evangelical Lutheran Church in Germany, although some voices were criticizing their moderate course (H. Diem).

4. Only a month after Dahlem a Provisional Directorate took over from the Council of the GEC. At its head was Bishop Marahrens (1875-1950) of Hannover, who came into conflict with the Fraternal Council by cooperating with the Committee of the National Church that followed the Reichsbischof. At the synod in Bad Oeynhausen, the Fraternal Council set up in opposition a second Provisional Directorate (composed of F. Müller, O. Fricke, M. Albertz, H. Böhm, and B. H. Forck), which in 1936 sent a bold protest to A. Hitler (1889-1945) against many wrongs. The intact churches held aloof from this body, and even more so from the liturgy used during the Czech crisis of 1938.

The Confessing Church was severely burdened when many within it accepted the → oath to Hitler in 1938. In spite of suppression, the directorate continued to work quietly (esp. K. Scharf and W. Rott) in concert with the Conference of Provincial Fraternal Councils and then with the movement toward unification initiated by Bishop Wurm (1868-1953) in 1942 with the church "center." The twelfth Prussian synod of the Confessing Church issued a last courageous word in 1943 on the basis of the Ten Commandments (→ Decalogue).

5. The Confessing Church received congregational support from many committed laypeople and held many confessional meetings. Its opposition was sustained by the struggle for inner church renewal (e.g., at the synod at Halle in 1937; → Eucharist). It made its own arrangements for the training of ministers, setting up seminaries and various seminars. Its confessing, however, was increasingly hampered by the → state (e.g., through censorship of speech, writing, and communication and through restriction of movement, including imprisonment), so that hardly any action did not conflict with some law or other. The Confessing Church even had its → martyrs (e.g., F. Weißler, P. Schneider, and W. Sylten for helping Jews; D. Bonhoeffer for political opposition).

6. After the war the Confessing Church issued the first call to repentance — the Stuttgart Declaration of Guilt — October, 19, 1945. In August 1945 the Fraternal Council handed over its functions to the Council of the Evangelical Church, and in July 1948 it repealed the emergency measure of 1934. Whereas the former Council of the Lutheran church helped to form the United Evangelical Lutheran Church, the Dahlem wing under M. Niemöller tried to maintain the influence of the Confessing Church in the new circumstances by means of the Fraternal Council of the Evangelical Church (→ Darmstadt Declaration of 1947; Word on the Jewish Question [1948]; Word on Rearmament [1950]). Its lack of support in the restoration of church and society, however, showed that people were generally oriented more to an earlier time than to the Confessing Church.

The strong impact of the Confessing Church on the → ecumenical movement, however, shows that the Confessing Church in fact transcended the time-bound occasion of its confession. It represented a new beginning for the church as one that would bear witness to the world on the basis of the → Word of God alone, thus revealing its significance for all Christians.

Bibliography: A. BOYENS, Kirchenkampf und Ökumene, 1933-1939. Darstellung und Dokumentation (Munich, 1969); idem, Kirchenkampf und Ökumene 1939-1945 (Munich, 1973) • J. S. CONWAY, The Nazi Persecution of the Churches, 1933-45 (Toronto, 1968) • E. C. HELMREICH, The German Churches under Hitler: Background, Struggle, and Epilogue (Detroit, 1979) • W. NIEMÖLLER, Die evangelische Kirche im Dritten Reich (Bielefeld, 1956) bibliography; idem, Kampf und Zeugnis der Bekennende Kirche (Bielefeld, 1949) • K. SCHOLDER, Die Kirchen und das Dritte Reich (Berlin, 1977ff.) bibliography. See also the bibliographies in "Barmen Declaration" and "Church Struggle."

EBERHARD BUSCH

Confession (as Christian Group) →
Denomination 1-5

Confession of Faith

1. The Nature and Task of Confession
2. Confession and Eschatology
3. Confession and Unity
4. The Public Nature of Confession
5. The Ecumenicity of Confession

1. The Nature and Task of Confession

In confession, the Christian community (→ Congregation) gives its expression to God's saving action and fellowship with Christ. It accepts God's saving action, his Word and → sacrament, and it confesses → Jesus Christ as the only basis of faith. In him the community also confesses God's comprehensive work as the → Trinity. Through confession, faith in Jesus Christ takes a binding communal form, even as it includes personal confession. It embraces → faith, life, and action. As a liturgical action in which God is praised (→ Doxology), confession has a place in → worship, → liturgy, the celebration of the → Eucharist, and → baptism. The church is a confessing church not merely in marking itself off from the world but in confessing God's unique act in Jesus Christ.

As the community responds to God's comprehensive work by its confession, it simultaneously makes confession of faith *(Credo)* and confession of sins *(Confiteor)* (cf. Ps. 42:5; Jer. 17:26). With such a response to God's work, the community is ministering God's Word, thereby witnessing to the → gospel in various specific situations. In the discharge of this task, confession is the norm of what is said about God and of the church's teaching. Confession thus embraces the church's teaching and life in all its multiplicity.

2. Confession and Eschatology

Confession occupies an → eschatological place, for it is grounded in God's promise and eschatological action (see Heb. 11:13; 13:14-15). In confession, the community enters into God's presence, in which the promise of God is fulfilled in the → Holy Spirit. The continuity and discontinuity of confession have their basis here, in this promise, for confession always occurs between past experience and the future expectation of God's working. It represents an integration into the experience of God, in which the church constantly knows its time-bound nature; and it is also an affirmation of the well-founded → hope, in which it achieves stability in ever-new confessing.

In confession, the church expresses definitively something that cannot come to an end within the limits of human recollection or expectation. Thus confession is the constant task of the community, in which it experiences God's faithfulness across the ages. Faithfulness to the apostolic confession and the expectation of new confession have their basis in this faithfulness of God. In new confession, the church enters into the fullness of God, responding to it in its own, new situation. As it continually develops and adapts to new situations, living confession is thus able constantly to confront error (→ Heresies and Schisms).

3. Confession and Unity

In confession, the church experiences and recognizes its → unity. Confession creates fellowship, for it represents agreement in response to the gospel and in fellowship with Christ. The unity of the church does not rest on confession, merely as a common set of obligatory dogmas or as a marking out of confessional differences. Confession, rather, expresses → consensus in the proclamation of the gospel and the use of the sacraments.

In the light of the consensus expressed in confession, one can recognize the unity — but also the disunity — of the church. In this sense confession can also be understood as the basis on which a particular church fellowship rests (→ Confessions and Creeds). Confession, however, must be protected from being misunderstood confessionalistically (i.e., simply as a statute). Taking up a confessional stance (→ Status confessionis) means not letting the truth be falsified in witness. This demarcation means more than simply establishing doctrinal differences but actually often points to a failure to achieve unanimity in faith. Only when confession is not tied to rigid confessional positions can it bear witness to the unity of faith against error, either of some disputable teaching or, more fundamentally, of denying what is said in the gospel.

Here again confession is in an eschatological situation in which a decision is taken about confessing or denying Jesus Christ. In this sense confession is necessary to salvation. Confession enters into God's judgment of condemnation and salvation, which establishes the contradiction that the church experiences in its disunity.

4. The Public Nature of Confession

As a witness to the gospel, confession is a proclamation, a public communication. The public nature of confession has its basis in the confession of Jesus Christ as Lord of the world. In confession, the public is established to which the Word of God is directed. It does not derive, then, from any sense of what might be proper to public opinion or to the nature of public action. Confession to others is a mark of the eschatological presence of the proclamation that is for all.

When the truth of the gospel is denied in a society, a case of confession (*casus confessionis*) may well lead to persecution and → suffering. To the degree that resistance to the gospel has political and ethical grounds, confession leads to → ethical decisions.

We must not view the given propositions that make up a confession as a shortcut to the discovery of truth. Rather, true confession demands that every possibility of understanding be explored in faith. It marks the frontier of human action in integration with God's action.

5. The Ecumenicity of Confession

In integration into fellowship with Christ, confession is always ecumenical, even where there is only imperfect agreement. In confession, the community confesses the one and undivided faith with respect to the whole → church. Thus confession promotes the → dialogue of the church, especially because differences become visible in it.

In the → ecumenical movement, well-founded hope is bound up with confession of the one apostolic faith, the hope that confession will be an expression of → unity. Even though unanimity has not yet been found in an explicit confession, in this hope the movement finds itself on the way to the unity of a fellowship of confessing churches. The question of conciliar confessing has taken on significance as a pointer to common confessing. Various efforts at common confessing in the form of bilateral conversations (e.g., on the meaning of the → *filioque*) and projects of → union (e.g., the Basis of Union in Australia [1974]) have led to progress.

The churches of Asia, Africa, and Latin America have increasingly contributed their own practice of confessing to the discussion. They have brought to light specific (new) features of confession as they have related confession to the living context of the church. They have rooted it as living confession in the worship and life of the community, relating it to the needs of the neighbor (e.g., in a social *Credo*). They have given it a missionary reference. In this regard they have fostered expectations that confession would be freed from the burden of confessionalism, which had caused many churches in their constitutions to call traditional confessions (e.g., the Augsburg Confession) the foundation of the faith, with little space left for their own personal confessing. Contextual confession and the apppeal to unity

in confession of the apostolic faith have thus taken their place among the central concerns in ecumenical work.

Bibliography: K. BARTH, *Das Bekenntnis der Reformation und unser Bekennen* (Munich, 1935) • J. BAUR, "Kirchliches Bekenntnis und neuzeitliches Bewußtsein," *Einsicht und Glaube* (Göttingen, 1978) 269-88 • G. BÉKÉS and H. MEYER, eds., *Den einen Glauben bekennen. Confessio fidei . . .* (Frankfurt, 1982) includes contributions from Asia and Latin America • U. DUCHROW, *Konflikt um die Ökumene. Christusbekenntnis–in welcher Gestalt der ökumenischen Bewegung?* (Munich, 1980; 2d ed., 1981) • N. EHRENSTRÖM and G. GASSMANN, eds., *Confessions in Dialogue: A Survey of Bilateral Conversations among World Confessional Families, 1959-74* (Geneva, 1975) • E. HULTSCH and K. LÜTHI, eds., *Bekennendes Bekenntnis. Form und Formulierung christliches Glaubens* (Gütersloh, 1982) • J. H. LEITH, ed., *Creeds of the Churches: A Reader in Christian Doctrine from the Bible to the Present* (3d ed.; Atlanta, 1982) • H. MEYER and H. SCHÜTTE, eds., *Confessio Augustana. Bekenntnis des einen Glaubens. Gemeinsame Untersuchung lutherischer und katholischer Theologen* (Paderborn, 1980) • G. SAUTER, "Bekenntnis heute–Erwartungen an die Theologie," *Erwartung und Erfahrung, Predigten, Vorträge und Aufsätze* (Munich, 1972) 208-41 • P. SCHAFF, *The Creeds of Christendom* (6th ed.; 3 vols.; New York, 1931) • M. SCHLOEMANN, "Der besondere Bekenntnisfall," *Politik als Glaubenssache? Beiträge zur Klärung des Status Confessionis im südlichen Afrika und in anderen soziologischen Kontexten* (ed. E. Lorenz; Erlangen, 1983) 48-98 • R. SLENCZKA, "Bekenntnis als Deutung, Gemeinschaft und Grenze des Glaubens," *KuD* 26 (1980) 245-61 • W. SPARN, "Evangelium und Norm. Über die Perfektibilität des Bekenntnis in den reformatorischen Kirchen," *EvT* 40 (1980) 494-516 • H. STOEVESANDT, *Die Bedeutung des Symbolums in Theologie und Kirche. Versuch einer dogmatisch-kritischen Ortsbestimmung aus evangelischer Sicht* (Munich, 1970) • J. TRACK, ed., *Lebendiger Umgang mit Schrift und Bekenntnis. Theologische Beiträge zur Beziehung von Schrift und Bekenntnis und zu ihrer Bedeutung für das Leben der Kirche* (Stuttgart, 1980) • V. VAJTA and H. WEISSGERBER, eds., *The Church and the Confessions* (Philadelphia, 1963) • WORLD COUNCIL OF CHURCHES, *Confessing the One Faith: An Ecumenical Explication of the Apostolic Faith As It Is Confessed in the Nicene-Constantinopolitan Creed (381)* (Geneva, 1993); idem, *Confession and Confessing: A Documentary and Bibliographical Survey* (Geneva, 1979).

HANS G. ULRICH

Confession of Sins

1. Biblical Background
2. Present-Day Practice
3. Pastoral Implications

"Confession" refers to an acknowledgment of sin by an individual or a group, made either privately or publicly. Its various forms include (1) individual private → prayer (spoken or unspoken); (2) spoken confession by individuals to a priest, followed by individual or group absolution; (3) spoken confession by an individual or by a group in the presence of the whole congregation; and (4) general confession by a priest (minister) or by the whole congregation as a part of public worship, followed typically by absolution from the priest. The common denominator in all these forms is that confession is always made (mediately or immediately) to God, that it requires a penitent state of mind, and that signs of repentance should follow through a changed pattern of behavior and a more forgiving attitude to others.

1. Biblical Background

1.1. Confession in the OT was both private (Ps. 32:1-6) and public (Lev. 16:21). A basic distinction in types of sin is made between sins of ignorance, which are remissible, and cases of malicious disobedience of the → law, which merit death (Num. 15:22-31). In the postexilic period, rites of reconciliation had developed using animal sacrifice, incense, and the aspersion of blood to reduce the "sins unto death" to sins that could be remitted (Leviticus 4–6; 16:12-14). Judaic practice at the time of Christ provided an annual occasion for the remission of even the most serious sins through the rite of Yom Kippur, entailing both sacrifices and a scapegoat. Sins could be remitted whether or not the sinners themselves were present, but true repentance of sin was regarded as necessary before such rites could be considered efficacious.

1.2. In the NT the distinction between sins worthy of death and sins of ignorance is continued (Heb. 10:26-31; 1 John 5:16-17; Matt. 12:31), but the death is now seen as spiritual rather than physical. Remission is gained through the new High Priest, Christ, but no reconciliation rite is described to replace the OT sacrifices. The power of Christ to forgive is witnessed to by the apostles (Matt. 16:19; 18:15-18), and the resurrected Christ, in giving his Spirit to the apostles, also gives the power to declare or withhold forgiveness (John 20:21-23). Nevertheless, no priestly office is defined in the NT in relation to remission of sins; rather, brotherly correction (Matt. 18:15-18) and confession to one another (Jas. 5:16) are advocated. Many passages in the Epistles make it plain that certain sins will exclude one from the kingdom (1 Cor. 6:9-10; Gal. 5:19-21; Eph. 5:5), and it remains unclear whether there are unforgivable sins (e.g., the "sin against the Holy Spirit"; see Matt. 12:31-32).

1.3. In the subsequent history of the church, controversy about the remission of postbaptismal sin (esp. the sin of apostasy) continued until John → Chrysostom, who stated the (eventually) normative view that God's mercy was unbounded toward those who truly repent. The subsequent historical development of penitential practice is described elsewhere (→ Penitence).

2. Present-Day Practice

Historically the Christian churches have been divided by acceptance or rejection of the sacrament of penance, a rite rejected by most of the → Reformers in the form that had developed in the Middle Ages. Historical traditions, however, are now under question. The major denominations are influenced by liturgical renewal and the rise of independent churches, especially those in non-Western cultures, which has introduced some intriguing variations.

2.1. Following → Vatican II, the → Roman Catholic Church has introduced a major revision of the rite of penance, which stresses more a reconciliation in the context of the hearing of God's Word than the recitation of specific sins. Nevertheless the need for "integrity" of confession (i.e., the confession of *all* known mortal sins) remains an unresolved issue. Local variations in the rite have been advocated, and liturgies for public services of reconciliation introduced.

2.2. In the Orthodox Church the ancient formularies are, as a rule, unchanged, but practice varies widely. Churches of the Byzantine Rite require individual confession four times a year (in the church or in the home), but in others it has become rare. Some Eastern rites (largely disused) include prostration before the altar and before the priest and kissing the priest's feet, while others emphasize general confession and general absolution. In most Oriental rites only married secular priests or monks hear confession as a general rule. All Orthodox rites, except those of the Oriental churches in union with Rome, use the *forma deprecativa* ("may the Lord forgive"), not *indicativa* ("I absolve you").

2.3. Churches in the → Anglican Communion and the → Lutheran churches have retained the possibility of private confession, but mostly they lay greater emphasis on public confession in new liturgical forms (see, e.g., *Lutheran Book of Worship* [Minneapolis, 1978]). The place of confession and absolution within the Eucharist has been questioned by some churches in the Anglican Communion (see *Handbook to Scottish Episcopal Liturgy* [Edinburgh, 1982]), and cosmic as well as individual dimensions of sin are now emphasized.

2.4. Churches in the Reformed tradition have tended to move from extemporaneous prayer by the minister to the more standard forms of confession developed within the prayer books of other traditions and derived from the historic documents of the early church. Personal responsibility for sin is sometimes counterbalanced by an emphasis on its tragic aspects.

2.5. The emergence of → independent churches and, in particular, the great expansion of Pentecostalism have led to a return to *individual* public confession, often within a context of high emotion. Purification of the worshiper is stressed, and the confession (which must be detailed and specific) draws → ecstatic responses from the congregation (see B. G. M. Sundkler). Apart from such independent churches, however, cultural variations in confessional practice are not as great as one might expect. It may be that the effect of the indigenization of the major denominations in Africa and Asia is yet to be seen. The practice of confession remains notably Western in character.

3. Pastoral Implications

3.1. Within traditions retaining private confession there has been a marked change of emphasis. In the revised Roman Rite three liturgies of penance are suggested: the reconciliation of individual penitents (which may take place in a "counseling style" environment rather than that of the confessional booth); the reconciliation of several penitents, each receiving individual absolution; a public liturgy of reconciliation, using a general confession and a general absolution. These changes potentially lead to a more personal form of self-evaluation and to a greater consciousness of group solidarity in sin and in penitence (see J. D. Crichton, vol. 2, chap. 11), but there is some concern that the practice of individual confession may decline.

3.2. The changes within the Roman Catholic Church are merely one sign that sin and → guilt now carry different connotations from those enshrined in ancient rites and liturgies. The effect of psychoanalysis and related schools of dynamic → psychology on contemporary consciousness is considerable. S. Freud (1856-1939), especially in his later writings on religion, argued that the guilt dealt with by religious practices, while an unfortunate necessity because of the repressive character of civilization, must

be deplored as infantile (see esp. his *Civilization and Its Discontents*). The Swiss minister and Freudian psychoanalyst Oskar Pfister wished to substitute a "religion of love" for a "religion of fear." Pfister could see no place for rituals of confession, since they dealt with only the surface of the person's guilt and created an undue dependence upon the priest or confessor. C. G. Jung (1875-1961), in a more positive assessment of religious confession, noted that Protestants appeared to be turning to psychotherapists for what Catholics could gain within the rituals of their own church.

3.3. Contemporary pastoral practice has incorporated and extended some of these insights from → psychotherapy. Guilt is no longer regarded as either helpful or harmful in itself. A distinction is drawn between pathological and normal guilt. Some guilt requires skilled therapeutic treatment, whereas some is the inevitable concomitant of being human and can lead to an increase in sensitivity and compassion. Confession within a pastoral relationship is necessary and restorative, provided regressive dependency and defensive → moralism are replaced by an identification of the true conflicts of loyalty in the individual's life. These distinctions have proved particularly important in guiding appropriate → pastoral care of adolescents, of those in marriage difficulties, and of the dying and the bereaved.

3.4. Confession may also be viewed from a sociopsychological perspective. W. Sargant has documented the effect of public rituals of confession in both political indoctrination and religious evangelism. M. Hepworth and B. S. Turner observe that confession seems inevitably "sociologically and culturally ambiguous." It preserves the freedom of the individual conscience, but it also induces conformity through public exposure of deviant behavior. (An interesting example may be seen in the use of confession to ensure conformity in Communist China during the period of the Cultural Revolution [1966-69].)

This sociopsychological perspective sheds light on liturgical reform. To what extent do confessional rituals enable Christians to act in a responsible way within society? Liturgical changes that stress reconciliation and the restoration of love of neighbor may be seen as attempts to counterbalance the individualism and sectarianism of some earlier practices.

3.5. The revaluation of confession in modern times and the flowering of a variety of forms thus appear to have positive and negative effects, ethically and pastorally. Primitive notions of cultic impurity, of unintentional transgressions, and of sins that cannot be forgiven linger on in folk religion and may be perceived in the cults flourishing in deprived areas of the world. Yet the more ordered rituals of the established denominations can merely create a sense of security that blunts moral sensitivity, especially toward political questions. The blend of emotion and reason in confession that may lead to genuine moral change has perhaps yet to take a powerful hold on the modern imagination and to find appropriate ritual form.

Bibliography: J. Chryssavgis, *Repentance and Confession in the Orthodox Church* (Brookline, Mass., 1990) • J. D. Crichton, *Christian Celebration* (London, 1982) • M. Hepworth and B. S. Turner, *Confession: Studies in Deviance and Religion* (London, 1982) • R. Janin, *Églises Orientales et Rites Orienteaux* (Paris, 1955) • L. Ligier, *Péché d'Adam et péché du monde* (Lyons, 1960) • V. Palachkovsky, *Sin in the Orthodox Church* (New York, n.d.) • C. J. Peter, "Confession," *NCE* 16.94-95 • O. Pfister, *Das Christentum und die Angst* (Zurich, 1944) • K. Rahner, "Penance," *SM(E)* 4.385-99 (full bibliography) • W. Sargant, *Battle for the Mind* (London, 1957) • G. Siegmund, "Die Beichte in der protestantischen Kirche," *TGl* 53 (1963) 16-28 • E. V. Stein, *Guilt: Theory and Therapy* (Philadelphia, 1968) • B. G. M. Sundkler, *Bantu Prophets in South Africa* (London, 1948) • T. Tentler, *Sin and Confession on the Eve of the Reformation* (Princeton, 1977).

Alastair V. Campbell and Gianfranco Tellini

Confessional, Confidentiality of the → Seal of the Confessional

Confessionalism → Denomination 4

Confessionality → Denomination 5.2

Confessions and Creeds

1. Confessions as Statements of Faith
2. Lutheran Confessions
3. Reformed Confessions

In one of its meanings, "confession" refers to a declaration of religious belief. It can be as simple as "Jesus is Lord" (1 Cor. 12:3) or as detailed as the Augsburg Confession (1530) or similar Protestant expressions of faith in the 16th and 17th centuries. "Creed" refers to a concise statement of Christian doctrine, typically produced by a council of the early church. The Apostles' Creed and Nicene Creed are perhaps the most famous of such statements.

1. Confessions as Statements of Faith

Christian confessions serve the purposes of acknowledgment, praise, and delimitation. At their center stands → Jesus of Nazareth, whose relation to God the creeds seek to present and establish.

Peter affirmed, "You are the Christ" (Mark 8:29). At least implicitly, this confession calls Jesus the Messiah (→ Christological Titles), acknowledges him to be the unique Word of God (John 1:14), recognizes him as Son of Man (on the basis of Dan. 7:13), and declares him to be Son of God (John 1:34). Belief in him as *kyrios* (1 Cor. 12:3 etc.) claims a predicate that was to attain special significance in the Greek-speaking world, as it cast doubt on the lordship of other so-called lords (→ Emperor Worship).

The NT contains a variety of Christian confessions, all centering on the one God (1 Cor. 8:6), who sent Jesus as Savior (1 Thess. 1:9-10). As Jesus was raised from the dead, so Christians expect the → resurrection of the dead (1 Cor. 15:1-34). Statements of confession, perhaps early hymns, appear in Rom. 1:3-4; 4:24-25; Phil. 2:5-11. Intimately connected with confession is personal belief (Rom. 10:9).

Confession also involved praise of the divine messenger from whom Christians received their name (Acts 11:26). It summed up briefly what they thought about Jesus. In so doing, it had also from the outset an element of delimitation. Those who would not join in praise of Jesus but cursed him (1 Cor. 12:3; → Curse) placed themselves outside the company of his followers (→ Discipleship). Very soon, however, Christians would be shown how necessary it was to stand by their confession (Heb. 4:14). In particular, they had to define the relation of Jesus to God more precisely, for Marcion (d. ca. 160) and → Gnosticism contested the equation of Creator and Redeemer. There was thus a need to say who the God is who has sent Jesus. Confession became the rule of faith. Confessions in this sense do not merely mark off opponents of Jesus but pronounce anathemas on those who do not preach the gospel as the community has received it (Gal. 1:9).

Statements of faith are also made about the Spirit (→ Holy Spirit), whose sending Jesus promised (John 16:13) and of whom it must be said in what relation he stands to the Father and the Son. These factors led to the making of Trinitarian confessions, formulated in various ways.

The variety relates to the different functions that

confessions had to serve. They had an important role in catechetical instruction to impart the faith to baptismal candidates (→ Baptism). Condensed, narrative forms (e.g., the → Apostles' Creed) were suitable for this purpose. To safeguard against heresy the → Niceno-Constantinopolitan Creed (381) could be used, with its related anathemas. Additionally, it was linguistically very well adapted for use in → worship. Finally, the church had an inner need to clarify questions of faith. Thus the → Athanasian Creed declares what one must believe to be saved.

The East at first had many creeds, but in the West the baptismal confession of the Roman church managed to achieve supremacy. Ultimately in the East, however, theological discussion led to a → consensus that found important expression at the Council of → Nicaea in 325 and then in an extended form in the Niceno-Constantinopolitan Creed. Here the Trinitarian-Christological → monotheism of early → orthodoxy found its most significant and influential expression. In the Orthodox Church the theological statements of the seven ecumenical → councils from Nicaea I (325) to Nicaea II (787) all have normative weight, but the form of the Nicene Creed as expanded at the First Council of Constantinople is regarded as a summary of the decisions of all these councils. This creed clearly has the best chance to gain ecumenical acceptance as a statement of faith that has characterized the church from 381 onward. It excludes not only pagans but also heretics who have departed from biblical Christianity (→ Heresies and Schisms).

In the Middle Ages the need to set a boundary against error led Pope → Innocent III (1198-1216) to propose a new confession at the Fourth Lateran Council in 1215. On the basis of the Nicene Creed it gave definitive answers to disputed questions regarding the → Trinity and the → Eucharist. The West accepted the rulings of the council, which were intended to promote a union with Orthodoxy, but the Orthodox Church would not go along with the later definitions of Florence.

In the Roman Catholic Church the three symbols (from Gk. *symbolon,* here meaning "sign of communion" or "summary") of the early church — the Apostles' Creed, the Nicene Creed, and the Athanasian Creed — are highly regarded, but what counts as → dogma is what the church defines as necessary to believe for → salvation. Thus the church can abandon a statement that it once thought to be very important, such as the → Anti-Modernist Oath of 1910. The Roman Church has no official list of creeds; the familiar *Enchiridion symbolorum* (DS) is a private collection.

2. Lutheran Confessions

At the time of the → Reformation many churches followed the preaching of M. → Luther (1483-1546) and his friends. Although Pope Leo X (1513-21) condemned what he considered the Lutheran → heresy, the Lutherans claimed that they were upholding orthodox doctrine. In the → Augsburg Confession (1530) they appealed to the Nicene Creed and the Apostles' Creed. This confession became the basis of the Schmalkaldic League. When a council was announced in 1536 (nine years before actually beginning in → Trent) and Evangelicals were invited to it, Luther composed as a personal testament the Schmalkaldic Articles in 1537.

Only one section of Protestants, however, subscribed to the Augsburg Confession, which was but one of many confessions. There were also attempted agreements, both in the eucharistic debate (Wittenberg Concord [1536]) and in the application and amendment of the Augsburg Confession (e.g., the *Confessio Augustana variata* of 1540). To supplement the confession, P. → Melanchthon (1497-1560), by special commission, wrote *Treatise on the Power and Primacy of the Pope* (1537).

The course of confessional development was determined when a specific attempt to bridge the gap between Roman Catholics and Protestants failed. The *Regensburg Book* (1541) was meant to be the basis of unity, but both Pope Paul III (1534-49) and Luther opposed it. The Council of Trent began in 1545 by formulating Roman Catholic belief over against Protestant doctrinal development and in distinction from it. The end of the council saw the *Professio fidei Tridentina* (1564). All church officials had to subscribe to it and pledge themselves by oath to obedience to the → pope.

The Peace of Augsburg (1555; → Augsburg, Peace of) granted security to those who followed the Augsburg Confession. Further attempts to restore church unity, as imperial law demanded, failed — not least because of differences among Protestants. For the latter, who viewed theological decisions as confessional matters, the debate about the Interim of Augsburg (1548) led to the influential slogan that there can be no adiaphora in a confessional situation.

Truth is always at issue in confessional statements. Its formulation in the Augsburg Confession, which became legally binding (→ Cuius regio eius religio), did not help to decide or mediate between the new opposing views. Authorities in the different states collected various other confessions and gave them the rank of → *corpora doctrinae.* Since the issue was that of what officeholders throughout a given state were required to teach, these territorially valid collections adopted explicit positions on the debated questions. Since there were so many states in Germany, this territorializing carried the danger of provincialism.

A more important point, however, is that the confessions now became viewed as final statements of faith. What had been spoken praise that gave liturgical expression to one's personal faith now became a written document that changed as one crossed a territorial boundary. These differences led inevitably to a relativizing that threatened to make truth unrecognizable.

German → Lutheranism tried to avoid this development by seeking theological agreement, and it succeeded to a large extent by securing general and lasting recognition for its Book of Concord in 1580. Faced with disputed questions, Lutherans were now to appeal to convincing criteria. They claimed the *sola Scriptura* of the Reformation in this connection. They could accept confessionally only what agreed with the → revelation that found expression in Holy Scripture. If the Bible forms the *norma normans* (the standardizing norm), to use later terminology, the confessions are the *normae normatae* (the standardized norms; → Formula of Concord, "Solid Declaration, The Summary Formulation, Basis, Rule, and Norm").

These confessions are witnesses to the true church in history, for they uphold prophetic and apostolic truth. In their Book of Concord, then, Lutherans collected the three creeds of the → early church (see 1), which take precedence. Then come the Reformation confessions: (1) Augsburg, (2) Melanchthon's Apology of the Augsburg Confession, (3) Luther's Schmalkaldic Articles, (4) Melanchthon's *Treatise on the Power and Primacy of the Pope*, and (5) Luther's Small and Large catechisms. The Formula of Concord regarded itself as a supplement to Augsburg, and it concluded the Book of Concord, apart from a *Catalogus testimoniorum*. The phenomenon of formalized confessions reached its climax with the Book of Concord, which pastors and state officials had to accept if they were to function in states that endorsed it.

From the 17th century, Pietism set the confession of the heart over that of the lips. With the theological changes brought about by the → Enlightenment, this priority weakened the allegiance given to confessions, which nontheologians in particular had always felt to be a burden.

Opposition to the Enlightenment and to the union of Lutheran and Reformed churches in the neoconfessionalism of the 19th century led to a rediscovery of confessions. K. → Barth's (1886-1968) opposition to liberal → Culture Protestantism also gave confessions a new importance. In the → church struggle in particular, people came to see how necessary it is to confess one's faith. Many new confessions came to be formulated between 1933 and 1935, which cooperation between the Lutherans and Reformed made possible.

In Germany, Reformed and Lutherans combined to draw up the → Barmen Declaration (1934), the most important confession in the church struggle. Some of the territorial churches accepted this document as a confession (as has, for example, the Presbyterian Church [USA]), while the Evangelical Church in Germany (EKD) and the United Evangelical Lutheran Church in Germany (VELKD) confined their approval to hailing its decisions and welcoming the fellowship to which it bore witness. Conversations between these denominations led in the → Leuenberg Agreement (1973) to the withdrawal of the anathemas that they had hurled at one another in the 16th century. Although an essential piece of confessional development did indeed take place here, this has not everywhere been recognized as such.

Bibliography: Primary sources: BSKORK • BSLK • *Doctrinal Declarations* (St. Louis, 1957) • DS • B. A. GERRISH, ed., *The Faith of Christendom* (New York, 1963) • J. N. KARMIRIS, ed., *Ta dogmatika kai symbolika mnēmeia tēs Orthodoxou Katholikēs Ekklēsias* (2 vols.; Athens, 1952-53; 3d ed., 1968-69) • J. H. LEITH, ed., *Creeds of the Churches* (rev. ed.; Atlanta, 1973) • H. LIETZMANN, ed., *Symbole der alten Kirche* (Berlin, 1906; 6th ed., 1968) • P. SCHAFF, ed., *The Creeds of Christendom* (3 vols.; New York, 1878; 5th ed., 1977-78) • H. STEUBING, ed., *Bekenntnisse der Kirche. Bekenntnistexte aus zwanzig Jahrhunderten* (Wuppertal, 1970) • T. G. TAPPERT, ed., *The Book of Concord* (Philadelphia, 1959).

Secondary works: M. BRECHT and R. SCHWARZ, eds., *Bekenntnisse und Einheit der Kirche. Studien zum Konkordienbuch* (Stuttgart, 1980) • W. KAHLE, "Die Bedeutung der Confessio Augustana für die Kirchen im Osten," *KO* 27 (1984) 9-35 • J. N. D. KELLY, *Early Christian Creeds* (2d ed.; London, 1960) • G. KRETSCHMAR, "Realpräsenz und Transsubstantiation. Der Reichstag von Regensburg 1541 und ökumenische Konsensdokumente der Gegenwart," *Praesentia Christi* (FS J. Betz; Düsseldorf, 1984) 208-39; idem, "Tradition und Erfahrung der reformatorischen Kirchen," *I simboli dell'iniziazione cristiana* (Rome, 1983) 157-92 • F. MILDENBERGER, *Theologie der Lutherischen Bekenntnisschriften* (Stuttgart, 1983) • J. WIRSCHING, "Bekenntnisschriften," *TRE* 5.487-511 • E. WOLF, "Bekenntnisschriften," *RGG* 1.1012-17.

GERHARD MÜLLER

3. Reformed Confessions

The development of the Reformed confession, unlike the Lutheran, has never reached any conclusion. It has no *corpus doctrinae* comparable to the Lutheran Book of Concord, and the various collections of Reformed confessional writings possess no official character. Count Palatine Johann Casimir's efforts at establishing a common confession for all European Reformed churches, prompted by the delimitation of Concordist → Lutheranism from Philippism and → Crypto-Calvinism, came to nothing (1577). Nor is the conflation of various Reformed confessions of faith into the *Harmonia Confessionum Fidei, Orthodoxarum et Reformatarum Ecclesiarum* (1581) comparable to the Book of Concord. Originally undertaken by Jean François Salvard with the participation of Theodore → Beza, this piece was continually expanded and served merely to illustrate the confessional unity of the various individual Reformed churches and their agreement with the original form of Lutheranism.

Commensurate with the basic distinction between older → Protestantism and neo-Protestantism, one can distinguish an earlier and a more recent epoch of confessional development. The earlier epoch can itself be subdivided into several stages. At the beginning we find the Zwinglian-influenced confessions of German-speaking Switzerland, after which John → Calvin established his own confessions in Geneva; Heinrich Bullinger then provided a unification between the traditions of Zurich and Geneva. Subsequent development is characterized by the expansion of → Calvinism and the emergence of Calvinist confessions in western and eastern Europe. By contrast, the specifically German Reformed tradition is characterized by an eventual alliance between Philippism and Calvinism following the exclusion of Philippism from Lutheranism. For this reason, the doctrine of → predestination never acquired the significance attaching to it in genuine Calvinism, which condemned humanistically inspired → Arminianism with the doctrinal decisions of the Synod of Dort. Developments in the English-speaking sphere were influenced by the resolutions of the Puritan → Westminster Assembly during the English civil war and the secession of Congregationalism from Presbyterianism. At the end of older Reformed orthodoxy, the Reformed confessional development returned once again to its point of departure. The formula of → consensus worked out in Zurich turned against all theological innovations of the sort represented especially by theologians of the Huguenot academy of Saumur.

3.1. The earliest Reformed confession is repre-sented by Ulrich → Zwingli's Theses (1523) for the First Zurich Disputation, which led to the reformation of the city by the city council. Zwingli's Berne Theses (1528) played a similar role. Typical of the early Zwinglian confessional writings is their emphasis on the sole authority of Scripture, whose center is Christ. Initially, no real distinction from Martin → Luther's position is discernible; a difference emerges only when under humanistic influence Zwingli interprets the → Eucharist in a purely symbolic fashion as a commemorative meal.

The dissent between Luther and Zwingli in the question of the Eucharist, articulated in the Marburg Articles (1529), resulted at the Diet of Augsburg (1530) not only in the Lutherans presenting the Confession of → Augsburg but also in four southern free imperial cities preparing the Tetrapolitan Confession and in Zwingli himself sending the emperor his own private confession, the *Fidei ratio.* Efforts by the southern Germans, led by Wolfgang Capito and Martin → Bucer from Strasbourg, to come to some compromise between Zwinglian and Lutheran understandings of the Eucharist finally resulted in the Concord of Wittenberg (1536), which, while indeed leading to an agreement between Luther and the southern Germans, constituted the final break between the Wittenberg and Swiss Reformations. For although the influence of the Strasbourg theologians did indeed exert itself in Switzerland in the Berne Synod (1532) after Zwingli's death as well as in the First → Helvetic Confession (Basle 1536), Luther was willing to conciliate with the Swiss only if the latter accepted the Concord of Wittenberg. The question of the Eucharist thus remained the decisive point of contention, rendering impossible any genuine confessional unity between Wittenberg and German-speaking Switzerland.

3.2. The First Helvetic Confession, signed by all the cities in German-speaking Switzerland that had gone over to the Reformation, constitutes the high point of the first, Zwinglian stage of confessional development. The second stage begins with Calvin's first Genevan Confession (1536), which although elevated to the basic religious state law of the Genevan republic, nonetheless lost its significance after Calvin's expulsion. After his return, Calvin resumed his reform work with the *Ordonnances ecclésiastiques* (1541) and the Genevan Catechism (1542 in French, 1545 in Latin). Precisely in the disputed question of the Eucharist, Calvin's contacts with Bucer and Philipp → Melanchthon brought him closer to Luther than to Zwingli, and Bullinger's retreat from the strictly Zwinglian doctrine of the Eucharist resulted in the Consensus Tigurinus (1549) in an agreement between Geneva and Zurich. Calvin's Consensus Genevensis (1552) countered Jerome Bolsec with a supralapsarian doctrine of predestination, but it was accepted only in Geneva itself. Here the doctrine of predestination became the center of attention for the first time within the context of the development of the Reformed confession.

Despite the agreement between Geneva and Zurich in the question of the Eucharist, the Zurich Reformation maintained its own character. Differently than in Geneva, where the independence of the church was maintained within the framework of a presbyterial ecclesiastical organization over against the municipal authorities, in Zurich the integrity of the state church was preserved; in addition, Bullinger's Second Helvetic Confession (1561, first published in 1566), which replaced the First Helvetic Confession, continued to be characterized by tempered Zwinglianism. Hence in Switzerland, Calvinism and Zwinglianism stood juxtaposed (→ Calvin's Theology; Zwingli's Theology), albeit without any schismatic consequences.

In the second half of the 16th century, Calvinism quickly spread from Geneva to other parts of western and eastern Europe. In France, various congregations formed an alliance for the first time as a Reformed → national church independent of the state, which established a presbyterial-synodal church order for itself in Paris and adopted the Gallican Confession (1559) worked out by Calvin and his pupil Antoine de la Roche Chandieu. Beyond emphasizing the sole authority of Scripture, it affirms the inspired nature of the canonical Scriptures.

The Belgic Confession (1561), drawn up by Guido de Brès, follows the Gallican Confession quite closely; it ultimately became the standard confession of the Dutch Reformed Church. It was first adopted by the refugee communities in the Netherlands at their synods in Wesel (1568) and Emden (1571), where the Dutch Reformed Church established its own presbyterial-synodal order.

The introduction of Calvinism in Scotland had particularly far-reaching consequences. Here the First Scottish Confession (1560), composed by John → Knox and characterized by biblical rigorism, became sanctioned by the state. After the establishment of the presbyterial-synodal church order in the Second Book of Discipline (1581), the king was required (1) to swear allegiance to the covenant (1581), called the Second Scottish Confession (or National Covenant), considered to be God's covenant with the Scottish people, and (2) to extricate himself from papism.

In eastern Europe, Calvinism took hold especially in Hungary and Poland. The theological imbalance of the Erlauthal Confession (1562), composed by Melanchthon's pupil Peter Melius, prompted the Synod of Tarczal to adopt a revised version of Beza's Confession of Christian Faith (1559) as the Hungarian Confession, though this remained in effect only until the adoption of the Second Helvetic Confession at the Synod of Debrecen (1567). Also in Poland, Bullinger's confession was adopted as the Reformed confession, and the Consensus Sandomiriensis (1570) even affirms Eucharistic fellowship between the Reformed, Lutheran, and → Bohemian Brethren.

In Germany, the expansion of Calvinism led to a renewed dispute with the Lutherans concerning the Eucharist. John Laski, who composed both the Emden Catechism (1554) and the doctrinal norm of the East Frisian Church, which was in effect along with the Augsburg Confession, first tried with Calvin to resolve the dispute on the basis of the *Confessio Augustana variata* (1540), presented by Melanchthon, which mitigates the Eucharist article in the sense of the Concord of Wittenberg. The unyielding posture of the Lutherans, however, ultimately led the electorate of the Palatinate to go over to the Reformed camp. The doctrinal standard here, in addition to the Augsburg Confession, was now the → Heidelberg Catechism (1563), composed by Zacharius Ursinus and Caspar Olevianus, which unites the Philippist, Zwinglian, and Calvinist spirit into a harmonious whole; it was accepted as normative not only in all the German territories that went over into the Reformed camp but also in the Dutch Reformed Church.

In reaction especially to the counterreformation conducted by the Jesuits, many German territories followed the lead of the Palatinate and experienced a so-called Second Reformation, in which the Philippists, having been accused of Crypto-Calvinism by the → Gnesio-Lutherans and expelled, played a major role. Christoph Pezel, a pupil of Melanchthon, composed the Nassau Confession (1578), which the Dillenburg Synod accepted along with the Heidelberg Catechism, as well as the Bremen Consensus (1595). In Anhalt the Philippist Anhalt Repetition (1579) and in Hesse-Kassel the Hessian Correctives (1607) signal the Second Reformation. The Sigismund Confession (1613), then, no longer represents a confession promulgated by territorial authorities for subjects, but rather a private confession of the Brandenburg prince elector. The subsequent confessional differences between the prince elector and his subjects explain the ensuing efforts at establishing a union undertaken in Brandenburg-Prussia. The Reformed confessions in Germany are characterized by a decreased emphasis on predestination; this shift reflects the enduring influence of Melanchthon, who rejected absolute predestination in favor of free will.

Prompted by the criticism of Calvin's and Beza's doctrine of predestination by Jacobus Arminius and his adherents in the Remonstrance (1610), a dispute arose in the Dutch Reformed Church between Calvinists and Arminians, culminating in the Synod of Dort (1618-19), which hosted representatives not only from the States General but also from the Palatinate, Nassau, Hesse, East Friesland, Bremen, England, Scotland, and Switzerland. This synod confirmed the Belgic Confession and the Heidelberg Catechism as the confessional writings of the Dutch Reformed Church and, in the Canons of Dort (1619), sanctioned the Calvinist doctrine of double predestination, albeit without taking the side of supralapsarianism. The Calvinist doctrine of predestination thus became the identifying feature of strict Reformed thinking. Accordingly, the Puritan-influenced Cambridge theologians also tried, without success, to complement the Thirty-Nine Articles (1563) with theses concerning double predestination in the Lambeth Articles (1595). The strict doctrine of predestination did, however, find its way into the Irish Articles (1615), composed by Archbishop Ussher.

In the course of the Puritan revolution, the Westminster Assembly was charged by the English Parliament with revising the Anglican articles in the spirit of Puritanism and with establishing a church order. Unification with Scotland merely reinforced the Presbyterian longing for uniformity in church order, → catechism, and confession of faith. Instead of concluding the reworking of the Anglican Thirty-Nine Articles, however, the Westminster Assembly composed the Westminster Confession (1647) and the two Westminster Catechisms (1647), with recourse to the Irish Articles. With its strictly presbyterian ecclesiology, this confession breathes the spirit of Calvinist orthodoxy, though the notion of predestination is subordinated to that of → covenant (§3). While the Westminster Confession remained without practical consequences for the English state church as a result of the Restoration, it was accepted by the state church in Scotland, where it replaced the Scottish Confession. The congregationalist → Puritans, unlike the Presbyterians, emphasized the independence of the individual congregation. In their own Savoy Declaration (1658) they adopted the Westminster Confession, altering only the particular article fixing the presbyterian church order. Presbyterian and Congregationalist immigrants from England and Scotland then contributed to the enormous spread of the two confessions in North America (→ Reformed and Presbyterian Churches; Congregationalism).

The conclusion to the earlier development of Reformed confessions is represented by the Helvetic Consensus Formula (1675), required by the Genevan Franciscus Turretinus as the universal Swiss confession, contra the teachings of the academy of Saumur. Although this formula does prescribe the orthodox doctrine of double predestination, of original sin, and of verbal inspiration, its author, the Zurich theologian Johann Heinrich Heidegger, circumvented the similarly required condemnation of the teachings of Johannes Cocceius and of René Descartes, both of whom had already mitigated the older versions of Reformed orthodoxy.

3.3. The dissolution of the authority of confessions in the Reformed churches signals the beginning of the new epoch of confessional development and initially involves recourse to the idea of the sole authority of Scripture already contained in the earlier confessions. Thus the Academy of Lausanne already advocated assent to the Helvetic Formula of Consensus only if it agreed with Scripture. This position, together with unionistic irenics found in the Reformed camp, ultimately led to the thesis of the fundamental agreement of the basic articles of the Reformed and Lutheran faiths, to the resultant tolerance between those confessions whose bases of faith were generally in agreement (tolerance demanded especially by the Congregationalists), and finally also to the suspension of compulsory confession and thus of confessional uniformity in the territories. The states of the early modern period also found such suspension of confessional uniformity necessary because of the disintegrating effects of the confessional wars on the identity of various countries (→ Union 2).

John Locke in England first developed the doctrine of state → tolerance of the various confessions, a doctrine then radicalized in the American Bill of Rights into the thesis of inherent religious freedom (→ Religious Liberty). The religious freedom and religious neutrality of the state anchored in the U.S. Constitution prompted the American Presbyterians to alter the articles of the Westminster Confession concerning the state and synods (1788). In Europe too, in the wake of the French Revolution, the demand for a separation of church and state was raised, one already raised by the Congregationalists, and Reformed free churches now arose in connection with the Awakening that either reaffirmed the older Reformed confessions (e.g., the Dutch Reformed Church) or introduced new confessions (e.g., that of the Free Church in Canton Vaud, as formulated by Alexandre Vinet in 1847).

In the course of territorial reorganization after the Congress of Vienna, unions emerged in Germany between Reformed and Lutheran churches, with the initiative coming from the Reformed. Consensus unions arose in Nassau, the Palatinate, Baden, and elsewhere. While the Palatinate Union Document (1818) recognized only Scripture itself as its doctrinal norm, the Baden Union Act (1821) accepted the Augsburg Confession, Luther's Small Catechism, and the Heidelberg Catechism as its common confessional basis. In Prussia, which had only a purely administrative union, the king was prompted to emphasize the continuation of the authority of the previous confessional writings. Union theologians, however, did resist, in the name of the sole authority of Scripture, any legal doctrinal authority of the symbolic books of the sort they found evident in emergent confessionalism (→ Denomination 4). Friedrich → Schleiermacher asserted that, not through Scripture, but only through the confessional writings could one demonstrate the Protestant nature of a doctrinal statement. The Protestant spirit of the confessional writings was decisive, he alleged; only that which was common to both Reformed and Lutheran confessional writings was essential to Protestantism. Accordingly, Reformed theologians of mediation such as Carl Ullmann and Alexander Schweizer criticized the articles of the older Reformed confessional writings. The spirit or principle of the confessions replaced the actual wording, with Ullmann distinguishing between (1) justification through faith alone as the *material principle* and (2) the sole authority of Scripture as the *formal principle*.

In Zurich, the free theologians' struggle against this denominational repristination of confessions of faith resulted in Alois Emanuel Biedermann effecting the separation of the territorial church from its previous confessional basis (1855). Given the individual character of religion, this view holds that there can be no binding confessions. Liberal theology thus could now view the various denominational confessions as only the obsolete, dogmatic expression of Protestant piety.

3.4. In connection with neoorthodoxy, however, Karl → Barth especially arrived at a positive estimation of the Reformed confessions. Although he referred to their spatial and temporal relativity in denying the possibility or even desirability of establishing any universal Reformed confession of faith, still in view of concrete historic situations, any given, individual Reformed church might find it necessary to present a new confession of faith. Barth found that such a situation had arisen through the → German Christian church politics of the Deutsche Evangelische Kirche (DEK). Following the Reformed Düsseldorf Theses (1933) and the Declaration on the Correct Understanding of Reformational Confessions in the DEK (1934), adopted by the Free Reformed Synod in Barmen, the → Barmen Declaration (1934) sanctioned a position that, with Barth, emphasizes the exclusivity of God's revelation in Jesus Christ and understands Jesus Christ, the one Word of God, not only as gospel but also as law. This position effectively proclaims the dominion of Christ over all spheres of life, including that of the state, and at the same time radically renounces the entirety of post-Enlightenment neo-Protestantism. Barth's confessional updating, as well as the Christological premise of his neoorthodox Word-of-God theology, was influential in the postwar development of Reformed confessions (→ Dialectical Theology; Word of God 3.3.4).

This renewed estimation of confessing in a fashion oriented toward the present, as well as of the acutely perceived insufficiency of the older Reformed confessions for the present, provides the background for understanding the declarations of faith of the English Presbyterians (1956), the Congregationalists of England and Wales (1967), the U.S. United Church of Christ (1959), and the United Presbyterian Church, USA (1967). This background also has influenced the numerous confessions of young Reformed churches in Latin America, Africa, and Asia such as those of the Presbyterian-Reformed Church in Cuba (1977), the Dutch Reformed Mission Church (1982), and the Presbyterian Church in the Republic of Korea (1976), and it has also influenced the various union documents of the postwar era. These new confessions usually involve declarations coupling a neoorthodox Word-of-God theology with Christologically based socioethical concerns. By contrast, the → Leuenberg Agreement (1973) among Reformational churches in Europe led to an ecclesiastical fellowship between Reformed and Lutherans among the signatories; it was characterized by German union theology, which assumes the unity of the Protestant confessions in its principles and thus considers the denunciations of the Reformation period to be no longer valid. Nonetheless, even those churches that formulate new confessions largely view the older Reformed confessions as norms subordinated to Scripture but as still valid.

Bibliography: Primary sources: BSRK • A. C. COCHRANE, ed., *Reformed Confessions of the Sixteenth Century* (London, 1966) • *The Constitution of the United Presbyterian*

Church in the U.S.A. (Philadelphia, 1967) • L. Vischer, ed., *Reformed Witness Today: A Collection of Contemporary Reformed Confessions* (Bern, 1982) • W. Walker, ed., *The Creeds and Platforms of Congregationalism* (2d ed.; Boston, 1960).

Secondary works: B. G. Armstrong, *Calvinism and the Amyraut Heresy* (London, 1969) • C. Bangs, *Arminius: A Study in the Dutch Reformation* (2d ed.; Grand Rapids, 1985) • P. Jacobs, *Theologie reformierter Bekenntnisschriften in Grundzügen* (Neukirchen, 1959) • J. H. Leith, *Assembly at Westminster: Reformed Theology in the Making* (Richmond, Va., 1973) • W. Neuser, "Dogma und Bekenntnis in der Reformation. Von Zwingli und Calvin bis zur Synode von Westminster," *HDThG* 2.165-352 • J. Rohls, *Theologie reformierter Bekenntnisschriften* (Göttingen, 1987) • M. Schneckenburger, *Vergleichende Darstellung des lutherischen und reformierten Lehrbegriffs* (Bern, 1855) • A. Schweizer, *Die Glaubenslehre der reformierten Kirche dargestellt und aus Quellen belegt* (Zurich, 1844-47); idem, *Die protestantischen Central-Dogmen in ihrer Entwicklung innerhalb der reformierten Kirche* (Zurich, 1854-56).

Jan Rohls

Confirmation

1. Baptism and Confirmation
2. Origin and Historical Development
   2.1. Early Stages
   2.2. The Reformation
   2.3. Further Development
3. Twentieth-Century Discussion
   3.1. Service
   3.2. Instruction
   3.3. Present Situation
4. Ecumenical Aspects

1. Baptism and Confirmation

Confirmation owes its existence to → baptism, regardless of whether it precedes or follows baptism, or whether it is viewed as the personal acceptance of what was done at baptism. In the → early church the sacrament of confirmation (→ Initiation Rites 2.3-4) administered by the → Roman Catholic Church developed out of baptism and originally was part of it. The baptizing presbyter or → bishop, after dipping in the water, conferred the gift of the → Holy Spirit by the → laying on of hands and → anointing. In the third century this conferral became a sacramental act on its own.

In criticism of the Roman Catholic view of confirmation as a → sacrament necessary to salvation, the Reformation churches developed their own doctrine and practice of confirmation. For them, confirmation had an independent function in the context of the whole catechetical process (→ Catechesis). Consistent with the early history of confirmation, there is renewed reflection today on the relation between baptism and confirmation. Some doctrinal schemes and approaches base confirmation and its instruction on the original baptismal command (Matt. 28:19-20).

2. Origin and Historical Development
2.1. Early Stages
Historically the path led from baptism by way of the laying on of hands and anointing to confirmation. As the anointing was increasingly detached from baptism, the latter came to be seen more and more as merely an act of washing, with anointing itself assuming the meaning of imparting the Spirit as a necessary completion of baptism. → Thomas Aquinas (1224/25-74) saw baptism as giving new life but also taught that strengthening by a further sacrament of confirmation was needed (→ Thomism). In 1439 the Council of Florence declared unequivocally that "the second sacrament is confirmation." In the Roman Catholic Church confirmation does not come until after First Communion (→ Initiation Rites 2.3.1) and can be administered only by a bishop. In the → Orthodox Church the sacrament of Holy Unction is still related directly to baptism. The → Cathari, → Waldenses, and → Bohemian Brethren all criticized the medieval practice, but it was left for the Reformers to make a breakthrough.

2.2. The Reformation
In controversy with the view of confirmation as a sacrament, M. → Luther (1483-1546) attacked the claim that it is necessary to → salvation, finding no basis for this belief in Scripture. Confirmation does not have the divine promise that is essential to the ordaining of a sacrament. As Luther saw it, confirmation devalues baptism, which already mediates all saving gifts. Confirmation was for him a deceitful mockery (WA 10/2.282). In the course of his pastoral → visitations, however, he saw the practical value of the → catechism. Hence his interest in confirmation was primarily catechetical, not sacramental. He wanted baptismal instruction to be repeated so that there would be the knowledge needed for intelligent partaking of the → Eucharist. For Luther it was essential that all who come to the Lord's Supper should know what they are doing. His theological understanding of confirmation thus was governed by its relation to baptism and the Eucharist. Luther had no great interest in the rite as such, but he did not object

to having a rite, viewing it as an act of blessing, and finding a place in it for intercession (→ Prayer; Luther's Theology).

M. → Bucer (1491-1551) did much to promote a wider use of confirmation. His main interest was in → church discipline. In controversy with the → Anabaptists, he wanted to strengthen infant baptism. He saw in confirmation a renewal of the baptismal confession (→ Confession of Faith) and tied it to the laying on of hands, prayer for the Holy Spirit, and admission to Holy Communion. This view found expression in the Ziegenhain Church Order of 1539. In effect, Bucer was the father of Protestant confirmation. He regarded it as a sacramental ceremony and influenced the form it took in England. With the laying on of hands the minister was to say, "Receive the Holy Spirit as protection and defense against all evil." The idea that Bucer's orders were the first ritual orders in the Protestant world has been corrected, however, by B. Hareide (p. 13), for confirmation had an independent place in churches associated with Wittenberg, not merely as a catechetical function, but with ritual elements as well as in orientation to the Eucharist. It should be noted that the focus was not simply on confirmation as a formal requirement for admission to Communion but as an invitation and introduction to it.

The Genevan Reformer J. → Calvin (1509-64) had a catechetical interest similar to Luther's. Each year he had four examination periods to determine whether those wishing to partake of the Eucharist had the necessary knowledge (→ Calvin's Theology). The catechetical and disciplinary type of confirmation spread rapidly. For all the differences in detail, the following features are common to the → Reformation views: (1) rejection of a sacramental understanding; (2) high regard for, and not devaluing, baptism; (3) a dominant catechetical interest, even concerning the Eucharist; and (4) intercession either with (Luther and Bucer) or without (Calvin and → Zwingli) the laying on of hands.

2.3. Further Development
Pietism and the → Enlightenment shared the Reformation view of confirmation but stressed more heavily the personal addressing of the candidates, with a view to their decision and confession; that is, it assumed their maturity. For the Pietists, the main aims of confirmation were penitence and → conversion (§1). It was a matter not of learning doctrine but of assimilating its contents. With the Enlightenment, confirmation became more of a social ritual to mark the end of school days and passage from → childhood to → adulthood. Admission to Communion was less important, but emphasis fell on the

confirming and renewing of baptism. → Pietism and the Enlightenment helped to spread confirmation as an institution.

In the 19th century, criticism of confirmation arose on a broad front. The Erlangen theologians J. C. K. von Hofmann (1810-77), T. Harnack (1817-89), and G. von Zezschwitz (1825-86) advocated reform by dividing confirmation into two acts: renewal of baptism and admission to full church membership. The first would be for all, the second only for those who were ready for true involvement in congregational life. The focus of J. H. Wichern (1808-81) was on the vitality of the → congregation. He sought to separate theory and practice and inquired into the confirmands and → pedagogy. On balance, however, efforts at reform changed little (see K. Frör, 43ff.).

3. Twentieth-Century Discussion
The question of the meaning and practice of confirmation was still a live one in the 20th century. Further proposals for reform have been made. During the period of the Third Reich in Germany, the catechumenate was rediscovered, and the whole confirmation process was appreciated anew (G. Adam 1984, 28ff.).

3.1. Service
After 1945 a concept of confirmation developed that is oriented to the Reformation catechism and sees confirmation instruction as the path needed to get from baptism to the Eucharist. Conclusions regarding the order and theology of confirmation have shaped the form of confirmation instruction.

In his work *Confirmatio,* Frör describes three main types of instruction for confirmation. If the stress is on the catechetical ministry of the church to the baptized, the ministry of the Word is the sustaining and determinative element, with preparation for the Eucharist and the recalling of baptism being central in the instruction. If the focus is on the Eucharist, then sacramental instruction is predominant. Confirmation may then be viewed as providing an orderly form of preparation for, and admission to, Communion. (If the stress falls on direct participation in the Eucharist, then the First Communion is the focus.) Finally, if the emphasis is placed on blessing and intercession by the congregation, then confirmation is primarily an act of congregational prayer, with the introduction of children to congregational life as the center.

3.2. Instruction
A new phase began in Germany in 1964 with W. Neidhart's analyses of confirmation instruction as an institution of the → people's church. Note is taken here of the reality of the people's church and

the significance of the understanding of the church in preparing candidates for confirmation. At the end of the 1960s, broad reforms were made in the instruction. The reasons for change included the weakness of the instruction presently being given, the lack of desire or readiness to learn on the part of the candidates, the absence of parental support, the increasing rigidity of instruction, and the inadequate pedagogical training of the ministers. Renewed effort was made to correct the last point (H. B. Kaufmann).

A common theme of all attempted reforms was a concern to engage the total → experience of the candidates. Faith and learning, rather than being opposed to one another dialectically and theologically, were constructively related. Rote learning was changed to include learning by head, heart, and hand. The term "comprehensive" summed up the new perspective. Specific possibilities of instruction were found in direct encounters with others, in the preparation of services (→ Worship), and in testing various expressions of the Christian faith. The period of confirmation instruction thus took on new intensity, rhythm, and variety with regard to its form (now involving traditional teaching as well as leisure-time activities, courses, practical diakonia, and liturgical projects), times and places, and teachers (teams made up of ministers, → church employees, and members of the congregation). The change may be seen in the use of the term "confirmation work" for the older "confirmation instruction" and the greater emphasis on → Christian education.

3.3. Present Situation

The question of the right age for confirmation has always been a starting point when reform has been under discussion. The model of adult confirmation was examined in Stuttgart-Rot after 1967 (Adam 1984, 114ff.). The problems of confirmation vows, however, did not disappear with postponement to the 18th year. Recently there has been a proposal to lower the age, but thus far it has been tried only in individual congregations. As the result of an investigation of Lutheran churches worldwide, R. Virkunnen states that the age of confirmation varies from 12 to 25, the lowest figures coming from Asia, the highest from Latin America and Holland, and the usual age being 15.

Another new feature has been greater sensitivity to handicapped young people in the matter of confirmation and its instruction (see R. Rogge in Comenius-Institut, 128ff.). An essential result of debate on this issue is that those with mental handicaps are no longer automatically excluded from confirmation (Adam 1986).

No sphere of congregational work reaches an age group so comprehensively today as does instruction for confirmation. In view of the modern situation, preparation for confirmation is no longer in many instances so much an agency of socialization as it is an agency of → mission to a secularized society (→ Secularization).

Confirmation is a voluntary creation of the church rather than a biblically ordained sacrament. There are different motivating forces behind it, theological and otherwise. On a Protestant view, it does not complete baptism or mediate new and fuller → grace. It is, however, a reminder of baptism and an act of intercession and blessing at a specific stage of life under the promise of the gospel. The question of confirmation → vows is still a difficult one. It does not affect the fact that the confirmed agree with the confession of the church to the best of their insight (Adam 1984, 64-68). The service seeks to give visible expression to the personal receiving of the young people, through naming, blessing, laying on of hands, and pronouncement. By intercession it sets their future course under God's protection.

4. Ecumenical Aspects

A glance at the ecumenical situation (→ Ecumenical Movement) shows that much is in flux. It is certainly no accident, but reflects the situation in many churches of the Reformation, that in the Lima Declaration ("Baptism," par. 14), so little could be said by way of consensus about confirmation.

A study of confirmation by the → Lutheran World Federation states that there is practically full agreement regarding the understanding and practice of catechetical instruction. The educational task of the church should be viewed as a lifelong affair, with confirmation seen not as the end of instruction but as only a single milestone in a longer process (R. Virkunnen, 4). The study also showed that for most Lutherans, confirmation is still basic to the understanding of Lutheran identity.

There have recently been forward-looking developments not only among Lutherans but also in the → Anglican Communion, → Methodist churches, and → Reformed churches, among others (Adam 1984, 249-61). For all these churches, confirmation is of great importance, but views of what it is and when it should be given vary. It is usually related to baptism and basic Christian instruction, also in many places to the Eucharist, with the problem being one of agreeing on how these various factors relate to one another (R. Virkunnen, 4).

There were few changes in confirmation instruction and the practice of confirmation up to the 1960s, but since then there have been many individual changes, the main common feature being a mounting tendency to detach confirmation from admission to Communion (D. R. Holeton; Initiation Rites 2.3.2). It is an open question how confirmation will be understood and practiced in the future.

→ Occasional Services; Socialization; Youth Work

Bibliography: G. ADAM, *Der Unterricht der Kirche. Studien zur Konfirmandenarbeit* (Göttingen, 1980; 3d ed., 1984); idem, "Zur Konfirmation Geistigbehinderter," *Danken und Dienen* (Diakonisches Werk; Stuttgart, 1986) 42-46 • C. BÄUMLER and H. LUTHER, eds., *Konfirmandenunterricht und Konfirmation Texte zu einer Praxistheorie im 20. Jahrhundert* (Munich, 1982) 345-78 • C. BIZER, "Konfirmandenunterricht," *Handbuch religiöser Erziehung* (ed. W. Böcker, H.-G. Heimbrock, and E. Kerhoff; Düsseldorf, 1987) 2.391-402 • D. C. BROCKOPP, B. L. HELGE, and D. G. TRUEMPER, eds., *Christian Initiation: Reborn of Water and Spirit* (Valparaiso, Ind., 1981) • COMENIUS-INSTITUT, *Handbuch für die Konfirmandenarbeit* (Gütersloh, 1984; 2d ed., 1985) • G. DIX, *The Theology of Confirmation in Relation to Baptism* (Westminster, Eng., 1953) • K. FRÖR, *Confirmatio. Forschungen zur Geschichte und Praxis der Konfirmation* (Munich, 1959) • B. HAREIDE, *Die Konfirmation in der Reformationszeit* (Göttingen, 1971) • D. R. HOLETON, "Konfirmation in den 80er Jahren," *Ökumenische Perspektiven von Taufe, Eucharistie und Amt* (ed. M. Thurian; Frankfurt, 1983) 87-109 • U. T. HOLMES, *Confirmation: The Celebration of Maturity in Christ* (San Francisco, 1975) • P. J. JAGGER, *Christian Initiation, 1552-1969: Rites of Baptism and Confirmation since the Reformation Period* (London, 1970) • H. B. KAUFMANN, "Didaktische Überlegungen zur Theorie des Konfirmandenunterrichts," *Theologie und Unterricht* (FS H. Stock; Gütersloh, 1969) 229-42 • T. A. MARSH, *Gift of Community: Baptism and Confirmation* (Wilmington, Del., 1984) • MURPHY CENTER FOR LITURGICAL RESEARCH, *Made, Not Born: New Perspectives on Christian Initiation and the Catechumenate* (Notre Dame, Ind., 1976) • W. NEIDHART, *Konfirmandenunterricht in der Volkskirche* (Zurich, 1964) • B. NEUNHEUSER, *Baptism and Confirmation* (New York, 1964) • R. R. OSMER, *Confirmation: Presbyterian Practices in Ecumenical Perspective* (Louisville, Ky., 1997) • E. SCHWERIN, *Evangelische Kinder- und Konfirmandenarbeit* (Würzburg, 1989) • R. VIRKUNNEN, *Konfirmation in den lutherischen Kirchen heute. Studien über die Konfirmation in den LWB-Mitgliedskirchen* (Geneva, 1987) • K. WEGENAST, "Konfirmandenunterricht und Konfirmation," *Gemeindepädagogisches Kompendium* (ed. G. Adam and R. Lachmann; Göttingen, 1987) 314-54 (bibliography).

GOTTFRIED ADAM

Conflict

Today the term "conflict" denotes a wide variety of collisions of impulses, interests, powers, and groups on the psychological, social, political, and international levels, with or without the use of force, and with or without a symmetry of the conflicting interests or parties. The exclusively negative evaluation of conflict today in popular parlance is only partly shared by → psychology (→ Psychotherapy) and not at all by → sociology. Since the term is used so broadly on so many different levels, which may be interrelated but cannot be reduced to a common denominator, no single theory of conflict has been able to establish itself. We may group the theories as follows.

1. Psychological theories relate to inner psychological and intrahuman relations. When applied to larger groups nationally or internationally, the theories require elaboration if they are to go beyond simplistic analogies.

Classic → psychoanalysis sees human development as driven by conflicts between inner impulses and outer obstacles. Conflicts between need and (moral) rules and prohibitions, once recognized, can be resolved. If the conflict is latent or suppressed, however, it can produce various physical and mental disturbances (→ Neurosis). While not disputing this conclusion, the generation of analysts after Freud (Karen Horney and Erich Fromm et al.) stress that there are fields of human development that, though essentially free of conflict (e.g., speech, physical achievement, curiosity), still have promoted art and science. Conflict arises, however, with the search for security.

Kurt Lewin (1890-1947) explained conflicts in human life along the lines of field theory. Followed by Neal E. Miller, he classified conflicts according to positive and negative desires and their collision.

Behavioral research (→ Behaviorism) investigates these types of conflict. It sees every conflict as a clash of behavioral trends that arises through attraction to the outside world. Since these trends (involving the opposites appetency and aversion) have been learned, they can be unlearned through conditioning therapy. Transfer of this theory directly to social conflicts can easily lead to political and ideological → manipulation. The theory is unsatisfying in leaving open the central question of the origin of → aggression (→ Evil).

2. Basic → anthropological questions of this kind occupied classic political → philosophy (Aristotle,

Hobbes, Kant, et al.). With a negative view of conflicts, however, this philosophy treated them in the context of questions of order, → authority, and → war. Only in the 18th century did the idea arise that → property is an important source of conflict — a theme systematized in the 19th century (→ Marxism).

Today distinction is made between behaviorist and systemic theories of conflict. The former starts with the notion of stimulus and response, the latter with self-definition in the role-conduct of a → system (i.e., seeking to discover how the parts of a system function, with some inherent "meaning" as the controlling device; → Political Parties). Conflicts are here seen as reaction conflicts (→ Peace Research).

3. Since the work of Georg Simmel (1858-1918), sociology has taken into account the stabilizing function of conflicts and analyzed their causes, intensity, and forms. The ambivalence of their integrative and dysfunctional effects in → society is still a matter of debate. Recent research (Lewis A. Coser) has identified basic social types. Conflicts may be guided and institutionalized best in pluralist societies (→ Pluralism 1), where they are stabilizing and permit change. In closed societies they are more intense but free of force. In totalitarian societies they simmer for a long time and then erupt violently (→ Revolution). An important modern insight is into asymmetrical conflicts between stronger and weaker parties (North-South conflict; → Dependence) and the necessary strategies of disengagement.

Although the discussion of ambivalence is still open, along with the question of social causes (for Marxists, property; for Ralf Dahrendorf, government), and though the debate continues regarding structural-functional theory, there is consensus that in the social and political field, as in psychotherapy, we must reject any harmony that is based on the repression of conflicts. Conflicts can be mastered, guided, and limited, but there is no benefit in trying to avoid them.

4. The → church can learn from these theories, especially the first and third. It has promoted the popular negative view of conflict with its reference to → love and → reconciliation. It has often contributed indeed to the avoidance of conflict. At the same time, the church and theology can also contribute important impulses toward the overcoming of social and political conflict. They can do so first by working out and taking seriously synodic and conciliar strategies for dealing with conflict. Yet they can also do so by taking as their point of departure the heart of the → gospel, which testifies of God's own reconciling act as an event that itself is profoundly characterized by conflict. The ministry of reconciliation (2 Cor. 5:18) does not ignore conflicts in church and society; rather, it faces them honestly in arbitration.

→ Anxiety; Dialogue; Disarmament and Armament; Group and Group Dynamics; Peace

Bibliography: "Conflict / Conflict of Interest / Conflict of Laws," *IESS* 220-53 • L. A. Coser, *The Functions of Social Conflict* (Glencoe, Ill., 1956) • R. Dahrendorf, *Gesellschaft und Freiheit* (Munich, 1961); idem, *Konflikt und Freiheit* (Munich, 1972) • J. Galtung, *Strukturelle Gewalt* (Reinbek, 1975) • A. Honneth, *The Struggle for Recognition: The Moral Grammar of Social Conflicts* (Cambridge, 1995) • K. S. Larsen, ed., *Conflict and Social Psychology* (London, 1993) • K. Lewin, *Field Theory in Social Science* (New York, 1951); idem, *Resolving Social Conflicts* (New York, 1948) • D. Senghaas, *Gewalt, Konflikt, Frieden* (Hamburg, 1974) • G. Simmel, "Der Streit," *Soziologie* (Berlin, 1918; 3d ed., 1926).

Dietrich Ritschl

Confucianism

The modern term "Confucianism" has no exact equivalent in traditional Chinese doxography. It denotes the sum of the officially sanctioned values and → norms that have influenced, and to some extent still influence, the fabric of Chinese social structure, visible, e.g., in → ancestor worship, subordination in the five key human relations (prince and subject, father and son, husband and wife, older brother and younger brother, teacher and student), and the governing of everyday life by moral concepts.

The nearest Chinese equivalent is the teaching of the Ju, cultured officials who in the unified Han dynasty (206 b.c.–a.d. 220) set up a unified cosmological, social, and political structure of thought that served as a basis for governing the country and controlling the theoretically omnipotent ruler. The Ju made the classics the orthodox canon, ascribing their redaction to Confucius (551-479). Confucius was viewed as the last *shengren,* or saint, who had handed down and systematized the teachings of earlier founders of culture. Ancestor worship and the hierarchy of the five relations had long been established by the time of Confucius, and he himself said little about them. For him the legitimacy of a regime rested on the satisfaction of the people.

The Ju appealed to a secret Confucianist tradition of yin and yang and the five elements, which they developed into a corresponding system. Heaven controls the ruler, with heavenly phenomena (eclipses etc.) providing direction and criticism. The Ju themselves observe and interpret them. Popular cults, magicians (→ Magic) with their promises of → immortality and journeys to paradise, and the → Taoists were their declared opponents, and the rulers constantly sought to establish direct access (beyond these groups) to the heavenly authority that these groups were popularly thought to personify. Although in many esoteric Ju texts Confucius is depicted as the son of the black (heavenly) emperor and therefore as a demigod, the imperial offerings made to him, later taken over by local authorities, were never more than commemorative offerings. The Ju did not try to meet their opponents on their own level.

With the collapse of the Han dynasty, the Ju system of teaching and interpretation, which had already split into two schools, also collapsed. Reformers of the ancient-text school prepared the way for the ontologically based political philosophy of Wang Pi (226-49). This philosophy left Confucius in his exalted position and derived itself from his classics but advocated the self-regulation of society with the ruler as no more than a nominal center.

The spread of → Buddhism among educated circles in the centuries that followed involved a crisis for Ju teaching. The Buddhist doctrine of retribution gave added force to the traditional canon of values and found ready acceptance. → Meditation came to be practiced by artists, writers, and philosophers, and Chinese culture was greatly enriched by the Buddhist legacy.

The revival of Confucianism began with the persecution of Buddhism demanded by Han Yü (768-824), a Ju writer. Measures against the Taoists quickly followed. The new Ju teaching (Neo-Confucianism) absorbed many elements, especially from Buddhism. Chu Hsi (1130-1200) systematized the teaching into a uniform philosophical canon incorporating simple primers of moral axioms, basic principles of government and cosmic order, and the self-education of scholars. A strong central state had by this time been set up again, and with it the influence of the Ju increased. This form of Ju teaching was also influential in tributary states (e.g., Korea and Viet Nam).

The dynasties that followed the Sung Dynasty (960-1279) supported and promoted the uniform establishment of teaching and examination according to this canon, even when the rulers belonged to other religions, such as the Ch'ing, who were adherents of Lamaism (→ Tibetan Religions). Ju doctrine seemed to fit in so well with the premises of enlightened absolutism in politics and rationalistic theology in religion that Confucianist China was found to be a distant model for Europe. Stimulated thus, Chinese reformers like K'ang Yu-wei (1858-1927), who wrote decisive reforming works in 1888 and 1895, proposed a constitution at the end of the imperial period in which Confucianism would be the state religion. This religion would unite core pieces of Christian → ethics with a purely Chinese tradition. The tradition has been continued in Taiwan, Singapore, and South Korea, where the state promotes Confucianism as the basis of public morality and the → family.

By contrast, Protestant evangelical missionaries (→ Revivals), the Chinese → Taiping Rebellion, and 20th-century students have held Confucianism responsible for "rationalistic unbelief" and "Chinese stagnation." Max → Weber (1864-1920) argued that Confucianism lacks the inner tension that has made Protestant ethics a driving force of → capitalism. In the People's Republic of China criticism of Confucianism continued. It was stated in 1972, for example, that Confucius had wanted to restore a society of slaveholders.

Confucius was rehabilitated as an educational reformer with the reforms that began in 1978. The upheavals and revolutions in 20th-century China have brought much change, yet the traditional values and behavioral norms associated with Confucianism have proved very persistent, both among the people and among the revolutionary leaders, who have grown into or been forced into the role of Ju officials that they earlier contested so bitterly. With the strengthening of the family among the latest reformers, the Confucianist elements are even clearer. In the long run, the Cultural Revolution (1966-69), which denounced leaders, parents, and teachers, has strengthened this role, while women, who were hailed as revolutionary heroes, have sunk back into their essentially traditional role with the end of the Cultural Revolution.

→ Asian Theology

Bibliography: W. T. DE BARY, *Neo-Confucian Orthodoxy and the Learning of the Mind-and-Heart* (New York, 1981) • H. G. CREEL, *Confucius: The Man and the Myth* (Chicago, 1949) • J. W. DARDESS, *Conquerors and Confucians* (New York, 1973) • J. DULL, "A Historical Introduction to the Apocryphal *(ch'anwei)* Texts of the Han Dynasty" (Diss., Washington, D.C., 1966) • W. EICHHORN, *Die Religionen Chinas* (Stuttgart, 1973) • J. LEGGE, *The Chinese Classics* (5 vols.; Hong Kong, 1861-65) • W. C. LIU, *A Short History of the Confucian Philosophy* (Harmondsworth, 1955) • T. METZGER, *Escape from Predicament* (New York, 1977) • M. WEBER, *Gesammelte Aufsätze zur Religionssoziologie* (vol. 1; Tübingen, 1922) • A. WRIGHT, ed., *The Confucian Persuasion* (Stanford, Calif., 1960).

RUDOLF G. WAGNER

Confutation → Augsburg Confession

Congo (Brazzaville)

	1960	1980	2000
Population (1,000s):	988	1,669	2,982
Annual growth rate (%):	2.35	2.84	2.72

Area: 342,000 sq. km. (132,047 sq. mi.)

A.D. *2000*

Population density: 9/sq. km. (23/sq. mi.)
Births / deaths: 4.05 / 1.34 per 100 population
Fertility rate: 5.45 per woman
Infant mortality rate: 87 per 1,000 live births
Life expectancy: 52.3 years (m: 50.0, f: 54.7)
Religious affiliation (%): Christians 90.8 (Roman Catholics 45.3, Protestants 18.4, unaffiliated 15.9, indigenous 10.7, other Christians 0.5), tribal religionists 4.8, nonreligious 2.3, Muslims 1.3, other 0.8.

1. General Situation
2. Religious Situation

1. General Situation

The Republic of Congo, whose capital is Brazzaville, is bordered by Gabon, Cameroon, and the Central African Republic, as well as by the former Zaire, known since May 1997 as the Democratic Republic of Congo. The most important tribal groups are the 10 groups of the Kongo peoples (840,000), 15 groups of Teke (490,000), 6 groups of Mboshi (195,000), and 6 groups of Mbete (140,000). There are altogether over 75 ethnic groups speaking 60 different languages.

Congo includes small percentages of other African peoples, as well as Europeans and Asians. French is the official language, with the trade languages Lingala and Munukutuba widely spoken. The chief crops are palm oil and kernels, cocoa, coffee, and tobacco. It has rich oil and mineral deposits, including gold, lead, copper, and zinc.

The Portuguese were the first Europeans to reach present-day Congo. Afonso I (1506/7-ca. 1550), ruler of the Kongo Kingdom (in present-day Zaire and Angola), demanded modernization and Christianization, but with only partial success. The territory came under French rule in the 19th century,

while Belgium claimed what became the Belgian Congo (later renamed Zaire). In 1960 Congo achieved independence, with Roman Catholic priest F. Youlou the first president (1960-63). Congo became a Marxist-Leninist state in 1970, but serious economic problems, including massive embezzlement of government funds, led eventually to a return of multiparty democracy in 1992.

2. Religious Situation

The success of → mission (§3) was considerable in the 16th century, but many of the churches declined with the collapse of the kingdom in the 17th and 18th centuries. The → Roman Catholic Church began new missionary work in 1883 and today claims a little under 50 percent of the people.

Protestant work began in 1909 under the aegis of Svenska Missionsförbundet (→ Scandinavian Missions). The mission's work resulted in the Église Évangélique du Congo, which became independent in 1961 and is the largest Protestant church in Congo, with 310,000 adherents in 1990. Somewhat less than one-fifth of the people are Protestant.

After 1926 there was a widespread movement of political and religious protest under the leadership of the former Roman Catholic catechist A. Matswa (1889-1942), which included the later president Youlou as an adherent. The → Salvation Army began work in 1935; in 1990 it was the second largest Protestant group, with 63,000 adherents. There also are smaller communities of Baptists and Assemblies of God in Congo.

The largest Independent Church in the Congo, as in Africa as a whole, is the → Kimbanguist Church (→ Independent Churches). In 1990 it numbered approximately 80,000 adherents in Congo; altogether in the country, adherents of African indigenous movements represent over one-sixth of the population (→ Guinea 2).

Congo also has a number of religious movements (→ Sect). The most active of these is Nzambi ya Bougie (God of Candles). Another is the Croix-Koma movement, which was founded by the Roman Catholic layman Ta Malanda in 1964 to root out → witchcraft. Before 1978 there were many other small groups, most of which the Communist government banned.

Other religious groupings include African traditional religions and Muslims (→ Islam), with much smaller numbers of → Baha'is and → Jehovah's Witnesses.

The → Salvation Army, Église Évangélique du Congo, and the Kimbanguist Church are members of the → All Africa Conference of Churches and the →

World Council of Churches. With the Église Baptiste du Congo Populaire (→ Baptists) and the Roman Catholic Church they also belong to the Fédération des Églises Chrétiennes du Congo-Brazzaville.

After a period of tension between → church and state during the Communist period, all restrictions on religious belief have now been removed. Growth of Christian churches has been steady — in some cases, dramatic.

→ African Theology

Bibliography: E. ANDERSON, Churches at the Grass-Roots: A Study in Congo-Brazzaville (London, 1968); idem, Messianic Popular Movements in the Lower Congo (Uppsala, 1958) • S. AXELSON, Culture and Confrontation in the Lower Congo (Stockholm, 1970) • D. BARRETT, ed., WCE 245-48 • D. LAGERGREN, Mission and State in the Congo (Uppsala, 1970) • M. SINDA, Le messianism congolais et ses incidences politiques (Paris, 1972) • W. USTORF, Afrikanische Initiative. Das aktive Leiden des Propheten Simon Kimbangu (Frankfurt, 1975).

THE EDITORS

Congregation

1. NT
    1.1. Term
    1.2. Beginnings
    1.3. Paul
2. Practical Thelogy
    2.1. Terms
    2.2. Structure and Organization
    2.3. Principles of Work
        2.3.1. Martyria
        2.3.2. Diakonia
        2.3.3. Koinonia
    2.4. Plural Form
    2.5. Unity
3. Sociology
4. Systematic Theology
    4.1. Biblical Foundations
    4.2. Historical Development
    4.3. Ecumenical Multiplicity
    4.4. Theological Criteria

1. NT

1.1. Term

The word "congregation" has become established alongside "church" as English translations of the central NT word "ecclesia" (Gk. ekklēsia, originally meaning "assembly, gathering"). In modern theology a distinction is seen that is materially, though not semantically, based on the NT but that raises ecu-menical problems. The congregation is the specific local assembly, whereas the church is the people of God as a universal entity and in its extralocal forms of organization.

1.2. Beginnings

In its beginnings, emerging Christianity was mostly organized locally, for which the → synagogue model was influential. The synagogue served the interests of community teaching and → prayer but had no theological relevance. At least before A.D. 70, the orientation to → Jerusalem as the one cultic center was normative in Israel's understanding of itself. Similarly, the first Christian communities were oriented to Jerusalem. The → early church there did not regard itself as a local entity but as the center of the eschatological people of God that the → Holy Spirit was gathering. The self-designation "ekklēsia of God," which was chosen quite early (see 1 Cor. 15:9), expresses a universal and eschatological self-understanding, for it has in view God's final promise, the gathering of his people in its eschatological totality.

1.3. Paul

It was → Paul who found in the local congregation a basic theological entity and who thus established the historical basis on which even today, in almost all churches, the local congregation has become the inalienable form of Christian life. The impulses in this direction appear in Paul's → Christology, his understanding of the sacraments, his pneumatology, and his self-understanding as an → apostle. By his death, Christ overcame inimical forces, especially the → law (Gal. 3:13; 4:5). Raised from the dead by God, he is the beginning of God's eschatological creation. Those who belong to him share already in the new reality of life (2 Cor. 5:17), not just by possessing individual salvation, but as those who are incorporated into a social sphere of life stamped by Christ and shaped by his power. They are "in Christ" (Gal. 3:28; Eph. 1:3-4, etc.).

Almost more important even than → baptism, in which they are set under Christ's power (Gal. 3:27), is the → Eucharist in Paul's view of the local church. By common reception of the gift whose content is the Lord giving himself for the many, these many are brought together into a fellowship in which the renewing power of this Lord is the determinative reality of life. They become "one body" (1 Cor. 10:17).

The congregation, then, is the body of Christ, a living organism, whose varied functions are interrelated as they signify the eschatological reality that is given in Christ (1 Cor. 12:12). Vital for the congregation is its coming together for → worship (1 Cor.

14:23). By what it receives here in Word and sacrament, it becomes what it is — a fellowship of life and witness in which people no longer rule over one another but serve one another after the manner of Jesus (Gal. 5:13), and in the liberating power of the → gospel bear witness by overcoming all human distinctions and barriers (Gal. 3:28).

Using the image of the temple, Paul expounds the pneumatological aspect of the church community. It is God's end-time temple, which the Holy Spirit is building, in which he dwells, and over whose holiness and purity he watches (1 Cor. 3:16). Hence Paul lays the sanctions of the Spirit on church members who disregard this holiness and purity and who persist impenitently in → sin (chap. 5).

Founding congregations is the goal of the apostolic commission (Rom. 1:5) and also the criterion for its fulfillment (2 Cor. 10:13-16). For the gospel that the apostle carries and represents is a powerful event that seeks physical manifestations. Because each local congregation is such a manifestation of the apostolic gospel, it is the ecclesia in the full sense. It does not become this only as it sees itself as a part or expression of a total church (represented, e.g., in Jerusalem). Certainly the universal dimension of the ecclesia is important for Paul, as his concern to bring collections of money to Jerusalem shows, but it is to be found in the fellowship of faith and love between the local assemblies, in each of which the essential Christian community takes concrete shape.

The later epistles modify this conception. Thus the ecclesiological statements in Colossians and Ephesians are interested in the ekklēsia as an overarching, worldwide entity in salvation history, with local congregations receiving less prominence.

Bibliography: N. A. DAHL, Das Volk Gottes. Eine Untersuchung zum Kirchenbewußtsein des Urchristentums (2d ed.; Darmstadt, 1963) • J. HAINZ, Ekklesia. Strukturen paulinischer Gemeinde-Theologie und Gemeinde-Ordnung (Regensburg, 1972) • B. HOLMBERG, Paul and Power: The Structure of Authority in the Primitive Church as Reflected in the Pauline Epistles (Lund, 1978) • W. KLAIBER, Rechtfertigung und Gemeinde. Eine Untersuchung zum paulinischen Kirchenverständnis (Göttingen, 1982) bibliography • T. W. MANSON, "The NT Basis of the Doctrine of the Church," JEH 1 (1950) 1-11 • J. L. MURPHY, "The Use of 'Ekklesia' in the NT," AEcR 140 (1959) 250-59, 325-32 • J. PFAMMATTER, Die Kirche als Bau (Rome, 1960) • R. SCHNACKENBURG, The Church in the NT (London, 1965) • W. SCHRAGE, " 'Ekklesia' und 'Synagoge.' Zum Ursprung des urchristlichen Kirchenbegriffs," ZTK 60 (1963) 178-202.

JÜRGEN ROLOFF

2. Practical Theology

2.1. Terms

"Congregation" is the term for the basic unit in church organization (→ Church; Church Government). It may be defined both geographically and legally, two aspects that are closely related.

We may also speak of "Christian community," which points to what believers in a given place hold in common, or that in which the members of a given congregation share both legally and geographically. → Luther had such emphases in view when he used Gemeinde (community, municipality, corporate body) to translate ekklēsia. The Christian community thus is the fellowship of those who, sharing and enjoying a common good in Christ, enter into a new relationship with one another. The theological formula for this aspect is the → priesthood of all believers. Common participation in Word and sacrament (→ Worship) creates a new inward and outward relationship. The secular sense of the term "community" is hereby radicalized. Women and children also enjoy the priestly dignity. Office means service — the service that all members of the congregation owe one another. In Reformation terms, the ministry of the Word is committed to the whole congregation. Filled out theologically, the parish has become the Christian community.

The term "parish" (Gk. paroikia) can also be defined geographically and legally. It originally meant a living abroad without civil rights or rights of domicile (TDNT 5.851). It was used first for the → house church or → diaspora in a pagan environment. A profound change came with the setting up of the state church in 381 (→ Early Church 2.3). The parish then became the basic civil and ecclesiastical district, in the midst of which was the church.

Roman Catholicism defines the parish (Lat. paroecia) as "a definite community of the Christian faithful established on a stable basis within a particular church; the pastoral care of the parish is entrusted to a pastor as its own shepherd under the authority of the diocesan bishop" (1983 CIC 515.1). A legally established parish is a legal entity (515.3). Although the term "parish" is still used in official language, Roman Catholic theology has to a large extent opted today for "community" (F. Klostermann, K. Lehmann, et al.). In interdenominational conversations the legal qualification of the local congregation is disputed. There is agreement, however, that it is the historically developed and theologically qualified basic unit of the church as the worldwide people of God.

Along with the local congregation, and partly within it, there are other forms of Christian community, such as the institutional, the personal, the para-church (note the discussions of the WCC Assembly at Delhi in 1961), the house church, and the → base community (Medellín 1968; → Latin American Councils 2). All of these point to reforming impulses in specific contexts but do not replace the basic form of the congregation. As practical theology reflects on the concept, it inquires into the ways in which normative concepts of community may be passed on in church practice, and also into the theological content of empirical analyses of present-day models against an ecumenical background.

2.2. Structure and Organization

In the NT we find the coexistence of various forms of church life (see 1). Materially, however, and usually even organizationally, all historically known models have → worship as their organizing center. Worship may take very different forms in the different denominational traditions, but it is the exemplary, if not the exclusive, touchstone whereby to test the governing structure of the congregation. The variety of forms reflects the variety of congregational models.

The difference in structures also depends on non-theological factors. Here John 1:14 suggests that great breadth is allowable, for the indigenization of structures corresponds in some sense to the → incarnation of the Word (see Augs. Conf. 7 and 15). Fundamentally, however, order is also a witness (Barmen, thesis 3). We must ask, then, whether structures and forms of organization reflect evangelical liberation from ungodly worldly ties, and whether they make the congregation capable of thankful ministry to God's creatures (Barmen, thesis 2).

We cannot discuss the congregation abstractly as a community of witness and service, removed from its historical setting. Yet its Christological definition as the body of Christ and its pneumatological definition as the temple of the Holy Spirit offer us perspectives on idealized aspects that must be constitutive, and that also are full of promise, for every congregation. Structures and forms of organization are not value-neutral and thus must be investigated critically. Even in NT days it was the church's eschatological self-understanding that made possible adjustment and contradiction, therefore allowing further development. This eschatological self-understanding will show itself in a critical and constructive relating of congregational structures to existing social models.

These insights are worked out differently in the different denominational traditions. The standard dogmatic differences (e.g., regarding church offices) should not be overrated as far as their respective impact on the reality of congregational life is concerned. Across all the dogmatic differences, forms may vary according to substantive issues, such as whether a more participatory or a more controlled structure should be sought.

2.3. Principles of Work

For all the local and denominational differences, three basic principles of congregational work have emerged. Each has assumed great significance in ecumenical discussion (highlighted at Nairobi 1975).

2.3.1. Martyria

The congregation is a witnessing and confessing fellowship. It constitutes itself by attesting to and confessing God's gracious lordship, doing so publicly and constantly, critically and constructively. There is a distinction between witness and confession (→ Confession of Faith). Witness is the personal response of individual Christians to God's address to them, whereas confession is the common word of the congregation. For the congregation as a whole to become a confessing community, individual members must have the opportunity to respond personally to the → Word of God. These responses must be stimulated, noted, and respected in their various forms of expression.

As a rule, then, the work of the congregation will be organized as a → system of communicating individuals and groups. Theologically, this system has worship as its inner core, for in this it articulates its common confession. Worship is in principle public, whereas groups have a tendency to be closed. In groups of manageable size, however (ideally 8-15 persons), each person can have a say. The important thing is that groups should communicate with one another. Empirically, the festivals in the → church year, as well as specific projects, form a focus for such → communication. Ideally the congregation constitutes itself in this way as a learning fellowship, a conciliar process, integrating individuals and groups, experts and ordinary members.

To initiate the learning process, or to keep it going, has traditionally been the task of church office-holders and coworkers. At root, however, the task of teaching and shaping (e.g., the conscience and consciousness) is entrusted to every member. It is the task of catechizing (→ Catechesis) or → religious education to see to this responsibility in detail. The competence of experts is needed for this ministry, but they must be aware of their ambivalent role. They must not allow their competence and authority to squelch the expression and initiative of ordinary members, yet they must seek to build a unified community out of the varied expressions.

The many testimonies need to come together in common confession, not merely in extreme political situations (e.g., Barmen 1934), but on the basis of the practice of → baptism. The sacrament of baptism establishes the fellowship of the church or the congregation. Though it may be administered only by a church officer who is properly authorized to do so, the congregation as a whole accepts responsibility for the baptized. Often it is hard to convey this plain theological connection in church practice. Baptism seems to be an official act, an act of ministry. The tension between popular practice, with fewer infant baptisms and more adult baptisms, and the theological validation of the sacrament is especially acute, and it shows a need to take baptismal practice seriously as a focal point for the process of learning and formation.

2.3.2. Diakonia

The congregation is a fellowship of service. It responds to God's address to it in the form of → diakonia, or → charity. Originally diakonia meant direct personal action, to which all Christians are called. Now, with the state typically caring for many human needs, a differentiated system of organized church aid has arisen. It has the power to accomplish a great deal and in some cases may receive financial help from the state, either directly or through tax relief. An element of professionalism has thus entered in, along with institutional expansion.

The same developments have affected the spheres of → pastoral care and → counseling, with reduction of face-to-face, spontaneous involvement the result. The ability to console and admonish (mutum colloquium fratrum) has become increasingly less common in the form of spontaneous Christian action. The extension of spheres of service is a phenomenon in every highly developed industrial state, and the church has a part in it (→ Service Society).

At the local level the professionalizing and institutionalizing of elementary forms of Christian conduct commonly lead to a polarization between those who care and those who are cared for. This unsatisfactory situation can be partly remedied by institutional cooperation with other agencies and the setting up of personal contacts. Basic diaconal and pastoral functions such as aiding neighbors, caring for the infirm, and visiting the sick certainly must be discharged. The local church, as "the church of short cuts" (H. Schröer), offers plenty of opportunities for renewal in these areas. The public credibility of the church in a secular social context depends essentially on whether a witness of love in these practical dimensions confirms the witness of faith.

2.3.3. Koinonia

The congregation is a fellowship of sharing in Word and sacrament. In its formation as a community of witness and service, the congregation is responding to God's call. It experiences this call in exemplary form in worship. The significance of worship for its work is apparent in the → Eucharist, which offers a demonstration of the love of God and opens the door for a family communion of saints.

The experience of God's self-communication in Word and sacrament can be a basic model for the communication of the gospel (E. Lange), far beyond the bounds of formal worship. Eucharistic participation in God's saving call is the motive for a structural repetition of this communication in the interpersonal sphere. Mutual participation and communication bring to light a structure of community that might be called participatory. Ideally, then, the result will be a structure that in principle is open for others — that is, a missionary structure. In real life the structure will be ambivalent, for those involved inevitably bring negative elements into the participation and communication.

2.4. Plural Form

The plurality of styles and focuses of the various congregations is to be regarded as a sign of vitality. It is desirable that congregations should develop different profiles, that they should create different identities, and that they should thus open up possibilities of choice. Membership as an act of conscious participation can succeed only when it is possible to share in different congregations and to participate conditionally for a period. This line of thought would suggest that all congregations should become voluntary, even within a → people's church. For good reason, however, congregations should normally be locally defined. Rooted to the soil, they can more easily resist the constant pressure to cater merely to a group of like-minded people.

With its variety, the congregation offers an alternative form of communication to the culture of the → mass media, which increasingly treats individuals and groups as merely passive recipients. Through its varied groups, local congregations can present their own independent ideas in opposition to the models of life and values promoted by the media. In so doing, they have the chance to help cultivate in every locality a public that will keep alive its own local memory and conscience. As yet, however, the church as a whole and local congregations have barely begun to accept the challenge of the age of mass media communication.

2.5. Unity

The various forms of the congregation raise the question of what constitutes its inalienable unity. The answer is that its unity exists in its everywhere embracing a variety of spiritual gifts, or → charismata.

To establish this unity is the prime task of the ministry.

The complexity of the fellowship makes a variety of forms necessary. The → elders have the task of shaping and organizing the various people and factors responsibly, perhaps as the advocates of minorities, providing for unavoidable differences. At the local level, ecumenical richness can be achieved by contacts and partnerships (→ Local Ecumenism). From these various angles the inalienable unity of the congregation develops as a project. In the task and goal of all congregational life, the unity shows itself materially in a liturgically inspired fellowship of witness and service.

→ Church Employees; Church Orders; Free Church; Occasional Services; Primitive Christian Community; Student Work; Youth Work

Bibliography: H. D. BASTIAN, ed., *Experiment Isolotto. Dokumentation einer neuen Gemeinde* (Munich, 1970) • C. BÄUMLER, *Kommunikative Gemeindepraxis. Eine Untersuchung ihrer Bedingungen und Möglichkeiten* (Munich, 1984) • P. C. BLOTH et al., eds., *HPTh(G),* vol. 3, *Praxisfeld: Gemeinden* (Gütersloh, 1983) • R. BODENSTEIN et al., eds., *Kirche als Lerngemeinschaft. Dokumente aus der Arbeit des Bundes der evangelischen Kirchen in der DDR* (FS D. Albrecht Schönherr; Berlin, 1981) • A. BURGSMÜLLER, ed., *Kirche als "Gemeinde von Brüdern" (Barmen III)* (2 vols.; Gütersloh, 1980-81) • J. W. CARROLL, C. S. DUDLEY, and W. MCKINNEY, eds., *Handbook for Congregational Studies* (Nashville, 1986) • W. DIRKS et al., *Die Chance der brüderlichen Gemeinde* (Mainz, 1970) • C. S. DUDLEY, ed., *Building Effective Ministry: Theory and Practice in the Local Church* (San Francisco, 1983) • H. FRANKEMÖLLE, ed., *Kirche von unten. Alternative Gemeinden* (Mainz, 1981) • G. A. GETZ, *Sharpening the Focus of the Church* (Chicago, 1974) • G. HOLTZ, *Die Parochie. Geschichte und Problematik* (Gütersloh, 1967) • W. HUBER, *Kirche* (Stuttgart, 1979) • V. L. HUNTER and P. JOHNSON, *The Human Church in the Presence of Christ* (Macon, Ga., 1985) • E. S. JONS, *The Reconstruction of the Church–on What Pattern?* (Nashville, 1970) • F. KLOSTERMANN, *Gemeinde–Kirche der Zukunft. Thesen, Dienste, Modelle* (2 vols.; Freiburg, 1974); idem, *Prinzip Gemeinde* (Vienna, 1965) • E. LANGE, *Chancen des Alltags. Überlegungen zur Funktion des christlichen Gottesdienstes in der Gegenwart* (ed. P. Cornehl; 2d ed.; Munich, 1984); idem, *Kirche für die Welt. Aufsätze zur Theorie kirchlichen Handelns* (ed. R. Schloz; Munich, 1981) • B. LEERS, L. BOFF, and U. ZANKANELLA, *Kirchliche Basisgemeinden* (2d ed.; Mettingen, 1984) • K. LEHMANN, "Gemeinde," *Christlicher Glaube in moderner Gesellschaft* (vol. 29; Freiburg, 1982) 6-65 (bibliography) • W. LÜCK, *Praxis:*

Kirchengemeinde (Stuttgart, 1978) • H. J. MARGULL, *Mission als Strukturprinzip* (Geneva, 1965) • N. METTE et al., *Volkskirche–Gemeindekirche–Parakirche* (= *ThBer* 10 [1981]) bibliography • G. MEYER-MINTEL, *Gemeindebilder in Theologie und kirchlicher Praxis* (Frankfurt, 1986) • C. MÖLLER, *Lehre vom Gemeindeaufbau,* vol. 1, *Konzepte, Programme, Wege* (Göttingen, 1987) • J. MÜLLER, *Gemeinde-Reform? Kritisches Korrektiv oder Zufluchtsort* (Vienna, 1983) • W. C. ROOF, *Community and Commitment: Religious Plausibility in a Liberal Protestant Church* (2d ed.; New York, 1983) • D. A. ROOZEN, W. MCKINNEY, and J. W. CARROLL, *Varieties of Religious Presence: Mission in Public Life* (New York, 1984) • L. SCHALLER, *Effective Church Planning* (Nashville, 1979); idem, *The Local Church Looks to the Future: A Guide to Church Planning* (Nashville, 1968) • M. SCHIBILSKY, *Alltagswelt und Sonntagskirche. Sozialethisch orientierte Gemeindearbeit im Industriegebiet* (Munich, 1983) • F. SCHWARZ, *Überschaubare Gemeinde* (3 vols.; Gladbeck, 1980-81) • E. SULZE, *Die evangelische Gemeinde* (Gotha, 1891) • T. SWEETSER, *Successful Parishes: How They Meet the Challenge of Change* (Minneapolis, 1983) • O. WEBER, *Versammelte Gemeinde. Beiträge zum Gespräch über Kirche und Gottesdienst* (2d ed.; Neukirchen, 1975) • H. WIEH, *Konzil und Gemeinde. Eine systematisch-theologische Untersuchung zum Gemeindeverständnis des Zweiten Vatikanischen Konzils in pastoraler Absicht* (Frankfurt, 1978) • E. WINKLER, *Die Gemeinde und ihr Amt* (Stuttgart, 1973) • WORLD COUNCIL OF CHURCHES, *"The Church for Others" and "The Church for the World": A Quest for Structures for Missionary Congregations* (Geneva, 1967) • P. M. ZULEHNER, "Gemeinde," *NHThG* (1st ed.) 2.52-65 (bibliography).

WOLFGANG GRÜNBERG and HORST ALBRECHT

3. Sociology

The local congregation, a basic locus of religious experience, is primarily an association of people. As such, it is a theme for → sociology.

In its primary significance the term "local congregation" denotes an association of believers or adherents living in the same place. In the great Roman Catholic and Protestant traditions, physical proximity was long the most important, though not the only, criterion of membership. It is a neutral criterion that makes no distinction between the inhabitants of the place. With the development of means of communication, this geographic criterion has changed, though it still persists, and it has been joined by others of a sociocultural character, or even opposed by them (e.g., nationality, similarity of intellectual goals, or shared religious interpretations). Along with the organization by territory, which typically encompasses culturally heterogeneous people, we now find, especially in cities, congregations defined by national group, → base communities, fellowships aligned behind a charismatic leader, and the like. These comprise groupings that in many cultural respects are more homogeneous than parish churches.

Apart from the criteria of association, the local congregation in hierarchically structured denominations (→ Hierarchy) forms a structural link between individuals and other geographic associations of the adherents of the denomination (cf. the → diocese, district, national church, universal church). It is the form of a religious movement that is closest to individuals. It provides them with the conditions, means, and activities that will be most immediately useful for them in their encounters with the holy.

Sociologically, the local congregation is a → system of social relationships and interpersonal connections. This system will be more or less integrated and unified according to the status and influence of the various factors that contribute to its development and continuance. Some of these are external, some internal.

External factors include the number of believers who live in the locality or whose cultural characteristics fall within the sphere tolerated by the congregation, as well as the topography and ecology of the area, especially the network of communications. The difference between rural and urban congregations is sociologically significant. We also need to know the prevailing mood (whether basically religious, agnostic, or atheistic), the various religious views held by the population, and the various individual and collective motivations in the search for the holy. For example, are people searching for God in order to find psychological peace? Are they interested in a life to come? Do they desire moral change? Is the real motive a spontaneous one, or does it have secular, cultural overtones? Is it to be found in the church, or is it socioreligious?

Internal factors, which involve the organization and work of the local congregation itself, concern the activities, roles, and structure of the whole nexus. Thus a congregation that stresses liturgical activities and the corresponding means of expression will not be structured or integrated in the same way as another that stresses good deeds or efficiency. The same applies to the roles of members. A pyramidal structure will produce a different kind of unity from a democratic structure, a charismatic leadership (→ Charisma) from an institutional leadership, an active membership from a passive membership with a consumer attitude. Also important is the structure — that is, the number of parts, subdivisions, and sub-

groups, as well as their integration, their orientation toward a common goal.

All these factors combine to give each local congregation its own distinctive profile. The variety enables us to construct ideal types, which allow us in turn to sketch the profile of real congregations. One type is (1) the local congregation to which those living within its domain belong but in which most of them do not participate. Another is (2) the congregation in which believers satisfy their religious needs but with no true → solidarity. Others are (3) the congregation as a local community comprising most of the civil community, (4) the congregation as a substitute fellowship that borrows its principle of cohesion from some other type of fellowship that is defective in some way, and (5) the congregation as the product of voluntary solidarity to achieve one or more goals. A final type is (6) the congregation as a fellowship in which the principle of fellowship and solidarity is not just the rendering of service, the achieving of one or more goals, or some factor borrowed from a secular environment but a common mind, a common → faith, a common mystique of intervention and engagement. This final type corresponds to the ideal model of congregational integration toward which those responsible for a religious association should strive.

No matter what form a particular congregation may take or what principle may underlie its unity, it will be in more or less frequent and intensive contact with other civil and religious groups. Some will include the congregation, while others will not. These contacts influence in their own way a given congregation's social system. Whether they are religious or secular, their influence depends on what they demand. If they recognize the distinctive features and the distinctive religious or secular functions of the congregation, it will have room to develop its own social system and to influence these other groups, even though the space granted might be partly or occasionally restricted, depending on the use that other groups make of it. If outside groups do not recognize the distinctiveness of the congregation, then its composition, the form of its contacts, and its social relations incur the danger of becoming dependent on external factors or at least of being strongly directed by them.

Though the goals that the local congregation sets may be high, its basis and function are always subject to the factors and laws that apply to any social group. For this reason, sociology can have something to say about it.

→ Church 4; Communication; Organization; Sociology of Churches; Sociology of Religion

Bibliography: H. Carrier, *The Sociology of Religious Belonging* (New York, 1965) • D. B. Clark, "The Sociological Study of the Parish," *ExpTim* 82 (1970/71) 296-300 • J. H. Fichter, *Social Relations in the Urban Parish* (4th ed.; Chicago, 1966) • J. Freytag, *Die Kirchengemeinde in soziologischer Sicht* (Hamburg, 1959) • F. Fürstenberg, "Soziologische Strukturprobleme der Kirchengemeinde," *ZEE* 7 (1963) 224-33 • N. Glatzel, *Gemeindebildung und Gemeindestruktur* (Munich, 1976) • D. Goldschmidt, F. Greiner, and H. Schelsky, eds., *Soziologie der Kirchengemeinde* (Stuttgart, 1960) • A. Greeley et al., *Parish, Priest, and People: New Leadership for the Local Church* (Chicago, 1981) • N. Greinacher, *Soziologie der Pfarrei* (Freiburg, 1955) • F. Houtart and E. Pin, *The Church and the Latin American Revolution* (New York, 1965) • R. König, *The Community* (New York, 1968); idem, ed., *Handbuch der empirischen Sozialforschung* (3d ed.; Stuttgart, 1974) 4.82-141 ("Soziologie der Gemeinde") • D. O. Moberg, *The Church as a Social Institution* (Englewood Cliffs, N.J., 1962) • J. Nuesse and T. J. Harte, eds., *The Sociology of the Parish: An Introductory Symposium* (Milwaukee, Wis., 1951) • E. Pin, "La paroisse urbaine peut-elle être une communauté?" *Essais de sociologie religieuse* (ed. H. Carrier and E. Pin; Paris, 1966) 473-510 • J. Rémy, J.-P. Hiernaux, and E. Servais, "Le phénomène paroissial aujourd'hui. Éléments pour une interrogation sociologique," *LV(L)* 25 (June/July 1975) 25-36 • L. Schneider, *Theologische Reflexionen zu Strukturuntersuchungen von Kirchgängergemeinden* (Munich, 1978).

Jean-Paul Rouleau

4. Systematic Theology

4.1. *Biblical Foundations*

Trying to find a biblical basis for the nature, function, and structure of the congregation runs into a twofold difficulty. First, the boundary between universal church and local congregation is fluid. The NT writings do not mark it out. All that they say about the *ekklēsia* can apply just as well to the local assembly of Christians, and yet the local congregation is never equated with the total church as such. The textual point that *ekklēsia* means both "church" and "local congregation" does not solve the theological question raised by the multiplicity of churches, their mutual relations, and their relation to the universal church (the sum of all of them?).

The second difficulty lies in the idea of a biblical "foundation." The existence of local congregations has no need of any justification. We can derive them historically from the first NT churches, which followed to some extent the model of the → synagogue. In considering their nature, functions, and structure,

are we to seek a biblical basis in the sense of subjecting them to biblical criticism, thus being able to say that one congregation is "more biblical" than another? Such judgments are possible only in a very limited way, for many forms of congregational life and structure are justifiable biblically, and only a few principles may be derived solely and strictly from the Bible. The important distinction between possible and necessary biblical justification, which is often overlooked in church history, makes theological and ecumenical discussion of the congregation, the ministry (→ Offices, Ecclesiastical), and the → sacraments uncommonly difficult.

In the Hebrew Bible the terms → "people of God" and → "covenant" are relevant, and so is the OT dialectic of gathering and sending, which the NT clearly adopts. The implied theological insights, however, might apply to both the universal church and the individual congregation. We cannot derive guidelines from the OT solely for the latter, the less so as Jewish congregations (→ Judaism) were also unable to claim such orientation after the destruction of Jerusalem in a.d. 70. In the → ecumenical movement this inability is not fully accepted, for the → Orthodox Church, and more cautiously the → Roman Catholic Church, attempts to base church rules and practices on OT passages (e.g., regarding → priests and eucharistic → sacrifice), often with the help of → allegorical exposition.

The NT statements are more directly relevant. Here, however, it is surprising how much more appeal there is to the letters of → Paul than to the other NT writings. NT scholarship has shown interest in the latter (e.g., in Matthew 18 as an early congregational order, or in the implicit theology of the Christian community in Revelation and John), and they have also found direct application in sermons, but Pauline concepts have dominated church orders and congregational orders.

4.2. *Historical Development*

We shall not sketch here the actual development of the understanding of the congregation. We simply point out that it involved tension between alternatives. First, the question arose whether the congregation is to be seen charismatically (→ Charisma), as a work of the Spirit, spontaneous, and free in its form of life, or whether it is to be seen legally as a sacramental or officially governed → institution. Second, the question also arose whether the congregation is the → base community, the fundamental form of the church, the place of God's presence in Christ by the Holy Spirit, or whether it is a branch of the true and universal church, a partial actualization of the whole, an offshoot of the real community.

Concerning the first question, nearly all reforming movements, especially in the → Reformation, at first opted for the first answer, although for sociological reasons they finally decided in favor of the second. In every movement from the → Bohemian Brethren to → Luther and → Calvin, for all the fear of anarchy, one finds very plainly a high regard for spontaneous congregational life (even to the point of the encouragement of → house churches by Luther; see also Calvin *Inst.* 4.1.1-7).

With regard to the second question, before the Reformation the decision usually went in favor of the second answer for reasons of historical and sociological development (→ Mission) as Christianity expanded from the cities to the countryside (→ Proprietary Church). The Reformation protest against this answer is important. It gave primacy to the local church, allowed it to choose its pastors, and charged it with the duty of overseeing doctrine. Overall, however, Protestant churches have implemented this answer only partially.

4.3. *Ecumenical Multiplicity*

The multiplicity in understanding the congregation is not so much an expression of deliberate theological decision as it is of finding theological justification of the respective historical decisions. We find conscious theological planning at best in the congregations that suffered under the Counter-Reformation (in Bohemia, Lower Rhineland, and France; cf. Scotland; → Catholic Reform and Counterreformation), in the → Confessing Church after 1934, and in the churches in Latin America (→ Liberation Theology). More common in the ecumenical world are historically developed structures and conceptions that are now the object of defense or theological criticism.

Three structural models predominate. The first is the *regionally structured denominational congregation.* This is mostly found outside Europe. A → denomination helps to plan it and at first to finance it, following a geographic plan as numbers allow, or attempting some approximation to the ubiquity of the European parishes. Basically, each congregation will be responsible for its own finances, though with some central funds available to help where needed (→ Church Finances). Membership is voluntary, is not dependent on the place of residence, and usually begins with confirmation (frequently not related to age) or transfer of membership after a change of residence (after the pattern of a society).

A second model is that of the *territorial church* in countries in which either one denomination is predominant (Scandinavia) or there are two strong denominations (Germany, Switzerland) to which

people belong by birth or migration. Typical in such cases is a division into parishes and central financing.

The third model is a *mixture* of the first two in countries that have had established churches (e.g., England), where nominal membership and the use of → occasional services still reflect the earlier situation.

Congregations in the churches of the ecumenical movement tend to focus theologically in one of two directions. One kind centers on the sacrament of the altar and the → priest. These are usually in episcopal denominations, in which the local church is strictly that of the → bishop (i.e., the → diocese). No matter what other work may be done in such congregations, the point of membership and → worship is not in the last resort → diakonia but the sacrament. We "bring" something into the church, ultimately ourselves as "a living sacrifice, holy and acceptable to God" (Rom. 12:1).

The second kind of congregation (a *creatura verbi* in the Reformation sense) centers on the pulpit, the Word, and pastoral care; in this kind, the pastor finds respect as a teacher, not as a priest. Those who worship want to receive something from the sermon, and those who are in need or sick are visited and counseled.

These two models confront one another in ecumenical discussion and seem to be irreconcilable, in view of the different conceptions of ministry (→ Pastor, Pastorate). Even the Lima Document of 1982 could not solve this problem.

To different degrees both might be seen to be compatible with the ideal of the congregation as a fellowship that discharges diakonia to its members by strengthening their ability to serve; with the missionary task of reaching outsiders, enlarging the congregation, and founding new ones (e.g., by radio and television; → Mass Media); with a political diakonia and social involvement, even at the risk of offending members; and finally with the idea of a pure service community that adjusts to the religious needs and expectations of the people.

4.4. *Theological Criteria*

In judging the various models, theological criteria have thus functioned mostly negatively. Critical norms have been taken from such basic ecclesiological insights as "church for others" or "church with others," "creatura verbi," "priesthood of all believers," "sending into all the world." These ideals have been used to criticize both national churches and free churches, as well as congregations devoted purely to service and those that focus on an ideal of Christian fellowship but are politically passive. None of these criticisms, however, is ultimately compelling. The model of autonomous local congregations in a loose synodal union (→ Congregationalism) seems to come closest to the churches of the NT age, although other forms involving special ministries, political action groups, middle-class suburban churches, and so forth can also find plausible theological justification.

Theology faces today a fresh demand to search critically for basic ecclesiological insights and in the light of these to establish trust between different congregations and their parent denominations; to make possible eucharistic fellowship, pulpit exchanges, and visits to other lands and cultures; and to promote a readiness to learn. The future center of gravity of the Christian church will probably be in Africa, North and South America, and the growing churches of other continents. An inquisitive critical search for other congregational forms might help us to move past the old alternatives. If Christ exists as community (D. → Bonhoeffer), then more than ever in the future we need to "learn Christ together" (L. Vischer) on our ever-shrinking earth.

→ Christology; Church Government; Church Membership; Church Orders; Eucharist; Gospel; Lay Movements; Local Ecumenism; Primitive Christian Community; Third World; Unity

Bibliography: K. Barth, "The Holy Spirit and Christian Faith," *CD* IV/1, 740-79; idem, "The Holy Spirit and the Upbuilding of the Christian Community," *CD* IV/2, 614-726; idem, "The Holy Spirit and the Sending of the Christian Community," *CD* IV/3b, 681-901 • E. Brunner, *The Misunderstanding of the Church* (London, 1952) • A. B. Come, *Agents of Reconciliation* (Philadelphia, 1960) • M. Geiger, *Wesen und Aufgabe kirchlicher Ordnung* (Zurich, 1954) • E. Geldbach, *Ökumene in Gegensätzen* (Göttingen, 1987) • *Gemeinsame Synode der Bistümer in der BRD* (Freiburg, 1976) 153-85, 637-77 • G. Hartmann, *Christliche Basisgruppen und ihre befreihende Praxis. Erfahrungen im Nordosten Brasiliens* (Munich, 1980) • Kirchenamt in Auftrag des Rates der EKD, *Christsein gestalten. Eine Studie zum Weg der Kirche* (4th ed.; Gütersloh, 1987) • H. Kotsonis, "Die Stellung der Laien innerhalb des kirchlichen Organismus," *Die orthodoxe Kirche in griechischer Sicht* (pt. 2; ed. P. I. Bratsiotis; 2d ed.; Stuttgart, 1970) 92-116 • E. Schweizer, *Church Order in the NT* (Naperville, Ill., 1961) • T. Sundermeier, "Konvivenz als Grundstruktur ökumenischer Existenz," *ÖEH* 1 (1986) 49-100 • World Council of Churches, *Baptism, Eucharist, and Ministry* (Geneva, 1982).

Dietrich Ritschl

Congregationalism

1. Polity
2. History

1. Polity

The term "Congregationalism" is used in both a more general and a more specific sense. In the former, it denotes a type of church polity in which episcopal and synodic elements have no place, with authority being concentrated in the local → congregation and with extralocal conferences having only an advisory function. Today most → Baptists, Quakers (→ Friends, Society of), the Disciples of Christ (→ Christian Church [Disciples of Christ]), and individual → free churches are Congregationalists in this sense (see 2).

In the more specific sense the reference is to a fellowship that arose historically in the 16th century and that consists of congregations that view themselves as churches in the full meaning of the term, uniting members under an elected minister according to the biblical model. Open from an ecumenical and missionary standpoint, the national unions of Congregationalists have often joined union churches (in England, Canada, the United States, and South India; → United and Uniting Churches), while still preserving their distinctiveness. The International Congregational Council, founded in 1891, joined the World Alliance of Reformed Churches in 1970, and this body now calls itself presbyterian and congregational (see 2).

→ Church Government

Herbert Frost

2. History

2.1. Congregationalism originated in the later 16th century in England. Many → Puritans were convinced that the English church settlement under Elizabeth I (1558-1603) was not adequately reformed on scriptural principles. An episcopal system dependent on state appointment was felt to be inimical to a pure and godly → church according to the NT, and a number of "Separatist" congregations started to meet in London and elsewhere.

In 1582 Robert Browne (ca. 1550-1633) in two books stated the "gathered church" principle, whereby the → kingdom of God is built not out of the territorially defined parish but out of the committed believers who → covenant with each other under God to form a congregation, independent of the → state and competent to govern itself. Browne retracted his radical views a few years later, but the name "Brownists" became attached to other leaders and congregations of similar opinion. The new leaders of the movement — John Greenwood, Henry Barrow (b. ca. 1550), and John Penry (b. 1559) — were imprisoned and then hanged (1593). Driven underground, the movement sought refuge in Leiden and Amsterdam.

Under the reign of the Stuarts, conditions remained difficult for religious → dissenters in England, but the Independents, as they were now known, grew in strength and numbers (as did the Baptists, who can be seen as a version of Congregationalism). During the civil war the movement was especially important in the parliamentary cause, and it was dominant under Oliver Cromwell (1599-1658). In the Savoy Declaration of 1658, representatives of 120 churches reaffirmed congregational (as distinct from → presbyterian) polity, while identifying closely with the Calvinism of the → Westminster Confession (1643).

On the restoration of the monarchy after the death of Cromwell, conditions worsened again for Independents and other dissenters under the Act of Uniformity (1662). They were somewhat mitigated, however, by the Toleration Act (1689), and Independency became strongly identified with the demand for political and → religious liberty. Meanwhile, of highest significance was the migration, in search of such liberty, of many Independents to America in the first half of the 17th century. W. Brewster (1567-1644) and younger members of his Leiden community were among the → Pilgrim Fathers who sailed to America in the *Mayflower* in 1620.

Early on, then, Congregationalist principles were firmly planted in the New World, though often in uneasy tension with Presbyterianism (→ Reformed and Presbyterian Churches) and → Anglicanism. Paradoxically, while English Independency included a rigorous independence from the state, Congregationalism in New England was happy to accept state patronage, as a legally established church, until the latter part of the 18th century, when the Great Awakening (→ Revivals 2.1; Theology of Revivals 2) advocated the separation of → church and state and → religious liberty. Congregationalists played an important part in the evangelical → revival, though they also came under the influence of the → Unitarians and theological → liberalism. Jonathan → Edwards (1703-58) in America and Philip Doddridge (1702-51) in England were supreme theological luminaries, while to Isaac Watts (1674-1748) we owe → hymns sustained by a profound → piety.

2.2. Congregationalists have generally combined a firm adherence to Scripture with a freedom from → dogmatism. They have tended to be more evangelical than the Presbyterians and more intellectually preoccupied than the → Baptists. The English Congregationalists formulated their understanding of faith, of "the → church order given by Jesus Christ" (→ Church Orders), and of → church membership in the Savoy Declaration, while the New England Congregationalists had already stated their principles of polity in the Cambridge Platform of 1648.

Although emphasizing the autonomy of each congregation under Christ, Congregationalism in the 18th century developed connectional structures on a regional basis for mutual support and common enterprises. The underlying conviction here was that the covenant with Christ links the congregations to one another as well. In England in 1832 the Congregational Union of England and Wales was formed. Congregationalists had also shared in the founding of the London Missionary Society (1795; → British Missions 1.2.1), which in due course became almost exclusively a Congregational enterprise working in China, Southeast Asia, the Pacific, and East Africa (→ Mission 3). By the end of the 19th century, through missionary work and migration, Congregationalism had become a worldwide fellowship.

2.3. Congregationalism has shared in many modern schemes of union (→ United and Uniting Churches), especially with churches of the Reformed tradition, as in the South India United Church of 1908 (which in turn joined with others to form the → Church of South India in 1947), the United Church of Canada (1925), the United Church of Christ (the result of a merger in 1957 in the United States between the Congregational Christian Churches and the Evangelical Reformed Church), and the United Reformed Church in England (with the Presbyterian Church of England, 1972). The United Church of Christ has achieved importance with its creative tension of social and individual impulses. The presupposition of the English union was that the autonomy of each congregation does not preclude a proper structure of oversight and support that is in no way coercive over the local church, so that a degree of presbyterial polity may be accommodated. A significant minority of English Congregational churches, however, felt unable to participate in such unions, associating instead as the Congregational Federation.

Parallel organizations exist elsewhere for similar reasons as a consequence of union schemes, and these are associated in the International Congregational Federation, with affiliated bodies in England, Wales, Australia, Greece, Guyana, Hong Kong, India, Korea, Nauru (Pacific), New Zealand, Nigeria, Samoa, and the United States. The ethos of such continuing Congregational churches and bodies tends to be evangelical (→ Evangelical Movement), with a wariness of centralization in both denominational and ecumenical structures. Yet it is by no means isolationist. The Congregational Federation in England, for example, while not a member of the → World Council of Churches (WCC), is a member of the British Council of Churches and of the Council for World Mission. Similarly, the International Congregational Federation is not a member of the WCC or of the World Alliance of Reformed Churches. In 1985 the Congregationalists claimed 2.9 million members worldwide.

Bibliography: "Congregationalism," *ODCC* 399-400 • R. W. DALE, *History of English Congregationalism* (London, 1907) • H. ESCOTT, *History of Scottish Congregationalism* (Glasgow, 1960) • F. L. FAGLEY, *Story of the Congregational Christian Churches* (Boston, 1941) • N. GOODALL, ed., *Der Kongregationalismus* (Stuttgart, 1973) • D. HORTON, "Kongregationalisten," *WKL* 768-71 • D. T. JENKINS, *Congregationalism: A Restatement* (London, 1954) • R. T. JONES, *Congregationalism in England, 1662-1962* (London, 1962) • A. D. MARTIN, *The Principle of the Congregational Churches* (New York, 1927) • E. ROUTLEY, *The Story of Congregationalism* (London, 1961) • A. P. F. SELL, *Saints: Visible, Orderly, and Catholic. The Congregational Idea of the Church* (Allison Park, Pa., 1986) • B. D. SPINKS, *Freedom or Order? The Eucharistic Liturgy in English Congregationalism, 1645-1980* (Allison Park, Pa., 1984).

KEITH W. CLEMENTS

Congregations → Orders and Congregations

Conscience

1. In Philosophy
   1.1. Definition and Terminology
   1.2. Conscience in the History of Philosophy
   1.3. Conscience in Modern Discussion
2. In Theology
   2.1. Ambivalence
   2.2. Contingency
   2.3. Freedom
   2.4. Individuality and Sociality
   2.5. Political Responsibility

1. In Philosophy

1.1. *Definition and Terminology*

"Conscience" (from Lat. *conscientia;* see also Lat. *synderesis* and Gk. *syneidēsis*) means (1) the faculty of human personality that decides the moral worth of actions, and (2) the making of such a judgment by comparing specific actions to general → norms. According to whether these norms are set by the self or by others, conscience is autonomous or authoritarian. According to the verdict, we have a good conscience or a bad conscience.

1.2. *Conscience in the History of Philosophy*

Plato (427-347 B.C.) and Aristotle (384-322 B.C.) did not use the term "conscience" (→ Platonism; Aristotelianism), but it occurs in later antiquity and the Fathers in two senses. On the one hand (in Epicurus, Cicero, and Seneca), in agreement with what later became the only relevant usage, it means the evaluative moral sense; on the other hand (in Epictetus, Marcus Aurelius, and → Origen), it means one's consciousness as the epitome of individual thoughts, feelings, and wishes, with no moral reference — that is, simply one's inner being *(intus hominis).* → Augustine (354-430) took the latter view, though he was also familiar with the former. → Thomas Aquinas (1224/25-74) defined *synderesis* as *habitus* (unlike Bonaventure [ca. 1217-74], who viewed it as *potentia affectiva*) and therefore viewed this conscience as a court of judgment, in contrast to *conscientia*, which as an act represents conscience as the making of the actual verdict (*Summa theol.* I, q. 79, arts. 12-13; → Thomism).

I. Kant (1724-1804) understood conscience not as the logical judging of individual actions according to their conformity to norms but in the moral verdict regarding whether the acts are evaluated with proper care, so that an erring conscience is impossible (→ Kantianism). G. W. F. Hegel (1770-1831) did not recognize any such duality of judgment, so that he could conceive of a mistaken conscience and always saw the possibility of a reversion to evil, since conscience represents formal subjectivity in the absolute (→ Hegelianism). As norm, the → categorical imperative necessarily lays the foundations of conscience. F. → Nietzsche (1844-1900) in his moral criticism found in conscience an early turning of the instinct of → aggression upon the self. M. Heidegger (1889-1976) defined conscience as a "call of anxiety" summoning existence from the "plunge into anonymity" to the authenticity of the self (→ Existentialism).

As for Cicero (106-43 B.C.) and Augustine, so for H. Kuhn, conscience was a divine voice. R. M. Hare, appealing to Kant's categorical imperative, stressed universalizability (i.e., application to anyone under similar conditions) as the basic premise of the judgment of conscience. W. D. Ross (1877-1971) distinguished between the right, which involves actions, and the good, which involves motives. The judgment of conscience concerns the → good.

1.3. Conscience in Modern Discussion

1.3.1. When, following S. Freud (1856-1939), conscience was understood as the superego, which results from parental moral demands, which punishes, and which thus gives rise to → anxiety (→ Psychoanalysis), questions arose as to the ontogenetic development of conscience. J. Piaget (1896-1980) and E. H. Erikson showed that we must not think of it as a fixed adoption of norms but that there is flexible interplay between external → authority and individual impulses.

1.3.2. Hegel's concept of morality raised the question of the admittance and/or need for social communication of norms that are the basis of conscience. H. Hofmeister made it clear that commitment to social judgment cannot remove the risk of individual action or absolve one from individual responsibility, with this → responsibility always arising for → family, → society, and the → state.

1.3.3. The → autonomy of conscience cannot be surrendered even in the name of → faith, and conscience cannot be defined as the voice of God without falling back below the level of the Kantian → emotive theory of ethics. Nevertheless, the unavoidable involvement of the conscience in → guilt means that it must find its true meaning on the level of faith.

→ Duty; Ethics 1; Evil; Freedom

Bibliography: J. Blühdorn, ed., *Das Gewissen in der Diskussion* (Darmstadt, 1976) bibliography • E. D'Arcy, *Conscience and Its Right to Freedom* (New York, 1961) • E. H. Erikson, *Childhood and Society* (2d ed.; New York, 1963) • S. Freud, *The Ego and the Id* (New York, 1962; orig. pub., 1923) • G. W. F. Hegel, *Elements of the Philosophy of Right* (Cambridge, 1991; orig. pub., 1821) §§129ff. • M. Heidegger, *On Being and Time* (London, 1962; orig. pub., 1927) • E. Heintel, *Logik der Dialektik* (vol. 2; Darmstadt, 1984) chap. 13 • H. Hofmeister, "Das Gewissen als Ort sittlicher Urteilsfindung," *ZEE* 25 (1981) 30-44 • I. Kant, "On the Failure of All Attempted Philosophical Theodicies," *Kant on History and Religion* (M. Despland; Montreal, 1973) 283-97; idem, *Religion within the Limits of Reason Alone* (trans. T. M. Greene and H. H. Hudson; New York, 1960; orig. pub., 1793) B287ff. • H. Kuhn, *Begegnung mit dem Sein* (Tübingen, 1954) • F. Nietzsche, *On the Genealogy of Morals* (New York, 1969; orig. pub., 1887) • J. Piaget, *The Moral Judgment of the Child* (London, 1977) • W. D. Ross, *The Right and the Good* (London, 1930).

Wolfgang Nikolaus

2. In Theology

2.1. Ambivalence

The lack of clarity in defining conscience stands in marked contrast to the general emphasis of our time on clear definition. Appeals to conscience are common, and the threat of a bad conscience has a place in → education and religious → socialization, but what is meant by "conscience" as a technical term is usually not very clear. Surprisingly, the criticism of conscience popularized by F. → Nietzsche (1844-1900) and S. Freud (1856-1939) has not eliminated the appeal to it (see 1). It is also surprising that in a → democracy the reference to freedom of conscience occurs at the very point where the dignity of the human person (→ Human Dignity) must be protected against inroads by the state.

In spite of all the ambivalence and criticism, the concept of conscience still points to the core of human → identity. Wherever the concept is cited, the fact that we are responsible for our life and actions, and that we are aware of this → responsibility, is stressed as a special characteristic of human personality. The use of the term "conscience" shows that this responsibility is viewed as primarily moral. Conscience is the moral sense. Yet it is more. A theological concept of conscience must also point to its transmoral quality. In this regard → Luther's understanding had epochal significance.

2.2. Contingency

The ambivalence of conscience is connected with the elementary fact that although the concept is a basic anthropological datum, the reality and concept of conscience enter the human consciousness only under specific historical conditions and in specific social forms. It is thus useless to try to grasp the nature of conscience independently of these forms of historical apprehension.

The idea of *syneidēsis* (knowing with, Lat. *conscientia*) developed only late in Greek history. The term might be rendered "consciousness" as well as "conscience." It denotes a thoughtful relation to the self that is the basis of theoretical as well as practical → reason. In the Jewish Hellenistic thinking of Philo (b. 15-10 b.c., d. a.d. 45-50) and also in → Paul and the Deutero-Paulines, the concept was linked to a form of thought that derived from the OT. The OT viewed the heart as the place where people are reached by the divine word. Those who find a response to that word in their hearts do what is right (see Deut. 30:14; Ezek. 36:26). This combination made "conscience" a key word in what D. Mieth has called a theonomous, responsive ethics. Tension between response and self-reflection would henceforth go hand in hand with the history of the concept.

The term "conscience" is relatively common in Paul (see Rom. 2:14-15; 1 Corinthians 8). → Faith and a good conscience come together later (1 Tim. 1:5, 19; 3:9; Heb. 10:22). Right doctrine and right conduct are constitutive marks of Christianity, thus preparing the way for the later moral emphasis on conscience.

→ Augustine (354-430) especially followed this path when he viewed the conscience as the place where we are conscious of sin and guilt (→ Augustine's Theology). Conscience is the innermost self, in which there is experience of standing *coram Deo* (before God). Already in Augustine the struggle for the doctrine of → justification was affecting the concept of conscience. In conscience we are aware of our → guilt and thus realize that we are thrown totally on the efficacy of divine → grace.

The understanding of the Greek → church fathers clung with the same intensity to both the biblical tradition and that of antiquity. The influence of the *logos* teaching of the → Stoics may be seen in the view of → Origen (ca. 185-ca. 254) that conscience is the witness of the indwelling divine Spirit (→ Origenism). This position led to a speculative view that plainly differs from the predominantly moral view of the West. Conscience is the place of faith, the organ of union with God. In this sense a pure conscience was for the Greek fathers the condition of sincere → prayer and participation in → worship. Along these lines the heart frequently replaced conscience in later Greek and Russian → Orthodoxy (§3). Modern Orthodox dogmatics is simply following the Eastern tradition when it defines the conscience as "transparency for God and others" (D. Staniloae).

Medieval development led to a distinction between *synderesis* (a misspelling of *syneidēsis* in → Jerome) and *conscientia*. Scholasticism saw in the former the human capacity to know primal moral certainties (i.e., the locus of moral ability). *Conscientia*, in contrast, was the court of judgment in specific cases. The high value placed on conscience may be seen especially in the fact that according to → Thomas Aquinas (1224/25-74), we are under obligation to follow a pronouncement of conscience, even when this objectively is an error (→ Thomism).

While Thomas stressed the fact that such a judgment can be rationally followed, the Franciscan school put more emphasis on the voluntaristic element in the concept (→ Scotism). This difference gave rise to a second basic tension that would remain in all future development, namely, the tension between an intuitional view, which protects a decision of conscience against intersubjective testing, and a rational view, according to which a judgment of conscience can be supported by rational argument.

2.3. *Freedom*

M. Luther (1483-1546) did not accept the scholastic distinctions but reinterpreted the concept of conscience in his relational → anthropology. As he saw it, conscience relates to the existence of the whole person rather than to the evaluation of individual actions. It originally is imprisoned, standing under the power of sin and death. It achieves freedom only through the liberating → Word of God. Only a good conscience, which is identical with → faith, produces good works.

The relation between the liberating Word and conscience means that the freedom of conscience and the binding of conscience condition, rather than exclude, one another. Intrinsic to freedom is the fact that the properly grounded conclusion of one's conscience is unconditionally binding. Not a timeless → norm but concrete address by God's Word in a specific situation makes it binding. For this new understanding of conscience, the conflict between Luther and the emperor at the Diet of Worms (1521) took on symbolic importance.

The modern demand for freedom of conscience is unthinkable without the impulse given by the Reformation. Yet it did not develop straightforwardly from it, for in this demand the element of self-reflection again came to the fore. In a classic definition, I. Kant (1724-1804) described conscience as the power to judge oneself (→ Kantianism). He found in it the awareness of an inner moral court (see 1). This approach raises the basic problem of the relation between self-reference and universality. The idealistic philosophy of Kant and Hegel insisted that the freedom of conscience is itself forfeited if it turns into caprice. This freedom is safeguarded only when there is a link to something universal (Kant's → categorical imperative or Hegel's morality).

Such a line of thought must be brought into harmony with the → autonomy of conscience to the degree that no external authority can have the right to govern the individual conscience and its decisions, which would mean a relapse into heteronomy. Because heteronomy is incompatible with human dignity, from the time of the → Enlightenment and the revolutions in America and France, protecting the freedom of conscience has been a basic motif in the concept of a constitutional state.

In the English tradition Edward Herbert, first Lord Herbert of Cherbury (1583-1648), viewed conscience as a natural instinct, thus presupposing that nature also lays down the norms (or "common notions") by which conscience makes decisions. In this way he opened up the way for an emphasis on the element of self-reflection with respect to conscience. English → empiricism broke with the idea of an innate morality and also with the dialogic view of conscience as the place of human response to a divine address. A. A. C. Shaftesbury (1671-1713) gave classic definition to conscience as "a natural sense of the odiousness of crime and injustice." J. Locke (1632-1704) stressed that conscience is no proof of an innate moral rule. As a judge, but not a lawgiver, it judges on the basis of obligations that derive from → education and social norms. This approach prepared the way for viewing the norms that conscience recognizes as resulting from processes of socialization and internalization.

The → analytic philosophy of the 20th century could take up the same tradition. It regarded conscience in terms of function rather than content. Conscience is the cognitive ability to reflect on one's past and future actions, to approve or disapprove actions and motivations, and finally to seek what is thought to be good and to avoid what is thought to be bad. Proponents of this school often fail to see that in formulating a linguistic standard, they are also laying down a standard of action. They can offer no information, however, as to the sources of the norms that may be appealed to in cases when a dominant standard is rejected on grounds of conscience. Such cases make clear that empiricism unleashed a development that does not give to the critical function of conscience the same importance as it receives in the theological tradition.

2.4. Individuality and Sociality

As it has been perceived in various forms from late antiquity, conscience is the result of an individualizing process. Individuals are no longer completely controlled by society, whether tribe or polis. Rather, they are granted the ability to weigh their own motives apart from the prevailing ethos. Only for this reason can they ascribe credit to themselves and accept responsibility for their actions.

Yet conscience transcends the sphere of mere individuality (G. Picht), for in conscience we are aware of a supraindividual duty. Theological thinking identifies this awareness as part of our relation to God. It finds supreme expression in the image of the → last judgment but is present in every reference to normative obligations. Freud in particular urged this position critically against the guilty conscience, in which the authority of the superego is internalized (→ Psychoanalysis).

Investigations have made it clear that conscience cannot be regarded as simply a private, human ability. It is also the result of a process of social communication. Sociology often concludes that the successful formation of the conscience leads to the development of a humanistic or ethical conscience that can critically overcome heteronomy or authoritarianism. It also stresses in its own way the need to see conscience against the background of an → anthropology of relation rather than of substance. Theological anthropology has an important contribution to make in this regard.

2.5. Political Responsibility

The common thesis that conscience belongs to the private sphere and is not politically relevant is part of the world of thought of enlightened absolutism. A democracy, however, accepts the claim that regard must be had to conscience as publicly relevant. Thus the protection of freedom of conscience, as the core of basic rights (→ Human and Civil Rights), is not just a negative or defensive matter. It gives rise to the positive demand that we use convictions of conscience to help shape public affairs.

A fundamental law in protecting freedom of conscience is the express recognition of → conscientious objection to military service. This conflict of conscience differs from others inasmuch as what is at issue here is something active rather than passive (i.e., killing or preparing to kill). Thus compulsory military service against one's conscience would violate in a particularly striking way the limit that must be set to state power. It is the more regrettable, then, that some democratic states do not recognize the general basic right of conscientious objection and that others fail to provide appropriate processes for recognizing conscientious objectors, at least from the standpoint of Protestant ethics.

The political relevance of conscience, however, goes further, requiring that any appeal to conscience in political → conflicts must not be used as an excuse for breaking off communication. Conscientious conviction does not express itself by refusing to advance arguments or to consider counterarguments. It expresses itself instead in recognition of the binding character of any insight into what is good and necessary for life in society. Those who try to bring the insight of conscience into the process of political communication will always leave room for the possibility that they are wrong. Yet they must always reckon also with the extreme situation that their conviction will not find a hearing, even though it is still a binding obligation for them. They will then have to make a protest, even though this action makes clear their minority position or places them in a situation of suffering. A democracy is characterized by the fact that it tries to avoid such conflicts. A mature political order, however, is also characterized by the fact that it does not rule out the unusual situation of civil disobedience or resistance for conscience' sake (→ Resistance, Right of).

→ Duty; Ethics; Moral Theology; Obedience

Bibliography: J. BLÜHDORN, ed., *Das Gewissen in der Diskussion* (Darmstadt, 1976) • J. BLÜHDORN et al., "Gewissen," *TRE* 13.192-241 (bibliography) • H. CHADWICK, *Betrachtungen über das Gewissen in der griechischen, jüdischen und christlichen Tradition* (Düsseldorf, 1974); idem, "Gewissen," *RAC* 10.1025-1107 • G. EBELING and T. KOCH, *Was ist das? Gewissen* (Hannover, 1984) • EVANGELISCHE ARBEITSGEMEINSCHAFT ZUR BETREUUNG DER KRIEGSDIENSTVERWEIGERER, *Wem das Gewissen schlägt. Zur Rechtsprechung über das Gewissen der Kriegsdienstverweigerer* (Bremen, 1984) • EVANGELISCHE BUND, *Gewissen* (Göttingen, 1982) • E. FROMM, *Psychoanalysis and Religion* (New Haven, 1950) • P. GLOTZ, ed., *Ziviler Ungehorsam* (Frankfurt, 1983) • R. M. HARE, *The Language of Morals* (Oxford, 1952) • C. G. JUNG, "Das Gewissen in psychologischer Sicht," *Das Gewissen* (Zurich, 1958) 185-207 • L. KOHLBERG, *The Psychology of Moral Development: The Nature and Validity of Moral Stages* (San Francisco, 1984) • D. MIETH, "Gewissen," *Christliche Glaube in moderner Gesellschaft* (vol. 12; Freiburg, 1981) 137-84 • R. MOKROSCH, *Das religiöse Gewissen* (Stuttgart, 1979) • C. E. NELSON, ed., *Conscience* (New York, 1973) • O. O'DONOVAN, *Resurrection and Moral Order* (Grand Rapids, 1986) esp. 114-20, 190-97 • S. PFÜRTNER, *Politik und Gewissen–Gewissen und Politik* (Zurich, 1976) • C. A. PIERCE, *Conscience in the NT* (London, 1955) • H. REINER, "Gewissen," *HWP* 3.574-92 • D. STANILOAE, *Orthodoxe Dogmatik* (Zurich, 1985).

WOLFGANG HUBER

Conscientious Objection

1. Term
2. Law
3. History
4. Pastoral Care
5. Organization

1. Term

As distinct from → "pacifism," the term "conscientious objection" denotes the individual refusal of military service. The expression came into use with World War I. A distinction is sometimes made between a strict conscientious objection, when a person refuses to engage in any form of defensive action, and a modified conscientious objection, when a person resists service only in the armed forces (→ Force and Nonviolence). In the United States objectors must demonstrate that they object to all war on religious or moral grounds, while Great Britain allows for objection to particular wars. Provisions for exemption from military service are even more lenient in the Scandinavian countries.

2. Law

In 1989 the Committee on Human Rights of the Economic and Social Council of the United Nations recognized conscientious objection as "a legitimate exercise of the right to freedom of thought, conscience and religion," but individual countries vary widely in how they treat conscientious objection. Some countries (e.g., Germany, Portugal, Spain, and, in the 1990s, Russia and some nations of the former Eastern bloc) give it a constitutional basis. Others (almost all Western democracies except Switzerland) allow it by law. Military dictatorships and Islamic countries strongly oppose it, as do countries in the → Third World. There is a growing movement to recognize it in Latin America.

Where there is universal conscription, a formal declaration of conscientious objection is usually required, and sometimes (e.g., in Germany and Austria) an application must be filled out, with reasons stated. Alternative forms of service are imposed, whether in the army (e.g., in medical corps) or in the social field (e.g., in development, civil defense, or hospital work). Alternative forms of service are usually similar to the military proper in their command structure, low pay, and restricted rights. Longer terms may also be imposed in some instances.

Conscientious objectors who refuse every type of service usually come under legal penalties. Where no provision is made for conscientious objection, they are subject to military prosecution when they do not register for service in the armed forces. During military service, some countries still allow the right to conscientious objection, though as a rule this does not apply in the case of a professional army. The United States is among the relatively few nations that allow discharge or transfer to noncombatant service for those who become conscientious objectors while in the service, although the process is complex and time consuming.

3. History

Conscientious objection may be traced back to various traditions of nonviolence, for example, in → Buddhism, Christianity, and → humanism. In the early Christian church, military service was generally opposed on the basis of such texts as Matt. 5:9, 21-26, 38-42; 26:52; Rom. 12:14, 17-21; 1 Pet. 3:9. In the long run, however, the compromise of the Synod of Arles (314) became normative, granting recognition to the army in time of peace and exempting the clergy as a sign of their ministry of peace.

From the time of the → Reformation the pacifist "left wing" (H. Fast) has been the most important champion of conscientious objection The → Anabaptists preached a nonviolent → discipleship of the cross. They suffered bloody persecution and often had to seek new places of refuge.

Especially significant in the Anglo-Saxon world were the declaration of the Quakers (→ Friends, Society of) in 1661 in favor of nonviolence and the work of William Penn (1644-1718). By their industry, peaceful way of life, piety, and readiness for martyrdom, the adherents of the → peace churches won respect and rights, the first right being that of emigration (1555). With local toleration (e.g., in Holland in 1557) came dearly bought written rights, for example, privileges for Mennonites in Schleswig-Holstein in 1623, the Palatinate in 1648, and Prussia in 1780, though these were sometimes annulled (e.g., by Germany in 1867 and Russia in 1917). Many who were persecuted for conscientious objection emigrated. The first permanent human rights go back to emigrants belonging to the peace churches (religious liberty as gained in Maryland in 1639, Rhode Island in 1641, New Jersey and Pennsylvania in 1681), finally making their way into the U.S. Declaration of Independence.

Along with the appeal to the → Sermon on the Mount and to → millenarian conscientious objection in some groups marginal to Christianity (→ Jehovah's Witnesses; Mormons), the ideals of humanism and the → Enlightenment worked in favor of conscientious objection and human rights and contributed to the founding of peace societies. Total → war and the development of → weapons of mass destruction gave a new turn to the question of conscientious objection from 1945 onward. Ecumenical discussion (→ Ecumenical Movement; SODEPAX) demands the outlawing of war and tends to favor conscientious objection, especially in the Protestant → free churches and the → Reformed churches. The → Roman Catholic Church clings to the traditional doctrine of legitimate defense under certain conditions *(bellum iustum)* but since → Vatican II has recognized that a decision for conscientious objection must be protected.

Under the impact of World War II and the bloody persecution of German conscientious objectors in the years 1933-45, Germany gave constitutional legitimacy to conscientious objection in response to millions of petitions from women's groups. Thus far,

however, the demands of the churches for discontinuing the tests of conscience, the recognition of situational conscientious objection, and the framing of substitute service as voluntary social service with no additional burdens have not been met.

4. Pastoral Care

Counseling on conscientious objection needs to be undertaken by educational institutions and the churches. Conscience is formed in the → family and small groups (confirmation instruction; → Youth Work). It is important that up-to-date information be available. Conversations with objectors and visits to alternative service sites are helpful. Special tasks are the counseling (→ Counseling Centers, Christian) and accompanying of objectors and the providing of → pastoral care for those doing alternative civilian work. Pastors are also qualified to offer counsel along with those specially trained and commissioned for the purpose. Roman Catholic dioceses offer similar services.

5. Organization

Several international organizations, as well as the historic peace churches, act on behalf of objectors. Especially noteworthy are War Resisters International, International Fellowship of Reconciliation, International Peace Bureau, and Service Civil International.

→ Brethren Churches; Disarmament and Armament; Hutterites; Mennonites; Peace; Peace Education; Peace Movement; Salvation Army

Bibliography: Periodicals: Bundesamt für den Zivildienst, *Der Zivildienst* • European Bureau for Conscientious Objection, *The Right to Refuse to Kill* • Evangelische Arbeitsgemeinschaft zur Betreuung der Kriegsdienstverweigerer, *Was uns betrifft* • Referat Katholische Zivildienstseelsorge, *Zivildienstleistende–Informationen.*

Other works: O. R. Barclay, ed., *Pacifism and War: When Christians Disagree* (Downers Grove, Ill., 1984) • P. Baumüller, R. Fritz, and B. Brunn, *Kriegsdienstverweigerungsgesetz* (2d ed.; Neuwied, 1985) • C. Bausenwein, *Dienen oder Sitzen* (Nürnberg, 1984) on total rejection • S. Biesemans, *The Right to Conscientious Objection and the European Parliament* (Brussels, 1995) • J. Callies, ed., *Peaceful Settlement of Conflicts: A Joint Task for a Civil Society* (Loccum, 1993-95) • J. Calliess and R. E. Lob, *Handbuch. Praxis der Umwelt- und Friedenserziehung* (3 vols.; Düsseldorf, 1987-88) • Conference of European Churches, *Conscientious Objection: A Human Right* (Geneva, 1996) • A. Eide and C. L. C. Mubanga-Chipoyá, *Conscien-*

tious Objection to Military Service (Geneva, 1997) • J. Finn, ed., *A Conflict of Loyalties: The Case for Selective Conscientious Objection* (New York, 1968) • E. Isakson, ed., *Women and the Military System* (New York, 1988) • B. de Ligt, *The Conquest of Violence: An Essay on War and Revolution* (London, 1989; orig. pub., 1937) • R. Seeley, *Advice for Conscientious Objectors in the Armed Forces* (Philadelphia, 1984); idem, *Handbook for Conscientious Objectors* (Philadelphia, 1981); idem, *Handbook of Nonviolence* (Westport, Conn., 1986) • R. J. Sider, *Christ and Violence* (Scottdale, Pa., 1979) • J. H. Yoder, *The Politics of Jesus* (3d ed.; Grand Rapids, 1975). See also the bibliographies in "Pacifism," "Peace," and "Violence and Nonviolence."

Ulrich Finckh

Conscientization → Literacy

Consecration

1. Consecrations are rites of → initiation that fundamentally alter the religious and/or social status of a person or that bestow a special dignity on a person's surroundings. Whereas secular understanding views consecrations as ceremonies of acceptance or maturity (e.g., → youth dedications), in religious communities this concept, which even in pre-Christian times occupied a central position, refers to liturgical services that place persons, things, or locales into a special relationship with the holy. The various understandings of church office (→ Offices, Ecclesiastical) and of → ordination determine which form religious consecrations ultimately take.

2. Against the background of a sharp OT separation between the sacred and the profane, consecrations are the dedicating of things to Yahweh by → anointing (§1) with holy oil (Exod. 30:22-33; 40:12-15). With → blessing (§2) and the → laying on of hands, spiritual power is conveyed to consecrated persons (Num. 27:18-23). The NT focuses on the gift of the Spirit (John 20:21-22; → Charisma 1) and on appointment to office (Acts 6:1-6; 13:1-3).

3. The doctrine of powers in the → Roman Catholic Church distinguishes the power of jurisdiction from the consecratory power of the → hierarchy, which is standardized as the episcopate (→ Bishop, Episcopate, 2), the presbytery (→ Priest, Priesthood, 3), and the diaconate (→ Deacon 1; 1983 CIC 1008ff.). Receiving the → sacrament of → ordination (§3.1) is a presupposition for exercising the ecclesiastical offices of sanctification, teaching, and leading, and it distinguishes the → clergy from the laity.

The consecration of bishops and priests irrevocably confers essential powers, especially the right to celebrate the → Eucharist (→ Mass). Episcopal consecration, which is subject to apostolic succession, gives the right to confer consecration as a decisive prerogative before presbyterial consecration. Church law distinguishes grades of consecration, but the consecration of deacons carries no special rights, being dependent on the jurisdictional transfer of ecclesiastical authority (→ Missio canonica).

A person must be baptized and male to be consecrated (can. 1050). The gender requirement obtains only by church law. With reference to the Congregation for the Doctrine of the Faith having addressed the question of admitting women to the priesthood (October 15, 1976), John Paul II in his apostolic letter *Ordinatio sacerdotalis* (May 22, 1994) maintained their exclusion from priestly → ordination (§1.5.2) once and for all. The question raised by the synod of bishops regarding women being admitted at least as deacons has been left unanswered.

A valid consecration presupposes that certain criteria have been met and that no impediments to consecration are in effect. Bishops must have papal consecration; a failure to meet this need is a permanent impediment to consecration and automatically means excommunication.

The rite of consecration in the Pontificale Romanum involves the → laying on of hands and → prayer. Since bishops are simultaneously admitted into the college of bishops, the consecrating bishop must have at least two other bishops as co-consecrators. The local bishop or someone properly charged is responsible for consecration. In the consecratory trial, the invalidity of consecration is established.

As holy places, → cathedrals and parish churches must be consecrated, and all other churches must be at least blessed (→ Benediction; Blessing 4). Things can be consecrated for holy purposes, and for secular purposes they may be blessed (→ Sacramentals).

4. According to the Orthodox view, a consecratory hierarchy is basic to the canonically legitimate existence of the church. Seven stages of consecration are functionally distinguished: bishops, priests, deacons, subdeacons, readers, singers, and sacristans. Consecrations take place in connection with the Eucharist in a fixed sequence and at a fixed time in the liturgy. The laity have a constitutive right to participate by → acclamation. Bearers of higher consecration must be unmarried, but priests and deacons may

maintain existing marriages. Women are admitted as deacons.

5. The → Anglican Communion has the three states of deacon, priest, and bishop, consecrated by separate rituals. Episcopal consecration holds to the notion of valid succession as a symbol of unity and continuity. Depending on the decisions of the variously independent ecclesiastical provinces, women are admitted to all levels of consecration.

6. The theological claim that all believers are → priests (§4) gave the Reformation doctrine of orders a functional concept of → ordination and vocation in debate with the medieval concept of a hierarchy. Ordination confers the power and the duty of purely proclaiming the → gospel and rightly administering the sacraments. The biblical sign of consecration is the laying on of hands by those who ordain. In Germany the ecclesiastical commissioning of future religious teachers (→ School and Church) is by vocation, and for other ministries there are possibilities of liturgical confirmation or presentation with duties and intercession before the congregation. Protestant forms of service (→ Liturgical Books 4-5) also have blessings for things (e.g., at dedications).

7. Free Churches, too, use consecrations as ceremonies for the assumption and transfer of offices. Centrally structured church communities, like the New Apostolic Church (→ Apostolic Churches), by the sacred blessing of their members or by the ordination of bishops and apostles simultaneously establish the authoritarian dependencies of their members and clergy.

Bibliography: A. BURGSMÜLLER and R. FRIELING, eds., Amt und Ordination im Verständnis evangelischer Kirchen und ökumenischer Gespräche (Gütersloh, 1974) • "Concerning the Reply of the Congregation for the Doctrine of the Faith on the Teaching Contained in the Apostolic Letter 'Ordinatio sacerdotalis,'" OR(E), November 22, 1995, 2, 9 • CONGREGATION FOR THE DOCTRINE OF THE FAITH, "Inter insigniores" (October 15, 1976), AAS 69 (1977) 98-116 • M. DAVIES, The Order of Melchisedech: A Defence of the Catholic Priesthood (Harrison, N.Y., 1993) • S. DOWELL, Bread, Wine, and Women: The Ordination Debate in the Church of England (London, 1994) • R. DREIER, Das kirchliche Amt (Munich, 1972) • K. FELMY, Die orthodoxe Theologie der Gegenwart (Darmstadt, 1990) 227-36 • E. GELDBACH, "Endgültiges Nein Roms zur Priesterweihe von Frauen," MD 4 (1994) 65-67 • JOHN PAUL II, "Ordinatio sacerdotalis" (May 22, 1994), AAS 86 (1994) 545-48 •

M. KANYORO, ed., In Search of a Round Table: Gender, Theology, and Church Leadership (Geneva, 1997) • R. LAURENTIN, The Meaning of Consecration Today: A Marian Model for a Secularized Age (San Francisco, 1992) • K. LÜDICKE and H. J. F. REINHARDT, "Die Weihe," Münsterischer Kommentar zum CIC (Essen, 1985ff.) cans. 1008ff. • J. RATZINGER and T. BERTONE, "Responsum ad dubia circa doctrinam in Epist. Ap. 'Ordinatio sacerdotalis' traditam" / "Reply to the 'Dubium' concerning the Teaching Contained in the Apostolic Letter 'Ordinatio sacerdotalis,'" OR(E), November 22, 1995, 2 • A. STEIN, Evangelisches Kirchenrecht (3d ed.; Neuwied, 1992) 102-17.

BERND T. DRÖSSLER

Consensus

1. Term
2. In Christian Tradition
3. Orthodox, Catholic, and Protestant Views
4. In Ecumenical Dialogue

1. Term

Derived from the Latin, the term "consensus" suggests agreement, union, and harmony. In → anthropology it is used for the unity of the senses and perception that influences the will and the → conscience. In social philosophy it denotes public opinion and common sense and expresses the desire for agreement in intrahuman relations and common enterprises. The reference may be to basic agreements or to the result of a search for understanding in face of a plurality of views.

There are many forms of consensus in → society, even though it may not be formulated explicitly or codified. There may also be an articulated consensus that hides controversies. In the legal area, consensus is what is law for all (→ Jurisprudence). In some sense consensus can also be a final authority in a relation by common understanding (e.g., in a contract or a → marriage). In sociology and politics the aim is to fix normatively the relation between consensus and → conflict. Consensus is present by definition in an authoritarian social order, but it must be mediated in a → pluralist society.

Since the French → Revolution certain basic → human rights have been seen as a matter of consensus and accepted by international agreement. Discussion of the various anthropological, philosophical, and natural foundations for basic values still continues. In detail, consensus is often achieved only by → compromise or by vote. In the latter case the majority must safeguard the rights of → minorities. The constitutions of countries and other → organizations and → institutions regulate the structures of consensus.

In theology consensus first denotes agreed concurrence with God's acts toward humanity and the world. Consensus bears witness to life by the → truth of God and is thus a category of Christian → faith. In distinction from social consensus as agreement about different options, theological consensus means acceptance of God's revelation as the determinative court of appeal. Theological diversity arises as we seek human assurance concerning faith in God's revelation. When we are confronted with the plurality of theologies and denominations (→ Pluralism 2), consensus means agreement in faith — in the search for truth, in the formulation of truth, or in common life and work.

2. In Christian Tradition

In the Christian tradition it has been taken for granted from the days of the primitive church that the consensus of Christians is not the result of a process of opinion-building by human decision. Rather, the truth that constitutes consensus is given by the revelation of God in Christ (→ Christology) and is communicated by the → Holy Spirit. The means used by the Holy Spirit is the proclamation of the → Word of God (the → gospel of Christ) by word and deed, including the administration of the → sacraments. The consensus of the Christian community of faith manifests itself in various ways, such as in → worship, confessions (→ Confession of Faith), joint action, lifestyle, and various customs. It finds fulfillment in the life of a local congregation that confesses and acknowledges together that God is here at work.

Because of the historicity of human life and of church life, the truth must be constantly articulated afresh in visible and explicit agreement. Consensus has a historical, dogmatic, and ecumenical function. It must demonstrate historical continuity with the → proclamation of the gospel in history. It responds dogmatically to questions of church proclamation today as new questions and conflicts continually demand new attempts at consensus, such as those surrounding → liberation theologies, → feminist theologies, and national theologies (→ Independent Churches). And the plurality of churches calls for ecumenical consensus, interdenominationally as well as internationally, intercontinentally, and interculturally. Many churches in the → Third World have the impression that the historical consensus of Western churches fails to represent them. They seek their own consensus in their own context and thus press for new ecumenical efforts to achieve consensus with the older churches.

Several historical and confessional features are relevant when describing the theological structure of consensus. Holy Scripture is the basic document of church consensus. All other actualizations of the Christian life find their norm here, at least in Protestant theology (→ Tradition). From the days of the so-called apostolic council (→ Acts of the Apostles §8), the church has found in → synods and → councils a suitable way to articulate consensus (note Acts 15:28: "It has seemed good to the Holy Spirit and to us . . ."). Consensus at a synod shows that the Holy Spirit has made possible a common mind and will. For church members this was to mean that the truth of God manifests itself in consensus. Truth leads to consensus, consensus to truth.

3. Orthodox, Catholic, and Protestant Views

The → Orthodox Church holds that the process of finding consensus ended with the first seven ecumenical councils (through the Second Council of Nicaea, in 787).

The → Roman Catholic Church acts on the principle that through the promise of the Holy Spirit, the totality of believers "cannot err in matters of belief" (→ Vatican II, *Lumen gentium* 12). More specifically, it teaches that the "supernatural appreciation of the faith" *(supernaturalis sensus fidei)* of the whole people can be articulated by the collegial magisterium of the bishops (e.g., at a council) and bindingly and infallibly by the pope (→ Teaching Office; Infallibility).

In Protestant churches the insight has held sway since the 16th-century → Reformation that even consensus does not protect against error. In commitment to → Jesus Christ, who is the heart of Scripture, the truth of faith is judge over the → unity of the church. The consensus of a council or a supreme teaching office is no infallible guarantee of truth and unity. This means that there is no necessary congruence of consensus and truth, though consensus is still valuable as a means of finding truth, as a norm of correct proclamation, and as a confirmation of fellowship in faith. The Reformation → confessions emphasize the great consensus (*magnus consensus,* i.e., the Augs. Conf., 1530) of Protestant churches in their teaching, and they seek to maintain full agreement with Holy Scripture and the "common Christian churches" *(gemeine christliche Kirchen).*

The term "consensus" from then on often appears in Protestant formulations of a confessional character, sometimes in the sense of concord. The thought is that a disagreement in faith and action has been discussed so long in a common listening to the gospel according to Scripture that a uniting and binding recognition of truth has finally been achieved. This understanding of consensus is the Protestant equivalent of the Roman Catholic magisterium (G. Sauter).

4. In Ecumenical Dialogue

The different emphases that appear in the concept of consensus have implications for ecumenical efforts to achieve it today (→ Ecumenical Movement; Ecumenical Theology). A legitimate variety in theology and liturgical, legal, and cultural expressions of the faith is nowhere denied. Some church leaders and theologians take it that full and articulated doctrinal consensus is needed for communion in Word and sacrament, whereas others regard it as sufficient if the churches recognize in one another a basic consensus and thus relativize earlier rejections that arose over specific articles and practice communion in sacrament and ministry in spite of the differences that remain.

The Rahner-Fries Theses demand epistemological tolerance beyond the basic consensus. No confession of a → dogma of another church is to be bindingly demanded. Further consensus must be left to the future. Since, however, the theses call for recognition of the papacy and the → hierarchical structure of the church (§3.2) by all churches, we can hardly envision a consensus here that will lead to church unity.

The Lima text of the → World Council of Churches on baptism, Eucharist, and ministry (1982) represents a significant step toward ecumenical consensus. Here the Faith and Order Commission, with the cooperation of Roman Catholic theologians, pinpoints "convergences" that are calculated to end the controversies that divide the churches. "Convergence" means that things previously separated are now moving toward each other. On the relevant themes the declarations show what agreements there are in faith, what legitimate variety might be possible, and what controversies still exist. The term "consensus" was deliberately avoided. The official responses of the churches give evidence both of basic agreement and of reservations. On the Protestant side, a main problem is whether consensus in the faith necessitates a universally binding church order. On the Roman Catholic side, an important question is whether convergences adequately restore the church's fundamental catholicity (→ Catholic, Catholicity; Reception).

In ecumenical dialogue consensus relates not merely to dogmatic formulations but more gener-ally to the process of mutual understanding in the common life of the church, for example, in ecumenical worship or in common witness and service at every level. The most significant ecumenical attempt at consensus is occurring in the conciliar process of the churches on behalf of "justice, peace, and the integrity of creation." In this process, for the first time since the great divisions, almost all world churches are trying to serve humanity by common proclamation of the will and → promises of God.

In this connection consensus means agreement that does not affect other differences. It has the force of a common denominator in spite of denominational variety. This understanding of consensus is valid to the degree that faith and unity in faith are a gift of God's → grace and thus precede all human and ecclesiastical attempts to achieve consensus. It becomes questionable when it aims only at minimal consensus, and beyond this leaves in abeyance the question of truth or understands truth and consensus as a mutual accommodation of previously divisive factors. The irreversible relation between truth and unity is vital to the oikoumene, and only within this particular horizon can there be consensus encompassing the multiplicity of spiritual life in truth.

→ Ecumenism

Bibliography: H. Fries and K. Rahner, *Einigung der Kirchen–reale Möglichkeit* (Freiburg, 1983) • P. Lengsfeld and H. G. Stobbe, eds., *Theologischer Konsens und Kirchenspaltung* (Stuttgart, 1981) • E. Lessing, *Konsensus in der Kirche* (Munich, 1977) • J. L. Leuba, "Wahrheit und Konsensus," *Freiheit in der Begegnung* (ed. J. L. Leuba and H. Stirnimann; Frankfurt, 1969) 165-80 • J.-B. Metz and E. Schillebeeckx, eds., *The Teaching Authority of Believers* (Edinburgh, 1985) • G. Sauter, "Consensus," *TRE* 8.182-89 • World Council of Churches, *Baptism, Eucharist, and Ministry* (Geneva, 1982).

Reinhard Frieling

Conservatism

1. Secular Usage
 1.1. Definitions
 1.2. Political Conservatism
 1.3. New Trends
 1.4. Neoconservatism
2. Christian Usage
 2.1. Religious Neoconservatism
 2.2. Neoconservatism in Roman Catholicism
 2.3. Neoconservatism in Protestantism

1. Secular Usage

1.1. *Definitions*

In its most common usage, the word "conservatism" refers to attitudes, → worldviews, → ideologies, organizations, groups, and social constructs that are fundamentally oriented to preserving the status quo. The specific positions taken vary depending on context, but common to them all are reactionary and defensive principles of resistance to change, → progress, and → emancipation, of trying to block the effects of the → Enlightenment and the expansion of political participation and social equality.

Conservatism took shape as a coherent political position at the end of the 18th century and the beginning of the 19th. The word itself has been used since 1830. Conservatism declined during the first half of the 20th century with the rise of the social state, which was organized, → capitalist, and regulatory, but the structural, systemic conservatism of the relevant social systems increased. Beginning in the 1970s, a new trend of neoconservatism arose in reaction to the rigidity of the regulatory and social state, which produced a constellation of economic and intellectual crises.

1.2. *Political Conservatism*

1.2.1. Among the most common types of political conservatism is the intransigent conservatism that wants no change but simply wishes to preserve the status quo. Reforming conservatism hopes to propagate gradual reforms so as to be able to preserve what is essential and stabilize what is threatened. It challenges a "progressive" politics of reform by trying to block fundamental change. The attempt to restore the past is no longer genuine conservatism.

The place of conservatism is right of center. It does not always include the entire Right, which includes not only conservative but also ultrareactionary or ostensibly modern populist, or → fascist, movements. Conservative politics will usually be the politics of those who have, in favor of those who have. It will claim the power of state as guarantor of the status quo in the distribution of property, capital, and opportunity. But it will not allow the state to be a rival in matters of trade, the market, profit, or distribution. It follows the principle of laying relatively greater burdens on those who have less, rather than on those who have more.

1.2.2. Political conservatism arose at the end of the 18th century in response to enlightened absolutism (J. Möser) and the French → Revolution (E. Burke and F. von Gentz). It aimed to defend the rights of autonomous local or territorial corporations and established class privileges. At first it was almost exclusively the mouthpiece of the interests of the nobility, the church, and the great landowners against constitutionalism, liberal politics, and capitalist thinking, as well as against the feared social consequences of early industrializing. But in western and central Europe, as the 19th century progressed and the middle class established itself, political conservatism joined liberalism in becoming the expression of middle-class politics. Instead of being on the offensive against crown, aristocracy, and class, it went on the defensive against the → labor movement.

Corresponding to this process was a reorientation of nationalism to the Right instead of the Left (→ Nation, Nationalism). In the Anglo-Saxon countries and revolutionary France a capitalist-oriented liberal conservatism came into being and was able to institutionalize itself in broadly reformist parliamentary parties (→ Political Parties) that could engage in conflict and compromise (note the Federalists, Burke, B. Disraeli, A. de Tocqueville). In preparliamentary Germany, which had had no revolution, conservatism, being closely tied to the great landed interests and to premodern, hierarchical forms of life, remained essentially antiliberal, anti–middle class, and antiparliamentary right up to 1945; in its rhetoric it was even in many cases anticapitalist (until → anti-Semitic agitation eased the situation after 1890).

1.2.3. The basic values of the older conservatism were → property, → family, personality (in class or corporation, not individuality; → Individualism), → freedom (not equality), life (not as abstract concept), religion, legitimacy, and → authority. What had come into being historically took precedence over speculative programs and abrupt change. Developments in Germany involved the early dialectical romanticizing and historicizing of older class thinking (A. Müller, G. W. F. Hegel, L. von Ranke) — an organizing and harmonizing terminology that could easily become biological under the influence of social Darwinism (→ Evolution) — as well as a narrow legitimism (K. L. von Haller, L. and E. Gerlach) and → denominational division.

Roman Catholic conservatives (J. Görres, F. Baader) stressed especially the corporate spheres of freedom (family and → church), while Protestants split over theological minutiae and the collective influence of Hegel (1770-1831; → Hegelianism), Haller (1768-1854), the → Pietists, and E. W. Hengstenberg's church newspaper *Evangelische Kirchen-Zeitung*. When the first conservative parties formed after 1848, the consensus of the Berlin legitimists consisted of a synthesis of → obedience to authority, the alliance of throne and altar, rule by the grace of God, antirationalist belief, a general doctrine of class, and a mystifying of the → Middle Ages (→ Church and State).

The final stage of the older conservative thinking (K. Mannheim) was reached when the Protestant conservatives who governed Prussia in the 1850s, especially through the efforts of F. J. Stahl (1802-61), became increasingly constitutional, though within the limits of the monarchical principle. These conservatives made their peace with the founding of the empire in the later 1870s, largely because of the dominant influence of O. von Bismarck (1815-98), who, with the founding of the German Conservative Party in 1876, united Roman Catholic and Protestant conservatives to fight the depression, forming a solid alliance in support of government policies and in favor of large-scale agriculture and big business. Reform conservatives (e.g., the Roman Catholics F. Baader and W. Ketteler and the Protestants V. A. Huber and A. H. G. Wagner), who to some extent favored the integration of the working class into society so as to ward off class conflict, and who tried to propagate a middle-class conservatism, were in a minority.

1.2.4. In Germany there have been two decisive changes in the historical place of conservatism.

1.2.4.1. The transition to nationalism between 1890 and 1918 and the extension of the franchise largely destroyed the older conservatism. The basic values of the new Right were national solidarity, the middle class, national labor in town and country, the fight for existence and preservation, and a policy of sound common sense. Conservatism became an ideology of national integration, stressing corporate elements, opposing liberalism and socialism, with adherents both among the aristocracy and in the lower middle class. As a result of experiences in World War I and its aftermath, there developed under the Weimar Republic a literary and aesthetic conservatism that advocated conservative revolution and, with its new state and new humanity, had radically nonconservative goals (E. Jünger, C. Schmitt, et al.). The prefascist new Right and the traditional conservative elite both contributed to the rise of National Socialism.

1.2.4.2. A second basic reorientation was the adoption of Anglo-Saxon models and aims after 1945. Under the influence of the Western Allies, the new conservative consensus combined the economic doctrine of neoliberalism with the concept of parliamentary → democracy (whose institutions were now unreservedly accepted for the first time). The panconfessional Christian Democrats, who became the representatives of this postwar conservatism, encompassed what was essentially a much broader political spectrum. Apart from emphasizing a free-market economy and anti-Communism, they mainly focused on ensuring the social and territorial status quo (favoring no "experiments"). Other features included stress on hierarchical models of behavior, criticism of culture, affirmation of the Christian West, family, education, health, the principle of → subsidiarity (as in Roman Catholic → social ethics), and policies extremely favorable to farmers and the middle class.

1.2.5. Conservatism in western and southern Europe was largely spared the historical deviations of German conservatism, for here liberal and republican movements were stronger, political systems more uniform (no federalism), and reactionary enclaves more limited; also, for a long time the political pressure of labor on the middle class was weaker. As a result, the traditional structures lasted longer, organized mass mobilization was less intense, the ability to make reforms and compromises was greater, parliamentarianism was accepted, and the transition to nationalistic new rights either followed later or was less drastic for traditional conservatism. In the United States, after the beginning of the interventionist New Deal, economic liberals (usually Republicans) were called conservative in a political sense inasmuch as they sought the restoration of a free market.

1.3. *New Trends*

From the middle of the 20th century, as the interventionist and social state gained increasing acceptance, traditional concepts of political conservatism, as well as of liberalism and → socialism, gradually dissolved. Their components have been put to arbitrary use and often combined with the general formulas of a politics of the center that embraces as many ideologies as possible, carries through minimal reforms, and, in view of the drastically reduced sphere of action, is often that of the lowest common denominator — tending in fact toward immobility.

Along with the increase of conservative elements in all politics, whether social democratic, progressive, or liberal, one might speak of a new systemic conservatism, of a structural tendency on the part of highly organized industrial-capitalist systems to preserve the status quo, to seek stability, to engage in strategies of avoidance. This tendency can find support in the technological possibilities now open to the → mass media for the mobilizing of the loyalty of the public and for depoliticization. The attempt in the 1960s to combine foreseeable developments with the principles of traditional conservatism into a technocratic conservatism that is systemic, contemporary, and oriented to effective initiatives and optimal functioning (H. Schelsky, H. Freyer, A. Gehlen) has been a failure.

1.4. Neoconservatism

Insight into the limitations of the modern interventionist and social state, as it had to face a growing economic crisis and shortage of resources, produced various reactions in the 1970s that shattered the consensus of the reformist welfare state and that are often known by the imprecise label "neoconservatism."

1.4.1. "Neoconservatism" denotes the attempt to combat the current crisis of the developed social state — a crisis that represents the clear abrogation of the modern interventionist state, with all its progress-oriented projects (→ Modernity) — with weapons drawn from the arsenal of Manchester liberalism and competitive capitalism. In this way it hopes to reverse the direction of all the development of the previous centuries. Out of consideration for society (H. Lübbe), state intervention in particular must be blocked, with all its → bureaucracies, instruments of planning, and social achievements. The great public (but not private) → organizations and structures that threaten to become unmanageable must be dismantled, replaced by smaller units. Market mechanisms and the principle of achievement need to be restored, supplemented by a monetarist economic policy oriented to supply.

These principles of an extreme neoliberal economy conflict with conservative values, although they go hand in hand with political programs focusing on family and workplace. Wherever they have been translated into politics (e.g., as Reaganomics or Thatcherism), they have been applied unevenly, leading to redistribution in favor of the wealthy and to social polarization. They have gained the support of North American intellectuals (often disillusioned leftists or New Dealers) who write in the very influential papers *Commentary* and *Public Interest* (e.g., I. Kristol, N. Podhoretz, N. Glazer, D. Bell, and S. Hook).

Among these authors and many of their followers in western Europe, neoliberalism carries with it a conservative, missionary-like criticism of culture that is aimed especially at the excesses of progress, equality, and democracy, which are seen as a threat to a liberal social order. Other factors include anti-Communism, the elite self-analysis of a new class of postmodern intellectual leaders, and a positivist belief in natural science. The last item manifests itself especially in the high regard for genetic explanations and the racist sociobiology of the French New Right, a well-organized and fashionable philosophical trend (e.g., *Groupement de Recherche et d'Études pour la Civilisation Européenne*) that, with its anti-Enlightenment and vitalist fea-

tures, appeals to German advocates of the conservative revolution.

1.4.2. Authors who have focused on the criticism of progress and culture (e.g., Lübbe, O. Marquard, R. Spaemann) have discussed North American neoconservatism and have again adopted the position of the older pre-Romantic German and European conservatism (Möser, Burke) and the anthropological approaches of Freyer (1887-1969) and Gehlen (1904-76). Value-conservative views (E. Eppler) that favor the conservation of resources and that prefer smaller units to larger organizations occur among movements of protest organized by ecologists and opponents of nuclear power (e.g., the Greens; → Counterculture; Ecology).

The policies of the Christian Democrats in the 1980s were only partially neoconservative. To a large extent they adopt traditional conservative concepts. The neoliberal accent has certainly gained in strength (with its call for less state intervention, privatization, and redistribution), but neoconservatism is less obvious than in other places, since many of the features were already part of the postwar conservative consensus (e.g., neoliberalism, anticollectivism, and the subsidiarity principle), and there have been limits to the dismantling of the interventionist, social state (limits set by various institutions or simply hallowed by tradition, or because of subsidies, entitlements, bureaucracies, and Roman Catholic social teaching). The mix of conservatism and neoconservatism may be seen in many contradictions, such as in the advocacy of a state that is simultaneously strong (in dealing with crime and security) and weak (in its economic policy and welfare and in deferring to individual initiative).

→ Moral Rearmament; Organism; Postmodernism; Radicalism of the Right

Bibliography: H. Dubiel, *Was ist Neokonservatismus?* (Frankfurt, 1985) • I. Fetscher, ed., *Neokonservative und "Neue Rechte"* (Munich, 1983) • M. Greiffenhagen, *Das Dilemma des Konservatismus in Deutschland* (Munich, 1971) • K. Mannheim, *Konservatismus* (Frankfurt, 1984; orig. pub., 1925) • H.-J. Puhle, "Conservatism in Modern German History," *JCH* 13 (1978) 689-720 • H. G. Schumann, ed., *Konservatismus* (2d ed.; Königstein, 1984; orig. pub., 1974).

Hans-Jürgen Puhle

2. Christian Usage

Since the 1970s the term "conservatism" or "neoconservatism" has assumed a new connotation in Christian usage. Neoconservatism is an international, interconfessional phenomenon expressed variously in different continents or churches. Neoconservatives judge that doctrinal integrity and ecclesiastical structures are being threatened by misguided enthusiasm, selective emphases, or ignorance. They possess an acute sense of → tradition and stress the value of established → institutions. They have a wary, cautious outlook on → pluralism. In pastoral strategy (→ Pastoral Care) they strive to protect the simple faithful from being disturbed by irresponsible theological speculations. Doctrinal conservatives may in fact be "liberal" in social or political matters. Protestant neoconservatism also includes the conservative concerns of the New Religious Right.

During the mid-1990s, U.S. national politics shifted notably toward conservatism. While representatives of this political shift often share with the Religious Right similar attitudes in regard to abortion, capital punishment, welfare programs, and armaments, still political conservatism and religious conservatism are separate and distinct entities.

2.1. Religious Neoconservatism

Neoconservatism reflects reactions to the social turmoil of the 1960s. In the → Roman Catholic Church it exhibits a concern about changes that followed → Vatican II (1962-65): the emergence of the laity (→ Clergy and Laity), theological dissent, the assertiveness of national conferences of bishops, and decline in vocations to the priesthood and religious orders. Neoconservatives argue that the → church has recently tolerated too much diversity and too much dissent from orthodox doctrine, especially by theologians obsessed with preoccupations about structural reform. Church life has neglected spiritual concerns and exaggerated particularist → acculturation of the → gospel. Christian social teaching and praxis have in some places become imbued with → Marxist → ideology because of → liberation theology. Furthermore, while official ecumenical dialogues are desirable, they should not proceed too quickly, and their proposals should be submitted to appropriate authorities for rigorous scrutiny.

One formulation of conservative worries is the 1975 "Hartford Appeal for Theological Affirmation" by a U.S. ecumenical group endorsing the views of Peter Berger, Richard Neuhaus, and others. Another expression of neoconservatism may be found in the objections by Edward Norman and Ernst W. Lefever to questionable social teachings (→ Social Ethics) of the → World Council of Churches, especially its Faith and Order Commission.

2.2. Neoconservatism in Roman Catholicism

Among some Roman Catholics a conservative reaction developed to the social programs of "conscientization" formulated, for example, by CELAM (Con-

ference of Latin American Catholic Bishops) at Medellín, Colombia, in 1968, and at the International Synod of Bishops in 1971. Neoconservatism has been supported by Pope John Paul II, who proceeds cautiously to appoint only → bishops who reflect doctrinal conservatism. This is described as a "restoration" agenda.

Neoconservatism differs from the disruptive and radical "Traditionalist" movement associated with the French archbishop Marcel Lefebvre, who judged that Vatican II's decisions on → religious liberty, → collegiality, and → ecumenism were capitulations to the secular goals of liberté, égalité, fraternité. The papal appointment of the German theologian and cardinal Joseph Ratzinger as prefect of the Congregation for the Doctrine of the Faith, the former Holy Office (→ Inquisition), has strengthened neoconservatist views. His pessimistic assessment of → Catholicism after Vatican II was published in the Ratzinger Report in 1985.

Vatican support of the personal prelacy → Opus Dei and international lay organizations (→ Lay Movements) such as Communione e Liberazione are institutional instances of neoconservatism. In the United States the foundation by H. Lyman Stebbins in 1968 of Catholics United for the Faith reflects its commitment to monitor doctrinal orthodoxy and fidelity to the ecclesiastical magisterium (→ Teaching Office).

Some have asked whether the modern charismatic renewal (→ Charismatic Movement) associated with the → "baptism in the Spirit" of Catholics in 1967 in Pittsburgh is an expression of neoconservatism. This movement, inspired by enthusiastic and sectarian → Pentecostalism, stresses biblical tradition, → prayer, and spiritual gifts of the → Holy Spirit as well as → obedience and institutional loyalty. Charismatics search for the plenitude of tradition, as do neoconservatives, but generally they are more optimistic and are not preoccupied with pursuing questionable theologians.

2.3. Neoconservatism in Protestantism

Among American Protestants since the 1970s, neoconservatism usually refers to a different phenomenon, specifically, the emergence of the New Religious Right (or New Christian Right), such as Jerry Falwell's former Moral Majority. It is new in that it encourages American evangelicals (→ Evangelical Movement) to be involved in the political processes, even in congressional lobbies, and not only to protect traditional religious values relating to → creationism or school prayers but also to articulate "Christian" concerns about capital → punishment, defense spending, → abortion, → homosexual rights, public aid to private education, and so forth. The New Religious Right shares with Catholic neoconservatives similar fears about the spiritual deterioration of → society. It dislays much of the same intensity, certitude, pessimism, and lack of humor as Roman Catholic neoconservatives.

→ Biblicism; Fundamentalism; Worldview

Bibliography: G. BAUM, ed., *Neo-Conservatism: Social and Religious Phenomenon* (Edinburgh, 1981) • P. BERGER and R. NEUHAUS, eds., *Against the World, for the World: The Hartford Appeal and the Future of American Religion* (New York, 1976) • M. CROMARTIE, ed., *Disciples and Democracy: Religious Conservatives and the Future of American Politics* (Washington, D.C., 1994); idem, ed., *No Longer Exiles: The Religious New Right in American Politics* (Washington, D.C., 1993) • M. S. EVANS, ed., *The Theme Is Freedom: Religion, Politics, and the American Tradition* (Washington, D.C., 1994) • G. FACKRE, *The Religious Right and Christian Faith* (Grand Rapids, 1982) • J. FALWELL, *Listen, America!* (New York, 1980) • S. S. HILL and D. E. OWEN, *The New Religious Political Right in America* (Nashville, 1982) • D. M. KELLEY, *Why Conservative Churches Are Growing* (New York, 1972) • H. KÜNG and L. SWIDLER, eds., *The Church in Anguish: Has the Vatican Betrayed Vatican II?* (San Francisco, 1987) • E. W. LEFEVER, *Amsterdam to Nairobi: The World Council of Churches and the Third World* (Washington, D.C., 1979) • R. C. LIEBMAN and R. WUTHNOW, eds., *The New Christian Right* (New York, 1983) • D. LOTZ, D. SHRIVER JR., and J. WILSON, eds., *Altered Landscapes: Christianity in America, 1935-1985* (Grand Rapids, 1989) • E. R. NORMAN, *Christianity and the World Order* (Oxford, 1979) • R. REED, ed., *Politically Incorrect: The Emerging Faith Factor in American Politics* (Dallas, 1994) • P. STEINFELS, *The Neoconservatives* (New York, 1979) • R. VEKEMANS, *Caesar and God: The Priesthood and Politics* (New York, 1972) • R. VIGUERIE, *The New Right* (Falls Church, Va., 1980).

MICHAEL A. FAHEY

Consolation, Comfort

In → pastoral care, consolation involves subjective experiences in which painful difficulties in relation to God, to others, and to the self are either overcome or are made bearable. The aim of comfort and consolation as a basic task of Christian pastoral care is to help people in situations of stress or crisis, such as in loss and distress through dying, → death, divorce (→ Marriage and Divorce), sickness (→ Health and Illness), and → handicaps, and to do so in such a way that people are able to resolve the crisis

conflicts actively on the basis of → faith, or at least consciously to live with unremitting suffering. Protestants define consolation as an experience of the relativizing of suffering by grounding identity in the sinners' justification by faith alone (→ Reformation Principles; Sin 3). The popularization of the → criticism of religion in the → modern period has discredited Christian solace as compensatory but illusory consolation in the hereafter. If the understanding and practice of consolation are to be cultivated anew and are to remain a theme of more than inner-church → piety, they need to be set in interdisciplinary → dialogue and marked off clearly from consolation as emotional release through reference to elements of an illusory experience of reality.

From a sociological perspective (→ Sociology), consolation is the stabilization of the social life of persons by means of actions that help to overcome experiences of contingency. Church rituals at birth (→ Baptism 4), marriage (→ Wedding Ceremony), and death (→ Funeral), for example, have served as rites of passage with a comforting integrative function in the uncertain situation of a social change of status (→ Initiation Rites 2).

Viewed psychoanalytically, consolation involves temporarily activating real earlier experiences, which then unburden a person from the acute pressure of suffering (regression in the service of the ego) and strengthen the power of the ego. Crises that, according to psychoanalytic theory, arise when individuals fail to solve problems, lead with continuing pressure to → anxiety, to helplessness, to a destabilization of the ego, and to disintegration of the → person (→ Crisis Intervention). People resort regressively to modes of behavior deriving from earlier oral, anal, or genital stages of development. Corresponding defense mechanisms come to expression in the comforting and consoling actions through which a person attempts to cope (e.g., sleep, excessive eating and drinking, transitional phenomena such as music, painting, → aggression or strict self-control, memories, tales, → humor). Effective consolation plays a role in pastoral crisis intervention. It leads to resolution of conflicts by temporarily, and in a way adequate to the situation, offering within the framework of a personal relationship religious or secular means of coping (e.g., by assurance, physical contact, the → Eucharist, → prayer, explanation of the suffering). Consolation must address regressive behavior, the type of crisis, and the momentary stage in the process by dealing with the sequential phases of uncertainty, certainty, aggression, negotiation, depression, acceptance, activity, or → solidarity (→ Dying, Aid for the).

At the heart of the biblical understanding of consolation is the experience of pain and death caused by God's turning away, and also by the vivifying renewal of God's presence when he turns back to us (Ps. 71:20-21; 119:76; Isa. 40:1; Job 38). The theology of → Paul unites the themes of pastoral care and → ethics in the concept of *paraklēsis* (i.e., consolation, admonition). The common root is God's compassion (Rom. 12:1-2), which is imparted to believers on the basis of → baptism (§2). A change of being is imparted to them in which, by their belonging to Christ, they pass over from sinful humanity to the status of those who are justified by → grace and see their suffering done away in the → hope of fellowship with Christ. Thus the Heidelberg Catechism describes belonging to Christ, which is our "only comfort in life and in death" (q. 1), as the basis of Christian identity.

M. → Luther's (1483-1546; Luther's Theology) concept of pastoral care understood consolation as a refuge from the assaults of → conscience with the promise of → forgiveness. The universal priesthood of believers finds expression in *mutuum colloquium et consolatio fratrum* (mutual encouragement and brotherly consolation; → Priest, Priesthood, 4). Protestant pastoral care has rightly retained this model. If we are not to miss the psychosocial reality of suffering people by clinging one-sidedly to → tradition, comfort must increasingly be an element in pastoral psychology.

→ Despair; Empathy; Grief; Guilt; Laughing and Crying; Pastoral Care of the Sick; Penitence

Bibliography: J. Bowlby, *Loss, Sadness, and Depression* (London, 1980) • D. Capps, *Agents of Hope: A Pastoral Psychology* (Minneapolis, 1994) • S. Hiltner, *Preface to Pastoral Theology* (New York, 1958) • R. Jerneizig, A. Langenmayr, and U. Schubert, *Leitfaden zur Trauerarbeit und Trauerbegleitung* (Göttingen, 1991) • M. Leist, *Kinder begegnen dem Tod* (Gütersloh, 1979) • R. Leuenberger and F. Meerwein, "Trauer und Trost," *CGG* 10.117-38 • C. Schneider-Harpprecht, *Trost in der Seelsorge* (Stuttgart, 1989) bibliography • E. Schuchardt, *Warum gerade ich . . . ? Behinderung und Glaube* (8th ed.; Göttingen, 1994) • Y. Spiegel, *Der Prozeß des Trauerns* (2 vols.; Munich, 1973) • D. K. Switzer, *The Minister as Crisis Counselor* (Nashville, 1974) • H. Tacke, *Glaubenshilfe als Lebenshilfe. Probleme und Chancen heutiger Seelsorge* (2d ed.; Neukirchen, 1979) • H. T. Weyhofen, *Trost. Modelle des religiösen und philosophischen Trostes und ihre Beurteilung durch die Religionskritik* (Frankfurt, 1983).

Christoph Schneider-Harpprecht

Constance, Council of → Reform Councils

Constitution

"Constitution" is a legal term with significance both for legislation and for the theory of norms (→ Law). It is used not only in connection with political states (i.e., governing the manner in which sovereign power is distributed) but also in Roman Catholic law (→ Church Law).

1. A constitution is a technical, legal way of publishing universal church legislation (→ Jurisdiction, Ecclesiastical). Along with the → motu proprio, the apostolic constitution issues basic papal laws (→ Pope, Papacy). The conciliar constitution (→ Councils of the Church) is a legal resolution on the part of an ecumenical council that has legal validity when it is passed by the representatives and confirmed and published by the pope (→ Codex Iuris Canonici). Because their form is problematic from the standpoint of legal use, the most important theological constitutions of → Vatican II (the pastoral, dogmatic, and liturgical constitutions) have an uncertain legal status.

2. "Constitution" may also refer to the legal act of establishment (e.g., of a religious order). According to the 1983 CIC, what is involved is the written recording of norms that must be approved when orders and societies for a consecrated or apostolic life, as well as secular institutes, draw up their own constitutions (→ Orders and Congregations).

→ Bulls and Briefs; Encyclicals

Bibliography: A. Erler, "Konstitution, constitutio," *HDRG* 2.1119-22 (on the history of the term).

On 1: J. Listl, "Die Rechtsnormen," *Handbuch des katholischen Kirchenrechts* (ed. J. Listl et al.; Regensburg, 1983) 83-98 • J. Neumann, "Die Verbindlichkeit der Beschlüsse," *Die Autorität der Freiheit* (vol. 1; ed. J. C. Hampe; Munich, 1967) 77-85 • H. Schmitz, "Der CIC und das konziliare und nachkonziliare Kirchenrecht," *Grundriß des nachkonziliaren Kirchenrechts* (ed. H. Schmitz et al.; Regensburg, 1980) 22-30.

On 2: M. Cerletty, "Some Practical Helps for the Development of Constitutions," *StCan* 14 (1980) 155-70 • D. F. O'Connor, "Constitutions and the Revised Code of Canon Law," *RfR(StM)* 42 (1983) 506-13.

Bernd T. Drössler

Consumption

1. Definition
2. As Individual Decision
3. As Social Phenomenon
4. Education and Policy
5. Goals and Forms of Restraint

1. Definition

1.1. In economic theory, consumption involves the use of goods and services in private households. Statistics cover only those goods acquired on regular markets and not the goods and services due to private initiative or private employment.

1.2. In terms of attitudes, consumption relates to the use of goods and services that meet human needs. Distinguishing these activities from productive private or leisure-time work is difficult.

2. As Individual Decision

2.1. Common to all of us is the fact that we have recurrent needs and attempt to satisfy them. The role of consumption here depends on economic and social data (availability of goods and social → norms) and also on individual attitude and the resulting behavior.

2.2. From the economic standpoint, individual consumption involves a process of decision. Many models of consumption theory rest on a supposed rationality of the act of consumption. Empirical research into human behavior (→ Behaviorism) shows, however, that consumers are not usually well informed about the market or the actual makeup of products; furthermore, they can be influenced in their purchases with relative ease. The theory and practice of marketing rest on these findings.

3. As Social Phenomenon

3.1. Industrialization entails a clear separation between the organized sphere of production and the domestic sphere of consumption. Increased productivity has brought more goods to market, and the activities of private households have increasingly been reduced to the sphere of pure consumption.

3.2. Expansion of industrial production brought changes in the social norms of needs and in what individuals would define as their needs. The rise in the standard of living results not merely from the greater availability of goods but is supported steadily by advertising. The advertisement of goods contains information about products, as well as influential statements about their alleged symbolic value (e.g., in terms of social prestige and aesthetic significance). Consumption, thus, provides an important index to the orientation and content of human life (→ Masses, The).

4. Education and Policy

4.1. To strengthen the market position of consumers, efforts are made to promote the critical awareness of individuals and the rationality of their decisions relative to consumption. This is done by way of information, advice, and consumer education in public schools and in adult classes (→ Continuing Education).

4.2. Another aspect is the strengthening of the collective market position by supporting consumer groups (e.g., tenant organizations) or larger associations that protect the interests of all consumers over against producers or in matters of legislation.

5. Goals and Forms of Restraint

5.1. Various negative consequences have brought into question the basic industrial value of constantly expanding production and consumption. The resultant new → ethics of consumer restraint has three sociopolitical thrusts. First, it involves rejection of a blatantly materialistic lifestyle. Then it stresses conservation of the natural → environment (→ Ecology). Third, it seeks to even out differences in the standard of living with regard to the → Third World.

5.2. Forms of restraint are the general reduction of expenditures on consumer goods, the partial or complete avoidance of specific goods, and the switching of consumption to other goods. Large-scale restraint of consumption could bring about profound economic and social changes. The modest beginnings thus far have primarily sent a signal, challenging the dominant social order and prevailing lifestyles, and also appealing for → solidarity with the exploited.

→ Economics, Ethics of; Economy; Everyday Life; Family; Meaning; Money; Symbol; Work

Bibliography: C. Améry, *Natur als Politik* (Hamburg, 1976) • R. Bahro, *Logik der Rettung. Wer kann die Apokalypse aufhalten?* (Stuttgart, 1987) • E. Fromm, *To Have or to Be?* (New York, 1976) • A. O. Herrera, *Grenzen des Elends* (Frankfurt, 1977) • S. Lebergott, *Pursuing Happiness: American Consumers in the Twentieth Century* (Princeton, 1993) • G. Scherhorn, *Verbraucherinteresse und Verbraucherpolitik* (Göttingen, 1975) • L. E. Schmidt, *Consumer Rites: The Buying and Selling of American Holidays* (Princeton, 1995) • A. B. Schmookler, *The Illusion of Choice: How the Market Economy Shapes Our Destiny* (Albany, N.Y., 1993) • C. F. von Weizsäcker, *Die Zeit drängt* (7th ed.; Munich, 1988) • K. E. Wenke and H. Zillessen, eds., *Neuer Lebensstil–verzichten oder verändern?* (Opladen, 1978).

Peter Hunziker

Contemplation

1. Term

The Latin word *contemplari* originally had to do with auguries in a context of sacrifice. It involved consultation in the sacred precincts. It became a religious term as a rendering of the (Neo-)Platonic word *theōreō*. According to Plotinus (ca. 205-70), each thing is contemplation of the divine according to the measure of its own essential truth. We ourselves experience oneness with all things in the ascent of contemplation (→ Platonism). This interpretation was gradually given a Christian twist by means of the message of love. As Hugh of St. Victor (1096-1141) put it, "Love enters in when the understanding remains outside."

From the very beginning, Christian *contemplari* oriented itself to the biblical word and the sacramental reality, where God might be seen in Jesus (the *Logos* as the *theōria* of God). The history and the questions of Christian → spirituality may be seen in the dialogue of the Christian message of love and the Neoplatonic schema of ascent. In this regard the term "contemplation" embraces the sphere of experience of God in a more nuanced way than the later word → "mysticism" (which we find beginning in the 17th cent.).

2. Aspects

Plotinus's → metaphysics of unity rests on an experience of religious crisis, notwithstanding the philosophical → hermeneutics. A related thought is that the Christian tradition of contemplation is important in dialogue with the experiential religions of Asia and Africa (→ Buddhism and Christianity; Hinduism and Christianity). In this article we discuss only that which is distinctively Christian.

Christian contemplation can be seen from six perspectives: (1) the primacy of → love, (2) darkness and suffering, (3) as a gift, (4) in relation to history, (5) in relation to activity, and (6) as personal analogy.

2.1. M. Buber (1878-1965) finds two roots for the contemplative experience of unity: experience of the self, and (self-forgetting) experience of encounter, with the "peak experience" of loving encounter. Christian contemplation often takes the route of self-experience (→ Teresa of Ávila [1515-82]) and retains certain features of this factor, but it is always open to the → experience (§2) of encounter.

2.2. This experience of encounter necessarily involves transcending the self. The other becomes the center of attention. The result might be emotional fulfillment, but it might also be the pain of self-renunciation. In Christian contemplation the way to contemplation can be that of → asceticism, first by the renunciation of sensual fulfillment (John of the Cross), then of intellectual and personal fulfillment for the sake of the other (the dark night of the soul). In contemplative experience, however, the ascent above experience also has an essential place. For this reason Buber hesitates to describe the encounter with God as experience. In the Christian evaluation of contemplation, the dark and painful hours of transcending the self are the criterion of the true experience of God. Passion mysticism (→ Suffering) as the high point of this contemplative ascent is a phenomenon that Christian mysticism shares with other theistic traditions (→ Sufism; Theism).

2.3. According to the Christian tradition, we ourselves cannot achieve the radical ascent above the self in contemplation. God himself must do it for us. It is experienced and theologically evaluated as a gift of → grace. C. Albrecht calls it the coming of the all-embracing. For this reason many Christian contemplatives hold aloof from any methodology of contemplation (e.g., Meister → Eckhart [ca. 1260-ca. 1328], according to A. M. Haas). Others, like Teresa of Ávila, value the fact that the high point of contemplation can never be forced but must always be received.

2.4. The darkness that comes with → faith shows that in spite of its high points (*Nunc stans,* Eckhart), experience is always immanent in time and history and holds out hope of future consummation (P. Teilhard de Chardin; → Eschatology; Future).

2.5. The essential transcending of the self is connected with action. In the tradition of Christian contemplation, Neoplatonism was an obstacle to the theoretical development of this fundamental unity. All the same, the contemplative ideal of encounter led necessarily in practice to activity on behalf of others (→ Bernard of Clairvaux; → Taizé Community). High points of reflection are Eckhart's second sermon on Mary and Martha, the contemplative in action of → Ignatius Loyola (1491-1556), and especially the evolutionary mysticism of Teilhard de Chardin (1881-1955).

2.6. The phenomenologically visible aspect of Christian contemplation is a deposit of the experience of the one personal → God in three persons: the mystery of origin, the visibility of encounter, and the immanence of experience (→ Trinity).

3. Classic Authors

The practice of contemplation covers the whole history of Christian mysticism (see the Ruhbach and Sudbrack items below). We find the beginnings in the Fathers (Gregory of Nyssa; → Cappadocian Fathers), with important contributions from the Eastern church (Simeon the New Theologian, Palamas; → Palamism), from German mysticism, and from the women. A high point is the Spanish mysticism of Teresa of Ávila, which was continued in French mysticism (Madame Guyon). Modern examples include some from → meditative and charismatic circles. The still-unresolved controversy between R. Garrigou-Lagrange (1877-1964) and A. Poulain (1836-1919; the former holding that only a gradual difference separates the grace of faith and mystical faith, the latter that the difference between the two is essential) raises the vital questions.

4. Related Concepts

It is hard to fix precise boundaries between contemplation, → prayer, meditation, and mysticism, with the differences being mostly a matter of different emphases. Prayer involves a simple Thou-relation. Meditation involves a methodology and collecting of experience. Mysticism finds a high point in concrete experiences. Contemplation has to do with a kind of viewing. Quite apart from these distinctions, we must also differentiate between the religiosity of Christianity (and other monotheistic religions) and that of religions that are not monotheistic.

Superficial similarities exist between Christian contemplation and religious-phenomenological parallels as well as psychological reductions to the immanence (or extension) of consciousness. Nevertheless, Christian contemplation has its own distinctiveness. Although it may include techniques of meditation or mystical speculation, the features to which we have drawn attention, and especially the inalienable role played by the reference to the → Jesus of Holy Scripture, constitute the norm for any serious religious dialogue.

→ Buddhism; Emanation; Piety; Yoga; Zen

Bibliography: H. U. VON BALTHASAR, Prayer (San Francisco, 1986) • M. CASEY, The Undivided Heart: The Western Monastic Approach to Contemplation (Petersham, Mass., 1994) • "Contemplation," DSp 2.1643-2193 • P. KING, Dark Night Spirituality: Thomas Merton, Dietrich Bonhoeffer, Etty Hillesum. Contemplation and the New Paradigm (London, 1995) • M. E. MASON, Active Life and Contemplative Life: A Study of the Concepts from Plato to the Present (Milwaukee, Wis., 1961) • "Mystique," DSp 10.1884-1984 • G. RUHBACH and J. SUD-BRACK, eds., Christliche Mystik. Texte aus zwei Jahrhunderten (Munich, 1989); idem, eds., Große Mystiker, Leben und Wirken (Munich, 1984) • J. SUDBRACK, Herausgefordert zur Meditation. Christliche Erfahrung im Gespräch mit dem Osten (Freiburg, 1977); idem, ed., Das Mysterium und die Mystik. Beiträge zu einer Theologie der christlichen Gotteserfahrung (Würzburg, 1974) • R. C. ZAEHNER, Mysticism, Sacred and Profane (New York, 1957).

JOSEF SUDBRACK

Contextual Theology

1. Term
2. Development
3. Theological Self-Understanding
4. Essential Criterion

1. Term

Contextual theology is → theology predicated with reference to its context. Contextuality, then, means relation to the substance and nature of the context, which goes beyond merely the literary setting to include geographic, linguistic, social, political, cultural, and ideological factors. Contextual theology is faith-knowledge on the basis of both the biblical → revelation and the contemporary reference. In contextual theology a text is not only a literary unit (e.g., from the tradition of the Bible or the church). Rather, it is the starting point or determinative factor in theological work done in light of its modern-day background.

Ecumenical discussion has talked about contextual theology since the 1960s. In deciding funding for theological education (→ World Council of Churches), Shoki Coe and Aharon Sapsezian further developed the term "context" after 1973. They argued that emphasis must be put on theological education in context as the only way in which theology can be truly evangelistic, namely, as a living encounter of the universal gospel with the realities that people face in their own settings (Nairobi Report [1976]). In the period that followed, contextuality was universally promoted, not only in → Third World theology but also in the theology of Europe and North America.

2. Development

Contextual theology has developed regionally. The → liberation theology of Latin America was basically formulated by the Roman Catholic bishops at Medellín, Colombia, in 1968. According to G. Gutiérrez, its concern is not so much with unbelievers as with nonpersons — that is, the poor and the oppressed.

The contextuality of this theology comes to light in its sociological analysis of the relevant social factors (including international → dependence) and in its resistance to a spiritualizing of poverty and a politicizing that ignores the people's faith.

The influence of Latin American theologians in Asia (e.g., in the Philippines) resulted in a recognition that poverty is a mark of the culture of many Asian peoples. Contextualization, then, means the rebirth of theology in the midst of Asia's poor (C. H. Abesamis, 1978). In 1978 liberation became the core concept in contextualizing. Contextual theology also took three other paths in Asia. First, there was dialogue with other faiths or religious traditions. Then there was dialogue with different cultures. Finally, South Korea (§2) in 1978 saw the emergence of minjung theology — that is, a people's theology that articulates confession of Christ in the contemporary political situation.

We owe the concept and origin of → black theology (§§1-2) to contextual theology in North America. In the context of black-white confrontation, J. H. Cone rejected the exclusiveness of this antithesis and constructed a larger frame of reference. For the process of liberation the starting point in racism would not be denied but strengthened if racism were linked to imperialism and sexism (Cone 1977). One might speak here of a contextual shift. Even the geographic context (North America) was broadened. In combination with other theologies in the → Third World, a transcontinental contextuality has arisen that finds a common starting point in the poor and the oppressed and therefore also in blacks.

In South Africa in particular, → black theology (§3.1) has been the most pregnant form of contextual theology (→ African Theology). It sees itself as a situational and liberation theology in the context of South Africa (A. Boesak, B. Khumalo, et al.) and as a contribution to nonviolent resistance. It thus finds expression in its alliance with the black awareness movement, reflecting the faith-practice of blacks in the experience of oppression by the apartheid regime (→ Racism). In both speech and method it stands in opposition to the discriminatory theology of whites.

In tropical Africa, contextual theology adopts various older and newer approaches, addressing common political and social problems and taking theological action to solve them. These different approaches mark the concern for an authentic new beginning of Christian theology in the existing situation, and also for dialogue with the religious traditions of Africa (J. S. Pobee; → Guinea 2).

In Germany, H. E. Tödt, W. Huber, U. Duchrow, and others are proponents of contextual theology.

H. Waldenfels sees it as → fundamental theology. Its significance for Christian and theological education and for the → people's church demands recognition. Such a recognition can hardly be expected, however, unless it finds reception in exegetical scholarship.

3. Theological Self-Understanding

The incarnation of God is the starting point for contextual theology's understanding of itself (O. E. Costas, C. S. Song). God has contextualized himself by the death and → resurrection of Jesus (→ Incarnation 3).

In its comparable motivation, the frame of reference of such a contextual theology displays a common note: the critique of the universalistic self-understanding of Western theology, including the effort to answer the different questions of the various churches (W. Freytag) in ways appropriate to each one (G. Söhngen). The → Ecumenical Association of Third World Theologians pursues this goal. Contextual theology tries to indigenize the → gospel by giving it fresh orientation (in detachment from Christian thought in the West) and in part a different accent. It thus is itself an expression of indigenization. Part of this effort involves a new approach to the Bible (K. H. Ting; → Hermeneutics) that sees it as testimony to wrestling with a specific background (e.g., the exodus, or the rich and the poor).

Regional development of contextual theology, which at times can assume very specific features (e.g., in minjung theology), shows that the problem is to relate the universality of Christ's rule to the particularity of contextual theology. This is the problem of catholicity and contextuality. European theology does not answer the difficult problem of universality but perpetuates it.

By developing the incarnation of God in a consistently Trinitarian way, contextual theology can give contextuality a stronger pneumatological basis. In the power of the Spirit, the church and theology can penetrate its particular context and shatter the dominion of secular powers. In this connection, contextual theology in part makes contact with its context and in part opposes it, as was shown at the Hong Kong conference Confessing Christ Today (1966).

→ Feminist theology (§4) views itself as a kind of contextual theology. Especially in the United States it has emerged with prominent aims.

4. Essential Criterion

The essential criterion of contextual theology is the extent to which a contextual understanding of the gospel leads people to Christ. When the second conference of Asian theologians at Hong Kong (1984) stated that theology must help to mobilize people and resources for the liberation of people from oppression, this type of contextual theology saw itself committed to the insight that being a Christian in any cultural and sociopolitical situation not only orients us to Jesus Christ but makes him the basis of decision in our specific contexts. Attachment to Jesus Christ in judgment and → grace is what proves characteristic of contextual theology (K. Blaser).

→ Acculturation; Biblical Theology 2; Culture and Christianity; Political Theology; Theology of Revolution

Bibliography: Asian Perspectives on Christian Thought: The Significance of Context for Doing Theology in Asia, Colloquia in Pattaya, 1980 (= SEAJT 21/22 [1980/81]) • K. BLASER, "Christliche Theologie vor der Vielfalt der Kontexte," ZMiss 10 (1984) 5-20; idem, "Kontextuelle Theologie als ökumenisches Problem," TZ 36 (1980) 220-35 • L. BOFF, Jesus Christ Liberator: A Critical Christology for Our Times (Maryknoll, N.Y., 1978) • L. BOFF and N. PORTO, Kreuzweg der Auferstehung (Düsseldorf, 1984) • G. CASALIS et al., Bibel und Befreiung (Fribourg, 1985) • Chinese Theological Review, Yearbook (Holland, Mich., 1985-) • S. COE, Contextualizing Theology (Dayton, Ohio, 1973) • J. H. CONE, "Black Theology and the Black Church: Where Do We Go from Here?" CrossCur 27 (1977) 147-56; idem, God of the Oppressed (Minneapolis, 1978) • J. M. ELA, My Faith as an African (Maryknoll, N.Y., 1988) • D. J. ELWOOD, ed., Asian Christian Theology: Emerging Themes (Philadelphia, 1980) • R. FRIEDLI, Mission oder Demission (Fribourg, 1982) • F. HERZOG, God-Walk: Liberation Shaping Dogmatics (Maryknoll, N.Y., 1988); idem, Justice Church: The New Function of the Church in North American Christianity (Maryknoll, N.Y., 1980) • W. HUBER, Folgen christlicher Freiheit (Neukirchen, 1985) • B. KAHL, Armenevangelium und Heidenevangelium (Berlin, 1987) • K. KOYAMA, No Handle on the Cross: An Asian Meditation on the Crucified Mind (Maryknoll, N.Y., 1977) • E. LANGE, Kirche für die Welt (Munich, 1981) • E. Y. LARTNEY, Pastoral Counselling in Inter-Cultural Perspective (Frankfurt, 1987) • J. Y. LEE, ed., An Emerging Theology in World Perspective (Mystic, Conn., 1988) • J. M. LOCHMAN, Christ and Prometheus? A Quest of Theological Identity (Geneva, 1988) • J. B. METZ, Faith in History and Society: Toward a Practical Fundamental Theology (New York, 1980) • J. MOLTMANN, ed., Minjung (Neukirchen, 1984) • A. PIERIS, An Asian Theology of Liberation (Maryknoll, N.Y., 1988) • K. PISKATY, The Process of Contextualization and Its Limits (= VSVD 24 [1983]) • J. S. POBEE, Toward an African Theology (Nashville, 1979) • D. RITSCHL, "Westliche Theologie im Licht der Kritik aus der Dritten Welt. Kritisches zum Begriff 'Indigenous Theology,'" EvT 39 (1979) 451-65 • D. SCHIRMER, ed., Die Bibel als politisches Buch (Stuttgart, 1982) • E. SCHÜSSLER FIORENZA, In Memory of Her: A Feminist Theological Reconstruction of Christian Origins (New York, 1983) • C. S. SONG, Theology from the Womb of Asia (London, 1988) • T. SUNDERMEIER, ed., Religionen–Mission–Ökumene (= VF 30/1 [1985]) • K. TAKIZAWA, Das Heil im Heute. Texte einer japanischen Theologie (Göttingen, 1987) • K. H. TING, How to Study the Bible (New York, 1981) • S. TORRES et al., eds., Dem Evangelium auf der Spur (Frankfurt, 1980) • S. TORRES and V. FABELLA, eds., The Emergent Gospel: Theology from the Underside of History (Maryknoll, N.Y., 1978) • D. M. B. TUTU, Versöhnung ist unteilbar (Wuppertal, 1977) • E. K. TWESIGYE, Common Ground: Christianity, African Religion, and Philosophy (New York, 1987) • S. VINAY and C. SUDGEN, eds., Der ganze Christus für eine geteilte Welt (Erlangen, 1987) • L. VISCHER, ed., Theologie im Entstehen (Munich, 1976) • H. WALDENFELS, Kontextuelle Fundamentaltheologie (Paderborn, 1985) • L. WIEDENMANN, ed., Theologie der Dritten Welt (7 vols.; Freiburg, 1981-89) • S. YAGI and U. LUZ, eds., Gott in Japan (Munich, 1973).

LOTHAR SCHREINER

Continuing Education

1. Term
2. Description
   2.1. Spread
   2.2. Tasks and Goals
   2.3. Structure and Organization
   2.4. Pedagogy
3. In the Churches
   3.1. Historical Roots
   3.2. Present-Day State
   3.3. Problems

1. Term

The term "continuing education" refers most broadly to formal study by adults, usually as part-time students. The men and women involved have gone beyond the earlier phase of their general education, where schooling represented a general preparation for life, and now are taking responsibility for their own choices about further instruction. Various institutions and voluntary groups offer the possibility of additional training or retraining in various spheres to meet the challenge of social change.

The phrase "continuing education" stands between a term such as "workers' education" (from the 19th cent.) and others denoting a combination of vocational and general education, with precise differentiation hardly possible.

2. Description

2.1. *Spread*

Continuing education is a worldwide phenomenon, though understood in various ways. It has its roots in the extension of the → industrial society (which brought to light the need for social change), decolonization (→ Colonialism), and the idea of a general establishment of → human rights. Several common, basic demands work in tension with one another: the need for lifelong learning, removal of the distinction between education and training, education for the nonprivileged, and greater state involvement. Differences arise for historical, cultural, social, and religious reasons, including discrepancies in overall → development. → Literacy programs and programs of basic education are typical in the → Third World, with a reconstruction of education as the goal. In industrialized states continuing education needs to be integrated into an established educational structure.

2.2. *Tasks and Goals*

Social change is both the basis and the general theme of continuing education (H. H. Groothoff), for which the → Enlightenment and industrialization have posed two tasks. Its offerings must correspond to individual needs that general life changes have revealed, and it must meet the demands of adjustment to social development. The education may take the form of fostering personal aptitudes, helping people in their → vocation, or teaching them to master social problems or to achieve social skills in such spheres as personal life, → family life, vocation, → leisure, public life, and social involvement on a global scale. Needs both are the result of adjustment and provide the demand for it. A sense of the need for self-determination, however, may provoke resistance to responding to a presumed need.

When the state promotes continuing education, the expectation arises that it will help people meet new qualifications demanded by the labor market (→ Work), that it will promote integration into society, and that it will help to avoid or settle social → conflicts. The increasing use of continuing education as a tool of the state is in tension with a concept of education oriented to self-education and self-determination. What H. Dauber calls "wilde Erwachsenbildung" (unmanaged continuing education) is a reaction to this situation of tension.

2.3. *Structure and Organization*

In the older industrial states, continuing education began with individual or group initiatives and led to the founding of organizations or free institutions devoted to it. More structured forms then followed, but it was only later that the state itself began to promote continuing education. Today the picture is complex, ranging from ad hoc courses and seminars to the offerings of organizations of various kinds and finally to the structured programs of community schools, colleges, universities, seminaries, and churches.

2.4. *Pedagogy*

Adults learn in the same way as children (→ Childhood) and young people but under different conditions and for different reasons. They themselves decide when, where, and why they will learn, making what H.-D. Raapke has called the didactic choice. They learn in the course of life, in a specific situation in which they sense the need for learning, using all previous life experiences as a foundation for their further education. A longer period of formal education makes participation in continuing education more likely, but for anyone, obstacles may exist in one's working life, requiring special efforts in the sphere of continuing education to achieve equality of opportunity (e.g., through the provision of study leaves). A general cultural problem is that learning is not traditionally viewed as something for adults (W. Schulenberg).

The special conditions of continuing education have led from the outset to forms of organization that differ from those of schools. Soon after World War I, which led to questioning of traditional education, the pedagogical issues of the goal, content, and form of continuing education came under discussion. The key concept has been that of a working partnership of equals.

After World War II group pedagogics took up this thought, but at first with a stronger emphasis on methodology, which came to be regarded as typical in some circles. With a realistic reversal around 1960, content came to the fore again. The pedagogical models of schools were modified to suit adults. Such models are adapted to processes that offer certifiable qualifications but not where offerings must be oriented to specific needs (e.g., the solution of problems).

In deciding its content, continuing education must engage the participants, giving them a role in defining the method and goal, helping to formulate in the process their own needs and solutions, and offering them the means to solve their own problems. This approach has led to the emphasis of important terms like → "experience," "conflict," "situation," "everyday world," and "mode of interpretation," which have become part of frank and uninhibited discussion that is also relevant for churches who sponsor continuing education (E. Lange, G. Strunk).

In the West, much of the discussion relates to institutional learning. In the Third World (I. Illich, P. Freire), orientation to the participants, in criticism of irrelevant institutions and professionalism, takes the form of self-direction and has been worked out in attempts at continuing education outside schools, which in turn have influenced those of industrialized countries (Dauber, E. Meueler).

3. In the Churches

3.1. *Historical Roots*

Continuing education in the church has a twofold origin. On the one hand, it arose from the close relation between → mission and the adult catechumenate (→ Catechesis). On the other hand, it has come from a desire to meet the challenges of the modern age, as also has been the motivation of the church's social work (e.g., A. Kolping, J. H. Wichern; → Diakonia).

3.2. *Present-Day State*

Development of continuing education by the church has been much the same in Europe and North America. The main difference is between a plural structure and a more centrally controlled structure, although both exist. Only with the former can the church take part in public continuing education. In situations where the education is more centrally controlled, the church is more limited, able to offer only a pedagogically sound adult catechumenate and to make a voluntary contribution to social dialogue.

In the Third World the churches and church institutions have taken the initiative in basic education. In Germany the churches share in public continuing education, though in the selection of contents and goals they focus on theological and personal education, educational questions, and social and political instruction (→ Development; Environment; Peace). They have achieved a certain competence in educating marginalized groups, offering courses on the national, state, diocesan, and local levels.

For reasons both of politics and of economics, the tendency recently has been to view continuing education less as a matter of public responsibility and more as simply education made available in the open market, which has led to an emphasis on vocational training. For their part, churches in their efforts in continuing education seek to have the state guarantee equal educational opportunities for all.

3.3. *Problems*

Continuing education must continually face questions about its theological and pedagogical basis and validity. It must maintain the delicate balance between its orientation to the proclamation of its message and its focus on the situation of the learners. Organizational issues also require attention, as do the problem of the nature of the church (the church for others, its role in → civil religion, the need for critical ferment) and the matter of how churches should relate to society (distinct from it? part of it?). A related issue concerning → anthropology asks how to interpret and respect human adulthood.

Discussion of these matters is forcing the churches to consider their unclarified relation to the dialectical legacy of the Enlightenment, which has such an impact on continuing education. It also keeps them open to the questions of their contemporaries regarding this life and the next, and encourages them to accept their maturity, to trust their tradition, and to prove themselves redemptive and helpful.

Bibliography: General reference works: C. Knapper, *Lifelong Learning and Higher Education* (London, 1989) • S. B. Merriam and P. M. Cunningham, eds., *Handbook of Adult and Continuing Education* (San Francisco, 1989) • F. Pöggeler, ed., *Handbuch der Erwachsenenbildung* (8 vols.; Stuttgart, 1974ff.) • E. Schmitz and H. Tietgens, eds., *Enzyklopädie Erziehungswissenschaft*, vol. 11, *Erwachsenenbildung* (Stuttgart, 1984) • R. Tippelt, ed., *Handbuch Erwachsenenbildung/Weiterbildung* (Opladen, 1994) • I. Wirth, ed., *Handwörterbuch der Erwachsenenbildung* (Paderborn, 1978).

On church-sponsored continuing education: G. Buttler et al., eds., *Lernen und Handeln. Bausteine zu einer Konzeption evangelischer Erwachsenenbildung* (Karlsruhe, 1980) • W. Deresch, *Handbuch für kirchliche Erwachsenenbildung* (Hamburg, 1973) • Deutsche evangelische Arbeitsgemeinschaft für Erwachsenenbildung, *Evangelische Erwachsenenbildung–ein Auftrag der Kirche* (Karlsruhe, 1983) • Kammer der EKD für Bildung und Erziehung, *Erwachsenenbildung als Aufgabe der evangelischen Kirche* (Gütersloh, 1983) • E. Lange, "Sprachschule für die Freiheit," *Bildung als Problem und Funktion der Kirche* (ed. R. Schloz; Munich, 1980) • C. Meier, *Kirchliche Erwachsenenbildung. Ein Beitrag zu ihrer Begründung* (Stuttgart, 1979) • G. Strunk, "Evangelische Erwachsenenbildung. Ziele–Inhalte–Formen," *HPTh(G)* 3.

Gottfried Buttler

Contraception, Contraceptives → Birth Control

Conversion

1. Conversion to Christian Faith

In Christian usage, but also in other religions, "conversion" denotes a sudden or longer process of complete reorientation on the part of individuals or groups. One might say that a person was converted to → Islam or that a tribe of Saxons was converted to Christianity. Conversion is from and to. It refers to a fundamental change of conviction that leads to visible results, such as joining another religious communion, changing one's lifestyle, or adopting a new self-understanding (including at times a new name). It might also entail a return, as, for example, in the proclamation of the OT → prophets, who summoned the apostate people to return to their → covenant with God. As a rule, conversion has a transcendent component. Especially in Christian usage the reorientation is always connected with faith in God.

In Christian usage, "conversion" primarily means acceptance of faith in Christ. In a narrower sense, however, it is also used for the change from one denomination to another. The first section of this article considers the former meaning; the second treats the latter.

1.1. Conversion, Mission, and Evangelism

Conversion is a leading concept in → mission. Traditionally, mission has aimed to convert pagans (including the adherents of other religions) to Christian faith (→ Gentiles, Gentile Christianity). When conversion takes place, it leads to → baptism. Conversion and baptism are the subjective and objective sides of the same process of mission. Yet there may be important differences in theological evaluation. Protestant missions normally regard conversion as the presupposition of baptism, but on the Roman Catholic view, a long process of Christian instruction might follow baptism. Some Protestant missions

stress individual conversion, but others seek tribal conversion on the ground that individual conversion is too much to ask of primitive peoples.

"Conversion" is also a leading term in → evangelism, occurring typically in the context of various efforts in Christianized countries to (re)awaken dead Christians to spiritual life (e.g., using tent missions, evangelistic campaigns, or → inner mission). Indeed, the focus of such efforts is conversion, which is usually understood as → regeneration. Here more strongly than in missions abroad, it is held that conversion is a clearly perceptible and datable turning point that manifests itself in the confession (public or private) of giving one's life to → Jesus Christ. Baptism is here presupposed.

A kind of ecumenical consensus has arisen regarding conversion. In the Roman Catholic view, the mediation of salvation involves a total and radical reorientation, a profound transformation in mind and heart (Paul VI, *Evangelii nuntiandi* 10). The evangelical Lausanne statement (1974) affirms that God wills that everyone should repent and be converted (§3). An ecumenical declaration on mission and evangelism (Geneva, 1982) states that the proclamation of the gospel carries with it the invitation to recognize and accept Christ's saving lordship in a personal decision (§10). Common to each of these statements is the belief that in every case → discipleship of Jesus Christ entails a personal conversion. (In ecumenical circles, "conversion" is not normally used to describe the transfer of Christians from their original confession to a new one or to a new communion. For a review of this usage, see 2.)

1.2. Biblical, Ecclesiastical, and
     Theological Aspects

1.2.1. The new ecumenical → consensus comes close to the biblical view of conversion. The summons to convert or return to God is a fundamental part of the OT message, especially in the Prophets. The prophets call upon the whole people, or later the faithful remnant or even individuals, to return to total → obedience. Returning is the presupposition of deliverance and → salvation.

Similarly, Jesus' preaching can be summarized as, "The kingdom of God has come near; repent, and believe in the good news" (Mark 1:15 and par.). The coming of the end time stresses the urgency of a change of mind (*metanoia*), of turning (*epistrephō*), of regeneration (in John). Explicitly or implicitly, the summons to make this decision runs through all the NT writings and is a constituent part of Paul's doctrine of → justification. There is no insistence, however, upon a fixed method or form of conversion.

1.2.2. This latitude helps to explain why, although

a concern for conversion runs like a red thread through the Fathers, its form and theological significance vary widely and often seem to be very indefinite. The list of model conversions goes from → Paul through → Augustine (354-430), M. → Luther (1483-1546), J. → Calvin (1509-64), Count N. L. von → Zinzendorf (1700-1760), J. → Wesley (1703-91), and to the present day, but there is no single pattern in each.

Every essay in dogmatics throughout the history of theology has a chapter on conversion and repentance (→ Penitence), but the contents vary between a traditional Roman Catholic emphasis on the liturgical and sacramental aspects, the Lutheran view of remorse and penitence as a daily exercise and ongoing attitude, and the → Pietist stress on a once-for-all and datable experience of conversion. In view of the deepening cleft between Christianity as a whole and the norms and values of a secular → industrial society, conversion has taken on new significance as the call to a self-conscious Christian lifestyle and a nonconforming attitude (e.g., note the emphasis on conversion in the report of the European Ecumenical Assembly on peace and justice, held in Basel in May 1989).

1.2.3. Theologically, conversion is often equated with repentance, although with a rather narrower reference than one finds in the Bible. Biblically, conversion consists primarily, not of turning *from* → sin, but of turning *to* → faith in Jesus Christ, which carries with it a total transformation. What is involved is a new manner of life that lines up with the aims and values of the kingdom of God as these manifest themselves in Jesus Christ. The personal component is important in this regard. Conversion is the answer of each → person to God's individual call. It marks the interaction between the divine work and the human response.

1.3. *Contextual Factors*
Because of the necessarily personal component, conversion always involves psychological, sociocultural, and political factors.

1.3.1. Conversion is especially common among young people (→ Youth) in the late stages of puberty, when they are seeking a steadying direction for life. Evangelists definitely make use of this factor, which can lead to phenomena governed by mass psychology.

1.3.2. Sociocultural factors also may be involved. In Latin America, for example, there is a relatively high rate of conversion to the → Pentecostal churches, with converts belonging, as a rule, to the upward-moving lower middle class. In and with their conversion, these people typically adopt a new ethic

of seriousness, industry, and asceticism (e.g., no smoking or drinking), which aids them in their social ascent. Similarly, mass conversions among the outcasts in India in the last century had something to do with the fact that these people, who were socially and culturally excluded from traditional → Hindu society, could better their social situation and cultural valuation by turning to Western Christianity.

1.3.3. Finally, conversion always has political implications. Thus in a → colonial context it could lead to shifts of power between different groups in the population. Under the banner of Pietism it might also involve a deliberate withdrawal from politics, which would in effect confirm the status quo. Conversely, the Latin American theology of → liberation speaks of a turning to the oppressed.

In the larger sense, the shaping of conversion by Western → anthropology and → culture as a result of the history of Christianity in Europe stands clearly in tension today with its original theological basis and goal. Because conversion always means both the act of faith and the outward expression of its implications, it can never be rid of this tension. It contains both the reorientation of conviction and the ethical and social implications of this reorientation.

Bibliography: W. BARCLAY, *Turning to God* (Philadelphia, 1964) • K. BARTH, *CD* IV/2, 305ff., 557ff. • *Christentum ohne Bekehrung?* (= *Das missionarische Wort* 3/74 [1974]) • W. CONN, *Christian Conversion: A Developmental Interpretation of Autonomy and Surrender* (New York, 1986); idem, ed., *Conversion: Perspectives on Personal and Social Transformation* (New York, 1978) • *Conversion* (= *ER* 19 [1967]) • P. LÖFFLER, "Conversion," *DEM* 229-30 • J. TRIEBEL, *Bekehrung als Ziel der missionarischen Verkündigung* (Erlangen, 1976).

PAUL LÖFFLER

2. Conversion as Denominational Change
Besides its reference to a personal affirmation of faith in Christ, the word "conversion" may also be used to describe a change of allegiance that a person makes within the larger Christian family. Roman Catholics used to reserve the term for transfer from another body to the → Roman Catholic Church, with any other change being called "perversion" (1917 CIC 1070.1; also 1060). → Vatican II suggested "reconciliation," but since strictly this term applied only to lapsed Roman Catholics, it was quickly replaced by "admission into the full communion of the Catholic Church" (*Directory on Ecumenism* [1967]).

2.1. *The Ecumenical Problem*
→ Neoscholastic Roman Catholic theology taught a divine duty of conversion to Roman Catholicism

(1917 CIC 1322; Encyclical *Mortalium animos* [1928]). Vatican II, however, regarded non–Roman Catholic churches as instruments of salvation and thus differentiated the reception of non–Roman Catholic Christians from the ecumenical task, stating clearly that the latter is not a means of conversion.

In the Protestant tradition the distinction between the invisible and the visible church has more easily carried with it an acknowledgment that there might be access to → salvation even in a false church. The thesis that affirmation of the doctrine of → justification necessarily implies conversion from Roman Catholicism had to be rejected because of its exclusive claim and also because of the deep commonalities in the understanding of Christian faith (→ Unity). It has seemed better to view denominational change as simply a change of fellowship within the church of Christ (R. Frieling).

Ecumenical studies oppose → proselytism, but ecclesiological differences have so far prevented churches from resolving the conflict between the duty of individual churches to bear witness to the truth and their ecumenical responsibility for one another (cf. the official reports of the → World Council of Churches [WCC] and the Roman Catholic Church in 1967 and 1971; → Ecumenical Theology).

→ Judaism makes no exclusive claim to salvation and thus has developed no systematic → mission. Those who adopt it become members of the Jewish people as well as the religious fellowship. → Islam tolerates Jews and Christians within the theocratic Islamic fellowship. According to the classic theory, death is the punishment for apostasy from Islam.

2.2. *In Practice*

For the most part, churches today refrain from wooing and winning but no longer find any ecumenical problem in conversions for reasons of conscience. Roman Catholic → church law recognizes, though with no more exact definition, a formal act of departure from the Roman Catholic Church, which liberates from specified legal obligations (1983 CIC 1086.1, 1117, 1124). Conditional → baptism is no longer imposed on non–Roman Catholic Christians who join the church (since 1967), nor is there now a lifting of excommunication, since these converts are not returning after sinful separation. Reception usually takes place during the → Eucharist and with a confession of faith (with the addition "I believe and profess all that the holy Catholic Church believes, teaches, and proclaims as revealed by God") and the → laying on of hands or confirmation (→ Initiation Rites 2). The ceremony is conducted by the → priest.

→ Orthodox churches, insofar as they are in fellowship with the WCC, are also content with confirmation in the case of the baptized who convert to them.

Protestant churches, too, have for the most part a liturgical act of reception in the presence of witnesses. There need not be an act of public confession similar to that made in confirmation. The real incorporation comes with admission to the Eucharist, or with partaking of it, although the mere fact that non-Protestants communicate does not of itself involve a denominational change.

In all churches, reception presupposes prior pastoral discussion that clarifies the motives and introduces the new member to the church's life. Dogmatic instruction alone does not do justice to the situation of those who are making the change or to the complexity of the → denominational problem. In countries like Germany, legal questions are involved, and care must be taken not to violate the constitutional freedom of religion (→ Religious Liberty). Arrangements for easier transfer have sometimes been made, for example, between certain territorial churches and the → free churches.

2.3. *Motives*

The actual motives involved in a denominational change are seldom fully identical with what is consciously felt and stated. Also to be noted is biographical stylization in the testimonies of converts. Social and psychological predispositions yield types of motivation that might vary from age to age.

We may ignore conversions that simply involve assimilation to a social background (e.g., through immigration or marriage), that are for political reasons (e.g., Henry of Navarre in 1593 or Augustus of Saxony in 1697), that are due to political pressure (e.g., forcible baptisms of Jews), or that are from non-Christian religions. There is a fluid boundary between normal denominational changes and those that lead from a previous indifference to committed Christianity and thus represent genuine conversions (see 1). The latter may involve a return in faith to one's own previous church (e.g., Paul Claudel in 1886).

Even today the conflict that the → Reformation initiated between the experience of justification and the ecclesiastical → institution lends an emancipatory character to conversion to Protestantism. As a rule, it is occasioned less by a positive ideal concept of Protestantism than by negative experiences with one's own church — for example, legalism in discipline, in the practice of penance (→ Penitent), or in moral teaching — or by criticism of its authoritarian structure.

If Protestantism seems more open, but also more

susceptible, to the spirit of the age, situations of historical crisis often cause conversions to the Roman Catholic Church. Roman Catholic canonizing of converts as saints (e.g., Edith Stein in 1987 or Niels Stensen in 1988) underlines its ecclesiological claim. Accounts of conversion state as typical reasons for change the search for → authority, certainty, and security. Where there has previously been a subjective Protestant Christianity, we find a turning to the objectivity of the church, which with its teaching (→ dogma instead of → confession [of faith], the magisterium, or → teaching office, instead of → pluralism), its dispensing of salvation (→ sacrament instead of Word-event), and its structure (→ hierarchy instead of uncontrollable → charisma) claims to embody the divine in the world and to bear witness to it in supratemporal ethical → norms, and which is thus constantly found to be bulwark against the → Enlightenment, → liberalism, and the decay of values (e.g., during the period after World War I and II; → Romanticism; Restoration).

Another motive among those who convert to the Catholic Church is the desire for palpability and religious experience. The pedagogically curative concepts of → grace and → sanctification seem to be more human than the doctrine of forensic justification, and the Roman Catholic → liturgy, along with its → piety, as in the veneration of → Mary, seems to meet a need for palpability and wholeness.

A third motive is the longing for continuity, unity, and fullness. Conversion means renunciation of the Protestant Scripture principle, confession of the NT church and the Fathers (H. Bürkle), and ecumenical signs (Anglo-Catholicism; → Una Sancta Movement).

When conversion is to the → free churches, the reasons include personal awakening, the striving for sanctification, and dissatisfaction with a lack of commitment. In Latin America the → Pentecostal churches are growing at a rate of 25 percent a year because the members of the lower classes in the cities, who are not reached by the pastoral ministry of the Catholic Church, are made aware of their → human dignity by the democratizing of the Word in theology and liturgy and are thus enabled to face their socioeconomic problems with a strictly spiritual interpretation.

Conversions from Christianity to Judaism may often be traced to decision for an ethical → monotheism without the burden of a historically compromised dogma of redemption (→ Christology), and also for a form of faith that has been proved in extreme situations (→ Diaspora; Holocaust) as well as in → everyday life.

Islam has had some successes in its missionary work in the West, for example among North American blacks and South American → Indians. It can claim some spectacular converts (e.g., some prominent American black athletes).

2.4. Evaluation

Describing sociologically and psychologically the types of piety that arise in the various denominations can help us better understand the process of conversion and defuse the → polemics, but it has only a limited value from the standpoint of explaining conversions. The denominations do not see themselves as merely the result of anthropological types or sociopsychological tendencies. Truly ecumenical → dialogue is not possible unless each church views itself as being related to the truth of the → gospel. Furthermore, most denominations offer a varied phenomenological picture that can lead to disappointment for converts who are seeking an ideal type.

The step taken, for example, by a couple entering a so-called → mixed marriage can express the precedence of a commonly lived-out faith over differing confessional statements. Converts who do not deny their inheritance can have the function of an ecumenical bridge, though the same motive can also cause those who are ready for conversion to stay in their own churches.

To the extent that converts see confessional differences more sharply, conversions are a warning against an ecumenism of compromise (F. Mußner). All the churches agree that conversions can sharpen the ecumenical task, although they themselves do not offer a solution.

Bibliography: K. ALAND, *Über den Glaubenswechsel in der Geschichte des Christentums* (Berlin, 1961) • "Evangelicals and Catholics Together: The Christian Mission in the Third Millennium," *First Things*, no. 43 (May 1994) 15-22 • R. FRIELING, *Konfessionswechsel heute* (Göttingen, 1979) • JOINT WORKING GROUP OF THE WORLD COUNCIL OF CHURCHES AND THE ROMAN CATHOLIC CHURCH, "Common Witness and Proselytism," *ER* 23 (1971) 9-20; idem, "Second Official Report," *ER* 19 (1967) 461-67 • A. T. KHOURY, *Toleranz im Islam* (Munich, 1980) • F. MUSSNER, "Warum noch Konversionen?" *IKaZ* 4 (1975) 331-38 • H.-J. PRIEN, *Die Geschichte des Christentums in Lateinamerika* (Göttingen, 1978) • L. I. RABINOWITZ and D. M. EICHHORN, "Proselytes," *EncJud* 13.1182-93 • K. RAHNER, "Konversion," *SM* 3.39-47 • W. SUCKER, "Konvertiten," *RGG* (3d ed.) 3.1795-98.

WALTER SCHÖPSDAU

Coptic Orthodox Church

1. Strictly speaking, the name "Coptic Orthodox Church" applies only to the ancient Oriental Orthodox Church in Egypt. It is wrongly used also for the → Ethiopian Orthodox Church. The head of the Coptic Orthodox Church is traditionally called the pope or → patriarch of → Alexandria. The title "pope" was used for the bishop of Alexandria before it came into use for the bishop of Rome (→ Pope, Papacy).

2. Tradition ascribes the origin of the Coptic Orthodox Church to St. Mark, whom it regards as the first → bishop of Alexandria. According to Egyptian sources, John Mark came from the Pentapolis and was one of the 70 disciples of → Jesus. By means of its catechetical school, Alexandria became the spiritual center of the Christian church. This school produced → Origen (ca. 185-ca. 254; → Origenism) and → Athanasius (ca. 297-373), two of its best-known teachers (→ Alexandrian Theology).

The Coptic Orthodox Church begins its reckoning of time with the Diocletian → persecution. St. Anthony the Egyptian (250?-356) probably moved off into the desert in 285. Around the year 305 he came out of isolation and organized the many who had fled to the desert during the persecution into a monastic community. → Martyrdom and → monasticism in the early fourth century, along with the scholarship of the catechetical schools, were significant for the character and → spirituality of the Coptic Orthodox Church.

The Council of Chalcedon (451) was the occasion of a deep-seated breach with the Byzantine imperial church, though this was due less to theological differences than to conflicts between → Hellenism and the culture of Africa and Asia Minor. In the fifth and sixth centuries the Byzantine emperors made repeated attempts at reconciliation but were rebuffed by the stubborn Copts. During the second half of the sixth century Jacob Baradai (ca. 500-578), bishop of Edessa, traveled around Egypt and Syria and consolidated the anti-Byzantine church of Africa and Asia Minor, which has wrongly been labeled → Monophysite or Jacobite (→ Oriental Orthodox Churches). The anti-Byzantine attitude of the Egyptians helped to make possible the Persian conquest of Egypt in 616, and a generation later the Arab conquest.

Under al-Ḥākim (caliph 996-1021), thousands of Coptic churches were destroyed and hundreds of thousands of Christians forced to convert to → Islam. Christianity to a large extent went under-

ground. In the 12th century the Coptic Orthodox Church suffered as a result of the → Crusades, though the Arab leader Saladin (d. 1193) later brought a semblance of justice (→ Righteousness, Justice) and order to the devastated land and founded the line of Ayyubid caliphs, who were for the most part tolerant. With incursions into Egypt from western Europe in the 16th century, the anti-Latin attitude became even more intense than the anti-Byzantine. The relation between Islam and Christianity has vacillated in Egypt between → tolerance and persecution. Attempts at mission, which the Copts rejected, led to controversies with France and Britain in the 19th century.

3. In 1968 three events brought new life and enthusiasm to the Coptic Orthodox Church: apparitions of → Mary at a church in Zaytūn, a suburb of Cairo; the return of the → relics of St. Mark from Venice to Egypt; and the dedication of the gigantic cathedral of St. Mark in Cairo.

In 1986 Amba Shenouda III (b. 1923, enthroned 1971), the pope and patriarch, the 117th successor of St. Mark, was placed under house arrest, along with the leaders of certain Islamic groups. After his release, however, he was able to resume his normal duties.

Today the Coptic Orthodox Church has over five million members, 60 bishops, 1,800 priests, and two large seminaries (in Cairo and Alexandria). For the most part the liturgy of St. Basil is used. → Worship takes place in a mixture of Coptic and Arabic. There are nine monasteries for men, with about 350 monks, and seven for women, with 200 nuns. The Coptic Orthodox Church is a member of the → World Council of Churches and other ecumenical organizations.

→ Nestorians; Orthodoxy 3

Bibliography: A. S. ATIYA, "Coptic Church," *EncRel(E)* 4.82-86; idem, *A History of Eastern Christianity* (London, 1968) 11-145; idem, ed., *The Coptic Encyclopedia* (8 vols.; New York, 1991) • N. VAN DOORN-HARDER and K. VOGT, *Between Desert and City: The Coptic Orthodox Church Today* (Oslo, 1997) • E. R. HARDY, *Christian Egypt* (Oxford, 1952) • O. MEINARDUS, *Christian Egypt, Ancient and Modern* (Cairo, 1965); idem, *Christian Egypt: Faith and Life* (Cairo, 1970) • T. H. PARTRICK, *Traditional Egyptian Christianity: A History of the Coptic Orthodox Church* (Greensboro, N.C., 1996) • P. VERGHESE, ed., *Koptisches Christentum. Die orthodoxe Kirchen Ägyptens und Äthiopiens* (Stuttgart, 1973) bibliography.

PAULOS MAR GREGORIOS

Corinthians, Epistles to the

1. Significance
2. History of the Corinthian Church
3. Literary Data
4. First Corinthians
5. Second Corinthians
6. Edition and Redaction

1. Significance

The Corinthian epistles of the apostle → Paul are a collection of letters from the middle of the first century A.D. This collection contains important documents that throw light on a decisive period of the history of the → primitive Christian community. The letters show that different Christian groups stood in opposition to each other and that firm theological and ethical positions had not been defined regarding the social, cultural, and religious situation in the cosmopolitan city of Corinth. In addition to helping us to see how Christian identity was developing, they also give evidence of the way in which Paul's own theology was taking shape in response to the demands posed by the → congregation and his opponents.

2. History of the Corinthian Church

The history of the church in Corinth can to a degree be gleaned from 1 and 2 Corinthians and from Acts 18:1-18 and 18:24–19:1.

2.1. Little is known about the origins of the Corinthian church. Luke's report in Acts 18:1-18 is probably based on the foundation account of that church. First and Second Corinthians presuppose that Paul was its sole founder, which does not rule out his having rivals for leadership (see 1 Cor. 3:5-15; 2 Cor. 10:13-16).

2.2. The epistles cover only a relatively short period in the church's history, probably A.D. 54/55-55/56. Problems had apparently arisen in the congregation very soon after its founding, which rapidly led to a crisis that threatened to destroy the new church. The problems may have been caused by the fact that in Corinth Paul's → mission came into contact for the first time with a highly civilized and sophisticated Hellenistic metropolis. The congregation consisted of several independent groups and individuals, some of whom proceeded to interpret Paul's → gospel in forms and life characteristic of Hellenistic religion, including → Gnostic trends.

Paul hoped to be able to overcome these problems by writing 1 Corinthians, but it is evident from 2 Corinthians that the crisis had intensified and taken a new turn. The details may be gleaned from the epistles only to a limited degree. We have gaps in our knowledge because other letters exchanged between Paul and the church have not been preserved, and also because some of the communications were oral (1 Cor. 1:11; 4:17; 16:10; 2 Cor. 7:6-7, etc.).

Whereas in 1 Corinthians questions of religious and moral conduct are to the fore, the focus in 2 Corinthians is on Paul's → apostleship; his person, qualifications, and integrity are challenged as well as his office. Second Corinthians shows Paul clearly on the defensive, an apostle who in his struggle is driven to using all the weapons of rhetoric and diplomacy at his command. Note should also be taken of the highly effective mediating ministry of his coworker Titus (2 Cor. 2:13; 7:6, 13-14; 8:6, 16, 23). From the so-called letter of reconciliation (see 5), we may gather that the Corinthians had been convinced by his arguments in his earlier "letter of tears" (see 5), so that he can express his joy at the restoration of harmony at the conclusion of the correspondence.

Chapters 8 and 9 are most probably fragments of originally independent letters, written for the purpose of recommencing and completing the collection for the church in → Jerusalem, which the crisis had interrupted. In Romans Paul can announce that the collection is now complete and that he is about to go to Jerusalem to deliver it (Rom. 15:23-33).

2.3. Paul's opponents play an important role in the Corinthian controversies, though it is not clear precisely what that role was. The "parties" (1 Cor. 1:10-15; 11:18; 12:25) seem linked to opposition to Paul only to a limited degree. Whether his opponents in 2 Corinthians are the same as in 1 Corinthians, or new ones, or a combination of both, is contested. Both the opponents and the points at issue have a somewhat different profile in the two epistles. In 1 Corinthians Paul offers the criticism that among the Corinthian Christians a wealth of eloquence and knowledge (1 Cor. 1:5; cf. 2 Cor. 8:7) is confused with a high degree of maturity in the faith. In 2 Corinthians, however, Paul rebuts charges of incompetence, corruption, and charlatanism that are brought against him.

2.4. Apart from brief references in Acts 20:2 and Rom. 15:25-28, little is known about further developments in the Corinthian church. *First Clement* (→ Apostolic Fathers 2.3.1) draws a warning example from the confusion at Corinth, but we cannot say whether the new problems in the church were causally related to the old (see *1 Clem.* 47:1-7).

3. Literary Data

Only a part of the total Corinthian correspondence has come down to us. The preserved letters include whole letters (1 Corinthians and the "letter of reconciliation"), but many scholars find fragments of other letters in 2 Corinthians. Their edition and redaction in 2 Corinthians require the assumption of a redactor in the post-Pauline period (see 6). We do not possess Paul's letter mentioned in 1 Cor. 5:9, 11, nor have the inquiries addressed to Paul been preserved (see 1 Cor. 7:1; 8:1; 12:1; 16:1, 12). It is quite likely that there were other letters of which there is no mention. The so-called 3 Corinthians is a later fabrication.

4. First Corinthians

First Corinthians was written from Ephesus (16:8) in about A.D. 55. Although its unity is accepted, there is scholarly debate about its composition and genre. The letter's argumentative structure is of the deliberative kind. Regarding its composition, the main features are fairly clear. The epistolary prescript (1:1-3) is followed by an exordium (1:4-9) and a *narratio* (1:10-17), in which the problem of the situation is set forth. The Corinthians can claim great riches in eloquence and knowledge (1:5), but they suffer from practical inadequacies regarding communal love (1:6-7), a dangerous discrepancy that Paul traces to the divisions in the congregation (1:10-17; 11:18; 12:25).

The argument contains a first, more theoretical section (1:18–4:21) consisting of a critical analysis of the Corinthians' self-appraisal in the light of the Pauline doctrine of → justification by faith.

The second main section (chaps. 5–15) is devoted to practical problems in the church resulting from the → freedom of the gospel (see 6:12; 10:23; 12:13). Questions of family ethics are dominant in chaps. 5–7. Chap. 5 deals with a striking example of a member of the church "living with his father's wife" (v. 1). In 6:1-11 the apostle deals with lawsuits between members of the church; in 6:12-20 the subject is → prostitution. Chap. 7 submits new regulations concerning → marriage and → celibacy. The following chapters discuss regulations concerning relations to pagan religion. Chap. 8 focuses on the implications of idol worship, especially → sacrifices made to idols (idol meats). Chap. 9 sets forth Paul's apostleship as a model of freedom and responsibility. In 10:1–11:1 Paul continues to establish rules regarding the attitude to pagan cultic meals (→ Gentiles, Gentile Christianity). In the comprehensive section 11:2–14:40 Paul then turns to questions of Christian → worship. The proper role of → women is the first issue (11:2-16), followed by directives concerning the celebration of the → Eucharist (11:17-34). The emphasis is on the phenomenon of "enthusiasm" at Corinth, including spiritual gifts (chap. 12), → glossolalia, and → prophecy (chap. 14). The hymn to love is interposed in chap. 13. In chap. 15 Paul presents a detailed argument justifying belief in the → resurrection from the dead (vv. 1-57), with the peroration of the argument coming in v. 58. Chap. 16 brings the customary closing regulations, travel information, and greetings.

5. Second Corinthians

Unlike 1 Corinthians, 2 Corinthians supports little scholarly consensus concerning its unity. Since the days of J. S. Semler (1776) there has been continuing debate about the number, extent, and chronological sequence of the assumed letters and letter fragments included in 2 Corinthians. The component elements can be summarized as follows. In 2:14–6:13 and 7:2-4, Paul offers a first apology, depicting himself as a herald at the head of a procession (2:14; 5:20-21; 6:11). What moved the apostle to write in this vein is not stated directly. Probably doubts had been raised about his fitness for the apostolic office (2:16; 3:5), compelling Paul to defend himself.

A second apology in 10:1–13:10, probably identical with the "letter of tears" (see 2:3-4), is much sharper in tone. If this is a later letter, it is assumed that the first apology (2:14–6:13 and 7:2-4) had not been successful. Paul quotes from an extremely negative assessment of his person (10:10; 11:6), which no doubt emanated from his opponents (10:10; cf. 2:5-7; 7:12). In answer he offers a brilliant defense sharpened by irony and sarcasm. At the heart of this defense is his "foolish discourse," a parody of himself as a fool (11:1–12:10). Here Paul displays the "signs of an apostle" that his opponents demanded of him (12:12). Demonstrating, however, that these signs can easily be faked, he disputes that they can serve to validate an apostle's credibility. If this apology was in a separate letter, it was probably carried to Corinth by Titus (7:6-7).

The "letter of reconciliation" (1:1–2:13 plus 7:5-16 and 13:11-13) expresses Paul's joy at the reconciliation that Titus has effected between the apostle and his church (2:13; 7:6, 13-15). Along with further details about the crisis, this letter contains an interpretation of the "letter of tears" (10:1–13:10) and the winning back of the community that it achieved, which Titus could report to Paul when he met him in Macedonia (7:6-13a).

Chaps. 8 and 9, in our view, represent fragments of two originally independent letters concerned with administration and fund-raising. The letter of chap. 8 legitimates the sending of Titus and two church members as delegates to Corinth to reactivate and complete the financial collection that had been interrupted by the crisis. Chap. 9 is a letter to the churches of Achaia asking for their sympathetic assistance to Corinth in bringing the collection to completion. In 9:6-14 we find a detailed explanation of the spiritual nature and purpose of this collection, which also offers evidence of the apostle's ecclesiastical strategies.

The section 6:14–7:1 presents a special problem in that many scholars do not attribute it to Paul. Rather, it seems to reflect a strictly Jewish-Christian theology (→ Jewish Christians 1) when it issues an uncompromising warning (directed at Paul?) against consorting with "unbelievers."

6. Edition and Redaction

If we have 1 and 2 Corinthians as a corpus of several letters, we apparently owe their present form and arrangement to an unknown editor or redactor. J. Weiß and others have postulated certain redactional changes in 1 Corinthians. If it is not an original unity, the arrangement of the letter fragments in 2 Corinthians must be the work of a post-Pauline redactor. The redactor took the "letter of reconciliation" (1:1–2:13 plus 7:5-16 and 13:11-13) as a frame, in which he inserted the various fragments at different places. The reasons for the specific placing of the insertions have yet to be fully explained; at any rate, the prescripts and postscripts of these inserted letters must have been omitted, as was the custom also in other editions of letters. The fact that the redactor believed 6:14–7:1 to be from Paul shows that he had a deutero-Pauline understanding of Paul.

Bibliography: Commentaries on 1 and 2 Corinthians: F. Lang (NTD; Göttingen, 1986) • H. Lietzmann and W. G. Kümmel (HNT; 5th ed.; Tübingen, 1969) • H. D. Wendland (NTD; Göttingen, 1980).

Commentaries on 1 Corinthians: C. K. Barrett (BNTC/HNTC; New York, 1973) • H. Conzelmann (Hermeneia; Philadelphia, 1975) • E. Fascher (THKNT; 3d ed.; Leipzig, 1984) chaps. 1-7 • G. D. Fee (NICNT; Grand Rapids, 1987) • W. Schrage, *Der erste Brief an die Korinther*, vol. 1, *1 Kor 1, 1–6, 11;* vol. 2, *1 Kor 6, 12–11, 16* (Zurich, 1991-95) • A. Strobel (ZBK; Zurich, 1989) • J. Weiss (KEK; Göttingen, 1910; repr., 1970) • C. Wolff (THKNT; 2d ed.; Leipzig, 1984) chaps. 8-16.

Commentaries on 2 Corinthians: C. K. Barrett (BNTC/HNTC; New York, 1973) • H. D. Betz, *2 Corinthians 8 and 9: Two Administrative Letters of the Apostle Paul* (Philadelphia, 1985) bibliography • R. Bultmann (Minneapolis, 1985) • M. Carrez (CNT; Geneva,

1986) • V. P. Furnish (AB; Garden City, N.Y., 1984) bibliography • H. J. Klauck (2d ed.; Würzburg, 1988) • R. H. Strachan (MNTC; London, 1935) • M. E. Thrall, *The Second Epistle to the Corinthians*, vol. 1, *Introduction and Commentary on II Corinthians I–VII* (Edinburgh, 1994) • H. Windisch (KEK; 9th ed.; Göttingen, 1970) with later bibliography.

Other works: K. Aland, "Die Entstehung des Corpus Paulinum," *Neutestamentliche Entwürfe* (Munich, 1979) 302-50 • C. K. Barrett, *Essays on Paul* (Philadelphia, 1982) • H. D. Betz, *Der Apostel Paulus und die sokratische Tradition* (Tübingen, 1972); idem, *Galatians* (Philadelphia, 1979) 329-30 on 2 Cor. 6:14–7:1; idem, *Paulinische Studien. Gesammelte Aufsätze* (vol. 3; Tübingen, 1994); idem, "The Problem of Rhetoric and Theology according to the Apostle Paul," *L'Apôtre Paul* (ed. A. Vanhoye; Louvain, 1986) 16-48; idem, "2 Cor. 6:14–7:1: An Anti-Pauline Fragment?" *JBL* 92 (1973) 88-108 • G. Bornkamm, "Die Vorgeschichte des sogenannten 2 Korintherbriefs," *Gesammelte Aufsätze* (vol. 4; Munich, 1971) 162-94 • R. Bultmann, *Exegetica* (Tübingen, 1967) • J.-F. Collange, *Énigmes de la deuxième épître de Paul aux Corinthiens* (Cambridge, 1972) • W. Deming, *Paul on Marriage and Celibacy: The Hellenistic Background of 1 Corinthians 7* (Cambridge, 1995) • D. Georgi, *The Opponents of Paul in Second Corinthians* (Philadelphia, 1986; orig. pub., 1957); idem, *Remembering the Poor: The History of Paul's Collection for Jerusalem* (Nashville, 1992; orig. pub., 1965) • J. A. Harrill, *The Manumission of Slaves in Early Christianity* (Tübingen, 1995) • R. F. Hock, *The Social Context of Paul's Ministry* (Philadelphia, 1980) • J. C. Hurd, *The Origin of 1 Corinthians* (London, 1965) • E. Käsemann, "Die Legitimität des Apostels. Eine Untersuchung zu II Kor 10–13," *ZNW* 41 (1942) 33-71 (repr. Darmstadt, 1956) • H.-J. Klauck, *Herrenmahl und hellenistischer Kult* (Münster, 1982) • G. Lüdemann, *Paulus, der Heidenapostel* (2 vols.; Göttingen, 1980-83) • W. A. Meeks, *The First Urban Christians: The Social World of the Apostle Paul* (New Haven, 1983) • M. M. Mitchell, *Paul and the Rhetoric of Reconciliation: An Exegetical Investigation of the Language and Composition of 1 Corinthians* (Tübingen, 1991) • W. Schmithals, *Gnosticism in Corinth* (Nashville, 1971) • J. Weiss, *Earliest Christianity: A History of the Period* A.D. *30-150* (New York, 1959; orig. pub., 1917) • L. L. Welborn, "On the Discord in Corinth: 1 Cor 1–4 and Ancient Politics," *JBL* 105 (1986) 85-111.

Hans Dieter Betz

Corpora doctrinae

Corpora doctrinae (collections of teaching) are proclamations or collections of creeds and confessions. These *corpora,* which included ancient and modern statements, some of which were local and others that were accepted more universally, together document the continuity of confession and functioned to safeguard the confessional status of various territories and cities in eastern, central, and northern Germany between 1560 and 1580.

Preliminary stages are the *Doctrinalia* and teaching rules in the → church orders from 1535. The idea of *corpus doctrinae* comes from P. → Melanchthon (1497-1560). As a term for a summary of valid doctrine consonant with Scripture, it appears first in the Frankfurt Compact of 1558 (CRef 9.494). Melanchthon initiated the short epoch of doctrinal collections with his *Corpus doctrinae Christianae,* which was published in German and Latin after his death in 1560. Along with the early creeds, the *Confessio Augustana variata* (the Latin version of the Augs. Conf., published in 1540), the Apology, and Melanchthon's *Loci,* it contains four (German) or five (Latin) other later works. As the so-called *Corpus doctrinae Philippicum/Misnicum,* it gained recognition in Pomerania (1561), the Electorate of Saxony (1566), and Bremen (1572), and it aroused sympathy in Anhalt, Hessen, Schleswig-Holstein, and Denmark. Because of its Melanchthonian slant, it stirred up opposition on the → Gnesio-Lutheran side and in 1570 even brought violent controversy to Brunswick-Wolfenbüttel.

A resolution of eight northern German Hanseatic cities at Lüneburg in July 1561, opposing the Naumburg Decree, took up the question of what a *corpus doctrinae* requires. In answer they established or codified an emphatically Lutheran *corpus doctrinae* over against → Crypto-Calvinist Philippism. Before its collapse in Saxony, this produced one other *corpus doctrinae* for Nürnberg (1573) and Brandenburg-Ansbach (1574) in the so-called Normal Books, which were a mixture of → Luther and Melanchthon. → Calvinism developed no *corpus doctrinae.*

Lutheran *corpora doctrinae* appeared in Hamburg and Lübeck in 1560, in Brunswick in 1563, in Pomerania (supplementing the *Corpus doctrinae Philippicum*) in 1564, in the Reussian lands and Prussia (with an appended elucidation of nine controversies) in 1567, in Göttingen in 1568, in Brunswick-Wolfenbüttel (as a list in the church orders) in 1569, in Ducal Saxony in 1570, in Brandenburg in 1572, in Brunswick-Lüneburg and Brunswick-Wolfenbüttel (as a book) in 1576, and in Hessen-Darmstadt in 1626. M. Chemnitz (1522-86) had a hand in publishing the *corpora doctrinae* in Prussia and the two Lower Saxonies.

The various → confessions and creeds of the Julium *corpus doctrinae,* minus two tractates by U. Rhegius (1489-1541) and M. Chemnitz, found their way into the Book of Concord (1580), which, as a work for the whole of Lutheranism, ended the era of territorial *corpora doctrinae.* Because of the Philippist associations, the term was now avoided. The idea of a doctrinal collection that Chemnitz and the Hanseatic cities supported, using a Lutheran *corpus doctrinae* as the basis and adding judgments on theological controversies, underlay the concord sought by Jakob Andreae (1528-90) after a first failure in 1569/70. Since this effort did not unite all Lutherans when painfully concluded in 1577-80, local *corpora doctrinae* remained in force (e.g., in Brunswick-Wolfenbüttel, and to some extent in Pomerania). Without the intervening period of *corpora doctrinae,* the partial unification of Lutheranism would probably have been much harder to attain.

→ Formula of Concord

Bibliography: W.-D. HAUSCHILD, "Corpus Doctrinae und Bekenntnisschriften," *Bekenntnis und Einheit der Kirche* (ed. M. Brecht and R. Schwarz; Stuttgart, 1980) 235-52 • H. HEPPE and G. KAWERAU, "Corpus doctrinae," *RE* 4.293-98 • I. MAGER, "Das Corpus Doctrinae der Stadt Braunschweig im Gefüge der übrigen niedersächsischen Lehrschriftensammlungen," *Die Reformation in der Stadt Braunschweig* (Brunswick, 1978) 111-22, 139-43 • K. MÜLLER, "Die Symbole des Luthertums," *PrJ* 63 (1889) 121-48 • L. W. SPITZ and W. LOHFF, eds., *Discord, Dialogue, and Concord: Studies in the Lutheran Reformation's Formula of Concord* (Philadelphia, 1977) • T. G. TAPPERT, ed., *The Book of Concord* (Philadelphia, 1959) • J. WIRSCHING, "Bekenntnisschriften," *TRE* 5.487-511 (esp. 499-501).

INGE MAGER

Corpus Christi, Feast of → Eucharistic Spirituality

Corpus Iuris Canonici

1. Contents
   1.1. Decretum Gratiani
   1.2. Liber Extra
   1.3. Liber Sextus
   1.4. The Clementines
   1.5. The Extravagantes of John XXII
   1.6. The Extravagantes Communes

2. The Roman Edition (1582) and
   Later Editions
3. Significance

1. Contents

The Corpus Iuris Canonici (Collection of canon law) is a set of six collections of law that functioned as the primary source of Roman Catholic church law from the Middle Ages until 1918, when it was superseded by the → Codex Iuris Canonici. The Corpus was first named as such in the brief *Cum pro munere pastorali* (1580) of Gregory XIII (1572-85). Along with Roman law, the elements of the Corpus had become a part of European common law.

1.1. *Decretum Gratiani*

The Decretum Gratiani (Decree of Gratiani), originally entitled *Concordia discordantium canonum*, came into being about 1140. It is a comprehensive collection of early church law in almost 4,000 chapters, with a commentary that attempts to reconcile the contradictions between individual texts. The sources are the canons of early and medieval councils, the decretals of the popes, including the approximately 400 forged Pseudo-Isidorian decretals of the ninth century (→ False Decretals), some 1,200 patristic texts, and Roman law. Gratian, their collector and commentator, apparently was a monk and a law professor at Bologna. The work is in three parts.

1.1.1. The first part contains 973 chapters, arranged in discussion of 101 *distinctiones* (divisions). The first 20 divisions present a doctrine of legal sources. The other divisions treat the doctrine of the → ordination of clergy and election to church offices (→ Offices, Ecclesiastical). It is cited by division and chapter (e.g., 20.2).

1.1.2. The second part deals with *negotia* (legal matters) affecting clergy and laypeople. The material appears in 2,576 chapters, grouped together under 36 fictitious *causae* (cases), which are in turn subdivided into specific *quaestiones* (questions). This comprehensive second part presents the church's law of procedure, property, marriage, and punishment. It is cited by case, question, and chapter (e.g., 32.2.11).

Within the second part, question 3 of case 33 became a separate treatise on the law of penance (*De penitentia;* → Penitence) in seven divisions. It apparently rests in part on later elaboration. It is cited by division and chapter, with the addition *de pen* (e.g., 1.88 *de pen.*).

1.1.3. A third part, *De consecratione,* presents laws governing the other → sacraments, especially rules for the consecrating of churches and church vessels and for observing the Eucharist, → baptism, and confirmation. Its 396 chapters are grouped under five divisions. It is cited by division and chapter, with the addition *de cons.* (e.g., 2.14 *de cons.*).

Immediately after its completion, the work of Gratian became the object of commentaries in glosses and *summae.* It gave canon law a uniform basis, even though it never received official papal sanction, and effectively began the story of European canon law. Very soon specific additions, the so-called *paleae,* were made to it.

1.2. *Liber Extra*

The Liber Extra (or *extravagantium decretalium*) is an official collection of papal law from 1140 to 1234. As a supplement to the Decretum Gratiani, the new law of decretals assumed great importance after about 1170 and soon was assembled in special collections. Five collections that supplement one another (1188-1226) became particularly significant as widely circulated texts for legal instruction and church courts (*compilationes antiquae*). These codes consisted mostly of individual decisions of the popes rather than abstract norms. Gregory IX (1227-41) had the most comprehensive texts of the five compilations put together in a single codex. Many of the texts were greatly revised, many were omitted, and new norms were appended for the settling of controversial questions.

The Gregorian codex is arranged in five systematically connected books containing 2,139 chapters, of which 195 come from Gregory himself. The pope entrusted the revision to the canonist Raymond of Penafort, a Dominican and the papal penitentiary. Gregory, who authenticated revisions of individual texts within the codex, promulgated the codex in 1234 and with it revoked the validity of all former collections other than Gratian's. Texts not included in it can no longer be adduced (the principle of exclusion). This work marks the high-water mark of papal legislation. Identified by "CorpIurCan X," it is usually cited with mention of book, title, and chapter (e.g., CorpIurCan X 3.1.15).

1.3. *Liber Sextus*

After 1234 several collections of later rulings appeared in the form of collections of constitutions of individual popes. A comprehensive codex of later law came out only under Boniface VIII (1294-1303). This contained some 359 chapters, of which two-thirds (251) were norms issued by Boniface himself. The editing in this case was more thorough, all the abstract norms were reworked, and their true source is often no longer recognizable.

Formally, the Liber Sextus is much more like a modern code than the Liber Extra. At the end, after the pattern of a digest, there are 88 *regulae iuris* (rules or principles of law). Like the Liber Extra, the work is divided into five books and numerous titles. The name shows that it has the function of a supplement to the books of the Extra, as Boniface sought to complete Gregory's five books (and it might also have something to do with the numbers of mysticism common in the Middle Ages). A comprehensive work, the Liber Sextus invalidates all the texts from 1234 to 1294 that are not incorporated in it. Its promulgation took place in 1298. It is cited as "Sext.," followed by book, title, and chapter (e.g., Sext 2.14.3).

1.4. The Clementines
This collection contains essentially the legislation of the Council of Vienne (1311-12) and the rulings of Clement V (1305-14). Official promulgation, which came only under John XXII in 1317, made it a universally valid papal code and gave authority to its 106 chapters, 52 titles, and 5 books. It did not claim to be an exclusively valid collection for the period from 1294 to 1314, so that the omission of the *Unam sanctam* of Boniface VIII did not affect the validity of this decree. If the collection has less importance than the Liber Sextus on this account, this is largely due to the relative weakness of the Avignon papacy. The Clementines are the last strictly papal code until the Codex of 1917. They are cited by book, title, and chapter (e.g., CorpIurCan Clem 3.7.1).

1.5. The Extravagantes of John XXII
The pontificate of John XXII (1316-34) did not produce any new book of official law, but the legislative activity of the papacy continued. Contemporary canonists commented on 20 laws of this pope, which were published by a private person in 1325 and which the schools of law perpetuated. These laws became called *extravagantes* (circulating outside), meaning that they appeared after a collection that was intended to be exclusive and final, such as the Liber Extra or Liber Sextus.

In 1500 the Paris canonist Jean Chappuis published an edition of church law in which he included these *extravagantes* of John XXII, arranging them under 14 titles and 20 chapters. By the 16th century they had become an official part of the Corpus Iuris Canonici. Citations of this collection mention title and chapter (e.g., CorpIurCanExtravag Jo XXII 4.1).

1.6. The Extravagantes Communes
This collection contains 74 decretals selected from those promulgated from the pontificate of Urban IV (1261-64) to that of Sixtus IV (1471-84). Chappuis included 70 of these in his 1500 edition, and then added four more for an edition he published in 1503. Chappuis arranged them in five books. The Extravagantes Communes, or "[Decretals] commonly circulating," are cited by book, title, and chapter (e.g., CorpIurCanExtravagCom 1.8.1). The two collections of *extravagantes* are not official documents but are the product of private editors.

2. The Roman Edition (1582) and Later Editions
The Roman edition of the Corpus Iuris Canonici was prepared by a papal commission of cardinals, the Correctores Romani, which, especially in the case of the Decretum Gratiani, made what are by modern standards dubious textual changes. The edition was published in 1582 and became the only binding text in the Roman Catholic Church. Later editions, which to some extent reflect progress in textual criticism, are the work of Justus Henning Böhmer (1747) and Emil Friedberg (1879-81). Modern research uses the Friedberg edition. The important medieval *Glossa ordinaria,* the quintessence of classical studies in canon law from the 12th to the 14th century, was added to the printed edition for the last time in 1671.

3. Significance
The texts of the Corpus Iuris Canonici are historically the most important sources of Western canon law and therefore one of the bases of European law. Since canon law shaped secular civil law, penal law, public law, and procedural law, it is one of the main sources of the development of secular law. Formally, the Corpus remained the valid church law for the Roman Catholic Church until the Codex came into force in 1918. Many of the rulings of the Corpus survive even in the revised Codex of 1983. The character of the norms is affected by the fact that they arose under the influence of a scientific study of law. Hence the style and thought forms deviate considerably from the traditions of Eastern church law, although a common basis with the East remains, due to the work of Gratian.

The → Reformation entailed a fairly strong rejection of the whole tradition and basic claim of canon law but could not wholly set aside its validity. In many matters that Protestant → church law has not regulated, the rulings of the Corpus still play a role.

Bibliography: General: G. LE BRAS, C. LEFEBVRE, and J. RAMBAUD, eds., *L'âge classique, 1140-1378. Sources et théorie du droit* (Paris, 1965) • J. A. BRUNDAGE, *Medieval Canon Law* (London, 1995) 44-57 • E. FRIEDBERG, *Corpus Iuris Canonici* (2 vols.; Leipzig, 1879-81) • J. GAUDEMET, *Les sources du droit canonique, VIIIe-XXe siècle* (Paris, 1993) 102-31 • S. KUTTNER, "Quelques observations sur l'autorité des collections canoniques dans le droit classique de l'église," *Medieval Councils, Decretals, and Collections of Canon Law* (London, 1980;

orig. pub., 1950) I.305-12 • A. M. Stickler, *Historia iuris canonici Latini*, vol. 1, *Historia fontium* (Turin, 1950) • A. Van Hove, *Prolegomena* (2d ed.; Mechelen, 1945).

On 1.1: S. Kuttner, *Gratian and the Schools of Law, 1140-1234* (London, 1983) • P. Landau, "Neue Forschungen zu vorgratianischen Kanonessammlungen und den Quellen des gratianischen Dekrets," *ICom* 11 (1984) 1-29 • J. T. Noonan, "Gratian Slept Here: The Changing Identity of the Father of the Systematic Study of Canon Law," *Tr.* 35 (1979) 145-72.

On 1.2: S. Kuttner, "Raymund of Penafort as Editor: The 'decretales' and 'constitutiones' of Gregory IX," *BMCL*, n.s., 12 (1982) 65-80.

On 1.3: S. Gagnér, *Studien zur Ideengeschichte der Gesetzgebung* (Stockholm, 1960).

On 1.4: E. Müller, *Das Konzil von Vienne, 1311-1312. Seine Quellen und seine Geschichte* (Münster, 1934).

On 1.5: Extravagantes Johannes XXII (ed. J. Tarrant; Vatican City, 1983).

On 2: K. Schellhass, "Wissenschaftliche Forschungen unter Gregor XIII für die Neuausgabe des gratianischen Dekrets," *Papsttum und Kaisertum* (FS P. Kehr; Munich, 1926; repr., Aalen, 1973) 674-90.

On 3: J. Heckel, "Das Decretum Gratiani und das evangelische Kirchenrecht," *StGra* 3 (1955) 483-537 • A. Pincherle, "Graziano e Lutero," ibid. 451-81 • R. Schäfer, "Die Geltung des kanonischen Rechts in der Evangelischen Kirche Deutschlands von Luther bis zur Gegenwart," *ZSRG.K* 5 (1915) 165-413 • U. Wolter, *Ius canonicum in iure civili* (Cologne, 1975).

Peter Landau

Correspondence Courses → Distance Education

Corruption

1. Term
2. In Non-Christian Religions
3. In the Bible
4. Significance

1. Term

The term "corruption" comes from Lat. *corrumpere* (break to pieces, spoil). Philosophers from Thucydides (ca. 460-ca. 400 B.C.) through Plato (427-347 B.C.) to F. → Nietzsche (1844-1900) have presented corruption as the negative side of teaching about the state. From the days of → Augustine (354-430), "cor-

ruption" has been a term in dogmatics for original → sin.

For investigative journalists in the United States, "corruption," ever since the 19th century, has been a term for bribery, the misuse of power and office, nepotism — in general, any conduct that deviates from responsible norms out of a personal desire for money or status (see Nye in A. Heidenheimer, 566-67). H. S. Alatas views corruption of this kind as a social sin, for which there exist legal penalties. It is the other side of → power (P. Noack) and always works to the detriment of a country's → development (Myrdal in Heidenheimer, 540).

2. In Non-Christian Religions

2.1. In → Hinduism, corruption is *a-dhārma*, which right-thinking people reject as sin. Its source is greed. Kauṭilya (fl. 300 B.C.) viewed it as a capital offense in the eyes of pure religion. According to M. Gandhi (1869-1948), it has its origin in the heart and is a social sin.

2.2. In → Buddhism, too, corruption is an expression of the evil in the human heart that can be overcome only by the good. The five rules and the Eightfold Path are the only remedy, according to S. Tachibana, who regards avarice or greed as its root.

2.3. In → Islam, corruption has been fought as a social sin from the days of Imam Aḥmad ibn Ḥanbal (780-855). According to al-Ghazālī (1058-1111), envy and the love of money are its main source. For Islam, bribery *(raswa)* is a sin.

2.4. In China, from the time of Confucius (551-479 B.C.; → Confucianism) corruption has been viewed as the opposite of doing right. Greed is its source. We must resist it on the basis of our implanted moral nature, which wills the good. According to Meng-tzu (d. ca. 289 B.C.), only the four cosmic potencies can protect the world against corruption, an opinion shared by Hsün-tzu (d. ca. 230 B.C.) and other philosophers. In the → Taiping Rebellion (1850-64), corruption was treated as a capital offense. In modern China corruption is seen as a great threat to the achievements of the social revolution.

2.5. In ancient Egypt, Amon-Re would accept no bribes; those who do nothing crooked are righteous before him. According to the Babylonian *Advice to Princes*, Babylon treated corruption *(datum)* as a capital offense.

3. In the Bible

3.1. A basic OT thesis is that → Yahweh is incorruptible (Deut. 10:17). Corruption means cutting the thread of life (*bṣ'*, "cut, break") through greed (Exod. 18:21 etc.). Corruption begins at the top, and like a cancer, it destroys the whole body of the people. It makes the seeing blind, perverts justice (Exod. 23:8), and brings ruin *(šḥd)*. The corrupt, then, are under a curse (Deut. 27:25).

A classic description of corruption appears in Mal. 3:14-15. The corrupt person *(ršʿ)* lives in inward disharmony and therefore does what is evil. The → prophets combat corruption as an offense against both God and neighbor (Mic. 2:1-11; chap. 3, etc.). Corruption also has consequences for → creation (Gen. 6:5, 11-12), for it breaks the basic order of change and conservation. The elders are to be on guard against corruption (Isa. 1:21-26; Micah 3).

The ones who renounce corruption have a place in the → kingdom of God (Isa. 33:15-16). Because corruption has its origin in the heart, in the new → covenant God gives a new heart (Jer. 31:33-34), for he wills a → life in which → righteousness and → peace kiss each other (Ps. 85:10). This is the ideal of the wise (e.g., Prov. 17:23; 19:9), who live uprightly in both great things and small.

3.2. This basic teaching is found also in the NT. → Jesus fights against the systemic corruption that is immanent in the Pax Romana, and also against corruption in the → temple. As the story of the temptation shows, Jesus himself cannot be corrupted. For him, corruption (the unjust mammon) is antigod. The → apostles continue his teaching (Rom. 1:18–3:20 etc.).

4. Significance

As an outworking of evil, corruption is a structural sin (G. Gutiérrez). It involves the exploitation of some people by others. It is the root of situations of injustice and an offense against God, for it produces real, objective death (one thinks of Archbishop Oscar Romero, slain in El Salvador in 1980) among its victims in many parts of the world. For this reason the → church, like its Lord, must be "on the watch at these otherwise unguarded gates" (R. Schutz, Taizé).

→ Capitalism; Church and State; Economics, Ethics of; Ethics; Money; Socialism; Society

Bibliography: H. S. ALATAS, *The Sociology of Corruption* (Singapore, 1968) • C. BRÜNNER, ed., *Korruption und Kontrolle* (Vienna, 1981) • A. HEIDENHEIMER, ed., *Political Corruption* (2d ed.; New Brunswick, N.J., 1978) • P. NOACK, *Die andere Seite der Macht* (Munich, 1987) • K. RENNSTICH, *Korruption als theologisches Problem und weltweite Herausforderung der Kirche Jesu Christi* (Basel, 1988) bibliography • W. SCHULER, ed., *Korruption im Altertum* (Konstanz Symposium; Munich, 1982) • S. TACHIBANA, *Ethics of Buddhism* (2d ed.; New York, 1975; orig. pub., 1926).

KARL RENNSTICH

Cosmological Argument → God, Arguments for the Existence of

Cosmology → Creation

Costa Rica

	1960	1980	2000
Population (1,000s):	1,236	2,284	3,798
Annual growth rate (%):	3.62	2.91	1.84

Area: 51,100 sq. km. (19,730 sq. mi.)

A.D. 2000

Population density: 74/sq. km. (192/sq. mi.)
Births / deaths: 2.24 / 0.40 per 100 population
Fertility rate: 2.78 per woman
Infant mortality rate: 11 per 1,000 live births
Life expectancy: 77.3 years (m: 75.0, f: 79.8)
Religious affiliation (%): Christians 96.4 (Roman Catholics 93.0, Protestants 10.5, marginal 2.4, indigenous 2.3, other Christians 0.4), nonreligious 1.7, Chinese folk religionists 1.1, other 0.8.

1. The Country and Its History
2. The Roman Catholic Church
3. Protestantism
4. Non-Christian Religions

1. The Country and Its History

Costa Rica is a Central American republic with neighbors Nicaragua to the north and Panama to the south. The people are mostly of Catalan, Basque, and Galician descent.

The first Europeans arrived in Costa Rica in 1502, and within the century the area had become part of the Viceroyalty of New Spain (→ Colonialism). In 1821 Costa Rica and other parts of Central America joined Mexico in declaring their independence from Spain. It later joined the Central American Federation (1823), but not long after it left this association to become fully independent (1838).

Early census figures show the preponderance of Native Americans. In 1569, for example, the country numbered 17,200 Indians, 113 Spaniards, 30 blacks, and 170 mestizos.

In the independent state that was formed after 1821, only 1.4 percent of the total area had been opened up economically. During the second half of the 19th century the development of the coffee industry brought concentration of the scattered property holdings. After 1880 capital from the United

States made possible an intensive cultivation of bananas, which led to mass migrations of the labor force and seasonal workers.

Increasing social tensions led to mass labor demonstrations in the years 1943-48, which resulted in new social legislation. A civil war was fought in 1948-49. The winner in the conflict was José Figueres Ferrer, who founded the socialist Partido de Liberación Nacional (PLN; Party of national liberation) and who led national politics for over two decades. Through his efforts, democracy flourished in Costa Rica, more so than in perhaps any other country of Central America.

In 1948 the government abolished Costa Rica's army, a move intended to prevent rightist coups. In 1959 industrialization began to replace the country's reliance on imports. The recession of 1975 led to a period of economic decline that lasted until 1988. The chief export in 1994 was coffee, with bananas, sugar, cocoa, cotton, and hemp also important. The land produces gold, salt, sulphur, and iron and has developed industries in furniture, food processing, aluminum, textiles, and fertilizers. Overall, Costa Rica has achieved a relatively high standard of living and social services. In 1994 the urban population represented 44 percent of the whole.

2. The Roman Catholic Church

San José became a bishopric in 1850 and an archbishopric in the 20th century. It comprises three dioceses and one apostolic vicariate. In 1991 the church numbered 2.5 million adherents, or 80 percent of the total population.

The relation between → church and state was marked by serious tensions between the liberals and the hierarchy. It became more relaxed in the 1940s, with social legislation inspired in part by Roman Catholic social teaching (→ Social Ethics) and the passing of the 1949 constitution, which guaranteed freedom of conscience and worship. The constitution made the Roman Catholic Church the state religion, put church marriage on an equality with the otherwise obligatory civil marriage, gave the Roman Catholic Church the right to provide religious instruction in the public schools, and freed it from all taxation. These privileges are features of a new-model Christendom, a repristination of the medieval *corpus Christianum* in the changed conditions of the 20th century.

The model resulted in considerable immobility on the part of the church, conditioned in part by the teaching and personality of Archbishop Carlos Humberto Rodríguez (1960-78), by the spiritualizing and otherworldly pastoral work of the middle-class secular clergy, and by the orders that came to Costa Rica after 1950. Having no knowledge of the decisive events of the 1940s, the orders typically identified themselves with the colonial mentality of the upper classes and devoted their energies to the education of the children of the rich.

The main cause of inertia, however, was the dissolution of the diaconal infrastructure of the church, which had been replaced by the welfare system set up by the PLN. Yet the clergy increasingly came to see themselves in different ways, leading to three distinct groups.

The first was strongly conservative. The second was reformist, convinced of the Christian inspiration of the welfare state, and content to leave matters of social concern to the state. The third was progressive, sympathizing with the struggles of the people (→ Liberation Theology) and making experiments in pastoral care among them. The last group sought to be present in a Christian sense in strategically important social strata (banana workers, seasonal workers, etc.). It understood its faith to involve an obligation of solidarity with the very poor and a struggle to transform society.

In keeping with the pastoral orientation of most of the clergy, much of the laity in Costa Rica manifested an individualistic, fervent devotion, for example, in the keeping of the sacraments and the observance of traditional forms of piety (15 percent attend mass weekly in the towns, 25 percent in the rural areas). An increasing number of people, however, have turned to Protestant churches (collectively representing about 11 percent of the population in 1990), where they often find more warmth and fellowship in worship and community life than in the Catholic Church. Others have become religiously indifferent, turning away from institutional Roman Catholicism because they find it outdated.

A visit by John Paul II in 1983 promoted the restriction of the church to pastoral and spiritual tasks and was thus in line with the new stage in the relation between church and state that was inaugurated with the election of Luis Alberto Monge Álvarez as president of the republic on February 7, 1982. The bishops, and especially Arrieta, supported almost unconditionally the economic measures taken by the government and its policy toward Nicaragua, which meant the toleration of subversive movements on the soil of Costa Rica. Oscar Arias Sánchez, who succeeded Monge as president in 1986, played a key role in ending the bloody struggles in nearby Nicaragua, El Salvador, and Guatemala, for which he received the Nobel Peace Prize in 1987.

3. Protestantism

When the → Congregationalists and → Methodists jointly built a church in San José in 1865, there were only 286 Protestants in the country. With the development of the banana industry at the end of the 19th century, there was an influx of workers from the Caribbean, which attracted → British missions to work among them. The Baptist Missionary Society of Jamaica came in 1887, and the Methodist Missionary Society in 1894. The Anglicans also came; the U.S. Episcopal Church later took over their work.

The first missionary society from the United States to do work in Costa Rica was the Central American Mission (1891), followed by the Methodists (1917), the Latin America Mission (1921), and then the Pentecostals (after 1930). A → charismatic movement of renewal outside the Pentecostal churches after 1969 spread to many Protestant congregations of various denominations.

In 1990 the largest Protestant group was the Assemblies of God (55,000 adherents), followed by the Seventh-day Adventists and Church of God (Cleveland, Tenn., each group with 29,000 adherents), as well as several smaller groups (primarily Pentecostal and Baptist).

In 1951 the Alianza Evangélica Costarricense was formed by 14 churches. This alliance, to which the Episcopalians, → Baptists, and → Adventists do not belong, was spurred on by the Seminario Latinoamericano, the leading evangelical seminary in Latin America. Harry Strachan of the Latin American Mission founded this seminary in 1960/61 to undertake a national Evangelism-in-Depth campaign, and also to initiate many diaconal projects, especially among the poverty-stricken of the population (→ Evangelical Movement).

In 1950 the Spanish Language Institute, which the United Presbyterians had originally established in Colombia, moved to San José. By 1967 it had trained 3,000 missionaries from over 100 societies for service in Latin America. There is no official Roman Catholic ecumenical organization, but there are interconfessional movements like the progressive group Éxodo (1971), which works with ISAL (Church and Society in Latin America) and the Departamento Ecuménico de Investigación.

4. Non-Christian Religions

In 1990 approximately 9 percent of the population was not Christian. The largest groups were the → Jehovah's Witnesses (36,000) and the → Mormons (13,000), with smaller numbers of Baha'is, → Indians belonging to animistic tribal religions (Bribri, Cabe-car, Boruca, Guatuso, Orotina), Rosicrucians, → Theosophists, → Spiritists, Jews, followers of → Krishna, and → Hindus.

→ Colonialism and Mission

Bibliography: D. Barrett, ed., *WCE* 249-52 • L. Bird, *Costa Rica: Unarmed Democracy* (London, 1984) • D. Boris and R. Rausch, eds., *Zentralamerika* (Cologne, 1983) • R. Cardenal, ed., *América Central,* vol. 6, *Historia general de la iglesia en América Latina* (Salamanca, 1985) • T. S. Creedman, *Historical Dictionary of Costa Rica* (2d ed.; Metuchen, N.J., 1991) • E. D. Miller, *A Holy Alliance? The Church and the Left in Costa Rica, 1932-1948* (Armonk, N.Y., 1996) • J. M. Paige, *Coffee and Power: Revolution and the Rise of Democracy in Central America* (Cambridge, Mass., 1997) • P. Richard and G. Meléndez, eds., *La iglesia de los pobres en América Central* (San Jose, 1982) • R. B. Segura, *Historia eclesiástica de Costa Rica, 1501-1850* (San José, 1967) • C. Stansifer, *Costa Rica* (2d ed.; Oxford, 1991) bibliography • V. Urbano, *Juan Vásquez de Coronado y su ética en la conquista de Costa Rica* (Madrid, 1968) • P. J. Williams, *The Catholic Church and Politics in Nicaragua and Costa Rica* (Pittsburgh, 1989).

Guillermo Meléndez and Hans-Jürgen Prien

Côte d'Ivoire → Ivory Coast

Councils of the Church

1. Term
2. Early Church
3. Middle Ages
4. Reformation
5. Modern Period
6. Roman Catholic Church Law
7. Orthodox Church
8. Protestantism
9. Ecumenical Movement
10. List of Ecumenical Councils

1. Term

"Council," as well as the originally synonymous "synod" (from Lat. *concilium* and Gk. *synodos,* both meaning "assembly"), refers to gatherings of church representatives for the purpose of discussing matters of faith and order, reaching decisions, and issuing decrees. The → Roman Catholic Church and the → Orthodox Church use the term "council" mainly for gatherings of → bishops. Modern usage, which distinguishes national and provincial *synods* from general *councils,* developed at a later date, with its beginnings in the Middle Ages.

The Orthodox Church recognizes only the seven councils of the fourth to eighth centuries as ecumenical. The Roman Catholic Church, however, views as ecumenical any medieval or modern council that is summoned or approved by the pope. According to the reckoning initiated by Robert → Bellarmine (1542-1621), the church now numbers 21 general councils (see 10). The historical problems involved in this listing, however, are now increasingly recognized.

2. Early Church

Regional synods were held in Asia Minor from as early as the second half of the second century. They grew out of efforts to settle local and regional conflicts and crises (e.g., over → Montanism) by concerted discussion and decision, to establish the church's unity in expressing what is correct belief, and to give uniformity to church customs and practices. In the third century, in parallelism with the development of metropolitan districts, synods became a fixed institution. After their beginning in the East, they spread to North Africa (perhaps in connection with Montanism), where synods were held at Carthage to decide the attitude of the church toward those who fell away (→ Lapsi) under the → persecution of Christians, and also to decide the issue of → heretical baptism. Synods were also held in Spain (Elvira, ca. 300) and Gaul.

Synods were primarily assemblies of bishops, though the transition from congregational gatherings was a gradual one, with → prophets and → martyrs, or confessors, at first playing an important part. The model was the so-called apostolic council of Acts 15 (→ Acts of the Apostles §8). As successors of the apostles, bishops claimed the assistance of the Holy Spirit (cf. Acts 15:28: "It has seemed good to the → Holy Spirit and to us"), who would manifest himself in the unanimity of the decisions reached.

For an ecclesiology that found the church's unity in the fellowship of bishops (→ Cyprian [d. 258]; Church 3.2), synods were the supreme authority, the only authority superior to that of the congregation. They ranked above individual bishops, whom they could on occasion depose. Their autonomy could be asserted even in opposition to the bishop of Rome (e.g., by a rejection of Roman practice).

Under Constantine (306-37) it became necessary to assemble bishops from the whole oikoumene (the world of the Roman Empire; cf. Luke 2:1) to deal with disputed issues at imperial synods. Constantine linked the church to the empire and the empire to

the church (E. Schwartz). It was in the interests of the state to settle church conflicts at the imperial level, for the unity of the church promoted that of the empire.

A beginning came in 314, when Constantine gathered the bishops of the western provinces at Arles to discuss the → Donatists, heretical baptism, and the date of Easter. The → Arian controversy that broke out in the East led to the summoning of the imperial synod of Nicaea (325), which is considered the first ecumenical council. The councils that followed up to the ninth century were all summoned by the Roman or Byzantine emperors and met under their protection and external direction (either personally or through their commissaries). Council decisions were promulgated as imperial laws. In the shifting power play of ecclesiastical politics, they determined the course of early church dogma and usually made disciplinary decisions.

Not all imperial synods attained ecumenical rank (e.g., Sardica [present-day Sofia] in 343, Ariminum [Rimini] and Seleucia in 359, Ephesus in 449, and Constantinople in 754). Seven usually rank as ecumenical: → Nicaea I (325), Constantinople I (381), Ephesus (431; → Ephesus, Council of), → Chalcedon (451), Constantinople II (553), Constantinople III (680-81), and Nicaea II (787). The first six formulated the doctrine of the → Trinity and Christological → dogma (→ Christology 2). The seventh legitimated the veneration of → images (→ Icon 2). An eighth council, Constantinople IV (869-70), which the Orthodox no longer regard as ecumenical, ended the schism of the Byzantine patriarch Photius (858-67 and 877-86) by means of his → excommunication (→ Byzantium 3).

Since all these councils took place in the East, the West was only weakly represented at them, or not at all in the case of Constantinople I and II. Decisive for their ecumenicity was not only the will of the emperor who summoned them or the sense of the assembled bishops that they were stating the traditional faith in their agreed teaching but also their ultimate → reception by the whole church. The → Nestorians and → Monophysites who were condemned at the Councils of Ephesus and Chalcedon refused to accept the decisions and thus separated dogmatically from the imperial church.

Universal reception, which was not approbation in the later sense, included the approval of the bishop of Rome, who did not participate in person in any of the early councils, but whose assent was essential in the West. Rome did not agree, in fact, to the detailed decisions of Constantinople I and Chalcedon regarding the legal position of the bishop of

Constantinople. In the course of developing claims to primacy, → Leo I (440-61) and Gelasius I (492-96) equated approval by Rome with reception by the whole church, so that reception was complete when the bishop of Rome at least subsequently joined in the universal approval.

Imperial synods were simply the culmination of a rich conciliar practice. Alongside them were provincial synods, which were to meet twice a year, according to the canon of Nicaea I. Then there were patriarchal synods at → Alexandria (→ Alexandrian Theology), → Antioch (→ Antiochian Theology), and Constantinople. All the North African bishops likewise held plenary synods. At first, even after Nicaea I, no distinction in theological significance was made between local and imperial synods. Only gradually did the ecumenical councils, especially the first four (some saw a parallel in them with the four gospels), acquire special theological status.

3. Middle Ages

The councils of the Christian empires in the early Middle Ages were provincial or national synods, often related to secular assemblies. The Council of Frankfurt summoned by Charlemagne (768-814) in 794 as a counter to Nicaea II did not achieve ecumenical ranking, in spite of its claims to universality. Imperial synods were used as an instrument of → church government. The Synod of Sutri assembled by Henry III (1039-56) in 1046, which deposed three rival popes, laid the foundations for the development of the reforming papacy and for a new type of papal general councils. Contributing also to this turn of events was the fact that with the breach with the East (the schism of 1054; → Heresies and Schisms), the West had lost the ecumenical dimension of the early church.

The papal general councils of the Middle Ages (Lateran I-IV, Lyons I-II, and Vienne) were marked by the dominance that the papacy had achieved as a result of the Gregorian reforms. It was now the pope who summoned and personally directed the councils and who enforced their decisions, even to the point of altering the wording of their decrees (in the case of Lyons II and Vienne). These councils developed out of the reform synods of the 11th century, which the popes as promoters of reform held at the Lateran Palace in Rome or at other places near Rome. The synods were instruments for reinforcing the stronger claim to primacy now being made by the popes.

Although the term "general council" (concilium generale or universale) at first denoted only a synod of several provincial churches, the growing number of participants and tasks gave rise to the idea of a fully universal council (generalissimae) that could make basic decisions and might rank with the early church councils. → Innocent III (1198-1216), when summoning Lateran IV, was the first deliberately to refer to the "ancient custom of the Holy Fathers." This council's → confession of faith, which headed its decisions and which formulated transubstantiation (→ Eucharist 3) as a dogma, was designed to underline the claim to equality of rank. Lateran I-III (in 1123, 1139, and 1179) were now, in retrospect, stated to be ecumenical.

In the 13th century the two councils of Lyons were added, and in the 14th that of Vienne. In keeping with the close interweaving of the medieval churches and → society (→ Empire and Papacy; Middle Ages 3), these councils dealt not only with questions of faith and church discipline (e.g., the duty of communicating at Easter and of yearly penance; → Penitence) but also with ecclesiastical and political issues such as the relation between spiritual and secular powers, the Peace of God, and the → Crusades. Besides bishops, now → abbots, representatives of → cathedral chapters and universities, and secular princes or their envoys also participated in discussion of the relevant issues.

The → reform councils of the 15th century were influenced by → conciliarism, which gave to general councils, as representative of the whole church, supreme authority and supremacy over the pope. Conciliarism assumed practical relevance with the start of the Great Schism in 1378 (→ Heresies and Schisms 3). When the council that the cardinals of both sides arranged at Pisa in 1409 failed to restore unity to the church, the Council of Constance (1414-18) in its decree Haec sancta solemnly proclaimed the supreme authority of councils and thus laid a foundation for the deposition or enforced resignation of the three rival popes, the election of a new pope that all would recognize, and the resultant restoration of the Western church's unity. The prosecution of J. → Hus (ca. 1372-1415; → Hussites) on a charge of heresy, which the council carried through without the pope, was also an expression of the council's understanding of itself.

The task of church reform in head and members was certainly tackled energetically, but with no lasting success. Failure was due to the fact that the periodic summoning of councils to exert constitutional control (as postulated in the decree Frequens) was obstructed by a newly strengthened papacy that opposed conciliarism.

This opposition came to light in the conflict between Eugenius IV (1431-47) and the Council of Basel (1431). When the pope moved the council to

Ferrara and Florence, it took the form of a papal general council. The Basel minority, which still saw itself as a reform council and elected a rival pope, could not prevail against the success of Eugenius in achieving reunion with the Greeks, Armenians, and Jacobites (→ Oriental Orthodox Churches; Uniate Churches).

Nevertheless, the idea of council linked to demands for reform lingered on and found expression in frequent appeals to a future council, which Pius II (1458-64) condemned as an execrable abuse in his 1460 → bull *Execrabilis*. Lateran V, which was summoned to counter the *Conciliabulum* at Pisa that France and opposition cardinals had arranged, was hardly more than an extended Roman synod.

4. Reformation

The continued existence of conciliar thinking formed the setting for M. → Luther's (1483-1546) two appeals to a general council, first in 1518 after the fruitless hearing before Cardinal Cajetan, and then in 1520 after he learned of the bull threatening excommunication. Conciliar thinking also lay behind the demand for a free council in Germany, which was taken up by the imperial estates in the imperial diets. Charles V (1519-56) at first based his religious policy on the holding of a council. In Rome, however, experiences with the reform councils and fear of conciliarism resulted in a curial policy of obstruction.

It was only after long hesitation that the Council of → Trent finally met, and attendance initially was poor. On the one hand, this council was a papal council of the medieval type, for the pope summoned it, his legates directed it, and the pope (Pius IV, 1559-65) confirmed its decrees (unaltered). On the other hand, this was a council like those of the early church, for only bishops could vote (apart from generals of → orders and two abbots of monastic congregations).

The decrees of Trent were in two senses a response to the → Reformation. In controverted dogmatic questions (the doctrine of → justification and the → sacraments, also Scripture and → tradition), the doctrinal decrees fixed the Roman Catholic position along the lines of → Scholasticism. At the same time, reforming decrees offered guidelines for a renewal of the Roman Catholic Church (→ Catholic Reform and Counterreformation).

Trent gave → Catholicism a new self-awareness and opened up a new epoch in Roman Catholic history that extended into the 20th century. The commitment of the popes to Tridentine reform resulted in an increasing regard for the papacy.

5. Modern Period

The two → Vatican Councils continued the type of council developed at Trent. There was a 300-year interval before Vatican I, the biggest gap between two general councils. → Pius IX (1846-78) summoned this council only after → Gallicanism and → episcopalianism had lost their political base and the papacy had experienced a brilliant resurgence (→ Ultramontanism). In its composition Vatican I differed from Trent in the twofold sense that representatives of the by-now secular states were not invited, but there were also far more participants (as many as 700).

Significant for the relation between pope and council was the fact that the agenda that the pope offered in advance gave the pope alone the right to propose matters for discussion (a disputed issue at Trent) and that the decisions of the council were published, like those of medieval councils, as papal constitutions, with a mere addition signifying the approval of the council *(sacro approbante concilio)*. The dogmatic definition of papal primacy and → infallibility, which was originally part of a more comprehensive constitution on the church, brought a provisional end to the century-long debate about the relation between pope and council, settled dogmatically the supremacy of the papacy, and expressly rejected the conciliarist contention that a council is superior to the pope. The relation between papal authority and that of the total episcopate remained unclear.

The dogmatic statements about the papal office, which were pushed through against the opposition of a considerable minority, led in Germany and Switzerland to the schism of the → Old Catholics, who contested the ecumenical character of Vatican I. The centralizing of authority in the papacy seemed to make future councils unnecessary. In 1854 Pius IX had already defined the immaculate conception of Mary as a dogma without the cooperation of a council, and in 1950 Pius XII (1939-58) did not consult a council when he defined as a dogma the bodily assumption of Mary into heaven (→ Mariology), announcing it merely in the form of an ex cathedra papal decision.

Nevertheless, forecasts that there would be no more general councils proved to be premature. → John XXIII (1958-63) surprised the world in 1959 by calling an ecumenical council whose main task would be to deal with problems of the day *(aggiornamento)*. Vatican II, the largest council thus far, with over 2,500 participants, initiated a new period in Roman Catholic history. Structurally it was still a papal council like Vatican I, but there were notable changes in the relation between pope and council. In the discussions the council developed its own dynamic and profile as an assembly that was not willing simply to add its approval to papal proposals but was prepared to decide according to its own judgment.

As "council of the church on the church" (K. → Rahner), it became the forum for fresh ecclesiological reflection. The college of bishops has supreme authority in the church, solemnly exercised at an ecumenical council, but only in organic combination with the pope as its head, never able to act without or against him, though the pope himself may act without the college. Papal prerogatives in calling, directing, and confirming councils remain untouched. This ecclesiological view came to expression in the modified formula used in promulgation of the decrees of the council. The pope now proclaimed them together with the council fathers (una cum sacrosancti concilii patribus).

6. Roman Catholic Church Law

Roman Catholic law pertaining to councils was laid down in 1983 CIC 337-41. Though the rules are embodied in the statements of Vatican II about the collegiality of bishops, the decisive principles are still those of 1917 CIC 222-29, which was governed by Vatican I. Only the pope has the right to summon an ecumenical council. The pope presides either in person or through legates. He must confirm the decrees. He can suspend or dismiss a council. He sets the agenda. If he dies during a council, as John XXIII did during Vatican II, it is automatically broken off until a successor either continues or ends it. Participation is for those who are members of the bishops' college by consecration; titular bishops without → jurisdiction are included. But the pope may also invite non-bishops, for example, heads of orders without episcopal consecration.

When the united bishops' college along with the pope definitively declares doctrines of faith and morals to be binding, their decision is infallible (1983 CIC 749.2). Rejection of a promulgated doctrine, advocacy of a rejected doctrine (can. 1371), and appeals from a decision of the pope to a general council are all punishable (can. 1372). There is no possibility of complaint against the decrees of a council.

7. Orthodox Church

The Orthodox Church accepts only the first seven councils as ecumenical. Other synods (in 879, 1341, and 1642) were meant to be ecumenical but were not received as such. Nor did the Orthodox Church receive the union supposedly settled at Ferrara-Florence.

During the 20th century, attempts have been made to summon a Pan-Orthodox or even an eighth ecumenical council, and preparatory discussions with this end in view are still being held. A preliminary conference at → Athos in 1930 and four preconciliar Pan-Orthodox conferences at Rhodes in 1961, 1963, and 1965 and at Geneva in 1968 have drawn up a list of theological themes (e.g., sources of revelation) and ecclesiastical issues (e.g., lay cooperation and disciplinary → dispensation) and have tried to determine future Orthodox relations with Roman Catholicism and → Protestantism. Preconciliar gatherings were also held at Chambésy, Switzerland, in 1976, 1982, and 1986.

8. Protestantism

In the framework of their new ecclesiological thinking, M. Luther, U. → Zwingli (1484-1531), and J. → Calvin (1509-64; → Luther's Theology; Zwingli's Theology; Calvin's Theology) all regarded councils as fallible human institutions that have no more than a derived authority to the extent that they correctly expound Scripture (as the first four councils did in their dogmatic decisions). The related discussions of Lutheran and Reformed dogmaticians regarding the place of a council (locus de conciliis) in the age of orthodoxy were no more than theoretical, with no possibility of practical application.

In the Reformed tradition especially there is some discrepancy between confidence that the Holy Spirit will be at work at a council of true Christians, thus making its decisions binding, and the right of all believers to examine whether these findings are in agreement with Scripture. Neither did the Synod of Dort (1618-19) — summoned as a Dutch national synod but attended by representatives of the Calvinist churches of western Europe — ever claim to be an ecumenical council. The church constitutions of many Protestant churches, however, especially those within the Reformed sphere, exhibited synodic structural elements from the very outset.

9. Ecumenical Movement

In the history of the → ecumenical movement, the holding of world church conferences is linked to conciliar structures. This is true of the Lambeth Conferences of the → Anglican Communion and the gatherings of the → Lutheran World Federation and the → World Alliance of Reformed Churches. In ecumenical discussion from the 1960s onward, the conciliar practice of the early church attracted increasing attention as a model for that of ecumenical encounter and cooperation. The term → "conciliarity" came into use for the conciliar process of common consultation and decision in which the fellowship of the churches would find expression as conciliar fellowship. The clarifying of historical differences, it is thought, might lead to the finding of → consensus in a process of growing convergence.

In the 1980s a proposal was made to plan and hold a common Christian council of peace. This proposal evoked extensive and intensive discussion. In view of Roman Catholic and Orthodox reservations about the term "council," which had become a fixed one in tradition and → church law, the alternative suggestion was made that there should be a world convocation of Christians for justice, peace, and the integrity of creation. Preparations were to be made for this by a conciliar process at every level. Europe held its own assembly at Basel in May 1989, and a world convocation took place at Seoul, Korea, in 1990.

10. List of Ecumenical Councils

10.1. The seven councils that are unanimously accepted by Christian churches as ecumenical councils are as follows:

1. Nicaea I (325): asserted the consubstantiality of the Son with the Father against Arius (→ God).
2. Constantinople I (381): upheld the deity of the Holy Spirit.
3. Ephesus (431): championed the *theotokos* against Nestorius.
4. Chalcedon (451): stated the two natures of the one person of Christ.
5. Constantinople II (553): condemned the Nestorian "Three Chapters."
6. Constantinople III (680-81): condemned Monothelitism and dealt with the question of Honorius.
7. Nicaea II (787): permitted and explained the veneration of images.

10.2. Roman Catholics also regard the following 14 councils as ecumenical:

8. Constantinople IV (869-70): ended the Photian schism.
9. Lateran I (1123): confirmed the Concordat of Worms, ending the Investiture Controversy.
10. Lateran II (1139): deposed the antipope Anacletus II (1130-38).
11. Lateran III (1179): decided for a two-thirds majority in papal elections, confirmed the Peace of Venice with Frederick I (Holy Roman emperor 1152-90), and took measures against Jews, Saracens, → Cathari, and → Waldenses.
12. Lateran IV (1215): defined transubstantiation, enjoined annual confession and Communion,

confirmed the election of Frederick II (Holy Roman emperor 1215-50), and called for a crusade.
13. Lyons I (1245): deposed Frederick II.
14. Lyons II (1274): passed the rule regarding the conclave, decided for union with the Greeks, and called for a crusade.
15. Vienne (1311-12): abolished the Templar order, dealt with the issue of the → Franciscans, and issued reforming decrees.
16. Constance (1414-18): ended the Great Schism, proclaimed the supremacy of councils over the pope, condemned → Wycliffe and Hus, and demanded periodic councils and other reforms.
17. Basel, Ferrara, Florence, Rome (1431-ca. 1445): established union with the Greeks, Armenians, and Jacobites, while the rump council in Basel (up to 1449) asserted the supremacy of councils as a dogma, elected the rival pope Felix V (1439-49), and issued reforming decrees.
18. Lateran V (1512-17): condemned conciliarism.
19. Trent (1545-63): issued dogmatic decrees on Scripture and tradition, original → sin, justification, the sacraments, and the veneration of → saints; issued reforming decrees on the duties of → cardinals and bishops, the conduct of diocesan and provincial synods, → visitation, and the orders.
20. Vatican I (1869-70): dealt with the natural knowledge of God and → revelation, faith and knowledge, and the primacy and infallibility of the pope.
21. Vatican II (1962-65): took up the issues of → liturgy, the → church, revelation, the church in the world today, means of → communication, → ecumenism (→ Ecumenical Theology), Oriental churches, the bishop's pastoral office, the religious, → lay apostolate, → missions, Christian → education, non-Christian → religions, → religious liberty, and the training, life, and ministry of → priests.

→ Ecumenical Symbols; Heresies and Schisms; Niceno-Constantinopolitan Creed

Bibliography: Primary sources: ACO • MANSI • N. P. TANNER, ed., *Decrees of the Ecumenical Councils* (2 vols.; London, 1990).

Secondary works: W. AYMANNS, *Das synodale Element in der Kirchenverfassung* (Munich, 1970) • H.-M. BARTH, "Die Weltversammlung der Christen. Vorbereitungen einer Friedenskonferenz zwischen Management und Inspiration," *MD* 38 (1987) 128-30 • W. BRANDMÜLLER, ed., *Konziliengeschichte* (Paderborn, 1980ff.) • L. D. DAVIS, *The First Seven Ecumenical Coun-*

cils (325-787): Their History and Theology (Wilmington, Del., 1987) • F. Dvornik, "Emperors, Popes, and General Councils," DOP 6 (1951) 1-23 • P. Hughes, The Church in Crisis: A History of the Twenty Great Councils (London, 1961) • P. Huizing and K. Wolf, The Ecumenical Council and the Church Constitution (Edinburgh, 1983) • M. Kessler, "Das synodale Prinzip. Bemerkungen zu seiner Entwicklung und Bedeutung," TQ 168 (1988) 43-60 • J. Listl et al., eds., Handbuch des katholischen Kirchenrechts (Regensburg, 1983) 38ff. • J. L. Murphy, The General Councils of the Church (Milwaukee, Wis., 1959) • Ökumene, Konzil, Unfehlbarkeit (Innsbruck, 1979) • R. Riemeck, Glaube–Dogma–Macht. Geschichte der Konzilien (Stuttgart, 1985) • G. Schwaiger, "Die konziliare Idee in der Geschichte der Kirche," RoJKG 5 (1986) 11-23 • H. J. Sieben, Die Konzilsidee des lateinischen Mittelalters (847-1378) (Paderborn, 1984); idem, Die Konzilsidee in der Alten Kirche (Paderborn, 1979) • P. Stockmeier, "Das Konzil in der Kirche. Erwartungen und Widerstände," MTZ 36 (1985) 168-85 • M. Wojtowytsch, Papsttum und Konzile von den Anfängen bis Leo I (440-461) (Stuttgart, 1981). See also the bibliography in "Chalcedon, Council of"; "Ephesus, Council of"; "Nicaea, Councils of"; "Reformed and Presbyterian Churches"; "Trent, Council of"; and "Vatican Council I and II."

HANS SCHNEIDER

Counseling

1. Definition
2. Counseling versus Therapy
3. Methods
4. Biblical Perspectives
5. Trends in the United States

1. Definition

In the broader sense, "counseling" refers to almost any oral or written assistance that is given by a qualified counselor to those who seek counsel. The spectrum reaches from educational and vocational counseling to medical consultation, marriage and family counseling, and family or individual → psychotherapy. The narrower technical sense relates less to the variety of those that seek counsel, or to the nature of their problems, and more to the actual process and goal of counseling. Here both the literature and practice bring to light problems and questions of competence that mark the boundaries between counseling and therapy. The narrower concept also forces theologians to clarify the relation between counseling and → pastoral care.

2. Counseling versus Therapy

Various theories of counseling are clearly reflected in differences in how counseling is distinguished from therapy. Only recently, however, have precise theories been offered (e.g., by A. Houben [b. 1919]). Nevertheless, for some decades analytically oriented and trained therapists have made a sharp distinction between counseling and therapy, at least as regards their psychoanalytically based reservations about direct "counsel" or friendly relations with the patient or client between sessions. At the same time, analytic therapists know that longer and more probing counseling can also go into conflicts in early childhood, which becomes psychotherapy. In the last resort, then, the distinction between counseling and therapy lies less in what takes place and more in the training and competence of the counselor or therapist. From the standpoint of the counselor who is not analytically oriented or trained, however, the distinction depends upon an understanding (sometimes dubious or superficial) of sickness (→ Health and Illness). Psychotherapy deals with sick patients, whereas counseling offers help to clients who are basically healthy but who are having problems. The same reasoning is used in relation to pastoral care.

In principle, there is indeed much truth in such a distinction, but in practice one may ask whether it is always possible to know in advance what element of sickness there is in a complex human problem, or especially who can know this — the one who seeks counsel or the counselor, who may not have the most adequate training. These questions have come under discussion with the development of new programs of counseling that are to some extent analytically oriented. In this connection we also find new concepts of pastoral training (→ Clinical Pastoral Education; Pastoral Care of the Sick; Pastoral Psychology; Rogerian Psychotherapy).

3. Methods

New methods of therapy — such as nondirective theories centered on the client or subject, psychodrama, and transactional analysis — are for their part rooted in the counseling experience of their authors (e.g., C. R. Rogers [1902-87]), although as psychotherapeutic methods, they also rest in part on the theory and practice of counseling. This is also true to some extent of work with groups and personal experience. In particular, counselors themselves profit from these concepts and are sensitized to the relation between themselves and their clients.

Rogers's nondirective method of counseling has strongly influenced modern concepts of pastoral care, at first, in the United States, also in a regrettably superficial use of the method of having the counselor or pastor "reflect back" what the client says. Despite protests raised by persons of unquestionable therapeutic and theological integrity, the beginnings of Clinical Pastoral Education in America have often been without therapeutic profile and theologically very much open to attack. This situation has undoubtedly changed, and today fully qualified supervisors are indispensable in the training of theological students (and other → church employees) in counseling and pastoral care.

4. Biblical Perspectives

The relation between (biblical) wisdom and counseling has not yet been clarified and raises even deeper questions than that between therapy and counseling. Perhaps the therapeutic → diakonia of the → church needs counselors who will give direction to wounded and suffering people, although in a catalytic, not an authoritarian, manner. The nondirective method, which requires all creativity to come from the client, could be considered a concealed form of an authoritarian lack of compassion. Perhaps the true model to which Christian counselors should orient themselves is not the clinical psychologist but the → rabbi, who knows the Bible and knows people. Counseling would then be a matter of seeking the practical wisdom of God.

→ Abortion Counseling; Counseling Centers, Christian

Bibliography: D. W. AUGSBURGER, *Pastoral Counseling across Cultures* (Philadelphia, 1986) • M. BALINT, *Der Arzt, sein Patient und die Krankheit* (Stuttgart, 1965) on the counselor-client relation • H. CLINEBELL, *Basic Types of Pastoral Care and Counseling* (Nashville, 1984) • E. FRIEDMAN, *Generation to Generation* (New York, 1985) • E. GUHR, *Personale Beratung* (Göttingen, 1981) bibliography • B. HOLIFIELD, *History of Pastoral Care in America* (Nashville, 1983) • A. HOUBEN, *Klinisch-psychologische Beratung* (Munich, 1975) • H. JUNKER, *Das Beratungsgespräch* (Munich, 1973) • M. KROEGER, *Themenzentrierte Seelsorge* (2d ed.; Stuttgart, 1976) • C. R. ROGERS, *Client-Centered Therapy* (Boston, 1951) • H. STROTZKA, ed., *Psychotherapie: Grundlagen, Verfahren, Indikationen* (Munich, 1978) • H. J. THILO, *Beratende Seelsorge* (2d ed.; Göttingen, 1975) • R. J. WICKS, R. D. PARSONS, and D. CAPPS, eds., *Clinical Handbook of Pastoral Counseling* (New York, 1993) • *WzM.*

DIETRICH RITSCHL

5. Trends in the United States

Influenced by the theology of → Paul Tillich in the 1950s, W. Oates and S. Hiltner developed methods that integrated theology and psychology. Oates's method was a theologically informed → psychoanalytic approach, and Hiltner's a psychologically informed theological method. In the late 1960s both called for the primacy of theology and the church as the context for pastoral counseling. Although neither was as influential as Rogers, this movement was revived by P. Pruyser, who developed a pastoral diagnostic method using theology rather than psychology as the discipline out of which human ills are understood and ministry defined.

Among evangelicals various bibliotherapeutic methods developed. The most visible authors are J. Adams (nouthetic counseling), L. Crabb (biblical counseling), and G. Collins (Christian counseling). In all these methods, biblical insight is normative for psychological methods.

Early in the 1990s a new method known as short-term or brief pastoral counseling was developed by B. H. Childs, H. Stone, and D. Benner. This approach stressed limited objectives, the use of homework, and a counseling sequence of not more than six sessions.

Bibliography: J. ADAMS, *Competent to Counsel* (Grand Rapids, 1970) • B. H. CHILDS, *Short-Term Pastoral Counseling* (Nashville, 1990) • E. B. HOLIFIELD, *A History of Pastoral Care in America* (Nashville, 1983) • P. PRUYSER, *The Minister as Diagnostician* (Philadelphia, 1976).

MELVIN D. HUGEN

Counseling Centers, Christian

1. Definition
2. Europe
3. United States and Canada
4. Latin America
5. Asia and Africa

1. Definition

Church counseling centers are church institutions at which those seeking advice are offered psychologically qualified → counseling in questions relating to education, partnership, marriage, and life in general.

2. Europe

In Germany 60 percent of those participating in a 1992 survey regarded Protestant church counseling centers as no less a function of the church than the traditional → preaching, → pastoral care, and → Christian education. Of those surveyed, 72 percent said that the church should care for the counseling of individuals, and 77 percent felt the church should care for the problems of those in social need. In 1995 there were more than 1,000 centers in Germany. On the basis of Christ's command in Matt. 10:7-8, their aim is to meet the growing demand for help in crises, → conflicts, and psychological difficulties. They do this by qualified counseling for individuals, married and unmarried couples, and families in specific cases of difficulty (→ Family 3.2). They also try to prevent problems through public lectures, seminars, and various publications (→ Family Education), by → supervision of professional and volunteer workers in the church, and by cooperation with → congregations and social services.

The varied nature of the problems that are raised demands a multiprofessional team of counselors and a multidimensional concept of counseling (including, for example, the cooperation of physicians, social workers, jurists, teachers in remedial education, and theologians with special training in educational counseling, child and youth psychology, marriage counseling, → psychotherapy, or family therapy).

It is essential that church counseling centers be readily accessible, with no financial, political, philosophical, or religious barriers. Information must be given voluntarily and in complete confidence.

Church counseling centers are partly financed by the churches and partly also by secular bodies. It is expected that the workers will have qualifications in psychological counseling but also a Christian commitment.

Church counseling centers are organized both at the territorial level and in a national conference. There is also a European conference and an international commission headquartered in Paris.

Most western European countries have church counseling centers. Switzerland with 85 counseling centers and 160 workers, Finland with 31 counseling centers and 91 mainly family counselors, Norway with 23 counseling centers and 240 workers, and Sweden with 24 counseling centers and 50 counselors operate in much the same way as Germany. Australia has adopted a similar procedure (17 centers and 200 workers).

In Ireland preventive work is done by 153 Roman Catholic centers (available to all residents within 20 miles) and 1,800 workers. The preparing of young people for marriage and the giving of information on → birth control, especially by natural methods, take precedence over the psychological counseling of couples in difficulties. Courses are also offered for married couples seeking marriage enrichment. In Italy, too, the main thrust is preventive (marriage preparation and enrichment, with medical advice on

family planning). Psychological counseling is mainly in the hands of nonchurch centers.

3. United States and Canada

In the United States and Canada there are many different types of church counseling centers, ranging from therapy to pastoral care. First are mental health centers, in which the only workers are psychologists, psychiatrists, and social workers, as well as pastoral counselors. Then there are centers for pastoral counseling run by one or more congregations on an ecumenical basis and using specialists in pastoral psychology and counseling, as well as some secular professionals. Pastors with clinical training offer pastoral-psychological counseling at the local church level. Some churches have teams of specialists. We also find centers for pastoral counseling and personal growth. These church counseling centers are marked by close interdenominational cooperation on the part of churches and social services, by the principle of teamwork, and by a commitment to supervision. Many church counseling centers must support themselves financially and thus advertise themselves, help being offered in this regard by a marketing society known as Samaritan. Some psychiatric hospitals either are operated by a certain denomination (e.g., one in Loma Linda, Calif., by Seventh-day Adventists) or have Christian roots (e.g., the Menninger Clinic, founded by Presbyterians).

In a study of Christian counseling in Canada (1985), J. Stewart and J. C. Carr concluded that church counselors are often isolated and receive inadequate support. They proposed that there should be more collegial cooperation and that the churches should do more to finance and refer clients. Counseling is 47 percent in the hands of professional therapists, 27 percent in the hands of pastoral psychologists, and 25 percent in the hands of voluntary workers.

4. Latin America

Most Latin American countries have church counseling centers for educational, marriage, and family counseling and enrichment. One such effort is Eirene, a society for family and pastoral counseling, with an institute at Quito, Ecuador. The main aim of Eirene is to offer training and further education to Christians by supervised courses in marriage and family counseling, by workshops, and by courses on family life and education from the standpoint of psychology and biblical theology. Counselors are taught at various centers and also by audio and video cassettes.

5. Asia and Africa

In several countries in Africa (Cameroon, Egypt, Ghana, Kenya, Sierra Leone, South Africa, and Zaire) and Asia (India and Sri Lanka), the churches are making some attempts to offer help to families by way of therapy, counseling, and education. The Centre Zairois de l'Enfant et de la Famille illustrates some of these efforts. The center, which was founded in 1986 at Kinshasa, is the first (and thus far the only) counseling center in Zaire. An interdisciplinary team of counselors, therapists, and coworkers, partly trained in Europe and the United States, and working in close association with the university faculties, offers help in therapy, pastoral psychology, and medicine, holds weekend seminars for married couples, counsels church and secular institutions, and trains marriage and family counselors and youth leaders. It also conducts research projects. Help is given to the so-called street children by a clinic and workshop.

As in this example, the aim is to find African answers to African problems in which existing resources are used (e.g., group-discussion therapy). The point of this is to resolve conflicts by bringing all the members of a family or extended family into common discussion. In this case, an ancient process provides the framework, to which principles of Western therapy have been adapted.

→ Abortion Counseling; Conscientious Objection; Crisis Intervention; Foreigners; Handicapped, The; Marginal Groups; Substance Abuse; Suicide; Telephone Ministry

Bibliography: J. C. CARR, J. E. HINKLE, and D. M. MOSS III, *The Organization and Administration of Pastoral Counseling Centers* (Nashville, 1981) • H. J. CLINEBELL, *Basic Types of Pastoral Care and Counseling: Resources for the Ministry of Healing and Growth* (rev. ed.; Nashville, 1984); idem, *Counseling for Spiritually Empowered Wholeness: A Hope-Centered Approach* (rev. ed.; New York, 1995) • A. HAID-LOH, F.-W. LINDEMANN, and M. MÄRTENS, *Familienberatung im Spiegel der Forschung* (Berlin, 1995) • H. HALBERSTADT, *Psychologische Beratungsarbeit in der evangelischen Kirche. Geschichte und Perspektiven* (Stuttgart, 1983) esp. 210-20, "Leitlinien für die psychologische Beratung in evangelischer Erziehungs-, Ehe-, Familien- und Lebensberatung" • E. B. HOLIFIELD, *A History of Pastoral Care in America: From Salvation to Self-Realization* (Nashville, 1983) • S. KEIL, ed., *Familien- und Lebensberatung. Ein Handbuch* (Stuttgart, 1975) • N. KLANN and K. HAHLWEG, *Beratungsbegleitende Forschung. Evaluation von Vorgehensweisen in der Ehe-, Familien- und Lebensberatung und ihre spezifischen Auswirkungen* (Stuttgart, 1994); idem, *Bestandsaufnahme in der Institutioneller Ehe-*, *Familien- und Lebensberatung* (Stuttgart, 1994) • M. KOSCHORKE, "Evangelische Beratung," *HPTh(G)* 4 • MASAMBA MA MPOLO and W. KALU, eds., *The Risks of Growth: Counselling and Pastoral Theology in the African Context* (Geneva, 1985) • J. PATTON, *Pastoral Counseling: A Ministry of the Church* (Nashville, 1983) • J. STEWART and J. C. CARR, *Counseling and Family Life Centre* (Vancouver, 1989).

FRIEDRICH-WILHELM LINDEMANN

Counterculture

1. Term
2. Historical Origins and Development
3. Spiritual Dimensions
4. Decline and Enduring Significance

1. Term

Since the 1970s the term "counterculture" has been applied to a number of late 20th-century sociopolitical movements opposed to capitalist, technological society (→ Capitalism; Technology). In common usage, however, the term is historically identified with the romantic, youth-based "hippie" movement of the 1960s and early 1970s, which embodied the dissatisfaction of a segment of the younger generation with the conformist, consumer ethos (→ Consumption) of postwar Western society — particularly as it developed in the United States. While the emergence of the hippie counterculture was generated by many of the same political, social, and cultural problems that gave rise to the radical New Left in the United States and the student leftist movements of France and West Germany, the two responses — counterculture and leftist politics — should properly be seen as two overlapping, yet distinct, movements. Indeed, the hippie → lifestyle attracted many adherents who were skeptical of the possibility of reforming modern Western culture or who were simply dedicated to dropping out of it altogether. Thus, although there were shared sentiments on some topics (e.g., opposition to the Viet Nam War), the countercultural mind-set was basically an apolitical mixture of good will, good times, and good humor that by turns exasperated and infuriated their politically radical peers.

Opposed to what they perceived as the "straight" world's mad race for status and material goods (→ Materialism), the hippies valued a holistic, expressive search for pleasure and inner meaning. Intrinsic to this quest was a permissive and experimental approach to → sexuality, as well as a near-sacramental view of the role of psychedelic drugs — marijuana and the mind-altering LSD in particular — in attaining emotional equilibrium and spiritual insight. With the medium of rock music serving as the disorganized movement's unifying force, the hippie counterculture moved beyond its bohemian enclaves and for a short period dominated the wider American, and world, youth cultures.

2. Historical Origins and Development

The origins of the counterculture of the 1960s lie deep within the historical and cultural fabric of both European and American society, harking back to early 19th-century critiques of the technologically dependent market society by figures such as William Blake, the → Romantic poets, Henry David Thoreau, and Walt Whitman. Within a purely American context, the counterculture's penchant for communal-style living arrangements (→ Commune) resonated with the earlier examples of the Shakers and experiments like Brook Farm (Mass.), New Harmony (Ind.), and the → Oneida (N.Y.) Community. In its rebellious emphasis on youth and sensual pleasure, the counterculture mirrored the bohemian artistic and literary culture of the 1920s. And in its conscious tendency to opt out of participation in a technologically based consumer society, the counterculture echoed the protests of interwar thinkers like the sociologist Herbert Marcuse.

The direct predecessor of the counterculture emerged after World War II in the United States in the rise of the protest group known as the Beats. Profoundly alienated from mainstream American culture, the Beats flaunted their estrangement from traditional values in their indulgent attitudes about alcohol, drugs, and sex (→ Substance Abuse), as well as in their emphasis on the bold, creative act of individuality (→ Individualism). Attracted to the marginal nature of urban African American culture, they embraced the "hip" language and music of jazz musicians and created a small subculture of nightclubs and coffeehouses in such "Beatnik" havens as New York's Greenwich Village and San Francisco. The movement's intellectual and inspirational leaders were largely literary figures such as poets Allen Ginsberg (*Howl* [1959]) and Lawrence Ferlinghetti (*A Coney Island of the Mind* [1958]) and novelist Jack Kerouac (*On the Road* [1957]). Their writings proved influential not only as exemplars of the 1950s Beat ideal but as background reading for the much larger number of youth in the 1960s who shared their disillusioned reaction to Western (and particularly American) society.

While there were undoubtedly continuities and parallels between the Beat movement and the counterculture of the 1960s, the two were quantitatively and qualitatively different from each other. The developing historical context of the 1960s — which included the growing strife over → civil rights, the Cuban missile crisis, the assassination of President John F. Kennedy, and the escalation of the Viet Nam War — pointed to a climate in the United States and the world that differed greatly from the secure confidence of the 1950s. As a result, a far greater number of young people questioned traditional values and lifestyles. Moreover, the tone of the developing new counterculture was very different. As observer Leonard Wolf pointed out in 1968: "Beat was dark, silent, moody, lonely, sad — and its music was jazz. Hippie is bright, vivacious, ecstatic, crowd-loving, joyful — and its music is rock. Beat was the *Lonely Crowd*; hippie, the crowd tired of being lonely" (p. xviii).

By the mid-1960s the emergence of this carefree, younger new counterculture was noticeable in several major cities, including New York, London, Amsterdam, West Berlin, and Paris. The city that took the lead, however, was undeniably San Francisco. As early as 1964, the city's Haight-Ashbury district became a regional locus for youthful bohemians. Playing a powerful role in this development were groups like novelist Ken Kesey's (*One Flew over the Cuckoo's Nest* [1961]) loose assemblage of kindred spirits, the Merry Pranksters. With a background in Beat literature, an interest in Zen Buddhism, and a new devotion to psychedelics (psilocybin, mescaline, peyote, but esp. LSD), Kesey and the Pranksters' part seminar/part carnival "acid tests" served as an early countercultural center around which a loose community developed. The defining moment of the new movement was the first of a series of "Human Be-Ins" held in Golden Gate Park on January 14, 1967. Following this seminal event was the "Summer of Love" — an open invitation to what the new hippies believed would be a course in the liberation of the human spirit. Food co-ops, free medical clinics, hip businesses and "head shops" (stores specializing in drug paraphernalia), underground newspapers like the *Oracle*, and a continuous broadcast soundtrack of "psychedelic rock" on local FM station KMPX made Haight-Ashbury an idyllic, self-contained countercultural community for much of that year.

The flood of national and international publicity, however, eventually proved too powerful a force. Along with an estimated 100,000 youthful seekers and busloads of tourists who came to gawk at the hippies came a variety of new problems: overcrowding, overpricing, and increasing violence connected with the drug trade and the exploitation of young runaways. Several hippie groups opted to leave San Francisco behind in favor of rural, communal settings. But even as Haight-Ashbury degenerated into a haven for drug addicts, prostitutes, and tourist-driven hippie-chic, the publicity surrounding the Summer of Love spawned replica hippie districts in cities throughout North America and Western Europe. "Hippie" had progressed from the rebellious style of a subcultural fringe to a pervasive generational rejection of the modern Western lifestyle.

3. Spiritual Dimensions

The quest for personal enlightenment played a major role in the lives of many people involved in the counterculture. This was evidenced not only in the use of psychedelic drugs like LSD but in a widespread fascination with exotic forms of religious knowledge and experiences that fed into the larger critique of modern Western culture. → Astrology, numerology, and the → occult were much-favored areas of hippie inquiry, as was Native American spirituality (→ Indians, American). Eastern forms of religious beliefs that emphasized the unity of creation with the discovery of the inner self — particularly → Zen Buddhism, Hare → Krishna and various forms of meditation, and the teachings of the I Ching — proved especially popular (→ New Religions).

Despite the wide interest in nontraditional religions, some members of the counterculture also expressed a renewed interest in Christianity. Attracted by the NT themes of good works, → pacifism, and communal living, some hippies found an appealing religious model in various → Anabaptist and Quaker (→ Friends, Society of) groups. Communes with strong countercultural roots that reflected this influence included Reba Place in Evanston, Illinois, and the Sojourners' Fellowship in Washington, D.C. (the latter particularly combined communal living with an ethic of political activism).

The most significant example of a countercultural move to Christianity, however, was the rise of the North American Jesus People movement. Conservative evangelicalism with its primitivist leanings, separatist mentality, and emphasis on apocalypticism and (particularly within → Pentecostal circles) → ecstatic religious experiences meshed nicely with various counterculture values and found a good reception among hippies disillusioned with the pathologies of drugs, sex, and the predatory habits of many of their peers. The movement first appeared in Haight-Ashbury during the 1967 Summer of Love with the establishment of the Living Room Coffeehouse by several hip converts and a team of local

evangelical pastors. Although Jesus People communes, coffeehouses, and newspapers sprang up in other regions of the United States and Canada, the movement did not establish a strong presence outside the West Coast until a flood of media coverage in 1971. The Jesus People were strongly criticized by fundamentalists and traditionalists, who opposed the movement on grounds of its theology (for strong Pentecostal leanings) and its culture (for acceptance of communes, long hair, hippie styles of dress, and use of rock music as an evangelistic and worship tool). Nonetheless, the movement gained wide acceptance among many evangelical youth (→ Youth Work 5), as well as among evangelical church and parachurch leaders who saw the movement as an effective means of reaching the young. Overall, the Jesus People movement flourished in North America as a separate evangelical youth subculture until well into the late 1970s. While much less successful outside of North America, the movement did encourage new forms of charismatic worship and the growth of a parallel evangelical youth culture in countries like the United Kingdom, where the Greenbelt music festivals were a direct link to touring American Jesus People groups of the early 1970s.

4. Decline and Enduring Significance

The countercultural phenomenon unraveled in the early 1970s almost as quickly as it had appeared in the mid-1960s. A number of factors are responsible, including the youthfulness of its constituency and the faddishness of much of its attraction; the winding down of the Viet Nam War; the unanticipated downsides of hippie enthusiasm for sex and drugs — psychological wounds and rampant venereal diseases, on the one hand, and, on the other, the horrors of "bad trips" and addiction; the backlash of government and law enforcement agencies tightening the clamps on hippie and radical "troublemakers"; and the crushing naïveté of the movement's belief in its own virtue and power to effect change in the world. Whatever the exact weight of the respective causes for its demise, by 1973 it was clear that the hippie experiment was largely over.

Despite the ephemeral nature of the movement, its impact has clearly been both widespread and long-lasting, not the least of which was a substantial conservative backlash in the 1980s. Certainly the counterculture had a major effect in popularizing the recreational use of psychedelic drugs as well as playing a major role in accelerating the so-called sexual revolution. The hippie emphasis on natural living and being in tune with nature also played an important role in promoting concern about healthy eating and physical fitness. Moreover, countercultural concern for the natural world has greatly strengthened interest in protecting the → environment — from grassroots recycling efforts in the American suburbs to international organizations like Greenpeace and Robin Wood. Indeed, the combination of countercultural pacifism, environmentalism, → feminism, and leftist politics now forms a substantial and widely accepted part of the agenda of "liberal" political movements throughout the West, reaching its most potent form in the emergence of the German Green Party and its international counterparts (ca. 1976).

Perhaps, however, the counterculture's strongest impact has been upon Western religion and spirituality. The hippie taste for the occult, Native American religion, and a panoply of Eastern religious philosophies and techniques has issued forth in the amorphous body of religious esoterica known as the → New Age movement. With a holistic, → pantheistic emphasis on personal development and fulfillment that squares nicely with environmentalism, modern therapeutic models, and entrepreneurial promotion, New Age philosophies and styles have proved remarkably portable and adaptable. As a result, what since the 19th century had been the spiritual fringe in Western society has been given a major push into the center of the religious marketplace, largely as a result of the countercultural experience.

The counterculture has had a profound effect upon the Christian church as well. Arguably, countercultural views on human sexuality, personal and community interaction, and the environment have gained a considerable following within sectors of Protestantism and Roman Catholicism. Even within conservative sectors of the church, however, the issues raised by the counterculture have attracted not only recrimination and backlash but a serious reexamination of attitudes toward → stewardship of the environment, the inner life of the church, and Western consumerism. The impact of the Jesus Movement is still particularly noticeable within North American evangelicalism. The growth of — and controversy over — informal, nontraditional "seeker services," the spread of charismatic-style worship, and the use of music based in rock-style idioms is all traceable in part to the influence of the counterculture mediated through the Jesus Movement.

Although the 1967 Summer of Love has long since faded into oblivion, the effects of the counterculture remain strong within North American and Western European culture. This is as true within the church as it is for secular society. It is clear that the forces put into motion by the counterculture in the 1960s will continue to form much of the social and cultural agenda for Western society well into the 21st century.

Bibliography: T. H. ANDERSON, *The Movement and the Sixties: Protest in Modern America from Greensboro to Wounded Knee* (New York, 1995) • R. S. ELWOOD, *The Sixties' Spiritual Awakening* (New Brunswick, N.J., 1994) • R. M. ENROTH, E. E. ERICKSON, and C. B. PETERS, *The Jesus People: Old-Time Religion in the Age of Aquarius* (Grand Rapids, 1973) • H. MARCUSE, *One Dimensional Man* (Boston, 1964) • T. MILLER, *The Hippies and American Values* (Knoxville, Tenn., 1991) • E. P. MORGAN, *The Sixties Experience: Hard Lessons about Modern America* (Philadelphia, 1991) • C. PERRY, *The Haight-Ashbury: A History* (New York, 1984) • C. REICH, *The Greening of America* (New York, 1970) • T. ROSZAK, *The Making of a Counterculture* (Garden City, N.Y., 1969) • R. J. SIDER JR., ed., *Lifestyle in the Eighties: An Evangelical Commitment to Simple Lifestyle* (Philadelphia, 1982) • J. STEVENS, *Storming Heaven: LSD and the American Dream* (New York, 1987) • L. WOLF, *Voices from the Love Generation* (Boston, 1968).

LARRY ESKRIDGE

Counter-Reformation → Catholic Reform and Counterreformation

Covenant

1. OT
    1.1. Translation and Usage
    1.2. Formula
    1.3. Development of the Theological Concept
        1.3.1. God's Self-Commitment
        1.3.2. Israel's Commitment
        1.3.3. Range of the Concept
    1.4. Post-OT Usage
2. NT
    2.1. Term, Usage, and Translation
    2.2. The Eucharistic Tradition
    2.3. Paul
    2.4. Hebrews
    2.5. Luke, Ephesians, Revelation
3. Dogmatic Aspects
    3.1. In the Federal Theology of the Sixteenth and Seventeenth Centuries
        3.1.1. Covenant as Alliance with God
        3.1.2. Covenant of Works and Covenant of Nature
        3.1.3. Cocceius
    3.2. Modern Discussion

1. OT

1.1. *Translation and Usage*

The Hebrew word *bĕrît*, "covenant," occurs 287 times in the OT, only in the singular. Even the latest attempts (e.g., by E. Kutsch) have not convincingly clarified its etymology. Showing a derivation from a Semitic root, however, would not necessarily throw light on its semantic function (J. Barr), which can and must be understood in terms of its semantic field and the relevant context.

In translation, the LXX does not use *synthēkē* (agreement, contract) but almost always *diathēkē* (last will and testament). The Vg (→ Jerome [ca. 345-420]), however, does not have *testamentum* but (except in the Psalms) mostly *foedus* (135 times) or *pactum* (96 times), which led J. Reuchlin (1455-1522) and M. → Luther (1483-1546) to choose *Bund* and the English translators to choose "covenant." This is in keeping with the secular use (e.g., the treaty between Hiram and Solomon in 1 Kgs. 5:12).

Theologically, the prepositions used in conjunction with "covenant" often suggest the idea of a bilateral covenant (Gen. 17:7: "I will establish my covenant between me and you"). But Kutsch definitely (and often rightly) takes the theological term to mean "commitment," with an accent on the expression of self-commitment on the part of the one who guarantees the covenant ("promise"), or the binding of the one on whom it is laid ("claim" or "demand"; → Law). Neither semantically nor theologically may one think of a (reciprocal) pact between God and us.

The verbs connected with *bĕrît* confirm these findings. The oldest and most common term for making a covenant is "cut [*kārat*] a *bĕrît*." An ancient Near Eastern ritual finds reflection in Gen. 15:10, 17-18 and Jer. 34:18-19. This type of dismemberment threatens those who break the *bĕrît*. Prepositions used with *kārat bĕrît* are *'et/'im* (with) and *lĕ* (for, on behalf of). These show that the phrase has a broad range of meaning.

The predominantly Priestly phrase *hēqîm bĕrît* (establish a covenant, set a covenant in force) shows the one-sidedness in the making of a *bĕrît*, as do two other verbs used with it: *nātan* (give) and *śîm* (establish). If there is already a commitment, God remembers *(zākar)* it. The human party can keep *(šāmar)*, break *(hēpēr)*, transgress *('ābar)*, or forget *(šākaḥ)* the covenant. Since most of these verbs frequently also have other expressions for command as objects, "covenant" rarely seems to be the translation. The usage changes with the literary sources, so that it is usually only from the context and semantic field that one may arrive at the proper rendering.

1.2. *Formula*

The OT seldom links *bĕrît* with other words, although we do find "the book of the *bĕrît*" (Exod. 24:7), "the ark of the *bĕrît*" (Josh. 3:6 etc.), "the tablets of the *bĕrît*" (Deut. 9:9-15), and "the blood of the *bĕrît*" (Exod. 24:8). Yet in the history of theology, "covenant" is used as a comprehensive category, and therefore (even though *bĕrît* may not be explicitly present) it is often put with other terms in phrases like "covenant law," "covenant worship," "feast of the covenant," "feast of the renewal of the covenant," "institution of the covenant," and "covenant formula" (R. Smend: "Yahweh as the God of Israel, and Israel as the people of Yahweh").

The idea of a covenant formula is an artificial one (N. Lohfink) that held the field in OT scholarship in the 1960s (K. Baltzer, D. J. McCarthy, M. Weinfeld). It denotes the idea that the form of the covenant, especially in Deuteronomy, followed the schemata of Hittite state treaties (from the 14th and 13th centuries B.C.) or Assyrian suzerainty treaties (8th and 7th centuries B.C.). In the OT, however, the formula was never complete, and the constituent elements (preface, commands, blessing, and cursing) may be explained from Israel's language and religion, quite apart from any appeals to Near Eastern political instruments. Furthermore, the total concept is hardly in keeping with the range of the term *bĕrît* in the OT.

1.3. *Development of the Theological Concept*

To define its relation to God, → Israel at first (in the Mosaic age) did not use *bĕrît*, doing so only toward the end of the monarchy (L. Perlitt). The uncontested focus of the OT theology of the covenant in the Deuteronomic tradition offers a decisive proof of its age (7th and 6th centuries B.C.). If we go back beyond this time, we come up against the silence of the 8th-century prophets regarding the covenant (Perlitt, though see H. Cazelles; Hos. 8:1 is the most debatable verse). Similarly, in the Sinai pericope (Exodus 19; 24; 34) we do not find *bĕrît* in the oldest sources but in the Deuteronomic interpolations (see M. Noth on Exod. 19:3-8; 24:3-8). The postexilic Priestly writing (→ Pentateuch) abandons a Sinai covenant in favor of the promise to Abraham (W. Zimmerli). It thus seems that at a time when Judah was under a growing political threat, the Deuteronomic theologians of the 7th century set Israel's relation to God under the many-layered concept of the *bĕrît*.

1.3.1. *God's Self-Commitment*

Theologically, the term *bĕrît* served first to express the self-commitment of → Yahweh to faithfulness to his people or their representatives. The recipients of this guarantee of the promise (esp. of the threatened land) to the three patriarchs were their descendants, whom → Moses addressed in Deuteronomy. As the means to guarantee the promise, we first have the word (Gen. 12:7), then the oath (24:7), and finally the *bĕrît:* "Yahweh made [or cut] a *bĕrît* with Abram [i.e., solemnly promised him], saying, 'To your descendants I give this land'" (Gen. 15:18). In Deuteronomy the theology of the *bĕrît* rests essentially on the fact that Yahweh guaranteed his gift and promises (i.e., increase of population, the land, his being Israel's God). This commitment to the promises is especially emphatic in the Priestly promise to → Abraham (Gen. 17:1-8) and retrospectively in the revelation to Moses (Exod. 6:3-5).

In Deuteronomistic texts the stability of his dynasty is also promised to → David, either by word (2 Samuel 7) or by oath and/or *bĕrît* (2 Sam. 23:5; Ps. 89:3). Finally, the Priestly promise of life to Noah and his sons extends under the rubric of *bĕrît* to the whole of the human race (Gen. 9:11). Everywhere the *bĕrît* denotes God's faithfulness to his own commitment, both in the present and the → future.

1.3.2. *Israel's Commitment*

Strangely enough, the same term can also denote what the giver of the *bĕrît* requires of the recipients. Thus in the Deuteronomistic writings *bĕrît* as a synonym of *tôrâ* can have the sense of law. Very influential was the localizing of the making of the demand at Horeb (Deuteronomy) or → Sinai (Exodus 19ff.). The so-called Moab *bĕrît* (Deut. 29:1) is thus a subsidiary feature in the Deuteronomistic redaction. In this regard *bĕrît* does not denote the act of the declaration of God's will but the content of this will, that is, the first commandment (worshiping other gods is a breach of the covenant), the → Decalogue (see Deut. 5:2-3, preceding vv. 6ff.), or the whole of Deuteronomy as a book of the law (see 2 Kgs. 23:2-3).

This theology has come into the older strata of the Sinai pericope. According to Exod. 24:7, after the reading of the law the people pledged themselves to obey all that Yahweh had commanded therein and therewith (cf. Exod. 19:5). At that Deuteronomistic stage the words of the *bĕrît* are the same as the words of the *tôrâ* (2 Kgs. 23:3, 24). They are now written in a book. They are read and commanded, heard and done. Obedience to this revealed will of God leads to → blessing and → life; disobedience, to → cursing and/or → death (Deuteronomy 28; 30).

Even the promise of the new covenant after the breaking of the old (Jer. 31:31-34) is simply the promise of a new and more inward commitment: "This is the [new] *bĕrît.* . . . I will put my law within them."

1.3.3. *Range of the Concept*

The broad theological use of the term *bĕrît* could easily lead to the mistaken view that the basic sense is that of a contract between Yahweh and Israel. But the recipients of a *bĕrît* are first blessed and then show themselves obedient. The word makes sense only if the sovereignty of the God who commits himself by giving and demanding remains inviolate. The term thus covers the whole area between → gospel and → law in the OT.

1.4. *Post-OT Usage*

In the post-OT Hebrew of the → Qumran writings, the term *bĕrît* is used almost as it is in the OT. God remembers his promise to Israel, the fathers, and David. He has laid upon Israel an obligation to do what he has commanded. In rabbinic Judaism, on the basis of Gen. 17:10, the focus in *bĕrît* is on → circumcision as a mark of belonging, so that *bĕnê bĕrît* (sons of the covenant) could become a term for Israelites. In the Aramaic of the Targums *bĕrît* is almost always translated *qĕyām* and denotes above all the obligation established by God.

Bibliography: K. BALTZER, *Das Bundesformular* (Neukirchen, 1960; 2d ed., 1964) • J. BARR, "Some Semantic Notes on the Covenant," *Beiträge zur alttestamentlichen Theologie* (FS W. Zimmerli; Göttingen, 1977) 23-38 • J. BEGRICH, "Berīt" (1944), *Gesammelte Studien zum Alten Testament* (Munich, 1964) 55-66 • H. CAZELLES, "La rupture de la *bᵉrît* selon des prophètes," *JJS* 33 (1982) 133-44 • W. GROSS, "Bundeszeichen und Bundesschluß in der Priesterschrift," *TTZ* 87 (1978) 98-115 • R. KRAETZSCHMAR, *Die Bundesvorstellung im Alten Testament in ihrer geschichtlichen Entwicklung* (Marburg, 1896) • E. KUTSCH, "Bund (Altes Testament bis Neues Testament)," *TRE* 7.397-410 (bibliography); idem, *Verheißung und Gesetz. Untersuchungen zum sogenannten Bund im Alten Testament* (Berlin, 1973) revision of six important essays, 1967-72 • C. LEVIN, *Die Verheißung des neuen Bundes* (Göttingen, 1985) • N. LOHFINK, *Die Landverheißung als Eid. Eine Studie zu Gn 15* (Stuttgart, 1967) • D. J. MCCARTHY, *Treaty and Covenant* (Rome, 1963; 2d ed., 1978) • G. E. MENDENHALL, "Covenant," *IDB* 1.714-23; idem, *Law and Covenant in Israel and the Ancient Near East* (Pittsburgh, 1955) • E. W. NICHOLSON, *God and His People: Covenant and Theology in the OT* (New York, 1986) • L. PERLITT, *Bundestheologie im Alten Testament* (Neukirchen, 1969) • R. SMEND, *Die Bundesformel* (Zurich, 1963) • M. WEINFELD, "בְּרִית *bᵉrîth*," *TDOT* 2.253-79 • W. ZIMMERLI, "Sinaibund und Abrahambund. Ein Beitrag zum Verständnis der Priesterschrift" (1960), *Gottes Offenbarung. Gesammelte Aufsätze* (Munich, 1963; 2d ed., 1969) 205-16.

LOTHAR PERLITT

2. NT

2.1. Term, Usage, and Translation

The translation of the NT term *diathēkē,* like that of the OT term *bĕrît,* is contested. The NT authors took over *diathēkē* as a rendering of *bĕrît* from the LXX. In classical and Hellenistic Greek this word usually has the sense of last will and testament. Never, or only marginally, does it mean "covenant" (debatable in Aristophanes). Yet many NT scholars firmly believe that "covenant" is the true meaning of *diathēkē* in the NT (e.g., U. Luz and H. Hegermann). E. Kutsch, in contrast, interprets it in agreement with his understanding of the OT *bĕrît,* philological findings, and incisive exegesis as "disposing" or "disposition" (of God).

What is indubitable is that in every reference to *diathēkē,* God's saving work is prominent. In the NT the correspondence between the indicative of the effected work of reconciliation and the resultant imperative may be essential, yet when *diathēkē* is at issue, there is normally no question of responsive human action. Thus Kutsch's interpretation is probably right in principle. Nevertheless, the question of the meaning of *diathēkē* cannot be answered by using a single English word for every NT instance of it. → Paul and Hebrews deliberately use the Greek term in such a way as to exploit its broad range of meaning in order to advance their own theological expositions.

2.2. The Eucharistic Tradition

The oldest *diathēkē* tradition in the NT is the saying about the blood or the cup in the story of the Last Supper (→ Eucharist 2). Yet in the phrase "blood of the *diathēkē*" (Mark 14:24; Matt. 26:28) or "new *diathēkē* in my blood" (1 Cor. 11:25; Luke 22:20), *diathēkē* might be a secondary interpretation. The phrase "blood of the *diathēkē*" takes up typologically (Kutsch; → Typology) the *to haima tēs diathēkēs* of Exod. 24:8, transcending and dissolving the → Sinai *diathēkē* as God sets up a new saving order of → reconciliation by the self-giving of Jesus.

2.3. Paul

It is hard to say whether Paul knew the idea of the *diathēkē* only from the eucharistic tradition and then used the term in different ways in his theological arguments. In Galatians he is engaged in a debate about the → law with the Judaizers, for whom Christianity is simply a messianically fulfilled → Judaism. The → Abraham *diathēkē* has for Paul both chronological and material priority over the Mosaic law (Gal. 3:15-19). Even if *diathēkē* has the sense "testament" here, its character as promise is decisive.

In Gal. 4:21–5:1 *diathēkē* almost has the sense of → religion. The Jewish religion of law as a religion of bondage and the Christian religion as one of →

freedom are mutually exclusive. The *diathēkē* symbolized by Hagar cannot be the covenant of God with → Israel at Sinai, for according to 3:19, God was not present when the law was given.

In 2 Cor. 3:6, 14 the contrast between the old and the new order of salvation is shown to be a very radical one as the contrast between letter and spirit, or between → death and → life. Thus the concept of the old *diathēkē* comes close to having the sense of the Scripture of the old order of salvation. Paul, however, regards himself as a servant of the new order of salvation, but with no mention of a written record in this case. He does not have in mind our usual description of the Bible as the Old and New Testaments.

According to Rom. 11:27 (cf. Isa. 59:21; 27:9) the forgiveness of sins is for Israel the new, not the renewed, covenant. Only the pl. *hai diathēkai* in Rom. 9:4 implies a more positive evaluation of OT dispositions in accordance with the generally more positive view of Israel and the law in this epistle. Here, the connotation of "dispositions" seems at least to be alluded to.

2.4. Hebrews

The word *diathēkē* is common in Hebrews, beginning in 7:22. It appears often in OT quotations, among which Jer. 31:31-34 occupies a special place theologically as the promise of the new *diathēkē* (Heb. 8:8-13; 10:16-17). In contrast to the old *diathēkē* that God made with → Moses (9:20; see also v. 4: "the tablets of the *diathēkē*" — the meaning "covenant" is present here), the "new" (8:8; 9:15; 12:24), "better" (7:22; 8:6), and "eternal" (13:20) *diathēkē* is grounded in the high-priestly ministry (→ High Priest) and expiatory death of Christ (→ Atonement). The *diathēkē* is God's disposition in pure grace, even though Christ is called its mediator (8:6; 9:15; 12:24). In 9:16-17 *diathēkē* has the sense "will" or "testament." The author of Hebrews plays on the term similar to the way Paul does.

2.5. Luke, Ephesians, Revelation

Luke uses *diathēkē* for the old order of salvation in Luke 1:72 ("his holy *diathēkē*"), Acts 3:25 ("You [Jews] are the descendants . . . of the *diathēkē,*" in the sense "descendants of the promise"), and Acts 7:8 ("*diathēkē* of → circumcision," where the meaning might well be "covenant"). In Eph. 2:12 the expression *tōn diathēkōn tēs epangelias* has primary reference to the OT promises given to Israel. Rev. 11:19 mentions the OT → ark of the covenant as an object of heavenly worship (cf. Heb. 9:4).

Bibliography: J. Behm, "Διαθήκη," *TDNT* 2.124-34 • E. Grässer, *Der Alte Bund im Neuen* (Tübingen, 1985) • H. Hegermann, "Διαθήκη," *EDNT* 1.299-301 •

H. Hübner, *Biblische Theologie des Neuen Testaments* (2 vols.; Göttingen, 1990-93) 1.77-100, 2.209-20 • G. D. Kilpatrick, "Διαθήκη in Hebrews," *ZNW* 68 (1977) 263-65 • E. Kutsch, "Bund III," *TRE* 7.406-9 (bibliography); idem, *Neues Testament–Neuer Bund? Eine Fehlübersetzung wird korrigiert* (Neukirchen, 1978) • F. Lang, "Abendmahl und Bundesgedanke im Neuen Testament," *EvT* 35 (1975) 524-38 • U. Luz, "Der alte und der neue Bund bei Paulus und im Hebr.," *EvT* 27 (1967) 318-36 • V. Wagner, "Der Bedeutungswandel von בְּרִית חֲדָשָׁה bei der Ausgestaltung der Abendmahlsworte," *EvT* 35 (1975) 538-44.

Hans Hübner

3. Dogmatic Aspects

3.1. *In the Federal Theology of the Sixteenth and Seventeenth Centuries*

The term "covenant" was central in the so-called federal theology of the 16th and 17th centuries. U. → Zwingli (1484-1531; → Zwingli's Theology) first introduced it in his controversy with the → Anabaptists. The → baptism (§2.2) of infants was for him a covenant sign like → circumcision in the OT.

3.1.1. *Covenant as Alliance with God*

With the extension of the covenant concept from the middle of the 16th century, the emphasis shifted. The covenant was now seen as a divinely instituted and legally regulated alliance whose conditions we are under obligation to observe. What caused the shift has not as yet been adequately explained. In part, a tendency to legalism seems to be involved, but it is more probable that in the sphere of Reformed theology, which was governed by J. → Calvin's (1509-64) doctrine of predestination, the concept of the covenant offered a needed counterpoise (→ Calvin's Theology; Predestination).

In favor of the latter view is the fact that in this area, Reformed theology received its decisive impulses, not from Calvin and his immediate followers, but from H. Bullinger (1504-75) in Zurich and from C. Olevianus (1536-87) and Z. Ursinus (1534-83), the authors of the → Heidelberg Catechism.

3.1.2. *Covenant of Works and Covenant of Nature*

The next step at the end of the 16th century and in the first decades of the 17th came with contributions from especially British theologians like R. Rollock (d. 1599) and W. Ames (1576-1633). A distinction was now made betwen the covenant of works (*foedus operum*) or covenant of nature (*foedus naturae*), which God made with → Adam before the fall, and the covenant of grace (*foedus gratiae*), which is to be found in Jesus Christ. As Jesus Christ took upon himself the penalty of death, which was necessarily imposed when the covenant of works was broken, he made possible a new covenant whereby the elect may again achieve salvation on the condition of → faith and repentance (→ Penitence). Yet the conditions of the covenant of works are still negatively in force. As the → Puritan J. Owen (1616-83) put it in the 17th century, for human beings in general, God is the just and wrathful Judge, and only for the elect is he a loving → Father. The reverse side of this position was a far-reaching → dualism of → nature and → grace, the results of which are comparable with the worst interpretations of a → two-kingdoms doctrine. (The ideology of apartheid in → South Africa [§3], for example, easily found theological support by playing on the distinction between the covenant of nature and the covenant of grace.)

3.1.3. *Cocceius*

Federal theology came to fruition in the truly magnificent work *Summa doctrinae de foedere et testamento Dei* (Comprehensive treatise on the doctrines of the covenant and testament of God; 1648) by J. Cocceius (1603-69), a disciple of Ames. In this context we can refer only to two aspects. First, Cocceius anchored the concept of the covenant in the nature of God himself. The covenant of grace rests on a covenant (of redemption) made in eternity between the Father and the Son. Second, he developed a large-scale theology of salvation history in which God's whole action toward us is characterized by the antithesis between the covenant of works and the covenant of grace, and by the successive abrogations of the former in favor of the latter. Although during his lifetime Cocceius was embroiled in constant controversy with more orthodox Calvinists, his schema was largely adopted in Reformed theology in Britain and North America.

3.2. *Modern Discussion*

It cannot be denied that this approach raises various problems. In particular, debates within Reformed theology in the 18th and 19th centuries showed that to attach conditions to the covenant of grace and to distinguish between the covenant of grace and the covenant of works or nature is to cause serious theological and pastoral difficulties. K. → Barth (1886-1968) offered a very promising solution to these difficulties when in *CD* III/1 he described the covenant of grace in Jesus Christ as "the internal basis of creation" and creation as "the external basis of the covenant." This insight may allow us to adopt and correct the concern of the older federal theology.

Future efforts in this direction, however, must also take another factor into account. In the light of modern biblical research it seems very doubtful whether the OT *běrît* and the NT *diathēkē* really have the same sense as a term like *foedus* (i.e., covenant in the sense of contract). The undoubtedly valuable associations of the term would better be expressed, perhaps, in some other way. The faithfulness of God, which is biblically attested and based, might well be best suited to render this necessary service.

→ Calvinism

Bibliography: P. Y. DE JONG, *The Covenant Idea in New England Theology, 1620-1847* (Grand Rapids, 1945) • J. F. G. GOETERS, "Föderaltheologie," *TRE* 2.246-52 • K. HAGEN, "From Testament to Covenant," *SCJ* 3 (1972) 1-24 • A. I. C. HERON, ed., *The Westminster Confession in the Church Today* (Edinburgh, 1982) bibliography • E. L. LUEKER, "Federal Theology," *LuthCyc* 294.

ALASDAIR I. C. HERON

Cranmer, Thomas

Born in 1489 at Aslockton, Nottinghamshire, second son of a minor squire, Thomas Cranmer completed a doctorate in divinity at Cambridge. There he acquired a knowledge of Scripture, respect for its authority, and interest in its plain exposition. → Luther's revolt had an impact in the 1520s, and papal resistance to reform convinced Cranmer that correction of abuses demanded elimination of the power of Rome.

In 1529, while discussing the crisis in Henry VIII's suit for marriage annulment, Cranmer suggested to two of the king's advisers that European faculties of → canon law should make the decision. The king liked the proposal and soon commissioned Cranmer to write an opinion, then present the case at Cambridge and abroad. In 1532 Henry recalled him as the new archbishop of Canterbury, a post he accepted only very reluctantly. As archbishop, Cranmer dissolved Henry's first marriage and ratified the new marriage to Ann Boleyn, also sponsoring the baby Elizabeth. Three times again he would have the unpleasant task of helping the king out of his matrimonial tangles. If his role was not heroic here, he followed law and precedent, suffered from an uneasy → conscience, and later tried to press for necessary canon revision.

Theologically, Cranmer made the case against papal supremacy, assailed private masses and purgatory, used the king's need for Lutheran allies to promote → justification by → faith (Ten Articles and Bishop's Book [1536]), and stressed the need for catechetical instruction. In 1534 Cranmer initiated a project of translating the Bible into English. Tradi-

tionalist bishops stalled this effort, but in 1537 Cranmer persuaded Thomas Cromwell and Henry to sponsor the so-called Matthew's Bible. Cranmer wrote a preface commending Bible reading, and in spite of restrictions later in Henry's reign, the Bible remained and became the basis of the Elizabethan Bishops' Bible and the definitive King James Version of 1611. Cranmer also introduced an official English → litany, which was the first part of the 1549 prayer book and was retained almost unchanged in all subsequent editions through that of 1662.

The last years of Henry were difficult for Cranmer. Three serious attempts were made to remove him, and only the king's intervention saved him. Significantly Henry turned finally to Cranmer for spiritual comfort. At the end the king had been contemplating more radical reform along with France, and his arrangements for the minority of his son Edward VI gave the archbishop new and greater freedom. Reforming work could now forge ahead more rapidly.

First Cranmer tried to improve parish ministry by publishing → Erasmus's *Paraphrases,* writing homilies for unlicensed ministers to read, putting the Gospels and Epistles in English, appointing reforming bishops, bringing in European scholars, and insisting that at least the rudiments of Christianity be taught.

An English Communion replaced the Latin → Mass in 1548. The first → Book of Common Prayer brought more comprehensive reform in 1549. Combining reforming and traditional elements, Cranmer displayed true liturgical genius in this work. Cranmer undertook more radical reform (esp. in → baptism and the → Eucharist) in the second prayer book (1552), which with slight changes eventually became the Elizabethan book and the basis of 1662, thus shaping → Anglican liturgical life for centuries.

Nor had Cranmer forgotten doctrine. Facing confused teaching in his own diocese, he drew up a list of authoritative articles that he brought to the bishops and council in 1551. After revision, they came out as an official statement, the Forty-Two Articles, in 1553. The aim was comprehension rather than exclusion, but only within limits. The main features are affirmation of the early creeds, acceptance of the Reformation view of Scripture and justification, advocacy of the Reformed teaching on the → sacraments (esp. the Eucharist), and rejection of traditionalist positions on, for example, masses and → purgatory. Cranmer expounded his eucharistic teaching in his main work, *The True and Catholic Doctrine of the Lord's Supper.*

In addition to giving the church the Bible and →

liturgy in English, and also a doctrinal statement, Cranmer sought a revision of canon law. The government, however, having no taste for → church discipline, successfully thwarted him in this field. As it was, he finished the doctrinal statement only just in time, for Edward died in July 1553, and Mary's accession ended the whole reforming movement. Unwillingly involved in the plot to oust Mary, Cranmer was speedily arrested, but it was finally on the charge of eucharistic heresy that he was tried, convicted, deposed, and, in 1556, burned at the stake. In his last months he was under unrelenting pressure to recant. In the end he seemed ready to yield, but at the stake, instead of reading the public recantation, he boldly recanted of the recantation, and as a gesture dramatically held out the hand that had signed it first to the flames.

Cranmer apparently died in failure. Mary repealed all reforming legislation, reformers were scattered or burned or became turncoats, and the mass of clergy and people had as yet no enthusiasm for the changes. Nevertheless, what Cranmer had done would have an enduring impact once Mary's unhappy regime came to a quick and ignominious close and the Elizabethan Settlement secured the place of the English Bible, restored the second prayer book, reintroduced the articles as the familiar Thirty-Nine Articles, and brought back reforming bishops. By his initiating of reform in → piety, → worship, doctrine, and pastoral practice, Cranmer had in fact bequeathed to his church a legacy both lasting and precious.

Bibliography: Primary sources: Works (ed. G. E. Duffield; Philadelphia, 1965) • *Works* (ed. H. Jenkyns; 4 vols.; 1833) • *Works* (ed. Parker Society; 2 vols.; 1844-46).

Secondary works: P. AYRIS and D. SELWYN, eds., *Thomas Cranmer: Churchman and Scholar* (Rochester, N.Y., 1993) • G. W. BROMILEY, *Thomas Cranmer, Theologian* (New York, 1956) • P. N. BROOKS, *Thomas Cranmer's Doctrine of the Eucharist* (2d ed.; Basingstoke, 1992) • D. MACCULLOCH, "Cranmer, Thomas," *OER* 1.448-50; idem, *Thomas Cranmer* (New Haven, 1996) • A. F. POLLARD, *Thomas Cranmer and the English Reformation, 1489-1556* (Hamden, Conn., 1904) • C. H. SMYTH, *Cranmer and the Reformation under Edward VI* (Cambridge, 1926) • J. STRYPE, *Memorials of Thomas Cranmer* (3 vols.; 1848).

GEOFFREY W. BROMILEY

Creation

1. In the History of Religion

1.1. Perspectives on Creation

Philosophy and natural science trace the origin of the world and humanity back to impersonal, law-governed causes. Religion, however, finds a suprahuman plan behind life and its foundations. In addition to the elementary language of confession (→ Confession of Faith), reflection on creation also can draw on philosophical and scientific argumentation, which makes use of elements and general concepts familiar from the world around us. It may also use the language of → myth, which presents creation in the story of a one-time, fundamental event. Myth and the religious confession make the regularity of the world dependent upon this event and put humanity in the center, whereas → philosophy uses myth in a conscious, nonmythical way to depict creation as a sequence in time, even though in truth it regards the world as timeless. For confession the world finds its inner basis and meaning in the central experience of the divine power's self-revelation as Creator. According to myth, today's order arose out of chaos and stagnation through the formative power of the Holy One. This order persists until it is overlayed, modified, or replaced by something new.

1.2. Creation in Middle Eastern Religions

1.2.1. Israel and Mesopotamia

The God of Israel and the Christian world miraculously created his people and, before that, the world itself as their dwelling, through his Spirit and his formative word (→ Primeval History). He made life out of dead chaos without reliance on any preceding structures. The Babylonian city god Marduk in the Akkadian epic *Enuma elish* (ca. 1100 B.C.), with which the biblical story shows several parallels, was the creator in a dramatic encounter with chaos (→ Babylonian and Assyrian Religion). Cosmogony is preceded here by a theogony with developments within the divine world itself. The Sumerians tell how the goddess of the primal ocean, Nammu, gave birth by parthenogenesis to An, the god of heaven, and Ki, the goddess of earth, and these two then gave birth to Enki, the king of the freshwater ocean and orderer of human civilization, and Enlil, the god of the air, who separates → heaven and earth. The Akkadians put Marduk in place of the latter, the supreme god who rules over destiny and who slays Tiamat, goddess of the primal ocean, and makes her body the vault of heaven and the earth.

Whereas the God of Israel is already recognized as the Creator of the great sea monsters and the Savior from the flood of chaos who has made his bow the → symbol (§2) of his divine lordship (→ Covenant), it is only by his bow that Marduk first gains victory over the divine-demonic flood of chaos. The sequence of creation in *Enuma elish* corresponds to what we find in the first biblical account, though the creation of man and woman is not the crowning medium for divine power on earth but an appendix of creation to the alliances and conflicts of the gods. For these gods, by the resolve of Marduk, humanity is created to render service. This is why, already in the Sumerian epos, human beings are rescued from the flood.

Whereas the God of Israel wills to dwell with his people, to bless them from his → sanctuary, and to bless the peace following the conclusion of creation, the gods freed by Marduk set up the sanctuary of his global dominion in Babylon. Among the Sumerians the → temple (§1) and city sanctify the world, and the king who dwells there, mediating between humanity and the gods, protects and defends the threatened world and brings it new life at each New Year's festival.

1.2.2. Egyptian Parallels

There are many parallels in Egyptian texts, though in their theology only one god can be the creator. Behind the texts stands the flooding of the Nile as an experience of the primal, divine power of Ka, who is the root of any individuality embodied in the soul of the dead Ba. The Creator here arose from himself. A nuanced plurality unfolds from him. At the end of the ages, when there will be no more sunrises, New Years, or renewals of the monarchy, the necessary repetition and confirmation of creation having ceased, all things will be put back together again as at the outset, and the Creator with them. An earlier time thus preceded creation.

The mythology of Heliopolis called this primal being Nu and its hiddenness Amoln. These, with their feminine counterparts, were embodiments of the primal chaos from which the city god Atum derived as the primal hill. Atum was the source of the first duality. Men and women are like him, and the world was created for their sake. At Hermopolis the crawling out of frogs and → serpents, cows and lotus from the water and the primitive ovum were depictions of the upheaval that took place as the primal time came to an end. The "invisible" Amon, revered as the city god of Thebes, hovers like a bird over the world of chaos and brings forth being through his creative cry.

Although creation in Egypt is largely viewed as an incomplete process into which human actions are also integrated, creation by Ptah, viewed more than an act (Ptah having established creation with great artifice through his word according to a plan devised in his heart), does exhibit the character of conclusion: "Ptah rested when he had created all things and all divine words." In Theban texts, the remoteness of the creator conceived as the sun god Re provides a less distinct kind of caesura between *creatio primordialis* and *creatio continua*. The creation of human beings is ascribed primarily to Khnum, the god of the cataract of Aswan, who creates from the loam of the ground (→ Egyptian Religion).

1.3. Worldwide Themes

1.3.1. Simplicity to Multiplicity

In India (→ Hinduism) creative activity belongs by nature to the lord of the world. Because he creates freely out of joy and will, "play" is often portrayed as the guiding motif in creation. Brahman, from whom all things come, is his own creator and, as such, makes himself into primal spirit and primal matter. Creation, after resting in him, proceeds forth from him, is upheld, and is then taken back by him as it dissolves. Primal unity is more superpersonal than impersonal. The will to create assumes concrete form as the personal creator of the world, Brahma, and the spirit as the begetter of all things, Prajāpati. Consciousness and the universe are both products of creative desire, as in concretions in later Sankhya → Yoga and → Buddhism. Viewed as his own → father, and identified with the universe, the year, and the fiery altar, the divine consumes itself in its creations. But the whole is an eternal process of creation from the being of the one, though the latter does not lose its transcendence (→ Immanence and Transcendence). As the spider produces threads (a motif found also in China, the islands of the Pacific, and the American Southwest), the earth its plants, and the flame its sparks, so all things have their origin in the incorruptible.

Other notions hold that the one god created heaven and earth from his own body; that the One created a second, and the father god joined himself to the daughter in a dangerous incest; that the all-soul in the form of the primal giant Purusha dissociates into a pair, and from their marriage all the species developed; that the primal giant gave birth to a feminine principle of creation that bore the world; that from the seemingly sleeping, indefinite, primal state the self-borne primal spirit emerged, itself undeveloped, developing the world and putting to flight the darkness, changing its creative power into the elements, and from its Self giving rise to the power of thought, and developing from this the concept of ego that produces ideas of itself.

A similar understanding of the primal creative ground may be found in Iran (→ Iranian Religions), with its infinite primal light that contains within itself all ideal and material creation, or in the primal god Zurvan, whose ambivalent thinking gives rise to the good creator god and his opponent. Note also Oceanos in Homer (end of the 8th cent. B.C.) or chaos in Hesiod (ca. 700 B.C.); the nonexistent supreme god of → Gnosis; the Ginnungagap of the Germans; the one, eternal Tao of China (→ Taoism and Chinese Popular Religion), which expresses itself in the polar opposites yin and yang; the chaos or nothingness that is simultaneously being-in-itself in Polynesian primal deities like Tangaroa, Kiho, or, among the Maori (→ New Zealand 8), in being-in-itself as pure thought that takes shape as both non-

being and being; the cosmic totality in the mouth of the water snake in Borneo; and the Taiowa of North American Hopi (→ Indians, American), who had the infinite world in mind and, in thinking of the finite, set forth an active power that formed the creative spider.

The natural-generative aspect of this basic motif of self-development is presented in many similes. The one hovering over the water like a shoot of gold in Vedic Indian thought is also the golden yolk that formed itself at the beginning, the creator god Prajāpati that is the equivalent of finite time (cf. the myths of the Chinese P'an Ku, the Iranian Zurvan, and the Polynesian Taaro, as well as those of Orphism and of the African Dogon). The feminine aspect is even more pronounced in the symbolism of the mussel (Polynesian), the cave of the earth (North America, Africa), or the rock or plant (Melanesia), from which all things come; or in the mother earth (→ Mother Goddesses), which generates itself from chaos and releases heaven from within itself as the principle of all further generation. This foundational motif expresses the notion of development and change within the deity. In a derivative form, → ancestors are understood as creative powers as well.

1.3.2. The Almighty and His Rivals

More strongly among gatherers, hunters, and herding farmers, we find a complex of motifs that are bound up with a primal father who is both self-sufficient and almighty. Creation among such groups is by thought and voice (Zoroaster, Gnosis, → Islam, the Polynesian Tuemotuans and Maori). The primal father is omnipotent on the basis of his wisdom; he knows the potentiality of every form and knows all the powers that would give them actuality independently of feminine matter. By his will we may also expect a renewal and refashioning of the world. Whereas this belief in a supreme god and → monotheism stresses the absoluteness of the god's power, myths of lesser male beings posit the presence of a capacity — one juxtaposed to the feminine capacity to give birth — to bring forth life from within a flood or to rescue the earth from feminine inundation (both in North America).

A direct conflict between hunters and gatherers, on the one hand, and emerging agricultural society or military invaders, on the other, seems to be reflected in the motif of the diver (North America, East Asia, eastern Europe, India). The matter that is capable of life is hidden in the water and must be brought to light by a cultural hero, usually an animal, so that it may undergo development. This often includes the motif of rival creators. The independent creative work attempted by the diver is disqualified in comparison with that of a higher ranking being, which explains the imperfection and evil that we find in the world. We find such myths in Gnosticism, in eastern Europe, and in northern Asia. Zoroaster probably expanded on this theme in his doctrine of the good spirit of Ahura Mazda and the destructive spirit, who, by the decision of his twin, became the → devil. In Iranian Zurvanism evil was created by the evil principle through self-sodomy.

1.3.3. *Admixture and Separation*

Often divine creation is depicted as sexual union, especially in India, where the personal deity joins his own, conscious creative power Shakti. In Tibetan-Lamaistic teaching (→ Tibetan Religions) the "second-world" of paradise is created from the coupling in the hearts of those who meditate (→ Meditation). This involves coupling of those that are sexually different, then separation on the basis of differences (Homer). The motif of violent severing (Hesiod) can also include the primal monster that tyrannically holds captive the forces of life and that is trampled and smashed. Thus the dragon Vṛtra is destroyed by the warrior god Indra in India, with parallels in the Iranian New Year's festival, and the stone monster Ullikummi is destroyed by the storm god Tešup among the Hittites.

The → sacrificial death of a positive divine being can also be the theme of creative separation. One form is the death in childbirth of the mother who releases her powers of fertility upon the world (North American Hurons, African Mande, also Japan). Or we may have the killing of the Indonesian Dema, or of Mediterranean mystery deities (→ Mystery Religions), which brings gain both in this world and in the beyond. Myths speak especially of the sacrificial death of a powerful primal giant (Indian Purusha, German Ymir, Chinese P'an Ku, Nommo of the African Dogon) whose power is transferred to the whole universe when he is slain and dismembered. The motif of a divine sacrifice is of basic significance in Indo-European cultures that see correspondence between parts of the body and parts of the cosmos and society and thus believe in a basic consubstantiality in a widespread and enduring hierarchical total system.

→ Confucianism; Demons; Emanation; Greek Religion; Hell; Hellenistic-Roman Religion; Innocence, State of; Life; Nature; Nature Religion; Ontology; Paradise; Roman Religion; Tribal Religions; Reincarnation; Time and Eternity

Bibliography: J. ASSMANN, "Schöpfergott, Schöpfung," *LÄ* 5.676-90 • H. BAUMANN, *Schöpfung und Urzeit des Menschen im Mythus der afrikanischen Völker* (2d ed.; Berlin, 1974) • J. BLACK and A. GREEN, *Gods, Demons, and Symbols of Ancient Mesopotamia* (Austin, Tex., 1992) • A. DUNDES, ed., *The Flood Myth* (Berkeley, Calif., 1988); idem, *Sacred Narrative* (Berkeley, Calif., 1984) • A. EHRHARDT, *The Beginning: A Study in the Greek Philosophical Approach to the Concept of Creation from Anaximander to St. John* (Manchester, 1968) • M. ELIADE, *Australian Religions* (Ithaca, N.Y., 1973); idem, *A History of Religious Ideas* (3 vols.; Chicago, 1979-85) • E. HORNUNG, *Idea into Image: Essays on Ancient Egyptian Thought* (New York, 1992) • O. A. ILOANUSI, *Myths of the Creation of Man and the Origin of Death in Africa* (Frankfurt, 1984) • B. LINCOLN, *Myth, Cosmos, and Society: Indo-European Themes of Creation and Destruction* (Cambridge, Mass., 1986) • H. LIXFELD, *Gott und Teufel als Weltschöpfer* (Munich, 1971) • C. H. LONG, "Cosmogony," *EncRel(E)* 4.94-100; idem, ed., *Alpha: The Myths of Creation* (New York, 1963) • R. A. MALL, *Indische Schöpfungsmythen* (Bonn, 1982) • U. MANN, *Schöpfungsmythen. Vom Ursprung und Sinn der Welt* (Stuttgart, 1982) • V. NOTTER, *Biblischer Schöpfungsbericht und ägyptische Schöpfungsmythen* (Stuttgart, 1974) • P. RICOEUR, *Symbolism of Evil* (Boston, 1969) • *Die Schöpfungsmythen. Ägypter, Sumerer, Hurriter, Hethiter, Kanaanier und Israeliten* (2d ed.; Zurich, 1991) • B. C. SPROUL, *Primal Myths: Creating the World* (2d ed.; San Francisco, 1980) • C. F. VON WEIZSÄCKER, *Die Tragweite der Wissenschaft,* vol. 1, *Schöpfung und Weltentstehung* (5th ed.; Stuttgart, 1976) • E. ZENGER, *Gottes Bogen in den Wolken* (Stuttgart, 1983).

CHRISTOPH ELSAS

2. OT

2.1. *Israelite Explanations of the Universe*

The ancient Israelites explained the origin of the universe in three different ways: through a struggle with chaos, through procreation, and by divine fiat.

2.1.1. Various poetic texts (e.g., Exodus 15; Psalms 18, 68, 104; Hab. 3:8; Job 38–41; Isa. 51:9-10) describe Yahweh's struggle against primordial foes to wrest order from chaos. Traditions vary about the ultimate fate of the defeated agents of chaos and their actual names. In some versions these foes (Rahab, Leviathan, *Tannîn* [dragon, NRSV]) were vanquished; in others, they were only restricted in activity. The actual creation accompanying this conflict is described in the language of shaping.

2.1.2. Because Yahweh lacked a consort, except in texts found in places like Kuntilet ʿal-Jirud (northern Sinai) and Elephantine (Egypt), only remnants of the sexual view survive. The epithet in Gen. 14:19 ("maker [*qōnēh*] of heaven and earth"), reminiscent of Ugaritic praise of El, preserves an echo of the sexual view of creation, as does the metaphor in Isa. 51:1 ("Look to the rock from which you were hewn").

2.1.3. The third view preserves divine transcendence, placed in jeopardy by images of an artisan who molded forms and enlivened them by the divine breath. The majestic deity merely spoke and the world appeared, the only connection between God and the cosmos being a verbal one (→ Word of God).

2.2. The Literary Traditions

2.2.1. Priestly

The initial biblical story, relatively late, contains the Priestly account of creation (Gen. 1:1–2:3[4a?]; → Pentateuch; Genesis; Primeval History). The verbs *bārā'* and *'āśâ* alternate here, with the subject of the former verb restricted to God. Somber repetition, measured cadence, and exalted images indicate liturgical use (→ Liturgy) and careful crafting. The creative acts are symmetrical; the first three days issued in the "locus" for the "inhabitants" mentioned in the following three days: (1/4) light and darkness/ heavenly luminaries, (2/5) firmament/sea creatures and birds, and (3/6) dry land and vegetation/land creatures and humans. God's oft-repeated declaration that everything was good extends beyond the moral realm to the aesthetic, and the divine image (→ Adam; Anthropology 3) points beyond physical resemblance to the human task of ruling the earth. The high points of this account elevate eros and → Sabbath rest above ordinary activity.

2.2.2. Yahwistic

The Yahwistic story of creation (Gen. 2:4–3:24), which is more anthropocentric, offers an entirely different rendering of origins. The reverse order of humans and → animals, necessitated by the different explanation for woman's derivation from the man's rib, finds a complement in the way water functions here as a catalyst rather than a foe. No hint of human dominance surfaces in this story, for men and women are entrusted with tilling the land, their source and destiny. Creation and fall (→ Sin 1) belong together in this version, with a solemn reminder of offense arising from hybris and self-centeredness.

2.2.3. Other

Other texts, dispersed throughout the Hebrew Bible, expand this picture of origins and bring into clearer focus the ordering of the universe, so that it coheres (Exodus 15; Deuteronomy 32–33; Judges 5; 2 Samuel 22; Psalm 29). Both the physical arena and the social entity constitute a cosmology, a universe sustained by its Creator and by human actions. The royal → covenant tradition stressed a correspondence between the order of the universe and political order (Psalms 74, 89), and the Wisdom tradition empha-

sized creation as the basis of an order that humans identify and act in accordance with for their own benefit. In this universe everything serves a meaningful purpose (Prov. 16:4; Eccl. 3:11; cf. Psalms 19, 104), for → Wisdom has functioned as an agent of creation (Prov. 8:25-27; Sir. 24:3, 9; Wis. 7:24-25; cf. Col. 1:15-16).

2.3. Israel's Neighbors

2.3.1. The three views of creation summarized above in §2.1 characterize texts from ancient Egypt, Canaan, and Mesopotamia. In Egypt (→ Egyptian Religion), the understanding of origins as a battle between the sun god Re and the nocturnal demon Apepi vied with Memphite theology, according to which a preexistent deity commanded the world into being. The struggle between Marduk and Tiamat in the Sumero-Babylonian (→ Babylonian and Assyrian Religion) account of creation contains echoes of verbal command amid sexual imagery in its portrayal of the mysteries of → nature. Some scholars deny a creation account to Ugarit, but the struggle between Baal and Mot or Yamm (gods of the dead and of the sea) issued in the ordering of society that accompanied the struggle against chaos in Egypt and Mesopotamia (specifically a triumphal procession, enthronement, promulgation of → law, and the dedication of a holy place).

2.3.2. Certain biblical ideas may polemicize against prevalent concepts among → Israel's neighbors, including the lack of a name for sun and moon, the menial task assigned to humans, and the concept of divine image. Nevertheless, many other ideas link Israel with the peoples of the ancient world, including creation from mud, clay, or dust; life-giving breath; a pun on the name for the earth creature; and the dark context for discussing creation and fall.

2.4. Theological Themes

2.4.1. The Nature of Creation

The grammar and syntax of Gen. 1:1 leave open the issue of a whether the beginning was absolute or temporal. Weighty arguments can be mustered on either side of the question. The idea of conflict presupposes primordial matter that the Creator overcame; this struggle provided a convenient explanation for the origin of → evil. In Israel, Deutero-Isaiah thought it necessary to affirm divine purpose, insisting that God created the universe for human habitation, not a chaos (Isa. 45:18). Eventually, an explicit claim of *creatio ex nihilo* surfaced (2 Macc. 7:28). In the version of creation that mentions no willful resistance, the presence of evil in the world presented an enigma at best, a problem at worst. How did evil enter a perfectly ordered universe? The association of → theodicy and creation in Wisdom literature accentuates the concerns of sages who pondered the meaning of existence in the context of survival.

2.4.2. The People of God

Israel's theologians associated creation with the beginnings of the people who emerged from bondage (Exod. 15:16; Deut. 32:6). → Mythical imagery about a struggle between order and chaos pointed to a deeper reality, namely, Yahweh's formation of a covenant people instructed by divine law (→ People of God). The focus of creation imagery thus became radically → soteriological; by defeating Pharaoh, Yahweh created a social and political entity.

The exact process by which the universe came into being never became a matter for creedal affirmation, although belief that Yahweh created and sustained the world was an essential theme of → biblical theology. For Qoheleth, divine indifference in an ordered universe exacerbated the problem of evil, whereas the author of the divine speeches in Job and Sirach surrendered before ultimate mystery. Sirach brought the Creator a step closer to the human community through the identification of divine wisdom and the → Torah. Other biblical texts entertained the possibility of a return to chaos (Jer. 5:22) and an entirely new creation (Isa. 65:17-25; 1 Enoch; Revelation 21).

→ Heaven; Hell; Paradise; Promise and Fulfillment; Time and Eternity

Bibliography: R. Albertz, Weltschöpfung und Menschenschöpfung (Neukirchen, 1974) • B. W. Anderson, ed., Creation in the OT (London, 1984) • Association Catholique Française pour l'Étude de la Bible, La création dans l'Orient Ancien (Paris, 1987) • G. May, Creatio ex nihilo. The Doctrine of "Creation out of Nothing" in Early Christian Thought (Edinburgh, 1994; orig. pub., 1978) • G. von Rad, "Das theologische Problem des alttestamentlichen Schöpfungsglaubens," Gesammelte Studien zum Alten Testament (vol. 1; 4th ed.; Munich, 1971) 136-47.

James L. Crenshaw

3. NT

3.1. Introduction

The NT never deals directly with the details of creation. In Heb. 11:3 and 2 Pet. 3:5 we read that God created the world by his → Word. It is taken to be self-evident that God is the Creator of concrete reality (Matt. 19:4; Mark 13:19; 1 Tim. 4:3, etc.). In this regard the NT relies on OT and Jewish models, with some input from Hellenistic Judaism and earlier → Stoic influences (1 Cor. 8:6; Rom. 1:19-20; Acts 17:24-28). Creation includes heaven, earth, and the underworld, yet not abstractly, but always in relation to the Creator, to whom they owe their being and before whom they are called to → responsibility. This creation lives as creatio continua by God's action, which creates out of nothing in time as well (Rom. 4:17; 2 Cor. 1:9; Luke 12:24; → Time and Eternity). Missionary preaching to the → Gentiles presents the one Creator God in contrast to the surrounding → polytheism (1 Thess. 1:9-10; Acts 14:15-17; Rom. 1:20). The special feature of the primitive Christian understanding of creation is that it relates it to → Christology and → eschatology.

3.2. Christology and Creation

Tradition saw in God the origin, upholding, and goal of creation (Rom. 11:36). But in the NT, on the basis of Jewish → Wisdom speculation (Prov. 8:22-31), Christ in his preexistence was seen to have the function of a mediator of creation, by whom all things were created (cf. the early confession in 1 Cor. 8:6, the hymns to Christ in Col. 1:15-20 [Eph. 1:9], Heb. 1:1-4, and the Johannine Prologue; → Confession of Faith). The question of why Christ's saving work was necessary if he is himself the mediator and sustainer of creation was not directly taken up. With his preexistent mediatorship and postexistent exaltation, he has a position of lordship over all creaturely powers (Col. 1:16; Phil. 2:10; 1 Cor. 15:24-28).

3.3. Eschatology and Creation

Primitive Christian eschatology and → apocalyptic viewed the present creation and its structures as temporary, their limit being the coming of the → kingdom of God and the parousia of Jesus Christ (e.g., Mark 12:25). Yet this view leaves room for different evaluations — such as, trust in God's future provision in light of his present creative activity (Jesus in Luke 12:22-31), the expectation of something totally new on the premise of destruction of the first creation (Rev. 21:1, 5), or the inclusion of the first creation in the future redemption (Romans 8; → Soteriology).

3.3.1. Jesus

Jesus proclaims the coming of God's reign (→ Kingdom of God 2) as a fulfilling of God's will as Creator and an establishing of his power. In the name of God, Jesus frees creation as it is from demonic forces (Luke 10:18; 11:20), appeals to the Creator's original will in forbidding divorce (Matt. 5:27-32; Mark 10:2-9), and seeks to give people confidence in the Creator's work in caring for living things (Matt. 6:25-34) and healing the sick (Matt. 11:5, → Health and Illness).

3.3.2. Paul

Paul expects the parousia of Christ in the near future (1 Thess. 4:15; 1 Cor. 15:51), which, among other things, will provide full fellowship with Christ. In the interval, a certain ambivalence marks the relation to the present creation. Instead of leaving the world in a burst of enthusiasm (see the charismatics at Corinth), Paul counsels staying within it and its structures (1 Corinthians 7; → Marriage and Divorce; Slavery). Yet "the present form of this world is passing away," and thus Christians should hold aloof from the present orders (vv. 29-31).

The Christian life now has its basis already in a sacramental reality (→ Sacrament) that transcends creaturely, ethnic, and social antitheses (Gal. 3:26-28). Hence there is a new creation in Christ on the basis of baptism and the gift of the Spirit (2 Cor. 5:17; Gal. 6:15; Col. 3:10; Eph. 2:15), one involving change and enlightenment (2 Cor. 3:18; 4:6). As the last Adam (1 Cor. 15:45), the firstborn (Rom. 8:29), and the unique image of God (2 Cor. 4:4), Christ guarantees the new creation, which believers have in virtue of their union with Christ. In Rom. 8:18-23 Paul links the state of Christians who still await redemption with that of all creation insofar as both now experience → suffering and await future liberation and redemption. In contrast to apocalyptic writings, Paul offers no positive description of the future but simply stresses that the power of God and his Son will be established (1 Cor. 15:24-28).

3.3.3. Revelation
Passages in Revelation depict the catastrophic harm done to creation before the judgment on Satan (6; 8:6–9:21; 16), which does not, however, lead to the conversion of the inhabitants. Hence the first creation is abandoned and replaced by the heavenly city (21:1-2), in which all alienation is ended between → nature, creatures, and God. This view of the future new creation rests on different premises, of course, from those of our modern ecological consciousness.

3.3.4. Early Missionary Preaching
Primitive Christian missionary preaching to the Gentiles turned references to God the Creator, his works, and his blessings into an appeal for conversion in face of coming judgment (Acts 14:15-17; 17:22-31; Rom. 1:18-20).

3.4. Later Themes
In the later NT and postapostolic age we find both an early Gnostic negating of creation and a Hellenistically oriented → natural theology. → Dualism relates → life, light, and → truth to the upper, heavenly sphere of God, and in turn → death, darkness, and falsehood to the lower, earthly sphere of the → devil (see John 5:21, 26; 8:44; 12:31). Whereas later → Gnosticism would see in creation the work of the Demiurge, not God, John holds fast to the unity of God as Creator and Redeemer (John 1:1-4).

Bibliography: J. Becker, "Geschöpfliche Wirklichkeit als Thema des Neuen Testaments," *Schöpfungsglaube und Umweltverantwortung* (ed. W. Lohff and H. C. Knuth; Hannover, 1985) 45-100 • C. Burger, *Schöpfung und Versöhnung* (Neukirchen, 1975) • O. Cullman, *Christ and Time: The Primitive Christian Conception of Time and History* (Philadelphia, 1950) • E. Grässer, "Neutestamentliche Erwägungen zu einer Schöpfungsethik," *WPKG* 68 (1979) 98-114 • H. Hegermann, *Die Vorstellung von Schöpfungsmittler im hellenistischen Judentum und Urchristentum* (Berlin, 1961) • G. W. H. Lampe, "Die neutestamentliche Lehre von der Ktisis," *KuD* 11 (1965) 21-32 • G. Lindeskog, *Studien zum neutestamentlichen Schöpfungsgedanken* (Uppsala, 1952) • U. Mell, *Neue Schöpfung* (Berlin, 1989) • K. H. Schelkle, *Theologie des Neuen Testaments* (vol. 1; Düsseldorf, 1968) • O. H. Steck, *Welt und Umwelt* (Stuttgart, 1978) • L. H. Taylor, *The New Creation: A Study of the Pauline Doctrine of Creation, Innocence, Sin, and Redemption* (New York, 1958).

Friedrich Wilhelm Horn

3.5. Ethical Implications
The NT teaching on creation highlights certain basic ethical implications. Jesus in Mark 10:5-6 bases monogamous → marriage of male and female on God's creation at the beginning. In this way he sets a divine pattern for Christian marriage and Christian sexual conduct, excluding extramarital sex, easy divorce, and supposed same-sex marriage.

Paul in Acts 17:26 proclaims the unity of the human race by creation. If his immediate aim to show that the → gospel is equally for all people, we may also infer a more general → equality by creation (prior to that by new creation, Gal. 3:28) that transcends antitheses of color, nationality, status, or endowment.

The divine plan to fulfill all things in Christ (Eph. 1:10) has plain, if usually ignored, → environmental and → ecological implications. The NT may not deal specifically with God's purpose for individual creatures or species, but it is surely out of the line of God's will to exploit, despoil, or destroy that which he aims to fulfill in either the present world or the future new creation.

Bibliography: D. S. Bailey, *The Man-Woman Relationship in Christian Thought* (London, 1959) • K. Barth, *CD* IV/3, §54.3 ("Near and Distant Neighbours") • D. C. Thomasma, *Human Life in the Balance* (Louisville, Ky., 1990) • L. Wilkinson, ed., *Earthkeeping: Christian Stewardship of Natural Resources* (Grand Rapids, 1980).

The Editors

4. Systematic Theology and Ethics

4.1. *Understandings of "Creation"*

What the church says about creation is not unequivocal. The term "creation" is often used today instead of → "nature," as if adding a subjective element to a general understanding of nature (e.g., → theistic faith in a first cause). "Creation" sometimes is used if a → teleological view of nature is replacing a purely causal view. The will of the Creator lies behind these ends, and therefore → ethics is given a standard. "Creation" can also refer to the basis of all life underlying the notion of elementary trust, a basis accessible in one's personal experience of creation. Finally, "creation" epitomizes the ordering of life, as in the doctrine of creation ordinances. Nor do these definitions cover all that → dogmatics has to say about creation.

4.2. *Creation in Church Doctrine*

In dealing with creation, church doctrine covers the four fields of (1) God as Creator, (2) creation out of nothing, (3) the world and human beings as creation, and (4) God's relation with his creation (→ Providence; Theodicy).

4.2.1. *God as Creator*

The orientation of the biblical witness regarding creation is to the Creator, and thus the created world is conceived as being contingent. Though the OT does attest something akin to an experience of creation, it does not allow us to move back from creation to the Creator. All that exists finds its true place and time only when seen against knowledge of the Creator. Later attempts at → natural theology must thus be read within the bracket of faith. Only the self-disclosure of the Creator makes experience of creation possible.

Within the history of Israel's faith the Creator is seen first in what he wills against his people. The goodness of his will allows one to hold onto faith in the goodness of his creation ordinances, even in experiences that seem to contradict it. Creation is thus linked to the covenant (K → Barth: as the external ground of that covenant which is the internal ground of creation). The Hebrew words for "create" may be used in part for human acts, but stress falls on the uniqueness of the divine creating.

God's will becomes clear in the sending of Jesus Christ, who thus reveals the meaning of creation, the inner relationship of all that was and is and will be (cf. Rom. 11:36 with 1 Cor. 8:6). Building on John 1:3, dogmatics clings to the fact that creation was through Christ. God did not need any demiurge. He is God, and he is so because in incomparable → freedom he seeks relation to others. Without → Christology, the relation of the Creator to the world tends to be impersonally pantheistic or deistic in a way that sets God at a distance from his creatures (→ Deism; Pantheism; Person).

4.2.2. *Creation out of Nothing*

The uniqueness of the Creator is that he has made the world out of nothing. This doctrine reflects the fact that God has no counterpart (e.g., shapeless matter). He himself freely creates all that is distinct from himself. Ezekiel 37 and 2 Macc. 7:28 may be adduced in support for this teaching. It is tied in with the → resurrection (§2) of the dead and with all that is impossible for us (→ Death). We can trace back what is truly new in relation to human death only to God. God is the → future of all futures. Ontologically, possibility precedes reality (E. Jüngel). This provides a connection with → justification insofar as sinners have nothing to claim before God, and it is from the same "nothing" that God has made the creature.

4.2.3. *The Elements of God's Creation*

We cannot consider creation and creatures apart from the Creator. Theology has often treated the creation of the world very speculatively (→ Speculative Theology), giving play to (Neo-)Platonic (→ Platonism) and → Stoic ideas. To stress God's perfection, → Origen (ca. 185-ca. 254; → Origenism) advocated the eternity of his work, which he located, not in the world of time and matter, but in the spiritual cosmos. → Augustine (354-430; → Augustine's Theology) set the spiritual creation before the temporal. → Evil, then, is the absence of the → good of the divine world of light. High medieval (→ Thomism) and the older Protestant theology (→ Orthodoxy 2.2) largely adopted the → Aristotelian doctrine of causes, viewing God as the First Cause, who has set in motion a system of secondary causes but who can also intervene in it (→ Miracle). The organization of the work of six days yielded to much more complex systems of organization. The theology of the → Enlightenment (→ Neology) especially linked God and his providence to purposive design in nature. The theory of → evolution and the claims of modern natural science robbed the Creator of his creation because the world of nature no longer reflected his work (→ Modern Period; Science and Theology). Dogmatics still had only an older concept of creation to offer. F. D. E. → Schleiermacher (1768-1834; → Schleiermacher's Theology) attempted a rescue operation by positing, within a feeling of absolute dependence, faith in an original perfection of the world. God is always present as cause, creation becoming thereby *creatio continua.*

Because of these problems, dogmatics now focuses primarily on the existential aspect of belief in creation and therefore on the human being as creature (→

Anthropology 3). What is bewailed as an anthropocentric understanding has thus gained in strength. M. → Luther (1483-1546; → Luther's Theology) in his Small Catechism, while confessing his faith that God has created *me,* insisted that he has created all other creatures as well. Only the second article qualifies this "me," and does so Christocentrically: "I believe that Jesus Christ . . . is *my* Lord." Both are subsumed by Luther's declaration in the third article: "I believe that by my own reason or strength I cannot believe in Jesus Christ." Thus the existential exposition of the article on creation presupposes the doctrine of the → Trinity. Only as theology became alienated from nature in the 19th century did anthropocentricity develop in relation to creation faith. The 20th century has made attempts to overcome this oversight (K. Heim and North American → process theology).

The → ecological crisis (L. White Jr.; → Environment) has forced theology to define more precisely what is meant by dominion over the earth (Gen. 1:28) and the image of God. Human dominion must correspond to the care the Creator has for his creation. God retains for himself basic control over the existence of all his creatures.

4.2.4. *God's Relation with His Creation*

The most influential motif in the doctrine of creation has always been that of divine → providence (→ Predestination). It finds its basis especially in OT → Wisdom literature. Providence implies prevision and the establishment of the divine will and ordering activity in the world. It manifests itself as divine preservation *(conservatio),* the influencing of causes within the world *(concursus),* and world sovereignty *(gubernatio).* God permits, executes, prevents, and establishes goals. The Bible can also speak of God's hiddenness in creation (Job 38–41) and of human → sin that has distorted the goodness of creation. In evil times there is often reference to the saying in Genesis that God saw that, "indeed, it was very good" (Gen. 1:31). Creation is thus not a matter of → metaphysics of providence, but rather of promise, a starting point — but one we must always discover afresh. Human beings occupy a special position only because they are open to this experience and can respond commensurately to it.

The question of → theodicy demanded a naive metaphysics of providence. G. W. Leibniz (1646-1716) could reconcile the good and evil in the world from God's perspective, but the crisis of the → Enlightenment has taught theology that we know God the Creator, not first on the basis of his eternal world sovereignty, but by his identification with the Crucified. No theoretical answer can really be given to the question of theodicy.

4.3. *Present Concepts*

Can we link the doctrine of creation to present concepts of nature and the world?

4.3.1. "Nature" and "world" are abstract terms. They denote a totality that cannot be the object of empirical knowledge and that is contingent. What exists in them is subject to time and space. Even though the → relativity theory has dissolved the idea of absolute time and space, events that take place within these relational systems do form a nexus. Like the elementary trustworthiness of the world's structures (→ Structuralism), this observation needs interpretation. The → process philosophy of A. N. Whitehead (1861-1947) has taught → process theology to find God in the dynamic of the process. God is not relative but "surrelative" (C. Hartshorne).

4.3.2. The nexus of the world consists of events, not substances (Whitehead). These are self-originating and, through their interrelations, grow together into a process. God gives actual entities the impetus that makes them self-creative. On this view, the structure of the world develops out of events themselves. C. F. von Weizsäcker thus makes this presupposition in the basic alternatives suggested by physics. Views of this kind do not constitute the premise for natural theology. They do, however, show how earlier experiences of creation can be made understandable when new questions arise about the cosmos and its nexus.

4.3.3. It is not helpful simply to insert into (the theory of) evolution a model of → teleology similar to that of Aristotle (384-322 B.C.), since this can only be a subjective addition to an objectified world. The (ambiguous) success of → technology demonstrates that nature is not controlled by a plan and an aim. This would merely impose aims on nature as a moral postulate (see 4.2.4 on the hiddenness of God).

4.4. *Biblical Issues*

4.4.1. What the Bible tells us about creation does not seek to expand the subjective statement that things simply were created. All that is real, however, is already encountered couched in a framework of interpretation. There is an eschatological component (→ Eschatology 1). As we see it, the "very good" of Gen. 1:31 has not yet been fulfilled. "Creation" also has concrete human existence in view. Isaiah 40ff. links liberation to creation. Creation also glorifies God (Psalms 29, 65, 147, etc.; → Doxology). It has received life as a gift from God. It is thus a mistake to limit creation to a fictitious beginning of all things.

4.4.2. Unsuccessful attempts to put creation into an → ontological framework, as in the problems of teleology, confirm the fact that we cannot reduce God or the world to formal structures. God creates as he speaks. The Logos is the mediator of creation (John 1:3). The verbal structure of creation shows itself in the fact that it addresses us (nonverbally) and that we can "respond" to it "responsibly" (→ Responsibility). That creation concerns us can be understood as God's indirect address to us. It summons our respect, allowing not unlimited experiments (→ Ethics) but, rather, careful investigation of creation's own processes. Barth's (1886-1968; → Dialectical Theology) use of the concept of parable (natural parables of the kingdom of God) means, not that the world reflects a Platonic idea, but that we need to hear imaginatively what is there in nature, reorientating ourselves to it and acting responsively with it.

4.4.3. The statements and the attitude of Jesus provide guidance for this discovery. They help us discover what is actually self-evident in the perverted relationships of life (e.g., learning about the humanity of our enemy from the sun and the rain, or about the gift of bread through parents) — and we discover these things in the light of a newly revealed future (→ Kingdom of God; New Self). Christology is another guide. God is not simply manifest but, rather, is to be perceived in that which is antithetical to what is God's, namely, in death (→ Theologia crucis). We can thus cling to the "very good" of Gen. 1:31, even though facts often seem to contradict it.

4.4.4. God is to be differentiated from both heaven and earth. → Heaven symbolizes infinity, the totality and nexus of all that is accessible through the senses. God relates to all his work both by creating *within* it and by resting *over* it (→ Sabbath; Sunday).

4.4.5. The Creator cannot be equated with the order or meaning of the whole ("heaven"). He shows himself in the → power with which he gives and takes concrete life in inadequately known contexts of meaning. He is thus not simply the motor of evolution leading up to a spiritual stage (P. Teilhard de Chardin) nor the unity and totality of nature and history anticipated by → reason (W. Pannenberg). He speaks, rather, through the → promise to which → faith clings and which permits new experiences. We can thus talk of a theology of nature but not of natural theology.

4.5. Ethical Perspectives

4.5.1. A theology of creation ordinances (P. Althaus, W. Elert, E. Brunner) shows how easy it is to justify temporally conditioned views by appeal to the Creator. We cannot simply equate what is natural with creation.

4.5.2. Charges of anthropocentricity are justified when creation is made existential or made into an element in human self-consciousness. But to talk of biocentricity or cosmocentricity is illusory. For what

stands outside the center? For the sake of the mystery of all being, we need to describe creation as theocentric.

4.5.3. In view of the most recent possibilities of invading the structure of being (→ Genetic Counseling; Medical Ethics), any reference to human cocreativity is extremely dangerous. To protect the gift and mystery of creation, we need to say with Luther that it is given to each one of us to be a *cooperator,* not a *concreator.*

4.5.4. Neither goals allegedly immanent in nature nor those set by human technology can do justice to creation or to its inherent promise. An ethics of creation thus must be an ethics of latitude that weighs the consequences in various comprehensive life systems and yet allows creation itself the possibility of providing answers.

4.5.5. "Peace" or "reconciliation with nature" (→ Conciliarity 3) can only be figurative expressions, although they do show us that humans themselves are affected by divine → reconciliation only within their social context with other creatures and that they ought to bear witness to this reconciliation by finding in creation the starting point of life.

Bibliography: K. Barth, *CD* III/2 • D. Bonhoeffer, *Act and Being* (New York, 1962) • J. B. Cobb, *A Christian Natural Theology* (Philadelphia, 1965) • C. Frey, "Theologie und Ethik der Schöpfung," *ZEE* 32 (1988) 47-62 • L. Gilkey, *Maker of Heaven and Earth* (Garden City, N.Y., 1959) • C. Hartshorne, *The Divine Relativity* (2d ed.; New Haven, 1964) • A. Heilmann, ed., *Texte der Kirchenväter* (vol. 1; Munich, 1963) 79-260 • J. Hübner, ed., *Der Dialog zwischen Theologie und Naturwissenschaft* (Munich, 1987) • E. Jüngel, *Unterwegs zur Sache* (Munich, 1972) 206-33 • G. W. Leibniz, *Theodicy* (Indianapolis, 1966; orig. pub., 1710) • G. Liedke, *Im Bauch des Fisches. Ökologische Theologie* (Stuttgart, 1979) • C. Link, *Schöpfung* (2 vols.; Gütersloh, 1991) • J. Moltmann, *God in Creation: A New Theology of Creation and the Spirit of God* (New York, 1985) • D. Sattler and T. Schneider, "Schöpfungslehre," *Handbuch der Dogmatik* (vol. 1; ed. T. Schneider; Düsseldorf, 1992) 120-238 • F. Schleiermacher, *The Christian Faith* (2 vols.; New York, 1963; orig. pub., 1821-22) §§40-49 • O. H. Steck, *Welt und Umwelt* (Stuttgart, 1978) • K. Tanner, *God and Creation in Christian Theology: Tyranny or Empowerment?* (New York, 1988) • C. F. von Weizsäcker, *The Unity of Nature* (New York, 1980) • C. Westermann, *Genesis* (2 vols.; 4th ed.; Darmstadt, 1989) • L. White jr., "The Historical Roots of Our Ecological Crisis," *Science* 155 (1967) 1203-7 • N. Young, *Creator, Creation, and Faith* (London, 1976).

Christofer Frey

Creationism

The contemporary North American usage of this term most frequently signifies the closely related movements known as *scientific creationism* (also called *creation science*) and *biblical creationism*. Essential to each of these perspectives is the belief that God brought instantaneously into being, in mature form and within an extraordinary period of six 24-hour days, a few (6-10) thousand years ago, each of the principal kinds of astronomical structures and bodies (e.g., galaxies, stars, and planets) and each distinct "kind" of life-form. Of comparable importance is the belief that the earth was subjected to a global flood (ca. 4,000-5,000 years ago) that destroyed most plant and animal life, killed all humans except eight, and formed the major geological structures now composing the earth's surface.

Proponents of *biblical creationism* hold that this scenario of God's creative work and judgment by flood is warranted by a faithful reading of Scripture, especially of the early chapters of Genesis, which are believed to constitute a factual chronicle of historical particulars that must be read in the literalistic manner generally associated with the conservative evangelical (or fundamentalist) expression of Christian belief. Typical arguments favoring such a "plain reading" of the text would be that it is (1) traditional, thereby constituting one of the "deliverances of the faith"; (2) accessible to the greatest number of ordinary believers; (3) free from strained reference to those cultural, historical, and literary considerations that characterize the work of most professional biblical scholars; and (4) unaffected by the influence of modern professional science, considered strongly biased toward philosophical naturalism.

Proponents of *scientific creationism* seek to demonstrate that this same recent, special-creationist picture of God's creative works can be derived from (or at least affirmed by) empirical data gathered by the natural sciences but interpreted without naturalistic bias. To this end, creationist organizations such as the Institute for Creation Research and the Creation Research Society carry out programs of investigation that seek to uncover empirical evidence indicating that (1) the universe and all basic life-forms were created suddenly; (2) natural processes are not sufficient for effecting the evolution of all life-forms from a single ancestral organism; (3) biological changes can take place only within the limits of the originally created kinds; (4) humans are not related to other creatures by common ancestry; (5) the earth's geological features were brought about primarily by catastrophic events, including a global flood; and (6)

the earth and all life-forms were brought into being relatively recently.

A third position, commonly called *progressive creationism*, accepts the idea of a continuous formative history for inanimate structures over many thousands of millions of years but still posits the existence of gaps in the developmental economy of the biotic world. Such gaps would make impossible the genealogical continuity envisioned in the macroevolutionary paradigm of modern biology and would thereby make necessary a series of "miraculous divine interventions" in the course of time (contrary to the manner in which → Augustine and Basil envisioned God's creative work) to bring the present array of life-forms into being.

All versions of creationism here described place a high value on the apologetic importance of discrediting the macroevolutionary paradigm (so that the inerrancy and scientific relevance of the Bible may be upheld) and of demonstrating that special creation provides the only means of giving a satisfactory account of the formation of the diversity of creatures, past and present.

→ Soul 2

Bibliography: *Scientific creationism:* H. M. MORRIS, *The Biblical Basis for Modern Science* (Grand Rapids, 1984); idem, *History of Modern Creationism* (San Diego, Calif., 1984) • H. M. MORRIS and G. E. PARKER, *What Is Creation Science?* (2d ed.; San Diego, Calif., 1987). Henry M. Morris is currently the chief proponent of scientific creationism.

Progressive creationism: B. RAMM, *The Christian View of Science and Scripture* (Grand Rapids, 1955).

Critical analyses of the modern creationist movement: R. A. EVE and F. B. HARROLD, *The Creationist Movement in Modern America* (Boston, 1991) • L. GILKEY, *Creationism on Trial* (Minneapolis, 1985) • R. NUMBERS, *The Creationists: The Evolution of Scientific Creationism* (New York, 1992) • H. J. VAN TILL et al., *Portraits of Creation: Biblical and Scientific Perspective on the World's Formation* (Grand Rapids, 1990) esp. chap. 6.

HOWARD J. VAN TILL

Creativity

1. Definition
2. The Humanities
3. Theological Discussion and Church Practice

1. Definition
In spite of intensive investigation of the phenomenon of creativity, no precise definition is yet possible.

Qualities of creativity such as novelty, originality, and uniqueness are helpful indicators but still do not yield an exact definition.

The starting point of a theological approach to the problem must be that in modern studies, interest focuses especially on humans as creative beings and on their creative production (→ Anthropology). Yet creativity can be relevantly treated theologically only in the context of God's relation to us. This means, on the one hand, a qualitative distinction between → creation out of nothing, which is posited in the biblical witness to God's creative action, and all human activity. On the other hand, the human characteristic of divine likeness also means a qualitative correspondence to the Creator himself (B. W. Liesch and T. J. Finley, A. Ganoczy and J. Schmid).

2. The Humanities

2.1. The concentration on creativity as an anthropological problem under the influence of the → Renaissance and the → Enlightenment was most fruitful for the older → pedagogy from the standpoint of natural philosophy. The approach of → Romanticism, however, also reflected a theology of creation (cf. F. Froebel's principle of self-activity, also M. Buber). In contrast, modern pedagogics in its empirical orientation has obviously ignored this historical link. Today, in light of questions of global survival, modern views of education and learning are discussed from the standpoint of innovation and the anticipation of possible crises (Club of Rome).

2.2. In the 20th century the conditions and characteristics of creative action have been investigated from various psychological angles (W. Matthäus; → Psychology). Research that focused on individual genius or artistic creativity has now been replaced with formal analysis — for example, in terms of phases (e.g., preparation, incubation, illumination, verification). Depth psychology stresses especially the affective dynamics and biographical context of creativity (H. Müller-Braunschweig, D. Winnicott; → Biography, Biographical Research).

3. Theological Discussion and Church Practice

3.1. In its reception of modern research, theology can learn from relevant empirical descriptions but must also consider the ambivalence of creativity (W. Härle) and raise critical questions to the approaches in the humanities. Thus a creativity that is promised to all in the divine likeness can hardly be compatible with the establishment of a creative elite in the interests of national policy (Matthäus, col. 1204). It is precisely to this elite, however, that psy-

chological research in the West is indebted. Ethically the reduction of creativity to scientific and technological utility must be also challenged, in view of the threat that humanity is posing to creation (G. Altner).

3.2. In spite of such criticisms, the modern interest in creativity significantly stimulates theological anthropology to reformulate its central conceptions. The psychological and pedagogical dimension of creativity as innovative action can be significant for a realistic explanation of the concept of repentance (→ Penitence). In an understanding of human → work from the standpoint of social ethics, the pneumatologically based creative aspect calls for notice, in contrast to the reproductive aspect that is so often stressed in Protestantism (Y. Spiegle; → Holy Spirit).

Finally, it is in the interests of "hominization," oriented to the humanity of Jesus Christ, to shed light on the creative aspect of → suffering over against a one-sided emphasis on production-oriented creativity (A. M. K. Müller).

3.3. The practical expression of the Christian → faith faces a twofold task. With reference to Scripture, it must bring to light, on the one hand, the salutary limitation of human → life in terms of creation theology. On the other hand, the appropriation of the biblical tradition and the framing of practical rules for living (→ Lifestyle) can and should be developed in evangelical → freedom under the banner of the promised gift of the Spirit. Here, then, we have both the limit and the basis of all creativity in the fields of the church's action. We are given perspectives for → religious instruction (H. Stock), for instruction in prayer (F. Oser), for the liturgical shaping of → worship, and so forth.

Pastoral practice alone, however, is not at issue. In addition, the work of the church must critically and constructively allow room for human creativity in the → everyday life of a → society that is increasingly under alien influences, even in the field of → leisure.

→ Imagination; Play

Bibliography: G. ALTNER, *Schöpfung am Abgrund* (Neukirchen, 1976) • T. M. AMABILE, *The Social Psychology of Creativity* (New York, 1983) • J. R. ANDERSON, *The Architecture of Cognition* (Cambridge, Mass., 1983) • J. W. BOTKIN, M. ELMANDJRA, and M. MALITZA, *No Limits to Learning: Bridging the Gap. A Report to the Club of Rome* (New York, 1979) • M. BUBER, "Über das Erzieherische" (1926; repr. in *Werke* [vol. 1; Munich, 1962] 787-808) • *Creativity Research Journal* (1988-) • M. CSIKSZENTMIHALYI, "Creativity," *EncHI* 1.298-306; idem, "Society, Culture, Person: A Systems View of Creativity," *The Nature of Creativity* (ed. R. J. Sternberg; Cambridge, 1988) 325-39 • A. GANOCZY and J. SCHMID, eds., *Schöpfung und Kreativität* (Düsseldorf, 1980) • W. HÄRLE, "Kreativität," *WzM* 30 (1978) 288-99 • H.-G. HEIMBROCK, ed., *Gottesdienst: Spielraum des Lebens. Sozial- und kulturwissenschaftliche Analysen zum Ritual in praktisch-theologischem Interesse* (Kampen, 1993) • B. W. LIESCH and T. J. FINLEY, "The Biblical Concept of Creativity: Scope, Definition, Criteria," *JPsT* 12 (1984) 188-97 • W. MATTHÄUS, "Kreativität," *HWP* 4.1194-1204 (bibliography) • A. M. K. MÜLLER, "Vom Sinn des Leidens," *Die vielen Namen Gottes* (FS G. Heinz-Mohr; Stuttgart, 1974) 311-25 • H. MÜLLER-BRAUNSCHWEIG, "Psychopathologie und Kreativität," *Psyche* 28 (1974) 600-634 • F. OSER, *Kreatives Sprach- und Gebetsverhalten in Schule und Religionsunterricht* (Olten, 1972) • M. A. RUNCO, "Creative and Imaginative Thinking," *EncHB* 2.11-16 • H. STOCK, *Evangelientexte in elementarer Auslegung* (Göttingen, 1981) • D. WINNICOTT, *Playing and Reality* (New York, 1971).

HANS-GÜNTER HEIMBROCK

Creed

A creed is a concise statement of Christian doctrine, typically produced by one of the → councils of the early church. In this encyclopedia, the fullest treatment of "creed" appears in "Confessions and Creeds."

→ Apostles' Creed; Athanasian Creed; Barmen Declaration; Darmstadt Declaration; Niceno-Constantinopolitan Creed

Bibliography: J. N. D. KELLY, ed., *Early Christian Creeds* (3d ed.; London, 1972) • J. H. LEITH, *Creeds of the Churches* (3d ed.; Atlanta, 1982).

THE EDITORS

Creed of Pius IV

Following up on a decision of → Trent (Session 24, "Decree on Reform," cans. 2 and 12), Pius IV in his → bull *Injunctum nobis* (November 13, 1564) required all → bishops and holders of pastoral benefices, before taking office, to make a profession of their Catholic → faith (→ Confession of Faith) according to an obligatory formula, often called the *Professio fidei Tridentina*. This formula contained the → Niceno-Constantinopolitan Creed plus the main doctrinal articles of the → Roman Catholic Church on Scripture and → tradition, the → sacraments, → justification, the sacrifice of the → Mass, Commu-

nion (→ Eucharist), purgatory (→ Hell), veneration of the → saints, → indulgences, the → church, and the papacy (→ Pope, Papacy). The text seems to have orginated with the Roman → Inquisition (H. Jedin).

In 1877 → Pius IX (1846-78) expanded this creed to include decisions made at → Vatican I, and in 1910 the → Antimodernist Oath was added (→ Modernism). By decrees of the Congregation for the Doctrine of the Faith (→ Curia 1.2.2), new formulas were introduced in 1967 and again in 1989 (*AAS* 59 [1967] 1058 and 81 [1989] 105; cf. 1983 CIC 833). A special oath of loyalty was also appended in 1989 (*AAS* 81 [1989] 106). Formally, these developments pushed the Creed of Pius IV into the background, although it remains the authentic statement of Roman Catholic faith.

Bibliography: Primary sources: DH 1862-70 • C. MIRBT (K. ALAND), *Quellen zur Geschichte des Papsttums und des römischen Katholizismus* (6th ed.; Tübingen, 1967) 1.649-51 • "The Tridentine Profession of Faith, 1564," *Documents of the Christian Church* (ed. H. S. Bettenson; 2d ed.; New York, 1963) 375-77.

Secondary works: H. JEDIN, "Zur Entstehung der Professio fidei Tridentina," *AHC* 6 (1974) 369-75 • H. SCHMITZ, "Professio fidei" und "Iusiurandum fidelitatis," *AKathKR* 157 (1988) 353-429 • G. THILS and T. SCHNEIDER, *Glaubensbekenntnis und Treueid* (Mainz, 1990).

HUBERT KIRCHNER

Crisis Cult

1. The phrase "crisis cult" refers broadly to a collective attempt to meet a crisis situation along cultic lines. It is not a matter of personal → religion in crises in individual → life but involves a group situation. Research into crisis cults is thus done by sociologists.

Crises affect not only religious groups but also political, racial, and social groups and involve political, military, economic, cultural, or religious reasons. In reality, there is seldom a single cause. Although a crisis is an acute situation whose outcome is uncertain, some scholars speak of permanent crises (e.g., → death, which in turn would make of every religion a crisis cult).

2. Crisis cults arose during → colonialism, when whites seemed to overpower nonwhites by their technology, → culture, and religion. Thus American → Indians tried to overcome the resultant crises by spirit dances, the Melanesians by → cargo cults, the

Africans by → prophetic movements or Mau-Mau. → Racism and social needs led to the rise of the Black Muslims in the United States and the → Rastafarians in Jamaica. Collective frustration could also result in crisis cults even in higher cultures, as in Japan.

3. Christianity has been viewed as a crisis cult that arose in the form of a movement of political resistance premised on an earthly Messiah (→ Messianism). As such, Christianity is only one of many messianic movements that have arisen in times of cultural crisis.

Pilate executed → Jesus as such a Messiah, along with two terrorists. According to this theory, the role of the Jews in rejecting Jesus for religious reasons was secondary. Under foreign occupation, the court of Herod had adopted more and more of the alien culture, which inevitably provoked the corresponding reaction among Jewish conservatives and revolutionaries. Europeans aroused similar reactions in 19th-century African colonies. Jesus confronting Pilate was like many a black prophet before a district officer.

4. In church history, reference might be made to the → Cathari, the democracy of G. Savonarola (1452-98), and the → Anabaptists in Münster as examples of crisis cults.

Bibliography: S. G. F. BRANDON, *Jesus and the Zealots* (Manchester, 1966); idem, "The Trial of Jesus," *Horizon* 9 (1967) 5-13; idem, "The Zealots: The Jewish Resistance against Rome, A.D. 6-73," *HT* 15 (1965) 632-41 • C. COLPE, "Krisenkulte," *TRT* 3.158-60 • W. LA BARRE, "Materials for a History of Studies of Crisis Cults: A Bibliographic Essay," *CA* 12 (1971) 3-44 • F. SIERKSMA, "Review of *The Religion of the Oppressed,* by V. Lanternari," *CA* 6 (1965) 455-56 • F. VALJAVEC, "Über die Selbstorganisation von Krisenkulten," *Soc.* 33 (1983) 1-24, 131-51.

HANS-JÜRGEN GRESCHAT

Crisis Intervention

1. Crisis intervention is a response to acute crises in human → life. It developed out of care for mourners (→ Grief), the → depressed, and potential → suicides but now covers many other crises. C. Kulessa categorizes the various crises as biological (somatopsychical and maturational), psychological (psychosomatic and psychosocial), and social (sociopsychiatric and sociopsychological). E. Erikson refers to development crises (oedipal, puberty, pregnancy, family; → Development 2). Severe crises may involve → neuroses, alcoholism, addictions (→ Substance

Abuse), and criminal acts, and they may ultimately lead to suicide. Crises, although very dangerous, offer great possibilities for personality reorientation.

2. Crises arise when people cannot adjust to difficult situations (first phase). If no solution is found, → anxiety becomes helplessness (second phase), which all outer and inner resources are deployed to overcome (third phase). If extraordinary reactions do not help, resignation and collapse follow (fourth phase). With outward pressure, confusion quickly mounts, and total disorientation results. The underlying complete disruption of → communication can be overcome only by helpers who can read the emergency signals.

3. Anyone who encounters a crisis situation can and should help, including → family members, fellow workers, emergency personnel, physicians, psychiatrists, psychotherapists, pastors, social workers, nurses, the police, and counselors. Diagnosis and prognosis must take account of the degree of isolation, the scope of the problem, the immediate cause of the crisis, previously observed factors, the overlapping crisis levels, the additional impact of alcohol or drugs (→ Substance Abuse), prior psychological sickness, special risk factors, and any presuicidal syndrome.

4. The aim of crisis intervention is to help those concerned and those around to help themselves, by means of a dynamic process of interaction. An important first step is the immediate prevention of deterioration, of further damage, of panic solutions, and of suicide. Evasion may alleviate the → suffering but ultimately hampers reconstruction.

Lengthy physical tests and investigations are not indicated. The helper or institution (in contrast to the technique in → psychotherapy) needs to act. → Conflict must be carefully brought out of the confusion of feelings, prejudices, and anxieties, and confrontation must occur. With the watchful support of the helper, clients should freely display their feelings of grief, pain, rage, and anger so as to achieve stability and to avoid repression of reality, with all its difficulties.

5. True crisis intervention is a dynamic process into which relatives may be drawn at a later stage so as to achieve what promises to be a successful restructuring of the personality (see H. Petzold's four-phase model). According to the nature of the crisis, it may take place in counseling, in psychotherapy, in clinics, or over the phone (→ Telephone Ministry). Reorientation should always be the positive result.

→ Counseling; Counseling Centers, Christian; Pastoral Care; Psychiatry

Bibliography: D. S. EVERSTINE and L. EVERSTINE, *People in Crisis* (New York, 1983) • K. GASTGEBER, "Pastorale Krisenberatung nach der Gestalttherapie," *Hilfe in Krisen. Wege und Chancen einer personalen Krisesintervention* (ed. H. Gastager and S. Gastager; Vienna, 1982) 117-35 • L. A. HOFF, *People in Crisis: Understanding and Helping* (2d ed.; Menlo Park, Calif., 1984) • C. KULESSA, "Zur Theorie der Krise," *Hilfe in Krisen. Wege und Chancen einer personalen Krisesintervention* (ed. H. Gastager and S. Gastager; Vienna, 1982) 67-93 • E. LINDEMANN, *Beyond Grief: Studies in Crisis Intervention* (New York, 1979) • H. G. PETZOLD, *Psychotherapie und Körperdynamik* (2d ed.; Paderborn, 1977) esp. 289-373; idem, ed., *Leiblichkeit* (Paderborn, 1985) esp. 374-81 • D. K. SWITZER, *The Minister as Crisis Counselor* (2d ed.; Nashville, 1986); idem, *Pastoral Care Emergencies: Ministering to People in Crisis* (New York, 1989) • S. L. TALLEY and M. C. KING, *Psychiatric Emergencies: Nursing Assessment and Intervention* (New York, 1984).

KARL GASTGEBER

Critical Theory

1. History
2. Development
    2.1. Main Motifs
    2.2. The Middle Phase of Critical Theory
    2.3. Second Generation
3. Critical Theory and Theology
4. International Reception of Critical Theory

1. History

Critical theory, or the Frankfurt school, is closely related in origin to the Frankfurt Institute for Social Research (founded in 1930) and the *Zeitschrift für Sozialforschung*. M. Horkheimer (1895-1976), T. W. Adorno (1903-69), H. Marcuse (1899-1979), and W. Benjamin (1892-1940) were the main representatives of the first generation. They were forced into exile under National Socialism, and only Horkheimer and Adorno returned to Germany after World War II.

Beginning in the 1960s, a group of social philosophers and sociologists that had been in contact with the first generation took up the cause. This second generation included A. Schmidt, C. Offe, O. Negt, A. Wellmer, and, its most outstanding representative, J. Habermas. Critical theory had great influence on the student movement that swept industrialized countries toward the end of the 1960s, although holding aloof from its more violent manifestations.

2. Development
2.1. *Main Motifs*
The term "Frankfurt school" is misleading in two respects. First, its chief members did not stand in a teacher-student relation to one another. Second, the interdisciplinary-oriented social philosophy of the institute, which involved politics, economics, psychoanalysis, and → aesthetics, was not based on a common body of opinions. Critical theory evolved instead within a research program that Horkheimer succinctly outlined in his 1937 essay "Traditionelle und kritische Theorie." In this essay he contrasted a contemplative, value-free theory in the Cartesian sense with critical theory, which takes into account the interest-driven presuppositions of academic systems, seeking to analyze the products of scholarship in the light of rational change in existing → society.

This view was inspired on the one hand by → Marx's (1818-83) *Kritik der politischen Ökonomie* (→ Marxism), and on the other hand by themes from the three Critiques of Kant (1724-1804; → Criticism; Kantianism). As Horkheimer saw it, in opposition to both a positivist worship of facts and a dogmatic → metaphysics, Kant had shown "the relation of the matter of apparently ultimate facts to human production."

2.2. *The Middle Phase of Critical Theory*
The trust of the older critical theory (up to the end of the 1930s) in the possibility of shaping history rationally began to wane in Horkheimer and Adorno, not least under the impact of → fascism and Stalinism. In their joint study *Dialektik der Aufklärung* (1944), they carried the critical concept a stage beyond Kant and Marx and argued that the modern subject has fallen victim to a destructive logic of self-aggrandizement that manifests itself in a purely instrumental use of → reason. Using this analysis, middle critical theory extended its critical negation of → capitalist societies to all social forms.

The study revolves around the question why in the process of → emancipation humanity sinks into a new form of barbarism instead of entering into a truly human state. In his *Negative Dialektik* (1966) Adorno attempted a more precise, nonsystematic, yet still philosophical development of this concept of criticism, which inspired all his analyses of enlightenment. In his work on the philosophy of history and aesthetics (published posthumously as *Ästhetische Theorie*), Adorno took up key motifs from Benjamin's radical criticism of → progress.

2.3. *Second Generation*
The critical understanding of middle critical theory suffered from the fact that it could not finally justify the critical standards it used. This came to light in

the so-called positivism conflict in German → sociology (1961), in which, after initial debate between the critical rationalists K. R. Popper and Adorno, Habermas began, in his controversy with H. Albert, to state more precisely the criteria that the older critical theory had used only implicitly. In pursuit of this issue, from the time of his inaugural lecture at Frankfurt ("Erkenntnis und Interesse" [1965]), and with a direct appeal to Horkheimer's original program, Habermas sought an epistemological basis for critical theory that would include considerations from the fields of philosophy of → language and → communication and that would free it from the difficulties of a "negative dialectics."

In his main work, *Theorie des kommunikativen Handelns* (1981), Habermas tackled the project of reconstructively finding conceptual foundations for a critical theory of society, studying the history of the formation of social theory (M. → Weber, É. Durkheim, T. Parsons). He also used the linguistic analysis of J. I. Austin and J. Searle (→ Analytic Philosophy), as well as the social psychology of G. H. Mead, to develop his "discourse theory." In the process the Kantian motif of "critique" was partially rehabilitated in the new dress of linguistic analysis. In his *Der philosophische Diskurs der Moderne* (1985), Habermas also defended the historical potential of Kant's and Hegel's "practical reason," in the main against the radical criticism of reason of the French neostructuralists (M. Foucault, J. Derrida, J.-F. Lyotard, and deconstruction; → Structuralism).

3. Critical Theory and Theology
The postulated → atheism of most of the adherents of critical theory was transcended in the works of some authors. We note especially Benjamin's attempt to link historical → materialism and → theology, and also comments in the later Horkheimer in which theology plays a hypothetical role in the context of the philosophy of history. Adorno's later work, in its aesthethic appeal to an absolute, also includes themes from a philosophy of religion, although in a postreligious form. For Habermas, however, the rational core of theology was dissolved in discursive rationality (→ Dialectic). In other words, there is no place in the theory of communicative action for a rational theology (e.g., in the sense of the Kantian doctrine of postulates). Recently, Habermas clearly revised one of the religiophilosophical theses of his "theory of communicative action" (H. Peukert; P. Lakeland) and speaks of the (perhaps yet unrealized) "semantic potential" of religious language (D. S. Browning and F. Schüssler Fiorenza).

4. International Reception of Critical Theory
Both the first and second generations of critical theory claimed attention especially in the Anglo-American world, but also in Scandinavia and France. M. Jay studied the early history of the Frankfurt school (1973), and R. Bernstein (1976) linked it to American → pragmatism and → phenomenology. D. Held (1980) gave a full account of the school from Horkheimer to Habermas. T. A. McCarthy (1978) and R. Geuss (1981) attempted a critical reconstruction of the main themes of Habermas along the lines of linguistic analysis. In 1984 M. Jay published a widely read monograph on Adorno. The Norwegian G. Skirbekk facilitated the Scandinavian discussion of pragmatism with detailed studies of Habermas and others. In the French-speaking sphere, G. Kortian (1979) promoted acquaintance with critical theory. S. Benhabib, S. White, and D. M. Rasmussen have analyzed important aspects of the recent development of Habermas's theory. Critical theory has also had a growing influence on postanalytic Anglo-American philosophy, which is still in process of formation.

→ Authority; Culture; Ideology; Institution; Rationalism

Bibliography: T. W. Adorno, *Ästhetische Theorie* (1970; ET *Aesthetic Theory* [London, 1984]); idem, *Negative Dialektik* (1966; ET *Negative Dialectics* [New York, 1973]) • S. Benhabib, *Critique, Norm, and Utopia: A Study of the Foundations of Critical Theory* (New York, 1986) • W. Benjamin, "Theses on the Philosophy of History," *Illuminations* (New York, 1968) 255-66 • R. J. Bernstein, *The Restructuring of Social and Political Theory* (Oxford, 1976) • D. S. Browning and F. Schüssler Fiorenza, eds., *Habermas, Modernity, and Public Theology* (New York, 1992) bibliography • H. Dubiel, *Theory and Politics: Studies in the Development of Critical Theory* (Cambridge, Mass., 1985) • R. Geuss, *The Idea of a Critical Theory: Habermas and the Frankfurt School* (Cambridge, 1981) • J. Habermas, *Der philosophische Diskurs der Moderne* (1985; ET *The Philosophical Discourse of Modernity: Twelve Lectures* [2d ed.; Cambridge, Mass., 1987]); idem, *Theorie des kommunikativen Handelns* (1981; ET *The Theory of Communicative Action* [Boston, 1981]) • D. Held, *Introduction to Critical Theory: Horkheimer to Habermas* (London, 1980) • M. Horkheimer, "Traditional and Critical Theory," *Critical Theory: Selected Essays* (New York, 1972) 188-243 • M. Horkheimer and T. W. Adorno, *Dialektik der Aufklärung* (1944; ET *Dialectic of Enlightenment* [New York, 1972]) • M. Jay, *Adorno* (London, 1984); idem, *The Dialectical Imagination: A History of the Frankfurt School and the Institute of Social*

Research, 1923-1950 (Boston, 1973) • G. KORTIAN, *Metacritique: The Philosophical Argument of Jürgen Habermas* (Cambridge, 1980; orig. pub., 1979) • P. LAKELAND, *Theology and Critical Theory: The Discourse of the Church* (Nashville, 1990) • T. A. McCARTHY, *The Critical Theory of Jürgen Habermas* (Cambridge, Mass., 1978) • L. NAGL, *Gesellschaft und Autonomie* (Vienna, 1981); idem, "Das verhüllte Absolute. Religionsphilosophische Motive bei Habermas und Adorno," *Mesotes* (Vienna, 1994) 2.176-93 • H. PEUKERT, *Science, Action, and Fundamental Theology* (Cambridge, Mass., 1986) • D. M. RASMUSSEN, *Reading Habermas* (Cambridge, Mass., 1990) • W. VON REIJEN, *Philosophie als Kritik. Einführung in die kritische Theorie* (Königstein, 1984) bibliography • G. SKIRBEKK, "Pragmatism in Habermas and Apel," *Essays in Pragmatic Philosophy* (ed. H. Høibraaten and I. Gullvåg; Oslo, 1985) • S. WHITE, *The Recent Work of Jürgen Habermas* (Cambridge, 1988) • R. WIGGERSHAUS, *Die Frankfurter Schule. Geschichte, theoretische Entwicklung, politische Bedeutung* (Munich, 1988) bibliography.

LUDWIG NAGL

Criticism

1. Term
2. Early History
3. Kant and Hegel
4. The Nineteenth Century
5. The Critical Faculty

1. Term

The term "criticism" (from Gk. *kritikos*, deriving from *krinō*, "discern; divide") already in Plato (427-347 B.C.; → Platonism) and Aristotle (384-322 B.C.; → Aristotelianism) had the two senses that it still bears today: the ability to make logical and legal judgments, and the art of rhetoric and philosophy. These two senses constitute the formal meaning. In the modern era the term also has a substantive meaning of its own.

2. Early History

In antiquity the Romans took the term in the narrower sense of the *ars iudicandi* as distinct from the *ars inveniendi* (Cicero [106-43 B.C.]). For the more rhetorical or philological component, the term *grammaticus* came into use. Appealing to the earlier history of the term, the → Renaissance, → humanism, and the early → modern period opened up new spheres of meaning.

With a straightforward antitheological thrust, criticism now became the power of philological judg-

ment, the *ars critica* that recognized no authority (A. Calepino [ca. 1440-1510]). In logic, criticism denoted the practice of logical analysis (P. Ramus [1515-72]), and Renaissance → aesthetics, which adopted Aristotelian concepts, viewed itself as a philosophically directed art of judgment (J. C. Scaliger [1484-1558]). In contrast, the criticism of Scripture, which was developing into the historical-critical method and which F. Bacon (1561-1626) and later G. B. Vico (1668-1744) declared to be typical of the modern scientific approach, was reclaimed by the new aesthetics, which was now trying to transform itself from an art into a sensitive science of knowledge (A. Baumgarten [1714-62]).

In the second half of the 18th century the term "criticism" became even broader. The formal sense was now generalized to denote the evaluation of all that people do or produce. There was thus a shift toward the negative. In dealing with texts, traditions, works of art, and logical arguments, the criticism of the → Enlightenment focused on the weaknesses, with a view, not to conserve, but to change.

3. Kant and Hegel

I. Kant (1724-1804; → Kantianism) defined criticism as the free and open testing to which everything must be subject. This definition contains less objective features that prepare the way for the emphatic substantive use in the 19th and 20th centuries. For one thing, Kant set the term in opposition to → dogmatism, using "criticism" in the sense of setting a limit. The critical use of theoretical → reason takes note of the boundaries of possible → experience, while the dogmatic use ignores them. Along the lines of the formal sense of antiquity, criticism takes place before the court of reason. Criticism, then, is not just a validating authority.

The concept of a process transcends the difference between formal and material criticism. No longer are certain contents (dogmas) ipso facto valid. Only that which derives from the process of transcendental reflection can be regarded as philosophically, scientifically, and ethically legitimate. In religion Kant seeks to use criticism to eliminate what is knowledge only in appearance in order to make way for → faith. Against the background of the historical development of the meaning of criticism, Kant's philosophy, which he himself called criticism, may be seen as such in three ways: in the criticism of logic and knowledge (→ Epistemology), of → ethics and action, and of aesthetics and → theology.

The philosophy of G. W. F. Hegel (1770-1831; → Hegelianism) is the second cornerstone in construction of the emphatic material sense of criticism. Although it does not bear the term "criticism," as a whole it must be seen as a methodical application of negation as the basic component of criticism, as a total → skepticism that results in the development of a system. Logically, then, the critical impulse leads to an acknowledgment of what is there, to a grasping of what is real.

4. The Nineteenth Century

The meanings of criticism underwent further development in the 19th century. In particular, the affirmative character of Hegel's understanding provoked varying reactions. Right-wing Hegelians, holding fast to the view found in the Gospels that there is a union of divine and human natures in Christ, also clung to Hegel's idea that criticism means overcoming what is partial and one-sided and achieving a grasp of the reconciled whole (J. K. F. Rosenkranz [1805-79]).

Left-wing Hegelians, on the basis of historical and philological biblical criticism (→ Exegesis, Biblical), raised → doubt about the → truth content of the accounts in the Gospels and, in their Christology, did not believe that the divine-human reconciliation had been achieved. Criticism thus became criticism of religion (L. A. Feuerbach [1804-72]). Religion was seen as a projection of human nature into divine attributes.

Critical criticism (B. Bauer [1809-82]) found in total negative criticism philosophy's final chance to free itself from the false and dazzling positive. The transition from this position to the idea of philosophy apart from Greek thought was represented by the demands that philosophy should take the form of a breakthrough to the masses (A. Ruge [1803-80]). When this purely intellectual postulate proved to be a failure, K. → Marx (1818-83; → Marxism) concluded that we must (1) secularize Christological salvation history (i.e., the story of the God who manifests himself; → History of Salvation) into the history of political economy, and (2) achieve philosophical criticism by the organizing of an international political movement, linking the weapon of criticism to the criticism of weapons.

Less spectacular and less influential from the standpoint of world history was the view of criticism adopted by → Kantianism (§3) and neo-Kantianism. This was for the most part a matter of methodology. The neo-Kantianism prominent in southwestern Germany investigated the boundaries between the natural and the social sciences as the natural sciences achieved their great triumphs (W. Windelband [1848-1915], H. Rickert [1863-1936]), while the neo-Kantianism of Marburg (H. Cohen [1842-1918], P. G. Natorp [1854-1924])

focused on Kant's idea that criticism can bring to light what is pure in reason and thus lay a foundation for science.

5. The Critical Faculty

Modern thinking, at least since the Enlightenment, has been typically marked by the conviction that there must be qualities in us that correspond to the emphatic concept of criticism. Since criticism in every form involves appraisal and evaluation, we must develop the faculty in order to engage in criticism. Kant viewed this kind of development as education for adulthood.

We also find variations on Kant's idea. In Hegel the consciousness undergoes a learning experience. In Feuerbach there is a gradual reappropriation of the humanity that has been projected on deity. In Marx we find → ideological criticism and the adoption of a → revolutionary consciousness. In the neo-Kantians there is a return to the idea of the pure elements in knowledge and action. In neo-Marxism we find critical theory as emancipation through reflection. Finally, critical → rationalism stresses the quality of letting oneself be criticized and of accepting what is fragmentary.

Today under the banner of a general critique of reason, there is no longer much confidence in the power of reason and its critical ability. Instead of lofty emancipatory claims, education in critical ability focuses more on dealing with the many forms of reason in a → pluralistic world. The same is true in religion and theology. Although we still find traces of an emancipatory theology linked to critical theory, as but one of many trends, this is integrated into the Christian view of the world, just as the Christian religion itself, after the disruption of the Enlightenment, sees itself as one option among many within the → postmodern technological age. In this context the critical faculty means subjecting the claim of Christianity that it has a monopoly of truth to the limits imposed by the existence of many such claims, yet without falling into → relativism.

→ Cartesianism; Dialectic; Dialogue; Empiricism; Illusion; Philosophy of History; Subjectivism and Objectivism

Bibliography: C. VON BORMANN, *Der praktische Ursprung der Kritik* (Stuttgart, 1974) • H. HOLZHEY, "Kritik," *HWP* 4.1267-82 • K. RÖTTGERS, "Kritik," *Geschichtliche Grundbegriffe* (ed. O. von Brunner et al.; Stuttgart, 1982) 3.651-75; idem, *Kritik und Praxis. Zur Geschichte des Kritikbegriffs von Kant bis Marx* (Berlin, 1975) • K. SCHNEID, "Erziehung zur Kritikfähigkeit," *Pädagogische Welt* 30 (1976) 493-95 • W. SCHNEIDERS,

"Vernünftiger Zweifel und wahre Eklektik. Zur Entstehung des modernen Kritikbegriffs," *StLeib* 17 (1985) 143-61 • J. A. SCHÜLEIN, "Soziologische und sozialpsychologische Aspekte von Kritik," *Soziale Welt* 30 (1979) 246-55 • H. SCHWEPPENHÄUSER, ed., *Krise und Kritik. Zur Aktualität der marxschen Theorie* (2d ed.; Lüneburg, 1987) • R. SIMON-SCHAEFER and W. C. ZIMMERLI, *Theorie zwischen Kritik und Praxis. Jürgen Habermas und die Frankfurter Schule* (Stuttgart, 1975) • R. C. SOLOMON and K. M. HIGGINS, eds., *The Age of German Idealism* (London, 1993) • H. THIELICKE, *Modern Faith and Thought* (Grand Rapids, 1990; orig. pub., 1983) • J. B. THOMPSON, *Critical Hermeneutics: A Study in the Thought of Paul Ricoeur and Jürgen Habermas* (New York, 1983) • W. C. ZIMMERLI, *Inwiefern wirkt Kritik systemkonstituierend?* (Bonn, 1980) 81-102.

WALTHER C. ZIMMERLI

Croatia

	1960	*1980*	*2000*
Population (1,000s):	4,045	4,377	4,485
Annual growth rate (%):	0.37	0.43	−0.16
Area: 56,538 sq. km. (21,829 sq. mi.)			

A.D. 2000
Population density: 79/sq. km. (205/sq. mi.)
Births / deaths: 1.09 / 1.25 per 100 population
Fertility rate: 1.60 per woman
Infant mortality rate: 9 per 1,000 live births
Life expectancy: 73.1 years (m: 69.1, f: 77.3)
Religious affiliation (%): Christians 93.4 (Roman Catholics 88.1, Orthodox 7.4, other Christians 1.1), Muslims 4.4, nonreligious 1.8, other 0.5.

Croatia (with provinces of Croatia proper, Dalmatia, the Dubrovnik region, Istria, and Slavonia) is a Mediterranean country situated on the Adriatic Sea. In 1991, when Croatia declared its independence from Yugoslavia, it had a population that the United Nations estimated at 4.5 million. Borders shifted in 1991, when one-third of Croatian land was captured by rebel Croatian Serbs, and again in 1995, when Croatia recaptured all but 5 percent of these lands. The ethnic composition of the country before the war in 1991 was 77.9 percent Croats, 12.2 percent Serbs, and 9.9 percent others. Because of the war, beginning in 1991, hundreds of thousands of Croats became displaced and refugees. Then the 1995 Croat liberation of West Slavonia and the Krajina region resulted in more than 100,000 Serbs leaving Croatia. As a result of the war in Bosnia, since 1992 almost half a million Bosnian Croats and Muslims have found refuge in Croatia.

Ancient Croatia was a part of the Western Roman Empire's province of Illyricum and was under the jurisdiction of the Roman Church. Christianity was introduced to this area as early as the first century through the missionary travels of the apostle Paul and his disciples. (Illyricum is mentioned in Rom. 15:19, and Dalmatia in 2 Tim. 4:10.) Croats, of South Slavic origin, settled in the areas of present-day Croatia and Bosnia in the seventh century A.D. Their arrival was followed by their conversion from the old Slavic nature-god religions to Roman Catholicism. Since that time and since the Great Schism in 1054 between Eastern and Western Christianity, Croatia has remained almost exclusively Roman Catholic. The Croatian church received the rare privilege from Rome of having the liturgy in its own language (Croatian) and was also permitted to use its own Glagolithic square script. This peculiarity of Croatian Catholicism has persisted to the present time.

Croatia became an independent kingdom in 925, when Pope John X crowned Tomislav as the first king of lands that included modern Croatia and Bosnia. In the 12th century the Croats united in one state with the Hungarians, another Catholic nation. Bosnia, however, remained a separate kingdom with an autonomous Bosnian church.

Protestant efforts to extend their influence in Croatia were moderately successful in the 16th century. The most prominent Croat Protestant theologian of that time was Matthias Flacius Illyricus (1520-75), a student of Luther. Protestants A. Jurij Dalmatin and S. Konzul Istranin worked on the first Croatian translation of the Bible. Ultimately, however, with the resurgence of Roman Catholicism, Protestantism was confined to a few small minorities, including Hungarians, Slovaks, and Germans.

From the mid-16th century until the end of the 17th century, most of Croatia came under Turkish rule, with the rest of the country joined to the Austro-Hungarian Empire. The Austrians created a military frontier in southeast Croatia called the Krajina region, where they settled thousands of Eastern Orthodox Serbs in order to form a barrier against the Turks. Since that time, Catholic Croatia has had a large Orthodox minority. Under the Turkish Ottoman Empire, Croats for the most part resisted the temptations of economic and political benefits that were presumably to accompany conversion to Islam. Croatia therefore, unlike Bosnia, never had a large Muslim population. The Turkish invasion of the Croatian lands, over time, resulted in the disappearance of the Bosnian church, successful Islamization in Bosnia, penetration of the Orthodox Christian Serbs deep into Bosnia and Croatia, some Catholics joining with Orthodox Christianity in the attempt to avoid Islamization, and some Orthodox joining the Catholic Church (often known as Greek Catholics).

The Turkish presence forced many Catholic Croats to find refuge outside Bosnia and Croatia. It is estimated that, since that time, 25 percent of the entire population left Croatia for neighboring countries. This emigration was caused by a combination of economic and political circumstances, including periods of Turkish rule, Hungarianization attempts, oppression by the Hapsburgs, dictatorship in the Kingdom of Yugoslavia, the Communist takeover, and Serbian aggression.

Croatia became part of Yugoslavia in 1918. Between the two world wars Yugoslavia was a kingdom ruled by a Serbian royal dynasty. Croatian dissatisfaction with the Serbian dictatorship found expression in 1941, when Croats took the opportunity under the Nazis of establishing their own state. The so-called Independent State of Croatia, which also included Bosnia, maintained its independence for only four years. During that time it was actually a Nazi puppet state, in which genocide was committed against Serbs, Jews, Gypsies, and anti-Nazi Croats.

After World War II, Croatia became one of the six republics of Communist Yugoslavia. In Croatia, Communist ideology was disproportionately more popular among Croat Serbs than among Croats, which led to a Serbian domination of the country, especially in politics, the military, the police, management-level positions, and the media. This discrepancy of power was a source of a continuing conflict between Croats and Serbs that finally erupted in 1991, when Croatia won international support for its independence but Croatian Serbs rebelled against Croatia. The four-year Serbian occupation of the Krajina region (which forms 20 percent of total Croatia) ended in 1995, when Croatia regained control.

Croatia is a country in transition. The religious situation in the country is characterized by a revival of Roman Catholicism, the influx of hundreds of thousands of Bosnian Muslim refugees, and a sudden decrease in the number of Serbian Orthodox Christians. All Protestants together constitute only 0.6 percent of the population, and evangelicals only 0.2 percent of the total population. After years of stagnation, Lutheran, Baptist, and Pentecostal churches in particular have begun to experience growth. Despite their small numbers, throughout this time of crisis evangelicals have made a notable effort to assist refugees and displaced people, to maintain church unity across ethnic lines, and to participate in the peacemaking efforts within the country.

Bibliography: S. Gaži, *A History of Croatia* (New York, 1973) • M. Korade et al., *Jesuits and Croatian Culture* (Zagreb, 1992) • I. Nizich, *Civil and Political Rights in Croatia* (New York, 1995) • S. P. Ramet, *Balkan Babel: Politics, Culture, and Religion in Yugoslavia* (Boulder, Colo., 1992) • R. Stallaerts and J. Laurens, *Historical Dictionary of the Republic of Croatia* (Metuchen, N.J., 1995) • M. Tanner, *Croatia: A Nation Forged in War* (New Haven, 1997) • Z. Tomac, *The Struggle for the Croatian State: Through Hell to Democracy* (Zagreb, 1993).

PETER KUZMIČ

Cross

1. General
2. Presuppositions
3. Forms
4. Methodology
5. Depictions

1. General

The prominence of the cross as a Christian → symbol is rooted in the NT account of the saving death of → Jesus on the cross at Golgotha. The wealth of the symbolism is due to the link with another line of interpretation that was originally independent, namely, the cross as an eschatological seal. In this view, the cross is a sign whose bearers commit themselves to the protection and possession of God at the last judgment. Basic here is the idea of sealing, which carries with it from the legal sphere the element of inviolability. The adoption of Ezek. 9:4 in Rev. 7:2 and elsewhere bears witness to the antiquity of this tradition. The crosses in Jewish graves give archaeological evidence of its impact upon → Judaism.

Most important for the image and concept of the cross was the need to wrestle with the "scandal" of the crucifixion of Jesus (see Gal. 5:11). The shame of crucifixion in the Roman empire as a capital punishment for slaves and criminals was the reason for the relatively late appearance of the cross in official art. The attempt to show that God willed the cross of Jesus, notwithstanding the curse of Deut. 21:23, initiated an early → theology of the cross and enriched cross iconography.

If the development is seen as a whole, for all the change of significance and the loss of value that the cross suffered as a cultic object at the → Reformation, the symbol of the cross has been historically most effective as an expression of the content of Christian faith, no other Christian symbol being comparable to it.

2. Presuppositions

The witness in the Bible, early writings, and the cultus is older than that in depictions of crosses.

2.1. The OT had a fruitful influence by means of typology. Although Deut. 21:23 worked negatively through the equation of the cross with the accursed tree (LXX *xylon*, Vg *lignum*), proof was also adduced for the positive character of the Christian cross as salvific and conferring blessing (Justin Martyr *Dial.* 89-91). The prefigurations demonstrating this positive meaning lived on in Christian art. The *xylon* was given a positive meaning as the Tree of Life and paradise (Gen. 2:9; 3:22, 24). This was the root of the symbolism of the cross as the Tree of Life (Ign. *Trall.* 11.2).

Ezek. 9:4 had even greater impact. At the last judgment the saved would be marked with a tau on the forehead. This was the last letter of the alphabet, which in ancient Hebrew had the form of a + or a ×. The concept made its way into Christianity, unmistakably in Rev. 7:2-3 and other passages. → Tertullian (ca. 160-ca. 225) quoted Ezek. 9:4 as a biblical argument in favor of marking a cross on the forehead; he found the cross in the *t*[*au*] of the Latin and Greek text of Ezekiel (*Adv. Marc.* 3.22). → Origen (ca. 185-ca. 254) saw the proof in the crosslike *tau* of the archaic letters (*Sel. in Ezech.* 9), which was known also to → Jerome (ca. 345-420; *In Hiez. comm.* 3:9). We have here a basic component of cross symbolism, namely, the cross as an eschatological seal (Gk. *sphragis*), a sign (Gk. *sēmeion*, Lat. *signum*) of possession, protection, and dedication. A related phenomenon may be the custom of apotropaic crosses (e.g., on the entrance door) or their use in → exorcism.

This line of understanding quickly joined hands with a second motif that had NT roots in the accounts of the historical *lignum* of Golgotha and the Easter story. Paul used "the word of the cross" as a phrase describing the whole salvation event, including → Easter. The idea implies victory (1 Cor. 1:18-25 etc.). In Eph. 2:16 and Col. 2:14 the cross is the mediator of → reconciliation and the liberator from → guilt. A link to its cosmological significance may be seen in Eph. 3:18 and 4:16 (cf. Justin Martyr *Apol.* 1.55).

The saying of Jesus about bearing the cross (Mark 8:34) became significant for the seeing of an attribute in the cross. Along with these texts that are oriented to the crucifixion, Matt. 24:30 was also an influential text for Christian symbolism, especially in the East

(→ Eschatology). The resplendent sign of the Son of Man was very soon interpreted as the cross (*Did.* 16.6), which at the → parousia goes before Christ as a sign of victory (*tropaion,* "trophy"; Cyril of Jerusalem *Cat.* 13.41).

2.2. The *Sitz im Leben* of the sign and symbolism of the cross was the → liturgy and cultus, and primarily → baptism (§1). In 2 Cor. 1:22 (cf. Eph. 1:13-14; 4:30) we perhaps have an early witness to a rite of marking with the cross *(sphragis)*. There might be a connection here with non-Christian rites of sealing. When Paul in Rom. 6:6-11 speaks of baptism as being crucified with Christ, we can see how the two components of interpretation of the cross come together — the cross as cultic *sphragis* and as historical *stauros.*

The gesture of crossing oneself, of which we have early attestation, also came to be linked to baptismal sealing. Pagan, magical, and apotropaic ideas might have had an influence at this point, with the power to terrify demons being ascribed to the cross (Origen *In Exod. hom.* 6.8; Cyril *Cat.* 4.13-14). Praying with outstretched arms was also regarded as a "type of a cross" *(typos staurou;* Justin Martyr *Apol.* 1.55).

Especially influential on art was the early turning to the east in prayer, for it was from the east that the parousia was expected (Matt. 24:27). This tradition produced the symbolism of the cross of → light and the crosses in church apses. At all these points we can see clearly the antiquity of the liturgical impact of the cross. Theological thinking on the cross and the liturgical sign of the cross converged in the act of baptism long before the symbol took actual shape.

3. Forms

Over the centuries, the cross has assumed many different forms, some of which appear in the accompanying figures.

1. The circular cross is commonly used in magic.
2. The ankh cross, or *crux ansata,* takes its form and meaning from the Egyptian hieroglyph for "life"; it was Christianized before A.D. 391.
3. The Greek cross is the *crux quadrata.*
4. The St. Andrew's cross (= the Greek cross on its side), or *crux decussata,* corresponds formally to the Hebrew tau and occurs also in Jewish art.
5. The Latin cross is the *crux immissa;* in the later fourth century it often appears with scalloped ends (cf. 11).
6. The staurogram, or (inaccurately) *crux monogrammatica,* seems to be the oldest Christian symbol. Consisting of the superimposed letters rho and tau, it was originally a pagan shorthand abbreviation but was adopted in Greek gospel

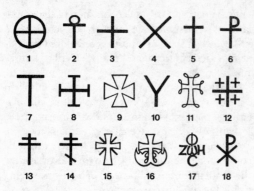

MSS about A.D. 200. The abbreviation was placed into the context of a word — C̅T̅O̅C̅ (= *stauros*) — and treated like a *nomen sacrum*.

7. The St. Anthony's cross, also known as the tau cross or the *crux commissa,* is based on the Greek tau and is thought to have been in the form of the cross at Golgotha (see Justin Martyr *Dial.* 91.2).

8. The crooked cross is common in texts.

9. The Maltese cross became the sign of the order.

10. The forked cross, or pestilence cross, was common in the later Middle Ages. It stressed the torment of the cross and, when depicted with branches, also symbolized the Tree of Life.

11. The (tear)drop cross, with its opening arms, denotes the victorious character of the cross.

12. The Jerusalem cross carries a suggestion of the five wounds of Christ.

13. The double cross, or the *crux gemina* — later the patriarchs' cross — carries the caption above the crossbar; with three crossbars, it becomes the papal cross.

14. The Russian cross has a footrest.

15. The cross of light, or *crux radiata,* is gold in color, or else four beams radiate from it.

16. The cross with floral motifs — the *crux florida,* or arborvitae cross — carries a reference to paradise (Rev. 22:2).

17. This cross combines the two NT motifs of light (ΦѠC / *phōs*) and life (ZѠH / *zōē;* see John 8:12), which also underlie numbers 15 and 16.

18. The Christogram and variants (→ Monogram of Christ) are not crosses in the strict sense, since they were originally signs for the name of Christ, not for the cross.

4. Methodology

In fixing the meaning of the cross, we must consider not only the fact that a symbol can have many senses but also the twofold iconological root of cross symbolism as both *signum* and *lignum crucis.* The inter-

relation of the two motifs greatly extends the range of what the cross expresses. To arrive at the dominant sense we have to take into account the setting and function. In the case of the cross at an entrance, the stress is on the sheltering aspect of the place; for a cross in the apse, the focus is on the room's consecrated aspect.

5. Depictions

5.1. In the → early church before Constantine, few crosses (mostly on graves; → Catacombs; Christian Art), apart from staurograms, are unquestionably Christian and can be dated with any precision. Under Constantine (306-37), the cross slowly made its way into the political sphere (e.g., appearing on coins), preceded by the Christogram. Representative Constantinian crosses have not been preserved, however, and the literary evidence is debatable. It is often said that there was a Constantinian memorial cross on Golgotha, but contemporary references are lacking. This would presuppose the ending of crucifixion as a punishment, which cannot be dated with any certainty.

Great influence was exerted by Constantine's vision of a heavenly sign promising victory before the decisive battle of A.D. 312, or by the later understanding of this sign as a cross (Rufinus *Hist. eccl.* 8.15). The motif of political victory was now added to that of theological victory. We know that the cross came into art by way of the idea of victory, the influence thus being hermeneutical rather than historical.

The first examples of the cross as an artistic theme of its own date from the middle of the fourth century on Roman passion sarcophagi. They depict triumphant crosses with laurel wreaths, in what is a diagram of the resurrection (H. von Campenhausen). In the Theodosian era the cross came to express the divinely given victorious power of the emperor, who included it in his insignia. After his victory over the Persians in 422, Theodosius II (emperor 408-50) set up a splendid cross on Golgotha that was often copied in later art.

The cult of the cross in → Jerusalem about the middle of the fourth century became a second creative force, along with → Byzantium, for the use of the cross in art. Cross → relics, legends regarding the finding of the true cross, pilgrimages to the holy places, feasts of the cross, and poems about it all gave rise to new depictions. Votive crosses, cross-decorated reliquaries, and devotionals of all types — sometimes with written references to the power of the cross to protect and bless, and simple or costly adornments — bear witness to private → piety alongside the official statements made by the church on sacred buildings, liturgical vessels, books, and textiles. The sarcophagi at Ravenna are examples of the funerary use of the cross. Express testimony to the development of the use of the cross even in → everyday life appears in Pseudo-Chrysostom (*PG* 48.825-27).

The theologically most significant conceptions of crosses represented in apses date from the days of Justinian, for example, S. Apollinare in Classe (ca. 549), outside Ravenna, and also the church at Sinai (548/565), where the cross is a subsidiary motif but integrates the whole composition. Findings of silver hoards from Syria show how costly the vessels were that were adorned with crosses from the fifth century to the seventh.

Monastic veneration of the cross in → meditation may be seen from wall paintings in Coptic monasteries. The cross played an important part in the iconoclastic controversy (→ Images 3.2) as the only permissible image in apses (e.g., in St. Irene, Constantinople, after 740).

5.2. In the early and high → Middle Ages, for all the richness and variety, the → doxological aspect remained dominant. As Ludwig of Bavaria wrote in his inscription to a poem by Rabanus Maurus on the holy cross (ca. 840), Christ's victory and salvation are in the cross. The ancient idea of the eschatological seal also persisted. The early Mozarabic Beatus Apocalypse of Gerona (10th cent.), for the sealing of the forehead in Rev. 7:2-3, shows an angel descending from the place of the sun, having the seal of the living God. The imperial cross of Conrad II (1024-39) refers to the power of the cross to ward off evil. Herrad von Landsberg (d. 1195) writes about the radiant cross of the end time in her *Hortus deliciarum:* "This cross is so bright that it obscures the splendor of the sun and moon with its brightness" (based on Rev. 21:23). The rite on the sending forth of → crusaders bears witness to the ongoing double meaning of the cross — for protection of body and soul, but also as a sign of the cross, passion, and death of Christ (Mark 8:34).

A new emphasis came in the High Middle Ages when the cross was given a place in depictions of the last judgment. The context of imagery (instruments of the passion and Christ's gesture of displaying his wounds) also interprets "the cross in relation to Christ's passion, that is, as both judgment and salvation" (B. Brenk). The new depiction of Christ as → suffering man rather than majestic God came to full development in the later Middle Ages as the cross came to be seen increasingly as a symbol of suffering. Beginning in the 11th century, a crucifix placed on the → altar expressed closeness to the → sacrament of → sacrifice (§1).

On the eve of the → Reformation the ideas of A. Dürer (1471-1528) are noteworthy. In his pen-and-ink drawing *Christ in Gethsemane* (1521), Christ's prostrating of himself in the form of a cross symbolizes unremitting acceptance by means of identification.

5.3. The Reformation brought significant changes in the use of the cross in art. In the → Roman Catholic Church there was no break with → tradition, but the cross lost its cultic character in → Protestantism. Creative depiction came now in audible rather than visible form, that is, in poetry and music (→ Hymnody; Theology and Music).

The 16th century saw examples of iconoclasm (→ Images 3.3). The attempt to detach → faith from the material, along the lines of the OT commandments, led the Reformed to an attitude of great reserve with respect to images, especially crucifixes (→ Church 3.5; Reformed and Presbyterian Churches). In contrast, M. → Luther (1483-1546; → Luther's Theology) thought that the crucifix should remain as a witness, for remembrance, as a sign (WA 18.80). More important for Luther was the spiritual place of the cross in its determinative significance for theology as *theologia crucis* (G. Ebeling).

5.4. In the → modern period ecclesiastically accepted forms of the cross have ceased to be binding. Instead we find individual conceptions that tend to stress also the human aspect. E. Barlach (1870-1938), for example, took up the theme of conformity to Christ in his 1932 *Pietà*. He used a strict form of the cross, yet also gave it relevance by transferring a medieval-type picture to a modern mother whose son was slain in war. Remnants of the ancient idea of the sign of the cross as protection live on, especially in popular custom (→ Piety). At the same time, the doxological symbolism in its many forms still has a firm place in the symbolic language of the → liturgy, especially in the → Orthodox Church.

→ Christian Art; Iconography; Sign of the Cross; Symbol

Bibliography: G. T. ARMSTRONG, "The Cross in the OT according to Athanasius," *Theologia Crucis, Signum Crucis* (FS E. Dinkler; Tübingen, 1979) 17-38 • B. BRENK, *Tradition und Neuerung in der christlichen Kunst des 1. Jahrhunderts* (Vienna, 1966) • H. VON CAMPENHAUSEN, "Zwingli und Luther zur Bilderfrage," *Das Gottesbild im Abendland* (Witten, 1957) 139-72 • E. DINKLER, "Zur Ikonographie des Kreuzes in der nubischen Kunst," *Nubia* (Warsaw, 1975) 22-30 • E. DINKLER and E. DINKLER–VON SCHUBERT, "Kreuz," *LCI* 2.562-90 • E. DINKLER, E. DINKLER–VON SCHUBERT, and G. GALAVARIS, "Kreuz," *RBK* 5.9-219 (bibliog-

raphy) • E. DINKLER–VON SCHUBERT, "ϹΤΑΥΡΟϹ: Vom
'Wort vom Kreuz' (1 Kor. 1,18) zum Kreuz-Symbol,"
Byzantine East, Latin West (FS K. Weitzmann; Princeton, 1995) 29-38; idem, "Zur Abschaffung der Kreuzi-
gungsstrafe in der Spätantike," *JAC* 35 (1990) 135-46 •
J. ENGEMANN, "Das Kreuz auf spätantiken Kopfbedek-
ungen," FS Dinkler, 137-53; idem, "Magische Übelab-
wehr in der Spätantike," *JAC* 18 (1975) 22-48; idem, "Zu
spätantiken Geräten des Alltagslebens," *JAC* 15 (1972)
154-73 • R. FARIOLI, "I sarcofagi ravennati con segni
cristologici," *FR* 4 (1978) 131-59 • V. GROSSI, "Croce,"
Dizionario patristico e di antichità christiana (1983)
864-67 (bibliography) • H. J. KLIMKEIT, "Das Kreuzes-
symbol in der zentralasiatischen Religionsbegegnung,"
ZRG 31 (1979) 99-115 • L. KÖTZSCHE-BREITENBRUCH,
"Pilgerandenken aus dem Heiligen Land," *Vivarium* (FS
T. Klauser; Münster, 1984) 220-46 • E. LUCCHESI PALLI,
"Bulla und Kreuzanhänger," FS Dinkler, 351-58 • P. VAN
MOORSEL, "The Worship of the Holy Cross in Saqqara,
Archaeological Evidence," FS Dinkler, 409-16 •
C. OAKES et al., "Cross," *DArt* 8.195-204 • M. RASSART-
DEBERGH, "La peinture copte avant le XIIᵉ siècle,"
Miscellanea Coptica (Rome, 1981) 221-85 •
K. SCHNEEMELCHER, "Das Kreuz Christi und die Dä-
monen," *Pietas* (FS B. Kötting; Münster, 1980) 381-92 •
W. C. VAN UNNIK, "Der Fluch der Gekreuzigten, Dt.
21,23," FS Dinkler, 483-99 • K. WEITZMANN, ed., *Age of
Spirituality: Late Antique and Early Christian Art, Third
to Seventh Century* (New York, 1979) bibliography •
W. WISCHMEYER, "Christogramm und Staurogramm in
den lateinischen Inschriften altkirchlicher Zeit," FS
Dinkler, 539-50.

ERIKA DINKLER–VON SCHUBERT

Cross, Sign of the → Sign of the Cross

Cross, Stations of the → Stations of the Cross

Crusades

1. Background
2. Cause and Progression
3. Perspectives
4. Evaluation

At a time when we have reason to be anxious about
world → peace, the Crusades epitomize the danger
that Christians will discount the way of reconciliation and trust in the naked → power of military
might (→ War). Though it is essential that we take
note of this temptation, we must be careful neither
to make "Crusades" a mere slogan in criticism of the
church nor to use the term uncritically for any good
cause. We must study the Crusades as a historical
phenomenon.

1. Background
The Crusades give their name to a whole epoch, for
they affected every sphere of life. Because of their
various forms and influences, we have thus far been
unable to arrive at a satisfactory definition of the
term. Among the immediate factors affecting the
crusade movement we must number, on the side of
→ Islam, the concentration and increase of power
of the Seljuk Turks, who had moved from central
Asia to the Mediterranean and were coming into
increasing opposition to → Byzantium. On the
Christian side, we must consider the increasing
importance of → pilgrimages to → Jerusalem, the
growing power and greater cohesion of the peoples
of the Christian West, the attempt to give visible
expression to this sense of community, and the
development of the idea of a → holy war against
heretics and heathen (→ Heresies and Schisms),
which made possible the recognition of a warrior
caste (knights) that had long been basically repudiated.

2. Cause and Progression
The immediate occasion for the Crusades was an
appeal for help sent by Emperor Alexius I of Byzantium (1081-1118) to Pope Urban II (1088-99), which
Urban then passed on to the assembled Council of
Clermont (1095). Urban's speech has come down to
us in several versions, making it difficult to decide
exactly which themes evoked the spontaneous enthusiasm of his listeners: the liberation of the Holy
Sepulchre, aid for Christians in the East, or the hope
of → union with the Greek church. Undoubtedly the
diversion of the warlike impulses of knights to external enemies played a role, as did also, as we see from
many districts in France, the prospect of ensuring for
many younger sons of nobles a patrimony of their
own. Finally, the love of adventure was also a factor.
The enthusiasm was increased by an external symbol
— the fabric cross that the pope allowed those who
were ready for battle to wear on their cloaks (which
ultimately gave the movement its name) — and by
the plenary → indulgence that was promised to all
crusaders. (Perhaps deliberately, this indulgence was
formulated only imprecisely.) The → cross was seen
both as a sign of victory and as a mark of meritorious
→ discipleship (see Matt. 16:24) for the hazarding of
life itself.

2.1. A crusade of commoners under Peter the Hermit (ca. 1050-1115, also known as Peter of Amiens) was launched in 1096, but it was a miserable failure. In 1097 five armies of knights set off, though with no unified command. The march through Byzantium was difficult, and campaigning through Asia Minor and Syria was slow and involved many casualties.

On July 15, 1099, however, Jerusalem fell into the hands of the crusaders. In the intoxication of victory, a bloodbath took place. The crusaders set up feudal estates in the conquered territories under general Frankish supervision. Ruins of their castles may be seen to this day. In Jerusalem itself the ruler Godfrey of Bouillon (ca. 1060-1100) took the title "defender of the Holy Sepulchre," which shows that the enterprise originally had a religious goal. His successor, Baldwin I (1058?-1118), took a further step, however, in having himself crowned "king of Jerusalem."

2.2. A new crusading wave in 1101 spent itself in Asia Minor. The original armies of knights were increasingly replaced by more spiritual knightly → orders charged to offer military protection. The first of these was the Order of the Knights Templar, given formal approval at the Council of Troyes (1128). → Bernard of Clairvaux (1090-1153) extolled the monastic knight as an avenger of Christ and a protector of Christians. When Edessa was lost in 1144, Bernard called upon the kings of Christendom to take up the cause. His preaching of repentance led both Germany and France to initiate crusades under royal leadership in 1146. National rivalries, however, led to the failure in Asia Minor of this Second Crusade. In the Holy Land itself, internal quarrels weakened the power of the crusading knights.

2.3. The thoughtlessly provoked battle of Hattin (1187), near the Sea of Galilee, against the strengthened Saracens under Sultan Saladin (1137/38-93) led to the collapse of the Jerusalem kingdom and the loss of the relic of the True Cross. This time Frederick I (1152-90) took charge. With the help of Pope Gregory VIII (1187) and his legate Henry of Albano (d. 1188), Frederick made preparations for a massive crusade. He found support at the Diet of Mainz in 1188 (which came to be known as the Diet of Jesus Christ). But the great joint campaign, in which the kings of France and England took part, going by ship (though this was regarded as less knightly!), broke up with the death of Frederick in Asia Minor. The only tangible result of this Third Crusade (1188-90) was the capture of Acre and Cyprus, which became important bases. King Richard I of England (1189-99) also secured access to the holy places by treaty (1192).

Frederick's son and successor, Henry VI (1190-97), assembled a new crusading army, though not now under imperial leadership, and organized it very effectively. But the army disintegrated when it heard of the sudden death of the emperor, for a struggle now broke out for the succession between Otto IV (1198-1215) and those who supported Henry's infant son, Frederick II (1215-50).

2.4. At the time of this power vacuum, one of the most energetic of all the medieval popes was elected. This was → Innocent III (1198-1216), who at once took the initiative and already in 1198 was calling for a fourth crusade. His call evoked a widespread response, but the crusade lacked both firm leadership (no kings took part) and money. The crusading army thus fell into the clutches of the powerful Republic of Venice, whose doge, Dandolo (d. 1205), used it to plunder the Adriatic port city of Zara, which was then in Hungarian hands. At the urging of Venice, the army in 1203 captured Constantinople, thus revealing that it had lost sight completely of its spiritual purpose. In their lust for → relics and treasures, the crusaders plundered this center of Eastern Christianity, which had been in schism since 1054. The founding of the Latin kingdom of Romania in 1204 sealed the misuse of the crusading army in the interests of power politics. The crusade itself was repudiated.

2.5. Innocent III again tried to initiate a new crusade in 1213, for which he drew Lateran IV (→ Councils of the Church) into his plans. With the pope's death in 1216, however, preparations continued only halfheartedly.

In 1220/21 an army set off for Damietta in Egypt but met with no success. Aid was sought from Frederick II, but it did not materialize. → Francis of Assisi (1181/82-1226; → Franciscans) made unsuccessful efforts to make peace between the warring parties. Cardinal Pelagius (named legate in 1218) and the sultan, al-Malik al-Kāmil (ruled 1218-38), received Francis respectfully but did not understand this "little brother" of the Crucified or his call to conversion. In 1228 the emperor redeemed his crusading vow, yet ultimately it was not by military might but by negotiations and a treaty in 1229 that he won back Jerusalem for Christendom. The time for war was past.

With the loss of Jerusalem in 1244, however, Louis IX ("St. Louis," 1226-70) of France launched new expeditions in 1249 and 1270. Both were unsuccessful. Acre, the last secure Christian foothold in the Holy Land, was lost in 1291. Crusading lasted for another century as small armies set out, but a terrible defeat at Nicopolis in 1396 ended all further zest for the venture.

The conflicts between the Islamic East and the Christian West now took the form of the Turkish wars against the West. Constantinople fell in 1453, and the age of the → Reformation was marked by fear of the Turks, whose advances were checked only in 1683 at the gates of Vienna.

The religious consequences of the Crusades in the East were negative for both Muslims and Christians. The economic and cultural impact in the West is the subject of debate. New plants came from the East, as did fabulous stories. In courtly poetry the chivalrous crusader and the noble heathen were important figures. G. E. Lessing (1729-81), in his parable of the ring, was the first to advocate the idea of the equal value of different religions (→ Tolerance).

3. Perspectives

The historical summary reveals a clear development. Initially, knights and barons supported the crusading movement with their enthusiasm. Kings in Germany and France then took the lead in the Second Crusade. The Third Crusade began as an imperial venture, though it was taken over by the English and French kings. The abortive crusade of 1197 was also an imperial crusade. The papacy headed the Fourth and Fifth Crusades as it reached the apogee of its medieval power under Innocent III (→ Empire and Papacy; Middle Ages 2). Yet the Fifth Crusade showed already that a strong secular ruler (Frederick II) was needed. The French king attempted to replace the emperor; finally all the efforts of Pope Gregory X (1271-76) to keep the crusading movement alive among Christians failed.

The organization and financing of the Crusades, and recruitment for them, underwent increasing improvement. The diet at Mainz under Barbarossa in 1188 did not merely serve the ends of propaganda but helped to mobilize the whole empire. Innocent III systematically united all the traditions of the 12th century and effectively exploited them. From this time onward there were taxes for crusades, precisely formulated indulgences, a central organization for recruiting, and proper protection for the rights of crusaders.

The idea of the Crusades also changed. A militant eschatological mood prevailed in the First Crusade. Bernard of Clairvaux then taught his generation to view a crusade as an opportunity for active → penitence. With a play on words, Innocent changed Bernard's slogan of *affectus* (affection) into *effectus* (success) — crusades had to show tangible results. Under papal leadership, Christians were to free the holy places for their liege-Lord Christ, who had been driven out. The pope summoned the faithful (*fideles*

Christi) to act on their Lord's behalf. Religiously, the *fideles* were believers, but in feudal law they were also liege men.

All other concerns — church union with the East, church reform, → mission, the politics of the Peace of the Land and the Peace of God — were now subjugated to that of success in the Crusades. Innocent impressed all these things into service in actualization of his idea of *christianitas* engaging in a crusade under papal leadership. With his successors, the Crusades thus fell into the swamp of politics, and religious enthusiasm waned in consequence.

4. Evaluation

In the Crusades, Christendom as a community of Christians and kingdoms engaged in the venture against the enemy according to the demands of the pope, the religious reward for which was the crusader indulgence. The enemy included the Moors in Spain, against whom a crusade was quickly organized. When Bernard stressed *affectus* in crusading, this could easily be directed against pagans in mission areas (e.g., the Wends in eastern Germany, Lithuanians, and Prussians), though the idea of a missionary crusade was plainly subordinate to the politics of colonization.

Ultimately, the pope saw in the crusades a final weapon against internal enemies. In 1208 the battle against heretics in the south of France (→ Cathari) was given the rank of a crusade. This weapon soon proved to be inappropriate and went out of use, being replaced by the → Inquisition. Nevertheless, the dam had been broken. It was only a tiny step to the purely political crusade. In 1234 a crusade was launched against the peasants who opposed the lordship of the archbishop of Bremen, though this weapon, too, was quickly blunted in the papacy's war of extermination against the Hohenstaufens. The misuse of crusades, along with the growing insight that mission to pagans, at least in Christ's sense, is more than their destruction in crusades, increasingly eroded any support for the concept of a crusade. The movement collapsed because it lost its resonance among Christian people.

In the 20th century the term "crusade" came into use in political propaganda for opposition to Bolshevism. In the Anglo-American world the term also occurs in some circles to denote evangelistic campaigns or charitable endeavors.

Bibliography: A. S. ATIYA, *The Crusades in the Later Middle Ages* (2d ed.; New York, 1965) • C. ERDMANN, *The Origin of the Idea of Crusade* (Princeton, 1977; orig. pub., 1935) • F. GABRIELI, *Die Kreuzzüge aus arabischer*

Sicht (Zurich, 1973) • R. Grousset, *Histoire des croisades et du royaume franc de Jérusalem* (3 vols.; Paris, 1934-36) • H. E. Mayer, *Bibliographie zur Geschichte der Kreuzzüge* (2d ed.; Hannover, 1965); idem, bibliography, *HZ* 3 (1969) 642-731; idem, *The Crusades* (2d ed.; New York, 1990) • J. Riley-Smith, *The Crusades: A Short History* (New Haven, 1987); idem, *What Were the Crusades?* (2d ed.; Basingstoke, 1992) • H. Roscher, *Papst Innocenz III. und die Kreuzzüge* (Göttingen, 1969) • S. Runciman, *A History of the Crusades* (3 vols.; Cambridge, 1951-54) • R. C. Schwinges, *Kreuzzugsideologie und Toleranz* (Stuttgart, 1977) • K. M. Setton, ed., *A History of the Crusades* (6 vols.; Madison, Wis., 1969-89) • F. W. Wentzlaff-Eggebert, *Kreuzzugsdichtung des Mittelalters* (Berlin, 1960).

Helmut Roscher

Crying → Laughing and Crying

Crypt

The word "crypt" (from Gk. *kryptō*, "conceal, cover over") was used in early Christian times for burial places in the → catacombs. It then came to denote a vaulted, sacred chamber under the church chancel, which in large churches might extend under the nave and transepts (→ Church Architecture). Reached by stairs, crypts served as sites in which to store and venerate → relics and to bury → saints. When furnished with → altars, they were also used as → chapels.

In the forms of crosses, crypts appeared by the fifth century in North Africa, southeastern Europe, and Asia Minor (e.g., St. Demetrius Church in Thessalonica, Studios Church and Chalcoprateia Church in Constantinople). In circular form, in which a gallery leads to the burial chamber from the semicircular entrance, they first appeared in Italy in the seventh century (e.g., St. Peter's Church in → Rome). The external crypt developed in the ninth century as an ancillary room appended to the ring crypt, forming thus the preliminary stage of the hall crypt, which as a structure with multiple naves became the prominent crypt form in the Romanesque period (e.g., the cathedrals of Auxerre and Speyer and St. Michael's at Hildesheim). The Gothic did not have crypts (→ Middle Ages 1).

→ Cathedral

Bibliography: J. S. Curl, *A Celebration of Death: An Introduction to Some of the Buildings, Monuments, and Settings of Funerary Architecture in the West European Tradition* (London, 1980) • S. Heywood, "Crypt," *DArt*

8.222-25 • R. Krautheimer, *Early Christian and Byzantine Architecture* (2d ed.; Harmondsworth, 1975) • E. H. Lemper, *Entwicklung und Bedeutung der Krypten, Unterkirchen und Crufträume von Ende der Romanik bis zum Ende der Gotik* (Leipzig, 1963) • M. Magni, "Cryptes du haut Moyen Age en Italie. Problèmes de typologie du IXe jusqu'au début du XIe siècle," *CAr* 28 (1979) 41-85 • W. Sanderson, "Monastic Reform in Lorraine and the Architecture of the Outer Crypt, 950-1100," *TAPhS*, n.s., 61/6 (1971) 3-36 • R. Wallrath, "Zur Entwicklungsgeschichte der Krypta," *JKGV* 22 (1940) 273-92.

Sabine Möllers

Crypto-Calvinism

1. Term
2. History
3. Aftermath

1. Term
The term "Crypto-Calvinism" (or secret Calvinism) came into use in the Protestant doctrinal controversies following the Interim of Augsburg (1548), when the → Gnesio-Lutherans (or genuine Lutherans) began calling the adherents of Philipp → Melanchthon (1497-1560) Philippists and also → Crypto-Calvinists. This polemical term arose in connection with the so-called second eucharistic controversy (→ Eucharist 3.3), which was stirred up by the Consensus Tigurinus, the Zurich agreement between H. Bullinger and J. → Calvin (→ Calvin's Theology 3.5; Helvetic Confession). The agreement represented a eucharistic teaching that affirmed the real presence of Christ in the Spirit but rejected the notion of real presence in the bread and wine and advocated a → Christology that found no place for the → ubiquity (omnipresence) of the exalted body of Christ. In essence, the Gnesio-Lutherans refused to accept Melanchthon's efforts at conciliation with the Calvinists.

2. History
The history of Philippism and so-called Crypto-Calvinism must be seen in the context of the confessional hardening of → Lutheranism and all the developments in the political and ecclesiastical spheres subsequent to the Peace of Augsburg (1555; → Augsburg, Peace of). Philippism at first consolidated itself in Electoral Saxony, but it collapsed after the scandal provoked by the *Exegesis perspicua . . . de sacra coena* (1574) of Joachim Curaeus (1532-73). In its wake Kaspar Peucer (1525-1602) and Christoph Pezel (1539-1604), who were responsible for the Wit-

tenberg Catechism (1571), which was branded as Crypto-Calvinist, were deprived, imprisoned, and exiled. This defeat for Philippism promoted unification in the → Formula of Concord (1577).

Crypto-Calvinism enjoyed a resurgence in Electoral Saxony under Elector Christian I (1586-91), supported by his chancellor, Nikolaus Crell (1550-1601). Upon Christian's death, however, Crell was deposed and, after a ten-year trial, beheaded.

3. Aftermath

As the doctrinal fronts hardened, many Philippists took refuge in Protestant areas that did not receive the Formula of Concord and became full adherents of → Calvinism. Outside Germany the followers of Melanchthon were also accused of Crypto-Calvinism. In Denmark, for example, the important theologian Niels Hemmingsen (1513-1600) was deprived of his professorship on this charge (1579).

→ Synergism

Bibliography: C. Andresen, ed., *HDThG* 2 • E. Bizer, *Studien zur Geschichte des Abendmahlsstreites im 16. Jahrhundert* (Gütersloh, 1940; repr., Darmstadt, 1962) • R. Calinich, *Kampf und Untergang des Melanchthonismus in Kursachsen, 1570-1574* (Leipzig, 1886) • H. Gollwitzer, *Coena Domini. Die altlutherische Abendmahlslehre in ihrer Auseinandersetzung mit dem Calvinismus, dargestellt an der lutherischen Frühorthodoxie* (Munich, 1937) • J. Moltmann, *Christoph Pezel (1539-1604) und der Calvinismus in Bremen* (Bremen, 1958) • L. D. Peterson, "The Philippist Theologians and the Interims of 1548: Soteriological, Ecclesiastical, and Liturgical Compromises and Controversies within German Lutheranism" (Diss., University of Wisconsin, 1974) • L. W. Spitz and W. Lohff, eds., *Discord, Dialogue, and Concord: Studies in the Lutheran Reformation's Formula of Concord* (Philadelphia, 1977) • H. E. Weber, *Reformation, Orthodoxie und Rationalismus* (I/2; Gütersloh; repr., Darmstadt, 1966).

Steffen Kjeldgaard-Pedersen

Cuba

1. Geography
2. Population
3. Mission and Historical Development
4. Churches and Religions
5. Revolution and Its Consequences

1. Geography

The subtropical island of Cuba was reached by Christopher Columbus (1451-1506) on October 27, 1492.

	1960	1980	2000
Population (1,000s):	6,985	9,710	11,201
Annual growth rate (%):	2.09	0.82	0.30
Area: 110,861 sq. km. (42,804 sq. mi.)			

A.D. 2000

Population density: 101/sq. km. (262/sq. mi.)
Births / deaths: 1.16 / 0.72 per 100 population
Fertility rate: 1.55 per woman
Infant mortality rate: 8 per 1,000 live births
Life expectancy: 76.7 years (m: 74.8, f: 78.7)
Religious affiliation (%): Christians 45.2 (Roman Catholics 41.3, Protestants 2.2, indigenous 1.4, marginal 1.1, other Christians 0.1), nonreligious 28.9, spiritists 17.9, atheists 7.3, other 0.7.

It is approximately 1,200 km. (750 mi.) long and averages 110 km. (68 mi.) wide. It is the largest of the Greater Antilles.

Cuba consists of mountains and plains and also embraces 1,600 islands. Pico Turquino, the highest mountain, reaches 1,947 m. (6,388 ft.). The south coast especially is swampy. The largest navigable river, the Canto, empties into the southern gulf.

2. Population

The population of Cuba consists for the most part of Spaniards, former African slaves, and a mixture of the two. In 1994 the population was 51 percent mulatto, 37 percent white, and 11 percent black. The annual growth rate (1988-93) was 0.9 percent per year. Of the original Taino people, which was estimated at 100,000 in 1492 and was linguistically related to the Aruaks, we now have only archaeological and biological remains.

3. Mission and Historical Development

The missionary work (→ Mission) of the → Dominicans, Mercedarians, and → Franciscans began with the occupation of the island in 1511 and ended with the extermination of the Tainos (→ Genocide). In 1537 there were 300 whites, 4,700 mostly mainland → Indians, and 800 African → slaves. Black slaves, belonging to Christian institutions or individuals, underwent forced baptism. From that time onward, Cuba was Roman Catholic.

As a docking and transit point, Cuba at first had only a small population (only 200,000 in 1777). Transient → bishops and → priests provided → pastoral care. Seminaries were founded at San Basilio in 1722 and San Carlos y San Ambrosio in 1772, and the university in 1728.

A sense of Cuban identity arose under the leadership of national clergy from the middle of the 18th century. This nationalism resulted in a slave revolt in 1812 and wars of independence in 1868-78 and 1895-98, with independence finally achieved in 1898.

Spain used the → patronage system in the church to oust Cubans from key positions, to close monasteries, and to abolish tithes (→ Church Finances). It reacted with oppression and then concessions to demands for political freedom (Creoles) and civil emancipation (slaves).

Slavery ended in 1880, and Cuba achieved provincial status and free trade. But the new sense of national identity was not satisfied by the weakened, royalist-dominated church, nor was it fostered by the new dependence brought about when the United States entered the war against Spain, since the armistice was arranged without Cuban participation. The Platt Amendment conferred a U.S. right of intervention (up to 1934), a perpetual lease had to be granted for the large Guantánamo naval base (114 sq. km. / 44 sq. mi.), and both political and a crushing economic dependence remained.

After 1901 the republic brought in stricter separation of church and state. The end of patronage made independent development possible. Dioceses were founded at Pinar del Rio and Cienfuegos in 1903 and at Camagüey and Matanzas in 1912. (The archbishoprics of Santiago and La Habana had been bishoprics since 1787; → Catholic Action.) Roman Catholicism also lost its monopoly position.

4. Churches and Religions

The → Anglicans gained a footing in 1741 in order to care for their own members. Through Cubans converted in the United States, the → Methodists came in 1883, the → Baptists in the same year, and the Presbyterians (→ Reformed and Presbyterian Churches) a year later. There are now over 50 churches, → denominations, and groups, with 15 mostly → North American missions at work.

In 1990 the largest Protestant church was the Iglesia Evangélica Pentecostal de Cuba (from 1920; → Pentecostal Churches), with 56,000 adherents. Other important groups were Assemblies of God, Seventh-day Adventists, Baptists, and Methodists. Perhaps as much as one-fourth of the population engages in occult practices. The respective cultic forms and membership correspond to the origins: Santería (Sudan), Naniguismo (Nigeria), Arara (Dahomey), and Mayombe and Ganga (Zaire). Members of the Communist Party — perhaps 10 percent of the population — are officially → atheists. Overall, roughly 41 percent of Cubans in 1991 were Catholic, and 3 percent were Protestant.

5. Revolution and Its Consequences

The triumph of the → revolution under Fidel Castro (January 1, 1959) over the dictator Fulgencio Batista (1952-59) was at first viewed positively by the churches. The development into a one-party Communist state with a monopoly of education and profound social changes, however, caught them unprepared. The emigration of the upper and middle classes (some 800,000), who supported the churches, and the financial dependence on the United States (esp. by Protestant churches) and Spain (esp. by Catholics) brought to light the churches' weakness. In 1961 the government closed the Catholic University of Villanueva, nationalized 350 Catholic schools, and expelled 136 priests. Anglicans and Episcopalians shrank from 75,000 to 12,000, and the Baptists were reduced by up to 90 percent by mass emigration after the imprisonment of 30 pastors in 1965.

Restrictive oppression continued until 1990, when the government began taking a less hostile position toward the churches. An amendment to the constitution in 1992 made discrimination against Christians illegal.

Events in Cuba in 1994-95 have suggested that the churches may be experiencing dramatic growth, even as the economic situation worsens. Cuban Methodists, for example, once down to 6,000 members, had grown to over 50,000 by 1994. Also, a rapidly growing → house church movement has been reported.

Ecumenically, the Roman Catholics have a national commission and study center for ecumenism (Havana), and the Protestants have the Ecumenical Council of Churches, with 13 member churches (Protestant and Orthodox; → National Councils of Churches), as well as a Union Seminary in Matanza (serving Methodist, Presbyterian, and Episcopal interests). There is a Protestant and Roman Catholic study center in Camagüey.

Bibliography: S. ARCE MARTINEZ, *The Church and Socialism: Reflections from a Cuban Context* (New York, 1985) • D. BARRETT, ed., *WCE* 252-55 • F. BETTO, *Nachtgespräche mit Fidel* (Berlin, 1987) • J. CLARK, *Religious Repression in Cuba* (Miami, 1986) • ENCUENTO NACIONAL ECLESIAL CUBANO, *Documento final e instrucción pastoral de los obispos* (Rome, 1987) • P. GHEDDO, "Kirche im revolutionären Kuba," *KM* 1 (1977) 13-16 • R. GOMEZ TRETO, *The Church and Socialism in Cuba* (Maryknoll, N.Y., 1988) • O. GORÍN, "Dialog mußten wir erst lernen," *Weltmission* 6 (1987) 8 • A. L. HAGEMAN and P. E. WHEATON, *Religion in Cuba Today: A New Church in a New Society* (New York, 1971) • J. M. KIRK, *Between God and the Party: Religion and Politics in Rev-*

olutionary Cuba (Tampa, Fla., 1989) • Lateinamerika-
Ploetz, Die ibero-amerikanische Welt. Geschichte, Pro-
bleme, Perspektiven (Freiburg, 1978) • O. Noggler,
"Kuba," Lateinamerika. Gesellschaft–Kirche–Theologie,
vol. 1, Aufbruch und Auseinandersetzung (ed. H.-J. Prien;
Göttingen, 1981) 273-303 • T. Oden, "The Church
Castro Couldn't Kill," ChrTo, April 25, 1994, 18-22 •
O. Ortega, "Die kubanische Kirche im Sozialismus,"
ZMiss 10 (1984) 205-11 • J. Ortega y Alamino, "Zur
Situation der Kirche in Kuba," WK 5 (1985) 321-23 •
M. A. Ramos, Protestantism and Revolution in Cuba
(Miami, 1989) • "Schlußbotschaft des Ersten National-
kongresses der Kirche in Kuba," WK 6 (1986) 59-60 •
T. Tschuy, Hundert Jahre kubanischer Protestantismus
(1868-1961) (Frankfurt, 1978).

Othmar Noggler, O.F.M.

Cuius regio eius religio

The slogan Cuius regio eius religio (whose the region,
his the religion) was coined at the beginning of the
17th century by the jurist J. Stephani (1544-1623) to
describe the right that the Peace of Augsburg (1555)
granted to secular rulers to determine the confession
that would be binding on all their subjects. This principle thus transferred to Protestant rulers both spiritual jurisdiction and episcopal power (→ Bishop,
Episcopate) along the lines of → Episcopalianism.

In a broader sense the formula formed part of the
ius reformandi that traditionalists brought to the
Augsburg deliberations, arguing for "one lord, one
religion" (cf. Eph. 4:5) against the demand of the
Protestant princes for general → religious liberty.
The right was finally restricted to those who opted
for either Roman Catholicism or the Augsburg Confession, but the restriction was softened by the concession that subjects might freely move from one
territory to another. The principle was open to interpretation and thus became the occasion for disagreements. Overall, however, it stabilized the secular
government of the church. At the cost of the question
of truth, it also guaranteed the officially recognized
confessions, to which the Reformed was added in
1648. In an increasingly weakened form, it controlled
the Confessional Age.
→ Denomination

Bibliography: M. Heckel, Staat und Kirche nach den
Lehren der evangelischen Juristen Deutschlands in der er-
sten Hälfte des 17. Jahrhunderts (Tübingen, 1968) •
R. Kolb, Luther's Heirs Define His Legacy (Brookfield,
Vt., 1996).

Manfred Biersack

Cultic Meal

1. A meal assumes a religious meaning if it is approached in a ritual manner, as indicated by the
specific food and drink used, as well as the occasion,
time, and other factors. Such meals function as rites
of communication between one person and another,
or between people and the divine. In the latter case
particularly, they are usually linked to → sacrifices
(sacrificial meals).

2. The social character predominates when the meals
relate to making or celebrating a covenant (e.g., wedding feasts or meals to strengthen kinship bonds).
When the covenant is with God, cultic meals may
also be called for.

3. At a cultic meal the deity may be thought of as a
participant by epiclesis (→ Eucharistic Prayer), for
example, at meal offerings (→ Greek Religion). The
deity may also be seen as the host and believers as
guests (later Serapis cult). In both cases the deity also
is strengthened by the shared meal.

The food that is consumed is not profane but is
holy as the venerated deity is holy (→ Sacred and
Profane). Among the Greeks and Romans, milk and
honey were regarded especially as the food of the
gods. An intoxicating drink (e.g., mead) could put
the participants in a state of ecstasy. The intoxicating
plant juice soma of ancient India, as well as the
Zoroastrian haoma, were regarded as divine. Communication between people and deity could then become communion. In place of the gods there could
be union with the deceased (at the → cemetery) or,
as with the Greeks, hero worship (→ Dead, Cult of
the).

4. In other types of cultic meals only humans participate. The food or drink is then viewed as holy or
even divine (hierophagy). The food used, which reflects the culture (whether gatherer, hunter, herder,
or farmer), might include plants, flesh and blood,
water, fruit, wine, milk, bread, or cakes. Small holy
objects such as sacred texts might also be eaten. Consuming does not automatically bring → salvation.
For example, if a person who has a ritual defect takes
part, such action might bring sickness or even →
death.

This kind of cultic meal was widespread. In ancient Egypt participation brought salvation and
union with the world of the divine (→ Egyptian
Religion).

5. Substantial union with the divine is seen most

clearly in the sacramental meal, even to the point of being considered theophagy (cf. the Dionysian orgies). The linking of the sacramental meal to the Savior God brings redemption, as in the mystery meals of the Hellenistic → mystery religions. The orientation of the sacramental meal may also be to future eternal life (e.g., in the later Attis and Orphic cults).

In the view of G. van der Leeuw (1890-1950), the sacrifice that establishes fellowship is central. What is offered belongs to the community and represents it, so that the community itself is offered and sustained. We find elements of the cultic meal in the → Eucharist inasmuch as it signifies communion (with the dying Christ) and, on many interpretations, is taken to one's condemnation by any who are in a state of → sin.

→ Cannibalism; Human Sacrifice

Bibliography: F. BAMMEL, *Das heilige Mahl im Glauben der Völker. Eine religionsphänomenologische Untersuchung* (Gütersloh, 1950) • *Feasts and Fasting* (= *Liturgy: Journal of the Liturgical Conference* 2/1 [1981]) • W. L. WILLIS, *Idol Meat in Corinth: The Pauline Argument in 1 Corinthians 8 and 10* (Chico, Calif., 1985).

JACQUES D. J. WAARDENBURG

Cultic Purity

1. Cultic purity primarily involves issues of contact and of purification that one who is part of the cultus must respect. Underlying the concept is a sense of the existence of clean and unclean as antithetical religious realities. Cultic purity is sought with reference to the teachings of the → religions, according to which pleasing God and maintaining positive dealings with higher powers demand a certain purity of both worshipers and the related cultic objects (→ Temple). At the same time, participation in the cultus deepens purity, which is ultimately the work of that which is regarded as divine. Cultic purity can even guarantee the presence and help of the deity. Purifications can be seen as communications of divine life (as in ancient Egypt; → Egyptian Religion). Imparted purity or purification always signifies a new beginning in relations with the deity.

2. In most cultures sex (→ Sexuality) and → death are particular sources of impurity. Some animals and plants (→ Dietary Laws) and things considered foreign (foreign gods in particular) also make one unclean. Some impurities are unavoidable, and purifications for them are necessary.

3. Distinction is typically made between cathartic → rites (which cleanse) and prophylactic rites (which prevent uncleanness). Purifications may be periodic or occasional. Apotropaic rites (to ward off impurity, and esp. to counter evil influences) are found everywhere. Special means may be used (e.g., oil, blood, → fire), along with total or partial abstinence (from sleep, food, or sexual intercourse; → Asceticism; Fasting).

4. The rules can apply to the broader circle of participants as well as to ministers, to the place (temple) and time, to offerings and vessels, to words and gestures, and also to the conditions of entry to the sacred site. Cultic purity may also be demanded outside the cultus. In ancient Egypt the dead had to be cultically clean (→ Dead, Cult of the). Early cultic regulations are often rules of purification with the character of → taboos, and these have in many cases made their way into sacred texts. The color white, light, and fire are symbols of cultic purity (e.g., in ancient Persia; → Iranian Religions).

5. Cultic purity can demand a specific lifestyle, which brings blessings such as health and insight. In the religions of ancient Persia and Israel, cultic purity was a condition for the required life according to → ethical commands. In → Islam distinction is made between cultic purity and ethical purity. In India → castes are graded according to their purity. The baptism of blood in the Attis and Mithras mysteries (→ Mystery Religions) counted as purification that brings redemption.

Some elements of cultic purity came into Christian → baptism and the → Eucharist, inasmuch as these impart or presuppose purification from → sin (upon → penitence).

→ Sacred and Profane

Bibliography: J. DÖLLER, *Die Reinheits- und Speisegesetze des Alten Testaments in religionsgeschichtlicher Beleuchtung* (Münster, 1917) • M. DOUGLAS, *Purity and Danger: An Analysis of the Concepts of Pollution and Taboo* (2d ed.; New York, 1970) • H. EILBERG-SCHWARTZ, *The Savage in Judaism: An Anthropology of Israelite Religion and Ancient Judaism* (Bloomington, Ind., 1990) • *Guilt or Pollution and Rites of Purification* (Proceedings of the XIth International Congress of the International Association for the History of Religions at Claremont, Calif., September 6-11, 1965; vol. 2; Leiden, 1968) • L. MOULINIER, *Le pur et l'impur dans la pensée des Grecs, d'Homère à Aristote* (Paris, 1952) • R. PARKER, *Miasma: Pollution and Purification in Early Greek Religion* (Oxford, 1983).

JACQUES D. J. WAARDENBURG

Culture

1. Term

The word "culture" (from Lat. *colo,* "till, cultivate, honor," and *cultura,* "cultivation, training"), even in antiquity, denoted both the outer cultivating of → nature and the inner cultivating of the mind and → soul *(cultura animi).* Up to the 18th century the primary reference was to the perfecting of one's physical, mental, and spiritual qualities.

In the 19th century another meaning was added to this more individual sense. "Culture" now came to embrace all kinds of human works and constructs, including the tending of nature, the raising of plants and animals, utensils, tools and machines, nourishment, practices of sleep and locomotion, types of human expression, → language, government, social institutions, customs, moral norms, mythical and religious ideas, magical and cultic practices (i.e., rituals and ceremonies), symbols, the knowledge and interpretation of reality in philosophy and → science, works of art, and educational ideals. Reference began to be made of the cultures of geographic or social units, of broader traditions (e.g., Western culture; → Tradition), of an epoch (e.g., the Middle Ages), or of a people or class.

Everyday language also employs a valuative concept of culture; only works of higher value are designated as culture. Such valuation is also at work in the distinction common in German between *Kultur* (intellectual culture) and *Zivilisation* (material culture).

2. Philosophy

Reflection on the philosophy of culture was long a branch of the philosophy of history; only in the modern period has it become an independent discipline. It harks back to G. W. F. Hegel's (1770-1831) philosophy of spirit (→ Hegelianism). In the objective spirit the subjective spirit loses its contingency (→ Chance) and subjectivity (→ Subjectivism and Objectivism), doing so via the objectivity of law, morality, and custom (→ Family; State). The process of the spirit coming to itself culminates in forms of the absolute spirit, namely, art, → religion, and philosophy. Hegel's philosophy made it plain that the objective spirit has a reality that is supraindividual (though not separate from the individual) because, taking precedence over individuals, it controls them and binds them to supraindividual claims and goals (→ Individualism).

With a reference back to Hegel and the historical school, W. Dilthey (1833-1911) founded the modern philosophy of culture, viewing history comprehensively from the standpoint of culture. In seeking to explain the nature of culture, he defined a cultural construct as a mental construct, as a process that is independent of the inner processes of its creator. Dilthey made an important contribution to the epistemology of the arts and cultural sciences by pointing to the understanding as the method that enables us to comprehend both historical individual experience and objective mental constructs.

H. Freyer (1887-1969) investigated the process of objectivation. For him, human experience is oriented to the contents of → meaning, which derive from acts of the psyche, take objective form, and finally become constructs. In the understanding of a construct, it often undergoes a change of meaning, a transformation even to the point of emptying it of meaning. Most constructs (e.g., → myth, speech, art, and knowledge) are symbolic forms (E. Cassirer). They mediate our relation to reality in knowledge and action. A human being is a "rational" and "symbolic animal."

Culture is human work detached from the nexus of individual experience and action, (consciously) given shape as a construct, to be appropriated in the understanding, and then passed on to others. It can be reproduced in their experience and deeds and can be transformed by them, but it also forms them. Through tradition there is an accumulation of culture. We are creators of culture but also its creatures (M. Landmann).

3. Morphology of Culture

Pioneers of a morphology of culture include the cyclical views of history of Ibn Khaldūn (1332-1406) and G. B. Vico (1668-1744) and, in a narrower sense, the theories of history of N. J. Danilevsky (1822-85), K. Lambrecht (1856-1915), and K. Breysig (1866-1940).

O. Spengler's (1880-1936) morphology of culture distinguishes eight great cultures (from the Egyptian to the Western, or Faustian, culture). For Spengler, cultures are like living creatures that go through the stages of → childhood, → youth, maturity, and old age. Our Western culture has entered the final stage, as we can learn from its ossification and its enchantment with a second religiosity (e.g., new religious movements, mysticism; → Gnosis).

A. J. Toynbee (1889-1975) finds 26 civilizations,

or cultures. The work of creative → minorities, each one assumes its distinctive characteristics in the interplay of challenge and response, of differentiation and integration. A culture decays when the dominant minority fails to meet historical demands, the majority refuses to follow it, and the cohesion of → society is lost as a result.

A morphology of culture on the basis of → ethnological research was developed by L. Frobenius (1873-1938), who viewed individual cultures as living entities with their own souls. He originated the notion of *Kulturkreise* (spheres or complexes of culture), each with its own material and intellectual features.

→ Aesthetics; Culture and Christianity; Development; Education; Evolution; Future; Pedagogy; Philosophy of Life; Subculture; Utopia; Worldview

Bibliography: E. Cassirer, *The Philosophy of Symbolic Forms* (3 vols.; New Haven, 1953-57) • W. Dilthey, *Der Aufbau der geschichtlichen Welt in den Geisteswissenschaften* (4th ed.; Frankfurt, 1970; orig. pub., 1910) • L. Frobenius, *Paideuma* (Munich, 1921) • N. Hartmann, *Das Problem des geistigen Seins* (2d ed.; Berlin, 1949; orig. pub., 1933) • G. W. F. Hegel, *Encyclopedia of the Philosophical Sciences* (New York, 1990; orig. pub., 1817) • M. Landmann, *Der Mensch als Schöpfer und Geschöpf der Kultur* (Munich, 1961) • P. A. Sorokin, *The Crisis of Our Age: The Social and Cultural Outlook* (New York, 1951); idem, *Social Philosophies of an Age of Crisis* (Boston, 1950) • O. Spengler, *The Decline of the West* (New York, 1962; orig. pub., 1918-22) • A. J. Toynbee, *A Study of History* (12 vols.; Oxford, 1934-61).

Herbert Zdarzil

4. Culture and Anthropology

Very generally, the → anthropology of culture is an integrative discipline that spans → ethnology, → sociology, → linguistics, history, → philosophy, human biology, and other disciplines. It examines the way in which we shape our world and culture. Historically, it has its roots in the → Enlightenment, when accounts of foreign lands (e.g., from Captian James Cook) made it necessary to test the notion that European culture and society was the only right one.

J. Locke (1632-1704) and others had prepared the philosophical ground for this new line of thinking with his view that moral principles are by no means absolute, since the human mind is at birth an "empty cabinet," "white paper," *tabula rasa;* for each person, cultural action is learned anew. This cultural relativism, which is closely related to the concept of → tolerance, led to intense discussion.

J. Turgot (1727-81) was another pioneer of the anthropology of culture with his emphasis on the importance of the existing culture for the development of the individual. Another important early writer is J.-F. Lafitau (1681-1746), a student of the Indians of North America, who attacked authors who described tribal peoples as godless and devoid of culture. Lafitau already had in view the modern anthropological idea that human beings universally have religion and naturally live in social orders.

I. Kant (1724-1804) was another important forerunner of cultural anthropology (→ Kantianism) with his view that it is the task of anthropology to ask what a human being is. In answering this question, Kant entered into ethnological and even physiological discussions. In the process, he postulated human → freedom and → equality.

Nevertheless, in the attempt to view humanity scientifically, there has been regression inasmuch as the concept of culture has been tied to that of race. The overhasty and fantastic theories advanced along these lines brought anthropology into discredit. A doctrine of race became the essential driving force that made "anthropology" a comprehensive science inquiring into human culture and origins.

Against this background, anthropological societies came into being in the mid-19th century that made it their aim to see the human race from a variety of perspectives (ethnological, archaeological, biological, and sociological). Finally, J. Frazer (1854-1941) made an essential contribution to the development of an anthropology of culture when in his two-volume *Golden Bough* (1890, expanded to 12 vols. in 1907-15) he assembled a wealth of cultural materials. Frazer in turn influenced the anthropology of S. Freud (1856-1939). É. Durkheim (1858-1917) and M. Mauss (1872-1950) were outstanding representatives of the anthropology of culture. The latter used sociology, ethnology, and social psychology in his descriptions and interpretations.

American cultural anthropology, as it was first represented by F. Boas (1858-1942) and then R. Benedict (1887-1948) and M. Mead (1901-78), was viewed in the European style as an interdisciplinary science in which symbols, culture (e.g., speech), social relations, biological aspects, and philosophical questions are all interwoven. In this sense mere description did not suffice. Universally valid pronouncements had to be made about cultural phenomena.

In setting its goals, the anthropology of culture received important support and enrichment from the discussions of philosophical → anthropology (§4). Along the lines of cultural anthropology, the latter inquires into the nature and overall "image" of humans. In its discussions it thus uses the findings of physical anthropology (human biology) and ethnology.

A. Gehlen (1904-76), building on H. Plessner (1892-1985) and M. Scheler (1874-1928), described human beings as open to the world and poor in instincts, hence defective in J. G. → Herder's sense. Human intelligence compensates for the lack of inborn and stereotyped forms of behavior (→ Behaviorism). Culture as altered nature (Gehlen) shapes human action and is thus the theme of cultural anthropology. Characteristic of this anthropology is its closeness to the understanding of sociology of M. → Weber (1864-1920), for whom we are active beings that shape our world (culture) and give it → meaning. As "symbolic animals" (E. Cassirer; see 2), we posit symbols in the process, and these connect us artificially to our environment (→ Symbol).

In this context R. König pleads for an empirical anthropology of culture that will deal with the different human cultures and cultural expressions. Its task is to inquire into intercultural → communication, especially with regard to the → Third World, the related interchange, and the resultant conflicts (→ Acculturation). This kind of anthropology might contribute to truly human intercommunication. Finally, the anthropology of culture shows that even single societies are not uniform. They consist of a variety of niches in which people have their own cultures with their own typical symbols and models of action, thus becoming a proper theme of cultural anthropology.

A pluralistic view of culture, toward which cultural anthropology is striving and which confronts human atomization, has the goal of going beyond the cultures, which are never completely isolated from one another and which always mutually affect one another, and inquiring into the nature of *Homo creator*. Related to this view is a humanistic outlook that in the sense of J. G. Herder (1744-1803) starts out from the fact that no single culture can lay claim to being the one true culture.

→ Culture and Christianity; Evolution; Future; Progress

Bibliography: F. Boas, *The Mind of Primitive Man* (New York, 1911) • E. Cassirer, *The Philosophy of Symbolic Forms* (3 vols.; New Haven, 1953-57) • A. Gehlen, *Anthropologische Forschung* (Reinbek, 1970); idem, *Urmensch und Spätkultur* (Frankfurt, 1964) • R. Girtler, *Die feinen Leute* (Frankfurt, 1989); idem, *Kulturanthropologie. Entwicklungslinien, Paradigmata und Methoden* (Munich, 1979); idem, *Die Methoden der qualitativen*

Sozialforschung (Vienna, 1984) • M. Harris, *Cultural Anthropology* (2d ed.; New York, 1987) • R. König and A. Schmalfuss, eds., *Kulturanthropologie* (Düsseldorf, 1972) • M. Mauss, *Sociology and Anthropology* (London, 1979) • W. E. Mühlmann, *Geschichte der Anthropologie* (Frankfurt, 1968) • W. E. Mühlmann and E. W. Müller, eds., *Kulturanthropologie* (Cologne, 1966) • S. Nanda, *Cultural Anthropology* (5th ed.; Belmont, Calif., 1994) • A. Schütz, *Der sinnhafte Aufbau der sozialen Welt* (Vienna, 1960) • J. Stagl, *Kulturanthropologie und Gesellschaft* (Munich, 1974) • M. Weber, *Gesammelte Aufsätze zur Wissenschaftslehre* (Tübingen, 1957).

Roland Girtler

5. Culture and Sociology

Sociology today uses a concept of culture that finds no opposition between culture and civilization (see 1), culture and → nature, or ideal and real factors. Instead, it stresses the integrative character and adaptability of culture in a changing environment and the high degree of cultural diffusion. It does not see culture as a complete, static entity but underlines the fact that it is a process that includes both creation and destruction. Cultures are not superorganic. They are not closed and do not share a common "style." There is necessary tension between the dominant culture and countercultures or subcultures, between the more lofty and the more everyday and popular. Instead of trying to engage in → criticism of culture, the → sociology of culture attempts to understand the basic processes of sociocultural change that are necessary to overcome culture crises or to bring about creative cultural change.

Cultural sociology studies the constitutive sociopsychological and sociostructural conditions of the formation and dynamics of cultures. If earlier the field was restricted to a doctrine of the stages of cultural objectivation — expressed, for example, in works of art, pottery, signs, or → language — or to a typology of cultural forms, such as middle class, industrial, → postmodern (P. Koslowski), or ideational/sensory, today what is sought is the structural *code* that is common to various cultural phenomena (I. Rossi).

In this regard one can hardly begin by postulating an equation of → society, → state, and culture, as though there were a state culture or a national culture. There are indeed such things as national cultures, but they are permeated by a common global culture. At the same time, more stress is being put on regional cultures, which often have a historical basis (H. Lübbe). An important theme is the dynamics of cultural change, which may be cyclical (J. Z.

Namenwirth) or quasi-evolutionary (C. J. Lumsden; → Evolution), or which may involve fluctuations even to the point of collapse (C. Renfrew), so that one can no longer speak of a uniform → development (§1), although there are many signs of globalization (M. Featherstone).

The sociology of culture that developed after World War I has split into four conflicting directions or schools: the → phenomenological (M. Scheler, K. Mannheim, A. Weber), the Marxist (G. Lukács, E. Bloch, H. Marcuse; → Marxism), the structural-genetic (A. Vierkandt, H. Freyer, A. Gehlen, H. Fischer), and the → psychoanalytic (S. Freud, E. Neumann, G. Roheim, E. Fromm). After World War II, and in a pragmatic-empirical turn influenced by American sociology (→ Pragmatism; Empiricism), cultural sociology avoided any all-too-ambitious attempts at cultural-sociological speculation, as well as any cultural criticism determined by political ressentiment. Only with the transition to a postindustrial society did there come new reflection on problems of cultural sociology, though it is hard to argue that the sociology of culture can be shown to be a special and independent discipline (see F. Neidhart volume).

→ Aesthetics; Anthropology; Behaviorism; Counterculture; Culture and Christianity; Functionalism; Future; Idealism; Lifestyle; Progress; Social Systems; Utopia; Worldview

Bibliography: W. L. Bühl, *Kulturwandel* (Darmstadt, 1987) • M. Featherstone, ed., *Global Culture* (London, 1990) • P. Koslowski, *Die postmoderne Kultur* (Munich, 1987) • H. Lübbe, *Zeit-Verhältnisse* (Graz, 1983) • C. J. Lumsden and E. O. Wilson, *Genes, Mind, and Culture* (Cambridge, Mass., 1981) • J. Z. Namenwirth and R. P. Weber, *Dynamics of Culture* (Winchester, 1987) • F. Neidhart, ed. *Kultur und Gesellschaft* (Opladen, 1986) • C. Renfrew and K. L. Cooke, eds., *Transformations: Mathematical Approaches to Culture Change* (New York, 1979) • I. Rossi, ed., *The Unconscious in Culture* (New York, 1974).

WALTER L. BÜHL

Culture and Christianity

1. Problem

The phrase "culture and Christianity" covers a broad and varied field that can be studied here only in terms of its relevance to → fundamental theology and in light of the actual state of the discussion in the ecumenical world. Culture is the shaping of human existence in this world, while Christianity bears witness to the lordship of Jesus Christ that is not of this world, though fully oriented to it. A Christianity without → culture or cultural impact is historically unknown and inconceivable. Conversely, Western cultures cannot be understood apart from their links to Christianity. Our problem is to correctly distinguish the two concepts and to consider both the positive and the negative aspects of their relationship.

In its origin, the Christian message is related to a specific culture. We thus must ask the nature of Christianity's tie to that original culture, whether it remains the same when immersed into changing cultures, and whether it can be reconciled with history (→ Acculturation). We must also inquire into the mediation of culture and Christianity and the role of the churches in the process. Are they a crucial part of the → gospel as the concrete form of its existence? We must consider, too, the significance of the cultural factor in theology. Even though the relationship involves problems, theology cannot repudiate culture. The problem is not with culture per se but with the self-assertion that a dominant culture typically displays.

2. Concept

2.1. The Plurality of Culture

Possible definitions of culture are so numerous that it might be better to use the plural "cultures." Cultures result from our encounter with → nature and generate our decisive values. The original sense of agrarian cultivation in the word "culture" has been extended to cover the most varied fields of human endeavor, yet it can also be restricted to intellectual and artistic activities (literature, painting, etc.). Since cultures are governed by the dynamics of the life and survival of human → societies, they can and must adjust to new situations and compensate for the loss of past values by new meanings and changes in the cultural system. In this regard → religion plays a vital part in all cultures and civilizations. If religion is lost, substitutes will be found.

In an age of intercultural give-and-take, cultures can never be totally domesticated by the individuals and groups that develop them. Nevertheless, the culture of a people is essentially determined and channeled by those in power. Globally, the dominant culture results in a culture of → poverty for two-thirds of the world population (→ Third World), who stand in need of total redemption from oppression and fatalism.

2.2. *The Multiformity of Christianity*

Christianity, too, must be seen in its different forms when we consider its relation to culture. Here we must distinguish between the gospel, Christian history, and → theology. The gospel denotes God's communication with us in the person, life, and history of the one who loved his own to the very end and who gave the → promise of the kingdom of God especially to the marginalized and to those without rights. The communication of the gospel through human word and cultures must be seen in the context of the condescension of God and the integration of the world into his plan. In any case, the → Christological determination precedes the cultural, though the gospel itself reaches us only by way of Jewish and Hellenistic culture, yet without ever imprisoning the Bible, the church, or its preachers. The actual process of assimilation, transformation, and contradiction has led to objectivizations that we call the Christian religion.

In the history of Christianity the gospel that has been handed down has entered into many new cultural arrangements. The result has been not merely Christian systems of thought that are culturally influenced but a variety of forms of Christianity with different churches, differences in → tradition, → liturgy, attitude toward the world, and so forth. Church history as a complex shaping, negation, denial, and confusion of the gospel is also the history of culture, that is, the attempt to frame life under constantly changing conditions and to seek to ensure its survival. When we speak about culture and Christianity, this is what we usually have in view. For the West, a scientific and technological culture has impressed upon its Christianity the stamp of superiority and even imperialism.

Less on the surface is the relation to theology as the work of reflection on the Christian message of → creation, → reconciliation, and redemption (→ Soteriology 2). In accordance with the prevailing consciousness, theology works out a theory both of understanding and of what is to be understood. Its history is a history in many different cultural contexts. Conversely, theologies also create cultures and in a distinctive version often lead the way for many generations.

If today the problem of the relation of all these components of culture is being discussed afresh, this is because, after many centuries of Latin captivity, the problem has become that of ecumenical Christianity. Now that the uniform culture of the Christian West is no longer a universally valid framework of orientation, and now that there is more intensive encounter with other cultures, Western culture and the Christianity that has grown up in it are no longer so significant or so formative. The rise of independent churches in other cultural contexts, and of theologians who seek to expound the gospel in and for a specific context without allowing Western thought to play its historically oppressive role, has made culture and Christianity a basic problem of ecumenical life that is more important than confessional differences, themselves in part culturally mediated (→ Denomination; Contextual Theology).

3. Ecumenical Debate

3.1. *Relations between Culture and Christianity*

Two trends, one which affirms culture, the other which criticizes it (→ Eschatology), run through the history of Christian thought and action. H. R. Niebuhr (1894-1962) saw five types of relation in his work *Christ and Culture* (1951), where he discussed "Christ against Culture," "The Christ of Culture," "Christ above Culture," "Christ and Culture in Paradox," and "Christ the Transformer of Culture." From this standpoint the issue brings us up against such basic problems as → immanence and transcendence, this-worldliness and otherworldliness, creation and redemption, religion and → revelation. As such, it is always a burning issue, as various considerations show.

How far, for instance, can pagan → philosophy help Christianity to explain or understand itself (note the *paideia* of the → apologists and the reconciliation with Hellenistic culture at → Alexandria)? Again, what social and economic changes were needed to give rise to the → universities and to theological scholarship in the Middle Ages? → Monasticism undoubtedly rejected conformity to the world, yet it created an imposing Christian culture (→ Church Architecture). Worldly → asceticism could well have contributed to the rise of → capitalism. → Pietism, too, renounced the wicked world but engaged in imposing works of love, → mission, and development.

The → Culture Protestantism of the later 19th century found the essence of Christianity in its history and in the culmination of this history in modern middle-class culture (→ Bourgeois, Bourgeoisie). → Dialectical theology, however, regarded this linkage and identification with cultural → progress as an assault upon God and an impermissible reduction of the message to human terms. Was not the call for desecularization after World War II simply a reaction to the disaster, just as the theology of → hope 20 years later spoke to the mood of reawakening after → Vatican II?

To the extent, however, that it is not a mere matter of superstructure, the question arises how the specifically Christian element can be sustained in these relationships. Along with questions of ideology and of the → sociology of knowledge, debate regarding this issue has been revisited in ecumenical circles by a readdressing of the problem of culture and Christianity (P. → Tillich).

3.2. The Reformation and the World Missionary Movement

M. → Luther (1483-1546) and the → Reformation introduced the thought of communicating the gospel in the language of the people, which ultimately had far-reaching consequences both inside and outside the church. In 1659 the Roman Catholic Congregation for Propagation warned the apostolic vicars against Europeanizing Christianity in the new mission fields and made a plea for the accommodation of → missionaries and their message to national rites and customs (→ Colonialism and Mission; Mission). In practice, however, the warning and the plea were often neglected, even though they represent the official Roman Catholic position.

To root the gospel in culture is not to imprison it in culture. Missionary practice, however, could appeal to traditions and theories that found in the non-Christianized world, especially the religious, no more than idolatry and the work of the devil. Such appeals harmonized far too conveniently with the European sense of superiority and lust for expansion.

The world mission conference at Jerusalem in 1928 (→ Missionary Conferences) expressly took up for the first time the issue of secular culture and the non-Christian religions and provoked a debate that reached a provisional climax at Tambaram ten years later in the thesis of H. Kraemer (1888-1965) that the Christian message cannot be reconciled to non-Christian religions. The impetus of dialectical theology and the fateful linkage of popular culture and Christianity in Nazi Germany then resulted in a moratorium. Such concepts as "point of contact," → natural theology, *praeparatio evangelica* (preparation for the gospel), and *pierres d'attente* (stepping-stones) are no longer open to discussion.

Things changed in this matter only when the ecumenical and missionary movements had found their Christological and Trinitarian orientation (→ Trinity 2), joined forces, and on this basis could address the urgent questions of society, → development, the non-Christian religions, and the diversity of regional interests. The problem of the gospel (or Christianity) and culture now came to the fore with increasing sharpness (e.g., as seen in the newly rekindled interest in E. → Troeltsch). Is it possible, for example, to be an African Christian if → faith in Christ means separation from the tribal community, conformity to imported forms of cultural expression, and being limited to conservative political solutions (→ African Theology; Faith 3.6)?

3.3. Roman Catholic Views

On the Roman Catholic side, Vatican II stressed the many links between the message of → salvation and culture, for God claimed the possibilities of cultural expression in a particular epoch in order to give to us a full revelation in his Son. The message of Christ constantly renews the life and culture of fallen humanity. It purifies and elevates the moral quality of nations and fructifies their → spirituality. The importance of a cultural legacy is expressly recognized here, for no peoples are without culture.

In his *Evangelii nuntiandi* (1975) Paul VI (1963-78) called the break between the gospel and culture the tragedy of our time. He made a plea, on the one hand, for the evangelizing of culture and, on the other, for the cultural transposition of the gospel. Culture thus became a matter of primary concern to the church. Inculturation (or interculturation, to use a more recent term) was defined as the effort of the church to bring the message of Christ into a specific sociocultural sphere by inviting people to believe in accordance with the values of that sphere, insofar as these are compatible with the gospel (International Commission of Theologians [1989]).

3.4. Ecumenical Statements

Within the non-Roman ecumenical world, the issue has been raised at every ecumenical conference and in every ecumenical pronouncement. As Bangkok 1973 put it, Christ became a real man. He identified himself fully with people of various tribes, races, colors, and cultures. Christ is also the one who frees and unites and who confirms as well as judges cultures (Nairobi 1975).

In the ecumenical statement on mission and evangelization issued in 1982, inculturation, inspired by the incarnation, is said to be the task and expression of Christian mission. The study "The Gospel and Culture" (cf. Riano Consultation [1984]) was initiated against the background of many situational forms of expressing the faith, including the battle of the church against → slavery and discrimination. Also part of the background were the aspirations of certain groups (e.g., → women), a new reading of the Bible (Latin American *releitura*), and grassroots theologies (→ Base Community). The San Antonio World Mission Conference (1989), following up on Nairobi and making common cause with some evangelical voices (see the 1978 Willowbank Report; → Evangelical Movement), again pointed out the oppressive features of culture (e.g., in relation to → minorities in South Africa) and warned against any absolutizing. It is an open question whether these debates are restricted to the literary North or also influence the Christianity of the South, with its more oral culture.

The most important results of the discussion are as follows (see A. Karamaga). First, the rooting of Christianity in a culture is harmful when the culture becomes archaic or evades the concrete demands of the poor.

Second, the relation between culture and Christianity is in constant flux as long as cultures are dynamic and a specific Christianity is not equated with the gospel. New possibilities of interpreting both one's own tradition and the gospel may be found in cultures and religions.

Third, only societies that can harmoniously overcome differences can meet the demands of a world that is deeply divided into the rich and the poor. These can no longer be concerned only about themselves if they want to serve the kingdom of God, including its causes of → love, → righteousness, and → peace. For the sake of their own → future and hope, the world and the church both need permeation by the gospel.

Finally, if inculturating the gospel is a matter ultimately for all existing churches, we still have to ask, Who is inculturating what? Is the gospel that is personified in → Jesus to be inculturated by people or a church? Do not such questions reveal a hidden Christian claim to control the gospel and culture as elements that can be subjected to analysis and made to serve a strategy? We need to define exactly both the subject and the object of the relation.

4. Perspectives

4.1. *"Culture" in Positive Light*
The problems of culture and Christianity are today finding both existential and conceptual formulation in contextual theologies. In keeping with missionary and ecumenical experiences, these have revised the judgment that culture, → science, philosophy, religion, and so forth cannot serve the gospel but only pervert it.

The churches of Africa and African theologies have posed the problem of the gospel and culture with a new urgency. They ask, for example, whether there is a bridge from Christ to ancestors, who for all Africans, including Christians, are part of living society (→ Ancestor Worship).

In Latin America, → liberation theology (→ Latin American Theology) and related movements in and outside the church have focused on the problem of → sociology and theology. Can — may — must theology serve sociology? If so, how? To what extent can sociological insight lead to words and action that truly conform with the gospel?

The experience of the churches and theologians of Asia (→ Asian Theology) has made it impossible to ignore the question of Christ and the religions. Is → dialogue possible? If so, on what basis? How are we to proclaim Christ amid the many religious offers of salvation? For example, is it permissible to see Christ less as a historical person and more as the Consummator of creation and the religions?

Perhaps we may agree that, for the sake of the effectiveness of the Christian message, we must face the question of how to communicate and give shape to this message in different cultural contexts. We still need to address, however, the problems that have arisen as Third World theologies have advocated various methods of mediating Christianity and culture.

4.2. *The Relativization of Western Culture*
The → Ecumenical Association of Third World Theologians admits openly that their aim is not merely to draw attention to their own context but to focus, too, on the Western context, which, being middle class and capitalist, is inclined to be oppressive and is entangled in historical injustices. A liberating theological impetus is thus to be at work in the center of → power.

The existence of different kinds of theology changes the whole historical picture. We may thus speak of "the Third World church with a Western prehistory" (J. B. Metz). The total Christian tradition is to be seen as a synchronous and diachronous series of local theologies that differ culturally, linguistically, and socially, that are partial traditions within the total tradition. The task is to recognize our own place in the ecumenical encounter, to live with this relativity, and to see our place as part of a relationship stamped by power structures.

4.3. *Theological Moorings*
The basic underlying question then arises: What can be the future of Christianity when it threatens to break up into many different culturally and contextually shaped Christianities and theologies? Two theological considerations are fundamental.

4.3.1. Only an ecumenical and multicultural (or intercultural) Christianity of the future is conceivable. Like the conciliar fellowship of churches (→ Conciliarity), which by way of mutual recognition of diversity is on the path to → unity, theology also must be a conciliar process in which contextual theologies bring their own identities, differences, functions, and talents; criticize others and let themselves be criticized; enrich others and let themselves be enriched by them. To this extent the synodic principle is a condition of survival, and "differentiated universality" (H.-W. Gensichen) is the goal. A dialogue and → pluralism that exclude all totalitarian and imperialistic forms of communication still will aim, however, to proclaim the commonly recognized → truth and the common commitment, namely, the Christ who unites and the righteousness of God's kingdom.

4.3.2. Ultimately, the criteria of Christian → identity will not be cultural, phenomenological, ecclesiological, or cultic features. The one criterion will be confession of the Jew Jesus Christ. Theologically, through all cultures and contexts, the decisive thing is attachment to Jesus as God present to save. Jesus is the possibility of a relation to the cultural context, which more recent Christian history has made clear. But he is also its limit, for being a Christian means orientation to him in any cultural or sociopolitical situation. *His* name is decisive. In this way the gospel maintains its freedom with respect to culture and Christianity while constantly fructifying and judging the relation.

→ Ecumenical Theology; Ecumenism; Ethnology

Bibliography: J. Agossou, *Christianisme africain* (Paris, 1987) • H. Balz, *Theologische Modelle der Kommunikation. Bastian–Kraemer–Nida* (Gütersloh, 1978) • K. Blaser, "Christliche Theologie vor der Vielfalt der Kontexte," *ZMiss* 10 (1984) 5-20 • R. H. Boyd, *India and the Latin Captivity of the Church: The Cultural Context of the Gospel* (Cambridge, 1975) • E. Burke-Leacock, ed., *The Culture of Poverty* (New York, 1971) • *Christian Faith and Culture* (= *IRM* 84 [1995]) • R. Friedli, "Interkulturelle Theologie," *Lexikon missionstheologischer Grundbegriffe* (1987) 181-85 • C. Geffré, ed., *Théologie et choc des cultures* (Paris, 1984) • H.-W. Gensichen, "Evangelium und Kultur," *ZMiss* 4 (1978) 197-214 • D. J. Hesselgrave, *Communicating Christ Cross-Culturally* (Grand Rapids, 1978) • W. J. Hollenweger, *Interkulturelle Theologie* (3 vols.; Munich, 1979-88) • A. Karamaga, *L'Evangile en Afrique. Ruptures et continuités* (Morges, 1990) • C. H. Kraft, *Christianity in Culture* (Maryknoll, N.Y., 1979) • A. L. Kroeber and C. Kluckhohn, *Culture: A Critical Review of Concepts and Definitions* (New York, 1963) • L. J. Luzbetak, *The Church and Cultures* (Techny, Ill., 1963) • J. Mbiti, *Afrikanische Religion und Weltanschauung* (Berlin, 1974) • Missions- wissenschafts Institut Missio, *Theologie der Dritten Welt* (Freiburg, 1980ff.) esp. vol. 4 (*Herausgefordert durch die Armen* [1983]) and vol. 10 (J. M. Ela, *Mein Glaube als Afrikaner* [1987]) • K. Müller, "Inkulturation," *Lexikon missionstheologischer Grundbegriffe* (1987) 176-80 • H. R. Niebuhr, *Christ and Culture* (New York, 1951) • E. Nunnenmacher, "Kultur," *Lexikon missionstheologischer Grundbegriffe* (1987) 235-39 • R. J. Schreiter, *Constructing Local Theologies* (New York, 1985) • P. Tillich, *The Theology of Culture* (New York, 1983) • H. Waldenfels, "Kontextuelle Theologie," *Lexikon missionstheologischer Grundbegriffe* (1987) 224-30.

Klauspeter Blaser

Culture Protestantism

1. Term
2. In History and in Society
3. Criticism
4. Culture Protestantism and
   Christian Freedom

1. Term

The term *Kulturprotestantismus,* or "culture Protestantism," common since at least 1870, has obscure origins. Seldom used in self-designation, it is often equated in popular parlance with → liberal theology or neo-Protestantism (→ Protestantism). Early → dialectical theology seems to have introduced this equation.

Although the term was little used before 1930 and has taken on many different senses, it has been useful for bringing into relief the consciousness of a postliberal epoch that, especially under the impact of World War I, no longer sees itself in the school of F. D. E. → Schleiermacher (1768-1834; → Schleiermacher's Theology) or the metaphysics of history of German → idealism. It identifies, rather, with S. → Kierkegaard (1813-55), F. W. → Nietzsche (1844-1900), and especially with a newly discovered M. → Luther and Paul. Theologically, it has come to view the → Word of God as a radical eschatological break with human self-assertion and world → immanence and therefore as critical of culture and religion (→ Religion, Criticism of).

2. In History and in Society

Culture Protestantism cannot be viewed as a distinct intellectual movement or focus. What is implied, rather, is some form of naive, optimistic belief in → progress that affirms the cultural achievements (→ Culture) of one's own denomination. Certain values that are traced back to the → Reformation (e.g., freedom from ecclesiastical tutelage, this-worldliness, national self-determination) are claimed with great assurance as defining conditions for the present and → future. Literary, artistic, and scientific culture, which is also traced back to the Reformation, is advanced and fostered as the horizon of one's → identity, so that religious sanction is found for a sense of historical superiority and a cultural self-confidence. The Prussian → Kulturkampf (ca. 1872-88) offers an illustration, as does the founding of the Protestantenverein (1863), which proclaimed a program for the Protestant shaping of the world in harmony with general cultural development and in opposition to political reaction and Romanizing trends.

Culture Protestantism was clearly a historical phenomenon. Sociologically, however, it was more a functional structural element of a historically oriented group identity than an explicit theological theory. For all its ambiguity, what is meant by the concept is best shown on the public level, both national and religious, by the formation of societies, the celebration of jubilees, and so forth. In seeking, or at least valuing, an ecclesiastical-political linkage of altar and throne, it came close to ideological abuse. Also relevant philosophically was its opposition to Darwinism and → evolutionism.

3. Criticism
By its very nature, and due to the systematic problems at issue with those theologians charged with being guilty of Culture Protestantism, the term has its limits. When used in demarcation, "Culture Protestantism" does not reflect the self-understanding of the position that is criticized. Rather than facilitating objective insight, it serves more as a foil, helping a younger theological generation (e.g., after World War I) to find its own identity.

The front against Culture Protestantism also contained in part some controversial theological concepts. Even in 1934, E. Hirsch (1888-1972) was describing the warding off of Culture Protestantism as the common concern of his theological generation. In contrast, the idea of a theology of culture as set forth in 1919 by the early P. → Tillich (1886-1965) shows how a criticism of Culture Protestantism and of the liberal concept of religion — criticism related to that of K. → Barth (1886-1968) — can go hand in hand with dialectical synthesis in which → religion is viewed as the substance of culture. Even a decided critic of Culture Protestantism like Barth could not escape the need to sketch out theologically a relationship between the church and culture (1926). Al-

though Barth does maintain eschatological reservations, he transcends complete disjunction by regarding culture as capable of offering us a parable.

When we look more closely at the theologians who were supposedly the most prominent champions of Culture Protestantism (e.g., A. Ritschl, A. Harnack, A. Stoecker, F. Naumann, and E. → Troeltsch), we find that they were already taking issue with it, opposing the position that there is no difference between the → gospel and culture, the kingdom of God and the shaping of the world. (See, for example, Harnack's *What Is Christianity?* [1900] lecture 7, §4.)

4. Culture Protestantism and Christian Freedom
Neither historically nor materially can we ignore the constructive task of developing a theological understanding of culture and of systematically defining its relation to the Protestant → faith and its institutions (→ Culture and Christianity). This implies a criticism of culture insofar as the latter is heralded as a substitute for religion. The significant relation between the Reformation and → humanism, with its historically influential effect upon modern culture and education (note Luther's translation of the Bible and his hymns, → Melanchthon's educational program, etc.), indicates and in part addresses the material problem.

In Schleiermacher's universal attempt to prevent a disintegration of Christianity and learning into barbarism and unbelief, as well as in idealistic conceptions (by J. G. Fichte, G. F. W. Hegel, F. W. J. von Schelling, and R. Rothe), themselves bolstered by certain affinities to Christianity, the aim is to overcome the difficulties of modern Enlightenment culture along Christian lines and at the same time to encourage a productive faith that is fully relevant to reality.

Expressing Christian freedom is the material problem of Culture Protestantism. In terms of the gospel and the corresponding relationship of → time and eternity, a purely negative demarcation is impossible. Our relation to the world — our knowledge of it and our creativity expressed in it — is transcended in the → kingdom of God, which maintains both detachment from culture and yet linkage with it. Christian faith, then, can and must deal constructively with culture. As Protestantism, especially under the conditions of a Christian world (T. Rendtorff), it can and must inwardly relate itself to culture (even when culture seems most autonomous), though not in principle exclusively identifying itself with it.

→ Liberalism; Theology in the Nineteenth and Twentieth Centuries

Bibliography: AMERICAN ACADEMY OF RELIGION, *Culture Protestantism and Catholic Modernism* (Berkeley, Calif., 1977) • H.-Y. BIRKNER, "Kulturprotestantismus und Zweireichelehre," *Gottes Wirken in seiner Welt* (vol. 1; ed. N. Hasselmann; Hamburg, 1980) 81-92 • E. HIRSCH, *Die gegenwärtige geistige Lage* (1934) 112; idem, *Geschichte der neuern evangelischen Theologie* (vol. 5; Gütersloh, 1954) 156 • H. M. MÜLLER, ed., *Kulturprotestantismus: Beiträge zu einer Gestalt des modernen Christentums* (Gütersloh, 1992) • J. RATHJE, *Die Welt des freien Protestantismus* (Stuttgart, 1952) • G. RUPP, *Culture Protestantism* (Missoula, Mont., 1977) • W. SCHUBRING, *Vom wahren Wesen und Wert des Kulturprotestantismus* (Berlin, 1926) • E. TROELTSCH, *Protestantism and Progress: A Historical Study of the Relation of Protestantism to the Modern World* (London, 1912).

JOACHIM RINGLEBEN

Curia

1. Papal Curia
  1.1. History
  1.2. In Church Law
    1.2.1. Secretariat of State
    1.2.2. Congregations
    1.2.3. Tribunals
    1.2.4. Councils
    1.2.5. Offices
    1.2.6. Other
2. Episcopal Curia

According to → canon law, the term "curia" refers to the administrative and judicial institutions in the → Roman Catholic Church that discharge the functions of the papacy (→ Pope, Papacy) for the whole church and of the → bishop for the → diocese.

1. Papal Curia

In the name and on the authority of the pope, the papal curia does its work for the benefit and in the service of the individual churches of the universal church. It is made up of a variety of departments, each with specific tasks and powers (1983 CIC 360; → Codex Iuris Canonici).

1.1. History

It was probably in 1089 that the term *Curia Romana* was first used instead of *Palatium Lateranense* for the papal court, but the beginnings of the papal curia may be traced back to the early days of the Roman church. The Presbytery of Rome and the bishops of neighboring dioceses from the beginning began doing tasks for the Roman church, which eventually led to the formation of the college of → cardinals. The seven → deacons, attested from the time of Fabian (236-50), did administrative work. Notaries prepared the Acts of the Martyrs (→ Martyrs, Acts of the) and then assumed other administrative duties. Even before → Gregory the Great (590-604) they constituted a college with a *primicerius notariorum* at its head. They were the earliest officials of the Apostolic Chancery.

Defensores (originally also lay) served as advocates in the church courts and assumed the function of lawyers in the jurisdiction conferred on the church since the time of Constantine (306-37). From the fourth century there was a department of finance and another of archives. Seven judges existed from the seventh century *(iudices de clero)*, later called *iudices palatini*.

The college of cardinals, attested as such from the time of Stephen III (768-72), assumed some administrative duties. It served from the 12th century in the so-called consistory, or papal governing body. In a very general way it reflects the secular curial concept (the Roman senate) and the practice of German, French, and Spanish courts.

Papal administration was reorganized by → Gregory VII (1073-85), who linked his reforms to the centralizing of papal power. The most important bodies now became the Apostolic Chancery, for general church business, and the Apostolic Chamber, the supreme financial body. From the 12th century, consistories (the solemn public curia consisting of cardinals, clergy, and laity, as well as the secret curia consisting only of cardinals) handled the tasks of government under the presidency of the pope. They dealt with matters of faith, morals, discipline, and investiture affecting the whole church.

In the period from the 12th to the 14th centuries there also developed the Apostolic Penitentiary for the granting of → dispensations (with general competence in the sphere of conscience), the Apostolic Datary (to confer nominations reserved for the pope), the Roman Rota as a papal court, and, with varied legal powers, the Apostolic Signatura.

After the Council of → Trent, Sixtus V (1585-90) undertook a first radical reform of the curia with the apostolic constitution *Immensae aeterni* of January 22, 1588. Pius X (1903-14) instigated further basic reform with the constitution *Sapienti consilio* of June 29, 1908, which was essentially put into effect in CIC (cans. 242-64), promulgated by Benedict XV in 1917.

The desire of → Vatican II to reform the curia and its modus operandi (see discussion of the decree *Christus Dominus*, arts. 8-10) led to the apostolic constitution *Regimini ecclesiae universae*, which

Paul VI (1963-78) promulgated on August 15, 1967. The reform that John Paul II announced on the basis of CIC 1983 was promulgated on June 28, 1988, in *Pastor bonus* and went into effect on March 1, 1989.

1.2. *In Church Law*

The 1983 CIC deals with the curia only in the basic statements of cans. 360-61. The detailed regulations are in *Pastor bonus* (*AAS* 80 [1988] 841-912). Also incorporated was the reform of the papal household by the *Pontificalis Dominus* of March 28, 1968 (*AAS* 60 [1968] 305-15).

The reorganized curia, with it various bodies under the presidency of a cardinal or archbishop, includes the Secretariat of State, 9 congregations, 3 tribunals, 11 councils, 3 offices, and various other agencies, commissions, and institutes, all accountable to the Holy See. In accordance with their importance, these are composed of cardinals, bishops (of the universal church), and other members. In most cases they also include international consultants chosen by the pope.

1.2.1. *Secretariat of State*

The secretariat is headed by a cardinal who is secretary of state and who functions as the pope's alter ego. His position terminates automatically with the pope's death.

Under the secretariat, the Section for General Affairs handles daily business (including papal correspondence, links to other bodies, and coordination of tasks) and oversees the *Acta Apostolicae Sedis* and *Annuario Pontificio*, as well as the Vatican Press Office and the Central Statistics Office. The secretariat's Section for Relations with States is responsible for all diplomatic and other relations with civil states (→ Concordat; Nuncio).

1.2.2. *Congregations*

The nine congregations are → collegial administrative organs, each headed by a cardinal as prefect. All have specific legislative powers (→ Church Law); some also possess judicial powers. They comprise papally elected cardinals and, as a rule, seven bishops and diocesan bishops from the church worldwide.

In 1995 the congregations included first the Congregation for the Doctrine of the Faith. This body goes back historically to the 13th century, when it was commissioned as the Holy Office of the Inquisition. It is responsible for safeguarding and promoting the doctrines of the faith as well as morals. It examines doctrines and can censor books or authors for doctrinal error (→ Censorship). The congregation can also dissolve nonsacramental marriages (*privilegium fidei*) and safeguards the dignity of the sacrament of penance. Related to it are the international commission of theologians set up by Paul VI

on April 11, 1969, and the papal Bible commission reinstituted on June 27, 1971.

The Congregation for the Oriental Churches deals with all personal, disciplinary, and ritual questions arising with regard to the Eastern Catholic churches (→ Uniate Churches). Its membership includes all patriarchs of these churches and major archbishops.

The Congregation for Bishops (formerly the Consistorial Congregation) is responsible, as far as the Congregation for the Propagation of the Faith does not take precedence, for setting up local churches, for → military chaplaincies, for establishing new dioceses, and for appointing coadjutor and auxiliary bishops. It also has oversight over bishops, local churches, and bishops' conferences and supervises the Pontifical Commission for Latin America.

The Congregation for Divine Worship and the Discipline of the Sacraments watches over the → liturgy (involving the issuing of → liturgical books and overseeing the legislation arising out of bishops' conferences) and control of the administration of the → sacraments (including dispensations, nullifying of marriages, and the validity of ordinations).

The Congregation for the Causes of Saints, which was reorganized by Paul VI in his *Sacra rituum congregatio* of May 8, 1969, has charge of the processes of beatification and sanctification. John Paul II revised this congregation and the procedures of canonization through his *Divinis perfectionis magister* of January 25, 1983 (→ Saints, Veneration of). This body also settles all matters relating to the keeping of → relics.

The Congregation for the Clergy was set up by Pius IV in 1564, originally as a congregation to put into effect the decisions of Trent. It is responsible for all matters affecting the discipline, lifestyle, training (→ Theological Education), and payment (→ Church Finances) of the clergy and the clerical life.

The Congregation for Institutes of Consecrated Life and Societies of Apostolic Life was at one time part of other congregations but was made autonomous by Pius X in 1908. It originally supervised religious orders but now covers the members, discipline, administration, and founding of all societies and institutions for a consecrated or apostolic life (→ Orders and Congregations).

The Congregation for Catholic Education (for Seminaries and Institutes of Study) was first set up by Sixtus V in 1588 to supervise the University of Rome, but then Pius X broadened it in 1908 to have oversight of all the church's universities and faculties. In 1915 Benedict XV gave it supreme authority in all matters of higher education. The whole of the church's educational enterprise (including its → universities, faculties, seminaries, schools, and educational institutes) is under its charge, especially spiritual and academic preparation for taking holy orders.

The Congregation for the Evangelization of Peoples, founded by Gregory XV in 1622, has responsibility for all missionary work and the → mission fields around the world. It is the highest commission for all papal missionary societies.

1.2.3. Tribunals

Three tribunals, or judicial agencies, are part of the papal curia.

The Apostolic Penitentiary, whose origin traces back to the 13th century, was set up as the court of the cardinal penitentiary for releasing from sins and church penalties from which the pope alone could grant absolution. It is responsible only for the "internal forum" (i.e., matters of conscience), involving the remission of sins and church penalties, as well as the granting and use of → indulgences.

The Apostolic Signatura, which Sixtus IV (1471-84) set up as a judicial and administrative court, originally prepared cases for the pope involving pardons or decisions in disputed legal cases. It was reorganized by Pius X in 1908 and is now the supreme court and highest judicial administration of the church and of Vatican City (can. 1445). It also supervises the Roman Rota in nullity cases and suits and acts as a final administrative court when appeal is made against the administrative decisions of the congregations.

The Roman Rota was set up in the 13th century with the appointment of permanent papal judges. As a court for the Papal States, it became redundant with their dissolution, but Pius X reorganized it in 1908 as the regular appeals court of the Apostolic See. It is active especially in questions of marriage (§2.2). Fundamentally a court of appeals, in certain cases it can also act as a primary court (cans. 1444.2 and 1445).

1.2.4. Councils

After Vatican II a number of councils were set up with a variety of promotional or special-interest functions. The 11 councils now are partly independent and partly under the congregations. In most cases, a cardinal serves as president of the council.

The Pontifical Council for the Laity addresses the apostolate of the laity and their overall participation in the church.

The Pontifical Council for Promoting Christian Unity deals with all ecumenical questions (→ Ecumenical Movement). It includes a commission for conversations with Jews (→ Jewish-Christian Dialogue).

The Pontifical Council for the Family seeks to promote the pastoral care of families. Members of this council include married couples and men and women from various countries and cultures around the world.

The Pontifical Council for Justice and Peace aims to use the teaching of the Gospels and of the church to promote worldwide justice and peace.

The Pontifical Council "Cor unum" coordinates the church's charitable work.

The Pontifical Council for Pastoral Care of Migrants and Itinerant People gives pastoral assistance to migrants, nomads, tourists, and air and sea travelers.

The Pontifical Council for Pastoral Assistance to Health Care Workers assists Roman Catholic organizations working in health care.

The Pontifical Council for the Interpretation of Legislative Texts was set up in 1984 by John Paul II to interpret the 1983 CIC. It now addresses the interpretation of all church laws.

The Pontifical Council for Interreligious Dialogue tries to promote dialogue that will lead to increased respect between Christians and non-Christians. It includes the Commission for Religious Relations with Muslims (→ Islam and Christianity).

The Pontifical Council for Culture seeks to develop the church's relations with the world of culture and with those who profess no religion. The council's functions reflect its expansion in 1993, when it absorbed the former Pontifical Council for Dialogue with Non-Believers.

The Pontifical Council for Social Communications works to see the Christian gospel penetrate civil culture.

1.2.5. Offices

The three curial offices, or specialized service agencies, were reorganized by Paul VI and John Paul II.

The Apostolic Chamber, or Apostolic Camara, with the cardinal chamberlain as its head, administers the finances of the Holy See when there is a vacancy (→ Pope, Papacy).

The Prefecture for the Economic Affairs of the Holy See supervises and coordinates all papal finances.

The Administration of the Patrimony of the Apostolic See handles the estate of the Holy See.

1.2.6. Other

Other curial institutions include the Prefecture of the Papal Household, which handles matters of protocol, audiences, ceremony, and papal escorts; and the Office for Liturgical Celebrations of the Supreme Pontiff, which prepares everything needed for the pope's own liturgial use. The curia also includes advocates to deal with judicial and administrative cases.

Also assisting in the exercise of the papacy, though not officially part of the curia, are institutions that oversee the secret archives, the promotion of learning and culture, the Vatican library, the papal academy, the Vatican press, the Vatican radio and television, and the administering of apostolic alms.

2. Episcopal Curia

According to 1983 CIC 469, the episcopal curia has charge of judicial and administrative affairs in a diocese. On the administrative side, it consists of the general vicariate under the bishop's vicar general with the necessary powers (cans. 135, 475-81). On the judicial side is the consistory under the officialis, or judicial vicar (can. 1420). The bishop appoints or releases the vicars. The vicar general loses his office when a vacancy occurs, but the vicar official remains in office until confirmation by the new bishop. Vatican II created the function of an episcopal vicar who does not have to be consecrated bishop but may take over some of the duties of pastoral care (cans. 134, and 476-81).

→ Catholic, Catholicity; Catholicism (Roman); Church 3.2; Church Government; Church Law; Offices, Ecclesiastical

Bibliography: 1983 CIC 360-61, 469-94 • H. E. FEINE, *Kirchliche Rechtsgeschichte. Die katholische Kirche* (5th ed.; Cologne, 1972) • F. A. FOY and R. M. AVATO, eds., *1997 Catholic Almanac* (Huntington, Ind., 1997) 144-50 • J. F. LAHEY, "Roman Curia," *HCEC* 1125-30 • J. J. MARKHAM, "Curia, Roman," *NCE* 4.539-40 • H. MÜLLER, "Die Diözesankurie," *Handbuch des katholischen Kirchenrechts* (ed. J. Listl et al.; Regensburg, 1983) 364-76 • J. PÉREZ DE HERDIA Y VALLE, "Die römische Kurie," ibid., 281-94 • W. M. PLÖCHL, *Geschichte des Kirchenrechts* (5 vols.; 2d ed.; Vienna, 1960-70) • H. SCHMITZ, *Kurienreform* (2 vols.; Trier, 1958-76).

HERIBERT HEINEMANN

Curse

1. As elsewhere in antiquity, so too in Israel the curse and its opposite (→ Blessing) were understood primarily as words of power that were thought to take effect magically. The curse was a materialized, harmful force that flew across the earth, overtook the one against whom it was uttered, and brought about his or her destruction (Zech. 5:1-4). To avert it, there was need of a countercurse (Gen. 27:29; Num. 24:9; Ps. 140:9-11) or of an opposing blessing (Judg. 17:2; 1 Kgs. 2:44-45). Fear of the automatic operation of a curse led to the use of "bless" as a euphemism for

"curse" (Job 1:5; 2:9) or to the omission of self-cursing in an oath.

As Israel's polytheistic neighbors placed the curse under one or another deity, so Israel placed it under → Yahweh as the one who enforces it (Josh. 6:26; 1 Sam. 17:43; 26:19; 2 Kgs. 2:24). In this way it was taken out of the domain of magic (Prov. 26:2). With the introduction of the divine name, the indicative formula *'ārûr 'attâ* ("cursed are you") changed into a wish or petition.

2. Originally the curse formula (which came from the seminomadic world or Gentile society) gave expression to the banishing of the cursed person from the place of blessing provided by a community (Gen. 3:14; 4:11). In the rural (and urban) world of the ancient Near East and Israel, however, the main effect of the curse lay in its effects upon individual life (Deut. 28:16-19). As in lists elsewhere (cf. *ANET* 538-41, 659-60), the effects of the curse are set out in long lists in the OT, the point being to cover as many aspects of life as possible (Lev. 26:14-39; Deut. 28:15-68). Curses of this kind often form the background of prophetic threats of disaster (cf. Jer. 5:6 with Lev. 26:22, Jer. 19:9 with Deut. 28:53-57, etc.; → Prophets).

3. The OT refers to the curse that is imposed by qualified speakers (Numbers 22–23; Job 3:8) as a magical ban on a people or by a military leader on a conquered city (Josh. 6:26; 1 Kgs. 16:34). The curse is also a weapon of revenge for one who is wounded in honor (2 Kgs. 2:23-24), persecuted, unjustly accused (Psalm 109; Jer. 18:18-23), or hurt by persons unknown (Lev. 5:1; Judg. 17:2; Prov. 29:24). As unconditional self-cursing, it expresses deep despair (Jer. 20:15-18; Job 3).

As in the ancient Near East, where curses often safeguard the observance of private compacts and treaties and the sanctity of inscriptions and tombs, so in Israel the curse is often found as a sacred sanction in various legal matters (Judg. 21:18; 1 Sam. 14:24; Jer. 48:10; *TSSI* 1.19-20, 23-24), especially along with an → oath (Neh. 5:12-13; 10:29). At a holy place a community periodically purged out with a curse those who were committing secret offenses (Deut. 27:15-26). Thus we find oaths of purification (Job 31) and ordeals (Num. 5:11-31, cf. 1 Kgs. 8:31-32 = 2 Chr. 6:22-23) along with the use of curse rituals.

In Genesis, → primeval history is a time of developing curse (Gen. 3:14-19; 4:11-12; 9:25-27). In contrast, the age of the patriarchs is that of the beginning of → blessing (Gen. 12:1-3 etc.).

4. The primitive Christian community uses the curse as a means of separating itself from false brethren (1 Cor. 16:22; Gal. 1:8-9). When persecutors curse believers, the latter reply with blessing in a context of showing love for → enemies (Matt. 5:44 and par.; Rom. 12:14). In expectation of the righteous judgment of God, believers renounce all attempts to exact vengeance or retribution on their own.

Bibliography: H. C. Brichto, *The Problem of "Curse" in the Hebrew Bible* (Philadelphia, 1963) • D. R. Hillers, *Treaty Curses and the OT Prophets* (Rome, 1964) • J. Scharbert, *Solidarität in Segen und Fluch im Alten Testament und in seiner Umwelt* (vol. 1; Bonn, 1958) • W. Schottroff, *Der altisraelitische Fluchspruch* (Neukirchen, 1969) bibliography.

Willy Schottroff†

Custom

1. Custom as a Social Phenomenon
2. Religious and Ecclesiastical Custom
3. Functions
4. Development
5. Change
6. Forms
7. Perspectives and Tasks

1. Custom as a Social Phenomenon

"Custom" is the general term for regular forms of social practice that are recognized by a → society and may be expected in it. It embodies social → norms with sanctions to enforce observance. For the most part, customs are less obligatory than laws. Laws are what one *must* do, customs what one *must* do or *ought* to do or *may* do.

The dominant morality of a society finds expression in custom as a collection of social norms. Even in older tradition, the conduct conforming to custom is viewed as moral conduct. Yet custom covers more than moral conduct. In it we often have the symbolic representation of social traditions. For this reason the term is sometimes synonymous with "habit."

Customs apply in different spheres, so that we may speak of the cultural sphere or of a regional or local sphere. → Families and other social groups may develop specific forms of custom. As culturally specific rules of social action, customs relate to elementary expressions of human life. They regulate the way that natural needs are met, including those for food, sleep, and sex. They find expression in → everyday rituals (e.g., specific customs at the beginning and ending of the day). They determine the

socially recognized annual cycle and special events within it. Rites of passage (birth, puberty, marriage, and death) are often elements in the social custom of a given time (→ Initiation Rites).

Customs are learned by imitation, and their content is often hard to teach cognitively. Yet they have a considerable impact on society, even to the point of establishing general cultural practice. One of the most important functions of custom, then, is to pass on prevailing values and norms.

Common custom has an integrative function and thus guarantees the unity of a society. Varieties of custom distinguish subgroups within a society. For individuals, custom has a liberating effect inasmuch as they are freed from having to set up rules for themselves. In contrast, in societies that place high value on individual decision, the tie of custom is often felt to be oppressive, as the compulsion of tradition. In such cases custom is seen as no more than convention.

2. Religious and Ecclesiastical Custom

Religious custom consists of socially recognized rules, especially rituals, that center on human experiences at which we learn to know the ultimate conditions of human existence. This happens when it is a matter of recalling critical or fortunate events in the history of a given social group. Religious custom is also anchored in the corresponding events in the lives of individuals that are significant for all the members of the group and for which specific forms of religious action have been developed (see 6). Older religious custom was to a high degree popular. When it had a public or political character, it was part of → civil religion (e.g., days of national mourning).

Religious custom is closely related to ecclesiastical custom. It embraces socially recognized rules of conduct that are in harmony with ecclesiastical norms or that represent them or that are designed to promote them. Ecclesiastical custom might be described as the participation of church members in liturgical life (P. Drews), but it is not restricted to this, since many other forms of custom center on this participation.

Participation in the → Eucharist plays a large part, which also involves customs relating to admission to the Eucharist and the way of administering it and distributing the elements. In a culturally confessional community some forms of church custom will be relatively uniform, but even then, local customs vary from place to place. Church orders (e.g., in the German territorial churches) might establish customs and enforce them by → church discipline.

When the churches are held in high esteem, ecclesiastical custom is part of social custom in general. But the more private religion becomes, and the more participation in church life is a matter for individual decision, the weaker is church custom, since it is binding only on those who consciously belong to the Christian community.

3. Functions
The functions of ecclesiastical custom are the same as those of custom in general. Besides providing norms of social conduct, it symbolizes important transitions and relieves individuals of the burden of decision. It offers forms by which to represent both individual and group problems. It binds the members of a group together, whether members of a congregation or a local society, thereby differentiating them from others.

State and church → institutions have had a particular interest in ecclesiastical customs and their stability in view of their normative force. Christian morality can have a great impact in the form of church custom. The interpretive power of Christian → symbols can develop great interpretive force through the forms of expression of ecclesiastical custom and practice.

4. Development
Local religious customs often have a very complex origin that in many cases defies explanation, especially when folk religion has influenced the custom. Local pastors play a large part both in forming customs and in changing or ending them. Since the days of the → Enlightenment, theologians have often advocated individual → piety and therefore challenged the validity of church custom.

Insofar as they regulate moral practice, ecclesiastical customs have their origin in the rules laid down for the churches in the NT. The Roman practice of penance (→ Penitence) and absolution supported these. Shared control at the local level also played a dominant part.

The → church orders and → visitation orders of the 16th century helped to develop Protestant customs. The aim of these was not merely to regulate → worship and liturgical actions but to shape the particular disposition of congregation members' participation in these services in the larger sense. In the moral field the orders dealt especially with → marriage. Moral lapses called for particular notice, such as the assigning of special seats to "fallen women."

The present century has still seen an institutional ordering of ecclesiastical custom. Experiences during the German → church struggle (1933-45) strength-

ened the concern to introduce regulations governing church life. It became clear that a definite lifestyle ought to mark off the Christian community from other social → groups. The aim, then, was to establish church custom. Special attention was paid to the ministry to → youth and the life of young people in the congregations, as well as to the question of withdrawal from the church (→ Church Membership 5) and readmission into membership.

A crucial difference between the new church orders and those of the Reformation, however, is that today the orders are not enforceable; no sanctions are available. For this reason, stress is laid on their pastoral character.

5. Change
Like all custom, ecclesiastical custom is subject to a process of social change. In the various industrialized societies of Europe, relations vary. In substantially Roman Catholic countries church custom is anchored in forms of → popular religion and can thus persist much longer than it does in Protestant areas. The loss of public recognition of ecclesiastical custom has not led to its general dissolution, but rather to the strengthening of local and regional differences and to a limited anchoring of custom in the family.

As congregational custom, ecclesiastical custom can achieve stability only in the → free churches (→ Church 3.5). In this sphere, attempts are also made to enforce it by sanctions. But today the situation in general is characterized by limited dissolution. Instead of the rituals that constitute church custom, we now have nonreligious rituals, both in western Europe and in the former Communist lands.

6. Forms
The three most important complexes of church custom relate to religious rituals covering the daily routine, the annual cycle, and life as a whole. Traditional daily Christian rituals include morning prayer, grace at meals, family → devotions, and evening → prayer. The vehicle for these forms of church custom is the Christian home. One must add, however, that considerable alterations have occurred here, in some cases even resulting in a specific practice being abandoned entirely. For a renewed religious ritualization of the course of daily life, we must turn to the new Protestant → orders. There Bible reading often occurs as a form of group custom in various circles, more recently in many youth groups.

The annual cycle is strongly anchored in folk religion, the emphasis falling on → Christmas, → Easter, → harvest festivals, and, in some countries, → All Saints' and All Souls' Days (→ Church Year).

Many practices are connected with these feasts. They are often preserved, even when their Christian roots are not recognized and their true content is no longer affirmed. Christmas in particular has become a family and children's festival.

Among church members, rituals marking the stages of life are still strong. Many forms of ecclesiastical (or more generally religious) custom cluster around them, though often with various changes. Thus it is no longer so common a practice to baptize infants in the first six weeks of life (→ Baptism). Children are often baptized today when of kindergarten age or at confirmation, though this may not become a lasting custom. It seems more likely that the time for baptism will be left to the decision of the parents or family.

Now as before, the life rituals of confirmation and burial remain part of church custom, while the significance of marriage has receded. New versions and interpretations are shaped by regional and local custom.

7. Perspectives and Tasks

Even if short-term changes in the forms of church participation are not to be expected, especially when they have no support in folk religion, church life in the future will depend to a large extent on social custom. Church regulations themselves are comparatively ineffective, their main function being to strengthen core groups whose common lifestyle differentiates them from the general mass of church members. The work of the church must reckon with this fact.

Where custom still influences participation in church life more generally, imposing or reinforcing common practice on the majority, we may expect this to continue, since the decision to participate is made easier for individuals and families. The function of custom is apparent at this point as it integrates individuals and their decisions into a social nexus that sustains them. The danger of a purely conventional orientation is present, however, and for this reason we must deal consciously with traditions in ecclesiastical custom, even where their validity seems (at least for the present) to be relatively unquestioned.

→ Ecumenical Theology; Ethics; Occasional Services 6; Religious Folklore; Sociology of Churches

Bibliography: J. Baumgartner, ed., *Wiederentdeckung der Volksreligiosität* (Regensburg, 1979) • R. Benedict, *Patterns of Culture* (Boston, 1934) • R. Bockock, *Ritual in Industrial Society* (London, 1974) • P. Bourdieu, *Distinction: A Social Critique of the Judgement of Taste* (Cambridge, Mass., 1984) • U. Brandt and B. Köhler, "Norm und Konformität," *HPs* 7/2, 1710-89 • P. Drews, ed., *Evangelische Kirchenkunde. Das kirchliche Leben der deutschen evangelischen Landeskirchen,* vol. 1, *Die Evangelisch-Lutherische Landeskirche des Königreichs Sachsen, dargestellt von P. Drews* (Tübingen, 1902) • M. N. Ebertz and F. Schultheis, eds., "Populare Religiosität in der modernen Gesellschaft–Kontinuität, Pluralität und Visibilität," *ÖZS* 11 (1986) 62-79; idem, *Volksfrömmigkeit in Europa* (Munich, 1986) • K. Egger, "Die anthropologische und theologische Bedeutung des Brauchtums," *LS* 37 (1986) 92-96 • N. Elias, *The Civilizing Process* (Oxford, 1994; orig. pub., 1939) • A. von Gennep, *The Rites of Passage* (Chicago, 1960; orig. pub., 1906) • W. Heim, *Volksbrauch im Kirchenjahr heute* (Basel, 1983) • H. Kirchhoff, *Christliches Brauchtum–von Advent bis Ostern* (Munich, 1984) • H. Kleger and A. Müller, eds., *Religion des Bürgers* (Munich, 1986) • R. M. MacIver, *Politics and Society* (ed. D. Spitz; New York, 1969) 150-69 • C. I. Nitzsch, *Praktische Theologie* (vol. 1; 2d ed.; Bonn, 1859) esp. §§84, 432ff. • T. Parsons, *The System of Modern Societies* (Englewood Cliffs, N.J., 1971) • M. Plathow, *Lehre und Ordnung im Leben der Kirche heute* (Göttingen, 1982) • M. Schian, *Grundriß der Praktischen Theologie* (3d ed.; Giessen, 1934) • G. Schmied, *Sterben und Traurern in der modernen Gesellschaft* (Opladen, 1985) esp. 143ff. • F. Tönnies, *Custom: An Essay on Social Codes* (New York, 1961; orig. pub., 1909) • M. Weber, *Economy and Society: An Outline of Interpretive Sociology* (2 vols.; Berkeley, Calif., 1978; orig. pub., 1922) chap. 1, §4.

Karl-Fritz Daiber

Cynicism

1. The ancient Cynics were shadowy figures. The word "cynic" has never been explained etymologically, though it was usually thought to be the teaching place of the founder of the school, Antisthenes (b. ca. 445 B.C., a student of Socrates, who taught in the gymnasium Kynosarges), or to be grounded on a nickname: with Diogenes of Sinope (d. ca. 320 B.C.), a shameless and sarcastic pupil of Antisthenes, philosophy seemed to have gone "to the dogs" (Gk. *kyōn,* adj. *kynikos*). As "Socrates gone mad," according to Plato, Diogenes attacked with a "quixotically evil tongue" (J. Burckhardt) "whatever was of most value in the civilization of Athens" (P. Sloterdijk).

Cynicism reacted to the social and political upheavals of the fourth century B.C. by giving a new polemical accent to the traditional ethical contrast between the natural *(physei dikaion)* and the conventional *(thesei;* → Ethics 1.3; Hellenism 2.4). The good life was for the Cynics a life of self-satisfaction *(autarkeia)* whose happiness resulted from complete renunciation ("prefer nothing to freedom"). Whereas culture thrives on heightening notoriously insatiable needs, Cynics demonstrate the possibilities for attaining satisfaction by decreasing one's needs (→ Fasting 1.2): minimal existence, reduced virtually to the point of addressing only minimal physical needs, as a philosophical form of life. As wandering beggars equipped only with a cloak, a purse, and a stick (to beat off unwanted adherents), Cynics revoked the difference between nature and culture, between intimacy and a public life (even to having sex on the market square), thus provoking the moral traditions of the polis. G. W. F. Hegel's (1770-1831; → Hegelianism) disparaging dictum that there was nothing particularly notable about the Cynics is correct only insofar as they declared as a general lifestyle their indifference to any particulars.

In Cynicism the anecdote became the medium of → philosophy. Diogenes is thus a disruptive entry in any lexicon, since one can only tell stories about him. His dismissive answer to Alexander the Great (336-323 B.C.), "Please get out of my sun," is one of the most popular narratives illustrating an exemplary instance of instruction in the → virtue of contented moderation. Expelled from home because of forgery, he was the first to view himself consciously as a "world citizen," whose reply to the charge that "the people of Sinope have condemned you to banishment" was "and I condemn them to remain at home." Parodying Socrates (ca. 470-399 B.C.), Diogenes also justified his own conduct with a saying from the Delphic oracle: "Set your own stamp on the coin." The programmatic demand to revalue all values remained influential up to F. → Nietzsche (1844-1900; → Nihilism).

Accustomed by Greek comedy to a display of the insolent, Cynic disregard of convention aimed at exposing illusory content and false philosophical certainties. It represents the continuation of a shadowy enlightenment with polemical means. Since philosophy does not cease when satire begins, Diogenes once provided the foil for the Platonic definition of humans (→ Platonism 2.2) as two-legged beings without feathers by the presentation of a plucked hen. He not only brought laughter to serious thinkers but enabled people to see that humans become ridiculous when they forget that they can → laugh — even though there is not always something to laugh at.

The cynical impulse lasted by way of Zeno of Citium (ca. 335-ca. 263 B.C.), a student of Diogenes' follower Crates of Thebes (4th cent. B.C.), on into → Stoicism (Cynic-Stoic popular philosophy). It was often watered down to a mild → hedonistic Cynicism, following the principle of live and let live, and finding a new blossoming in this form in later antiquity.

2. The → ascetic life and inner → freedom from public institutions made the Cynics of some interest to Christians. Gregory of Nazianzus (329/30-389/90; → Cappadocian Fathers), an important theologian of the Trinity, viewed them as models of the good life *(In Praise of Maximus)* and as allies against the Neoplatonism (→ Platonism) established by Emperor Julian the Apostate (361-63), which Julian dismissed by distinguishing strictly between contemporary and original Cynicism (see Julian's address against the "uneducated dogs"). Historically the emperor was probably right, for the idea of a synthesis between Christianity and Cynicism rests on a general appreciation of Cynic-Stoic motifs in the fourth century A.D. rather than on any specific affinity to Diogenes in the fourth century B.C. Yet from an external perspective such affinity continued to be noted (though cf. R. Bultmann, 1910). According to F. Schlegel (1772-1829; → Romanticism), "Christianism . . . is universal Cynicism" insofar as it rejects any sort of self-glorifying luster; and Sloterdijk finds typical cynical elements both in → Jesus and in M. → Luther (1483-1546; → Luther's Theology), whose Protestantism itself is called to be basically an insolent act. What is rightly seen here is that Protestant criticism of the religious consciousness can also be a disrespectful disillusionment such as we already find prefigured in the prophetic criticism of religion (Isa. 44:9ff.; → Religion, Criticism of, 2.2).

3. Cynicism is a healthy → compromise between the lofty (esp. moral) claims and the fun recognized by R. Musil (1880-1942) "in tripping up that loftiness and seeing it fall on its face." If cynicism heightens this contrast, it becomes "well-formulated baseness" (Sloterdijk); if it ameliorates it, it betrays "delight in its own shabbiness" (K. Kraus). The "uninhibited uncovering of the painful reverse side of grand ideal claims" (H. Schmitz), however, can also systematically close itself off from a liberating insight and become self-induced embarrassment. This blockade produces a cynical attitude. The term "cynicism" thus comes into pejorative use:

Perverse directors of Caritas
   fly first-class to Eritrea
   and have themselves photographed by the world
      press
   with the starving.

The pope gives a so-called hot meal for the
　　homeless
　　in his chambers
　　and lets the fact be known worldwide
　　a cynical world
　　the whole world is nothing but cynicism.
　　　　　　　　　　　　　　　　(T. Bernhard)

Not just the shameless misuse of the → good is
cynical, but so also is that particular form of → evil
intensified by its malice. A lack of feeling for suffering
can become a *déformation professionelle*. It is no accident that the oldest examples of a pejorative use
are in Jean Paul's (J. P. F. Richter, 1763-1825) account
of a physician in *Dr. Katzenbergers Badereise* and in
the assertion that "the gentlemen are doctors, which
means cynics" (J. I. Baggesen, 1804). Nietzsche
coined the word "medicynics." → Psychoanalytic explanations speak of a demonstrative lack of feeling
that is a self-protective mechanism, an avoidance of
→ depression by → aggression (M. Grotjahn). But
we find it not merely in medicine, for in → theology
and the → church as well, cynicism finds ideal conditions for development, often as a travesty of official
→ soteriology.

The transition from cynical accusation to the
typically cynical art can be seen in O. Wilde (1854-
1900), who pejoratively defined a cynic as "one who
knows the price of everything and the value of nothing," stands juxtaposed with the cynical claim "I am
not cynical; I merely have experience." The cynic
deals with the ambivalent factors in human life, such
as we find in the soteriological considerations especially of P. → Tillich (1886-1965). His theology of
the new being also insists, "Cynically speaking, it is
true to life to be cynical about it."

4. There is a sharp distinction between this kind of
cynicism and real cynicism, as pointed out by Sloterdijk in his *Critique of Cynical Reason,* which finds the
two related only by an inexplicable caprice in the
term's history. The prominence of modern rationality of purpose (→ Rationalism 1), instrumental
→ reason, the modern Machiavellianism of the →
state, the social democracy of H. Schmidt (German
chancellor, 1974-82), functional systems theory (→
Social Systems), and the routine dealing with the
factual in the → mass media may all be diagnosed as
forms of expression of a kind of cynicism of "the
masters of the universe." They give evidence that insolence has changed sides. The powerful know (cynically) the despicable nature of their means, enlightened citizens are aware of uneasiness within
their own culture, and yet all agree (cynically) to
"keep going." Cynicism seems to be a modern mass

phenomenon of abiding the worst at an ironic and
sarcastic distance. Sloterdijk develops a phenomenology of the false consciousness that is determined
largely by the prospect that a cynicism of means can
be compensated by a cynicism of ends. To that extent,
in his criticism of culture he sets forth with epic
breadth a picture of successful life that has fled from
the contemporary ethical debate to programmatic
moral disarmament. There is a countermovement
here to the kind of moral indignation we find in K. R.
Popper's (1902-94) *Gegen den Zynismus in der Interpretation der Geschichte.*

5. Cynicism tests the → truth of things by the
amount of mockery they can bear, as not just Sloterdijk but long before him A. A. Cooper, third earl of
Shaftesbury (1671-1713), recommended in his "Ridicule as Manner of Proof" (1709). Whatever stands
the test allows a treatment "with cynicism and innocence" (F. Nietzsche). Cynicism is thus not → skepticism but loyal opposition to regnant certainties. If
it slips over from critical self-reflection to aggression,
then such "cynicism in social intercourse is . . . a sign
that in our loneliness we are treating ourselves like
dogs" (Nietzsche). In the face of their dissatisfaction
with life's contrariness, moderate cynics risk a joke
at the expense of satisfaction in order to gain advantage from the situation.

Bibliography: Primary sources: Diogenes Laertius, *Peri
biōn* 6.25-69 • Epictetus, *Discourses* 3.
　　Secondary works: T. BEWES, *Cynicism and Postmoder-
nity* (New York, 1997) • M. BILLERBECK, ed., *Die Kyniker
in der modernen Forschung. Aufsätze mit Einführung und
Bibliographie* (Amsterdam, 1991) • R. BULTMANN, *Der
Stil der paulinischen Predigt und die kynisch-stoische Dia-
tribe* (Göttingen, 1910) • L. E. NAVIA, *The Philosophy of
Cynicism: An Annotated Bibliography* (New York, 1995)
• H. NIEHUES-PRÖBSTING, "Der 'kurze Weg': Nietzsches
'Cynismus,'" *ABG* 24 (1980) 103-22; idem, *Der Ky-
nismus des Diogenes und der Begriff des Zynismus* (2d
ed.; Frankfurt, 1988) • P. SLOTERDIJK, *Critique of Cynical
Reason* (Minneapolis, 1987).

MICHAEL MOXTER

Cyprian of Carthage

Caecilius Cyprianus became → bishop of Carthage
in North Africa in late 248 or early 249. If he was
then middle-aged, a birth date of approximately 200
may be conjectured. Little is known of his early life,
but it is generally surmised that he was from a
wealthy Carthaginian family, had acquired a reputa-

tion as a rhetorician, and was among the intellectual elite of the city. Influenced by the presbyter Caecilius, Cyprian became a Christian at Easter 246, giving away much if not all of his property, embracing → celibacy, and undertaking extensive reading of the Scriptures and the works of → Tertullian, his theological master. Soon afterward he was ordained presbyter (→ Elder); on the death of the bishop Donatus, he was popularly acclaimed bishop over more senior clergy.

Despite conflicts in Carthage, he quickly established himself as a leader among the African bishops and a forceful counterpart to the bishop of Rome. In the plague of 252 he organized relief for both pagans and Christians in the city. Exiled to nearby Curubis on the Gulf of Hammamet during → persecution in 257, Cyprian was → martyred at Carthage on September 14, 258. Sources for his life include an effusive biography by his deacon Pontius, the acts of his trial and martyrdom, an account of his → conversion addressed to a friend named Donatus, and a collection of 82 letters, 66 written by Cyprian.

In the year 250, early in Cyprian's episcopate, the emperor Decius ordered that all inhabitants of the empire certify that they had sacrificed to the gods. Many Christians in Carthage and elsewhere obeyed the order, others falsely obtained certificates of sacrifice; all were regarded as having lapsed from the faith (→ Lapsi). Christians who refused to sacrifice were imprisoned, tortured, or sent into exile (known collectively as confessors); others were executed.

Cyprian avoided confrontation and withdrew from the city, directing the church by letter from his hiding place. His authority was challenged by confessors who claimed the right to forgive the lapsed and receive them back into communion. Reluctant either to forgive → apostasy or to yield to the confessors, Cyprian urged that the matter await the common decision of the bishops once persecution had ended. Returning to Carthage after Easter 251, he wrote *On the Lapsed,* which was read to the African bishops assembled there in council later that spring. The council approved a process of penance and reconciliation of the lapsed overseen by the bishop, and it → excommunicated recalcitrant presbyters and confessors, leading to schism in Carthage (→ Heresies and Schisms).

At the same time, controversy arose in Rome around the presbyter Novatian, who opposed restoration of the lapsed. Recently disappointed in his quest for episcopal office and objecting to the liberal policies of the bishop, Cornelius, Novatian was joined by other rigorists in establishing a rival see in the city.

With both the Roman and Carthaginian schisms in mind, Cyprian wrote his most influential treatise, *On the Unity of the Catholic Church,* arguing for the necessity of visible → unity, the authority of the rightful bishop, and the importance of charity as the bond of peace in the church. A disputed text about the primacy of the Roman bishop as the successor of Peter (chap. 4) exists in two versions in MSS of the treatise. Contemporary scholarship generally regards the "primacy text" as earlier and the "received text" as a later revision by Cyprian to prevent Stephen of Rome from using it to his advantage in the baptismal controversy. Historically, the variant texts have been cited in support of contrasting views of the Roman bishop's role in the church.

As Novatian's movement lost ground, his followers sought admission to the larger church, raising questions about the validity of their → baptism. Cyprian affirmed traditional North African practice, arguing that baptism outside the unity of the church was not efficacious, so that converts from schism or heresy were to be baptized — not again, but for the first time. Stephen, bishop of Rome, asserted his church's tradition of recognizing the validity of schismatic, or → heretical, baptism and receiving such converts into the church as penitents. The African Council of 255 upheld Cyprian's position, as did the bishops of Egypt and parts of Asia Minor. Councils meeting in Carthage in the spring and fall of 256 continued to insist that schismatics be (re)baptized, but they allowed for difference in practice among bishops.

Unwilling to tolerate such diversity, Stephen threatened to excommunicate all who differed with him. In a series of letters (*Epp.* 69-75), Cyprian opposed Stephen's theology and practice. The conflict was never resolved, though schism was averted by the renewal of persecution under the emperors Valerian and Gallienus in 257: Stephen was martyred that August, and Cyprian was exiled until his return and execution the following year. → Donatist schismatics in the fourth century cited Cyprian in support of their view of sacramental efficacy; against them → Augustine appealed to the example of Cyprian's charity in not breaking communion but rejected his theology.

Cyprian's writings on the lapsed, the unity of the church, and the baptismal controversy are crucial to the historical development of Western ecclesiology and sacramental theology. His letters and treatises offer a vivid picture of church life in mid-third-century North Africa. In his extensive citation of scriptural texts, Cyprian is an important witness to early Latin versions of the Bible.

Bibliography: Texts (treatises and letters): W. HARTEL, ed., *Opera omnia* (3 vols.; 1868-71).

Texts (treatises): M. BÉVENOT, ed., *Cyprian: De lapsis; De ecclesiae catholicae unitate* (Oxford, 1971) • M. SIMONETTI and C. MORESCHINI, eds., *Sancti Cypriani episcopi. Opera* (pt. 2; Turnhout, 1976) • R. WEBER and M. BÉVENOT, eds., *Sancti Cypriani episcopi. Opera* (pt. 1; Turnhout, 1972).

Translations: M. BÉVENOT, ed., *St. Cyprian: The Lapsed; The Unity of the Catholic Church* (Westminster, Md., 1957) • G. W. CLARKE, ed., *The Letters of St. Cyprian of Carthage* (4 vols.; New York, 1984-89) with heavy annotation • R. J. DEFERRARI, ed., *St. Cyprian, Treatises* (New York, 1958) does not include the *Testimonia.* • M. M. MÜLLER and R. J. DEFERRARI, eds., "Life of St. Cyprian, by Pontius," *Early Christian Biographies* (New York, 1952) 1-24 • H. MUSURILLO, ed., "Acta proconsularia Sancti Cypriani / The Acts of St. Cyprian," *The Acts of the Christian Martyrs* (Oxford, 1972) 168-75 (official account of Cyprian's trial and martyrdom).

Secondary works: A. D'ALÈS, *La théologie de Saint Cyprien* (2d ed.; Paris, 1922) • E. W. BENSON, *Cyprian: His Life, His Times, His Work* (London, 1897) • M. BÉVENOT, *St. Cyprian's "De unitate" Chapter 4 in the Light of the MSS* (Rome, 1937) • M. A. FAHEY, *Cyprian and the Bible: A Study in Third-Century Exegesis* (Tübingen, 1971) • P. HINCHLIFF, *Cyprian of Carthage and the Unity of the Christian Church* (London, 1974) • H. KOCH, *Cyprianische Untersuchungen* (Bonn, 1926) • P. MONCEAUX, *Histoire littéraire de l'Afrique chrétienne depuis les origines jusqu'à l'invasion arabe,* vol. 2, *Saint Cyprien et son temps* (Paris, 1902) • M. M. SAGE, *Cyprian* (Cambridge, 1975) • C. SAUMAGNE, *Saint Cyprien, évêque de Carthage, "Pape" d'Afrique* (Paris, 1975) • G. S. M. WALKER, *The Churchmanship of St. Cyprian* (Richmond, Va., 1969).

FRANCINE CARDMAN

Cyprus

Cyprus (Heb. *Kittim,* after the harbor Citium, mentioned often by the Phoenicians and the site of present-day Larnaca), from the Greek "Kypros" (etymology unknown), is a Mediterranean island 100 km. (60 mi.) west of the Syrian coast and 65 km. (40 mi.) south of the coast of Turkey.

1. Late Paleolithic and Neolithic settlement of Cyprus before the fourth millennium B.C. points to close relations with the Near East. During the third and second millennia the Copper and Bronze Age of Egypt, Crete, Mycenae, Syria, and Anatolia made Cyprus, with its rich metal and smithy work, a great

	1960	1980	2000
Population (1,000s):	442	454	608
Annual growth rate (%):	0.32	1.16	0.98
Area: 5,916 sq. km. (2,284 sq. mi.)			

A.D. 2000

Population density: 103/sq. km. (266/sq. mi.)
Births / deaths: 1.55 / 0.75 per 100 population
Fertility rate: 2.24 per woman
Infant mortality rate: 6 per 1,000 live births
Life expectancy: 78.3 years (m: 76.0, f: 80.7)
Religious affiliation (%): Christians 94.1 (Orthodox 89.3, marginal 1.6, Roman Catholics 1.6, other Christians 1.6), nonreligious 4.0, Muslims 1.0, other 0.9.
Note: Figures do not include Northern Cyprus.

center of trade. The original population, which spoke remnants of a language similar to Hurrian, to which Hittites and Egyptians might have already been added, was supplanted around the 15th century B.C. by early Greeks from Mycenae, who learned the Akkadian form of inscription and developed from its syllabic principle a Cyprian-Mycenaean script not unlike Cretan A linear writing. Assyrian rule in the 8th and 7th centuries was followed by Egyptian, and then Persian. After the battle of Issus in 333 B.C., Cyprus fell under the regime of Alexander the Great (336-323 B.C.). The Ptolemies exercised control from 294 to 258, when the Roman province of Cilicia assumed dominance. After the division of the Roman Empire in A.D. 395, Cyprus remained under → Byzantine control until the Arab conquests from 647 to 965 (→ Islam 2).

2. Cyprus has had many religious traditions. Women figurines from the Neolithic Age point to an Aegean–Near Eastern mother-goddess cult as a background for the changes in the main sanctuary at Paphos, which lasted from the early Greek period to the Hellenistic age. Then Cyprus became the home of Aphrodite. During the imperial age Hellenistic city culture provided it with agoras, gymnasiums, libraries, and temples of every cult. A Jewish diaspora that began in the fifth century B.C. became so large after the Jewish war of 66-70 that it played a great part in the war against Trajan (98-117; → Roman Empire 2.1) in 116/17.

Retribution by the Romans helped the Christians, who after the persecution of Stephen had found a home in Cyprus and converted many Jews, in whose synagogue Paul and Barnabas preached (Acts 11:19; 13:4-12; → Paul 2.3; Persecution of Christians 2). By the fourth century most of the people had become

Christian. Resisting the claims of the patriarchate of → Antioch (→ Patriarch, Patriarchate), the church gained → autocephaly in 488 and still retains it today.

3. The threat of Muslim possession made Cyprus a goal in the → Crusades. The English king Richard the Lion-Hearted (1189-99) gave the nominal crown to → Jerusalem, which had been won back from Saladin (1171-93). In 1489, however, Venice took the island, but the Ottoman Turks recaptured it in 1570/71. They introduced their own Cypriot Turkish population.

4. Sultan Abdülhamid II (1842-1918, ruled 1876-1909), after losing a war with Russia in 1878, ceded Cyprus to Great Britain, which practically annexed it during World War I and made it a colony in 1924. The Greek → Orthodox Church, however, fostered the idea of union with Greece, and after World War II Archbishop Makarios III (1913-77) became the political leader of the Greek party. With the desire for independence he found support in the anti-British Ethniki Organosis Kiprion Agoniston (National organization of Cypriot combatants), though this group did not offer resistance to the Turks. In 1959 Great Britain, Greece, and Turkey united with both groups to set up military points for all three in promising independence. Although independence was officially proclaimed by Makarios as the elected president on August 16, 1960, it was challenged between 1962 and 1965 by a "colonels' junta" that had come to power in Greece through a coup d'état. This ultimately led in 1974 to the flight of Makarios and to a Turkish military invasion that drove 200,000 Greeks from the northeastern part of the island. The divisions of the country were united in 1975 in a Turkish-Cypriot state, though they are in fact two, with R. Denktash elected as president of the Turkish partial state, and S. Kyprianou as president of the Greek. On November 15, 1983, the Turkish Republic of Northern Cyprus was proclaimed, though the United Nations Security Council condemned it as an illegal act of secession and only Turkey recognizes it. Its constitution does not permit reunion but calls for a bi-zonal federation with the Greek Cypriot state. Talks to end the division have taken place in the → United Nations in 1984, 1985, and 1988, but the idea of union under a common superstructure has not been successful, and there has been no revision of boundaries in the actual division.

5. In 1989 the Republic of Cyprus (Gk. Kypriaki Dimokratia, Turk. Kıbrıs Cumhuriyeti) plus Northern Cyprus had a combined population of 695,000, of which 79 percent were Greeks, 18 percent Turks, 3

percent Armenians, and the rest various other nationalities. The Orthodox Church claimed 77 of the population, 5 percent belonged to various other churches (Armenian, Maronite, Anglican, Roman Catholic; → Armenian Apostolic Church; Anglican Communion; Roman Catholic Church; Uniate Churches), and 18 percent were Muslims (→ Islam). In 1990 Cyprus was accepted into the European Union, with which it had had a customs agreement since 1987.

6. According to 1995 figures, the Turkish Republic of Northern Cyprus (Turk. Kuzey Kıbrıs Türk Cumhuriyeti) covers an area of 3,335 sq. km. (1,288 sq. mi.) and has a population of 134,000. The residents consist of a small number of Turkish Cypriots, with the majority of settlers from Anatolia. There are also some 700 Greek Cypriots. Among the Muslims the main group is the Hanifite branch of → Sunna, with a mufti in the Turkish portion of the capital, Nicosia.

Bibliography: T. BAHCHELI, *Greek-Turkish Relations since 1955* (San Francisco, 1990) • A. S. BANKS, ed., *Political Handbook of the World: 1992* (New York, 1992) 190-97 • *The Europa World Year Book* (London, 1992) 1.866-77 • G. HILL, *A History of Cyprus* (4 vols.; Cambridge, 1949-52) • B. HUNTER, ed., *The Statesman's Year-Book . . . for the Year 1992-1993* (New York, 1992) 466-73 • E. KIRSTEN, "Cyprus," *RAC* 3.481-99 • G. T. KURIAN, ed., *Encyclopedia of the First World* (New York, n.d.) 1.193-217 • K. P. KYRRIS, *History of Cyprus* (Nicosia, 1985) • E. MEYER, "Kypros," *KP* 3.404-8 • A. J. PEASLEE, *Constitutions of Nations* (3d ed.; The Hague, 1968) 3.132-37 • M. STEARNS, *Entangled Allies: U.S. Policy toward Greece, Turkey, and Cyprus* (New York, 1992) • J. WHITAKER, *An Almanac for the Year of Our Lord 1993* (London, 1992) 830-31 • J. WIESNER, "Zypern," *BHH* 3.2252-54.

CARSTEN COLPE

Cyril of Alexandria

1. Life
2. Writings

1. Life

Few facts are known with certainty about Cyril's early life, but it appears that he was born in the town of Theodosian (near the present-day Egyptian city of Mahalla al-Kubra) sometime around 375 C.E. Cyril's mother was the sister of Theophilus, the bishop of → Alexandria. Cyril was initially educated in the classical Greek fashion, but after learning how to read and interpret secular texts, he continued his education by focusing on the Bible, theology, and Christian disciplines. This phase of Cyril's education may have occurred under the tutelage of Didymus the Blind (d. 398), the last head of the catechetical school in Alexandria, but it is more likely that Cyril went through a period of spiritual apprenticeship at a monastic community located in the Egyptian desert near Mount Nitria.

When Cyril had completed both his classical and his spiritual education, Theophilus brought him to Alexandria as a special assistant. Severus suggests that Cyril lived in the same cell as his uncle and functioned as an amanuensis and reader. Cyril himself says little about this period of his life other than indicating that he accompanied Theophilus to the Synod of the Oak in 403, where he says he played only a minor role in this council, which condemned John → Chrysostom. While functioning as Theophilus's assistant, Cyril had garnered enough support within the ecclesiastical community in Alexandria so that, after a brief power struggle, he was elected → bishop in 412 when Theophilus died.

Cyril's bishopric was defined by a series of adversarial confrontations. The first of these involved an acrimonious battle with his Jewish contemporaries. Defending his actions on the basis of his interpretation of Scripture, Cyril viciously attacked the Jews of Alexandria. The church historian Socrates Scholasticus says that Cyril was instrumental in instigating riots against the Jews of the city, stripping them of their property, and expelling all of them from Alexandria. A more sober analysis of the situation, however, suggests that despite Cyril's vociferous attacks on the Jews, he succeeded in forcing no more than a handful of Jews out of the city.

Cyril's overt hostility toward the Jews and the lawless behavior of his followers caused Orestes, the governor, to condemn Cyril's actions. Cyril, being disinclined to accept criticism graciously, may have retaliated by masterminding the brutal murder of a local pagan philosopher named Hypatia. Having apparently incurred Cyril's wrath merely because she was a close and influential friend of Orestes, Hypatia was abducted by a band of Christians, dragged through the streets to a local church, stripped, beaten, and murdered. Although Socrates does not directly accuse Cyril of being a member of the murderous gang, he clearly believes that Cyril was ultimately responsible.

The final confrontation of Cyril's episcopate was a heated theological and political battle with Nestorius (→ Nestorians), who was appointed bishop of Constantinople in 428. The theological portion of the battle was Christological. For philosophical reasons, Nestorius wanted to maintain a clear distinction between the divine and human natures in Christ,

while Cyril argued that the divine and human had been united into one nature in Christ. Although the debate was theological, it often deteriorated into a series of exchanges in which Cyril's brilliant theological insights were sullied by a superabundance of vitriolic calumny against Nestorius.

Although his caustic attitude caused many of his fellow churchmen to dislike him, Cyril's theological position was confirmed by the Council of Ephesus in 431, which deposed Nestorius and his followers. John, the bishop of Antioch, who had been delayed and arrived in → Ephesus four days late, refused to accept the verdict of the council. He counterattacked by convening a synod composed of Nestorius's friends and followers that deposed and excommunicated Cyril. After a brief period of imprisonment, both Cyril and Nestorius returned to their homes, but the animosity between the two factions continued unabated until 433.

An uneasy truce was reached in 433 when Cyril accepted a formula for reconciliation that was proffered by John of Antioch. In this formula, the Antiochenes acknowledged the condemnation of Nestorius in exchange for Cyril's commitment to certain theological points concerning the Virgin → Mary. Despite the apparent reconciliation, the Christological debate was still unsettled when Cyril died in 444. When the Council of → Chalcedon clarified the church's perspective on → Christology in 451, however, it reasserted Cyril's orthodoxy and used his second letter to Nestorius as the basis for its doctrinal statement.

2. Writings

Cyril was one of the most prolific writers of the early church. His writings before 424 were primarily exegetical. Cyril's earliest writings were two topical expositions of the → Pentateuch entitled *De adoratione in spiritu et veritate* (On worship and adoration in spirit and truth) and *Glaphyra* (Polished comments). He later wrote verse-by-verse commentaries on many of the other books of the Old and New Testaments, which may have grown out of a series of instructional lectures for his clergy on the principles of → exegesis. Unfortunately, only his commentaries on the Minor Prophets, Isaiah, and John survive in more than fragmentary form.

Beginning around 424, Cyril's writings began to focus on theological and → polemical issues. His first theological treatises *(De Trinitate* and the *Thesaurus)* were refutations of → Arian thought, but after 428 Cyril's writing centered on his debate with Nestorius. He used a variety of forms such as letters, essays, and anathemas to express his opinions. During the final years of his life, Cyril devoted a great deal of energy to produce a volume entitled *Contra Julianum* in which he refuted the attacks on Christianity that had been made by Julian the Apostate some 80 years earlier.

→ Monophysites

Bibliography: Primary sources: G. M. DE DURAND, trans., *Cyrille d'Alexandrie. Deux dialogues christologiques* (Paris, 1964); idem, *Cyrille d'Alexandrie. Dialogues sur la Trinité* (Paris, 1976-78) • J. McENERNEY, trans., *The Letters of Cyril of Alexandria* (Washington, D.C., 1987) • *PG* 68-77 • P. E. PUSEY, ed., *Sancti Patris Nostri Cyrilli Archiepiscopi Alexandrini in XII Prophetas* (2 vols.; Brussels, 1965) • R. P. SMITH, trans., *Commentary on the Gospel of St. Luke by St. Cyril, Patriarch of Alexandria* (Oxford, 1859) • L. WICKHAM, trans., *Select Letters of Cyril of Alexandria* (Oxford, 1983).

Secondary works: L. M. ARMENDARIZ, *El Nuevo Moisés. Dinámica cristocéntrica en la tipología de Cirolo Alejandrino* (Madrid, 1962) • A. GRILLMEIER, *Christ in Christian Tradition* (2d ed.; vol. 1; Atlanta, 1975) 414-84 • A. KERRIGAN, *St. Cyril of Alexandria: Interpreter of the OT* (Rome, 1952) • J. KOPALLIK, *Cyrillus von Alexandrien* (Mainz, 1881) • J. LIEBAERT, *La doctrine christologique de s. Cyrille d'Alexandrie avant la querelle nestorienne* (Lille, 1951) • SEVERUS, *The History of the Patriarchs of the Coptic Church of Alexandria* (trans. B. Evetts; Paris, 1948-59) • R. L. WILKEN, *Judaism and the Early Christian Mind: A Study of Cyril of Alexandria's Exegesis and Theology* (New Haven, 1971).

J. DAVID CASSEL

Czech Republic

1. Historical Survey
2. Religious Groups
   2.1. Roman Catholic Church
   2.2. Old Catholic Church
   2.3. Orthodox Church
   2.4. Hussite Church
   2.5. Protestants
   2.6. Others
3. Interchurch Relations
4. Theological Education
5. Church and State

After the collapse of the Austrian Empire in 1918, what is now the Czech Republic formed part of the independent state of Czechoslovakia. With an interruption during the German occupation (1939-45) and throughout the period of Communist rule (1948-89), this situation continued until the peaceful separation from Slovakia in 1993. Prague, the largest city, is the capital.

	1960	1980	2000
Population (1,000s):	9,552	10,283	10,195
Annual growth rate (%):	0.34	0.04	−0.13
Area: 78,864 sq. km. (30,450 sq. mi.)			

A.D. *2000*

Population density: 129/sq. km. (335/sq. mi.)
Births / deaths: 1.05 / 1.19 per 100 population
Fertility rate: 1.40 per woman
Infant mortality rate: 8 per 1,000 live births
Life expectancy: 73.8 years (m: 70.8, f: 76.8)
Religious affiliation (%): Christians 65.9 (Roman Catholics 45.4, unaffiliated 10.3, Protestants 6.9, indigenous 2.2, other Christians 1.2), nonreligious 30.1, atheists 3.9, other 0.1.

1. Historical Survey

After a short but important period of → Slavic mission in the ninth century, the inhabitants of what is now the Czech Republic came under the political, cultural, and ecclesiastical influence of the West, but with no complete suppression of the older Slavic legacy. The native reformation of the → Hussites and → Bohemian Brethren prepared the way for the European → Reformation, but it was reversed after 200 years (1620), and the mostly Protestant country was then almost fully recatholicized as a result of the Counter-Reformation policies of the ruling Hapsburgs (→ Catholic Reform and Counterreformation).

The interweaving of → Catholicism with Hapsburg interests explains the relatively early date (late 19th cent.) and rapid progress of the → secularization of public life and national culture. Recatholicizing by force resulted finally in distrust of all religion. Nor could the achieving of independence in 1918 essentially alter this development. The → democratic state granted full → religious liberty, but hopes that the liberated people would return to the "faith of their fathers" came to nothing.

The experience of the Munich Pact (1938) and of → fascism during the German occupation of Bohemia and Moravia (1939-45) pushed the people toward the → socialist alternative, with all that it meant for the value placed on → religion in Czech society. In late 1989 the fall of the regime brought the dismantling of the Communist system. The → Roman Catholic Church had never officially accepted the regime and had suffered severely from 1950 to 1989 with the prohibition of orders and schools along with episcopal vacancies.

Protestant churches had varying relations to socialism. None proclaimed its ideology, but against the background of their history certain Protestants had some understanding of the positive socialist goals. In the debate with socialism and the Christian-Marxist dialogue of the 1960s (→ Marxism and Christianity; Church in a Socialist Society), J. L. Hromádka (1889-1969) played a leading but disputed role. The invasion of Czechoslovakia by Warsaw Pact troops in August 1968 shattered hopes of a humanizing of the Communist system.

2. Religious Groups
2.1. *Roman Catholic Church*
In 1993, with 4 million members in seven → dioceses (increased to eight by 1997), the Roman Catholic Church is still the largest church in the Czech Republic and is involved in many ways in the country's history and culture. Members take part in church activities in various ways in different parts of the land. Secularization and → atheistic propaganda have not been without influence on the popular shape of the church, and in many places there is a thrust toward a community church. Much effort goes into → diakonia and education. The Greek Catholic Church, with 9,000 members, is united with Rome.

2.2. *Old Catholic Church*
The Old Catholic Church has only about 2,500 members in eight congregations. It gained its first supporters in the 1870s among Germans in northern Bohemia. A distinctive feature is its relation to the theological and liturgical (→ Liturgy) traditions of the Hussites (see 2.4).

2.3. *Orthodox Church*
In 1993 the → Orthodox Church had some 20,000 members. Previously under the → jurisdiction of the Serbian → patriarchate, it received → autocephalous status from Moscow in 1951. After World War I its numbers grew, thanks in part to the missionary work of Bishop Gorazd (1870-1942) and in part to the flood of Russian refugees into what was then Czechoslovakia. In 1950 the church united with the Uniate Orthodox, but this union did not last, for many Uniate groups split off again in 1968.

2.4. *Hussite Church*
The Czechoslovak Hussite Church inherited the aspirations of the Czech reformers, especially the Hussites. It arose in 1920 out of the movement of reform in the Roman Catholic Church (→ Modernism). Although repudiated by Benedict XV (1914-22), a group of priests led by K. Farský (1880-1927) founded a new church with a new program, including offering the cup to the laity, worship in the language of the people, marriage of priests, and openness to modern social and cultural strivings. The new church adopted a combined episcopal-presbyterian struc-

ture and a liturgical form of worship. The separation from Rome in 1920 brought in hundreds of thousands of members, but their ideas were by no means as clear as those of the founders. The first decade was marked by a search for identity in which both orthodox and → Unitarian trends were present. Inner consolidation came through the biblical and → Trinitarian liturgy of Farský, who saved the church for ecumenical Christianity and helped to promote new theological reflection. In 1993 the church had 170,000 members in 355 congregations and 5 dioceses.

2.5. *Protestants*
In their modern forms, the Protestant churches are all creations of the last 200 years. The edict of toleration in 1781 (→ Josephinism 4) removed the illegal status from the decimated remnants of earlier churches and made possible the limited but tolerated existence of the two churches of the → Augsburg and → Helvetic Confessions. Only in 1861 were they granted equal status and the possibility of public activity. They were wholly Austrian in organizational structure, so that they had to engage in reconstruction after the 1918 collapse, amid severe debates regarding nationality.

This was especially the situation in the Silesian Evangelical Church of the Augsburg Confession, in view of the mixture of Germans, Czechs, and Poles in its territory. The German congregations split off after 1918, and the Polish and Czech congregations set up an independent system, but the state did not recognize their → constitution. During World War II they were put under the Breslau consistory and largely Germanized. Only the settling of the question of national identity after 1945 made possible the consolidation of this church and gave it its present form. Two languages (Czech and Polish) are spoken by the 50,000 members in the 19 congregations.

The Evangelical Church of the Czech Brethren originated in 1918 with the union of Reformed and Lutheran congregations in Bohemia and Moravia (→ United and Uniting Churches). This church claims to be heir to the native reformation. It adopted the Confessio Bohemica of 1575 and the Brethren Confession of 1662, though without renouncing ties to the European Reformation, which came to expression in its endorsing of the Augsburg and Second Helvetic Confessions in 1945. Since most of the congregations were Reformed and had stronger links to Reformed churches abroad, the church has a Reformed character and belongs to the → World Alliance of Reformed Churches. In 1993 it had 190,000 members in 270 congregations.

Other Protestant churches arose mostly under the influence of foreign denominations that gained adherents in the Czech Republic. The Moravian Brethren began work in the land of their fathers in 1861, and in what is now an autonomous province have about 4,500 members. The Brethren Church arose out of the work of American → Congregationalists and a spontaneous → revival in eastern Bohemia. With 5,000 full members it represents the revivalist and → free church legacy. The Baptists (from 1885) have 2,000 full members, the Evangelical Methodists 4,500 members (→ Methodist Churches). Relief work by American Methodists after 1918 gave rise to the latter group. The Seventh-day → Adventists began their work in 1919 and are now a growing church with 7,500 baptized members. Christian Fellowships form another body with 3,200 members (at work since 1918, legalized in 1957), and there are also various → Pentecostal churches.

2.6. Others

Also officially registered by the state are the Religious Fellowship of Unitarians (5,000 members) and Jewish synagogues with 2,700 members (→ Judaism). Groups that have been seeking official status since 1989 include the → Mormons, → Jehovah's Witnesses, Muslims, and the → Unification Church.

3. Interchurch Relations

Twelve of the churches mentioned belong to the Ecumenical Council of Churches in the Czech Republic (→ National Councils of Churches), successor to the Czechoslovak Council founded in 1955 and dissolved in 1993. Roman Catholics, Anglicans, Adventists, and Jews have observer status on this council. The Alliance of Protestant Churches founded in 1926 was a predecessor. The council promotes interchurch relations at home and abroad and coordinates efforts in publicity, diakonia, and education. It holds conferences and sponsors study and work among young people and → women. Member churches also belong to the → World Council of Churches, the confessional families of the → Conference of European Churches, the → Leuenberg Fellowship, and other international organizations. To stimulate → local ecumenism there are ecumenical weeks of prayer and occasional joint services in which Roman Catholics also take part.

An important ecumenical achievement was the common Czech translation of the Bible (1979), in which all denominations, including Roman Catholics, had a hand. It was published by the Czech Bible Society.

The Kostnicka Jednota, founded in 1905, is an older ecumenical organization uniting Czech and Slovak Protestants and sponsoring publications, conferences, and lectures to heighten ecumenical consciousness.

Local interchurch relations differ from area to area and denomination to denomination. Often the more distant (Counter-Reformation; see 1) or more recent past (Uniates; see 2.3) hampers them. But the → diaspora situation and the churches' new tasks favor closer cooperation in catechesis, diakonia, and other functions.

4. Theological Education

Theological education currently is given by five theological faculties (three Roman Catholic) that after 1990 were incorporated into the universities of Prague, Olomouc, and České Budějovice. Some individual churches also have their own colleges or programs to train church workers.

5. Church and State

The Czech Republic did not accept the principle of separation of church and state, even though some leading intellectuals, including the first president, T. G. Masaryk (1850-1937), advocated it. Even the Communist state supported the churches financially, and by the church law of 1949 the state undertook to remunerate ministers in return for the nationalizing of church property. In this way the state gained fuller control over church life and ministry and was able to impede the churches' public work. Religious instruction at public schools was still possible in principle but hard to give in practice.

Restrictions were set aside when the Communist regime collapsed. The laws now allow the churches to function in all sectors of public life. A new regulation governing relations between church and state was in the process of being formulated in 1995.

Bibliography: D. Capek, Fellowship of Service: Life and Work of Protestant Churches in Czechoslovakia (Prague, 1961) • P. Filipi, P. Pokorný, M. Salajka, and J. M. Svoboda, eds., Tschechischer Ökumenismus. Historische Entwicklungen (Prague, 1977) • J. Otter, The First Unified Church in the Heart of Europe: The Evangelical Church of Czech Brethren (Prague, 1992) • M. Salajka and J. Svoboda, eds., Czech Ecumenical Fellowship (Prague, 1981) • F. Seibt, ed., Bohemia Sacra. Das Christentum in Böhmen, 973-1973 (Düsseldorf, 1974) • F. Siegmund-Schultze, ed., Ekklesia. Eine Sammlung von Selbstdarstellungen der christlichen Kirchen, vol. 5, Osteuropäische Länder, fasc. 20, Die Kirchen der Tschechoslowakei (Leipzig, 1937) • R. Urban, Die Tschechoslowakische Hussitische Kirche (Marburg, 1973) • A. Wondruschka and P. Urbanitsch, eds., Die Habsburger Monarchie, 1848-1918, vol. 4, Die Konfessionen (Vienna, 1985).

Pavel Filipi

D

Dance

1. History of Religion

Dance, the rhythmic movement of the body to the accompaniment of music (G. van der Leeuw, "the oldest of the arts"), has been considered a sacred activity from the dawn of time. Spanish cave paintings of the late Paleolithic age depict hunting dances, indicating their connection with sympathetic → magic (i.e., the imitation of a chase in dance is believed to ensure its success). A similar understanding is discernible in the war dances of the Greeks and Romans.

1.1. *Classical Period*

From Plato onward many writers refer to dance as instituted by the deities, as something that they enjoy doing, and as a way to attract their presence. Narrative dances were also common, which related the deeds of the deities for edification and for promoting a worshipful response.

1.2. *Eastern Religions*

The recalling of the sacred myths in dance is normal in the major Eastern religions. Indeed, the → Hindu Siva, in one respect, is the Lord of the Dance, who has devised a dance as a model for adoration. The masked figures in the Tibetan devil dance impersonate lamas and bodhisattvas struggling with → demons and putting the opponents of → Buddhism to flight. In the → Shinto shrines of Japan ritual dance is common, as it is in both → Confucian and → Taoist centers. In Islam the → Sufis regard dance as a spiritual exercise whereby the body becomes a channel for the descent of the divine power. They disregard the mimetic possibilities of dance, believing that dance in itself is a form of prayerful self-offering. The → Sunnites, however, condemn dance, although neither the Koran nor the traditions forbid it.

2. Scripture

Numerous OT references indicate how dance was a valued feature of Hebrew religion. There is, for example, the victory dance of Miriam expressing joyful thanksgiving for the overthrow of Pharaoh (Exod. 15:20-21). David demonstrated his delight in Yahweh by dancing before the ark (2 Sam. 6:14) — indeed, the exhortation of the psalmist may be taken as exemplary: "Let them praise his name with dancing" (Ps. 149:3).

There is little on the subject in the NT; it is neither

condemned nor approved. Its joyful character was recognized by Jesus when he referred to the music and dancing that greeted the return of the Prodigal Son (Luke 15:25; cf. Mark 6:22 and par.), and dancing figures in the saying in Matt. 11:17, but there is no dance at worship.

It is the Hasidim in particular who resort to dancing as a form of devotion, although synagogue services in general are often marked by swaying (Yid. *shoveling*). There are special dances for the death of a *zaddik* (spiritual leader). At the celebration of the Feast of Tabernacles, each one dances with a Torah roll as a partner.

3. Church

3.1. *Dance in Church History*
Virtually without exception, the patristic writers (→ Early Church) condemned all dancing, no doubt in reaction to the contemporary cultural situation. No self-respecting citizen, whether Christian or not, would indulge in what had become a debauched pastime. Moreover, dancing was practiced by heretical groups such as the Gnostics, from whom the church wished to distance itself. Hence the councils of Aquileia (381), Toledo (589), and Constantinople (680) all condemned it. Nevertheless there was some dancing at the sanctuaries of the → martyrs (→ Saints, Veneration of).

By the → Middle Ages the cultural situation had changed, and dancing became widespread in churches and cathedrals, especially at Christmas and Easter. The → Reformers did not favor dance, and → Pietism regarded it as sinful. The → Puritans, however, allowed dance if done to the glory of God or for edification or as a recuperation from labor. In the Russian Orthodox Church (→ Orthodox Church 2.4), dance makes possible ecstatic experiences at worship.

3.2. *Dance in Missionary Settings*
Dance became a missionary problem in Latin America. → Indian cultic dances were partly forbidden because of their pagan character and partly permitted to prevent slipping back into the older religion or as a means of adjusting piety to culture. Dance is now an element of folk religion and is practiced at Marian cultic centers (→ Mary, Devotion to, 3) in the form of impressive native dances.

The Mar Thomas Christians in → India (§3.1) have developed the art of dance in tandem with religious song. Since the 1930s, Roman Catholic missionaries in India have adopted the traditional symbolic dance with Indian music as a culturally appropriate medium of Christian → proclamation. In Zaire, dance and song have had a place in eucharis-

tic liturgy since 1988. The Constitution on the Sacred Liturgy of → Vatican II addressed the possibility of bringing liturgical dance into worship insofar as it is "not indissolubly bound up with superstition and error" (*Sacrosanctum concilium* 37).

3.3. *Current Use*
Dancing to the glory of God has remained a feature of the ritual of the → Ethiopian Orthodox Church, at which the music of drums and cymbals and the clapping of the congregation accompany the dancing of the psalm-singing priests. The dance is also habitual in the → Pentecostal churches and many African → Independent Churches, and it has become a mark of the worship of the Shakers in the United States (→ Modern Church History 2.4.2), signifying a gift of the Holy Spirit and a natural expression of → joy.

In mainline churches, dance was featured at the 1967 consecration of the Liverpool Roman Catholic cathedral, and there was dancing at the saying of the → Lord's Prayer in Uppsala cathedral at a 1983 peace conference. Dance figures, too, at the German Kirchentag. This modern development has been much influenced by modern cultural changes and by the pioneering work of such dancers as Isidora Duncan, Ted Shawn, Ruth St. Denis, Martha Graham, Mary Wigman, and Doris Humphrey, with encouragement from the Sacred Dance Guild in the United States (1958) and the Christian Dance Fellowship in Australia (1978).

4. Liturgy
Dance as an element in Christian corporate worship — as well as a form of individual meditation — can enable worship to be incarnational and complete, in that it possesses a sacramental quality and is the offering of spiritual/physical beings in their entirety. As such, it rejects an antibiblical dualism (→ Anthropology 2.3 and 3.2; Soul). It can be a way of glorifying God in the body (1 Cor. 6:20) and a celebration of salvation *for* the world, not *from* it (→ Soteriology). Liturgical dance is in itself an act of thanksgiving, praise, and joy; at the same time, it is a means of presenting and exploring the meaning of the biblical narrative and of promoting the unity of the fellowship of believers in the Body of Christ.

Bibliography: D. ADAMS, *Congregational Dance in Christian Worship* (Austin, Tex., 1980) • N. CHALLINGWORTH, *Liturgical Dance Movement: A Practical Guide* (New York, 1982) • J. G. DAVIES, *Liturgical Dance: An Historical, Theological, and Practical Handbook* (London, 1984) • G. VAN DER LEEUW, *Phänomenologie der Religionen* (4th ed.; Tübingen, 1977) • M. F. TAYLOR, *A Time to*

Dance: Symbolic Movement in Worship (Austin, Tex., 1976) • F. Weege, *Der Tanz in der Antike* (Hildesheim, 1976).

J. G. Davies†

Dance Macabre

Dance macabre (or "dance of death"; Ger. *Totentanz*) is an allegorical theme in European art of the late Middle Ages. Typically involving the juxtaposed portrayal of either a clergyman or a layperson (→ Clergy and Laity) shown dancing with a dead person or with → death itself, personified as a skeleton, it consists ideally of a picture and text (at first monologic, later dialogic) and is widespread throughout Europe both inside and outside of churches and also in MSS and books.

We do not know the origin of the dance macabre (Spain, France, or Germany?), nor do we know the time it began (ca. 1350? or only in the 15th cent.?), the occasion (the Black Death?), the earlier forms (Vado mori? the legend of the three living and the three dead persons? a pictorial broadsheet?), or even the etymology of the French term "macabre" itself (Arab. *maqabir* = graves? Maccabees?). These and many other questions remain unanswered. The only sure thing is that the oldest dance macabre, found in a print from 1485 as well as in several MSS, can be dated to the year 1424 (Paris, S. Innocents) but was probably not, as long assumed, composed by Jean le Fèvre (14th cent.). That a Latin text preserved only in a more recent MS from 1443/47 actually provides the background to this particular French dance macabre is just as uncertain as the widespread assumption that the original form of the oldest "upper-German, four-line dance macabre," also preserved in this MS, was composed as early as 1350 in Dominican circles in Würzburg under the impact of the plague of 1348. The traditional view that the dance macabre was a reaction to the plague probably does apply to the best-known representation in monument form, namely, the Basel Dance Macabre, which was perhaps created by Konrad Witz (d. ca. 1445) around 1425.

The intellectual and spiritual background that explains the rapid rise of dance macabre, even independent of plagues, was the general feeling of crisis and of the end time (caused also by the Hundred Years' War, 1337-1453; → Middle Ages 2.4.2) that characterized the late 14th and early 15th centuries (→ Middle Ages 1.4), as well as church reforms such as the Council of Basel (1431-39; → Reform Councils 2.3) and the → penitential literature prompted by

these developments. The dance of death gave assurance that in death all social distinctions would be abolished. But it also carried the warning that the more decisive inequality determining the ultimate fate of one's soul would be set up between those who have done good works and atoned for their → sins and those who are unprepared and go to meet the → last judgment with a great list of sins. The dance macabre, propagated especially by the → Franciscans and → Dominicans and often introduced with a commentary delivered by a mendicant friar (→ Monasticism), offered the opportunity both for harsh class criticism, especially of the church's office-holders (→ Offices, Ecclesiastical; Religion, Criticism of), and also for general admonition on regulations affecting the relation between temporal and eternal life (→ Time and Eternity).

Further development of the dance macabre led away from the class principle and penitential exhortation to the individual representation of a dramatic conflict with one's own death (Hans Holbein the Younger). The 19th and 20th centuries have seen a much-changed revival of the dance macabre in both art (F. Pocci, A. Rethel, A. Böcklin, A. Hrdlicka, H. Naegeli) and literature (H. von Hofmannsthal, H. H. Jahnn).

Bibliography: A. Breeze, "The Dance of Death," *CMCS* 13 (1987) 87-96 • J. M. Clark, *The Dance of Death in the Middle Ages and Renaissance* (Glasgow, 1950) • G. Kaiser, ed., *Der tanzende Tod* (Frankfurt, 1982) • L. P. Kurtz, *The Dance of Death and the Macabre Spirit in European Literature* (New York, 1934) • H. Rosenfeld, *Der mittelalterliche Totentanz* (3d ed.; Vienna, 1974) • B. Schulte, *Die deutschsprachigen spätmittelalterlichen Totentänze* (Cologne, 1990).

Jens Haustein

Daniel, Book of

The Book of Daniel was the first apocalypse — and the only one to find its way into the OT canon. Other apocalypses exist but belong to the → pseudepigrapha. Earlier forms in the OT prophets (Ezekiel, Zechariah, Isaiah 24–27) share with true → apocalyptic (§2) only the means of presentation. Hence the origin of apocalyptic must be sought in terms of the theological and historical subject matter of the Book of Daniel, namely, the *status confessionis* of the religious persecutions under the Seleucid Antiochus IV Epiphanes (175-164 B.C.). This setting explains the statements of Daniel, which in turn determine the nature of apocalyptic.

1. The contemporary period of suffering no longer belonged to the time when → revelation appeared in Israel. Thus the author Daniel — a name handed down with Noah and Job in Ezekiel (14:14, 20; 28:3) as that of a mythical wise and righteous figure — is probably identical with the righteous judge Danel in the Ugaritic Aqhat epic. This name is brought back to the age of the empires of the Babylonians (Nebuchadnezzar in Dan. 1:1; 2:1; 3:1; 4:1; Belshazzar in 5:1; 7:1; 8:1), the Medes (the legendary Darius in 6:1; 9:1), and the Persians (Cyrus in 10:1). The contemporary history of the Macedonian rule of Alexander the Great to Antiochus IV appears only in concealed form as prophecy (2:33-35, 40-45; 7:7-27; 8:7-26; 9:25b-27; 11:3–12:13).

The fictive history revealed in Daniel acquires the character of legend, which becomes relevant through the use of motifs of contemporary persecution. As a true prophet, Daniel resists ungodly power; he must deal with Nebuchadnezzar's dream of four empires (chaps. 1–2), Nebuchadnezzar's madness (4), and Belshazzar's blasphemy (5). Daniel and his companions are persecuted for the sake of the → law in the incidents of the three men in the fiery furnace (3) and of Daniel in the lions' den (6).

The actual history of the period of persecution, told in disguised form as prophecy, focuses on two events: the desecration of the temple at Jerusalem, called "an abomination that desolates" (9:27; 11:31; 12:11; cf. 8:11-14), which took place in the summer of 167 B.C.; and the temple's yet anticipated restoration on the death of the desecrator at the end of 164 B.C. (7:11, 25-27; 8:9-26; 9:26-27; 11:30-45). This period of three and a half years (7:25; 8:14; 12:7, 11-12), as the last half of a week of years (9:26), is the origin of the apocalyptic interpretation of the 70 years of exile in the prophecy of Jeremiah (9:2; Jer. 25:11-12; 29:10) as 70 weeks of years (Dan. 9:24).

This formal structure is filled out historically only in the great "audition" in chap. 11, which presents the early history of Macedonian-Ptolemaic-Seleucid rule (vv. 3-20), the history of religious persecution under the Seleucids and of the Jewish resistance and inner purification (21-39), and expectation of the thus not realized end (40-45). Such a schema offers a timely application for the time the book received its final redaction.

2. The internal relationship between legend and prophecy comes about by means of the doctrine of four world empires in the sequence of Babylonians, Medes, Persians, and Macedonians. This sequence links the legendary section with the prophetic section in two ways: by a framework connecting the individual testimonies, and by the repetition of the dream of the four empires (chap. 2) in the → vision of the four beasts (chap. 7).

The doctrine of the empires is a genuine element in Israelite apocalyptic. It entails a transferring of the idea of the increasing degeneracy of the ages to the sequential world empires and its eschatological orientation to the royal dominion of Yahweh, embodied in the stone that crushes the empires (2:34-35, 44-45), in "the holy ones of the Most High" portrayed in the coming of the Son of Man (7:9-14, 21-22, 26-27), and in the host of the righteous who are raised again to everlasting life (12:1-3).

3. The traditions that underlie the apocalyptic statement of Daniel have their origin in Israel and the OT traditions concerning the fall of → Jerusalem and the exile (1:1-3), Jeremiah's prophecy of the 70 years (9:1-2), and the form of lamentation (9:4-19). But traditions from outside Israel can also be demonstrated, including the doctrine of world epochs (cf. the idea of the four yugas in Hindu thought; also cf. Hesiod), as well as that of world empires, which as a principle of historiographical grouping first appears in the sequence Assyrians-Medes-Persians in Ctesias, the historian of Artaxerxes II (reigned 404-359/58 B.C.).

The origin of the idea of the Son of Man is much debated. The only certain point is that in Daniel the early Israelite form of the concept in Ezekiel played some part. With regard to the legend of Nebuchadnezzar's madness, the Nabonidus text found in Cave 4 of → Qumran shows that in Israel, traditions concerning the last ruler of the Babylonian empire were transferred to Nebuchadnezzar.

It is not clear how the Book of Daniel achieved the form it now has in the Masoretic canon. It is impossible to establish any chronological movement within contemporary history from vision to vision, since the differences in the historical statements are only formal, not material. Furthermore, differences in reckoning the last half-week of years point only to the final stages of redaction at the end of 164 B.C. The two languages (1:1–2:4a in Hebrew, 2:4b–7:28 in Aramaic, 8:1–12:13 in Hebrew) are no criterion for composition, for they cut across the two main portions. Secondary translation back into Hebrew cannot be ruled out. There is a material reason for the first shift, for the sages of Babylon speak Aramaic.

4. Like Revelation, the only NT apocalypse, Daniel, the only OT apocalypse, has had a profound influence on the history and theology of the Christian church. Commentaries have been written mostly in

times of persecution — for example, those of Hippolytus (the first Christian commentary) and of → Luther and → Calvin.

Jewish tradition (Josephus) related the last empire to Rome. With the adoption of this interpretation, the doctrine of the four kingdoms became the principle of eschatologically oriented Christian → historiography. Only since the end of the Middle Ages has this view of history been challenged, on historical grounds.

Bibliography: Commentaries: A. Bentzen (HAT 1/19; 2d ed.; Tübingen, 1952) • J. Calvin (Grand Rapids, 1993; orig. pub., 1561) • J. J. Collins (Minneapolis, 1993) • P. R. Davies (Sheffield, 1988) • M. Delcor (SB; Paris, 1971) • L. F. Hartman and A. A. Di Lella (AB; Garden City, N.Y., 1978) • K. Koch (BK; Stuttgart, 1986ff.) • A. Lacocque (Atlanta, 1979) • J.-C. Lebram (ZBK; Zurich, 1984) • J. A. Montgomery (ICC; New York, 1927) • O. Plöger (KAT; Gütersloh, 1965) • W. Porteous (OTL; Philadelphia, 1965) • H. O. Thompson (GRLH; New York, 1993).

Other works: W. Baumgartner, *Das Buch Daniel* (Giessen, 1926); idem, "Ein Vierteljahrhundert Danielforschung," *TRu* 11 (1939) 59-83, 125-44, 201-28 • M. Casey, *Son of Man: The Interpretation and Influence of Daniel 7* (London, 1979) • C. Colpe, "Ὁ υἱὸς τοῦ ἀνθρώπου," *TDNT* 8.400-477 • R. Hanhart, "Die Heiligen des Höchsten," *Hebräische Wortforschung* (FS W. Baumgartner; Leiden, 1967) 90-101 • A. Klempt, *Die Säkularisierung der universalhistorischen Auffassung* (Göttingen, 1960) • K. Koch, *Das Buch Daniel* (Darmstadt, 1980) • J. Lebram, "Daniel / Danielbuch," *TRE* 7.325-49 (bibliography) • E. Marsch, *Biblische Prophetie und chronographische Dichtung* (Berlin, 1972) • A. Mertens, *Das Buch Daniel im Lichte der Texte vom Roten Meer* (Stuttgart, 1971) • R. Meyer, *Das Gebet des Nabonid* (Leipzig, 1962) • M. Noth, "The Understanding of History in OT Apocalyptic" and "The Holy Ones of the Most High," *The Laws in the Pentateuch and Other Studies* (Edinburgh, 1966) 194-214 and 215-28 • R. Reitzenstein and H. H. Schaeder, *Studien zum antiken Synkretismus aus Iran und Griechenland* (Leipzig, 1926; repr., 1965).

Robert Hanhart

Darmstadt Declaration

The Darmstadt Declaration was issued on August 8, 1947, by the Bruderrat (leaders of the → Confessing Church), concerning "the political path of our people." It was based on drafts by H. J. Iwand (1899-1960), M. → Niemöller (1892-1984), and K. → Barth (1886-1968). It followed up on the Stuttgart Declaration of Guilt (1945) but dealt with the causes

of the → guilt of church and people in the time of National Socialist rule (→ Fascism; Church Struggle). It found these in the older political mistakes of accepting power politics, of forming fronts "of the good against the evil," and of the → conservatives' rejection of the needed social reorganization and ignoring the cause of the poor and the needy.

A confession of the reconciliation of the world with God in Christ (→ Confession of Faith) precedes the confession of guilt. Then follows a resolve to undertake "a new and better ministry to the glory of God and the eternal and temporal → salvation of men." The Darmstadt Declaration rejects the understanding of National Socialist dictatorship as an unfortunate accident. It focuses, rather, on the political structures that made it possible. It withstands any restoration of these among either church or people after 1945 and calls for a radically new outlook and order.

The declaration initially encountered heavy opposition. H. Asmussen (1898-1968) and W. Künneth (1901-97) charged it with relapsing into a theology that favored → socialism. In the years that followed, it was largely forgotten or ignored.

The Darmstadt Declaration deserves to be remembered, however. It recognizes that the daily repentance (→ Penitence) of the church entails a readiness to change its structures, and it contains insight into what the church must do and refrain from doing relative to its political responsibility.

Bibliography: H. Ludwig, *Die Entstehung der Darmstädter Erklärung* (= *JK* nos. 8/9 [1977] supp.) text and historical commentary.

Eberhard Busch

Darwinism → Evolution

Daughter Church → Filiation

David

1.1. The historical traditions about David (whose name means "beloved"), Israel's most important king, appear in the → Deuteronomistic history, whose author incorporated into the work the earlier stories of David's rise (1 Sam. 16:14–2 Sam. 5:10) and of his reign and succession (2 Samuel 9–20 and 1 Kings 1–2). Further material about David — lists, anecdotes, annals, stories, and poems (see 2 Sam. 5:11–8:18 and chaps. 21–24) — also entered the work in the course of redaction.

1.2. The story of David's rise is composite. It developed over a long and indefinite period in Judah and Jerusalem after the death of Solomon. Its theological aim is to give a divine legitimation to David's rise. Only critically can it also be used as a historical source.

1.3. The story of David's succession seems more unified than the story of his rise to power, though the former is not entirely free from later elaborations. Thus, for example, the theological judgments in 2 Sam. 11:27; 12:24; and 17:14 were not found in the original. Furthermore, in the original work Solomon's birth is depicted as the fruit of David's adultery with Bathsheba (ignoring 2 Sam. 12:1-24abα), and his accession to the throne in 1 Kings 1–2 comes by way of a palace intrigue. Originally the story probably goes back to dissidents in → Jerusalem in Solomon's own day.

2. The time of David's reign can be roughly dated from 1004/1003 to 965/964 B.C., for we know that Solomon died in 926/925 and that he (1 Kgs. 11:42), like David (2 Sam. 5:4), reigned some 40 years (a round number!).

3. The significance of David in world politics lies in his founding the first relatively large independent kingdom in Syria and Palestine. After gathering a small mercenary army around him (1 Sam. 22:2) and serving for a time as a vassal of the → Philistines (chaps. 27–29), he united the southern tribes under his rule as Judah (2 Sam. 2:4a). After the short reign of Ishbaal, a son of Saul (vv. 8-10), the northern tribes were ready to conclude a royal treaty with David (2 Sam. 5:3). David took into account the rivalry between North and South when he chose the neutral city of Jerusalem as his capital (vv. 6-9) and, by bringing up the → ark there (chap. 6), made a connection with the sacred traditions of the northern tribes.

The presuppositions of David's foreign policy were the ending of Philistine domination in → Palestine (2 Sam. 8:1) and the incorporation of the Canaanite city-states (see 1 Kgs. 4:9-12). Further steps concerned Moab, Aram, and Edom, which to various degrees David subjected to his rule (2 Samuel 8). Ammon was directly integrated into David's kingdom (12:29-31). His sway thus extended from the southern border of Palestine to Middle Syria.

4. David's kingdom was too much his own personal achievement to endure. After Solomon's death the northern tribes broke away from the personal union, and only Judah and Benjamin remained faithful to David's house (1 Kings 12). The dynasty lasted in Jerusalem until the destruction of Judah and Jerusalem in 587 B.C.

5. More lasting was the royal ideology that formed around the palace at Jerusalem and found expression especially in the royal psalms (see Psalms 2; 18; 20–21; 45; 72; 101; 110). The Deuteronomistic theology took up the related concepts and integrated them into the ancient credo of Israel. The hope thus arose that the dynasty would last forever (e.g., 2 Samuel 7; Psalms 89; 132), and the foundation was laid for messianic expectations that would sometimes take a more dynastic form (e.g., Isa. 9:2-7; Jer. 33:14-26; Amos 9:11-15; Hag. 2:23; Zech. 12:7-10) and sometimes a more individualistic form (e.g., Isa. 11:1-9; Jer. 23:5-6; Mic. 5:2-6; Zech. 9:9-10). These found a direct continuation in early Jewish sources, in which the expected Messiah bears not only the traditional designation "shoot of David" (e.g., *T. Jud.* 24:4-5; 4QPBless 3-4; 4QFlor 1.11) but also the title "son of David" (*Pss. Sol.* 17:21).

6. In NT telling, the birth of "Jesus the Messiah, the son of David" (Matt. 1:1) occurs significantly in Bethlehem, "the city of David" (Luke 2:4).

→ Christological Titles; Israel; Monarchy in Israel; Tribes of Israel

Bibliography: S. AMSLER, *David, roi et messie* (Neuchâtel, 1963) • R. C. BAILEY, *David in Love and War: The Pursuit of Power in 2 Samuel 10–12* (Sheffield, 1990) • D. BARTHÉLEMY et al., *The Story of David and Goliath: Textual and Literary Criticism* (Göttingen, 1986) • W. BRUEGGEMANN, *David's Truth: In Israel's Imagination and Memory* (Philadelphia, 1985) • R. A. CARLSON, *David, the Chosen King: A Traditio-Historical Approach to the Second Book of Samuel* (Stockholm, 1964) • J. W. FLANAGAN, *David's Social Drama: A Hologram of Israel's Early Iron Age* (Sheffield, 1988) • J. H. GRØNBÆK, *Die Geschichte vom Aufstieg Davids* (Copenhagen, 1971) • D. M. GUNN, *The Story of King David: Genre and Interpretation* (Sheffield, 1982) • T. ISHIDA, ed., *Studies in the Period of David and Solomon and Other Essays* (Winona Lake, Ind., 1982) • F. LANGLAMET, "Pour ou contre Salomon? La rédaction prosalomonienne de I Rois I–II," *RB* 83 (1976) 321-79, 481-528 (bibliography) • T. VEIJOLA, *David* (Helsinki, 1990); idem, *Die ewige Dynastie* (Helsinki, 1975); idem, *Verheißung in der Krise* (Helsinki, 1982) bibliography • E. WÜRTHWEIN, *Die Erzählung von der Thronfolge Davids–theologische oder politische Geschichtsschreibung?* (Zurich, 1974).

TIMO VEIJOLA

Days of Prayer and Repentance

Israel has its yearly Yom Kippur (day of atonement), with → sacrifices for the sins of the people (Leviticus 16). In times of crisis a → fast or day of prayer and repentance might also be proclaimed (Judg. 20:26; 1 Sam. 7:5-6; 31:13; Joel 1:13-14, etc.).

The Western church developed weekly fasts on Wednesday and Friday, the Lenten fast before → Easter, and in a limited sense the Advent fast and seasonal Ember Days based on pagan models. The authorities might also order fasts for special occasions.

In Europe and America the Protestant churches followed this tradition. New England Puritans especially held many special days of repentance, or celebration, for the two centuries from 1620 to 1833. Throughout Western Christendom, however, their influence gradually dwindled. Instead, occasional days of prayer and repentance have become more important — for example, Good Friday, the third Sunday in September, or the last Wednesday in the church's year. In contrast to the votive → mass in Roman Catholic circles, periods of prayer (→ Hours, Canonical) are more common in the Protestant world. Apart from personal → penitence and → confession of sin, the focus is on national guilt before God, the church's role as watchkeeper of the sins of the day, and intercession for the public, nations, and churches.

Bibliography: K. Dienst, "Buß- und Bettage," *RGG* (3d ed.) 1.1539-41 • P. Graff, *Geschichte der Auflösung der alten gottesdienstlichen Formen in der evangelischen Kirche Deutschlands* (2 vols.; Göttingen, 1937-39) 1.221-36, 2.164-69 • G. Kunze, "Die gottesdienstliche Zeit," *Leit.* 1.486-87 • W. D. Love, *The Fast and Thanksgiving Days of New England* (Boston, 1895) • L. Schmidt, "Buße VIII: Kirchliche Buß- und Bettage," *TRE* 7.492-96 • H. S. Stout, *The New England Soul: Preaching and Religious Culture in Colonial New England* (New York, 1986) • E. Weismann, "Der Predigtgottesdienst und die verwandten Formen," *Leit.* 3.88-93.

Hans-Christoph Schmidt-Lauber

Deacon, Deaconess

1. Definition
    1.1. Those Named Deacons
    1.2. Deacons under Other Names
2. Forms
    2.1. Liturgical-Sacramental
    2.2. Social Service
    2.2.1. Civil Servant Pattern
    2.2.2. Institutional-Clerical Pattern
    2.2.3. Local Congregational "Lay" Pattern
    2.3. Combined Forms
3. Ecumenical Situation
    3.1. Developments
    3.2. Challenges

Over the centuries, the definitions of deacon and deaconess have changed and developed, producing the present complex situation in which varied (sometimes overlapping) forms exist simultaneously in different (or occasionally the same) Christian bodies. Although there are some indications of convergence, the evolution also continues today in the worldwide ecumenical church.

1. Definition

Defining "deacon" is often very confusing because the word is used for a number of different concepts that are usually not clearly distinguished, and in some cases people function as deacons without bearing the title. The primary focus here are those called deacons and deaconesses, but some attention is also given those devoted to recognized ecclesiastical → diakonia under other titles.

1.1. *Those Named Deacons*

At least five factors shape the varied definitions of those called deacon: function, training and time commitment, ecclesial locale, ministerial status, and qualifications of candidates. What is the primary function of deacons: social or liturgical-sacramental? What kind of training do deacons receive, and what is the time commitment of their service: professional or voluntary? full-time or part-time? What is the geographic-ecclesiastical locale and relationship of deacons to other ministers: diocesan (or regional), subordinate to → bishop or conference? or elected by and responsible to the → congregation? What is the ministerial status and tenure of deacons: ordained or not, lifetime or term? Who are considered suitable candidates: men only? either men or women? celibate, married, or either?

These factors are combined in various ways in different Christian communities. Not all forms can be described, but a general historical picture can suggest the most common patterns. There are two very typical forms. The work of "transitional" deacons is sacramental-liturgical, under episcopal authority; they are ordained and usually → celibate men who will later become → priests and whose work is normally a full-time profession. Some churches ordain married men; some allow women to fill this role.

The work of what we might call "Protestant" deacons is social–community service and is under the local congregation. They are "ordained lay" people, usually both men and women, without regard for marital status, elected by a local congregation for part-time voluntary service. → Ordination is for life; active service may be continuous or for designated terms.

1.2. Deacon under Other Names

Several other groups of persons should be included in a definition of "deacons," although they do not have this title. Typical patterns are religious orders or parachurch agencies whose primary functions are service ministries, although other Christians engaged in regular service ministries in local congregations should also be counted in this context. Defining the boundaries is difficult, though often issues of training, time commitment, and church calling or recognition play a vital role in determining who is considered a deacon.

2. Forms

2.1. Liturgical-Sacramental

In many Christian communions deacons are primarily concerned with liturgical-sacramental functions. For Orthodox, Roman Catholics, Anglicans, Methodists, and some others, deacons are a transitional rank in the ministry of → Word and → sacraments, being trained for ordination as priests (presbyters, → elders). Orthodox and Roman Catholics ordain only men, while Anglicans and others usually ordain both men and women without regard to marital status.

Women deaconesses, as a separate order from male deacons and having a significant liturgical role, were known in the → early church. For example, in third-century Syria deaconesses had special roles in sacramental acts such as the instruction and → baptism of adult women. With changing circumstances (infant baptism replacing adult baptism, imperial influences on church hierarchy, the growing monastic movement), deaconesses and the related order of widows gradually developed into orders of nuns.

2.2. Social Service

For many Christian communities, the primary functions of deacons are related to social or material service (→ Diakonia), whether within the Christian body or beyond its bounds.

The diaconal functions of deacons in the early church were gradually diffused among varied individuals and groups, as the deacons themselves became more involved in sacramental ministries. Organized groups that carried out diaconal ministries (e.g., monastic bodies) usually did so not as deacons per se but alongside their primary functions of prayer

and meditation. Gradually, mostly lay groups (e.g., confraternities) were formed that served particular charitable purposes such as feeding the poor, housing travelers or the sick, caring for orphans or widows, and so forth, as well as benefiting their members spiritually. The understanding of deacons as ministers of material service was revived in the early modern West. Particularly important were Protestant views of the priesthood of believers and a new sense, shared by Roman Catholics and Protestants, that social activity in the world is a form of ministry. Essentially three patterns of deacons emerged: (1) a civil-servant pattern, which eventually became dissociated from the church as such; (2) professional institutional diaconal orders; and (3) congregational or local church lay ecclesiastical offices of deacons (the only ones consistently given the name).

2.2.1. Civil Service Pattern

Many established non-Catholic churches (e.g., Lutheran, Zwinglian, Church of England) organized diaconal work as part of the responsibility of the Christian ruler, although usually these civil servants were not called deacons. In time, especially by the 18th and 19th centuries, this form of diaconal organization became for practical purposes a branch of the state government, with no connection to the church, and other forms of church diaconate were developed, on the model of the Roman Catholic religious orders.

2.2.2. Institutional-Clerical Pattern

Roman Catholics established institutional or professional orders for the purpose of service, although again these were not usually called deacons. Some 16th-century → communities brought together laity and clergy without formal vows or training, but most diaconal groups were religious orders of celibate men or women under lifetime vows, whose service activities were usually teaching or ministries to the sick.

Led by German Lutherans, 19th-century Protestants established orders of deaconesses, especially for hospital work and teaching, although other ministries in local parishes were possible. These women were unmarried but not bound by permanent vows. The deaconess movement spread widely among many different confessions and across Europe to North America and through the British Empire. Expansion continued well into the 20th century, although the appeal of the deaconess orders declined after World War II. Today parachurch service agencies of various kinds provide a somewhat analogous form of ministry for Christians of many confessions.

These organized institutional diaconal bodies have been related to established church structures of ministry in varied ways, from close links or supervision by diocesan authorities to no formal connection at all.

2.2.3. *Local Congregational "Lay" Pattern*

Among some Protestants (esp. Calvinist Reformed) and → Anabaptist reformers (e.g., → Mennonites and → Hutterites), a new form of deacon or deaconess was established in the local congregation. Usually these deacons were elected by and responsible to the local church community. Primary tasks were care for the poor and afflicted and administration of the church's charitable budget, although some confessions (e.g., Calvinists) also gave deacons limited liturgical roles. Their service might be voluntary part-time or full-time and supported by the community, exercised in limited or repeated terms of office or for life, but they were considered lay ecclesiastical ministers, set apart for a church ministry. Calvinists were quite willing to recognize or cooperate with civil diaconal ministries as long as deacons were understood as first an office of the church and not primarily civil servants, while Anabaptist churches rejected any association with civil government. Although occasionally women deacons or deaconesses were chosen in the early period, men were dominant among both Calvinists and Anabaptists. Normally deacons were married or widowed, but this was not a requirement.

In the modern period, the local congregational lay pattern has developed various forms among Protestants groups such as → Baptists and others who follow a more → congregationalist or "free church" form of polity. Traditionally, deacons are responsible for charitable or benevolent activities but not governing functions, but in some → free church communities deacons may combine these roles and also share in pastoral leadership. Today, in many though not all Protestant churches that have congregational deacons, both men and women, married or not, may be elected, sometimes for life, sometimes for a specified term, and many churches practice ordination of deacons.

2.3. *Combined Forms*

In the second half of the 20th century, some Christian communities that have traditionally practiced a transitional diaconate have added a new form of "permanent" diaconate that combines features of both liturgically and socially oriented functions. The → Vatican II reforms of the → Roman Catholic Church have established a "permanent deacon" form for married men. The office combines sacramental duties with social action, although deacons may have more liturgical responsibilities in places where priests are few. A similar form of diaconate has developed in some parts of the → Anglican Communion, which, however, ordains women as well as men to this diaconate. Although they may work in varied or regional ministries, these deacons are frequently assigned by the bishop to particular parishes.

3. Ecumenical Situation

3.1. *Developments*

There has been something of an ecumenical revival of interest in deacons in the later 20th century, as the new permanent diaconates illustrate, but there is also continuing development. One form of this discussion is a reassessment of the appropriateness of having two forms of the diaconate. Some of those who have traditionally had a transitional diaconate but have recently instituted a new permanent diaconate (e.g., Anglicans and → Methodists) are discussing the wisdom of direct ordination to the priesthood and having only one form of deacon, effectively eliminating a transitional diaconate.

The single most important ecumenical statement about ministry, the Lima document *Baptism, Eucharist, and Ministry* (*BEM;* 1982), gives some attention to deacons as the traditional third order of Christian ministry (after bishops and priests; see "Ministry," par. 31). The description of deacons is somewhat loose and wide-ranging, capable of covering most of the different views of the five factors noted above. In working to apply *BEM*'s understanding of the diaconate, some churches have begun to gather under the name "deacon" or "diaconal ministry" a variety of ministries, from Christian education and music to church administration and home missions, along with more traditional community service. Two examples of this are found in the new diaconal ministries of the United Methodist Church (in the United States) and the Evangelical Lutheran Church in America, although these bodies do not presently ordain diaconal ministers.

3.2. *Challenges*

Although it provides exciting opportunities, the new ecumenical work on the diaconate also poses some challenges. Perhaps the most difficult one may be finding a way to define "deacon" that does not result in the word meaning nothing because it can mean everything. However, it is also significant that the door is open to finding a recognizable ministerial status for many forms of service that have been neglected or denigrated because they have not been labeled as ministries.

In addition, some of the continuing challenges revolve around relating deacons (however broadly they are defined) to other dimensions of Christian life. These challenges include finding ways to relate diaconal ministries at different geographic and ecclesiastical levels (from local to worldwide) to each other, ways to relate civil and ecclesiastical service ministries, ways to relate deacons to the diaconal ministries of other Christians (esp. "laity"), and means for relating diaconal and pastoral ministries in new ways (→ Clergy and Laity).

Bibliography: P. CRAIGHILL, ed., *Diaconal Ministry: Past, Present, and Future* (Providence, R.I., 1994) • J. G. DA-VIES, "Deacon, Deaconess, and the Minor Orders in the Patristic Period," *JEH* 14 (1963) 1-15 • E. A. McKEE, *Diakonia in the Classical Reformed Tradition and Today* (Grand Rapids, 1989) • J. OLSON, *One Ministry, Many Roles: Deacons and Deaconesses through the Centuries* (St. Louis, 1992) • J. ROLOFF, "Amt / Ämter / Amtsverständnis IV-VIII," *TRE* 2.509-622 • H. SCHWENDENWEIN, "Der ständige Diakon," *Handbuch des katholischen Kirchenrechts* (ed. J. Listl et al.; Regensburg, 1983) 229-38 • R. ZIEGERT and H. KRAMER, "Diakonat I-II," *ÖL* 240-43.

ELSIE ANNE McKEE

Dead, Cult of the

→ Death is part of the order of this world. Almost without exception, however, people have protested against its dominion, refused to acknowledge it, and even denied it. Accounts like that in Gen. 25:8, according to which people die contentedly after becoming sated with → life, or the idea of a "good death" after a fulfilled life (→ Confucianism), are the exception. The protest against death underlies the cult of the dead, and at the same time these cults aid in coming to terms with the psychological and social → conflicts among the survivors that are called forth by death (→ Grief). Finally, the concentration of many people together, especially in cities, demanded a regular form of burial (→ Funeral). All that accompanies a person's transition from the land of the living to the status of the dead forms a part of the cult of the dead.

1. → Archaeological findings suggest that today's burials in the ground and cremation are the oldest forms of disposing of the corpse. But people have also been buried on trees or frames, as in Siberia, or on the "towers of silence" for the vultures to eat, as in → Iranian religions. In Tibet, too, corpses were sometimes left at certain places for dogs and birds to eat (→ Tibetan Religions). We also find burying in water, as in burials at sea or the setting out of the dead in a boat on the sea or on some other body of water. Occasional instances of → cannibalism probably cannot be shown to represent any regularly occurring custom. Mummification (in Egypt) and other forms of conserving the dead are also found. Another common custom is burying the dead in natural or artificial caves (→ Catacombs) or in what are often grandiose buildings like mausoleums or pyramids. Various forms of burial might be practiced simultaneously or combined, as in ancient → Rome, where a pontifical rescript said that after burial by fire, at least one part of the body should be buried in the earth. Cities almost everywhere developed cemeteries, grave precincts, or a necropolis, usually outside the city.

2. The nature of the grave, grave accompaniments, obsequies, and mourning varied according to the social status and wealth of the deceased. → Slaves and uninitiated children were often buried with little ceremony. The callous burying of slaves, however, as in Jamaica or the West Indies in the 17th and 18th centuries, was exceptional. Unbaptized and → excommunicated persons were refused burial in a Christian cemetery, even into the 20th century. Today most burials are under state regulation.

3. The funeral, grave accompaniments, mourning ceremonies, laudation of the deceased, as well as mourning regulations all derive from the understanding of death itself within a given culture, an understanding that as a rule is also linked to religion. Yet many older elements often survive precisely in the cult of the dead. It is still problematic, however, to what extent a certain type of burial, lacking other evidence, allows us to conclude the presence of a specific understanding of death (e.g., to what extent an embryonic interment in crouching position in prehistoric graves allows us to conclude the presence of a belief in rebirth).

It is said of some → tribal religions that a natural death is not accepted; death must be traced back to witchcraft or to cultic errors. Commensurately, observation of the corpse or of similar phenomena allegedly enables one to determine from whom the magic came or what cultic errors were committed. Many peoples have tales of the origin of death through a → mythical conflict, deception, mistake, or error of a hero or god; through a false human choice; or as a → punishment inflicted on the world. Mourning laments occasionally accompanied by rented mourning women are also common. Depending on the tradition, burial takes place at once or after a fixed number of days, and until then, and occasionally for some time afterward, at least the nearest relatives are considered cultically unclean (→ Cultic Purity). The body is wrapped in linens, laid in a coffin or something similar, and then buried or burned.

4. Most tribal religions have little idea of a personal life after death for individuals. Only as long as people are still alive who knew the deceased are the latter remembered in one form or another. But then the deceased either disappear entirely or become one of the usually anonymous ancestors who are the basis of the social order through → ancestor worship (→ Shamanism).

H. Spencer (1820-1903) found the origin of all religion in the cult of the dead. After human beings became sedentary, the cult of the dead, of ancestors and heroes acquired a certain stability, and ancestors were successively transformed into gods (as in euhemerism). Some support for this thesis might be found in the fact that among the ancient Romans a grave became a holy place after the rites were fulfilled. The relation to the dead and to their afterlife — however understood — may well be important in religion. It is still a one-sided approach, however, to understand religion, which always concerns the whole of life, as having arisen simply out of the cult of the dead. Research occasionally supports one-sidedness, since for some religions we have more information about the cult of the dead than about everyday religious life.

5. The presupposition of survival after death is the idea of a → soul that is independent of the body, which leaves the body at death, and which must be led into the hereafter, the netherworld (Hades, Sheol), the eternal hunting grounds, the isles of the blessed, or → paradise. More exact ideas about the way, the next world, or the measures to be undertaken by the survivors were worked out in some circles (Egyptian and Tibetan books of the dead; → Egyptian Religion). Concerning survival after death, in addition to the notions already discussed from tribal religion and the areligious view that a person lives on only through fame or in the memory of survivors, we also have the idea of rebirth (→ Hinduism; Karma; Reincarnation) and the Christian doctrine of the → resurrection of the body and eternal → life (see 1; → Eschatology). Rebirth or resurrection is not always dependent upon a moral life that is pleasing to God. Many religions also offer measures through which a person can shorten postmortal punishment in → hell or ensure an immediate entry into paradise (→ Indulgence).

6. Burial accompaniments are quite varied. They may include the weapons, tools, or adornment of a person, but also food offerings (which are occasionally to be repeated), money, and, in Hinduism, the immolation of the widow. A king might even have his following go with him into death so as to serve him in the hereafter as they did on earth (Assyria).

Funeral speeches praising the merits of the deceased and offering comfort to those left behind are very common. The fulfilling of the rituals for the dead usually prescribe a mourning period of various lengths for the nearest relatives, with some restriction on daily life. The deceased are remembered on the day of their death or, as in ancient Rome (though also in contemporary cultures), on fixed days (Parentalia [observed February 13-21] and Lemuria [May 9, 11, and 13]; → Church Year).

7. Almost always the cult includes an element to prevent the return of the dead. In Rome, for example, the dead were laid out in state with their feet toward the door, and elsewhere their bones were broken or chained down and the grave blocked by heavy stones. Burial vaults could sometimes serve the same purpose, albeit in an unspoken fashion, honoring the dead but also ensuring their rest and, accordingly, also the rest of the living. In these ideas, which combine tender memories with resistance to any return of the dead, we find an in part unconscious, ambiguous attitude on the part of the living that underlies all burial cults. As a rule, cults conducted by the living focus more on dealing with their own → anxiety, → fear, and → love than on the dead. Burial rites offer an enormous release in overcoming these conflicts for individuals. Even nonreligious people are usually content to follow the traditional → rites.

→ Animism; Fetishism; Immortality; Requiem; Sacrifice; Spiritism; Taboo; Totemism

Bibliography: P. Ariès, *The Hour of Our Death* (New York, 1981) • E. Bendam, *Death Customs* (London, 1969; orig. pub., 1930) • F. Boas, "The Origin of Death," *JAF* 30 (1917) 486-91 • C. C. Clemen, *Das Leben nach dem Tode im Glauben der Menschheit* (Bonn, 1920) • E. von Dassow, ed., *The Egyptian Book of the Dead* (San Francisco, 1994) • M. Fortes, "Some Reflections on Ancestor Worship," *African Systems of Thought* (ed. M. Fortes and G. Dieterlein; London, 1965) 122-44 • A. Hahn, *Einstellungen zum Tode und ihre soziale Bedingtheit* (Frankfurt, 1968) • E. S. Hartland et al., "Death and Disposal of the Dead," *ERE* 4.411-511 • H. J. Klimkeit, *Tod und Jenseits im Glauben der Völker* (Wiesbaden, 1978) • K. Preuss, *Tod und Unsterblichkeit im Glauben der Naturvölker* (Tübingen, 1930) • H. Spencer, *The Principles of Sociology* (Westport, Conn., 1975; orig. pub., 1879-93) • G. Stephenson, *Leben und Tod in den Religionen. Symbol und Wirklichkeit* (Darmstadt, 1980) • E. B. Tylor, *Primitive Culture* (New York, 1976; orig. pub., 1871).

Hartmut Zinser

Dean → Rural Dean; Superintendent

Death

1. State of the Problem
2. Biblical Data
3. Philosophical Aspects
4. Theological Aspects

1. State of the Problem

All societies share the basic experience of death, yet they respond to it in different ways in their thinking and customs (→ Dead, Cult of the). We find ideas ranging from self-evident certainty of the presence of the dead (→ Ancestor Worship; Demons) to preparation for the journey of the dead to their new home and hope of redemption in a new life beyond the present course. The various theories of the relation to death that are also found in → society and → religion do not allow of systematization. Even the idea of a development from a "primitive" to a "higher" view of death (→ Evolution 4; Animism) is not tenable. In the various → rites and views of death, we find a knowledge of → life that can enrich our relation to both life and death and that is at times preserved in the Christian tradition in customs relating to both death and burial (→ Funeral).

2. Biblical Data

2.1. A characteristic mark of the biblical understanding of death is that it did not simply adopt the views found in surrounding cultures. Neither the varied and developed Egyptian view (→ Egyptian Religion) nor the rites of Canaan became relevant for the OT. The speculations and practices of the world of the great religions relating to death were, indeed, totally incompatible with faith in Yahweh. Classification of contact with the dead and with graves as unclean (→ Cultic Purity) ruled out any → magical practices or ritual glorification connected with death. The story of Samuel's visit with the witch of Endor (1 Samuel 28) does not provide evidence of belief in the spirits of the dead so much as it does that of a strict prohibition (and teaching about the uselessness) of any contacts with them. Disinterest in the graves of the mighty men of → Israel (Deut. 34:6; 1 Kgs. 2:10) bears witness to this rejection of overvaluation of the dead. To this religious depreciation there corresponds a solemn warning about death, which does not soften its harshness and cruelty but can still accept it as the limit set to creaturely life, and with it such hindrances of life as

sickness, weakness, and so forth (→ Health and Illness).

The OT deals only incidentally with death. → Yahweh is the Lord of life and therefore also the Lord of death. Because the OT views Yahweh centrally as the Lord of life and its gifts, it treats death as the sphere in which fellowship with Yahweh is broken. The deepest terror of death lies in the loss of fellowship with God (Ps. 88:5). It can thus be seen as the consequence of → sin (Eccl. 7:17 and esp. Ezekiel) and as God's → punishment. The question of the state of life after death is thus of little consequence for the OT. Most of the sayings about a realm of the dead (Sheol; → Hell) cannot be systematized. Death as the irrevocable end of life becomes a problem only when there is an interest in questioning God's → righteousness in view of the good fortune of the wicked and the bad fortune of the righteous. The destruction of death as the last victory of God and the → resurrection to judgment and eternal life are found clearly only in Dan. 12:2.

2.2. Because the cross and resurrection of → Jesus Christ are central in the NT, its theological understanding of death is determined by the → Easter triumph over it. If the death of Jesus is unique, the saving significance of the cross (→ Soteriology) sets the death of all others in a new light. The view of death follows the lines laid down in the OT but, when necessary, transforms them in the light of the → gospel. Along these lines the NT can adopt later OT and Jewish theological developments and motifs. Hellenistic influences have little effect. Death is not made heroic, and the thought of an → immortality of the → soul that is proper to humanity itself is as alien to the NT as it is to the OT.

In the NT, theological reflection on death has a soteriological basis. → Salvation has taken place in the resurrection of Jesus Christ from the dead. This does not mean that the death of Jesus is a model. The fruit of his death, however, is for all of us. The nature of this fruit is the object of the NT theology of death. → Paul sees death as the consequence of the sin of → Adam (Rom. 5:12-21), and he calls death the wages of sin (Rom. 6:23) in contrast to the gift of eternal life. → Justification is directly linked to the overcoming of death. The NT, then, views turning from God as death and returning to him as → regeneration. But it neither does away with physical death nor spiritualizes the resurrection. The new life involves → hope of the → eschatological overcoming of death as the last enemy (1 Cor. 15:26), which will reveal the → glory of the God who vanquishes the → suffering of every age (Rev. 21:5; → Time and Eternity).

3. Philosophical Aspects

Plato (427-347 B.C.; → Platonism) long influenced philosophical thinking about death with his view of death as the separation of the body and the intelligible soul. When received into Christian theology, this theory gave thinking about death its normative form. For Plato, following the Greek mysteries, death was also a liberation because the immortal soul that makes us human is hampered by the body in its upward ascent. → Gnosticism took up this thought, but because of its esoteric character (→ Esotericism) with its denial of the experience of death, it made little impact on Christian theology, especially as it was in contradiction with the doctrine of → creation. R. Descartes (1596-1650; → Cartesianism) renewed the → dualism of body and soul. For him, death is simply the end of the bodily machine. We see in Descartes the modern attempt to overcome death by means of knowledge and → science (→ Epistemology; Modern Period). I. Kant (1724-1804; → Kantianism) opposed proofs of → immortality (→ God, Arguments for the Existence of) but still regarded immortality as indispensable for → reason because death does not allow happiness to be in proportion to morality. For → idealism, death was the taking up of the individual into the eternity of the spirit.

A change in philosophical thinking about death was prepared by A. Schopenhauer (1788-1860) and S. → Kierkegaard (1813-55), with M. Heidegger (1889-1976). If death is nothingness and the destruction of all meaning, existence for Heidegger finds its authenticity only in the face of death. But French → existentialism protested against treating death as the condition of proper life. Falling victim to death, it thought, proved the absurdity of life. The same is true of → critical theory, which after the → Holocaust treats every attempt to find meaning in death as simply cynical. In opposition to the intolerable thought of allowing destruction the last word, the negative dialectic of T. W. Adorno (1903-69) insisted on the hope of a physical resurrection, though not along Judeo-Christian lines.

4. Theological Aspects

Death is not a proper theme in → dogmatics or an object in confessional statements (→ Confessions and Creeds). It is theologically relevant only in relation to sin, the → last judgment, the resurrection, and so forth. Because it is not a primary theme in → theology, there is openness to its terrible power, which resists all attempts to explain or understand it. No reflection can rob us of the speechlessness that grips us in face of death. Only the gospel of the death of death in the cross and resurrection of Jesus Christ can break through the deadly silence. "Death has been swallowed up in victory. . . . Where, O death, is your sting?" (1 Cor. 15:54-55). Yet the power of death is not negated. It is still the last enemy.

A theology of death cannot for this reason be a theory that puts death at a distance. It is a preparation for dying and a pronouncement of the → promise. Death is still the most serious test case of all theology. M. → Luther's (1483-1546; Luther's Theology) question of finding a gracious God was really a question about death. The irrevocability of death makes the question of sin and judgment especially urgent because death blocks any prospect of removing → guilt. This does not mean that only death gives individual life its true uniqueness and meaning. The risen Lord, not death, is the Lord of life. Death is eschatologically robbed of its power, and so too are → anxiety and → despair. A proof of the → truth (§2) of faith, then, is that it means → consolation in both life and death. Death should neither be disparaged nor made heroic. → Faith can accept it as the end of this life and therefore demands a humane form of dying (*ars moriendi;* → Dying, Aid for the; Euthanasia; Pastoral Care of the Dying).

→ Denominations differ on the question of the state after death and on the → immortality of the soul, which the Orthodox and Roman Catholics accept but some modern Protestant dogmatics does not. The differences are relative, however, for in → Orthodoxy (§3) and → Roman Catholic teaching there is emphasis that the immortality of the soul is not a part of human → nature but is a result of Christ's saving work. The protest against the immortality of the soul is grounded in the protest against making death, → war, → genocide, and the destruction of the → environment (→ Ecology) less harmful, but also individual → grief for dead loved ones makes any belittling of death illegitimate. The anthropological presuppositions of the doctrine of the immortality of the soul are also problematic, for insight into the essential corporeality of life seems to make inconceivable a survival of the soul that has no physical references or means of → communication (→ Anthropology).

It is theologically advisable, then, not to try to say too much about death or the state after death. Christian comfort in face of death can be neither explanation nor doctrine but only reiteration of the promise that "neither death, nor life . . . will be able to separate us from the love of God in Christ Jesus our Lord" (Rom. 8:38-39). In the thinking of the God who raised Christ from the dead, earthly life is preserved and will be reestablished in God's eternity.

Bibliography: G. ALTNER, *Tod, Ewigkeit und Überleben. Todeserfahrung und Todesbewältigung im nachmetaphysischen Zeitalter* (Heidelberg, 1981) • P. ARIÈS, *The Hour of Our Death* (New York, 1981) • H. BECKER et al., eds., *Im Angesicht des Todes. Ein interdisziplinäres Kompendium* (2 vols.; St. Ottilien, 1987) • H. EBELING, *Der Tod in der Moderne* (Königstein, 1979) • H. FRANK, *Leben angesichts des Todes. Beiträge zum theologischen Problem des Todes* (Tübingen, 1968) • S. HAUERWAS, *Naming the Silences: God, Medicine, and the Problem of Suffering* (Grand Rapids, 1990) • J. HICK, *Death and Eternal Life* (2d ed.; London, 1985) • E. JÜNGEL, *Tod* (Stuttgart, 1971) • H. KÜNG, *Eternal Life? Life after Death as a Medical, Philosophical, and Theological Problem* (Garden City, N.Y., 1984) • V. LIDZ et al., "Death," *EncBio* 1.477-523 • K. RAHNER, *On the Theology of Death* (New York, 1973) • G. SCHERER, *Das Problem des Todes in der Philosophie* (Darmstadt, 1979) • W. THIEDE, *Auferstehung der Toten–Hoffnung ohne Attraktivität?* (Göttingen, 1994); idem, *Die mit dem Tod spielen. Okkultismus–Reinkarnation–Sterbeforschung* (Gütersloh, 1994).

WOLFGANG SCHOBERTH

Death, Dance of → Dance Macabre

Death of God Movement → God Is Dead Theology

Death Penalty

1. Biblical Data
2. In Theology and Church History
3. Ethical Reflections

Many peoples and civilizations have had → punishments involving the → death penalty. They usually leave it to a judicial court made up of competent persons who judge publicly according to fair and well-regulated procedures.

1. Biblical Data

Whereas the OT bears witness to the death penalty as an accepted judicial institution, there is little mention of it in the NT.

1.1. Gen. 4:10b-14 tells the relatives of a murdered person to avenge the blood of the dead, which cries out to God for vengeance. They can evade this duty if the slayer flees, but only if the killing has been involuntary or accidental. The history of → Israel (§1) according to the → Pentateuch shows how in-

creasingly and with the proper differentiation a written code replaced family vengeance. Decreeing the death penalty is left to the rulers and taken away from the family or clan. Examples may be found in the Deuteronomic texts.

Revenge for purposeful slaying in Gen. 9:5-6 is enhanced by the "second → law" (§1.2.2) to cover idolatry, blasphemy, severe cases of → Sabbath misuse, rebellion against parents, certain cases of adultery on the part of women (→ Marriage and Divorce 3.2), incest, sodomy, and bestiality as crimes worthy of death. It is important that the people remain pure before → Yahweh and keep themselves from all that might disrupt the covenant relation between God and his people (→ Covenant 1.3.1; cf. Deut. 13:5-11). The lex talionis, or law of eye for eye and tooth for tooth, must be set in this theological context. It is not blind cruelty but a historical step toward a humanization of law. The law cannot act without restraint but must use the offense (→ Evil) as a measure or reference for punishment.

The law of retaliation allows an individualized application of punishment by forbidding the exacting of punishment on innocent people of some other clan. The principle of individual → guilt begins to penetrate both thinking and customs (Deut. 19:21 and Exod. 21:23-25). To prevent other abuses of the death penalty without being untrue to blood revenge, the right of → asylum is also instituted (1 Kgs. 1:50-53; 2:28-35). The prophetic literature (→ Prophet 2) still contains many elements of collective → responsibility but also those that foretell a future of personal responsibility (Jer. 18:21-23; 31:29-30). Later → Judaism became much more reserved in applying the death penalty. Various Sanhedrin sources show that they were proud of applying the death penalty only rarely, if at all.

1.2. Apart from Rom. 13:4, the NT never discusses the death penalty as an ethical problem. It simply mentions its existence (see John 8:1-11). We have here less an instance of new → norms and more a radical questioning of the ideology of blood revenge. The way of thinking that appeals to biological and/or cosmic elements is finally desacralized by the message of → Jesus as we have it in the → Synoptics. We cannot overcome evil by bloodthirsty → force but only by a fellowship of → love that embraces friend and foe like. The → Sermon on the Mount does not negate the lex talionis on casuistic grounds with a new set of norms but replaces it with the forgiving love of God, which makes possible human → forgiveness (Matt. 5:38-39; Luke 6:29-30). The judgment of God (→ Last Judgment) is full of compassion and relativizes every human judgment and the absolute claim related to it (Matt. 7:1-5; Luke 6:37-38, 41-42).

Romans 13 seems to uphold the power of human governments over the life and death of all who break the law. Yet → Paul's purpose here is not to validate the death penalty but to correct Christians who believe that the message of the coming → kingdom of God relieves them of all duties as citizens. He neither maintains nor denies that the death penalty is justified. The Synoptic tradition affirms that with reference to the kingdom of God, Christ did not set his → hope on the powers of avenging justice and the lex talionis but on the power of a renunciation of law. The → righteousness of God drives out the law of revenge in human justice.

2. In Theology and Church History

2.1. In → Tertullian (ca. 160-ca. 225), Minucius Felix (2d/3d cent.), the *Canons of St. Hippolytus* (Hippolytus ca. 170-ca. 236), and Lactantius (ca. 250-ca. 325), we find statements forbidding killing either personally or by the authorities. A historical-critical investigation of these texts underlines their polemical element. These theologians wanted to question both pagan customs and the imperial cult. Expectation of the immediacy of God's kingdom influenced them.

After Constantine the problem of the death penalty had a place in the discourse of political → ethics; the relation between → church and state had now radically changed. The state came to be understood as an *instrumentum regni*, as a possible tool for the coming of the kingdom of God. This relation explains the uncertainty of many theologians regarding the death penalty. → Augustine (354-430; → Augustine's Theology) argued on the basis of Romans 13 that the state has the right to use the sword against evildoers, but the right of life and death should be modified by the intervention of the → bishop. As a new criterion in justifying the death penalty, he claimed that it was the task of the political power to help the church in its fight against heretics (→ Heresies and Schisms).

2.2. In the → Middle Ages we find the older reservations against the death penalty in the division made between spiritual and secular authorities. *Ecclesia non sitit sanguinem* (The church is not bloodthirsty); it must not execute the death penalty directly, but in cases where it is concerned (e.g., heresy), it should leave the carrying out of the sentence to the secular arm. Yet there are signs of a relapse into earlier thinking. In a letter to Bulgaria, Pope Nicholas II (1059-61) expresses thanks that in its laws the Bulgarians have not omitted → torture and the death penalty. The Synod of Rouen in 1190

forbade holding trials that might bring a death penalty in church buildings, as well as warning clergy not to engage in duels or tournaments. The power of the sword was radically unleashed only against heretical groups (e.g., the → Cathari and the → Waldenses).

Academic theology from the 13th century onward (→ Middle Ages 1.3.3) took up the polemic against Waldensian radicalism and gave it a systematic form that would persist in handbooks of all the Christian confessions. → Thomas Aquinas (1224/25-74; → Thomism) went beyond the voluntarist perspective of Augustine and offered a rationalistic and secular evaluation of the problem. "The good of the community surpasses a particular good of the individual. Therefore the particular good must give way, that the common good may be maintained. Now, the life of a few pestilential individuals is a hindrance to the common good, which is the harmony of the human community. Therefore such men should be cut off by death from the society of their fellows" (*Summa c. Gent.* 3.146).

The voluntarist elements of the Augustinian tradition, however, were not forgotten. A reminder of the demand of the divine will in applying the death penalty played an increasing role when Duns Scotus (ca. 1265-1308; → Scotism) opposed the death penalty in matters not covered in the biblical tradition (which included, for example, theft and adultery).

2.3. The → Reformers at times followed the lines set down in the Middle Ages. M. → Luther (1483-1546; → Luther's Theology) dealt with the suspicions that had affected medieval theory and practice. For Luther, the basic flaw in medieval theology was that the → two kingdoms often became confused (*commixtio regnum*). He thus attacked corporal punishment and especially the death penalty against heretics ("Here God's Word must work. If it cannot succeed, neither will the secular power"). U. → Zwingli (1484-1531) and J. → Calvin (1509-64) were not opposed to the execution of heretics, arguing that they were dangerous to the well-being of political society (→ Zwingli's Theology; Calvin's Theology). The arguments of Luther on the death penalty caused R. → Bellarmine (1542-1621; → Church 2.2.7.1) to oppose him in his *Disputationes de controversiis Christianae fidei*.

2.4. The real challenge to the death penalty, and the radical questioning of it, came with the philosophy of the → Enlightenment. Especially the work *Dei delitti e delle pene* (Of crimes and punishments) of C. Beccaria (1738-94) unleashed the controversy throughout Europe and made a vigorous case against the death penalty. The Roman Catholic Church reacted negatively, placing Beccaria's book on the Index (→ Censorship; Inquisition 2). Then in the 19th century F. D. E. → Schleiermacher (1768-1834; → Schleiermacher's Theology) criticized theologically the theory of retribution and the death penalty, regarding it as a demand for → suicide.

In the 20th century sensitivity has grown regarding the issue of the state's moral right to conduct a violent attack on individuals. Yet denominations have produced no basic critique of the death penalty, expressing only opinions about how it should be used. A significant exception was Karl → Barth (1886-1968; → Dialectical Theology), who, unlike the Enlightenment, argued Christologically that after the death of Christ, no atonement or redeeming dimension of punishment is needed, for the works of human atonement cannot add anything to the atoning and redeeming work of the Son of God (→ Soteriology).

3. Ethical Reflections

In discussing the death penalty, the usual arguments relating to the meaning and basis of → punishment (§§1-2) are used, but with added force.

3.1. Those who justify punishment ethically on the ground of its resocializing role (→ Rehabilitation) of making good or compensating obviously cannot defend the moral justice of the death penalty, which clearly proclaims in a bloody way the definitive desocialization of the delinquent. He or she is forcibly removed from human → society without any alternative, unless we view "entry into the fellowship of the saints" as a kind of "socialization a posteriori," which has been done.

3.2. Arguments and justifications on the ground of making any repetition impossible can appeal neither to ethics nor to logic. The irreversible loss of free will (→ Freedom 1.2 and 2.7) certainly means that the delinquent can no longer harm anyone after death, but it is impossible to say whether or not he or she might have committed any further crimes.

3.3. If we expand the argument to include the factors of prevention or general deterrence, the discussion becomes more difficult. We must distinguish here between a normative (i.e., legal and ethical) and an empirical → legitimation. In the latter case empirical research reveals that the death penalty has little deterrent effect. The assurance that might be gained in this way is not great enough to prevent many sociologists from holding a contrary opinion. We should not forget, however, that empirical investigation itself cannot provide the basis for a moral justification or rejection (a so-called naturalistic mistake).

3.4. If the death penalty is defended on the ground that it is a necessary means to enforce "moral order" in an exemplary way, serious difficulties arise. Even if we could prove empirically that the death penalty raises the moral level of a people, this is not enough to prove its necessity, urgency, or moral force. No means are either good or justifiable in achieving an ethically incontestable end. If it is not proved for certain that the death penalty is the only means to achieve peace and security, we should hesitate and perhaps choose less bloody means to attain the same end. This is the practice today in almost all societies in which the political machinery has enough technical means to ensure and guarantee security without resorting to the death penalty.

3.5. There remains the idea of punishment as retribution. This legitimation, which is called absolute, still has various weaknesses and involves the danger of misuse. Misuse appears most clearly when we argue for reasons of state. Ethically it can be used only in case of serious emergency, for example, in a → war of defense into which one is forced. In relation to all these arguments we come up against the irreversible possibility of an error in justice.

Bibliography: P. ALTHAUS, "Die Todesstrafe als Problem der christlichen Ethik," *SBAW*, 1955, 3-35 • H. A. BEDAU, ed., *The Death Penalty in America: Current Controversies* (New York, 1997) • A. BERISTAIN, "Katholizismus und Todesstrafe," *ZGSRW* 27 (1977) 215-38 • F. BOCKLE and J. M. POHIER, eds., *The Death Penalty and Torture* (New York, 1979) • A. BONDOLFI, " 'Ecclesia non sitit sanguinem.' Die Ambivalenz von Theologie und Kirche in der Frage nach der Legitimation der Todesstrafe," *Strafe und Todesstrafe* (Fribourg, 1993) 41-54; idem, *Pena e pena di morte* (Bologna, 1985); "Straftheorien und Strafrechtsbegründungen. Schwierigkeiten einer ethischen Neubesinnung," *ZEE* 27 (1983) 375-90 • H. CANCIK, "Christentum und Todesstrafe. Zur Religionsgeschichte der legalen Gewalt," *Angst und Gewalt. Ihre Präsenz und ihre Bewältigung* (ed. H. Stietenaar; Düsseldorf, 1979) 312-51 • M. GEIGER, G. STRATENWERTH, and H. SANER, *Nein zur Totesstrafe* (Basel, 1978) • M. KRONENWETTER, *Capital Punishment: A Reference Handbook* (Santa Barbara, Calif., 1993) • J. A. McCAFFERTY, comp., *Capital Punishment* (New York, 1974) • S. NATHANSON, *An Eye for an Eye? The Morality of Punishing by Death* (Totowa, N.J., 1987) • H. ROTTER, "Todesstrafe," *KSL* 3056-60 • T. SORELL, "Death Penalty," *EncBio* 1.592-96 • C. W. TRICHE, *The Capital Punishment Dilemma, 1950-1977: A Subject Bibliography* (Troy, N.Y., 1979).

ALBERTO BONDOLFI

Decalogue

1. The Decalogue (Greek for "ten words") has come down to us in the OT in two places: Exod. 20:2-17 and Deut. 5:6-21. It has often been called the classic Decalogue, as distinct from the ethical, or Elohistic, Decalogue in Exod. 34:10-26. In both books the Decalogue shows itself to be an independent entity. This is especially clear in exodus, for the preceding verses in Exodus 19 do not prepare the ground for it, nor do the succeeding verses in 20:18-21 relate to it. They form a transition instead to the → Book of the Covenant that follows. In virtue of the location of the Decalogue in Exodus 20, it is the first and thus the most important expression of the law of God revealed at → Sinai. In Deuteronomy the Decalogue comes in the parting address of → Moses before Israel's entry into the promised land. It is here a decisive expression of the divine command. Deuteronomy is indeed an exposition of the Decalogue.

2. The two versions of the Decalogue are substantially the same in wording, but apart from purely stylistic variations, there are some important differences. Most of them are in the Sabbath commandment.

The version in Deuteronomy contains three additions beyond what appears in Exodus: "as the Lord your God commanded you" (v. 12); "or your ox or your donkey, or any of [your livestock]" (v. 14); and "that your male and female slave may rest as well as you" (v. 14). The beginning is also different, as Exod. 20:8 has *zākôr* (remember), but Deut. 5:12 has *šāmôr* (observe). Most striking is the different reason given for the commandment. Exod. 20:11 refers back to the conclusion of the Priestly creation story (see Gen. 2:2-3) and bases the Sabbath rest on God's own resting after finishing his work of → creation. Deut. 5:15, however, offers a basis in social ethics by referring, as Deuteronomy often does, to Israel's experience of slavery in Egypt.

Other differences occur in the commandment to honor one's parents and the commandment not to covet. In the latter, the order of the words "house" and "wife" is changed. (Does this indicate a higher regard for wives in Deuteronomy?) As a rule, extensions would seem to suggest a later form. But this can hardly apply to the Sabbath commandment, for the Priestly theologoumenon in Exod. 20:11 is surely not as early as the characteristic statement in Deut. 5:15. Hossfeld has thus come to the opposite conclusion that the version in Deuteronomy is older and that the Exodus version has been set alongside it as a deliberate reshaping. It is an open question whether

this thesis will become accepted. It is at any rate noteworthy that so important an OT text is present in two versions with no attempt at reconciliation.

3. Formally the Decalogue is not a unity. In this regard it differs from other collections of apodictic law. One formal difference is that the first part is God's direct speech (Exod. 20:2-6), but in the second part God appears in the third person. Most of the commandments are negative; only the two about the Sabbath and about parents have a positive form. Originally these might have had a negative form as well (but cf. E. Gerstenberger). According to W. H. Schmidt, the transformation into the positive form of the commandments made possible an expansion of their content.

The differing lengths of the commandments call for comment. Three consecutive commandments contain only two words each in the Hebrew (Exod. 20:13-15), whereas the Sabbath commandment spans several verses. The differences in form lead to the conclusion that the Decalogue resulted from a period of development. The process no doubt began, not with what was earlier called an "original Decalogue" *(Urdekalog)*, but with preliminary stages — small groups of two or three members each.

4. The decisive principle in the construction of the Decalogue is that the more specifically theological commandments precede the ethical commandments. The order, however, is not to be understood as implying a ranking among the ten. The distinctive feature of the Decalogue, rather, is the indissoluble relation between the commandments of the so-called first table and those of the so-called second table (on this idea and terminology, see Exod. 24:12; 31:18; 34:1-4; Deut. 10:1-5). Also significant, however, is the preamble that introduces the Decalogue (Exod. 20:2), which provides the theological setting for the commands of the Decalogue. God gives before he demands. He demands as the one who has already shown himself to be the God of liberation.

5. To what period does the Decalogue belong? Authorship by Moses, which earlier was often claimed, is ruled out. Some elements might come from the early nomadic age of Israel. Thus the form of the so-called prohibitives might have been connected with the instruction of the nomadic tribes (Gerstenberger), and some of the short series of prohibitions could be of similar age.

The Decalogue as a whole, however, is later. The → prophets of the eighth century do not explicitly mention it, although Hos. 4:2 seems to show some knowledge of one of its early components. Thus a later preexilic date seems likely (F. Crüsemann). Discussions of the traditions that shaped the individual commandments or groups of commandment point in a similar direction (Schmidt).

6. On the basis of the preamble and the first commandment, which is a norm for all that follows, the Decalogue gives human faith and action a place and direction in a way that is consistent with the whole OT. This does not involve the casuistic restriction of a full list of commandments (note the omissions stressed by Crüsemann) but a focusing on what is essential. Divine and human relations are kept equally in view. The decisive point, however, is that the human task is grounded in the prior divine gift.

Bibliography: C. M. CARMICHAEL, *Law and Narrative in the Bible: The Evidence of the Deuteronomic Laws and the Decalogue* (Ithaca, N.Y., 1985); idem, *The Origins of Biblical Law: The Decalogues and the Book of the Covenant* (Ithaca, N.Y., 1992) • F. CRÜSEMANN, *Bewahrung der Freiheit. Das Thema des Dekalogs in sozialgeschichtlicher Perspektive* (Munich, 1983) • J. DAVIDMAN, *Smoke on the Mountain: An Interpretation of the Ten Commandments* (Philadelphia, 1954) • G. FOHRER, "Das sogenannte apodiktische formulierte Recht und der Dekalog," *KuD* 11 (1965) 49-74 (repr., *Studien zur alttestamentlichen Theologie und Geschichte* [Berlin, 1969] 120-48) • E. GERSTENBERGER, *Wesen und Herkunft des "apodiktischen Rechts"* (Neukirchen, 1965) • F. L. HOSSFELD, *Der Dekalog. Seine späten Fassungen, die originale Komposition und seine Vorstufen* (Freiburg, 1982) • P. L. LEHMANN, *The Decalogue and a Human Future: The Meaning of the Commandments for Making and Keeping Human Life Human* (Grand Rapids, 1995) • L. PERLITT, "Dekalog I," *TRE* 8.408-13 • A. C. J. PHILLIPS, *Ancient Israel's Criminal Law: A New Approach to the Decalogue* (Oxford, 1970) • W. H. SCHMIDT, "Überlieferungsgeschichtliche Erwägungen zur Komposition des Dekalogs," *Congress Volume, Uppsala, 1971* (Leiden, 1972) 201-20 • W. H. SCHMIDT, with H. DELKURT and A. GRAUPNER, *Die Zehn Gebote im Rahmen alttestamentlicher Ethik* (Darmstadt, 1993) • H. SCHÜNGEL-STRAUMANN, *Der Dekalog—Gottes Gebote?* (2d ed.; Stuttgart, 1980) • J. J. STAMM, with M. E. ANDREW, *The Ten Commandments in Recent Research* (2d ed.; London, 1967).

HANS JOCHEN BOECKER

Decree → Calvin's Theology; Predestination

Decretals → Corpus Iuris Canonici

Deification → Theosis

Deism

Until the 18th century, the term "deism" (from Lat. *deus*, a god, God) was interchangeable with → "theism." It was used for the first time by the Swiss theologian P. Viret (Geneva, 1564), who spoke with abhorrence of people who called themselves deists to emphasize that, in contrast to → atheists, they believed in God, even though they accepted nothing of Christ and his teaching. Some writers (e.g., C. Blount and M. Tindal) explicitly confessed deism, but many deists avoided the term because of its negative connotation for their orthodox opponents.

Later, deism increasingly became a philosophical position to the effect that → God is the Creator but then does not intervene in → nature or history. (In a common image, the world is likened to a clock. Both have a creator; once put in motion, each runs perfectly well without further reference to its maker.) Yet this description does not adequately represent the most important views of various authors who, especially in the 17th and 18th centuries, under the impact of changes in scientific and philosophical thinking and in the midst of violent religious controversies, were seeking rational foundations for faith.

This movement reached a climax in England at the end of the 17th century and the beginning of the 18th (Blount and Tindal, and also A. Collins and T. Woolston; see especially the debate about J. Toland's *Christianity Not Mysterious* [1696]). From England the influence of the movement spread to France (Voltaire), Germany (Reimarus), and the United States (T. Paine). It finally collapsed in the 19th century, stripped of its most important presuppositions (i.e., natural → religion and the possibilities of theoretical → reason) by the radical criticism of D. Hume and I. Kant (→ Kantianism).

It has proved almost impossible to define deism in a way that includes all its advocates. Edward Herbert, first Lord Herbert of Cherbury, who is regarded as the father of English deism, proposed five criteria in his work *De veritate* (1624) whereby to distinguish true religion from false. These basic truths, which all "normal" people supposedly share, are (1) the existence of a supreme God, (2) the duty of worshiping God, (3) moral → virtue as the most important element of religious practice, (4) the possibility of atoning for past → sin by penitence, and (5) reward and → punishment in a future life.

Such a list, however, can hardly serve as a common creed for all deists. What unites most of them is trust in reason as an adequate instrument by which to answer religious questions. Deists were critical of the historical phenomena of religion. They sharply attacked all → superstition, all → revelation that could not be tested by reason, ecclesiastical → authority, the → priesthood, intolerance (→ Tolerance), and religious persecution.

Positively, deists tried to construct a natural religion that would be free from all superstition and self-evident to all people who think rationally. This would serve as a test for Christianity and lead back to the original religion of Christ — or it would totally replace it. Decisive in this regard was their belief in an autonomous morality that is independent of revelation (→ Ethics), common to all people, and the instrument of what is in some cases vehement criticism of the Bible (e.g., in Voltaire).

Bibliography: G. GAWLICK, "Der Deismus als Grundzug des Religionsphilosophie der Aufklärung," *Hermann Samuel Reimarus (1694-1768)* (Göttingen, 1973) • P. GAY, *Deism: An Anthology* (Princeton, 1968) • G. V. LECHLER, *Geschichte des englischen Deismus* (2 vols.; Stuttgart, 1841; repr., Hildesheim, 1965) • H. M. MORAIS, *Deism in Eighteenth Century America* (New York, 1934) • H. REVENTLOW, *The Authority of the Bible and the Rise of the Modern World* (Philadelphia, 1984) 289-410 • H. SCHOLZ, "Zur ältesten Begriffsgeschichte von Deismus und Pantheismus," *PrJ* 142 (1910) 318ff. • L. STEPHEN, *A History of English Thought in the Eighteenth Century* (2 vols.; London, 1876; repr., New York, 1963) 1.74-277 • R. E. SULLIVAN, *John Toland and the Deist Controversy: A Study in Adaptations* (Cambridge, Mass., 1982) • N. TORREY, *Voltaire and the English Deists* (Hamden, Conn., 1967; orig. pub., 1930) • E. TROELTSCH, "Der Deismus," *Gesammelte Schriften* (vol. 4; Tübingen, 1925) 429-87.

RUURD VELDHUIS

Delegation

Delegation is the handing over of tasks to another person (the delegate) to discharge on his or her own responsibility. This may be done in a general way, as when a Catholic bishop commits questions of penance (→ Confession of Sins) or → marriage to priests, or in special cases, as when a parish priest leaves a matter to an assistant. Roman Catholic → canon law lays down rules for delegation (1983 CIC 131-42), and the church may step in when mistakes are made or substantial doubts arise (can. 144).

In Protestant church law, delegation occurs particularly in → occasional services when, at the request of those concerned, one who is not the regular minister of the Word acts instead of the local pastor. In such cases, appropriate notice must be secured from the latter (→ Dimissorial).

Bibliography: W. AYMANS, *Kanonisches Recht* (Paderborn, 1991) 425-35.

ALBERT STEIN

Democracy

1. Term and History
2. Concepts and Problems
    2.1. Modern Problems
    2.2. The Concept of Substantive Democracy
    2.3. The Concept of Formal Democracy
    2.4. Democratization
3. Democracy and Christianity

1. Term and History

The term "democracy," which comes from ancient Greece, literally means "rule by the people." In political → philosophy, democracy was viewed as a form of government. It stood between aristocracy (the rule of the elite) and the negatively viewed ochlocracy (mob rule; Aristotle *Pol.*).

Classical Greece — or more narrowly the city-state of Athens in the fifth and fourth centuries B.C. up to its subjugation by Philip II of Macedonia and the end of its independence in 338 B.C. — ranked as a model democracy. In Athens male citizens had the right to vote at popular assemblies that made political decisions. The sphere of political decisions embraced potentially all areas of social life. There was no sharing of power in the modern sense, nor did the popularly elected executive make use of any → bureaucratic machinery. This was a → society that acted by word of mouth, everyone knew everyone else, and almost every citizen (→ Bourgeois, Bourgeoisie) at some time held some public office in the city *(polis)*.

The limits of this direct democracy, in which all were potentially informed and competent and in which the place of assembly (i.e., the agora) was easily and on short notice accessible, were as follows. This was a purely male democracy. It also rested in part on → slavery and on an economy supported by residents who were not recognized as full citizens. It existed as the center of a loose area of trade and government.

Nevertheless, this first recognized and self-styled democracy in history can still teach us many things about political theory and citizen participation (M. J.

Finley, C. Meier). Undoubtedly in other cultures as well (e.g., in early Europe) a high measure of general participation characterized other political forms, even greater than that in classical Athens. Primitive societies and their modern offshoots offer many examples (S. Diamond, F. Kramer, and C. Sigrist). In early and medieval European history there were numerous movements and uprisings that sought more participation by those who had neither property nor noble rank, or any other enhancement of power.

Though we can learn from this history "from below," and especially from primitive societies and their forms of association that have no special centers of power, it is by no means accidental that the idea and reality of democracy were more or less lost for 2,000 years in the "world history of Europe" (H. Freyer). Apart from the classical model, it was only in modern times in Europe, from the 18th and 19th centuries, that democracy became a positive, if contested, political concept. Now clear demands for democracy are widespread. In the 20th century it has become an almost universal test of the legitimacy of all government (J. Dunn).

2. Concepts and Problems

There are various reasons why democracy was so late in becoming a leading concept in political debate and a benchmark of political organization. Government now extends over wider areas and has become more concentrated (N. Elias 1976). Forms of economic production change. The capitalist-industrial mode of production (→ Capitalism), which helps to promote the modern → state and vice versa, demands more regulation and mobilization. With universal → secularization and rationalization, the problem of the justification of government and inequality arises afresh. The participation of the people, which is now economically and militarily more important, has become in part a requirement and even more so a demand of groups that have broken free from traditional ties and acquired a new self-consciousness — first the middle class, and then the → proletariat. Democracy, which became a guiding concept in the 18th and 19th centuries, faces quantitatively and qualitatively greater problems at the end of the 20th century.

2.1. *Modern Problems*

The first problem is that of size. How can the people (i.e., all adults) participate in making regular choices and decisions in societies that number millions of citizens spread over large areas, and in which a host of decisions must be made daily because of the complex interaction of the multifarious workforce and an economy oriented to exchange? The citizens cannot all meet in a popular assembly, nor can they all take part in every decision. Even in political decisions there must be sharing. But this situation leads to political inequality, for instead of the people ruling themselves, there arises rule by representatives.

A related problem is that of competence. Is it possible that all should be informed about every question and thus equipped to make complex decisions? Do we not need professional politicians and a political machine? But what if these achieve autonomy and become, in effect, an oligarchy and a self-standing → bureaucracy?

A third, related problem is that democracy is demanded and developed as a form of the modern state, but no matter what form this state might take, "it commands a monopoly of legitimate physical force" (M. → Weber). By means of the bureaucracy in general, and the military and the police in particular, it issues sanctions that threaten to undermine democracy by superior force and by the power of regulation. It has always been a mark of bureaucracy, the military, and the police that they are not structured democratically. Can democratic quality be achieved, then, by normative and controlling bodies of this kind?

A fourth problem is that of the sphere of democracy. Democracy is not only a form of the state that does not prevent this state monopoly of power. It also — to the extent it is actualized today — occurs in capitalist societies, where democratic decision making typically applies only in matters of government. According to a mistaken belief, only such areas are truly political. The economic system and many other social processes are regarded as private and thus beyond the reach of the democratic will. But can democracy arise or persist if society as a whole is not organized on democratic principles? For this reason those who draw up the program of the → labor movement demand both → socialism and democracy, that is, the socializing of the economy in the sense of economic self-determination for direct producers (i.e., the workers). But even in countries that pride themselves on being socialistic, this goal has not been achieved. The two main concepts of democratic orientation try to solve these problems in different ways.

2.2. *The Concept of Substantive Democracy*

The best-known pioneer of this approach is J.-J. Rousseau (1712-78), who began his *Social Contract*, "Man is born free; and everywhere he is in chains." To secure human freedom again in civilization, what is needed is the only legitimate form of government — self-government. The people's government of itself, averse to every form of representation, demands its consistent participation in all planning and decision making, and also in the overturning of decisions. Four things are thus necessary.

First, all social spheres must be democratized. Where greater organizations are unavoidable, there must be democracy within parties and societies.

Second, if society at large cannot be split up in principle, then it must be divided into several small areas that are as autonomous and self-governing as possible so that a high measure of direct democracy is possible. This is the constant goal. All delegation must justify itself. With the dividing of society into autonomous spheres, we can change many social relations that otherwise are undemocratic.

Third, democratically excluded spheres, especially bureaucracy and the apparatus of monopoly, must be returned to democratic control.

Fourth, where common decisions are unavoidable, there must be added protection for minorities, and the process of decision by majorities must be supplemented by other forms of expressing the democratic will (e.g., with plebiscites). The demands of this concept lead to "daring more democracy" (W. Brandt), as well as to aiding the orientation of society toward its roots.

Difficulties arise in practical matters. Organizationally, it is hard to see how participation can be preserved on the abstract level of reaching decisions (social synthesis) or how the development of political hierarchies can be avoided except at the price of inefficiency and local dependence.

2.3. *The Concept of Formal Democracy*

This view is largely followed in the Western democracies (E. Fraenkel). Ideologically, its proponents follow Montesquieu's (1689-1755) idea of the balance of powers, as well as the principle of representation, which traces back to J. Locke (1632-1704) and E. Burke (1729-97). In view of the problems mentioned earlier, this concept holds that direct democracy is impossible and even dangerous. It does not work in larger areas in which important and difficult matters require decision. The same holds true even in the individual professional sphere. Direct democracy leads easily to totalitarianism, for the incompetent → masses are easily led astray.

Essentially, then, democracy is simply a process for appointing political leaders. It is best to characterize it as "temporary rule" (T. Heuss). The people have a voice in periodic elections, in which they vote for candidates who are picked in various ways, usually by the → political parties. For the rest, the representatives decide policy (J. A. Schumpeter 1950), but only in matters of state.

Other decisions are governed by the politically valid principle of the market (i.e., competition) and by the guarantee that a plurality of participants will be maintained. Politically, this means that along with free elections there must be a system of two or more parties and the possibility of organization in favor of various interests. Otherwise, a simple division is made between professional politicians and private citizens, who awaken from their nonpolitical slumbers only when elections are held.

Proponents of this more realistic view, which limits democracy to a few ground rules, resist any excessive demands made of a representative democracy, as it is now called, by popular groups. Reforming proposals relate to the correction of representative institutions.

The problem with this concept is that it can lead to a greatly attenuated idea of democracy. In particular, there is the very present danger that the very narrow process of forming the representative will can easily be overwhelmed by a public and private bureaucracy. The representatives also seem to be so far above the represented that the gulf between them can be bridged only through stereotypical preconceptions or mass media.

2.4. *Democratization*

Where it is held that democracy is practiced today, there is an unmistakable tendency for it to become no more than "politics as ritual" (M. Edelman), a propagandist formula of legitimation, a process that serves the disenfranchising of citizens rather than their participation. If, however, there is to be any possibility of peacefully resolving issues that cause conflict between societies or within a single society, it seems that an extension of democracy is indispensable. The more abstractly organizational the government becomes in economically and technologically highly developed countries, the more the arrogance and irresponsibility of power grow, no matter who the representatives are, and the more helpless and dependent citizens become, who end up viewing politics only as a matter of prejudice.

Democracy, however, is not necessary merely to avoid the solutions of conflicts by force. Democracy is the demand of the hour from the standpoint of human rights. It is needed equally in every land. For even if → human rights take specific cultural forms, it is only democratically that they are possible. If democracy does not orient itself to human rights and all other valid rights, if it does not try to put them into practice, then it degenerates into an external mechanism, into an → ideology that gives a false sense of legitimacy.

A warning must be issued against the material

forces that representatives of the formal concept of democracy accept too readily, in a way that favors the rule of the elite, as though they were beyond the reach of social regulation. Mostly it is just a matter of protecting strongly vested interests. Greater decentralization and extended participation have yet to be tested. It would be worth making the experiment, even though it would not be fully successful and could not be undertaken without conflict. For the possibility of achieving human rights peacefully at the political level does not lie with a world government but with the overthrowing of inequality within given local societies and, even more so, between different societies. Enhanced participation would be a good place to start.

Bibliography: S. DIAMOND, Kritik der Zivilisation. Anthropologie und die Wiederentdeckung der Primitiven (Frankfurt, 1976) • J. DUNN, Western Political Theory in the Face of the Future (Cambridge, 1979) • M. EDELMANN, Politik als Ritual (Frankfurt, 1978) • N. ELIAS, Über den Prozeß der Zivilisation (2 vols.; Frankfurt, 1976) • J. B. ELSHTAIN, Democracy on Trial (New York, 1995) • M. J. FINLEY, Antike und moderne Demokratie (Stuttgart, 1980) • B. GUGGENBERGER and C. OFFE, eds., Grenzen der Mehrheitsdemokratie (Frankfurt, 1984) • F. KRAMER and C. SIGRIST, eds., Gesellschaften ohne Staat (2 vols.; Frankfurt, 1978) • C. B. MACPHERSON, Vergangenheit und Zukunft der liberalen Demokratien (Frankfurt, 1983) • C. MEIER, Die Entstehung des Politischen bei den Griechen (Frankfurt, 1983) • W.-D. NARR and F. NASCHOLD, Theorie der Demokratie (Stuttgart, 1971) • E. A. PURCELL JR., The Crisis of Democratic Theory: Scientific Naturalism and the Problem of Value (Lexington, Ky., 1973) • J. A. SCHUMPETER, Kapitalismus, Sozialismus und Demokratie (Bern, 1950) • A. DE TOCQUEVILLE, Democracy in America (orig. pub., 1835-40).

WOLF-DIETER NARR

3. Democracy and Christianity

The theme of democracy arose with Christianity — at first only implicitly — as it made its way into the world of peoples and through the epochs of history. Primitive Christianity was subject to three forces. In the old covenant the people had a sovereign charge from God to set up judges and officials and to base all order on the law that God had given. The older Israelite → theocracy, however, undoubtedly had democratic features. The → monarchy, which came under prophetic criticism, was also the product of a divinely concluded → covenant that "the whole assembly made . . . with the king" (2 Chr. 23:3).

Second, classical Athenian democracy (see 1) en-

trusted power to all citizens and decided all important questions at least once a month by majority vote. Although it had largely decayed by NT times, it was preserved theoretically in the Aristotelian typology of government.

Finally, the world power of Rome, under which Christianity developed, had dismantled its democratic elements or institutions and transformed itself into an imperial monarchy.

In the NT, government and reality were reflected in the sign of the → kingdom of God, which comes with Christ, and for this reason concrete recommendations for the conduct of the community with respect to existing political authorities predominated (Rom. 13:1-7). Nevertheless, the inner structure of the community as a reflection of the heavenly polis became the norm for human life together as renewed by God in Christ (Mark 10:42-43). In this life → righteousness, → freedom, → peace, brotherly → love, and service were dominant as epitomizing life with Christ.

The community of free adults called itself by the term ekklēsia, which in the cities of late antiquity was the word for the people's self-determination. This ecclesia, or → church, was the gathering of God's people in each place. Christ was the head, and its life was regulated by various charisms and offices (→ Charisma; Offices, Ecclesiastical). Precisely this open structure, and the lack of any broad theoretical basis, exposed the church after Constantine to various governmental and hierarchical influences (→ Early Church). These in turn continually provoked countermovements or individual critics that kept the theme of democracy alive as a political and ecclesiastical problem.

In the High Middle Ages the development of partially democratic city constitutions gave concrete form to Christian motifs that derived from the tradition of the ancient polis and Jerusalem and that had crystallized for the first time in the idea of the civitas Dei (→ Augustine; Augustine's Theology). The acceptance of Aristotle (→ Aristotelianism; Scholasticism) and the general theological use of ancient sources led, esp. in → Thomas Aquinas (1224/25-74), to the development of a Christian political → ethics that increasingly expressed democratic ideas and brought them into union with the lex divina.

Popular sovereignty as well as the framework of local meetings and elections was put under the rule that what concerns all must be considered and approved by all. This approach strengthened parliamentary and conciliar movements and the freedom of cities beginning in the 13th century. In 1275 and 1295 Edward I of England summoned parliaments.

Marsilius of Padua and William of Ockham supported the idea of democratic legitimacy. Nicholas of Cusa (1401-64) laid it down as a theological principle that even after the fall, all have equal rights and are equally free by nature, so that law and government achieve legitimacy only by election and consent (→ Natural Law).

Later Spanish Scholasticism, centered at the University of Salamanca (Francisco de Vitoria, Navarrus, Covarruvias, and F. Vásquez), established in the 16th century the constitutional, political form of the modern idea of legitimacy by natural law. Cross-connections with the → Reformation, especially → Calvinism, have been demonstrated (E. Reibstein). T. → Beza, J. → Calvin's colleague and successor in the Geneva church and in the French Reformation, combined the traditions of the Bible and natural law in his *De iure magistratum* (1579), thereby making possible a strict theological and ethical grounding of popular sovereignty, government by consent, and human rights.

Reformed theology from the time of U. → Zwingli and Calvin, by actualizing the biblical idea of the covenant *(mutua obligatio;* → Covenant 3) and a binding concept of the congregation, helped to establish democratic principles (Beza, Danaeus, Cocceius). M. → Luther's biblical understanding led him to the royal priesthood of all believers (shaped in part by conciliar ideas), to the theology of Christian liberty, and to the cooperation of the justified in the orders of state, economy, and church. Education and culture thus should lead to the point where ordinary people and those of lowly birth should be able to rule (WA 30.367.4ff. and 576.4ff.). The *politia Christi* seeks the transforming of the existing order into God's kingdom. This view leads to a political ethics that is shaped by the concept of office, though this position could be only partially maintained in the age that followed.

J. Althusius (1557-1638), H. Grotius (1583-1645), and S. Pufendorf (1632-94) are the most important representatives of a political doctrine of natural law under Reformation influence that helped to shape the principles of → human dignity and popular sovereignty, along with democratic institutions. John Wise of Ipswich, Massachusetts (pastor 1680-1725), who was influenced by Pufendorf, regarded the democratic constitution of his own Congregational church (→ Congregationalism) as the original form for a state and the one best suited to political order. He had a decisive impact on the development of the American constitution. The influence of this document on the French declaration of human rights has been well documented.

Democratic movements in Germany (esp. 1815-48) enjoyed strong theoretical and theological support (e.g., from I. Kant and F. D. E. → Schleiermacher; note → religious socialism and the Evangelical Social Congress). F. Naumann (1860-1919), E. → Troeltsch (1865-1923), and A. Harnack (1851-1930) helped to shape the Weimar democracy. Yet the church authorities and denominational groupings (F. J. Stahl; cf. the encyclicals of → Leo XIII) rejected modern democracy on philosophical grounds; they saw it as incompatible with the idea of a supreme order validated by God himself. A. Vilmar could even interpret democracy apocalyptically as a sign of the end time.

After the → Barmen Declaration (see esp. theses 3-5) the Fraternal Councils of the → Confessing Church brought a fresh orientation, as did → Vatican II in the → Roman Catholic Church. K. → Barth (1886-1968) established "an affinity between the Christian community and the civil community of free peoples." The recognition that democracy had essentially developed apart from Christianity (although influenced by it) posed the task of constructive appropriation and promotion, especially in a movement from the informal to the social constitutional state (E. Wolf, H. Simon). The theme of economic democracy that Naumann had espoused was developed in social ethics in terms of codetermination, the humanity of → work, and → social partnership (H. D. Wendland, H. Rich).

The demand arose for a democratizing of the church as an implication of the priesthood of all believers and of Barmen (which described the church as a community of brothers and sisters). The official church hesitantly responded by increasing the participation of the laity and introducing elections. → Lay movements in all denominations pressed for Christian rights in analogy to human rights, including the right of access to the faith and the right to → unity, → love, freedom of conscience and opinion, personal integrity, → equality, and participation in decision making. Democratic structures of church order and a congregational structure that emphasizes communication correspond to a → people's church in this sense. Along these lines, the inner order of the congregation might assume exemplary significance for constitutional democracy at the state level.

→ Church and State; Social Ethics

Bibliography: C. Bäumler, *Kommunikative Gemeindepraxis. Eine Untersuchung ihrer Bedingungen von Möglichkeiten* (Munich, 1984) • G. E. Davie, *The Democratic Intellect* (Edinburgh, 1961) • A. A. T. Ehrhardt, *Politische Metaphysik von Solon bis Augustin* (2 vols.; Tübingen, 1959) • *Evangelische Kirche und freiheitliche Demokratie–eine Denkschrift der EKD* (Gütersloh, 1985) • W. HUBER and H. E. TÖDT, *Menschenrechte. Perspektiven einer menschlichen Welt* (2d ed.; Stuttgart, 1978) • R. J. NEUHAUS, *The Naked Public Square* (Grand Rapids, 1986) • M. NOVAK, *The Spirit of Democratic Capitalism* (New York, 1982) • E. REIBSTEIN, *Johannes Althusius als Fortsetzer der Schule von Salamanca. Untersuchungen zur Ideengeschichte des Rechtsstaats und zur altprotestantischen Naturrechtslehre* (Karlsruhe, 1955) • G. SCHARF-FENORTH, "Politik bei Luther. Römer 13 in der Geschichte des politischen Denkens" (Diss., Heidelberg, 1967) • Q. SKINNER, *The Foundation of Modern Political Thought* (2 vols.; Cambridge, 1978) • T. STROHM and H. D. WENDLAND, eds., *Kirche und moderne Demokratie* (Darmstadt, 1970); idem, eds., *Politik und Ethik* (Darmstadt, 1969) • H. E. TÖDT, "Demokratie I," *TRE* 8.434-52 • H. WELZEL, *Naturrecht und Materiale Gerechtigkeit* (4th ed.; Göttingen, 1962).

THEODOR STROHM

Democratic Republic of the Congo → Zaire

Demons

As personal spiritual beings of varied origin, midway between divine and human beings, demons appear in the mythologies both of the so-called → tribal religions and of the great world religions (→ Hinduism; Buddhism; Islam), though their significance differs in the two cases. Fundamentally, they are morally ambivalent, but they belong for the most part to the sphere of → evil, and in this sense they have a harmful influence on humans, animals, and nature. To ward off their influence, the religions use various rites and techniques that break their power, including → magic, → fasting, and especially → exorcism. These means can be either preventive (e.g., powerful amulets that hold demons at bay) or therapeutic (e.g., the direct driving out of demons). The idea that demons are a personal representation of evil expresses the conviction that evil is a cosmic force that rules over humanity and nature and is not a constituent part of them.

The Judeo-Christian tradition also finds a place for demons. In this framework their significance can be adequately grasped only when we take into account the dominant → monotheism and specific → eschatology.

In contrast to the surrounding Canaanite world, OT → Israel lay under the claim of the first commandment (Exod. 20:2-3) and thus was prohibited from making representations of demons. Instead, the demonic was consistently integrated into the belief in Yahweh, so that the God of Israel was the author of both good and bad. Sometimes in ancient traditional writings there lurks the figure of a demon (e.g., Gen. 32:22-32), and certain rites very likely initially had an apotropaic character (e.g., the sprinkling of the doorposts with blood, Exod. 12:7, 13, 22-23) or presuppose a specific concept of demons (e.g., a possible sacrifice to the desert demon Azazel as the basis of the offering of the scapegoat at Yom Kippur, Lev. 16:8, 10, 26). Strict faith in Yahweh, however, so overlaid any demonic background as to empty it of all significance. Many amulets have been found, however, which enable us to conclude that a belief in demons was more active in the popular religion of Israel than the canonical tradition would lead us to suppose.

As distinct from the earlier OT tradition, the situation changes in the postexilic period and the age of early Judaism. With the development of an → apocalyptic view of the world and history, ideas arose about demons and their influence on people and on the course of history, even though demons were seldom named individually (an exception is the wicked demon Asmodeus in Tob. 6:16-17). Particularly in connection with → dualistic conceptions (→ Qumran), demons become the opponents of God and his → angels (1QS 3:13/4:26). Satan (or Belial) is now the head of the demons.

Apart from these theological ideas, the intertestamental writings tell us little about the existing beliefs in demons in the popular religion of the Jews. Early Jewish conceptions of demons survive in the Talmudic period. The most common terms for "demon" in the Jerusalem → Talmud are *mazzîkîm*, *šēdîm*, and *rûḥôt*. There is no uniform view of their origin (the fall, the Tower of Babel, God), but Satan is still the head of these adversaries of God. Demons are invisible and dwell in the atmosphere. They particularly like unclean places (burial grounds, toilets, drains), and they congregate under palm trees. The night is when they are active. They harm people, but incantations and magic can offer protection against them. For the rabbis, obedience to the Torah and → prayer are the most effective weapons against demons. The ideas of the Talmud survive in the medieval → cabala, but an effort is now made to arrive at a systematic demonology. Some non-Jewish elements have been adopted, including popular Arab, Christian, German, and Slavic beliefs.

When the authors of the NT speak about demons *(daimonia)*, they presuppose the ideas about demons that were current in the Jewish world of their day. For them, demons stand between God and humans; they are opponents of the former and harmful to the latter. (Acts 17:18 is an exception, for there, in an allusion to the trial of Socrates, alien, non-Athenian gods are meant.) In a hierarchical order, the demons are subject to the devil *(diabolos)*, or Satan *(satanas)*. On one occasion Beelzebul is called their chief *(archōn,* Matt. 12:24). They attack people and take possession of them. They cause illnesses (Mark 1:32-34 and par.; Matt. 9:32-34; 12:22-24 and par.) or destroy the → self, so that it is finally they who speak through those possessed by them (Luke 4:33-37 and par.).

The decisive point in the NT understanding is that the NT speaks about demons from an eschatological standpoint. In the Synoptic Gospels → Jesus confronts demons as the end-time emissary of God. His work in casting out demons is a sign of the imminent coming of God's kingdom (Matt. 12:28 and par.). Logically, the → disciples too, in their eschatological mission, have power to drive out demons (Matt. 10:1-16 and par.). Ephesians proclaims the exalted Christ as Lord over all powers, both in this world and in the world to come (1:20-22).

With reference to the NT message, Christian theologians — making use of mythological speech — can speak about demons only in broken fashion. On the one hand, they must take their destructive power seriously and see in them the working of transpersonal evil. On the other hand, they must publish the claim of the → gospel that Christ's own claim to lordship has shattered their power. Christian missionary proclamation in religious areas dominated by demons thus can always be a liberating proclamation. → Preaching takes away people's → anxiety. → Pastoral care to the possessed or to those suffering from the powerful constraints of → superstition must take the form of a promise that → faith in Christ means God's deliverance from evil.

Bibliography: O. Böcher, *Christus exorcista* (Stuttgart, 1972); idem, *Dämonenfurcht und Dämonenabwehr* (Stuttgart, 1970) • C. Colpe et al., "Geister, Dämonen, Engel," *RAC* 9.546-797 • R. Detweiler and W. G. Doty, *The Daemonic Imagination: Biblical Text and Secular Story* (Atlanta, 1990) • W. Kasper et al., eds., *Teufel, Dämonen, Besessenheit. Zur Wirklichkeit des Bösen* (Mainz, 1978) • H. A. Kelly, *The Evil, Demonology, and Witchcraft* (New York, 1968) • E. Langton, *Essentials of Demonology* (London, 1949) • M. Limbeck, "Die Wurzeln der biblischen Auffassung vom Teufel und den Dämonen," *Conc(D)* 11 (1975) 161-68 • H. Mode, *Fabeltiere und Dämonen* (2d ed.;

Leipzig, 1977) • B. Noack, *Satanás und Sotería. Untersuchungen zur neutestamentlichen Dämonologie* (Copenhagen, 1948).

Wolfgang G. Röhl

Demythologizing

In 1941 Rudolf Bultmann (1884-1976) wrote a programmatic essay "Neues Testament und Mythologie. Das Problem der Entmythologisierung der neutestamentlichen Verkündigung" (NT and mythology. The problem of demythologizing the NT proclamation). Only after World War II, however, did a full-scale discussion — often embittered — of demythologizing take place. Other themes have replaced it now; it is no longer a main subject of ecclesiastical and theological debate. For the foreseeable future, however, it will undoubtedly be recognized as an important theological issue.

According to Bultmann, the presentation of the event of salvation, which is the true content of NT proclamation, is in terms of an outdated, mythical → worldview of the NT to which we can no longer return. Examples of mythical accounts are the stories of Christ's descent into → hell and ascension (→ Heaven), the expectation of the returning Son of Man (→ Parousia), and a doctrine like that of substitutionary → atonement with its "primitive" and "outmoded" concepts of God, → guilt, and → righteousness. But we are not to eliminate mythical ideas. → Myth speaks in worldly terms about the unworldly, in human terms about the gods. Rather, we are to interpret myth according to its true purpose, inquiring into the view of existence that it expresses. In its real intention, demythologizing is a mode of interpretation, which, following M. Heidegger (1889-1976), Bultmann calls existential interpretation.

Although widely misunderstood, existential interpretation is for Bultmann not just a method suggested by myth but the hermeneutical principle by which to understand all texts, including those that are not mythological. Whereas the existential interpretation of Heidegger seeks to bring to light the general structures of being within a basic → ontology, that of Bultmann is an interpretation of texts — especially demythologizing as the interpretation of mythological texts — based on Heidegger.

A more fundamental issue is whether Bultmann's methodology presupposes Heidegger's philosophy. The introduction to Bultmann's book on Jesus, which Bultmann wrote before he "knew anything about Heidegger or his philosophical ideas" (as he stated in a letter to the author dated June 5, 1971), gives evidence already of his mode of existential interpretation. One suspects that the philosophy of W. Dilthey (1833-1911) influenced some of the passages in it.

When Bultmann states that the critical research of the 19th century eliminated NT mythology but that our task today is critically to interpret it, this is not entirely correct. I. Kant (1724-1804) in his work on religion (pp. 106-14) had already offered a kind of existential interpretation of the NT idea of substitutionary atonement. D. F. Strauss (1808-74), in §145 of *Das Leben Jesu* (The life of Jesus), had taken up this approach and given it a Hegelian twist. In opposition to rationalistic historicizing → exegesis (§2), he had also noted the constitutive significance of myth and the need to interpret it.

Much of the attack on Bultmann's theology of demythologizing failed to see its philosophical basis, especially in Heidegger's philosophy. But precisely in this failure there comes to light a sense that in Bultmann's distinction between "existential" and "existentiell" interpretation — the former in terms of the underlying view of human existence and the latter in terms of the personal application — there lies the true problem of reliance on Heidegger. Basic criticism of Heidegger's *Being and Time* (→ Existentialism) would have to ask whether the purely existential approach in the first sense does not involuntarily carry with it elements of the second, the "existentiell." Much of the misunderstanding of demythologizing is probably due to the fact that Bultmann did not fully think through this distinction. Fresh attention to this point would perhaps give new systematic worth to the little-noted discussion between Karl Jaspers and Bultmann (see H.-W. Bartsch, vol. 3). Shortsighted criticism such as the unjust charge of "individualistic restriction" in demythologizing (e.g., by D. Sölle) carries little weight.

For a time, a branch of Bultmann's school (esp. through E. Fuchs and G. Ebeling) gained a hearing as it continued the program with borrowings from the later Heidegger (e.g., *Unterwegs zur Sprache* [On the way to language]). In this New Hermeneutics, exposition is no longer oriented to the understanding of existence but to → language. We do not expound the text, including the text of myth; the text expounds us. In this regard Fuchs refers to the language-event, Ebeling to the word-event. Some American theologians took up this program, especially J. M. Robinson, J. B. Cobb Jr. (who spoke of the cultural conditioning of all statements), and A. Wilder (language-event and speech as meaning).

The New Hermeneutics, however, gained little support. Modern hermeneutical discussion, insofar as hermeneutically intended procedures are practiced at all, follows the French approach, in which the introduction of psychoanalytic (P. Ricoeur) and structuralist (C. Lévi-Strauss) elements not only epistemologically broadens the interpretation of myth but also assumes that Bultmann's whole putting of the question has been decisively outdated.

Certain essays in the Bultmann *Gedenkschrift* of 1984 probed into Bultmann's program with commendable depth (see Hübner 1985). Theological discussion would be enriched at a central point if attention were paid to them.

→ Hermeneutics

Bibliography: G. Backhaus, *Kerygma und Mythos bei David Friedrich Strauss und Rudolf Bultmann* (Hamburg-Bergstedt, 1956) • H.-W. Bartsch et al., eds., *Kerygma und Mythos* (6 vols.; Hamburg-Bergstedt, 1948ff.) • R. Bultmann, *Jesus Christ and Mythology* (New York, 1958); idem, "NT and Mythology" (1941) and "On the Problem of Demythologizing" (1952), *NT and Mythology and Other Basic Writings* (ed. S. M. Ogden; Philadelphia, 1984) 1-43 and 95-130 • M. van Esbroeck, *Hermeneutik, Strukturalismus und Exegese* (Munich, 1968) on P. Ricoeur and C. Lévi-Strauss • E. Fuchs, *Programm der Entmythologisierung* (3d ed.; Bad Cannstadt, 1967); idem, *Zum hermeneutischen Problem in der Theologie* (2d ed.; Tübingen, 1965) • G. Gloege, *Mythologie und Luthertum. Recht und Grenze der Entmythologisierung* (3d ed.; Göttingen, 1963) • E. M. Good, "The Meaning of Demythologization," *The Theology of Rudolf Bultmann* (ed. C. W. Kegley; New York, 1966) 21-40 • M. Heidegger, *On the Way to Language* (New York, 1982; orig. pub., 1959) • H. Hübner, *Biblische Theologie des Neuen Testaments* (3 vols.; Göttingen, 1990-95); idem, *Politische Theologie und existentiale Interpretation. Zur Auseinandersetzung Dorothee Sölles mit Rudolf Bultmann* (Witten, 1973); idem, "Rückblick auf dem Bultmann-Gedenkjahr," *TLZ* 110 (1985) 641-52; idem, "Rudolf Bultmanns Herkunft und Hin-Kunft," *TLZ* 120 (1995) 3-22 • M. Huppenbauer, *Mythos und Subjektivität. Aspekte neutestamentlicher Entmythologisierung im Anschluß an Rudolf Bultmann und Georg Picht* (Tübingen, 1992) • B. Jaspert, ed., *Bibel und Mythos. Fünfzig Jahre nach Rudolf Bultmanns Entmythologisierungsprogramm* (Göttingen, 1991); idem, ed., *Rudolf Bultmanns Werk und Wirkung* (Darmstadt, 1984) • R. A. Johnson, *The Origins of Demythologizing: Philosophy and Historiography in the Theology of Rudolf Bultmann* (Leiden, 1974) • G. Jones, *Bultmann: Towards a Critical Theology* (Oxford, 1991) • O. Kaiser, ed., *Gedenken an Rudolf Bultmann* (Tübingen, 1977) • I. Kant, *Religion within the Limits of Reason Alone* (trans. T. M. Greene and H. H.

Hudson; New York, 1960; orig. pub., 1793) • J. MAC-QUARRIE, *The Scope of Demythologizing* (New York, 1960) • R. MARLÉ, *Bultmann et l'interprétation du Nouveau Testament* (Aubier, 1956) on which see R. Bultmann, *Glauben und Verstehen* 3.178-89 • J. M. ROBINSON and J. B. COBB JR., eds., *New Frontiers in Theology*, vol. 1, *The Later Heidegger and Theology;* vol. 2, *The New Hermeneutic* (New York, 1963-64) • W. SCHMITHALS, *An Introduction to the Theology of Rudolf Bultmann* (London, 1968) esp. 249-72; idem, "Glaubensgewißheit bei Rudolf Bultmann," *BTZ* 2 (1985) 317-32 • G. SINN, *Christologie und Existenz. Rudolf Bultmanns Interpretation des paulinischen Christuszeugnisses* (Tübingen, 1991) • D. SÖLLE, *Politische Theologie, Auseinandersetzung mit Rudolf Bultmann* (Stuttgart, 1971) • H. WEDER, *Neutestamentliche Hermeneutik* (Zurich, 1986) 405-11.

HANS HÜBNER

Denmark

	1960	1980	2000
Population (1,000s):	4,581	5,123	5,274
Annual growth rate (%):	0.76	−0.04	0.12
Area: 43,094 sq. km. (16,639 sq. mi.)			

A.D. 2000

Population density: 122/sq. km. (317/sq. mi.)
Births / deaths: 1.24 / 1.16 per 100 population
Fertility rate: 1.89 per woman
Infant mortality rate: 7 per 1,000 live births
Life expectancy: 76.1 years (m: 73.5, f: 78.8)
Religious affiliation (%): Christians 91.5 (Protestants 89.2, unaffiliated 1.5, other Christians 2.3), nonreligious 5.3, atheists 1.5, Muslims 1.4, other 0.3.

1. The Evangelical Lutheran Church (Folkekirke)
  1.1. The Lutheran Church, 1536-1849
  1.2. The Folkekirke after 1849
    1.2.1. Organization and Finances
    1.2.2. Church and State
    1.2.3. Theological Basis
    1.2.4. Church Practice
    1.2.5. Ecumenical Relations
2. Other Churches and Communions

1. The Evangelical Lutheran Church (Folkekirke)

1.1. *The Lutheran Church, 1536-1849*

After the victory of the Danish king over a revolt of peasants and citizens, the Lutheran Church became established in Denmark in 1536/37. It served as a religious department of state, though the congregations could choose their pastors and the city pastors their bishops. The office of → bishop remained as an administrative one.

The confessional allegiance of the church was at first unclear, but in the → Crypto-Calvinist debates it viewed the → Augsburg Confession as a norm. In 1683 Danish law defined the "religion of the king" as agreeing with the Bible, the three early creeds, the Augsburg Confession, and M. → Luther's Small Catechism. The constitution of 1849 describes the church as Evangelical Lutheran.

In the days of absolutism the church was governed in practice by the royal chancellery. Danish was the official language in Denmark, and German in Schleswig-Holstein. Confessional adherence was strictly enforced. Roman Catholics who belonged to foreign embassies enjoyed → religious liberty, and for economic reasons concessions were made to the Reformed and Jews in the late 17th century.

1.2. *The Folkekirke after 1849*

The constitution of 1849 granted full religious freedom but not religious equality. The state church became the Folkekirke, with 99.5 percent of the people as members (90 percent in 1990). The law conferred on it certain rights, and the state gave it moral, if not always economic, support.

1.2.1. *Organization and Finances*

Attempts to establish a representative and synodal church constitution (→ Church Government) remained unsuccessful. The Parliament (originally *Reichstag;* after 1953, *Folketing*) did not want any legislative body apart from itself, and the church's financial arrangements were and are obscure. The king must be a member of the Folkekirke. General legislation governs the church's external affairs, while its internal affairs (e.g., preaching; → Liturgy) are controlled by a body of specialists whose work the minister for church affairs presents to the king for implementation. There are ten dioceses ruled by bishops and provosts. These contain over 2,000 churches with about 1,800 pastors. The churches in Greenland and the Faeroe Islands come formally under the jurisdiction of the Diocese of Copenhagen but have their own vice-bishops.

The coming of parliamentary democracy in 1901 brought a good deal of decentralization to the church, along with extensive self-government. Almost all the church buildings are now owned congregationally, rather than privately. An endowment has replaced tithes, and a church tax the former general tax (→ Church Finances). This church tax is levied only on members. Some 85 percent of the church's income derives from it, about 3 to 4 percent from older sources (tithes and property), and the rest from the state in payment for services rendered for marriages and burials (→ Church Registers). The faculties of theology at Copenhagen and Århus are devoted solely to the training of pastors (→ Theological Education). The number of theological students is increasing sharply. In 1947 women were accepted as pastors, though this issue is still a subject of intense theological and ecclesiastical debate. It is projected that women soon will staff more than half the parishes.

1.2.2. *Church and State*

The coming of democracy has brought constant controversy concerning the separation of → church and state. The Social Democrats were at first very anticlerical but changed in the 1930s and now favor the Folkekirke. Politicians of every type are wary lest the church try to exert political pressure. Most church groups, however, think the Folkekirke is adaptable and, in the last resort, find security in state control.

1.2.3. *Theological Basis*

For the most part, theological development has been the same as in Germany. Philippism ruled in the 16th century (→ Crypto-Calvinism), → orthodoxy (§1) and reform orthodoxy in the 17th. Halle-type → Pietism became a kind of state religion in the 18th century and brought with it a good deal of reforming legislation (in church discipline, confirmation, education, and the law concerning conventicles). The Herrnhut movement (→ Moravian Church) quietly influenced many circles.

The first dominating force in the 19th century was speculative, idealistic theology in the spirit of → Romanticism. Then came → empiricism — as it was taught, for example, in Erlangen. There was also a close connection with religious revivals, which the state church and clergy viewed as controversial.

N. F. S. Grundtvig (1783-1872), a pastor, author, and historian, developed an understanding of the church in distinction from both → biblicism and → rationalism and made his mark in confrontation with the established church. In contrast with his view of → baptism and the Lord's Supper (→ Eucharist) as elements that constitute and sustain the church, and the Apostles' Creed, to which he assigned a key function, Grundtvig argued that Scripture is of secondary importance. Along with his idea of a free state church, Grundtvig championed voluntary residential folk high schools as a basis of national education; he viewed national life as a divinely given reality. In the middle of the 19th century the followers of Grundtvig split into two wings: a church wing, influenced by the clergy; and a national wing, based on the idea of national folk high schools.

In the first third of the 20th century → liberal theology penetrated every aspect of the church. In the 1920s, however, → Barth's → dialectical theology made an impact, as did the Lutheran renaissance. At the universities theology followed German trends, but the church's preaching was strongly colored by Grundtvig and S. → Kierkegaard (1813-55). After World War II, study of these two theologians was taken up again in earnest.

1.2.4. *Church Practice*

In the 19th century the church sought models for its practical ministry in England rather than Germany. The idea of societies caught on in the form of Bible societies, missionary societies, and church societies (→ Societies and Associations, Ecclesiastical). → Missions overseas, especially in Asia and Africa, were carried on by many private societies, coordinated in part by the Danish Missionary Council.

In the cities, work was done according to the English and in part the German model of city missions (→ Inner Mission).

The various trends in the revivals have hardened into fairly rigid groups, but their impact continues both nationally and locally. General leveling — both socially and culturally — has meant that theological innovations do not affect the population at large. Liberal theology, the theology of K. Barth and the journal *Tidehverv* (begun in 1926), and High Church theology according to the Anglican or Roman Catholic model may have a decisive influence on preaching, but they are movements of clergy rather than popular movements in the true sense. In contrast, one may perhaps say that the new religious interest of the last part of the 20th century is a kind of awakening. This interest represents a varied and indeterminate phenomenon that combines Indian → mysticism, → Yoga, popular initiatives (→ Social Movements), a protest against boredom, and a fear of natural science with its technological threats to life (e.g., pollution, dissipation of resources, the urban mentality, and world armaments).

The → secularization of society and the protest against, or abandonment of, the established church are reflected in the decrease in → occasional services. About 82 percent of the children are baptized, about 75 percent are confirmed, and about 55 percent of the weddings and 90 percent of the funerals take place in church. Lately the percentages of baptisms and weddings have begun to rise again, but the number of those at Sunday services has declined to less than 5 percent in most parishes, although participation in the Eucharist is increasing.

Within church circles a certain pull to the right may be observed. The development of Bible → fundamentalism in protest against historicocritical → exegesis, liberal theology, or the → existential theology influenced by Kierkegaard has resulted in the formation of free theological faculties, which for now at least are private. The → charismatic movement has also spread and influenced some circles.

For a long time the church has made little impact on the universities, high schools, or teacher-training colleges. Up to 1933 the pastor was chairman of the local school board. High value was placed on confessionally oriented → religious instruction. In 1975, however, a more broadly religious orientation replaced the confessional orientation in the school curricula, with Christianity as the central theme.

→ Worship in the Folkekirke shows clear traces of the German mass and other German → church orders, with a High Church flavor. The Kierkeritual (church order) of 1685 forms the basis. Today, however, there are many variants: High Church, charismatic, local forms, and forms influenced by revival generally. After 1970 some attempt was made to introduce order into the liturgical chaos.

Among the many organizations that are nationally significant, Det Kobenhavnske Kirkefond (The Copenhagen church fund; 1896) deserves special notice. It has promoted the construction of some 50 churches, helped to divide up parishes that have become unmanageably large, and promoted other activities.

In close cooperation with the Ministry for Church Affairs (after 1940), the financing of church construction by the church tax has made extension easier. Important, too, is the Folkekirkens Nødjælp (The state church emergency aid), which with state support oversees a worldwide, comprehensive aid program.

1.2.5. Ecumenical Relations

After World War I the Folkekirke has played an unofficial role in ecumenical activity (its constitution forbids official involvement; → Ecumenical Movement; Local Ecumenism). The Mellemkirkelige Råd (Interchurch council) was set up in 1954 to strengthen relations with other Danish churches. There is also active cooperation with church organizations in other Scandinavian countries. The theological faculties supervise special research centers (financed by the state) for → ecumenical theology, and a semiofficial Danish organization takes part in the → World Council of Churches and the → Lutheran World Federation.

2. Other Churches and Communions

Many communions enjoy recognition by the state. Their clergy receive accreditation, and they may thus perform valid marriages and provide similar services. This is especially true in the case of traditional churches, including the Norwegian and Swedish Lutheran churches, the Anglican congregation (some 220 families), and the → Roman Catholic Church.

After suffering almost total loss to the Reformation, the Catholic Church received recognition in the constitution of 1849; since 1892 there has been a Danish bishopric. Most of the Roman Catholic clergy are from abroad, and foreign workers (esp. Germans and Poles) often make up the congregations, though the church has firm roots in the middle class and to some extent in the upper classes. In 1992 the church numbered 31,000 members in 50 parishes. There were 94 priests as well as several schools, homes for the elderly, and hospitals. The church also maintains 3 monasteries, 5 orders, 16 convents, and various publishing houses and conference centers.

The Pentecostal movement (→ Pentecostal Churches) subdivides into three branches with a total of 9,000 members in 1990.

The → Baptists first came into Denmark illegally in 1839 and suffered some persecution (e.g., the forcible baptism of their children). With religious freedom they grew, partly because of sharp criticism of the Folkekirke for social as well as religious reasons. The Baptist Church was the last to be officially recognized (1952). Strict → church discipline led to divisions and stagnation. In 1992 the Baptist Union of Denmark numbered 6,000 baptized members. Closely related to it is the Danske Missionsforbund (Danish mission), which is at work especially in Jutland.

Most of the approximately 5,000 members of the → Salvation Army (from 1887) also belong to the Folkekirke, which imitates its social work in the towns with an organization known as the Kirkens Korshaer (The church's army of the cross).

→ Adventists (1877) number some 3,900 baptized adults and about 1,800 children and young people.

The → Methodist Church was founded in 1858 and officially recognized in 1865. In 1990 it numbered over 2,500 adherents.

The → Reformed churches consist of a German-speaking and a French-speaking group. They are located chiefly in Copenhagen and Fredericia and have some 800 members.

The Greek → Orthodox Church is also officially recognized. Founded in 1880, it has about 400 members and comes under the patriarchate of Constantinople. Guest workers have increased its numbers.

The Unitas Fratrum (→ Bohemian Brethren) forms the background of the Folkekirke societies for Lutheran Missions and the Brethren colony in Christiansfeld (some 260 members). A Free Evangelical

Lutheran Church was founded in 1855 in protest against the lack of discipline in the Folkekirke; it has some 180 members. There are also various Free Evangelical Lutheran congregations of Grundtvigian origin, many of them founded in political protest against state rule and working in close cooperation with Grundtvigian groups in the Folkekirke.

There are also small groups of Quakers (about 60 members; → Friends, Society of).

Free Churches have never found conditions very favorable in Denmark. The Baptists found themselves opposing Grundtvig's view of baptism, and the Inner Mission, which itself sometimes showed Methodist tendencies, acted as a buffer in relation to Anglo-American groups. Free church influence, however, is greater than their relatively small numbers would suggest.

→ Jehovah's Witnesses are organized in 230 groups, with 27,000 adherents in 1990. Since 1850 the → Mormons have persuaded about 15,000 Danes to emigrate to Utah. They have approximately 4,000 followers in Denmark. Much smaller groups of Unitarians and Christian Science (from 1920) are also represented.

More recently, immigrants have brought → Islamic communities into Denmark, with → mosques and culture centers. The largest group is the Turks (30,000 as of 1990), with smaller numbers of Iranians, Arabs, and workers and refugees from the former Yugoslavia.

Bibliography: J. L. BALLING and P. G. LINDHARDT, *Den nordiske kirkes historie* (4th ed.; Copenhagen, 1979) • H. FLEDELINS, *Freedom of Religion in Denmark* (Copenhagen, 1992) • N. F. S. GRUNDTVIG, *Tradition und Erneuerung* (ed. C. Thodberg and A. P. Thyssen; Copenhagen, 1983) • P. HARTLING, ed., *The Danish Church* (Copenhagen, 1964) • H. KOCH and B. KORNERUP, eds., *Den danske kirkes historie* (8 vols.; Copenhagen, 1950ff.) vol. 3, *Reformationen indtil 1536* (P. G. Lindhardt); vol. 4, *1537 til c. 1700* (B. Kornerup and U. Schrøder); vol. 5, *Det 18. århundrede* (J. Pedersen and B. Kornerup); vol. 6, *1800-1849* (H. Koch); vol. 7, *1849-1901* (P. G. Lindhardt); vol. 8, *1901-1965* (P. G. Lindhardt) • P. G. LINDHARDT, *Kirchengeschichte Skandinaviens* (Göttingen, 1983); idem, *Skandinavische Kirchengeschichte seit dem 16. Jahrhundert* (Göttingen, 1982) • K. E. MILLER, *Denmark: A Troubled Welfare State* (Boulder, Colo., 1991) • M. N. NEIIENDAM, *Frikirker og sekter* (4th ed.; Copenhagen, 1958) • P. SALOMONSEN, "Contemporary Religious Attitudes in Denmark: A Qualitative Description Based on Empirical Research," *Contemporary Metamorphosis of Religion* (ed. L. Laeyendecker et al.; Lille, 1973) 451-66; idem, "Religion in a Welfare State," *Religion and Social Change* (ed. J. Aranguren et al.; Lille, 1975) 433-39 • T. R. SKARSTEN, *The Scandinavian Reformation: A Bibliographical Guide* (St. Louis, 1985).

POUL GEORG LINDHARDT

Denomination

1. Terminology
2. Churches and the Various Confessions and Denominations
 2.1. In Church History Generally
 2.2. Since the Sixteenth Century
3. The Denominational Problem
 3.1. The Ecumenical Problem
 3.2. Present Situation
 3.3. Reformulation
4. Confessionalism and Denominationalism
 4.1. Concepts
 4.2. In Church History
 4.3. Rise and Structure
 4.4. Limitation as Stigma
5. Recent Discussion
 5.1. Denominational Identity
 5.2. Confessionality
6. Sociological Perspectives

1. Terminology

The term "denomination" refers broadly to any class of persons called, or denominated, by the same name. In the context of Christianity, "denomination" may be defined as "an organized Christian church or tradition or religious group or community of believers or aggregate of worship centers or congregations, usually within a specific country, whose component congregations and members are called by the same name in different areas, regarding themselves as an autonomous Christian church distinct from other denominations, churches and traditions" (*WCE*, 824). In 1985 David Barrett could count 22,150 distinct denominations worldwide. A shorter characterization, one that equally highlights sociological factors, describes denominations as "juridically self-governing, doctrinally autonomous, and legally erected bodies" (*NCE*, 4.772). In terms of their view of the church, the → Roman Catholic Church and the → Orthodox Church prefer not to think of themselves as denominations but reserve the term for others.

A conceptually related but much more specific term is "confession" (from Lat. *confessio,* "confession, admission"). When used of church bodies, it refers to "a large family of distinct or different autonomous churches or denominations around the world which are linked by similar ecclesiastical tradition, history, polity and name, and often by some informal or formal organization. Confessions include: Anglicanism, Greek Orthodoxy, Lutheranism, Methodism, Roman Catholicism, and 40 or so others" (*WCE*, 85). Since 1979 it has been common to refer to confessional bodies as → Christian World Communions (→ Anglican Communion; Lutheran World Federation; Reformed Alliance).

Theologically, "confession" refers to the → confession of faith. In the → early church, those Christians who were willing to be martyred for their → faith were called *confessores* (→ Martyrs). The *Confessions* of → Augustine (354-430; → Augustine's Theology) is essentially confession and praise. The confession of sin in the → liturgy is called *confiteor* (Lat. "I confess") or *confessio generalis* (open guilt), and auricular confession (→ Confession of Sins) is called *confessio oralis*. In public legal proceedings, the *confessio iudicalis* (oral or written admission) enjoys the status of legal proof (1983 CIC 1535-36). During the Reformation, the word *confessio* came to refer to a summary of the beliefs of "religions," "religious groups," or "church groups," as for example the Augsburg Confession (1530), the First Helvetic Confession (1536), the Gallican Confession (1559), and the Belgic Confession (1561; → Confession of Faith). These groups themselves came to be known as confessions only in the 19th century.

2. Churches and the Various Confessions and Denominations

2.1. *In Church History Generally*

Many churches have arisen in the course of church history. Though all regard themselves as manifestations of the one holy church attested in their creeds, through mutual division and condemnations (→ Heresies and Schisms) they have in fact discriminated against and hampered the → unity of the church of Christ in which they profess to believe. The unity has not been a historical possibility.

Some of the churches have shrunk and perished, others have become established and → traditional, and new ones have arisen. The development of → free churches, national church movements, overseas churches as a result of → mission (§3), and dissenting bodies because of crises and disagreements (→ Church 5) has enriched the denominational spectrum. It is the task of the comparative study of denominations to describe the situation (→ Ecumenical Theology).

2.2. *Since the Sixteenth Century*

Historically, the term "confession" has been applied especially to the types of churches that arose with the 16th century → Reformation and the development of a confessional sense. These were formed as the doctrinal absolutism of the Reformers became the doctrinal particularism of Protestant → orthodoxy (§§1-2; → Calvinism; Lutheranism), as the Roman Catholic Church consolidated itself apologetically (→ Catholic Reform and Counterreformation), and as schism took place from Rome for reasons of ecclesiastical policy (e.g., the Church of England). As the Reformation progressed, territorial churches came into being. Reaction against the Reformation led Rome into the development of a conservative denomination of its own. In England the repudiation of papal authority produced a national church with some traditional features, and further splits resulted in the → free church type (→ Church 3.6; Congregationalism; Dissenters).

Denominational structuring and the stabilizing of separate churches now became features of the visible church (even geographically). They involved a passionate insistence on the unfalsified truth of the → gospel and pure doctrine, and a passionate struggle to separate clearly the true church from the false and to promote specific modes of conduct, both within and without the church (→ Catholicism [Roman]; Protestantism). At the same time, political means and even force were used to establish denominations. Every sphere of life was affected, including the → social movements in the lower classes (→ Peasants' War) and the interests of the middle classes and nobility. A denominational milieu developed that had dogmatic, spiritual, and moral aspects and was motivated originally by a desire for church renewal. It also had legal, administrative, and economic elements, which gave the churches of a given denomination their distinctive forms and influenced them. State law recognized and guaranteed their existence (→ Cuius regio eius religio; Church and State). The denominations demonstrated their spirit and power in → culture and → society.

3. The Denominational Problem

The rise and perpetuation of denominations has produced the denominational, or confessional, problem. Traditionally, this is the problem of how to justify and to limit denominations. The solution has been to demonstrate the "essential" church in the "manifest" churches. This issue is debated in → polemics.

3.1. *The Ecumenical Problem*

The contemporary → ecumenical movement has made the fellowship of churches its dominant theme. Theological interest focuses on "church unity" as the "ecumenical problem." Reference is made to the already given → unity of the body of Christ and the testimony of the early creeds to the one → church (§1.1) and to the obligation that these factors place on existing churches for the sake of the credibility of that witness.

The making visible of the one church of Christ in which we believe is the theme of → ecumenical theology. In theology that is primarily concerned with this problem, the experienced reality of the complex phenomenon of the church is to a large extent neglected. Hence the ecumenical idea, based as it is on the insight of faith, seems largely unaffected by the actual ambivalence of the phenomenon of the church, its elementary disparity, and its inherent tensions (→ Church 1.2-3).

3.2. *Present Situation*

The change of themes and theological shortsightedness have pushed the earlier problem into the background but have not been able to solve it. The problem manifests itself again when the actual churches cling to their denominational identity (see 4 and 5), and this fact clearly slows the ecumenical process. We cannot ignore the historical and material reasons for denominations, their relevance and legitimacy. Real relations in the churches and their role in society (cf. church splits and the inadequacy and minimal impact of the churches in their sociocultural nexus; → Church 1.4.1.4-5) unavoidably pose the problem of their function and value in their existing context. When we consider that there is now a worldwide, diverse Christianity with ecclesiological, socioethical, and contextual fields of tension and disagreement but also unmistakable expansionist trends (→ Church 5; European Theology; Third World; Third World Theology), we have also to ask what causes and impulses produced and fostered this heterogeneous picture of Christianity and what factors direct it. With such questions, which take into account the different forms of denominationalism (see 5.2), the denominational problem again becomes an urgent one.

3.3. *Reformulation*

In the necessary reformulating of this problem, it is not enough merely to recall the older question of the legitimacy and limit of confessions and denominations. In light of the actual reality of the church, we must ask what conditions make possible and permissible the confessional and cultural particularity, pluralism, and variety of Christianity. With regard to ecclesiological problems, we must also seek the reasons for the existing ambivalence and distinctiveness of the phenomenon of the church and explain how and why its present forms are legitimate and relevant.

In this new inquiry we must take into account

not only the empirical facts but also the insights of faith into the relation (and also the permanent distinction) between the unconditioned action of God on the one side and conditioned human action on the other. The relation means that an act of faith based on the contingency of the → revelation of God, the election of a → people of God, and the saving message of Jesus of Nazareth is not something that we can pick and choose at will. What is here believed affects the life of those who believe it, and it is here that they must demonstrate it. The difference means that the act of faith must occur under the presuppositions of life in the human world and with the means at the disposal of human thought and action. It is constituted in part by the experiences of everyday life, which are not always and everywhere the same.

The reformulated denominational problem finds a relevant answer in an understanding of the church that can reconcile the insights of faith with the data of empirical reality and thus apprehend the ambivalence of the phenomenon of the → church (§1.4). An ecclesiology of this type sees that the church in all its manifestations, both theoretically and practically, is subject to change. It points out that under the conditions of human history and possibilities a variable actualization of the saving message of Jesus is unavoidable and that denominational differentiation can be justified (→ Church 5.4).

4. Confessionalism and Denominationalism

4.1. *Concepts*

The term "confessionalism" denotes a theological or philosophical system that rests on a specific confession of faith or comparable formula, forms the basis for a corresponding confessional consciousness and conduct, and makes delimitation possible. Claiming correctness of belief, this system is normative and can thus be made the standard for everything Christian and argued polemically against other positions. With the demarcation that the confession articulates, that which is distinctive and specific comes to expression and governs the teaching, order, and practice that are necessary to perpetuate and identify (→ Identity) the system.

"Denominationalism" has similar uses, although the defining feature is not necessarily a specific confession of faith but any element of doctrine, practice, or tradition in terms of which the particular denomination defines itself. The term currently often has negative connotations (e.g., as "the emphasizing of denominational differences to the point of being narrowly exclusive," *WCE*, 824), although originally — particularly in the 18th-century Evangelical revival in Great Britain — it was a neutral, nonjudgmental term (W. S. Hudson, 292-93).

4.2. In Church History

Church history displayed confessional tendencies from the outset in the encounter between → orthodoxy and → heresy (see 2). These tendencies became dominant in the 16th century with the establishment of confessional churches, the battle between irreconcilable dogmatic systems (→ Ecumenical Theology 4.2), and the absolutizing of one's own confession or denomination and the negation of others.

Although we might call this tendency confessionalism or denominationalism, this concept applies especially to the ecclesiastical, theological, cultural, and political attitude that not only revived and strengthened the denominational sense in the 19th-century controversies but organized it and made it militant. On the basis of the inherited confessions, this attitude opposed the leveling influences of the → Enlightenment, → rationalism, and → Pietism; fought against church → union; championed a repristination of revealed doctrine; and made common cause with politically conservative forces in the fight against → revolution and → liberalism (→ Theology in the Nineteenth and Twentieth Centuries; Modern Church History; Restoration).

Confessional positions played a large part in the 20th-century → church struggle and the reconstitution of the German churches after World War II. In the decades that followed, a confessional movement developed within the → evangelical movement. A similar traditionalist movement arose in the → Roman Catholic Church. Denominationalist ideas represent a potential for criticism in the → ecumenical movement and also in antiecumenical organizations (e.g., the → International Council of Christian Churches). We may see here a reaction to the decay of traditional belief (→ Fundamentalism) and to present-day → pluralism. As in the 19th century, they are part of the spectrum of → conservatism.

4.3. Rise and Structure

All forms of confessionalism or denominationalism show common features in development and structure. These show that denominational positions represent a constantly recurring historical phenomenon and help us to understand the polemical attitude that seems to be typical.

4.3.1. The rise of denominationalism presupposes (1) the theological and intellectual possibility of the development of the specific, along with intellectual competition; and (2) an element of threat, relativizing, or suppression that creates anxiety and triggers defense mechanisms.

These two factors combine to produce denominationalism. As historical changes take place that set the whole nexus of life in motion, these stir up sterile teachings and practices to engage in self-correction and to challenge older authorities. What has been neglected or perverted is recalled and stated, as well as what must be preserved and what promises to be useful. Special emphasis is put on specific teachings, norms, and values. The reacquired or new insights lead to reinterpretation of the whole nexus of experience and to modes of conduct that compete with Christianity as it is understood by the bearers of power and tradition. If the opposing positions prove to be irreconcilable, → conflicts occur in which identity must be established. This is done by a selection and differentiation that aims at something unique and bases denominational existence on opposition to other groups. The confession or doctrinal formula orients as well as delimits by stressing the distinctive insight and rejecting what is in opposition to it. The desire for orthodoxy comes to light in the proof that is offered from Scripture and in the agreement claimed with the original gospel.

4.3.2. In the long run, the various assertions and denominational claims cannot be upheld or secured without a comprehensive doctrinal structure. The resulting systematization is dependent on the questions that characterized the conflict while others were ignored. It also reflects the situation that provoked the confession. The genesis and conceptual or doctrinal result coincide; the system stabilizes both. It elevates the insight that the confession formulates ("I believe . . .") to the level of reflection and makes it methodologically accessible. Confessional identity can thus be transferred to a collective ("The church believes . . ."). It is institutionalized (→ Institution 1.1).

With "pure doctrine" (or → dogma), the confessional or denominational self-understanding can claim to be true, lasting, objective, and universally valid. This dogmatically fixed orthodoxy offers a norm for assessing those outside and is the only possible basis for → consensus with them. It is also a standard for the piety of its own members. Doctrine is what binds the collective together. The latter is subject to doctrinal authority and is hierarchically structured (→ Hierarchy). The dogmatic a priori sets limits for every branch of knowledge. In principle it cannot be challenged by insight into its own history, for the system guarantees regulated (salvation) history (→ History of Salvation).

4.4. Limitation as Stigma

Limitation is the stigma attaching to the setting of denominational norms and the construction of denominational systems. It arises from the fact that we cannot stretch the particular into a universal. One denominational position always implies another, as we see from the mutual doctrinal condemnations of the 16th century (→ Reformation). Yet it is the very delimitation (with differentiation, maybe denunciation) that gives profile and permanence to denominationalism. Its strategy is also one of stabilization, though success depends on whether the conflict can reproduce itself and the particular insight can still be attractive in an increasingly complex set of relations. The stigma of limitation also characterizes churches of denominations that follow the structural model of confessionalism, along with more recent confessionalistic thinking.

5. Recent Discussion

In modern discussion of the problem of denominations we find the concepts of denominational identity and confessionality. While the former considers the actual denominations and their self-consciousness, the latter aims at a transcending of denominational or confessional interests.

5.1. Denominational Identity

The expression "denominational identity" involves the various responses to the divine message of salvation. The personal and collective practice of inner decision for Christ, of the confession "Jesus is Lord," finds varying formal and material expression in liturgical life (→ Worship) and → church government, in the working out of the divine salvific will in everyday life and its manifold relationships (e.g., in → work, → marriage, → family, and → society), and in the doctrinal presentation of the good news and its defense against both inward doubts and outward attacks. In this practical and theoretical response to the reality of redemption in Christ as experienced in faith, there come to expression the concrete occasion and measure of involvement (knowledge of sin, knowledge of God, conversion), the agreement and fellowship with other believers (consensus in acknowledged truth, spiritual communication in praise, thanksgiving, prayer, and listening), the claim to orthodoxy in thought and action (orthodoxy and orthopraxis), and the desire to give permanence to the experience of faith (institutionalizing), to pass it on, and to promote it (→ Evangelization; Mission).

Denominational identity shows how the original event of salvation is being communicated by contingent experiences. Inasmuch as a concrete expression of faith is involved, it may be defined materially. It can thus serve to distinguish different expressions of faith.

5.2. Confessionality

Concern for a visible unity of the churches aims, on the one hand, to overcome denominationalism, abandoning denominational identities in favor of an embracing and unifying Christian identity. On the other hand, the distinctive denominational elements that find expression in the doctrine, worship, organization, and piety of the various churches must not be lost but, rather, respected, for they contribute to catholic fullness and give evidence of the riches of the one church.

To provide a common perspective for the two goals, the term "confessionality" has been coined in ecumenical discussion. This recognizes that confessing is one of the necessary marks of Christian faith both individually and collectively. What is specifically confessional as well as every other manner of witnessing can be identified; one's faith and things that differ may be acknowledged as being of the same quality. Confessionality is demonstrated, first, by confessional churches that link their origin and self-understanding to historical confessional documents, develop their basic documents in dogmatic teaching, and lay claim to orthodoxy and catholicity. It is demonstrated, second, by individual and collective expressions of faith that are not tied to specific confessional documents but abandon doctrinal systems for the sake of other modes of confessional expression, either in one confessional church or in several at once (e.g., with a pietist, evangelical, High Church, traditional, or social ethics orientation), or perhaps by establishing themselves by separation from an existing church. Third, it is demonstrated by expressions of faith that cross confessional boundaries, finding herein their character as witness, engaging in various ecumenical activities (→ local ecumenism, ecumenical worship, etc.), showing a concern for intraconfessional doctrinal formulas (→ Consensus; Dialogue), participating in transdenominational movements, or taking form in union churches (→ United and Uniting Churches).

Confessionality is a concept that is purely formal, and thus it can take concrete form in many different ways. It seems well adapted to show how necessary confessing and differentiating are, but also how dubious and limited are all denominations. Yet it offers no more than a framework within which to discuss denominational and ecumenical problems.

Bibliography: H. Dombois, "Konfessionelle Auseinandersetzung als hermeneutisches Problem," ZTK 60 (1963) 122-31 • G. Ebeling, "Zur Geschichte des konfessionellen Problems," Wort Gottes und Tradition (Göttingen, 1964) 41-55 • E. Fahlbusch, "Abschied von der Konfessionskunde. Überlegungen zu einer Phäno-menologie der universalen Christenheit," *Evangelisch und Ökumenisch* (ed. G. Maron; Göttingen, 1986) 456-93 (reformulation of the confessional problem) • K. Haendler, "'Haben wir nicht alle einen Gott?' Überlegungen zum Konfessionsproblem," *EvT* 29 (1969) 534-54 • W. S. Hudson, "Denominationalism," *EncRel(E)* 4.292-98 • P. Lengsfeld, ed., *Ökumenische Theologie* (Stuttgart, 1980) bibliography • H. Meyer, "Konfession," *ÖL* 701-8 (bibliography); idem, "Konfessionalität und ökumenische Gemeinschaft," *ILRef* 16 (1973) 60-81 (bibliography) • K. Raiser, "Die Identität der Kirche in ökumenischer Sicht," *LR* 26 (1976) 50-55 • W. Reinhard, "Konfession und Konfessionalisierung in Europa," *Bekenntnis und Geschichte* (ed. W. Reinhard; Munich, 1981) 165-89 • R. E. Richey, ed., *Denomi-nationalism* (Nashville, 1977) • K. G. Steck, "Konfes-sionskirchen," *EKL* (1st/2d ed.) 2.884-87 (bibliography) • V. Vajta, "Das Bekenntnis der Kirche als öku-menisches Anliegen," *Das Bekenntinis im Leben der Kirche* (ed. V. Vajta and H. Weissgerber; Berlin, 1963) 245ff. • L. Vischer, "Neues Bekenntnis und neues Bekennen," *ÖR* 17 (1968) 64ff. • E. W. Zeeden, *Die Entstehung der Konfessionen. Grundlagen und Formen der Konfessionsbildung im Zeitalter der Glaubenskämpfe* (Munich, 1965); idem, *Konfessionsbildung. Studien zur Reformation, Gegenreformation und katholischen Reform* (Stuttgart, 1985).

Erwin Fahlbusch

6. Sociological Perspectives

"Denomination" (from the Lat. verb *denomino*, "name") is a neutral term for a confession or its adherents. Theologically and sociologically, it has a specific content, which, however, is subject to aca-demic debate.

Theological and sociological differences between religious groups led to the construction of a typology with → church and → sect as the two basic forms. Normative here was the view of E. → Troeltsch (1865-1923). As he saw it, a *church* is predominantly conservative; it "to a certain extent accepts the secular order, and dominates the masses; in principle, there-fore, it is universal" — that is, it seeks to cover the whole community. It has an objective, institutional character, and one is born into it. A *sect*, in contrast, is "a voluntary community whose members join it of their own free will [i.e., intentionally]. The very life of the sect, therefore, depends on actual personal service and co-operation"; the sect, according to Troeltsch, gathers an elite from among the elect (331, 339).

This description of two ideal types, however, does not do justice to the many variations in practice.

Troeltsch himself added another type: → *mysticism*, which stresses the "direct inward and present reli-gious experience." In mysticism, the world of ideas that had become rigid in ritual and doctrine is trans-formed into a purely personal and inward possession of the soul. The individualism of mysticism, however, "differs entirely from that of the sect," for it involves a "purely spiritual fellowship, known to God alone." Mystics cultivate "intimate circles for edification" (730, 743-46, 993).

Troeltsch also mentioned the → *free church* sys-tem, which in essence implies the disintegration of "the mediaeval and early Protestant idea of a social order welded together by one uniform State Church." It champions religious → subjectivism and → rela-tivism; similar to the sects, it shifts the decision to join a church to the will of the individual; and from the external and legal standpoint, it considers the church a society, without dismissing its dogmatic and ethical implications (656-57).

In the further development of this typology, the term *denomination* (H. Richard Niebuhr; J. Wach 1944) has come to denote a middle position between church and sect. The denomination differs from the church in that it makes no universal claim, and from the sect in that it imposes less stringent rules of con-duct; it thus does not represent a society of the "re-ligiously fully qualified" (M. → Weber). Other dif-ferences are also important, such as in regard to the ministry (→ Offices, Ecclesiastical), → eschatology, and the → sacraments (D. A. Martin).

The position of the denomination as an interme-diate link raises the question of its dynamic relation to the other two types. After Niebuhr, the view has gained ground that the denomination is the product of a process by which sects become adjusted and institutionalized (→ Institution). As the members of sects have children, they relax the standards of ad-mission. Moral strictness lessens in the second generation, and routinization sets in. The standards and values of the social and religious environment are accepted. A more comprehensive organization and the appointment of full-time employees become necessary. This view, however, is only partly tenable, for some sects have maintained their specific charac-ter for several generations (e.g., the Society of → Friends), whereas many denominations (e.g., → Methodists and → Baptists) have arisen as such.

Of particular importance today is the transition of the universal or national churches to denomina-tions. It is connected with the fact that national churches are losing members on a massive scale, their norms and values are causing problems of identifi-cation, and their political position is weakening while religious → pluralism is advancing. This situation necessitates a moderation of exclusive claims and promotes an increasing measure of → tolerance and openness. The Roman Catholic Church in the Netherlands offers a good example. It shows that the process in which the various confessions draw nearer to one another goes together with a more personal relationship with one's own church (O. Schreuder).

The denomination is primarily an Anglo-Saxon phenomenon, a fact that is connected in general with a cultural emphasis on → individualism. In the United States it also is the result of the policy adopted after the American Revolution of granting equal recognition before the law to all religious groups (→ Religious Liberty).

Bibliography: D. A. MARTIN, "The Denomination," *BJS* 13 (1962) 1-14 • S. E. MEAD, "Denominationalism: The Shape of Protestantism in America," *CH* 23 (1954) 291-320 • H. R. NIEBUHR, *The Social Sources of Denominationalism* (Magnolia, Mass., 1984; orig. pub., 1929) • O. SCHREUDER, "Von der Volkskirche zur Freiwilligkeitskirche," *Gestaltwandel der Kirche* (Freiburg, 1967) • E. TROELTSCH, *The Social Teaching of the Christian Churches* (New York, 1956; orig. pub., 1923) • J. WACH, *The Sociology of Religion* (Chicago, 1944); idem, *Types of Religious Experience: Christian and Non-Christian* (Chicago, 1951) • M. WEBER, *Gesammelte Aufsätze zur Religionssoziologie* (vol. 1; 3d ed.; Tübingen, 1934) • B. R. WILSON, *Religion in Sociological Perspective* (Oxford, 1982).

LEO LAEYENDECKER

Deontology

The term "deontology" comes from the Gk. *to deon,* meaning "what is required; duty." J. Bentham (1748-1832) was the first to use the term. He denoted by it the whole complex of his utilitarian theory, which is oriented to a balance of → duty and self-interest.

Since the time of Bentham the usage has changed. "Deontology" now denotes normative ethical theories (→ Norms; Metaethics) that assess moral actions (or judgments or rules, e.g., the rule that promises must be kept) solely in terms of themselves. Quite apart from any positive or negative consequences, qualities inherent in the actions have an intersubjective binding character, which constitutes their morality. Deontological → ethics thus stands over against the ethics of teleology (from Gk. *telos,* "end, aim"), in which nonmoral values — such as the happiness, pleasure, or profit that the actions bring (→ Fate and [Good] Fortune), or that are intended by them — serve as criteria in evaluating their morality, so that

the good or bad consequences of actions or rules play a decisive part in judging their moral quality (egoism; → Utilitarianism).

According to the function that rules have in the theories, a distinction is made between act-deontology (→ Act) and rule-deontology. For the former, moral judgments have their basis in individual situations. For the latter, general rules or principles are the basis of the morality of moral decisions. The ethics of intuitionism (→ Analytic Ethics) and of → existentialism are examples of act-deontology; prominent proponents of rule-deontology are W. D. Ross (1877-1971) and, in a classic form, I. Kant (1724-1804), with his → categorical imperative (→ Kantianism).

Deontological theories usually include teleological considerations, for example, by formulating the principle of promoting the well-being of others. Without some deontological elements, it is hard to present morality, since it is only deontologically and not from a standpoint of social utility that one can find a basis for justice and respect for human dignity.

Deontological logic is a special discipline. It analyzes the formal → logic of normative statements and rules and sets up rules for valid inferences regarding commands, prohibitions, dispensations, and rights. Since it deals with every kind of prescriptive or evaluative → language, its range is broader than that of ethics.

Bibliography: J. BENTHAM, *Deontology* (New York, 1983) • D. BIRNBACHER and N. HOERSTER, eds., *Texte zur Ethik* (Munich, 1976) 230-69 • R. B. BRANDT, *Ethical Theory* (Englewood Cliffs, N.J., 1959) • W. K. FRANKENA, *Ethics* (Englewood Cliffs, N.J., 1963) • R. M. HARE, *The Language of Morals* (Oxford, 1952) • G. H. VON WRIGHT, *Handlung, Norm und Intention* (Berlin, 1977).

WERNER SCHWARTZ

Dependence

1. Term
2. Theories of Dependence
   2.1. Historical and Theoretical Context
   2.2. Explanatory Force and Limits
3. Strategies to Overcome Dependence
4. Dependence in the Context of the Church

1. Term

The term "dependence," especially after World War II, refers to relations of subordination among nations. The point of using this term is to stress the fact that the underdevelopment of the → Third

World results, not from a general economic backwardness in the sense of being on a lower rung of social → development, but from the centuries-long dependence of the periphery on the countries of the → capitalist center.

"Dependence" implies the penetration of dependent societies at every social level. Thus there is *political and military penetration,* involving → colonialism, the political domination of industrial lands in important international institutions (→ Industrial Society), and the military superiority of industrial powers, especially the United States. There also is *economic and technological penetration,* such as in dependence on the export of a few products, mostly raw materials; the concentration of trade with a few partners; the high proportion of foreign capital, especially in modern industries; and extensive technological dependence. Finally, there is *cultural dependence,* which appears in the dependence of the media on imported broadcast and foreign press agencies, the suppression of national cultures, and the adoption of foreign consumerism (→ Consumption).

As a result of dependent development, deformed social structures have arisen (→ Society) in which the interplay between production for export and production for domestic luxury consumption forms the central axis of economic development and blocks any deepening of the capitalist process of development in terms of mass consumption. The marginalizing of great sections of the population, structural heterogeneity (the coexistence of different modes and forms of production, in which capitalist accumulation uses traditional elements but also tends to destroy them), and national disintegration (with the modern sector of a country typically linked with the internationalized core of the total world economic system and at the same time increasingly alienated from the country's traditional sector) constitute the most important characteristics of this deformation. For this dependent development France has coined the phrase "peripheral capitalism," which now plays a significant part in Western discussion.

2. Theories of Dependence
2.1. *Historical and Theoretical Context*
Since the mid-1960s the term "dependence" has been the focal point of criticism in discussions of the dominant model of development in Latin America, namely, the model of *desarrollismo,* or the state-promoted policy of modernization on the basis of imported industrialization, initiated with the UN Economic Commission for Latin America and the Caribbean and promoted by Kennedy's Alliance for Progress.

This criticism has moved in two directions. The first is middle-class and nationalist. It focuses chiefly on the structures of dependence in the international sphere and seeks reform by a policy of national reintegration (C. Furtado, P. González Casanova, O. Sunkel, et al.).

The second is radical and in part Marxist. It stresses the involvement of middle-class forces with multinational companies and the world market and thus views a revolutionary break with the capitalist world market as the necessary presupposition of successful national development (A. G. Frank, R. M. Marini, T. Dos Santos, A. Córdova, A. Quijano, and, with reservations, F. H. Cardoso and E. Faletto). At the beginning of the 1970s these concerns were picked up in North America and Europe, especially by critical sociologists, who have had considerable influence on further discussion of the theory of development.

2.2. *Explanatory Force and Limits*
Two aspects of the discussion of dependence have had a decisive influence on the theory of development. The first is its *global perspective.* One can give a meaningful analysis of underdevelopment only in the context of the processes of global development. The second is its *holistic perspective.* Underdevelopment is not just an "economic," "politological," or "sociological" phenomenon. It can be understood only as a single complex problem that embraces every human dimension.

The approach by way of dependence, however, does not question the concept of development in the theory of modernization. It simply offers an analysis showing why the proposed strategies (essentially the imitation of industrial countries) cannot reach the set goals (growth, industrialization, raising the standards of living, etc.). The problems of → ecology, lifestyle, and so on are not taken into account. Further points calling for criticism are the focus on circulation (trade, movements of capital, neglect of the sphere of production), the reduction of the many capitalist societies to two polar types, and the economist-type character of the analysis, which simply regards the state and politics as a reflection and instrument of economic interests. The widespread failure of dissociative development strategies, the debt crisis, the breakdown of socialist systems, and the success of the world-market-oriented strategy of East Asian countries have led to a loss of importance of dependence theory in the discussion of development, though its basic explanatory contributions are still important for critical development thinking (C. Leys).

3. Strategies to Overcome Dependence
If dependence results from integration into the world

market, more or less radical dissociation from this world market is needed to overcome it. It has been shown that radical national dissociation (e.g., China, North Korea, Albania, and, to a lesser degree, Cuba) has not been the result of deliberate strategy but the result of the reaction of capitalist countries to revolutionary processes in countries of the Third World.

From the analysis made in the theory of dependence, some partial strategies have emerged that have had considerable impact on the political discussion of development. These strategies have included local control or nationalization of affiliates of multinational companies, the adjustment of imported technology to local situations, the development of a special adjusted technology, the promotion of national technological capacities, greater independence in growing food, improvement of terms of trade in relations with industrial countries, and cooperation between developing countries. The idea of overcoming dependence has taken on decisive importance as a perspective that can unite the countries of the Third World in the framework of the North-South conflict. Although national strategies to overcome development have in recent years been oriented primarily toward improving world-market competitiveness, elements of dependency thinking continue to play an important role in fostering cooperation among southern nations in global conferences.

4. Dependence in the Context of the Church

Up to the 1960s the structures of socioeconomic dependence were reflected in the churches as well. In the 19th century the → Roman Catholic Church ceased to be the church of the colonial power (→ Colonialism and Mission) and became the church of the national oligarchy, whose economic dependence corresponded to the dependence of the church on the Vatican. Illustrating this situation in 1967 was the fact that 36 percent of all the priests at work in Latin America were foreigners (in some countries as many as 80 percent). The Protestant churches also depended heavily on other lands, whether as churches of immigrants or as missionary churches financed especially from North America (→ Mission).

In the 1950s the churches began a process of adjustment to the strategies of modernization (e.g., the founding of the → Latin American Council of Bishops [CELAM], with a social but anti-Communist perspective), though this was increasingly challenged in the next decade. → Vatican II, the model of the Cuban revolution, the struggle of the priest Camillo Torres (killed as a Colombian guerrilla), and the inclusion of the church in resistance movements led to an intensive battle against dependence in the church sphere and to the beginnings of a theology of liberation (note the documents of CELAM at Medellín in 1968). Although conservative criticism (including from within the churches) of thinking inspired by dependence theory has grown — in particular, criticism of the theology of liberalization — the dependency approach still has a powerful influence on church involvement in the field of development NGOs.

→ Acculturation; Contextual Theology; Liberation Theology

Bibliography: F. H. Cardoso and E. Faletto, *Abhängigkeit und Entwicklung in Lateinamerika* (Frankfurt, 1976) • A. G. Frank, *Kapitalismus und Unterentwicklung in Lateinamerika* (Frankfurt, 1969) • B. Goudzwaard, *Beyond Poverty and Affluence: Toward an Economy of Care with a Twelve-Step Program for Economic Recovery* (Grand Rapids, 1995) • T. Hurtienne, "Peripherer Kapitalismus und autozentrierte Entwicklung," *ProKla,* no. 44 (1981) 105-36; idem, "Zur Ideologiekritik der lateinamerikanischen Theorien der Unterentwicklung und Abhängigkeit," ibid., no. 14/15 (1974) 213-83 • C. Leys, *The Rise and Fall of Development Theory* (London, 1996) • H.-J. Prien, *Die Geschichte des Christentums in Lateinamerika* (Göttingen, 1978); idem, ed., *Lateinamerika. Gesellschaft, Kirche, Theologie* (2 vols.; Göttingen, 1981) • D. Senghaas, ed., *Imperialismus und strukturelle Gewalt* (Frankfurt, 1972); idem, ed., *Peripherer Kapitalismus* (Frankfurt, 1974) • E. Weede, *Economic Development, Social Order, and World Politics, with Special Emphasis on War, Freedom, the Rise and Decline of the West, and the Future of East Asia* (Boulder, Colo., 1996).

Wolfgang Hein

Depression

1. Definition
2. Symptoms and Course
3. Causes and Classification
4. Therapy
5. Depression and Faith

1. Definition

In psychiatry, depression (Lat. *deprimo,* "press down, depress") denotes a state of severe mental and physical loss of confidence and vigor, usually lasting for a limited period. Allowing for variation, depression differs from ordinary sadness or dispiritedness, on the one hand, and, on the other, from what is called a depressive personality structure.

2. Symptoms and Course

Depression manifests itself fundamentally as a combination of individual depressive symptoms (depressive syndrome) that form a unified syndrome at the mental and physical levels. Mental symptoms include melancholy, an incapacity for → joy, a sense of inner loss, difficulty in thinking and deciding, → anxiety, feelings of worthlessness and → guilt, a loss of social contact and → libido, hopelessness, and even thoughts of → suicide, suicidal impulses, and depressive illusions. Physical symptoms include weakened vitality, loss of energy, feelings of oppression and constriction, pain, loss of appetite and weight, insomnia, impotence, menstrual disruption, and irregular heartbeat.

The main effect on behavior is a depressive disruption of initiative. This may take the form of a reduction of behavior (the "minus symptom"), such as apathy even to the point of stupor; or it may take the form of an excess of initiative (the "plus symptom"), such as a tormenting unrest and anxious busyness. Socially, as depression increases, it becomes impossible to meet daily demands (through depressive inhibition or withdrawal). Thoughts of suicide are always to be taken seriously, but the degree of the danger depends on the depth and nature of the depression as well as the social situation.

The course of the depression is determined by various causes and influences and varies greatly. There may be only a few hours or days of attacks, or there may be a chronic state that lasts for years. Most episodes, however, last for several weeks or months, and they usually lead back to the former level of psychological health. The danger of a relapse, or of fresh depressive episodes, will always be present as long as the pathogenic constellation does not change. For most depressives the intensity of a depression fluctuates even between morning and evening on a single day. According to the estimates of the World Health Organization, the total number of people afflicted by the condition amounts to 3-5 percent of the population.

3. Causes and Classification

The causes of depression may be either psychological (psychosocial) or physical (organic), and completing the so-called etiologic triad, inherited (genetic) factors may also play a part. The modern view generally is that the onset is multicausal. In the case of extreme psychogenic depression, a distinction is made between reactive depression (failure to cope with an experience), depressive developments (due to difficult permanent situations), and neurotic depression (unconscious failure to work through problems, esp.

in early childhood). Usually even before the onset of depression, those affected manifest a depressive personality structure (e.g., restraint of aggression, inclination to withdraw, perfectionism, fear of separation).

Known physical ailments (infection, brain tumors, arteriosclerosis, etc.) are present in the case of those suffering from somatogenic (organic) depression. Among those with endogenous depression, the diagnosis of which is the subject of much debate, we find in a marked way the classic phases, the onset coming at a fixed time each year (spring or fall), with typical variations occurring during the day (the "morning low"). Melancholia, which has been described since antiquity, corresponds to this form. Among some patients there are also manic phases with symptoms opposite to those of depression (the manic-depressives).

4. Therapy

The therapy for depression is multidimensional, in keeping with our understanding of the various pathogenic factors in the condition. The various standpoints, presuppositions, and practical possibilities of therapy lead in practice, however, to very different forms of treatment. Whether a stationary or ambulatory therapy is indicated depends on the severity of the depression, the danger of suicide, the background, and the therapeutic goals. Simply improving or removing symptoms is done relatively quickly (in weeks or months), but dealing with typical underlying structures and factors causing the depression requires a long-range perspective.

Among physical or medical methods of treatment, the chief is the use of antidepressants. This is especially important in the case of severe and predominantly endogenous depression. Medications can also have some prophylactic effects. The large field of → psychotherapeutic possibilities includes depth psychology, psychoanalysis, and cognitive, supportive, suggestive, and behavior-changing procedures. Important, too, is a structured activity-therapy (e.g., a structured day and occupational therapy). Sociotherapy enlists relatives (marriage or family therapy) and deals with the patient's environment (e.g., living conditions at home, the situation at work). All the therapeutic methods work together, supplementing one another.

5. Depression and Faith

The loss of vitality and of a positive approach to life that people suffer in depression can lead to such extensive apathy and inner emotional draining that it affects religious experience. Patients suffer a loss of the ability to believe (→ Faith), along with added feelings of guilt and fear of sinning (→ Sin). They can no longer pray or confess, and they feel hopelessly far from God. In a carefully accepting and supportive way, → pastoral care must take this inability into account. Only occasionally does a moderate depression lead to an enhanced intensity of faith.

Bibliography: V. FAUST and G. HOLE, eds., *Depressionen* (Stuttgart, 1983) • H. J. HAASE, *Depressive Verstimmungen* (Stuttgart, 1980) • G. HOLE, *Der Glaube bei Depressiven* (Stuttgart, 1977) • E. S. PAYKEL, *Handbook of Affective Disorders* (Edinburgh, 1982) • H. TELLENBACH, *Melancholie* (Berlin, 1961; 3d ed., 1976).

GÜNTER HOLE

Depth-Psychological Exegesis

1. Depth-psychological exegesis is any exposition of the Bible (→ Exegesis, Biblical) that uses depth-psychological concepts, theories, or methods. In European usage, as distinct from American, depth psychology denotes all psychological trends using the unconscious, especially → psychoanalysis, the analytic psychology of C. G. Jung (1875-1961), and its further developments (→ Ego Psychology; Identity; Psychotherapy). As such, it is merely one form of psychological exegesis (G. Theissen, K. Berger). Depth-psychological theories vary so much, as do the stages of interrelation between → psychology and exegesis (from the use of simple concepts to depth-psychological method), that we have here a complex phenomenon. Depth-psychological exegesis can take the form of meditative personal dealing with the Bible, → preaching, bibliodramatic theater, scientific discussion of the historical sense of the texts, or the reflection of psychotherapists (see the bibliography in E. Nase and J. Scharfenberg).

2. In the area of biblical scholarship, depth-psychological exegesis is based on a threefold hermeneutical framework.

2.1. In its historical-critical mode, depth-psychological exegesis attempts to identify, analyze, and evaluate the theories of behavior and religious experience implicit in the text. This is then tested by scientific psychology and at times improved. In the process, new questions are usually raised (O. Pfister 1920, Theissen, T. Callan). Especially this question has been fruitful: What could have been the cognitive and emotional reactions of the first readers of the NT (T. Vogt; H. Raguse)?

2.2. We then have a therapeutic and critical psychoanalytic exegesis. Psychologically problematic traditions are evaluated from a psychoanalytic perspective (Pfister 1985, K. Niederwimmer).

2.3. Most publications of depth-psychological exegesis, however, are devoted to what the biblical texts bring to us today. In this applicative exegesis, which establishes identity, the use of depth-psychology is justified through various interrelated arguments.

The premise of the "wisdom" argument is that the Bible contains many profound truths concerning human existence (F. Dolto and G. Séverin), the meaning of → suffering, the secrets of → healing (H. Hark), and so forth. Dialogue with depth psychology can uncover these truths.

A universal identification theory finds in biblical figures identification possibilities for people today.

The normative concept of identity of H. Wolff portrays the historical → Jesus as a model for an integrated humanity that is binding for all (individuation).

The premise of the symbol-didactic concept is that biblical → symbols provide an essential aid to attaining fully mature human existence (M. Kassel).

The most developed form of depth-psychological exegesis is the archetypal → hermeneutics of E. Drewermann. This has as its goal the continuation of existential interpretation (→ Existential Theology 2), as indicated already by Niederwimmer and Kassel. → Archetypes replace existentials as anthropological constants (J. Fischer).

3. No uniform judgment of depth-psychological exegesis can be given, but the following points are worth noting (see M. Leiner).

3.1. On a positive note, depth-psychological exegesis directs attention to unconscious dimensions of the biblical statements. In particular, identification with biblical personages, the meaning of symbols, the emotional dynamics of the texts, and unusual experiences (such as → visions) are expounded through depth-psychological exegesis. The principled antipsychologism of → dialectical theology does not stand up to a critical test.

3.2. But the following questions have to be put to any psychological exegesis. What understanding of reality and what implicit values does it draw from depth psychology? For example, is transcendence identified with the unconscious, and are ecstatic experiences interpreted pathologically? Second, are connections attempted with other exegetical methods? Is sufficient attention paid to historical and social references in the Bible? Third, are the depth-psychological theories empirically and theoretically valid (A. Bucher)?

4. In Germany and France, depth-psychological exegesis achieved great publicity in the dispute about the loss of E. Drewermann's teaching position on October 7, 1991. Drewermann intended to replace historical with depth-psychological exegesis.

Bibliography: K. BERGER, *Historische Psychologie des Neuen Testaments* (Stuttgart, 1991) • A. BUCHER, *Bibel-Psychologie* (Stuttgart, 1992) • T. CALLAN, *Psychological Perspectives on the Life of Paul* (Lewiston, N.Y., 1990) • F. DOLTO and G. SÉVÉRIN, *L'évangile au risque de la psychanalyse* (2 vols.; Paris, 1977) • E. DREWERMANN, *Tiefenpsychologie und Exegese* (2 vols.; Olten, 1974-85) • J. FISCHER, *Heilendes Bild oder Wirklichkeit schaffendes Wort? Glaube und Erkenntnis* (Munich, 1989) 119-48 • P. VON GEMÜNDEN, "La culture des passions à l'époque du Nouveau Testament," *ETR* 70/3 (1995) 335-48 • A. GÖRRES and W. KASPER, eds., *Tiefenpsychologische Deutung des Glaubens?* (Freiburg, 1988) • D. J. HALPERIN, *Seeking Ezekiel: Text and Psychology* (University Park, Pa., 1993) • H. HARK, *Jesus der Heiler* (Olten, 1988); idem, *Religiöse Traumsymbolik* (Frankfurt, 1980) • M. KASSEL, *Biblische Urbilder* (Munich, 1980) • D. A. KILLE, "Jacob: A Study in Individuation," *Jung and the Interpretation of the Bible* (ed. D. L. Miller; New York, 1995) 40-54 • M. LEINER, *Psychologie und Exegese* (Gütersloh, 1995) • D. MERKUR, "Prophetic Initiation in Israel and Judah," *The Psychoanalytic Study of Society* (ed. L. B. Boyer and S. A. Grolnick; Hillsdale, N.J., 1988) 37-67 • S. D. MOORE, "Psychoanalytic Criticism," *The Postmodern Bible* (ed. E. A. Castelli et al.; New Haven, 1995) 187-224 • E. NASE and J. SCHARFENBERG, eds., *Psychoanalyse und Religion* (Darmstadt, 1977) • K. NIEDERWIMMER, "Tiefenpsychologie und Exegese," *WzM* 22 (1970) 257-72 • O. PFISTER, *Die Angst und das Christentum* (Frankfurt, 1985; orig. pub., 1940); idem, "Die Entwicklung des Apostels Paulus," *Imago* 6 (1920) 243-90 • H. RAGUSE, *Psychoanalyse und biblische Interpretation* (Stuttgart, 1993) • I. N. RASHKOW, *The Phallacy of Genesis: A Feminist-Psychoanalytic Approach* (Louisville, Ky., 1993) • W. G. ROLLINS, *Jung and the Bible* (Atlanta, 1983) • R. RUBENSTEIN, *My Brother Paul* (New York, 1972) • Y. SPIEGEL, ed., *Doppeldeutlich* (Munich, 1978) • G. THEISSEN, *Psychological Aspects of Pauline Theology* (Philadelphia, 1986) • T. VOGT, *Angstbefähigung und Identitätsbildung im Markusevangelium* (Fribourg, 1993) • W. WINK, *The Powers* (3 vols.; Philadelphia, 1984-92) • H. WOLFF, *Jesus der Mann* (10th ed.; Stuttgart, 1990) • D. ZELIGS, *Psychoanalysis and the Bible: A Study in Depth of Seven Leaders* (New York, 1974).

MARTIN LEINER

Descartes, René → Cartesianism

Descent into Hell

According to the Apostles' Creed, Jesus Christ "descended into hell." The statement that between his → death (§2.2) and → resurrection came his descent *ad inferna* or *ad infernos* was adopted into the confession only around A.D. 400, probably to stress the full humanity of Christ, both body and soul, in opposition to heretical views (e.g., of Arius and Apollinarius; → Arianism; Christology 2). The descent, however, had already been associated with ideas that would greatly affect its interpretation in personal piety, literature, and art.

In the NT the basis was found partly in such texts as Matt. 12:40; Acts 2:24-25; Rom. 10:7; Eph. 4:9; and Heb. 13:20. The primary source, however, was 1 Pet. 3:18-20; 4:4-6, in which Christ visited the souls in prison to proclaim → salvation to the disobedient of the generation of the flood. Rev. 1:18, taken together with Matt. 16:18, might also be understood to mean that Christ's crucifixion itself vanquished death and hades as an → eschatological anticipation of the → last judgment.

The preaching to the dead and the liberation of the patriarchs found particularly clear expression in the *anastasis* of the Eastern church, in which Christ lifts → Adam by hand out of → hell. The storming of the gates of hell is the theme of Western presentations of the Savior defeating the → devil and hell with the → cross (→ Symbol). In literature the two motifs (with undeniable pagan parallels) go back to the → early church. An especially good example appears in the third-century Gospel of Nicodemus.

In comparison, the church's dogmatic tradition is fairly restrained. The medieval Western church emphasized (against Abelard) that Christ descended in soul and not just *per potentiam* (DH 738). Also rejected were the universalistic notions that Christ led *all* out of hell or that he *destroyed* the lower hell (DH 587, 1077). The nuanced analysis of High → Scholasticism appears in → Thomas Aquinas (*Summa theol.* III, q. 52; → Thomism).

New thinking on the meaning of the descent into hell came with M. → Luther (→ Luther's Theology), who stressed Christ's suffering of the hellish torments of despair and → temptation but who also stressed a triumphant descent after death. The → Formula of Concord (art. 9) followed suit. In contrast, J. → Calvin (→ Calvin's Theology) retained only the first aspect, as did the → Heidelberg Catechism (q. 44). The result in the age of → orthodoxy was the dispute whether the descent into hell was part of Christ's humiliation (the Reformed view) or of his exaltation (the Lutheran view). K. → Barth offered the correction that both views demanded (*CD* IV/1, 132ff.).

Bibliography: H. U. VON BALTHASAR, *Mysterium Paschale: The Theology of the Easter Mystery* (Edinburgh, 1990) 148-88 • W. BIEDER, *Die Vorstellung von der Höllenfahrt Jesu Christi* (Zurich, 1949) • J. FRIEDMAN, "Christ's Descent into Hell and Redemption through Evil," *ARG* 76 (1985) 217-30 • F. C. GRANT et al., "Höllenfahrt" and "Höllenfahrt Christi," *RGG* (3d ed.) 3.407-11 • E. KOCH, "Höllenfahrt Christi," *TRE* 15.455-61 • W. MAAS, *Gott und die Hölle. Studien zum Descensus Christi* (Einsiedeln, 1979) • R. MURRAY, *Symbols of Church and Kingdom: A Study in Early Syriac Tradition* (Cambridge, 1975) 231-36, 299-301, 324-29 • W. PANNENBERG, *Jesus—God and Man* (Philadelphia, 1968) 269-74 • B. REICKE, *The Disobedient Spirits and Christian Baptism* (Copenhagen, 1946) • H. J. VOGELS, *Christi Abstieg ins Totenreich* (Freiburg, 1976) • D. D. WALLACE, "Puritan and Anglican: The Interpretation of Christ's Descent into Hell," *ARG* 69 (1978) 248-87.

ALASDAIR I. C. HERON

Design, Argument from → God, Arguments for the Existence of

Despair

1. In Psychology
2. Situational Neurosis
3. In Theology and Philosophy

Despair is a state that, like → anxiety or a feeling of → guilt, affects a person's whole experience. It may derive from differing situations, depending on whether the psychological nature of → conflict, the state of the nervous system, or existence as a → metaphysical problem is dominant. The loss of all → hope of well-being causes despair to seem related to sadness and depression, though in reality it represents a radical heightening of the latter within experience. In older → psychiatry (J.-É.-D. Esquirol, F. C. A. Heinroth, K. W. Ideler) despair was subsumed under melancholy, but in modern psychology of the self (H. Kohut; → Psychoanalysis 2.2) it appears when a severe objective loss is also a severe loss of → self. To understand its nature the following distinctions may be formulated: (1) despair as a phenomenon of sickness or of the human situation generally, (2) despair as human alienation or creative suffering, and (3) despair as falling away from God or as distress because of God. The word "or" in these phrases does not refer to any absolute antithesis but, rather, to the possibility of partial intersection.

1. In Psychology

Despair as a phenomenon of sickness runs right through psychiatry as fever does through medicine. There is thus no particular syndrome called despair. We find it in endogenous melancholy, in psychoreactive depression, in schizophrenia, and in → neurosis. It is less common in sicknesses of the brain because it involves psychological self-observation, unlike somatically induced anxiety or unrest. Despair can take many forms, affecting the whole ego as in depression or giving people different personages as in schizophrenia (e.g., as when a person's verbal expressions are despairing while his or her gestures are indifferent).

The phenomenon of sickness becomes increasingly "the human situation" when there is no biological or psychopathological reason for it. Despair arises in this case when people are unable to solve vital conflicts and when this failure severely affects self-identity (→ Identity). In this setting it spans the two different genetic poles of → traumatic external experience and the inner experience that is rooted in the structure of the personality. Psychologically it is then understood as an unconscious state of failure with underlying pathogenic ideas and longings that can be brought to light and overcome in an illuminating relationship.

2. Situational Neurosis

A dynamic pair of contrasts is that of despair as human alienation and as creative suffering. The former occurs when, in situations of psychological collapse, people are lost even to the point of → suicide, for they feel nothing beneath them, they cannot accept themselves, and they can no longer find any possibility of identification with others.

Creative despair, however, has a positive future because the wounded sensitiveness from which it derives may have the self as its object insofar as this self takes seriously a universal situation of human need like its own and finds it intolerable. Even where such despair is not overcome (as, in literature, the blinded Oedipus or the dying Lear), it bears witness to a creative longing for right and freedom.

As in the dynamic contrast of psychological sickness and the human situation, antitheses here, too, may touch each other, for the creative variant is not always present from the outset but arises only out of the particular kind of encounter with others.

3. In Theology and Philosophy

3.1. In biblical usage the word "despair" is fairly uncommon (as a noun in Ps. 69:20, Eccl. 2:20, Isa. 19:9, Ezek. 7:27, and 2 Cor. 4:8; as a verb only in

1 Sam. 27:1, Job 15:22 and 24:22, and 2 Cor. 1:8), but the phenomenon arises as a result of (either subjectively or collectively perceived) feeling of abandonment by God. It finds expression as lament (Ps. 22:1 = Mark 15:34; Job 3), as protest (Job 7:17-20; Psalm 88), or as acceptance of the inevitable and thus as resignation (Eccl. 2:4-11; → Wisdom Literature), which frequently appears as pious resignation in God (e.g., Ps. 42:6-11).

3.2. In → Scholastic theology despair is regarded as → sin (§3) against the Holy Spirit because it views the operation of grace as impossible and thus means the loss of all hope. For → Thomas Aquinas (1224/25-74; → Thomism), "despair is more dangerous [than even unbelief or hatred of God], since hope withdraws us from → evils and induces us to seek for → good things, so that when hope is given up, men rush headlong into sin, and are drawn away from good works" (*Summa theol.* II of II, q. 20, art. 3c).

3.3. In the → Reformation understanding (→ Calvin's Theology; Zwingli's Theology), despair is a result of → sin, which can be described as radical self-absorption. Picking up on Romans 7, M. → Luther (1483-1546; → Luther's Theology) describes the sinner as *homo in se ipsum incurvatus* ("a person incurved into himself"), who in such a state loses sight of his or her → neighbor, the world, and even God. Instead, he becomes a victim of the → devil, who reproaches him with his sins, provoking thus a bad → conscience, which itself ultimately drives the sinner to despair (see WA.*TR* 6.6827.215.40–216.9).

For Luther, however, this fixation on oneself and on one's own works, which are to serve self-redemption before God, has been sundered theologically. The → incarnation, death, and → resurrection of Jesus Christ bring about a "joyous change" (see WA 43.582; WA.*TR* 2.1351.66.1-7). That is, Christ takes the sins of the world on himself; delivers human beings from the curse of the → law, which makes (excessive) demands on them; and thus renders possible good works for one's fellow human beings (→ Law and Gospel).

3.4. One contemporary view of despair, oriented toward the → reconciliation of God with the world (2 Cor. 5:19-20) as the basis for → justification, advocates the acknowledgment and acceptance of the desperate instead of their condemnation (D. Stollberg). This attitude of → empathy and participative → solidarity has also been quite influential on the church's → pastoral care. Such an understanding of faith and life can help others who under inner and outer pressure suffer or despair of themselves, their lives, or their world. Pastoral comforting, personal empathy, and individual help can be given so that they can accept their situation, come to terms with it, and find possibilities of action. It is essential, however, that we bring to light, criticize, and change the structures in the church and society that make people, accidentally or systematically, the victims of despair.

3.5. The concept of despair played an especially important role in the thinking of S. → Kierkegaard (1813-55). In his *Sickness unto Death* (1849) he explained the human self as a synthesis of → immanence and transcendence, of body and → soul. This self is not posited by itself but by another transcendent self — by God. The relation of the individual self to the transcendent self determines our → health or sickness. Affirmation of being posited by a transcendent self (i.e., by God), and gratitude for it, is the posture of faith. Where there is doubt about this relation, however, we have the phenomenon of despair, which can express itself in three ways: (1) in despair not being conscious of having a self (inauthentic despair); (2) in despair not wanting to be one's self (despair of weakness); and (3) in despair wanting to be one's self (defiance). The last two forms count as sin if they take place in the presence of God. Relating sin, the self, and despair in this way, Kierkegaard succeeds through philosophical reflection in regaining the "transmoral character" (C. H. Ratschow) of the concept of sin such as we find in the theological accounts given by Paul and Luther.

→ Doubt 2; Penitence; Psychoanalysis; Psychosis; Salvation; Temptation

Bibliography: G. BENEDETTI, "The Irrational in the Psychotherapy of Psychosis," *Psychotherapy of Schizophrenia* (Northvale, N.J., 1995) 139-46; idem, *Todeslandschaften der Seele* (3d ed.; Göttingen, 1991) • A. M. CARRÉ, *Espérance et désespoir* (Paris, 1954) • A. HAYNAL, *Depression and Creativity* (New York, 1985) • S. KIERKEGAARD, *Gesammelte Werke* (trans. H. Gottsched and C. Schrempf; 12 vols.; Jena, 1909-22) • B. MEERPOHL, *Verzweiflung als metaphysisches Phänomen in der Philosophie Sören Kierkegaards* (Würzburg, 1934) • U. RAUCHFLEISCH, *Leiden–verzweifeln–hoffen* (Freiburg, 1991) • M. THEUNISSEN, *Der Begriff Verzweiflung. Korrekturen an Kierkegaard* (Frankfurt, 1993).

GAETANO BENEDETTI and EKKEHARD STARKE

Deus absconditus, Deus revelatus → God 7

Deutero-Isaiah → Isaiah, Book of, 3.2

Deuteronomistic History

1. In the Hebrew Bible the first part of the → canon (§1) — the → Law and the Former Prophets, or the books from Genesis to Kings — contains a consecutive narrative from the → creation to the Babylonian exile. Not merely by canonical arrangement or in terms of content but also in view of its historical development, there are good reasons to divide it into two parts. The first part consists of the → Pentateuch, which ends with the death of → Moses and therefore with the conclusion of the age of the founding of the people → Israel, which reached a climax with the giving of the law at Sinai. The second part consists of the Books of Joshua, Judges, Samuel, and Kings, which recount the history of the people in the promised land.

At the junction of the two parts stands Deuteronomy, which in its opening chapters gives a kind of résumé of past events, but for the rest looks ahead no less than backward. In his long parting address Moses has in view the land beyond the Jordan, into which his people will now go without him. Again, the books from Joshua to Kings also look back a great deal to Deuteronomy, to its announcements as well as its statutes. Even where this does not take place explicitly, there are single verses or longer passages that in form and content remind us so much of the characteristic historical, theological, and hortatory style of Deuteronomy that scholars have long called them Deuteronomistic. There is undoubtedly a literary connection.

According to M. Noth, "a writer of Deuteronomistic history" compiled the books Deuteronomy through Kings. He used extensive older materials, yet did not simply edit them superficially, but independently and deliberately conformed them to ideas that we find expressed in some of the basic parts that he himself formulated. These include the parting address of Moses beginning with the backward look in Deuteronomy 1–3, the introduction to the story of the conquest and the summary of it in Joshua 1 and 12, the parting address of Joshua in Joshua 23, the survey of the age of the Judges in Judg. 2:11-19, the speech of Samuel after the inauguration of the monarchy in 1 Samuel 12, the speech and prayer of Solomon at the dedication of the temple in 1 Kings 8, and the epilogue to the northern kingdom in 2 Kgs. 17:7-23.

The schematization of events according to the Deuteronomistic theology of history comes out most plainly in the depiction of the age of the judges and the monarchy. The judges schema has the following elements: Israel's disobedience, Yahweh's anger, oppression by enemies, Israel's cry for help, the raising up of a deliverer (judge) by Yahweh, and a period of rest following deliverance (e.g., see Judg. 3:7-11, the elements of which occur in the ensuing stories).

The monarchy schema (e.g., 1 Kings 15) gives the dates of the reign; the obedience or (more often, and always so in the North) disobedience of the kings, which consists of idolatry (as in the age of the judges) or, after the erection of the → temple, of "the sin of Jeroboam" (i.e., the cultic worship of Yahweh outside → Jerusalem); then, in the northern kingdom, the threat of punishment as delivered by the → prophets; and finally an account of the fulfillment of the threat (1 Kgs. 16:1-4, 11-13, etc.). After → David, only Hezekiah and → Josiah in the South receive a totally positive report (2 Kgs. 18:3-6; 22:2; 23:25).

2. The Deuteronomistic author or historian probably wrote during the Babylonian exile. The grace shown by the Babylonian king Evil-merodach to the imprisoned Judean king Jehoiachin in 560 B.C., with which the work significantly closes (2 Kgs. 25:27-30), seems to be for the writer an event that has just taken place.

How far theologizing compilations of greater parts of the material were already present prior to the exile is much debated. Certainly there were various later revisions, so that it is the fashion to speak of a "nomistic" and a "prophetic" Deuteronomist. Important features are the increasing emphasis on the law and the negative evaluation of the monarchy (see the additions Josh. 1:7-8 and 1 Sam. 8:6-22a).

In the strata of the work we find the trend within the Deuteronomic-Deuteronomistic school that in the face of an uncertain future at the time of the exile was trying to summarize the experiences of Israel with its God. The work of this school covered several generations, and it had an impact not only on historical writing (Genesis–Numbers, as well as Deuteronomy–Kings; → Historiography 1) but particularly also on the prophetic literature (e.g., Jeremiah).

Bibliography: W. DIETRICH, *Prophetie und Geschichte* (Göttingen, 1972) • R. E. FRIEDMAN, *The Exile and Biblical Narrative* (Chico, Calif., 1981) • S. L. MCKENZIE and M. P. GRAHAM, eds., *The History of Israel's Traditions* (Sheffield, 1994) • A. D. H. MAYES, *The Story of Israel between Settlement and Exile: A Redactional Study of the Deuteronomistic History* (London, 1983) • R. D. NELSON, *The Double Redaction of the Deuteronomistic History* (Sheffield, 1981) • M. NOTH, *The Deuteronomistic History* (Sheffield, 1981) • M. A. O'BRIEN, *The Deuteronomistic History Hypothesis* (Freiburg, 1989) •

W. Roth, "Deuteronomistisches Geschichtswerk / Deuteronomistische Schule," *TRE* 6.543-52 (bibliography) • T. Veijola, *Die ewige Dynastie. David und die Entstehung seiner Dynastie nach der deuteronomistischen Darstellung* (Helsinki, 1975); idem, *Das Königtum in der Beurteilung der deuteronomistischen Historiographie* (Helsinki, 1977); idem, *Verheißung in der Krise* (Helsinki, 1982) • E. Würthwein, *Studien zum deuteronomistischen Geschichtswerk* (Berlin, 1994).

RUDOLF SMEND

Deuteronomy, Book of

1. Name
2. Form
3. Contents
    3.1. Law
    3.2. Parenetic Framework
    3.3. Historical Framework
4. Date

1. Name

Deriving from the LXX, "Deuteronomy" is the name for the fifth book of the → Pentateuch. On the basis of Deut. 17:18, it has the sense "repetition of the law" (i.e., of that given in Exodus–Numbers). This is a mistaken rendering, however, of the Heb. *mišnēh hattôrâ*, "copy of the law."

2. Form

In its form, Deuteronomy is largely the parting address of → Moses, structured in several sections. He gave this address to the Israelites in Moab, east of the Jordan (1:1, 5; 29:1), immediately before the conquest of the promised land (Joshua 1–12). This stylistic device forces the author and redactors into several literary and historical inconsistencies.

3. Contents

We best grasp the contents of Deuteronomy by considering the formal and material features of the various sections and the probable sequence of their compilation.

3.1. Law

The core consists of the law in chaps. 12–25 (with two liturgical appendixes in 26). The various statutes display no uniform form or content. Neither is there any obvious arrangement of the laws, which we may divide roughly into (1) cultic laws (12:1–16:17), (2) laws of office (16:18–18:22), and (3) mixed public and private law (19–25).

Notable themes of the cultic laws are the central-

ization of the cult at "the place that the LORD your God will choose . . . [for] his name" (12:5, 11) and the calendar of feasts (16:1-17). The laws of office include instructions about judges (16:18-20; 17:8-13), kings (17:14-20), → priests (18:1-8), and → prophets (18:9-22). The third group includes the laws of warfare (20), community law (23:2-8), and various laws about sex and the family (scattered throughout 21–25). Several of these laws give humanitarian and religious depth to the corresponding laws in the → Book of the Covenant, but their different structure argues against direct dependence. The law in Deuteronomy is a compilation of what are in part smaller, pre-Deuteronomic collections.

There is a formal diversity in Deuteronomic law. Alongside apodictic commands that often have a parenetic basis (e.g., 15:1-11), we find, especially in chaps. 19 and 21–25, casuistic rulings in various forms ("if someone . . . ," "if you . . ."). The alternation of themes and forms shows that the Deuteronomic law was collected and edited for generations.

3.2. *Parenetic Framework*

The Deuteronomic theologians have put this law in a parenetic framework. Furthermore, these exhortations, compressed into chaps. 5–11, are not all of a piece. The common change in number in the form of address, the motivation for which is seldom obvious, itself gives evidence of development (note connected Deuteronomistic pieces, mostly in the pl., in 9:7–10:11; 10:12–11:32). Though the addresses are repetitive in style and content, they contain a concentrate of Deuteronomic theology, especially (in various strata and hence with different emphases) such themes or concepts as → promise, election, → covenant, the gift of the land, the conquest, the people of God, → Israel and the nations, command, and → obedience.

The pre-Deuteronomistic Deuteronomy probably began with 6:4 and following verses. There is disagreement regarding when the → Decalogue and its parenetic framework (5:1–6:3) was put before it, thus making all of Deuteronomy appear as an exposition of the Decalogue. Deuteronomistic continuations of parenesis, in part alluding to the exile, occur in the related framework — chaps. 4 and 29, and 30. The respective results of obedience and disobedience are set forth at the end in → blessing and → cursing (28). The developing theology of the Deuteronomic and Deuteronomistic school kept giving Deuteronomy a new shape, with the result that throughout 4–30 one can distinguish the earliest Deuteronomic from the latest Deuteronomistic strata.

3.3. *Historical Framework*

At a later stage in this process the parenetically extended law was put in a historical framework provided by chaps. 1–3 and 31–34 (separate traditions include the Song of Moses and Moses' blessing in 32–33). These framing sections, which point beyond Deuteronomy, constitute the beginning of → Deuteronomistic history. In retrospect in 1–3, Moses brings himself and Israel once again (following themes in Exodus and Numbers) from Horeb to the Jordan. There he gives his address just before the conquest, for he himself may not enter the promised land. References forward and back forge a link between Deuteronomy 1–3 and the early chapters of Joshua (Deut. 3:21-28; 31:1-8; 32:45-52; Josh. 1:1-3).

4. Date

The linguistic and thematic connection between Deuteronomy and the books Joshua–Kings gives us a decisive hint as to the date of both Deuteronomy and the Deuteronomistic history. The depiction, which goes up to the exile, carries the historical and religious experiences of that later age back into the account of the time of Moses. Thus Deuteronomy in its canonical form can hardly have taken shape before the sixth century, if not considerably later.

The age of the legislative collections in Deuteronomy is harder to determine. They probably come from some time during the eighth through sixth centuries. Especially debated is the time of composition of the pre-Deuteronomistic, but already parenetically extended, Book of the Law (12–26? 5–26?). Already the → early church took a view for which the 19th century gave good scholarly reasons, namely, that this book (the so-called Ur-Deuteronomy of older research) lay behind the reforms of Josiah in 622 B.C. (2 Kings 22–23), for the individual reforms correspond to Deuteronomic cultic statutes at many points, especially the law of the central sanctuary (Deuteronomy 12). The Deuteronomic Book of the Law can hardly be much older than the situational context in which it first played a role.

As regards authorship, scholarship has achieved no consensus (priests? elders? Levites?). The process of composition and the impact of Deuteronomy on the OT suggest → Jerusalem in the seventh or sixth century. From a literary standpoint, Deuteronomy plays a crucial role — perhaps *the* crucial role — in historical criticism of the Pentateuch and Deuteronomistic history. Theologically, as G. von Rad has observed, it is "the heart of the OT."

Bibliography: *Commentaries:* S. R. DRIVER (ICC; 3d ed.; New York, 1902) • A. D. H. MAYES (NCB; London, 1979) • E. NIELSEN (HAT; Tübingen, 1995) • A. PHILLIPS (CBC; Cambridge, 1973) • G. VON RAD (OTL; London, 1966) • K. STEUERNAGEL (HKAT; 2d ed.; Göttingen, 1923) • M. WEINFELD (AB; New York, 1991).

Other works: A. ALT, "Die Heimat des Deuteronomiums," *Kleine Schriften* (vol. 2; Munich, 1953) 250-75 • F. GARCÍA MARTÍNEZ et al., eds., *Studies in Deuteronomy* (Leiden, 1994) • F. HORST, *Das Privilegrecht Jahwes. Rechtsgeschichtliche Untersuchungen zum Deuteronomium* (Göttingen, 1930; repr. *Gottes Recht* [Munich, 1961] 17-154) • F.-L. HOSSFELD, *Der Dekalog* (Göttingen, 1982) • N. LOHFINK, *Das Hauptgebot. Eine Untersuchung . . . zu Deuteronomium 5–11* (Rome, 1963); idem, *Studien zum Deuteronomium und zur deuteronomistischen Literatur* (3 vols.; Stuttgart, 1990-95) • J. G. MCCONVILLE, *Law and Theology in Deuteronomy* (Sheffield, 1984) • E. W. NICHOLSON, *Deuteronomy and Tradition* (Oxford, 1967) • L. PERLITT, *Bundestheologie im Alten Testament* (Neukirchen, 1969); idem, *Deuteronomium-Studien* (Tübingen, 1994) • H. D. PREUSS, *Deuteronomium* (Darmstadt, 1982) • G. VON RAD, *Studies in Deuteronomy* (London, 1953; orig. pub., 1947) • G. SEITZ, *Redaktionsgeschichtliche Studien zum Deuteronomium* (Stuttgart, 1971) • M. WEINFELD, *Deuteronomy and the Deuteronomic School* (Oxford, 1972).

LOTHAR PERLITT

Deutsche Christen → German Christians

Development

1. Socioeconomic Development
   1.1. Theory
   1.2. Underdevelopment and Developing
      Countries
   1.3. Strategies
   1.4. Aid
2. Psychological Development
3. Religious Development

1. Socioeconomic Development

Descriptively, the term "development" denotes historical changes made to produce the form of → society desired by its members; normatively, it denotes the structural changes made toward this goal. Whether the development or its basic mechanisms represent → progress in some absolute sense is immaterial. In the normative sense, socioeconomic developments are the processes that can bring a poor society closer to its desired form. Politically, various indicators stand in the forefront, including gross national product (GNP) and the satisfaction of primary needs.

In the 19th century, theories predominately arranged the different cultures on a single ladder of development (evolutionism). Similar ideas are found in K. → Marx (1818-83; → Marxism). The 20th century, in contrast, has stressed the equal value of the various cultures (→ Functionalism; Relativism). But it has also called → poverty (or "underdevelopment," for Marxists and others) the result of international exploitation or imperialism.

Not only Marxists have advanced the theory that continued growth in political and economic → dependence can lead only to underdevelopment. The international boom after World War II made a theory of modernization plausible, namely, development following the European model with the creation of the "correct" sociocultural presuppositions. But the decreasing possibilities of self-determination and social self-renewal in developing countries have become an argument against dependence. The rapid development of some previously dependent countries (e.g., Japan and other countries on the rim of Asia) shows that certain endogenous presuppositions of development, such as also characterized Europe, must carry greater weight in a general theory of development.

1.1. *Theory*

Overall, a theory of development must take account of the unique character of each society; that is, it must leave room for what we could call endogenous presuppositions.

Trade between societies, even as it increases, must include a sense of its rightful limitation. Not everything can be traded. A society engaging in trade must maintain a mutuality, even with anonymous outsiders (within itself or beyond its borders). In Europe in the Middle Ages, as in → Third World countries today, there was exchange not merely of goods in daily use but also of intangible social factors like → love, justice, and divine → grace. Development seen too narrowly inevitably reaches a dead end.

The development of → communication and markets has as its central presupposition the development of the modern → state and the related civilized restraint of → force (N. Elias). An increasing monopolizing of force by the state frees greater areas from violence, which is a key condition for commercial expansion. Failure to accomplish this level of protection is one of the biggest problems in developing countries.

A key process is putting the culture in writing. This makes possible a quicker spread of innovations, longer chains of command and their control (a prerequisite for any expansion of rule), and the accumulation of knowledge beyond the limitations of memory. In turn, → institutions are needed that will promote the use of writing, in spite of its formality.

Development in the 20th century is dominated by a qualitative advance in handling → energy and a changed attitude toward the → environment. The decreased need for land in the industrialized agriculture of a modern → industrial society has its cost — namely, by consuming more energy resources and irreversibly poisoning the environment, we become increasingly at odds with future generations (→ Ecology).

The developing countries often have found that their own presuppositions make it difficult to use the technologies of industrial countries. Countries that have articulated their own models of political and economic organization, however, even though they have begun efforts involving outsiders who perhaps use unfamiliar assumptions in solving technological problems, can ultimately arrive at productive and stable processes of development if they are open to possibilities of variation and selection. This combination has been called "social → evolution" (N. Luhmann). Although the linking of pluralist → democracy with freedom of information is not the only possibility for achieving this, it is probably the one least susceptible to violence.

1.2. *Underdevelopment and Developing Countries*

Underdevelopment is a state of general poverty that is rooted in the structures of a country and its dependence on other countries for its own development. The term is misleading inasmuch as the cultures of these countries are just as old and developed as those of wealthy lands, and their structures are formed by the same process of development as those that brought wealth to other lands.

Leaving aside all theoretical terms, we must remember simply that underdeveloped countries are poor. Their average income is clearly lower than that of the industrialized countries. Such criteria as literacy or life expectancy may parallel the level of income, but still income is the decisive criterion.

High subsistence production, which is hard to measure statistically, may give → farmers better nourishment and a higher life expectancy, even when they have little cash income, than would a better income from the production of goods under the compulsion of debts. The GNP says nothing about distribution. If, as in Zaire, or earlier in Nicaragua, a single family owns more than half of the industrial capacity, their wealth would count in the GNP but would tell us nothing about the well-being of the people.

The gap between the poorest or least developed

countries (→ Third World 1.1) and the other developing countries has widened considerably in recent years. Countries like Brazil, Singapore, and Taiwan, because of factors like industrialization, are now on the threshold between the developing countries and the poorer industrialized countries.

Earlier, underdeveloped countries were said to be marked by dualism between a modern sector and a traditional sector. Elements in the latter, because of traditionalism, wrong emphases, or lack of ability to compete, resisted modernization of the economy. Such theories, however, are no longer tenable. As a reaction to the uncertainties of the marketplace, it may make more sense to invest less money in productive capacity and more in building up and improving social relations (e.g., involving ceremonial tasks, the creation of new kinds of extended families, the founding of ethnic societies with self-help aspects). In view of the traditional forms of agriculture and domestic and social structures, many observers favor a subsistence economy.

In the 20th century the breakdown of traditional forms of social control means that it is hard to restrain the invasion of social relations by → money. Often, then, the social structure is undermined by financial factors. In the bride price system (→ Family 1.7), in religious rituals involving money, and in political corruption, there is, from an individual standpoint, much more opportunity for profit than in the economy in the strict sense (e.g., from work in agriculture). An agricultural policy that holds down prices in favor of a city elite and labor, or that shows a preference for metropolitan or state industrial projects, helps to put the rural majority on the economic periphery. In this way, traditional structures are both undermined and perpetuated by their entanglement with modern market and state structures. The dubious legacy of → colonialism and imperialism exists in the creation of such structures that hamper development, rather than in overt economic exploitation per se.

1.3. Strategies

Various strategies have emerged from the respective theories and interests. The strategy of *unbalanced growth* is based on European and North American experience. Discrepancies between strongly expanding and lagging economic sectors supposedly demand special economic incentives. But it may be asked whether such incentives for the domestic market can now work, in view of lower costs of international trade and the great advances being made by leading nations.

The strategy of *balanced growth* has in view the problem of social tensions because of economic disparities.

Some threshold countries have enjoyed success with a strategy of *developing exports.* But it is doubtful that this approach would work for all countries.

The strategy of *self-centered development* gives more weight to replacing imports. Precedence should be given to the stimulation and integration of existing resources (D. Senghaas).

Strategies oriented to *financial criteria* like the GNP or balance of trade take too little account of providing for the basic needs of the people. Another problem is that of growth by exhausting resources at the expense of future generations.

The strategy of *ecodevelopment* (I. Sachs) tries to deal with problems of this kind. It relates value-use to economic calculations and stresses self-regulation by self-organized units.

1.4. Aid

The aid in question is foreign aid. From the time of Frederick the Great (king of Prussia, 1740-86), subsidies have been used politically as a means of securing and protecting zones of influence. During World War II the United States built up a system of lend-lease contracts, and in 1943 it provided the stimulus for the founding of the United Nations Relief and Rehabilitation Administration. In 1946 the UN founded the International Bank for Reconstruction and Development. After 1949, when the Chinese Communists triumphed and Britain and France began to withdraw from Asia, the developing countries of Asia became the main recipients of aid in Truman's Four Point Program. From the time of colonialism, and in veiled reaction to it, Christian → missions also supported aid programs (→ Colonialism and Mission).

Aid may be divided into capital aid (credits, subsidies) and technical and personal aid (ostensibly to introduce technological innovations but in fact to take charge of infrastructures). Humanitarian motives, security interests, economic interests, and prestige are closely interwoven in the giving of aid. The last two mean that small countries (which have an equal vote in the UN and count for just as much in public opinion) receive proportionately more aid per capita than large countries.

Several supranational agencies are active in granting aid, including the UN's Food and Agriculture Organization (FAO); the UN Educational, Scientific, and Cultural Organization (UNESCO); the UN Development Programme (UNDP); and the Development Assistance Committee (DAC) for the Organisation for Economic Co-operation and Development (OECD). In addition, many countries have their own aid agencies. Nongovernmental organizations (NGOs) are more effective with fewer means at their disposal. In this regard, we could note church and church-related organizations such as Bread for the World, Eirene, Misereor, Oxfam, and World Vision. In some cases the multiplicity of organizations and the uncoordinated efforts of foreign agencies have forced the receiving countries to try to coordinate the work or to impose restrictions.

Bibliography: J. W. BENNET, *The Ecological Transition* (New York, 1976) • W. BRANDT, ed., *Das Überleben sichern. Gemeinsame Interessen der Industrie- und Entwicklungsländer. Bericht der Nord-Süd-Kommission* (Cologne, 1980) • R. CHILCOTE and D. JOHNSON, eds., *Theories of Development: Mode of Production or Dependency?* (Beverly Hills, Calif., 1983) • H. D. EVERS, D. SENGHAAS, and H. WIENHOLTZ, eds., *Auf dem Weg zu einer neuen Weltwirtschaftsordnung?* (Baden-Baden, 1983) • K. GRIMM, *Theorien der Unterentwicklung und Entwicklungsstrategien* (Opladen, 1979) • D. LEHMANN, ed., *Development Theory* (London, 1979) • I. SACHS, ed., *Initiation à l'écodéveloppement* (Toulouse, 1981) • A. SCHMIDT, ed., *Strategien gegen Unterentwicklung* (Frankfurt, 1976) • M. SCHULZ, ed., *Europäische Gemeinschaft und Entwicklungsländer* (Frankfurt, 1978) • T. SKOCPOL, *States and Revolutions* (Cambridge, 1979) • E. SOTTAS, *The Least Developed Countries* (New York [UN], 1984) • P. SPITZ et al., *Il faut manger pour vivre. . . . Controverses sur les besoins fondamentaux et le développement* (Paris, 1980) • R. STRAHM, *Warum sie so arm sind* (Wuppertal, 1985).

GEORG ELWERT

2. Psychological Development

The term "development" became important in the 19th century in the humanities, partly through the influence of G. W. F. Hegel (1770-1831; → Hegelianism), and in the natural sciences, especially through C. Darwin (1809-82; → Evolution). Before 1900 → psychology became systematically interested in the development of the child, and around 1920 in that of youth.

Around 1950 developmental psychology began to study the individual lifespan as a whole. Persons were seen to be beings that learn throughout life (→ Anthropology). In → childhood and → youth the focus is on bodily growth and the associated maturing of functions. In this sphere the point of interest is the way in which individual functions (e.g., intellectual) ripen. Various stages are studied and compared, and standards are fixed. Research into adulthood follows individual life histories, which can be compared only in a limited sense because personal experiences and decisions differ.

Throughout, our bipolarity as biological and psy-

chological beings is apparent. Development is thus the actualizing of genetic programs and personal decisions in the context of → environment, destiny, and tasks (→ Socialization).

→ Psychotherapies work on blocks and other detriments to development and provide important insights about its nature. The model of *psychoanalysis* (S. Freud et al.) deals with → neurotic misdevelopment and claims that in such cases development comes to a halt in all spheres either totally or partially at early childhood stages (oral, anal, and phallic stages with regard to the id sphere, specific defense mechanisms with regard to the ego sphere, orientation to need with regard to objective relations). Normal development involves the genital organization of the id, the free functioning of the ego, and an independently related and life-affirming superego.

Individual psychology (A. Adler et al.) orients itself to meaningful goals and the development of social interests. A natural human lack of self-worth can be overcome by achievement and fellowship, but false development can lead to a complex that disguises itself through overcompensation.

Analytic psychology (C. G. Jung et al.) relates development especially to the second half of life. The goal is wholeness of personality by the integration of polar opposites (individuation). By this process the personality acquires an expanded consciousness that transcends social convention.

Development as the meaning of life is advocated by *humanistic psychology,* which is rooted philosophically in → humanism and → existentialism (S. → Kierkegaard et al.). Many psychotherapists now view the human person as a meaningful whole (C. Rogers et al.). At the heart of this view of development are such concepts as self-actualization, self-fulfillment, personality growth, → meaning, → creativity, encounter, and → love.

Transcendental and esoteric psychologies go a step further in consciousness-development and focus on transcendental experiences (→ Immanence and Transcendence).

Psychological → counseling deals especially with people in the crises of life and of development, which offer opportunities for further development. Progressive development leads to more → autonomy. Fear (→ Anxiety) of → freedom and → responsibility causes stagnation of development or regression to childlike dependence and reduced responsibility. In partners this leads to destructive "games" (as discussed in transactional analysis). Opposition may be stronger in the system of → marriage and → family, and disruption may result.

Because of anxiety, many people do not reach full

maturity in an emotional and spiritual sense, and even hinder others from developing fully. Within societies and social groups, other individual hindrances to development can be fostered by certain leadership styles (authoritarian as well as antiauthoritarian). Prompted by experiences with the → fascist dictatorships in Europe, this nexus of relationships was investigated and brought into the light of consciousness. Although the practical results of this work are certainly discernible in the Western democracies in an increased emphasis on codetermination and partnership, such results nonetheless still lag behind original expectations.

The ideal goals of human development are autonomy and love. The research of J. Piaget, L. Kohlberg, R. Selman, and others shows in their multistep models of intellectual development a steady increase in autonomy and social competence, which we thus can identify as the presuppositions for reaching the ideal goals of development. Thus far, however, their achievement has been only fragmentary or limited to a relative few.

→ Biography, Biographical Research; Education; Identity

Bibliography: P. BALTES, ed., *Entwicklungspsychologie der Lebensspanne* (Stuttgart, 1979) • H. BARTZ, *Stichwort: Selbstverwirklichung* (Stuttgart, 1982) • C. BÜHLER and M. ALLEN, *Einführung in die humanistische Psychologie* (Frankfurt, 1983) • R. CASE, *Intellectual Development: Birth to Adulthood* (New York, 1985) • L. KOHLBERG, *Zur kognitiven Entwicklung des Kindes* (Frankfurt, 1974) • B. LIEVEGOED, *Lebenskrisen — Lebenschancen* (3d ed.; Munich, 1983) • J. PIAGET, *The Moral Judgment of the Child* (London, 1977) • R. SELMAN, *Die Entwicklung des sozialen Verstehens* (Frankfurt, 1984) • G. STEINER, ed., *Entwicklungspsychologie* (Weinheim, 1984) • H. THOMAE, ed., *Entwicklungspsychologie* (2d ed.; Göttingen, 1972) • H. M. WELLMAN, *Children's Theories of Mind* (Cambridge, Mass., 1990).

GÜNTER HOPPE

3. Religious Development

In the → psychology of religion, as distinct from the → philosophy of religion, religious development has to do with the ontogenetic forms of experience, perception, cognition, and so forth, insofar as they relate to what children, young people, and adults regard as transcendent (→ Immanence and Transcendence). For the most part, attempts to view religious development psychologically date only from the late 19th and early 20th centuries (E. D. Starbuck, W. James, G. Bohne).

We may distinguish concept-oriented, cognitive-developmental, and psychoanalytic approaches. The first deals with individual ideas (e.g., understanding of God), using an inductive process (M. P. Strommen, A. Vergote).

The second (J. Piaget) stresses the step-by-step development of cognitive structures, worldviews, and moral judgment from an egocentric form of reflection to one based on the group and society, and then to one determined by individual judgment (L. Kohlberg). A corresponding development is seen in religious thinking from a mythological unity of transcendence and immanence to a sharp separation critical of tradition, and finally to a reuniting (R. Goldman; F. Oser and P. Gmünder). J. W. Fowler even speaks of a "development of faith."

Psychoanalytic religious psychology (S. Freud) was strongly influenced by criticism of religion and focused on experiences with one's → father. The implied view of religious development was soon worked out independently by C. G. Jung but aroused serious attention only in the interpretation of ego psychology (E. H. Erikson). Only later was a comprehensive interpretation of religious development attempted in all its stages from childhood (→ Narcissism) to old age (A.-M. Rizzuto).

In → pastoral care and → religious educational theory (F. Schweitzer) the investigation of religious development is of great help toward understanding learning processes and learning tasks that condition development (K. E. Nipkow). Yet the understanding of religious psychology is not in full accord with that of theology. The idea of a development of → faith in the sense of a better faith is incompatible with the doctrine of → justification, as is also an understanding of faith as a mere product of development. At the same time, the definition of faith as "experience with experience" (G. Ebeling, E. Jüngel) shows that the forms of → experience can also be significant for → theology.

Bibliography: J. W. FOWLER, *Stages of Faith: The Psychology of Human Development and the Quest for Meaning* (San Francisco, 1981) • R. GOLDMAN, *Religious Thinking from Childhood to Adolescence* (London, 1964) • K. E. HYDE, *Religion in Childhood and Adolescence* (Birmingham, Ala., 1990) • L. KOHLBERG, *Essays on Moral Development,* vol. 1, *The Philosophy of Moral Development: Moral Stages and the Idea of Justice* (San Francisco, 1981) • K. E. NIPKOW, *Grundfragen der Religionspädagogik,* vol. 3, *Gemeinsam leben und glauben lernen* (Gütersloh, 1982) • F. OSER and P. GMÜNDER, *Religious Judgment: A Developmental Perspective* (Birmingham, Ala., 1991; orig. pub., 1984) • A.-M. RIZZUTO, *The Birth of the Living God: A Psychoanalytic Study* (Chicago, 1979) •

F. Schweitzer, *Die Religion des Kindes* (Gütersloh, 1992) • M. P. Strommen, ed., *Research on Religious Development: A Comprehensive Handbook* (New York, 1971) • A. Vergote, *Religionspsychologie* (Olten, 1970).

Friedrich Schweitzer

Development Education

1. History
2. Concepts and Methods

1. History

Development education arose in the 1970s as a relatively independent activity alongside → mission and aid. The economic growth of the period, as well as the widening gulf between rich and poor countries (→ Third World), posed a demand for information as well as assistance. Wrestling with the causes of the gulf would also bring an awareness of existing problems. Working parallel to, and sometimes in conjunction with, such international bodies as the UN's Food and Agriculture Organization (FAO), the UN Educational, Scientific, and Cultural Organization (UNESCO), the UN Conference on Trade and Development (UNCTAD), and the UN Development Programme (UNDP), the churches have done pioneering work in this area, including the Conference on Church and Society (Geneva 1966), the papal → encyclical *Populorum progressio* (1967), and the decision of the German Evangelical Church in 1968 not only to give money to overcome → poverty and → hunger but also to inform the congregations as clearly as possible about the need to do so. After 1973 awareness of development education grew, and it seemed to register itself in the conscience of the church at large.

2. Concepts and Methods

2.1. Two concepts are to be distinguished. The first is development education as *a developing of awareness among the rich*. From the outset it was designed to probe the motives of giving. But as the causes of underdevelopment (→ Development 1) were understood more clearly, the philanthropic aspect receded and the self-critical question of structural conditions arose. Riches, the acquisition of capital, became the problem, not poverty and its elimination (→ Capitalism). Today development education is usually an independent activity teaching us how to work together for liberation, bringing to light conflicts of interest, contesting the unjust distribution of → power, and showing how to resolve → conflicts without concealing differences to the profit of the strong.

Methods include teaching weeks, dissemination of information, discussions, role-playing, plans for new lifestyles, solidarity campaigns for the disadvantaged at home and abroad, debate, influencing teaching plans, and training development helpers. In view of the increasingly close relation between economic and military interests, there is cooperation with the work of → peace education. In both cases the aim is to uncover the structural → forces behind society with a view to changing it. In the field of → ecumenical learning the churches have an important role to play.

2.2. The second concept is that of *attempting to liberate the disadvantaged,* an effort that is ineffective unless accompanied by reflection. A → pedagogy of the oppressed demands education concerning the causes of alienation. Hence various forms of educational work have developed, including → literacy campaigns, analysis of new organizational models, suitable technology, and forms of independent management and financing such as cooperatives. → Education itself, often an instrument of the ruling class, comes under critical evaluation.

Methods in these cases include exchanges of information, the development of alternative models of education, and involvement in specific projects. Attempts are made to forward the work of education and make it more effective by the building of networks. The Third World has established contacts with groups for study and action in the industrialized lands. The churches can provide the setting for sharing the experiences of these groups via development education in wealthy lands.

The increasing internationalization of underdevelopment, which has an effect on almost every country, leads to various transnational contacts between disadvantaged groups and peoples. Precisely at this point the churches, because of their international structures and contacts, can contribute to development education theologically by means of biblical input regarding → righteousness, → peace, and the wholeness of → creation. They can also spread it by their own involvement, bringing into their → spirituality the → suffering of people in their own and other lands.

Bibliography: R. Burns, *The Formation and Legitimation of Development Education* (Melbourne, 1979) special consideration of Australia and Sweden • H. Dauber and W. Simpfendörfer, *Eigener Haushalt and bewohnter Erdkreis* (Wuppertal, 1981) • R. D. N. Dickinson, *Poor, Yet Making Many Rich* (Geneva, 1983)

• P. Freire, *Pädagogik der Unterdrückten* (Frankfurt, 1980) • S. Lindholm, *Seeing for Oneself: A Report on an Experiment in Development Education* (Stockholm, 1975) • G. Linnenbrink, "15 Jahre kirchlicher Entwicklungsdienst," *Der Überblick* 4 (1983) • J. Lissner, *The Politics of Altruism* (Geneva, 1976) • R. Pradervand, "Development Education" (MS; Bern, 1982) survival and development in the 20th cent. • R. Traitler, *Leaping over the Wall* (Geneva, 1982) an evaluation of ten years of development education.

Coenraad M. Boerma

Development Services → Christian Development Services

Developmental Psychology → Development 2

Devil

1. Concept
2. Early Forms in Judaism
3. Development
   3.1 Early Christianity
   3.2. Islam
   3.3. Early Modern Age
4. Relation to Faith
5. Roman Catholic Exorcism
6. Satanism in Literature; Satanic Groups

1. Concept

1.1. Gk. *diabolos,* from which the Eng. "devil" is derived, is the usual LXX translation of *śāṭān* (adversary). In the NT it is used more in the Greek sense as "accuser" or "slanderer." By way of the Gothic Bible it was taken over in Frankish, Anglo-Saxon, and German. It has retained its full meaning only as a Christian term, which also refers to the leader and representative of unbelief and heresy (→ Heresies and Schisms) and to the seducer and perverse paramour of witches (→ Witchcraft). To this extent, as one might say also of "God" (G. van der Leeuw, *Phänomenologie der Religion* [4th ed.; Tübingen, 1977] 103), the devil is "a latecomer in the history of religion."

1.2. The → history of religion can thus only inquire how certain negative features successively accumulated in his person. Similarly, attempts that try to disclose the earliest manifestations of the devil as such are inappropriate, as are those that by using his appellative as a genre designation try to make the devil into the special case either of one or of a plurality of universally occurring → evil spirits.

1.3. In most ancient cultures, certain gods or spirits stand over against other gods and thus also over against human beings (e.g., Pali *Māra,* → "death" — allegorically, the worldly sensuality that seeks to thwart the enlightening → meditation of Buddha; → Buddhism), though without → dualism characterizing the worldview as a whole. These divine enemies always include various wild → animals that are hostile to us. These included very early the → serpent, whose bad relationship with human beings the biblical story of paradise so deepens that it becomes the symbol of our failure to respond appropriately to the question of the origin of sin or of evil. Later, too, there were the toad, the ram, the ape, and others (→ Symbolism of Animals). Behind all these ideas are elementary notions that play a part in finding roles for the following figures.

2. Early Forms in Judaism

2.1. According to Zech. 3:1-2 (520/518 B.C.), *Śāṭān,* the "adversary," complains to → Yahweh concerning the → high priest Joshua in order to stop the rebuilding of the → temple (§2) and to thwart the community in → Jerusalem. In Job 1–2 (5th-4th cent. B.C.), Yahweh permits the same figure to test a person as an antagonist. In both cases he usurps functions that previously could be ascribed to God (e.g., the sending of an evil spirit in 1 Sam. 16:14 and Judg. 9:23 and the demand for a census in 1 Chr. 21:1 [cf. 2 Sam. 24:1]).

2.2. In the following period, especially in intertestamental literature, including the → Qumran writings, new personifications of uselessness and destruction accrue to the devil (*Běliyyā'al,* Nah. 1:11), including hostility (*Maśṭēmâ,* since Hos. 9:7-8) and arrogated power (*Zěbulâ, Zěbul,* Hab. 3:11; note *Ba'al,* "lord," later *Beelzebu, Beelzebub*). These developments may also reflect a desire on the part of the Jews to give formative expression to their own experiences of the evil of this world, and to do so quite apart from the manifestations of falsehood with which they too might have become quite familiar during the postexilic period under Persian rule.

2.3. This is suggested in the NT, not only by the presence of most of the names just mentioned, but also by the addition of new ones, such as "tempter" (Matt. 4:3), "deceiver of the whole world" (Rev. 12:9; see also 20:10), "murderer from the beginning" (John 8:44), "roaring lion . . . looking for someone to devour" (1 Pet. 5:8), "ruler of this world" (John 12:31; 14:30; 16:11), and "god [!] of this world" (2 Cor. 4:4).

3. Development

3.1. Early Christianity

These various personifications, to the extent they had not already become a (smaller number of) figure(s), probably coalesced into the figure of the devil/Satan as early as the first two Christian generations (30/35-65/70 and 65/70-95/100). This likely took place under the considerable weight of → apocalyptic influences that in many places were prompted by Jesus' proclamation of the commencing kingdom of God. This proclamation could be perceived in its full import only if the eschatological counterfigure, later to be served by the antichrist, was not fragmented into many different powers but, rather, reduced to one. The alien beasts in the Revelation of John were drawn into this unifying tendency, the ten-horned and seven-headed beasts of chap. 13 being monsters of Satan, and the dragon or serpent in chaps. 12 and 20 (→ Iranian Religions 9) Satan himself.

The early Jewish-Christian → Gnostic response to the challenge posed by the Persian Ahriman was to hypostasize evil into a universal figure (Aram. *bîšā;* Gk. *to ponēron*). The early church appropriated this idea from Jewish prayer as the seventh petition in the → Lord's Prayer (Matt. 6:13b), such that it could now also coincide with sin, which previously had merely intersected it at certain points (*hamartiai, opheilēmata, paraptōmata*). Since then, the Syrian church has always understood it as the devil (most pronounced in Ephraem Syrus [ca. 306-73]), while the Greek and Latin churches have frequently understood it in this way (in all three instances as masc. gender). → Baptism, whose purpose is to extinguish sin, thus simultaneously serves to drive out or expel the devil, who in his own turn then acquires even more pronounced contours in the → exorcism ritual developed especially for this purpose beginning in the second century.

Against the background of early Jewish views of the fall of → angels and a new → Platonic scheme of devolution, → Origen (ca. 185-ca. 254; → Origenism) compared Lucifer the "Lightbearer" (as his Latin translator T. Rufinus called the morning star in *De princ.* 1.5.5, following the Vg) with a Babylonian king who first occupied and then fell from heaven (Isa. 14:12). He then combined all this with comparisons of Satan with a bolt of lightning from heaven (Luke 10:18), thus creating numerous interpretive possibilities for following generations (e.g., of the devil as a fallen angel, or in truth as a bringer of illumination withheld by God, etc.).

→ Augustine (354-430) sexualized the devil by making the devil, in his anti-Pelagian writings (→ Pelagianism), the author of the sexual impulse (= *voluptas, concupiscentia carnis, pudenda libido),* by means of which sin is inherited (→ Augustine's Theology 5).

3.2. Islam

Arabic borrowed Gk. *diabolos* as *Iblīs* (→ Islam 7), which can also be given a new etymology in newer contexts. Among other things, the → Koran already contains the → midrash that before → Adam all the angels except Iblīs had prostrated themselves, and for his resistance God cursed him (2:34; 7:11-18; 15:26-48; 17:61-65; 18:50-51; 38:71-85). Later he succeeded in leading many people astray into unbelief (34:20-21). On the Last Day he will be cast into hellfire along with them (26:91-104; Islam 3).

3.3. Early Modern Age

To the extent that the ascendancy of Christianity prompted the ancient religions (→ Greek Religion; Roman Religion) to be regarded as pagan (→ Gentiles, Gentile Christianity), the gods came to be associated with the devil, especially within the monastic-ascetic controversy with paganism, or became concentrated in paganism, beginning with the altar of Zeus at Pergamum being called "Satan's throne" (Rev. 2:13). Christians also called the evil one, or the archenemy, the Black One; they vilified him as a persecutor of Christians, battled against him in the heretic, and experienced him as their adversary in → everyday life. "What the Christians believed about the devil received at the hands of the heathen a twofold enlargement: heathen gods and spirits already malign and gloomy in themselves readily dropped into the Christian category of devilish beings; with greater difficulty and more resistance from public opinion nevertheless the transmutation of the good gods of old into specters and demons was effected" (J. Grimm, 3.985-86, modernized slightly).

Something of the same is added in the rejection of → Judaism, the Jews in Smyrna being the "synagogue of Satan" as early as Rev. 2:9. Up to the time following the Renaissance, and especially then, the many devils in Satan's entourage distorted or acquired artificial Hebrew names, imitating but not following the Jewish demonology of late antiquity (→ Demons). The chief devil was called Breaker, Invalidator, Faithless One (*mēpēr,* hiphil part. of *prr*), or Speaker of Nonsense or Defiler (*tōpēl,* qal part. of *tpl* or *ṭpl*), which is Mephistopheles. Walpurgis Night, or some other special night, when witches fly to a cannibalistic feast and → dancing and sex with the devil, became the witches' Sabbath (→ Sabbath; Witchcraft). By adopting this expression uncritically as a reference to any event at which the devil is venerated in this way, academic and popular usage both increase and veil → anti-Semitism.

In the 10th century the devil was often understood as a repugnant mixed form, as attributes of ancient → mythical monsters were attributed to him, for example, horns, often like the Minotaur (→ Greek Religion 2), or ram's feet like Azazel (→ Demons), or an ass's tail, possibly like the slayer of Osiris, Seth, who was later identified with the Greek monster Typhon (→ Egyptian Religion 1.1).

By the 13th century the devil had taken full shape. The → Inquisition presupposed it, thus strengthening certain notions of him and transforming him into a social reality.

4. Relation to Faith
The history of religion and of the church would be uncritical if, in a way recalling analogous criticism of the proofs of God (→ God, Arguments for the Existence of), it were driven to try to prove the imagined existence or nonexistence of the devil. Results of research must be formulated such that theology, if it desires, has the possibility of speaking of the devil as a → symbolic figure occurring at all times and in all religions. This is especially so in interpretations of Jewish-Christian tradition, for example, that takes the serpent in Gen. 3:1 and in Rev. 20:2 as one and the same, and the devil can accordingly manifest himself in it both at the beginning of history and at the end.

5. Roman Catholic Exorcism
The → Roman Catholic Church incorporated → exorcism (§2.1) into the Rituale Romanum in 1614 in the version of the reforming Pope Paul V (1566-72), after it had been transformed in the early church from the expulsion of evil spirits within the ritual of baptism into the more specialized and independent ritual of an expulsion of the devil. Pius XII (1939-58) accommodated it to the statutes of the → Codex Iuris Canonici, according to which → priests (§1.2) need special qualifications if they are called upon as exorcists and occasionally even carry out this rite after a bishop examines all the attendant circumstances.

6. Satanism in Literature; Satanic Groups
Literary Satanism blossomed in the 19th century, especially in France. It uses all the motifs of the literature and theology of the devil from preceding centuries to illustrate the modern understanding of evil. Satanic groups and sects feel the need today to express their experience of → sexuality as something evil and are thereby occasionally led in fact into evil (→ Superstition 5).

Bibliography: K. BERGER, *Das Buch der Jubiläen* (Gütersloh, 1981) entry "Mastema" • J. W. BOYD, *Satan and Māra: Christian and Buddhist Symbols of Evil* (Leiden, 1975) • C. COLPE, "Ahriman, oder Der Unheil bringende Geist Zarathustras," *Das Böse. Eine historische Phänomenologie der Unerklärlichen* (ed. W. Schmidt-Biggemann; Frankfurt, 1993); idem, "Das Böse bei Gnostikern und syrischen Kirchenvätern. Aus der Geschichte des Teufels im Abendland," ibid. • M. ELIADE, *The Two and the One* (New York, 1965) • H.-J. FABRY, "נָחָשׁ *nāḥāš*," *TWAT* 5.384-97 • N. FORSYTH, *The Old Enemy: Satan and the Combat Myth* (Princeton, 1987) • K. R. H. FRICK, *Satan und die Satanisten* (3 vols.; Graz, 1982-86) • J. GRIMM, *Teutonic Mythology* (4 vols.; New York, 1966; trans. of 4th Ger. ed., 1875-78) • P. HABERMEHL, *Perpetua und die Ägypter oder Bilder der Bösen im frühen afrikanischen Christentum* (Berlin, 1992) • H. A. KELLY, *Towards the Death of Satan: The Growth and Decline of Christian Demonology* (London, 1968) • E. LOHSE, *Synagoge des Satans und Gemeinde Gottes* (Münster, 1992) • J. MARTIKAINEN, *Das Böse und der Teufel in der Theologie Ephraems des Syrers* (Turku, 1978) • G. ROSKOFF, *Geschichte des Teufels* (2 vols.; Aalen, 1967; orig. pub., 1869) • J. B. RUSSELL, *The Devil: Perceptions of Evil from Antiquity to Primitive Christianity* (Ithaca, N.Y., 1977); idem, *Lucifer: The Devil in the Middle Ages* (Ithaca, N.Y., 1984); idem, *Mephistopheles: The Devil in the Modern World* (Ithaca, N.Y., 1986); idem, *The Prince of Darkness* (Ithaca, N.Y., 1988); idem, *Satan: The Early Christian Tradition* (Ithaca, N.Y., 1981) • A. SHARMA, "Satan," *EncRel(E)* 13.81-84 • G. SIEGMUND, ed., *Der Exorzismus der katholischen Kirche* (Stein, 1981) • W. SPEYER, "Gottesfeind," *RAC* 11.996-1043 • B. TEYSSÈDRE, *Le diable et l'enfer au temps de Jésus* (Paris, 1985); idem, *Naissance du diable. De Babylone aux grottes de la mer Morte* (Paris, 1985) • I. TIEMANN, "Die Deutung des Minotauros von den ältesten Quellen bis zum frühen Mittelalter" (Diss., Utrecht, 1992) • A. J. WENSINCK, "Iblīs," *HIsl* 181-82 • "Die Wiederkehr des Teufels," *Der Spiegel*, December 22, 1986, 148-63 • G. ZACHARIAS, *Satanskult und Schwarze Messe* (3d ed.; Wiesbaden, 1992).

CARSTEN COLPE

Devil's Advocate → Promotor fidei

Devotion, Devotions

The term "devotion" denotes the fixing of one's senses and mind totally on God and the things of God. The pl. "devotions" denotes various private and public exercises aimed at giving a spiritual orientation to life, at enhancing one's devotion. These may be at set times of the week or of the day (morning or evening), or they may be customized for specific groups (e.g., in schools and hospitals). Devotions may reflect the → church year (e.g., at Advent or Holy Week) and may be conducted through the media (radio or television). They typically give church groups and circles an evangelical flavor. They occur especially in churches and in → evangelization and express a → piety that is the work of the Spirit and that has its basis in Holy Scripture. In the Society of → Friends, worship often consists of quiet devotion in which the congregation silently waits upon God.

The forms and content of devotion have changed considerably during the course of church history. In the Middle Ages it typically took the form of contemplating images (e.g., Henry Suso; → Mysticism) or saying the → rosary (from the 12th cent.). By the monotony of a rhythm of prayer, believers should get focused on the mysteries of the person of → Jesus or → Mary. The methodical devotional exercises of Thomas à Kempis (1379/80-1471) and the *Spiritual Exercises* of → Ignatius Loyola (1491-1556) found a doctrinally established place in Roman Catholic piety.

Along with the canonical → hours of the clergy, popular devotions also developed in the West (including, e.g., the Salve Regina and the benediction). The liturgical reforms of → Vatican II in no way weakened the firm place of devotions in the life of the → Roman Catholic Church. The stations of the cross, the rosary, and devotions to Mary and the Sacred Heart of Jesus are all exercises "of devout people that are followed by custom or by episcopal appointment according to duly authorized practice. They flow from the sacred → liturgy and lead people to it" (SC 13). They can assume special significance at services where there is no priest.

M. → Luther (1483-1546) opposed a self-created pious disposition. "Not your zeal," he said, "but God's Word and promise render your prayer good. This faith, based on God's words, is also the true worship" (*LuthW* 42.77 = WA 2.127-28, in exposition of the Lord's Prayer). He gave an example of devotion in keeping with the gospel in the morning and evening blessings of his Small Catechism. During the 16th and 17th centuries family devotions became the custom in both towns and villages as supplements to public worship. Bells sometimes summoned people to these devotions as a parallel to the Roman Catholic ringing of the Angelus.

In → Pietism private devotion as an institution assumed a new significance as compared with public worship. *Collegia pietatis* (schools of piety) as programs of devotional exercises supplemented public worship (P. J. Spener). Many widely circulated books of devotion (by A. H. → Francke, N. L. von → Zinzendorf, F. C. Oetinger, J. F. Stark, et al.) offered direction and examples, and these were followed by the devotional books of the → Moravian Church, Christian tear-off calendars, and schedules for Bible reading (→ Devotional Literature 3).

The fact that devotions took place primarily in the family or in closed religious circles long prevented them from being the theme of scholarly investigation. Thus we have no monographs on early devotional practice and no explicit discussions in the handbooks of practical theology from the 19th and 20th centuries. Only later in the 20th century — and largely because they had become less popular as family devotions — did personal devotions become increasingly important in the → congregation and its various subgroups. The devotions manifest the Christian character of these groups for the participants. For this very reason, however, devotion is always in danger of being taken for granted and becoming routine.

For lack of other models, theologians and nontheologians alike tend to practice devotions unreflectingly as merely a shorter form of public worship. Always, however, the devotions could be shaped to become more sensitive, more personal, and more oriented to the group. They become vital when they include attentive meditation on Scripture in light of the participants' actual life situation. This is consistent with the basic definition of fixing the senses totally on God. Spiritual discussion, hymns, → prayers, stillness, and location can all contribute to this end. An advantage of devotions is that they are flexible in liturgical structure (→ Liturgy). A fixed order can be helpful, although devotions must always be seen in the context of the worship, teaching, and fellowship of the whole congregation.

Bibliography: D. Lonsdale, *Eyes to See, Ears to Hear: An Introduction to Ignatian Spirituality* (Chicago, 1990) • J. Grotz, "Andacht," *LTK* (2d ed.) 1.502-4 • A. E. McGrath, *Spirituality in an Age of Change: Rediscovering the Spirit of the Reformers* (Grand Rapids, 1994) • F. Merkel, "Andacht, eine vernachlässigte 'kleine Form,'" *PThI* 1 (1983) 21-38 • H. B. Meyer, "Andachten und Wortgottesdienste," *LJ* 24 (1974) 157-75 • B. Olsson and G. Neumann, "Devotional Literature," *ELC* 1.687-96 • L. Richter and M. Mezger, "Andacht," *RGG* (3d ed.) 1.360-63 • W. Schütz, "Andacht," *HWP* 1.295-96 • *WDCS*.

Friedemann Merkel

Devotion to Mary → Mary, Devotion to

Devotional Images

Devotional images are cultic objects that believers piously venerate in holy places and from which, as representations of the → saints (DH 1823), they expect → miracles and → salvation (→ Piety). → Pilgrimages to devotional images sprang up besides pilgrimages to places of remembrance, graves, and → relics of saints. Veneration of → Mary, which developed from the 12th century and was promoted by the → orders and later by the Counter-Reformation, especially the → Jesuits, greatly increased pilgrimages to devotional images, since Mary was not a → martyr, and there were no bodily relics of Mary.

Devotional images may take the form of two-dimensional → icons or of sculpture, and copies of them may be distributed. They are set up in special places (chapels) and are protected by the faithful when in danger. In many places there are legends about their miraculous preservation or deliverance.

Bibliography: H. BELTING, Likeness and Presence: A History of the Image before the Era of Art (Chicago, 1994) • H. DÜNNINGER, "Wahres Abbild. Bildwallfahrt und Gnadenbildkopie," Wallfahrt kennt keine Grenzen (ed. L. Kriss-Rettenbeck and G. Möhler; Munich, 1984) 274-83 • H. GRAEF, Mary: A History of Doctrine and Devotion (2 vols.; New York, 1963-65) • J. N. GROU, Marks of True Devotion (Springfield, Ill., 1962) • K. KOLB, Mariengnadenbilder. Marienverehrung heute (Würzburg, 1976); idem, "Typologie der Gnadenbilder," Handbuch der Marienkunde (ed. W. Beinert and H. Petri; Regensburg, 1984) 849-82 • B. KÖTTING, "Wallfahrt III," LTK (2d ed.) 10.942-46.

JOHANNES SCHILLING

Devotional Literature

1. Term
2. History
    2.1. Early Church and Middle Ages
    2.2. Luther and the Post-Reformation Period
    2.3. Baroque and Pietism
    2.4. Enlightenment and Revival
3. Moravian Daily Texts

1. Term

Over the centuries the phrase "devotional literature" has continually expanded its reference, today being used for any kind of literature that helps to promote piety as an overall religious attitude (R. Mohr) or that strengthens the religious aspirations of believers (S. Ringler) or that leads to a fuller life of Christian → virtue. In short, it has become an omnibus term for religious writing.

1.1. The first reference of devotional literature was to the works of → Pietism. Then by way of Roman Catholic ascetic literature, the term came to be used for the religious writings of the → Middle Ages and the → early church, though without sufficient attention to the aims of these works as stated in the works themselves. The surprising rise of devotional literature around 1600 corresponds to the desire for a reform of church life and the awakening of a "sluggish Christianity" (J. Arndt) to a new → piety. This desire arose out of the dissatisfaction of the post-Reformation generation with a gospel that was stunted by pure but dead doctrine (→ Orthodoxy 1-2). The demand was for the building up of an effective → faith that would shape life deeply and permanently by the experience of true → penitence and → regeneration. Devotional literature, in short, was designed to promote "true Christianity."

1.2. This demand led to a devotional literature that addressed the inner piety of the individual in relation to God and not Christians as members of a congregation. In seeking thus to promote an individual appropriation of salvation, the literature in effect bypassed or relativized the role of the church in mediating salvation. As in the poems of Angelus Silesius (1624-77), it thus became a companion and tended to take over the office of spiritual director and to offer the cure of souls, which those who turned to it felt they needed for self-awareness and inner vision.

Essential to devotional literature, then, is the idea of a spiritual goal (the "way of the soul to God") and the willingness to pursue this goal. It serves to promote spiritual progress through fairly specific directions. The presupposition is that readers will identify completely with the devotional content. To be critical or aloof renders it ineffectual. Because the content is so much at the service of the goal, it is difficult to speak in isolation of literary genres.

1.3. The following literary forms might be called typical. Some texts are written in the first person, inviting readers to apply the "I" directly to themselves (prayers, hymns, devotional works). Others are contemplative works that invite meditation (often exegetical, though also dealing with overall biblical themes or themes from salvation history). Others are in the form of proverbs, epigrams, and aphorisms that lead to "divine contemplation" (Angelus Silesius), while others are biographies that lead to → discipleship and provide readers with an account they can use as a mirror to reveal "what they lack, how near they are to God's kingdom, or how far they are from it" (J. H. Reitz). Typical for a (daily) →

devotion is a combination of a song, a → meditation, a → prayer, and often the inclusion of a devotional picture (see 3).

1.4. "Devotional literature" can be defined only functionally. No genre is edifying as such. What constitutes devotional literature in the narrower sense is the purpose of the author, and in a wider sense the intention of the mature reader, who ultimately can turn everything to spiritual profit. As a rule, apologetic, polemical, purely dogmatic, and purely speculative theological writings are not edifying, nor are those that are predominantly moral, didactic, liturgical, or entertaining.

2. History

2.1. *Early Church and Middle Ages*
Since the rise of devotional literature is linked to a markedly individual devotional sense found only in the late Middle Ages, one may wonder whether it makes much sense to speak of devotional literature in the early church. Yet in light of their influence, we should at least mention the lives and apothegmatic writings of early → monasticism (*Vitae* and *Apophthegmata Patrum,* Cassian's *Collationes,* etc.) and also → Augustine's *Confessions,* which presents sections from his life as stages in the search for God. We may consider these writings the foreshadowing of devotional literature proper.

Works intended to edify arose in quantity only during the late Middle Ages. Many, for example, aimed at *moral asceticism,* giving comprehensive instruction and exhortation, often in the form of dialogues (*aedificatio* in such works means "betterment"). These works include tractates on parts of the catechism (e.g., Marquard von Lindau on the Decalogue), as well as teaching on conscience, penance, sins (Martin von Amberg, Heinrich von Langenstein), and the doctrine of salvation (*Speculum humanae salvationis*). Other works focused on the spiritual pilgrimage (Stephan von Landskron) and the *ars moriendi* (art of dying [well]), which often included the *ars bene vivendi* (art of living well; e.g., Geiler von Kaysersberg's "Sterbe-ABC").

Other examples of devotional literature sought primarily to promote Christian → salvation in the context of the church or through an emphasis on → dogma and morality (P. E. Weidenhiller). Some of these aimed at *mystical asceticism,* and some had inner exercises (*aedificatio* here is the development of spiritual powers). This kind of devotional literature arose within the monastic theology of the 12th and 13th centuries (→ Bernard of Clairvaux, also Bonaventure and Pseudo-Augustinian works) and blossomed in the popular mysticism of the 14th cen-

tury (J. Tauler, Henry Suso, J. Ruysbroeck, lives and revelations of nuns).

In many different forms in the 15th century — including translations, revisions of Latin texts, and compilations — this literature aimed at the laity. Its themes are (1) the mystical way and the contemplative life, God's love and goodness and our love for God (bride-mysticism); (2) the passion and death of Christ (Henry Suso's *Little Book of Eternal Wisdom,* Ludolf von Sachsen, Jordan von Quedlinburg) and the sorrows of Mary; (3) human sufferings and temptations, life as imitation of Christ, inward consolation and resignation, self-knowledge, penitence and → humility (Suso's *Vita,* Thomas à Kempis's *Imitation of Christ,* J. von Staupitz); and (4) contemplation of the "four last things" (Gerhard von Vliederhoven). Various works include one or more of these themes.

Especially in the 15th century the *Devotio moderna* (Modern devotion) helped to turn prayer books and catechetical writings into devotional works along the lines of mystical edification (Weidenhiller, B. Adam). In the "Twenty-four Ancients" of Otto von Passau and many allegorical writings (e.g., "The Spiritual Chariot," "Christ and the Seven Arks"), we again find a fusion of the catechetical and the mystically edifying. It is not easy to categorize the legends that also serve to entertain (e.g., *Legenda aurea* of Jacobus de Voragine). They have edifying value in their call to discipleship and in their "inflaming of believers with gratitude and enthusiastic praise of God for the gracious possibility of achieving the divine likeness" (S. Ringler).

2.2. *Luther and the Post-Reformation Period*
Reformers such as T. Müntzer and S. Franck adopted the term "edification" from the tradition of late medieval mysticism. M. → Luther, however, had reservations about using the term in reference to his popular works, many of which would be considered devotional literature. If the essence of pious edification lies in application to piety (A. H. → Francke), then Luther indeed is almost a stranger to it. His exegetical and theological concern is application to faith.

The closeness of many of Luther's writings to devotional literature, however, results from the practical function that is also peculiar to them. Readers are to relate what the works say to themselves, recognizing the personal application that lies there for them. In this existential character of → Luther's theology one sees the edifying element in his works. Luther is well aware of the need to practice faith. But he speaks about this need only in relation to its constant perversion by the assault of the → law, in which faith must continually be won afresh. Designed to help regain an evangelical faith, Christian exercises must be restricted to devotional immersion in Holy Scripture or in parts of the → catechism (M. Nicol), and then the living voice of the gospel will itself speak to us.

Luther indeed — though seldom — mentioned conscious devotional exercises preparatory to receiving God's Word. With one exception, these references occur in early works that follow late medieval traditions (e.g., a sermon in 1519 on contemplating the passion, in preparation for penance; a sermon, also from 1519, in preparation for death, with contemplation of the sacrament a preparation for death; a consolatory work in 1520 urging contemplation of seven good and evil things, leading to a final picture of the risen Christ). The one later example is in the work *A Simple Way to Pray, for a Good Friend* (1535), which explains in detail Luther's personal habit of meditation on the Ten Commandments, the Lord's Prayer, and the creed by a fourfold approach involving reflection on doctrine and then thanksgiving, confession, and petition.

In the second half of the 16th century, Protestant devotional literature — oriented at first, after the pattern of Luther, to the Bible, the church, and the creed — increasingly came to be fascinated by the question of what means would appropriate salvation and shape the inner life of faith. Words like "meditation," "devotion," and "worship" (P. Althaus) appear in the titles and show that the aim of this literature is to kindle and nurture devotion. → Contemplation focuses increasingly on *novissima* (last things, eschatology).

Most influential were the readoption of texts from the early church, medieval mysticism (M. Moller), and contemporary Roman Catholicism (A. Musculus, L. Rabe, J. Mynsinger). The → Jesuits (Loyola's *Spiritual Exercises* and the prayer books of P. Canisius and P. Michaelis) had shaped Roman Catholic devotional literature from the middle of the century, and they had an impact on Protestant devotional literature toward the end of the century as Protestants adopted the methods of prayer and meditation and divided the materials of meditation into fixed periods (J. Habermann, P. Kegel). These developments led to the devotional literature of → baroque, which reached a high point at the beginning of the 17th century.

2.3. Baroque and Pietism

Evangelical devotional literature is one of "the most impressive achievements of Protestantism" in the 17th century (W. Zeller). At the beginning of an important list of names stands that of J. Arndt, whose main works *Four Books on True Christianity* (1606-10, based on sermons), the prayer book *A Little Garden of Paradise* (1612), and "postils" (short homilies on texts from the Gospels and Epistles) represent the

three basic types of devotional literature in the period. In *Four Books* Arndt links together related devotional sequences that build on one another (theme, scriptural text, exposition, prayer). The first three books correspond to the mystical way of penitence, illumination, and sanctification. The aim is by methodical exercising of the affective powers of the soul (will and love) in meditative contemplation to reach an → experience of God's gracious working in the soul, from which the power is derived to press on to → sanctification.

Spiritually akin to Arndt are J. Gerhard (*Meditationes sacrae* [1606] and *Schola pietatis* [1622/23]), J. Lütkemann, H. Müller, and C. Scriver, who in his devotional work *Gottholds zufälliger Andachten . . .* (1671?) adopted the English concept of edification by an allegorizing contemplation of nature. Hymns also blossomed at this period (e.g., by P. Gerhardt, P. Fleming, J. Neander, F. Spee von Langenfeld, S. von Birken, P. von Zesen, J. Rist, M. Opitz, Q. Kuhlmann, Angelus Silesius, C. R. von Greiffenberg, G. Arnold, G. Tersteegen, N. L. von → Zinzendorf, and K.-H. von Bogatzky). They promote private devotion and the "practice of divine blessedness" (J. Crüger, *Praxis pietatis melica* [1647]), though often edification becomes no more than a momentary uplifting of the pious mind.

Like Dutch Pietism, English → Puritanism also produced after 1600 a wealth of devotional literature that promoted the searching of the conscience and penitential seriousness. It in turn influenced German Pietism by way of translations. Along with L. Bayly's *Practice of Piety* (3d ed., 1613), John Bunyan's *Pilgrim's Progress* (1678) is especially noteworthy, being an → allegory of the conversion and life of a regenerate person that addresses the theme of Christian pilgrimage and warfare.

Along with their work of editing and translating (from Spanish and French mystics as well as Dutch and English Pietists), German Pietists contributed to devotional literature especially in two areas: (1) work on the Bible, including its propagation, reading, and exposition (A. H. Francke, the Canstein Bible publishing house, J. A. Bengel's *Gnomon* [1742] and *Sixty Edifying Discourses on Revelation*, and the Ebersdorf, Marburg, and Berleburg Bibles); and (2) → biographies (§3). The biography became a paradigm of the divine work of salvation, "God's process with the souls of his children," which is "not uniform but varied" and which the individual may experience concretely and then share to the edification of others (J. H. Reitz, *Historie der Wiedergebohrnen* [1698ff.]; also Tersteegen, F. C. Oetinger, and E. H. Graf Henckel).

2.4. *Enlightenment and Revival*

Historically, Pietism is "an initial religious stage in the emancipation of spiritual experience" (A. Langen). Once discovered, the capacity for spiritual experience bursts its religious banks. Then begins the process of secularizing devotional literature (→ Secularism; Secularization) by giving the experience of edification an aesthetic and moral character (casting it primarily as an experience of nature or of what is artistically beautiful or lofty). In the contemplation of nature in particular, one may see the steady development of an allegorical or symbolic exegesis of the book of nature into a depiction of authentic and moving impressions of nature.

The spirit of the → Enlightenment, with its stress on the God of creation (Milton, *Paradise Lost* [1667]; → Deism) and on the human striving for virtue, influenced devotional literature from the middle of the 18th century (C. F. Gellert, "The Glory of God in Nature," from *Spiritual Odes and Songs* [1757]). The lines between poetry and religious devotional literature are often hard to draw in the second half of the 18th century (B. H. Brockes, F. G. Klopstock, M. Claudius, J. C. Lavater; see also orthodox writers like M. Goeze and B. Schmolck). Literature increasingly acquired a function of edification. Goethe's *Werther* (1774), a modern passion story, signals the end of what has thus far been ordinary devotional literature (R. Mohr). → Catholicism, however, was less influenced by the Enlightenment, and it continued the tradition of medieval and baroque mysticism without a break (e.g., see the book of prayers by J. M. Sailer [1751-1832]).

Pietism had shown some concern for education and mission (note esp. Francke's Institutes, later called the Franckesche Stiftungen). Toward the end of the 18th century the → revivals took up the concern for inner mission, for the → conversion (§1) of an indifferent population alien to the church, and set it on a new foundation by adopting a position in opposition to the Enlightenment. → Methodism came first (John and Charles Wesley) and had a strong influence on churches in the United States. Along with individuals who wrote edifying works in opposition to the spirit of the age, which was colored by the Enlightenment (e.g., J. H. Jung-Stilling, A. Tholuck, C. Harms), we find Protestant societies and missions that devoted themselves to the production and planned distribution of devotional literature, often without charge. Many classics of devotional literature were also reprinted.

The end of the 19th century, however, had little to show in the way of creative achievement. For the most part, well-tested models were followed; in content, there was a looking to the past. During this time, devotional literature essentially became popular religious literature. The single, but significant, exception is S. → Kierkegaard's varied attempt to claim the empty content of edification for his own theological concern (*Edifying Discourses* [1843-44], *Sickness unto Death* [1849], etc.).

Bibliography: P. ALTHAUS, *Forschungen zur evangelischen Gebetsliteratur* (Gütersloh, 1927) • E. AXMACHER, *"Aus Liebe will mein Heyland sterben." Untersuchungen zum Wandel des Passionsverständnisses im frühen 18. Jahrhundert* (Neuhausen, 1984); idem, *Praxis Evangeliorum. Theologie und Frömmigkeit bei Martin Moller (1547-1606)* (Göttingen, 1989) • L. DUPRE, D. E. SALIERS, and J. MEYENDORFF, eds., *Christian Spirituality: Post-Reformation and Modern* (New York, 1989) • G. EBELING, *Luthers Seelsorge. Theologie in der Vielfalt der Lebenssituationen an seinen Briefen dargestellt* (Tübingen, 1997) • P. C. ERB, ed., *Pietists: Selected Writings* (New York, 1983) • D. L. JEFFREY, ed., *A Burning and a Shining Light* (Grand Rapids, 1987; reissued in 1994 as *English Spirituality in the Age of Wesley*); idem, ed., *The Law of Love: English Spirituality in the Age of Wyclif* (Grand Rapids, 1987) • A. LANGEN, "Pietismus," *RDL* 1.103-14 • B. McGINN and J. MEYENDORFF, eds., *Christian Spirituality: Origins to the Twelfth Century* (New York, 1985) • A. E. McGRATH, *Spirituality in an Age of Change: Rediscovering the Spirit of the Reformers* (Grand Rapids, 1994) • U. MENNECKE-HAUSTEIN, "Erbauungsliteratur," *Literatur-Lexikon* (ed. V. Meid; Gütersloh, 1992) 13.233-39; idem, *Luthers Trostbriefe* (Gütersloh, 1989) • M. NICOL, *Meditation bei Luther* (Göttingen, 1984) • M. C. O'CONNOR, *The Art of Dying Well: The Development of the "ars moriendi"* (New York, 1966) • D. PIEL, "Erbauungsliteratur," *Das Fischer Lexikon Literatur* (ed. U. Ricklefs; Frankfurt, 1996) 1.571-93 • J. PROCOPÉ, R. MOHR, and H. WULF, "Erbauungsliteratur," *TRE* 10.28-83 • J. RIATT, B. McGINN, and J. MEYENDORFF, eds., *Christian Spirituality: High Middle Ages and Reformation* (New York, 1987) • S. RINGLER, "Zur Gattung Legende," *Würzburger Prosastudien* (FS K. Ruh; vol. 2; Munich, 1975) 225-70 • R. RUDOLF and R. MOHR, "Ars moriendi," *TRE* 4.143-54 • A. SANN, *Bunyan in Deutschland. Studien zur literarischen Wechselbeziehung zwischen England und dem deutschen Pietismus* (Giessen, 1951) • S. SCHEDL and D.-R. MOSER, "Erbauungsliteratur," *Reallexikon der deutschen Literaturwissenschaft* (Berlin, 1997) 1.484-88 • I. SCHEITLER, *Das geistliche Lied im deutschen Barock* (Berlin, 1982) • H.-J. SCHRADER, ed., *Nachwort zu J. H. Reitz, "Historie der Wiedergebohrnen"* (4 vols.; Tübingen, 1982) 4.127-203 • F. SCHULZ, "Gebetbücher II," *TRE* 12.105-19 • W. STAMMLER, "Mittelalterliche Prosa in deutscher

Sprache," *Philologie im Aufriß* (2d ed.; Berlin, 1960) 2.749-1102 • A. Völker, "Gesangbuch," *TRE* 12.547-65 • W. Zeller, *Theologie und Frömmigkeit. Gesammelte Aufsätze* (2 vols.; ed. B. Jaspert; Marburg, 1971-78).

UTE MENNECKE-HAUSTEIN

3. Moravian Daily Texts

The Moravian Daily Texts (in the U.K.: Daily Watchwords; in Germany: Losungen) are among the most widely read daily devotional guides in the world. They are especially popular in Germany, where publication ran to 1.7 million copies in 1997. Altogether they appeared in 43 different languages, including Eskimo (Labrador), Miskito (Central America), Sepedi (South Africa), and Tibetan.

The idea of uniting the → congregation through a daily "watchword" arose in Herrnhut in 1728 (→ Moravian Church). At a hymn-singing service on May 3, Count → Zinzendorf (1700-1760; → Pietism) chose the short verse of a hymn as the watchword for the next day. Short and succinct verses from the Bible and hymns (→ Hymnbook) then came to be chosen each day as the word for the next day and were taken from house to house. In 1731 watchwords for the whole year were published in book form, either chosen in advance by Zinzendorf or taken from constantly revised collections of sayings. Zinzendorf then gave expression to a didactic concern by publishing further daily texts, out of which there developed the "daily doctrinal texts" of 1771. From the mid-19th century the two groups of daily readings have been combined.

Out of some 1,800 OT readings 365 watchwords are drawn three years in advance from Herrnhut. The additional NT texts as well as the verses from hymns or → prayers are selected and are related to the OT watchwords or to the → church year. The goal is to gather daily, under one God-given biblical saying, Christians of many different languages and denominations.

→ Meditation; Piety

Bibliography: *Daily Watchwords 1998* (London, 1997) • DIREKTION DER BRÜDER-UNITÄT HERRNHUT, *Alle Morgen neu. Die Herrnhuter Losungen von 1791 bis heute* (Berlin, 1976) • H.-W. HEIDLAND, *Die Losungen im Ringen des Glaubens heute. Überlegungen zu ihrem Selbstverständnis* (Hamburg, 1980) • *Moravian Daily Texts 1998: Bible Texts with Hymn Verses and Prayers for Every Day in the Year* (Bethlehem, Pa., 1997) • H. RENKEWITZ, *Die Losungen. Entstehung und Geschichte eines Andachtsbuches* (2d ed.; Hamburg, 1967).

HELMUT BINTZ

Diaconate → Deacon, Deaconess; Diakonia

Diakonia

1. Theological Basis
2. Forms and Agents
   2.1. Institutions
   2.2. Homes
   2.3. Aid for Seniors
   2.4. Child Care
   2.5. Congregational Diakonia
   2.6. Counseling
   2.7. Group Care
   2.8. Ecumenical Diakonia
   2.9. International Cooperation
3. Church and State
4. Historical Development and Ecclesiological Significance
   4.1. The Early Church and Orthodox Christendom
   4.2. Middle Ages and Roman Catholic Developments
4.3. Reformation

1. Theological Basis

Diakonia (from Gk. *diakoneō*, "serve") has been described as "the responsible service of the Gospel by deeds and by words performed by Christians in response to the needs of people" (T. G. White, 276). Like → mission, diakonia exists in a contemporary social context and expresses the life and nature of the church. Particularly because of the social demands of the → Third World, the church in the modern age has reached an unprecedented degree of consensus regarding diakonia. Face to face with rapid social change in the countries of Africa, Asia, and Latin America, the problems of the poor and of refugees, of exploitation and → hunger, the churches worldwide have declared their solidarity with the poor. Christians like Mother Teresa of Calcutta, who have sought out the poorest of the poor in the slums, have served as an example of modern Christian → discipleship. By living with the victims of need, they show that God's → salvation is for a lost world and that it embraces both physical and spiritual needs.

Theologically, diakonia starts in the local → congregation and indeed may be defined as the social presence of the local worshiping community. The new ecumenical awareness of this service becomes a Christian challenge for churches that use a comprehensive diakonia to secure for themselves a clear role in → society.

Western industrial states possess a broad net of

social security. Legal measures of various kinds provide justice and help for those in need. In the West, it can almost seem that specialized help exists for every emergency. The question arises, then, how in such cases the eucharistic community can still be the basis of a true diakonia. For it to be so, the members must have a responsible attitude toward the comprehensive social orientation needed.

The demand today is for a Christian answer to the trends toward disintegration inherent in modern → industrial society. This society has loosened the once-firm network of family, neighborhood, job, and personal interests that formerly united old and young. It is breaking up even the ties that hold the nuclear → family together. Insecurity is damaging human relations, which manifests itself nowadays even in the care of infants; continues in problems of school, education, and marriage; and finds expression as well in dealings with the old, the sick, the neighborhoods, and → foreigners.

A special demand is made upon the Christianity of professionals, who need an approach to the principles of the Christian faith that is appropriate to their specialized world. Their expertise and → piety ought not to be in conflict. "The point of intersection of these two dimensions ideally defines the tone and scope of diaconal action. In this grid of spiritual coordinates, the vertical axis is the promise, power, and performance of faith, while the horizontal axis is the ability to listen to the other, an authentic application of the → gospel in everyday theological practice, and an acceptance of the other without prejudice" (T. Schober).

To meet such concerns there have been ecumenical efforts to renew the diaconate (→ Deacon, Deaconess), as may be seen in the 1982 Lima text *Baptism, Eucharist, and Ministry* ("Ministry," par. 31). Impulses in this direction are part of the movement to unite the churches (note esp. the → Church of South India; → United and Uniting Churches). → Vatican II also spoke of renewing the diaconate within the Roman Catholic Church (see *Lumen gentium* 3.29).

2. Forms and Agents

The diaconal work of the churches takes many forms in both Protestant and Roman Catholic churches.

2.1. *Institutions*

Diaconal institutions include hospitals, facilities for the handicapped, maternity homes, and many others. The methods of operation have changed, since the institutions do not now serve only the poor. The most up-to-date medical standards are demanded, and the personnel must be specialists. The dominance of medical technique raises the problem whether Christian institutions can integrate modern medical standards and still provide total therapy and truly Christian help to the sick and dying. The new aim in ministering to those with → handicaps is to rehabilitate and reintegrate them rather than simply providing homes or places of refuge.

2.2. *Homes*

Special homes mostly serve the purpose of providing education for neglected children, the educationally disadvantaged, the psychologically sick, and delinquents. This form of diakonia traces back to the days of J. A. Comenius (1592-1670) and A. H. → Francke (1663-1727). In this area also there are revolutionary changes. How meaningful is education apart from home and family? Economic factors have also made radical reorientation necessary. The need for small-group pedagogy, specialization, and differentiation has led to smaller homes, work among parents, and the follow-up of those who are sent back to their own homes (→ Youth Work).

2.3. *Aid for Seniors*

Diakonia involving senior citizens takes various forms, but the idea of merely caring for the elderly is yielding to that of strengthening their desire for independence. Gerontology has paved the way for new forms of aid such as self-help groups, senior citizens' clubs, and care of the sick at home. Planning is still needed to make it possible for the elderly to continue to live in their familiar setting. It is important, too, that the church should develop a theology of aging, which will help to bring the young and the old together in a truly biblical ethics (→ Old Age).

2.4. *Child Care*

The churches provide many of the day-care centers for children that are now so greatly needed. New emphases are work among foreign children, aid for children from dysfunctional families, and the integrating of children with handicaps into regular centers.

2.5. *Congregational Diakonia*

The congregation can play its part in such fields as care of children and the sick and youth work, with centers to improve care of the sick and elderly. Yet many churches are not yet equal to the new social demands, especially in cities, where the social structures are breaking down. They prefer to leave such tasks to the city missions instead of taking the initiative and setting up the group services that could be the catalysts for new social integration (→ Social Services).

2.6. *Counseling*

Counseling services deal with various personal problems and promote social reintegration. Nevertheless, the pastoral relevance of much of this work is open to question. It is all too possible for various concepts and methods (e.g., group dynamics) and views of → anthropology that are alien to the gospel (e.g., humanism, positivism) to intrude surreptitiously into the church's proclamation.

What is the proper relation between → counseling and → pastoral care? The best answer will be a context in which the congregation is taken seriously as a social form of the gospel. The new social psychiatry (note esp. Basaglia in Italy), which brings the community into the picture, is a promising beginning in the psychiatric field.

2.7. Group Care
Special forms of diakonia occur in the care provided for specific groups, such as in missions to → seamen, actors, and Gypsies (→Roma), and in such → leisure activities as camping and vacation chaplaincies. Integrating pastoral care with diakonia, these ministries are an answer to progressive social disintegration. Mobility often characterizes these special groups, which lends itself to ecumenical cooperation in service.

2.8. Ecumenical Diakonia
Diakonia involves not only the needy in one's own land but distant neighbors in other lands and continents. Ecumenical diakonia has been systematically developed by the churches since World War II and now provides aid programs in cases of need, sends help to refugees and the victims of disasters, and works on behalf of → human rights. It seeks to help forward → development in the countries of the → Third World, working especially among the poorest of the poor, → marginal groups, the illiterate (→ Literacy), those who live in the slums, the → unemployed, women, the aged, and the handicapped.

Now that there is specialized knowledge of the causes of underdevelopment, the roots of need are also being tackled. For this reason programs and projects that are designed to move toward self-help must fit into the social, economic, and cultural situations of the recipients. The receiving churches, and if possible the groups concerned, should have a voice in both the planning and implementation of the various projects.

2.9. International Cooperation
The diakonia in one country is not separate from that in other churches and countries. Thus the European churches both east and west coordinate much of their work, and Protestant churches often keep in close touch with the → Roman Catholic Church. Above all, the churches work closely together with the → World Council of Churches in Geneva, whose program unit Sharing and Service is concerned with promoting solidarity by the sharing of resources and with fostering a comprehensive diakonia.

3. Church and State
The extent of diaconal work in a given country depends on the existing relation between church and → state in that country.

3.1. In many countries, even from the period before World War I, cities and regions had begun to set up their own social programs (e.g., in health care and in youth programs). The state, too, with its measures for social security, laid the foundation of a general system of social security and finally claimed much of the responsibility for caring for needs in this area.

The churches with their diakonia have become partners in this system, helping the state to carry out its tasks, so that in the field of social activity there is now a whole web of cooperative and coordinated effort embracing voluntary societies, the churches, and the state. This partnership ensures and opens up for the diakonia, thanks to financial grants, a whole area of social activity. It also highlights the duty not to become dependent but to defend the freedom and autonomy of its own institutions.

Problems naturally arise, and in the attempt to maintain the church's diaconal independence, different emphases surface. The Catholic Church tends to stress the → subsidiary nature of the church's work; Protestant churches stress the church's autonomy and freedom of choice for individual citizens relative to the social work or institution that best meets their own specific situation. In fact, the state regulation of social aid has tended to increase with new claims.

The degree to which diakonia can maintain its own special orientation and freedom of ministry depends on its awareness of its own autonomy and inner vitality. In its social and political concerns, the church must have a social or political diakonia, and it must make basic public statements in which it takes up a position relative to problems in social ethics.

3.2. Social aid is less closely integrated in the United States. In accord with its society's greater emphasis on individuality in various spheres of life, the social work of the church in the United States has been more free and independent and also more sacrificial. → Religious liberty means that the denominations are more on their own. They organize various forms of social aid, including → community service, church schools, hospitals, and homes for the elderly, all of which they support by their voluntary giving (→ Stewardship). There are also many publicly financed and administered schemes at the state and federal levels.

To support their witness regarding social issues,

the larger denominations have created their own organizations for social work. Societies for social action sharpen the social conscience with a view to solving social and educational problems in ways consistent with Christian ethics.

3.3. Opportunities for the development of diakonia have emerged in the former socialist countries where, before the political changes, the state bore sole responsibility for addressing social and health concerns. The present democratic governments, concerned as they are with economic and political restructuring, are anticipating help in this area from the social engagement of church diakonia. Hospitals, children's homes, and nursing homes, all of which were formerly under the purview of the socialist states, have been returned to the oversight of churches and new institutions assigned to the churches. Ecumenical aid reinforces the capabilities of such church diakonia, providing not only financial resources but also experience in social work, though the overall effectiveness of such aid is still dependent on the development of social structures by the state. To strengthen their own diakonia, minority churches in Hungary and Romania have developed common centers of diakonia: AIDROM in Romania and the Ecumenical Aid Organization in Hungary. Orthodox churches, especially the Russian church, define service to those in distress as the "liturgy after the Liturgy." One task of a theology of diakonia is to mediate this understanding of diakonia with the standards and expectations of western European social work.

3.4. Where ecumenical diakonia does not make possible the churches' own projects and institutions, the question constantly arises whether Christian social service in the Third World would not have greater missionary force if church members would discharge their diaconal ministry through state institutions. For many Third World churches, "nation building" in fact ranks as an essential aspect of Christian ministry.

4. Historical Development and Ecclesiological Significance

How the concern of Christian love manifests itself is a question that has arisen not merely in the encounter or coexistence of diakonia, church, and state in modern times. Throughout church history, the people of God have taken seriously the burden of the diakonia. Various epochs and churches, however, have had to carry this burden in different ways.

4.1. The Early Church and Orthodox Christendom

When Constantine in the fourth century laid upon the church some of the social tasks of the state, he started a trend that not only would affect the whole of Christianity for centuries but would leave its mark even today in the sphere of Orthodox Christendom. In the time of Constantine the church became a state church. Two and a half centuries before, it had developed its daily diakonia out of the common meals of the congregation (Acts 6). It had then organized a kind of episcopal-congregational diakonia by placing under the bishop deacons who would care for social concerns. But this church that had lived in the power of a fellowship of faith was now to take over the role of a state-privileged diaconal organization.

Answering the demands of the new situation, the church in the following decades created welfare institutions like hospitals, for which Basil the Great (ca. 330-79) provided a model, and the developing → monasteries took over responsibility. In the ensuing period, and later still in Russian Orthodoxy, monastic diakonia was the only form of centralized charitable activity, though it was not the only form of diakonia in general. In keeping with the early-church principle of the "symphony" of church and state (→ Early Church), the → Orthodox Church cared for its own people in Greece, up to supporting the war of independence against Turkey in the 1820s. These churches never forgot their obligation to minister to the world. Even individuals, although rooted in a liturgical type of piety, practiced as self-evident an everyday diakonia. Helping others, showing sympathy and kindness to the unfortunate and suffering, was a fundamental part of a → spirituality that followed the great example of Orthodox saints.

4.2. Middle Ages and Roman Catholic Developments

In the West, too, monastic diakonia developed after the pattern of Basil. In the later Middle Ages it was supplemented by the charitable work of spiritual fellowships (→ Orders and Congregations), which linked spiritual concerns to organized aid for the needy and suffering. Yet these efforts were not yet the basis of later charitable enterprise. Only after the Council of → Trent did C. Borromeo (1538-84) and Vincent de Paul (1581-1660) set a new direction with their charitable work.

The Caritas movement of the 19th century completely reshaped the social contribution of the Roman Catholic Church. New orders arose to deal with specific social evils. An organization comparable to that of the Inner Mission developed, along with various societies. Especially noteworthy was the Society of St. Vincent de Paul, founded by A. F. Ozanam (1813-53) in France, which sharpened the social conscience of Roman Catholics. The German

Caritas Society was founded at Freiburg im Breisgau in 1897 by L. Werthmann (1858-1921). The international organ of the movement is the Caritas Internationalis in Rome.

4.3. *Reformation*

Did the Reformation mean a new beginning for diakonia? M. → Luther himself was ambivalent. He believed that care for the body as well as the soul was part of the duty of good Christian order, but he did not have in mind the creation of a congregational diakonia. Measures were passed that made it a Christian obligation of the authorities to help the poor, the sick, widows, and orphans. Even in countries where the Reformed tradition revived the diaconate with the doctrine of a fourfold office, the government would still play the major role in regard to the social task.

A change came only with → Pietism. A. H. Francke (1663-1727) in Halle, Count N. L. von → Zinzendorf (1700-1760) in Herrnhut, and J. F. Oberlin (1740-1826) in Steintal were all responsible for innovative foundations that went far beyond existing public welfare. The → Inner Mission continued the movement in the 19th century, with parallels in other countries like Britain and the United States. Confronted with crying mass poverty as a result of industrialization, the diaconate set up institutions and organizations that recruited workers from training colleges for deacons and deaconesses. This movement spread also to → free churches in other countries. The mission was the common instrument and resource for innovative action (→ Societies and Associations, Ecclesiastical). In Germany the various efforts found a focal point in the Central Board of the Inner Mission, which J. H. Wichern (1808-81) set up at the Wittenberg Kirchentag in 1848.

Whether or not this development helped to renew the established churches is in retrospect a moot point. Wichern wanted such a renewal in the spirit of the love of Jesus. Against the background of the establishment, however, the new societies seem to have been a substitute for the congregation or an addition to it. Diakonia still has not manifested itself fully as an expression of the church's life and nature.

The churches have been seeking to make this a concern with their new approaches to diakonia. The University of Heidelberg, for example, has set up an Institute of Diaconal Science, which makes diakonia a subject of instruction. Other faculties and churches have offered sporadic courses in diaconal practice in order to foster a sharper diaconal consciousness. The subject has also claimed the interest of young people.

Many contemporaries understand the witness of a practical faith better than they do the church's preaching. For individual congregations, much will depend on whether the church of the future becomes a church of diakonia.

Bibliography: E. T. BACHMANN et al., eds., *Churches and Social Welfare* (3 vols.; New York, 1955-56) • E. BEYREUTHER, *Geschichte der Diakonie und Inneren Mission in der Neuzeit* (3d ed.; Berlin, 1983) • J. N. COLLINS, *Diakonia: Re-Interpreting the Ancient Resources* (New York, 1990) • *Diakonie in Europa* (Stuttgart, 1977) • M. GERHARD, *Ein Jahrhundert Innere Mission* (2 vols.; Gütersloh, 1948) • P. GREGORIOS, *The Meaning and Nature of Diakonia* (Geneva, 1988) • J. VAN KLINKEN, *Diakonia: Mutual Helping with Justice and Compassion* (Grand Rapids, 1989) • H. KRIMM, ed., *Das diakonische Amt der Kirche* (2d ed.; Stuttgart, 1965); idem, ed., *Das diakonische Amt der Kirche im ökumenischen Bereich* (Stuttgart, 1960) • W. C. MÜLLER, *Wie Helfen zum Beruf wurde. Eine Methodengeschichte der Sozialarbeit* (Weinheim, 1982) • T. SCHOBER et al., eds., *Handbuch für Zeugnis und Dienst der Kirche* (7 vols.; Stuttgart, 1978-83) • H. SEIBERT, *Diakonie–Hilfehandeln Jesu und soziale Arbeit des diakonischen Werkes* (Gütersloh, 1983) • T. G. WHITE, "Diakonia," *DEM* 275-80.

RICHARD BOECKLER

Dialectic

1. Etymology and History
2. Systematics

1. Etymology and History

1.1. The term "dialectic" comes from the Greek phrase *hē dialektikē technē* or *epistēmē* (the art or knowledge of discussion by question and answer), and specifically, the verb *dialegomai* (discuss, dispute). In Plato (→ Platonism) dialectic is thus the knowledge that is achieved by (Socratic) → dialogue. In contrast, Aristotle (→ Aristotelianism) opposed the apodictic proofs of analytic to the probability proofs of dialectic. Ever since, the term has been ambiguous. In the Middle Ages it was often equated with → logic and then defined as the art or science of distinguishing the true from the false. But often, too, it was opposed to logic and understood as the science of probability argumentation.

1.2. From an early time (Cicero, Boethius, Ramus, etc.) dialectic was defined as the doctrine of the invention of new arguments. I. Kant (→ Kantianism) viewed it ambivalently as the process of → reason by which reason entangles itself in contradictions, and yet also as the doctrine of solving contradictions by means of the use of transcendental analysis (→ Criticism; Epistemology). J. G. Fichte and G. W. F. Hegel, however, restored it to a place of honor. Hegel (→ Hegelianism) gave it ontic and not just conceptual significance. For him it was not just a way of doing philosophy, but it could claim to be expressing the thing itself. This view had an abiding influence on theology, for it opened up the prospect that human talk about God might be God's own Word.

1.3. → Marxism adopted the formal structure of Hegelian dialectic but turned it on its head. As → Marx himself stated, he did not merely differ from Hegel at the very root; rather, he taught the exact opposite. For Marx, the ideal was simply the material as the human mind transformed and translated it (afterword to 2d ed. of *Das Kapital*). The priority of thought and ideas yields to a dialectic of history and the economic forces of production at work in it. Dialectic was thus brought into relation with → materialism, which views concepts materialistically as the reflection of real things, instead of viewing real things as the reflection of various stages of the absolute concept. Dialectic thus amounted to no more than the science of the general laws of movement, both in the external world and in human thought (Marx and Engels, 26.383-84).

In Marxism, however, the nature of dialectic is debated. Engels (Marx and Engels, 25.313-14, 356-57) defined it in terms of the "most general" laws of nature, describing its three most important aspects as follows: (1) the changing of quantity into quality and vice versa (i.e., not merely quantitative change in development but the unity of quantity and quality, of evolution and revolution, of continuity and discontinuity); (2) the mutual interpenetration of polar opposites and their turning into one another when carried to extremes (so that the contradictions in things are the impelling forces in every movement and development, development being self-development according to the law of the unity and conflict of opposites); and (3) development by contradiction, or the negation of negation in spiral forms of evolution (in which the old is not destroyed but a higher development transcends earlier stages and thus takes up what is positive and capable of development in them). J. Stalin abandoned the idea of the negation of negation, but it was rehabilitated after his death in 1953.

1.4. Marxist-Leninist philosophy accepts these three basic laws and adds other laws, for example, the connection between essence and appearance, content and form, reality and possibility, necessity and accident, the general and the individual. The theory of objective dialectic in the movement and development of the external world, which takes place apart

from our consciousness, differs from the theory of subjective dialectic. This is predominantly an epistemology and seeks the dialectical connection between theory and practice, absolute and relative truth, the abstract and the concrete, the logical and the historical, along with the associated dialectical principles of unity.

Dialectic is thus used as a method as its laws and principles are systematically and deliberately applied to the mastering of the material world both practically and theoretically. In this regard it is not possible to see things or phenomena in isolation or unhistorically. They must always be viewed in the process of movement and change, and their inner contradictions and mutual connections are to be investigated. In comprehensive analysis the unity in the opposing parts will come to light.

1.5. In the → process philosophy of A. N. Whitehead, the process is dialectical in nature. For Whitehead, a person's "prehension" of a fact or object (i.e., a "mere taking account of," without conscious awareness of, its essential character) leads to its transformation into something new.

1.6. In his existential dialectic, S. → Kierkegaard opposed the mediating Hegelian dialectic, which no longer distinguished sharply between concepts and facts. He pointed to the radical contrast between the various stages of existence. In the *aesthetic* stage the attainment of happiness is the supreme goal of one's existence. In the *ethical* stage we see the distinction between good and bad and set ourselves under the norm of the divine law. But our glorying in being able to keep God's requirements is broken when we have to admit our failure or guilt. Remorse and suffering mark the *religious* stage. Only by a "leap," a decision for which there neither is nor can be any basis, can we move from one stage to another.

Christian faith is shaped by this dialectic, which aims to shatter illusions and to achieve a relation to God in very truth. There is an infinitely qualitative distinction between God and humankind, between God and the world. Thus only indirectly can we speak about the world of God. We believe against reason; we surrender our will and rights to God without reservation. → Dialectical theology (e.g., of K. → Barth, E. Brunner, F. Gogarten, and R. Bultmann) adopted these thoughts of Kierkegaard.

2. Systematics

Dialectic necessarily builds on classical logic. It plays a role only where a dynamic that classical logic can no longer control is important. In general we may distinguish three types of dialectic.

2.1. There is the dialectic of the *infinite* or →

absolute, which is also called Platonic dialectic. This permits deduction from the relative to the absolute. Everything relative and limited presupposes something absolute and unlimited.

2.2. There is a dialectic of *polarity.* This type appears, for example, in the Pythagoreans (→ Greek Philosophy), in the philosophies of the Far East, and in Germany (e.g., J. W. von Goethe). Here the world is viewed as a totality of irreducible polarities — hot and cold, north and south, male and female, yang and yin, and so forth.

2.3. There is finally the dialectic of *synthesis.* The world process moves by opposites that are dissolved in something new, as in Fichte, Hegel, Marxism, and other philosophies. Several traditional themes of dialectic are dealt with in classical logic, including the doctrine of induction and abduction (C. Peirce, U. Eco). The distinction between conceptual dialectic and real dialectic is significant only where the reality of the world is regarded as a problem.

Bibliography: T. W. ADORNO, *Negative Dialektik* (Frankfurt, 1966) • W. BECKER and W. K. ESSLER, eds., *Konzepte der Dialektik* (Frankfurt, 1981) • J. N. FINDLAY, *Hegel: A Re-Examination* (London, 1958) • E. HEINTEL, *Grundriß der Dialektik,* vol. 1, *Zwischen Wissenschaftstheorie und Theologie;* vol. 2, *Zum Logos der Dialektik und zu seiner Logik* (Darmstadt, 1984) • R. HEISS, *Wesen und Formen der Dialektik* (Cologne, 1959) • W. JANKE, *Historische Dialektik. Destruktion dialektischer Denkformen von Kant bis Marx* (Berlin, 1977) • K. KOSIK, *Dialectics of the Concrete* (Hingam, Mass., 1976) • J. McTAGGERT, *Studies in Hegelian Dialectic* (Cambridge, 1896; 2d ed., New York, 1964) • K. MARX and F. ENGELS, *Collected Works* (trans. R. Dixon et al.; New York, 1975ff.) • W. RISSE et al., "Dialektik," *HWP* 2.164-226 (historical survey and bibliography) • W. RÖD, *Dialektische Philosophie der Neuzeit* (Munich, 1974) • R. SIMON-SCHAEFFER, *Dialektik. Kritik eines Wortgebrauchs* (Stuttgart, 1973) • W. VAN DOOREN, *Dialektiek* (Assen, 1977) • W. VIERTEL, *Eine Theorie der Dialektik* (Königstein, 1983).

HUBERTUS G. HUBBELING†

Dialectical Theology

1. The Phrase

"Dialectical theology" is the name for a movement that after World War I initiated a new period in theology and the church, first of all in Germany. It found expression in the journal *Zwischen den Zeiten* (Between the times; 1923-33), produced by Karl → Barth (1886-1968), Friedrich Gogarten (1887-1967), Georg Merz (1892-1959), and Eduard Thurneysen (1888-1974). Coworkers were Rudolf Bultmann (1884-1976) and Emil Brunner (1889-1966); for a time, Paul → Tillich (1886-1965) was also in dialogue with them.

1.1. Purpose

What the proponents of the trend had in mind can hardly be gleaned from the phrase "dialectical theology," which did not come from their own ranks but was a designation meant critically, apparently coined by Leonhard Ragaz (1868-1945), a Swiss → religious socialist. Barth, Bultmann, and Gogarten adopted the label from time to time and tried to relate it to their own aims, but with different explanations and no common denominator. They were united only in opposition to → Culture Protestantism and its false → reconciliation of the world with God.

In 1920 Barth wrote that God's → truth is "the living → dialectic of all worldly reality inasmuch as it questions its supposed answers and answers its real questions." → Theology, which relates to this truth, should never want to have the last word but always needs supplementing and must always remain open. It must speak about the incarnation of God in Jesus Christ (→ Christology), which does not remove the distinction between God and the world but is the basis for making it truly plain. Thus theology (as Barth explained in 1922) must adopt the dialectical method, a way of thought that does not lead to a set result but follows the answer that God has given. In all that it says, theology must remember that only God can speak the decisive word about our human → life and → death.

Bultmann interpreted dialectical theology in 1924 as an attack on the → liberal theology that makes humanity and not God its theme. In opposition to so-called positive theology, the opponent of liberalism, Bultmann held that → God cannot be directly an object of human speech and the thinking based upon it. Theology has to do with human beings to whom the Word of God comes — the message of the cross, of the → justification of the sinner — and who themselves decide to accept this decision made about them. In 1928 Bultmann described dialectical theology as talk about God that is fully aware of human finitude and of the possibilities of human language.

Gogarten thought that all theology is dialectical from the outset insofar as it does not try to control God's Word and does not consist only of an intellectual and religious mastering of existence.

1.2. Dialectical Theology and Philosophical Dialectic

Many of these descriptions remind us of the → dialectic of the → Platonic dialogues. There is also an affinity with the existential dialectic of S. → Kierkegaard (1813-55) and his criticism of G. W. F. Hegel's (1770-1831) dialectical mediation of God and the world. Over against this, Kierkegaard set the → paradox of the incarnation of God, which demands the decision of → faith and which we can communicate only indirectly by pointing to a truth beyond our control. Apart from these echoes, however, dialectical theology does not pay heed to the history of philosophical dialectic, nor does it consider earlier examples of dialectical speech in theology.

1.3. Dialectical Theology as Dialectical Speech about God and Humanity

Dialectical theology takes up the divine contradiction of ungodly self-assertion, maintaining that human thought cannot reconcile God and humanity, → time and eternity, → grace and → sin. God's creative contradiction breaks open human reflection and gives it a movement that must find expression in dialectical speech. Dialectical theology opposes any tradition of theological thought that appeals to our God-consciousness or to any other religious data.

2. Tasks

Gogarten's manifesto "Zwischen den Zeiten" (*ChW* 34 [1920]) led the discussion with its prophetic conclusion that "we are so deeply sunk in the human that we have lost God . . . yes, really lost him; there is no longer any thought in us that reaches him." Face to face with this situation, dialectical theology regards itself as an attempt to speak as we hear God's Word addressed to us, and on this basis to think afresh. The origin of theology (as distinct from its historically datable beginnings) lies in God's speaking. It begins with the presupposition that we do not know God but that he has made himself known to us in Jesus Christ. This once-for-all → revelation

takes place in the act of proclamation with which God sovereignly addresses us and claims our whole life, doing so with an overarching sense of promise.

2.1. Proclamation as a Basis

With all of its arguments and methodological views, dialectical theology contradicts the idea that the Christ-event empirically changed the course of history and God's relationship to humanity (i.e., that the Christ-event can be proved or disproved through historical methods). According to that idea, theology would only be reporting the transformation and its historical effects, while → preaching would only communicate news of the change and indicate its results. In contrast, dialectical theology rests on the task of proclamation. (Barth and later Bultmann in particular preferred to speak of → kerygma, the message of salvation that we can only deliver and never develop or concoct from our own experience.)

2.2. Tradition

Apart from Bultmann, the proponents of dialectical theology did not follow ordinary academic careers. For all their criticism of contemporary academic theology, however, they did not abandon theological work to focus instead on practical and social demands of church work. But they sought to set theology on new foundations — those that had been accepted up to modern times, but then abandoned by → Enlightenment → piety, partly also by → Pietism, and definitely by → liberalism. In laying this new foundation, they would not simply repeat classic insights but would try to define them afresh under conditions that had been radically altered by the war and its consequences. Especially they were aware of the distant, unknown God, the "Wholly Other," who will not let himself be defined within the concept of history (→ Theology of History).

The new approach of dialectical theology opposed any sense of standing in an ongoing nexus of tradition. It thus broke with a tradition that rested on the significance of Christianity in the march of humanity to establish the → kingdom of God on earth. The confidence in such a march was completely lost with the outbreak of World War II. Even concepts of social criticism like religious socialism, to which Barth and Thurneysen originally gave their support, seemed to be inadequate. Proclaiming God's judgment on the world, dialectical theology gave its own expression to the crisis in Western culture, of which everyone was aware. But when Tillich called it the theology of crisis in 1923, this was only partially apt, for dialectical theology did not want to be viewed as an answer to the demands of the situation. It uncompromisingly thought of itself as theology (specifically, theo-logy, word about God), sharply differentiated from any explanation along the lines of religious sociology, psychology, or history.

2.3. *Philosophy of Science*

Rejecting the established classification of theology as a part of the humanities, dialectical theology still had to deal with questions of → epistemology, but did so only in a preliminary way. Unlike in the thought of F. D. E. → Schleiermacher, it did not trace the uniqueness of theology back to the independence of → religion. Yet God himself cannot be objectified in theology, and the → Word of God can be the theme of theology only if we remember the infinite distance between theological statements and the reality stated in them. Nevertheless, the → axiom of theology is *that* God has spoken (Barth). Bultmann and Gogarten rejected → subjectivism no less than objectifying thinking; unlike Barth, they were interested in a prior philosophical clarification of theological concepts.

3. Further Development and Result

Because of these differences, which reflected fundamental and unbridgeable conflicts, Gogarten and Bultmann drew increasingly further away from Barth. In 1933 Barth declared that their partnership in work and warfare was at an end for theological reasons, describing it as a productive misunderstanding. It remained fruitful, however, as an aesthetic revolution in theology that found for it a new foundation and permanently changed its mode of presentation. Yet it was also a misunderstanding, for lack of agreement about how to carry out the project threw doubt on agreement about the foundations.

3.1. *Bultmann, Gogarten, and Barth*

Barth charged Bultmann, Gogarten, and especially Brunner with returning to an anthropological basis instead of seeking the basis of theology exclusively in Christology. Behind the divergences there lay opposing views of the central theological problems and their priorities.

Bultmann maintained most consistently the early insights. Christian faith cannot be justified by a reconstruction of its tradition. But when theology uses reconstruction, it must make unrestricted use of the historico-critical method (→ Exegesis, Biblical). Bultmann found a need for existential interpretation to understand the kerygma, and he turned to M. Heidegger's (1889-1976) existential philosophy for help. The → demythologizing of biblical texts will liberate faith from all regard for traditional ideas.

Gogarten's main interest focused on the debate of faith with intellectual history. With its immoderate striving, humanity is destroying itself and the world. It must rediscover its creatureliness under God, the Creator (→ Anthropology). To make this critique of culture clear, Gogarten took a different path from Barth in both ecclesiastical and national politics.

Barth wanted to replace the misleading title "dialectical theology" with "theology of the Word of God," which he developed as a → dogmatic task. All the other demands that others might make on theology (e.g., concern about the difficulties that face us moderns in matters of faith) he regarded as secondary and even epistemologically misleading, as he emphasized against Brunner.

3.2. *Impact*

3.2.1. *In Germany*

Apart from its thematic influence, the main effect on the German church was to present the unity of theology "from text to preaching." Dialectical theology brought together the individual branches of theological work, bridged the gap between theological theory and church practice, and drew pastors into theological discussion. In its call for theological decisions, it also supported the → church struggle, though here it did not maintain a closed front but entered into new alliances with former opponents. The → Barmen Declaration was prepared and shaped in accordance with Barth's conception. The two also remained in alliance through their ecumenical impact.

3.2.2. *In the Church at Large*

Barth never viewed himself confessionally as Reformed. Yet he referred back to the principles of the Reformed tradition and had the greatest influence in → Reformed churches, notably in Holland (K. H. Miskotte, G. C. Berkouwer, H. Berkhof), Hungary (I. Török), Scotland (T. F. Torrance), and the United States (J. A. Mackay in the Presbyterian Church, K. Ernst in the Reformed Church, H. Frey at Yale). Scandinavia, which was more oriented to a comparative religion view, was less open to the impulses of dialectical theology (R. Prenter, critically G. Wingren). In the United States R. → Niebuhr in his criticism of culture appealed to a dialectical theology of sin and grace, which for all its differences was similar at many points to the renewal of the basic thoughts of the Reformation in German dialectical theology.

Barth's leading role in the church struggle both supported and strengthened his ecumenical contacts, and it also strengthened these, as in his support for the Czech theologian J. L. Hromádka. At the first full meeting of the → World Council of Churches at Amsterdam in 1948, Barth gave a keynote address that was wholly in keeping with the intentions of dialectical theology.

Gogarten found international recognition only with his later work, but Bultmann soon gained fame as an exegete, and his ideas made an ecumenical impact with the increasing influence of → hermeneutics. Brunner's works found a better reception in the English-speaking world than in the German.

3.3. Results

Dialectical theology made an impact as theological renewal in the spirit of the Reformation. It attracted attention even outside → Protestantism and beyond the boundaries of the church. The direct recourse to the Bible, to the ideas of → Luther and → Calvin — and also, with Barth, to the → church fathers, → Scholasticism, and Reformed → orthodoxy — was either hailed as an advance or attacked as a relapse into traditionalism. Yet a purely historical evaluation would not be in the spirit of dialectical theology. Its question about the basis of theology (prior to all theological work), its proclamation of the freedom of faith from all criteria of public plausibility, and not least its adoption and reformulation of urgent questions of the day in terms of the → hope grounded in God's judgment — all these things live on, even in the form of attacks on what dialectical theology set in motion.

Bibliography: Primary sources: K. Barth, *CD* I/1; idem, *Die christliche Dogmatik im Entwurf*, vol. 1, *Prolegomena* (Munich, 1927; 2d ed., Zurich, 1982); idem, *The Epistle to the Romans* (London, 1957; orig. pub., 1919; 2d ed., 1922); idem, *The Göttingen Dogmatics: Instruction in the Christian Religion* (vol. 1; ed. H. Reiffen; Grand Rapids, 1991; orig. pub., 1924) • K. Barth and E. Thurneysen, *Briefwechsel*, vol. 1, *1913-1921*; vol. 2, *1921-1930* (Zurich, 1973-74) • R. Bultmann, *Faith and Understanding* (ed. R. W. Funk; New York, 1969; orig. pub., 1933) • W. Fürst, ed., *"Dialektische Theologie" in Scheidung und Bewährung, 1933-1936* (Munich, 1966) • F. Gogarten, *Ich glaube an den dreieinigen Gott* (Jena, 1926) • J. Moltmann, ed., *The Beginnings of Dialectic Theology* (Richmond, Va., 1968) • G. Sauter, ed., *Theologie als Wissenschaft* (Munich, 1971) • E. Thurneysen, *Das Wort Gottes und die Kirche* (Munich, 1971).

Secondary works: M. Beintker, *Die Dialektik in der "dialektischen Theologie" Karl Barths* (Munich, 1987) • W. Härle, "Dialektische Theologie," *TRE* 8.683-96 (bibliography) • E. Jüngel, *Barth-Studien* (Zurich, 1982) • D. Korsch, *Dialektische Theologie nach Karl Barth* (Tübingen, 1996) • W. Pannenberg, "Dialektische Theologie," *RGG* (3d ed.) 2.168-74 • G. Sauter, "Die 'dialektische Theologie' und das Problem der Dialektik in der Theologie," *Erwartung und Erfahrung* (Munich, 1972) 108-46 • *ZDT*.

Gerhard Sauter

Dialogue

1. Philosophy
2. Ecumenical Context
   2.1. Term
   2.2. Dialogue between Denominations and Religions
   2.3. Subjects and Results

1. Philosophy

Deriving from the Gk. *dialogos* (conversation), the term "dialogue" has become a key term in 20th-century philosophy, though used in different ways. In the history of philosophy it has played a leading role since Plato (→ Platonism), mainly as a literary genre. Yet the form Plato chose was connected with his conviction that we can reach true insight only in a conversation that does justice to opposing views and seeks agreement step by step.

The term took on philosophical significance only in the 20th century. It did so first, out of anthropological and ontological interest, in the so-called dialogic philosophy espoused by Jewish and Christian thinkers like H. Cohen, F. Ebner, F. Rosenzweig, G. Marcel, and M. Buber (→ Jewish Philosophy). Buber parted company with earlier Western philosophy (esp. → idealism), which had been mostly an isolated monologue, apart from some beginnings of dialogue in F. H. Jacobi, L. A. Feuerbach, and S. → Kierkegaard.

In contrast, Buber stressed the primacy of the relationship that is given a priori with being human. "There is no 'I' as such, only the 'I' in a basic I-Thou and I-It relation" (*Werke* 1.79). The isolation of the Westerner, who reduces everything (including the other person) to the world of the I-It, can be broken only by a reversal, by an encounter with the Thou in which I lovingly recognize the Thou in its own → freedom. All systematic theorizing inevitably founders on the nonobjectifiability of this event. This led to the criticism that Buber was fixated on the prophetic but developed no explicit → ontology.

E. Lévinas, who stressed the asymmetrical element in the intersubjective relation more strongly than Buber, emphasized the impossibility of describing the otherness of the other ontologically. One can describe subjectivity only in ethical terms. The face of the other that looks on me cannot be an object of thought, but it lays upon me a responsibility for this other. In this sense, diakonia precedes dialogue.

A very different interest in dialogue emerged in discussions of → epistemology and → philosophy of science. On the one hand, stress falls on the limits of dialogue between those who hold different paradigms (note T. Kuhn's thesis of incommensurability). On the other hand, there is great confidence in dialogue as an instrument to provide a basis for certain claims to validity (note the consensus, or discourse, theory of truth [J. Habermas], as well as the dialogic, or constructivist, theory of truth [K. Lorenz]). To engage in rational dialogue it is necessary to describe and establish exactly the initial situation, the basic positions of the partners, and the rules and strategies. In → ethics, too, there has been an attempt to justify moral → norms in neutral dialogue (e.g., B. Ackermann). In the so-called dialogic → logic an attempt is made to replace the → axiomatic construction of a logical system by a social contract about rules for critical dialogue.

Bibliography: E. M. Barth and E. C. W. Krabbe, *From Axiom to Dialogue* (New York, 1982) • M. Buber, *Werke* (vol. 1; Munich, 1962) • E. Lévinas, *Ethics and Infinity* (Pittsburgh, 1985); idem, *Otherwise Than Being; or, Beyond Essence* (Hingham, Mass., 1981) • P. Lorenzen and K. Lorenz, *Dialogische Logik* (Darmstadt, 1978) • F. Reynolds and D. Tracy, eds., *Discourse and Practice* (Albany, N.Y., 1992) • H. H. Schrey, *Dialogisches Denken* (Darmstadt, 1970; 2d ed., 1983) • M. Theunissen, *The Other: Studies in the Social Ontology of Husserl, Heidegger, Sartre, and Buber* (Cambridge, Mass., 1984).

Ruurd Veldhuis

2. Ecumenical Context

2.1. *Term*

Dialogue is a basic human reality because we can be truly human only with others and because in this togetherness with others we are oriented to → truth and possible → meaning. The question of truth and meaning permeates our common work and our concern for the survival of individuals and the species. Ontologically, human history as a whole is essentially a nexus of relations and encounters, either profound or superficial, which sometimes succeed and sometimes fail. In the 20th century M. Buber reflected philosophically on the basic reality of dialogue, influencing decisively the use of the term (see 1).

We must construe the term "dialogue" as broadly as possible. Dialogue may be verbal and intellectual. But it may take place simply within life itself as different people, societies, or cultures live together and are open to one another. Thus the final document of the → World Council of Churches (WCC) conference at Chiang Mai, Thailand, in 1977 bore the title "Dialogue in Community." The implication is that we must understand simple daily fellowship itself as dialogue.

2.2. *Dialogue between Denominations and Religions*

In recent decades we have become aware in a new way of the basic reality of dialogue in the field of religion, where it has become a key theme. This awareness has taken place especially in Christian thought as the different denominations and traditions began to come closer together (as happened at the founding of the WCC and at → Vatican II). Opening up in dialogue has gone beyond the circle of Christianity. As a result of Vatican II, for example, the Roman curia established three secretariats (later, pontifical councils) specifically to promote dialogue — with other Christians (Pontifical Council for Promoting Christian Unity), with non-Christian religions (Pontifical Council for Interreligious Dialogue), and with unbelievers (Pontifical Council for Culture). Parallel bodies exist in the WCC.

2.2.1. The sociocultural constellation of our times has brought about this opening up to dialogue in concentric circles. In a world of growing dependence and interconnection, a lack of interest in other beliefs, whether in other denominations or in other religions, is hardly right or appropriate.

2.2.2. Specific differences exist between dialogue with other denominations and dialogue with other religions. In spite of many structural similarities, one cannot view the latter as a mere extension or broadening of the former.

Dialogue between denominations, or ecumenical dialogue, seeks step by step, by recourse to an originally common → tradition and basic faith, to restore the visible → unity and harmony of Christianity (of the one → church of Christ), which denominational division has destroyed. Participants can view this process as the fulfillment of a common task. The visible unity sought, however, is not uniformity. In the underlying harmony of the body of Christ, the different traditions concerning rites, forms of organization, and doctrinal accents all have their place.

2.2.3. In contrast, the goal of dialogue between religions is much less clear, for it does not rest on an inheritance that all regard as normative, nor is there a consensus regarding the need to pursue this task. John 17:21, the charter of modern → ecumenism, does not apply here. This dialogue rests on a realization of the fact that God's reality is greater than human forms and formulations. This perspective gives believers an awareness that God might have something to say to them through those who belong to other religious faiths.

2.3. *Subjects and Results*

In both cases, whether denominations or different religions are in dialogue, the essence of the process is openness. It allows of neither programs nor prognostications. Its results are unpredictable.

2.3.1. Dialogue can lead to → consensus in the sense that earlier differences are no longer regarded as divisive, as in the dialogue between Roman Catholics and Protestants about → justification, Scripture and tradition, purgatory (→ Hell), or even → Mariology and the veneration of → saints; or in the dialogue between the Eastern and Western churches about the → *filioque* clause. This is the form of ecumenical dialogue within Christianity. It has a goal, namely, the → unity of the church, and to this extent it is itself a transitional stage.

We must remember that (1) the goal itself is not fully defined (dialogue is also needed for deciding the nature of the unity that we seek) and (2) dialogue must continue, even when a new form of the church's visible unity has been achieved at some future time. Thus it is common today to say that the church is always conciliar by nature.

The individual denominations also pursue ecumenical dialogue either in a bilateral or a multilateral form, either at the global or at the regional and local levels. The subjects in this dialogue are usually doctrines that have traditionally brought division. The results, or provisional results, usually come in the form of statements of agreement or convergence, as in the Lima texts of 1982 regarding the understanding of baptism, the Eucharist, and church offices.

2.3.2. Dialogue can also lead, however, to an awareness that we do not have to occupy opposing positions but that we stand before an open question (e.g., dialogue about the nature of the sacraments). Or it may lead to the result that by meeting different forms of the faith, we see our own tradition in a new light and thus gain a deeper understanding of the faith. In most cases, dialogue between religions has this desirable effect.

2.3.3. In any case, dialogue demands a new style of theology, one that is dialogic, as distinct from positional.

→ Jewish-Christian Dialogue

Bibliography: H. Fries and K. Rahner, *Unity of the Churches: An Actual Possibility* (Philadelphia, 1985) • F. von Hammerstein, *Von Vorurteilen zum Verständnis. Dokumente zum jüdischen-christlichen Dialog* (Frankfurt, 1976) • S. S. Samartha, *Courage for Dialogue* (Geneva, 1981); idem, ed., *Faith in the Midst of Faiths: Reflections on Dialogue in Community* (Geneva, 1977) official report of Chiang Mai consultation • E. Valyi-Nagy, "Das dialogische Wesen der Kirche" (Diss., Basel, 1965) • V. Vayta, *Zur ekklesiologischen Bedeutung des Dialogs, Oecumenica 1969* (Strasbourg, 1969) • L. Vischer, *Überlegungen nach dem vatikanischen Konzil* (Zurich, 1966) • World Council of Churches, *Ecumenical Considerations on Jewish-Christian Dialogue* (Geneva, 1983); idem, *Guidelines on Dialogue with People of Living Faith and Ideologies* (Geneva, 1979).

Heinrich Ott

Diaspora

1. Term
2. Diaspora and Ecumenism

1. Term

Etymologically, "diaspora" is from Gk. *diaspeirō* (scatter); semantically, its usage derives from Jewish tradition.

1.1. In the LXX the term describes the fate of Jews outside Palestine. As traders, hired workers, captives, slaves, and colonists, they were "scattered" over three continents (Isa. 11:11). Although diaspora and exile are not synonymous, yet for the prophets they are closely related. Divine judgment has scattered the disobedient; divine mercy will gather the dispersed (e.g., Ezek. 22:15; 37:21). In Isa. 49:6 Israel is the light of the Gentiles.

In the NT the "new" Israel takes over diaspora from the old. The first reference of diaspora is to churches outside Palestine (1 Pet. 1:1; Jas. 1:1). Then Acts 8:1, 4 describes diaspora as an opportunity for → mission, obviously with the certainty that as the seed is scattered, it will grow. Up to the time of Constantine, diaspora was important in this regard. After that time, however, the term vanished for a long period from the church and theology. The word next found color and significance only with M. → Luther's lectures on the Psalms, in which he speaks of the church as hidden and very dispersed (on Psalm 40).

1.2. New perspectives on diaspora have arisen through confessional developments in and after the → Reformation. Thus in Germany → Protestantism took a territorial form. In the course of the Counterreformation (→ Catholic Reform and Counterreformation), confessional → minorities arose that were recognized at the Peace of Augsburg (1555; → Augsburg, Peace of) and the Peace of Westphalia (1648; → Thirty Years' War 2). Dispersed churches then came into being with the development of toleration. Immigrants also formed diaspora churches in such places as Russia, North America, Latin America, and Australia. Displacement of the population with the onset of industrialization led to the same result. Finally, the great uprooting and movement of people after World War II brought new situations of diaspora.

1.3. A further shift in the understanding of diaspora came in the latter part of the 20th century. In many places an awareness developed that Christianity as a whole has become a minority. The situation of diaspora, however, is "the original situation of the church" (G. Niemeyer). Fundamentally, "the community of Jesus Christ is on the road to diaspora" (W. Krusche). All over the world such movements as → secularism, urbanization (→ City), and ideologization (→ Ideology) are isolating both individual Christians and Christian churches.

1.4. In discussion within Protestantism, the term "diaspora" has become unfortunately imprecise as a result of these processes. "It may be asked whether a return to the confessional use would not give it clearer contours" (C. E. Schott). Ecumenical observations, however, show how little chance such an effort has of arresting developments.

1.5. Diaspora has also taken on importance in the → Roman Catholic Church. At first only traces of the Protestant understanding might be found, but especially in Karl → Rahner's theological interpretation of the position of Christians in the modern world, the new view of diaspora has come also into Roman Catholic theology, and the idea of the church as diaspora has produced the concept of the *sacramentum mundi*. "As a description of the situation, diaspora is the starting point for a new depiction of the basic position of the church in relation to the world. The Catholic Church must move out boldly from its Roman Catholic ghetto into the open country of a pluralistic society" (L. Ullrich).

2. Diaspora and Ecumenism

Minority churches are in danger of being left behind on the way to an ecumenical consciousness. Wounds that small diaspora churches have suffered from the large churches in the past are an impediment in this regard. To overcome wounds and anxieties, diaspora needs an eschatological and universal horizon. Hope for the gathering of the dispersed comes from biblical statements such as John 11:52, Mark 10:45, and 1 Tim. 2:1-6, in which "many" — indeed "all" — will be brought to → salvation in Christ. On the way to this insight, small diaspora churches need the attentive understanding and active help of larger partner churches.

2.1. Small diaspora churches keep a stronger confessional sense than larger churches. The result is a greater fear of losing their → identity and an inclination to withdraw from the surrounding world. In diaspora aid, confession has played a big part from the time of Count N. L. von → Zinzendorf and A. H. → Francke.

2.2. In diaspora work, partner churches evaluate confession variously. Thus some societies will help only Lutherans, others Protestants in a broader sense, while Roman Catholics take care of their own diaspora churches.

2.3. In diaspora relief, more than money is needed. Important, too, are kindness, understanding, and encouragement. Small groups must be enabled to stand firm against elimination (H. Hoekendijk).

2.4. In the relation between diaspora and mission (see 1.1), there is a place both for concern to keep confessional peace and for respect for the faith of others. The task today is not so much to bring the gospel to other Christians as to work with them to take it to the world.

2.5. The legal aspects of diaspora may be seen especially in minorities that enjoy the protection of both → church law and civil law. Foreign congregations are in a special situation. They have legal, personal, and financial ties with the home churches, even while they strive to maintain good relations with the churches in their countries of residence.

2.6. Diaspora ought not to become a matter of condescension but an opportunity for learning. From it we may gain a better perception both of urgent and difficult tasks and of the problems and opportunities of ecumenism (→ Ecumenical Movement). In both theology and church we need to realize that diaspora is not just a catchword from the past but a key to the future.

Bibliography: S. Appelbaum, "The Organization of the Jewish Communities in the Diaspora," *The Jewish People in the First Century* (vol. 1; ed. S. Safrai and M. Stern; Assen, 1974) 464-503 • G. Besch, "Theologie des Diaspora?" *EvDia* 46 (1976) 31-38 • D. Biale, *Power and Powerlessness in Jewish History* (New York, 1986) • O. Dibelius, *Die Bedeutung der Diaspora* (Kassel, 1952) • B. Kresing, *Für die Vielen* (Paderborn, 1984) • W. Krusche, "Die Gemeinde Jesu Christi auf dem Weg in den Diaspora," *EvDia* 45 (1975) 56-82 • F. Lau, "Diaspora II," *RGG* (3d ed.) 2.177-80 • G. Niemeier, "Diaspora als Gestalt kirchliches Seins und kirchlicher Sendung," *EvT* 7 (1947/48) • H. Reiss, "Abscondita ecclesia et valde dispersa," *Reformation und praktische Theologie* (FS W. Jetter; Göttingen, 1983); idem, ed., *In der Liebe lebt Hoffnung* (Kassel, 1982) • G. Sheffer, ed., *Modern Diasporas in International Politics* (New York, 1986) • C. E. Schott, "Diaspora II," *TRE* 8.717-18 • R. Segal, *The Black Diaspora* (New York, 1995) • M. Stern, "The Jewish Diaspora," Safrai and Stern, *Jewish People*, 117-83.

Hermann Riess†

Didactics

1. The word "didactics" comes from Lat. *(ars) didactica,* which is based on Gk. *didaktikē technē* (the art of teaching). → Baroque → pedagogy popularized it, especially the famous *Didactica magna* of J. A. Comenius (Czech 1632, Latin 1657). Most of the languages of western Europe use a cognate (e.g., Fr. *didactique*), though English prefers to speak of "educational psychology" or "instructional theory" for the formal and methodological aspects of teaching, and "curriculum (development)" for content. The art of teaching originally comprised rules for successful teaching and the mastering of these rules. "Didactics" today, however, has the broader sense of theory of instruction. "Teaching" is the promotion of learning.

Descriptively, "didactics" means the deriving of general structures and laws of teaching from the observation of concrete processes (empirical research on teaching). The results obtained provide the basis for *prescriptive didactics,* which aims at elaborating criteria for the organization of teaching-learning processes.

2. The basic structure of teaching processes points to several problem areas and divisions of the field: individuals or groups (the teaching side) familiar with the subject matter work with others less informed (the learning side) to improve their abilities and/or attitudes (didactic goals). Taking into account preexisting dispositions of learning, the teachers devise schemes appropriate to promoting the learners toward these ends.

General didactics makes statements relatively independent of content, while *special didactics* relates exclusively to specific content. *Formative didactics* investigates the conditions of a formative encounter with cultural materials and proposes criteria for selecting such materials. At the heart of *curricular didactics* stands the positing and validating of didactic goals, and the elements of instruction are means to achieve these goals. *Structural didactics* concentrates on elucidating formal relations between the elements of the instructional setting and the best way to make the other elements serve the goals. *Communicative didactics* stresses the relation between students and teachers, while *activity didactics* aims at offering students learning opportunities to be used according to their own preferences and initiatives.

→ Religious Instruction

Bibliography: H. GLÖCKEL, *Vom Unterricht* (Bad Heilbrunn, 1990) • M. E. GREDLER, *Learning and Instruction* (Upper Saddle River, N.J., 1997) • A. MacKEOUGH, *Toward the Practice of Theory-Based Instruction* (Hillsdale, N.J., 1991) • C. J. MacMILLAN and J. W. GARRISON, *A Logical Theory of Teaching* (Dordrecht, 1988) • A. C. ORNSTEIN, *Teaching* (Boston, 1995) • W. H. PETERSSEN, *Lehrbuch allgemeiner Didaktik* (Munich, 1983) • G. SCHRÖTER, *Strömungen der Gegenwartsdidaktik* (Düsseldorf, 1980) • W. SÜNKEL, *Phänomenologie des Unterrichts. Grundriß der theoretischen Didaktik* (Munich, 1996).

GÜNTER R. SCHMIDT

Dietary Laws

In the ancient Orient (e.g., Egypt, Persia), as in all cultures, dietary laws were common. Being → taboos, they defy rational explanation. In the OT they apply primarily to animals used for food. Deuteronomy 14 and Leviticus 11 contain systematic lists of clean and unclean animals of the land, sea, and air. Animals that chew the cud and have cloven hoofs are clean, as are most birds, all fish that have fins and scales, and, among insects, grasshoppers. Unclean are cloven-hoofed animals that do not chew the cud, various birds, fish without fins and scales, almost all insects, small mammals, amphibians, and reptiles. Eating blood is strictly forbidden, since it is → life (Lev. 17:10-16; Deut. 12:23-25). It also is a means of → atonement (e.g., Lev. 3:8; 4:5-7) and must be poured out on the ground when animals are slaughtered (Deut. 12:15-16). Extraneous fat must be offered to → Yahweh as a burnt offering (Lev. 3:14-17; → Sacrifice). Dead animals and those torn by beasts of prey are unclean. It is forbidden to boil a lamb in its mother's milk (Exod. 23:19; 34:26; Deut. 14:21) or to slaughter mother and offspring on the same day (Lev. 22:28). With the joining of the Festival of Unleavened Bread to the → Passover (Deut. 16:1-4), only unleavened bread was to be eaten during Passover week (Lev. 23:6; → Jewish Practices 2.1).

In early → Judaism dietary laws were further developed to differentiate Jews from Gentiles (e.g., see Dan. 1:18 and esp. the tractate *Ṭoharot* in the → Mishnah). → Jesus, however, set himself above dietary laws (Mark 7:15 and par.). → Paul saw no problem in eating meats that had been offered to idols, for false gods have no existence (1 Cor. 8:4-6). He thus stressed freedom of → conscience (10:25) but also urged restraint on behalf of those who were weak in faith (8:7-13; Rom. 14:1-3). The apostolic council (→ Acts of the Apostles §8) enjoined → Gentile Christians to refrain from eating blood and the meat of strangled animals (Acts 15:20, 29). Conflicts between Jewish and Gentile Christians could break out at meals (Gal. 2:11-13).

In the Christian churches, vegetarian movements have arisen at times, and rules have been set for → fasting (→ Montanism; Adventists; Monasticism), but OT dietary laws have never been seen as binding on Christians. Dedication to God and his service, however, poses the need for a sensible and healthy diet according to individual circumstances.

→ Cultic Meal; Cultic Purity; Sacred and Profane

Bibliography: M. Boyce, *A History of Zoroastrianism* (vol. 1; Leiden, 1975) 294-324 • Y. A. Cohen, "Dietary Laws and Food Customs," *NEBrit* (1985) 26.861-68 • J. Döller, *Die Reinheits- und Speisegesetze des Alten Testaments in religionsgeschichtlicher Beleuchtung* (Münster, 1917) • M. Douglas, *Purity and Danger: An Analysis of Concepts of Pollution and Taboo* (2d ed.; London, 1969) • S. H. Dresner, S. Siegel, and D. M. Pollock, eds., *The Jewish Dietary Laws: A Guide to Observance* (rev. and exp. ed.; New York, 1982) • W. Kornfield, "Reine und unreine Tiere im Alten Testament," *Kairos* 7 (1965) 134-47 • J. Milgrom, "The Biblical Diet Laws as an Ethical System," *Studies in Cultic Theology and Terminology* (Leiden, 1983) 104-18 • H. Rabinowicz, "Dietary Laws," *EncJud* 6.26-45 • B. Reicke, "Speisegesetze," *BHH* 3.1828-29 • R. Schlichting, "Speisege- und verbote," *LÄ* 5.1126-28 • S. Stein, "The Dietary Laws in Rabbinic and Patristic Literature," *StPatr* 2 (1957) 141-54 • K. Wigand, "Die altisraelitische Vorstellung von unreinen Tieren," *ARW* 17 (1914) 413-36.

Henning Graf Reventlow

Dignity → Human Dignity

Dimissorial

A dimissorial, also *(Littera) Dimissoria* (from Lat. *dimitto,* "release"), is a certificate of discharge or release that one principal sends to another on behalf of certain individuals. In various forms it is customary in most Christian churches (→ Church Law). It approves or requests the giving of the sacraments or the performance of → occasional services by another ordained person, presupposing the fulfillment of all preconditions and the making of a report. In some countries it is also important in relation to standing and income (→ Pastor, Pastorate).

Present-day mobility makes the dimissorial more necessary than ever, and it can be refused only for very serious reasons. It is especially necessary in the case of → baptism (required, except in emergencies,

by Orthodox, Catholic, and Protestant), confirmation (Catholic, Protestant), ordination of deacons and priests (Orthodox, Catholic [1983 CIC 1015-23, 1052.2; → Codex Iuris Canonici]), → weddings (Orthodox, Catholic [1983 CIC 1115], Protestant), and → funerals (Orthodox, Catholic, Protestant).

In the territorial churches, or where there is no church connection, members often do not know whether a person belongs to a particular → congregation, parish, or → diocese, and information must be sought. In some cases the requested dimissorial will have to be sent; in others the information can be given orally. Those who send a dimissorial should take note of it and revoke it if they do not hear of its being used. The dimissorial is indispensable if church records are to be reliable and complete.

Heiner Grote†

Diocese

The Greek word *dioikēsis* (housekeeping, government) quickly found its way into the official vocabulary of the Roman Empire in the sense of an administrative district. It first denoted individual parts of a province, then a larger unit consisting of several provinces. In the East the latter sense came into use for a division of the church. In the West the church retained the older Roman understanding and used the term for a bishopric (→ Bishop, Episcopate).

Today the word has become a technical term in canon law and ecclesiology. For the → Roman Catholic Church, local, or "particular," churches — "in which and from which exists the one and unique Catholic Church" (1983 CIC 368) — are primarily the dioceses. These units are described as "a portion of the people of God which is entrusted for pastoral care to a bishop with the cooperation of the presbyterate so that, adhering to its pastor and gathered by him in the Holy Spirit through the gospel and the Eucharist, it constitutes a particular church in which the one, holy, catholic and apostolic Church of Christ is truly present and operative" (can. 369). The synonym "bishopric" well expresses the implied relation between the bishop and God's people. Similar local churches may be found in the areas administered by prelates and → abbots, and also — usually preparatory to the formation of dioceses — in the areas under the supervision of apostolic administrators, prefects, or vicars, as well as in independent missions.

The → Orthodox Church calls the sphere supervised by a bishop an eparchy or exarchate. Reformation churches that understand the bishop's office in a Reformed sense, or that give a different form to the tasks of care, supervision, and administration, use not only "diocese" but also "bishopric" and various equivalents. In a derived sense, even words like "synod," "conference," or "assembly" sometimes have a territorial connotation.

Bibliography: 1983 CIC 368-74 • "Diocese," *ODCC* 482 • A. STEIN, *Evangelisches Kirchenrecht* (2d ed.; Neuwied, 1985) 150-56.

HEINER GROTE†

Diplomacy → History, Auxiliary Sciences to, 6

Diptych

The term "diptych," from Greek, literally denotes something that is folded double. It was first used for two tablets that were laid together, which in antiquity were in common use as a kind of notebook. In many cases they were decorated with artwork, often with portraits of Roman consuls, who would send them as gifts to friends when taking office.

Quite early the diptych came into church use, for commemorations for the eucharistic → liturgy (→ Eucharist) could be noted in them. Christian themes that often bear witness to their provenance were depicted on the outside. These church diptychs often contained three or more tablets, so that strictly they were polyptychs. They served to embellish the → altar on which they were displayed.

They found their true use, however, in the → anaphora (note esp. the Orthodox liturgies of St. James and Basil the Great), the central prayer in the eucharistic liturgy, for in both origin and significance, diptychs cannot be distinguished from the prayer of the faithful. The diptychs list the names of living and dead Christians (including the saints and even Mary) for whom special intercession was made. Such commemorations, which are now themselves called diptychs, occur in all rites. In the Roman canon they come before the account of the institution, in the Alexandrian group after the Sanctus, and in the Antiochene and Byzantine rites after the epiclesis and before the final doxology (cf. the new Roman high-prayers).

Diptychs are canonically as well as liturgically important. Naming the members of the hierarchy of an → autocephalous church denotes for Orthodoxy both fellowship with and dependence upon the → bishop mentioned and is thus a guarantee of the validity of the liturgy and the dispensing of the mysteries. Being struck from the diptych, then, means

revocation of church fellowship (→ Excommunication). In the Munich report of the Roman-Orthodox dialogue of 1982, the explicit statement that the Eucharist of each local church is in full communion with the whole church clarified afresh the significance of the diptych.

Bibliography: V. E. BISHOP, *The Diptychs* (Cambridge, 1909) 97-117 • R. DELBRÜCK, *Die Consular-Diptychen* (Berlin, 1929) • DONATI, *De dittici degli antichi profani e sacri* (Lucca, 1753) • R. KACZYNSKI, "Die Interzessionen im Hochgebet," *Gemeinde im Herrenmahl. Zur Praxis der Meßfeier* (ed. T. Maas-Ewert and K. Richter; Freiburg, 1976) 303-13 • N. J. MORGAN, "Diptych," *DArt* 9.3-5 • R. F. TAFT, *A History of the Liturgy of St. John Chrysostom,* vol. 4, *The Diptychs* (Rome, 1991)

ARCHBISHOP LONGIN

Disarmament and Armament

1. Political Aspects
2. Theological and Ethical Aspects
    2.1. In Church Discussions
    2.2. In Secular Discussions

1. Political Aspects

In an international → society that might be described as a mitigated → anarchy, power relations between states have a central role. Although other means of exerting → force are of increasing importance, military → power is still seen as decisive. The question of the relation of armaments to the possibility of → war has not yet been satisfactorily answered by → peace research. Two contrary positions are adopted. The first takes the old view that if one wants → peace (§1), one must prepare for war. The second maintains that armaments not only are wasteful of resources (→ Ecology; Environment) but lead to arms races and thus increase the danger of war.

→ Technology has had an increasingly major impact on the development of armaments potential since the 19th century, whether in means of transport (e.g., steamships, railroads, airplanes) or in such things as dynamite, the machine gun, and the tank, followed later by electronics, rockets, and nuclear → weapons. Qualitative factors, not mere quantity, have always had greater influence on the dynamics of armament.

Until the end of the cold war, the overall burden of armaments increased continually (between 1960 and 1990, an increase of 250 percent). The United States and the Soviet Union and their allies shouldered an average 75 percent of the burden, but

→ Third World countries, pushed by a relentless arms trade, claimed an increasingly large share. Since the demise of world Communism and the implosion of the Soviet Union, the pattern has changed significantly. Between 1987 and 1994, overall expenditures worldwide (with regional exceptions) decreased by some 35 percent, including those in Third World countries (the so-called peace dividend). Arms sales decreased by some 50 percent in the same period. While not identical with disarmament, this process implied a considerable reduction of the military burden.

Two theoretical models are used to explain the dynamics of armaments. The one rests on the notion of the security dilemma that involves international processes of action and reaction. The other begins with internal factors — specifically, the material interests of the military-industrial complex, linked to an ideologically based belief (→ Ideology) in the necessity of military power.

Often, but incorrectly, the term "disarmament" is equated with armaments control, that is, with measures to limit or control armaments in order to promote military stability and to limit the risk and the costs of possible war. With few significant exceptions, all that has been achieved in this whole field comes under the heading of arms control. Disarmament, however, involves the renouncing of military power, the disbanding of troops, and the destroying of weapons and weapon systems. It may be unilateral, multilateral, or the result of tacit reciprocity. A distinction may also be made between quantitative and qualitative, or between total and partial, disarmament. The latter may relate to specific weapons (e.g., nuclear bombs or medium-range missiles), territories (e.g., Europe, the Antarctic, or the seabed), or countries (e.g., the United States and Russia).

We cannot count as disarmament in the narrower sense the limitations or demilitarizing imposed by victors in a war (e.g., upon Germany by the 1919 Versailles Treaty, or upon Iraq after the 1991 Gulf War), the voluntary renunciation by a country of arms that it does not possess (e.g., the renunciation of nuclear weapons by East Germany in the 1954 Paris Treaties), or international agreements to forbid certain weapons or technologies of warfare on humanitarian grounds (e.g., by the Hague agreement of 1907 or the prohibition of chemical weapons in 1925).

From the beginning of the 20th century (notably at the Hague peace conferences of 1899 and 1907), serious attempts have been made at disarmament. Thus far, however, they have been largely unsuccessful. Causes of failure are (1) the persistent anarchy of the international system, (2) the demands of national states (→ Nation, Nationalism), (3) domestic forces that are interested in maintaining a high level of armaments, and (4) technical factors, including issues of definitions, numbers, inequalities, and inspections.

The effort to achieve disarmament was institutionalized in the framework of the League of Nations. In the context of the → United Nations, founded in 1945, the goal of disarmament only gradually assumed more importance. At the beginning of the 1960s, general and full disarmament was the goal. But then the less ambitious goal of arms control replaced it, as we see in the banning of certain research on nuclear weapons in the Limited Test Ban Treaty (1963), in the Nuclear Nonproliferation Treaty (1968), and in the series of limited bilateral agreements between the United States and the USSR — including the Strategic Arms Limitation Treaty (SALT I in 1972, SALT II in 1979) and the Strategic Arms Reduction Treaties (START I in 1991, START II in 1993) — which aim at the limiting of strategic nuclear weapons. In 1972 a treaty was signed that forbade the making, storing, and use of biological weapons.

Reforms after 1985 in the former Soviet Union and a better international climate made possible a treaty in 1987 for the banning of intermediate-range nuclear forces (INF) in Europe, the first agreement for the actual destruction of existing weapons under international supervision. Since that time the technically and politically vexing problem of inspection and verification has become much less difficult. Along with gradually increasing economic pressures, this led to a series of successful disarmament negotiations and agreements, including a drastic reduction of heavy weapons in Europe (through the Conventional Forces in Europe [CFE] Treaty of 1990) and of nuclear weapons of the United States and the former USSR (START I and II).

In the wake of the dissolution of the Soviet Union, nuclear weapons were also removed from the territories of Belarus, Ukraine, and Kazakhstan. The implementation of the concluded treaties required major financial efforts, especially in view of the need to avoid further harm to the environment and to restore the extensive damage already done.

In 1995 the Nuclear Nonproliferation Treaty was renewed indefinitely. A treaty banning the manufacture, possession, and use of chemical weapons was agreed to in 1992 and came into force in 1997. In 1996 a treaty banning all nuclear tests (except simulation experiments) was agreed upon, but it required the cooperation of potential nuclear-weapons states to become effective.

Especially after a verdict in 1996 of the International Court of Justice on the illegality of nuclear weapons, it was argued increasingly that the discriminatory nature of existing arms-control treaties should be ended — that is, that the five recognized nuclear powers should finally start to disarm before further progress in the field could be made. This thinking also affected the willingness to negotiate other agreements, like a ban on land mines and a prohibition of the production of fissile materials.

Efforts to limit or reduce conventional weapons and the trade in these weapons have so far been unsuccessful, despite the fact that these are the weapons actually used in killing people.

→ Conflict; Force and Nonviolence; Genocide; International Law; Pacifism; Peace Education; Peace Movement

Bibliography: The following yearly publications consider the sociological aspects of disarmament and armament: *SIPRI* [Stockholm International Peace Research Institute] *Yearbook on World Armament and Disarmament* (Stockholm and Oxford, 1969-) • *Strategic Survey* (London, 1971-) • *World Military and Social Expenditures* (Leesburg, Va., 1981-).

PHILIP P. EVERTS

2. Theological and Ethical Aspects

No sphere of → politics has so drastically revealed the embarrassing weakness of religions and churches as that of disarmament and armament. For decades the budgets of most states have included increasing amounts for military purposes, even as the rhetoric of disarmament has been heard at international conferences. For years most churches have demanded in vain an overcoming of the dilemmas posed by nuclear strategy, an end to arms races, and a limitation on the arms trade. They have published many proposals and suggestions, which have been well received but for the most part disregarded in practice. Only the collapse of the Communist dictatorships in eastern Europe at the end of the 1980s (→ Socialism) brought with it a radically new situation that has opened up opportunities for creating new forms for ensuring peace. Whether anything will in fact be achieved is still completely uncertain.

2.1. *In Church Discussions*

The 20th century has witnessed a flood of statements on disarmament by churches and church groups. In this section we classify these efforts in terms of the recent history of international negotiations for disarmament and arms control.

2.1.1. The views of → church and → theology, as well as in → jurisprudence and → philosophy, depend upon the prior understanding of → force, → peace, → war, and → power. For centuries it was assumed that although wars perhaps could be limited, they could never be totally eliminated from this world. They have their root in the human capacities for power and in the human → freedom to do what is → evil. Opposition to force where necessary, and under certain conditions, was the theme of teaching about defense, → resistance, and so-called just war. Such teachings have come down to us from antiquity.

Only in the past 100 years or so, however, has there been the demand for a fundamental outlawing and overcoming of war by means of a prohibition of international law. A disarmament manifesto by Czar Nicholas II (1894-1917) in 1898 led to the first Hague Peace Conference (1899), and this in turn to the establishing of the Hague Tribunal (1901), or the Permanent Court of Arbitration. The nations involved now demanded obligatory arbitration in case of conflict, the prohibition of aerial bombing, the prohibition of the use of poison gas, and similar controls.

At the second Hague Peace Conference (1907) Protestant, Roman Catholic, and Jewish (→ Judaism) representatives petitioned together for the first time for an end to the arms race. The German-English Committee and the World Alliance for Promoting Friendship through the Churches, founded at the beginning of World War I with F. Siegmund-Schultze as its general secretary, followed up on these beginnings and formed a bridge to the early → ecumenical movement. It worked especially with the Life and Work movement, whose leader, Swedish archbishop N. Söderblom, won the Nobel Peace Prize in 1930. Efforts at disarmament in the framework of the League of Nations were only partially successful, however, ultimately failing as the Third Reich made military might its goal (→ Fascism).

2.1.2. In the first years after World War II the existence of nuclear weapons brought a new situation with the cold war. Apart from the historic → peace churches, no church wanted to make a plea for unilateral disarmament; instead, many declarations appeared containing urgent warnings about the dangers of a nuclear war and the arms race.

The Commission of the Churches on International Affairs (CCIA) played an important role in shaping ethical judgment at the ecumenical level. It consulted scientists, politicians, soldiers, jurists, and theologians in arriving at its pronouncements, and in its demands it oriented itself to the principles of the UN charter. It repeatedly brought forward its own proposals and memoranda at international disarmament conferences. Important demands were the ending, or at least the limiting, of nuclear tests; the renouncing by treaty of the threat and use of nuclear, biological, and chemical weapons; and the reduction and control of arms exports. The full assemblies of the → World Council of Churches (WCC) adopted many of the CCIA positions and regularly asked for studies from it.

2.1.3. In the first two decades after the war, initiatives for a general and full disarmament all failed. Reasons included the worldwide strategic situation, military-political doctrines, the strategic possibilities, but especially the opposing interests and convictions, all of which led to a sense of being under threat on all sides (→ Aggression). Scholars and the churches had little power to influence politics in a way that transcended the opposing blocs, but they constantly sought to relativize the views taken of → enemies and to plead on behalf of human survival. Beginning in 1957 at a meeting in Pugwash, Nova Scotia, the Conference on Science and World Affairs (the Pugwash Conferences) has consistently engaged leading scholars from around the world in efforts to reduce the arms race.

Only in the 1960s, after the Cuban missile crisis, did people begin to see what the conditions are for the survival of the race. The resultant negotiations for missile control had the limited aims of ensuring more stability (they included Test Stop, hot line, ABM treaty, nonproliferation of nuclear technology, and a halt to the stationing of missiles). In general, these steps were consistent with what the CCIA had been insisting upon for some years.

2.1.4. Partial agreements of this kind could not prevent the escalation, quantitatively as well as qualitatively, of the arms race. The studies conducted by the Institute for Peace Research, which was founded in the 1960s and with which many churches cooperated closely, documented regularly the account of its development (SIPRI yearbook, IISS studies, peace documents).

The popes and especially the papal commission Iustitia et Pax after → Vatican II issued warnings against the continuation of the arms race and the terrible destruction of human and material resources (→ Genocide). They pointed especially to the devastating effect of armaments on the Third World (→ Dependence), increasingly challenged the validity of nuclear terror as a deterrent, and in special UN assemblies called emphatically for comprehensive dis-

armament. John Paul II took this approach in his addresses and → encyclicals (e.g., *Redemptor hominis* [1979] and *Dives in misericordia* [1980]).

2.1.5. On the basis of CCIA proposals, the Fifth Assembly of the WCC, at Nairobi in 1975, analyzed the world arms situation and, with prompting especially from the Netherlands, adopted a program against militarism and the arms race. It expressly demanded that attention be given to the experiences of the historic peace churches, that an international disarmament conference be summoned, and that studies be made of the possibilities of arms conversion. A special appeal was made to the churches to stress the church's readiness to live without the protection of weapons and to take up significant initiatives that would exert pressure for effective disarmament (D. M. Paton, 124, 169-75, 181-82).

2.1.6. A new stage in the threat came in the late 1970s when the USSR deployed new medium-range missiles and NATO announced its response in the so-called twin-track decision of December 1979. Out of this development arose a new global → peace movement. Some groups were unequivocally pacifist, like those in West Germany that committed themselves to the maxim of living without armaments. Others demanded a policy of common security such as that promoted by the Independent Commission on Disarmament and Security Issues, or the Palme Commission (→ Pacifism). This concept involved a cooperatively controlled disarmament that would take into account the sense of threat and the valid security interests of both sides. It thus would allow only typical defensive systems in conventional weapons and only a minimal deterrent in the sphere of nuclear weapons, at the same time ruling out any incentives for first use of nuclear weapons and gradually declaring more and more areas to be nuclear free.

Many initiatives on the part of the churches had prepared the ground for the concept of common security, but the churches then adopted and developed the concept (see the peace memoranda), and mass peace movement demonstrations in the fall of 1981 supported it. In November of that year, at an international hearing in Amsterdam, the WCC presented related initiatives from many lands and churches (see P. Abrecht and N. Koshy). It is not clear, however, whether all these initiatives and proposals could have made any difference had it not been for the readiness of the USSR (→ Soviet Union) under M. Gorbachev to pursue disarmament and the dissolution of the Eastern bloc and its Warsaw Pact.

2.2. *In Secular Discussions*

Meanwhile NATO had begun to modify its military and especially its nuclear strategy. As the INF treaty put an end to the medium-range missile threat, the time became ripe for the reduction of conventional forces as well. The reduction of strategic nuclear arsenals also became a possibility. Strategy was changed accordingly to rule out an early deployment of nuclear weapons (NATO Doc. MC400, May 1992), and reliance upon them for defensive purposes was greatly reduced. Such weapons, however, are still the main pillar of a last-resort policy in view of an enlarged field of possible risks. In relation to such crisis regions as the Near East and the area of the Commonwealth of Independent States, NATO planning includes a list of options, including the nuclear option. This extension of strategic goals could very well trigger further development of armaments in connection with the need for modernization, mobility, and flexibility.

2.2.1. Nevertheless, an opportunity for true and stable disarmament does now exist. In 1989 the UN General Assembly in resolution 44/116J asked all states to report regularly to the UN secretary-general on measures and experiences in the field of arms conversion. This position is in keeping with the earlier demands of the churches.

For economic reasons the successor states of the USSR are interested in the converting of their armaments industry. It is to be noted, however, that although some military budgets allow much less for procurement, they still spend as much and even more on research and development. In the 1991 Gulf War modern weapon systems were used for the first time, which since then have been in high demand. This situation poses a new threat to the chances for disarmament.

2.2.2. Disarmament, which is pledged to the goal of a just peace, must include more than a quantitative reduction of available weapons. For this reason older proposals for a comprehensive peace structure in the later → Middle Ages, the → Renaissance, and the early → modern period (e.g., by P. Dubois, D. → Erasmus, J. A. Comenius, and I. Kant) all related disarmament to legal principles and a corresponding moral education.

In his philosophical work *Zum ewigen Frieden* (Project for a perpetual peace; 1795), Kant argued for the disbanding of all standing armies in the broader context of an order of → international law that would include all states. He also stressed the need for a free republican constitution in all states and the prohibition of states' squandering their resources for the purposes of building up their armaments. He saw, too, that there would have to be an international law to cover the rights of aliens in accordance with the idea of a common world citizenship. All these things,

he argued, must be grounded in universal moral principles (→ Ethics; Kantianism).

2.2.3. Kant's proposal makes it plain that military disarmament alone brings no security and offers no adequate guarantee of peace. If we do not succeed in eliminating the causes of war (including → hunger, unjust division of resources, and oppression) and in solving economic, political, and cultural → conflicts by submitting them to international arbitration, then incentives for rearmament and arms races will inevitably bring new threats to peace. True disarmament requires an order of international law that will limit state sovereignty, and international law in turn demands the consensus of the international legal community, which in the long run can come only as the result of true → peace education.

→ Christian Peace Conference

Bibliography: P. ABRECHT and N. KOSHY, eds., *Before It's Too Late: The Challenge of Nuclear Disarmament* (Geneva, 1983) • E. BAHR and D. S. LUTZ, *Gemeinsame Sicherheit* (2 vols.; Baden-Baden, 1987) • *Bericht der Unabhängigen Kommission für Abrüstung und Sicherheit "Common Security"* (Berlin [Palme Commission], 1982) • R. D. BURNS, ed., *Encyclopedia of Arms Control and Disarmament* (New York, 1993) • J. DELBRÜCK et al., eds., *Friedensdokumente aus fünf Jahren. Abrüstung, Kriegsverhütung, Rüstungskontrolle* (2 vols.; Kehl, 1984) • *Dienst am Frieden. Stellungnahmen der Päpste, des II. Vatikanischen Konzils und der Bischofssynode von 1963 bis 1980* (Bonn, 1980) • M. EFINGER, "Wettrüsten–Rüstungskontrolle–Abrüstung," *Handbuch Praxis der Umwelt- und Friedenserziehung* (ed. J. von Calließ and E. Lob; Düsseldorf, 1988) 3.584-97 (bibliography) • P. K. GHOSH, ed., *Disarmament and Development: A Global Perspective* (Westport, Conn., 1984) • W. GRAF VON BAUDISSIN, "Abrüstung," *EStL* 1.18-28 (bibliography) • W. HUBER and H.-R. REUTER, *Friedensethik* (Stuttgart, 1990) bibliography • N. KOSHY, ed., *Disarmament: Prospects and Problems* (Geneva, 1990) • B. MOLTMANN, ed., *Militarismus und Rüstung. Beiträge zur ökumenischen Diskussion* (Heidelberg, 1981) • D. M. PATON, ed., *Breaking Barriers, Nairobi 1975* (Grand Rapids, 1976) • *Peace and Disarmament: Documents of the World Council of Churches and the Roman Catholic Church* (Geneva and Vatican City, 1982) • H. RUH and J.-L. BLONDEL, "Ethische Kriterien für Rüstung und Abrüstung," *HCE* 3.448-64 (bibliography) • F. SIEGMUND-SCHULTZE, *Friedenskirche, Kaffeeklappe und die ökumenische Vision* (Munich, 1990) • R. STEINWEG, ed., *Das kontrollierte Chaos: Die Krise der Abrüstung* (Frankfurt, 1980) • J. A. VIERA GALLO, ed., *The Security Trap: Arms Race, Militarism, and Disarmament* (Rome, 1982).

WOLFGANG LIENEMANN

Discalced Friars

The discalced friars are religious orders whose members wear nothing on their feet but sandals (→ Franciscans) or who go totally barefoot (Carmelites). Biblical reasons and precedents include → poverty (Isa. 20:2-4), → reverence (Exod. 3:5; Josh. 5:15), and → penitence (2 Sam. 15:30).

The underlying idea is that in the spirit of → discipleship of Jesus, the discalced friars observe a rule Jesus once gave prohibiting the use of shoes (see Matt. 10:10). Observants, Capuchins, Camaldolese, Servites, and Passionists are some of the orders of male religious involved. Women's orders include the Poor Clares, as well as women Capuchins, Carmelites, and → Augustinians.

→ Orders and Congregations

Bibliography: C. W. Currier, *Carmel in America: A Centennial History of the Discalced Carmelites in the United States* (Baltimore, 1890) • M. Heimbucher, *Die Orden und Kongregationen der katholischen Kirche* (3d ed.; Paderborn, 1933-34; repr., 1965).

Johannes Schilling

Disciple

The word "disciple" comes from Lat. *discipulus*. Both terms are used for the Gk. *mathētēs* (pupil), which refers especially to the disciples of → Jesus and then, in a way that transcends the mere teacher-student relation, to the followers and admirers of a religious leader or to the younger members of a religious group. The NT itself speaks not only of the disciples of Jesus but also of the disciples of → Moses (John 9:28; cf. 1 Cor. 10:2), of the → Pharisees (Matt. 22:15-16; Mark 2:18 and par.), of → John the Baptist (Matt. 11:2; Mark 6:29 and par.), and of → Paul (Acts 9:25).

1. In the OT we might think first of the → prophetic groups (1 Sam. 10:5, 10; 19:20; 1 Kgs. 13:11; 2 Kgs. 2:3, 5; Mic. 3:5), which one might join in youth (2 Kgs. 5:22; 9:4). → Elijah had a disciple in → Elisha (2 Kings 2), who gathered around him a host of disciples (2 Kings 4–6). The fellowship of prophetic disciples (e.g., in Bethel [2 Kgs. 2:3] or Jericho [v. 5]) was characterized by monastic simplicity and sharing (2 Kgs. 4:1-7, 38-44; 6:5). In a broader sense the Rechabites were prophetic disciples whose fellowship, marked by abstinence from wine and from ownership of property, might well go back to Elijah (Jer. 35:8-10; cf. Zech. 13:5).

Josephus mentions a prophetic group of Pharisees (*Ant.* 17.41-45; cf. Matt. 22:15-16; Mark 2:18 and par.). The Teacher of Righteousness (1QpHab 7:1-6, based on Hab. 2:2-3) might also have been a prophet, and the Essenes or the people of → Qumran his disciples in a community life marked by abstinence from wine and meat (Josephus *J.W.* 2.160-61; 1QS 6:4-5; 1QSa 2:17-21).

John the Baptist also called and baptized disciples (John 1:35, 37; 3:25-26; 4:1; → Baptism; Discipleship), among them Jesus of Nazareth (Mark 1:9-11 and par.). The Baptist obviously gave his disciples some rules of purification (John 3:25), fasting (Mark 2:18 and par.), and prayer (Luke 5:33; 11:1). The disciples of John came to question Jesus (Matt. 11:2-6 and par.) and buried their master (Matt. 14:12 and par.). Apart from Jesus, Andrew (John 1:40) and Apollos (Acts 18:24-25) were originally disciples of John, and Paul met some of John's disciples in → Ephesus (Acts 19:1-7).

2. Jesus had both a narrower and a broader circle of followers. The Gospels call members of both groups disciples (Matt. 10:1; Mark 3:7, etc.; cf. Luke 6:13, 17; 19:37, 39; John 6:60, 66; 7:3; 8:31; 19:38). The inner circle, whose numbers Jesus himself limited, was made up of the → Twelve, who in post-Pauline times were called → apostles (cf. Mark 3:14, 16 with Matt. 10:1-2 and par.) and who were regarded as the foundation of the → church (Rev. 21:14; cf. Eph. 2:20). Jesus called Simon → Peter, Andrew, → James, John, and Levi-Matthew away from their jobs and told them to follow him (Mark 1:16-20 and par.; 2:14 and par.). He chose 12 disciples, corresponding to the number of the → tribes of Israel (Mark 3:13-19 and par.). He sent them out two by two to preach repentance and to heal the sick (Mark 6:7-13 and par.). He appointed them the eschatological regents of the renewed people of God (Matt. 19:28 and par.; → Kingdom of God).

In the broader circle of disciples, though they are not specifically called such, we might number the 500 "brothers" who are mentioned in 1 Cor. 15:6, the many who heard the preaching of Jesus and ate with him (see Mark 6:32-44 and par.), and especially the women who followed him (Mark 15:40-41 and par.; Luke 8:1-3; John 20:1-2, 11-18), including Mary and Martha (Luke 10:38-42; John 11:1-44; 12:1-3). Tabitha was the first actually to be called *mathētria* (disciple [fem.], Acts 9:36; cf. Vg. *discipula*). Luke in his gospel knows only the 72 (Luke 10:1-12, 17-20); however, in Acts (6:1-2, 7; 9:10, 19, 26; 11:26, 29, etc.) he describes all members of the Christian community as disciples (→ Congregation).

Bibliography: E. Best, "Disciples and Discipleship," *Studies in the Gospel according to Mark* (Edinburgh, 1986) • H. D. Betz, *Nachfolge und Nachahmung Jesu Christi im Neuen Testament* (Tübingen, 1967) • F. Hahn, "Die Nachfolge Jesu in vorösterlicher Zeit," *Die Anfänge der Kirche im Neuen Testament* (ed. P. Rieger; Göttingen, 1967) 7-36 • M. Hengel, *Nachfolge und Charisma* (Berlin, 1968) • P. Nepper-Christensen, "Μαθητής, μαθητεύω," *EDNT* 2.372-74 • K. H. Rengstorf, "Μανθάνω κτλ.," *TDNT* 4.390-461 • J. Roloff, "Apostel / Apostolat / Apostolizität I," *TRE* 3.430-45.

OTTO BÖCHER

Disciples of Christ → Christian Church (Disciples of Christ)

Discipleship

1. NT
2. Systematic Theology

1. NT

1.1. The Greek verb *akoloutheō,* "follow," has a specifically religious sense only in the Gospels (apart from Rev. 14:4) and relates exclusively to → Jesus, never to God.

1.2. The call of Jesus, "Follow me" (Mark 1:17), which is always directed to individuals, initiates discipleship. The announcing of the imminence of the → kingdom of God, with the ensuing demand for conversion and → faith in the → gospel (cf. v. 15), gives urgency to the summons. Those who heed the call renounce existing ties (1:18; 10:28; Luke 9:61-62), receive a share in the future → salvation that the person of Jesus makes present, receive → wisdom instruction, and are commissioned to proclaim the kingdom of God. Following Jesus, the → disciples are representatives of the new Israel and will judge the 12 → tribes of Israel (Matt. 19:28; Luke 22:30; → Twelve, The). In the post-Easter community, wandering charismatics and settled teachers continued to proclaim the binding nature of discipleship and its claim over all spheres of human life.

1.3. Presupposing the situation after Easter, the Gospels, despite their historical framework as a life of Jesus, make clear the relevance of the discipleship of the Twelve for the life of the early Christian community (→ Congregation). *Mark* works the thought of discipleship into his motif of the messianic secret. We must follow the hidden Messiah on his way to the cross (→ Theologia crucis).

Matthew links the summons to discipleship with the unconditional requirement of → love and → righteousness (→ Sermon on the Mount), even to the point of self-denial and readiness for → martyrdom (10:38-39; 16:24-25).

Luke uses the term "discipleship" only relative to the earthly life of Jesus (not in Acts) and has a hortatory concern (→ Parenesis). The call of Jesus demands → obedience and changes our attitude to possessions (18:22, 28-30). Women "follow" Jesus from Galilee to Jerusalem (23:49, 55; cf. 8:2-3). In discipleship the community practices merciful love and generosity (10:29-37; 11:41; 12:33).

In *John* discipleship is the acceptance of → revelation in faith (8:12). To follow is the same as to believe (see 12:44). Discipleship is the same as being in the light and not walking in darkness, a teaching that does not involve any → Docetic spiritualizing. John can speak concretely of the discipleship of the followers of Jesus (1:37-39) or of the people (6:2). Discipleship implies readiness for serving the Revealer and for self-sacrifice (12:26; 13:36-37), even in the period after Easter (21:19-23).

Revelation uses the term for the endtime 144,000 who are without fault and who follow the Lamb wherever he goes (14:4).

While the term does not occur in the rest of the NT in the theological sense, the subject itself — a vital fellowship with Christ — is present, described in other terms ("in Christ," 1 Thess. 4:16; "imitation," *mimeomai,* 2 Thess. 3:7, 9; Heb. 13:7; 3 John 11, elsewhere common elements in apostolic parenesis). It is part of the larger subject of NT → ethics.

Bibliography: F. W. Horn, *Glaube und Handeln in der Theologie des Lukas* (2d ed.; Göttingen, 1986) esp. 189-203 • H.-W. Kuhn, "Nachfolge nach Ostern," *Kirche* (FS G. Bornkamm; Tübingen, 1980) 105-32 • G. Lohfink, *Was hat Jesus Gemeinde gewollt? Zur gesellschaftlichen Dimension des christlichen Glaubens* (Freiburg, 1982) • G. Schneider, "Ἀκολουθέω," *TDNT* 1.49-52 (bibliography) • G. Strecker, *Der Weg der Gerechtigkeit* (3d ed.; Göttingen, 1971) esp. 230-32.

GEORG STRECKER†

2. Systematic Theology

2.1. When the → parousia of Christ did not materialize as expected in the lifetime of the first Christian communities (→ Congregation 1), a problem arose. What would following Christ as his disciple look like when he who had issued the summons was no longer present? How could it still be personal following? In the later periods, many forms of discipleship thus developed.

In the first centuries the → martyrs who accepted persecution, → suffering, and → death for their witness to the gospel were regarded as the true followers of Christ. On their view, imitation (*mimēsis*) of Christ would finally lead to deification (→ *theōsis*). This thought, central to all the → church fathers along the line from → Irenaeus (ca. 130-ca. 200) by way of → Athanasius (ca. 297-373) to → Cyril of Alexandria (ca. 375-444), had great influence on the theology of the Eastern church (→ Orthodoxy 3). But soon there came the devout ascetic or monk (→ Asceticism; Monasticism), who attempted an authentic discipleship in the form of personal renunciation, flight from the world, and radical → obedience.

In the → Middle Ages the → poverty movements and mendicant orders followed, making the abandonment of → property and possessions the standard of discipleship. With → Francis of Assisi (1181/82-1226; → Franciscans) it became an issue how far a rich and powerful church could credibly preach and display discipleship (→ Power 3). A similar theme appeared in the preaching of John → Wycliffe (ca. 1330-84) in England, who demanded a poor apostolic church. In controversy with the Franciscans in the 1320s, John XXII (1316-34) managed to control those particular impulses of Francis that were critical of the church and was able instead to present as a model for believers Francis's advocacy of → poverty, → humility, obedience, and renunciation of power. In addition, the renunciation of possessions by a great many individuals — renunciation prompted by just this presentation — resulted in a not inconsiderable enhancement of the church's own wealth.

A further type of discipleship as imitation of Christ crystallized in → mysticism (§2). The effort was made in stages to achieve conformity to Christ in total inwardness, with roots reaching back to Neoplatonic ideas, to → Origen (ca. 185-ca. 254; → Origenism), and to → Augustine (354-430; → Augustine's Theology). In Germany this idea of the inner ascent often went hand in hand with a passion mysticism (Henry Suso, Mechthild of Magdeburg) that found true imitation in repetition of the passion of Christ. An influential presentation of medieval ideas of discipleship appears in the *Imitation of Christ,* ascribed to Thomas à Kempis (1379/80-1471). Often on the basis of mystical experiences an understanding of following Christ also developed that aimed at the reshaping of political and social relations (Joachim of Fiore, J. → Hus) and that culminated in a radical declaration of war on the ungodly (T. Müntzer; → Millenarianism).

2.2. The → Reformation brought an incisive change in the understanding of discipleship. With his thesis of → justification (§2) by faith and grace alone *(sola fide, sola gratia),* M. → Luther (1483-1546; → Luther's Theology) radically challenged the idea that the state of alienation from God that resulted from original → sin (§§2-3) could be removed by meritorious works. Hence he viewed the types of discipleship by imitation mentioned above as well-meaning but needlessly self-torturing attempts at self-justification. According to Luther, imitation does not make sons, but sonship makes imitators (WA 2.518.16).

For Luther, focusing on the cross of Christ is ecclesiologically relevant and allows him to lump together Jews, enthusiasts, papists, Turks, and heretics as people who all try to set their own meritorious works in opposition to the → grace of God. Freed from the need to justify themselves, the Reformers (including also J. → Calvin and U. → Zwingli) could give concrete form to discipleship in every personal and social relation (→ Two Kingdoms Doctrine; Vocation).

2.3. The relation to the world that was defined at the Reformation was again relativized or partially abandoned in the period that followed (see John Bunyan's *Pilgrim's Progress;* → Dissenters). The theology of the cross degenerated into pious → edification, and in → Pietism and the → Enlightenment the historical Jesus, in the tradition of → humanism, became a moral example for imitation and witness (→ Diakonia; Mission 1). After the baroque manner (note the arias and chorales of Bach's *St. Matthew's Passion*), Christ was often no longer viewed as the Crucified who therefore justifies but as the unselfish and patient Man of Sorrows, and hence as the object of an often naive piety of the heart (as in many of P. Gerhardt's hymns).

Finally, I. Kant (1724-1804; → Kantianism), with his attempted refutation of the cosmological and ontological proofs of God, left no place for God in the world even philosophically but set him in transcendent spheres (→ God, Arguments for the Existence of; Transcendental Philosophy). Instead of suffering and acting in the world, God thus became a moral postulate (see E. Jüngel, §§8-12) that served as a basis for civil morality.

The distinction of a heroic Jesus and a Christ who is remote from the world characterizes the → liberal theology of the 18th and 19th centuries, even though in this case, as in Britain and the United States, a middle-class → optimism of → progress developed, along with philanthropic and social concern for the victims of emergent → capitalism (→ Proletariat), for example, in the → Social Gospel movement (→

Methodism 2.4; North American Theology). Accompanying this moral trend was more intensive research into the historical Jesus (→ History of Religions School) and a subjective focus on the suffering of a fully dehistoricized Christ (as in S. → Kierkegaard, for whom discipleship brings self-destruction).

2.4. Against this background, it represented a → hermeneutical revival of the Reformation concern for theologians like M. Kähler (1835-1912), K. → Barth (1886-1968), P. → Tillich (1886-1965), and D. → Bonhoeffer (1906-45) to discuss again the distinction of → law and gospel and to emphasize that true discipleship, no matter how worthy or full of good intentions, must always orient itself to the cross and therefore to suffering. Discipleship takes place in the world and not in the heart, but it must never be equated or confused with individual achievements. In this context every subsequent theology of existence or experience must be asked how far it is not again individualizing, dehistoricizing, or ethicizing discipleship.

2.5. In ecumenical discussion (→ Dialogue; Ecumenical Movement) the issue of authentic discipleship again has become an important theme. → Vatican II and the pastoral constitution *Gaudium et spes* (1965) encouraged increasing discussion in Roman Catholic moral theology (A. Auer, B. Häring, F. Schillebeeckx). It was worked out in different ways internationally — for example, as a struggle for social justice in the Latin American → liberation theology (→ Humanity; Righteousness, Justice); in the concern to abolish apartheid in South Africa; in minjung theology (→ Asian Theology 4.2) and its question of the importance of the poor in salvation history, or in the development of a "theology of the pain of God" (K. Kitamori) in Asian theology; in the battle for equal rights for women and blacks (→ Emancipation; Equality; Racism) and the protest against nuclear → weapons (→ Disarmament and Armament) in the United States; and in the search for a new identity of church and people in the former socialist states of eastern Europe. The end of establishment and the emergence of new social problems makes the issue of authentic discipleship an urgent one from many different angles.

2.6. A distinctively Protestant view of discipleship cannot be static or unhistorical, since the idea of discipleship appears in many → religions and → worldviews. It can take different forms in different historical and cultural circumstances. The decisive point, however, is that it must do so in the coordinates of the theology of the cross and justification, seeking neither to downplay suffering (note Bonhoeffer's warning about "cheap grace") nor to be-

come absorbed in it. Autonomous ways of redemption (e.g., through political activism or individual piety) stand under the → eschatological caveat and are not as such discipleship. "Only discipleship in → everyday life, however, justifies our → dogmatics to the world" (E. Käsemann).

→ Beguines; Brethren of the Common Life; Cathari; Contextual Theology; Dialectical Theology; Dominicans; Gospel; Lifestyle; Orders and Congregations; Waldenses

Bibliography: K. Barth, "The Call to Discipleship," *CD* IV/2, 533-53 • D. Bonhoeffer, *The Cost of Discipleship* (3d ed.; New York, 1960) • V. Guroian, *Incarnate Love: Essays in Orthodox Ethics* (Notre Dame, Ind., 1987) • E. Jüngel, *God as the Mystery of the World* (Grand Rapids, 1983) • E. Käsemann, "For and against a Theology of Resurrection," *Jesus Means Freedom: A Polemical Survey of the NT* (London, 1969) • S. Kierkegaard, *Training in Christianity* (2d ed.; Princeton, 1964; orig. pub., 1850) • K. Kitamori, *Theology of the Pain of God* (Richmond, Va., 1965) • M. Luther, *Lectures on Galatians* (1535 and 1519) (St. Louis, 1963-64) • J. Moltmann, ed., *Nachfolge und Bergpredigt* (2d ed.; Munich, 1982) • T. Münzer, "Von dem gedichteten Glauben," *Schriften und Briefe* (ed. G. Wehr; Gütersloh, 1978) 44-50 • W. Nethöfel, *Moraltheologie nach dem Konzil. Personen, Programme, Positionen* (Göttingen, 1987) • E. Schillebeeckx, *Christ: The Experience of Jesus as Lord* (New York, 1981) • Thomas à Kempis, *The Imitation of Christ* (trans. J. N. Tylenda; Wilmington, Del., 1984) • E. J. Tinsley, *The Imitation of God in Christ: An Essay on the Biblical Basis of the Christian Spirituality* (London, 1960).

Ekkehard Starke

Dispensation

A dispensation is a grant of relief from an ordinance in individual cases, a means for the church to give spiritual direction in particular matters affecting an individual. In canon law the dispensation presupposes the presence of adequate legal grounds (1983 CIC 90). A dispensation from divine law is impossible. The cases of dispensation today are primarily in relation to hindrances to marriage or ordination. Except when the privilege is reserved for the papacy (e.g., see discussion of → celibacy, can. 291), diocesan bishops grant the dispensation, although with → delegation to parish priests in the case of → mixed marriage. A different basis for a dispensation is the recognition that those who framed the law did not mean it to be valid in a given instance.

"Economy" in the law of the → Orthodox Church

is closely akin (R. Slenczka). In Protestant church law a related idea is that there may be exception to ecclesiastical rules for reasons of Christian → love.

The concept of dispensation developed in the Middle Ages and has passed over from → canon law into administrative law in general.

→ Economy (Orthodox Theology)

Bibliography: W. Aymans, *Kanonisches Recht* (Paderborn, 1991) 269-82 • Church of England, *Dispensation in Practice and Theory, with Special Reference to the Anglican Churches* (London, 1944) • 1983 CIC 85-93 • J. Listl et al., eds., *Handbuch des katholischen Kirchenrechts* (Regensburg, 1983) • R. Slenczka, *Ostkirche und Ökumene* (Göttingen, 1962) 234ff. • W. J. Sparrow-Simpson, *Dispensations* (London, 1935) • A. Stein, *Evangelisches Kirchenrecht–Lernbuch* (3d ed.; Neuwied, 1992) 43-45; idem, "Freiheit und Bindung im evangelischen Agendenrecht," *ZEvKR* 26 (1981) 279-84.

Albert Stein

Dispensationalism

1. J. N. Darby
2. American Dispensationalism
3. Revised Dispensationalism
4. Progressive Dispensationalism

Dispensationalism is a → tradition in evangelical orthodoxy that interprets the Bible — and indeed all history — in terms of a series of God's dispensations. Originating in Britain in the 1830s, this approach, while showing variations over time, has consistently emphasized the → authority of Scripture, discontinuities in the divine administration of history, the uniqueness of the → church and of certain features of → grace for the dispensation of the church (which began at pentecost), the practical significance of the universal church, the theological relevance of biblical → apocalyptic and → prophecy, a futurist premillennialism, the imminent return of Christ, and a national future for → Israel (see C. Blaising and D. Bock 1993, 13-21; → Millenarianism; Parousia).

1. J. N. Darby
The originator of this tradition of biblical interpretation is John Nelson Darby (1800-1882), who was the leader of a group of → separatist believers who later became known as the Plymouth Brethren. Darby, a former → Anglican priest, was a "futurist" in his → eschatology (i.e., the biblical prophecies of the last days were yet to be fulfilled), rejecting the "historicist" viewpoint then popular in British millennial-

ism, which saw present fulfillment of those prophecies.

In the 1830s and 1840s Darby developed two distinctive additions to futurist thinking (Sandeen, 38): (1) the church age was a "parenthesis" between the 69th and 70th "weeks" of years in Dan. 9:25-27, and (2) there would be a rapture (so-called from the Vg term for "caught up" in 1 Thess. 4:17) of believers from the earth to heaven by Christ before the 70th week of Daniel 9, the "great tribulation" of divine → wrath poured out on human wickedness and unbelief. These two affirmations seem to be genuine novelties in the history of theology, though some have claimed to find seminal elements of them in earlier thinkers.

Darby developed these ideas from his concept of the apostate organized church. This notion derived from an anthropological dualism; namely, the true church is heavenly and invisible (and thus separate from "Christendom"), in contrast to God's earthly, visible people — Israel. Promises and prophecies for Israel will be fulfilled on earth during the Millennium and the eternal state, but the church will not participate in their fulfillment, nor will Israel share the church's future blessings in heaven.

2. American Dispensationalism
In the second half of the 19th century, premillennial ideas, including the dispensational form, became widespread in America. Darby himself made seven trips to America, where he was well received, particularly for his prophetic teaching. To his chagrin, Americans discarded his fundamental doctrine, the apostasy of the organized church. Most American → fundamentalists were committed, rather, to purifying or restoring an organized Christianity, whether denominational or not. Thus dispensationalism in America was and is an eschatological perspective built upon an ecclesiology quite different from the earlier British Brethren version.

The growth of dispensationalism in North America was fostered by a series of Bible and prophecy conferences, the most famous of which was held at Niagara-on-the-Lake, Ontario (1883-97). This stage and its legacy in the participants' later work (e.g., of J. H. Brookes, A. J. Gordon, and C. I. Scofield) and in later men (e.g., A. C. Gaebelein, J. M. Gray, and L. S. Chafer) can be called the classic stage of American dispensationalism. These Americans, with the debacle of W. Miller's failed predictions for Christ's return in 1844 still fresh in their memories (→ Adventists), were as adamantly futurist and antihistoricist as their British counterparts. They maintained the anthropological dualism, contrasting a heavenly people with an earthly people. They emphasized biblical authority, the "Spirit-filled" life of holiness and → obedience, and world → evangelization. Though a spectrum of denominations was represented, → Presbyterians, → Episcopalians, and → Congregationalists were prominent among the conference speakers. By the second half of the 20th century, → Baptists and nondenominational churches (esp. "Bible" churches) had become the most common ecclesiastical affiliations for dispensationalists.

The most important publication of this classic form of dispensationalism was the *Scofield Reference Bible*, an edition of the King James Bible published in successive editions by C. I. Scofield in 1909 and 1917. Already a prominent teacher in the movement for years, as well as a longtime Congregational pastor in Dallas, Texas, Scofield gained his reputation primarily as the result of the success of this study Bible. The technical quality of the publication, the venerable reputation of its publisher (Oxford University Press), and the general usefulness of many of the notes and cross-references combined to promote an enormous readership, many of whom may not have been previously committed to Scofield's distinctive views. Under the influence of this study Bible, "Scofieldism" came to denote this form of premillennialism, a term replaced in the 1940s by "dispensationalism."

Dispensational teaching dominated the emerging Bible school movement. Dallas Theological Seminary, founded by Scofield's disciple L. S. Chafer, has been the leading dispensational seminary. Chafer's eight-volume *Systematic Theology* (1948) was the most developed form of classic dispensationalism.

3. Revised Dispensationalism

The next generation, including Chafer's students J. F. Walvoord, J. D. Pentecost, and C. C. Ryrie, all made significant modifications in classic dispensational thought. The most visible indication of the changes was the 1967 publication of the *Revised Scofield Bible*. Some of the most controversial notes were changed, many others were modified, and many new notes added. This edition continues to sell well, thus carrying the revision to more readers each year.

Though the revised stage continues to be futurist, among some there has been increasing inclination to suggest possible alignments of contemporary world events with biblical prophecy (the most extreme example is H. Lindsey, author of the best-selling *The Late Great Planet Earth*). Always insistently stopping short of "date-setting," this practice is nonetheless inconsistent with the futurist view.

4. Progressive Dispensationalism

Within a decade of these revisions, additional changes were proposed. In articles and books from the mid-1970s through the 1980s, suggestions came for further developments. The most significant characteristics of this stage of American dispensationalism are the greater emphasis upon the continuity or progression between the dispensations and a greater emphasis upon the present inauguration of the eschatological blessings of the messianic era, which will culminate in the Millennium and the eternal state. R. L. Saucy, C. A. Blaising, and D. L. Bock are the most prominent representatives of the "progressive" stage.

Bibliography: C. Bass, *Backgrounds to Dispensationalism* (Grand Rapids, 1960; repr., 1977) • C. A. Blaising and D. Bock, *Progressive Dispensationalism* (Wheaton, Ill., 1993); idem, eds., *Dispensationalism, Israel, and the Church* (Grand Rapids, 1992) • L. V. Crutchfield, *The Origins of Dispensationalism: The Darby Factor* (Lanham, Md., 1992) • C. N. Kraus, *Dispensationalism in America* (Richmond, Va., 1958) • G. Marsden, *Fundamentalism and American Culture* (New York, 1980) • V. S. Poythress, *Understanding Dispensationalism* (2d ed.; Phillipsburg, N.J., 1994) • C. C. Ryrie, *Dispensationalism* (rev. ed.; Chicago, 1995); idem, *Dispensationalism Today* (Chicago, 1965) • E. R. Sandeen, *The Roots of Fundamentalism: British and American Millenarianism, 1800-1930* (Chicago, 1970; repr., Grand Rapids, 1978) • R. Saucy, *The Case for Progressive Dispensationalism* (Grand Rapids, 1994) • S. R. Spencer, "Reformed Theology, Covenant Theology, and Dispensationalism," *Integrity of Heart, Skillfulness of Hands* (ed. C. Dyer and R. B. Zuck; Grand Rapids, 1994) 238-54 • T. P. Weber, *Living in the Shadow of the Second Coming: American Premillennialism, 1875-1982* (Grand Rapids, 1983) • W. R. Willis, J. R. Master, and C. C. Ryrie, eds., *Issues in Dispensationalism* (Chicago, 1994).

Stephen R. Spencer

Dissenters

1. British Protestant Christians who worship outside the Church of England (→ Anglican Communion) have been designated at different times as Anabaptists, Brownists, Separatists, Dissenters, Nonconformists, and Free Churchmen. Those in the 16th century who inherited Lollard attitudes and heterodox opinions from the Netherlands were called Anabaptists. The Brownists and Separatists, losing hope of → Puritan reform in the church, met in secret conventicles in the late 16th and early 17th centuries.

Dissenters were those who would not accept the Act of Uniformity of 1662 and included some who had refused to conform even to the reformed establishment of the Commonwealth. The term "Nonconformist" gained greater currency in the 19th century, though by then it was applied to many Methodists (→ Methodism) who conformed to the → Book of Common Prayer. The term "Free Churchmen" was more apt to the aggressive voluntaryist politics of many. The growth of ecumenical sentiments since 1920 has weakened the force of even this description of nonepiscopal communities, some of which have lately expressed a willingness to take episcopacy into their system (→ Episcopalianism; Bishop, Episcopate).

For a time in the late 17th century, English Dissenters formed religious establishments in America, with Quakers (→ Friends, Society of) settling in Pennsylvania, Presbyterians and → Congregationalists in New England. In America, however, their special privileges were removed piecemeal between 1692 and 1833.

The establishment of the Presbyterian Church of Scotland in 1688 left the Episcopalians as the chief dissenting body there, but they were soon outnumbered by the emergence of numerous dissenting Presbyterian communions unwilling to accept various features of the establishment.

The persistence of a Roman Catholic community in Britain since the → Reformation is another form of religious dissent. Catholics, however, termed "recusants" in the 16th century, are not normally known as Dissenters.

2. The term "Dissenter" was principally current from 1662 to about 1850. The Dissenters' main political achievement, a reward for their support of the Protestant constitution against the Catholic James II (1685-88), was the Toleration Act of 1689. This granted them only second-class citizenship, and they remained in a minority position.

In the early 18th century dissenting families made up some 6 percent of the population, and even in 1850 only about 20 percent worshiped in chapels, though that number was not much below those appearing in a church. Nevertheless, even as a minority, they had considerable influence. Their tenacity ensured that the effort to create a confessional state in England was brief and inglorious. The covenant theology (→ Calvinism; Covenant 3) of the Calvinist Dissenters underlay the political thought of J. Locke (1632-1704), the constitutions of New England, and, eventually, the American apologetic for → revolution.

During the 18th century the old Presbyterians and Quakers declined in numbers (though not in influence). The Congregationalists and → Baptists were reconstructed from within under the influence of the Evangelical → Revival, which also added Methodist denominations to the Dissenter strength.

Bibliography: D. HEMPTON, *Religion and Political Culture in Britain and Ireland* (Cambridge, 1996) • E. PAYNE, *The Free Church Tradition in the Life of England* (London, 1944) • M. R. WATTS, *The Dissenters* (2 vols.; Oxford, 1978-95).

W. REGINALD WARD

Distance Education

1. The phrase "distance education" refers to various forms of nontraditional learning that often present a confusing picture with great differences but that also share some common features. The term includes, for example, external programs set up at a distance from the main center, correspondence courses for work at home, part-time study in conjunction with a job (→ Vocation), independent learning, teletuition, and radio and television instruction. The extension of possibilities is reflected in the change of the name of the worldwide organization for distance education from International Council for Correspondence Education to International Council for Distance Education.

1.1. Common to all these types of nontraditional education is their seeking to be less formal, to be open to all who want to learn, and especially to serve adults who for various reasons seek more training. They offer great freedom regarding the time, place, goals, content, and pace of education. Above all, this education is meant to be relevant to the student, offering further training in various fields, including courses preparing a student for college (→ University) and courses for both serious study and as a hobby (→ Leisure).

1.2. Various means are used to bridge the distance between teacher and student: printed matter (still used in 95 percent of the cases), audiovisual media, radio, television (→ Mass Media), and up-to-date techniques involving videos and home computers.

1.3. Didactically (→ Didactics), distance education is increasingly understood as *directed self-study*. Direction is given by more or less highly structured material or by personal or group supervision. Individual direction designed to make itself superfluous is didactically more important in distance education than the element of distance per se. It makes it possible for adults to be far more independent of institutionalized pedagogy and allows more flexibility with the goal of learning independence and thus achieving self-determination by meaningful education.

1.4. As a consequence of the information explosion, the spreading of information technologies, the changing nature of work, and changing learner populations, education, schooling, and training on all levels are also undergoing a paradigm shift worldwide that makes fundamental changes in distance education necessary. In an information society the characteristic feature is the dominance of information instead of material products. To use its potential in a humane way, the information society needs to develop a new "learner paradigm," which means lifelong learning for all and learner-centeredness, which requires new roles for all involved in learning processes.

The present understanding of distance education comes remarkably near this shift: It includes informal, incidental, everyday learning modes; it is enhanced by a general move away from objective toward constructed knowledge, from providing instruction to promoting learning; and it gives a more prominent role to technology in mediating the processes of communication and learning. Here we must acknowledge the rapidly expanding role of the worldwide internet.

Institutions of distance education, as well as distance-education students themselves, are in the midst of developing open, integrated, networked models that give learners (esp. adults) the possibility of taking initiative in their learning and of gaining access to the necessary learning resources. In these models the learning exchange is not one-sided and one-dimensional but interactive, participatory, and lifelong; the learning "customer" is in an ongoing dialogue with his or her educational process, listening to many voices from outside, only one of which may be the pedagogically qualified teacher. The locus of control of the learning activity moves away from formal institutions and the isolated classroom to a variety of other learning environments, including the home and the workplace. The main task of educational institutions is not so much to provide instruction as it is to foster learning, especially by using specific didactic methods to overcome learning barriers. One implication of these shifts is that the distinction between distance education and new learning is blurring. Distance education in the 1990s is, and for the foreseeable future will continue to be, in the mainstream of education. It has the potential to contribute effectively to developing a truly learning society.

2. The types of organization vary widely across the globe. Distance education may be sponsored by the state or by private institutions. It may occur in conjunction with high schools, by colleges offering on-campus as well as correspondence instruction, or, with a minimum of institutional structure, by radio and television colleges.

3. In many cases distance education plays a remedial role, helping students overcome deficiencies in specific fields such as mathematics or science. It has also served to introduce people to the new math or to give vocational preparation. In many cases it is designed to orient teachers to educational, social, and international problems.

4. The churches likewise long ago grasped the significance of distance education both in training their own teachers and in adult education. In Germany and other countries Protestant and Catholic churches have cooperated with other agencies to train religious teachers at all levels (→ Religious Educational Theory; Religious Instruction; Continuing Education) and to offer more general programs on themes relating to religion, theology, or the church that will appeal to more heterogeneous groups. Specific courses have also been devised for theological students.

In → Third World lands distance education by the church is especially important in raising the level of general education (→ Literacy) and in giving initial or further instruction to → pastors, teachers, → catechists, and hospital personnel.

→ Education; Theological Education

Bibliography: B. COLLIS, *Tele-Learning in a Digital World: The Future of Distance Learning* (London, 1996) • D. CORRIGAN, *The Internet University: College Courses by Computer* (Harwich, Mass., 1996) • DANISH MINISTRY OF EDUCATION, *Technology-Supported Learning (Distance Learning)* (Copenhagen, 1993) • R. M. DELLING, *Fernstudium–Fernunterricht,* vol. 1, *Bibliographie deutschsprachiger Texte von 1897-1974;* vol. 2, *Bibliographie deutschsprachiger Texte von 1975-1978 und Nachträge aus früheren Jahren* (Weinheim, 1977-82) • G. DOHMEN, C. A. WEDEMEYER, and K. REBEL, *Offenes Lernen und Fernstudium* (Weinheim, 1976) • T. EVANS, *Reforming Open and Distance Education: Critical Reflections from Practice* (London, 1993); idem, *Understanding Learners in Open and Distance Education* (London, 1994) • K. HARRY, M. MAGNUS, and D. KEEGAN, eds., *Distance Education: New Perspectives* (London, 1993) • H.-B. KAUFMANN and H. SCHULTZE, "Fortbildung–Fernstudium–Medienverbund," *Neue Aufgaben für die Kirche* (Gütersloh, 1971) • D. KEEGAN, ed., *Theoretical*

Principles of Distance Education (London, 1993) •
F. Lockwood, ed., *Open and Distance Learning Today*
(London, 1995) • R. Mason, *Using Communications
Media in Open and Flexible Learning* (London, 1994) •
M. G. Moore, *On the Theory of Independent Study*
(Hagen, 1977) • M. Moore and G. Kearsley, *Distance
Education: A Systems View* (Belmont, Calif., 1996) • L. R.
Porter, *Creating the Virtual Classroom: Distance Learn-
ing with the Internet* (New York, 1997) • K. Rebel, "Das
Lernen Erwachsener im Fernstudium," *KatBl* 102
(1977) 997-1007 • R. J. Seidel and P. R. Chatelier,
eds., *Learning without Boundaries: Technology to Support
Distance/Distributed Learning* (New York, 1994) • C. A.
Wedemeyer, *Learning at the Back Door: Reflections on
Non-Traditional Learning in the Lifespan* (Madison,
Wis., 1981) • R. Zemsky and W. F. Massy, *Using Infor-
mation Technology to Enhance Academic Productivity*
(Washington, D.C., 1995).

                                                    Karlheinz Rebel

Divination

1. Term
2. Social Practice
    2.1. Oracles
    2.2. Diviners
    2.3. Social Setting
    2.4. Belief System
3. Motifs, Needs, Functions
4. Biblical Assessment

1. Term

The term "divination" comes from Lat. *divinatio,*
meaning "divine inspiration; soothsaying." Divination is a social practice of choosing and evaluating
→ signs. It is related to such phenomena as the interpretation of events, the seeking of causes (diagnosis), and the planning of action (prognosis). But it
also carries with it the extraordinary claim of being
the disclosure of what is hidden (→ Apocalypticism
1), of having privileged access to a special "pool" of
signs (e.g., the anatomy of sheep livers), and of
having unquestionable authority. Divination practices thus usually have a sacral relation and form a
constitutive part of religious systems (e.g., as they did
in ancient Rome). But they also engage in private
consultations and deal with everyday matters as in
giving advice on love or in publishing horoscopes in
daily newspapers. When we look at divination as a
social fact or action, we need to distinguish it clearly
from parapsychology, in which there can be a super-
sensible perception of present or future events (second sight, clairvoyance, precognition).

It should be expressly emphasized that divination
in the more comprehensive sense of mantic (from
Gk. *mantikē* [*technē*], "[art of] divination"), as distinct from a narrower understanding of both the
concept and its practice in modern → industrial
societies, does not deal exclusively or even primarily
with foretelling the → future ("What is to happen?")
but can also relate to other temporal dimensions of
life in society, as, for example, to a present situational
understanding of a person's character or actions
("Who am I?" and "Is my action right?") or to the
investigation of causes ("Who or what is/was guilty
here?") with regard to the past (cf. the African witch
doctor; → Witchcraft).

2. Social Practice

The social practice contains four main elements:
oracles, diviners, the social setting, and the underlying belief system.

2.1. Oracles

One aspect is the technique of oracles. This consists
of (1) a precisely limited and materially or in-
spirationally generated class of objects (birds, coffee
grounds in a cup, wooden rods; → Dream), by observing which one acquires a "code" as a material
interpretive basis; (2) rules and interpretive models
by which to achieve decoding; and (3) rituals (→
Rite), which help either in interpretation or in its
public presentation.

According to the constitution of these classes of
signs, two forms of discovery and symbolic handling
may be distinguished. Signs may be present ("oblative divination"), or they are to be sought out and
constructed ("impetretive divination"). The first
group includes all kinds of "superpregnant" (A. Gehlen) events — that is, extraordinary, threatening, or
unnatural events such as bolts of lightning, earth-
quakes, meteors, and births of misformed animals or
humans, all of which divination discloses as omens
or prodigies or monsters (from Lat. *monstrum,*
"warning") in need of interpretation and then makes
collectively "intelligible."

The second group, which uses signs produced by
specific rituals, has been subdivided from the time of
Plato (427-347 B.C.; *Phdr.* 244B-C; → Platonism; cf.
also Cicero *De div.* 1.11 and 2.26; and today
A. Bouché-Leclerq) into divinations that use natural
or artificial objects (e.g., the stars; → Astrology) in
what is called inductive mantic (*divinatio artificiosa*),
and divinations that rely on the stimulation of the
imagination and on exceptional psychic states such as
trances, dreams, or hallucinations (intuitive mantic,
divinatio naturale; Ecstasy; Inspiration; Shamanism).
The choice of objects seems to be unlimited in variety

(for surveys, see A. Caquot and M. Leibovici, J. Bottéro, D. Harmening, M. Loewe and C. Blacker), though each one has a specific historical and cultural background.

2.2. *Diviners*

Diviners serve as a medium. As communicators, such specialists in interpreting signs have a double role. They produce the message, and they also "send" it. But the role as sender claims little attention in the divinatory construction of faith. The role is understood "merely" as that of personified transmitters, channels, or mediums. Only an implementation of the role makes it possible for the diviner to adopt the authoritative desires projected onto him or her by the public.

The specialists are of two kinds. First are those who act as "freelancers" in the marketplace, in private practice, or as itinerants; second is an established cultic personnel. The trend toward professional independence also affects content, for divinatory systems are occasionally developed into organizational patterns so complex that in their virtuosity and interpretive wealth they form independent paradisciplines (e.g., astrology and → occultism). Ethnic specializations such as that found today among the Gypsies are both striking and conducive to the formation of stereotypes. Within → monotheistic religions that claim a monopoly of revelation (Muḥammad as the "seal of the prophets" in → Islam), a certain, in part considerable rivalry develops between the established clergy and popular soothsayers such as wise women or clairvoyants (→ Magic; Popular Religion).

The form for the publishing of divination is the word or, less frequently, writing (→ Prophet, Prophecy). The history of the dissemination of divinatory proclamation reflects a broad spectrum of social possibilities: from the decisive yes or no answer using lots from oracles to requests about conduct, including responses to desires for counsel in life matters, to nuanced forms in written replies (such as those given by the Etruscan viewing of livers or production of horoscopes), dialogically obtained diagnoses of problems in a therapeutic setting (the reading of cards or crystals), and enigmatic oracles that leave the burden of interpretation to the clients (the highest virtuosity of which was demonstrated by the Delphic oracle).

2.3. *Social Setting*

On the one side is the public (crisis) management of oblative divination. The state or public organs could interpret unusual signs such as thunderstorms or comets or UFOs as messages from outside prompting various interpretations, but they could also ignore them. In particular, the ritual neutralizing ("atoning") of signs of misfortune by society could yield an emphatic dramatization of → solidarity (processions in expiation or for intercession). Impetative divinations, for their part, could take place in a setting in a fixed time or place characterized by the question-and-answer pattern. Privately or publicly a client with a specific concern would come to a specialist and find an answer with the help of the divinatory ritual. According to the need and the degree of social institutionalization, the settings will differ in function.

2.3.1. For private persons they will be means of conflict resolution, seances of healing, or cathartic trance therapies (→ Shamanism).

2.3.2. Cultic personnel (e.g., the cult prophets in Jerusalem) can offer political decisions but also deal with private clients, as did the ancient oracle at Delphi through the medium Pythia.

2.3.3. Legal divination in the form of divine judgment (→ Ordeal) can be understood as a symbolically enacted pronouncement of sentence with whose help societies with weakly developed legal systems sanction collectively accepted but unproven judgments (motto: "The choice of [divinatory] means determines the outcome").

2.3.4. Court or state divination by official functionaries can serve as a means of power and of legitimation for central political and military authorities (e.g., the Roman consulting of auguries, the Tibetan state oracle, and the use of court astrologers by the Ottoman sultans).

2.4. *Belief System*

The heart of divinatory practice guaranteed the credibility of the statements by constructing an imaginary sender (the helping spirit[s], God, or fortune). Only the cultural setting can tell us whether this had a mythological religious origin (the "divinatory" god Apollo, → Yahweh, a particular illness demon) or whether it was a background ideology such as diffuse → fatalism or an idea of foreordination (→ Predestination). The typical wishes of the clientele for a hard determinism find theological form in myths of the all-determinative will or the holistic nexus of all things on which divinatory practice found basic consensus. In this way, everything can become a sign (of God, etc.); the (surrounding) world becomes pan-semiotically readable.

3. Motifs, Needs, Functions

Human beings have a basic need for certainty regarding the future consequences of their actions and clarity concerning the causes of → chance occurrences. Hence the desire for special — or indeed even total — care and assurance is a driving motif behind the attractiveness of soothsayers. Negatively, this means help in anxiety concerning the unfathomability of the risks of life. In practice, being freed from → responsibility in the uncertainty of decision making prepares a psychological mechanism that encourages the overcoming of anxiety and the resolution of conflicts, though the result is that the decisions are not our own (i.e., they are externally guided) and that our free will is at least in part abandoned. Here the practice of divination resembles a kind of rudimentary behavior therapy (→ Behaviorism). The danger of such an identificatory release lies in the generation of "secondary anxieties" (B. Gladigow). The disaster that is vaguely foretold might in extreme cases become a self-fulfilling prophecy as fear calls forth what is feared (e.g., → voodoo death).

But we must not explain divination simply in terms of anxiety and conflicts. The mixture of contingency, firm rules, and a role for interpretation and action points to another anthropological universal — that of → play. Divination is also a playful probing of the unconscious, a curious searching of the possibilities of desire and resolve, an instructive conceptual game concerning fortune (→ Fate and [Good] Fortune), the end of the world, or → death; it is a small drama on the stage of life. Though many forms of divination have been rationalized away in modern industrial societies or overtaken by scientific prognosis (as, for instance, in medicine), some of the fragmentary divinatory systems of earlier high cultures (including those of the East like the I Ching) and some divinatory techniques still enjoy wide support. As social games (moving objects) or as elements of entertainment in the mass media, they inherit traditional divinatory practice in dealing with the risks and the turning points of life (birth, marriage, change of spouse, career, and death).

→ Prophet, Prophecy, 1; Superstition

Bibliography: J. Bottéro, "Symptômes, signes, écritures en Mésopotamie ancienne," Divination et rationalité (ed. J.-P. Vernant et al.; Paris, 1974) 70-197 • A. Bouché-Leclerq, Histoire de la divination dans l'antiquité (4 vols.; Paris, 1879-82) • A. Caquot and M. Leibovici, eds., La divination (2 vols.; Paris, 1968) • J. Cohen, Behaviour in Uncertainty and Its Social Implications (London, 1964) • F. H. Cryer, Divination in Ancient Israel and Its Near Eastern Environment: A Socio-Historical Investigation (Sheffield, 1994) • E. E. Evans-Pritchard, Witchcraft, Oracles, and Magic among the Azande (Oxford, 1937) • T. Fahd, La divination arabe. Études religieuses, sociologiques et folkloriques sur le milieu natif de l'Islam (Leiden, 1966) • A. Gehlen, Urmensch und Spätkultur (3d ed.; Wiesbaden, 1976) esp. §29 • B. Gladigow, "Konkrete Angst und offene Furcht. Am Beispiel des Prodigienwesens in Rom," Angst und Gewalt. Ihre Präsenz und ihre Bewältigung in den Religionen (ed. H. von Stietencron; Düsseldorf, 1979) 61-77 • D. Harmening, Superstitio. Überlieferungs- und theoriegeschichtliche Untersuchungen zur kirchlich-theologischen Aberglaubensliteratur des Mittelalters (Berlin, 1979) • M. Loewe and C. Blacker, eds., Oracles and Divination (Boulder, Colo., 1981) • A. S. Lyons, Der Blick in die Zukunft. Eine illustrierte Kulturgeschichte (Cologne, 1991) • O. K. Moore, "Divination: A New Perspective," AmA 59 (1957) 69-74 (cf. L. G. Vollweiler, "Divination: 'Adaptive' from Whose Perspective?" Ethnology 22 [1983] 193-209) • W. Nöth, "Magische Kommunikation," Handbuch der Semiotik (Stuttgart, 1985) 244-50 • G. K. Park, "Divination and Its Social Contexts," JRAI 93 (1963) 195-209 • R. J. Smith, Fortune-Tellers and Philosophers: Divination in Traditional Chinese Society (Boulder, Colo., 1991) • K. Thomas, Religion and the Decline of Magic: Studies in Popular Beliefs in Sixteenth- and Seventeenth-Century England (London, 1971) • C. Thulin, Die Etruskische Disciplin (Darmstadt, 1968; orig. pub., 1905-9) • A. Warburg, Heidnisch-antike Weissagung in Wort und Bild zu Luthers Zeiten (Heidelberg, 1920) • F. Welte, Der Gnâwa-Kult. Trancespiele, Geisterbeschwörung und Besessenheit in Marokko (Frankfurt, 1990).

HUBERT MOHR

4. Biblical Assessment

The Bible strongly criticizes and condemns divination. God, it is true, uses many of the forms of divination, speaking through → dreams to Joseph, to Daniel, and to the NT Joseph and also giving his revealed work, including a foretelling of the future, through the seers and the prophets. Nevertheless, he holds up to ridicule the magicians (→ Magic) of Egypt and the → astrologers and stargazers of Babylon (Exod. 8:18-19; Isa. 47:12-13), warns Israel against divination and → witchcraft (Deut. 18:10), promises that no enchantment used against his people will prosper (Num. 23:23), though he himself may use divination for his own purposes (Ezek. 21:21-22), sharply rebukes the false prophets who gave cultic divination to the kings of Israel and Judah (Jer. 27:9), and by means of the apostle Paul rescues the girl who brought her owners much gain by soothsaying (Acts 16:16-18). The answer to the problems of life — → anxiety about an unknown future and the need for guidance in decision making — is to be found in God alone.

Bibliography: D. E. Aune, "Divination," ISBE 1.971-74.

THE EDITORS

Divine Light Mission

The Divine Light Mission originated as a humanitarian organization seeking to propagate a method of meditation for the achievement of "perfect knowledge." It was founded in 1960 at Patna (Bihar, India) by Shree Hans (Skt. *haṇsá*, "goose," symbol of the white color of the soul and the migratory bird), who died in 1965.

At the funeral of Shree Hans, his son, Prem Pal Singh Rawat, who was born on December 10 or 16, 1957, in Hardwar (Uttar Pradesh, India), comforted those who mourned his father's death with the thought that they still had perfect knowledge with them. The son himself had become the subject of this knowledge, the perfect master, in the place of his father, and he took the title "guru" and the name Maharaj Ji, or Great King, a title of respect, to which other titular names were often added.

The honors paid him by his followers gave him the characteristics of a messianic child. These were supposedly his by nature, and they helped him to eliminate rival claims from his own family. The efficacy of rites and the success of → meditation were linked to his office as master. As a guru, he was equal to a god and even above "God," since God has prepared a → hell for people, but Shree Guru Maharaj Ji took from them all fear and plunged them into the sea of universal → love.

Meditation involves a fourfold technique and leads to divine light, music, nectar, and word. Nectar, which points to the sacred pool at Amritsar, as well as the use of "nectar" water from the "lotus" pool for ritual drinking and symbolic purifications, veneration of the guru and Rama, the concept of creation, the doctrine of light, and hymns, all of which perhaps have connections with → Sikh religion. Various traditions, especially from → Yoga, still remain to be elucidated.

Maharaj Ji began traveling to the West in 1969. He made a spectacular appearance in London in June 1971. His mission won 1.2 million followers by 1974 (12,000 in Europe; the figure of 5 million for India is probably exaggerated). Centers of information and meditation were set up in 55 countries, along with a Divine United Organization and a World Peace Corps. Since then the organization has been largely dismantled and the number of adherents has declined, although exact statistics are not available. The movement lives on, however, and with its cultic festivals in various cities attracts many who find something uncomplicated in the world peace that such organizations promise.

Bibliography: S. COLLIER, *Soul Rush: The Odyssey of a Young Woman of the '70s* (New York, 1978) • J. V. DOWNTON JR., *Sacred Journeys: The Conversion of Young Americans to Divine Light Mission* (New York, 1979). See also brochures published by the Divine Light Mission in Denver and Munich.

CARSTEN COLPE

Divinization → Theosis

Divorce → Marriage and Divorce

Djibouti

	1960	1980	2000
Population (1,000s):	83	281	687
Annual growth rate (%):	5.27	6.59	2.43
Area: 23,200 sq. km. (8,950 sq. mi.)			

A.D. 2000
Population density: 30/sq. km. (77/sq. mi.)
Births / deaths: 3.67 / 1.37 per 100 population
Fertility rate: 4.98 per woman
Infant mortality rate: 97 per 1,000 live births
Life expectancy: 52.3 years (m: 50.7, f: 54.0)
Religious affiliation (%): Muslims 93.2, Christians 5.4 (Orthodox 3.8, Roman Catholics 1.5, other Christians 0.1), nonreligious 1.3, other 0.1.

Ruled by France as a base from 1888, Djibouti became an independent republic in 1977. Because of its harbor on the west coast of Africa and the railroad that runs to Addis Ababa, Ethiopia, it has an importance that its relatively small population and area would not otherwise warrant.

The → nomads of the Afar and Issa tribes (the former of Ethiopian origin, the latter from Somalia), who inhabit the desert that borders Eritrea, Djibouti, and Somalia, have been exposed to Islamic influence since the ninth century. Even in the 1990s the native population is over 90 percent Islamic (→ Sunna). As of 1993, France was maintaining a naval base in Djibouti, as well as supporting a force of 4,000 troops. French presence protects the independence of Djibouti against stronger neighbors that have claimed the area (Somalia) and that exert political and economic pressure (Ethiopia) or religious and ideological influence (Saudi Arabia).

With French rule, Roman Catholic → priests came to Djibouti. In 1914 they were placed under the vicariate of Galla (i.e., Oromo) because Roman Catholic missionaries (Capuchins) had worked since 1846 among the Oromo of southern Ethiopia, a people close to the Issa and related to them. In 1955 the → Diocese of Djibouti was placed directly under Rome. In 1992 the Catholic Church numbered 8,000 members and five priests in Djibouti.

The church of the small Greek colony also serves the needs of the Ethiopian Orthodox Christians (approximately 600 adherents; → Ethiopian Orthodox Church). In 1984 the Ethiopian head of state Mengistu laid the foundation stone of an Ethiopian Orthodox church, which was felt to be very odd, since at the same time his Communist regime had closed at least 1,000 Protestant churches in Ethiopia. For Protestant aliens in Djibouti there is a church center (1940) with a Reformed pastor from France.

Whereas the above churches care mainly for the needs of their own people, the Red Sea Mission Team came to Djibouti in 1975 with the aim of → mission among Muslims. In an arrangement with the government that relates primarily to economic projects, it has been granted the right to preach.

Since the Ogaden War of 1977-78 between neighboring Ethiopia and Somalia, as well as a period of droughts in the early 1980s, Djibouti has suffered from a continuous influx of → refugees. Humanitarian and church organizations from western Europe and the United States have helped to care for these homeless, leading to an unusually large number of foreign organizations present in the capital city Djibouti. In 1984, in cooperation with the United Nations High Commissioner for Refugees, the government of Djibouti announced a program of repatriation for the 35,000 Ethiopian refugees then in the country. Approximately half this number returned to Ethiopia later that year. A further agreement in 1986 with the Ethiopian government, again under UN aegis, led to some lessening of the problem. By 1990, however, 30,000 Somali refugees had fled to Djibouti, a number that had tripled by 1992. Whereas all the churches cooperate in helping refugees, → Islam is rather restrained, since it does not have a tradition of institutionalized aid.

Bibliography: P. J. SCHRAEDER, comp., *Djibouti* (Oxford, 1991) bibliography • R. THOLOMIER, *Djibouti, Pawn of the Horn of Africa* (Metuchen, N.J., 1981) • V. THOMPSON and R. ADLOFF, *Djibouti and the Horn of Africa* (Stanford, Calif., 1968).

GUNNAR HASSELBLATT†

Docetism

The term "Docetism" (from Gk. *dokeō*, "seem") includes a variety of meanings throughout the history of dogma, covering heretical (→ Heresies and Schisms) claims and doctrines about Christ (→ Christology). At the root of all of them lies the denial of the truth and reality of the material, earthly, and corporal existence of Christ, with the concurrent assumption that he lived among humans only in appearance, our perception of him being no more than a delusion of the senses.

The earliest reference to this concept is found in the letters of Ignatius of Antioch (d. ca. 107) to the churches of Asia Minor, in which he warns them to beware of false teachers who maintain that Jesus Christ "only appeared to suffer" and thus to undergo birth, eating and drinking, persecution and crucifixion under Pontius Pilate, and resurrection in appearance only. In contrast, Ignatius stresses the connection that exists between the historical reality of Christ's earthly life and his own martyrdom and hope of resurrection, and beyond that the faith and life of all Christians in general. Such false doctrine is already rejected in 1 John 4:2-3 and 2 John 7 with the confession that "Jesus Christ has come in the flesh." It can therefore be assumed that the earliest amplifications of the Christological confession were added in order to refute Docetism.

This denial of the reality of the incarnation is probably connected to influences, on the one hand, of the Jewish tradition stressing the sublime transcendence of God (→ Immanence and Transcendence) and, on the other hand, of Hellenistic views, according to which there exists a strong contrast between the spirit and things corporeal. Thus → Irenaeus (d. ca. 200) cites John 1:14 as the one criterion distinguishing Christian teachings over against any number of different kinds of views (see *Adv. haer.* 3.11.3), all of which (Cerdo, Saturninus, Cerinthus, Marcion, Basilides, and Valentinians) he identifies as → Gnostic views. Certainly Docetism has never been a clearly defined and unified doctrine (variously asserting appearance in a nonmaterial body, appearance as an → angel, an indwelling of divine power in the son of Joseph brought about at his baptism, a clothing of this power under the cover of an earthly body). Moreover, recent studies of Gnostic texts have shown that some of the Gnostics defend themselves against the charge that their teachings are Docetist.

At the beginning of the third century, the term "Docetist" was being applied to a specific breed of heretics of Valentinian derivation; their belief that Christ's life on earth had no reality served them as an argument for a rigorous → asceticism (such as the Encratites practiced). Furthermore, throughout church history the accusation of Docetism has been made against any Christological construct in which Jesus was not clearly understood as the incarnate Son of God.

Bibliography: G. Bardy, "Docétisme," DSp 3.1461-68 • N. Brox, "Doketismus–eine Problemanzeige," ZKG 95 (1984) 301-14 • J. G. Davies, "The Origins of Docetism," StPatr 6 (1962) 13-35 • G. Salmon, "Docetae and Docetism," DCB 1.865-70 • M. Slusser, "Docetism: A Historical Definition," SecCent 1 (1981) 163-72 • K. W. Tröger, "Doketistische Christologie in Nag-Hammadi-Texten. Ein Beitrag zum Doketismus in frühchristlicher Zeit," Kairos 19 (1977) 45-52 • P. Weigandt, "Der Doketismus im Urchristentum und in der theologischen Entwicklung des zweiten Jahrhunderts" (Diss., Heidelberg, 1961).

Ekkehard Mühlenberg

Doctrine → Dogmatics

Dogma

1. History of the Term
2. Material Sense
3. Confessional Forms
   3.1. Early Church
   3.2. Orthodox
   3.3. Catholic
   3.4. Protestant and Anglican
4. Ecumenical Focus
5. Specifically Christian?
6. Critical Evaluation

1. History of the Term

Like the verb dokeō, its cognate noun dogma in classical Greek has a double sense: (1) from the transitive "believe, think," it may denote a way of thinking (in philosophy, medicine, or law); (2) from the intransitive "seem good," it may denote a resolution or edict. Thus the LXX, Philo, and Josephus use it with reference to the → law, and Luke uses it both for imperial edicts (Luke 2:1; Acts 17:7; see also Heb. 11:23 var.) and for the resolutions of the apostolic council (note the use of dokeō in Acts 15:22-29, dogma in 16:4), with an emphasis on universality and authority. According to Col. 2:14 and Eph. 2:15, Christ abolished the law with its dogmata, which were against us.

The → Apostolic Fathers relate dogma sporadically to the ordinances of creation (1 Clem. 20.4;

27.5); to the loyalty that is demanded to bishop, presbyters, and deacons (Ign. Magn. 13.1; cf. Trall. 7.1); to the treatment that the gospel prescribes for wandering apostles (Did. 11.3); and to a true walk in → hope, → righteousness, and → love (Barn. 1.6).

The → apologists (esp. Justin Martyr and Tatian) use the term more often. In their discussions of → Stoicism, "dogma" denotes that which is inaccessible to the senses and which, midway between mere opinion and radical skepticism, makes a religious ethos possible. Tatian relates it to the church in speaking of "our dogmas" and "the dogmas of the barbarians."

Clement and → Origen (→ Origenism) make a place for the term "dogma" in → Alexandrian theology. In the acts of councils it denotes decisions, canons, or teachings. Eusebius of Caesarea connects resolutions and teachings either in detail (pl.) or in their totality (sing.). Between Constantine and Theodosius the legal aspect becomes sharper. Justinian sets the dogmas of the four ecumenical → councils alongside Scripture. The law against heretics henceforth concerns the → Trinity, → Christology, and → Mariology. A singular distinction is that made by Basil between the public → kerygma and arcane dogma (De Spir. S. 27.66; Ep. 125).

The West was hesitant to adopt the alien term "dogma" and along with it uses words like decreta, placita, and scita. → Tertullian, Ambrose, → Augustine, → Leo the Great, and → Gregory the Great use "dogma" almost exclusively for heretical or philosophical teachings. Isidore of Seville derives it from putare (Etym. 8.2).

Only Vincent of Lérins in his Commonitoria (434) gives it the rank of a rule of faith that will overthrow → heresy. The deposit of faith (1 Tim. 6:20), which has been handed down in the world church (universitas) from the apostles (antiquitas) and which is preserved in the consent of the bishops (consensio), is a "dogma divinum . . . caelestis philosophiae, ecclesiae, Christianae religionis" — in short, dogma catholicum (M. Elze, 435, with examples). Vincent's position here represents only a development (profectus) in insight, not a change (permutatio) in content (→ Tradition). As a Semi-Pelagian whom Prosper of Aquitaine had refuted (→ Pelagianism), Vincent remained unknown in the Middle Ages. The Commonitoria was edited only in 1528, but it went through 35 editions and 22 translations in the 16th century. In the battle between the → Reformation and the Counter-Reformation (→ Catholic Reform and Counterreformation), the phrase dogmata fidei (dogmas of the faith) established itself. Distinction was made between fides dogmatica and historica, between traditiones dogma-

ticae and *historicae,* and between a *theologia dogmatica* and *historiae* or *moralis.*

2. Material Sense
The term "dogma," then, has three different senses: (1) in the singular, it signifies the epitome of the knowledge of faith disclosed in God's → revelation; (2) in the plural, it refers to doctrines authorized by the church; and (3) in either the singular or the plural, it can refer to an arbitrary and untested opinion.

Deriving from the → early church (through the concepts of the canon of truth and the exposition of the faith), the first sense became current in the Middle Ages *(articulus fidei, doctrina catholica)* and was radicalized by M. → Luther. As a product of the → gospel, the church confessed only the self-disclosure of God the Father through the Son in the Holy Spirit, as attested by the Scriptures. The → Apostles' Creed formed a brief summary of dogma in this sense, and the four ecumenical councils defended it. It was established sacramentally and fixed legally in the Middle Ages. Both teaching and practice were to be shaped according to the one gospel of Christ.

The Council of → Trent prepared the ground for the second sense, and it was fixed at → Vatican I (DH 3011). Dogma is "the explicit and definitive adoption of a statement as a revealed truth by the church" — a truth that is part of the "divine, official, public Christian revelation" and that is contained in the "Word of God as it has come down to us in Scripture and/or tradition" (*MySal* 1.655).

The underlying sense of "human desires or opinions" (Marcellus of Ancyra *Frg.* 86) is reflected in the modern revolution in → metaphysics (R. Descartes, I. Kant), which has led to the third sense of "dogma." On the one hand, there is denunciation of the dogmatic superstructure as a Hellenistic alienation of the simple message of Jesus (from J. F. W. Jerusalem to A. Harnack). On the other hand, there is transposition of the creative dynamic of the Spirit (John 16:12-13) to the cosmic evolution of life.

3. Confessional Forms
3.1. *Early Church*
The primitive Christian confession contains a mixture of the basic forms of theological statement: witness, → prayer, → doxology, and teaching (E. Schlink; → Confession of Faith). A saying of Jesus that has been handed down four times (Luke 12:8-9; Matt. 10:32-33; Mark 8:38; Luke 9:26) and that is often echoed opposes confession of Jesus to denial and relates both to the → eschatological forum of God. In → baptism the church relates commitment to the triune God with renunciation of the powers of Satan. The early Christian rule of faith sets confession of Christ against an apocalyptic background and gives it a Trinitarian structure. The early creeds express the rule of faith in hymnic and doxological forms, which they superimpose on the original basis *(archē).* Ancient metaphysics is used for the purpose.

3.2. *Orthodox*
The → Orthodox Church keeps the orientation of the early church. It sets the seven ecumenical councils (up to Nicaea II, in 787) alongside Scripture and the Fathers. The church on earth joins with the church in heaven in the celebration of the → liturgy and the veneration of → images. Byzantine developments of dogma in, for example, the mysticism of Simeon the New Theologian (949-1022), the doctrine of divine energies of Gregory Palamas (ca. 1296-1359; → Palamism), and the solemn rejection of the → *filioque* find universal acceptance. Confessions and catechisms, however, that were drawn up in the 16th and 17th centuries as fruit of the struggles among Rome, Wittenberg, and Geneva are totally rejected as foreign, Western products.

3.3. *Catholic*
The → Roman Catholic Church shifted its emphasis from direct confession — from the "we believe" or "we confess" of the original creeds — to the "we teach that this is to be confessed" (DH 300*) of → Chalcedon, and then to the "whoever will be saved, above all things it is necessary that he hold the Catholic faith" (DH 75*) of the → Athanasian Creed.

In the Middle Ages the creed of the congregation and the oath of the clergy parted company. The former led to the penance of the confessional, and the latter concentrated on the sacramental mediation of grace. In the definitions of Lateran IV (1215; DH 800-802) against the Albigenses and → Cathari, in the subscription that the Council of Lyons II (1274; DH 851-61) demanded of the envoys of Emperor Michael Palaeologus, and in the corresponding oaths and creedal expositions, the sacraments were increased to seven and the papal office was emphasized (→ Pope, Papacy).

The Tridentine oath (1564; DH 1862-70) extended and sharpened this development in an anti-Reformation direction. The combining of the early creeds with the sacramental system still marks the creed of Paul VI (1968) and the first short formula of K. → Rahner (*Theological Investigations* 9.117-26). Both medieval → Scholasticism and the controversial theology of Trent tried to deduce this new dogmatic complex from the articles of the Apostles' Creed. The more difficult this proved, the stronger was the stress on the → teaching office of the papacy (esp. M. Cano *De locis theol.* 12.5.6).

The Roman Catholic Tübingen School of the 19th century (J. S. von Drey, J. A. Möhler, J. E. von Kuhn), as well as J. H. → Newman, taught the idea of doctrinal development. With J. G. → Herder, F. D. E. → Schleiermacher, and G. W. F. Hegel, they changed the traditional relationship of reason and revelation into one of revelation and history. A preparatory commission (G. Perrone, C. Passaglia) supported the dogma of the immaculate conception (1854; DH 2800-2804) by the church's infallible dogmatic sense, in view of the absence of biblical testimony and the defectiveness of tradition (→ Mariology). The declaration of the teaching → infallibility and comprehensive headship of the pope (1870; DH 3050-75), followed by the dogma of the assumption of Mary (1950; DH 3900-3904), gave added weight to authoritarianism.

Vatican II confirmed this trend but put it in an ecclesial context. *Dei verbum* (November 18, 1965), the dogmatic constitution on divine revelation, inclines back to Scripture as the "soul" of theology and calls for the renewal of the church by the Word of God. In unclarified tension with Trent, which refers only in the plural to traditions not included in Scripture (DH 1501; cf. 3006), it speaks of tradition in the singular, leaving undecided the debate kindled by J. R. Geiselmann's interpretation of the Tübingen school about whether the original tradition came fully into the canon or not. The guiding principle of ongoing dogmatic progress mediates between the primitive biblical tradition and the new dogmas. The reality of sin and error becomes less prominent, however, and the judicial function of Scripture is reduced (see the criticism of J. Ratzinger).

3.4. *Protestant and Anglican*

In the Protestant churches, the → Reformers went back to Scripture and developed dogma Christocentrically in terms of → law and → gospel, → grace and judgment. In his "short form" of instruction (1520; *WLuth* 2.354-84 = WA 7.204-29), Luther follows the eschatological orientation of the medieval symbols and under the "for me" brings the anthropological schema of his tractate on freedom into the Apostles' Creed. In the 1528 confession (*LuthW* 37.360-72 = WA 26.499-509), the model for Reformation confessions, he presses the *particula exclusiva* (→ Reformation Principles) eschatologically against the medieval additions.

The → Augsburg Confession (1530) follows the movement of Scripture and the rule of faith from the creation to the resurrection of the dead (arts. 1-17). It accepts the doctrinal decisions of the early church — the Trinity (art. 1), the Augustinian doctrine of original sin (art. 2), and the two natures of Christ (art. 3) — leads on from these to → justification and

the new → obedience under the law and gospel (arts. 2-6, 18-20), and defends the resultant form of the church (arts. 7-15, 22-28). The dominant terms are "confession," "doctrine," "faith," and "articles of faith," with "dogma" occurring hardly at all (cf. WA 18.604.3-4). Reformation → catechisms shape the practice. The confessions emphasize either eschatological accountability (Lutheran → Formula of Concord) or consistent instruction from Scripture (Reformed confessions).

The → Anglican Church has oriented itself more strongly to the → Book of Common Prayer (1549 and 1552) than to the Thirty-Nine Articles (1563 and 1571), which were based on the Forty-Two Articles of 1553. In particular, John Jewel (1522-71) and Richard Hooker (ca. 1554-1600) viewed Anglicanism as a *via media* between Rome and Geneva. The 17th-century Caroline divines and the 19th-century → Oxford Movement emphasized agreement with the early, undivided church. In the struggle with → deism, George Berkeley (1685-1753) and Joseph Butler (1692-1752) shattered an unbroken trust in reason and linked the revelation in Christ to an empirical, rational starting point.

With such roots, Anglicanism has combined an Anglo-Catholic insistence on the fundamental → unity of the church, an evangelical call for renewal of life through an experience of grace, and a liberal rejection of dogmatic narrowness along with an opening up of the → incarnation to the evolutionary process. The Lambeth Quadrilateral (1888) regards four points as essential: (1) the Bible as the basis of doctrine; (2) the Apostles' Creed as a valid baptismal symbol and the → Niceno-Constantinopolitan Creed as a universal and sufficient confession of faith; (3) the central sacraments of → baptism and the → Eucharist; and (4) the historic episcopate (→ Bishop, Episcopate).

Neo-Protestantism (→ Protestantism), following F. Schleiermacher (1768-1834), brought to the Reformation struggle for certainty the new method of "logically ordered reflection upon the immediate utterances of the religious self-consciousness" (*The Christian Faith*, postscript to §16). The Neo-Lutheranism of Erlangen (→ Lutheranism) and A. Ritschl (1822-89) and his followers all accepted this approach and saw in Schleiermacher "the reformer of theology" (W. Herrmann). Dogma was discredited as a doctrinal system and abandoned as a concept (P. → Tillich).

4. Ecumenical Focus

The basis of the → World Council of Churches (1948, expanded in 1961 to include reference to the Bible and to the Trinity), interconfessional agreements — whether universal, multinational (e.g., the document of union of the → Church of South India in 1947 or the → Leuenberg Agreement of 1973), or national (e.g., the → Barmen Declaration of 1934 and the Arnoldshain Theses on the Lord's Supper of 1957) — and bilateral conversations (→ Dialogue), especially with the Roman Catholic Church after Vatican II, have all resulted in a concentration on what is elementary and fundamental. The classic points at issue are still debated, but in Faith and Order the focus is on baptism, Eucharist, and ministry (Lima 1982) and on a creed that will be a form of the Niceno-Constantinopolitan Creed appropriate for the present-day world situation.

There are two possibilities in this regard. One is to follow the Reformers in a search for "the heart of the gospel" (Malta Report, 24-25) through a hierarchy of truths (Ecumenism Decree) that will lead by way of confession and proclamation to the gospel of Christ (O. Weber, E. Kinder, W. Kasper, K. Lehmann). The other is to pledge all churches afresh to "the basic truths of Christianity as we have them in Holy Scripture, the Apostles' Creed, and the Niceno-Constantinopolitan Creed" (H. Fries, K. Rahner).

Dogma is oriented either to the kerygma and preaching or to the rule of faith and doxology. K. → Barth finds in it an eschatological "concept of relation." For him, it aims to compare the proclamation of the church with Holy Scripture, making sure that the two agree (*CD* I/1, 287). T. F. Torrance identifies dogma (sing.) with God's self-revelation in Jesus Christ as the basis of the church's existence; dogmas (pl.) expound this core both in development and in defense. D. Ritschl makes a similar distinction between creeds, dogmas, and theological doctrines. E. Schlink refers the → canon, dogma, and → church order to the church's preservation by its Lord but distinguishes dogma and order, which are open, from the canon, which is closed, and sketches the basic outlines of a dogmatic hermeneutics (*Ökumenische Dogmatik*, chap. 21).

5. Specifically Christian?

Christian dogma differs both from revelation in → Islam and from Eastern religions as a whole. This is because God's final revelation came in a Jewish man and was developed in reflective witness against the background of human and cosmic destiny. The core confession of Islam ("There is no God but Allah, and Muḥammad is his prophet") is dogmatically purely speculative as far as Allah is concerned, although strictly revelatory with respect to the Prophet. In → Buddhism intellectually fixed convictions that are

handed down as doctrines are left behind on the way to enlightenment.

6. Critical Evaluation

The core question is, How, in agreement with those who have gone before us and those who are beside us, do we discover what it is that we are to witness to God and the world today in the struggle between belief and unbelief? This question forces upon us a → hermeneutics that combines philological and historical investigation of traditions with a systematic inquiry into the central witness of Scripture, and yet at the same time responds critically to our own situation. The ecumenical thrust toward what is elementary and fundamental should loosen confessional narrowness without leveling down differences in an unhealthy way.

The kerygmatic, doxological, catechetical, communicative, and legal functions of dogma are always oriented to God's own self-disclosure. The personal truth of the Reconciler seeks to make itself known in the servant form of factual and propositional statements. Acceptance and rejection, maranatha and anathema, are all ultimately accountable before the forum of God. When it loses this reference, Christian dogma no longer has any meaning or function.

Bibliography: C. ANDRESEN, ed., *HDThG* • K. BEYSCHLAG, *Grundriß der Dogmengeschichte* (Darmstadt, 1982) 1-54 • H. VON CAMPENHAUSEN, "Das Bekenntnis im Urchristentum," *ZNW* 63 (1972) 210-53 • CHURCH OF ENGLAND, DOCTRINE COMMISSION, *Christian Believing: The Nature of the Christian Faith and Its Expression in Holy Scripture and Creeds* (London, 1976) • *Doctrine in the Church of England* (2d ed.; Essex, 1957) • A. DULLES, *The Survival of Dogma* (New York, 1971) • M. ELZE, "Der Begriff des Dogma in der alten Kirche," *ZTK* 61 (1964) 421-38 • H. FRIES and K. RAHNER, *Einigung der Kirchen–reale Möglichkeit* (Freiburg, 1983) • J. R. GEISELMANN, "Dogma," *HThG* 1.225-41 • A. HARNACK, *Die Entstehung der christlichen Theologie und des christlichen Dogmas* (Gotha, 1927) • L. HÖDL, "Articulus fidei," *Einsicht und Glaube* (FS G. Söhngen; Freiburg, 1962) 358-76 • E. HULTSCH and K. LÜTHI, eds., *Bekennendes Bekenntnis* (FS W. Dantine; Gütersloh, 1982) • A. JEFFNER, *Kriterien christlicher Glaubenslehre* (Göttingen, 1977) • W. KASPER, *Dogma unter dem Worte Gottes* (Mainz, 1965) • G. KITTEL, "Δόγμα, δογματίζω," *TDNT* 2.230-32 • G. LANCZKOWSKI et al., "Glaubensbekenntnis(se)," *TRE* 13.384-446 • G. MENSCHING and G. GLOEGE, "Dogma," *RGG* (3d ed.) 2.220-25 • H. MEYER, H. J. URBAN, and I. VISCHER, eds., *Dokumente wachsender Übereinstimmung* (Paderborn, 1983) • W. PANNENBERG, *Basic Questions in Theology* (2 vols.; Philadelphia, 1970-71); idem, "Was ist eine dogmatische Aussage?" *KuD* 8 (1962) 81-99 • A. PETERS, *Rechenschaft des Glaubens* (Göttingen, 1984) • K. RAHNER, *Theological Investigations* (vols. 4-5; Baltimore, 1966) • K. RAHNER and K. LEHMANN, "Geschichtlichkeit der Vermittlung," *MySal* 1.727-87; idem, *Kerygma and Dogma* (New York, 1969) • C. H. RATSCHOW and U. WICKERT, "Dogma," *TRE* 9.36-41 • J. RATZINGER, "Kommentar" (on chaps. 1-2 of *Dei Verbum*), *LTK, Das zweite vatikanische Konzil*, 2.509, 513, 518, 520-21, 524-28 • W. E. REISER, *What Are They Saying about Dogma?* (New York, 1978) • D. RITSCHL, *The Logic of Theology* (Philadelphia, 1987) • E. SCHLINK, *Ökumenische Dogmatik* (Göttingen, 1983); idem, "Die Struktur der dogmatischen Aussage als ökumenisches Problem," *KuD* 3 (1957) 251-306 (repr., *Der kommende Christus und die kirchlichen Traditionen* [Göttingen, 1961] 24-79) • P. SCHRODT, *The Problem of the Beginning of Dogma in Recent Theology* (Frankfurt, 1978) • T. F. TORRANCE, *Theological Science* (London, 1969) • H. J. URBAN, *Bekenntnis, Dogma, Kirchliches Lehramt* (Wiesbaden, 1972) • H. VORGRIMLER, K. RAHNER, and W. LOHFF, "Dogma," *LTK* (2d ed.) 3.438-46 • WORLD COUNCIL OF CHURCHES, *Baptism, Eucharist, and Ministry* (Geneva, 1982) the so-called Lima text.

ALBRECHT PETERS†

Dogma, History of

The task of the history of dogma is to trace the development of the dogmas that the church has formulated. The task is closely tied to that of the history of theology, for theologians have influenced the formulation of the dogmas.

No history of dogma was possible in the → early church or the Middle Ages because the content of the Christian → faith was then regarded as unalterably fixed from the beginning. This immutability was presupposed even in the → heresies that were combatted, for, in the eyes of the orthodox, heretics were always ultimately the same, opposing the true faith for the same reasons.

The → Reformation, however, subjected → dogma to the Bible and thus challenged the infallibility of dogma, although accepting dogma as corresponding to the Bible. It denied that the teachers of the church had taught the same thing throughout the centuries. The → Reformers could be sharply critical of the → Scholastics and even of the → church fathers, including → Augustine. In this way a history of dogma became theologically possible. Yet in fact the Reformers and Orthodox (→ Orthodoxy 3) were

content for the most part simply to collect → patristic texts that supported their positions against those of Roman Catholics (→ Catholicism [Roman]).

→ Anti-Trinitarians and the theologians of the Enlightenment (e.g., M. Servetus, J. Clericus, J. L. von Mosheim) were to different degrees cautiously critical of the content of dogma and tried to show that it was influenced by → Greek philosophy and opposed to a true biblical and rational faith. Christianity, they argued, had undergone Hellenization. Such a position opened the door to the history of dogma, though, like the collections of quotations, it remained in the sphere of the theological controversies of the time (the anti-Trinitarians and theologians of the Enlightenment vs. the orthodox and Roman Catholics). The emphasis on development in the history of dogma was new, but the Reformers and humanists had prepared the way for it with their theory of depravation — the view that pure doctrine had been increasingly obscured over the course of the centuries.

The end of the 18th century and beginning of the 19th saw some basic work in the history of dogma (S. G. Lange, F. C. Münter, W. Münscher). The most important writings of the 19th century were those of F. C. Baur (1792-1860) and A. Harnack (1851-1930). Under the influence of G. W. F. Hegel (1770-1831), Baur regarded the history of dogma as a strictly logical and necessary process of the religious consciousness. In fact, he was closer to the orthodox view than were the theologians of the Enlightenment, who bewailed dogmatic development as a decline from biblical and rational faith. Nevertheless, Baur's starting point — the conflict between → Jesus and → Paul — was unacceptable to → orthodoxy (§§1-2).

Influenced by A. Ritschl (1822-89), Harnack, along with R. Seeberg and F. Loofs, restored to individuals a greater historical significance and, in so doing, pointed out that dogmas have only a time-bound validity. Yet in this regard the later sections of Harnack's work are milder and more differentiated, so that ultimately Harnack differed from Baur less than Harnack initially wanted his readers to believe. Following the Reformation in the spirit of the modern age, Harnack set the → gospel of Jesus Christ in antithesis to dogma, which for him was an inadequate (although not incorrect) rendering of the gospel. According to Harnack, the gospel has a critical function in history relative to the church's dogmatic structure. In this regard Harnack influenced the → dialectical theology of K. → Barth and E. Brunner, who at first vehemently opposed him. Here again the distinction in positions was ultimately not as great as it appeared to be at first. Later efforts (e.g., by W. Köhler and M. Werner) have not gone far beyond Harnack's depiction, for in spite of their criticisms of Harnack, their positions are similar to his.

The 20th century has largely overcome the polemical emphasis in the history of dogma. Almost all theological camps and confessions (→ Denomination) recognize the fallibility of dogma, or at least of the human ability to interpret it. They also refrain from speculating on the way in which history ought to have moved instead of the way it did. As a result of specialization, the history of dogma has increasingly become a historical rather than a theological discipline. The facts and development are put in specific periods, but it is no longer thought possible to gain a total view and to present a theological evaluation. Thus the influence of the history of dogma on modern theology is relatively slight, and dogmatic historians are no longer leading among the theologians. The interest of systematic theologians will determine the future of the history of dogma, aided by the measure of interest that dogmatic historians will be able to generate in theology.

Bibliography: C. Andresen, ed., *HDThG* • F. C. Baur, *Lehrbuch der christlichen Dogmengeschichte* (Darmstadt, 1979; orig. pub., 1847) • K. Beyschlag, *Grundriß der Dogmengeschichte* (vol. 1; Darmstadt, 1982) • A. von Harnack, *History of Dogma* (7 vols.; New York, 1961; orig. pub., 1886-90) • W.-D. Hauschild, "Dogmengeschichtsschreibung," *TRE* 9.116-25 (bibliography) • F. Loofs, *Leitfaden zum Studium der Dogmengeschichte* (Halle, 1889; 5th ed., 1950) • J. Pelikan, *Historical Theology: Continuity and Change in Christian Doctrine* (New York, 1971) • M. Schmaus et al., eds. *HDG* (5 vols.; Freiburg, 1956ff.) • R. Seeberg, *Textbook of the History of Doctrines* (Grand Rapids, 1958).

Eginhard P. Meijering

Dogmatics

1. Concept

Protestant theology, unlike Roman Catholic theology, has not developed any clear-cut concept of → dogma and hence has not achieved any precise definition of dogmatics. Instead, many different accents exist. At the same time, some basic lines of understanding have emerged from the various practices of dogmatics. According to the assumptions and conditions of modern critical consciousness, dogmatics is the theological discipline that, on the basis of the biblical witness and against the background of church tradition, thinks through and systematically presents the → truth of the Christian faith in its central contents (dogmas), adopting a scientific and critical method and taking into account the contemporary situation.

Dogmatics forms an underlying unity with theological → ethics. Neither derives from the other. Both relate equally to God's saving work in Christ and reflect upon it — the one in terms of understanding, the other in terms of the required action. Since the 17th century, it has been customary to deal with the two separately, but it is with good reason that some have sought either to integrate ethics into dogmatics (M. Kähler, E. Hirsch, K. → Barth) or to see dogmatics from the standpoint of ethical questions (R. Rothe, W. Herrmann, T. Rendtorff). Systematic theology is the discipline embracing both dogmatics and ethics.

Dogmatics presupposes biblical → exegesis, yet does not attempt a historical reconstruction of biblical theology but expounds the biblical witness to God's saving acts in terms of the modern experience of faith. It presupposes historical theology (i.e., the history of the church and its dogmas and the wider history of thought and culture), for faith and action — and reflection on them — always take place under certain historical presuppositions and conditions. Dogmatics as a function of the church relates in many ways to its needs, and thus it is tied also to → practical theology.

2. History

As a thoughtful presentation of the fundamental statements of the biblical message and the Christian faith, dogmatics was present long before the term came into use. There were instead such terms as *sententiae, summa theologiae,* or, from the 16th century, *loci theologici.* Although the Greek terms for dogma or dogmatics go back to the pre-Christian era, we first encounter the term "dogmatics" in a title like *Theologia dogmatica* only in the 17th century. The adjective serves the cause of precision and theological differentiation. G. Calixtus (→ Orthodoxy 1) seems to have been the first to speak of *theologia dogmatica* as distinct from *theologia moralis* (in his work *Epitome theologiae moralis* [1634]). In 1635 J. H. Alting used *theologia dogmatica* in distinction from *theologia historica.* The term then appeared without differentiation in L. F. Reinhart's *Synopsis theologia Christianae dogmaticae* (1659). This usage established itself with the works of C. M. Pfaff and J. F. Buddeus. Also in the 17th century Roman Catholics took it over from the Lutherans.

2.1. *Reformation and Older Protestantism*

M. → Luther (→ Luther's Theology) never presented his new theological insights systematically. In its form and purpose, even his Schmalkaldic Articles (1537) has a different orientation. Generally speaking, P. → Melanchthon's *Loci communes* (1521) is the first Protestant dogmatics (→ Reformers). This work is meant as an introduction to the study of Scripture and expounds certain central and controverted themes *(loci)* but manifests no systematic concern. Only from the second edition of 1535 did Melanchthon complete and systematize his material. The last edition (1559) bore the title *Loci praecipui theologici.* → Calvin's *Institutio Christianae religionis* (→ Calvin's Theology), the Reformed equivalent of Melanchthon's *Loci,* also only in its later editions (last ed., 1559) asumed a systematic character, oriented to the → Apostles' Creed. In structure, the first edition of 1536 resembles Luther's catechisms.

Alongside these classic expositions of Reformation teaching, the → confessions gave stability to the new understanding of the → gospel. On the Lutheran side this process reached a climax in 1580 with the Book of Concord, which led to the development of the second generation of Protestant dogmatics in Lutheran and Reformed versions. The older scholastic orthodoxy worked out the newly discovered truth of Scripture against the background of the Reformation legacy and the decisions reached in the confessions, with increasing openness again to (Aristotelian) philosophy (→ Orthodoxy 1-2).

Early and high orthodoxy followed Melanchthon in using the method of *loci* and related the themes to one another only very loosely. For the Lutherans, the salvation-event and its appropriation in → faith (→ Justification) stood at the center. For the Reformed, the central matter was the divine decrees and their actualization in salvation history (→ Predestination). The federal theology of J. Cocceius (→ Covenant 3) represented a particular form of reformed scholastic orthodoxy.

Later orthodoxy followed the so-called analytic method. It expounded the biblical statements from the standpoint of the goal, object, and means of salvation, thus proceeding systematically and providing a structure for the individual doctrines. In content, changes came about as the adoption of → Aristotelianism (and → Cartesianism on the Reformed side) opened up afresh the problems of → natural theology. High orthodoxy was represented on the Lutheran side by L. Hutter and J. Gerhard, and on the Reformed side by J. Wollebius and G. Voetius. Later orthodoxy found its champions in the Lutherans J. A. Quenstedt and D. Hollaz and the Reformed J. H. Heidegger. The age of orthodoxy ended with the rise of two new movements, the → Enlightenment and → Pietism, which increasingly influenced the theological debate.

2.2. *Neo-Protestantism*

F. D. E. → Schleiermacher (1768-1834) discussed the problems posed by Pietism, the Enlightenment, → idealistic philosophy, and → Romanticism. He became the leading figure in Protestant theology during the 19th century, and on into the early 20th century in the German sphere. He established the independence of religion from morality and → metaphysics by anchoring it in "feeling," in the "direct self-consciousness." In writing dogmatic statements, Schleiermacher thus appealed not so much to Scripture as to Christian self-awareness, as this has been shaped by Scripture and church tradition. By his definition, dogmatic statements are "accounts of the Christian religious affections set forth in speech" (*The Christian Faith,* §15). Dogmatics changes to analysis of the historically mediated → experience of faith. This basic change in the dogmatic task is reflected in the title of his work *Der christliche Glaube nach den Grundsätzen der evangelischen Kirche im Zusammenhange dargestellt* (The Christian faith, presented systematically according to the fundamental doctrines of the Evangelical church; 1821-22; 2d ed., 1830-31).

In the second half of the 19th century A. Ritschl gave dogmatic work some characteristic emphases, especially in his basic work *Rechtfertigung und Versöhnung* (Justification and reconciliation; 3 vols., 1870-74; 3d ed., 1888-89). Ritschl addressed Reformation themes on a biblical basis and with an ethical orientation. In his *Ethik* (1901; 6th ed., 1921), W. Herrmann sharpened the ethical components of theology apparent in Ritschl. As the teacher of R. Bultmann and K. Barth, Herrmann had a major, so far largely unexplored influence on 20th-century theology.

E. → Troeltsch boldly tackled the problems of history in theology and became the dogmatician of the so-called → history-of-religions school (*Glaubenslehre,* published posthumously in 1925). Like Ritschl, M. Kähler (*Die Wissenschaft der christlichen Lehre* [1883; 3d ed., 1905]) developed Christian dogma on the basis of the chief Reformation article of justification, but he took a less critical view of the biblical witness and traditional teaching. Kähler's distinction between the "historical Jesus" and the "biblical Christ" influenced R. Bultmann's → Christology. Kähler's significance in the thought of his student P. → Tillich is still unclear.

2.3. The New Era
World War I marked an important break in German-speaking Protestant theology. Representatives of the → dialectical theology (K. Barth, E. Brunner, F. Gogarten, and, to some extent, R. Bultmann), along with other important 20th-century systematicians such as P. Althaus, W. Elert, E. Hirsch, and P. Tillich, clearly distinguished themselves from the preceding theology, which they viewed as Culture Protestantism. Only in working out a positive understanding of theology and dogmatics did differences increasingly come to light. K. Barth and his followers viewed theology strictly as an intellectual following of God's → revelation in Jesus Christ; even in the title of his major work, *Church Dogmatics,* Barth stressed the relation of dogmatics to the church.

In contrast, another type of theology emerged — unified in orientation but differing in detail — which found its theme in the tension between God's self-disclosure and human reality, thus opening up dogmatics to the sense of reality and truth (P. Althaus, E. Brunner, F. Buri, W. Elert, F. Gogarten, E. Hirsch, P. Tillich, M. Werner). This approach raised new questions and problems. Most impressively, P. Tillich methodically developed and championed this view of systematic (dogmatic) theology.

Although new fields have opened up and antitheses are frequently covered over, modern discussion constantly proceeds in terms of these alternatives.

3. Current Protestant Dogmatics
Since the 19th century, Protestants have followed orthodox Protestantism in dividing dogmatics into prolegomena and dogmatics in the specific sense. The latter usually follows Lombard's scheme: God, creation, humanity and sin, Christ, church, and es-

chatology. It may take an overtly Trinitarian shape (presently, by W. Trillhaas, H. Thielicke, and G. Ebeling), or it may be indirectly Trinitarian (K. Barth, E. Brunner, and P. Tillich). Schleiermacher represents a major exception, for he adopted a completely different structure, but he founded no school.

In the non-German-speaking world, Protestant systematic theology, for geographic and historical reasons, shows closeness to German-speaking theology (in Holland, Scotland, and Scandinavia) but also independence of it (England, America, and, to some extent, Sweden). (On this matter, see *TRE* 9.77-116.)

3.1. Germany
German Protestantism, unlike Roman Catholicism, → Orthodoxy (§3), and Anglicanism, does not make → tradition dogmatically binding. It is from the outset a theology of the Word of God, for which Scripture alone is normative. The Reformation principle of *sola Scriptura* (→ Reformation Principles) has contributed directly and indirectly to the development of historicocritical research. Specific problems have arisen for the church and theology with the application of this principle to Scripture.

3.1.1. Nature
Theology is a function of the church (Schleiermacher, Barth, Tillich, Brunner), which is true particularly of dogmatic theology. Dogmatics (along with theological ethics) is the part of systematic theology that reflects on the truth of God's revealing and reconciling work in Jesus Christ, according to the biblical testimony, in terms of the experience of faith, elucidates it as teaching (dogma), and presents it systematically. In this view, the mutual relationship of → revelation and → faith is presupposed (see Tillich, *Systematic Theology* 1.135). Dogmatic theology is not the same as faith and must be strictly differentiated from it as a form of reflection. Presupposing faith, it is not itself an act of faith (cf. Barth, *CD* I/1, §1.3).

As faith expresses itself in confession (→ Confession of Faith), dogmatic reflection follows this thread. Insofar as the event of faith is embedded in a specific historical situation, this context forms part of dogmatic reflection. (Tillich speaks of the polar tension between the message and the situation.) The resultant dogma is not, as on the Roman Catholic view, a doctrinal law or a law of faith. Rather, it is an objective expression of the certainty and truth of faith, for which the individual is responsible.

3.1.2. Basic Problem
Historical criticism threatens the foundations of a theology of God's Word based on Scripture. Awareness of this problem characterizes modern theology and dogmatics. Many theologians no longer view the

older doctrine of → inspiration as a viable possibility, not even Barth (see *CD* I/1, 112-13). The different thrusts of modern Protestant theology are all attempts at dealing with this basic problem of the relationship of faith and history. How are binding dogmatic statements still possible?

With the theologians of the → Enlightenment (→ Neology), one may try to harmonize the biblical truth of revelation with → reason. With Kant (→ Kantianism), one may stop at the moral truths of Christianity. Like Schleiermacher, one may use historically mediated → experience as a methodological principle. Like Barth, one may make the → Word of God in its threefold form — proclaimed, written, and revealed (*CD* I/1, §4) — the criterion of dogmatics. In each case, however, the issue ultimately is that of solving the problem raised by the historical dimension of Scripture. Common to all such attempts are two points: (1) dogma and dogmatics are human talk about God and his saving work in Christ rather than, as in Catholic and Orthodox theology, themselves divine revelation; (2) dogmatics is no longer, as in the days of orthodoxy, taken directly from Scripture but from Scripture as viewed from a specific angle. Subjectivity is a constant threat that can be averted only by a steady concern for the center of Scripture.

The terms "dogma" and "dogmatics" have thus come under a cloud and are either seldom used or avoided altogether. We see the change in the title of Schleiermacher's work, although he himself could still use the term "dogmatics." Tillich expresses his reservations about the concept (*Systematic Theology* 1.41), but Barth and Brunner still use the older term, and Ebeling tries to bring out the tension between tradition and present responsibility by combining the older and newer titles in his *Dogmatik des christlichen Glaubens* (Dogmatics of Christian faith).

3.2. Holland
The main feature of theological discussion in Holland is a wrestling with Barth's theology. The neo-Calvinism (→ Calvinism) deriving from A. → Kuyper has been critical (K. Schilder, G. C. Berkouwer), but other thinkers have been receptive (T. L. Haitjema, K. H. Miskotte).

3.3. Scotland
Reformed theology in Scotland has been influenced by that of Germany and Switzerland. The brothers J. and D. M. Baillie attempted to combine the liberal legacy with the new insights of dialectical theology (e.g., see D. M. Baillie, *God Was in Christ* [1948]). T. F. Torrance, more strongly influenced by Barth, was concerned to overcome the gulf between the theology of revelation and modern science, which in his judgment had been

based on a false view of nature that modern physics has now rendered outdated. The sharp alternatives of German theology are alien to the Scots.

3.4. Scandinavia
In the Scandinavian countries Luther research has been important, but with different emphases. In Denmark K. E. Lögstrup's *Etiske fordring* (The ethical demand; 1956) set the ethical demand in the light of belief in creation, clearly differentiating his understanding from the supposed Platonizing of Christianity in S. → Kierkegaard (→ Platonism). In Sweden N. Söderblom approached the science of religion (→ Religious Studies) as it relates to the → philosophy of religion.

For the rest, we find a distinctively polar development. On the one hand, some thinkers have demonstrated a firmer attachment to Luther and → Lutheranism, with a basing of dogmatics on the theology of creation (G. Wingren); on the other hand, some have oriented themselves toward Anglo-Saxon analytic and antimetaphysical philosophy. In the latter field interest focuses on the scientific possibility of theological statements, with critical reservations regarding traditional dogmatics (A. Gyllenkrog, A. Jeffner).

3.5. England
The tradition of empirical philosophy in England renewed itself in the 20th century (B. Russell, G. E. Moore) and took a new turn in logical positivism and linguistic philosophy (L. Wittgenstein, J. L. Austin; → Analytic Philosophy). This development has had an impact on theology. Efforts were made to show that Christian truth is rational, whether in relation to Bultmann's demythologizing or in view of the demands of linguistics (A. Flew, A. MacIntyre, R. Hepburn). Under the influence of such demands, theories arose that would no longer allow religious statements a cognitive status but would regard them as meaningful and necessary on other grounds (R. B. Braithwaite, R. M. Hare). According to I. T. Ramsey, we can espouse religious statements only when they bring to light new situations or materials.

3.6. North America
The situation in North America is so complex that this brief survey of the understanding of theology and dogmatics scarcely does it justice. Neoorthodoxy and → fundamentalism exist alongside theological liberalism and the → Social Gospel. P. Tillich has made a great impact, and so have the brothers H. Richard and Reinhold → Niebuhr, with their criticism of belief in progress and their → social ethics, which includes the → dialectic of God and humanity, eternity and history, and sin and grace, and which causes a radical change in theological awareness.

The lines of development are complicated by the fact that the views of many theologians have changed, so that different ideas are linked to their names. In a strange reversal, the Christological concentration of K. Barth led in the 1960s to the proposal of a death-of-God theology (T. J. J. Altizer, P. M. Van Buren, W. Hamilton, G. Vahanian; → God Is Dead Theology). Other motifs inclined in the same direction, especially analytic (linguistic) philosophy, which made a great impact on America, the implications of which were drawn out by Van Buren. He has tried to redefine the task of Christian dogmatics through his multivolume systematic theology entitled *A Theology of the Jewish-Christian Reality.*

Along with G. Kaufman's new version of the doctrine of → God, special note should be taken of G. Wainwright's dogmatics in the light of → doxology.

The → process philosophy of A. N. Whitehead and C. Hartshorne has also gained in importance for theological thinking. The so-called → process theology adopts insights from Bultmann's → existential theology (S. M. Ogden) but also addresses the world of nature and in a formal theology of nature tries to explain the evolutionary development of the cosmos in terms of God's creative action (J. B. Cobb). Criticism focuses on the inadequate account of God's transcendence (L. Gilkey, R. C. Neville; → North American Theology).

3.7. *Latin American Liberation Theology*

→ Liberation theology arose out of the special problems and needs of Latin America (→ Latin American Theology), to which it primarily relates. But it also uses impulses from J. Moltmann's theology of hope and from → political theology, thus showing the influence of western Europe and North America. It reflects not only the ecclesiastical and theological but especially the social and political situation of Latin America, partly also of Asia, and tries to indicate ways of liberation motivated by Christianity and based upon it.

Although liberation theology has been developed particularly by Roman Catholic thinkers (G. Gutiérrez, C. and L. Boff), Protestants have also been active in its development, as it has had an impact beyond Latin America (→ Third World Theology). We cannot equate its problems with confessional distinctions; there is within it an organic move to → ecumenical theology. Roman Catholicism has criticized its recourse to elements in the → Marxist analysis of society and has likewise expressed reservations concerning various teachings in the spheres of Christology, ecclesiology, and anthropology, raising the suspicion of heresy.

4. Roman Catholic

On the Roman Catholic view, dogma is "a truth directly revealed by God and clearly and definitively proclaimed by the church's → teaching office as something in the divine and catholic faith that all Christians must accept" (F. Diekamp, 1.12). This definition goes back to the ruling of → Vatican I (D 3011 = NR 1971, no. 34; see also 1917 CIC 1323.1 = 1983 CIC 750). Dogma is didactic law, a law of faith. Dogmatics in the strict sense is the science of dogmas. More generally, it deals with "the church's total proclamation." It is "the scientific establishment, discussion, and presentation of the saving truths imparted to us by God's self-revelation and is attested, guaranteed, and set forth by the church" (Schmaus, *Katholische Dogmatik,* 1.67). It includes the basic principles of → moral theology. Its relation to clearly defined dogma limits the possibilities of reflection and statement. There can be no modification, criticism, or revision of dogma either for internal theological reasons or because of external ecclesiastical factors.

Dogma, however, is open to interpretation. An impressive example is the attempt to see dogma in terms of salvation history in the work *Mysterium salutis.* Along with this basic enterprise in modern Roman Catholic theology, the theological writings of K. → Rahner show how the space thus opened up can be put to use, while those of H. Küng show where the line must be drawn.

5. Eastern Orthodox

In much the same way as Roman Catholicism, Eastern Orthodoxy (→ Orthodoxy 3) views dogmas as divinely revealed truths with "divine, absolute, and eternal validity for all believers" (J. N. Karmiris, in P. Bratsiotis, 16). Dogmas are necessary to salvation. Their source and basis is the divine revelation contained in Holy Scripture and the sacred tradition. They were definitively formulated at the seven ecumenical councils (held in A.D. 325, 381, 431, 451, 553, 680-81, and 787) and are comprehensively summed up in the → Niceno-Constantinopolitan Creed.

The truth stated in these sources has always been taught and is recognized by the whole church (*plērōma*). "The dogmatic teaching of the Orthodox Catholic Church is identical with that of the ancient, united, undivided church, and Orthodoxy has preserved it intact and unfalsified throughout the centuries" (ibid., 15). There is no need of a supreme teaching office. The fixing of dogma by synod, being done by common consent, is something more or less accidental.

Central to Orthodox teaching are the doctrines of

the → incarnation and the → Trinity. The so-called → *filioque* (the proceeding of the Spirit from both Father and Son), which the Eastern church rejected, was the occasion rather than the final reason for the definitive breach with Rome in 1054. The intellectualism of Western theology is alien to the Eastern church.

The main locus of its dogmas is in its liturgical life and → doxology. Although Christian dogma is fixed, the theology of the Eastern church reacts critically with that of the Western church in ecumenical → dialogue and is pressing on to fresh interpretations of doctrine (N. A. Nissiotis).

6. Anglican

The self-understanding of → Anglicanism appears especially in the → Book of Common Prayer (1549, 1552, 1662) and the Thirty-Nine Articles (1563, 1571). Acceptance of an episcopal form of government goes hand in hand with Reformation teaching (e.g., on justification, the Eucharist, and the papacy). The combination has given Anglicanism something of a mediating position in debates with Roman Catholicism and also within Protestantism.

The Lambeth Quadrilateral of 1888 lays down four basic principles: (1) Holy Scripture as the foundation of faith and doctrine; (2) the Nicene and Apostles' Creeds; (3) the sacraments of → baptism and the → Eucharist; and (4) the historic episcopate. These were intended at first as minimal conditions for the reunion of the English free churches and the Church of England, but they have taken on wider significance in the ecumenical search for unity. They allow considerable breadth in doctrinal statement.

Tolerance is a typical feature of Anglican theology, which comprises liberal as well as Anglo-Catholic and evangelical elements. Alongside a concern for ecumenical → unity, the concern exists to harmonize Scripture and tradition with modern thought.

7. Contemporary Themes and Tasks

New developments in philosophy (critical rationalism; → Positivism; Analytic Philosophy; Critical Theory) have led to a new definition of the scientific status of theology (and dogmatics; Philosophy of Science) and of its relation to other sciences (W. Pannenberg, G. Sauter, H. Peukert). Interdisciplinary interest gives a key position to theological → anthropology (Pannenberg) and focuses fresh attention on the concept of experience. The ecumenical enlargement of theology has brought with it the discussion of themes that in origin and in their more specific forms reflect the experiences and problems of the → Third World (→ Black Theology; Liberation Theol-

ogy; Programme to Combat Racism; Theology of Revolution). In general, questions of ethics, especially → social ethics, are to the fore. T. Rendtorff has tried to reckon with the idea of an "ethical theology."

Interdenominational exchanges, which used to be highly → polemical, have now become true → dialogue and, with the wider possibilities of communication in the 20th century, have broadened out into multilateral ecumenical conversations. Ecumenical theology itself is done mostly at conferences and aims at convergence or → consensus. Only tentatively does dogmatics take up these matters. E. Schlink's attempt at an "ecumenical dogmatics" (1983) oriented itself to the classic themes of dogmatics and dealt only indirectly with the results of ecumenical dialogue.

On the whole, a growing awareness of the fullness and variety of problems in dogmatics seems to inhibit the venturing of new, comprehensive conceptions. The present-day stress seems to be on monographs (esp. in → anthropology, → Christology, ecclesiology, and the doctrine of → God), whether in the Protestant sphere (Pannenberg, Moltmann, E. Jüngel) or in the Roman Catholic world (W. Kasper, H. Küng, E. Schillebeeckx). Even Rahner has engaged only in *Schriften zur Theologie* (Writings on theology; ET *Theological Investigations*). His *Grundkurs des Glaubens* is not a dogmatics in the usual sense but a more modest "introduction to the concept of Christianity."

Bibliography: On 1: W. PANNENBERG, *Theology and the Philosophy of Science* (Philadelphia, 1976) 346-423 • O. RITSCHL, "Literarische Beobachtungen über die Nomenklatur der theologischen Disziplinen im 17. Jahrhundert" (FS T. Haering; Tübingen, 1918) 76-85; idem, "Das Wort dogmaticus in der Geschichte des Sprachgebrauchs bis zum Aufkommen des Ausdrucks theologia dogmatica" (FS J. Kaftan; Tübingen, 1920) 260-72.

On 2: H. FISCHER, *Systematische Theologie, Konzeptionen und Probleme im 20. Jahrhundert* (Stuttgart, 1992) extensive bibliography • G. GLOEGE, "Dogmatik," *RGG* (3d ed.) 2.225-30 • F. MILDENBERGER, *Geschichte der deutschen evangelischen Theologie im 19. und 20. Jahrhundert* (Stuttgart, 1981) • K. RAHNER and W. LOHFF, "Dogmatik," *LTK* (2d ed.) 3.446-56 • G. SAUTER, "Dogmatik I," *TRE* 9.41-77 (bibliography) • F. SCHLEIERMACHER, *The Christian Faith* (2 vols.; New York, 1963; orig. pub., 1821-22) • H. THIELICKE, *Modern Faith and Thought* (Grand Rapids, 1990) • H. ZAHRNT, *Die Sache mit Gott. Die protestantische Theologie im 20. Jahrhundert* (7th ed.; Munich, 1970).

On 3.1: R. A. HARRISVILLE and W. SUNDBERG, *The*

Bible in Modern Culture: Theology and Historical-Critical Method from Spinoza to Käsemann (Grand Rapids, 1995) • W. Pannenberg, *Theology and the Philosophy of Science* (Philadelphia, 1976) • C. H. Ratschow, ed., *Handbuch systematischer Theologie* (18 vols.; Gütersloh, 1979ff.). See also the bibliography on 2.

On 3.2: H. Bavinck, *Gereformeerde dogmatik* (4 vols.; 4th ed.; Kampen, 1928-30) • G. C. Berkouwer, *Karl Barth* (Kampen, 1936); idem, *The Triumph of Grace in the Theology of Karl Barth* (Grand Rapids, 1956) • T. L. Haitjema, "Abraham Kuyper und die Theologie des holländischen Neucalvinismus," *ZZ* 9 (1931) 331-54; idem, "Der Kampf des holländischen Neu-Calvinismus gegen die dialektische Theologie," *Theologische Aufsätze* (FS K. Barth; Munich, 1936) 571-89 • H. M. Kuitert, *Gott in Menschengestalt* (Munich, 1967) • A. Kuyper, *Encyclopaedie de heilige godgeleerdheid* (2d ed.; Amsterdam, 1908); idem, *De gemeene gratie* (3 vols.; Amsterdam, 1902-5) • K. H. Miskotte, *Über Karl Barths Kirchliche Dogmatik* (Munich, 1961) • R. Schilder, *Heidelbergsche Catechismus* (4 vols.; Goes, 1947-52).

On 3.3-5: A. Heron, "Dogmatik III," *TRE* 9.92-104 • A. Jeffner, "Dogmatik II," ibid. 77-92 • K. E. Lögstrup, *The Ethical Demand* (Philadelphia, 1971).

On 3.6: J. B. Cobb and D. R. Griffin, *Process Theology: An Introductory Exposition* (Brescia, 1976) • E. Farley, *Ecclesiastical Reflection: An Anatomy of Theological Method* (Philadelphia, 1982) • F. Herzog, "Dogmatik IV," *TRE* 9.104-16 • P. C. Hodgson and R. H. King, eds., *Christian Theology: An Introduction to Its Traditions and Tasks* (Philadelphia, 1982) • P. L. Holmer, *The Grammar of Faith* (New York, 1978) • G. A. Lindbeck, *The Nature of Doctrine: Religion and Theology in a Postliberal Age* (Philadelphia, 1984) • J. Macquarrie, *Principles of Christian Theology* (New York, 1966) • P. M. Van Buren, *A Christian Theology of the People Israel* (New York, 1983); idem, *Discerning the Way: A Theology of the Jewish-Christian Reality* (New York, 1980) • G. Wainwright, *Doxology: The Praise of God in Worship, Doctrine, and Life* (New York, 1980).

On 3.7: H. Assmann, *Theology for a Nomad Church* (Maryknoll, N.Y., 1975) • C. Boff, *Theology and Praxis* (Maryknoll, N.Y., 1987) • R. Frieling, *Befreiungstheologien* (Göttingen, 1984) • G. Gutiérrez, *A Theology of Liberation: History, Politics, and Salvation* (Maryknoll, N.Y., 1988) • M. Hofmann, *Identifikation mit den Anderen. Theologische Themen und ihr hermeneutischer Ort bei lateinamerikanischen Theologen der Befreiung* (Stockholm, 1978).

On 4: J. Auer and J. Ratzinger, *Kleine katholische Dogmatik* (9 vols.; Regensburg, 1970ff.) • B. Bartmann, *Lehrbuch der Dogmatik* (2 vols.; 8th ed.; Freiburg, 1932) • DH • F. Diekamp, *Katholische Dogmatik nach den Grundsätzen des heiligen Thomas* (3 vols.; 13th ed.; ed. K. Jüssen; Münster, 1958-62; orig. pub., 1912-14) • J. Feiner and M. Löhrer, eds., *Mysterium salutis. Grundriß heilsgeschichtlicher Dogmatik* (5 vols.; Einsiedeln, 1965-76) • G. Hasenhüttl, *Kritische Dogmatik* (Graz, 1979) • J. Neuner and H. Roos, *The Teaching of the Catholic Church As Contained in Her Documents* (Staten Island, N.Y., 1967) • L. Ott, *Grundriß der katholischen Dogmatik* (9th ed.; Freiburg, 1976) • K. Rahner, *Foundations of Christian Faith* (New York, 1978); idem, "'Mysterium ecclesiae': On the Declaration Made by the Congregation for the Doctrine of the Faith on the Doctrine of the Church," *Theological Investigations* (London, 1981) 17.139-55, esp. 148-55 • M. J. Scheeben, *Handbuch der katholischen Dogmatik* (I/1–IV/2 [IV by L. Atzberger]; 2d ed.; Freiburg, 1948-61) • M. Schmaus, *Der Glaube der Kirche. Handbuch katholischer Dogmatik* (2 vols.; Munich, 1969-70; 2d ed.; 6 vols.; St. Ottilien, 1979-82); idem, *Katholische Dogmatik* (5 vols.; Munich, 1937-55)

On 5: P. Bratsiotis, ed., *Die orthodoxe Kirche in griechischer Sicht* (2d ed.; Stuttgart, 1970) • N. A. Nissiotis, *Die Theologie der Ostkirche im ökumenischen Dialog* (Stuttgart, 1968) • C. G. Patelos, ed., *The Orthodox Church in the Ecumenical Movement: Documents and Statements, 1902-1975* (Geneva, 1978).

On 6: H. H. Harms, ed., *Die Kirche von England und die anglikanische Kirchengemeinschaft* (Stuttgart, 1966) • S. Neill, *Anglicanism* (4th ed.; Oxford, 1977); idem, "Anglikanische (Kirchen-)Gemeinschaft," *TRE* 2.713-23 (bibliography).

On 7: C. Andresen, ed., *HDThG* 3 • W. Pannenberg, *Anthropology in Theological Perspective* (Philadelphia, 1985); idem, *What Is Man?* (Philadelphia, 1970) • G. Sauter et al., *Wissenschaftstheoretische Kritik der Theologie* (Munich, 1973) • E. Schlink, *Ökumenische Dogmatik* (Göttingen, 1983).

Hermann Fischer

Dogmatism

1. Philosophy
2. Theology

1. Philosophy

The term "dogmatism" was coined in French philosophy and was understood by M. de Montaigne and B. → Pascal as the opposite of → skepticism. Dogmatism denotes the uncritical appeal to a doctrine whose truth has not been demonstrated and whose presuppositions have not been adequately evaluated. Thus the German → Enlightenment saw dogmatism in the pedantic → metaphysics of the schools that built on principles that were part of an outdated philosophical approach. Of the many meanings of the term → "dogma," dogmatism stresses the pejorative one of an unproved opinion.

In the epistemology of I. Kant (1724-1804) dogmatism is viewed as the prejudice of metaphysics whereby the latter "gets along without a critique of pure reason"; Kant criticizes the blind confidence that believes it can expand principles of the transcendental use of the understanding and of reason (of the conditioned possibility of → experience) to include uses transcending experience itself (→ Epistemology; Kantianism). As far as philosophy itself is concerned, Kant concludes that a critique of the faculty of understanding must precede any systematic exposition of philosophy. His followers in German → idealism then attempted to regard this critique not only as this sort of presupposition but also as philosophy that is already part of the system itself.

J. G. Fichte (1762-1814) went beyond Kant insofar as he classified → realism together with dogmatism because the latter assumes, according to the schema of affection, that the non-ego exerts an influence on the ego, whereas Fichte himself views the non-ego as being constituted in the first place only through the ego. Fichte also diagnoses dogmatism in the sphere of → ethics insofar as there the ultimate ground of what is actually in the ego itself is posited outside it. It is through precisely this notion that dogmatism reduces morality to a natural science, whereas its real principle, namely, → freedom, can be found only within the sphere of the ego.

G. W. F. Hegel (1770-1831; → Hegelianism) tried to find a way of synthesizing the philosophy of the schools (which taught a "metaphysics of objectivity") and that of Kant and Fichte (who held a "metaphysics of subjectivity"). If for Kant the misuse of the principles that constitute experience leads to dogmatism, much the same is true for Hegel, for whom the essence of dogmatism is that it posits something finite as absolute. In Hegel's *Phenomenology of the Spirit* dogmatism is characterized as a way of thinking for which what is true resides in a statement that produces a certain result or that is known directly.

F. W. J. von Schelling (1775-1854) viewed the term differently in his philosophy of identity. For him, "dogmatism" concerns a synthesis of the criticism of Kant and the realism of B. Spinoza (→ Spinozism). It thus loses its pejorative sense; "dogmaticism" is the word for the pejorative element in it.

In → Marxist philosophy there is a basic rejection of dogmatism on the ground that it contradicts the historical and dialectical character of reality (→ Dialectic). Nevertheless, in practice the teaching in → socialist countries shows strong dogmatic tendencies. Quotations from the classics of Marxist-Leninism play a decisive role as the basis of argumentation.

In modern French → phenomenology (M. Merleau-Ponty) "dogmatism" denotes a position in which one stands unwittingly in a historical tradition that is open to question. The term underwent a similar development in theological thought. Finally, in neoscholasticism it denotes the necessary presuppositions of basic truths of faith — presuppositions that for their part are no longer subject to proof.

Bibliography: J. G. FICHTE, *The Science of Ethics As Based on the Science of Knowledge* (2d ed.; London, 1907; orig. pub., 1798); idem, *The Science of Knowledge: Wissenschaftslehre* (ed. P. Heath and J. Lachs; New York, 1970; orig. pub., 1794) • G. W. F. HEGEL, *Werke* (ed. H. Glockner; Stuttgart, 1929) vols. 1 and 18 • I. KANT, *Critique of Pure Reason* (trans. N. K. Smith; New York, 1987; orig. pub., 1781; rev., 1787) • M. MERLEAU-PONTY, *Phenomenology of Perception* (London, 1962; orig. pub., 1945) • F. W. J. SCHELLING, "Vom Ich als Prinzip der Philosophie" (1795), *Ausgewählte Werke* (I/1; Stuttgart, 1856-57) 29-124.

HUBERTUS G. HUBBELING†

2. Theology

Modern discussions of dogmatism are largely governed by sociological questions. T. Adorno and his fellow workers have set up decisive methodological principles on a psychodynamic basis in their studies of the authoritarian character. M. Rokeach in the framework of a cognitive theory of personality and S. Ertel with the help of linguistic analysis have continued and modified this approach. On these views "dogmatism" denotes a system of ideas that is (1) marked by rigid → socialization, (2) manifested in dichotomous structures of conviction, (3) strongly actualized in threatening situations, (4) either political or religious in content, and (5) expressive of an excessive individual need for uniformity and delimitation both as a framework of orientation and as a defensive mechanism.

In the relation between dogmatism and theology the problem arises how far an individual theological style of thinking and writing (→ Language) determines a theology and its practical → communication. New empirical research has not confirmed the current preconception that theologians manifest a particularly high degree of dogmatism. Typical Protestant theologians, at least in Europe, do not provide support for the view that there is a connection between dogmatism, → fundamentalism, and → conservatism.

The investigation of dogmatism has posed several new tasks for theology. In the systematic consideration of its subject matter, it must learn to distinguish between the dogmatic content of thought and what we might call a dogmatistic style of thought. Academic forms of instruction must be found that will make possible a critical acceptance of the biblical and church → tradition with a balance of openness and confidence. In church work and → pastoral care, special attention will have to be paid to dealing with members who manifest an authoritarian character structure.

→ Authority; Dogmatics

Bibliography: K.-F. DAIBER and M. JOSUTTIS, eds., *Dogmatismus. Studien über den Umgang der Theologen mit Theologie* (Munich, 1985) bibliography • J. NOLTE, *Dogma in Geschichte* (Freiburg, 1971).

MANFRED JOSUTTIS

Dominic

Domingo de Guzmán, founder of the Order of Friars Preachers (the Dominicans), was born about 1170 at Caleruega, Castile, and died on August 6, 1221, at Bologna. He was canonized on July 3, 1234.

Dominic, born of the lowest rank of nobility, was educated in the arts and theology at the cathedral school of Palencia. Ordained a → priest, he joined the cathedral chapter at Osma about 1196, where he lived the monastic life of an → Augustinian canon regular and ministered in the → cathedral. In the early 1200s, however, his cloistered life changed into an active one when he accompanied his → bishop on an embassy to Denmark for the king of Castile. As he passed through southern France, the problem of the Albigensians stimulated in him the → preaching → vocation. It is likely that Pope → Innocent III requested him to assist the preaching band organized in 1203 to deflect the threat of heterodoxy in Languedoc.

Dominic adopted a mendicant form of life to counteract the Albigensian claim to be the only authentic observance of gospel life. More basic, his sermons and public debates aimed to expose the non-Christian, neo-Manichaean → Cathari dogma. Laboring for years in this mission, Dominic concluded that a permanent preaching corps grounded in theology was needed instead of random recruitment of clerics not properly prepared for such a doctrinal mission. By 1214 he headed a small band of preachers, and in 1215 Bishop Foulques of Toulouse approved them as a diocesan religious community.

Gradually Dominic came to think of the preaching corps as having a universal rather than a local mission. This became fully conscious when he accompanied Bishop Foulques to the Fourth Lateran Council in 1215. There he requested papal confirmation of the Toulouse preachers. When the council prohibited the formation of new religious orders, he returned to Toulouse, and the Foundation Chapter of 1216 adopted the approved rule of St. → Augustine and the strict form of conventual life of Prémontré. On December 22, 1216, Pope Honorius III approved the institute as canons regular and shortly after granted them the title and function of preachers, giving them a share in this aspect of the episcopal office.

In 1217 Dominic dispersed his preachers to make new foundations in Spain and in the university cities of Paris and Bologna, which became centers for the friars' study of dogmatic → theology, → canon law, and → pastoral theology. As growth of members and priories was rapid, in 1218-19 Dominic made a long visitation journey to France, Spain, and Italy, planning further expansion and foundations. Upon his return, Bologna became his base in the last two years of his life.

Dominic was the preacher personified, devoting himself entirely to it from 1206 to his death. He was a preacher of power, totally orthodox, loyal to church and magisterium (→ Teaching Office), able to move hearts to → conversion and to form both laity and his own friars in a fervent life. Deeply spiritual, devoted to → prayer and severe → asceticism, Dominic at the same time was engaging and cheerful. A man of vision, vigor, decisiveness, and prudence, he had a special genius for organization, as the order he founded testifies.

His order is a model of constitutional government, representational, like a "finely regulated republic," with powers distributed between chapters and superiors in three strata. For the first time in monastic history the chapter had a role that was legislative, not merely advisory. The superb organization was not an end in itself but served to free the friars from internal problems, lest they be deflected from preaching.

Preaching was popular yet doctrinal, expounding Catholic truth both to refute heterodoxy and to strengthen the Catholic faithful. Conversion after preaching was followed by sacramental and → pastoral care, spiritual guidance, and the fostering of a popular devotion suitable for urban dwellers. Dominic directed itinerant preaching and lay piety aspirations into orthodox channels, relieving the church of anxieties that had beset it.

The Friars Preachers were the prototype and pattern of all subsequent active religious → orders — a universal organism under one head, unlike the independent house ideal of monk and canon. As the → Benedictines are the classical monks, so the → Dominicans are the classic form of friars.

Bibliography: Primary sources: GERARD DE FRACHET, Lives of the Brethren of the Order of Preachers (New York, 1955) • JORDAN OF SAXONY, On the Beginnings of the Order of Preachers (ed. S. Tugwell; Dublin, 1982) by Dominic's direct successor • V. J. KOUDELKA, "Notes sur le cartulaire de S. Dominique," AFP 28 (1958) 92-114; 33 (1963) 89-120; 34 (1964) 5-44 • F. C. LEHNER, ed., St. Dominic: Biographical Documents (Washington, D.C., 1964) • MOFPH vols. 15-16, Monumenta historica S. P. N. Dominici (Paris and Rome, 1933-35); vol. 25, Monumenta diplomatica S. Dominici (Rome, 1966).

Secondary works: G. BEDOUELLE, St. Dominic: The Grace of the Word (San Francisco, 1987) • H. CLERISSAC, The Spirit of St. Dominic (ed. B. Delany; London, 1939) • B. JARRETT, Life of St. Dominic (2d ed.; London, 1934) • P. MANDONNET, St. Dominic and His Work (trans. M. B. Larkin; St. Louis, 1948) • L. VON MATT, St. Dominic: A Pictorial Biography (Chicago, 1957) • M. H. VICAIRE, "Dominic, St.," NCE 4.964-65; idem, St. Dominic and His Times (trans. K. Pond; New York, 1964) the definitive biography; idem, S. Dominique d'après les documents du XIIIe siècle (Paris, 1955).

JOHN F. HINNEBUSCH, O.P.

Dominican Republic

	1960	1980	2000
Population (1,000s):	3,231	5,697	8,495
Annual growth rate (%):	3.27	2.25	1.43
Area: 48,443 sq. km. (18,704 sq. mi.)			

A.D. 2000

Population density: 175/sq. km. (454/sq. mi.)
Births / deaths: 2.18 / 0.52 per 100 population
Fertility rate: 2.57 per woman
Infant mortality rate: 30 per 1,000 live births
Life expectancy: 72.2 years (m: 70.2, f: 74.5)
Religious affiliation (%): Christians 95.4 (Roman Catholics 88.6, Protestants 4.9, indigenous 1.9, other Christians 1.0), spiritists 2.2, nonreligious 1.7, other 0.7.

1. The island of Hispaniola, later to be divided into the Spanish-speaking Dominican Republic and the French Creole–speaking Republic of Haiti, was the first territory to be settled by Spain following discovery by Columbus in 1492 and settlement the following year. Santo Domingo, its capital city, was established in 1497 and became the principal center for launching the exploration, conquest, and evangelization of Latin America.

The full horror of Spanish rule, and the tension between → colonialism and mission, manifested itself already in the first decades. In Santo Domingo in 1511 the Dominicans protested against the reign of terror that Antonio de Montesinos established over the Taino (→ Indians, American), but the protest was vehemently rejected by the Spaniards and by other church leaders. The result was that after 20 years of colonial rule, 90 percent of the Taino had perished, and within a few decades practically the whole original population of the Antilles had disappeared. The church made not even a minimal protest against its massive replacement by black → slaves.

2. The → Roman Catholic Church was the only religious institution permitted to function during the Spanish → colonial period. When the eastern part of the island managed to free itself from the yoke of Haiti in 1844, the first constitution of the Dominican Republic provided for → religious liberty. Nevertheless, it also declared Roman Catholicism to be the religion of the state and granted special privileges to the church. Intervention and occupation by the United States from 1916 to 1924, and American economic control during the years that followed, led to an increasing expansion of Protestantism.

Except for the period of rapid institutional development during the first half of the 16th century, the Roman Catholic Church, alienated from social reality, suffered from an acute lack of personnel and economic resources up to the dictatorship of R. Trujillo (1930-61). Since 1954 relations between church and state have been regularized through a → concordat signed by Trujillo and the papacy. This made the church a suitable instrument to give the dictatorship validity, even to the point of saying nothing about the massacre of some 20,000 Haitians in a frontier area in 1937.

Since 1954, however, substantial government subventions, charitable contributions, and a major influx of foreign priests and religious personnel have permitted considerable institutional growth in pastoral care, education, rural ministry, and health care. When the church began to oppose Trujillo in 1960, out of fear of Communism it held aloof from revolutionary attempts to change unjust social structures. Most of the clergy approved of military intervention by the United States in 1965. Although the decisions of Medellín (1968) have had some influence, as did the official papal nuncio Emanuele Clarizo up to 1967, after 1970 the church shifted the accent from the defense of human rights to defense of the rights of the church and to pastoral renewal.

3. The story of Protestantism in the Dominican Republic begins with the invasion and occupation by Haiti (1822-44). Responding to an invitation from the government of Haiti, several thousand African Americans, including some freed slaves, settled on the northeast coast in 1824. Clergy of the African Methodist Episcopal Church accompanied the group. Methodist missionaries began their efforts among English-speaking immigrants in 1841 (→ Methodism), making Spanish the official language in 1844.

Numerous denominations from the United States established mission work in the Dominican Republic during the 20th century. The Free Methodist Church (1908) was the first to begin → evangelization of Spanish-speaking Dominicans and founded a school in conjunction with its churches. The Seventh-day → Adventists followed a similar pattern. While the Episcopal Church originally came to minister to English-speaking immigrants from the West Indies (1821), today it addresses itself to the whole nation. Other denominations include the Assemblies of God (1916), Plymouth Brethren (1921), Church of God (1940), Southern Baptists (1962), and numerous conservative evangelical groups after 1970 (→ Evangelical Movement).

In 1990 the largest Protestant groups were the Seventh-day Adventists (73,000 affiliated), Assemblies of God (72,000), Church of God of Prophecy (40,000), Church of God (Cleveland, Tenn., 30,000), Church of the Nazarene (22,000), and Free Methodist Church (21,000).

4.1. A significant interdenominational effort was begun by the U.S. Methodist, Presbyterian, and → Brethren churches in cooperatively founding and supporting the Dominican Evangelical Church (1916). The Social Service of the Dominican Churches, an interdenominational organization, was founded in 1962 for the purpose of providing a Christian response to human need. Two smaller organizations created by conservative evangelicals and → Pentecostals also provide relief and welfare.

4.2. Initially, Protestant churches were disparaged by the Roman Catholic Church as sects and met with various hindrances, in spite of the constitutional guarantee of freedom of religion. In general, however, relations between the denominations have now become more cordial.

5. Other religious groups include → Jehovah's Witnesses, → Mormons, and a number of sects based on Oriental religious precepts. → Voodoo, a syncretistic religion combining African and Christian elements, is widely practiced, particularly in the rural areas (→ Afro-American Cults).

Bibliography: A. C. GONZÁLEZ, *El marco historico de la pastoral dominicana* (Santo Domingo, 1983) • G. LOCKWARD, *El Protestantismo en Dominicana* (Santo Domingo, 1976) • W. L. WIPFLER, *The Church as a Socio-Political Factor in the Dominican Republic* (Ann Arbor, Mich., 1978); idem, *The Churches of the Dominican Republic in the Light of History* (Cuernavaca, Mex., 1966).

WILLIAM L. WIPFLER

Dominicans

1.1. The Dominican preaching order (Ordo Fratrum Praedicatorum, O.P.) arose between 1206 and 1217 through the vision of → Dominic (originally Domingo de Guzmán). Dominic was born in approximately 1170 at Caleruega, Castile, and before 1200 was a canon at the cathedral of Osma. In 1206, with Bishop Diego of Osma, he was in the south of France along with papal legates in the struggle against heresy. Struck by the religious need, he and his bishop aimed to make → conversions (§§1-2) and began to preach in the voluntary → poverty commended by → Innocent III. When Diego returned to Spain, where he died on December 30, 1207, Dominic continued the work and gathered followers.

In June 1215 Bishop Foulques of Toulouse gave Dominic's group a position as diocesan preachers, with the Romanus church in Toulouse as a center and a source of income. In December 1216 Honorius III took the fellowship under papal protection, confirmed their possessions, and accepted their lifestyle according to the → Augustinian Rule. They thus secured a legal basis for multidiocesan extension. Honorius confirmed their work (preaching) and name (preaching brothers) with the *Gratiarum omnium* of January 1217, and he followed up this document with letters of recommendation to the bishops. In August 1217 Dominic sent some of the brothers to set up work in Paris, Bologna, Rome, and Spain. In 1220 the first General Chapter was set up. Dominic died on August 6, 1221, in Bologna and was canonized on July 3, 1234. He had already sketched the basic outlines of the goals and constitution of the order and clarified them to the extent that a smooth transition was made by his successor, Jordan of Saxony (1222-37).

1.2. Various interrelated factors determined the goal and structure of the order. First was the tradition of monastic, ascetic self-understanding, involving ascetic sanctification according to a rule of life. Next was the religious movement of the age, with its apostolic, ascetic ideal of the disciples of Jesus as wandering preachers (→ Discipleship). Third were the religious and ecclesiastical needs of deeper religious instruction and of special cultic communities alongside the parish church, along with the socioeconomic possibilities of city life. (With economic development came more alms and more willingness to spend, with alms becoming a means of support.) Fourth, there was the intellectual revolution with the academic teaching of theology, leading to the rise of the universities. The final factor was the development of Petrine apostolic ecclesiology, which made it possible for the → pope to act as *episcopus orbis* (bishop at large) and to commission itinerant preachers across → diocesan boundaries. These five factors all came together in the mendicant orders to produce a new form of monastic life focused on the → city.

The Dominicans soon manifested three characteristics that became particularly significant for later developments. First, they *accepted a lack of communal property* and the principle of support by alms in return for pastoral services. To put this into practice, they set aside their existing property and assured source of income in 1220/21, restricting their property to a church, a residence, and a garden. This exception distinguished them legally from the poverty of the → Franciscans. (The Dominican ban on property was often broken by the end of the 13th cent., and finally was lifted in 1475.)

Second, within the total church corporation headed by the pope, they *set up a corporate society that was not tied to any particular place* and in which each member, no matter where he resided, was directly linked to the head of the order. This head was elected at a General Chapter, provincial heads were elected at provincial chapters, and priors by house chapters. The various chapters were oriented to control and administration, with the General Chapter also having a legislative function. Even in pastoral work the order was an → exempt society. This characteristic soon led to differences with the parish clergy, which in turn resulted in many controversies about the mendicant orders.

Third, the Dominicans *combined pastoral work and study* in an ascetic lifestyle. This feature led to an organization of studies related to the universities by way of the *studia generalia.*

2.1. In accordance with the aims of the Dominicans, extension in the Middle Ages took place exclusively in the cities. Later, considerably weakened in standing and numbers by the → Reformation, the order found a center in Italy and especially Spain. The closing of cloisters from the 18th to the 19th century left only a few remnants, but reorganization took place in the first half of the 19th century, which led to a gradual upsurge. The Dominicans, however, never regained their former significance in the church. The order now exists in 40 provinces and has about 7,000 members. The original corporative constitution is still in force. A new set of constitutions was issued in 1968.

2.2. The goals of the order and the needs of the church guided the work of the Dominicans in the Middle Ages. From the time of the later Middle Ages, special → devotions came into use. The → rosary was one of the first, and it is now the most common (→ Mary, Devotion to). The Dominicans wrote and circulated much of the pastoral literature of the Middle Ages. Especially in pastoral work among women there arose a mystical literature, which in the German sphere included that of Meister → Eckhart (d. ca. 1328), J. Tauler (d. 1361), and Henry Suso (d. 1366).

The scholarly orientation of the Dominicans led to great achievements, especially with the adoption of Aristotle by Albertus Magnus (d. 1280) and → Thomas Aquinas (d. 1274) (→ Aristotelianism; Scholasticism; Thomism). The influence of Thomas on the theology of the order was palpable and increased sharply in the 15th century, though it was only later that the order developed an exclusive commitment to Thomism (General Chapter of 1615).

In connection with the establishment of a special → Inquisition, Gregory IX appointed individual Dominicans as inquisitors from 1231; in the course of the 13th century, most diocesan courts were entrusted to the Dominicans. The medieval orders believed that fighting heresy was one of their most important tasks, and they identified themselves with the Inquisition in spite of some tensions with personnel exempt from the control of the order. The strong medieval presence of the Dominicans in Greece and the Near East aimed primarily at the winning back of the "Greeks." In modern times missionary activity (→ Mission) began to follow Spanish and Portuguese conquests and helped to Latinize the native peoples. (B. de Las Casas was unusual in resisting exploitation by the church.) In the Chinese

Rites Controversy of the 17th and 18th centuries, the Dominicans and other medicant orders championed a conservatism focused on relations with Europe.

The widespread activity of the order today is shaped by the varying needs and possibilities in different countries. The recent General Chapters have made support for the poor and social justice a special priority.

3. Like other orders, the medieval Dominicans had clusters of societies around them. Thus already in the 13th century we find early forms of → Tertiaries, now called the Dominican Lay Society. Out of these there also developed societies of women Dominicans under rule of life. These mostly came into being in the 19th century as congregations for teaching and care of the sick. There are now some 40 independent convents and over 130 congregations with about 50,000 members.

From Dominic's concern for women there also came the beginnings of the Second Order, formed by nuns living in seclusion. Most of the medieval cloisters arose in connection with the religious movement among women and owe their legal and spiritual link with the order to papal recommendation and local circumstances. There are still some 200 convents with about 5,000 nuns. Some of these houses are not legally under the order but under episcopal or papal rule, which is even more true of the congregations.

Bibliography: Primary sources: AFP (the most important periodical on the history of the order) • T. KAPPELI, ed., *Scriptores Ordinis Praedicatorum medii aevi* (Rome, 1970ff.) catalog of authors • MOFPH (edition of all important sources concerning origins) • QGDOD (important contributions on the Dominicans in Germany).

Secondary works: B. M. ASHLEY, *The Dominicans* (Collegeville, Minn., 1990) • G. BEDOUELLE, *St. Dominic: The Grace of the Word* (San Francisco, 1987) • I. W. FRANK, "Die Verbreitung der Dominikaner bis 1303," *Großer historischer Weltatlas. Erläuterungen* (vol. 2; ed. E. W. Zeeden; Munich, 1983) 128-30 • H. GRUNDMANN, *Religiöse Bewegungen im Mittelalter* (2d ed.; Darmstadt, 1961) • W. A. HINNEBUSCH, "Dominicans," *NCE* 4.974-82; idem, *The Dominicans: A Short History* (New York, 1975); idem, *The History of the Dominican Order: Origins and Growth to 1500* (2 vols.; New York, 1965-73) bibliography • A. H. THOMAS, *De oudste Constituties van de Dominicanen* (Louvain, 1965) • M.-H. VICAIRE, *Dominicains* (Paris, 1980); idem, *St. Dominic and His Times* (New York, 1964) • A. M. WALZ, *Compendium historiae Ordinis Praedicatorum* (2d ed.; Rome, 1948).

ISNARD W. FRANK, O.P.

Donation of Constantine

The Donation of Constantine (*Constitutum* or *Donatio Constantini*) was a document forged sometime between roughly A.D. 750 and 850, probably with the participation of the Roman clergy. It is first attested in the → False Decretals (ca. 850, attributed to Isidore of Seville), then in many versions and MSS. It is linked to a fifth-century story involving Pope Sylvester I (314-35) and Emperor Constantine (306-37). According to the story, Constantine was healed of leprosy and, in gratitude, became a Christian and gave the Roman → church under Sylvester many lavish gifts. Furthermore, when Constantine made → Byzantium (Constantinople) his new capital, he handed over → Rome, Italy, and all the West to the rule of the → pope.

The Donation of Constantine contains two parts that are sometimes treated separately. The first part, which has no legal significance, consists of the story of the emperor's conversion and healing and his confession of faith. The second part is the Donation proper. It lists the privileges of the Roman bishop. The Salvator Church in the Lateran, for example, is to be "the head of all churches worldwide," and the emperor's possessions are made over to the pope and his successors, along with the imperial insignia.

The Donation is part of → canon law, having appeared in various versions since about 850. The second part appears in the Decretum Gratiani (96.13-14) of the → Corpus Iuris Canonici. In this way it achieved canonical authority.

Before the → Investiture Controversy (→ Middle Ages 2) the popes made only tentative use of the Donation of Constantine, but debate regarding it became intense during the controversies regarding the relation between secular and spiritual power (→ Empire and Papacy) and the primacy of the pope. Jurists cast doubt on the authenticity and validity of the Donation. Theologians criticized the secularization of the church and argued that the pope should be Christ's follower, not Constantine's.

For the most part, the Donation was accepted as genuine throughout the → Middle Ages. The first to argue its inauthenticity was Nicholas of Cusa (1401-64), in a work presented to the Council of Basel in 1433 (*De concordantia catholica*). Nicholas stressed the lack of authentic sources. Sometime around 1449 the English bishop Reginald Pecock (ca. 1393-1461) also contested the authenticity of the Donation.

Finally, using the methods of historical and philological criticism, Lorenzo Valla (1407-57) proved that the Donation was a forgery in his work *De falso credita et ementita Constantini donatione*, which he wrote in April–May 1440, probably in connection with the transactions at the Council of Florence (1439-43; → Reform Councils). First printed in 1506, this work made a great impact through an edition put out with a preface in 1518 or 1519 by Ulrich von Hutten (1488-1523). M. → Luther (1483-1546) knew it in 1520 through this edition, and in 1537 he denounced the Donation as "clear papal falsehood" (WA 50.70). Valla's case was so strong that even the papacy has eventually had to admit the Donation's inauthenticity.

Bibliography: H. FUHRMANN, "Constitutum Constantini," *TRE* 8.196-202; idem, ed., *Das Constitutum Constantini (Konstantinische Schenkung)* (Hannover, 1968; ET in *Church and State through the Centuries* [ed. S. Z. Ehler and J. B. Morrall; Westminster, Md., 1954] 15-22) • W. SETZ, *Lorenzo Vallas Schrift gegen die konstantinische Schenkung* (Tübingen, 1975) • W. ULLMANN, *The Growth of Papal Government in the Middle Ages* (London, 1955) 74-86 • L. VALLA, *The Treatise of Lorenzo Valla on the Donation of Constantine* (2d ed.; ed. C. B. Coleman; New York, 1971) • J. VAN ENGEN, "Donation of Constantine," *DMA* 4.257-59.

JOHANNES SCHILLING

Donatists

1. The Donatists were a North African schismatic church of the fourth and early fifth centuries. They fell into schism because, against the realities of their own time, they wished to be loyal to the ancient principles inherited from → Tertullian (ca. 160-ca. 225) and → Cyprian (ca. 200-258). With naive enthusiasm they clung to the ideal of a Spirit-filled church of saints and → martyrs that could not tolerate anything unclean and that therefore had to suffer persecution. The main period also saw an infusion of social and revolutionary elements. Ethnic and cultural antitheses between the rural Berber provinces of Numidia and Mauritania and the urban, Romanized province of *Africa proconsularis* played a role but did not affect the essential issue, plain though the rivalry was between the Diocese of Numidia and that of Carthage.

2. The history of the Donatists is that of their attempt to see themselves as a church that is persecuted because of its purity. Their beginnings reach back to the time of the → persecution under Diocletian (284-305). Either directly or tacitly, some clergy obeyed the imperial edict demanding the handing over of the Scriptures. A stricter party viewed this action as

basically → apostasy. After the death of the Carthaginian bishop Mensurius, the ordination of Caecilian in 311 met with resistance on the ground that it was invalid and that it had not been agreed upon by the Diocese of Numidia. Caecilian himself was also alleged to be unacceptably cool toward martyrdom. The Numidian bishops mustered strong opposition at a synod in Carthage, where Majorinus (d. ca. 311) was elected as a rival bishop. His successor was the purposeful Donatus (d. ca. 355), who gave his name to the rigorist faction.

State patronage of the church under Constantine (306-37) sharpened the conflict, for both groups laid claim to being catholic. In 313 Constantine commissioned an ecclesiastical court of inquiry in Rome. This body ruled in favor of Caecilian and, in accordance with the Roman concept of the sacraments, condemned Donatus for rebaptizing and reordaining. When the Donatists appealed against the decision, the emperor summoned the great Western Council of Arles (314), which ratified the Roman decision. Yet this did not solve the matter in Africa. When political attempts to impose a settlement failed, Constantine let the schism take its course.

In the period that followed, the Donatists grew in numbers. From about 340, the Circumcellions joined them. The latter were wandering and often armed bands, which combined revolutionary traits with a fanatical religious zeal for martyrdom. Their name shows that they met "around a *cella*," which was probably a martyr chapel containing a storeroom. (Alternatively, their name has been interpreted as reflecting their encircling attacks on their opponents' dwellings.) Under Constans I (337-50) a wave of persecution in 347 seemed as though it might restore unity to the church, but the religious policy of Julian (361-63) led to reverses, so that the Donatists were able to maintain their strong, distinct position even under his successors.

The Donatists began to weaken when a split came after the death of Bishop Parmenian (391/92), who had succeeded Donatus in 355. The Catholic side rallied under → Augustine (354-430) and Aurelius of Carthage (d. ca. 430) and pushed the Donatists into a corner. Discussions, polemical writings, and numerous synods were designed to win them back. Augustine even went so far as to sanction the use of force against them. Measures of suppression eventually led to the dissolution of the Donatist church. These measures were sanctioned at a discussion in Carthage in 411 and rigorously applied.

3. The Donatists were living in the past. For them the one holy → church manifested itself in the bish-

op's office, whose holder must display exemplary personal purity. A sinful → bishop excluded himself from the church, lost the ability to dispense valid sacraments, and polluted those who were in fellowship with him. The thought was Cyprianic. The beginnings of further theological work by Tyconius (d. before 400) and Parmenian led to a crisis, and at the same time Augustine clarified his ecclesiology relative to the question. The Donatists shut themselves off from developments in the church's life. Augustine clarified his own ecclesiology through the confrontation with the Donatists, who, even had they weathered their violent suppression, probably could not have long survived.

Bibliography: J.-P. BRISSON, Autonomisme et christianisme dans l'Afrique romaine de Septime Sévère à l'invasion vandale (Paris, 1958) • H. DÖRRIES, "Konstantinische Wende und Glaubensfreiheit," Wort und Stunde (vol. 1; Göttingen, 1966) 1-117 • W. H. C. FREND, The Donatist Church: A Movement of Protest in Roman North Africa (3d ed.; Oxford, 1985) • A. SCHINDLER, "Afrika I," TRE 1.640-700 (extensive bibliography) • G. G. WILLIS, St. Augustine and the Donatist Controversy (London, 1950).

DIETMAR WYRWA

Doubt

1. Philosophical Aspects
2. Theological Aspects

1. Philosophical Aspects

1.1. As a look at everyday usage shows (→ Language 1), the "language game" (L. Wittgenstein) of doubt is very diverse. One may doubt the → truth of a statement, the rightness of a decision to act, the motives of actions, one's own feelings or those of others, perceptions of meaning, and religious or other beliefs of every kind. Philosophical tradition has taken over the broad claim that the essential meaning of doubt lies in the subjective impossibility of assessing truth claims definitively. Doubt, then, has to do in the main with the problem of knowing the truth of human knowledge. The same holds true in the theological attitude to doubt (see 2) insofar as the grounds of knowledge touch directly on the relation of the needed assurance of the central truths of the faith to the "natural" possibility of human knowledge (→ Anthropology 3-4; Epistemology).

1.2. Philosophical handling of doubt is closely linked to the tradition of → skepticism. In its more developed Pyrrhonian form, ancient skepticism argued for a need to withhold all unconditional judg-

ments. It ruled out the dogmatic assertion that a true judgment is not possible in principle. There may be true judgments, but they are always open to doubt. Christian → apologetic literature hardly discussed this Pyrrhonian skepticism. → Augustine (354-430; → Augustine's Theology) pointed out that skeptics cannot doubt that they doubt, and thus doubt presupposes the truth already. He thus opposed a dogmatic skepticism that insists that the truth is unknowable in principle.

1.3. The powerful renaissance of the skeptical, especially the Pyrrhonian, arguments in the 16th and 17th centuries is related to criticism of the truth claims of traditional → Aristotelian knowledge. Especially in its → metaphysical criticism, it could refer to late → nominalist tendencies. It is clear already in M. de Montaigne (1533-92) that the skeptical doubt of reaching objectively valid truth meant theologically an option either for radical fideism or for an attack on the truth claims of the → church. Counterreformation authors (→ Catholic Reform and Counterreformation) used skeptical doubt polemically, pointing to the inability of the human intellect as an argumentative weapon against subjective certainty as a criterion of truth in matters of faith.

1.4. Against the background of the criticism of metaphysics, and to establish a new way of arriving at the truth, F. Bacon (1561-1626) and Galileo (1564-1642) pointed to the need for doubting the tradition as the starting point of a new → philosophy of nature.

Doubt played an important role for R. Descartes (1596-1650; → Cartesianism) in an argument to find assurance for human truth claims. Methodical doubt of the subject's reference to the world (→ Worldview), which he stylized dramatically as self-experience in a way that reminds us of Augustine, led him to the invincible certainty of the *sum cogitans*. This in turn became the starting point for a proof of God that points to God alone as the guarantor of the objective truth of all judgments resting on "clear and distinct" insights (→ Subjectivism and Objectivism; God, Arguments for the Existence of). This strategy of profound doubt of the possibility of true knowledge stands clearly in the broad context of a replacement of objective truth by a methodical certainty of knowledge (*certitudo objecti* by *certitudo procedendi*) that does not have the criterion of subjective evidence. Skeptical doubt questions the attainability of subjective certainty or deplores the lack of a reliable criterion of truth, and it plays a role in basic procedures during the → modern period.

In Descartes's attempt to move, with the help of

radical doubt, to a foundation of sure and certain knowledge beyond all possibilities of doubt, there is an increasing dissolving of the originally ethical and practical motives of the skeptical cultivation of doubt in favor of dealing with epistemological problems. Similarly, the so-called metaphysical doubt evoked by Descartes (*Med.* 3.5) — that is, doubt of the knowability and existence of objective facts — was much more fundamental than the argument of the skeptical tradition that all human perception is subject to illusion and that human judgments are irreducibly diverse.

The metaphysical fundamentality of Descartes's argument from doubt aroused direct criticism. G. W. Leibniz (1646-1716) put it in a form that still influences modern debates about radical Cartesian doubt, namely, relating to a world that is outside our perception, or to the reality of what is psychologically alien. Descartes's skepticism demands a certainty withstanding any doubt that no one can have. For if we are so exposed to illusion that even judgments that seem to be evident as, for example, the elementary truths of mathematics, still come under the reservation of doubt in principle, then all experience of evidence is undermined. In this sense Cartesian doubt is unanswerable, but methodically it makes no sense, for the nature of evidence is against it, and the experiences and results of one's whole life prove the contrary. Like B. → Pascal (1623-62), Leibniz points out that even well-founded knowledge does not ideally derive from indisputable presuppositions. In the history of epistemology this argument marks the beginning of a tradition whereby science seeks its own autonomy by throwing off the demand for absolute proofs according to the ideal of metaphysical certainty. The corresponding relativization (→ Relativism) of the exemplary character of the geometric method of proof leads at the same time to an appreciation of the epistemic and practical value of statements that have only doubtful value in this sense.

1.5. To the extent that skeptical doubt opposes any absolutely certain foundation of theoretical knowledge, modern sciences hardly offer it any point of attack. But doubt of the proof of truth claims occurs in philosophical attempts to meet the demands of radical skepticism by pointing to insights that are absolutely certain. For D. Hume (1711-76), an analysis of human understanding showed that evidence that is free from doubt is not attainable. Judgments based on experiences do not amount to certainty but rest on blind subjection to the natural tendency of the understanding to relate sensory perceptions to an apparently valid objective context. For I. Kant (1724-1804; → Kantianism), who regarded

the necessity of → experience as a basic condition, the skeptical method of transcendentally rational criticism leads to a certainty of a priori knowledge free from all doubt (→ Transcendental Philosophy). While Kant encountered skeptical doubt in his epistemology, G. W. F. Hegel (1770-1831; → Hegelianism) made it an element in the development of the spirit, whose one-sidedness and abstraction is overcome in the superior knowledge of → philosophy completed as a system (→ Social Systems).

1.6. An incisive criticism of the idea that subjective certainty can be articulated in the assertion of knowledge that is free from doubt is given by L. Wittgenstein (1889-1951; → Analytic Philosophy). A basis of his argument is defense of the thesis that statements of the form "I know that . . ." can make sense only when there is possibility of error. A precondition of knowledge is that it be exposed to reasonable doubt. If such doubt is excluded, we do not encounter absolute certainty, but certainties without foundation in which an intersubjective form of life finds expression. This means also that when doubt is well founded, we can still speak sensibly, for radical Cartesian doubt falls under suspicion of nonsense. "If you tried to doubt everything you would not get as far as doubting anything. The game of doubting itself presupposes certainty" (*On Certainty*, §115).

Bibliography: G. P. BAKER and P. M. HACKER, *Scepticism, Rules, and Language* (New York, 1986) • I. HACKING, *The Emergence of Probability* (Cambridge, 1975) • M. HOSSENFELDER, *Die Philosophie der Antike. Stoa, Epikureismus und Skepsis* (Munich, 1985) • P. KONDYLIS, *Die Aufklärung im Rahmen des neuzeitlichen Rationalismus* (Stuttgart, 1981); idem, *Neuzeitliche Metaphysikkritik* (Stuttgart, 1990) • K. LÖWITH, *Wissen, Glaube, Skepsis* (Göttingen, 1956) = *Werke* (vol. 3; Stuttgart, 1985) • L. LÜTTERFELDS, "Die Lebensform–ein System der Evidenz. L. Wittgenstein 'Über Gewißheit,'" *WJP* 20 (1988) 213-29 • R. H. POPKIN, *The History of Scepticism from Erasmus to Spinoza* (Berkeley and Los Angeles, 1979) • SEXTUS EMPIRICUS, *Outlines of Pyrrhonism* (Buffalo, N.Y., 1990) • B. J. SHAPIRO, *Probability and Certainty in Seventeenth-Century England* (Princeton, 1983) • L. WITTGENSTEIN, *On Certainty* (New York, 1972); idem, *Philosophical Investigations* (3d ed.; New York, 1973).

HELMUT MAYER

2. Theological Aspects

Because Christian → faith is a genuine form of knowledge (→ Epistemology), it is accompanied by doubt. This doubt accompanies faith from without as a contesting of its → truth (§2), and the theological efforts of → apologetics seek to meet it. But doubt also encounters the faith of believers themselves. It is a threat and temptation here to faith, and at the same time an element of faith itself. The → dialectic of doubt in relation to faith finds expression in the NT in the sense that the verb *diakrinō* and its related noun *diakrisis* can mean the overthrow of faith (Rom. 4:20) but also the critical task of exposition and the distinguishing of spirits (1 Cor. 12:10), both of which are essential to the faith.

In its primary relation to the character of faith as knowledge, doubt stands in contrast to the → temptation that comes to believers from God and that may be understood as → anxiety before the → wrath of God (§3) and the → last judgment. Such temptation does not dispute the certainty of faith but involves an existential threat (→ Assurance of Salvation 3). If doubt is existential, it is mostly less evident and may lead to an imperceptible loss of → hope (§2). Doubt is a threat to faith when it leaves no room for the hope of faith that is rooted in the assurance of faith. The NT warning has this element of doubt in view, as we see from the Greek *diakrinō*, when the orientation of life to the assurance that is promised to faith is lost in two equally apparent possibilities, between which the thinking "I" (→ Reason) must finally choose. The → promise of faith, however, cannot be experienced in the resultant hesitation between alternatives. It is simply a reference to the necessary implication of doubt when M. → Luther (1483-1546; → Luther's Theology) says, "One must know how one stands with God, if the conscience is to be joyful and be able to stand. For when a person doubts this and does not steadfastly believe that he has a gracious God, then he actually does not have a gracious God" (*LuthW* 51.59 = WA 2.249). Doubt does not obliterate the → grace of God, though it hampers its appropriation and the possibility that it can sustain life in human perception as well.

Doubt can also serve the assurance of faith by questioning the language of believers (→ Language and Theology), critically asking whether or not it corresponds to what it seeks to attest. This critical doubt links the knowledge unique to faith with that of philosophy and science by inquiring into the truth of faith's various assertions. The doubt associated with faith is different from philosophy and science, however, insofar as it has no possibilities for securing any firm grounding for itself. The critical doubt of faith lives from the fact that the certainty or assurance it envisions does not stand at the end of its attempts to arrive at knowledge, attempts first set in motion by doubt itself (as was paradigmatically the case with

R. Descartes [1596-1650]; → Cartesianism); rather, it is to precisely this certainty that doubt owes its own existence. Because the certainty of faith is not that of subjective consciousness, doubt is part of this certainty itself rather than a contradiction for it.

The Reformation distinction (→ Reformers) between *securitas* (the security one attempts to attain through one's own efforts and yet ultimately never reaches) and *certitudo* (the certainty that precedes and is granted to all knowledge and doubt; → Assurance of Salvation 2) can help clarify this dialectic of doubt. Over against the critical doubt that begins and ends with the certainty of faith there stands the doubt whose search for security necessarily always hovers in a way distancing it from the promise of faith. Hence although faith is indeed familiar with temptation and doubt, recognizing both as parts of itself, it excludes the attitude of methodical doubting such as that characterizing → skepticism.

Bibliography: C. Barrett, *Understanding the Christian Faith* (London, 1980) 129-76 • K. Barth, *Einführung in die evangelische Theologie* (2d ed.; Gütersloh, 1977) 96-104 • I. U. Dalferth, "Zweifel," *TRT* (4th ed.) 5.325-28 • G. MacGregor, "Doubt and Belief," *EncRel(E)* 4.424-30 • P. Tillich, *Dynamics of Faith* (New York, 1958).

Wolfgang Schoberth

Dove

In religion the dove has been viewed as a → symbol of the vital spirit or → soul and also of → virtues and female deities. In Israel it was an animal to be sacrificed (Lev. 12:8). At Jesus' → baptism (Mark 1:10 and par.) the dove appeared as an embodiment of the → Holy Spirit. The dove represents innocence in Matt. 10:16. Early Christian art first depicted it as the bird of the soul, then on the basis of Gen. 8:11 as a → sign (§2) of → peace and of God's will for → creation. From the early Middle Ages onward, it came to represent the Holy Spirit (obligatorily so for Roman Catholics since 1745). The "Eucharistic dove" is a receptacle for the Host (→ Tabernacle 2).

→ Symbolism of Animals

Bibliography: G. Cansdale, "Pigeons and Doves," *Animals of the Bible Lands* (Exeter, 1970) 169-73 • K. Goldammer, "Taube," *RGG* (3d ed.) 6.622 • H. Greeven, "Περιστερά, τρυγών," *TDNT* 6.63-72 • G. F. Hasel, "Dove," *ISBE* 1.987-89 • R. K. Murton, "Birds: Columbiformes," *NEBrit* (1985) 15.64-68 • O. Schilling and B. Briesenick, "Taube," *LTK* (2d ed.) 9.1307-8.

Thaddeus A. Schnitker

Doxology

1. Literally an address of praise, the doxology in the narrower sense, which occurs in all major religions, is a magnifying of deity in short formulas either at the beginning or at the conclusion of acts of prayer. It is often oriented to → acclamation by the worshipers (→ Prayer). In the OT, doxologies occur at the latest in the postexilic temple and in the prayer psalms of the developing synagogue (e.g., Neh. 8:6; Ps. 106:1; Isa. 25:1; 37:15-20). This cultic form was cultivated in early Judaism and adopted directly by the NT congregation. Along with the doxology of the → Lord's Prayer in Matt. 6:13b (var.) and also Acts 4:24 and Luke 2:14, the many liturgical scenes in Revelation are noteworthy, which at least partially reflect the liturgical life of the primitive church. Passages like Rom. 11:36; Eph. 1:3; 1 Pet. 1:3 show that doxology also provides a framework for → preaching.

In the postcanonical period there are doxologies not only to God and Christ but also to the Trinity, especially in the *Gloria Patri*, which became customary at the end of psalms. Quite early in both East and West the *trisagion* of Isa. 6:3, along with the Benedictus of Matt. 21:9b, was made part of the celebration of the → Eucharist. The *Gloria in excelsis* (Luke 2:14) was adopted in the West from the eighth century, and the → Nicene Creed, understood as a doxology, from the end of the first millennium. Intercessions and the eucharistic → eulogia had closed with a doxology from as early as the third century. The conclusion of the Roman collect, which is found from the fifth century, should also be understood as a doxology. Final doxological verses also appear in most of the → hymns of the Latin church.

2. In a broader sense, "doxology" applies to anything that takes place with a view to glorifying God. Thus we read of a doxology of judgment in exposition of scenes like Josh. 7:19 or texts like Isaiah 12, Ezra 9:5-15, and Psalm 78. In the → Orthodox Church, all theological work, if it is to be legitimate, is doxology; it goes beyond knowledge to the praise of the great acts of God. In a general sense, those who pray are participating in the ongoing praise of the heavenly world and anticipating the → eschatological consummation.

→ Benediction; Liturgy; Trinity

Bibliography: P. Brunner, "Zur Lehre vom Gottesdienst der im Namen Jesu versammelten Gemeinde," *Leit.* 1.83-361 (esp. 261ff.) • G. Wainwright, *Doxology: The Praise of God in Worship, Doctrine, and Life* (New York,

1980) • C. Westermann, *Lob und Klage in den Psalmen* (Göttingen, 1977).

Albert Mauder†

Drama → Religious Drama

Dream

1. Biblical Data
  1.1. OT
  1.2. NT
2. Origin and Psychological Meaning
  2.1. In History
  2.2. Modern Dream Research
3. Religious Functions and
  Theological Relevance

1. Biblical Data

Biblical accounts of dreams are set in the context of the ancient Near Eastern understanding (K. Seybold), which viewed dreams according to basic types. One kind was the → revelation (§1) or message dream, which was immediately understandable, like the "orthodox" → theophanies of the official → religion (e.g., that of Thutmose IV [1425-1417 B.C.], who once was told in a dream to clear sand away from the great Sphinx). Other types were the symbolic riddle dream (→ Symbol 3), which was indirect and needed illumination (e.g., in → myths and epics); the dream understood as an omen in the narrower sense, as in the "if-then" schema of dialectic (e.g., the Assyrian Book of Dreams); and the anonymous or so-called bad dreams, which, though seldom recorded because this was forbidden by religious and literary convention, were found to be anxiety-causing and confusing and needed specific cultural and religious → rites to interpret them.

1.1. OT

The dream, at times numinous and frightening (Job 7:13-14), serves in the biblical texts as a locus of revelation, as a legitimate means to question God (1 Sam. 28:6, 15) and to learn his will (Gen. 31:10-13; 46:1-4). → Jacob's dream at Bethel is a typical example of a revelation dream (Gen. 28:10-15). As a theophany dream, it is a classic sacred story of the → sanctuary. The account combines two versions (audition and → vision) from different phases of the tradition and compresses it in a stylized manner according to the theological insights of the priests. The vision, which is formed according to classical Sumerian and Mesopotamian models, underlies the glory of the Bethel → temple (§1; → Pentateuch). Similar accounts of revelation dreams appear in Gen. 20:3-7, 1 Sam. 3:3-14, and 1 Kgs. 3:5-14 (the only biblical instance of incubation). Riddle dreams (Gen. 37:5-11; 40:1-23; 41:1-36; Judg. 7:13-14) must be interpreted by a charismatically wise man (Dan. 1:17; 5:12) and are legitimated by repetition (a favorite motif; see Gen. 41:32) or by accompanying → signs.

The dream motif is used as a background in the Joseph stories. Three pairs of dreams, each dreamed by a different person, push forward the action. The dreams have no religious introduction or → allegory and emphasize a central idea almost dispassionately, using symbolism from everyday life. The possibility is artfully suggested that they may not be prophetic but simply dreams of desire or → anxiety. → Joseph, a pious young man of charismatic gifts, the ideal of Wisdom education, overshadows the magi of Egypt. Their art of interpreting dreams is both explicitly and implicitly derided. Interpreting dreams, given here in two forms, cannot be learned; it is a → charisma.

For theological motifs (Deut. 13:1-5) → prophecy came into conflict with the dream mantic, which also was widespread in → Israel (§1). The claims of direct revelation had to be rejected (Num. 12:6-8). God could not be experienced directly in dreams (Jer. 23:16-32; 27:9-10; 29:8-9 in the fight against "lying prophets"; see also Zech. 10:2).

In → Wisdom thought, anxiety at the frightening prospect of dreams yields to reflection on their fleeting appearance (Job 20:8, also Ps. 73:20), which may be precisely depicted (Job 4:12-21), which may be interpreted (a woman's dream of love as in the lyrical dramatizing of feelings and moods in Canticles 3), and which may have different functions (Job 33:13-18, and the dream as wish fulfillment in Isa. 29:7-8). Later Wisdom shows some skepticism (Eccl. 5:3, 7; Sir. 34:1-8) but still retains some knowledge of the nature of the dream. In Daniel 2, 4, and 7 a dream vision forms the schema for a universal and apocalyptic interpretation of history (→ Apocalypticism 2). Dreams are reckoned an eschatological gift (→ Eschatology 1) in Joel 2:28 (also Ps. 126:1).

1.2. NT

In the NT, dreams are important only in Matthew and Acts, though contemporary literature takes full account of the phenomenon (Philo, Josephus, rabbinic Judaism). For Matthew the dream is a sign pointing the way ahead. The dreams of Joseph in 1:20-23 and 2:13, of the wise men in 2:12, and of the wife of Pilate in 27:19 all involve the protection of → Jesus. In Acts, dreams (usually in the form of visions, as in 10:1-16) play the role of encouragement at various points in the history of the → church (16:9-10) or its missionaries (18:9-10; 23:11; 27:23-

24). → Paul himself in his letters does not mention dreams. The variously formed dreams mentioned in the Bible allow us to draw no firm conclusion about the dreams of everyday life.

2. Origin and Psychological Meaning
2.1. In History

On the origin and psychological significance of dreams, European cultural history (→ Culture) has had a wide variety of views. In antiquity we find widespread religious significance attached to dreams and a systematic effort to interpret them, which, like fortune-telling (→ Divination), was a way of foretelling the → future (e.g., the Oneirocritica [Interpretation of dreams] of Artemidorus Daldianus in the 2d cent. A.D.). But we also find sharp criticism of dreams (Cicero), an attempt to give a psychological explanation (Aristotle), and a therapeutic use (Hippocrates). These positions were influential in later centuries, for example, in new editions of the Oneirocritica, in the distinction between divine and natural dreams in Albertus Magnus and → Thomas Aquinas, and in the the importance of dreams in the lives of the great figures of church history such as → Augustine, → Gregory I ("the Great"), and Ambrose.

M. → Luther (1483-1546; → Luther's Theology) argued against the importance of dreams for → faith in opposition to "monks' dreams" (→ Monasticism) and radical groups of → Anabaptists, who, in criticism of the church, viewed dreams as direct revelation (see H. J. Goertz). P. → Melanchthon (1497-1560) wrote a tractate specifically on "God-fearing" interpretation of dreams for a German edition of Artemidorus's Oneirocritica. → Rationalism saw in dreams an expression of a confused life of the → soul (§2), but books of dreams were still common among the people. → Romanticism valued dreams as a revelation of the unconscious and related them to myths and fairy stories.

2.2. Modern Dream Research

Basic to scientific research into dreams was the work of S. Freud (1856-1939) on the interpretation of dreams (1900), although earlier steps had been taken by, among others, K. A. Scherner in 1861 and A. Maury in 1865. In an epochal essay Freud managed to explain dreams as full-scale psychological phenomena and to point out that they are a way to knowledge of the unconscious in the life of the soul. The dream is a clothed, hallucinatory fulfilling of a suppressed desire (infantile → sexuality and → aggression), a way of compromising between the violence of impulse and → censorship. By the mechanisms of the dream (compression, displacement, secondary outworking, symbolism), a latent content becomes a manifest dream content and an attraction that spoils our sleep is set aside (the dream as watcher over sleep). Free association forms the basis of the interpretation, whose orientation is the suppressed wish.

For C. G. Jung (1875-1961), dreams are not a superficial facade but a valid, goal-directed expression of the unconscious. Their function is to compensate for one's consciousness by helping forward the process of individuation as they work toward integrating divided psychological complexes. The symbols in dreams have both individual and collective signficance. Dreams of great religious significance bring the dreamer into contact with → archetypal, psychological forces of overriding cultural and historical importance (anima/animus, image of God; → Self). As numinous → experience, they can have life-giving power on the way to psychological wholeness.

Following and criticizing Freud and Jung are new forms of the therapeutic use of dreams, namely, analytically in various ways (see R. Battegay and A. Trenkel; → Psychoanalysis); phenomenologically in L. Binswanger and M. Boss; in the context of → groups in Battegay, M. Ullmann, and N. Zimmermann; and in identificatory actualization in → Gestalt psychology (e.g., F. S. Perls and others).

Systematic empirical research into dreams received decisive impulses through electroencephalographic techniques (cf. I. Strauch and B. Meier), which show that sleep is not a simple state but involves several different stages in a cyclic process. We dream intensively (though not exclusively) in a phase of sleep that is marked by rapid eye movement (the REM phase). Excitement of physiological processes such as breathing, the heartbeat, and sexual reactions, as well as the relaxing of the muscles, characterizes this state (discovered by E. Aserinski and N. Kleitman). Some 20 percent of the time sleeping is spent in dreaming, with the times for dreaming lasting between 5 and 30 minutes. The systematic and regular frequency of dreaming has presumably influenced human and higher animal evolution. The neuro- and cognitive-psychological functions of dreaming (→ Cognition) are postulated in all work on → information processing and storage.

Research into the contents of dreams shows that most people dream each day (→ Everyday Life), and only occasionally do the dreams contain bizarre actions, persons, or scenarios. Most dreams are "I"-dreams that are aware of life in the world, react to it emotionally, and think along a single track. The contents and structures develop with age and are dependent on the social and cultural environment. Research into daydreams and the like (e.g., hypnagogic images) shows that it is hard to distinguish psychologically among daydreams, dreams, hallucinations, and visions.

3. Religious Functions and Theological Relevance

Most religions have given dreams various functions (in the cultus, in the form of "rites of passage" [→ Initiation Rites 1], as access to changed states of consciousness; see B. Tedlock). A popular form of interpreting dreams may be found as a type of everyday psychologizing apart from therapy (→ Psychotherapy) and science. It is a broad area of interest, often as a way to self-discovery in connection with religious needs (see K. Bulkeley; G. Schmidtchen).

We must consider the religious functions of dreams in a critical theory of → religion and make them fruitful also for → theology. As an independent experience of reality, dreams demand a theological interpretation in the context of → faith (E. Jüngel). The systematic investigation of religious dreams has only just begun but will be important for an empirically based → pastoral theology (H. Hark, C. Morgenthaler). A critical analysis of the principles and → norms of the religious interpretation of dreams can enlighten the → hermeneutical strategies of the self, which takes shape in dreams and their interpretation. Religious dreams can also be analyzed inasmuch as they structure contents according to religious judgment, bring the conscious and the unconscious into systematic harmony, and thereby develop the self. They display the creative, poetic, and rhetorical abilities (→ Rhetoric 2) of the religious self, which is at work in the → metaphoric sphere of religious dream interpretation, which transforms itself, and which in dreams attaches itself to cultural and religious traditions.

Dreams are also important in → pastoral care (cf. J. A. Sanford, Hark) as a stimulus and element in pastoral discussion (often in connection with the crises of sickness and → death), as a discussion tool in group counseling, and in creative work on diaries (I. Progoff). In a counseling relation they must be taken very seriously as intimate disclosures, whose interpretation must ultimately be left to the dreamer. Often the dreams that a person selects to tell say something about the relation to the counselor. The manner of telling them is usually as important as the dream itself.

→ Magic; Mysticism; Witchcraft

Bibliography: ARTEMIDORUS, *The Interpretation of Dreams* (trans. R. J. White; Park Ridge, N.J., 1975) • R. BATTEGAY and A. TRENKEL, eds., *Der Traum aus der*

Sicht verschiedener psychotherapeutischer Schulen (2d ed.; Bern, 1987) • K. BULKELEY, *The Wilderness of Dreams: Exploring the Religious Meanings of Dreams in Modern Western Culture* (New York, 1994) • D. FOULKES, *A Grammar of Dreams* (New York, 1978) • S. FREUD, *The Interpretation of Dreams* (trans. J. Strachey; New York, 1965) • H. J. GOERTZ, "Träume, Offenbarungen und Visionen in der Reformation," *Reformation und Revolution* (FS R. Wohlfeil; ed. R. Postel and F. Kopitzsch; Stuttgart, 1989) 171-92 • H. HARK, *Der Traum als Gottes vergessene Sprache. Symbolpsychologische Deutung biblischer und heutiger Träume* (Olten, 1982) • C. G. JUNG, *Allgemeine Gesichtspunkte zur Psychologie des Traumes* (1916; repr. in *Gesammelte Werke* [vol. 8; Olten, 1982] 263-308) • E. JÜNGEL, "Der Traum vom wachen Leben," *Ich habe einen Traum. Visionen und Wirklichkeiten* (ed. M. Krauss; Stuttgart, 1978) 47-92 • C. MORGENTHALER, *Der religiöse Traum. Erfahrung und Deutung* (Stuttgart, 1992) • F. S. PERLS, *Gestalt Therapy Verbatim* (New York, 1971) • I. PROGOFF, *At a Journal Workshop: The Basic Text and Guide for Using the Intensive Journal Process* (New York, 1975) • J. A. SANFORD, *Dreams: God's Forgotten Language* (San Francisco, 1989) • G. SCHMIDTCHEN, *Sekten und Psychokultur. Reichweite und Attraktivität von Jugendreligionen in der Bundesrepublik Deutschland* (Freiburg, 1987) • K. SEYBOLD, "Der Traum in der Bibel," *Traum und Träumen. Traumanalysen in Wissenschaft, Religion und Kunst* (Göttingen, 1984) • I. STRAUCH and B. MEIER, *Den Träumen auf der Spur. Ergebnisse der experimentellen Traumforschung* (Bern, 1992) • B. TEDLOCK, *Dreaming: Anthropological and Psychological Interpretations* (Cambridge, 1987) • M. ULLMANN and N. ZIMMERMANN, *Working with Dreams* (New York, 1979).

CHRISTOPH MORGENTHALER

Drugs → Substance Abuse

Dualism

Dualism, in contrast to → monism, assumes that two antagonistic principles underlie existence. It found classic expression in Zoroastrianism, in some tendencies in early → Judaism, and in → Gnosticism and its aftermath. In milder form it also appears implicitly in the worldviews of prescientific cultures. A characteristic of modern scientific culture is to find in such hostile factors as disasters and illnesses a challenge to human knowledge and ability. Prescientific cultures, however, push such anomalies into the realm of the unclean (see R. Horton on African

worldviews). They thereby give the anomalous a place and significance and master it by bringing it under personal or abstract control.

At this point M. → Weber (1864-1920) built a bridge from the level of existential experience to the history of religion. He found in the problem of experience of the irrationality of the world the driving force behind all religious development. As he saw it, the Indian doctrine of → karma, Persian dualism, original sin, → predestination, and the *Deus absconditus* all grew out of this experience (p. 178). Later, C. Geertz gave a similar description of the connection between → culture and the → experience of anomaly. But not only personal experiences like ignorance, → suffering, and injustice need explanation. We often find social and political irrationalities that have collective consequences. If civilization is the ideal order that a real → society prescribes for itself, then it must explain disorder in some way. Only when it succeeds to some extent in doing so can it function as a model of integration.

When we turn from this sketch of the problem to religious testimonies to dualism, three aspects become important: (1) how the two opposing forces are conceived, (2) what experiences they represent, and (3) how they are institutionalized. Dualism as a kind of basic thought may be worked out systematically in many different ways. In the *Gathas*, Zoroaster taught that there is an unceasing battle between two spirits that are subject to the deity Ahura Mazda — namely, the → good and the → evil in thought, word, and deed (*Yasna* 30). The magi replaced this ethical dualism between → truth *(asha)* and falsehood *(druj)* by a cosmological dualism between Ahura Mazda himself and the evil deity Ahriman (*Yasht* 13.77; Diogenes Laertius *Peri biōn*, intro. 8).

The → Qumran Essenes (1st cent. before and after Christ) also taught an ethical dualism. God has ordained for us two spirits *(rûḥôt)* to walk in — "the spirits of truth [*'ĕmĕt*] and of error [*'āwĕl*]" (1QS 3:17-19). The Gnostics who flourished in the middle of the second century A.D. promoted an anthropological dualism with cosmological implications, teaching that the divine spirit fell involuntarily into the human body (see → Irenaeus *Adv. haer.* 1.23.2-4).

Dualistic conceptions have helped believers to explain the absurd and to formulate experiences of the irrational. What has to be represented in this way must be a subject of separate study in the case of each religion. In other words, the absurd is not in any sense thought of abstractly and impersonally. What is antithetical may be depicted and identified. Thus it is possible that Zoroaster's dualism stood for an ecological conflict between settled peasants and

thieving → nomads. Unquestionably the →
Manichees viewed not only their persecutions but
also → war, property, and → sexuality as powers of
darkness. Finally, the peasant → Cathari regarded the
battle of their own village communities against the
concentrated forces of the papacy (→ Pope, Papacy),
the church, the → Inquisition, and the emperor as
the battle between light and darkness. The more
plainly dualistic conceptions are seen to be representative in this way, the clearer is their setting.

The institutionalizing of dualism is the final
aspect. Dualistic worldviews can be a purely cognitive
conception of intellectuals without practical consequences. We may think of philosophical schemata
like that of *nous* and *hylē* in middle → Platonism
(Plutarch *De Is. et Os.* 45ff.). But things are different
with the Gnostics, Manichees, and Cathari. These
groups exemplified the struggle of light against darkness by abstaining from flesh and wine, avoiding sex,
and renouncing homes and property (→ Asceticism).

Dualistic conceptions could also be institutionalized in other ways, for example, in collective rituals.
Thus the Semitic New Year festival represents the
annual transition from chaos to cosmos (A. J. L.
Wensinck). We find the same phenomenon in the
story of → Iranian religion. Among the → Shiites in
Iran the conflict between imams and their mortal
enemies is fought out afresh every year in the Ashura
festival, in which the rivalries between different city
wards play a part.

Bibliography: U. BIANCHI, "Dualism," *EncRel(E)* 4.506-
12 • C. COLPE, "Die griechische, die synkretistische und
die iranische Lehre von der kosmischen Mischung,"
OrSuec 27/28 (1978-79) 132-47; idem, "Lichtsymbolik
im alten Iran und antiken Judentum," *StGen* 18 (1965)
116-33 • C. GEERTZ, *Dichte Beschreibung* (Frankfurt,
1983) 44-95 • R. HORTON, "African Traditional
Thoughts and Western Science," *Rationality* (ed. B. Wilson; Oxford, 1970) 131-71 • H. G. KIPPENBERG, ed.,
*Struggles of Gods: Papers of the Groningen Work Group
for the Study of the History of Religions* (Berlin, 1984) •
P. VON DER OSTEN-SACKEN, *Gott und Belial. Traditions-
geschichtliche Untersuchungen zum Dualismus in den
Texten von Qumran* (Göttingen, 1969) • M. WEBER,
Soziologie–weltgeschichtliche Analysen–Politik (Stuttgart,
1968) • A. J. L. WENSINCK, "The Semitic New Year and
the Origin of Eschatology," *AcOr* 1 (1923) 158-99.

HANS G. KIPPENBERG

Dutch Missions

1. History and Current Situation
2. The Missionary Task

1. History and Current Situation

1.1. Christianity came rather late to the Netherlands, being introduced by the English missionaries
Willibrord (658-739) and Wynfrith Boniface (ca.
675-754). In the → Middle Ages the Dutch church
did not produce any significant missionaries, nor did
it have, like Spain and Portugal, any missionary commission from the papacy, since before achieving independence from Spain, Holland did not engage in
any voyages of discovery or conquest (→ Colonialism).

The → Reformation brought a Calvinist state
church (→ Reformed Churches) to the Netherlands,
which from the very first had a sense of responsibility
to → mission. Outstanding missionary theologians
were A. Walaeus (1573-1639), J. Heurnius (1587-
1652), and G. Voetius (1589-1676). Missionary work
was closely bound up with the activities of the East
and West Indies Companies (→ Colonialism and
Mission). In the 17th and 18th centuries the fields
were Indonesia (from 1598), Taiwan (1624), India
(1633), Brazil (1640), and South Africa (1652).
Reverses came in the 18th century because of wars
with Britain, France, and Spain and because of the
occupation of Holland by Napoleon.

1.2. A law establishing → religious liberty was
passed in 1848, and in 1853 the → Roman Catholic
Church restored its → hierarchy. Two → Moravian
churches had been founded in the 18th century, and
from the outset the one at Zeist engaged in impressive missionary work in Suriname.

→ Pietism and → revivals gave a new impulse to
mission in the early 19th century and led to the
ending of the tie to the colonial authorities. A. →
Kuyper (1837-1920) was an outspoken critic of
colonial policies, arguing that the colonial powers
should be no more than trustees for the dependent
countries and had a duty to lead them to freedom.

Although the Gereformeerde Kerken in Nederland (GKN) and the Nederlandse Hervormde Kerk
(NHK) accepted their missionary responsibilities by
synod decision only in 1896 and 1950 respectively,
missionary societies had been founded in the late
18th and mid-19th centuries: the Nederlandse Zen-
delingsgenootschap in 1797, the Nederlandse
Zendingsvereniging in 1858, the Utrecht Zendingsvereniging in 1859, and the Gereformeerde Zendingsvereniging in the same year. The Nederlands
Bijbelgenootschap was organized in 1815.

Indonesia was the main mission field, but denominational strife and the colonial authorities hampered the work in the 19th century. The first Javanese Bible translation (→ Bible Versions), for example, was confiscated because the authorities were opposed to missionary work. In the early 20th century, leading advocates of Dutch missions (e.g., H. Kraemer, C. van Doorn, J. Verkuyl) opposed colonialism. Most missionaries to Indonesia resumed their work after the interruption caused by World War II. Almost all of them supported the cause of Indonesian independence in the 1945-50 conflict. Even high-placed Islamic officials recognized the distinction between the missionaries and the colonial authorities.

The Indonesian churches began to achieve independence in the 1930s (→ Third World 2). Rejecting paternalism, they adopted the motto "Partners in Responsibility." The Council of Churches in Indonesia was founded in 1950. Christianity enjoyed increasingly rapid growth from 11 million members in 1970 (9 percent of the population) to 17 million in 1980 (11 percent), with a projected 29 million (14 percent) by 2000.

1.3. In the late 20th century new mission fields were opened up. The NHK is at work in Cameroon, Nigeria, Ghana, and Senegal, and the Gereformeerde Bond in Kenya and Peru. The GKN does work in Rwanda, Argentina, Brazil, Pakistan, and Bangladesh. Other Reformed churches are active in South Africa, Brazil, Suriname, and the Antilles, as are the → Lutheran Church in Tanzania; the Remonstrant Brotherhood in Ghana; the → Baptists in Cameroon, Sierra Leone, and Zaire; and the Evangelical Brethren in Suriname and the Antilles. In addition, many → evangelical missions work together under the aegis of the Zendings Alliantie. The NHK and the GKN have almost completely joined forces in Indonesia.

The central organ of Dutch Roman → Catholic Missions is the Nederlandse Missie Raad (NMR), which is under the bishops' conference. In spite of problems, this body works well with the Protestant Nederlandse Zendings Raad (NZR), and they publish a joint paper. There is also joint work on the theological faculties (→ Theological Education) in the Instituut voor Missiologie at Leiden and the Instituut voor Oecumenica at Utrecht. Coordination for global diaconal work (→ Diakonia) is achieved by the Beraad Internationale Dienst, while the Oecumenische Missionair Beraad brings together agencies for home → evangelization. Home and foreign mission is seen as a single task, and in the 1970s an international team was set up to explore ways of expressing their dependence on one another.

2. The Missionary Task

In 1986 the NMR, with substantial agreement from many Protestant churches, formulated the task of mission in terms of the proclamation of the gospel, the promotion of → unity among the Christian churches (→ Ecumenical Learning), → dialogue with other → religions and → worldviews, development aid and liberation for all peoples, and the promotion of justice (→ Righteousness, Justice) and peace. After much discussion the insight gained ground that there should be coordination of → proclamation, diaconal activities, and the work of development. The missionary responsibility of local churches was recognized.

The NZR and the NMR have declared → solidarity with the poor (→ Poverty) throughout the world and thus opposed exploitation, injustice, → racism, and oppression in every form, as well as new forms of colonialism (→ Dependence). In 1986 the churches urged the Dutch government to impose sanctions on South Africa. Conversion, the saving of souls, and the planting of new churches are still goals of mission (Voetius), but witness is to be given with "heart and hands and voices," which means that people should be helped to form new social groups and political structures that will effect positive change and thus bring new hope and liberation. In this way → salvation will be given its full biblical meaning.

Bibliography: A. J. J. M. van den Eerenbeemt, *De missie-actie in Nederland, 1600-1940* (Nijmegen, 1945) • I. H. Enklaar, with J. Verkuyl, *Onze blijvende opdracht. De Nederlandse deelname aan wereldzending en werelddiakonaat in een nieuwe tijd* (Kampen, 1968) • R. S. Kipp, *The Early Years of a Dutch Colonial Mission: The Karo Field* (Ann Arbor, Mich., 1990) • A. Mulders, *De missie in tropisch Nederland* ('s Hertogenbosch, 1940) • T. Müller-Krüger, *Der Protestantismus in Indonesien* (Stuttgart, 1968) • *De Nederlandse Missie Raad. Een terugblik over 18 jaar beleid* (The Hague, 1985) • J. H. Roes, *Het grote missie uur 1915-1940, op zoek naar de missie-motivatie van de Nederlandse Katholieken* (Bilthoven, 1974) • E. C. Smith, *God's Miracles: Indonesian Church Growth* (South Pasadena, Calif., 1970). A brief survey of missionary work appears in *Evangelijke Zendingsalliantie* (1986).

Anton G. Honig

Duty

1. In everyday parlance, "duty" denotes what we ought to do because an inner as well as an outer legal code of what is expected in social relations prescribes it, irrespective of our own subjective inclinations (→ Action Theory).

2. → Stoicism introduced the term into the discussion of philosophical ethics, arguing that what is fitting for us (Gk. *to kathēkon*) is to act in harmony with the laws of → nature and of the universe, which are reflected in human → reason. By way of Cicero (106-43 B.C.), the concept of duty (Lat. *officium*, "dutiful or respectful action") found its way into Christian → ethics.

Already in → patristics (by → Tertullian and Ambrose) a distinction was proposed between the canon of ordinary duties that ought to govern all moral actions and the additional special duties incumbent on the wise. This distinction led in the → Middle Ages and the → moral theology of Roman Catholicism even today (→ Modern Period) to the further distinction between general *precepts* (i.e., God's commandments) and the *counsels* that apply to specific people and that go beyond the general commandments. In this way ethical thought could find a basis in → natural law and could take the material form of describing duties, often with the help of a developed → casuistry.

3. Duty assumed central importance for ethical thinking with I. Kant (1724-1804; → Kantianism), but as a formal, not a material, principle. Material norms for Kant were oriented to an attainable state or object, for example, the ideal state of happiness. They are thus related to human desires, and so they are both empirical and subjective.

In accordance with his → epistemological analysis, Kant tried to ground morality a priori, rationally, and formally in the → freedom and → autonomy of the acting subject. Mere agreement with a norm cannot make an action moral, only legal. Its morality depended for Kant on the formal principle of performing an action as a duty. We recognize the need for the action out of regard for the moral law and perform it "as a duty" that derives from the moral law as our own moral disposition. This → law must be generalized, and it is binding on all who freely decide to be part of a moral society. Kant formulated the basic rule of this moral law in terms of the → categorical imperative. Not subjective inclination, but → conscience governed by pure practical reason compels those who judge or act morally to give unconditional obedience to this law.

4. Kant's view of duty influenced German-speaking philosophical and theological ethics and all middle-class ethics in 19th- and 20th-century → Protestantism, even though later criticism of the rigorous formalism of Kant called into question the building of ethics on the concept of duty (A. Schopenhauer, F. → Nietzsche). The Anglo-Saxon tradition, in contrast, remained more closely tied to empiricism and → utilitarianism (D. Hume, J. Bentham). It was left for → analytic ethics (→ Analytic Philosophy) expressly to develop a formal line of argument close to that of Kant, to which has been given the label → "deontology" (W. D. Ross, R. M. Hare, et al.).

5. The impact of → existentialism and → dialectical theology reduced the importance of the concept of duty in 20th-century theological ethics. Stress now fell instead on the unconditional command of God, though this focus opens up the danger of decisionism in ethics. Also to the fore was the concept of → responsibility, which shows how ethics is conditioned materially and historically and takes into account the context of ethical judgments and actions, though not without → teleological considerations. One of the lasting results of the discussion of duty in ethics seems to be the consensus that ethics can have no basis apart from the reference to a rationally necessary and unconditional obligation and apart from some standard of universal applicability such as we find in Kant's categorical imperative. We see similar elements in the Christian command of love or the → Golden Rule.

Bibliography: Cicero, *De officiis* • S. Engstrom and J. Whiting, eds., *Aristotle, Kant, and the Stoics: Rethinking Happiness and Duty* (Cambridge, 1996) • C. Frey, *Theologische Ethik* (Neukirchen, 1990) 197-212 • R. M. Hare, *Essays on Religion and Education* (Oxford, 1992) • S. Hauerwas, *Christians among the Virtues: Theological Conversations with Ancient and Modern Ethics* (Notre Dame, Ind., 1997) • A. Hügli, "Pflichtenkollision," *HWP* 7.440-56 • I. Kant, *Critique of Practical Reason* (trans. L. W. Beck; New York, 1993; orig. pub., 1788); idem, *Foundations of the Metaphysics of Morals* (New York, 1969; orig. pub., 1785) • W. Kersting, "Pflicht, Pflichten, Pflichtethik," *HWP* 7.406-39, 456-60 (bibliography) • J. J. Kotva, *The Christian Case for Virtue Ethics* (Washington, D.C., 1996) • H. Reiner, *Pflicht und Neigung* (Meisenheim, 1951; 2d ed., 1974, with title *Die Grundlagen der Sittlichkeit*) • W. D. Ross, *Foundations of Ethics* (Oxford, 1939).

Werner Schwartz

Dying, Aid for the

1. Concept

The phrase "aid for the dying" variously conveys (1) simply being there for them, (2) care and medical measures to make dying easier, and (3) refraining from medical measures to keep the dying alive. From all these forms of passive aid we must theoretically distinguish active aid in the form of hastening death (i.e., so-called assisted suicide; see 3 below), which ethically and legally counts as homicide, whether on request or not. The meaning of the phrase "aid for the dying" overlaps with that of "euthanasia" but pertains only to the dying. It is open to debate when the process of dying begins, whether only with a final comatose condition or with the onset of a fatal disease (→ Health and Illness). We call people dying when an irreversible process begins that will lead to death in a foreseeable time.

Also debated is when the process ends in → death. On the basis of pragmatic questions involving the removal of organs, the ending of intensive treatment, or the replacement of organs (→ Organ Transplants), the death of one part — namely, the brain — has been isolated from the process and equated with the death of the whole person, since it involves the inevitable destruction of the → organism and since the brain is what makes the organism human. The latter conclusion is a debatable judgment. The → Cartesian separation of mind and body meant that the body itself was no longer regarded as the bearer of personhood and dignity (→ Person; Human Dignity; Anthropology 3). Important for aid to the dying is patients' subjective awareness of their own imminent death, even if this is not always in accord with the objective findings.

2. Aid

2.1. *The Hospice Movement*

Radical changes in social structure, along with the growing ability of medicine to combat serious illnesses, have meant that dying often takes place in hospitals. But hospitals are organized to fight illness, and there the mortally sick are often treated as if death could be averted. Hospitals, then, can neither accept death nor meet the needs of the dying. This situation led the English physician C. Saunders in 1967 to found a "hospice" for the dying. This insti-

tution soon led to a hospice movement that spread quickly in Britain and the United States and then to countries like Germany. The hospice does not fight the disease but focuses on care, alleviation of suffering, and pastoral help (→ Pastoral Care of the Sick), involving the aid of relatives as far as possible. The aim is to permit death at home if possible. For this reason, ambulatory work is important.

2.2. *Withholding of Life-Sustaining Treatment*

If death is construed as brain death, this means that the body is to be regarded up to this point as that which sustains → life. It is to be treated as such, all its basic needs being met in the same way as those of an infant (e.g., by providing food, washing, alleviation of pain, and loving attention). These needs must be met even when dying is prolonged. Withholding things of this sort that make dying easier diminishes human dignity. It does not follow, however, that every possible measure must be taken to fight an inevitably fatal sickness. A basic ethical principle of medicine is to help without doing more harm than good (see the Hippocratic oath; → Medical Ethics).

Withholding heroic medical measures creates no legal problem as long as patients request it, for the law gives precedence to self-determination over the duty of physicians to keep people alive. Problems arise only if patients can no longer make free decisions or make them known clearly. Then physicians must decide whether it is their duty to help, not in prolonging life, but in easing what may otherwise be simply a painful process of dying. The will of patients conveyed either in writing or on the credible testimony of close relatives may not be absolutely binding, but in most countries it gives legal protection to physicians should conflicts arise. A difficult situation is when death comes at once when measures are withheld, and the impression might be given that death was caused and not just allowed.

A Christian view is that we are created with a limited span of life on this earth. Hence it is not the duty of physicians to fight death as such but only to see to it that conditions exist for a tolerable life. Even if it is not for us as creatures to make a final judgment about the meaning and value of our lives, nevertheless it is primarily for the sick themselves to decide what forms of life-fulfillment to claim. If they are ready for death and do not want life prolonged, they are not making a judgment about the value of life but recognizing that an irrevocable decision concerning their lives has already been made. By accepting death, Christians acknowledge God's control over their lives.

3. Assisted Suicide

Christians view their lives as standing under the prohibition of murder. Ending life by → suicide, at one's own hand or with the assistance of others, means regarding incurable, severe suffering as meaningless and valueless. → Nietzsche and others have argued that to accept that we are not in final control of our own lives devalues us by subjecting us to a blind natural fate, which religious people view rather as divine overruling. In contrast, a human right exists to a self-determined, kindly death (→ Adulthood). Christians, however, maintain that there is no more lack of dignity in experiencing the end of life than in its beginning, even to the loss of the powers of personhood (→ Fatalism; Suffering), and that we may safely entrust the self in dying, too, to the action of God (Rom. 8:31-37) until he brings life to an end.

In extreme cases of severe pain a cry for release might come (→ Despair) without any → autonomous self-determination or evaluation of the value of life. If in fighting pain, life might then be unintentionally shortened as a side effect, or even if helplessness might lead to the use of means that do intentionally shorten life, such cases do not fall under the usual rules (→ Norms). Those who take such action must answer with their own → consciences to God alone and accept, if need be, the → guilt and the legal consequences. It is hard to objectify such cases legally and ethically, and we may not use them to erode the basic prohibition of death that protects human life.

Philosophers from the days of antiquity have demanded active aid to the dying as a right and a duty. The → Stoics advocated self-determined dying and made a plea for killing, if necessary, by their own hands or those of others. T. More (1478-1535), J. G. Fichte (1762-1814), F. Nietzsche (1844-1900), and others (→ Humanism; Idealism; Renaissance 6-7) also espoused "free death" and putting to death on request or out of pity.

The churches, however, have always rejected active aid to the dying. Thus far only the synods of the Gereformeerde and Hervormde churches in the Netherlands have declared (1985) that deciding to end one's own life, or have it ended, is consistent with the Christian faith as an act of → freedom and → love (H. M. Kuitert; U. Eibach 1988). → Judaism (→ Life 1.1) and → Islam resolutely reject active aid to the dying. → Hinduism and → Buddhism teach that by suicide, assisted or not, none of us can escape our own → karma.

In keeping with the Hippocratic oath, the organization Weltärtzebund has thus far been opposed to assisted suicide. Almost all Western countries, however, have euthanasia societies that support the withholding of heroic measures and favor assisted suicide on request and often even the killing of those who are incapable of deciding but may not necessarily be dying. In most countries attempts to legalize active aid have thus far failed. The Netherlands, however, passed a law in 1993 that exempted from any legal penalties the ending of life on request under specific conditions. In the United States, Jack Kevorkian, the so-called suicide doctor, has assisted in several well-publicized suicides and, through the legal challenge that his actions pose, is forcing the courts to define more carefully the legal boundaries of this whole issue.

Tendencies are also apparent toward the extension of the idea of assisted suicide in cases of people who from birth or because of accident or senility are → handicapped in such a way that life is seen to be valueless and they are simply a burden to themselves and others. Many who do not accept a religious basis for the prohibition of homicide support moves in this direction.

Bibliography: T. Bastian, ed., *Denken, schreiben, töten* (Stuttgart, 1990) • F. L. Beauchamp and L. Walters, eds., *Contemporary Issues in Bioethics* (4th ed.; Belmont, Calif., 1994) 351-512 • B. A. Brody, ed., *Suicide and Euthanasia* (Dordrecht, 1989) • A. Eser and G. H. Koch, eds., *Materialien zur Sterbehilfe. Eine internationale Dokumentation* (Freiburg, 1991) • U. Eibach, *Medizin und Menschenwürde* (Wuppertal, 1976; 4th ed., 1993); idem, *Sterbehilfe–Tötung auf Verlangen?* (Wuppertal, 1988; 2d ed., 1997) • V. Guroian, *Life's Living toward Dying* (Grand Rapids, 1996) • Y. Keown, *Euthanasia Examined* (Cambridge, 1995) • H. M. Kuitert, *Der gewünschte Tod* (Gütersloh, 1991) • Linacre Centre, *Euthanasia and Clinical Practice: Trends, Principles, and Alternatives* (London, 1982) • M. von Lutteroti, *Menschenwürdiges Sterben* (Freiburg, 1986) • S. B. Nuland, *How We Die* (New York, 1994) • J. Rachels, *The End of Life: Euthanasia and Morality* (Oxford, 1986) • C. H. Ratschow, *Wenn Sterbehilfe töten darf* (Wuppertal, 1992) • F. Rest, *Das kontrollierte Töten* (Gütersloh, 1992) • M. A. Simpson, *Dying, Death, and Grief: A Critical Bibliography* (Pittsburgh, 1987) • P. Singer, *Rethinking Life and Death* (Oxford, 1995) • C. Stadler, *Sterbehilfe–gestern und heute* (Bonn, 1991) • J. Student, ed., *Das Hospiz-Buch* (Freiburg, 1989; 2d ed., 1991) • R. F. Weir, ed., *Ethical Issues in Death and Dying* (New York, 1977).

Ulrich Eibach